TRAVELING WITH YOUR PET
THE AAA PETBOOK®

The AAA guide to more than 12,000
pet-friendly, AAA-RATED® lodgings
across the United States and Canada

6th Edition

AAA PUBLISHING

President & CEO	**Robert Darbelnet**
Executive Vice President, Publishing & Administration	**Rick Rinner**
Managing Director, Travel Information	**Bob Hopkins**
Director, Product Development & Sales	**Bill Wood**
Director, Publishing Marketing	**Patty Wight**
Director, Manufacturing & Quality	**Susan Sears**
Director, Tourism Information Development (TID)	**Michael Petrone**
Director, Publishing Operations/Travel Information	**Jeff Zimmerman**
Director, Publishing/GIS Systems & Development	**Ramin Kalhor**
Director, GIS/Cartography	**Jan Coyne**
Director, Purchasing & Corporate Services	**Becky Barrett**
Director, Business Development	**Gary Sisco**
Product Manager	**Lisa Spence**
Manager, Business Line Publicity	**Janie Graziani**
Print Buyer	**Bob Bailes**
TID Regional Managers	**Lisa Brenneman, Todd Cronson, Michel Mousseau, Stacy Mower, Patrick Schardin**
TID Field Operations Manager	**Laurie DiMinico**
Manager, Travel Information Operations	**Brenda Daniels**
Publishing Business Manager	**Linda Indolfi**
Manager, Electronic Media Design	**Mike McCrary**
Manager, Pre-Press/Photo Services & Product Support	**Tim Johnson**
Manager, Graphic Communication Services	**Yvonne Macklin**
Manager, Application Development	**Scott Chrisien**
Development Editor	**Greg Weekes**
Art Director and Cover Design	**Barbra Natali**
Photo Research	**Diane Norden**
Quality Services	**Andrea Payne-Lecky**
Paginator	**Christine Carter**
Technical Specialist	**Roland Levett**
System Analyst	**Samuel Allen**
Programmer	**James Cothrine**
Data Processors	**Dawn Garrison, Kelly Giewont, Jan Roza, Andrea Tlumacki, Susan Trapp**
Proofreader	**Janet D'Amico**

AAA wishes to acknowledge the following for their assistance:
American Boarding Kennels Association, American Veterinary Medical Association, Dogpark.com®, Humane Society of the United States, National Association of Professional Pet Sitters, Pet Sitters International, U.S. Department of Agriculture-Animal & Plant Health Inspection Services

Cover Photos

Couple walking dog on beach	**© ICS/Photo Network**
Camping	**© Tom Stewart/Corbis**
Dog wearing snorkeling gear	**© Stephen Frink/Corbis**

Published by AAA Publishing
1000 AAA Drive, Heathrow, Florida 32746

Sixth Edition Copyright © 2004 AAA Publishing. All rights reserved.
ISBN 1-56251-406-7 Stock Number 552204
Printed in the USA by Dickinson Press

TRAVELING WITH YOUR PET PHOTO CONTEST ENTRY FORM

The next time you go on vacation with your pet, be sure to take along your camera. The winning entry in AAA's PetBook Photo Contest will appear on the cover of the 7th edition of *Traveling With Your Pet: The AAA PetBook®*. The winner also will receive five complimentary copies of the book as well as some handy pet travel accessories.

Please print

Name:

Address:

City: **State:**   **Zip code:**

Daytime phone: **Evening phone:**

Pet's name: **Animal breed:**

Please answer the following questions:

*1. Why do you travel with your pet?

*2. What is your favorite place or city to take your pet, and why?

3. Tell us about an adventure you had while traveling with your pet.

*Required answer

Official Rules

1. Email digital photos to Petbookcontest@national.aaa.com. Please send the photo as a .jpeg file attachment no larger than 2 MB, and include the information requested on the entry form in the body of the email. The digital photo must have a minimum resolution of 1200 pixels by 1600 pixels. The entry form information (name, address, phone, pet's name, animal breed and answers to questions) must be included in the email for contest consideration. Minor digital enhancement for cropping, red-eye removal, filters and correction functions are permitted, but images that are determined to be significantly altered will be disqualified. Photographers are not permitted to place borders or frames around their image or to place a watermark, signature, date or copyright notices on the image.

2. Send printed photos that are in focus, color and no larger than 8" x 10" unmounted along with the completed entry form to:

   PetBook Photo Contest
   AAA
   1000 AAA Drive, MS 64
   Heathrow, FL 32746

Official Rules *continued*

3. Photos must be postmarked by Nov. 22, 2004, and received by Nov. 30, 2004, to be eligible for the contest.

4. Photos must feature at least one pet and have a travel theme.

5. The entrant must be the person who took the photo and who has full rights to the photo.

6. The entrant must obtain full consent from all models or persons appearing in the photo for full use of the photo, including use and publishing in this contest and the other uses stated herein.

7. More than one photo may be entered, but a separate, completed entry form must accompany each photo. (This includes photos sent digitally.)

8. The photos become the property of AAA and will not be returned. The prize-winning photo, including all rights of every kind therein, will become the sole and exclusive property of AAA.

9. A panel of judges will choose the winning photo based on the following qualities: impact, lighting, composition and effectively conveying the idea that Traveling With Your Pet: The AAA PetBook® is about traveling on vacation with your pet. Posed or studio photographs are not preferred.

10. The winner will be notified **by mail** by Dec. 17, 2004.

Disclaimer

By participating, entrants agree that: (i) these rules and the decisions of AAA shall be final in all respects, and (ii) AAA may put the winner's photo on the front or back cover or spine of the 7th edition of Traveling With Your Pet: The AAA PetBook®. The winner grants AAA the right to use his or her name, likeness, portrait, picture, photo, answers on entry form and/or prize information for advertising, publicity and promotional purposes relating to the contest without compensation or permission (unless prohibited by law). The winner agrees to hold harmless and release AAA from any injuries, losses or damages of any kind that may result from taking a photo intended to be submitted. The pet travel accessories prize will be selected at the sole discretion of AAA. The winner agrees to hold harmless and release AAA from use of the pet travel accessories. AAA is not responsible for late, lost or misdirected entries or mail; for technical, hardware or software malfunctions, lost or unavailable network connections, or failed, incorrect, inaccurate, incomplete, garbled or delayed electronic communications, whether caused by the sender or by any of the equipment or programming associated with or utilized in this promotion, or by any human error that may occur in the processing of entries; or for loss of or damage to any entries. AAA retains the right to not award the prize should no acceptable photos be received.

Eligibility

No purchase is necessary to enter the contest or claim the prize. Open to U.S. or Canadian residents 18 years or older except for employees of AAA, CAA and their clubs.

By submitting an entry I agree that I have read the Contest Rules, assent thereto, and submit the enclosed picture in accordance therewith; I attest that I own all rights to the picture and it has not been published or accepted for publication in any medium; and if the picture portrays any living person or persons, I have secured a model release or releases. I further agree that should my entry be chosen as the winning entry I will execute all necessary paperwork/releases as requested by AAA.

ABOUT THIS BOOK

Welcome to the 6th edition of ***Traveling With Your Pet — The AAA PetBook***®. *Traveling With Your Pet* is a must for the traveler who's also an animal lover. This comprehensive book provides all the information you need to know about taking a four-legged friend on the road. Will Spot be a good car passenger? Is it safe to take Snowball on a plane? What are the important rules of pet etiquette? Is pet insurance a good idea? *Traveling With Your Pet* answers all of these questions and more. Here are just some of the features covered:

- Dog parks where you and your furry friends can play, exercise or just relax.

- An extensive listing of animal clinics compiled by the Veterinary Emergency & Critical Care Society. Names, addresses and phone numbers provide valuable information for unexpected or emergency situations, both en route and at your destination.

- A roundup of pet-friendly attractions.

- National public lands in the United States and Canada that allow pets, along with recreation information.

- Border crossing procedures and tips for travelers — both entering Canada from the United States and vice versa.

- Policies pertaining to service animals.

Traveling With Your Pet lists more than 12,000 AAA-RATED® lodgings. And the listings show AAA's trustworthy diamond ratings, the traveler's assurance of quality. Other handy features include:

- Informative highway directions.

- Specific information about lodgings' pet policies: deposits and fees (rounded to the nearest dollar), housekeeping service, designated rooms and other stipulations relating to travelers with pets.

- Additional details about the lodgings themselves, including icons for amenities, recreation, dining and accessibility.

- Icons designating AAA's member discount programs.

All of this valuable information is packaged in a contemporary, easy-to-read format, making *Traveling With Your Pet — The AAA PetBook* as indispensable an on-the-road companion as Spot's water dish or Snowball's litter box. Don't leave home without it, and remember: It always pays to *Travel With Someone You Trust*®.

TABLE OF CONTENTS

Traveling With Pets

Pet-Friendly Places in the U.S. and Canada

Pet-Friendly Lodgings

U.S. Lodgings

Canadian Lodgings

Many people view their pets as full-fledged members of the family. Spot and Snowball often have their own beds, premium-quality foods, a basketful of toys and a special place in their humans' hearts.

Until it's time to go on vacation, that is. Then the family dog or cat is consigned to "watching the fort" at home while everyone else experiences the joy of traveling. Many pet lovers hesitate to take their animals with them because they don't think they'll be able to find accommodations that accept four-legged guests. Others aren't sure how — or if — their furry friends will adapt.

The truth is, including a pet in the family vacation is fairly easy, so long as you plan ahead. Most pets respond well to travel, a fact that isn't lost on the tourism industry. More than 12,000 AAA-RATED® hotels and motels from coast to coast are pet-friendly, and airline bookings for pet passengers are on the rise. Great companions at home, pets are earning their stripes on the road, too.

So if you've been longing to hit the trail with a canine or feline companion, read the tips on the following pages. You may find that a getaway can be far more enjoyable with than without your pet.

Should Your Pet Travel?

Before you make reservations, determine if your pet is able to travel. Most animals can and do make the most of the experience, but a small percentage simply are not cut out for traveling. Illness, physical condition and temperament are important factors, as is your pet's ability to adjust to such stresses as changes to his environment and routine. When in doubt, check with your veterinarian. If you feel your pet isn't up to the trip, it's better for everyone if he stays home.

❧ **Rule 1: Pets who are very young, very old, pregnant, sick, injured, prone to biting or excessive vocalizing, or who cannot follow basic obedience commands should not travel.**

Even if Spot and Snowball are seasoned travelers, take into account the type of vacation and activities you have planned. No pet is going to be happy (or safe) cooped up in a car or hotel room. Likewise, the family dog may love camping and hiking, but the family cat may not. Putting a little thought toward your animal's needs and safety will pay off in a more enjoyable vacation for everyone.

❧ **Rule 2: If your pet can't actively participate in the trip, she should stay home.**

Most of the information in this book pertains to cats and dogs. If you own a bird, hamster, pig, ferret, lizard or other exotic creature, remember that unusual animals are not always accepted as readily as more conventional pets. Always specify the type of pet you have when making arrangements.

Also check states' animal policies. **Hawaii** imposes 5-, 30- and 120-day quarantines for all imported carnivorous animals to prevent the importation of rabies. Guide dogs and other service animals are exempt from the quarantine (issued not more than 14 days prior to arrival in Hawaii) provided they have a standard health certificate and a current rabies vaccination with documentation of the product name, lot or serial number and the lot expiration date. Upon arrival they still must be examined for external parasites and undergo serum antibody testing and microchip identification. For additional details, obtain the brochure Animal Quarantine Station Rabies Information Brochure from the Hawaii Department of Agriculture, Animal Quarantine Station, 99-951 Halawa Valley St., Aiea, HI 96701-5602; phone (808) 483-7151, fax (808) 483-7161. The website address is www.hawaiiag.org/hdoa/ai_aqs_info.htm.

North Carolina has stringent restrictions regarding pets in lodgings. Make certain you understand an accommodation's specific policies before making reservations.

❧ **Rule 3: Be specific when making travel plans that include your pet. Nobody wants unpleasant surprises on vacation.**

If Spot and Snowball stay behind, leave them in good hands while you're gone. **Family, friends and neighbors** make good sitters (provided they're willing), especially if they know your pet and can care for him in your home. Provide detailed instructions for feeding, exercise and medication, as well as phone numbers for your destination, your veterinarian and your local animal emergency clinic.

Professional pet sitters offer a range of services, from feeding and walking your pet daily to full-time house sitting while you are gone. Interview several candidates, and always check credentials and references. For additional information, contact the National Association of Professional Pet Sitters or Pet Sitters International. *(See sidebars below and on p. 9.)*

Kennels board many animals simultaneously and generally are run by professionals who will provide food and exercise according to your instructions. Pets usually are kept in a run (dogs) or cage (cats and small dogs) and may not get the same level of human interaction as at home. **Veterinary clinics** also board pets and may be the best choice if yours is sick, injured or needs special medical care. For further information on how to select a kennel, contact the American Boarding Kennels Association.

Veterinarians, fellow pet owners and professional associations are a good source of referrals for sitters and kennels.

❀ **Rule 4: Never leave your pet with someone you don't trust.**

CHOOSING A PET SITTER

Before hiring a pet sitter, ask:
- Is he or she insured (for commercial liability) and bonded?
- What is included in the fee?
- Does the sitter require that your pet have a current vaccination?
- What kind of animals does the sitter typically care for?
- How will a medical, weather or home emergency be handled?
- Does he or she fully understand your pet's medical or dietary needs?
- How much time will be spent with your pet?

The pet sitter should:
- Have a polished, professional attitude.
- Provide references.
- Have a standard contract outlining terms of service.
- Have experience in caring for animals.
- Insist on current vaccinations.
- Ask about your pet's health, temperament, schedule and needs.
- Visit and interact with your pet before you leave.
- Devote time and attention to your pet.
- Be affiliated with pet care organizations.

Be sure you:
- Explain your pet's personality — favorite toys, good and bad habits, hiding spots, general health, etc.
- Leave care instructions, keys, food and water dishes, extra supplies (food, medication, etc.), and phone numbers for your veterinarian and an emergency contact.
- Bring pets inside before leaving.

CHOOSING A KENNEL

Before reserving a kennel, ask:
- What is included in the fee?
- Do they require current vaccinations?
- What kind of animals do they board?
- How will they handle a medical or weather emergency?
- Will your pet be kept in a cage or run?
- Will your pet receive daily exercise?
- Do they fully understand your pet's medical or dietary needs?
- How and how often will they interact with your pet?

The kennel should:
- Require proof of current vaccinations.
- Be clean, well-ventilated and offer adequate protection from the elements.
- Have separate areas for dogs, cats and other animals, with secure fencing and caging.
- Clean and disinfect facilities daily.
- Give your pet his regular food on his regular schedule.
- Provide soft bedding in runs/cages.
- Understand your pet's medical needs.
- Provide or obtain veterinary care if necessary.
- Offer sufficient supervision.
- Have a friendly, animal-loving staff.

Be sure you:
- Notify staff of behavior quirks (dislike of other animals, children, etc.).
- Provide food and medication.
- Leave a familiar object with your pet.
- Leave phone numbers for your veterinarian and an emergency contact.
- Spend time with your pet before boarding him.

Travelers Who Have Disabilities

Individuals with disabilities who own service animals to assist them with everyday activities undoubtedly face challenges, but traveling should not be one of them. Service animals (the accepted term for animals trained to help people with disabilities) are not pets and thus are not subject to many of the laws or policies pertaining to pets.

The Americans With Disabilities Act (ADA) defines a service animal as "any guide dog, signal dog or other animal individually trained to provide assistance to an individual with a disability." ADA regulations stipulate that public accommodations are required to modify policies, practices and procedures to permit the use of a service animal by an individual with a disability.

The purpose of these regulations is to provide equal access opportunities for people with disabilities and to ensure that they are not separated from their service animals. A tow truck operator, for example, must allow a service animal to ride in the truck with her owner rather than in the towed vehicle.

Public accommodations may charge a fee or deposit to an individual who has a disability — provided that fee or deposit is required of all customers — but no fees or deposits may be charged for the service animal, even those normally charged for pets.

The handler (the animal's owner) is responsible for her care and behavior; if she creates an altercation or poses a direct threat, the handler may be required to remove the animal from the premises and pay for any resulting damages.

The **Delta Society,** an organization devoted to companion and service animals, has information about laws that affect people and service animals in public accommodations. Phone (425) 226-7357 for a catalog, or visit www.deltasociety.org.

Preparing Your Pet for Travel

Happily, many vacations can be planned to include fun activities for pets. Trips to parks, nature trails, the ocean or lakes offer exposure to the world beyond the window or fence at home, as well as the chance to explore new sights

CONTACT INFORMATION

The following organizations offer information, tips, brochures and other travel materials designed to help you and your pet enjoy a happy and safe vacation.

American Animal Hospital Association
12575 W. Bayaud Ave., Lakewood, CO 80228
(303) 986-2800 — www.healthypet.com

American Boarding Kennels Association
1702 East Pikes Peak Ave.
Colorado Springs, CO 80909
(719) 667-1600 — www.abka.com

American Society for the Prevention of Cruelty to Animals
424 E. 92nd St., New York, NY 10128-6804
(212) 876-7700 — www.aspca.org

American Veterinary Medical Association
1931 N. Meacham Rd., Suite 100
Schaumburg, IL 60173
(847) 925-8070 — www.avma.org

Dogpark.com®
716 Fourth St., San Rafael, CA 94901
www.dogpark.com

Humane Society of the United States
2100 L St. NW, Washington, DC 20037
(202) 452-1100 — www.hsus.org

National Association of Professional Pet Sitters
17000 Commerce Pkwy., Suite C
Mt. Laurel, NJ 08054
(856) 439-0324 — www.petsitters.org

PetGroomer.com
P.O. Box 2489
Yelm, WA 98597
(360) 446-5348 — www.petgroomer.com

Pet Sitters International
201 E. King St., King, NC 27021-9161
(336) 983-9222 — www.petsit.com

USDA-APHIS
Deputy Administrator
USDA-APHIS-Animal Care
4700 River Rd.
Riverdale, MD 20737
(301) 734-4981 — www.aphis.usda.gov/ac

and sounds. Even the streets of an unfamiliar city can provide a smorgasbord of discoveries for your animal friend to enjoy.

Once you decide Spot and Snowball are ready to hit the road, plan accordingly:

🐾 **Get a clean bill of health from the veterinarian.** Update your pet's vaccinations, check his general physical condition and obtain a health certificate showing proof of up-to-date inoculations, particularly rabies, distemper and kennel cough. Such documentation will be necessary if you cross state or country lines, and also may come in handy in the unlikely event your pet gets lost and must be retrieved from the local shelter. Don't forget to ask the doctor about potential health risks at your destination (Lyme disease, heartworm infection) and the necessary preventive measures.

If your pet is taking prescribed medicine pack a sufficient supply, plus a few days' extra. Also take the prescription in case you need a refill. Be prepared for emergencies by getting the names and numbers of clinics or doctors at your destination from your veterinarian or the American Animal Hospital Association **Hint:** Obtain these references before you leave and keep them handy throughout the trip.

Make sure your pet is in good physical shape overall, especially if you are planning an active vacation. If your animal is primarily sedentary or overweight, he may not be up to lengthy hikes through the woods.

Note: Some owners believe a sedated animal will travel more easily than one that is fully aware, but this is rarely the case. In fact, tranquilizing an animal can make travel much more stressful. Always consult a veterinarian about what is best for your pet, and administer sedatives only under the doctor's direction. In addition, never give an animal medication that is specifically prescribed for humans. The dosage may be too high for an animal's much smaller body mass, or may cause dangerous side effects.

🐾 **Acclimate your pet to car travel.** Even if you're flying, your pet will have to ride in the car to get to the airport or terminal, and you don't want any unpleasant surprises before departure.

Some animals are used to riding in the car and even enjoy it. But most associate the inside of the carrier or the car with one thing only: the annual visit to the V-E-T. Considering that these visits usually end with a jab from a sharp needle, it's no wonder that some pets forget their training and act up in the car. If this is your situation, you will have to re-train your animal to view a drive as a reward, not a punishment.

Begin by allowing your pet to become used to the car without actually going anywhere. Then take short trips to places that are fun for animals, such as the park or the drive-through window at a fast-food restaurant. (Keep those indulgent snacks to a minimum!) Be sure to praise her for good behavior with words, petting and healthy treats. It shouldn't take long before you and your furry friend are enjoying leisurely drives without incident. *(See Traveling by Car, p. 13.)*

🐾 **Brush up on behavior.** Will Snowball make a good travel companion? Or will he be an absolute terror on the road? Don't wait until the vacation is already under way to find out; review general behavioral guidelines with respect to your animal, keeping in mind that the unfamiliarity of travel situations may test the temperament of even the most well-behaved pet.

It's a good idea to socialize Spot by exposing her to other people and animals (especially if she normally stays inside). You're likely to encounter both on your trip, and it is important that she learns to behave properly in the company of strangers. Make her introduction to the outside world gradual, such as a walk in a new neighborhood or taking her along while you run errands. Exposure to new situations will help reduce fear of the unknown and result in more socially acceptable behavior.

Is your pet housebroken? How is he around children? Does he obey vocal commands? Be honest about your animal's ability to cope in unfamiliar surroundings. Depending on the length and nature of the trip and your pet's level of command response, an obedience refresher course might be a good idea.

🐾 **Learn about your destination.** Check into quarantines or other restrictions well in advance, and make follow-up calls as your departure date approaches. Find out what types of documentation will be required — not just en route, but on the way home as well.

Be aware of potential safety or health risks where you're going, and plan accordingly. For example, the southeastern United States — particularly Florida — is home to alligators and heartwormcarrying mosquitoes, and many mountainous and wooded areas may harbor ticks that transmit Lyme disease.

Confirm all travel plans within a few days of your departure, especially with lodgings and airlines; their policies may have changed after you made the reservations. If you plan to visit state parks or attractions that accept pets on the premises, obtain their animal regulations in advance.

❀ **Determine the best mode of transportation.** Most people traveling with pets drive. Many airlines do accept animals in the passenger cabin or cargo hold, and as more people choose to fly with their pet airlines are becoming more pet-conscious. Restrictions vary as to the type and number of pets an airline will carry, however, so inquire about animal shipping and welfare policies before making reservations. If your pet must travel in the cargo hold, heed the cautionary advice in the Traveling by Air section. *(See p. 14.)*

Flying is really the only major option to car travel. Amtrak, as well as Greyhound and other inter-state bus lines, do not accept pets. **Note:** Seeing-eye dogs and other service animals are exempt from the regulations prohibiting pets on Amtrak and interstate bus lines. Local rail and bus companies may allow pets in small carriers, but this is an exception rather than a rule.

The only cruise ship that permits pets is the Cunard Line's *Queen Elizabeth 2* (on trans-Atlantic crossings); kennels are provided, but animals are accepted on a very limited basis. Several charter and sightseeing boat companies permit pets onboard, however.

A word of advice: Never try to sneak your pet onto any mode of public transportation where she is not permitted. You may face legal action or fines, and the animal may be confiscated if discovered.

❀ **Pack as carefully for your pet as you do for yourself.** *(See checklist, below.)* Make sure she has a collar with a license tag and ID tag(s) listing her name and yours, along with your

WHAT TO TAKE

- ☐ Carrier or crate. *(See Selecting a Carrier or Crate, p. 12, for specifications.)*
- ☐ Nylon or leather collar or harness, license tag, ID tag(s) and leash. All should be sturdy and should fit your pet properly.
- ☐ Food and water dishes.
- ☐ Can opener and spoon (for canned food).
- ☐ An ample supply of food, plus a few days' extra.
- ☐ Bottled water from home. (Many animals are finicky about their drinking water.)
- ☐ Cooler with ice.
- ☐ Healthy treats.
- ☐ Medications, if necessary.
- ☐ Health certificate and other required documents.
- ☐ A blanket or other bedding. (If your pet is used to sleeping on the furniture, bring an old blanket or sheet to place on top of the hotel's bedding.)
- ☐ Litter supplies (for cats or other small animals), a scooper and plastic bags (for dogs).
- ☐ Favorite toys.
- ☐ Carpet deodorizer.
- ☐ Chewing preventative.

- ☐ A recent photograph and a written description including name, breed, gender, height, weight, coloring and distinctive markings.
- ☐ Grooming supplies:
  comb/brush
  nail clippers
  shampoo
  towels
  cotton balls/tissues
  paper towels
- ☐ First-aid kit:
  gauze
  bandages and adhesive tape
  towels
  hydrogen peroxide
  rubbing alcohol
  ointment
  muzzle
  scissors
  tweezers (for removing ticks, burrs, splinters, etc.)
  local emergency phone numbers
  first-aid guide (such as *Pet First Aid: Cats & Dogs,* published by The Humane Society of the United States and the American Red Cross)

address and phone number. As an added precaution, some owners outfit their dog with a second tag listing the name and number of a contact person at home. Popular backup identification methods are to have your animal tattooed with an ID number (usually a social security number) or to implant a microchip under her skin.

If your pet requires medication, make sure that is specified on his tag. This helps others understand your animal's needs and also may prevent people from keeping a found pet or from stealing one to sell.

Note: Choke chains, collars that tighten when they are pulled, may be useful during training sessions, but they do not make good full-time collars. If the chain catches on something, your pet could choke herself trying to pull free. For regular wear, use a harness or a conventional collar made of nylon or leather.

Selecting a Carrier or Crate

This is one of the most important steps in ensuring your pet's safety when traveling. A good-quality carrier not only contains your pet during transit, it also gives him a safe, reassuring place to stay when confinement is necessary at your destination. Acclimate the animal before the trip so he views the crate as a cozy den, not a place of exile.

If you plan to travel by car, a carrier will confine your pet en route, and also may come in handy if Spot or Snowball must stay in the room unsupervised. A secured crate will prevent your pet from escaping from the room when the cleaning staff arrives, or at night if camping in the open. *(See At Your Destination, p. 17.)*

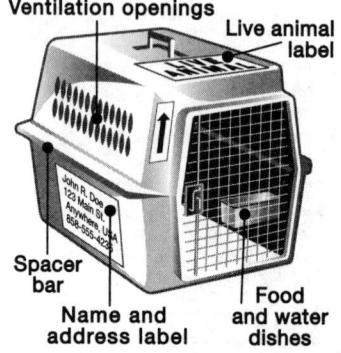

Ventilation openings

Live animal label

John R. Doe
123 Main St
Anywhere, USA
958-565-4258

Spacer bar

Name and address label

Food and water dishes

Some airlines allow small pets to travel in the passenger cabin as carry-on luggage. There are no laws dictating the type of carrier to use, but remember that it must be small enough to fit under a standard airplane seat, usually **13 by 9 by 23 inches or 10 by 16 by 24 inches.** If your pet will be flying in the cargo hold, you must use a carrier that meets U.S. Department of Agriculture Animal and Plant Health Inspection Service (USDA-APHIS) specifications. *(See Traveling by Air, p. 14.)*

Crates are available at pet supply stores; some airlines also sell carriers. Soft-sided travel bags are handy for flyers with small pets. The Sherpa Bags sold by Sherpa's Pet Trading Co. are approved by most major airlines and are available in three sizes for animals weighing up to 6, 16 and 22 pounds; phone (800) 743-7723 for information, or visit their website: www.sherpapet.com.

Even if you never take to the skies, these common-sense guidelines provide a good rule of thumb in selecting a crate for other uses. USDA-APHIS rules stipulate the following:

❧ The crate must be enclosed, but with ventilation openings occupying at least 14 percent of total wall space, at least one-third of which must be located on the top half of the kennel. A three-quarter-inch lip or rim must surround the exterior to prevent air holes from being blocked.

❧ The crate must open easily, but must be sufficiently strong to hold up during normal cargo transit procedures (loading, unloading, etc.).

❧ The floor must be solid and leakproof, and must be covered with an absorbent lining or material (such as an old towel or litter).

❧ The crate must be just large enough to allow the animal to turn freely while standing, and to have a full range of normal movement while standing or lying down.

❧ The crate must offer exterior grips or handles so that handlers do not have to place their hands or fingers inside.

❧ If the carrier has wheels, they must be removed or immobilized prior to loading.

❧ One-inch lettering stating "Live Animal" or "Wild Animal" must be placed visibly on the exterior, and must be accompanied by directional arrows showing the crate's proper orientation. It also is a good idea to label the crate with your name, home address and home phone number, as well as an address and phone number where you can be reached during the trip. (Hint: Use an adhesive label or an indelible marker and write directly on the crate, as paper may be ripped off accidentally in transit.)

❧ Attach a list of care instructions (feeding, watering, etc.) for a 24-hour period to the exterior of the carrier. This will help airport workers care for your pet if he is sent to the wrong destination.

❧ If you are traveling with multiple pets, note that crates may contain only one animal whose weight exceeds 20 pounds. Smaller animals may travel together under the following guidelines: one species to a crate, except compatible dogs and cats of similar size; two puppies or kittens under 6 months of age; 15 guinea pigs or rabbits; 50 hamsters. **Note:** These are federal limits; airlines may impose more stringent regulations.

Traveling by Car

The first step in ensuring your pet's well-being during a vacation is to train her to ride in the car. For safety reasons, pets should be confined to the back seat, either in a carrier or a harness attached to the car's seat belt. This keeps the animal from interfering with or distracting the driver, and also may save her life in the event of an accident. And a restrained animal will not be able to break free and run away the second the car door is opened.

To help prevent car sickness, feed your pet a light meal four to six hours before departing. Do not give an animal food or water in a moving vehicle.

Never allow your pet to ride in the bed of a pickup truck. It's illegal in some states; he also can jump out or be thrown, endangering himself and others on the road. Harnessing or leashing him to the truck bed is not advisable either: If he tries to jump out, he could be dragged along the road or the restraint could become a noose. Avoid placing animals in campers or trailers as well. **If your pet cannot ride in the car with you, leave him at home.**

HEATSTROKE AND HYPOTHERMIA

The best way to treat heatstroke or hypothermia is to prevent it. Do not leave pets unattended in a car, even if only for a few minutes. Also heed airlines' restrictions on pet travel, and carefully investigate animal welfare policies to make certain the airline has safeguards to protect your pet from both conditions.

Other preventive measures are to avoid strenuous exercise — including such activities as hiking and "fetch" — when the sun is strongest (10 a.m.-2 p.m.), and to provide your pet access to clean, fresh drinking water at all times.

Following are the warning signs and basic first aid for heatstroke and hypothermia. Always be alert to your pet's physical condition and watch for symptoms — immediate attention to the situation may mean the difference between life and death. If your pet is struck with either disorder, take him to an animal hospital or veterinarian as fast as safely possible.

HEATSTROKE

Symptoms
- rapid, shallow breathing
- excessive salivation
- heavy panting
- hot to the touch
- glazed eyes
- unsteadiness, dizziness
- deep red or purple tongue or gums
- vomiting
- body temperature of 104 F or higher

First Aid
- place pet in the shade
- quickly dampen with cool water, especially on the head and neck
- give small amounts of water

HYPOTHERMIA

Symptoms
- shivering
- weakness
- lethargy
- cold to the touch
- body temperature of 95 F or lower

First Aid
- place in a warm area
- wrap in towels or a blanket
- quickly warm by gently massaging the head, chest and extremities

Don't let your dog stick her head out the window, no matter how enjoyable it seems. Road debris and other flying objects can injure delicate eyes and ears, and the animal is at greater risk for severe injury if the vehicle should stop suddenly or be struck. If it is hot outside, run the air conditioner instead of opening the windows, and be sure that the air flow is reaching your pet.

AAA recommends that drivers stop every two hours to stretch their legs and take a quick break from driving. Your pet will appreciate the same break. Plan to visit a rest stop every four hours or so to let him have a drink and a chance to answer the call of nature. (Cat owners should bring along a litter box; dog owners should clean up afterward.)

Be sure your pet is leashed before opening the car door. This is not merely a courtesy to fellow travelers; it will prevent her from unexpectedly breaking free and running away. Keep in mind that even the most obedient pet may become disoriented during travel or in strange places and set off for home. **Hint:** If your pet is not used to traveling, use a harness instead of a collar; it is more difficult for an animal to wriggle out of a harness.

NEVER leave an animal in a parked car, even if the windows are partially open. Even on pleasant days the temperature inside a car can soar to well over 100 degrees in less than 10 minutes, placing your pet at risk for heatstroke and possibly death. On very cold days, hypothermia is a risk. Also, animals left unattended in parked cars frequently are stolen.

Traveling by Air

(Service animals are normally exempt from most of the regulations and fees specified in this section. Check policies with the airline when making reservations.)

Opinion is divided as to whether air travel is truly safe for pets. Statistically, it is less dangerous than being a passenger in a car, but some experts warn of potentially deadly conditions for animals. The truth lies somewhere in between: Most pets arrive at their destination in fine condition, but death or injury is always a possibility. Before you decide to fly, know the risk factors and the necessary precautions to keep your pet safe.

❖ **Determine whether your pet is fit to fly.** The Animal Welfare Act (AWA), administered by USDA-APHIS, specifies that dogs and cats must be at least eight weeks old and weaned at least five days before air travel. Animals that are very young, very old, pregnant, ill or injured should not fly at all. Cats, snub-nosed dogs (pugs, boxers, etc.) and long-nosed dogs (shelties, collies, etc.) are prone to severe respiratory difficulties in an airplane's poorly ventilated cargo hold and should travel only in the passenger cabin (if size allows) with their owner.

❖ **Decide where your pet will fly.** Most animals fly in the hold as checked baggage when traveling with their owners, or as cargo when they are unaccompanied. The AWA was enacted to ensure animals traveling in this manner are treated humanely and are not subjected to dangerous or life-threatening conditions. For specific requirements pertaining to your animal, check with the airline in advance, as policies vary. Some airlines will not ship dogs as checked baggage, and United Airlines will only accept dogs shipped as cargo from "known shippers"; i.e., commercial shippers or licensed pet breeders.

Items classified as "dangerous goods" (dry ice or toxic chemicals, for example) must be transported in a different part of the hold from where live animals are carried. Some planes are designed to have separate hold areas, but so-called "people mover" airlines that are primarily interested in getting human passengers from one point to another as quickly as possible may not give priority to this feature. Check your airline's specific baggage policies so you know exactly where in the hold your pet will be traveling.

Small pets may be taken into the passenger cabin with you as carry-on luggage. This places the animal's welfare squarely in your hands but is feasible only if he is very well-behaved and fits comfortably in a container that meets standard carry-on regulations. *(See Selecting a Carrier or Crate, p. 12.)* Keep in mind that the carrier — with the animal inside — must be kept under the seat in front of you throughout the flight. **Note:** AWA regulations do not apply to animals traveling in the cabin.

❖ **Do your homework.** Investigate the airline's animal transport and welfare policies, especially if you are flying with a small or commuter airline. All airlines are subject to the basic regulations of the AWA, but specific standards of care vary greatly from one company to another. Do your research well in advance and confirm the information 24-48 hours before departing.

The more information an airline provides, the better care your pet is likely to receive. Beware of companies that have vague animal welfare guidelines, or none at all. All major airlines provide information about pet transport on their websites. Also talk to fellow travelers and pet owners about their experiences. Finally, keep in mind that airlines are not required to transport live animals and can refuse to carry them for any reason.

❖ **Protect your investment.** Most people think of their pets as part of the family, but the legal system assigns them the same value as a piece of luggage. Inquire about insurance — an airline that won't insure animals in its care may not be the right one for your pet. (Always read the fine print before purchasing any insurance policy.) Also ask if the airline's workers are trained to handle animals. Few are, but it doesn't hurt to check. Remember, it's up to you to choose an airline that values pets and will treat yours with care.

❖ **Understand the potential hazards.** Because a plane's cargo hold is neither cooled nor heated until takeoff, the most dangerous time for your pet is that spent on the ground in this unventilated compartment. In summer the space absorbs heat while the plane sits on the tarmac; the reverse is true in winter, when it is no warmer inside the hold than outside. Both instances expose pets to the possibility of serious injury or death from heatstroke or hypothermia. **Note:** The latter also may be a concern during flight if the hold's heater is disabled or turned off, allowing the temperature to drop to near-freezing levels.

To minimize these risks, USDA-APHIS rules prohibit animals from being kept in the hold or on the tarmac for more than 45 minutes when temperatures are above 85 F or below 45 F. Some airlines impose even tighter temperature restrictions and may not permit animals to fly on planes going to cities where the ground temperatures may exceed these limits. American and Delta, for example, do not carry animals in their cargo holds May 15 through Sept. 15. (Exceptions may be made for animals whose veterinarians certify they are acclimated to colder temperatures, but never warmer.)

❖ **Make stress-free travel arrangements.** Once you decide to fly, reserve space for Spot or Snowball when you arrange your own tickets, preferably well in advance of your travel date. Airlines accept only a limited number of animals per flight — usually two to four in the passenger cabin and one pet per passenger — on a first-come, first-served basis. More animals are generally allowed in the cargo hold.

Prepare to pay an additional fee, about $75-$100 each way; the cost is often greater for large animals traveling on a flight without their owner. (Unfortunately, pets are not eligible for frequent flyer miles.) Always reconfirm your reservations and flight information 24-48 hours before departure.

If your pet will be flying in the hold, travel on the same plane and reserve a nonstop flight. This not only reduces the danger of heatstroke or hypothermia during layovers, it also eliminates the possibility that she will be placed on the wrong connecting flight. In summer, fly during the early

PET INSURANCE

Just like their owners, pets can experience major medical problems at some point in their lifetime—even those that live indoors. And if illness strikes while you're on the road, it may be necessary to obtain care quickly. As a result, more and more people who travel with their devoted companion are considering pet health insurance.

Insurance plans run the gamut from basic coverage and routine care for illness and injury to comprehensive health maintenance, vaccinations and exams. Annual premiums range from less than $100 to more than $350, depending on the type of pet and plan. When choosing your plan, consider the following:

- What are the enrollment guidelines (age, breed, specific restrictions, etc.)?
- Which expenses are covered and which are excluded?
- What is the plan's policy concerning existing health problems?
- Does the plan allow you to use your own veterinarian?
- How are veterinary fees paid?
- Is a multiple pet discount offered?

If you're thinking about pet insurance for your dog or cat, contact AAA Insurance Services for more information; phone (407) 444-8608.

morning or late evening when temperatures are cooler. Because of large crowds and the chance of heavy air traffic causing delays, avoid holiday travel whenever possible.

Additional precautions may be necessary when traveling outside the United States and Canada. Other countries may impose lengthy quarantines, and airline workers outside North America may not be bound by animal welfare laws. *(See International Travel, p. 20.)*

❧ **Play an active role in your pet's well-being.** Flying safely with your pet requires careful planning and attention to his welfare. See the veterinarian within 10 days of departure for a health certificate (required by most airlines) and a pre-flight check-up.

Address any concerns you have about your pet traveling by air, especially if you are considering tranquilization. Sedation usually is not recommended for cats and dogs, regardless of whether they fly in the cabin or in the hold. Exposure to increased altitude pressure can create respiratory and cardiovascular problems; animals with short, wide heads are particularly susceptible to disorientation and possible injury. Sedation should never be administered without your veterinarian's approval.

Obtain an airline-approved carrier and acclimate your pet to its presence by leaving it open with a familiar object inside. A sturdy, well-ventilated crate adds an additional measure of protection.

Because animals are classified as luggage, they may be loaded on the plane via conveyor belt. If the crate falls off the belt, your pet could be injured or released. Ask that she be hand-carried on and off the plane, and that you be permitted to watch both procedures. Also ask about "counter-to-counter" shipping, in which the animal is loaded immediately before departure and unloaded immediately after arrival. There usually is an additional fee for this service.

Make sure you will have access to your pet if there is a lengthy layover or delay. Think twice about flying on an airline that won't allow you to check on your animal under such circumstances.

❧ **Prepare for the flight.** Keep in mind that traveling with an animal will require additional pre-flight time and preparation on your part. Exercise your pet before the flight, and arrive at least two but not more than four hours before departure. If he is traveling as carry-on luggage, check-in is normally at the passenger terminal; if he is traveling as checked baggage or as cargo in the cargo hold, proceed to the airline's cargo terminal, which is often in a different location. Find this out when making reservations and again when confirming flight information.

Make sure your animal's crate is properly labeled and secured, but do not lock it in case airline personnel have to provide emergency care. Include an ice pack for extra comfort on a hot day or a hot water bottle on a cold day. **Hint:** Wrap in a towel to prevent leaking.

Do not feed your pet less than four hours before departure, but provide water up until boarding.

AIRLINE CONTACT INFORMATION

Following is a list of the major North American airlines and their toll-free reservation numbers.

Website addresses have been given for those airline websites that include information about flying with animals. Hint: Look under links for baggage, cargo or programs and services, or do a site search for "pets."

Air Canada . . . . (888) 247-2262
www.aircanada.ca

Alaska Airlines . . . . (800) 252-7522
www.alaskaair.com

America West Airlines . . . (800) 235-9292
www.americawest.com

American Airlines . . . . . . (800) 433-7300
www.americanair.com

Continental Airlines . . . . . (800) 523-3273
www.continental.com

Delta Airlines . . . . (800) 221-1212
www.delta.com

Northwest Airlines . . . . . . (800) 225-2525
www.nwa.com

Southwest Airlines . . . . . (800) 435-9792
www.iflyswa.com

(Accepts service animals only.)

United Airlines . . . . (800) 864-8331
www.ual.com

US Airways . . . . (800) 428-4322
www.usair.com

Hint: Freeze water in the bowl so that it melts throughout the trip, providing a constant drinking source.

Spot or Snowball should wear a sturdy collar (breakaway collars are recommended for cats) and two identification tags marked with your name, home address and phone number, and travel address and phone number. It's also a good idea to clip your pet's nails before departure so they won't accidentally get caught on any part of the carrier.

Note: You may be required to take your pet out of the carrier as you pass through security on your way to the gate. Make sure the animal is wearing a collar and leash or harness.

Attach food and water dishes inside the carrier so that airline workers can reach them without opening the door. If the trip will take longer than 12 hours, also attach a plastic bag with at least one meal's worth of dry food. Animals under 16 weeks of age must be fed every 12 hours, adult animals every 24 hours. Water must be provided at least every 12 hours, regardless of the animal's age.

Allow your pet to answer the call of nature before boarding, but do not take her out of the carrier while in the terminal. As a courtesy, wait until you are outside and away from fellow travelers. Keep her leash with you — do not leave it inside or attached to the kennel.

If your pet is traveling as carry-on luggage, let the passenger sitting next to you know. Someone with allergies may want to change seats.

Perhaps the most important precaution is to alert the flight crew and the captain that your pet is aboard. The pilot must activate the heater for the cargo hold; make sure this is done once you are in the air. If there are layovers or delays, ask the flight crew to be sure your pet has adequate shelter and/or ventilation; better yet, ask them to allow you to check in person.

If you have arranged to watch your pet being unloaded, ask a flight attendant to call the baggage handlers and let them know you are on the way. Above all, do not hesitate to voice any concerns you have for your pet's welfare — it is your responsibility to do so.

❧ **Be prepared for emergencies.** In the unlikely event your pet gets lost en route, contact the airline, local humane shelters, animal control agencies or USDA-APHIS. Many airlines can trace a pet that was transferred to the wrong flight. If your pet is injured in transit, proceed to the nearest animal hospital; register any complaints with USDA-APHIS. **Hint:** Carry a list of emergency contact numbers and a current photograph of your pet in your wallet or purse, just in case.

At Your Destination

How well you and your companion behave on the road directly affects the way future furry travelers will be treated. Always clean up after your pet and keep him under your control. This is not only a courtesy to fellow human travelers; it's the surest way to enjoy a safe and happy vacation.

Inquire about pet policies before making lodging reservations. Properties may impose restrictions on the type or size of pet allowed, or they may designate only certain rooms, such as smoking rooms, for travelers with animals. If you have a dog, get a room on the first floor with direct access outside, preferably near a walking area; keep her leashed on any excursion.

Lodgings may have supervision policies requiring that pets be crated when unattended or that they may not be left alone at all. Allow your pet only in designated exercise or animal-approved areas; never take him into such off-limits places as the lobby, pool area, patio or restaurant. Prepare to receive limited housekeeping service, or none at all.

Expect to pay some type of additional charge, which may be per room or per pet and may include any of the following: refundable deposit, non-refundable deposit, daily fee, weekly fee.

If staying with friends or relatives, make certain your pet is a welcome guest. Know and respect their "house rules," especially if they have small children or pets of their own.

Once in the room, check for such hazards as chemically treated toilet water, hiding spaces and electrical cords before freeing your pet. Give her time to adjust to her new surroundings under your supervision.

Above all, practice good "petiquette":

❧ Try not to leave your pet alone, but if you must, crate or otherwise confine her.

❧ Crate at night as well.

❁ To keep your pet and the housekeeper from having an unexpected encounter, leave the "Do Not Disturb" sign on the door when you go out without him.

❁ Barking dogs make poor hotel neighbors — keep your pet quiet.

❁ Don't allow your pet on the furniture. If she insists on sleeping on the bed, bring a bedspread or sheet from home and place that on top of the hotel bedding.

❁ Clean up after your pet immediately — inside the room and out — and leave no trace of him behind when checking out.

❁ Dispose of litter and other "accidents" properly — check with housekeeping.

❁ Notify the management immediately if something is damaged, and be ready to pay for repairs.

❁ Add a little extra to the housekeeping tip.

❁ When you take your pet out of the room, keep her leashed, especially in wilderness areas and around small children. No matter how obedient she is at home, new stimuli and distractions may cause her to forget or ignore vocal commands. Know and obey animal policies at parks, beaches and other public areas. Check before arriving to make certain animals still are welcome, even if you've been there before — the rules may have changed.

❁ Look for outdoor cafes when selecting restaurants. For health reasons, pets are not permitted inside eating establishments, but many restaurants allow animals to sit quietly with their owners at outdoor tables. Drive-through restaurants are another alternative.

In Case of Emergency

Be prepared for any turn of events by knowing how to get to the nearest animal hospital. *(See Animal Clinics, p. 50.)* Also have the name and number of a local animal shelter and a local veterinarian handy — ask your veterinarian for a recommendation. Take first-aid supplies with you and know how to use them. An animal in pain may become aggressive, so exercise caution at all times.

Emergency evacuation shelters do not accept pets, and domesticated animals do not fare well if left to weather an emergency on their own, especially when far from home. Avert a potential tragedy by planning in advance where you will go with your pet in case of evacuation. Use the listings in this book to find other lodgings willing to take you and your pet. Above all, don't wait for disaster to strike. Leave as soon as the evacuation order is announced, and take your animal with you.

The Great Outdoors

Travelers planning an active or camping vacation should make some additional preparations. Check in advance to be sure your pet is permitted at campgrounds, parks, beaches, trails and anywhere else you will be visiting. If there are restrictions — and there usually are — follow them. Remember that pets other than service animals usually are not allowed in public buildings.

Note: It is not advisable to take animals other than dogs into wilderness areas. For example, bringing a pet is not recommended at some national parks in Alaska. Also keep in mind that rural areas often have few veterinarians and even fewer boarding kennels.

Use common sense. Clean up after your pet, do not allow excessive vocalizing and keep her under your control. If the property requires your pet to be leashed or crated at all times, do so. Few parks or natural areas will allow a pet to be unattended, even when chained — the risk of disagreeable encounters with other travelers or wildlife is too great. The National Park Service may confiscate pets that harm wildlife or other visitors.

If camping, crate your pet at night to protect him from the elements and predators. (Chaining confines the animal but won't keep him from becoming a midnight snack.)

When hiking, stick to the trail and keep your pet on a short leash. It is all too easy for an unleashed pet to wander off and get lost or fall prey to a larger animal. Keep an eye out for such wildlife as alligators, bears, big cats, porcupines and skunks, and avoid other dogs and small children. Be aware of indigenous poisonous plants, such as English ivy and oleander, or those causing physical injury, such as cactus, poison ivy or stinging nettle. Your veterinarian or local poison control center should be able to give you a full list of hazardous flora.

Before setting out on the trail, make sure both of you are in good physical shape. An animal that rarely exercises at home will not suddenly be ready for a 10-mile trek across uneven terrain. Plan a hike well within the limits of your pet's endurance, and don't push — remember, if Spot gets too tired to make it back on her own, you'll have to carry her.

Carry basic first-aid supplies, including a first-aid guide. *(See What to Take, p. 11.)* Also carry fresh drinking water for both of you — "found" water may contain harmful germs or toxins. Drink often, not just when thirst strikes, and have your pet do the same. Watch for signs of dehydration, leg or foot injuries, heat exhaustion or heatstroke. Stop immediately and return home or to camp if any of these occur.

Note: Dogs can carry their own backpacks (check your local pet store for specially designed packs), but should never carry more than one-third of their body weight. Train the dog to accept the pack beforehand, and only use it with a strong, healthy animal in excellent physical condition.

No matter where or how you spend your vacation, visit the veterinarian when you return home to check for injuries, parasites and general health.

Note: Most campgrounds accept pets. The AAA CampBook guides are an excellent source for obtaining detailed information regarding pet policies, restrictions and extra charges for campgrounds in the United States and Canada. AAA members may obtain complimentary copies of the CampBook guides at their local AAA club.

Traveling Between the U.S. and Canada

Traveling across the international border with your pet — either from the United States into Canada or from Canada into the United States — should prove largely hassle-free, although some basic regulations need to be kept in mind.

Passports to enter Canada or return to the United States are not required for native-born citizens of either country. Proof of citizenship is required; a birth or baptismal certificate and a photo ID (a driver's license, which also establishes proof of residence) normally are sufficient. Naturalized citizens should carry their naturalization certificate, and U.S. resident aliens must have an Alien Registration Receipt Card (Green Card).

U.S. Customs grants returning U.S. citizens who stay in Canada more than 48 hours an individual $800 exemption (if not used within the prior 30 days). Any amount over the $800 exemption is subject to duty.

The exemption is based on fair retail value and applies to goods acquired for personal or household use or as gifts but not intended for sale. All items for which the exemption is claimed must accompany you upon return. A $200 exemption is granted for stays of less than 48 hours.

A 7 percent Goods and Service Tax (GST) is levied on most items sold and most services rendered in Canada. In Nova Scotia, New Brunswick and Newfoundland, a Harmonized Sales Tax (HST) of 15 percent (which includes the GST) is charged on goods and services. Rebates can be claimed on some items. Brochures that explain the GST and contain a rebate form are available at tourist information centers, customs offices and duty free shops at the border and in airports.

U.S. citizens taking pet cats and dogs three months of age and older into Canada must carry a health certificate signed by a licensed veterinarian that describes the animal and provides proof of rabies vaccination within the past 12 or 36 months, depending on the type of vaccine. Collar tags are not sufficient proof of immunization. The certificate also is needed to bring a pet back into the United States; make sure the vaccination doesn't expire while you're in Canada.

Service animals are exempt from these rules. Also exempt are up to two puppies or kittens under three months old; obtain a certificate of health from your veterinarian indicating that the animal is too young to vaccinate. **Note:** Pets entering Canada through Newfoundland require a certificate and entry permit, which must be obtained in advance. For details, contact the Canadian Embassy; 501 Pennsylvania Ave. N.W., Washington, DC 20001; phone (202) 682-1740. The website address is www.canadianembassy.org.

The Canadian Food Inspection Agency (CFIA) provides additional pet information; phone (613) 225-2342. If you need assistance while in Canada, contact the U.S. Embassy, 490 Sussex Dr., Ottawa, ON, Canada K1N 1G8; phone (613) 238-5335.

Canadian Customs allows Canadian citizens to bring back from the United States, duty and tax free, goods valued up to $200 any number of times per year, provided the visit is 48 hours or more. A $50 exemption, excluding alcoholic beverages and tobacco products, may be claimed if the visit is 24 hours or more and no other exemption is being used. If returning from a visit of seven days or more (not counting the day of departure from Canada), the exemption goes up to $750.

Canadian travelers may take pet cats and dogs into the United States with no restrictions, but U.S. Customs requires that dogs have proof of rabies vaccination no less than 30 days before arrival. For additional information on U.S. regulations, contact the Animal and Veterinary Services department of the USDA-APHIS National Center for Import and Export, (301) 734-3277.

International Travel

If you plan to travel abroad with Spot or Snowball, prepare for a lengthy flight and at least a short quarantine period. Be aware that airline and animal workers in other countries may not be bound by the same animal welfare laws that exist in the United States and Canada. Contact the embassy or consulate at your destination for information about documentation and quarantine requirements, animal control laws and animal welfare regulations.

As with any trip, have your pet checked by your regular veterinarian within 10 days of departure to obtain a health certificate showing proof of rabies and other inoculations. If you are traveling with an animal other than a domesticated dog or cat, check with USDA-APHIS for restrictions or additional documentation required.

The booklet "Pets and Wildlife" has general information about traveling abroad with animals; write U.S. Customs & Border Protection, 1300 Pennsylvania Ave. NW, Room 34A, Washington, D.C. 20229.

Note: Many island nations, such as Australia and the United Kingdom, are rabies-free and impose a quarantine on animals brought in from the United States and Canada. Hawaii imposes 5-, 30- and 120-day quarantines for all imported animals except guide dogs.

Loss Prevention Tips

Searching the woods or an unfamiliar town for a missing pet is easily prevented by following these helpful tips:

* Have your pet wear a sturdy nylon or leather collar with current ID and rabies tags firmly attached. Be sure the ID tag includes the phone number of an emergency contact.

* Keep your pet on a leash or harness. Even trained animals can become agitated or disoriented in unfamiliar surroundings and fail to obey vocal commands.

* Attach the leash or harness while your pet is still inside the closed car or crate.

* Do not leave your pet unattended at any time, anywhere. A stolen pet is extremely difficult to recover.

* Escape-proof your hotel room by crating your pet and asking hotel management to make certain no one enters your room while you are gone. (Inform the property that you're traveling with an animal when making reservations.)

* Take along a recent picture and a detailed written description of your pet.

If your pet gets lost these steps will improve your chances of recovery:

* If your pet is lost in transit, contact the airline immediately. Ask to trace the animal via the airline's automated baggage tracking system.

* Contact local police, animal control, animal shelters, humane organizations and veterinary clinics with a description and a recent photograph. Stay in contact until your pet is found, and provide your home and destination phone numbers.

* Post signs and place an ad in the local newspaper so that anyone who comes across your pet knows she is lost and how to reach you.

The Last Word

You are ultimately responsible for your pet's welfare and behavior while traveling. Since animals cannot speak for themselves, it is up to you to focus on your pet's well-being every step of the way. It also is important to make sure he conducts himself properly so that other pets will be welcome visitors in the future. Following the common-sense information in this book will help ensure that both you and your animal companion have a safe and happy trip.

PET-FRIENDLY
PLACES
IN THE U.S. AND CANADA

Dog Parks
Attractions
National Public Lands
Animal Clinics

DOG PARKS

A dog park is a place where people and their dogs can play together. These places offer dogs an area to play, exercise and socialize with other dogs while their owners enjoy the park-like setting. Dog park size and features vary greatly from location to location, from several hundred square feet in urban areas to several hundred acres in the suburbs and rural locations. Dog owners should remember to always keep their animal leashed until they reach the dog park entrance, to maintain voice control of their animal at all times, to bring their own supply of bags for picking up after their pet (and to be diligent in doing so), and to always have fresh water available for their dog. Please observe all dog park rules.

This list of dog parks in the United States and Canada is provided by Dogpark.com®. Dogpark.com is all about dogs — all breeds, all mixes of breeds, and all shapes, sizes and dispositions. It provides articles and information about dogs and their care, health and play. Online, visit www.dogpark.com.

The dog parks listed here welcome people who travel with their dogs; private parks or parks requiring local residency are not included. **Note:** Fence types and heights vary, and some areas have no fencing at all, requiring that the dog be under firm voice control.

United States

ARIZONA

Chaparral Park - Scottsdale
5401 N. Hayden Rd., (at the southeast corner of McDonald Drive and Hayden Road)
Daily sunrise-9 p.m.
2.2 acres, fenced, separate small and large dog areas, shade, water, benches, restroom.

Horizon Park - Scottsdale
15444 N. 100th St. (Thompson Peak Parkway and 100th Street, east of SR 101 off Frank Lloyd Wright Boulevard)
Daily sunrise-10:30 p.m.
Fenced, benches, tables, disposal bags, parking, phones, restrooms, lighted, trash cans, bring your own water, little shade.

Vista del Camino Park - Scottsdale
7700 East Pierce St.; take Pierce Street heading west from Hayden Road
Daily sunrise-10:30 p.m.
Drinking fountains (one for people and one for pooches), benches, mutt mitt stations, lighted. The fenced-in area is all turf and just under an acre in size. Restroom facilities nearby.

Creamery Park - Tempe
tempe.gov/pkrec/parkfacil/offleash.htm
8th Street and Una Avenue (just south of University near Rural)
Daily 6 a.m.-midnight
Fenced, benches, disposal bags, parking, lighted, water, trash cans.

Jaycee Park - Tempe
tempe.gov/pkrec/parkfacil/offleash.htm
5th Street and Hardy Drive
Daily 6 a.m.-midnight
Fenced, benches, disposal bags, trees, parking, lighted, water, trash cans. Access for the disabled.

Mitchell Park - Tempe
tempe.gov/pkrec/parkfacil/offleash.htm
Mitchell Drive and 9th Street
Daily 6 a.m.-midnight
Fenced, benches, disposal bags, trees, parking, lighted, water, trash cans. Access for the disabled.

Papago Park - Tempe
tempe.gov/pkrec/parkfacil/offleash.htm
Curry Road and College Avenue
Daily 6 a.m.-midnight
Fenced, disposal bags, trees, parking, lighted, water, trash cans. Access for the disabled.

CALIFORNIA

Calabasas Bark Park - Calabasas
ci.calabasas.ca.us/recreation/barkpark.html
4232 Las Virgenes Rd., south of the Las Virgenes Municipal Water District (approximately 2 miles west of US 101 on the south side)
Daily 5 a.m.-9 p.m.
Fenced, benches, trees, parking, lighted, water, trash cans, scoops, doggie drinking fountain.

Claremont Pooch Park - Claremont
ClaremontPOOCHPark.org
100 S. College Ave. (just north of Arrow Highway)
Daily 7 a.m.-9 p.m.
Tree-lined park, fully fenced with double-gated entry. Ample parking, lots of benches, water, disposal bags and trash cans provided. Access for the disabled.

Costa Mesa Bark Park - Costa Mesa
cmbarkpark.org, hotline (949) 733-4101
Arlington Drive and Newport Boulevard, across from the Orange County Fairgrounds Equestrian Center
Wed.-Mon. dawn-dusk; phone ahead in rainy conditions
Fenced, benches, tables, disposal bags, trees, parking, restrooms, water, trash cans, grass surface, 2.1 acres. Access for the disabled.

Elizabeth Anne Perrone Dog Park - Glen Ellen
sonoma-county.org/PARKS/foundation/
perrone_dog_park.htm
13630 Sonoma Hwy. in Sonoma Valley Regional Park
(SR 12 between Arnold Drive and Madrone Road)
Daily sunrise-sunset
Fully fenced, 1 acre, double-gated entry, doggy
drinking fountain.

Huntington Dog Beach - Huntington Beach
dogbeach.org
Pacific Coast Highway between 21st and Seapoint
streets
Daily 5 a.m.-8 p.m.
Benches and tables on the bluffs above the beach,
disposal bags, metered parking, restrooms, trash cans.
Dogs may be off leash in the water and on the wet
sand. Access for the disabled to the sand.

Laguna Niguel Pooch Park - Laguna Niguel
ci.laguna-niguel.ca.us/index.asp?SID=481
31461 Golden Lantern near Chapparosa Park
Tues.-Thurs. and Sat. 7 a.m.-dusk, Sun. 8 a.m.-dusk,
Mon. and Fri. noon-dusk
Fenced, landscaped, water source, 1.1 acres.

Long Beach Recreation Dog Park - Long Beach
geocities.com/lbdogpark
5201 East 7th St. at Park
Daily sunrise-10 p.m.; closed Mon. until noon for
regular maintenance
Fenced, benches, tables, disposal bags, trees,
parking, lighted, water, trash cans, separate fenced
area for small dogs, crushed-granite ground cover.
Access for the disabled.

Palm Springs Dog Park - Palm Springs
ci.palm-springs.ca.us/dogpark.html
222 Civic Dr. North, behind City Hall
Daily dawn-10 p.m.
Fenced, benches, tables, disposal bags, trees,
parking, phones, lighted, water, trash cans, shelter.
Beautiful fence designed and built by sculptor Phill
Evans; dual-level drinking fountains, large and small
dog areas, antique fire hydrants. Access for the
disabled.

**Rancho Cucamonga Dog Park - Rancho
Cucamonga**
North end of East Avenue north of Summit Avenue;
the dog park is part of Etiwanda Creek Park
Daily dawn-dusk
Fences, trees, parking, phones, restrooms, water, dog
washing facility, puppy/small dog area.

Redondo Beach Dog Park - Redondo Beach
rbdogpark.com
Located on the southeast corner of 190th Street and
Flagler Lane
Daily dawn-dusk.; closed Wed. dawn-noon for
maintenance
Fences, benches, disposal bags, trees, parking,
phones, water, trash cans, separate fenced small dog
area. Access for the disabled.

Bannon Creek Dog Park - Sacramento
cityofsacramento.org/parksandrecreation/parks/
dogpark1.htm
In Bannon Creek Park on Bannon Creek Drive, off of
Azevedo Drive (near West El Camino)
Daily sunrise-10 p.m.
Well-fenced, about a half-acre, bench, water spigot for
dogs, trash cans, disposal bags. Access for the
disabled.

Granite Dog Park - Sacramento
cityofsacramento.org/parksandrecreation/parks/
dogpark1.htm
On Ramona Avenue off Power Inn Road (in Granite
Regional Park)
Daily sunrise-10 p.m.
Fenced, 2 acres, bench, water spigot for dogs, trash
cans, disposal bags. Access for the disabled.

Partner Park - Sacramento
cityofsacramento.org/parksandrecreation/parks/
dogpark1.htm
5699 South Land Park Dr. (at Fruitridge Road), behind
Belle Cooledge Community Center
Daily sunrise-10 p.m.
Fenced, lighted, over 2 acres, landscaped with turf
and mature trees, bench, water spigot for dogs, trash
cans, disposal bags. Access for the disabled.

Balboa Park - San Diego
ci.san-diego.ca.us/park-and-recreation/general-info/
dogs.shtml
There are two off-leash areas within Balboa Park:
Nate's Point at El Prado, on the south side of Cabrillo
Bridge; and Morley Field, northwest of the tennis
courts.
Daily 24 hours
Large field.

Cadman Community Park - San Diego
ci.san-diego.ca.us/park-and-recreation/general-info/
dogs.shtml
4280 Avati Dr.
During the school year: daily 7:30-10 a.m. and 4:30-7
p.m. Summer vacation: daily 7-9:30 a.m. and 5-7:30
p.m. There are no leash-free hours on July 4th and
Saturdays from March 1-June 15.
Unfenced.

Dog Beach - San Diego
ci.san-diego.ca.us/park-and-recreation/general-info/
dogs.shtml
Beach area is located in Ocean Beach at the west
end of Voltaire Street; enter the parking lot at the west
end of Voltaire Street.
Daily 24 hours
Disposal bags, trash cans, water, restrooms nearby.
Access for the disabled.

Fiesta Island - San Diego
ci.san-diego.ca.us/park-and-recreation/general-info/
dogs.shtml
This island in Mission Bay Park allows dogs anywhere
outside the fenced areas.
Daily 6 a.m.-10 p.m.

Grape Street Park - San Diego
ci.san-diego.ca.us/park-and-recreation/general-info/
dogs.shtml
Grape Street and Granada Avenue
Mon.-Fri. 7:30-10 a.m. and 4-9 p.m., Sat.-Sun. and
holidays 9-11 a.m. and 4-9 p.m.
Benches, tables, trees, parking, restrooms, lighted,
water, trash cans.

Alamo Square Park - San Francisco
sfgov.org/site/recpark_index.asp?id=1448
Western half of the park, along Scott Street between
Hayes and Fulton streets
Daily 6 a.m.-10 p.m.
Unfenced; dogs must be under firm voice control.

Alta Plaza Park - San Francisco
sfgov.org/site/recpark_index.asp?id=14486
Second terrace of park, on Clay Street between Scott
and Steiner streets
Daily 6 a.m.-10 p.m.
Unfenced; dogs must be under firm voice control.

Bernal Heights - San Francisco
sfgov.org/site/recpark_index.asp?id=1448
Top of the hill (the entire section bounded by Bernal
Heights Boulevard)
Daily 6 a.m.-10 p.m.
Unfenced; dogs must be under firm voice control.

Buena Vista Park - San Francisco
sfgov.org/site/recpark_index.asp?id=1448
Buena Vista West at Central Avenue
Daily 6 a.m.-10 p.m.
Unfenced; dogs must be under firm voice control.

Corona Heights - San Francisco
sfgov.org/site/recpark_index.asp?id=14486
Field area next to Randall Museum at Roosevelt Way
and Museum Way
Daily 6 a.m.-10 p.m.
Fenced area.

Crocker Amazon Playground - San Francisco
sfgov.org/site/recpark_index.asp?id=1448
Northern portion of park, between LaGrande and
Dublin streets, adjacent to community garden
Daily 6 a.m.-10 p.m.
Unfenced; dogs must be under firm voice control.

Dolores Park - San Francisco
sfgov.org/site/recpark_index.asp?id=1448
South of the tennis courts between Church and
Dolores streets
Daily 6 a.m.-10 p.m.
Unfenced; dogs must be under firm voice control.

Douglass Park - San Francisco
fgov.org/site/recpark_index.asp?id=1448
Upper field at 27th and Douglass streets
Daily 6 a.m.-10 p.m.
Unfenced; dogs must be under firm voice control.

Eureka Valley Recreation Center - San Francisco
sfgov.org/site/recpark_index.asp?id=1448
On Collingwood side of park, adjacent to the tennis
courts.
Daily 6 a.m.-10 p.m.
Fenced area.

Golden Gate Park - San Francisco
sfgov.org/site/recpark_index.asp?id=1448
Southeast section bounded by Lincoln Way, King
Drive and 2nd and 7th avenues
Northeast section at Stanyan and Grove streets
South-central area bounded by Martin Luther King Jr.
Drive, Middle Drive and 34th and 38th avenues
Fenced dog training area near 38th Avenue and
Fulton Street.

Lafayette Park - San Francisco
sfgov.org/site/recpark_index.asp?id=1448
Near Sacramento Street, between Octavia and Gough
streets
Daily 6 a.m.-10 p.m.
Unfenced; dogs must be under firm voice control.

Lake Merced - San Francisco
sfgov.org/site/recpark_index.asp?id=1448
Northern lake area at Lake Merced Boulevard and
Middlefield Drive
Daily 6 a.m.-10 p.m.
Unfenced area; dogs must be under firm voice control.

McKinley Square - San Francisco
sfgov.org/site/recpark_index.asp?id=1448
San Bruno Avenue and 20th Street, on the west slope
Daily 6 a.m.-10 p.m.
Unfenced area; dogs must be under firm voice control.

McLaren Park - San Francisco
sfgov.org/site/recpark_index.asp?id=1448
The area bounded by Shelly Drive and Mansell
Avenue at the top of the hill
Daily 6 a.m.-10 p.m.
Unfenced area; dogs must be under firm voice control.

Mountain Lake Park - San Francisco
sfgov.org/site/recpark_index.asp?id=1448
East end of park, north of Lake Street at 8th Avenue
Daily 6 a.m.-10 p.m.
Unfenced area; dogs must be under firm voice control.

Pine Lake Park - San Francisco
sfgov.org/site/recpark_index.asp?id=1448
Second terrace of park, west of and contiguous to
Stern Grove, and adjacent to the parking lot entered
via Crestlake and Vale streets
Daily 6 a.m.-10 p.m.
Unfenced area; dogs must be under firm voice control.

Potrero Hill Mini Park - San Francisco
sfgov.org/site/recpark_index.asp?id=1448
22nd Street between Arkansas and Connecticut
streets
Daily 6 a.m.-10 p.m.
Unfenced area; dogs must be under firm voice control.

Stern Grove - San Francisco
sfgov.org/site/recpark_index.asp?id=1448
North side, along Wawona Street between 21st and
23rd avenues
Daily 6 a.m.-10 p.m.
Unfenced area; dogs must be under firm voice control.

St. Mary's Recreation Center - San Francisco
sfgov.org/site/recpark_index.asp?id=1448
Lower terrace of park (enter at Justin and Benton
Streets)
Daily 6 a.m.-10 p.m.
Fenced area.

Upper Noe Recreation Center - San Francisco
sfgov.org/site/recpark_index.asp?id=1448
30th Street between Church and Sanchez streets,
behind and along the baseball field
Daily 6 a.m.-10 p.m.
Fenced area.

Field of Dogs - San Rafael
fieldofdogs.org
3540 Civic Center Dr. near the intersection of US 101
and North San Pedro Road
Daily sunrise-sunset
Fenced, double-gated entry, parking, benches, tables,
disposal bags, trees, parking, water, trash cans,
shelter. Access for the disabled.

DeTurk Roundbarn Park - Santa Rosa
ci.santa-rosa.ca.us/rp/
819 Donahue St. between West 8th and 9th streets
Daily during daylight hours
Fenced, water. This is a small neighborhood park.

Doyle Park Dog Park - Santa Rosa
ci.santa-rosa.ca.us/rp/
700 Hoen Ave. within Doyle Park (Enter via Hoen
Avenue, go west on Sonoma, turn left on Hoen and

Off-leash, unfenced, under voice control areas:

Doyle Park - Santa Rosa
ci.santa-rosa.ca.us/rp/
Mon.-Fri. 6-9 a.m.
Dogs may be off leash but under voice control in the
area in front of the caretaker's residence (designated
by signs and maps in the parking lot).

700 Doyle Park Drive - Santa Rosa
ci.santa-rosa.ca.us/rp/
Enter on Hoen Avenue, go west on Sonoma, turn left
on Hoen and then turn right into the parking lot. There
is an unfenced, off-leash area to the right of the
fenced dog park.
Daily 6-9 a.m., early Apr.-late Oct.

Franklin Park - Santa Rosa
ci.santa-rosa.ca.us/rp/
2095 Franklin Ave.
Daily 6-8 a.m.

Southwest Community - Santa Rosa
ci.santa-rosa.ca.us/rp/
1698 Hearn Ave.
Daily 6-8 a.m.

Youth Community - Santa Rosa
ci.santa-rosa.ca.us/rp/
1725 Fulton Rd.
Daily 6-8 a.m.

Remington Dog Park - Sausalito
dogpark-sausalito.com
Ebbtide at Bridgeway
Mon.-Fri. 7-7, Sat.-Sun. 8-7
Fully fenced with safety gated entrance, water, tents
for shelter, parking, scoops and scooper cleaning
station, trash cans, lighted, tennis balls and racquets
provided, picnic tables and benches.

Sierra Madre Dog Park - Sierra Madre
*ci.sierra-madre.ca.us/departments/
administrative_services/licenses_detail.asp?ID=279*
611 East Sierra Madre Blvd.
Daily 6 a.m.-10 p.m.
Fenced, double-gated entry, benches, disposal bags,
trees, parking, phones, restrooms, lighted, water, trash
cans, separate fenced areas for large/active dogs and
"special needs" dogs. Access for the disabled.

COLORADO

Grandview Off-Leash Dog Park - Aurora
For additional information phone (303) 739-7160
17900 E. Quincy Ave. (west of Quincy Reservoir and
just east of Pitkin Street)
Daily dawn-dusk
Fenced, parking, water, trash cans.

Dog Park - Boulder
fidos.org
Valmont and Airport roads
Daily dawn-dusk
Fenced, disposal bags, parking, trash cans, water.
Access for the disabled.

East Boulder Community - Boulder
fidos.org
5660 Sioux Dr.
Daily dawn-dusk
Fenced, disposal bags, parking, water, trash cans, fenced-off swimming area. Access for the disabled.

Howard H. Hueston Park
fidos.org
34th Street near O'Neal Parkway
Daily dawn-dusk
Benches, tables, trees, parking, trash cans. Access for the disabled.

Palmer Park - Colorado Springs
ci.colospgs.co.us/Page.asp?NavID=2723
At Maizeland Road and Academy Boulevard
Daily 5 a.m.-11 p.m., May-Oct.; 5 a.m.-9 p.m., rest of year
Fenced, benches, tables, parking, water, trash cans, disposal bags, restrooms. Access for the disabled.

Rampart Dog Park - Colorado Springs
ci.colospgs.co.us/Page.asp?NavID=2723
8270 Lexington Dr. (from the intersection of Lexington Drive and N. Union Boulevard, go north on Lexington, then turn left into the park entrance)
Daily 5 a.m.-11 p.m., May-Oct.; 5 a.m.-9 p.m., rest of year
Fenced, benches, trees, parking, disposal bags, water, trash cans. Access for the disabled.

Denver Off-Leash Dog Park - Denver
denvergov.org or email kelledl@ci.denver.co.us for additional information
678 South Jason St. (the large area directly behind the Denver Municipal Animal Shelter)
Daily sunrise-sunset
Fenced, parking, grass, toys. Access for the disabled.

FLORIDA

Happy Tails Canine Park - Bradenton
51st Street West at G.T. Bray Park, about halfway between Manatee Avenue and Cortez Road
Daily dawn-dusk
Approximately 3 acres, 8-foot fence, benches, tables, parking (including handicapped spaces), disposal bags, trees, restrooms (a short walk outside the park), water, trash cans.

Dr. Paul's Pet Care Center Dog Park - Coral Springs
TopPetCare.com
Off Sportsplex Drive in the Sportsplex Regional Park Complex (park off Sportsplex Drive at the west pedestrian entrance)
Daily 7:30 a.m.-sunset
Enclosed, paved running path, watering area, dog shower, dog statues, dog and people water fountains, landscaping, disposal bag dispensers, trash barrels, picnic table, weatherproof dog agility equipment, gazebo, trees, shaded area, restroom adjacent.

The Dog Park in Lake Ida Park - Delray Beach
co.palm-beach.fl.us/parks
2929 Lake Ida Rd. (take the Atlantic Avenue West exit off I-95, proceed west to Congress Avenue, go north on Congress for 1 mile, turn right onto Lake Ida Road, proceed east just past I-95, park entrance is on the left)
Daily sunrise-sunset; closed Thurs. noon-3 for maintenance
2.5 acres, separate fenced areas for large and small dogs, two canine drinking stations, dog washing area, eight shaded sitting areas, partial paved pathway, dispensers and receptacles for disposal bags, restrooms and parking areas nearby, information kiosk.

Bark Park at Snyder Park - Fort Lauderdale
ci.fort-lauderdale.fl.us/cityparks/snyder/barkpark
3299 S.W. 4th Ave. (dogs must remain in the car until arrival at the Bark Park and are not permitted in the remainder of Snyder Park)
Daily 7-7, early Apr.-late Oct.; 7-6:30, rest of year
Fee Mon.-Fri. $1.50; ages 6-12, $1. Fee Sat.-Sun. and holidays $2, $3 including dog swim; ages 6-12, $1.50.
Fenced, benches, trees, disposal bags, parking, restrooms, water, trash cans, agility equipment, separate small dog area, two hose stations, drinking fountains, two open-air pavilions, small nature area with more than 20 labeled native trees. Freshwater dog swim Sat.-Sun. and holidays 10-5, Mar.-Dec. Access for the disabled.

Dog Wood Off-Leash Park - Gainesville
dogwoodpark.com
5505 S.W. Archer Rd., 1 mile west of I-75
Sun. noon-5
Fee $8.25 plus tax for the first dog, $2.50 plus tax for each additional dog
Approximately 15 acres, 6-foot-high chain link fence, double-gated entrances and exits, jogging trail, hammocks, picnic tables, lounge chairs, swinging benches, regular benches, two huge dog swimming ponds, kiddie pools, fountain, gazebo, agility course, sunny and shady small dog areas, dog shower, indoor restrooms, soft drinks for sale, free bottled water, agility equipment, park-provided tennis balls, multiple clean-up stations with disposal bags. Dog Wood Park also offers a do-it-yourself dog wash, a doggie boutique, dog day care, a dog photography studio, and agility and obedience training.

Paw Park of Historic Sanford - Sanford
pawparksanford.org
427 French Ave. (US 17/92) in Sanford's Historic District. From I-4, take the SR 46 exit (exit 101C, Sanford/Mount Dora), proceed east on SR 46 approximately 4 miles to French Avenue, turn right (southbound) and get into the left-thru lane; the Paw Park is on the left just past the Burger King.
Daily 7:30 a.m.-8 p.m.
Fenced, double-gated entrance, benches, tables, self-watering bowls, dog showers, small dog area, disposal bag dispensers, parking, community bulletin board, historic lighting, 20 minutes north of downtown Orlando. Access for the disabled.

Lakeview Park - Sarasota
co.sarasota.fl.us/parks/pawpark.asp
7150 Lago St.
Daily dawn-dusk
Six-foot fence, benches, tables, disposal bags, many trees, parking, restrooms, water, trash cans, dog shower, community bulletin board, small dog area, double-gated entrance. Access for the disabled.

Sarasota Paw Park - Sarasota
co.sarasota.fl.us/parks/pawpark.asp
4570 17th St.
Daily dawn-midnight (lighted)
Approximately 6 acres, 6-foot fence, lighted, benches, tables, disposal bags, trees, parking, restrooms, water, trash cans, dog shower, small dog area, double-gated entrance, community bulletin board. Access for the disabled.

Brohard Beach - Venice
co.sarasota.fl.us/parks/pawpark.asp
1600 Harbor Dr.
Daily dawn-dusk
Boardwalk to beach, parking, trash cans.

Brohard Paw Park - Venice
co.sarasota.fl.us/parks/pawpark.asp
1600 Harbor Dr.
Daily dawn-dusk
Six-foot fence, benches, tables, shelter, disposal bags, trees, parking, water, trash cans, small dog area, dog shower, community bulletin board. Access for the disabled.

Woodmere Paw Park - Venice
co.sarasota.fl.us/parks/pawpark.asp
3951 Merewood Blvd. (at Alligator Creek near Jacaranda)
Daily dawn-dusk
Fenced, double-gated entrance, benches, tables, disposal bags, trees, parking, restrooms, water, trash cans, double-gated small dog section near the front gate, dog shower, community bulletin board. Access for the disabled.

MICHIGAN

Orion Oaks Bark Park - Lake Orion
co.oakland.mi.us/parksrec/activities/bark_pk.html
Off Joslyn Road, south of Clarkston Road (park at the north Joslyn Road entrance and follow the signs)
Daily half an hour before sunrise-half an hour after sunset
A park pass is required. A daily pass is available at the Lake Orion Township office (open Mon.-Fri.), located on Joslyn Road south of the park; or at Independence Oaks County Park (open daily), located on Sashabaw Road 2 1/2 miles north of I-75. Resident fee $5 per day, $28 for an annual pass. Non-resident fee $10 per vehicle for daily entry, $49 for an annual pass; over 62, $3 per vehicle for daily entry, $23 for an annual pass. Fenced, 7 acres, benches, tables, disposal bags, trees, water source, parking, Portajohns, trash cans. Access for the disabled. A portion of Lake Sixteen is reserved for canine swimmers.

Lyon Oaks Bark Park - Lyon Township
co.oakland.mi.us/parksrec/activities/bark_pk.html
Pontiac Trail, between Wixom and Old Plank roads
Daily half an hour before sunrise-half an hour after sunset
A park pass is required; daily and annual passes are available at the park. Resident fee $5 per day, $28 for an annual pass. Non-resident fee $10 per vehicle for daily entry, $49 for an annual pass; over 62, $3 per vehicle for daily entry, $23 for an annual pass. 13 acres, fenced, benches, tables, disposal bags, parking, restrooms, trash cans, open fields, water pump available spring 2004.

MINNESOTA

Note: In the greater Minneapolis area there are eight off-leash sites located within a 15-minute drive of downtown Minneapolis/St. Paul. There are an additional seven sites located in rural/suburban areas of the seven-county metropolitan area. Some sites require permits for off-leash use and/or parking; others have no permit requirements. Please read descriptions carefully.

Minneapolis dog parks: All Minneapolis dog parks require a permit for use. The Minnehaha site also requires a permit for parking. For Minneapolis dog park permit information phone (612) 348-4250. Nearby dog parks in St. Paul, Maplewood, Shoreview, Roseville and Bloomington do not require a permit for use.

Bloomington Off-Leash Area - Bloomington (south metro suburb)
ci.bloomington.mn.us/cityhall/dept/commserv/parkrec/parks/sigsites/offleash.htm
111th and Nesbitt
Daily dawn-10 p.m.
Approximately 25 acres, partially fenced, tables, disposal bags, trees, parking, trash cans, swimming hole available. Access for the disabled.

Alimagnet Dog Park - Burnsville (south metro suburb)
alimagnetdogpark.org
1200 Alimagnet Pkwy. (Cross street is County Road 11; from central St. Paul, proceed south on I-35E to the County Road 42 exit. Proceed east to County Road 11, then go north on County Road 11 to Alimagnet Parkway and turn right. The dog park will be on the right.)
Daily 5 a.m.-10 p.m.
7 acres, fenced, benches, tables, disposal bags, trees, water, phones, restrooms, parking, trash cans, pond, wooded areas, open field, mowed prairie grass trail, double-gated entrance. A permit is required; phone the Recreation Department at (952) 895-4500.

Elm Creek Park Reserve - Dayton (northwest metro rural)
threeriversparkdistrict.org/trails/trails_pet.cfm
Daily 5 a.m.-sunset
Fenced, tables, trees, parking, restrooms, trash cans. Over 30 acres with mowed trail through area. Use is by permit only; day permits are available at the site. For an annual special use permit phone Park Guest Services at (763) 559-9000.

Battle Creek Off-Leash Site - Maplewood (east central metro)
co.ramsey.mn.us/parks/parks/offleash.asp
Lower Afton and McKnight
Daily sunrise-sunset
12 acres, partially fenced, tables, parking, trash cans. No permit required.

Columbia Park - Minneapolis
dogromp.org
St. Anthony Parkway off Central Avenue
Daily 6 a.m.-10 p.m.
Approximately 2 acres, double-gated entry at the east and west ends of the park, fully fenced, parking, disposal bag dispensers, bench.

Franklin Terrace - Minneapolis
dogromp.org
Franklin Terrace and 30th Avenue S.
Daily 6 a.m.-10 p.m.
2.6 acres, fully fenced, double-gated entry at the east and west ends of the site, disposal bag dispensers, bench, on-street parking.

Lake of the Isles Park - Minneapolis
dogromp.org
Lake of the Isles Parkway and W. 28th Street
Daily 6 a.m.-10 p.m.
2.6 acres, fully fenced, two double-gated entry vestibules at the northern end of the site, lighted at the southern end, disposal bag dispensers, benches.

Minnehaha Park - Minneapolis
dogromp.org
Minnehaha Avenue and E. 54th Street
Daily 6 a.m.-10 p.m.
Approximately 4.2 acres along the Mississippi River (where dogs can swim), partially fenced, disposal bag dispensers, lighted parking area (permit required), Portajohn in parking area.

Egan Park's Off-Leash Area - Plymouth
http://www2.ci.plymouth.mn.us, Parks & Recreation Dept. phone (763) 509-5200
Located in northwest Plymouth on the south side of County Road 47, about two blocks west of Dunkirk Lane
Daily sunrise-sunset
10 acres, unfenced area, trash cans, bring your own water. No permit required.

Cleary Lake Regional Park - Prior Lake (south metro rural)
threeriversparkdistrict.org/trails/trails_pet.cfm
Daily 5 a.m.-sunset
35 acres with pond, fenced, tables, parking, restrooms, trash cans. Trails are mowed in summer, packed in winter. Annual pet exercise area permit or daily use fee required; day permits are available at the site. For an annual special use permit phone Park Guest Services at (763) 559-9000.

Lake Sarah Regional Park - Rockford (west metro rural)
threeriversparkdistrict.org/trails/trails_pet.cfm
Approximately 30 miles west of Minneapolis and east of County Road 92 (Take US 55 west to County Road 92, proceed south to Lake Sarah Drive, turn left and then turn left again onto the first gravel road; the parking lot for the off-leash area is on the left-hand side.)
Daily 5 a.m.-sunset
Trees, parking, restrooms, trash cans. Over 30 acres with mowed parking area. Use is by permit only; day permits are available at the site. For an annual special use permit phone Park Guest Services at (763) 559-9000.

Crow-Hassan Park Reserve - Rogers (northwest metro rural)
threeriversparkdistrict.org/trails/trails_pet.fmc
West of Rogers on Sylvan Lake Road (From I-94, take the Rogers exit and go south through town to the T intersection. Turn right on County Road 116 and proceed to County Road 203. Turn left and follow County Road 203 to the park entrance.)
Daily 5 a.m.-sunset
Fenced, tables, trees, parking, restrooms, trash cans. Over 30 acres with a mowed trail through the area. Use is by permit only; day permits are available at the site. For an annual special use permit phone Park Guest Services at (763) 559-9000.

Woodview Dog Park - Roseville (central)
co.ramsey.mn.us/parks/parks/offleash.asp
Located off Larpenteur Avenue, just east of Dale Street (access gate to main off-leash area is about 100 yards down the bike trail)
Daily sunrise-sunset
Partially fenced (along bike trail only), 3 acres, disposal bags, trees, water, tables, parking, trash cans. Small dog area (fenced). Access for the disabled. No permit required.

Rice Creek Off-Leash Site - Shoreview (northeast metro)
co.ramsey.mn.us/parks/parks/offleash.asp
Located just south of County Road J on Lexington Avenue
Daily sunrise-sunset
12 acres, not fenced, tables, parking, trash cans, flat with prairie vegetation, small pond. No permit required.

Arlington-Arkwright (ArlArk) Dog Park - St. Paul
dogromp.org
Located on Arkwright Street at Arlington Avenue (From I-35E, take the Maryland Avenue exit east to Arkwright Street, then go north; the park is on the right-hand side.)
Daily sunrise-9 p.m.
Fenced, 4.5-acre site with trails and woods, disposal bags, tables, parking, trash cans. There are multiple entrances, and park users sometimes leave the gates open; be sure you have voice control of your dog to prevent escapes. No permit required.

NEVADA

Desert Breeze Park - Las Vegas
accessclarkcounty.com, (702) 455-8200
8425 W. Spring Mountain Rd. (at Durango)
Daily 6 a.m.-11 p.m.
Three dog runs, two open at any one time (one for large and one for small dogs). Runs are fenced and include benches, lights and water.

Desert Inn Dog Park - Las Vegas
accessclarkcounty.com, (702) 455-8200
3570 Vista del Monte
Daily 6 a.m.-11 p.m.
Fenced, water, benches.

Dog Fancier's Park - Las Vegas
accessclarkcounty.com, (702) 455-8200
5800 E. Flamingo Rd. (cross streets Flamingo and Stepanie)
Daily 6 a.m.-11 p.m.
12-acre park used for dog shows and training. There is a separate fenced dog run area.
Groups often reserve the park for dog shows and related activities including canine trials, agility training and club meetings. For information on upcoming events, phone the 24-hour Dog Fancier's hotline at (702) 564-3647. To reserve the park for a canine-related event, leave a message for Patti Pickerd at (702) 367-6796.

Shadow Rock Dog Park - Las Vegas
accessclarkcounty.com, (702) 455-8200
2650 Los Feliz (cross streets Lake Mead past Hollywood)
Daily dawn-dusk
Fenced dog run is located east of the park area. Benches, trash cans, water.

Silverado Ranch Park Dog Park (Central SE) - Las Vegas
accessclarkcounty.com, (702) 455-8200
9855 S. Gillespie
Daily 6 a.m.-11 p.m.
Dog runs are fenced and include benches, lights and water. Two runs are available, one for dogs under 30 pounds and the other for dogs over 30 pounds.

Sunset Park (SE) - Las Vegas
accessclarkcounty.com, (702) 455-8200
2601 E. Sunset Rd.
Daily 6 a.m.-11 p.m.
Two dog runs for large and small breeds. Fenced, benches, tables, nearby restrooms, lights, water. The closest parking to the dog park is off Eastern between Sunset Road and Warm Springs Road.

NEW YORK

New York City (Manhattan & boroughs)
urbanhound.com
nycgovparks.org/sub_things_to_do/facilities/af_dog_runs.html

Ewen Park ("John's Run"), Riverdale - Bronx
Riverdale to Johnson avenues, south of West 232nd Street and down the steps in the clearing on the right
Daily dawn-dusk
Plastic lawn furniture, scenic views.

Seton Park, Riverdale - Bronx
West 235th Street and Independence Avenue (west of Independence on 235th Street, near the Spuyten Duyvil Library)
Daily dawn-dusk

Canine Court, Van Cortlandt Park - Bronx
West 252nd Street and Broadway (enter on the path on 252nd and follow it about 100 feet to the left)
Daily dawn-dusk
Two huge runs, a basic dog run and a canine agility playground with a teeter-totter, hurdles, a ladder, three chutes and a hanging tire.

Owl's Head Park, Bay Ridge - Brooklyn
68th Street and Shore Road
Disposal bags, tree, grass surface.

Hillside Park, Brooklyn Heights - Brooklyn
Columbia Heights and Middagh Street
Daily 24 hours
Fenced.

Palmetto Playground, Brooklyn Heights - Brooklyn
Columbia Place and State Street (in a corner by the BQE)
Daily 24 hours
Water supply, four benches, one park light.

Prospect Park, Brooklyn Heights - Brooklyn
fidobrooklyn.org, 888-604-3422
Grand Army Plaza and Flatbush; off-leash areas may be accessed from all park entrances
Off-leash times: daily 9 p.m.-9 a.m., Apr.-Oct.; 5 p.m.-9 a.m., rest of year (in the 80-acre Long Meadow and 6-acre Peninsula Meadow). Dogs may be off-leash in the 15-acre Nethermead Mon.-Fri. 5 p.m -9 a.m. year-round (except holidays). On holidays and weekends, the hours above apply to Nethermead as well. At all other times, dogs must be on a leash; minimum fine for non-compliance is $100. There are no fenced or small dog areas. There is a small swimming area in the Long Meadow near the 9th Street entrance. Trees, restrooms (at Long Meadow only; may not be available early in the morning), water (some fountains equipped with troughs for dogs).
Note: Use of the area is at the dog owner's risk. Dogs may be off-leash with appropriate supervision in three large meadows at the hours specified above; please observe all off-leash rules. Dogs must be on a leash at all other places and times.

Carl Shurz Park, Upper East Side - Manhattan
East 86th Street at East End Avenue
Daily dawn-1 a.m.
Benches, scoops, pea gravel surface. Past the main run, toward the East River, is a second run for small dogs that has a superb view of the river and the 59th Street Bridge.

Fishbridge Park, Lower East Side - Manhattan
Dover Street at Pearl Street, just south of the Brooklyn Bridge
Daily dawn-dusk
Water hose, wading pool (summer only), benches, lockbox for toys, lockbox with newspapers for picking up after your dog.

**J. Hood Wright Park, Inwood/Ft. George/
Washington Heights - Manhattan**
West 173rd Street between Fort Washington Avenue
and Haven Avenue

**Madison Square Park, Gramercy/Flatiron/Union
Square - Manhattan**
East 24th Street at Fifth Avenue
Daily 6 a.m.-midnight
Disposal bags, water supply, benches, trees.

Peter Detmold Park, Midtown East - Manhattan
East 49th Street at FDR Drive (behind Beeckman
Place)
Daily dawn-9 p.m., June-Sept.; dawn-8 p.m., Mar.-May
and Oct.-Nov.; dawn-7 p.m., rest of year
Benches, disposal bags, trees, historical lamps.

**Riverside Park at 72nd Street, Upper West
Side/Morningside Heights - Manhattan**
West 72nd Street
Daily 6 a.m.-1 a.m.
Bench, disposal bags, scoopers, hanging flowerpots.

**Riverside Park at 87th Street, Upper West
Side/Morningside Heights - Manhattan**
West 87th Street
Daily dawn-dusk
Separate large and small dog areas, fountain and
hose.

**Riverside Park at 105th Street, Upper West
Side/Morningside Heights - Manhattan**
riversidedog.org
West 105th Street, Riverside Park Central Promenade
Daily dawn-dusk
Water fountain for dogs, small dog area, disposal bag
dispensers, benches, trees, crushed granite surface.

**Theodore Roosevelt Park, Upper West Side/
Morningside Heights - Manhattan**
West 81st Street at Columbus Avenue
Daily 8 a.m.-10 p.m.
Water faucets for dogs, a water fountain for humans,
many benches, a separate run for small dogs, shade
trees.

Thomas Jefferson Park, Harlem - Manhattan
East 112th Street at First Avenue
Daily 24 hours
Benches, wood chips.

Tompkins Square Park, East Village - Manhattan
East 9th Street at Avenue B
Daily 6 a.m.-midnight
Benches, picnic tables, water, a dog memorial.

Washington Square Park, West Village - Manhattan
West 4th Street at Thompson Street
Daily 6 a.m.-midnight
Benches, trees, water hose, water bowls, scoopers,
pea gravel surface.

Doughboy Plaza, Woodside - Queens
Windmuller Park
Woodside Avenue from 54th to 56th streets (also
south of Woodside at 56th Street)
Daily dawn-dusk
Fenced, trash can.

NORTH CAROLINA

French Broad River Link Dog Park - Asheville
ci.asheville.nc.us/parks/parks&play_areas.htm
Within French Broad River Link Park (closest cross
streets are Amboy and Lyman)
Daily dawn-dusk
Fenced, benches, disposal bags, trees, parking,
restrooms, water, trash cans, scenic views of the
French Broad River, convenient to downtown
Asheville.

OHIO

Mt. Airy Dog Park - Cincinnati
cincinnati-oh.gov/parks
Located within Mt. Airy Forest's Highpoint Picnic Area
on Westwood Northern Boulevard, between Montana
Avenue and North Bend Road
Daily dawn-dusk
Fenced, benches, tables, trees, parking, restrooms,
water, trash cans, shelter. Access for the disabled.

Upper Arlington (all city public parks)
ua-ohio.net
Daily after 8 p.m., early Apr.-late Oct.; after 5 p.m.,
rest of year
No fenced areas; dogs must be under voice control at
all times when off-leash, and owners must bring their
own disposal bags.

OREGON

Alton Baker Park - Eugene
ci.eugene.or.us
South of Leo Harris Parkway
Daily 6 a.m.-11 p.m.
Fenced, parking, water, disposal bag receptacles,
benches and/or tables and simple shelters for
protection from sun/rain. Park in the lot south of
Autzen Stadium and cross the pedestrian bridge to
the dog park.

Amazon Park - Eugene
ci.eugene.or.us
East of 29th Street and Amazon Parkway
Daily 6 a.m.-11 p.m.
Fenced, water, disposal bag receptacles, benches
and/or tables and simple shelters for protection from
sun/rain, parking nearby.

Morse Ranch - Eugene
ci.eugene.or.us
Crest Drive and Lincoln Street (park in the main
parking area at 595 Crest Dr. and take the trail east)
Daily 6 a.m.-11 p.m.
Fenced, water, disposal bag receptacles, benches
and/or tables and simple shelters for protection from
sun/rain.

Chimney Park - Portland
*parks.ci.portland.or.us/DogsinParks/yes_sites/
Chimney.htm*
9360 N. Columbia Blvd.
6 acres of off-leash meadow and trails. Not fenced;
dogs should be under excellent voice command.

East Delta Park - Portland
parks.ci.portland.or.us/DogsinParks/yes_sites/Eastdelta.htm
N. Denver and Martin Luther King Jr. Boulevard
5-acre, fenced field with trees and benches is located off I-5 exit 307 on I-5 across from the East Delta Sports Complex. Water is not available. Open during dry season only, May-October. Dogs are not allowed on the sports fields.

Gabriel Park - Portland
parks.ci.portland.or.us/DogsinParks/yes_sites/Gabriel.htm
S.W. 45th Street and Vermont
The 1.5-acre, fenced, off-leash area has trees, picnic tables, and water. Open during dry season only, May-October. Dogs must remain leashed when not in the off-leash area.

West Delta Park - Portland
parks.ci.portland.or.us/DogsinParks/yes_sites/Westdelta.htm
North Expo and Broadacre roads (located just north of Portland International Raceway)
Off-leash site, large open field, not fenced; dogs should be under excellent voice command.

TEXAS

White Rock Lake Dog Park - Dallas
dallasdogparks.org
Mockingbird Point within White Rock Lake Park
Tues.-Sun. 5 a.m.-midnight
Approximately 2 1/2 acres, fenced, benches, disposal bags, trees, parking, restrooms, trash cans, water fountains.

VIRGINIA

Ben Brenman Park - Alexandria
ci.alexandria.va.us/recreation/parks/dogpark.html#fenced
Along Backlick Creek
Daily 6 a.m.-10 p.m.
Fenced, trash bins, parking, disposal bag dispensers.

Dog Park - Alexandria
ci.alexandria.va.us/recreation/parks/dogpark.html#fenced
5000 block of Duke Street east of the Charles E. Beatley, Jr. Library
Daily 6 a.m.-10 p.m.
Fenced, trash bins, parking, disposal bag dispensers.

Montgomery Park - Alexandria
ci.alexandria.va.us/recreation/parks/dogpark.html#fenced
At the corner of Fairfax and 1st streets
Daily 6 a.m.-10 p.m.
Fenced, trash bins, parking, disposal bag dispensers.

Simpson Stadium Park - Alexandria
ci.alexandria.va.us/recreation/parks/dogpark.html#fenced
At Monroe Avenue
Daily 6 a.m.-10 p.m.
Fenced, trash bins, parking, disposal bag dispensers, dog-accessible water fountains.

Off-leash, unfenced, under voice control areas:

Chinquapin Park - Alexandria
ci.alexandria.va.us/recreation/parks/dogpark.html#unfenced
At the east end of the loop road
Daily 6 a.m.-10 p.m.
Unfenced site.

Hooff's Run - Alexandria
ci.alexandria.va.us/recreation/parks/dogpark.html#unfenced
East of Commonwealth Avenue between Oak and Chapman streets
Daily 6 a.m.-10 p.m.
Unfenced site. Please note area is marked by bollards.

Monticello Park - Alexandria
ci.alexandria.va.us/recreation/parks/dogpark.html#unfenced
Area to the east of the entrance
Daily 6 a.m.-10 p.m.
Unfenced 50-foot by 200-foot site. Please note area is marked by bollards.

Tarleton Park - Alexandria
ci.alexandria.va.us/recreation/parks/dogpark.html#unfenced
Along Old Mill Run west of Gordon Street
Daily 6 a.m.-10 p.m.
Unfenced site.

WindMill Hill Park - Alexandria
ci.alexandria.va.us/recreation/parks/dogpark.html#unfenced
Gibbon and Union streets
Daily 6 a.m.-10 p.m.
Unfenced site.

Dog exercise area - Alexandria
ci.alexandria.va.us/recreation/parks/dogpark.html#unfenced
Northeast corner of Founders Park (at Oronoco Street and the Potomac River)
Daily 6 a.m.-10 p.m.
Unfenced 100-foot by 100-foot site. Please note area is marked by bollards.

Dog exercise area - Alexandria
ci.alexandria.va.us/recreation/parks/dogpark.html#unfenced
Southeast corner of Braddock Road and Commonwealth Avenue
Daily 6 a.m.-10 p.m.
Unfenced site.

Dog exercise area - Alexandria
ci.alexandria.va.us/recreation/parks/dogpark.html#unfenced
Area between Ft. Williams and New Ft. Williams Parkway
Daily 6 a.m.-10 p.m.
Unfenced site. Please note area is marked by bollards.

Dog exercise area - Alexandria
ci.alexandria.va.us/recreation/parks/dogpark.html#unfenced
Southeast corner of Armistead and Beauregard streets
Daily 6 a.m.-10 p.m.
Unfenced site.

Dog exercise area - Alexandria
ci.alexandria.va.us/recreation/parks/
dogpark.html#unfenced
Along Chambliss Street, south of the tennis courts at
Grigsby Avenue
Daily 6 a.m.-10 p.m.
Unfenced site. Please note area is marked by
bollards.

Dog exercise area - Alexandria
ci.alexandria.va.us/recreation/parks/
dogpark.html#unfenced
East side of entrance to Fort Ward Park
Daily 6 a.m.-10 p.m.
Unfenced 100-foot by 100-foot site. Please note area
is marked by bollards.

Dog exercise area - Alexandria
ci.alexandria.va.us/recreation/parks/
dogpark.html#unfenced
From Median to Timberbranch Parkway between
Braddock Road and Oakley Place
Daily 6 a.m.-10 p.m.
Unfenced site. Please note area is marked by
bollards.

Dog exercise area - Alexandria
ci.alexandria.va.us/recreation/parks/
dogpark.html#unfenced
Area west of the Edison Street cul-de-sac, between
the bike trail and Berkey Photo Processing
Daily 6 a.m.-10 p.m.
Unfenced site. Please note area is marked by
bollards.

Dog exercise area - Alexandria
ci.alexandria.va.us/recreation/parks/
dogpark.html#unfenced
200 feet of the W&OD Railroad right-of-way located
south of Raymond Avenue
Daily 6 a.m.-10 p.m.
Unfenced site. Please note area is marked by
bollards.

Benjamin Banneker Park - Arlington County
arlingtondogs.org
1600 block of North Sycamore Street (Take I-66 west
to Sycamore Street/exit 69. Turn left on Sycamore
and proceed past the East Falls Church Metro Station.
Turn right onto North 16th Street and take the first
right, which dead-ends at the dog exercise area.)
Daily sunrise to a half-hour after sunset
Fully fenced, water source, picnic table and benches.

Fort Barnard Park - Arlington County
arlingtondogs.org
Corner of South Pollard Street and South Walter Reed
Drive (From Route 50, take Glebe Road south. Turn
right on South Walter Reed Drive and proceed to
Pollard Street; the park is on the right-hand side.)
Daily sunrise to a half-hour after sunset
Fully fenced, water source, picnic table and benches.

Glencarlyn Park - Arlington County
arlingtondogs.org
301 South Harrison St. (From Route 50, head west to
the Carlin Springs Road exit. Exit right and then turn
left at the stop sign. Pass under Route 50 and follow
Carlin Springs to 4th Street. Turn left on 4th Street
and proceed five blocks until the road ends at the
Glencarlyn Park sign. Follow the park road until it
ends. Park and walk over a small bridge and stream
to the exercise area.)
Daily sunrise to a half-hour after sunset
Unfenced area located near a creek and woods,
picnic table and benches.

Madison Community Center - Arlington County
arlingtondogs.org
3829 North Stafford St. (From Lee Highway/US 29
northbound or southbound, turn onto Military Road
and follow it to the end. Turn left onto Old Glebe
Road; the exercise area is on the left. Drive past and
turn left into the Community Center entrance. Park in
the center's front lot and walk to the left of the
building to enter the area.)
Daily sunrise to a half-hour after sunset
Fully fenced.

Shirlington Park - Arlington County
arlingtondogs.org
2601 S. Arlington Mill Dr. (The dog area is located
along the bicycle path behind a storage facility that
borders South Four Mile Run, between Shirlington
Road and South Walter Reed Drive; it is close to but
not in Jennie Dean Park. Heading east on South Four
Mile Run, take a right on Nelson; if heading west on
South Four Mile Run, take a left. Proceed on Nelson
and park behind the storage facility. The dog area is
between the facility and the water; there is no signage
indicating its location.)
Daily sunrise to a half-hour after sunset
Partially fenced, water source, picnic table and
benches.

Utah Park - Arlington County
arlingtondogs.org
3308 S. Stafford St. (From I-395 North or South, take
the Shirlington exit and follow signs to Quaker Lane.
From Quaker Lane, take the first right onto 32nd
Road S. Take the next right onto S. Stafford Street
and follow the curve to the yield sign. At the sign, turn
left onto 32nd Street. Park at the bottom of the hill or
along the street. The dog exercise area is on the far
side of the softball diamond from the parking lot.)
Daily sunrise to a half-hour after sunset
Fully fenced, water source, picnic table and benches.

Blake Lake Park - Oakton
10033 Blake Ln. (near Bushman Drive)
Daily sunrise-sunset
Approximately 1/3 acre, fully fenced, benches, parking,
trash cans. Children under 9 are not permitted.
Capacity limited to 25 dogs. Please bring water and
disposal bags. Parking is available at the Recycling
Center on Blake Lane.

Red Wing Park - Virginia Beach
vbgov.com/e-gov/vbcsg/faqinfo/0,1172,5353,00.html
1398 General Booth Blvd.
Daily 7:30 a.m.-sunset; closed Jan. 1, Martin Luther King Day, Veterans Day, Thanksgiving and Dec. 25
Fenced, benches, disposal bags, parking, restrooms, water. Access for the disabled.
Annual fee $3 for first-time visitors, who must register at the park office, show proof of their pet's rabies shot and vaccines, and obtain a city dog license.

Woodstock Community Park - Virginia Beach
vbgov.com/e-gov/vbcsg/faqinfo/0,1172,5353,00.html
5709 Providence Rd.
Daily 7:30 a.m.-sunset; closed Jan. 1, Martin Luther King Day, Veterans Day, Thanksgiving and Dec. 25
Fenced, benches, disposal bags, parking, restrooms. Access for the disabled.
Annual fee $3 for first-time visitors, who must register at the park office, show proof of their pet's rabies shot and vaccines, and obtain a city dog license.

WASHINGTON

Dr. Jose Rizal Park - Seattle
coladog.org
1008 12th Ave. South, on North Beacon Hill (off-leash area is in the lower portion of the park)
Daily 6 a.m.-11 p.m.
4 acres, fenced, double-gated entry, parking, beautiful view of downtown, doggie drinking fountain.

Genesee Park - Seattle
coladog.org
46th Avenue South and South Genesee Street
Daily 6 a.m.-11 p.m.
Fenced, double-gated entry, disposal bags, doggie drinking fountain, parking.

Golden Gardens Park - Seattle
coladog.org
8498 Seaview Pl. N.W. in Ballard
Daily 6 a.m.-11 p.m.
Fenced, lighted, parking, doggie drinking fountain. The off-leash area is located in the upper (eastern) portion of the park, not in the lower beach area. Please note that dogs are not allowed on the beach.

I-90 "Blue Dog Pond" - Seattle
coladog.org
Martin Luther King Jr. Way and South Massachusetts Street, on the northwest corner
Daily 6 a.m.-11 p.m.
Fenced, parking, sculpture of large blue dog, doggie drinking fountain. Note: There are no off-leash areas in I-90 Lid Park, located just east of Blue Dog Pond.

Magnuson Park - Seattle
coladog.org
6500 Sandpoint Way N.E.
Daily 6 a.m.-11 p.m.
Parking, shelter, double-gated entry, doggie drinking fountain. The off-leash area is located along the eastern and northern boundary of the park, with some beach access in the park's northeast corner.

Northacres Park - Seattle
coladog.org
West of I-5 at North 130th Street
Daily 6 a.m.-11 p.m.
Fenced, double-gated entry, parking, doggie drinking fountain. The off-leash area is in the northeast corner of the park at 12530 Third Ave. N.E., north of the ball field. Parking is available on the west side of the park along 1st Street N.E. and on the south side along North 125th Street.

Westcrest Park - Seattle
coladog.org
8806 8th Ave. S.W. in West Seattle
Daily 6 a.m.-11 p.m.
Unfenced site, parking, doggie drinking fountain. The off-leash area is located along the southern and western border of the reservoir.

Woodland Park - Seattle
coladog.org
West of the tennis courts on West Green Lake Way North
Daily 6 a.m.-11 p.m.
Fenced, doggie drinking fountain, parking.

Canada

ALBERTA

91 Street Right of Way - Edmonton
gov.edmonton.ab.ca (780) 496-1475
Berm east of 91 Street, starting at 10 Avenue and extending north to Whitemud Freeway and east to 76 Street
Unfenced site.

Buena Vista Great Meadow - Edmonton
gov.edmonton.ab.ca (780) 496-1475
North of Laurier Park and Buena Vista Drive and south of Melton Ravine (in the vicinity of 88 Avenue)
Unfenced site. Does not include the pedestrian bridge access trail, Yorath property or the trail north to McKenzie Ravine. This is a hot-air balloon site, so please leash your dog when balloons launch.

Hermitage Park North - Edmonton
gov.edmonton.ab.ca (780) 496-1475
129 Avenue to 137 Avenue, also 22 Street along the riverbank where signs designate an off-leash area. Unfenced site. This is a multi-use area in the valley north of the park's fishing pond and picnic area.

Jackie Parker Park - Edmonton
gov.edmonton.ab.ca (780) 496-1475
Whitemud Freeway and 50th Street
Unfenced site. Includes the area south of the 44 Avenue entrance. Does not include golf course.

Keehewin Blackmud - Edmonton
gov.edmonton.ab.ca (780) 496-1475
Pipeline corridor, 104 Street and 20 Avenue to the south end of 109 Street (excludes Bearspaw Drive West and Blackmud Creek and Ravine)
Unfenced site.

Kennedale - Edmonton
gov.edmonton.ab.ca (780) 496-1475
Ravine west of the 40 Street loop, west to 47 Street and the top of the bank
Unfenced site.

Lauderdale - Edmonton
gov.edmonton.ab.ca (780) 496-1475
South end of Grand Trunk Park, from 127 to 129 Avenue and 113A to 109 Street
Unfenced site.

Mill Creek Ravine - Edmonton
gov.edmonton.ab.ca (780) 496-1475
Access is from 68 Avenue and 93 Street (west side of Argyll Park) or from the north side of Argyll Park
Unfenced site. A granular trail along the bottom of the ravine leads to the Whyte (82) Avenue overpass.

Terwillegar Park - Edmonton
gov.edmonton.ab.ca (780) 496-1475
Park access via Rabbit Hill Road
Unfenced site. This is a multi-use area.

MANITOBA

Bourkevale Park - Winnipeg
city.winnipeg.mb.ca/publicworks/parks/fieldsforfido.asp
Area south of the dike, along the riverbank
Daily 6 a.m.-10 p.m.
Unfenced site, trash cans, parking, bring your own disposal bags.

Juba Park & Pioneer Avenue - Winnipeg
city.winnipeg.mb.ca/publicworks/parks/fieldsforfido.asp
All vacant land west of the walkway to Juba Park
Daily 6 a.m.-10 p.m.
Unfenced site, trash cans, parking, bring your own disposal bags.

Kil-Cona Park - Winnipeg
city.winnipeg.mb.ca/publicworks/parks/fieldsforfido.asp
The area north of the west parking lot
Daily 6 a.m.-10 p.m.
Unfenced site, trash cans, parking, bring your own disposal bags.

King's Park - Winnipeg
city.winnipeg.mb.ca/publicworks/parks/fieldsforfido.asp
South end of park, south of the lake
Daily 6 a.m.-10 p.m.
Unfenced site, trash cans, parking, bring your own disposal bags.

Maple Grove Park - Winnipeg
city.winnipeg.mb.ca/publicworks/parks/fieldsforfido.asp
North area of park
Daily 6 a.m.-10 p.m.
Unfenced site, trash cans, parking, bring your own disposal bags.

Westview Park - Winnipeg
city.winnipeg.mb.ca/publicworks/parks/fieldsforfido.asp
Entire park is an off-leash area
Daily 6 a.m.-10 p.m.
Unfenced site, trash cans, parking, bring your own disposal bags.

ATTRACTIONS

United States

CALIFORNIA

 Disneyland® Resort

(714) 781-4565, 1313 S. Harbor Blvd. via I-5
Disneyland Drive and Disney Way exits, Anaheim
Disneyland® Resort consists of two family-oriented
theme parks — Disneyland Park and Disney's
California Adventure Park — and the shops,
restaurants and entertainment of Downtown Disney®.
Indoor kennel facilities $10. Mon.-Fri. 10-8, Sat. 9
a.m.-midnight, Sun. 9 a.m.-10 p.m. Extended hours in
summer; phone ahead to confirm. Admission to either
park $47; over 60, $45; ages 3-9, $37. Parking fee.
disneyland.disney.go.com

 **SeaWorld Adventure Park**

(619) 226-3901 or (800) 257-4268, 500 SeaWorld Dr.,
San Diego
SeaWorld offers four major animal shows, rides and
playgrounds, a marina and exhibits featuring marine
creatures from around the world. Pet facility provided
for a nominal charge on a first-come, first-serve basis.
Opens daily at 9, mid-June through Labor Day; at 10,
rest of year. Closing times vary. Admission $46.95;
ages 3-9, $37.95. Parking fee.
www.seaworld.com/ca

 Universal Studios Hollywood

(800) 864-8377, 100 Universal City Plaza, Universal
City
In addition to thrill rides and arcade games, Universal
Studios gives visitors a behind-the-scenes look at the
workings of a major film and TV studio.
Complimentary kennel service. Daily 9-9 in summer,
10-6 rest of year. Box office closes at 5 in summer, at
4 rest of year. Hours may vary; phone ahead to
confirm. Closed Thanksgiving and Dec. 25. Admission
$49; over 59, $47; under 48 inches tall $39. Parking
fee. themeparks.universalstudios.com

DISTRICT OF COLUMBIA

 Washington Monument

(202) 426-6841, 15th Street and Constitution Avenue
N.W., Washington, D.C.
This instantly recognizable 555-foot marble obelisk
commemorates our nation's first president and is
surrounded by grounds that extend for several blocks.
Pets on leash. Daily 9-5; closed Dec. 25. Free.
www.nps.gov/wamo

FLORIDA

 Busch Gardens Tampa Bay

(866) 353-8622, 3000 E. Busch Blvd., Tampa
This African-themed family entertainment park and
outstanding zoological facility features all kinds of thrill
rides and numerous opportunities for animal
observation. Outdoor kennel facilities. Generally open
daily at 9 a.m.; closing times vary. Phone ahead to
confirm hours. Admission $53.95; ages 3-9, $44.95.
Parking fee. www.buschgardens.com

 SeaWorld Orlando

(407) 351-3600 or (800) 327-2424, 7007 SeaWorld Dr.
at I-4 and SR 528 (Bee Line Expressway), Orlando
A research facility as well as a theme park, SeaWorld
Orlando presents crowd-pleasing animal shows
starring a family of performing killer whales.
Air-conditioned kennels. Generally opens daily at 9;
closing times vary. Phone ahead to confirm hours.
Admission $53.95; ages 3-9, $44.95.
Parking fee. www.seaworld.com

 Universal Orlando

(866) 353-8622, off I-4 exit 75A (eastbound) or 74B
(westbound) following signs, Orlando
At Universal Orlando you can "ride the movies" at the
Universal Studios theme park, cavort with superheroes
and cartoon characters at the Islands of Adventure
theme park, or visit the specialty shops,
celebrity-themed restaurants and entertainment venues
at CityWalk. Air-conditioned and outdoor kennels.
Theme parks open daily at 9 a.m.; closing times vary
by season. Phone ahead to confirm hours. CityWalk
open daily 11 a.m.-2 a.m. Admission to both theme
parks $53.95; ages 3-9, $44.95. Individual CityWalk
venue charges vary. Parking fee.
themeparks.universalstudios.com

Walt Disney World® Resort

(407) 824-4321, theme parks accessible from US 192,
Osceola Parkway and several I-4 exits, Lake Buena
Vista
Walt Disney World has — count 'em — four theme
parks: Magic Kingdom® Park, Epcot®, Disney's Animal
Kingdom® Theme Park and Disney-MGM Studios,
plus shopping, dining and entertainment at the
Downtown Disney® Area. Air-conditioned and outside
kennels. Theme parks generally open daily at 9 a.m.,
closing times vary. One-day, one-park admission $52;
ages 3-9, $42. Parking fee. disneyworld.disney.go.com

GEORGIA

 Six Flags Over Georgia

(770) 948-9290, 275 Riverside Pkwy. (off I-20), Austell
Six Flags offers more than 100 rides, attractions and
shows, a 12,000-seat concert amphitheater,
Broadway-style musical shows and a nightly summer
fireworks display. Kennel facilities (water provided, but
no food). Open daily at 10 a.m., late May to mid-Aug.;
Sat.-Sun. at 10, mid-Mar. to late May and mid-Aug. to
late Oct. Closing times vary. Admission $42.99, over
54 and under 49 inches tall $25.99, under 2 free.
Parking fee. www.sixflags.com

ILLINOIS

 Six Flags Great America

(847) 249-4636, 542 N. Route 21, Gurnee
Batman the Ride, Iron Wolf and Raging Bull are
among the thrill rides at this family theme park, which
also has a section of rides and attractions for children
under 55 inches tall. Kennel facilities. Open daily at 10
a.m., early May-late Aug.; Sat.-Sun. at 10, early-late
May and first 2 weekends in Sept.; Fri.-Sun. at 10, in
Oct. Closing times vary; phone ahead to confirm
hours. Admission $41.99, over 60 and under 55
inches tall $29.99, under 3 free. Parking fee.
www.sixflags.com

IOWA

 Pella Historical Village

(641) 628-2409 or 628-4311, 507 Franklin St., Pella
A country store, log cabin, grist mill, windmill, smithy
and other buildings (including Wyatt Earp's boyhood
home) are reminders of this town's Dutch Heritage.
Pets on leash (grounds only). Mon.-Fri. 9-5 (also Sat.
9-5, Apr.-Dec.). Admission $7; ages 5-18, $1.

MASSACHUSETTS

 Bunker Hill Monument

(617) 242-5641, in Monument Square on Breed's Hill,
Charlestown
Part of Boston National Historical Park, this
221-foot-tall granite obelisk commemorates the site of
the Battle of Bunker Hill on June 17, 1775. Pets on
leash (grounds only); must pick up after pet. Visitor
lodge and exhibits daily 9-5. Free. www.nps.gov/bost/
Bunker_Hill/htm

MISSISSIPPI

 Vicksburg National Military Park

(601) 636-0583, 3201 Clay St. (entered on the eastern
edge off US 80)
More than 1,260 memorials, monuments, statues and
markers honor the Union and Confederate troops who
engaged in the siege of Vicksburg in 1863. Pets on
leash. Grounds open daily dawn-dusk; visitor center
daily 8-5. Admission $5 per private vehicle.
www.nps.gov/vick

MISSOURI

 The Gateway Arch

(877) 982-1410, Memorial Drive and Market Street, St.
Louis
This curved, stainless steel monument soars 630 feet
high and symbolizes the gateway to the West. A tram
ride takes visitors to an observation deck. Pets on
leash (grounds only). Tram ticket center open daily
8:20 a.m.-9:10 p.m., Memorial Day-Labor Day; 9-5,
rest of year. Closed Jan. 1, Thanksgiving and Dec.
25. Tram ride $8; ages 13-16, $5; ages 3-12, $3.
www.gatewayarch.com

NEW YORK

 Fort Ticonderoga

(518) 585-2821, about 1 mile east on SR 74,
Ticonderoga
Built by the French in 1755, this restored fort on Lake
Champlain once controlled the connecting waterway
between Canada and the American Colonies. Pets on
leash (designated areas only).
Site open daily 9-5, early May-late Oct. Admission
$12; over 60, $10.80; ages 7-12, $6.
www.fort-ticonderoga.org

NORTH CAROLINA

 Paramount's Carowinds Theme Park

(704) 588-2600 in N.C., (803) 548-5300 or (800)
888-4386, 10 miles south on I-77 to exit 90, Charlotte
Themed areas at this park depict the past and
present of the Carolinas, and offer roller coasters and
water rides, children's play areas and other family
entertainment. Air-conditioned kennels. Open daily,
Jun.-Jul.; various times from late Mar. through May 31
and Aug. 1 to early Oct. Hours vary seasonally; phone
ahead. Admission $42.99; over 55 and ages 3-6 or
under 48 inches tall, $27.99. Parking fee.
www.carowinds.com

OHIO

 Paramount's Kings Island

(513) 754-5700 or (800) 288-0808, Kings Island Drive
(off I-71 exits 24 and 25), Kings Mills
Kings Island is a family entertainment park featuring
12 hair-raising roller coasters; WaterWorks, a water
recreation playground; costumed cartoon characters;
and a variety of live shows. Outdoor kennel
facilities (fee). Open daily at 9 a.m., late May-late Aug. and
Aug. 31-Sept. 2; Sat.-Sun. at 9 a.m., early
Apr. to mid-May. Phone ahead to confirm hours.
Admission $42.99; over 59, ages 3-6 or under 48
inches tall, $25.99. Parking fee. www.pki.com

PENNSYLVANIA

Hersheypark

(800) 437-7439, 100 W. Hersheypark Dr. (just off SR 743 and US 422), Hershey
The emphasis is on thrill rides at Hersheypark, plus live entertainment that includes a marine mammal show, song and dance reviews and big-name performers. Air-conditioned kennels. Open daily at 10 a.m., mid-May to mid-Sept.; Fri.-Sun. at 10, selected weekends in May; Sat.-Sun at 10, selected weekends in Sept. Closing times vary; phone ahead to confirm hours. Admission $37.95; over 54 and ages 3-8, $21.95; 70 and over $15.95.
Parking fee. www.hersheypark.com

TEXAS

SeaWorld San Antonio

(210) 523-3611 or (800) 722-2762, 10500 Sea World Dr. (off SR 151 at the junction of Westover Hills Boulevard and Ellison Drive), San Antonio
Killer and beluga whales, sea lions, otters, walruses and dolphins perform at this marine life park, which also has shark exhibits, a penguin habitat and a children's playground. Outdoor kennel facilities (owner must provide food and water containers). Open daily at 10 a.m., early Mar.-Nov. 30; closing times vary. Admission $41.99; ages 3-9, $31.99 (phone to confirm times and admission). www.buschgardens.com/seaworld/tx

Six Flags Over Texas

(817) 530-6000, 2201 Road to Six Flags (at the junction of I-30 and SR 360 exit 30), Arlington
Themed areas, each featuring thrill rides, food and entertainment, depict Texas under six different flags: Spain, France, Mexico, the Republic of Texas, the Confederate States of America and the United States. Air-conditioned kennels. Open daily, June 1 to mid-Aug.; Sat.-Sun and Labor Day, late Mar. through May 31, mid-Aug. through Oct. 31 and early to mid-Dec. Hours vary; phone ahead to confirm schedule. Admission $39.99; over 54, the physically impaired and under 48 inches tall, $24.99; under 3 free. Parking fee. www.sixflags.com

VIRGINIA

Busch Gardens Williamsburg

(800) 343-7946, 3 miles east on US 60 or off I-64 exit 242A, Williamsburg[<]1This European-themed adventure park offers something for the entire family, from thrill rides to dance and music shows to villages representing England, Germany, France and other nations. Outdoor kennel facilities (England parking lot); fee $4 per pet per day. Open daily at 10 a.m., early May-Labor Day; closing times vary. Open at 10, late Mar.-early May and day after Labor Day-late Oct.; days and closing times vary. Admission $46.99; ages 3-6, $39.99. Parking fee. www.buschgardens.com

Paramount's Kings Dominion

(804) 876-5000, 16000 Theme Park Way (on SR 30 1/2 mile east off I-95 exit 98), Doswell
Eight themed areas make up Kings Dominion, a full-scale theme park with thrill rides, kiddie play areas, costumed characters, live shows and specialty shopping. Kennels. Park open daily, Memorial Day-Labor Day; Sat.-Sun., late Mar.-day before Memorial Day and first Sat. after Labor Day-early Oct. Hours vary seasonally; phone ahead. Admission $41.99; over 54, $36.99; ages 3-6, $27.99. Parking fee. www.kingsdominion.com

WASHINGTON

Hovander Homestead

(360) 384-3444, 1 mile south via Hovander Road, Ferndale
This restored house, dating from 1903 and furnished with antiques, is within a large park encompassing gardens, picnic sites and a children's farm zoo. Pets on leash (grounds only). Grounds open daily 8 a.m.-dusk; house open Thurs.-Sun. noon-4:30, June 1-Labor Day. Grounds $4 per private vehicle. House $1; ages 5-12, 50 cents.

Canada

ONTARIO

Upper Canada Village

(613) 543-4328 or (800) 437-2233, 7 miles (11 kilometers) east on CR 2 off Hwy. 401, Morrisburg
Upper Canada Village re-creates life during the 1860s through a working community of artisans and costumed interpreters who perform chores typical of the era. Pets on leash (grounds only). Daily 9:30-5, Victoria Day weekend-Oct. 6. Village admission $16.95; over 65, $15.95; students with ID $10.50; ages 5-12, $7.50. www.uppercanadavillage.com

Paramount Canada's Wonderland

(905) 832-7000 or 832-8131, off Hwy. 400 (Rutherford Road exit northbound or Major Mackenzie Drive E. exit southbound) at 9580 Jane St., Vaughan
Thrill rides at this theme park include the Top Gun coaster and Drop Zone, a free-fall plunge, while Scooby Doo's Haunted Mansion and Hanna-Barbera Land will entertain little ones. Air-conditioned kennels (fee). Open daily at 10 a.m., late May-Labour Day; some weekends early to late May and day after Labour Day-second Mon. in Oct. Closing times vary. Grounds admission $24.99. Grounds and rides passport $46.99; over 59 and ages 3-6, $23.49. Parking fee. www.canadas-wonderland.com

The National Public Lands listed below permit pets on a leash. Keep in mind that animals may be prohibited from entering public buildings and even some areas outdoors, particularly those that are ecologically sensitive. Specific pet policies vary from park to park and are subject to change. Always check in advance regarding any applicable regulations and to confirm that pets are still permitted where you are going.

Never leave your pet unattended. Keep him leashed or crated at all times. Follow park guidelines faithfully, and monitor your pet's behavior; the National Park Service may confiscate pets that harm wildlife or other visitors. *For additional information on outdoor vacations, see The Great Outdoors, p. 18.*

United States

ALABAMA

Conecuh National Forest
On the Alabama-Florida border.
(334) 222-2555
🚲 🔺 🚶 🌳 🏊

Horseshoe Bend National Military Park
12 mi. north of Dadeville on SR 49.
(256) 234-7111
🚶 🌳 🏊 👥

Talladega National Forest
In central Alabama.
(256) 362-2909
🔺 🚶 🌳 🏊

Tuskegee National Forest
Northeast of Tuskegee.
(334) 727-2652
🔺 🚶 🌳

William B. Bankhead National Forest
In northwestern Alabama.
(205) 489-5111
🚲 🔺 🚶 🌳 🏊

ALASKA

Chugach National Forest
Along the Gulf of Alaska from Cape Suckling to Seward.
(907) 743-9500
🔺 🚶 🌳 👥

Denali National Park and Preserve
In south-central Alaska.
(907) 683-2294
🔺 🚶 🌳 👥 🍽

Glacier Bay National Park and Preserve
North of Cross Sound to the Canadian border.
(907) 697-2230
🔺 🚶 👥 🍽

Kenai Fjords National Park
Southeastern side of the Kenai Peninsula.
(907) 224-3175 or 224-2132
🔺 🚶 🌳 👥

Lake Clark National Park and Preserve
In southern Alaska.
(907) 271-3751
🔺 👥

Tongass National Forest
In southeastern Alaska.
(907) 586-8751 or 228-6220
🔺 🚶 🌳 👥

Wrangell-St. Elias National Park and Preserve
In southeastern Alaska, northwest of Tongass National Forest.
(907) 822-5234
🔺 🚶 🌳 👥

ARIZONA

Apache-Sitgreaves National Forests
In east-central Arizona.
(928) 333-4301
🚲 🔺 🚶 🌳 👥 🍽

Coconino National Forest
In northern Arizona.
(928) 527-3600
🔺 🚶 🌳 🏊 🍽

Coronado National Forest
In southeastern Arizona and southwestern New Mexico.
(520) 670-4552
🚲 🔺 🚶 🌳 👥

Glen Canyon National Recreation Area
In north-central Arizona.
(928) 608-6404 or 608-6200
🔺 🚶 🌳 🏊 👥 🍽

Grand Canyon National Park
In northwestern Arizona.
(928) 638-7888
🔺 🚶 🌳 👥 🍽

🚲 Bicycling   🔺 Camping   🚶 Hiking   🌳 Picnicking
🏊 Swimming   👥 Visitor center   🍽 Food service

Kaibab National Forest
In north-central Arizona.
(928) 635-4061 or (800) 863-0546
▲ 🏕 🎣 🚻 🔭

Lake Mead National Recreation Area
In northwestern Arizona.
(702) 293-8906
▲ 🏕 🎣 🚣 🚻 🔭

Petrified Forest National Park
In east-central Arizona, east of Holbrook.
(928) 524-6228
🏕 🎣 🚻 🔭

Prescott National Forest
In central Arizona.
(928) 771-4700 or TDD (928) 771-4792
▲ 🏕 🎣 🔭

Saguaro National Park
Two districts, 15 mi. east and west of Tucson.
(520) 733-5153
♿ ▲ 🏕 🎣 🚻

Tonto National Forest
In central Arizona.
(602) 225-5200
♿ ▲ 🏕 🎣 🚣 🔭

ARKANSAS

Buffalo National River
In northwestern Arkansas.
(870) 741-5443
▲ 🏕 🎣 🚣 🚻 🔭

Felsenthal National Wildlife Refuge
7 mi. west of Crossett on US 82.
(870) 364-3167
▲ 🏕 🎣 🚻

Hot Springs National Park
In western Arkansas.
(501) 624-3383
▲ 🏕 🎣 🚻

Ouachita National Forest
In west-central Arkansas and southeastern Oklahoma.
(501) 321-5202
♿ ▲ 🏕 🎣 🚣 🚻 🔭

Ozark National Forest
In northwestern Arkansas.
(479) 968-2354
♿ ▲ 🏕 🎣 🚣 🚻

St. Francis National Forest
In east-central Arkansas.
(870) 295-5278
▲ 🏕 🎣 🚣

CALIFORNIA

Angeles National Forest
In southern California.
(626) 574-5200
♿ ▲ 🏕 🎣 🚣 🚻 🔭

Cleveland National Forest
In southwestern California.
(858) 673-6180
♿ ▲ 🏕 🎣 🚻 🔭

Death Valley National Park
Along the Nevada border in east-central California.
(760) 786-2331
▲ 🏕 🎣 🚣 🚻 🔭

Eldorado National Forest
In central California.
(530) 644-6048
♿ ▲ 🏕 🎣 🚣 🚻 🔭

Golden Gate National Recreation Area
North of the Golden Gate Bridge and in northern and western San Francisco.
(415) 561-4700
♿ ▲ 🏕 🎣 🚣 🚻 🔭

Inyo National Forest
In central California.
(760) 873-2400
♿ ▲ 🏕 🎣 🚣 🚻 🔭

Joshua Tree National Park
East of Desert Hot Springs.
(760) 367-5500
▲ 🏕 🎣 🚻

Klamath National Forest
In northern California.
(530) 842-6131
♿ ▲ 🏕 🎣 🚣 🚻

Lassen National Forest
In northern California.
(530) 257-2151
♿ ▲ 🏕 🎣 🚣 🚻 🔭

Lassen Volcanic National Park
In northeastern California.
(530) 595-4444
▲ 🏕 🎣 🚣 🚻 🔭

Los Padres National Forest
In southern California.
(805) 968-6640 or 968-6790
♿ ▲ 🏕 🎣 🚣

Mendocino National Forest
In northwestern California.
(530) 934-2350 or 934-3316, or TDD (530) 934-7724
♿ ▲ 🏕 🎣 🚣 🚻 🔭

Modoc National Forest
In northeastern California.
(530) 233-5811
♿ ▲ 🏕 🎣 🚣 🚻

Mojave National Preserve
Between I-15 and I-40 in southeastern California.
(760) 733-4040
▲ 🏕 🎣 🚻 🔭

Plumas National Forest
In northern California.
(530) 283-2050
♿ ▲ 🏕 🎣 🚣 🚻 🔭

Point Reyes National Seashore
Along the California coast just north of San Francisco.
(415) 464-5100
🚲 🏕 🥾 🧺 👥 🍴

Redwood National Park
On the northern California coast.
(707) 464-6101, ext. 5064 or 5265
🚲 🏕 🥾 🧺 🏊 👥 🍴

San Bernardino National Forest
In southern California.
(909) 383-5588
🚲 🏕 🥾 🧺 🏊 👥 🍴

Santa Monica Mountains National Recreation Area
West from Griffith Park in Los Angeles to the Ventura County line.
(805) 370-2301 or 370-2300 in Calif.
🚲 🏕 🥾 🧺 🏊 👥 🍴

Sequoia and Kings Canyon National Parks
In east-central California.
(559) 565-3341
🏕 🥾 🧺 👥 🍴

Sequoia National Forest
In south-central California.
(559) 784-1500
🚲 🏕 🥾 🧺 🏊 👥 🍴

Shasta-Trinity National Forests
In northern California.
(530) 244-2978
🏕 🥾 🧺 🏊 👥 🍴

Sierra National Forest
In central California.
(559) 297-0706
🚲 🏕 🥾 🧺 🏊 👥 🍴

Six Rivers National Forest
In northwestern California.
(707) 441-3523
🚲 🏕 🥾 🧺 🏊 👥 🍴

Smith River National Recreation Area
Within Six Rivers National Forest in northwestern California.
(707) 457-3131
🚲 🏕 🥾 🧺 🏊

Stanislaus National Forest
In central California.
(209) 532-3671
🚲 🏕 🥾 🧺 🏊 🍴

Tahoe National Forest
In north-central California.
(530) 265-4531
🏕 🥾 🧺 🏊 👥 🍴

Whiskeytown-Shasta-Trinity National Recreation Area
North and west of Redding.
(530) 242-3400
🚲 🏕 🥾 🧺 🏊 👥 🍴

Yosemite National Park
In central California.
(209) 372-0200
🚲 🏕 🥾 🧺 🏊 👥 🍴

COLORADO

Arapaho and Roosevelt National Forests
In north-central Colorado.
(970) 498-2770 or TDD 498-2707
🚲 🏕 🥾 🧺 🏊 👥

Arapaho National Recreation Area
In north-central Colorado.
(970) 887-4100 or TDD 887-4101
🚲 🏕 🥾 🧺 🏊 👥

Black Canyon of the Gunnison National Park
In western Colorado.
(970) 641-2337
🏕 🥾 🧺 👥 🍴

Curecanti National Recreation Area
In south-central Colorado between Gunnison and Montrose, paralleling US 50.
(970) 641-2337
🏕 🥾 🧺 🏊 👥 🍴

Grand Mesa-Uncompahgre-Gunnison National Forests
In west-central Colorado.
(970) 874-6600
🚲 🏕 🥾 🧺 🍴

Mesa Verde National Park
In southwestern Colorado.
(970) 529-4465
🏕 🥾 🧺 👥 🍴

Pike National Forest
In central Colorado.
(719) 553-1400
🚲 🏕 🥾 🧺 👥 🍴

Rio Grande National Forest
In south-central Colorado.
(719) 852-5941
🚲 🏕 🥾 🧺 👥

Rocky Mountain National Park
In north-central Colorado.
(970) 586-1206 or 586-1333
🏕 🥾 🧺 👥 🍴

Routt National Forest
In northwestern Colorado.
(970) 879-1870
🚲 🏕 🥾 🧺 🏊 👥

🚲 Bicycling   🏕 Camping   🥾 Hiking   🧺 Picnicking
🏊 Swimming   👥 Visitor center   🍴 Food service

San Isabel National Forest
In south-central Colorado.
(719) 553-1400
▲ 🐟 🎋 🏕 🍴

San Juan National Forest
In southwestern Colorado.
(970) 247-4874
♿ ▲ 🐟 🎋 🚤 🏕 🍴

White River National Forest
In west-central Colorado.
(970) 945-2521
♿ ▲ 🐟 🎋 🚤 🏕 🍴

FLORIDA

Ocala National Forest
In north-central Florida.
(352) 236-0288
♿ ▲ 🐟 🎋 🚤 🏕 🍴

GEORGIA

Chattahoochee and Oconee National Forests
In central and northern Georgia.
(770) 297-3000
▲ 🐟 🎋 🚤 🏕

Chattahoochee River National Recreation Area
North of Atlanta.
(770) 399-8070, ext. 236
♿ 🐟 🎋 🍴

IDAHO

Boise National Forest
In south-central Idaho.
(208) 373-4007
♿ ▲ 🐟 🎋 🚤 🏕 🍴

Caribou National Forest
In southeastern Idaho.
(208) 524-7500
▲ 🐟 🎋 🚤

Clearwater National Forest
In northeastern Idaho.
(208) 476-4541
▲ 🐟 🎋 🚤 🏕

Hells Canyon National Recreation Area
In western Idaho and northeastern Oregon.
(509) 758-0616 or 758-1957
♿ ▲ 🐟 🎋 🏕

Idaho Panhandle National Forest
In northern and northwestern Idaho.
(208) 765-7223
♿ ▲ 🐟 🎋 🚤

Nez Perce National Forest
In north-central Idaho.
(208) 983-1950
♿ ▲ 🐟 🎋 🚤 🏕

Payette National Forest
In west-central Idaho.
(208) 634-0700
♿ ▲ 🐟 🎋 🚤 🏕

Salmon-Challis National Forest
In east-central Idaho.
(208) 756-5100
▲ 🐟 🎋 🚤 🍴

Sawtooth National Forest
In south-central Idaho.
(208) 737-3200 or TDD (208) 737-3235
♿ ▲ 🐟 🎋 🚤 🏕 🍴

Sawtooth National Recreation Area
In south-central Idaho.
(208) 727-5013 or (800) 260-5970
♿ ▲ 🐟 🎋 🚤 🏕 🍴

Targhee National Forest
In southeastern Idaho.
(208) 624-3151
▲ 🐟 🎋 🚤 🍴

ILLINOIS

Shawnee National Forest
In southern Illinois.
(618) 253-7114 or (800) 699-6637
▲ 🐟 🎋 🚤

INDIANA

Hoosier National Forest
In southern Indiana.
(812) 275-5987
♿ ▲ 🐟 🎋 🚤

Indiana Dunes National Lakeshore
On the southern shore of Lake Michigan.
(219) 926-7561, ext. 225
♿ ▲ 🐟 🎋 🚤 🏕

KENTUCKY

Big South Fork National River and Recreation Area
In southeastern Kentucky and northeastern Tennessee.
(423) 286-7275 or (606) 376-5073
♿ ▲ 🐟 🎋 🚤 🏕

Daniel Boone National Forest
In eastern Kentucky.
(859) 745-3100
▲ 🐟 🎋 🚤 🏕

Daniel Boone National Forest (Laurel River Lake)
In southeastern Kentucky west of Corbin.
(859) 745-3100
▲ 🐟 🎋 🚤

Daniel Boone National Forest (Rockcastle)
In southeastern Kentucky 22 mi. southwest of London via SR 192/3497.
(859) 745-3100
▲ 🐟 🎋 🚤

Land Between the Lakes National Recreation Area
In western Kentucky and Tennessee.
(270) 924-2000 or (800) 525-7077
♿ ▲ 🐟 🎋 🚤 🏕

Mammoth Cave National Park
In south-central Kentucky 10 mi. west of Cave City.
(270) 758-2180
🚴 📷 🚶 ⛺ 🏊 👫 🍽️

LOUISIANA

Bayou Sauvage National Wildlife Refuge
Within the New Orleans city limits.
(985) 882-2000
🚶 ⛺

Kisatchie National Forest
In central and northern Louisiana.
(318) 473-7160
📷 🚶 ⛺ 🏊

Sabine National Wildlife Refuge
8 mi. south of Hackberry on SR 27.
(337) 762-3816
🚶 👫

MAINE

Acadia National Park
Along the Atlantic coast southeast of Bangor.
(207) 288-3338
🚴 📷 🚶 ⛺ 🏊 👫 🍽️

MARYLAND

Assateague Island National Seashore
In southeastern Maryland south of Ocean City.
(410) 641-1441 or 641-3030
🚴 📷 🚶 ⛺ 🏊 👫

MICHIGAN

Hiawatha National Forest
In Michigan's Upper Peninsula.
(906) 786-4062
🚴 📷 🚶 ⛺ 🏊 👫

Huron-Manistee National Forests
In the northern part of the Lower Peninsula.
(231) 775-2421 or (800) 821-6263
🚴 📷 🚶 ⛺ 🏊 👫

Ottawa National Forest
In Michigan's Upper Peninsula.
(906) 932-1330
🚴 📷 🚶 ⛺ 🏊 👫

Pictured Rocks National Lakeshore
Along Lake Superior in Michigan's Upper Peninsula.
(906) 387-2607
📷 🚶 ⛺ 🏊 👫

Sleeping Bear Dunes National Lakeshore
Along Lake Michigan in the northwestern part of the
Lower Peninsula.
(231) 326-5134
📷 🚶 ⛺ 🏊 👫

MINNESOTA

Chippewa National Forest
In north-central Minnesota.
(218) 335-8600 or TDD (218) 335-8632
🚴 📷 🚶 ⛺ 🏊 👫 🍽️

Superior National Forest
In northeastern Minnesota.
(218) 626-4300
🚴 📷 🚶 ⛺ 🏊 👫 🍽️

MISSISSIPPI

Bienville National Forest
In central Mississippi.
(601) 469-3811
📷 🚶 ⛺ 🏊 👫

Gulf Islands National Seashore
Along the Gulf of Mexico in southern Mississippi.
(228) 875-9057
📷 ⛺ 🏊 👫 🍽️

MISSOURI

Mark Twain National Forest
In southern Missouri.
(573) 364-4621
🚴 📷 🚶 ⛺ 🏊

Mark Twain National Forest (Big Bay)
1 mi. southeast of Shell Knob on SR 39, then 3 mi.
southeast on CR YY.
(573) 364-4621
📷 ⛺ 🏊

Mark Twain National Forest (Crane Lake)
12 mi. south of Ironton off SR 49 and CR E.
(573) 364-4621
🚴 🚶 ⛺

Mark Twain National Forest (Fourche Lake)
18 mi. west of Doniphan on SR 160.
(573) 364-4621
🚶 ⛺

Mark Twain National Forest (Noblett Lake)
8 mi. west of Willow Springs on SR 76, then 1.5 mi.
south on SR 181, 3 mi. southeast on CR AP and 1
mi. southwest on FR 857.
(573) 364-4621
🚴 📷 🚶 ⛺

Mark Twain National Forest (Pinewoods Lake)
2 mi. west of Ellsinore on SR 60.
(573) 364-4621
🚴 🚶 ⛺ 🏊

Mark Twain National Forest (Red Bluff)
1 mi. east of Davisville on CR V, then 1 mi. north on
FR 2011.
(573) 364-4621
📷 🚶 ⛺ 🏊

🚴 Bicycling   📷 Camping   🚶 Hiking   ⛺ Picnicking
🏊 Swimming   👫 Visitor center   🍽️ Food service

Ozark National Scenic Riverways
In southeastern Missouri.
(573) 323-4236
🔺 👟 🌲 ⛵ 🚻 🍴

MONTANA

Beaverhead-Deerlodge National Forest Area
In southwestern Montana.
(406) 683-3900
♿ 🔺 👟 🌲 ⛵

Bighorn Canyon National Recreation Area
In southern Montana and northern Wyoming.
(406) 666-2412
🔺 👟 🌲 ⛵ 🚻 🍴

Bitterroot National Forest
In western Montana.
(406) 363-7161
🔺 👟 🌲 ⛵ 🚻

Custer National Forest/Dakota Prairie Grasslands
In southeastern Montana.
(406) 657-6200
♿ 🔺 👟 🌲 ⛵ 🍴

Flathead National Forest
In northwestern Montana.
(406) 758-5204
♿ 🔺 👟 🌲 ⛵ 🚻

Gallatin National Forest
In south-central Montana.
(406) 522-2520
♿ 🔺 👟 🌲 ⛵ 🚻 🍴

Glacier National Park
In northwestern Montana.
(406) 888-7800
🔺 👟 🌲 ⛵ 🚻 🍴

Helena National Forest
In west-central Montana.
(406) 449-5201
🔺 👟 🌲 ⛵

Kootenai National Forest
In northwestern Montana.
(406) 293-6211
♿ 🔺 👟 🌲 ⛵ 🚻 🍴

Lewis and Clark National Forest
In central Montana.
(406) 791-7700
🔺 👟 🌲 ⛵

NEBRASKA

Nebraska National Forest
In central and northwestern Nebraska.
(308) 432-0300 or TDD (308) 432-0304
🔺 👟 🌲 ⛵

Oglala National Grassland
In northwestern Nebraska, 6 mi. north of Crawford via SR 2.
(308) 432-4475 or 665-3900
🔺 👟 🌲 🚻

NEVADA

Great Basin National Park
In central Nevada, 5 mi. west of Baker near the Nevada-Utah border.
(775) 234-7331
🔺 👟 🌲 🚻 🍴

Lake Mead National Recreation Area
In southeastern Nevada.
(702) 293-8906
♿ 🔺 👟 🌲 ⛵ 🚻 🍴

Humboldt-Toiyabe National Forest
In central, western, northern and southern Nevada and eastern California.
(775) 331-6444
♿ 🔺 👟 🌲

NEW HAMPSHIRE

White Mountain National Forest
In northern New Hampshire.
(603) 528-8721 or TDD (603) 528-8722
♿ 🔺 👟 🌲 ⛵ 🚻

NEW JERSEY

Gateway National Recreation Area
In northeastern New Jersey (Sandy Hook Unit).
(732) 872-5970
👟 🌲 ⛵ 🚻 🍴

NEW MEXICO

Carson National Forest
In north-central New Mexico.
(505) 758-6200
♿ 🔺 👟 🌲 🚻

Chaco Culture National Historical Park
In northwestern New Mexico.
(505) 786-7014
♿ 🔺 👟 🌲 🚻

Cibola National Forest
In central New Mexico.
(505) 346-3900
♿ 🔺 👟 🌲 ⛵ 🚻 🍴

Gila National Forest
In southwestern New Mexico.
(505) 388-8201
🔺 👟 🌲 ⛵ 🚻

Lincoln National Forest
In south-central New Mexico.
(505) 434-7200 or TTY (505) 434-7296
♿ 🔺 👟 🌲 🍴

Santa Fe National Forest
In north-central New Mexico between the San Pedro Mountains and the Sangre de Cristo Mountains.
(505) 438-7840
♿ 🔺 👟 🌲 🚻

NEW YORK

Finger Lakes National Forest
In north-central New York on a ridge between Seneca and Cayuga lakes, via I-90, I-81 and SR 17.
(607) 546-4470
[▲] [𝄜] [⌐π]

Fire Island National Seashore
In southeastern New York on Fire Island, off the south shore of Long Island.
(631) 289-4810
[▲] [𝄜] [⌐π] [⌐] [👥] [🍴]

Gateway National Recreation Area (Jamaica Bay District)
On Brooklyn and Queens boroughs in New York City.
(718) 354-4606
[🚲] [𝄜] [⌐π] [👥] [🍴]

Gateway National Recreation Area (Staten Island Unit)
On Staten Island borough in New York City.
(718) 354-4606
[🚲] [𝄜] [⌐π] [⌐] [👥] [🍴]

NORTH CAROLINA

Cape Hatteras National Seashore
In eastern North Carolina along the Outer Banks.
(252) 473-2111 or 441-5711
[▲] [𝄜] [⌐π] [⌐] [👥]

Croatan National Forest
In southeastern North Carolina.
(252) 638-5628
[▲] [𝄜] [⌐π] [⌐]

Great Smoky Mountains National Park
In western North Carolina.
(865) 436-1200
[▲] [𝄜] [⌐π] [⌐] [👥]

Nantahala National Forest
At North Carolina's southwestern tip.
(828) 257-4200 or 526-3765
[🚲] [▲] [𝄜] [⌐π] [⌐]

Nantahala National Forest (Hanging Dog)
5 mi. northwest of Murphy on SR 1326.
(828) 257-4200 or 526-3765
[▲] [𝄜]

Nantahala National Forest (Jackrabbit Mountain)
10 mi. northeast of Hayesville via US 64, SR 175 and SR 1155.
(828) 257-4200 or 526-3765
[▲] [𝄜] [⌐π] [⌐]

Nantahala National Forest (Standing Indian Mountain)
9 mi. west of Franklin on US 64, then 2 mi. east on old US 64 and 2 mi. south on FR 67.
(828) 257-4200 or 526-3765
[▲] [𝄜] [⌐π]

Pisgah National Forest
In western North Carolina.
(828) 257-4200
[🚲] [▲] [𝄜] [⌐π] [⌐] [👥] [🍴]

Pisgah National Forest (Lake Powhatan)
7 mi. southwest of Asheville on SR 191 and FR 3484.
(828) 257-4200
[🚲] [▲] [𝄜] [⌐π] [⌐]

Pisgah National Forest (Rocky Bluff)
3 mi. south of Hot Springs on SR 209.
(828) 257-4200
[▲] [𝄜] [⌐π]

Uwharrie National Forest
In central North Carolina.
(910) 576-6391
[▲] [𝄜] [⌐π] [⌐]

NORTH DAKOTA

Theodore Roosevelt National Park (North Unit)
In western North Dakota.
(701) 623-4466
[▲] [𝄜] [⌐π] [👥]

Theodore Roosevelt National Park (South Unit)
In western North Dakota.
(701) 623-4466
[▲] [𝄜] [⌐π] [👥]

Note: Leashed pets allowed in front country only; some restrictions apply.

OHIO

Cuyahoga Valley National Park
In northeastern Ohio.
(216) 524-1497
[🚲] [𝄜] [⌐π] [👥]

OKLAHOMA

Chickasaw National Recreation Area
In south-central Oklahoma.
(580) 622-3165
[▲] [𝄜] [⌐π] [⌐] [👥]

Ouachita National Forest
In southeastern Oklahoma and west-central Arkansas.
(501) 321-5202
[🚲] [▲] [𝄜] [⌐π] [⌐] [👥] [🍴]

OREGON

Crater Lake National Park
On the crest of the Cascade Range off SR 62.
(541) 594-3100
[🚲] [▲] [𝄜] [⌐π] [👥] [🍴]

Deschutes National Forest
In central Oregon 6 mi. south of Bend via US 97.
(541) 383-5300
[🚲] [▲] [𝄜] [⌐π] [⌐] [👥] [🍴]

🚲 Bicycling   ▲ Camping   𝄜 Hiking   ⌐π Picnicking
⌐ Swimming   👥 Visitor center   🍴 Food service

Fremont National Forest
In south-central Oregon.
(541) 947-2151

Hells Canyon National Recreation Area
In northeastern Oregon and western Idaho.
(541) 523-3356 or (800) 523-1235

Malheur National Forest
In eastern Oregon.
(541) 575-3000

Mount Hood National Forest
In northwestern Oregon.
(888) 622-4822

Ochoco National Forest
In central Oregon off US 26.
(541) 416-6500

Oregon Dunes National Recreation Area
Between North Bend and Florence.
(541) 271-3611

Rogue River National Forest
In southwestern Oregon off I-5 from Medford.
(541) 858-2200

Siskiyou National Forest
In southwestern Oregon.
(541) 471-6500

Siuslaw National Forest
In western Oregon.
(541) 750-7000

Umatilla National Forest
In northeastern Oregon.
(541) 278-3716

Umpqua National Forest
In southwestern Oregon 33 mi. east of Roseburg on SR 138.
(541) 672-6601 or TDD (541) 957-3459

Wallowa-Whitman National Forest
In northeastern Oregon.
(541) 523-6391

Willamette National Forest
In western Oregon.
(541) 465-6521

Winema National Forest
In south-central Oregon off US 97N or 140W from Klamath Falls.
(541) 883-6714

PENNSYLVANIA

Allegheny National Forest
In northwestern Pennsylvania.
(814) 723-5150 or TDD (814) 726-2710

Delaware Water Gap National Recreation Area
In eastern Pennsylvania and northwestern New Jersey.
(570) 588-2451

SOUTH CAROLINA

Francis Marion National Forest
On the Coastal Plain north of Charleston.
(803) 561-4000

Sumter National Forest
In western South Carolina.
(803) 561-4000

SOUTH DAKOTA

Badlands National Park
In southwestern South Dakota.
(605) 433-5361, ext. 100

Black Hills National Forest
In southwestern South Dakota.
(605) 673-9200 or TDD (605) 673-4954

Custer National Forest/Dakota Prairie Grasslands
In northwestern South Dakota.
(605) 797-4432

Wind Cave National Park
In southwestern South Dakota.
(605) 745-4600

TENNESSEE

Big South Fork National River National Recreation Area
In northeastern Tennessee and southeastern Kentucky.
(423) 286-7275 or (606) 376-5073

Cherokee National Forest
In eastern Tennessee.
(423) 476-9700

Great Smoky Mountains National Park
In eastern Tennessee.
(865) 436-1200

Land Between the Lakes National Recreation Area
In western Kentucky and Tennessee.
(270) 924-2000 or (800) 525-7077
🚴 🅰 🥾 ⛲ 🏊 👥 🍴

TEXAS

Amistad National Recreation Area
Northwest of Del Rio via US 90.
(830) 775-7491
🅰 🥾 ⛲ 🏊

Angelina National Forest
In east Texas.
(936) 897-1068
🅰 🥾 ⛲ 🏊

Big Bend National Park
Southeast of Alpine on SR 118 and US 385.
(432) 477-2251
🅰 🥾 ⛲ 👥 🍴

Davy Crockett National Forest
In east Texas.
(936) 655-2299
🅰 🥾 ⛲ 🏊 🍴

Guadalupe Mountains National Park
110 mi. east of El Paso on US 62/180.
(915) 828-3251
🅰 🥾 ⛲ 👥

Lake Meredith National Recreation Area
45 mi. northeast of Amarillo and 9 mi. west of Borger via SR 136.
(806) 857-3151
🅰 ⛲ 🏊

Padre Island National Seashore
On Padre Island paralleling the Texas coast between Port Isabel and Corpus Christi.
(361) 949-8068
🅰 🥾 ⛲ 🏊 👥 🍴

Sabine National Forest
In east Texas.
(409) 787-3870
🅰 🥾 ⛲ 🏊

Sam Houston National Forest
40 mi. north of Houston in east Texas.
(936) 344-6205
🚴 🅰 🥾 ⛲ 🏊 🍴

UTAH

Arches National Park
5 mi. northwest of Moab on US 191.
(435) 719-2100 or TTY (435) 259-5279
🅰 🥾 ⛲ 👥

Ashley National Forest
In northeastern Utah.
(435) 789-1181
🚴 🅰 🥾 ⛲ 🏊 👥 🍴

Bryce Canyon National Park
26 mi. southeast of Panguitch via US 89 and SRs 12 and 63.
(435) 834-5322
🅰 🥾 ⛲ 👥 🍴

Canyonlands National Park
In southeastern Utah.
(435) 259-7164
🅰 🥾 ⛲ 👥

Capitol Reef National Park
5 mi. east of Torrey on SR 24.
(435) 425-3791
🚴 🅰 🥾 ⛲ 👥

Dixie National Forest
In southwestern Utah.
(435) 865-3700
🚴 🅰 🥾 ⛲ 🏊 👥 🍴

Fishlake National Forest
In south-central Utah.
(435) 896-9233
🚴 🅰 🥾 ⛲ 👥 🍴

Flaming Gorge National Recreation Area
In northeastern Utah.
(435) 784-3445
🚴 🅰 🥾 ⛲ 🏊 👥 🍴

Glen Canyon National Recreation Area
In south-central Utah.
(928) 608-6404 or 608-6200
🅰 🥾 ⛲ 🏊 👥 🍴

Manti-La Sal National Forest
In southeastern Utah.
(435) 637-2817
🅰 🥾 ⛲ 🍴

Uinta National Forest
In central Utah.
(801) 377-5780
🚴 🅰 🥾 ⛲ 🏊 👥

Wasatch-Cache National Forest
In north-central and northeastern Utah.
(801) 524-3900
🚴 🅰 🥾 ⛲ 🏊

Zion National Park
In southwestern Utah.
(435) 772-3256
🅰 🥾 ⛲ 👥 🍴

VERMONT

Green Mountain National Forest
In south-central Vermont.
(802) 747-6700
🅰 🥾 ⛲ 🏊

🚴 Bicycling 🅰 Camping 🥾 Hiking ⛲ Picnicking
🏊 Swimming 👥 Visitor center 🍴 Food service

VIRGINIA

George Washington and Jefferson National Forests
In western Virginia and the eastern edge of West Virginia.
(888) 265-0019

Mount Rogers National Recreation Area
In southwestern Virginia.
(276) 783-5196 or (800) 628-7202

Shenandoah National Park
In western Virginia.
(540) 999-3500

WASHINGTON

Gifford Pinchot National Forest
In southwestern Washington.
(360) 891-5000

Lake Roosevelt National Recreation Area
In northeastern Washington.
(509) 633-9441

Mount Baker-Snoqualmie National Forest (Douglas Fir)
2 mi. east of Glacier on SR 542.
(425) 775-9702 or (800) 627-0062, ext. 0

Mount Baker-Snoqualmie National Forest (Horseshoe Cove)
14 mi. north of Concrete on Baker Lake.
(425) 775-9702 or (800) 627-0062, ext. 0

Mount Baker-Snoqualmie National Forest (Shannon Creek)
24 mi. north of Concrete on Baker Lake.
(425) 775-9702 or (800) 627-0062, ext.0

Olympic National Forest
In northwestern Washington.
(360) 956-2400

WEST VIRGINIA

Monongahela National Forest
In eastern West Virginia.
(304) 636-1800 (voice and TDD)

New River Gorge National River
Between Fayetteville and Hinton.
(304) 465-0508

Spruce Knob-Seneca Rocks National Recreation Area
In east-central West Virginia.
(304) 567-2827

WISCONSIN

Apostle Islands National Lakeshore
Off northern Wisconsin's Bayfield Peninsula in Lake Superior.
(715) 779-3397

Chequamegon-Nicolet National Forest
In north-central and northeastern Wisconsin.
(715) 762-2461 or TTY (715) 762-5701 (Chequamegon), (715) 362-1300 or TTY (715) 362-1383 (Nicolet)

St. Croix National Scenic Riverway
Running 252 mi. from Cable to Prescott.
(715) 483-3284

WYOMING

Bighorn Canyon National Recreation Area
In Montana and northern Wyoming.
(307) 548-2251

Bighorn National Forest
In north-central Wyoming.
(307) 674-2600

Devils Tower National Monument
Between Sundance and Hulett.
(307) 467-5283

Flaming Gorge National Recreation Area
On the Wyoming-Utah border.
(435) 784-3445

Fossil Butte National Monument
14 mi. west of Kemmerer on US 30.
(307) 877-4455

Grand Teton National Park
In northwestern Wyoming.
(307) 739-3300

Medicine Bow National Forest
In eastern Wyoming.
(307) 745-2300

Shoshone National Forest
In northwestern Wyoming.
(307) 527-6241
🚲 ⛺ 🥾 🪑 ⚓ 🏠 🍽️

Yellowstone National Park
In northwestern Wyoming.
(307) 344-7311
⛺ 🥾 🪑 🏠 🍽️

Canada

ALBERTA

Elk Island National Park
In central Alberta, east of Edmonton.
(780) 992-2950
⛺ 🥾 🪑 🏠 🍽️

Jasper National Park
In west-central Alberta along the British Columbia border.
(780) 852-6161
🚲 ⛺ 🥾 🪑 ⚓ 🏠 🍽️

Waterton Lakes National Park
In Alberta's southwestern corner.
(403) 859-5133, or 859-2224 during the winter
⛺ 🥾 🪑 ⚓ 🏠 🍽️

BRITISH COLUMBIA

Glacier National Park
In southeastern British Columbia.
(250) 837-7500
⛺ 🥾 🪑 🏠 🍽️

Kootenay National Park
In southeastern British Columbia.
(250) 347-9615 or (800) 748-7275
🚲 ⛺ 🥾 🪑 ⚓ 🏠 🍽️

Mount Revelstoke National Park
In southeastern British Columbia.
(250) 837-7500
🥾 🪑

Pacific Rim National Park Reserve
On the southwestern coast of Vancouver Island.
(250) 726-7721 or 726-4212, Jun. 1 to mid-Sept.
⛺ 🥾 🪑 ⚓ 🏠

Yoho National Park
On the British Columbia-Alberta border.
(250) 343-6783
🚲 ⛺ 🥾 🪑 🏠 🍽️

MANITOBA

Riding Mountain National Park
In western Manitoba.
(204) 848-7275 or (800) 707-8480
🚲 ⛺ 🥾 🪑 ⚓ 🏠 🍽️

NEW BRUNSWICK

Fundy National Park
On Hwy. 114, 130 km. southwest of Moncton.
(506) 887-6000
⛺ 🥾 🪑 ⚓ 🏠 🍽️

Kouchibouguac National Park
On Hwy. 134, north of Moncton.
(506) 876-2443 or TDD (506) 876-4205
🚲 ⛺ 🥾 🪑 ⚓ 🏠 🍽️

NEWFOUNDLAND

Gros Morne National Park
On Newfoundland's western coast.
(709) 458-2417, 458-2066 or TDD (709) 772-4564
⛺ 🥾 🪑 ⚓ 🏠

Terra Nova National Park
In eastern Newfoundland.
(709) 533-2801
⛺ 🥾 🪑 ⚓ 🏠 🍽️

NORTHWEST TERRITORIES

Nahanni National Park Reserve
145 km. west of Fort Simpson in western Northwest Territories.
(867) 695-3151
⛺ 🥾 🪑 ⚓ 🏠

Wood Buffalo National Park
On the Northwest Territories-Alberta border.
(867) 872-7960
⛺ 🥾 🪑 ⚓ 🏠

NOVA SCOTIA

Cape Breton Highlands National Park
5 km. northeast of Chéticamp on Cabot Tr.
(902) 224-2306 or (888) 773-8888
⛺ 🥾 🪑 ⚓ 🏠 🍽️

Kejimkujik National Park and National Historic Site
In southwestern Nova Scotia off Hwy. 8 at Maitland Bridge.
(902) 682-2772
⛺ 🥾 🪑 ⚓ 🏠 🍽️

🚲 Bicycling ⛺ Camping 🥾 Hiking 🪑 Picnicking
⚓ Swimming 🏠 Visitor center 🍽️ Food service

ONTARIO

Bruce Peninsula National Park
In southwestern Ontario.
(519) 596-2233 or 596-2263
🅰 🚶 🛖 🛶 🏕

PRINCE EDWARD ISLAND

Prince Edward Island National Park
Along the island's northern shore.
(902) 566-7050
♿ 🅰 🚶 🛖 🛶 🏕 🍽

QUEBEC

Forillon National Park
20 km. northeast of Gaspé via Hwy. 132.
(418) 368-5505 or (800) 463-6769
♿ 🅰 🚶 🛖 🛶 🏕 🍽

La Mauricie National Park of Canada
North of Trois Rivières via Hwy. 55.
(819) 538-3232 or (800) 463-6769
♿ 🅰 🚶 🛖 🛶 🏕 🍽

SASKATCHEWAN

Grasslands National Park
Between Val Marie and Killdeer in southern
Saskatchewan.
(306) 298-2257
🅰 🚶 🛖 🏕

Prince Albert National Park
In central Saskatchewan.
(306) 663-4522
♿ 🅰 🚶 🛖 🛶 🏕 🍽

ANIMAL CLINICS

This list of animal clinics in the United States and Canada is provided by the Veterinary Emergency & Critical Care Society as a service to the community for information purposes only. This is not to be construed as a certification or an endorsement of any clinic listed. For further information, contact the society at (210) 698-5575 or online at http://veccs.org. Note: Hours frequently change, and not all clinics are open 24 hours or in the evening. In addition, not all facilities listed here are emergency clinics. In non-emergency situations, it's best to call first.

If you are traveling to an area not covered in this list, be prepared for an emergency by asking your regular veterinarian to recommend a clinic or veterinarian at your destination. The American Animal Hospital Association also provides a veterinary locator service to clinics that meet the association's high standards for veterinary care. Contact the association at (303) 986-2800 or online at www.healthypet.com.

United States

ALABAMA

Village Veterinary Clinic
403 Opelika Rd., Auburn
(334) 821-7730

Emergency and Specialty Animal Medical Center
2864 Acton Rd., Birmingham
(205) 967-7389

Lakeview Pet Wellness Center
3222 6th Ave. S., Birmingham
(205) 323-1536

Emergency Clinic of North Alabama
2306-A Memorial Pkwy. SW, Huntsville
(256) 533-7600

Rehm Animal Clinic
951 Hillcrest Rd., Mobile
(251) 639-9120

Carriage Hills Animal Clinic
3200 E. Bypass, Montgomery
(334) 277-2867

ALASKA

Pet Emergency Treatment
3315 Fairbanks St., Anchorage
(907) 274-5636

ARIZONA

East Valley Veterinary Hospital
1721 E. University Dr., Mesa
(480) 890-8283

Emergency Animal Clinic
1235 S. Gilbert Rd., Ste. 24, Mesa
(480) 497-0222

Mesa Veterinary Hospital
858 N. Country Club Dr., Mesa
(480) 833-7330

Emergency Animal Clinic
9875 W. Peoria Ave., Peoria
(623) 974-1520

Emergency Animal Clinic
2260 West Glendale Ave., Phoenix
(602) 995-3757

Palo Verde Animal Hospital
1215 E. Northern Ave., Phoenix
(602) 944-9661

Emergency Animal Clinic
14202 N. Scottsdale Rd., Suite 163, Scottsdale
(480) 949-8001

Paradise Valley Emergency Animal Clinic
6969 E. Shea Blvd., #225, Scottsdale
(480) 991-1845

Animal Emergency Service
4832 E. Speedway St., Tucson
(520) 327-5624

Grant Road Small Animal Hospital
1675 West Grant Rd., Tucson
(520) 792-1858

ARKANSAS

Animal Emergency Clinic
8735 Sheltie Dr., Maumelle
(501) 224-3784

CALIFORNIA

Animal Hospital of Antioch
2204 A St., Antioch
(925) 754-6700

Antioch Veterinary Hospital
1432 West 10th St., Antioch
(925) 757-2233

Central Coast Pet Emergency Clinic
1558 W. Branch St., Arroyo Grande
(805) 489-6573

Animal Emergency and Urgent Care
4300 Easton Dr., #1, Bakersfield
(661) 322-6019

Pet Emergency Treatment Service Inc.
1048 University Ave., Berkeley
(510) 548-6684

United Emergency Animal Clinic
1657 S. Bascom Ave., Campbell
(408) 371-6252

Acacia Veterinary Hospital
479 East Ave., Chico
(530) 345-1338

Contra Costa Veterinary Emergency Center
1410 Monument Blvd., Concord
(925) 798-2900

Solano Pet Emergency Clinic
4437 Central Pl., Cordelia
(707) 864-1444

East Valley Emergency Pet Clinic
938 N. Diamond Bar Blvd., Diamond Bar
(909) 861-5737

Dublin Veterinary Hospital
7410 Amador Valley Blvd., #D, Dublin
(925) 828-5520

Emergency Pet Clinic of San Gabriel Valley
3254 Santa Anita Ave., El Monte
(626) 579-4550

Greenback Veterinary Hospital
8311 Greenback Ln., Fair Oaks
(916) 725-1541

All Care Animal Referral Center
18440 E. Amistad St., Fountain Valley
(714) 963-0909

Central Veterinary Hospital & Emergency Service
5245 Central Ave., Fremont
(510) 797-7387

Veterinary Emergency Services
1639 N. Fresno St., Fresno
(559) 486-0520

Orange County Emergency Pet Clinic
12750 Garden Grove Blvd., Garden Grove
(714) 537-3032

Pet Medical Center Chatoak
17659 Chatsworth St., Granada Hills
(818) 363-7444

Animal Emergency Clinic
12022 La Crosse Ave., Grand Terrace
(909) 825-9350

North Orange County Emergency Pet Clinic
1474 S. Harbor Blvd., La Habra
(714) 441-2925

Pet Emergency & Specialty Center
5232 Jackson Dr., #105, La Mesa
(619) 462-4800

Loomis Basin Veterinary Clinic
3901 Sierra College Blvd., Loomis
(916) 652-5816

Adobe Animal Hospital
396 First St., Los Altos
(650) 948-9661

Animal Emergency Facility
1736 South Sepulveda Blvd., #A, Los Angeles
(310) 473-1561

Eagle Rock Emergency Pet Clinic
4254 Eagle Rock Blvd., Los Angeles
(323) 254-7382

VCA/West Los Angeles Animal Hospital
1818 South Sepulveda Blvd., Los Angeles
(310) 473-2951

Animal Urgent Care
28085 Hillcrest, Mission Viejo
(949) 364-6228

Monterey Animal Hospital Inc.
725 Foam St., Monterey
(831) 373-0711

Crossroads Animal Emergency & Referral Center
11057 E. Rosecrans Ave., Norwalk
(562) 863-2522

South Peninsula Veterinary Emergency Clinic
3045 Middlefield Rd., Palo Alto
(650) 494-1461

Animal Emergency Clinic of Pasadena
2121 Foothill Blvd., Pasadena
(626) 564-0704

McClave Vet Hospital
6950 Reseda Blvd., Reseda
(818) 881-5102

Rimforest Animal Hospital
1299 Bear Springs Rd., Rimforest
(909) 337-8589

Animal Care Center of Sonoma County
6470 Redwood Dr., Rohnert Park
(707) 584-4343

Emergency Animal Clinic of Sacramento
9700 Business Park Dr., #404, Sacramento
(916) 362-3111

Sacramento Emergency Veterinary Clinic
2201 El Camino Ave., Sacramento
(916) 922-3425

San Clemente Veterinary Hospital
1833 South El Camino Real, San Clemente
(949) 492-5777

VCA Hillcrest Animal Center
246 W. Washington St., San Diego
(619) 299-7387

Emergency Animal Hospital & Referral Center
2317 Hotel Cir. South, San Diego
(619) 299-2400

All Animals Emergency Hospital
1333 9th Ave., San Francisco
(415) 566-0531

Mission Pet Hospital
720 Valencia St., San Francisco
(415) 552-1969

Pets Unlimited
2343 Fillmore St., San Francisco
(415) 563-6700

South Bay Veterinary Specialists
5440 Thornwood Dr., #E, San Jose
(408) 363-8066

Bay Area Veterinary Medical Group
14790 Washington Ave., San Leandro
(510) 352-6080

California Veterinary Specialist
100 N. Rancho Santa Fe Rd., San Marcos
(760) 734-4433

Northern Peninsula Veterinary Emergency Clinic
227 N. Amphlett Blvd., San Mateo
(650) 348-2575

Santa Cruz Veterinary Hospital
2585 Soquel Dr., Santa Cruz
(831) 475-5400

North Bay Animal Emergency Hospital
1304 Wilshire Blvd., Santa Monica
(310) 451-8962

Pet Care Veterinary Hospital
1370 Fulton Rd., Santa Rosa
(707) 579-5900

Beverly Oaks Animal Hospital
14302 Ventura Blvd., Sherman Oaks
(818) 788-2022

American Veterinary Hospital
2109 Tapo St., #3, Simi Valley
(805) 581-9111

Rancho Sequoia Veterinary Hospital
3380 Los Angeles Ave., Simi Valley
(805) 522-7476

Animal Emergency Center
11740 Ventura Blvd., Studio City
(818) 760-3882

Emergency Pet Clinic of the Inland Empire
27443 Jefferson Ave., Temecula
(909) 695-5044

Pet Emergency Clinic of Thousand Oaks
2967 North Moorpark Rd., Thousand Oaks
(805) 492-2436

Animal Emergency Clinic of the Desert
72-374 Ramon Rd., Thousand Palms
(760) 343-3438

Emergency Pet Clinic of South Bay
2325 Torrance Blvd., Torrance
(310) 320-8300

Central Animal Hospital
281 North Central Ave., Upland
(909) 981-2855

Pet Emergency Clinic of Ventura
2301 S. Victoria Ave., Ventura
(805) 642-8562

Washington Blvd. Animal Hospital
12116 East Washington Blvd., Whittier
(562) 693-8233

COLORADO

All Pets Veterinary Clinic
5290 Manhattan Cir., Boulder
(303) 499-5335

Boulder Emergency Pet Clinic
1658 30th St., Boulder
(303) 440-7722

Animal Emergency Care Center
5752 North Academy Blvd., Colorado Springs
(719) 260-7141

Animal Emergency Care Center
3775 Airport Ave., Colorado Springs
(719) 578-9300

Alameda East Animal Hospital
9870 E. Alameda Ave., Denver
(303) 366-2639

Colorado State University Veterinary Teaching Hospital
300 W. Drake Rd., Fort Collins
(970) 221-4535

Centennial Veterinary Clinic
5151 S. Federal Blvd., Littleton
(303) 795-0130

Wheat Ridge Animal Hospital
3695 Kipling St., Wheat Ridge
(303) 424-3325

CONNECTICUT

East of the River Veterinary Emergency Clinic
222 Boston Tpk., Bolton
(860) 646-6134

Shoreline Animal Emergency Clinic
7365 Main St., Stratford
(203) 375-6500

Animal Emergency Care of West Hartford County
41 Prospect Ave., West Hartford
(860) 233-8564

FLORIDA

Veterinary Emergency Clinic
195 Concord Dr., Casselberry
(407) 644-4449

Volusia Animal Emergency Clinic
US 92, Daytona Beach
(386) 252-4300

Animal Emergency Clinic of Deerfield
103 N. Powerline Rd., Deerfield Beach
(954) 428-9888

Animal Emergency and Referral Center
3984 S. US 1, Fort Pierce
(772) 466-3441

Affiliated Pet Emergency
7520 W. University Ave., Gainesville
(352) 373-4444

Chasewood Animal Clinic
6390 Indiantown Rd., #15, Jupiter
(561) 745-4944

Veterinary Emergency Clinic
3609 Hwy. 98 S., Lakeland
(863) 665-3199

Lantana Animal Clinic
3530 Lantana Rd., Lantana
(561) 439-0694

Promenade Animal Hospital
4424 N. University Dr., Lauderhill
(954) 748-9600

Animal Emergency Clinic South
8429 S.W. 132nd St., Miami
(305) 251-2096

Knowles Emergency Clinic
1000 N.W. 27th Ave., Miami
(305) 649-1234

Knowles Snapper Creek Animal Clinic
9933 Sunset Dr., Miami
(305) 279-2323

Emergency Veterinary Clinic Okaloosa/Walton
210 A Government Ave., Niceville
(850) 729-3335

Veterinary Emergency Clinic
2080 Principal Row, Orlando
(407) 438-4449

Pet Emergency & Critical Care Clinic
3816 Northlake Blvd., Palm Beach Gardens
(561) 691-9999

Emergency Animal Clinic
6602 Pines Blvd., Pembroke Pines
(954) 962-0300

Animal Hospital
8560 N. Davis Hwy., Pensacola
(850) 479-9484

Animal Emergency Clinic of Pasco
8740 US Hwy. 19 N., Port Richey
(727) 841-6575

Emergency Veterinary Clinic of Sarasota
7517 S. Tamiami Tr., #107, Sarasota
(941) 923-7260

Animal Emergency of Hernando
3496 Deltona Blvd., Spring Hill
(352) 666-0904

Animal Emergency Clinic of St. Petersburg
3165 22nd Ave. N., St. Petersburg
(727) 323-1311

Allied Veterinary Emergency Hospital
401 East 9th Ave., Tallahassee
(850) 222-0123

Northwood Animal Hospital
1881-B North Martin Luther King Jr. Blvd., Tallahassee
(850) 385-8181

Murphy Animal Hospital
6845 N. Dale Mabry, Tampa
(813) 879-6090

American Animal Emergency Clinic
3425 Forest Hill Blvd., West Palm Beach
(561) 433-2244

Summit Boulevard Animal Hospital
1000 S. Military Tr., #B and C, West Palm Beach
(561) 439-7900

GEORGIA

Animal Emergency Clinic of Sandy Springs
228 Sandy Springs Pl., Atlanta
(404) 252-7881

Augusta Animal Emergency
208 Hudson Trace, Augusta
(706) 733-7458

Animal Emergency Care
2009 Mercer University Dr., Macon
(478) 750-0911

Cobb Emergency Veterinary Clinic
630 Cobb Pkwy. N., Ste. C, Marietta
(770) 424-9157

Peachtree Corners Animal Clinic
4020 Holcomb Bridge Rd., Norcross
(770) 448-0700

Animal Emergency Center of North Fulton
900 Mansell Rd., #19, Roswell
(770) 594-2266

Chattahoochee Animal Clinic
1176 Alpharetta St., Roswell
(770) 993-6329

Savannah Veterinary Emergency and Specialty Referral Center
317 Eisenhower Dr., Savannah
(912) 355-6113

ILLINOIS

Animal Emergency Center
2005 Mall St., Collinsville
(618) 346-1843

Emergency Veterinary Care South
13715 S. Cicero Ave., Crestwood
(708) 388-3771

Animal Emergency and Treatment Center
1810 Belvidere Rd., Grayslake
(847) 548-5300

Emergency Veterinary Services
820 Ogden Ave., Lisle
(630) 960-2900

Animal Emergency and Critical Care Center
1810 Frontage Rd., Northbrook
(847) 564-5775

Emergency Pet Care Center
530 Dunham Rd., St. Charles
(630) 584-7447

INDIANA

All Pet Emergencies Clinic
104B South Heidelbach, Evansville
(812) 422-3300

Emergency Animal Clinic
5818 Maplecrest Rd., Fort Wayne
(260) 426-1062

Indianapolis Veterinary Emergency Center
5245 Victory Dr., Indianapolis
(317) 782-4418

Veterinary Centers of America
4030 W. 86th St., Indianapolis
(317) 872-0200

New Carlisle Animal Clinic
8935 East US 20, New Carlisle
(574) 654-3129

Calumet Emergency Veterinary Clinic
216 W. Lincoln Hwy., Schererville
(219) 865-0970

Arbor View Animal Hospital
244 W. US Hwy. 6, Valparaiso
(219) 762-6586

IOWA

Animal Emergency Clinic & Referral Center of Central Iowa
6110 Crescent Ave., Des Moines
(515) 280-3051

KANSAS

Mission Medvet
5914 Johnson Dr., Mission
(913) 722-5566

Veterinary Specialty & Emergency Center
11950 W. 110th St., Overland Park
(913) 642-9563

Wichita Emergency Veterinary Clinic
737 S. Washington, Wichita
(316) 262-5321

KENTUCKY

Colonial Animal Clinic
1601 Argillite Rd., Flatwoods
(606) 836-8112

Hagyard Davidson McGee Veterinarians
4250 Ironworks Pike, Lexington
(859) 255-8741

Jefferson Animal Hospital & Emergency Center
4504 Outer Loop, Louisville
(502) 966-4104

LOUISIANA

Buccaneer Villa Vet
8220 W. Judge Perez Dr., Chalmette
(504) 271-1234

Westbank Pet Emergency Clinic, Inc.
403 Lapalco Blvd., Gretna
(504) 392-1932

Animal Emergency Clinic
1955 Veterans Memorial Blvd., Metairie
(504) 835-8508

Gentilly Veterinary Hospital
7006 Read Ln., New Orleans
(504) 242-4200

MAINE

Animal Emergency Clinic of Mid Maine
37 Strawberry Ave., Lewiston
(207) 777-1110

Norway Veterinary Hospital
Route 26, 10 Main St., Norway
(207) 743-6384

Animal Emergency Clinic
352 Warren Ave., Portland
(207) 878-3121

MARYLAND

Anne Arundel Veterinary Emergency Clinic, Inc.
808 Bestgate Rd., Annapolis
(410) 224-0331

Emergency Veterinary Clinic
32 Mellor Ave., Catonsville
(410) 788-7040

Veterinary Referral Associates, Inc.
15021 Dufief Mill Rd., Gaithersburg
(301) 340-3129

Beltway Emergency Animal Hospital
11660 Annapolis Rd., Glenn Dale
(301) 464-3737

Emergency Animal Center, Inc.
1896 Urbana Pike, #23, Hyattstown
(301) 831-1088

Metropolitan Emergency Animal Clinic
12106 Nebel St., Rockville
(301) 770-5225

Animal Emergency Center and Chesapeake Veterinary Referral
1209 Cromwell Bridge Rd., Towson
(410) 252-8387

Southern Maryland Veterinary Referral Center and Emergency
3 Rockefeller Ct., Waldorf
(301) 638-0988

Westminster Veterinary Hospital-Emergency Trauma Center
269 W. Main St., Westminster
(410) 848-3363

MASSACHUSETTS

Angell Memorial Animal Hospital
350 S. Huntington Ave., Boston
(617) 522-7282

Roberts Animal Hospital
516 Washington St., Hanover
(781) 826-2306

Holyoke Animal Hospital
320 Easthampton Rd., Holyoke
(413) 538-8700

Animal Health Care Associates
Martha's Vineyard Airport, Martha's Vineyard
(508) 693-6515

Highland Animal Hospital
1299 Highland Ave., Needham
(781) 433-0467

Tufts University School Of Veterinary Medicine
200 Westboro Rd., North Grafton
(508) 839-5395

South Deerfield Veterinary Clinic
Elm Street and Route 5 & 10, South Deerfield
(413) 665-3626

Veterinary Associates of Cape Cod
16 Commonwealth Ave., South Yarmouth
(508) 394-3566

Angell Animal Medical Center
171 Union St., Springfield
(413) 785-1221

VCA/Wakefield Animal Hospital
19 Main St., Wakefield
(781) 245-0045

MICHIGAN

Lansing Veterinary Urgent Care
5133 S. Martin Luther King Jr. Blvd., Lansing
(517) 393-9200

Veterinary Medical Center
243 N. Jebavy Dr., Ludington
(231) 845-0585

Veterinary Emergency Service & Critical Care
28223 John R Rd., Madison Heights
(248) 547-4677

Veterinary Emergency Service West
40850 Ann Arbor Rd., Plymouth
(734) 207-8500

Michigan Veterinary Emergency Care
21600 West Eleven Mile Rd., Southfield
(248) 354-6660

Affiliated Veterinary Emergency Services
14085 Northline Rd., Southgate
(734) 284-1700

Union Lake Veterinary Hospital
6545 Cooley Lake Rd., Waterford
(248) 363-1508

MINNESOTA

South Metro Animal Emergency Care Clinic
14690 Pennock Ave., Apple Valley
(952) 953-3737

Emergency Veterinary Service
1615 Coon Rapids Blvd., Coon Rapids
(763) 754-9434

Emergency Veterinary Service
4708 Olson Memorial Hwy., Golden Valley
(763) 529-6560

Animal Emergency Clinic
301 University Ave., St. Paul
(651) 293-1800

MISSISSIPPI

Bienville Animal Hospital
1524 Bienville Blvd., Ocean Springs
(228) 872-1231

MISSOURI

Animal Emergency Clinic
12501 Natural Bridge Rd., Bridgeton
(314) 739-1500

Animal Emergency Clinic
9937 Big Bend Blvd., St. Louis
(314) 822-7600

MONTANA

Animal Medical Clinic
5100 9th Ave. South, Great Falls
(406) 761-8183

NEBRASKA

VCA-Rohrig Animal Hospital
8022 W. Dodge Rd., Omaha
(402) 399-8100

NEVADA

Carson Tahoe Veterinary Hospital
3389 S. Carson St., Carson City
(775) 883-8238

Animal Emergency Center
1914 E. Sahara Ave., Las Vegas
(702) 457-8050

Painted Desert Animal Hospital
4601 N. Rancho Dr., Las Vegas
(702) 645-2543

Animal Emergency Center
6425 S. Virginia St., Reno
(775) 851-3600

NEW HAMPSHIRE

Animal Emergency Clinic
2626 Brown Ave., Pine Island Plaza, Manchester
(603) 666-6677

State Line Veterinary Hospital
325 S. Daniel Webster Hwy., Nashua
(603) 888-2751

Animal Medical Center
1550 Woodbury Ave., Portsmouth
(603) 436-4922

NEW JERSEY

Ocean County Veterinary Hospital
838 River Ave., Lakewood
(732) 363-7202

Oradell Animal Hospital
580 Winters Ave., Paramus
(201) 262-0010

Alliance Emergency Veterinary Clinic
540 Route 10 West, Randolph
(973) 328-2844

NEW MEXICO

Albuquerque Animal Emergency Clinic
5005 Prospect Ave. N.E., Albuquerque
(505) 884-3433

Great Plains Veterinary Clinic
2720 Lovington Hwy., Hobbs
(505) 392-5513

Ruidoso Animal Clinic
160 Sudderth, Ruidoso
(505) 257-4027

Emergency Veterinary Clinic of Santa Fe
1311 Calle Nava, Santa Fe
(505) 984-0625

NEW YORK

Central Veterinary Hospital
388 Central Ave., Albany
(518) 434-2115

Greater Buffalo Veterinary Services
4949 Main St., Amherst
(716) 839-4043

Bayside Animal Clinic
36-43 Bell Blvd., Bayside
(718) 224-4451

Bellerose Animal Hospital
242-01 Jamaica Ave., Bellerose
(718) 347-1057

Brooklyn Veterinary Emergency Service
453 Bay Bridge Ave., Brooklyn
(718) 748-5180

Far Rockaway Animal Hospital
1833 Cornaga Ave., Far Rockaway
(718) 327-0256

Boulevard Animal Clinic
112-49 Queens Blvd., Forest Hills
(718) 261-1231

Terrace Animal Clinic
501 Great Neck Rd., Great Neck
(516) 466-9191

Homer Animal Clinic
66 S. West St., Homer
(607) 749-7223

Queens Veterinary Emergency Clinic
187-11 Hillside Ave., Jamaica
(718) 454-4141

Hilton Hospital for Animals
120 Merrick Rd., Lynbrook
(516) 887-2914

Animal Medical Center/Bobst Hospital
510 East 62nd St., New York
(212) 838-8100

VCA/Manhattan Veterinary Group
240 East 80th St., New York
(212) 988-1000

Riverside Animal Hospital
250 West 100th St., New York
(212) 865-2224

Orchard Park Veterinary Medical Center
3507 Orchard Park Rd., Orchard Park
(716) 662-6660

Animal Emergency Clinic of Hudson Valley
84 Patrick Ln., Poughkeepsie
(845) 471-8242

Animal Hospital Group of Staten Island
640 Willowbrook Rd., Staten Island
(718) 494-0050

Veterinary Emergency Center
1293 Clove Rd., Staten Island
(718) 720-4211

Animal Emergency Clinic
2612 Erie Blvd. East, Syracuse
(315) 446-7933

Valley Cottage Animal Hospital
202 Route 303, Valley Cottage
(845) 268-9263

Central Veterinary Associates
73 W. Merrick Rd., Valley Stream
(516) 825-3066

Animal Care Hospital
4535 Old Vestal Rd., Vestal
(607) 770-9999

Schroon River Animal Hospital
150 Schroon River Rd., Warrensburg
(518) 623-3181

Nassau Animal Emergency Clinic
740 Old Country Rd., Westbury
(516) 333-6262

NORTH CAROLINA

Freedom Animal Hospital
3055 Freedom Dr., Charlotte
(704) 399-6534

Triangle Pet Emergency Treatment Service
3319 Chapel Hill Blvd., Durham
(919) 489-0615

Veterinary Emergency Clinic of Gaston County
728 E. Franklin Blvd., Gastonia
(704) 866-7918

Cabarrus Emergency Veterinary Clinic
1317 S. Cannon Blvd., Kannapolis
(704) 932-1182

Emergency Veterinary Clinic
2440 Plantation Center Dr., Matthews
(704) 844-6440

After Hours Small Animal Emergency Clinic
409 Vick Ave., Raleigh
(919) 781-5145

Ansede Animal Hospital
3535 South Wilmington St., #107, Raleigh
(919) 661-1515

Wilmington Animal Emergency Clinic
5333 Oleander Dr., Wilmington
(910) 791-7387

Forsyth After Hours Veterinary Emergency Clinic
7781 Northpoint Blvd., Winston-Salem
(336) 896-0902

OHIO

Animal Emergency & Specialty Clinic
5320 West 140th St., Cleveland
(216) 362-6000

Dayton Emergency Veterinary Clinic
2714 Springboro West, Dayton
(937) 293-2714

Animal Medical & Emergency Hospital
2527 West Dublin-Granville Rd., Dublin
(614) 889-2556

Lorain County Animal Emergency Center
1909 North Ridge Rd., Lorain
(440) 240-1400

County Animal Hospital
1185 Reading Rd., Mason
(513) 398-8000

Aaron Animal Clinic and Emergency Hospital
7640 Broadview Rd., Parma
(216) 901-9980

Columbus Veterinary Emergency Service
300 E. Wilson Bridge Rd., Worthington
(614) 846-5800

OKLAHOMA

Midtown Animal Hospital
1101 S.W. Park Ave., Lawton
(580) 353-3438

Veterinary Emergency and Critical Care Hospital
1800 W. Memorial Rd., Oklahoma City
(405) 749-6989

Animal Emergency Center
7220 E. 41st St., Tulsa
(918) 665-0508

OREGON

Willamette Veterinary Clinic
650 S.W. Third St., Corvallis
(541) 753-2223

Dove Lewis Emergency Animal Hospital
1984 N.W. Pettygrove St., Portland
(503) 228-7281

Salem Veterinary Emergency Clinic
450 Pine St. N.E., Salem
(503) 588-8082

Emergency Veterinary Clinic
19314 S.W. Mohave Ct., Tualatin
(503) 691-7922

PENNSYLVANIA

Providence Veterinary Hospital
24th and Providence Ave., Chester
(610) 872-4000

Animal Emergency & Critical Care Service
2010 Cabot Blvd., Langhorne
(215) 750-2774

St. Francis Veterinary Hospital
18200 Conneaut Lake Rd., Meadville
(814) 337-3271

Metropolitan Veterinary Center
560 McNeilly Rd., Pittsburgh
(412) 344-6888

Allegheny Veterinary Emergency Associates
1810 Rte. 286, Pittsburgh
(724) 325-1881

Castle Shannon Veterinary Hospital
3610 Library Rd., Pittsburgh
(412) 885-2500

Tri-County Veterinary Emergency Service
2250 Old Bethlehem Pike, North Quakertown
(215) 536-6245

Valley Central Emergency Veterinary Hospital
210 Fullerton Ave., Whitehall
(610) 435-5588

Animal Emergency Clinic
3256 Susquehanna Tr., York
(717) 767-5355

RHODE ISLAND

North Kingstown Animal Hospital
3736 Quaker Ln., North Kingstown
(401) 295-9777

Animal Care Services
135 Meadow St., Warwick
(401) 738-6695

Warwick Animal Hospital
1950 Elmwood Ave., Warwick
(401) 785-2222

SOUTH CAROLINA

South Carolina Veterinary Emergency Care Center
132 Stonemark Ln., Columbia
(803) 798-3837

Animal Hospital of North Myrtle Beach
2501 Hwy. 17 S., North Myrtle Beach
(843) 272-8121

Veterinary Emergency Clinic of Spartanburg
1291 Ashville Hwy., Spartanburg
(864) 591-1923

TENNESSEE

Keith Street Animal Clinic
1990 Keith St., Cleveland
(423) 476-1804

After Hours Pet Emergency Clinic
215 Center Park Dr., Knoxville
(865) 966-3888

TEXAS

I-20 Animal Medical Center
5820 I-20 West, Arlington
(817) 478-9238

Animal Emergency Hospital of Austin
4106 N. Lamar Blvd., Austin
(512) 459-4336

Emergency Animal Hospital of Austin
4434 Frontier Tr., Austin
(512) 899-0955

Emergency Animal Clinic of Northwest Austin
12034 Research Blvd., #8, Austin
(512) 331-6121

North Texas Emergency Pet Clinic
1712 W. Frankford Rd., Carrollton
(972) 323-1310

Emergency Animal Clinic
12101 Greenville Ave., #118, Dallas
(972) 994-9110

Whiterock Animal Hospital
11414 East Northwest Hwy., Dallas
(214) 328-3255

El Paso Animal Emergency Center
2101 Texas Ave., El Paso
(915) 545-1148

Airport Freeway Animal Emergency Clinic
411 N. Main St., Euless
(817) 571-2088

Fort Worth Animal Medical Center
8329 W. Freeway, Fort Worth
(817) 560-8387

Animal Emergency Clinic
8921 Katy Frwy., Houston
(713) 932-9589

Animal Emergency Clinic Southeast
1100 Gulf Frwy. S., #104, League City
(281) 332-1678

Lake Olympia Animal Hospital
3603 Glenn Lakes, Missouri City
(281) 499-7242

Permian Basin Emergency Veterinary Clinic
13528 W. US Hwy. 80, Odessa
(432) 561-8301

Emergency Pet Clinic
8503 Broadway, #105, San Antonio
(210) 822-2873

Southwest Freeway Animal Hospital & Emergency Center
15575 Southwest Frwy., Sugar Land
(281) 491-8387

UTAH

Animal Medical Services
469 W. Center St., Orem
(801) 225-3346

Central Valley Emergency Animal Clinic
55 E. Miller Ave., Salt Lake City
(801) 487-1325

VERMONT

Lamoille Valley Veterinary Services
278 Vermont #15 East, Hyde Park
(802) 888-7911

VIRGINIA

Virginia-Maryland Veterinary Emergency Service
2660 Duke St., Alexandria
(703) 823-3601

Albemarle Veterinary Hospital
445 Westfield Rd., Charlottesville
(434) 973-6146

Animal Emergency Clinic of Fredericksburg
1210 Snowden St., Fredericksburg
(540) 371-0554

Animal Emergency Hospital & Referral Center
2 Cardinal Park Dr., #101B, Leesburg
(703) 777-5755

Animal Emergency Clinic of Central Virginia
1000 Miller Park Sq., Lynchburg
(434) 846-1504

Veterinary Internal Medicine Practice
8610 Centreville Rd., Manassas
(703) 631-1030 (referrals only)

Veterinary Emergency Center
3312 W. Cary St., Richmond
(804) 353-9000

Springfield Emergency Veterinary Hospital
6651-F Backlick Rd., Springfield
(703) 451-8900

Silver Spring Veterinary Hospital
241 Garber Ln., Winchester
(540) 662-2301

WASHINGTON

Auburn Veterinary Hospital
718 Auburn Way N., Auburn
(253) 833-4510, after hours 939-6272

Aerowood Animal Hospital
2975 156th St. S.E., Bellevue
(425) 746-6557

Snoqualmie Valley Animal Hospital
32020 S.E. 40th St., Fall City
(425) 222-7220

Vista Veterinary Hospital
5603 W. Canal Dr., Kennewick
(509) 783-2131

Animal Emergency & Referral Center
19511 24th Ave. W., Lynnwood
(425) 697-6106

Animal Emergency and Trauma Center
19494 7th Ave. N.E., #F, Poulsbo
(360) 697-7771

Emerald City Emergency Clinic
4102 Stone Way N., Seattle
(206) 634-9000

Five Corners Veterinary Hospital
15707 1st Ave. S., Seattle
(206) 243-2982

Pet Emergency Clinic
21 E. Mission Ave., Spokane
(509) 326-6670

Animal Emergency Clinic
5608 South Durango, Tacoma
(253) 474-0791

Emergency Veterinary Service
6818 E. 4th Plain Blvd., Vancouver
(360) 694-3007

WEST VIRGINIA

Middletown Animal Clinic
1615 Bobbeck Ln., Fairmont
(304) 366-6130

Kanawha Valley Animal Emergency Clinic
5304 MacCorkle Ave. S.W., South Charleston
(304) 768-2911

WISCONSIN

Fox Valley Animal Referral Center
842 Westhill Blvd., Appleton
(920) 993-9193

Animal Emergency Center
2100 W. Silver Spring Dr., Glendale
(414) 540-6710

Emergency Clinic for Animals
229 W. Beltline Hwy., Madison
(608) 274-7772

Animal Clinic
2734 Calumet Dr., Sheboygan
(920) 458-3636

Emergency Veterinary Service
360 Bluemound Rd., Waukesha
(262) 542-3241

Canada

BRITISH COLUMBIA

Animal Emergency Clinic
#103-6337 198th St., Langley
(604) 514-1711

Animal Emergency Clinic
1590 West 4th Ave., Vancouver
(604) 734-5104

ONTARIO

Park Animal Hospital
1958 Burnham Thorpe Rd. E., Mississauga
(905) 625-5222

Niagara Veterinary Emergency Clinic
2F Tremont Dr., #1, St. Catharines
(905) 641-3185

PET-FRIENDLY LODGINGS

How to Use the Listings
U.S. Lodgings
Canadian Lodgings

How to Use the Listings

Some 12,000 AAA-RATED® properties across North America accept traveling pets. This guide provides listings for those lodgings in the United States and Canada that roll out the welcome mat for pets as well as the people who love them.

For the purpose of this book, "pets" are domestic cats or dogs. If you are planning to travel with any other kind of animal — particularly such exotic pets as birds or reptiles — check with the property before making definite plans. If you are taking a nontraditional pet, expect to keep her crated at all times.

Note: Always inform the management that you are traveling with an animal; you may be fined if you do not declare your pet. Many properties require guests with pets to sign a waiver or release form and to pay for the room with a credit card. Of course, whether you pay in cash or by credit card, you will be held liable for any damages caused by your pet, even if the property does not charge a deposit or pet fee. It is not a good idea to leave your pet unattended in the room, but if you must, crate him and notify the management. When in public areas, keep your pet leashed and do not allow him to disturb other guests.

About the Listings

Geographic listings are used for accuracy and consistency; lodgings are listed under the city or town in which they physically are located — or in some cases under the nearest recognized city or town. For a complete list of all cities within a state or province, see the comprehensive City Index at the beginning of the corresponding section.

U.S. properties are given first, followed by Canadian properties. Most listings are alphabetically organized by state or province, city and establishment name. Reflecting contemporary travel patterns, properties in some cities or towns may instead be listed within destination cities or areas. Such "vicinity cities" and their listings will be shown alphabetically in the destination city or area, and the vicinity city also will appear in alphabetical order in the City Index, along with the page number on which the listings begin.

Each listing provides the following information (see sample listing, next page):

❶ Symbol denoting Official Appointment (OA) properties. The OA program permits properties to display and advertise the Ⓐ or Ⓐ logo. OAs have a special interest in serving AAA/CAA members. Ask if they offer special member amenities such as free breakfast, early check-in/late checkout, free room upgrade, free local phone calls, etc.

❷ Diamond rating. *See next page.*

❸ Property name.

❹ Lodging classification. *See p. 62.*

❺ Special amenities offered. These properties provide an additional benefit to pets, such as treats, toys or gifts, pet sitting and/or walking, a pet menu, food/water dishes, pet sheets or pillows, pet beds or other extras.

❻ Telephone number.

❼ Two-person (2P) rate year-round, and cancellation notice validity period (if more than 48 hours). Rates listed are usually daily, but weekly rates also may be listed. **Note:** Most properties accept any or all of the major credit cards, including American Express, MasterCard and VISA. If a property accepts only cash, the phrase "(no credit cards)" follows the rates.

❽ Physical address and highway location. If no physical address was available, the phrase "call for directions" appears.

❾ Exterior or interior corridors.

❿ Pet policies. If the phrase "pets accepted" appears, the property does accept pets but specific information was unavailable at press time. Otherwise, pet-specific policies are denoted as follows:

Size. "Very small" denotes pets weighing up to 10 pounds; "small," up to 25 pounds; "medium," up to 50 pounds; and "large," up to 100 pounds. If no size is specified, the property accepts pets of all sizes.

Species. "Other" indicates the property accepts animals other than dogs and cats. Always call ahead and specify the type of pet you plan to bring.

Deposits and fees. Includes the dollar amount, the type of charge (refundable deposit or nonrefundable fee), the frequency of the charge and whether the charge is per pet or per room.

Designated rooms. Guests with pets are placed in certain rooms, often smoking rooms or those on the ground floor.

Housekeeping service. The phrase "service with restrictions" denotes properties that require the pet to be crated, removed or attended by the owner during housekeeping service.

Supervision. The pet is required to be supervised at all times.

Crate. The pet must be crated when the owner is not present. If this policy applies only to cats, the phrase "(cats only)" will follow.

⓫ Property discounts and amenities:

    🆂🅰🆅🅴 Minimum 10% discount.

    🅰🆂🅺 May offer discount.

    🆂🅳 Senior discount.

    ✕ Non-smoking rooms.

    🆂🅼 Semi-accessible or 🅵🅼 fully accessible.

    🖉 Hearing impaired.

    🚿 Roll-in showers.

    🞏 Refrigerator.

    🞐 Coffee maker.

    🍴 Restaurant on premises.

    🏊 Pool.

    🞐 Recreational activities.

    🅀 No air conditioning.

    🆃🆅 No TV.

    🅃 No telephones.

Please note: Some in-room amenities represented by the icons in the listings may be available only in selected rooms, and may incur an extra fee. Please inquire when making your reservations.

It is important to remember that animal policies do change; always confirm policies, restrictions and fees with the lodging when making reservations and again 1-2 days before departure.

Listing information is subject to change. All listing information was accurate at press time. However, lodging rates and policies change and the publisher cannot be held liable for changes occurring after publication.

AAA Diamond Ratings

Before a property is listed by AAA, it must satisfy a set of minimum standards regarding basic lodging needs as identified by AAA members. If a property meets those requirements, it is assigned a diamond rating reflecting the overall quality of the establishment.

AAA ratings range from one to five diamonds and indicate the property's physical and service standards as measured against the standards of each diamond level. The rating process takes into account the property's classification; i.e., its physical structure and style of operation.

▼ Properties meet all listing requirements. They are clean and well-maintained.

▼▼ Properties maintain the attributes offered at the one-diamond level while showing noticeable enhancements in room decor and quality of furnishings.

▼▼▼ Properties show a marked upgrade in physical attributes, services and comfort. Additional amenities, services and facilities may be offered.

◆◆◆◆ Properties reflect an exceptional degree of hospitality, service and attention to detail while offering upscale facilities and a variety of amenities.

◆◆◆◆◆ Property facilities and operations exemplify an impeccable standard of excellence while exceeding guest expectations in hospitality and service. These renowned properties are both striking and luxurious, offering many extra amenities.

Lodging Classifications

BB Bed & Breakfast: Usually smaller establishments emphasizing a more personal relationship between operators and guests, leading to an "at home" feeling. Guest units tend to be individually decorated. Rooms may not include some modern amenities such as televisions and telephones, and may have a shared bathroom. Usually owner-operated, with a common room or parlor separate from the innkeeper's living quarters, where guests and operators can interact during evening and breakfast hours. Evening office closures are normal. A continental or full, hot breakfast is served and is included in the room rate.

CA Cabin/Cottage: Vacation-oriented, small-scale, freestanding houses or cabins. Units vary in design and decor and often contain one or more bedrooms, living room, kitchen, dining area and bathroom. Studio-type models combine the sleeping and living areas into one room. Typically, basic cleaning supplies, kitchen utensils, and complete bed and bath linens are supplied. The guest registration area may be located off-site.

CI Country Inn: Although similar in definition to a bed and breakfast, country inns are usually larger in size, provide more spacious public areas and offer a dining facility that serves at least breakfast and dinner. May be located in a rural setting or downtown area.

CO Condominium: Establishments that primarily offer guest accommodations that are privately owned by individuals and available for rent. These can include apartment-style units or homes. A variety of room styles and decor treatments as well as limited housekeeping service is typical. May have off-site registration.

LH Large-scale Hotel: A multistory establishment with interior room entrances. A variety of guest unit styles is offered. Public areas are spacious and include a variety of facilities such as a restaurant, shops, fitness center, spa, business center or meeting rooms.

M Motel: Low-rise or multistory establishment offering limited public and recreational facilities.

RA Ranch: Often offers rustic decor treatments and food and beverage facilities. Entertainment and recreational activities are geared to a Western-style adventure vacation. May provide some meeting facilities.

SH Small-scale Hotel: A multistory establishment typically with interior room entrances. A variety of guest unit styles is offered. Public areas are limited in size and/or the variety of facilities available.

VH Vacation Home: Vacation-oriented or extended-stay, large-scale, freestanding houses that are routinely available for rent through a management company. Houses vary in design and décor and often contain two or more bedrooms, living room, full kitchen, dining room and multiple bathrooms. Typically, basic cleaning supplies, kitchen utensils, and complete bed and bath linens are supplied. The guest registration area may be located off-site.

United States

ALABAMA

ABBEVILLE

◈◈ Best Western-Abbeville Inn 🅂🄷
(334) 585-5060. **$55-$65.** 1237 US 431. At jct SR 27. Ext corridors. **Pets:** $8 daily fee/pet. Service with restrictions, supervision.
[ASK] [S⬩] [✕] [⦿] [⬛] [⥲]

ALBERTVILLE

◈◈ Jameson Inn 🅂🄷
(256) 891-2600. **$67-$72.** 315 Martling Rd. On US 431; center. Ext corridors. **Pets:** Small. Service with restrictions, crate.
[✕] [⬩] [⦿] [⬛] [⥲]

ALEXANDER CITY

◈◈ Jameson Inn 🅂🄷
(256) 234-7099. **$68-$73.** 4335 US Hwy 280. US 280, just s of jct SR 22; just w of jct SR 63. Ext corridors. **Pets:** Small. Service with restrictions, crate.
[✕] [⬩] [⦿] [⬛] [⥲]

ANDALUSIA

◈◈ Days Inn 🅂🄷
(334) 427-0050. **$50-$75, 7 day notice.** 1604 E Bypass Hwy 84. Just s of US 84. Ext corridors. **Pets:** Medium, other species. $6 daily fee/room. Service with restrictions.
[ASK] [S⬩] [✕] [⦿] [⬛] [⥲]

ARAB

◈◈ Jameson Inn 🅂🄷
(256) 586-5777. **$65-$70.** 706 N Brindlee Mountain Pkwy (US 231). 0.5 mi sw of SR 69. Ext corridors. **Pets:** Small. Service with restrictions, crate.
[✕] [⬩] [⦿] [⬛] [⥲]

ARDMORE

◍◍◍ ◈◈◈ Budget Inn Ⓜ
(256) 423-6699. **$59-$69.** I-65 & Hwy 53. I-65, exit 365, just se. Ext corridors. **Pets:** Accepted.
[SAVE] [S⬩] [✕] [⦿]

ATHENS

◍◍◍ ◈◈◈ Best Western Anthens Inn 🅂🄷 ❀
(256) 233-4030. **$49-$99, 3 day notice.** 1329 Hwy 72. I-65, exit 351, just w. Ext corridors. **Pets:** Small, dogs only. $10 daily fee/pet. Designated rooms, service with restrictions, supervision.
[SAVE] [S⬩] [✕] [⦿] [⬛] [⥲]

◈◈ Country Hearth Inn 🅂🄷
(256) 232-1520. **$59-$99.** 1500 Hwy 72 E. I-65, exit 351, just se. Ext corridors. **Pets:** Small, other species. $10 daily fee/room. Service with restrictions, supervision.
[ASK] [S⬩] [✕] [⬛] [⥲]

◈◈ Days Inn Athens 🅂🄷
(256) 233-7500. **$45-$50.** 1322 Hwy 72 W. I-65, exit 351, just nw. Ext corridors. **Pets:** Accepted.
[ASK] [S⬩] [✕] [⦿] [⬛] [⥲]

◈◈◈ Hampton Inn-Athens 🅂🄷
(256) 232-0030. **$70-$85.** 1488 Thrasher Blvd. I-65, exit 351, just ne. Ext corridors. **Pets:** Other species. $10 one-time fee/room. Service with restrictions.
[ASK] [S⬩] [✕] [⦿] [⬛] [⥲]

◈◈ Sleep Inn 🅂🄷
(256) 232-4700. **$54-$89.** 1115 Audubon Ln. I-65, exit 351, just nw. Int corridors. **Pets:** $10 daily fee/pet. Service with restrictions, supervision.
[ASK] [S⬩] [✕] [⬩] [⬛] [⥲]

◈◈ Super 8 🅂🄷
(256) 233-1446. **$40-$60.** 1325 Hwy 72. I-65, exit 351, just w. Int corridors. **Pets:** Accepted.
[ASK] [S⬩] [✕] [⦿] [⬛]

ATTALLA

◍◍◍ ◈◈◈ Econo Lodge 🅂🄷
(256) 538-9925. **$49-$64.** 507 Cherry St. I-59, exit 183, just nw. Ext/int corridors. **Pets:** Small. $25 deposit/pet. Service with restrictions, supervision.
[SAVE] [S⬩] [✕] [⦿] [⬛] [🍴] [⥲]

◍◍◍ ◈◈◈ Holiday Inn Express Gadsden/Attalla 🅂🄷 ❀
(256) 538-7861. **$74.** 801 Cleveland Ave. I-59, exit 183, just e. Ext corridors. **Pets:** Other species. $10 one-time fee/room. Service with restrictions, supervision.
[SAVE] [S⬩] [✕] [⬩] [⦿] [⬛] [⥲]

AUBURN

◍◍◍ ◈◈◈ Auburn University Hotel & Dixon Conference Center 🄻🄷
(334) 821-8200. **$89-$179.** 241 S College St. I-85, exit 51, 3.5 mi w. Int corridors. **Pets:** Accepted.
[SAVE] [S⬩] [✕] [⬩M] [⊘] [⦿] [⬛] [🍴] [⥲]

AAA ▼▼ **Best Western University Convention Center** SH
(334) 821-7001. **$66-$162, 7 day notice.** 1577 S College. I-85, exit 51, 1.4 mi w. Ext corridors. **Pets:** Accepted.
SAVE S⚫ ✕ 🔒 📞 🍴 🏊

▼▼ **Jameson Inn** SH
(334) 502-5020. **$68-$73.** 1212 Mall Pkwy. I-85, exit 58, 1.5 mi w on US 280, then 2.9 mi sw on US 29/SR 14. Ext corridors. **Pets:** Small. Service with restrictions, crate.
✕ 🔒 📞 🏊

BIRMINGHAM METROPOLITAN AREA

BESSEMER

AAA ▼▼▼ **Best Western Hotel & Suites** SH
(205) 481-1950. **$84-$104.** 5041 Academy Ln. I-20/59, exit 108, just sw. Int corridors. **Pets:** Other species. $10 daily fee/pet. Service with restrictions, supervision.
SAVE S⚫ ✕ ♿ 🔒 📞 🏊

▼▼ **Comfort Inn** SH
(205) 428-3999. **$69-$155.** 5051 Academy Ln. I-20/59, exit 108, just sw. Int corridors. **Pets:** Other species. Supervision.
ASK S⚫ ✕ ♿ 🔒 📞 🏊

▼▼ **Jameson Inn** SH
(205) 428-3194. **$69-$74.** 5021 Academy Ln. I-20/59, exit 108, just sw. Ext corridors. **Pets:** Small, other species. Service with restrictions, crate.
✕ ♿M 🔊 ♿ 🔒 📞 🏊

BIRMINGHAM

AAA ▼▼▼ **AmeriSuites (Birmingham/Inverness)** SH
(205) 995-9242. **$109.** 4686 Hwy 280 E. I-459, exit 19 (US 280), 1.7 mi e. Int corridors. **Pets:** Small, dogs only. $25 deposit/room. Service with restrictions, supervision.
SAVE S⚫ ✕ ♿M ♿ 🔒 📞 🏊

▼▼ **Baymont Inn & Suites Birmingham** SH
(205) 995-9990. **$49-$64.** 513 Cahaba Park Cir. I-459, exit 19 (US 280), 1.2 mi e. Int corridors. **Pets:** Accepted.
ASK S⚫ ✕ 🔒 📞

▼▼ **Best Inn & Suites** SH
(205) 836-5400. **$65.** 9225 Parkway E. I-59, exit 134, just w, then just s on US 11. Ext corridors. **Pets:** Medium. $25 deposit/pet. Service with restrictions, supervision.
ASK S⚫ ✕ 🔒 📞 🏊

▼▼▼ **Drury Inn & Suites-Birmingham Southeast** SH
(205) 967-2450. **$82-$102.** 3510 Grandview Pkwy. I-459, exit 19 (US 280), southeast corner. Int corridors. **Pets:** Large, other species. Service with restrictions, supervision.
ASK ✕ ♿ 🔒 📞 🏊

AAA ▼▼▼ **Embassy Suites Birmingham** LH
(205) 879-7400. **$139-$249.** 2300 Woodcrest Pl. Just n of jct US 31 and 280, exit 21st Ave southbound, then 0.3 mi s. Int corridors. **Pets:** $300 deposit/room. Service with restrictions, supervision.
SAVE S⚫ ✕ 🔊 🔒 📞 🍴 🏊 ✕

▼▼▼ **Holiday Inn-Airport** SH
(205) 591-6900. **$74-$89, 30 day notice.** 5000 10th Ave N. I-20/59, exit 129, just s. Int corridors. **Pets:** Small. $25 daily fee/room. Service with restrictions, supervision.
ASK S⚫ ✕ 📞 🍴 🏊

▼▼ **Homestead Studio Suites Hotel-Birmingham/ Perimeter Park South** SH ❀
(205) 967-3800. **$50-$75.** 12 Perimeter Park S. I-459, exit 19 (US 280), 0.5 mi e, then just s. Ext corridors. **Pets:** Medium, other species. $25 daily fee/room. Service with restrictions, crate.
ASK S⚫ ✕ ♿M 🔊 ♿ 🔒 📞

▼▼▼ **La Quinta Inn-Birmingham** SH
(205) 324-4510. **$65-$85.** 905 11th Ct W. I-20/59, exit 123, just sw. Ext/int corridors. **Pets:** Accepted.
✕ 🔒 📞 🏊

▼▼▼ **Pickwick Hotel** SH
(205) 933-9555. **$80-$169.** 1023 20th St S. 1.5 mi s of downtown (Five Points area). Int corridors. **Pets:** Accepted.
ASK S⚫ ✕ 🔒 📞

▼▼▼ **Residence Inn By Marriott** SH
(205) 991-8686. **$69-$115.** 3 Green Hill Pkwy. I-459, exit 19 (US 280), 2 mi e. Ext corridors. **Pets:** Accepted.
ASK S⚫ ✕ ♿ 🔒 📞 🏊 ✕

AAA ▼▼▼ **The Tutwiler-A Wyndham Historic Hotel** LH
(205) 322-2100. **$119-$169.** 2021 Park Pl N. Downtown. Int corridors. **Pets:** Accepted.
SAVE S⚫ ✕ 🔊 🔒 📞 🍴

CALERA

▼▼ **Holiday Inn Express** SH
(205) 668-3641. **$79.** 357 Hwy 304. I-65, exit 231, just se. Ext corridors. **Pets:** Accepted.
✕ ♿ 🔒 📞 🏊

HOMEWOOD

AAA ▼▼▼ **La Quinta Inn & Suites-Birmingham Homewood** SH
(205) 290-0150. **$89-$119.** 60 State Farm Pkwy. I-65, exit 255, 0.9 mi on northwest frontage road. Int corridors. **Pets:** Accepted.
SAVE ✕ ♿ 🔒 📞 🏊

▼▼▼ **Microtel** SH
(205) 945-5550. **$48-$58.** 251 Summit Pkwy. I-65, exit 256 northbound; exit 256A southbound, just w. Int corridors. **Pets:** Other species. $10 one-time fee/room. Service with restrictions, supervision.
ASK S⚫ ✕ ♿

AAA ▼▼ **Red Roof Inn** M
(205) 942-9414. **$44-$59.** 151 Vulcan Rd. I-65, exit 256 northbound; exit 256A southbound, just nw. Ext corridors. **Pets:** Accepted.
SAVE ✕

▼▼▼▼ Residence Inn by Marriott SH
(205) 943-0044. **$146-$195.** 50 State Farm Pkwy. I-65, exit 255, 1 mi on northwest frontage road. Int corridors. **Pets:** Medium. $165 one-time fee/room. Service with restrictions, crate.
(ASK) (S6) (✕) (ᵢ) (🛏) (💻) (≈) (✕)

▼▼▼ Shoney's Inn & Suites SH
(205) 916-0464. **$59-$79.** 226 Summit Pkwy. I-65, exit 256 northbound; exit 256A southbound, just w. Int corridors. **Pets:** Medium, other species. No service, supervision.
(ASK) (S6) (✕) (🛏) (💻) (≈)

▲▲▲ ▼▼▼ Super 8 Motel SH
(205) 945-9888. **$47-$53, 7 day notice.** 140 Vulcan Rd. I-65, exit 256 northbound; exit 256A southbound, just nw. Int corridors. **Pets:** Small, other species. $5 daily fee/pet. Service with restrictions, supervision.
(SAVE) (S6) (✕) (🛏) (💻)

▼▼▼▼ TownePlace Suites by Marriott SH
(205) 943-0114. **$89.** 500 Wildwood Cir. I-65, exit 255, 0.6 mi w, then just n. Int corridors. **Pets:** Accepted.
(✕) (ᴹ) (ᵢ) (🛏) (💻) (≈)

HOOVER

▲▲▲ ▼▼▼▼ AmeriSuites (Birmingham/Riverchase) SH
(205) 988-8444. **$89-$94.** 2980 John Hawkins Pkwy. I-459, exit 13, 0.5 mi s on US 31, then 0.8 mi w on SR 150. Int corridors. **Pets:** Small. Designated rooms, service with restrictions, supervision.
(SAVE) (S6) (✕) (ᵢ) (🛏) (💻) (≈)

▲▲▲ ▼▼▼ La Quinta Inn & Suites-Birmingham Hoover SH
(205) 403-0096. **$71-$101.** 120 Riverchase Pkwy E. I-65, exit 247 (Valleydale Rd), just w. Int corridors. **Pets:** Other species. Service with restrictions, supervision.
(SAVE) (✕) (ᵢ) (🛏) (💻) (≈)

IRONDALE

▲▲▲ ▼▼▼▼ Best Western Rime Garden Inn & Suites SH
(205) 951-1200. **$99.** 5320 Beacon Dr. I-20, exit 133 westbound, just sw. Ext corridors. **Pets:** Small, dogs only. $25 one-time fee/room. Service with restrictions, supervision.
(SAVE) (S6) (✕) (🛏) (💻) (¶) (≈)

LEEDS

▲▲▲ ▼▼▼ Days Inn of Leeds M
(205) 699-9833. **$54-$140.** 1835 Ashville Rd. I-20, exit 144A eastbound; exit 144B westbound, then just s. Ext corridors. **Pets:** Medium, other species. $7 daily fee/pet. Service with restrictions, supervision.
(SAVE) (S6) (✕) (🛏) (≈)

MOODY

▼▼▼ Super 8 Motel M
(205) 640-7091. **$50-$55.** 2451 Moody Pkwy. I-20, exit 144, 1 mi n on US 411. Ext corridors. **Pets:** Accepted.
(ASK) (✕) (🛏)

ONEONTA

▼▼▼▼ Best Western Colonial Inn SH
(205) 274-2200. **$53-$129.** 293 Valley Rd. On SR 75, 0.5 mi ne of jct US 231. Ext corridors. **Pets:** Very small, other species. $8 daily fee/pet.
(ASK) (S6) (✕) (ᵢ) (🛏) (💻) (≈)

PELHAM

▲▲▲ ▼▼▼ Best Western at Oak Mountain SH
(205) 982-1113. **$69.** 100 Bishop Cir. I-65, exit 246, just sw, then just s on State Park Rd. Int corridors. **Pets:** Medium. Designated rooms, service with restrictions, supervision.
(SAVE) (S6) (✕) (ᵢ) (🛏) (💻) (≈)

TRUSSVILLE

▼▼▼ Jameson Inn SH
(205) 661-9323. **$71-$76.** 4730 Norrell Dr. I-59, exit 141, just ne. Ext corridors. **Pets:** Small. Service with restrictions, crate.
(✕) (ᵢ) (🛏) (💻) (≈)

VESTAVIA HILLS

▼▼▼ Hampton Inn South SH
(205) 822-2224. **$62-$87.** 1466 Montgomery Hwy. I-65, exit 252 (US 31), 0.5 mi e. Ext corridors. **Pets:** Accepted.
(ASK) (S6) (✕) (💻) (≈)

❀   END METROPOLITAN AREA   ❀

BOAZ

▼▼▼ Key West Inn SH
(256) 593-0800. **$48-$125.** 10535 SR 168. 0.5 mi w of jct US 431. Ext corridors. **Pets:** $3 daily fee/pet. Service with restrictions, crate.
(ASK) (S6) (✕) (🛏) (💻)

▼▼▼ Rodeway Inn SH
(256) 593-8410. **$35-$50.** 751 Hwy 431 S. On US 431. Ext/int corridors. **Pets:** Accepted.
(ASK) (S6) (✕) (🛏) (💻) (≈)

CLANTON

▲▲▲ ▼▼▼▼ Best Western Inn SH
(205) 280-1006. **$65-$80, 5 day notice.** 801 Bradberry Ln. I-65, exit 205, 0.5 mi e. Ext corridors. **Pets:** Small. $6 daily fee/pet. Service with restrictions, supervision.
(SAVE) (✕) (ᵢ) (🛏) (💻) (≈)

▼▼▼ Days Inn SH
(205) 755-0510. **$48-$85.** 2000 Big M Blvd. I-65, exit 205, just ne. Ext corridors. **Pets:** Accepted.
(ASK) (S6) (✕) (🛏) (≈)

▼▼ ▼▼ **GuestHouse International Inn** 🆂🅷
(205) 280-0306. **$53-$65.** 946 Lake Mitchell Rd. I-65, exit 208, just w. Ext corridors. **Pets:** Medium. $20 deposit/room. Service with restrictions, crate.
🅰🆂🅺 ✕ 💻 🍴 🏊

▼▼ ▼▼ **Key West Inn** Ⓜ
(205) 755-8500. **$46-$50, 7 day notice.** 2045 7th St S. I-65, exit 205, just w on US 31 and SR 22. Ext corridors. **Pets:** Accepted.
🅰🆂🅺 ✕ 🛏 💻

CULLMAN

🄰🄰🄰 ▼▼▼▼ **Best Western Fairwinds Inn** 🆂🅷
(256) 737-5009. **$49-$98.** 1917 Commerce Ave NW. I-65, exit 310, just e. Ext corridors. **Pets:** Other species. $9 daily fee/room. Crate.
🆂🅰🆅🅴 🆂📶 ✕ 🛏 💻 🏊

▼▼ ▼▼ **Comfort Inn** 🆂🅷
(256) 734-1240. **$68-$73.** 5917 Alabama Hwy 157 NW. I-65, exit 310, just e. Ext corridors. **Pets:** Accepted.
🅰🆂🅺 🆂📶 ✕ 🛏 💻 🏊

▼▼ ▼▼ **Days Inn** 🆂🅷
(256) 739-3800. **$53.** 1841 4th St SW. I-65, exit 308 (US 278), just e. Ext corridors. **Pets:** Large, other species. $5 daily fee/room. Service with restrictions.
🅰🆂🅺 🆂📶 ✕ 🛏 🏊

🄰🄰🄰 ▼▼ **Super 8 Motel** Ⓜ
(256) 734-8854. **$40-$50, 7 day notice.** 6349 Alabama Hwy 157. I-65, exit 310, just w. Ext corridors. **Pets:** Small. $10 daily fee/room. No service, supervision.
🆂🅰🆅🅴 🆂📶 ✕ 🏊

DALEVILLE

▼▼ ▼▼ **The Lodge** Ⓜ
(334) 598-6304. **$43-$45, 5 day notice.** 444 N Daleville Ave. 1 mi n of jct US 84 and SR 85. Ext corridors. **Pets:** Other species. $15 one-time fee/room. Service with restrictions, crate.
🆂📶 ✕ 🛏 💻 🏊

DECATUR

▼▼▼▼ **Comfort Inn** 🆂🅷
(256) 355-1037. **$59-$125.** 3239 Point Mallard Pkwy. I-65, exit 334, just w. Int corridors. **Pets:** Very small. $10 daily fee/room. Service with restrictions, supervision.
🅰🆂🅺 🆂📶 ✕ 🕱 🖉 🛏 💻 🏊

▼▼▼▼ **Comfort Inn & Suites** 🆂🅷
(256) 355-1999. **$59-$79, 30 day notice.** 2212 Danville Rd SW. SR 67; at intersection with Beltline Rd SW. Int corridors. **Pets:** Other species. $35 deposit/pet, $10 daily fee/pet. Service with restrictions, supervision.
🅰🆂🅺 🆂📶 ✕ 🖉 🛏 💻 🏊

▼▼ ▼▼ **Jameson Inn** 🆂🅷
(256) 355-2229. **$67-$72.** 2120 Jameson Pl SW. SR 67, 1.6 mi s of jct US 72A, 3.9 mi n of jct US 31. Ext corridors. **Pets:** Small. Service with restrictions, crate.
✕ 🖉 🛏 💻 🏊

▼▼ ▼▼ **Microtel Inn & Suites** 🆂🅷
(256) 301-9995. **$49-$59.** 2226 Beltline Rd SW. On SR 67, 4 mi w of jct US 31; I-65, exit 334, 8 mi w. Int corridors. **Pets:** Small, dogs only. $50 one-time fee/room. Service with restrictions, supervision.
🅰🆂🅺 🆂📶 ✕ 🕱 🖉 🖉 🛏 💻

▼▼▼▼ **Ramada Limited** 🆂🅷 ❀
(256) 353-0333. **$47-$57, 3 day notice.** 1317 Hwy 67 E. I-65, exit 334, 4 mi w; 0.4 mi e of jct US 31. Ext corridors. **Pets:** Other species. $10 one-time fee/pet. Service with restrictions, supervision.
🅰🆂🅺 🆂📶 ✕ 🛏 💻 🏊

DEMOPOLIS

▼▼ ▼▼ **Days Inn** 🆂🅷
(334) 289-2500. **$51-$70.** 1005 Hwy 80 E. 0.5 mi e of jct US 43. Ext corridors. **Pets:** Accepted.
🅰🆂🅺 🆂📶 ✕ 🛏 💻 🏊

DOTHAN

🄰🄰🄰 ▼▼▼ **Best Value Inn & Suites** 🆂🅷
(334) 793-5200. **$42.** 2901 Ross Clark CIR. On US 231 Bypass. Ext corridors. **Pets:** Accepted.
🆂🅰🆅🅴 🆂📶 ✕ 🛏 💻

🄰🄰🄰 ▼▼▼▼ **Comfort Inn** 🆂🅷
(334) 793-9090. **$75-$92.** 3593 Ross Clark Cir. Just sw of jct US 231 N. Int corridors. **Pets:** Medium, other species. $10 daily fee/pet. Service with restrictions, supervision.
🆂🅰🆅🅴 🆂📶 ✕ 🕱 🖉 🛏 💻 🏊

▼▼ ▼▼ **Days Inn** 🆂🅷
(334) 793-2550. **$46-$51.** 2841 Ross Clark Cir. 2 mi sw on US 231 Bypass. Ext corridors. **Pets:** Small, other species. $5 daily fee/pet. Service with restrictions, supervision.
🅰🆂🅺 🆂📶 ✕ 🛏 💻 🏊

🄰🄰🄰 ▼▼▼▼ **Holiday Inn Express** 🆂🅷
(334) 671-3700. **$55-$79.** 3071 Ross Clark Cir. US 231 Bypass at jct US 84 W. Ext corridors. **Pets:** Other species. $15 one-time fee/pet. Service with restrictions.
🆂🅰🆅🅴 🆂📶 ✕ 🕱 🖉 💻

▼▼▼▼ **Holiday Inn-South** 🆂🅷
(334) 794-8711. **$66-$93, 60 day notice.** 2195 Ross Clark Cir SE. 2 mi s on US 231 Bypass at jct US 84 W. Ext corridors. **Pets:** Small, other species. $15 one-time fee/room. Service with restrictions, supervision.
🅰🆂🅺 🆂📶 ✕ 🕱 🖉 🛏 💻 🍴 🏊

▼▼▼▼ **Howard Johnson Express Inn** 🆂🅷
(334) 792-3339. **$49-$60.** 2244 Ross Clark Cir. On US 231 Bypass. Ext corridors. **Pets:** Medium, other species. $10 daily fee/pet. Service with restrictions, supervision.
🅰🆂🅺 🆂📶 ✕ 🛏 💻 🏊 ✕

🄰🄰🄰 ▼▼▼▼ **Quality Inn** 🆂🅷
(334) 794-6601. **$55-$79.** 3053 Ross Clark Cir. 2 mi w on US 231 Bypass; just s of jct US 84 W. Ext corridors. **Pets:** Accepted.
🆂🅰🆅🅴 🆂📶 ✕ 🕱 🖉 🖉 🛏 💻 🍴 🏊

▼▼ Ramada Inn 🆂🅷
(334) 792-0031. **$65-$120.** 3011 Ross Clark Cir. US 231 Bypass at jct US 84 W. Ext/int corridors. **Pets:** Medium, other species. $15 one-time fee/room. Designated rooms, service with restrictions, crate.

🅰🆂🅺 🆂🅾 ⊠ 🛏 🖥 🍽 🏊

ENTERPRISE

▼▼◆ Comfort Inn 🆂🅷
(334) 393-2304. **$72.** 615 Boll Weevil Cir. On SR 167, 0.5 mi s of jct US 84/SR 248. Ext corridors. **Pets:** Other species. $25 one-time fee/pet. Designated rooms, service with restrictions.

🅰🆂🅺 🆂🅾 ⊠ 🕁 🛏 🖥 🏊

▼▼ Ramada Inn 🆂🅷
(334) 347-6262. **$58.** 630 Glover Ave. On SR 248, 0.5 mi w of jct US 84/SR 167. Ext corridors. **Pets:** Accepted.

🅰🆂🅺 🆂🅾 ⊠ 🕁 🖫 🛏 🖥 🏊

EUFAULA

▼▼▼ Comfort Suites 🆂🅷
(334) 616-0114. **$80-$101.** 12 Paul Lee Pkwy. On US 431, 1.5 mi s of jct US 82. Int corridors. **Pets:** Other species. $25 one-time fee/room. Service with restrictions, crate.

🅰🆂🅺 🆂🅾 ⊠ 🖫 🛏 🖥 🏊 ⊠

▼▼ Jameson Inn 🆂🅷
(334) 687-7747. **$66-$71.** 136 Towne Center Blvd. On US 431, 1.1 mi s of US 82. Ext corridors. **Pets:** Small. Service with restrictions, crate.

⊠ 🛏 🖥 🏊

▼▼ Ramada Inn 🆂🅷
(334) 687-2021. **$45-$60.** 631 E Barbour St. On US 82, 0.5 mi e of jct US 431. Ext corridors. **Pets:** Other species. No service.

🅰🆂🅺 🆂🅾 ⊠ 🖥 🍽 🏊

EVERGREEN

🅰🅰🅰 ▼▼◆ Comfort Inn 🆂🅷
(251) 578-4701. **$70, 10 day notice.** 198 Bates Rd. I-65, exit 96 (SR 83), on southwest service road. Ext corridors. **Pets:** Accepted.

🆂🅰🆅🅴 🆂🅾 ⊠ 🕁 🛏 🖥 🏊

▼▼ Days Inn of Evergreen 🅼
(251) 578-2100. **$48-$85.** I-65, exit 96 (SR 83), just w. Ext corridors. **Pets:** $10 daily fee/pet. Designated rooms, service with restrictions, supervision.

🅰🆂🅺 🆂🅾 ⊠ 🛏

FAIRHOPE

▼▼ Key West Inn 🅼
(251) 990-7373. **$64-$114.** 231 S Greeno Rd (Hwy 98). I-10, exit 35A, 9.7 mi s on US 98, on the east side. Ext corridors. **Pets:** Small. $10 daily fee/pet. Designated rooms, service with restrictions, supervision.

🅰🆂🅺 🆂🅾 ⊠ 🖫 🛏 🖥 🏊

FLORENCE

▼ Days Inn-Florence 🅼
(256) 766-2620. **$50-$70.** 1915 Florence Blvd. On US 72. Ext corridors. **Pets:** Small, other species. $20 deposit/room. Service with restrictions, supervision.

🅰🆂🅺 🆂🅾 ⊠ 🛏 🏊

▼▼ Homestead Executive Inn 🆂🅷
(256) 766-2331. **$38-$54.** 505 S Court St. US 43/72 at jct SR 17 and 157. Ext corridors. **Pets:** Small, other species. $10 daily fee/pet. Service with restrictions, crate.

🅰🆂🅺 🆂🅾 ⊠ 🛏 🖥 🏊

▼▼ Jameson Inn 🆂🅷
(256) 764-5326. **$67-$72.** 115 Ana Dr. On US 43/72, just nw of jct SR 113 (Cox Creek Pkwy). Ext corridors. **Pets:** Small. Service with restrictions, crate.

⊠ 🖫 🛏 🖥 🏊

🅰🅰🅰 ▼ Super 8 Motel 🅼 🐾
(256) 757-2167. **$49-$58.** 101 Hwy 72 & 43 E. 3.8 mi e on US 43/72 from jct SR 133. Ext corridors. **Pets:** $20 deposit/ room, $10 daily fee/pet. Designated rooms, service with restrictions, supervision.

🆂🅰🆅🅴 🆂🅾 ⊠ 🛏 🏊

FOLEY

🅰🅰🅰 ▼▼◆ Holiday Inn Express 🆂🅷
(251) 943-9100. **$60-$170.** 2682 S McKenzie St. SR 59, 1.9 mi s of jct US 98. Ext corridors. **Pets:** Small, other species. $20 one-time fee/room. Service with restrictions.

🆂🅰🆅🅴 🆂🅾 ⊠ 🕃 🕁 🖫 🛏 🖥 🏊

▼▼ Key West Inn 🅼
(251) 943-1241. **$44-$109.** 2520 S McKenzie St. SR 59, 1.8 mi s of jct US 98. Ext corridors. **Pets:** Medium. $10 daily fee/pet. Service with restrictions, crate.

🅰🆂🅺 🆂🅾 ⊠ 🛏 🖥 🏊

FORT PAYNE

🅰🅰🅰 ▼▼◆ Days Inn 🆂🅷 🐾
(256) 845-2085. **$65-$85.** 1416 Glenn Blvd SW. I-59, exit 218, just w. Ext corridors. **Pets:** Large, other species. $10 daily fee/pet. Designated rooms.

🆂🅰🆅🅴 🆂🅾 ⊠ 🛏 🖥 🏊

GADSDEN

▼▼ Red Roof Inn 🆂🅷
(256) 543-1105. **$49-$59.** 1600 Rainbow Dr. I-759, exit 4A, just s on US 411. Ext corridors. **Pets:** Accepted.

⊠ 🕁 🏊

GREENVILLE

🅰🅰🅰 ▼▼◆ Best Western Inn 🆂🅷
(334) 382-9200. **$52-$75.** 56 Cahaba Rd. I-65, exit 130, just w on SR 185. Ext corridors. **Pets:** Small. $5 daily fee/pet. Service with restrictions, supervision.

🆂🅰🆅🅴 🆂🅾 ⊠ 🕁 🛏 🖥 🏊

⚠️ ▼▼▼▼ Comfort Inn 🆂🅷
(334) 383-9595. **$55-$85.** 1029 Fort Dale Rd. I-65, exit 130, just w. Int corridors. **Pets:** Small. $5 daily fee/pet. Service with restrictions, supervision.
🆂🅰️ 🆂🔟 ❌ 🔼M ② 🅰️ 🅱️ 💻 ➿

⚠️ ▼▼▼ Econo Lodge 🅼
(334) 382-3118. **$60-$65, 4 day notice.** 946 Fort Dale Rd. I-65, exit 130, just ne on SR 185. Ext corridors. **Pets:** $10 daily fee/pet. Service with restrictions, supervision.
🆂🅰️ 🆂🔟 ❌ 🅱️ 💻

▼▼ Jameson Inn 🆂🅷
(334) 382-6300. **$67-$72.** 71 Jameson Ln. I-65, exit 130, just n on SR 185. Ext corridors. **Pets:** Small. Service with restrictions, crate.
❌ 🅱️ 💻 ➿

GUNTERSVILLE

⚠️ ▼▼▼ Super 8 Motel-Guntersville 🅼
(256) 582-8444. **$41-$86.** 14341 Hwy 431 S. 2 mi s of jct SR 69. Ext corridors. **Pets:** $10 daily fee/room. Designated rooms, service with restrictions, supervision.
🆂🅰️ 🆂🔟 ❌ 🅱️

HAMILTON

▼▼ Country Hearth Inn 🆂🅷
(205) 921-7831. **$50-$55.** 2031 Military St S. US 78, exit 14, 1 mi n, then 1 mi w on US 43. Ext corridors. **Pets:** Accepted.
🅰️🆂🅺 ❌ 🅱️ 💻 🍴 ➿

⚠️ ▼▼▼ Days Inn 🆂🅷
(205) 921-1790. **$53-$69.** 1849 Military St S. US 78, exit 14, 1 mi n, then 1 mi w on US 43. Ext corridors. **Pets:** $10 daily fee/pet. Service with restrictions, supervision.
🆂🅰️ 🆂🔟 ❌ 🔼 🅰️ 🅱️ 💻 ➿

HUNTSVILLE

⚠️ ▼▼▼▼ Baymont Inn & Suites Huntsville 🆂🅷
(256) 830-8999. **$64-$89.** 4890 University Dr. US 72, 5 mi w of jct US 231. Int corridors. **Pets:** Accepted.
🆂🅰️ 🆂🔟 ❌ 🅱️ 💻 ➿

▼▼▼▼ GuestHouse Suites Plus 🆂🅷
(256) 837-8907. **$85-$105.** 4020 Independence Dr. US 72, just w of jct SR 53. Ext corridors. **Pets:** Large. $50 one-time fee/room. Service with restrictions.
🅰️🆂🅺 🆂🔟 ❌ 🅱️ 💻 ➿ ❌

▼▼▼▼ Hilton Huntsville 🅻🅷
(256) 533-1400. **$69-$139.** 401 Williams Ave. Downtown. Int corridors. **Pets:** Accepted.
🅰️🆂🅺 ❌ 💻 🍴 ➿ ❌

⚠️ ▼▼▼▼ La Quinta Inn-Huntsville Research Pk 🆂🅷
(256) 830-2070. **$65-$85.** 4870 University Dr. US 72, 5 mi w of US 231. Ext corridors. **Pets:** Accepted.
🆂🅰️ ❌ 🅱️ 💻 ➿

⚠️ ▼▼▼▼ La Quinta Inn-Huntsville Space Center 🆂🅷
(256) 533-0756. **$65-$85.** 3141 University Dr. US 72, 1.3 mi w of jct US 231/431. Ext corridors. **Pets:** Other species. Service with restrictions, crate.
🆂🅰️ ❌ 💻 ➿

JASPER

▼▼▼ Jameson Inn 🆂🅷
(205) 387-7710. **$69-$74.** 1100 Hwy 118. SR 118, 1.8 mi w of jct SR 69. Ext corridors. **Pets:** Small. Service with restrictions, crate.
❌ 🔼M 🅰️ 🅱️ 💻 ➿

MADISON

▼▼ Motel 6-1087 🅼
(256) 772-7479. **$39-$52.** 8995 Madison Blvd. I-565, exit 8, just nw. Ext corridors. **Pets:** Accepted.
🆂🔟 ❌ 🅰️ 🅱️ ➿

MOBILE

▼▼▼▼ Best Suites of America 🆂🅷
(251) 343-4949. **Call for rates.** 150 S Beltline Hwy. I-65, exit 4, 0.5 mi s on west service road. Int corridors. **Pets:** Small, other species. $8 daily fee/room. Service with restrictions, supervision.
❌ 🅱️ 💻 ➿

▼▼▼▼ Drury Inn 🆂🅷
(251) 344-7700. **$82-$102.** 824 W I-65 Service Rd S. I-65, exit 3 (Airport Blvd), just sw on service road. Int corridors. **Pets:** Large, other species. Service with restrictions, supervision.
🅰️🆂🅺 ❌ 🅱️ 💻 ➿

▼▼ GuestHouse Inn of Mobile 🆂🅷
(251) 660-1520. **$50.** 5472A Inn Rd. I-10, exit 15B, just nw on service road. Ext corridors. **Pets:** Accepted.
🅰️🆂🅺 ❌ 🅱️ 💻 ➿

▼▼▼▼ Holiday Inn-Bellingrath Gardens 🆂🅷 🐾
(251) 666-5600. **$87-$88.** 5465 Hwy 90 W. I-10, exit 15B, just ne. Int corridors. **Pets:** Large, other species. $25 deposit/room. Designated rooms, service with restrictions, supervision.
🅰️🆂🅺 🆂🔟 ❌ ② 🔼 🅱️ 💻 🍴 ➿

▼▼ Lafayette Plaza Hotel 🆂🅷
(251) 694-0100. **$59-$99, 3 day notice.** 301 Government St. Downtown. Int corridors. **Pets:** Accepted.
🅰️🆂🅺 🆂🔟 ❌ 🅱️ 💻 🍴 ➿

⚠️ ▼▼▼▼ La Quinta Inn-Mobile 🅼
(251) 343-4051. **$65-$85.** 816 W I-65 Service Rd S. I-65, exit 3 (Airport Blvd), just s on west service road. Ext corridors. **Pets:** Accepted.
🆂🅰️ ❌ 🅱️ 💻 ➿

⚠️ ▼▼ Olsson's Motel 🅼
(251) 661-5331. **$35-$45, 10 day notice.** 4137 Government Blvd. I-65, exit 1B, 2 mi w on US 90. Ext corridors. **Pets:** Accepted.
🆂🅰️ ❌ 🅱️

▼▼▼ Ramada Inn-I-65 🆂🅷
(251) 342-3220. **$85.** 850 W I-65 Service Rd S. I-65, exit 3 (Airport Blvd), 0.5 mi sw on west service road. Ext corridors. **Pets:** Accepted.
🅰🅂🅺 🆂🅾 ✕ ▣ 🍽 🌊

🅐🅐🅐 ▼▼▼ Red Roof Inn-North 🆂🅷
(251) 476-2004. **$44-$55.** 33 S Beltline Hwy. I-65, exit 4, just s on east service road. Ext corridors. **Pets:** Large, other species. Service with restrictions.
🆂🅰🆅🅴 ✕

🅐🅐🅐 ▼▼▼ Red Roof Inn-South 🆂🅷
(251) 666-1044. **$39-$52.** 5450 Coca Cola Rd. I-10, exit 15B, just ne on service road. Ext corridors. **Pets:** Medium, other species. Service with restrictions, crate.
🆂🅰🆅🅴 ✕ 🌊

▼▼▼▼ Residence Inn by Marriott Mobile 🆂🅷
(251) 304-0570. **$109-$139.** 950 W I-65 Service Rd S. I-65, exit 3 (Airport Blvd), 0.5 mi s on west service road. Int corridors. **Pets:** Other species. $125 one-time fee/room.
🅰🅂🅺 🆂🅾 ✕ ⚙ 🅼 ▣ 🌊 ✕

▼▼▼▼ TownPlace Suites by Marriott 🆂🅷
(251) 345-9588. **$59-$129.** 1075 Montlimar Dr. I-65, exit 3 (Airport Blvd), 0.5 mi w, then 0.5 mi s. Int corridors. **Pets:** Other species. $75 one-time fee/room. Service with restrictions, crate.
🅰🅂🅺 🆂🅾 ✕ 🗂 ▣ 🌊

MONROEVILLE

▼▼▼▼ Holiday Inn Express 🆂🅷
(251) 743-3333. **$55-$125.** 120 Hwy 21 S. On SR 21, just s of jct US 84. Int corridors. **Pets:** Accepted.
🅰🅂🅺 🆂🅾 ✕ 🅼 🖏 🗂 ▣ 🌊

MONTGOMERY

🅐🅐🅐 ▼▼▼ Baymont Inn & Suites Montgomery 🆂🅷
(334) 277-6000. **$61-$89.** 5225 Carmichael Rd. I-85, exit 6, just sw. Int corridors. **Pets:** Accepted.
🆂🅰🆅🅴 🆂🅾 ✕ 🅼 ⚙ 🗂 ▣ 🌊

▼▼ Best Inn and Suites 🆂🅷
(334) 288-5740. **$45-$56, 3 day notice.** 977 W South Blvd. I-65, exit 168, just e. Ext corridors. **Pets:** Other species. $10 daily fee/pet. Service with restrictions.
🅰🅂🅺 🆂🅾 ✕ 🗂 ▣ 🌊

▼▼▼ Best Inns of America-Montgomery 🆂🅷
(334) 270-9199. **$66-$96.** 5135 Carmichael Rd. I-85, exit 6, just sw. Int corridors. **Pets:** Accepted.
🅰🅂🅺 🆂🅾 ✕ ⚙ 🖏 🗂 ▣ 🌊

🅐🅐🅐 ▼▼▼ Best Western Monticello Inn 🆂🅷
(334) 277-4442. **$70-$75.** 5837 Monticello Dr. I-85, exit 6, just ne. Ext corridors. **Pets:** Medium. $10 daily fee/pet. Designated rooms, no service, crate.
🆂🅰🆅🅴 ✕ 🗂 ▣ 🌊

▼▼ Days Inn Airport 🆂🅷 🐾
(334) 281-8000. **$52-$55.** 1150 W South Blvd. I-65, exit 168, just w. Ext corridors. **Pets:** Other species. $10 one-time fee/pet. Service with restrictions, crate.
🅰🅂🅺 🆂🅾 ✕ 🗂 🌊

▼▼▼ Econo Lodge 🅼
(334) 284-3400. **$50-$60.** 4135 Troy Hwy. On US 82 and 231, 0.5 mi se of jct South and East blvds. Ext corridors. **Pets:** Very small. $10 daily fee/pet. Designated rooms, service with restrictions, supervision.
🅰🅂🅺 🆂🅾 ✕ 🗂 ▣ 🌊

▼▼▼▼ Holiday Inn-East 🆂🅷
(334) 272-0370. **$90.** 1185 Eastern Bypass. I-85, exit 6, just ne. Ext/int corridors. **Pets:** Accepted.
🅰🅂🅺 🆂🅾 ✕ 🅼 ⚙ 🖏 🗂 ▣ 🍽 🌊 ✕

🅐🅐🅐 ▼▼▼▼ La Quinta Inn-Montgomery 🆂🅷
(334) 271-1620. **$59-$79.** 1280 East Blvd. I-85, exit 6, just sw. Ext corridors. **Pets:** Service with restrictions, supervision.
🆂🅰🆅🅴 ✕ ▣ 🌊

▼▼▼▼ Residence Inn by Marriott 🆂🅷
(334) 270-3300. **$145-$165.** 1200 Hilmar Ct. I-85, exit 6, 0.4 mi se on Carmichael Rd. Ext/int corridors. **Pets:** Accepted.
🅰🅂🅺 ✕ ⚙ 🖏 🗂 ▣ 🌊 ✕

▼▼▼▼ TownePlace Suites by Marriott 🆂🅷
(334) 396-5505. **$94.** 5047 Townplace Dr. I-85, exit 6, just sw, off Carmichael Rd. Int corridors. **Pets:** Accepted.
🅰🅂🅺 🆂🅾 ✕ 🅼 ⚙ 🖏 🗂 ▣ 🌊

OPELIKA

▼▼▼ Travelodge 🅼
(334) 749-1461. **$40-$43, 14 day notice.** 1002 Columbus Pkwy. I-85, exit 62, just w. Ext corridors. **Pets:** Accepted.
🅰🅂🅺 🆂🅾 ✕ 🗂 ▣ 🌊

OPP

▼▼ Executive Inn 🆂🅷
(334) 493-6399. **$55-$60.** 812 Florala Hwy 331 S. On US 331, 0.9 mi s of jct US 84. Ext corridors. **Pets:** Accepted.
🅰🅂🅺 ✕ 🗂 ▣ 🌊

OXFORD

🅐🅐🅐 ▼▼▼ Best Western-Anniston/Oxford 🆂🅷
(256) 831-3410. **$49-$89.** US 78 & SR 21. I-20, exit 185, just n. Ext corridors. **Pets:** Other species. Designated rooms, service with restrictions, crate.
🆂🅰🆅🅴 🆂🅾 ✕ 🗂 ▣ 🌊 ✕

▼▼▼ Jameson Inn Oxford 🆂🅷
(256) 835-2170. **$69-$150.** 161 Colonial Dr. I-20, exit 188, just nw. Ext corridors. **Pets:** Small. Service with restrictions, crate.
✕ 🖏 🗂 ▣ 🌊

OZARK

🅐🅐🅐 ▼▼▼ All American Ozark Inn 🅼 🐾
(334) 774-5166. **$52-$60.** Deese Rd, US 231 S. 0.5 mi s of jct US 231 and SR 249. Ext corridors. **Pets:** Medium, other species. Service with restrictions, supervision.
🆂🅰🆅🅴 🆂🅾 ✕ 🗂 ▣ 🌊

▼▼ Jameson Inn 🆂🅷
(334) 774-0233. **$64-$69.** 1360 S US Hwy 231. 0.4 mi s of jct SR 249. Ext corridors. **Pets:** Small. Service with restrictions, crate.
🗙 🔣 🛏 🖵 🛬

▼▼▼ Quality Inn & Suites-Ozark/Ft Rucker 🆂🅷
(334) 774-7300. **$70.** 151 Hwy 231 N. US 231, 0.3 mi n of jct SR 249. Ext corridors. **Pets:** Accepted.
🅰🆂🅺 🆂🅾 🗙 🛏 🖵 🍴 🛬

PHENIX CITY

▼▼ Holiday Inn Express 🆂🅷
(334) 298-9321. **$89-$99.** 1700 E US 280 Bypass. US 280/431 Bypass. Ext corridors. **Pets:** Service with restrictions, supervision.
🅰🆂🅺 🆂🅾 🗙 🛏 🖵 🛬

PRATTVILLE

▼▼ Jameson Inn 🆂🅷
(334) 361-6463. **$68-$73.** 104 Jameson Ct. I-65, exit 179, 1 mi w. Ext corridors. **Pets:** Small. Service with restrictions, crate.
🗙 🎲 🔣 🛏 🖵 🛬

PRICEVILLE

▼▼ Days Inn 🆂🅷
(256) 355-3297. **$39-$99.** 63 Marco Dr. I-65, exit 334, just e. Ext corridors. **Pets:** Medium. $10 daily fee/room. Service with restrictions, crate.
🅰🆂🅺 🆂🅾 🗙 🔣 🛏 🖵 🛬

SCOTTSBORO

▼▼▼ Best Western Scottsboro 🆂🅷
(256) 259-4300. **$50-$55.** 46 Micah Way. US 72 at jct SR 35. Ext corridors. **Pets:** Accepted.
🅰🆂🅺 🆂🅾 🗙 🛏 🖵 🛬

▼▼▼ Jameson Inn 🆂🅷
(256) 574-6666. **$67-$72.** 208 Micah Way. US 72 at jct SR 35. Ext corridors. **Pets:** Very small. Service with restrictions, crate.
🗙 🔣 🛏 🖵 🛬

SELMA

▼▼ Comfort Inn 🆂🅷
(334) 875-5700. **$60-$70.** 1812 Hwy 14 E. Jct SR 14 and US 80 Bypass. Int corridors. **Pets:** Accepted.
🅰🆂🅺 🆂🅾 🗙 🛏 🖵 🛬

▼▼ Holiday Inn 🆂🅷
(334) 872-0461. **$58-$65.** 1710 W Highland Ave. 2.3 mi w on US 80. Ext corridors. **Pets:** Other species. Service with restrictions, supervision.
🅰🆂🅺 🆂🅾 🗙 🎲 🛏 🖵 🍴 🛬

▼▼ Jameson Inn 🆂🅷
(334) 874-8600. **$65-$70.** 2420 Broad St. SR 22, just n of jct US 80. Ext corridors. **Pets:** Small. Service with restrictions, crate.
🗙 🔣 🛏 🖵 🛬

SYLACAUGA

▼▼ Jameson Inn 🆂🅷
(256) 245-4141. **$69-$74.** 89 Gene Stewart Blvd. Off US 280, just s. Ext corridors. **Pets:** Small. Service with restrictions, crate.
🗙 🔣 🛏 🖵 🛬

TROY

▼▼ Holiday Inn Express 🆂🅷
(334) 670-0012. **$65-$70.** Hwy 231 (US 29). On US 231, just n of jct US 29. Ext corridors. **Pets:** Other species. Service with restrictions, supervision.
🅰🆂🅺 🆂🅾 🗙 🛏 🖵

TUSCALOOSA

◆◆ Jameson Inn 🆂🅷
(205) 345-5018. **$71-$76.** 5021 Oscar Baxter Rd. I-59/20, exit 71A, just s. Ext corridors. **Pets:** Small. Service with restrictions, crate.
🗙 🔣 🛏 🖵 🛬

🆎🆎🆎 ▼▼▼ La Quinta Inn-Tuscaloosa 🆂🅷
(205) 349-3270. **$55-$75.** 4122 McFarland Blvd E. I-59/20, exit 73, just sw on US 82. Ext corridors. **Pets:** Accepted.
🆂🅰🆅🅴 🗙 🛏 🖵 🛬

🆎🆎🆎 ▼ Masters Inn 🅼
(205) 556-2010. **$38-$58.** 3600 McFarland Blvd. I-59/20, exit 73, just nw on US 82. Ext corridors. **Pets:** Accepted.
🆂🅰🆅🅴 🆂🅾 🗙 🛏 🛬

▼▼ Shoney's Inn-Tuscaloosa 🆂🅷
(205) 556-7950. **$45-$125.** 3501 McFarland Blvd. I-59/20, exit 73, just ne on US 82. Ext corridors. **Pets:** Accepted.
🅰🆂🅺 🆂🅾 🗙 🖵 🍴 🛬

VANCE

🆎🆎🆎 ▼▼▼ Wellesley Inn & Suites 🆂🅷
(205) 556-3606. **$79.** 11170 Will Walker Rd/Daimler Benz Blvd. I-59/20, exit 89 southbound, just s; northbound, 0.8 mi n on Mercedes Dr, 0.3 mi w, then just s. Int corridors. **Pets:** Small. $15 one-time fee/pet. Designated rooms, service with restrictions, supervision.
🆂🅰🆅🅴 🆂🅾 🗙 🔣 🔣 🛏 🖵

YORK

🆎🆎🆎 ▼▼▼ Days Inn-York 🆂🅷
(205) 392-9675. **$44.** 17700 SR 17. I-59/20, exit 8, just se. Ext corridors. **Pets:** Accepted.
🆂🅰🆅🅴 🆂🅾 🗙 🔣 🛏 🖵

ALASKA

ANCHORAGE

Best Western Barratt Inn SH
(907) 243-3131. **$89-$199.** 4616 Spenard Rd. International Airport Rd, just w of jct Jewel Lake and Spenard rds. Ext/int corridors. **Pets:** Other species. $50 deposit/room. Service with restrictions, crate.

Comfort Inn Ship Creek SH
(907) 277-6887. **$69-$239.** 111 W Ship Creek Ave. At 3rd and E sts, 0.3 mi n on E St, across the railway, just e on Ship Creek Ave (formerly Warehouse Ave); downtown. Int corridors. **Pets:** Medium. $10 daily fee/pet. Designated rooms, service with restrictions, supervision.

Holiday Inn Express Anchorage Airport SH
(907) 248-8848. **$109-$199.** 4411 Spenard Rd. 0.5 mi ne of Jewell Lake and International Airport rds. Int corridors. **Pets:** $10 daily fee/pet. Designated rooms, service with restrictions, supervision.

Long House Alaskan Hotel SH
(907) 243-2133. **$62-$139.** 4335 Wisconsin St. International Airport Rd, 1.5 mi ne on Spenard Rd, nw on Wisconsin St at 43rd Ave, then just e. Int corridors. **Pets:** Large, other species. $50 deposit/pet, $10 daily fee/pet. Designated rooms, service with restrictions, supervision.

Merrill Field Inn M
(907) 276-4547. **$60-$156.** 420 Sitka St. 1 mi e via US 1 (Glenn Hwy). Ext corridors. **Pets:** Other species. $7 daily fee/pet. Service with restrictions, supervision.

Microtel Inn & Suites SH
(907) 245-5002. **$70-$150.** 5205 Northwood Dr. 1.7 mi e of airport. Int corridors. **Pets:** Medium. $10 daily fee/room. Designated rooms, service with restrictions, supervision.

Millennium Alaskan Hotel Anchorage LH
(907) 243-2300. **$149-$270.** 4800 Spenard Rd. International Airport Rd, just ne from jct Jewel Lake and Spenard rds. Int corridors. **Pets:** Other species. $50 deposit/room. Supervision.

Parkwood Inn M
(907) 563-3590. **$69-$140.** 4455 Juneau St. Jct International Airport Rd and Old Seward Hwy, 0.4 mi n on Old Seward Hwy, just e on 45th St. Ext corridors. **Pets:** Other species. $50 deposit/room. Supervision.

Residence Inn by Marriott CO
(907) 563-9844. **$116-$310.** 1025 E 35th Ave. Corner of US 1 (New Seward Hwy) and 36th Ave. Int corridors. **Pets:** Accepted.

Super 8 Motel-Anchorage SH
(907) 276-8884. **$72-$150.** 3501 Minnesota Dr. At 36th Ave, just n of Spenard Rd. Int corridors. **Pets:** Accepted.

CANTWELL

Backwoods Lodge M
(907) 768-2232. **$90-$150, 10 day notice.** Denali Hwy MM 133.8. George Parks Hwy, (Milepost 210), just e on Denali Hwy. Ext corridors. **Pets:** Medium. Service with restrictions, supervision.

DENALI NATIONAL PARK AND PRESERVE

McKinley Chalet Resort LH
(907) 683-8200. **$165-$220, 7 day notice.** Milepost 238 (George Parks Hwy). Milepost 238.5 SR 3 (George Parks Hwy). Ext corridors. **Pets:** Service with restrictions, supervision.

EAGLE RIVER

Eagle River Motel M
(907) 694-5000. **$49-$100, 3 day notice.** 11111 Old Eagle River Rd. Glenn Hwy, exit Eagle River, just e; center. Ext corridors. **Pets:** Other species. $7 daily fee/pet. Designated rooms, service with restrictions, crate.

FAIRBANKS

Comfort Inn-Chena River SH
(907) 479-8080. **$79-$169.** 1908 Chena Landings Loop. Airport Way, just n on Peger Rd, then just e on Phillips Field Rd, follow signs in wooded area south of road. Int corridors. **Pets:** $10 daily fee/room. Designated rooms, service with restrictions, crate.

Super 8 Motel M
(907) 451-8888. **$64-$143.** 1909 Airport Way. Airport Way at Wilbur St. Int corridors. **Pets:** Accepted.

GUSTAVUS

▼▼▼▼ Glacier Bay's Bear Track Inn Ⓜ
(907) 697-3017. **$704, 61 day notice.** 255 Rink Creek Rd. 7 mi e of airport; at the end of Rink Creek Rd. Int corridors. **Pets:** Accepted.

[ASK] [S☉] [✕] [❄] [✕] [𝕂] [𝕎] [☎]

HAINES

Ⓐ ▼ Captain's Choice Inc Motel Ⓜ
(907) 766-3111. **$80-$113.** 108 2nd Ave N. Jct 2nd Ave and Dalton St. Ext corridors. **Pets:** Other species. $10 one-time fee/room. Service with restrictions, supervision.

[SAVE] [✕] [⊟] [▦] [𝕂]

HOMER

Ⓐ ▼▼▼ Best Western Bidarka Inn Ⓜ
(907) 235-8148. **$89-$174.** 575 Sterling Hwy. 0.3 mi n on Sterling Hwy (SR 1). Ext/int corridors. **Pets:** Other species. $10 daily fee/room. Designated rooms, service with restrictions, supervision.

[SAVE] [S☉] [✕] [⊟] [▦] [❄] [𝕂]

JUNEAU

Ⓐ ▼▼▼ Frontier Suites Airport Hotel 🆂🅷
(907) 790-6600. **$89-$159.** 9400 Glacier Hwy. At Juneau International Airport. Ext/int corridors. **Pets:** Small, dogs only. Service with restrictions.

[SAVE] [S☉] [✕] [♿] [⊟] [▦] [❄] [✕] [𝕂]

▼ Juneau Super 8 🆂🅷
(907) 789-4858. **$85-$110.** 2295 Trout St. At airport, just nw to Glacier Hwy, just e. Int corridors. **Pets:** Accepted.

[ASK] [S☉] [✕] [𝕂]

Ⓐ ▼▼▼ Westmark Baranof 🆂🅷
(907) 586-2660. **$107-$116.** 127 N Franklin St. At 2nd and Franklin sts; downtown. Int corridors. **Pets:** Dogs only. $100 deposit/room, $10 daily fee/pet. Service with restrictions, crate.

[SAVE] [S☉] [✕] [⊘] [⊟] [▦] [❄] [𝕂]

KETCHIKAN

Ⓐ ▼▼▼ Best Western Landing 🆂🅷
(907) 225-5166. **$115-$182.** 3434 Tongass Ave. Across from the Alaska Marine Hwy ferry terminal. Ext/int corridors. **Pets:** Other species. $50 deposit/room, $10 daily fee/room. Designated rooms, service with restrictions.

[SAVE] [✕] [⊟] [▦] [❄]

▼ Ketchikan Super 8 Motel 🆂🅷
(907) 225-9088. **$85-$116.** 2151 Sea Level Dr. From Alaska Marine Hwy ferry terminal, 0.9 mi se to Washington St, then just s; from airport ferry terminal, 1.3 mi se. Int corridors. **Pets:** Accepted.

[ASK] [S☉] [✕] [⊟] [𝕂]

KODIAK

Ⓐ ▼▼▼ Best Western Kodiak Inn 🆂🅷 ✿
(907) 486-5712. **$99-$149.** 236 W Rezanof Dr. 0.3 mi w of ferry terminal; center. Ext/int corridors. **Pets:** $50 deposit/room, $25 one-time fee/room. Designated rooms, service with restrictions, supervision.

[SAVE] [S☉] [✕] [⊘] [⊟] [▦] [❄] [𝕂]

SITKA

▼▼▼ Super 8 Motel-Sitka 🆂🅷
(907) 747-8804. **$90-$127.** 404 Sawmill Creek Rd. Just e from corner of Lake St and Halibut Point/Sawmill Creek rds; center. Int corridors. **Pets:** Small. $6 daily fee/pet. Service with restrictions, supervision.

[ASK] [S☉] [✕] [⊘] [⊟]

SKAGWAY

▼▼▼ Westmark Inn Skagway 🆂🅷
(907) 983-6000. **$99.** 3rd & Spring St. Downtown. Ext/int corridors. **Pets:** Accepted.

[ASK] [S☉] [✕] [♿] [⊟] [▦] [❄] [𝕂]

TOK

Ⓐ ▼▼▼ Cleft of the Rock Bed & Breakfast 🅲🅰
(907) 883-4219. **$55-$135, 3 day notice.** MM 0.5 Sundog Tr. Jct SR 1 and 2 (Alaskan Hwy), 3 mi w on SR 2 (Alaskan Hwy) to Sundog Tr, then 0.5 mi n. Ext/int corridors. **Pets:** Other species. $5 daily fee/pet. Service with restrictions, supervision.

[SAVE] [✕] [⊟] [▦] [✕] [𝕂]

Ⓐ ▼▼▼ Westmark Tok Ⓜ
(907) 883-5174. **$109.** Jct Alaska Hwy & Glenn Hwy. On SR 1; at jct SR 2 (Alaskan Hwy). Ext corridors. **Pets:** Accepted.

[SAVE] [S☉] [✕] [▦] [❄] [𝕂]

TRAPPER CREEK

▼▼ Gate Creek Cabins 🅲🅰
(907) 733-1393. **$90-$250, 10 day notice.** Mile 10.5 Petersville Rd. From MM 114 (Parks Hwy), 10.5 mi w at Petersville Rd. Ext corridors. **Pets:** Accepted.

[ASK] [✕] [⊟] [▦] [✕] [𝕂] [☎]

VALDEZ

Ⓐ ▼▼▼ Best Western Valdez Harbor Inn 🆂🅷
(907) 835-3434. **$89-$149.** 100 Harbor Dr. Just s at Meals Dr. Int corridors. **Pets:** Small. $50 deposit/room, $25 one-time fee/pet. Designated rooms, service with restrictions, supervision.

[SAVE] [S☉] [✕] [⊘] [⊟] [▦] [❄] [𝕂]

WASILLA

Ⓐ ▼▼▼▼ Best Western Lake Lucille Inn 🆂🅷
(907) 373-1776. **$79-$189.** 1300 W Lake Lucille Dr. George Parks Hwy (SR 3), just w on Hallea Ln; center. Int corridors. **Pets:** Medium. $10 daily fee/pet. Designated rooms, service with restrictions, supervision.

[SAVE] [S☉] [✕] [⊘] [⊟] [▦] [❄] [✕] [𝕂]

Ⓐ ▼▼▼ Pioneer Ridge B & B Inn 🅱🅱
(907) 376-7472. **$65-$155, 7 day notice.** 2221 Yukon Cir. Jct George Parks Hwy (SR 3), 1.5 mi s on Fairview Loop Rd, follow signs onto Lin-Lu Rd and onto Yukon. Int corridors. **Pets:** $5 daily fee/pet. Service with restrictions, supervision.

[SAVE] [✕] [⊟] [▦] [✕] [𝕂] [𝕎]

WILLOW

▼▼ Alaskan Host Bed & Breakfast 🅱🅱
(907) 495-6800. **$90-$100, 15 day notice.** Mile 66.5 Old Parks Hwy. Parks Hwy (Mile 66), 1 mi e at Old Parks Hwy. Ext/int corridors. **Pets:** Dogs only. Supervision.

[✕] [⊟] [✕] [𝕂] [☎]

CITY INDEX

AJO

 La Siesta Motel M
(520) 387-6569. **$42-$54.** 2561 N Ajo-Gila Bend Hwy. On SR 85, 1.8 mi n of town plaza. Ext corridors. **Pets:** Accepted.

Marine Motel M
(520) 387-7626. **$41-$65.** 1966 N 2nd Ave. On SR 85, 1 mi n of town plaza. Ext corridors. **Pets:** Accepted.

BELLEMONT

 Bellemont Microtel Inn M
(928) 556-9599. **$49-$79.** 12380 W Interstate Hwy 40. I-40, exit 185. Int corridors. **Pets:** $10 daily fee/pet. Designated rooms, service with restrictions, supervision.

BENSON

Best Western Quail Hollow Inn M
(520) 586-3646. **$60-$75.** 699 N Ocotillo Ave. I-10, exit 304, just s. Ext corridors. **Pets:** $10 daily fee/pet. Designated rooms, service with restrictions, supervision.

Motel 6 Benson #4036 SH
(520) 586-0066. **$41-$65.** 637 S Whetstone Commerce Dr. I-10, exit 302, just s to Frontage Rd, then just e. Int corridors. **Pets:** Small. Service with restrictions, supervision.

Super 8 Motel M
(520) 586-1530. **$53-$90.** 855 N Ocotillo Ave. I-10, exit 304, just n. Ext corridors. **Pets:** Accepted.

BISBEE

Audrey's Inn CO ❀
(520) 227-6120. **$85.** 20 Brewery Ave. SR 80, just n; center of downtown. Int corridors. **Pets:** Dogs only. $25 deposit/pet. Designated rooms, service with restrictions.

San Jose Lodge M
(520) 432-5761. **$75-$125, 3 day notice.** 1002 Naco Hwy. SR 80, take SR 92, 2.5 mi sw, then 1.5 mi s. Ext corridors. **Pets:** Medium, dogs only. $10 daily fee/pet. Designated rooms, service with restrictions, supervision.

BULLHEAD CITY

Best Western Bullhead City Inn SH ❀
(928) 754-3000. **$44-$99.** 1126 Hwy 95. 1.8 mi s of Laughlin Bridge. Ext corridors. **Pets:** $10 one-time fee/pet. Service with restrictions, supervision.

Lake Mohave Resort M
(928) 754-3245. **$95-$105, 3 day notice.** Katherine Landing. 1.5 mi n of Laughlin Bridge on SR 95 to CR 68, then 4.6 mi on Lake Mead/Katherine Landing turn off, follow signs. Ext corridors. **Pets:** Accepted.

CAMP VERDE

Comfort Inn SH
(928) 567-9000. **$49-$99.** 340 N Industrial Dr. I-17, exit 287, just e, then just s. Int corridors. **Pets:** Other species. $15 one-time fee/room. Supervision.

Days Inn & Suites of Camp Verde SH
(928) 567-3700. **$54-$75.** 1640 W Finnie Flat Rd. I-17, exit 287, just e, then just n. Int corridors. **Pets:** Other species. $10 one-time fee/room. Designated rooms, service with restrictions, supervision.

CASA GRANDE

Best Western Casa Grande M
(520) 836-1600. **$69-$129.** 665 Via Del Cielo. I-10, exit 194 (SR 287), 1 mi w. Ext corridors. **Pets:** Accepted.

▼▼ ▼▼ **Holiday Inn Casa Grande** SH
(520) 426-3500. **$83-$99.** 777 N Pinal Ave. I-10, exit 194 (SR 287), 3.9 mi w. Int corridors. **Pets:** Other species. Service with restrictions, supervision.
ASK ⊠ ⟲ 🖥 💻 ⊪ ⇌

▼▼ **Motel 6–1263** M
(520) 836-3323. **$39-$63.** 4965 N Sunland Gin Rd. I-10, exit 200. Ext corridors. **Pets:** Accepted.
S6 ⊠ ⟲ 🖥 ⇌

④④④ ▼▼▼ **Super 8 Motel** SH
(520) 836-8800. **$42-$125.** 2066 E Florence Blvd. I-10, exit 194 (SR 287), 0.6 mi w on SR 187. Int corridors. **Pets:** $10 daily fee/pet. No service, supervision.
SAVE S6 ⊠ ⟲ 🖥 ⇌

CHAMBERS

④④④ ▼▼▼ **Chieftain Inn** M
(928) 688-2754. **$60-$130.** I-40 & State 191. I-40, exit 333, just n at jct US 191. Ext corridors. **Pets:** Accepted.
SAVE S6 ⊠ ⟲ 💻 ⊪ ⇌

CHINLE

④④④ ▼▼▼▼ **Best Western Canyon de Chelly Inn** M
(928) 674-5875. **$69-$119.** 100 Main St, Rt 7. US 191, just e. Ext corridors. **Pets:** Medium. $5 daily fee/pet. Designated rooms, service with restrictions, supervision.
SAVE S6 ⊠ 🖥 ⊪ ⇌

COTTONWOOD

④④④ ▼▼▼ **Budget Inn & Suites** M
(928) 634-3678. **$49-$99.** 1089 Hwy 260. On SR 260, just e of jct SR 89A. Ext corridors. **Pets:** Small. $7 daily fee/pet. Service with restrictions, supervision.
SAVE S6 ⊠ 🖥 💻

④④④ ▼▼ **Little Daisy Motel** M
(928) 634-7865. **$48-$52.** 34 S Main St. On SR 89A, just n of jct SR 89A. Ext corridors. **Pets:** Other species. $20 deposit/room, $3 daily fee/room. Service with restrictions, crate.
SAVE S6 ⊠ 🖥

④④④ ▼▼ **The Pines Motel** M
(928) 634-9975. **$49-$69.** 920 S Camino Real. Jct SR 260, just nw on SR 89A, then just s. Ext corridors. **Pets:** $10 one-time fee/room. Service with restrictions, supervision.
SAVE S6 ⊠ 🖥 ⇌

④④④ ▼▼ **The View Motel** M
(928) 634-7581. **$48-$58.** 818 S Main St. On SR 89A, 0.4 mi nw of jct SR 260. Ext corridors. **Pets:** Accepted.
SAVE ⊠ 🖥 ⇌

EAGAR

④④④ ▼▼▼▼ **Best Western Sunrise Inn** M
(928) 333-2540. **$59-$99.** 128 N Main St. SR 260, just n; US 60, 1.5 mi s. Ext corridors. **Pets:** Small. $25 deposit/room. Designated rooms, service with restrictions, supervision.
SAVE S6 ⊠ ⟲ 🖥 💻

EHRENBERG

④④④ ▼▼▼ **Best Western Flying J Motel** SH
(928) 923-9711. **$69-$199.** S Frontage Rd. I-10, exit 1, just s; 0.5 mi e of the Colorado River. Int corridors. **Pets:** Accepted.
SAVE S6 ⊠ 🖥 💻 ⇌

ELOY

④④④ ▼▼ **Super 8 Motel** M
(520) 466-7804. **$49-$99.** 3945 W Houser Rd. I-10, exit 203 (Toltec Rd), just e, then just s. Ext corridors. **Pets:** Accepted.
SAVE S6 ⊠ 🖥 ⇌

FLAGSTAFF

④④④ ▼▼▼▼ **AmeriSuites (Flagstaff/Interstate Crossroads)** SH
(928) 774-8042. **$59-$129.** 2455 S Beulah Blvd. I-40, exit 195B, just n to Forest Meadows St, just w, then just s. Int corridors. **Pets:** Small. Service with restrictions, supervision.
SAVE S6 ⊠ ⟲ ⟲ 🖥 💻 ⇌

④④④ ▼▼▼ **Best Western Kings House Motel** M
(928) 774-7186. **$44-$119.** 1560 E Route 66. I-40, exit 198 (Butler Ave), just w, then 1 mi n on Enterprise. Ext corridors. **Pets:** Medium. $10 daily fee/pet. Designated rooms, service with restrictions, supervision.
SAVE S6 ⊠ 🖥 ⇌

④④④ ▼▼▼ **Budget Host Saga Motel** M
(928) 779-3631. **$28-$46.** 820 W Route 66. I-40, exit 195B westbound, 1.5 mi n on Milton Rd, then just w; exit 191 eastbound, just n. Ext corridors. **Pets:** Other species. $6 daily fee/pet. Designated rooms, service with restrictions, crate.
SAVE S6 ⊠ 🖥 💻 ⇌

④④④ ▼▼ **Canyon Inn** M
(928) 774-7301. **$34-$125.** 501 S Milton Rd. I-40, exit 195B, 1.5 mi n. Ext corridors. **Pets:** Accepted.
SAVE S6 ⊠ 🖥 💻

④④④ ▼▼▼ **Comfort Inn I-17/I-40** SH
(928) 774-2225. **$59-$139.** 2355 S Beulah Blvd. I-40, exit 195B, just n to Forest Meadows St, then 1 blk w. Int corridors. **Pets:** Accepted.
SAVE S6 ⊠ ⟲ 🖥 💻 ⇌

④④④ ▼▼▼ **Days Inn Flagstaff Hwy 66** M
(928) 774-5221. **$39-$139, 3 day notice.** 1000 W Route 66. I-40, exit 195B, 1.5 n on Milton Rd, then just w. Ext corridors. **Pets:** Small. $10 daily fee/room. Service with restrictions, crate.
SAVE S6 ⊠ ⟲ ⇌

▼▼ ▼▼ **Econo Lodge** SH
(928) 774-7701. **$50-$109.** 2480 E Lucky Ln. I-40, exit 198 (Butler Ave), just e. Int corridors. **Pets:** Very small. $10 daily fee/pet. Designated rooms, service with restrictions, supervision.
ASK S6 ⊠ 🖥 💻 ⇌ ⊠

Econo Lodge-University M
(928) 774-7326. **$43-$99.** 914 S Milton Rd. I-40, exit 195B, 1.2 mi n. Ext corridors. **Pets:** Other species. Service with restrictions, supervision.

Embassy Suites-Flagstaff/Grand Canyon SH
(928) 774-4333. **$109-$149.** 706 S Milton Rd. I-40, exit 195B, 1.5 mi n. Int corridors. **Pets:** Accepted.

Family Inn M
(928) 774-8820. **$32-$115.** 121 S Milton Rd. I-40, exit 195B, 2.5 mi n. Ext corridors. **Pets:** Small. $10 deposit/pet. No service, supervision.

Flagstaff Travelodge M
(928) 526-1399. **$29-$99.** 2610 E Route 66. I-40, exit 201, 1.3 mi w on US 180, 89 and I-40 business loop. Ext corridors. **Pets:** $10 daily fee/pet. Service with restrictions, supervision.

Holiday Inn Flagstaff/Grand Canyon SH
(928) 714-1000. **$89-$119.** 2320 E Lucky Ln. I-40, exit 198 (Butler Ave), just n. Int corridors. **Pets:** Other species. $25 one-time fee/room. Service with restrictions, supervision.

Howard Johnson Inn M
(928) 526-1826. **$39-$89.** 3300 E Route 66. I-40, exit 201, 1.7 mi w. Ext corridors. **Pets:** Other species. $7 one-time fee/room. Service with restrictions, supervision.

InnSuites Hotel & Suites Flagstaff/ Grand Canyon SH
(928) 774-7356. **$54-$129.** 1008 E Route 66. I-40, exit 198 (Butler Ave), 1 mi n on Milton Rd/SR 89A, then just e. Ext corridors. **Pets:** Accepted.

La Quinta Inn & Suites SH
(928) 556-8666. **$62-$129.** 2015 S Beulah Blvd. I-40, exit 195B, just n to Forest Meadow St, then just w. Int corridors. **Pets:** Medium, other species. Service with restrictions.

Quality Inn SH
(928) 774-8771. **$34-$99.** 2000 S Milton Rd. I-40, exit 195B, 0.5 mi n. Int corridors. **Pets:** Other species. $10 one-time fee/room. Supervision.

Quality Inn-Lucky Lane M
(928) 226-7111. **$42-$69, 7 day notice.** 2501 E Lucky Ln. I-40, exit 198 (Butler Ave). Ext corridors. **Pets:** Medium, other species. $5 one-time fee/room. Service with restrictions, supervision.

Radisson Woodlands Hotel Flagstaff LH
(928) 773-8888. **$69-$179.** 1175 W Route 66. I-40, exit 195B westbound, 1.5 mi n on Milton Rd, then 0.5 mi w; exit 191 eastbound, then 2 mi e. Int corridors. **Pets:** Medium, other species. $20 one-time fee/room. Designated rooms, service with restrictions, supervision.

Ramada Limited-Lucky Lane M
(928) 779-3614. **$49-$69, 7 day notice.** 2350 E Lucky Ln. I-40, exit 198 (Butler Ave). Ext corridors. **Pets:** Small, other species. $5 one-time fee/room. Service with restrictions, supervision.

Ramada Limited West SH
(928) 773-1111. **$44-$129.** 2755 S Woodlands Village Blvd. I-40, exit 195, just n to Forest Meadows St, then w to Beulah Blvd, then just w. Ext corridors. **Pets:** Medium. $10 daily fee/room. Service with restrictions.

Red Roof Inn M
(928) 779-5121. **$40-$79.** 2520 E Lucky Ln. I-40, exit 198 (Butler Ave), just n, then just e. Ext corridors. **Pets:** Accepted.

Residence Inn by Marriott Flagstaff SH
(928) 526-5555. **$79-$175.** 3440 N Country Club Dr. I-40, exit 201, just s. Ext corridors. **Pets:** Medium, other species. $10 daily fee/room. Designated rooms, service with restrictions, supervision.

Rodeway Inn East SH
(928) 526-2200. **$39-$99.** 2650 E Route 66. I-40, exit 201, 0.5 mi n, then 0.5 mi w. Ext corridors. **Pets:** Very small. $10 one-time fee/pet. Service with restrictions, supervision.

Sleep Inn M
(928) 556-3000. **$55-$105.** 2765 S Woodlands Village Blvd. I-40, exit 195, just n to Forest Meadows St, then w to Beaulah Rd, then just w. Int corridors. **Pets:** Other species. $50 deposit/room. Service with restrictions, crate.

Super 8 Motel M
(928) 774-4581. **$45-$125.** 602 W Route 66. I-40, exit 195B, 1.5 mi n on SR 89A, then just w. Ext corridors. **Pets:** Accepted.

Travel Inn M
(928) 774-3381. **$24-$69.** 801 W Route 66. I-40, exit 191, 2 mi e. Ext corridors. **Pets:** Accepted.

Travelodge Hotel SH
(928) 779-6944. **$34-$120.** 2200 E Butler Ave. I-40, exit 198 (Butler Ave), just nw. Int corridors. **Pets:** Accepted.

FOREST LAKES

ⒶⒶⒶ ◆◆ Forest Lakes Lodge Ⓜ
(928) 535-4727. **$49-$69.** On SR 260. Ext corridors.
Pets: Small, dogs only. $10 one-time fee/pet. Service with restrictions, supervision.
(SAVE) (S⌀) (✕) (📶) (Ⓧ)

GILA BEND

ⒶⒶⒶ ◆◆◆ Best Western Space Age Lodge Ⓜ
(928) 683-2273. **$59-$99.** 401 E Pima St. Business Loop I-8; center. Ext corridors. **Pets:** Other species. Service with restrictions, crate.
(SAVE) (S⌀) (✕) (📶) (💻) (🍽) (🏊)

◆◆ Super 8 Motel Ⓜ
(928) 683-6311. **$60-$70.** 2888 Butterfield Tr. I-8, exit 119, just w. Int corridors. **Pets:** Other species. $10 one-time fee/room. Service with restrictions, supervision.
(ASK) (S⌀) (✕) (📶) (💻) (🏊)

GLOBE

◆◆ Comfort Inn Ⓜ
(928) 425-7575. **$69-$89.** 1515 South St. On US 60, 1 mi e of town. Ext corridors. **Pets:** Other species. $10 daily fee/pet. Service with restrictions, supervision.
(ASK) (S⌀) (✕) (📶) (💻) (🏊)

◆◆ Motel 6 #4223 Ⓜ
(928) 425-5741. **$45-$84.** 1699 E Ash St. On US 60, 1.3 mi e of town. Ext/int corridors. **Pets:** Accepted.
(ASK) (S⌀) (✕) (🐾) (📶) (🏊)

ⒶⒶⒶ ◆◆◆ Travelodge ⓈⒽ
(928) 425-7008. **$50-$70.** 2119 Hwy 60. On US 60, 4 mi w of town. Int corridors. **Pets:** Medium, other species. $10 daily fee/pet. Designated rooms, service with restrictions, supervision.
(SAVE) (S⌀) (✕) (🐾) (🐾) (📶)

GRAND CANYON NATIONAL PARK

◆◆◆ Grand Hotel ⓈⒽ
(928) 638-3333. **$99-$139.** On SR 64; 2 mi s of South Rim entrance. Int corridors. **Pets:** Accepted.
(ASK) (S⌀) (✕) (🐾) (📶) (💻) (🍽) (🏊)

ⒶⒶⒶ ◆◆ Rodeway Inn-Red Feather Lodge ⓈⒽ
(928) 638-2414. **$49-$129.** On SR 64; 2 mi s of South Rim entrance. Ext/int corridors. **Pets:** Other species. $50 deposit/room, $10 daily fee/pet. Service with restrictions, supervision.
(SAVE) (S⌀) (✕) (🐾) (📶) (💻) (🏊) (✕)

HOLBROOK

ⒶⒶⒶ ◆◆ Best Inn Ⓜ
(928) 524-2654. **$40-$52.** 2211 E Navajo Blvd. I-40, exit 289, 1 mi w. Ext corridors. **Pets:** Accepted.
(SAVE) (S⌀) (✕) (📶)

ⒶⒶⒶ ◆◆ Best Western Adobe Inn Ⓜ
(928) 524-3948. **$40-$55.** 615 W Hopi Dr. I-40, exit 285, 1 mi e on US 180. Ext corridors. **Pets:** Accepted.
(SAVE) (S⌀) (✕) (💻) (🏊)

ⒶⒶⒶ ◆◆ Best Western Arizonian Inn ⓈⒽ
(928) 524-2611. **$60-$87.** 2508 Navajo Blvd. I-40, exit 289, 0.5 mi w. Ext corridors. **Pets:** Medium, dogs only. $30 deposit/room. Service with restrictions.
(SAVE) (S⌀) (✕) (📶) (💻) (🏊)

ⒶⒶⒶ ◆◆◆ Comfort Inn ⓈⒽ
(928) 524-6131. **$59-$75.** 2602 E Navajo Blvd. I-40, exit 289, just w. Ext corridors. **Pets:** Accepted.
(SAVE) (S⌀) (✕) (📶) (💻) (🏊)

ⒶⒶⒶ ◆◆◆ Econo Lodge ⓈⒽ
(928) 524-1448. **$40-$50.** 2596 E Navajo Blvd. I-40, exit 289, just w. Ext corridors. **Pets:** Accepted.
(SAVE) (S⌀) (✕) (📶) (💻) (🏊)

◆◆◆◆ Holbrook Holiday Inn Express Ⓜ
(928) 524-1466. **$69-$78.** 1308 E Navajo Blvd. I-40, exit 289, just n. Int corridors. **Pets:** Other species. $10 one-time fee/pet. Designated rooms, no service, supervision.
(ASK) (S⌀) (✕) (📶) (💻) (🏊)

ⒶⒶⒶ ◆◆ Holbrook Inn Ⓜ
(928) 524-3809. **$26-$30.** 235 W Hopi Dr. I-40, exit 285, 1.5 mi e on US 180. Ext corridors. **Pets:** Other species. $10 deposit/room. No service, supervision.
(SAVE) (S⌀) (✕) (📶) (💻)

ⒶⒶⒶ ◆◆ Relax Inn Ⓜ
(928) 524-6815. **$35.** 2418 E Navajo Blvd. I-40, exit 289, 0.4 mi w. Ext corridors. **Pets:** Small. $5 daily fee/pet. Designated rooms, service with restrictions, supervision.
(SAVE) (S⌀) (✕) (📶)

JEROME

◆◆◆◆ Connor Hotel of Jerome ⓈⒽ
(928) 634-5006. **$90-$115, 3 day notice.** 164 Main St. Center. Int corridors. **Pets:** Other species. Service with restrictions, supervision.
(ASK) (S⌀) (✕) (📶) (💻)

KAYENTA

◆◆◆ Hampton Inn of Kayenta ⓈⒽ
(928) 697-3170. **$65-$115.** Hwy 160. On US 160, just w. Int corridors. **Pets:** Accepted.
(ASK) (✕) (🐾) (📶) (💻) (🍽) (🏊)

KINGMAN

ⒶⒶⒶ ◆◆◆◆ Best Western A Wayfarer's Inn ⓈⒽ
(928) 753-6271. **$70-$87.** 2815 E Andy Devine Ave. I-40, exit 53, 0.5 mi sw on I-40 business loop (US 93 and SR 66). Ext corridors. **Pets:** Accepted.
(SAVE) (S⌀) (✕) (🐾) (📶) (💻) (🏊)

ⒶⒶⒶ ◆◆◆◆ Best Western King's Inn & Suites ⓈⒽ
(928) 753-6101. **$72-$110.** 2930 E Route 66. I-40, exit 53, 0.3 mi sw on I-40 business loop and SR 66. Ext corridors. **Pets:** Small. Designated rooms, service with restrictions, supervision.
(SAVE) (S⌀) (✕) (🐾) (🐾) (📶) (💻) (🏊)

⚠⚜⚜ Brunswick Hotel 🆂🅷
(928) 718-1800. **$55-$75.** 315 E Andy Devine Ave. On SR 66; downtown. Int corridors. **Pets:** Medium. $10 one-time fee/pet. No service.
(SAVE) (S🄳) (✕) (🗲) (🛏) (🍽)

⚠⚜⚜ Days Inn West 🅼
(928) 753-7500. **$29-$89, 3 day notice.** 3023 E Andy Devine Ave. I-40, exit 53, just sw on I-40 business loop (US 93 and SR 66). Ext corridors. **Pets:** Accepted.
(SAVE) (S🄳) (✕) (🛏) (≈)

⚠⚜ Hill Top Motel 🅼
(928) 753-2198. **$36-$70, 3 day notice.** 1901 E Andy Devine Ave. I-40, exit 53, 2 mi sw on I-40 business loop (US 93 and SR 66). Ext corridors. **Pets:** Dogs only. Service with restrictions, supervision.
(SAVE) (S🄳) (✕) (🛏) (≈)

⚜ Motel 6–1114 🅼
(928) 753-9222. **$42-$57.** 424 W Beale St. I-40, exit 48, just se on Busines Loop I-40/US 93. Ext corridors. **Pets:** Accepted.
(S🄳) (✕) (🖉) (🗲) (≈)

⚠⚜⚜ Quality Inn 🅼
(928) 753-4747. **$59-$79.** 1400 E Andy Devine Ave. I-40, exit 48, 2 mi se on I-40 business loop (US 93 and SR 66). Ext corridors. **Pets:** Other species. $10 one-time fee/room. Service with restrictions, supervision.
(SAVE) (S🄳) (✕) (🖉) (🛏) (💻) (≈) (✕)

⚠⚜⚜ Super 8 Motel 🆂🅷
(928) 757-4808. **$36-$69.** 3401 E Andy Devine Ave. I-40, exit 53, 0.3 mi ne on SR 66. Int corridors. **Pets:** Accepted.
(SAVE) (S🄳) (✕) (🛏)

LAKE HAVASU CITY

⚠⚜⚜ Best Western Lake Place Inn 🆂🅷
(928) 855-2146. **$55-$250.** 31 Wing's Loop. 1 mi e of SR 95 via Swanson Ave; downtown. Ext corridors. **Pets:** Medium. $5 daily fee/pet. Service with restrictions, supervision.
(SAVE) (S🄳) (✕) (🛏) (💻) (≈)

⚜⚜⚜ Holiday Inn 🅻🅷
(928) 855-4071. **$73-$111.** 245 London Bridge Rd. 0.5 mi n of London Bridge. Int corridors. **Pets:** Accepted.
(A$K) (S🄳) (✕) (🖉) (🗲) (🛏) (💻) (🍽) (≈) (✕)

⚠⚜⚜ Island Inn Hotel 🆂🅷
(928) 680-0606. **$55-$300, 3 day notice.** 1300 W McCulloch Blvd. 0.7 mi w of London Bridge/SR 95. Int corridors. **Pets:** Medium. $10 one-time fee/pet. Service with restrictions, supervision.
(SAVE) (S🄳) (✕) (🛏) (🍽) (≈)

⚜ Lake Havasu City Super 8 🅼
(928) 855-8844. **$46-$100.** 305 London Bridge Rd. Just w of SR 95, exit Palo Verde; 0.5 mi n of London Bridge. Int corridors. **Pets:** Other species. $50 deposit/room. Service with restrictions, supervision.
(A$K) (✕) (≈)

⚜ Motel 6 Lake Havasu 🅼
(928) 855-3200. **$46-$187, 21 day notice.** 111 London Bridge Rd. 0.3 mi n of London Bridge. Int corridors. **Pets:** Medium. $50 deposit/pet. Service with restrictions, supervision.
(A$K) (S🄳) (✕)

⚠⚜⚜ Ramada Inn 🅼
(928) 855-1111. **$70-$196.** 271 S Lake Havasu Ave. SR 95, just e on Swanson Ave, then just s. Ext corridors. **Pets:** Medium. $50 deposit/pet, $20 daily fee/room. Designated rooms, service with restrictions, supervision.
(SAVE) (S🄳) (✕) (🖉) (🗲) (🛏) (💻) (🍽) (≈)

MUNDS PARK

⚠⚜⚜ Motel In The Pines 🅼
(928) 286-9699. **$35-$89.** 80 W Pinewood Rd. I-17, exit 322, just e. Ext corridors. **Pets:** Medium, other species. $30 deposit/room, $5 daily fee/pet. Designated rooms, service with restrictions, supervision.
(SAVE) (S🄳) (✕) (🛏) (💻)

NOGALES

⚜ Motel 6 Nogales #71 🅼
(520) 281-2951. **$41-$57, 3 day notice.** 141 W Mariposa Rd. I-19, exit 4, 0.9 mi e. Ext corridors. **Pets:** Accepted.
(S🄳) (✕) (🗲) (🛏) (≈)

PAGE

⚜⚜⚜ Best Western Arizona Inn 🆂🅷
(928) 645-2466. **$44-$119.** 716 Rimview Dr. 0.7 mi e of US 89 via SR 89L, Lake Powell Blvd. Int corridors. **Pets:** Accepted.
(A$K) (S🄳) (✕) (🖉) (🛏) (💻) (≈)

⚠⚜ Budget Host Economy Inn 🅼
(928) 645-2488. **$35-$64, 3 day notice.** 121 S Lake Powell Blvd. 1.3 mi e of US 89/SR 89L. Ext corridors. **Pets:** Small. $5 one-time fee/pet. Designated rooms, no service, supervision.
(SAVE) (S🄳) (✕) (≈)

⚠⚜⚜⚜ Lake Powell Days Inn 🆂🅷
(928) 645-2800. **$59-$109.** 961 N Hwy 89. Just s. Int corridors. **Pets:** Other species. $10 daily fee/pet. Designated rooms, service with restrictions, supervision.
(SAVE) (S🄳) (✕) (🖉) (🗲) (🛏) (≈)

⚜⚜ Linda's Lake Powell Condos 🅲🅾
(928) 353-4591. **$78-$114, 3 day notice.** 1019 Tower Butte. 6 mi n on US 89. Ext corridors. **Pets:** Accepted.
(A$K) (✕) (🛏) (💻)

⚠⚜⚜ Motel 6–Page/Lake Powell–4013 🆂🅷
(928) 645-5888. **$39-$69, 3 day notice.** 637 S Lake Powell Blvd. On Business Loop SR 89L, just e of US 89. Int corridors. **Pets:** Small. Designated rooms, no service, supervision.
(SAVE) (S🄳) (✕) (🗲) (≈)

⚠⚜⚜ Quality Inn, At Lake Powell 🆂🅷
(928) 645-8851. **$40-$100.** 287 N Lake Powell Blvd. 0.8 mi e of US 89/SR 89L. Int corridors. **Pets:** Other species. Designated rooms, service with restrictions.
(SAVE) (S🄳) (✕) (🖉) (🛏) (💻) (🍽) (≈)

(AAA) ♦♦♦ Wahweap Lodge 🔲
(928) 645-2433. **$109-$155.** 100 Lakeshore Dr. 4 mi n of
Glen Canyon Dam via US 89. Int corridors. **Pets:** Accepted.
(SAVE) 🔲 🔲 🔲 🔲 🔲 🔲 🔲 🔲

PARKER

(AAA) ♦♦♦ Best Western Parker Inn 🔲
(928) 669-6060. **$49-$110.** 1012 Geronimo Ave. SR 95, just
e. Int corridors. **Pets:** Small. Designated rooms, service
with restrictions.
(SAVE) 🔲 🔲 🔲 🔲 🔲

PAYSON

(AAA) ♦♦ Best Value Inn 🔲
(928) 474-2283. **$45-$99.** 811 S Beeline Hwy (SR 87). On
SR 87, 0.5 mi s of SR 260. Ext/int corridors. **Pets:** Small.
$5 daily fee/pet. Designated rooms, service with restrictions,
supervision.
(SAVE) 🔲 🔲 🔲 🔲

(AAA) ♦♦♦ Best Western Payson Inn 🔲
(928) 474-3241. **$69-$149.** 801 N Beeline Hwy. On SR 87,
0.5 mi n of SR 260. Ext corridors. **Pets:** Dogs only. $10
daily fee/room. Service with restrictions, supervision.
(SAVE) 🔲 🔲 🔲 🔲 🔲 🔲 🔲

(AAA) ♦♦♦ Comfort Inn 🔲
(928) 474-5241. **$49-$129.** 809 E Hwy 260. 0.8 mi e of SR
87. Ext corridors. **Pets:** Small, dogs only. $10 daily fee/pet.
Designated rooms, service with restrictions, supervision.
(SAVE) 🔲 🔲 🔲

(AAA) ♦♦♦ Days Inn & Suites 🔲 🐾
(928) 474-9800. **$59-$129.** 301-A S Beeline Hwy (SR 87).
On SR 87, just s of SR 260. Int corridors. **Pets:** Small,
other species. $10 daily fee/pet. Designated rooms, service
with restrictions, supervision.
(SAVE) 🔲 🔲 🔲 🔲 🔲

♦♦♦ Majestic Mountain Inn 🔲
(928) 474-0185. **$69-$160.** 602 E Hwy 260. 0.5 mi e of SR
87. Ext corridors. **Pets:** Accepted.
(ASK) 🔲 🔲 🔲 🔲 🔲 🔲

♦♦ Motel 6 #4201 🔲
(928) 474-4526. **$45-$86.** 101 W Phoenix St. On SR 87, 1.3
mi s of SR 260. Int corridors. **Pets:** Accepted.
🔲 🔲 🔲

(AAA) ♦♦♦ Paysonglo Lodge 🔲
(928) 474-2382. **$65-$140.** 1005 S Beeline Hwy (Hwy 87).
On SR 87, 1 mi s of SR 260. Ext corridors. **Pets:** Medium.
Designated rooms, no service, crate.
(SAVE) 🔲 🔲 🔲 🔲 🔲

PHOENIX METROPOLITAN AREA

APACHE JUNCTION

(AAA) ♦♦ Apache Junction Motel 🔲 🐾
(480) 982-7702. **$38-$66, 3 day notice.** 1680 W Apache Tr.
US 60, exit 195, 2 mi n, just w. Ext corridors. **Pets:** Very
small, dogs only. $15 one-time fee/pet. Designated rooms,
service with restrictions, supervision.
(SAVE) 🔲 🔲 🔲 🔲

(AAA) ♦♦♦ Apache Junction Super 8 🔲
(480) 288-8888. **$59-$89.** 251 E 29th Ave. US 60, exit 196
(Idaho Rd/SR 8 E), just n. Ext/int corridors. **Pets:** Dogs
only. $20 deposit/room, $5 daily fee/room. Designated
rooms, service with restrictions, supervision.
(SAVE) 🔲 🔲 🔲 🔲 🔲 🔲

♦♦♦ Gold Canyon Golf Resort 🔲
(480) 982-9090. **$135-$310, 3 day notice.** 6100 S Kings
Ranch Rd. US 60, exit Kings Ranch Rd, 1 mi n. Ext corridors. **Pets:** Large. $75 one-time fee/room. Service with
restrictions, supervision.
(ASK) 🔲 🔲 🔲 🔲 🔲 🔲 🔲 🔲

BUCKEYE

(AAA) ♦♦♦ Days Inn-Buckeye 🔲
(623) 386-5400. **$69-$199.** 25205 W Yuma Rd. I-10, exit 114
(Miller Rd), just sw. Ext corridors. **Pets:** Medium, other species. $20 deposit/room. Service with restrictions, supervi-
sion.
(SAVE) 🔲 🔲 🔲 🔲 🔲 🔲

CAREFREE

(AAA) ♦♦♦♦ The Boulders Resort & Golden
Door Spa-A Wyndham Luxury
Resort 🔲
(480) 488-9009. **$169-$495, 21 day notice.** 34631 N Tom
Darlington Dr. Scottsdale Rd, 11 mi n of Bell Rd to Carefree
Hwy, then just n. Ext corridors. **Pets:** Accepted.
(SAVE) 🔲 🔲 🔲 🔲 🔲 🔲 🔲

CHANDLER

(AAA) ♦♦♦ Chandler Super 8 🔲
(480) 961-3888. **$49-$76.** 7171 W Chandler Blvd. I-10, exit
160 (Chandler Blvd), just e. Int corridors. **Pets:** Other species. $5 one-time fee/pet. Service with restrictions, supervi-
sion.
(SAVE) 🔲 🔲 🔲 🔲

♦♦♦ Comfort Inn 🔲
(480) 705-8882. **$59-$99.** 255 N Kyrene Rd. I-10, exit 160
(Chandler Blvd), 1.5 mi e, just n. Int corridors.
Pets: Accepted.
(ASK) 🔲 🔲 🔲 🔲 🔲 🔲 🔲

♦♦♦♦ Hawthorn Suites Ltd 🔲
(480) 705-8881. **$129-$159.** 5858 W Chandler Blvd. I-10,
exit 160 (Chandler Blvd), 1.5 mi e. Int corridors. **Pets:** Other
species. $25 one-time fee/pet. Service with restrictions,
crate.
(ASK) 🔲 🔲 🔲 🔲 🔲 🔲 🔲

▼▼▼▼ Homewood Suites by Hilton 🆂🅷
(480) 753-6200. **$81-$129.** 7373 W Detroit St. I-10, exit 160
(Chandler Blvd), 0.4 mi e, n on 54th St. Int corridors.
Pets: Accepted.

🅰🆂🅺 💲🗐 ✕ 🔛 🗐 🗐 🗐 🗳 🗐

🅰🅰🅰 ▼▼▼ Red Roof Inn-Chandler 🆂🅷
(480) 857-4969. **$44-$69.** 7400 W Boston St. I-10, exit 160
(Chandler Blvd), just e, then s on Southgate Dr. Int corridors. **Pets:** Accepted.

💲🗐 ✕ 🔛 🗐 🗐 🗐 🗳

▼▼▼▼ Residence Inn-Chandler 🆂🅷 🐾
(480) 782-1551. **$94-$179, 3 day notice.** 200 N Federal St.
I-10, exit 160 (Chandler Blvd), 4.2 mi e; Loop 101 (Price
Rd), exit Chandler Blvd, just w. Int corridors. **Pets:** Medium,
other species. $150 one-time fee/room. Service with restric-
tions, crate.

🅰🆂🅺 💲🗐 ✕ 🔛 🗐 🗐 🗐 🗳 🗐

▼▼▼▼ San Marcos Golf Resort and Conference
Center 🅻🅷
(480) 812-0900. **$85-$119, 3 day notice.** 1 San Marcos Pl.
Just s of Chandler Blvd on Arizona Ave. Ext corridors.
Pets: Accepted.

🅰🆂🅺 💲🗐 ✕ 🗐 🗐 🗐 🗳 🗐

🅰🅰🅰 ▼▼▼▼ Windmill Suites of
Chandler 🆂🅷 🐾
(480) 812-9600. **$69-$129.** 3535 W Chandler Blvd. I-10, exit
160 (Chandler Blvd), 3.9 mi e, corner of Country Club Way.
Int corridors. **Pets:** Other species. Service with restrictions,
supervision.

💲🗐 🗐 ✕ 🗐 🗐 🗳 🗐

GLENDALE

▼▼▼▼ Holiday Inn Express Arrowhead 🆂🅷
(623) 412-2000. **$62-$71.** 7885 W Arrowhead Towne Ctr Dr.
Loop 101, exit 14 (Bell Rd), 0.3 mi e, then just n on 79th
Ave. Ext corridors. **Pets:** Accepted.

🅰🆂🅺 💲🗐 ✕ 🗐 🗐 🗐 🗳

GOODYEAR

🅰🅰🅰 ▼ Best Western Phoenix Goodyear
Inn 🅼 🐾
(623) 932-3210. **$69-$104.** 55 N Litchfield Rd. I-10, exit 128,
0.8 mi s. Ext/int corridors. **Pets:** Other species. $10 daily
fee/room. Supervision.

💲🗐 🗐 ✕ 🗐 🗐 🗐 🗳

▼▼▼▼ Hampton Inn & Suites 🆂🅷
(623) 536-1313. **$89-$179.** 2000 N Litchfield Rd. I-10, exit
128, 0.5 mi n. Int corridors. **Pets:** Medium, other species.
$25 deposit/room. Service with restrictions, supervision.

🅰🆂🅺 💲🗐 ✕ 🔛 🗐 🗐 🗳 🗐

▼▼▼▼ Holiday Inn Express 🆂🅷
(623) 535-1313. **$89-$169.** 1313 Litchfield Rd. I-10, exit 128,
just n. Int corridors. **Pets:** Accepted.

🅰🆂🅺 💲🗐 ✕ 🗐 🗐 🗐 🗳

🅰🅰🅰 ▼▼▼▼ Wingate Inn & Suites 🆂🅷
(623) 547-1313. **$99-$169.** 1188 N Dysart Rd. I-10, exit 129
(Dysart Rd), just n. Int corridors. **Pets:** Small, other species.
$25 deposit/pet. Service with restrictions, crate.

💲🗐 🗐 ✕ 🗐 🗐 🗐 🗳

MESA

🅰🅰🅰 ▼▼▼▼ Arizona Golf Resort & Conference
Center 🅻🅷 🐾
(480) 832-3202. **$99-$179.** 425 S Power Rd. 1.3 mi n of US
60 (Superstition Frwy), exit 188 (Power Rd); southeast corner of Broadway and Power rds; entrance on Broadway Rd.
Ext corridors. **Pets:** Other species. Service with restrictions.

💲🗐 🗐 ✕ 🗐 🗐 🗐 🗐 🗳 🗐

🅰🅰🅰 ▼▼▼▼ Best Western Dobson Ranch Inn
Resort 🆂🅷 🐾
(480) 831-7000. **$60-$180.** 1666 S Dobson Rd. Just s of US
60 (Superstition Frwy), exit 177 (Dobson Rd). Ext/int corridors. **Pets:** Dogs only. Service with restrictions, supervision.

💲🗐 🗐 ✕ 🗐 🗐 🗳

🅰🅰🅰 ▼▼▼ Best Western Mesa Inn 🆂🅷
(480) 964-8000. **$45-$85.** 1625 E Main St. 2 mi n of US 60
(Superstition Frwy), exit Stapley Dr, 0.5 mi e. Ext corridors.
Pets: Other species. $10 one-time fee/room. Service with
restrictions.

💲🗐 🗐 ✕ 🗐 🗐 🗳

🅰🅰🅰 ▼▼▼ Best Western Mezona Inn 🆂🅷 🐾
(480) 834-9233. **$49-$139.** 250 W Main St. Just e of Country
Club Dr; downtown. Ext corridors. **Pets:** Dogs only. Service
with restrictions, supervision.

💲🗐 🗐 ✕ 🗐 🗐 🗳

🅰🅰🅰 ▼▼▼▼ Best Western Superstition Springs Inn
& Suites 🆂🅷
(480) 641-1164. **$49-$109.** 1342 S Power Rd. Just n of US
60 (Superstition Frwy), exit 188 (Power Rd), on the northwest corner of Power Rd and Hampton Ave. Ext corridors.
Pets: Medium. $10 daily fee/pet. Designated rooms, service
with restrictions, supervision.

💲🗐 🗐 ✕ 🗐 🗐 🗐 🗳

▼▼ Days Inn 🆂🅷
(480) 844-8900. **$49-$99.** 333 W Juanita. US 60 (Superstition Frwy), exit 179 (Country Club Dr), just s, then just e. Int
corridors. **Pets:** Other species. $10 one-time fee/room.
Service with restrictions, supervision.

🅰🆂🅺 💲🗐 ✕ 🗐 🗐 🗐 🗳 🗐

🅰🅰🅰 ▼▼▼▼ Hampton Inn Phoenix/Mesa 🆂🅷
(480) 926-3600. **$69-$119.** 1563 S Gilbert Rd. US 60
(Superstition Frwy), exit 182 (Gilbert Rd), just ne. Int corridors. **Pets:** Accepted.

💲🗐 🗐 ✕ 🗐 🗐 🗳

🅰🅰🅰 ▼▼▼ Holiday Inn Express Hotel and
Conference Center 🆂🅷
(480) 985-3600. **$59-$119.** 5750 E Main St. 0.7 mi e of
Higley Rd. Ext corridors. **Pets:** Accepted.

💲🗐 🗐 ✕ 🗐 🗐 🗐 🗳

▼▼▼ **Holiday Inn Hotel & Suites** 🏨
(480) 964-7000. **$59-$119.** 1600 S Country Club Dr. US 60
(Superstition Frwy), exit 179 (Country Club Dr), just sw.
Ext/int corridors. **Pets:** Medium. $20 one-time fee/room.
Service with restrictions, crate.
🅰🆂🅺 🆂🔟 ✖ 🐾 🛏 💻 🍴 🏊

▼▼ **Homestead Studio Suites Hotel-East**
  Phoenix/Tempe 🏨 ✿
(480) 752-2266. **$39-$83.** 1920 W Isabella. Just s of US 60
(Superstition Frwy), exit 177 (Dobson Rd). Ext corridors.
Pets: Medium, other species. $25 daily fee/room. Service
with restrictions, crate.
🅰🆂🅺 🆂🔟 ✖ 🐾 🛏 💻

▼▼▼ **La Quinta Inn & Suites-Mesa** 🏨
(480) 844-8747. **$50-$88.** 902 W Grove Ave. US 60 (Superstition Frwy), exit 178 (Alma School Rd), just n, then just e.
Int corridors. **Pets:** Accepted.
🅰🆂🅺 🆂🔟 ✖ 🐕 🐾 🛏 💻 🏊

▼▼▼ **La Quinta Inn & Suites-Mesa East** 🏨
(480) 654-1970. **$56-$120.** 6530 E Superstition Springs Blvd.
US 60 (Superstition Frwy), exit 187 (Superstition Springs
Blvd) eastbound, just se; exit 188 (Power Rd) westbound,
just sw. Int corridors. **Pets:** Accepted.
🅰🆂🅺 🆂🔟 ✖ ♿ 🐕 🐾 🛏 💻 🏊

▼ **Motel 6-Mesa North #378** Ⓜ
(480) 844-8899. **$40-$63.** 336 W Hampton Ave. US 60
(Superstition Frwy), exit 179 (Country Club Dr), just n, then
just e. Ext corridors. **Pets:** Accepted.
🆂🔟 ✖ 🐾 🛏 🏊

▼ **Motel 6–Mesa South** Ⓜ
(480) 834-0066. **$40-$63.** 1511 S Country Club Dr. US 60
(Superstition Frwy), exit 179 (Country Club Dr), northeast
corner. Ext corridors. **Pets:** Accepted.
🆂🔟 ✖ 🐾 🛏 🏊

▼▼▼ **Residence Inn by Marriott Mesa** 🏨
(480) 610-0100. **$59-$169.** 941 W Grove Ave. US 60 (Superstition Frwy), exit 178 (Alma School Rd), just n, then just e.
Int corridors. **Pets:** Large. $10 daily fee/pet, $50 one-time
fee/pet. Service with restrictions, supervision.
🅰🆂🅺 🆂🔟 ✖ ♿ 🐕 🐾 🛏 💻 🏊

𝔸𝔸𝔸 ▼▼▼ **Sheraton Phoenix East Hotel** 🏨
(480) 898-8300. **$59-$110.** 200 N Centennial Way. US 60
(Superstition Frwy), exit 180 (Mesa Dr), 2 mi n, just w on
Main St, then just n. Int corridors. **Pets:** Accepted.
🆂🅰🆅🅴 🆂🔟 ✖ 🐾 🛏 💻 🍴 🏊

▼▼ **Sleep Inn of Mesa** 🏨
(480) 807-7760. **$59-$109.** 6347 E Southern Ave. US 60
(Superstition Frwy), exit 188 (Power Rd), 0.8 mi n, then 0.4
mi w to mall entrance west. Int corridors. **Pets:** Small, other
species. $25 deposit/room. Designated rooms, service with
restrictions, crate.
🅰🆂🅺 🆂🔟 ✖ 🐾 🛏 💻 🏊

𝔸𝔸𝔸 ▼▼▼ **Super 8 Motel-Mesa/Gilbert Rd** 🏨
(480) 545-0888. **$44-$79, 5 day notice.** 1550 S Gilbert Rd.
US 60 (Superstition Frwy), exit 182 (Gilbert Rd), then 1 blk
n. Int corridors. **Pets:** Medium. $5 daily fee/pet. Service with
restrictions, supervision.
🆂🅰🆅🅴 🆂🔟 ✖ 🐾 🛏 🏊

▼▼ **Travelodge Suites Mesa** 🏨
(480) 832-5961. **$39-$79.** 4244 E Main St. US 60, exit 185
(Greenfield Rd), 2 mi n, then just w. Ext corridors.
Pets: $10 daily fee/pet. Designated rooms, service with
restrictions, supervision.
🅰🆂🅺 🆂🔟 ✖ 🐾 🛏 💻 🏊

NEW RIVER

𝔸𝔸𝔸 ▼▼▼ **Comfort Suites at Anthem** 🏨
(623) 465-7979. **$59-$139.** 42415 N 41st Dr. I-17, exit 229
(Anthem Way), just w. Int corridors. **Pets:** Small, other species. $10 daily fee/room. Designated rooms, service with
restrictions, supervision.
🆂🅰🆅🅴 🆂🔟 ✖ 🐾 🛏 💻 🏊

PARADISE VALLEY

▼▼▼▼ **Doubletree La Posada**
  Resort–Scottsdale 🏨
(602) 952-0420. **$59-$235, 3 day notice.** 4949 E Lincoln Dr.
Southeast corner of Lincoln Dr and Tatum Blvd; enter from
Lincoln Dr. Ext corridors. **Pets:** Other species.
🅰🆂🅺 🆂🔟 ✖ 🐕 ♿ 💻 🍴 🏊 ✖

▼▼▼▼ **Hermosa Inn** 🏨
(602) 955-8614. **$89-$600, 3 day notice.** 5532 N Palo Cristi
Rd. 1 mi s of Lincoln Dr, corner of Stanford Dr. Ext corridors. **Pets:** Medium, other species. $50 one-time fee/room.
Service with restrictions.
🅰🆂🅺 🆂🔟 ✖ 💻 🍴 🏊 ✖

▼▼▼ **Marriott's Mountain Shadows Resort and**
  Golf Club 🏨
(480) 948-7111. **$89-$249.** 5641 E Lincoln Dr. 1 mi e of
Tatum Blvd, on south side of Lincoln Dr. Ext corridors.
Pets: Small, dogs only. $50 one-time fee/room. Service with
restrictions, supervision.
🅰🆂🅺 🆂🔟 ✖ 🐕 ♿ 🛏 💻 🍴 🏊 ✖

𝔸𝔸𝔸 ▼▼▼▼ **Sanctuary Camelback**
  Mountain 🏨
(480) 948-2100. **$225-$595, 7 day notice.** 5700 E
McDonald Dr. US 101, exit McDonald Dr, 3.9 mi w. Ext
corridors. **Pets:** Large, other species. Service with restrictions, supervision.
🆂🅰🆅🅴 ✖ ♿ 💻 🍴 🏊 ✖

PEORIA

𝔸𝔸𝔸 ▼▼▼ **Baymont Inn & Suites**
  Phoenix-Peoria 🏨
(623) 933-1633. **$59-$149.** 16771 N 84th Ave. Loop 101, exit
14 (Bell Rd), just w. Int corridors. **Pets:** Accepted.
🆂🅰🆅🅴 🆂🔟 ✖ ♿ 🛏 💻 🏊

▼▼▼ **Comfort Suites Peoria Sports**
  Complex 🏨
(623) 334-3993. **$49-$159.** 8473 W Paradise Ln. Loop 101,
exit 14 (Bell Rd), just e to 83rd Ave, then just s. Int corridors. **Pets:** Accepted.
🅰🆂🅺 🆂🔟 ✖ 🐕 ♿ 🛏 💻 🏊

▼▼▼▼ **La Quinta Inn & Suites Phoenix Peoria West** SH
(623) 487-1900. **$68-$156.** 16321 N 83 Ave. Loop 101, exit 14 (Bell Rd), just e, then just s. Int corridors. **Pets:** Other species. Service with restrictions, crate.

A$K S6 ✕ 🏊 🖥 🖨 🛏 🏊

▼▼▼▼ **Residence Inn by Marriott** SH
(623) 979-2074. **$84-$259.** 8435 W Paradise Ln. Loop 101, exit 14 (Bell Rd), just e, then just s on 83rd Ave. Int corridors. **Pets:** Accepted.

A$K S6 ✕ 🖥 🖨 🛏 🏊 ✕

PHOENIX

AAA ▼▼▼▼ **AmeriSuites (Phoenix/Metro Center)** SH
(602) 997-8800. **$79-$134.** 10838 N 25th Ave. I-17, exit 208 (Peoria Ave), just e, then 0.3 mi n. Int corridors. **Pets:** Accepted.

SAVE S6 ✕ 🖥 🖨 🛏 🏊

AAA ▼▼▼ **Best Western Airport Inn** M
(602) 273-7251. **$58-$119.** 2425 S 24th St. I-10, exit 150B westbound, just s; exit 151 eastbound (University Dr), just n to I-10 westbound, 1 mi w to exit 150B (24th St), just s. Ext/int corridors. **Pets:** Small. $10 daily fee/pet. Designated rooms, service with restrictions, crate.

SAVE S6 ✕ 🏊 🖥 🖨 🛏 🍴 🏊

AAA ▼▼▼ **Best Western Bell Hotel** SH
(602) 993-8300. **$50-$95.** 17211 N Black Canyon Hwy. I-17, exit 212, just e, then just n. Ext corridors. **Pets:** Accepted.

SAVE S6 ✕ 🏊 🖥 🖨 🛏 🏊

AAA ▼▼▼▼ **Best Western InnSuites Hotel Phoenix Northern/Airport** SH
(602) 997-6285. **$59-$109.** 1615 E Northern Ave. Loop 51, 0.3 mi w. Ext corridors. **Pets:** Medium. $25 one-time fee/pet. Designated rooms, service with restrictions, crate.

SAVE S6 ✕ 🏊 🖥 🖨 🛏 🏊 ✕

AAA ▼▼▼ **Comfort Inn Black Canyon** M
(602) 242-8011. **$39-$129.** 5050 N Black Canyon Hwy. I-17, exit 203 (Camelback Rd), just w, then just n on west side of freeway. Ext corridors. **Pets:** Accepted.

SAVE S6 ✕ 🖥 🖨 🛏 🏊

▼▼ **Comfort Inn Phoenix North** SH
(602) 866-2089. **$49-$79.** 1711 W Bell Rd. I-17, exit 212 (Bell Rd), 1 mi e. Ext corridors. **Pets:** Small, other species. $25 deposit/room, $10 daily fee/room. Service with restrictions, supervision.

A$K S6 ✕ 🏊 🖥 🖨 🛏 🏊

▼▼▼▼ **Comfort Suites** SH ❀
(602) 861-3900. **$49-$129.** 10210 N 26th Dr. I-17, exit 208 (Peoria Ave), just e, just s on 25th Ave, then 0.3 mi w on W Beryl Ave. Int corridors. **Pets:** Large, other species. $50 one-time fee/room. Service with restrictions, crate.

A$K S6 ✕ ♿ 🖥 🖨 🛏

AAA ▼▼▼▼ **Crowne Plaza North Phoenix** SH
(602) 943-2341. **$59-$119.** 2532 W Peoria Ave. I-17, exit 208 (Peoria Ave), just e. Int corridors. **Pets:** Accepted.

SAVE S6 ✕ 🖢M 🏊 🖥 🖨 🛏 🍴 🏊

AAA ▼▼▼ **Days Inn-Airport** M
(602) 244-8244. **$49-$99.** 3333 E Van Buren. Loop 202, exit 1C (32nd St), 0.6 mi s, then just e. Ext/int corridors. **Pets:** Small, dogs only. $20 one-time fee/room. Designated rooms, service with restrictions, supervision.

SAVE S6 ✕ 🖥 🖨 🛏 🍴 🏊

▼▼▼ **Econo Lodge Inn & Suites-Downtown** SH
(602) 528-9100. **$59-$119.** 202 E McDowell Rd. Just e of Central Ave. Int corridors. **Pets:** Medium. $25 deposit/pet. Service with restrictions, supervision.

A$K S6 ✕ 🖥 🖨 🛏 🏊

AAA ▼▼▼▼ **Embassy Suites Airport at 44th St** SH
(602) 244-8800. **$69-$243.** 1515 N 44th St. Loop 202, exit 2 (44th St), 0.3 mi n on east side. Ext corridors. **Pets:** Accepted.

SAVE S6 ✕ 🏊 🖥 🖨 🛏 🍴 🏊

▼▼▼▼ **Embassy Suites Phoenix Airport at 24th St** SH
(602) 957-1910. **$69-$189.** 2333 E Thomas Rd. Just w of 24th St. Ext corridors. **Pets:** Small. $15 daily fee/room. Service with restrictions, supervision.

A$K S6 ✕ 🏊 🖥 🖨 🛏 🏊

▼▼▼▼ **Embassy Suites Phoenix-Biltmore** SH 🐾
(602) 955-3992. **$89-$260.** 2630 E Camelback Rd. Just n of Camelback Rd on 26th St. Int corridors. **Pets:** Medium, other species. $25 one-time fee/pet. Designated rooms, service with restrictions, crate.

A$K S6 ✕ 🏊 🖥 🖨 🛏 🏊

▼▼▼▼ **Hampton Inn I-17 Phoenix Metro Center** SH
(602) 864-6233. **$49-$89, 5 day notice.** 8101 N Black Canyon Hwy. I-17, exit 206 (Northern Ave), just e, then just n; on east side of freeway. Ext corridors. **Pets:** Other species. $25 one-time fee/pet. Service with restrictions, supervision.

A$K S6 ✕ 🏊 🖥 🖨 🛏 🏊

▼▼▼▼ **Hampton Inn Phoenix I-10 West** SH
(602) 484-7000. **$59-$129.** 5152 W Latham St. I-10, exit 139 (51st Ave), just sw. Int corridors. **Pets:** Medium, other species. $25 deposit/room. Service with restrictions, supervision.

A$K S6 ✕ ♿ 🖥 🖨 🛏 🏊

AAA ▼▼▼▼ **Hilton Suites-Phoenix** LH
(602) 222-1111. **$89-$229.** 10 E Thomas Rd. Just e of Central Ave; in Phoenix Plaza. Int corridors. **Pets:** Accepted.

SAVE S6 ✕ 🖢M 🏊 ♿ 🖥 🖨 🛏 🍴 🏊 ✕

AAA ▼▼▼▼ **Holiday Inn Express Hotel & Suites** SH
(480) 785-8500. **$89-$119.** 15221 S 50th St. I-10, exit 160 (Chandler Blvd), just w. Int corridors. **Pets:** Small, other species. Designated rooms.

SAVE S6 ✕ ♿ 🖥 🖨 🛏

▼▼▼▼ **Holiday Inn Express Hotel & Suites** SH
(602) 453-9900. **$59-$139.** 3401 E University Dr. I-10, exit 151 (University Dr), just n. Int corridors. **Pets:** Accepted.

A$K S6 ✕ ♿ 🖥 🖨 🛏 🏊

AAA ▼▼▼ Holiday Inn Select-Airport SH
(602) 273-7778. **$64-$103.** 4300 E Washington St. Loop 202, exit 2 (44th St), 0.7 mi s. Int corridors. **Pets:** Accepted.
[SAVE] [S6] [✕] [🎧] [&] [🛏] [💻] [¶] [⊃]

AAA ▼▼▼ Holiday Inn West SH
(602) 484-9009. **$129-$159.** 1500 N 51st Ave. I-10, exit 139 (51st Ave), just n. Int corridors. **Pets:** Medium. $25 one-time fee/pet. Service with restrictions, supervision.
[SAVE] [S6] [✕] [&M] [🎧] [&] [🛏] [💻] [¶] [⊃]

▼▼▼ Homestead Studio Suites Hotel-North Phoenix/Metro M ❀
(602) 944-7828. **$39-$66.** 2102 W Dunlap Ave. I-17, exit 207, 0.7 mi e. Ext corridors. **Pets:** Medium, other species. $25 daily fee/room. Service with restrictions, crate.
[ASK] [S6] [✕] [&] [🛏]

AAA ▼▼▼ Homewood Suites Hotel SH
(602) 674-8900. **$69-$139.** 2536 W Beryl Ave. I-17, exit 208 (Peoria Ave), just e, just s on 25th Ave, then just w. Int corridors. **Pets:** Accepted.
[SAVE] [S6] [✕] [&M] [&] [🛏] [💻] [⊃]

AAA ▼▼▼ Howard Johnson Phoenix Airport M
(602) 220-0044. **$43-$73.** 124 S 24th St. I-10, exit 150B (24th St) westbound, 1.5 mi n; exit 151 (University Dr) eastbound, 1 mi w to 24th St, then 1.7 mi n. Ext corridors. **Pets:** Medium. $25 one-time fee/room. Service with restrictions, supervision.
[SAVE] [S6] [✕] [🛏] [💻] [¶] [⊃]

▼▼▼ La Quinta Inn & Suites-Chandler SH
(480) 961-7700. **$66-$115.** 15241 S 50th St. I-10, exit 160 (Chandler Blvd), just w, then just n. Int corridors. **Pets:** Small. Service with restrictions.
[ASK] [S6] [✕] [&M] [🎧] [&] [🛏] [💻] [⊃]

AAA ▼▼ La Quinta Inn-Phoenix Airport North SH
(602) 956-6500. **$65-$109.** 4727 E Thomas Rd. Just w of 48th St. Ext/int corridors. **Pets:** Medium. $50 deposit/room. Service with restrictions, supervision.
[SAVE] [S6] [✕] [🛏] [💻] [⊃]

AAA ▼▼▼ La Quinta Inn Thomas Rd M
(602) 258-6271. **$58-$102.** 2725 N Black Canyon Hwy. I-17, exit 201 (Thomas Rd), just e, then just s on east side of freeway. Ext corridors. **Pets:** Accepted.
[SAVE] [S6] [✕] [🛏] [💻] [⊃]

AAA ▼▼▼ La Quinta Phoenix North SH
(602) 993-0800. **$59-$115.** 2510 W Greenway Rd. I-17, exit 211, just e. Ext corridors. **Pets:** Small, dogs only. Service with restrictions, supervision.
[SAVE] [S6] [✕] [🎧] [&] [🛏] [💻] [⊃] [✕]

AAA ▼▼▼ Premier Inns M ❀
(602) 943-2371. **$44-$79.** 10402 N Black Canyon Hwy. I-17, exit 208 (Peoria Ave), 0.3 mi w to 28th Dr, just s, just e on Metro Pkwy E, then just n on 27th Ave. Ext corridors. **Pets:** Small. Service with restrictions, supervision.
[SAVE] [S6] [✕] [🛏] [💻] [⊃]

AAA ▼▼▼ Quality Inn South Mountain SH
(480) 893-3900. **$59-$104.** 5121 E La Puenta Ave. I-10, exit 157 (Elliot Rd), just w, just n on 51st St, then just e. Ext corridors. **Pets:** Accepted.
[SAVE] [S6] [✕] [🛏] [💻] [¶] [⊃] [✕]

▼▼▼ Ramada Inn Phoenix North SH
(602) 866-7000. **$59-$159.** 12027 N 28th Dr. I-17, exit 209 (Cactus Rd), just w, then just s. Int corridors. **Pets:** Accepted.
[ASK] [S6] [✕] [🎧] [🛏] [💻] [¶] [⊃]

AAA ▼▼▼ Red Roof Inn SH
(602) 233-8004. **$47-$69.** 5215 W Willetta. I-10, exit 139 (51st Ave), just n, just e on McDowell Rd, then just s. Int corridors. **Pets:** Accepted.
[SAVE] [✕] [&M] [&] [🛏] [⊃]

▼▼ Red Roof Inn-Camelback SH
(602) 264-9290. **$55-$85.** 502 W Camelback Rd. I-17, exit 203 (Camelback Rd), 1.8 mi e. Int corridors. **Pets:** Medium. Service with restrictions, supervision.
[ASK] [S6] [✕] [🛏] [¶] [⊃]

AAA ▼▼▼ Red Roof Inn-Phoenix SH
(602) 866-1049. **$48-$71.** 17222 N Black Canyon Hwy. I-17, exit 212, just w, then just n. Int corridors. **Pets:** Large, other species. Service with restrictions.
[SAVE] [✕] [🎧] [&] [🛏] [⊃]

▼▼▼ Residence Inn By Marriott SH
(602) 864-1900. **$69-$179.** 8242 N Black Canyon Hwy. I-17, exit 207 (Dunlap Ave), just w, then 0.8 mi s. Ext/int corridors. **Pets:** Large. $25 daily fee/room. Service with restrictions.
[ASK] [S6] [✕] [&M] [🎧] [&] [🛏] [💻] [⊃] [✕]

▼▼▼ Residence Inn by Marriott Phoenix Airport SH ❀
(602) 273-9220. **$80-$179.** 801 N 44th St. Loop 202, exit 152 (40th and 44th sts) eastbound; exit 152 (44th St) westbound, just s. Int corridors. **Pets:** Large, other species. $6 daily fee/pet, $50 one-time fee/room. Service with restrictions.
[ASK] [S6] [✕] [&M] [&] [🛏] [💻] [⊃] [✕]

AAA ▼▼ Rodeway Inn-Airport M
(602) 685-9911. **$45-$105.** 3541 E Van Buren St. Loop 202 E, exit 1C, 0.6 mi s, 0.4 mi e. Ext corridors. **Pets:** Other species. $6 daily fee/pet. Service with restrictions, supervision.
[SAVE] [S6] [✕] [🛏] [💻] [⊃]

AAA ▼▼▼ ▼▼▼ Royal Palms Resort and Spa LH ❀
(602) 840-3610. **$179-$395, 7 day notice.** 5200 E Camelback Rd. Just e of 52nd St. Ext/int corridors. **Pets:** Small, dogs only. $100 deposit/room, $100 one-time fee/room. Designated rooms, crate.
[SAVE] [✕] [&] [🛏] [💻] [¶] [⊃] [✕]

▼▼▼ Sheraton Crescent Hotel LH
(602) 943-8200. **$69-$229.** 2620 W Dunlap Ave. I-17, exit 207 (Dunlap Ave), just e. Int corridors. **Pets:** Accepted.
[ASK] [S6] [✕] [&M] [🎧] [&] [🛏] [💻] [¶] [⊃] [✕]

Sleep Inn Phoenix North SH
(602) 504-1200. **$50-$115.** 18235 N 27th Ave. I-17, exit 214A, just w, then just s. Int corridors. **Pets:** Other species. $25 deposit/room, $5 daily fee/room. Designated rooms, service with restrictions, crate.

🅰🆂$ 🆂💰 ⊗ 🚿 🛎 🍴 💻 ⛵

Sleep Inn Sky Harbor Airport SH
(480) 967-7100. **$89-$99.** 2621 S 47th Pl. I-10, exit 151 (University Dr), 2 mi n, then just w. Int corridors. **Pets:** Medium. $25 one-time fee/pet.

💰 🆂💰 ⊗ 🍴 💻 ⛵

SpringHill Suites-Phoenix/Metro Center SH
(602) 943-0010. **$59-$129.** 9425 N Black Canyon Hwy. I-17, exit 207, just e, then 0.3 mi n. Int corridors. **Pets:** Accepted.

🅰🆂$ 🆂💰 ⊗ 🍴 🛎 💻 ⛵

Studio 6 Phoenix-Deer Valley #6030 SH
(602) 843-1151. **$45-$73.** 18405 N 27th Ave. I-17, exit 214A (Union Hills Dr), just w, then just s. Ext corridors. **Pets:** Accepted.

⊗ 🍴 🛎 💻

Sunshine Hotel & Suites SH
(602) 248-0222. **$45-$145.** 3600 N 2nd Ave. Just n of Osborn Rd, 0.5 mi s of Indian School; downtown. Ext/int corridors. **Pets:** Accepted.

🅰🆂$ 🆂💰 ⊗ 🍴 🛎 💻 🍴 ⛵ ⊠

TownePlace Suites-Phoenix SH
(602) 943-9510. **$39-$90.** 9425 N Black Canyon Hwy. I-17, exit 207, just e, then 0.3 mi n. Int corridors. **Pets:** Accepted.

🅰🆂$ 🆂💰 ⊗ 🛎 💻 ⛵

Travelers Inn SH
(602) 233-1988. **$40-$75.** 5102 W Latham St. I-10, exit 139 (51st Ave), just sw. Ext corridors. **Pets:** Large. Service with restrictions, supervision.

💰 🆂💰 ⊗ 🛎 💻 ⛵

Wellesley Inn & Suites (Phoenix/Airport) SH
(602) 225-2998. **$54-$74.** 4357 E Oak St. Loop 202, exit 2 (44th St), just e, then 1 mi n. Ext corridors. **Pets:** Other species. $25 one-time fee/room. Service with restrictions, supervision.

💰 🆂💰 ⊗ 🚿 🛎 💻 ⛵

Wellesley Inn & Suites (Phoenix/Chandler) SH
(480) 753-6700. **$45-$72.** 5035 E Chandler Blvd. I-10, exit 160 (Chandler Blvd), just w. Ext corridors. **Pets:** Medium, other species. $25 one-time fee/room. Service with restrictions, crate.

💰 🆂💰 ⊗ 🚿 🛎 💻 ⛵

Wellesley Inn & Suites (Phoenix/Metro Center) SH
(602) 870-2999. **$39-$49.** 11211 N Black Canyon Hwy. I-17, exit 208 (Peoria Ave), just e, then 0.3 mi n on east side of freeway. Ext corridors. **Pets:** Medium, other species. Service with restrictions.

💰 🆂💰 ⊗ 🚿 🛎 💻 ⛵ ⊠

Wellesley Inn & Suites (Phoenix/Midtown) SH
(602) 279-9000. **$54-$154, 17 day notice.** 217 W Osborn Rd. Just w of Central Ave, between Indian School and Thomas rds. Int corridors. **Pets:** Small. Service with restrictions, supervision.

💰 🆂💰 ⊗ 🚿 🍴 🛎 💻 ⛵

SCOTTSDALE

AmeriSuites (Scottsdale/Old Town) SH
(480) 423-9944. **$49-$149.** 7300 E 3rd Ave. Just e of Scottsdale Rd. Int corridors. **Pets:** Small, other species. Service with restrictions, supervision.

💰 🆂💰 ⊗ 🚿 🍴 🛎 💻 ⛵

Chaparral Suites Resort SH
(480) 949-1414. **$149-$199.** 5001 N Scottsdale Rd. At Chaparral Rd. Ext corridors. **Pets:** Medium, dogs only. $25 one-time fee/room. Service with restrictions, crate.

💰 🆂💰 ⊗ 🍴 🚿 🛎 💻 🍴 ⛵

Country Inn & Suites By Carlson SH
(480) 314-1200. **$62-$120.** 10801 N 89th Pl. Just n of Shea Blvd, just e of Pima Rd. Int corridors. **Pets:** Medium. $50 one-time fee/pet. Service with restrictions, supervision.

🅰🆂$ 🆂💰 ⊗ 🍴 🚿 🛎 💻 ⛵

The Fairmont Scottsdale Princess LH
(480) 585-4848. **$179-$589, 14 day notice.** 7575 E Princess Dr. 0.6 mi n of Bell Rd, 0.5 mi e of Scottsdale Rd, on south side of Princess Dr. Ext/int corridors. **Pets:** Accepted.

💰 🆂💰 ⊗ 🚿 🍴 🚿 🛎 💻 🍴 ⛵ ⊠

Four Seasons Resort Scottsdale at Troon North LH 🐾
(480) 515-5700. **$195-$4000, 7 day notice.** 10600 E Crescent Moon Dr. Pima Rd, 2 mi e on Happy Valley, then 1.5 mi n on Alma School Rd. Ext corridors. **Pets:** Small. Service with restrictions, supervision.

💰 ⊗ 🚿 🍴 🚿 🛎 💻 🍴 ⛵ ⊠

Hampton Inn-Oldtown/Fashion Square Scottsdale SH
(480) 941-9400. **$59-$159.** 4415 N Civic Center Plaza. Scottsdale Rd, just e on Camelback Rd, just s on 75th St. Ext/int corridors. **Pets:** $50 one-time fee/room. Service with restrictions.

🅰🆂$ 🆂💰 ⊗ 🚿 🍴 🚿 🛎 💻 ⛵

Holiday Inn Express Hotel & Suites-Scottsdale SH
(480) 675-7665. **$69-$289.** 3131 N Scottsdale Rd. Northeast corner of Scottsdale Rd and Earll Dr. Int corridors. **Pets:** Small, other species. $50 deposit/room. Designated rooms, service with restrictions, crate.

💰 🆂💰 ⊗ 🚿 🍴 🛎 💻 ⛵

▼▼ **Homestead Studio Suites**
   Hotel-Scottsdale SH ❀
(480) 994-0297. **$46-$87.** 3560 N Marshall Way. Just w of Scottsdale Rd on Goldwater, then just s. Ext corridors. **Pets:** Medium, other species. $25 daily fee/room. Service with restrictions, crate.

[ASK] [🛏] [✕] [🖥] [📶] [🛗] [💻] [🏊]

▲▲▲ ▼▼▼ **Hospitality Suite Resort** SH
(480) 949-5115. **$49-$119.** 409 N Scottsdale Rd. Just n of McKellips Rd, on east side of Scottsdale Rd. Ext corridors. **Pets:** Accepted.

[SAVE] [🛏] [✕] [🛗] [💻] [🍴] [🏊] [✕]

▼▼ **The Inn at Pima** CO
(480) 948-3800. **$45-$244.** 7330 N Pima Rd. 0.4 mi n of Indian Bend Rd, on west side of Pima Rd. Ext/int corridors. **Pets:** Accepted.

[ASK] [🛏] [✕] [📶] [🛗] [💻] [🏊] [✕]

▲▲▲ ▼▼ **InnSuites Hotels & Suites Scottsdale**
   Eldorado Park Resort SH
(480) 941-1202. **$49-$109.** 7707 E McDowell Rd. Just w of Hayden Rd, on south side of McDowell Rd. Ext corridors. **Pets:** Medium, other species. $25 one-time fee/pet. Designated rooms, service with restrictions, crate.

[SAVE] [🛏] [✕] [📶] [🛗] [💻] [🍴] [🏊] [✕]

▲▲▲ ▼▼▼ **James Hotel-Scottsdale** SH
(480) 994-9203. **$169-$299.** 7353 E Indian School Rd. Just e of Scottsdale Rd, on south side of Indian School Rd. Ext corridors. **Pets:** Accepted.

[SAVE] [🛏] [✕] [📶] [🛗] [💻] [🏊] [✕]

▲▲▲ ▼▼▼▼ **La Quinta Inn & Suites** SH
(480) 614-5300. **$66-$139.** 8888 E Shea Blvd. Loop 101, exit Shea Blvd, northeast corner. Int corridors. **Pets:** Other species. Service with restrictions.

[SAVE] [🛏] [✕] [📶] [📶] [🛗] [💻] [🏊]

▲▲▲ ▼▼▼▼▼ **Marriott's Camelback Inn Resort,**
   Golf Club & Spa LH
(480) 948-1700. **$129-$439, 10 day notice.** 5402 E Lincoln Dr. 0.5 mi e of Tatum Blvd, on north side of Lincoln Dr. Ext corridors. **Pets:** Small. $100 deposit/room. Service with restrictions, supervision.

[SAVE] [🛏] [✕] [📶] [📶] [🛗] [🛗] [💻] [🍴] [🏊] [✕]

▲▲▲ ▼▼▼ ▼▼▼ **The Phoenician** LH
(480) 941-8200. **$275-$725, 7 day notice.** 6000 E Camelback Rd. 0.5 mi w of 64th St. Ext/int corridors. **Pets:** Accepted.

[SAVE] [🛏] [✕] [📶] [📶] [🛗] [💻] [🍴] [🏊] [✕]

▲▲▲ ▼▼▼▼ **Renaissance Scottsdale Resort** LH
(480) 991-1414. **$89-$229.** 6160 N Scottsdale Rd. Just n of McDonald Dr, on the west side of Scottsdale Rd. Ext corridors. **Pets:** Accepted.

[SAVE] [✕] [📶] [📶] [🛗] [🛗] [💻] [🍴] [🏊] [✕]

▼▼▼▼ **Residence Inn by Marriott** SH
(480) 948-8666. **$59-$159.** 6040 N Scottsdale Rd. Just n of McDonald Dr. Ext/int corridors. **Pets:** $6 daily fee/pet, $50 one-time fee/room. Designated rooms, service with restrictions, supervision.

[ASK] [🛏] [✕] [📶] [📶] [🛗] [🛗] [💻] [🏊] [✕]

▲▲▲ ▼▼▼ **Rodeway Inn of Scottsdale** M ❀
(480) 946-3456. **$35-$139.** 7110 E Indian School Rd. Just w of Scottsdale Rd, on north side of Indian School Rd. Ext corridors. **Pets:** Medium. $10 daily fee/room. Service with restrictions, supervision.

[SAVE] [🛏] [✕] [📶] [🛗] [🛗] [💻] [🏊]

▲▲▲ ▼▼▼ ▼▼▼ **Scottsdale Marriott at McDowell**
   Mountains SH
(480) 502-3836. **$219-$299.** 16770 N Perimeter Dr. Loop 101, exit 36 (Princess Dr), just w to Perimeter Dr, then 0.6 mi s. Int corridors. **Pets:** Accepted.

[SAVE] [🛏] [✕] [🛗] [📶] [🛗] [🛗] [💻] [🍴] [🏊] [✕]

▲▲▲ ▼▼▼▼ **Scottsdale Park Apts. & Inn** SH
(480) 949-8637. **$49-$129.** 1251 N Miller Rd. 0.5 mi e of Scottsdale Rd on McDowell Rd, then just s. Ext corridors. **Pets:** Accepted.

[SAVE] [✕] [🛗] [💻] [🏊] [✕]

▲▲▲ ▼▼▼ **Sleep Inn** SH ❀
(480) 998-9211. **$42-$119.** 16630 N Scottsdale Rd. Just s of Bell Rd. Int corridors. **Pets:** Medium, other species. $10 daily fee/pet. Designated rooms, service with restrictions, supervision.

[SAVE] [🛏] [✕] [🛗] [🛗] [💻] [🏊]

▼▼▼▼ **Summerfield Suites by**
   Wyndham-Scottsdale SH
(480) 946-7700. **$89-$189, 3 day notice.** 4245 N Drinkwater Blvd. 0.3 mi e of Scottsdale Rd. Ext corridors. **Pets:** Accepted.

[ASK] [🛏] [✕] [📶] [🛗] [🛗] [💻] [🏊] [✕]

▼▼ ▼▼ **TownePlace Suites by Marriott** SH
(480) 551-1100. **$59-$159.** 10740 N 90th St. Loop 101, exit Shea Blvd, just e to 90th St, then just n. Int corridors. **Pets:** Accepted.

[✕] [🛗] [📶] [📶] [🛗] [💻] [🏊]

▲▲▲ ▼▼▼ ▼▼▼ **The Westin Kierland Resort &**
   Spa LH ❀
(480) 624-1000. **$109-$599, 7 day notice.** 6902 E Greenway Pkwy. 0.5 mi w of Scottsdale Rd. Int corridors. **Pets:** Designated rooms.

[SAVE] [🛏] [✕] [📶] [💻] [🍴] [🏊] [✕]

SURPRISE

▲▲▲ ▼▼▼ **Best Inn & Suites** SH
(623) 933-4000. **$49-$119.** 12477 W Bell Rd. US 60 (Grand Ave), 1.1 mi e, just s on Greasewood St. Int corridors. **Pets:** Small, other species. $25 one-time fee/pet. Service with restrictions, supervision.

[SAVE] [🛏] [✕] [📶] [🛗] [💻] [🏊]

▲▲▲ ▼▼▼▼ **Windmill Suites at Sun City**
   West SH ❀
(623) 583-0133. **$69-$149.** 12545 W Bell Rd. US 60 (Grand Ave), 1 mi e. Int corridors. **Pets:** Designated rooms, service with restrictions, supervision.

[SAVE] [🛏] [✕] [📶] [🛗] [🏊] [✕]

TEMPE

AAA ▼▼▼ **AmeriSuites (Tempe/Arizona Mills)** SH
(480) 831-9800. **$62-$116.** 1520 W Baseline Rd. I-10, exit 155 (Baseline Rd), 0.4 mi e. Int corridors. **Pets:** Accepted.
SAVE Sfb ⊠ &'• ♿ ◻ ➔

AAA ▼▼▼ **AmeriSuites (Tempe/Phoenix Airport)** SH
(480) 804-9544. **$59-$109.** 1413 W Rio Salado Pkwy. Just w of Priest Dr. Int corridors. **Pets:** Small, other species. Service with restrictions, supervision.
SAVE Sfb ⊠ ♿ ◻ ➔

AAA ▼▼▼ **Best Western Inn of Tempe** SH
(480) 784-2233. **$61-$119.** 670 N Scottsdale Rd. SR 202 Loop (Red Mountain Frwy), exit 7, just s. Int corridors. **Pets:** Accepted.
SAVE Sfb ⊠ &'• ♿ ◻ ➔

▼▼▼ **Country Inn & Suites By Carlson** SH
(480) 345-8585. **$50-$110.** 1660 W Elliot Rd. I-10, exit 157, just e. Ext corridors. **Pets:** Medium, other species. $100 deposit/pet. Service with restrictions, crate.
ASK Sfb ⊠ ♿ ◻ ➔

AAA ▼▼▼ **Fiesta Inn Resort** LH
(480) 967-1441. **$125-$135.** 2100 S Priest Dr. I-10, exit 153 (Broadway Rd), 0.5 mi e. Ext corridors. **Pets:** Small, other species. $100 deposit/room. Designated rooms, no service, supervision.
SAVE Sfb ⊠ ♿ &'• ♿ ◻ ⦿ ➔ ⊠

▼▼▼ **Hampton Inn & Suites** SH
(480) 675-9799. **$71-$116.** 1429 N Scottsdale Rd. SR 202 (Red Mountain Frwy), exit 7, 0.5 mi n. Ext corridors. **Pets:** Accepted.
ASK Sfb ⊠ ♿ &'• ♿ ◻ ➔ ⊠

AAA ▼▼▼ **Holiday Inn** SH
(480) 968-3451. **$49-$99.** 915 E Apache Blvd. US 60 (Superstition Frwy), exit 174 (Rural Rd), 2 mi n. Int corridors. **Pets:** Medium. $25 one-time fee/room. No service, crate.
SAVE Sfb ⊠ ♿ &'• ♿ ◻ ⦿ ➔ ⊠

▼▼▼ **Holiday Inn Express/Tempe** SH
(480) 820-7500. **$59-$109.** 5300 S Priest Dr. I-10, exit 155 (Baseline Rd), 0.4 mi e, then just s. Int corridors. **Pets:** Accepted.
ASK ⊠ ♿ ◻ ➔

▼▼▼ **Homestead Studio Suites Hotel-Phoenix/Airport/Tempe** SH ❀
(480) 557-8880. **$58-$104.** 2165 W 15th St. I-10, exit 153 (Broadway Rd), 0.3 mi ne, then just nw on S 52nd St, just w. Int corridors. **Pets:** Medium, other species. $25 daily fee/room. Service with restrictions, crate.
ASK Sfb ⊠ &'• ♿ ◻ ➔

AAA ▼▼▼ **InnSuites Hotels & Suites Tempe/ Phoenix Airport** M
(480) 897-7900. **$55-$99.** 1651 W Baseline Rd. I-10, exit 155 (Baseline Rd), just e. Ext corridors. **Pets:** Accepted.
SAVE Sfb ⊠ ♿ ◻ ⦿ ➔ ⊠

▼▼▼ **La Quinta Inn** SH
(480) 967-4465. **$58-$105.** 911 S 48th St. I-10, exit 153 (Broadway Rd) eastbound; exit 153A (University Dr) westbound, 0.8 mi n, on south side of University Dr and east side of SR 143 (Hohokam Expwy). Ext corridors. **Pets:** Accepted.
ASK Sfb ⊠ ♿ ◻ ➔

▼▼ **Quality Inn Airport/ASU** SH
(480) 774-2500. **$69-$129.** 1375 E University Dr. 0.5 mi e of Rural Rd. Int corridors. **Pets:** Medium, other species. Service with restrictions, supervision.
ASK Sfb ⊠ &'• ♿ ◻ ➔

AAA ▼▼ **Ramada Limited** SH ❀
(480) 413-1188. **$51-$76.** 1701 W Baseline Rd. I-10, exit 155 (Baseline Rd), just e. Ext corridors. **Pets:** Medium. Service with restrictions, crate.
SAVE Sfb ⊠ ♿ &'• ♿ ◻ ➔

AAA ▼▼▼ **Red Roof Inn Phoenix Airport** SH
(480) 449-3205. **$46-$64.** 2135 W 15th St. I-10, exit 153 (Broadway Rd), just nw on S 52nd St, just w. Int corridors. **Pets:** Accepted.
SAVE ⊠ &'• ♿ ◻ ➔

▼▼ **Residence Inn by Marriott** SH
(480) 756-2122. **$79-$169.** 5075 S Priest Dr. I-10, exit 155 (Baseline Rd), 0.4 mi e, then just n. Ext/int corridors. **Pets:** Other species. $6 daily fee/pet, $50 one-time fee/ room. Service with restrictions.
ASK Sfb ⊠ ♿ &'• ♿ ◻ ➔ ⊠

▼▼ **Rodeway Inn Tempe Airport East** M
(480) 967-3000. **$39-$89.** 1550 S 52nd St. I-10, exit 153 (Broadway Rd), 0.3 mi ne. Ext corridors. **Pets:** Accepted.
ASK Sfb ⊠ ♿ ◻ ◻ ➔

AAA ▼▼▼ **Tempe Mission Palms Hotel** SH
(480) 894-1400. **$99-$199.** 60 E 5th St. Just e of Mill Ave, 0.3 mi n of University Dr; downtown. Int corridors. **Pets:** Accepted.
SAVE Sfb ⊠ ♿ &'• ♿ ◻ ⦿ ➔ ⊠

▼▼ **Tempe Super 8** M
(480) 967-8891. **$39-$115.** 1020 E Apache Blvd. Just e of Rural Rd. Ext corridors. **Pets:** Large, other species. $15 one-time fee/room. Designated rooms, service with restrictions, supervision.
ASK ⊠ ♿

AAA ▼▼▼▼ Wyndham Buttes Resort 🆂🅷
(602) 225-9000. **$99-$199.** 2000 Westcourt Way. I-10, exit 153 (Broadway Rd) westbound, 0.8 mi w to 48th St, 0.3 mi s; exit 48th St eastbound, 0.5 mi s. Int corridors. **Pets:** Small. $35 one-time fee/pet. Supervision.
🆂🅰🆅🅴 🆂🔊 ☒ 🖉 🖵 🍴 ➹ ☒

YOUNGTOWN

AAA ▼▼▼ Best Western Inn & Suites of Sun City 🆂🅷
(623) 933-8211. **$61-$126.** 11201 Grand Ave. On US 60, just se of 113th Ave. Ext/int corridors. **Pets:** Medium, other species. Designated rooms, service with restrictions, supervision.
🆂🅰🆅🅴 🆂🔊 ☒ 🖉 🅕 🖵 ➹

❖ **END METROPOLITAN AREA** ❖

PINETOP-LAKESIDE

▼▼ Best Western Inn of Pinetop Ⓜ
(928) 367-6667. **$89-$109.** 404 E White Mountain Blvd. On SR 260. Ext corridors. **Pets:** Medium. $10 daily fee/pet. Service with restrictions, supervision.
🅰🆂🅺 🆂🔊 ☒ 🅕 🖵

▼▼ Lakeside Inn 🆂🅷
(928) 368-6600. **$54-$142.** 1637 W White Mountain Blvd. On SR 260. Int corridors. **Pets:** Accepted.
🅰🆂🅺 🆂🔊 ☒ 🅕 🖵

▼▼ Lazy Oaks Resort 🅲🅰
(928) 368-6203. **$67-$82 (no credit cards), 21 day notice.** 1075 Larson Rd. SR 260, 0.8 mi s on Rainbow Lake Dr, 0.6 mi w. Ext corridors. **Pets:** Medium. No service, supervision.
🅕 🖵 ☒ 🅚 🆉

▼▼▼ Northwoods Resort 🅲🅰
(928) 367-2966. **$79-$149, 14 day notice.** 165 E White Mountain Blvd. On SR 260. Ext corridors. **Pets:** Accepted.
☒ 🅕 🖵 ☒ 🅚 🆉

AAA ▼▼▼ Woodland Inn & Suites Ⓜ
(928) 367-3636. **$62-$129, 3 day notice.** 458 E White Mountain Blvd. On SR 260. Ext corridors. **Pets:** Medium. $50 deposit/room, $10 daily fee/room. Service with restrictions, supervision.
🆂🅰🆅🅴 🆂🔊 ☒ 🅕 🖵

PRESCOTT

▼▼▼ Arizona Vacation Lodging 🅲🅰
(928) 778-9573. **$110-$200, 14 day notice.** 5555 Onyx Dr. Jct SR 89, 5 mi e on SR 69, 0.4 mi s on dirt/gravel road. Ext corridors. **Pets:** Other species. $10 daily fee/pet. No service, crate.
☒ 🅕 🖵 ☒

▼▼ Best Western Prescottonian Motel Ⓜ
(928) 445-3096. **$69-$89.** 1317 E Gurley St. On SR 89, just s of jct SR 69. Ext corridors. **Pets:** Accepted.
🅰🆂🅺 🆂🔊 ☒ 🖉 🅕 🖵 🍴 ➹

AAA ▼▼▼▼ Comfort Inn of Prescott Ⓜ
(928) 778-5770. **$60-$160.** 1290 White Spar Rd. On SR 89, 1.5 mi s of town center. Ext corridors. **Pets:** Small, dogs only. $10 daily fee/pet. Designated rooms, service with restrictions, supervision.
🆂🅰🆅🅴 🆂🔊 ☒ 🅕 🖵

▼▼ Lynx Creek Farm Bed & Breakfast 🅱🅱
(928) 778-9573. **$75-$170, 14 day notice.** 5555 Onyx Dr. Jct SR 89, 5 mi e on SR 69, 0.4 mi s on dirt/gravel road. Ext corridors. **Pets:** Other species. $10 daily fee/pet. No service, crate.
☒ 🅕 🖵 ➹ ☒ 🅦 🆉

▼▼ Prescott Super 8 Motel Ⓜ
(928) 776-1282. **$50-$70.** 1105 E Sheldon St. 0.4 mi e of jct SR 89. Int corridors. **Pets:** Medium, dogs only. $10 one-time fee/room. Service with restrictions, supervision.
🅰🆂🅺 🆂🔊 ☒ 🖉 🅕 🖵 ➹

AAA ▼▼▼▼ Quality Inn & Suites 🆂🅷
(928) 777-0770. **$89-$209.** 4499 Hwy 69. On SR 69, 3.6 mi e of jct SR 89. Int corridors. **Pets:** Accepted.
🆂🅰🆅🅴 🆂🔊 ☒ 🖉 🅕 🖵 🍴 ➹ ☒

PRESCOTT VALLEY

AAA ▼▼▼ Days Inn/Prescott Valley Ⓜ
(928) 772-8600. **$69-$119.** 7875 E Hwy 69. On SR 69, corner of Windsong Rd. Ext corridors. **Pets:** Other species. $50 deposit/room. Service with restrictions.
🆂🅰🆅🅴 🆂🔊 ☒ 🅕 🖵

RIO RICO

AAA ▼▼▼▼ Rio Rico Resort & Country Club 🅻🅷
(520) 281-1901. **$107-$143.** 1069 Camino Caralampi. I-19, exit 17 (Rio Rico Dr), 0.5 mi w. Ext corridors. **Pets:** Accepted.
🆂🅰🆅🅴 🆂🔊 ☒ 🅶ᴹ 🖉 🅕 🖵 🍴 ➹ ☒

SAFFORD

AAA ▼▼▼ Best Western Desert Inn Ⓜ
(928) 428-0521. **$60-$70.** 1391 W Thatcher Blvd. US 191, 1 mi w of US 70. Ext corridors. **Pets:** Accepted.
🆂🅰🆅🅴 🆂🔊 ☒ 🅕 🖵 ➹

▼▼ Comfort Inn Ⓜ
(928) 428-5851. **$66-$96.** 1578 W Thatcher Blvd. US 191, 1.3 mi w on US 70. Ext corridors. **Pets:** Small. $10 daily fee/room. Service with restrictions, supervision.
🅰🆂🅺 🆂🔊 ☒ 🅕 🖵 ➹

AAA ▼▼▼ Days Inn Ⓜ
(928) 428-5000. **$77-$85.** 520 E Hwy 70. US 191, 0.5 mi e. Ext corridors. **Pets:** Accepted.
🆂🅰🆅🅴 🆂🔊 ☒ 🅶ᴹ 🖉 🅕 🖵 ➹ ☒

▼ Econo Lodge M
(928) 348-0011. **$60.** 225 E Hwy 70. Just e of jct US 191 and 70. Ext corridors. **Pets:** Accepted.
(ASK) (S) (X) (B) (⌐)

▲▲▲ ▼▼▼▼ Quality Inn & Suites SH
(928) 428-3200. **$110-$165.** 420 E Hwy 70. US 191, 0.5 mi e. Ext/int corridors. **Pets:** Accepted.
(SAVE) (S) (X) (L) (B) (⌐) (⌐) (X)

SEDONA

▼▼ A Touch of the Southwest Suites M
(928) 282-4747. **$109-$175, 3 day notice.** 410 Jordan Rd. SR 179, 0.3 mi n on SR 89A, then just w. Ext corridors. **Pets:** Accepted.
(ASK) (S) (X) (B) (⌐)

▲▲▲ ▼▼▼▼ Best Western Inn of
Sedona SH ❀
(928) 282-3072. **$99-$174.** 1200 W Hwy 89A. Jct SR 179, 1.2 mi w. Ext corridors. **Pets:** Large. $10 daily fee/room. Designated rooms, service with restrictions.
(SAVE) (S) (X) (L) (B) (⌐) (⌐)

▲▲▲ ▼▼▼▼ Desert Quail Inn M
(928) 284-1433. **$69-$139.** 6626 Hwy 179. On SR 179, 6.9 mi s of jct SR 89A. Ext corridors. **Pets:** Small, dogs only. $10 daily fee/pet. Designated rooms, service with restrictions, supervision.
(SAVE) (S) (X) (⌐) (L) (B) (⌐) (⌐)

▼▼▼▼ El Portal Sedona BB ❀
(928) 203-9405. **$200-$400, 15 day notice.** 95 Portal Ln. Jct SR 89A, just s on SR 179, just w. Ext/int corridors. **Pets:** Medium, other species. Designated rooms, service with restrictions, supervision.
(X) (L) (B)

▲▲▲ ▼▼▼▼ Hilton Sedona Resort &
Spa LH ❀
(928) 284-4040. **$149-$429, 3 day notice.** 90 Ridge Trail Dr. Jct SR 89A, 7.3 mi s on SR 179. Int corridors. **Pets:** $50 one-time fee/room. Service with restrictions, supervision.
(SAVE) (S) (X) (L) (B) (⌐) (¶) (⌐) (X)

▼▼▼▼ The Lodge at Sedona BB ❀
(928) 204-1942. **$160-$325, 14 day notice.** 125 Kallof Pl. SR 179, 1.8 mi w on SR 89A, then just s. Ext/int corridors. **Pets:** Dogs only. $150 deposit/room, $30 daily fee/pet. Designated rooms, service with restrictions, supervision.
(X) (L) (X) (☎)

▲▲▲ ▼▼▼▼ Matterhorn Lodge M ❀
(928) 282-7176. **$69-$129.** 230 Apple Ave. SR 89A, just w; uptown. Ext corridors. **Pets:** Large, other species. Designated rooms, service with restrictions, crate.
(SAVE) (S) (X) (B) (⌐) (⌐)

▲▲▲ ▼▼ Red Rock Inn M
(928) 284-2487. **$59-$135.** 65 E Cortez Dr. 6.9 mi s on SR 179, from jct SR 89A, just e. Ext corridors. **Pets:** Accepted.
(SAVE) (X) (B)

▲▲▲ ▼▼▼▼ Sedona Real Inn SH
(928) 282-1414. **$87-$270.** 95 Arroyo Pinon. On SR 89A, 3 mi w of jct SR 179. Ext corridors. **Pets:** Small, other species. $20 one-time fee/pet. Designated rooms, service with restrictions, supervision.
(SAVE) (S) (X) (B) (⌐) (⌐)

▲▲▲ ▼▼▼ Sedona Super 8 SH ❀
(928) 282-1533. **$65-$89.** 2545 W Hwy 89A. On SR 89A, 2.4 mi w of jct SR 179. Int corridors. **Pets:** Medium. $10 one-time fee/pet. Designated rooms, service with restrictions, supervision.
(SAVE) (X) (∅) (B) (⌐)

▲▲▲ ▼▼▼▼ Sky Ranch Lodge M
(928) 282-6400. **$80-$200.** Airport Rd. SR 179, 1 mi w on SR 89A, 1 mi s on Airport Rd, on west side. Ext corridors. **Pets:** Accepted.
(SAVE) (X) (B) (⌐) (⌐)

▲▲▲ ▼▼▼ Village Lodge M
(928) 284-3626. **$49-$59.** 78 Bell Rock Blvd. Jct SR 89A, 6 mi s on SR 179, then just w. Ext/int corridors. **Pets:** Medium, other species. Supervision.
(SAVE) (S) (X) (B) (⌐)

SELIGMAN

▲▲▲ ▼ Historic Route 66 Motel M
(928) 422-3204. **$62-$67.** 500 W Hwy 66. I-40, exit 121, 1.1 mi n, follow signs to I-40 business loop and SR 66, then 0.3 mi e. Ext corridors. **Pets:** Medium, dogs only. $25 deposit/pet. Service with restrictions, supervision.
(SAVE) (S) (X) (B)

SHOW LOW

▲▲▲ ▼▼▼▼ Best Western Paint Pony
Lodge M
(928) 537-5773. **$85-$110.** 581 W Deuce of Clubs Ave. On US 60 and SR 260. Ext corridors. **Pets:** Other species. $50 deposit/room, $10 daily fee/pet. Designated rooms, service with restrictions, supervision.
(SAVE) (X) (B) (⌐)

▲▲▲ ▼▼▼ Days Inn M
(928) 537-4356. **$62-$76.** 480 W Deuce of Clubs Ave. On US 60 and SR 260. Ext/int corridors. **Pets:** Medium. $10 one-time fee/room. Service with restrictions, supervision.
(SAVE) (S) (X) (L) (B) (¶) (⌐)

▲▲▲ ▼▼ Kiva Motel M
(928) 537-4542. **$46-$58.** 261 E Deuce of Clubs Ave. On US 60 and SR 260. Ext corridors. **Pets:** Small, dogs only. $5 daily fee/pet. No service, supervision.
(SAVE) (S) (X) (B) (⌐)

▲▲▲ ▼▼▼ Sleep Inn SH
(928) 532-7323. **$74-$115.** 1751 W Deuce of Clubs Ave. On SR 260, 0.5 mi w of US 60. Int corridors. **Pets:** Other species. $10 daily fee/pet. Service with restrictions, supervision.
(SAVE) (S) (X) (M) (∅) (L) (B) (⌐) (⌐)

SIERRA VISTA

Best Western Mission Inn M
(520) 458-8500. **$59-$79.** 3460 E Fry Blvd. Just w of jct SR 90 and 92. Ext corridors. **Pets:** Medium, other species. Service with restrictions, supervision.
(SAVE) (S6) (X) (&M) (H) (P) (≈)

Quality Inn SH
(520) 458-7900. **$64-$69.** 1631 S Hwy 92. On SR 92, 1 mi s of jct SR 90. Int corridors. **Pets:** Accepted.
(SAVE) (S6) (X) (H) (P) (≈)

Sierra Suites SH
(520) 459-4221. **$79-$99.** 391 E Fry Blvd. SR 90 and 92, 2.5 mi w. Ext corridors. **Pets:** Very small. $25 one-time fee/room. Designated rooms, service with restrictions.
(SAVE) (S6) (X) (H) (P) (≈) (X)

Super 8 Motel M
(520) 459-5380. **$50-$70.** 100 Fab Ave. Jct Business SR 90 and Fry Blvd, then just e; east of main entrance to Fort Huachuca. Ext corridors. **Pets:** Accepted.
(ASK) (S6) (X) (∅) (H) (P) (≈)

Windemere Hotel & Conference Center SH
(520) 459-5900. **$89, 3 day notice.** 2047 S Hwy 92. 1.5 mi s of jct SR 90. Int corridors. **Pets:** Accepted.
(ASK) (S6) (X) (H) (P) (¶) (≈)

TAYLOR

Silver Creek Inn M
(928) 536-2600. **$53-$69.** 825 N Main St. On SR 77. Ext corridors. **Pets:** Accepted.
(SAVE) (S6) (X) (H) (P)

TOMBSTONE

Best Western Lookout Lodge SH
(520) 457-2223. **$69-$90.** US Hwy 80 W. On SR 80, 1 mi n. Ext corridors. **Pets:** Accepted.
(SAVE) (X) (H) (P) (≈)

Tombstone Motel M
(520) 457-3478. **$42-$79.** 502 E Fremont St. On SR 80; center. Ext corridors. **Pets:** Small. $50 deposit/pet. No service.
(SAVE) (S6) (X)

Trail Riders Inn M
(520) 457-3573. **$45.** 13 N 7th St. Just e; center. Ext corridors. **Pets:** Medium, dogs only. $5 daily fee/pet. Designated rooms, service with restrictions, supervision.
(SAVE) (X)

TUBA CITY

Quality Inn SH ❀
(928) 283-4545. **$78-$138.** Main St & Moenave Rd. 1 mi n of US 160. Int corridors. **Pets:** Medium. $20 deposit/pet. Designated rooms, service with restrictions, supervision.
(SAVE) (S6) (X) (H) (P) (¶)

TUCSON METROPOLITAN AREA

GREEN VALLEY

Baymont Inn & Suites SH
(520) 399-3736. **$62-$109.** 90 W Esperanza Blvd. I-19, exit 65, just w. Int corridors. **Pets:** Small, dogs only. $50 deposit/pet. Designated rooms, service with restrictions, supervision.
(SAVE) (S6) (X) (∅) (☼) (H) (P) (≈)

Best Western Green Valley SH
(520) 625-2250. **$65-$115.** 111 S La Canada Dr. I-19, exit 65, just w, then just s. Int corridors. **Pets:** Medium. $25 one-time fee/pet. Service with restrictions, supervision.
(SAVE) (S6) (X) (H) (P) (¶) (≈)

MARANA

Days Inn &
Suites-Tucson/Marana SH
(520) 744-6677. **$39-$129.** 8370 N Cracker Barrel Rd. I-10, exit 246 (Cortaro Rd), just w. Int corridors. **Pets:** $10 daily fee/pet. Service with restrictions, supervision.
(SAVE) (S6) (X) (☼) (H) (P) (≈)

Red Roof Inn Tucson North SH
(520) 744-8199. **$42-$78.** 4940 W Ina Rd. I-10, exit 248 (Ina Rd), just w. Int corridors. **Pets:** Small, other species. No service, supervision.
(SAVE) (X) (☼) (≈)

ORO VALLEY

Hilton Tucson El Conquistador
Golf & Tennis Resort LH
(520) 544-5000. **$89-$289, 3 day notice.** 10000 N Oracle Rd. I-10, exit 248 (Ina Rd), 5.4 mi e, then 4.4 mi n. Ext/int corridors. **Pets:** Accepted.
(SAVE) (S6) (X) (&M) (☼) (H) (P) (¶) (≈) (X)

TUCSON

AmeriSuites (Tucson/Airport) SH
(520) 295-0405. **$69-$129.** 6885 S Tucson Blvd. Just n of Tucson International Airport. Int corridors. **Pets:** Service with restrictions.
(SAVE) (S6) (X) (&M) (∅) (☼) (H) (P) (≈)

Best Value Inn-Tucson M
(520) 884-5800. **$46-$120.** 810 E Benson Hwy. I-10, exit 262, just s. Ext corridors. **Pets:** Medium, other species. $25 deposit/pet. Service with restrictions.
(SAVE) (S6) (X) (H) (P) (≈)

Best Western Executive Inn SH
(520) 791-7551. **$39-$89.** 333 W Drachman St. I-10, exit 257 (Speedway Blvd), 0.4 mi e to Main St, then 0.3 mi n. Int corridors. **Pets:** Large. $35 one-time fee/room. No service.
(SAVE) (S6) (X) (∅) (H) (P) (¶) (≈)

♥♥ ♥♥ **Best Western Inn At The Airport** 🄢🄷
(520) 746-0271. **$59-$119.** 7060 S Tucson Blvd. At entrance to Tucson International Airport. Int corridors. **Pets:** Accepted.

🄰🄢🄚 🅂🄳 ⊠ 🄷 🄻 🄹 🖚 ⊠

♦♦♦ **♥♥▼♥** **Best Western InnSuites Hotel & Suites Tucson-Catalina Foothills** 🄢🄷
(520) 297-8111. **$59-$109.** 6201 N Oracle Rd. I-10, exit 250 (Orange Grove Rd), 4 mi e, then just s. Ext corridors. **Pets:** Medium. $25 one-time fee/room. Designated rooms, service with restrictions.

🅂🄰🅅🄴 🅂🄳 ⊠ 🄷 🄻 🖚 ⊠

♦♦♦ **♥▼♥** **Clarion Hotel-Randolph Park** 🄢🄷
(520) 795-0330. **$69-$129.** 102 N Alvernon. Jct Campbell Rd, 2.2 mi e on Broadway, just n. Ext/int corridors. **Pets:** Small. $20 one-time fee/room. Designated rooms, service with restrictions, supervision.

🅂🄰🅅🄴 🅂🄳 ⊠ 🄷 🄻 🖚 ⊠

♥▼♥▼♥ **Clarion Santa Rita Hotel & Suites** 🄢🄷
(520) 622-4000. **$89-$129.** 88 E Broadway Blvd. I-10, exit 258 (Broadway Blvd/Congress St), 0.6 mi e. Ext/int corridors. **Pets:** Medium. $25 one-time fee/pet. Designated rooms, service with restrictions, supervision.

🄰🄢🄚 🅂🄳 ⊠ 🄷 🄻 🖚 ⊠

♦♦♦ **♥▼♥▼♥** **Comfort Suites** 🄢🄷
(520) 295-4400. **$79-$109.** 6935 S Tucson Blvd. Just n of Tucson International Airport. Int corridors. **Pets:** Small, other species. $25 one-time fee/room. Service with restrictions, supervision.

🅂🄰🅅🄴 🅂🄳 ⊠ 🄻 🄷 🄻 🖚

♥▼♥ **Comfort Suites at Tucson Mall** 🄢🄷
(520) 888-6676. **$69-$140.** 515 W Auto Mall Dr. I-10, exit 254 (Prince Rd), 1.9 mi e, then 1.2 mi n. Int corridors. **Pets:** Other species. $10 one-time fee/pet. Service with restrictions, supervision.

🄰🄢🄚 🅂🄳 ⊠ 🄻 🄷 🄻 🖚 ⊠

♦♦♦ **♥▼♥▼♥** **Country Inn & Suites By Carlson** 🄢🄷
(520) 575-9255. **$59-$139.** 7411 N Oracle Rd. SR 77 (Oracle Rd), just n of Ina Rd. Ext corridors. **Pets:** Medium. $25 one-time fee/room. Service with restrictions.

🅂🄰🅅🄴 🅂🄳 ⊠ 🄼 🄿 🄻 🄷 🄻 🖚 ⊠

♦♦♦ **♥▼♥▼♥** **Doubletree Hotel at Reid Park** 🄻🄷
(520) 881-4200. **$64-$260, 3 day notice.** 445 S Alvernon Way. I-10, exit 259 (22nd St), 4 mi e, then just n. Ext/int corridors. **Pets:** Accepted.

🅂🄰🅅🄴 ⊠ 🄿 🄻 🄷 🄻 🄹 🖚 ⊠

♦♦♦ **♥▼** **Econo Lodge** 🄼
(520) 622-6714. **$49-$69.** 1136 N Stone Ave. I-10, exit 257 (St Mary Speedway) eastbound, just e, then just n. Ext corridors. **Pets:** Dogs only. $20 deposit/room. Designated rooms, service with restrictions, crate.

🅂🄰🅅🄴 🅂🄳 ⊠ 🄷 🖚

♦♦♦ **♥▼** **Econo Lodge Inn & Suites** 🄢🄷
(520) 747-1440. **$45-$90, 3 day notice.** 1440 S Craycroft Rd. I-10, exit 265 (Alvernon Way), 4 mi n to Golf Links Rd, 2 mi e, 0.7 mi n. Ext corridors. **Pets:** Accepted.

🅂🄰🅅🄴 🅂🄳 ⊠ 🄻 🄷 🖚

♦♦♦ **♥▼♥▼♥** **Embassy Suites Hotel @ Tucson International Airport** 🄢🄷
(520) 573-0700. **$189-$339.** 7051 S Tucson Blvd. At entrance to Tucson International Airport. Ext corridors. **Pets:** $50 deposit/room. Supervision.

🅂🄰🅅🄴 🅂🄳 ⊠ 🄻 🄷 🄻 🄹 🖚 ⊠

♥▼♥ **Ghost Ranch Lodge** 🄼
(520) 791-7565. **$46-$106.** 801 W Miracle Mile. I-10, exit 255 (Miracle Mile), 1 mi e, just w of Oracle Rd (SR 77). Ext corridors. **Pets:** Large, other species. $75 deposit/room. Designated rooms, service with restrictions, supervision.

🄰🄢🄚 🅂🄳 ⊠ 🄷 🄻 🄹 🖚 ⊠

♦♦♦ **♥▼♥▼♥** **Hampton Inn North** 🄢🄷
(520) 206-0602. **$74-$149.** 1375 W Grant Rd. I-10, exit 256 (Grant Rd), just w. Int corridors. **Pets:** Medium, other species. $10 one-time fee/room. Designated rooms, service with restrictions, supervision.

🅂🄰🅅🄴 🅂🄳 ⊠ 🄻🄼 🄻 🄷 🄻 🖚

♦♦♦ **♥▼♥▼♥** **Holiday Inn Express Hotel & Suites Tucson Airport** 🄢🄷
(520) 889-6600. **$79-$149.** 2548 E Medina Rd. 0.5 mi n of entrance to Tucson International Airport. Int corridors. **Pets:** Medium. $50 deposit/room. Service with restrictions, supervision.

🅂🄰🅅🄴 🅂🄳 ⊠ 🄻🄼 🄻 🄷 🄻 🖚

♥▼♥▼♥ **Holiday Inn Express on Grant** 🄢🄷
(520) 624-3200. **$89-$170.** 1560 W Grant Rd. I-10, exit 256, just w. Int corridors. **Pets:** Accepted.

🄰🄢🄚 🅂🄳 ⊠ 🄻 🄷 🄻 🖚

♦♦♦ **♥▼♥** **Howard Johnson Midtown** 🄢🄷
(520) 622-5871. **$49-$129.** 1010 S Freeway. I-10, exit 259 (Starr Pass Blvd), just w to Farmington, then just n. Ext corridors. **Pets:** Medium, other species. $10 daily fee/pet. Service with restrictions, supervision.

🅂🄰🅅🄴 🅂🄳 ⊠ 🄷 🄻 🖚

♦♦♦ **♥▼♥** **InnSuites Hotels & Suites Tucson City Center** 🄢🄷
(520) 622-3000. **$59-$139.** 475 N Granada Ave. I-10, exit 258 (Broadway Blvd/Congress St), just e, then 0.4 mi n. Ext/int corridors. **Pets:** Accepted.

🅂🄰🅅🄴 🅂🄳 ⊠ 🄷 🄻 🄹 🖚 ⊠

♥▼♥▼♥ **La Posada Lodge & Casitas** 🄢🄷
(520) 887-4800. **$99-$229.** 5900 N Oracle Rd. 0.5 mi s of Orange Grove Rd. Ext corridors. **Pets:** Service with restrictions.

🄰🄢🄚 ⊠ 🄷 🄻 🖚

♦♦♦ **♥▼♥▼♥** **La Quinta Inn & Suites Airport** 🄢🄷
(520) 573-3333. **$62-$165.** 7001 S Tucson Blvd. Just n of Tucson International Airport. Int corridors. **Pets:** Medium. Service with restrictions.

🅂🄰🅅🄴 🅂🄳 ⊠ 🄻🄼 🄿 🄻 🄷 🖚

♥▼♥▼♥ **La Quinta Inn-East** 🄢🄷
(520) 747-1414. **$65-$115.** 6404 E Broadway. Just e of Wilmot Rd. Ext corridors. **Pets:** Small. Service with restrictions, supervision.

🄰🄢🄚 🅂🄳 ⊠ 🄷 🄻 🖚

Lodge on the Desert SH
(520) 325-3366. **$95-$299.** 306 N Alvernon Way. I-10, exit 258 (Broadway/Congress St), 4 mi e, then just n. Ext corridors. **Pets:** Accepted.

Loews Ventana Canyon Resort LH
(520) 299-2020. **$85-$425, 7 day notice.** 7000 N Resort Dr. I-10, exit 256 (Grant Rd), 8.6 mi e, 0.6 mi ne on Tanque Verde Rd, 2 mi n on Sabino Canyon Rd, then 3.5 mi n on Kolb Rd. Ext/int corridors. **Pets:** Other species.

The Pueblo Inn SH
(520) 622-6611. **$69-$159.** 350 S Freeway. I-10, exit 158 (Broadway/Congress St), just w, then 0.4 mi s. Ext/int corridors. **Pets:** Accepted.

Quality Inn Tucson Airport SH
(520) 623-7792. **$59-$139.** 1025 E Benson Hwy. I-10, exit 262, just s. Int corridors. **Pets:** Accepted.

Radisson Hotel City Center Tucson LH
(520) 624-8711. **$89-$249.** 181 W Broadway. I-10, exit 258 (Broadway Blvd/Congress St), just e. Int corridors. **Pets:** Accepted.

Ramada Inn & Suites Foothills Resort SH
(520) 886-9595. **$49-$169.** 6944 E Tanque Verde Rd. Jct Campbell Ave, 5.5 mi e on Grant Rd, then just ne. Ext corridors. **Pets:** Small. $25 one-time fee/pet. Service with restrictions, crate.

Ramada Inn & Suites/Palo Verde SH
(520) 294-5250. **$50-$109.** 5251 S Julian Dr. I-10, exit 264A, 0.4 mi s. Ext/int corridors. **Pets:** Accepted.

Ramada Limited West M
(520) 622-6491. **$66-$115.** 665 N Frwy. I-10, exit 257 (St Mary's Rd/Speedway), just s. Ext corridors. **Pets:** Other species.

Red Roof Inn-Tucson South M
(520) 571-1400. **$43-$66.** 3704 E Irvington Rd. I-10, exit 264 westbound; exit 264B eastbound. Ext corridors. **Pets:** Medium. Service with restrictions, supervision.

Residence Inn By Marriott SH
(520) 721-0991. **$79-$172, 10 day notice.** 6477 E Speedway Blvd. Just e of Wilmot Rd. Ext corridors. **Pets:** Other species. $50 one-time fee/room. Service with restrictions.

Rodeway Inn I-10 & Grant Rd M
(520) 622-7791. **$64-$139, 3 day notice.** 1365 W Grant Rd. I-10, exit 256 (Grant Rd), just w. Ext corridors. **Pets:** Accepted.

Sheraton Tucson Hotel & Suites SH
(520) 323-6262. **$84-$179.** 5151 E Grant Rd. Jct Campbell Ave, 3.6 mi e. Ext/int corridors. **Pets:** Large, dogs only. Service with restrictions, crate.

Studio 6 Extended Stay #6002 M
(520) 746-0030. **$47-$93.** 4950 S Outlet Center Dr. I-10, exit 264B eastbound, just s, then just n; exit 264A westbound, just e. Ext corridors. **Pets:** Accepted.

Super 8 Motel M
(520) 622-8089. **$39-$109.** 1000 S Freeway. I-10, exit 259 (22nd St), just w, then just n. Int corridors. **Pets:** $10 daily fee/pet. Service with restrictions, supervision.

TownePlace Suites by Marriott SH
(520) 292-9697. **$49-$159.** 405 W Rudasill Rd. Jct of Orange Grove Rd, 0.5 mi s on Oracle Rd, then just e. Int corridors. **Pets:** $10 daily fee/pet. Designated rooms, service with restrictions.

Vagabond Plaza Hotel SH
(520) 740-0123. **$45-$89.** 1601 N Oracle Rd. I-10, exit 256 (Grant Rd), 0.8 mi e, then 0.6 mi s. Ext/int corridors. **Pets:** Other species. $25 deposit/room. Service with restrictions, supervision.

Westward Look Resort LH
(520) 297-1151. **$109-$309, 3 day notice.** 245 E Ina Rd. I-10, exit 248 (Ina Rd), 6 mi e, then just n on Westward Look Dr. Ext corridors. **Pets:** $50 one-time fee/room. Designated rooms, service with restrictions, supervision.

Windmill Suites at St. Philip's Plaza SH
(520) 577-0007. **$79-$169.** 4250 N Campbell Ave. I-10, exit 254 (Prince Rd), 4 mi e, then 1 mi n. Int corridors. **Pets:** Accepted.

❖ **END METROPOLITAN AREA** ❖

WICKENBURG

Best Western Rancho Grande SH
(928) 684-5445. **$69-$123.** 293 E Wickenburg Way. On US 60; center. Ext corridors. **Pets:** Accepted.

Super 8 Motel M
(928) 684-0808. **$65.** 975 N Tegner Rd. 1 mi n of US 60 and 93. Ext/int corridors. **Pets:** Accepted.

WILLCOX

Days Inn M
(520) 384-4222. **$55.** 724 N Bisbee Ave. I-10, exit 340, just s. Ext corridors. **Pets:** Medium. $5 daily fee/pet. Service with restrictions, supervision.

WILLIAMS

A Westerner Motel M
(928) 635-4312. **$24-$48.** 530 W Route 66. I-40, exit 161, 1.3 mi e. Ext corridors. **Pets:** Accepted.

Budget Host Inn M
(928) 635-4415. **$18-$48.** 620 W Route 66. I-40, exit 161, 1 mi e. Ext corridors. **Pets:** Very small, dogs only. $5 daily fee/pet. Designated rooms, service with restrictions, supervision.

The Canyon Motel M
(928) 635-9371. **$45-$75.** 1900 E Rodeo Rd/Route 66. I-40, exit 165 (Grand Canyon), 1.4 mi s on Buisness Loop 40, just w. Ext corridors. **Pets:** Other species. $7 daily fee/pet. Designated rooms, no service, crate.

Days Inn M
(928) 635-4051. **$52-$102.** 2488 W Route 66 Ave. I-40, exit 161, 0.3 mi e on I-40 business loop. Int corridors. **Pets:** Small. $20 deposit/room. Service with restrictions, supervision.

El Rancho Motel M ❀
(928) 635-2552. **$32-$63.** 617 E Route 66. I-40, exit 163, 0.8 mi s, then just e. Ext corridors. **Pets:** Dogs only. $5 daily fee/pet. Designated rooms, service with restrictions, supervision.

Highlander Motel M
(928) 635-2541. **$25-$48.** 533 W Route 66. I-40, exit 161, 1.2 mi e. Ext corridors. **Pets:** Accepted.

Holiday Inn Williams SH
(928) 635-4114. **$49-$109.** 950 N Grand Canyon Blvd. I-40, exit 163. Int corridors. **Pets:** Large, other species. Service with restrictions.

Motel 6-4122 M
(928) 635-4464. **$32-$58.** 710 W Route 66 Ave. I-40, exit 161, 1 mi e on I-40 business loop. Int corridors. **Pets:** Accepted.

Quality Inn Mountain Ranch Resort SH
(928) 635-2693. **$59-$109.** 6701 E Mountain Ranch Rd. I-40, exit 171 (Deer Farm Rd), just s. Ext corridors. **Pets:** $20 one-time fee/room. Service with restrictions, supervision.

Ramada Inn Grand Canyon SH
(928) 635-4431. **$66-$86.** 642 E Route 66. I-40, exit 163, 0.6 mi s, then just e. Ext corridors. **Pets:** Dogs only. $50 deposit/pet. Designated rooms, service with restrictions, supervision.

Rodeway Inn M
(928) 635-9127. **$30-$79.** 750 N Grand Canyon Blvd. I-40, exit 163, just s. Int corridors. **Pets:** Accepted.

Travelodge Williams M
(928) 635-2651. **$35-$85.** 430 E Route 66. I-40, exit 161, 2 mi e on I-40 business loop. Ext corridors. **Pets:** Accepted.

WINDOW ROCK

Navajo Nation Inn SH
(928) 871-4108. **$67-$77.** 48 W Hwy 264. Center. Ext corridors. **Pets:** Small. $50 deposit/pet. Service with restrictions, supervision.

WINSLOW

Best Western Adobe Inn SH
(928) 289-4638. **$67-$95.** 1701 N Park Dr. I-40, exit 253. Int corridors. **Pets:** Small, other species. $10 daily fee/pet. Service with restrictions, supervision.

Days Inn SH
(928) 289-1010. **$50-$80.** 2035 W Hwy 66. I-40, exit 252, just s. Int corridors. **Pets:** Other species. $10 one-time fee/room. Service with restrictions, supervision.

Econo Lodge SH
(928) 289-4687. **$49-$89.** 1706 North Park Dr. I-40, exit 253. Ext corridors. **Pets:** Small, other species. $5 one-time fee/room. Service with restrictions, supervision.

Holiday Inn Express- Winslow SH
(928) 289-2960. **$99.** 816 Transcon Ln. I-40, exit 255, just n. Int corridors. **Pets:** $10 daily fee/pet. Service with restrictions, supervision.

▼▼▼▼ **La Posada Hotel** 🆂🅷
(928) 289-4366. **$89-$129, 3 day notice.** 303 E 2nd St. I-40, exit 252, s to Route 66, then 0.5 mi e; downtown. Int corridors. **Pets:** Other species. $10 one-time fee/room. Designated rooms, service with restrictions, supervision.

(A$K) 🆂 ✕ 🖥 ❚❙ 🖼

🔷🔷 ▼▼▼ **Motel 6 Winslow 4012** Ⓜ
(928) 289-9581. **$39-$57.** 520 W Desmond St. I-40, exit 253, just w on North Park Dr. Int corridors. **Pets:** Accepted.

(SAVE) 🆂 ✕ 🖮 🖥 ⌣

🔷🔷 ▼▼▼ **Super 8 Motel** Ⓜ
(928) 289-4606. **$48-$78.** 1916 W Third St. I-40, exit 252, just e. Int corridors. **Pets:** Other species. $10 one-time fee/pet. Service with restrictions, supervision.

(SAVE) 🆂 ✕

🔷🔷 ▼▼▼ **Travelodge Townhouse of Winslow** Ⓜ ❁
(928) 289-4611. **$50-$65.** 1914 W Third St. I-40, exit 252, 0.5 mi e. Ext corridors. **Pets:** Other species. $5 daily fee/pet. Service with restrictions, supervision.

(SAVE) 🆂 ✕ 🖥 🖳 ⌣

YUMA

🔷🔷 ▼▼▼ **Airport Travelodge** Ⓜ
(928) 726-4721. **$55-$89.** 711 E 32nd St. I-8, exit 3E (SR 280), 1.2 mi s, then 1.9 mi w. Ext corridors. **Pets:** Accepted.

(SAVE) 🆂 ✕ 🖮 🖥 🖳 ❙❙ ⌣

🔷🔷 ▼▼▼ **Best Western Coronado Motor Inn** Ⓜ
(928) 783-4453. **$69-$120.** 233 4th Ave. I-8, exit 4th Ave eastbound, 0.5 mi s; exit 1 (Giss Pkwy) westbound, 0.5 mi w. Ext corridors. **Pets:** Medium. Designated rooms, service with restrictions, supervision.

(SAVE) 🆂 ✕ 🖥 🖳 ❙❙ ⌣

🔷🔷 ▼▼▼ **Best Western InnSuites Hotel Yuma-Castle Dome** 🆂🅷
(928) 783-8341. **$59-$109.** 1450 Castle Dome Ave. I-8, exit 2 (16th St/US 95), just ne. Ext corridors. **Pets:** Accepted.

(SAVE) 🆂 ✕ 🗾 🖥 🖳 ❙❙ ⌣ ⨉

▼▼ **Comfort Inn** 🆂🅷
(928) 782-1200. **$59-$105, 14 day notice.** 1691 S Riley Ave. I-8, exit 2 (16th St/US 95), just w. Int corridors. **Pets:** Medium. $10 daily fee/room. Service with restrictions, supervision.

(A$K) 🆂 ✕ 🖫ᴹ 🖥 🖳 ⌣

▼▼▼ **Holiday Inn Express** 🆂🅷
(928) 344-1420. **$64-$93, 7 day notice.** 3181 S 4th Ave. I-8, exit 3E (SR 280 S), 1 mi s to 32nd St, then 2 mi w. Ext corridors. **Pets:** Accepted.

(A$K) 🆂 ✕ 🖥 🖳 ⌣

🔷🔷 ▼▼▼ **La Fuente Inn & Suites** 🆂🅷
(928) 329-1814. **$93-$119.** 1513 E 16th St. I-8, exit 2 (16th St/US 95), just e. Ext corridors. **Pets:** Medium. Designated rooms, service with restrictions, crate.

(SAVE) 🆂 ✕ 🖥 🖳 ⌣ ⨉

▼▼ **Microtel Inn & Suites** 🆂🅷
(928) 345-1777. **$47-$99.** 11274 S Fortuna Rd, Suite H. I-8, exit 12 (Fortuna Rd), just s, then w on Frontage Rd. Int corridors. **Pets:** Small. Service with restrictions, supervision.

(A$K) ✕ 🗾 🖥 🖳 ⌣

▼▼ **Oak Tree Inn** 🆂🅷
(928) 539-9000. **$69-$79.** 1730 Sunridge Dr. I-8, exit 2 (16th St/US 95), just e, then just s. Int corridors. **Pets:** $10 one-time fee/room. No service, supervision.

(A$K) 🆂 ✕ 🖥 🖳 ⌣

🔷🔷 ▼▼▼▼ **Radisson Suites Inn Yuma** 🆂🅷
(928) 726-4830. **$73-$189.** 2600 S 4th Ave. I-8, exit 2 (16th St) eastbound, 1 mi w, then 1.3 mi s; exit 3 (SR 280) westbound, 0.5 mi s, then 2 mi w. Ext corridors. **Pets:** Accepted.

(SAVE) 🆂 ✕ 🗾 🖥 🖳 ⌣

🔷🔷 ▼▼▼ **Ramada Inn Chilton Conference Center** 🆂🅷
(928) 344-1050. **$69-$119, 3 day notice.** 300 E 32nd St. I-8 business loop, 2.3 mi s of jct US 95. Ext corridors. **Pets:** Accepted.

(SAVE) 🆂 ✕ 🖥 🖳 ❙❙ ⌣

▼▼ **Shilo Inn Hotel-Yuma** 🆂🅷
(928) 782-9511. **$84-$129.** 1550 S Castle Dome Rd. I-8, exit 2 (16th St/US 95), just ne. Int corridors. **Pets:** Accepted.

(A$K) 🆂 ✕ 🗾 🖥 🖳 ❙❙ ⌣ ⨉

🔷🔷 ▼▼▼ **Yuma Cabana Motel** Ⓜ
(928) 783-8311. **$40-$69.** 2151 S 4th Ave. I-8, exit 2 (16th St/US 95), 1 mi w, then 0.5 mi s. Int corridors. **Pets:** Accepted.

(SAVE) 🆂 ✕ 🖥 ⌣

▼▼ **Yuma Super 8 Motel** 🆂🅷
(928) 782-2000. **$49-$90, 14 day notice.** 1688 S Riley Ave. I-8, exit 2 (16th St/US 95), just w. Int corridors. **Pets:** Accepted.

(A$K) 🆂 ✕ 🖫ᴹ 🗾 🖥 🖳 ⌣

ARKANSAS

CITY INDEX

ALMA

Howard Johnson Express Inn SH
(479) 632-4141. **$49-$80.** 439 Hwy 71 N. I-40, exit 13, just n.
Ext/int corridors. **Pets:** Other species. Designated rooms,
service with restrictions, supervision.

ARKADELPHIA

Best Western-Continental Inn SH
(870) 246-5592. **$49-$99.** 136 Valley St. I-30, exit 78. Ext
corridors. **Pets:** Accepted.

Super 8 Motel SH
(870) 246-8585. **$49-$65.** 118 Valley St. I-30, exit 78. Ext
corridors. **Pets:** Small, other species. $15 daily fee/pet.
Service with restrictions, supervision.

BATESVILLE

Ramada Inn of Batesville SH
(870) 698-1800. **$74-$84.** 1325 N St Louis St. 1 mi n on US
167. Ext corridors. **Pets:** Medium. Service with restrictions,
supervision.

BEEBE

Days Inn SH
(501) 882-2008. **$49-$125.** 100 Tammy Ln. US 67/167, exit
28, just e. Ext corridors. **Pets:** Small. $10 daily fee/pet.
Service with restrictions, supervision.

BENTON

Best Inn SH
(501) 776-1515. **$39-$55.** 1221 Hot Springs Rd. I-30, exit
117. Int corridors. **Pets:** $5 daily fee/pet. Service with
restrictions, supervision.

Days Inn SH ❖
(501) 776-3200. **Call for rates.** 17701 I-30. I-30, exit 118, on
east service road. Ext corridors. **Pets:** Other species. $5
daily fee/pet, $5 one-time fee/pet. Service with restrictions,
supervision.

BLYTHEVILLE

Comfort Inn of Blytheville SH
(870) 763-7081. **Call for rates.** 1520 E Main. I-55, exit 67,
just w. Ext corridors. **Pets:** Accepted.

Hampton Inn SH
(870) 763-5220. **$69-$79.** 301 N Access Rd. I-55, exit 67,
just nw. Ext corridors. **Pets:** Accepted.

Holiday Inn SH
(870) 763-5800. **$80-$100.** 1121 E Main. I-55, exit 67, just w.
Ext/int corridors. **Pets:** Small. $60 deposit/pet, $15 one-time
fee/pet. Designated rooms, service with restrictions, supervision.

Pear Tree Inn-Blytheville SH
(870) 763-2300. **$58-$78.** 239 N Service Rd. I-55, exit 67,
just nw. Int corridors. **Pets:** Large, other species. Service
with restrictions, supervision.

BRINKLEY

Best Western Brinkley SH ❖
(870) 734-1650. **$54-$59.** 1306 Hwy 17 N. I-40, exit 216, just
s. Ext corridors. **Pets:** Other species.

Days Inn M
(870) 734-1052. **Call for rates.** 2203 N Main St. I-40, exit
216, just n. Ext corridors. **Pets:** Accepted.

BRYANT

Super 8 Motel M
(501) 847-7888. **$52-$56.** 201 Dell Dr. I-30, exit 123, just e.
Ext corridors. **Pets:** Dogs only. $20 deposit/room. Service
with restrictions, supervision.

CABOT

Days Inn of Cabot M
(501) 843-0145. **$55-$60.** 1114 W Main St. US 67/167, exit
19 (SR 89), just e. Ext corridors. **Pets:** Accepted.

▼▼ ▼▼ **Super 8 of Cabot** 🆂🅷
(501) 941-3748. **$55-$60.** 15 Ryeland Dr. US 67/167, exit 19
(SR 89), just e. Ext corridors. **Pets:** $5 daily fee/pet. Service
with restrictions, supervision.
ⒶⓈⓀ 🆂 ⊠ 🛏 ⇌

CAMDEN

▼▼▼▼ **Holiday Inn Express** 🆂🅷 🐾
(870) 836-8100. **$75-$85.** 1450 Hwy 278 SW. 1 mi w of jct
US 79 and 278. Int corridors. **Pets:** Small. Service with
restrictions, supervision.
ⒶⓈⓀ 🆂 ⊠ 🛏 🖵 ⇌

CARLISLE

ⒶⒶⒶ ▼▼▼ **Best Western Carlisle** 🆂🅷
(870) 552-7566. **$59-$79, 14 day notice.** 1505 Bankhead
Dr. I-40, exit 183, just s. Ext corridors. **Pets:** Accepted.
🆂🅐🆅🅴 🆂 ⊠ 🖵 ⇌

CLARKSVILLE

ⒶⒶⒶ ▼▼▼▼ **Best Western Sherwood Motor**
Inn 🆂🅷
(479) 754-7900. **$39-$59, 10 day notice.** 1203 S Rogers
Ave. I-40, exit 58, just n. Ext corridors. **Pets:** Other species.
Service with restrictions, supervision.
🆂🅐🆅🅴 🆂 ⊠ 🛏 🖵 ⇌

ⒶⒶⒶ ▼▼▼▼ **Comfort Inn** 🆂🅷
(479) 754-3000. **$54-$105.** 1167 S Rogers Ave. I-40, exit 58,
just n. Ext corridors. **Pets:** Medium. $10 daily fee/pet. Des-
ignated rooms, service with restrictions, supervision.
🆂🅐🆅🅴 🆂 ⊠ 🛏 🖵 ⇌

CONWAY

ⒶⒶⒶ ▼▼▼▼ **Comfort Inn** 🆂🅷
(501) 329-0300. **$57-$74.** 150 Hwy 65 N. I-40, exit 125, just
n. Ext corridors. **Pets:** Small, other species. $20 one-time
fee/room. Service with restrictions.
🆂🅐🆅🅴 🆂 ⊠ ⟲ 🛏 🖵 ⇌

ⒶⒶⒶ ▼▼▼▼ **Days Inn** 🆂🅷
(501) 450-7575. **$49-$55, 7 day notice.** 1002 E Oak St.
I-40, exit 127, just n. Ext corridors. **Pets:** Small, other species. $20 one-time fee/room. Service with restrictions.
🆂🅐🆅🅴 🆂 ⊠ 🛏 🖵 ⇌

▼▼ **Motel 6 #260** 🅼
(501) 327-6623. **$37-$51.** 1105 Hwy 65 N. I-40, exit 125, just
se. Ext corridors. **Pets:** Accepted.
🆂 ⊠ ⟲ ✦ ⇌

ⒶⒶⒶ ▼▼▼ **Ramada Inn** 🆂🅷
(501) 329-8392. **$57-$74.** 815 E Oak St. I-40, exit 127. Ext
corridors. **Pets:** Small, other species. $20 one-time fee/
room. Service with restrictions.
🆂🅐🆅🅴 🆂 ⊠ ⟲ 🛏 🖵 🍴 ⇌

DARDANELLE

ⒶⒶⒶ ▼▼ **Economy Inn** 🅼
(479) 229-4118. **$40-$45.** 503 Hwy 22. I-40, exit 81, 7 mi s
on US 7; jct SR 7, 22 and 27. Ext corridors.
Pets: Accepted.
🆂🅐🆅🅴 🆂 ⊠ 🛏 ⇌

DUMAS

▼▼▼ **Days Inn** 🆂🅷
(870) 382-4449. **$50-$55.** 501 Hwy 65 S. On US 65. Ext
corridors. **Pets:** Accepted.
ⒶⓈⓀ ⊠ ✦ 🛏 ⇌

EUREKA SPRINGS

ⒶⒶⒶ ▼▼▼▼ **1886 Crescent Hotel & Spa** 🆂🅷
(479) 253-9766. **$99-$239, 3 day notice.** 75 Prospect Ave.
Jct US 62 W and SR 23 N, 0.4 mi w on US 62 W to US
62B Historic Loop, then 0.9 mi n. Int corridors. **Pets:** Small.
$50 deposit/room. Service with restrictions.
🆂🅐🆅🅴 🆂 ⊠ 🛏 🖵 🍴 ⇌ ⊠

ⒶⒶⒶ ▼▼▼ **Basin Park Hotel** 🆂🅷
(479) 253-7837. **$89-$229, 3 day notice.** 12 Spring St. 0.7
mi n of jct US 62 via SR 23 N; downtown. Int corridors.
Pets: Small, other species. Service with restrictions.
🆂🅐🆅🅴 🆂 ⊠ 🛏 🖵 🍴

ⒶⒶⒶ ▼▼▼ **Best Western Inn of the**
Ozarks 🆂🅷 🐾
(479) 253-9768. **$49-$109.** 207 W Van Buren St. On US 62,
0.5 mi w of jct SR 23. Ext corridors. **Pets:** Large, dogs only.
$5 daily fee/room. Service with restrictions, supervision.
🆂🅐🆅🅴 🆂 ⊠ ⟲ ✦ 🛏 🖵 🍴 ⇌ ⊠

ⒶⒶⒶ ▼▼▼ **Colonial Mansion Inn** 🆂🅷
(479) 253-7300. **$38-$98, 3 day notice.** 154 Huntsville Rd.
Just s of jct US 62 and SR 23. Ext/int corridors.
Pets: Small. Crate.
🆂🅐🆅🅴 🆂 ⊠ 🛏 🖵 ⇌

▼▼ ▼▼ **Days Inn** 🅼
(479) 253-8863. **$49-$190, 3 day notice.** 120 W Van Buren
St. On US 62, just w of jct SR 23 N. Ext corridors.
Pets: Small, dogs only. $15 daily fee/room. Service with
restrictions, supervision.
ⒶⓈⓀ 🆂 ⊠ 🛏 🖵 ⇌

▼▼▼ **Eureka Springs Swiss Holiday Resort &**
Visitor Center 🆂🅷
(479) 253-9501. **$39-$129, 3 day notice.** 2015 E Van Buren
St. Just nw of jct US 62 and SR 23 S. Ext corridors.
Pets: Small. Service with restrictions, crate.
ⒶⓈⓀ 🆂 ⊠ 🛏 🖵 ⇌

ⒶⒶⒶ ▼▼▼▼ **Howard Johnson Express** 🆂🅷
(479) 253-6665. **$49-$110.** 4042 E Van Buren St. 1.8 mi e of
jct US 62 and SR 23. Ext corridors. **Pets:** Accepted.
🆂🅐🆅🅴 🆂 ⊠ 🖵 ⇌

ⒶⒶⒶ ▼▼▼ **The Joy Motel** 🅼
(479) 253-9568. **$50-$125, 3 day notice.** 216 W Van Buren
St. 0.5 mi w of jct US 62 and SR 23. Ext corridors.
Pets: Accepted.
🆂🅐🆅🅴 🖵 ⇌

▼▼▼ **Lazee Daze Log Cabin Resort** 🅲🅰
(479) 253-7026. **$130-$275, 10 day notice.** 5432 Hwy 23 S. 6.1 mi s of jct US 62 and SR 23. Ext corridors. **Pets:** Large, dogs only. $20 one-time fee/room. No service, supervision.
⊠ 🛅 💻 ☎

▼ **Road Runner Inn** Ⓜ
(479) 253-8166. **$40-$50, 3 day notice.** 3034 Mundell Rd. On US 62, 4.3 mi w, 3.9 mi s on SR 187, then 3 mi se. Ext corridors. **Pets:** Medium, dogs only. $50 deposit/pet. Service with restrictions, crate.
🛅 💻 ☎

🅐🅐🅐 ▼▼▼ **Travelers Inn** Ⓜ
(479) 253-8386. **$32-$58, 3 day notice.** 2044 E Van Buren St. On US 62, just e of jct US 62 and SR 23. Ext corridors. **Pets:** Small, dogs only. Service with restrictions, supervision.
🆂🅰🆅🅴 💲 ⊠ 🛅 ➦

🅐🅐🅐 ▼▼ **Travelodge** 🆂🅷
(479) 253-8992. **$38-$120.** 110 Huntsville Dr. Jct US 62 and SR 23. Ext corridors. **Pets:** Accepted.
🆂🅰🆅🅴 💲 ⊠ 🛅 💻 ➦

FAYETTEVILLE

🅐🅐🅐 ▼▼▼▼ **Best Western Windsor Suites** 🆂🅷
(479) 587-1400. **$60-$199, 3 day notice.** 1122 S Futrall Dr. I-540, exit 62, just se. Ext corridors. **Pets:** Small, other species. $10 one-time fee/room. Designated rooms, service with restrictions.
🆂🅰🆅🅴 💲 ⊠ 🛅 💻 ➦

🅐🅐🅐 ▼▼▼ **Days Inn** 🆂🅷
(479) 443-4323. **$70-$100.** 2402 N College Ave. I-540, exit 67, 1.6 mi e, 1.9 mi s on US 71B. Ext corridors. **Pets:** Accepted.
🆂🅰🆅🅴 💲 ⊠ 🛅 💻 ➦

▼▼ **Quality Inn** 🆂🅷
(479) 444-9800. **$68.** 523 S Shiloh Dr. I-540, exit 62, just w. Ext corridors. **Pets:** Medium. $15 one-time fee/room. Designated rooms, service with restrictions, supervision.
🅰🆂🅺 💲 ⊠ 🛅 💻 ➦

▼▼▼ **Radisson Hotel Fayetteville** 🅻🅷
(479) 442-5555. **$83-$135.** 70 N East Ave. Just w of US 71B and SR 471; downtown. Int corridors. **Pets:** Medium. $50 deposit/room, $5 daily fee/room. Service with restrictions, supervision.
🅰🆂🅺 💲 ⊠ 🛅 💻 🍴 ➦

▼▼ **Sleep Inn** 🆂🅷 🐾
(479) 587-8700. **$69-$124.** 728 Millsap Rd. I-540, exit 67, 1.6 mi e, then just s on US 71B. Int corridors. **Pets:** Small. $10 deposit/room. Service with restrictions, supervision.
🅰🆂🅺 💲 ⊠ 🛅 💻

FORREST CITY

▼▼▼ **Days Inn** 🆂🅷
(870) 633-0777. **Call for rates.** 350 Barrow Hill Rd. I-40, exit 241B, just n. Ext corridors. **Pets:** Accepted.
⊠ 🛅 💻 ➦

▼▼▼ **Holiday Inn** 🆂🅷
(870) 633-6300. **$70-$80.** 200 Holiday Dr. I-40, exit 241B, just n. Ext corridors. **Pets:** Accepted.
🅰🆂🅺 💲 ⊠ 🛅 💻 🍴 ➦

FORT SMITH

🅐🅐🅐 ▼▼▼ **Baymont Inn & Suites Fort Smith** 🆂🅷 🐾
(479) 484-5770. **$59-$89.** 2123 Burnham Rd. I-540, exit 8A (Rogers Ave), just w. Int corridors. **Pets:** Other species. Service with restrictions.
🆂🅰🆅🅴 💲 ⊠ 🛅Ⓜ 🐾 🛅 💻 ➦

🅐🅐🅐 ▼▼▼ **Best Western Kings Row Inn & Suites** 🆂🅷
(479) 452-4200. **$61-$66.** 5801 Rogers Ave. I-540, exit 8A (Rogers Ave), just w. Ext corridors. **Pets:** Medium, dogs only. $10 deposit/pet. Service with restrictions.
🆂🅰🆅🅴 💲 ⊠ 🐾 🛅 💻 ➦

▼▼▼ **Comfort Inn** 🆂🅷
(479) 484-0227. **$69-$89.** 2120 Burnham Rd. I-540, exit 8A (Rogers Ave), just w. Int corridors. **Pets:** Other species. Service with restrictions, supervision.
🅰🆂🅺 💲 ⊠ 🐾 🛅 💻 ➦

▼▼▼ **Holiday Inn Fort Smith City Center** 🅻🅷
(479) 783-1000. **$85-$109.** 700 Rogers Ave. Just s of US 64 (Garrison Ave); downtown. Int corridors. **Pets:** Accepted.
🅰🆂🅺 💲 ⊠ 🛅Ⓜ 🐾 🛅 💻 🍴 ➦ ⊠

🅐🅐🅐 ▼▼▼ **Super 8** Ⓜ
(479) 646-3411. **$50-$57.** 3810 Towson Ave. 2 mi s of SR 22. Ext corridors. **Pets:** Very small, dogs only. $5 one-time fee/pet. Designated rooms, service with restrictions, supervision.
🆂🅰🆅🅴 💲 ⊠ 🐾 🛅 ➦

GAMALIEL

▼ **Twin Gables Resort** 🅲🅰
(870) 467-5686. **$62, 5 day notice.** 3166 Hwy 101. Jct CR 806. Ext corridors. **Pets:** Small. $10 daily fee/pet. Service with restrictions, supervision.
🅰🆂🅺 💲 ⊠ 🛅 ⊠ ☎

GENTRY

▼▼▼ **Apple Crest Inn Bed & Breakfast** 🅱🅱
(479) 736-8201. **$85-$155, 7 day notice.** 12758 S Hwy 59. On SR 59, 1 mi s. Int corridors. **Pets:** Accepted.
🅰🆂🅺 💲 ⊠

GLENWOOD

▼▼ **Riverwood Inn** Ⓜ
(870) 356-4567. **$55-$70.** 363 Hwy 70 E. On US 70, 0.5 mi e. Ext corridors. **Pets:** Accepted.
⊠ ➦

HARRISON

▼▼▼ **Comfort Inn** 🆂🅷
(870) 741-7676. **$60-$85.** 1210 Hwy 62/65 N. 1 mi n on US 62/65/412. Ext/int corridors. **Pets:** Small. $20 one-time fee/room. Service with restrictions, supervision.
🅰🆂🅺 💲 ⊠ 🐾 🛅 💻 ➦

AAA ♥♥◆ Family Budget Inn M ✿
(870) 743-1000. **$37-$40.** 401 S Main (Hwy 65B S). 1 mi s
on US 65B from jct SR 7. Ext corridors. **Pets:** Small. $3
daily fee/room. Designated rooms, no service, supervision.
[SAVE] [S▢] [✕] [🛏] [💻] [🏊]

HAZEN

♥♥ Super 8 Motel SH
(870) 255-2888. **$55-$75, 4 day notice.** 2809 Hwy 63. I-40,
exit 193, just s. Ext corridors. **Pets:** Accepted.
[ASK] [S▢] [✕] [🛏] [💻] [🏊]

HETH

♥ Super 8 Motel M
(870) 657-2101. **$45-$55.** 453 Hwy 149 N. I-40, exit 260, just
n. Ext corridors. **Pets:** Accepted.
[ASK] [S▢] [✕] [🛏] [🏊]

HOPE

AAA ♥♥ Best Western of Hope SH ✿
(870) 777-9222. **$55-$60.** 1800 Holiday Dr. I-30, exit 30, just
nw. Ext corridors. **Pets:** Other species. Service with restrictions.
[SAVE] [S▢] [✕] [🛏] [💻] [🏊]

♥♥♥ Holiday Inn Express SH
(870) 722-6262. **Call for rates.** 2600 N Hervey. I-30, exit 30,
just w. Int corridors. **Pets:** Accepted.
[✕] [🌀] [🐕] [🛏] [💻] [🏊]

HOT SPRINGS

♥♥♥ Baymont Inn & Suites SH
(501) 520-5522. **$84-$149.** 5321 Central Ave. 4 mi s of jct
US 270 and SR 7. Int corridors. **Pets:** Accepted.
[ASK] [S▢] [✕] [⛎M] [🐕] [🛏] [💻] [🏊]

AAA ♥♥♥ Clarion Resort SH
(501) 525-1391. **$69-$159.** 4813 Central Ave. 5.5 mi s of jct
US 270 and SR 7. Int corridors. **Pets:** Medium, other species. $10 daily fee/room. Service with restrictions.
[SAVE] [S▢] [✕] [🐕] [🛏] [💻] [🍴] [🏊] [✕]

♥♥♥ Lake Hamilton Resort SH
(501) 767-8606. **$84-$104.** 2803 Albert Pike Rd. 5 mi w on
US 270. Int corridors. **Pets:** Accepted.
[ASK] [S▢] [✕] [🛏] [💻] [🍴] [🏊] [✕]

AAA ♥ Margarete Motel M
(501) 623-1192. **$45-$75.** 217 Fountain St. Just e of jct SR
7. Ext corridors. **Pets:** Other species. $10 deposit/pet.
[SAVE] [S▢] [✕] [🛏] [💻]

AAA ♥♥♥ Quality Inn SH
(501) 624-3321. **$65-$135.** 1125 E Grand Ave. 1.1 mi e of jct
US 270B and 70. Ext corridors. **Pets:** $10 daily fee/pet.
[SAVE] [S▢] [✕] [🌀] [🐕] [🛏] [💻] [🍴] [🏊]

AAA ♥ Travelier Inn M
(501) 624-4681. **$48-$67.** 1045 E Grand Ave. 1 mi e of jct
US 270B and 70. Ext corridors. **Pets:** Other species. Service with restrictions.
[SAVE] [S▢] [✕] [🛏] [💻] [🏊]

AAA ♥♥♥ Velda Rose Resort Hotel & Spa LH
(501) 623-3311. **$85.** 217 Park Ave. On US 70B and SR 7;
center. Int corridors. **Pets:** Medium, other species. Service
with restrictions.
[SAVE] [S▢] [✕] [🛏] [💻] [🍴] [🏊]

JACKSONVILLE

♥♥ Days Inn M
(501) 982-1543. **$50-$60.** 1414 John Harden Dr. US 67/167,
exit 10B southbound; exit 11 northbound. Ext corridors.
Pets: $6 daily fee/pet. Designated rooms, service with
restrictions, supervision.
[ASK] [S▢] [✕] [🛏] [🏊]

JONESBORO

♥♥ Comfort Inn & Suites SH
(870) 972-9000. **Call for rates.** 2911 Gilmore Dr. US 63, exit
Stadium Blvd/Caraway Rd, just n. Int corridors. **Pets:** Small,
dogs only. $10 daily fee/pet. Service with restrictions, super-
vision.
[✕] [🌀] [🛏] [💻] [🏊]

♥♥♥ Holiday Inn Express SH
(870) 932-5554. **$80-$90.** 2407 Phillips Dr. US 63, exit Stadium Blvd/Caraway Rd, just n. Int corridors.
Pets: Accepted.
[ASK] [S▢] [✕] [🐕] [🛏] [💻] [🏊]

♥♥♥ Holiday Inn of Jonesboro SH
(870) 935-2030. **$80-$140.** 3006 S Caraway Rd. US 63, exit
Stadium Blvd/Caraway Rd, just n. Ext/int corridors.
Pets: Accepted.
[ASK] [S▢] [✕] [🐕] [🛏] [💻] [🍴] [🏊]

AAA ♥♥♥ Ramada Limited SH
(870) 932-5757. **$67-$74.** 3000 Apache Dr. US 63, exit Stadium Blvd/Caraway Rd, just n on Stadium Blvd. Ext/int
corridors. **Pets:** Small, other species. $10 one-time fee/pet.
Designated rooms, service with restrictions, crate.
[SAVE] [S▢] [✕] [🛏] [💻] [🏊]

LITTLE ROCK

**AAA ♥♥♥ AmeriSuites (Little Rock/Financial
       Center) SH**
(501) 225-1075. **$76-$81.** 10920 Financial Center Pkwy. Jct
I-430 and 630, exit Shackleford Rd. Int corridors.
Pets: Accepted.
[SAVE] [S▢] [✕] [🛏] [💻] [🏊]

**AAA ♥♥♥ Baymont Inn & Suites Little Rock
       West SH**
(501) 225-7007. **$61-$81.** 1010 Breckenridge Rd. I-430, exit
8, just e to Breckenridge Rd, then just s. Int corridors.
Pets: Other species. $50 deposit/room. Service with restric-
tions, crate.
[SAVE] [S▢] [✕] [🌀] [🛏] [💻]

AAA ♥♥♥ Hampton Inn Little Rock I-30 SH
(501) 562-6667. **$72-$82.** 6100 Mitchell Dr. I-30, exit 133. Int
corridors. **Pets:** Very small. $25 daily fee/pet. Service with
restrictions, supervision.
[SAVE] [S▢] [✕] [💻] [🏊]

▼▼▼ Holiday Inn Select **SH**
(501) 223-3000. **$114-$129.** 201 S Shackleford Rd. Jct I-430 and 630. Ext/int corridors. **Pets:** Accepted.
(ASK) (S⌀) (✕) (𝄢) (🛏) (💻) (🍴) (🏊)

AAA ▼▼▼ La Quinta Inn-Fair Park **SH**
(501) 664-7000. **$59-$75.** 901 Fair Park Blvd. I-630, exit 4, just s. Ext corridors. **Pets:** Medium. Designated rooms, service with restrictions, supervision.
(SAVE) (S⌀) (✕) (🛗M) (𝄢) (🛏) (💻) (🏊)

AAA ▼▼▼ La Quinta Inn-Otter Creek **SH**
(501) 455-2300. **$59-$75.** 11701 I-30. I-30, exit 128. Ext corridors. **Pets:** Small.
(SAVE) (S⌀) (✕) (🛏) (💻) (🍴) (🏊)

AAA ▼▼▼ La Quinta Inn-West **SH**
(501) 224-0900. **$59-$79.** 200 S Shackleford Rd. I-430, exit 6; I-630, exit Shackleford Rd N; jct I-430 and 630. Ext corridors. **Pets:** Accepted.
(SAVE) (S⌀) (✕) (🛏) (💻) (🏊)

AAA ▼▼▼ Residence Inn **SH**
(501) 312-0200. **$119-$159.** 1401 S Shackleford Rd. I-430, exit 5, just n. Int corridors. **Pets:** Other species. $100 one-time fee/room. Service with restrictions.
(SAVE) (S⌀) (✕) (🛗M) (𝄢) (⛳) (🛏) (💻) (🏊) (✕)

LONOKE

AAA ▼▼ Days Inn **SH**
(501) 676-5138. **$65.** 105 Dee Dee Ln. I-40, exit 175, just n. Ext corridors. **Pets:** Small. $5 daily fee/pet. Designated rooms, service with restrictions, supervision.
(SAVE) (S⌀) (✕) (⛳) (🛏) (💻) (🏊)

▼▼ Super 8 Motel **SH**
(501) 676-8880. **$59-$64.** 102 Dee Dee Ln. I-40, exit 175, just n. Int corridors. **Pets:** Small. $10 one-time fee/pet. Service with restrictions, supervision.
(ASK) (S⌀) (✕) (🛏) (💻) (🏊)

MAGNOLIA

▼▼ Best Western-Coachman's Inn **SH**
(870) 234-6122. **$65-$79.** 420 E Main St. 1.3 mi w of jct US 79 and 82B. Ext corridors. **Pets:** Small. Service with restrictions, supervision.
(✕) (🛏) (💻) (🍴) (🏊)

MARION

▼▼ Best Western-Regency Motor Inn **SH**
(870) 739-3278. **$65-$85, 7 day notice.** 3635 I-55. I-55, exit 10, just nw. Ext corridors. **Pets:** Very small, other species. Service with restrictions, supervision.
(ASK) (S⌀) (✕) (𝄢) (🛏) (💻) (🏊)

MAUMELLE

▼▼▼ Comfort Suites **SH**
(501) 851-8444. **$69-$149.** 14322 Frontier Dr. I-40, exit 142, just sw. Int corridors. **Pets:** Small. $10 one-time fee/pet. Designated rooms, service with restrictions, supervision.
(ASK) (S⌀) (✕) (𝄢) (⛳) (🛏) (💻) (🏊)

▼▼▼ Super 8 Motel of Maumelle **SH**
(501) 851-3500. **$55-$65.** 14325 Frontier Dr. I-40, exit 142, just sw. Ext corridors. **Pets:** Medium. $10 one-time fee/room. Designated rooms, service with restrictions, crate.
(ASK) (S⌀) (✕) (🛏) (🏊)

MOUNTAIN HOME

▼▼ Best Western Carriage Inn **SH** ❀
(870) 425-6001. **$52-$75.** 963 Hwy 62 E. 1.3 mi e on US 62B. Ext corridors. **Pets:** Small. $50 deposit/pet. Designated rooms, service with restrictions, supervision.
(ASK) (S⌀) (✕) (💻) (🏊)

AAA ▼▼▼ Teal Point Resort **CA**
(870) 492-5145. **$66-$126, 45 day notice.** 715 Teal Point Rd. 7 mi e on US 62, 0.6 mi n on CR 406, follow signs. Ext corridors. **Pets:** $7 daily fee/pet. Designated rooms, service with restrictions, supervision.
(SAVE) (🛏) (💻) (🏊) (✕) (🏇)

MOUNTAIN VIEW

▼▼ Best Western Fiddlers Inn **M**
(870) 269-2828. **$48-$90.** 601 Sylomore. 1 mi n on SR 5, 9 and 14. Ext corridors. **Pets:** Small, dogs only. $5 one-time fee/room. Supervision.
(ASK) (S⌀) (✕) (🛏) (💻) (🏊)

NEWPORT

AAA ▼▼▼ Park Inn **M**
(870) 523-5851. **$60-$65.** 901 Hwy 367 N. US 67, exit 83, 1 mi w, 0.3 mi n. Ext corridors. **Pets:** Other species. Service with restrictions, crate.
(SAVE) (S⌀) (✕) (🛏) (💻) (🏊)

NORTH LITTLE ROCK

AAA ▼▼▼ Baymont Inn & Suites North Little Rock **SH**
(501) 758-8888. **$59-$79.** 4311 Warden Rd. US 67/167, exit 1B northbound; exit 1 southbound. Int corridors. **Pets:** Accepted.
(SAVE) (S⌀) (✕) (𝄢) (⛳) (🛏) (💻) (🏊)

▼▼ Days Inn **M**
(501) 945-4100. **$45-$65.** 5800 Pritchard Dr. I-40, exit 157. Ext corridors. **Pets:** $10 daily fee/pet. No service, supervision.
(ASK) (✕) (🛏)

▼▼▼ Days Inn **SH**
(501) 851-3297. **$50.** 7200 Bicentennial Rd. I-40, exit 142. Ext corridors. **Pets:** Small, dogs only. $10 daily fee/pet. Designated rooms, service with restrictions, supervision.
(ASK) (S⌀) (✕) (𝄢) (🛏)

▼▼▼ Hampton Inn **SH**
(501) 771-2090. **$79-$89.** 500 W 29th St. I-40, exit 152. Int corridors. **Pets:** Very small, other species. $25 one-time fee/pet. Supervision.
(ASK) (S⌀) (✕) (𝄢) (💻) (🏊)

Holiday Inn SH
(501) 758-1851. **$68.** 120 W Pershing Blvd. I-40, exit 152 westbound; exit 153A eastbound. Int corridors. **Pets:** Accepted.
[ASK] [S] [X] [◻] [¶] [≈]

La Quinta North SH
(501) 945-0808. **$65-$75.** 4100 E McCain Blvd. Jct US 67/167, exit 1A northbound; exit 1 southbound. Ext corridors. **Pets:** Accepted.
[SAVE] [S] [X] [◻] [≈]

Red Roof Inn SH
(501) 945-0080. **$55.** 5711 Pritchard Dr. I-40, exit 157, just s. Int corridors. **Pets:** Small. Service with restrictions, supervision.
[ASK] [S] [X] [◻] [≈]

Residence Inn by Marriott-North SH
(501) 945-7777. **$89-$109, 14 day notice.** 4110 Healthcare Dr. I-40, exit 156. Int corridors. **Pets:** Medium, other species. $100 one-time fee/room. Service with restrictions, crate.
[ASK] [S] [X] [◻] [◻] [≈] [X]

Rest Inn SH
(501) 537-3106. **$40-$60.** 5801 Pritchard Dr. I-40, exit 157, just s. Ext corridors. **Pets:** $10 one-time fee/pet. Service with restrictions, supervision.
[ASK] [X]

Super 8 North Little Rock M
(501) 945-0141. **$43-$52, 5 day notice.** 1 Gray Rd. I-40, exit 157. Ext/int corridors. **Pets:** Medium. $5 daily fee/pet. No service, supervision.
[ASK] [S] [X] [≈]

Travelodge M
(501) 758-8110. **$50-$60, 5 day notice.** 3100 N Main. I-40, exit 153A eastbound, just n; exit SR 107 westbound, just w. Ext corridors. **Pets:** Accepted.
[ASK] [S] [X] [◻] [◻] [≈]

OSCEOLA

Best Western Inn SH
(870) 563-3222. **$59-$64.** 4635 W Keiser. I-55, exit 48. Ext corridors. **Pets:** Accepted.
[SAVE] [S] [X] [◻] [◻] [¶] [≈]

OZARK

Oxford Inn M
(479) 667-1131. **$40.** 305 N 18th St. I-40, exit 35, 3 mi s on SR 23, just n of jct US 64. Ext corridors. **Pets:** Medium, other species. $10 daily fee/room. Service with restrictions, supervision.
[ASK] [S] [X] [◻] [≈]

PARAGOULD

Ramada Inn SH
(870) 239-2121. **$75-$78.** 2310 W Kingshighway. 0.8 mi w of jct US 412 and 49. Ext/int corridors. **Pets:** Small. $20 daily fee/pet. Service with restrictions, supervision.
[ASK] [S] [X] [◻] [◻] [¶] [≈]

PINE BLUFF

Best Western Pines SH
(870) 535-8640. **Call for rates.** 2700 E Harding. I-530, exit 46, just n. Ext corridors. **Pets:** Accepted.
[X] [◻] [◻] [¶] [≈]

Hampton Inn Pine Bluff SH
(870) 850-0444. **$75.** 3103 E Market St. I-530, exit 46, just n. Int corridors. **Pets:** Small. Service with restrictions, supervision.
[X] [S] [◻] [◻] [◻] [◻] [≈]

Holiday Inn Express Hotel & Suites SH
(870) 879-3800. **$90-$100.** 3620 Camden Rd. I-530, exit 39, just sw. Int corridors. **Pets:** Small. $25 one-time fee/pet. Designated rooms, service with restrictions, supervision.
[ASK] [X] [S] [◻] [◻] [◻] [≈]

POCAHONTAS

Days Inn & Suites SH
(870) 892-9500. **$75, 10 day notice.** 2805 Hwy 67 S. 1.7 mi s. Int corridors. **Pets:** $25 deposit/pet, $10 daily fee/pet. Designated rooms, service with restrictions, crate.
[ASK] [S] [X] [◻] [◻] [≈]

ROGERS

AmeriSuites (Rogers/Bentonville) SH
(479) 633-8555. **$118-$127.** 4610 W Walnut. I-540, exit 85, just e. Int corridors. **Pets:** Medium, other species. Service with restrictions, crate.
[ASK] [S] [S] [◻] [◻] [◻] [◻] [≈]

Embassy Suites Northwest Arkansas LH
(479) 254-8400. **$87-$179.** 3303 Pinnacle Hills Pkwy. I-540, exit 83, just w, 0.6 mi s. Int corridors. **Pets:** Medium. $50 one-time fee/room. Service with restrictions, crate.
[ASK] [S] [X] [S] [◻] [◻] [◻] [◻] [◻] [¶] [≈] [X]

RUSSELLVILLE

Comfort Inn M
(479) 967-7500. **$60-$95.** 3019 E Parkway Dr. I-40, exit 84, just s. Ext corridors. **Pets:** Medium. $10 daily fee/pet. Service with restrictions, supervision.
[ASK] [S] [X] [◻] [◻] [≈]

Holiday Inn SH
(479) 968-4300. **$70.** 2407 N Arkansas Ave. I-40, exit 81, just s. Ext corridors. **Pets:** Accepted.
[SAVE] [S] [X] [◻] [◻] [¶] [≈]

Park Motel M
(479) 968-4862. **$30-$44.** 2615 W Main St. I-40, exit 81, 2 mi s on SR 7, 1.6 mi w on US 64. Ext corridors. **Pets:** Other species. Service with restrictions.
[ASK] [S] [X] [◻] [≈]

SEARCY

Royal Inn M
(501) 268-3511. **$49-$59.** 2203 E Race Ave. US 67, exit 46, 1.1 mi w. Ext corridors. **Pets:** Accepted.
[SAVE] [S] [X] [◻] [◻]

SILOAM SPRINGS

▼▼ ◆◆ Super 8 Motel Ⓜ
(479) 524-8898. **$51-$54.** 1800 Hwy 412 W. Center. Ext
corridors. **Pets:** Accepted.
(A$K) (S🐾) (✕) (🐾) (📶) (💻) (🚭)

SPRINGDALE

🅐🅐🅐 ▼◆◆◆ Baymont Inn & Suites
                   Springdale 🆂🅷
(479) 751-2626. **$69-$89.** 1300 S 48th St. I-540, exit 72, just
e on US 412. Int corridors. **Pets:** Medium, other species.
Service with restrictions, crate.
(SAVE) (S🐾) (✕) (🐾) (🐾) (🐾) (📶) (💻) (🚭) (✕)

🅐🅐🅐 ▼◆◆ Best Western Heritage Inn 🆂🅷
(479) 751-3100. **$60-$80.** 1394 W Sunset Ave. I-540, exit 72,
2.4 mi e on US 412. Ext/int corridors. **Pets:** Accepted.
(SAVE) (S🐾) (✕) (📶) (💻) (🚭)

🅐🅐🅐 ▼◆◆◆ Hampton Inn & Suites 🆂🅷
(479) 756-3500. **$56-$106, 30 day notice.** 1700 S 48th St.
I-540, exit 72, just e. Int corridors. **Pets:** Accepted.
(SAVE) (S🐾) (✕) (🐾) (🐾) (🐾) (📶) (💻) (🚭)

🅐🅐🅐 ▼◆◆◆ Holiday Inn Northwest AR Hotel &
                   Convention Center 🅻🅷 🐾
(479) 751-8300. **$149-$179.** 1500 S 48th St. I-540, exit 72,
just e on US 412. Int corridors. **Pets:** Large, other species.
Service with restrictions, supervision.
(SAVE) (S🐾) (✕) (🐾) (🐾) (📶) (💻) (🍴) (🚭) (✕)

▼◆◆ Residence Inn by Marriott 🆂🅷
(479) 872-9100. **$119.** 1740 S 48th St. I-540, exit 72, e to
48th St, then 0.5 mi s. Int corridors. **Pets:** Medium, other
species. $8 daily fee/room, $50 one-time fee/pet. Service
with restrictions, crate.
(A$K) (S🐾) (✕) (🐾) (📶) (💻) (🚭) (✕)

STUTTGART

▼◆◆◆ Holiday Inn Express 🆂🅷
(870) 673-3616. **$69-$124.** 708 W Michigan. On US 79, just
w. Ext corridors. **Pets:** Medium, dogs only. $5 daily fee/pet.
Designated rooms, service with restrictions, supervision.
(A$K) (S🐾) (✕) (📶) (💻) (🚭)

TEXARKANA

🅐🅐🅐 ▼◆◆ Baymont Inn & Suites Texarkana 🆂🅷
(870) 773-1000. **$49-$69.** 5102 N State Line Ave. I-30, exit
223B, just n. Int corridors. **Pets:** Other species. Service with
restrictions, supervision.
(SAVE) (S🐾) (✕) (🐾) (📶) (💻) (🚭)

🅐🅐🅐 ▼◆◆ Best Western Kings Row Inn &
                   Suites Ⓜ
(870) 774-3851. **$60-$65.** 4200 N State Line Ave. I-30, exit
223A, just s. Ext/int corridors. **Pets:** Accepted.
(SAVE) (S🐾) (✕) (📶) (💻) (🍴) (🚭)

▼◆◆ Holiday Inn Texarkana 🆂🅷
(870) 774-3521. **$98, 7 day notice.** 5100 N State Line Ave.
I-30, exit 223B, just n. Int corridors. **Pets:** $25 one-time
fee/room. Service with restrictions.
(A$K) (S🐾) (✕) (🐾) (📶) (💻) (🍴) (🚭) (✕)

🅐🅐🅐 ▼◆◆ Quality Inn 🆂🅷
(870) 772-0070. **$49-$79.** 5210 N State Line Ave. I-30, exit
223B, just n. Ext corridors. **Pets:** Accepted.
(SAVE) (S🐾) (✕) (📶) (💻) (🚭)

VAN BUREN

▼◆◆ Comfort Inn 🆂🅷
(479) 474-2223. **$55-$80.** 3131 Cloverleaf. I-540, exit 2A,
just s. Int corridors. **Pets:** Medium, dogs only. $15 one-time
fee/pet. Service with restrictions, supervision.
(A$K) (S🐾) (✕) (📶) (💻) (🚭)

▼◆◆ Holiday Inn Express 🆂🅷
(479) 474-8100. **$68.** 1903 N 6th St. I-40, exit 5, just n. Ext
corridors. **Pets:** Accepted.
(A$K) (S🐾) (✕) (💻) (🚭)

▼◆ Super 8 Motel 🆂🅷
(479) 471-8888. **$55-$70.** 106 North Plaza Ct. I-40, exit 5,
just s. Ext/int corridors. **Pets:** Medium, dogs only. $15 one-
time fee/pet. Service with restrictions, supervision.
(A$K) (S🐾) (✕) (📶) (💻) (🚭)

WEST HELENA

🅐🅐🅐 ▼◆◆◆ Best Western Inn 🆂🅷
(870) 572-2592. **$55.** 1053 Hwy 49 W. US 49, 3 mi w. Ext
corridors. **Pets:** Accepted.
(SAVE) (S🐾) (✕) (📶) (💻) (🚭)

CALIFORNIA

CITY INDEX

ALTURAS

 Best Western Trailside Inn 🅼
(530) 233-4111. **$75-$80, 7 day notice.** 343 N Main St. On
US 395. Ext corridors. **Pets:** Accepted.

ANAHEIM

🆅 Anaheim Comfort Inn 🅼
(714) 635-6461. **$55-$99.** 1251 N Harbor Blvd. SR 91, exit
Harbor Blvd, just s. Ext corridors. **Pets:** Accepted.

▲▲▲ ▽▽▽ Anaheim Marriott Hotel LH
(714) 750-8000. **$149-$199.** 700 W Convention Way. I-5, exit Katella Ave, 0.6 mi w to Harbor Blvd, 0.3 mi s, then just w. Int corridors. **Pets:** Accepted.
SAVE ⊠ &M 🛏 📶 🔋 📺 ⁍ ⋙ ⊠

▲▲▲ ▽▽ Anaheim Plaza Hotel & Suites SH
(714) 772-5900. **$99-$119.** 1700 S Harbor Blvd. I-5, exit Katella Ave, 0.5 mi w, then just n. Ext corridors. **Pets:** Small. $50 deposit/room. Designated rooms, service with restrictions, supervision.
SAVE S⋄ ⊠ 🔋 📺 ⁍ ⋙

▲▲▲ ▽▽▽ Anaheim Quality Inn M ❀
(714) 750-5211. **$59-$109.** 2200 S Harbor Blvd. I-5, exit Chapman Ave, 1.5 mi w, just n. Ext corridors. **Pets:** Small, dogs only. $100 deposit/room, $25 one-time fee/pet. Service with restrictions, crate.
SAVE S⋄ ⊠ 🔋 📺 ⋙

▲▲▲ ▽▽▽ Anaheim Towneplace Suites By Marriott M
(714) 939-9700. **$69-$129.** 1730 S State College Blvd. I-5, exit Katella Ave, 0.5 mi e, then just n. Int corridors. **Pets:** Accepted.
SAVE S⋄ ⊠ 🔋 📺 ⋙

▲▲▲ ▽▽▽ Best Western Anaheim Stardust M
(714) 774-7600. **$68-$119.** 1057 W Ball Rd. I-5, exit Ball Rd, just w. Ext corridors. **Pets:** Accepted.
SAVE S⋄ ⊠ 🔋 📺 ⋙

▲▲▲ ▽▽▽ Clarion Hotel Anaheim Resort LH
(714) 750-3131. **$99-$149.** 616 Convention Way. I-5, exit Katella Ave, 0.6 mi w to Harbor Blvd, then 0.3 mi s. Int corridors. **Pets:** Medium. $10 daily fee/room, $25 one-time fee/room. Designated rooms, service with restrictions, supervision.
SAVE S⋄ ⊠ 🔋 📺 ⁍ ⋙

▲▲▲ ▽▽▽ Coast Anaheim Hotel LH ❀
(714) 750-1811. **$89-$139, 3 day notice.** 1855 S Harbor Blvd. I-5, exit Katella Ave, 0.6 mi w, then just s. Int corridors. **Pets:** Large, other species. Designated rooms, service with restrictions, crate.
SAVE S⋄ ⊠ 🔋 📺 ⁍ ⋙

▲▲▲ ▽▽▽ Embassy Suites Hotel Anaheim-North Near Disneyland Resort LH
(714) 632-1221. **$119-$204.** 3100 E Frontera St. SR 91, exit Glassell St, just se. Int corridors. **Pets:** Medium. $50 one-time fee/room. Service with restrictions.
SAVE S⋄ ⊠ 🔋 📺 ⁍ ⋙ ⊠

▽▽▽ Hawthorn Suites, Ltd Anaheim SH
(714) 635-5000. **$85-$139.** 1752 S Clementine St. I-5, exit Katella Ave, just n. Int corridors. **Pets:** Medium. $100 deposit/room, $50 one-time fee/room. Service with restrictions, crate.
ASK S⋄ ⊠ 🔋 📺 ⋙

▲▲▲ ▽▽▽ Hilton Anaheim LH
(714) 750-4321. **$99-$299, 3 day notice.** 777 Convention Way. I-5, exit Katella Ave, just w to Harbor Blvd, just s, then just w. Int corridors. **Pets:** Accepted.
SAVE ⊠ &M 🛏 📶 🔋 📺 ⁍ ⋙ ⊠

▲▲▲ ▽▽▽ Residence Inn By Marriott SH
(714) 533-3555. **$189-$209.** 1700 S Clementine St. I-5, exit Katella Ave, just sw. Ext corridors. **Pets:** Accepted.
SAVE ⊠ 🔋 📺 ⋙ ⊠

▲▲▲ ▽▽▽ Staybridge Suites by Holiday Inn-Anaheim Resort SH
(714) 748-7700. **$109-$229.** 1855 S Manchester Ave. I-5, exit Katella Ave, just s, adjacent to west side of freeway. Int corridors. **Pets:** Accepted.
SAVE S⋄ ⊠ 🔋 📺 ⋙ ⊠

ANAHEIM HILLS

▽▽▽ Best Western Anaheim Hills M
(714) 779-0252. **$64-$74.** 5710 E La Palma Ave. SR 91, exit Imperial Hwy, 0.3 mi n. Ext/int corridors. **Pets:** Accepted.
ASK S⋄ ⊠ 🔋 📺 ⋙ ⊠

ANDERSON

▽▽▽ AmeriHost Inn-Anderson M
(530) 365-6100. **$72-$79.** 2040 Factory Outlet Dr. I-5, exit Factory Outlet Dr, just w. Int corridors. **Pets:** Medium. $10 daily fee/pet. Supervision.
ASK S⋄ ⊠ &M 🛏 🔋 📺 ⋙ ⊠

▲▲▲ ▽▽▽ Best Western Knights Inn M
(530) 365-2753. **$60-$80.** 2688 Gateway Dr. I-5, exit Central Anderson eastbound; exit Lassen Park westbound, just e. Ext corridors. **Pets:** Accepted.
SAVE S⋄ ⊠ 🔋 📺 ⋙

ANGELS CAMP

▽▽▽ Angels Hacienda BB
(209) 785-8533. **$129-$179, 14 day notice.** 7 mi on SR 4, then 5 mi. Int corridors. **Pets:** Accepted.
ASK S⋄ ⊠ 🔋 ⋙ ⌖

▲▲▲ ▽▽▽ Angels Inn Motel M
(209) 736-4242. **$75-$105.** 600 N Main St. SR 49, north end of town. Ext corridors. **Pets:** Dogs only. $50 deposit/room, $10 daily fee/room. Designated rooms, service with restrictions, supervision.
SAVE S⋄ ⊠ 🔋 📺 ⋙

▲▲▲ ▽▽▽ Best Western Cedar Inn & Suites M
(209) 736-4000. **$89-$169.** 444 S Main St. On SR 49; center of town. Ext/int corridors. **Pets:** Dogs only. $10 daily fee/pet. Designated rooms, supervision.
SAVE S⋄ ⊠ &M 🛏 🔋 📺 ⋙ ⊠

▲▲▲ ▽▽▽ Jumping Frog Motel M
(209) 736-2191. **$41-$108.** 330 Murphys Grade Rd. SR 49, n of Angels Camp Center, just left. Ext corridors. **Pets:** Accepted.
SAVE S⋄ ⊠ 📺

ARCATA

▲▲▲ ▽▽▽ Arcata Super 8 SH
(707) 822-8888. **$45-$90.** 4887 Valley West Blvd. US 101, exit Guintoli Ln, 2 mi n. Int corridors. **Pets:** Medium. $50 deposit/room, $5 daily fee/pet. Service with restrictions, supervision.
SAVE S⋄ ⊠ 🔋

Best Western Arcata Inn M
(707) 826-0313. **$62-$103.** 4827 Valley West Blvd. US 101, exit Guintoli Ln, 2 mi n. Ext corridors. **Pets:** Medium. $10 daily fee/pet. Service with restrictions, supervision.

Comfort Inn M
(707) 826-2827. **$60-$99.** 4701 Valley West Blvd. US 101, exit Guintoli Ln, 2 mi n. Ext corridors. **Pets:** Small, dogs only. $5 daily fee/pet. Service with restrictions, supervision.

Hotel Arcata SH
(707) 826-0217. **$80-$130.** 708 9th St. At Central Plaza. Int corridors. **Pets:** Other species. $50 deposit/pet, $5 daily fee/pet. Service with restrictions, supervision.

Quality Inn-Arcata SH
(707) 822-0409. **$59-$139.** 3535 Janes Rd. US 101, exit Guintoli Ln/Janes Rd, 2 mi n. Int corridors. **Pets:** $10 daily fee/pet. Service with restrictions, supervision.

ARROYO GRANDE

Best Western Casa Grande Inn M
(805) 481-7398. **$69-$198.** 850 Oak Park Rd. US 101, exit Oak Park Rd, just e. Ext/int corridors. **Pets:** Medium, dogs only. $10 daily fee/pet. Designated rooms, service with restrictions, supervision.

Premier Inns M
(805) 481-4774. **$40-$110.** 555 Camino Mercado. US 101, exit Oak Park Rd, just e. Ext corridors. **Pets:** Medium, other species. Service with restrictions, supervision.

AUBURN

Best Western Golden Key M
(530) 885-8611. **$79-$115.** 13450 Lincoln Way. I-80, exit Foresthill Rd. Ext corridors. **Pets:** Medium, other species. $15 one-time fee/pet. Designated rooms, service with restrictions, supervision.

Foothills Motel M
(530) 885-8444. **$55-$95.** 13431 Bowman Rd. I-80, exit Foresthill Rd. Ext corridors. **Pets:** Dogs only. $10 daily fee/pet. Designated rooms, service with restrictions, supervision.

Holiday Inn-Auburn M
(530) 887-8787. **$119-$159.** 120 Grass Valley Hwy. Jct I-80 and SR 49. Int corridors. **Pets:** Small, dogs only. $20 daily fee/pet. Service with restrictions, supervision.

Travelodge M
(530) 885-7025. **$60-$85.** 13490 Lincoln Way. I-80, exit Foresthill Rd. Ext/int corridors. **Pets:** Very small. $10 daily fee/pet. Designated rooms, service with restrictions, supervision.

BAKERSFIELD

Bakersfield Red Lion Hotel SH
(661) 327-0681. **$71-$152.** 2400 Camino Del Rio Ct. SR 99, exit SR 58 (Rosedale Hwy), just s. Ext/int corridors. **Pets:** Accepted.

Best Inn M
(661) 764-5221. **$49-$59.** 200 Trask St. I-5, exit Stockdale Hwy, 15 mi w. Ext corridors. **Pets:** Medium, other species. $5 daily fee/pet. Designated rooms, service with restrictions, supervision.

Best Western Crystal Palace Inn & Suites SH
(661) 327-9651. **$59-$99.** 2620 Buck Owens Blvd. SR 99, exit Buck Owens Blvd northbound; exit Rosedale Hwy southbound. Int corridors. **Pets:** Small. $10 daily fee/pet. Designated rooms, service with restrictions, supervision.

Best Western Heritage Inn M
(661) 764-6268. **$79-$109.** 253 Trask St. I-5, exit Stockdale Hwy, 15 mi w. Ext corridors. **Pets:** Accepted.

Best Western Hill House SH
(661) 327-4064. **$59-$99.** 700 Truxtun Ave St. SR 99, exit California Ave, just e, just n on Oak St, then 1.5 mi e. Int corridors. **Pets:** Medium. $10 daily fee/pet. Service with restrictions, supervision.

Days Inn M
(661) 324-5555. **$79-$109.** 4500 Buck Owens Blvd. SR 99, exit SR 58 (Rosedale Hwy) southbound, just e to Pierce Rd, then 0.7 mi n; exit Airport Dr northbound to Buck Owens Blvd, then just s. Ext corridors. **Pets:** Accepted.

Doubletree Hotel LH
(661) 323-7111. **$89-$165.** 3100 Camino Del Rio Ct. SR 99, exit SR 58 (Rosedale Hwy), just w. Int corridors. **Pets:** Other species. $15 one-time fee/room. Supervision.

Holiday Inn Select Convention Center LH
(661) 323-1900. **$85-$119.** 801 Truxtun Ave. SR 99, exit California Ave, 1.2 mi e, then 0.4 mi n on Chester Ave; downtown. Int corridors. **Pets:** $150 deposit/room, $50 one-time fee/room. Designated rooms, service with restrictions.

(AAA) ◆◆◆◆ La Quinta Inn M ❀
(661) 325-7400. **$81-$91.** 3232 Riverside Dr. SR 99, exit SR 58 (Rosedale Hwy) southbound; exit Buck Owens Blvd northbound, just n of Rosedale Hwy. Ext corridors. **Pets:** Medium. Service with restrictions, supervision.

[SAVE] [⊠] [🖒M] [🕮] [📞] [🖵] [➔]

(AAA) ◆◆ Liberty Inn Motel M
(661) 366-1630. **$52-$55.** 8230 E Brundage Ln. SR 99, 7 mi e on SR 58, exit SR 284 (Weed Patch Hwy), just n, then just e. Int corridors. **Pets:** Accepted.

[SAVE] [S🖒] [⊠] [📞] [➔]

(AAA) ◆◆◆◆ Quality Inn M
(661) 325-0772. **$66-$130.** 1011 Oak St. SR 99, exit California Ave, just e, then just s. Ext/int corridors. **Pets:** Accepted.

[SAVE] [S🖒] [⊠] [📞] [🖵] [➔]

◆◆◆◆ Residence Inn by Marriott SH
(661) 321-9800. **$124-$146.** 4241 Chester Ln. SR 99, exit California Ave, just w, then just n. Ext corridors. **Pets:** Accepted.

[ASK] [⊠] [🖒M] [🕮] [🖒'] [📞] [🖵] [➔] [⊠]

◆◆ Rio Bravo Resort LH
(661) 872-5000. **$85-$119.** 11200 Lake Ming Rd. SR 99, exit SR 178, 12 mi e, then 2.5 mi n on Alfred Harrell Hwy. Int corridors. **Pets:** Accepted.

[ASK] [S🖒] [⊠] [📞] [🖵] [🍽] [➔] [⊠]

(AAA) ◆◆ Royal Oak Inn M
(661) 324-9686. **$42-$68.** 889 Oak St. SR 99, exit California Ave, then just se. Ext corridors. **Pets:** Accepted.

[SAVE] [⊠] [📞] [🖵] [➔]

◆◆ Super 8 Motel Bakersfield M
(661) 322-1012. **$60-$70.** 901 Real Rd. SR 99, exit California Ave, just w, then just s. Ext corridors. **Pets:** Small. $10 daily fee/pet. Service with restrictions, supervision.

[ASK] [S🖒] [⊠] [📞] [➔]

(AAA) ◆◆◆ Vagabond Inn North M
(661) 392-1800. **$42.** 6100 Knudsen Dr. SR 99, exit Olive Dr, west side. Ext corridors. **Pets:** Accepted.

[SAVE] [S🖒] [⊠] [📞] [🖵] [➔]

(AAA) ◆◆◆ Vagabond Inn South M
(661) 831-9200. **$42.** 6501 Colony St. SR 99, exit Panama Ln, just e, then just s. Ext corridors. **Pets:** Accepted.

[SAVE] [S🖒] [⊠] [📞] [🖵] [➔]

BANNING

(AAA) ◆◆◆ Banning Travelodge M
(909) 849-1000. **$57-$199.** 1700 W Ramsey St. I-10, exit 22nd St, 0.5 mi e, just n. Ext corridors. **Pets:** Medium. $5 daily fee/pet. Designated rooms, service with restrictions, supervision.

[SAVE] [⊠] [📞] [🖵] [➔]

◆◆ Days Inn M
(909) 849-0092. **$57-$160.** 2320 W Ramsey St. I-10, exit 22nd St, just n, then just w. Ext corridors. **Pets:** Small. $10 daily fee/pet. Supervision.

[ASK] [S🖒] [⊠] [📞] [🖵] [➔]

(AAA) ◆◆ Super 8 Motel M
(909) 849-8888. **$65-$199.** 1690 W Ramsey St. I-10, exit 22nd St, just n, then 0.4 mi e. Int corridors. **Pets:** Medium. $5 daily fee/pet. Designated rooms, service with restrictions, supervision.

[SAVE] [⊠] [📞] [🖵] [➔]

BARSTOW

(AAA) ◆◆◆ Barstow-Super 8 Motel M
(760) 256-8443. **$58-$72.** 170 Coolwater Ln. I-15/40, exit E Main St, 0.3 mi w, then just s. Ext corridors. **Pets:** Medium. $5 daily fee/pet. Service with restrictions, supervision.

[SAVE] [S🖒] [⊠] [📞] [🖵] [➔]

◆◆ Best Motel M ❀
(760) 256-6836. **$33-$36.** 1281 E Main St. I-15/40, exit E Main St, 0.5 mi w. Ext corridors. **Pets:** Other species. $5 daily fee/pet.

[ASK] [S🖒] [⊠] [📞] [🖵] [➔]

(AAA) ◆◆◆ Best Western Desert Villa Inn M
(760) 256-1781. **$59-$139.** 1984 E Main St. I-15/40, exit Main St westbound; exit Montara eastbound, 0.5 mi e of I-15. Ext corridors. **Pets:** $10 daily fee/room. Service with restrictions, supervision.

[SAVE] [S🖒] [⊠] [🖒M] [🕮] [🖒'] [📞] [🖵] [🍽] [➔]

(AAA) ◆◆◆ Days Inn M
(760) 256-1737. **$49-$59.** 1590 Coolwater Ln. I-15/40, exit E Main St, just w, then just s on Roberta St. Ext corridors. **Pets:** Medium. $10 one-time fee/pet. Service with restrictions, supervision.

[SAVE] [S🖒] [⊠] [📞] [➔]

(AAA) ◆◆ Econo Lodge M
(760) 256-2133. **$44-$64.** 1230 E Main St. I-15/40, exit E Main St, 0.8 mi w. Ext corridors. **Pets:** Accepted.

[SAVE] [S🖒] [⊠] [📞] [🖵] [➔]

(AAA) ◆◆ Executive Inn M
(760) 256-7581. **$35-$60.** 1261 E Main St. I-15/40, exit E Main St, 0.8 mi w. Ext corridors. **Pets:** Accepted.

[SAVE] [S🖒] [⊠] [📞] [➔]

(AAA) ◆◆ Gateway Motel M
(760) 256-8931. **$31-$85.** 1630 E Main St. I-15/40, exit E Main St, just e. Ext corridors. **Pets:** Accepted.

[SAVE] [S🖒] [⊠] [📞] [➔]

◆◆◆ Holiday Inn Express, Barstow-Historic Route 66 SH
(760) 256-1300. **$89-$109.** 1861 W Main St. I-15/40, exit W Main St, 0.8 mi ne. Int corridors. **Pets:** Other species. $20 deposit/room. Service with restrictions, supervision.

[ASK] [S🖒] [⊠] [📞] [➔]

◆◆◆ Holiday Inn Express Hotel & Suites SH
(760) 253-9200. **$89-$159.** 2700 Lenwood Rd. I-15/40, exit Lenwood Rd, just e, then 0.5 mi s. **Pets:** Other species. $25 deposit/room. Service with restrictions, supervision.

[ASK] [S🖒] [⊠] [🖒M] [🕮] [🖒'] [📞] [➔]

▼▼ **Motel 6 Barstow** **M**
(760) 256-1752. **Call for rates.** 150 N Yucca Ave. I-15/40, exit E Main St, 0.5 mi w, then just s. Ext corridors. **Pets:** Medium, other species. Service with restrictions, supervision.
⊠ ⌂

▲▲▲ ▼▼▼ **Oak Tree Inn** **SH**
(760) 254-1148. **$65-$70.** 35450 Yermo Rd. I-15/40, exit Ghost Town Rd, just e, then just s. Int corridors. **Pets:** Other species. $10 daily fee/pet. Service with restrictions.
SAVE ⌂ ⊠ ⊟ ⌨ ⌂

▲▲▲ ▼▼▼ **Quality Inn** **M**
(760) 256-6891. **$35-$75.** 1520 E Main St. I-15/40, exit E Main St, 0.3 mi w. Ext corridors. **Pets:** Medium, other species. $10 one-time fee/pet. Service with restrictions, supervision.
SAVE ⌂ ⊠ ⊟ ⌨ ⌁ ⌂

▼▼ ▼▼ **Ramada Inn** **SH**
(760) 256-5673. **$89-$99.** 1511 E Main St. I-15/40, exit E Main St, 0.3 mi w. Int corridors. **Pets:** Medium. $20 one-time fee/room. Service with restrictions, supervision.
ASK ⌂ ⊠ ⌁M ⊟ ⌨ ⌁ ⌂

▲▲▲ ▼▼ **Stardust Inn** **M**
(760) 256-7116. **$35-$50.** 901 E Main St. I-15/40, exit Barstow Rd, 0.8 mi n, then 0.4 mi e. Ext corridors. **Pets:** Small, dogs only. $10 one-time fee/pet. Service with restrictions, supervision.
SAVE ⌂ ⊠ ⊟ ⌂

BEAUMONT

▲▲▲ ▼▼ **Best Value Inn** **M**
(909) 845-2185. **$70-$95.** 625 E 5th St. I-10, exit SR 79 (Beaumont Ave), just n. Ext corridors. **Pets:** Small. $5 daily fee/pet. Service with restrictions, supervision.
SAVE ⌂ ⊠ ⊟ ⌂

▲▲▲ ▼▼▼ **Best Western El Rancho Motor Inn** **M**
(909) 845-2176. **$65-$100.** 480 E 5th St. I-10, exit SR 70 (Beaumont Ave), just n, then just e. Ext corridors. **Pets:** Very small. $10 daily fee/pet. Designated rooms, service with restrictions, supervision.
SAVE ⌂ ⊠ ⊟ ⌨ ⌁ ⌂

BENICIA

▲▲▲ ▼▼▼ **Best Western Heritage Inn** **SH**
(707) 746-0401. **$80-$120.** 1955 E 2nd St. I-780, exit Central Benicia/E 2nd St, just e. Int corridors. **Pets:** Small. $25 one-time fee/pet. Service with restrictions, supervision.
SAVE ⌂ ⊠ ⊟ ⌨ ⌂

BERRY CREEK

▼▼ ▼▼ **Lake Oroville Bed & Breakfast** **BB** ✿
(530) 589-0700. **$125-$165, 5 day notice.** 240 Sunday Dr. SR 162, exit SR 70, 15 mi e on SR 162 to Bell Ranch Rd, 0.5 mi w. Int corridors. **Pets:** Other species. $10 daily fee/pet. Supervision.
ASK ⌂ ⊠ ⌁M ⌂ ⊟

BIG BEAR LAKE

▼▼▼ **Alpine Village Suites Lodge** **M** ✿
(909) 866-5460. **$98-$189, 7 day notice.** 546 Pine Knot Ave. SR 18 business route. Ext/int corridors. **Pets:** Medium, other species. $100 deposit/room. Service with restrictions.
ASK ⌂ ⊠ ⊟ ⌨ ⌂

▼▼▼▼ **Best Western Big Bear Chateau** **SH** ✿
(909) 866-6666. **$79-$400, 3 day notice.** 42200 Moonridge Rd. SR 18, 1.5 mi e of Pine Knot Ave, then 0.5 mi s. Int corridors. **Pets:** Dogs only. $15 daily fee/pet, $30 one-time fee/pet. Service with restrictions.
ASK ⊠ ⊟ ⌨ ⌁ ⌂ ⊠

▲▲▲ ▼▼▼ **Cozy Hollow Lodge** **CA**
(909) 866-9694. **$49-$249, 15 day notice.** 40409 Big Bear Blvd. SR 18, 0.8 mi w. Ext corridors. **Pets:** Accepted.
SAVE ⌂ ⊠ ⊟ ⌨ ⊠ ⌂

▼▼▼ **Eagle's Nest Bed & Breakfast** **BB** ✿
(909) 866-6465. **$85-$165, 5 day notice.** 41675 Big Bear Blvd. SR 18, 1 mi e of Pine Knot Ave. Ext/int corridors. **Pets:** Other species. Designated rooms, service with restrictions, supervision.
ASK ⌂ ⊠ ⊟ ⌨ ⌂

▲▲▲ ▼▼▼ **Golden Bear Cottages** **CA**
(909) 866-2010. **$80-$109, 30 day notice.** 39367 Big Bear Blvd. SR 18, 2 mi w of village. Ext corridors. **Pets:** Other species. $10 one-time fee/pet. Designated rooms, service with restrictions, crate.
SAVE ⌂ ⊠ ⊟ ⌨ ⌁ ⊠ ⌂

▲▲▲ ▼▼▼ **Grey Squirrel Resort** **CA**
(909) 866-4335. **$76-$85, 14 day notice.** 39372 Big Bear Blvd. SR 18, 2.5 mi w of village. Ext corridors. **Pets:** Other species. $100 deposit/room, $10 daily fee/pet. Service with restrictions, supervision.
SAVE ⌂ ⊠ ⊟ ⌨ ⌁ ⊠ ⌂

▲▲▲ ▼▼▼ **Honey Bear Lodge** **M**
(909) 866-7825. **$49-$269, 7 day notice.** 40994 Pennsylvania Ave. SR 18 business route (Pine Knot Ave), just e. Ext corridors. **Pets:** Accepted.
SAVE ⌂ ⊠ ⊟ ⌨ ⌂

▼▼▼ **Majestic Moose Lodge** **CA**
(909) 866-2435. **$79-$209, 14 day notice.** 39328 Big Bear Blvd. SR 18, 2.5 mi w of village. Ext/int corridors. **Pets:** $100 deposit/room, $10 daily fee/pet. Service with restrictions, supervision.
ASK ⌂ ⊠ ⊟ ⌨ ⌁ ⊠ ⌂

▼▼▼ **Pine Knot Guest Ranch** **CA** ✿
(909) 866-6500. **$79-$179, 7 day notice.** 908 Pine Knot Ave. Just s of SR 18 business route and downtown area. Ext corridors. **Pets:** Other species. $10 daily fee/pet. Designated rooms.
ASK ⌂ ⊠ ⊟ ⌨

▲▲▲ ▼▼▼ **Shore Acres Lodge** **CA**
(909) 866-8200. **$105-$295, 14 day notice.** 40090 Lakeview Dr. SR 18, 0.5 mi w of Pine Knot Ave, then 0.7 mi nw. Ext corridors. **Pets:** Other species. $10 daily fee/pet.
SAVE ⌂ ⊠ ⊟ ⌨ ⌁ ⊠ ⌂

ⒶⒶⒶ ♦♦♦ Stage Coach Lodge 🇨🇦
(909) 878-3008. **$89-$165, 14 day notice.** 652 Jeffries Rd. SR 18, 0.5 mi e of Pine Knot Ave, 0.3 mi s. Ext corridors. **Pets:** Other species. $10 daily fee/pet. Designated rooms, service with restrictions, supervision.
[SAVE] [S🐾] 🍴 💻 🐾 🐾

ⒶⒶⒶ ♦♦♦ Timber Haven Lodge 🇨🇦
(909) 866-3568. **$99-$189, 14 day notice.** 877 Tulip Ln. SR 18, 1.8 mi w of Pine Knot Ave, then 0.4 mi s. Ext corridors. **Pets:** Dogs only. $10 daily fee/pet. Designated rooms, service with restrictions, supervision.
[SAVE] [S🐾] 🐾 🍴 💻 🐾 🐾

ⒶⒶⒶ ♦♦♦ The Timberline Lodge 🇨🇦
(909) 866-4141. **$79-$459, 10 day notice.** 39921 Big Bear Blvd. SR 18, 1.5 mi w of Pine Knot Ave. Ext corridors. **Pets:** Other species. $10 daily fee/pet.
[SAVE] [S🐾] 🐾 🍴 💻 🐾 🐾 🐾

BIG PINE

ⒶⒶⒶ ♦ Big Pine Motel Ⓜ
(760) 938-2282. **$42-$62.** 370 S Main. On US 395. Ext corridors. **Pets:** Accepted.
[SAVE] 🐾 🍴 💻

ⒶⒶⒶ ♦ Bristlecone Motel Ⓜ
(760) 938-2067. **$40-$68.** 101 N Main St. On US 395. Ext corridors. **Pets:** Other species. $4 one-time fee/pet. Service with restrictions, supervision.
[SAVE] [S🐾] 🐾 🍴 💻

BISHOP

ⒶⒶⒶ ♦♦♦ Best Western Bishop Holiday Spa Lodge Ⓜ
(760) 873-3543. **$79-$119.** 1025 N Main St. On US 395. Ext corridors. **Pets:** Medium, other species. Designated rooms, service with restrictions, supervision.
[SAVE] [S🐾] 🐾 🍴 💻 🐾 🐾

ⒶⒶⒶ ♦♦♦ Best Western Creekside Inn 🅂🄷
(760) 872-3044. **$109-$189.** 725 N Main St. On US 395. Int corridors. **Pets:** Accepted.
[SAVE] 🐾 🐾 🍴 💻 🐾

ⒶⒶⒶ ♦♦♦ Comfort Inn Ⓜ
(760) 873-4284. **$79-$109.** 805 N Main St. On US 395. Ext corridors. **Pets:** Medium. $5 daily fee/pet. Designated rooms, service with restrictions, supervision.
[SAVE] [S🐾] 🐾 🍴 💻 🐾

♦♦♦ Motel 6-4094 Ⓜ
(760) 873-8426. **$49-$89.** 1005 N Main St. On US 395. Ext corridors. **Pets:** Designated rooms, service with restrictions, supervision.
🐾 🍴 🐾

♦♦♦ Ramada Limited Ⓜ 🐾
(760) 872-1771. **$69-$89.** 155 E Elm St. On US 395, just e. Ext corridors. **Pets:** Medium, other species. $15 one-time fee/pet. Service with restrictions, supervision.
[A$K] [S🐾] 🐾 [🐾M] 🐾 🍴 💻 🐾

♦♦ Thunderbird Motel Ⓜ
(760) 873-4215. **$55-$150.** 190 W Pine St. On US 395, just w. Ext corridors. **Pets:** Accepted.
[A$K] [S🐾] 🐾 🍴 💻

ⒶⒶⒶ ♦♦♦ Vagabond Inn Ⓜ 🐾
(760) 873-6351. **$90.** 1030 N Main St. On US 395. Ext corridors. **Pets:** Large, other species. $5 daily fee/pet. Service with restrictions, supervision.
[SAVE] [S🐾] 🐾 🍴 💻 🐾 🐾

BLYTHE

ⒶⒶⒶ ♦♦♦ Best Western Sahara Motel Ⓜ
(760) 922-7105. **$79-$169.** 825 W Hobsonway. I-10, exit Lovekin Blvd, just n, then just w. Ext corridors. **Pets:** Medium. Service with restrictions, supervision.
[SAVE] [S🐾] 🐾 🍴 💻 🐾

ⒶⒶⒶ ♦♦♦ Legacy Inn Ⓜ
(760) 922-4146. **$55-$115.** 903 W Hobsonway. I-10, exit Lovekin Blvd, just n, then just w. Ext corridors. **Pets:** Accepted.
[SAVE] [S🐾] 🐾 🍴 💻 🐾

ⒶⒶⒶ ♦♦♦ Travelers Inn Express Ⓜ
(760) 922-3334. **$60-$129.** 1781 E Hobsonway. I-10, exit Intake Blvd, just n, then just w. Ext corridors. **Pets:** Designated rooms, service with restrictions, supervision.
[SAVE] [S🐾] 🐾 🍴 💻 🐾

BORREGO SPRINGS

ⒶⒶⒶ ♦♦♦ Borrego Springs Resort Hotel 🅂🄷 🐾
(760) 767-5700. **$94-$135.** 1112 Tilting T Dr. SR 22, 1.5 mi s on Borrego Valley Rd, just w. Int corridors. **Pets:** Very small. $50 deposit/pet. Designated rooms, service with restrictions, crate.
[SAVE] [S🐾] 🐾 🐾 🍴 💻 🍴 🐾 🐾

BREA

♦♦ Homestead Studio Suites Hotel-Brea/Anaheim Ⓜ 🐾
(714) 528-2500. **$74-$95.** 3050 E Imperial Hwy. SR 57, 1.4 mi e. Ext corridors. **Pets:** Medium, other species. $25 daily fee/room. Service with restrictions.
[A$K] [S🐾] 🐾 🍴 💻

ⒶⒶⒶ ♦ Hyland Motel Ⓜ
(714) 990-6867. **$50-$60, 3 day notice.** 727 S Brea Blvd. SR 57, exit Imperial Hwy, 1 mi w, then 0.7 mi s. Ext corridors. **Pets:** Very small, dogs only. Designated rooms, service with restrictions, supervision.
[SAVE] 🐾 🍴 💻

♦♦ Woodfin Suite Hotel Ⓜ
(714) 579-3200. **$115-$165, 3 day notice.** 3100 E Imperial Hwy. SR 57, 1.5 mi e. Ext corridors. **Pets:** Other species. $5 daily fee/pet. Service with restrictions, crate.
[A$K] [S🐾] 🐾 🍴 💻 🐾

BRIDGEPORT

AAA ▼▼▼ **Best Western Ruby Inn** Ⓜ
(760) 932-7241. **$90-$150.** 333 Main St. On US 395; center. Ext corridors. **Pets:** Accepted.
[SAVE] [S⊘] [✕] [⊟] [🖵]

AAA ▼▼ **Redwood Motel** Ⓜ ✿
(760) 932-7060. **$56-$149.** 425 Main St. On US 395; at the north side of town. Ext corridors. **Pets:** Other species. $5 daily fee/pet. Designated rooms, service with restrictions, supervision.
[SAVE] [S⊘] [✕] [✍] [⊟] [🖵]

AAA ▼▼ **Silver Maple Inn** Ⓜ
(760) 932-7383. **$75-$95, 3 day notice.** 310 Main St. On US 395; center. Ext corridors. **Pets:** Other species. $25 one-time fee/pet. Service with restrictions, supervision.
[SAVE] [S⊘] [✕] [⊟] [🖵] [🎾]

AAA ▼▼ **Walker River Lodge** Ⓜ
(760) 932-7021. **$55-$145.** 100 Main St. US 395; at south end of town. Ext corridors. **Pets:** Other species. Supervision.
[SAVE] [S⊘] [✕] [🎧] [⊟] [🖵] [🌊] [✕]

BUELLTON

AAA ▼▼ **Rodeway Inn** Ⓜ
(805) 688-0022. **$59-$149, 7 day notice.** 630 Ave of Flags. US 101, exit first Buellton southbound; exit Frontage Rd northbound, just w over the freeway. Ext/int corridors. **Pets:** Accepted.
[SAVE] [S⊘] [✕] [⊟]

BUENA PARK

AAA ▼▼▼ **Best Western InnSuites Hotel Buena Park** Ⓜ
(714) 522-7360. **$59-$119.** 7555 Beach Blvd. SR 91, exit Beach Blvd, just s. Ext corridors. **Pets:** Accepted.
[SAVE] [S⊘] [✕] [⊟] [🖵] [🌊] [✕]

AAA ▼▼ **Days Inn** Ⓜ
(714) 828-5211. **$48-$58.** 8580 Stanton Ave. SR 91, exit Beach Blvd, 1.6 mi s, just e on Crescent Ave, then just s. Ext corridors. **Pets:** Accepted.
[SAVE] [S⊘] [✕] [⊟] [🌊]

BURNEY

AAA ▼▼ **Burney Motel** Ⓜ
(530) 335-4500. **$45-$79, 3 day notice.** 37448 Main St. 0.8 mi e on SR 299. Ext corridors. **Pets:** Accepted.
[SAVE] [✕] [⊟] [🖵] [✕]

AAA ▼ **Charm Motel** Ⓜ ✿
(530) 335-2254. **$46-$82, 3 day notice.** 37363 Main St. 0.8 mi e on SR 299. Ext corridors. **Pets:** $5 daily fee/pet. Service with restrictions, supervision.
[SAVE] [S⊘] [✕] [⊟] [🖵]

AAA ▼ **Green Gables Motel** Ⓜ ✿
(530) 335-2264. **$46-$82, 3 day notice.** 37385 Main St. 0.8 mi e on SR 299. Ext corridors. **Pets:** Other species. $5 one-time fee/pet. Service with restrictions, supervision.
[SAVE] [S⊘] [✕] [⊟] [🖵] [🌊]

AAA ▼▼ **Shasta Pines Motel** Ⓜ
(530) 335-2201. **$46-$95, 5 day notice.** 37386 Main St. 0.8 mi e on SR 299. Ext corridors. **Pets:** Very small. $100 deposit/pet. No service, supervision.
[SAVE] [S⊘] [✕] [⊙M] [⊟] [🖵] [🌊] [✕]

BUTTONWILLOW

▼ **Super 8 Motel** Ⓜ
(661) 764-5117. **$42-$49.** 20681 Tracy Ave. I-5, exit SR 58. Ext corridors. **Pets:** Small, dogs only. $10 daily fee/room. Designated rooms, service with restrictions, supervision.
[ASK] [S⊘] [✕] [✍] [⊟] [🌊]

CALIMESA

AAA ▼▼ **Calimesa Inn Motel** Ⓜ
(909) 795-2536. **$65-$70.** 1205 Calimesa Blvd. I-10, exit Calimesa Blvd, just ne. Ext corridors. **Pets:** Small. $6 daily fee/pet. Designated rooms, service with restrictions, crate.
[SAVE] [S⊘] [✕] [⊟] [🌊]

CALIPATRIA

▼▼▼ **Calipatria Inn** Ⓜ ✿
(760) 348-7348. **$66-$150.** 700 N Sorenson. On SR 111. Ext corridors. **Pets:** Large, other species. $10 deposit/room. Service with restrictions, supervision.
[ASK] [S⊘] [✕] [⊟] [🌊]

CAMBRIA

▼▼ **Cambria Shores Inn** Ⓜ ✿
(805) 927-8644. **$105-$180, 7 day notice.** 6276 Moonstone Beach Dr. SR 1, exit Moonstone Beach Dr, just w, then 0.8 mi s. Ext corridors. **Pets:** Dogs only. Service with restrictions, supervision.
[✕] [⊟] [🖵] [🎾]

▼▼▼ **Fog Catcher Inn** Ⓜ
(805) 927-1400. **$119-$309, 3 day notice.** 6400 Moonstone Beach Dr. SR 1, exit Moonstone Beach Dr, just w, then 0.7 mi s. Ext corridors. **Pets:** Other species. $25 daily fee/pet. Designated rooms, no service, supervision.
[ASK] [S⊘] [✕] [🖵] [🎾]

AAA ▼▼ **Mariners Inn by the Sea** Ⓜ ✿
(805) 927-4624. **$79-$239, 5 day notice.** 6180 Moonstone Beach Dr. SR 1, exit Moonstone Beach Dr, just w, then 1 mi s. Ext corridors. **Pets:** Dogs only. $15 daily fee/pet. Designated rooms, service with restrictions, supervision.
[SAVE] [✕] [⊟] [🎾]

▼▼▼ **Sea Otter Inn** Ⓜ
(805) 927-5888. **$99-$259, 3 day notice.** 6656 Moonstone Beach Dr. SR 1, exit Moonstone Beach Dr, just w, then 0.5 mi s. Ext corridors. **Pets:** Large, other species. $25 daily fee/pet. Designated rooms, service with restrictions, supervision.
[ASK] [S⊘] [✕] [⊟] [🖵] [🌊] [🎾]

CAMERON PARK

▼▼▼ **Best Western Cameron Park Inn** Ⓜ
(530) 677-2203. **$79-$149.** 3361 Coach Ln. 12 mi w of Placerville on US 50, exit Cameron Park Dr. Ext corridors. **Pets:** Accepted.
[ASK] [S⊘] [✕] [⊙M] [⊟] [🖵] [🌊]

CAMINO

▼▼ ▼▼ Camino Hotel-Seven Mile House 🅱🅱
(530) 644-7740. **$68-$98, 7 day notice.** 4103 Carson Rd.
US 50, exit at Camino, just n. Int corridors. **Pets:** Accepted.
Ⓐ🅂🄺 🅂🄳 ☒ 🄺 🄿 ☎

CAMPBELL

▼▼▼▼ Residence Inn By Marriott-San
        Jose Ⓜ ❀
(408) 559-1551. **$149-$179.** 2761 S Bascom Ave. SR 17,
exit Camden Ave E, just n. Ext corridors. **Pets:** Other species. $20 daily fee/room, $75 one-time fee/room. Service
with restrictions.
Ⓐ🅂🄺 🅂🄳 ☒ 💻 ☎

CAPITOLA

🅐🅐🅐 ▼▼▼▼ Best Western Capitola By-the-Sea Inn
        & Suites 🆂🄷 ❀
(831) 477-0607. **$79-$199.** 1435 41st Ave. SR 1, exit 41st
Ave, 4 blks w. Int corridors. **Pets:** Dogs only. $10 daily
fee/pet. Service with restrictions.
🆂🄰🅅🄴 🅂🄳 ☒ 🄼 🄹 🎫 💻 ☎

▼▼ ▼▼ Capitola Inn Ⓜ
(831) 462-3004. **$80-$135.** 822 Bay Ave. SR 1, exit Bay Ave,
just w. Ext/int corridors. **Pets:** Small, dogs only. $20 one-
time fee/pet. Designated rooms, service with restrictions,
supervision.
Ⓐ🅂🄺 🅂🄳 ☒ 🎫 ☎

CARLSBAD

🅐🅐🅐 ▼▼▼▼▼ Four Seasons Resort
        Aviara 🅻🅷 ❀
(760) 603-6800. **$405-$525, 3 day notice.** 7100 Four Seasons Point. I-5, exit Poinsettia Ln/Aviara Pkwy, 1 mi e on
Poinsettia Ln, then 1 mi s on Aviara Pkwy. Int corridors.
Pets: Small. $100 one-time fee/room. Service with restric-
tions.
🆂🄰🅅🄴 ☒ 💻 🄹 ☎ 🄭

🅐🅐🅐 ▼▼ ▼▼ Inns of America Ⓜ ❀
(760) 931-1185. **$89-$129.** 751 Raintree Dr. I-5, exit Poin-
setta Ln, just w to Ave Encinas, then just n. Ext corridors.
Pets: Medium, other species. $5 daily fee/pet. Service with
restrictions, supervision.
🆂🄰🅅🄴 🅂🄳 ☒ 🎫 🄹 ☎

▼▼ Motel 6–1021 Ⓜ
(760) 434-7135. **$47-$65.** 1006 Carlsbad Village Dr. I-5, exit
Carlsbad Village Dr, just w. Ext corridors. **Pets:** Accepted.
🅂🄳 ☒

CARPINTERIA

🅐🅐🅐 ▼▼▼▼▼ Comfort Suites 🆂🄷
(805) 566-9499. **$99-$199.** 5606 Carpinteria Ave. US 101,
exit Casitas Pass Rd, just s, then just e. Int corridors.
Pets: Accepted.
🆂🄰🅅🄴 🅂🄳 ☒ 🎫 💻 ☎

CASTAIC

🅐🅐🅐 ▼▼ ▼▼ Comfort Inn Ⓜ
(661) 295-1100. **$64-$94.** 31558 Castaic Rd. I-5, exit Parker
Rd northbound, 0.3 mi ne; exit Lake Hughes Rd southbound, 0.5 mi se. Ext corridors. **Pets:** $10 one-time fee/
room. Designated rooms, no service, supervision.
🆂🄰🅅🄴 🅂🄳 ☒ 🏊 🎫 💻 ☎

CATHEDRAL CITY

🅐🅐🅐 ▼▼ ▼▼ Comfort Suites Ⓜ
(760) 324-5939. **$49-$199.** 69-151 E Palm Canyon Dr. I-10,
exit Date Palm Dr, 5 mi s, then just e. Ext corridors.
Pets: Small. $10 daily fee/pet. Service with restrictions,
supervision.
🆂🄰🅅🄴 🅂🄳 ☒ 🎫 💻 ☎

🅐🅐🅐 ▼▼▼▼▼ Doral Desert Princess Resort, Palm
        Springs 🅻🅷
(760) 322-7000. **$69-$149, 3 day notice.** 67-967 Vista
Chino. I-10, exit Date Palm Dr, 0.5 mi s, then 1 mi w. Int
corridors. **Pets:** Small. $50 one-time fee/room. Designated
rooms, service with restrictions, supervision.
🆂🄰🅅🄴 🅂🄳 ☒ 🎫 💻 🄹 ☎ 🄭

CAYUCOS

▼▼▼▼ Cayucos Beach Inn Ⓜ ❀
(805) 995-2828. **$75-$175.** 333 S Ocean Ave. On SR 1
business route. Ext corridors. **Pets:** Other species. $10
daily fee/room. Crate.
☒ 🎫 💻

🅐🅐🅐 ▼▼ Cypress Tree Motel Ⓜ ❀
(805) 995-3917. **$39-$97.** 125 S Ocean Ave. On SR 1 business route. Ext corridors. **Pets:** Other species. $10 one-
time fee/room. Service with restrictions, crate.
🆂🄰🅅🄴 🅂🄳 ☒ 🎫 💻 🄺

🅐🅐🅐 ▼▼ Dolphin Inn Ⓜ
(805) 995-3810. **$59-$149, 3 day notice.** 399 S Ocean Ave.
On SR 1 business route. Ext corridors. **Pets:** Dogs only.
$10 one-time fee/pet. Service with restrictions, supervision.
🆂🄰🅅🄴 🅂🄳 ☒ 🎫 💻 🄺

🅐🅐🅐 ▼▼ Estero Bay Motel Ⓜ
(805) 995-3614. **$49-$145, 3 day notice.** 25 S Ocean Ave.
On SR 1 business route. Ext corridors. **Pets:** Medium. $15
one-time fee/pet. Service with restrictions, supervision.
🆂🄰🅅🄴 🅂🄳 ☒ 🎫 💻 🄺

🅐🅐🅐 ▼▼ Shoreline Inn Ⓜ
(805) 995-3681. **$80-$160.** 1 N Ocean Ave. On SR 1 business route. Ext corridors. **Pets:** $10 one-time fee/room.
Supervision.
🆂🄰🅅🄴 🅂🄳 ☒ 🎫 💻 🄺

CEDARVILLE

🅐🅐🅐 ▼▼ ▼▼ Sunrise Motel Ⓜ
(530) 279-2161. **$55-$60.** 54889 Hwy 299. 0.5 mi w on SR
299. Ext corridors. **Pets:** Small. $25 deposit/room, $10 daily
fee/pet. Designated rooms, service with restrictions, supervision.
🆂🄰🅅🄴 🅂🄳 ☒ 🎫 💻

CHICO

⚠ ▼▼▼ Deluxe Inn Ⓜ
(530) 342-8386. **$39-$69, 7 day notice.** 2507 Esplanade. 2 mi n on SR 99 business route. Ext corridors. **Pets:** Accepted.
⟦SAVE⟧ ⟦S⟧ ⟦✕⟧ ⟦🛏⟧ ⟦≈⟧

▼▼▼ Oxford Suites Ⓢ ❖
(530) 899-9090. **$79-$159.** 2035 Business Ln. SR 99, exit 20th St E. Int corridors. **Pets:** Small, dogs only. $25 one-time fee/pet. Service with restrictions, supervision.
⟦ASK⟧ ⟦S⟧ ⟦✕⟧ ⟦♿⟧ ⟦▣⟧ ⟦🛏⟧ ⟦▭⟧ ⟦≈⟧

⚠ ▼ Safari Garden Motel Ⓜ
(530) 343-3201. **$48.** 2352 Esplanade. 2 mi n on SR 99 business route. Ext corridors. **Pets:** Small, dogs only. Designated rooms, service with restrictions, supervision.
⟦SAVE⟧ ⟦S⟧ ⟦✕⟧ ⟦🛏⟧ ⟦▭⟧ ⟦≈⟧

⚠ ▼▼▼ Super 8 Motel Ⓜ
(530) 345-2533. **$70-$150.** 655 Manzanita Ct. Just w of SR 99, via Cohasset Rd. Int corridors. **Pets:** Small. $4 daily fee/pet. Designated rooms, no service, supervision.
⟦SAVE⟧ ⟦S⟧ ⟦✕⟧ ⟦🛏⟧ ⟦▭⟧ ⟦≈⟧

CHOWCHILLA

⚠ ▼▼ Days Inn Ⓜ
(559) 665-4821. **$58-$68.** 220 E Robertson Blvd. SR 99, exit Robertson Blvd W. Ext corridors. **Pets:** Other species. $10 daily fee/pet. Service with restrictions.
⟦SAVE⟧ ⟦S⟧ ⟦✕⟧ ⟦🛏⟧ ⟦▭⟧ ⟦≈⟧

CITRUS HEIGHTS

⚠ ▼▼▼▼ Olive Grove Inn & Suites Ⓜ
(916) 725-0100. **$99-$150.** 6143 Auburn Blvd. I-80, exit Greenback Ln, 1 mi s. Ext corridors. **Pets:** Accepted.
⟦SAVE⟧ ⟦S⟧ ⟦✕⟧ ⟦♿⟧

CLIO

▼▼ Molly's Bed & Breakfast Ⓑ ❖
(530) 836-4436. **$90-$110, 7 day notice.** 276 Lower Main St. Just e of SR 89. Int corridors. **Pets:** Large, dogs only. $10 daily fee/pet. Designated rooms, service with restrictions, supervision.
⟦ASK⟧ ⟦✕⟧ ⟦Ⓦ⟧ ⟦☎⟧

COALINGA

⚠ ▼▼▼▼ Best Western Big Country Inn Ⓜ
(559) 935-0866. **$79-$129.** 25020 W Dorris Ave. I-5, exit SR 198/Hanford-Lemoore, just w. Ext corridors. **Pets:** Small. $10 one-time fee/pet. Service with restrictions, supervision.
⟦SAVE⟧ ⟦S⟧ ⟦✕⟧ ⟦🛏⟧ ⟦▭⟧ ⟦≈⟧

⚠ ▼▼▼▼ The Inn at Harris Ranch Ⓢ
(559) 935-0717. **$116-$250.** 24505 W Dorris Ave. I-5, exit SR 198, just e; at Hanford-Lemoore off-ramp. Ext/int corridors. **Pets:** Accepted.
⟦SAVE⟧ ⟦S⟧ ⟦✕⟧ ⟦♿⟧ ⟦▭⟧ ⟦¶⟧ ⟦≈⟧

COLUMBIA

▼ Columbia Gem Motel Ⓒ
(209) 532-4508. **$79-$139, 7 day notice.** 22131 Parrotts Ferry Rd. 3 mi n of Sonora; 1 mi from Columbia State Historic Park. Ext corridors. **Pets:** Dogs only. Service with restrictions, supervision.
⟦✕⟧ ⟦🛏⟧ ⟦≈⟧

CONCORD

⚠ ▼▼▼▼ Holiday Inn Concord Ⓢ
(925) 687-5500. **$89-$129.** 1050 Burnett Ave. I-680, exit E Concord Ave, Diamond Ave S, Burnett Ave W. Ext/int corridors. **Pets:** $10 daily fee/room. Service with restrictions, supervision.
⟦SAVE⟧ ⟦S⟧ ⟦✕⟧ ⟦🛏⟧ ⟦▭⟧ ⟦¶⟧ ⟦≈⟧

⚠ ▼▼ Premier Inns Ⓜ
(925) 674-0888. **$57-$80.** 1581 Concord Ave. SR 242, exit Clayton Rd northbound; exit Concord Ave southbound, just e. Ext corridors. **Pets:** Accepted.
⟦SAVE⟧ ⟦S⟧ ⟦✕⟧ ⟦▣⟧ ⟦🛏⟧ ⟦≈⟧

CORNING

⚠ ▼▼▼ Amerihost Inn-Corning Ⓜ
(530) 824-5200. **$69-$99.** 910 Hwy 99 W. I-5, exit 631 (Solano St), just e. Int corridors. **Pets:** Accepted.
⟦SAVE⟧ ⟦S⟧ ⟦✕⟧ ⟦♿⟧ ⟦▣⟧ ⟦🛏⟧ ⟦▭⟧ ⟦≈⟧

⚠ ▼▼▼ Best Western Inn Corning Ⓜ
(530) 824-2468. **$65-$99.** 2165 Solano St. I-5 E, exit Corning, 1 blk e. Ext corridors. **Pets:** Medium. $10 daily fee/room. Designated rooms, service with restrictions, supervision.
⟦SAVE⟧ ⟦S⟧ ⟦✕⟧ ⟦♿⟧ ⟦🛏⟧ ⟦▭⟧ ⟦≈⟧

⚠ ▼▼▼ Days Inn Ⓜ ❖
(530) 824-2000. **$50-$130.** 3475 Hwy 99 W. I-5, exit South Ave, 0.3 mi s. Int corridors. **Pets:** Other species. $5 daily fee/pet. Service with restrictions, supervision.
⟦SAVE⟧ ⟦S⟧ ⟦✕⟧ ⟦♿⟧ ⟦▣⟧ ⟦🛏⟧ ⟦≈⟧

CORONA

⚠ ▼▼▼ Dynasty Suites Corona Ⓜ
(909) 371-7185. **$66-$78.** 1805 W 6th St. SR 91, exit 6th St eastbound; exit Maple St westbound, just s. Ext corridors. **Pets:** Accepted.
⟦SAVE⟧ ⟦S⟧ ⟦✕⟧ ⟦🛏⟧ ⟦▭⟧ ⟦≈⟧

COSTA MESA

▼▼▼ Costa Mesa Marriott Suites Ⓛ
(714) 957-1100. **$179-$189.** 500 Anton Blvd. I-405, exit Bristol St, just n, then 3 blks e. Int corridors. **Pets:** Accepted.
⟦S⟧ ⟦✕⟧ ⟦♿⟧ ⟦▨⟧ ⟦🛏⟧ ⟦▭⟧ ⟦≈⟧ ⟦⊠⟧

▼▼▼ Hilton Costa Mesa Ⓛ
(714) 540-7000. **$89-$240, 3 day notice.** 3050 Bristol St. I-405, exit Bristol St, just s. Int corridors. **Pets:** Accepted.
⟦ASK⟧ ⟦S⟧ ⟦✕⟧ ⟦🛏⟧ ⟦▭⟧ ⟦¶⟧ ⟦≈⟧ ⟦⊠⟧

La Quinta Inn M
(714) 957-5841. **$71-$86.** 1515 South Coast Dr. I-405, exit Harbor Blvd, just n, then just w. Ext corridors. **Pets:** Accepted.

[SAVE] [X] [🔌] [💻] [≈]

Ramada Limited & Suites SH
(949) 645-2221. **$94-$124.** 1680 Superior Ave. Just w of SR 55 (Newport Blvd) at 17th St. Ext corridors. **Pets:** Accepted.

[SAVE] [S&] [X] [🔌] [💻] [≈]

Residence Inn by Marriott SH ✿
(714) 241-8800. **$139-$199.** 881 W Baker St. SR 73, exit Bear St; SR 55, exit Baker St. Ext corridors. **Pets:** Other species. $10 daily fee/pet, $100 one-time fee/room. Designated rooms, service with restrictions, supervision.

[S&] [X] [🔌] [💻] [≈] [X]

Vagabond Inn M ✿
(714) 557-8360. **$63-$89.** 3205 Harbor Blvd. I-405, exit Harbor Blvd, just s; entrance from Gisler Ave, just w of Harbor. Ext corridors. **Pets:** Small. $5 daily fee/pet. Service with restrictions, supervision.

[ASK] [S&] [X] [🔌] [💻] [≈]

The Westin South Coast Plaza Hotel LH ✿
(714) 540-2500. **$320.** 686 Anton Blvd. I-405, exit Bristol St, just n, then just e. Int corridors. **Pets:** Medium. Service with restrictions, crate.

[ASK] [S&] [X] [💻] [🍴] [≈] [X]

Wyndham Orange County Airport LH
(714) 751-5100. **$84-$144.** 3350 Ave of the Arts. I-405, exit Bristol St, n to Anton Blvd, just e, then just n. Int corridors. **Pets:** Other species. $150 one-time fee/room. Designated rooms, service with restrictions, crate.

[SAVE] [S&] [X] [🎮] [🔌] [💻] [🍴] [≈]

CRESCENT CITY

Best Value Inn M
(707) 464-4141. **$55-$84.** 440 Hwy 101 N. On US 101. Ext corridors. **Pets:** Dogs only. $5 daily fee/pet. Service with restrictions, crate.

[ASK] [S&] [X] [🔌] [💻] [🐾]

Hiouchi Motel M
(707) 458-3041. **$55-$65.** 2097 Hwy 199. US 101, exit US 199, 5 mi e. Ext corridors. **Pets:** Accepted.

[ASK] [S&] [X] [🎮] [🐾] [🏊]

Super 8 M ✿
(707) 464-4111. **$45-$85.** 685 Hwy 101 S. E of US 101 S. Ext corridors. **Pets:** Small, dogs only. $10 daily fee/pet. Designated rooms, service with restrictions, supervision.

[SAVE] [S&] [X] [💻] [🐾]

CROMBERG

Long Valley Resort CA
(530) 836-0754. **$55-$75, 14 day notice.** 59532 Hwy 70. SR 70. Ext corridors. **Pets:** Other species. $7 daily fee/pet. Designated rooms, no service, supervision.

[X] [L&M] [🎮] [🔌] [💻] [X] [☎]

CYPRESS

Homestead Studio Suites Hotel-Cypress/Long Beach SH ✿
(714) 761-2766. **$84-$104.** 5990 Corporate Ave. I-605, exit Katella Ave, 3 mi e, 0.4 mi n on Valley View Ave, just w. Int corridors. **Pets:** Medium, other species. $25 daily fee/room. Service with restrictions, crate.

[ASK] [S&] [X] [🔌] [💻]

Woodfin Suite Hotel-Cypress SH
(714) 828-4000. **Call for rates.** 5905 Corporate Ave. I-605, exit Katella Ave, 3 mi e, then 0.4 mi n on Valley View Ave, just w. Int corridors. **Pets:** Accepted.

[S&] [X] [🔌] [💻] [≈]

DANA POINT

Laguna Cliffs Marriott Resort LH ✿
(949) 661-5000. **$298-$418, 3 day notice.** 25135 Park Lantern. I-5, exit Pacific Coast Hwy, just w on Harbor Dr. Int corridors. **Pets:** Large, other species. $75 one-time fee/room. Designated rooms, service with restrictions, supervision.

[SAVE] [S&] [X] [🔌] [💻] [🍴] [≈] [X]

The St. Regis Monarch Beach Resort & Spa LH ✿
(949) 234-3200. **$405-$875, 7 day notice.** One Monarch Beach Resort. I-5, exit Pacific Coast Hwy northbound, 3 mi n; exit Crown Valley Pkwy southbound, 3 mi s on Coast Hwy. Int corridors. **Pets:** Small, other species. Supervision.

[SAVE] [S&] [X] [L&M] [🎮] [🎮] [🍴] [≈] [X]

DAVIS

Best Western University Lodge M
(530) 756-7890. **$75-$95.** 123 B St. Just e of University of California Campus. Ext corridors. **Pets:** $10 daily fee/pet. Service with restrictions, supervision.

[SAVE] [S&] [X] [L&M] [🔌] [💻] [X]

Howard Johnson Hotel M
(530) 792-0800. **$79-$109.** 4100 Chiles Rd. I-80, exit Mace Blvd, just s, then 0.3 mi w. Int corridors. **Pets:** Medium, dogs only. $15 daily fee/room. Designated rooms, service with restrictions, supervision.

[SAVE] [S&] [X] [L&M] [🎮] [🔌] [💻] [🍴] [≈]

DELANO

Comfort Inn M
(661) 725-1022. **$60-$70.** 2211 Girard St. SR 99, exit County Line Rd, just e. Ext corridors. **Pets:** Very small. $10 daily fee/pet. No service, supervision.

[SAVE] [S&] [X] [🔌] [💻] [≈]

DIXON

Best Western Inn Dixon M
(707) 678-1400. **$95-$135.** 1345 Commercial Way. I-80, exit Pitt School Rd, 8 mi w of University of California Davis Campus. Ext/int corridors. **Pets:** Medium. $10 one-time fee/room. Designated rooms, service with restrictions, supervision.

[SAVE] [S&] [X] [L&M] [🎮] [🔌] [💻] [≈]

DOWNIEVILLE

◆ Riverside Inn **M**
(530) 289-1000. **$63-$70, 3 day notice.** 206 Commercial St. Downieville Hwy 49; center of town. Ext corridors. **Pets:** Other species. $10 one-time fee/pet. Service with restrictions, supervision.

DUBLIN

◆◆◆ ◆◆◆ AmeriSuites (San Francisco/Dublin) **SH**
(925) 828-9006. **$162.** 4950 Hacienda Dr. I-580, exit Hacienda Dr, then n. Int corridors. **Pets:** Supervision.

◆◆◆ ◆◆◆ Radisson Dublin **SH**
(925) 828-7750. **$109-$149.** 6680 Regional St. At northwest quadrant of I-580 and 680. Int corridors. **Pets:** $35 one-time fee/room. Designated rooms, service with restrictions, supervision.

DUNNIGAN

◆◆ Best Value Inn **M**
(530) 724-3333. **$63-$100.** 3930 Road 89. I-5, exit Dunnigan. Int corridors. **Pets:** Accepted.

◆◆◆ ◆◆◆ Best Western Country **M**
(530) 724-3471. **$69-$125.** 3930 Road 89. I-5, exit Dunnigan. Ext corridors. **Pets:** Accepted.

◆ Budget 8 Motel **M**
(530) 724-3411. **$45-$55.** 4930 CR 99 W. I-5, exit CR 8, just e. Ext corridors. **Pets:** Medium. $5 daily fee/pet. Service with restrictions, supervision.

DUNSMUIR

◆◆◆ ◆◆◆ Caboose Motel-Railroad Park Resort **M** ✿
(530) 235-4440. **$75-$100.** 100 Railroad Park Rd. I-5, exit 778 (Railroad Park Rd), 1 mi s. **Pets:** $10 daily fee/pet. Service with restrictions, supervision.

◆◆◆ ◆◆◆ Cedar Lodge Motel **M**
(530) 235-4331. **$52-$75, 4 day notice.** 4201 Dunsmuir Ave. I-5, exit 730 (Dunsmuir/Siskiyou), 0.5 mi w. Ext corridors. **Pets:** Accepted.

EL CENTRO

◆◆◆ ◆◆◆ Barbara Worth Golf Resort and Convention Center **SH**
(760) 356-2806. **$93-$99.** 2050 Country Club Dr. I-8, exit Bowker Rd, 2 mi n, then 3 mi e on CR S-80; 9 mi e of SR 86. Ext/int corridors. **Pets:** Small, other species.

◆◆◆ ◆◆◆ Ramada Inn El Centro **M**
(760) 352-5152. **$77.** 1455 Ocotillo Dr. I-8, exit Imperial Ave, just n, then just e. Ext corridors. **Pets:** Medium. Service with restrictions, supervision.

◆◆ Vacation Inn **M**
(760) 352-9700. **$59-$69, 3 day notice.** 2015 Cottonwood Cir. I-8, exit Imperial Ave, just n, then just w. Ext corridors. **Pets:** Small. $100 deposit/room. Service with restrictions, supervision.

EL PORTAL

◆◆◆ ◆◆◆ Yosemite View Lodge **M**
(209) 379-2681. **$85-$249, 7 day notice.** 11136 Hwy 140. Just w of Yosemite National Park West Gate. Ext corridors. **Pets:** Other species. $10 daily fee/pet. Service with restrictions, supervision.

ENCINITAS

◆◆◆ ◆◆◆ Best Western Encinitas Inn & Suites at Moonlight Beach **M**
(760) 942-7455. **$120-$150, 3 day notice.** 85 Encinitas Blvd. I-5, exit Encinitas Blvd, just w. Ext corridors. **Pets:** $50 one-time fee/room. Designated rooms, service with restrictions, supervision.

ESCONDIDO

◆◆◆ ◆◆◆ Best Western Escondido **SH**
(760) 740-1700. **$79-$119, 7 day notice.** 1700 Seven Oaks Rd. I-15, exit El Norte Pkwy, just e. Int corridors. **Pets:** Small. $25 one-time fee/room.

◆◆◆ ◆◆ Rodeway Inn **M**
(760) 746-0441. **$54-$120.** 250 W El Norte Pkwy. I-15, exit El Norte Pkwy, 1 mi e. Ext corridors. **Pets:** Medium. $100 deposit/room, $18 daily fee/pet. Designated rooms, service with restrictions, supervision.

◆◆◆ ◆◆◆ Welk Resort-San Diego **LH**
(760) 749-3000. **$120-$375, 3 day notice.** 8860 Lawrence Welk Dr. I-15, exit Deer Springs Rd northbound, just e, 2.7 mi n on Champagne Ave, then just e; exit Old Castle Rd southbound, just e, 1.5 mi s on Champagne Ave, then just e. Ext corridors. **Pets:** Accepted.

ETNA

◆ Motel Etna **M**
(530) 467-5330. **$42.** 317 Collier Way. Just w of SR 3. Ext corridors. **Pets:** Accepted.

EUREKA

◆◆◆ Bayview Motel **M** ✿
(707) 442-1673. **$75-$150.** 2844 Fairfield St. E of US 101, exit Henderson, at top of hill, just n. Ext corridors. **Pets:** Small. $5 daily fee/room. Designated rooms, service with restrictions, supervision.

▲▲▲ ◆◆◆ Best Western Bayshore Inn M ❀
(707) 268-8005. **$88-$149.** 3500 Broadway. US 101, s of Bayshore Mall. Ext corridors. **Pets:** Large, dogs only. $20 one-time fee/pet. Designated rooms, service with restrictions, supervision.
〔SAVE〕 〔S⬆〕 ✕ 〔✍〕 🖥 🖵 〔¶〕 ⇆ ✕

▲▲▲ ◆◆ Eureka Ramada Limited M
(707) 443-2206. **$69-$81.** 270 5th St. On US 101 northbound. Int corridors. **Pets:** Small. $25 deposit/room, $8 daily fee/pet. Service with restrictions, supervision.
〔SAVE〕 〔S⬆〕 ✕ 🖥 🖵 〔✍〕

▲▲▲ ◆ Eureka Town House Motel M
(707) 443-4536. **$45-$85.** 933 4th St. US 101 southbound, corner of 4th and K sts. Ext corridors. **Pets:** Medium, dogs only. $5 daily fee/pet. Designated rooms, service with restrictions, supervision.
〔SAVE〕 〔S⬆〕 ✕ 🖥 🖵 〔✍〕

◆◆ Eureka Travelodge M
(707) 443-6345. **$54-$150, 10 day notice.** 4 4th St. On US 101; corner of 4th and B sts. Ext corridors. **Pets:** Small, dogs only. $10 daily fee/pet. Designated rooms, service with restrictions, supervision.
〔ASK〕 〔S⬆〕 ✕ 🖥 🖵 ⇆ 〔✍〕

▲▲▲ ◆◆◆ Quality Inn Eureka M
(707) 443-1601. **$75-$200.** 1209 4th St. US 101 southbound, between M and N sts. Ext corridors. **Pets:** Accepted.
〔SAVE〕 〔S⬆〕 ✕ 🖥 🖵 ⇆ 〔✍〕

▲▲▲ ◆◆◆ Red Lion Hotel M ❀
(707) 445-0844. **$169-$179.** 1929 4th St. US 101 southbound; between T and V sts. Int corridors. **Pets:** Medium, other species. $15 one-time fee/room. Designated rooms, service with restrictions, supervision.
〔SAVE〕 〔S⬆〕 ✕ 〔✍〕 🖥 🖵 〔¶〕 ⇆

▲▲▲ ◆◆ Sunrise Inn & Suites M
(707) 443-9751. **$45-$69.** 129 4th St. US 101, exit C St southbound; exit C St W northbound; downtown. Ext corridors. **Pets:** $6 daily fee/pet. Service with restrictions, supervision.
〔SAVE〕 〔S⬆〕 ✕ 🖥 〔✍〕

FALLBROOK

▲▲▲ ◆◆◆ Best Western Franciscan Inn M
(760) 728-6174. **$73-$125.** 1635 S Mission Rd. I-15, exit CR S-13, 6.5 mi sw. Ext corridors. **Pets:** Small, other species. $10 one-time fee/room. Service with restrictions, supervision.
〔SAVE〕 〔S⬆〕 ✕ 🖥 🖵 ⇆

FALL RIVER MILLS

▲▲▲ ◆ Hi-Mont Motel M ❀
(530) 336-5541. **$45-$87, 3 day notice.** 43021 Bridge St. 1 mi w on SR 299. Ext corridors. **Pets:** Other species. $5 daily fee/pet. Service with restrictions, supervision.
〔SAVE〕 〔S⬆〕 ✕ 〔✍〕 🖥 🖵

◆◆ Pit River Lodge 〔CI〕
(530) 336-5005. **$115-$150, 14 day notice.** 24500 Pit One PowerHouse Rd. I-299 E, exit Pit One PowerHouse Rd. Int corridors. **Pets:** Accepted.
〔ASK〕 〔S⬆〕 ✕ 🖥 🖵 〔¶〕 〔▷〕

FERNDALE

◆◆◆ Collingwood Inn Bed & Breakfast 〔BB〕 ❀
(707) 786-9219. **$99-$203, 14 day notice.** 831 Main St. US 101, exit Ferndale, 5 mi w. Int corridors. **Pets:** Other species. $25 daily fee/pet. Crate.
〔ASK〕 〔S⬆〕 ✕ 〔✍〕 〔▷〕

FISH CAMP

◆◆◆ Apple Tree Inn 〔CA〕
(559) 683-5111. **$99-$209.** 1110 Hwy 41. 2 mi from South Gate to Yosemite National Park. Ext corridors. **Pets:** $50 one-time fee/pet. Designated rooms, service with restrictions, supervision.
〔ASK〕 〔S⬆〕 ✕ 〔M⬆〕 〔🅿〕 🖵 ⇆ ✕ 〔✍〕

◆◆ The Narrow Gauge Inn M ❀
(559) 683-7720. **$79-$195, 4 day notice.** 48571 Hwy 41. 4 mi from South Gate to Yosemite National Park. Ext corridors. **Pets:** Other species. $25 one-time fee/pet. Designated rooms, service with restrictions, supervision.
✕ 🖥 🖵 〔¶〕 ⇆

FORTUNA

▲▲▲ ◆◆◆ Best Western Country Inn M
(707) 725-6822. **$64-$110.** 2025 Riverwalk Dr. US 101, exit Kenmar Rd/Riverwalk Dr, just w. Ext corridors. **Pets:** Medium, dogs only. $10 one-time fee/room. Designated rooms, service with restrictions, supervision.
〔SAVE〕 〔S⬆〕 ✕ 〔M⬆〕 〔🅿〕 〔✍〕 🖥 🖵 ⇆

▲▲▲ ◆◆ Fortuna Super 8 M
(707) 725-2888. **$55-$95.** 1805 Alamar Way. US 101, exit Kenmar Rd/Riverwalk Dr, just w. Ext corridors. **Pets:** Small, dogs only. $10 daily fee/pet. Designated rooms, service with restrictions, supervision.
〔SAVE〕 〔S⬆〕 ✕ 〔✍〕 🖥 🖵

▲▲▲ ◆◆◆ Holiday Inn Express M ❀
(707) 725-5500. **$74-$179.** 1859 Alamar Way. US 101, exit Kenmar Rd/Riverwalk Dr, just w. Ext corridors. **Pets:** Small, dogs only. $20 deposit/pet, $10 daily fee/pet. Designated rooms, service with restrictions, supervision.
〔SAVE〕 〔S⬆〕 ✕ 🖥 🖵 ⇆ ✕

FOUNTAIN VALLEY

▲▲▲ ◆◆◆ Ramada Limited-Huntington Beach/ Fountain Valley M
(714) 847-3388. **$79-$89.** 9125 Recreation Cir. I-405, exit Warner Ave W northbound; exit Magnolia southbound, just w. Ext corridors. **Pets:** Medium. $25 deposit/pet, $20 daily fee/pet. Designated rooms, service with restrictions, supervision.
〔SAVE〕 〔S⬆〕 ✕ 🖥 🖵 ⇆

▼▼▼▼ **Residence Inn by Marriott** SH
(714) 965-8000. **$149-$199.** 9930 Slater Ave. I-405, exit Brookhurst St, just n, then just w. Ext corridors. **Pets:** Small. $10 daily fee/pet, $100 one-time fee/room.

[SAVE] [S🐾] [✕] [🖥] [💻] [�"] [✕]

FREMONT

▲▲▲ ▼▼▼▼ **AmeriSuites (Silicon Valley/Fremont)** SH 🐾
(510) 623-6000. **$69-$109.** 3101 W Warren Ave. I-880, exit Warren Ave/Mission Blvd, just w. Int corridors. **Pets:** Medium, other species. $25 one-time fee/room. Designated rooms, service with restrictions, supervision.

[SAVE] [S🐾] [✕] [&ᴹ] [🐾] [🖥] [💻] [�"]

▲▲▲ ▼▼▼▼ **Best Western Garden Court Inn** SH 🐾
(510) 792-4300. **$79-$159.** 5400 Mowry Ave. I-880, exit Mowry Ave, just e. Int corridors. **Pets:** Medium. $10 daily fee/room. Service with restrictions, supervision.

[SAVE] [S🐾] [✕] [🖥] [💻] [�"]

▼▼▼▼▼ **Crawford Suites** SH
(510) 651-7373. **$129-$189.** 42200 Albrae St. I-880, exit Automall Pkwy, just w, n on Christy, then e. Int corridors. **Pets:** $50 one-time fee/pet. Service with restrictions, crate.

[ASK] [S🐾] [✕] [🖥] [💻] [�"]

▲▲▲ ▼▼▼▼▼ **Fremont Marriott** LH
(510) 413-3700. **$69-$139.** 46100 Landing Pkwy. I-880, exit Fremont Blvd/Cushing Pkwy, then w. Int corridors. **Pets:** Small. $15 deposit/pet. Service with restrictions, crate.

[SAVE] [✕] [🐾] [🖥] [💻] [🍴] [�"]

▼▼▼▼ **Homestead Studio Suites Hotel-Fremont** SH 🐾
(510) 353-1664. **$77-$97.** 46080 Fremont Blvd. I-880, exit Fremont Blvd/Cushing Pkwy, just w. Int corridors. **Pets:** Medium, other species. $25 daily fee/room. Service with restrictions, crate.

[ASK] [S🐾] [✕] [🐾] [💻]

▼▼▼▼▼ **La Quinta Inn & Suites** SH 🐾
(510) 445-0808. **$90-$119.** 46200 Landing Pkwy. I-880, exit Fremont Blvd/Cushing Pkwy, just w. Int corridors. **Pets:** Other species. Service with restrictions.

[✕] [🐾] [🖥] [💻] [�"]

▼▼▼▼ **Residence Inn By Marriott** M
(510) 794-5900. **$129.** 5400 Farwell Pl. I-880, exit Mowry Ave, just e. Ext corridors. **Pets:** Accepted.

[ASK] [S🐾] [✕] [💻] [�"] [✕]

FRESNO

▲▲▲ ▼▼▼ **Days Inn-Parkway** M
(559) 268-6211. **$49-$99.** 1101 N Parkway Dr. SR 99, exit Olive St, just w. Ext corridors. **Pets:** Medium. $5 daily fee/pet. Service with restrictions, supervision.

[SAVE] [S🐾] [✕] [🖥] [�"]

▲▲▲ ▼▼▼▼ **Holiday Inn Express-Barcus** M
(559) 277-5700. **$99-$119.** 5046 N Barcus. SR 99, exit Shaw Ave, just e. Int corridors. **Pets:** Small. $20 one-time fee/room. Service with restrictions, supervision.

[SAVE] [S🐾] [✕] [&ᴹ] [🐾] [🖥] [💻] [�"]

▲▲▲ ▼ **Knights Inn** M 🐾
(559) 275-7766. **$49-$69.** 3093 N Parkway. SR 99, exit Shields Ave eastbound; exit Clinton northbound, just w. Ext corridors. **Pets:** $5 daily fee/pet. Designated rooms, service with restrictions, supervision.

[SAVE] [S🐾] [✕] [&ᴹ] [🖥] [💻] [�"]

▲▲▲ ▼▼▼▼ **La Quinta Inn** M
(559) 442-1110. **$72-$86.** 2926 Tulare St. SR 99, exit Fresno St, 2 mi e. Ext corridors. **Pets:** Medium. Service with restrictions, crate.

[SAVE] [✕] [&ᴹ] [🐾] [🖥] [💻] [�"]

▼▼ **Quality Inn** M
(559) 275-2727. **$99-$129.** 4278 W Ashlan Ave. SR 99, exit Ashlan Ave, just w. Ext corridors. **Pets:** Medium, dogs only. $20 daily fee/room. Designated rooms, service with restrictions.

[ASK] [S🐾] [✕] [🖥] [💻] [�"]

▼▼▼▼ **Radisson Hotel** LH
(559) 268-1000. **$104-$154.** 2233 Ventura St. SR 99, exit Ventura St, just e. Int corridors. **Pets:** Large. $50 one-time fee/room. Designated rooms, service with restrictions.

[ASK] [S🐾] [✕] [&ᴹ] [🐾] [🐾] [🖥] [💻] [🍴] [🚂] [✕]

▲▲▲ ▼▼▼ **Red Roof Inn** M
(559) 431-3557. **$50-$80.** 6730 N Blackstone Ave. SR 41, exit Herndon Ave, then w. Ext corridors. **Pets:** Service with restrictions, crate.

[SAVE] [S🐾] [✕] [🖥] [🚂]

▲▲▲ ▼ **Red Roof Inn** M
(559) 276-1910. **$56-$59.** 5021 N Barcus Ave. SR 99, exit Shaw Ave. Ext corridors. **Pets:** Small. Service with restrictions, supervision.

[SAVE] [S🐾] [✕] [🖥] [🚂]

▼▼▼▼ **Residence Inn by Marriott** M
(559) 222-8900. **$119-$124.** 5322 N Diana Ave. SR 41, exit Shaw Ave, 0.3 mi w, n on Blackstone Ave, then e on Barstow Ave. Int corridors. **Pets:** Other species. $5 daily fee/pet, $25 one-time fee/pet. Service with restrictions, supervision.

[ASK] [S🐾] [✕] [&ᴹ] [🐾] [🐾] [💻] [🚂] [✕]

▲▲▲ ▼▼▼ **Super 8-Downtown** M
(559) 268-0621. **$60-$80, 3 day notice.** 2127 Inyo St. SR 99, exit Ventura St, 0.5 mi e. Ext corridors. **Pets:** Very small. $10 daily fee/pet. Designated rooms, service with restrictions, crate.

[SAVE] [S🐾] [✕] [🐾] [🖥] [💻] [🚂]

▲▲▲ ▼▼▼ **Super 8-Parkway** M
(559) 268-0741. **$55-$85.** 1087 N Parkway Dr. SR 99, exit Olive Ave, just w. Ext corridors. **Pets:** $10 daily fee/pet. Service with restrictions, supervision.

[SAVE] [S🐾] [✕] [🖥] [💻] [🚂]

AAA ▼▼▼ TownePlace Suites by Marriott M
(559) 435-4600. **$69-$129.** 7127 N Fresno St. SR 41, exit Herndon Ave E. Int corridors. **Pets:** Accepted.
🅂🅰🅴 ⬛ ⬛ ⬛ ⬛ ⬛ ⬛ ⬛ ⬛

AAA ▼▼ Travelodge M
(559) 276-7745. **$64-$129.** 3093 N Parkway. SR 99, exit Sheilds Ave southbound; exit Clinton northbound, just w. Ext corridors. **Pets:** Accepted.
🅂🅰🅴 ⬛ ⬛ ⬛ ⬛ ⬛

AAA ▼ University Inn M
(559) 294-0224. **$52-$85.** 2655 E Shaw Ave. SR 41, exit Shaw Ave, 1.5 mi e. Ext corridors. **Pets:** Accepted.
🅂🅰🅴 ⬛ ⬛ ⬛ ⬛

AAA ▼ Villager Lodge M
(559) 233-3913. **$35-$45.** 933 N Parkway Dr. SR 99, exit Olive Ave, then w. Ext corridors. **Pets:** Small, dogs only. $5 daily fee/room. Designated rooms, service with restrictions, crate.
🅂🅰🅴 ⬛ ⬛

FULLERTON

AAA ▼▼▼ Fullerton Inn M
(714) 773-4900. **$65-$75.** 2601 W Orangethorpe Ave. SR 91, exit Magnolia Ave, just n, then just e. Ext corridors. **Pets:** Very small. $10 daily fee/pet. Designated rooms, service with restrictions, supervision.
🅂🅰🅴 ⬛ ⬛ ⬛ ⬛

▼▼▼ Fullerton Marriott Hotel at California State Univ SH
(714) 738-7800. **$79-$149.** 2701 E Nutwood Ave. SR 57, just w. Int corridors. **Pets:** Accepted.
🄰🅂🄺 ⬛ ⬛ ⬛ ⬛ ⬛ ⬛ ⬛ ⬛

GALT

AAA ▼ Royal Delta Inn M
(209) 745-9181. **$51.** 1040 N Lincoln Way. SR 99, exit Pringle Ave. Ext corridors. **Pets:** Small, dogs only. Service with restrictions, supervision.
🅂🅰🅴 ⬛ ⬛ ⬛

GARBERVILLE

AAA ▼▼▼ Best Western Humboldt House Inn M
(707) 923-2771. **$85-$125.** 701 Redwood Dr. US 101, 1st exit. Ext corridors. **Pets:** Other species. Designated rooms, service with restrictions, supervision.
🅂🅰🅴 ⬛ ⬛ ⬛ ⬛ ⬛

AAA ▼▼ Motel Garberville M
(707) 923-2422. **$49-$79.** 948 Redwood Dr. On US 101 business route. Ext corridors. **Pets:** Accepted.
🅂🅰🅴 ⬛ ⬛ ⬛ ⬛

AAA ▼▼▼ Sherwood Forest Motel M
(707) 923-2721. **$76-$96.** 814 Redwood Dr. On US 101 business route. Ext corridors. **Pets:** Small. Designated rooms, no service, supervision.
🅂🅰🅴 ⬛ ⬛ ⬛ ⬛ ⬛

GARDEN GROVE

▼▼▼ Anaheim Marriott Suites SH
(714) 750-1000. **$119-$199.** 12015 Harbor Blvd. I-5, exit Chapman Ave, 1.5 mi w, then just s. Int corridors. **Pets:** Other species. $15 daily fee/pet. Designated rooms, service with restrictions, supervision.
🄰🅂🄺 ⬛ ⬛ ⬛ ⬛ ⬛ ⬛ ⬛

▼▼▼ Candlewood Suites Anaheim-South SH
(714) 539-4200. **$110-$170.** 12901 Garden Grove Blvd. SR 22, exit Haster St westbound, just w; exit Fairview St eastbound, just nw. Int corridors. **Pets:** Large, other species. $75 one-time fee/pet. Service with restrictions, supervision.
🄰🅂🄺 ⬛ ⬛ ⬛ ⬛

AAA ▼▼▼ Residence Inn Anaheim Resort Area SH ✿
(714) 591-4000. **$129-$369, 3 day notice.** 11931 Harbor Blvd. I-5, exit The City Dr/Chapman Ave, 1 mi w on Chapman Ave, then just n. Int corridors. **Pets:** Large. $10 daily fee/room, $150 one-time fee/room. Service with restrictions, crate.
🅂🅰🅴 ⬛ ⬛ ⬛ ⬛ ⬛ ⬛ ⬛ ⬛ ⬛

GILROY

AAA ▼▼▼ Comfort Inn M
(408) 848-3500. **$59-$159.** 8292 Murray Ave. US 101, exit Leavesley Rd, just w. Ext corridors. **Pets:** Accepted.
🅂🅰🅴 ⬛ ⬛ ⬛ ⬛ ⬛ ⬛

AAA ▼▼▼ Leavesley Inn M
(408) 847-5500. **$68-$75.** 8430 Murray Ave. US 101, exit Leavesley Rd, just w. Ext corridors. **Pets:** Accepted.
🅂🅰🅴 ⬛ ⬛ ⬛ ⬛

GLENNVILLE

▼▼ The Bunkhouse Motel M
(661) 536-9100. **$65-$75.** 12044 Hwy 15 S. On SR 155 at Granite Rd. Ext corridors. **Pets:** $10 deposit/pet. Service with restrictions, supervision.
🄰🅂🄺 ⬛ ⬛ ⬛ ⬛ ⬛

GRASS VALLEY

AAA ▼▼▼ Alta Sierra Village Inn M ✿
(530) 273-9102. **$64-$185, 10 day notice.** 11858 Tammy Way. 6 mi s, 1.1 mi e on Alta Sierra Dr, 0.8 mi w on Norlene, 0.5 mi e on Tammy, follow signs to Alta Sierra Country Club. Ext corridors. **Pets:** $10 one-time fee/room. Designated rooms, service with restrictions, supervision.
🅂🅰🅴 ⬛ ⬛ ⬛ ⬛ ⬛

AAA ▼▼▼ Best Western Gold Country Inn M
(530) 273-1393. **$98-$119.** 11972 Sutton Way. SR 20 and 49, exit Brunswick Rd, just e; midway between Grass Valley and Nevada City. Ext corridors. **Pets:** Medium, other species. $10 daily fee/pet. Service with restrictions, supervision.
🅂🅰🅴 ⬛ ⬛ ⬛ ⬛ ⬛ ⬛

🏛 ▼ Coach N' Four Motel M
(530) 273-8009. **$60-$122, 3 day notice.** 628 S Auburn St. SR 49, exit E Empire St, 0.3 mi e, then just s. Ext corridors. **Pets:** Medium, other species. $50 deposit/room, $10 one-time fee/pet. Designated rooms, service with restrictions, supervision.
SAVE S6 ✕ ⅏ᴹ 🖩

🏛 ▼ Golden Chain Resort Motel M
(530) 273-7279. **$62-$102.** 13413 SR 49. 2.5 mi s on SR 49. Ext corridors. **Pets:** Medium. $10 one-time fee/room. Service with restrictions, supervision.
SAVE S6 ✕ ⅏ᴹ 🖩 🖳 ⇌

▼▼▼ Grass Valley Courtyard Suites M ❀
(530) 272-7696. **$115-$260, 3 day notice.** 210 N Auburn St. SR 49, exit Central Grass Valley. Ext corridors. **Pets:** Dogs only. $25 one-time fee/pet. Service with restrictions, supervision.
ASK S6 ✕ ⅏ᴹ 🖫 🖩 🖳 ⇌ ✕

GRIDLEY

🏛 ▼▼ Gridley Inn M
(530) 846-4520. **$69-$89.** 1490 Hwy 99, Suite A. 1 mi s on SR 99. Ext corridors. **Pets:** Accepted.
SAVE S6 ✕ 🖩 🖳 ⇌

🏛 ▼▼ Pacific Motel M
(530) 846-4580. **$50-$60.** 1308 Hwy 99. 1 mi s on SR 99. Ext corridors. **Pets:** Accepted.
SAVE ✕ 🖩 🖳 ⇌

GROVELAND

🏛 ▼▼ Best Value Yosemite Westgate BuckMeadows Lodge M
(209) 962-5281. **$69-$179, 3 day notice.** 7633/7647 Hwy 120. On SR 120, 12 mi e. Ext corridors. **Pets:** Large. $10 daily fee/room. Designated rooms, service with restrictions, supervision.
SAVE S6 ✕ 🖩 🖳 ⇌

🏛 ▼▼▼ Groveland Hotel at Yosemite National Park CI
(209) 962-4000. **$165.** 18767 Main St. Center. Int corridors. **Pets:** Accepted.
SAVE ✕ 🖳 🍽

HANFORD

🏛 ▼▼▼ Sequoia Inn SH
(559) 582-0338. **$65-$105.** 1655 Mall Dr. SR 198, exit 12th Ave, then n. Int corridors. **Pets:** $100 deposit/room. Service with restrictions, crate.
SAVE S6 ✕ 🖩 🖳 ⇌

HAYWARD

🏛 ▼▼▼ La Quinta Inn & Suites SH
(510) 732-6300. **$79-$109.** 20777 Hesperian Blvd. I-880, exit A St, 0.5 mi w. Int corridors. **Pets:** Accepted.
SAVE S6 ✕ 🖫 🖩 🖳 ⇌

🏛 ▼▼▼ MainStay Suites SH
(510) 731-3571. **$69-$129.** 835 West A St. I-880, exit A St, just w. Int corridors. **Pets:** Other species. $100 deposit/room, $15 daily fee/pet. Service with restrictions.
SAVE S6 ✕ 🖫 🖳 ⇌

HEMET

🏛 ▼▼▼ Best Western Inn of Hemet M
(909) 925-6605. **$70-$94.** 2625 W Florida Ave. 2.4 mi w of SR 79 N (San Jacinto St) on SR 74/79. Ext corridors. **Pets:** Medium. $20 one-time fee/pet. Service with restrictions, supervision.
SAVE S6 ✕ 🖩 🖳 ⇌ ✕

🏛 ▼▼ Coach Light Motel M
(909) 658-3237. **$50-$59.** 1640 W Florida Ave. 1.7 mi w of SR 74 N (San Jacinto St) on SR 74/79. Ext corridors. **Pets:** Dogs only. $5 daily fee/pet. No service, supervision.
SAVE S6 ✕ 🖩 ⇌

HESPERIA

🏛 ▼▼▼ Days Inn Suites-Hesperia/Victorville M
(760) 948-0600. **$59-$89.** 14865 Bear Valley Rd. I-15, exit Bear Valley Rd, 0.5 mi e of Victor Valley Mall. Ext corridors. **Pets:** Accepted.
SAVE S6 ✕ 🖩 🖳

▼▼▼ Holiday Inn Express Hotel & Suites SH
(760) 244-7674. **$59-$119.** 9750 Key Point Ave. I-15, exit Main St, just w, then just n. Int corridors. **Pets:** Accepted.
ASK S6 ✕ ⅏ᴹ ⌨ 🖫 🖩 🖳 ⇌

🏛 ▼▼▼ Super 8 Motel M
(760) 949-3231. **$49-$89, 3 day notice.** 12033 Oakwood Ave. I-15, exit Bear Valley Rd, just se. Ext corridors. **Pets:** $10 one-time fee/pet. Service with restrictions, supervision.
SAVE S6 ✕ 🖩 🖳 ⇌

HUNTINGTON BEACH

🏛 ▼▼▼ ▼▼▼ Hilton Waterfront Beach Resort LH
(714) 845-8000. **$189-$329, 3 day notice.** 21100 Pacific Coast Hwy. I-405, exit Beach Blvd, 6 mi s, then just w. Int corridors. **Pets:** Very small. $100 deposit/pet. Service with restrictions, supervision.
SAVE ✕ 🖩 🖳 🍽 ⇌ ✕

IDYLLWILD

▼▼ Fireside Inn CA
(909) 659-2966. **$60-$125, 10 day notice.** 54540 N Circle Dr. From SR 243 and town center, 0.3 mi ne. Ext corridors. **Pets:** Other species. Supervision.
✕ 🖩 🖳 🖫

IMPERIAL

▼▼ Imperial Valley Inn M
(760) 355-4500. **$59-$79.** 1093 Airport Blvd. On SR 86. Ext corridors. **Pets:** Accepted.
ASK S6 ✕ 🖩 🖳 🍽 ⇌ ✕

INDEPENDENCE

(AAA) 🔷 Ray's Den Motel M
(760) 878-2122. **$49-$72.** 405 N Edwards. On US 395. Ext corridors. **Pets:** Dogs only. $6 daily fee/room. Service with restrictions, supervision.
[SAVE] [S💰] [✕] [📵] [💻]

INDIO

(AAA) 🔷🔷 Best Western Date Tree
Hotel M ❀
(760) 347-3421. **$49-$150.** 81-909 Indio Blvd. I-10, exit Monroe St westbound, 0.5 mi s; exit Indio Blvd eastbound, 2.4 mi s. Int corridors. **Pets:** Large. $50 deposit/room, $10 one-time fee/pet. Designated rooms, service with restrictions, supervision.
[SAVE] [S💰] [✕] [📵] [💻] [🔜] [✕]

🔷🔷 Palm Shadow Inn M
(760) 347-3476. **$59-$144.** 80-761 Hwy 111. I-10, exit Jefferson Ave, 2.5 mi s, then 0.7 mi e. Ext corridors. **Pets:** Accepted.
[ASK] [S💰] [✕] [📵] [💻] [🔜] [✕]

(AAA) 🔷🔷 Quality Inn M
(760) 347-4044. **$79-$159.** 43-505 Monroe St. I-10, exit Monroe St, 0.5 mi s. Int corridors. **Pets:** $10 daily fee/room. Service with restrictions, supervision.
[SAVE] [S💰] [✕] [📵] [💻] [🔜]

🔷🔷 Royal Plaza Inn SH
(760) 347-0911. **$49-$129, 3 day notice.** 82-347 Hwy 111. I-10, exit Monroe St, 1.8 mi s, then 0.4 mi e. Int corridors. **Pets:** Medium, other species. $5 daily fee/pet. Service with restrictions, supervision.
[ASK] [S💰] [✕] [📵] [🍴] [🔜]

(AAA) 🔷 Super 8 Motel M
(760) 342-0264. **$55-$120.** 81753 Hwy 111. I-10, exit Monroe St, 1.8 mi s, 0.5 mi w. Ext corridors. **Pets:** Other species. $50 deposit/pet, $10 daily fee/pet. Service with restrictions, supervision.
[SAVE] [S💰] [✕] [📵] [💻] [🔜]

IRVINE

🔷🔷🔷 Candlewood Suites-Irvine Spectrum SH
(949) 788-0500. **$79-$149.** 16150 Sand Canyon Ave. I-5, exit Sand Canyon Ave, 1.4 mi w to Hospital Rd, 0.3 mi s. Int corridors. **Pets:** Medium. $150 one-time fee/pet. Service with restrictions, supervision.
[ASK] [S💰] [✕] [📵] [💻] [✕]

(AAA) 🔷🔷🔷 Hilton Irvine/Orange County
Airport LH ❀
(949) 833-9999. **$164-$234.** 18800 MacArthur Blvd. I-405, exit MacArthur Blvd, 0.5 mi s. Int corridors. **Pets:** Large. $50 one-time fee/room. Designated rooms, service with restrictions.
[SAVE] [✕] [📵] [💻] [🍴] [🔜] [✕]

🔷🔷🔷 Irvine Marriott Hotel LH
(949) 553-0100. **$189-$209.** 18000 Von Karman Ave. I-405, exit Jamboree Rd, 0.3 mi s to Michelson Dr, 0.4 mi w, then just n. Int corridors. **Pets:** Accepted.
[S💰] [✕] [📵] [💻] [🍴] [🔜] [✕]

🔷🔷🔷 La Quinta Inn Irvine Spectrum M
(949) 551-0909. **$86-$102.** 14972 Sand Canyon Ave. I-5, exit Sand Canyon Ave, just w. Ext/int corridors. **Pets:** Accepted.
[✕] [📵] [💻] [🔜]

🔷🔷🔷 Residence Inn by Marriott-Irvine
Spectrum SH
(949) 380-3000. **$149-$199.** 10 Morgan. I-5, exit Alton Pkwy, 2 mi e. Ext corridors. **Pets:** Medium, other species. $10 daily fee/pet, $60 one-time fee/room. Service with restrictions.
[S💰] [✕] [📵] [💻] [🔜] [✕]

JACKSON

(AAA) 🔷 Amador Motel M ❀
(209) 223-0970. **$54-$66, 5 day notice.** 12408 Kennedy Flat Rd. 1.5 mi n at jct SR 49 and 88 on Frontage Rd. Ext corridors. **Pets:** Large, other species. Service with restrictions, supervision.
[SAVE] [✕] [📵] [💻] [🔜]

(AAA) 🔷🔷🔷 Best Western Amador Inn SH
(209) 223-0211. **$85-$119.** 200 S Hwy 49. On SR 49. Int corridors. **Pets:** Small, dogs only. $10 daily fee/pet. Service with restrictions, supervision.
[SAVE] [S💰] [✕] [📵] [💻] [🔜]

JAMESTOWN

(AAA) 🔷🔷🔷 1859 Historic National Hotel, A
Country Inn CI ❀
(209) 984-3446. **$90-$140, 3 day notice.** 18183 Main St. Downtown. Int corridors. **Pets:** Medium. $10 daily fee/pet. Service with restrictions, supervision.
[SAVE] [✕] [🍴]

🔷🔷🔷 Country Inn Sonora M
(209) 984-0315. **$64-$159.** 18730 Hwy 108. On SR 108 and 49, 1 mi e of town. Ext corridors. **Pets:** Medium. $10 daily fee/pet. Designated rooms, service with restrictions.
[ASK] [S💰] [✕] [📵] [🔜]

(AAA) 🔷 Jamestown Railtown Motel M
(209) 984-3332. **$69-$85, 3 day notice.** 10301 Willow St. Just s of Main St. Ext corridors. **Pets:** Medium, dogs only. $10 one-time fee/pet. Designated rooms, crate.
[SAVE] [S💰] [✕] [📵] [🔜]

JULIAN

(AAA) 🔷🔷🔷 The Julian Homestead BB
(760) 765-1536. **$135-$200, 7 day notice.** 4924 Hwy 79. 4.5 mi s of SR 78. Ext/int corridors. **Pets:** Accepted.
[SAVE] [S💰] [✕] [W] [Z]

JUNE LAKE

(AAA) 🔷🔷🔷 Double Eagle Resort/Spa,
Inc CA ❀
(760) 648-7004. **$287-$319, 30 day notice.** 5587 Hwy 158. On SR 158, 3 mi w of the village. Ext corridors. **Pets:** $15 daily fee/pet. Service with restrictions, supervision.
[SAVE] [S💰] [✕] [📵] [💻] [🍴] [🔜] [✕] [🎾]

▼▼ **Gull Lake Lodge** Ⓜ
(760) 648-7516. **$65-$149, 14 day notice.** 132 Leonard Ave. Just n of SR 158; via Knoll and Bruce sts. Ext corridors. **Pets:** Other species. Designated rooms, service with restrictions, supervision.

✕ 🛏 📋 Ⓚ Ⓩ

KERNVILLE

🔷🔷🔷 🔷🔷🔷 **River View Lodge** Ⓜ ❀
(760) 376-6019. **$79-$129, 14 day notice.** 2 Sirretta St. On Kernville Rd, at the bridge; center. Ext corridors. **Pets:** Medium, dogs only. $10 one-time fee/pet. Designated rooms, service with restrictions, supervision.

SAVE Sᴅ ✕ 🛏

KETTLEMAN CITY

🔷🔷🔷 🔷🔷🔷 **Best Western Kettleman Inn and Suites** Ⓜ ❀
(559) 386-0804. **$72-$159.** 33410 Powers Dr. E of and adjacent to I-5, exit SR 41 N, 0.3 mi to Bernard, then 0.3 mi n. Ext corridors. **Pets:** Medium, other species. $6 daily fee/pet. Service with restrictions.

SAVE Sᴅ ✕ 🛏 📋 🖘

▼▼ **Super 8** Ⓜ ❀
(559) 386-9530. **$55-$65.** 33415 Powers Dr. E of and adjacent to I-5, exit SR 41 N, 0.3 mi to Bernard, then 0.3 mi n. Ext corridors. **Pets:** Other species. $40 deposit/room. Service with restrictions, supervision.

ASK Sᴅ ✕ Ⓕ 🖘

KING CITY

▼▼ **Courtesy Inn** Ⓜ ❀
(831) 385-4646. **$39-$119.** 4 Broadway Cir. US 101, exit Broadway, just w. Ext corridors. **Pets:** Small. $10 daily fee/room. Designated rooms, service with restrictions, supervision.

ASK Sᴅ ✕ ♿ᴹ 🐾 Ⓕ 🛏 📋 🖘

KINGSBURG

🔷🔷🔷 🔷🔷🔷 **Swedish Inn** Ⓜ
(559) 897-1022. **$68-$129.** 401 Conejo St. SR 99, exit Conejo St, just w. Ext corridors. **Pets:** Medium, other species. $50 deposit/pet. Designated rooms, service with restrictions, supervision.

SAVE Sᴅ ✕ 🛏 📋 🖘

KLAMATH

🔷🔷🔷 🔷🔷🔷 **Motel Trees** Ⓜ
(707) 482-3152. **$48-$86.** 15495 Hwy 101 N. 4 mi n on US 101. Ext corridors. **Pets:** $20 daily fee/pet. Service with restrictions, supervision.

SAVE Sᴅ ✕ 🛏 📋 Ⓚ

KYBURZ

🔷🔷🔷 🔷🔷🔷 **Kyburz Resort Motel** Ⓜ
(530) 293-3382. **$60-$90.** 13660 Hwy 50. On US 50, halfway between Placerville and South Lake Tahoe. Ext corridors. **Pets:** Accepted.

SAVE ✕ ♿ᴹ Ⓚ

LAGUNA BEACH

🔷🔷🔷 🔷🔷🔷🔷 **Best Western Laguna Brisas Spa Hotel** Ⓜ
(949) 497-7272. **$99-$269.** 1600 S Coast Hwy. SR 133, 1 mi s on SR 1. Ext/int corridors. **Pets:** Small. $50 daily fee/pet. Service with restrictions, supervision.

SAVE Sᴅ ✕ 🛏 📋 🖘

🔷🔷🔷🔷 **The Carriage House-Bed & Breakfast** Ⓑ Ⓑ
(949) 494-8945. **$140-$180, 3 day notice.** 1322 Catalina St. SR 133, 1 mi s on S Coast Hwy to Cress St, then just e. Ext corridors. **Pets:** $10 daily fee/pet. Service with restrictions, supervision.

✕ 🛏 📋 Ⓚ Ⓩ

🔷🔷🔷 🔷🔷🔷 **Casa Laguna Inn** Ⓑ Ⓑ ❀
(949) 494-2996. **$105-$350, 5 day notice.** 2510 S Coast Hwy. SR 133, 1.3 mi s on SR 1. Ext corridors. **Pets:** Other species. $25 daily fee/pet. Service with restrictions, supervision.

SAVE Sᴅ ✕ 🛏 📋 🖘

LAKE ARROWHEAD

🔷🔷🔷 🔷🔷🔷🔷 **Arrowhead Saddleback Inn** Ⓒ Ⓘ
(909) 336-3571. **$89-$218, 7 day notice.** On SR 173, jct SR 189; across from entrance to Lake Arrowhead Village. Ext/int corridors. **Pets:** Other species. $8 daily fee/pet. Designated rooms, service with restrictions, supervision.

SAVE ✕ 🛏 📋 🍴

🔷🔷🔷🔷 **Chateau du Lac Bed & Breakfast Inn** Ⓑ Ⓑ
(909) 337-6488. **$159-$225, 7 day notice.** 911 Hospital Rd. 3 mi ne of Lake Arrowhead Village via SR 173. Ext/int corridors. **Pets:** Accepted.

ASK Sᴅ ✕ ✕ Ⓚ

🔷🔷🔷🔷 **Fleur de LAC European Inn** Ⓑ Ⓑ
(909) 336-4612. **$153-$252.** 285 Hwy 173. Just s of SR 189 via Mittry Ln. Ext corridors. **Pets:** Accepted.

ASK Sᴅ ✕ Ⓚ Ⓩ

🔷🔷🔷 **Lake Arrowhead Resort** Ⓛ Ⓗ
(909) 336-1511. **$119-$209, 7 day notice.** 27984 Hwy 189. Just w of SR 173; in Lake Arrowhead Village. Int corridors. **Pets:** Medium. Designated rooms, service with restrictions.

ASK Sᴅ ✕ 🛏 📋 🍴 🖘 ✕

🔷🔷🔷🔷 **Storybook Inn** Ⓑ Ⓑ ❀
(909) 337-0011. **$89-$299, 7 day notice.** 28717 SR 18. SR 18, 1.1 mi e of jct SR 173. Ext/int corridors. **Pets:** Other species.

ASK Sᴅ ✕ 🍴 ✕ Ⓚ

LAKE FOREST

🔷🔷🔷🔷 **Candlewood Suites-Irvine East** Ⓢ Ⓗ
(949) 598-9105. **$108-$169.** 3 S Pointe Dr. I-5, exit Bake Pkwy, 2.6 mi e, just s. Int corridors. **Pets:** Accepted.

ASK Sᴅ ✕ 🛏 📋

LAKE TAHOE AREA

KINGS BEACH

🆎 🚩 Stevenson's Holliday Inn Ⓜ
(530) 546-2269. **$69-$129, 7 day notice.** 8742 N Lake Blvd. SR 28, 1 mi e of SR 267. Ext corridors. **Pets:** Accepted.

[SAVE] [S🔟] [✕] [🔟M] [🔟] [🔟] [🔟]

SOUTH LAKE TAHOE

🆎 🚩🚩 3 Peaks Resort & Beach Club Ⓜ
(530) 544-4131. **$69-$199, 10 day notice.** 931 Park Ave. 6 blks w of casino center; 2 blks n off US 50 toward lake at Park and Manzanita aves. Ext corridors. **Pets:** Accepted.

[SAVE] [✕] [🔟] [🔟] [🔟] [🔟]

🆎 🚩🚩 Alder Inn Ⓜ ❀
(530) 544-4485. **$65-$140, 15 day notice.** 1072 Ski Run Blvd. 2.5 blks s off US 50 on Ski Run Blvd; 0.8 mi below Heavenly Valley ski lift terminal. Ext corridors. **Pets:** Other species. Supervision.

[SAVE] [S🔟] [✕] [🔟] [🔟] [🔟] [🔟]

🆎 🚩🚩 Alpenrose Inn Ⓜ
(530) 544-2985. **$50-$130, 7 day notice.** 4074 Pine Blvd. 0.3 mi n of US 50 via Park Ave. Ext corridors. **Pets:** Accepted.

[SAVE] [S🔟] [✕] [🔟] [🔟]

🆎 🚩🚩 Ambassador Motor Lodge Ⓜ
(530) 544-6461. **$45-$110.** 4130 Manzanita Ave. Just s of US 50 on Stateline Ave. Ext corridors. **Pets:** Medium. $10 daily fee/pet. Designated rooms, no service, supervision.

[SAVE] [✕] [🔟] [🔟] [🔟] [🔟]

🆎 🚩🚩🚩 Best Western Timber Cove Lodge Ⓜ
(530) 541-6722. **$79-$215.** 3411 Lake Tahoe Blvd. 1.5 mi w of casino center, 0.5 mi w of Ski Run Blvd. Ext corridors. **Pets:** Accepted.

[SAVE] [S🔟] [✕] [🔟M] [🔟] [🔟] [🔟] [🔟] [🔟]

🆎 🚩🚩 Blue Jay Lodge Ⓜ
(530) 544-5232. **$59-$109.** 4133 Cedar Ave. 2 blks from casino center. Ext corridors. **Pets:** Accepted.

[SAVE] [S🔟] [✕] [🔟M] [🔟] [🔟] [🔟] [🔟]

🆎 🚩 Budget Inn Ⓜ
(530) 544-2834. **$35-$150, 3 day notice.** 3496 Lake Tahoe Blvd. On US 50, 1.5 mi w of casino center. Ext corridors. **Pets:** Medium, dogs only. $50 deposit/pet. Designated rooms, service with restrictions, supervision.

[SAVE] [S🔟] [✕] [🔟] [🔟]

🆎 🚩 Cal Va Rado Motel Ⓜ
(530) 541-3900. **$39-$79.** 988 Stateline Ave. Just n of US 50; near casino center. Ext corridors. **Pets:** Medium, other species. Designated rooms, service with restrictions, supervision.

[SAVE] [S🔟] [✕] [🔟] [🔟]

🆎 🚩 Capri Motel Ⓜ
(530) 544-3665. **$45-$100.** 932 Stateline Ave. Just s of US 50. Ext corridors. **Pets:** Medium. $10 daily fee/pet. Designated rooms, no service.

[SAVE] [✕] [🔟] [🔟] [🔟] [🔟]

🆎 🚩 Cedar Inn & Suites Ⓜ
(530) 543-0159. **$49-$139.** 890 Stateline Ave. US 50, 2 blks n, at Stateline and Manzanita aves. Ext corridors. **Pets:** $10 daily fee/pet. No service, supervision.

[SAVE] [S🔟] [✕] [🔟] [🔟] [🔟]

🆎 🚩 Cedar Lodge Ⓜ
(530) 544-6453. **$40-$100.** 4069 Cedar Ave. N off US 50, toward the lake; at Cedar and Friday aves; 3 blks from the casino center. Ext corridors. **Pets:** Dogs only. $40 deposit/room, $10 one-time fee/room. Designated rooms, service with restrictions, supervision.

[SAVE] [✕] [🔟] [🔟] [🔟]

🆎 🚩🚩 Days Inn-Casino Area/South Lake Tahoe Ⓜ
(530) 541-4800. **$41-$199, 3 day notice.** 968 Park Ave. 3 blks w of casino center, 1 blk n off US 50 toward lake at Park and Cedar aves. Int corridors. **Pets:** Medium. $10 daily fee/pet. Designated rooms, service with restrictions, supervision.

[SAVE] [S🔟] [✕] [🔟] [🔟]

🚩🚩 Fireside Lodge B & B 🅱🅱
(530) 542-1717. **$69-$155, 30 day notice.** 515 Emerald Bay Rd. SR 89, 1 mi n of US 50. Ext corridors. **Pets:** Accepted.

[ASK] [S🔟] [✕] [🔟] [🔟] [🔟] [🔟]

🆎 🚩🚩 High Country Lodge Ⓜ
(530) 541-0508. **$35-$150, 3 day notice.** 1227 Emerald Bay Rd. US 50, 0.5 mi n of airport. Ext corridors. **Pets:** Accepted.

[SAVE] [S🔟] [✕] [🔟] [🔟] [🔟]

🆎 🚩🚩🚩 Inn By The Lake Ⓜ ❀
(530) 542-0330. **$98-$228.** 3300 Lake Tahoe Blvd. US 50, 2 mi s of casino center. Int corridors. **Pets:** Dogs only. $20 daily fee/pet. Designated rooms, supervision.

[SAVE] [S🔟] [✕] [🔟M] [🔟] [🔟] [🔟] [🔟]

🚩🚩 Lampliter Inn Ⓜ
(530) 544-2936. **$49-$199.** 4143 Cedar Ave. 2 blks n of US 50. Ext corridors. **Pets:** Accepted.

[ASK] [S🔟] [✕] [🔟] [🔟]

🆎 🚩 Ridgewood Inn Ⓜ
(530) 541-8589. **$49-$135, 3 day notice.** 1341 Emerald Bay Rd. US 50, 0.5 mi n of airport. Ext corridors. **Pets:** Other species. $50 deposit/room, $10 daily fee/room. Designated rooms, service with restrictions, supervision.

[SAVE] [S🔟] [✕] [🔟] [🔟] [🔟]

🆎 🚩 Tahoe Colony Inn Ⓜ ❀
(530) 544-6481. **$60-$80.** 3794 Montreal Rd. Just s of US 50. Int corridors. **Pets:** Large, other species. $40 deposit/pet. Service with restrictions, supervision.

[SAVE] [S🔟] [✕] [🔟] [🔟] [🔟]

◊◊◊ ▼▼▼▼ Tahoe Keys Resort 🆑 ❄
(530) 544-5397. **$100-$1300.** 599 Tahoe Keys Blvd. US 50, exit Tahoe Keys Blvd, 1 mi w. Ext corridors. **Pets:** Other species. $100 deposit/pet, $25 one-time fee/pet. Designated rooms, service with restrictions, supervision.
[SAVE] [S🐾] [✕] [🛏] [💻] [🍽] [✕] [🐾]

◊◊◊ ▼ Tahoe Sundowner Motel 🅼
(530) 541-2282. **$35-$250, 5 day notice.** 1211 Emerald Bay Rd. US 50, 0.5 mi n of airport. Ext corridors. **Pets:** Accepted.
[SAVE] [S🐾] [✕] [🐾]

◊◊◊ ▼ Tahoe Valley Lodge 🅼
(530) 541-0353. **$95-$295, 7 day notice.** 2241 Lake Tahoe Blvd. 0.5 mi e of jct US 50 and SR 89, at Tahoe Keys Blvd. Ext corridors. **Pets:** Accepted.
[SAVE] [S🐾] [✕] [🛏] [💻] [🍽]

TAHOE VISTA

▼ Holiday House 🅼 ❄
(530) 546-2369. **$115-$215, 14 day notice.** 7276 N Lake Blvd. SR 28, 1 mi w of SR 267. Ext corridors. **Pets:** Other species. $100 deposit/room, $10 daily fee/pet, $30 one-time fee/pet. Service with restrictions, supervision.
[✕] [🐾] [💻] [🐾]

TRUCKEE

▼ Alpine Country Lodge 🅼 ❄
(530) 587-3801. **$60-$160.** 12260 Deerfield Dr. I-80, exit Donner Pass Rd, just s. Ext corridors. **Pets:** Other species. $10 daily fee/room. Designated rooms, service with restrictions, supervision.
[ASK] [S🐾] [✕] [🐾] [🛏] [💻] [🐾]

▼▼ The Inn at Truckee 🅼 ❄
(530) 587-8888. **$79-$135, 3 day notice.** 11506 Deerfield Dr. I-80, exit SR 89, just s. Int corridors. **Pets:** Other species. $11 daily fee/room. Supervision.
[ASK] [S🐾] [✕] [🐾] [🛏] [💻]

❖ END AREA ❖

LANCASTER

◊◊◊ ▼▼▼ Best Western Antelope Valley Inn 🅼
(661) 948-4651. **$95-$110.** 44055 N Sierra Hwy. SR 14, exit Ave K, 2.3 mi e. Ext/int corridors. **Pets:** Small. $35 one-time fee/room. Service with restrictions, supervision.
[SAVE] [S🐾] [✕] [🛏] [💻] [🍴] [🐾]

▼▼▼▼ Oxford Inn & Suites 🅼
(661) 949-3423. **$89-$119.** 1651 W Ave K. SR 14, exit Ave K, just w. Int corridors. **Pets:** Large. $50 one-time fee/pet. Service with restrictions, crate.
[ASK] [S🐾] [✕] [🛏] [💻] [🐾]

LA PALMA

▼▼▼▼ La Quinta Inn & Suites-La Palma Conference Center 🆂🅷
(714) 670-1400. **$100-$130.** 3 Center Pointe Dr. SR 91, exit Orangethorpe Ave/Valley View St, just n. Int corridors. **Pets:** Service with restrictions.
[✕] [🐾] [🛏] [💻] [🐾] [✕]

LATHROP

▼▼ Days Inn 🅼
(209) 982-1959. **$75-$82.** 14750 S Harlan Rd. I-5, exit Lathrop Rd. Int corridors. **Pets:** Accepted.
[ASK] [S🐾] [✕] [🐾] [🛏] [🐾]

LEBEC

▼▼ Best Rest Inn 🅼 ❄
(661) 248-2700. **$49-$75.** 51541 N Peace Valley Rd. I-5, exit Frazier Park, just w. Int corridors. **Pets:** Other species. $10 daily fee/room. Designated rooms, service with restrictions, supervision.
[ASK] [S🐾] [✕] [🐾] [🛏] [💻] [🍴] [🐾]

◊◊◊ ▼▼▼▼ Ramada Limited Country Inn 🅼
(661) 248-1530. **$75-$90.** 9000 Country Side Ct. I-5, exit Grapevine, just w. Ext corridors. **Pets:** Large, other species. $5 daily fee/pet. Designated rooms, service with restrictions, supervision.
[SAVE] [S🐾] [✕] [🐾] [🐾] [🛏] [💻] [🐾]

LEE VINING

◊◊◊ ▼▼▼ Murphey's Motel 🅼
(760) 647-6316. **$53-$108.** 51493 Hwy 395. On US 395; in town. Ext corridors. **Pets:** Small. $5 daily fee/room. Service with restrictions, supervision.
[SAVE] [✕] [🛏] [💻]

LEMOORE

◊◊◊ ▼▼▼ Best Western Vineyard Inn 🅼 ❄
(559) 924-1261. **$85-$95.** 877 East D St. SR 198, exit Houston St, 0.8 mi nw. Ext corridors. **Pets:** Other species. $50 deposit/pet. Service with restrictions, supervision.
[SAVE] [S🐾] [✕] [🐾] [🛏] [💻] [🐾] [✕]

LINDSAY

◊◊◊ ▼▼▼ Super 8 Motel 🅼
(559) 562-5188. **$65-$95.** 390 N Hwy 65. On SR 65. Ext corridors. **Pets:** Accepted.
[SAVE] [✕] [🛏] [🐾]

LIVERMORE

▼▼▼ Residence Inn By Marriott 🅼
(925) 373-1800. **$119-$174.** 1000 Airway Blvd. I-580, exit Airway/Collier Canyon Rd, just n. Ext corridors. **Pets:** Accepted.
[ASK] [S🐾] [✕] [💻] [🐾] [✕]

LODI

El Rancho Motel M ❀
(209) 368-0651. **$55.** 603 N Cherokee Ln. SR 99, exit Turner Rd, just s. Ext corridors. **Pets:** Very small. $25 deposit/pet. Service with restrictions, supervision.

LOMPOC

Motel 6 M
(805) 735-7631. **$41-$55.** 1521 N H St. On SR 1, 2 mi n of Ocean Ave. Ext corridors. **Pets:** Accepted.

Quality Inn & Executive Suites SH
(805) 735-8555. **$79-$109, 7 day notice.** 1621 North H St. On SR 1, 1.8 mi n. Int corridors. **Pets:** Other species. $25 one-time fee/pet. Designated rooms, service with restrictions, crate.

Vagabond Inn M
(805) 735-7744. **$59-$129.** 1122 N H St. SR 1, 1.2 mi n. Ext/int corridors. **Pets:** Large. $25 one-time fee/room. Service with restrictions, crate.

LONE PINE

Best Western Frontier Motel M
(760) 876-5571. **$49-$103.** 1008 S Main St. On US 395, at south end of town. Ext corridors. **Pets:** Other species. Service with restrictions, supervision.

Comfort Inn SH
(760) 876-8700. **$59-$129.** 1920 S Main St. US 395, 1.5 mi s of town. Int corridors. **Pets:** Accepted.

Dow Villa Motel M
(760) 876-5521. **$60-$92.** 310 S Main St. On US 395. Ext corridors. **Pets:** Medium, dogs only. $50 deposit/room. Designated rooms, service with restrictions, supervision.

Lone Pine Budget Inn Motel M
(760) 876-5655. **$45-$99, 3 day notice.** 138 W Willow St. US 395, just w. Ext corridors. **Pets:** Accepted.

National 9 Trails Motel M
(760) 876-5555. **$45-$99, 3 day notice.** 633 S Main St. On US 395. Ext corridors. **Pets:** Medium, dogs only. $10 daily fee/pet. Designated rooms, service with restrictions, supervision.

LOS ALAMITOS

Residence Inn by Marriott-Cypress/Orange County SH
(714) 484-5700. **$139-$189.** 4931 Katella Ave. I-605, exit Katella Ave, 1.5 mi e. Int corridors. **Pets:** Medium. $10 daily fee/pet, $75 one-time fee/room.

LOS ANGELES METROPOLITAN AREA

ARCADIA

Residence Inn by Marriott SH ❀
(626) 446-6500. **$149-$189.** 321 E Huntington Dr. I-210, exit Huntington Dr, 0.5 mi w, then just n on Gateway Dr. Ext corridors. **Pets:** Other species. Service with restrictions.

BEVERLY HILLS

Avalon Hotel SH
(310) 277-5221. **$195-$255.** 9400 W Olympic Blvd. I-10, exit Robertson Blvd, 1.7 mi n, then 0.8 mi w. Ext/int corridors. **Pets:** Accepted.

The Beverly Hills Hotel LH ❀
(310) 276-2251. **$410-$470.** 9641 Sunset Blvd. I-405, exit Sunset Blvd, 3.7 mi w. Int corridors. **Pets:** Small, dogs only. $200 one-time fee/pet. Designated rooms, supervision.

Beverly Hilton LH
(310) 274-7777. **$205-$329.** 9876 Wilshire Blvd. I-405, exit Wilshire Blvd, 2.2 mi e. Int corridors. **Pets:** Medium. $25 daily fee/room. Service with restrictions.

Luxe Hotel Rodeo Drive SH
(310) 273-0300. **$400.** 360 N Rodeo Dr. I-405, exit Wilshire Blvd, 4.4 mi e, then just n. Int corridors. **Pets:** Very small, other species. $250 deposit/room, $200 one-time fee/room. Service with restrictions, supervision.

The Peninsula Beverly Hills SH
(310) 551-2888. **$395-$3000.** 9882 S Santa Monica Blvd. I-405, exit Santa Monica Blvd, 2.2 mi e at Wilshire Blvd. Int corridors. **Pets:** Accepted.

Raffles L'Ermitage Beverly Hills SH ❀
(310) 278-3344. **$418-$448.** 9291 Burton Way. I-10, exit Robertson Blvd, 3.1 mi n, then just w. Int corridors. **Pets:** Medium. $150 one-time fee/room. Service with restrictions, supervision.

Regent Beverly Wilshire LH ❀
(310) 275-5200. **$385-$7500.** 9500 Wilshire Blvd. I-405, exit Wilshire Blvd, 4.5 mi e. Int corridors. **Pets:** Small. Service with restrictions, supervision.

BURBANK

▼▼▼▼ **Burbank Airport Hilton & Convention Center** 🄻🄷
(818) 843-6000. **$119-$269.** 2500 Hollywood Way. I-5, exit Hollywood Way, 1 mi s. Int corridors. **Pets:** Accepted.
(ASK) 🆂🄳 ☒ 🛢 💻 🍴 🏊

🄰🄰🄰 ▼▼▼▼ **The Coast Anabelle Hotel** 🅂🄷
(818) 845-7800. **$116-$169.** 2011 W Olive Ave. I-5, exit Olive Ave, 1.3 mi sw. Int corridors. **Pets:** Other species. $100 deposit/pet. Service with restrictions, supervision.
(SAVE) 🆂🄳 ☒ 🆕🄼 🎨 💺 🛢 💻 🍴 🏊

▼▼▼▼ **The Graciela Burbank** 🅂🄷 🐾
(818) 842-8887. **$190-$240.** 322 N Pass Ave. SR 134, exit Hollywood Way westbound, just w on Alameda, 0.5 mi n on Pass Ave; exit Pass Ave eastbound, 0.5 mi n. Ext corridors. **Pets:** Small. $150 one-time fee/room. Service with restrictions.
(ASK) 🆂🄳 ☒ 🛢 💻 🍴 ☒

🄰🄰🄰 ▼▼▼▼ **Safari Inn, A Coast Hotel** 🄼
(818) 845-8586. **$83-$169.** 1911 W Olive Ave. I-5, exit Olive Ave, 1.3 mi sw. Ext corridors. **Pets:** Other species. $100 deposit/pet. Service with restrictions, supervision.
(SAVE) 🆂🄳 ☒ 🎨 💺 🛢 💻 🍴 🏊

CHATSWORTH

▼▼ **Ramada Inn** 🅂🄷
(818) 998-5289. **$78-$88, 7 day notice.** 21340 Devonshire St. SR 118, exit De Soto Ave, 1.5 mi s, then 0.5 mi w. Int corridors. **Pets:** Very small. $50 deposit/room, $10 daily fee/pet. Designated rooms, service with restrictions, supervision.
(ASK) ☒ 🛢 💻 🍴 🏊

🄰🄰🄰 ▼▼▼▼ **Staybridge Suites** 🅂🄷
(818) 773-0707. **$119-$159.** 21902 Lassen St. SR 118, exit Topanga Canyon Blvd, 2 mi s, then just e. Ext corridors. **Pets:** Accepted.
(SAVE) 🆂🄳 ☒ 🛢 💻 🏊 ☒

CULVER CITY

▼▼▼▼ **Four Points by Sheraton Culver City** 🄻🄷
(310) 641-7740. **$89.** 5990 Green Valley Cir. I-405, exit Sepulveda Blvd, just n, then just e. Int corridors. **Pets:** Small, other species. $25 one-time fee/pet. Designated rooms, service with restrictions, supervision.
(ASK) 🆂🄳 ☒ 🛢 💻 🍴 🏊

🄰🄰🄰 ▼▼▼▼ **Radisson Hotel-LA Westside** 🄻🄷
(310) 649-1776. **$105-$129.** 6161 W Centinela Ave. I-405, exit Jefferson Blvd, just s, then just nw. Int corridors. **Pets:** $100 deposit/room, $50 one-time fee/room. Service with restrictions.
(SAVE) 🆂🄳 ☒ 🛢 💻 🍴 🏊

DOWNEY

🄰🄰🄰 ▼▼▼▼ **Embassy Suites Hotel** 🄻🄷
(562) 861-1900. **$139-$182.** 8425 Firestone Blvd. I-605, exit Firestone Blvd, 2 mi w. Int corridors. **Pets:** Medium. $25 daily fee/pet. Service with restrictions, crate.
(SAVE) 🆂🄳 ☒ 🛢 💻 🍴 🏊 ☒

EL SEGUNDO

▼▼▼▼ **Embassy Suites-LAX South** 🄻🄷
(310) 640-3600. **$99-$209.** 1440 E Imperial Ave. I-405, exit Imperial Hwy, 1.6 mi w. Int corridors. **Pets:** Accepted.
(ASK) 🆂🄳 ☒ 🛢 💻 🍴 🏊

▼▼▼▼ **Homestead Studio Suites Hotel-LAX/El Segundo** 🄼 🐾
(310) 607-4000. **$79-$99.** 1910 E Mariposa Ave. I-105, exit Sepulveda Blvd, 1 mi s. Ext corridors. **Pets:** Medium, other species. $25 daily fee/room. Service with restrictions, crate.
(ASK) 🆂🄳 ☒ 🆕🄼 🎨 💺 🛢 💻

▼▼▼▼ **Summerfield Suites by Wyndham-El Segundo** 🄼
(310) 725-0100. **$99-$159.** 810 S Douglas St. I-405, exit Rosecrans Ave, 0.5 mi e, then just n. Ext/int corridors. **Pets:** Accepted.
(ASK) 🆂🄳 ☒ 🆕🄼 🎨 💺 🛢 💻 🏊 ☒

GLENDALE

▼▼▼▼ **Homestead Studio Suites Hotel-Glendale/Burbank** 🅂🄷 🐾
(818) 956-6665. **$95-$115.** 1377 W Glenoaks Blvd. I-5, exit Western Ave, 0.4 mi e, then 0.6 mi s. Int corridors. **Pets:** Medium, other species. $25 daily fee/room. Service with restrictions, crate.
(ASK) 🆂🄳 ☒ 🆕🄼 🎨 💺 🛢 💻

▼▼▼▼ **Los Angeles Days Inn-Glendale** 🅂🄷
(818) 956-0202. **$80-$144, 3 day notice.** 450 W Pioneer Dr. SR 134, exit Pacific Ave, just s, then just e. Int corridors. **Pets:** Medium. $50 deposit/room. Designated rooms, service with restrictions, supervision.
(ASK) 🆂🄳 ☒ 🛢 💻 🍴 🏊

🄰🄰🄰 ▼▼▼ **Vagabond Inn** 🄼
(818) 240-1700. **$89-$94.** 120 W Colorado St. SR 134, exit Brand Blvd, 1 mi s, then just w. Ext corridors. **Pets:** Medium. $10 daily fee/pet. Service with restrictions, supervision.
(SAVE) 🆂🄳 ☒ 🛢 💻 🏊

HAWTHORNE

▼▼▼▼ **TownePlace Suites by Marriott** 🄼
(310) 725-9696. **Call for rates.** 14400 Aviation Blvd. I-405, exit Rosecrans Ave, 0.4 mi w. Int corridors. **Pets:** Accepted.
☒ 🛢 💻 🏊

HOLLYWOOD

🄰🄰🄰 ▼▼ **Motel 6** 🄼
(323) 464-6006. **$56-$82, 30 day notice.** 1738 N Whitley Ave. US 101, exit Cahuenga Blvd, 0.5 mi s to Hollywood Blvd, just w, then just n. Int corridors. **Pets:** Small. Service with restrictions, supervision.
(SAVE) 🆂🄳 ☒

INDUSTRY

▼▼▼▼ **Pacific Palms Conference Resort** 🄻🄷
(626) 810-4455. **$159.** One Industry Hills Pkwy. SR 60, exit Azusa Ave, 1.3 mi n, 0.5 mi w. Int corridors. **Pets:** Small, other species. $50 deposit/pet, $25 one-time fee/pet.
(ASK) 🆂🄳 ☒ 💻 🍴 🏊 ☒

LA MIRADA

▼▼▼ **Residence Inn by Marriott** 🆂🅷 ❖
(714) 523-2800. **$149-$189.** 14419 Firestone Blvd. I-5, exit Valley View, just n, then 0.5 mi e. Ext corridors. **Pets:** Small, other species. $6 daily fee/pet, $75 one-time fee/pet. Service with restrictions.
A$K 🆂🔟 ✕ 🖥 🖵 ➳ 🚫

LONG BEACH

🆎🆎 ▼▼▼ **Days Inn-City Center** 🅼
(562) 591-0088. **$70-$75.** 1500 E Pacific Coast Hwy. I-710, exit SR 1 (Pacific Coast Hwy), 2 mi e. Ext corridors. **Pets:** Accepted.
🆂🅰🆅🅴 ✕ 🅶🅼 ✍ 🖥 🖵

🆎🆎 ▼▼▼ **GuestHouse Hotel Long Beach** 🅼
(562) 597-1341. **$89.** 5325 E Pacific Coast Hwy. I-405, SR 22 (Long Beach) northbound, 2 mi nw; exit Lakewood Blvd southbound, 2 mi se on SR 1. Ext corridors. **Pets:** $10 one-time fee/room. Service with restrictions, crate.
🆂🅰🆅🅴 🆂🔟 ✕ ✎ 🅶 🖥 🖵 ➳

▼▼▼ **Hilton Long Beach** 🅻🅷
(562) 983-3400. **$94-$295.** Two World Trade Center. I-710, exit Broadway/Downtown, just e to Daisy Ave, just s to Ocean Blvd, then just w. Int corridors. **Pets:** Small. $100 deposit/room. Service with restrictions.
🆂🔟 ✕ 🖥 🍴 ➳ 🚫

🆎🆎 ▼▼▼ **Holiday Inn-Long Beach Airport** 🅻🅷
(562) 597-4401. **$79-$129.** 2640 Lakewood Blvd. I-405, exit Lakewood Blvd, just s. Ext/int corridors. **Pets:** Accepted.
🆂🅰🆅🅴 🆂🔟 ✕ 🖥 🖵 🍴 ➳

LOS ANGELES

🆎🆎 ▼ **Beverly Laurel Motor Hotel** 🅼
(323) 651-2441. **$84-$94.** 8018 Beverly Blvd. I-10, exit Fairfax Ave, 2.8 mi n, then just w. Ext corridors. **Pets:** $15 daily fee/pet. Service with restrictions, supervision.
🆂🅰🆅🅴 ✕ 🖥 🍴 ➳

▼▼▼ **Century Plaza Hotel & Spa** 🅻🅷 ❖
(310) 277-2000. **$435-$455.** 2025 Avenue of the Stars. I-10, exit Robertson Blvd, 2.7 mi n to Olympic Blvd, 1.9 mi w, then just n. Int corridors. **Pets:** Medium, other species. $30 deposit/pet. Service with restrictions.
A$K 🆂🔟 ✕ 🅶🅼 ✍ 🅶 🖥 🍴 ➳ 🚫

🆎🆎 ▼▼▼ **Four Points by Sheraton LAX** 🅻🅷
(310) 645-4600. **$79-$175.** 9750 Airport Blvd. I-405, exit Century Blvd, 1.5 mi w, then just n. Ext/int corridors. **Pets:** Accepted.
🆂🅰🆅🅴 🆂🔟 ✕ 🖥 🖵 🍴 ➳

🆎🆎 ▼▼▼ **Four Seasons Hotel** 🅻🅷 ❖
(310) 273-2222. **$330-$460.** 300 S Doheny Dr. I-10, exit Robertson Blvd, 3 mi n to Burton Way, then just w. Int corridors. **Pets:** Very small. Service with restrictions, supervision.
🆂🅰🆅🅴 ✕ 🖵 🍴 ➳ 🚫

▼▼▼ **Furama Hotel Los Angeles** 🅻🅷
(310) 670-8111. **$59-$89.** 8601 Lincoln Blvd. I-405, exit La Tijera Blvd, 1.2 mi sw, then 1.6 mi w. Int corridors. **Pets:** Other species. $75 deposit/room, $10 daily fee/pet. Service with restrictions, supervision.
A$K 🆂🔟 ✕ 🖥 🖵 🍴 ➳

🆎🆎 ▼▼▼ **Holiday Inn Brentwood/Bel-Air** 🅻🅷
(310) 476-6411. **$99-$119.** 170 N Church Ln. I-405, exit Sunset Blvd, just w, then just n. Int corridors. **Pets:** Accepted.
🆂🅰🆅🅴 🆂🔟 ✕ 🖥 🖵 🍴 ➳

▼▼▼ **Hotel Bel-Air** 🆂🅷
(310) 472-1211. **$385-$3000, 3 day notice.** 701 Stone Canyon Rd. I-405, exit Sunset Blvd, 2 mi e, then 0.8 mi n. Ext corridors. **Pets:** Accepted.
🚫 🖥 🍴 ➳

▼▼▼ **Le Meridien at Beverly Hills** 🅻🅷
(310) 247-0400. **$290-$450.** 465 S La Cienega Blvd. I-10, exit La Cienega Blvd, 2.5 mi n. Ext corridors. **Pets:** Accepted.
A$K 🆂🔟 ✕ 🅶🅼 ✍ 🅶 🖥 🍴 ➳ 🚫

▼▼▼ **Los Angeles Airport Hilton & Towers** 🅻🅷
(310) 410-4000. **$79-$149.** 5711 W Century Blvd. I-405, exit Century Blvd, 0.8 mi w. Int corridors. **Pets:** Accepted.
A$K ✕ 🖥 🖵 🍴 ➳ 🚫

🆎🆎 ▼▼▼ **Quality Hotel-Los Angeles Airport** 🅻🅷
(310) 645-2200. **$70-$130.** 5249 W Century Blvd. I-405, exit Century Blvd, just w. Int corridors. **Pets:** Accepted.
🆂🅰🆅🅴 🆂🔟 ✕ 🖵 🍴 ➳

🆎🆎 ▼▼▼ **Radisson Hotel at Los Angeles Airport** 🅻🅷
(310) 670-9000. **$99-$210, 3 day notice.** 6225 W Century Blvd at Sepulveda Blvd. I-405, exit Century Blvd, 1.6 mi w. Int corridors. **Pets:** $50 deposit/room. Service with restrictions, crate.
🆂🅰🆅🅴 ✕ 🖵 🍴 ➳ 🚫

▼▼▼ **Residence Inn by Marriott-Beverly Hills** 🆂🅷
(310) 277-4427. **$119-$159.** 1177 S Beverly Dr. I-10, exit Robertson Blvd, 1.6 mi n to Pico Blvd, then 0.6 mi w. Int corridors. **Pets:** Accepted.
🚫 🖥 🖵

▼▼▼ **St Regis Hotel Los Angeles** 🅻🅷 ❖
(310) 277-6111. **$485-$650.** 2055 Avenue of the Stars. I-10, exit Robertson Blvd, 2.7 mi n to Olympic Blvd, 1.9 mi w, then just n. Int corridors. **Pets:** Accepted.
🚫 🅶🅼 ✍ 🖵 🍴 ➳ 🚫

🆎🆎 ▼▼▼ **Travelodge Hotel at Lax** 🆂🅷
(310) 649-4000. **$54-$89.** 5547 W Century Blvd. I-405, exit Century Blvd, 0.5 mi w. Ext/int corridors. **Pets:** Other species. $10 daily fee/pet. Service with restrictions, crate.
🆂🅰🆅🅴 🆂🔟 ✕ 🖥 🖵 🍴 ➳

🆎🆎 ▼▼▼ **Vagabond Inn** 🅼
(213) 746-1531. **$80-$85.** 3101 S Figueroa St. SR 110, exit Adams Blvd, 0.5 mi s. Ext corridors. **Pets:** Accepted.
🆂🅰🆅🅴 🆂🔟 ✕ 🖥 🖵 ➳

▼▼▼ **The Westin Hotel-Los Angeles Airport** 🏨 ✿
(310) 216-5858. **$89-$239.** 5400 W Century Blvd. I-405, exit Century Blvd, just w. Int corridors. **Pets:** Medium, dogs only. $25 deposit/pet. Service with restrictions, supervision.
🅰🅢 🆂🅑 ⊠ 🖵 🖳 🍴 🗯 🗶

MANHATTAN BEACH

▼▼▼ **Residence Inn by Marriott** 🆂🅷
(310) 546-7627. **$278-$299.** 1700 N Sepulveda Blvd. I-405, exit Rosecrans Ave, 1.5 mi w, then 1 mi s on SR 1. Ext corridors. **Pets:** Small. $8 daily fee/pet, $100 one-time fee/room. Service with restrictions.
🅰🅢 🆂🅑 ⊠ 🖥 🖳 🗯 🗶

MONROVIA

▼▼▼ **Homestead Studio Suites Hotel-Monrovia/Pasadena** 🆂🅷 ✿
(626) 256-6999. **$86-$106.** 930 S Fifth Ave. I-210, exit Huntington Dr, just w, then just n. Int corridors. **Pets:** Medium, other species. $25 daily fee/room. Service with restrictions, crate.
🅰🅢 🆂🅑 ⊠ 🅰🅼 🅰🅵 🖥 🖳

PASADENA

🅰🅰🅰 ▼▼ **Quality Inn Pasadena** 🅼
(626) 796-9291. **$65-$75.** 3321 E Colorado Blvd. I-210, exit Madre St, just s, then 0.3 mi e. Ext corridors. **Pets:** Medium. $10 daily fee/room. Designated rooms, service with restrictions, crate.
🆂🅰🆅🅴 🆂🅑 ⊠ 🖥 🖳 🗯

🅰🅰🅰 ▼◆▼▼ **The Ritz-Carlton, Huntington Hotel & Spa** 🏨
(626) 568-3900. **$325-$3000.** 1401 S Oak Knoll Ave. I-210, exit Lake Ave, 2 mi s. Ext/int corridors. **Pets:** Small.
🆂🅰🆅🅴 ⊠ 🖥 🖳 🍴 🗯 🗶

🅰🅰🅰 ▼ **Super 8** 🅼
(626) 449-3020. **$56-$95.** 2863 E Colorado Blvd. I-210, exit San Gabriel Blvd, 0.3 mi s, then just e. Ext corridors. **Pets:** Very small. $10 daily fee/pet. Designated rooms, service with restrictions, supervision.
🆂🅰🆅🅴 🆂🅑 ⊠ 🖥 🗯

🅰🅰🅰 ▼▼ **Vagabond Inn** 🅼
(626) 449-3170. **$68-$95.** 1203 E Colorado Blvd. I-210, exit Hill St, just s, then just w. Ext/int corridors. **Pets:** Medium. $10 daily fee/pet. Designated rooms, service with restrictions, supervision.
🆂🅰🆅🅴 🆂🅑 ⊠ 🖥 🖳 🗯

🅰🅰🅰 ▼▼ **Westway Inn** 🅼
(626) 304-9678. **$75-$350, 31 day notice.** 1599 E Colorado Blvd. I-210, exit Allen Ave westbound; exit Hill Ave eastbound, 0.8 mi s. Ext corridors. **Pets:** Medium. $10 daily fee/pet. Designated rooms, service with restrictions, supervision.
🆂🅰🆅🅴 ⊠ 🖥 🖳 🗯

POMONA

▼◆ **Sheraton Suites Fairplex** 🏨 ✿
(909) 622-2220. **$95-$99.** 601 W McKinley Ave. I-10, exit White Ave eastbound, 0.5 mi n, just w; exit Faiplex Dr westbound, 1 mi n, 0.7 mi e. Int corridors. **Pets:** Other species. Service with restrictions, crate.
🅰🅢 🆂🅑 ⊠ 🖥 🖳 🍴 🗯 🗶

SAN DIMAS

▼▼ **Red Roof Inn** 🅼
(909) 599-2362. **$54-$99.** 204 N Village Ct. I-210, exit Arrow Hwy, just e. Ext corridors. **Pets:** Accepted.
⊠ 🅰🅼 🅰🅵 🖥 🗯

SAN PEDRO

🅰🅰🅰 ▼▼▼ **Hilton Port of Los Angeles San Pedro** 🏨
(310) 514-3344. **$209.** 2800 Via Cabrillo Marina. I-110, exit Gaffey St, 1.5 mi s, then 0.5 mi e on 22nd St. Int corridors. **Pets:** Medium. $25 one-time fee/room. Service with restrictions, supervision.
🆂🅰🆅🅴 ⊠ 🖥 🖳 🍴 🗯 🗶

🅰🅰🅰 ▼◆▼ **Holiday Inn San Pedro-LA Harbor** 🆂🅷
(310) 514-1414. **$99-$119.** 111 S Gaffey St. I-110, exit Gaffey St, just s. Int corridors. **Pets:** Other species. $25 daily fee/pet. Supervision.
🆂🅰🆅🅴 ⊠ 🖥 🖳 🍴 🗯

🅰🅰🅰 ▼ **Vagabond Inn** 🅼
(310) 831-8911. **$69.** 215 S Gaffey St. I-110, exit Gaffey St, just s from terminus. Ext corridors. **Pets:** $10 deposit/pet. Service with restrictions, supervision.
🆂🅰🆅🅴 🆂🅑 ⊠ 🖥 🖳 🗯

SANTA MONICA

🅰🅰🅰 ▼▼▼▼ **The Fairmont Miramar Hotel Santa Monica** 🏨
(310) 576-7777. **$209-$299.** 101 Wilshire Blvd. I-10, exit Lincoln Blvd, 0.6 mi n, then 0.6 mi w. Ext/int corridors. **Pets:** Accepted.
🆂🅰🆅🅴 ⊠ 🖳 🍴 🗯 🗶

▼▼▼ **The Georgian** 🆂🅷
(310) 395-6333. **$235-$285.** 1415 Ocean Ave. I-10, exit Lincoln Blvd, just n, then 0.5 mi w on Broadway. Int corridors. **Pets:** Accepted.
🅰🅢 🆂🅑 ⊠ 🖥 🖳 🍴

🅰🅰🅰 ▼▼▼▼ **Le Merigot, A JW Marriott Beach Hotel and Spa** 🏨 ✿
(310) 395-9700. **$299-$479.** 1740 Ocean Ave. I-10, exit Lincoln Blvd, 0.3 mi s, 0.6 mi w on Pico Blvd, then just n. Int corridors. **Pets:** Large. $150 deposit/room, $25 one-time fee/room. Service with restrictions.
🆂🅰🆅🅴 🆂🅑 ⊠ 🍴 🗯 🗶

(AAA) ▼▼▼ Loews Santa Monica Beach Hotel [H]
(310) 458-6700. **$212-$325.** 1700 Ocean Ave. I-10, exit Lincoln Blvd, 0.3 mi s, 0.6 mi w on Pico Blvd, then just n. Int corridors. **Pets:** Accepted.
[SAVE] [S⊘] [✕] [&M] [⊘] [🐾] [❨❩] [🏊] [⊠]

SHERMAN OAKS

(AAA) ▼▼▼ Best Western Carriage Inn [M]
(818) 787-2300. **$99-$169.** 5525 Sepulveda Blvd. I-405, exit Burbank Blvd, just e, then just s. Ext/int corridors. **Pets:** Accepted.
[SAVE] [S⊘] [✕] [⊘] [🐾] [⊟] [⊞] [❨❩] [🏊]

TARZANA

▼▼ St. George Motor Inn [M]
(818) 345-6911. **$70-$82.** 19454 Ventura Blvd. US 101, exit Tampa Ave, just s, then just w. Ext corridors. **Pets:** Accepted.
[ASK] [S⊘] [✕] [⊟] [⊞] [🏊]

TORRANCE

▼▼ Homestead Studio Suites Hotel-Torrance/ Redondo Beach [SH] ❁
(310) 543-0048. **$80-$100.** 3995 Carson St. I-405, exit Hawthorne Blvd, 3.6 mi s; I-110, exit Carson St, 4.5 mi w. Int corridors. **Pets:** Medium, other species. $25 daily fee/room. Service with restrictions, crate.
[ASK] [S⊘] [✕] [&M] [⊘] [🐾] [⊟] [⊞]

(AAA) ▼▼▼ Residence Inn by Marriott [SH]
(310) 543-4566. **$79-$149.** 3701 Torrance Blvd. I-405, exit Hawthorne Blvd, 3.2 mi s, then just e. Ext corridors. **Pets:** Medium. $8 daily fee/pet, $75 one-time fee/room. Service with restrictions, supervision.
[SAVE] [✕] [⊟] [⊞] [🏊] [⊠]

(AAA) ▼▼▼ Staybridge Suites [M]
(310) 371-8525. **$99-$145.** 19901 Prairie Ave. I-405, just s to 190th St, 1 mi w, then just s. Ext/int corridors. **Pets:** Accepted.
[SAVE] [S⊘] [✕] [⊟] [⊞] [🏊] [⊠]

WEST COVINA

(AAA) ▼▼▼ Hampton Inn [SH]
(626) 967-5800. **$89.** 3145 E Garvey Ave N. I-10, exit Barranca St, just n, then just e. Int corridors. **Pets:** Accepted.
[SAVE] [S⊘] [✕] [&M] [⊘] [⊟] [⊞] [🏊]

WEST HOLLYWOOD

▼▼▼ Argyle Hotel [SH] ❁
(323) 654-7100. **$265-$330.** 8358 Sunset Blvd. I-10, exit La Cienega Blvd, 4.4 mi n, then just e. Int corridors. **Pets:** Other species. Service with restrictions.
[ASK] [S⊘] [✕] [❨❩] [🏊]

▼▼▼ The Grafton on Sunset [SH]
(323) 654-4600. **$150-$310.** 8462 Sunset Blvd. I-10, exit La Cienega Blvd, 4.4 mi n, then just e. Int corridors. **Pets:** Small. $100 one-time fee/room. Designated rooms, service with restrictions, supervision.
[ASK] [S⊘] [✕] [&M] [⊘] [🐾] [⊟] [❨❩] [🏊]

▼▼▼ Le Montrose Suite Hotel [SH] ❁
(310) 855-1115. **$165-$440.** 900 Hammond St at Cynthia St. I-10, exit La Cienega Blvd, 2.6 mi n to San Vicente Blvd, 1.3 mi nw, then just w on Cynthia St. Int corridors. **Pets:** Small. $100 one-time fee/room.
[ASK] [S⊘] [✕] [⊟] [⊞] [❨❩] [🏊] [⊠]

▼▼▼ Le Parc Suite Hotel [H]
(310) 855-8888. **$330-$440.** 733 N West Knoll Dr. I-10, exit La Cienega Blvd, 3.5 mi n, just w on Melrose Ave, then just n. Int corridors. **Pets:** Medium. $75 one-time fee/room. Designated rooms, service with restrictions.
[ASK] [S⊘] [✕] [⊟] [⊞] [❨❩] [🏊] [⊠]

(AAA) ▼▼▼ Wyndham Bel Age [H] ❁
(310) 854-1111. **$169-$189.** 1020 N San Vicente Blvd. I-10, exit La Cienega Blvd, 2.6 mi n, then 1.5 mi nw. Int corridors. **Pets:** Medium, other species. $100 deposit/pet, $50 one-time fee/pet. Service with restrictions, supervision.
[SAVE] [S⊘] [✕] [⊞] [❨❩] [🏊]

WHITTIER

(AAA) ▼▼▼ Vagabond Inn [M]
(562) 698-9701. **$65-$80.** 14125 E Whittier Blvd. I-605, exit Whittier Blvd, 3.5 mi e. Ext corridors. **Pets:** Medium, other species. $10 daily fee/pet. Designated rooms, service with restrictions, crate.
[SAVE] [S⊘] [✕] [⊟] [⊞] [🏊]

❁ **END METROPOLITAN AREA** ❁

LOS BANOS

(AAA) ▼▼▼ Best Western Executive Inn [SH]
(209) 827-0954. **$65-$75.** 301 W Pacheco Blvd. On SR 152. Int corridors. **Pets:** Medium. $10 one-time fee/pet. Service with restrictions, supervision.
[SAVE] [S⊘] [✕] [&M] [⊘] [⊟] [⊞] [🏊] [⊠]

(AAA) ▼▼ Regency Inn [M]
(209) 826-3871. **$49-$55.** 349 W Pacheco Blvd. On SR 152; center of town. Ext corridors. **Pets:** Medium. $20 deposit/pet, $5 daily fee/pet. Service with restrictions, supervision.
[SAVE] [S⊘] [✕] [⊟] [⊞] [🏊]

LOS GATOS

Los Gatos Lodge M
(408) 354-3300. **$109-$159.** 50 Los Gatos-Saratoga Rd. SR 17, exit E Los Gatos, just e. Ext/int corridors. **Pets:** Accepted.

LOST HILLS

Days Inn of Lost Hills M
(661) 797-2371. **$44-$98.** 14684 Aloma St. I-5, exit SR 46, just w. Ext corridors. **Pets:** Accepted.

MADERA

Best Western Madera Valley Inn M
(559) 664-0100. **$79-$109.** 317 North G St. SR 99, exit Central Madera, just e. Int corridors. **Pets:** Other species. $5 daily fee/room, $20 one-time fee/room. Service with restrictions, supervision.

Liberty Inn M
(559) 675-8697. **$53-$85, 3 day notice.** 22683 Ave 18 1/2. SR 99, exit Ave 18 1/2, just w. Int corridors. **Pets:** Accepted.

Super 8 M
(559) 661-1131. **$65.** 1855 W Cleveland Ave. SR 99, exit Cleveland Ave, just w. Ext corridors. **Pets:** $5 daily fee/pet. Service with restrictions, supervision.

MAMMOTH LAKES

Discovery 4 Condominiums CO
(760) 934-6410. **$115-$280, 30 day notice.** 25 Lee Rd. Old Mammoth Rd, take SR 203 (Main St) and Lake Mary Rd, 1.5 mi w, just nw on Davidson Rd, then just s. Ext corridors. **Pets:** Dogs only. $20 daily fee/pet. Designated rooms, supervision.

Econo Lodge Wildwood Inn M
(760) 934-6855. **$69-$149, 7 day notice.** 3626 Main St. SR 203 (Main St), 0.7 mi w of Old Mammoth Rd. Ext corridors. **Pets:** Medium. $10 daily fee/pet. Designated rooms, service with restrictions, supervision.

Mammoth Ski & Racquet Club CO
(760) 934-7368. **$105-$322, 28 day notice.** 248 Mammoth Slopes Dr. From Old Mammoth Rd, take SR 203, 1 mi w; SR 203, just n, Canyon Blvd, 0.8 mi w, then just s. Int corridors. **Pets:** Dogs only. $20 daily fee/pet. Designated rooms, no service, supervision.

Royal Pines Resort M
(760) 934-2306. **$79-$139, 7 day notice.** 3814 View Point Rd. Adjacent to SR 203, 0.8 mi w of Old Mammoth Rd. Ext/int corridors. **Pets:** Accepted.

Sierra Lodge SH
(760) 934-8881. **$69-$179.** 3540 Main St. SR 203, 0.6 mi w of Old Mammoth Rd. Int corridors. **Pets:** Other species. $10 daily fee/pet. Designated rooms, service with restrictions.

Sierra Nevada Rodeway Inn SH
(760) 934-2515. **$89-$249.** 164 Old Mammoth Rd. Just s of SR 203. Ext/int corridors. **Pets:** Large. Designated rooms, service with restrictions.

Swiss Chalet Motel M
(760) 934-2403. **$65-$120, 7 day notice.** 3776 Viewpoint Rd. Adjacent to SR 203, 0.7 mi w of Old Mammoth Rd. Ext corridors. **Pets:** Dogs only. $5 one-time fee/pet. Designated rooms, service with restrictions, supervision.

Travelodge SH
(760) 934-8892. **$79-$149, 5 day notice.** 54 Sierra Blvd. Just n of SR 203, 0.6 mi w of Old Mammoth Rd. Int corridors. **Pets:** Accepted.

MANTECA

Best Western Executive Inn & Suites M
(209) 825-1415. **$73-$89.** 1415 E Yosemite Ave. Jct SR 99 and 120, exit Yosemite Ave. Ext corridors. **Pets:** Small. $25 one-time fee/room. Designated rooms, no service, supervision.

MARIPOSA

Best Value Mariposa Lodge M
(209) 966-3607. **$49-$129.** 5052 Hwy 140. Center. Ext corridors. **Pets:** Medium. $10 daily fee/pet. Service with restrictions, supervision.

Best Western Yosemite Way Station Motel M
(209) 966-7545. **$44-$96.** 4999 Hwy 140. SR 140 at SR 49 S. Ext corridors. **Pets:** Small. $10 daily fee/pet. Designated rooms, service with restrictions, supervision.

Miners Inn M
(209) 742-7777. **$55-$69.** 5181 Hwy 49 N. On SR 49, n at SR 140. Ext/int corridors. **Pets:** $10 daily fee/pet. Designated rooms, service with restrictions, supervision.

MARYSVILLE

Best Value Inn M
(530) 743-1531. **$50-$80.** 904 E St. Jct SR 70 and 20. Ext corridors. **Pets:** Medium, dogs only. $7 one-time fee/pet. Service with restrictions, supervision.

MERCED

Merced-Yosemite Travelodge M
(209) 722-6224. **$45-$75.** 1260 Yosemite Pkwy. SR 99, exit SR 140, just e. Ext corridors. **Pets:** Medium. $10 daily fee/pet. Service with restrictions, supervision.

MILPITAS

Best Western Brookside Inn M
(408) 263-5566. **$89-$119.** 400 Valley Way. I-880, exit Calaveras Blvd (SR 237/N Abbott Ave), just e. Ext/int corridors. **Pets:** $15 one-time fee/room. Service with restrictions.

Candlewood Suites-Milpitas/Silicon Valley SH ❖
(408) 719-1212. **$69-$139.** 40 Ranch Dr. SR 237, exit McCarthy, just n. Int corridors. **Pets:** Medium. $75 one-time fee/room. Service with restrictions, supervision.

Homestead Studio Suites Hotel-Milpitas/Silicon Valley M ❖
(408) 433-9700. **$86-$106.** 330 Cypress Dr. SR 237, exit McCarthy S. Ext/int corridors. **Pets:** Medium, other species. $25 daily fee/room. Service with restrictions, crate.

Inns of America M
(408) 946-8889. **$69-$109.** 270 S Abbott Ave. I-880, exit Calaveras Blvd (SR 237), just e. Ext corridors. **Pets:** Small. $10 one-time fee/room. Service with restrictions, supervision.

Residence Inn By Marriott SH
(408) 941-9222. **$99-$139.** 1501 California Cir. I-880, exit Dixon Landing Rd E, just s. Int corridors. **Pets:** Medium, other species. $75 one-time fee/room.

TownePlace Suites by Marriott SH
(408) 719-1959. **$59-$119.** 1428 Falcon Dr. I-880, exit Montague Expwy, e to Great Mall Pkwy, turn left; turn right on Mustang Dr, right on Great Mall Dr, then just right. Int corridors. **Pets:** Medium. $75 one-time fee/pet. Supervision.

MIRANDA

Miranda Gardens Resort CO
(707) 943-3011. **$55-$225, 7 day notice.** 6766 Avenue of the Giants. US 101, exit Avenue of the Giants E. **Pets:** Accepted.

MI-WUK VILLAGE

Mi-Wuk Village Inn & Resort M ❖
(209) 586-3031. **$98-$160, 7 day notice.** 24680 SR 108. 15 mi e of Sonora. Ext corridors. **Pets:** Dogs only. $150 deposit/room, $20 one-time fee/pet. Designated rooms, service with restrictions, supervision.

MODESTO

Best Western Town House Lodge M
(209) 524-7261. **$78-$85.** 909 16th St. SR 99, exit Central Modesto at I St, 1 mi e. Ext corridors. **Pets:** $10 one-time fee/pet. Designated rooms, service with restrictions, supervision.

Chalet Motel M
(209) 529-4370. **$60.** 115 Downey Ave. Downtown. Ext corridors. **Pets:** Small. $20 one-time fee/room. Supervision.

DoubleTree LH
(209) 526-6000. **$69-$169.** 1150 9th St. SR 99 exit Central Modesto northbound; exit Maze Blvd southbound. Int corridors. **Pets:** Accepted.

Howard Johnson Express Inn M
(209) 537-4821. **$65-$90.** 1672 Herndon Rd. SR 99, exit Hatch Rd, then s. Ext corridors. **Pets:** Small, other species. $50 deposit/pet. Designated rooms, service with restrictions, supervision.

Microtel Inn & Suites M
(209) 538-6466. **$79-$99.** 1760 Herndon Rd. SR 99, exit Hatch Rd E, then just s. Int corridors. **Pets:** Small, other species. $75 deposit/pet. Service with restrictions, supervision.

Travelodge M
(209) 524-3251. **$50-$75.** 722 Kansas Ave. SR 99, exit Kansas Ave, then w. Ext corridors. **Pets:** Accepted.

MOJAVE

Best Value Inn M
(661) 824-9317. **$55-$65.** 16532 Sierra Hwy. On SR 14 and 58. Ext corridors. **Pets:** Other species. $5 daily fee/pet. Service with restrictions, supervision.

Best Western Desert Winds M
(661) 824-3601. **$70-$75.** 16200 Sierra Hwy. On SR 14 and 58. Ext corridors. **Pets:** Medium. $10 one-time fee/pet. Service with restrictions, supervision.

Desert Inn M
(661) 824-2518. **$46-$54.** 1954 Hwy 58. Just e of SR 14. Ext corridors. **Pets:** Medium. Service with restrictions, crate.

AAA WWW Econo Lodge M
(661) 824-2463. **$39-$69.** 2145 Hwy 58. Just e of SR 14. Ext corridors. **Pets:** Other species. $5 daily fee/pet. Service with restrictions, supervision.
SAVE S X 🖶 🖵 ≈

AAA WWWW Mariah Country Inn & Suites SH
(661) 824-4980. **$95.** 1385 Hwy 58. 1.5 mi e of SR 14. Int corridors. **Pets:** Medium, other species. $10 one-time fee/ room. Service with restrictions, supervision.
SAVE S X ᴸM 🖋 ⚡ 🖶 🖵 ¶ ≈

MONTEREY PENINSULA AREA

CARMEL-BY-THE-SEA

AAA WWWW Best Western Carmel Mission Inn SH
(831) 624-1841. **$79-$329.** 3665 Rio Rd. 1 mi s on SR 1. Ext/int corridors. **Pets:** Medium. $35 one-time fee/pet. Designated rooms, service with restrictions, supervision.
SAVE S X 🖶 🖵 ¶ ≈

AAA WWWW Briarwood Inn BB
(831) 626-9056. **$110-$235, 7 day notice.** 3 blks n off Ocean Ave at San Carlos St and 4th Ave. Ext corridors. **Pets:** Medium. $25 daily fee/pet. Service with restrictions, supervision.
SAVE S X 🖶 🖵 ⚡

WWWW Carmel Country Inn BB 🐾
(831) 625-3263. **$150-$325, 7 day notice.** 4 blks n of Ocean Ave at Dolores St and 3rd Ave. Ext corridors. **Pets:** Other species. $20 daily fee/pet. Designated rooms, service with restrictions, supervision.
ASK X 🖶 🖵 ⚡

AAA WWWW Carmel Fireplace Inn M
(831) 624-4862. **$99-$285, 7 day notice.** 3 blks n off Ocean Ave at San Carlos St and 4th Ave. Ext corridors. **Pets:** Medium. $25 daily fee/pet. Service with restrictions, supervision.
SAVE S X 🖶 🖵 ⚡

AAA WWW Carmel Garden Court BB
(831) 624-6926. **$150-$245, 7 day notice.** 3 blks n off Ocean Ave, at 4th Ave and Torres St. Ext corridors. **Pets:** Large. $50 one-time fee/pet. Service with restrictions, supervision.
SAVE X 🖶 🖵 ⚡

AAA WWW Carmel River Inn M
(831) 624-1575. **$125-$250, 3 day notice.** 1 mi s on SR 1, n of Carmel River Bridge at Oliver Rd. Ext corridors. **Pets:** Other species. $25 daily fee/pet. Designated rooms.
SAVE S X 🖶 🖵 ≈ ⚡

WWWW Carmel Tradewinds Inn M
(831) 624-2776. **$150-$475.** 4 blks n off Ocean Ave; at Mission St and 3rd Ave. Ext corridors. **Pets:** Accepted.
X 🖶 🖵 ⚡

AAA WWWW Coachman's Inn M 🐾
(831) 624-6421. **$135-$425, 3 day notice.** Just s of Ocean Ave, San Carlos St between 7th and 8th aves. Ext corridors. **Pets:** Medium, dogs only. $25 daily fee/pet. Designated rooms, service with restrictions, supervision.
SAVE S X ᴸM 🖶 🖵 ⚡

WWWW Cypress Inn SH 🐾
(831) 624-3871. **$125-$395, 3 day notice.** Just s off Ocean Ave at Lincoln St and 7th Ave. Ext/int corridors. **Pets:** $20 daily fee/pet. Service with restrictions, supervision.
X ⚡

AAA WWWW Wayside Inn M
(831) 624-5336. **$99-$299, 7 day notice.** 1 blk s off Ocean Ave, at Mission St and 7th Ave. Ext corridors. **Pets:** Medium, other species. Designated rooms, service with restrictions, supervision.
SAVE S X 🖶 🖵 ⚡

CARMEL VALLEY

AAA WWWW Carmel Valley Lodge M 🐾
(831) 659-2261. **$149-$219, 7 day notice.** 8 Ford Rd. 11.5 mi e of SR 1; at Carmel Valley and Ford rds. Ext corridors. **Pets:** Dogs only. $10 daily fee/pet. Service with restrictions, supervision.
SAVE S X 🖋 🖶 🖵 ≈ X ⚡

AAA WWWW Los Laureles Lodge M
(831) 659-2233. **$105-$155, 3 day notice.** 313 W Carmel Valley Rd. 10.5 mi e of SR 1. Ext corridors. **Pets:** Medium. $20 daily fee/pet. Service with restrictions, supervision.
SAVE S X 🖶 🖵 ¶ ≈ ⚡

MONTEREY

AAA WWWW Bay Park Hotel SH 🐾
(831) 649-1020. **$89-$249.** 1425 Munras Ave. SR 1, exit Munras Ave, just w. Int corridors. **Pets:** Small, other species. $20 daily fee/room. Designated rooms, service with restrictions, supervision.
SAVE S X ᴸM 🖋 ⚡ 🖶 🖵 ¶ ≈

AAA WWW Best Western The Beach Resort SH 🐾
(831) 394-3321. **$99-$389.** 2600 Sand Dunes Dr. SR 1, exit Del Rey Oaks, just w. Ext corridors. **Pets:** Medium, other species. $25 daily fee/pet. Service with restrictions, supervision.
SAVE S X 🖶 🖵 ¶ ≈

AAA WWWW Best Western Victorian Inn M
(831) 373-8000. **$125-$369.** 487 Foam St. SR 1, exit Monterey, 3.4 mi w. Ext/int corridors. **Pets:** Accepted.
SAVE S X ᴸM 🖋 ⚡ 🖶 🖵 ⚡

AAA WW El Adobe Inn M
(831) 372-5409. **$45-$175, 3 day notice.** 936 Munras Ave. SR 1, exit Munras Ave, 0.6 mi w. Ext corridors. **Pets:** Accepted.
SAVE X 🖋 🖶 🖵 ⚡

[AAA] ♦♦♦ Hyatt Regency-Monterey Resort & Conference Center [LH] 🐾
(831) 372-1234. **$109-$295.** 1 Old Golf Course Rd. SR 1, exit Aguajito Rd northbound; exit Monterey southbound, just e. Int corridors. **Pets:** Other species. $50 one-time fee/room. Designated rooms, service with restrictions, crate.
[SAVE] ⊠ ♿ 👂 ♿ ▣ 📺 🍴 🏊 ⊗ [AC]

[AAA] ♦♦ Monterey Fireside Lodge [M]
(831) 373-4172. **$69-$309, 3 day notice.** 1131 10th St. SR 1, exit Aguajito Rd or Monterey, just w. Ext corridors. **Pets:** Other species. $20 daily fee/pet. Designated rooms, service with restrictions, supervision.
[SAVE] ⊠ ▣ [AC]

PACIFIC GROVE

[AAA] ♦♦ Bide-A-Wee Inn & Cottages [M]
(831) 372-2330. **$69-$149, 3 day notice.** 221 Asilomar Ave. 1 mi n of SR 68. Ext corridors. **Pets:** Large, dogs only. $15 daily fee/pet. Designated rooms, service with restrictions, supervision.
[SAVE] [SD] ⊠ ▣ 📺 [AC]

[AAA] ♦♦ Olympia Motor Lodge [M]
(831) 373-2777. **$88-$160, 3 day notice.** 1140 Lighthouse Ave. 1 mi w. Ext corridors. **Pets:** Medium. $20 one-time fee/room. Service with restrictions, crate.
[SAVE] [SD] ⊠ ▣ 🏊 [AC]

♦ Pacific Grove Motel [M] 🐾
(831) 372-3431. **$59-$169.** 1101 Lighthouse Ave. Just w of Seventeen Mile Dr. Ext corridors. **Pets:** Large. $25 one-time fee/pet. Designated rooms, service with restrictions, supervision.
[A$K] [SD] ⊠ ▣ 📺 🏊 [AC]

♦♦ Sea Breeze Inn and Cottages [M] 🐾
(831) 372-7771. **$69-$189.** 1100 Lighthouse Ave. Just w of Seventeen Mile Dr; Lighthouse and Grove Acre. Ext/int corridors. **Pets:** Large. $25 one-time fee/pet. Designated rooms, service with restrictions, supervision.
[A$K] [SD] ⊠ ▣ 📺 [AC]

PEBBLE BEACH

♦♦♦♦ The Lodge at Pebble Beach [LH] 🐾
(831) 624-3811. **$425-$1650, 3 day notice.** Seventeen Mile Dr. Off SR 1. Ext/int corridors. **Pets:** Medium, dogs only. Service with restrictions, crate.
⊠ ♿ 👂 ♿ 📺 🍴 🏊 ⊗ [AC]

SEASIDE

[AAA] ♦♦ Econo Lodge Bay Breeze [M]
(831) 899-7111. **$49-$249.** 2049 Fremont Blvd. SR 1, exit Sand City/Seaside, just e. Ext/int corridors. **Pets:** Small. Designated rooms, service with restrictions, supervision.
[SAVE] [SD] ⊠ ▣ [AC]

🐾 END AREA 🐾

MORGAN HILL

[AAA] ♦♦ Best Western Country Inn [M]
(408) 779-0447. **$59-$109.** 16525 Condit Rd. US 101, exit Tennant Ave or E Dunne Ave, just e. Int corridors. **Pets:** Other species. $10 daily fee/pet. Designated rooms, service with restrictions, supervision.
[SAVE] [SD] ⊠ ▣ 📺 🏊

♦♦♦ Residence Inn by Marriott [SH]
(408) 782-8311. **$108-$138.** 18620 Madrone Pkwy. US 101, exit Cochrane W, just n. Int corridors. **Pets:** Accepted.
[A$K] ⊠ ▣ 📺 🏊

MORRO BAY

[AAA] ♦♦ Best Western El Rancho [M]
(805) 772-2212. **$59-$149.** 2460 Main St. SR 1, exit SR 41, 0.5 mi n. Ext corridors. **Pets:** Other species. $10 one-time fee/pet. No service, supervision.
[SAVE] [SD] ⊠ ▣ 📺 🍴 🏊 [AC]

[AAA] ♦♦ Morro Bay Sandpiper/Keystone Inn [M]
(805) 772-7503. **$49-$169, 3 day notice.** 540 Main St. SR 1, exit Morro Bay Blvd, 0.7 mi w, then 0.4 mi s. Ext corridors. **Pets:** Medium, dogs only. $10 daily fee/pet. Designated rooms, no service, supervision.
[SAVE] [SD] ⊠ ▣ 📺 [AC]

[AAA] ♦ Sundown Motel [M]
(805) 772-7381. **$38-$135.** 640 Main St. SR 1, exit Morro Bay Blvd, 0.7 mi w, then just s. Ext corridors. **Pets:** Accepted.
[SAVE] ⊠ ▣ 📺 [AC]

MOUNTAIN VIEW

♦♦ Homestead Studio Suites Hotel-Mountain View/Silicon Valley [M] 🐾
(650) 962-1500. **$100-$120.** 190 E El Camino Real. On SR 82, just w of SR 85. Ext corridors. **Pets:** Medium, other species. $25 daily fee/room. Service with restrictions, crate.
[A$K] [SD] ⊠ ♿ ▣ 📺

[AAA] ♦♦ Tropicana Lodge [M]
(650) 961-0220. **$75-$105.** 1720 El Camino Real W. US 101, exit Shoreline Blvd, 2 mi to SR 82, just n. Ext/int corridors. **Pets:** Designated rooms, service with restrictions, supervision.
[SAVE] [SD] ⊠ ♿ ▣ 📺 🏊

MOUNT SHASTA

[AAA] ♦♦♦ Best Western Tree House Motor Inn [M]
(530) 926-3101. **$91-$159.** 111 Morgan Way. I-5, exit Central Mt Shasta (2nd exit), just e. Ext/int corridors. **Pets:** Medium, other species. $10 daily fee/pet. Service with restrictions, supervision.
[SAVE] [SD] ⊠ 👂 ▣ 📺 🍴 🏊

(AAA) ▼▼▼ Econo Lodge M
(530) 926-3145. **$55-$85.** 908 S Mt Shasta Blvd. I-5, exit Central, 0.5 mi e, then 0.5 mi s. Ext corridors. **Pets:** Medium. $10 one-time fee/pet. Service with restrictions, supervision.
SAVE S✆ ✕ 🛏 💻 ➤

(AAA) ▼▼ Evergreen Lodge M
(530) 926-2143. **$59-$79, 3 day notice.** 1312 S Mt Shasta Blvd. I-5, exit McCloud/SR 89, just n at first left, then 1 mi. Ext corridors. **Pets:** Very small, dogs only. $10 daily fee/pet. Designated rooms, service with restrictions, supervision.
SAVE S✆ ✕ 🛏 ➤

(AAA) ▼▼ Swiss Holiday Lodge M ❀
(530) 926-3446. **$48-$75.** 2400 S Mt Shasta Blvd. I-5, exit McCloud/SR 89, just n at first left. Ext corridors. **Pets:** Small, other species. $5 daily fee/pet. Service with restrictions, supervision.
SAVE S✆ ✕ 🛏 ➤

NEEDLES

(AAA) ▼▼▼ Best Western Colorado River Inn M
(760) 326-4552. **$55-$75, 7 day notice.** 2371 W Broadway. I-40, exit W Broadway/River Rd, 0.3 mi e; on Business Loop I-40. Ext corridors. **Pets:** Small. $30 deposit/room. Designated rooms, no service, supervision.
SAVE S✆ ✕ 🛏 💻 ➤

(AAA) ▼▼▼ Best Western Royal Inn M
(760) 326-5660. **$55-$75, 7 day notice.** 1111 Pashard St. I-40, exit W Broadway. Ext corridors. **Pets:** Small. $30 deposit/room. Designated rooms, no service, supervision.
SAVE S✆ ✕ 🛏 💻 ➤

(AAA) ▼▼ Days Inn & Suites M
(760) 326-5836. **$45-$60.** 1215 Hospitality Ln. I-40, exit J St, just se. Ext corridors. **Pets:** Accepted.
SAVE S✆ ✕ ✍ 🛏 ➤

▼▼ Super 8 Motel of Needles M
(760) 326-4501. **$49-$59.** 1102 E Broadway. I-40, exit US 95 (E Broadway), just sw. Ext corridors. **Pets:** Accepted.
ASK S✆ ✕ 🛏 ➤

(AAA) ▼▼ Travelers Inn M
(760) 326-4900. **$35-$65, 7 day notice.** 1195 3rd St Hill. I-40, exit J St, just e, then just s. Ext corridors. **Pets:** $30 deposit/room. Designated rooms, no service, supervision.
SAVE S✆ ✕ ✍ 🛏 ➤

NEVADA CITY

(AAA) ▼ Nevada City Inn M
(530) 265-2253. **$59-$139, 5 day notice.** 760 Zion St. SR 20 and 49, exit Gold Flat/Ridge Rd, 0.3 mi w, then 0.3 mi n. Ext corridors. **Pets:** $10 daily fee/pet. Service with restrictions, supervision.
SAVE S✆ ✕ 🛏 💻

NEWARK

▼▼▼ Homewood Suites by Hilton SH
(510) 791-7700. **$129.** 39270 Cedar Blvd. I-880, exit Mowry Ave, w to Cedar Blvd, then 0.3 mi s. Int corridors. **Pets:** Accepted.
ASK S✆ ✕ ♿ 🛏 💻 ➤ ✕

▼▼▼ Residence Inn by Marriott Newark/Silicon Valley SH 🐾
(510) 739-6000. **$89-$159.** 34566 Dumbarton Ct. SR 84, exit Newark Blvd, just s. Int corridors. **Pets:** Medium, other species. $10 daily fee/pet, $75 one-time fee/pet. Supervision.
ASK S✆ ✕ ⬆M ✍ 💻 ➤

▼▼▼ TownePlace Suites Newark SH
(510) 657-4600. **$89-$119.** 39802 Cedar Blvd. I-880, exit Mowry Ave, just w to Cedar, then s. Int corridors. **Pets:** Accepted.
ASK S✆ ✕ 💻 ➤

▼▼ Woodfin Suites M
(510) 795-1200. **$89-$129.** 39150 Cedar Blvd. I-880, exit Mowry Ave, just w, 0.3 mi s. Ext corridors. **Pets:** Other species. $50 one-time fee/pet. Supervision.
ASK S✆ ✕ ✍ 💻 ➤

NEWBURY PARK

▼ Motel 6 Thousand Oaks M
(805) 499-0711. **$46-$60.** 1516 Newbury Rd. US 101, exit Ventu Park Rd, just w, then just n. Ext corridors. **Pets:** Accepted.
✕ ➤

(AAA) ▼▼ Premier Inns M
(805) 499-0755. **$39-$75.** 2434 W Hillcrest Dr. US 101, exit Borchard Rd, just e, then just n. Ext corridors. **Pets:** Accepted.
SAVE S✆ ✕ 🛏 ➤

NEWPORT BEACH

(AAA) ▼▼▼▼ Four Seasons Hotel Newport Beach LH
(949) 759-0808. **$325-$355.** 690 Newport Center Dr. SR 73, exit MacArthur Blvd northbound, 3 mi s to San Joaquin Hills Rd, then 0.5 mi w; exit Jamboree Rd southbound, 2.5 mi s to San Joaquin Hills Rd, then 0.5 mi e. Int corridors. **Pets:** Accepted.
SAVE ✕ ⬆M 🍴 ✍ 💻 🍴 ➤ ✕

▼▼▼ The Sutton Place Hotel LH
(949) 476-2001. **$129-$169.** 4500 MacArthur Blvd. I-405, exit MacArthur Blvd, 1 mi s. Int corridors. **Pets:** Accepted.
✕ 🛏 💻 🍴 ➤ ✕

NIPOMO

▼ Kaleidoscope Inn & Gardens B&B BB
(805) 929-5444. **$125, 7 day notice.** 130 E Dana St. US 101, exit Tefft St, 0.7 mi e, just s on Thompson Rd, then just e. Ext/int corridors. **Pets:** Other species. Designated rooms, service with restrictions, crate.
✕ 🐾 🛏 🗲

NOVATO

ⒶⒶⒶ ▼▼▼ Inn Marin Ⓜ ❀
(415) 883-5952. **$89-$139.** 250 Entrada Dr. US 101, exit Ignacio Blvd, just w, then just n on Enfrente Rd. Ext corridors. **Pets:** Other species. $20 one-time fee/pet. Service with restrictions, crate.
[SAVE] [S🔥] [✕] [🔥M] [🔥] [🔥] [💻] [≈]

ⒶⒶⒶ ▼ Novato Travelodge Ⓜ
(415) 892-7500. **$69-$89.** 7600 Redwood Blvd. US 101, exit San Marin Dr, just w. Ext corridors. **Pets:** Small. $10 daily fee/pet. Designated rooms, service with restrictions, supervision.
[SAVE] [S🔥] [✕] [🔥M] [🔥] [💻] [≈]

OAKHURST

ⒶⒶⒶ ▼▼▼ Best Western Yosemite Gateway Inn Ⓜ
(559) 683-2378. **$49-$102.** 40530 Hwy 41. SR 49, 0.8 mi n. Ext corridors. **Pets:** Small, dogs only. Designated rooms, service with restrictions, supervision.
[SAVE] [S🔥] [✕] [🔥M] [🔥] [🔥] [🔥] [💻] [≈] [✕]

ⒶⒶⒶ ▼▼▼ Comfort Inn-Oakhurst Ⓜ
(559) 683-8282. **$49-$109.** 40489 Hwy 41. SR 49, 0.5 mi n. Ext corridors. **Pets:** Other species. $10 daily fee/pet. Service with restrictions, supervision.
[SAVE] [✕] [🔥] [🔥] [💻] [≈]

OAKLAND

▼▼▼ Clarion Suites Lake Merritt Hotel 🆂🅷
(510) 832-2300. **$199-$319.** 1800 Madison St. I-880, exit Broadway, 0.8 mi e to 17th St, then just s. Int corridors. **Pets:** Accepted.
[ASK] [S🔥] [✕] [🔥] [💻] [🔥] [🔥]

ⒶⒶⒶ ▼▼▼ Hilton Oakland Airport 🅛🅗
(510) 635-5000. **$89-$189.** 1 Hegenberger Rd. I-880, exit Hegenberger Rd, 1 mi w, 1.3 mi e of Oakland Airport. Int corridors. **Pets:** Accepted.
[SAVE] [✕] [🔥] [🔥] [💻] [🔥] [≈]

▼▼▼ Homewood Suites 🆂🅷
(510) 663-2700. **$169-$299.** 1103 Embarcadero. I-880, exit 5th/Embarcadero southbound; exit 16th/Embarcadero northbound. Int corridors. **Pets:** Accepted.
[ASK] [S🔥] [✕] [🔥] [💻] [≈]

OCEANSIDE

ⒶⒶⒶ ▼▼▼ Oceanside Marina Suites Ⓜ ❀
(760) 722-1561. **$135-$400.** 2008 Harbor Dr N. I-5, exit Oceanside Harbor Dr, just sw, then 1 mi around the harbor to the end of Harbor Dr N. Ext/int corridors. **Pets:** Small, dogs only. $100 one-time fee/pet. Designated rooms, service with restrictions, supervision.
[SAVE] [S🔥] [✕] [🔥] [💻] [≈] [✕] [🔥]

OJAI

ⒶⒶⒶ ▼▼▼ Best Western Casa Ojai Ⓜ ❀
(805) 646-8175. **$85-$199.** 1302 E Ojai Ave. 0.8 mi e on SR 150. Ext corridors. **Pets:** $10 daily fee/pet. Designated rooms, supervision.
[SAVE] [S🔥] [✕] [🔥] [💻] [≈]

▼▼▼ Blue Iguana Inn Ⓜ ❀
(805) 646-5277. **$105-$145, 7 day notice.** 11794 N Ventura Ave. 2.5 mi w of town on SR 33. Ext corridors. **Pets:** Medium, dogs only. $20 daily fee/pet. Service with restrictions, supervision.
[ASK] [S🔥] [✕] [🔥] [💻] [≈]

ⒶⒶⒶ ▼▼▼ Oakridge Inn Ⓜ
(805) 649-4018. **$75-$125.** 780 N Ventura Ave. In Oak View; 4 mi s on SR 33; 2 mi e of Lake Casitas. Ext corridors. **Pets:** Small, dogs only. $10 one-time fee/pet. Designated rooms, service with restrictions, supervision.
[SAVE] [S🔥] [✕] [🔥] [💻] [≈]

ⒶⒶⒶ ▼▼▼ ▼▼▼ Ojai Valley Inn & Spa 🅛🅗 ❀
(805) 646-1111. **$299-$455, 3 day notice.** 905 Country Club Rd. 1 mi w on SR 150, 0.3 mi s. Ext/int corridors. **Pets:** Small. $35 daily fee/room. Designated rooms, service with restrictions.
[SAVE] [✕] [🔥M] [🔥] [🔥] [🔥] [💻] [🔥] [≈] [✕]

ONTARIO

ⒶⒶⒶ ▼▼▼ AmeriSuites (Los Angeles/Ontario Mills) 🆂🅷
(909) 980-2200. **$79-$159, 3 day notice.** 4760 E Mills Cir. I-10, exit Milliken Ave, just n, then 0.5 mi e on Ontario Mills Dr. Int corridors. **Pets:** Small. $50 one-time fee/room. Service with restrictions, supervision.
[SAVE] [S🔥] [✕] [🔥M] [🔥] [🔥] [💻] [≈]

ⒶⒶⒶ ▼▼▼ Country Inn & Suites by Carlson Ⓜ
(909) 937-6000. **$114-$194.** 231 N Vineyard Ave. I-10, exit Vineyard Ave, just s. Ext corridors. **Pets:** Accepted.
[SAVE] [S🔥] [✕] [🔥] [🔥] [💻] [≈] [✕]

ⒶⒶⒶ ▼▼▼ Doubletree Hotel Ontario 🅛🅗
(909) 937-0900. **$94-$254.** 222 N Vineyard Ave. I-10, exit Vineyard Ave, 0.4 mi s. Int corridors. **Pets:** Small, dogs only. $15 daily fee/pet. Service with restrictions, crate.
[SAVE] [✕] [🔥M] [🔥] [🔥] [💻] [🔥] [≈]

▼▼▼ Hilton Ontario Airport 🅛🅗
(909) 980-0400. **$99-$219.** 700 N Haven Ave. I-10, exit Haven Ave, just n. Int corridors. **Pets:** Small. $100 deposit/room. Designated rooms, service with restrictions, crate.
[ASK] [S🔥] [✕] [🔥M] [🔥] [💻] [🔥] [≈] [✕]

ⒶⒶⒶ ▼▼▼ Holiday Inn Hotel & Suites Airport 🆂🅷
(909) 466-9600. **$79-$139.** 3400 Shelby St. I-10, exit Haven Ave, just n to Inland Empire Blvd, w to Lotus Ave, then just s. Ext/int corridors. **Pets:** Small. $25 one-time fee/room. Designated rooms, service with restrictions, supervision.
[SAVE] [S🔥] [✕] [🔥] [💻] [🔥] [≈] [✕]

▼▼▼ La Quinta Inn & Suites 🆂🅷
(909) 476-1112. **$100-$140.** 3555 Inland Empire Blvd. I-10, exit Haven Ave, just n, then just e. Int corridors. **Pets:** Small, other species. Service with restrictions, crate.
[✕] [🔥M] [🔥] [🔥] [💻] [≈]

▼▼▼▼ Residence Inn by Marriott 🆂🅷 ❀
(909) 937-6788. **$135-$161.** 2025 Convention Center Way. I-10, exit Vineyard Ave, just s, then 1 blk e. Ext corridors. **Pets:** Small, other species. $10 daily fee/room, $100 one-time fee/room. Service with restrictions, supervision.
(A$K) (S🔒) (✕) 🔒 🖥 ⊃ ⊠

ORANGE

🔷 ▼▼▼▼ Hilton Suites Anaheim/Orange 🆂🅷
(714) 938-1111. **$95-$225.** 400 N State College Blvd. I-5, exit State College Blvd, just s. Int corridors. **Pets:** Small. $50 deposit/room. Service with restrictions, supervision.
(SAVE) (S🔒) (✕) 🔒 🖥 🍴 ⊃ ⊠

ORLAND

🔷 ▼▼ Amber Light Inn Motel Ⓜ ❀
(530) 865-7655. **$49-$54.** 828 Newville Rd. I-5, exit Chico (SR 32), 0.3 mi e. Ext corridors. **Pets:** Small. $5 one-time fee/pet. Service with restrictions, supervision.
(SAVE) (S🔒) (✕) 🔒 ⊃

🔷 ▼▼ Orland Inn Ⓜ
(530) 865-7632. **$53-$59.** 1052 South St. I-5, exit South St, 0.5 mi s; northbound exit I-5 E via Orland-Fairgrounds; southbound exit I-5 E via CR 16. Ext corridors. **Pets:** Large, other species. $5 one-time fee/pet. Service with restrictions, supervision.
(SAVE) (S🔒) (✕) (L🔒M) 🔒 ⊃

OROVILLE

🔷 ▼▼▼ Best Value Inn Ⓜ ❀
(530) 533-7070. **$65-$110.** 580 Oro Dam Blvd. SR 70, exit Oroville Dam Blvd, 0.3 mi e. Ext corridors. **Pets:** Other species. $20 deposit/room, $6 daily fee/pet. Designated rooms, service with restrictions, supervision.
(SAVE) (S🔒) (✕) 🔒 🖥

🔷 ▼▼▼▼ Comfort Inn Ⓜ
(530) 533-9673. **$74-$89.** 1470 Feather River Blvd. SR 70, exit E Montgomery St. Int corridors. **Pets:** Accepted.
(SAVE) (S🔒) (✕) (L🔒M) (🔒) 🔒 🖥 ⊃ ⊠

🔷 ▼▼ Days Inn-Oroville Ⓜ
(530) 533-3297. **$55-$75.** 1745 Feather River Blvd. SR 70, exit E Montgomery St, just e to Feather River Blvd, then 0.5 mi s. Ext corridors. **Pets:** Medium, dogs only. $10 daily fee/pet. Service with restrictions, supervision.
(SAVE) (S🔒) (✕) 🔒 🖥 ⊃

🔷 ▼ Sunset Inn Ⓜ
(530) 533-8201. **$45-$150.** 1835 Feather River Blvd. SR 70, exit E Montgomery St, 0.5 mi s. Ext corridors. **Pets:** $7 daily fee/pet. Service with restrictions, supervision.
(SAVE) (S🔒) (✕) 🔒 🖥 ⊃

OXNARD

🔷 ▼▼▼▼ Best Western Oxnard Inn Ⓜ
(805) 483-9581. **$99-$109.** 1156 S Oxnard Blvd. US 101, exit Vineyard Ave northbound; exit Oxnard Blvd southbound, 3 mi s. Ext corridors. **Pets:** Small. $20 one-time fee/room. Supervision.
(SAVE) (S🔒) (✕) 🔒 🖥 ⊃

▼▼▼▼ Residence Inn At River Ridge 🆂🅷
(805) 278-2200. **$128-$167.** 2101 W Vineyard Ave. US 101, exit Vineyard Ave, 1.8 mi w. Ext corridors. **Pets:** $5 daily fee/pet, $100 one-time fee/pet. Service with restrictions, supervision.
(A$K) (S🔒) (✕) (🔒) 🔒 🖥 ⊃ ⊠

🔷 ▼▼▼ Vagabond Inn Ⓜ
(805) 983-0251. **$64-$74.** 1245 N Oxnard Blvd. US 101, exit Vineyard Ave northbound, exit Oxnard Blvd southbound, 1.5 mi s. Ext corridors. **Pets:** Accepted.
(SAVE) (S🔒) (✕) 🔒 🖥 ⊃

PALMDALE

▼▼▼▼ Residence Inn by Marriott 🆂🅷
(661) 947-4204. **$140-$180.** 514 W Ave P. SR 14, exit Ave P, just w. Int corridors. **Pets:** Accepted.
(A$K) (S🔒) (✕) (L🔒M) (🔒) (🔒) 🔒 🖥 ⊃ ⊠

PALM DESERT

🔷 ▼▼▼ Comfort Suites Ⓜ
(760) 360-3337. **$69-$149.** 39-585 Washington St. I-10, exit Washington St, just n. Int corridors. **Pets:** Accepted.
(SAVE) (S🔒) (✕) 🔒 🖥 ⊃ ⊠

▼▼🔷 Desert Patch Inn Ⓜ ❀
(760) 346-9161. **$47-$124, 7 day notice.** 73758 Shadow Mountain Dr. I-10, exit Cook St, 4.4 mi s to SR 111, 1.2 mi w to San Luis Rey Ave, just s, then just e. Ext corridors. **Pets:** Other species. Designated rooms.
(✕) 🔒 🖥 ⊃

🔷 ▼▼▼ The Inn at Deep Canyon Ⓜ
(760) 346-8061. **$47-$127, 3 day notice.** 74470 Abronia Tr. I-10, exit Cook St, 4.4 mi s to SR 111, 0.5 mi w, then just s on Deep Canyon Rd. Ext corridors. **Pets:** Large, other species. $10 daily fee/room. Designated rooms, service with restrictions.
(SAVE) (S🔒) (✕) 🔒 🖥 ⊃

▼▼▼▼ Residence Inn by Marriott 🆂🅷
(760) 776-0050. **$89-$199.** 38-305 Cook St. I-10, exit Cook St, 0.8 mi s. Ext corridors. **Pets:** Medium, other species. $10 daily fee/pet, $75 one-time fee/pet. Service with restrictions, supervision.
(A$K) (✕) 🔒 🖥 ⊃ ⊠

PALM SPRINGS

▼▼ A Place In The Sun Ⓜ ❀
(760) 325-0254. **$69-$179, 7 day notice.** 754 San Lorenzo Rd. Just e of Palm Canyon Dr via Mesquite Ave and Random Rd. Ext corridors. **Pets:** Other species. $15 daily fee/pet. Service with restrictions.
(✕) 🔒 🖥 ⊃ ⊠

▼▼ Caliente Tropics Resort Ⓜ ❀
(760) 327-1391. **$65-$225, 3 day notice.** 411 E Palm Canyon Dr. 1.5 mi s of Tahquitz Canyon Way. Ext corridors. **Pets:** $20 daily fee/pet. Designated rooms, service with restrictions, supervision.
(A$K) (S🔒) (✕) 🔒 🍴 ⊃ ⊠

▼▼ **Casa Cody Country Inn** M
(760) 320-9346. **$59-$189, 3 day notice.** 175 S Cahuilla Rd. SR 111, just w on Tahquitz Canyon Way, then just s. Ext corridors. **Pets:** Other species. $10 daily fee/pet. Service with restrictions, supervision.

🖥 💻 🛁

▼▼ **Comfort Inn Resort** M
(760) 778-3699. **$69-$159, 3 day notice.** 390 S Indian Canyon Dr. 0.5 mi s of Tahquitz Canyon Way. Ext corridors. **Pets:** Small. $35 one-time fee/pet. Designated rooms, service with restrictions.

ASK 🖥 ✕ 🖥 💻 🛁

▼▼▼ **Hilton Palm Springs Resort** LH
(760) 320-6868. **$98-$189, 3 day notice.** 400 E Tahquitz Canyon Way. Just e of Indian Canyon Dr. Int corridors. **Pets:** Other species. $100 deposit/room, $20 one-time fee/pet. Designated rooms, service with restrictions, supervision.

✕ 🖥 💻 🍽 🛁 ✕

▼▼▼ **La Mancha Private Villas & Spa Resort** SH
(760) 323-1773. **$99-$499, 3 day notice.** 444 N Avenida Caballeros. 0.6 mi e of Palm Canyon Dr, on Tahquitz Canyon Way, then 0.5 mi n. Ext corridors. **Pets:** Accepted.

ASK 🖥 ✕ 🖥 💻 🛁 ✕

▼▼▼ **Le Parker Meridian Palm Springs** SH ❀
(760) 770-5000. **Call for rates.** 4200 E Palm Canyon Dr. 4.5 mi se on Palm Canyon Dr. Ext/int corridors. **Pets:** Other species. $100 one-time fee/room. Designated rooms, service with restrictions, supervision.

🖥 ✕ 🖥 💻 🍽 🛁 ✕

▼▼▼ **Palm Springs Riviera Resort** LH ❀
(760) 327-8311. **$89-$269.** 1600 N Indian Canyon Dr. 1.5 mi n of Tahquitz Canyon Way. Int corridors. **Pets:** Medium, dogs only. $200 deposit/room, $20 daily fee/room. Designated rooms, service with restrictions, supervision.

ASK 🖥 ✕ 🖥 🖥 💻 🍽 🛁 ✕

▼▼▼ **Quality Inn Resort** M
(760) 323-2775. **$49-$169.** 1269 E Palm Canyon Dr. 2.3 mi se of Tahquitz Canyon Way. Ext corridors. **Pets:** Large, dogs only. Designated rooms, service with restrictions.

ASK 🖥 ✕ 🖥 💻 🍽 🛁

▼▼▼ **Ramada Resort Inn & Conference Center** SH
(760) 323-1711. **$59-$179.** 1800 E Palm Canyon Dr. 2.7 mi se of Tahquitz Canyon Way. Ext/int corridors. **Pets:** Other species. $20 daily fee/room. Designated rooms, service with restrictions, crate.

SAVE 🖥 ✕ 🖥 💻 🍽 🛁 ✕

▼ **Super 8 Lodge** M
(760) 322-3757. **$45-$85.** 1900 N Palm Canyon Dr. 1.4 mi n of Tahquitz Canyon Way. Ext corridors. **Pets:** Accepted.

ASK 🖥 ✕ 🖥 💻 🛁

▼▼ **Villa Rosa Inn** M
(760) 327-5915. **$109-$165, 3 day notice.** 1577 S Indian Tr. 2 mi se of Tahquitz Canyon Way, then just n. Ext corridors. **Pets:** Accepted.

ASK ✕ 🖥 💻 🛁

PALO ALTO

▼▼▼ **Crowne Plaza Hotel and Resort Cabana Hotel** SH
(650) 857-0787. **$99-$279.** 4290 El Camino Real. US 101, exit San Antonio Rd, 0.4 mi n. Ext/int corridors. **Pets:** Accepted.

ASK 🖥 ✕ 🖥 🎿 🖥 🖥 💻 🍽 🛁 ✕

▼▼▼ **Sheraton Palo Alto Hotel** SH
(650) 328-2800. **$299.** 625 El Camino Real. US 101, exit Embarcadero W to SR 82, then 0.5 mi n. Int corridors. **Pets:** Medium, dogs only.

ASK 🖥 ✕ 🖥 🖥 💻 🍽 🛁

▼▼ **Travelodge Palo Alto** M
(650) 493-6340. **$89.** 3255 El Camino Real. US 101, exit Oregon Expwy, 2 mi w to SR 82. Ext corridors. **Pets:** Accepted.

ASK 🖥 ✕ 🖥 🖥 💻 🛁

PARADISE

🅰🅰🅰 ▼▼▼ **Comfort Inn** M
(530) 876-0191. **$69-$94.** 5475 Clark Rd. SR 191, 0.5 mi s of Pearson Rd. Int corridors. **Pets:** $6 daily fee/pet. Service with restrictions, supervision.

SAVE 🖥 ✕ 🖥 🖥 💻 🛁

🅰🅰🅰 ▼▼▼ **Ponderosa Gardens Motel** M
(530) 872-9094. **$78-$105.** 7010 Skyway. 2 blks e; center. Ext corridors. **Pets:** Accepted.

SAVE ✕ 🖥 🖥 🖥 💻 🛁

PASO ROBLES

▼▼▼ **Hampton Inn & Suites** SH
(805) 226-9988. **$85-$154.** 212 Alexa Ct. US 101, exit SR 46 W, just sw. Int corridors. **Pets:** Small. $50 deposit/room. Service with restrictions, supervision.

ASK 🖥 ✕ 🖥 💻 🛁

PHELAN

🅰🅰🅰 ▼▼▼ **Best Western Cajon Pass** M
(760) 249-6777. **$59-$109.** 8317 US Hwy 138. I-15, exit Silver Lake/US 138, just w. Ext corridors. **Pets:** Small. $20 deposit/room. Designated rooms, service with restrictions, supervision.

SAVE 🖥 ✕ 🖥 💻 🛁

PISMO BEACH

🅰🅰🅰 ▼▼▼ **Cottage Inn by the Sea** M
(805) 773-4617. **$89-$249.** 2351 Price St. US 101, exit Shell Beach Rd northbound, just w, 0.5 mi s; exit Price St southbound, just w, then just s. Ext corridors. **Pets:** Other species. $10 one-time fee/room. Designated rooms, service with restrictions, supervision.

SAVE 🖥 ✕ 🖥 💻 🛁 🐾

🅰🅰🅰 ▼▼▼ **Oxford Suites Resort** SH ❀
(805) 773-3773. **$99-$179.** 651 Five Cities Dr. US 101, exit 4th St, just w, then just n. Ext corridors. **Pets:** Medium, other species. $10 daily fee/pet. Designated rooms, service with restrictions, supervision.

SAVE 🖥 ✕ 🖥 💻 🛁

(AAA) ▼▼▼ Sandcastle Inn **M**
(805) 773-2422. **$99-$329.** 100 Stimson Ave. US 101, exit Price St northbound, 0.3 mi s, just w; exit Hinds Ave southbound, just w, then just s. Ext/int corridors. **Pets:** $10 daily fee/pet. Designated rooms, service with restrictions, supervision.
[SAVE] [S🐾] [✕] [🛏] [💻]

▼▼ Sea Gypsy Motel **CO**
(805) 773-1801. **$50-$165.** 1020 Cypress St. US 101, exit Price St northbound, 0.5 mi n to Pismo Ave, then just w; exit Hines Ave southbound, 0.3 mi w, then just n. Ext/int corridors. **Pets:** Medium, other species. $15 daily fee/pet. Service with restrictions, supervision.
[✕] [🛏] [💻] [🏊] [🐾]

(AAA) ▼ Shell Beach Motel **M**
(805) 773-4373. **$71-$169.** 653 Shell Beach Rd. US 101, exit Shell Beach Rd northbound, just w, then 1.2 mi s; exit Price St southbound, just w, then 1 mi n. Ext corridors. **Pets:** $15 daily fee/pet. Service with restrictions, supervision.
[SAVE] [S🐾] [✕] [🛏] [💻] [🏊] [🐾]

(AAA) ▼▼▼ Spyglass Inn **SH**
(805) 773-4855. **$79-$239.** 2705 Spyglass Dr. US 101, exit Spyglass Dr northbound; exit Shell Beach Rd southbound, just w, then just n. Ext corridors. **Pets:** Other species. $10 one-time fee/pet. Designated rooms, service with restrictions, supervision.
[SAVE] [S🐾] [✕] [🛏] [💻] [🍴] [🏊] [🐾]

PLACENTIA

▼▼▼ Residence Inn by Marriott **SH**
(714) 996-0555. **$124.** 700 W Kimberly Ave. SR 57, exit Orangethorpe Ave, just w, just n on Placentia Ave, then just e. Ext corridors. **Pets:** Small, other species. $10 daily fee/pet, $150 one-time fee/room. Service with restrictions.
[ASK] [S🐾] [✕] [🛏] [💻] [🏊] [🐾]

PLACERVILLE

(AAA) ▼▼ Mother Lode Motel **M**
(530) 622-0895. **$44-$62, 3 day notice.** 1940 Broadway. 2 mi e, adjacent to US 50, exit Point View Dr. Ext corridors. **Pets:** Small. $10 daily fee/pet. Designated rooms, service with restrictions, supervision.
[SAVE] [✕] [♿] [🛁] [🛏] [💻] [🏊]

PLEASANT HILL

▼▼▼ Residence Inn By Marriott-Pleasant Hill **M** ✿
(925) 689-1010. **$89-$179.** 700 Ellinwood Way. I-680, exit Willow Pass Rd to Taylor W; S Contra Costa Blvd, e on Ellinwood Dr, then n. Ext/int corridors. **Pets:** Other species. $75 one-time fee/pet.
[ASK] [S🐾] [✕] [💻] [🏊] [🐾]

▼▼▼ Summerfield Suites by Wyndham-Pleasant Hill **SH**
(925) 934-3343. **$104-$169.** 2611 Contra Costa Blvd. I-680, exit Contra Costa Blvd, then w. Int corridors. **Pets:** Accepted.
[ASK] [S🐾] [✕] [♿] [🛁] [💻] [🏊] [🐾]

PLEASANTON

(AAA) ▼▼▼ Candlewood Suites **SH**
(925) 463-1212. **$129.** 5535 Johnson Dr. I-580, exit Hopyard Rd S, w on Owen. Int corridors. **Pets:** Accepted.
[SAVE] [S🐾] [✕] [💻]

▼▼ Ramada Inn **M**
(925) 463-1300. **$59-$109.** 5375 Owens Ct. I-580, exit Hopyard Rd, just s. Ext corridors. **Pets:** Accepted.
[ASK] [S🐾] [✕] [🛏] [💻] [🏊]

(AAA) ▼▼▼ Residence Inn by Marriott **SH**
(925) 227-0500. **$69-$139.** 11920 Dublin Canyon Rd. I-580, exit Foothill Blvd S, then w. Int corridors. **Pets:** Accepted.
[SAVE] [S🐾] [✕] [♿] [🛁] [💻] [🏊] [🐾]

▼▼▼ Summerfield Suites by Wyndham-Pleasanton **M**
(925) 730-0070. **$99-$199.** 4545 Chabot Dr. I-580, exit Hopyard Rd, 1 mi s, e on Stoneridge Dr, then s. Ext corridors. **Pets:** Small, other species. $150 one-time fee/room. Service with restrictions.
[ASK] [S🐾] [✕] [♿] [🛁] [💻] [🏊] [🐾]

POLLOCK PINES

(AAA) ▼▼▼ Best Western Stagecoach Inn **M**
(530) 644-2029. **$99-$129.** 5940 Pony Express Tr. US 50, exit Pollock Pines eastbound, 1 mi e; exit Sly Park westbound; 12 mi e of Placerville. **Pets:** Accepted.
[SAVE] [S🐾] [♿] [💻] [🏊]

▼▼▼ Westhaven Inn **M**
(530) 644-7800. **Call for rates.** 5658 Pony Express Tr. US 50, exit Pollock Pines, just n. Ext corridors. **Pets:** Accepted.
[S🐾] [✕] [♿] [🛏] [💻]

PORTOLA

▼ Sleepy Pines Motel **M**
(530) 832-4291. **$61-$120.** 74631 Hwy 70. On SR 70. Ext corridors. **Pets:** Dogs only. Supervision.
[✕] [🛏] [💻] [🏊]

QUINCY

(AAA) ▼ Pine Hill Motel **M**
(530) 283-1670. **$65-$75.** 42075 Hwy 70. 1 mi s. Ext corridors. **Pets:** Medium. $5 daily fee/pet. Service with restrictions, supervision.
[SAVE] [✕] [🛏] [🐾]

RANCHO CORDOVA

(AAA) ▼▼▼ AmeriSuites (Sacramento/Rancho Cordova) **SH** ✿
(916) 635-4799. **$129.** 10744 Gold Center Dr. US 50, exit Zinfandel Dr, just s. Int corridors. **Pets:** Other species. Supervision.
[SAVE] [S🐾] [✕] [♿] [🛁] [🛏] [💻] [🏊]

(AAA) ▼▼▼ Best Western Heritage Inn **M**
(916) 635-4040. **$99.** 11269 Point East Dr. US 50, exit Sunrise Blvd S; 12 mi e of Sacramento. Int corridors. **Pets:** Small, other species. $25 one-time fee/room. Designated rooms, service with restrictions, supervision.
[SAVE] [S🐾] [✕] [♿] [🛏] [💻] [🍴] [🏊]

(AAA) ▽▽◇ Inns of America M
(916) 351-1213. **$69-$77.** 12249 Folsom Blvd. US 50, exit Hazel Ave, then just s. Ext corridors. **Pets:** Medium. Service with restrictions, supervision.
[SAVE] [S☉] [✕] [🛏] [🔌] [➤]

▽▽▽▽ Residence Inn M
(916) 851-1550. **$130-$170.** 2779 Prospect Park Dr. US 50, exit Zinfandel Dr. Int corridors. **Pets:** Large, other species. $10 daily fee/pet, $100 one-time fee/room. Service with restrictions, supervision.
[ASK] [S☉] [✕] [⚷M] [✂] [🔌] [➤] [✕]

RED BLUFF

(AAA) ▽▽◇ Best Value Inn & Suites M ✿
(530) 529-2028. **$55-$75, 3 day notice.** 30 Gilmore Rd. I-5, exit SR 36 W (Central District), just s. Ext corridors. **Pets:** Medium. $5 daily fee/pet. Designated rooms, service with restrictions, supervision.
[SAVE] [S☉] [✕] [🛏] [🔌] [➤]

(AAA) ▽▽ Cinderella Riverview Motel M
(530) 527-5490. **$45-$65, 3 day notice.** 600 Rio St. I-5, exit SR 36 W (Central District), 0.4 mi w on Antelope Blvd. Ext corridors. **Pets:** Medium, other species. $6 daily fee/pet. Designated rooms, service with restrictions, supervision.
[SAVE] [S☉] [✕] [➤]

(AAA) ▽▽▽ Days Inn & Suites M
(530) 527-6130. **$55-$95.** 5 John Sutter St. I-5, exit S Main St southbound, just right; exit S Main St northbound, cross over bridge, just right. Ext corridors. **Pets:** Accepted.
[SAVE] [S☉] [✕] [🛏] [➤]

▽▽ River Inn M
(530) 528-8890. **$45-$90.** 1142 N Main St. I-5, exit 351 northbound, just s; exit Antelope Blvd southbound, 0.5 mi w, then just n. Ext corridors. **Pets:** Other species. $5 daily fee/pet.
[ASK] [S☉] [✕] [🛏] [🔌] [➤]

(AAA) ▽▽ Sportsman Lodge M
(530) 527-2888. **$50-$100, 3 day notice.** 768 Antelope Blvd. I-5, exit Susanville/Lassen Park, 1.5 mi e. Ext corridors. **Pets:** Other species. $5 daily fee/pet. No service, supervision.
[SAVE] [S☉] [✕] [🛏] [🔌] [➤]

(AAA) ▽▽▽ Super 8 Motel M
(530) 527-8882. **$60-$90.** 203 Antelope Blvd. I-5, exit Susanville/Lassen Park. Int corridors. **Pets:** Large, other species. $5 daily fee/pet. Service with restrictions, crate.
[SAVE] [S☉] [✕] [🛏] [➤]

(AAA) ▽▽◇ Travelodge Red Bluff M ✿
(530) 527-6020. **$55-$75.** 38 Antelope Blvd. I-5, exit 36 W (Central District), just w. Ext corridors. **Pets:** Medium. $5 daily fee/pet. Designated rooms, service with restrictions, supervision.
[SAVE] [✕] [🛏] [🔌] [➤]

(AAA) ▽▽ Villager Lodge M
(530) 527-3545. **$50-$100.** 250 S Main St. I-5, exit SR 36 W (Central District), 0.5 mi w on Antelope Blvd, then 0.7 mi s. Ext corridors. **Pets:** Other species. $5 daily fee/pet. No service, supervision.
[SAVE] [S☉] [✕] [🛏] [➤]

REDCREST

(AAA) ▽▽▽ Redcrest Resort CA ✿
(707) 722-4208. **$55-$115, 14 day notice.** 26459 Avenue of the Giants. US 101, exit Redcrest, just n. Ext corridors. **Pets:** $5 daily fee/pet. Designated rooms, no service, supervision.
[SAVE] [✕] [🛏] [🔌] [✕] [⚷] [☎]

REDDING

(AAA) ▽▽▽ Best Western Hospitality House M
(530) 241-6464. **$66-$95.** 532 N Market St. I-5, exit Lake Blvd northbound, just w, 0.5 mi to Market St, then 0.5 mi s; exit Market St southbound, then 2 mi s. Ext corridors. **Pets:** Small, dogs only. $10 daily fee/pet. Designated rooms, service with restrictions, supervision.
[SAVE] [S☉] [✕] [🛏] [🔌] [🍴] [➤]

(AAA) ▽▽▽ Best Western Ponderosa Inn M
(530) 241-6300. **$59-$70.** 2220 Pine St. I-5, exit Cypress Ave, 1.5 mi w. Ext corridors. **Pets:** Small, other species. $15 one-time fee/pet. Service with restrictions, supervision.
[SAVE] [S☉] [✕] [🛏] [🔌] [➤]

(AAA) ▽▽▽ Comfort Inn M
(530) 221-6530. **$79-$109.** 2059 Hilltop Dr. I-5, exit Cypress Ave E, 0.3 mi n. Ext corridors. **Pets:** Accepted.
[SAVE] [S☉] [✕] [🛏] [🔌] [➤]

(AAA) ▽▽◇ Holiday Inn Express M
(530) 241-5500. **$94-$140.** 1080 Twin View Blvd. I-5, exit Twin View Blvd, just w. Int corridors. **Pets:** Accepted.
[SAVE] [S☉] [✕] [⚷M] [🛏] [🔌] [➤]

(AAA) ▽▽▽ La Quinta Inn M
(530) 221-8200. **$75-$115.** 2180 Hilltop Dr. I-5, exit Cypress Ave E, 0.5 mi n. Int corridors. **Pets:** Accepted.
[SAVE] [✕] [⚷] [🛏] [🔌] [➤]

▽▽▽▽ Oxford Suites M
(530) 221-0100. **$88-$135.** 1967 Hilltop Dr. I-5, exit Cypress Ave E, 0.5 mi n. Ext/int corridors. **Pets:** Small. $25 one-time fee/pet. Service with restrictions, supervision.
[ASK] [S☉] [✕] [🛏] [🔌] [➤]

(AAA) ▽▽◇▽ Ramada Limited M
(530) 246-2222. **$81-$111.** 1286 Twin View Blvd. I-5, exit Twin View Blvd E, just n. Int corridors. **Pets:** Other species. $15 one-time fee/room. Service with restrictions, crate.
[SAVE] [S☉] [✕] [⚷M] [⚷] [🛏] [🔌] [➤]

(AAA) ▽▽◇▽ Redding TraveLodge M
(530) 243-5291. **$65-$105.** 540 N Market St. I-5, exit Lake Blvd southbound, 1 mi to Market St, then make left; exit SR 273 northbound, SR 90 S 2 mi. Ext corridors. **Pets:** Accepted.
[SAVE] [S☉] [✕] [⚷] [🛏] [🔌] [➤]

▽▽▽▽ Red Lion Hotel M
(530) 221-8700. **$109-$124.** 1830 Hilltop Dr. I-5, exit SR 44 and 299 (Hilltop Dr). Int corridors. **Pets:** $50 deposit/room. Service with restrictions, supervision.
[ASK] [S☉] [✕] [⚷] [🛏] [🔌] [🍴] [➤]

River Inn M
(530) 241-9500. **$65-$85, 7 day notice.** 1835 Park Marina Dr. I-5, exit SR 299 W; 1 mi w, exit Park Marina Dr. Ext corridors. **Pets:** Accepted.

REDLANDS

Best Western Sandman Motel M
(909) 793-2001. **$59-$99.** 1120 W Colton Ave. I-10, exit Tennessee St, just s, then just e. Ext corridors. **Pets:** Accepted.

Dynasty Suites-Redlands M
(909) 793-6648. **$66-$78.** 1235 W Colton Ave. I-10, exit Tennessee St, just s, then just w. Ext corridors. **Pets:** Very small. $15 daily fee/pet. Designated rooms, service with restrictions, supervision.

REDWAY

Dean Creek Resort M
(707) 923-2555. **$55-$130, 3 day notice.** 4112 Redwood Dr. US 101, exit Redwood Dr northbound; exit Redway/Shelter Cove southbound, just w. Ext corridors. **Pets:** $100 deposit/pet. Service with restrictions, supervision.

REDWOOD CITY

Hotel Sofitel San Francisco Bay at Redwood Shores LH ✿
(650) 598-9000. **$99-$349.** 223 Twin Dolphin Dr. US 101, exit Marine World Pkwy E, 0.5 mi s. Int corridors. **Pets:** Medium. $25 one-time fee/room. Service with restrictions.

TownePlace Suites by Marriott M
(650) 593-4100. **$69-$179.** 1000 Twin Dolphin Dr. US 101, exit Redwood Shores Pkwy, 0.3 mi s, then just s. Int corridors. **Pets:** Accepted.

REEDLEY

Edgewater Inn M
(559) 637-7777. **$74-$84.** 1977 W Manning Ave. 12 mi e of SR 99 via Manning Ave. Ext corridors. **Pets:** Medium, dogs only. $8 daily fee/pet. Designated rooms, service with restrictions, supervision.

RIDGECREST

Best Western China Lake Inn M
(760) 371-2300. **$77.** 400 S China Lake Blvd. On US 395 business route. Ext corridors. **Pets:** Small. $10 one-time fee/pet. Service with restrictions, supervision.

Carriage Inn M ✿
(760) 446-7910. **$120-$180.** 901 N China Lake Blvd. On SR 178 and US 395 business route. Ext corridors. **Pets:** Large. $25 one-time fee/room. Designated rooms, service with restrictions, crate.

Econo Lodge M
(760) 446-2551. **$55-$70.** 201 Inyokern Rd. On SR 178 and US 395 business route, just w of China Lake Blvd. Ext corridors. **Pets:** Small, dogs only. Designated rooms, service with restrictions, supervision.

Heritage Inn & Suites SH
(760) 446-7951. **$75-$88.** 1050 N Norma. On US 395 business route, just w. Int corridors. **Pets:** Medium. $100 deposit/room. Service with restrictions, crate.

Quality Inn M
(760) 375-9731. **$79-$89.** 507 S China Lake Blvd. On US 395 business route. Ext corridors. **Pets:** Small. $50 deposit/pet. Designated rooms, service with restrictions, supervision.

Vagabond Inn M ✿
(760) 375-2220. **$70-$75.** 426 China Lake Blvd. On US 395 business route. Ext corridors. **Pets:** Medium. $10 one-time fee/pet. Service with restrictions, supervision.

RIO DELL

Humboldt Gables Motel M
(707) 764-5609. **$50-$58.** 40 W Davis St. US 101, exit Rio Dell/Davis St W. Ext corridors. **Pets:** Medium, dogs only. Service with restrictions, supervision.

RIVERSIDE

Best Western of Riverside M
(909) 359-0770. **$80-$140.** 10518 Magnolia Ave. SR 91, exit Tyler St, 0.5 mi nw, then 0.3 mi sw. Ext corridors. **Pets:** Medium, other species. $10 daily fee/pet. Designated rooms, service with restrictions, crate.

Dynasty Suites Riverside M
(909) 369-8200. **$66-$78.** 3735 Iowa Ave. I-215 and SR 60, exit University Ave, just w, then just n. Ext corridors. **Pets:** Accepted.

ROCKLIN

Howard Johnson Hotel M
(916) 624-4500. **$84-$114.** 4420 Rocklin Rd. I-80 E, exit Rocklin Rd. Int corridors. **Pets:** Small, other species. $100 deposit/room, $20 one-time fee/room. Service with restrictions, supervision.

Ramada Limited M
(916) 632-3366. **$53-$93.** 4480 Rocklin Rd. I-80, exit Rocklin Rd. Int corridors. **Pets:** Accepted.

ROSEVILLE

♣♣♣ ▼▼▼ Best Western Roseville Inn M
(916) 782-4434. **$80-$90, 5 day notice.** 220 Harding Blvd.
I-80, exit Douglas Blvd, just w, then just n. Ext corridors.
Pets: Medium. $10 daily fee/pet. Designated rooms, service
with restrictions, supervision.
⟦SAVE⟧ ⟦S⟧ ⟦✕⟧ ⟦&M⟧ ⟦🛄⟧ ⟦💻⟧ ⟦☎⟧

▼▼▼ Oxford Suites M
(916) 784-2222. **$89-$149.** 130 N Sunrise Ave. I-80, exit
Douglas Blvd, just e, then 0.3 mi n. Ext/int corridors.
Pets: Large, other species. $15 one-time fee/room. Service
with restrictions, supervision.
⟦ASK⟧ ⟦S⟧ ⟦✕⟧ ⟦&M⟧ ⟦🛄⟧ ⟦💻⟧ ⟦☎⟧

▼▼▼▼ Residence Inn SH
(916) 772-5500. **$134-$179.** 1930 Taylor Rd. I-80, exit
Eureka-Taylor Rd, just s. Int corridors. **Pets:** Accepted.
⟦ASK⟧ ⟦S⟧ ⟦✕⟧ ⟦&M⟧ ⟦📷⟧ ⟦💻⟧ ⟦☎⟧ ⟦✕⟧

SACRAMENTO

♣♣♣ ▼▼▼ Best Western Expo Inn M
(916) 922-9833. **$85-$150.** 1413 Howe Ave. Jct SR 16 and
US 50, exit Howe Ave, 2.5 mi n. Int corridors. **Pets:** Large.
$50 deposit/room. Designated rooms, service with restric-
tions, crate.
⟦SAVE⟧ ⟦S⟧ ⟦✕⟧ ⟦&M⟧ ⟦🛄⟧ ⟦💻⟧ ⟦☎⟧

♣♣♣ ▼▼▼▼ Best Western Harbor Inn &
Suites M
(916) 371-2100. **$79-$159.** 1250 Halyard Dr. 4 mi w; exit
Business Rt 80 via Harbor Blvd. Ext/int corridors.
Pets: Accepted.
⟦SAVE⟧ ⟦S⟧ ⟦✕⟧ ⟦&M⟧ ⟦🛄⟧ ⟦💻⟧ ⟦☎⟧

♣♣♣ ▼▼▼▼ Candlewood Suites SH
(916) 646-1212. **$124-$149.** 555 Howe Ave. US 50, exit
Howe Ave, 1.5 mi n. Int corridors. **Pets:** Medium, other
species. $75 one-time fee/room. Service with restrictions.
⟦SAVE⟧ ⟦S⟧ ⟦✕⟧ ⟦&M⟧ ⟦📷⟧ ⟦🛄⟧ ⟦💻⟧

▼▼ Canterbury Inn M
(916) 927-0927. **$59-$89.** 1900 Canterbury Rd. Business Rt
80, exit Exposition Blvd, 0.4 mi w to Leisure Ln, then just n
of SR 160. Ext corridors. **Pets:** $5 daily fee/pet. Service
with restrictions, supervision.
⟦✕⟧ ⟦&M⟧ ⟦💻⟧ ⟦☎⟧

▼▼ Doubletree Hotel LH ❖
(916) 929-8855. **$89-$225.** 2001 Point West Way. 1 blk off
Business Rt 80, exit via Arden Way, 3 mi e. Int corridors.
Pets: Small. $50 deposit/room. Service with restrictions,
supervision.
⟦ASK⟧ ⟦S⟧ ⟦✕⟧ ⟦&M⟧ ⟦📷⟧ ⟦🛄⟧ ⟦💻⟧ ⟦🍴⟧ ⟦☎⟧

♣♣♣ ▼▼▼ Econo Lodge M
(916) 443-6631. **$60-$119.** 711 16th St. Business Rt 80, exit
15th St eastbound; exit 16th St westbound; I-5, exit J St.
Ext corridors. **Pets:** Other species. $6 daily fee/pet. Desig-
nated rooms, service with restrictions.
⟦SAVE⟧ ⟦S⟧ ⟦✕⟧ ⟦&M⟧ ⟦🛄⟧

♣♣♣ ▼▼▼ Good Nite Inn M
(916) 386-8408. **$53.** 25 Howe Ave. Southwest corner of jct
SR 50 and Howe Ave. Ext corridors. **Pets:** Accepted.
⟦SAVE⟧ ⟦S⟧ ⟦✕⟧ ⟦&M⟧ ⟦🛄⟧ ⟦☎⟧

▼▼ ▼▼ Homestead Studio Suites
Hotel-Sacramento M ❖
(916) 564-7500. **$77-$97.** 2810 Gateway Oaks Dr. I-5, exit
W El Camino Ave, just w, then 0.4 mi n. Ext corridors.
Pets: Medium, other species. $25 daily fee/room. Service
with restrictions, crate.
⟦ASK⟧ ⟦S⟧ ⟦✕⟧ ⟦&M⟧ ⟦📷⟧ ⟦💻⟧

▼▼ ▼▼ Host Airport Hotel M
(916) 922-8071. **$80-$140.** 6945 Airport Blvd. 11 mi nw of
state capitol; 6 mi nw of I-80, off I-5. Ext corridors.
Pets: Large. $50 one-time fee/room. Designated rooms,
service with restrictions, supervision.
⟦✕⟧ ⟦&M⟧ ⟦💻⟧

▼▼▼▼ La Quinta Inn-North M
(916) 348-0900. **$86-$101.** 4604 Madison Ave. I-80, exit
Madison Ave, 9 mi e. Ext corridors. **Pets:** Other species.
Service with restrictions.
⟦✕⟧ ⟦&M⟧ ⟦💻⟧ ⟦☎⟧

▼▼▼▼ La Quinta Inn-Sacramento Downtown M
(916) 448-8100. **$92-$121.** 200 Jibboom St. I-5, exit Richards Blvd W, 2.3 mi nw of Business Loop 80. Ext corridors.
Pets: Small. Service with restrictions, supervision.
⟦✕⟧ ⟦&M⟧ ⟦🛄⟧ ⟦💻⟧ ⟦☎⟧

▼▼▼▼ Marriott Residence Inn M
(916) 920-9111. **$159.** 1530 Howe Ave. 2.5 mi n of jct SR 16
and US 50, exit Howe Ave. Ext corridors. **Pets:** Accepted.
⟦ASK⟧ ⟦S⟧ ⟦✕⟧ ⟦&M⟧ ⟦📷⟧ ⟦🛄⟧ ⟦💻⟧ ⟦☎⟧

▼▼ ▼▼ Quality Inn Hotel & Conference Center M
(916) 487-7600. **$64-$69.** 2600 Auburn Blvd. Business Rt
80, exit Fulton Ave. Int corridors. **Pets:** Accepted.
⟦ASK⟧ ⟦S⟧ ⟦✕⟧ ⟦&M⟧ ⟦🛄⟧ ⟦💻⟧ ⟦🍴⟧ ⟦☎⟧

♣♣♣ ▼▼▼▼ Radisson Hotel SH
(916) 922-2020. **$105-$185.** 500 Leisure Ln. Business Rt 80,
exit Exposition Blvd, 0.4 mi w. Ext corridors. **Pets:** Small.
$50 deposit/pet, $50 one-time fee/pet. Designated rooms,
service with restrictions, supervision.
⟦SAVE⟧ ⟦S⟧ ⟦✕⟧ ⟦&M⟧ ⟦📷⟧ ⟦📷⟧ ⟦💻⟧ ⟦🍴⟧ ⟦☎⟧ ⟦✕⟧

♣♣♣ ▼▼▼▼ Red Lion Hotel Sacramento M
(916) 922-8041. **$129-$159.** 1401 Arden Way. Exit Business
Rt 80 via Arden Way. Ext/int corridors. **Pets:** Accepted.
⟦SAVE⟧ ⟦S⟧ ⟦✕⟧ ⟦&M⟧ ⟦🛄⟧ ⟦💻⟧ ⟦🍴⟧ ⟦☎⟧ ⟦✕⟧

▼▼▼▼ Residence Inn by Marriott M ❖
(916) 649-1300. **$154-$184.** 2410 W El Camino Ave. I-5, exit
W El Camino Ave. Ext corridors. **Pets:** $6 daily fee/room,
$50 one-time fee/room.
⟦ASK⟧ ⟦S⟧ ⟦✕⟧ ⟦&M⟧ ⟦🛄⟧ ⟦💻⟧ ⟦☎⟧

♣♣♣ ▼▼▼ Vagabond Executive Inn M
(916) 446-1481. **$88-$90.** 909 3rd St. I-5, exit J St (Old
Sacramento), 8 blks w of capitol. Ext corridors. **Pets:** Small.
$5 daily fee/pet. Designated rooms, service with restrictions,
supervision.
⟦SAVE⟧ ⟦S⟧ ⟦✕⟧ ⟦&M⟧ ⟦📷⟧ ⟦🛄⟧ ⟦💻⟧ ⟦☎⟧

SALINAS

(AAA) 🛇🛇🛇 Ramada Limited M
(831) 424-4801. **$69-$159.** 109 John St. US 101, exit John St, 0.7 mi w. Ext corridors. **Pets:** Small, other species. $25 deposit/pet. Service with restrictions, supervision.
[SAVE] [S6] [X] [🐾] [🕯] [💻]

(AAA) 🛇 Vagabond Inn M
(831) 758-4693. **$70-$170.** 131 Kern St. US 101, exit Market St, just e. Ext corridors. **Pets:** Accepted.
[SAVE] [S6] [X] [&M] [🕯] [💻] [🔀]

SAN ANDREAS

🛇🛇🛇 The Robins Nest BB ✦
(209) 754-1076. **$90-$150, 7 day notice.** 247 W St. Charles St. SR 49; north end of town. Int corridors. **Pets:** Other species. Designated rooms, service with restrictions, supervision.
[ASK] [S6] [X] [🕯] [💻] [X]

SAN BERNARDINO

🛇🛇🛇 La Quinta Inn M
(909) 888-7571. **$95-$117.** 205 E Hospitality Ln. I-10, exit Waterman Ave, just n, then 0.3 mi w. Ext corridors. **Pets:** Accepted.
[X] [🕯] [💻] [🔀]

SAN CLEMENTE

🛇🛇🛇 Casa de Elena BB
(949) 940-9099. **$139-$350.** 516 Elena Ave. I-5, exit Avenida Palizada, just w, just s on El Camino Real to Del Mar, then 1.1 mi w. Ext/int corridors. **Pets:** Accepted.
[ASK] [S6] [X] [X] [K] [🐾]

🛇🛇🛇 Holiday Inn-San Clemente Resort SH
(949) 361-3000. **$139-$199, 3 day notice.** 111 S Avenida de la Estrella. I-5, exit Avenida Palizada southbound; exit Avenida Presidio northbound, just s, then just w. Int corridors. **Pets:** Other species. $10 daily fee/pet. No service.
[ASK] [S6] [X] [🕯] [💻] [🍴] [🔀]

SAN DIEGO METROPOLITAN AREA

CHULA VISTA

🛇🛇🛇 La Quinta Inn M
(619) 691-1211. **$110-$130.** 150 Bonita Rd. I-805, exit E St/Bonita Rd, just w. Ext corridors. **Pets:** Accepted.
[X] [💻] [🔀]

🛇 Motel 6 San Diego-Chula Vista #1037 M
(619) 422-4200. **$56-$75.** 745 E St. I-5, exit E St, just e. Ext corridors. **Pets:** Medium, other species. Service with restrictions, supervision.
[X] [🔀]

CORONADO

🛇🛇🛇 Coronado Island Marriott Resort LH
(619) 435-3000. **$229-$304.** 2000 2nd St. I-5, exit Coronado Bridge (toll), 1.5 mi w to Glorietta Blvd, then just ne. Ext corridors. **Pets:** Small. Service with restrictions, crate.
[ASK] [S6] [X] [🕯] [💻] [🍴] [🔀] [X]

🛇🛇 Crown City Inn M ✦
(619) 435-3116. **$99-$239.** 520 Orange Ave. I-5, exit Coronado Bridge (toll), 1.5 mi w, then just s. Ext corridors. **Pets:** Medium, other species. $8 daily fee/pet. Designated rooms, service with restrictions, supervision.
[X] [&M] [🐾] [🕯] [💻] [🍴]

(AAA) 🛇🛇🛇 Loews Coronado Bay Resort LH ✦
(619) 424-4000. **$155-$255.** 4000 Coronado Bay Rd. I-5, exit Coronado Bridge (toll), 1.7 mi w to Orange Ave, 1 mi sw to Silver Strand Blvd, then 4.5 mi s to Coronado Cays. Ext/int corridors. **Pets:** Other species.
[SAVE] [S6] [X] [🕯] [💻] [🍴] [🔀] [X]

DEL MAR

(AAA) 🛇🛇🛇 Best Western Stratford Inn M
(858) 755-1501. **$99-$249, 3 day notice.** 710 Camino Del Mar. I-5, exit Del Mar Heights Rd, 1 mi w, then 0.3 mi n. Int corridors. **Pets:** Accepted.
[SAVE] [S6] [X] [&M] [🌐] [🐾] [💻] [🔀]

(AAA) 🛇🛇🛇 Del Mar Inn, A Clarion Carriage House SH
(858) 755-9765. **$94-$194, 3 day notice.** 720 Camino Del Mar. I-5, exit Del Mar Heights Rd, 1 mi w, 0.3 mi n. Int corridors. **Pets:** Accepted.
[SAVE] [S6] [X] [🕯] [🔀]

IMPERIAL BEACH

(AAA) 🛇🛇🛇 Hawaiian Gardens Suite-Hotel M
(619) 429-5303. **Call for rates.** 1031 Imperial Beach Blvd. I-5, exit Coronado Ave, 2 mi w. Ext corridors. **Pets:** Accepted.
[X] [🔀] [K]

LA JOLLA

(AAA) 🛇🛇 La Jolla Village Lodge M
(858) 551-2001. **$69-$289.** 1141 Silverado St. I-5, exit La Jolla Pkwy northbound, 1.5 mi w to Torrey Pines Rd, 1 mi w, then 0.8 mi sw; exit La Jolla Village Dr southbound, 1 mi w to Torrey Pines Rd, 3.6 mi sw. Ext corridors. **Pets:** Other species. $20 one-time fee/pet. Service with restrictions, supervision.
[SAVE] [S6] [X] [🕯] [💻]

🛇🛇🛇 La Valencia Hotel LH
(858) 454-0771. **$275-$3500.** 1132 Prospect St. I-5, exit La Jolla Pkwy northbound, 1.5 mi w to Torrey Pines Rd, 1 mi w, then 0.6 mi sw; exit La Jolla Village Dr southbound, 1 mi w to Torrey Pines Rd, 2.7 mi sw, 0.6 mi sw. Ext/int corridors. **Pets:** Accepted.
[X] [🕯] [💻] [🍴] [🔀] [X]

🛇🛇🛇 Residence Inn by Marriott La Jolla SH
(858) 587-1770. **$149-$199.** 8901 Gilman Dr. I-5, exit Gilman Dr, 1.5 mi nw. Ext corridors. **Pets:** Other species. $10 daily fee/room, $150 one-time fee/room. Service with restrictions.
[ASK] [X] [💻] [🔀] [X]

WWW San Diego Marriott La Jolla 🔲
(858) 587-1414. **$179.** 4240 La Jolla Village Dr. I-5, exit La Jolla Village Dr, 0.5 mi e. Int corridors. **Pets:** Accepted.
🆎 🔲 ⊠ 🔲 🔲 🔲 🔲 🔲 🔲 🔲

LA MESA

WW Motel 6 San Diego-La Mesa #1319 🔲
(619) 464-7151. **Call for rates.** 7621 Alvarado Rd. I-8, exit Fletcher Pkwy, just s, then just w. Ext corridors. **Pets:** Accepted.
⊠

NATIONAL CITY

🔺🔺🔺 WWW Red Lion Inn & Suites San Diego/
South Bay 🔲
(619) 336-1100. **$69-$139.** 801 National City Blvd. I-5, exit 8th St southbound; exit Plaza Blvd northbound. Ext corridors. **Pets:** Other species. $30 deposit/pet. Supervision.
🔲 🔲 ⊠ 🔲 🔲 🔲 🔲

POWAY

WW Best Western Country Inn 🔲
(858) 748-6320. **$65-$99.** 13845 Poway Rd. I-15, exit Poway Rd, 4 mi e. Ext corridors. **Pets:** Accepted.
🆎 🔲 ⊠ 🔲 🔲 🔲

🔺🔺🔺 WW Ramada Limited 🔲
(858) 748-7311. **$79-$109.** 12448 Poway Rd. I-15, exit Poway Rd, 3 mi e. Ext corridors. **Pets:** Small. $50 deposit/pet, $10 daily fee/pet. Service with restrictions, supervision.
🔲 🔲 ⊠ 🔲 🔲 🔲

RANCHO BERNARDO

🔺🔺🔺 WWW La Quinta Inn 🔲
(858) 484-8800. **$86-$115.** 10185 Paseo Montril. I-15, exit Rancho Penasquitos Blvd, just w. Ext corridors. **Pets:** Medium, other species. Service with restrictions, crate.
🔲 ⊠ 🔲 🔲 🔲 🔲

🔺🔺🔺 WWWW Rancho Bernardo Inn 🔲
(858) 487-1611. **$259-$379, 3 day notice.** 17550 Bernardo Oaks Dr. I-15, exit Rancho Bernardo Rd, 1 mi e, then 1 mi n. Ext/int corridors. **Pets:** Medium. $100 one-time fee/room. Service with restrictions, supervision.
🔲 🔲 ⊠ 🔲 🔲 🔲 🔲

WW Rancho Bernardo Travelodge 🔲
(858) 487-0445. **$77-$90.** 16929 W Bernardo Dr. I-15, exit Rancho Bernardo Rd, just w, then just s. Ext corridors. **Pets:** Small. $10 daily fee/pet. Designated rooms, service with restrictions, crate.
🆎 🔲 ⊠ 🔲 🔲 🔲

WWWW Residence Inn San Diego Rancho
Bernardo/Carmel Mountain
Ranch 🔲
(858) 673-1900. **$139-$219.** 11002 Rancho Carmel Dr. I-15, exit Carmel Mountain Rd, just e. Ext/int corridors. **Pets:** Other species. $10 daily fee/pet, $150 one-time fee/room. Designated rooms, supervision.
🆎 ⊠ 🔲 🔲 🔲 🔲

WWWW Staybridge Suites by Holiday Inn Carmel
Mountain 🔲
(848) 487-0900. **$156-$200.** 11855 Ave of Industry. I-15, exit Carmel Mountain Rd, 1 mi ne to second Rancho Carmel Dr, just w to Innovation Dr, just n, then just e. Int corridors. **Pets:** Medium, other species. $150 one-time fee/room. Service with restrictions.
🆎 ⊠ 🔲 🔲 🔲 🔲 🔲 🔲

RANCHO SANTA FE

WWWW The Inn at Rancho Santa Fe 🔲
(858) 756-1131. **$185-$275, 3 day notice.** 5951 Linea del Cielo. I-5, exit Lomas Sante Fe Dr, 4 mi e on CR S-8. Ext/int corridors. **Pets:** Other species. Designated rooms, service with restrictions.
🔲 🔲 🔲 🔲 🔲

SAN DIEGO

🔺🔺🔺 WWW Best Western Lamplighter Inn &
Suites 🔲
(619) 582-3088. **$75-$130.** 6474 El Cajon Blvd. I-8, exit 70th St, 0.5 mi s, then 1 mi w. Ext corridors. **Pets:** $10 daily fee/pet. Service with restrictions, supervision.
🔲 🔲 ⊠ 🔲 🔲 🔲

🔺🔺🔺 WWW The Bristol 🔲
(619) 232-6141. **$239-$259.** 1055 First Ave. I-5, exit Front St, 0.5 mi s at C St; downtown. Int corridors. **Pets:** Other species. Designated rooms, service with restrictions, supervision.
🔲 🔲 ⊠ 🔲 🔲 🔲

🔺🔺🔺 WWW Crown Point View Suite-Hotel 🔲
(858) 272-0676. **$48-$76, 14 day notice.** 4088 Crown Point Dr. I-5, exit Garnet Ave, 1 mi e to Morrell St, then 0.5 mi s. Ext corridors. **Pets:** Accepted.
🔲 🔲 🔲 🔲 🔲

🔺🔺🔺 WWWW DoubleTree Club Hotel San Diego
Zoo/SeaWorld Area 🔲
(619) 881-6900. **$109-$149, 3 day notice.** 1515 Hotel Cir S. I-8, exit Hotel Cir, south side. Int corridors. **Pets:** Accepted.
🔲 🔲 ⊠ 🔲 🔲 🔲 🔲 🔲

🔺🔺🔺 WWWW Doubletree Hotel San Diego-Mission
Valley 🔲
(619) 297-5466. **$142-$230.** 7450 Hazard Center Dr. SR 163, exit Friars Rd, 0.3 mi e to Frazee Rd, then just s. Int corridors. **Pets:** Accepted.
🔲 🔲 ⊠ 🔲 🔲 🔲 🔲 🔲

WWWW Hampton Inn SeaWorld/Airport 🔲
(619) 299-6633. **$89-$128.** 3888 Greenwood St. I-8, exit Sports Arena Blvd, 0.5 mi s, 0.3 mi e on Hancock St, then 0.4 mi s on Kurtz St. Int corridors. **Pets:** Accepted.
🆎 🔲 ⊠ 🔲 🔲 🔲

🔺🔺🔺 WWWW Holiday Inn on the Bay 🔲
(619) 232-3861. **$99-$169.** 1355 N Harbor Dr at Ash St. I-5, exit B St northbound, 1.8 mi w to India St, just n to Ash St, then just w; exit Front Ave southbound, 0.5 mi s to Ash St, then just w. Int corridors. **Pets:** Accepted.
🔲 🔲 ⊠ 🔲 🔲 🔲 🔲

▼▼ Homestead Studio Suites Hotel-San
Diego/Mission Valley [M] ❖
(619) 299-2292. **$76-$96.** 7444 Mission Valley Rd. SR 163, exit Friars Rd, 1 mi ne via Mission Center Dr. Ext corridors. **Pets:** Medium, other species. $25 daily fee/room. Service with restrictions, crate.
[ASK] [🛏] [✕] [🖨] [💻]

▼▼ Homestead Studio Suites Hotel-San
Diego/Sorrento Mesa [M] ❖
(858) 623-0100. **$89-$109.** 9880 Pacific Heights Blvd. I-805, exit Mira Mesa Blvd, 1 mi e. Ext corridors. **Pets:** Medium, other species. $25 daily fee/room. Service with restrictions, crate.
[ASK] [🛏] [✕] [&M] [🔌] [👍] [🖨] [💻]

[AAA] ▼▼▼ Horton Grand Hotel [SH]
(619) 544-1886. **$129-$189.** 311 Island Ave. I-5, exit Front St southbound, 1.2 mi s, then just e; exit J St northbound, 1 mi w, just n on 3rd Ave, then just e. Int corridors. **Pets:** Accepted.
[SAVE] [🛏] [✕] [🖨] [💻] [🍴]

▼ Motel 6 San Diego-Downtown #1419 [M]
(619) 236-9292. **Call for rates.** 1546 2nd Ave. I-5, exit 6th Ave northbound, 0.3 mi w, then just s; exit 2nd Ave southbound, just s. Int corridors. **Pets:** Accepted.
[✕]

▼ Motel 6 San Diego North #1020 [M]
(858) 268-9758. **Call for rates.** 5592 Clairemont Mesa Blvd. I-805, exit Clairemont Mesa Blvd, just w. Ext corridors. **Pets:** Accepted.
[✕]

[AAA] ▼▼ Ocean Villa Inn [M]
(619) 224-3481. **$70-$150, 3 day notice.** 5142 W Point Loma Blvd. I-8, exit Sunset Cliff Blvd, 1.5 mi sw. Ext corridors. **Pets:** $100 deposit/room, $25 one-time fee/room. Service with restrictions, crate.
[SAVE] [🛏] [✕] [🖨] [➰]

[AAA] ▼▼ Old Town Inn [M]
(619) 260-8024. **$60-$140.** 4444 Pacific Hwy. I-5, exit Sea-World Dr, just w, then 1 mi s. Ext corridors. **Pets:** $10 daily fee/pet. Service with restrictions, supervision.
[SAVE] [🛏] [✕] [&M] [🔌] [🖨] [➰]

[AAA] ▼▼ Premier Inns [M]
(619) 291-8252. **$44-$124.** 2484 Hotel Circle Pl. I-8, exit Taylor St, just n. Ext corridors. **Pets:** Medium, dogs only. $20 deposit/pet. Designated rooms, service with restrictions, supervision.
[SAVE] [🛏] [✕] [🖨] [➰]

[AAA] ▼▼▼ Radisson Hotel-San Diego [LH]
(619) 260-0111. **$219-$249.** 1433 Camino Del Rio S. I-8, exit Mission Center Rd, south side. Int corridors. **Pets:** Accepted.
[SAVE] [🛏] [✕] [🖨] [💻] [🍴] [➰]

▼▼▼ Red Lion Hanalei Hotel [LH] ❖
(619) 297-1101. **$99-$169.** 2270 Hotel Cir S. I-8, exit Tayor St, just n, then just e. Ext corridors. **Pets:** Medium. $50 deposit/room. Service with restrictions, supervision.
[ASK] [🛏] [✕] [&M] [🔌] [👍] [🖨] [💻] [🍴] [➰] [✕]

▼▼▼ Residence Inn by Marriott San Diego
Downtown [SH] ❖
(619) 338-8200. **$159-$219.** 1747 Pacific Hwy. I-5, exit Front St southbound, just s to Grape St, 0.3 mi w, then just n; exit Hawthorn St northbound, 0.4 mi w, then just s. Int corridors. **Pets:** Medium, other species. $100 one-time fee/pet.
[ASK] [🛏] [✕] [🖨] [💻] [➰]

[AAA] ▼▼▼ Residence Inn San Diego/Mission
Valley/SeaWorld Area [SH] ❖
(619) 881-3600. **$139-$359, 3 day notice.** 1865 Hotel Cir S. I-8, exit Hotel Cir, south side. Int corridors. **Pets:** Other species. $150 one-time fee/room. Designated rooms, service with restrictions.
[SAVE] [🛏] [✕] [&M] [🔌] [👍] [🖨] [💻] [➰] [✕]

▼▼▼ Residence Inn San Diego-Sorrento Mesa [SH]
(858) 552-9100. **$139-$159.** 5995 Pacific Mesa Ct. I-805, exit Mira Mesa Blvd, 1.5 mi e. Int corridors. **Pets:** Other species. $10 daily fee/pet, $150 one-time fee/room. Service with restrictions, supervision.
[ASK] [✕] [🖨] [💻] [➰] [✕]

▼▼ ▼▼▼ San Diego Marriott Hotel & Marina [LH] ❖
(619) 234-1500. **$365-$385.** 333 W Harbor Dr. I-5, exit Front St, 1.3 mi s, then just w. Int corridors. **Pets:** Other species. Service with restrictions, crate.
[✕] [🖨] [💻] [🍴] [➰] [✕]

▼▼ San Diego Marriott Mission Valley [LH]
(619) 692-3800. **$159-$228.** 8757 Rio San Diego Dr. I-8, exit Qualcomm Way, just n. Int corridors. **Pets:** Small. $100 deposit/room, $50 one-time fee/room. Designated rooms, service with restrictions, supervision.
[✕] [💻] [🍴] [➰] [✕]

[AAA] ▼▼▼ Shelter Pointe Hotel & Marina [SH]
(619) 221-8000. **$139-$219.** 1551 Shelter Island Dr. I-5, exit Rosecrans St southbound, 3 mi sw; exit Hawthorn St northbound, 3 mi nw on Harbor Dr to Scott Rd, then 0.5 mi w. Ext/int corridors. **Pets:** Accepted.
[SAVE] [🛏] [✕] [🖨] [💻] [🍴] [➰] [✕]

[AAA] ▼▼▼ Sheraton Suites San Diego [LH] ❖
(619) 696-9800. **$369.** 701 A St/7th Ave. I-5, exit Front St, 0.5 mi s. Int corridors. **Pets:** Medium. Service with restrictions, supervision.
[SAVE] [🛏] [✕] [&M] [🔌] [👍] [💻] [🍴] [➰]

[AAA] ▼▼▼ Sommerset Suites Hotel [SH]
(619) 692-5200. **$79-$279.** 606 Washington St. SR 163, just w. Ext/int corridors. **Pets:** Small, other species. $35 one-time fee/pet. Service with restrictions, supervision.
[SAVE] [🛏] [✕] [➰]

▼▼▼ Staybridge Suites by Holiday Inn-Sorrento
Mesa [SH]
(858) 453-5343. **$107-$207.** 6639 Mira Mesa Blvd. I-805, exit Mira Mesa Blvd, 2.3 mi e. Int corridors. **Pets:** Accepted.
[ASK] [🛏] [✕] [&M] [🔌] [👍] [🖨] [💻] [➰]

[AAA] ▼▼ Vagabond Inn-Point Loma [M]
(619) 224-3371. **$64-$79.** 1325 Scott St. I-8, exit Nimintz Blvd, 2 mi s to Rosecrans St, just w to Jarvis St, then just s. Ext corridors. **Pets:** Large, other species. $10 daily fee/room. Service with restrictions, supervision.
[SAVE] [🛏] [✕] [🖨] [💻] [➰]

SAN FRANCISCO METROPOLITAN AREA

BELMONT

▼▼▼ **Summerfield Suites by Wyndham-Belmont/Redwood Shores** Ⓜ
(650) 591-8600. **$79-$139.** 400 Concourse Dr. US 101, exit Marine World Pkwy, just e, then just n on Oracle Pkwy. Ext corridors. **Pets:** Accepted.
ASK Só ✕ &M 🐾 ▤ ⇌

BURLINGAME

▼▼▼ **Crowne Plaza** ⅬⒽ 🐾
(650) 342-9200. **$249-$349.** 1177 Airport Blvd. US 101, exit Broadway-Burlingame or Old Bayshore, just e. Int corridors. **Pets:** Medium. $100 deposit/pet. Service with restrictions, supervision.
ASK Só ✕ &M 🐾 🖥 ▤ ❙❙ ⇌

⟐ ▼▼▼ **Doubletree Hotel-San Francisco Airport** ⅬⒽ 🐾
(650) 344-5500. **$79-$149.** 835 Airport Blvd. US 101, exit Broadway-Burlingame or Anza Blvd, just e. Int corridors. **Pets:** Medium, other species. $20 one-time fee/room. Designated rooms, service with restrictions, supervision.
SAVE Só ✕ &M 🐾 🖥 🖥 ❙❙

⟐ ▼▼▼▼ **Embassy Suites-SFO** ⅬⒽ
(650) 342-4600. **$119-$199.** 150 Anza Blvd. US 101, exit Broadway-Burlingame or Anza Blvd, just e. Int corridors. **Pets:** Accepted.
SAVE Só ✕ &M 🐾 🖥 🖥 ▤ ❙❙ ⇌ ✕

⟐ ▼▼▼ **Red Roof Inn** Ⓜ 🐾
(650) 342-7772. **$59-$89.** 777 Airport Blvd. US 101, exit Broadway-Burlingame or E Anza Blvd; just s of airport. Ext corridors. **Pets:** Other species. Service with restrictions, supervision.
SAVE ✕ &M 🐾 🖥 ⇌

▼▼▼▼ **San Francisco Airport Marriott** ⅬⒽ
(650) 692-9100. **$99-$229.** 1800 Old Bayshore Hwy. US 101, exit Millbrae Ave, just e. Int corridors. **Pets:** No service, supervision.
ASK Só ✕ &M 🐾 🖥 🖥 ▤ ❙❙ ⇌ ✕

⟐ ▼▼▼ **Vagabond Inn-Airport** Ⓜ
(650) 692-4040. **$60-$80.** 1640 Bayshore Hwy. US 101, exit Millbrae Ave, just e. Ext corridors. **Pets:** Accepted.
SAVE Só ✕ &M 🖥 ▤

CORTE MADERA

⟐ ▼▼▼ **Marin Suites Hotel** Ⓜ
(415) 924-3608. **$154-$220.** 45 Tamal Vista Blvd. US 101, exit Tamalpais Rd/Paradise Dr. Ext corridors. **Pets:** Other species. $10 daily fee/pet. Service with restrictions, supervision.
SAVE Só ✕ &M 🐾 ▤ ⇌ ✕

HALF MOON BAY

⟐ ▼▼▼ **Harbor View Inn** Ⓜ
(650) 726-2329. **$86-$176.** 51 Ave Alhambra. 4 mi n of jct SR 92 and 1; e of SR 1. Ext corridors. **Pets:** Accepted.
SAVE Só ✕ 🖥 ✕

⟐ ▼▼▼ **Holiday Inn Express** Ⓜ 🐾
(650) 726-3400. **$99-$139.** 230 S Cabrillo Hwy. On SR 1, just s of SR 92. Ext corridors. **Pets:** $10 daily fee/pet. Designated rooms, service with restrictions, supervision.
SAVE Só ✕ 🖥 ▤

⟐ ▼▼▼ **Miramar Lodge & Conference Center** Ⓜ
(650) 712-1999. **$89-$189.** 2930 N Cabrillo Hwy. On SR 1. Ext corridors. **Pets:** Accepted.
SAVE Só ✕ 🖥 ▤

▼▼ **Ramada Limited** Ⓜ
(650) 726-9700. **$70-$325.** 3020 N Cabrillo Hwy. 2 mi n of jct SR 92 and 1, w of SR 1. Ext corridors. **Pets:** Accepted.
ASK Só ✕ 🖥 ▤

MILLBRAE

▼▼▼ **Clarion Hotel-San Francisco Airport** ⅬⒽ
(650) 692-6363. **$99-$129.** 401 E Millbrae Ave. US 101, exit Millbrae Ave, just e. Int corridors. **Pets:** Accepted.
ASK Só ✕ &M 🖥 ▤ ❙❙ ⇌

▼▼▼ **The Westin Hotel-San Francisco Airport** ⅬⒽ 🐾
(650) 692-3500. **$299-$319.** 1 Old Bayshore Hwy. Just e of US 101, exit Millbrae Ave. Int corridors. **Pets:** Medium, dogs only. $100 deposit/pet. Service with restrictions, supervision.
ASK Só ✕ &M 🐾 🖥 🖥 ▤ ❙❙ ⇌ ✕

SAN BRUNO

⟐ ▼▼▼ **Regency Inn** Ⓜ
(650) 589-7535. **$75.** 411 E San Bruno Ave. US 101, exit San Bruno Ave, 0.4 mi w. Ext corridors. **Pets:** Medium, other species. $15 daily fee/pet. Designated rooms, service with restrictions, supervision.
SAVE Só ✕ &M 🖥 ▤

⟐ ▼▼▼ **Staybridge Suites** Ⓜ
(650) 588-0770. **$89-$139.** 1350 Huntington Ave. I-380, exit El Camino Real N, e on Sneath Ln. Ext corridors. **Pets:** Other species. $200 one-time fee/room.
SAVE Só ✕ &M 🖥 ▤ ⇌ ✕

SAN CARLOS

▼▼ **Homestead Studio Suites Hotel-San Carlos/Redwood Shores** Ⓜ 🐾
(650) 368-2600. **$100-$120.** 3 Circle Star Way. US 101, exit Whipple Ave, w to Industrial, then just n. Int corridors. **Pets:** Medium, other species. $25 daily fee/room. Service with restrictions, crate.
ASK Só ✕ &M 🖥 🖥 ▤

SAN FRANCISCO

AAA ▼▼▼▼ **Beresford Arms** 🆂🅷 ❀
(415) 673-2600. **$99-$129.** 701 Post St. 3 blks w of Union Square. Int corridors. **Pets:** Other species. Designated rooms, service with restrictions, supervision.
[SAVE] [🛏] [✕] [🖬] [🔒] [🖬] [🖵] [✗]

AAA ▼▼▼ **Best Western Tuscan Inn at**
Fisherman's Wharf 🆂🅷 ❀
(415) 561-1100. **$169-$269.** 425 Northpoint St. Just s of Fisherman's Wharf at Mason St. Int corridors. **Pets:** Large, other species. $25 one-time fee/room. Service with restrictions, crate.
[SAVE] [🛏] [✕] [🖬] [🖵] [🍴]

▼▼▼▼ **Campton Place Hotel** 🆂🅷 ❀
(415) 781-5555. **$335-$470.** 340 Stockton St. Just n of Union Square. Int corridors. **Pets:** Other species. $35 daily fee/room.
[ASK] [🛏] [✕] [🖬] [🍴]

▼▼ **Cartwright Hotel** 🆂🅷
(415) 421-2865. **$99-$139.** 524 Sutter St. Union Square at Powell St. Int corridors. **Pets:** Accepted.
[ASK] [🛏] [✕] [🖬]

AAA ▼▼▼ **Clarion Hotel Cosmo** 🆂🅷 ❀
(415) 673-6040. **$89-$159.** 761 Post St. 3 1/2 blks w of Union Square. Int corridors. **Pets:** Other species. Designated rooms, service with restrictions, supervision.
[SAVE] [🛏] [✕] [🖵] [🍴] [✗]

AAA ▼▼▼▼ **Crowne Plaza Union Square** 🅻🅷
(415) 398-8900. **$139-$309.** 480 Sutter St. Just n off Union Square; corner of Powell St. Int corridors. **Pets:** Medium. $106 deposit/pet. Designated rooms, service with restrictions, supervision.
[SAVE] [🛏] [✕] [🖬] [🔒] [🖬] [🖵] [🍴]

AAA ▼▼▼▼ **Executive Hotel Vintage**
Court 🆂🅷 ❀
(415) 392-4666. **$109-$179.** 650 Bush St. 2 blks n of Union Square. Int corridors. **Pets:** Other species. $50 deposit/room. Service with restrictions.
[SAVE] [🛏] [✕] [🖬]

▼▼▼▼ **The Fairmont San Francisco** 🅻🅷
(415) 772-5000. **$189-$289.** 950 Mason St. Atop Nob Hill at California St. Int corridors. **Pets:** Accepted.
[ASK] [✕] [🖬] [🔒] [🖬] [🍴]

▼▼▼▼ **Four Seasons San Francisco** 🅻🅷
(415) 633-3000. **$469-$600.** 757 Market St. Between 3rd and 4th sts. Int corridors. **Pets:** Accepted.
[ASK] [✕] [🖬] [🔒] [🍴] [➤] [✗]

AAA ▼▼▼ **Harbor Court Hotel** 🆂🅷
(415) 882-1300. **$120-$235.** 165 Steuart St. On Embarcadero; between Howard and Mission sts. Int corridors. **Pets:** Accepted.
[SAVE] [🛏] [✕] [🖬] [🍴] [➤]

AAA ▼▼▼ **Holiday Inn Civic Center** 🅻🅷
(415) 626-6103. **$94-$229.** 50 8th St. 2 blks from civic auditorium; just s of Market St and BART Station. Int corridors. **Pets:** Small. $75 one-time fee/room. Service with restrictions.
[SAVE] [🛏] [✕] [🖬] [🖬] [🔒] [🖬] [🖵] [🍴] [➤]

AAA ▼▼▼ **Holiday Inn Select & Spa**
Downtown 🅻🅷
(415) 433-6600. **$119-$279.** 750 Kearny St. Adjacent to North Beach. Int corridors. **Pets:** Accepted.
[SAVE] [🛏] [✕] [🖬] [🖬] [🔒] [🖬] [🖵] [🍴] [➤]

AAA ▼▼▼ **Hotel Beresford** 🆂🅷 ❀
(415) 673-9900. **$87-$119.** 635 Sutter St. 1 blk nw of Union Square at Mason St. Int corridors. **Pets:** Other species. Designated rooms, service with restrictions, supervision.
[SAVE] [🛏] [✕] [🖬] [🍴] [✗]

AAA ▼▼▼▼ **Hotel Juliana** 🆂🅷
(415) 392-2540. **$169-$219.** 590 Bush St. Downtown. Int corridors. **Pets:** Accepted.
[SAVE] [🛏] [✕] [🖬] [🖵]

▼▼ **Hotel Metropolis** 🆂🅷 ❀
(415) 775-4600. **Call for rates.** 25 Mason St. US 101, exit Market St, just w. Int corridors. **Pets:** Medium, other species. $50 one-time fee/room. Service with restrictions.
[✕] [🔒] [✗]

AAA ▼▼▼ ▼▼▼ **Hotel Monaco** 🅻🅷 ❀
(415) 292-0100. **$170-$359.** 501 Geary St. Just w of Union Square at Taylor St. Int corridors. **Pets:** Dogs only. Designated rooms, service with restrictions, supervision.
[SAVE] [🛏] [✕] [🖬] [🔒] [🖵] [🍴] [✗]

AAA ▼▼▼ ▼▼▼ **Hotel Nikko** 🅻🅷
(415) 394-1111. **$175.** 222 Mason St. 3 blks w of Union Square. Int corridors. **Pets:** Small, dogs only. $50 deposit/room. Service with restrictions, supervision.
[SAVE] [🛏] [✕] [🖬] [🔒] [🖵] [➤] [✗]

AAA ▼▼▼ ▼▼▼ **Hotel Palomar** 🆂🅷 ❀
(415) 348-1111. **$169-$349.** 12 Fourth St. At Market St; downtown. Int corridors. **Pets:** Dogs only. Service with restrictions, crate.
[SAVE] [✕] [🖬] [🔒] [🖬] [🍴]

AAA ▼▼▼ **Hotel Triton** 🆂🅷
(415) 394-0500. **$139-$199.** 342 Grant Ave. Near Union Square at Bush St. Int corridors. **Pets:** Accepted.
[SAVE] [🛏] [✕] [🖬] [🖵]

▼▼▼ **Hotel Union Square** 🆂🅷
(415) 397-3000. **$79-$165.** 114 Powell St. US 101, exit Market E to Powell St, just n of cable car turnaround. Int corridors. **Pets:** Medium, other species. $50 one-time fee/pet. Service with restrictions, supervision.
[ASK] [🛏] [✕] [✗]

▼▼ **Kensington Park Hotel** 🆂🅷 ❀
(415) 788-6400. **$125-$159.** 450 Post St. US 101, exit 5th St, r to Ellis St, r on Taylor St. Int corridors. **Pets:** Other species. $50 one-time fee/room. Service with restrictions.
[ASK] [🛏] [✕] [🖬] [🍴] [✗]

▼▼▼▼ The Laurel Inn M ❖
(415) 567-8467. **$150-$185.** 444 Presidio Ave. 1 mi w of US 101 (Van Ness Ave), 1 mi e of Park Presidio Blvd (SR 1) at California St. Int corridors. **Pets:** Service with restrictions, supervision.
[SAVE] [X] [&M] [⌂] [🛏] [💻] [/K]

▼▼▼▼ Mandarin Oriental, San Francisco LH ❖
(415) 276-9888. **$495-$745.** 222 Sansome St. US 101, s on Lombard St, e on Bush, then s. Int corridors. **Pets:** Small, dogs only. $25 daily fee/pet. Service with restrictions, supervision.
[ASK] [S6] [X] [⌂] [💻] [⑪] [🐾]

▲▲ ▼▼▼ Monticello Inn SH
(415) 392-8800. **$129-$199.** 127 Ellis St. Just w of Union Square. Int corridors. **Pets:** Accepted.
[SAVE] [S6] [X] [💻] [⑪]

▼▼▼ Omni San Francisco Hotel LH ❖
(415) 677-9494. **$159-$299.** 500 California St. Downtown financial district; at Montgomery St. Int corridors. **Pets:** Small. $50 one-time fee/room. Service with restrictions, supervision.
[ASK] [S6] [X] [💻] [⑪]

▲▲ ▼▼▼ Pacific Heights Inn M
(415) 776-3310. **$85-$150.** 1555 Union St. Just w of US 101 (Van Ness Ave). Ext corridors. **Pets:** Medium.
[SAVE] [S6] [X] [&M] [⌂] [🛏] [💻] [/K]

▼▼▼▼ The Pan Pacific Hotel LH
(415) 771-8600. **$265-$365.** 500 Post St. Just w of Union Square at Mason St. Int corridors. **Pets:** Accepted.
[ASK] [S6] [X] [&M] [⌂] [⑪]

▲▲ ▼▼▼▼ The Prescott Hotel LH
(415) 563-0303. **$275-$1200.** 545 Post St. Just w of Union Square. Int corridors. **Pets:** Accepted.
[SAVE] [S6] [X] [⑪]

▼▼▼ San Francisco Marriott Fisherman's Wharf LH
(415) 775-7555. **$169-$239.** 1250 Columbus Ave. Just s of Fisherman's Wharf at Bay St. Int corridors. **Pets:** Medium, dogs only. $100 one-time fee/room. Service with restrictions, supervision.
[ASK] [X] [&M] [⌂] [⌂] [🛏] [💻] [⑪]

▲▲ ▼▼▼ Serrano Hotel SH ❖
(415) 885-2500. **$179-$219.** 405 Taylor St. Just w of Union Square. Int corridors. **Pets:** Other species. $50 deposit/room. Service with restrictions, supervision.
[SAVE] [X] [&M] [⌂] [⑪] [🐾]

▲▲ ▼▼▼▼ Sir Francis Drake Hotel LH
(415) 392-7755. **$149-$239.** 450 Powell St. Just off Union Square at Sutter St. Int corridors. **Pets:** Small. Designated rooms, service with restrictions, supervision.
[SAVE] [S6] [X] [⑪]

▲▲ ▼▼▼ Travelodge By The Bay M ❖
(415) 673-0691. **$79-$119.** 1450 Lombard St. On US 101 (Van Ness Ave). Ext corridors. **Pets:** Other species. $20 daily fee/pet. Designated rooms, supervision.
[SAVE] [S6] [X] [&M] [⌂] [💻]

▲▲ ▼▼▼▼ The Westin St. Francis LH ❖
(415) 397-7000. **$129-$569.** 335 Powell St. On Union Square. **Pets:** Medium, dogs only. $75 one-time fee/pet. Designated rooms, service with restrictions, supervision.
[SAVE] [S6] [X] [💻] [⑪] [🐾]

SAN MATEO

▼▼ Homestead Studio Suites Hotel-San Mateo/SFO M ❖
(650) 574-1744. **$91-$111.** 1830 Gateway Dr. SR 92, exit Edgewater Blvd, se of jct US 101 and SR 92. Ext corridors. **Pets:** Medium, other species. $25 daily fee/room. Service with restrictions, crate.
[ASK] [S6] [X] [&M] [⌂] [🛏] [💻]

▼▼▼ Radisson Villa Hotel SH
(650) 341-0966. **$185.** 4000 S El Camino Real. 8 mi s of San Francisco International Airport; US 101, exit W Hillsdale Blvd, 0.5 mi s on SR 82. Ext/int corridors. **Pets:** Medium. $150 deposit/room. Service with restrictions, supervision.
[ASK] [S6] [X] [&M] [⌂] [🛏] [💻] [⑪] [🏊]

▼▼▼ Residence Inn by Marriott M
(650) 574-4700. **$104-$151.** 2000 Winward Way. 0.8 mi se from jct US 101 and SR 92; exit SR 92 via Edgewater Blvd. Ext corridors. **Pets:** Other species. $10 daily fee/pet, $75 one-time fee/room. Designated rooms.
[ASK] [S6] [X] [&M] [⌂] [🛏] [💻] [🏊]

SAN RAFAEL

▼▼ Villa Inn M
(415) 456-4975. **$65-$90.** 1600 Lincoln Ave. Off US 101 at Lincoln Ave off-ramp; exit Central San Rafael northbound, 0.3 mi w on Fourth St, 0.5 mi n. Ext corridors. **Pets:** Medium, dogs only. $20 deposit/pet. Designated rooms, service with restrictions, supervision.
[X] [&M] [⌂] [🛏] [💻] [🏊]

SOUTH SAN FRANCISCO

▲▲ ▼▼▼ Howard Johnson Express Inn M
(650) 589-9055. **$49-$119.** 222 S Airport Blvd. US 101, exit S Airport Blvd, just e. Ext corridors. **Pets:** Accepted.
[SAVE] [S6] [X] [&M] [🛏] [💻]

▲▲ ▼▼▼ La Quinta Inn M
(650) 583-2223. **$100-$169.** 20 S Airport Blvd. US 101, exit S Airport Blvd, just w. Int corridors. **Pets:** Accepted.
[SAVE] [X] [&M] [⌂] [🛏] [💻] [🏊]

❖   **END METROPOLITAN AREA**   ❖

SAN JOSE

(AAA) ◆◆◆◆ Doubletree Hotel LH
(408) 453-4000. **$79-$259.** 2050 Gateway Pl. 0.3 mi e of San Jose International Airport via Airport Blvd; w of US 101, exit N 1st St; US 101 northbound, exit Brokaw Rd. Int corridors. **Pets:** Other species. $50 deposit/room. Service with restrictions, supervision.
SAVE 🛏 ✕ 🖥 💻 🍴 🏊

◆◆◆◆ The Fairmont San Jose LH
(408) 998-1900. **Call for rates.** 170 S Market St. At Fairmont Plaza. Int corridors. **Pets:** Small, other species. $25 one-time fee/room. Service with restrictions, supervision.
✕ 🍴 🏊 🏊

(AAA) ◆◆◆◆ Hilton San Jose & Towers LH
(408) 287-2100. **$89-$249.** 300 Almaden Blvd. Downtown. Int corridors. **Pets:** Accepted.
SAVE 🛏 ✕ 🖥 💻 🍴 🏊

◆◆ Homestead Studio Suites Hotel-San Jose SH 🐾
(408) 573-0648. **$95-$115.** 1560 N 1st St. 1 mi e of San Jose International Airport; US 101, exit N 1st St, then s. Int corridors. **Pets:** Medium, other species. $25 daily fee/room. Service with restrictions, crate.
ASK 🛏 ✕ 💻

◆◆◆ Homewood Suites by Hilton M
(408) 428-9900. **$159-$199.** 10 W Trimble Rd. 2 mi ne of San Jose International Airport; US 101, exit Trimble Rd, 1.3 mi e. Ext/int corridors. **Pets:** Accepted.
ASK 🛏 ✕ 💻 🏊 🏊

◆◆◆◆ Residence Inn by Marriott SH
(408) 226-7676. **Call for rates.** 6111 San Ignacio Ave. US 101, exit Bernal Rd, then e. Int corridors. **Pets:** Medium, other species. $10 daily fee/room, $75 one-time fee/room. Service with restrictions.
✕ 💻 🖥 🍴 💻 🏊 🏊

(AAA) ◆◆◆ Staybridge Suites M 🐾
(408) 436-1600. **$89-$159.** 1602 Crane Ct. US 101, exit Brokaw Rd E, 0.4 mi to Bering S, then 0.5 mi. Ext corridors. **Pets:** Medium. $150 one-time fee/room. Service with restrictions.
SAVE 🛏 ✕ 🖥 💻 🏊

(AAA) ◆ Vagabond M
(408) 453-8822. **$59-$89.** 1488 N 1st St. I-880, exit N 1st St, then w. Ext corridors. **Pets:** Other species. $20 deposit/room. Service with restrictions, supervision.
SAVE 🛏 ✕ 🖥 💻 🏊

SAN JUAN BAUTISTA

(AAA) ◆◆◆ San Juan Inn M
(831) 623-4380. **$79-$99.** 410 The Alameda. Jct SR 156. Ext corridors. **Pets:** Medium. $15 daily fee/room.
SAVE 🛏 ✕ 🖥 💻 🏊

SAN JUAN CAPISTRANO

(AAA) ◆◆◆ Best Western Capistrano Inn M
(949) 493-5661. **$89-$179, 3 day notice.** 27174 Ortega Hwy. I-5, exit SR 74 (Ortega Hwy), just e. Ext corridors. **Pets:** Accepted.
SAVE 🛏 ✕ 🖥 💻 🏊

SAN LUIS OBISPO

(AAA) ◆◆◆ Best Western Royal Oak Hotel M
(805) 544-4410. **$79-$150.** 214 Madonna Rd. US 101, exit Madonna Rd, just s. Ext/int corridors. **Pets:** Medium. $10 one-time fee/pet. Service with restrictions, supervision.
SAVE 🛏 ✕ 🖥 💻 🏊

(AAA) ◆◆◆ Days Inn M
(805) 549-9911. **$69-$189.** 2050 Garfield St. US 101, exit Monterey St, just sw. Ext corridors. **Pets:** Small, dogs only. $10 daily fee/pet. Designated rooms, service with restrictions, supervision.
SAVE 🛏 ✕ 🖥 💻 🏊

◆◆◆ Heritage Inn Bed & Breakfast BB 🐾
(805) 544-7440. **$85-$185, 7 day notice.** 978 Olive St. US 101, exit SR 1/Morro Bay northbound, just w on Santa Rosa St, then just s; exit Santa Rosa St southbound, just ne. Int corridors. **Pets:** Medium, other species. $100 deposit/room. Designated rooms, service with restrictions, supervision.
✕ 🐕 📺 📻

(AAA) ◆◆◆ Holiday Inn Express SH
(805) 544-8600. **$99-$219.** 1800 Monterey St. US 101, exit Monterey St, just w. Int corridors. **Pets:** Medium. $25 one-time fee/room. Service with restrictions, supervision.
SAVE 🛏 ✕ 🖥 💻 🍴 🏊

(AAA) ◆◆◆ Ramada Inn Olive Tree M
(805) 544-2800. **$69-$199, 3 day notice.** 1000 Olive St. US 101, exit Morro Bay northbound, just w on Santa Rosa St, then just s; exit Santa Rosa St southbound, just ne. Ext corridors. **Pets:** Accepted.
SAVE 🛏 ✕ 🖥 💻 🏊

(AAA) ◆◆◆ Sands Suites & Motel M
(805) 544-0500. **$59-$219.** 1930 Monterey St. US 101, exit Monterey St, just sw. Ext corridors. **Pets:** Other species. $10 one-time fee/pet. Designated rooms, service with restrictions, supervision.
SAVE 🛏 ✕ 🖥 💻 🏊

(AAA) ◆◆◆ Super 8 Motel M
(805) 544-6888. **$59-$129.** 1951 Monterey St. US 101, exit Monterey St, just e. Ext corridors. **Pets:** Small, dogs only. $10 daily fee/pet. Designated rooms, service with restrictions, supervision.
SAVE 🛏 ✕ 🖥 🏊

SAN MARCOS

▲▲▲ ▼▼▼ Quails Inn Hotel Lake San Marcos Resort 🆂🅷

(760) 744-0120. **$119-$149.** 1025 La Bonita Dr. SR 78, exit Rancho Santa Fe Rd, 2 mi s, 0.5 mi e via Lake San Marcos Dr and San Marino Dr; at Lake San Marcos. Ext/int corridors. **Pets:** Medium, other species. $10 daily fee/pet. Service with restrictions, crate.

🆂🅰🆅🅴 ⊠ 🄴 ▣ 🍴 🛁 ⊠

SAN RAMON

▼▼ Homestead Studio Suites Hotel-San Ramon 🄼 🐾

(925) 277-0833. **$95-$145.** 18000 San Ramon Valley Blvd. I-680, exit Bollinger Canyon Rd E, just n. Ext corridors. **Pets:** Medium, other species. $25 daily fee/room. Service with restrictions, crate.

🄰🆂🅺 🆂🄳 ⊠ 🄴 ▣

▼▼▼ Residence Inn by Marriott 🆂🅷 🐾

(925) 277-9292. **$199-$249.** 1071 Market Pl. I-680, exit Bollinger Canyon Rd E, 0.5 mi e. Ext corridors. **Pets:** Other species. $5 daily fee/pet, $125 one-time fee/room. Supervision.

🄰🆂🅺 🆂🄳 ⊠ 🄴 ▣ 🛁 ⊠

▼▼▼ San Ramon Marriott at Bishop Ranch 🅻🅷

(925) 867-9200. **$79-$199.** 2600 Bishop Dr. I-680, exit Bollinger Canyon E, n on Sunset, then just w. Int corridors. **Pets:** Medium, other species. $75 one-time fee/room. Service with restrictions, crate.

⊠ 🄴 ▣ 🍴 🛁 ⊠

SAN SIMEON

▼▼ Motel 6 Premiere–1212 🆂🅷

(805) 927-8691. **$45-$95.** 9070 Castillo Dr. Just e of SR 1. Int corridors. **Pets:** Accepted.

🆂🄳 ⊠ 🍴 🛁

▲▲▲ ▼▼▼ Silver Surf Motel 🄼 🐾

(805) 927-4661. **$39-$176.** 9390 Castillo Dr. Just e of SR 1. Ext corridors. **Pets:** $10 daily fee/pet. Designated rooms, service with restrictions, supervision.

🆂🅰🆅🅴 🆂🄳 ⊠ 🄴 ▣ 🛁 🎿

SANTA ANA

▼ Motel 6 🄼

(714) 558-0500. **$46-$56.** 1623 E 1st St. I-5, exit 4th St, just s on Mabury St, then just w. Ext corridors. **Pets:** Other species. Service with restrictions, supervision.

⊠ 🛁

▲▲▲ ▼▼▼ Quality Suites-Orange County Airport 🄼

(714) 957-9200. **$109-$159.** 2701 Hotel Terrace Dr. SR 55, exit Dyer Rd W, just w. Ext corridors. **Pets:** Small, other species. $25 one-time fee/room. Service with restrictions, supervision.

🆂🅰🆅🅴 🆂🄳 ⊠ 🄴 ▣ 🛁

▼▼ Red Roof Inn 🄼

(714) 542-0311. **$54-$74.** 2600 N Main St. I-5, exit Main St, 0.3 mi n. Ext/int corridors. **Pets:** Medium, other species. Designated rooms, service with restrictions, supervision.

⊠ 🄴 🛁

SANTA BARBARA

▼▼▼▼ Bacara Resort & Spa 🅻🅷 🐾

(805) 968-0100. **$425-$5000, 3 day notice.** 8301 Hollister Ave. US 101, exit Winchester Ganyon Rd northbound, just w, Calle Rd just w, then 0.5 mi n. Ext/int corridors. **Pets:** Small, dogs only. $175 one-time fee/room. Supervision.

🄰🆂🅺 ⊠ ▣ 🍴 🛁 ⊠

▲▲▲ ▼▼▼ Best Western Beachside Inn 🄼

(805) 965-6556. **$135-$279.** 336 W Cabrillo Blvd. US 101, exit Bath St northbound, just w on Haley St to Castillo St, 0.4 mi s; exit Castillo St southbound, 0.3 mi s. Ext corridors. **Pets:** Other species. $20 daily fee/pet. Designated rooms, service with restrictions, supervision.

🆂🅰🆅🅴 🆂🄳 ⊠ 🄴 ▣ 🛁

▲▲▲ ▼▼ Blue Sands Motel 🄼

(805) 965-1624. **$75-$205, 3 day notice.** 421 S Milpas St. US 101, exit Milpas St, 0.3 mi s. Ext corridors. **Pets:** Accepted.

🆂🅰🆅🅴 🆂🄳 ⊠ 🄴 ▣ 🛁 🎿

▲▲▲ ▼▼ El Prado Inn 🄼

(805) 966-0807. **$85-$180.** 1601 State St. US 101, exit Mission St, 0.4 mi e, then 0.3 mi s. Ext corridors. **Pets:** Accepted.

🆂🅰🆅🅴 🆂🄳 ⊠ 🄴 ▣ 🛁

▼▼▼ Fess Parker's Doubletree Resort 🅻🅷 🐾

(805) 564-4333. **$380-$417, 3 day notice.** 633 E Cabrillo Blvd. US 101, exit Milpas St, just s, then just w. Ext/int corridors. **Pets:** Other species. Designated rooms, service with restrictions, supervision.

🄰🆂🅺 ⊠ 🄴 ▣ 🍴 🛁 ⊠

▼▼▼ Four Seasons Biltmore 🅻🅷 🐾

(805) 969-2261. **$490-$675, 3 day notice.** 1260 Channel Dr. US 101, exit Olive Mill Rd, 0.3 mi s. Ext/int corridors. **Pets:** Other species. Designated rooms, service with restrictions, crate.

🄰🆂🅺 ⊠ 🄴 ▣ 🍴 🛁 ⊠

▼▼▼ Marina Beach Motel 🄼

(805) 963-9311. **$79-$275.** 21 Bath St. US 101, exit Haley St northbound, just w to Castillo St, 0.3 mi s to Natoma St, just e, then just s; exit Castillo St southbound, 0.3 mi s to Natoma St, just e, then just s. Ext corridors. **Pets:** Small. $15 daily fee/pet. Service with restrictions, supervision.

🆂🄳 ⊠ 🄴 ▣

▲▲▲ ▼▼▼ Pacifica Suites 🆂🅷

(805) 683-6722. **$119-$259.** 5490 Hollister Ave. US 101, exit Patterson Ave, 0.5 mi s, then 0.5 mi w. Ext/int corridors. **Pets:** Large, other species. $10 one-time fee/pet. Designated rooms, service with restrictions, supervision.

🆂🅰🆅🅴 🆂🄳 ⊠ 🄴 ▣ 🛁

SANTA CATALINA ISLAND

AAA ▼▼▼▼ Best Western Catalina Canyon Hotel & Spa M
(310) 510-0325. **$79-$299, 3 day notice.** 888 Country Club Dr. 0.5 mi from the harbor via Sumner Ave. Ext corridors. **Pets:** Accepted.
[SAVE] [S⊘] [✕] [▦] [¶] [⌕ᴹ] [⊠]

SANTA CLARA

AAA ▼▼▼▼ GuestHouse International Inn & Suites-Silicon Valley USA M
(408) 241-3010. **$89-$145, 3 day notice.** 2930 El Camino Real. SR 82, 0.5 mi w of San Tomas Expwy; US 101, exit S Bowers Ave. Ext corridors. **Pets:** Other species. $10 daily fee/pet.
[SAVE] [S⊘] [✕] [⌕ᴹ] [▦] [▦] [⌕ᴹ]

AAA ▼▼▼ Santa Clara Marriott Hotel LH
(408) 988-1500. **$80-$229.** 2700 Mission College. 0.5 mi e off US 101, exit Great America Pkwy; 0.8 mi s of Great America Theme Park. Int corridors. **Pets:** Accepted.
[SAVE] [✕] [▦] [▦] [¶] [⌕ᴹ] [⊠]

AAA ▼▼▼ The Vagabond Inn M
(408) 241-0771. **$44-$109.** 3580 El Camino Real. On SR 82, southeast corner of Lawrence Expwy cloverleaf. Ext corridors. **Pets:** Medium. $10 daily fee/pet. Service with restrictions, crate.
[SAVE] [S⊘] [✕] [▦] [▦] [⌕ᴹ]

AAA ▼▼▼ Wellesley Inn (Santa Clara) SH
(408) 257-8600. **$79-$89.** 5405 Stevens Creek Blvd. I-280 and Lawrence Expwy, exit Stevens Creek Blvd, just w. Int corridors. **Pets:** Small, other species. Designated rooms, service with restrictions, supervision.
[SAVE] [S⊘] [✕] [▦] [▦] [⌕ᴹ]

▼▼ ▼▼▼ The Westin Hotel-Santa Clara LH ❖
(408) 986-0700. **$99-$239.** 5101 Great America Pkwy. 0.8 mi e off US 101, exit Great America Pkwy. Int corridors. **Pets:** Medium, dogs only. Service with restrictions, supervision.
[ASK] [S⊘] [✕] [⌕ᴹ] [⊘] [▦] [▦] [¶] [⌕ᴹ] [⊠]

SANTA CRUZ

AAA ▼▼▼ Bay Front Inn M
(831) 423-8564. **$48-$185.** 325 Pacific Ave. 6 blks se of SR 1. Ext corridors. **Pets:** Accepted.
[SAVE] [S⊘] [✕] [▦] [⌕ᴹ]

AAA ▼▼▼▼ Coast Santa Cruz Hotel SH
(831) 426-4330. **$129-$289.** 175 W Cliff Dr. At the Wharf. Int corridors. **Pets:** Large, other species. $10 daily fee/pet. Service with restrictions, supervision.
[SAVE] [✕] [▦] [▦] [¶] [⌕ᴹ]

AAA ▼▼▼ Continental Inn M
(831) 429-1221. **$75-$260, 7 day notice.** 414 Ocean St. 5 blks from beach; between Broadway and Soquel aves. Ext corridors. **Pets:** $10 daily fee/pet. Designated rooms, service with restrictions, supervision.
[SAVE] [S⊘] [✕] [▦] [▦] [⌕ᴹ]

AAA ▼▼▼ GuestHouse International Pacific Inn M
(831) 425-3722. **$69-$199.** 330 Ocean St. 1 mi from jct SR 1 and 17. Int corridors. **Pets:** Dogs only. $10 daily fee/pet. Service with restrictions, supervision.
[SAVE] [S⊘] [✕] [▦] [▦] [⌕ᴹ]

AAA ▼▼▼▼ Ocean Pacific Lodge M ❖
(831) 457-1234. **$60-$140.** 120 Washington. SR 1 and 17, exit w via Ocean St, 1 mi w to Broadway, turn right, left on Front St to Pacific Ave, then just right. Ext corridors. **Pets:** Small, dogs only. $20 one-time fee/pet. Designated rooms, supervision.
[SAVE] [S⊘] [✕] [▦] [⌕ᴹ]

SANTA MARIA

AAA ▼▼▼ Best Western Big America M
(805) 922-5200. **$89-$149.** 1725 N Broadway. US 101, exit Broadway, 0.5 mi w. Ext corridors. **Pets:** Medium. Service with restrictions, supervision.
[SAVE] [S⊘] [✕] [▦] [▦] [⌕ᴹ]

AAA ▼▼▼ Comfort Inn M
(805) 922-5891. **$69-$179.** 210 S Nicholson Ave. US 101, exit Main St, just e, then just s. Int corridors. **Pets:** Accepted.
[SAVE] [S⊘] [✕] [▦] [▦] [⌕ᴹ]

▼▼▼ Historic Santa Maria Inn LH
(805) 928-7777. **$119-$149, 7 day notice.** 801 S Broadway. US 101, exit Main St, 1 mi w, then 0.5 mi s. Int corridors. **Pets:** Medium. $50 one-time fee/room. Service with restrictions, supervision.
[ASK] [S⊘] [✕] [▦] [▦] [¶] [⌕ᴹ] [⊠]

SANTA NELLA

AAA ▼▼▼ Best Western Andersen's Inn M
(209) 826-5534. **$68-$95.** 12367 Hwy 33 S. I-5, exit SR 33, just e. Ext corridors. **Pets:** Small, dogs only. $10 daily fee/pet. Designated rooms, service with restrictions, supervision.
[SAVE] [S⊘] [✕] [▦] [⌕ᴹ]

AAA ▼▼▼ Comfort Inn M
(209) 827-8700. **$59-$80, 14 day notice.** 28821 W Gonzaga Rd. 3 mi w of I-5; SR 152, exit Gonzaga Rd, just s. Ext corridors. **Pets:** Other species. $10 daily fee/room. Service with restrictions, crate.
[SAVE] [S⊘] [✕] [▦] [▦] [⌕ᴹ]

AAA ▼▼▼▼ Holiday Inn Express M
(209) 826-8282. **$65-$85.** 28976 W Plaza Dr. I-5, exit SR 33, just e. Ext corridors. **Pets:** Medium. Designated rooms, service with restrictions, supervision.
[SAVE] [S⊘] [✕] [▦] [▦] [⌕ᴹ]

▼▼ Ramada Inn Mission de Oro ⚓
(209) 826-4444. **$67-$91.** 13070 Hwy 33 S. I-5, exit SR 33, just w. Ext/int corridors. **Pets:** Large, other species. $10 daily fee/room. Designated rooms, service with restrictions, supervision.
(ASK) (S✿) (✕) (▮) (▣) (▥) (≈)

SCOTTS VALLEY

(AAA) ▼▼▼ Hilton San Jose South/Scotts
Valley ⚓
(831) 440-1000. **$119-$349.** 6001 La Madrona Dr. SR 17, exit Mt Hermon Rd. Int corridors. **Pets:** Other species. $25 daily fee/pet. Service with restrictions, supervision.
(SAVE) (S✿) (✕) (✿M) (▮) (▣) (▥) (≈)

SELMA

(AAA) ▼ Super 8 Motel ⚓
(559) 896-2800. **$58-$70.** 3142 S Highland Ave. SR 99, exit Floral Ave. Int corridors. **Pets:** Accepted.
(SAVE) (S✿) (✕) (≈)

SHASTA LAKE

(AAA) ▼▼ Bridge Bay Resort M ❖
(530) 275-3021. **$78-$175, 3 day notice.** I-5, exit 690, e of I-5, exit Bridge Bay Rd; 12 mi n of Redding. Ext corridors. **Pets:** $50 deposit/pet. Designated rooms, service with restrictions, supervision.
(SAVE) (S✿) (✕) (▮) (▣) (▥) (≈) (⊠)

(AAA) ▼▼ Fawndale Lodge & RV Resort M
(530) 275-8000. **$59-$87, 4 day notice.** I-5, exit 689, 1 mi s of Shasta Lake; e of I-5, exit Fawndale Rd; 10 mi n of Redding. Ext corridors. **Pets:** Small. $50 deposit/pet, $6 daily fee/pet. Service with restrictions.
(SAVE) (S✿) (✕) (▮) (▣) (≈) (⊠)

SHAVER LAKE

▼▼ Dinkey Creek Inn & Chalets CA
(559) 841-3435. **$85-$100.** 53861 Dinkey Creek Rd. SR 168, 13.5 mi e. Ext corridors. **Pets:** Dogs only. $25 one-time fee/room. No service, supervision.
(✕) (▮) (▣) (▥) (⊠) (▧) (⊡)

SHELTER COVE

(AAA) ▼▼▼ Shelter Cove Motor Inn M
(707) 986-7521. **$75-$120.** 205 Wave Dr. 23 mi w of US 101 via Shelter Cove Rd, 1 mi n on Upper Pacific Rd, w on Lower Pacific Rd. Ext corridors. **Pets:** Other species. $10 daily fee/pet. Supervision.
(SAVE) (S✿) (▮) (▣) (▧) (⊡)

SIERRA CITY

(AAA) ▼▼▼ Herrington's Sierra Pines M
(530) 862-1151. **$65-$89, 7 day notice.** 104 Main St. 0.5 mi w on SR 49. Ext corridors. **Pets:** Other species. Supervision.
(SAVE) (S✿) (✕) (▣) (▥) (▧) (⊡)

SMITH RIVER

▼▼ Ship Ashore Motel M
(707) 487-3141. **$60-$90.** 12370 Hwy 101. 2.8 mi n on US 101; 3 mi s of OR-CA state line. Ext corridors. **Pets:** Accepted.
(S✿) (✕) (▮) (▣) (▥) (▧)

SOLEDAD

(AAA) ▼▼▼ Best Western Valley Harvest
Inn M
(831) 678-3833. **$79-$170.** 1155 Front St. US 101, exit Soledad, just e. Ext/int corridors. **Pets:** Small. $300 deposit/ pet, $10 daily fee/pet. Designated rooms, service with restrictions, supervision.
(SAVE) (S✿) (✕) (▮) (▣) (▥) (≈)

SOLVANG

▼▼ Meadowlark Inn M
(805) 688-4631. **$130, 7 day notice.** 2644 Mission Dr. On SR 246, 1.6 mi e. Ext corridors. **Pets:** Accepted.
(ASK) (S✿) (✕) (▮) (▣)

(AAA) ▼▼▼ Royal Copenhagen Inn M ❖
(805) 688-5561. **$69-$165, 3 day notice.** 1579 Mission Dr. On SR 246. Ext/int corridors. **Pets:** Designated rooms, service with restrictions, supervision.
(SAVE) (S✿) (✕) (▮) (▣) (≈)

SONORA

(AAA) ▼▼▼ Aladdin Motor Inn M ❖
(209) 533-4971. **$76-$102.** 14260 Mono Way (Hwy 108). On SR 108, 3.5 mi e. Ext/int corridors. **Pets:** Medium, other species. $5 one-time fee/pet. Service with restrictions, supervision.
(SAVE) (✕) (▮) (▣) (≈)

(AAA) ▼▼▼ Best Western Sonora
Oaks M ❖
(209) 533-4400. **$79-$95.** 19551 Hess Ave. 3.5 mi e on SR 108. Ext/int corridors. **Pets:** Medium, dogs only. $20 daily fee/room. Designated rooms, service with restrictions, supervision.
(SAVE) (S✿) (✕) (🅰) (▮) (▣) (≈)

(AAA) ▼ Miners Motel M
(209) 532-7850. **$59-$75, 3 day notice.** 18740 SR 108. On SR 108 and 49, 1 mi e of Jamestown. Ext corridors. **Pets:** Medium, dogs only. $5 daily fee/pet. Service with restrictions, supervision.
(SAVE) (S✿) (✕) (▮) (▣) (≈)

(AAA) ▼▼▼ Sonora Days Inn M
(209) 532-2400. **$73-$93.** 160 S Washington St. Downtown. Ext/int corridors. **Pets:** Medium. $10 one-time fee/pet. Designated rooms, service with restrictions, supervision.
(SAVE) (S✿) (✕) (▮) (▣) (▥) (≈)

(AAA) ▼ Sonora Gold Lodge M
(209) 532-3952. **$49-$109.** 480 Stockton St. 0.5 mi sw on SR 108 business route and 49. Ext corridors. **Pets:** Other species. $10 one-time fee/room. Service with restrictions, supervision.
(SAVE) (✕) (▮) (≈) (⊠)

STOCKTON

Econo Lodge of Stockton M
(209) 466-5741. **$55-$62.** 2210 S Manthey Rd. I-5, exit 8th St, 0.3 mi s of jct SR 4. Int corridors. **Pets:** Very small, dogs only. $50 deposit/room. Designated rooms, no service, supervision.

Howard Johnson Express Inn-Marina M
(209) 948-6151. **$65-$75.** 33 N Center St. 1 blk n; w off El Dorado St via Weber; SR 99 southbound, exit Wilson Way; SR 99 northbound, w via Mariposa Rd to Charter Way; I-5, exit downtown. Ext corridors. **Pets:** Small. $10 daily fee/pet. Designated rooms, service with restrictions, supervision.

La Quinta Inn M
(209) 952-7800. **$86-$101.** 2710 W March Ln. I-5, exit March Ln, just w. Ext corridors. **Pets:** Accepted.

Residence Inn by Marriott SH
(209) 472-9800. **$139-$279.** 3240 W March Ln. I-5, exit March Ln, 0.5 mi w. Int corridors. **Pets:** Accepted.

SUN CITY

Travelodge M
(909) 679-1133. **$69.** 27955 Encanto Dr. I-215, exit McCall Blvd, just e, then just s. Ext corridors. **Pets:** Accepted.

SUNNYVALE

Homestead Studio Suites Hotel-Sunnyvale/ Santa Clara M
(408) 734-3431. **$91-$111.** 1255 Orleans Dr. N of SR 237, exit Mathilda Ave, then e on Moffett Park Dr. Ext corridors. **Pets:** Medium, other species. $25 daily fee/room. Service with restrictions, crate.

Quality Inn-Sunnyvale SH
(408) 744-1100. **$65-$165.** 1280 Persian Dr. US 101, exit Lawrence Expwy N, 1 mi n to Persian Dr, then 0.3 mi w. Int corridors. **Pets:** Small. $50 deposit/pet, $10 daily fee/pet. Designated rooms, service with restrictions, supervision.

Radisson Inn-Sunnyvale SH
(408) 247-0800. **$79-$149.** 1085 E El Camino Real. SR 82; 0.3 mi w of Lawrence Expwy. Int corridors. **Pets:** Medium, other species. $10 daily fee/pet.

Residence Inn by Marriott M
(408) 720-8893. **$79-$169.** 1080 Stewart Dr. US 101, exit Lawrence Expwy S, Duane Ave W. Ext corridors. **Pets:** Accepted.

Residence Inn by Marriott M
(408) 720-1000. **$159.** 750 Lakeway Dr. US 101, exit Lawrence Expwy S, then e on Oakmead. Ext corridors. **Pets:** Accepted.

Staybridge Suites M
(408) 745-1515. **$89-$129.** 900 Hamlin Ct. SR 237, exit Mathilda Ave S, w on Ross. Ext corridors. **Pets:** Accepted.

Vagabond Inn M
(408) 734-4607. **$54-$209.** 816 Ahwanee Ave. US 101, exit Mathilda Ave S, then s. Ext corridors. **Pets:** $10 daily fee/pet. Service with restrictions, supervision.

Woodfin Suites M
(408) 738-1700. **$99-$189.** 635 E El Camino Real. US 101, exit Fair Oaks, 2.5 mi w to SR 82 E. Ext corridors. **Pets:** Medium, other species. $5 daily fee/pet. Service with restrictions.

SUSANVILLE

America's Best Inns M
(530) 257-4522. **$46-$60.** 2705 Main St. 1.5 mi e on SR 36. Ext corridors. **Pets:** Accepted.

River Inn M ❖
(530) 257-6051. **$46-$58.** 1710 Main St. 0.8 mi e on SR 36. Ext corridors. **Pets:** Medium. $10.80 daily fee/pet. Designated rooms, service with restrictions, supervision.

Super 8 Motel M
(530) 257-2782. **$54-$64.** 2975 Johnstonville Rd. SR 36, 1.8 mi e. Ext corridors. **Pets:** Large. $5.40 one-time fee/pet. Designated rooms, service with restrictions, supervision.

TEHACHAPI

Best Western Mountain Inn M
(661) 822-5591. **$79-$89.** 418 W Tehachapi Blvd. SR 58, exit SR 202, then 1 mi e. Ext corridors. **Pets:** Other species. Designated rooms.

Tehachapi Summit Travelodge M
(661) 823-8000. **$78.** 500 Steuber Rd. SR 58, exit Monolith eastbound; exit Tehachapi Blvd westbound. Int corridors. **Pets:** Other species. $7 one-time fee/room. Designated rooms, service with restrictions, supervision.

THOUSAND OAKS

Thousand Oaks Inn SH
(805) 497-3701. **$90-$115.** 75 W Thousand Oaks Blvd. US 101, exit Moorpark Rd, just n, then just w. Ext corridors. **Pets:** Small. $75 one-time fee/room. Designated rooms, service with restrictions, crate.

THOUSAND PALMS

Red Roof Inn M ❖
(760) 343-1381. **$52-$79.** 72-215 Varner Rd. I-10, exit Ramon Rd, just n, then just w. Ext corridors. **Pets:** Medium, other species. Designated rooms, no service, supervision.

THREE RIVERS

ⒶⒶⒶ ▽▽▽ Best Western Holiday Lodge Ⓜ
(559) 561-4119. **$69-$129.** 40105 Sierra Dr. SR 198, 2 mi sw of town center. Ext corridors. **Pets:** Medium. $5 daily fee/pet. Service with restrictions, supervision.
[SAVE] [S6] [✕] [🛏] [💻] [🏊] [✕]

ⒶⒶⒶ ▽▽▽ Buckeye Tree Lodge Ⓜ
(559) 561-5900. **$69-$118, 3 day notice.** 46000 Sierra Dr. SR 198, 6 mi ne of town center; 0.5 mi sw of entrance to Sequoia National Park. Ext corridors. **Pets:** Accepted.
[SAVE] [S6] [✕] [🛏] [💻] [🏊]

ⒶⒶⒶ ▽▽▽ Gateway Lodge Ⓜ
(559) 561-4133. **$69-$119, 3 day notice.** 45978 Sierra Dr. SR 198, 6 mi ne of town center; 0.5 mi sw of entrance to Sequoia National Park. Ext corridors. **Pets:** Other species. $10 one-time fee/pet.
[SAVE] [S6] [✕] [🛏] [💻] [🍴] [🅿]

ⒶⒶⒶ ▽▽▽ Lazy J Ranch Motel Ⓜ ❀
(559) 561-4449. **$85-$105, 3 day notice.** 39625 Sierra Dr. SR 198, 2.5 mi sw of town center. Ext corridors. **Pets:** $5 one-time fee/pet. Service with restrictions, supervision.
[SAVE] [S6] [✕] [🛏] [💻] [🏊] [✕]

ⒶⒶⒶ ▽▽▽ Sequoia Village Inn Ⓒ
(559) 561-3652. **$69-$249, 14 day notice.** 45971 Sierra Dr. SR 198, 6 mi ne of town center; 0.5 mi sw of entrance to Sequoia National Park. Ext corridors. **Pets:** $5 daily fee/pet. Service with restrictions, supervision.
[SAVE] [S6] [✕] [🛏] [💻] [🏊] [🅿]

ⒶⒶⒶ ▽▽▽ Sierra Lodge Ⓜ
(559) 561-3681. **$46-$96, 14 day notice.** 43175 Sierra Dr. SR 198, 1 mi se of town center; 3 mi sw of entrance to Sequoia National Park. Ext corridors. **Pets:** Accepted.
[SAVE] [S6] [✕] [🛏] [💻] [🏊]

TRACY

ⒶⒶⒶ ▽▽▽ Best Western Luxury Inn Ⓜ
(209) 832-0271. **$79-$99, 3 day notice.** 811 W Clover Rd. I-205, exit Central Tracy. Int corridors. **Pets:** Accepted.
[SAVE] [S6] [✕] [LM] [🅿] [🛏] [💻] [🏊] [✕]

ⒶⒶⒶ ▽▽▽ Phoenix Lodge Ⓜ
(209) 835-1335. **$56-$81, 3 day notice.** 3511 N Tracy Blvd. I-205, exit Central Tracy. Int corridors. **Pets:** Accepted.
[SAVE] [S6] [✕] [LM] [🛏] [💻] [🏊]

TRINIDAD

ⒶⒶⒶ ▽▽▽ Bishop Pine Lodge Ⓒ
(707) 677-3314. **$80.** 1481 Patricks Point Dr. Just w on US 101, exit Trinidad northbound, then 2 mi n; exit Seawood southbound, then 1 mi s. Ext corridors. **Pets:** Accepted.
[SAVE] [S6] [✕] [🛏] [💻] [🐾]

ⒶⒶⒶ ▽▽▽ Trinidad Inn Ⓜ
(707) 677-3349. **$75-$90, 5 day notice.** 1170 Patricks Point Dr. US 101, exit Trinidad northbound, 1.5 mi w; exit Seawood southbound, 1.5 mi s. Ext corridors. **Pets:** Dogs only. $10 one-time fee/pet. Service with restrictions, supervision.
[SAVE] [✕] [🛏] [💻] [🐾]

TULARE

ⒶⒶⒶ ▽▽▽ Best Western Town & Country Lodge Ⓜ
(559) 688-7537. **$70-$150.** 1051 N Blackstone St. SR 99, exit Prosperity Ave, just w. Int corridors. **Pets:** Accepted.
[SAVE] [S6] [✕] [🅿] [🛏] [💻] [🏊]

ⒶⒶⒶ ▽▽▽ Charter Inn Ⓢ𝐇
(559) 685-9500. **$69-$109.** 1016 E Prosperity Ave. SR 99, just e. Int corridors. **Pets:** Small, other species. $100 deposit/room, $5 daily fee/pet. Service with restrictions, supervision.
[SAVE] [S6] [✕] [🍴] [🅿] [🛏] [💻] [🏊]

ⒶⒶⒶ ▽▽▽ Days Inn Ⓜ
(559) 686-0985. **$60.** 1183 N Blackstone St. SR 99, exit Prosperity Ave, just w. Ext corridors. **Pets:** $5 one-time fee/pet. Designated rooms, service with restrictions, supervision.
[SAVE] [S6] [✕] [🛏] [🏊]

ⒶⒶⒶ ▽▽▽ Quality Inn Ⓜ
(559) 686-3432. **$69-$75.** 1010 E Prosperity Ave. SR 99, exit Prosperity Ave, just e. Int corridors. **Pets:** Small, dogs only. $10 daily fee/pet. Service with restrictions, supervision.
[SAVE] [S6] [✕] [🅿] [🛏] [💻] [🏊] [✕]

TURLOCK

ⒶⒶⒶ ▽▽▽ The Tree Inn Ⓜ
(209) 668-3400. **$64-$75.** 201 W Glenwood Ave. SR 99, exit Lander. Ext corridors. **Pets:** Small, dogs only. Designated rooms, service with restrictions, supervision.
[SAVE] [S6] [✕] [LM] [🅿] [🛏] [💻] [🏊]

TWENTYNINE PALMS

ⒶⒶⒶ ▽▽▽ Best Western Gardens Inn & Suites Ⓜ
(760) 367-9141. **$79-$90.** 71487 Twentynine Palms Hwy. On SR 62; 1.8 mi w of town center. Ext/int corridors. **Pets:** Accepted.
[SAVE] [S6] [✕] [🛏] [💻] [🏊]

▽▽▽ Circle C Lodge Ⓜ
(760) 367-7615. **$80-$90.** 6340 El Rey Ave. On SR 62, just n; 1.5 mi w of town center. Ext corridors. **Pets:** Accepted.
[ASK] [S6] [✕] [🛏] [💻] [🏊]

▽▽ Sunnyvale Garden Suites Hotel Ⓒ
(760) 361-3939. **$69-$89, 7 day notice.** 73843 Sunnyvale Dr. SR 62, 0.7 mi n on Adobe Rd, just e on S Slope, just n on Ocotillo, then just e. Ext corridors. **Pets:** Accepted.
[ASK] [S6] [✕] [🛏] [💻] [✕]

VACAVILLE

ⒶⒶⒶ ▽▽▽ Best Western Heritage Inn Ⓜ
(707) 448-8453. **$78-$100.** 1420 E Monte Vista Ave. I-80, exit Monte Vista Ave, just n. Ext corridors. **Pets:** Medium. Designated rooms, service with restrictions, supervision.
[SAVE] [S6] [✕] [LM] [🛏] [💻] [🏊]

▼▼▼▼ Residence Inn by Marriott SH
(707) 469-0300. **$122-$152.** 360 Orange Dr. I-80, exit Orange Dr eastbound, 0.5 mi; exit Monte Vista westbound, freeway overpass to E Nut Tree Pkwy. Int corridors. **Pets:** Accepted.
(ASK) ⊠ ⑥M ⑥° 🖥 🖵 🏊 ⊠

▼▼ Vacaville Super 8 M
(707) 449-8884. **$64-$84.** 101 Allison Ct. I-80, exit Monte Vista Ave, just n. Int corridors. **Pets:** Medium, dogs only. $10 one-time fee/room. Service with restrictions, supervision.
(ASK) SD ⊠ ⑥M 🖵 🏊

VALLEJO

**▲▲▲ ▼▼▼▼ Holiday Inn at Napa
Gateway** SH ❧
(707) 644-1200. **$109-$149.** 1000 Fairgrounds Dr. I-80, exit Marine World Pkwy (SR 37), 0.3 mi n. Int corridors. **Pets:** Medium, other species. $25 one-time fee/room. Service with restrictions, crate.
(SAVE) SD ⊠ ⑥M ⑥° 🖥 🖵 🍴 🏊

▼▼ Ramada Inn M
(707) 643-2700. **$99-$109.** 1000 Admiral Callaghan Ln. I-80 S, exit Columbus Pkwy, 0.5 mi w. Ext corridors. **Pets:** Accepted.
(ASK) SD ⊠ ⑥M 🖥 🖵 🏊

VENTURA

▲▲▲ ▼▼▼▼ Best Western Inn of Ventura M
(805) 648-3101. **$99-$149.** 708 E Thompson Blvd. US 101, exit California St northbound, just e; exit Ventura Ave southbound, then 0.5 mi e. Ext corridors. **Pets:** Medium. $20 daily fee/room. Service with restrictions, supervision.
(SAVE) SD ⊠ 🖥 🖵 🏊

▲▲▲ ▼▼▼▼ La Quinta Inn M
(805) 658-6200. **$83-$97.** 5818 Valentine Rd. US 101, exit Victoria Ave, just s, then just n. Ext/int corridors. **Pets:** Medium, other species. Service with restrictions, supervision.
(SAVE) ⊠ ⑥M 🌀 🖥 🖵 🏊

▼▼▼ Marriott Ventura Beach Hotel LH
(805) 643-6000. **$229.** 2055 Harbor Blvd. US 101, exit Seaward Ave, just w, then 0.5 mi n. Int corridors. **Pets:** Other species. $75 one-time fee/room. Service with restrictions.
(ASK) SD ⊠ 🖥 🖵 🍴 🏊

▲▲▲ ▼▼▼ Vagabond Inn M
(805) 648-5371. **$69-$159.** 756 E Thompson Blvd. US 101, exit California St northbound, just n, then just e; exit Ventura Ave southbound, 0.6 mi e. Ext corridors. **Pets:** Other species. $10 daily fee/room. Service with restrictions, supervision.
(SAVE) SD ⊠ 🖥 🖵 🍴 🏊

VICTORVILLE

▲▲▲ ▼▼ Budget Inn M
(760) 241-8010. **$42-$47.** 14153 Kentwood Blvd. I-15, exit SR 18 W (Palmdale Rd), just w. Ext corridors. **Pets:** Very small, dogs only. $10 deposit/room. Service with restrictions, supervision.
(SAVE) SD ⊠ 🖥

▲▲▲ ▼▼▼ Howard Johnson Express Inn M
(760) 243-7700. **$60-$70.** 16868 Stoddard Wells Rd. I-15, exit Stoddard Wells Rd, just w. Ext corridors. **Pets:** Other species. $10 daily fee/pet. Service with restrictions, supervision.
(SAVE) ⊠ 🖥 🖵 🏊

▲▲▲ ▼▼▼ Ramada Inn SH
(760) 245-6565. **$85-$90.** 15494 Palmdale Rd. I-15, exit SR 18 W (Palmdale Rd), just w. Int corridors. **Pets:** Other species. $25 one-time fee/room. Designated rooms, service with restrictions.
(SAVE) SD ⊠ 🖥 🖵 🍴 🏊

▼▼ Red Roof Inn M
(760) 241-1577. **$55-$99.** 13409 Mariposa Rd. I-15, exit Bear Valley Rd northbound, just e, then 1.5 mi n; exit Green Tree Blvd southbound, just e, then 1.5 mi s. Ext corridors. **Pets:** Accepted.
⊠ 🖥 🖵 🏊

▲▲▲ ▼▼▼ Travelodge Victorville M
(760) 241-7200. **$52-$72.** 12175 Mariposa Rd. I-15, exit Bear Valley Rd, 0.2 mi e, then just n. Ext corridors. **Pets:** Medium, dogs only. $6 one-time fee/pet. Service with restrictions, supervision.
(SAVE) SD ⊠ 🖥 🏊

VISALIA

▲▲▲ ▼▼▼ Best Western Visalia Inn M
(559) 732-4561. **$79-$85.** 623 W Main St. SR 198, exit Mooney Blvd, just n, then just 0.9 mi e. Ext corridors. **Pets:** Small, dogs only. $10 daily fee/pet. Designated rooms, service with restrictions, supervision.
(SAVE) SD ⊠ 🖥 🖵 🏊

**▲▲▲ ▼▼▼▼ Visalia Holiday Inn Hotel &
Conference Center** LH ❧
(559) 651-5000. **$109-$159.** 9000 W Airport Dr. SR 99, exit SR 198, just e to Plaza Dr. Int corridors. **Pets:** $25 one-time fee/pet. Designated rooms, service with restrictions, supervision.
(SAVE) SD ⊠ 🖥 🖵 🍴 🏊

VISTA

▼▼▼ La Quinta Inn M
(760) 727-8180. **$92-$126.** 630 Sycamore Ave at Thibodo Rd. SR 78, exit Sycamore Ave, just sw. Ext/int corridors. **Pets:** Accepted.
⊠ 🖥 🖵 🏊

WALNUT CREEK

▲▲▲ ▼▼▼▼ Holiday Inn Walnut Creek SH ❧
(925) 932-3332. **$79-$199.** 2730 N Main St. I-680, exit N Main St, just n. Int corridors. **Pets:** Medium. $6 daily fee/pet, $50 one-time fee/pet. Designated rooms, service with restrictions, crate.
(SAVE) SD ⊠ 🖥 🖵 🍴 🏊

WATSONVILLE

▲▲▲ ▼▼▼ Best Western Rose Garden Inn M
(831) 724-3367. **$69-$129.** 740 Freedom Blvd. On SR 152. Ext corridors. **Pets:** Accepted.
(SAVE) SD ⊠ 🖥 🖵 🏊

▼▼ Red Roof Inn SH ❀
(831) 740-4520. **$75-$90.** 1620 W Beach St. SR 1, exit Riverside Dr (SR 129), just w. Int corridors. **Pets:** Other species. Service with restrictions, supervision.
[A$K] [S♦] [✕] [🖪] [⬛] [🏊]

WEAVERVILLE

▲▲▲ ▼▼▼▼ Best Western Weaverville Victorian Inn M
(530) 623-4432. **$65-$198.** 1709 Main St. On SR 299. Ext corridors. **Pets:** Accepted.
[SAVE] [S♦] [✕] [🖉] [🖪] [⬛] [🍴] [🏊]

▲▲▲ ▼ Motel Trinity M ❀
(530) 623-2129. **$40-$90, 3 day notice.** 1112 Main St. Ext corridors. **Pets:** Medium. $5 daily fee/pet. Service with restrictions, supervision.
[SAVE] [S♦] [✕] [🖪] [⬛] [🏊]

▼ Red Hill Motel CA
(530) 623-4331. **$35-$75.** Red Hill Rd. SR 299, just w of SR 3. Ext corridors. **Pets:** Other species. $5 one-time fee/pet. Service with restrictions, supervision.
[🖪] [⬛]

WEED

▲▲▲ ▼▼▼▼ Comfort Inn M
(530) 938-1982. **$69-$99.** 1844 Shastina Dr. I-5, exit S Weed, just e. Int corridors. **Pets:** Large, other species. $100 deposit/room, $10 daily fee/room. Designated rooms, service with restrictions, supervision.
[SAVE] [✕] [🗗] [🖪] [⬛] [🏊]

▲▲▲ ▼▼▼▼ Holiday Inn Express M
(530) 938-1308. **$80-$89.** 1830 Black Butte Dr. Just e of I-5, in town. Int corridors. **Pets:** $10 one-time fee/pet. Designated rooms, no service, supervision.
[SAVE] [S♦] [✕] [🖪]

▲▲▲ ▼▼ Sis-Q-Inn Motel M
(530) 938-4194. **$100.** 1825 Shastina Dr. I-5, exit S Weed. Int corridors. **Pets:** Accepted.
[SAVE] [S♦] [✕] [🖪]

WESTLEY

▲▲▲ ▼▼▼ Econo Lodge M
(209) 894-3900. **$65-$90, 3 day notice.** 7100 McCracken Rd. I-5, exit Westley E. Ext corridors. **Pets:** $10 daily fee/pet. No service, supervision.
[SAVE] [S♦] [✕] [🖪] [⬛] [🏊]

WESTMORLAND

▼▼ Super 8 Motel M
(760) 351-7100. **$65.** 351 W Main St. On SR 86. Int corridors. **Pets:** Medium, other species. $10 daily fee/pet. Designated rooms, no service, supervision.
[A$K] [S♦] [✕] [🖪] [🏊]

WILLIAMS

▲▲▲ ▼▼ Comfort Inn M
(530) 473-2381. **$70-$85.** 400 C St. I-5, exit Williams, just w on E St, then just n on 4th St. Ext corridors. **Pets:** Accepted.
[SAVE] [S♦] [✕] [♿M] [🖪] [⬛] [🏊]

▲▲▲ ▼▼▼▼ Granzella's Inn M
(530) 473-3310. **$75-$100.** 391 6th St. I-5, exit Williams, 0.5 mi w. Int corridors. **Pets:** $10 daily fee/pet. Service with restrictions, supervision.
[SAVE] [S♦] [✕] [♿M] [🗗] [🖪] [⬛] [🍴] [🏊]

▲▲▲ ▼ Stage Stop Inn M
(530) 473-2281. **$43-$50.** 300 N 7th St. I-5, exit SR 20 business route, 3 blks w. Ext corridors. **Pets:** Accepted.
[SAVE] [S♦] [✕] [🖪] [🏊]

WILLOW CREEK

▲▲▲ ▼ Bigfoot Motel M
(530) 629-2142. **$55-$95.** 39039 Hwy 299. SR 299; center of town. Ext corridors. **Pets:** Large. $50 deposit/pet. Designated rooms, service with restrictions, supervision.
[SAVE] [✕] [🖪] [🏊]

WILLOWS

▲▲▲ ▼▼▼ Best Value Inn M ❀
(530) 934-7026. **$44-$119.** 452 N Humboldt Ave. I-5, exit Willow-Elk Creek-Glenn Rd, just e. Ext corridors. **Pets:** Other species. $7 daily fee/pet. Service with restrictions, supervision.
[SAVE] [S♦] [✕] [🖪] [🏊]

▲▲▲ ▼▼▼▼ Best Western Golden Pheasant Inn M
(530) 934-4603. **$79-$150.** 249 N Humboldt Ave. I-5, exit Willow-Elk Creek-Glenn Rd, just e. Ext corridors. **Pets:** Accepted.
[SAVE] [✕] [♿M] [🖪] [⬛] [🍴] [🏊]

▼▼ Super 8 Motel of Willows M
(530) 934-2871. **$49-$57.** 457 Humboldt Ave. I-5, exit Willow-Elk Creek-Glenn Rd. Int corridors. **Pets:** Accepted.
[A$K] [S♦] [✕] [🖪] [🏊]

WINE COUNTRY AREA

BODEGA BAY

▲▲▲ ▼▼▼▼ Bodega Coast Inn M
(707) 875-2217. **$159-$279.** 521 SR 1 N. 2 blks s. Ext corridors. **Pets:** Accepted.
[SAVE] [S♦] [✕] [♿M] [🖪] [⬛] [🎿]

CALISTOGA

▼▼ Washington Street Lodging CA ❀
(707) 942-6968. **$95-$140 (no credit cards), 3 day notice.** 1605 Washington St. On SR 29. Ext corridors. **Pets:** Other species. $15 one-time fee/pet. Service with restrictions.
[✕] [♿M] [🖪] [⬛] [🔲]

FORT BRAGG

⚫⚫⚫ ◆◆◆◆ Beachcomber Motel M ❖
(707) 964-2402. **$59-$250.** 1111 N Main St. Ext corridors.
Pets: Other species. $10 daily fee/pet. Designated rooms,
service with restrictions, supervision.
[SAVE] [S👁] [✕] [📶] [💻] [🐾]

⚫⚫⚫ ◆◆◆◆ Beach House Inn M
(707) 961-1700. **$79-$175.** 100 Pudding Creek Rd. 0.7 mi n
on SR 1. Int corridors. **Pets:** Medium. $20 daily fee/pet.
Designated rooms, service with restrictions, supervision.
[SAVE] [S👁] [✕] [📶] [💻] [🐾]

◆◆◆ Cleone Gardens Inn M
(707) 964-2788. **$86-$140, 3 day notice.** 24600 N Hwy 1. 3
mi n on SR 1. Ext corridors. **Pets:** Service with restrictions,
supervision.
[✕] [📶] [💻] [🐾]

⚫⚫⚫ ◆◆◆ Old Stewart House Inn BB ❖
(707) 961-0775. **$100-$145, 7 day notice.** 511 Stewart St.
Just w of SR 1 via Pine St. Ext/int corridors. **Pets:** Dogs
only. $10 daily fee/pet. Designated rooms, supervision.
[SAVE] [✕] [📶] [🐾] [🔧]

⚫⚫⚫ ◆◆◆ Seabird Lodge M
(707) 964-4731. **$70-$110.** 191 South St. 0.8 mi n of Noyo
River Bridge; 1 blk e off SR 1. Ext corridors. **Pets:** Medium.
$8 daily fee/pet. Designated rooms, service with restrictions,
supervision.
[SAVE] [S👁] [✕] [📶] [💻] [🏊] [🐾]

⚫⚫⚫ ◆◆◆◆ Tradewinds Lodge M
(707) 964-4761. **$49-$150.** 400 S Main St. 6 blks s on SR 1.
Ext corridors. **Pets:** Other species. $10 daily fee/room. Des-
ignated rooms, supervision.
[SAVE] [S👁] [✕] [📶] [💻] [🍴] [🏊] [🐾] [🔧]

GUALALA

◆◆◆ Gualala Country Inn M
(707) 884-4343. **$110-$165, 3 day notice.** 47955 Center St.
East side of SR 1. Ext/int corridors. **Pets:** Other species.
$10 one-time fee/pet. Service with restrictions, supervision.
[✕] [📶] [💻] [🔧]

◆◆◆ Surf Motel M
(707) 884-3571. **$95-$179.** 39170 S Hwy 1. West side of SR
1. Ext corridors. **Pets:** Other species. $10 one-time fee/pet.
Service with restrictions, supervision.
[✕] [📶] [💻] [🔧]

GUERNEVILLE

◆◆◆ Ferngrove Cottages CA ❖
(707) 869-8105. **$79-$219, 3 day notice.** 16650 Hwy 116.
On SR 116. Ext corridors. **Pets:** Large, other species. $15
daily fee/pet. Service with restrictions, crate.
[✕] [S,M] [📶] [💻] [🏊] [🐾] [🔧] [🔧]

HEALDSBURG

⚫⚫⚫ ◆◆◆◆ Best Western Dry Creek Inn M
(707) 433-0300. **$84-$199.** 198 Dry Creek Rd. US 101, exit
Dry Creek Rd, just e. Ext corridors. **Pets:** $20 daily fee/pet.
Designated rooms, service with restrictions, supervision.
[SAVE] [S👁] [✕] [S,M] [🐕] [📶] [💻] [🏊]

◆◆◆◆ Duchamp CA
(707) 431-1300. **$225-$375, 14 day notice.** 421 Foss St. US
101, exit Central Healdsburg. Ext corridors. **Pets:** Medium,
dogs only. $500 deposit/room. Designated rooms, supervi-
sion.
[✕] [S,M] [📶] [🐾]

⚫⚫⚫ ◆◆◆◆ Fairview Motel M
(707) 433-5548. **$59-$139.** 74 Healdsburg Ave. US 101, exit
Central Healdsburg, just e; exit N Guernville/Westside Rd.
Ext corridors. **Pets:** Small, dogs only. $10 daily fee/pet.
Designated rooms, service with restrictions, supervision.
[SAVE] [✕] [S,M] [📶] [💻] [🐾]

JENNER

◆◆◆ Jenner Inn CI ❖
(707) 865-2377. **$98-$268, 10 day notice.** 10400 Hwy 1. On
SR 1 at jct SR 116. Ext corridors. **Pets:** Large, dogs only.
$35 one-time fee/pet. Designated rooms, service with
restrictions, supervision.
[S👁] [✕] [S,M] [📶] [💻] [🍴] [🔧] [📺]

KELSEYVILLE

◆◆◆ Bell Haven Resort CA
(707) 279-4329. **$95-$125, 15 day notice.** 3415 White Oak
Way. SR 29, exit SR 281, 6 mi e. Ext corridors. **Pets:** Other
species. $10 daily fee/pet. No service, supervision.
[✕] [📶] [💻] [🏊] [🔧] [🔧]

LITTLE RIVER

**⚫⚫⚫ ◆◆◆◆ The Inn at Schoolhouse
Creek BB** ❖
(707) 937-5525. **$130-$175, 14 day notice.** 7051 N Hwy 1.
3 mi s of Mendocino; e of Coast Hwy. Ext corridors.
Pets: Other species. $50 one-time fee/room.
[SAVE] [S👁] [✕] [📶] [💻] [🔧]

MENDOCINO

⚫⚫⚫ ◆◆◆◆ Blackberry Inn M
(707) 937-5281. **$90-$180, 4 day notice.** 44951 Larkin Rd.
SR 1, exit Larkin Rd, just e. Ext corridors. **Pets:** Accepted.
[SAVE] [S👁] [✕] [📶] [💻] [🔧]

◆◆◆◆ Hill House Inn CI
(707) 937-0554. **$117-$250, 5 day notice.** 10701 Pallette Dr.
SR 1, exit Little Lake St, just w to stop sign, right to
entrance. Ext/int corridors. **Pets:** Medium, other species.
$15 daily fee/pet. Designated rooms, supervision.
[ASK] [S👁] [✕] [📶] [💻] [🍴] [🔧]

◆◆◆◆ MacCallum House Inn BB ❖
(707) 937-0289. **$120-$295, 7 day notice.** 45020 Albion St.
Center. Ext/int corridors. **Pets:** Other species. $25 daily
fee/pet. Designated rooms.
[ASK] [S👁] [✕] [📶] [💻] [🍴] [🔧]

**⚫⚫⚫ ◆◆◆◆ Mendocino Seaside
Cottages BB** ❖
(707) 485-0239. **$187-$391 (no credit cards), 14 day
notice.** 10940 Lansing St. SR 1, exit Little Lake Rd; exit
Lansing St, 0.6 mi nw. Ext/int corridors. **Pets:** Other species. $80 deposit/pet. Designated rooms, crate.
[SAVE] [S👁] [✕] [📶] [💻] [🔧]

(AAA) ▼▼▼ ▼▼▼ Stanford Inn by the Sea-Big River Lodge 🆑 ✿
(707) 937-5615. **$225-$465, 7 day notice.** SR 1, exit Comptche-Ukiah Rd, 0.5 mi e. Ext corridors. **Pets:** Other species. $25 one-time fee/room. Supervision.
[SAVE] [✕] [⛷M] [🐾] [🛏] [💻] [¶] [🏊] [⊠] [♨]

NAPA

(AAA) ▼▼▼ The Napa Inn 🅱🅱
(707) 257-1444. **$120-$295.** 1137 Warren St. SR 29, exit 1st St, 0.5 mi e, 0.3 mi n. Int corridors. **Pets:** $20 daily fee/room. Designated rooms, service with restrictions, supervision.
[SAVE] [✕] [🛏] [💻]

▼▼▼ Napa River Inn 🅼 ✿
(707) 251-8500. **$159-$399.** 500 Main St. Downtown. Int corridors. **Pets:** Medium. $25 daily fee/pet. Designated rooms, service with restrictions, supervision.
[ASK] [⛷] [✕] [⛷M] [🐾] [🛏] [💻]

(AAA) ▼ Napa Valley Redwood Inn 🅼 ❀
(707) 257-6111. **$67-$150.** 3380 Solano Ave. Just w off SR 29 via Redwood Rd, then just s. Ext corridors. **Pets:** $10 one-time fee/room. Service with restrictions, supervision.
[SAVE] [⛷] [✕] [⛷M] [🐾] [🛏]

OCCIDENTAL

(AAA) ▼▼▼ Occidental Lodge 🅼
(707) 874-3623. **$58-$119.** 3610 Bohemian Hwy. In the village. Ext corridors. **Pets:** Medium. $8 daily fee/pet. Designated rooms, service with restrictions, supervision.
[SAVE] [⛷] [✕] [⛷M] [💻] [🏊] [♨]

PETALUMA

(AAA) ▼▼▼ Quality Inn-Petaluma 🅼
(707) 664-1155. **$90-$180.** 5100 Montero Way. US 101, exit Old Redwood Hwy-Penngrove northbound; exit Petaluma Blvd N-Penngrove southbound (east side). Ext/int corridors. **Pets:** Large, other species. $15 daily fee/room. Service with restrictions, supervision.
[SAVE] [⛷] [✕] [⛷M] [🐾] [🛏] [💻] [🏊] [⊠]

ROHNERT PARK

(AAA) ▼▼▼ Best Western Inn 🅼
(707) 584-7435. **$73-$89, 3 day notice.** 6500 Redwood Dr. US 101, exit Rohnert Park Expwy, just w. Ext corridors. **Pets:** Large. Service with restrictions, supervision.
[SAVE] [⛷] [✕] [⛷M] [🛏] [💻] [🏊]

ST. HELENA

▼▼▼ El Bonita Motel 🅼
(707) 963-3216. **$89-$289, 3 day notice.** 195 Main St. 0.8 mi s on SR 29. Ext corridors. **Pets:** Medium, other species. $5 daily fee/pet. Service with restrictions.
[✕] [⛷M] [🐾] [🛏] [💻] [🏊]

(AAA) ▼▼▼ ▼▼▼ Harvest Inn 🆂🅷
(707) 963-9463. **$249-$675, 7 day notice.** One Main St. 1.5 mi s on SR 29. Ext corridors. **Pets:** Accepted.
[SAVE] [⛷] [✕] [⛷M] [🐾] [🛏] [💻] [🏊]

SANTA ROSA

(AAA) ▼▼▼ Best Western Garden Inn 🅼
(707) 546-4031. **$79-$129.** 1500 Santa Rosa Ave. US 101, exit Baker Ave northbound; exit Corby Ave southbound. Ext corridors. **Pets:** Accepted.
[SAVE] [⛷] [✕] [⛷M] [🐾] [🛏] [💻] [¶] [🏊]

(AAA) ▼▼▼ Santa Rosa Motor Inn 🅼
(707) 523-3480. **$65-$89.** 1800 Santa Rosa Ave. US 101, northbound exit Baker Ave; southbound exit Corby Ave. Ext corridors. **Pets:** $50 deposit/room, $10 one-time fee/pet. Service with restrictions, crate.
[SAVE] [⛷] [✕]

(AAA) ▼▼▼ Vineyard Lodge 🅼
(707) 542-3472. **$69-$99.** 1815 Santa Rosa Ave. 1.5 mi s on US 101 business route; exit US 101 via Baker Ave northbound; exit Santa Rosa Ave-Corby southbound. Ext corridors. **Pets:** Accepted.
[SAVE] [⛷] [✕] [⛷M] [🛏] [💻] [🏊]

SONOMA

(AAA) ▼▼▼ Best Western Sonoma Valley Inn 🅼 ✿
(707) 938-9200. **$114-$314, 3 day notice.** 550 2nd St W. 1 blk w of Town Plaza. Ext corridors. **Pets:** $30 one-time fee/room. Designated rooms, crate.
[SAVE] [⛷] [✕] [⛷M] [🐾] [🛏] [💻] [🏊]

UKIAH

(AAA) ▼▼▼ Days Inn 🅼
(707) 462-7584. **$60-$129, 7 day notice.** 950 N State St. US 101, exit N State St, 0.5 mi s. Ext corridors. **Pets:** Other species. $10 daily fee/room. Designated rooms, service with restrictions, supervision.
[SAVE] [⛷] [✕] [🛏] [💻] [🏊]

▼▼▼ Hampton Inn Ukiah 🆂🅷 ✿
(707) 462-6555. **$89-$199.** 1160 Airport Park Blvd. US 101, exit Talmage Rd W. Int corridors. **Pets:** Large, other species. $200 deposit/room.
[ASK] [⛷] [🐾] [🛏] [💻] [🏊] [⊠]

(AAA) ▼▼▼ Super 8 Motel 🅼
(707) 462-6657. **$59-$125.** 1070 S State St. US 101, exit Talmage Rd, 1 mi w. Ext corridors. **Pets:** Accepted.
[SAVE] [⛷] [✕] [🛏] [🏊]

(AAA) ▼▼▼ Western Traveler Motel 🅼
(707) 468-9167. **$49-$79.** 693 S Orchard Ave. US 101, exit Gobbi St W. Ext corridors. **Pets:** Medium, other species. $5 daily fee/pet. Designated rooms, service with restrictions, supervision.
[SAVE] [⛷] [✕] [🛏] [💻] [🏊]

WESTPORT

(AAA) ▼▼▼ De Haven Valley Farm 🅱🅱
(707) 961-1660. **$89-$144.** 39247 N Hwy 1. SR 1, 18 mi n of jct SR 20, just n of Branscomb Rd. Ext/int corridors. **Pets:** Designated rooms, supervision.
[SAVE] [✕] [🛏] [💻] [♨] [♨]

WILLITS

▼▼▼▼ Baechtel Creek Inn & Spa M ❀
(707) 459-9063. **$69-$150.** 101 Gregory Ln. US 101, just w.
Ext corridors. **Pets:** Small, dogs only. $10 one-time fee/pet.
Designated rooms, service with restrictions, supervision.
ASK S✓ ✕ 🛋 ⊃

YOUNTVILLE

◈◈◈ ▼▼▼ ▼▼ Vintage Inn SH ❀
(707) 944-1112. **$215-$430, 7 day notice.** 6541 Washington
St. SR 29, exit Yountville; center. Ext corridors. **Pets:** $35
one-time fee/room. Service with restrictions, crate.
SAVE S✓ ✕ 🛋 🔌 🛋 💻 ⊃ ✕

❀ **END AREA** ❀

WOODLAND

◈◈◈ ▼▼▼ Days Inn M
(530) 666-3800. **$65-$95.** 1524 E Main St. I-5, exit Main St
(Woodland) northbound; exit SR 113 (Davis) southbound.
Int corridors. **Pets:** Medium, dogs only. $10 daily fee/pet.
No service, supervision.
SAVE S✓ ✕ 🛋 🛋 ⊃

YOSEMITE NATIONAL PARK

▼▼ The Redwoods In Yosemite VH
(209) 375-6666. **$135-$672, 10 day notice.** 8038 Chilnualna
Falls Rd. 6 mi inside the southern entrance via SR 41 and
Chilnualna Falls Rd. Ext corridors. **Pets:** Accepted.
ASK S✓ ✕ 🛋 💻

YREKA

◈◈◈ ▼▼▼▼ AmeriHost Inn-Yreka M
(530) 841-1300. **$69-$90.** 148 Moonlit Oaks Ave. I-5, exit SR
3 (Fort Jones Rd). Int corridors. **Pets:** Medium. $10 one-
time fee/room. Service with restrictions, supervision.
SAVE S✓ ✕ 🔌 🛋 💻 ⊃ ✕

◈◈◈ ▼▼▼ Best Western Miner's Inn M
(530) 842-4355. **$75-$99.** 122 E Miner St. I-5, exit Central
Yreka, just w. Ext corridors. **Pets:** Medium. Service with
restrictions, supervision.
SAVE S✓ ✕ 🔌 🛋 💻 ⊃

◈◈◈ ▼▼▼ Comfort Inn M
(530) 842-1612. **$69-$99.** 1804-B Fort Jones Rd. I-5, exit SR
3 (Fort Jones Rd). Int corridors. **Pets:** Medium. $20 deposit/
room, $10 daily fee/pet. Designated rooms, service with
restrictions, supervision.
SAVE S✓ ✕ 🛋 ⊃

◈◈◈ ▼▼▼ Economy Inn M
(530) 842-4404. **$44-$99.** 526 S Main St. I-5, exit Central
Yreka, 0.3 mi s. Ext corridors. **Pets:** Other species. $5 daily
fee/pet. Designated rooms, service with restrictions, supervision.
SAVE ✕ 🛋 ⊃

◈◈◈ ▼▼▼ Super 8-Yreka M
(530) 842-5781. **$51-$61.** 136 Montague Rd. I-5, exit Montague Rd, just w. Ext corridors. **Pets:** $25 deposit/pet, $5
one-time fee/pet. Service with restrictions, supervision.
SAVE S✓ ✕ 🛋 💻 ⊃

◈◈◈ ▼▼ Wayside Inn M
(530) 842-4412. **$45-$78.** 1235 S Main St. I-5, SR 3 (Fort
Jones Rd) northbound, 1 mi n; exit Central Yreka southbound, 1 mi s. Ext corridors. **Pets:** Other species. $4 daily
fee/pet. Service with restrictions, supervision.
SAVE S✓ ✕ 🛋 💻 ⊃

YUBA CITY

▼▼ Comfort Inn M
(530) 674-1592. **$65-$99.** 730 Palora Ave. SR 99, exit Bridge
St, 0.5 mi s of jct SR 20. Int corridors. **Pets:** Accepted.
ASK S✓ ✕ 🛋 🔌 🛋 💻 ⊃

◈◈◈ ▼▼ Days Inn-Downtown-Yuba City M
(530) 674-1711. **$45-$80.** 700 N Palora Ave. SR 99, exit
Bridge St, 0.5 mi s of SR 20. Ext corridors. **Pets:** Accepted.
SAVE S✓ ✕ 🛋 🔌 🛋 💻 ⊃

YUCCA VALLEY

◈◈◈ ▼▼▼ Oasis of Eden Inn & Suites M
(760) 365-6321. **$69-$140.** 56377 Twentynine Palms Hwy. 1
mi w of Jct SR 62 and 247. Ext corridors. **Pets:** Medium.
$10 daily fee/pet. Designated rooms, service with restric-
tions, supervision.
SAVE S✓ ✕ 🛋 💻 ⊃

◈◈◈ ▼▼▼ Super 8 Motel M
(760) 228-1773. **$59-$99.** 57096 Twentynine Palms Hwy. On
SR 62, 0.3 mi w of jct SR 247. Int corridors.
Pets: Accepted.
SAVE S✓ ✕ 🛋 💻 ⊃

◈◈◈ ▼ Yucca Inn & Suites M
(760) 365-3311. **$49-$149.** 7500 Camino Del Cielo. Just n of
SR 62. Ext corridors. **Pets:** Medium, other species. $50
deposit/room. Service with restrictions, supervision.
SAVE S✓ ✕ 🛋 💻 🍴 ⊃

COLORADO

CITY INDEX

ALAMOSA

🐾 Best Western Alamosa Inn SH
(719) 589-2567. **$90-$100.** 2005 W Main St. 1 mi w on US 160 and 285. Ext corridors. **Pets:** Accepted.
SAVE 🛇 ✕ 💻 🌊

Comfort Inn of Alamosa SH
(719) 587-9000. **$60-$110,** 14 day notice. 6301 Rd 107 S. 2.3 mi w on US 160. Int corridors. **Pets:** Accepted.
SAVE 🛇 ✕ 🍴 💻 🌊

Inn of the Rio Grande SH
(719) 589-5833. **$60-$85.** 333 Sante Fe Ave. Just e of jct SR 17 on US 160. Int corridors. **Pets:** Accepted.
SAVE 🛇 ✕ 🔊 🗮 🍴 💻 🏊 🌊 ✕

ASPEN

Aspen Meadows Resort A Dolce Conference Destination LH
(970) 925-4240. **$99-$300,** 14 day notice. 845 Meadows Rd. 3 blks e of SR 82 via 7th Ave. Ext/int corridors. **Pets:** Accepted.
SAVE 🛇 ✕ 🎾 🍴 💻 🍴 🏊 ✕ 🎿

Aspen Mountain Lodge SH
(970) 925-7650. **$89-$259,** 30 day notice. 311 W Main St. Just w on SR 82, between 2nd and 3rd sts. Int corridors. **Pets:** $20 daily fee/room. Service with restrictions, supervision.
SAVE 🛇 ✕ 🍴 💻 🌊

Hotel Aspen SH
(970) 925-3441. **$89-$399,** 30 day notice. 110 W Main St. On SR 82, just w. Ext/int corridors. **Pets:** $20 daily fee/room. Designated rooms, service with restrictions.
ASK 🛇 ✕ 🍴 💻 🌊

Hotel Jerome SH 🐾
(970) 920-1000. **$235-$1360,** 30 day notice. 330 E Main St. On SR 82; downtown. Int corridors. **Pets:** $75 one-time fee/room. Service with restrictions.
SAVE 🛇 ✕ 🍴 🌊 ✕

Hotel Lenado BB 🐾
(970) 925-6246. **$125-$495,** 30 day notice. 200 S Aspen St. Just s of SR 82 via Aspen St at jct of Hopkins St. Ext/int corridors. **Pets:** Medium. $200 deposit/room. Designated rooms, service with restrictions, supervision.
ASK ✕ 🍴 💻

Limelite Lodge M
(970) 925-3025. **$68-$359,** 30 day notice. 228 E Cooper Ave. Just s of SR 82 at Monarch and Cooper sts. Ext corridors. **Pets:** Other species. Supervision.
SAVE 🛇 ✕ 🔊 🗮 🍴 💻 🌊

The Little Nell LH 🐾
(970) 920-4600. **$250-$4450,** 30 day notice. 675 E Durant Ave. Beside the gondola at the base of Aspen Mountain. Int corridors. **Pets:** Other species. Service with restrictions, supervision.
🛇 🍴 🍴 🌊 ✕

St. Regis Aspen LH 🐾
(970) 920-3300. **$250-$725,** 14 day notice. 315 E Dean St. SR 82, s on Monarch St, then just e. Int corridors. **Pets:** Other species. $100 one-time fee/room. Service with restrictions, supervision.
✕ 🔊 🍴 🌊 ✕

Sky Hotel LH 🐾
(970) 925-6760. **$139-$599,** 14 day notice. 709 E Durant Ave. At base of Aspen Mountain. Ext/int corridors. **Pets:** Other species. Service with restrictions, crate.
SAVE 🛇 ✕ 🗮 💻 🍴 🌊 ✕

BEAVER CREEK

Comfort Inn-Vail/Beaver Creek SH 🐾
(970) 949-5511. **$69-$199.** 161 W Beaver Creek Blvd. I-70, exit 167, just s, then w. Int corridors. **Pets:** Medium, other species. $25 one-time fee/room. Designated rooms, service with restrictions, supervision.
ASK 🛇 ✕ 🔊 🍴 💻 🌊

▼▼ ▼▼ The Ritz-Carlton, Bachelor Gulch 🅛🅗 ❀
(970) 748-6200. **$195-$700, 60 day notice.** 0130 Daybreak
Ridge. I-70, exit 167, s on Avon and Village rds beyond
gatehouse, w on Prater Rd, follow signs to Bachelor Gulch.
Int corridors. **Pets:** Dogs only. $35 one-time fee/room. Serv-
ice with restrictions.

⊠ 🅼 🗐 🖪 🖵 🍴 🐾 🗶

BOULDER

🅐🅐🅐 ▼▼▼ Best Western Boulder Inn 🆂🅷
(303) 449-3800. **$74-$109.** 770 28th St. US 36 at Baseline
Rd. Int corridors. **Pets:** Medium. $100 deposit/room. Desig-
nated rooms, supervision.

🆂🅰🆅🅴 🆂🅳 ⊠ 🖪 🖵 🍴 🐾 🗶

▼▼▼ Boulder Broker Inn 🆂🅷
(303) 444-3330. **$129-$139.** 555 30th St. US 36 (28th St),
exit Baseline Rd, 0.3 mi e to 30th St, then just s. Int
corridors. **Pets:** Medium. Designated rooms, service with
restrictions, supervision.

🅰🆂🅺 🆂🅳 ⊠ 🖪 🖵 🍴 🐾 🗶

▼▼ ▼▼ Boulder Outlook Hotel & Suites 🆂🅷 ❀
(303) 443-3322. **$79-$159, 30 day notice.** 800 28th St. US
36 (28th St), exit Baseline Rd via Frontage Rd. Ext/int
corridors. **Pets:** Large, other species. $10 daily fee/room.
Designated rooms, service with restrictions.

🅰🆂🅺 🆂🅳 ⊠ 🗐 🖪 🖵 🍴 🐾 🗶

🅐🅐🅐 ▼▼▼ Foot of The Mountain Motel 🅜
(303) 442-5688. **$70-$85.** 200 Arapahoe Ave. 1.8 mi w of US
36 (28th St). Ext corridors. **Pets:** $50 deposit/room, $5 daily
fee/pet. Service with restrictions, supervision.

🆂🅰🆅🅴 🖪 🗶 🅺

▼▼▼ Homewood Suites by Hilton 🆂🅷
(303) 499-9922. **$129-$250.** 4950 Baseline Rd. 0.3 mi e of
US 36; SR 157 (Foothills Pkwy), exit Baseline Rd, just w;
entry off Baseline Rd. Ext/int corridors. **Pets:** Accepted.

🅰🆂🅺 🆂🅳 ⊠ 🗐 🖪 🖵 🐾 🗶

🅐🅐🅐 ▼▼▼ Millennium Harvest House
Boulder 🅛🅗
(303) 443-3850. **$139-$219.** 1345 28th St. Just s of intersection Arapahoe Rd and 28th St (US 36). Int corridors.
Pets: Accepted.

🆂🅰🆅🅴 🆂🅳 ⊠ 🗐 🖵 🍴 🐾 🗶

▼▼▼ Residence Inn by Marriott 🆂🅷
(303) 449-5545. **$80-$152.** 3030 Center Green Dr. 0.5 mi e
of US 36 (28th St); on Valmont Rd at corner of Foothills
Pkwy. Ext corridors. **Pets:** Accepted.

🅰🆂🅺 🆂🅳 ⊠ 🗐 🖪 🖵 🐾 🗶

▼▼ ▼▼ Super 8 of Boulder 🅜 ❀
(303) 443-7800. **$55-$115.** 970 28th St. On US 36 (28th St).
Ext corridors. **Pets:** Other species. $50 deposit/room, $5
daily fee/pet. Service with restrictions, supervision.

🅰🆂🅺 🆂🅳 ⊠ 🖪 🖪 🖵 🐾

BRECKENRIDGE

▼▼▼ Wildwood Suites 🅒🅞
(970) 453-0232. **$95-$415, 30 day notice.** 120 Sawmill Rd.
From SR 9, just w on Ski Hill Rd, then just s. Int corridors.
Pets: Accepted.

🅰🆂🅺 🆂🅳 ⊠ 🖪 🖵 🗶 🅺

BROOMFIELD

🅐🅐🅐 ▼▼▼ Omni Interlocken
Resort 🅛🅗 ❀
(303) 438-6600. **$199-$239.** 500 Interlocken Blvd. US 36
(Boulder Tpke), exit Interlocken Loop, then w, just s via
signs. Int corridors. **Pets:** Medium, other species. $50 one-
time fee/room. Service with restrictions, crate.

🆂🅰🆅🅴 🆂🅳 ⊠ 🅼 🗐 🖪 🖪 🖵 🍴 🐾 🗶

▼▼▼ TownePlace Suites by Marriott
Boulder/Broomfield 🆂🅷 ❀
(303) 466-2200. **$99-$149.** 480 Flat Iron Blvd. US 36 W
(Boulder Tpke), Interlocken Loop, to first traffic light, w on
Interlocken Blvd, then s. Int corridors. **Pets:** Medium. $25
daily fee/room, $200 one-time fee/room. Service with
restrictions, supervision.

🅰🆂🅺 🆂🅳 ⊠ 🅼 🗐 🖪 🖪 🖵 🐾

BRUSH

🅐🅐🅐 ▼▼▼ Best Western Brush 🆂🅷 ❀
(970) 842-5146. **$58-$79.** 1208 N Colorado Ave. I-76, exit
90B, just n. Ext/int corridors. **Pets:** $10 daily fee/pet. Serv-
ice with restrictions, supervision.

🆂🅰🆅🅴 🆂🅳 ⊠ 🖪 🖵 🐾

▼▼▼ Microtel Inn 🆂🅷
(970) 842-4241. **$52-$72.** 975 N Colorado Ave. I-76, exit
90A, just s. Int corridors. **Pets:** Dogs only. $20 deposit/
room, $15 daily fee/pet. Designated rooms, service with
restrictions, supervision.

🅰🆂🅺 🆂🅳 ⊠ 🖪 🖵 🐾

BUENA VISTA

🅐🅐🅐 ▼▼ Alpine Lodge 🅜
(719) 395-2415. **$45-$65, 15 day notice.** 12845 Hwy 24 &
285. 2 mi s on US 24, 0.5 mi e on US 24 and 285. Ext
corridors. **Pets:** Accepted.

🆂🅰🆅🅴 🆂🅳 ⊠ 🖪

🅐🅐🅐 ▼▼▼ Best Western Vista Inn 🅜
(719) 395-8009. **$67-$139.** 733 US Hwy 24 N. 0.5 mi n. Int
corridors. **Pets:** Medium, dogs only. $50 deposit/room, $7
daily fee/pet. Designated rooms, service with restrictions,
supervision.

🆂🅰🆅🅴 🆂🅳 ⊠ 🗐 🖪 🖵

BURLINGTON

▼▼▼ Burlington Comfort Inn 🆂🅷
(719) 346-7676. **$69-$99.** 282 S Lincoln St. I-70, exit 437,
just n on US 385. Int corridors. **Pets:** Large. $50 deposit/
room, $10 daily fee/room. Designated rooms, service with
restrictions, supervision.

🅰🆂🅺 🆂🅳 ⊠ 🖪 🖪 🖵 🐾

🅐🅐🅐 ▼▼▼ Chaparral Motor Inn 🅜 ❀
(719) 346-5361. **$45-$59.** 405 S Lincoln St. I-70, exit 437,
just n on jct US 385. Ext corridors. **Pets:** Small, other
species. $7 daily fee/pet. Service with restrictions, crate.

🆂🅰🆅🅴 🆂🅳 ⊠ 🖵 🐾

⟡⟡⟡ Sloans Motel M
(719) 346-5333. **$35-$60.** 1901 Rose Ave. I-70, exit 437, 0.5 mi n on US 385, just e on US 24; exit 438 westbound, 1 mi w on US 24. Ext corridors. **Pets:** Accepted.
[SAVE] [S🐾] [✕] [🔥M] [🔊] [▤] [🏊]

CANON CITY

⟡⟡⟡ Best Western Royal Gorge Motel M
(719) 275-3377. **$50-$120.** 1925 Fremont Dr. 0.8 mi e on US 50. Ext/int corridors. **Pets:** Accepted.
[SAVE] [S🐾] [✕] [🔥] [▤] [🍴] [🏊] [✕]

⟡⟡⟡⟡ Canon Inn-Quality Inn & Suites M
(719) 275-8676. **$64-$99.** 3075 E Hwy 50. 2 mi e of jct SR 115 and US 50; center. Int corridors. **Pets:** Other species. Designated rooms, service with restrictions, supervision.
[SAVE] [S🐾] [✕] [🔥] [▤] [🍴] [🏊]

⟡⟡⟡ Comfort Inn SH
(719) 276-6900. **$82-$99.** 311 Royal Gorge Blvd. On US 50, just w of downtown. Int corridors. **Pets:** Other species. $10 one-time fee/pet. Service with restrictions, supervision.
[SAVE] [S🐾] [✕] [🔥M] [🔊] [🔥] [▤] [🏊]

⟡⟡⟡ Royal Gorge Inn M
(719) 269-1100. **$42-$80.** 217 N Raynolds Ave. 1 mi e on US 50, just n. Int corridors. **Pets:** Accepted.
[SAVE] [S🐾] [✕] [🔥] [🏊]

CARBONDALE

⟡⟡⟡⟡ Comfort Inn & Suites SH ❀
(970) 963-8880. **$79-$159.** 920 Cowen Dr. Jct of SR 82 and 133, just s via signs. Int corridors. **Pets:** Other species. $10 one-time fee/pet. Supervision.
[SAVE] [S🐾] [✕] [🔊] [🔥] [▤] [🏊] [✕]

⟡⟡⟡⟡ Days Inn-Carbondale SH
(970) 963-9111. **$69-$129, 3 day notice.** 950 Cowen Dr. Jct SR 82 and 133. Int corridors. **Pets:** Accepted.
[SAVE] [S🐾] [✕] [🔊] [🔥] [🏊] [✕]

⟡⟡⟡ Thunder River Lodge M ❀
(970) 963-2543. **$40-$77.** 179 Hwy 133. Just s on SR 133 from jct SR 82. Ext corridors. **Pets:** Other species. $20 deposit/room, $5 daily fee/pet. Designated rooms, service with restrictions, supervision.
[SAVE] [✕]

CASTLE ROCK

⟡⟡⟡⟡ Best Western Inn & Suites of Castle Rock SH
(303) 814-8800. **$69-$109.** 595 Genoa Way. I-25, exit 184 (Meadows Pkwy), just w to Castleton Way, then s and e on Genoa Way. Int corridors. **Pets:** Medium. $15 daily fee/pet. Designated rooms, service with restrictions, supervision.
[SAVE] [S🐾] [✕] [🔊] [🔥] [▤] [🏊]

⟡⟡⟡ Comfort Suites SH ❀
(303) 814-9999. **$59-$149.** 4755 Castleton Way. I-25, exit 184 (Meadows Pkwy), w to Castleton Way; entry on eastside. Int corridors. **Pets:** Other species. $10 daily fee/room. Service with restrictions.
[SAVE] [S🐾] [✕] [🔥M] [🔊] [🔥] [▤] [🏊]

⟡⟡⟡ Holiday Inn Express SH
(303) 660-9733. **$79-$119.** 884 Park St. I-25, exit 182, just w. Int corridors. **Pets:** Accepted.
[A$K] [S🐾] [✕] [🔊] [🔥] [▤] [🏊]

CEDAREDGE

⟡⟡⟡ Howard Johnson Express Inn M
(970) 856-7824. **$69-$119.** 530 S Grand Mesa Dr. Just s on SR 65. Int corridors. **Pets:** $10 daily fee/pet. Designated rooms, supervision.
[SAVE] [S🐾] [✕] [🔥] [▤] [🏊]

COLORADO SPRINGS METROPOLITAN AREA

CALHAN

⟡⟡⟡ Calhan Inn M
(719) 347-9589. **$55-$77.** 15 5th St, Hwy 24. On US 24, e of downtown. Ext corridors. **Pets:** Accepted.
[SAVE] [S🐾] [✕] [🔊]

COLORADO SPRINGS

⟡⟡⟡⟡ AmeriSuites (Colorado Springs/ Garden of the Gods) SH
(719) 265-9385. **$69-$125.** 503 W Garden of the Gods Rd. I-25, exit 146, just w. Int corridors. **Pets:** Accepted.
[SAVE] [S🐾] [✕] [🔊] [🔥] [▤] [🏊]

⟡⟡⟡ Apollo Park Executive Suites CO
(719) 634-0286. **$85-$105.** 805 S Circle Dr, 2-B. I-25, exit 138, 2.5 mi e. Int corridors. **Pets:** Accepted.
[SAVE] [S🐾] [✕] [🔥] [▤] [🏊]

⟡⟡⟡⟡ Best Western Airport Inn SH
(719) 574-7707. **$49-$99.** 1780 Aeroplaza Dr. I-25, exit 139 (US 24 Bypass), 4 mi e on Fountain Blvd. Int corridors. **Pets:** Designated rooms.
[SAVE] [S🐾] [✕] [🔥M] [🔥] [▤] [🏊] [✕]

⟡⟡⟡ Chief Motel M
(719) 473-5228. **$27-$65.** 1624 S Nevada Ave. I-25, exit 140A northbound; exit 140B southbound. Ext corridors. **Pets:** Other species. $20 deposit/room, $5 daily fee/pet. Supervision.
[SAVE] [S🐾] [✕] [🔥]

⟡⟡⟡⟡ Comfort Inn North SH ❀
(719) 262-9000. **$49-$139.** 6450 Corporate Dr. I-25, exit 149 (Woodmen Rd), just w to second light, then 0.3 mi s. Int corridors. **Pets:** Medium. $20 one-time fee/room. Service with restrictions, supervision.
[SAVE] [S🐾] [✕] [🔥M] [🔊] [🔥] [▤] [🏊] [✕]

△△△ ▽▽▽▽ Comfort Suites SH
(719) 536-0731. **$59-$119.** 1055 Kelly Johnson Blvd. I-25, exit 150, just s on Academy Blvd to Kelly Johnson Blvd, then w. Int corridors. **Pets:** Large. $25 deposit/pet. Service with restrictions, crate.
SAVE S☐ ☒ &M ☐ ☐ ☐ ☐

△△△ ▽▽▽ Days Inn-Air Force Academy SH
(719) 266-1317. **$49-$94.** 8350 Razorback Rd. I-25, exit 150, just s, then e. Int corridors. **Pets:** Small. $10 daily fee/pet. Service with restrictions, supervision.
SAVE S☐ ☒ &M ☐ ☐ ☐

△△△ ▽▽▽▽ Doubletree Hotel Colorado Springs, World Arena SH ❀
(719) 576-8900. **$89-$189.** 1775 E Cheyenne Mountain Blvd. I-25, exit 138, just w. Int corridors. **Pets:** Medium, other species. $10 daily fee/pet. Service with restrictions, supervision.
SAVE S☐ ☒ &M ☐ ☐ ☐ ☐ ☐ ☐

▽▽▽▽ Drury Inn-Pikes Peak SH
(719) 598-2500. **$65-$109.** 8155 N Academy Blvd. I-25, exit 150, just s, then e. Int corridors. **Pets:** Large, other species. Service with restrictions, supervision.
ASK ☒ ☐ ☐ ☐ ☐

△△△ ▽▽ Econo Lodge Inn & Suites World Arena SH
(719) 632-6651. **$50-$95.** 1623 S Nevada Ave. I-25, exit 140, just s. Ext corridors. **Pets:** Other species. $10 deposit/pet, $10 one-time fee/pet. Service with restrictions, supervision.
SAVE S☐ ☒ ☐ ☐ ☐ ☐ ☐

▽▽▽▽ Hampton Inn Colorado Springs South SH
(719) 579-6900. **$59-$129.** 1410 Harrison Rd. I-25, exit 138 (Circle Dr), just w to Rand Rd, then ne. Int corridors. **Pets:** Other species. Service with restrictions.
ASK S☐ ☒ ☐ ☐ ☐

△△△ ▽▽▽ Holiday Inn Garden of the Gods LH
(719) 598-7656. **$69-$89.** 505 Pope's Bluff Tr. I-25, exit 146, just w, then n on Hilton Pkwy. Int corridors. **Pets:** Accepted.
SAVE S☐ ☒ &M ☐ ☐ ☐ ☐ ☐ ☐

▽▽▽▽ Homewood Suites by Hilton SH
(719) 265-6600. **$109-$209.** 9130 Explorer Dr. I-25, exit 151, 0.8 mi e; across from Focus on the Family. Int corridors. **Pets:** Accepted.
ASK S☐ ☒ &M ☐ ☐ ☐ ☐ ☐

△△△ ▽▽▽▽ La Quinta Inn & Suites SH
(719) 527-4788. **$70-$120.** 2750 Geyser Dr. I-25, exit 138 (Circle Dr), just w to Cheyenne Mountain Blvd, then just s. Int corridors. **Pets:** Accepted.
SAVE ☒ &M ☐ ☐ ☐ ☐

△△△ ▽▽▽▽ La Quinta Inn Garden of the Gods SH
(719) 528-5060. **$60-$90.** 4385 Sinton Rd. I-25, exit 146, just e. Ext/int corridors. **Pets:** Medium. Service with restrictions, supervision.
SAVE ☒ ☐ ☐ ☐ ☐

▽▽▽▽ Le Baron Hotel, Downtown Colorado Springs SH
(719) 471-8680. **$71-$98.** 314 W Bijou St. I-25, exit 142, northwest corner. Int corridors. **Pets:** Other species. $50 deposit/pet. Service with restrictions, crate.
ASK S☐ ☒ ☐ ☐ ☐ ☐ ☐

▽▽▽▽ Marriott TownePlace Suites Colorado Springs SH ❀
(719) 594-4447. **$69-$149.** 4760 Centennial Blvd. I-25, exit 146 (Garden of the Gods Rd), 1 mi w, n on Centennial Blvd, then first left. Int corridors. **Pets:** Other species. $25 daily fee/pet, $25 one-time fee/room. Service with restrictions.
ASK S☐ ☒ &M ☐ ☐ ☐ ☐

△△△ ▽▽▽▽ Quality Inn & Suites SH
(719) 576-2371. **$79-$160.** 1440 Harrison Rd. I-25, exit 138 (Circle Dr), just w, on northwest corner of interchange; entry through restaurant. Int corridors. **Pets:** $50 deposit/pet, $5 daily fee/pet. Designated rooms, service with restrictions, supervision.
SAVE S☐ ☒ &M ☐ ☐ ☐ ☐

▽▽▽▽ Quality Inn-Garden of the Gods SH ❀
(719) 593-9119. **$59-$139.** 555 W Garden of the Gods Rd. I-25, exit 146, just w. Int corridors. **Pets:** Other species. $50 deposit/room. Service with restrictions, crate.
ASK S☐ ☒ ☐ ☐ ☐ ☐

△△△ ▽▽▽▽ Radisson Inn & Suites LH
(719) 597-7000. **$88-$126, 7 day notice.** 1645 N Newport Rd. I-25, exit 139, 4 mi e on US 24 Bypass (Fountain Blvd). Int corridors. **Pets:** Other species. $100 deposit/room. Service with restrictions, crate.
SAVE S☐ ☒ &M ☐ ☐ ☐ ☐ ☐ ☐ ☐

△△△ ▽▽▽▽ Radisson Inn Colorado Springs North LH
(719) 598-5770. **$79-$169.** 8110 N Academy Blvd. I-25, exit 150, just s. Int corridors. **Pets:** Small. $50 deposit/room. Service with restrictions, crate.
SAVE S☐ ☒ &M ☐ ☐ ☐ ☐ ☐ ☐

△△△ ▽▽▽ Rainbow Motel M ❀
(719) 632-4545. **$53-$95, 7 day notice.** 3709 W Colorado Ave. I-25, exit 141, 2.5 mi w on US 24, just n on 31st, then 0.7 mi w. Ext corridors. **Pets:** Small, dogs only. $25 deposit/pet. Service with restrictions, supervision.
SAVE S☐ ☒ ☐ ☐

△△△ ▽▽▽ Ramada Inn-North SH
(719) 633-5541. **$49-$129.** 3125 Sinton Rd. I-25, exit 145, just e, then just n. Ext/int corridors. **Pets:** Accepted.
SAVE S☐ ☒ ☐ ☐ ☐ ☐ ☐ ☐

▽▽▽ Ramada Limited East-Airport SH ❀
(719) 596-7660. **$59-$89.** 520 N Murray Blvd. I-25, exit 141, e to Wahsatch, s to Platte, 3.8 mi e to Murray Blvd, then just n. Ext/int corridors. **Pets:** Other species. $50 deposit/room. Service with restrictions, supervision.
ASK S☐ ☒ ☐ ☐ ☐ ☐

▼▼▼▼ **Residence Inn by Marriott-Central** 🆂🅷
(719) 574-0370. **$99-$139.** 3880 N Academy Blvd. I-25, exit 146, 6 mi e on Austin Bluffs Pkwy to Academy Blvd (SR 83), 0.3 mi s. Ext corridors. **Pets:** Other species. $50 one-time fee/room. Service with restrictions, crate.

ⒶⓈⓀ 🆂🅾 ✕ 🌀 🛏 🍴 💻 ⤳ ✕

▼▼▼▼ **Residence Inn by Marriott Colorado Springs North Interquest** 🆂🅷
(719) 388-9300. **$99-$249.** 9805 Federal Dr. I-25, exit 153, just e, then s. Int corridors. **Pets:** Medium, other species. $75 one-time fee/room.

ⒶⓈⓀ 🆂🅾 ✕ 🅜 🍴 🛏 💻 ⤳ ✕

▼▼▼▼ **Residence Inn by Marriott-South** 🆂🅷 ❀
(719) 576-0101. **$69-$189.** 2765 Geyser Dr. I-25, exit 138 (Circle Dr), just w to E Cheyenne Mountain Blvd, then just s. Int corridors. **Pets:** Other species. $50 one-time fee/room. Service with restrictions.

ⒶⓈⓀ 🆂🅾 ✕ 🅜 🍴 🛏 💻 ⤳ ✕

▼▼ **Rodeway Inn** 🆂🅷
(719) 471-0990. **$60-$147.** 2409 E Pikes Peak Ave. I-25, exit 143, e on Uintah to Union, s to Pikes Peak, then e; exit 138, ne on Circle Dr to Pikes Peak Ave, then w. Ext corridors. **Pets:** Accepted.

ⒶⓈⓀ 🆂🅾 ✕ 🛏 💻 ⤳

▼▼ **Sleep Inn** 🆂🅷
(719) 260-6969. **$39-$99.** 1075 Kelly Johnson Blvd. I-25, exit 150, just s on Academy Blvd to Kelly Johnson Blvd, then w. Int corridors. **Pets:** Large. $25 deposit/pet. Service with restrictions, crate.

ⒶⓈⓀ 🆂🅾 ✕ 🅜 🍴 💻

ⒶⒶⒶ ▼ **Stagecoach Motel** 🅼 ❀
(719) 633-3894. **$39-$69.** 1647 S Nevada Ave. I-25, exit 140A or 140B, just s. Ext corridors. **Pets:** Small, other species. $5 daily fee/pet. Service with restrictions, supervision.

🆂🅰🆅🅴 🆂🅾 ✕ 🛏

ⒶⒶⒶ ▼▼▼ **Staybridge Suites-Air Force Academy** 🆂🅷
(719) 590-7829. **$69-$199.** 7130 Commerce Center Dr. I-25, exit 149, just w, then n. Int corridors. **Pets:** Accepted.

🆂🅰🆅🅴 🆂🅾 ✕ 🅜 🌀 🍴 🛏 💻 ⤳ ✕

ⒶⒶⒶ ▼▼ **Travel Inn** 🅼
(719) 636-3986. **$27-$65.** 512 S Nevada Ave. I-25, exit 141, just e to Nevada Ave, then just s. Ext/int corridors. **Pets:** Other species. $20 deposit/room, $5 daily fee/pet. Supervision.

🆂🅰🆅🅴 🆂🅾 ✕ 🛏

ⒶⒶⒶ ▼▼ **Travelodge** 🆂🅷
(719) 632-4600. **$40-$85.** 2625 Ore Mill Rd. I-25, exit 141, 2.3 mi nw on US 24; entry via 26th St. Int corridors. **Pets:** Small. $20 daily fee/room. Service with restrictions, supervision.

🆂🅰🆅🅴 🆂🅾 ✕ 🛏 💻 ⤳

ⒶⒶⒶ ▼▼▼▼ **Wyndham Colorado Springs** 🅻🅷 ❀
(719) 260-1800. **$89-$109.** 5580 Tech Center Dr. I-25, exit 147 (Rockrimmon Blvd), 0.5 mi w. Int corridors. **Pets:** Other species. $250 deposit/room, $25 one-time fee/room.

🆂🅰🆅🅴 🆂🅾 ✕ 🌀 🛏 💻 🍴 ⤳ ✕

MANITOU SPRINGS

ⒶⒶⒶ ▼▼▼ **Park Row Lodge** 🅼
(719) 685-5216. **$59-$89, 3 day notice.** 54 Manitou Ave. I-25, exit 141, 4 mi nw on US 24, exit Manitou Ave, then just se. Ext corridors. **Pets:** Accepted.

🆂🅰🆅🅴 🆂🅾 ✕ 🛏

ⒶⒶⒶ ▼▼ **Red Wing Motel** 🅼
(719) 685-5656. **$42-$68.** 56 El Paso Blvd. I-25, exit 141, 4 mi w on US 24, just e to Beckers Ln, then n. Ext corridors. **Pets:** Accepted.

🆂🅰🆅🅴 🆂🅾 ✕ 🛏 💻 ⤳

❀   END METROPOLITAN AREA   ❀

COPPER MOUNTAIN

▼▼▼▼ **Copper Mountain Resort** 🅲🅾
(970) 968-2882. **$79-$1029, 14 day notice.** 0508 Copper Rd. I-70, exit 195. Int corridors. **Pets:** Accepted.

ⒶⓈⓀ ✕ 🛏 💻 🍴 ⤳ ✕ 🕪

CORTEZ

ⒶⒶⒶ ▼▼▼ **Anasazi Motor Inn** 🅼
(970) 565-3773. **$55-$71.** 640 S Broadway. 0.5 mi sw on US 160 and 491. Ext corridors. **Pets:** Other species. $50 deposit/room. Service with restrictions, crate.

🆂🅰🆅🅴 🆂🅾 ✕ 🍴 ⤳ ✕

ⒶⒶⒶ ▼▼▼ **Best Western Sands** 🅼
(970) 565-3761. **$50-$92.** 1120 E Main St. 0.3 mi e on US 160. Ext/int corridors. **Pets:** Accepted.

🆂🅰🆅🅴 🆂🅾 ✕ 🛏 💻 ⤳

ⒶⒶⒶ ▼▼▼▼ **Best Western Turquoise Inn & Suites** 🆂🅷
(970) 565-3778. **$64-$129.** 535 E Main St. On US 160. Ext corridors. **Pets:** Other species. $15 one-time fee/room. Service with restrictions, supervision.

🆂🅰🆅🅴 🆂🅾 ✕ 🛏 💻 ⤳

ⒶⒶⒶ ▼▼▼ **Budget Host Inn** 🅼
(970) 565-3738. **$38-$78.** 2040 E Main St. 1.3 mi e on US 160, w of jct SR 145. Ext corridors. **Pets:** Other species. $5 daily fee/pet. Designated rooms, service with restrictions, supervision.

🆂🅰🆅🅴 🆂🅾 ✕ 🛏 💻 ⤳

ⒶⒶⒶ ▼▼▼▼ **Comfort Inn** 🆂🅷
(970) 565-3400. **$69-$129.** 2321 E Main St. 1.3 mi e on US 160. Ext/int corridors. **Pets:** Accepted.

🆂🅰🆅🅴 🆂🅾 ✕ 🛏 💻 ⤳

(AAA) ▼▼ Days Inn SH
(970) 565-8577. **$49-$99.** 1.5 mi e on US 160, at jct SR 145. Ext/int corridors. **Pets:** Accepted.
[SAVE] [S🐾] [✕] [🔧] [🍽] [≈]

▼▼ Econo Lodge M 🌼
(970) 565-3474. **$49-$99.** 2020 E Main St. 1.3 mi e on US 160. Ext corridors. **Pets:** Designated rooms, service with restrictions, supervision.
[ASK] [S🐾] [✕] [🔧] [💻] [≈]

▼▼▼ Holiday Inn Express SH 🌼
(970) 565-6000. **$79-$149.** 2121 E Main St. 1.3 mi e on US 160. Int corridors. **Pets:** Other species. Designated rooms, service with restrictions, supervision.
[ASK] [S🐾] [✕] [🗇] [🔧] [≈] [✕]

(AAA) ▼▼ Tomahawk Lodge M
(970) 565-8521. **$37-$73.** 728 S Broadway. 1 mi sw on US 160 and 491. Ext corridors. **Pets:** Accepted.
[SAVE] [S🐾] [✕] [≈]

▼▼ Travelodge M
(970) 565-7778. **$45-$79.** 440 S Broadway. 0.8 mi sw on US 160 and 491. Ext corridors. **Pets:** Accepted.
[ASK] [S🐾] [✕] [🔧] [💻] [≈]

CRAIG

(AAA) ▼▼ Black Nugget Motel M
(970) 824-8161. **$40-$65.** 2855 W Victory Way. 1.5 mi w on US 40, 0.3 mi w of jct SR 13. Ext corridors. **Pets:** Other species. $5 daily fee/pet. Supervision.
[SAVE] [S🐾] [✕] [🔧] [💻] [✕]

▼▼▼ Craig Holiday Inn SH
(970) 824-4000. **$84-$139.** 300 S Hwy 13. 0.3 mi s on SR 13 from jct US 40. Int corridors. **Pets:** Small, other species. Service with restrictions, supervision.
[ASK] [S🐾] [✕] [🗇] [🔧] [💻] [🍽] [≈] [✕]

(AAA) ▼▼▼▼ Deer Park Inn and Suites SH
(970) 824-9282. **$79-$139.** 262 Commerce St. Jct US 40, just 0.3 mi s on SR 13. Int corridors. **Pets:** Large. $50 deposit/room. Service with restrictions, supervision.
[SAVE] [S🐾] [✕] [🗇] [🔧] [≈]

CRESTED BUTTE

▼▼ Old Town Inn SH
(970) 349-6184. **$58-$98, 14 day notice.** 708 6th St. Se on SR 135. Int corridors. **Pets:** Accepted.
[ASK] [S🐾] [✕]

▼▼▼▼ Sheraton Crested Butte Resort LH 🌼
(970) 349-8000. **$69-$239.** 6 Emmons Rd. 2.5 mi n on SR 135. Int corridors. **Pets:** $30 daily fee/room. Designated rooms, service with restrictions, supervision.
[ASK] [S🐾] [✕] [🗇] [🔧] [💻] [🍽] [≈] [✕] [AC]

CRIPPLE CREEK

▼▼▼ Double Eagle Hotel/Casino SH
(719) 689-5000. **$60-$140.** 442 E Bennett Ave. On SR 67; at nw entry to town diagonal from Cripple Creek Museum. Int corridors. **Pets:** Accepted.
[ASK] [S🐾] [✕] [🗇] [🔧] [💻] [🍽]

DELTA

(AAA) ▼▼▼ Best Western Sundance M
(970) 874-9781. **$75-$95, 14 day notice.** 903 Main St. 0.5 mi s on US 50. Ext corridors. **Pets:** Other species. $10 daily fee/room. Service with restrictions, crate.
[SAVE] [S🐾] [✕] [🔧] [💻] [🍽] [≈]

(AAA) ▼▼▼ Comfort Inn M
(970) 874-1000. **$63-$90.** 180 Gunnison River Dr. Just n, then w of jct US 50 and 92. Int corridors. **Pets:** $5 daily fee/pet. Designated rooms, service with restrictions, supervision.
[SAVE] [S🐾] [✕] [🔧] [💻]

(AAA) ▼▼▼ South Gate Inns M
(970) 874-9726. **$45-$79.** 2124 S Main St. 1.5 mi s on US 50. Ext corridors. **Pets:** Accepted.
[SAVE] [S🐾] [✕] [🔧] [💻] [≈]

DENVER METROPOLITAN AREA

AURORA

(AAA) ▼▼▼▼ AmeriSuites (Denver/Airport) SH
(303) 371-0700. **$89-$107.** 16250 E 40th Ave. I-70, exit 283 (Chambers Rd), just n, then 0.5 mi e. Int corridors. **Pets:** Service with restrictions, supervision.
[SAVE] [S🐾] [✕] [5.M] [🗇] [🔧] [💻] [≈]

▼▼ The Hearthside by Villager SH 🌼
(303) 481-0379. **$39, 14 day notice.** 14090 E Evans. I-225, exit 5, e to Blackhawk St, then 0.4 mi nw. Int corridors. **Pets:** $100 deposit/room, $50 one-time fee/room. Designated rooms, service with restrictions.
[ASK] [S🐾] [✕] [🔧] [💻]

(AAA) ▼▼▼ Holiday Inn DIA LH
(303) 371-9494. **$79-$94.** 15500 E 40th Ave. I-70, exit 283 (Chambers Rd), just n, then just e. Int corridors. **Pets:** Medium. $50 deposit/room, $25 one-time fee/room. Designated rooms, service with restrictions, supervision.
[SAVE] [S🐾] [✕] [5.M] [🗇] [🔧] [💻] [🍽] [≈] [✕]

▼▼ Homestead Studio Suites Hotel-Denver/Aurora M 🌼
(303) 750-9116. **$46-$66.** 13941 E Harvard Ave. I-225, exit 5, just e on E Iliff Ave to Blackhawk St, then just s. Ext corridors. **Pets:** Medium, other species. $25 daily fee/room. Service with restrictions, crate.
[ASK] [S🐾] [✕] [5.M] [🗇] [🔧] [💻]

WWWW La Quinta Inn-Aurora M
(303) 337-0206. **$65-$80.** 1011 S Abilene St. I-225, exit 7, just e, then n. Ext corridors. **Pets:** Other species. Service with restrictions, supervision.
[SAVE] [X] [&M] [🐾] [💻] [≈]

WW Sleep Inn Denver International Airport SH
(303) 373-1616. **$59-$99.** 15900 E 40th Ave. I-70, exit 283, from airport, Pena Blvd s to 40th Ave W. Int corridors. **Pets:** Accepted.
[SAVE] [So] [X] [&M] [🐾] [🐕] [🔋] [💻] [≈]

WWW Wellesley Inn & Suites (Denver/Aurora) SH
(303) 337-7000. **$64-$99.** 14095 E Evans Ave. I-225, exit 5 (E Iliff Ave), just e to Blackhawk St, then just n. Int corridors. **Pets:** Small, other species. Service with restrictions, supervision.
[SAVE] [X] [&M] [🐾] [🐕] [🔋] [💻] [≈]

CENTENNIAL

WWWW TownePlace Suites Denver Tech Center SH 🐾
(720) 875-1113. **$47-$85.** I-25, exit 196, just w to Chester St, then 0.3 mi s. Int corridors. **Pets:** Other species. $25 daily fee/room. Service with restrictions.
[SAVE] [So] [X] [&M] [🐕] [🔋] [💻] [≈]

DENVER

WW Best Western Central Denver SH
(303) 296-4000. **$45-$95.** 200 W 48th Ave. I-25, exit 215 northbound; exit 214B southbound. Int corridors. **Pets:** Medium, other species. $10 daily fee/room. Service with restrictions, supervision.
[ASK] [So] [X] [🔋] [💻] [🍴] [≈]

WWWW Brown Palace Hotel LH
(303) 297-3111. **$279-$1199.** 321 17th St, Tremont & Broadway. I-25, exit 210 (E Colfax Ave), to Lincoln St, n to Tremont, then just w. Int corridors. **Pets:** Accepted.
[SAVE] [So] [X] [🐾] [🐕] [🔋] [🍴] [X]

WW Cameron Motel M
(303) 757-2100. **$45-$55.** 4500 E Evans Ave. I-25, exit 203, then w. Ext corridors. **Pets:** $5 daily fee/pet. Designated rooms, service with restrictions, supervision.
[SAVE] [So] [X] [🔋]

WWWW Comfort Inn Downtown Denver SH 🐾
(303) 296-0400. **$62-$134.** 401 17th St. I-25, exit 210 (E Colfax Ave) to Lincoln St, n to Tremont, then just w; opposite Brown Palace Hotel. Int corridors. **Pets:** Medium, dogs only. $50 one-time fee/room. Supervision.
[SAVE] [So] [X] [🐾] [💻] [🍴]

WWWW Denver Marriott Hotel City Center LH
(303) 297-1300. **$152-$169.** 1701 California St at 17th St. I-25, exit 210 (E Colfax Ave) to Welton St, 0.5 mi ne, nw on 18th, then 1 blk. Int corridors. **Pets:** Accepted.
[ASK] [So] [X] [🐾] [🐕] [🔋] [💻] [🍴] [≈] [X]

WWWW Denver Marriott Southeast Hotel LH
(303) 758-7000. **$98.** 6363 E Hampden Ave. I-25, exit 201, just e. Ext/int corridors. **Pets:** Accepted.
[ASK] [So] [X] [&M] [🐾] [🐕] [💻] [🍴] [≈] [X]

WWWW Denver Marriott Tech Center LH
(303) 779-1100. **$149, 3 day notice.** 4900 S Syracuse St. I-25, exit 199, exit Bellview e to Syracuse St, then just n. Int corridors. **Pets:** Accepted.
[ASK] [So] [X] [&M] [🐾] [🐕] [🔋] [💻] [🍴] [≈]

WWWW DoubleTree Hotel Denver LH
(303) 321-3333. **$79-$179.** 3203 Quebec St. I-70, exit 278, 0.5 mi s; I-270, exit 4. Int corridors. **Pets:** Accepted.
[ASK] [So] [X] [🐾] [🐕] [🔋] [💻] [🍴] [≈] [X]

WWWW Drury Inn-Denver East SH
(303) 373-1983. **$72-$92.** 4380 E Peoria St. I-70, exit 281, just n. Int corridors. **Pets:** Large, other species. Service with restrictions, supervision.
[ASK] [X] [🐾] [🔋] [💻] [≈]

WWWW Embassy Suites Hotel Denver Aurora LH
(303) 375-0400. **$109-$179.** 4444 N Havana St. I-70, exit 280, just n. Int corridors. **Pets:** Medium. $25 deposit/pet. Service with restrictions, supervision.
[SAVE] [So] [X] [&M] [🐾] [🔋] [💻] [🍴] [≈] [X]

WWWW Four Points by Sheraton at Denver University-a Barcelo Hotel SH 🐾
(303) 757-8797. **$55-$169.** 1475 S Colorado Blvd. I-25, exit 204, 0.5 mi n; entry on Arkansas St. Int corridors. **Pets:** Large. $35 one-time fee/pet. Designated rooms, service with restrictions.
[SAVE] [So] [X] [&M] [🐾] [🐕] [🔋] [💻] [🍴] [≈]

WWW Guesthouse Hotel Denver Stapleton SH
(303) 388-6161. **$60-$100.** 3737 Quebec St. I-70, exit 278, just s. Int corridors. **Pets:** Small. $15 daily fee/pet. Designated rooms, service with restrictions, crate.
[SAVE] [So] [X] [🔋] [💻] [🍴] [≈]

WWWW Hampton Inn & Suites Denver Tech Center SH
(303) 804-9900. **$99-$119.** 5001 S Ulster St. I-25, exit 199, e to Ulster St, then just n. Int corridors. **Pets:** Small. Designated rooms, supervision.
[ASK] [So] [X] [&M] [🐾] [🐕] [🔋] [💻] [≈]

WWWW Holiday Chalet A Victorian Bed & Breakfast BB
(303) 437-8245. **$90-$145.** 1820 E Colfax Ave. I-25, exit 210, 1.3 mi e on US 40. Int corridors. **Pets:** Dogs only. Service with restrictions, supervision.
[SAVE] [So] [X] [🔋] [💻]

WWWW Holiday Inn-Denver North Coliseum LH
(303) 292-9500. **$98-$109.** 4849 Bannock St. I-25, 215 northbound; exit 214B southbound, 1 mi s. Ext/int corridors. **Pets:** Small. $50 deposit/room. Designated rooms, service with restrictions, supervision.
[ASK] [So] [X] [&M] [🐾] [🐕] [🔋] [💻] [🍴] [≈]

▼▼ **Homestead Studio Suites Hotel-Denver/Tech Center-North** SH 🐾
(303) 689-9443. **$42-$62.** 4885 S Quebec St. I-25, exit 199, just w to Quebec St, then just n; next to Mountain View Golf Course. Ext corridors. **Pets:** Medium, other species. $25 daily fee/room. Service with restrictions, crate.
(ASK) (S🛏) (✕) (&M) (🐾) (&) 🔒 💻

▲▲ ▼▼▼▼ **Hotel Monaco Denver** SH 🐾
(303) 296-1717. **$159-$269.** 1717 Champa St. I-25, exit 212A (Speer Blvd S), s to Curtis St, w to 19th St, 1 blk s to Champa St, then 2 blks w. Int corridors. **Pets:** Other species. Service with restrictions, supervision.
(SAVE) (S🛏) (✕) (&M) (🐾) (&) 💻 (▮▮) (✕)

▲▲ ▼▼▼▼ **Hotel Teatro** SH 🐾
(303) 228-1100. **$225-$395.** 1100 14th St. I-25, exit 212 (Speer Blvd), s at jct Arapahoe St to Lawrence St, then e to 14th; exit Auraria Pkwy northbound. Int corridors. **Pets:** Dogs only.
(SAVE) (S🛏) (✕) (🐾) (&) 🔒 💻 (▮▮) (✕)

▼▼▼▼ **La Quinta Inn & Suites DIA** SH
(303) 371-0888. **$70-$110.** 6801 Tower Rd. I-70, exit 286, 4.2 mi n; 0.8 mi s of Pena Blvd. Int corridors. **Pets:** Accepted.
(✕) (&M) (🐾) (&) 🔒 💻 🔜 (✕)

▲▲ ▼▼▼▼ **La Quinta Inn-Cherry Creek** SH 🐾
(303) 758-8886. **$60-$80.** 1975 S Colorado Blvd. I-25, exit 204, just s. Ext corridors. **Pets:** Small. No service, supervision.
(SAVE) (✕) (🐾) 💻 🔜

▼▼▼▼ **La Quinta Inn-Downtown** SH
(303) 458-1222. **$73-$100.** 3500 Park Ave W. I-25, exit 213, take 38th Ave, just s, left at Fox St, left on Park to 2nd light, then U-turn. Ext/int corridors. **Pets:** Accepted.
(✕) (&M) (🐾) 💻 🔜

▼▼▼▼ **Magnolia Hotel-Downtown** SH 🐾
(303) 607-9000. **$220-$290.** 818 17th St. I-25, exit 212A (Speer Blvd S) to Market St, e to 17th St, then s to jct 17th and Stout sts. Int corridors. **Pets:** Accepted.
(ASK) (S🛏) (✕) (&M) (🐾) (&) 🔒 💻

▲▲ ▼▼▼▼ **Ramada Inn Denver Downtown** LH 🐾
(303) 831-7700. **$69-$179, 3 day notice.** 1150 E Colfax Ave. I-25, exit 210 (E Colfax Ave), 1 mi e on US 40; 0.5 mi e of State Capitol. Int corridors. **Pets:** Other species. $100 deposit/room. Service with restrictions.
(SAVE) (S🛏) (✕) (&) 🔒 💻 (▮▮) 🔜

▼▼▼▼ **Red Lion Denver Central** SH
(303) 321-6666. **$89-$139.** 4040 Quebec St. I-70, exit 278, just s. Ext/int corridors. **Pets:** Other species. $50 deposit/room. Designated rooms, service with restrictions.
(ASK) (S🛏) (✕) (&) 🔒 💻 (▮▮) 🔜

▲▲ ▼▼▼▼ **Red Lion Hotel Denver Downtown at Invesco Field** SH
(303) 433-8331. **$109-$129.** 1975 Bryant St. I-25, exit 210B, just w. Int corridors. **Pets:** $50 deposit/room, $10 daily fee/pet. Service with restrictions, supervision.
(SAVE) (S🛏) (✕) 💻 (▮▮) 🔜

▲▲ ▼▼▼▼ **Red Roof Inn & Suites** SH
(303) 371-5300. **$62-$68.** 6890 Tower Rd. I-70, exit 286, 4.2 mi n; 0.8 mi s of Pena Blvd. Int corridors. **Pets:** Accepted.
(SAVE) (S🛏) (✕) (&M) (🐾) (&) 🔒 💻 🔜

▼▼▼▼ **Residence Inn by Marriott Denver Downtown** SH
(303) 458-5318. **$119-$199.** 2777 Zuni St. I-25, exit 212B, just w. Ext corridors. **Pets:** Large, other species. $75 one-time fee/pet. Service with restrictions.
(ASK) (S🛏) (✕) (🐾) 🔒 💻 🔜 (✕)

▼▼▼▼ **TownePlace Suites by Marriott-Denver Southeast** SH 🐾
(303) 759-9393. **$47-$66.** 3699 S Monaco Pkwy. I-25, exit 201, just e to Monaco Pkwy, then s. Int corridors. **Pets:** Other species. $25 daily fee/room. Service with restrictions, crate.
(ASK) (S🛏) (✕) (&) 🔒 💻 🔜

▼▼▼▼ **TownePlace Suites by Marriott Downtown Denver** SH
(303) 722-2322. **$59-$149.** 685 Speer Blvd. I-25, exit Speer Blvd S, 1.5 mi s, stay in right lane, just past second Bannock St, exit towards Broadway, right onto Acoma St. Int corridors. **Pets:** Accepted.
(ASK) (S🛏) (✕) (&M) (&) 🔒 💻

▼▼▼▼ **The Warwick Hotel-Denver** SH
(303) 861-2000. **$149-$210.** 1776 Grant St at 18th Ave. I-25, exit 210 (E Colfax Ave) to Logan, n to 18th, then just w. Int corridors. **Pets:** Accepted.
(ASK) (S🛏) (✕) (🐾) (&) 💻 (▮▮) 🔜

▲▲ ▼▼▼▼ **The Westin Tabor Center Denver** LH 🐾
(303) 572-9100. **$279-$299.** 1672 Lawrence St. I-25, exit 212A (Speer Blvd S) to Lawrence St, then e. Int corridors. **Pets:** Dogs only. Designated rooms, service with restrictions, supervision.
(SAVE) (S🛏) (✕) (&M) (🐾) (&) 💻 (▮▮) 🔜 (✕)

ENGLEWOOD

▲▲ ▼▼▼▼ **AmeriSuites (Denver/Tech Center)** SH
(303) 804-0700. **$55-$115.** 8300 E Crescent Pkwy. I-25, exit 199 (Bellview Ave), 0.4 mi e to Crescent Pkwy, then s. Int corridors. **Pets:** Medium. Service with restrictions.
(SAVE) (S🛏) (✕) (🐾) (&) 🔒 💻 🔜

▼▼▼▼ **Drury Inn & Suites-Denver Near the Tech Center** SH
(303) 694-3400. **$82-$97.** 9445 E Dry Creek Rd. I-25, exit 196, just w, on northwest corner. Int corridors. **Pets:** Large, other species. Service with restrictions, supervision.
(ASK) (✕) (&) 🔒 💻 🔜 (✕)

▼▼▼▼ **Holtze Executive Village** SH
(303) 290-1100. **Call for rates.** 6380 S Boston St. I-25, exit 197, just e, then just n. Ext corridors. **Pets:** Accepted.
(✕) 🔒 💻 🔜 (✕)

♦♦ **Homestead Studio Suites Hotel-Denver/Tech South/Inverness** [M] 🐾
(303) 708-8888. **$46-$66.** 9650 E Geddes Ave. I-25, exit 196 (Dry Creek Rd), just e, then n on S Clinton St. Ext corridors. **Pets:** Medium, other species. $25 daily fee/room. Service with restrictions, crate.
[ASK] [S/D] ⊠ 🦻 ♿ ▣ 🖥

♦♦♦ **Quality Suites-Englewood** [SH]
(303) 858-0700. **$79-$99.** 7374 S Clinton St. I-25, exit 196 (Dry Creek Rd), just e, then n. Int corridors. **Pets:** Accepted.
[ASK] [S/D] ⊠ ♿M 🦻 ♿ ▣ 🖥 🏊

♦♦♦ **Residence Inn by Marriott-Denver Tech Center** [SH]
(303) 740-7177. **$99-$139.** 6565 S Yosemite St. I-25, exit 197, just w on Arapahoe Rd, then n. Ext corridors. **Pets:** Accepted.
[ASK] [S/D] ⊠ 🦻 ▣ 🖥 🏊 🏋

♦♦♦ **Residence Inn Park Meadows** [SH]
(720) 895-0200. **$89-$119.** 8322 S Valley Hwy. I-25, exit 195 (County Line Rd), just e to S Valley Hwy, then just s. Int corridors. **Pets:** Other species. $100 one-time fee/pet. Service with restrictions, crate.
[ASK] [S/D] ⊠ ♿M ♿ ▣ 🖥 🏊 🏋

GLENDALE

♦♦♦ **Four Points Cherry Creek Denver** [SH]
(303) 757-3341. **$79-$119.** 600 S Colorado Blvd. I-25, exit 204, 1 mi n. Int corridors. **Pets:** Accepted.
⊠ 🖥 🍴 🏊

♦♦ **Homestead Studio Suites Hotel-Denver/Cherry Creek** [SH] 🐾
(303) 388-3880. **$65-$85.** 4444 Leetsdale Dr. I-25, exit 204, 1.2 mi n to E Virginia Ave, just e to S Birch St, then just n. Ext corridors. **Pets:** Medium, other species. $25 daily fee/room. Service with restrictions, crate.
[ASK] [S/D] ⊠ ♿M ♿ ▣ 🖥

[AAA] ♦♦♦♦ **Loews Denver Hotel** [SH] 🐾
(303) 782-9300. **$95-$140.** 4150 E Mississippi Ave. I-25, exit 204, 1 mi n on Colorado Blvd, then just e. Int corridors. **Pets:** Other species. $5 deposit/room. Service with restrictions, supervision.
[SAVE] [S/D] ⊠ ♿M 🦻 ♿ ▣ 🖥 🍴

♦♦♦ **Staybridge Suites** [SH] 🐾
(303) 321-5757. **$119-$179.** 4220 E Virginia Ave. I-25, exit 204, 1.2 mi n on Colorado Blvd to Virginia Ave, then just e. Int corridors. **Pets:** $75 one-time fee/room. Designated rooms, service with restrictions, supervision.
[ASK] [S/D] ⊠ ♿M 🦻 ♿ ▣ 🖥 🏋

GOLDEN

♦♦♦ **Denver Marriott West** [LH]
(303) 279-9100. **$180.** 1717 Denver W Blvd. I-70, exit 263, just n, then w. Int corridors. **Pets:** Accepted.
⊠ ♿M 🦻 ♿ 🖥 🍴 🏊 🏋

♦♦♦ **Holiday Inn Golden** [LH] 🐾
(303) 279-7611. **$79.** 14707 W Colfax Ave. I-70, exit 262 (Colfax Ave), just e. Ext/int corridors. **Pets:** Other species. $250 deposit/room. Designated rooms, service with restrictions.
[ASK] [S/D] ⊠ ♿M 🦻 🖥 🍴 🏊 🏋

[AAA] ♦♦♦ **La Quinta Inn-Golden** [SH]
(303) 279-5565. **$63-$80.** 3301 Youngfield Service Rd. I-70, exit 264 (32nd Ave), just w, then n. Ext corridors. **Pets:** Accepted.
[SAVE] ⊠ 🖥 🏊

♦♦♦ **Residence Inn Denver West/Golden** [SH]
(303) 271-0909. **$79-$139.** 14600 W 6th Ave Frontage Rd. US 6, exit Indiana Ave to frontage road, just e. Int corridors. **Pets:** Accepted.
[ASK] ⊠ ♿M ♿ ▣ 🖥 🏊 🏋

[AAA] ♦♦♦ **Table Mountain Inn** [SH] 🐾
(303) 277-9898. **$99-$172.** 1310 Washington Ave. US 6, exit 19th St, 0.5 mi n to Washington Ave, 0.5 mi w; downtown, just s of arch. Int corridors. **Pets:** Other species. $50 deposit/room. Service with restrictions.
[SAVE] [S/D] ⊠ ♿M ♿ ▣ 🖥 🍴

GREENWOOD VILLAGE

♦♦♦ **Hampton Inn Southeast** [SH]
(303) 792-9999. **$69-$99.** 9231 E Arapahoe Rd. I-25, exit 197, just e. Int corridors. **Pets:** Accepted.
[ASK] [S/D] ⊠ ♿M 🦻 ▣ 🖥 🏊

♦♦♦ **Homestead Studio Suites Hotel-Denver/Tech South/Greenwood Village** [SH] 🐾
(303) 858-1669. **$50-$70.** 9253 E Costilla St. I-25, exit 197, just e on Arapahoe Rd, se on Clinton St to Costilla St, then w. Int corridors. **Pets:** Medium, other species. $25 daily fee/room. Service with restrictions, crate.
[ASK] [S/D] ⊠ ♿M 🦻 ♿ ▣ 🖥

[AAA] ♦♦♦ **La Quinta Inn & Suites Denver Tech Center** [SH]
(303) 649-9969. **$80-$100.** 7077 S Clinton St. I-25, exit 197, e to Clinton St, then s. Int corridors. **Pets:** Small, other species. Service with restrictions, crate.
[SAVE] ⊠ ♿M 🦻 ♿ ▣ 🖥 🏊

♦♦♦ **Sheraton Denver Tech Center Hotel** [SH] 🐾
(303) 799-6200. **$199, 3 day notice.** 7007 S Clinton St. I-25, exit 197, e on Arapahoe Rd, then s. Int corridors. **Pets:** Supervision.
[ASK] [S/D] ⊠ ♿M 🦻 ♿ 🖥 🍴 🏊

♦♦ **Sleep Inn Denver Tech Center** [SH]
(303) 662-9950. **$49-$59.** 9257 Costilla Ave. I-25, exit 197, just e to Clinton St, s to Costilla Ave, then w. Int corridors. **Pets:** Other species. $25 one-time fee/pet. Service with restrictions.
[ASK] [S/D] ⊠ ♿M 🦻 ♿ ▣ 🖥 🏊

[AAA] ♦♦♦ **Summerfield Suites by Wyndham-Denver Tech Center** [SH]
(303) 706-1945. **$88-$108.** I-25, exit 197, e to Clinton St, just s. Int corridors. **Pets:** Medium, other species. $150 one-time fee/room. Service with restrictions, crate.
[SAVE] [S/D] ⊠ ♿M 🦻 ♿ ▣ 🖥 🏊 🏋

♦♦♦ **Woodfield Suites Denver-Tech Center** [SH] 🐾
(303) 799-4555. **$89-$129.** 9009 E Arapahoe Rd. I-25, exit 197, just e. Int corridors. **Pets:** Other species. $50 deposit/pet. Service with restrictions, supervision.
[ASK] [S/D] ⊠ ♿M 🦻 ♿ ▣ 🖥 🏊 🏋

HIGHLANDS RANCH

▼▼▼▼ Residence Inn Denver South Highlands Ranch SH ❀
(303) 683-5500. **$134.** 93 Centennial Blvd. C-470, exit Broadway, just s, then w. Int corridors. **Pets:** $100 one-time fee/room. Service with restrictions, crate.

(ASK) ⊠ &M ☑ 🖑 🚪 🖵 ➤ ⊠

LAKEWOOD

▼▼▼▼ Comfort Suites SH
(303) 231-9929. **$75-$95.** US 6, exit Simms/Union, westbound travelers must turn right at stop light, but do not use right turn lane, follow signs to frontage road. Int corridors. **Pets:** $10 daily fee/pet. Designated rooms, service with restrictions, supervision.

(ASK) 🏊 ⊠ &M 🖑 🚪 🖵 ➤ ⊠

▼▼▼ Days Inn-Lakewood SH
(303) 989-5500. **$49-$69.** 3440 S Vance St. Just ne of jct US 285 (Hampden Ave) and S Wadsworth Blvd, e on Girton Dr, then just s. Int corridors. **Pets:** Medium. $25 one-time fee/room. Service with restrictions, supervision.

(ASK) 🏊 ⊠ 🚪 🖵 ➤

▼▼▼ Holiday Inn Lakewood SH
(303) 980-9200. **$69.** 7390 W Hampden Ave. Just se of jct US 285 (W Hampden Ave) and Wadsworth Blvd, e on Jefferson Ave, then n on frontage road. Int corridors. **Pets:** Small. $50 one-time fee/pet. Designated rooms, service with restrictions, supervision.

(ASK) 🏊 ⊠ ☑ 🖑 🚪 🖵 🍴 ➤ ⊠

🆔 ▼▼▼▼ La Quinta Inn & Suites Ⓜ
(303) 969-9700. **$70-$90.** 7190 W Hampden Ave. Just se of jct US 285 (W Hampden Ave) and Wadsworth Blvd, e on Jefferson Ave, just n, then e on frontage road. **Pets:** Accepted.

(SAVE) ⊠ &M 🖑 🖑 🚪 🖵 ➤

▼▼▼▼ Quality Suites Lakewood SH
(303) 988-8600. **$69-$119.** 7260 W Jefferson Ave. Just se of US 285 (W Hampden Ave) and Wadsworth Blvd, then e. Int corridors. **Pets:** Other species. $10 daily fee/pet. Designated rooms, service with restrictions, crate.

(ASK) 🏊 ⊠ 🖑 🚪 🖵 ➤

▼▼▼▼ Residence Inn by Marriott Denver SW/Lakewood SH
(303) 985-7676. **$99-$109.** 7050 W Hampden Ave. Just se of jct US 285 (W Hampden Ave) and Wadsworth Blvd, e on Jefferson Ave, then n on frontage road. Int corridors. **Pets:** Large, other species. $50 one-time fee/room. Service with restrictions.

(ASK) 🏊 ⊠ &M 🖑 🖑 🚪 🖵 ➤ ⊠

▼▼▼ TownePlace Suites by Marriott-Lakewood SH ❀
(303) 232-7790. **$89-$112.** 800 Tabor St. US 6, exit Simms/Union, just n to 8th, then w. Int corridors. **Pets:** Large. $20 daily fee/room. Service with restrictions, crate.

(ASK) 🏊 ⊠ &M 🖑 🚪 🖵 ➤

▼▼▼▼ Travelodge Denver West SH
(303) 238-7751. **$59-$89.** 11595 W 6th Ave. I-70, exit 261, 3 mi e on US 6. Ext/int corridors. **Pets:** Other species. $15 one-time fee/room. Designated rooms, service with restrictions, crate.

(ASK) 🏊 ⊠ 🚪 🖵 🍴 ➤

LITTLETON

▼▼▼▼ Marriott Denver South SH
(303) 925-0004. **$49-$179.** 10345 Park Meadows Dr. I-25, exit 193 (Lincoln Ave), just w to Park Meadows Dr, then n and e. Int corridors. **Pets:** Accepted.

(ASK) 🏊 ⊠ &M 🖑 🖑 🚪 🖵 🍴 ➤

LONE TREE

🆔 ▼▼▼ AmeriSuites (Denver/Park Meadows) SH
(303) 662-8500. **$99-$109.** 9030 E Westview Rd. I-25, exit 195 (County Line Rd), 0.5 mi w to Yosemite, then s & e to Parkland; or take Yosemite if eastbound on C-470. Int corridors. **Pets:** Small, other species. Service with restrictions, crate.

(SAVE) 🏊 ⊠ 🖑 🚪 🖵 ➤

▼▼▼▼ Staybridge Suites Denver South-Lone Tree SH
(303) 649-1010. **$94-$166.** 7820 Park Meadows Dr. I-25, exit 195, w on County Line Rd to Acres Green, s to E Park Meadows Dr, then just w; Quebec St exit off C-470, just se. Int corridors. **Pets:** Accepted.

(ASK) 🏊 ⊠ &M 🖑 🚪 🖵 ➤

NORTHGLENN

🆔 ▼▼▼▼ Holiday Inn Denver-Northglenn SH
(303) 452-4100. **$94-$114.** 10 E 120th Ave. I-25, exit 223, just e. Int corridors. **Pets:** $15 one-time fee/room. Designated rooms, service with restrictions, supervision.

(SAVE) 🏊 ⊠ &M 🖑 🖑 🚪 🖵 🍴 ➤ ⊠

THORNTON

🆔 ▼▼▼ Sleep Inn North Denver SH
(303) 280-9818. **$54-$104.** 12101 Grant St. I-25, exit 223, e to Grant St, then n. Int corridors. **Pets:** Accepted.

(SAVE) 🏊 ⊠ &M 🖑 🖑 🖵 ➤

WESTMINSTER

▼▼▼▼ DoubleTree Hotel Denver/Boulder SH
(303) 427-4000. **$59-$169.** 8773 Yates Dr. US 36 (Boulder Tpke), exit Sheridan Ave, n to 92nd Ave, e to Yates Dr, then 0.5 mi s. Int corridors. **Pets:** Medium, other species. Service with restrictions, crate.

⊠ 🖑 🖑 🖵 🍴 ➤ ⊠

🆔 ▼▼▼▼ La Quinta Inn & Suites Westminster Promenade SH
(303) 438-5800. **$69-$89.** 10179 Church Ranch Way. US 36 (Boulder Tpke), exit Church Ranch Blvd, just s to 103rd Pl, then e. Int corridors. **Pets:** Accepted.

(SAVE) 🏊 ⊠ &M 🖑 🚪 🖵 ➤

AAA ▼▼▼▼ La Quinta Inn-Denver North SH
(303) 252-9800. **$63-$80.** 345 W 120th Ave. I-25, exit 223, just w. Ext/int corridors. **Pets:** Other species. Service with restrictions, crate.
SAVE ⊠ 🗗 🖃 🏊

AAA ▼▼▼▼ La Quinta Inn-Westminster Mall SH
(303) 425-9099. **$63-$80.** 8701 Turnpike Dr. US 36 (Boulder Tpke), exit Sheridan Ave, just s, then left on Turnpike Dr at 87th Ave. Ext/int corridors. **Pets:** Accepted.
SAVE ⊠ 🗗ᴹ 🗗 🖃 🖃 🏊

▼▼▼▼ Residence Inn by
Marriott-Westminster SH
(303) 427-9500. **$129.** 5010 W 88th Pl. US 36 (Boulder Tpke), exit Sheridan Ave, n to 92nd Ave, e to Yates Dr, then s. Int corridors. **Pets:** Accepted.
A$K S❺ ⊠ 🗗ᴹ 🗗 🖃 🖃 🏊 ⊠

▼▼▼▼ Super 8 Motel/Denver North SH
(303) 451-7200. **$67-$87.** 12055 Melody Dr. I-25, exit 223, just w. Int corridors. **Pets:** $5 daily fee/room. Service with restrictions, crate.
A$K S❺ ⊠ 🗗 🗗 🖃 🖃 ⊠

▼▼▼▼ The Westin Westminster LH ❖
(303) 410-5000. **$99-$219.** 10600 Westminster Blvd. US 36 (Boulder Tpke), exit 104th Ave, just n. Int corridors. **Pets:** Other species. Service with restrictions, supervision.
A$K S❺ ⊠ 🗗ᴹ 🗗 🗗 🖃 🖃 🍴 🏊 ⊠

❖ **END METROPOLITAN AREA** ❖

DILLON

AAA ▼▼▼▼ Best Western Ptarmigan Lodge SH
(970) 468-2341. **$60-$145, 7 day notice.** 652 Lake Dillon Dr. I-70, exit 205, 1.3 mi se on US 6, then 0.3 mi s. Ext/int corridors. **Pets:** Other species. $15 one-time fee/pet. Designated rooms, service with restrictions, supervision.
SAVE S❺ ⊠ 🗗 🖃 ⊠ 🅐

AAA ▼ Dillon Super 8 Motel SH
(970) 468-8888. **$70-$135.** 808 Little Beaver Tr. I-70, exit 205, just s, then e. Int corridors. **Pets:** $15 one-time fee/pet. Service with restrictions, supervision.
SAVE S❺ ⊠ 🗗 🖃

DURANGO

AAA ▼▼▼ Adobe Inn M
(970) 247-2743. **$35-$89.** 2178 Main Ave. On US 550, 1.4 mi n of jct US 160. Ext corridors. **Pets:** Other species. $20 deposit/room, $5 one-time fee/room. Service with restrictions, supervision.
SAVE S❺ ⊠ 🏊

AAA ▼▼▼ Alpine Inn M
(970) 247-4042. **$38-$84.** 3515 N Main Ave. 2.7 mi n of jct US 160 W and 550, on US 550. Ext corridors. **Pets:** Other species. Service with restrictions, supervision.
SAVE S❺ ⊠ 🗗

AAA ▼ Caboose Motel M
(970) 247-1191. **$38-$88.** 3363 Main Ave. 2.5 mi n of jct US 550 and 160. Ext corridors. **Pets:** Dogs only. $3 one-time fee/pet. Designated rooms, service with restrictions, supervision.
SAVE S❺ ⊠ 🗗 🖃

▼▼ Days Inn Durango M
(970) 259-1430. **$59-$109.** 1700 CR 203. 4.5 mi n on US 550; entry just s of establishment, then w. Int corridors. **Pets:** Other species. Designated rooms, service with restrictions, supervision.
A$K S❺ ⊠ 🖃 🏊 ⊠

▼▼▼ DoubleTree Hotel Durango SH ❖
(970) 259-6580. **$69-$229.** 501 Camino Del Rio. Jct US 160 and 550. Int corridors. **Pets:** $15 daily fee/room. Service with restrictions, supervision.
A$K S❺ ⊠ 🗗ᴹ 🗗 🗗 🖃 🖃 🍴 🏊 ⊠

AAA ▼▼▼ Holiday Inn SH
(970) 247-5393. **$68-$139.** 800 Camino Del Rio. On US 550, just n of jct US 160. Ext corridors. **Pets:** $10 daily fee/pet. Service with restrictions, crate.
SAVE ⊠ 🗗 🗗 🖃 🍴 🏊 ⊠

AAA ▼▼▼ Iron Horse Inn M
(970) 259-1010. **$64-$109.** 5800 N Main Ave. 4.5 mi n on US 550. Ext corridors. **Pets:** Medium. $50 deposit/room. Designated rooms, service with restrictions, supervision.
SAVE S❺ ⊠ 🗗 🖃 🍴 🏊 ⊠

▼ National 9 Inn M
(970) 247-2653. **$49-$89.** 2855 N Main Ave. 2.2 mi n of jct US 160 and 550, on US 550. Ext corridors. **Pets:** Accepted.
A$K S❺ ⊠ 🗗 🖃 🏊

AAA ▼▼▼▼ Quality Inn & Suites SH
(970) 259-7900. **$89-$159.** 455 S Camino Del Rio. On US 160, 1.5 mi e of jct US 550. Int corridors. **Pets:** Large. $50 deposit/room, $10 daily fee/room. Designated rooms, service with restrictions, supervision.
SAVE S❺ ⊠ 🗗ᴹ 🗗 🗗 🖃 🏊 ⊠

▼▼▼▼ Residence Inn by Marriott SH
(970) 259-6200. **$94-$224, 3 day notice.** 21691 Hwy 160 W. On US 160, just w. Int corridors. **Pets:** Accepted.
A$K S❺ ⊠ 🗗 🗗 🖃 🏊 ⊠

▼▼▼ The Rochester Hotel BB ❖
(970) 385-1920. **$129-$219, 14 day notice.** 726 E 2nd Ave. Just e of Main Ave via 7th St, then just n. Int corridors. **Pets:** Other species. $20 daily fee/pet. Designated rooms, crate.
S❺ ⊠ 🗗

⬥⬥ ▼▼ Rodeway Inn M ❀
(970) 259-2540. **$39-$109.** 2701 Main Ave. On US 550, 2 mi n of jct US 160. Ext corridors. **Pets:** Dogs only. $7 daily fee/pet. Service with restrictions, crate.
[SAVE] [S♦] [✕] [📶] [🏊]

⬥⬥ ▼ Siesta Motel M ❀
(970) 247-0741. **$30-$75.** 3475 N Main Ave. 2.6 mi n of jct US 160 W and 550, on US 550. Ext corridors. **Pets:** Medium, dogs only. $10 daily fee/pet. Service with restrictions, supervision.
[SAVE] [S♦] [✕] [📶] [🏊]

⬥⬥ ▼▼ Travelodge M
(970) 247-1741. **$78-$129.** 2970 Main Ave. 2.2 mi n jct US 160 and 550, on US 550. Ext corridors. **Pets:** Other species. $8 daily fee/pet. Designated rooms, service with restrictions.
[SAVE] [S♦] [✕] [📶] [🏊]

EAGLE

▼▼▼ Americinn Lodge & Suites SH
(970) 328-5155. **$89-$139.** 0085 Pond Rd. I-70, exit 147, just n, then w. Int corridors. **Pets:** Small. $25 one-time fee/room. Designated rooms, service with restrictions, supervision.
[ASK] [S♦] [✕] [&M] [🅿] [&] [📶] [🏊] [✕]

⬥⬥ ▼▼▼ Best Western Eagle Lodge & Suites SH
(970) 328-6316. **$75-$145.** 200 Loren Ln. I-70, exit 147, just s. Int corridors. **Pets:** Large, other species. $50 deposit/pet, $10 one-time fee/pet. Designated rooms, service with restrictions, supervision.
[SAVE] [S♦] [✕] [&] [📶] [🏊] [✕]

▼▼▼ Holiday Inn Express SH
(970) 328-8088. **$60-$129.** 0075 Pond Rd. I-70, exit 147, just n, then w. Int corridors. **Pets:** $20 one-time fee/room. Designated rooms, service with restrictions, supervision.
[ASK] [S♦] [✕] [&M] [🅿] [&] [📶] [🏊]

EDWARDS

▼▼▼ Inn and Suites at Riverwalk SH
(970) 926-0606. **$85-$200, 14 day notice.** 27 Main St. I-70, exit 163, 0.3 mi s. Int corridors. **Pets:** Large, other species. $25 one-time fee/room. Service with restrictions, supervision.
[ASK] [S♦] [✕] [🅿] [📶] [🍴] [🏊] [✕]

ESTES PARK

⬥⬥ ▼▼ Budget Host Four Winds Motor Lodge M ❀
(970) 586-3313. **$43-$130.** 1120 Big Thompson Ave. 1 mi e on US 34. Ext corridors. **Pets:** Medium. $15 daily fee/pet. Service with restrictions, supervision.
[SAVE] [S♦] [✕] [📶] [🏊] [✕]

⬥⬥ ▼▼▼ Castle Mountain Lodge CA ❀
(970) 586-3664. **$70-$215.** 1520 Fall River Rd. 1 mi w on US 34. Ext corridors. **Pets:** Dogs only. $15 daily fee/pet. Designated rooms, service with restrictions, supervision.
[SAVE] [S♦] [📶] [✕] [🐾] [📷]

⬥⬥ ▼▼▼ Holiday Inn SH
(970) 586-2332. **$89-$299.** 101 S St Vrain Ave. 0.5 mi se; on SR 7 at jct US 36. Int corridors. **Pets:** Accepted.
[SAVE] [S♦] [✕] [&M] [🅿] [&] [📶] [🏊] [🍴] [🏊] [✕]

⬥⬥ ▼▼▼ Lake Estes Inn & Suites M
(970) 586-3386. **$99-$349, 7 day notice.** 1650 Big Thompson Ave. 1.7 mi e on US 34. Ext corridors. **Pets:** Accepted.
[SAVE] [S♦] [✕] [📶] [🏊] [🏊] [✕] [🐾]

⬥⬥ ▼▼▼ Silver Moon Inn M
(970) 586-6006. **$64-$130, 30 day notice.** 175 Spruce Dr. Just w on US 34 business route, then just ne. Ext corridors. **Pets:** Other species. Designated rooms, service with restrictions, supervision.
[SAVE] [✕] [📶] [🏊] [🏊]

▼▼ Timber Creek Chalets CA
(970) 586-8803. **$55-$265.** 2115 Fall River Rd. Jct US 34 and 36, 2.9 mi w. Ext corridors. **Pets:** Accepted.
[✕] [📶] [🏊] [🐾]

EVANS

⬥⬥ ▼▼▼ Sleep Inn Greeley/Evans SH
(970) 356-2180. **$75-$90.** 3025 8th Ave. Just sw of jct US 34 and 85 Bypass. Int corridors. **Pets:** Other species. $15 one-time fee/room. Service with restrictions, crate.
[SAVE] [S♦] [✕] [&M] [🅿] [&] [📶] [🏊] [🏊]

EVERGREEN

▼▼▼ Quality Suites Evergreen SH ❀
(303) 526-2000. **$80-$100.** I-70, exit 252 (Evergreen Pkwy), on west side of El Rancho Restaurant; exit 251 eastbound. Int corridors. **Pets:** Other species. $50 deposit/room. Designated rooms, service with restrictions, supervision.
[ASK] [S♦] [✕] [&M] [&] [📶] [🏊] [🏊] [✕]

FAIRPLAY

⬥⬥ ▼▼ The Western Inn M ❀
(719) 836-2026. **$53-$75.** 490 Hwy 285. US 285, 0.3 mi n of jct SR 9. Ext corridors. **Pets:** Large, other species. $5 one-time fee/pet. Supervision.
[SAVE] [S♦] [✕] [📶] [🏊] [🐾]

FORT COLLINS

⬥⬥ ▼▼ Best Western University Inn M
(970) 484-1984. **$74-$125.** 914 S College Ave. I-25, exit 268, 4 mi w to College, just n on US 287. Ext/int corridors. **Pets:** Other species. $10 daily fee/pet. Service with restrictions, crate.
[SAVE] [S♦] [✕] [📶] [🏊] [🏊]

▼▼▼ Comfort Suites-Fort Collins SH
(970) 206-4597. **$69-$109.** 1415 Oakridge Dr. I-25, exit 265, 3.3 mi w to McMurray Ave, just s, then w. Int corridors. **Pets:** Accepted.
[ASK] [S♦] [✕] [🅿] [&] [📶] [🏊] [🏊]

▼▼▼ Courtyard by Marriott SH
(970) 282-1700. **$79-$120.** 1200 Oakridge Dr. I-25, exit 265, 3.3 mi w; entry via Lemay Ave. Int corridors. **Pets:** $25 daily fee/room. Designated rooms, service with restrictions, supervision.
[ASK] [S♦] [✕] [&M] [🅿] [&] [📶] [🏊] [🍴] [🏊] [✕]

▼▼▼▼ Hampton Inn SH
(970) 229-5927. **$99-$114.** 1620 Oakridge Dr. I-25, exit 265, 3.3 mi w, s on McMurray Ave to Oakridge Dr, then just e. Int corridors. **Pets:** Large. $25 one-time fee/room. Service with restrictions, supervision.

ASK SD X GM ⚐ ⊟ ⊡ ➤

▲▲▲ ▼▼▼▼ Holiday Inn University Park SH
(970) 482-2626. **$99-$149.** 425 W Prospect Rd. I-25, exit 268, 4 mi w. Int corridors. **Pets:** Service with restrictions.
SAVE SD X ⚐ ⚐ ⊡ ♈ ➤ X

▲▲▲ ▼▼▼▼ Quality Inn & Suites SH
(970) 282-9047. **$99-$134.** 4001 S Mason St. I-25, exit 265, 4.6 mi w to Mason St, then 0.5 mi n. Int corridors. **Pets:** $25 deposit/room. Designated rooms, service with restrictions, supervision.
SAVE SD X ⚐ ⚐ ⊟ ⊡ ➤

▼▼▼▼ Residence Inn Fort Collins SH ✿
(970) 223-5700. **$114-$169.** 1127 Oakridge Dr. I-25, exit 265, 3.3 mi w on Harmony Rd to Lemay Ave, then s to Oakridge Dr. Int corridors. **Pets:** Other species. $25 one-time fee/pet. Designated rooms, service with restrictions.
ASK SD X ⚐ ⊟ ⊡ ➤ X

▼▼▼ Sleep Inn SH ✿
(970) 484-5515. **$70-$120.** 3808 E Mulberry St. I-25, exit 269B, just nw. Int corridors. **Pets:** Large, other species. $10 daily fee/room. Designated rooms, service with restrictions, crate.
ASK SD X ⚐ ⊟ ⊡

▼▼▼▼ Super 8 Motel SH
(970) 493-7701. **$45-$105, 14 day notice.** 409 Centro Way. I-25, exit 269B, just w. Int corridors. **Pets:** Medium. $5 daily fee/pet. Service with restrictions, supervision.
ASK SD X ⊟

FORT MORGAN

▼▼ ▼▼ Best Western Park Terrace Inn SH
(970) 867-8256. **$53-$80.** 725 Main St. I-76, exit 80, 0.5 mi s. Ext corridors. **Pets:** Other species. $10 one-time fee/room. Service with restrictions, crate.
ASK SD X ⊟ ⊡ ♈ ➤

▲▲▲ ▼▼▼ Central Motel M
(970) 867-2401. **$44-$61.** 201 W Platte Ave. I-76, exit 80, 0.6 mi s, then w on US 34. Ext corridors. **Pets:** Other species. $5 one-time fee/room. Supervision.
SAVE SD X ⊟ ⊡

FRISCO

▲▲▲ ▼▼▼▼ Best Western Lake Dillon Lodge SH
(970) 668-5094. **$69-$199, 7 day notice.** 1202 Summit Blvd. I-70, exit 203, just s. Int corridors. **Pets:** Medium. $15 one-time fee/room. Designated rooms, service with restrictions, supervision.
SAVE SD X ⊟ ⊡ ♈ ➤ X

▲▲▲ ▼▼▼▼ Holiday Inn-Frisco SH
(970) 668-5000. **$55-$165.** 1129 N Summit Blvd. I-70, exit 203, just s. Ext/int corridors. **Pets:** Other species. $20 one-time fee/room. Designated rooms, service with restrictions, supervision.
SAVE SD X GM ⚐ ⚐ ⊟ ⊡ ♈ ➤ X

▲▲▲ ▼▼▼ New Summit Inn SH
(970) 668-3220. **$50-$145.** 1205 N Summit Blvd. I-70, exit 203, just s, then just e. Int corridors. **Pets:** $10 daily fee/pet. Service with restrictions, supervision.
SAVE SD X ⊟

▲▲▲ ▼▼▼ Snowshoe Motel M
(970) 668-3444. **$45-$125, 14 day notice.** 521 Main St. I-70, exit 203 westbound, 1 mi s to Main St, just w; exit 201 eastbound. Ext corridors. **Pets:** $10 deposit/pet, $10 one-time fee/pet. Designated rooms, service with restrictions, supervision.
SAVE X ⊟ ⊡ ⚿

FRUITA

▲▲▲ ▼▼ Balanced Rock Motel M
(970) 858-7333. **$40-$55.** 126 S Coulson. I-70, exit 19, just n to Aspen Ave, then just w. Ext corridors. **Pets:** Dogs only. $5 daily fee/pet. Service with restrictions, supervision.
SAVE X ⊟

▲▲▲ ▼▼ H-Motel M ✿
(970) 858-7198. **$35-$55, 3 day notice.** 333 Hwy 6 & 50. I-70, exit 19, 0.5 mi e. Ext corridors. **Pets:** Large. $5 daily fee/pet. Service with restrictions, supervision.
SAVE X ⊟

▲▲▲ ▼▼▼ Super 8 SH
(970) 858-0808. **$45-$70.** 399 Jurassic Ave. I-70, exit 19, 0.3 mi s; just e of Dinosaur Discovery Museum. Int corridors. **Pets:** Accepted.
SAVE SD X GM ⚐ ⚐ ⊟ ➤

GEORGETOWN

▲▲▲ ▼▼▼ Georgetown Mountain Inn M
(303) 569-3201. **$51-$69.** 1100 Rose St. I-70, exit 228, just s, then 0.3 mi w. Ext corridors. **Pets:** Other species. $10 one-time fee/room. Designated rooms, service with restrictions, supervision.
SAVE SD X ⊟ ➤ X ⚿

GLENWOOD SPRINGS

▼▼▼ Caravan Inn M
(970) 945-7451. **$55-$109.** 1826 Grand Ave. I-70, exit 116, 1.3 mi s on SR 82. Ext corridors. **Pets:** Other species. $5 daily fee/pet. Designated rooms, service with restrictions, crate.
ASK SD X ⊟ ➤

▲▲▲ ▼▼▼▼ Hotel Colorado SH
(970) 945-6511. **$139-$169.** 526 Pine St. I-70, exit 116, just ne. Int corridors. **Pets:** Accepted.
SAVE SD X ⊟ ⊡ ♈ X ⚿

▼▼▼ Quality Inn & Suites 🆂🅷
(970) 945-5995. **$59-$149.** 2650 Gilstrap. I-70, exit 114, just s, then w. Int corridors. **Pets:** Accepted.
🅰🆂🅺 🆂🛅 ❌ 🔊 📶 🎬 🍴 📖 ➿ ❌

▼▼▼ Ramada Inn & Suites 🆂🅷
(970) 945-2500. **$69-$149.** 124 W 6th St. I-70, exit 116, just w. Ext/int corridors. **Pets:** Accepted.
🅰🆂🅺 🆂🛅 ❌ 🍴 📖 🍴 ➿

🔷 ▼▼ Silver Spruce Motel Ⓜ 🐾
(970) 945-5458. **$49-$110.** 162 W 6th St. I-70, exit 116, just w on frontage road. Ext corridors. **Pets:** Other species. $5 daily fee/pet. Designated rooms, service with restrictions.
🆂🅰🆅🅴 🆂🛅 ❌ 🍴

GRAND JUNCTION

🔷 ▼▼▼ Best Western Horizon Inn 🆂🅷
(970) 245-1410. **$55-$84.** 754 Horizon Dr. I-70, exit 31, 0.3 mi n. Ext corridors. **Pets:** Large. Designated rooms, service with restrictions, supervision.
🆂🅰🆅🅴 🆂🛅 ❌ 🔊 🎬 🍴 📖 ➿

🔷 ▼▼▼ Budget Host Inn Ⓜ
(970) 243-6050. **$55-$75.** 721 Horizon Dr. I-70, exit 31, 0.3 mi s. Ext corridors. **Pets:** $50 deposit/room. Service with restrictions, crate.
🆂🅰🆅🅴 🆂🛅 ❌ 🍴 📖 ➿

🔷 ▼▼▼ Days Inn of Grand Junction 🆂🅷
(970) 245-7200. **$55-$80.** 733 Horizon Dr. I-70, exit 31, just s. Int corridors. **Pets:** $50 deposit/room. Designated rooms, service with restrictions, supervision.
🆂🅰🆅🅴 🆂🛅 ❌ 🍴 📖 🍴 ➿

🔷 ▼▼▼ Grand Junction Super 8 🆂🅷
(970) 248-8080. **$45-$70.** 728 Horizon Dr. I-70, exit 31, just s. Int corridors. **Pets:** Accepted.
🆂🅰🆅🅴 🆂🛅 ❌ 🍴 ➿

🔷 ▼▼▼▼ Grand Vista Hotel 🆂🅷
(970) 241-8411. **$75-$82.** 2790 Crossroads Blvd. I-70, exit 31, 0.3 mi n. Int corridors. **Pets:** Small. $10 daily fee/room. Designated rooms, service with restrictions, supervision.
🆂🅰🆅🅴 🆂🛅 ❌ 🍴 📖 🍴 ➿ ❌

▼▼▼ Hampton Inn 🆂🅷
(970) 243-3222. **$95.** 205 Main St. At 2nd and Main sts; downtown. Int corridors. **Pets:** Medium. $25 daily fee/pet. Service with restrictions, supervision.
🅰🆂🅺 🆂🛅 ❌ 🔊 📶 🎬 🍴 📖 ➿ ❌

▼▼▼ Hawthorn Suites 🆂🅷
(970) 242-2525. **$99-$209.** 225 Main St. At 2nd and Main sts; downtown. Int corridors. **Pets:** Other species. $25 daily fee/pet. Supervision.
🅰🆂🅺 🆂🛅 ❌ 🔊 🎬 🍴 📖 ➿ ❌

🔷 ▼▼▼ Holiday Inn 🆂🅷
(970) 243-6790. **$84-$109.** 755 Horizon Dr. I-70, exit 31, northwest corner. Ext/int corridors. **Pets:** Other species. Service with restrictions, supervision.
🆂🅰🆅🅴 🆂🛅 ❌ 📶 🎬 🍴 📖 🍴 ➿ ❌

🔷 ▼▼▼ La Quinta Inns & Suites 🆂🅷
(970) 241-2929. **$83-$100.** 2761 Crossroads Blvd. I-70, exit 31, n to Crossroads Blvd, just w. Int corridors. **Pets:** Service with restrictions, crate.
🆂🅰🆅🅴 ❌ 🎬 📶 🍴 🍴 📖 ➿

🔷 ▼▼ Mesa Inn Ⓜ
(970) 245-3080. **$40-$75.** 704 Horizon Dr. I-70, exit 31, 0.5 mi s. Ext corridors. **Pets:** $50 deposit/room. Designated rooms, service with restrictions, supervision.
🆂🅰🆅🅴 🆂🛅 ❌ 🍴 📖 ➿

🔷 ▼▼▼ Ramada Inn Ⓜ 🐾
(970) 243-5150. **$54-$84.** 752 Horizon Dr. I-70, exit 31, just n. Int corridors. **Pets:** Other species. $10 one-time fee/room. Service with restrictions.
🆂🅰🆅🅴 🆂🛅 ❌ 📖 🍴 ➿

🔷 ▼▼ West Gate Inn Ⓜ
(970) 241-3020. **$54-$74.** 2210 Hwy 6 & 50. I-70, exit 26, 0.3 mi se. Ext corridors. **Pets:** $50 deposit/room. Designated rooms, service with restrictions, crate.
🆂🅰🆅🅴 🆂🛅 ❌ 📖 🍴 ➿

GRAND LAKE

🔷 ▼▼ Spirit Lake Lodge Ⓜ
(970) 627-3344. **$55-$160, 7 day notice.** 829 Grand Ave. Just e of US 34; downtown. Ext corridors. **Pets:** $10 daily fee/pet. Designated rooms, no service, supervision.
🆂🅰🆅🅴 🆂🛅 ❌ 🍴 ➿ 🎾

GREAT SAND DUNES NATIONAL MONUMENT

▼▼ Great Sand Dunes Lodge Ⓜ
(719) 378-2900. **$85.** 7900 Hwy 150 N. From Alamosa, 16 mi e on US 160, 16 mi n on SR 150; at entrance to Great Sand Dunes National Monument. Ext corridors. **Pets:** $10 one-time fee/pet. Service with restrictions, supervision.
❌ ➿

GREELEY

🔷 ▼▼▼ Best Western Regency Hotel 🆂🅷
(970) 353-8444. **$79-$249.** 701 8th St. On US 85 business route; downtown. Int corridors. **Pets:** Small. $25 one-time fee/room. Service with restrictions, crate.
🆂🅰🆅🅴 🆂🛅 ❌ 🔊 📶 🎬 🍴 📖 🍴 ➿

🔷 ▼▼▼ Country Inn & Suites By Carlson 🆂🅷
(970) 330-3404. **$72-$99.** 2501 W 29th St. US 34 Bypass, exit 23rd Ave, just s. Int corridors. **Pets:** Small, other species. $10 daily fee/pet. Designated rooms, service with restrictions, supervision.
🆂🅰🆅🅴 🆂🛅 ❌ 🔊 🍴 📖 ➿

▼▼▼ Holiday Inn Express 🆂🅷
(970) 330-7495. **$64-$95.** 2563 W 29th St. US 34 Bypass, exit 23rd Ave, just s, then w. Int corridors. **Pets:** Accepted.
🅰🆂🅺 🆂🛅 ❌ 🔊 📶 🍴 📖 ➿ ❌

GUNNISON

△△△ ▽▽▽ ABC Motel M
(970) 641-2400. **$48-$69.** 212 E Tomichi Ave. On US 50; near Western State College. Ext corridors. **Pets:** Medium. $5 daily fee/pet. Designated rooms, service with restrictions, supervision.
[SAVE] [S/D] [X] [🔔]

△△△ ▽▽▽ Hylander Inn M
(970) 641-0700. **$55-$75.** 412 E Tomichi Ave. On US 50; near Western State College. Ext corridors. **Pets:** Dogs only. $5 daily fee/pet. Designated rooms, service with restrictions, supervision.
[SAVE] [S/D] [X] [🔔]

HOTCHKISS

△△△ ▽▽▽ Hotchkiss Inn M
(970) 872-2200. **$59-$65, 3 day notice.** 406 Hwy 133. 0.3 mi e jct SR 92 and 133. Ext corridors. **Pets:** Accepted.
[SAVE] [S/D] [X] [🔔]

HOT SULPHUR SPRINGS

△△△ ▽▽ Canyon Motel M ❀
(970) 725-3395. **$54-$84.** 221 Byers Ave. On US 40. Ext corridors. **Pets:** Other species. $10 daily fee/room. Supervision.
[SAVE] [S/D] [X] [🔔] [💻] [K]

JULESBURG

△△△ ▽▽ Budget Host Platte Valley Inn SH
(970) 474-3336. **$44-$60.** 15225 Hwy 385 & I-76. I-76, exit 180, just n. Ext corridors. **Pets:** Dogs only. $7 one-time fee/pet. Designated rooms, service with restrictions, supervision.
[SAVE] [S/D] [X] [💻] [🍴] [🏊]

KEYSTONE

△△△ ▽▽▽▽ The Inn at Keystone SH
(970) 496-4825. **$153-$336, 30 day notice.** 23044 Hwy 6. I-70, exit 205, 6.5 mi e on US 6; at Keystone Ski Area. Int corridors. **Pets:** Large, other species. $20 daily fee/room. Designated rooms, service with restrictions.
[SAVE] [X] [≈] [🔔] [💻] [🍴] [K]

LA JUNTA

▽▽▽▽ Holiday Inn Express M ❀
(719) 384-2900. **$79-$99.** 27994 US Hwy 50 Frontage Rd. 0.8 mi w on US 50. Int corridors. **Pets:** $10 daily fee/room. Service with restrictions, supervision.
[ASK] [S/D] [X] [≈] [🖋] [🔔] [💻] [🏊]

△△△ ▽▽ Travel Inn M
(719) 384-2504. **$40-$48.** 110 E 1st St. On US 50. Ext corridors. **Pets:** Dogs only. $8 one-time fee/pet. Designated rooms, service with restrictions, supervision.
[SAVE] [S/D] [X] [🔔]

LAKE CITY

△△△ ▽▽ Matterhorn Mountain Motel M
(970) 944-2210. **$60-$79, 7 day notice.** 409 Bluff St. SR 149, just w via 4th St. Ext corridors. **Pets:** Other species. $10 one-time fee/pet. No service, supervision.
[SAVE] [X] [🖋] [🔔] [💻] [K] [🏊]

LAKE GEORGE

△△△ ▽▽▽ Mule Creek Outfitters/M Lazy C Ranch RA
(719) 748-3398. **$65-$95.** 801 CR 453. 5 mi w on US 24, then 0.8 mi n on dirt road. Ext corridors. **Pets:** Accepted.
[SAVE] [X] [🔔] [💻] [🖋] [K] [W] [🏊]

LAMAR

△△△ ▽▽▽ Best Western Cow Palace Inn M
(719) 336-7753. **$84-$114.** 1301 N Main St. 0.8 mi n on US 50 and 287. Ext/int corridors. **Pets:** Other species. No service, supervision.
[SAVE] [S/D] [X] [≈] [🖋] [🔔] [💻] [🍴] [🏊]

△△△ ▽▽▽ Blue Spruce Motel M
(719) 336-7454. **$49-$69.** 1801 S Main St. 1.3 mi s on US 287 and 385. Ext corridors. **Pets:** Medium, other species. $5 daily fee/pet. Service with restrictions, supervision.
[SAVE] [S/D] [X] [🔔] [💻] [🏊]

▽▽ Passport Inn M
(719) 336-7746. **$40-$45.** 113 N Main St. Jct US 50 and 385, just e. Ext corridors. **Pets:** Other species. $5 daily fee/pet. Service with restrictions, crate.
[ASK] [S/D] [X] [🔔]

LAS ANIMAS

△△△ ▽▽▽▽ Best Western Bent's Fort Inn M
(719) 456-0011. **$59-$69.** 10950 E US 50. On US 50, 1.5 mi e. Int corridors. **Pets:** Other species. Service with restrictions.
[SAVE] [S/D] [X] [🔔] [💻] [🍴] [🏊]

LEADVILLE

△△△ ▽▽▽ Alps Motel M
(719) 486-1223. **$59-$109, 3 day notice.** 207 Elm St. Just s on US 24. Int corridors. **Pets:** Accepted.
[SAVE] [X] [🔔] [K]

LIMON

△△△ ▽▽▽▽ Best Western Limon Inn SH
(719) 775-0277. **$60-$100.** 925 T Ave. I-70, exit 359. Int corridors. **Pets:** Other species. $10 one-time fee/room. Designated rooms, service with restrictions, supervision.
[SAVE] [S/D] [X] [💻] [🏊]

△△△ ▽▽▽ Safari Motel M
(719) 775-2363. **$38-$76.** 637 Main St. I-70, exit 361, 0.8 mi w. Ext corridors. **Pets:** Other species. $5 one-time fee/pet. Service with restrictions, supervision.
[SAVE] [S/D] [X] [🏊]

(AAA) ☗☗☗ Super 8 Motel SH
(719) 775-2889. **$44-$68, 5 day notice.** 937 Hwy 24. I-70, exit 359, just s. Int corridors. **Pets:** Accepted.
SAVE ☒

(AAA) ☗☗☗ Tyme Square Inn SH
(719) 775-0700. **$59-$85.** 2505 6th St. I-70, exit 359, then s. Int corridors. **Pets:** Large, other species. $10 one-time fee/pet. Service with restrictions, supervision.
SAVE ☒ ☒ ☒ ☒ ☒ ☒ ☒ ☒ ☒ ☒

LONGMONT

☗☗☗ Hawthorn Suites SH
(303) 774-7100. **$162-$295.** 2000 Sunset Way. 1 mi s on US 287, 1.3 mi sw on SR 119. Int corridors. **Pets:** Accepted.
ASK ☒ ☒ ☒ ☒ ☒ ☒ ☒ ☒ ☒

☗☗☗ Radisson Hotel and Conference Center-Longmont SH ☜
(303) 776-2000. **$169.** 1900 Ken Pratt Blvd. 1 mi s on US 287, 1.3 mi sw on SR 119. Int corridors. **Pets:** Large. $50 deposit/room. Designated rooms, service with restrictions, crate.
ASK ☒ ☒ ☒ ☒ ☒ ☒ ☒ ☒ ☒ ☒

☗☗☗ Residence Inn by Marriott Boulder/Longmont SH
(303) 702-9933. **$99-$149.** 1450 Dry Creek Dr. I-25, exit 235, jct Hover Rd and SR 119. Int corridors. **Pets:** Other species. $50 one-time fee/room. Service with restrictions, supervision.
ASK ☒ ☒ ☒ ☒ ☒ ☒ ☒ ☒ ☒

☗☗ Super 8 Motel SH
(303) 772-0888. **$53-$88.** 10805 Turner Blvd. I-25, exit 240, jct SR 119; 7 mi e of town. Int corridors. **Pets:** Accepted.
ASK ☒ ☒

LOUISVILLE

(AAA) ☗☗☗☗ Comfort Inn of Boulder County SH ☜
(303) 604-0181. **$64-$134.** 1196 Dillon Rd. US 36 (Boulder Tpke), exit Superior (SR 170), just n on McCaslin Blvd, then just w. Int corridors. **Pets:** $100 deposit/room. Designated rooms, service with restrictions, supervision.
SAVE ☒ ☒ ☒ ☒ ☒ ☒ ☒

(AAA) ☗☗☗☗ La Quinta Inn-Boulder Louisville Area SH
(303) 664-0100. **$70-$110.** 902 Dillon Rd. US 36 (Boulder Tpke), exit Superior (SR 170), just n on McCaslin Blvd, then e. Int corridors. **Pets:** Medium. Service with restrictions, supervision.
SAVE ☒ ☒ ☒ ☒ ☒ ☒ ☒

☗☗☗☗ Residence Inn by Marriott-Boulder/Louisville SH ☜
(303) 665-2661. **$116-$134.** 845 Coal Creek Cir. US 36 (Boulder Tpke), exit Superior (SR 170), n on McCaslin Blvd to Dillon Rd, then 0.6 mi e. Int corridors. **Pets:** $100 one-time fee/room. Service with restrictions.
ASK ☒ ☒ ☒ ☒ ☒ ☒ ☒ ☒ ☒ ☒

LOVELAND

(AAA) ☗☗☗ Best Western Coach House SH ☜
(970) 667-7810. **$74-$94.** 5542 E US Hwy 34. I-25, exit 257B, just w. Ext/int corridors. **Pets:** Other species. $15 one-time fee/room. Service with restrictions, supervision.
SAVE ☒ ☒ ☒ ☒ ☒

(AAA) ☗☗ Budget Host Exit 254 Inn M ☜
(970) 667-5202. **$49-$76.** 2716 SE Frontage Rd. I-25, exit 254, just e. Ext corridors. **Pets:** Medium, dogs only. $5 daily fee/pet. Service with restrictions, supervision.
SAVE ☒ ☒ ☒ ☒

MARBLE

☗☗☗ Ute Meadows Inn Bed & Breakfast BB ☜
(970) 963-7088. **$110-$159, 14 day notice.** 2880 CR 3. SR 133, 3 mi to town. Int corridors. **Pets:** Dogs only. $15 daily fee/pet. Crate.
ASK ☒ ☒ ☒ ☒ ☒ ☒ ☒

MESA VERDE NATIONAL PARK

(AAA) ☗☗☗ Far View Lodge in Mesa Verde M
(970) 529-4421. **$93-$123.** 1 Navajo Hill. 10 mi e of Cortez; 8 mi w of Mancos on US 160, then 15 mi within the park; near park visitors center. Ext corridors. **Pets:** Accepted.
SAVE ☒ ☒ ☒ ☒ ☒ ☒ ☒ ☒ ☒

MONTE VISTA

(AAA) ☗☗☗☗ Best Western Movie Manor Motor Inn SH
(719) 852-5921. **$55-$110.** 2830 W Hwy 160. On US 160, 2 mi w. Ext corridors. **Pets:** Accepted.
SAVE ☒ ☒ ☒ ☒

(AAA) ☗☗☗ Comfort Inn M
(719) 852-0612. **$80-$105.** 1519 Grande Ave. 0.3 mi e on US 160. Int corridors. **Pets:** Other species. Service with restrictions, supervision.
SAVE ☒ ☒ ☒

MONTROSE

(AAA) ☗☗☗ Best Western Red Arrow SH ☜
(970) 249-9641. **$69-$109.** 1702 E Main St. 1 mi e on US 50. Ext/int corridors. **Pets:** $8 one-time fee/room. Service with restrictions.
SAVE ☒ ☒ ☒ ☒ ☒ ☒ ☒

(AAA) ☗☗☗ Black Canyon Motel M
(970) 249-3495. **$45-$95.** 1605 E Main St. 1 mi e on US 50. Ext corridors. **Pets:** $5 daily fee/pet. Designated rooms, service with restrictions, supervision.
SAVE ☒ ☒ ☒ ☒ ☒ ☒

(AAA) ☗☗☗ Canyon Trails Inn M ☜
(970) 249-3426. **$36-$58.** 1225 E Main St. 0.8 mi e on US 50. Ext corridors. **Pets:** Small, other species. Service with restrictions, supervision.
SAVE ☒ ☒ ☒

▼▼▼ **Comfort Inn** 🄢🄗

(970) 240-8000. **$60-$95.** 2100 E Main St. 1.3 mi e on US 50. Int corridors. **Pets:** Medium, dogs only. $10 daily fee/pet. Designated rooms, service with restrictions, supervision.

🄐🄢🄚 🕉 ⊠ 🖫 🖥 🖵 🏊

▼▼ 🔷 **Days Inn** 🄢🄗

(970) 249-3411. **$39-$75.** 1655 E Main St. 1 mi e on US 50. Int corridors. **Pets:** Accepted.

🄐🄢🄚 🕉 ⊠ 🖥 🖵 🏊

🄐🄐🄐 ▼▼▼ **Holiday Inn Express Hotel & Suites** 🄢🄗

(970) 240-1800. **$89-$149.** 1391 S Townsend Ave. 1 mi s on US 550, e on Niagara Ave. Int corridors. **Pets:** Designated rooms, service with restrictions, supervision.

🅂🄰🅅🄴 🕉 ⊠ 🖫 ⊘ 🖥 🖵 🏊

▼▼▼ 🔷 **Quality Inn & Suites-Montrose** 🄢🄗

(970) 249-1011. **$59-$99.** 2751 Commercial Way. 1.5 mi s on US 550, w on Odello Rd. Int corridors. **Pets:** $5 one-time fee/pet. Designated rooms, service with restrictions, supervision.

🄐🄢🄚 🕉 ⊠ ⊘ 🖫 🖥 🖵 🏊

🄐🄐🄐 ▼▼▼ **San Juan Inn** 🄼

(970) 249-6644. **$50-$75.** 1480 S Townsend Ave. 1 mi s on US 550. Ext corridors. **Pets:** Small. $6 daily fee/pet. Designated rooms, service with restrictions, supervision.

🅂🄰🅅🄴 🕉 ⊠ 🖥 🏊 ⊠

▼▼ 🔷 **Uncompahgre Bed & Breakfast** 🄱🄱 ❁

(970) 240-4000. **$57-$77.** 21049 Uncompahgre Rd. 8 mi s on US 550. Int corridors. **Pets:** Large, dogs only. Service with restrictions, supervision.

🕉 ⊠ ⊠ 🖫 ☎

🄐🄐🄐 ▼▼▼ **Western Motel** 🄼

(970) 249-3481. **$42-$90.** 1200 E Main St. 0.8 mi e on US 50. Ext corridors. **Pets:** Small, dogs only. $25 deposit/room, $5 daily fee/pet, $5 one-time fee/pet. Designated rooms, service with restrictions, supervision.

🅂🄰🅅🄴 🕉 ⊠ 🖥 🖵 🏊

NEW CASTLE

▼▼▼ 🔷 **Comfort Inn** 🄢🄗

(970) 984-2363. **$49-$109.** 781 Burning Mountain Rd. I-70, exit 105, just n, then w. Int corridors. **Pets:** Accepted.

🄐🄢🄚 🕉 ⊠ ⊘ 🖥 🖵 🏊

OURAY

🄐🄐🄐 ▼▼▼ **Rivers Edge Motel** 🄼

(970) 325-4621. **$50-$112.** 110 7th Ave. Just w of US 550 (Main St) via 7th Ave. Ext corridors. **Pets:** Dogs only. $10 daily fee/room. Supervision.

🅂🄰🅅🄴 🕉 ⊠ 🖥 🖵 ⊠ 🄐

🄐🄐🄐 ▼▼▼ **Riverside Inn** 🄼 ❁

(970) 325-4061. **$50-$95, 14 day notice.** 1805 N Main St. Just n on US 550. Ext corridors. **Pets:** Dogs only. $25 deposit/pet. Designated rooms, service with restrictions, supervision.

🅂🄰🅅🄴 🕉 ⊠ 🖥 🖵

PAGOSA SPRINGS

🄐🄐🄐 ▼▼▼ **Best Value High Country Lodge** 🄼 ❁

(970) 264-4181. **$65-$91.** 3821 E Hwy 160. On US 160, 3 mi e. Ext/int corridors. **Pets:** Other species. $15 one-time fee/room. Service with restrictions, crate.

🅂🄰🅅🄴 🕉 ⊠ 🖥 🖵 ⊠

🄐🄐🄐 ▼▼▼ **Best Western Oak Ridge Lodge** 🄼

(970) 264-4173. **$53-$120, 3 day notice.** 158 Hot Springs Blvd. Just s of US 160. Int corridors. **Pets:** Other species. $100 deposit/pet, $15 one-time fee/pet. Service with restrictions, supervision.

🅂🄰🅅🄴 🕉 ⊠ 🖥 🖵 🍴 🏊 ⊠

▼▼ **Econo Lodge** 🄼

(970) 731-2701. **$59-$109.** 315 Navajo Trail Dr. 4 mi w on US 160. Int corridors. **Pets:** Accepted.

🄐🄢🄚 🕉 ⊠ ⊘ 🖥 🏊

▼▼ **Fireside Inn Cabins** 🄒🄐

(970) 264-9204. **$85-$144, 15 day notice.** 1600 E Hwy 160. 1.3 mi e on US 160. Ext corridors. **Pets:** $5 daily fee/pet. No service, supervision.

🄐🄢🄚 🕉 ⊠ 🖥 🖵 🄐

▼▼▼ 🔷 **Pagosa Springs Inn & Suites** 🄢🄗

(970) 731-3400. **$61-$89.** 519 Village Dr. 3.8 mi w on US 160. Int corridors. **Pets:** Other species. $10 daily fee/pet. Designated rooms, service with restrictions, supervision.

🄐🄢🄚 🕉 ⊠ 🖥 🖵 🏊 ⊠

🄐🄐🄐 ▼▼ **Super 8 Motel** 🄼

(970) 731-4005. **$40-$100.** 8 Solomon Dr. 2.5 mi w on US 160. Ext/int corridors. **Pets:** Accepted.

🅂🄰🅅🄴 🕉 ⊠ 🖥

PUEBLO

🄐🄐🄐 ▼▼▼ **Best Western Town House Motel** 🄼

(719) 543-6530. **$60-$75, 3 day notice.** 730 N Santa Fe Ave. I-25, exit 99B, just w, then just s. Ext corridors. **Pets:** $10 one-time fee/room. Service with restrictions.

🅂🄰🅅🄴 🕉 ⊠ ⊘ 🖫 🖥 🖵 🍴 🏊

▼▼▼ **Hampton Inn** 🄢🄗 ❁

(719) 544-4700. **$75-$90.** 4703 N Freeway. I-25, exit 102, just w. Ext corridors. **Pets:** Small, other species. $25 one-time fee/room. Designated rooms, service with restrictions, supervision.

🄐🄢🄚 🕉 ⊠ 🖥 🖵 🏊

🄐🄐🄐 ▼▼▼ **Holiday Inn Pueblo** 🄼 ❁

(719) 543-8050. **$69-$99, 7 day notice.** 4001 N Elizabeth St. I-25, exit 101 (US 50 W), 0.3 mi n on service road. Ext/int corridors. **Pets:** $25 deposit/room. Service with restrictions, supervision.

🅂🄰🅅🄴 🕉 ⊠ 🖥 🖵 🍴 🏊 ⊠

▼▼▼ 🔷 **La Quinta Inn & Suites** 🄢🄗

(719) 542-3500. **$69-$99.** 4801 N Elizabeth St. I-25, exit 102, just nw. Int corridors. **Pets:** Accepted.

⊠ ⊘ ⊘ 🖥 🖵 🏊

AAA ▼▼▼ Microtel Inn & Suites **M**
(719) 242-2020. **$54-$74.** 3343 Gateway Dr. I-25, exit 94. Int corridors. **Pets:** Other species. $50 deposit/room, $10 one-time fee/room. Service with restrictions, supervision.
SAVE So X &M 🐾 🖥 💻

PUEBLO WEST

▼▼▼▼ Inn at Pueblo West **M**
(719) 547-2111. **$47-$74.** 201 S McCulloch Blvd. I-25, exit 101, 8 mi w on US 50, then 0.5 mi s. Ext/int corridors. **Pets:** Accepted.
ASK So X &M 🐾 🖥 💻 🏊

PURGATORY

AAA ▼▼▼▼ Inn at Durango Mountain **M**
(970) 247-9669. **$69-$350, 30 day notice.** 49617 US 550 N. On US 550. Int corridors. **Pets:** Accepted.
SAVE So X 🖥 💻 🍴 🏊 🐕 🐾

RIDGWAY

AAA ▼▼▼▼ Chipeta Sun Lodge and Spa **BB**
(970) 626-3737. **$95-$215, 30 day notice.** 304 S Lena St. Jct US 550, just w on SR 62, then just s. Ext/int corridors. **Pets:** Medium, dogs only. $35 one-time fee/pet. Designated rooms, service with restrictions, supervision.
SAVE So X 🖥 💻 🏊 🐕 🐾

AAA ▼▼▼ Ridgway-Telluride Super 8 Lodge **M**
(970) 626-5444. **$55-$99.** 373 Palomino Tr. US 550, at jct SR 62. Int corridors. **Pets:** $10 daily fee/pet. Designated rooms, service with restrictions, supervision.
SAVE So X 🖥 🏊 🐕

RIFLE

AAA ▼▼▼ Rusty Cannon Motel **M**
(970) 625-4004. **$68-$76, 7 day notice.** 701 Taughenbaugh Blvd. I-70, exit 90, just s. Ext corridors. **Pets:** Dogs only. $20 deposit/pet. Designated rooms, service with restrictions, supervision.
SAVE So X 🖥 💻 🏊

SALIDA

AAA ▼▼▼ Aspen Leaf Lodge **M**
(719) 539-6733. **$49-$69.** 7350 W Hwy 50. Just w of Hot Springs Pool. Ext corridors. **Pets:** Small, other species. $5 daily fee/room. Service with restrictions, supervision.
SAVE So X 🖥

AAA ▼▼▼▼ Best Western Colorado Lodge **M**
(719) 539-2514. **$49-$85.** 352 W Rainbow Blvd. On US 50. Ext corridors. **Pets:** Accepted.
SAVE So X 🖥 💻 🏊 🐕

AAA ▼▼ Circle R Motel **M**
(719) 539-6296. **$33-$76.** 304 E US Hwy 50 Blvd. Ext corridors. **Pets:** Service with restrictions, supervision.
SAVE So X 🖥 💻

AAA ▼▼▼ Days Inn **SH**
(719) 539-6651. **$49-$99.** 407 Hwy 50 E. US 50. Int corridors. **Pets:** $10 one-time fee/pet. Designated rooms, service with restrictions, supervision.
SAVE So X 🖥

AAA ▼▼▼▼ Econo Lodge **SH**
(719) 539-2895. **$49-$119.** 1310 E Hwy 50. Ext corridors. **Pets:** Medium, dogs only. $10 daily fee/pet. Designated rooms, service with restrictions, supervision.
SAVE So X 🖥

AAA ▼▼▼ Silver Ridge Lodge **M** 🐾
(719) 539-2553. **$45-$85, 3 day notice.** 545 W Rainbow Blvd. US 50, just w of Chamber of Commerce. Ext corridors. **Pets:** Medium. $10 daily fee/pet. Designated rooms, service with restrictions, supervision.
SAVE So X 🖥 💻 🏊

AAA ▼▼▼ Super 8 Motel **M** 🐾
(719) 539-6689. **$59-$119.** 525 W Rainbow Blvd. On US 50. Ext corridors. **Pets:** Medium. Supervision.
SAVE So X 🖥 💻 🏊

AAA ▼▼▼ Travelodge **M**
(719) 539-2528. **$59-$109.** 7310 Hwy 50. US 50 W. Ext corridors. **Pets:** Other species. $5 daily fee/pet.
SAVE So X 🖥 💻 🏊

AAA ▼▼▼ Woodland Motel **M** 🐾
(719) 539-4980. **$41-$99.** 903 W 1st. US 50 westbound, 1.5 mi on SR 291; eastbound, 1 mi ne on G St, then 6 blks w on SR 291; US 285 southbound, 8 mi s on SR 291, then e. Ext corridors. **Pets:** Other species.
SAVE X 🖥 💻

SILVERTHORNE

▼▼▼ Days Inn Summit County **SH**
(970) 468-8661. **$59-$229, 3 day notice.** 580 Silverthorne Ln. I-70, exit 205, just n on SR 9, just e on Rainbow Dr, then just e on Tanglewood Ln. Int corridors. **Pets:** Other species. $10 daily fee/pet. Service with restrictions, supervision.
ASK So X &M 🕐 🖥 🏊

▼▼▼ Four Points by Sheraton Silverthorne **SH**
(970) 468-6200. **$80-$152.** 560 Silverthorne Ln. I-70, exit 205, just n on SR 9, just e on Rainbow Rd, then just e on Tanglewood Ln. Int corridors. **Pets:** Small, dogs only. $25 one-time fee/pet. Service with restrictions, supervision.
ASK So X &M 🕐 🖥 🖥 💻 🍴 🏊 🐕

▼▼▼▼ Quality Inn & Suites **SH**
(970) 513-1222. **$70-$130.** 530 Silverthorne Ln. I-70, exit 205, just n on SR 9, just e on Rainbow Rd, then just e on Tanglewood Ln. Int corridors. **Pets:** $50 deposit/room, $10 daily fee/room. Designated rooms, service with restrictions.
ASK So X &M 🕐 🖥 🖥 💻 🏊

SILVERTON

AAA ▼▼▼ Silverton's Inn of the Rockies at the Historic Alma House **BB**
(970) 387-5336. **$80-$130, 7 day notice.** 220 E 10th St. SR 110, off US 550 to 10th St, then just se. Int corridors. **Pets:** Accepted.
SAVE So X 🐕 🏊 🔑

▼▼ Villa Dallavalle B & B 🅑🅑 ❧
(970) 387-5555. **$79-$125, 7 day notice.** 1257 Blair. SR
110, off US 550, se on 12th to Blair St, then just n. Int
corridors. **Pets:** Very small, dogs only. $5 daily fee/pet.
Designated rooms, service with restrictions.
(A$K) (S6) (✕) (💻) (🛗)

⧫⧫ ▼▼ The Wyman Hotel & Inn 🅑🅑 ❧
(970) 387-5372. **$120-$215, 14 day notice.** 1371 Greene
(Main) St. Northeast corner of Greene (Main) and 14th sts.
Int corridors. **Pets:** Other species. $25 one-time fee/room.
Designated rooms, service with restrictions, supervision.
(SAVE) (✕) (🛗) (🍽) (🛗)

SNOWMASS VILLAGE

▼▼▼ Silvertree Hotel 🅛🅗
(970) 923-3520. **$98-$535.** 100 Elbert Ln. 4 mi sw of SR 82
via Brush Creek and Snowmelt rds, Lot 8. Int corridors.
Pets: Accepted.
(A$K) (S6) (✕) (🅰) (🛗) (💻) (🍽) (≈) (🛗)

⧫⧫ ▼▼▼ Snowmass Mountain Chalet 🅢🅗
(970) 923-3900. **$59-$325, 45 day notice.** 115 Daly Ln. 4 mi
sw of SR 82 via Brush Creek and Lower Village rds, Lot 5.
Ext/int corridors. **Pets:** Accepted.
(SAVE) (✕) (🛗) (≈) (🛗) (🛗)

SOUTH FORK

⧫⧫ ▼ Budget Host Ute Bluff Lodge 🅜
(719) 873-5595. **$49-$64, 14 day notice.** 27680 W Hwy
160. 2 mi e of jct US 160 and SR 149. Ext corridors.
Pets: Medium, dogs only. $5 one-time fee/pet. Designated
rooms, service with restrictions, supervision.
(SAVE) (S6) (✕) (🛗) (💻) (🛗)

⧫⧫ ▼▼▼ Comfort Inn 🅜
(719) 873-5600. **$79-$150.** 0182 E Frontage Rd. On US
160. Int corridors. **Pets:** Accepted.
(SAVE) (S6) (✕) (🛗) (💻) (≈)

⧫⧫ ▼▼▼ Wolf Creek Ski Lodge 🅜
(719) 873-5547. **$55-$80, 15 day notice.** 31042 Hwy 160 W.
On US 160. Ext corridors. **Pets:** Accepted.
(SAVE) (S6) (✕) (🛗) (💻) (🛗)

STEAMBOAT SPRINGS

⧫⧫ ▼▼ The Alpiner Lodge 🅜
(970) 879-1430. **$99-$139, 3 day notice.** 424 Lincoln Ave.
US 40, just w of Hot Springs Pool. Ext/int corridors.
Pets: Large, dogs only. $15 one-time fee/pet. Supervision.
(SAVE) (S6) (✕) (🛗) (💻)

**⧫⧫ ▼▼▼ Best Western Ptarmigan
Inn** 🅢🅗 ❧
(970) 879-1730. **$79-$245, 14 day notice.** 2304 Apres Ski
Way. 2.3 mi e on US 40, 0.8 mi n on Mt Werner Rd, then
take Apres Ski Way. Int corridors. **Pets:** $25 one-time fee/
room. Service with restrictions, supervision.
(SAVE) (S6) (✕) (🛗) (💻) (🍽) (≈) (🛗)

▼▼ Comfort Inn 🅢🅗 ❧
(970) 879-6669. **$69-$289.** 1055 Walton Creek Rd. 2.8 mi e
on US 40. Int corridors. **Pets:** $100 deposit/room, $10 daily
fee/room. No service.
(A$K) (S6) (✕) (🅼) (🅲) (🛗) (💻) (≈) (🛗)

▼▼▼▼ Fairfield Inn by Marriott 🅢🅗
(970) 870-9000. **$79-$129.** 3200 S Lincoln Ave. 3 mi e on
US 40. Int corridors. **Pets:** Accepted.
(A$K) (S6) (✕) (🅼) (🅰) (🅲) (🛗) (💻) (≈) (🛗)

⧫⧫ ▼▼▼▼ Hampton Inn & Suites 🅢🅗
(970) 871-8900. **$99-$329.** 725 S Lincoln Ave. 1.1 mi e on
US 40. Int corridors. **Pets:** Other species. $10 daily fee/
room. Designated rooms, service with restrictions, supervision.
(SAVE) (S6) (✕) (🅼) (🅰) (🅲) (🛗) (💻) (≈) (🛗)

⧫⧫ ▼▼▼ Holiday Inn Steamboat 🅢🅗 ❧
(970) 879-2250. **$99-$169, 3 day notice.** 3190 S Lincoln
Ave. 3 mi e on US 40. Int corridors. **Pets:** Other species.
$25 deposit/room, $10 daily fee/room. Service with restrictions, supervision.
(SAVE) (S6) (✕) (🅼) (🅰) (🅲) (🛗) (💻) (🍽) (≈) (🛗)

**⧫⧫ ▼▼▼ Iron Horse Inn-Steamboat
Springs** 🅢🅗
(970) 879-6505. **$95-$200, 3 day notice.** 333 S Lincoln Ave.
1 mi e on US 40. Ext/int corridors. **Pets:** Accepted.
(SAVE) (✕) (🛗) (💻) (🛗)

⧫⧫ ▼▼▼ Rabbit Ears Motel 🅜
(970) 879-1150. **$69-$129, 3 day notice.** 201 Lincoln Ave.
Just e on US 40. Ext corridors. **Pets:** $12 one-time fee/
room. Service with restrictions, supervision.
(SAVE) (S6) (✕) (🛗) (💻)

▼▼ Super 8 Motel 🅢🅗
(970) 879-5230. **$59-$109.** 3195 S Lincoln Ave. 3 mi e on
US 40. Int corridors. **Pets:** Large, dogs only. $20 deposit/
room. Designated rooms, service with restrictions, supervision.
(A$K) (S6) (✕) (≈)

STERLING

⧫⧫ ▼▼▼ Best Western Sundowner 🅜
(970) 522-6265. **$89-$149.** 125 Overland Trail St. I-76, exit
125, just w. Ext/int corridors. **Pets:** Accepted.
(SAVE) (S6) (✕) (💻) (≈)

⧫⧫ ▼ Colonial Motel 🅜
(970) 522-3382. **$41-$60.** 915 S Division. I-76, exit 125, 1.8
mi w on US 6 to 2nd traffic light (4th St), then s. Ext
corridors. **Pets:** Dogs only. $5 daily fee/pet. No service,
supervision.
(SAVE) (S6) (✕) (🛗)

⧫⧫ ▼▼▼ Ramada Inn 🅢🅗
(970) 522-2625. **$70-$100.** 22140 E Hwy 6. I-76, exit 125,
0.5 mi e on US 6. Ext/int corridors. **Pets:** Other species.
$25 deposit/room. Designated rooms, service with restric-
tions, supervision.
(SAVE) (S6) (✕) (🅰) (🛗) (💻) (🍽) (≈) (🛗)

STRATTON

🛆🛆🛆 ▽▽▽ Best Western Golden Prairie Inn 🆂🅷
(719) 348-5311. **$65-$99.** 700 Colorado Ave. I-70, exit 419, just n. Ext corridors. **Pets:** Accepted.
SAVE S🐾 ✕ 🔲 🖵 🍴 ⤻

TELLURIDE

🛆🛆🛆 ▽▽▽ Hotel Columbia 🆂🅷 ❀
(970) 728-0660. **$140-$450, 45 day notice.** 300 W San Juan Ave. Just s of SR 145 Spur at Aspen St and San Juan Ave; opposite gondola. Int corridors. **Pets:** Dogs only. $15 daily fee/room. Designated rooms, service with restrictions.
SAVE S🐾 ✕ 🔲 🖵 🍴 ✕

▽▽▽ The Hotel Telluride 🆂🅷
(970) 369-1188. **$149-$1099, 30 day notice.** 199 N Cornet St. Just n of jct SR 145 (Colorado Ave). Int corridors. **Pets:** Accepted.
ASK S🐾 ✕ 🅜 ⌘ 🎱 🔲 🖵 🍴 ✕

🛆🛆🛆 ▽▽▽▽ Wyndham Peaks Resort & Golden Door (R) Spa 🅻🅷
(970) 728-6800. **$199-$299, 30 day notice.** 136 Country Club Dr. 1.8 mi s of jct SR 145 (Colorado Ave) and 145 Spur; in Telluride Mountain Village. Int corridors. **Pets:** Accepted.
SAVE S🐾 ✕ 🅜 🖵 🍴 ⤻ ✕ 🎿

TRINIDAD

🛆🛆🛆 ▽▽▽ Best Western Trinidad Inn 🅼
(719) 846-2215. **$59-$109.** 900 W Adams St. I-25, exit 13A, uphill and across bridge. Ext corridors. **Pets:** Medium, other species. Service with restrictions, crate.
SAVE S🐾 ✕ 🔲 🖵 🍴 ⤻

🛆🛆🛆 ▽▽▽ Budget Host Derrick Motel 🅼
(719) 846-3307. **$59-$89.** 10301 Santa Fe Trail Dr. I-25, exit 11, just ne. Ext corridors. **Pets:** Small. $10 daily fee/room. Service with restrictions, supervision.
SAVE S🐾 ✕ 🔲 🖵

▽▽▽ Budget Summit Inn 🅼
(719) 846-2251. **$45-$60.** 9800 Santa Fe Trail Dr. I-25, exit 11, just se. Ext/int corridors. **Pets:** Medium, dogs only. $10 one-time fee/room. Designated rooms, service with restrictions, supervision.
ASK S🐾 ✕ ⌘ 🎱 🔲

▽▽▽ Holiday Inn 🅼
(719) 846-4491. **Call for rates.** 3125 Toupal Dr. I-25, exit 11. Int corridors. **Pets:** Accepted.
✕ 🔲 🖵 🍴 ⤻ ✕

▽▽▽ Super 8 Motel 🅼
(719) 846-8280. **$55-$80, 20 day notice.** 1924 Freedom Rd. I-25, exit 15. Int corridors. **Pets:** Medium. $10 one-time fee/room. Designated rooms, service with restrictions, supervision.
ASK S🐾 ✕ 🔲 🖵

VAIL

🛆🛆🛆 ▽▽▽ Antlers at Vail 🄲🄾
(970) 476-2471. **$160-$415, 60 day notice.** 680 W Lionshead Pl. I-70, exit 176, 0.5 mi w, just s on Lionshead Cir. Ext corridors. **Pets:** Other species. $15 daily fee/pet. Designated rooms, service with restrictions.
SAVE ✕ 🎱 🔲 🖵 ⤻ ✕ 🎿

▽▽▽ ▽▽▽ Sonnenalp Resort of Vail 🅻🅷
(970) 476-5656. **$200-$975, 14 day notice.** 20 Vail Rd. I-70, exit 176, just s. Int corridors. **Pets:** Accepted.
✕ 🎱 🍴 ⤻ ✕

WALSENBURG

🛆🛆🛆 ▽▽ Anchor Motel 🅼
(719) 738-2800. **$35-$65.** 1001 Main St. I-25, exit 49, 0.5 mi nw. Ext corridors. **Pets:** Small, other species. Designated rooms, service with restrictions, supervision.
SAVE S🐾 ✕ 🔲

🛆🛆🛆 ▽▽ Best Western Rambler 🆂🅷
(719) 738-1121. **$62-$97.** 457 US Hwy 85-87. I-25, exit 52, just w. Ext corridors. **Pets:** Accepted.
SAVE S🐾 ✕ 🖵 🍴 ⤻

🛆🛆🛆 ▽▽ Country Budget Host Motel 🅼
(719) 738-3800. **$42-$64.** 553 US Hwy 85 & 87. I-25, exit 52, 0.3 mi w. Ext corridors. **Pets:** Accepted.
SAVE S🐾 ✕

WINDSOR

🛆🛆🛆 ▽▽▽ AmericInn Lodge & Suites 🆂🅷
(970) 226-1232. **$89-$164.** 7645 Westgate Dr. I-25, exit 262, just se off SR 392. Int corridors. **Pets:** Small. $10 daily fee/pet. Designated rooms, service with restrictions, supervision.
SAVE S🐾 ✕ 🅜 ⌘ 🎱 🔲 🖵 ⤻ ✕

▽▽ Super 8 Motel 🆂🅷
(970) 686-5996. **$66-$76, 10 day notice.** 1265 Main St. I-25, exit 262, 3.8 mi e; in shopping/restaurant complex. Int corridors. **Pets:** Accepted.
ASK ✕ 🅜 🔲 🖵

WINTER PARK

🛆🛆🛆 ▽▽▽ Winter Park Mountain Lodge 🆂🅷
(970) 726-4211. **$50-$300, 3 day notice.** 81699 US Hwy 40. 2.3 mi se on US 40; near ski area. Int corridors. **Pets:** Accepted.
SAVE S🐾 ✕ 🅜 ♿ 🔲 🖵 🍴 ⤻ ✕

YAMPA

🛆🛆🛆 ▽▽▽ Oak Tree Inn 🆂🅷
(970) 638-1000. **$75, 3 day notice.** 98 Moffat Ave. Just off SR 131. Int corridors. **Pets:** $10 one-time fee/room. Service with restrictions, supervision.
SAVE S🐾 ✕ 🔲 🍴

BETHEL

Microtel Inn & Suites SH ❖
(203) 748-8318. **$72-$102, 30 day notice.** 80 Benedict Rd. I-84, exit 8, 1 mi e on US 6. Int corridors. **Pets:** Medium, other species. $100 deposit/room, $10 daily fee/pet. Service with restrictions, supervision.

BRANFORD

Days Inn & Conference Center M
(203) 488-8314. **$69-$199.** 375 E Main St. I-95, exit 55, just n on US 1. Ext/int corridors. **Pets:** Dogs only. $20 one-time fee/room. Designated rooms, service with restrictions, supervision.

Motel 6–1279 SH
(203) 483-5828. **$45-$67.** 320 E Main St. I-95, exit 55, 0.3 mi n on US 1. Int corridors. **Pets:** Accepted.

BRIDGEPORT

Bridgeport Holiday Inn & Convention Center SH
(203) 334-1234. **$109-$159.** 1070 Main St. SR 8 northbound, exit 2, 0.7 mi se; SR 8 southbound, exit 2, just s, then just e. Int corridors. **Pets:** Small, other species. $50 deposit/room. Service with restrictions, supervision.

BROOKFIELD

Twin Tree Inn M
(203) 775-0220. **$85-$95.** 1030 Federal Rd (Rt 7 & 202). Jct SR 25 and US 202, 1 mi n. Int/ext corridors. **Pets:** Other species. $10 one-time fee/room. Designated rooms, service with restrictions, crate.

DANBURY

Holiday Inn SH ❖
(203) 792-4000. **$109-$113.** 80 Newtown Rd. I-84, exit 8 (Newtown Rd), 0.5 mi s on US 6 W. Int corridors. **Pets:** Other species. $15 deposit/room. Designated rooms, service with restrictions, crate.

Maron Hotel & Suites Danbury SH
(203) 791-2200. **$109.** 42 Lake Ave Extension. I-84, exit 4, 0.5 mi w on US 6 and 202. Int corridors. **Pets:** Accepted.

Residence Inn by Marriott SH
(203) 797-1256. **$109-$139.** 22 Segar St. I-84, exit 4 eastbound, just n; westbound, just e on Lake Ave Extension, then just s. Int corridors. **Pets:** Accepted.

Wellesley Inn (Danbury) SH
(203) 792-3800. **$89-$129.** 116 Newtown Rd. I-84, exit 8 (Newtown Rd), northeast corner. Int corridors. **Pets:** Accepted.

DAYVILLE

Holiday Inn Express SH
(860) 779-3200. **$120-$140.** 16 Tracy Rd. I-395, exit 94, just w. Int corridors. **Pets:** Medium, dogs only. $10 one-time fee/room. Service with restrictions, crate.

GRISWOLD

AmericInn Lodge & Suites SH
(860) 376-3200. **$69-$269.** 375 Voluntown Rd. I-395, exit 85, w on SR 138. Int corridors. **Pets:** Small. $100 deposit/pet. Designated rooms, service with restrictions, supervision.

GROTON

Clarion Inn SH
(860) 446-0660. **$59-$199.** 156 Kings Hwy. I-95, exit 86, 0.3 mi ne on SR 184. Int corridors. **Pets:** Medium, dogs only. $10 daily fee/pet. Designated rooms, service with restrictions, crate.

HARTFORD METROPOLITAN AREA

BERLIN

⚠ ▼▼▼▼ Best Western New England Inn & Suites 🆂🅷
(860) 828-3000. **$79-$219.** 2253 Wilbur Cross Pkwy. I-91, exit 17 northbound, 4.9 mi n on SR 15 (Berlin Tpke); exit 22 N southbound, 2.5 mi n on SR 9 to exit 22, follow signs onto US 5 and SR 15 S (Berlin Tpke) for 2.8 mi. Int corridors. **Pets:** Small. $25 daily fee/pet. Designated rooms, service with restrictions, crate.
🆂🅰 ⊠ 🅼 ✄ 🛢 🖵 🏊

⚠ ▼▼▼ Hawthorne Inn 🆂🅷 ❁
(860) 828-4181. **$99-$194.** 2387 Wilbur Cross Pkwy. I-91, exit 17 northbound, 4.7 mi n on SR 15 (Berlin Tpke); exit 22N southbound, 2.5 mi n on SR 9 to exit 22, follow signs onto US 5 and SR 15 S (Berlin Tpke) for 3 mi. Int corridors. **Pets:** Other species. Service with restrictions.
🆂🅰 ⊠ 🛢 🍴 🏊 ⊠

CROMWELL

▼▼ Comfort Inn 🆂🅷 ❁
(860) 635-4100. **$59-$99.** 111 Berlin Rd. I-91, exit 21, just e on SR 372. Int corridors. **Pets:** Large, other species. $15 daily fee/room. Service with restrictions, crate.
🅰🆂🅺 🆂🅰 ⊠ 🛢 🖵

▼▼▼ Radisson Hotel and Conference Center Cromwell/Hartford South 🅻🅷
(860) 635-2000. **$79-$158.** 100 Berlin Rd. I-91, exit 21, just e on SR 372. Int corridors. **Pets:** Large. $25 daily fee/room. Service with restrictions, supervision.
🅰🆂🅺 🆂🅰 ⊠ 🅼 🛢 🖵 🍴 🏊 ⊠

EAST HARTFORD

⚠ ▼▼▼▼ Holiday Inn 🆂🅷
(860) 528-9611. **$75-$195.** 363 Roberts St. I-84, exit 58, just w. Int corridors. **Pets:** Small. $25 one-time fee/room. Service with restrictions, supervision.
🆂🅰 ⊠ 🌀 ✄ 🛢 🖵 🍴 🏊

EAST WINDSOR

▼▼▼ Holiday Inn Express Hartford Airport Area 🅼
(860) 627-6585. **$79-$99.** 260 Main St. I-91, exit 44, just s. Int corridors. **Pets:** Accepted.
⊠ 🅼 🌀 ✄ 🛢 🖵

ENFIELD

⚠ ▼▼▼ Radisson Hotel Springfield-Enfield 🆂🅷
(860) 741-2211. **$150-$180.** 1 Bright Meadow Blvd. I-91, exit 49, just e on service road. Int corridors. **Pets:** $50 one-time fee/room. Service with restrictions, supervision.
🆂🅰 ⊠ 🅼 🌀 ✄ 🛢 🖵 🍴 🏊 ⊠

⚠ ▼▼▼ Red Roof Inn 🅼
(860) 741-2571. **$46-$74.** 5 Hazard Ave. I-91, exit 47. Ext corridors. **Pets:** Accepted.
🆂🅰 ⊠ 🅼 🌀 ✄ 🛢

⚠ ▼▼▼ Super 8 Motel-Enfield 🅼
(860) 741-3636. **$59-$109.** 1543 King St. I-91, exit 46, 0.3 mi n on US 5. Ext corridors. **Pets:** $10 daily fee/room. Service with restrictions, supervision.
🆂🅰 ⊠ 🛢 🖵

FARMINGTON

▼▼▼ Centennial Inn Suites 🅲🅾
(860) 677-4647. **$129-$239.** 5 Spring Ln. US 6, 0.3 mi e of jct SR 177. Ext/int corridors. **Pets:** Other species. $15 daily fee/pet. Service with restrictions, crate.
🅰🆂🅺 🆂🅰 ⊠ 🅼 ✄ 🛢 🖵 🏊 ⊠

▼▼▼ Homewood Suites by Hilton 🆂🅷
(860) 321-0000. **$149-$200.** 2 Farm Glen Blvd. I-84, exit 39, 0.6 mi e on SR 4. Int corridors. **Pets:** Large, other species. $200 one-time fee/room. Service with restrictions, supervision.
🅰🆂🅺 🆂🅰 ⊠ 🅼 ✄ 🛢 🖵 🏊

HARTFORD

▼▼▼ Crowne Plaza Hartford Downtown 🅻🅷
(860) 549-2400. **$129-$199.** 50 Morgan St. I-91, exit 32B; I-84, exit 50 eastbound; exit 52 westbound. Int corridors. **Pets:** Very small. $50 one-time fee/pet. Designated rooms, service with restrictions, crate.
🅰🆂🅺 🆂🅰 ⊠ 🅼 🌀 ✄ 🛢 🖵 🍴 🏊

▼▼▼ Goodwin Hotel 🆂🅷
(860) 246-7500. **$209-$309.** 1 Haynes St. Downtown; entrance on Asylum St. Int corridors. **Pets:** Small, dogs only. $250 deposit/room. Service with restrictions, crate.
🅰🆂🅺 🆂🅰 ⊠ 🅼 ✄ 🛢 🍴

⚠ ▼▼▼ Residence Inn by Marriott Downtown Hartford 🅻🅷
(860) 524-5550. **$99.** 942 Main St. I-91, exit 29A northbound; exit 31 southbound. Int corridors. **Pets:** Accepted.
🆂🅰 ⊠ ✄ 🛢 🖵

MANCHESTER

▼▼▼ Residence Inn Manchester 🆂🅷
(860) 432-4242. **$149-$164.** 201 Hale Rd. I-84, exit 63, 0.5 mi nw, then 0.6 mi sw. Int corridors. **Pets:** Other species. $8 daily fee/room, $75 one-time fee/room. Service with restrictions, crate.
🅰🆂🅺 🆂🅰 ⊠ 🅼 🌀 ✄ 🛢 🖵 🏊 ⊠

MILLDALE

▼ Days Inn 🆂🅷
(860) 621-9181. **$45-$99.** 1845 Meriden Waterbury Tpke. I-84, exit 28, just e on SR 322. Int corridors. **Pets:** Other species. $10 daily fee/room. Service with restrictions, crate.
🅰🆂🅺 🆂🅰 ⊠ 🛢 🖵

OLD SAYBROOK

(AAA) ▼▼▼ ▼▼▼ Saybrook Point Inn & Spa SH ❀
(860) 395-2000. **$159-$799, 3 day notice.** 2 Bridge St. On
SR 154, 2.2 mi s of jct US 1; at Saybrook Point. Int corridors Small, dogs only. $50 one-time fee/room. Designated
rooms, service with restrictions, supervision.
[SAVE] [ASK] [✕] [✕] [⛅M] [🔌] [📱] [🅱] [🖥] [🍴] [🏊] [✕]
[🎞] [♨] [🆎]

SIMSBURY

(AAA) ▼▼▼ The Ironhorse Inn M
(860) 658-2216. **$86-$96.** 969 Hopmeadow St. On US
202/SR 10, 0.4 mi n. Int corridors. **Pets:** $15 one-time
fee/pet. Designated rooms, service with restrictions, supervision.
[SAVE] [🔌] [✕] [🅱] [🏊]

WINDSOR

▼▼▼▼ The Residence Inn by Marriott
Hartford-Windsor CO
(860) 688-7474. **$159-$229.** 100 Dunfey Ln. I-91, exit 37,
just w on SR 305 to Dunfey Ln, then 0.3 mi n. Ext corridors.
Pets: Other species. $20 daily fee/room. Service with
restrictions.
[ASK] [🔌] [✕] [⛅M] [🔌] [🅱] [🖥] [🏊] [✕]

WINDSOR LOCKS

(AAA) ▼▼▼ Baymont Inn & Suites
Hartford-Airport SH ❀
(860) 623-3336. **$89-$94.** 64 Ella T Grasso Tpke. I-91, exit
40, 2.5 mi w on SR 20, then just n on SR 75. Int corridors.
Pets: Medium, other species. Service with restrictions,
supervision.
[SAVE] [🔌] [✕] [⛅M] [🔌] [🅱] [🖥]

▼▼▼ Homewood Suites by Hilton SH
(860) 627-8463. **$149.** 65 Ella T Grasso Tpke. I-91, exit 40,
2.5 mi w on SR 20, then just n on SR 75. Ext/int corridors.
Pets: Accepted.
[ASK] [🔌] [✕] [⛅M] [🔌] [🅱] [🖥] [🏊] [✕]

▼▼▼ Ramada Inn Bradley International
Airport SH ❀
(860) 623-9494. **$89-$139.** 5 Ella T Grasso Tpke. I-91, exit
40, 2.5 mi w on SR 20, then just n on SR 75. Int corridors.
Pets: $10 daily fee/pet. Designated rooms, supervision.
[ASK] [🔌] [✕] [🅱] [🖥] [🍴] [🏊]

▼▼▼▼ Sheraton Hotel At Bradley International
Airport LH
(860) 627-5311. **$89-$215.** 1 Bradley International Airport. At
Bradley International Airport terminal. Int corridors.
Pets: Medium. Service with restrictions, supervision.
[ASK] [🔌] [✕] [⛅M] [🔌] [🅱] [🖥] [🍴] [🏊]

❀ END METROPOLITAN AREA ❀

IVORYTON

(AAA) ▼▼▼ The Copper Beech Inn CI
(860) 767-0330. **$165-$475.** 46 Main St. SR 9, exit 3, 1.7 mi
w. Int corridors. **Pets:** Medium, dogs only. $25 daily fee/pet.
No service, supervision.
[SAVE] [✕] [🍴]

LAKEVILLE

(AAA) ▼▼▼▼ Inn at Iron Masters M
(860) 435-9844. **$95-$195.** 229 Main St (Rt 44 & 41). 0.5 mi
ne. Ext corridors. **Pets:** Accepted.
[SAVE] [✕] [🅱] [🖥] [🏊]

(AAA) ▼▼▼▼ Interlaken Inn Resort and Conference
Center SH ❀
(860) 435-9878. **$139-$339, 7 day notice.** 74 Interlaken Rd.
On SR 112, 0.5 mi w of jct SR 41. Ext/int corridors.
Pets: Other species. $10 daily fee/room. Designated
rooms, service with restrictions.
[SAVE] [✕] [🔌] [🅱] [🖥] [🍴] [🏊] [✕]

LEDYARD

▼▼▼ The Mare's Inn B & B BB
(860) 572-7556. **$100-$199, 14 day notice.** 333 Colonel
Ledyard Hwy. I-95, exit 89, 1 mi n to Gold Star Hwy, 0.6 mi
w, then 0.7 mi n. Int corridors. **Pets:** Designated rooms, no
service, supervision.
[✕] [🅱] [🖥] [🆎]

MERIDEN

▼▼▼▼ Ramada Plaza Hotel & Conference
Center SH
(203) 238-2380. **$99-$109.** 275 Research Pkwy. I-91, exit 17
southbound; exit 16 northbound, 0.5 mi e, then 0.5 mi s. Int
corridors. **Pets:** Other species. Designated rooms, supervision.
[ASK] [🔌] [✕] [⛅M] [🔌] [🅱] [🖥] [🍴] [🏊] [✕]

▼▼▼▼ Residence Inn by Marriott SH
(203) 634-7770. **$129-$139.** 390 Bee St. I-91, exit 17 northbound, just e on E Main St, then 0.7 mi n. Ext/int corridors.
Pets: Accepted.
[✕] [⛅M] [🔌] [🅱] [🖥] [🏊] [✕]

MILFORD

▼▼▼ Comfort Inn SH
(203) 877-9411. **$70-$79.** 278 Old Gate Ln. I-95, exit 40, just
s. Int corridors. **Pets:** Other species. $10 one-time fee/
room. Service with restrictions, supervision.
[ASK] [🔌] [✕] [🅱] [🖥]

MYSTIC

(AAA) ▼▼▼ AmeriSuites (Mystic/I-95 &
Seaport) SH
(860) 536-9997. **$109-$224.** 224 Greenmanville Ave. I-95,
exit 90, just se. Int corridors. **Pets:** Small. Service with
restrictions, supervision.
[SAVE] [🔌] [✕] [⛅M] [🔌] [🅱] [🖥] [🏊]

AAA ▼▼▼ Residence Inn by Marriott SH
(860) 536-5150. **$129-$359.** 40 Whitehall Ave. I-95, exit 90, just n on SR 27. Int corridors. **Pets:** Other species. $5 daily fee/room, $75 one-time fee/room.
SAVE ⬛ ⊠ 🏷 ⬛ 🖥 ⬅ ⊠

NEW HAVEN

AAA ▼▼▼▼ Omni New Haven Hotel at Yale LH
(203) 772-6664. **$219.** 155 Temple St. Center of downtown. Int corridors. **Pets:** Medium. $50 one-time fee/room. Service with restrictions, supervision.
SAVE ⬛ ⊠ ⬛ 🏷 ⬛ 🖥 🍴

▼▼▼ Residence Inn by Marriott M
(203) 777-5337. **$129-$189.** 3 Long Wharf Dr. I-95, exit 46, 0.6 mi nw. Ext corridors. **Pets:** Accepted.
ASK ⊠ 🏷 ⬛ 🖥 ⬅ ⊠

NEW LONDON

AAA ▼ Red Roof Inn M 🐾
(860) 444-0001. **$52-$96.** 707 Colman St. I-95, exit 82A northbound, 0.8 mi n, just w, then 0.6 mi on Bayonet St; exit 83 southbound, 0.6 mi s. Ext corridors. **Pets:** Large. Service with restrictions, supervision.
SAVE ⊠ 🏷

NEW MILFORD

AAA ▼▼▼ The Homestead Inn BB
(860) 354-4080. **$104-$148.** 5 Elm St. Just e of village green off Main St; center. Ext/int corridors. **Pets:** Other species. $10 daily fee/pet. Designated rooms, service with restrictions, supervision.
SAVE ⬛ ⊠ ⬛

NORTH HAVEN

AAA ▼▼▼ Holiday Inn SH
(203) 239-4225. **$99-$109.** 201 Washington Ave. I-91, exit 12, on US 5. Int corridors. **Pets:** Accepted.
SAVE ⬛ ⊠ ⬛ ⬛ 🖥 🍴 ⬅ ⊠

NORTH STONINGTON

▼▼▼ Antiques and Accommodations BB 🐾
(860) 535-1736. **$99-$229, 14 day notice.** 32 Main St. I-95, exit 92, 2.5 mi nw on SR 2, then 0.3 mi n. Int corridors. **Pets:** Large. $50 deposit/pet. Designated rooms, service with restrictions, crate.
ASK ⬛ ⊠ ⬛ 🖥 📠

AAA ▼▼▼ Cedar Park Inn & Whirlpool Suites M 🐾
(860) 535-7829. **$79-$229.** 85 Norwich Westerly Rd. I-95, exit 92, 1 mi w on SR 2. Ext corridors. **Pets:** $50 deposit/room. Designated rooms, no service, supervision.
SAVE ⬛ ⊠ ⬛ 🏷 ⬛ 🖥

▼▼ The Inn at Lower Farm BB
(860) 535-9075. **$95-$140, 7 day notice.** 119 Mystic Rd. I-95, exit 90, 1.5 mi n on SR 27, 1.4 mi e on SR 184, then 3.4 mi n on SR 201. Int corridors. **Pets:** Medium, dogs only. Designated rooms, supervision.
ASK ⬛ ⊠ 📺 📠

NORWALK

▼▼ Homestead Studio Suites Hotel-Norwalk SH 🐾
(203) 847-6888. **$100-$155.** 400 Main Ave. I-95, exit 15, 3.5 mi n via US 7, just e, then 1 mi s. Int corridors. **Pets:** Medium, other species. $25 daily fee/room. Service with restrictions, crate.
ASK ⬛ ⊠ 🏷 🎾 ⬛ 🖥

OLD LYME

AAA ▼▼▼ Old Lyme Inn CI
(860) 434-2600. **$135-$185, 10 day notice.** 85 Lyme St. I-95, exit 70 northbound, just n on SR 156, then 0.5 mi e on US 1; exit southbound, just n. Int corridors. **Pets:** Other species. Designated rooms, service with restrictions, supervision.
SAVE ⊠ ⬛ 🍴

PUTNAM

AAA ▼▼ King's Inn SH
(860) 928-7961. **$68-$98.** 5 Heritage Rd. I-395, exit 96, just w. Int corridors. **Pets:** Medium. Service with restrictions, supervision.
SAVE ⬛ ⊠ ⬛ 🖥 🍴 ⬅

RIVERTON

▼▼ Old Riverton Inn CI
(860) 379-8678. **$90-$145, 10 day notice.** 436 E River Rd (SR 20). Center. Int corridors. **Pets:** Medium. $20 daily fee/pet. Designated rooms, no service, supervision.
⊠ ⬛ 🍴

SHELTON

AAA ▼▼▼ AmeriSuites (Shelton/Corporate Towers) SH
(203) 925-5900. **$109-$159.** 695 Bridgeport Ave. SR 8, exit 12, 0.3 mi w, then just s. Int corridors. **Pets:** Accepted.
SAVE ⬛ ⊠ ⬛ 🏷 🎾 ⬛ 🖥 ⬅ ⊠

▼▼▼ Homestead Studio Suites Hotel-Shelton SH 🐾
(203) 926-6868. **$100-$109.** 945 Bridgeport Ave. SR 8, exit 11, 0.5 mi w. Int corridors. **Pets:** Medium, other species. $25 daily fee/room. Service with restrictions, crate.
ASK ⬛ ⊠ ⬛ 🎾 ⬛ 🖥

AAA ▼▼▼ Ramada Plaza Hotel SH
(203) 929-1500. **$99-$139.** 780 Bridgeport Ave. SR 8, exit 12, 0.3 mi w. Int corridors. **Pets:** Other species. $25 one-time fee/pet. Service with restrictions, supervision.
SAVE ⬛ ⊠ ⬛ 🖥 🍴 ⬅ ⊠

▼▼▼ Residence Inn by Marriott M
(203) 926-9000. **$129-$169.** 1001 Bridgeport Ave. SR 8, exit 11, 0.3 mi w. Ext corridors. **Pets:** Other species. $200 one-time fee/room. Service with restrictions, crate.
ASK ⬛ ⊠ ⬛ 🖥 ⬅ ⊠

SOUTHBURY

▼▼▼ **Hilton Southbury** SH
(203) 598-7600. **$109-$134.** 1284 Strongtown Rd. I-84, exit 16, just n on SR 188. Int corridors. **Pets:** Other species. Service with restrictions, supervision.

[ASK] [S🔒] [✕] [&M] [🛏] [📺] [🍴] [🏊] [🚫]

STAMFORD

(AAA) ▼▼▼ **Super 8 Motel** SH
(203) 324-8887. **$79-$89.** 32 Grenhart Rd. I-95, exit 6, just n. Int corridors. **Pets:** Large, other species. $20 one-time fee/room. Designated rooms, service with restrictions, supervision.

[SAVE] [S🔒] [✕] [🛏]

STRATFORD

▼▼▼▼ **Staybridge Suites by Holiday Inn** SH
(203) 377-3322. **$139-$169.** 6905 Main St. SR 15, exit 53, just n. Int corridors. **Pets:** Medium. $250 one-time fee/pet. Service with restrictions, supervision.

[ASK] [S🔒] [✕] [&M] [🐾] [🛏] [📺] [🏊] [🚫]

TORRINGTON

(AAA) ▼▼▼ **Days Inn** M
(860) 496-8808. **$90-$253, 3 day notice.** 395 Winsted Rd. SR 8 N, exit 45, just w, then 0.6 mi s. Ext corridors. **Pets:** Large. $15 daily fee/pet. Designated rooms, service with restrictions, supervision.

[SAVE] [S🔒] [✕] [🐾] [🛏] [📺] [🏊]

WATERBURY

▼▼▼ **House on the Hill Bed & Breakfast** BB 🐾
(203) 757-9901. **$150-$200, 7 day notice.** 92 Woodlawn Terrace. I-84, exit 21, 0.6 mi n on Meadow St, then 0.4 mi ne on Pine St. Int corridors. **Pets:** Service with restrictions, supervision.

[✕] [🛏]

WATERFORD

(AAA) ▼▼▼ **Oakdell Motel** M
(860) 442-9446. **$60-$150.** 983 Hartford Rd. I-95, exit 82, 2 mi n on SR 85. Ext/int corridors. **Pets:** Medium.

[SAVE] [🛏] [🏊]

WESTBROOK

▼▼▼ **Beach Plum Inn** M
(860) 399-9345. **$80-$450, 14 day notice.** 1935 Boston Post Rd. I-95, exit 65, 1.5 mi e of jct SR 153 on US 1. Ext corridors. **Pets:** Other species. Designated rooms, service with restrictions, supervision.

[ASK] [✕] [🛏] [📺] [🏊] [🚫]

WILLINGTON

▼▼ **Econo Lodge** SH
(860) 684-1400. **$69-$104.** 327 Ruby Rd. I-84, exit 71, just s. Int corridors. **Pets:** Accepted.

[ASK] [S🔒] [✕] [&M] [🐾] [🐾] [🏊]

DELAWARE

CLAYMONT

AAA ◆◆◆◆ **Holiday Inn Select Wilmington** LH
(302) 792-2700. **$79-$149.** 630 Naamans Rd. I-95, exit 11, just w on SR 92; I-495, exit 6 (Naamans Rd). Int corridors. **Pets:** Other species. $50 one-time fee/room. Service with restrictions, crate.

DEWEY BEACH

AAA ◆◆◆ **Atlantic Oceanside Motel** M ❀
(302) 227-8811. **$35-$199, 7 day notice.** 1700 Hwy 1. Jct SR 1 and McKinley St. Ext corridors. **Pets:** Other species. $5 daily fee/pet. Service with restrictions.

◆◆ **Bellbuoy Motel** M
(302) 227-6000. **Call for rates.** 21 Van Dyke St. SR 1, on oceanside block of Van Dyke St. Ext corridors. **Pets:** Accepted.

AAA ◆◆ **Best Western Gold Leaf Inn** SH
(302) 226-1100. **$69-$289, 3 day notice.** 1400 Hwy 1. Center. Int corridors. **Pets:** Other species. $20 daily fee/pet. Designated rooms, no service, crate.

DOVER

◆◆◆ **Little Creek Inn** BB
(302) 730-1300. **$150-$195.** 2623 N Little Creek Rd. SR 1, exit 98, 1 mi e on SR 8; 2.2 mi e of jct US 13. Int corridors. **Pets:** Large, dogs only. Designated rooms, supervision.

◆◆ **Red Roof Inn Dover** SH
(302) 730-8009. **$70-$250, 30 day notice.** 652 N DuPont Hwy. SR 1, exit 104, 2.7 mi s on US 13. Int corridors. **Pets:** Accepted.

FENWICK ISLAND

◆◆ **Atlantic Coast Inn** M
(302) 539-7673. **$42-$159, 5 day notice.** Lighthouse Rd & Coastal Hwy. Jct SR 1 and 54. Ext corridors. **Pets:** Accepted.

GEORGETOWN

◆◆◆ **Comfort Inn-Georgetown** SH
(302) 854-9400. **$69-$179.** 507 N DuPont Hwy. On US 113, 0.5 mi n of jct SR 404. Int corridors. **Pets:** Accepted.

HARRINGTON

◆◆◆ **AmericInn Lodge & Suites of Harrington** SH ❀
(302) 398-3900. **$77-$107.** 1259 Corn Crib Rd. On US 13, 0.6 mi s of jct SR 14. Int corridors. **Pets:** Dogs only. $20 daily fee/pet. Service with restrictions, supervision.

LEWES

AAA ◆◆◆ **The Inn at Canal Square** SH
(302) 644-3377. **$110-$230, 7 day notice.** 122 Market St. On the canal. Int corridors. **Pets:** Accepted.

AAA ◆◆◆ **Sleep Inn & Suites** SH ❀
(302) 645-6464. **$59-$209.** 1595 Hwy 1. On SR 1, 1.5 mi s. Int corridors. **Pets:** Other species. $15 daily fee/pet. Service with restrictions, supervision.

NEWARK

AAA ◆◆◆ **Best Western Delaware Inn and Conference Center-Wilmington/Newark** SH
(302) 738-3400. **$69-$79.** 260 Chapman Rd. I-95, exit 3 southbound; exit 3A northbound, 0.3 mi e on SR 273 E, then just n. Int corridors. **Pets:** Accepted.

◆◆◆ **Hilton Wilmington/Christiana** LH ❀
(302) 454-1500. **$89-$199.** 100 Continental Dr. I-95, exit 4B, 0.3 mi n on SR 7, exit 166, 0.4 mi w on SR 58 (Churchman's Rd). Int corridors. **Pets:** Medium, other species. Service with restrictions.

◆◆ **Homestead Studio Suites Hotel-Newark/Christiana** SH ❀
(302) 283-0800. **$77-$102.** 333 Continental Dr. I-95, exit 4B, 0.3 mi n on SR 7, exit 166, 0.4 mi w on SR 58 (Churchman's Rd). Int corridors. **Pets:** Medium, other species. $25 daily fee/room. Service with restrictions, crate.

AAA ◆◆◆ **Howard Johnson Inn & Suites–Wilmington/Newark** SH
(302) 368-8521. **$55-$99.** 1119 S College Ave. I-95, exit 1B southbound; exit 1 northbound, 0.3 mi n on SR 896. Int corridors. **Pets:** Accepted.

⚫⚫⚫ ▼▼▼ Quality Inn by Choice Hotels-University M
(302) 368-8715. **$49-$84.** 1120 S College Ave. I-95, exit 1B southbound; exit 1 northbound, 0.3 mi n on SR 896. Ext corridors. **Pets:** Medium, other species. $10 one-time fee/room. Designated rooms, service with restrictions, supervision.

SAVE S🄳 ✕ 🄷 🄿 🄳 ⤶

⚫⚫⚫ ▼▼ Red Roof Inn-Wilmington M
(302) 292-2870. **$54-$64.** 415 Stanton Christiana Rd. I-95, exit 4B, 0.5 mi n on SR 7. Ext corridors. **Pets:** Other species. Service with restrictions, supervision.

SAVE ✕ 🄿

▼▼▼ Residence Inn by Marriott SH
(302) 453-9200. **$129-$179.** 240 Chapman Rd. I-95, exit 3 southbound; exit 3A northbound, 0.3 mi e on SR 273 E, then 0.5 mi s. Ext corridors. **Pets:** Other species. $50 daily fee/room. Service with restrictions.

ASK S🄳 ✕ 🄿 🄳 🄷 🄿 🄳 ⤶ 🄿

▼▼ Sleep Inn-Newark SH
(302) 453-1700. **$59-$169.** 630 S College Ave. I-95, exit 1B southbound; exit 1 northbound, 0.8 mi n on SR 896. Int corridors. **Pets:** Accepted.

ASK S🄳 ✕ 🄿 🄳 🄷 🄿

NEW CASTLE

⚫⚫⚫ ▼▼▼ Quality Inn Skyways M 🐾
(302) 328-6666. **$85-$104.** 147 N DuPont Hwy. I-95, exit 5A, 0.8 mi s on SR 141, exit 1B, 0.5 mi s on US 13, 40 and 301; I-295, exit New Castle Airport/US 13 S, 1.8 mi s on US 13, 40 and 301. Ext/int corridors. **Pets:** Medium. $10 one-time fee/room. Designated rooms, service with restrictions, supervision.

SAVE S🄳 ✕ 🄿 🄳 🄷 🄿 ⤶

▼▼ Rodeway Inn M 🐾
(302) 328-6246. **$65.** 111 S DuPont Hwy. I-295, exit Dover/Shore Points, 2.5 mi s on US 13, 40 and 301. Ext corridors. **Pets:** Other species. $10 daily fee/room. Service with restrictions, supervision.

ASK ✕ 🄷 🄿

REHOBOTH BEACH

▼▼▼ AmericInn Lodge & Suites of Rehoboth Beach SH
(302) 226-0700. **$79-$259.** 329Z Airport Rd. Just w of SR 1, 1.3 mi n of jct with SR 1A. Int corridors. **Pets:** Accepted.

✕ 🄻🄼 🄿 🄳 🄷 🄿 ⤶

▼▼ Atlantic Budget Inn-Downtown M
(302) 227-9446. **$59-$249, 7 day notice.** 154 Rehoboth Ave. At Rehoboth Ave and 2nd St; downtown. Ext corridors. **Pets:** Dogs only. $10 daily fee/pet. No service, supervision.

ASK S🄳 ✕ 🄷 🄿 ⤶

⚫⚫⚫ ▼▼◆ The Breakers Hotel & Suites M
(302) 227-6688. **$55-$299, 3 day notice.** 105 2nd St. Just n of Rehoboth Ave. Ext corridors. **Pets:** Large. $10 daily fee/pet. Designated rooms, service with restrictions, supervision.

SAVE S🄳 ✕ 🄷 🄿 ⤶

⚫⚫⚫ ▼▼▼ Sea-Esta IV M
(302) 227-5882. **$39-$169, 3 day notice.** 3101 Hwy 1. 1 mi s. Ext corridors. **Pets:** Other species. $8 daily fee/pet.

SAVE S🄳 ✕ 🄷 ⤶

WILMINGTON

⚫⚫⚫ ▼▼◆ Best Western Brandywine Valley Inn M
(302) 656-9436. **$99-$139.** 1807 Concord Pike. I-95, exit 8, 1 mi n on US 202. Ext corridors. **Pets:** Small. Designated rooms, service with restrictions, supervision.

SAVE S🄳 ✕ 🄿 🄷 🄿 ⤶

⚫⚫⚫ ▼▼▼ Days Inn Wilmington M 🐾
(302) 478-0300. **$69-$125.** 5209 Concord Pike. I-95, exit 8, 4 mi n on US 202, jct SR 92 (Naamans Rd). Ext corridors. **Pets:** Other species. $10 daily fee/pet. Service with restrictions, crate.

SAVE S🄳 ✕ 🄿 🄷 🄿

⚫⚫⚫ ▼▼▼▼ Wyndham Wilmington LH
(302) 655-0400. **$109-$159.** 700 N King St. King and 7th sts; downtown. Int corridors. **Pets:** Accepted.

SAVE S🄳 ✕ 🄻🄼 🄿 🄿 🄷 🄿 🍴 ⤶

WASHINGTON

(AAA) ☆☆☆ Best Western-New Hampshire Suites Hotel SH
(202) 457-0565. **$179, 3 day notice.** 1121 New Hampshire Ave NW. Just ne of 22nd and L sts NW. Int corridors. **Pets:** Medium, other species. Designated rooms, service with restrictions, crate.
SAVE S X 🗆 🗆 🗆 🗆

(AAA) ☆☆☆ Capitol Hill Suites SH
(202) 543-6000. **$85-$219.** 200 C St SE. 2 blks from Capitol grounds. Int corridors. **Pets:** Accepted.
SAVE S X 🗆 🗆 🗆 🗆

☆☆☆ Doubletree Guest Suites, Washington DC SH
(202) 785-2000. **$109-$279.** 801 New Hampshire Ave NW. Just sw at Washington Circle. Int corridors. **Pets:** Small. $20 daily fee/pet. Service with restrictions, supervision.
X 🗆 🗆 🗆 🗆 🗆 🗆

(AAA) ☆☆☆ ☆☆☆ The Fairmont Washington, DC LH ❀
(202) 429-2400. **$169-$379.** 2401 M St NW. 24th and M sts NW. Int corridors. **Pets:** Large. Service with restrictions.
SAVE S X 🗆 🗆 🗆 🗆 🗆 🗆 🗆

(AAA) ☆☆☆☆ Four Seasons Hotel Washington LH ❀
(202) 342-0444. **$490-$660.** 2800 Pennsylvania Ave NW. Located in Georgetown. Int corridors. **Pets:** Small. Designated rooms, service with restrictions, supervision.
SAVE X 🗆 🗆 🗆 🗆 🗆 🗆

(AAA) ☆☆☆ Hamilton Crowne Plaza Hotel and Resort Washington LH
(202) 682-0111. **$305-$345, 3 day notice.** 1001 14th St NW. 14th and K sts NW. Int corridors. **Pets:** Accepted.
SAVE S X 🗆 🗆 🗆 🗆 🗆

☆☆☆ ☆☆☆ The Hay-Adams SH
(202) 638-6600. **$545-$915.** 1 Lafayette Square NW. 16th and H sts NW, just n of the White House. Int corridors. **Pets:** Accepted.
X 🗆 🗆 🗆 🗆

☆☆☆ ☆☆☆ Henley Park Hotel SH
(202) 638-5200. **$129-$199.** 926 Massachusetts Ave NW. 10th St and Massachusetts Ave NW. Int corridors. **Pets:** Accepted.
ASK S X 🗆 🗆

☆☆☆ ☆☆☆ Hilton Washington LH
(202) 483-3000. **$119-$369.** 1919 Connecticut Ave NW. Just n of DuPont Circle at T St NW. Int corridors. **Pets:** Small, other species. $30 one-time fee/pet. Service with restrictions.
X 🗆 🗆 🗆 🗆 🗆 🗆 🗆

(AAA) ☆☆☆ ☆☆☆ Holiday Inn-Central LH
(202) 483-2000. **$189-$209.** 1501 Rhode Island Ave NW. Just e of Scott Circle. Int corridors. **Pets:** Small, dogs only. $250 deposit/room, $75 one-time fee/room. Service with restrictions, crate.
SAVE S X 🗆 🗆 🗆 🗆 🗆 🗆

(AAA) ☆☆☆ ☆☆☆ Holiday Inn Downtown LH
(202) 737-1200. **$169-$259, 3 day notice.** 1155 14th St NW. Massachusetts Ave, at Thomas Circle NW. Int corridors. **Pets:** Small, other species. $45 one-time fee/pet. Designated rooms, service with restrictions, supervision.
SAVE S X 🗆 🗆 🗆 🗆 🗆 🗆

(AAA) ☆☆☆ ☆☆☆ Hotel Helix SH
(202) 462-9001. **$199-$319.** 1430 Rhode Island Ave NW. Just e of Scott Circle. Int corridors. **Pets:** Accepted.
SAVE S X 🗆 🗆 🗆 🗆 🗆

☆☆☆ ☆☆☆ Hotel Madera SH ❀
(202) 296-7600. **$119-$259.** 1310 New Hampshire Ave NW. Between 20th and N sts NW. Int corridors. **Pets:** Service with restrictions, crate.
ASK S X 🗆 🗆 🗆 🗆 🗆

(AAA) ☆☆☆ ☆☆☆ Hotel Monaco Washington DC LH
(202) 628-7177. **$349-$399.** 700 F St NW. Between 7th and 8th sts NW. Int corridors. **Pets:** Accepted.
SAVE S X 🗆 🗆 🗆 🗆

(AAA) ☆☆☆ ☆☆☆ Hotel Rouge SH ❀
(202) 232-8000. **$109-$229.** 1315 16th St NW. Just n of Scott Circle. Int corridors. **Pets:** Other species. Service with restrictions, supervision.
SAVE S X 🗆 🗆 🗆 🗆 🗆

(AAA) ☆☆☆ Hotel Washington LH
(202) 638-5900. **$195-$275.** 515 15th St NW. 1 blk e of the White House at Pennsylvania Ave and 15th St NW; 2 blks from Metro Center. Int corridors. **Pets:** Accepted.
SAVE S X 🗆 🗆 🗆 🗆

☆☆☆ ☆☆☆ The Jefferson, A Loews Hotel SH ❀
(202) 347-2200. **$179-$369.** 1200 16th St NW. 16th and M sts NW. Int corridors. **Pets:** Other species. Service with restrictions.
ASK S X 🗆 🗆 🗆 🗆 🗆

(AAA) ☆☆☆ Lincoln Suites Downtown SH
(202) 223-4320. **$115-$185.** 1823 L St NW. Between 18th and 19th sts NW. Int corridors. **Pets:** Small. $25 daily fee/pet. Designated rooms, service with restrictions, crate.
SAVE S X 🗆 🗆 🗆 🗆 🗆

(AAA) ☆☆☆ Loews L'Enfant Plaza Hotel LH ❀
(202) 484-1000. **$219-$289.** 480 L'Enfant Plaza SW. I-395, exit L'Enfant Plaza/12th St. Int corridors. **Pets:** Other species.
SAVE X 🗆 🗆 🗆 🗆 🗆 🗆

AAA ▼▼▼ Marriott Wardman Park Hotel LH
(202) 328-2000. **$119-$229.** 2660 Woodley Rd NW. Just w of Connecticut Ave. Int corridors. **Pets:** Small. Service with restrictions, supervision.
SAVE 🐾 ✕ 🛏 🎦 📶 🛎 💻 🍽 🏊 ✕

▼▼▼ The Melrose Hotel Washington LH
(202) 955-6400. **$99-$199.** 2430 Pennsylvania Ave NW. Between 24th and 25th sts NW. Int corridors. **Pets:** Accepted.
ASK 🐾 ✕ 🎦 📶 💻 🍽

▼▼▼ Morrison-Clark Historic Inn and Restaurant SH
(202) 898-1200. **$109-$199.** 1015 L St NW. 11th and L sts NW, just n of Massachusetts Ave. Ext/int corridors. **Pets:** Accepted.
ASK 🐾 ✕ 🍽

▼▼ ▼▼ Omni Shoreham Hotel LH
(202) 234-0700. **$309-$319.** 2500 Calvert St NW. Just w of Connecticut Ave. Int corridors. **Pets:** Small. $50 one-time fee/room. Designated rooms, service with restrictions, crate.
ASK 🐾 ✕ 🎦 📶 🛎 💻 🍽 🏊 ✕

AAA ▼▼ ▼▼ Park Hyatt Washington, D.C. LH
(202) 789-1234. **$195-$370.** 1201 24th St NW. 24th and M sts NW. Int corridors. **Pets:** Accepted.
SAVE ✕ 🛏 🎦 📶 🍽 🏊 ✕

AAA ▼▼ ▼▼ Red Roof Inn Downtown SH
(202) 289-5959. **$89-$144.** 500 H St NW. At 5th and H sts NW. Int corridors. **Pets:** Accepted.
SAVE ✕ 🎦 📶 🛎 💻 🍽

AAA ▼▼ ▼▼ Renaissance Mayflower Hotel LH
(202) 347-3000. **$129-$339.** 1127 Connecticut Ave NW. Just n of K St NW. Int corridors. **Pets:** Accepted.
SAVE 🐾 ✕ 🛏 🎦 🍽

AAA ▼▼ ▼▼ Residence Inn by Marriott-Dupont Circle LH
(202) 466-6800. **$159-$299.** 2120 P St NW. Between 21st and 22nd sts NW, just w of DuPont Circle. Int corridors. **Pets:** Medium. $200 one-time fee/room.
SAVE 🐾 ✕ 📶 🛎 💻 🍽

AAA ▼▼ ▼▼ Residence Inn by Marriott-Washington DC-Vermont Ave LH
(202) 898-1100. **$229.** 1199 Vermont Ave NW. Jct 14th St and Vermont Ave NW, at Thomas Circle. Int corridors. **Pets:** $8 daily fee/pet, $150 one-time fee/room. Service with restrictions.
SAVE 🐾 ✕ 🛏 🎦 📶 🛎 💻

▼▼ ▼▼ Ritz Carlton Georgetown SH ❀
(202) 912-4100. **$271-$428.** 3100 South St. Just s of jct M St and Wisconsin Ave, off Wisconsin, just e. Int corridors. **Pets:** Medium, other species. $30 daily fee/room. Supervision.
ASK ✕ 🎦 📶 🛎 🍽 ✕

AAA ▼▼ ▼▼ The Ritz-Carlton, Washington, DC LH
(202) 835-0500. **$259-$775.** 1150 22nd St NW. At 22nd and M sts NW. Int corridors. **Pets:** Accepted.
SAVE ✕ 🎦 📶 🛎 💻 🍽 🏊 ✕

AAA ▼▼ ▼▼ The River Inn SH
(202) 337-7600. **$109-$159.** 924 25th St NW. Between K and I sts NW. Int corridors. **Pets:** Small. $150 one-time fee/room. Service with restrictions.
SAVE 🐾 ✕ 🎦 🛎 💻 🍽

▼▼ ▼▼ The St. Regis LH
(202) 638-2626. **$245.** 923 16th St NW. Just n of the White House, 16th and K sts. Int corridors. **Pets:** Accepted.
ASK 🐾 ✕ 🎦 📶 🍽

AAA ▼▼ ▼▼ Topaz Hotel SH ❀
(202) 393-3000. **$119-$239.** 1733 N St NW. Just e of Connecticut Ave. Int corridors. **Pets:** Service with restrictions, supervision.
SAVE 🐾 ✕ 🎦 📶 🍽

▼▼ ▼▼ Travelodge Gateway SH
(202) 832-8600. **$95.** 1917 Bladensburg Rd NE. US 50 and Alternate Rt 1; just w of entrance to Baltimore-Washington Pkwy, New York Ave. Ext/int corridors. **Pets:** Large, other species. $75 deposit/room. Service with restrictions, supervision.
ASK 🐾 ✕ 🎦 📶 🛎 💻 🍽 🏊

▼▼ ▼▼ The Washington Court Hotel LH
(202) 628-2100. **$139-$189.** 525 New Jersey Ave NW. 3 blks from Capitol grounds. Int corridors. **Pets:** Accepted.
ASK 🐾 ✕ 🛎 💻 🍽

AAA ▼▼ ▼▼ Washington Suites Georgetown SH ❀
(202) 333-8060. **$140-$175.** 2500 Pennsylvania Ave NW. Jct 25th St NW and Pennsylvania Ave; 2 blks from Foggy Bottom Metro Station. Int corridors. **Pets:** Large, other species. $20 daily fee/pet. Designated rooms, service with restrictions.
SAVE 🐾 ✕ 📶 🎦 🛎 💻

▼▼ ▼▼ The Westin Embassy Row LH ❀
(202) 293-2100. **$99-$229.** 2100 Massachusetts Ave NW. Just w of DuPont Circle; at 21st St. Int corridors. **Pets:** Medium, dogs only. Service with restrictions, supervision.
ASK 🐾 ✕ 🎦 💻 🍽 ✕

▼▼ ▼▼ The Willard InterContinental LH ❀
(202) 628-9100. **$480.** 1401 Pennsylvania Ave NW. Just e of the White House. Int corridors. **Pets:** Medium, other species. Service with restrictions, supervision.
ASK 🐾 ✕ 🛏 📶 🎦 🍽

FLORIDA

CITY INDEX

ALACHUA

Comfort Inn/FL-339 [SH]
(386) 462-2414. **$75.** 15920 NW US Hwy 441. I-75, exit 399, just e. Ext corridors. **Pets:** Small. $10 daily fee/pet. Designated rooms, service with restrictions, supervision.

Days Inn of Alachua [M]
(386) 462-3251. **$55-$125, 3 day notice.** 16100 NW Hwy 441. I-75, exit 399, just w. Ext corridors. **Pets:** Accepted.

Quality Inn Alachua [SH]
(386) 462-2244. **$70-$80.** 15960 NW Hwy 441. I-75, exit 399, just e. Ext corridors. **Pets:** Accepted.

APALACHICOLA

The Gibson Inn [CI]
(850) 653-2191. **$85-$120.** Market St & Ave C. On US 98 at west end of bridge. Int corridors. **Pets:** Accepted.

ARCADIA

Best Western Arcadia Inn [M]
(863) 494-4884. **$50-$105.** 504 S Brevard Ave. 0.6 mi s of SR 70 on US 17. Ext corridors. **Pets:** Other species. $15 one-time fee/room. Service with restrictions, crate.

BOCA RATON

Homestead Studio Suites Hotel-Boca Raton/Commerce [M]
(561) 994-2599. **$58-$119.** 501 NW 77th St. I-95, exit 50, just s on Congress Ave to NW 6th Ave. Ext corridors. **Pets:** Medium, other species. $25 daily fee/room. Service with restrictions, crate.

Radisson Suite Hotel Boca Raton [SH]
(561) 483-3600. **$179-$289.** 7920 Glades Rd. Florida Tpke, exit 75 (SR 808/Glades Rd). Int corridors. **Pets:** Accepted.

Renaissance Boca Raton Hotel [LH]
(561) 368-5252. **$89-$209.** 2000 NW 19th St. I-95, exit 45 (SR 808/Glades Rd), just w to NW 19th St. Int corridors. **Pets:** Very small. $25 daily fee/pet. Designated rooms, service with restrictions, supervision.

Residence Inn-By Marriott-Boca Raton [SH]
(561) 994-3222. **$119-$199.** 525 NW 77th St. I-95, exit 50, just w of Congress Ave. Ext corridors. **Pets:** Accepted.

▼▼▼ **TownePlace Suites by Marriott** SH ❀
(561) 994-7232. **$59-$159.** 5110 NW 8th Ave. I-95, exit 48
(Yamato Rd), just w. Int corridors. **Pets:** Large, other species. $3 daily fee/room, $70 one-time fee/room. Service with
restrictions, crate.
ASK Sᴅ ✕ ᴋᴍ 🍽 🕹 🛋 💻 ➹

BONITA SPRINGS

▼▼▼ **AmericInn Hotel & Suites** SH
(239) 495-9255. **$59-$109.** 28600 Trails Edge Blvd. I-75, exit
116, 0.7 mi s of Bonita Beach Rd on US 41. Int corridors.
Pets: Small, dogs only. $10 daily fee/room. Designated
rooms, supervision.
ASK Sᴅ ✕ ᴋᴍ 🍽 🕹 🛋 💻 ➹

▼▼▼ **Staybridge Suites by Holiday Inn** SH
(239) 949-5913. **$54-$169.** 8900 Brighton Ln. I-75, exit 116,
3.5 mi w on CR 865, 1.4 mi n on US 41, then e on
Highland Woods Blvd. Int corridors. **Pets:** Medium. $100
one-time fee/pet. Service with restrictions, crate.
ASK Sᴅ ✕ ᴋᴍ 🍽 🕹 🛋 💻 ➹

BRADENTON

🆔 ▼▼▼ **Comfort Inn & Suites** SH
(941) 795-4633. **$69-$159, 3 day notice.** 4450 47th St W.
Just s of jct SR 684 (Cortez Rd). Int corridors. **Pets:** Very
small. $10 daily fee/room. Service with restrictions, crate.
SAVE Sᴅ ✕ 🍽 🕹 🛋 💻 ➹

▼▼ **Days Inn Bradenton** M
(941) 746-1141. **$62-$99.** 3506 1st St W. On US 41, just e of
jct US 301. Ext corridors. **Pets:** Medium. $50 deposit/room,
$10 daily fee/room. Designated rooms, service with restric-
tions, crate.
ASK Sᴅ ✕ 🛋 🍽 ➹

🆔 ▼▼▼ **Econo Lodge Airport** M
(941) 758-7199. **$45-$90.** 6727 14th St W. US 41, 2 mi s of
jct SR 70. Ext corridors. **Pets:** $5 daily fee/pet. Designated
rooms, service with restrictions, supervision.
SAVE Sᴅ ✕ 🛋 💻 ➹

BRADENTON BEACH

🆔 ▼▼▼▼ **Tortuga Inn Beach Resort** M
(941) 778-6611. **$109-$329, 14 day notice.** 1325 Gulf Dr N.
On SR 789, 0.3 mi n of jct SR 684. Ext corridors.
Pets: Medium, other species. $25 one-time fee/room. Des-
ignated rooms, service with restrictions, supervision.
SAVE ✕ 🛋 💻 ➹ ✕

🆔 ▼▼▼ **Tradewinds Resort** M
(941) 779-0010. **$99-$318, 14 day notice.** 1603 Gulf Dr N.
On SR 789, 0.5 mi n of jct SR 684. Ext corridors.
Pets: Small. $25 one-time fee/room. Designated rooms,
service with restrictions.
SAVE Sᴅ ✕ 🛋 💻 ➹

BROOKSVILLE

🆔 ▼▼▼▼ **Best Western Brooksville I-75** M ❀
(352) 796-9481. **$64-$99.** 30307 Cortez Blvd. I-75, exit 301,
just w on SR 50/US 98. Ext corridors. **Pets:** Other species.
$25 one-time fee/room. Designated rooms, service with
restrictions, supervision.
SAVE ✕ ᴋᴍ 🕹 🛋 💻 🍽 ➹

▼▼▼ **Days Inn Heritage Inn** M ❀
(352) 796-9486. **$59-$69.** 6320 Windmere Rd. I-75, exit 301,
just e on SR 50/US 98. Ext corridors. **Pets:** $15 one-time
fee/pet. Service with restrictions, crate.
ASK Sᴅ ✕ ᴋᴍ 🍽 🕹 🛋 💻 🍽 ➹

BUSHNELL

🆔 ▼▼▼ **Best Western Guest House Inn** M
(352) 793-5010. **$55-$85.** 2224 W Hwy 48. I-75, exit 314,
just e. Ext corridors. **Pets:** Other species. $20 daily fee/pet.
Service with restrictions, supervision.
SAVE Sᴅ ✕ 🛋 💻 ➹

CAPE CORAL

▼▼▼ **Quality Inn-Nautilus** SH
(239) 542-2121. **$55-$125.** 1538 Cape Coral Pkwy. Jct Del
Prado Blvd. Int corridors. **Pets:** Accepted.
ASK Sᴅ ✕ 🍽 🛋 💻 ➹ ✕

CARRABELLE

▼▼▼ **The Moorings At Carrabelle** SH
(850) 697-2800. **$90-$150.** 1000 US 98. US 98, just e of
bridge. Ext corridors. **Pets:** Other species. $10 daily fee/pet.
Service with restrictions, supervision.
ASK 🛋 💻 ➹ ✕

CEDAR KEY

🆔 ▼▼▼ **Park Place Motel &**
Condominiums M
(352) 543-5737. **$65-$90.** 211 2nd St. At A St. Ext corridors.
Pets: Small, other species. $7 one-time fee/pet. Designated
rooms, service with restrictions, supervision.
SAVE ✕ 🛋 💻

CHARLOTTE HARBOR

▼ **Banana Bay Waterfront Motel** M
(941) 743-4441. **$46-$92.** 23285 Bayshore Rd. Jct US 41.
Ext corridors. **Pets:** Small. $4 daily fee/pet. Service with
restrictions, supervision.
ASK ✕ 🛋 ✕

CHIEFLAND

🆔 ▼▼▼ **Best Western Suwannee Valley**
Inn SH
(352) 493-0663. **$72.** 1125 N Young Blvd. On US 19/98,
just n of jct US 129. Ext corridors. **Pets:** Small. $15 daily
fee/room. Service with restrictions, crate.
SAVE Sᴅ ✕ 🛋 💻 ➹

▼▼▼ **Holiday Inn Express** SH
(352) 493-9400. **$72.** 809 NW 21st Ave. US 19/98, 1.5 mi n
of jct US 129. Ext corridors. **Pets:** Small, other species. $15
daily fee/pet. Designated rooms, service with restrictions,
supervision.
ASK Sᴅ ✕ ᴋᴍ 🍽 🕹 🛋 ➹

CHIPLEY

▼▼ ▼▼ **Super 8 Motel M**
(850) 638-8530. **$45-$75.** 1700 Main St. I-10, exit 120, just n. Ext corridors. **Pets:** Other species. $5 daily fee/pet. Service with restrictions.

A$K S⬛ ⊠ ☎

COCOA

⬤⬤ ▼▼ ▼▼ **Best Western Cocoa Inn SH** ❀
(321) 632-1065. **$59-$89.** 4225 W King St. I-95, exit 201 (SR 520), 0.3 mi e. Ext corridors. **Pets:** $6 daily fee/room. Service with restrictions, crate.

SAVE S⬛ ⊠ ☎ ⌨ ☎ ▣ ⬳

▼▼ ▼▼ **Econo Lodge-Space Center SH**
(321) 632-4561. **$48-$150.** 3220 N Cocoa Blvd. US 1, just n of jct SR 528. Ext corridors. **Pets:** Accepted.

A$K S⬛ ⊠ ☎ ☎ ▣ ⏀ ⬳

⬤⬤ ▼▼ ▼▼ **Ramada Inn Cocoa Beach Area/KSC SH** ❀
(321) 631-1210. **$49-$99.** 900 Friday Rd. I-95, exit 202 (SR 524), just w. Ext corridors. **Pets:** Small. $50 deposit/room, $5 daily fee/pet. Service with restrictions, crate.

SAVE S⬛ ⊠ ☎ ☎ ▣ ⏀ ⬳ ⊠

⬤⬤ ▼▼ ▼▼ **Super 8 Motel Cocoa Beach Area/KSC M** ❀
(321) 631-1212. **$39-$89.** 900A Friday Rd. I-95, exit 202, 0.5 mi sw. Ext corridors. **Pets:** Small. $50 deposit/room, $5 daily fee/pet. Service with restrictions, crate.

SAVE S⬛ ⊠ ☎ ☎ ⬳ ⊠

COCOA BEACH

⬤⬤ ▼▼▼▼ **Best Western Oceanfront Resort SH**
(321) 783-7621. **$79-$209.** 5600 N Atlantic Ave. SR A1A, 0.8 mi n of jct SR 520. Ext/int corridors. **Pets:** Medium. Designated rooms, service with restrictions, supervision.

SAVE S⬛ ⊠ ⬛M ☎ ⌨ ☎ ▣ ⬳ ⊠

⬤⬤ ▼▼▼▼ **Days Inn Cocoa Beach SH**
(321) 784-2550. **$139.** 5500 N Atlantic Ave. SR A1A, 0.8 mi n of jct SR 520. Ext corridors. **Pets:** Medium. Service with restrictions, supervision.

SAVE S⬛ ⊠ ☎ ☎ ▣ ⬳ ⊠

⬤⬤ ▼▼▼▼ **Holiday Inn Cocoa Beach Oceanfront Resort SH**
(321) 783-2271. **$120-$300.** 1300 N Atlantic Ave. SR A1A, 1.8 mi s of jct SR 520. Ext corridors. **Pets:** Medium. $25 daily fee/pet. Service with restrictions, supervision.

SAVE S⬛ ⊠ ⬛M ☎ ⌨ ☎ ▣ ⏀ ⬳ ⊠

▼▼ ▼▼ **South Beach Inn M**
(321) 784-3333. **$70-$130, 10 day notice.** 1701 S Atlantic Ave. SR A1A northbound, 5 mi s of jct SR 520 at Indian Village Tr; 1.5 mi n of Patrick AFB. Ext corridors. **Pets:** Medium. $15 daily fee/pet. No service, supervision.

A$K ☎ ▣

▼▼ ▼▼ **Surf Studio Beach Resort M**
(321) 783-7100. **$70-$175, 7 day notice.** 1801 S Atlantic Ave. SR A1A northbound, 5 mi s of jct SR 520 at Francis St; 1.3 mi n of Partrick AFB. Ext corridors. **Pets:** Medium, other species. $20 daily fee/pet. Service with restrictions, supervision.

☎ ☎ ▣ ⬳ ⊠

CRESCENT BEACH

⬤⬤ ▼▼ ▼▼ **Beacher's Lodge SH**
(904) 471-8849. **$53-$249.** 6970 A1A S. Just s of jct SR 206. Ext corridors. **Pets:** Accepted.

SAVE S⬛ ⊠ ☎ ▣ ⬳

CRESCENT CITY

▼▼ ▼▼ **Lake View Motel M**
(386) 698-1090. **$55-$80.** 1004 N Summit St. 1 mi n on US 17. Ext corridors. **Pets:** Medium, dogs only. $5 daily fee/pet. Designated rooms, service with restrictions, supervision.

⊠ ☎ ▣ ⬳

CRESTVIEW

▼▼ ▼▼ **Holiday Inn SH**
(850) 682-6111. **$69-$89.** 4050 S Ferdon Blvd. I-10, exit 56, 0.5 mi s. Ext corridors. **Pets:** Small, other species. $25 one-time fee/room. Service with restrictions.

A$K S⬛ ⊠ ⌨ ☎ ▣ ⏀ ⬳

▼▼▼▼ ▼▼ **Jameson Inn SH**
(850) 683-1778. **$76-$81.** 151 Cracker Barrel Dr. I-10, exit 56, just s. Int corridors. **Pets:** Small. Service with restrictions, crate.

⊠ ☎ ▣ ⬳

⬤⬤ ▼▼ ▼▼ **Super 8 Motel M**
(850) 682-9649. **$43-$62.** 3925 S Ferdon Blvd. I-10, exit 56, 0.3 mi s. Ext corridors. **Pets:** $5 one-time fee/room. Designated rooms, service with restrictions, crate.

SAVE S⬛ ⊠ ☎

CROSS CITY

⬤⬤ ▼▼ ▼▼ **Carriage Inn M**
(352) 498-0001. **$40-$52.** 280 E Main (US 19/98/27A). 0.5 mi s on US 19, 27A and 98. Ext corridors. **Pets:** Small. $10 daily fee/pet. Service with restrictions, supervision.

SAVE S⬛ ⊠ ⬳

CRYSTAL RIVER

⬤⬤ ▼▼ ▼▼ **Best Western Crystal River Resort SH**
(352) 795-3171. **$82-$120.** 614 NW Hwy 19. On US 19/98, 0.8 mi n of jct SR 44. Ext corridors. **Pets:** Small, other species. $3 daily fee/pet. Service with restrictions, supervision.

SAVE S⬛ ⊠ ☎ ⌨ ☎ ▣ ⬳ ⊠

DAYTONA BEACH

▼▼ ▼▼ **Aruba Inn M**
(386) 253-5643. **$40-$200, 15 day notice.** 1254 N Atlantic Ave. On SR A1A, 1.5 mi n of jct US 92. Ext corridors. **Pets:** Accepted.

A$K S⬛ ☎ ▣ ⬳

Breakers Beach Oceanfront Motel M
(386) 252-0863. **$52-$95, 30 day notice.** 27 S Ocean Ave. Just n of US 92, 1 blk e of SR A1A. Ext corridors. **Pets:** Accepted.
(ASK) (S6) (X) (B) (≈)

Days Inn Speedway M
(386) 255-0541. **$49-$249, 7 day notice.** 2900 W International Speedway Blvd. I-95, exit 261B southbound; exit 261 northbound, just w on US 92. Ext corridors. **Pets:** Medium. $10 daily fee/pet. No service, supervision.
(SAVE) (S6) (X) (B) (¶) (≈)

La Quinta Inn M
(386) 255-7412. **$71-$101.** 2725 W International Speedway Blvd. I-95, exit 261 northbound; exit 261B southbound, just e. Int corridors. **Pets:** Accepted.
(SAVE) (X) (6M) (∅) (¢) (B) (●) (≈)

Ramada Inn Speedway SH
(386) 255-2422. **$83-$249.** 1798 W International Speedway Blvd. I-95, exit 261, 2 mi e on US 92. Ext corridors. **Pets:** Large, other species. $25 one-time fee/room.
(ASK) (S6) (X) (∅) (B) (●) (¶) (≈)

Scottish Inns M
(386) 258-5742. **$39-$195.** 1515 S Ridgewood Ave. I-95, exit 260A, 2.5 mi e on SR 400, just n on US 1. Ext corridors. **Pets:** Very small, dogs only. $8 one-time fee/pet. Designated rooms, service with restrictions, supervision.
(SAVE) (S6) (X) (B) (≈)

DAYTONA BEACH SHORES

Atlantic Ocean Palm Inn M
(386) 761-8450. **$39-$99, 30 day notice.** 3247 S Atlantic Ave. On SR A1A, 5 mi s of jct US 92. Ext corridors. **Pets:** Small, dogs only. $15 one-time fee/pet. Designated rooms, service with restrictions, supervision.
(SAVE) (S6) (X) (B) (●) (≈)

Quality Inn Ocean Palms SH
(386) 255-0476. **$65-$200.** 2323 S Atlantic Ave. On SR A1A, 2.5 mi s of jct US 92. Ext corridors. **Pets:** Other species. $10 daily fee/room. Designated rooms, service with restrictions, crate.
(SAVE) (S6) (X) (6M) (∅) (¢) (B) (●) (≈)

DE FUNIAK SPRINGS

Best Western Crossroads Inn SH
(850) 892-5111. **$59-$99.** 2343 Freeport Rd. I-10, exit 85, just s. Ext/int corridors. **Pets:** Accepted.
(ASK) (S6) (X) (B) (●) (¶) (≈)

Days Inn SH
(850) 892-6115. **$55-$60.** 472 Hugh Adams Rd. I-10, exit 85, just n. Ext corridors. **Pets:** Accepted.
(SAVE) (S6) (X) (B) (≈)

DELAND

Holiday Inn SH
(386) 738-5200. **$69-$129.** 350 E International Speedway Blvd. 0.3 mi ne on US 92 from jct US 17. Int corridors. **Pets:** Small. $10 daily fee/pet. Service with restrictions, crate.
(SAVE) (S6) (X) (∅) (¢) (B) (●) (¶) (≈)

University Inn M
(386) 734-5711. **$59-$175.** 644 N Woodland Blvd. US 17, 0.9 mi n of jct SR 44. Ext corridors. **Pets:** Dogs only. $25 daily fee/room. Designated rooms, service with restrictions, supervision.
(SAVE) (S6) (X) (¢) (B) (●) (≈)

DELRAY BEACH

The Colony Hotel & Cabana Club SH
(561) 276-4123. **$85-$245, 3 day notice.** 525 E Atlantic Ave. On SR 806 at US 1 northbound; center. Int corridors. **Pets:** Accepted.
(SAVE) (X) (∅) (¢) (B) (≈)

Residence Inn Delray Beach SH
(561) 276-7441. **$109-$349.** 1111 E Atlantic Ave. I-95, exit 52, 1.7 mi e. Int corridors. **Pets:** Accepted.
(ASK) (S6) (X) (6M) (∅) (¢) (B) (●) (≈) (✗)

ELKTON

Comfort Inn St. Augustine SH
(904) 829-3435. **$54-$189, 5 day notice.** 2625 SR 207. I-95, exit 311, just w. Ext corridors. **Pets:** Medium, other species. $15 one-time fee/room. Designated rooms, service with restrictions, supervision.
(SAVE) (S6) (X) (B) (●) (≈)

ELLENTON

Ramada Limited-Ellenton M
(941) 729-8505. **$70-$110, 7 day notice.** 5218 17th St E. I-75, exit 224, 0.3 mi s on US 301, just w on 51st Ave E, then just n. Ext corridors. **Pets:** Large, other species. $10 one-time fee/room. Service with restrictions, crate.
(ASK) (S6) (X) (B) (●) (≈)

Sleep Inn & Suites M
(941) 721-4933. **$70-$135.** 5605 18th St E. I-75, exit 224, just n on US 301, just e on 19th St E, then 0.3 mi sw. Int corridors. **Pets:** Accepted.
(ASK) (S6) (X) (6M) (¢) (B) (●) (≈)

FLAGLER BEACH

Beach Front Motel M
(386) 439-0089. **$45-$68, 3 day notice.** 1544 S A1A. On SR A1A, 1 mi s of SR 100. Ext corridors. **Pets:** Medium, dogs only. $15 one-time fee/pet. Service with restrictions, supervision.
(SAVE) (S6) (X) (B) (●)

Topaz Motel SH
(386) 439-3301. **$55-$175, 14 day notice.** 1224 S Oceanshore Blvd. On SR A1A, 0.5 mi s of SR 100. Ext/int corridors. **Pets:** Accepted.
(SAVE) (X) (B) (●) (≈)

FLORAL CITY

Moonrise Resort CA
(352) 726-2553. **$60-$85 (no credit cards), 14 day notice.** 8801 E Moonrise Ln, Lot 18. Just e on CR 48, 1.5 mi n on Old Floral City Rd. Ext corridors. **Pets:** Medium, other species. $20 daily fee/pet. No service.
(B) (●) (✗) (✓)

THE FLORIDA KEYS AREA

ISLAMORADA

⚑⚑⚑ ▼▼ Sands of Islamorada M
(305) 664-2791. **$99-$260, 3 day notice.** 80051 Overseas
Hwy. US 1 at MM 80. Ext corridors. **Pets:** Accepted.

KEY LARGO

**⚑⚑⚑ ▼▼▼ Howard Johnson Resort Key
Largo SH**
(305) 451-1400. **$115-$179.** 92000 Overseas Hwy. US 1 at
MM 102 (Bayside). Int corridors. **Pets:** Other species. $10
daily fee/room. Designated rooms, service with restrictions,
supervision.

▼▼▼▼ Marina Del Mar Resort & Marina SH
(305) 451-4107. **$100-$190, 3 day notice.** 527 Caribbean
Dr. US 1 at MM 100. Ext corridors. **Pets:** Accepted.
[A$K] [S☉] [✕] [✐] [▤] [▦] [¶] [➤] [✕]

KEY WEST

**⚑⚑⚑ ▼▼▼ Ambrosia Too At Fleming
St BB ❀**
(305) 296-9838. **$120-$425, 30 day notice.** 622 Fleming St.
Just n of Simonton St. Ext corridors. **Pets:** Other species.
$25 one-time fee/room. Service with restrictions.
[SAVE] [✕] [▤] [▦] [➤]

**▼▼▼▼ Center Court Historic Inn &
Cottages BB ❀**
(305) 296-9292. **$98-$238, 30 day notice.** 915 Center St.
0.5 mi n of jct US 1, between Duval and Simonton sts.
Ext/int corridors. **Pets:** Other species. $10 daily fee/pet.
Designated rooms, service with restrictions.
[✕] [▤] [➤] [✕]

⚑⚑⚑ ▼▼▼▼ Chelsea House BB ❀
(305) 296-2211. **$79-$250, 10 day notice.** 707 Truman Ave.
Corner of Elizabeth St and Truman Ave. Ext/int corridors.
Pets: Other species. $15 daily fee/room. Designated
rooms.
[SAVE] [✕] [▤] [▦] [➤]

**⚑⚑⚑ ▼▼ Courtney's Place Historic Cottages &
Inn CA ❀**
(305) 294-3480. **$75-$300, 21 day notice.** 720 Whitmarsh
Ln. Just e from jct Petronia and Simonton sts. Ext corridors.
Pets: Other species. $25 one-time fee/pet. Designated
rooms, service with restrictions.
[SAVE] [✐] [▤] [▦] [➤]

▼▼▼ The Cuban Club Suites M
(305) 294-5269. **$159-$399, 14 day notice.** 1108 Duval St.
Corner of Duval and Amelia sts. Int corridors.
Pets: Accepted.
[A$K] [S☉] [✕] [▤] [➤]

⚑⚑⚑ ▼▼▼▼ Curry Mansion Inn BB
(305) 294-5349. **$145-$325.** 511 Caroline St. Just n of jct
Duval St. Ext/int corridors. **Pets:** Small. Supervision.
[SAVE] [✕] [▤] [➤]

⚑⚑⚑ ▼▼▼▼ Frances Street Bottle Inn BB
(305) 294-8530. **$89-$189, 14 day notice.** 535 Frances St.
From US 1/Roosevelt Blvd, w on White St, then just s on
Southard St; corner of Frances and Southard sts. Int corridors. **Pets:** Other species. $25 one-time fee/pet. Desig-
nated rooms.
[SAVE] [✕] [▤] [✐]

⚑⚑⚑ ▼▼▼ The Palms Hotel BB
(305) 294-3146. **$95-$195, 14 day notice.** 820 White St.
Just w of Truman Ave. Ext corridors. **Pets:** Medium, other
species. Designated rooms, service with restrictions, supervision.
[SAVE] [S☉] [➤] [✕]

**▼▼/▼ Travelers Palm Inn &
Guesthouses BB ❀**
(305) 294-9560. **$58-$178, 30 day notice.** 915 Center St.
US 1, just n. Ext corridors. **Pets:** Other species. $10 daily
fee/pet. Designated rooms, service with restrictions.
[✕] [▤] [▦] [➤]

MARATHON

**⚑⚑⚑ ▼▼▼ Ramada Marathon Oceanview Florida
Keys SH**
(305) 743-8550. **$59-$159.** 13351 Overseas Hwy. On US 1
at MM 54. Int corridors. **Pets:** Accepted.
[SAVE] [S☉] [✕] [▤] [▦] [➤]

❀ END AREA ❀

FORT LAUDERDALE METROPOLITAN AREA

CORAL SPRINGS

Coral Springs Marriott Hotel Golf Club & Convention Center LH
(954) 753-5598. **$89-$169.** 11775 Heron Bay Blvd. Sawgrass Expwy/SR 869, exit Coral Ridge Dr N, 0.3 mi w on Heron Bay Blvd, then first right. Int corridors. **Pets:** Accepted.

La Quinta Inn SH
(954) 753-9000. **$71-$121.** 3701 University Dr. SR 817, just n of jct Sample Rd (SR 834). Int corridors. **Pets:** Accepted.

Studio 6 #6027 M
(954) 796-0011. **$61-$91.** 5645 University Dr. SR 869 (Sawgrass Expwy), exit 12 (University Dr), just s. Ext corridors. **Pets:** Medium, other species. $10 daily fee/pet. Service with restrictions, supervision.

Wellesley Inn (Coral Springs) SH
(954) 344-2200. **$79-$99.** 3100 N University Dr. SR 817, just s of jct Sample Rd (SR 834). Int corridors. **Pets:** Accepted.

DANIA BEACH

Sheraton Fort Lauderdale Airport Hotel LH
(954) 920-3500. **$89-$159.** 1825 Griffin Rd. I-95, exit 23. Int corridors. **Pets:** Accepted.

DAVIE

Homestead Studio Suites Hotel-Plantation/Davie M ❖
(954) 476-1211. **$59-$105.** 7550 SR 84 E. I-595, exit University Dr/SR 817, 0.3 mi. Ext corridors. **Pets:** Medium, other species. $25 daily fee/room. Service with restrictions, crate.

DEERFIELD BEACH

Comfort Suites SH
(954) 570-8887. **$85-$145.** 1040 E Newport Center Dr. I-95, exit 41, jct SW 10th St to SW 12th Ave, then s. Ext corridors. **Pets:** Small. $25 one-time fee/room. Designated rooms, supervision.

La Quinta Inn M
(954) 421-1004. **$59-$109.** 351 W Hillsboro Blvd. I-95, exit 42A, 0.3 mi e on SR 810. Ext corridors. **Pets:** Medium. Service with restrictions, crate.

Ramada Inn Deerfield Beach/Boca Raton SH
(954) 427-2200. **$30-$125.** 1250 W Hillsboro Blvd. I-95, exit 42B, just w on SR 810 (Hillsboro Blvd), then just s on 12th Ave SW. Ext corridors. **Pets:** Accepted.

Ramada Inn Deerfield Beach East M
(954) 421-5000. **$50-$99.** 1401 S Federal Hwy. On US 1, 1.3 mi s of jct SR 810 (Hillsboro Blvd). Ext/int corridors. **Pets:** Medium. $10 daily fee/pet. Designated rooms, service with restrictions, supervision.

Wellesley Inn (Deerfield Beach) SH
(954) 428-0661. **$45-$109.** 100 12th Ave SW. I-95, exit 42A, just w on SR 810 (Hillsboro Blvd), then just s. Int corridors. **Pets:** Medium. $10 daily fee/pet. Designated rooms, service with restrictions, supervision.

FORT LAUDERDALE

AmeriSuites (Fort Lauderdale/17th Street) SH
(954) 763-7670. **$89-$125.** 1851 SE Tenth Ave. SR A1A/17th St Cswy, just s. Int corridors. **Pets:** Small. Service with restrictions, crate.

Birch Patio Motel M
(954) 563-9540. **$35-$105, 14 day notice.** 617 N Birch Rd. 0.4 mi s on SR A1A from jct SR 838 (Sunrise Blvd), w on Aurumar St. Ext corridors. **Pets:** $10 daily fee/pet. Designated rooms, service with restrictions.

The Doubletree Guest Suites/Galleria/Intracoastal Waterway SH
(954) 565-3800. **$75-$198, 3 day notice.** 2670 E Sunrise Blvd. Intracoastal Bridge on SR 838 (Sunrise Blvd), 3 blks w of jct SR A1A. Int corridors. **Pets:** $15 daily fee/pet. Designated rooms, service with restrictions.

Eighteenth Street Inn BB
(954) 467-7841. **$110-$185, 21 day notice.** 712 SE 18th St. I-95, exit 25 (SR 84 E), 1.9 mi e to US 1, 0.4 mi n, then just e. Ext corridors. **Pets:** Accepted.

Fort Lauderdale Marriott North LH
(954) 771-0440. **$89-$199.** 6650 N Andrews Ave. I-95, exit 33B, just nw, 0.5 mi n of jct Cypress Creek Rd. Int corridors. **Pets:** Medium, dogs only. $75 deposit/room, $75 one-time fee/room. Service with restrictions, supervision.

Hampton Inn Fort Lauderdale Airport North SH
(954) 524-9900. **$94-$149.** 2301 SW 12th Ave. I-95, exit 25 (SR 84), 0.7 mi e to SW 12th Ave, just n. Int corridors. **Pets:** Accepted.

(AAA) ▼▼▼▼ La Quinta Inn-Cypress Creek SH
(954) 491-7666. **$66-$126.** 999 W Cypress Creek Rd. I-95, exit 33 southbound, 0.8 mi; exit 33B northbound, at Powerline Rd. Int corridors. **Pets:** Other species. Service with restrictions, supervision.
SAVE ⊠ 🕅 🖬 💻 ➔

▼ Motel 6-55 SH
(954) 760-7999. **$45-$79.** 1801 SR 84. I-95, exit 25 (SR 84 E), just e, then U-turn at light. Int corridors. **Pets:** Accepted.
S🔊 ⊠ 🕅 ➔

(AAA) ▼▼ Red Roof Inn SH
(954) 776-6333. **$51-$85.** 4800 Powerline Rd. I-95, exit 32, just sw of jct Commercial Blvd. Int corridors. **Pets:** Accepted.
SAVE ⊠ 🕅 👍 ➔

(AAA) ▼▼ Royal Saxon Apartments M
(954) 566-7424. **$65-$175, 14 day notice.** 551 Breakers Ave. Just w of SR A1A, 0.5 mi s of SR 838 (Sunrise Blvd), corner of Breakers Ave and Terranar St. Ext corridors. **Pets:** Large, other species. $50 one-time fee/room. Service with restrictions, supervision.
SAVE 🖬 ➔

▼▼▼ TownePlace Suites by Marriott SH
(954) 484-2214. **$49-$139.** 3100 Prospect Rd. I-95, exit 33, 2.7 mi w, then 0.5 mi s on NW 31st St. Int corridors. **Pets:** Other species. $3 daily fee/room, $70 one-time fee/ room. Service with restrictions.
ASK S🔊 ⊠ 🕅 👍 🖬 💻 ➔

▼▼▼ The Westin, Fort Lauderdale LH ❀
(954) 772-1331. **$99-$269.** 400 Corporate Dr. I-95, exit 33 southbound, then e; exit 33A northbound. Int corridors. **Pets:** Medium. $50 one-time fee/room. Service with restrictions, supervision.
ASK S🔊 ⊠ 🕅 👍 🖬 💻 🍽 ➔ ⊠

HOLLYWOOD

(AAA) ▼▼▼ Comfort Inn-Airport/Cruise Port South M
(954) 922-1600. **$69-$139.** 2520 Stirling Rd. I-95, exit 22, just e, 2 mi s of airport. Ext corridors. **Pets:** Accepted.
SAVE S🔊 ⊠ 🖹 🕅 👍 🖬 💻 🍽 ➔

▼▼▼ Days Inn Fort Lauderdale/Hollywood Airport South SH
(954) 923-7300. **$69-$199.** 2601 N 29th Ave. I-95, exit 21, just nw on SR 822 (Sheridan St). Int corridors. **Pets:** Accepted.
ASK S🔊 ⊠ 🕅 🖬 💻 ➔

▼▼▼ La Quinta Inn & Suites SH
(954) 922-2295. **$96-$131.** 2620 N 26th Ave. I-95, exit 21 (Sheridan St/SR 822), just e to Oakwood, then just left. Int corridors. **Pets:** Accepted.
⊠ 🖹 🕅 🖬 💻 ➔ ⊠

LAUDERDALE-BY-THE-SEA

(AAA) ▼▼ The Pier Point Resort SH
(954) 776-5121. **$69-$249.** 4320 El Mar Dr. From Commerical Blvd (SR 870), just s. Ext corridors. **Pets:** Other species.
SAVE S🔊 ⊠ 🖬 💻 ➔

PLANTATION

(AAA) ▼▼▼ Holiday Inn Plantation/Sawgrass SH
(954) 472-5600. **$69-$119.** 1711 N University Dr. SR 817, just s of jct SR 838 (Sunrise Blvd). Ext/int corridors. **Pets:** Accepted.
SAVE S🔊 ⊠ 🖹 🖬 💻 🍽 ➔

▼▼▼ La Quinta Inn & Suites SH
(954) 476-6047. **$79-$99.** 8101 Peters Rd. I-595, exit 5 (University Dr/SR 817 N), just w. Int corridors. **Pets:** Accepted.
⊠ 🖹 🕅 🖬 💻 ➔

▼▼▼ Residence Inn by Marriott-Plantation SH
(954) 723-0300. **$89-$219.** 130 N University Dr. University Dr (SR 817), just n of jct Broward Blvd (SR 842). Int corridors. **Pets:** Medium, other species. $30 daily fee/pet. Service with restrictions.
ASK S🔊 ⊠ 🖹 🕅 🖬 💻 ➔ ⊠

(AAA) ▼▼▼ Sheraton Suites-Plantation LH
(954) 424-3300. **$209-$249.** 311 N University Dr. On SR 817 (University Dr), 0.3 mi n of jct SR 842 (Broward Blvd). Int corridors. **Pets:** Accepted.
SAVE S🔊 ⊠ 🕅 🖹 💻 🍽 ➔ ⊠

(AAA) ▼▼▼ Staybridge Suites by Holiday Inn Ft Lauderdale-Plantation SH
(954) 577-9696. **$109-$179.** 410 N Pine Island Rd. I-595, exit 4, 1.7 mi n. Int corridors. **Pets:** Large, other species. $70 deposit/pet, $30 one-time fee/pet. Service with restrictions.
SAVE S🔊 ⊠ 🖹 🕅 🖹 👍 🖬 💻 ➔ ⊠

(AAA) ▼▼▼ Wellesley Inn (Plantation) SH
(954) 473-8257. **$79-$109.** 7901 SW 6th St. 0.3 mi w of University Dr (SR 817); 0.5 mi sw of jct Broward Blvd (SR 842). Int corridors. **Pets:** Small, other species. Service with restrictions, supervision.
SAVE S🔊 ⊠ 🕅 🕅 👍 🖬 💻 ➔

POMPANO BEACH

(AAA) ▼▼▼ Sea Castle Resort Inn M
(954) 941-2570. **$48-$240.** 730 N Ocean Blvd. SR A1A, 1 mi n of jct SR 814 (Atlantic Blvd). Ext corridors. **Pets:** Accepted.
SAVE ⊠ 🖬 💻 ➔

(AAA) ▼▼▼ Wellesley Inn & Suites (Ft. Lauderdale/Cypress Creek) SH
(954) 783-1050. **$71-$99.** 1401 SW 15th St. I-95, exit 33B (Cypress Creek Rd) to Andrews Ave, just s, left on McNab St. Int corridors. **Pets:** Small. Service with restrictions, supervision.
SAVE S🔊 ⊠ 🕅 👍 🖬 💻 ➔

SUNRISE

AAA ▼▼▼▼ **Baymont Inn & Suites Sunrise at Sawgrass** SH
(954) 846-1200. **$69-$89.** 13651 NW 2nd St. SW 136th Ave, 0.3 mi n of jct I-595, exit 1A and SR 84; 0.5 mi e of jct I-75 and Sawgrass Expwy. Int corridors. **Pets:** Medium, other species. $50 deposit/pet. Designated rooms, service with restrictions, crate.

SAVE S X A G B P A

AAA ▼▼▼▼ **Wellesley Inn & Suites (Sunrise)** SH
(954) 845-9929. **$65-$119.** 13600 NW 2nd St. SW 136th Ave, 0.3 mi n of jct I-595, exit 1A and SR 84; 0.5 mi e of jct I-75 and Sawgrass Expwy. Int corridors. **Pets:** Accepted.

SAVE S X A G B P A

TAMARAC

AAA ▼▼▼ **Baymont Inn & Suites Ft. Lauderdale** SH
(954) 485-7900. **$49-$84.** 3800 W Commercial Blvd. On SR 870 (Commercial Blvd), 0.8 mi e of Florida Tpke, exit 62, just e of jct SR 7 and US 441. Int corridors. **Pets:** Medium. $50 deposit/room. Designated rooms, service with restrictions, supervision.

SAVE S X A B P A

▼▼▼ **Homestead Studio Suites Hotel-Ft Lauderdale/Tamarac** M ❀
(954) 733-6644. **$59-$99.** 3873 W Commercial Blvd. SR 870 (Commercial Blvd), 0.7 mi e of Florida Tpke, exit 62, then just e of jct US 441 and SR 7. Ext corridors. **Pets:** Medium, other species. $25 daily fee/room. Service with restrictions, crate.

ASK S X A G B P

WESTON

AAA ▼▼▼▼ **AmeriSuites (Ft. Lauderdale/Weston)** SH
(954) 659-1555. **$89-$129.** 2201 N Commerce Pkwy. I-75, exit 15, 0.5 mi w on Arvida Pkwy to Weston Rd, n to N Commerce Pkwy, then just e. Int corridors. **Pets:** Small. Service with restrictions, supervision.

SAVE S X &M A G B P A

▼▼▼▼ **Residence Inn by Marriott Weston** SH
(954) 659-8585. **$109-$129.** 2605 Weston Rd. I-75, exit 15 (Arvida Pkwy E) to Weston Rd, then just s. Int corridors. **Pets:** Other species. $10 daily fee/room, $75 one-time fee/room. Service with restrictions.

ASK X B P A X

▼▼▼▼ **Towneplace Suites by Marriott Weston** SH ❀
(954) 659-2234. **$69-$159.** 1545 Three Village Rd. I-75, exit 15, 1 mi e on Arvida Pkwy to Bonaventure Blvd, n to Three Village Rd, then w. Int corridors. **Pets:** Other species. $50 deposit/room, $75 one-time fee/room. Designated rooms, service with restrictions.

ASK S X B P A X

❀   **END METROPOLITAN AREA**   ❀

FORT MYERS

▼▼▼ **Best Western Airport Inn** SH
(239) 561-7000. **$69-$169.** 8955 Daniels Pkwy. I-75, exit 131, 0.6 mi w. Int corridors. **Pets:** Small. $10 daily fee/pet. Designated rooms, service with restrictions.

ASK S X G B P A

AAA ▼▼▼ **Best Western Springs Resort** M ❀
(239) 267-7900. **$67-$134.** 18051 S Tamiami Tr. On US 41 at Constitution Blvd. Ext corridors. **Pets:** Medium. $15 daily fee/pet. Service with restrictions, supervision.

SAVE S X B P ❘❘ A X

▼▼▼▼ **Comfort Inn-Ft. Myers** SH
(239) 694-9200. **Call for rates.** 4171 Boatways Rd. I-75, exit 141, just e on SR 80, then just s on Orange River Blvd. Int corridors. **Pets:** Small. $10 one-time fee/room. Service with restrictions, crate.

X &M A G B P A

AAA ▼▼▼ **Comfort Suites Airport/University** M
(239) 768-0005. **$89-$169.** 13651A Indian Paint Ln. I-75, exit 131, just w. Int corridors. **Pets:** Accepted.

SAVE S X A G B P A

AAA ▼▼▼▼ **Country Inn & Suites By Carlson Sanibel-Gateway** SH
(239) 454-9292. **$79-$199.** 13901 Shell Point Plaza. Jct McGregor Blvd. Int corridors. **Pets:** Medium, other species. $100 one-time fee/room. Service with restrictions, crate.

SAVE S X &M A G B P A

AAA ▼▼▼ **Days Inn Fort Myers South** M
(239) 936-1311. **$39-$139.** 11435 S Cleveland Ave. On US 41 at Beacon Manor Dr. Ext corridors. **Pets:** Accepted.

SAVE S X A B P A

▼▼▼ **Homewood Suites by Hilton-Ft. Myers** SH
(239) 275-6000. **$99-$244.** 5255 Big Pine Way. Just e of jct US 41. Int corridors. **Pets:** Medium. $75 one-time fee/room. Service with restrictions.

ASK S X &M A G B P A X

Howard Johnson-Fort Myers M
(239) 936-3229. **Call for rates.** 4811 Cleveland Ave. On US 41, just s of jct N Airport Rd. Ext corridors. **Pets:** Other species. $25 one-time fee/pet. Designated rooms, service with restrictions, crate.

La Quinta Inn M
(239) 275-3300. **$75-$141.** 4850 S Cleveland Ave. On US 41, just s of jct N Airport Rd. Ext corridors. **Pets:** Accepted.

Quality Hotel Historic District SH
(239) 332-3232. **$57-$155.** 2431 Cleveland Ave. On US 41, just n. Int corridors. **Pets:** Small. $10 daily fee/pet. Designated rooms, service with restrictions, crate.

Radisson Inn Sanibel Gateway SH
(239) 466-1200. **$74-$199.** 20091 Summerlin Rd SW. Jct John Morris Rd. Ext corridors. **Pets:** Accepted.

Residence Inn by Marriott SH
(239) 936-0110. **$99-$164.** 2960 Colonial Blvd. I-75, exit 136, 3.8 mi w on SR 884. **Pets:** Other species. $125 one-time fee/room. No service.

Sleep Inn Airport/University M
(239) 561-1117. **$65-$140.** 13661 Indian Paint Ln. I-75, exit 131, just w. Int corridors. **Pets:** Accepted.

Suburban Extended Stay Hotel SH
(239) 938-0100. **$50-$125.** 10150 Metro Pkwy. I-75, exit 136, 3.5 mi w on Colonial Blvd. Int corridors. **Pets:** Medium. $25 one-time fee/pet. Designated rooms, service with restrictions, supervision.

Ta Ki-Ki Riverfront Inn M
(239) 334-2135. **$46-$105, 7 day notice.** 2631 First St. I-75, exit 141, 4.5 mi w on SR 80. Ext corridors. **Pets:** Accepted.

Wynstar Inn & Suites SH
(239) 791-5000. **$69-$199.** 10150 Daniels Pkwy. I-75, exit 131, just e. Int corridors. **Pets:** Accepted.

FORT MYERS BEACH

Best Western Beach Resort SH
(239) 463-6000. **$109-$239.** 684 Estero Blvd. 0.4 mi n of Matanzas Pass Bridge. Ext corridors. **Pets:** Small. $10 daily fee/pet. Designated rooms, service with restrictions, supervision.

Casa Playa Hotel M ❀
(239) 765-0510. **$90-$300, 30 day notice.** 510 Estero Blvd. 0.5 mi n of Matanzas Pass Bridge via 5th St. Ext corridors. **Pets:** $15 daily fee/pet. Designated rooms, service with restrictions, supervision.

Lighthouse Resort Inn & Suites SH
(239) 463-9392. **$52-$250, 7 day notice.** 1051 5th St. Jct of SR 865 and 5th St; at south end of Matanzas Pass Bridge. Ext corridors. **Pets:** Very small. $20 daily fee/room. Designated rooms, service with restrictions, supervision.

Silver Sands Villas SH
(239) 463-6554. **$75-$197, 21 day notice.** 1207 Estero Blvd. Just s of Matanzas Pass Bridge. Ext corridors. **Pets:** Medium, other species. $50 one-time fee/room. No service.

Sun Deck Resort M
(239) 463-1842. **$49-$189.** 1051 Third St. Just s of Matanzas Pass Bridge. Ext corridors. **Pets:** Accepted.

FORT PIERCE

Days Inn SH
(772) 466-4066. **$42-$89.** 6651 Darter Ct. I-95, exit 129, just e. Ext corridors. **Pets:** Other species. $10 daily fee/pet. Service with restrictions.

Days Inn Hutchinson Island M
(772) 461-8737. **$95.** 1920 Seaway Dr. SR A1A southbound, Hutchinson Island, 2.5 mi e of jct US 1. Ext/int corridors. **Pets:** Medium, other species. $10 daily fee/pet. Designated rooms, service with restrictions, supervision.

Holiday Inn Express SH
(772) 464-5000. **$69-$109.** 7151 Okeechobee Rd. I-95, exit 129, 0.7 mi w on SR 70; Florida Tpke, exit 152. Ext corridors. **Pets:** Small. $25 one-time fee/room. Service with restrictions, supervision.

Royal Inn M
(772) 464-0405. **$50-$90.** 222 Hernando St. 2.5 mi e on SR A1A southbound to Hernando St, just s. Ext corridors. **Pets:** Accepted.

FORT WALTON BEACH

Marina Motel & Marina M
(850) 244-1129. **$47-$99, 3 day notice.** 1345 Miracle Strip Pkwy SE. 1 mi e on US 98. Ext/int corridors. **Pets:** Accepted.

GAINESVILLE

Baymont Inn & Suites-Gainesville SH
(352) 376-0004. **$79-$159.** 3905 SW 43rd St. I-75, exit 384, just w. Int corridors. **Pets:** Medium, other species. $10 daily fee/room. Designated rooms, service with restrictions, supervision.

⚠ ▽▽▽▽ Best Western Gateway Grand SH
(352) 331-3336. **$79-$99.** 4200 NW 97th Blvd. I-75, exit 390, just n of SR 222, just w. Int corridors. **Pets:** Large, other species. $15 one-time fee/pet.
SAVE S✪ ✕ ⅗M ✪ ❶ 💻 ❚❚ ⇆ ✕

▽▽▽▽ Comfort Inn West SH
(352) 264-1771. **$69-$109.** 3440 SW 40th Blvd. I-75, exit 384, just e, then just n. Int corridors. **Pets:** Accepted.
ASK S✪ ✕ ⅗M ✪ ❶ 💻 ⇆

⚠ ▽▽ Econo Lodge University M
(352) 373-7816. **$41-$104.** 2649 SW 13th St. I-75, exit 382, 2 mi e on SR 331, then 0.5 mi n on US 441. Ext corridors. **Pets:** Small. $10 deposit/room. Designated rooms, service with restrictions, supervision.
SAVE S✪ ✕ ❶ 💻 ⇆

▽▽▽▽ La Quinta Inn SH
(352) 332-6466. **$73-$86.** 920 NW 69th Terrace. I-75, exit 387, just e, then just n. Ext corridors. **Pets:** Accepted.
✕ ✪ ❶ 💻 ⇆

⚠ ▽▽▽ Red Roof Inn-Gainesville SH
(352) 336-3311. **$45-$55.** 3500 SW 42nd St. I-75, exit 384, just e. Int corridors. **Pets:** Medium. Service with restrictions, supervision.
SAVE ✕ ⅗M ✪ ✪ ❶ ⇆

HAINES CITY

⚠ ▽▽▽▽ Best Western Lake Hamilton M
(863) 421-6929. **$64-$91.** 605 B Moore Rd. On US 27, just s of jct SR 544, 2 mi s of jct US 17-92. Ext corridors. **Pets:** Other species. $5 daily fee/pet. Designated rooms, service with restrictions, supervision.
SAVE S✪ ✕ ⅗M 💻 ⇆ ✕

⚠ ▽▽▽ Howard Johnson Inn M
(863) 422-8621. **$49-$69.** 33224 Hwy 27 S. On US 27, 1.8 mi s of jct US 17-92. Ext corridors. **Pets:** Accepted.
SAVE S✪ ✕ ✪ ❶ 💻 ❚❚ ⇆

HERNANDO

▽▽▽▽ Best Western Citrus Hills Lodge SH
(352) 527-0015. **$78-$103.** 350 E Norvell Bryant Hwy. CR 486 at Citrus Hills Blvd, 3.3 mi w of US 41. Ext corridors. **Pets:** Small. $10 daily fee/pet. Designated rooms, service with restrictions, supervision.
ASK S✪ ✕ ⅗M ✪ ❶ 💻 ❚❚ ⇆

HOMOSASSA

▽▽ Park Inn SH
(352) 628-4311. **$69-$89.** 4076 S Suncoast Blvd. Just s of jct CR 490 and US 19. Ext corridors. **Pets:** Other species. $15 daily fee/pet. Service with restrictions.
ASK S✪ ✕ ❶ 💻 ⇆

INDIALANTIC

⚠ ▽▽▽ GuestHouse International Inn M
(321) 779-9994. **$79-$525.** 2900 N A1A Hwy. 0.4 mi s of SR 518 (Eau Gallie Cswy). Ext corridors. **Pets:** Accepted.
SAVE ✕ ❶ ❚❚ ⇆

▽▽▽▽ Hilton Melbourne Beach Oceanfront SH
(321) 777-5000. **$130-$210.** 3003 N SR A1A. N SR A1A, 3 mi n of jct US 192. Int corridors. **Pets:** Accepted.
ASK S✪ ✕ ✪ ❶ 💻 ❚❚ ⇆ ✕

▽▽▽ Melbourne Quality Suites Oceanfront Hotel SH
(321) 723-4222. **$119-$209.** 1665 N SR A1A. SR A1A, 1.5 mi n of jct US 192. Ext corridors. **Pets:** Medium. $11 daily fee/pet, $25 one-time fee/room. Designated rooms, service with restrictions, supervision.
ASK S✪ ✕ ✪ ❶ 💻 ❚❚ ⇆ ✕

▽▽▽▽ Oceanfront Cottages CA
(321) 725-8474. **$650-$1190 (weekly), 60 day notice.** 612 Wavecrest Ave. Just s of east end of US 192. Ext corridors. **Pets:** Small. $50 one-time fee/room. No service, supervision.
✕ ❶ 💻 ⇆

INDIAN HARBOUR BEACH

▽▽ Travelodge M
(321) 773-0325. **$59-$79.** 1894 S Patrick Dr. I-95, exit 183, 8 mi e, 1 mi n on SR 513. Int corridors. **Pets:** Small. $25 one-time fee/pet. Service with restrictions, crate.
ASK S✪ ✕ ✪ ✪ ❶ 💻 ⇆ ✕

INVERNESS

▽▽▽▽ Van der Valk Inverness VH
(352) 637-1140. **$1130-$1600 (weekly), 28 day notice.** 4555 E Windmill Dr. 2.7 mi n on US 41. **Pets:** Accepted.
ASK ✕ ❶ 💻 ⇆

JACKSONVILLE METROPOLITAN AREA

BALDWIN

⚠ ▽▽▽ Best Western Baldwin Inn M
(904) 266-9759. **$55-$160.** 1088 US 301 & I-10. I-10, exit 343, just s. Ext corridors. **Pets:** Small, other species. $8 daily fee/pet. Service with restrictions, supervision.
SAVE S✪ ✕ 💻 ⇆

FERNANDINA BEACH

⚠ ▽▽▽▽ Florida House Inn CI
(904) 261-3300. **$89-$199, 7 day notice.** 22 S 3rd St. In Fernandina Beach; just s of Centre St. Ext/int corridors. **Pets:** Accepted.
SAVE S✪ ✕ 💻 ❚❚

JACKSONVILLE

AAA ▼▼▼ **AmeriSuites**
(Jacksonville/Baymeadows) **SH**
(904) 737-4477. **$77-$86.** 8277 Western Way Cir. I-95, exit 341, just e. Int corridors. **Pets:** Accepted.
[SAVE] [S₆] [✕] [🐾] [🖼] [🔒] [💻] [🛏]

▼▼ **Baymont Inn & Suites Jacksonville** **SH**
(904) 268-9999. **$59-$74.** 3199 Hartley Rd. I-295, exit 5A northbound; exit 5 southbound at SR 13. Int corridors. **Pets:** Accepted.
[ASK] [S₆] [✕] [🐾] [🔒] [💻] [🛏]

AAA ▼▼▼ **Best Western Hotel**
JTB/Southpoint [LH] ❋
(904) 281-0900. **$59-$149.** 4660 Salisbury Rd. I-95, exit 344, just e. Int corridors. **Pets:** Small. $10 daily fee/pet. Designated rooms, service with restrictions, supervision.
[SAVE] [S₆] [✕] [🐾] [🔒] [💻] [🍴] [🛏] [✕]

▼▼▼ **Candlewood Suites** **SH**
(904) 296-7785. **$89-$149.** 4990 Belfort Rd. I-95, exit 344, e to Belfort Rd, just s. Int corridors. **Pets:** Accepted.
[ASK] [S₆] [✕] [🅼] [🐾] [🔒] [🔒] [💻]

AAA ▼▼▼ **Hampton Inn Jacksonville**
Airport **M**
(904) 741-4980. **$64-$94.** 1170 Airport Entrance Rd. I-95, exit 363, jct Airport Rd. Ext corridors. **Pets:** Accepted.
[SAVE] [S₆] [✕] [🅼] [🐾] [🔒] [💻] [🛏]

▼▼▼ **Holiday Inn Airport** **SH**
(904) 741-4404. **$129.** 14670 Duval Rd. I-95, exit 363, just w. Ext/int corridors. **Pets:** Medium, other species. Designated rooms, service with restrictions.
[ASK] [S₆] [✕] [🐾] [🔒] [🔒] [💻] [🍴] [🛏] [✕]

▼▼▼ **Holiday Inn Baymeadows** **SH**
(904) 737-1700. **$59-$89.** 9150 Baymeadows Rd. I-95, exit 341, 0.3 mi e. Ext/int corridors. **Pets:** Medium, other species. Service with restrictions, crate.
[ASK] [S₆] [✕] [🐾] [🔒] [💻] [🍴] [🛏]

▼▼▼ **Homestead Studio Suites**
Hotel-Jacksonville/Baymeadows **SH** ❋
(904) 739-1881. **$59-$69.** 8300 Western Way. I-95, exit 341, just e to Western Way, then just s. Int corridors. **Pets:** Medium, other species. $25 daily fee/room. Service with restrictions, crate.
[ASK] [S₆] [✕] [🐾] [🔒] [🔒] [💻]

▼▼▼ **Homestead Studio Suites**
Hotel-Jacksonville/Southeast **SH** ❋
(904) 296-0661. **$89-$99.** 4693 Salisbury Rd S. I-95, exit 344, e on J Turner Butler Blvd, then just s. Int corridors. **Pets:** Medium, other species. $25 daily fee/room. Service with restrictions, crate.
[ASK] [S₆] [✕] [🅼] [🐾] [🔒] [🔒] [💻] [🛏]

▼▼ **Homestead Studio Suites**
Hotel-Jacksonville/Southside **M** ❋
(904) 642-9911. **$64-$74.** 10020 Skinner Lake Dr. I-95, exit 344, 3.5 mi on J Turner Butler Blvd to Gate Pkwy, just n, then just w. Ext corridors. **Pets:** Medium, other species. $25 daily fee/room. Service with restrictions, crate.
[ASK] [S₆] [✕] [🅼] [🔒] [🔒] [💻]

▼▼▼ **Homewood Suites by Hilton** **SH**
(904) 733-9299. **$129-$159.** 8737 Baymeadows Rd. I-95, exit 341, 0.3 mi w. Ext/int corridors. **Pets:** Medium, other species. $75 one-time fee/pet. Service with restrictions, crate.
[ASK] [S₆] [✕] [🔒] [💻] [🛏] [✕]

▼▼▼ **La Quinta Inn & Suites** **SH**
(904) 296-0703. **$77-$112.** 4686 Lenoir Ave S. I-95, exit 344, northwest corner. Int corridors. **Pets:** Service with restrictions.
[✕] [🅼] [🐾] [🔒] [🔒] [💻] [🛏]

▼▼▼ **La Quinta Inn-Baymeadows** **M**
(904) 731-9940. **$68-$88.** 8255 Dix Ellis Tr. I-95, exit 341, southwest corner. Ext corridors. **Pets:** Accepted.
[✕] [🔒] [💻] [🛏]

AAA ▼▼▼ **La Quinta Inn-Jacksonville/Orange**
Park **SH**
(904) 778-9539. **$67-$87.** 8555 Blanding Blvd. I-295, exit 12, just s on SR 21. Ext corridors. **Pets:** Accepted.
[SAVE] [S₆] [✕] [🐾] [🔒] [💻] [🛏]

▼▼▼ **La Quinta Inn-North** **SH**
(904) 751-6960. **$72-$87.** 812 Dunn Ave. I-95, exit 360, southwest corner. Ext corridors. **Pets:** Accepted.
[✕] [🐾] [🔒] [💻] [🛏]

▼▼ **Masters Inn** **SH**
(904) 741-1133. **$45-$59, 7 day notice.** 14585 Duval Rd. I-95, exit 363B, just sw. Int corridors. **Pets:** Accepted.
[ASK] [S₆] [✕] [🔒]

AAA ▼▼ **Masters Inn JTB** **M**
(904) 281-2244. **$51-$69, 7 day notice.** 4940 Mustang Rd. I-95, exit 344, just w, then just n. Int corridors. **Pets:** Small, other species. $5 daily fee/pet. Supervision.
[SAVE] [S₆] [✕] [🅼] [🔒] [🔒]

AAA ▼▼▼ **Ramada Inn Conference**
Center **SH** ❋
(904) 268-8080. **$76-$77.** 3130 Hartley Rd. I-295, exit 5A northbound; exit 5 southbound, just n on SR 13. Ext corridors. **Pets:** Medium. $50 one-time fee/room. Service with restrictions, crate.
[SAVE] [S₆] [✕] [🐾] [🔒] [💻] [🍴] [🛏]

AAA ▼▼▼ **Red Roof Inn** **SH**
(904) 296-1006. **$49-$59.** 6969 Lenoir Ave E. I-95, exit 344, northwest corner. Int corridors. **Pets:** Medium. Service with restrictions, supervision.
[SAVE] [✕] [🐾] [🔒] [🔒] [🛏]

AAA ▼▼▼ **Red Roof Inn-Airport** **M**
(904) 741-4488. **$44-$54.** 14701 Airport Entrance Rd. I-95, exit 363. Ext corridors. **Pets:** Accepted.
[SAVE] [✕] [🛏]

AAA ▼▼▼ **Red Roof Inn-South** **M**
(904) 777-1000. **$43-$55.** 6099 Youngerman Cir. I-295, exit 12. Ext corridors. **Pets:** Medium, other species. Service with restrictions, crate.
[SAVE] [✕] [🛏]

▼▼▼▼ Residence Inn by Marriott [SH]
(904) 733-8088. $69-$159. 8365 Dix Ellis Tr. I-95, exit 341, sw off Baymeadows Rd. Ext corridors. Pets: $75 one-time fee/room. Service with restrictions, supervision.
[ASK] [S★] [✕] [🐾] [💺] [🏋] [💻] [🍴] [✕]

▼▼▼▼ Residence Inn by Marriott [SH]
(904) 996-8900. $124-$169. 10551 Deerwood Park Blvd. I-95, exit 344, 3.5 mi e on J Turner Butler Blvd to Gate Blvd, just s, then just w. Int corridors. Pets: Other species. $150 one-time fee/room. Service with restrictions, crate.
[ASK] [S★] [✕] [CM] [🐾] [💺] [🏋] [💻] [🍴] [✕]

JACKSONVILLE BEACH

AAA ▼▼▼ Surside Inn [M]
(904) 246-1583. $69-$169. 1236 N 1st St. 1.2 mi n of Beach Blvd (US 90). Ext corridors. Pets: Medium. $15 daily fee/pet. Designated rooms, service with restrictions, supervision.
[SAVE] [S★] [✕] [🏋] [💻] [🍴]

ORANGE PARK

▼▼▼▼ Comfort Inn [SH] ❀
(904) 264-3297. $79-$99. 341 Park Ave. I-295, exit 10, just s on US 17. Ext corridors. Pets: Small. $25 one-time fee/pet. Designated rooms, service with restrictions, crate.
[ASK] [S★] [✕] [🏋] [💻] [🍴]

▼▼▼ Days Inn [SH]
(904) 269-8887. $59-$89. 4280 Eldridge Loop. I-295, exit 10, just s on US 17. Int corridors. Pets: Small. $25 one-time fee/pet. No service, supervision.
[ASK] [S★] [✕] [🏋] [💻]

PONTE VEDRA BEACH

AAA ▼▼▼▼ The Sawgrass Marriott Resort & Beach Club [LH]
(904) 285-7777. $119-$229. 1000 PGA Tour Blvd. 2.5 mi s of J Turner Butler Blvd. Int corridors. Pets: $75 deposit/room, $25 one-time fee/pet. Designated rooms, supervision.
[SAVE] [S★] [✕] [🏋] [💻] [🍴] [🍴] [✕]

━━━━━━━━━ ❀ END METROPOLITAN AREA ❀ ━━━━━━━━━

JENSEN BEACH

▼▼▼▼ River Palm Cottages [CA] ❀
(772) 334-0401. $119-$209. 2325 NE Indian River Dr. On SR 707 (NE Indian River Dr), 1.4 mi s of jct SR 732. Ext corridors. Pets: Other species. $10 daily fee/pet. Designated rooms.
[ASK] [✕] [🏋] [💻] [🍴]

JUNO BEACH

▼▼▼▼ Holiday Inn Express-North Palm Beach [SH]
(561) 622-4366. $50-$259. 13950 US Hwy 1. Jct Donald Ross Rd. Ext/int corridors. Pets: Large, other species. $25 one-time fee/room. Service with restrictions, supervision.
[ASK] [S★] [✕] [🐾] [💺] [🏋] [💻] [🍴]

JUPITER

AAA ▼▼▼▼ The Jupiter Beach Resort [LH] ❀
(561) 746-2511. $115-$525, 7 day notice. 5 N A1A. SR A1A, 1 mi se of jct US 1; jct SR 706 (Indiantown Rd). Int corridors. Pets: Small, dogs only. $200 deposit/room, $25 daily fee/pet. Designated rooms, no service, supervision.
[SAVE] [S★] [✕] [💺] [🏋] [💻] [🍴] [🍴] [✕]

AAA ▼▼▼▼ Wellesley Inn (Jupiter) [SH]
(561) 575-7201. $79-$129. 34 Fishermans Wharf. SR 706 (Indiantown Rd); 0.3 mi w of jct US 1. Int corridors. Pets: Accepted.
[SAVE] [S★] [✕] [🐾] [💺] [🏋] [💻] [🍴]

LAKE CITY

AAA ▼▼▼▼ Best Western Inn [SH]
(386) 752-3801. $50-$95. 3598 W US Hwy 90. I-75, exit 427, just w. Ext corridors. Pets: Small. $5 daily fee/pet. Designated rooms, service with restrictions, supervision.
[SAVE] [S★] [✕] [🏋] [💻] [🍴] [✕]

▼▼ Days Inn I-10 [SH]
(386) 758-4224. $50-$75. US 441. I-10, exit 303, just s. Ext corridors. Pets: Accepted.
[ASK] [S★] [✕] [🏋] [💻] [🍴]

AAA ▼▼▼ Driftwood Inn [M]
(386) 755-3545. $33-$60. 2764 W US Hwy 90. I-75, exit 427, 0.7 mi e. Ext corridors. Pets: Small. $5 daily fee/pet. Designated rooms, service with restrictions, supervision.
[SAVE] [✕] [🏋]

AAA ▼▼▼ Econo Lodge South [M]
(386) 755-9311. $42-$49, 7 day notice. I-75, exit 414, at US 441. Ext corridors. Pets: Small. Designated rooms, service with restrictions, supervision.
[SAVE] [S★] [✕] [💻] [🍴]

▼▼▼ Jameson Inn [SH]
(386) 758-8440. $74-$79. 1393 Commerce Blvd. I-75, exit 427, just e, then just s. Int corridors. Pets: Small. Service with restrictions, crate.
[✕] [CM] [🐾] [💺] [🏋] [💻] [🍴]

AAA ▼▼▼ Rodeway Inn [M]
(386) 755-5203. $35-$55. 205 SW Commerce Dr. I-75, exit 427, just e. Ext corridors. Pets: Other species. $5 daily fee/pet. Designated rooms, service with restrictions.
[SAVE] [S★] [✕] [🏋] [💻]

AAA ▼▼▼ Scottish Inns [M]
(386) 755-0230. $39-$49. 2916 W US Hwy 90. I-75, exit 427, 0.6 mi e. Ext corridors. Pets: Medium. $5 daily fee/pet. Designated rooms, service with restrictions, crate.
[SAVE] [S★] [✕] [🏋]

LAKELAND

▲▲▲ ▼▼▼ AmeriSuites (Lakeland Center) SH
(863) 413-1122. **$79-$159.** 525 W Orange St. I-4, exit 32, 3.2 mi s on US 98, just w. Int corridors. **Pets:** Small. Designated rooms, service with restrictions, supervision.
🆂🅰🆅🅴 🆂🅳 ✖ 🦽ᴹ 🐾 🄴 🛏 💻 🏊

▲▲▲ ▼▼▼ Ampak Lakeland Mall Inn SH
(863) 859-0100. **$55-$85, 7 day notice.** 3520 Hwy US 98 N. I-4, exit 32, just nw. Int corridors. **Pets:** Medium, other species. $25 one-time fee/room. Service with restrictions, supervision.
🆂🅰🆅🅴 🆂🅳 ✖ 🦽ᴹ 🐾 🄴 🛏 💻 🏊

▲▲▲ ▼▼▼ Baymont Inn & Suites Lakeland SH
(863) 815-0606. **$49-$99.** 4315 Lakeland Park Dr. I-4, exit 33; jct SR 33, just nw. Int corridors. **Pets:** Medium, other species. $20 one-time fee/room. Designated rooms, service with restrictions, supervision.
🆂🅰🆅🅴 🆂🅳 ✖ 🦽ᴹ 🐾 🄴 🛏 💻 🏊

▼▼▼ Jameson Inn SH
(863) 858-9070. **$76-$81.** 4375 Lakeland Park Dr. I-4, exit 33, just nw. Int corridors. **Pets:** Small. Service with restrictions, crate.
✖ 🦽ᴹ 🐾 🄴 🛏 💻 🏊

▼▼▼ Lakeland Residence Inn by Marriott SH
(863) 680-2323. **$119-$189.** 3701 Harden Blvd. I-4, exit 27 (Polk Pkwy), se on SR 570 (toll) to exit 5, then just n. Int corridors. **Pets:** Accepted.
🄰🆂🄺 🆂🅳 ✖ 🐾 🄴 🛏 💻 🏊 🏋

▲▲▲ ▼▼▼ La Quinta Inn & Suites SH
(863) 859-2866. **$75-$105.** 1024 Crevasse St. I-4, exit 32, just n on US 98. Int corridors. **Pets:** Accepted.
🆂🅰🆅🅴 ✖ 🦽ᴹ 🐾 🄴 🛏 💻 🏊

▼▼▼ Motel 6 #0677 Lakeland FL SH
(863) 682-0643. **$45-$61.** 3120 US Hwy 98 N. I-4, exit 18, just e. Ext corridors. **Pets:** Accepted.
🆂🅳 ✖ 🐾 🄴 🛏 🏊

▲▲▲ ▼▼▼ Super 8 Motel SH ❀
(863) 683-5961. **$54-$95.** 601 E Memorial Blvd. Just e of jct SR 33. Ext/int corridors. **Pets:** Small. $10 daily fee/room. Designated rooms, service with restrictions, crate.
🆂🅰🆅🅴 ✖ 🛏 🏊

▼▼ Travelers Inn M
(863) 688-9221. **$55-$90.** 1817 E Memorial Blvd. 2 mi e of jct US 98 and 92. Ext corridors. **Pets:** Accepted.
🄰🆂🄺 🆂🅳 ✖ 🛏 💻 🏊

LAKE WORTH

▲▲▲ ▼▼▼ Lago Motor Inn M
(561) 585-5246. **$60-$75, 7 day notice.** 714 S Dixie Hwy. I-95, exit 63, 0.7 mi e, then just s on US 1; US 1, just s of jct 6th Ave S. Ext corridors. **Pets:** Medium. $10 deposit/pet. No service, supervision.
🆂🅰🆅🅴 ✖ 🛏 🏊

▲▲▲ ▼▼ Martinique Motor Lodge M
(561) 585-2502. **$55-$95, 7 day notice.** 801 S Dixie Hwy. I-95, exit 63, 0.5 mi e on 6th Ave S, just s. Ext corridors. **Pets:** Medium, dogs only. $10 daily fee/pet. No service, supervision.
🆂🅰🆅🅴 🆂🅳 🛏

▼▼▼ Parador Inn of the Palm Beaches BB
(561) 540-1443. **$75-$150, 14 day notice.** 1000 S Federal Hwy. I-95, exit 63, 1 mi e on 6th Ave S, then 0.5 mi s on SR 5 (Federal Hwy). Ext/int corridors. **Pets:** Medium, other species. Service with restrictions.
🄰🆂🄺 🆂🅳 ✖ 🛏 💻 🆉

LIVE OAK

▲▲▲ ▼▼▼ Econo Lodge SH ❀
(386) 362-7459. **$45-$99.** 6811 N US 129 & I-10. I-10, exit 283, just s. Ext corridors. **Pets:** Other species. $10 one-time fee/room. Service with restrictions.
🆂🅰🆅🅴 🆂🅳 ✖ 🛏 💻 🏊

▲▲▲ ▼▼▼ Suwannee River Best Western Inn SH
(386) 362-6000. **$40-$130, 7 day notice.** 6819 US 129 N. I-10, exit 283, 0.3 mi s. Ext corridors. **Pets:** Accepted.
🆂🅰🆅🅴 ✖ 🛏 💻 🏊

LONGBOAT KEY

▲▲▲ ▼▼▼▼ Hilton Longboat Key Beachfront Resort SH
(941) 383-2451. **$125-$350.** 4711 Gulf of Mexico Dr. On SR 789, 6.2 mi n of New Pass Bridge. Ext/int corridors. **Pets:** Small, dogs only. $100 one-time fee/room. Service with restrictions.
🆂🅰🆅🅴 🆂🅳 ✖ 🐾 🄴 🛏 💻 🍴 🏊 🏋

▼▼▼ Riviera Beach Resort M
(941) 383-2552. **$640-$1195 (weekly), 60 day notice.** 5451 Gulf of Mexico Dr. On SR 789, 5 mi s of jct SR 684 (Cortez Rd). Ext corridors. **Pets:** Accepted.
🄰🆂🄺 🆂🅳 🛏 💻 🏊 🏋

MACCLENNY

▲▲▲ ▼▼▼ Econo Lodge M
(904) 259-3000. **$45-$89.** 151 Woodlawn Rd. I-10, exit 335, just s of jct SR 121. Ext corridors. **Pets:** Other species. $10 one-time fee/room. Service with restrictions.
🆂🅰🆅🅴 🆂🅳 ✖ 🛏 💻 🏊

MARIANNA

▲▲▲ ▼▼▼ Best Western Marianna Inn SH
(850) 526-5666. **$49-$79.** 2086 Hwy 71 S. I-10, exit 142, 0.3 mi s. Ext corridors. **Pets:** Other species. $500 daily fee/pet. Service with restrictions, supervision.
🆂🅰🆅🅴 🆂🅳 ✖ 🛏 💻 🏊

▲▲▲ ▼▼▼ Comfort Inn SH ❀
(850) 526-5600. **$59-$89.** 2175 Hwy 71 S. I-10, exit 142, just n. Ext corridors. **Pets:** Small. $12 daily fee/pet. Designated rooms, service with restrictions, supervision.
🆂🅰🆅🅴 🆂🅳 ✖ 🛏 💻 🏊

MELBOURNE

Baymont Inn & Suites Melbourne SH
(321) 242-9400. **$59-$79.** 7200 George T Edwards Dr. I-95, exit 191 (CR 509), just w. Int corridors. **Pets:** Accepted.
SAVE 🐾 ⊠ 🖊 🖨 🛏 💻 ⊷

Best Western Harborview SH
(321) 724-4422. **$59-$79.** 964 S Harbor City Blvd. 1 mi n of US 192 on US 1, jct Nasa Blvd. Int corridors.
Pets: Accepted.
SAVE 🐾 ⊠ 🖊 🖨 🛏 💻 🍴 ⊷

Crane Creek Inn Waterfront Bed & Breakfast BB
(321) 768-6416. **$100-$175, 14 day notice.** 907 E Melbourne Ave. Jct US 192, just s on Babcock, then 0.9 mi e. Ext/int corridors. **Pets:** Dogs only. $10 daily fee/pet. Supervision.
⊠ 🛏 💻 ⊷ ⊠

Hilton Melbourne Rialto Place SH ❖
(321) 768-0200. **$99-$229.** 200 Rialto Pl. 1 mi w of US 1, 0.8 mi n of US 192. Int corridors. **Pets:** Medium, other species. $50 deposit/room. Service with restrictions.
SAVE 🐾 ⊠ 🖊 🖨 🛏 💻 🍴 ⊷ ⊠

Ramada Inn SH
(321) 723-5320. **$60-$80.** 420 S Harbor City Blvd. US 1, 1.7 mi n of US 192. Ext corridors. **Pets:** Accepted.
ASK 🐾 ⊠ 🖊 🖨 🛏 💻 🍴 ⊷

Super 8 M
(321) 723-4430. **$45-$59.** 1515 S Harbor City Blvd. I-95, exit 180, 7 mi e to US 1 on SR 192, then 0.5 mi n. Int corridors. **Pets:** Other species. $20 deposit/pet. Service with restrictions, supervision.
SAVE 🐾 ⊠ 🖊 🖨

MIAMI-MIAMI BEACH METROPOLITAN AREA

AVENTURA

Residence Inn by Marriott-Aventura Mall SH ❖
(786) 528-1001. **$119-$399.** 19900 W Country Club Dr. 0.5 mi w of SR A1A via SR 856; from US 1 at NE 199th St and Biscayne Blvd. Int corridors. **Pets:** Medium. $20 daily fee/room. Crate.
ASK 🐾 ⊠ 🖨 🛏 💻 ⊷ ⊠

COCONUT GROVE

Mayfair House Hotel SH
(305) 441-0000. **$129-$419.** 3000 Florida Ave. At Florida Ave and Virginia St; center. Ext/int corridors. **Pets:** Accepted.
SAVE 🐾 ⊠ 🖊 🖨 🛏 🍴 ⊠

Residence Inn by Marriott SH
(305) 285-9303. **$99-$149.** 2835 Tigertail Ave. From S Bayshore Dr, w on SW 27th Ave/Cornelia Dr, then s. Ext corridors. **Pets:** Accepted.
ASK 🐾 ⊠ 🖨 🛏 💻 ⊷

The Ritz-Carlton, Coconut Grove LH ❖
(305) 644-4680. **$195-$575.** 3300 SW 27th Ave. Bayshore Dr, just w. Int corridors. **Pets:** Small, dogs only. $500 deposit/pet. Service with restrictions, supervision.
⊠ 🖊 🖨 🛏 🍴 ⊷

CUTLER RIDGE

Baymont Inn & Suites Miami-Cutler Ridge SH
(305) 278-0001. **$59-$89.** 10821 Caribbean Blvd. Florida Tpke, exit 12 (US 1), northwest corner. Int corridors. **Pets:** Medium. $50 deposit/room. Designated rooms, service with restrictions, supervision.
SAVE 🐾 ⊠ 🖊M 🖊 🖨 🛏 💻 ⊷

FLORIDA CITY

Coral Roc Motel M
(305) 246-2888. **$32-$99, 3 day notice.** 1100 N Krome Ave. On SR 997; just w of US 1, 0.5 mi s of Homestead. Ext corridors. **Pets:** Medium. $50 deposit/pet. Designated rooms, service with restrictions, supervision.
SAVE 🐾 ⊠ 🛏 ⊷

Hampton Inn M
(305) 247-8833. **$70-$125.** 124 E Palm Dr. On US 1, 0.3 mi s of Florida Tpke terminus. Ext corridors. **Pets:** Other species.
ASK 🐾 ⊠ 🖊 🛏 💻 ⊷

HIALEAH

Days Inn Miami Lakes/Westland Mall SH
(305) 823-2121. **$79-$89.** 1950 W 49th St. SR 826 (Palmetto Expwy), exit NW 103rd St, just e. Int corridors. **Pets:** Medium. $25 deposit/pet, $10 daily fee/pet. Designated rooms, service with restrictions.
SAVE 🐾 ⊠ 🛏 💻

Ramada Inn-Miami Airport North SH
(305) 823-2000. **$69-$99.** 1950 W 49th St. SR 826 (Palmetto Expwy), exit NW 103rd St, just e. Int corridors. **Pets:** Medium. $25 deposit/pet, $10 daily fee/pet. Designated rooms, service with restrictions.
SAVE 🐾 ⊠ 🖊 🖨 🛏 💻 🍴 ⊷

HOMESTEAD

Days Inn Homestead M
(305) 245-1260. **$65-$139, 3 day notice.** 51 S Homestead Blvd. US 1, 1.2 mi n of Florida Tpke, jct 320 St SW and US 1. Ext corridors. **Pets:** Small. $10 daily fee/pet. Designated rooms, service with restrictions, supervision.
ASK 🐾 ⊠ 🛏 🍴 ⊷

Everglades Motel M
(305) 247-4117. **$32-$95.** 605 S Krome Ave. Just w of US 1; between Lucy and 6th sts; on SR 997, 0.5 mi s of center of town. Ext corridors. **Pets:** Medium. $50 deposit/pet. Designated rooms, service with restrictions, supervision.

KENDALL

AmeriSuites (Miami/Kendall) SH
(305) 279-8688. **$119-$179.** 11520 SW 88th St. Florida Tpke, exit 20 (SW 88th/Kendall Dr), just e on SR 94, 0.3 mi s. Int corridors. **Pets:** Small. Service with restrictions, crate.

Wellesley Inn (Miami/Kendall) SH
(305) 270-0359. **$99-$109.** 11750 Mills Dr. Florida Tpke, exit 20, SW 88th (Kendall Dr), 0.3 mi e on SR 94, 0.3 mi n on SW 117 Ave. Int corridors. **Pets:** Accepted.

MIAMI

AmeriSuites (Miami/Airport West) SH
(305) 718-8292. **$84-$159.** 3655 NW 82nd Ave. 0.4 mi w on NW 36th St from jct SR 826 (Palmetto Expwy). Int corridors. **Pets:** Small. Service with restrictions, supervision.

AmeriSuites (Miami/Blue Lagoon) SH
(305) 265-0144. **$72-$108.** 6700 NW 7th St. SR 836, exit NW 72nd Ave S. Int corridors. **Pets:** Medium. $100 deposit/room. Service with restrictions.

Best Inn-Miami Airport M
(305) 592-5440. **$49-$89.** 7330 NW 36th St. Just e of jct SR 826 (Palmetto Expwy). Int corridors. **Pets:** Accepted.

Candlewood Suites Miami Airport West SH
(305) 591-9099. **$99-$149.** 8855 NW 27th St. SR 826 (Palmetto Expwy), 0.8 mi w on nw 36th St, 0.4 mi s. Int corridors. **Pets:** Accepted.

Hampton Inn-Miami Airport West SH
(305) 513-0777. **$71-$99.** 3620 NW 79th Ave. SR 826 (Palmetto Expwy), exit NW 36th St, just s of jct NW 58th St, exit s. Int corridors. **Pets:** Accepted.

Homestead Studio Suites Hotel-Miami/Airport/Blue Lagoon M ✿
(305) 260-0085. **$59-$89.** 6605 NW 7th St. SR 836 (Dolphin Expwy), exit Milam Dairy Rd S, 0.3 mi e. Ext corridors. **Pets:** Medium, other species. $25 daily fee/room. Service with restrictions, crate.

Homestead Studio Suites Hotel-Miami/Airport/Doral M ✿
(305) 436-1811. **$59-$89.** 8720 NW 33rd St. SR 826 (Palmetto Expwy), 0.8 mi w on NW 36th St, just s. Ext corridors. **Pets:** Medium, other species. $25 daily fee/room. Service with restrictions, crate.

Homewood Suites by Hilton-Miami Blue Lagoon SH
(305) 261-3335. **$116-$188.** 5500 Blue Lagoon Dr. Se of jct SR 836 (Dolphin Expwy), exit Red Rd. Int corridors. **Pets:** Other species. $20 daily fee/pet. Designated rooms, service with restrictions, crate.

La Quinta Inn & Suites SH
(305) 436-0830. **$75-$115.** 8730 NW 27th St. SR 836 (Dolphin Expwy), just n on 87th NW Ave. Int corridors. **Pets:** Accepted.

La Quinta Inn Miami Airport North M
(305) 599-9902. **$74-$104.** 7401 NW 36th St. Just e of jct SR 826 (Palmetto Expwy). Ext corridors. **Pets:** Accepted.

Mandarin Oriental, Miami LH ✿
(305) 913-8288. **$425-$5000.** 500 Brickell Key Dr. US 1 (Brickell Ave), just e on SE 8th St (Brickell Key Dr). Int corridors. **Pets:** Small. $100 deposit/pet, $100 one-time fee/pet. Service with restrictions, supervision.

Miami River Inn BB ✿
(305) 325-0045. **$79-$199, 3 day notice.** 118 SW South River Dr. I-95, exit 1B (SW 7th St), just w to SW 5th Ave, just n to SW 2nd St, then e. Ext/int corridors. **Pets:** $25 daily fee/room.

Quality Inn-South M
(305) 251-2000. **$76-$145.** 14501 S Dixie Hwy (US 1). US 1 at SW 145th St. Ext corridors. **Pets:** Other species. Service with restrictions.

Radisson Kendall Hotel & Suites Miami SH
(305) 279-7700. **$114-$215.** 9100 N Kendall Dr. Florida Tpke, exit 20, 3 mi e; SR 874 (Don Shula) 0.6 mi e; US 1, 1.8 mi w. Int corridors. **Pets:** Accepted.

Residence Inn Miami Airport by Marriott SH
(305) 591-2211. **$127-$165.** 1212 NW 82nd Ave. SR 836 (Dolphin Expwy), exit 87th Ave NW, just n to NW 82nd Ave, then e. Ext corridors. **Pets:** Other species. $6 daily fee/pet, $60 one-time fee/pet. Service with restrictions, crate.

▼▼▼ **Staybridge Suites Miami-Airport West** 🅂🅷 🐾
(305) 500-9100. **$109-$189.** 3265 NW 87th Ave. 0.4 mi s of jct NW 36th St. Int corridors. **Pets:** Medium. $125 one-time fee/pet. Service with restrictions, supervision.

🅰🆂🅺 🆂🔗 ✕ 🕖 🔲 🔳 ⊷ ✕

🅐🅐🅐 ▼▼▼ **Summerfield Suites by Wyndham-Miami Airport** 🅂🅷
(305) 269-1922. **$94-$140.** 5710 Blue Lagoon Dr. 2.5 mi sw of airport entrance; se of jct SR 836 (Dolphin Expwy), exit Red Rd, just w. Int corridors. **Pets:** Small. $150 one-time fee/room. Service with restrictions.

🆂🅰🆅🅴 🆂🔗 ✕ 🔗M 🕖 🔳 🔲 🔳 ⊷ ✕

▼▼▼ **TownePlace Suites by Marriott** 🅂🅷
(305) 718-4144. **$89-$109.** 10505 NW 36th St. Florida Tpke, exit 29, 1.2 mi e to 107th Ave, just s. Int corridors. **Pets:** Other species. $6 daily fee/room, $75 one-time fee/room.

🅰🆂🅺 🆂🔗 ✕ 🕖 🔲 🔳 ⊷

MIAMI BEACH

▼▼▼ **Abbey Hotel** 🅂🅷
(305) 531-0031. **$89-$205.** 300 21st St. Collins Ave, just w. Int corridors. **Pets:** Other species. $5 daily fee/room, $25 one-time fee/room. Service with restrictions, supervision.

🅰🆂🅺 🆂🔗 ✕ 🍽

▼▼▼ **Century Hotel** 🅂🅷
(305) 674-8855. **$75-$135.** 140 Ocean Dr. Just e of SR A1A (Collins Ave), just s of 2nd St. Int corridors. **Pets:** Accepted.

🅰🆂🅺 🆂🔗 🍽

🅐🅐🅐 ▼▼▼ **Comfort Inn Oceanfront Miami Beach** 🅂🅷
(305) 868-1200. **$115-$169.** 6261 Collins Ave. SR A1A/Collins Ave at 63rd St. Int corridors. **Pets:** Accepted.

🆂🅰🆅🅴 🆂🔗 ✕ 🕖 🔲 🔳 ⊷

▼▼ **Days Inn Oceanside** 🅂🅷
(305) 673-1513. **$69-$149.** 4299 Collins Ave. On SR A1A, corner of 43rd St. Int corridors. **Pets:** Accepted.

🅰🆂🅺 🆂🔗 ✕ 🔲 🔳 🍽 ⊷

▼▼▼ **Eden Roc Miami Beach A Renaissance Resort & Spa** 🅻🅷
(305) 531-0000. **$179-$319, 3 day notice.** 4525 Collins Ave. SR A1A (Collins Ave), just n of 41st St. Int corridors. **Pets:** Small, dogs only. $50 deposit/room. Service with restrictions.

🅰🆂🅺 🆂🔗 ✕ 🕖 🔳 🔲 🔳 🔳 🍽 ⊷ ✕

▼▼▼ **Fontainebleau Hilton Resort** 🅻🅷
(305) 538-2000. **$189-$569, 5 day notice.** 4441 Collins Ave. On SR A1A. Int corridors. **Pets:** Accepted.

🅰🆂🅺 ✕ 🕖 🔳 🔲 🔳 🔳 🍽 ⊷ ✕

▼▼▼ **Hotel Ocean** 🅂🅷 🐾
(305) 672-2579. **$179-$600, 3 day notice.** 1230 Ocean Dr. E of jct SR A1A (Collins Ave) and 12th St. Int corridors. **Pets:** Other species. $15 daily fee/pet.

🅰🆂🅺 🆂🔗 ✕ 🔳 🍽

▼▼▼ **The Kent** 🅂🅷
(305) 604-5068. **$130-$145.** 1131 Collins Ave. On SR A1A, at Collins Ave and 11th St. Int corridors. **Pets:** Small. $50 one-time fee/pet. Service with restrictions, crate.

✕ 🕖 🔗

🅐🅐🅐 ▼▼▼ ▼▼▼ **Loews Miami Beach Hotel** 🅻🅷 🐾
(305) 604-1601. **$189-$459, 3 day notice.** 1601 Collins Ave. On SR A1A, at Collins and 16th aves. Int corridors. **Pets:** Large, other species.

🆂🅰🆅🅴 🆂🔗 ✕ 🔗M 🕖 🔗 🔳 🔲 🍽 ⊷ ✕

▼▼▼ **The Marlin** 🅂🅷
(305) 604-5063. **$210-$415, 3 day notice.** 1200 Collins Ave. On SR A1A, at Collins Ave and 12th St. Int corridors. **Pets:** Accepted.

🕖 🔳 🔲 🍽 ✕

▼▼▼ **The Tides Hotel** 🅂🅷 🐾
(305) 604-5070. **$395-$650, 3 day notice.** 1220 Ocean Dr. E of jct SR A1A (Collins Ave) and 12th St. Int corridors. **Pets:** Medium, other species. $100 one-time fee/pet. Service with restrictions, supervision.

🅰🆂🅺 🆂🔗 ✕ 🔗M 🕖 🔗 🔳 🍽 ⊷

MIAMI LAKES

▼▼▼ **TownePlace Suites by Marriott** 🅂🅷
(305) 512-9191. **$79-$109, 3 day notice.** 8079 NW 154th St. SR 826 (Palmetto Expwy), exit 154th St, 0.4 mi w. Int corridors. **Pets:** Accepted.

🅰🆂🅺 🆂🔗 ✕ 🔳 🔲 ⊷

🅐🅐🅐 ▼▼▼ **Wellesley Inn (Miami Lakes)** 🅂🅷
(305) 821-8274. **$89-$99.** 7925 NW 154th St. Jct SR 826 (Palmetto Expwy), just w. Int corridors. **Pets:** Accepted.

🆂🅰🆅🅴 🆂🔗 ✕ 🕖 🔗 🔳 🔲 ⊷

MIAMI SPRINGS

▼▼ **Airways Inn & Suites** 🅼
(305) 883-4700. **$40-$79.** 5001 NW 36th St. Between SR 953 (Le Jeune Rd) and SR 826 (Palmetto Expwy). Ext/int corridors. **Pets:** Accepted.

🅰🆂🅺 🆂🔗 ✕ 🔳 🍽 ⊷

🅐🅐🅐 ▼▼▼ **Baymont Inn & Suites Miami-Airport** 🅂🅷
(305) 871-1777. **$59-$89.** 3501 NW Le Jeune Rd. SR 953 (Le Jeune Rd) at jct SR 112. Int corridors. **Pets:** Accepted.

🆂🅰🆅🅴 🆂🔗 ✕ 🕖 🔳 🔲 ⊷

🅐🅐🅐 ▼▼▼ **Comfort Inn & Suites-Miami International Airport** 🅂🅷
(305) 871-6000. **$99-$209.** 5301 NW 36th St. Between Le Jeune Rd and SR 826 (Palmetto Expwy). Int corridors. **Pets:** Accepted.

🆂🅰🆅🅴 🆂🔗 ✕ 🕖 🔳 🔲 🍽 ⊷ ✕

🅐🅐🅐 ▼▼▼ **Holiday Inn Express Miami International Airport** 🅂🅷
(305) 887-2153. **$109-$159.** 5125 NW 36th St. Between Le Jeune Rd and SR 826 (Palmetto Expwy). Int corridors. **Pets:** Accepted.

🆂🅰🆅🅴 🆂🔗 ✕ 🕖 🔗 🔳

▼▼◆▼ Homestead Studio Suites Hotel-Miami/
Airport/Miami Springs 🆂🅷 ❀
(305) 870-0448. **$94-$109.** 101 Fairway Dr. I-95 to SR 112
W, exit NW 36th St, then w, right on Palmetto Dr, then w;
behind Clarion Hotel; between Le Jeune Rd and SR 826
(Palmetto Expwy). Int corridors. **Pets:** Medium, other species. $25 daily fee/room. Service with restrictions, crate.
🅰🆂🅺 🆂💰 ☒ ⟋ 🔲 💻 ⇌ ⊠

🅰🅰🅰 ▼▼◆▼ Red Roof Inn Miami Airport 🆂🅷
(305) 871-4221. **$62-$85.** 3401 NW Le Jeune Rd. On SR
953 at SR 112; 0.5 mi n of airport entrance. Int corridors.
Pets: Accepted.
🆂🅰🆅🅴 ☒ ⟋ ⇌

🅰🅰🅰 ▼▼◆▼ Sleep Inn-Miami Airport 🆂🅷
(305) 871-7553. **$69-$159.** 105 Fairway Dr. I-95 to SR 112
W, exit NW 36th St, then w, right on Palmetto Dr, then w;
between Le Jeune Rd and SR 826 (Palmetto Expwy). Int
corridors. **Pets:** Medium. $10 daily fee/pet, $25 one-time
fee/pet. Designated rooms, service with restrictions, supervision.
🆂🅰🆅🅴 🆂💰 ☒ ⟋ 🔲 💻 ⇌ ⊠

SUNNY ISLES BEACH

▼▼◆▼ Homewood Suites by Hilton Sunny Isles
Beach 🆂🅷
(305) 932-8900. **$134-$215, 7 day notice.** 18100 N Bay Rd.
I-95, exit 16; SR 856, 0.6 mi s on SR A1A/Collins Ave to
183rd St, just w to N Bay Rd, then just s. Ext/int corridors.
Pets: Accepted.
🅰🆂🅺 🆂💰 ☒ 🅻🅼 ⟋ 🅻 🔲 💻 ⇌

🅰🅰🅰 ▼▼◆▼ Newport Beachside Hotel &
Resort 🅻🅷
(305) 949-1300. **$109-$209.** 16701 Collins Ave. SR A1A, jct
SR 826 and Sunny Isles Blvd. Int corridors. **Pets:** Small.
Service with restrictions, supervision.
🆂🅰🆅🅴 🆂💰 ☒ ⟋ 🔲 💻 🍴 ⇌ ⊠

▼▼◆▼ Trump International Sonesta Beach
Resort 🅻🅷 ❀
(305) 692-5600. **$180-$445, 3 day notice.** 18001 Collins
Ave. On SR A1A, just s of The William Lehman Cswy. Int
corridors. **Pets:** Medium, dogs only. $100 one-time fee/
room. Service with restrictions.
🅰🆂🅺 ☒ 🔲 💻 🍴 ⇌ ⊠

❀ **END METROPOLITAN AREA** ❀

MILTON

▼▼ Comfort Inn 🆂🅷
(850) 623-1511. **$49-$89.** 4962 S Hwy 87. I-10, exit 31, just
s. Int corridors. **Pets:** Accepted.
🅰🆂🅺 🆂💰 ☒ 🔲 💻 ⇌

▼▼ Red Roof Inn & Suites 🆂🅷
(850) 995-6100. **$54-$104, 3 day notice.** 2672 Avalon Blvd.
I-10, exit 22, just s. Int corridors. **Pets:** Large, other species.
Service with restrictions, supervision.
🅰🆂🅺 🆂💰 ☒ 🅻🅼 🅻 🔲 💻 ⇌

MOSSY HEAD

▼▼ Ramada Limited 🆂🅷
(850) 951-9780. **$54-$60.** 326 Green Acres Dr. I-10, exit 70,
just s. Ext corridors. **Pets:** Accepted.
🅰🆂🅺 🆂💰 ☒ 💻 🍴

NAPLES

🅰🅰🅰 ▼▼◆▼ Baymont Inn & Suites Naples 🆂🅷
(239) 352-8400. **$49-$99.** 185 Bedzel Cir. I-75, exit 101, just
w. Int corridors. **Pets:** Medium, other species. Designated
rooms, service with restrictions, supervision.
🆂🅰🆅🅴 🆂💰 ☒ 🅻🅼 ⟋ 🅻 🔲 💻 ⇌

🅰🅰🅰 ▼▼◆▼ The Fairways Resort 🅼
(239) 597-8181. **$50-$175, 3 day notice.** 103 Palm River
Blvd. I-75, exit 111, 2.2 mi w on CR 846. Ext corridors.
Pets: Accepted.
🆂🅰🆅🅴 🆂💰 ☒ 🔲 💻 ⇌ ⊠

🅰🅰🅰 ▼▼◆▼ The Hawthorn Suites of Naples 🆂🅷
(239) 593-1300. **$64-$204.** 3557 Pine Ridge Rd. I-75, exit
107, 0.7 mi w. Int corridors. **Pets:** Medium, other species.
$125 one-time fee/pet. Designated rooms, service with
restrictions, crate.
🆂🅰🆅🅴 🆂💰 ☒ 🅻🅼 ⟋ 🅻 🔲 💻 ⇌ ⊠

🅰🅰🅰 ▼▼◆▼ Holiday Inn 🅼
(239) 263-3434. **$79-$159.** 1100 Tamiami Tr N. I-75, exit
107, 3.8 mi w on CR 896, then 3.8 mi s on Tamiami Tr (US
41). Ext corridors. **Pets:** Medium, other species. $20 daily
fee/room. Designated rooms, service with restrictions,
supervision.
🆂🅰🆅🅴 🆂💰 ☒ 🔲 💻 🍴 ⇌

🅰🅰🅰 ▼▼ Red Roof Inn 🅼
(239) 774-3117. **$49-$87.** 1925 Davis Blvd. I-75, exit 101, 6.5
mi w on SR 84; just e of jct US 41. Ext corridors.
Pets: Accepted.
🆂🅰🆅🅴 ☒ 🅻 🔲 💻 ⇌

▼▼◆▼ Residence Inn by Marriott, Naples 🆂🅷
(239) 659-1300. **$69-$259.** 4075 Tamiami Tr N. I-75, exit
107, 3.8 mi w on CR 896 (Pine Ridge Rd), then 1 mi s on
US 41 (Tamiami Tr). Int corridors. **Pets:** Large, other species. $3 daily fee/room, $85 one-time fee/room. Service with
restrictions, crate.
🅰🆂🅺 🆂💰 ☒ 🅻🅼 ⟋ 🅻 🔲 💻 ⇌ ⊠

▼▼◆▼ Staybridge Suites by Holiday
Inn 🆂🅷 ❀
(239) 643-8002. **$79-$139.** 4805 Tamiami Tr N. I-75, exit
107, 3.8 mi w on Pine Ridge Rd to US 41 (Tamiami Tr),
then just s. Int corridors. **Pets:** Other species. $75 one-time
fee/room. Service with restrictions.
🅰🆂🅺 🆂💰 ☒ 🅻🅼 ⟋ 🅻 🔲 💻 ⇌ ⊠

[AAA] ◆◆ **Wellesley Inn (Naples)** [SH]
(239) 793-4646. **$69-$109.** 1555 5th Ave S. I-75, exit 101, 6.5 mi w on SR 84. Int corridors. **Pets:** Small, other species. Service with restrictions, supervision.
[SAVE] [S/D] ⊠ 🦻 ♿ ▣ 🖥 🏊

NEW SMYRNA BEACH

◆ **Buena Vista Inn and Apartments** [M]
(386) 428-5565. **$65-$85, 14 day notice.** 500 North Cswy. 2 mi e on Business 44, at west end of North Cswy Bridge. Ext corridors. **Pets:** Accepted.
[A$K] [S/D] ⊠ ▣ 🖥 🎾

NICEVILLE

◆◆◆ **Holiday Inn Express** [SH]
(850) 678-9131. **$79-$85.** 106 Bayshore Dr. SR 85, just se on jct SR 20. Int corridors. **Pets:** Small. $25 one-time fee/room. Service with restrictions, crate.
[A$K] [S/D] ⊠ ♿ ▣ 🖥 🏊

NORTH FORT MYERS

[AAA] ◆◆ **Econo Lodge** [M] 🐾
(239) 995-0571. **$48-$135.** 13301 N Cleveland Ave. On US 41, 1.1 mi n of Caloosahatchee Bridge. Ext corridors. **Pets:** $5 daily fee/pet. No service, supervision.
[SAVE] [S/D] ⊠ ▣ 🖥 🏊

OCALA

[AAA] ◆◆ **Budget Host Inn** [M]
(352) 732-6940. **$45-$72.** 4013 NW Bonnie Heath Blvd. I-75, exit 354, 0.3 mi n on US 27. Ext corridors. **Pets:** Medium. $5 daily fee/pet. Service with restrictions, supervision.
[SAVE] [S/D] ⊠ ▣

[AAA] ◆◆ **Comfort Inn** [M]
(352) 629-8850. **$65-$150.** 4040 W Silver Springs Blvd. I-75, exit 352, just w on SR 40. Ext corridors. **Pets:** Medium, other species. $5 daily fee/pet. Designated rooms, service with restrictions.
[SAVE] [S/D] ⊠ ▣ 🖥 🍴 🏊

[AAA] ◆ **Days Inn** [SH]
(352) 629-7041. **$60-$125, 3 day notice.** 3811 NW Bonnie Heath Blvd. I-75, exit 354, just n on US 27. Ext/int corridors. **Pets:** $5 daily fee/pet. Service with restrictions, supervision.
[SAVE] [S/D] ⊠ ▣ 🖥 🏊

◆◆◆ **Hilton Ocala** [LH] 🐾
(352) 854-1400. **$79-$159.** 3600 SW 36th Ave. I-75, exit 350, 0.3 mi e on SR 200. Int corridors. **Pets:** Large, other species. Service with restrictions, supervision.
[A$K] [S/D] ⊠ 🦻 ▣ 🖥 🍴 🏊 🎾

[AAA] ◆◆ **Howard Johnson Inn** [M] 🐾
(352) 629-7021. **$50-$200.** 3951 NW Blitchton Rd. I-75, exit 354, just w. Ext corridors. **Pets:** $10 daily fee/pet. Service with restrictions, crate.
[SAVE] [S/D] ⊠ ▣ 🖥 🍴 🏊

[AAA] ◆◆◆ **La Quinta Inn & Suites** [SH]
(352) 861-1137. **$79-$109.** 3530 SW 36th Ave. I-75, exit 350, just e on SR 200. Int corridors. **Pets:** Accepted.
[SAVE] ⊠ [♿M] 🦻 ♿ ▣ 🖥 🏊

◆◆ **Ocala Plaza** [SH]
(352) 629-0381. **$35-$98.** 3621 W Silver Springs Blvd. I-75, exit 352, just e on SR 40. Ext corridors. **Pets:** Accepted.
[A$K] [S/D] ⊠ ▣ 🖥 🍴 🏊

◆◆◆ **Red Roof Inn & Suites** [SH]
(352) 732-4590. **$59-$129.** 120 NW 40th Ave. I-75, exit 352, just w. Int corridors. **Pets:** Accepted.
[A$K] [S/D] ⊠ ▣ 🖥 🏊

[AAA] ◆◆◆ **Steinbrenner's Ramada Inn & Conference Center** [SH]
(352) 732-3131. **$69-$139.** 3810 NW Bonnie Heath Blvd. I-75, exit 354, just w. Ext corridors. **Pets:** Medium. $25 one-time fee/pet. Service with restrictions, supervision.
[SAVE] [S/D] ⊠ ♿ ▣ 🖥 🍴 🏊 🎾

OKEECHOBEE

[AAA] ◆◆ **Budget Inn** [M] 🐾
(863) 763-3185. **$49-$119.** 201 S Parrott Ave (US 441). US 98 and 441, just s of jct SR 70. Ext corridors. **Pets:** Small, dogs only. $10 daily fee/pet. Designated rooms, service with restrictions, supervision.
[SAVE] [S/D] ⊠ ▣ 🏊

[AAA] ◆ **Economy Inn** [M]
(863) 763-1148. **$45-$89.** 507 N Parrott Ave. US 441, 0.3 mi n of jct SR 70. Ext corridors. **Pets:** $10 daily fee/pet. Service with restrictions, supervision.
[SAVE] [S/D] ⊠ ▣

◆◆◆ **Holiday Inn Express** [SH]
(863) 357-3529. **$89-$175.** 3975 Hwy 441 S. US 98 and 441, 3 mi s of jct SR 70, 0.3 mi n of Lake Okeechobee and jct SR 78. Ext corridors. **Pets:** Accepted.
[A$K] [S/D] ⊠ [♿M] 🦻 ▣ 🏊

OLD TOWN

[AAA] ◆◆ **Suwanee Gables Motel** [M] 🐾
(352) 542-7752. **$75-$85, 14 day notice.** HC 3, Box 208. US 19, 98 and 27A; 2 mi s of jct SR 349. Ext corridors. **Pets:** Small. $8 daily fee/pet. Designated rooms, service with restrictions, supervision.
[SAVE] [S/D] ⊠ ▣ 🏊

ORLANDO METROPOLITAN AREA

ALTAMONTE SPRINGS

▼▼▼▼ Candlewood Suites SH
(407) 767-5757. **$79-$99.** 644 Raymond Ave. I-4, exit 92, just w to Douglas Ave, 0.8 mi n to Central Pkwy, just e. Int corridors. **Pets:** Accepted.

(ASK) (S6) (X) (6M) (7) (6) (B) (IMG) (2)

AAA ▼▼▼▼ Embassy Suites Orlando North SH
(407) 834-2400. **$109-$179.** 225 E Altamonte Dr. I-4, exit 92, 0.3 mi e on SR 436, just n on North Lake Blvd. Int corridors. **Pets:** Accepted.

(SAVE) (S6) (X) (6M) (7) (6) (B) (IMG) (TI) (2) (X2)

▼▼▼▼ Hampton Inn SH
(407) 869-9000. **$86-$96.** 151 N Douglas Ave. I-4, exit 92, just nw. Ext corridors. **Pets:** Medium, other species. $60 one-time fee/room. Service with restrictions.

(ASK) (S6) (X) (6M) (7) (6) (B) (IMG) (2)

AAA ▼▼▼▼ Holiday Inn of Altamonte
Springs SH ❀
(407) 862-4455. **$69-$89.** 230 W SR 436. I-4, exit 92, just sw. Ext/int corridors. **Pets:** Medium. $40 one-time fee/room. Designated rooms, service with restrictions.

(SAVE) (S6) (X) (6M) (7) (6) (B) (IMG) (TI) (2)

▼▼▼▼ Homestead Studio Suites Hotel-Orlando/
Altamonte Springs SH ❀
(407) 332-9300. **$59-$74.** 302 S North Lake Blvd. I-4, exit 92, just e, then 0.3 mi s. Int corridors. **Pets:** Medium, other species. $25 daily fee/room. Service with restrictions, crate.

(ASK) (S6) (X) (6M) (7) (6) (B) (IMG)

▼▼▼▼ La Quinta Inn-Orlando North SH
(407) 788-1411. **$65-$85.** 150 S Westmonte Dr. I-4, exit 92, 0.3 mi w, just s of SR 436. Ext corridors. **Pets:** Other species. Service with restrictions, supervision.

(X) (7) (6) (B) (IMG) (2)

▼▼▼▼ Residence Inn by Marriott SH
(407) 788-7991. **$79-$159.** 270 Douglas Ave. I-4, exit 92, just w on SR 436, then just n. Ext corridors. **Pets:** Medium. $5 daily fee/room, $150 one-time fee/room. Service with restrictions.

(ASK) (S6) (X) (6M) (7) (6) (B) (IMG) (2) (X2)

CLERMONT

▼▼▼▼ Florida Destinations, Inc.-Highlands
Reserve VH
(863) 424-3300. **$65-$195, 14 day notice.** 9230 US Hwy 192. On US 192, 1 mi e of US 27. Ext corridors. **Pets:** Accepted.

(ASK) (B) (IMG) (2) (X2)

DAVENPORT

AAA ▼▼▼▼ Best Western Central
Florida SH ❀
(863) 424-2596. **$59-$119.** 2425 Frontage Rd. I-4, exit 55, just s on US 27. Ext corridors. **Pets:** Service with restrictions.

(SAVE) (S6) (X) (6M) (7) (B) (IMG) (2)

▼▼▼▼ Calabay Parc VH
(407) 846-1722. **$980-$1575 (weekly), 30 day notice.** 3479 W Vine St. I-4, exit 68, 3.5 mi s on SR 535, then 3.8 mi e on US 192. Ext corridors. **Pets:** Accepted.

(ASK) (X) (B) (IMG) (2)

▼▼▼ Castaways Hotel & Resort SH
(863) 424-2811. **$40-$100.** 44089 US 27. I-4, exit 55, just w. Ext corridors. **Pets:** Accepted.

(ASK) (S6) (X) (7) (B) (IMG) (2)

▼▼▼ Esprit-Absolute Premier Vacation
Homes VH
(407) 396-2401. **$105-$235, 30 day notice.** 3160 Vineland Rd, Suite 1. I-4, exit 68, 2.5 mi e on SR 535 (Apopka-Vineland Rd). Ext corridors. **Pets:** Accepted.

(ASK) (S6) (X) (B) (IMG) (2)

▼▼▼▼ Greater Groves-Absolute Premier Vacation
Homes VH
(407) 396-2401. **$105-$235, 30 day notice.** 3160 Vineland Rd, Suite 1. I-4, exit 68, 2.5 mi e on SR 535 (Apopka-Vineland Rd). Ext corridors. **Pets:** Accepted.

(ASK) (S6) (X) (B) (IMG) (2)

▼▼▼▼ Hampton Inn Orlando-S of Walt Disney
Resort SH
(863) 420-9898. **$79-$119.** 5530 US Hwy 27 N. I-4, exit 55, just nw. Int corridors. **Pets:** Accepted.

(ASK) (S6) (X) (7) (6) (B) (IMG) (2)

▼▼▼▼ Southern Dunes-The Florida Store VH
(407) 846-1722. **$901-$1575 (weekly), 30 day notice.** 3479 W Vine St. I-4, exit 68, 3.5 mi s on SR 535, then 3.8 mi e on US 192; in gated community. Ext corridors. **Pets:** Accepted.

(ASK) (X) (B) (IMG) (TI) (2) (X2)

▼▼▼ Super 8 Motel Maingate South SH
(863) 420-8888. **$39-$120.** 44199 Hwy 27. I-4, exit 55, 0.5 mi n. Ext corridors. **Pets:** Other species. $10 daily fee/room. Designated rooms, service with restrictions, crate.

(ASK) (S6) (X) (7) (6) (B) (IMG) (2)

KISSIMMEE

AAA ▼▼▼▼ AmeriSuites (Orlando/Lake Buena
Vista South) SH
(407) 997-1300. **$79-$149.** 4991 Calypso Cay Way. I-4, exit 68, 3 mi s on SR 535, just s of Osceola Pkwy and just n of US 192. Int corridors. **Pets:** Accepted.

(SAVE) (S6) (X) (6M) (7) (6) (B) (IMG) (2) (X2)

AAA ▼▼▼ Best Western-Eastgate SH
(407) 396-0707. **$42-$138.** 5565 W Irlo Bronson Memorial Hwy. I-4, exit 64A, 2 mi e on US 192. Ext corridors. **Pets:** Other species. $15 daily fee/room. Service with restrictions.

(SAVE) (S6) (X) (7) (B) (IMG) (TI) (2) (X2)

▼▼▼▼ **Clear Creek-The Florida Store** VH
(407) 846-1722. **$910-$1435 (weekly), 30 day notice.** 3479 W Vine St. I-4, exit 68, 3.5 mi s on SR 535, then 3.8 mi e on US 192. Ext corridors. **Pets:** Accepted.
ASK ✕ ⊟ ⌨ ⇌

⚫⚫⚫ ▼▼▼ **Country Inn & Suites** SH
(407) 997-1400. **$79-$149, 3 day notice.** 5001 Calypso Cay Way. I-4, exit 68, 3 mi s on SR 535, just s of Osceola Pkwy, just n of US 192. Int corridors. **Pets:** Accepted.
SAVE S⊡ ✕ ⚒M ⌂ ⚿ ⊟ ⌨ ⇌ ⚔

▼ ▼ **Days Inn-Kissimmee** SH
(407) 846-7136. **$29-$189.** 2095 E Irlo Bronson Memorial Hwy. Florida Tpke, exit 244, 0.8 mi w on US 192. Ext corridors. **Pets:** Accepted.
ASK S⊡ ✕ ⊟ ⍟ ⇌

⚫⚫⚫ ▼▼ **Dorsan Suites Health Spa & Resort** SH
(407) 846-1530. **$199-$299.** 201 Simpson Rd. Florida Tpke, exit 244, 0.3 mi w on US 192, just n. Ext corridors. **Pets:** Accepted.
SAVE S⊡ ✕ ⌂ ⊟ ⌨ ⇌

⚫⚫⚫ ▼▼▼ **Econo Lodge Maingate Resort** SH
(407) 396-2000. **$29-$49.** 7514 W Hwy 192. I-4, exit 64B, 2.4 mi w, 1 mi w of Disney main gate. Ext corridors. **Pets:** Medium, dogs only. $25 deposit/room, $25 one-time fee/room. Designated rooms, service with restrictions, crate.
SAVE S⊡ ✕ ⌂ ⊟ ⌨ ⍟ ⇌ ⚔

⚫⚫⚫ ▼▼▼▼ **Fantasy World Club Villas** CO
(407) 396-1808. **$165-$195.** 5005 Kyngs Heath Rd. I-4, exit 64A, 3.5 mi e on US 192 and just n; at MM 11. Ext corridors. **Pets:** Small, dogs only. $30 daily fee/pet. Designated rooms, no service.
SAVE S⊡ ✕ ⊟ ⌨ ⇌ ⚔

⚫⚫⚫ ▼▼▼ **Flamingo Inn** M
(407) 846-1935. **$27-$37, 3 day notice.** 801 E Vine St. 0.3 mi e of jct US 441 and 192 on US 192. Ext corridors. **Pets:** Small. $8 daily fee/pet. Designated rooms.
SAVE ✕ ⌂ ⚿ ⊟ ⇌

▼▼▼▼ **Florida Pines-The Florida Store** VH
(407) 846-1722. **$910-$1295 (weekly), 30 day notice.** 3479 W Vine St. I-4, exit 68, 3.5 mi s on SR 535, then 3.8 mi e on US 192. Ext corridors. **Pets:** Accepted.
ASK ✕ ⊟ ⌨ ⇌

▼▼▼▼ **Hampton Lakes-The Florida Store** VH
(407) 846-1722. **$980-$1575 (weekly), 30 day notice.** 3479 W Vine St. I-4, exit 68, 3.5 mi s on SR 535, then 3.8 mi e on US 192. Ext corridors. **Pets:** Accepted.
ASK ✕ ⊟ ⌨ ⇌

▼▼▼▼ **Holiday Inn Hotel & Suites Main Gate East** SH
(407) 396-4488. **$59-$109.** 5678 W Irlo Bronson Memorial Hwy. I-4, exit 64A; between MM 9 and 10. Ext corridors. **Pets:** Small, dogs only. $15 daily fee/pet. Designated rooms, service with restrictions.
ASK S⊡ ✕ ⚒M ⌂ ⚿ ⊟ ⌨ ⍟ ⇌ ⚔

⚫⚫⚫ ▼▼▼ **Holiday Inn Kissimmee Downtown** SH
(407) 846-2713. **$69-$99, 7 day notice.** 2009 W Vine St. I-4, exit 64A, 8 mi e on US 192; 1.4 mi w of jct US 17-92 and 441. Ext corridors. **Pets:** Medium, other species. $8 daily fee/pet. Service with restrictions, crate.
SAVE S⊡ ✕ ⌂ ⊟ ⌨ ⍟ ⇌ ⚔

⚫⚫⚫ ▼▼▼▼ **Holiday Inn Maingate West** SH
(407) 396-1100. **$49-$109.** 7601 Black Lake Rd. I-4, exit 64B, 2.9 mi w on US 192, then just n; 1 mi w of Disney World main gate access road. Ext corridors. **Pets:** Medium, dogs only. $50 deposit/room, $25 one-time fee/room. Designated rooms, service with restrictions, crate.
SAVE S⊡ ✕ ⌂ ⚿ ⊟ ⌨ ⍟ ⇌ ⚔

⚫⚫⚫ ▼▼▼ **Homewood Suites by Hilton** SH
(407) 396-2229. **$69-$129.** 3100 Parkway Blvd. I-4, exit 64A, 0.3 mi n on US 192, 0.5 mi n. Ext/int corridors. **Pets:** Accepted.
SAVE S⊡ ✕ ⊟ ⌨ ⇌ ⚔

⚫⚫⚫ ▼▼▼ **Howard Johnson Express Inn Parkside** SH 🐾
(407) 396-7100. **$50-$100.** 4311 W Vine St/W Hwy 192. I-4, exit 64A, 3.5 mi w of jct US 17-92 and 441. Ext corridors. **Pets:** Large. $10 daily fee/pet. Supervision.
SAVE S⊡ ✕ ⊟ ⌨ ⇌

▼▼ **Howard Johnson Hotel** SH
(407) 846-4900. **$36-$50.** 2323 E Irlo Bronson Memorial Hwy. US 192 and 441; Florida Tpke, exit 244, just e. Int corridors. **Pets:** Accepted.
ASK S⊡ ✕ ⌂ ⚿ ⊟ ⌨ ⍟ ⇌

⚫⚫⚫ ▼▼ **Howard Johnson Maingate Resort West** M 🐾
(407) 396-4500. **$35-$62.** 8660 W Irlo Bronson Memorial Hwy. I-4, exit 64B, 5.6 mi w on SR 192. Ext corridors. **Pets:** Small. $25 one-time fee/pet. Designated rooms, service with restrictions, supervision.
SAVE S⊡ ✕ ⌂ ⚿ ⊟ ⌨ ⍟ ⇌ ⚔

▼▼◆▼ **Indian Creek-Absolute Premier Vacation Homes** VH
(407) 396-2401. **$105-$235, 30 day notice.** 3160 Vineland Rd, Suite 1. I-4, exit 68, 2.5 mi e on SR 535 (Apopka-Vineland Rd). Ext corridors. **Pets:** Accepted.
ASK S⊡ ✕ ⌂ ⊟ ⊟ ⇌

▼▼◆▼ **Indian Creek-The Florida Store** VH
(407) 846-1722. **$980-$1575 (weekly), 30 day notice.** 3479 W Vine St. I-4, exit 68, 3.5 mi s on SR 535, then 3.8 mi e on US 192. Ext corridors. **Pets:** Accepted.
ASK ✕ ⊟ ⌨ ⇌

▼▼◆▼ **Indian Point-Absolute Premier Vacation Homes** VH
(407) 396-2401. **$105-$235, 30 day notice.** 3160 Vineland Rd, Suite 1. I-4, exit 68, 2.5 mi e on SR 535 (Apopka-Vineland Rd). Ext corridors. **Pets:** Accepted.
ASK S⊡ ✕ ⊟ ⌨ ⇌

▼▼▼ **Indian Ridge Oaks-Absolute Premier Vacation Homes** 🏠
(407) 396-2401. **$105-$235, 30 day notice.** 3160 Vineland Rd, Suite 1. I-4, exit 68, 2.5 mi e on SR 535 (Apopka-Vineland Rd). Ext corridors. **Pets:** Accepted.
ASK 🛇 ✕ 🖅 💲 ⇌

◆◆◆ ▼▼▼▼ **La Quinta Inn & Suites Orlando/Maingate** 🏨
(407) 997-1700. **$79-$149, 3 day notice.** 3484 Polynesian Isle Blvd. I-4, exit 68, s on SR 535, just e. Int corridors. **Pets:** Accepted.
SAVE 🛇 ✕ 🗗 🖅 💲 ⇌ ✕

◆◆◆ ▼▼▼▼ **La Quinta Inn Lakeside** 🏨
(407) 396-2222. **$59-$109.** 7769 W Irlo Bronson Memorial Hwy. I-4, exit 64B westbound on US 192; exit 64A eastbound, 3 mi w; 1.8 mi w of Disney World main gate. Ext corridors. **Pets:** Small. $25 one-time fee/room. Designated rooms, service with restrictions, supervision.
SAVE ✕ 🛇ᴹ 🗗 🖅 🖅 💲 🍽 ⇌ ✕

◆◆◆ ▼ **Magic Castle Inn & Suites Eastgate** 🄼
(407) 396-1212. **$32-$50.** 4559 W Hwy 192. 4.5 mi w of US 17-92 and 441; 6.5 mi e of Disney/Epcot entrance. Ext corridors. **Pets:** Medium. $25 deposit/pet, $6 daily fee/pet. Designated rooms, service with restrictions.
SAVE 🛇 ✕ 🗗 🖅 💲 ⇌

◆◆◆ ▼ **Magic Castle Inn & Suites Maingate** 🏨
(407) 396-2212. **$35-$53.** 5055 W Irlo Bronson Memorial Hwy. I-4, exit 64A, 3.2 mi w on US 192; between MM 10 and 11. Ext corridors. **Pets:** Medium. $25 deposit/pet, $6 daily fee/pet. Designated rooms, service with restrictions.
SAVE 🛇 ✕ 🖅 💲 ⇌

◆◆◆ ▼▼▼ **Masters Inn-Kissimmee** 🄼
(407) 396-4020. **$34-$44, 7 day notice.** 5367 W Irlo Bronson Memorial Hwy. I-4, exit 25, 2.5 mi e on US 192. Ext corridors. **Pets:** Small, other species. $20 one-time fee/pet. Service with restrictions, supervision.
SAVE 🛇 ✕ 🗗 🖅 ⇌

◆◆◆ ▼▼▼ **Masters Inn-Main Gate** 🏨
(407) 396-7743. **$39-$59, 7 day notice.** 2945 Entry Point Blvd. I-4, exit 25, 2.5 mi w on US 192; 1 mi w of Disney World main gate. Ext corridors. **Pets:** Small. $20 one-time fee/pet. Service with restrictions, crate.
SAVE 🛇 ✕ 🗗 🖅 ⇌

▼ **Motel 6-#0436** 🏨
(407) 396-6422. **$35-$50.** 7455 W Irlo Bronson Memorial Hwy. I-4, exit 64B, 1.3 mi w on US 192. Ext corridors. **Pets:** Accepted.
🛇 ✕ 🗗 🖅 ⇌

▼ **Motel 6-#0464** 🄼
(407) 396-6333. **$35-$50.** 5731 W Hwy 192. I-4, exit 64A, 2 mi e on US 192. Ext corridors. **Pets:** Small. Designated rooms, service with restrictions, supervision.
🛇 ✕ 🛇ᴹ 🗗 🖅 🖅 ⇌

◆◆◆ ▼▼▼ **Park Inn & Suites Orlando Maingate East** 🏨
(407) 396-6100. **$49-$89.** 6075 W Irlo Bronson Memorial Hwy. I-4, exit 64A, 1 mi e on US 192; between MM 8 and 9. Ext corridors. **Pets:** Accepted.
SAVE 🛇 ✕ 🗗 🖅 💲 🖅 🍽 ⇌ ✕

◆◆◆ ▼▼▼ **Ramada Inn Resort Eastgate** 🏨 ❀
(407) 396-1111. **$49-$79.** 5150 W Irlo Bronson Memorial Hwy. I-4, exit 64A, 2.8 mi e on US 192. Int corridors. **Pets:** Medium, other species. $25 one-time fee/pet. Service with restrictions, supervision.
SAVE 🛇 ✕ 🗗 🖅 💲 🖅 🍽 ⇌ ✕

◆◆◆ ▼▼▼▼ **Ramada Plaza Hotel and Inn Gateway** 🏨
(407) 396-4400. **$59-$129, 3 day notice.** 7470 W Irlo Bronson Memorial Hwy. I-4, exit 64B, 2.3 mi w on US 192; 1 mi w of Disney World main gate. Ext/int corridors. **Pets:** Accepted.
SAVE 🛇 ✕ 🗗 🖅 💲 🖅 🍽 ⇌ ✕

◆◆◆ ▼▼▼▼ **Royal Oaks of Kissimmee-Magical Memories Vacation Rentals** 🄲🄾
(407) 390-8200. **$99-$129, 14 day notice.** 5075 W Irlo Bronson Memorial Hwy. I-4, exit 64A, 3.1 mi e on US 192. Ext corridors. **Pets:** Small. $50 one-time fee/room. Supervision.
SAVE 🛇 ✕ 💲 ⇌

◆◆◆ ▼▼▼▼ **Summerfield Condo Resort** 🄲🄾
(407) 847-7222. **$99-$159, 14 day notice.** 2422 Summerfield Way. SR 423 (John Young Pkwy), 0.8 mi n of US 192; Florida Tpke, exit 249, 2.5 mi w, 1.7 mi s. Ext corridors. **Pets:** Accepted.
SAVE ✕ 🗗 🖅 💲 ⇌ ✕

▼▼▼ **Sunset Lakes-Absolute Premier Vacation Homes** 🏠
(407) 396-2401. **$105-$235, 30 day notice.** 3160 Vineland Rd, Suite 1. I-4, exit 68, 2.5 mi e on SR 535 (Apopka-Vineland Rd). Ext corridors. **Pets:** Accepted.
ASK 🛇 ✕ 🖅 💲 ⇌

◆◆◆ ▼▼▼ **Super 8 Motel Maingate** 🏨
(407) 396-8883. **$35-$69.** 5875 W Irlo Bronson Hwy. I-4, exit 64A, 1.5 mi e on SR 192. Ext corridors. **Pets:** Accepted.
SAVE 🛇 ✕ 🗗 🖅 ⇌

◆◆◆ ▼▼▼ **Travelodge Hotel Maingate East** 🏨
(407) 396-4222. **$39-$69.** 5711 W Irlo Bronson Memorial Hwy. I-4, exit 64A, 2 mi e on SR 192. Int corridors. **Pets:** Accepted.
SAVE 🛇 ✕ 🗗 🖅 💲 ⇌ ✕

▼▼▼ **Windsor Palms-Absolute Premier Vacation Homes** 🏠
(407) 396-2401. **$105-$235, 30 day notice.** 3160 Vineland Rd, Suite 1. I-4, exit 68, 2.5 mi e on SR 535 (Apopka-Vineland Rd). Ext corridors. **Pets:** Accepted.
ASK 🛇 ✕ 🖅 💲 ⇌

LADY LAKE

▼▼▼▼ Holiday Inn Express Hotel & Suites 🆂🅷
(352) 750-3888. **$80-$90.** 1205 Avenida Central N. Just n on
US 441. Int corridors. **Pets:** $35 one-time fee/room. Desig-
nated rooms, service with restrictions, supervision.
ASK 🆂 ⊠ 🔒 🖵 🏊

▼▼ Microtel Inn & Suites 🆂🅷
(352) 259-0184. **$64-$84.** 850 US 27/441. 1 mi s. Int corridors. **Pets:** Small. $25 one-time fee/pet. Service with
restrictions, supervision.
⊠ 🔒 🖵 🏊

LAKE BUENA VISTA

**♦♦♦ ▼▼ Comfort Inn Lake Buena
        Vista** 🆂🅷 ❀
(407) 996-7300. **$49-$89.** 8442 Palm Pkwy. I-4, exit 68, 0.6
mi n on SR 535, 0.5 mi e. Ext corridors. **Pets:** Medium,
other species. $6 daily fee/pet. Service with restrictions.
SAVE 🆂 ⊠ 🔥 🕐 🔒 🖵 🍽 🏊

**♦♦♦ ▼▼▼▼ Holiday Inn-SunSpree Resort-Lake
        Buena Vista** 🅻🅷
(407) 239-4500. **$69-$109.** 13351 SR 535. I-4, exit 68, 0.3
mi se. Ext corridors. **Pets:** Accepted.
SAVE 🆂 ⊠ 🔥 🕐 🔒 🖵 🍽 🏊 ⊠

**▼▼▼▼ Marriott Residence Inn Lake Buena Vista
        North** 🆂🅷
(407) 465-0075. **$89-$189.** 11450 Marbella Palms Ct. I-4,
exit 68, 0.6 mi n on SR 535, then 0.5 mi e on Palm Pkwy.
Int corridors. **Pets:** Medium. $150 one-time fee/room. Serv-
ice with restrictions.
ASK 🆂 ⊠ 🔥 🕐 🔒 🖵 🏊 ⊠

LAKE MARY

**▼▼▼▼ Homestead Studio Suites Hotel-Orlando/
        Lake Mary** 🆂🅷 ❀
(407) 829-2332. **$99-$155.** 1040 Greenwood Blvd. I-4, exit
98, 0.5 mi s on Lake Emma Rd; in Commerce Park. Int
corridors. **Pets:** Medium, other species. $25 daily fee/room.
Service with restrictions, crate.
ASK 🆂 ⊠ 🔥 🕐 🔒 🔒 🖵 🏊

♦♦♦ ▼▼▼▼ La Quinta Inn & Suites 🆂🅷
(407) 805-9901. **$69-$109.** 1060 Greenwood Blvd. I-4, exit
98, just se via Lake Mary Blvd. Int corridors. **Pets:** Other
species. Service with restrictions, supervision.
SAVE ⊠ 🔥 🕐 🔒 🔒 🖵 🏊

LEESBURG

**♦♦♦ ▼▼▼ GuestHouse International Inn &
        Suites** 🆂🅷
(352) 787-1210. **$47-$68.** 1308 N 14th St. Jct US 27 and
441. Ext corridors. **Pets:** Small. $25 one-time fee/room.
Service with restrictions, supervision.
SAVE 🆂 ⊠ 🕐 🔒 🖵 🏊

♦♦♦ ▼▼▼ Super 8 Motel 🅼
(352) 787-6363. **$50-$100.** 1392 North Blvd W. Jct US 27
and 441. Int corridors. **Pets:** Other species. $10 daily fee/
pet. Service with restrictions, supervision.
SAVE 🆂 ⊠ 🔥 🕐 🔒 🏊

MAITLAND

▼▼▼▼ Homewood Suites Orlando North 🆂🅷
(407) 875-8777. **$139-$189.** 290 Southhall Ln. I-4, exit 90,
just w, then just s on Lake Destiny. Int corridors.
Pets: Accepted.
ASK 🆂 ⊠ 🔥 🕐 🔒 🔒 🖵 🏊

OCOEE

▼▼ Red Roof Inn Orlando West 🆂🅷
(407) 347-0140. **$61-$88, 7 day notice.** 11241 W Colonial
Dr. I-4, exit 84, 10 mi w on SR 50; 0.6 mi e of Florida Tpke,
exit 267. Int corridors. **Pets:** Accepted.
ASK ⊠ 🕐 🔒 🏊

ORLANDO

**♦♦♦ ▼▼▼▼ AmeriSuites (Orlando
        Airport/Northeast)** 🆂🅷
(407) 240-3939. **$77-$104.** 7500 Augusta National Dr. SR
528 (Bee Line Expwy), exit 11, 0.5 mi n on SR 436, just e
on TG Lee Blvd, then just s. Int corridors. **Pets:** Accepted.
SAVE 🆂 ⊠ 🕐 🔒 🔒 🖵 🏊

**♦♦♦ ▼▼▼▼ AmeriSuites (Orlando
        Airport/Northwest)** 🆂🅷
(407) 816-7800. **$99-$179.** 5435 Forbes Pl. SR 528 (Bee
Line Expwy), exit 11, 0.5 mi n on SR 436, just w. Int
corridors. **Pets:** Accepted.
SAVE 🆂 ⊠ 🔥 🕐 🔒 🔒 🖵 🏊

♦♦♦ ▼▼▼▼ AmeriSuites (Orlando/Universal) 🆂🅷
(407) 351-0627. **$89-$129.** 5895 Caravan Ct. I-4, exit 75B,
0.6 mi ne. Int corridors. **Pets:** Small, other species. Designated rooms, service with restrictions, crate.
SAVE 🆂 ⊠ 🔥 🕐 🔒 🔒 🖵 🏊

**♦♦♦ ▼▼▼ Baymont Inn & Suites Orlando
        South** 🆂🅷
(407) 240-0500. **$59-$79.** 2051 Consulate Dr. US 17-92 and
441, just s of SR 528 (Bee Line Expwy), off Florida Tpke,
exit 254. Int corridors. **Pets:** Accepted.
SAVE 🆂 ⊠ 🕐 🔒 🔒 🖵 🏊

♦♦♦ ▼▼▼ Best Western Orlando West 🆂🅷
(407) 841-8600. **$69-$125.** 2014 W Colonial Dr. I-4, exit 84,
1.5 mi w on SR 50, 0.4 mi e of SR 423. Int corridors.
Pets: Accepted.
SAVE 🆂 ⊠ 🕐 🔒 🔒 🖵 🍽 🏊

♦♦♦ ▼▼▼ Comfort Inn-North 🆂🅷
(407) 629-4000. **$65-$90.** 830 Lee Rd. I-4, exit 88, 0.4 mi w
on SR 423. Int corridors. **Pets:** Accepted.
SAVE 🆂 ⊠ 🕐 🔒 🔒 🖵 🏊 ⊠

▼▼ Crestwood Suites-UCF 🆂🅷
(407) 249-0044. **$109.** 11424 University Blvd. 2 mi e of SR
417. Int corridors. **Pets:** Other species. $25 daily fee/pet.
Service with restrictions, supervision.
ASK ⊠ 🕐 🔒 🖵

(A) ▼▼ Days Inn Maingate To Universal 🆂🅷
(407) 351-3800. **$39-$99, 3 day notice.** 5827 Caravan Ct. I-4, exit 75B, 0.5 mi n on SR 435 (Kirkman Rd), then just e. Ext corridors. **Pets:** Small. $10 daily fee/pet. Service with restrictions, supervision.
🆂🅰🆅🅴 🆂🄳 ⊠ 🔗 📶 ⊷

(A) ▼▼▼ Days Inn North of Universal 🆂🅷
(407) 841-3731. **$42-$69.** 2500 W 33rd St. I-4, exit 79, just e. Ext corridors. **Pets:** Medium. $10 one-time fee/pet. Designated rooms, service with restrictions, crate.
🆂🅰🆅🅴 🆂🄳 ⊠ 🔗 🅩 📶 🍴 ⊷

(A) ▼▼▼ Days Inn Orlando Lakeside 🆂🅷
(407) 351-1900. **$39-$99, 3 day notice.** 7335 Sand Lake Rd. I-4, exit 74A, just w. Ext corridors. **Pets:** Small, other species. $10 daily fee/room, $35 one-time fee/room. No service, crate.
🆂🅰🆅🅴 🆂🄳 ⊠ 🚹 🔗 🅩 📶 🍴 ⊷ ⊠

(A) ▼▼▼▼ Hawthorn Suites Orlando Airport 🆂🅷
(407) 438-2121. **$69-$109.** 7450 Augusta National Dr. SR 528 (Bee Line Expwy), exit 11, 0.5 mi n on SR 436, just e, then just s. Int corridors. **Pets:** Small, dogs only. $25 one-time fee/room. Designated rooms, no service, supervision.
🆂🅰🆅🅴 🆂🄳 ⊠ 🚹 🔗 🅩 📶 📺 ⊷ ⊠

(A) ▼▼▼ Holiday Inn & Suites At Universal Orlando 🆂🅷
(407) 351-3333. **$99-$159.** 5905 S Kirkman Rd. I-4, exit 75B, 0.5 mi n on SR 435 (Kirkman Rd). Int corridors. **Pets:** Medium, other species. $50 one-time fee/room. Service with restrictions, crate.
🆂🅰🆅🅴 🆂🄳 ⊠ 🚹 🔗 🅩 📶 📺 🍴 ⊷

(A) ▼▼▼ Holiday Inn Express International Drive Ⓜ
(407) 351-4430. **$79-$129.** 6323 International Dr. I-4, exit 74A, just e on SR 482 (Sand Lake Rd), then 0.7 mi n. Int corridors. **Pets:** Accepted.
🆂🅰🆅🅴 🆂🄳 ⊠ 🚹 🔗 🅩 📶 📺 ⊷

(A) ▼▼▼▼ Holiday Inn-International Drive Resort Ⓜ ❀
(407) 351-3500. **$79-$99.** 6515 International Dr. I-4, exit 74A, just e on SR 482 (Sand Lake Rd), then 0.5 mi n. Ext/int corridors. **Pets:** Large, other species. $25 deposit/room. Service with restrictions.
🆂🅰🆅🅴 🆂🄳 ⊠ 🚹 🔗 🅩 📶 📺 🍴 ⊷ ⊠

▼▼▼▼ Homestead Studio Suites Hotel-Orlando/South Ⓜ ❀
(407) 352-5577. **$59-$69.** 4101 Equity Row. Just sw of jct SR 423 (John Young Pkwy) and 482 (Sand Lake Rd). Int corridors. **Pets:** Medium, other species. $25 daily fee/room. Service with restrictions, crate.
🅰🆂🅺 🆂🄳 ⊠ 🚹 🔗 🅩 🔗 📶

▼▼ Howard Johnson Plaza Resort Universal Gateway 🆂🅷
(407) 351-2000. **$55-$109, 3 day notice.** 7050 S Kirkman Rd. I-4, exit 75A, 0.8 mi s on SR 435 (Kirkman Rd). Int corridors. **Pets:** Small. $10 daily fee/room. Service with restrictions, crate.
🅰🆂🅺 🆂🄳 ⊠ 🔗 🅩 📶 📺 🍴 ⊷ ⊠

(A) ▼▼▼▼ La Quinta Inn Airport West 🆂🅷
(407) 857-9215. **$59-$79.** 7931 Daetwyler Dr. SR 528 (Bee Line Expwy), exit 9 (Tradeport), via McCoy Rd. Ext corridors. **Pets:** Other species. Service with restrictions, supervision.
🆂🅰🆅🅴 🔗 📶 🍴 ⊷

(A) ▼▼▼▼ La Quinta Inn & Suites 🆂🅷
(407) 345-1365. **$82-$109.** 8504 Universal Blvd. I-4, exit 74A, 0.5 mi e on SR 482 (Sand Lake Rd), then 0.5 mi s. Int corridors. **Pets:** Other species. Service with restrictions, supervision.
🆂🅰🆅🅴 ⊠ 🚹 🔗 🅩 🔗 📶 ⊷

▼▼▼▼ La Quinta Inn & Suites Orlando Airport North 🆂🅷
(407) 240-5000. **$65-$95.** 7160 N Frontage Rd. SR 528 (Bee Line Expwy), exit 11, 0.5 mi n on SR 436, just w. Int corridors. **Pets:** Service with restrictions, supervision.
⊠ 🚹 🔗 🅩 🔗 📶 ⊷

▼▼▼▼ La Quinta Inn & Suites UCF 🆂🅷
(407) 737-6075. **$75-$115.** 11805 Research Pkwy. Just se of jct University Blvd and SR 434 (Alafaya Tr). Int corridors. **Pets:** Other species. Service with restrictions, supervision.
⊠ 🚹 🔗 🔗 📶 ⊷

(A) ▼▼▼▼ La Quinta Inn-Orlando International Drive 🆂🅷
(407) 351-1660. **$79-$99.** 8300 Jamaican Ct. I-4, exit 74A, just e on SR 482 (Sand Lake Rd), then just s on International Dr. Ext corridors. **Pets:** Other species. Service with restrictions, supervision.
🆂🅰🆅🅴 ⊠ 🚹 🔗 🔗 📶 📺 ⊷ ⊠

(A) ▼▼▼ Masters Inn International Drive 🆂🅷
(407) 345-1172. **$44-$79, 7 day notice.** 8222 Jamaican Ct. I-4, exit 74A, e on SR 482 (Sand Lake Rd), then just s on International Dr. Ext corridors. **Pets:** Medium. $20 one-time fee/room. Designated rooms, service with restrictions, supervision.
🆂🅰🆅🅴 🆂🄳 ⊠ 🔗 🔗 ⊷

(A) ▼▼▼ ▼▼▼ Portofino Bay Hotel a Loews Hotel at Universal Orlando 🅻🅷 ❀
(407) 503-1000. **$259-$549, 5 day notice.** 5601 Universal Blvd. I-4, exit 74B westbound; exit 75A eastbound, 1 mi n, follow signs. Int corridors. **Pets:** Large, other species. Designated rooms, service with restrictions.
🆂🅰🆅🅴 🆂🄳 ⊠ 🚹 🔗 🔗 📶 📺 🍴 ⊷ ⊠

▼▼ ▼▼ Quality Inn International 🆂🅷
(407) 996-1600. **$50-$80.** 7600 International Dr. I-4, exit 74A, just e on SR 482 (Sand Lake Rd), then just n. Ext corridors. **Pets:** Small. $10 daily fee/pet. Service with restrictions, crate.
🅰🆂🅺 🆂🄳 ⊠ 🚹 🔗 🔗 📶 📺 🍴 ⊷

▼▼ ▼▼ Quality Inn-Plaza Ⓜ
(407) 996-8585. **$39-$99.** 9000 International Dr. I-4, exit 74A, just e on SR 482 (Sand Lake Rd), then 1 mi s. Ext corridors. **Pets:** Medium, other species. $50 deposit/room, $10 daily fee/room. Service with restrictions, supervision.
🅰🆂🅺 🆂🄳 ⊠ 🚹 🔗 🔗 📶 📺 🍴 ⊷ ⊠

Ramada Inn at International Drive SH
(407) 351-4410. **$62-$89.** 5858 International Dr. I-4, exit 75A, just s on (SR 435 (Kirkman Rd), then just w. Ext corridors. **Pets:** Small. $50 deposit/room, $10 daily fee/room. Service with restrictions, crate.
SAVE 🛇 ⊠ 🗲 🏷 🖬 🖵 ⇔

Red Horse Inn SH
(407) 351-4100. **$49-$89, 3 day notice.** 5825 International Dr. I-4, exit 30A, just w of SR 435 (Kirkman Rd). Ext corridors. **Pets:** Small. $10 daily fee/pet. Designated rooms, service with restrictions, crate.
SAVE 🛇 ⊠ 🗲 🖬 ⇔

Red Roof Inn Convention Center SH
(407) 352-1507. **$39-$99.** 9922 Hawaiian Ct. I-4, exit 72, 0.9 mi e on SR 528 (Bee Line Expwy) to exit 1, then just n. Ext corridors. **Pets:** Small. Service with restrictions, supervision.
SAVE ⊠ 🗲M 🗲 🖬 ⇔

Red Roof Inn Universal Studios SH
(407) 313-3100. **$49-$69.** 5621 Major Blvd. I-4, exit 75B, just n, then just e. Int corridors. **Pets:** Accepted.
ASK 🛇 ⊠ 🗲M 🗲 🖬 ⇔

Renaissance Orlando Resort at SeaWorld LH
(407) 351-5555. **$107-$179, 3 day notice.** 6677 Sea Harbor Dr. I-4, exit 72, just e on Central Florida Pkwy, 0.3 mi n or 0.7 mi w of International Dr. Int corridors. **Pets:** Accepted.
SAVE 🛇 ⊠ 🗲M 🗲 🖬 🖵 🍴 ⇔ 🎾

Residence Inn by Marriott Orlando Convention Center SH
(407) 226-0288. **$89-$189.** 8800 Universal Blvd. I-4, exit 74A, 0.5 mi e on SR 482 (Sand Lake Rd). Int corridors. **Pets:** Small, other species. $75 one-time fee/pet. Service with restrictions, supervision.
ASK 🛇 ⊠ 🗲M 🗲 🖬 🖵 ⇔ 🎾

Residence Inn by Marriott/Orlando East SH
(407) 513-9000. **$89-$139.** 11651 University Blvd. 2.2 mi e of SR 417 on University Blvd, just w of SR 434 (Alafaya Tr). Int corridors. **Pets:** Accepted.
ASK 🛇 ⊠ 🗲 🗲 🖬 🖵 ⇔ 🎾

Residence Inn by Marriott-Orlando International Dr SH
(407) 345-0117. **$89-$209.** 7975 Canada Ave. I-4, exit 74A, just e on SR 482 (Sand Lake Rd). Ext corridors. **Pets:** $200 one-time fee/room. Service with restrictions.
SAVE 🛇 ⊠ 🗲 🗲 🖬 🖵 ⇔ 🎾

Residence Inn by Marriott Sea World International Center SH
(407) 313-3600. **$87-$209.** 11000 Westwood Blvd. I-4, exit 72. Int corridors. **Pets:** Medium. $150 one-time fee/room. Service with restrictions, supervision.
ASK ⊠ 🗲M 🗲 🗲 🖬 🖵 🍴 ⇔ 🎾

Rodeway Inn International M
(407) 996-4444. **$36-$69, 3 day notice.** 6327 International Dr. I-4, exit 74A, just e on SR 482 (Sand Lake Rd), then 0.7 mi n. Ext/int corridors. **Pets:** Medium. $10 daily fee/pet. Service with restrictions, crate.
ASK 🛇 ⊠ 🗲M 🗲 🖬 🖵 🍴 ⇔

Suburban Lodge of Orlando South Florida Mall SH
(407) 251-1110. **$249-$259.** 9435 Delegates Dr. Just s of SR 528 (Bee Line Expwy), exit 4; just w of US 17-92 and 441; just s of Florida Tpke, exit 244. Ext corridors. **Pets:** Accepted.
SAVE 🛇 ⊠ 🗲 🗲 🖬 🖵 ⇔

TownePlace Suites by Marriott SH
(407) 243-6100. **$119-$159.** 11801 High Tech Ave. 2.2 mi e of SR 417 on University Blvd. Int corridors. **Pets:** Other species. $20 daily fee/room. Service with restrictions.
ASK 🛇 ⊠ 🗲M 🗲 🖬 🖵 ⇔

Travelodge Orlando Downtown M
(407) 423-1671. **$55-$90.** 409 N Magnolia Ave. Corner of Magnolia, Rosalind aves and Livingston St. Ext/int corridors. **Pets:** Medium, other species. $10 daily fee/pet. No service, supervision.
ASK 🛇 ⊠ 🗲 🖬 🖵 🍴 ⇔

Universal's Hard Rock Hotel LH 🌤
(407) 503-2000. **$209-$539, 5 day notice.** 5800 Universal Blvd. I-4, exit 75A. Int corridors. **Pets:** Other species. Designated rooms, service with restrictions.
SAVE 🛇 ⊠ 🗲M 🗲 🗲 🖬 🖵 🍴 ⇔ 🎾

Universal's Royal Pacific Resort LH 🌤
(407) 503-3000. **$179-$609, 5 day notice.** 6312 Hollywood Way. I-4, exit 75A. Int corridors. **Pets:** Large, other species. Designated rooms, service with restrictions.
ASK 🛇 ⊠ 🗲 🖬 🖵 🍴 ⇔ 🎾

Ventura Resort Rentals-Kissimmee VH
(407) 273-8770. **$69-$195.** 5946 Curry Ford Rd. 0.6 mi e of SR 436. Ext corridors. **Pets:** Small, other species. $100 deposit/pet, $100 one-time fee/pet. Designated rooms, service with restrictions.
ASK 🛇 🗲 🖬 🖵 ⇔

Ventura Resort Rentals Orlando CO
(407) 273-8770. **$51-$195.** 5946 Curry Ford Rd. 0.6 mi e of SR 436. Ext corridors. **Pets:** Accepted.
ASK 🛇 🗲 🖬 🖵 ⇔ 🎾

Wellesley Inn & Suites (Orlando/Maitland) SH
(407) 659-0066. **$79-$89.** 1951 Summit Tower Blvd. I-4, exit 90, 1 mi w. Int corridors. **Pets:** Accepted.
SAVE 🛇 ⊠ 🗲M 🗲 🗲 🖬 🖵 ⇔

Wellesley Inn & Suites (Orlando/Southpark) SH
(407) 248-8010. **$85-$119.** 8687 Commodity Cir. Just sw of jct SR 423 (John Young Pkwy) and 482 (Sand Lake Rd). Int corridors. **Pets:** Small. Service with restrictions, supervision.
SAVE 🛇 ⊠ 🗲 🗲 🖬 🖵 ⇔

⚠ ▽▽▽▽ **Wellesley Inn (Orlando/International Drive)** 🆂🅷
(407) 345-5340. **$69-$99.** 6500 International Dr. I-4, exit 75A, 0.8 mi s. Ext corridors. **Pets:** Medium. $50 deposit/room. Designated rooms, service with restrictions.
🆂🅰🆅🅴 🆂🖼 ⊘ 🐾 🍴 💻 🏊

⚠ ▽▽▽▽ **Wyndham Orlando Resort** 🅻🅷
(407) 351-2420. **$79-$156, 3 day notice.** 8001 International Dr. I-4, exit 74A, just e at SR 482 (Sand Lake Rd). Ext/int corridors. **Pets:** Accepted.
🆂🅰🆅🅴 🆂🖼 ✕ 🖐 ⊘ 🐾 🍴 💻 🏊 🏊 ✕

ST. CLOUD

⚠ ▽▽▽ **Budget Inn of St Cloud** 🅼
(407) 892-2858. **$35-$45, 3 day notice.** 602 13th St. On US 192, 0.5 mi e of The Water Tower, 2 mi w of jct CR 15. Ext corridors. **Pets:** Very small, dogs only. Crate.
🆂🅰🆅🅴 🆂🖼 ✕ ⊘ 🍴 💻

SANFORD

▽▽ **Best Western Marina Hotel & Conference Center** 🆂🅷
(407) 323-1910. **$59-$140, 3 day notice.** 530 N Palmetto Ave. I-4, exit 101C, 4.8 mi e. Ext corridors. **Pets:** Small. $20 one-time fee/room. Service with restrictions, crate.
🅰🆂🅺 🆂🖼 ✕ 💻 🍴 🏊

🐾 END METROPOLITAN AREA 🐾

ORMOND BEACH

⚠ ▽▽▽ **Comfort Inn On The Beach** 🅼
(386) 677-8550. **$75-$195, 10 day notice.** 507 S Atlantic Ave. On SR A1A, 1 mi s of jct SR 40. Ext corridors. **Pets:** Very small. $10 daily fee/pet. Designated rooms, service with restrictions, supervision.
🆂🅰🆅🅴 🆂🖼 ✕ 🍴 💻 🏊

⚠ ▽▽▽ **Driftwood Beach Motel** 🅼
(386) 677-1331. **$45-$165, 14 day notice.** 657 S Atlantic Ave. On SR A1A, 1.5 mi s of jct SR 40. Ext corridors. **Pets:** Very small, other species. $20 daily fee/pet. Service with restrictions, supervision.
🆂🅰🆅🅴 🍴 💻 🏊

▽▽▽ **Jameson Inn** 🆂🅷
(386) 672-3675. **$80-$85.** 175 Interchange Blvd. I-95, exit 268, just w, then just s. Int corridors. **Pets:** Small. Service with restrictions, crate.
✕ 🖐 ⊘ 🐾 🍴 💻 🏊

OSPREY

⚠ ▽▽▽ **Ramada Inn-Sarasota South** 🅼 🐾
(941) 966-2121. **$50-$120.** 1660 S Tamiami Tr. On US 41, 1.8 mi n of jct SR 681. Ext/int corridors. **Pets:** Medium. $25 one-time fee/pet. Designated rooms, service with restrictions, supervision.
🆂🅰🆅🅴 🆂🖼 ✕ 🍴 💻 🍴 🏊

▽▽▽ **Rose Cottage Inn** 🅱🅱
(407) 323-9448. **$85-$155, 30 day notice.** 1301 Park Ave. From 1st St, 0.8 mi s on Park Ave; downtown. Int corridors. **Pets:** Accepted.
🅰🆂🅺 🆂🖼 ✕ 🍴 🍴 📺 ☎

TAVARES

▽▽ **Budget Inn** 🅼
(352) 343-4666. **$46-$79, 14 day notice.** 101 W Burleigh Blvd. On US 441, 0.3 mi e of jct SR 19 S. Ext corridors. **Pets:** Accepted.
🅰🆂🅺 🆂🖼 ✕ 🍴 💻 🏊

⚠ ▽▽▽▽ **Inn On The Green** 🅼
(352) 343-6373. **$65-$135.** 700 E Burleigh Blvd. On US 441, 1 mi e of jct SR 19. Ext corridors. **Pets:** Medium, other species. $10 daily fee/room.
🆂🅰🆅🅴 ✕ 🍴 💻 🏊 ✕

PALM BAY

▽▽▽ **Jameson Inn** 🆂🅷
(321) 725-2952. **$80-$85.** 890 Palm Bay Rd. I-95, exit 176. Int corridors. **Pets:** Small. Service with restrictions, crate.
✕ 🖐 ⊘ 🐾 🍴 💻 🏊

PALM BEACH

⚠ ▽▽▽▽ **The Chesterfield Hotel** 🆂🅷 🐾
(561) 659-5800. **$139-$1500, 3 day notice.** 363 Cocoanut Row. Just w of SR A1A; at Australian Ave and Cocoanut Row. Int corridors. **Pets:** Medium. $100 deposit/room, $50 one-time fee/room. Designated rooms, service with restrictions, supervision.
🆂🅰🆅🅴 🆂🖼 ✕ ⊘ 🍴 🍴 🏊 ✕

⚠ ▽▽▽▽▽ **The Four Seasons Resort, Palm Beach** 🅻🅷 🐾
(561) 582-2800. **$415-$750, 7 day notice.** 2800 S Ocean Blvd. On SR A1A, 0.3 mi n of jct SR 802. Int corridors. **Pets:** Small. Service with restrictions, supervision.
✕ 🖐 ⊘ 🐾 💻 🏊 ✕

▽▽▽▽ **Heart of Palm Beach Hotel** 🆂🅷
(561) 655-5600. **$109-$350, 3 day notice.** 160 Royal Palm Way. Just e of SR A1A; center. Int corridors. **Pets:** Accepted.
🅰🆂🅺 🆂🖼 ✕ ⊘ 🍴 🍴 🏊 ✕

▼▼▼ Plaza Inn SH ❀
(561) 832-8666. **$125-$275, 7 day notice.** 215 Brazilian Ave.
At Brazilian Ave and SR A1A (S County Rd); center. Int
corridors. **Pets:** Medium. Designated rooms, service with
restrictions, supervision.
(ASK) ⊠ 🐾 🛏 🔀

PALM BEACH GARDENS

♠♠♠ ▼▼▼ Doubletree Hotel In The
Gardens LH
(561) 622-2260. **$129-$259.** 4431 PGA Blvd. I-95, exit 79B
northbound; exit 79AB southbound; 1.8 mi e of Florida
Tpke, exit 109. Int corridors. **Pets:** Accepted.
(SAVE) 🐾 ⊠ 🖏 🐾 🅿 🛏 🔳 ❚❙ 🔀 ⊠

♠♠♠ ▼▼▼ Inns of America M
(561) 626-4918. **$65-$139.** 4123 Northlake Blvd. I-95, exit
77, just e. Ext corridors. **Pets:** Small. $10 daily fee/pet.
Service with restrictions, supervision.
(SAVE) 🐾 ⊠ 🛏 🔀

PALM BEACH SHORES

♠♠♠ ▼▼ Best Western Seaspray Inn SH
(561) 844-0233. **$70-$180, 14 day notice.** 123 S Ocean
Ave. On Singer Island; 0.5 mi s of SR A1A. Int corridors.
Pets: Accepted.
(SAVE) 🐾 ⊠ 🛏 🔳 ❚❙ 🔀

▼▼ Sailfish Marina & Resort M
(561) 844-1724. **$89-$139.** 98 Lake Dr. US 1, 1 mi e, then
0.4 mi s. Ext corridors. **Pets:** Accepted.
(ASK) 🐾 ⊠ 🛏 🔳 ❚❙ 🔀 ⊠

PALM COAST

▼▼ Microtel Inn & Suites SH
(386) 445-8976. **$59-$199.** 16 Kingswood Dr. I-95, exit 289,
just e, then just s. Int corridors. **Pets:** Accepted.
(ASK) 🐾 ⊠ 🖏 🐾 🛏 🔳 🔀

♠♠♠ ▼▼▼ Palm Coast Villas M
(386) 445-3525. **$55-$150.** 5454 N Oceanshore Blvd. I-95,
exit 289, 2.8 mi e to SR A1A, 1.8 mi n. Ext corridors.
Pets: Small. $5 daily fee/pet. Designated rooms.
(SAVE) 🐾 ⊠ 🛏 🔳 🔀

PANAMA CITY

♠♠♠ ▼▼▼ Days Inn Bayside SH
(850) 763-4622. **$55-$145.** 711 W Beach Dr. Business US
98, 0.5 mi w of jct US 231. Ext corridors. **Pets:** Accepted.
(SAVE) 🐾 ⊠ 🛏 🔳 ❚❙ 🔀

▼▼ Howard Johnson Inn SH
(850) 785-0222. **$89, 14 day notice.** 4601 W Hwy 98. US
98, 0.8 mi e of Hathaway Bridge. Ext/int corridors.
Pets: Small. $25 one-time fee/pet. Designated rooms, serv-
ice with restrictions, supervision.
(ASK) 🐾 ⊠ 🛏 🔳 ❚❙ 🔀

♠♠♠ ▼▼▼ La Quinta Inn & Suites SH
(850) 914-0022. **$102-$112.** 1030 E 23rd St. Jct US 231 and
CR 390A. Int corridors. **Pets:** Accepted.
(SAVE) 🐾 ⊠ 🖏 🐾 🛏 🔳 🔀

▼▼ Super 8 Motel M
(850) 784-1988. **$45-$99.** 207 Hwy 231 N. Just n of jct US
98. Ext/int corridors. **Pets:** Small, dogs only. $10 daily fee/
pet. Service with restrictions.
(ASK) 🐾 ⊠ 🛏 🔀

PENSACOLA

▼▼▼ Ashton Inn & Suites SH ❀
(850) 454-0280. **$69-$199.** 4 New Warrington Rd. Just n of
jct US 98 and SR 292. Int corridors. **Pets:** Other species.
$20 one-time fee/room. Crate.
(ASK) 🐾 ⊠ 🛏 🔳 🔀

♠♠♠ ▼▼▼ Comfort Inn-NAS Corry SH ❀
(850) 455-3233. **$59-$70.** 3 New Warrington Rd. Just n of jct
US 98 and SR 292. Ext corridors. **Pets:** Other species. $25
one-time fee/room. Service with restrictions.
(SAVE) 🐾 ⊠ 🛏 🔳 🔀

▼▼◆▼ Crowne Plaza Hotel and Resort Pensacola
Grand LH
. (850) 433-3336. **$135-$260.** 200 E Gregory St. Jct I-110 and
US 98. Int corridors. **Pets:** Accepted.
(ASK) 🐾 ⊠ 🛏 🔳 ❚❙ 🔀

♠♠♠ ▼◆ Days Inn North SH
(850) 476-9090. **$45-$89.** 7051 Pensacola Blvd. I-10, exit
10A, 0.3 mi s on US 29. Int corridors. **Pets:** Other species.
$10 daily fee/pet. Service with restrictions, supervision.
(SAVE) 🐾 ⊠ 🛏 🔀

▼▼ Hospitality Inn SH
(850) 477-2333. **$99, 3 day notice.** 6900 Pensacola Blvd.
I-10, exit 10A, 0.5 mi s on US 29. Ext/int corridors.
Pets: Medium. $25 one-time fee/room. Designated rooms,
no service, supervision.
(ASK) 🐾 ⊠ 🛏 🔳 🔀

♠♠♠ ▼▼◆▼ La Quinta Inn SH
(850) 474-0411. **$65-$85.** 7750 N Davis Hwy. I-10, exit 13,
just n. Ext corridors. **Pets:** Accepted.
(SAVE) ⊠ 🐾 🛏 🔳 🔀

♠♠♠ ▼▼ Quality Inn SH
(850) 477-0711. **$60-$75.** 6550 N Pensacola Blvd. I-10, exit
10, 1.2 mi s on US 29. Ext corridors. **Pets:** Other species.
$25 one-time fee/pet. Service with restrictions.
(SAVE) 🐾 ⊠ 🛏 🔳 ❚❙ 🔀

♠♠♠ ▼▼▼ Ramada Inn Bayview SH ❀
(850) 477-7155. **$59-$119.** 7601 Scenic Hwy. I-10, exit 17,
just s on US 90. Int corridors. **Pets:** Medium, other species.
$25 one-time fee/pet. Designated rooms, service with
restrictions, crate.
(SAVE) 🐾 ⊠ 🛏 🔳 ❚❙ 🔀

♠♠♠ ▼▼▼ Red Roof Inn M
(850) 476-7960. **$41-$61.** 7340 Plantation Rd. I-10, exit 13,
just s. Ext corridors. **Pets:** Medium. Service with restrictions, supervision.
(SAVE) ⊠ 🛏

▼▼ Travelodge Inn & Suites SH
(850) 473-0222. **$32-$149.** 6950 Pensacola Blvd. I-10, exit 10A, just s on US 29. Int corridors. **Pets:** Large, other species. $10 one-time fee/room. Service with restrictions.
ASK SD X 🗋 🖵 ⇌

PENSACOLA BEACH

▲▲▲ ▼▼▼ Beachside Resort & Conference Center SH
(850) 932-5331. **$69-$179.** 14 Via De Luna Dr. SR 399, just e of traffic light. Int corridors. **Pets:** Other species. $50 one-time fee/room. No service, supervision.
SAVE SD X ⛱ 🗋 🖵 ⑪ ⇌

PERRY

▲▲▲ ▼ Best Budget Inn M
(850) 584-6231. **$39.** 2220 US 19 S. US 19 and 98, 0.4 mi s jct US 221. Ext corridors. **Pets:** Accepted.
SAVE SD X ⇌

PORT CHARLOTTE

▼▼ Days Inn of Port Charlotte SH
(941) 627-8900. **$47-$119.** 1941 Tamiami Tr. On US 41, just s of jct Toledo Blade Blvd. Ext corridors. **Pets:** Accepted.
ASK SD X 🕖 🗋 🖵 ⇌

PUNTA GORDA

▲▲▲ ▼▼▼ Best Western Waterfront SH
(941) 639-1165. **$69-$148.** 300 Retta Esplanade. On US 41; just s of Peace River Bridge. Int corridors. **Pets:** Other species. $25 one-time fee/pet. Service with restrictions, supervision.
SAVE SD X 🕖 🗋 🖵 ⑪ ⇌ ⊠

▲▲▲ ▼▼▼ Holiday Inn Harborside M
(941) 639-2167. **$69-$159.** 33 Tamiami Tr. On US 41; at Peace River Bridge. Int corridors. **Pets:** Medium. $40 one-time fee/pet. Designated rooms, supervision.
SAVE SD X ⛱M ⛱ 🗋 🖵 ⑪ ⇌ ⊠

QUINCY

▼▼▼ Allison House Inn BB ❀
(850) 875-2511. **$80-$110, 14 day notice.** 215 N Madison St. Just e of town center. Int corridors. **Pets:** Small, dogs only. Designated rooms, service with restrictions, crate.
ASK SD X

ST. AUGUSTINE

▲▲▲ ▼▼ Best Western St. Augustine I-95 SH
(904) 829-1999. **$55-$99.** 2445 SR 16. I-95, exit 318, southwest corner. Ext corridors. **Pets:** Small, dogs only. $10 daily fee/room. Designated rooms, service with restrictions.
SAVE SD X 🖵 ⇌

▼▼ Conch House Marina Resort SH
(904) 829-8646. **$90-$250, 7 day notice.** 57 Comares Ave. 1 mi s of Bridge of Lions on SR A1A, then 0.3 mi n. Ext corridors. **Pets:** Other species. $50 one-time fee/pet. Service with restrictions, crate.
🗋 🖵 ⑪ ⇌ ⊠ ⓩ

▼▼ The Cozy Inn M ❀
(904) 824-2449. **$49-$99.** 202 San Marco Ave. 0.3 mi s of jct SR 16. Ext corridors. **Pets:** Other species. $200 deposit/room, $25 one-time fee/room. Service with restrictions, crate.
ASK SD X 🗋 🖵

▲▲▲ ▼▼ Days Inn Historic SH ❀
(904) 829-6581. **$52-$94.** 2800 N Ponce de Leon Blvd. US 1 at SR 16. Ext corridors. **Pets:** Medium. $10 daily fee/pet. Designated rooms, service with restrictions, crate.
SAVE SD X 🕖 🗋 ⑪ ⇌

▼▼ Days Inn-West SH
(904) 824-4341. **$45-$150.** 2560 SR 16. I-95, exit 318, northwest corner. Ext corridors. **Pets:** Large, dogs only. $25 daily fee/pet. Designated rooms, service with restrictions, supervision.
ASK X 🗋 🖵 ⑪ ⇌

▲▲▲ ▼▼▼ La Quinta Inn SH
(904) 824-3383. **$69-$150.** 1300 Ponce de Leon Blvd. US 1, 1 mi n. Ext corridors. **Pets:** Small, dogs only. $10 daily fee/room. Designated rooms, service with restrictions, supervision.
SAVE X ⛱ 🗋 🖵 ⑪ ⇌

▲▲▲ ▼▼▼ Ramada Limited SH
(904) 829-5643. **$49-$169.** 2535 SR 16. I-95, exit 318, just w. Ext corridors. **Pets:** Medium, other species. $15 one-time fee/pet. Service with restrictions.
SAVE SD X 🗋 ⇌

▼▼▼ St. Francis Inn BB
(904) 824-6068. **$109-$229, 7 day notice.** 279 St George St. Just s. Ext/int corridors. **Pets:** Small, other species. $10 one-time fee/pet. Designated rooms, service with restrictions, crate.
ASK X 🗋 🖵 ⇌ ⊠

▲▲▲ ▼▼▼ Scottish Inns M
(904) 824-2871. **$40-$89.** 110 San Marco Ave. Old Mission and San Marco aves; center. Ext corridors. **Pets:** Small. $10 one-time fee/pet. No service, crate.
SAVE SD X ⇌

ST. AUGUSTINE BEACH

▲▲▲ ▼▼▼ Holiday Inn-St Augustine Beach SH
(904) 471-2555. **$104-$149.** 860 A1A Beach Blvd. On Business Rt A1A, 1.8 mi s of jct SR 312 and A1A. Ext/int corridors. **Pets:** Small, other species. $20 daily fee/pet. Designated rooms, service with restrictions, supervision.
SAVE SD X ⛱ 🗋 🖵 ⑪ ⇌

▲▲▲ ▼▼▼ Super 8 By The Beach SH ❀
(904) 471-2330. **$49-$199.** 311 A1A Beach Blvd. On Business Rt A1A, 1 mi s of jct SR 312 and A1A. Ext corridors. **Pets:** Other species. $15 daily fee/room. Service with restrictions, supervision.
SAVE SD X 🕖 🗋 🖵 ⇌

SARASOTA

AAA ▼▼▼ The Calais Motel-Apartments **M**
(941) 921-5797. **$54-$110, 3 day notice.** 1735 Stickney Point Rd. On SR 72, 0.3 mi sw of jct US 41. Ext corridors. **Pets:** Accepted.
[SAVE] [🛏] [✕] [🖁] [💻] [🏊]

AAA ▼▼▼ Comfort Inn **SH**
(941) 921-7750. **$59-$125.** 5778 Clark Rd. I-75, exit 205, just w on SR 72. Int corridors. **Pets:** Small. $10 daily fee/pet. Designated rooms, service with restrictions, supervision.
[SAVE] [🛏] [✕] [🖊] [🖁] [💻] [🏊]

AAA ▼▼▼ Coquina on the Beach
             Resort **SH** ✿
(941) 388-2141. **$89-$349, 14 day notice.** 1008 Benjamin Franklin Dr. On St. Armands Key of Lido Beach, 0.9 mi s of St. Armands Circle. Ext corridors. **Pets:** Other species. $35 one-time fee/room. Service with restrictions.
[SAVE] [🛏] [🖁] [💻] [🏊]

▼▼▼ Country Inn & Suites By Carlson **SH**
(941) 925-0631. **$79-$179.** 5730 Gantt Rd. I-75, exit 205, 0.3 mi w on SR 72 (Clark Rd), just n. Int corridors. **Pets:** Accepted.
[ASK] [🛏] [✕] [🖙] [🖊] [🖁] [🖁] [💻] [🏊]

AAA ▼▼▼ Days Inn-Airport **M**
(941) 355-9721. **$59-$109.** 4900 N Tamiami Tr. On US 41, just s of jct University Pkwy. Ext corridors. **Pets:** Small, dogs only. $6 daily fee/pet. Designated rooms, no service, supervision.
[SAVE] [🛏] [✕] [🖊] [🖁] [💻] [🍴] [🏊] [✕]

AAA ▼▼▼ Ramada Limited **SH**
(941) 921-7812. **$79-$129.** 5774 Clark Rd. I-75, exit 205, just w on SR 72. Int corridors. **Pets:** Medium, dogs only. $10 daily fee/pet. Designated rooms, service with restrictions, supervision.
[SAVE] [🛏] [✕] [🖊] [🖙] [🖁] [💻] [🏊]

▼▼▼ The Ritz-Carlton, Sarasota **LH** ✿
(941) 309-2000. **$149-$375.** 1111 Ritz-Carlton Dr. I-75, exit 210, just w of jct US 41; center. Int corridors. **Pets:** Medium, other species. $125 deposit/pet, $125 one-time fee/pet. Service with restrictions, crate.
[ASK] [✕] [🖙] [🖊] [🖁] [🍴] [🏊] [✕]

▼▼ The Sunset Lodge Motel **M**
(941) 925-1151. **$60-$95, 45 day notice.** 1765 Dawn St. 0.3 mi sw of jct US 41 on SR 72, just s on Ave C, then just w. Ext corridors. **Pets:** Accepted.
[✕] [🖁] [💻] [🏊] [✕]

▼▼ The Tides Inn **M**
(941) 924-7541. **$60-$120, 28 day notice.** 1800 Stickney Point Rd. On SR 72, 0.3 mi sw of jct US 41. Ext corridors. **Pets:** Small, dogs only. $5 daily fee/pet, $15 one-time fee/pet. Designated rooms, service with restrictions, supervision.
[✕] [🖁] [🏊] [✕]

SATELLITE BEACH

AAA ▼▼▼ Days Inn **M**
(321) 777-3552. **$70-$100.** 180 SR A1A. 0.3 mi s of jct SR 404. Ext corridors. **Pets:** Accepted.
[SAVE] [🛏] [✕] [🖙] [🖁] [🏊] [✕]

SEBRING

▼▼▼ The Chateau Elan Hotel & Spa **SH**
(863) 655-6252. **$69-$149, 3 day notice.** 150 Midway Dr. From US 27, 2.2 mi e on SR 98; at entrance to Sebring International Raceway. Int corridors. **Pets:** Small, other species. $50 one-time fee/room. Service with restrictions, supervision.
[ASK] [🛏] [✕] [🖊] [🖙] [💻] [🍴] [🏊] [✕]

AAA ▼▼▼ Inn On The Lakes **SH**
(863) 471-9400. **$69-$99.** 3100 Golfview Rd. On US 27, 1.5 mi n of jct SR 17. Ext/int corridors. **Pets:** Medium. $40 one-time fee/room. Designated rooms, service with restrictions, supervision.
[SAVE] [🛏] [✕] [🖁] [💻] [🍴] [🏊] [✕]

AAA ▼▼▼ Quality Inn & Suites Conference
             Center **SH** ✿
(863) 385-4500. **$59-$259.** 6525 US 27 N. On US 27, 7 mi n of jct SR 17. Ext corridors. **Pets:** Small, other species. $20 daily fee/pet. Designated rooms, service with restrictions, supervision.
[SAVE] [🛏] [✕] [🖙] [🖊] [🖁] [💻] [🍴] [🏊]

SIESTA KEY

AAA ▼▼▼ Tropical Breeze Resort of Siesta
             Key **M**
(941) 349-1125. **$79-$379.** 5150 Ocean Blvd. Jct Avenida Messina; center. Ext corridors. **Pets:** $40 one-time fee/pet. Designated rooms.
[SAVE] [🛏] [✕] [🖁] [🍴] [🏊] [✕]

AAA ▼▼▼ Turtle Beach Resort **M**
(941) 349-4554. **$215-$425.** 9049 Midnight Pass Rd. 2.8 mi s of jct SR 72. Ext corridors. **Pets:** $31 one-time fee/room.
[SAVE] [✕] [🖁] [💻] [🏊] [✕]

SILVER SPRINGS

▼▼ Days Inn **M**
(352) 236-2891. **$50-$85, 3 day notice.** 5001 E Silver Springs Blvd. SR 40, 0.5 mi w of jct CR 35. Ext corridors. **Pets:** Medium. $7 daily fee/pet. Designated rooms, service with restrictions, supervision.
[ASK] [🛏] [✕] [🖁] [💻] [🏊]

AAA ▼▼ Sun Plaza Motel **M**
(352) 236-2343. **$54-$74, 3 day notice.** 5461 E Silver Springs Blvd. SR 40 at jct CR 35. Ext corridors. **Pets:** Accepted.
[SAVE] [🛏] [✕] [🖁] [💻] [🏊]

STARKE

(AAA) ▼▼▼ Best Western Motor Inn 🆂🅷
(904) 964-6744. **$60-$70, 30 day notice.** 1290 N Temple Ave. 1 mi n on US 301 from jct SR 100. Ext corridors. **Pets:** Small. $10 daily fee/pet. Designated rooms, service with restrictions, supervision.
[SAVE] [🗄] [✕] [🗄] [💻] [🏊]

▼▼ Days Inn 🆂🅷
(904) 964-7600. **$60-$125, 3 day notice.** 1101 N Temple Ave. 10 mi s of jct SR 16. Ext corridors. **Pets:** Accepted.
[A$K] [🗄] [✕] [🗄] [🗄] [🍴] [🏊]

STEINHATCHEE

▼▼▼ Steinhatchee Landing Resort 🄲🄾
(352) 498-3513. **$120-$385, 14 day notice.** SR 51 N. SR 51, 8 mi w of jct US 19/98. Ext corridors. **Pets:** Small, dogs only. $100 deposit/pet. Designated rooms, service with restrictions.
[A$K] [✕] [🗄] [💻] [🏊] [🗙]

▼▼ Steinhatchee River Inn 🅼
(352) 498-4049. **$65-$89, 28 day notice.** 1111 Riverside Dr. Center. Ext corridors. **Pets:** Accepted.
[✕] [🗄] [💻] [🏊]

STUART

▼▼▼ Hutchinson Island Marriott Beach Resort & Marina 🅻🅷
(772) 225-3700. **$139-$229, 3 day notice.** 555 NE Ocean Blvd. 4 mi ne on SR A1A, on south end of Hutchinson Island at east end of causeway. Ext/int corridors. **Pets:** Accepted.
[A$K] [🗄] [✕] [♿] [♿] [🗄] [💻] [🍴] [🏊] [🗙]

(AAA) ▼▼▼ Pirate's Cove Resort & Marina 🆂🅷
(772) 287-2500. **$110-$175.** 4307 SE Bayview St. 0.3 mi e of SR A1A. Ext corridors. **Pets:** Other species. $20 daily fee/pet. Service with restrictions.
[SAVE] [🗄] [♿] [🗄] [💻] [🍴] [🏊] [🗙]

TALLAHASSEE

(AAA) ▼▼▼ Best Western Seminole Inn 🅼
(850) 656-2938. **$65-$139, 7 day notice.** 6737 Mahan Dr. I-10, exit 31A, just w on US 90. Ext corridors. **Pets:** Small, dogs only. $5 daily fee/pet. Supervision.
[SAVE] [🗄] [✕] [🗄] [💻] [🏊]

(AAA) ▼▼▼ Econo Lodge 🅼
(850) 385-6155. **$48-$99.** 2681 N Monroe St. I-10, exit 199, 0.5 mi s. Ext corridors. **Pets:** Medium. $10 one-time fee/ room. No service, crate.
[SAVE] [🗄] [✕] [🗄] [💻]

▼▼▼ Homewood Suites by Hilton 🆂🅷
(850) 402-9400. **$89-$139.** 2987 Apalachee Pkwy. US 27, 3.5 mi s. Int corridors. **Pets:** Accepted.
[A$K] [🗄] [✕] [🗄] [💻] [🏊] [🗙]

(AAA) ▼▼▼ Howard Johnson Express Inn 🅼
(850) 386-5000. **$45-$65.** 2726 N Monroe St. I-10, exit 199, 0.5 mi s. Ext corridors. **Pets:** Other species. $10 daily fee/ pet. Service with restrictions, supervision.
[SAVE] [🗄] [✕] [🗄] [💻] [🏊]

▼▼▼ La Quinta Inn-North 🆂🅷
(850) 385-7172. **$76-$98.** 2905 N Monroe St. I-10, exit 199, just s on US 27. Ext corridors. **Pets:** Accepted.
[✕] [🗄] [💻] [🏊]

(AAA) ▼▼▼ La Quinta Inn-Tallahassee South 🆂🅷
(850) 878-5099. **$72-$106.** 2850 Apalachee Pkwy. 3 mi se on US 27. Ext corridors. **Pets:** Accepted.
[SAVE] [🗄] [✕] [♿] [♿] [♿] [🗄] [💻] [🏊]

▼▼ Motel 6–420 🅼
(850) 668-2600. **$43-$55.** 1481 Timberlane Rd. I-10, exit 203, just n, w on Timberlane Rd. Ext corridors. **Pets:** Service with restrictions, supervision.
[🗄] [✕] [🏊]

▼▼ Shoney's Inn & Suites 🅼
(850) 386-8286. **$49-$59.** 2801 N Monroe St. I-10, exit 199, just s. Ext corridors. **Pets:** Accepted.
[✕] [🗄] [💻] [🏊]

(AAA) ▼▼ Super 8 Motel 🆂🅷
(850) 386-8818. **$45-$120.** 2702 N Monroe St. I-10, exit 199, 0.4 mi s on US 27. Int corridors. **Pets:** Accepted.
[SAVE] [🗄] [✕] [🗄]

TAMPA BAY METROPOLITAN AREA

APOLLO BEACH

(AAA) ▼▼▼ Ramada Inn on Tampa Bay 🅼
(813) 641-2700. **$59-$149.** 6414 Surfside Blvd. I-75, exit 246, 1.8 mi w on CR 672; 1.8 mi s on US 41, 2.4 mi w on Apollo Beach Blvd. Ext corridors. **Pets:** Small. $15 daily fee/pet. Service with restrictions, supervision.
[SAVE] [🗄] [✕] [♿] [🗄] [💻] [🍴] [🏊] [🗙]

BRANDON

▼▼▼ Behind the Fence Bed & Breakfast 🅱🅱
(813) 685-8201. **$79-$89 (no credit cards), 10 day notice.** 1400 Viola Dr. I-75, exit 254, just s on US 301 northbound; 1.5 mi s on US 301 southbound, 2.5 mi e on Bloomingdale Ave, just n on Country Side St. Ext/int corridors. **Pets:** $10 one-time fee/room. Service with restrictions, crate.
[A$K] [🗄] [✕] [🗄] [💻] [🏊]

▼▼▼ **Homestead Studio Suites Hotel-Tampa/Brandon** M ❧
(813) 643-5900. **$67-$82.** 330 Grand Regency Blvd. I-75, exit 257, just e on SR 60, 0.4 mi n. Ext corridors. **Pets:** Medium, other species. $25 daily fee/room. Service with restrictions, crate.

ASK SB ✕ 🖋M 🐾 ✒ 🔒 🖳

(AAA) ▼▼▼▼ **La Quinta Inn & Suites** SH ❧
(813) 643-0574. **$79-$119.** 310 Grand Regency Blvd. I-75, exit 257, just e on SR 60, 0.5 mi n. Int corridors. **Pets:** Other species. Service with restrictions.

SAVE ✕ 🖋M 🐾 ✒ 🔒 🖳 ⤳

CLEARWATER

▼▼▼ **Homestead Studio Suites Hotel-Tampa/Clearwater** SH ❧
(727) 572-4800. **$54-$87.** 2311 Ulmerton Rd. I-275, exit 31B southbound; exit 30 northbound, 1.5 mi w on SR 688. Ext corridors. **Pets:** Medium, other species. $25 daily fee/room. Service with restrictions, crate.

ASK SB ✕ 🐾 ✒ 🔒 🖳

▼▼▼ **Homewood Suites by Hilton** SH
(727) 573-1500. **$99-$129.** 2233 Ulmerton Rd. I-275, exit 31B, 1.3 mi w on SR 688. Int corridors. **Pets:** Accepted.

ASK SB ✕ 🖋M 🐾 ✒ 🔒 🖳 ⤳

(AAA) ▼▼▼▼ **La Quinta Inn Clearwater-Airport** SH
(727) 572-7222. **$79-$99.** 3301 Ulmerton Rd. I-275, exit 31B, 1.7 mi w on SR 688. Int corridors. **Pets:** Other species. Service with restrictions.

SAVE ✕ 🐾 ✒ 🔒 🖳 ⤳ ✕

▼▼▼▼ **Radisson Hotel Clearwater Central** SH
(727) 799-1181. **$99-$135.** 20967 US 19 N. Just n of jct SR 60. Ext/int corridors. **Pets:** Accepted.

ASK SB ✕ 🖋M 🐾 ✒ 🔒 🖳 🍴 ⤳ ✕

▼▼▼ **Ramada Inn Countryside** SH
(727) 796-1234. **$69-$99.** 26508 US 19 N. On US 19; just s of jct SR 580. Int corridors. **Pets:** Small. $10 daily fee/pet. Designated rooms, service with restrictions, supervision.

ASK SB ✕ 🐾 🔒 🖳 🍴 ⤳ ✕

▼▼▼▼ **Residence Inn by Marriott** SH ❧
(727) 573-4444. **$125-$189.** 5050 Ulmerton Rd. On SR 688, 1 mi e of jct US 19. Ext corridors. **Pets:** Medium, other species. $150 one-time fee/room. Service with restrictions.

ASK ✕ 🐾 ✒ 🔒 🖳 ⤳ ✕

(AAA) ▼▼▼ **Super 8 Clearwater/St. Petersburg Airport** SH ❧
(727) 572-8881. **$45-$89.** 13260 34th St N. I-275, exit 31B southbound; exit 30 northbound, 1.8 mi w on SR 688, just s. Int corridors. **Pets:** Medium. $8 daily fee/pet. Designated rooms, no service, supervision.

SAVE SB ✕ 🔒 ⤳

▼▼▼ **TownePlace Suites by Marriott St. Petersburg/Clearwater** SH
(727) 299-9229. **$69-$159.** 13200 49th St N. I-275, exit 31B southbound; exit 30 northbound, 3 mi w on SR 688, just s. Int corridors. **Pets:** Other species. $75 deposit/room, $10 daily fee/room. Service with restrictions.

ASK SB ✕ 🖋M 🐾 ✒ 🔒 🖳 ⤳

HOLIDAY

(AAA) ▼▼▼ **Best Western-Tahitian Resort** M
(727) 937-4121. **$49-$99, 3 day notice.** 2337 US 19. On US 19, 3 mi n of jct SR 582, 1.5 mi s of jct SR 54. Ext corridors. **Pets:** Other species. $5 daily fee/pet. Designated rooms, service with restrictions, supervision.

SAVE SB ✕ 🐾 🔒 🖳 ⤳

INDIAN ROCKS BEACH

▼▼ **Sea Star Motel & Apartments** M ❧
(727) 596-2525. **$250-$485, 60 day notice.** 1805 Gulf Blvd. On SR 699, 1.2 mi n of jct SR 688 (Walsingham Rd). Ext corridors. **Pets:** Other species. $10 daily fee/pet. Designated rooms, no service, crate.

ASK ✕ 🔒 ✕ ⊠

MADEIRA BEACH

(AAA) ▼▼▼ **Snug Harbor Inn Waterfront Bed & Breakfast** M ❧
(727) 395-9256. **$50-$90, 14 day notice.** 13655 Gulf Blvd. On SR 699, 0.9 mi s of jct Tom Stuart Cswy. Ext corridors. **Pets:** Other species. Service with restrictions.

SAVE ✕ 🔒 🖳 ⤳ ✕

NEW PORT RICHEY

(AAA) ▼▼▼ **Econo Lodge** M
(727) 845-4990. **$45-$90.** 7631 US 19. 0.8 mi n of jct Main St. Ext corridors. **Pets:** Small. $6 daily fee/room. Designated rooms, no service, supervision.

SAVE SB ✕ 🔒 🖳 ⤳

PALM HARBOR

(AAA) ▼▼▼▼ **Four Points By Sheraton Tarpon Springs** SH
(727) 942-0358. **$59-$109.** 37611 US 19 N. On US 19, 3 mi s of jct SR 582. Ext corridors. **Pets:** Other species. $10 daily fee/pet. Designated rooms, service with restrictions, crate.

SAVE ✕ ✒ 🔒 🖳 🍴 ⤳ ✕

▼▼ **Knights Inn-Clearwater/Palm Harbor** M
(727) 789-2002. **$35-$105.** 34106 US 19 N. 1.8 mi n of CR 752 (Tampa Rd). Ext corridors. **Pets:** Other species. $10 daily fee/room. Service with restrictions.

ASK SB ✕ 🔒 🖳 ⤳

(AAA) ▼▼▼▼ **Red Roof Inn** M
(727) 786-2529. **$52-$87.** 32000 US 19 N. On US 19, 0.4 mi s of jct CR 752 (Tampa Rd). Ext corridors. **Pets:** Accepted.

SAVE SB ✕ 🐾 ✒ 🔒 🖳 ⤳

PINELLAS PARK

▼▼▼▼ La Quinta Inn-Pinellas Park SH
(727) 545-5611. **$69-$89.** 7500 US Hwy 19 N. I-275, exit 28, 1.4 mi s on Gandy Blvd (SR 694), just n. Ext/int corridors. **Pets:** Accepted.

PLANT CITY

▼▼ Days Inn Plant City M
(813) 752-0570. **$55-$115.** 301 S Frontage Rd. I-4, exit 21, just e via Frontage Rd. Ext corridors. **Pets:** $10 one-time fee/room. Service with restrictions, supervision.

PORT RICHEY

▼▼▼ Comfort Inn M
(727) 863-3336. **$50-$89.** 11810 US 19. On US 19, just s of jct SR 52. Ext corridors. **Pets:** $6 daily fee/pet. Service with restrictions, supervision.
ASK 🛇 ☒ 🎵 🔒 💻 ➔

▼▼ Travelodge Suites SH
(727) 863-1502. **$60-$80, 5 day notice.** 11736 US Hwy 19 N. On US 19, just s of jct SR 52. Ext corridors. **Pets:** Other species. $5 daily fee/pet. Designated rooms, service with restrictions.
ASK 🛇 ☒ 🔒 💻 🍴 ➔

REDINGTON SHORES

▼▼ San Remo Resort CO
(727) 320-9306. **$550-$1450 (weekly), 7 day notice.** 18320 Gulf Blvd. On SR 699, 0.6 mi s of jct Park Blvd (CR 694). Int corridors. **Pets:** Accepted.
ASK 🛇 ☒ 🔒 ➔

RUSKIN

▼▼▼ Bahia Beach Island Resort & Marina M
(813) 645-3291. **$79-$250.** 611 Destiny Dr. 3.5 mi w of US 41 via Shell Point Rd, follow signs. Ext/int corridors. **Pets:** Very small, other species. $25 one-time fee/room. Designated rooms, service with restrictions, supervision.
ASK 🛇 ☒ ☒ 🎵 🔒 💻 🍴 ➔ ☒

SAFETY HARBOR

◆◆◆ ▼▼▼ Safety Harbor Resort and Spa on Tampa Bay SH
(727) 726-1161. **$89-$209, 3 day notice.** 105 N Bayshore Dr. Jct SR 590 (Main St); downtown. Int corridors. **Pets:** Medium. $25 daily fee/pet. Service with restrictions, supervision.
SAVE 🛇 ☒ ☒ 🎵 ☒ 🔒 💻 🍴 ➔ ☒

ST. PETE BEACH

◆◆◆ ▼▼▼ Lamara Motel Apartments M
(727) 360-7521. **$55-$85, 7 day notice.** 520 73rd Ave. Just w of Gulf Blvd (SR 699). Ext corridors. **Pets:** Small, dogs only. $8 daily fee/pet. Designated rooms, service with restrictions.
SAVE 🛇 ☒ 🔒 ➔ ☒

▼▼ Ritz Motel M
(727) 360-7642. **$49-$95, 14 day notice.** 4237 Gulf Blvd. SR 699, 0.5 mi n of Pinellas Bayway. Ext corridors. **Pets:** Accepted.
🔒 ➔ ☒

ST. PETERSBURG

◆◆◆ ▼▼ Days Inn of St. Petersburg M
(727) 522-3191. **$45-$86.** 2595 54th Ave N. I-275, exit 26 southbound; exit 26B northbound, 0.3 mi w. Ext corridors. **Pets:** Accepted.
SAVE 🛇 ☒ 🎵 🔒 🍴 ➔ ☒

▼▼▼ La Quinta Inn M
(727) 527-8421. **$69-$89.** 4999 34th St N. I-275, exit 26 southbound; exit 26B northbound, just w on 54th Ave N, just s on US 19. Ext corridors. **Pets:** Other species. Service with restrictions, crate.
☒ 🛇 🎵 ☒ 🔒 💻 ➔

◆◆◆ ▼▼▼ Mansion House B & B and The Courtyard on Fifth BB ❀
(727) 821-9391. **$99-$220, 30 day notice.** 105 5th Ave NE. 0.5 mi n at jct 1st St N; downtown. Ext/int corridors. **Pets:** Small, dogs only. $150 deposit/pet, $20 daily fee/pet. Designated rooms, service with restrictions, crate.
SAVE ☒ 🔒 ➔

▼▼▼▼ St. Petersburg Bayfront Hilton LH
(727) 894-5000. **$159-$290.** 333 1st St S. I-275, exit 22, 1.5 mi s on 5th Ave, then just e. Int corridors. **Pets:** Accepted.
ASK 🛇 ☒ ☒ 🎵 ☒ 🔒 💻 🍴 ➔ ☒

SUN CITY CENTER

▼▼ Sun City Center Inn M
(813) 634-3331. **$49-$79.** 809 W Pebble Beach Blvd. I-75, exit 240A southbound; exit 240 northbound, 2.1 mi e on SR 674. Ext corridors. **Pets:** Accepted.
ASK 🛇 ☒ 🎵 ☒ 🔒 💻 ➔ ☒

TAMPA

◆◆◆ ▼▼▼ AmeriSuites (Tampa Airport/Westshore) SH
(813) 282-1037. **$119-$135.** 4811 W Main St. I-275, exit 40A, 0.5 mi w on Westshore; exit 39A northbound, 1 mi n on Kennedy Blvd, 1 mi w on Westshore. Int corridors. **Pets:** Very small, dogs only. Designated rooms, service with restrictions, supervision.
SAVE 🛇 ☒ ☒ 🎵 ☒ 🔒 💻 ➔

◆◆◆ ▼▼▼ AmeriSuites (Tampa near Busch Gardens) SH
(813) 979-1922. **$109-$119.** 11408 N 30th St. I-275, exit 51, 1.8 mi e on SR 582, just s. Int corridors. **Pets:** Small. Designated rooms, service with restrictions, supervision.
SAVE 🛇 ☒ ☒ 🎵 ☒ 🔒 💻 ➔

AmeriSuites (Tampa/Sabal Corp. Park) SH
(813) 622-8557. **$99-$119.** 10007 Princess Palm Ave. I-75, exit 260 southbound; exit 260B northbound, 0.5 mi w on SR 574, just s on Falkenburg Rd, just w. Int corridors. **Pets:** Small, other species. Service with restrictions, supervision.

Baymont Inn & Suites Tampa-Brandon SH
(813) 684-4007. **$69-$99.** 602 S Falkenburg Rd. I-75, exit 257, just w on SR 60. Int corridors. **Pets:** Large, other species. $10 daily fee/room. Service with restrictions, supervision.

Baymont Inn & Suites Tampa/near Busch Gardens SH
(813) 930-6900. **$59-$94.** 9202 N 30th St. I-275, exit 50, 2 mi e on SR 580, just n. Ext corridors. **Pets:** Medium, other species. Designated rooms, service with restrictions, crate.

Baymont Inn Tampa-Fairgrounds M
(813) 626-0885. **$54-$99.** 4811 US 301 N. I-4, exit 6 westbound; exit 6A eastbound, just se. Int corridors. **Pets:** Accepted.

Best Western-The Westshore Hotel LH
(813) 282-3636. **$75-$119, 3 day notice.** 1200 N Westshore Blvd. I-275, exit 40A southbound, 0.4 mi n; exit 39A northbound, 0.5 mi e on Kennedy Blvd, 1.2 mi n. Int corridors. **Pets:** Medium, other species. $25 one-time fee/pet. Designated rooms, service with restrictions, crate.

Chase Suite Hotel by Woodfin M
(813) 281-5677. **$89-$199.** 3075 N Rocky Point Dr. I-275, exit 39 southbound; exit 39B northbound, 3 mi w on SR 60, just n. Ext corridors. **Pets:** Accepted.

Comfort Inn and Conference Center Near Busch Gardens SH
(813) 933-4011. **$59-$89.** 820 E Busch Blvd. I-275, exit 50, just e on SR 580. Ext/int corridors. **Pets:** Small, other species. $25 one-time fee/room. Designated rooms.

Days Inn Airport Stadium M
(813) 877-6181. **$85-$149.** 2522 N Dale Mabry Hwy. I-275, exit 41B, 0.6 mi ne on US 92. Ext corridors. **Pets:** Accepted.

Hampton Inn Veterans Expressway SH
(813) 901-5900. **$109-$139.** 5628 W Waters Ave. SR 589 (Veteran's Expwy), exit 6A, just e on CR 584. Int corridors. **Pets:** $8 daily fee/room. Service with restrictions, supervision.

Holiday Inn Express Hotel & Suites Tampa Stadium/Airport M
(813) 877-6061. **$98-$139.** 4732 N Dale Mabry Hwy. I-275, exit 41B, 2 mi n. Ext corridors. **Pets:** Other species. $35 one-time fee/room. Service with restrictions.

Holiday Inn Tampa Near Busch Gardens SH
(813) 971-4710. **$129-$169.** 2701 E Fowler Ave. I-275, exit 51, 1.5 mi e on SR 582. Ext/int corridors. **Pets:** Small. $25 one-time fee/pet. Service with restrictions.

Homestead Studio Suites Hotel-Tampa/North Airport M
(813) 243-1913. **$44-$54.** 5401 Beaumont Ctr Blvd. SR 589 (Veterans Expwy), exit 4, just w on SR 580. Ext corridors. **Pets:** Medium, other species. $25 daily fee/room. Service with restrictions, crate.

La Quinta Inn & Suites USF SH
(813) 910-7500. **$85-$125.** 3701 E Fowler. I-275, exit 265, 2.2 mi e on SR 582. Int corridors. **Pets:** Accepted.

La Quinta Inn Tampa Airport M
(813) 287-0440. **$79-$109.** 4730 Spruce St. I-275, exit 40A southbound; exit 39A northbound (Westshore Blvd), 0.8 mi w. Ext corridors. **Pets:** Other species. Service with restrictions, supervision.

Motel 6 #1192 M
(813) 628-0888. **$41-$57.** 6510 US 301 N. I-4, exit 6 westbound; exit 6B eastbound, 0.7 mi n. Ext corridors. **Pets:** Accepted.

Motel 6–483 M
(813) 932-4948. **$41-$55.** 333 E Fowler Ave. I-275, exit 51, just w on SR 582. Ext corridors. **Pets:** Accepted.

Park Plaza Tampa Airport Westshore LH
(813) 289-1950. **$79-$159.** 5303 W Kennedy Blvd. I-275, exit 40A, 0.4 mi e on Westshore Blvd, 0.5 mi s; exit 39A northbound, just e. Ext/int corridors. **Pets:** Medium. $25 one-time fee/room. Service with restrictions, crate.

Red Roof Inn M
(813) 932-0073. **$34-$69.** 2307 E Busch Blvd. I-275, exit 50, 1.4 mi e on SR 580. Ext corridors. **Pets:** Accepted.

Red Roof Inn-Brandon M
(813) 681-8484. **$47-$87.** 10121 Horace Ave. I-75, exit 257, just w to S Falkenberg Rd, just n. Ext corridors. **Pets:** Medium, other species. Supervision.

Red Roof Inn-Fairgrounds M
(813) 623-5245. **$39-$79.** 5001 N US 301. I-4, exit 7 westbound; exit 7A eastbound, just se. Ext corridors. **Pets:** Accepted.
SAVE ✕ 🐾 🛋️

Residence Inn by Marriott SH
(813) 221-4224. **$119-$179.** 101 E Tyler St. I-275, exit 44, 0.5 mi se via Tampa St; downtown. Int corridors. **Pets:** Accepted.
ASK 🛏️ ✕ 🛋️ 🐾 🖥️ 📺 🍽️

Residence Inn by Marriott Sabal Park SH
(813) 627-8855. **$99-$169.** 9719 Princess Palm Ave. I-75, exit 260 southbound; exit 260B northbound, just w on SR 574, just s on Falkenburg Rd, then 0.4 mi w. Int corridors. **Pets:** Accepted.
ASK 🛏️ ✕ 🛋️ 🐾 🖥️ 📺 🍽️ 🏊

Tahitian Inn M 🐾
(813) 877-6721. **$99-$199.** 601 S Dale Mabry Hwy. I-275, exit 41A, 1.1 mi s. Ext corridors. **Pets:** Small, other species. $25 one-time fee/room. Service with restrictions.
SAVE 🛏️ ✕ 🖥️ 📺 🍽️

Wellesley Inn & Suites (Tampa/Westshore) SH
(813) 637-8990. **$89-$129.** 1805 N Westshore Blvd. I-275, exit 40A southbound, 0.5 mi n; exit 39A northbound, 0.5 mi e on Kennedy Blvd, 1.3 mi n. Int corridors. **Pets:** Accepted.
SAVE 🛏️ ✕ 🛋️ 🐾 🖥️ 📺

Wingate Inn-USF Near Busch Gardens SH
(813) 979-2828. **$79-$129.** 3751 E Fowler Ave. I-275, exit 51, 2.2 mi e on SR 582. Int corridors. **Pets:** Accepted.
ASK 🛏️ ✕ 🛋️ 🐾 🖥️ 📺 🍽️

TEMPLE TERRACE

Residence Inn by Marriott Tampa North SH 🐾
(813) 972-4400. **$129-$169.** 13420 N Telecom Pkwy. I-75, exit 266, 1.1 mi w on Fletcher Ave (CR 582A). Int corridors. **Pets:** Other species. $125 one-time fee/room. Service with restrictions, supervision.
ASK 🛏️ ✕ 🛋️ 🐾 🖥️ 📺 🍽️

TREASURE ISLAND

Best Western Sea Castle Suites M
(727) 367-2704. **$69-$165, 3 day notice.** 10750 Gulf Blvd. On SR 699, jct Treasure Island Cswy. Ext corridors. **Pets:** Very small. $50 deposit/room. Service with restrictions, crate.
SAVE 🛏️ ✕ 🖥️ 📺 🍽️

WESLEY CHAPEL

Masters Inn Tampa North SH
(813) 973-0155. **$49-$69.** 27807 SR 54 W. I-75, exit 279, just w. Ext corridors. **Pets:** Medium, other species. $10 one-time fee/pet. Designated rooms, service with restrictions, supervision.
SAVE 🛏️ ✕ 🛋️ 🖥️ 🍴 🍽️

❖ **END METROPOLITAN AREA** ❖

TITUSVILLE

Best Western Space Shuttle Inn SH 🐾
(321) 269-9100. **$69-$135.** 3455 Cheney Hwy. I-95, exit 215, just e on SR 50. Ext corridors. **Pets:** Other species. $10 daily fee/room. Designated rooms, service with restrictions.
SAVE 🛏️ ✕ 🛋️ 🖥️ 📺 🍴 🍽️

Comfort Inn Titusville SH
(321) 269-7110. **$59-$175.** 3655 Cheney Hwy. I-95, exit 215, just w. Ext corridors. **Pets:** Medium. $10 daily fee/pet. Service with restrictions, supervision.
SAVE 🛏️ 🖥️ 📺

Days Inn-Kennedy Space Center SH 🐾
(321) 269-4480. **$59-$135.** 3755 Cheney Hwy. I-95, exit 215 (SR 50). Ext corridors. **Pets:** Other species. $10 daily fee/room. Service with restrictions, crate.
ASK 🛏️ ✕ 🛋️ 🖥️ 📺 🍽️

Holiday Inn Riverfront-Kennedy Space Center SH 🐾
(321) 269-2121. **$74-$135.** 4951 S Washington Ave. US 1, 0.5 mi s of jct SR 50; 1.7 mi n of jct SR 405. Ext corridors. **Pets:** $25 one-time fee/room. Service with restrictions, supervision.
SAVE 🛏️ ✕ 🛋️ 🐾 🖥️ 📺 🍴 🍽️

Ramada Inn & Suites-Kennedy Space Center SH
(321) 269-5510. **$99-$109.** 3500 Cheney Hwy. I-95, exit 215, just e on SR 50. Int corridors. **Pets:** Other species. $10 one-time fee/room. Service with restrictions, supervision.
SAVE 🛏️ ✕ 🛋️ 🖥️ 📺 🍴 🍽️

VENICE

Holiday Inn Venice M
(941) 485-5411. **$109-$189.** 455 US 41 Bypass N. On US 41 Bypass, 0.5 mi s of jct US 41. Ext/int corridors. **Pets:** Small. $30 one-time fee/room. Designated rooms.
SAVE 🛏️ ✕ 🛋️ 🐾 🖥️ 📺 🍴 🍽️

▼▼▼ Horse and Chaise Inn A Bed &
Breakfast 🅱🅱
(941) 488-2702. **$95-$125.** 317 Ponce de Leon. Jct Venice
Ave, just s on Nassau St, then just sw; downtown. Ext/int
corridors. **Pets:** Accepted.
🄰🅂🄺 🆂📀 ☒ 🔟 🛇

▼▼ Motel 6–364 Ⓜ
(941) 485-8255. **$43-$79.** 281 US 41 Bypass N. On US 41,
just n of jct Venice Ave. Ext corridors. **Pets:** Accepted.
🆂📀 ☒ 🔟 🖋 🔜

VERO BEACH

▼▼ Vero Beach Resort 🆂🄷
(772) 562-9991. **$54-$67.** 8800 20th St. I-95, exit 147 (SR
60), 0.5 mi e. Ext corridors. **Pets:** Accepted.
🄰🅂🄺 🆂📀 ☒ 🔟 🔟 💻 🍴 🔜

WEEKI WACHEE

🄰🄰🄰 ▼▼▼ Best Western Weeki Wachee
Resort Ⓜ
(352) 596-2007. **$65-$80.** 6172 Commercial Way. On US 19,
jct SR 50 (Cortez Blvd). Ext corridors. **Pets:** Other species.
Service with restrictions, supervision.
🆂🄰🅅🄴 🆂📀 ☒ 🔟 💻 🔜

WEST MELBOURNE

▼▼ Howard Johnson 🆂🄷
(321) 768-8877. **$69-$129, 10 day notice.** 4431 W New
Haven Ave. I-95, exit 180, just e on SR 192. Ext corridors.
Pets: Other species. $20 one-time fee/room. Designated
rooms, service with restrictions, crate.
🄰🅂🄺 🆂📀 ☒ 🔟 💻 🔜

▼▼ Ramada Limited West Melbourne 🆂🄷
(321) 724-2051. **$55-$125.** 4500 W New Haven Ave. I-95,
exit 180, just e. Ext corridors. **Pets:** Accepted.
🄰🅂🄺 🆂📀 ☒ 🔟 🖋 💻

WEST PALM BEACH

🄰🄰🄰 ▼▼▼▼ Comfort Inn-Palm Beach Lakes Ⓜ
(561) 689-6100. **$65-$139.** 1901 Palm Beach Lakes Blvd.
I-95, exit 71, just w. Int corridors. **Pets:** Medium. $10 daily
fee/room, $25 one-time fee/room. Designated rooms, serv-
ice with restrictions, supervision.
🆂🄰🅅🄴 🆂📀 ☒ 🔟 🔟 💻 🍴 🔜

▼▼▼▼ Hibiscus House Bed & Breakfast 🅱🅱
(561) 863-5633. **$75-$190, 14 day notice.** 501 30th St. 1.2
mi n on Flagler Dr from jct Palm Beach Lakes Blvd, 0.3 mi
w. Int corridors. **Pets:** Other species.
🄰🅂🄺 🆂📀 ☒ 🔟 🔜

🄰🄰🄰 ▼▼▼▼ Radisson Suite Inn Palm Beach
Airport 🆂🄷
(561) 689-6888. **$129-$149.** 1808 Australian Ave S. I-95, exit
69, 0.5 mi w on Belvedere Rd, then 0.5 mi n. Int corridors.
Pets: Large. $75 one-time fee/room. Designated rooms,
service with restrictions.
🆂🄰🅅🄴 🆂📀 ☒ 🔟🄼 🖋 💻 🍴 🔜 ☒

🄰🄰🄰 ▼▼▼ Red Roof Inn-West Palm Beach Ⓜ
(561) 697-7710. **$47-$94.** 2421 Metro Center Blvd E. I-95,
exit 74 (45th St), just w on CR 702. Ext/int corridors.
Pets: Accepted.
🆂🄰🅅🄴 ☒ 🔟🄼 🖋 🔟 🔟 🔜

▼▼▼▼ Residence Inn by Marriott West Palm
Beach 🆂🄷
(561) 687-4747. **$135-$229.** 2461 Metrocenter Blvd. I-95,
exit 74, just w on 45th St. Int corridors. **Pets:** Accepted.
🄰🅂🄺 🆂📀 ☒ 🔟🄼 🖋 🔟 🔟 💻 🔜 ☒

▼▼▼ Studio 6 Extended Stay #6026 Ⓜ 🐾
(561) 640-3335. **$63-$93.** 1535 Centrepark Dr N. I-95, exit
69 (Belvedere Rd), w to Australian Ave, n to Centrepark Dr,
then e straight ahead. Ext corridors. **Pets:** Medium, other
species. $10 daily fee/pet. Service with restrictions.
☒ 🔟🄼 🖋 🔟 💻

🄰🄰🄰 ▼▼▼ Wellesley Inn (West Palm Beach) 🆂🄷
(561) 689-8540. **$69-$159.** 1910 Palm Beach Lakes Blvd.
I-95, exit 71, just w. Int corridors. **Pets:** Accepted.
🆂🄰🅅🄴 🆂📀 ☒ 🔟 🖋 🔟 💻 🔜

WILLISTON

▼ Williston Motor Inn Ⓜ
(352) 528-4801. **$35-$192.** 606 W Noble Ave. 0.5 mi n on
US 27 Alternate. Ext corridors. **Pets:** Accepted.
☒ 🔟 💻 🍴 🔜

WINTER HAVEN

🄰🄰🄰 ▼▼▼ Best Western Admiral's Inn 🆂🄷
(863) 324-5950. **$74-$167, 30 day notice.** 5665 Cypress
Gardens Blvd. SR 540, 3 mi e of jct US 17; 3.9 mi w of jct
US 27. Ext/int corridors. **Pets:** Small, other species. $15
one-time fee/room. Designated rooms, service with restrictions, supervision.
🆂🄰🅅🄴 🆂📀 ☒ 🔟 🔟 💻 🍴 🔜 ☒

▼▼ Cypress Motel Ⓜ
(863) 324-5867. **$50-$80.** 5651 Cypress Gardens Rd. 1.7 mi
w of US 27 on SR 540; or 2 mi e of Cypress Gardens
Theme Park, then 500 yds n. Ext corridors. **Pets:** Small.
$10 one-time fee/pet. Service with restrictions, crate.
🄰🅂🄺 🆂📀 ☒ 🔟 🔟 💻 🔜 ☒

GEORGIA

ADAIRSVILLE

▲▲▲ ▼▼ Comfort Inn SH
(770) 773-2886. **$50-$85.** 107 Princeton Blvd. I-75, exit 306, just w. Ext corridors. **Pets:** Small. $5 daily fee/pet. Service with restrictions, supervision.
SAVE SO X LM C H P

▼▼▼ Ramada Ltd SH
(770) 769-9726. **$59-$94.** 500 Georgia North Cir. I-75, exit 306, 0.3 mi w. Ext corridors. **Pets:** Accepted.
ASK SO X LM C H P

ADEL

▼▼▼ Hampton Inn SH
(229) 896-3099. **$72.** 1500 W 4th St. I-75, exit 39, just w. Int corridors. **Pets:** Other species. $10 daily fee/pet. Designated rooms, service with restrictions, supervision.
ASK SO X LM C H P

▼▼ Super 8 Motel I-75 SH
(229) 896-2244. **$39-$49.** 1103 W 4th St. I-75, exit 39, just e. Ext corridors. **Pets:** Accepted.
ASK SO X

ALBANY

▼▼ Jameson Inn SH
(229) 435-3737. **$69-$74.** 2720 Dawson Rd. 0.5 mi s of jct US 82 and SR 520. Ext corridors. **Pets:** Small. Service with restrictions, crate.
X H P

▼ Motel 6 SH
(229) 439-0078. **$36-$189.** 201 S Thorton Dr. Just e of US 19/82. Ext corridors. **Pets:** Accepted.
X

▼▼▼ Wingate Inn SH
(229) 883-9800. **$103.** 2735 Dawson Rd. Jct US 82 and SR 520, 0.4 mi s. Int corridors. **Pets:** Other species. $50 one-time fee/room. No service, crate.
ASK SO X H P

AMERICUS

▼▼▼ 1906 Pathway Inn Bed & Breakfast BB ☙
(229) 928-2078. **$89-$145.** 501 S Lee St. 0.5 mi s of US 280 on SR 377. Int corridors. **Pets:** Small. $50 deposit/room, $20 daily fee/pet. Designated rooms, supervision.
ASK SO X

ASHBURN

▲▲▲ ▼▼▼ Best Western Ashburn Inn SH
(229) 567-0080. **$46-$55.** 820 Shoney's Dr. I-75, exit 82, just w. Ext corridors. **Pets:** Very small. $5 daily fee/pet. Designated rooms, service with restrictions, supervision.
SAVE X H P

▲▲▲ ▼▼▼ Days Inn SH ☙
(229) 567-3346. **$42-$45.** 823 E Washington Ave. I-75, exit 82, just w on SR 112. Ext corridors. **Pets:** Small. $5 daily fee/pet. Service with restrictions, supervision.
SAVE X H

ATHENS

▲▲▲ ▼▼▼ Best Western-Colonial Inn SH
(706) 546-7311. **$59-$99.** 170 N Milledge Ave. Jct US 78 business route (Broad St), 0.5 mi w on SR 15. Ext corridors. **Pets:** Accepted.
SAVE SO X H P

▼▼▼ Holiday Inn SH
(706) 549-4433. **$89-$119.** 197 E Broad St. On US 78 business route (Broad St); center. Ext/int corridors. **Pets:** Accepted.
ASK SO X C H P H

▼▼▼ Holiday Inn Express SH
(706) 546-8122. **$85.** 513 W Broad St. On US 78 business route (Broad St); center. Int corridors. **Pets:** Small. $25 one-time fee/room. Designated rooms, service with restrictions, supervision.
ASK SO X LM C H P

ATLANTA METROPOLITAN AREA

ACWORTH

Best Western Frontier Inn SH
(770) 974-0116. **$55-$65.** 5155 Cowan Rd. I-75, exit 277, just w. Ext corridors. **Pets:** Accepted.
SAVE ⊠ 🖥 💻 ➾

Days Inn M
(770) 974-1700. **$50.** 5035 Cowan Rd. I-75, exit 277, just w. Ext corridors. **Pets:** Accepted.
SAVE S⊘ ⊠ ➾

Econo Lodge SH
(770) 974-1922. **$50.** 4980 Cowan Rd. I-75, exit 277, just w. Ext corridors. **Pets:** Accepted.
SAVE S⊘ ⊠ 💻 ➾

Red Roof Inn M
(770) 974-5400. **$44-$55, 3 day notice.** 5320 Glade Rd. I-75, exit 278, just w. Ext corridors. **Pets:** Accepted.
SAVE S⊘ ⊠ 🚳 🖥 ➾

Super 8 Motel SH
(770) 966-9700. **$45-$79.** 4970 Cowan Rd. I-75, exit 277, just w. Ext corridors. **Pets:** Large. $8 daily fee/pet. Service with restrictions, supervision.
SAVE S⊘ ⊠ 🚳 🖥 ➾

ALPHARETTA

AmeriSuites (Atlanta Alpharetta/Cingular Way) SH
(678) 339-0505. **$109.** 12505 Cingular Way. SR 400, exit 11, 0.5 mi w. Int corridors. **Pets:** Medium, dogs only. $10 one-time fee/pet. Service with restrictions, crate.
SAVE S⊘ ⊠ 🚳 🚳 🖥 💻 ➾

AmeriSuites (Atlanta Alpharetta/North Point Mall) SH
(770) 594-8788. **$79-$99.** 7500 North Point Pkwy. SR 400, exit 8, just e to North Point Pkwy, just n. Int corridors. **Pets:** Accepted.
SAVE S⊘ ⊠ 🚳 🚳 🖥 💻 ➾

AmeriSuites (Atlanta Alpharetta/Windward Parkway) SH
(770) 343-9566. **$89-$149.** 5595 Windward Pkwy. SR 400, exit 11, just w. Int corridors. **Pets:** Small. Service with restrictions, supervision.
SAVE S⊘ ⊠ 🚳 🚳 🖥 💻 ➾

Homewood Suites SH
(770) 998-1622. **$69-$89.** 10775 Davis Dr. SR 400, exit 8, northwest corner. Int corridors. **Pets:** Accepted.
SAVE S⊘ ⊠ 🚳 🚳 🚳 🖥 💻 ➾

La Quinta Inn & Suites SH
(770) 754-7800. **$79-$99.** 1350 North Point Dr. SR 400, exit 9, 0.5 mi e. Int corridors. **Pets:** Accepted.
SAVE S⊘ ⊠ 🚳 🚳 🖥 💻 ➾

Residence Inn by Marriott SH
(770) 664-0664. **$109-$155.** 5465 Windward Pkwy W. SR 400, exit 11, 0.4 mi w. Ext/int corridors. **Pets:** Accepted.
ASK S⊘ ⊠ 🚳 🚳 🚳 🖥 💻 ➾ ⊠

Staybridge Suites SH
(770) 569-7200. **$129-$169.** 3980 North Point Pkwy. SR 400, exit 10, 0.5 mi e. Int corridors. **Pets:** Other species. $150 one-time fee/pet. Service with restrictions.
ASK ⊠ 🚳 🚳 🚳 🖥 💻 ➾

TownePlace Suites by Marriott SH
(770) 664-1300. **$84-$109.** 7925 S Westside Pkwy. SR 400, exit 9, 0.3 mi w. Int corridors. **Pets:** Accepted.
ASK S⊘ ⊠ 🚳 🚳 🚳 🖥 💻 ➾

Wellesley Inn & Suites (Atlanta/Alpharetta) SH
(770) 569-1730. **$49-$129.** 3329 Old Milton Pkwy. SR 400, exit 10, just e. Int corridors. **Pets:** Other species. $25 deposit/room.
SAVE S⊘ ⊠ 🚳 🚳 🚳 🖥 💻 ➾

ATLANTA

AmeriSuites (Atlanta/Buckhead) SH
(404) 869-6161. **$124-$134.** 3242 Peachtree Rd NE. Jct Peachtree and Piedmont rds NE, just s. Int corridors. **Pets:** Medium, other species. Service with restrictions, supervision.
SAVE S⊘ ⊠ 🚳 🚳 🚳 🖥 💻 ➾

AmeriSuites (Atlanta/Perimeter Center) SH
(770) 730-9300. **$71-$90.** 1005 Crestline Pkwy. SR 400, exit 5A (Dunwoody), 0.3 mi e. Int corridors. **Pets:** Small, other species. Service with restrictions.
SAVE S⊘ ⊠ 🚳 🚳 🚳 🖥 💻 ➾

Baymont Inn & Suites Atlanta-Lenox/Buckhead SH
(404) 321-0999. **$64-$84.** 2535 Chantilly Dr NE. I-85, exit 88 southbound; exit 86 northbound, 2 mi on Buford Hwy to Lenox Rd, just e, under highway. Int corridors. **Pets:** Accepted.
ASK S⊘ ⊠ 🚳 🖥 💻

Best Western Granada Suite Hotel SH
(404) 876-6100. **$85-$209.** 1302 W Peachtree St. I-75/85, exit 250 (14th St), just e, then just n on W Peachtree St to 16th St. Int corridors. **Pets:** Small. $50 one-time fee/pet. Service with restrictions, supervision.
SAVE S⊘ ⊠ 🚳 🖥 💻

Best Western Inn at the Peachtrees SH
(404) 577-6970. **$81-$209.** 330 W Peachtree St. I-75/85, exit 248C northbound, 0.4 mi w to Peachtree St, 0.3 mi n; exit 249C southbound, just s to Peachtree Pl, then just e. Ext/int corridors. **Pets:** Large, other species. $50 one-time fee/pet. Service with restrictions, supervision.
SAVE S⊘ 🚳 🖥 💻

▼▼ Beverly Hills Inn 🅱🅱
(404) 233-8520. **$119-$165, 3 day notice.** 65 Sheridan Dr NE. Jct Piedmont and Peachtree rds, 1.1 mi s on Peachtree Rd to Sheridan Dr, just e. Int corridors. **Pets:** Large, other species. $50 one-time fee/pet. Service with restrictions, supervision.
(ASK) 🆂 🛢 🖵

▼▼▼ Crowne Plaza Atlanta-Buckhead 🅻🅷
(404) 264-1111. **$169-$229.** 3377 Peachtree Rd NE. I-85, exit 88, n on Lenox Rd to Peachtree Rd NE, 0.3 mi sw. Int corridors. **Pets:** Accepted.
(ASK) 🆂 ✕ 🔧 🎵 🎬 🛢 🖵 🍴

▼▼▼ Crowne Plaza Atlanta Perimeter NW 🅻🅷
(770) 955-1700. **$100-$200.** 6345 Powers Ferry Rd NW. I-285, exit 22, southeast corner. Int corridors. **Pets:** Small. $75 one-time fee/room. Service with restrictions.
(ASK) 🆂 ✕ 🔧 🎵 🎬 🛢 🖵 🍴 🏊

🅐🅐🅐 ▼▼▼▼ Four Seasons Hotel Atlanta 🆂🅷 ✿
(404) 881-9898. **$265-$3000.** 75 14th St. I-75/85, exit 250 (10th/14th St), 0.3 mi e. Int corridors. **Pets:** Small. Service with restrictions, supervision.
✕ 🔧 🎵 🎬 🍴 🏊 🚫

🅐🅐🅐 ▼▼▼ ▼▼ Grand Hyatt Atlanta 🅻🅷
(404) 365-8100. **$110-$265.** 3300 Peachtree Rd. Corner of Peachtree and Piedmont rds. Int corridors. **Pets:** Accepted.
(SAVE) 🆂 ✕ 🔧 🎵 🎬 🛢 🖵 🍴 🏊 🚫

▼▼▼ Hawthorn Suites-Atlanta NW 🆂🅷
(770) 952-9595. **$55-$95.** 1500 Parkwood Cir. I-75, exit 260 (Windy Hill Rd), 0.5 mi e, 0.3 mi s on Powers Ferry Rd. Ext corridors. **Pets:** Accepted.
(ASK) 🆂 ✕ 🎬 🛢 🖵 🏊 🚫

▼▼ Holiday Inn Select Atlanta Perimeter 🆂🅷
(770) 457-6363. **$109-$149.** 4386 Chamblee-Dunwoody Rd. I-285, exit 30 eastbound, southwest corner; westbound, follow access road 1.3 mi to Chamblee-Dunwoody Rd, just s. Int corridors. **Pets:** Accepted.
(ASK) 🆂 ✕ 🔧 🎵 🎬 🛢 🖵 🍴 🏊

▼▼ Homestead Studio Suites Hotel-Atlanta/North Druid Hills 🆂🅷 ✿
(404) 325-1223. **$69-$84.** 1339 Executive Park Dr NE. I-85, exit 89, just e to Executive Park Dr, then just s. Ext corridors. **Pets:** Medium, other species. $25 daily fee/room. Service with restrictions, crate.
✕ 🔧 🎵 🎬 🛢 🖵

▼▼▼ Homestead Studio Suites Hotel-Atlanta/Perimeter 🆂🅷 ✿
(770) 522-0025. **$59-$74.** 1050 Hammond Dr. I-285, exit 26 eastbound, 0.5 mi n to Hammond Dr, 0.5 mi e; exit 28 westbound, just n to Hammond Dr, then just w. Ext corridors. **Pets:** Medium, other species. $25 daily fee/room. Service with restrictions, crate.
✕ 🔧 🎵 🎬 🛢 🖵

▼▼▼ Homewood Suites-Atlanta Buckhead 🆂🅷
(404) 365-0001. **$116, 7 day notice.** 3566 Piedmont Rd. SR 400, exit 2, 1 mi n. Int corridors. **Pets:** Medium. $150 one-time fee/room. Designated rooms, service with restrictions, supervision.
(ASK) 🆂 ✕ 🔧 🎵 🎬 🛢 🖵 🏊

▼▼▼▼ Homewood Suites-Cumberland 🆂🅷
(770) 988-9449. **$79-$189.** 3200 Cobb Pkwy SW. I-285, exit 19 eastbound; exit 20 westbound, 0.7 mi se on US 41. Ext/int corridors. **Pets:** Other species. $150 one-time fee/room. Service with restrictions.
(ASK) 🆂 ✕ 🔧 🎵 🛢 🖵 🏊 🚫

▼▼▼▼ La Quinta Inn & Suites 🆂🅷
(770) 801-9002. **$69-$99.** 2415 Paces Ferry Rd SE. I-285, exit 18, just w. Int corridors. **Pets:** Accepted.
(ASK) 🆂 ✕ 🔧 🎵 🎬 🛢 🖵 🏊

🅐🅐🅐 ▼▼▼ La Quinta Inn & Suites-Perimeter 🆂🅷
(770) 350-6177. **$65-$89.** 6260 Peachtree-Dunwoody. I-285, exit 28 westbound, 0.7 mi n; exit 26 eastbound, 0.5 mi n to Hammond Dr, 0.7 mi e, then 0.5 mi n. Int corridors. **Pets:** Accepted.
(SAVE) 🆂 ✕ 🔧 🎵 🎬 🛢 🖵 🏊

▼▼▼ Omni Hotel at CNN Center 🅻🅷
(404) 659-0000. **$150-$380.** 100 CNN Center. I-75/85, exit 248C northbound, 0.8 mi w; exit 249C southbound to International Blvd, 0.5 mi w. Int corridors. **Pets:** Accepted.
(ASK) 🆂 ✕ 🎬 🛢 🖵 🍴

▼▼ Ramada Inn & Conference Center 🆂🅷
(404) 873-4661. **$69-$99.** 418 Armour Dr NE. I-85, exit 86 to Monroe Dr, just e to Armour Dr, 0.3 mi w. Ext corridors. **Pets:** Accepted.
(ASK) 🆂 ✕ 🔧 🎵 🎬 🛢 🖵 🍴 🏊

🅐🅐🅐 ▼▼▼ Red Roof Inn-Druid Hills 🅼
(404) 321-1653. **$54-$69.** 1960 N Druid Hills Rd. I-85, exit 89, just w. Ext corridors. **Pets:** Accepted.
(SAVE) ✕ 🎵

▼▼▼ Residence Inn Atlanta Midtown at 17th Street 🆂🅷
(404) 745-1000. **$89-$265.** 1365 Peachtree St. I-75/85, exit 250 (14th St), 0.5 mi e to Peachtree St, then 0.3 mi n. Int corridors. **Pets:** Medium. $150 one-time fee/room. Service with restrictions, supervision.
(ASK) 🆂 ✕ 🔧 🎵 🎬 🛢 🖵

▼▼▼ Residence Inn-Buckhead/Lenox 🆂🅷
(404) 467-1660. **$155-$170.** 2220 Lake Blvd. I-85, exit 89, 1.6 mi w on N Druid Hills which becomes E Roxboro, just n on Lenox Park Blvd. Int corridors. **Pets:** Accepted.
(ASK) 🆂 ✕ 🔧 🎵 🎬 🛢 🖵 🏊 🚫

▼▼▼ Residence Inn by Marriott-Atlanta/Buckhead 🆂🅷
(404) 239-0677. **$69-$194.** 2960 Piedmont Rd NE. Jct Piedmont and Pharr rds, just s. Ext corridors. **Pets:** Accepted.
(ASK) 🆂 ✕ 🎵 🎬 🛢 🖵 🏊 🚫

▼▼▼ Residence Inn by Marriott-Atlanta Downtown 🆂🅷
(404) 522-0950. **$160.** 134 Peachtree St NW. I-75/85, exit 248C northbound, 0.4 mi w, then just s; exit 249A southbound to International Blvd, just w, then just s. Int corridors. **Pets:** Accepted.
(ASK) 🆂 ✕ 🎵 🎬 🛢 🖵

Residence Inn by Marriott Atlanta Dunwoody SH ❀
(770) 455-4446. **$69-$99.** 1901 Savoy Dr. I-285, exit 30, just e. Ext corridors. **Pets:** Large, other species. $100 one-time fee/room. Supervision.

(ASK) (S6) (X) (🔊) (🔔) (🍴) (💻) (🏊) (🚫)

Residence Inn by Marriott Midtown SH
(404) 872-8885. **$189.** 1041 W Peachtree St. I-75/85, exit 250 (14th St), just e to W Peachtree St, just n; corner of 11th St. Int corridors. **Pets:** Other species. $100 one-time fee/pet. Service with restrictions, crate.

(ASK) (S6) (X) (&M) (🔊) (🔔) (🍴) (💻)

Residence Inn by Marriott-Perimeter West SH ❀
(404) 252-5066. **$74-$159.** 6096 Barfield Rd. I-285, exit 26 eastbound, 0.5 mi n on Glenridge to Hammond, 0.3 mi e to Barfield Rd; exit 28 westbound (Peachtree-Dunwoody Rd), 0.5 mi n to Hammond Dr, just w. Ext corridors. **Pets:** Small, other species. $100 one-time fee/room. Service with restrictions.

(SAVE) (X) (🔊) (🔔) (🍴) (💻) (🏊) (🚫)

The Ritz-Carlton, Buckhead LH ❀
(404) 237-2700. **$195-$335.** 3434 Peachtree Rd NE. I-85, exit 86, 1.8 mi n on Cheshire Bridge-Lenox Rd. Int corridors. **Pets:** Small. $250 one-time fee/room. Service with restrictions, supervision.

(SAVE) (S6) (X) (🔊) (🔔) (🍴) (💻) (🍽) (🏊) (🚫)

Staybridge Suites SH
(404) 842-0800. **$105-$154.** 540 Pharr Rd. Jct Pharr and Piedmont rds, just w. Int corridors. **Pets:** Small. $150 one-time fee/pet. Service with restrictions.

(ASK) (S6) (X) (🔊) (🔔) (🍴) (💻) (🏊) (🚫)

Staybridge Suites Atlanta Perimeter SH
(678) 320-0111. **$149-$189.** 4601 Ridgeview Rd. I-285, exit 29, 0.5 mi n, 0.5 mi w on Perimeter Center W to Crowne Pointe Dr, then just n. Int corridors. **Pets:** Medium. $75 one-time fee/room. Service with restrictions, supervision.

(ASK) (S6) (X) (&M) (🔊) (🔔) (🍴) (💻) (🏊)

Summerfield Suites by Wyndham-Atlanta/Buckhead SH
(404) 262-7880. **$84-$119.** 505 Pharr Rd. Jct Pharr Rd and Maple Dr, just w of Piedmont Rd. Ext/int corridors. **Pets:** Accepted.

(SAVE) (S6) (X) (🔊) (🔔) (🍴) (💻) (🏊) (🚫)

Summerfield Suites by Wyndham-Atlanta/Perimeter SH
(404) 250-0110. **$84-$119.** 760 Mt Vernon Hwy NE. I-285, exit 25, 0.8 mi n on Roswell Rd, 1 mi e. Ext/int corridors. **Pets:** Accepted.

(SAVE) (S6) (X) (🔊) (🔔) (🍴) (💻) (🏊) (🚫)

Super 8 Motel M
(404) 873-5731. **$69-$99.** 1641 Peachtree St NE. I-75/85, exit 250 (14th St), 0.3 mi e to W Peachtree St, then 1 mi n. Ext/int corridors. **Pets:** Accepted.

(ASK) (S6) (X) (🔔) (🍴)

Swissotel LH ❀
(404) 365-0065. **$159-$359.** 3391 Peachtree Rd NE. Adjacent to Lenox Mall. Int corridors. **Pets:** Medium, dogs only. Service with restrictions, crate.

(SAVE) (S6) (X) (🔊) (🔔) (🍴) (💻) (🍽) (🏊) (🚫)

University Inn at Emory SH ❀
(404) 634-7327. **$89-$144.** 1767 N Decatur Rd. I-85, exit 91, 3.8 mi s on Clairmont Rd to N Decatur Rd, then 0.8 mi w. Ext corridors. **Pets:** Small, other species. $20 one-time fee/ room.

(SAVE) (S6) (X) (🔊) (🔔) (🍴) (💻) (🏊)

W Atlanta LH ❀
(770) 396-6800. **$179-$359.** 111 Perimeter Center W. I-285, exit 29, 0.3 mi n. Int corridors. **Pets:** $25 daily fee/room. Service with restrictions, supervision.

(ASK) (S6) (X) (&M) (🔊) (🔔) (🍴) (💻) (🍽) (🏊) (🚫)

Wellesley Inn & Suites (Atlanta/Windy Hill) SH
(770) 226-0242. **$72-$82.** 2225 Interstate North Pkwy. I-75, exit 260 (Windy Hill Rd), just e to Interstate North Pkwy, then just s. Int corridors. **Pets:** Accepted.

(SAVE) (S6) (X) (&M) (🔊) (🔔) (🍴) (💻) (🏊)

The Westin Atlanta North LH
(770) 395-3900. **$114-$259.** 7 Concourse Pkwy. I-285, exit 28 westbound; exit 26 eastbound, 0.5 mi n to Hammond Dr, then 0.4 mi e. Int corridors. **Pets:** Accepted.

(ASK) (S6) (X) (🔊) (🔔) (🔔) (💻) (🍽) (🏊) (🚫)

AUSTELL

La Quinta-Atlanta West/Six Flags SH
(770) 944-2110. **$65-$105.** 7377 Six Flags Dr. I-20, exit 46 eastbound; exit 46B westbound, just n. Ext/int corridors. **Pets:** Accepted.

(ASK) (S6) (X) (🔊) (🔔) (💻) (🏊)

COLLEGE PARK

AmeriSuites (Atlanta/Airport) SH
(770) 994-2997. **$79-$89.** 1899 Sullivan Rd. I-85, exit 71, just e to Sullivan Rd, then just s; I-285, exit 60 (Riverdale Rd N), 1 mi to Sullivan Rd, just s. Int corridors. **Pets:** Accepted.

(SAVE) (S6) (X) (&M) (🔊) (🔔) (💻) (🏊)

Atlanta Airport Marriott LH
(404) 766-7900. **$89-$189, 3 day notice.** 4711 Best Rd. I-85, exit 71, just w, se on access road to Best Rd, then just s. Int corridors. **Pets:** Medium. $85 one-time fee/pet. Service with restrictions, supervision.

(ASK) (S6) (X) (&M) (🔊) (🔔) (🔔) (💻) (🍽) (🏊) (🚫)

Howard Johnson Express Inn SH
(404) 766-0000. **$55-$75, 7 day notice.** 2480 Old National Pkwy. I-285, exit 62, just s. Int corridors. **Pets:** Accepted.

(ASK) (S6) (X) (🔔) (💻)

Motel 6-1487 Atlanta Airport M
(404) 761-9701. **$43-$55.** 2471 Old National Pkwy. I-85, exit 69; I-285, exit 62, just s. Ext corridors. **Pets:** Accepted.

(S6) (X) (🔊)

Ramada Hotel Atlanta Airport South SH
(770) 996-4321. **$69-$89.** 1551 Phoenix Blvd. I-285, exit 60 (Riverdale Rd N), just sw. Ext/int corridors. **Pets:** Other species. Designated rooms, service with restrictions.
ASK S⭤ ✕ 🌮 🗟 🍴 🖥 📺 ⚓

DECATUR

Days Inn I-20 East SH
(770) 981-5670. **$59-$69.** 4300 Snapfinger Woods Dr. I-20, exit 68, just e. Ext corridors. **Pets:** Accepted.
ASK S⭤ ✕ 🖾 🗟 🍴 🖥 ⚓

DORAVILLE

Masters Inn M
(770) 454-8373. **$43-$53.** 3092 Presidential Pkwy. I-85, exit 94, just e, then n. Ext corridors. **Pets:** Accepted.
SAVE S⭤ ✕ 🌮 🍴 ⚓

DOUGLASVILLE

Comfort Inn SH
(678) 504-2000. **$59-$129.** 5487 Westmoreland Plaza. I-20, exit 37, northeast corner. Int corridors. **Pets:** Accepted.
SAVE S⭤ ✕ 🌮 🍴 🖥 ⚓

DULUTH

AmeriSuites (Atlanta/Duluth-John's Creek) SH
(770) 622-5858. **$99.** 11505 Medlock Bridge Rd. Jct SR 141 and 120, 0.7 mi n. Int corridors. **Pets:** Accepted.
SAVE S⭤ ✕ 🖾 🌮 🍴 🖥 ⚓

AmeriSuites (Atlanta/Gwinnett Mall) SH
(770) 623-9699. **$69-$99.** 3530 Venture Pkwy. I-85, exit 104, just w to Venture Pkwy, then just n. Int corridors. **Pets:** Accepted.
SAVE S⭤ ✕ 🖾 🌮 🍴 🖥 ⚓

Candlewood Suites-Atlanta SH
(678) 380-0414. **$63-$119.** 3665 Shackleford Rd. I-85, exit 104, just e, then just s. Int corridors. **Pets:** Accepted.
✕ 🖾 🌮 🗟 🍴 🖥

Days Inn Gwinnett Place SH
(770) 476-8700. **$69-$120.** 1920 Pleasant Hill Rd. I-85, exit 104; northwest corner. Int corridors. **Pets:** Small. $25 deposit/pet, $10 daily fee/pet. Service with restrictions, crate.
SAVE S⭤ ✕

Hampton Inn & Suites-Gwinnett SH
(770) 931-9800. **$99.** 1725 Pineland Rd. I-85, exit 104, 0.3 mi e to Crestwood, then just s. Int corridors. **Pets:** Accepted.
SAVE S⭤ ✕ 🖾 🌮 🗟 🍴 🖥 ⚓

Residence Inn-Atlanta Gwinnett SH ✿
(770) 921-2202. **$119-$154.** 1760 Pineland Rd. I-85, exit 104, just e to Shackleford Rd, just s to Pineland Rd, then just e. Int corridors. **Pets:** Medium, other species. $125 one-time fee/room.
ASK S⭤ ✕ 🖾 🌮 🗟 🍴 🖥 ⚓ ✕

Studio 6 #6023 SH
(770) 931-3113. **$48-$62.** 3525 Breckenridge Blvd. I-85, exit 104, just e to Breckenridge Blvd, then just n. Ext corridors. **Pets:** Accepted.
✕ 🖾 🍴 🖥

Wellesley Inn & Suites (Atlanta/Gwinnett Mall) SH
(770) 623-6800. **$59-$99.** 3390 Venture Pkwy NW. I-85, exit 104, just w to Venture Pkwy, then just n. Int corridors. **Pets:** Accepted.
SAVE S⭤ ✕ 🖾 🌮 🍴 🖥 ⚓

EAST POINT

Crowne Plaza Hotel and Resort Atlanta Airport LH
(404) 768-6660. **$169.** 1325 Virginia Ave. I-85, exit 73 southbound; exit 73B northbound, just w. Int corridors. **Pets:** Accepted.
SAVE S⭤ ✕ 🖾 🌮 🗟 🍴 🖥 🍴 ⚓

Drury Inn & Suites Atlanta Airport SH
(404) 761-4900. **$93-$113.** 1270 Virginia Ave. I-85, exit 73 southbound; exit 73A northbound, just e. Int corridors. **Pets:** Large, other species. Service with restrictions, supervision.
ASK ✕ 🖾 🌮 🗟 🍴 🖥 ⚓

Holiday Inn Atlanta Airport North LH
(404) 762-8411. **$129.** 1380 Virginia Ave. I-85, exit 73 southbound; exit 73B northbound, just w. Ext/int corridors. **Pets:** Accepted.
SAVE S⭤ ✕ 🖾 🌮 🗟 🍴 🖥 🍴 ⚓ ✕

Red Roof Inn-Atlanta Airport North SH
(404) 209-1800. **$79-$84.** 1200 Virginia Ave. I-85, exit 73 southbound; exit 73A northbound, just e. Int corridors. **Pets:** Accepted.
ASK S⭤ ✕ 🖾 🌮 🗟 ⚓

Wellesley Inn (Atlanta/Hartsfield Int'l Airport) SH
(404) 762-5111. **$70-$90.** 1377 Virginia Ave. I-85, exit 73 southbound; exit 73B northbound, just w. Int corridors. **Pets:** Small. Service with restrictions, supervision.
SAVE S⭤ ✕ 🌮 🗟 🍴 🖥 🍴 ⚓

FOREST PARK

Motel 6 M
(404) 363-6429. **$48-$57.** 5060 Frontage Rd. I-75, exit 237, southeast corner. Int corridors. **Pets:** Accepted.
SAVE S⭤ ✕

Super 8 Motel SH
(404) 363-8811. **$45-$55.** 410 Old Dixie Way. I-75, exit 235, just e. Ext corridors. **Pets:** Accepted.
SAVE ✕ 🗟 🍴 ⚓

HAPEVILLE

(AAA) ▼▼▼▼ Hilton Atlanta Airport LH
(404) 767-9000. **$89-$219.** 1031 Virginia Ave. I-85, exit 73 southbound; exit 73A northbound, just e. Int corridors. **Pets:** Large. $100 deposit/room. Service with restrictions, crate.

SAVE ⊠ &M 🐾 🛢 💻 🍴 ⊰ ⊠

▼▼▼▼ Residence Inn Atlanta Airport SH
(404) 761-0511. **Call for rates.** 3401 International Blvd. I-85, exit 73 southbound; exit 73A northbound, 0.5 mi e to International Blvd, then just n. Ext/int corridors. **Pets:** Accepted.

⊠ 🐾 🐾 🛢 💻 ⊰ ⊠

JONESBORO

**(AAA) ▼▼▼ Holiday Inn Atlanta South
Jonesboro** SH
(770) 968-4300. **$63-$99.** 6288 Old Dixie Hwy. I-75, exit 235, just w. Int corridors. **Pets:** Large, other species. $15 one-time fee/room. No service, supervision.

SAVE S🔒 ⊠ &M 🐾 🐾 🛢 💻 🍴 ⊰

▼▼▼ Shoneys Inn-Atlanta South SH ✿
(770) 968-5018. **$54-$59, 14 day notice.** 6358 Old Dixie Rd. I-75, exit 235, just w. Ext corridors. **Pets:** Medium. $25 deposit/room, $6 daily fee/pet. Designated rooms, service with restrictions, supervision.

ASK S🔒 ⊠ 🛢 💻 ⊰

KENNESAW

(AAA) ▼▼ Best Western Kennesaw Inn SH
(770) 424-7666. **$60-$74.** 3375 Busbee Dr. I-75, exit 271, just e. Ext corridors. **Pets:** Medium, other species. $10 daily fee/pet. Designated rooms, service with restrictions, supervision.

SAVE S🔒 ⊠ 🛢 💻 ⊰

**(AAA) ▼▼▼ Country Inn & Suites By
Carlson** SH
(770) 423-7105. **$79-$99, 3 day notice.** 3192 Barrett Lakes Blvd. I-75, exit 271, just w to Barrett Lakes Blvd, then just s. Int corridors. **Pets:** Small. $15 daily fee/pet. Designated rooms, service with restrictions, supervision.

SAVE S🔒 ⊠ 🐾 🛢 💻 ⊰

(AAA) ▼▼▼ Days Inn SH
(770) 419-1576. **$50-$99, 7 day notice.** 760 Cobb Place Blvd. I-75, exit 269, just w. Ext corridors. **Pets:** Medium, other species. $15 daily fee/room. Service with restrictions.

SAVE S🔒 ⊠ 🐾 🛢 💻 ⊰

(AAA) ▼▼▼ Ramada Limited SH
(770) 419-1530. **$50-$94, 7 day notice.** 750 Cobb Place Blvd. I-75, exit 269, just w. Ext corridors. **Pets:** Medium, other species. $15 daily fee/room. Service with restrictions.

SAVE S🔒 ⊠ 🐾 🛢 💻 ⊰

(AAA) ▼▼▼ Red Roof Inn-Town Center Mall M
(770) 429-0323. **$44-$54.** 520 Roberts Ct NW. I-75, exit 269, southeast corner. Ext corridors. **Pets:** Accepted.

SAVE ⊠ &M 🐾 🐾 🛢

**▼▼▼▼ Residence In by Marriott Town
Center** SH ✿
(770) 218-1018. **$82-$134.** 3443 Busbee Dr. I-75, exit 271, just e. Int corridors. **Pets:** Medium. $100 one-time fee/room. Designated rooms, service with restrictions.

ASK S🔒 ⊠ &M 🐾 🐾 🛢 💻 ⊰ ⊠

(AAA) ▼▼▼ Rodeway Inn M
(770) 590-0519. **$43-$60.** 1460 George Busbee Pkwy. I-75, exit 273, just e. Ext corridors. **Pets:** Accepted.

SAVE S🔒 ⊠ 🛢 💻 ⊰

▼▼▼▼ TownePlace Suites by Marriott SH
(770) 794-8282. **$119.** 1074 Cobb Place Blvd NW. I-75, exit 269, 1.1 mi w to Second Cobb Place Blvd entrance. Int corridors. **Pets:** Accepted.

ASK S🔒 ⊠ &M 🐾 🐾 🛢 💻 ⊰

LAWRENCEVILLE

▼▼▼▼ Hampton Inn SH
(770) 338-9600. **$89.** 1135 Lakes Pkwy. I-85, exit 106 northbound, 4 mi e to Riverside Pkwy, just n; exit 115 southbound, 4.4 mi s on SR 20 to SR 316, 1.1 mi w. Int corridors. **Pets:** Accepted.

ASK S🔒 ⊠ &M 🐾 🐾 🛢 💻 ⊰

LITHONIA

**(AAA) ▼▼▼▼ AmeriSuites (Lithonia/Stonecrest
Mall)** SH
(770) 484-4384. **$109-$149.** 7900 Mall Ring Rd. I-20, exit 75, just s on Turner Hill Rd, 0.7 mi w. Int corridors. **Pets:** Accepted.

SAVE S🔒 ⊠ 🛢 💻

▼▼▼▼ Motel 6 SH
(770) 981-6411. **$60-$76.** 2859 Panola Rd. I-20, exit 71, just n. Ext/int corridors. **Pets:** Small, other species. Service with restrictions, supervision.

ASK S🔒 ⊠ 🐾 🛢 💻 ⊰

MARIETTA

(AAA) ▼▼▼▼ Comfort Inn-Marietta SH
(770) 952-3000. **$79-$109.** 2100 Northwest Pkwy. I-75, exit 261, 0.3 mi w to Franklin Rd, just s. Ext corridors. **Pets:** Accepted.

SAVE S🔒 ⊠ 🐾 🛢 💻 ⊰

▼▼▼▼ Drury Inn & Suites-Atlanta Northwest SH
(770) 612-0900. **$77-$97.** 1170 Powers Ferry Pl. I-75, exit 261, just e. Int corridors. **Pets:** Large, other species. Service with restrictions, supervision.

ASK ⊠ &M 🐾 🐾 🛢 💻 ⊰

(AAA) ▼▼▼ Econo Lodge Northwest SH
(770) 952-0052. **$49-$99.** 1940 Leland Dr. I-75, exit 260, just e, then 0.3 mi n. Ext/int corridors. **Pets:** Medium. Service with restrictions.

SAVE ⊠ 🛢 💻

🔺 ▼▼▼ **Holiday Inn Hotel & Suites**
Atlanta-Marietta 🆂🅷
(770) 952-7581. **$119.** 2265 Kingston Ct. I-75, exit 261, 0.3 mi w to Franklin Rd, just n to Kingston Ct, just e. Int corridors. **Pets:** Accepted.
[SAVE] [🆂] [✕] [👪ᴹ] [🐾] [👶] [🛏] [💻] [🍽] [➰]

▼▼▼ **Homestead Studio Suites Hotel-Atlanta/**
Powers Ferry/Galleria Area 🆂🅷 🐾
(770) 303-0043. **$54-$69.** 2239 Powers Ferry Rd. I-285, exit 22, just n. Int corridors. **Pets:** Medium, other species. $25 daily fee/room. Service with restrictions, crate.
[✕] [👪ᴹ] [🐾] [👶] [🛏] [💻]

🔺 ▼▼▼ **La Quinta Inn Marietta** 🆂🅷
(770) 951-0026. **$53-$69.** 2170 Delk Rd. I-75, exit 261, 0.3 mi w. Ext/int corridors. **Pets:** Accepted.
[SAVE] [🆂] [✕] [🐾] [🛏] [💻] [➰]

🔺 ▼ **Masters Inn Marietta** 🅼
(770) 951-2005. **$43-$53.** 2682 Windy Hill Rd. I-75, exit 260, just w to Circle 75 Pkwy, then just w. Ext corridors. **Pets:** Small. $5 daily fee/pet. Designated rooms, service with restrictions, supervision.
[SAVE] [🆂] [✕]

🔺 ▼▼ **Quality Inn** 🆂🅷
(770) 955-0004. **$59-$99.** 1255 Franklin Rd. I-75, exit 261, 0.3 mi w to Franklin Rd, then just s. Int corridors. **Pets:** Accepted.
[SAVE] [🆂] [✕] [🐾] [🛏] [💻] [➰]

🔺 ▼▼▼ **Ramada Limited Suites** 🆂🅷
(770) 919-7878. **$45-$54.** 630 Franklin Rd. I-75, exit 263, 0.3 mi w to Franklin Rd, then 0.3 mi s. Ext corridors. **Pets:** Accepted.
[SAVE] [🆂] [✕] [🐾] [👶] [🛏] [💻] [➰]

🔺 ▼▼▼ **Super 8 Motel** 🆂🅷
(770) 919-2340. **$45-$54.** 610 Franklin Rd. I-75, exit 263, 0.3 mi w to Franklin Rd, then 0.3 mi s. Ext corridors. **Pets:** Accepted.
[SAVE] [🆂] [✕] [🐾] [🛏] [➰]

🔺 ▼▼▼ **Wyndham Garden Hotel-Atlanta**
Northwest 🆂🅷
(770) 428-4400. **$69-$109.** 1775 Parkway Pl NW. I-75, exit 263, southwest corner. Int corridors. **Pets:** Large. $50 one-time fee/room.
[SAVE] [🆂] [✕] [👪ᴹ] [🐾] [🛏] [💻] [🍽] [➰]

MORROW

🔺 ▼▼ **Best Western Southlake Inn** 🆂🅷
(770) 961-6300. **$64-$79.** 6437 Jonesboro Rd. I-75, exit 233, just e. Ext corridors. **Pets:** Accepted.
[SAVE] [✕] [🛏] [💻] [➰]

▼▼▼ **Drury Inn & Suites-Atlanta South** 🆂🅷
(770) 960-0500. **$82-$102.** 6520 S Lee St. I-75, exit 233, just e. Int corridors. **Pets:** Large, other species. Service with restrictions, supervision.
[ASK] [✕] [👪ᴹ] [🐾] [👶] [🛏] [💻] [➰]

🔺 ▼▼▼ **Quality Inn & Suites** 🆂🅷
(770) 960-1957. **$59-$79.** 6597 Hwy 54. I-75, exit 233, just w. Ext corridors. **Pets:** Accepted.
[SAVE] [🆂] [✕] [🛏] [💻] [➰]

🔺 ▼▼ **Red Roof Inn-South** 🅼
(770) 968-1483. **$44-$64.** 1348 Southlake Plaza Dr. I-75, exit 233, just e to Southlake Plaza Dr, then just n. Ext corridors. **Pets:** Accepted.
[SAVE] [✕] [🐾] [🛏]

🔺 ▼▼ **Sleep Inn** 🆂🅷
(770) 472-9800. **$59-$149, 3 day notice.** 2185 Mt Zion Pkwy. I-75, exit 231, just w to Mt Zion Pkwy, then just s. Int corridors. **Pets:** Small. $10 daily fee/pet. Designated rooms, service with restrictions, supervision.
[SAVE] [🆂] [✕] [👪ᴹ] [🛏] [💻] [➰]

NORCROSS

🔺 ▼▼▼ **Amberley Suite Hotel** 🆂🅷
(770) 263-0515. **$65-$75.** 5885 Oakbrook Pkwy. I-85, exit 99, 0.5 mi e to Live Oak Pkwy, 0.8 mi n, then w. Int corridors. **Pets:** Large. $50 one-time fee/room. Designated rooms, service with restrictions, supervision.
[SAVE] [✕] [👪ᴹ] [🐾] [🛏] [💻] [🍽] [➰] [✕]

🔺 ▼▼▼ **AmeriSuites (Atlanta/Peachtree**
Corners) 🆂🅷
(770) 416-7655. **$99.** 5600 Peachtree Pkwy. I-285, exit 31B, 4 mi n on SR 141, 1 mi n. Int corridors. **Pets:** Medium. $25 one-time fee/room. Designated rooms, service with restrictions, crate.
[SAVE] [🆂] [✕] [👪ᴹ] [🐾] [👶] [🛏] [💻] [➰]

🔺 ▼▼▼ **ClubHouse Inn & Suites** 🆂🅷
(770) 368-9400. **$79-$109.** 5945 Oakbrook Pkwy. I-85, exit 99, 0.5 mi e to Live Oak Pkwy, 0.8 mi w. Int corridors. **Pets:** Accepted.
[SAVE] [🆂] [✕] [👶] [🛏] [💻] [➰]

🔺 ▼▼▼ **Days Inn Atlanta NE** 🆂🅷
(770) 368-0218. **$59-$79.** 5990 Western Hills Dr. I-85, exit 99, 0.8 mi w to Norcross Tucker Rd to Western Hills Dr, then just n. Ext corridors. **Pets:** Medium, other species. $10 daily fee/pet. Service with restrictions, supervision.
[SAVE] [🆂] [✕] [🛏] [➰]

▼▼▼ **Drury Inn & Suites-Atlanta Northeast** 🆂🅷
(770) 729-0060. **$77-$97.** 5655 Jimmy Carter Blvd. I-85, exit 99, just w. Int corridors. **Pets:** Large, other species. Service with restrictions, supervision.
[ASK] [✕] [👪ᴹ] [🐾] [👶] [🛏] [💻] [➰]

▼▼ **GuestHouse Inn** 🆂🅷
(770) 564-0492. **$49-$59.** 2050 Willowtrail Pkwy. I-85, exit 101, just e. Ext corridors. **Pets:** Small. $20 deposit/room. Service with restrictions, supervision.
[ASK] [🆂] [✕] [🛏] [💻] [➰]

🔺 ▼▼▼ **Hilton Atlanta Northeast** 🅻🅷
(770) 447-4747. **$79-$145.** 5993 Peachtree Industrial Blvd. I-285, exit 31B, 4.5 mi ne. Int corridors. **Pets:** Medium. $25 one-time fee/room. Service with restrictions, supervision.
[SAVE] [🆂] [✕] [👪ᴹ] [🛏] [💻] [🍽] [➰] [✕]

▼▼▼▼ **Homestead Studio Suites**
Hotel-Atlanta/Norcross 🆂🅷 ❀
(770) 449-9966. **$44-$54.** 7049 Jimmy Carter Blvd. I-85, exit 99, 4 mi n; I-285, exit 31B, 4 mi n. Ext corridors. **Pets:** Medium, other species. $25 daily fee/room. Service with restrictions, crate.

❌ 🏋 📣 🔌 💻

🅐🅐🅐 **▼▼▼▼** **La Quinta Inn-Jimmy Carter** 🆂🅷
(770) 448-8686. **$60-$76.** 6187 Dawson Blvd. I-85, exit 99, just e to McDonough Dr, then just s. Ext corridors. **Pets:** Accepted.

🆂🅰🆅🅴 🆂🔟 ❌ 💻 🏊

▼▼▼▼ **La Quinta Inn-Peachtree** 🆂🅷
(770) 449-5144. **$54-$64.** 5375 Peachtree Industrial Blvd. I-285, exit 31B, 5.5 mi n; I-85, exit 99, 4 mi w to Peachtree Industrial Blvd, 1.5 mi n. Ext/int corridors. **Pets:** Accepted.

🅰🆂🅺 🆂🔟 ❌ 🏋 🔌 💻 🏊

▼▼ **Ramada Limited** 🆂🅷
(770) 449-7322. **$79-$89.** 6045 Oakbrook Pkwy. I-85, exit 99, just e to Live Oak Pkwy, 1 mi n, then w. Ext/int corridors. **Pets:** Accepted.

🅰🆂🅺 🆂🔟 ❌ 🔌 💻 🏊

▼▼ **Red Roof Inn & Suites** 🆂🅷
(770) 446-2882. **$45-$75.** 5395 Peachtree Industrial Blvd. I-285, exit 31B, 5.5 mi n; I-85, exit 99, 4 mi w to Peachtree Industrial Blvd, 1.5 mi n. Int corridors. **Pets:** Medium, other species. Service with restrictions, supervision.

🅰🆂🅺 🆂🔟 ❌ 🏋 🔌 💻 🏊

🅐🅐🅐 **▼▼▼** **Red Roof Inn-Indian Trail** Ⓜ
(770) 448-8944. **$43-$53.** 5171 Brook Hollow Pkwy. I-85, exit 101, just w to Brook Hollow Pkwy, just s. Ext corridors. **Pets:** Medium, other species. Service with restrictions, supervision.

🆂🅰🆅🅴 ❌ 🏋 📣

ROSWELL

🅐🅐🅐 **▼▼▼▼** **Baymont Inn & Suites**
Atlanta-Roswell 🆂🅷
(770) 552-0200. **$55-$72.** 575 Old Holcomb Bridge Rd. SR 400, exit 7B, just w. Int corridors. **Pets:** Small. Designated rooms, service with restrictions, supervision.

🆂🅰🆅🅴 🆂🔟 ❌ 🏋 📣 🔌 💻 🏊

🅐🅐🅐 **▼▼▼▼** **Best Western Roswell Suites** 🆂🅷
(770) 552-5599. **$74.** 907 Holcomb Bridge Rd. SR 400, exit 7B, 0.7 mi w. Int corridors. **Pets:** Small. $25 one-time fee/pet. Service with restrictions, supervision.

🆂🅰🆅🅴 🆂🔟 ❌ 🏋 📣 🔌 💻 🏊

▼▼▼▼ **Brookwood Inn** 🆂🅷
(770) 587-5161. **$45-$79.** 9995 Old Dogwood Rd. SR 400, exit 7B, just w to Old Dogwood Rd, just n. Ext corridors. **Pets:** Accepted.

🅰🆂🅺 🆂🔟 ❌ 📣 🔌 💻 🏊

▼▼ **Studio 6 #6025** Ⓜ
(770) 992-9449. **$53-$63.** 9955 Old Dogwood Rd. SR 400, exit 7B, just w. Ext corridors. **Pets:** Other species. $10 daily fee/pet. Service with restrictions.

📣 🔌 🔌 💻

SMYRNA

🅐🅐🅐 **▼▼▼** **AmeriHost Inn-Smyrna** 🆂🅷
(404) 794-1600. **$74-$119.** 5130 S Cobb Dr. I-285, exit 15, 0.3 mi w. Int corridors. **Pets:** Accepted.

🆂🅰🆅🅴 🆂🔟 ❌ 🏋 📣 🔌 🔌 💻 🏊 ❌

🅐🅐🅐 **▼▼▼▼** **AmeriSuites (Atlanta/Galleria)** 🆂🅷
(770) 384-0060. **$59-$149.** 2876 Springhill Pkwy. I-285, exit 20 westbound; exit 19 eastbound, just n to Spring Rd, then just w. Int corridors. **Pets:** Accepted.

🆂🅰🆅🅴 🆂🔟 ❌ 🏋 📣 🔌 💻 🏊

▼▼▼▼ **Comfort Inn & Suites-Smyrna** 🆂🅷
(678) 309-1200. **$45-$95.** 2800 Highlands Pkwy. I-285, exit 15, just w to Highlands Pkwy, then just s. Int corridors. **Pets:** Medium, other species. $10 one-time fee/pet. Designated rooms, service with restrictions, supervision.

🅰🆂🅺 🆂🔟 ❌ 🏋 📣 🔌 🔌 💻 🏊

▼▼▼ **Country Inn & Suites By Carlson Atlanta**
Northwest 🆂🅷
(770) 541-1499. **$55-$104.** 2221 Corporate Plaza. I-75, exit 260, just w. Int corridors. **Pets:** Accepted.

🅰🆂🅺 🆂🔟 ❌ 🏋 📣 🔌 🔌 💻 🏊 ❌

▼▼▼ **Homestead Studio Suites**
Hotel-Atlanta/Cumberland 🆂🅷 ❀
(770) 432-4000. **$49-$59.** 3103 Sports Ave. I-285, exit 20 westbound; exit 19 eastbound, just n to Spring Rd, 0.3 mi w. Ext corridors. **Pets:** Medium, other species. $25 daily fee/room. Service with restrictions, crate.

🅰🆂🅺 🆂🔟 ❌ 🏋 📣 🔌 🔌

🅐🅐🅐 **▼▼▼** **Red Roof Inn-North** Ⓜ
(770) 952-6966. **$45-$55.** 2200 Corporate Plaza. I-75, exit 260, just w to Corporate Plaza, just s. Ext corridors. **Pets:** Medium, other species. Service with restrictions, supervision.

🆂🅰🆅🅴 ❌ 🏋 📣 🔌

▼▼▼▼ **Residence Inn-Atlanta**
Cumberland 🆂🅷 ❀
(770) 433-8877. **$103-$123.** 2771 Cumberland Blvd. I-285, exit 20 westbound; exit 19 eastbound, just n to Spring Rd, 0.3 mi w w to Cumberland Blvd, then just n. Ext corridors. **Pets:** Medium. $75 one-time fee/room. Service with restrictions.

🅰🆂🅺 ❌ 🏋 📣 🔌 🔌 💻 🏊 ❌

SUWANEE

🅐🅐🅐 **▼▼▼** **Comfort Inn** 🆂🅷
(770) 945-1608. **$59-$81.** 2945 Hwy 317. I-85, exit 111, just e. Ext corridors. **Pets:** Medium, other species. $25 one-time fee/room. Service with restrictions, crate.

🆂🅰🆅🅴 🆂🔟 ❌ 🔌 💻 🏊

▼▼▼ **Park Inn Atlanta NE/Suwanee** 🆂🅷
(770) 945-4921. **$70-$100, 30 day notice.** 2955 Hwy 317. I-85, exit 111. Ext corridors. **Pets:** Accepted.

❌ 🏋 🔌 💻 🍴 🏊

TUCKER

▼▼▼ **Atlanta Northlake TownePlace Suites** SH
(770) 938-0408. **$62-$116.** 3300 Northlake Pkwy. I-285, exit 36 southbound, just w; exit 37 northbound, just w to Parklake Dr, 0.5 mi n, then just w. Int corridors. **Pets:** Accepted.
[ASK] [✕] [&M] [🔊] [🖟] [🛏] [💻] [➳]

▼▼▼ **Comfort Suites-Northlake** SH
(770) 496-1070. **$59-$79.** 2060 Crescent Centre Blvd. I-285, exit 37, 0.5 mi se. Int corridors. **Pets:** Accepted.
[ASK] [S▵] [✕] [&M] [🔊] [🛏] [💻] [➳]

▲ ▼▼ **Econo Lodge** M
(770) 939-8440. **$42-$48.** 1820 Mountain Industrial Blvd. US 78, exit 4, just n. Int corridors. **Pets:** Small. $5 daily fee/pet. Designated rooms, service with restrictions, supervision.
[SAVE] [S▵] [✕] [🛏]

▲ ▼▼ **Masters Inn Tucker** M
(770) 938-3552. **$43-$53.** 1435 Montreal Rd. I-285, exit 38, just w. Ext corridors. **Pets:** Accepted.
[SAVE] [S▵] [✕] [🛏] [➳]

▲▲ **▼▼▼** **Red Roof Inn-Atlanta Tucker NE** M
(770) 496-1311. **$40-$50.** 2810 Lawrenceville Hwy. I-285, exit 38, just w. Ext corridors. **Pets:** Accepted.
[SAVE] [✕] [🔊]

UNION CITY

▼▼▼ **Holiday Inn Express Hotel & Suites** SH
(770) 969-4567. **$59-$129.** 6743 Shannon Pkwy. I-85, exit 64, 0.3 mi w, just n. Int corridors. **Pets:** Small, other species. Service with restrictions, crate.
[ASK] [S▵] [✕] [&M] [🔊] [🖟] [🛏] [💻] [➳]

▲▲ **▼▼** **Ramada Limited** SH
(770) 964-5100. **$54.** 7420 Oakley Rd. I-85, exit 64, just e. Ext corridors. **Pets:** Accepted.
[SAVE] [S▵] [✕] [🛏] [💻] [➳]

▼▼ **Red Roof Inn** SH
(770) 306-7750. **$55-$65.** 6710 Shannon Pkwy. I-85, exit 64, 0.3 mi w, just n. Int corridors. **Pets:** Accepted.
[ASK] [S▵] [✕] [🖟] [🛏] [➳]

❀ END METROPOLITAN AREA ❀

AUGUSTA

▲▲ **▼▼▼▼** **AmeriSuites (Augusta/River Watch Pkwy)** SH
(706) 733-4656. **$70-$90.** 1062 Claussen Rd. I-20, exit 200 westbound, 0.4 mi sw on service road; exit 199 eastbound, 0.3 mi w, then 0.6 mi nw on service road. Int corridors. **Pets:** Small. $30 one-time fee/room. Service with restrictions, supervision.
[SAVE] [S▵] [✕] [&M] [🔊] [🖟] [🛏] [💻] [➳] [✕]

▲▲ **▼▼▼** **Augusta Suites Inn** SH
(706) 868-1800. **$99.** 3038 Washington Rd. I-20, exit 199 (Washington Rd), just w. Ext corridors. **Pets:** Small. $25 one-time fee/pet. Service with restrictions, supervision.
[SAVE] [S▵] [✕] [🛏] [💻] [🍴] [➳]

▲▲ **▼▼▼** **Comfort Inn** SH
(706) 855-6060. **$56.** 629 Frontage Rd NW. I-20, exit 196B, 0.3 mi n to Scott Nixon Memorial, just w, then 0.3 mi s. Int corridors. **Pets:** $25 one-time fee/room. Service with restrictions.
[SAVE] [S▵] [✕] [🛏] [💻] [➳]

▲▲ **▼▼▼** **Comfort Inn Medical Center** SH
(706) 722-2224. **$59-$62.** 1455 Walton Way. I-20, exit 199 (Washington Rd), 4.5 mi e on SR 28, then just sw on 15th St. Ext corridors. **Pets:** Small, other species. $50 deposit/pet. Service with restrictions, crate.
[SAVE] [S▵] [✕] [🖟] [🛏] [💻] [➳]

▲▲ **▼▼▼** **Country Suites Augusta Riverwalk** SH
(706) 774-1400. **$129.** 3 Ninth St. I-20, exit 200 (River Watch Pkwy), 5.4 mi se, then just n. Int corridors. **Pets:** Medium. Designated rooms, service with restrictions, crate.
[SAVE] [S▵] [✕] [&M] [🔊] [🖟] [🛏] [💻] [➳]

▲▲ **▼▼▼▼** **Holiday Inn Augusta-West** SH
(706) 738-8811. **$49-$79.** 1075 Stevens Creek Rd. I-20, exit 199 (Washington Rd), just w, then n. Ext corridors. **Pets:** Small. $25 one-time fee/room. Designated rooms, service with restrictions, supervision.
[SAVE] [S▵] [✕] [🖟] [🛏] [💻] [🍴] [➳] [✕]

▼▼▼ **Holiday Inn Gordon Highway at Bobby Jones** SH
(706) 737-2300. **$59-$99.** 2155 Gordon Hwy. I-520, exit 3A (US 78), just w. Ext corridors. **Pets:** Accepted.
[ASK] [S▵] [✕] [🛏] [💻] [🍴] [➳]

▼▼ **Howard Johnson Inn** M
(706) 863-2882. **$45-$50.** 601 Frontage Rd NW. I-20, exit 196B (Bobby Jones Hwy), just nw. Ext corridors. **Pets:** Small. $7 daily fee/pet. Designated rooms, service with restrictions, crate.
[ASK] [S▵] [✕] [🛏] [💻] [➳]

▲▲ **▼▼▼▼** **La Quinta Inn** SH
(706) 733-2660. **$56-$66.** 3020 Washington Rd. I-20, exit 199 (Washington Rd), just w. Ext/int corridors. **Pets:** Accepted.
[SAVE] [S▵] [✕] [&M] [🔊] [🛏] [💻] [➳]

▼▼▼ **The Partridge Inn** SH
(706) 737-8888. **$109-$139.** 2110 Walton Way. 1.3 mi w off 15th St. Int corridors. **Pets:** Accepted.
[ASK] [S▵] [✕] [🛏] [💻] [🍴] [➳]

▲▲ **▼▼▼▼** **Radisson Riverfront Hotel** LH
(706) 722-8900. **$129.** 2 10th St. I-20, exit 200 (River Watch Pkwy), 5.4 mi se, then just n; downtown. Int corridors. **Pets:** Medium. Designated rooms, service with restrictions, crate.
[SAVE] [S▵] [✕] [&M] [🔊] [🛏] [💻] [🍴] [➳]

(AAA) ▼▼▼▼ Sheraton Augusta Hotel SH

(706) 855-8100. **$99-$149.** 2651 Perimeter Pkwy. I-520, exit 1C (Wheeler Rd), just w to Perimeter Pkwy, then just n. Int corridors. **Pets:** Accepted.

[SAVE] [S⊘] [✕] [&M] [🛏] [▦] [¶] [✈] [⊠]

BAINBRIDGE

▼▼ Jameson Inn SH

(229) 243-7000. **$64-$66.** 1403 Tallahassee Hwy. Just s of US 84 Bypass on US 27. Ext corridors. **Pets:** Small. Service with restrictions, crate.

[✕] [&] [🛏] [▦] [✈]

BAXLEY

▼ Scottish Inn M

(912) 367-3652. **$40-$50.** 1179 Hatch Pkwy S. Jct US 1 and SR 15, just s. Ext corridors. **Pets:** Accepted.

[ASK] [S⊘] [✕] [🛏]

BLUE RIDGE

▼▼ Douglas Inn & Suites M

(706) 258-3600. **$39-$89.** 1192 Windy Ridge Rd. Just off SR 515 and US 76. Ext corridors. **Pets:** Accepted.

[ASK] [S⊘] [✕] [🛏] [▦] [✈]

BREMEN

▼▼ Days Inn SH ❁

(770) 537-4646. **$35-$165, 21 day notice.** 35 Price Creek Rd. I-75, exit 11, just n. Ext corridors. **Pets:** Other species. $5 daily fee/pet. Service with restrictions, crate.

[ASK] [S⊘] [✕] [🛏] [▦] [✈]

BRUNSWICK

(AAA) ▼▼▼ Baymont Inn & Suites Brunswick SH

(912) 265-7725. **$49-$89.** 165 Warren Mason Blvd. I-95, exit 36A (New Jesup Hwy/US 25), just se, then sw on Tourist Dr. Int corridors. **Pets:** Accepted.

[SAVE] [S⊘] [✕] [⏺] [🛏] [▦] [✈]

(AAA) ▼▼▼▼ Best Western Brunswick Inn SH

(912) 264-0144. **$68-$78.** 5323 New Jesup Hwy. I-95, exit 36B (New Jesup Hwy/US 25), just nw. Ext corridors. **Pets:** Medium, other species. Service with restrictions.

[SAVE] [S⊘] [✕] [🛏] [▦] [¶] [✈]

▼▼▼▼ Embassy Suites Hotel SH

(912) 264-6100. **$109-$179.** 500 Mall Blvd. I-95, exit 38 (Golden Isles Pkwy), 2 mi se, then just e. Int corridors. **Pets:** Medium. $15 daily fee/room. Service with restrictions, supervision.

[ASK] [S⊘] [✕] [⏺] [🛏] [▦] [✈]

(AAA) ▼▼▼▼ Holiday Inn I-95 SH

(912) 264-4033. **$79-$109.** 5252 New Jesup Hwy. I-95, exit 36B (New Jesup Hwy/US 25), just nw. Ext corridors. **Pets:** Accepted.

[SAVE] [S⊘] [✕] [&] [🛏] [▦] [¶] [✈]

▼▼ Jameson Inn Brunswick SH

(912) 267-0800. **$66-$76.** 661 Scranton Rd. I-95, exit 38 (Golden Isles Pkwy), 1.6 mi se, then just sw. Ext corridors. **Pets:** Small. Service with restrictions, crate.

[✕] [🛏] [▦] [✈]

▼ Knights Inn M

(912) 267-6500. **$44-$56.** 450 Warren Mason Blvd. I-95, exit 36A (New Jesup Hwy/US 25), just se on US 25, then just ne. Ext corridors. **Pets:** Medium. $5 daily fee/pet. Designated rooms, service with restrictions, supervision.

[ASK] [S⊘] [✕] [🛏] [✈]

▼ Motel 6 M

(912) 264-8582. **$39-$52.** 403 Butler Dr. I-95, exit 36B (New Jesup Hwy/US 25), just nw, then sw on I-95 south entrance service road. Ext corridors. **Pets:** Small. Service with restrictions, supervision.

[✕] [✈]

(AAA) ▼▼▼▼ Ramada Inn I-95 SH

(912) 264-3621. **$59-$99.** 3040 Scarlet St. I-95, exit 36A (New Jesup Hwy/US 25), just e. Ext corridors. **Pets:** Small, other species. $20 one-time fee/room. Service with restrictions, supervision.

[SAVE] [S⊘] [✕] [⏺] [🛏] [▦] [¶] [✈]

▼▼▼ Red Roof Inn & Suites I-95 SH

(912) 264-4720. **$58-$89.** 25 Tourist Dr. I-95, exit 36A (New Jesup Hwy/US 25), just se. Int corridors. **Pets:** Other species. Service with restrictions, supervision.

[ASK] [S⊘] [✕] [⏺] [🛏] [✈]

▼▼ Super 8 Motel M

(912) 264-8800. **$51-$61, 7 day notice.** 5280 New Jesup Hwy. I-95, exit 36B (New Jesup Hwy/US 25), just nw. Int corridors. **Pets:** Small, dogs only. $10 daily fee/pet. Supervision.

[ASK] [S⊘] [✕] [🛏]

BYRON

(AAA) ▼▼▼ Best Western Inn and Suites SH ❁

(478) 956-3056. **$56.** 101 Dunbar Rd (Hwy 49). I-75, exit 149 (SR 49), just ne. Ext corridors. **Pets:** Medium. $10 daily fee/room. Designated rooms, service with restrictions, supervision.

[SAVE] [S⊘] [✕] [&] [🛏] [▦] [✈]

CALHOUN

(AAA) ▼▼ Best Inns M

(706) 625-1511. **$40-$50, 7 day notice.** 1438 US Hwy 41 N. I-75, exit 318, just w. Ext corridors. **Pets:** Large. $5 daily fee/pet, $5 one-time fee/pet. Designated rooms, no service, supervision.

[SAVE] [S⊘] [✕] [🛏] [▦] [✈]

(AAA) ▼▼▼ Budget Host Shepherd Motel M

(706) 629-8644. **$39-$46.** 1007 Fairmount Hwy SE. I-75, exit 312, just e. Ext corridors. **Pets:** Large, other species.

[SAVE] [S⊘] [✕] [&] [🛏] [✈]

▼▼ Comfort Inn SH

(706) 629-8271. **$55-$60.** 742 Hwy 53 SE. I-75, exit 312, just w. Ext corridors. **Pets:** Other species. $4 daily fee/pet. Service with restrictions, crate.

[ASK] [S⊘] [✕] [🛏] [▦] [¶] [✈]

▼▼ Jameson Inn SH
(706) 629-8133. **$68-$73.** 189 Jameson St. I-75, exit 312, just w. Ext corridors. **Pets:** Small, other species. Service with restrictions.

⊠ ⒥ ⒨ ⒢ 🖵 ⇌

▼▼ Knights Inn of Calhoun M
(706) 629-4521. **$40-$44.** 2261 US 41 NE. I-75, exit 318, just e. Ext corridors. **Pets:** Accepted.

ASK S⒪ ⊠

▲▲▲ ▼▼ Quality Inn SH ✿
(706) 629-9501. **$55-$65.** 915 Hwy 53 E SE. I-75, exit 312, just e. Ext corridors. **Pets:** Small. $5 daily fee/pet. Service with restrictions.

SAVE S⒪ ⊠ ⒢ 🖵 ⒴ ⇌

▲▲▲ ▼▼ Ramada Limited SH
(706) 629-9207. **$45-$69.** 1204 Red Bud Rd NE. I-75, exit 315, just w. Ext corridors. **Pets:** Accepted.

SAVE S⒪ ⊠ ⒥ ⒢ 🖵 ⇌

CARROLLTON

▼▼ Country Hearth Inn SH
(770) 834-2001. **$57-$77.** 901 US 27 S. Just s of downtown. Ext corridors. **Pets:** Accepted.

ASK S⒪ ⊠ ⒢ 🖵 ⇌

▼▼ Jameson Inn SH
(770) 834-2600. **$67-$69.** 700 S Park St. On US 27, just s of downtown. Ext corridors. **Pets:** Small. Service with restrictions, crate.

⒢⒨ ⒨ ⒢ 🖵 ⇌

▼▼▼ Quality Inn & Suites SH
(770) 832-2611. **$49-$119.** 1202 S Park St. Jct US 27 and SR 166. Ext corridors. **Pets:** Accepted.

ASK S⒪ ⊠ ⒢ 🖵 ⒴ ⇌

CARTERSVILLE

▼ Budget Host Inn M
(770) 386-0350. **$36.** 851 Cass-White Rd. I-75, exit 296, just w. Ext corridors. **Pets:** Medium, other species. $3 one-time fee/pet. No service, supervision.

ASK S⒪ ⊠ ⇌

▲▲▲ ▼▼ Comfort Inn SH
(770) 387-1800. **$45-$60.** 28 SR 20 Spur. I-75, exit 290, 0.3 mi se. Ext corridors. **Pets:** Medium. $5 daily fee/pet. Service with restrictions, supervision.

SAVE S⒪ ⊠ ⒢ 🖵 ⇌

▼▼▼ Country Inn & Suites By Carlson SH
(770) 386-5888. **$75-$85.** 43 SR 20 Spur. I-75, exit 290, 0.3 mi se. Int corridors. **Pets:** Accepted.

ASK S⒪ ⊠ ⒢⒨ ⒨ ⒢ 🖵 ⇌

▲▲▲ ▼▼▼ Days Inn-Cartersville SH
(770) 382-1824. **$44-$88, 7 day notice.** 5618 Hwy 20 SE. I-75, exit 290, just w. Ext corridors. **Pets:** Very small. $10 daily fee/pet. Service with restrictions.

SAVE S⒪ ⊠ ⇌

▼▼▼ Holiday Inn SH
(770) 386-0830. **$62-$68.** 2336 Hwy 411 NE. I-75, exit 293, southwest corner. Int corridors. **Pets:** Accepted.

ASK S⒪ ⊠ ⒢⒨ ⒥ ⒢ 🖵 ⒴ ⇌

▲▲▲ ▼▼▼ Howard Johnson Express M
(770) 386-0700. **$50-$70.** 25 Carson Loop NW. I-75, exit 296, northwest corner. Ext corridors. **Pets:** Other species. $5 daily fee/pet. Designated rooms, service with restrictions, crate.

SAVE S⒪ ⊠ ⒢ 🖵 ⇌

▲▲▲ ▼▼▼ Knights Inn M
(770) 386-7263. **$50-$70.** 420 E Church St. I-75, exit 288, 1.5 mi w. Ext corridors. **Pets:** Medium. $10 one-time fee/pet. Service with restrictions, supervision.

SAVE S⒪ ⊠ ⒢ ⇌

▼▼ Motel 6-4046 M
(770) 386-1449. **$42-$46.** 5657 Hwy 20 NE. I-75, exit 290, 0.3 mi e. Ext corridors. **Pets:** Medium, other species. Service with restrictions, supervision.

ASK S⒪ ⊠ ⒥ ⇌

▲▲▲ ▼▼▼ Quality Inn SH
(770) 386-0510. **$57-$61.** 235 Dixie Ave. I-75, exit 288, 2.5 mi w. Ext corridors. **Pets:** Small. $5 daily fee/pet. Designated rooms, supervision.

SAVE S⒪ ⊠ ⒢ 🖵 ⒴ ⇌

▼▼ Super 8 Motel M
(770) 382-8881. **$40-$55.** 41 SR 20 Spur SE. I-75, exit 290, 0.3 mi e. Int corridors. **Pets:** Large, other species. $5 daily fee/pet. Service with restrictions, supervision.

ASK S⒪ ⊠ ⒥ ⒢

CHATSWORTH

▼▼ Key West Inn M
(706) 517-1155. **$49-$55.** 501 GI Maddox Pkwy. Jct SR 76 and US 411. Ext corridors. **Pets:** Accepted.

ASK S⒪ ⊠ ⒢

CLAYTON

▼▼▼ GuestHouse Inn & Suites SH
(706) 782-2214. **$59-$99.** 834 Hwy 441 S. 0.8 mi s. Ext corridors. **Pets:** Small. $25 daily fee/pet. Designated rooms, no service, supervision.

ASK S⒪ ⊠ ⒢ 🖵 ⇌

▲▲▲ ▼ Regal Inn M
(706) 782-4269. **$37-$95, 3 day notice.** 707 Hwy 441 S. 0.8 mi s. Ext corridors. **Pets:** Small, dogs only. $5 daily fee/pet. Designated rooms, service with restrictions, crate.

SAVE S⒪ ⊠ ⒢

▲▲▲ ▼▼ Stonebrook Inn SH
(706) 782-4702. **$37-$99.** 698 Hwy 441 S. 0.8 mi s. Int corridors. **Pets:** Small. $50 deposit/pet, $6 daily fee/pet. Service with restrictions, supervision.

SAVE S⒪ ⊠ ⒢ 🖵

COLUMBUS

(AAA) ▼▼▼▼ Baymont Inn & Suites Columbus 🆂🅷 🐾
(706) 323-4344. **$64-$79.** 2919 Warm Springs Rd. I-185, exit 7 southbound; exit 7A northbound, just e. Int corridors. **Pets:** Medium, other species. Service with restrictions, supervision.
🆂🅰🆅🅴 🆂🅰 ⊠ 🎛 🖥 💻 🏊

▼▼▼▼ Four Points-Sheraton Columbus Airport 🆂🅷
(706) 327-6868. **$89-$119.** 5351 Sidney Simons Blvd. I-185, exit 8, just w. Int corridors. **Pets:** Accepted.
🅰🆂🅺 🆂🅰 ⊠ 🎛 🕹 🎛 💻 🍴 🏊 ⊠

▼▼ Howard Johnson Inn & Suites 🆂🅷
(706) 322-6641. **$70-$77.** 1011 Veterans Pkwy. I-185, exit 7 southbound; exit 7A northbound, 1.2 mi w to Veterans Pkwy, 3.2 mi s. Ext corridors. **Pets:** Large. $25 one-time fee/room. Service with restrictions, supervision.
🅰🆂🅺 🆂🅰 ⊠ 🕹 🎛 💻 🍴 🏊

▼▼▼▼ La Quinta Inn 🆂🅷
(706) 568-1740. **$75-$89.** 3201 Macon Rd. I-185, exit 6, just w. Ext corridors. **Pets:** Other species. Service with restrictions, crate.
🅰🆂🅺 🆂🅰 ⊠ 🎛 🎛 💻 🏊

▼ Motel 6 #058 Ⓜ
(706) 687-7214. **$43-$55.** 3050 Victory Dr. I-185, exit 1B, 3 mi w. Ext corridors. **Pets:** Small, other species. Service with restrictions, supervision.
🆂🅰 ⊠ 🕹 🏊

▼▼ Super 8 Motel of Columbus Ⓜ 🐾
(706) 322-6580. **$45-$85.** 2935 Warm Springs Rd. I-185, exit 7 southbound; exit 7A northbound, just e. Int corridors. **Pets:** Small. Service with restrictions, supervision.
🅰🆂🅺 🆂🅰 ⊠ 🕹 🎛

COMMERCE

▼▼ Comfort Inn 🆂🅷
(706) 335-9001. **$65-$75.** 165 Eisenhower Dr. I-85, exit 149, just nw. Ext corridors. **Pets:** Accepted.
🅰🆂🅺 ⊠ 🎛 🎛 🏊

(AAA) ▼ GuestHouse Inn Ⓜ
(706) 335-5147. **$42-$100.** 30934 US 441 S. I-85, exit 149, 0.3 mi e. Ext corridors. **Pets:** Medium, other species. $10 one-time fee/pet. Service with restrictions, supervision.
🆂🅰🆅🅴 🆂🅰 ⊠ 🎛 🏊

▼▼▼▼ Holiday Inn Express 🆂🅷
(706) 335-5183. **$65-$125.** 30747 US 441 S. I-85, exit 149, just e. Ext corridors. **Pets:** Other species. $25 one-time fee/room. Supervision.
🅰🆂🅺 🆂🅰 ⊠ 🅻🅼 🎛 🎛 💻 🏊

▼▼ Howard Johnson Inn & Suites 🆂🅷
(706) 335-5581. **$39-$65.** 148 Eisenhower Dr. I-85, exit 149, just w. Ext corridors. **Pets:** Medium. $10 one-time fee/pet. Service with restrictions, supervision.
🅰🆂🅺 🆂🅰 ⊠ 🎛 🎛 💻 🏊

▼▼ Super 8 Motel 🆂🅷
(706) 336-8008. **$39-$65.** 152 Eisenhower Dr. I-85, exit 149, just w. Ext corridors. **Pets:** Medium. $10 one-time fee/pet. Service with restrictions, supervision.
🅰🆂🅺 🆂🅰 ⊠ 💻

CONYERS

(AAA) ▼▼▼▼ Comfort Inn 🆂🅷
(770) 760-0300. **$69-$99.** 1363 Klondike Rd. I-20, exit 80. Int corridors. **Pets:** Accepted.
🆂🅰🆅🅴 🆂🅰 ⊠ 🅻🅼 🎛 💻 🏊

▼▼▼▼ Hampton Inn 🆂🅷
(770) 483-8838. **$85-$95.** 1340 Dogwood Dr. I-20, exit 82, just n, then just e. Int corridors. **Pets:** Small, other species. $25 one-time fee/pet. Service with restrictions, crate.
🅰🆂🅺 🆂🅰 ⊠ 🅻🅼 🕹 🕹 💻 🏊

▼▼▼▼ Jameson Inn 🆂🅷
(770) 760-1230. **$69-$71.** 1164 Dogwood Dr. I-20, exit 82, just n to Dogwood Dr, then just w. Ext corridors. **Pets:** Small. Service with restrictions, crate.
⊠ 🎛 💻 🏊

▼▼▼▼ La Quinta Inn & Suites 🆂🅷
(770) 918-0092. **$75-$105.** 1184 Dogwood Dr. I-20, exit 82, just n to Dogwood Dr, then just w. Int corridors. **Pets:** Other species. Service with restrictions, supervision.
🅰🆂🅺 🆂🅰 ⊠ 🅻🅼 🕹 🕹 🎛 💻 🏊

▼▼▼▼ Ramada Limited 🆂🅷
(770) 760-0777. **$55-$99.** 1070 Dogwood Dr. I-20, exit 82, just n to Dogwood Dr, 0.5 mi w. Ext corridors. **Pets:** Accepted.
🅰🆂🅺 🆂🅰 ⊠ 🅻🅼 🎛 💻 🏊

CORDELE

(AAA) ▼▼▼▼ Best Western Colonial Inn 🆂🅷
(229) 273-5420. **$59.** 1706 E 16th Ave (US 280). I-75, exit 101 (US 280), just w. Ext/int corridors. **Pets:** Accepted.
🆂🅰🆅🅴 🆂🅰 ⊠ 🎛 🏊

(AAA) ▼▼▼▼ Ramada Inn 🆂🅷
(229) 273-5000. **$60.** 2016 E 16th Ave (US 280). I-75, exit 101 (US 280), just e. Ext corridors. **Pets:** Small. $10 daily fee/pet. Service with restrictions, crate.
🆂🅰🆅🅴 🆂🅰 ⊠ 🎛 💻 🍴 🏊

▼ Super 8 Ⓜ
(229) 273-2456. **$45-$55.** 1618 E 16th Ave. I-75, exit 101 (US 280), just w. Ext corridors. **Pets:** Small. Service with restrictions, crate.
🅰🆂🅺 🆂🅰 ⊠ 🎛

COVINGTON

(AAA) ▼▼▼ Best Western Colonial Inn 🆂🅷 🐾
(770) 786-5800. **$55-$150.** 10130 Alcovy Rd. I-20, exit 92, just n. Ext corridors. **Pets:** Small. $10 daily fee/pet, $50 one-time fee/pet. Designated rooms, service with restrictions, supervision.
🆂🅰🆅🅴 🆂🅰 ⊠ 🎛 💻 🏊

▼▼▼▼ Holiday Inn Express 🆂🅷
(770) 787-4900. **$78-$85, 14 day notice.** 10111 Alcovy Rd.
I-20, exit 92, just n. Ext corridors. **Pets:** Accepted.
🅰🆂🅺 🆂🅾 ⊠ 🖋🅼 📷 🖋 🎁 💷 🏊

▼▼ Jameson Inn 🆂🅷
(770) 784-1849. **$63-$70.** 10225 Hwy 142 N. I-20, exit 93,
just s. Ext corridors. **Pets:** Small. Service with restrictions,
crate.
🅰🆂🅺 🆂🅾 ⊠ 🖋🅼 🎁 💷 🏊

DALTON

▼▼▼ Best Inns 🆂🅷
(706) 226-1100. **$45-$55.** 1529 W Walnut Ave. I-75, exit 333,
just e. Ext corridors. **Pets:** Small. $20 deposit/room. Service
with restrictions, supervision.
🆂🅰🆅🅴 🆂🅾 ⊠ 📷 🎁 💷 🏊

▼▼ Best Value Inn 🆂🅷
(706) 278-4300. **$35-$45.** 2007 Tampico Way. I-75, exit 336,
just e. Int corridors. **Pets:** Very small. $10 one-time fee/pet.
Designated rooms, service with restrictions, supervision.
🅰🆂🅺 🆂🅾 ⊠ 🎁 💷 🏊

▼▼▼ Best Western Inn of Dalton 🆂🅷
(706) 226-5022. **$49-$64.** 2106 Chattanooga Rd. I-75, exit
336, just w. Ext corridors. **Pets:** Small. $5 daily fee/pet.
Service with restrictions, supervision.
🆂🅰🆅🅴 🆂🅾 ⊠ 🎁 💷 🏊

▼▼▼ Comfort Inn & Suites 🆂🅷
(706) 259-2583. **$69-$95.** 905 Westbridge Rd. I-75, exit 333,
just w to Westbridge Rd, then just s. Int corridors.
Pets: Accepted.
🆂🅰🆅🅴 🆂🅾 ⊠ 🖋🅼 📷 🖋 🎁 💷 🏊

▼▼▼ Holiday Inn 🆂🅷
(706) 278-0500. **$67.** 515 Holiday Dr. I-75, exit 333, north-
west corner. Ext corridors. **Pets:** Accepted.
🆂🅰🆅🅴 🆂🅾 ⊠ 📷 🎁 💷 🍴 🏊

▼▼▼ Jameson Inn 🆂🅷
(706) 281-1880. **$69-$71.** 422 Holiday Dr. I-75, exit 333, just
w, then 0.3 mi n. Ext corridors. **Pets:** Small. Service with
restrictions, crate.
🆂🅰🆅🅴 ⊠ 📷 🖋 🎁 💷 🏊

DARIEN

▼▼▼ Comfort Inn 🆂🅷
(912) 437-4200. **$89-$129.** 703 Frontage Rd. I-95, exit 49
(SR 251), just nw. Int corridors. **Pets:** Medium. $10 daily
fee/pet. Service with restrictions, supervision.
🆂🅰🆅🅴 🆂🅾 ⊠ 🖋 🎁 💷 🏊

▼▼▼ Holiday Inn Express 🆂🅷
(912) 437-5373. **$64.** I-95 & SR 251. I-95, exit 49 (SR 251),
just nw. Int corridors. **Pets:** Accepted.
🅰🆂🅺 🆂🅾 ⊠ 📷 🎁 🏊

DAWSONVILLE

**🅰🅰🅰 ▼▼▼ Best Western (Dawson Village
        Inn)** 🆂🅷
(706) 216-4410. **$55-$99.** 76 N Georgia Ave. Jct SR 400 and
53, 0.5 mi s. Int corridors. **Pets:** Small, other species. No
service, supervision.
🆂🅰🆅🅴 🆂🅾 ⊠ 🖋🅼 🖋 🎁 💷 🏊

▼▼▼ Comfort Inn 🆂🅷
(706) 216-1900. **$62-$71.** 127 Beartooth Pkwy. Jct SR 400
and 53, 0.5 mi s. Int corridors. **Pets:** Other species. $5 daily
fee/pet. Service with restrictions.
🅰🆂🅺 🆂🅾 ⊠ 🎁 💷 🏊

DILLARD

🅰🅰🅰 ▼▼▼ Dillard House 🆂🅷
(706) 746-5348. **$59-$149.** 768 Franklin St. US 441, just e
via Old Dillard Rd. Ext corridors. **Pets:** Accepted.
🆂🅰🆅🅴 ⊠ 🖋 🎁 💷 🍴 🏊 🐾

🅰🅰🅰 ▼▼▼ Ramada Limited 🅼
(706) 746-5321. **$49-$149.** 3 Best Inn Way. Center. Ext corridors. **Pets:** Accepted.
🆂🅰🆅🅴 🆂🅾 ⊠ 🎁 💷 🏊

DOUGLAS

▼▼ Jameson Inn 🅼
(912) 384-9432. **$64-$67.** 1628 S Peterson Ave. Jct US 221/
441/SR 31 and SR 206/353, just s. Ext corridors.
Pets: Small. Service with restrictions, crate.
⊠ 🎁 💷 🏊

DUBLIN

**🅰🅰🅰 ▼▼▼ Best Western Executive Inn &
        Suites** 🆂🅷
(478) 275-2650. **$59.** 2121 Hwy 441 S. I-16, exit 51 (US
441), 0.5 mi n. Ext corridors. **Pets:** Accepted.
🆂🅰🆅🅴 🆂🅾 ⊠ 📷 🎁 💷 🏊

▼▼ Econo Lodge 🅼
(478) 296-1223. **$45-$100.** 2184 Hwy 441 S. I-16, exit 51
(US 441), just n. Ext corridors. **Pets:** Accepted.
🅰🆂🅺 🆂🅾 ⊠ 🎁

▼▼ Jameson Inn 🆂🅷
(478) 275-3008. **$66-$71.** 100 PM Watson Dr. I-16, exit 51
(US 441), just n. Ext corridors. **Pets:** Small. Service with
restrictions, crate.
⊠ 🎁 💷 🏊

EASTMAN

▼▼ Jameson Inn 🆂🅷
(478) 374-7925. **$66-$71.** 103 Pine Ridge Rd. 1.6 mi se on
US 341 and 23. Ext corridors. **Pets:** Small. Service with
restrictions, crate.
⊠ 🎁 💷 🏊

FITZGERALD

♦♦♦ Country Hearth Inn SH
(229) 409-9911. **$40-$65.** 125 Stuart Way. Just n of US 319/107, just e. Int corridors. **Pets:** Small, other species. Service with restrictions, supervision.
ASK S⊘ ✕ 🖪 💻

♦♦ Jameson Inn SH
(229) 424-9500. **$64-$68.** 111 Bull Run Rd. Just n of US 319/107, on US 129. Ext corridors. **Pets:** Small. Service with restrictions, crate.
✕ 🖪 💻 ➰

FORSYTH

♦♦♦ Econo Lodge SH ❄
(478) 994-5603. **$48-$60.** 320 Cabiness Rd. I-75, exit 187 (SR 83), just ne. Int corridors. **Pets:** Small. No service, supervision.
SAVE S⊘ 💻 ➰

♦♦♦ Hampton Inn SH ❄
(478) 994-9697. **$67-$77.** 520 Holiday Cir. I-75, exit 186 (Juliette Rd), just w, then just s on Aaron St. Int corridors. **Pets:** Large, other species.
ASK S⊘ ✕ ⭕M 🖪 💻

♦♦♦ Holiday Inn Forsyth SH
(478) 994-5691. **$63-$74.** 480 Holiday Cir. I-75, exit 186 (Juliette Rd), just w, then just s on Arron St. Ext corridors. **Pets:** $25 one-time fee/room. Designated rooms, service with restrictions, crate.
ASK S⊘ ✕ ⭕ ⓢ 🖪 💻 ⅋ ➰

GAINESVILLE

♦♦♦♦ GuestHouse Inn SH ❄
(770) 535-8100. **$55-$70.** 520 Queen City Pkwy SW. I-985, exit 20, 1.8 mi nw on SR 60. Ext corridors. **Pets:** Small. $10 daily fee/pet. Service with restrictions, supervision.
SAVE S⊘ ✕ 🖪 💻 ➰

GARDEN CITY

♦♦♦ Masters Inn Garden City SH
(912) 964-4344. **$43-$63.** 4200 Augusta Rd. I-95, exit 109 (SR 21), 6.7 mi s. Ext/int corridors. **Pets:** Small. $5 daily fee/room. No service, supervision.
SAVE S⊘ ✕ ⓢ 🖪 ⅋ ➰

GLENNVILLE

♦♦♦ Cheeri-O Inn M
(912) 654-2176. **$40-$42, 7 day notice.** 820 Musgrove St. 0.8 mi s on US 25 and 301. Ext corridors. **Pets:** Medium. $5 daily fee/pet. Designated rooms, service with restrictions, supervision.
SAVE S⊘ ✕ 🖪 💻

GOLDEN ISLES AREA

JEKYLL ISLAND

♦♦♦♦♦ Clarion Resort Buccaneer SH
(912) 635-2261. **$45-$230, 3 day notice.** 85 S Beachview Dr. Jct Ben Fortson Pkwy (SR 50)/Beachview Dr, 0.5 mi s. Ext/int corridors. **Pets:** Accepted.
SAVE S⊘ ✕ ⭕ ⓢ 🖪 💻 ⅋ ➰ ✕

♦♦♦ Quality Inn & Suites SH
(912) 635-2202. **$79-$209, 7 day notice.** 700 N Beachview Dr. Jct Ben Fortson Pkwy (SR 50)/Beachview Dr, 1.5 mi n. Ext corridors. **Pets:** Small, other species. $10 daily fee/room. Service with restrictions, supervision.
SAVE S⊘ ✕ ⓢ 🖪 💻 ➰ ✕

❖ END AREA ❖

GRAY

♦♦ Days Inn M
(478) 986-4200. **$55-$58.** 288 W Clinton St. Jct SR 44/US 129, 0.9 mi w on US 129. Ext/int corridors. **Pets:** Accepted.
ASK S⊘ ✕ ⓢ 🖪 ➰

GREENSBORO

♦ Microtel Inn SH
(706) 453-7300. **$44-$57.** 2470 Old Eatonton Hwy. I-20, exit 130, just n. Int corridors. **Pets:** Accepted.
ASK S⊘ ✕ ⭕M ⭕ ⓢ 🖪

GRIFFIN

♦♦♦ Howard Johnson Inn & Suites SH
(770) 227-1516. **$59-$179.** 1690 N Expressway. 1.5 mi n on US 41 and 19. Ext corridors. **Pets:** Very small. $25 one-time fee/pet. Designated rooms, service with restrictions, supervision.
ASK S⊘ ✕ ⓢ 🖪 💻 ⅋ ➰

GROVETOWN

♦♦ Motel 6 of Augusta SH
(706) 651-8300. **$45-$47.** 459 Parkwest Dr. I-20, exit 194 (SR 383), just s, then w. Int corridors. **Pets:** Accepted.
ASK ✕ ⓢ 🖪 ➰

HAHIRA

▼▼ **Super 8 Motel I-75** 🆂🅷
(229) 794-8000. **$39-$46.** 1300 Georgia Hwy 122 W. I-75, exit 29, just w. Ext corridors. **Pets:** Accepted.
🅰🆂🅺 🆂🅾 ✖

HARTWELL

▼▼ **Jameson Inn** 🆂🅷
(706) 376-7298. **Call for rates.** 1091 E Franklin St. Jct SR 366/US 29, 1.2 mi e on US 29 (E Franklin St). Ext corridors. **Pets:** Small. Service with restrictions, crate.
✖ 🅼 🔋 ⊇

HELEN

🆀🅰🅰 ▼▼▼▼ **A Premier Vacation Rentals Inc** 🆅🅷
(706) 348-8323. **$95-$795, 14 day notice.** 5156 Helen Hwy. 3.5 mi s on SR 75. Ext corridors. **Pets:** Medium, dogs only. $15 daily fee/pet. No service, supervision.
🆂🅰🆅🅴 🔋 💻

🆀🅰🅰 ▼ **Econo Lodge** 🅼
(706) 878-2141. **$39-$225.** 749 Bruken Stasse. 0.3 mi s; center. Ext corridors. **Pets:** Accepted.
🆂🅰🆅🅴 🆂🅾 ✖ 🔋 💻 ⊇

▼▼ **The Helendorf River Inn & Conference Center** 🆂🅷
(706) 878-2271. **$34-$104, 10 day notice.** 33 Munichstrasse. SR 17 and 75; center. Ext corridors. **Pets:** Other species. $10 daily fee/pet. Designated rooms, service with restrictions, supervision.
✖ 🔋 💻 ⊇

▼▼ **Kountry Peddler Tanglewood Resort Cabins** 🅲🅰 🐾
(706) 878-3286. **$113-$175.** 3387 Hwy 356. 1 mi n on SR 75, then 3 mi ne on SR 356. Ext corridors. **Pets:** Medium, other species. $25 one-time fee/pet. Service with restrictions, supervision.
🅰🆂🅺 🆂🅾 ✖ 🔋 💻 ✖

HIAWASSEE

▼▼ **Enota B & B, Cabins & Conference Lodge** 🅲🅰
(706) 896-9966. **$40-$245.** 1000 Hwy 180. E on US 76 to SR 75/15, 6 mi s to SR 180, 3 mi w. Ext corridors. **Pets:** Accepted.
✖ 🔋 💻 ✖ 📷

HINESVILLE

▼▼▼ **Hampton Inn** 🆂🅷
(912) 876-4466. **$55.** 706 E Oglethrope Hwy. Just sw of jct US 84 and SR 38C. Ext corridors. **Pets:** Accepted.
🅰🆂🅺 🆂🅾 ✖ 🎱 🎱 🔋 💻 ⊇

HIRAM

▼▼▼ **Country Inn & Suites By Carlson** 🆂🅷
(770) 222-0456. **$59-$150.** 70 Enterprise Path. Jct SR 92/6 and US 278, 0.3 mi w. Int corridors. **Pets:** Accepted.
🅰🆂🅺 🆂🅾 ✖ 🎱 🔋 💻 ⊇

HOGANSVILLE

▼▼ **Days Inn** 🆂🅷
(706) 637-5400. **Call for rates.** 1630 Bass Cross Rd. I-85, exit 28, just w. Ext corridors. **Pets:** Accepted.
✖ 🔋 ⊇

🆀🅰🅰 ▼▼ **Econo Lodge** 🆂🅷
(706) 637-9395. **$50-$90.** 1888 E Main St. I-85, exit 28, just w. Ext corridors. **Pets:** Small, dogs only. $5 daily fee/pet. Designated rooms, service with restrictions, supervision.
🆂🅰🆅🅴 🆂🅾 ✖ 🔋 💻 ⊇

JEFFERSONVILLE

▼▼ **Jeffersonville Inn** 🅼
(478) 945-3785. **$55-$70.** 5193 Hwy 96. I-16, exit 24 (SR 96), just s. Ext corridors. **Pets:** Accepted.
🅰🆂🅺 🆂🅾 ✖ ⊇

JESUP

▼▼ **Jameson Inn of Jesup** 🅼
(912) 427-6800. **$66-$71.** 205 N Hwy 301. Jct US 341, just n. Ext corridors. **Pets:** Small. Service with restrictions, crate.
✖ 🎱 🔋 💻 ⊇

KINGSLAND

🆀🅰🅰 ▼▼▼▼ **Best Western/Kings Bay Inn** 🆂🅷
(912) 729-7666. **$62-$85.** 1353 Hwy 40 E. I-95, exit 3 (SR 40), just se, then ne. Ext corridors. **Pets:** Small. $7 one-time fee/pet. Service with restrictions, supervision.
🆂🅰🆅🅴 🆂🅾 ✖ 🎱 🔋 💻 ⊇

▼▼ **Econo Lodge** 🅼
(912) 673-7336. **$42-$52.** 1135 E King Ave. I-95, exit 3 (SR 40), just nw. Ext corridors. **Pets:** Small. $5 daily fee/pet. Service with restrictions, crate.
🅰🆂🅺 🆂🅾 ✖ 🅼 🎱 🎱 🔋 💻 ⊇

▼▼ **Jameson Inn** 🆂🅷
(912) 729-9600. **$67-$73.** 105 May Creek Blvd. I-95, exit 3 (SR 40), just nw, then s at Boone Ave. Ext corridors. **Pets:** Small. Service with restrictions, crate.
✖ 🅼 🔋 💻 ⊇

🆀🅰🅰 ▼▼▼ **Ramada Inn & Suites** 🆂🅷
(912) 729-3000. **$45-$75.** 930 Hwy 40 E. I-95, exit 3 (SR 40), just nw. Ext corridors. **Pets:** Other species. $10 daily fee/pet. Service with restrictions.
🆂🅰🆅🅴 🆂🅾 ✖ 🎱 🔋 💻 ⊇

🆀🅰🅰 ▼ **Super 8 Motel** 🆂🅷
(912) 729-6888. **$35-$85.** 120 Edenfield Dr. I-95, exit 3 (SR 40), just se. Int corridors. **Pets:** Medium. $5 daily fee/pet. Service with restrictions, supervision.
🆂🅰🆅🅴 ✖ 🔋

LA FAYETTE

🆀🅰🅰 ▼▼ **Days Inn** 🆂🅷
(706) 639-9362. **$50-$65, 7 day notice.** 2209 N Main St. 2.5 mi n on US 27. Ext corridors. **Pets:** Other species. $10 daily fee/pet. Service with restrictions, supervision.
🆂🅰🆅🅴 🆂🅾 ✖ 🔋 ⊇

LAGRANGE

⬥⬥⬥ ▽▽▽▽ Best Western Lafayette Garden Inn SH
(706) 884-6175. **$69-$89.** 1513 Lafayette Pkwy. I-85, exit 18 (Lafayette Pkwy), just w. Ext corridors. **Pets:** Small, dogs only. $25 daily fee/pet. Designated rooms, service with restrictions, supervision.
[SAVE] [S🏊] [✕] [🛏] [💻] [🍴] [➰]

⬥⬥⬥ ▽▽▽ Days Inn-LaGrange/Callaway Gardens SH ❀
(706) 882-8881. **$55.** 2606 Whitesville Rd. I-85, exit 13, just e. Ext corridors. **Pets:** Small. $50 deposit/pet, $6 daily fee/pet. Service with restrictions, supervision.
[SAVE] [S🏊] [✕] [🐾] [🛏] [💻] [➰]

⬥⬥⬥ ▽▽▽ Econo Lodge SH
(706) 882-9540. **$55-$79.** 1601 LaFayette Pkwy. I-85, exit 18 (Lafayette Pkwy), just e. Ext corridors. **Pets:** Other species. $10 one-time fee/room. Service with restrictions, crate.
[SAVE] [S🏊] [✕] [🛏] [💻] [➰]

▽▽ Jameson Inn LaGrange SH
(706) 882-8700. **$67-$73.** 110 Jameson Dr. I-85, exit 18 (Layafette Pkwy), 0.3 mi w. Ext corridors. **Pets:** Small. Service with restrictions, crate.
[✕] [♿M] [🐾] [🛏] [💻] [➰]

LAKE PARK

▽▽▽ Best Western Lake Park Inn SH
(229) 559-4939. **$49-$79.** 6972 Bellville Rd. I-75, exit 2, just w. Ext corridors. **Pets:** Accepted.
[ASK] [S🏊] [✕] [💻] [➰]

▽▽ Days Inn SH
(229) 559-0229. **$49-$59.** 4913 Timber Dr. I-75, exit 5, just w, then n. Ext corridors. **Pets:** Accepted.
[ASK] [S🏊] [✕] [🛏] [➰]

▽▽ Holiday Inn Express SH
(229) 559-5181. **$60-$80.** 1198 Lakes Blvd. I-75, exit 5, just e. Ext corridors. **Pets:** Accepted.
[ASK] [S🏊] [✕] [🛏] [💻] [➰]

⬥⬥⬥ ▽▽▽ Super 8 Motel SH
(229) 559-8111. **$45-$65.** 4907 Timber Dr. I-75, exit 5, just w, then n. Ext corridors. **Pets:** Very small. $10 daily fee/pet. Designated rooms, service with restrictions, supervision.
[SAVE] [S🏊] [✕] [🛏]

▽▽▽ Travelodge SH
(229) 559-0110. **$46-$58.** 4912 Timber Dr. I-75, exit 5, just w, just n. Int corridors. **Pets:** Service with restrictions, supervision.
[ASK] [✕] [♿M] [🛏] [💻] [➰]

LAVONIA

⬥⬥⬥ ▽▽▽ GuestHouse International Inn SH
(706) 356-8848. **$59-$69.** 14227 Jones St. I-85, exit 173, just w. Ext corridors. **Pets:** Other species. $10 daily fee/room. Service with restrictions, supervision.
[SAVE] [S🏊] [✕] [♿M] [🎣] [🐾] [🛏] [💻] [➰]

LOCUST GROVE

⬥⬥⬥ ▽▽▽ Econo Lodge M
(770) 957-2601. **$45-$100, 3 day notice.** 4829 Bill Gardner Pkwy. I-75, exit 212, just e. Ext corridors. **Pets:** Very small. $5 daily fee/pet. Designated rooms, service with restrictions, supervision.

⬥⬥⬥ ▽▽▽▽ Red Roof Inn & Suites SH ❀
(678) 583-0004. **$54-$94.** 4832 Bill Gardner Pkwy. I-75, exit 212, just e. Int corridors. **Pets:** Large, other species. No service, supervision.
[SAVE] [S🏊] [✕] [♿M] [🎣] [🐾] [🛏] [💻] [➰]

LOUISVILLE

⬥⬥⬥ ▽▽▽ Louisville Motor Lodge M
(478) 625-7168. **$43-$48.** 308 Hwy 1 Bypass. US 1 Bypass, 1 mi ne of center. Ext corridors. **Pets:** Accepted.
[SAVE] [✕] [🛏]

MACON

▽▽▽ Best Inns & Suites M
(478) 405-0106. **$49.** 130 Holiday North Dr. I-75, exit 169 (Arkwright Rd), just sw to US 23 (Riverside Dr), just se to Holiday North Dr, then just sw. Ext corridors. **Pets:** Accepted.
[ASK] [S🏊] [✕] [🛏] [💻]

⬥⬥⬥ ▽▽▽▽ Best Western Inn & Suites of Macon SH ❀
(478) 781-5300. **$56.** 4681 Chambers Rd. I-475, exit 3 (Eisenhower Pkwy/US 80), just ne, then just se. Ext corridors. **Pets:** Medium, other species. $10 daily fee/pet. Service with restrictions, supervision.
[SAVE] [S🏊] [✕] [🎣] [🛏] [💻] [➰]

▽▽▽▽ Comfort Inn-North SH
(478) 746-8855. **$69.** 2690 Riverside Dr. I-75, exit 167 (Riverside Dr), just nw. Ext/int corridors. **Pets:** Large. $25 one-time fee/room. Service with restrictions, supervision.
[ASK] [S🏊] [✕] [♿M] [🎣] [🛏] [💻] [➰]

⬥⬥⬥ ▽▽▽ Crowne Plaza Hotel LH
(478) 746-1461. **$119-$139.** 108 First St. Between Walnut St and Riverside Dr; downtown. Int corridors. **Pets:** Accepted.
[SAVE] [✕] [🛏] [💻] [🍴] [➰] [✕]

⬥⬥⬥ ▽▽▽ Econo Lodge M 🐾
(478) 474-1661. **$42-$50.** 4951 Romeiser Dr. I-475, exit 3 (Eisenhower Pkwy/US 80), just sw, then s. Ext corridors. **Pets:** Other species. $10 daily fee/room. Designated rooms, no service, crate.
[SAVE] [S🏊] [✕] [🛏] [➰]

▽▽▽ Hampton Inn I-75 SH
(478) 471-0660. **$72.** 3680 Riverside Dr. I-75, exit 169, just sw to Riverside Dr, then just se. Ext corridors. **Pets:** Accepted.
[ASK] [S🏊] [✕] [🛏] [💻] [➰]

Hawthorn Inn & Suites SH
(478) 471-2121. **$69.** 107 Holiday North Dr. I-75, exit 169, just sw to Riverside Dr, then just se. Ext corridors. **Pets:** Medium, other species. $25 one-time fee/pet. Service with restrictions, crate.
[ASK] [S$] [X] [🛏] [📺] [🏊]

Holiday Inn Express SH
(478) 743-1482. **$58-$64.** 2720 Riverside Dr. I-75, exit 167 (Riverside Dr), just nw. Int corridors. **Pets:** Accepted.
[ASK] [S$] [X] [&M] [🐾] [🛏] [📺] [🏊]

Holiday Inn Macon Conference Center SH
(478) 474-2610. **$72.** 3590 Riverside Dr. I-75, exit 169 (Arkwright Rd), just sw, then just se. Ext corridors. **Pets:** Accepted.
[ASK] [S$] [X] [🛏] [📺] [🍴] [🏊]

Howard Johnson Inn SH
(478) 746-7671. **$49, 10 day notice.** 2566 Riverside Dr. I-75, exit 167 (Riverside Dr), just sw. Ext/int corridors. **Pets:** Very small. $10 one-time fee/pet. Service with restrictions, supervision.
[ASK] [S$] [X] [📺] [🏊]

Jameson Inn M
(478) 474-8004. **$64-$69.** 150 Plantation Inn Dr. I-475, exit 9 (Zebulon Rd), just e to Peace Rd, then just s. Ext corridors. **Pets:** Small. Service with restrictions, crate.
[S$] [X] [🛏] [📺] [🏊]

La Quinta Inn & Suites SH 🐾
(478) 475-0206. **$75-$105.** 3944 River Place Dr. I-75, exit 169 (Arkwright Rd), just n, then e. Int corridors. **Pets:** Other species. Service with restrictions, crate.
[SAVE] [S$] [X] [&M] [🐾] [🛏] [📺] [🏊]

Motel 6 M
(478) 474-2870. **$30-$36.** 4991 Harrison Rd. I-475, exit 3 (Eisenhower Pkwy/US 80), just ne, then n. Ext corridors. **Pets:** Medium. Service with restrictions, crate.
[S$] [X] [🛏] [🏊]

Quality Inn & Conference Center SH 🐾
(478) 781-7000. **$45-$65.** 4630 Chambers Rd. I-475, exit 3 (Eisenhower Pkwy/US 80), just ne, then just se. Ext corridors. **Pets:** Medium. $10 daily fee/pet. Service with restrictions, supervision.
[ASK] [S$] [X] [🛏] [📺] [🏊]

Ramada Inn and Conference Center SH
(478) 474-0871. **$45-$50.** 5009 Harrison Rd. I-475, exit 3 (Eisenhower Pkwy/US 80), just ne, then just nw. Ext corridors. **Pets:** Very small. $15 daily fee/pet. Designated rooms, supervision.
[ASK] [S$] [X] [🛏] [📺] [🏊]

Red Roof Inn SH
(478) 477-7477. **$40-$50.** 3950 River Place Dr. I-75, exit 169 (Arkwright Rd), just n, then e. Int corridors. **Pets:** Medium, other species. Service with restrictions.
[SAVE] [X] [🐾] [🛏] [🏊]

Rodeway Inn SH 🐾
(478) 781-4343. **$45.** 4999 Eisenhower Pkwy. I-475, exit 3 (Eisenhower Pkwy/US 80), just ne. Ext corridors. **Pets:** Medium. $10 daily fee/room. Service with restrictions, crate.
[SAVE] [S$] [X] [🛏] [📺] [🏊]

Sleep Inn I-475 SH 🐾
(478) 476-8111. **$69.** 140 Plantation Inn Dr. I-475, exit 9 (Zebulon Rd), just e, then just s on Peake Rd. Int corridors. **Pets:** $10 daily fee/pet. Designated rooms, service with restrictions, crate.
[ASK] [S$] [X] [&M] [🐾] [🐾] [🛏] [📺] [🏊]

MADISON

Days Inn SH
(706) 342-1839. **$44-$54.** 2001 Eatonton Hwy. I-20, exit 114, just n. Ext corridors. **Pets:** $10 one-time fee/room. Service with restrictions, supervision.
[SAVE] [S$] [X] [🛏] [📺] [🏊]

Super 8 Motel SH
(706) 342-7800. **$42-$59.** 2091 Eatonton Hwy. I-20, exit 114, 0.3 mi s. Int corridors. **Pets:** Medium. $10 daily fee/pet. Service with restrictions, supervision.
[ASK] [S$] [X] [🛏]

MANCHESTER

Western Inn & Suites M
(706) 846-4410. **$42-$59, 3 day notice.** 1119 Warm Springs Hwy. On 5th Ave (SR 41), 1.1 mi n of town center. Ext corridors. **Pets:** Accepted.
[SAVE] [S$] [X] [🛏] [🏊]

MCDONOUGH

Comfort Inn SH
(770) 954-9110. **$75-$80.** 80 Hwy 81 W. I-75, exit 218, just nw. Ext corridors. **Pets:** Medium. $6 daily fee/pet. Designated rooms, service with restrictions, supervision.
[SAVE] [S$] [X] [🐾] [🛏] [📺] [🏊]

Days Inn SH
(770) 957-5261. **$60-$68.** 744 SR 155 S & I-75. I-75, exit 216, just e. Ext corridors. **Pets:** Medium. $8 daily fee/pet. Service with restrictions, supervision.
[SAVE] [S$] [X] [🐾] [🛏] [📺] [🏊]

Holiday Inn McDonough SH
(770) 957-5291. **$89.** 930 Hwy 155 S. I-75, exit 216, just w. Ext corridors. **Pets:** Medium. Service with restrictions, crate.
[SAVE] [S$] [X] [&M] [🐾] [🛏] [📺] [🍴] [🏊]

Masters Inn M
(770) 957-5818. **$40-$120.** 1311 Hampton Rd. I-75, exit 218, just w. Ext corridors. **Pets:** Small, dogs only. $5 daily fee/pet. Service with restrictions, supervision.
[SAVE] [S$] [X] [🛏] [🏊]

Super 8 Motel M
(770) 957-2458. **$50.** 1170 Hampton Rd. I-75, exit 218, just e. Ext/int corridors. **Pets:** Accepted.
[SAVE] [X] [🛏]

MILLEDGEVILLE

Holiday Inn Express SH ❀
(478) 454-9000. **$67-$85.** 1839 N Columbia St. Jct Business Rt US 441 and 441 Bypass on north side of city, just se. Int corridors. **Pets:** Small. Designated rooms, no service, supervision.

MONROE

Country Hearth Inn SH
(770) 207-1977. **$65-$70.** 1222 W Spring St. 1 mi w of downtown on Business Rt SR 10. Int corridors. **Pets:** Very small, dogs only. $10 daily fee/room. Service with restrictions, supervision.

NEWNAN

Best Western-Shenandoah Inn SH
(770) 304-9700. **$60-$69.** 620 Hwy 34 E. I-85, exit 47, just w. Ext corridors. **Pets:** Small, other species. $10 daily fee/pet. Service with restrictions, crate.

Jameson Inn SH
(770) 252-1236. **$74-$79.** 40 Lakeside Way. I-85, exit 47, 0.6 mi e. Int corridors. **Pets:** Small. Service with restrictions, crate.

Ramada Limited SH
(770) 683-1499. **$52.** 1310 Hwy 29 S. I-85, exit 41, just w. Ext corridors. **Pets:** Other species. $10 daily fee/pet. Service with restrictions, crate.

OAKWOOD

Country Inn & Suites By Carlson SH
(770) 535-8080. **$75-$165.** 4535 Oakwood Rd. I-985, exit 16, just sw. Int corridors. **Pets:** Accepted.

Jameson Inn of Oakwood/Gainesville SH
(770) 533-9400. **$57.** 3780 Merchants Way. I-985, exit 16, 0.4 mi sw. Ext corridors. **Pets:** Small. Service with restrictions, crate.

PERRY

Best Western Bradbury Inn & Suites SH
(478) 218-5200. **$62-$82.** 205 Lect Dr. I-75, exit 135 (US 41), just e on US 41, then just n. Int corridors. **Pets:** Accepted.

Comfort Inn Perry SH ❀
(478) 987-7710. **$45-$80.** 1602 Sam Nunn Blvd. I-75, exit 136 (Sam Nunn Blvd), just nw. Ext corridors. **Pets:** Small. $15 one-time fee/pet. Service with restrictions, supervision.

Hampton Inn SH
(478) 987-7681. **$65-$70.** 102 Hampton Ct. I-75, exit 136 (Sam Nunn Blvd), just se. Int corridors. **Pets:** Accepted.

Henderson Village CI
(478) 988-8696. **$175-$205.** 125 S Langston Cir. I-75, exit 127 (SR 26), 1.3 mi w. Ext/int corridors. **Pets:** Designated rooms, no service.

Jameson Inn-Perry SH
(478) 987-5060. **$64-$68.** 200 Market Place Dr. I-75, exit 136 (Sam Nunn Blvd), just se, then sw. Ext corridors. **Pets:** Small. Service with restrictions, crate.

New Perry Hotel SH ❀
(478) 987-1000. **$52-$125.** 800 Main St. I-75, exit 136 (Sam Nunn Blvd) southbound, 1.2 mi se on US 341, then just w; exit 135 (US 41) northbound, 1.5 mi ne, then just s. Ext/int corridors. **Pets:** Other species. $20 one-time fee/room. Service with restrictions, supervision.

Quality Inn SH
(478) 987-1345. **$57-$75.** 1504 Sam Nunn Blvd. I-75, exit 136 (Sam Nunn Blvd), just nw. Ext corridors. **Pets:** Accepted.

Super 8 Motel SH ❀
(478) 987-0999. **$50-$65, 3 day notice.** 102 Plaza Dr. I-75, exit 136 (Sam Nunn Blvd), just se. Ext corridors. **Pets:** Other species. $10 daily fee/room. Service with restrictions, crate.

PINE MOUNTAIN

Days Inn SH
(706) 663-2121. **$55-$79.** 368 S Main Ave. Just s on US 27 and SR 18. Ext corridors. **Pets:** Other species. $5 daily fee/pet. Designated rooms, no service, supervision.

POOLER

Best Western Bradbury Suites SH ❀
(912) 330-0330. **$69-$129.** 155 Bourne Ave. I-95, exit 102 (US 80), just e. Int corridors. **Pets:** Small. Designated rooms, service with restrictions, supervision.

Comfort Inn and Suites Conference Center SH
(912) 748-6464. **Call for rates.** 301 Governor Treutlen Dr. I-95, exit 102 (US 80), just nw, then just se. Int corridors. **Pets:** Accepted.

Econo Lodge–Savannah Pooler M ❀
(912) 748-4124. **$47-$70, 15 day notice.** 500 E Hwy 80. I-95, exit 102 (US 80), just nw. Ext corridors. **Pets:** Large, other species. $10 daily fee/room. Designated rooms, service with restrictions.

▼▼▼▼ **Jameson Inn** 🆂🅷
(912) 748-0017. **$78-$83.** 125 Bourne Ave. I-95, exit 102 (US 80), just e. Int corridors. **Pets:** Small. Service with restrictions, crate.
❎ 🗂 &⛎ 🛏 💻 🏊

▼▼ **Red Roof Inn & Suites** 🆂🅷
(912) 748-4050. **$60-$90.** 20 Mill Creek Cir. I-95, exit 104 (Pooler Pkwy), just w. Int corridors. **Pets:** Medium. Designated rooms, service with restrictions, supervision.
🅰🆂🅺 🆂🔟 ❎ 🗂 ⛎ 🛏 💻 🏊

▼▼▼▼ **Travelodge Suites** 🆂🅷
(912) 748-6363. **$59-$79.** 130 Continental Blvd. I-95, exit 102 (US 80), just e. Int corridors. **Pets:** Medium. $10 deposit/pet. Supervision.
❎ ⛎ 🛏 💻 🏊

RINCON

▼▼ ▼▼ **Days Inn** 🆂🅷
(912) 826-6966. **$49-$99.** 582 Columbia Ave. I-95, exit 109 (SR 21), 6.1 mi nw. Ext corridors. **Pets:** Small, other species. $10 daily fee/pet. Designated rooms, service with restrictions, supervision.
🅰🆂🅺 🆂🔟 ❎ ⛎ 🛏 💻 🏊

RINGGOLD

▼▼ ▼▼ **Super 8 Motel** Ⓜ
(706) 965-7080. **$47-$56.** 5400 Alabama Hwy. I-75, exit 348, just e. Ext corridors. **Pets:** Accepted.
🅰🆂🅺 🆂🔟 ❎ 🛏 🏊

ROME

▼▼▼▼ **Holiday Inn-Sky Top Center** 🆂🅷
(706) 295-1100. **$75.** 20 US 411 E. 2 mi e. Ext corridors. **Pets:** Medium. $15 one-time fee/room. Service with restrictions, crate.
🅰🆂🅺 🆂🔟 ❎ &⛎ 🗂 🛏 💻 🍽 🏊

▼▼ ▼▼ **Howard Johnson Express Inn of Rome** Ⓜ 🐾
(706) 291-1994. **$63-$140, 3 day notice.** 1610 Martha Berry Blvd. 2 mi n on US 27. Ext corridors. **Pets:** Small. $5 daily fee/pet. Designated rooms, service with restrictions.
🅰🆂🅺 🆂🔟 ❎ 🗂 🛏 💻 🏊

▼▼▼▼ **Jameson Inn** 🆂🅷
(706) 291-7797. **$65-$70.** 40 Grace Dr. On US 411, 2.2 mi e. Int corridors. **Pets:** Very small, other species. Service with restrictions, crate.
🅰🆂🅺 🆂🔟 ❎ &⛎ &⛎ 🛏 💻 🏊

SANDERSVILLE

🅐🅐🅐 ▼▼▼▼ **Villa South Motor Inn** 🆂🅷
(478) 552-1234. **$51-$57.** 725 S Harris St. Jct SR 15/242, just s on SR 15. Ext corridors. **Pets:** Accepted.
🆂🅰🆅🅴 🆂🔟 ❎ 🛏 💻 🍽 🏊

SAVANNAH

🅐🅐🅐 ▼▼▼▼ ▼▼▼▼ **Ballastone Inn** 🅱🅱
(912) 236-1484. **$215-$415, 15 day notice.** 14 E Oglethorpe Ave. Between Bull and Drayton sts. Int corridors. **Pets:** Accepted.
🆂🅰🆅🅴 ❎

🅐🅐🅐 ▼▼ ▼▼ **Baymont Inn & Suites Savannah** 🆂🅷
(912) 927-7660. **$59-$84.** 8484 Abercorn St. 2.4 mi s of jct SR 21/204 (Abercorn St). Int corridors. **Pets:** Other species. Service with restrictions, supervision.
🆂🅰🆅🅴 🆂🔟 ❎ 🗂 🛏 💻 🏊

🅐🅐🅐 ▼▼ ▼▼ **Best Value Inn** Ⓜ
(912) 927-2999. **$45-$55.** 390 Canebrake Rd. I-95, exit 94 (SR 204), just e, then just s. Ext corridors. **Pets:** Small, other species. $5 daily fee/pet. Service with restrictions, supervision.
🆂🅰🆅🅴 🆂🔟 ❎ 🗂 🛏 💻 🏊

🅐🅐🅐 ▼▼ ▼▼ **Best Western Central** 🆂🅷
(912) 355-1000. **$69-$89.** 45 Eisenhower Dr. 1.3 mi s of jct SR 21/204 (Abercorn St), then just w. Ext corridors. **Pets:** Medium, other species. $25 one-time fee/room. Designated rooms, service with restrictions, crate.
🆂🅰🆅🅴 🆂🔟 ❎ 🗂 🛏 💻 🏊

▼▼▼▼ **Catherine Ward House Inn** 🅱🅱
(912) 234-8564. **$139-$300, 14 day notice.** 118 E Walburg St. Between Drayton and Abercorn sts. Ext/int corridors. **Pets:** Accepted.
🅰🆂🅺 ❎ 🛏

▼▼▼▼ **ClubHouse Inn & Suites** 🆂🅷
(912) 356-1234. **$74-$104.** 6800 Abercorn St. 1 mi s of jct SR 21 and 204 (Abercorn St). Int corridors. **Pets:** Accepted.
🅰🆂🅺 🆂🔟 ❎ 🛏 💻 🏊

🅐🅐🅐 ▼▼▼▼ **East Bay Inn** 🅲🅸
(912) 238-1225. **$159-$199, 7 day notice.** 225 E Bay St. I-16, exit 167 (Montgomery St), 0.8 mi ne, then 0.8 mi se. Int corridors. **Pets:** Small, dogs only. $35 one-time fee/pet. Designated rooms, service with restrictions, supervision.
🆂🅰🆅🅴 🆂🔟 ❎ 💻 🍽

▼▼ ▼▼ **Econo Lodge Gateway** Ⓜ 🐾
(912) 925-2280. **$55-$120.** 7 Gateway Blvd W. I-95, exit 94 (SR 204), just nw, then just ne. Ext corridors. **Pets:** Medium. $5 daily fee/pet. Designated rooms, service with restrictions, supervision.
🅰🆂🅺 🆂🔟 ❎ 🛏 💻 🍽 🏊

▼▼▼▼ **Homewood Suites by Hilton** 🆂🅷
(912) 353-8500. **$139.** 5820 White Bluff Rd. Jct SR 21/204, 0.5 mi s. Ext/int corridors. **Pets:** Medium, other species. $45 one-time fee/room. Service with restrictions, supervision.
🅰🆂🅺 🆂🔟 ❎ 🛏 💻 🏊 🈂

🅐🅐🅐 ▼▼▼▼ **Howard Johnson Express Inn** Ⓜ
(912) 925-7050. **$55-$89.** 17003 Abercorn St. I-95, exit 94 (SR 204), just e. Ext corridors. **Pets:** Medium. $10 daily fee/pet. Service with restrictions, supervision.
🆂🅰🆅🅴 🆂🔟 ❎ &⛎ 🛏 💻 🏊

▼▼▼▼ Joan's on Jones B & B 🅱🅱 🐾
(912) 234-3863. **$145-$160 (no credit cards), 7 day notice.**
17 W Jones St. Between Whitaker and Bull sts. Ext corridors. **Pets:** Dogs only. $50 one-time fee/room. Designated rooms, crate.
🅧 📷 💻

▼▼▼▼ La Quinta Inn 🆂🅷
(912) 355-3004. **$67-$87.** 6805 Abercorn St. 1 mi s of jct SR 21/204 (Abercorn St). Ext/int corridors. **Pets:** Accepted.
🅰🆂🅺 🆂 🅧 🌀 📷 💻 ⇌

🅐🅐🅐 ▼▼▼ La Quinta Inn-Savannah I-95 Ⓜ
(912) 925-9505. **$60-$80.** 6 Gateway Blvd S. I-95, exit 94 (SR 204), just e, then s. Ext corridors. **Pets:** Service with restrictions, supervision.
🆂🅰🆅🅴 🆂 🅧 🅼 🌀 🅺 💻 ⇌

▼▼▼▼ The Olde Georgian Inn 🅱🅱
(912) 236-2911. **$105-$195, 7 day notice.** 212 W Hall St. Between Jefferson and Barnard sts, just w of Forsyth Park. Ext/int corridors. **Pets:** Accepted.
🅰🆂🅺 🅧 📷 💻 ✍

🅐🅐🅐 ▼▼▼▼ Olde Harbour Inn 🅱🅱
(912) 234-4100. **$169-$239, 7 day notice.** 508 E Factors Walk. Lincoln St ramp off E Bay St. Ext corridors. **Pets:** Small, other species. $35 one-time fee/pet. Designated rooms, service with restrictions, supervision.
🆂🅰🆅🅴 🆂 🅧 📷 💻

🅐🅐🅐 ▼▼▼ Quality Inn Savannah South Ⓜ 🐾
(912) 925-2770. **$55-$79.** 3 Gateway Blvd S. I-95, exit 94 (SR 204), just e, then just s. Ext corridors. **Pets:** Medium. $10 daily fee/pet. Service with restrictions, supervision.
🆂🅰🆅🅴 🆂 🅧 🌀 💻 🍽 ⇌

▼▼▼ Red Roof Inn 🆂🅷
(912) 920-3535. **$56-$76.** 405 Al Henderson Blvd. I-95, exit 94 (SR 204), just e. Int corridors. **Pets:** Small, other species. Service with restrictions, supervision.
🅰🆂🅺 🆂 🅧 🅼 🅺 📷 💻 ⇌

▼▼▼▼ Savannah Residence Inn by
Marriott 🆂🅷 🐾
(912) 356-3266. **$149-$179.** 5710 White Bluff Rd. Jct SR 21 and White Bluff Rd, 0.5 mi s. Int corridors. **Pets:** Medium, other species. $125 one-time fee/room. Service with restrictions, supervision.
🅰🆂🅺 🆂 🅧 🅺 📷 💻 ⇌ 🅧

🅐🅐🅐 ▼▼▼ Travelodge Ⓜ
(912) 925-2640. **$45-$179.** 1 Fort Argyle Rd. I-95, exit 94 (SR 204), just w. Ext corridors. **Pets:** Small. $10 daily fee/pet. Designated rooms, service with restrictions, supervision.
🆂🅰🆅🅴 🆂 🅧 🅺 📷 💻 ⇌

STATESBORO

▼▼▼ Best Western University Inn 🆂🅷
(912) 681-7900. **$58-$75.** 1 Jameson Ave. Jct US 25 and 301, 1 mi ne on US 25. Ext corridors. **Pets:** Accepted.
🅧 📷 💻 ⇌

▼▼▼ Hometown Inn Ⓜ
(912) 681-4663. **$59-$99.** 126 Rushing Ln. Jct US 301 Bypass and SR 67, just w. Ext corridors. **Pets:** Accepted.
🅰🆂🅺 🆂 🅧 🅺 📷 💻

▼▼▼▼ Statesboro Inn & Restaurant Ⓒ🅸
(912) 489-8628. **$85-$150.** 106 S Main St. US 301/25, just s of town center; downtown. Int corridors. **Pets:** Accepted.
🆂 🅧 📷 💻 🍽

STOCKBRIDGE

▼▼▼ Best Western Atlanta South 🆂🅷
(770) 474-8771. **$55-$100.** 619 Hwy 138. I-75, exit 228, just e; I-675, exit 1, 0.5 mi w. Ext corridors. **Pets:** Medium. $15 daily fee/room. Designated rooms, service with restrictions, supervision.
🅰🆂🅺 🆂 🅧 📷 💻 🍽 ⇌

▼ Motel 6-1117 Ⓜ 🐾
(770) 389-1142. **$43-$55.** 7233 Davidson Pkwy N. I-675, exit 1, northeast corner; I-75, exit 228, 1 mi e. Ext corridors. **Pets:** Small, other species. Service with restrictions, supervision.
🆂 🅧 🌀 🅺 📷

▼▼ Shoney's Inn 🆂🅷
(770) 389-5179. **$40.** 110 Hwy 138. I-675, exit 1, just e; I-75, exit 228, 1.1 mi e. Ext corridors. **Pets:** Accepted.
🅰🆂🅺 🆂 🅧 📷 💻 ⇌

🅐🅐🅐 ▼▼▼ Super 8 Motel Atlanta South 🆂🅷
(770) 474-5758. **$55-$65.** 1451 Hudson Bridge Rd. I-75, exit 224, just w. Ext corridors. **Pets:** Accepted.
🆂🅰🆅🅴 🆂 🅧 📷 💻 ⇌

SWAINSBORO

🅐🅐🅐 ▼▼▼ Bradford Inn 🆂🅷
(478) 237-2400. **$55-$84.** 688 S Main St. I-16, exit 90 (US 1), 12.4 mi n. Ext corridors. **Pets:** Small, dogs only. $6 daily fee/pet. Service with restrictions, supervision.
🆂🅰🆅🅴 🆂 🅧 📷 💻

TALLAPOOSA

▼▼▼▼ Comfort Inn 🆂🅷
(770) 574-5575. **$50-$200.** 788 Hwy 100. I-20, exit 5, just s. Int corridors. **Pets:** Accepted.
🅰🆂🅺 🆂 🅧 🅼 🅺 📷 💻 ⇌

THOMASTON

🅐🅐🅐 ▼▼▼ Best Western Thomaston Inn 🆂🅷
(706) 648-2900. **$50-$70.** 1207 Hwy 19 N. 2.8 mi n; center of town. Ext corridors. **Pets:** Small. $8 one-time fee/pet. Service with restrictions, supervision.
🆂🅰🆅🅴 🆂 🅧 📷 💻 ⇌

▼▼ Jameson Inn 🆂🅷
(706) 648-2232. **$64-$68.** 1010 Hwy 19 N. Jct SR 74, 2.3 mi n. Ext corridors. **Pets:** Small. Service with restrictions, crate.
🅧 📷 💻 ⇌

THOMASVILLE

WWW Hampton Inn Thomasville SH
(229) 227-0040. **$82-$87.** 1950 GA Hwy 122 (Pavo Rd). Jct of SR 300/I-19 and I-84 and SR 122, southeast corner. Int corridors. **Pets:** $50 deposit/pet.
ASK S♦ X ⬤M ⬤ ⬤ ⬤ ⬤ X

WW Jameson Inn SH
(229) 227-9500. **$66-$71.** 1670 Remington Ave. US 19, just w on CR 122. Ext corridors. **Pets:** Small. Service with restrictions, crate.
X ⬤M ⬤ ⬤ ⬤ ⬤ ⬤

WWWW Quality Inn & Suites Conference Center SH
(229) 225-2134. **$73.** 15138 Hwy 19 S. 0.3 mi s of US 319. Ext corridors. **Pets:** Other species. Service with restrictions, crate.
ASK S♦ X ⬤M ⬤ ⬤ ⬤ ⬤ T ⬤

THOMSON

AAA WWW Best Western White Columns Inn SH
(706) 595-8000. **$53-$139.** 1890 Washington Rd. I-20, exit 172 (US 78), just s. Ext corridors. **Pets:** Other species. $10 daily fee/room. Designated rooms, service with restrictions, crate.
SAVE S♦ X ⬤ ⬤ ⬤ T ⬤ X

AAA W Days Inn M
(706) 595-2262. **$49-$55.** 2658 Cobbham Rd. I-20, exit 175 (SR 150), just n. Ext corridors. **Pets:** Small. $15 daily fee/pet. Supervision.
SAVE S♦ X ⬤

TIFTON

AAA WW Family Values Inn SH
(229) 386-9558. **$36-$48.** 1103 King Rd. I-75, exit 63A (W 2nd St), just w. Ext corridors. **Pets:** Accepted.
SAVE S♦ X ⬤ ⬤ ⬤

WWW Hampton Inn SH
(229) 382-8800. **$87-$95.** 720 Hwy 319 S. I-75, exit 62, just e. Ext corridors. **Pets:** Medium, other species. $10 one-time fee/room. Service with restrictions, supervision.
ASK S♦ X ⬤ ⬤ ⬤

AAA WWW Holiday Inn SH
(229) 382-6687. **$80-$89.** 1208 Hwy 82 W. I-75, exit 62, at jct US 82 and 319. Ext corridors. **Pets:** Service with restrictions, supervision.
SAVE S♦ X ⬤ ⬤ ⬤ T ⬤

WW Microtel Inns & Suites SH
(229) 387-0112. **$39-$68.** 196 S Virginia Ave. I-75, exit 62, just n. Int corridors. **Pets:** Medium. $10 one-time fee/room. Service with restrictions, supervision.
ASK S♦ X ⬤M ⬤ ⬤ ⬤ ⬤

AAA W Motel 6 SH
(229) 388-8777. **$38-$51.** 579 Old Omega Rd. I-75, exit 61, just w. Int corridors. **Pets:** Small. Service with restrictions, supervision.
SAVE S♦ X ⬤

TOWNSEND

W Days Inn M
(912) 832-4411. **$56-$60.** I-95, exit 58 (SR 57), just nw. Ext corridors. **Pets:** Small. $10 daily fee/pet. Designated rooms, no service, supervision.
ASK S♦ X ⬤

UNADILLA

AAA W Scottish Inn M ✿
(478) 627-3228. **$39-$46.** 1062 Pine St (US 41). I-75, exit 121 (US 41), just ne. Ext corridors. **Pets:** Small. $5 daily fee/pet. Service with restrictions, supervision.
SAVE S♦ X ⬤

VALDOSTA

AAA WWW Best Western King of the Road SH
(229) 244-7600. **$59-$65.** 1403 N St Augustine Rd. I-75, exit 18, just w off of SR 94. Ext corridors. **Pets:** Accepted.
SAVE S♦ X ⬤ ⬤ ⬤ ⬤ T ⬤

AAA WWW Comfort Inn Conference Center SH
(229) 242-1212. **$64-$130.** 2101 W Hill Ave. I-75, exit 16, just w. Ext/int corridors. **Pets:** Accepted.
SAVE S♦ X ⬤ ⬤ T ⬤

WW Days Inn Conference Center SH
(229) 249-8800. **$44-$54.** 1827 W Hill Ave. I-75, exit 16, just e. Ext corridors. **Pets:** Other species. $5 daily fee/pet. Service with restrictions, supervision.
ASK S♦ X ⬤M ⬤ ⬤ ⬤ ⬤

WW Days Inn I-75 North SH
(229) 244-4460. **$41-$51.** 4598 N Valdosta Rd. I-75, exit 22, just w. Ext corridors. **Pets:** Accepted.
ASK S♦ X ⬤ ⬤

AAA WW Holiday Inn SH
(229) 242-3881. **$62-$80.** 1309 St Augustine Rd. I-75, exit 18, just e on SR 94. Ext corridors. **Pets:** Medium, dogs only. $10 daily fee/pet. Designated rooms, service with restrictions, supervision.
SAVE S♦ X ⬤ ⬤ ⬤ T ⬤

WW Jameson Inn SH
(229) 253-0009. **$70-$75.** 1725 Gornto Rd. I-75, exit 18, 0.3 mi e on north side of SR 94. Ext corridors. **Pets:** Small. Service with restrictions, crate.
X ⬤ ⬤ ⬤ ⬤

AAA WWW Quality Inn North SH
(229) 244-8510. **$49-$55.** 1209 St Augustine Rd. I-75, exit 18, 0.3 mi e on SR 94. Ext corridors. **Pets:** Small, dogs only. $25 one-time fee/room. Service with restrictions, crate.
SAVE S♦ X ⬤ ⬤ ⬤ ⬤ X

WW Quality Inn South SH ✿
(229) 244-4520. **$42-$59.** 1902 W Hill Ave. I-75, exit 16, just e on US 84. Ext corridors. **Pets:** Medium, other species. Service with restrictions, crate.
ASK S♦ X ⬤ ⬤ ⬤

◆◆◆ Ramada Limited SH ❀
(229) 242-1225. **$65, 7 day notice.** 2008 W Hill Ave. I-75, exit 16, just e on US 84. Ext corridors. **Pets:** Other species. $5 daily fee/room. Service with restrictions.
ASK S☐ ✕ ☐ ☐ 🏊

◆◆◆ Super 8 Motel I-75 SH
(229) 249-8000. **$44-$54.** 1825 W Hill Ave. I-75, exit 16, just e. Int corridors. **Pets:** Accepted.
ASK S☐ ✕ ☐ ☐ ☐ 🏊

VIDALIA

♦♦♦ ◆◆◆ Days Inn SH
(912) 537-9251. **$50-$56, 7 day notice.** 1503 Lyons E. 1 mi e on US 280. Ext corridors. **Pets:** Small. $10 daily fee/room. Service with restrictions, supervision.
SAVE S☐ ✕ ☐ ☐ ☐ 🏊

WARM SPRINGS

♦♦♦ ◆◆◆◆ Best Western White House Inn SH
(706) 655-2750. **$69-$150.** 2526 White House Pkwy. Jct US 41/27, 1.4 mi s. Ext/int corridors. **Pets:** Accepted.
SAVE ✕ ☐ ☐ ☐ ☐ 🏊

WARNER ROBINS

♦♦♦ ◆◆◆ Best Western Peach Inn SH
(478) 953-3800. **$46-$59.** 2739 Watson Blvd. I-75, exit 146 (SR 247C), 4.1 mi e. Ext corridors. **Pets:** Small, other species. $6 daily fee/pet. Designated rooms, service with restrictions, crate.
SAVE S☐ ✕ ☐ ☐ ☐ 🏊

♦♦♦ ◆◆◆◆ Comfort Inn & Suites SH
(478) 922-7555. **$63-$135.** 95 S Hwy 247. Jct SR 247C and US 129/SR 247, 1.6 mi s on US 129/SR 247. Ext/int corridors. **Pets:** Small, other species. $25 one-time fee/room.
SAVE S☐ ✕ ☐ ☐ ☐ ☐ 🏊

◆◆◆ Jameson Inn-Warner Robins SH
(478) 953-5522. **$61-$66.** 2731 Watson Blvd. I-75, exit 146 (SR 247C), 4.1 mi e. Ext corridors. **Pets:** Small. Service with restrictions, crate.
✕ ☐ ☐ ☐ 🏊

◆◆◆ Ramada Inn & Conference Center SH
(478) 953-3000. **$66-$89.** 2725 Watson Blvd. I-75, exit 146 (SR 247C), 4.1 mi e. Int corridors. **Pets:** $15 daily fee/room. Service with restrictions, crate.
ASK S☐ ✕ ☐ ☐ ☐ ☐ ☐ 🏊

♦♦♦ ◆◆ ◆ SuiteOne of Warner Robins SH
(478) 329-9222. **$59-$239.** 2103 Moody Rd. Jct US 129/SR 247 and Russell Pkwy; 1.8 mi e on Russell Pkwy, then just n. Ext corridors. **Pets:** Accepted.
SAVE S☐ ✕ ☐ ☐ ☐

◆ Super 8 Motel SH
(478) 923-8600. **$35-$57.** 105 Woodcrest Blvd. I-75, exit 146, 5.7 mi e, then just n. Int corridors. **Pets:** $5 daily fee/pet. Service with restrictions, supervision.
ASK S☐ ✕ ☐ ☐

WAYCROSS

◆◆ ◆ Days Inn M
(912) 285-4700. **$40-$65.** 2016 Memorial Dr. Jct US 1 and 82, 0.5 mi se, east of city. Ext corridors. **Pets:** Small, dogs only. $10 daily fee/pet. Designated rooms, no service.
ASK S☐ ✕ ☐ 🏊

◆◆◆ Holiday Inn Waycross SH
(912) 283-4490. **$70-$80.** 1725 Memorial Dr. Jct US 1 and 82. Ext corridors. **Pets:** Medium. $15 one-time fee/room. Service with restrictions, supervision.
ASK S☐ ✕ ☐ ☐ ☐ ☐ ☐ ☐ 🏊 ☐

◆◆ ◆ Jameson Inn M
(912) 283-3800. **$64-$68.** 950 City Blvd. Between US 1 and 82, east of city. Ext corridors. **Pets:** Small. Service with restrictions, crate.
✕ ☐M ☐ ☐ ☐ 🏊

WAYNESBORO

♦♦♦ ◆◆◆◆ Best Western Executive Inn SH
(706) 554-0806. **$57-$62.** 1224 N Liberty St. 0.8 mi n of downtown center on US 25. Int corridors. **Pets:** Accepted.
SAVE S☐ ✕ ☐ ☐ 🏊

♦♦♦ ◆◆ ◆ Days Inn-Waynesboro M
(706) 554-9941. **$55-$65.** 225 S Liberty St. US 25/SR 21, 0.7 mi se of center. Ext corridors. **Pets:** Medium. $7 daily fee/pet. Designated rooms, service with restrictions, supervision.
SAVE S☐ ✕ ☐ ☐

◆◆ ◆ Jameson Inn M
(706) 437-0500. **$65-$70.** 1436 N Liberty St. 1.2 mi n of downtown center on US 25. Ext corridors. **Pets:** Very small. Service with restrictions, crate.
✕ ☐ ☐ ☐ ☐ 🏊

WEST POINT

◆◆ ◆ Travelodge M
(706) 643-9922. **$51, 30 day notice.** 1870 SR 18. I-85, exit 2, just e. Int corridors. **Pets:** Accepted.
ASK S☐ ✕ ☐ ☐ 🏊

WINDER

◆◆ ◆ Jameson Inn SH
(770) 867-1880. **$67-$72.** 9 Stafford St. Jct SR 81, 11, 53 and 8; center. Ext corridors. **Pets:** Small. Service with restrictions, crate.
✕ ☐ ☐ ☐ 🏊

WOODSTOCK

♦♦♦ ◆◆ ◆ SuiteOne of Woodstock SH
(770) 592-7848. **$54-$79.** 470 Parkway 575. I-575, exit 7, just n. Ext corridors. **Pets:** Small. $100 one-time fee/pet. Service with restrictions, supervision.
SAVE S☐ ✕ ☐M ☐ ☐ ☐

HAWAII

HILO

**⚏⚏⚏ ◈◈ Hale Kai Hawaii (Bjornen) Bed &
Breakfast** BB
(808) 935-6330. **$95-$115 (no credit cards), 14 day notice.**
111 Honolii Pali. 2 mi n on SR 19, e on Paukaa Rd
(towards ocean), just right. Int corridors. **Pets:** Accepted.
SAVE ⊠ ⊟ ⇌ AC

HONOLULU

⚏⚏⚏ ◈◈◈ Halekulani LH
(808) 923-2311. **$325-$520, 3 day notice.** 2199 Kalia Rd.
Just s of Kalakaua Ave via Lewers St. Int corridors.
Pets: Accepted.
SAVE ⊠ ⚅ᴹ ⊘ ⚇ ⊟ ⊟ ¶ ⇌ ⊠

KAUPULEHU

**⚏⚏⚏ ◈◈◈◈ Four Seasons Resort Hualalai at
Historic Ka'upulehu** LH ✿
(808) 325-8000. **$520-$785.** 100 Ka'upulehu Dr. Off SR 19;
6 mi n of Kona International Airport. Ext corridors.
Pets: Small, other species. Service with restrictions, supervision.
SAVE ⊠ ⚅ᴹ ⊘ ⚇ ⊟ ¶ ⇌ ⊠

VOLCANO

⚏⚏⚏ ◈◈ Volcano Inn BB
(808) 967-7293. **$95-$138, 14 day notice.** 19-3820 Old Volcano Hwy. On SR 11 at MM 26, just w on Pearl Ave, then
just n on Old Volcano Hwy to the end. Ext/int corridors.
Pets: Accepted.
SAVE ⊠ ⊟ ⊟ AC

WAILEA

**⚏⚏⚏ ◈◈◈◈ Four Seasons Resort, Maui at
Wailea** LH ✿
(808) 874-8000. **$335-$770, 14 day notice.** 3900 Wailea
Alanui Dr. From end of SR 31, 0.5 mi s. Int corridors.
Pets: Small. Service with restrictions, supervision.
SAVE ⊠ ⚅ᴹ ⊘ ⚇ ⊟ ⊟ ¶ ⇌ ⊠

BLACKFOOT

Best Western Blackfoot Inn
(208) 785-4144. **$55-$99, 30 day notice.** 750 Jensen Grove Dr. I-15, exit 93, just e on Bergener, 0.4 mi n on Parkway. Int corridors. **Pets:** Other species. Service with restrictions, supervision.

BLISS

Amber Inn Motel
(208) 352-4441. **$39.** 17286 US Hwy 30. I-84, exit 141, just s. Int corridors. **Pets:** Medium. $6 daily fee/pet. Service with restrictions, supervision.

BOISE

AmeriSuites (Boise/Towne Square Mall)
(208) 375-1200. **$99-$109.** 925 N Milwaukee St. I-84, exit 49 (Franklin St), just w, 0.5 mi n. Int corridors. **Pets:** Small, other species. Service with restrictions, supervision.

Best Western Safari Motor Inn
(208) 344-6556. **$72-$84.** 1070 Grove St. At 11th and Grove sts; center. Int corridors. **Pets:** Designated rooms, service with restrictions, supervision.

Boise Super 8 Motel
(208) 344-8871. **$54-$79.** 2773 Elder St. I-84, exit 53 (Vista Ave), just n. Int corridors. **Pets:** Other species. $25 deposit/room. Service with restrictions, supervision.

Budget Host Inn
(208) 322-4404. **$60-$70.** 8002 Overland Rd. I-84, exit 50A westbound, just s, just w, then just n; exit 50B eastbound, just w, then just n. Ext corridors. **Pets:** $10 one-time fee/pet. Service with restrictions, crate.

Doubletree Club Hotel
(208) 345-2002. **$69-$174.** 475 W Parkcenter Blvd. I-84, exit 54 (Broadway Ave), 2 mi n, 0.3 mi e on Beacon and Parkcenter Blvd. Int corridors. **Pets:** Accepted.

Doubletree Hotel Riverside
(208) 343-1871. **$69-$179.** 2900 Chinden Blvd. I-184, exit Fairview Ave, just n, then just w on Garden. Int corridors. **Pets:** Accepted.

Econo Lodge Boise
(208) 344-4030. **$65-$75.** 4060 Fairview Ave. I-184, exit Fairview Ave, just n. Int corridors. **Pets:** Medium, dogs only. $10 one-time fee/pet. No service, supervision.

Hampton Inn
(208) 331-5600. **$74-$129.** 3270 S Shoshone St. I-84, exit 53 (Vista Ave), just n to Elder St, then just w. Int corridors. **Pets:** Medium, other species. $10 daily fee/room. Designated rooms, service with restrictions, supervision.

Holiday Inn Boise Airport
(208) 343-4900. **$75-$92.** 3300 Vista Ave. I-84, exit 53 (Vista Ave), just n. Int corridors. **Pets:** $25 one-time fee/room. Designated rooms, supervision.

Owyhee Plaza Hotel
(208) 343-4611. **$95-$145.** 1109 Main St. At 11th and Main sts; center. Ext/int corridors. **Pets:** Accepted.

Red Lion Hotel Boise Downtowner
(208) 344-7691. **$69-$119.** 1800 Fairview Ave. I-184, exit Fairview Ave, 1 mi n. Int corridors. **Pets:** Accepted.

Red Lion ParkCenter Suites–Boise
(208) 342-1044. **$79-$119.** 424 E Parkcenter Blvd. I-84, exit 54 (Broadway Ave), 2.3 mi n, just e on Beacon and Parkcenter Blvd. Int corridors. **Pets:** Other species. $10 daily fee/room. Service with restrictions, supervision.

Residence Inn by Marriott
(208) 344-1200. **$125-$175.** 1401 Lusk Ave. I-84, exit 53, 2.5 mi n, just w. Ext corridors. **Pets:** Other species. $20 daily fee/pet.

Rodeway Inn of Boise
(208) 376-2700. **$65-$100.** 1115 N Curtis Rd. I-184, exit 2, just se. Ext/int corridors. **Pets:** Large, other species. $25 deposit/room, $10 one-time fee/room. Designated rooms, service with restrictions, supervision.

BONNERS FERRY

Best Western Kootenai River Inn & Casino SH
(208) 267-8511. **$79-$119.** 7169 Plaza St. On US 95; city center. Int corridors. **Pets:** Small. Service with restrictions, supervision.

BURLEY

Best Western Burley Inn & Convention Center SH
(208) 678-3501. **$60-$73.** 800 N Overland Ave. I-84, exit 208, just s. Ext/int corridors. **Pets:** Accepted.

Budget Motel M
(208) 678-2200. **$50-$68.** 900 N Overland Ave. I-84, exit 208, just s. Ext corridors. **Pets:** Accepted.

CALDWELL

Best Western Caldwell Inn & Suites M
(208) 454-7225. **$64-$154.** 908 Specht Ave. I-84, exit 29, just s. Int corridors. **Pets:** Other species. $50 deposit/pet. Service with restrictions, supervision.

La Quinta Inn M
(208) 454-2222. **$65-$120.** 901 Specht Ave. I-84, exit 29, just s. Int corridors. **Pets:** Accepted.

COEUR D'ALENE

Best Western Coeur d'Alene Inn & Conference Center SH
(208) 765-3200. **$79-$159.** W 414 Appleway Ave. I-90, exit 12, just nw. Int corridors. **Pets:** Dogs only. $25 one-time fee/pet. Service with restrictions, supervision.

The Coeur d'Alene Resort LH
(208) 765-4000. **$99-$549, 7 day notice.** 115 S 2nd St. I-90, exit 11, 2 mi s. Ext/int corridors. **Pets:** Accepted.

Days Inn-Coeur d'Alene SH
(208) 667-8668. **$49-$109, 30 day notice.** 2200 Northwest Blvd. I-90, exit 11, just se. Int corridors. **Pets:** Other species. $5 one-time fee/pet. Service with restrictions, supervision.

La Quinta Inn SH
(208) 765-5500. **$43-$160.** 280 W Appleway Ave. I-90, exit 12, just ne. Int corridors. **Pets:** Service with restrictions, supervision.

La Quinta Inn & Suites SH
(208) 667-6777. **$39-$179.** 2209 E Sherman Ave. I-90, exit 15 (Sherman Ave), just s. Int corridors. **Pets:** Other species. Service with restrictions, supervision.

Rodeway Inn Pines Resort M
(208) 664-8244. **$50-$99.** 1422 Northwest Blvd. I-90, exit 11, 0.8 mi s. Ext corridors. **Pets:** Designated rooms, service with restrictions, supervision.

The Roosevelt, A Bed & Breakfast Inn BB
(208) 765-5200. **$79-$289, 14 day notice.** 105 Wallace Ave. I-90, exit 13, 2 mi s, then just w; downtown. Int corridors. **Pets:** Accepted.

DRIGGS

Best Western Teton West Motel SH
(208) 354-2363. **$70-$110.** 476 N Main St. 0.7 mi n on SR 33. Int corridors. **Pets:** Accepted.

GRANGEVILLE

Monty's Motel M
(208) 983-2500. **$46-$55.** W 700 Main. Jct SR 13 and US 95. Ext corridors. **Pets:** Service with restrictions, supervision.

Super 8 Motel SH
(208) 983-1002. **$65-$128.** 801 SW 1st St. Jct SR 95 and 13. Int corridors. **Pets:** Other species. $10 daily fee/room. Designated rooms, service with restrictions, supervision.

HAGERMAN

Hagerman Valley Inn M
(208) 837-6196. **$48-$52.** 661 Frog's Landing. South end of town on US 30. Ext/int corridors. **Pets:** Medium. $5 daily fee/pet. No service, supervision.

HAILEY

Airport Inn M
(208) 788-2477. **$78-$110, 7 day notice.** 820 4th Ave S. Just n of SR 75 at 4th Ave; near airport. Ext corridors. **Pets:** Accepted.

Wood River Inn SH
(208) 578-0600. **$92-$97.** 603 N Main. Just n of downtown on SR 75. Int corridors. **Pets:** $25 one-time fee/room. Service with restrictions, supervision.

HEYBURN

▼▼ ▼▼ Super 8–Burley 🆂🅷
(208) 678-7000. **$56-$86.** 336 S 600 W. I-84, exit 208, just n. Int corridors. **Pets:** Other species. $5 daily fee/pet. Supervision.

🅰🆂🅺 🆂🏀 ⊠ 🛎M 🐾 🐕 🅷 🏊

IDAHO FALLS

🆔 ▼▼▼▼ Best Western Driftwood Inn 🆂🅷
(208) 523-2242. **$69-$119.** 575 River Pkwy. I-15, exit 118 (Broadway), 0.5 mi e, then 0.3 mi n. Ext corridors. **Pets:** Accepted.

🆂🅰🆅🅴 🆂🏀 ⊠ 🅷 🖥 🏊 🗵

▼▼▼▼ Comfort Inn 🆂🅷
(208) 528-2804. **$59-$89, 14 day notice.** 195 S Colorado Ave. I-15, exit 118 (Broadway), just w to Colorado Ave, then just s. Int corridors. **Pets:** Other species. $10 daily fee/pet. Supervision.

🅰🆂🅺 🆂🏀 ⊠ 🐕 🅷 🖥 🏊

🆔 ▼▼▼▼ Le Ritz Hotel & Suites 🆂🅷 ❀
(208) 528-0880. **$69-$99.** 720 Lindsay Blvd. I-15, exit 118 (Broadway), 0.5 mi e, then just n. Int corridors. **Pets:** Small. $15 daily fee/pet. Designated rooms, service with restrictions, supervision.

🆂🅰🆅🅴 🆂🏀 ⊠ 🅷 🖥 🏊

🆔 ▼▼▼ National 9 Executive Inn 🆂🅷
(208) 523-6260. **$55-$95.** 850 Lindsay Blvd. I-15, exit 119, just e. Ext/int corridors. **Pets:** Small. $25 deposit/room, $5 daily fee/pet. Designated rooms, service with restrictions, supervision.

🆂🅰🆅🅴 🆂🏀 ⊠ 🅷 🖥 🍽 🏊

▼▼▼▼ Red Lion Hotel on the Falls 🆂🅷
(208) 523-8000. **$89-$109.** 475 River Pkwy. I-15, exit 118 (Broadway), 0.5 mi e, then just n. Ext/int corridors. **Pets:** Other species. $100 deposit/room. Designated rooms, service with restrictions.

🅰🆂🅺 🆂🏀 ⊠ 🐕 🅷 🖥 🍽 🏊 🗵

JEROME

🆔 ▼▼▼▼ Best Western Sawtooth Inn and Suites 🆂🅷
(208) 324-9200. **$79-$99.** 2653 S Lincoln. I-84, exit 168, just n on SR 79. Int corridors. **Pets:** Other species. $50 deposit/room. Designated rooms, service with restrictions, supervision.

🆂🅰🆅🅴 🆂🏀 ⊠ 🐕 🅷 🖥 🏊

KAMIAH

▼▼ ▼▼ Lewis-Clark Resort & Motel 🅼
(208) 935-2556. **$41-$50.** 1.5 mi e on US 12. Ext corridors. **Pets:** Service with restrictions, supervision.

🅰🆂🅺 🆂🏀 ⊠ 🐕 🅷 🖥 🍽 🏊 🗵

KELLOGG

▼▼ Silverhorn Motor Inn 🆂🅷 ❀
(208) 783-1151. **$53-$71.** 699 W Cameron Ave. I-90, exit 49, just ne. Int corridors. **Pets:** Other species. Supervision.

⊠ 🅷 🍽

🆔 ▼▼▼ Super 8 Motel-Kellogg 🆂🅷
(208) 783-1234. **$50-$64.** 601 Bunker Ave. I-90, exit 49, 0.5 mi s. Int corridors. **Pets:** Other species. $25 deposit/room. Supervision.

🆂🅰🆅🅴 🆂🏀 ⊠ 🛎M 🐾 🅷 🏊

KETCHUM

🆔 ▼▼▼▼ Best Western Tyrolean Lodge 🆂🅷
(208) 726-5336. **$85-$169, 3 day notice.** 260 Cottonwood. South end of town, just w of SR 75 (Main St) on Rivers St, just s on 3rd Ave. Int corridors. **Pets:** Medium. $10 daily fee/pet. Service with restrictions.

🆂🅰🆅🅴 🆂🏀 ⊠ 🅷 🖥 🏊 🗵

▼▼▼▼ Clarion Inn of Sun Valley 🆂🅷
(208) 726-5900. **$100-$210, 3 day notice.** 600 N Main St. North end of town on SR 75 (Main St), corner of 6th and Main sts. Ext/int corridors. **Pets:** $25 one-time fee/room. Designated rooms, service with restrictions, supervision.

🅰🆂🅺 🆂🏀 ⊠ 🐕 🅷 🖥 🏊

KOOSKIA

🆔 ▼▼▼▼ Reflections Inn (formerly Looking Glass Inn) 🅱🅱
(208) 926-0855. **$65-$89, 3 day notice.** HCR 75, Box 32, US Hwy 12. 11 mi e on US 12 (between MM 84 and 85). Ext corridors. **Pets:** Medium, dogs only. $10 daily fee/pet. Designated rooms, supervision.

🆂🅰🆅🅴 ⊠ 🅷 🖥 🗵 🆆 🅳

LEWISTON

▼▼▼▼ Comfort Inn 🆂🅷
(208) 798-8090. **$69-$139.** 2128 8th Ave. 1.2 mi s on US 12 from jct US 95, just s on 21st St. Int corridors. **Pets:** Small. $10 daily fee/room. Service with restrictions, supervision.

🅰🆂🅺 🆂🏀 ⊠ 🛎M 🐾 🐕 🅷 🏊

▼▼▼▼ Holiday Inn Express 🆂🅷
(208) 750-1600. **$89-$94.** 2425 Nez Perce Dr. 1.2 mi s on US 12 from jct US 95, 1.2 mi s on 21st St, just e. Int corridors. **Pets:** Accepted.

🅰🆂🅺 🆂🏀 ⊠ 🛎M 🐾 🐕 🅷 🖥 🏊

▼▼▼▼ Howard Johnson Express 🅼
(208) 743-9526. **$48-$78.** 1716 Main St. 1.6 mi s on US 12 from jct US 95. Ext corridors. **Pets:** Accepted.

🅰🆂🅺 🆂🏀 ⊠ 🅷 🖥

▼▼▼▼ Red Lion Hotel 🆂🅷
(208) 799-1000. **$69-$89.** 621 21st St. 1.2 mi s on US 12 from jct US 95, just s. Int corridors. **Pets:** Other species. Designated rooms, service with restrictions, crate.

🅰🆂🅺 🆂🏀 ⊠ 🛎M 🐾 🐕 🅷 🖥 🍽 🏊 🗵

🆔 ▼▼▼ Sacajawea Motor Inns 🅼
(208) 746-1393. **$63-$66.** 1824 Main St. 1.5 mi s on US 12 from jct US 95. Ext/int corridors. **Pets:** $2 daily fee/pet. Designated rooms, service with restrictions, supervision.

🆂🅰🆅🅴 🆂🏀 ⊠ 🐾 🐕 🅷 🍽 🏊

▼▼ Super 8 Motel 🅼
(208) 743-8808. **$42-$45.** 3120 North & South Hwy. Just e on US 12 from jct US 95. Int corridors. **Pets:** Accepted.

🅰🆂🅺 🆂🏀 ⊠ 🅷

LUCILE

▼▼ Steelhead Inn M
(208) 628-3044. **$55.** 5 mi n on US 95 at MM 210. Ext corridors. **Pets:** Accepted.
[ASK] [S⊘] [✕] [🖥] [▣]

MACKAY

▼ Wagon Wheel Motel M
(208) 588-3331. **$40-$80.** 809 W Custer. 0.3 mi n on US 93. Ext corridors. **Pets:** Accepted.
[S⊘] [✕] [🖥] [▣] [✕] [🐾]

MCCALL

(AAA) ▼▼▼ Best Western McCall SH
(208) 634-6300. **$55-$95.** 415 3rd St. SR 55, just s of jct with Lake St. Ext/int corridors. **Pets:** Accepted.
[SAVE] [S⊘] [✕] [♿] [🗝] [🖥] [▣] [🌊]

(AAA) ▼▼▼ McCall Super 8 Lodge M ♣
(208) 634-4637. **$55-$94.** 303 S 3rd St. South end of town on SR 55. Int corridors. **Pets:** Other species. $5 daily fee/pet. Service with restrictions, supervision.
[SAVE] [S⊘] [✕] [♿] [🗝] [🖥] [▣]

MONTPELIER

(AAA) ◆▼▼ Best Western Clover Creek Inn SH ♣
(208) 847-1782. **$67-$99.** 243 N 4th St. Just n on US 30 from jct US 89 S. Ext corridors. **Pets:** Dogs only. $10 one-time fee/pet. Service with restrictions, supervision.
[SAVE] [S⊘] [✕] [🖥] [▣]

(AAA) ▼▼ The Fisher Inn M
(208) 847-1772. **$33-$52.** 601 N 4th St. 0.8 mi n on US 30 from jct of US 89 S. Ext corridors. **Pets:** Accepted.
[SAVE] [✕] [🖥] [🌊]

MOSCOW

(AAA) ◆▼◆▼ Best Western University Inn SH
(208) 882-0550. **$90-$135, 3 day notice.** 1516 Pullman Rd. Jct US 95, 1 mi w on SR 8. Int corridors. **Pets:** Small, other species. $25 daily fee/room. Designated rooms, service with restrictions, crate.
[SAVE] [S⊘] [✕] [♿] [🗐] [🖥] [▣] [🍴] [🌊] [✕]

(AAA) ▼▼ Mark IV Motor Inn M ♣
(208) 882-7557. **$49-$129, 14 day notice.** 414 N Main St. Jct SR 8, 0.4 mi n on US 95. Ext/int corridors. **Pets:** Other species. $10 daily fee/room. Designated rooms, crate.
[SAVE] [S⊘] [✕] [🗐] [🖥] [🍴] [🌊]

MOUNTAIN HOME

(AAA) ◆▼◆▼ Best Western Foothills Motor Inn SH
(208) 587-8477. **$67-$84.** 1080 Hwy 20. I-84, exit 95, just n. Ext corridors. **Pets:** $5 daily fee/pet. Service with restrictions, supervision.
[SAVE] [S⊘] [✕] [♿] [🗐] [🗝] [🖥] [▣] [🌊]

▼▼ Sleep Inn SH
(208) 587-9743. **$65-$77.** 1180 Hwy 20. I-84, exit 95, just n. Int corridors. **Pets:** $5 daily fee/pet. Service with restrictions, supervision.
[ASK] [S⊘] [✕] [🖥] [▣]

NAMPA

▼▼ Sleep Inn-Nampa SH
(208) 463-6300. **$69-$89.** 1315 Industrial Rd. I-84, exit 36, just s. Int corridors. **Pets:** Accepted.
[ASK] [S⊘] [✕] [♿] [🗐] [🗝] [🖥] [▣] [🌊]

NEW MEADOWS

(AAA) ▼▼▼ Hartland Inn & Motel M
(208) 347-2114. **$59-$150, 3 day notice.** 211 Norris St. US 95, just n of jct SR 55. Ext/int corridors. **Pets:** Large. $10 one-time fee/pet. Designated rooms, service with restrictions, supervision.
[SAVE] [S⊘] [✕] [🗝] [🖥] [▣] [✕]

OROFINO

(AAA) ▼▼▼ Konkolville Motel M
(208) 476-5584. **$50-$55.** 2000 Konkolville Rd. 2.7 mi e on Michigan Ave. Ext corridors. **Pets:** Dogs only. $10 daily fee/pet. Service with restrictions, supervision.
[SAVE] [S⊘] [✕] [🖥] [▣] [🌊]

POCATELLO

(AAA) ▼▼▼ Best Western CottonTree Inn SH
(208) 237-7650. **$64-$69, 7 day notice.** 1415 Bench Rd. I-15, exit 71, just e. Int corridors. **Pets:** Accepted.
[SAVE] [S⊘] [✕] [🖥] [▣] [🌊] [✕]

◆▼◆▼ Comfort Inn SH
(208) 237-8155. **$56-$89.** 1333 Bench Rd. I-15, exit 71, just e. Int corridors. **Pets:** Other species. $7 daily fee/pet. Service with restrictions, supervision.
[ASK] [S⊘] [✕] [🗐] [🖥] [▣] [🌊]

▼▼ Econo Lodge-University SH
(208) 233-0451. **$50-$70.** 835 S 5th Ave. I-15, exit 67, 1.8 mi n. Int corridors. **Pets:** Accepted.
[ASK] [S⊘] [✕] [🖥] [▣] [🍴]

◆▼◆▼ Holiday Inn-Pocatello SH ♣
(208) 237-1400. **$59-$76.** 1399 Bench Rd. I-15, exit 71, just e. Ext/int corridors. **Pets:** Medium, other species. $10 one-time fee/room. Designated rooms, service with restrictions, supervision.
[✕] [🗐] [🗝] [🖥] [▣] [🍴] [🌊] [✕]

(AAA) ▼▼▼ Pocatello Super 8 Motel SH
(208) 234-0888. **$52-$79.** 1330 Bench Rd. I-15, exit 71, just e. Int corridors. **Pets:** Accepted.
[SAVE] [S⊘] [✕] [🗝] [🖥]

▼▼ Ramada Inn & Convention Center SH
(208) 237-0020. **$52-$70.** 133 W Burnside. I-86, exit 61, just n. Int corridors. **Pets:** Small. $25 deposit/room. Designated rooms, service with restrictions, supervision.
[ASK] [S⊘] [✕] [🖥] [▣] [🍴] [🌊] [✕]

▼▼ ▼▼ **Red Lion Hotel Pocatello** 🆂🅷
(208) 233-2200. **$65-$75.** 1555 Pocatello Creek Rd. I-15, exit 71, just e. Int corridors. **Pets:** Medium. Designated rooms, service with restrictions, supervision.
🅰🆂🅺 💲🔟 ✕ 📶 🛏 🍽 〰 ✕

▼▼ **Thunderbird Motel** 🅼
(208) 232-6330. **$46-$55.** 1415 S 5th Ave. I-15, exit 67, 1.3 mi n; just s of Idaho State University. Ext corridors. **Pets:** Other species. $5 daily fee/room. Service with restrictions, supervision.
🅰🆂🅺 💲🔟 ✕ 🛏 〰

POST FALLS

🔺 ▼▼ ▼▼ **Holiday Inn Express** 🆂🅷 ✿
(208) 773-8900. **$69-$109.** 3175 E Seltice Way. I-90, exit 7, just sw. Int corridors. **Pets:** Large, other species. $25 one-time fee/room. Service with restrictions, supervision.
🆂🅰🆅🅴 💲🔟 ✕ 🔶🅼 🎦 🛏 📶

🔺 ▼▼ ▼▼ **Howard Johnson Express** 🆂🅷
(208) 773-4541. **$64-$139.** 3647 W 5th Ave. I-90, exit 2, just ne. Int corridors. **Pets:** Medium. $10 daily fee/pet. Service with restrictions, supervision.
🆂🅰🆅🅴 💲🔟 ✕ 🔶🅼 🎦 🎛 🛏 📶 〰

🔺 ▼▼▼▼ **Red Lion Templin's Hotel on the River–Post Falls** 🆂🅷
(208) 773-1611. **$85-$139.** 414 E First Ave. I-90, exit 5 east-bound, just s to First Ave; exit 6 westbound, 0.7 mi w on Seltice Way to Spokane St, 0.5 mi s, then just e. Int corridors. **Pets:** Medium, other species. $5 daily fee/pet. Designated rooms, service with restrictions, supervision.
🆂🅰🆅🅴 💲🔟 ✕ 🔶🅼 🎦 🎛 🛏 📶 🍽 〰 ✕

🔺 ▼▼ ▼▼ **Sleep Inn** 🆂🅷
(208) 777-9394. **$49-$129.** 157 S Pleasant View Rd. I-90, exit 2, just s. Int corridors. **Pets:** Accepted.
🆂🅰🆅🅴 💲🔟 ✕ 🎦 🎛 📶 〰

PRIEST RIVER

▼▼ ▼▼ **Eagle's Nest Motel** 🅼
(208) 448-2000. **$45-$85.** 1007 Albeni Hwy (US 2). US 2, 0.5 mi w. Ext corridors. **Pets:** Dogs only. $5 daily fee/room. Designated rooms, service with restrictions, supervision.
🅰🆂🅺 ✕ 🔶🅼 🎦 🎛 🛏 📶

REXBURG

🔺 ▼▼▼▼ **Best Western CottonTree Inn** 🆂🅷
(208) 356-4646. **$77-$107.** 450 W 4th St S. US 20, exit S Rexburg, 1 mi e. Int corridors. **Pets:** Accepted.
🆂🅰🆅🅴 💲🔟 ✕ 🛏 📶 🍽 〰

🔺 ▼▼▼▼ **Comfort Inn** 🆂🅷 ✿
(208) 359-1311. **$55-$99, 30 day notice.** 885 W Main St. Just e of jct of US 20, exit Salmon/Rexburg and SR 33. Int corridors. **Pets:** Other species. Service with restrictions, supervision.
🆂🅰🆅🅴 💲🔟 ✕ 🛏 📶 〰

🔺 ▼▼▼▼ **Days Inn** 🅼
(208) 356-9222. **$55-$80.** 271 S 2nd W. US 20, exit S Rexburg, 1.8 mi e, just n. Ext corridors. **Pets:** Accepted.
🆂🅰🆅🅴 💲🔟 ✕ 🛏 〰

RIGGINS

▼▼ ▼▼ **Best Western Salmon Rapids Lodge** 🆂🅷 ✿
(208) 628-2743. **$73-$115.** 1010 S Main St. Just e of US 95; downtown. Int corridors. **Pets:** $15 daily fee/pet. Designated rooms, service with restrictions, supervision.
🅰🆂🅺 💲🔟 ✕ 🎛 🛏 📶 〰

▼▼ **Pinehurst Resort Cottages** 🅲🅰
(208) 628-3323. **$45-$65, 7 day notice.** MM 182 on US 95. 13 mi s on US 95. Ext corridors. **Pets:** Accepted.
✕ 🛏 ✕ 🎞 🎦 🆉

SAGLE

▼▼ ▼▼ **Bottle Bay Resort & Marina** 🅲🅰
(208) 263-5916. **$75-$95, 60 day notice.** 115 Resort Rd. 8.3 mi e on Bottle Bay Rd from US 95. Ext corridors. **Pets:** $8 daily fee/pet. Service with restrictions, supervision.
🛏 📶 🍽 ✕ 🎞 🆉

ST. ANTHONY

▼▼▼▼ **Best Western Henry's Fork Inn** 🆂🅷
(208) 624-3711. **$50-$79.** 115 S Bridge St. US 20, exit St. Anthony, just w. Ext corridors. **Pets:** Accepted.
🅰🆂🅺 💲🔟 ✕ 📶 🍽

SALMON

▼▼ **Motel DeLuxe** 🅼
(208) 756-2231. **$40-$45, 7 day notice.** 112 S Church St. Just s of Main St; downtown. Ext corridors. **Pets:** Other species. Service with restrictions, supervision.
🅰🆂🅺 💲🔟 ✕ 🛏

SANDPOINT

▼▼▼▼ **Best Western Edgewater Resort** 🆂🅷
(208) 263-3194. **$79-$149.** 56 Bridge St. Just e of US 95 N; downtown. Int corridors. **Pets:** Accepted.
🅰🆂🅺 💲🔟 ✕ 🛏 📶 🍽 〰 ✕

🔺 ▼▼ **The K2 Inn** 🅼 ✿
(208) 263-3441. **$28-$64.** 501 N Fourth Ave. US 95, just e. Ext corridors. **Pets:** Dogs only. $10 daily fee/room. Supervision.
🆂🅰🆅🅴 💲🔟 ✕ 🛏 📶

🔺 ▼▼▼▼ **La Quinta Inn** 🆂🅷
(208) 263-9581. **$89-$139.** 415 Cedar St. Jct US 95 and 2; downtown. Ext/int corridors. **Pets:** Accepted.
🆂🅰🆅🅴 💲🔟 ✕ 🔶🅼 🎦 🎛 🛏 📶 🍽

🔺 ▼▼ ▼▼ **Monarch Mountain Lodge** 🆂🅷
(208) 263-1222. **$49-$89.** 363 Bonner Mall Way. 0.5 mi n on US 95 N from jct SR 200. Int corridors. **Pets:** Accepted.
🆂🅰🆅🅴 💲🔟 ✕ 🛏 📶

▼▼ ▼▼ **Quality Inn Sandpoint** 🆂🅷
(208) 263-2111. **$49-$89.** 807 N 5th. US 2/95, just s of jct SR 200. Int corridors. **Pets:** Other species. $5 daily fee/pet. Service with restrictions, supervision.
🅰🆂🅺 💲🔟 ✕ 🎛 🛏 📶 🍽 〰

▼▼ ▼▼ **Sandpoint Motel 6–4163** 🆂🅷
(208) 263-5383. **$45-$55.** 477255 Hwy 95 N. 1.2 mi n on US 95 from jct SR 200. Int corridors. **Pets:** Other species. Service with restrictions, supervision.
Ⓐ$Ⓚ 🆂🔹 ⊠ 🅚🅜 🔻

▼▼ ▼▼ **Super 8 Motel** 🆂🅷
(208) 263-2210. **$46-$63.** 476841 Hwy 95 N. 0.7 mi n on US 95 from jct SR 200. Int corridors. **Pets:** Other species. $25 one-time fee/room. Service with restrictions, supervision.
Ⓐ$Ⓚ 🆂🔹 ⊠ 🅚🅜 🔻

SODA SPRINGS

🔸🔸🔸 ▼ **J-R Inn** Ⓜ
(208) 547-3366. **$47.** 179 W 2nd S. US 30. Ext corridors. **Pets:** Accepted.
🆂🅰🆅🅴 ⊠ 🔻 🅚

STANLEY

▼▼ ▼ **Mountain Village Lodge** 🆂🅷
(208) 774-3661. **$54-$121, 14 day notice.** Corner US 75 & SR 21. Jct US 75 and SR 21. Ext corridors. **Pets:** Accepted.
⊠ 🔻 🔲 🍴 🅚

🔸🔸🔸 ▼ **Salmon River Cabins & Motel** 🅲🅰
(208) 774-2290. **$75-$95.** 1 mi n on US 75 from jct SR 21. Ext corridors. **Pets:** Small, dogs only. $10 daily fee/pet. Service with restrictions, supervision.
🆂🅰🆅🅴 ⊠ 🔻 🔲 🅚

TETONIA

🔸🔸🔸 ▼▼▼ **Teton Mountain View Lodge** Ⓜ
(208) 456-2741. **$38-$89.** 510 Egbert Ave (Hwy 33). On SR 33. Ext corridors. **Pets:** Medium. $6 daily fee/pet. Service with restrictions, supervision.
🆂🅰🆅🅴 🆂🔹 ⊠ 🔻 🅧

TWIN FALLS

🔸🔸🔸 ▼▼▼ **Best Western Apollo Motor Inn** Ⓜ
(208) 733-2010. **$54-$80.** 296 Addison Ave W. I-84, exit 173, 5.7 mi s on US 93, 1.2 mi w. Ext corridors. **Pets:** Small, other species. $50 deposit/room. Designated rooms, service with restrictions, supervision.
🆂🅰🆅🅴 🆂🔹 ⊠ 🔻 🔲 ⇒

▼▼▼▼ **Comfort Inn** Ⓜ
(208) 734-7494. **$79-$149.** 1893 Canyon Springs Rd. I-84, exit 173, 3.5 mi s on US 93. Int corridors. **Pets:** Accepted.
Ⓐ$Ⓚ 🆂🔹 ⊠ 🔻 🔲 ⇒

🔸🔸🔸 ▼▼ ▼▼ **Days Inn** Ⓜ
(208) 324-6400. **$55-$65.** 1200 Centennial Spur. I-84, exit 173, just n on US 93. Int corridors. **Pets:** Medium, other species. $10 daily fee/pet. Designated rooms, service with restrictions, supervision.
🆂🅰🆅🅴 🆂🔹 ⊠ 🅚 🔻 🔲 🅧

🔸🔸🔸 ▼▼▼▼ **Red Lion Hotel Canyon Springs** 🆂🅷
(208) 734-5000. **$61-$84.** 1357 Blue Lakes Blvd N. I-84, exit 173, 4 mi s on US 93. Int corridors. **Pets:** Accepted.
🆂🅰🆅🅴 🆂🔹 ⊠ 🅚🅜 🎵 🔻 🔲 🍴 ⇒ 🅧

WALLACE

▼▼▼▼ **Best Western Wallace Inn** 🆂🅷 ✿
(208) 752-1252. **$72-$94.** 100 Front St. I-90, exit 61 (Business Rt 90), just se. Int corridors. **Pets:** Other species. $15 daily fee/pet. Service with restrictions, supervision.
Ⓐ$Ⓚ 🆂🔹 ⊠ 🅚🅜 🅚 🔻 🔲 🍴 ⇒ 🅧

▼▼ ▼▼ **Stardust Motel** Ⓜ ✿
(208) 752-1213. **$46-$64.** 410 Pine St. I-90, exit 61 (Business Rt 90), 0.7 mi e; downtown. Ext corridors. **Pets:** Other species. $15 daily fee/pet. Service with restrictions, supervision.
Ⓐ$Ⓚ 🆂🔹 ⊠ 🔻 🔲

WORLEY

🔸🔸🔸 ▼▼▼▼ **Coeur d'Alene Casino Resort Hotel** 🆂🅷
(208) 686-0248. **$65-$300.** 27068 S Hwy 95. On US 95, 3 mi n. Int corridors. **Pets:** Medium. $25 deposit/room, $5 daily fee/pet. Service with restrictions, supervision.
🆂🅰🆅🅴 🆂🔹 ⊠ 🅚 🔻 🔲 🍴 ⇒ 🅧

ILLINOIS

CITY INDEX

ALTON

AAA ♦♦♦ Comfort Inn SH
(618) 465-9999. **$81-$95.** 11 Crossroads Ct. Off SR 3, jct SR 140. Int corridors. **Pets:** Other species. Service with restrictions, supervision.
[SAVE] [S❄] [✕] [⌖M] [⌖] [🔧] [📺] [⇌]

♦♦ Super 8 Motel SH
(618) 465-8885. **$61-$80.** 1800 Homer Adams Pkwy. On SR 111, 1.8 mi e of jct US 67. Int corridors. **Pets:** Medium. $50 deposit/room. Service with restrictions, supervision.
[ASK] [S❄] [✕] [⌖M] [🔧] [📺]

ARCOLA

♦♦♦ Comfort Inn SH
(217) 268-4000. **$39-$99, 10 day notice.** 610 E Springfield Rd. I-57, exit 203, just w. Int corridors. **Pets:** Medium. $10 daily fee/pet. Service with restrictions, crate.
[ASK] [S❄] [✕] [⌖] [🔧] [📺] [⇌]

BEARDSTOWN

♦♦ Super 8 Motel SH
(217) 323-5858. **$48-$71.** 9918 Grand Ave. US 67, just w from SR 125. Int corridors. **Pets:** Accepted.
[ASK] [S❄] [✕] [🔧] [⇌]

BELLEVILLE

AAA ♦♦♦ The Shrine Hotel SH ✿
(618) 397-1162. **$63-$73.** 451 S Demazenod Dr. I-255, exit 17A, 1 mi e on SR 15. Int corridors. **Pets:** Small, other species. Service with restrictions, crate.
[SAVE] [S❄] [✕] [📺]

♦♦ Super 8 Motel SH
(618) 234-9670. **$50.** 600 E Main St. 0.4 mi e from SR 159. Ext corridors. **Pets:** Accepted.
[ASK] [S❄] [✕] [🔧]

BLOOMINGTON

♦♦♦ The Chateau LH
(309) 662-2020. **$117-$167.** 1601 Jumer Dr. I-55, exit 167, follow I-55 business route (Veterans Pkwy); 1.3 mi n of jct SR 9; 1 mi s of jct I-55. Int corridors. **Pets:** Accepted.
[ASK] [S❄] [✕] [⌖] [🔧] [📺] [🍴] [⇌] [⊗]

♦♦♦ Country Inn & Suites By Carlson
Bloomington/Normal-Airport SH ✿
(309) 662-3100. **$89-$106.** 2403 E Empire St. Jct I-55 business route (Veterans Pkwy) and SR 9 (Empire St), 0.8 mi e. Int corridors. **Pets:** Other species. Service with restrictions, crate.
[ASK] [S❄] [✕] [⌖] [⌖] [🔧] [📺] [⇌]

♦♦♦ Country Inn & Suites By Carlson
Bloomington/Normal-West SH ✿
(309) 828-7177. **$86-$101.** 923 Maple Hill Rd. I-55/74, exit 160B (SR 9), 0.3 mi w to Wylie Dr, just n, then just e. Int corridors. **Pets:** Medium. $10 daily fee/room. Designated rooms, service with restrictions, crate.
[ASK] [S❄] [✕] [⌖M] [⌖] [🔧] [📺] [⇌]

♦♦ Days Inn-Bloomington SH
(309) 829-6292. **$60-$90.** 1707 W Market St. I-55/74, exit 160A (SR 9), 0.5 mi e. Int corridors. **Pets:** Supervision.
[ASK] [S❄] [✕] [⌖M] [🔧] [⇌]

♦♦ Prospect Center Inn SH ✿
(309) 663-1361. **$53-$59.** 1803 E Empire St. SR 9, just e of I-55 business route (Veterans Pkwy). Int corridors. **Pets:** Other species. $6 one-time fee/room. Designated rooms, service with restrictions, crate.
[ASK] [S❄] [✕] [⌖] [🔧] [📺]

▼▼▼▼ **Radisson Hotel & Conference**
Center-Bloomington 🄻🄷
(309) 664-6446. **$135.** 10 Brickyard Dr. I-55 business route
(Veterans Pkwy), just n of US 150. Int corridors.
Pets: Small, other species. $25 deposit/room. Service with
restrictions, crate.

ASK 🅂🄾 ✕ 🄳 🄴 🄷 🄿 🍽 ⚠

▼▼ **Ramada Limited & Suites**
Bloomington/Normal-West 🄢🄷
(309) 828-0900. **$70-$77.** 919 Maple Hill Rd. I-55/74, exit
160B (SR 9), 0.3 mi w to Wylie Rd, just n, then just e. Int
corridors. **Pets:** $10 daily fee/room. Designated rooms,
service with restrictions, supervision.

ASK 🅂🄾 ✕ 🄷 🄿 🍽

▼▼▼ **Wingate Inn** 🄢🄷
(309) 820-9990. **$79-$89.** 1031 Wylie Dr. I-55/74, exit 160B
(SR 9), just w, then just n. Int corridors. **Pets:** Accepted.

ASK 🅂🄾 ✕ 🄳 🄴 🄷 🄿 🍽

BOURBONNAIS

▼▼▼ **Hampton Inn** 🄢🄷
(815) 932-8369. **$80-$127.** 60 Ken Hayes Dr. I-57, exit 315
(SR 50). Int corridors. **Pets:** Accepted.

ASK 🅂🄾 ✕ 🄴 🄷 🄿 🍽

▼▼▼▼ **Holiday Inn Express Hotel & Suites** 🄢🄷
(815) 932-4411. **$89-$94.** 62 Ken Hayes Dr. I-57, exit 315
(SR 50). Int corridors. **Pets:** Small, dogs only. $100 deposit/
room, $25 one-time fee/room. Service with restrictions,
supervision.

ASK 🅂🄾 ✕ 🄴🄼 🄳 🄷 🄿 🍽

CARBON CLIFF

▼▼ **Super 8 Motel-East Moline** 🄢🄷
(309) 796-1999. **$57, 7 day notice.** 2201 John Deere Rd.
I-80, exit 4A (John Deere Rd), 5.5 mi w on SR 5. Int
corridors. **Pets:** Accepted.

ASK 🅂🄾 ✕ 🄷

CARBONDALE

▼▼▼ **Hampton Inn** 🄢🄷
(618) 549-6900. **$78-$125.** 2175 Reed Station Pkwy. I-57,
exit 54B, 12 mi w on SR 13. Int corridors. **Pets:** Accepted.

ASK 🅂🄾 ✕ 🄴🄼 🄳 🄴 🄷 🄿 🍽

▼ **Motel 6** 🄼
(618) 466-8356. **$33-$49.** 700 E Main St. 1 mi e on SR 13.
Ext corridors. **Pets:** Accepted.

ASK 🅂🄾 ✕ 🄷

▼▼ **Super 8 Motel** 🄢🄷
(618) 457-8822. **$54-$75.** 1180 E Main St. 1 mi e on SR 13.
Int corridors. **Pets:** Accepted.

ASK 🅂🄾 ✕ 🄳 🄷 🄿

CARLINVILLE

▼▼ **Best Value Inn-Carlin Villa** 🄼
(217) 854-3201. **$39-$115, 7 day notice.** 18891 Rt 4. Jct SR
4 and 108, 0.5 mi s. Ext/int corridors. **Pets:** Accepted.

ASK 🅂🄾 ✕ 🄷 🄿 🍽

▼▼▼ **Holiday Inn-Carlinville** 🄢🄷
(217) 324-2100. **$69-$81.** 19067 W Frontage Rd. I-55, exit
60 (SR 108), just w. Int corridors. **Pets:** Accepted.

ASK 🅂🄾 ✕ 🄴🄼 🄷 🄿 🍽 🍽 ⚠

CASEY

🄰🄰🄰 ▼▼▼ **Comfort Inn** 🄢🄷
(217) 932-2212. **$58-$70.** 933 SR 49. I-70, exit 129, 0.3 mi
se. Int corridors. **Pets:** Accepted.

SAVE 🅂🄾 ✕ 🄷 🄿 🍽

CASEYVILLE

🄰🄰🄰 ▼▼▼ **Best Inns** 🄢🄷
(618) 397-3300. **$45-$70.** 2423 Old Country Inn Dr. I-64, exit
9 (SR 157), just s. Int corridors. **Pets:** Medium. Service with
restrictions, supervision.

SAVE 🅂🄾 ✕ 🄳 🄴 🄷 🍽

CENTRALIA

▼▼ **Bell Tower Inn** 🄢🄷
(618) 533-1300. **$49-$69.** 200 E Noleman St. Jct US 51 S
and SR 161. Int corridors. **Pets:** Accepted.

ASK 🅂🄾 ✕ 🄳 🄷 🄿 🍽

CHAMPAIGN

🄰🄰🄰 ▼▼▼▼ **Baymont Inn & Suites** 🄢🄷
(217) 356-8900. **$70-$125.** 302 W Anthony Dr. I-74, exit 182
(Neil St), just nw. Int corridors. **Pets:** Accepted.

SAVE 🅂🄾 ✕ 🄳 🄷 🄿

▼▼▼▼ **Drury Inn & Suites-Champaign** 🄢🄷
(217) 398-0030. **$87-$109.** 905 W Anthony Dr. I-74, exit 181
(Prospect Blvd). Int corridors. **Pets:** Large, other species.
Service with restrictions, supervision.

ASK ✕ 🄴🄼 🄳 🄴 🄷 🄿 🍽

🄰🄰🄰 ▼▼▼ **La Quinta Inn** 🄢🄷
(217) 356-4000. **$55-$80.** 1900 Center Dr. I-74, exit 182B
(Neil St), just n. Int corridors. **Pets:** Small. Service with
restrictions, supervision.

SAVE 🅂🄾 ✕ 🄴🄼 🄳 🄷 🄿 🍽

🄰🄰🄰 ▼▼▼ **Microtel Inn** 🄢🄷
(217) 398-4136. **$52-$105.** 1615 Rion Dr. I-57, exit 238, just
w. Int corridors. **Pets:** Small. $10 one-time fee/room. Serv-
ice with restrictions, supervision.

SAVE 🅂🄾 ✕

🄰🄰🄰 ▼▼▼ **Red Roof Inn #170** 🄢🄷
(217) 352-0101. **$41-$63.** 212 W Anthony Dr. I-74, exit 182B
(Neil St), just n to Anthony Dr, then just w. Ext corridors.
Pets: Accepted.

SAVE ✕ 🄳 🄷

CHICAGO METROPOLITAN AREA

ALSIP

▼▼ Baymont Inn-Chicago Midway South SH
(708) 597-3900. **$59-$94.** 12801 S Cicero Ave. I-294, exit Cicero Ave S. Int corridors. **Pets:** Accepted.
ASK SO ⊠ ⊘ ⌨ 🛏 💻

▼▼ Days Inn M
(708) 371-5600. **$72-$159.** 5150 W 127th St. I-294, exit Cicero Ave S, 0.3 mi w. Ext corridors. **Pets:** Accepted.
ASK ⊠

▲▲▲ ▼▼▼ Radisson Hotel-Alsip LH
(708) 371-7300. **$159.** 5000 W 127th St at Cicero Ave. I-294, exit Cicero Ave S, just w. Int corridors. **Pets:** Accepted.
SAVE SO ⊠ ⌖M 🛏 💻 🍴 ➳

ANTIOCH

▲▲▲ ▼▼▼ Best Western Regency Inn SH
(847) 395-3606. **$85-$145, 3 day notice.** 350 Rt 173. SR 173, 0.5 mi w of jct SR 83. Int corridors. **Pets:** Medium. $25 deposit/room. Designated rooms, service with restrictions, supervision.
SAVE SO ⊠ 🛏 💻 ➳

ARLINGTON HEIGHTS

▲▲▲ ▼▼▼ AmeriSuites (Chicago/Arlington Heights) SH
(847) 956-1400. **$89-$99.** 2111 S Arlington Heights Rd. I-90, exit Arlington Heights Rd, 0.6 mi n. Int corridors. **Pets:** Medium. Designated rooms, service with restrictions, crate.
SAVE SO ⊠ ⊘ ⌨ 🛏 💻 ⊠

▼ Best Value Inn SH
(847) 255-2900. **$55-$74.** 948 E Northwest Hwy. US 14 (Northwest Hwy), just e of Arlington Heights Rd; downtown. Ext corridors. **Pets:** Medium, dogs only. Service with restrictions, supervision.
ASK SO ⊠ 🛏 💻 🍴 ➳

▼▼▼▼ La Quinta Inn-Arlington Heights SH
(847) 253-8777. **$79-$109.** 1415 W Dundee Rd. SR 53, exit Dundee Rd, just e. Int corridors. **Pets:** Other species. Service with restrictions.
⊠ ⊘ 🛏 💻 ➳

▼ Motel 6-1048 SH
(847) 806-1230. **$45-$63.** 441 W Algonquin Rd. I-90, exit Arlington Heights Rd, 0.5 mi n, then 0.5 mi w. Int corridors. **Pets:** Accepted.
SO ⊠ ⌖M

▲▲▲ ▼▼▼ Radisson Hotel Arlington Heights LH
(847) 364-7600. **$55-$109.** 75 W Algonquin Rd. I-90, exit Arlington Heights Rd, just n to Algonquin Rd, then just w. Int corridors. **Pets:** Accepted.
SAVE SO ⊠ ⊘ 🛏 💻 🍴 ➳ ⊠

▲▲▲ ▼▼▼ Red Roof Inn #7102 M
(847) 228-6650. **$50-$71.** 22 W Algonquin Rd. I-90, exit Arlington Heights Rd, 0.5 mi n, then just w. Ext corridors. **Pets:** Accepted.
SAVE ⊠ ⌨

BANNOCKBURN

▼▼▼ Woodfield Suites Chicago-Bannockburn/Deerfield SH
(847) 317-7300. **$69-$109.** 2000 Lakeside Dr. I-94, exit Half Day Rd (SR 22), just e to Lakeside Dr, then just s. Int corridors. **Pets:** Accepted.
ASK SO ⊠ ⌖M ⊘ ⌨ 🛏 💻 ➳ ⊠

BLOOMINGDALE

▼▼▼ Residence Inn by Marriott Bloomingdale SH
(630) 893-9200. **$129-$149, 14 day notice.** 295 Knollwood Dr. I-355, exit Army Trail Rd, 4 mi w, then just n. Int corridors. **Pets:** Accepted.
ASK SO ⊠ ⊘ ⌨ 🛏 💻 ➳ ⊠

BOLINGBROOK

▼▼▼ Holiday Inn Hotel & Suites LH
(630) 679-1600. **$129-$179.** 205 Remington Blvd. I-55, exit 267, just n, then 0.4 mi sw. Int corridors. **Pets:** Medium. $35 one-time fee/room. Service with restrictions, supervision.
ASK SO ⊠ ⊘ ⌨ 🛏 💻 🍴 ➳ ⊠

BRIDGEVIEW

▲▲▲ ▼▼▼ Exel Inn of Bridgeview SH
(708) 430-1818. **$67-$87.** 9625 S 76th Ave. I-294, exit 95th St, just s. Int corridors. **Pets:** Accepted.
SAVE SO ⊠ 🛏 💻

CALUMET CITY

▼▼ Baymont Inn & Suites Chicago-Calumet City SH
(708) 891-2900. **$89-$99.** 510 E End Ave. I-94, exit 71B (Sibley Blvd), just e. Int corridors. **Pets:** Medium. Service with restrictions, supervision.
ASK SO ⊠ ⌖M ⊘ ⌨ 🛏 💻 ➳

CALUMET PARK

▼▼ Super 8 Motel Chicago Southwest SH
(708) 385-9100. **$59-$119.** 12808 S Ashland Ave. I-57, exit 353, just e. Int corridors. **Pets:** Small. Designated rooms, no service, supervision.
ASK SO ⊠ ⌖M ⊘ ⌨ 🛏

CHICAGO

▲▲▲ ▼▼▼ Allegro Chicago, A Kimpton Boutique Hotel LH
(312) 236-0123. **$109-$129.** 171 W Randolph St. Jct La Salle St. Int corridors. **Pets:** Accepted.
SAVE SO ⊠ 🛏 💻 🍴

Best Western Hawthorne Terrace 🆂🅷
(773) 244-3434. **$149-$195.** 3434 N Broadway St. Between Belmont Ave and Addison St. Int corridors. **Pets:** Medium. $250 deposit/room. Designated rooms, service with restrictions.

SAVE 🆂🅾 ⊠ 🔳 🔲 ⊠

Carlton Inn Midway 🅼 ❀
(773) 582-0900. **$69-$129.** 4944 S Archer Ave. I-55, exit 287, 1.8 mi s to Archer Ave, just e. Ext corridors. **Pets:** Medium. $50 deposit/pet. Designated rooms, service with restrictions, supervision.

SAVE 🆂🅾 ⊠ 🔳 🔲

Chicago Mart Plaza Holiday Inn 🅻🅷
(312) 836-5000. **$129-$239.** 350 N Orleans. Atop the Apparel Center; 14th thru 23rd floors. Int corridors. **Pets:** Medium, other species. $50 deposit/pet. Service with restrictions, crate.

SAVE 🆂🅾 ⊠ 🔳 🔲 🔳 🔲 🔲 🔲 ⊠

Claridge Hotel 🆂🅷
(312) 787-4980. **$139-$169.** 1244 N Dearborn St. Just s of Goethe St. Int corridors. **Pets:** Accepted.

ASK 🆂🅾 ⊠ 🔲 🔲

Clarion Barcelo Hotel O'Hare International 🆂🅷
(773) 693-5800. **$99-$129.** 5615 N Cumberland Ave. I-90, exit N Cumberland Ave S, just s. Int corridors. **Pets:** Small, other species. $50 deposit/room. Designated rooms, service with restrictions, supervision.

SAVE 🆂🅾 ⊠ 🔲 🔲 🔲 🔳 🔲 🔲 🔲

The Drake Hotel, Chicago 🅻🅷 ❀
(312) 787-2200. **$199-$379.** 140 E Walton Pl. N Michigan Ave at Lake Shore Dr and Walton Pl. Int corridors. **Pets:** Small. $200 deposit/room. Designated rooms, service with restrictions, supervision.

ASK ⊠ 🔲 🔲 🔳 🔲

The Fairmont Chicago 🅻🅷
(312) 565-8000. **$109-$369.** 200 N Columbus Dr. Jct Michigan Ave and Wacker Dr, just e. Int corridors. **Pets:** Accepted.

ASK ⊠ 🔲 🔲

Four Seasons Hotel Chicago 🅻🅷
(312) 280-8800. **$430-$3500, 3 day notice.** 120 E Delaware Pl. Jct Michigan Ave, just nw of the John Hancock building. Int corridors. **Pets:** Accepted.

SAVE ⊠ 🔲 🔲 🔲 🔲 🔲 🔲 🔲 ⊠

Hilton Chicago 🅻🅷
(312) 922-4400. **$154-$354.** 720 S Michigan Ave. I-290 (Congress Pkwy), just s. Int corridors. **Pets:** Accepted.

SAVE 🆂🅾 ⊠ 🔲 🔲 🔲 🔲 🔲 ⊠

Hilton Chicago O'Hare Airport 🅻🅷
(773) 686-8000. **$124-$284.** Opposite and connected to terminal buildings at O'Hare International Airport, accessed via I-190. Int corridors. **Pets:** Accepted.

SAVE 🆂🅾 ⊠ 🔲 🔲 🔲 🔲 ⊠

Holiday Inn O'Hare Kennedy 🆂🅷
(773) 693-2323. **$89-$169.** 8201 W Higgins Rd. I-90, exit 79B (Cumberland Ave N), just n to Higgins Rd (SR 72), just e. Int corridors. **Pets:** Accepted.

ASK 🆂🅾 ⊠ 🔲 🔲 🔲 🔲 🔲

House of Blues Hotel, A Loews Hotel 🅻🅷
(312) 245-0333. **$249-$369.** 333 N Dearborn St. Between Dearborn and State sts. Int corridors. **Pets:** Accepted.

SAVE 🆂🅾 ⊠ 🔲 🔲 🔲 🔲 🔲 ⊠

Le Meridien Chicago 🅻🅷
(312) 645-1500. **$209-$329.** 521 N Rush St at Michigan Ave. Jct Grand Ave. Int corridors. **Pets:** Accepted.

ASK 🆂🅾 ⊠ 🔲M 🔲 🔲 🔲 🔲 🔲 ⊠

Omni Ambassador East 🅻🅷
(312) 787-7200. **$169-$279.** 1301 N State Pkwy. Jct Goethe St and N State Pkwy. Int corridors. **Pets:** Small. $50 one-time fee/room. Designated rooms, service with restrictions, supervision.

SAVE 🆂🅾 ⊠ 🔲 🔲 🔲 🔲 ⊠

Omni Chicago Hotel 🅻🅷
(312) 944-6664. **$319-$399.** 676 N Michigan Ave. Jct Huron St. Int corridors. **Pets:** Small. $50 one-time fee/pet. Service with restrictions, supervision.

ASK 🆂🅾 ⊠ 🔲M 🔲 🔲 🔲 🔲 🔲 ⊠

The Palmer House Hilton 🅻🅷
(312) 726-7500. **$154-$294.** 17 E Monroe St. Between State St and Wabash Ave. Int corridors. **Pets:** Accepted.

SAVE 🆂🅾 ⊠ 🔲 🔲 🔲 🔲 🔲 ⊠

Park Hyatt Chicago 🅻🅷
(312) 335-1234. **$225-$425.** 800 N Michigan Ave. Jct Chicago and Michigan aves at Water Tower Square. Int corridors. **Pets:** Accepted.

SAVE ⊠ 🔲 🔲 🔲 🔲 ⊠

The Peninsula Chicago 🅻🅷 ❀
(312) 337-2888. **$405-$495.** 108 E Superior St. Jct Michigan Ave. Int corridors. **Pets:** Small.

SAVE 🆂🅾 ⊠ 🔲 🔲 🔲 🔲 🔲 ⊠

Radisson Hotel & Suites Chicago 🅻🅷
(312) 787-2900. **$299-$339.** 160 E Huron St. Just e of N Michigan Ave. Int corridors. **Pets:** Accepted.

SAVE 🆂🅾 ⊠ 🔲 🔲 🔲 🔲 🔲

Red Roof Inn 🆂🅷
(312) 787-3580. **$86-$126.** 162 E Ontario St. Just e of Michigan Ave. Int corridors. **Pets:** Medium, other species. $25 deposit/pet. No service, supervision.

SAVE ⊠ 🔲 🔲

Renaissance Chicago Hotel 🅻🅷 ❀
(312) 372-7200. **$249-$319.** 1 W Wacker Dr. Jct State St. Int corridors. **Pets:** Medium. $45 one-time fee/pet. Service with restrictions.

SAVE 🆂🅾 ⊠ 🔲M 🔲 🔲 🔲 🔲 🔲 ⊠

▼▼▼ Residence Inn by Marriott Chicago
Downtown SH
(312) 943-9800. $119-$199. 201 E Walton St. Just e of Michigan Ave at Mies van der Rohe. Int corridors. Pets: Accepted.

⊠ 🐾 🛏 🛎 🖵

AAA ▼▼▼ Sheraton Chicago Hotel &
Towers LH ❧
(312) 464-1000. $199-$239. 301 E North Water St. Columbus Dr at the Chicago River, just e of Michigan Ave. Int corridors. Pets: Dogs only. Designated rooms, service with restrictions, crate.

SAVE ⊠ 🐾 🛏 🖵 🍴 🏊 ⊠

AAA ▼▼▼ ▼ Sofitel Chicago Water
Tower LH ❧
(312) 324-4000. $299-$379. 20 E Chestnut St. Jct Wabash Ave and Chestnut St, 0.5 blk w of Rush St. Int corridors. Pets: Small, dogs only. Service with restrictions, supervision.

SAVE S⊄ ⊠ ⚙M 🐾 🛏 🍴

AAA ▼▼▼ ▼▼▼ The Sutton Place Hotel LH
(312) 266-2100. $135-$265. 21 E Bellevue Pl. Jct Rush St. Int corridors. Pets: Small, other species. $200 deposit/pet. Supervision.

SAVE S⊄ ⊠ 🐾 🛏 🍴

▼▼▼ ▼▼▼ W Chicago City Center LH ❧
(312) 332-1200. $289. 172 W Adams St. Between La Salle and Wells sts. Int corridors. Pets: $100 one-time fee/room. Service with restrictions.

S⊄ ⊠ 🐾 🛏 🛎 🖵 🍴 ⊠

▼▼▼ ▼▼▼ W Chicago Lakeshore LH
(312) 943-9200. $200-$400. 644 N Lake Shore Dr. Jct Ontario St. Int corridors. Pets: Accepted.

⊠ 🐾 🛏 🖵 🍴 🏊

AAA ▼▼▼ ▼▼▼ Westin Chicago River
North LH ❧
(312) 744-1900. $149-$179. 320 N Dearborn St. Just n of the Chicago River; between Dearborn and Clark sts. Int corridors. Pets: Small. Service with restrictions, crate.

SAVE ⊠ 🐾 🛏 🛎 🖵 🍴 ⊠

AAA ▼▼▼ ▼▼▼ The Westin Michigan Avenue
Chicago LH ❧
(312) 943-7200. $169-$199. 909 N Michigan Ave. Across from John Hancock Center. Int corridors. Pets: Medium, dogs only. $25 deposit/room. Service with restrictions, supervision.

SAVE ⊠ ⚙M 🐾 🛏 🖵 🍴 ⊠

AAA ▼▼▼ ▼▼▼ The Whitehall Hotel SH
(312) 944-6300. $159-$389. 105 E Delaware Pl. Just w of Michigan Ave. Int corridors. Pets: Very small. $100 deposit/pet. Service with restrictions, crate.

SAVE S⊄ ⊠ 🍴

CRYSTAL LAKE

▼▼ ▼▼ Comfort Inn SH
(815) 444-0040. $69-$72. 595 E Tracy Tr. Jct US 14 and SR 31, 0.4 mi w, then just s on Pingree St. Int corridors. Pets: Medium. $10 daily fee/pet. Service with restrictions, supervision.

ASK S⊄ ⊠ 🐾 🛏 🖵 🏊

DEERFIELD

▼▼▼ Residence Inn by Marriott SH
(847) 940-4644. $109-$279. 530 Lake Cook Rd. I-94, exit Lake Cook Rd, 1.8 mi e, 3 blks n on Corporate 500 Dr access road. Ext corridors. Pets: Accepted.

ASK S⊄ ⊠ 🐾 🛏 🖵 🏊 ⊠

DES PLAINES

▼▼ O'Hare Travelodge M
(847) 296-5541. $59-$99. 3003 Mannheim Rd. US 12 and 45 (Mannheim Rd), just n of jct SR 72 (Higgins Rd). Ext/int corridors. Pets: Accepted.

ASK S⊄ ⊠ 🛏 🖵 🏊

DOWNERS GROVE

AAA ▼▼ Red Roof Inn M
(630) 963-4205. $44-$69. 1113 Butterfield Rd. I-355, exit Butterfield Rd (SR 56), on frontage road; I-88, exit Highland Ave N, just w. Ext corridors. Pets: Other species. Service with restrictions, crate.

SAVE ⊠ 🐾

ELGIN

▼▼ ▼▼ Best Western-Elgin SH
(847) 695-5000. $79-$89. 345 W River Rd. I-90, exit SR 31 S, just s to W River Rd, then 0.5 mi e. Int corridors. Pets: Small. $50 one-time fee/pet. Designated rooms, service with restrictions, supervision.

ASK S⊄ ⊠ 🐾 🛏 🖵 🍴 🏊 ⊠

AAA ▼▼ ▼▼ Elgin Quality Inn SH ❧
(847) 931-4800. $65-$75. 500 Tollgate Rd. I-90, exit SR 31 N, just n. Int corridors. Pets: Other species. $10 daily fee/pet. Service with restrictions.

SAVE S⊄ ⊠ ⚙M 🐾 🛏 🖵

ELK GROVE VILLAGE

AAA ▼▼ Exel Inn of Elk Grove Village SH
(847) 895-2085. $56-$76. 1000 W Devon Ave. I-290, exit Thorndale Ave, 0.5 mi w to Rohlwing Rd, 0.3 mi n to Devon Ave, then 0.3 mi e. Int corridors. Pets: Small, other species. Designated rooms, service with restrictions, supervision.

SAVE S⊄ ⊠ 🐾 🛏 🖵

AAA ▼▼ ▼▼ Exel Inn of O'Hare SH
(847) 803-9400. $65-$85. 2881 Touhy Ave. Jct SR 72 (Higgins Rd) and 83 (Busse Rd), 1.5 mi e on SR 72 (Higgins Rd). Int corridors. Pets: Small, other species. Designated rooms, service with restrictions, supervision.

SAVE S⊄ ⊠ 🐾 🛏 🖵

▼▼ ▼▼ Holiday Inn of Elk Grove LH
(847) 437-6010. $79-$129. 1000 Busse Rd. 0.3 mi s of jct SR 72 (Higgins Rd). Int corridors. Pets: Accepted.

ASK S⊄ ⊠ 🐾 🛏 🖵 🍴 🏊 ⊠

▼▼▼ La Quinta Inn O'Hare Airport **SH**
(847) 439-6767. **$79-$109.** 1900 Oakton St. Jct SR 72 (Higgins Rd) and 83 (Busse Rd). Int corridors. **Pets:** Accepted.
✕ 🔒 💻 ⊇

▼▼▼ Sheraton Suites Elk Grove
            Village **LH** ❀
(847) 290-1600. **$69-$219, 3 day notice.** 121 Northwest Point Blvd. I-90, exit Arlington Heights Blvd, just s. Int corridors. **Pets:** Other species.
(ASK) ✕ 🖳M 🔊 💻 🍴 ⊇ ✕

▼▼▼ Super 8 Motel O'Hare **SH**
(847) 827-3133. **$69-$89.** 2951 Touhy Ave. Jct SR 72 (Higgins Rd) and 83 (Busse Rd), 1.5 mi e on SR 72 (Higgins Rd). Int corridors. **Pets:** Accepted.
(SAVE) (S∆) ✕ 🖳M 🔊 🖫 🔒 💻 ⊇

ELMHURST

▲▲▲ ▼▼▼▼ AmeriSuites (Chicago/Elmhurst-O'Hare
            South) **SH**
(630) 782-6300. **$69-$129.** 410 W Lake St. I-290, exit 12, just w on US 20 (Lake St). Int corridors. **Pets:** Very small. $150 deposit/room. Service with restrictions, crate.
(SAVE) (S∆) ✕ 🖳M 🔊 🖫 🔒 💻 ⊇

▲▲▲ ▼▼▼▼ Holiday Inn Chicago-Elmhurst **SH**
(630) 279-1100. **$99-$149.** 624 N York St. I-290, exit 12, just n. Int corridors. **Pets:** Large. $100 deposit/pet. Designated rooms, service with restrictions, supervision.
(SAVE) (S∆) ✕ 🔊 🔒 💻 🍴 ⊇ ✕

EVANSTON

▼▼▼▼ Omni Orrington Hotel **LH** ❀
(847) 866-8700. **$152-$161.** 1710 Orrington Ave. Jct Church St. Int corridors. **Pets:** Small, other species. $25 one-time fee/room. Service with restrictions, crate.
✕ 🔊 🔒 💻 🍴

FRANKLIN PARK

▲▲▲ ▼▼▼ Comfort Inn **SH**
(847) 233-9292. **$99-$119.** 3001 N Mannheim Rd. Jct US 12/45 (Mannheim Rd) and Grand Ave, just n. Int corridors. **Pets:** Accepted.
(SAVE) (S∆) ✕ 🖫 🔒 💻 ⊇

▲▲▲ ▼▼▼ Super 8 O'Hare South **SH**
(847) 288-0600. **$59-$89.** 3010 N Mannheim Rd. Jct US 12/45 (Mannheim Rd) and Grave Ave, just n. Int corridors. **Pets:** Small, dogs only. $20 one-time fee/room. Designated rooms, service with restrictions.
(SAVE) (S∆) ✕ 🔒

GLEN ELLYN

▼▼▼ Holiday Inn-Glen Ellyn **SH**
(630) 629-6000. **$75-$125.** 1250 Roosevelt Rd. I-355, exit Roosevelt Rd, 0.8 mi e on SR 38. Int corridors. **Pets:** Small, other species. $25 one-time fee/room. Service with restrictions, supervision.
(ASK) (S∆) ✕ 🖳M 🔊 🖫 🔒 💻 🍴 ⊇

GLENVIEW

▲▲▲ ▼▼▼ Baymont Inn & Suites
            Chicago-Glenview **SH**
(847) 635-8300. **$69-$89.** 1625 Milwaukee Ave. I-294, exit Willow Rd, 0.4 mi e to Landwehr Rd, 1.3 mi s to Lake Ave, then 0.5 mi w. Int corridors. **Pets:** Accepted.
(SAVE) (S∆) ✕ 🔊 🔒 💻

GURNEE

▲▲▲ ▼▼▼ Baymont Inn & Suites
            Chicago-Gurnee **SH**
(847) 662-7600. **$66-$125.** 5688 N Ridge Rd. I-94, exit Grand Ave (SR 132 E), just e via service road. Int corridors. **Pets:** Medium. $50 deposit/room. Designated rooms, service with restrictions, supervision.
(SAVE) (S∆) ✕ 🖳M 🔊 🖫 🔒 💻 ⊇

▼▼▼ Comfort Suites **SH**
(847) 782-0890. **$79-$139.** 5430 Grand Ave. I-94, exit Grand Ave (SR 132 E), 0.5 mi e. Int corridors. **Pets:** Small, other species. $30 one-time fee/room. Designated rooms, service with restrictions, crate.
(ASK) (S∆) ✕ 🖳M 🔊 🖫 🔒 💻 ⊇ ✕

▼▼▼ Country Inn & Suites By Carlson **SH**
(847) 625-9700. **$79-$139.** 5420 Grand Ave. I-94, exit Grand Ave (SR 132 E), 0.5 mi e. Int corridors. **Pets:** Small, other species. $30 one-time fee/room. Designated rooms, service with restrictions, crate.
(ASK) (S∆) ✕ 🖳M 🔊 🖫 🔒 💻 ⊇

HOFFMAN ESTATES

▲▲▲ ▼▼▼ AmeriSuites (Chicago/Hoffman
            Estates) **SH**
(847) 839-1800. **$115.** 2750 Greenspoint Pkwy. I-90, exit Barrington Rd westbound, 0.3 mi s; exit SR 59 eastbound, 0.5 mi n to SR 72 (Higgins Rd), 2 mi e to Barrington Rd, then just n. Int corridors. **Pets:** Small. Designated rooms, service with restrictions, supervision.
(SAVE) (S∆) ✕ 🔊 🖫 🔒 💻 ⊇

▲▲▲ ▼▼▼ Baymont Inn & Suites Chicago-Hoffman
            Estates **SH**
(847) 882-8848. **$79-$99.** 2075 Barrington Rd. I-90, exit Barrington Rd westbound, 0.3 mi s; exit SR 59 eastbound, 0.5 mi n to SR 72 (Higgins Rd), 2 mi e to Barrington Rd, then just n. Int corridors. **Pets:** Medium. $50 deposit/room. Designated rooms, service with restrictions, supervision.
(SAVE) (S∆) ✕ 🔊 🔒 💻

▼▼▼ La Quinta Inn **SH**
(847) 882-3312. **$79-$109.** 2280 Barrington Rd. I-90, exit Barrington Rd westbound, 0.3 mi s; exit SR 59 eastbound, 0.5 mi n to SR 72 (Higgins Rd), 2 mi e to Barrington Rd, then just n. Int corridors. **Pets:** Accepted.
✕ 🔊 🖫 🔒 💻 ⊇

▲▲▲ ▼▼▼ Red Roof Inn **M**
(847) 885-7877. **$51-$85.** 2500 Hassell Rd. I-90, exit Barrington Rd westbound, 0.3 mi s; exit SR 59 eastbound, 0.5 mi n to SR 72 (Higgins Rd), 2 mi e to Barrington Rd, then just n. Ext corridors. **Pets:** Accepted.
(SAVE) ✕ 🔊 🔒

ITASCA

[AAA] ♦♦♦ **AmeriSuites (Chicago/Itasca)** [SH]
(630) 875-1400. **$107-$116.** 1150 Arlington Heights Rd. I-290, exit Thorndale Ave, 0.6 mi e on Thorndale Heights Rd, then 0.5 mi n. Int corridors. **Pets:** Small, other species. Designated rooms, service with restrictions, crate.
[SAVE] [SD] ☒ ♿M 🦻 ♿ 🗄 💻 🏊

JOLIET

♦♦ **Comfort Inn-Joliet South** [SH]
(815) 744-1770. **$55-$75.** 135 S Larkin Ave. I-80, exit 130B, 0.5 mi n. Int corridors. **Pets:** Other species. Service with restrictions.
[A$K] [SD] ☒ 🦻 🗄 💻 🏊

♦♦ **Comfort Inn North** [SH]
(815) 436-5141. **$55-$75.** 3235 Norman Ave. I-55, exit 257, just e. Int corridors. **Pets:** Accepted.
[A$K] [SD] ☒ 🦻 🗄 💻 🏊

♦♦♦ **Holiday Inn Express-Joliet** [SH]
(815) 729-2000. **$69-$169.** 411 S Larkin Ave. I-80, exit 130B. Int corridors. **Pets:** Small, dogs only. Designated rooms, service with restrictions, supervision.
[A$K] [SD] ☒ ♿M ♿ 🗄 🏊

♦ **Motel 6 Joliet I-55–1296** [SH]
(815) 439-1332. **$39-$55.** 3551 Mall Loop Dr. I-55, exit 257, 0.4 mi e on US 30, then 0.4 mi s. Int corridors. **Pets:** Accepted.
[SD] ☒ ♿M 🦻 ♿

[AAA] ♦♦ **Red Roof Inn** [M] 🐾
(815) 741-2304. **$40-$69.** 1750 McDonough St. I-80, exit 130B, just off Larkin Ave. Ext corridors. **Pets:** Other species. Service with restrictions, crate.
[SAVE] ☒ 🦻 🗄

[AAA] ♦♦ **Super 8 Motel I-55 North** [SH]
(815) 439-3838. **$59-$77.** 3401 Mall Loop Dr. I-55, exit 257, 0.4 mi e on US 30, then just s. Int corridors. **Pets:** Accepted.
[SAVE] [SD] ☒ 🦻 ♿ 🗄 🏊

LANSING

[AAA] ♦♦ **Red Roof Inn** [M]
(708) 895-9570. **$44-$77.** 2450 E 173rd St. I-80/94, exit 161 (Torrence Ave), just n. Ext corridors. **Pets:** Large, other species. Service with restrictions.
[SAVE] ☒ 🦻 🗄

LIBERTYVILLE

♦♦ **Candlewood Suites Chicago-Libertyville** [SH]
(847) 247-9900. **$99.** 1100 N US 45. I-94, exit SR 137 (Buckley Rd), 5.6 mi w to US 45, then 1.4 mi s. Int corridors. **Pets:** Accepted.
[A$K] [SD] ☒ ♿M 🦻 ♿ 🗄 💻

♦♦ **Days Inn** [SH]
(847) 816-8006. **$65-$99.** 1809 N Milwaukee Ave. Jct SR 21 and 137 (Buckley Rd). Int corridors. **Pets:** Medium. $5 daily fee/pet. Designated rooms, service with restrictions, supervision.
[A$K] [SD] ☒ 🦻 🗄 💻 🏊

♦♦♦ **Holiday Inn Express Hotel & Suites** [SH]
(847) 549-7878. **$89-$168.** 77 W Buckley Rd. I-94, exit SR 137 (Buckley Rd), 2.3 mi w. Int corridors. **Pets:** Accepted.
[A$K] [SD] ☒ ♿ 🗄 💻 🏊

LINCOLNSHIRE

[AAA] ♦♦♦♦ **Marriott's Lincolnshire Resort** [LH]
(847) 634-0100. **$89-$199.** 10 Marriott Dr. I-94, exit Half Day Rd, 2 mi w to jct US 45, SR 21 and 22, then just s. Int corridors. **Pets:** Small. $75 one-time fee/room. Service with restrictions, crate.
[SAVE] [SD] ☒ ♿M 🦻 ♿ 🗄 💻 🍴 🏊 ✂

LOMBARD

[AAA] ♦♦♦ **AmeriSuites (Chicago/Lombard/Oakbrook)** [SH]
(630) 932-6501. **$89-$99.** 2340 S Fountain Square Dr. I-88, exit Highland Ave, just n to Butterfield Rd (SR 56), 0.9 mi e, then just n. Int corridors. **Pets:** Accepted.
[SAVE] [SD] ☒ ♿M 🦻 ♿ 🗄 💻 🏊

♦♦♦ **Homestead Studio Suites Hotel-Chicago/Lombard/Oak Brook** [SH] 🐾
(630) 928-0202. **$69-$84.** 2701 Technology Dr. I-88, exit Highland Ave, just n, 0.6 mi e on Butterfield Rd (SR 56), then just s. Int corridors. **Pets:** Medium, other species. $25 daily fee/room. Service with restrictions, crate.
[A$K] [SD] ☒ ♿M 🦻 ♿ 🗄 💻

MATTESON

[AAA] ♦♦ **Baymont Inn & Suites Chicago-Matteson** [SH]
(708) 503-0999. **$79-$119.** 5210 W Southwick Dr. I-57, exit 340A, 0.3 mi e on US 30, 0.3 mi s on Cicero Ave. Int corridors. **Pets:** Medium. $50 deposit/pet. Service with restrictions, supervision.
[SAVE] [SD] ☒ 🦻 🗄 💻

MONEE

[AAA] ♦♦ **Best Western Monee Inn** [SH]
(708) 534-3500. **$55-$89.** 5815 W Monee-Manhattan Rd. I-57, exit 335, 0.3 mi e. Int corridors. **Pets:** Small. $20 deposit/pet, $6 daily fee/pet. Designated rooms, service with restrictions, supervision.
[SAVE] [SD] ☒ 🗄 💻 🏊

♦♦ **Super 8 Motel** [SH]
(708) 534-1900. **$49-$89, 3 day notice.** 5825 W Monee-Manhattan Rd. I-57, exit 335, 0.3 mi e. Int corridors. **Pets:** Small. $20 deposit/pet, $6 daily fee/pet. Designated rooms, service with restrictions, supervision.
[A$K] [SD] ☒

MUNDELEIN

▼▼▼ Crowne Plaza Chicago-North
Shore SH ❄️
(847) 949-5100. **$89-$119.** 510 SR 83 E. Jct US 45 and SR 83. Int corridors. **Pets:** Other species. Service with restrictions, supervision.

(ASK) (S🐾) (✕) (🐕) (🛏️) (🖥️) (🍴) (🚮) (✕)

🏧 ▼▼ 💎 Super 8 Motel SH
(847) 949-8842. **$55-$73.** 1950 S Lake St. Jct US 45, SR 60 and 83. Int corridors. **Pets:** Medium, dogs only. $6 daily fee/room. Service with restrictions, supervision.

(SAVE) (S🐾) (✕) (🛏️)

NAPERVILLE

▼▼▼ Country Inn & Suites By Carlson SH
(630) 548-0966. **$70-$105.** 1847 W Diehl Rd. I-88, exit SR 59, just s. Int corridors. **Pets:** Very small. $10 daily fee/pet. Service with restrictions, supervision.

(ASK) (S🐾) (✕) (🛏️M) (🐕) (🐾) (🛏️) (🖥️) (🚮)

🏧 ▼▼▼ Exel Inn of Naperville SH
(630) 357-0022. **$56-$76.** 1585 N Naperville/Wheaton Rd. I-88, exit Naperville Rd, 0.5 mi s. Int corridors. **Pets:** Small, other species. Designated rooms, service with restrictions, supervision.

(SAVE) (S🐾) (✕) (🛏️) (🖥️)

▼▼▼ Hawthorn Suites-Naperville SH
(630) 548-0881. **$99-$169.** 1843 W Diehl Rd. I-88, exit SR 59, just s to Diehl Rd, then just w. Int corridors. **Pets:** Medium, other species. $100 one-time fee/room. Service with restrictions, supervision.

(ASK) (S🐾) (✕) (🐕) (🐾) (🛏️) (🖥️) (🚮) (✕)

▼▼▼ Homestead Studio Suites
Hotel-Chicago/Naperville SH ❄️
(630) 577-0200. **$74-$89.** 1827 Centre Point Cir. I-88, exit Naperville Rd, just s to Diehl Rd, 0.8 mi w, then just n. Int corridors. **Pets:** Medium, other species. $25 daily fee, crate. Service with restrictions, crate.

(ASK) (S🐾) (✕) (🛏️M) (🐕) (🐾) (🛏️) (🖥️)

🏧 ▼ Red Roof Inn M
(630) 369-2500. **$55-$84.** 1698 W Diehl Rd. I-88, exit SR 59, just s. Ext corridors. **Pets:** Large, other species. Service with restrictions, supervision.

(SAVE) (✕) (🛏️)

NORTH AURORA

🏧 ▼▼▼ Baymont Inn & Suites North
Aurora SH
(630) 897-7695. **$79-$139.** 308 S Lincoln Way. I-88, exit SR 31. Int corridors. **Pets:** Service with restrictions, supervision.

(SAVE) (S🐾) (✕) (🐾) (🛏️) (🖥️) (🚮)

NORTHBROOK

🏧 ▼ Red Roof Inn M
(847) 205-1755. **$51-$76.** 340 Waukegan Rd. I-94, exit SR 43 (Waukegan Rd). Ext corridors. **Pets:** Large, other species. Service with restrictions, crate.

(SAVE) (✕)

OAK BROOK

▼▼▼ Residence Inn Chicago/Oak Brook SH
(630) 571-1200. **$149-$169.** 790 Jorie Blvd. I-88, exit Midwest Rd eastbound, just n to 22nd St (Cermak Rd), 1.7 mi to Jorie Blvd, then just sw; exit 22nd St (Cermak Rd) westbound, 0.4 mi e to Jorie Blvd. Int corridors. **Pets:** Accepted.

(✕) (🛏️M) (🐕) (🐾) (🛏️) (🖥️) (🚮) (✕)

OAKBROOK TERRACE

🏧 ▼▼▼ La Quinta Inn-Oakbrook Terrace SH
(630) 495-4600. **$69-$99.** 1 S 666 Midwest Rd. I-88, exit Midwest Rd, 0.4 mi n, just n of 22nd St (Cermak Rd). Int corridors. **Pets:** Small. Designated rooms, service with restrictions, supervision.

(SAVE) (✕) (🐕) (🛏️) (🖥️) (🚮)

PROSPECT HEIGHTS

🏧 ▼▼ Exel Inn of Prospect Heights SH
(847) 459-0545. **$51-$71.** 540 Milwaukee Ave. Jct SR 21 and US 45. Int corridors. **Pets:** Small. Designated rooms, service with restrictions, crate.

(SAVE) (S🐾) (✕) (🐕) (🛏️) (🖥️)

ROSEMONT

🏧 ▼▼▼ Embassy Suites Hotel O'Hare
Rosemont LH
(847) 678-4000. **$109-$325.** 5500 N River Rd. I-190, exit 1B, just s. Int corridors. **Pets:** Medium, other species. $100 deposit/room, $25 one-time fee/room. Service with restrictions, crate.

(SAVE) (S🐾) (✕) (🐕) (🐾) (🛏️) (🖥️) (🍴) (🚮) (✕)

🏧 ▼▼▼ Holiday Inn O'Hare International LH
(847) 671-6350. **$169-$199, 3 day notice.** 5440 N River Rd. I-190, exit 1B, just s. Int corridors. **Pets:** Accepted.

(SAVE) (S🐾) (✕) (🛏️M) (🐕) (🐾) (🛏️) (🖥️) (🍴) (🚮) (✕)

🏧 ▼▼▼ Radisson Hotel O'Hare
Chicago-Rosemont LH
(847) 297-1234. **$189-$209.** 6810 N Mannheim Rd. On US 12 and 45, just n of SR 72 (Higgins Rd). Int corridors. **Pets:** Medium. $50 deposit/room. Service with restrictions, supervision.

(SAVE) (S🐾) (✕) (🐕) (🖥️) (🍴) (🚮) (✕)

▼▼▼ Residence Inn by Marriott
Chicago-O'Hare SH ❄️
(847) 375-9000. **$139-$169.** 7101 Chestnut St. US 12 and 45, 3 mi n of O'Hare Airport. Int corridors. **Pets:** Large, other species. $5 daily fee/pet, $50 one-time fee/room.

(ASK) (S🐾) (✕) (🐕) (🐾) (🛏️) (🖥️) (🚮) (✕)

🏧 ▼▼▼ Sofitel Chicago O'Hare LH ❄️
(847) 678-4488. **$99-$279.** 5550 N River Rd. I-190, exit 1B, just s. Int corridors. **Pets:** Dogs only. $100 deposit/pet, $25 one-time fee/pet. Service with restrictions, supervision.

(SAVE) (S🐾) (✕) (🐕) (🛏️) (🍴) (🚮) (✕)

🏧 ▼▼▼▼ The Westin O'Hare LH ❄️
(847) 698-6000. **$109-$209.** 6100 N River Rd. I-190, exit 1B, just n. Int corridors. **Pets:** Medium, dogs only. Service with restrictions, supervision.

(SAVE) (S🐾) (✕) (🛏️M) (🐕) (🐾) (🖥️) (🍴) (🚮) (✕)

ST. CHARLES

AAA ♦♦♦ Best Western Inn of St. Charles SH
(630) 584-4550. **$79-$89.** 1635 E Main St. On SR 64, 0.5 mi
e of SR 25. Ext/int corridors. **Pets:** Dogs only. $50 deposit/
room. Service with restrictions, supervision.

[SAVE] [S₆] [X] [🅱] [💻] [🔁]

AAA ♦♦♦ Super 8 Motel-St. Charles SH
(630) 377-8388. **$64-$78.** 1520 E Main St. On SR 64, 1 mi
e. Int corridors. **Pets:** Small. $50 deposit/room, $6 daily
fee/pet. Designated rooms, crate.

[SAVE] [X] [🅱]

SCHAUMBURG

AAA ♦♦♦ AmeriSuites
(Chicago/Schaumburg) SH ☙
(847) 330-1060. **$79-$134.** 1851 McConnor Pkwy. I-290, exit
1A (Woodfield/Golf rds) northbound, just n to Golf Rd, just w
to McConnor Pkwy, then just n; exit 1B (Woodfield/Golf rds)
southbound. Int corridors. **Pets:** Small, other species. $25
one-time fee/pet. Designated rooms, service with restrictions, crate.

[SAVE] [S₆] [X] [&M] [🔁] [🅱] [💻] [🔁]

♦♦♦♦ Chicago Marriott Schaumburg LH
(847) 240-0100. **$79-$159.** 50 N Martingale Rd. I-290, exit
Higgins Rd (SR 72) westbound, 0.5 mi s. Int corridors.
Pets: Accepted.

[X] [&M] [🔁] [🅱] [💻] [🍽] [🔁] [X]

♦♦♦♦ Drury Inn-Schaumburg SH
(847) 517-7737. **$103-$133.** 600 N Martingale Rd. I-290, exit
Higgins Rd (SR 72) westbound, just w, then just n. Int
corridors. **Pets:** Large, other species. Service with restrictions, supervision.

[ASK] [X] [🔁] [🅱] [💻] [🔁] [X]

♦♦♦ Hawthorn Suites SH
(847) 706-9007. **$119.** 1251 E American Ln. I-290, exit 1A
(Woodfield/Golf rds), 0.5 mi w to Meacham Rd, just n to
American Ln, then just w. Int corridors. **Pets:** Accepted.

[ASK] [S₆] [X] [&M] [🔁] [🅱] [💻] [X]

♦♦♦ Holiday Inn Schaumburg/Hoffman
Estates SH
(847) 310-0500. **$79-$119.** 1550 N Roselle Rd. I-90, exit
Roselle Rd, 0.8 mi s. Int corridors. **Pets:** Medium. Service
with restrictions, crate.

[ASK] [S₆] [X] [🔁] [🅱] [💻] [🍽] [🔁]

♦♦♦ Homestead Studio Suites
Hotel-Chicago/Schaumburg SH ☙
(847) 882-6900. **$94-$104.** 51 E State Pkwy. I-90, exit
Roselle Rd, 0.8 mi s, then just e. Int corridors.
Pets: Medium, other species. $25 daily fee/room. Service
with restrictions, crate.

[ASK] [S₆] [X] [&M] [🔁] [🔁] [🅱] [💻]

♦♦♦ Homewood Suites Schaumburg SH
(847) 605-0400. **$97-$139.** 815 E American Ln. I-290, exit
Higgins Rd (SR 72), 0.5 mi w, 0.8 mi n on Meacham Rd,
then 0.8 mi w. Ext/int corridors. **Pets:** Accepted.

[ASK] [S₆] [X] [&M] [🔁] [🅱] [💻] [🔁] [X]

AAA ♦♦♦ La Quinta Inn Schaumburg SH
(847) 517-8484. **$79-$109.** 1730 E Higgins Rd. I-290, exit
Higgins Rd (SR 72) westbound, just w. Int corridors.
Pets: Other species. Service with restrictions, supervision.

[SAVE] [X] [🔁] [🅱] [💻] [🔁]

AAA ♦♦♦♦ Radisson Hotel Schaumburg SH
(847) 397-1500. **$55-$109.** 1725 E Algonquin Rd. SR 53,
exit Algonquin Rd (SR 62), 0.5 mi w. Int corridors.
Pets: Medium. Service with restrictions, supervision.

[SAVE] [S₆] [X] [&M] [🔁] [🔁] [🅱] [💻] [🍽] [🔁] [X]

♦♦♦♦ Residence Inn by
Marriott-Chicago/Schaumburg SH ☙
(847) 517-9200. **$159, 3 day notice.** 1610 McConnor Pkwy.
I-290, exit 1A (Woodfield/Golf rds) northbound, follow signs
just n to Golf Rd, just w to McConnor Pkwy, then just n; exit
1B (Woodfield/Golf rds) southbound. Int corridors.
Pets: Medium, other species. $100 one-time fee/room.
Service with restrictions, crate.

[ASK] [X] [&M] [🔁] [🔁] [🅱] [💻] [🔁] [X]

AAA ♦♦♦♦ Staybridge Suites SH ☙
(847) 619-6677. **$109-$139.** 901 E Woodfield Office Ct. Jct
SR 53, 1.5 w on SR 72 (Higgins Rd), then 0.3 mi n on
Plum Grove Rd. Ext/int corridors. **Pets:** Medium, other species. $200 one-time fee/room. Service with restrictions.

[SAVE] [S₆] [X] [🔁] [🅱] [💻] [🔁] [X]

SCHILLER PARK

AAA ♦♦♦ Twelve Oaks Suites at O'Hare SH
(847) 725-2210. **$89-$300.** 9450 W Lawrence Ave. 0.5 mi e
of US 12 and 45. Int corridors. **Pets:** Accepted.

[SAVE] [S₆] [X] [🅱] [💻]

SKOKIE

AAA ♦♦♦ Holiday Inn North Shore SH
(847) 679-8900. **$95-$179.** 5300 W Touhy Ave. I-94, exit
39A, 0.5 mi w. Ext/int corridors. **Pets:** Small. $25 one-time
fee/room. Designated rooms, service with restrictions, crate.

[SAVE] [S₆] [X] [🔁] [🔁] [🅱] [💻] [🍽] [🔁] [🔁]

AAA ♦♦♦ Howard Johnson Hotel-Skokie SH
(847) 679-4200. **$135-$165.** 9333 Skokie Blvd. I-94, exit Old
Orchard Rd, 0.4 mi e to Skokie Blvd (US 41), then 0.3 mi s.
Int corridors. **Pets:** Accepted.

[SAVE] [S₆] [X] [🔁] [🅱] [💻] [🍽] [🔁] [X]

SOUTH HOLLAND

♦ Motel 6-1483 M ☙
(708) 331-1621. **$42-$55.** 17301 S Halsted St. I-80/294, exit
Halsted St northbound. Ext corridors. **Pets:** Small, other
species. Service with restrictions, supervision.

[S₆] [X]

TINLEY PARK

AAA ♦♦♦ Baymont Inn & Suites Chicago-Tinley
Park SH
(708) 633-1200. **$69-$99.** 7255 W 183rd St. I-80, exit 148B,
0.5 mi n to 183rd St, just w to North Creek Business
Center. Int corridors. **Pets:** Medium. $50 deposit/room. Des-
ignated rooms, service with restrictions, supervision.

[SAVE] [S₆] [X] [&M] [🔁] [🅱] [💻] [🔁]

VERNON HILLS

▼▼▼ **Homestead Studio Suites Hotel-Chicago/**
Vernon Hills/Lincolnshire SH ❖
(847) 955-1111. **$77-$92.** 675 Woodlands Pkwy. I-94, exit SR
60 (Town Line Rd), 2.1 mi w to SR 21 (Milwaukee Ave), 1.9
mi s to Woodlands Pkwy, then just w. Int corridors.
Pets: Medium, other species. $25 daily fee/room. Service
with restrictions, crate.
ASK S⊘ ✕ ⌀ ☁ ⊟ ▦

WAUKEGAN

▼▼▼ **Candlewood Suites**
Chicago/Waukegan SH
(847) 578-5250. **$105-$135.** 1151 S Waukegan Rd. I-94, exit
Buckley Rd (SR 137), 0.5 mi e to SR 43 (Waukegan Rd),
then 1.9 mi n. Int corridors. **Pets:** Accepted.
ASK S⊘ ✕ ⌀ ☁ ⊟ ▦

▼▼▼ **Residence Inn by Marriott-Waukegan** SH
(847) 689-9240. **$113-$189.** 1440 S White Oak Dr. I-94, exit
SR 137 (Buckley Rd), 0.5 mi e to SR 43 (Waukegan Rd),
1.5 mi n to Lakeside Dr, then just e. Int corridors.
Pets: Accepted.
ASK ✕ ⌂ ⌀ ☁ ⊟ ▦ ⇌ ⊠

WEST DUNDEE

▼▼▼ **TownePlace Suites by Marriott** SH ❖
(847) 608-6320. **$94.** 2185 Marriott Dr. I-90, exit SR 31, 0.4
mi n to Marriott Dr, then just e. Int corridors. **Pets:** Large.
$100 one-time fee/room. Service with restrictions, crate.
ASK ✕ ☁ ⊟ ▦ ⇌

WESTMONT

▼▼▼ **ClubHouse Inn & Suites** SH
(630) 920-2200. **$89.** 630 Pasquinelli Dr. Just off US 34, 0.3
mi nw of jct SR 83. Int corridors. **Pets:** Small. $25 deposit/
room. Designated rooms, service with restrictions, supervision.
ASK S⊘ ✕ ⌀ ⊟ ▦ ⇌

▼▼ ▼▼ **Homestead Studio Suites Hotel-Chicago/**
Westmont/Oak Brook SH ❖
(630) 323-9292. **$64-$79.** 855 Pasquinelli Dr. SR 83, exit
Ogden Ave (US 34), just w to Pasquinelli Dr, 0.5 mi n. Int
corridors. **Pets:** Medium, other species. $25 daily fee/room.
Service with restrictions, crate.
ASK S⊘ ✕ ⌂ ⌀ ☁ ⊟ ▦

WILLOWBROOK

ⒶⒶⒶ ▼▼▼ **Baymont Inn & Suites**
Chicago-Willowbrook SH
(630) 654-0077. **$79-$94.** 855 79th St. I-55, exit 274, just n.
Int corridors. **Pets:** Medium. $25 deposit/room. Designated
rooms, service with restrictions, supervision.
SAVE S⊘ ✕ ⌀ ⊟ ▦

ⒶⒶⒶ ▼▼▼ **Red Roof Inn** Ⓜ ❖
(630) 323-8811. **$54-$87.** 7535 Kingery Hwy. I-55, exit 274,
0.5 mi n on SR 83. Ext corridors. **Pets:** Large, other species. Service with restrictions, supervision.
SAVE ✕ ⌀ ⊟

WOODSTOCK

▼ **Super 8 Motel** SH
(815) 337-8808. **$55-$205, 7 day notice.** 1220 Davis Rd. On
SR 47, s of jct US 14. Int corridors. **Pets:** Accepted.
ASK S⊘ ✕ ⊟

❖   **END METROPOLITAN AREA**   ❖

CHILLICOTHE

▼▼ **Super 8 Motel** SH
(309) 274-2568. **$55-$75.** 615 S Fourth St. 1.1 mi s on SR
29. Int corridors. **Pets:** Large, other species. $5 daily fee/
pet. Service with restrictions, crate.
ASK S⊘ ✕ ⊟

COLLINSVILLE

ⒶⒶⒶ ▼▼▼ **Best Western/Pear Tree**
Inn-Collinsville SH
(618) 345-9500. **$57-$91.** 552 Ramada Blvd. I-55/70, exit 11
(SR 157), just s. Ext corridors. **Pets:** Accepted.
SAVE ✕ ⌂ ⌀ ☁ ⊟ ▦ ⇌

▼▼▼▼ **Drury Inn St. Louis/Collinsville** SH
(618) 345-7700. **$84-$110.** 602 N Bluff Rd. I-55/70, exit 11
(SR 157), just n. Int corridors. **Pets:** Large, other species.
Service with restrictions, supervision.
ASK ✕ ⌂ ⌀ ⊟ ▦ ⇌

ⒶⒶⒶ ▼▼▼ **Holiday Inn Collinsville/St.**
Louis SH
(618) 345-2800. **$89-$129.** 1000 Eastport Plaza Dr. I-55/70,
exit 11 (SR 157), just nw. Int corridors. **Pets:** Accepted.
SAVE S⊘ ✕ ⊟ ▦ 🍴 ⇌ ⊠

▼▼▼ **Motel 6-1133** SH
(618) 345-2100. **$39-$57.** 295A N Bluff Rd. I-55/70, exit 11
(SR 157), just s. Int corridors. **Pets:** Accepted.
S⊘ ✕ ⌀ ☁ ⇌

DANVILLE

Best Western Regency Inn 🅂🄷
(217) 446-2111. **$75-$95.** 360 Eastgate Dr. I-74, exit 220 (Lynch Dr), just n. Ext/int corridors. **Pets:** Medium. $10 daily fee/pet. Designated rooms, service with restrictions, supervision.

Best Western Riverside Inn 🅂🄷
(217) 431-0020. **$70-$90.** 57 S Gilbert St. I-74, exit 215, 0.8 mi n, on US 150 and SR 1. Ext/int corridors. **Pets:** Medium. $10 daily fee/pet. Designated rooms, service with restrictions, supervision.

Comfort Inn 🅂🄷
(217) 443-8004. **$55-$96.** 383 Lynch Dr. I-74, exit 220 (Lynch Dr), just n. Int corridors. **Pets:** Accepted.

Sleep Inn & Suites 🅂🄷
(217) 442-6600. **$59-$99.** 361 Lynch Dr. I-74, exit 220 (Lynch Dr), just n, then just e. Int corridors. **Pets:** Small, dogs only. $10 daily fee/pet. Designated rooms, service with restrictions, supervision.

Super 8-Danville 🅂🄷
(217) 443-4499. **$51-$60.** 377 Lynch Dr. I-74, exit 220 (Lynch Dr), just n. Int corridors. **Pets:** Accepted.

DECATUR

Baymont Inn Decatur 🅂🄷
(217) 875-5800. **$54-$74.** 5100 Hickory Point Frontage Rd. I-72, exit 141B (US 51 N), s on frontage road. Int corridors. **Pets:** Accepted.

Country Inn & Suites By Carlson 🅂🄷
(217) 872-2402. **$79.** 5150 Hickory Point Frontage Rd. I-72, exit 141B (US 51 N), s on frontage road. Int corridors. **Pets:** Accepted.

Ramada Limited Decatur 🅂🄷
(217) 876-8011. **$73-$79.** 355 E Hickory Point Rd. I-72, exit 141B (US 51 N), just n, then s via frontage road. Int corridors. **Pets:** Medium. Service with restrictions.

Sleep Inn of Decatur 🅂🄷
(217) 872-7700. **$59-$80, 7 day notice.** 3920 E Hospitality Ln. I-72, exit 144 (SR 48), just s to Brush College Rd, then just e. Int corridors. **Pets:** Medium. $10 one-time fee/room. Service with restrictions, crate.

Super 8 Motel-Decatur 🅂🄷
(217) 877-8888. **$60, 5 day notice.** 3141 N Water St. I-72, exit 141A (US 51 S), 1.8 mi s; downtown. Int corridors. **Pets:** Accepted.

Wingate Inn 🅂🄷
(217) 875-5500. **$89-$109.** 5170 Wingate Dr. I-72, exit 38B, 0.5 mi n on US 51, just e. Int corridors. **Pets:** Other species. $10 daily fee/pet. Service with restrictions, crate.

DEKALB

Best Western DeKalb Inn & Suites 🅂🄷
(815) 758-8661. **$79-$85.** 1212 W Lincoln Hwy. I-88, exit Annie Glidden Rd, 2 mi n to W Lincoln Hwy (SR 38), then just w. Ext/int corridors. **Pets:** Medium. $10 one-time fee/room. Service with restrictions, crate.

DIXON

Best Western Reagan Hotel 🅂🄷
(815) 284-1890. **$49-$59.** 443 IL Rt 2. SR 2, 3.6 mi w of jct SR 26. Int corridors. **Pets:** Accepted.

Comfort Inn 🅂🄷
(815) 284-0500. **$64-$75.** 136 Plaza Dr. I-88, exit SR 26, n, then just e. Int corridors. **Pets:** Medium, other species. $100 deposit/room, $15 daily fee/pet. Service with restrictions, supervision.

Quality Inn & Suites 🅂🄷
(815) 288-2001. **$74-$86.** 154 Plaza Dr. I-88, exit SR 26, n, then just e. Int corridors. **Pets:** Medium, other species. $100 deposit/room, $15 daily fee/pet. Service with restrictions, supervision.

EAST PEORIA

Super 8 Motel 🅂🄷
(309) 698-8889. **$55-$85.** 725 Taylor St. I-74, exit 96, just e. Int corridors. **Pets:** Accepted.

EFFINGHAM

Best Western Raintree Inn 🅂🄷
(217) 342-4121. **$48-$65, 10 day notice.** 1811 W Fayette Ave. I-57/70, exit 159. Ext/int corridors. **Pets:** Medium. Designated rooms, service with restrictions, supervision.

Comfort Inn 🅂🄷
(217) 347-5050. **$59-$75.** 1304 W Evergreen Dr. I-57/70, exit 160 (SR 32/33), just e, then just n. Int corridors. **Pets:** Accepted.

Comfort Suites 🅂🄷
(217) 342-3151. **$59-$89.** 1310 W Fayette Ave. I-57/70, exit 159, 0.4 mi e. Int corridors. **Pets:** Accepted.

Days Inn 🄼
(217) 342-9271. **$55-$85.** 1412 W Fayette Ave. I-57/70, exit 159, just e. Ext corridors. **Pets:** $5 daily fee/pet. Service with restrictions, supervision.

▼▼▼ Holiday Inn Express 🆂🅷
(217) 540-1111. **$69-$90.** 1103 Ave of Mid-America. I-57/70, exit 160 (SR 32/33), just n. Int corridors. **Pets:** Other species. $10 one-time fee/room. Designated rooms, service with restrictions, supervision.
🅰🆂🅺 S🐾 ✕ 🛋M 🖥 💻 🍽

🆀🆀🆀 ▼ Paradise Inn Ⓜ
(217) 342-2165. **$39-$45.** 1000 W Fayette Ave. I-57/70, exit 159, 1 mi e. Ext corridors. **Pets:** Small. $6 daily fee/pet. Designated rooms, no service, supervision.
SAVE S🐾 ✕ 🖥

▼▼ Super 8 Motel-Effingham Ⓜ 🐾
(217) 342-6888. **$60-$90.** 1400 Thelma Keller Ave. I-57/70, exit 160 (SR 32/33), 0.5 mi n. Int corridors. **Pets:** Other species. Service with restrictions, supervision.
🅰🆂🅺 S🐾 ✕ 🅕 🖥 💻

FAIRVIEW HEIGHTS

▼▼▼ Drury Inn & Suites Fairview Heights 🆂🅷
(618) 398-8530. **$90-$110.** 12 Ludwig Dr. I-64, exit 12 (SR 159). Int corridors. **Pets:** Large, other species. Service with restrictions, supervision.
🅰🆂🅺 ✕ 🖥 💻 🍽

🆀🆀🆀 ▼▼▼ Ramada Inn Fairview Heights 🅻🅷
(618) 632-4747. **$79-$99.** 6900 N Illinois Ave. I-64, exit 12 (SR 159), just n. Int corridors. **Pets:** Medium, other species. $15 one-time fee/room. Service with restrictions, crate.
SAVE S🐾 ✕ 🖥 💻 🍴 🍽

▼▼ Super 8 Motel 🆂🅷
(618) 398-8338. **$65-$88.** 45 Ludwig Dr. I-64, exit 12 (SR 159). Int corridors. **Pets:** Other species. Service with restrictions, supervision.
🅰🆂🅺 S🐾 ✕ 🅕 🖥

FLORA

▼▼▼ Best Western 🆂🅷
(618) 662-3054. **$64-$84.** 201 Gary Hagen Dr. Jct US 45 and 50. Int corridors. **Pets:** Accepted.
🅰🆂🅺 S🐾 ✕ 🛋M 🖥 💻

FORSYTH

▼▼ Comfort Inn of Forsyth 🆂🅷
(217) 875-1166. **$59.** 134 Barnett Ave. I-72, exit 141B (US 51), 0.5 mi n. Int corridors. **Pets:** Accepted.
🅰🆂🅺 S🐾 ✕ 🅕 🖥 💻 🍽

FREEPORT

🆀🆀🆀 ▼▼▼ AmeriHost Inn & Suites-Freeport 🆂🅷
(815) 599-8510. **$73-$89.** 1060 Riverside Dr. Jct US 20 Bypass and SR 26, just s. Int corridors. **Pets:** Small. $25 one-time fee/room. Service with restrictions, supervision.
SAVE S🐾 ✕ 🖥 💻 🍽

GALENA

🆀🆀🆀 ▼▼▼ Best Western Quiet House Suites 🆂🅷 🐾
(815) 777-2577. **$97-$202.** 9915 US 20 W. 1 mi e. Ext/int corridors. **Pets:** Other species. $15 daily fee/pet. Designated rooms, supervision.
SAVE S🐾 ✕ 🖥 💻 🍽

🆀🆀🆀 ▼▼▼ Eagle Ridge Inn & Resort 🅻🅷
(815) 777-2444. **$149-$289, 7 day notice.** 444 Eagle Ridge Dr. 6 mi e on US 20, then 4.5 mi n. Ext/int corridors. **Pets:** Medium, dogs only. $75 one-time fee/room. Designated rooms, service with restrictions, crate.
SAVE ✕ 🅐 🖥 💻 🍴 🍽 🍽

GALESBURG

🆀🆀🆀 ▼▼▼ Best Western Prairie Inn 🆂🅷
(309) 343-7151. **$86-$157.** 300 S Soangetaha Rd. I-74, exit 48 (Main St), just e, then just s. Int corridors. **Pets:** Small. $25 deposit/room. Designated rooms, service with restrictions, supervision.
SAVE S🐾 ✕ 🅐 🅕 🖥 💻 🍴 🍽 🍽

▼▼▼ Comfort Inn 🆂🅷
(309) 344-5445. **$64-$84.** 907 W Carl Sandburg Dr. US 34, exit 150 E. Int corridors. **Pets:** Other species. $15 one-time fee/room. Service with restrictions, crate.
🅰🆂🅺 S🐾 ✕ 🛋M 🅐 🖥 💻

▼▼▼ Holiday Inn Express 🆂🅷
(309) 343-7100. **$77-$117.** 2285 Washington St. I-74, exit 48A (US 150), just w to Michigan Ave, just s to Washington St, then just e. Int corridors. **Pets:** Accepted.
🅰🆂🅺 S🐾 ✕ 🛋M 🅔 🖥 💻

GILMAN

🆀🆀🆀 ▼▼▼ Super 8 Motel 🆂🅷
(815) 265-7000. **$59-$69.** 1301 S Crescent St. I-57, exit 283, 0.3 mi n. Int corridors. **Pets:** Accepted.
SAVE S🐾 ✕ 🅐 🖥

▼▼ Travel Inn Ⓜ
(815) 265-7283. **$65.** 834 Hwy 24 W. I-57, exit 283, just e. Ext/int corridors. **Pets:** $5 daily fee/room. Designated rooms, service with restrictions, supervision.
🅰🆂🅺 S🐾 ✕ 🍽

GREENVILLE

🆀🆀🆀 ▼▼▼ Best Western Country View Inn 🆂🅷
(618) 664-3030. **$50-$80.** Rt 127 & I-70. I-70, exit 45, just n. Ext/int corridors. **Pets:** Other species. $5 one-time fee/room. Designated rooms, service with restrictions, supervision.
SAVE S🐾 ✕ 🅐 🖥 💻 🍽

🆀🆀🆀 ▼▼▼ Budget Host Inn 🆂🅷
(618) 664-1950. **$30-$47.** 1525 SR 127 S. I-70, exit 45, 0.3 mi n. Ext corridors. **Pets:** $5 daily fee/pet. Service with restrictions, supervision.
SAVE S🐾 ✕ 🅕 🖥 💻 🍽

HIGHLAND

Holiday Inn Express SH
(618) 651-1100. **$69-$80.** 20 Central Blvd. I-70, exit 24 (SR 143), 4 mi s. Int corridors. **Pets:** Accepted.

JACKSONVILLE

Starlite Motel M
(217) 245-7184. **$43-$49.** 1910 W Morton Ave. On US 67/SR 104, 1.8 mi w. Ext corridors. **Pets:** Accepted.

LINCOLN

Holiday Inn Express SH
(217) 735-5800. **$82-$94.** 130 Olson Dr. I-55, exit 126 (US 121), just e to Heitman Dr, just w to Olson Dr, then just n. Int corridors. **Pets:** Accepted.

LITCHFIELD

Baymont Inn-Litchfield SH
(217) 324-4556. **$72-$87.** 1405 W Hudson Dr. I-55, exit 52 (SR 16), just e to Ohren Ln, just s to W Hudson Dr, then just w. Int corridors. **Pets:** Medium, dogs only. Designated rooms, service with restrictions, supervision.

Litchfield Comfort Inn SH
(217) 324-9260. **$70-$75.** 1010 E Columbian Blvd N. I-55, exit 52 (SR 16), 0.7 mi e to Old SR 66, then 0.3 mi n. Int corridors. **Pets:** Accepted.

MACOMB

Super 8 Motel SH
(309) 836-8888. **$49-$125, 7 day notice.** 313 University Dr. 1.1 mi n on US 67 to University Dr, 0.5 mi w. Int corridors. **Pets:** Accepted.

MANTENO

Comfort Inn SH
(815) 468-8657. **$70-$86.** 157 Cypress. I-57, exit 322. Int corridors. **Pets:** Designated rooms, service with restrictions, supervision.

Country Inn & Suites by Carlson SH
(815) 468-2600. **$80-$130.** 380 S Cypress St. I-57, exit 322, just se via frontage road. Int corridors. **Pets:** Medium. $15 daily fee/room. Designated rooms, service with restrictions, supervision.

MARION

Drury Inn-Marion SH
(618) 997-9600. **$77-$99.** 2706 W DeYoung St. I-57, exit 54B (SR 13), 0.5 mi w. Int corridors. **Pets:** Large, other species. Service with restrictions, supervision.

Motel 6 #1174 SH
(618) 993-2631. **$40-$55.** 1008 Halfway Rd. I-57, exit 54B (SR 13), 0.3 mi w. Ext corridors. **Pets:** Small, other species. Service with restrictions, supervision.

Super 8 Motel SH
(618) 993-5577. **$56-$80.** 2601 W DeYoung St. I-57, exit 54B (SR 13), just w. Int corridors. **Pets:** Accepted.

METROPOLIS

Isle of View Bed & Breakfast BB
(618) 524-5838. **$95-$135, 7 day notice.** 205 Metropolis St. I-24, exit 37, 3 mi w, 0.3 mi s of US 45. Int corridors. **Pets:** Accepted.

Super 8 SH
(618) 524-8200. **$51-$87.** 2055 E 5th St. I-24, exit 37, just w. Int corridors. **Pets:** Accepted.

MONTICELLO

Best Western Monticello Gateway Inn SH
(217) 762-9436. **$74-$110.** 805 Iron Horse Pl. I-72, exit 166, just s. Ext/int corridors. **Pets:** Other species. $15 daily fee/pet. Designated rooms, service with restrictions, supervision.

MORRIS

Days Inn & Suites SH
(815) 942-9000. **$60-$70.** 80 Hampton Rd. I-80, exit 112, just n. Int corridors. **Pets:** Other species. Service with restrictions.

Holiday Inn SH
(815) 942-6600. **$90-$102.** 200 Gore Rd. I-80, exit 112, 0.3 mi nw. Int corridors. **Pets:** Other species. Designated rooms, service with restrictions, supervision.

MORTON

Best Western Ashland House Inn & Conference Center SH
(309) 263-5116. **$64-$84.** 201 E Ashland St. I-74, exit 102, 0.3 mi ne. Int corridors. **Pets:** Very small. $50 deposit/pet. Designated rooms, service with restrictions, supervision.

Comfort Inn SH
(309) 266-8888. **$55-$60.** 210 E Ashland St. I-74, exit 102, 0.4 mi ne. Int corridors. **Pets:** Accepted.

Holiday Inn Express SH
(309) 266-8310. **$65-$85.** 115 E Ashland St. I-74, exit 102B, just w. Ext/int corridors. **Pets:** Accepted.

MOUNT VERNON

◆◆ Best Inns of America Ⓜ ✿
(618) 244-4343. **$45-$51, 30 day notice.** 222 S 44th St. I-57/64, exit 95 (SR 15), just e to 44th St, then just s. Ext corridors. **Pets:** Other species. $10 one-time fee/room. Designated rooms, service with restrictions, supervision.
🅰🆂🅺 🆂🄳 ⊠ 🎬 💻 ➿

◆◆◆ Drury Inn-Mount Vernon 🆂🄷
(618) 244-4550. **$77-$99.** 145 N 44th St. I-57/64, exit 95 (SR 15), just e, then just n (entry through restaurant parking lot). Int corridors. **Pets:** Large, other species. Service with restrictions, supervision.
🅰🆂🅺 ⊠ 🎬 🎬 💻 ➿

◆◆◆ Holiday Inn 🄻🄷
(618) 244-7100. **$95-$150.** 222 Potomac Blvd. I-57/64, exit 95 (SR 15), just w to Potomac Blvd, then just n. Int corridors. **Pets:** Accepted.
🅰🆂🅺 🆂🄳 ⊠ 🆂🄼 🎬 🎬 🎬 💻 🍽 ➿ ⊠

◆ Motel 6-1180 🆂🄷
(618) 244-2383. **$37-$53.** 333 S 44th St. I-57/64, exit 95 (SR 15), just e to Mateer Dr, then 0.4 mi s. Ext corridors. **Pets:** Other species. Service with restrictions, supervision.
🆂🄳 ⊠ ➿

◆◆ Super 8 Motel 🆂🄷 ✿
(618) 242-8800. **$54-$84.** 401 S 44th St. I-57/64, exit 95 (SR 15), just e, then just s. Int corridors. **Pets:** Medium, other species. Service with restrictions, supervision.
⊠ 🎬 💻

◆◆ Thrifty Inn-Mt. Vernon 🆂🄷
(618) 244-7750. **$62-$72.** 100 N 44th St. I-57/64, exit 95 (SR 15), just e. Ext corridors. **Pets:** Large, other species. Service with restrictions, supervision.
🅰🆂🅺 ⊠ 🎬

NASHVILLE

ⒶⒶⒶ ◆◆◆ Best Western U S Inn 🆂🄷
(618) 478-5341. **$55-$65.** 11640 SR 127. I-64, exit 50 (SR 127), 0.3 mi s. Int corridors. **Pets:** Accepted.
🆂🄰🆅🄴 🆂🄳 ⊠ 🆂🄼 🎬 🎬 💻 ➿

NORMAL

ⒶⒶⒶ ◆◆◆ Best Western University Inn 🆂🄷
(309) 454-4070. **$59-$89.** 6 Traders Cir. I-55, exit 165A (US 51), just s, then return on frontage road. Int corridors. **Pets:** Other species. Service with restrictions, supervision.
🆂🄰🆅🄴 🆂🄳 ⊠ 🎬 🎬 💻 ➿

◆◆◆ Comfort Suites of Bloomington 🆂🄷
(309) 452-8588. **$75-$155.** 310 B Greenbriar Dr. I-55, exit 167, follow I-55 business route (Veterans Pkwy), 1.3 mi s; jct Fort Jesse Rd. Int corridors. **Pets:** Accepted.
🅰🆂🅺 🆂🄳 ⊠ 🆂🄼 🎬 🎬 💻 ➿

◆◆ Holiday Inn Bloomington-Normal 🆂🄷
(309) 452-8300. **$109-$115.** 8 Traders Cir. I-55, exit 165A, 0.5 mi e, return on service road. Int corridors. **Pets:** Large. $15 one-time fee/room. Service with restrictions, crate.
🅰🆂🅺 🆂🄳 ⊠ 🎬 🎬 🎬 💻 🍽 ➿ ⊠

◆◆◆ Holiday Inn Express Hotel & Suites 🆂🄷 ✿
(309) 862-1600. **$69-$129.** 1715 Parkway Plaza Dr. I-55, exit 167, follow I-55 business route (Veterans Pkwy), 1.7 mi s to Parkway Plaza Dr, then just e. Int corridors. **Pets:** Other species. $10 deposit/room. Service with restrictions.
🅰🆂🅺 🆂🄳 ⊠ 🎬 🎬 🎬 💻 ➿ ⊠

◆◆ Signature Inn-Normal 🆂🄷
(309) 454-4044. **$71-$79.** 101 S Veterans Pkwy. I-55, exit 167; I-55 business route (Veterans Pkwy), 1.5 mi s. Int corridors. **Pets:** Small. Service with restrictions, crate.
⊠ 🎬 🎬 💻 ➿

O'FALLON

ⒶⒶⒶ ◆◆◆ Comfort Inn 🆂🄷 ✿
(618) 624-6060. **$65-$129.** 1100 Eastgate Dr. I-64, exit 19B (SR 158), 0.5 mi n, then just sw. Int corridors. **Pets:** Other species. $50 deposit/pet. Service with restrictions.
🆂🄰🆅🄴 🆂🄳 ⊠ 🎬 💻 ➿

◆◆ Econo Lodge 🆂🄷
(618) 628-8895. **$55-$105.** 1409 W Hwy 50. I-64, exit 14 (US 50), 0.4 mi w. Int corridors. **Pets:** Other species. $40 deposit/room, $5 daily fee/room, $10 one-time fee/room. Designated rooms, service with restrictions, supervision.
🅰🆂🅺 🆂🄳 ⊠ 🎬 🎬 💻 ➿

OGLESBY

◆◆◆ Holiday Inn Express 🆂🄷
(815) 883-3535. **$82-$90.** 900 Holiday St. I-39, exit 54, just e. Int corridors. **Pets:** Accepted.
🅰🆂🅺 🆂🄳 ⊠ 🎬 💻 ➿

OTTAWA

◆◆◆ Hampton Inn 🆂🄷
(815) 434-6040. **$87-$117.** 4115 Holiday Ln. I-80, exit 90 (SR 23), just n. Int corridors. **Pets:** Designated rooms, service with restrictions, crate.
🅰🆂🅺 🆂🄳 ⊠ 🆂🄼 🎬 🎬 🎬 💻 ➿ ⊠

◆◆ Holiday Inn Express 🆂🄷
(815) 433-0029. **$82-$119.** 120 W Stevenson Rd. I-80, exit 90 (SR 23), just n. Int corridors. **Pets:** Other species. Designated rooms, service with restrictions, supervision.
🅰🆂🅺 🆂🄳 ⊠ 🎬 💻 ➿

PEKIN

◆◆ Comfort Inn 🆂🄷
(309) 353-4047. **$62-$85.** 3240 Vandever Ave. Just n of SR 9, 3 mi e from jct SR 29. Int corridors. **Pets:** Accepted.
🅰🆂🅺 🆂🄳 ⊠ 🎬 🎬 💻 ➿

PEORIA

ⒶⒶⒶ ◆◆◆◆ AmericInn Lodge & Suites 🆂🄷
(309) 692-9200. **$88-$139.** 9106 N Lindbergh Dr. SR 6, exit 6, 0.5 mi s. Int corridors. **Pets:** Small. $50 deposit/room. Designated rooms, service with restrictions, supervision.
🆂🄰🆅🄴 🆂🄳 ⊠ 🎬 🎬 🎬 💻 ➿

▼▼▼▼ Best Western Signature Inn 🆂🅷
(309) 685-2556. **$71-$79.** 4112 N Brandywine Dr. I-74, exit 89 (US 150/War Memorial Dr), just e, then just n. Int corridors. **Pets:** Accepted.

🅇 🎢 🛏 💻 ⇋

▼▼▼ Comfort Suites 🆂🅷
(309) 688-3800. **$70-$110.** 1812 N War Memorial Dr. I-74, exit 89 (US 150/War Memorial Dr), just e, then just s. Int corridors. **Pets:** Medium. Designated rooms, service with restrictions, supervision.

🅰🆂🅺 🆂🅾 🅇 🎢 🛏 💻 ⇋

🄰🄰🄰 ▼▼▼▼ Holiday Inn City Centre 🅻🅷
(309) 674-2500. **$129-$300.** 500 Hamilton Blvd. I-74, exit 92 (Glendale Ave) eastbound, just se; exit Jefferson St westbound, just nw; downtown. Int corridors. **Pets:** Accepted.

🆂🅰🆅🅴 🆂🅾 🅇 🎢 🛏 💻 🍴 ⇋ 🅇

▼▼▼▼ Holiday Inn Peoria I-74 at Northwoods Mall 🅻🅷
(309) 686-8000. **$87-$99.** 4400 N Brandywine Dr. I-74, exit 89 (US 150/War Memorial Dr), just nw. Int corridors. **Pets:** Accepted.

🅰🆂🅺 🆂🅾 🅇 🛏 💻 🍴 ⇋ 🅇

🄰🄰🄰 ▼▼▼▼ Jumer Hotel-Castle Lodge 🅻🅷
(309) 673-8040. **$85-$159.** 117 N Western Ave. I-74, exit 91 (University St), 1 mi s to Moss, then 0.7 mi w. Int corridors. **Pets:** Accepted.

🆂🅰🆅🅴 🆂🅾 🅇 🎢 🛏 💻 🍴 ⇋ 🅇

▼▼▼▼ Mark Twain Hotel 🆂🅷
(309) 676-3600. **$109-$119.** 225 NE Adams St. I-74, exit 98B (Adams St) westbound, just w; exit 93 eastbound; downtown. Int corridors. **Pets:** Accepted.

🅰🆂🅺 🆂🅾 🅇 🛏 💻 🍴 🅇

🄰🄰🄰 ▼▼▼ Red Roof Inn 🅼
(309) 685-3911. **$47-$63.** 4031 N War Memorial Dr. I-74, exit 89 (US 150/Memorial Dr), just e. Ext corridors. **Pets:** Medium. Service with restrictions, supervision.

🆂🅰🆅🅴 🅇 🎢 🅲 🛏

▼▼▼▼ Residence Inn by Marriott 🆂🅷
(309) 681-9000. **$109.** 4201 N War Memorial Dr. I-74, exit 89 (US 150/War Memorial Dr), just w. Int corridors. **Pets:** $10 daily fee/room, $25 one-time fee/room. Service with restrictions, crate.

🅰🆂🅺 🆂🅾 🅇 🎢 🛏 💻 ⇋ 🅇

▼▼ Sleep Inn & Suites 🆂🅷
(309) 682-3322. **$58-$78.** 4244 Brandywine Dr. I-74, exit 89 (US 150/Memorial Dr), just w to Brandywine Dr, then just ne. Int corridors. **Pets:** Small. Designated rooms, service with restrictions, supervision.

🅰🆂🅺 🆂🅾 🅇 🅴🅼 🎢 🅲 🛏 💻 ⇋

▼▼▼▼ Staybridge Suites Peoria-Downtown 🆂🅷
(309) 673-7829. **$69-$199.** 300 W Romeo B Garrett Ave. I-74, exit 92 (Glendale Ave), 0.5 mi w (Glendale Ave becomes William Kumpf St), then just w on Fourth Ave. Int corridors. **Pets:** Small, dogs only. $75 one-time fee/pet. Designated rooms, service with restrictions, crate.

🅰🆂🅺 🆂🅾 🅇 🛏 💻 ⇋ 🅇

▼▼ Super 8 Motel 🆂🅷
(309) 688-8074. **$62-$82.** 4025 N War Memorial Dr. I-74, exit 89 (US 150/War Memorial Dr), just e. Int corridors. **Pets:** Other species. $50 deposit/pet. Service with restrictions, supervision.

🅰🆂🅺 🆂🅾 🅇 🎢 🛏 💻

PERU

▼▼▼▼ La Quinta Inn 🆂🅷
(815) 224-9000. **$67-$77.** 4389 Venture Dr. I-80, exit 75 (SR 251), 0.4 mi s to 38th St, just w to Venture Dr, then 0.4 mi nw. Int corridors. **Pets:** Accepted.

🅰🆂🅺 🅇 🛏 💻 ⇋ 🅇

PONTOON BEACH

🄰🄰🄰 ▼▼▼ Best Western Camelot Inn 🆂🅷
(618) 931-2262. **$59-$79, 7 day notice.** 1240 E Old Chain of Rocks Rd. I-270, exit 6B (SR 111), just n. Int corridors. **Pets:** Small. $10 daily fee/pet. Designated rooms, service with restrictions, supervision.

🆂🅰🆅🅴 🆂🅾 🅇 🛏 💻 ⇋

QUAD CITIES AREA

MOLINE

🄰🄰🄰 ▼▼ Exel Inn of Moline 🆂🅷
(309) 797-5580. **$44-$64.** 2501 52nd Ave. I-280/74, exit 18A eastbound; exit 5B westbound, just s on US 6 and 150, then 1 mi nw on 27th St. Int corridors. **Pets:** Accepted.

🆂🅰🆅🅴 🆂🅾 🅇 🛏 💻

▼▼▼▼ Hampton Inn-Airport 🆂🅷
(309) 762-1711. **$79.** 6920 27th St. I-280/74, exit 18A eastbound; exit 5B westbound, just s on US 6 and 150, then just nw. Int corridors. **Pets:** Accepted.

🅰🆂🅺 🆂🅾 🅇 🎢 🛏 💻 ⇋

▼▼ Holiday Inn Express-Moline Airport 🆂🅷
(309) 762-8300. **$109.** 6910 27th St. I-280/74, exit 18A eastbound; exit 5B westbound, just s on US 6 and 150, then just nw. Int corridors. **Pets:** Medium, other species. $5 daily fee/pet. Service with restrictions.

🅰🆂🅺 🆂🅾 🅇 🎢 🛏 💻

◆◆ **Holiday Inn-Moline Convention Center Airport** [SH]
(309) 762-8811. **$79-$119.** 6902 27th St. I-280/74, exit 18A eastbound; exit 58 westbound, just s on US 6 and 150, just nw. Int corridors. **Pets:** Medium. Designated rooms, service with restrictions, supervision.
[ASK] [SD] ☒ ☎ ♿ ▣ ☕ 🍴 🏊 🏋

[AAA] ◆◆◆ **La Quinta Inn** [SH] 🐾
(309) 762-9008. **$66-$72.** 5450 27th St. I-280/74, exit 18A eastbound; exit 5B westbound, just s on US 6 and 150 to traffic light, then just nw. Int corridors. **Pets:** Other species. Service with restrictions.
[SAVE] ☒ ☎ ▣ ☕ 🏊

🐾 **END AREA** 🐾

QUINCY

◆◆ **Comfort Inn** [SH]
(217) 228-2700. **$55-$100.** 4122 Broadway. I-172, exit 14 (SR 104), 1.3 mi w. Int corridors. **Pets:** Other species. $10 daily fee/pet. Service with restrictions, supervision.
[ASK] [SD] ☒ ▣ ☕ 🏊

◆◆ **Super 8 Motel** [SH]
(217) 228-8808. **$43-$49.** 224 N 36th St. I-172, exit 14 (SR 104), 1.8 mi w, then just s. Int corridors. **Pets:** Accepted.
[ASK] [SD] ☒ ♿[M] ▣

RANTOUL

[AAA] ◆◆◆ **Best Western Heritage Inn** [SH]
(217) 892-9292. **$55-$85.** 420 S Murray Rd. I-57, exit 250 (US 136), 0.5 mi e, then just s. Ext corridors. **Pets:** Medium. $10 one-time fee/room. Service with restrictions, crate.
[SAVE] [SD] ☒ ▣ ☕ 🏊

◆◆ **Super 8 Motel** [SH]
(217) 893-8888. **$54-$84.** 207 S Murray Rd. I-57, exit 250 (US 136), just e. Int corridors. **Pets:** Small, dogs only. $5 daily fee/pet. Designated rooms, service with restrictions, supervision.
☒ ▣

ROBINSON

◆◆◆ **Best Western Robinson Inn** [SH]
(618) 544-8448. **$64-$105.** 1500 W Main St. 1 mi w on SR 33. Int corridors. **Pets:** Other species. $5 daily fee/pet. Service with restrictions.
[ASK] [SD] ☒ ☎ ▣ ☕

ROCHELLE

[AAA] ◆◆◆ **Comfort Inn & Suites** [SH]
(815) 562-5551. **$74-$184.** 1131 N 7th St. I-39, exit 99 (SR 38), 2.5 mi w; jct SR 38 and 251; downtown. Int corridors. **Pets:** Accepted.
[SAVE] [SD] ☒ ▣ ☕ 🍴 🏊 🏋

ROCK FALLS

[AAA] ◆◆◆ **Holiday Inn Rock Falls/Sterling** [SH]
(815) 626-5500. **$105-$125.** 2105 First Ave. I-88, exit 41 (SR 40), 0.4 mi n. Int corridors. **Pets:** Medium, other species. $20 one-time fee/room. Designated rooms, service with restrictions, crate.
[SAVE] ☒ ▣ ☕ 🍴 🏊 🏋

◆ **Rock Falls Super 8** [SH]
(815) 626-8800. **$50-$60.** 2100 First Ave. I-88, exit 41 (SR 40), 0.3 mi n, just w on W 21st St. Int corridors. **Pets:** $10 one-time fee/room. Service with restrictions, supervision.
[ASK] [SD] ☒ ▣

ROCKFORD

[AAA] ◆◆◆ **Baymont Inn & Suites Rockford** [SH]
(815) 229-8200. **$66-$150.** 662 N Lyford Rd. I-90, exit US 20 business route, just e, then just n. Int corridors. **Pets:** Accepted.
[SAVE] [SD] ☒ ▣ ☕ 🏊

[AAA] ◆ **Exel Inn of Rockford** [SH]
(815) 332-4915. **$46-$79.** 220 S Lyford Rd. I-90, exit US 20 business route, just e, then just s. Int corridors. **Pets:** Small, other species. Designated rooms, service with restrictions, supervision.
[SAVE] [SD] ☒ ▣ ☕

[AAA] ◆◆◆ **Quality Suites** [SH] 🐾
(815) 227-1300. **$70-$189.** 7401 Walton St. I-90, exit US 20 business route, just w to Bell School Rd, then just s. Int corridors. **Pets:** Medium. Service with restrictions, supervision.
[SAVE] [SD] ☒ ☎ ♿ ▣ ☕ 🏊 🏋

[AAA] ◆ **Red Roof Inn** [M]
(815) 398-9750. **$44-$76.** 7434 E State St. I-90, exit US 20 business route, just w. Ext corridors. **Pets:** Accepted.
[SAVE] ☒ ☎ ▣

◆◆◆ **Residence Inn by Marriott** [SH]
(815) 227-0013. **$110-$120.** 7542 Colosseum Dr. I-90, exit US 20 business route, just w. Int corridors. **Pets:** Medium. $200 one-time fee/room. Service with restrictions, crate.
[ASK] [SD] ☒ ☎ ♿ ▣ ☕ 🏊 🏋

[AAA] ◆◆ **Sleep Inn-Rockford** [SH]
(815) 398-8900. **$84-$129.** 725 Clark Dr. I-90, exit US 20 business route, just w to Bell School Rd, just n to Clark Dr, then 0.4 mi ne. Int corridors. **Pets:** Medium. $15 daily fee/room. Designated rooms, service with restrictions, supervision.
[SAVE] [SD] ☒ ♿ ▣ ☕

[AAA] ◆◆ **Travelodge** [SH]
(815) 398-5050. **$49-$99.** 4850 E State St. I-90, exit US 20 business route, 3.5 mi w. Int corridors. **Pets:** $10 daily fee/pet. Service with restrictions, supervision.
[SAVE] [SD] ☒ ☎ ▣ ☕ 🏊

SALEM

▼▼ **Super 8 Motel of Salem** SH
(618) 548-5882. **$62-$85.** 118 Woods Ln. I-57, exit 116 (US 50), just w. Ext/int corridors. **Pets:** Other species. Service with restrictions, supervision.
[ASK] [S🐾] [✕] [🕭M] [🕭] [🍽] [💻]

SAVOY

🆎 ▼▼ **Best Western Paradise Inn** SH
(217) 356-1824. **$69-$79, 3 day notice.** 1001 N Dunlap. I-57, exit 229, 1 mi e to US 45, then 2.5 mi n. Ext corridors. **Pets:** Small. $5 daily fee/pet. Service with restrictions, crate.
[SAVE] [S🐾] [✕] [🍽] [💻] [➿]

SOUTH JACKSONVILLE

🆎 ▼▼▼ **Comfort Inn-South Jacksonville** SH
(217) 245-8372. **$79-$109.** 200 Comfort Dr. I-72, exit 64, just n. Int corridors. **Pets:** Accepted.
[SAVE] [S🐾] [🍽] [💻] [➿]

SPRINGFIELD

▼▼▼ **Baymont Inn Springfield** SH 🐾
(217) 529-6655. **$75, 3 day notice.** 5871 S 6th St. I-55, exit 90 (Toronto Rd), just e to 6th St, then just n. Int corridors. **Pets:** Small, dogs only. Service with restrictions, supervision.
[ASK] [S🐾] [✕] [🕭M] [🕭] [🍽] [💻] [➿]

▼▼ **Comfort Inn** SH
(217) 787-2250. **$68-$90.** 3442 Freedom Dr. I-72, exit 93 (Veterans Pkwy), 0.7 mi n to Lindbergh Blvd, just w to Freedom Dr, then just s. Int corridors. **Pets:** Accepted.
[ASK] [S🐾] [✕] [🍽] [🕭] [💻] [➿]

▼▼ **Days Inn** M
(217) 529-0171. **$66-$79, 3 day notice.** 3000 Stevenson Dr. I-55, exit 94 (Stevenson Dr), just w. Ext corridors. **Pets:** $5 daily fee/pet. Service with restrictions, crate.
[ASK] [S🐾] [✕] [🍽] [🕭] [💻] [➿]

▼▼▼ **Drury Inn & Suites-Springfield** SH
(217) 529-3900. **$87-$107.** 3180 S Dirksen Pkwy. I-55, exit 94 (Stevenson Dr), just w to Dirksen Pkwy, then just n. Int corridors. **Pets:** Large, other species. Service with restrictions, supervision.
[ASK] [✕] [🕭M] [🍽] [🍽] [🕭] [💻] [➿] [🍽]

▼▼ **Howard Johnson Inn & Suites** M
(217) 541-8762. **$79-$130.** 1701 J David Jones Pkwy. 1.5 mi s of Capital Airport on SR 29; opposite west entrance to Lincoln's tomb. Ext corridors. **Pets:** Medium. $25 deposit/pet. Service with restrictions, supervision.
[ASK] [S🐾] [✕] [🕭] [💻] [🍴] [➿]

🆎 ▼▼▼ **Mansion View Inn & Suites** SH
(217) 544-7411. **$79-$129.** 529 S 4th St. I-55, exit 92 (6th St), 3.9 mi n to Edwards St, then just w, follow signs. Ext/int corridors. **Pets:** Accepted.
[SAVE] [S🐾] [✕] [🍽] [🕭] [💻]

▼▼ **Pear Tree Inn by Drury-Springfield** SH
(217) 529-9100. **$60-$86.** 3190 S Dirksen Pkwy. I-55, exit 94 (Stevenson Dr), just w. Int corridors. **Pets:** Accepted.
[ASK] [✕] [🍽] [💻]

🆎 ▼▼▼▼ **Quality Inn & Suites-State House** SH
(217) 528-5100. **$79-$99.** 101 E Adams St. Jct 1st and Adams sts; just n of the State House. Int corridors. **Pets:** Accepted.
[SAVE] [S🐾] [✕] [🕭M] [🍽] [🍽] [🕭] [💻]

▼▼ **Ramada Limited (South)** SH
(217) 529-1410. **$55-$69.** 5970 S 6th St. I-55, exit 90 (Toronto Rd), 0.3 mi e. Int corridors. **Pets:** Accepted.
[ASK] [S🐾] [✕] [🕭] [💻] [➿]

🆎 ▼ **Red Roof Inn** M
(217) 753-4302. **$44-$61.** 3200 Singer Ave. I-55, exit 96B, just w. Ext corridors. **Pets:** Medium. Service with restrictions, supervision.
[SAVE] [✕] [🍽] [🍽]

▼▼▼ **Signature Inn & Conference Center** SH
(217) 529-6611. **$71-$79.** 3090 Stevenson Dr. I-55, exit 94 (Stevenson Dr), just w. Int corridors. **Pets:** Small. Service with restrictions, crate.
[✕] [🕭M] [🍽] [🍽] [🕭] [💻] [➿] [🍽]

▼▼ **Sleep Inn** SH
(217) 787-6200. **$55-$75.** 3470 Freedom Dr. I-72, exit 93 (Veterans Pkwy), 0.7 mi n to Lindbergh Blvd, just w to Freedom Dr, then just s. Int corridors. **Pets:** Other species. $25 one-time fee/room. Service with restrictions, crate.
[ASK] [S🐾] [✕] [🍽] [🍽] [🕭] [💻]

▼▼ **Super 8 Springfield South** SH
(217) 529-8898. **$44-$54.** 3675 S 6th St. I-55, exit 92A (Business Rt US 55), just n to Hazel Bell, just w to Access Rd, then just n. Int corridors. **Pets:** $25 deposit/room, $5 daily fee/pet. No service, crate.
[ASK] [S🐾] [✕] [🕭] [💻]

STAUNTON

▼▼ **Staunton Super 8** SH
(618) 635-5353. **$51-$53.** 1527 Herman Rd. I-55, exit 41, 0.3 mi w. Int corridors. **Pets:** Other species. Designated rooms, service with restrictions, crate.
[ASK] [S🐾] [✕] [🍽] [🕭] [💻]

SYCAMORE

▼▼ **Microtel Inn & Suites** SH
(815) 899-6500. **$54-$64.** 1860 Dekalb Ave. On SR 23, 0.9 mi s of Peace Rd. Int corridors. **Pets:** Accepted.
[ASK] [S🐾] [✕] [🕭M] [🍽] [🕭] [💻]

TROY

▼▼ **Red Roof Inn** SH
(618) 667-2222. **$39-$99.** 2030 Formosa Rd. I-55/70, exit 18, just w. Int corridors. **Pets:** Large, other species. Service with restrictions, supervision.
[ASK] [S🐾] [✕] [🕭M] [🍽] [🍽] [🕭] [➿]

TUSCOLA

▼▼▼ Holiday Inn Express SH
(217) 253-6363. **$72-$99.** 1201 Tuscola Blvd. I-57, exit 212
(US 36), 0.3 mi w to Progress Blvd, just s to Tuscola Blvd,
then 0.4 mi se. Int corridors. **Pets:** Other species. Designated rooms, service with restrictions, supervision.
ASK SÁ ✕ Ꮭᴹ 📶 💻 ≈

▼▼▼ Super 8 Motel-Tuscola SH
(217) 253-5488. **$55.** 1007 E Hwy 36. I-57, exit 212 (US 36),
0.4 mi w. Int corridors. **Pets:** Accepted.
ASK SÁ ✕ 📶 💻

URBANA

⚑⚑ ▼▼▼ Ramada
Limited-Urbana/Champaign SH ✿
(217) 328-4400. **$75-$92.** 902 W Killarney St. I-74, exit 183
(Lincoln Ave), just s to Killarney St, then just w. Int corridors.
Pets: $50 deposit/room. Service with restrictions, supervision.
SAVE SÁ ✕ 📶 💻 ≈

▼▼ Sleep Inn SH ✿
(217) 367-6000. **$67-$115.** 1908 N Lincoln Ave. I-74, exit
183 (Lincoln Ave), 0.5 mi s. Int corridors. **Pets:** Other species. $6 one-time fee/room. Service with restrictions.
ASK SÁ ✕ 🛋 📶 💻 ≈

VANDALIA

⚑⚑ ▼▼▼ Days Inn M
(618) 283-4400. **$60-$78.** 1920 Kennedy Blvd. I-70, exit 63
(US 51), 0.6 mi n. Ext corridors. **Pets:** Medium, other species. $10 deposit/room. Designated rooms, service with
restrictions, supervision.
SAVE SÁ ✕ 📶 💻 ≈

⚑⚑ ▼▼▼ Jay's Inn M
(618) 283-1200. **$48-$60.** 720 Gochenour St. I-70, exit 63
(US 51), just s. Ext corridors. **Pets:** Other species. Service
with restrictions.
SAVE SÁ ✕ 📶 💻

⚑⚑ ▼▼▼▼ Ramada Limited Vandalia SH
(618) 283-1400. **$51-$65.** 2707 Veterans Ave. I-70, exit 61,
just s. Int corridors. **Pets:** Other species. $10 one-time fee/
room. Designated rooms, crate.
SAVE SÁ ✕ 📶 💻 ≈

▼▼▼ Travelodge of Vandalia M
(618) 283-2363. **$43-$66.** 1500 N 6th St. I-70, exit 63 (US
51), just s. Ext corridors. **Pets:** Other species. $3 daily
fee/pet. Service with restrictions, supervision.
ASK SÁ ✕ 📶 💻 ≈

WASHINGTON

▼▼ Super 8 Motel SH
(309) 444-8881. **$49-$69.** 1884 Washington Rd. On Business Rt SR 24, 1.5 mi w. Int corridors. **Pets:** Medium. $5
daily fee/pet. Designated rooms, service with restrictions,
supervision.
ASK SÁ ✕ 📶

WATSEKA

⚑⚑ ▼▼▼ Super 8 Motel SH
(815) 432-6000. **$60-$70.** 710 W Walnut. On US 24; center
of downtown. Int corridors. **Pets:** Medium, other species. $3
daily fee/pet. Service with restrictions, supervision.
SAVE SÁ ✕ 📶

WEST CITY

▼▼ Days Inn of Benton/West City SH
(618) 439-3183. **$50-$89.** 711 W Main St. I-57, exit 71 (SR
14), just e. Int corridors. **Pets:** Small. $10 daily fee/pet.
Service with restrictions, supervision.
ASK SÁ ✕ Ꮭᴹ 🛋 📶 🍴

▼▼ Super 8 Motel of Benton/West City SH
(618) 438-8205. **$50-$89.** 711 1/2 W Main St. I-57, exit 71
(SR 14), just e. Int corridors. **Pets:** Small. $10 daily fee/pet.
Service with restrictions, supervision.
ASK SÁ ✕ 🛋 📶

INDIANA

CITY INDEX

ANGOLA

Best Western Angola Inn M
(260) 665-9561. **$55-$90, 15 day notice.** 3155 W US 20. I-69, exit 148 (US 20). Ext corridors. **Pets:** Medium. $7 one-time fee/room. Service with restrictions, supervision.

Ramada Inn SH
(260) 665-9471. **$75-$135.** 3855 N SR 127. I-69, exit 154, just e, then 0.4 mi s. Int corridors. **Pets:** Medium. $25 one-time fee/room. Service with restrictions, supervision.

AUBURN

Holiday Inn Express SH
(260) 925-1900. **$88.** 404 Touring Dr. I-69, exit 129, just e off SR 8. Int corridors. **Pets:** Other species. Designated rooms, service with restrictions, supervision.

La Quinta Inn-Auburn SH
(260) 920-1900. **Call for rates.** 306 Touring Dr. I-69, exit 129, 0.5 mi e on SR 8. Int corridors. **Pets:** Other species. Designated rooms, service with restrictions, supervision.

Super 8 Motel-Auburn SH
(260) 927-8800. **$68-$74, 30 day notice.** 503 Ley Dr. I-69, exit 129, just e. Int corridors. **Pets:** $50 deposit/room, $10 one-time fee/pet. Designated rooms, service with restrictions, crate.

BEDFORD

Bedford Super 8 SH
(812) 275-8881. **$60-$150.** 501 Bell Back Rd. Jct SR 37 and 58, just e on SR 58. Int corridors. **Pets:** $10 daily fee/pet. No service.

Holiday Inn Express SH
(812) 279-1206. **$85-$99.** 2800 Express Ln. On US 50/SR 37, 1.4 mi s from jct SR 450. Int corridors. **Pets:** Small, dogs only. $10 daily fee/pet. Service with restrictions, crate.

BLOOMINGTON

Hampton Inn SH
(812) 334-2100. **$80-$170, 30 day notice.** 2100 N Walnut St. 1 mi e of jct SR 37 on SR 45/46 Bypass, just s on College Ave/Walnut St. Int corridors. **Pets:** Medium. Designated rooms, service with restrictions, crate.

TownePlace Suites By Marriott SH
(812) 334-1234. **$89-$199.** 105 S Franklin Rd. Just e from SR 37 at Third St, 0.3 mi n. Int corridors. **Pets:** Medium. $75 one-time fee/room. Service with restrictions.

BLUFFTON

Budget Inn M
(260) 824-0820. **$38-$42.** 1090 N Main St. Jct SR 1 and 116; north side of town. Ext corridors. **Pets:** Accepted.

BRAZIL

Howard Johnson Express Inn M
(812) 446-2345. **$40-$100.** 935 W SR 42. I-70, exit 23, just s to SR 42, then just e. Ext corridors. **Pets:** Accepted.

CHESTERTON

Super 8 Motel SH
(219) 929-5549. **$58-$76, 5 day notice.** 418 Council Dr. I-94, exit 26A, just s, just e on Indian Boundary Rd, then just s; I-80/90, exit 31, 3 mi n on SR 49, then just se. Int corridors. **Pets:** Accepted.

NEARBY OHIO
CINCINNATI METROPOLITAN AREA

LAWRENCEBURG

▼▼▼▼ Quality Inn & Suites SH
(812) 539-4770. **$79-$169.** 1000 E Eads Pkwy. I-275, exit 16, 0.5 mi w on US 50. Int corridors. **Pets:** Medium. $20 daily fee/room. Service with restrictions, supervision.
(ASK) [S] [X] [✦] [🛏] [💻] [➤]

❈ END METROPOLITAN AREA ❈

CLARKSVILLE

▼▼ Best Western Green Tree Inn M
(812) 288-9281. **$69-$89.** 1425 Broadway St. I-65, exit 4, just w. Ext corridors. **Pets:** Small, dogs only. Designated rooms, service with restrictions.
(ASK) [S] [X] [🛏] [💻] [➤]

CLOVERDALE

▼▼▼ Holiday Inn Express SH
(765) 795-5050. **$80-$89, 7 day notice.** 1017 N Main St. I-70, exit 41. Int corridors. **Pets:** Other species. $10 one-time fee/room. Designated rooms, service with restrictions, crate.
(ASK) [S] [X] [✦M] [🐾] [🛏] [💻] [➤]

▼▼ Super 8 Motel Cloverdale/Greencastle SH
(765) 795-7373. **$50-$135.** 1020 N Main St. I-70, exit 41, just s. Int corridors. **Pets:** Accepted.
(ASK) [S] [X] [✦] [🛏] [💻] [➤]

COLUMBIA CITY

AAA ▼▼▼▼ AmeriHost Inn & Suites SH
(260) 248-4551. **$75-$87.** 701 W Connexion Way. 1 mi w, just off US 30. Int corridors. **Pets:** Accepted.
(SAVE) [S] [X] [✦M] [✦] [🛏] [💻] [➤] [X]

COLUMBUS

AAA ▼▼▼▼ Columbus Holiday Inn and Conference Center SH
(812) 372-1541. **$80-$120.** 2480 Jonathan Moore Pike. I-65, exit 68, just e on SR 46. Ext/int corridors. **Pets:** Accepted.
(SAVE) [S] [X] [✦M] [🐾] [🛏] [💻] [🍴] [➤] [X]

AAA ▼▼▼ Days Inn Columbus SH
(812) 376-9951. **$59-$94.** 3445 Jonathan Moore Pike. I-65, exit 68, just w. Int corridors. **Pets:** Accepted.
(SAVE) [S] [X] [🛏] [💻] [➤]

▼▼▼ Ramada Inn SH
(812) 376-3051. **$89-$119.** 2485 Jonathan Moore Pike. I-65, exit 68, just e on SR 46. Int corridors. **Pets:** Large, other species. $35 deposit/room. Service with restrictions, crate.
(ASK) [S] [X] [🛏] [💻] [➤]

CRAWFORDSVILLE

AAA ▼▼▼▼ Comfort Inn SH
(765) 361-0665. **$79-$150.** 2991 N Gandhi Dr. I-74, exit 34, just s on US 231. Int corridors. **Pets:** Very small. $10 daily fee/pet. Designated rooms, service with restrictions, supervision.
(SAVE) [S] [X] [🛏] [💻] [➤]

▼▼▼▼ Holiday Inn-Crawfordsville SH
(765) 362-8700. **$62-$135.** 2500 N Lafayette Rd. I-74, exit 34, 0.3 mi s on US 231. Ext corridors. **Pets:** Small. $10 daily fee/room. Designated rooms, service with restrictions, supervision.
(ASK) [S] [X] [✦M] [🐾] [✦] [🛏] [💻] [🍴] [➤]

DALE

▼▼▼ Baymont Inn & Suites Dale SH
(812) 937-7000. **$70-$230.** 20857 N US 231. I-64, exit 57 (US 231), just s. Int corridors. **Pets:** $50 deposit/room. Designated rooms, service with restrictions, supervision.
(ASK) [S] [X] [✦M] [✦] [🛏] [💻] [➤]

▼ Motel 6 #4068 SH
(812) 937-2294. **$46-$116.** 20840 N US Hwy 231. I-64, exit 57 (US 231), just s. Int corridors. **Pets:** Medium, other species. No service, supervision.
(ASK) [X] [🛏] [➤]

DECATUR

AAA ▼▼ AmeriHost Inn Decatur SH
(260) 728-4600. **$72-$75.** 1201 S 13th St. On US 27 and 33, 1 mi s of jct US 224. Int corridors. **Pets:** Medium, other species. Service with restrictions, crate.
(SAVE) [X] [✦M] [🐾] [✦] [🛏] [💻] [➤]

▼▼ Comfort Inn of Decatur SH ❈
(260) 724-8888. **$69-$89.** 1302 S 13th St. 1 mi s on US 27 and 33. Int corridors. **Pets:** Small, dogs only. $5 daily fee/pet. Designated rooms, service with restrictions, crate.
(ASK) [S] [X] [✦M] [🐾] [✦] [🛏] [💻] [➤]

▼▼ Days Inn SH
(260) 728-2196. **$55.** 1033 N 13th St. On US 27 and 33, 0.5 mi n of jct US 224. Ext/int corridors. **Pets:** Accepted.
(ASK) [S] [X] [🛏] [💻] [➤]

ELKHART

AAA ▼▼▼ Econo Lodge **M**
(574) 262-0540. **$35-$59, 7 day notice.** 3440 Cassopolis St. I-80/90, exit 92, 0.3 mi n. Ext corridors. **Pets:** Large. $5 daily fee/pet. Service with restrictions, supervision.
SAVE S X 🖶 💻

▼▼▼▼ Quality Inn & Suites **SH**
(574) 264-0404. **$69-$165.** 3321 Plaza Ct. I-80/90, exit 92, just n. Int corridors. **Pets:** Small. $10 one-time fee/pet. No service.
ASK S X 🖶 💻 ≈

AAA ▼▼▼ Red Roof Inn-Elkhart **M**
(574) 262-3691. **$46-$74.** 2902 Cassopolis St. I-80/90, exit 92, 0.5 mi s. Ext corridors. **Pets:** Large, other species. Service with restrictions.
SAVE X 🖉 🔌 🖶

▼▼▼ Signature Inn Elkhart **SH**
(574) 264-7222. **$78-$87.** 3010 Brittany Ct. I-80/90, exit 92, 0.3 mi s on SR 19. Int corridors. **Pets:** Small. Service with restrictions, crate.
X 🖉 🖶 💻 ≈

▼▼ Super 8 Motel-Elkhart **SH**
(574) 264-4457. **$49-$80, 7 day notice.** 345 Windsor Ave. I-80/90, exit 92, 0.3 mi s on SR 19. Int corridors. **Pets:** Accepted.
ASK S X 🖶 💻

EVANSVILLE

AAA ▼▼▼▼ Baymont Inn & Suites Evansville East **SH** ❀
(812) 477-2677. **$59-$63.** 8005 E Division St. I-164, exit 7B (SR 66/Lloyd Expwy), 0.5 mi w to Cross Pointe Blvd, just n to Division St, then 0.5 mi e. Int corridors. **Pets:** Very small. Designated rooms, service with restrictions, supervision.
SAVE S X 🖳 🔌 🖶 💻 ≈

AAA ▼▼▼▼ Baymont Inn & Suites Evansville West **SH**
(812) 421-9773. **$89-$99.** 5737 Pearl Dr. Jct US 41 and SR 62, 5.7 mi w on SR 62, just s on Boehne Camp Rd. Int corridors. **Pets:** Medium. $15 one-time fee/room. Service with restrictions, supervision.
SAVE S X 🖳 🔌 🖶 💻 ≈

AAA ▼▼▼▼ Casino Aztar Hotel **LH**
(812) 433-4000. **$74-$114.** 421 NW Riverside Dr. SR 62 (Lloyd Expwy), just s on Fulton. Int corridors. **Pets:** Small, dogs only. $100 deposit/pet. Service with restrictions.
SAVE S X 🖳 🔌 🖶 💻 🍴

▼▼▼▼ Comfort Inn East **SH**
(812) 476-3600. **$58-$61.** 8331 E Walnut St. I-164, exit 7B (SR 66/Lloyd Expwy), 0.5 mi w to Eagle Crest Blvd, 0.3 mi se to Fuquay St, just s to Walnut St, then 0.4 mi e. Int corridors. **Pets:** Medium. $10 daily fee/room. Service with restrictions, crate.
ASK S X 🖳 🖉 🔌 🖶 💻 ≈

▼▼▼▼ Drury Inn & Suites Evansville East **SH**
(812) 471-3400. **$77-$97.** 100 Cross Pointe Blvd. I-164, exit 7B (SR 66/Lloyd Expwy). 0.5 mi w. Int corridors. **Pets:** Large, other species. Service with restrictions, supervision.
ASK X 🖳 🖉 🔌 🖶 💻 ≈

▼▼▼▼ Drury Inn-Evansville North **SH**
(812) 423-5818. **$69-$91.** 3901 US 41 N. On US 41, 2.5 mi n of jct SR 62 and 66 (Lloyd Expwy), 3.3 mi sw of Regional Airport entrance. Int corridors. **Pets:** Large, other species. Service with restrictions, supervision.
ASK X 🖶 💻 ≈ ⊗

▼▼ Econo Lodge East **SH**
(812) 477-2211. **$55-$60.** 5006 Morgan Ave. I-164, exit 9, 1.5 mi w on SR 62. Int corridors. **Pets:** Accepted.
ASK S X 🖶 💻 ≈

▼▼ Evansville Microtel Inn & Suites **SH**
(812) 471-9340. **$44-$84.** 1930 Cross Pointe Blvd. I-164, exit 9, just w. Int corridors. **Pets:** Accepted.
ASK S X 🖶 💻

▼▼▼ HomeLife Studios & Suites **M**
(812) 475-1700. **$44-$54.** 100 S Green River Rd. I-164, exit 7B (SR 66/Lloyd Expwy), 2 mi w to Green River Rd, then just s. Ext corridors. **Pets:** Medium. Designated rooms, service with restrictions, crate.
X 🖉 🔌 🖶 💻 ≈

AAA ▼▼▼▼ Quality Inn & Suites East **SH** ❀
(812) 471-3414. **$89-$169.** 8015 E Division St. I-164, exit 7B (SR 66/Lloyd Expwy), 0.5 mi w to Cross Pointe Blvd, just n, then 0.5 mi e. Int corridors. **Pets:** Small, other species. $10 daily fee/room. Service with restrictions, supervision.
SAVE S X 🖳 🔌 🖶 💻 ≈

▼▼▼▼ Residence Inn Hotel **SH**
(812) 471-7191. **$104, 10 day notice.** 8283 E Walnut St. I-164, exit 7B (SR 66/Lloyd Expwy), 0.5 mi w to Eagle Crest Blvd, 0.3 mi se to Fuquay St, then 0.3 mi e. Int corridors. **Pets:** Medium, other species. $200 one-time fee/pet. Service with restrictions, crate.
ASK S X 🖳 🖉 🔌 🖶 💻 ≈ ⊗

▼▼ Signature Inn Evansville **SH**
(812) 476-9626. **$71-$79.** 1101 N Green River Rd. I-164, exit 9 (SR 62 E/Morgan Ave), 1.5 mi w on SR 62, then just s. Int corridors. **Pets:** Small. Service with restrictions, crate.
X 🖉 🖶 💻 ≈

▼▼ Super 8 **SH**
(812) 476-4008. **$48-$70.** 4600 Morgan Ave. I-164, exit 9 (SR 62 E/Morgan Ave), 1.7 mi w on SR 62. Int corridors. **Pets:** Accepted.
ASK S X 🖶

FORT WAYNE

AAA ▼▼▼▼ AmeriSuites (Ft Wayne) **SH**
(260) 471-8522. **$69-$99.** 111 W Washington Center Rd. I-69, exit 112A, just w of Coldwater Rd. Int corridors. **Pets:** Accepted.
SAVE S X 🖶 💻 ≈

▼▼ Baymont Inn Fort Wayne 🆂🅷
(260) 489-2220. **$50-$75.** 1005 W Washington Center Rd. I-69, exit 111B, 0.5 mi e. Int corridors. **Pets:** Accepted.

A$K 🆂🔟 ✖ 🔊 🎮 🛑 🖭

▼▼▼ Fort Wayne Marriott 🅻🅷
(260) 484-0411. **$179.** 305 E Washington Center Rd. I-69, exit 112A. Int corridors. **Pets:** $50 one-time fee/room. Service with restrictions, supervision.

A$K ✖ 🔊 🖭 🍽 🏊 ✖

▼▼ Lees Inn & Suites 🆂🅷
(260) 489-8888. **$84-$89.** 5707 Challenger Pkwy. I-69, exit 111B, just n on SR 3, then just w. Int corridors. **Pets:** Accepted.

A$K 🆂🔟 ✖ 🛑 🖭 🏊

▲▲▲ ▼▼▼ Red Roof Inn-Fort Wayne 🅼 🐾
(260) 484-8641. **$46-$66.** 2920 Goshen Rd. I-69, exit 109A, jct US 30 Bypass. Ext corridors. **Pets:** Medium. Service with restrictions, crate.

SAVE ✖ 🔊

▼▼▼▼ Residence Inn by Marriott North 🆂🅷
(260) 484-4700. **$79-$109.** 4919 Lima Rd. I-69, exit 111A, just s. Ext corridors. **Pets:** Other species. $50 one-time fee/room. Service with restrictions.

A$K 🆂🔟 ✖ 🛑 🖭 🏊 ✖

▼▼▼▼ Residence Inn Southwest 🆂🅷
(260) 432-8000. **$99-$139.** 7811 W Jefferson Blvd. I-69, exit 102. Int corridors. **Pets:** Medium. $200 one-time fee/room. Service with restrictions, supervision.

A$K 🆂🔟 ✖ 🔊 🛑 🖭 🏊 ✖

▼▼ Signature Inn Fort Wayne 🆂🅷
(260) 489-5554. **$71-$79.** 1734 W Washington Center Rd. I-69, exit 111B. Int corridors. **Pets:** Small. Service with restrictions, crate.

✖ 🔊 🛑 🖭 🏊

FRANKFORT

▼▼▼▼ Holiday Inn Express 🆂🅷
(765) 659-4400. **$85.** 592 S CR 200 W. I-65, exit 158, 6.1 mi e; jct US 421/SR 38/39, 1.8 mi w. Int corridors. **Pets:** Designated rooms, service with restrictions, supervision.

A$K 🆂🔟 ✖ 🔊 🔊 🖭 🏊

GAS CITY

▼▼ Super 8 Motel Gas City 🆂🅷
(765) 998-6800. **$45-$65.** 5172 S Kaybee Dr. I-69, exit 59. Int corridors. **Pets:** Other species. $15 one-time fee/pet. Service with restrictions, crate.

A$K 🆂🔟 ✖ 🔊

GEORGETOWN

▼▼ Motel 6-4097 🆂🅷
(812) 923-0441. **$52-$56.** 1079 N Luther Rd. I-64, exit 118, just w on SR 64. Int corridors. **Pets:** Other species. Service with restrictions, supervision.

A$K ✖ 🔊 🛑 🏊

GOSHEN

▲▲▲ ▼▼▼ Best Western Inn 🅼
(574) 533-0408. **$69.** 900 Lincolnway E. 1 mi se on US 33. Ext corridors. **Pets:** Designated rooms, service with restrictions, supervision.

SAVE 🆂🔟 ✖ 🖭

GREENCASTLE

▲▲▲ ▼ College Inn 🅼
(765) 653-4167. **$41-$56.** 315 Bloomington St. I-70, exit 41, 8 mi n on US 231. Ext corridors. **Pets:** Accepted.

SAVE 🆂🔟 ✖ 🛑

GREENSBURG

▼▼▼▼ Holiday Inn Express 🆂🅷
(812) 663-5500. **$79-$99.** 915 Ann Blvd. I-74, exit 134A, 1.4 mi s on SR 3. Int corridors. **Pets:** Other species. Service with restrictions, supervision.

A$K 🆂🔟 ✖ 🔊 🛑 🖭 🏊

HAMMOND

▼▼▼▼ Best Western Northwest Indiana Inn 🆂🅷
(219) 844-2140. **$78-$88.** 3830 179th St. I-80/94, exit 5 (Cline Ave), 0.6 mi s to frontage road, then 0.6 mi n. Int corridors. **Pets:** Medium. $30 deposit/room, $5 one-time fee/pet. Designated rooms, service with restrictions, supervision.

A$K 🆂🔟 ✖ 🔊 🛑 🖭 🍽 🏊

▼▼▼▼ Residence Inn by Marriott 🆂🅷
(219) 844-8440. **$129-$169.** 7740 Corinne Dr. I-80/94, exit 3 (Kennedy Ave S), just s. Int corridors. **Pets:** Accepted.

A$K ✖ 🎮 🔊 🔊 🛑 🖭 🏊 ✖

HAUBSTADT

▲▲▲ ▼▼▼ Quality Inn Evansville North 🆂🅷 🐾
(812) 768-5878. **$70-$103.** RR 1, Box 252 (Hwy 41 & I-64). I-64, exit 25B, 0.4 mi n on US 41 to Warrenton Rd, just w to frontage road, then 0.3 mi s. Int corridors. **Pets:** $15 one-time fee/room. Service with restrictions, crate.

SAVE 🆂🔟 ✖ 🔊 🛑 🖭 🏊

HOWE

▲▲▲ ▼▼▼ Super 8 Motel 🆂🅷
(260) 562-2828. **$64-$99.** 7333 N SR 9. I-80/90, exit 121, 0.5 mi s. Int corridors. **Pets:** Large. Service with restrictions, supervision.

SAVE 🆂🔟 ✖ 🎮 🔊 🔊 🛑

INDIANAPOLIS METROPOLITAN AREA

ANDERSON

▼▼ Best Inns SH ☙
(765) 644-2000. **$38-$43.** 5706 Scatterfield Rd. I-69, exit 26, just w on SR 9. Int corridors. **Pets:** Medium. $5 daily fee/room. Service with restrictions, supervision.

ASK S⊘ ✕ 🕸 🖵

▼▼ Econo Lodge SH
(765) 644-4422. **$45-$60.** 2205 E 59th St. I-69, exit 26, on SR 9. Int corridors. **Pets:** Accepted.

ASK S⊘ ✕ 🕸 🔔 🖵 ➢

▼▼ Hampton Inn SH
(765) 622-0700. **$79-$139.** 2312 Hampton Dr. I-69, exit 26, just e. Int corridors. **Pets:** Small. $35 one-time fee/pet. Service with restrictions, supervision.

ASK S⊘ ✕ ♿M 🕸 🔔 🖵 ➢

▼▼ Super 8 Motel SH
(765) 642-2222. **$50-$56.** 2215 E 59th St. I-69, exit 26. Int corridors. **Pets:** Medium, other species. $8 daily fee/pet. Service with restrictions, crate.

ASK S⊘ ✕ 🔔 🖵 ➢

CARMEL

▼▼▼ Country Inn & Suites By Carlson-Indianapolis North SH
(317) 876-0333. **$84-$159.** 9797 N Michigan Rd. I-465, exit 27, 0.3 mi n on US 421. Int corridors. **Pets:** Medium. $50 daily fee/pet. Designated rooms, service with restrictions, supervision.

ASK S⊘ ✕ ♿M 🕸 🔔 🖵 ➢

▼▼▼ Residence Inn by Marriott Indianapolis/Carmel SH
(317) 846-2000. **$119-$209.** 11895 N Meridian St. I-465, exit 31, 2 mi n on US 31, just e on 116th St, then just n on Pennsylvania Rd. Int corridors. **Pets:** Accepted.

ASK S⊘ ✕ 🕸 🔔 🖵 ➢ ✕

▼▼ Signature Inn Carmel SH
(317) 816-1616. **$84-$94.** 10201 N Meridian St. I-465, exit 31, 0.3 mi n on US 31. Int corridors. **Pets:** Small. Service with restrictions, crate.

✕ 🕸 🔔 🖵 ➢ ✕

CHESTERFIELD

▼▼ Super 8 Motel SH
(765) 378-0888. **$47-$57.** 15701 W Commerce Rd. I-69, exit 34, just w. Ext/int corridors. **Pets:** $25 deposit/room, $5 one-time fee/room. Service with restrictions, supervision.

ASK S⊘ ✕

EDINBURGH

⬥⬥⬥ ▼▼▼ Best Western Horizon Inn SH
(812) 526-9883. **$55-$149.** 11780 N US 31. I-65, exit 76B, just n. Int corridors. **Pets:** Dogs only. $10 one-time fee/room. Service with restrictions, supervision.

SAVE S⊘ ✕ 🔔 🖵 ➢

FISHERS

▼▼▼ Frederick-Talbott Inn BB
(317) 578-3600. **$99-$150, 7 day notice.** 13805 Allisonville Rd. I-465, exit 35 (Allisonville Rd), 6.2 mi n; I-69, exit 5, 1.8 mi w on 116th St to Allisonville Rd, then 2.2 mi n. Int corridors. **Pets:** Medium, dogs only. Designated rooms, service with restrictions, supervision.

ASK S⊘ ✕

▼▼▼ Residence Inn by Marriott Indianapolis/Fishers SH ☙
(317) 842-1111. **$109-$159.** 9765 Crosspoint Blvd. I-69, exit 3, just nw. Int corridors. **Pets:** Other species. $75 daily fee/pet, $150 one-time fee/pet. Service with restrictions, crate.

ASK S⊘ ✕ ♿M 🕸 🕮 🔔 🖵 ➢ ✕

▼▼▼ Staybridge Suites Indianapolis-Fishers SH
(317) 577-9500. **$95-$105.** 9780 Crosspoint Blvd. I-69, exit 3, just nw. Int corridors. **Pets:** Medium. $75 one-time fee/room. Service with restrictions, crate.

ASK S⊘ ✕ ♿M 🕸 🕮 🔔 🖵 ➢ ✕

GREENFIELD

⬥⬥⬥ ▼▼ Comfort Inn-Greenfield/Indianapolis SH
(317) 467-9999. **$79-$189.** 178 E Martindale Dr. I-70, exit 104. Int corridors. **Pets:** Accepted.

SAVE S⊘ ✕ 🔔 🖵 ➢

GREENWOOD

▼▼ Comfort Inn Greenwood M
(317) 887-1515. **$59-$250.** 110 Sheek Rd. I-65, exit 99. Ext corridors. **Pets:** Accepted.

ASK S⊘ ✕ 🔔 🖵 ➢

▼▼▼ Lees Inn & Suites SH
(317) 865-0100. **$89.** 1281 S Park Dr. I-65, exit 99. Int corridors. **Pets:** Accepted.

ASK S⊘ ✕ ♿M 🕸 🕮 🔔 🖵 ➢

INDIANAPOLIS

⬥⬥⬥ ▼▼▼ AmeriSuites (Indianapolis/Airport-Speedway) SH
(317) 227-0950. **$89-$109.** 5500 Bradbury Ave. I-465, exit 11A, 0.3 mi e on Airport Expwy to Executive Dr exit. Int corridors. **Pets:** Accepted.

SAVE S⊘ ✕ ♿M 🕸 🔔 🖵 ➢

⬥⬥⬥ ▼▼▼ AmeriSuites (Indianapolis/Keystone) SH
(317) 843-0064. **$105-$115.** 9104 Keystone Crossing. I-465, exit 33, 0.5 mi s on SR 431, just e on 86th St, then 0.5 mi n. Int corridors. **Pets:** Accepted.

SAVE S⊘ ✕ 🕸 🕮 🔔 🖵 ➢

Baymont Inn & Suites Indianapolis-Airport SH
(317) 244-8100. **$79-$99.** 2650 Executive Dr. I-465, exit 11, 0.3 mi e. Int corridors. **Pets:** Accepted.

Baymont Inn & Suites Indianapolis East SH
(317) 897-2300. **$79-$99.** 2349 Post Dr. I-70, exit 91 (Post Rd), just n. Int corridors. **Pets:** Accepted.

Best Western Airport Suites SH
(317) 246-1505. **$69-$89.** 55 S High School Rd. I-465, exit 13B. Int corridors. **Pets:** Accepted.

Best Western Castleton Inn SH
(317) 842-9190. **$53-$199.** 8300 Craig St. I-69, exit 1, 0.5 mi w to Craig St, then just n. Int corridors. **Pets:** Large, other species. $25 one-time fee/room. Service with restrictions.

Comfort Inn & Suites City Centre SH
(317) 631-9000. **$119-$300.** 530 S Capitol Ave. Just s of South St. Int corridors. **Pets:** Other species. Designated rooms, service with restrictions, supervision.

Comfort Suites SH
(317) 578-1200. **$69-$109.** 9760 Crosspoint Blvd. I-69, exit 3, just w on 96th St, then just n. Int corridors. **Pets:** Other species. $10 daily fee/room. Service with restrictions.

Drury Inn-Indianapolis SH
(317) 876-9777. **$72-$90.** 9320 N Michigan Rd. I-465, exit 27, just s. Int corridors. **Pets:** Large, other species. Service with restrictions, supervision.

Four Points by Sheraton Indianapolis East SH
(317) 897-4000. **$69-$109.** 7701 E 42nd St. I-465, exit 42 (Pendleton Pike), just e. Int corridors. **Pets:** Accepted.

Hawthorn Suites East SH
(317) 322-0011. **$90-$95, 7 day notice.** 7035 Western Select Dr. I-70, exit 89; 0.5 mi w of jct I-465. Int corridors. **Pets:** Accepted.

Holiday Inn East SH
(317) 359-5341. **$89-$109.** 6990 E 21st St. I-70, exit 89, 0.5 mi w of jct I-465. Int corridors. **Pets:** Accepted.

Holiday Inn-Southeast SH
(317) 783-7751. **$89.** 5120 Victory Dr. I-465, exit 52 (Emerson Ave). Int corridors. **Pets:** Small. $20 daily fee/room. Service with restrictions, supervision.

Homestead Studio Suites Hotel-Indianapolis/Northwest SH
(317) 334-7829. **$84-$99.** 8520 Northwest Blvd. I-465, exit 23, just e. Int corridors. **Pets:** Medium, other species. $25 daily fee/room. Service with restrictions, crate.

Indianapolis Marriott East LH
(317) 352-1231. **$89-$139.** 7202 E 21st St. I-70, exit 89, 0.3 mi se; 0.5 mi w of jct I-465. Int corridors. **Pets:** Other species. $100 deposit/room, $10 daily fee/room. Service with restrictions, crate.

La Quinta Inn-Airport SH
(317) 247-4281. **$89-$99.** 5316 W Southern Ave. I-465, exit 11A, 0.5 mi e on Airport Expwy to Lynhurst Dr exit. Int corridors. **Pets:** Small. Service with restrictions, crate.

La Quinta Inn-East SH
(317) 359-1021. **Call for rates.** 7304 E 21st St. I-70, exit 89, just s, then just e; 0.5 mi w of jct I-465. Int corridors. **Pets:** Medium, other species. Service with restrictions, crate.

Microtel Inn & Suites SH
(317) 870-7765. **$45-$130.** 9140 N Michigan Rd. I-465, exit 27, just s. Int corridors. **Pets:** Small. $25 one-time fee/room. Designated rooms, service with restrictions, supervision.

Omni Indianapolis North Hotel LH
(317) 849-6668. **$184.** 8181 N Shadeland Ave. I-69, exit 1, just e. Int corridors. **Pets:** Medium, dogs only. $50 one-time fee/pet. Service with restrictions, supervision.

Omni Severin Hotel LH
(317) 634-6664. **$139-$219.** 40 W Jackson Pl. Opposite Union Station. Int corridors. **Pets:** Small. $50 one-time fee/room. Service with restrictions, crate.

Quality Inn & Suites Airport SH
(317) 381-1000. **$89-$99.** 2631 S Lynhurst Dr. I-465, exit 11A, 0.5 mi e on Airport Expwy to Lynhurst Dr. Int corridors. **Pets:** Accepted.

Red Roof Inn-South M
(317) 788-9551. **$43-$59.** 5221 Victory Dr. I-465/74, exit 52 (Emerson Ave). Ext corridors. **Pets:** Accepted.

Red Roof Inn-Speedway M
(317) 293-6881. **$43-$59.** 6415 Debonair Ln. I-465, exit 16A, just se. Ext corridors. **Pets:** Accepted.

▼▼▼ **Residence Inn by Marriott/Indianapolis Airport** 🆂🅷 ❀
(317) 244-1500. **$79-$129.** 5224 W Southern Ave. I-465, exit 11A, 0.5 mi e on Airport Expwy to Lynhurst Dr exit. Int corridors. **Pets:** Medium, other species. $75 one-time fee/room. Service with restrictions.

ASK 🖪 ⊠ 🔊 🕹 🖥 💻 ⊇ ⊠

▼▼▼ **Residence Inn Indianapolis on the Canal** 🆂🅷
(317) 822-0840. **$179-$199.** 350 W New York St. At New York St and Senate Ave. Int corridors. **Pets:** Accepted.

ASK ⊠ 🔊 🕹 🖥 💻 ⊇ ⊠

▼▼▼ **Sheraton Indianapolis Hotel & Suites** 🅻🅷 ❀
(317) 846-2700. **$119-$214.** 8787 Keystone Crossing. I-465, exit 33, jct SR 431. Int corridors. **Pets:** Medium, dogs only. Service with restrictions, crate.

ASK 🖪 ⊠ 🕹 🔊 🖥 💻 ⧺ ⊇ ⊠

▼▼ **Signature Inn-Castleton** 🆂🅷
(317) 849-8555. **$78-$87.** 8380 Kelly Ln. I-465, exit 35 (Allisonville Rd). Int corridors. **Pets:** Small. Service with restrictions, crate.

⊠ 🔊 🖥 💻 ⊇

▼▼▼ **Signature Inn-Indianapolis East** 🆂🅷
(317) 353-6966. **$78-$87.** 7610 Old Trails Rd. I-465, exit 46, just sw. Int corridors. **Pets:** Small. Service with restrictions, crate.

⊠ 🔊 🖥 💻 ⊇

▼▼ **Signature Inn-South** 🆂🅷
(317) 784-7006. **$71-$79.** 4402 E Creekview Dr. I-65, exit 103. Int corridors. **Pets:** Small. Service with restrictions, crate.

⊠ 🔊 🖥 💻 ⊇

▼▼ **Super 8 Indianapolis-Northeast** 🆂🅷
(317) 841-8585. **$55-$59.** 7202 E 82nd St. I-69, exit 1, 0.3 mi e to Clear Vista, just n, then just w on Clear Vista Ln. Ext corridors. **Pets:** Accepted.

ASK 🖪 ⊠ 🕹 🖥 💻 ⊇

▲▲▲ ▼▼ **Wellesley Inn & Suites (Indianapolis/Airport)** 🆂🅷
(317) 241-0700. **$79-$109.** 5350 W Southern Ave. I-465, exit 11A, just e to Lynhurst Dr, just s, then just w. Int corridors. **Pets:** $25 one-time fee/room. Service with restrictions, crate.

SAVE 🖪 ⊠ 🔊 🕹 🖥 💻 ⊇

▲▲▲ ▼▼▼ **The Westin Indianapolis** 🅻🅷 ❀
(317) 262-8100. **$149-$329.** 50 S Capitol Ave. At Washington and Maryland sts and Capitol Ave. Int corridors. **Pets:** Medium. Service with restrictions, supervision.

SAVE 🖪 ⊠ 🔊 🕹 🖥 💻 ⧺ ⊇

LEBANON

▲▲▲ ▼▼▼ **Comfort Inn** 🆂🅷
(765) 482-4800. **$68-$205, 3 day notice.** 210 N Sam Ralston Rd. I-65, exit 140. Int corridors. **Pets:** $20 daily fee/pet. Service with restrictions, supervision.

SAVE 🖪 ⊠ 🖥 💻 ⊇

▼▼ ▼▼ **Super 8 Motel** 🆂🅷
(765) 482-9999. **$55-$59, 7 day notice.** 405 N Mount Zion Rd. I-65, exit 140, just w. Int corridors. **Pets:** Accepted.

ASK 🖪 ⊠ 🖥 ⊇

PLAINFIELD

▲▲▲ ▼▼▼ **Days Inn-Plainfield/Indianapolis** 🅼
(317) 839-5000. **$55-$225, 14 day notice.** 2245 Hadley Rd. I-70, exit 66. Ext corridors. **Pets:** Other species. $6 daily fee/room. Service with restrictions, crate.

SAVE 🖪 ⊠ 🔊 🖥 💻

▼▼▼ ▼▼ **Lees Inn & Suites** 🆂🅷
(317) 837-9000. **$99.** 6010 Gateway Dr. I-70, exit 66, just n. Int corridors. **Pets:** Accepted.

ASK 🖪 ⊠ 🔊 🕹 🖥 💻 ⊇

SHELBYVILLE

▼▼ ▼▼ **Lees Inn** 🆂🅷
(317) 392-2299. **$84.** 111 Lee Blvd. I-74, exit 116. Int corridors. **Pets:** Small. Designated rooms, service with restrictions, supervision.

ASK 🖪 ⊠ 🔊 🖥 💻

❀   **END METROPOLITAN AREA**   ❀

JASPER

▼▼ ▼▼ **Days Inn Jasper** 🆂🅷
(812) 482-6000. **$59-$129.** 272 Brucke Strasse. On SR 162 and 164, 0.5 mi e of jct US 231. Ext/int corridors. **Pets:** Medium. $10 daily fee/pet. Service with restrictions, crate.

ASK 🖪 ⊠ 🔊 🖥 💻 ⧺ ⊇ ⊠

JEFFERSONVILLE

▼▼◆▼▼ **TownePlace Suites by Marriott** 🆂🅷
(812) 280-8200. **$79.** 703 N Shore Dr. I-65, exit 0, just w. Int corridors. **Pets:** $10 daily fee/room. Service with restrictions.

ASK 🖪 ⊠ 🕹 🖥 💻 ⊇

KOKOMO

Best Western Signature Inn Kokomo SH
(765) 455-1000. **$71-$79.** 4021 S LaFountain St. US 31, 2.5 mi s of jct US 35. Int corridors. **Pets:** Accepted.
[SAVE] [X] [🐾] [🖥] [🖵] [🏊] [🐾]

Comfort Inn SH
(765) 452-5050. **$55-$75.** 522 Essex Dr. US 31, just n of jct US 35. Int corridors. **Pets:** Large. $25 deposit/room. Designated rooms, service with restrictions, supervision.
[ASK] [🐾] [X] [🐾] [🖥] [🖵] [🏊]

Days Inn & Suites M
(765) 453-7100. **$57-$87, 7 day notice.** 264 S 00 EW. US 31, 2.8 mi s of US 35. Ext corridors. **Pets:** Medium. $10 one-time fee/pet. Service with restrictions, supervision.
[ASK] [🐾] [X] [🐾] [🖥] [🖵] [🍴] [🏊]

Hampton Inn & Suites SH
(765) 455-2900. **$89-$99.** 2920 S Reed Rd (US Hwy 31). US 31, 2 mi s of jct US 35. Int corridors. **Pets:** Other species. Designated rooms, service with restrictions, crate.
[ASK] [🐾] [X] [🐾ᴹ] [🐾] [🐾] [🖥] [🖵] [🏊]

Super 8 Motel SH
(765) 455-3288. **$55-$75.** 5110 Clinton Dr. US 31, 2.8 mi s of jct US 35. Int corridors. **Pets:** Medium, other species. $50 deposit/room. Service with restrictions, crate.
[ASK] [🐾] [X] [🐾] [🖥] [🖵] [🏊]

LAFAYETTE

Budget Inn of America M
(765) 447-7566. **$50-$95.** 139 Frontage Rd. I-65, exit 172. Ext corridors. **Pets:** Small, other species. Designated rooms, no service, supervision.
[SAVE] [🐾] [X]

Comfort Suites SH
(765) 447-0016. **$85-$150.** 31 Frontage Rd. I-65, exit 172, just e. Int corridors. **Pets:** Other species. $10 one-time fee/pet. Designated rooms, service with restrictions, supervision.
[SAVE] [🐾] [X] [🐾ᴹ] [🐾] [🐾] [🖥] [🖵] [🏊] [🐾]

Days Inn & Suites SH
(765) 446-8558. **$48-$65.** 151 Frontage Rd. I-65, exit 172, just e. Int corridors. **Pets:** Accepted.
[ASK] [🐾] [X] [🖥] [🖵]

Holiday Inn Express SH
(765) 449-4808. **$60-$90.** 201 Frontage Rd. I-65, exit 172, just e. Int corridors. **Pets:** Accepted.
[SAVE] [🐾] [X] [🖵]

Homewood Suites by Hilton SH
(765) 448-9700. **$119-$204.** 3939 SR 26 E. I-65, exit 172, 0.8 mi w. Ext/int corridors. **Pets:** Accepted.
[X] [🐾] [🖥] [🖵] [🏊] [🐾]

Lees Inn & Suites SH
(765) 447-3434. **$89-$99.** 4701 Meijer Ct. I-65, exit 172, just e on SR 26. Int corridors. **Pets:** Accepted.
[ASK] [🐾] [X] [🐾] [🐾] [🖥] [🖵] [🏊]

Loeb House Inn BB
(765) 420-7737. **$85-$175, 5 day notice.** 708 Cincinnati St. SR 38, 0.4 mi n on 9th St, just w. Int corridors. **Pets:** Small. Crate.
[ASK] [🐾] [X]

Radisson Inn-Lafayette SH
(765) 447-0575. **$78-$199.** 4343 SR 26 E. I-65, exit 172, just n. Int corridors. **Pets:** Small. $15 daily fee/room. Designated rooms, service with restrictions, supervision.
[SAVE] [🐾] [X] [🐾] [🐾] [🖥] [🖵] [🍴] [🏊] [🐾]

Red Roof Inn-Lafayette M
(765) 448-4671. **$45-$65.** 4201 SR 26 E. I-65, exit 172, 0.3 mi w. Ext corridors. **Pets:** Accepted.
[SAVE] [X] [🐾]

Signature Inn Lafayette SH
(765) 447-4142. **$78-$87.** 4320 SR 26 E. I-65, exit 172. Int corridors. **Pets:** Small. Service with restrictions, crate.
[X] [🐾] [🖥] [🖵] [🏊]

TownePlace Suites by Marriott SH
(765) 446-8668. **$89-$144.** 163 Frontage Rd. I-65, exit 172, just e. Int corridors. **Pets:** Accepted.
[ASK] [🐾] [X] [🖥] [🖵] [🏊]

LOGANSPORT

Holiday Inn SH
(574) 753-6351. **$81-$87.** 3550 E Market St. 1.5 mi e on Business Rt US 24. Int corridors. **Pets:** Medium. Designated rooms, service with restrictions, supervision.
[ASK] [🐾] [X] [🐾ᴹ] [🐾] [🖵] [🍴] [🏊]

MADISON

Super 8 Motel SH
(812) 273-4443. **$55-$70.** 3767 Clifty Dr. Jct SR 56/62/256. Int corridors. **Pets:** Dogs only. $10 daily fee/pet. Service with restrictions, supervision.
[SAVE] [🐾] [X] [🐾] [🖥] [🖵] [🏊]

MARION

Comfort Suites SH
(765) 651-1006. **$79-$125.** 1345 N Baldwin Ave. 1.5 mi n of jct SR 9 and 18. Int corridors. **Pets:** Other species. $10 daily fee/room. Designated rooms, service with restrictions, supervision.
[SAVE] [🐾] [X] [🐾] [🐾] [🖥] [🖵] [🏊] [🐾]

Country Inn & Suites SH
(765) 664-5840. **$89.** 6138 E Corridor Dr. I-69, exit 64, just w. Int corridors. **Pets:** Medium, dogs only. $10 daily fee/pet. Service with restrictions, supervision.
[SAVE] [🐾] [X] [🐾ᴹ] [🖥] [🖵] [🏊]

MARKLE

Super 8 Motel Fort Wayne South/Markle SH
(260) 758-8888. **$56-$85.** 610 Annette Dr. I-69, exit 86, just e. Int corridors. **Pets:** Medium. $7 daily fee/pet. No service, supervision.
[ASK] [🐾] [X] [🖥] [🖵]

MERRILLVILLE

⬥⬥⬥ ▽▽▽▽ La Quinta Inn SH
(219) 738-2870. **$65-$79.** 8210 Louisiana St. I-65, exit 253A (US 30), 0.3 mi se. Int corridors. **Pets:** Medium, other species. Service with restrictions, crate.
SAVE ⊠ 🐾 🖥 💻 🏊

⬥⬥⬥ ▽▽▽ Red Roof Inn-Merrillville M
(219) 738-2430. **$46-$68.** 8290 Georgia St. I-65, exit 253B (US 30), 0.3 mi sw. Ext corridors. **Pets:** Other species. No service, supervision.
SAVE ⊠ 🐾 🖥 💻

▽▽▽ Residence Inn by Marriott SH
(219) 791-9000. **$129-$189.** 8018 Delaware Pl. I-65, exit 253B (US 30). Int corridors. **Pets:** Medium, other species. $5 daily fee/room, $75 one-time fee/room. Service with restrictions.
ASK 🐾 ⊠ 🏋M 🖥 🖥 💻 🏊 ⊠

⬥⬥⬥ ▽▽▽ Super 8 Motel SH
(219) 736-8383. **$44-$65, 8 day notice.** 8300 Louisiana St. I-65, exit 253A (US 30), 0.5 mi se. Int corridors. **Pets:** Accepted.
SAVE 🐾 ⊠ 🏋M 🖥

MICHIGAN CITY

⬥⬥⬥ ▽▽▽ Red Roof Inn-Michigan City M
(219) 874-5251. **$47-$84.** 110 W Kieffer Rd. I-94, exit 34B, 0.3 mi n on US 421. Ext corridors. **Pets:** Accepted.
SAVE ⊠ 🖥

MISHAWAKA

▽▽▽ Super 8 Motel M
(574) 247-0888. **$50-$70.** 535 W University Dr. I-80/90, exit 83 to SR 23, 1.6 mi sw to Main St, just s, then just w. Int corridors. **Pets:** Accepted.
ASK 🐾 ⊠ 🏋M 🖥 💻

MONTGOMERY

▽▽▽▽ Gasthof Village Inn SH
(812) 486-2600. **Call for rates.** CR 650 E. US 50, 1 mi n on First St. Int corridors. **Pets:** Accepted.
⊠ 🐾 🖥 💻 🍴 🏊 ⊠

MONTICELLO

⬥⬥⬥ ▽▽▽ Best Western Brandywine Inn & Suites SH
(574) 583-6333. **$63-$135.** 728 S 6th St. SR 24, just s. Int corridors. **Pets:** Other species. $20 deposit/room, $5 daily fee/room. Service with restrictions, supervision.
SAVE ⊠ 🏋M 🖥 💻 🏊 ⊠

MOUNT VERNON

▽▽ Four Seasons Motel M 🐾
(812) 838-4821. **$56-$99.** 70 Hwy 62 W. 1.8 mi w of jct SR 69 N. Ext corridors. **Pets:** Small, other species. $25 deposit/pet. Service with restrictions, supervision.
ASK 🐾 ⊠ 🖥 💻 🏊

▽▽ Super 8 Motel SH
(812) 838-8888. **$56-$61.** 6225 Hwy 69 S. On SR 69 Bypass, just n of SR 62. Int corridors. **Pets:** Accepted.
ASK 🐾 ⊠ 🖥 🏊

MUNCIE

▽▽ Comfort Inn SH
(765) 282-6666. **$55-$110, 30 day notice.** 4011 W Bethel Ave. I-69, exit 41, 6.3 mi e on SR 332, then just n. Int corridors. **Pets:** $15 one-time fee/room. Service with restrictions, supervision.
ASK 🐾 ⊠ 🖥 💻 🏊

▽▽ Muncie Days Inn SH
(765) 288-2311. **$49-$74.** 3509 N Everbrook Ln. I-69, exit 41, 6.3 mi e on SR 332, then just n. Int corridors. **Pets:** Other species. $10 one-time fee/room. Service with restrictions, supervision.
ASK 🐾 ⊠ 🖥 💻

▽▽▽▽ Radisson Hotel Roberts LH
(765) 741-7777. **$99.** 420 S High St. Opposite Horizon Convention Center. Int corridors. **Pets:** Accepted.
ASK 🐾 ⊠ 🖥 💻 🍴 🏊

▽▽▽ Signature Inn-Muncie SH
(765) 284-4200. **$78-$87.** 3400 N Chadam Ln. I-69, exit 41, 6.3 mi e on SR 332. Int corridors. **Pets:** Small. Service with restrictions, crate.
⊠ 🐾 🖥 💻 🏊

▽▽ Super 8 Motel SH
(765) 286-4333. **$50-$70, 7 day notice.** 3601 W Fox Ridge Ln. I-69, exit 41, 6.3 mi e on SR 332. Int corridors. **Pets:** Large. Service with restrictions, supervision.
ASK 🐾 ⊠ 🖥

NEW CASTLE

⬥⬥⬥ ▽▽▽ Best Western Raintree Inn SH
(765) 521-0100. **$65-$79, 10 day notice.** 2836 S SR 3. I-70, exit 123, 2.5 mi n. Ext/int corridors. **Pets:** Other species. $20 one-time fee/pet. Service with restrictions, supervision.
SAVE ⊠ 🐾 🖥 💻 🍴 🏊 ⊠

NORTH VERNON

▽▽▽▽ Comfort Inn SH
(812) 352-9999. **$70-$74, 7 day notice.** 150 FDR Dr. Jct US 50, 0.6 mi n on SR 7. Int corridors. **Pets:** Accepted.
ASK 🐾 ⊠ 🐾 🖥 💻 🏊

PERU

▽▽▽ Best Western Circus City Inn SH
(765) 473-8800. **$81-$150.** 2642 Business 31 S. Just e of jct US 31. Int corridors. **Pets:** Other species. $50 deposit/room. Service with restrictions.
ASK 🐾 ⊠ 🐾 🐾 🖥 💻 🏊

PLYMOUTH

▽▽▽ Super 8 Motel SH
(574) 936-8856. **$61-$125.** 2160 N Oak Rd. US 30, just s. Int corridors. **Pets:** Accepted.
ASK 🐾 ⊠ 🖥 💻 🏊

PORTAGE

▼▼ Super 8 Motel SH
(219) 762-8857. **$60-$84.** 6118 Melton Rd. I-94, exit 19, 0.5 mi w on US 20. Int corridors. **Pets:** Accepted.
ASK SO X ⊞ ▣

PORTER

▼▼▼ Spring House Inn SH
(219) 929-4600. **$79-$129.** 303 N Mineral Springs Rd. I-94, exit 22B, 1.5 mi ne on SR 20, follow signs. Int corridors. **Pets:** Accepted.
ASK X ▣ ⇌ ✕

PORTLAND

▼▼ Hoosier Inn M 🐾
(260) 726-7113. **$45-$60.** 1620 Meridian St. 1.4 mi n on US 27. Ext corridors. **Pets:** Dogs only. $4 daily fee/pet. Service with restrictions, supervision.
ASK SO X ⊞ ▣

REMINGTON

▼▼ Super 8 Motel-Remington SH
(219) 261-2883. **$63-$75.** 4278 W US 24. I-65, exit 201, just w. Int corridors. **Pets:** Accepted.
ASK SO X ⊞ ▣ ⇌

RENSSELAER

🔺 ▼▼▼ Holiday Inn Express SH
(219) 866-7111. **$82, 10 day notice.** 4788 Nesbitt Dr. I-65, exit 215, just e. Int corridors. **Pets:** Accepted.
SAVE X ⛾ ⛾

RICHMOND

🔺 ▼▼ Best Western Imperial Motor Lodge SH
(765) 966-1505. **$47-$87.** 3020 E Main St. I-70, exit 156A, 2 mi w. Ext corridors. **Pets:** Other species. $5 daily fee/pet. Service with restrictions, crate.
SAVE SO X ⛾ ⊞ ▣ ⇌

▼▼ Days Inn M
(765) 966-4900. **$55-$75.** 5775 National Rd E. I-70, exit 156A, just s. Ext corridors. **Pets:** Large. $10 daily fee/pet. Service with restrictions, crate.
ASK SO X

▼▼▼ Holiday Inn-Richmond SH 🐾
(765) 966-7511. **$99-$150.** 5501 National Rd E. I-70, exit 156A, 0.3 mi w. Ext corridors. **Pets:** $15 daily fee/pet. Designated rooms, service with restrictions, supervision.
ASK SO X ⛾ ⛾ ⛾ ⊞ ▣ ⛁ ⇌ ✕

▼▼▼ Lees Inn & Suites SH
(765) 966-6559. **$84-$104.** 6030 National Rd E. I-70, exit 156A, jct US 40. Int corridors. **Pets:** Accepted.
ASK SO X ⊞ ▣ ⇌

▼▼ Motel 6 Richmond #4170 M 🐾
(765) 966-6682. **$45-$79.** 419 Commerce Dr. I-70, exit 156A, just s on US 40. Ext corridors. **Pets:** Large. Designated rooms, service with restrictions, supervision.
X ⊞ ⇌

ROCKVILLE

🔺 ▼▼▼ Billie Creek Village & Inn SH 🐾
(765) 569-3430. **$59-$129, 3 day notice.** 1659 E US Hwy 36. 1.4 mi e on US 36. Int corridors. **Pets:** Other species. $10 daily fee/room. Designated rooms, service with restrictions.
SAVE X ⛾ ⇌

ROSELAND

🔺 ▼▼▼ Comfort Suites SH
(574) 272-1500. **$84-$165.** 52939 SR 933 N. I-80/90, exit 77, just e to Business Rt US 31/33, then 1 mi n. Int corridors. **Pets:** Accepted.
SAVE SO X ⛾ ⊞ ▣ ⇌ ✕

▼▼ Holiday Inn-University Area SH
(574) 272-6600. **$69-$239, 30 day notice.** 515 Dixie Way N. I-80/90, exit 77, on US 31 and SR 933, 0.8 mi n. Ext/int corridors. **Pets:** Accepted.
ASK SO X ⛾ ▣ ⛁ ⇌ ✕

▼▼ Ramada Inn South Bend SH
(574) 272-5220. **$69-$89.** 52890 SR 933 N. I-80/90, exit 77, 1 mi n. Ext/int corridors. **Pets:** Accepted.
ASK X ⊞ ▣ ⛁ ⇌

SCOTTSBURG

🔺 ▼▼▼ Mariann Travel Inn M
(812) 752-3396. **$53-$56.** SR 56. I-65, exit 29A, just e. Ext corridors. **Pets:** Accepted.
SAVE SO X ⛁ ⇌

SELLERSBURG

▼▼ Home Lodge SH
(812) 246-6332. **$249-$399 (weekly).** 363 Triangle Dr. I-65, exit 9, just e. Int corridors. **Pets:** Accepted.
ASK SO X ⛾ ⊞ ▣

🔺 ▼▼▼ Ramada Limited & Suites SH
(812) 246-3131. **$99.** 360 Triangle Dr. I-65, exit 9, just e. Int corridors. **Pets:** Accepted.
SAVE SO X ⊞ ▣ ⇌

SEYMOUR

▼ Motel 6 Seymour #4153 SH
(812) 524-7443. **$40-$43.** 365 Tanger Blvd. I-65, exit 50A. Int corridors. **Pets:** Medium, other species. Designated rooms, service with restrictions, supervision.
ASK SO X ⛾ ⛾ ⊞ ▣ ⇌

SHIPSHEWANA

🔺 ▼▼▼ Super 8 Motel SH
(260) 768-4004. **$55-$130.** 740 S Van Buren St. US 20, 0.8 mi n on SR 5. Int corridors. **Pets:** Medium, other species. $8 daily fee/pet. Service with restrictions, supervision.
SAVE SO X ⛾ ⊞ ▣

SOUTH BEND

▼▼▼▼ The Oliver Inn Bed & Breakfast BB
(574) 232-4545. $95-$165, 14 day notice. 630 W Washington St. 0.3 mi w of US 31. Int corridors. Pets: Accepted.
(ASK) (S&) (X)

STACER

▼▼▼ Holiday Inn Express SH
(812) 867-1100. $72. I-64, exit 25A (US 41), 0.5 mi s. Int corridors. Pets: Accepted.
(ASK) (S&) (X) (&M) (&) (🛏) (🍽) (⟿)

TAYLORSVILLE

▼▼ Comfort Inn M
(812) 526-9747. $58-$185. 10330 US 31. I-65, exit 76A, just s. Ext corridors. Pets: Medium. Service with restrictions, supervision.
(ASK) (S&) (X) (🛏) (🍽) (⟿)

TELL CITY

▼▼▼▼ Ramada Limited SH
(812) 547-3234. $62-$89. 235 Orchard Hill Dr. Just off SR 66, 1.7 mi se of jct SR 37. Int corridors. Pets: Other species. $50 deposit/pet. Service with restrictions, supervision.
(ASK) (S&) (X) (&M) (&) (🛏) (🍽) (⟿)

TERRE HAUTE

▼▼▼ Comfort Suites SH
(812) 235-1770. $69-$135, 3 day notice. 501 E Margaret Ave. I-70, exit 7 (US 41/150), just ne. Int corridors. Pets: Other species. $15 one-time fee/pet. Designated rooms, service with restrictions, supervision.
(ASK) (S&) (X) (&M) (🛏) (🍽) (⟿)

▼▼▼▼ Drury Inn-Terre Haute SH
(812) 238-1206. $83-$103. 3040 Hwy 41 S. I-70, exit 7 (US 41/150), just n. Int corridors. Pets: Large, other species. Service with restrictions, supervision.
(ASK) (X) (&M) (&) (🛏) (🍽) (⟿) (X)

▲▲▲ ▼▼▼▼ Holiday Inn SH
(812) 232-6081. $119-$180. 3300 US 41 S. I-70, exit 7 (US 41/150), just s. Ext/int corridors. Pets: Small, other species. Service with restrictions, supervision.
(SAVE) (X) (🌀) (🛏) (🍽) (🍴) (⟿) (X)

▼▼ Knights Inn M
(812) 234-9931. $53-$125. 401 E Margaret Ave. I-70, exit 7 (US 41/150), just n, then e. Ext corridors. Pets: Medium. Service with restrictions.
(ASK) (S&) (X) (🛏) (🍽) (⟿)

▼▼ ▼▼ Pear Tree Inn by Drury-Terre Haute SH
(812) 234-4268. $71-$87. 3050 US 41 S. I-70, exit 7 (US 41/150), just n. Int corridors. Pets: Large, other species. Service with restrictions, supervision.
(ASK) (X) (&) (🍽)

▼▼ ▼▼ Super 8 Motel-Terre Haute SH
(812) 232-4890. $45-$65. 3089 S 1st St. I-70, exit 7 (US 41/150), just nw. Int corridors. Pets: Accepted.
(ASK) (S&) (X)

VALPARAISO

▼▼ Holiday Inn Express SH
(219) 464-8555. Call for rates. 760 Morthland Dr. 0.8 mi e on US 30. Ext/int corridors. Pets: Other species. $15 daily fee/pet.
(X) (&)

WARREN

▼▼▼▼ La Quinta Inn SH
(260) 375-4800. Call for rates. 7275 S CR 75 E. I-69, exit 78, just n on SR 5. Int corridors. Pets: Accepted.
(X) (&M) (&) (🛏) (🍽) (⟿)

WARSAW

▲▲▲ ▼▼▼▼ Hampton Inn & Suites SH
(574) 269-6655. $72-$123. 3328 E Center St. 3.2 mi e of SR 15 on US 30. Int corridors. Pets: Accepted.
(SAVE) (S&) (X) (🌀) (&) (🛏) (🍽) (⟿) (X)

▲▲▲ ▼▼▼▼ Ramada Plaza Hotel of Warsaw SH
(574) 269-2323. $108-$115. 2519 E Center St. 2.8 mi e of SR 15 on US 30, just s. Int corridors. Pets: Other species. Service with restrictions, crate.
(SAVE) (S&) (X) (🛏) (🍽) (🍴) (⟿) (X)

WASHINGTON

▼▼▼▼ Baymont Inn & Suites Washington SH
(812) 254-7000. $57-$79. 7 Cumberland Dr. Just ne of jct US 50 and SR 57. Int corridors. Pets: Accepted.
(ASK) (S&) (X) (🌀) (🛏) (🍽) (⟿) (X)

WEST LAFAYETTE

▼▼ Super 8 Motel-West Lafayette SH
(765) 567-7100. $49-$119. 2030 Northgate Dr. I-65, exit 178, just n on SR 43. Int corridors. Pets: Accepted.
(ASK) (S&) (X) (&M) (&) (🛏) (🍽)

IOWA

ADAIR

⬥⬥ Adair Budget Inn Ⓜ
(641) 742-5553. **$39-$45.** 100 S 5th St. I-80, exit 76. Ext corridors. **Pets:** $20 deposit/room. Designated rooms, service with restrictions, supervision.
SAVE 🆂ⓓ ✖

⬥⬥ Adair Super 8 🆂🅷
(641) 742-5251. **$49-$69.** 111 S 5th St. I-80, exit 76, just n. Int corridors. **Pets:** Very small. $20 deposit/room. Service with restrictions, supervision.
ASK 🆂ⓓ ✖ 🖥 💻

ALBIA

⬥⬥ Indian Hills Inn 🆂🅷
(641) 932-7181. **$56-$92.** 100 Hwy 34 E. Just e of jct US 34 and SR 5. Ext/int corridors. **Pets:** $6 daily fee/pet. Designated rooms, service with restrictions, supervision.
SAVE ✖ 🖥 💻 🍴 🏊

ALTOONA

⬥⬥ Heartland Inn-Altoona 🆂🅷
(515) 967-2400. **$74-$92.** 5000 NE 56 St. I-80, exit 142, 0.5 mi s. Int corridors. **Pets:** $5 daily fee/room. Designated rooms, service with restrictions, supervision.
ASK 🆂ⓓ ✖ 🖥 💻 🏊 ✖

⬥⬥ Motel 6 Des Moines East #1420 🆂🅷
(515) 967-5252. **$45-$63.** 3225 Adventureland Dr. I-80, exit 142A. Int corridors. **Pets:** Accepted.
🆂ⓓ ✖ 🖥 💻 🏊

⬥⬥⬥ Settle Inn & Suites-Altoona 🆂🅷
(515) 967-7888. **$69-$99.** 2101 Adventureland Dr. I-80, exit 142A, just se. Int corridors. **Pets:** Accepted.
ASK 🆂ⓓ ✖ ⟲ 🖥 💻 🏊

AMANA COLONIES AREA

AMANA

⬥⬥⬥ Amana Holiday Inn 🆂🅷
(319) 668-1175. **$71-$159.** 2211 U Ave. I-80, exit 225 (US 151). Int corridors. **Pets:** Accepted.
ASK 🆂ⓓ ✖ ⟲ 🖥 💻 🍴 🏊 ✖

⬥⬥⬥ Comfort Inn Amana Colonies 🆂🅷
(319) 668-2700. **$69-$110.** 2185 U Ave. I-80, exit 225 (US 151), just n. Int corridors. **Pets:** Accepted.
ASK 🆂ⓓ ✖ 🆜ᴹ 🖥 💻 🏊

HOMESTEAD

⬥⬥ Die Heimat Country Inn & Bed & Breakfast 🅱🅱
(319) 622-3937. **$65-$89, 7 day notice.** 4430 V St. Just s of US 6, e on Main St, then just e of jct US 151. Int corridors. **Pets:** Medium, dogs only. $10 daily fee/pet. Designated rooms, supervision.
✖ 🖥 ☎

🐾 END AREA 🐾

AMES

⬥⬥⬥ Baymont Inn & Suites 🆂🅷
(515) 296-2500. **$74-$89.** 2500 Elwood Dr. I-35, exit 111B, 3.7 mi w. Int corridors. **Pets:** Medium. Service with restrictions, supervision.
SAVE 🆂ⓓ ✖ 🖥 💻 🏊

⬥⬥ Comfort Inn-Ames 🆂🅷
(515) 232-0689. **$55-$80.** 1605 S Dayton Ave. Jct I-35 and US 30, just nw. Int corridors. **Pets:** Medium. $5 daily fee/pet. Designated rooms, service with restrictions, supervision.
ASK 🆂ⓓ ✖ 🖥 💻 🏊

(AAA) ▼◆◆▼ Comfort Suites 🆂🅷
(515) 268-8808. **$69-$109.** 2609 Elwood Dr. Jct I-35 and US 30, 3.5 mi w on US 30, exit 146 (Elwood Dr), then just s. Int corridors. **Pets:** Medium. $10 one-time fee/pet. Designated rooms, service with restrictions, supervision.
🆂🅰🆅🅴 🆂🔌 ✖ 🔥Ⓜ 🐾 🔌 🔒 💻 ➿ ✖

▼◆ ◆▼ Heartland Inn-Ames 🆂🅷
(515) 233-6060. **$73-$83.** 2600 SE 16th St. Jct I-35 and US 30, just nw. Int corridors. **Pets:** $5 daily fee/room. Designated rooms, service with restrictions, supervision.
🅰🆂🅺 🆂🔌 ✖ 🔒 💻 ➿

▼◆◆▼ The Hotel at Gateway Center 🅻🅷
(515) 292-8600. **$99-$149, 7 day notice.** US 30 & Elwood Dr. Jct I-35 and US 30, 3.5 mi w on US 30, exit 146 (Elwood Dr). Int corridors. **Pets:** Accepted.
🅰🆂🅺 🆂🔌 ✖ 🔥Ⓜ 🐾 🔌 🔒 💻 🍴 ➿ ✖

(AAA) ▼◆ ◆▼ Howard Johnson Express Inn 🆂🅷
(515) 232-8363. **$70-$75.** 1709 S Duff Ave. Jct US 30 and exit 148 (Duff Ave), just n. Ext corridors. **Pets:** Small. $10 daily fee/pet. Designated rooms, supervision.
🆂🅰🆅🅴 🆂🔌 ✖ 🔒 💻 ➿

(AAA) ▼◆ ◆▼ Quality Inn & Suites Starlite Village Conference Center 🆂🅷
(515) 232-9260. **$69-$99.** 2601 E 13th St. I-35, exit 113 (US 30), 0.5 mi w. Int corridors. **Pets:** Medium. $10 daily fee/room. Service with restrictions.
🆂🅰🆅🅴 🆂🔌 ✖ 🐾 🔥 🔌 🔒 💻 🍴 ➿ ✖

ANAMOSA

▼◆ ◆▼ Super 8 Motel-Anamosa 🆂🅷
(319) 462-3888. **$50-$70.** 100 Grant Wood Dr. Just e on US 64 from US 151. Int corridors. **Pets:** Accepted.
🅰🆂🅺 🆂🔌 ✖ 🐾

ANKENY

(AAA) ▼◆◆▼ Best Western Metro North 🆂🅷 ❀
(515) 964-1717. **$65-$78, 30 day notice.** 133 SE Delaware Ave. I-35, exit 92, just w. Int corridors. **Pets:** $10 one-time fee/room. Designated rooms, service with restrictions, crate.
🆂🅰🆅🅴 🆂🔌 ✖ 🔒 💻 🍴 ➿ ✖

▼◆ ◆▼ Heartland Inn 🆂🅷
(515) 964-8202. **$74-$84.** 201 SE Delaware Ave. I-35, exit 92, just w. Int corridors. **Pets:** $5 daily fee/room. Designated rooms, service with restrictions, supervision.
🅰🆂🅺 🆂🔌 ✖ 🐾 🔒 💻 ➿

ARNOLDS PARK

▼◆◆▼ Fillenwarth Beach 🆂🅷
(712) 332-5646. **$275-$3800 (weekly) (no credit cards), 21 day notice.** 87 Lake Shore Dr. West Lake Okoboji; just w of US 71. Ext corridors. **Pets:** Other species.
🔒 💻 ➿ ✖

ATLANTIC

▼◆ ◆▼ Econo Lodge 🆂🅷
(712) 243-4067. **$44-$69.** 64968 Boston Rd. I-80, exit 60 (US 71), 0.5 mi s. Int corridors. **Pets:** Accepted.
🅰🆂🅺 🆂🔌 ✖ 💻 ➿

▼◆◆▼ Super 8 Motel 🆂🅷
(712) 243-4723. **$54-$69.** 1902 E 7th St. I-80, exit 60, 6 mi s on US 71, then 2 mi w; east side of town. Int corridors. **Pets:** Small, other species. $25 deposit/pet. Designated rooms, service with restrictions, supervision.
🅰🆂🅺 🆂🔌 ✖ 🔥 🔒 💻 ➿

BURLINGTON

(AAA) ▼◆◆▼ Best Western Pzazz Motor Inn 🆂🅷
(319) 753-2223. **$86-$95.** 3001 Winegard Dr. Jct US 61 and 34, just n. Int corridors. **Pets:** Other species. Service with restrictions.
🆂🅰🆅🅴 🆂🔌 ✖ 🔥Ⓜ 🐾 🔥 🔒 💻 🍴 ➿ ✖

▼◆ ◆▼ Comfort Inn-Burlington 🆂🅷
(319) 753-0000. **$50-$80.** 3051 Kirkwood Ave. US 61, just n of jct US 34. Int corridors. **Pets:** Accepted.
🅰🆂🅺 🆂🔌 ✖ 🔥 🔒 💻 ➿

▼◆ ◆▼ Super 8 Motel-Burlington 🆂🅷
(319) 752-9806. **$55-$72.** 3001 Kirkwood Ave. US 61, just n of jct US 34. Int corridors. **Pets:** $10 daily fee/room. Service with restrictions, supervision.
🅰🆂🅺 🆂🔌 ✖ 🔒

CARROLL

▼◆ ◆▼ Super 8 Motel 🆂🅷
(712) 792-4753. **$53-$61.** 1757 US 71 N. Just n of jct US 30 and 71. Int corridors. **Pets:** Service with restrictions, supervision.
🅰🆂🅺 🆂🔌 ✖

CEDAR FALLS

(AAA) ▼◆ ◆▼ University Inn Ⓜ ❀
(319) 277-1412. **$39-$112.** 4711 University Ave. 2 mi w of US 63. Ext/int corridors. **Pets:** $30 deposit/pet, $5 one-time fee/pet. Designated rooms, service with restrictions, crate.
🆂🅰🆅🅴 🆂🔌 ✖ 🔒 💻 ✖

CEDAR RAPIDS

(AAA) ▼◆◆▼ Best Western Cooper's Mill Hotel & Restaurant 🆂🅷
(319) 366-5323. **$64-$74.** 100 F Ave NW. I-380, exit 19C northbound, take a right at end of the exit, make an immediate U-turn and go under I-380; exit 20A southbound, cross river, right on 1st St NW. Int corridors. **Pets:** $5 daily fee/pet. Crate.
🆂🅰🆅🅴 🆂🔌 ✖ 🔒 💻 🍴 ➿ ✖

(AAA) ▼◆◆▼ Best Western Longbranch Hotel & Convention Center 🆂🅷
(319) 377-6386. **$79-$89.** 90 Twixt Town Rd NE. I-380, exit 24A (SR 100/Collins Rd), 2.5 mi e, then just n. Int corridors. **Pets:** $5 daily fee/room. Service with restrictions, supervision.
🆂🅰🆅🅴 🆂🔌 ✖ 🔒 💻 🍴 ➿ ✖

🆔 ▼▼▼▼ Clarion Hotel & Convention Center 🅻🅷
(319) 366-8671. **$60-$105.** 525 33rd Ave SW. I-380, exit 17 (33rd Ave SW), just w. Int corridors. **Pets:** $25 deposit/room. Service with restrictions, crate.
[SAVE] [🆓] [✕] [🖉] [🅴] [💻] [🍴] [🏊] [✕]

🆔 ▼▼▼▼ Collins Plaza Hotel & Convention Center 🅻🅷
(319) 393-6600. **$80-$111.** 1200 Collins Rd NE. I-380, exit 24A (SR 100/Collins Rd), 1 mi e. Int corridors. **Pets:** Accepted.
[SAVE] [🆓] [✕] [🖉] [🅴] [💻] [🍴] [🏊] [✕]

▼▼▼▼ Comfort Inn of Cedar Rapids North 🆂🅷
(319) 393-8247. **$64-$84.** 5055 Rockwell Dr. I-380, exit 24A (SR 100/Collins Rd), 1.3 mi e. Int corridors. **Pets:** Accepted.
[ASK] [🆓] [✕] [🖉] [💻]

▼▼ Comfort Inn-South 🆂🅷
(319) 363-7934. **$64-$84.** 390 33rd Ave SW. I-380, exit 17 (33rd Ave SW), just w. Int corridors. **Pets:** Medium, other species. $10 one-time fee/room. Designated rooms, service with restrictions, supervision.
[ASK] [🆓] [✕] [💻]

▼▼▼▼ Days Inn of Cedar Rapids 🆂🅷
(319) 365-4339. **Call for rates.** 3245 Southgate Pl SW. I-380, exit 17 (33rd Ave SW), just w. Int corridors. **Pets:** Accepted.
[✕] [🖉] [💻]

🆔 ▼▼ Exel Inn of Cedar Rapids 🆂🅷
(319) 366-2475. **$41-$61.** 616 33rd Ave SW. I-380, exit 17 (33rd Ave SW), 0.3 mi w. Int corridors. **Pets:** Small, other species. Designated rooms, service with restrictions, supervision.
[SAVE] [🆓] [✕] [💻]

🆔 ▼▼▼▼ GuestHouse International Inns & Suites 🆂🅷
(319) 378-3948. **$64-$104.** 2215 Blairs Ferry Rd NE. I-380, exit 24B, just e. Int corridors. **Pets:** Medium. $25 deposit/pet. Designated rooms, service with restrictions, supervision.
[SAVE] [🆓] [✕] [🅼] [💻]

▼▼▼▼ Hawthorn Suites Ltd 🆂🅷
(319) 294-8700. **$83-$93.** 4444 Czech Ln NE. I-380, exit 24A (SR 100/Collins Rd), just s. Int corridors. **Pets:** Accepted.
[✕] [🅼] [🖉] [🅴] [💻]

▼▼ Heartland Inn 🆂🅷
(319) 362-9012. **$73-$83.** 3315 Southgate Ct SW. I-380, exit 17 (33rd Ave SW), just sw. Int corridors. **Pets:** Small, dogs only. $5 daily fee/pet. Designated rooms, service with restrictions, supervision.
[ASK] [🆓] [✕] [🖉] [💻] [✕]

▼▼▼▼ Howard Johnson Airport Express Inn & Suites 🆂🅷
(319) 363-3789. **$89-$119.** 9100 Atlantic Dr SW. I-380, exit 13, just w. Int corridors. **Pets:** Other species. $10 daily fee/room. Service with restrictions, crate.
[ASK] [🆓] [✕] [🅼] [🅴] [💻] [✕]

▼▼▼▼ Mainstay Suites 🆂🅷
(319) 363-7829. **$69-$129.** 5145 Rockwell Dr NE. I-380, exit 24A (SR 100/Collins Rd), 1 mi e, then just n. Int corridors. **Pets:** Other species. $50 deposit/room, $10 daily fee/pet. Designated rooms, service with restrictions, supervision.
[ASK] [🆓] [✕] [🅼] [🖉] [💻] [✕]

▼▼ Motel 6 #1485 🅼
(319) 366-7523. **$37-$47.** 3325 Southgate Ct SW. I-380, exit 17 (33rd Ave SW), just sw. Ext corridors. **Pets:** Accepted.
[🆓] [✕] [🅼] [🖉]

▼▼▼▼ Residence Inn 🆂🅷
(319) 395-0111. **$79-$129.** 1900 Dodge Rd NE. I-380, exit 24A (SR 100/Collins Rd), just e. Int corridors. **Pets:** Other species. $5 daily fee/room, $50 one-time fee/room. Service with restrictions.
[ASK] [🆓] [✕] [🖉] [🅴] [💻] [🏊] [✕]

▼▼ Super 8 Motel 🆂🅷
(319) 363-1755. **$65.** 400 33rd Ave SW. I-380, exit 17 (33rd Ave SW), just w. Int corridors. **Pets:** Small. $10 daily fee/room, service with restrictions, supervision.
[ASK] [🆓] [✕] [🖉]

▼▼ Super 8 Motel 🆂🅷
(319) 362-6002. **$61-$69.** 720 33rd Ave SW. I-380, exit 17 (33rd Ave SW), 0.4 mi w. Int corridors. **Pets:** Medium, other species. $10 daily fee/room. Designated rooms, service with restrictions, supervision.
[ASK] [🆓] [✕] [🅼] [🖉]

CHEROKEE

🆔 ▼▼▼▼ Best Western La Grande Hacienda 🆂🅷
(712) 225-5701. **$74-$84, 3 day notice.** 1401 N 2nd St. Jct US 59 and SR 2, 0.4 mi s. Int corridors. **Pets:** Accepted.
[SAVE] [🆓] [✕] [🅼] [🖉] [💻] [🍴] [🏊]

CLARINDA

▼▼▼ Clarinda Super 8 Motel 🆂🅷
(712) 542-6333. **$55-$60.** 1203 S 12th St. Jct US 71 and SR 2, just e. Int corridors. **Pets:** Other species. Service with restrictions, supervision.
[ASK] [🆓] [✕] [🅼] [🅴] [💻]

CLEAR LAKE

🆔 ▼▼▼ Best Western Holiday Lodge 🆂🅷
(641) 357-5253. **$69-$89.** 2023 7th Ave N. I-35, exit 194 (US 18), 0.3 mi w. Ext/int corridors. **Pets:** Large. $10 daily fee/pet. Designated rooms, service with restrictions, supervision.
[SAVE] [🆓] [✕] [🅼] [🅴] [💻] [🍴] [🏊] [✕]

🆔 ▼▼▼ Budget Inn 🆂🅷
(641) 357-8700. **$40-$69.** 1306 N 25th St. I-35, exit 194 (US 18), just nw. Int corridors. **Pets:** Medium. Supervision.
[SAVE] [🆓] [✕] [💻]

▼▼ **Heartland Inn** SH
(641) 357-5123. **$73-$115.** 1603 S Shore Dr. I-35, exit 193, 1.3 mi w to S Shore Dr, then 1 mi s. Int corridors. **Pets:** Medium, dogs only. $5 daily fee/room. Service with restrictions, supervision.

[ASK] [S&] [✕] [♿] [📺] [🛬] [✕]

▼▼ **Lake Country Inn** M
(641) 357-2184. **$35-$40.** 518 Hwy 18 W. I-35, exit 194 (US 18), 2 mi w. Ext corridors. **Pets:** Other species. Supervision.

[ASK] [✕] [♿]

▼▼ **Microtel Inn** SH
(641) 357-0966. **$55-$63.** 1305 N 25th St. I-35, exit 194 (US 18), just nw. Int corridors. **Pets:** Other species. Service with restrictions, crate.

[ASK] [S&] [✕] [♿M] [✑] [♿] [📺]

▼▼ **Super 8 Motel** SH
(641) 357-7521. **$46-$54.** 2908 4th Ave S. I-35, exit 193, just e. Int corridors. **Pets:** Other species. $10 deposit/room. Service with restrictions, supervision.

[ASK] [S&] [✕]

CLINTON

⍟⍟ ▼▼▼ **Best Western-Frontier Motor Inn** SH
(563) 242-7112. **$79-$95.** 2300 Lincoln Way. On US 30, just e of jct US 30 and 67. Ext/int corridors. **Pets:** Small. Service with restrictions, supervision.

[SAVE] [S&] [✕] [✎] [✑] [♿] [📺] [🍴] [🛬] [✕]

⍟⍟ ▼▼▼ **Country Inn & Suites By Carlson** SH
(563) 244-9922. **$79-$95.** 2224 Lincoln Way. On US 30, just e of jct US 30 and 67. Int corridors. **Pets:** Small. $10 daily fee/pet. Service with restrictions, supervision.

[SAVE] [S&] [✕] [♿M] [✎] [✑] [♿] [📺] [🛬]

▼▼ **Super 8 Motel-Clinton** SH ❀
(563) 242-8870. **$49-$72.** 1711 Lincoln Way. On US 30 and 67, 2.4 mi w. Int corridors. **Pets:** Large, other species. $10 one-time fee/room. Service with restrictions, crate.

[ASK] [S&] [✕] [♿M] [✎] [♿]

CLIVE

⍟⍟ ▼▼▼ **Baymont Inn & Suites West Des Moines-Clive** SH
(515) 221-9200. **$69-$99.** 1390 NW 118th St. I-80/35, exit 124 (University Ave). Int corridors. **Pets:** Accepted.

[SAVE] [S&] [✕] [♿M] [✎] [✑] [♿] [📺] [🛬]

▼▼▼ **Chase Suite Hotel by Woodfin** M
(515) 223-7700. **$148-$198.** 11428 Forest Ave. I-80/35, exit 124 (University Ave), just ne. Ext corridors. **Pets:** Accepted.

[ASK] [S&] [✕] [✎] [✑] [♿] [📺] [🛬] [✕]

▼▼▼ **Clarion Hotel West** SH
(515) 278-5575. **$62-$92.** 11040 Hickman Rd. I-80/35, exit 125, 0.3 mi e. Int corridors. **Pets:** Accepted.

[ASK] [S&] [✕] [♿M] [✎] [✑] [♿] [📺] [🍴] [🛬] [✕]

▼▼ **Heartland Inn-West Des Moines** SH
(515) 226-0414. **$76-$86.** 11414 Forest Ave. I-80/35, exit 124 (University Ave), just e. Int corridors. **Pets:** $5 daily fee/room. Designated rooms, service with restrictions, supervision.

[ASK] [S&] [✕] [♿] [📺] [✕]

COLUMBUS JUNCTION

▼▼ **Columbus Motel** M
(319) 728-8080. **$48.** 265 Colonels Dr. Just e of jct US 92 and SR 70 on US 92. Int corridors. **Pets:** Accepted.

[✕] [♿] [📺]

CORALVILLE

▼▼▼ **AmericInn Motel & Suites** SH
(319) 625-2400. **$73-$90, 3 day notice.** 2597 Holiday Rd. I-80, exit 240, just n. Int corridors. **Pets:** Small. $6 one-time fee/pet. Designated rooms, service with restrictions, supervision.

[ASK] [S&] [✕] [♿M] [✑] [♿] [📺] [🛬]

▼▼ **Comfort Inn of Coralville** SH
(319) 351-8144. **$69-$109.** 209 W 9th St. I-80, exit 242, just s. Int corridors. **Pets:** Medium. Designated rooms, service with restrictions, supervision.

[ASK] [S&] [✕] [✎] [♿] [📺] [🛬]

▼▼ **Days Inn** M
(319) 354-4400. **Call for rates.** 205 2nd St. I-80, exit 242, 1 mi s to 2nd St, then just w. Ext corridors. **Pets:** Accepted.

[✕] [♿]

▼▼ **Heartland Inn** SH
(319) 351-8132. **$76-$86.** 87 2nd St. I-80, exit 242, 1 mi s on US 6, then just e. Int corridors. **Pets:** $5 daily fee/room. Designated rooms, service with restrictions, supervision.

[ASK] [S&] [✕] [✎] [♿] [📺] [🛬]

▼▼ **Super 8 Motel-Iowa City** SH
(319) 337-8388. **$56-$88.** 611 1st Ave. I-80, exit 242, 0.4 mi s. Int corridors. **Pets:** Accepted.

[ASK] [S&] [✕] [♿M] [✎]

COUNCIL BLUFFS

⍟⍟ ▼▼ **Best Western Crossroads of the Bluffs** SH
(712) 322-3150. **$59-$99.** 2216 27th Ave. I-80, exit 1B (24th St). Int corridors. **Pets:** Accepted.

[SAVE] [S&] [✕] [✎] [✑] [♿] [📺] [🛬] [✕]

⍟⍟ ▼▼▼ **Comfort Suites** SH
(712) 323-9760. **$67-$129.** 1801 S 35th St. I-29, exit 52. Int corridors. **Pets:** $10 daily fee/room. Designated rooms, service with restrictions, supervision.

[SAVE] [S&] [✕] [♿M] [✎] [✑] [♿] [📺] [🛬]

▼▼ **Days Inn** SH
(712) 366-9699. **Call for rates.** 3208 S 7th St. I-80, exit 3, just s. Int corridors. **Pets:** Accepted.

[✕] [✎] [♿] [📺]

▼▼ **Days Inn** SH
(712) 323-2200. **$59-$79.** 3619 9th Ave. I-29, exit 53A (9th Ave). Int corridors. **Pets:** Accepted.

[ASK] [S&] [✕] [✎] [♿] [📺]

▼▼ Heartland Inn SH
(712) 322-8400. **$76-$86.** 1000 Woodbury Ave. I-80, exit 5 (Madison Ave). Int corridors. **Pets:** $5 daily fee/pet. Designated rooms, service with restrictions, supervision.
ASK S🐾 ✕ 🐾 🛏 🖵 🏊

▼▼ Motel 6 Council Bluffs, IA #1153 SH
(712) 366-2405. **$47-$67.** 3032 S Expressway St. I-29/80, exit 3 (US 92). Int corridors. **Pets:** Medium. Service with restrictions, supervision.
S🐾 ✕ 🐾 🖵 🛏 🏊

▼▼▼ Quality Inn Metro SH ❧
(712) 328-3171. **Call for rates.** 3537 W Broadway. I-29, exit 53A (9th Ave), just e, 0.5 mi n on S 35th St, then just w. Ext/int corridors. **Pets:** Other species. Designated rooms, service with restrictions.
✕ 🐾 🖵 🛏 🖵 🏊

▼ Super 8 Motel SH
(712) 322-2888. **$55-$63.** 2712 S 24th St. I-80, exit 1B (24th St). Int corridors. **Pets:** Service with restrictions, supervision.
ASK S🐾 ✕ 🐾

AAA ▼▼▼ Western Inn SH
(712) 322-4499. **$68-$88.** 1842 Madison Ave. I-80, exit 5 (Madison Ave). Int corridors. **Pets:** Small, other species. $10 one-time fee/room. Service with restrictions, supervision.
SAVE S🐾 ✕ 🖵 🏊

CRESCO

AAA ▼ Cresco Motel M
(563) 547-2240. **$47-$90.** 620 2nd Ave SE. On SR 9; on east side of town. Ext corridors. **Pets:** Large, other species. $7.50 daily fee/room. Supervision.
SAVE S🐾 ✕ 🖵M 🖵 🛏

DECORAH

▼▼ Heartland Inn SH
(563) 382-2269. **$72-$82.** 705 Commerce Dr. Jct US 52, 1.8 mi e on SR 9. Int corridors. **Pets:** $5 daily fee/room. Designated rooms, service with restrictions, supervision.
ASK S🐾 ✕ 🛏 🖵 🏊

DENISON

▼▼ Denison Super 8 SH ❧
(712) 263-5081. **Call for rates.** 502 Boyer Valley Rd. Jct US 30/59 and SR 141, 0.3 mi sw. Int corridors. **Pets:** $5 daily fee/pet. Service with restrictions, supervision.
✕ 🛏

DES MOINES

▼▼ American Inn & Suites M
(515) 265-7511. **$51-$61.** 5020 NE 14th St. I-80/35, exit 136 (US 69), just n. Ext/int corridors. **Pets:** Accepted.
ASK S🐾 ✕ 🖵 🏊

▼▼ Bavarian Inn SH
(515) 265-5611. **$59-$69.** 5220 NE 14th St. I-80, exit 136 (US 69), 0.3 mi n. Int corridors. **Pets:** Small. $25 deposit/room. Service with restrictions, supervision.
ASK S🐾 ✕ 🛏 🖵 🍴 🏊

▼▼ Comfort Inn SH
(515) 287-3434. **$64-$89.** 5231 Fleur Dr. Across from airport. Int corridors. **Pets:** Accepted.
ASK S🐾 ✕ 🖵M 🐾 🛏 🖵 🏊

AAA ▼▼▼ Des Moines Marriott Downtown LH
(515) 245-5500. **$99-$189.** 700 Grand Ave. I-235, exit 7th St, 0.5 mi s. Int corridors. **Pets:** Accepted.
SAVE ✕ 🖵M 🐾 🖵 🛏 🖵 🍴 🏊 ✕

▼▼ Heartland Inn-Airport SH ❧
(515) 256-0603. **$78-$88.** 1901 Hackley Ave. Across from airport. Int corridors. **Pets:** $5 daily fee/pet. Service with restrictions, supervision.
ASK S🐾 ✕ 🐾 🖵 🛏 🖵 🏊

▼ Hickman Motor Lodge M
(515) 276-8591. **$44-$54, 7 day notice.** 6500 Hickman Rd. I-80/35, exit 125, 2.5 mi e. Ext corridors. **Pets:** Accepted.
ASK S🐾 ✕

AAA ▼▼▼ Holiday Inn-Merle Hay SH
(515) 278-0271. **$79-$99.** 5000 Merle Hay Rd. I-80/35, exit 131 (Merle Hay Rd), just s. Ext/int corridors. **Pets:** Small, other species. $20 one-time fee/pet. Service with restrictions, supervision.
SAVE S🐾 ✕ 🖵M 🛏 🖵 🍴 🏊 ✕

▼▼ Motel 6-30 M
(515) 287-6364. **$42-$55.** 4817 Fleur Dr. I-35, exit 68 (SR 5/Army Post Rd), 5 mi e to Fleur Dr (exit 97), then 2 mi n. Ext corridors. **Pets:** Accepted.
S🐾 ✕ 🖵

▼▼▼ Quality Inn & Suites SH
(515) 278-2381. **$59-$135.** 4995 Merle Hay Rd. I-80/35, exit 131 (Merle Hay Rd), just s. Int corridors. **Pets:** Other species. Supervision.
ASK S🐾 ✕ 🖵M 🐾 🖵 🛏 🖵 🏊 ✕

AAA ▼▼▼ Quality Inn & Suites Iowa Event Center LH
(515) 282-5251. **$74-$98.** 929 3rd St. I-235, exit 3rd St; downtown. Int corridors. **Pets:** Medium. $10 daily fee/pet. Service with restrictions, supervision.
SAVE S🐾 ✕ 🐾 🛏 🖵 🍴 🏊

▼▼▼ Red Roof Inn & Suites SH
(515) 266-6800. **$65-$80.** 4950 NE 14th St. I-80, exit 136. Int corridors. **Pets:** Large. Service with restrictions, supervision.
ASK ✕ 🛏 🖵 🏊

▼▼ Super 8 Lodge SH
(515) 278-8858. **$54-$64.** 4755 Merle Hay Rd. I-80/35, exit 131 (Merle Hay Rd), just s. Int corridors. **Pets:** Other species. $25 deposit/room. Crate.
ASK S🐾 ✕ 🛏 🖵

DE SOTO

▼ Edgetowner Motel M
(515) 834-2641. **$40-$60.** 804 Guthrie. I-80, exit 110, just s. Ext corridors. **Pets:** Accepted.
✕

DUBUQUE

Best Western Dubuque Inn 🔲
(563) 556-7760. **$79-$129.** 3434 Dodge St. US 20, 3 mi w of jct US 52/61/151 and Mississippi Bridge. Int corridors. **Pets:** Small. $10 daily fee/pet. Designated rooms, service with restrictions, crate.
🆚 🔲 ⊠ 🕖 📦 💻 🍴 🐾 🔀

Best Western Midway Hotel 🔲
(563) 557-8000. **$89-$125.** 3100 Dodge St. US 20, 2.3 mi w of jct US 52/61/151 and Mississippi Bridge. **Pets:** Medium, other species. Designated rooms, service with restrictions, supervision.
🆚 🔲 ⊠ 🕖 📦 💻 🍴 🐾 🔀

Comfort Inn of Dubuque 🔳
(563) 556-3006. **$59-$99.** 4055 McDonald Dr. US 20, 3.8 mi w of jct US 52/61/151 and Mississippi Bridge. Int corridors. **Pets:** Accepted.
🆎 🔲 ⊠ 🕖 📦 💻 🐾

Days Inn-Dubuque 🔳
(563) 583-3297. **$49-$99.** 1111 Dodge St. US 20, 0.8 mi w of jct US 52/61/151 and Mississippi Bridge, exit Hill/Bryant. Ext corridors. **Pets:** Other species. $5 daily fee/pet. Designated rooms, service with restrictions.
🆎 🔲 ⊠ 📦 💻 🍴 🐾

Heartland Inn-South 🔳
(563) 556-6555. **$70-$80.** 2090 Southpark Ct. US 151 and 61 at jct US 52; 2.5 mi s of jct US 20 and Mississippi Bridge. Int corridors. **Pets:** $5 daily fee/room. Designated rooms, service with restrictions, supervision.
🆎 🔲 ⊠ 📦 💻

Heartland Inn-West 🔳
(563) 582-3752. **$70-$80.** 4025 McDonald Dr. US 20, 3.8 mi w of jct US 52/61/151 and Mississippi Bridge. Int corridors. **Pets:** $5 daily fee/room. Designated rooms, service with restrictions, supervision.
🆎 🔲 ⊠ 🕖 📦 💻 🐾 🔀

Holiday Inn Dubuque/Galena 🔲
(563) 556-2000. **$89-$109.** 450 Main St. At Main and 4th sts; downtown. Int corridors. **Pets:** Accepted.
🆚 🔲 ⊠ 🅼 🔑 📦 💻 🍴 🐾 🔀

MainStay Suites 🔳
(563) 557-7829. **$69-$120.** 1275 Associates Dr. Just n of jct US 20 and NW Arterial Rd. Int corridors. **Pets:** Medium. $25 one-time fee/pet. Designated rooms, service with restrictions, crate.
🆎 🔲 ⊠ 🅼 🔑 📦 💻

DYERSVILLE

Comfort Inn-Dyersville 🔳
(563) 875-7700. **$65-$155.** 527 16th Ave SE. US 20, exit 294, just nw. Int corridors. **Pets:** Medium. $50 deposit/room, $15 one-time fee/room. Designated rooms, service with restrictions, supervision.
🆎 🔲 ⊠ 🅼 🔑 📦 💻 🐾 🔀

Super 8 Motel-Dyersville 🔳
(563) 875-8885. **$49-$59.** 925 15th Ave SE. SR 136, just n of jct US 20. Int corridors. **Pets:** Accepted.
🆎 🔲 ⊠ 🅼

ELDRIDGE

Quality Inn & Suites 🔳
(563) 285-4600. **$61-$81, 14 day notice.** 1000 E Iowa St. Just w of jct US 61 and CR F45. Int corridors. **Pets:** Medium. $50 deposit/room. Service with restrictions.
🆎 🔲 ⊠ 🔑 📦 💻 🐾

EVANSDALE

Ramada Limited 🔳
(319) 235-1111. **$62-$150.** 450 Evansdale Dr. I-380, exit 68, just n. Int corridors. **Pets:** Other species. $30 deposit/room, $5 one-time fee/room. Service with restrictions, supervision.
🆎 🔲 ⊠ 🅼 📦 💻 🐾

FAIRFIELD

Best Western Fairfield Inn 🔳
(641) 472-2200. **$65-$76.** 2200 W Burlington Ave. On US 34, 1 mi w of jct SR 1. Int corridors. **Pets:** Small, other species. Designated rooms, service with restrictions, supervision.
🔲 ⊠ 🔑 📦 💻 🍴 🐾

FORT DODGE

Arbor Inn 🔳
(515) 576-8000. **$43.** 3040 5th Ave S. US 20, exit 124 (Coalville), 3.7 mi n on CR P59, 1.2 mi w on Business Rt US 20. Int corridors. **Pets:** Small, dogs only. $6 daily fee/pet. Designated rooms, service with restrictions, supervision.
🆎 🔲 ⊠ 🔑 📦 💻

Comfort Inn 🔳
(515) 573-3731. **$65-$80, 7 day notice.** 2938 5th Ave S. US 20, exit 124 (Coalville), 6 mi n on CR P59, 2 mi w on 5th Ave and Business Rt US 20. Int corridors. **Pets:** Accepted.
🆚 🔲 ⊠ 🅼 🕖 📦 💻 🐾

Holiday Inn 🔳
(515) 955-3621. **$50-$60.** 2001 US 169 S. US 20, 2 mi n. Ext/int corridors. **Pets:** Accepted.
🆎 🔲 ⊠ 🅼 📦 💻 🍴 🐾 🔀

FORT MADISON

The Madison Inn Motel 🅜
(319) 372-7740. **$52-$85.** 3440 Ave L. US 2 and 61, 2 mi w. Ext corridors. **Pets:** $10 daily fee/pet. Designated rooms, service with restrictions, supervision.
🆚 🔲 ⊠ 📦 💻

Super 8 Motel-Ft Madison 🔳
(319) 372-8500. **$49-$59.** US 61 W, 5107 Ave O. US 61, 1 mi e of jct US 61 and SR 2. Ext/int corridors. **Pets:** Accepted.
🆎 🔲 ⊠ 🕖 📦

GLENWOOD

Lincoln Bluff View Motel 🅜
(712) 622-8191. **Call for rates.** 57902 190 St. I-29, exit 35 (US 34). Int corridors. **Pets:** Accepted.
⊠ 📦 🍴

GRIMES

▼▼▼ AmericInn Motel & Suites **SH**
(515) 986-9900. **$69-$164.** 251 Gateway. Just sw of jct US 44 and SR 144. Int corridors. **Pets:** $50 deposit/room, $10 daily fee/room. Designated rooms, service with restrictions, supervision.

⊠ ᏦM ⟨° ⊟ 🖵 ⌦ ⊠

HAMPTON

▼▼▼ AmericInn Lodge & Suites **SH**
(641) 456-5559. **$81-$127.** 702 Central Ave W. On SR 3 (Central Ave W), 0.7 mi w of jct US 65 and SR 3. Int corridors. **Pets:** Other species. $100 deposit/pet. Designated rooms, service with restrictions, supervision.

A$K ᏚᏅ ⊠ ⟨ᴹ ⟨° ⊟ 🖵 ⌦ ⊠

IDA GROVE

▼ Delux Motel **M**
(712) 364-3317. **$45-$60.** 5981 US Hwy 175. Jct US 59 S and 175. Ext corridors. **Pets:** Large. $10 daily fee/pet. Designated rooms, service with restrictions, supervision.

⊠ ⊟

INDEPENDENCE

▼▼ Super 8 Motel **SH**
(319) 334-7041. **$60-$125.** 2000 1st St W. US 20, exit 252, 1.4 mi n. Int corridors. **Pets:** Small. $10 daily fee/pet. Designated rooms, service with restrictions, supervision.

A$K ᏚᏅ ⊠ ᏦM ⊟

IOWA CITY

▲▲▲ ▼▼▼ Quality Inn & Suites **LH**
(319) 354-2000. **$79-$109.** 2525 N Dodge. I-80, exit 246, just ne. Int corridors. **Pets:** Small. $10 deposit/room. Designated rooms, service with restrictions, supervision.

SAVE ᏚᏅ ⊠ ⟨° ⊟ 🖵 ⊩ ⌦ ⊠

▼▼▼ Travelodge **SH** ❦
(319) 351-1010. **$74-$129.** 2216 N Dodge St. I-80, exit 246, just sw on SR 1. Ext/int corridors. **Pets:** $5 daily fee/pet. Designated rooms, service with restrictions, supervision.

A$K ᏚᏅ ⊠ ᏦM ⟨♪ ⟨° ⊟ 🖵 ⌦

IOWA FALLS

▼▼▼ AmericInn Iowa Falls **SH**
(641) 648-4600. **$70-$130.** 810 S Oak St. 1 mi s of jct US 65/20 and Washington Ave; south side of town. Int corridors. **Pets:** Other species. $50 deposit/pet. Service with restrictions, supervision.

⊠ ⟨° ⊟ 🖵 ⌦ ⊠

JEFFERSON

▲▲▲ ▼ The Redwood Motel **M**
(515) 386-3116. **$37-$46.** 209 E Gallup Rd. Just e of jct US 30 and SR 4. Ext corridors. **Pets:** Accepted.

SAVE ⊠

JOHNSTON

▼▼ Best Inns of America **SH**
(515) 270-1111. **$50-$74.** 5050 Merle Hay Rd. I-80/35, exit 131 (Merle Hay Rd), just n. Int corridors. **Pets:** Other species. $10 one-time fee/pet. Service with restrictions, supervision.

A$K ᏚᏅ ⊠ ᏦM ⟨♪ ⊟ 🖵 ⌦

▲▲▲ ▼▼▼ Ramada Inn-Des Moines
North **SH** ❦
(515) 276-5411. **$79-$99, 3 day notice.** 5055 Merle Hay Rd. I-80/35, exit 131 (Merle Hay Rd), just n. Int corridors. **Pets:** $30 deposit/pet, $10 daily fee/room. Designated rooms, service with restrictions, crate.

SAVE ᏚᏅ ⊠ ⟨♪ ⊟ 🖵 ⊩ ⌦

KEOKUK

▼ Super 8 Motel-Keokuk **SH**
(319) 524-3888. **$49-$59.** 3511 Main St. US 218, 2 mi nw. Int corridors. **Pets:** Accepted.

A$K ᏚᏅ ⊠ ᏦM ⊟ 🖵

LE CLAIRE

▲▲▲ ▼▼▼▼ Comfort Inn Riverview **SH**
(563) 289-4747. **$65-$85.** 902 Mississippi View Ct. I-80, exit 306 (US 67), 0.5 mi n to Eagle Ridge Rd, then just sw. Int corridors. **Pets:** Medium. $10 daily fee/room. Service with restrictions, supervision.

SAVE ᏚᏅ ⊠ ᏦM ⟨° ⊟ 🖵 ⌦

▲▲▲ ▼▼▼ Super 8 of LeClaire **SH**
(563) 289-5888. **$60-$70.** 1552 Welcome Center Dr. I-80, exit 306 (US 67), 0.5 mi n to Eagle Ridge Rd, then just sw to Mississippi View Ct. Int corridors. **Pets:** Accepted.

SAVE ᏚᏅ ⊠ ᏦM ⟨° ⊟ 🖵

LE MARS

▼▼ Super 8 Motel **SH**
(712) 546-8800. **$55-$65.** 1201 Hawkeye Ave SW. 1.2 mi s of jct US 75/SR 3, on US 75; south end of town. Int corridors. **Pets:** Other species. $6 daily fee/room. Designated rooms, service with restrictions, supervision.

A$K ᏚᏅ ⊠ ᏦM 🖵 ⌦

MANCHESTER

▼▼ Super 8 of Manchester **SH**
(563) 927-2533. **$58-$96.** 1020 W Main. Jct US 20 and SR 13, exit 275, 1.3 mi n, then 0.3 mi e. Int corridors. **Pets:** Accepted.

A$K ᏚᏅ ⊠ ᏦM ⊟ 🖵

MARION

▼▼ Microtel Inn & Suites **SH**
(319) 373-7400. **$59-$64.** 5500 Dyer Ave. Jct US 151 and SR 13. Int corridors. **Pets:** Other species. $25 deposit/room. Service with restrictions, crate.

A$K ᏚᏅ ⊠ ᏦM ⟨° ⊟ 🖵

MARSHALLTOWN

▼▼◆◆ Best Western Regency Inn 🆂🅷
(641) 752-6321. **$74-$99, 14 day notice.** 3303 S Center St. Jct US 30 and SR 14. Int corridors. **Pets:** Other species. $10 one-time fee/room. Service with restrictions, supervision.

▼▼◆◆ Comfort Inn 🆂🅷
(641) 752-6000. **$63-$88, 14 day notice.** 2613 S Center St. 0.5 mi n of jct US 30 and SR 14. Int corridors. **Pets:** Other species. $10 one-time fee/room. Service with restrictions, supervision.

▼▼ Econo Lodge 🆂🅷
(641) 753-3333. **$50-$70, 14 day notice.** 3315 S Center St. Just n of jct US 30 and SR 14. Int corridors. **Pets:** Other species. $10 one-time fee/room. Service with restrictions, supervision.

[A$K] [S6] [✕] [🐾] [🍴] [💻]

MASON CITY

▼▼ Days Inn Mason City 🆂🅷
(641) 424-0210. **$55-$76.** 2301 4th St SW. I-35, exit 194 (SR 122), 6 mi e. Int corridors. **Pets:** Small, other species. $10 daily fee/pet. No service, supervision.

[A$K] [S6] [✕] [🐾] [🍴] [💻]

◆◆◆ ▼▼◆◆ Holiday Inn 🆂🅷
(641) 423-1640. **$59-$79.** 2101 4th St SW (Hwy 122). 1.5 mi w of jct US 18 and 65, on SR 122; 8 mi e of jct I-35 and US 18. Ext/int corridors. **Pets:** Medium. $10 one-time fee/room. Service with restrictions, supervision.

[SAVE] [S6] [✕] [🐾] [🍴] [💻] [🍽] [🍴] [🍽] [✕]

▼▼ Mason City Super 8 Motel & Suites 🆂🅷
(641) 423-8855. **$65-$70.** 3010 4th St SW. I-35, exit 194 (SR 122), 6 mi e. Int corridors. **Pets:** Large, other species. $5 daily fee/pet. Service with restrictions.

[A$K] [S6] [✕] [🐾] [🍴] [🍽] [💻] [🍽]

◆◆◆ ▼▼◆◆ Thriftlodge 🅼
(641) 424-2910. **$55-$75, 15 day notice.** 24 5th St SW. Just w of jct US 65 and SR 122 (Business Rt 18). Ext/int corridors. **Pets:** Accepted.

[SAVE] [S6] [✕] [🍴] [🍽]

MONTICELLO

▼▼◆◆ The Blue Inn 🆂🅷
(319) 465-6116. **$55-$100.** 250 N Main St. North end of town on US 151. Int corridors. **Pets:** $20 deposit/room, $6 one-time fee/pet. Designated rooms, service with restrictions, supervision.

[A$K] [S6] [✕] [💻] [🍴] [🍽]

MOUNT PLEASANT

▼▼ Heartland Inn 🆂🅷
(319) 385-2102. **$70-$80.** 810 N Grand Ave. US 218/27, exit 45, 0.6 mi s. Int corridors. **Pets:** $5 daily fee/room. Designated rooms, service with restrictions, supervision.

[A$K] [S6] [✕] [🍴] [💻] [🍽] [✕]

▼▼◆◆ Ramada Limited 🆂🅷
(319) 385-0571. **$71-$88.** 1200 E Baker. US 218/27, exit 45, 0.6 mi s on Grand Ave. Int corridors. **Pets:** Medium, other species. $8 daily fee/room. Service with restrictions, supervision.

[A$K] [S6] [✕] [🐾] [🍴] [🍴] [💻] [🍽] [✕]

▼▼ Super 8 Motel-Mt Pleasant 🆂🅷
(319) 385-8888. **$46-$85.** 1000 N Grand Ave. US 218/27, exit 45, 0.6 mi s. Int corridors. **Pets:** Other species. $10 one-time fee/room. Service with restrictions, supervision.

[A$K] [S6] [✕] [🍴] [🍴]

MUSCATINE

▼▼▼ Holiday Inn Muscatine 🆂🅷
(563) 264-5550. **$95.** 2915 N Hwy 61. Jct US 61 and SR 38, just n. Int corridors. **Pets:** Accepted.

[A$K] [S6] [✕] [🍴] [🍴] [🍴] [💻] [🍽] [✕]

▼▼ Super 8 Motel-Muscatine 🆂🅷
(563) 263-9100. **$46-$69.** 2900 N Hwy 61. Jct US 61 and SR 38. Int corridors. **Pets:** Accepted.

[A$K] [S6] [✕] [🐾] [🍴]

NEWTON

▼▼ Days Inn of Newton 🆂🅷
(641) 792-2330. **$54-$69.** 1605 W 19th St S. I-80, exit 164 (SR 14), just n. Int corridors. **Pets:** Other species. $10 daily fee/pet. Service with restrictions, supervision.

[A$K] [S6] [✕] [🍴] [🍴] [💻]

◆◆◆ ▼▼◆◆ Holiday Inn Express 🆂🅷
(641) 792-7722. **$69-$129.** 1700 W 19th St S. I-80, exit 164 (SR 14), just nw. Int corridors. **Pets:** Medium. $20 daily fee/room. Service with restrictions, supervision.

[SAVE] [S6] [✕] [🍴] [🍴] [💻] [🍽]

◆◆◆ ▼▼▼ Ramada Limited 🆂🅷
(641) 792-8100. **$70-$85, 15 day notice.** 1405 W 19th St S. I-80, exit 164 (SR 14), just n. Int corridors. **Pets:** Small. $10 daily fee/pet. Designated rooms, service with restrictions, supervision.

[SAVE] [S6] [✕] [🍴] [💻]

OKOBOJI

▼▼▼ AmericInn Lodge & Suites 🆂🅷
(712) 332-9000. **$75-$165, 7 day notice.** 1005 Brooks Park Dr. Jct US 71 and SR 9, 2.5 mi s on US 71. Int corridors. **Pets:** Large. $50 deposit/room, $10 one-time fee/room. Service with restrictions, supervision.

[✕] [🍴] [🍴] [🍴] [💻] [🍽] [✕]

▼▼◆◆ Arrowwood Resort & Conference Center 🆂🅷
(712) 332-2161. **$79-$209, 7 day notice.** 1405 US 71. Jct US 71 and SR 9, 3 mi s. Ext/int corridors. **Pets:** Designated rooms, service with restrictions, supervision.

[A$K] [S6] [✕] [🍴] [🐾] [🍴] [🍴] [💻] [🍴] [🍽] [✕]

OSCEOLA

▼▼▼▼ AmericInn Motel & Suites SH
(641) 342-9400. **$74-$154.** 111 Ariel Cir. I-35, exit 33. Int corridors. **Pets:** Small. $50 deposit/room, $10 one-time fee/room. Designated rooms, service with restrictions, supervision.
ASK S🐾 ✕ 🔥M 🐾 🔋 🖵 🏊

OSKALOOSA

▼▼▼▼ Comfort Inn SH
(641) 672-0375. **$75-$109.** 2401 A Ave W. Just e of jct SR 163, exit 57 (SR 92). Int corridors. **Pets:** Medium. Designated rooms, service with restrictions, supervision.
ASK S🐾 ✕ 🔥 🔋 🖵 🏊 ✕🍴

AAA ▼▼▼ Rodeway Inn M
(641) 673-8351. **$55-$75.** 1315 A Ave E. SR 92 E. Ext/int corridors. **Pets:** Medium. Designated rooms, service with restrictions, supervision.
SAVE S🐾 ✕ 🔋 🖵

OTTUMWA

▼ Colonial Motor Inn M
(641) 683-1661. **$40-$46.** 1534 Albia Rd. W on US 34, s at Quincy St, 0.5 mi to Albia Rd, then just w. Ext/int corridors. **Pets:** Accepted.
ASK S🐾 ✕ 🔋

▼▼ Heartland Inn SH ✿
(641) 682-8526. **$73-$83.** 125 W Joseph Ave. 2 mi n on US 63. Int corridors. **Pets:** Medium. $5 daily fee/pet. Service with restrictions, supervision.
ASK S🐾 ✕ 🐾 🔋 🖵 🏊

PELLA

▼▼ Super 8 Motel-Pella SH
(641) 628-8181. **$49-$59.** 105 E Oskaloosa St. SR 163, exit 42, 1 mi n, then 0.5 mi e. Int corridors. **Pets:** $5 daily fee/pet. Designated rooms, service with restrictions, supervision.
ASK S🐾 ✕ 🔥M 🐾 🔋 🖵

PERCIVAL

▼▼ Nebraska City Super 8 Motel SH
(712) 382-2828. **$56-$76.** 2103 249th St. I-29, exit 10, just w. Int corridors. **Pets:** Small, dogs only. $5 one-time fee/pet. Designated rooms, service with restrictions, supervision.
ASK S🐾 ✕ 🔥 🔋 🖵

QUAD CITIES AREA

BETTENDORF

▼▼▼ Heartland Inn-Bettendorf SH
(563) 355-6336. **$72-$82.** 815 Golden Valley Dr. I-74, exit 2, just e, just n on Utica Ridge Rd, then just w. Int corridors. **Pets:** $5 daily fee/room. Designated rooms, service with restrictions, supervision.
ASK S🐾 ✕ 🔋 🖵 🏊 ✕🍴

▼▼▼▼ Holiday Inn Hotel & Suites-Bettendorf SH
(563) 355-4761. **Call for rates.** 909 Middle Rd. I-74, exit 3, just w. Int corridors. **Pets:** Accepted.
✕ 🔥 🔋 🖵 🍴 🏊 ✕🍴

▼▼▼▼ The Lodge-Bettendorf LH
(563) 359-7141. **$77-$126.** 900 Spruce Hills Dr. I-74, exit 2, just e, 3 mi s of jct I-74 and 80. Int corridors. **Pets:** Small, other species. $25 deposit/pet. Designated rooms, service with restrictions.
ASK S🐾 ✕ 🐾 🔋 🖵 🍴 🏊 ✕🍴

▼▼▼ Signature Inn Bettendorf SH
(563) 355-7575. **$71-$79.** 3020 Utica Ridge Rd. I-74, exit 2, just e. Int corridors. **Pets:** Small. Service with restrictions, crate.
✕ 🔥M 🔋 🖵 🏊

DAVENPORT

AAA ▼▼▼▼ Baymont Inn & Suites Davenport SH
(563) 386-1600. **$69-$89.** 400 Jason Way Ct. I-80, exit 295A (US 61), just s to 65th St, then 0.5 mi ne on frontage road. Int corridors. **Pets:** Other species. Designated rooms, no service, supervision.
SAVE S🐾 ✕ 🐾 🔥 🔋 🖵 🏊

AAA ▼▼▼▼ Best Western SteepleGate Inn SH
(563) 386-6900. **$99-$119.** 100 W 76th St. I-80, exit 295A (US 61), 0.5 mi s to 65th St and frontage road entrance, then just nw. Int corridors. **Pets:** Medium. $10 daily fee/pet. Designated rooms, service with restrictions, supervision.
SAVE S🐾 ✕ 🐾 🔋 🖵 🍴 🏊 ✕🍴

▼▼ Comfort Inn Davenport SH ✿
(563) 391-8222. **$60-$75.** 7222 Northwest Blvd. I-80, exit 292 (Northwest Blvd), 0.3 mi s. Ext corridors. **Pets:** $5 daily fee/room. Service with restrictions.
ASK S🐾 ✕ 🔥 🔋 🖵

▼▼▼ Country Inn & Suites By Carlson SH
(563) 388-6444. **$74-$99.** 140 E 55th St. I-80, exit 295A (US 61), 1.4 mi s. Int corridors. **Pets:** Accepted.
ASK S🐾 ✕ 🔥M 🔥 🔋 🖵 🏊

▼▼▼ Davenport Holiday Inn SH
(563) 391-1230. **$70-$105.** 5202 Brady St. I-80, exit 295A (US 61), 1.6 mi s. Int corridors. **Pets:** Medium. $10 one-time fee/pet. Service with restrictions, supervision.
ASK S🐾 ✕ 🔥M 🔥 🔋 🖵 🍴 🏊 ✕🍴

AAA ▼▼▼ **Davenport Super 8 Motel** SH
(563) 388-9810. **$44-$94.** 410 E 65th St. I-80, exit 295A (US 61), just e. Int corridors. **Pets:** Very small. $5 daily fee/pet. Service with restrictions, supervision.
SAVE S6 ✕ &M 🖬

AAA ▼▼▼ **Exel Inn of Davenport** SH
(563) 386-6350. **$42-$62.** 6310 N Brady St. I-80, exit 295A (US 61), 0.5 mi s. Int corridors. **Pets:** Small, other species. Designated rooms, service with restrictions, supervision.
SAVE S6 ✕ 🐾 🖬 🖵

▼▼▼ **Hampton Inn-Davenport** SH
(563) 359-3921. **$89-$175.** 3330 E Kimberly Rd. I-74, exit 2, just w, then just s. Int corridors. **Pets:** Accepted.
ASK S6 ✕ 🖬 🖵 🏊 ✕

▼▼▼ **Heartland Inn** SH 🐾
(563) 386-8336. **$72-$82.** 6605 Brady St. I-80, exit 295A (US 61), just se. Int corridors. **Pets:** Medium, other species. $5 one-time fee/pet. Designated rooms, service with restrictions, supervision.
ASK S6 ✕ 🖬 🖵 🏊 ✕

🐾 **END AREA** 🐾

RED OAK

AAA ▼▼▼ **Super 8–Red Oak** SH
(712) 623-6919. **$55-$75.** 800 Senate Ave. Just e of jct US 34 and SR 48 on US 34. Int corridors. **Pets:** Accepted.
SAVE S6 ✕ 🖬 🏊

SIBLEY

▼▼ **Super 8 Motel** SH
(712) 754-3603. **$65-$80.** 1108 2nd Ave. On SR 60. Int corridors. **Pets:** Accepted.
ASK ✕ 🖬

SIOUX CITY

▼▼▼ **AmericInn Lodge & Suites** SH 🐾
(712) 255-1800. **$75-$90, 7 day notice.** 4230 S Lewis Blvd. I-29, exit 143, just e. Int corridors. **Pets:** Other species. $50 deposit/room, $10 daily fee/room. Designated rooms, service with restrictions, supervision.
ASK S6 ✕ &M 🐾 🖬 🖵 🏊 ✕

▼▼▼ **Best Western City Centre** SH
(712) 277-1550. **$65-$77.** 130 Nebraska St. I-29, exit 147B, just w on Gordon Dr, then just n. Int corridors. **Pets:** $10 daily fee/pet. Designated rooms, service with restrictions.
ASK S6 ✕ 🖬 🖵 🏊

▼▼▼ **Comfort Inn** SH
(712) 274-1300. **$69-$89.** 4202 S Lakeport St. I-29, exit 144A, 1 mi e on US 20, just s; do not use Business Rt US 20. Int corridors. **Pets:** Other species. $10 daily fee/room. Service with restrictions, supervision.
ASK S6 ✕ 🐾 🖬 🖵 🏊

▼ **Motel 6–45** SH
(712) 277-3131. **$35-$55.** 6166 Harbor Dr. I-29, exit 141, just w. Int corridors. **Pets:** Accepted.
S6 ✕ 🐾 🏊

AAA ▼▼▼ **Plaza Hotel & Conference Center** LH
(712) 277-4101. **$79.** 707 4th St. Downtown. Int corridors. **Pets:** Accepted.
SAVE S6 ✕ 🐾 🖬 🖵 🍴 🏊 ✕

▼▼ **Super 8 Motel** M
(712) 274-1520. **$50-$68, 7 day notice.** 4307 Stone Ave. I-29, exit 144A, 4.2 mi e on US 20, 1.2 mi n on SR 12 (Gordon Dr). Int corridors. **Pets:** Small, other species. $10 daily fee/pet. Designated rooms, service with restrictions, supervision.
ASK S6 ✕ &M 🖬 🖵

SLOAN

▼▼ **Winna Vegas Inn** SH
(712) 428-4280. **$58-$64.** 1862 Hwy 141. I-29, exit 127, just e. Int corridors. **Pets:** Accepted.
ASK S6 ✕ &M 🐾 🖬 🖵

SPIRIT LAKE

▼ **Oaks Motel** M
(712) 336-2940. **$33-$95, 10 day notice.** 1701 Chicago. Jct US 71 and SR 9, just e. Ext corridors. **Pets:** Other species. $20 deposit/room. Designated rooms, service with restrictions, crate.
✕

▼ **Shamrock Inn** M
(712) 336-2668. **$60-$115, 3 day notice.** 1905 18th St. 0.6 mi e on SR 9 and US 71; from the w jct of SR 9 and US 71. Ext/int corridors. **Pets:** Medium, other species. $10 daily fee/room. Designated rooms, service with restrictions.
ASK S6 ✕ 🖬 🖵 🏊

▼▼ Spirit Lake Super 8 SH
(712) 336-4901. **$55-$120, 5 day notice.** 2203 Circle Dr W.
Jct US 71 and SR 9. Int corridors. **Pets:** $50 deposit/room,
$10 one-time fee/room. Service with restrictions, supervi-
sion.

A$K S⁄∂ ⊠ 🔥M 🔒 🖥

STORY CITY

▼▼ Viking Motor Inn M
(515) 733-4306. **$50-$54.** 1520 Broad St. I-35, exit 124, just
w. Int corridors. **Pets:** Small, other species. Service with
restrictions, supervision.

A$K S⁄∂ ⊠ 🔒 ≈

STUART

▼▼ Super 8 Motel SH
(515) 523-2888. **Call for rates.** 203 SE 7th St. I-80, exit 93.
Int corridors. **Pets:** Accepted.

⊠ 🔥M 🔒 🖥 ≈

TOLEDO

🅰🅰🅰 ▼▼ Days Inn SH
(641) 484-5678. **$51-$60.** 403 US 30 W. On US 30, just w of
jct US 63 and 30. Int corridors. **Pets:** Other species. $10
one-time fee/room. Designated rooms, supervision.

SAVE S⁄∂ ⊠ 🔒 ≈

▼▼ Super 8 Motel-Toledo SH
(641) 484-5888. **$49-$69.** 207 Hwy 30 W. On US 30, just w
of jct US 63 and 30. Ext/int corridors. **Pets:** Accepted.

A$K S⁄∂ ⊠ 🔥M 🔒 🖥

URBANDALE

🅰🅰🅰 ▼▼ Comfort Inn-Merle Hay SH
(515) 270-1037. **$64-$84.** 5900 Sutton Dr. I-80, exit 131, just
s, then w. Int corridors. **Pets:** Other species. $5 daily fee/
pet. Service with restrictions, supervision.

SAVE S⁄∂ ⊠ 🔥 🔒 🖥 ≈ ⊠

▼▼ Microtel Inn and Suites SH
(515) 727-5424. **$65.** 8711 Plum Dr. I-35/80, exit 129. Int
corridors. **Pets:** Other species. $25 deposit/room. Service
with restrictions, crate.

A$K S⁄∂ ⊠ 🔥M 🔥 🔒 🖥

▼▼ Sleep Inn SH
(515) 270-2424. **$75-$95.** 11211 Hickman Rd. I-35/80, exit
125 (Hickman Rd), just ne. Int corridors. **Pets:** Medium,
other species. $5 daily fee/pet. Designated rooms, service
with restrictions, supervision.

A$K S⁄∂ ⊠ 🔥M 🔥 🔥 🔒 🖥 ≈ ⊠

WALNUT

▼▼ Super 8 Motel SH
(712) 784-2221. **$50-$90.** 2109 Antique City Dr. I-80, exit 46,
just n. Int corridors. **Pets:** Other species. Designated
rooms, service with restrictions, supervision.

A$K S⁄∂ ⊠ 🔥 ≈

WASHINGTON

▼▼ Super 8 Motel-Washington M
(319) 653-6621. **$58-$61.** 119 Westview Dr. 1.5 mi w on SR
1 and 92. Int corridors. **Pets:** Accepted.

A$K S⁄∂ ⊠ 🔒

WATERLOO

▼▼ Comfort Inn of Waterloo SH
(319) 234-7411. **$64-$94.** 1945 La Porte Rd. I-380 N, exit 72
(E San Marnan). Int corridors. **Pets:** $75 deposit/room.
Designated rooms, service with restrictions, crate.

A$K S⁄∂ ⊠ 🔥 🔒 🖥 ≈

▼▼ Heartland Inn-Crossroads SH ☙
(319) 235-4461. **$74-$84.** 1809 La Porte Rd. I-380, exit 72
(E San Marnan), just nw. Int corridors. **Pets:** Medium. $5
daily fee/room. Service with restrictions, supervision.

A$K S⁄∂ ⊠ 🔥 🔒 🖥 ≈

▼▼ Heartland Inn-Greyhound Park SH
(319) 232-7467. **$74-$84.** 3052 Marnie Ave. US 63, exit 227,
1 mi n of jct US 20 and 63. Int corridors. **Pets:** $5 daily
fee/room. Designated rooms, service with restrictions,
supervision.

A$K S⁄∂ ⊠ 🔒 🖥 ≈ ⊠

🅰🅰🅰 ▼▼▼ Holiday Inn Express SH
(319) 233-9191. **$79-$150.** 2141 La Porte Rd. I-380, exit 72
(E San Marnan). Int corridors. **Pets:** Accepted.

SAVE S⁄∂ ⊠ 🔥 🔒 🖥 ≈ ⊠

▼▼▼ Motel 6-4081 SH
(319) 236-3238. **$52-$58.** 2343 Logan Ave. On US 63, 2.5
mi n of jct US 218 and 63. Int corridors. **Pets:** Accepted.

S⁄∂ ⊠ 🔥M 🔒 🖥 ≈

▼▼▼ Quality Inn & Suites SH
(319) 235-0301. **$75-$160.** 226 W 5th St. Downtown. Int
corridors. **Pets:** Accepted.

A$K S⁄∂ ⊠ 🔥M 🔥 🔒 🖥

▼▼▼ Ramada Inn & 5 Sullivan Brothers
Convention Center LH
(319) 233-7560. **$89-$149.** 205 W 4th St. 4th and Commercial sts; downtown. Int corridors. **Pets:** Other species. Service with restrictions.

A$K S⁄∂ ⊠ 🔥M 🔥 🔒 🖥 🍴 ≈ ⊠

WAVERLY

▼▼▼ AmeriHost Inn-Waverly SH
(319) 352-0399. **$73-$149, 7 day notice.** 404 29th Ave SW.
US Business Rt 218, exit 198, 0.5 mi n. Int corridors.
Pets: Medium. $10 daily fee/pet. Designated rooms, service
with restrictions, supervision.

A$K S⁄∂ ⊠ 🔥M 🔥 🔒 🖥 ≈ ⊠

▼▼▼ Red Fox Inn SH
(319) 352-5330. **$65-$170.** 1900 Heritage Way. On SR 3, 2
mi e of jct US 218 and SR 3. Ext/int corridors.
Pets: Medium. $5 daily fee/room. Service with restrictions.

A$K S⁄∂ ⊠ 🔥 🔒 🖥 🍴 ≈ ⊠

▼▼▼ Super 8 Waverly 🆂🅷
(319) 352-0888. **$55-$95.** 301 13th Ave SW. US Business Rt 218 S, exit 198, 1.2 mi n. Int corridors. **Pets:** Accepted.
🄰🅂🄺 🆂🄳 ⊠ 🄻🄼 📶

WEBSTER CITY

▼▼ The Executive Inn 🆂🅷
(515) 832-3631. **$54-$74.** 1700 Superior St. Jct US 20 and SR 17, exit 140, 0.5 mi n. Int corridors. **Pets:** Medium. $35 deposit/room. Designated rooms, service with restrictions.
🄰🅂🄺 🆂🄳 ⊠ 📶 💻 ➳

WEST BURLINGTON

▼▼▼ AmericInn Motel & Suites 🆂🅷 ❀
(319) 758-9000. **$63-$83.** 628 S Gear Ave. US 34, exit 260 (Gear Ave), just ne. Int corridors. **Pets:** Large, other species. Designated rooms, service with restrictions, supervision.
⊠ 🄻🄼 🎬 🄲 📶 💻 ➳ 🆇

WEST DES MOINES

▼▼▼ Candlewood Suites-West Des Moines 🆂🅷
(515) 221-0001. **$85-$114.** 7625 Office Plaza Dr N. I-80, exit 121 (74th St), just sw. Int corridors. **Pets:** Accepted.
🄰🅂🄺 🆂🄳 ⊠ 🄻🄼 🄲 📶 💻

▼▼▼ Hawthorn Suites Ltd 🆂🅷
(515) 223-0000. **$92-$102.** 6905 Lake Dr. I-80, exit 121 (74th St), just ne. Int corridors. **Pets:** Accepted.
⊠ 🄲 📶 💻 ➳ 🆇

▲▲▲ ▼▼▼ Holiday Inn-University Park 🅻🅷
(515) 223-1800. **$79-$159.** 1800 50th St. I-80/35, exit 124 (University Ave), just e. Int corridors. **Pets:** Medium. $50 one-time fee/room. Designated rooms, service with restrictions, supervision.
🆂🄰🅅🄴 🆂🄳 ⊠ 🄻🄼 🎬 🄲 📶 💻 🍴 ➳ 🆇

▼▼ Motel 6–1408 🆂🅷
(515) 267-8885. **$41-$57.** 7655 Office Plaza Dr N. I-80, exit 121 (74th St), just sw. Int corridors. **Pets:** Accepted.
🆂🄳 ⊠ 🄻🄼 🄲 ➳

▲▲▲ ▼▼▼ Quality Suites by Choice Hotels 🆂🅷
(515) 223-9005. **$89-$129.** 1236 74th St. I-80, exit 121 (74th St), just s. Int corridors. **Pets:** Small. Designated rooms, service with restrictions, supervision.
🆂🄰🅅🄴 🆂🄳 ⊠ 🄻🄼 🎬 🄲 📶 💻 ➳ 🆇

▼▼▼ Valley West Inn 🆂🅷
(515) 225-2524. **$85-$139.** 3535 Westown Pkwy. I-235, exit 1 (35th St), just n. Int corridors. **Pets:** Accepted.
🄰🅂🄺 🆂🄳 ⊠ 🎬 📶 💻 🍴 ➳ 🆇

▲▲▲ ▼▼▼▼ West Des Moines Marriott 🅻🅷
(515) 267-1500. **$79-$109.** 1250 74th St. I-80, exit 121 (74th St). Int corridors. **Pets:** Medium. $50 one-time fee/room. Service with restrictions, supervision.
🆂🄰🅅🄴 🆂🄳 ⊠ 🄻🄼 🄲 📶 💻 🍴 ➳ 🆇

WEST LIBERTY

▼▼ Econo Lodge 🄼
(319) 627-2171. **$51-$69.** 1943 Garfield Ave. I-80, exit 259, just sw. Int corridors. **Pets:** Medium. $5 daily fee/pet. Service with restrictions, supervision.
🄰🅂🄺 ⊠ 💻

WILLIAMS

▼▼ Best Western Norseman Inn 🄼
(515) 854-2281. **$50-$56.** 3086 220th St. I-35, exit 144, just e. Int corridors. **Pets:** Medium, dogs only. Service with restrictions, supervision.
🄰🅂🄺 🆂🄳 ⊠ 📶 💻

WILLIAMSBURG

▲▲▲ ▼▼▼ Best Western Quiet House Suites 🆂🅷
(319) 668-9777. **$83-$115.** 1708 N Highland St. I-80, exit 220, 0.8 mi n. Int corridors. **Pets:** Other species. $17 daily fee/pet. Designated rooms, service with restrictions, supervision.
🆂🄰🅅🄴 🆂🄳 ⊠ 🎬 🄲 📶 💻 ➳

▲▲▲ ▼▼▼ Crest Country Inn 🄼
(319) 668-1522. **$45-$57.** 340 W Evans St. I-80, exit 220, just nw. Ext corridors. **Pets:** Small. $5 daily fee/pet. Designated rooms, supervision.
🆂🄰🅅🄴 ⊠ 🄲

▲▲▲ ▼▼▼ Super 8 Motel 🆂🅷
(319) 668-9718. **$69-$82.** 1708 N Highland St. I-80, exit 220, 0.8 mi n. Ext/int corridors. **Pets:** Other species. $17 daily fee/pet. Designated rooms, service with restrictions, supervision.
🆂🄰🅅🄴 🆂🄳 ⊠ 🎬

WINTERSET

▼▼ Village View Motel 🄼
(515) 462-1218. **$54-$72.** 711 SR 92 E. Jct N US 169 and SR 92, 0.3 mi e. Int corridors. **Pets:** Accepted.
🄰🅂🄺 🆂🄳 ⊠ 📶

KANSAS

ABILENE

◇◇◇ Best Western President's Inn SH
(785) 263-2050. **$44-$58.** 2210 N Buckeye. I-70, exit 275.
Ext corridors. **Pets:** Service with restrictions, supervision.
[SAVE] [icons]

◇◇ Days Inn-Abilene Pride SH
(785) 263-2800. **Call for rates.** 1709 N Buckeye Ave. I-70,
exit 275, 0.5 mi s. Ext/int corridors. **Pets:** Accepted.
[icons]

◇◇◇ Diamond Motel M ✿
(785) 263-2360. **$36-$44.** 1407 NW 3rd St. I-70, exit 275,
1.3 mi s, then 1 mi w. Ext corridors. **Pets:** Medium, other
species. $5 one-time fee/pet. Service with restrictions, crate.
[SAVE] [icons]

◇◇◇◇ Holiday Inn Express Hotel & Suites SH
(785) 263-4049. **$79-$94.** 110 E Lafayette Ave. I-70, exit
275, just n. Int corridors. **Pets:** Accepted.
[ASK] [icons]

◇◇ Super 8 Motel SH
(785) 263-4545. **$51-$69.** 2207 N Buckeye. I-70, exit 275,
just s. Int corridors. **Pets:** Other species. $50 deposit/room,
$10 daily fee/pet. Service with restrictions, supervision.
[ASK] [icons]

ATCHISON

◇◇◇◇ Comfort Inn SH
(913) 367-7666. **Call for rates.** 509 S 9th. Just s of jct US
59, on US 73. Int corridors. **Pets:** Accepted.
[icons]

BAXTER SPRINGS

◇◇ Baxter Inn-4-Less SH
(620) 856-2106. **$40-$50.** 2451 Military Ave. On US 69 Alternate, 1 mi s from jct US 166. Int corridors. **Pets:** Small. $20
deposit/pet. No service, supervision.
[ASK] [icons]

BELOIT

◇◇ Super 8 Motel-Beloit SH
(785) 738-4300. **$45-$86.** 205 W Hwy 24. Just e of jct SR
14. Ext/int corridors. **Pets:** Medium. Designated rooms,
service with restrictions, supervision.
[icons]

BURLINGTON

◇◇ Country Haven Inn SH
(620) 364-8260. **$60-$67.** 207 Cross St. Just e of US 75; 1
mi n of center. Int corridors. **Pets:** Small, dogs only. $25
deposit/pet. Supervision.
[ASK] [icons]

CHANUTE

◇◇◇ Guest House Motor Inn M
(620) 431-0600. **$33-$36.** 1814 S Santa Fe. US 169, exit
35th St, 2.5 mi ne. Ext corridors. **Pets:** Small. $5 daily
fee/pet. Service with restrictions.
[SAVE] [icons]

CLAY CENTER

◇◇ Cedar Court Motel M
(785) 632-2148. **$40-$59.** 905 Crawford. 0.5 mi e on US 24.
Ext corridors. **Pets:** Very small, dogs only. Designated
rooms, service with restrictions, supervision.
[ASK] [icons]

COFFEYVILLE

◇◇◇ Appletree Inn M
(620) 251-0002. **$67-$73.** 820 E 11th St. 0.8 mi e of center.
Int corridors. **Pets:** Small. $3 daily fee/pet. Designated
rooms, service with restrictions, supervision.
[SAVE] [icons]

◇◇◇ Super 8 M
(620) 251-2250. **$56-$62, 7 day notice.** 104 W 11th St. On
US 169 and 166; center. Ext corridors. **Pets:** Accepted.
[SAVE] [icons]

COLBY

◇◇◇ Best Western Crown Motel M ✿
(785) 462-3943. **$60-$85.** 2320 S Range. I-70, exit 53 (SR
25), just s. Ext corridors. **Pets:** Other species.
[SAVE] [icons]

◇◇◇◇ Comfort Inn SH ✿
(785) 462-3833. **$69-$119.** 2225 S Range. I-70, exit 53 (SR
25), just s. Int corridors. **Pets:** Large, other species. $5 daily
fee/pet. Designated rooms, service with restrictions, supervision.
[SAVE] [icons]

(AAA) ▼▼▼ Days Inn SH
(785) 462-8691. **$50-$70.** 1925 S Range. I-70, exit 53 (SR 25), 0.3 mi n. Int corridors. **Pets:** Other species. $5 daily fee/pet. Service with restrictions, supervision.
SAVE S☐ ✕ ☐ ☐ ☐ ▱

(AAA) ▼▼▼▼ Holiday Inn Express Hotel & Suites SH
(785) 462-8787. **$80-$110.** 645 W Willow. I-70, exit 53 (SR 25), just ne. Int corridors. **Pets:** Small. $10 one-time fee/pet. Service with restrictions, supervision.
SAVE S☐ ✕ ☐ ☐ ☐ ☐ ▱

▼▼ Motel Super 8 SH
(785) 462-8248. **$47-$65.** 1040 Zelfer Ave. I-70, exit 53 (SR 25), 0.3 mi n, then just w. Int corridors. **Pets:** Accepted.
A$K S☐ ✕

(AAA) ▼▼ Quality Inn SH
(785) 462-3933. **$55-$85, 7 day notice.** 1950 S Range. I-70, exit 53 (SR 25). Ext/int corridors. **Pets:** Accepted.
SAVE S☐ ✕ ☐ ☐ ☐ ▱

COTTONWOOD FALLS

(AAA) ▼▼▼▼ Grand Central Hotel CI
(620) 273-6763. **$140-$180.** 215 Broadway. Just w of US 177; center of downtown. Int corridors. **Pets:** Small, dogs only. Service with restrictions, supervision.
SAVE S☐ ✕ ☐ ☐ ☐

COUNCIL GROVE

(AAA) ▼▼▼ The Cottage House Hotel & Motel SH
(620) 767-6828. **$60-$95, 7 day notice.** 25 N Neosho. Just n of Main St; downtown. Ext/int corridors. **Pets:** Accepted.
SAVE S☐ ✕ ☐ ☐

DODGE CITY

▼▼ Best Western Silver Spur Lodge SH
(620) 227-2125. **$63-$75.** 1510 W Wyatt Earp Blvd. 1 mi w on US 50 business route. Ext/int corridors. **Pets:** Other species. $15 daily fee/room. Designated rooms.
A$K S☐ ✕ ☐ ☐ ☐ ▱

▼▼ Econo Lodge of Dodge City SH
(620) 225-0231. **$51-$65.** 1610 W Wyatt Earp Blvd. 1 mi w on US 50 business route. Int corridors. **Pets:** Medium. $5 daily fee/pet. Designated rooms, service with restrictions, supervision.
A$K ✕ ☐ ☐ ☐ ☐ ▱

▼▼▼▼ Holiday Inn Express SH
(620) 227-5000. **$87-$91.** 2320 W Wyatt Earp Blvd. 1.4 mi w on US 50 business route. Int corridors. **Pets:** Medium. Service with restrictions, supervision.
A$K S☐ ✕ ☐ ☐ ☐ ☐ ▱

▼▼ Super 8 Motel SH
(620) 225-3924. **$60-$80.** 1708 W Wyatt Earp Blvd. 1.2 mi w on US 50 business route. Int corridors. **Pets:** Other species. Service with restrictions, supervision.
A$K S☐ ✕ ☐ ☐ ☐ ▱

EL DORADO

(AAA) ▼▼▼ Best Western Red Coach Inn SH 🐾
(316) 321-6900. **$63-$110.** 2525 W Central Ave. I-35, exit 71, 0.5 mi e. Ext corridors. **Pets:** Medium. Service with restrictions, supervision.
SAVE S☐ ✕ ☐ ☐ ☐ ☐ ▱ ☒

(AAA) ▼▼ Heritage Inn M
(316) 321-6800. **$50-$55, 3 day notice.** 2515 W Central Ave. I-35, exit 71, 0.5 mi e. Ext corridors. **Pets:** Medium. $25 deposit/room. Designated rooms, service with restrictions, supervision.
SAVE S☐ ✕ ☐

ELLSWORTH

(AAA) ▼▼▼ Best Western Garden Prairie Inn SH 🐾
(785) 472-3116. **$69-$76.** 1400 N Hwy 156. 1 mi ne on SR 140 at jct SR 156. Ext/int corridors. **Pets:** Service with restrictions, crate.
SAVE S☐ ✕ ☐ ☐ ☐ ▱

EMPORIA

▼▼ Days Inn SH
(620) 342-6800. **$55-$65.** 3032 W Hwy 50. I-35, exit 127, 0.5 mi e. Ext/int corridors. **Pets:** Accepted.
A$K S☐ ✕ ☐ ☐ ☐ ▱

▼ Motel 6 #4148 SH
(620) 343-1240. **$40-$59.** 2630 W 18th Ave. I-35, exit 128 (Industrial St), just s, then e. Int corridors. **Pets:** Accepted.
A$K S☐ ✕ ☐

▼▼ Ramada Inn & Conference Center SH
(620) 343-2200. **$69-$89.** 2700 W 18th Ave. I-35, exit 128 (Industrial St). Ext/int corridors. **Pets:** Accepted.
A$K S☐ ✕ ☐ ☐ ☐ ▱ ☒

▼ Super 8 Motel M
(620) 342-7567. **$52-$62.** 2913 W Hwy 50. I-35, exit 127, 0.8 mi e. Int corridors. **Pets:** Accepted.
A$K S☐ ✕ ☐

FORT SCOTT

▼ 1st Interstate Inn M
(620) 223-5330. **$44-$59, 15 day notice.** 2222 1/2 S Main. On US 69, 2.5 mi s of US 54. Int corridors. **Pets:** Small, dogs only. $5 one-time fee/pet. Service with restrictions, supervision.
A$K S☐ ✕ ☐ ☐

▼▼ Best Western Fort Scott Inn SH
(620) 223-0100. **Call for rates.** 101 State St. On US 69 Bypass, exit US 54 southbound; exit 3rd St northbound. Ext/int corridors. **Pets:** Accepted.
✕ ☐ ☐ ☐ ▱ ☒

GARDEN CITY

▼▼▼ **AmericInn Lodge & Suites** 🆂🅷 ✿
(620) 272-9860. **$85.** 3020 E Kansas Ave. Jct US 50, 83 and
SR 156. Int corridors. **Pets:** $50 deposit/room. Service with
restrictions, supervision.

🄰🅂🄺 🆂🄳 ⊠ 🕖 Ⓒ 🎀 🖵 ⇆ ⊠

🄰🄰🄰 ▼▼▼ **Best Western Red Baron Hotel** 🆂🅷
(620) 275-4164. **$63-$73.** Jct US 50 & 83. 2.3 mi e on US
50 business route, at US 83 Bypass. Ext corridors. **Pets:** Service with restrictions, supervision.

🆂🄰🅅🄴 🆂🄳 ⊠ 🕖 🎀 🖵 🍴 ⇆

🄰🄰🄰 ▼▼▼ **Best Western Wheat Lands Hotel &
Conference Center** 🆂🅷 ✿
(620) 276-2387. **$65-$89.** 1311 E Fulton. 1 mi e on US 50
business route. Ext corridors. **Pets:** Large, other species.
Service with restrictions, crate.

🆂🄰🅅🄴 🆂🄳 ⊠ 🕖 🎀 🖵 🍴 ⇆

▼▼▼ **Comfort Inn** 🆂🅷
(620) 275-5800. **$55-$86.** 2608 E Kansas Ave. Jct US 50, 83
and SR 156. Int corridors. **Pets:** Very small, other species.
$10 daily fee/pet. Service with restrictions, supervision.

🄰🅂🄺 🆂🄳 ⊠ Ⓒ 🎀 🖵 ⇆ ⊠

▼▼▼ **Holiday Inn Express Hotel & Suites** 🆂🅷
(620) 275-5900. **$85-$91.** 2502 E Kansas Ave. Jct US 50, 83
and SR 156. Int corridors. **Pets:** Large, other species. Service with restrictions, crate.

🄰🅂🄺 🆂🄳 ⊠ 🕖 Ⓒ 🎀 🖵 ⇆ ⊠

▼▼ **National 9 Inn** 🄼
(620) 275-0677. **$51-$61.** 123 Honey Bee Ct. 2.3 mi e on
US 50 business route, at US 83 Bypass. Ext corridors.
Pets: Accepted.

🄰🅂🄺 🆂🄳 ⊠ 🎀 ⇆

▼▼ **Plaza Hotel** 🆂🅷
(620) 275-7471. **$76-$83.** 1911 E Kansas. 0.5 mi w of US 50
and 83 Bypass on SR 156. Int corridors. **Pets:** Other species. Supervision.

🄰🅂🄺 🆂🄳 ⊠ Ⓒ 🎀 🖵 🍴 ⇆ ⊠

▼▼ **Super 8 Motel-Garden City** 🄼
(620) 275-9625. **$45-$65.** 2808 N Taylor. 0.7 mi s of jct US
50 and 83 on US 83 business route. Int corridors.
Pets: Accepted.

🄰🅂🄺 🆂🄳 ⊠ 🕖 🎀 🖵

GOODLAND

🄰🄰🄰 ▼▼▼ **Best Western Buffalo Inn** 🆂🅷
(785) 899-3621. **$59-$85.** 830 W Hwy 24. I-70, exit 17 or 19,
n to jct US 24 and SR 27. Ext corridors. **Pets:** Other
species. Designated rooms, service with restrictions, supervision.

🆂🄰🅅🄴 🆂🄳 ⊠ 🖵 🍴 ⇆

🄰🄰🄰 ▼▼▼▼ **Comfort Inn** 🆂🅷
(785) 899-7181. **$85-$90.** 2519 Enterprise Rd. I-70, exit 17,
just n. Int corridors. **Pets:** Accepted.

🆂🄰🅅🄴 🆂🄳 ⊠ Ⓜ Ⓒ 🎀 🖵 ⇆

GREAT BEND

🄰🄰🄰 ▼▼▼ **Best Western Angus Inn** 🆂🅷
(620) 792-3541. **$75.** 2920 10th St. 0.8 mi w on US 56.
Ext/int corridors. **Pets:** Accepted.

🆂🄰🅅🄴 🆂🄳 ⊠ 🕖 🎀 🖵 🍴 ⇆ ⊠

🄰🄰🄰 ▼▼▼ **Highland Hotel and Convention
Center** 🆂🅷
(620) 792-2431. **$72-$90.** 3017 10th St. 1 mi w on US 56.
Ext/int corridors. **Pets:** Medium. $10 daily fee/room. Designated rooms, service with restrictions, supervision.

🆂🄰🅅🄴 🆂🄳 ⊠ Ⓒ 🎀 🖵 🍴 ⇆ ⊠

▼▼ **Super 8 Motel-Great Bend** 🄼
(620) 793-8486. **$45-$60.** 3500 10th St. 1.2 mi w on US 56.
Int corridors. **Pets:** Medium, dogs only. $10 one-time fee/
room. Service with restrictions, supervision.

🄰🅂🄺 🆂🄳 ⊠ 🖵 ⇆

GREENSBURG

▼▼ **Best Western J-Hawk Motel** 🆂🅷
(620) 723-2121. **$68-$78.** 515 W Kansas Ave. 0.3 mi w on
US 54. Ext corridors. **Pets:** Service with restrictions, supervision.

🄰🅂🄺 🆂🄳 ⊠ 🎀 🖵 ⇆

HAYS

▼▼ **Best Western Vagabond Motel** 🄼
(785) 625-2511. **$55-$73.** 2524 Vine St. I-70, exit 159 (US
183), 1 mi s. Ext corridors. **Pets:** Other species. Service
with restrictions, supervision.

🄰🅂🄺 🆂🄳 ⊠ Ⓒ 🎀 🖵 🍴 ⇆

▼▼▼ **Hampton Inn-Hays** 🆂🅷
(785) 625-8103. **$59-$77.** 3801 Vine St. I-70, exit 159 (US
183), just sw. Ext/int corridors. **Pets:** Other species. No
service, supervision.

🄰🅂🄺 🆂🄳 ⊠ 🕖 Ⓒ 🖵

▼ **Motel 6–167** 🄼
(785) 625-4282. **$43-$58.** 3404 Vine St. I-70, exit 159 (US
183), 0.3 mi s. Ext corridors. **Pets:** Accepted.

🆂🄳 ⊠ ⇆

HAYSVILLE

🄰🄰🄰 ▼ **Haysville Inn** 🄼
(316) 522-1000. **$42-$48.** 301 E 71st St. I-35, exit 39, just w.
Ext corridors. **Pets:** Medium. Service with restrictions,
supervision.

🆂🄰🅅🄴 🆂🄳 ⊠ Ⓒ 🎀

HESSTON

▼▼ **AmericInn Lodge & Suites-Hesston** 🆂🅷
(620) 327-2053. **$68-$129.** 2 Leonard Ct. I-135, exit 40, just
e. Int corridors. **Pets:** Other species. Service with restrictions, supervision.

🄰🅂🄺 🆂🄳 ⊠ 🎀 🖵 ⇆

HILLSBORO

▼▼ Country Haven Inn SH
(620) 947-2929. **$55-$59, 3 day notice.** 804 Western Heights. On US 56; center. Int corridors. **Pets:** Small, other species. $10 one-time fee/pet. Designated rooms, service with restrictions, supervision.

A$K S✿ ✕ 🛗

HUTCHINSON

⬥⬥ Astro Motel M
(620) 663-1151. **$50-$70.** 15 E 4th Ave. Just e of Main St. Ext corridors. **Pets:** Small, dogs only. $5 one-time fee/pet. Service with restrictions, crate.

SAVE S✿ ✕ 🛗 ⇆

▼▼ Comfort Inn SH
(620) 663-7822. **$69-$99.** 1621 Super Plaza. 3 mi ne, just w of jct SR 61 and N 17th Ave. Int corridors. **Pets:** Small, other species. $5 daily fee/pet. Designated rooms, service with restrictions, supervision.

A$K S✿ ✕ 🗘 🖵 🛗 🖵 ⇆

▼▼ Econo Lodge SH
(620) 663-1211. **$79-$119.** 15 W 4th Ave. Just e of SR 96; downtown. Ext corridors. **Pets:** Small, other species. $4 daily fee/room. Designated rooms, service with restrictions, supervision.

A$K S✿ ✕ 🗘 🛗 🖵 ⇆

⬥▼▼ Holiday Inn Express Hotel & Suites SH
(620) 669-5200. **$81-$91.** 1601 Super Plaza. 3 mi ne, just w of SR 61. Int corridors. **Pets:** Designated rooms, service with restrictions, crate.

A$K S✿ ✕ 🖵M 🗘 🖵 🛗 🖵 ⇆

▼▼ Microtel Inn & Suites SH
(620) 665-3700. **$61-$92.** 1420 N Lorraine. Jct SR 61 and N 11th Ave, 2.5 mi n. Int corridors. **Pets:** Other species. Service with restrictions, crate.

A$K S✿ ✕ 🛗 🖵

▼ Super 8 Motel-Hutchinson M
(620) 662-6394. **$45-$65.** 1315 E 11th Ave. 2.5 mi ne at jct SR 61. Int corridors. **Pets:** Medium, dogs only. $10 one-time fee/room. Service with restrictions, supervision.

A$K S✿ ✕ 🗘 🖵

INDEPENDENCE

▼▼▼ Appletree Inn SH
(620) 331-5500. **$68-$72.** 201 N 8th St. At 8th and Laurel sts. Ext/int corridors. **Pets:** Service with restrictions, supervision.

✕ 🛗 ⇆

⬥⬥ ▼▼▼▼ Glencliff Farm Bed, Breakfast & Spa BB 🐾
(620) 331-1277. **$79, 14 day notice.** 448 Glencliff Rd. 1.5 mi n on US 75. Int corridors. **Pets:** $20 one-time fee/pet. Designated rooms, service with restrictions, supervision.

SAVE ✕ 🛗 🖵 ⇆ ✕

▼▼ Knights Inn SH
(620) 331-7300. **$49-$59.** 3222 W Main St. 1.4 mi e of jct US 75 and 160. Ext corridors. **Pets:** Small. $10 one-time fee/pet. Supervision.

A$K S✿ ✕ 🛗 🖵 ⇆

▼▼ Microtel Inn & Suites SH
(620) 331-0088. **$57-$73.** 2917 W Main St. 1.2 mi e of jct US 75 and 160. Int corridors. **Pets:** Other species. $6 one-time fee/room. No service, supervision.

A$K S✿ ✕ 🖵M 🗘 🖵 🛗 🖵

IOLA

⬥⬥ ▼▼ Best Western Inn M
(620) 365-5161. **$54-$58.** 1315 N State. Ext corridors. **Pets:** Accepted.

SAVE S✿ ✕ 🖵M 🗘 🖵 🛗 🖵 🍴 ⇆

JUNCTION CITY

▼▼ Days Inn SH
(785) 762-2727. **$58-$65, 3 day notice.** 1024 S Washington St. I-70, exit 296, just n. Ext/int corridors. **Pets:** Other species. Designated rooms, service with restrictions, supervision.

A$K S✿ ✕ 🗘 🛗 🖵 ⇆ ✕

⬥⬥ ▼▼ Econo Lodge M
(785) 238-8181. **$35-$80.** 211 Flint Hills Blvd. I-70, exit 299 (Grandview Plaza). Int corridors. **Pets:** Medium, other species. Designated rooms, service with restrictions, crate.

SAVE S✿ ✕ 🛗 🖵

⬥⬥ ▼ Golden Wheat Budget Host M
(785) 238-5106. **$30-$75, 3 day notice.** 820 S Washington St. I-70, exit 296, 0.5 mi n. Ext corridors. **Pets:** Small, dogs only. $5 daily fee/pet. Designated rooms, service with restrictions, crate.

SAVE S✿ ✕ 🛗

▼▼▼ Holiday Inn Express SH
(785) 762-4200. **$79-$105.** 120 N East St. I-70, exit 298, just nw. Int corridors. **Pets:** Accepted.

A$K S✿ ✕ 🖵M 🗘 🛗 🖵 ⇆ ✕

▼▼ Ramada Limited SH
(785) 238-1141. **$62-$77, 3 day notice.** 1133 S Washington St. I-70, exit 296. Ext corridors. **Pets:** Medium. $5 daily fee/pet. Designated rooms, service with restrictions, supervision.

A$K S✿ ✕ 🛗 🖵

KANSAS CITY METROPOLITAN AREA

DE SOTO

Super 8 Motel SH
(913) 583-3880. **$52-$64, 7 day notice.** 34085 Commerce Dr. Just ne of jct SR 10 and DeSoto exit. Int corridors. **Pets:** Small. $50 deposit/room, $10 one-time fee/room. Designated rooms, service with restrictions, supervision.

GARDNER

Super 8 SH
(913) 856-8887. **$45-$75.** 2001 E Santa Fe. I-35, exit 210. Int corridors. **Pets:** Accepted.

KANSAS CITY

Best Western Inn and Conference Center SH
(913) 677-3060. **$89-$99.** 501 Southwest Blvd. I-35, exit 234 (7th St), just s. Int corridors. **Pets:** Designated rooms, service with restrictions, crate.

Microtel Inn & Suites at the Speedway SH
(913) 334-3028. **$69-$89.** 7721 Elizabeth St. I-70, exit 414 (78th St N), just ne. Int corridors. **Pets:** Accepted.

LENEXA

Days Inn Lenexa M
(913) 492-7200. **$55-$65.** 9630 Rosehill Rd. I-35, exit 224 (95th St), just e. Ext corridors. **Pets:** Accepted.

La Quinta Inn SH
(913) 492-5500. **$69-$89.** 9461 Lenexa Dr. I-35, exit 224 (95th St), just ne; entrance left on Monrovia Rd, off 95th St. Int corridors. **Pets:** Other species. Service with restrictions, supervision.

Wellesley Inn & Suites (Kansas City/Lenexa)
(913) 894-5550. **$59-$69.** 8015 Lenexa Dr. I-35, exit 227 (75th St), 1 mi s on east frontage road. Ext corridors. **Pets:** Small, other species. Service with restrictions, supervision.

MERRIAM

Comfort Inn-Merriam SH
(913) 262-2622. **$35-$79.** 6401 E Frontage Rd. I-35, exit 228B (Shawnee Mission Pkwy), just se. Int corridors. **Pets:** Small. $5 daily fee/pet. Designated rooms, service with restrictions, supervision.

Drury Inn Merriam/Shawnee Mission Parkway SH
(913) 236-9200. **$75-$100.** 9009 W Shawnee Mission Pkwy. I-35, exit 228B (Shawnee Mission Pkwy). Int corridors. **Pets:** Large, other species. Service with restrictions, supervision.

Homestead Studio Suites Hotel-Kansas City/Shawnee Mission M
(913) 236-6006. **$73-$83.** 6451 E Frontage Rd. I-35, exit 228B (Shawnee Mission Pkwy), just se. Ext corridors. **Pets:** Medium, other species. $25 daily fee/room. Service with restrictions, crate.

OLATHE

Sleep Inn SH
(913) 390-9500. **$65-$75.** 20662 W 151st St. I-35, exit 215 (151st St), 0.4 mi sw. Int corridors. **Pets:** Medium, other species. $10 one-time fee/pet. Designated rooms, service with restrictions, supervision.

OVERLAND PARK

AmeriSuites (Overland Park/Metcalf) SH
(913) 451-2553. **$69-$149.** 6801 W 112th St. I-435, exit 79 (Metcalf Ave), 0.6 mi s. Int corridors. **Pets:** Accepted.

Candlewood Suites SH
(913) 469-5557. **$69-$110.** 11001 Oakmont. I-435, exit 82 (Quivira Rd), 0.5 mi s, 0.3 mi w on College Ave, then just n. Int corridors. **Pets:** Accepted.

Chase Suites by Woodfin SH
(913) 491-3333. **$69-$129.** 6300 W 110th. I-435, exit 79 (Metcalf Ave), 0.3 mi s on US 169, 0.5 mi e on College Blvd to Lamar Ave, then just n. Ext corridors. **Pets:** $150 deposit/pet, $10 daily fee/pet. Service with restrictions, crate.

Drury Inn & Suites-Overland Park SH
(913) 345-1500. **$90-$110.** 10963 Metcalf Ave. I-435, exit 79 (Metcalf Ave), just se. Int corridors. **Pets:** Large, other species. Service with restrictions, supervision.

Holiday Inn of Mission-Overland Park LH
(913) 262-3010. **$69-$99.** 7240 Shawnee Mission Pkwy. I-35, exit 228B (Shawnee Mission Pkwy), 1 mi e. Ext/int corridors. **Pets:** Accepted.

Holtze Executive Village SH
(913) 344-8100. **$109-$209.** 11400 College Blvd. I-435, exit 82 (Quivira Rd), 0.5 mi s, then just e. Ext/int corridors. **Pets:** $200 deposit/pet. Service with restrictions.

▼▼▼ Homestead Studio Suites Hotel-Kansas City/Overland Park SH ❀
(913) 661-7111. **$59-$79.** 5401 W 110th St. I-435, exit 77B (Nall Ave), just s. Int corridors. **Pets:** Medium, other species. $25 daily fee/room. Service with restrictions, crate.
ASK SD ✕ ᵫM ⬚ 🛢 🛢

▼▼ Microtel Inn and Suites of Overland Park/Lenexa SH
(913) 541-2664. **$54-$89.** 8750 Ballentine St. I-35, exit 225A, just se of jct. Int corridors. **Pets:** Accepted.
ASK SD ✕ ᵫM ⬚ 🛢 🖵 ⤳

▼▼▼ Pear Tree Inn-Overland Park SH
(913) 451-0200. **$70-$90.** 10951 Metcalf Ave. I-435, exit 79 (Metcalf Ave/US 169), just se. Int corridors. **Pets:** Large, other species. Service with restrictions, supervision.
ASK ✕ ᵫM 🐾 🛢 🖵 ⤳

⬥⬥⬥ ▼▼ Red Roof Inn-Overland Park M
(913) 341-0100. **$44-$61.** 6800 W 108th St. I-435, exit 79 (Metcalf Ave/US 169), just ne. Ext corridors. **Pets:** Accepted.
SAVE ✕ ᵫM ⬚

▼▼ Super 8 Motel SH
(913) 341-4440. **$44-$94.** 10750 Barkley St. I-435, exit 79 (Metcalf Ave/US 169), just n to 107th St, then just e. Int corridors. **Pets:** Small. $25 one-time fee/room. Service with restrictions, supervision.
ASK SD ✕ ᵫM ⬚

⬥⬥⬥ ▼▼▼ Wellesley Inn & Suites (Kansas City/Overland Park) SH
(913) 642-2299. **$69-$79.** 7201 W 106th St. I-435, exit 79 (Metcalf Ave/US 169), just nw. Int corridors. **Pets:** Small, other species. Service with restrictions, supervision.
SAVE SD ✕ ᵫM ⬚ 🛢 🛢

▼▼▼ White Haven Motor Lodge M
(913) 649-8200. **$54-$60.** 8039 Metcalf Ave. I-435, exit 79 (Metcalf Ave/US 169), 3.5 mi n. Ext corridors. **Pets:** Medium. Service with restrictions, supervision.
✕ ⬚ 🛢 ⤳

❀   **END METROPOLITAN AREA**   🐾

LANSING

⬥⬥⬥ ▼▼ Econo Lodge SH
(913) 727-2777. **$52-$56, 7 day notice.** 504 N Main. I-70, exit Leavenworth, 10 mi n on US 73 and SR 7. Int corridors. **Pets:** $25 deposit/pet, $5 daily fee/pet. Service with restrictions, crate.
SAVE SD ✕ 🛢 🖵

▼▼▼ Holiday Inn Express Hotel & Suites SH
(913) 250-1000. **$83-$90.** 120 Express Dr. On SR 7, just s of jct SR 5; downtown. Int corridors. **Pets:** Other species. $20 one-time fee/pet. Designated rooms, service with restrictions, supervision.
✕ ᵫM ⬚ 🛢 🖵 ⤳ ✕

LARNED

⬥⬥⬥ ▼▼▼ Best Western Townsman Inn SH
(620) 285-3114. **$57-$65.** 123 E 14th. Jct US 56 and SR 156. Ext corridors. **Pets:** Small. Service with restrictions, supervision.
SAVE SD ✕ 🐾 🛢 🖵 ⤳

LAWRENCE

⬥⬥⬥ ▼▼▼ Best Value Hallmark Inn M
(785) 841-6500. **$49-$125.** 730 Iowa St. I-70, exit 202, 1 mi s. Ext corridors. **Pets:** Large. $10 daily fee/room. Designated rooms, no service, supervision.
SAVE SD ✕ 🛢 🖵

⬥⬥⬥ ▼▼▼ Days Inn SH
(785) 843-9100. **$64-$99.** 2309 Iowa St. On US 59 at jct SR 10. Ext/int corridors. **Pets:** Other species. Designated rooms, service with restrictions, supervision.
SAVE SD ✕ ᵫM ⬚ 🛢 🖵 ⤳

▼▼ Super 8 Motel SH
(785) 842-5721. **$60-$70.** 515 McDonald Dr. I-70, exit 202, on McDonald Dr (US 59), 1 mi s. Int corridors. **Pets:** Accepted.
ASK SD ✕ 🖵

⬥⬥⬥ ▼▼▼ Westminster Inn & Suites M
(785) 841-8410. **$54-$85.** 2525 W 6th St. I-70, exit 202, 1 mi s, 0.3 mi w on US 40 (6th St). Ext corridors. **Pets:** Accepted.
SAVE SD ✕ 🛢 🖵 ⤳

LEAVENWORTH

▼▼ Days Inn M
(913) 651-6000. **$55-$65, 7 day notice.** 3211 S 4th St. On US 73 and SR 7. Ext corridors. **Pets:** Accepted.
ASK SD ✕ 🛢 🖵 ⤳

LIBERAL

⬥⬥⬥ ▼▼▼ Best Western LaFonda Motel SH
(620) 624-5601. **$49-$59.** 229 W Pancake Blvd. Just w of jct US 54 and 83B (Kansas Ave). Ext corridors. **Pets:** Small. Service with restrictions, supervision.
SAVE SD ✕ 🐾 🛢 🖵 🍴 ⤳

▼▼ Cimarron Inn M
(620) 624-6203. **$45.** 564 E Pancake Blvd. 0.8 w of jct US 54 and 83. Ext corridors. **Pets:** $5 one-time fee/pet. Designated rooms, service with restrictions, supervision.
ASK SD ✕ 🛢 🖵

⬥⬥⬥ ▼▼ Liberal Inn SH
(620) 624-7254. **$55-$69.** 603 E Pancake Blvd. 0.5 mi w of jct US 54 and 83. Int corridors. **Pets:** Medium, other species. Service with restrictions, crate.
SAVE SD ✕ 🛢 🖵 🍴 ⤳

LINDSBORG

▼▼▼ Viking Motel **M**
(785) 227-3336. **$52-$58.** 446 Harrison. 1 mi ne on Business Loop I-135 and SR 4. Ext corridors. **Pets:** Accepted.
⊠ ⊶

LYONS

▼▼ Lyons Inn **M**
(620) 257-5185. **Call for rates.** 817 W Main. 0.8 mi w on SR 96 and US 56. Int corridors. **Pets:** Other species. Service with restrictions, crate.
⊠ ▤

MANHATTAN

▼▼▼ Hampton Inn **SH**
(785) 539-5000. **$74-$85.** 501 E Poyntz Ave. SR 177, 0.3 mi e on US 24 (Frontage Rd). Int corridors. **Pets:** Medium, other species. Supervision.
A$K S▧ ⊠ ⅏ ⟨° ▤ ▢ ⊶

▼▼▼▼ Holiday Inn/Holidome **LH**
(785) 539-5311. **$81-$169.** 530 Richards Dr. 2.5 mi sw on SR 18 (Ft Riley Blvd), 0.3 mi e of jct SR 113. Ext/int corridors. **Pets:** Medium. $20 one-time fee/room. Designated rooms, service with restrictions, supervision.
SAVE S▧ ⊠ ⟨° ▤ ▢ ⅋ ⊶ ⊠

▼ Motel 6–152 **M**
(785) 537-1022. **$41-$57.** 510 Tuttle Creek Blvd. 0.3 mi ne on US 24 (Frontage Rd) and SR 177. Ext corridors. **Pets:** Small, other species. Service with restrictions, supervision.
S▧ ⊠ ⅏ ⟨ ⟨° ⊶

▼▼▼▼ Ramada Plaza Hotel **SH**
(785) 539-7531. **$75-$149.** 1641 Anderson. 1 mi n of SR 18. Int corridors. **Pets:** Other species. $10 daily fee/pet. Service with restrictions, supervision.
A$K S▧ ⊠ ▤ ▢ ⅋ ⊶

MARYSVILLE

▼▼ Best Western Surf Motel **SH**
(785) 562-2354. **$54-$75.** 2105 Center St. 1 mi e on US 36 (Pony Express Hwy). Ext/int corridors. **Pets:** Accepted.
A$K S▧ ⊠ ⟨° ▤ ▢ ⊠

▼▼▼ Oak Tree Inn-Marysville **SH**
(785) 562-1234. **$60.** 1127 Pony Express Hwy. 1.6 mi e on US 36 (Pony Express Hwy). Int corridors. **Pets:** Accepted.
SAVE S▧ ⊠ ⅏ ⟨° ▤ ▢ ⅋

▼▼ Super 8 Motel **SH**
(785) 562-5588. **$55-$60.** 1155 Pony Express Hwy. 2 mi e on US 36 (Pony Express Hwy). Int corridors. **Pets:** Other species. $10 one-time fee/room. Designated rooms, service with restrictions, supervision.
A$K S▧ ⊠ ▤

MCPHERSON

▼▼ Best Western Holiday Manor Motel **SH**
(620) 241-5343. **$56-$66.** 2211 E Kansas Ave. I-135, exit 60, just w. Ext/int corridors. **Pets:** Medium. $20 daily fee/pet. Service with restrictions, crate.
A$K S▧ ⊠ ⟨ ▤ ▢ ⅋ ⊶

▼▼ McPherson Super 8 Motel **M**
(620) 241-8881. **$45-$60.** 2110 E Kansas. I-135, exit 60, just w. Int corridors. **Pets:** Accepted.
A$K S▧ ⊠ ⅏ ⟨° ▢

▼▼▼ Red Coach Inn **SH**
(620) 241-6960. **$54.** 2111 E Kansas Ave. I-135, exit 60, just w. Ext/int corridors. **Pets:** Other species. $15 one-time fee/room. Designated rooms, service with restrictions, supervision.
SAVE S▧ ⊠ ⅋ ⊶ ⊠

MEADE

▼▼▼ Dalton's Bedpost Motel **M**
(620) 873-2131. **$40-$44.** 519 Carthage. On US 54. Ext corridors. **Pets:** Accepted.
SAVE ⊠

NEWTON

▼▼▼ Best Western Red Coach Inn **SH**
(316) 283-9120. **$65-$89.** 1301 E 1st St. I-135, exit 31. Ext/int corridors. **Pets:** Other species. Service with restrictions, supervision.
SAVE S▧ ⊠ ⟨ ▤ ▢ ⅋ ⊶ ⊠

▼▼ Days Inn Newton **SH** ❀
(316) 283-3330. **$63-$65.** 105 Manchester St. I-135, exit 31, just e. Int corridors. **Pets:** Other species. $10 daily fee/room. Service with restrictions, supervision.
A$K S▧ ⊠ ▤ ▢ ⊶

▼▼ Newton Super 8 Motel **M**
(316) 283-7611. **$45-$60.** 1620 E 2nd St. I-135, exit 31, just e. Int corridors. **Pets:** Accepted.
A$K S▧ ⊠ ⟨° ▢

OAKLEY

▼▼▼ 1st Travel Inn **SH**
(785) 672-3226. **$38-$60.** 708 Center Ave. Center. Ext corridors. **Pets:** Large. $4 daily fee/pet. Service with restrictions, crate.
SAVE S▧ ⊠ ⅋ ⊶

▼▼▼ Best Western Golden Plains Motel **M**
(785) 672-3254. **$58-$65.** 3506 US 40. I-70, exit 76, 1.7 mi w. Ext corridors. **Pets:** Small. Service with restrictions, supervision.
A$K S▧ ⊠ ▢ ⊶

OBERLIN

▼▼ Frontier Motel **M**
(785) 475-2203. **$35-$69.** 207 E Frontier Pkwy. On US 36, 0.5 mi e of jct US 83. Ext corridors. **Pets:** Service with restrictions, supervision.
A$K S▧ ⊠ ▤ ⅋ ⊶

OTTAWA

▼▼▼ Days Inn **M**
(785) 242-4842. **$50-$90, 7 day notice.** 1641 S Main. I-35, exit 183 (US 59), 1 mi n. Ext corridors. **Pets:** Accepted.
SAVE S▧ ⊠ ⅏ ▤ ▢

▽▽▽ Econo Lodge SH
(785) 242-3400. **$40-$80, 7 day notice.** 2331 S Cedar Rd.
I-35, exit 183 (US 59). Int corridors. **Pets:** Accepted.
SAVE (S⬛) (✕) (▣) (≈)

▽▽▽▽ Holiday Inn Express SH
(785) 242-2224. **$70-$100.** 606 E 23rd St. I-35, exit 183 (US
59). Ext corridors. **Pets:** Small. Designated rooms, service
with restrictions, supervision.
(ASK) (S⬛) (✕) (&M) (📧) (▣) (≈)

▽▽ Travelodge M
(785) 242-7000. **$69.** 2209 S Princeton Rd. I-35, exit 183
(US 59). Ext corridors. **Pets:** Accepted.
(ASK) (S⬛) (✕) (📧) (▣) (≈)

PARSONS

▽▽ Super 8 Motel-Parsons SH
(620) 421-8000. **$62-$72.** 229 E Main. 1.3 mi e of jct US 400
and 59. Int corridors. **Pets:** Very small. $50 deposit/room.
Service with restrictions, crate.
(ASK) (S⬛) (✕) (📧) (▣) (≈)

PHILLIPSBURG

▽▽▽ Cottonwood Inn M
(785) 543-2125. **$67-$97, 7 day notice.** 1200 State St. 2 mi
e on US 36. Ext corridors. **Pets:** Accepted.
SAVE (S⬛) (✕) (🖨) (≈)

PRATT

▽▽ Best Western Hillcrest Motel SH
(620) 672-6407. **$60.** 1336 E 1st St. 1 mi e on US 54. Ext
corridors. **Pets:** Medium, dogs only. $5 daily fee/pet. Desig-
nated rooms, service with restrictions, supervision.
(ASK) (S⬛) (✕) (📧) (▣) (≈)

▽▽▽ Days Inn SH ❀
(620) 672-9465. **$45-$85.** 1901 E 1st St. 1.7 mi e on US 54.
Ext corridors. **Pets:** Medium. $3 daily fee/pet. Designated
rooms, service with restrictions, supervision.
SAVE (S⬛) (✕) (📧) (▣) (≈)

▽ Economy Inn M
(620) 672-5588. **$36-$50.** 1401 E 1st St. 1 mi e on US 54.
Ext corridors. **Pets:** Medium. $5 daily fee/room. Designated
rooms, service with restrictions, supervision.
(ASK) (S⬛) (✕) (📧) (≈)

▽ Evergreen Inn M
(620) 672-6431. **$40.** 20001 W US Hwy 54. On US 54, 3 mi
w. Ext corridors. **Pets:** Accepted.
(✕) (📧) (≈)

▽▽▽ Holiday Inn Express SH
(620) 672-9433. **$78-$89.** 1401 W Hwy 54. On US 54, 2 mi
w. Int corridors. **Pets:** Other species. Service with restrictions, supervision.
(ASK) (S⬛) (✕) (🍥) (🖨) (📧) (▣) (≈)

▽▽ Super 8 Motel of Pratt SH
(620) 672-5945. **$53-$66.** 1906 E 1st St. 1.7 mi e on US 54.
Int corridors. **Pets:** Accepted.
(ASK) (S⬛) (✕)

QUINTER

▽▽ Budget Host Q Motel M
(785) 754-3337. **$50-$58.** 1202 Castle Rock St. I-70, exit
107, just n. Ext corridors. **Pets:** Accepted.
(ASK) (S⬛) (✕) (🍴)

RUSSELL

▽▽ Days Inn M
(785) 483-6660. **$54-$67.** 1225 S Fossil St. I-70, exit 184
(US 281), just n. Ext corridors. **Pets:** Other species. $5
daily fee/pet. Service with restrictions, supervision.
(ASK) (S⬛) (✕) (📧) (≈)

SALINA

▽ 1st Inn Gold M
(785) 827-5511. **$45-$54.** 2403 S 9th St. I-135, exit 90 (Magnolia), just e. Int corridors. **Pets:** Accepted.
(ASK) (✕) (📧) (▣) (≈)

▽▽▽▽ Baymont Inn & Suites SH
(785) 493-9800. **$50-$95.** 745 W Schilling Rd. I-135, exit 89
(Schilling Rd), just w. Int corridors. **Pets:** Medium, other
species. $50 deposit/room, $10 daily fee/room. Designated
rooms, service with restrictions, supervision.
SAVE (S⬛) (✕) (&M) (🍥) (📧) (▣) (≈) (✕)

▽▽▽ Best Inn-Salina SH
(785) 825-2500. **$45-$50.** 429 W Diamond Dr. I-70, exit 252,
just n, then just w. Int corridors. **Pets:** Large, other species.
$5 one-time fee/room. Designated rooms, service with
restrictions, supervision.
(ASK) (S⬛) (✕) (📧)

▽▽▽ Best Western Mid-America Inn SH
(785) 827-0356. **$62-$66.** 1846 N 9th St. I-70, exit 252, just
s. Ext corridors. **Pets:** Other species. $50 deposit/pet. Des-
ignated rooms, service with restrictions, crate.
SAVE (S⬛) (✕) (&M) (🍥) (▣) (🍴) (≈)

▽▽ Budget King Motel M
(785) 827-4477. **$36, 3 day notice.** 809 N Broadway. I-70,
exit 252, 1.5 mi s, then just e. Ext corridors.
Pets: Accepted.
SAVE (S⬛) (✕) (📧)

▽▽▽ Candlewood Suites SH ❀
(785) 823-6939. **$49-$99.** 2650 Planet Ave. I-135, exit 89
(Schilling Rd), just e to S 9th St, 0.5 mi n to Belmont, then
just w. Int corridors. **Pets:** Medium. $25 deposit/room. Serv-
ice with restrictions, supervision.
(ASK) (✕) (🍥) (🍥) (📧) (▣)

▽▽ Comfort Inn SH
(785) 826-1711. **$70.** 1820 W Crawford St. I-135, exit 92, just
e. Int corridors. **Pets:** Small, dogs only. $20 one-time fee/
pet. Service with restrictions, supervision.
(ASK) (S⬛) (✕) (🍥) (📧) (▣) (≈)

▽▽▽▽ Hampton Inn-Salina M
(785) 823-9800. **$92-$102.** 401 W Schilling Rd. I-135, exit 89
(Schilling Rd), just e. Int corridors. **Pets:** Small, other species. $10 one-time fee/room. Service with restrictions,
supervision.
SAVE (S⬛) (✕) (&M) (🍥) (🍥) (📧) (▣) (≈)

▼▼▼ **Holiday Inn Express Hotel & Suites-Salina** 🆂🅷
(785) 827-9000. **$58-$99.** 201 E Diamond Dr. I-70, exit 252, just ne. Int corridors. **Pets:** Other species. $25 one-time fee/room. Service with restrictions, crate.
Ⓐ🆂🅺 ⊠ 🔊🅼 🕖 👟 🚪 💻 ≈

▼▼▼ **Holiday Inn of Salina** 🆂🅷
(785) 823-1739. **$119.** 1616 W Crawford St. I-135, exit 92, 0.5 mi e. Int corridors. **Pets:** Medium. $25 one-time fee/pet. Service with restrictions, supervision.
Ⓐ🆂🅺 🔊 ⊠ 🕖 👟 🚪 💻 🍴 ≈ ⊠

🔼🔼🔼 ▼▼▼ **Red Coach Inn** 🆂🅷
(785) 825-2111. **$60-$125.** 2110 W Crawford St. I-135, exit 92, just w. Int corridors. **Pets:** Small, other species. $15 one-time fee/pet. Designated rooms, service with restrictions, supervision.
🅂🄰🅅🄴 🔊 ⊠ 🕖 👟 🚪 🍴 ≈ ⊠

🔼🔼🔼 ▼▼▼ **Super 8 I-70** 🆂🅷 🐾
(785) 823-8808. **$55-$75.** 120 E Diamond Dr. I-70, exit 252, just ne. Int corridors. **Pets:** Other species. $5 daily fee/pet. Crate.
🅂🄰🅅🄴 🔊 ⊠ ♿ 🚪 💻 ≈

🔼🔼🔼 ▼▼▼ **TraveLodge** 🆂🅷
(785) 825-8211. **$58-$65.** 1949 N 9th St. I-70, exit 252, just s. Ext corridors. **Pets:** Accepted.
🅂🄰🅅🄴 🔊 ⊠ 💻 🍴 ≈

SHARON SPRINGS

▼▼ **Oak Tree Inn** 🆂🅷
(785) 852-4664. **$72-$79.** 801 N Hwy 27. Jct US 40 and SR 27. Ext/int corridors. **Pets:** Other species. $5 daily fee/pet. Service with restrictions, supervision.
Ⓐ🆂🅺 🔊 ⊠ 🕖 👟 🚪 💻 🍴 ⊠

TOPEKA

🔼🔼🔼 ▼▼▼▼ **AmeriSuites (Topeka/Northwest)** 🆂🅷
(785) 273-0066. **$79-$129.** 6021 SW Sixth Ave. I-70, exit 356 (Wanamaker Rd). Int corridors. **Pets:** Accepted.
🅂🄰🅅🄴 🔊 ⊠ 🔊🅼 👟 🚪 💻 ≈

▼▼ **Best Western Candlelight Inn** Ⓜ
(785) 272-9550. **$52-$110.** 2831 SW Fairlawn Rd. I-470, exit 3. Ext corridors. **Pets:** Small. $8 daily fee/pet. Designated rooms, service with restrictions, supervision.
Ⓐ🆂🅺 🔊 ⊠ 👟 🚪 💻 ≈ ⊠

🔼🔼🔼 ▼▼▼▼ **Best Western Meadow Acres Motel** Ⓜ
(785) 267-1681. **$68-$94.** 2950 S Topeka Blvd. I-470, exit 6, 1.5 mi n. Ext corridors. **Pets:** Other species. $8 daily fee/pet. Designated rooms, service with restrictions, supervision.
🅂🄰🅅🄴 🔊 ⊠ 🚪 💻 ≈

🔼🔼🔼 ▼▼▼▼ **Capitol Plaza Hotel** 🅻🅷
(785) 431-7200. **$79-$134.** 1717 SW Topeka Blvd. I-70, exit SE 8th Ave, 1.6 mi s; I-470, exit Topeka Blvd, 2.9 mi n. Int corridors. **Pets:** Large, other species. Service with restrictions, supervision.
🅂🄰🅅🄴 🔊 ⊠ 🔊🅼 🕖 👟 🚪 💻 🍴 ≈ ⊠

▼▼▼▼ **ClubHouse Inn & Suites** 🆂🅷
(785) 273-8888. **$89-$125.** 924 SW Henderson. I-70, exit 356 (Wanamaker Rd). Int corridors. **Pets:** Accepted.
Ⓐ🆂🅺 🔊 ⊠ 🕖 👟 🚪 💻 ≈

▼▼ **Comfort Inn** 🆂🅷
(785) 273-5365. **$69-$114.** 1518 SW Wanamaker Rd. I-470, exit 1 (Wanamaker Rd). Int corridors. **Pets:** Other species. $10 daily fee/pet. Designated rooms, service with restrictions, supervision.
Ⓐ🆂🅺 🔊 ⊠ 👟 💻 ≈

▼▼▼▼ **Country Inn & Suites By Carlson-Topeka-West** 🆂🅷
(785) 478-9800. **$79-$150.** 6020 SW 10th St. I-70, exit 356 (Wanamaker Rd). Int corridors. **Pets:** Medium, other species. $50 deposit/room, $10 daily fee/room. Designated rooms, service with restrictions, supervision.
Ⓐ🆂🅺 🔊 ⊠ 🔊🅼 👟 🚪 💻 ≈

🔼🔼🔼 ▼▼▼▼ **Quality Inn** 🆂🅷
(785) 273-6969. **$59-$129.** 1240 SW Wanamaker Rd. I-470, exit 1 (Wanamaker Rd), just ne; I-70, exit 356A, 1 mi s. Int corridors. **Pets:** Very small, other species. $5.50 daily fee/pet. Designated rooms, no service, supervision.
🅂🄰🅅🄴 🔊 ⊠ 👟 🚪 💻 ≈

▼▼ **Ramada Inn Topeka Downtown** 🅻🅷
(785) 234-5400. **$71.** 420 SE Sixth St. I-70, exit 362B, just e. Int corridors. **Pets:** Medium. Designated rooms, service with restrictions, crate.
Ⓐ🆂🅺 🔊 ⊠ 🔊🅼 👟 🚪 💻 🍴 ≈

▼▼▼▼ **Residence Inn** 🆂🅷
(785) 271-8903. **$89-$139.** 1620 SW Westport Dr. I-470, exit 1 (Wanamaker Rd). Int corridors. **Pets:** Accepted.
Ⓐ🆂🅺 ⊠ 🔊🅼 🕖 👟 🚪 💻 ≈ ⊠

ULYSSES

▼▼▼▼ **Single Tree Inn** 🆂🅷
(620) 356-1500. **$65-$71.** 2033 W Oklahoma St. 1.5 mi w on US 160. Int corridors. **Pets:** Other species. $25 deposit/room. Service with restrictions, supervision.
Ⓐ🆂🅺 🔊 ⊠ 🕖 👟 💻

WAMEGO

🔼🔼🔼 ▼▼ **Simmer Motel** Ⓜ
(785) 456-2304. **$48.** 1215 Hwy 24 W. Jct SR 99, 0.5 mi w on US 24. Ext corridors. **Pets:** Accepted.
🅂🄰🅅🄴 ⊠ 👟 💻 ≈

WELLINGTON

🔼🔼🔼 ▼▼▼ **Oak Tree Inn** 🆂🅷
(620) 326-8191. **$60-$66.** 1177 E Hwy 160. I-35, exit 19, 2 mi w on US 160. Ext corridors. **Pets:** Accepted.
🅂🄰🅅🄴 🔊 ⊠ 👟 🚪 💻

WICHITA

🔼🔼🔼 ▼▼▼▼ **Best Western Airport Inn & Convention Center** 🆂🅷
(316) 942-5600. **$89, 5 day notice.** 6815 W Kellogg. I-235, exit 7A or 7B, 0.6 mi w on US 54 (S Frontage Rd). Int corridors. **Pets:** Small, dogs only. $100 deposit/pet, $25 daily fee/pet. Designated rooms, service with restrictions, supervision.
🅂🄰🅅🄴 🔊 ⊠ 👟 🚪 💻 🍴 ≈ ⊠

Best Western Governors Inn & Suites SH
(316) 522-0775. **$69-$79.** 4742 S Emporia. I-135, exit 16, just sw. Int corridors. **Pets:** Accepted.
ASK SO X I I I ⇌

Best Western Wichita North/Park City SH
(316) 832-9387. **$81-$89.** 915 E 53rd St N. I-135, exit 13, just w. Ext/int corridors. **Pets:** Large, other species. $15 one-time fee/room. Service with restrictions, crate.
ASK SO X I I I I ⇌ X

Candlewood Suites-Wichita Northeast SH
(316) 634-6070. **$99-$109.** 3141 N Webb Rd. SR 96, exit Webb Rd, just nw. Int corridors. **Pets:** Medium, other species. $75 one-time fee/pet. Service with restrictions, supervision.
ASK SO X M I I I I

ClubHouse Inn & Suites SH
(316) 684-1111. **$69-$94.** 515 S Webb Rd. I-35, exit 50, just e. Int corridors. **Pets:** Accepted.
ASK SO X I I I I ⇌

Comfort Inn SH
(316) 522-1800. **$60.** 4849 S Laura. I-135, exit 1A/B (47th St S), just e. Int corridors. **Pets:** Other species. $10 daily fee/room. Service with restrictions, crate.
SAVE SO X I I I I ⇌

Comfort Inn SH
(316) 686-2844. **$74-$94.** 9525 E Corporate Hills. I-35, exit 50, just ne. Int corridors. **Pets:** Accepted.
ASK SO X I I I I ⇌

Comfort Suites Airport SH
(316) 945-2600. **$81-$139.** 658 Westdale. Jct I-235 and US 54. Int corridors. **Pets:** Small, other species. $10 one-time fee/pet. Designated rooms, service with restrictions.
SAVE SO X I I I I ⇌

Days Inn Wichita North M 🐾
(316) 832-1131. **$58-$63, 3 day notice.** 901 E 53rd St N. I-135, exit 13, just w. Int corridors. **Pets:** $10 daily fee/room. Designated rooms, service with restrictions, crate.
SAVE SO X I

Four Points By Sheraton SH
(316) 942-7911. **$109.** 5805 W Kellogg. I-235, exit 7A or 7B, just w. Int corridors. **Pets:** Small, other species. $25 one-time fee/pet. Designated rooms, service with restrictions, crate.
SAVE SO X I I I I I I ⇌

Hampton Inn SH
(316) 686-3576. **$79-$99.** 9449 E Corporate Hills. I-35, exit 50, just ne. Int corridors. **Pets:** Other species. Service with restrictions, supervision.
ASK SO X M I I I I I ⇌

Hawthorn Suites at Reflection Ridge SH
(316) 729-5700. **$92-$119.** 2405 N Ridge Rd. I-235, exit 10, 1.7 mi w on Zoo Blvd/21st St N, just n. Int corridors. **Pets:** Other species. $20 one-time fee/room. Service with restrictions, crate.
ASK SO X I I I I X

Holiday Inn Express-North Wichita SH
(316) 634-3900. **$79-$99.** 7824 E 32nd St N. SR 96 E, exit Rock Rd, just sw. Int corridors. **Pets:** Accepted.
ASK SO X I I I I ⇌

Holiday Inn Select LH
(316) 686-7131. **$79-$139.** 549 S Rock Rd. I-35, exit 50, 0.5 mi w. Ext/int corridors. **Pets:** Accepted.
SAVE SO X I I I I I I ⇌

Holiday Inn Wichita/Airport SH
(316) 943-2181. **$79-$99.** 5500 W Kellogg. I-235, exit 7, just w. Int corridors. **Pets:** Small, other species. $25 one-time fee/room. Service with restrictions, crate.
ASK X I I I I I I I ⇌

The Inn at Willowbend BB
(316) 636-4032. **$89-$159.** 3939 Comotara. SR 96, exit Rock Rd, 0.5 mi n to 37th St, 0.3 mi e, then just n. Int corridors. **Pets:** Accepted.
SAVE SO X I I I

The Kansas Inn SH
(316) 269-9999. **$59.** 1011 N Topeka Ave. I-135, exit 8 (13th St), 0.7 mi w, then 0.3 mi s. Int corridors. **Pets:** Other species. $5 daily fee/pet. Designated rooms, service with restrictions, crate.
SAVE SO X I I I

La Quinta Inn SH
(316) 681-2881. **$59-$79.** 7700 E Kellogg. I-35, exit 50, 0.5 mi w. Int corridors. **Pets:** Accepted.
ASK SO X I I I I ⇌

Quality Inn-Airport SH
(316) 722-8730. **$50-$60, 3 day notice.** 600 S Holland. I-235, exit 7, 1.1 mi w on US 54. Int corridors. **Pets:** Other species. $10 one-time fee/room. Service with restrictions, crate.
SAVE SO X I I I ⇌

Residence Inn by Marriott SH
(316) 686-7331. **$95-$98.** 411 S Webb Rd. I-35, exit 50, just ne. Ext corridors. **Pets:** Accepted.
ASK SO X I I I ⇌ X

WINFIELD

Comfort Inn SH
(620) 221-7529. **$71-$155.** Hwy 77 at Quail Ridge Dr. On US 77, 1 mi s. Ext/int corridors. **Pets:** Medium. $10 daily fee/pet. Designated rooms, service with restrictions, crate.
ASK SO X I I I ⇌

YATES CENTER

Star Motel M
(620) 625-2175. **$32-$37.** 206 S Fry. On US 54 at jct US 75. Ext corridors. **Pets:** Medium. Service with restrictions, crate.
X

ASHLAND

Knights Inn M

(606) 928-9501. **$45-$60, 7 day notice.** 7216 US Rt 60. I-64, exit 185, 5 mi sw on US 60, then 4.3 mi n. Ext corridors. **Pets:** Small, other species. $5 daily fee/room. Service with restrictions, supervision.

BARDSTOWN

Bardstown-Parkview Motel M

(502) 348-5983. **$50-$60.** 418 E Stephen Foster Ave. 0.5 mi e on US 150; e of jct US 62. Ext corridors. **Pets:** Service with restrictions, supervision.

Best Western General Nelson Motel SH

(502) 348-3977. **$59-$79.** 411 W Stephen Foster Ave. 0.5 mi w on US 62. Ext corridors. **Pets:** Small, other species. Service with restrictions, crate.

Days Inn-Bardstown SH

(502) 348-9253. **$59.** 1875 New Haven Rd. Bluegrass Pkwy, exit 21. Ext corridors. **Pets:** Small. $10 one-time fee/pet. Service with restrictions, supervision.

Hampton Inn SH

(502) 349-0100. **$80-$150.** 985 Chambers Blvd. Just s of US 245. Int corridors. **Pets:** Accepted.

Old Kentucky Home Motel M

(502) 348-5979. **$35-$75.** 414 W Stephen Foster Ave. 0.5 mi w on US 62. Ext corridors. **Pets:** Medium, other species. $20 deposit/pet. Service with restrictions, crate.

Ramada Inn SH

(502) 349-0363. **$65-$85.** 523 N 3rd St. 0.5 mi n on US 150. Ext corridors. **Pets:** Other species. $10 daily fee/room. Service with restrictions, supervision.

BEAVER DAM

Days Inn Beaver Dam SH

(270) 274-0851. **$64-$69.** 1750 US Hwy 231. Kentucky Pkwy, exit 75, just n. Int corridors. **Pets:** $10 daily fee/pet. Service with restrictions, supervision.

BENTON

Holiday Inn Express Hotel & Suites SH

(270) 527-5300. **$80-$85, 7 day notice.** 173 Carroll Rd. Purchase Pkwy, exit 47. Int corridors. **Pets:** Accepted.

BEREA

Boone Tavern Hotel-Berea College SH

(859) 985-3700. **$85-$110.** 100 Main St. I-75, exit 76, 1.5 mi ne on SR 21. Int corridors. **Pets:** Accepted.

Comfort Inn & Suites SH

(859) 985-5500. **$59-$89.** 1003 Paint Lick Rd. I-75, exit 76, just w. Int corridors. **Pets:** Small. $5 daily fee/pet. Service with restrictions, supervision.

Knights Inn Berea M

(859) 986-2384. **$40-$60, 7 day notice.** 715 Chestnut St. I-75, exit 76, 0.3 mi e. Ext corridors. **Pets:** Other species. $5 daily fee/pet. Supervision.

Super 8 Motel SH

(859) 986-8426. **$45-$64.** 196 Prince Royal Dr. I-75, exit 76, 0.3 mi e. Ext corridors. **Pets:** Accepted.

BOWLING GREEN

Baymont Inn & Suites-Bowling Green SH

(270) 843-3200. **$54-$99.** 165 Three Springs Rd. I-65, exit 22 (Scottsville Rd), 0.3 mi w. Int corridors. **Pets:** Accepted.

AAA ▼▼ **Best Value Inn** 🆂🅷
(270) 781-9594. **$44-$90, 5 day notice.** 250 Cumberland Trace Rd. I-65, exit 22 (Scottsville Rd), just ne. Int corridors. **Pets:** Medium. $7 one-time fee/pet. Service with restrictions, supervision.
🆂🅰🆅🅴 💲 ✖ 🔽🅼 🔒 ⊇

AAA ▼▼▼ **Continental Inn** 🆂🅷
(270) 781-5200. **$49-$65.** 700 Interstate Dr. I-65, exit 28, 0.3 mi w; across from National Corvette Museum. Ext corridors. **Pets:** Accepted.
🆂🅰🆅🅴 💲 ✖ 💻 ⊇

▼▼ **Country Hearth Inn** 🆂🅷
(270) 783-4443. **$54-$64.** 395 Corvette Dr. I-65, exit 28, just w. Int corridors. **Pets:** Accepted.
🅰🆂🅺 ✖ 🔽🅼 🔒 💻

AAA ▼▼ **Days Inn** 🆂🅷
(270) 781-6470. **$35-$130.** 4617 Scottsville Rd. I-65, exit 22 (Scottsville Rd), 0.3 mi e. Int corridors. **Pets:** Medium. $10 daily fee/pet. Designated rooms, no service, supervision.
🆂🅰🆅🅴 💲 ✖ 🗝 🔒 💻 ⊇

▼▼▼ **Drury Inn-Bowling Green** 🆂🅷
(270) 842-7100. **$80-$93.** 3250 Scottsville Rd. I-65, exit 22 (Scottsville Rd), just w. Int corridors. **Pets:** Large, other species. Service with restrictions, supervision.
🅰🆂🅺 ✖ 🔽🅼 🗝 🔒 💻 ⊇

AAA ▼▼▼▼ **Holiday Inn University Plaza** 🅻🅷
(270) 745-0088. **$79-$119.** 1021 Wilkinson Trace. I-65, exit 22 (Scottsville Rd), 2.5 mi w, then just n. Int corridors. **Pets:** Large, other species. $25 one-time fee/pet. Service with restrictions, supervision.
🆂🅰🆅🅴 💲 ✖ 🗝 🔒 💻 🍴 ⊇ ✖

AAA ▼▼▼ **News Inn of Bowling Green** 🅼
(270) 781-3460. **$45-$69.** 3160 Scottsville Rd. I-65, exit 22 (Scottsville Rd). Ext corridors. **Pets:** Medium. $5 daily fee/pet. Service with restrictions, supervision.
🆂🅰🆅🅴 💲 ✖ 🔒 ⊇

▼▼ **Travelodge Hotel** 🆂🅷
(270) 781-6610. **$65.** 1000 Executive Way. I-65, exit 22 (Scottsville Rd), just ne. Int corridors. **Pets:** Accepted.
🅰🆂🅺 💲 ✖ 💻 🍴 ⊇

CADIZ

▼▼▼▼ **Holiday Inn Express** 🆂🅷
(270) 522-3700. **$70-$75.** 153 Broad Bent Blvd. I-24, exit 65, just s. Int corridors. **Pets:** Accepted.
🅰🆂🅺 💲 ✖ 🔒 ⊇

▼▼ **Super 8 Motel** 🆂🅷
(270) 522-7007. **$54.** 154 Hospitality Ln. I-24, exit 65. Ext corridors. **Pets:** Accepted.
🅰🆂🅺 💲 ✖ ⊇

CAMPBELLSVILLE

AAA ▼▼▼ **Best Western Campbellsville Lodge** 🆂🅷
(270) 465-7001. **$65-$71.** 1400 E Broadway. 2 mi e on US 68 and SR 55. Int corridors. **Pets:** Very small, other species. $10 daily fee/pet. Service with restrictions, supervision.
🆂🅰🆅🅴 💲 ✖ 🔒 💻 ⊇

CARROLLTON

▼▼▼ **Best Western Executive Inn** 🆂🅷
(502) 732-8444. **$59-$109, 7 day notice.** 10 Slumber Ln. I-71, exit 44, just nw. Int corridors. **Pets:** Accepted.
🅰🆂🅺 💲 ✖ 🔽🅼 🗝 🔒 💻 ⊇

AAA ▼▼▼ **Days Inn Carrollton** 🆂🅷
(502) 732-9301. **$59-$99.** 61 Inn Rd. I-71, exit 44, just nw. Int corridors. **Pets:** Accepted.
🆂🅰🆅🅴 💲 ✖ 🔒 💻 ⊇

▼▼ **Super 8 Carrollton** 🆂🅷
(502) 732-0252. **$55-$99.** 130 Slumber Ln. I-71, exit 44, just nw. Int corridors. **Pets:** Accepted.
🅰🆂🅺 💲 ✖ 🔒

CAVE CITY

AAA ▼▼▼ **Best Western Kentucky Inn** 🆂🅷
(270) 773-3161. **$29-$125.** 1009 Doyle Ave. I-65, exit 53, just e. Ext corridors. **Pets:** Accepted.
🆂🅰🆅🅴 💲 ✖ 🔒 💻 ⊇

AAA ▼▼▼ **Comfort Inn** 🆂🅷
(270) 773-2030. **$45-$115.** 801 Mammoth Cave Rd. I-65, exit 53, just ne. Ext corridors. **Pets:** Very small. $5 daily fee/pet. Designated rooms, service with restrictions, supervision.
🆂🅰🆅🅴 💲 ✖ 🗝 🔒 💻 ⊇

▼▼ **Quality Inn** 🆂🅷
(270) 773-3101. **$35-$59.** 102 Happy Valley Rd. I-65, exit 53, just e. Ext corridors. **Pets:** Accepted.
🅰🆂🅺 💲 ✖ 🗝 🔒 💻 ⊇

AAA ▼▼▼ **Super 8 Motel** 🆂🅷
(270) 773-2500. **$39-$129.** 799 Mammoth Cave Rd. I-65, exit 53, just ne. Ext corridors. **Pets:** Small. $7 daily fee/pet. Service with restrictions, supervision.
🆂🅰🆅🅴 💲 ✖ 🔽🅼 🗝 🔒 💻 ⊇

CORBIN

AAA ▼▼▼▼ **Baymont Inn & Suites-Corbin** 🆂🅷
(606) 523-9040. **$49-$89.** 174 Adams Rd. I-75, exit 29. Int corridors. **Pets:** Accepted.
🆂🅰🆅🅴 💲 ✖ 🔽🅼 🗝 🗝 🔒 💻 ⊇

AAA ▼▼▼ **Best Western-Corbin Inn** 🆂🅷
(606) 528-2100. **$50-$90.** 2630 Cumberland Falls Hwy. I-75, exit 25. Ext corridors. **Pets:** $10 daily fee/pet. Designated rooms, service with restrictions, supervision.
🆂🅰🆅🅴 💲 ✖ 🔒 💻 ⊇

COVINGTON

▼▼◆▼ **Embassy Suites Cincinnati RiverCenter** 🔲
(859) 261-8400. **$149-$209.** 10 E RiverCenter Blvd. I-71/75, exit 192, 0.8 mi e on 5th St, 0.3 mi n on Madison. Int corridors. **Pets:** Accepted.
(ASK) (S✿) (✕) (占M) (⌁) 🔲 🔲 (¶) 🔄 (✕)

DANVILLE

▼▼◆▼ **Holiday Inn Express-Danville** 🔲
(859) 236-8600. **$59-$79, 14 day notice.** 96 Daniel Dr. Just e of US 127 on US 150 Bypass. Int corridors. **Pets:** Accepted.
(ASK) (S✿) (✕) (占M) (⌁) 🔲 🔄

◆◆ ▼ **Super 8 Motel** 🔲
(859) 236-8881. **$49-$66.** 3663 Hwy 150/127 Bypass. Just e of US 127 on US 150 Bypass. Int corridors. **Pets:** Medium. $10 one-time fee/pet. Designated rooms, service with restrictions, supervision.
(SAVE) (S✿) (✕) (⌁) 🔲

DRY RIDGE

▼▼◆▼ **Holiday Inn Express** 🔲
(859) 824-7121. **$62-$72.** 1050 Fashion Ridge Rd. I-75, exit 159, just nw. Int corridors. **Pets:** Small. $5 one-time fee/pet. Designated rooms, service with restrictions, supervision.
(ASK) (S✿) (✕) (⌁) 🔲 🔲

▼▼◆▼ **Microtel Inn and Suites** 🔲
(859) 824-2000. **$45-$60.** 79 Blackburn Ln. I-75, exit 159, just ne. Int corridors. **Pets:** Large, other species. $5 one-time fee/pet. Service with restrictions, crate.
(ASK) (S✿) (✕) (⌁) 🔲 🔲

EDDYVILLE

▼▼ **Holiday Hills Townhouses** 🅼
(270) 388-7236. **$185, 45 day notice.** 5631 Kentucky 93 S. I-24, exit 45, 2 mi s. Ext corridors. **Pets:** Medium, dogs only. $10 daily fee/pet. Service with restrictions, crate.
🔲 🔲 🔄 (✕) (⌖)

ELIZABETHTOWN

▼▼ **Best Western Cardinal Inn** 🔲
(270) 765-6139. **$75-$109, 7 day notice.** 642 E Dixie Ave. I-65, exit 91 (US 31 W), 0.3 mi nw. Ext/int corridors. **Pets:** Accepted.
(ASK) (S✿) (✕) 🔲 🔄

▼▼ **Comfort Inn Atrium Gardens** 🔲
(270) 769-3030. **$69-$129.** 1043 Executive Dr. I-65, exit 94, just nw. Int corridors. **Pets:** Accepted.
(ASK) (S✿) (✕) 🔲 🔲 🔄

◆◆ ▼▼ **Days Inn** 🔲 🐾
(270) 769-5522. **$69.** 2010 N Mulberry St. I-65, exit 94, just ne. Ext corridors. **Pets:** Small. $10 one-time fee/room. Service with restrictions, crate.
(SAVE) (S✿) (✕) 🔲 🔲 🔄

▼▼ **Holiday Inn** 🔲
(270) 769-2344. **$84.** 1058 N Mulberry St. I-65, exit 94, just nw. Ext corridors. **Pets:** Accepted.
(ASK) (S✿) (✕) (⌁) 🔲 🔲 (¶) 🔄

▼▼▼ **Quality Inn & Suites** 🔲
(270) 765-4166. **$69-$99.** 2009 N Mulberry St. I-65, exit 94, just sw. Int corridors. **Pets:** Small, other species. $10 daily fee/room. Service with restrictions, supervision.
(SAVE) (S✿) (✕) (占M) (⌁) 🔲 🔲 🔄

▼▼ **Super 8 Motel** 🔲
(270) 737-1088. **$49-$75.** 2028 N Mulberry St. I-65, exit 94, just ne. Int corridors. **Pets:** Accepted.
(✕) (占M) (⌁) 🔲 🔄

ERLANGER

◆◆ ▼▼▼ **Baymont Inn & Suites Cincinnati-Airport (Erlanger, KY)** 🔲
(859) 746-0300. **$79-$99.** 1805 Airport Exchange Blvd. I-275, exit 2. Int corridors. **Pets:** Other species. Service with restrictions, crate.
(SAVE) (S✿) (✕) (占M) (⌁) (⌁) 🔲 🔲 🔄

▼▼◆▼ **Residence Inn by Marriott, Cincinnati Airport** 🔲
(859) 282-7400. **$99-$199.** 2811 Circleport Dr. I-275, exit 2. Int corridors. **Pets:** Accepted.
(ASK) (S✿) (✕) (占M) (⌁) 🔲 🔲 🔄 (✕)

FLORENCE

◆◆ ▼▼◆▼ **AmeriSuites (Cincinnati/Airport)** 🔲
(859) 647-1170. **$79-$99.** 300 Meijer Dr. I-71/75, exit 182, 0.4 mi sw. Int corridors. **Pets:** Small. Service with restrictions, supervision.
(SAVE) (S✿) (✕) (占M) (⌁) (⌁) 🔲 🔲 🔄

▼▼◆▼ **Ashley Quarters** 🔲
(859) 525-9997. **$74-$98.** 4880 Houston Rd. I-71/75, exit 182, 0.6 mi w on Turfway and Houston rds. Int corridors. **Pets:** Medium. $50 one-time fee/room. Designated rooms, service with restrictions.
(ASK) (S✿) (✕) (⌁) 🔲 🔲 🔄

◆◆ ▼▼◆▼ **Best Western Inn Florence** 🔲
(859) 525-0090. **$60-$100.** 7821 Commerce Dr. I-71/75, exit 181, just ne. Int corridors. **Pets:** Other species. $20 daily fee/pet. Service with restrictions, supervision.
(SAVE) (S✿) (✕) (占M) (⌁) 🔲 🔲 🔄

◆◆ ▼▼◆▼ **Florence Super 8** 🔲 🐾
(859) 283-1221. **$44-$79.** 7928 Dream St. I-71/75, exit 180, just e on US 42, then just n. Int corridors. **Pets:** Medium. $5 one-time fee/pet. Service with restrictions, supervision.
(SAVE) (S✿) (✕) 🔲

◆◆ ▼▼◆▼ **Knights Inn Florence** 🅼
(859) 371-9711. **$35-$99.** 8049 Dream St. I-71/75, exit 180, just e on US 42, then just n. Ext corridors. **Pets:** Accepted.
(SAVE) (S✿) (✕) 🔲 🔄

▼▼ **Motel 6-Florence** 🔲
(859) 283-0909. **$35-$56.** 7937 Dream St. I-75/71, exit 180, just e on US 42, then just n. Ext corridors. **Pets:** Small, other species. Service with restrictions, supervision.
(S✿) (✕) (占M) (⌁) 🔄

▼▼ ▼▼ **Ramada Inn** SH
(859) 371-4700. **$64-$89.** 7915 US Hwy 42. I-71/75, exit 180, just e. Int corridors. **Pets:** Medium. $10 daily fee/pet. Designated rooms, service with restrictions, supervision.
ASK S6 ✕ 🖥 💻 ➡

▼▼ **Red Roof Inn** M
(859) 647-2700. **$45-$72.** 7454 Turfway Rd. I-71/75, exit 182, 0.8 mi sw. Int corridors. **Pets:** Medium. Service with restrictions, supervision.
ASK S6 ✕ 🖥 💻

▼▼ **Travelodge of Florence** SH 🐾
(859) 371-0227. **$49-$60.** 8075 Steilen Dr. I-71/75, exit 180, just w. Int corridors. **Pets:** Small. $10 daily fee/room. Service with restrictions, supervision.
ASK S6 ✕ 🖥 💻

FORT MITCHELL

▲▲▲ ▼▼▼▼ **Holiday Inn Fort Mitchell** SH
(859) 331-1500. **$79-$119.** 2100 Dixie Hwy. I-71/75, exit 188, just w. Int corridors. **Pets:** Accepted.
SAVE S6 ✕ 6M 🖳 🖥 💻 ⅂⅂ ➡ ✕

FRANKFORT

▲▲▲ ▼▼ **Bluegrass Inn** M
(502) 695-1800. **$48-$64.** 635 Versailles Rd. I-64, exit 58, 1 mi n on US 60. Ext corridors. **Pets:** Medium. $10 daily fee/pet. Designated rooms, service with restrictions, supervision.
SAVE S6 ✕ 🖥 ➡

▲▲▲ ▼▼▼▼ **Holiday Inn Capital Plaza** LH
(502) 227-5100. **$79-$109.** 405 Wilkinson Blvd. Adjacent to Frankfort Civic Center. Int corridors. **Pets:** Accepted.
SAVE S6 ✕ 6M 🖳 🖥 💻 ⅂⅂ ➡

▼▼ **Super 8 Motel** SH
(502) 875-3220. **$45-$60.** 1225 US Hwy 127 S. I-64, exit 53B, 1.2 mi n. Int corridors. **Pets:** Accepted.
ASK S6 ✕ 💻

FRANKLIN

▲▲▲ ▼▼▼▼ **Best Western Franklin Inn** SH
(270) 598-0070. **$37-$75.** 162 Anand Dr. I-65, exit 2, just w. Ext corridors. **Pets:** Accepted.
SAVE S6 ✕ 6M 🖳 💻 ➡

▲▲▲ ▼▼▼ **Comfort Inn** SH
(270) 586-6100. **$45-$99.** 3794 Nashville Rd. I-65, exit 2. Ext corridors. **Pets:** Medium. $5 daily fee/pet. Service with restrictions, supervision.
SAVE S6 ✕ 6M 🖥 💻 ➡

▲▲▲ ▼▼▼▼ **Days Inn** SH
(270) 598-0163. **$50-$70, 3 day notice.** 103 Trotter Ln. I-65, exit 6, just w. Ext corridors. **Pets:** Other species. $5 daily fee/pet. Service with restrictions.
SAVE S6 ✕ 6M 🖳 🖥 ➡

▼▼▼ **Holiday Inn Express** SH
(270) 586-5090. **$55-$71.** 3811 Nashville Rd. I-65, exit 2, just w. Ext corridors. **Pets:** Accepted.
ASK S6 ✕ 6M 🖥 💻 ➡

GEORGETOWN

▲▲▲ ▼▼▼ **Days Inn of Georgetown** M
(502) 863-5000. **$35-$65.** 385 Cherry Blossom Way. I-75, exit 129, just se. Ext corridors. **Pets:** Other species. $5 daily fee/pet. Service with restrictions, supervision.
SAVE S6 ✕ 🖳 🖥 💻 ➡

▼▼ **Super 8 Motel** SH
(502) 863-4888. **$44-$104, 5 day notice.** 250 Shoney Dr. I-75, exit 126. Ext/int corridors. **Pets:** Accepted.
ASK S6 ✕ 6M 🖥 ➡

GLASGOW

▼▼ **Comfort Inn** SH
(270) 651-9099. **$51-$61.** 210 Calvary Dr. Cumberland Pkwy, exit 11, just n. Ext corridors. **Pets:** Medium. $10 daily fee/room. Designated rooms, service with restrictions, supervision.
ASK S6 ✕ 🖳 🖥 💻 ➡

GRAND RIVERS

▲▲▲ ▼▼▼ **Best Western Kentucky-Barkley Lakes Inn** SH
(270) 928-2700. **$52-$80.** 720 Complex Dr. I-24, exit 31 (SR 453), just s. Ext/int corridors. **Pets:** Medium. $5 daily fee/pet. Designated rooms, service with restrictions, crate.
SAVE ✕ 🖥 💻 ➡

▼▼ **Microtel Inn & Suites** SH
(270) 928-2740. **$49-$73.** 1017 Dover Rd. I-24, exit 31 (SR 453), just n. Int corridors. **Pets:** Accepted.
ASK S6 ✕ 6M 🖉 🖳 🖥 ➡

GRAYSON

▼▼ **Super 8 Motel** SH
(606) 474-8811. **$38-$88, 10 day notice.** 125 Super 8 Ln. I-64, exit 172, just s. Int corridors. **Pets:** Small, other species. $5 daily fee/pet. Designated rooms, service with restrictions, supervision.
ASK ✕ 6M 🖉 🖳 🖥 💻

HARLAN

▼▼▼ **Holiday Inn Express Harlan** SH
(606) 573-3385. **$69-$99, 14 day notice.** 2608 S Hwy 421. On US 421, 2.8 mi s. Int corridors. **Pets:** Accepted.
ASK S6 🖉 🖳 🖥 💻 ➡

HARRODSBURG

▼▼ **Country Hearth Inn** SH
(859) 734-2400. **$54-$70.** 105 Commercial Dr. 0.6 mi n on College St. Int corridors. **Pets:** Small. $20 one-time fee/pet. Service with restrictions, supervision.
ASK S6 ✕ 🖥 💻

HEBRON

▼▼▼▼ **Radisson Hotel Cincinnati Airport** LH
(859) 371-6166. **$89-$139.** Cincinnati N KY Airport. I-71 and 75 via I-275, 4 mi w, exit 4B from I-275 (SR 212), 1.3 mi w on SR 212. Int corridors. **Pets:** Small, other species. Service with restrictions, crate.
ASK S6 ✕ 🖉 🖥 💻 ⅂⅂ ➡ ✕

HOPKINSVILLE

▼▼▼ Holiday Inn 🆂🅷
(270) 886-4413. **$80.** 2910 Ft Campbell Blvd. Pennyrile Pkwy, exit 7A, 0.6 mi n on US 41A. Int corridors. **Pets:** Medium, other species. Service with restrictions, supervision.
🅰🆂🅺 🆂⬦ ⌧ 🍴 💻 🍴 ⮆ ⌧

⬩⬩⬩ ▼▼▼▼ Hopkinsville Best Western 🆂🅷 🐾
(270) 886-9000. **$69-$79.** 4101 Ft Campbell Blvd. Pennyrile Pkwy, exit 7A, just s on US 41A. Int corridors. **Pets:** Very small, dogs only. $10 daily fee/pet. Designated rooms, service with restrictions, supervision.
🆂🅰🆅🅴 🆂⬦ ⌧ 🍴 💻 ⮆

HORSE CAVE

⬩⬩⬩ ▼▼▼ Budget Host Inn 🆂🅷 🐾
(270) 786-2165. **$33-$77.** I-65 & Hwy 218. I-65, exit 58, just ne. Ext corridors. **Pets:** Small. $5 daily fee/pet. Designated rooms, service with restrictions, supervision.
🆂🅰🆅🅴 ⌧ 🍴 🍴 ⮆

▼▼▼▼ Hampton Inn 🆂🅷
(270) 786-5000. **$79.** 750 Flint Ridge Rd. I-65, exit 58, just nw. Int corridors. **Pets:** Small. Service with restrictions, crate.
🅰🆂🅺 🆂⬦ ⌧ 🍴 💻 ⮆

IRVINE

▼▼ Oak Tree Inn 🆂🅷
(606) 723-2600. **$40-$65.** 1075 Richmond Rd. 1 mi w on SR 52. Ext corridors. **Pets:** $25 deposit/pet, $7 daily fee/room. Service with restrictions, crate.
🅰🆂🅺 🆂⬦ ⌧ 🍴

KUTTAWA

▼▼ Days Inn 🆂🅷
(270) 388-4060. **$58-$73.** 139 Days Inn Dr. I-24, exit 40 (US 62), just s. Ext corridors. **Pets:** $10 one-time fee/room. Service with restrictions, crate.
🅰🆂🅺 🆂⬦ ⌧ 🅼⬦ 🅺⬦ 🍴 💻 ⮆

LEBANON

▼▼ Country Hearth Inn 🆂🅷
(270) 692-4445. **$56-$125.** 720 W Main St. 1.4 mi s on SR 55 and US 68. Int corridors. **Pets:** $15 daily fee/room. Service with restrictions, crate.
🅰🆂🅺 🆂⬦ ⌧ 🅼⬦ 🍴 💻

LEITCHFIELD

▼▼ Hatfield Inn 🆂🅷
(270) 259-0464. **$40-$69.** 769 White St. Western Kentucky Pkwy, exit 107, just nw. Int corridors. **Pets:** Other species. $10 daily fee/pet. Service with restrictions, supervision.
🅰🆂🅺 🆂⬦ ⌧ 🍴 💻

LEWISPORT

▼▼▼ Best Western Hancock Inn 🅼
(270) 295-3234. **$62.** 9040 US Hwy 60 W. On US 60. Int corridors. **Pets:** Other species. $50 deposit/pet. Service with restrictions, supervision.
⌧ 🍴 💻 ⮆

LEXINGTON

⬩⬩⬩ ▼▼▼ Days Inn-South 🆂🅷
(859) 263-3100. **$47-$69.** 5575 Athens-Boonesboro Rd. I-75, exit 104, just e. Ext corridors. **Pets:** Small. $5 daily fee/pet. Designated rooms, service with restrictions, supervision.
🆂🅰🆅🅴 🆂⬦ ⌧ 🅼⬦ 🍴 💻

⬩⬩⬩ ▼▼▼▼ Hampton Inn I-75 🆂🅷 🐾
(859) 299-2613. **$69-$119.** 2251 Elkhorn Rd. I-75, exit 110, 0.4 mi nw. Int corridors. **Pets:** Service with restrictions, crate.
🆂🅰🆅🅴 🆂⬦ ⌧ 🅼⬦ 🍴 💻 ⮆

⬩⬩⬩ ▼▼▼▼ Holiday Inn-Lexington North 🆂🅷 🐾
(859) 233-0512. **$99-$159.** 1950 Newtown Pike. I-75/64, exit 115, just s. Int corridors. **Pets:** Small. $25 one-time fee/room. Service with restrictions, crate.
🆂🅰🆅🅴 🆂⬦ ⌧ 🅼⬦ 🅺⬦ 🍴 💻 🍴 ⮆ ⌧

⬩⬩⬩ ▼▼▼▼ Holiday Inn Lexington South 🆂🅷
(859) 263-5241. **$79-$99.** 5532 Athens-Boonesboro Rd. I-75, exit 104, just e. Int corridors. **Pets:** Accepted.
🆂🅰🆅🅴 🆂⬦ ⌧ 🅺⬦ 💻 🍴 ⮆ ⌧

⬩⬩⬩ ▼▼▼▼ La Quinta Inn 🆂🅷
(859) 231-7551. **$72-$92.** 1919 Stanton Way. I-75/64, exit 115, just se off SR 922. Int corridors. **Pets:** Other species. Service with restrictions, supervision.
🆂🅰🆅🅴 ⌧ 🍴 💻 ⮆

⬩⬩⬩ ▼▼▼▼▼ Marriott's Griffin Gate Resort 🅻🅷
(859) 231-5100. **$89-$199.** 1800 Newtown Pike. I-75/64, exit 115, 0.5 mi sw. Int corridors. **Pets:** Accepted.
🆂🅰🆅🅴 ⌧ 🅼⬦ 🅺⬦ 🅺⬦ 🍴 💻 🍴 ⮆ ⌧

▼▼ Microtel Inn 🆂🅷
(859) 299-9600. **$41-$80.** 2240 Buena Vista Rd. I-75, exit 110, just w. Int corridors. **Pets:** Small, other species. $25 one-time fee/room. Service with restrictions, crate.
⌧

▼▼ Quality Inn Northwest 🆂🅷
(859) 233-0561. **$49-$79.** 750 Newtown Ct. I-75/64, exit 115, 1.5 mi w on SR 922. Ext corridors. **Pets:** Accepted.
🅰🆂🅺 🆂⬦ ⌧ 🍴 💻 ⮆

⬩⬩⬩ ▼▼▼ Radisson Plaza Hotel Lexington 🅻🅷
(859) 231-9000. **$89.** 369 W Vine St. Corner of Vine St and Broadway. Int corridors. **Pets:** Medium, dogs only. $60 deposit/room, $40 one-time fee/room. Service with restrictions, supervision.
🆂🅰🆅🅴 🆂⬦ ⌧ 🅼⬦ 🅺⬦ 🅺⬦ 🍴 💻 🍴 ⮆ ⌧

⬩⬩⬩ ▼▼▼ Red Roof Inn-North 🆂🅷
(859) 293-2626. **$42-$62.** 1980 Haggard Ct. I-75/64, exit 113, 0.3 mi nw. Ext corridors. **Pets:** Large, other species. Service with restrictions, supervision.
🆂🅰🆅🅴 ⌧

⬩⬩⬩ ▼▼▼ Red Roof Inn South 🆂🅷
(859) 277-9400. **$54-$67.** 2651 Wilhite Dr. Jct US 27 and SR 4. Ext corridors. **Pets:** Medium, other species. Service with restrictions, supervision.
🆂🅰🆅🅴 ⌧ 🅼⬦ 🍴

▼▼ Red Roof Inn Southeast 🆂🅷
(859) 543-1877. $49-$69. 100 Canebrake Dr. I-75, exit 104,
just e. Int corridors. Pets: Medium. No service, supervision.
ⒶⓈⓀ 🆂 ⓧ 🔲 💻 🏊

▼▼▼ Residence Inn by Marriott 🆂🅷 🐾
(859) 231-6191. $109-$149. 1080 Newtown Pike. I-75/64,
exit 115, 1 mi s on SR 922. Ext corridors. Pets: Other
species. $100 one-time fee/room.
ⒶⓈⓀ 🆂 ⓧ 🅻 🔲 💻 🏊 ⓧ

🅰🅰🅰 ▼▼▼ Sleep Inn Lexington 🆂🅷 🐾
(859) 543-8400. $54-$99. 1920 Plaudit Pl. I-75, exit 108, just
sw. Int corridors. Pets: Other species. $15 one-time fee/
room. Designated rooms, service with restrictions, supervision.
🆂🅰🆅🅴 🆂 ⓧ 🅻 🔲 💻 🏊

LIBERTY

🅰🅰🅰 ▼ Royal Inn Express 🆂🅷
(606) 787-6224. $42-$44. 579 N Wallace Wilkinson Blvd. 1
mi n on US 127; 0.5 mi n of jct SR 70. Ext corridors.
Pets: $5 daily fee/pet. Service with restrictions, supervision.
🆂🅰🆅🅴 🆂 ⓧ 🔲 🏊

LONDON

▼ Budget Host Westgate Inn 🆂🅷 🐾
(606) 878-7330. $45-$54, 3 day notice. 254 W Daniel
Boone Pkwy. I-75, exit 41, just w on SR 80. Ext/int corridors. Pets: Other species. Service with restrictions, supervision.
🆂 ⓧ 🅻 🅻 🔲 🏊

▼▼ Park Inn 🆂🅷
(606) 878-7678. $55-$115. 400 GOP St. I-75, exit 41. Ext
corridors. Pets: Small. Service with restrictions.
ⒶⓈⓀ 🆂 ⓧ 🔲 💻 🏊

🅰🅰🅰 ▼▼▼ Red Roof Inn 🆂🅷
(606) 862-8844. $54-$70. 110 Melcon Ln. I-75, exit 41,
southwest corner. Int corridors. Pets: Small. $6 daily fee/
room. Designated rooms, service with restrictions, supervision.
🆂🅰🆅🅴 🆂 ⓧ 🅻 🔲 💻 🏊

━━━━━━━━━ **LOUISVILLE METROPOLITAN AREA** ━━━━━━━━━

BROOKS

▼▼▼ Comfort Inn 🆂🅷
(502) 957-6900. $75, 15 day notice. 149 Willabrook Dr. I-65,
exit 121, just nw. Int corridors. Pets: Accepted.
ⒶⓈⓀ 🆂 ⓧ 🔲 💻 🏊

HURSTBOURNE

▼▼▼ Drury Inn & Suites-Louisville 🆂🅷
(502) 326-4170. $82-$107. 9501 Blairwood Rd. I-64, exit 15.
Int corridors. Pets: Large, other species. Service with
restrictions, supervision.
ⒶⓈⓀ ⓧ 🅻 🍽 🅻 🔲 💻 🏊

🅰🅰🅰 ▼ Red Roof Inn Louisville–East #034 🆂🅷
(502) 426-7621. $41-$61. 9330 Blairwood Rd. I-64, exit 15,
0.3 mi nw of Hurstbourne Pkwy. Ext corridors.
Pets: Accepted.
🆂🅰🆅🅴 ⓧ 🅻

JEFFERSONTOWN

🅰🅰🅰 ▼▼▼ AmeriSuites (Louisville/East) 🆂🅷
(502) 426-0119. $78-$88. 701 S Hurstbourne Pkwy. I-64, exit
15, 1 mi n. Int corridors. Pets: Accepted.
🆂🅰🆅🅴 🆂 ⓧ 🍽 🔲 💻 🏊

▼▼▼ Comfort Suites 🆂🅷
(502) 266-6509. $59-$99. 1850 Resource Way. I-64, exit 17,
0.5 mi s of Blankenbaker Rd. Int corridors. Pets: Accepted.
ⒶⓈⓀ 🆂 ⓧ 🅻 🔲 💻 🏊

🅰🅰🅰 ▼▼▼ Holiday Inn-Hurstbourne 🅻🅷
(502) 426-2600. $69-$99. 1325 S Hurstbourne Pkwy. I-64,
exit 15. Ext/int corridors. Pets: Accepted.
🆂🅰🆅🅴 🆂 ⓧ 🍽 🔲 💻 🍴 🏊 ⓧ

▼▼▼ Homestead Studio Suites
Hotel-Louisville/East 🆂🅷 🐾
(502) 267-4454. $80-$95. 1650 Alliant Ave. I-64, exit 17, just
s. Int corridors. Pets: Medium, other species. $25 daily
fee/room. Service with restrictions, crate.
ⒶⓈⓀ 🆂 ⓧ 🅻 🅻 🔲 💻 🏊

🅰🅰🅰 ▼▼▼ Microtel Inn 🆂🅷
(502) 266-6590. $50-$65. 1221 Kentucky Mills Dr. I-64, exit
17. Int corridors. Pets: Small. $20 one-time fee/pet. Service
with restrictions, supervision.
🆂🅰🆅🅴 🆂 ⓧ 🅻 🍽 🅻

▼▼ Sleep Inn 🆂🅷
(502) 266-6776. $59-$199. 1850 Priority Way. I-64, exit 17,
0.5 mi s of Blankenbaker Rd. Int corridors. Pets: Accepted.
ⒶⓈⓀ ⓧ 🔲 💻

▼▼ Super 8 Motel 🆂🅷
(502) 267-8889. $50-$100. 1501 Alliant Ave. I-64, exit 17,
just e. Int corridors. Pets: Medium, other species. $10 daily
fee/pet. Designated rooms, no service, supervision.
ⒶⓈⓀ 🆂 ⓧ 🅻 🅻 🔲 🏊

LA GRANGE

▼▼▼ Comfort Suites 🆂🅷
(502) 225-4125. $69-$99. 1500 Crystal Dr. I-71, exit 22, just
e. Int corridors. Pets: Accepted.
ⒶⓈⓀ 🆂 ⓧ 🅻 🅻 🔲 💻 🏊 ⓧ

LOUISVILLE

Airport & Expo Best Suites SH ❖
(502) 368-0007. **$89-$129.** 4125 Preston Hwy. I-65, exit 130, 1 mi w. Int corridors. **Pets:** Medium. $15 daily fee/room. Designated rooms, service with restrictions, supervision.
SAVE 🔊 ✕ 🛗 📶 💺 🛗 💻

Aleksander House Bed and Breakfast BB
(502) 637-4985. **$95-$169, 3 day notice.** 1213 S 1st St. I-65, exit 135 (St Catherine St), just s. Int corridors. **Pets:** Accepted.
ASK 🔊 ✕ 🛗 💻

Breckinridge Inn LH
(502) 456-5050. **$79-$95.** 2800 Breckinridge Ln. I-264, exit 18A, just s. Int corridors. **Pets:** Accepted.
ASK 🔊 ✕ 🛗 💻 🛂 ✕

Doubletree Club Hotel LH
(502) 585-2200. **$79-$179.** 101 E Jefferson St. I-65, exit 136C (Jefferson St) southbound; exit Brook St northbound. Int corridors. **Pets:** Large. $25 deposit/pet. Service with restrictions, supervision.
SAVE 🔊 ✕ 💺 🛗 💻 🍽 🛂

Executive West LH
(502) 367-2251. **$99-$129.** 830 Phillips Ln. I-264, exit 11 (Fairgrounds/Expo Center Main Gate). Int corridors. **Pets:** Other species. $100 one-time fee/room. Service with restrictions.
ASK ✕ 📶 🛗 💻 🍽 🛂 ✕

Holiday Inn Airport East SH
(502) 452-6361. **$122-$151.** 4004 Gardiner Point Dr. I-264, exit 15B westbound; exit 15 eastbound. Int corridors. **Pets:** Medium, dogs only. $25 one-time fee/pet. Designated rooms, service with restrictions, supervision.
SAVE 🔊 ✕ 💺 🛗 💻 🍽 🛂

Holiday Inn Louisville (Downtown) SH
(502) 582-2241. **$130.** 120 W Broadway. Just w on US 60 business route and 150. Int corridors. **Pets:** Medium. Service with restrictions, crate.
SAVE 🔊 ✕ 📶 💺 💻 🍽 🛂

Holiday Inn South-Airport LH
(502) 964-3311. **$105-$145.** 3317 Fern Valley Rd. I-65, exit 128 (Fern Valley Rd), northeast corner. Int corridors. **Pets:** Large. $35 one-time fee/room. Service with restrictions, supervision.
ASK 🔊 ✕ 💺 📶 💺 🛗 💻 🍽 🛂 ✕

Red Roof Inn-Airport-Fairgrounds SH
(502) 968-0151. **$40-$69.** 4704 Preston Hwy. I-65, exit 130, northeast corner. Ext corridors. **Pets:** Accepted.
SAVE ✕

Red Roof Inn-Southeast-Fairgrounds SH
(502) 456-2993. **$42-$63.** 3322 Red Roof Inn Pl. I-264, 15B westbound, 0.3 mi s; exit 15 eastbound. Ext corridors. **Pets:** Accepted.
SAVE ✕

Residence Inn by Marriott SH
(502) 363-8800. **$89-$139.** 700 Phillips Ln. I-264, exit 11 (Fairgrounds/Expo Center Main Gate), 0.4 mi w. Int corridors. **Pets:** Large, other species. $100 one-time fee/room. Service with restrictions, crate.
ASK 🔊 ✕ 💺 📶 💺 🛗 💻 🛂 ✕

Residence Inn by Marriott-Louisville NE SH
(502) 412-1311. **$59-$189.** 3500 Springhurst Commons Dr. I-265, exit 32, 0.5 mi w on Westport Rd, just n. Int corridors. **Pets:** Accepted.
ASK 🔊 ✕ 💺 💺 🛗 💻 🛂

Residence Inn Louisville East SH
(502) 425-1821. **$59-$189.** 120 N Hurstbourne Pkwy. I-64, exit 15, 1.8 mi n. Ext corridors. **Pets:** Other species. $135 one-time fee/room. Service with restrictions.
✕ 🛗 💻 🛂 ✕

The Seelbach Hilton Louisville LH
(502) 585-3200. **$99-$189.** 500 4th St. I-65, exit 136C (Muhammad Ali), 0.3 mi w, then just s. Int corridors. **Pets:** Other species. $50 deposit/room. Service with restrictions, crate.
SAVE 🔊 ✕ 💺 📶 💺 🛗 💻 🍽 ✕

Signature Inn South SH
(502) 968-4100. **$92-$97.** 6515 Signature Dr. I-65, exit 128 (Fern Valley Rd), southeast corner. Int corridors. **Pets:** Small. Service with restrictions, crate.
ASK 🔊 ✕ 🛗 💻 🛂

Sleep Inn Fairgrounds SH
(502) 368-9597. **$59-$150, 7 day notice.** 3330 Preston Hwy. I-264, exit 11 (Fairgrounds/Expo Center Main Gate), 0.5 mi e on Phillips Ln, then just n. Int corridors. **Pets:** Accepted.
ASK 🔊 ✕ 💺 🛗 💻

SHEPHERDSVILLE

Best Western South SH
(502) 543-7097. **$62-$79, 30 day notice.** 211 S Lakeview Dr. I-65, exit 117 (SR 44 W), just se. Int corridors. **Pets:** Small. Service with restrictions, supervision.
SAVE 🔊 ✕ 💻 🛂

SHIVELY

Holiday Inn-Southwest LH
(502) 448-2020. **$99-$139.** 4110 Dixie Hwy. I-264, exit 8B, just n on US 31 W and 60. Int corridors. **Pets:** Medium. $25 one-time fee/room. Service with restrictions, crate.
SAVE 🔊 ✕ 📶 🛗 💻 🍽 🛂

❖ **END METROPOLITAN AREA** ❖

MADISONVILLE

▼▼ **Days Inn Madisonville** SH
(270) 821-8620. **$65-$71.** 1900 Lantaff Blvd. Pennyrile Pkwy, exit 44. Int corridors. **Pets:** Accepted.
ASK S❄ ✕ ⊘ 🗎 💻 🍴 ⇌

MAYSVILLE

▼▼ **Super 8 Motel, Maysville KY** SH
(606) 759-8888. **$57-$67, 5 day notice.** 550 Tucker Dr. Just e of US 68. Int corridors. **Pets:** Accepted.
ASK S❄ ✕ 🗎

MOREHEAD

⬥ ▼▼▼ **Comfort Inn & Suites** SH 🐾
(606) 780-7378. **$55-$115.** 2650 Kentucky 801 N. I-64, exit 133, just s. Int corridors. **Pets:** Other species. $100 deposit/room, $10 daily fee/room. Service with restrictions, crate.
SAVE S❄ ✕ ⤵M 🐕 🗎 💻 ⇌

▼▼▼ **Holiday Inn Express of Morehead** SH
(606) 784-5796. **$69-$89, 7 day notice.** 110 Toms Dr. I-64, exit 137 (SR 32), just sw. Int corridors. **Pets:** Medium, other species. $10 daily fee/pet. Service with restrictions, supervision.
ASK S❄ ✕ ⤵M 🐕 🗎 💻 ⇌

MORGANTOWN

▼▼ **Motel 6 #4120** SH
(270) 526-9481. **$49-$55.** 1460 S Main St. From William H Natcher Pkwy, exit 26, just w. Int corridors. **Pets:** Accepted.
ASK S❄ ✕ ⤵M 🗎 💻 ⇌

MORTONS GAP

⬥ ▼▼ **Best Western Pennyrile Inn** SH
(270) 258-5201. **$54-$74.** White City Rd. Pennyrile Pkwy, exit 37 (US 41). Ext corridors. **Pets:** Accepted.
SAVE S❄ ✕ 🗎 ⇌

MOUNT VERNON

⬥ ▼ **Kastle Inn Motel** M
(606) 256-5156. **$52-$70, 3 day notice.** Hwy 25 S. I-75, exit 59. Ext corridors. **Pets:** Medium. Supervision.
SAVE S❄ ✕ 🍴 ⇌

MURRAY

▼▼ **Days Inn-Murray, KY** SH
(270) 753-6706. **$49-$59.** 517 S 12th St. 1 mi s on US 641. Ext corridors. **Pets:** Other species. $10 daily fee/pet. Service with restrictions, supervision.
ASK S❄ ✕ 🗎 💻 ⇌

⬥ ▼ **Murray Plaza Court** SH
(270) 753-2682. **$36-$39.** 504 12th St. 1 mi s on US 641. Ext corridors. **Pets:** Service with restrictions, supervision.
SAVE ✕ 🗎

OAK GROVE

⬥ ▼▼▼ **Comfort Inn-Oak Grove** SH
(270) 439-3311. **$64-$79.** 201 Auburn St. I-24, exit 86, just s. Ext corridors. **Pets:** Other species. $10 daily fee/pet. Designated rooms, no service, supervision.
SAVE S❄ ✕ ⤵M ⊘ 🐕 🗎 💻 ⇌

▼▼ **Days Inn Ft. Campbell** SH
(270) 640-3888. **$49-$65.** 212 Auburn St. I-24, exit 86, just s. Ext corridors. **Pets:** Accepted.
ASK S❄ ✕ ⤵M ⊘ 🗎 ⇌

▼▼▼ **Holiday Inn Express** SH
(270) 439-0022. **$69-$99.** 12759 Ft Campbell Blvd. I-24, exit 86. Int corridors. **Pets:** $7 daily fee/pet. Designated rooms, service with restrictions, crate.
ASK S❄ ✕ ⤵M ⊘ 🗎 💻 ⇌

OWENSBORO

▼ **Motel 6 #205** SH
(270) 686-8606. **$41-$53.** 4585 Frederica St. US 60 Bypass, exit 4 at jct US 431, just n. Ext corridors. **Pets:** Small, other species. Service with restrictions, supervision.
S❄ ✕ ⤵M ⊘ 🗎 ⇌

▼▼▼ **Super 8 Motel-Owensboro** SH
(270) 685-3388. **$55.** 1027 Goetz Dr. US 60 Bypass, exit 4 at jct US 431. Int corridors. **Pets:** Small, other species. $5 daily fee/pet. Service with restrictions, crate.
ASK S❄ ✕ ⤵M 🗎 ⇌

PADUCAH

⬥ ▼▼▼ **Baymont Inn-Paducah** SH 🐾
(270) 443-4343. **$49-$89.** 5300 Old Cairo Rd. I-24, exit 3 (SR 305), just w. Int corridors. **Pets:** Small. $50 deposit/pet. Service with restrictions, supervision.
SAVE S❄ ✕ ⊘ 🐕 🗎 💻

▼▼ **Days Inn** SH
(270) 442-7501. **$50-$90.** 3901 Hinkleville Rd. I-24, exit 4 (US 60), just e. Ext corridors. **Pets:** Small, dogs only. $10 deposit/room. Designated rooms, service with restrictions, supervision.
ASK S❄ ✕ 🗎 💻 ⇌

▼▼▼ **Drury Inn-Paducah** SH
(270) 443-3313. **$79-$96.** 3975 Hinkleville Rd. I-24, exit 4 (US 60), just e. Int corridors. **Pets:** Large, other species. Service with restrictions, supervision.
ASK ✕ 🐕 🗎 💻 ⇌

▼▼▼ **Drury Suites-Paducah** SH
(270) 441-0024. **$92-$102.** 2930 James-Sanders Blvd. I-24, exit 4 (US 60), just w. Int corridors. **Pets:** Large, other species. Service with restrictions, supervision.
ASK ✕ ⤵M 🐕 🗎 💻 ⇌ ✕

▼▼▼ **Hampton Inn-Paducah** SH
(270) 442-4500. **$88-$103.** 5006 Hinkleville Rd. I-24, exit 4 (US 60), just w. Int corridors. **Pets:** Accepted.
ASK ✕ ⤵M ⊘ 💻 ⇌

▼▼▼ **Holiday Inn Express** SH
(270) 442-8874. **$84-$112.** 3994 Hinkleville Rd. I-24, exit 4 (US 60), just e. Int corridors. **Pets:** Accepted.
ASK S❄ ✕ 🗎 💻 ⇌

▼▼ Pear Tree Inn-Paducah SH
(270) 444-7200. **$62-$77.** 5002 Hinkleville Rd. I-24, exit 4 (US 60), just w. Ext corridors. **Pets:** Large, other species. Service with restrictions, supervision.
ASK ⊠ 🖪 ⌫

PRESTONSBURG

▼▼ Super 8 Prestonsburg M
(606) 886-3355. **$49-$64.** 550 US 23 S. Jct US 114 and US 23. Int corridors. **Pets:** Accepted.
ASK 🖪 ⊠ 🖳

RICHMOND

▼▼▼ Holiday Inn Express Hotel & Suites SH
(859) 624-4005. **$72-$149.** 1990 Colby Taylor Dr. I-75, exit 87, just w. Int corridors. **Pets:** Other species. $10 daily fee/pet. Supervision.
ASK 🖪 ⊠ 🖳 🖫 🖪 🖪 ⌫

▼▼▼ Jameson Inn SH
(859) 623-0063. **$60-$71.** 1007 Colby Taylor Dr. I-75, exit 87, just e. Int corridors. **Pets:** Small. Service with restrictions, crate.
⊠ 🖳 🖫 🖪 🖪 ⌫

▲▲▲ ▼▼▼ La Quinta Inn-Richmond SH
(859) 623-9121. **$59.** 1751 Lexington Rd. I-75, exit 90 northbound; exit 90A southbound. Int corridors. **Pets:** Small. $5 one-time fee/pet.
SAVE ⊠ 🖫 🖪 🖪 ⌫

▼▼ Red Roof Inn M
(859) 625-0084. **$49-$69.** 111 Bahama Ct. I-75, exit 90 northbound; exit 90A southbound. Int corridors. **Pets:** Large. Service with restrictions, supervision.
ASK 🖪 ⊠ 🖪 🖪 ⌫

▲▲▲ ▼▼▼ Super 8 Motel SH
(859) 624-1550. **$55-$60, 7 day notice.** 107 N Keeneland Dr. I-75, exit 90. Int corridors. **Pets:** Very small. $7 daily fee/pet. Designated rooms, service with restrictions, supervision.
SAVE 🖪 ⊠ 🖪 🖪 🖳

SCOTTSVILLE

▲▲▲ ▼▼▼ Executive Inn SH
(270) 622-7770. **$55.** 57 Burnley Rd. US 31 E, jct SR 231 and 980. Ext corridors. **Pets:** Small. $6 one-time fee/pet. Service with restrictions.
SAVE 🖪 ⊠ 🖪 ⌫

SHELBYVILLE

▲▲▲ ▼▼▼ Best Western Shelbyville Lodge SH
(502) 633-4400. **$64-$135.** 115 Isaac Shelby Dr. I-64, exit 32, 0.5 mi n on SR 55. Int corridors. **Pets:** Other species. Service with restrictions, supervision.
SAVE 🖪 ⊠ 🖪 🖳 ⌫

▼▼ Days Inn Shelbyville SH ✿
(502) 633-4005. **$50-$109, 30 day notice.** 101 Howard Dr. I-64, exit 32, 0.8 mi n on SR 55. Ext corridors. **Pets:** Medium, other species. $10 one-time fee/room. Designated rooms, service with restrictions, crate.
ASK 🖪 ⊠ 🖪

▼▼▼ Holiday Inn Express SH
(502) 647-0109. **$80-$100.** 110 Club House Dr. I-64, exit 35, just s. Int corridors. **Pets:** Other species. Supervision.
ASK 🖪 ⊠ 🖳 🖫 🖪 🖪 ⌫

SMITHS GROVE

▲▲▲ ▼▼ Bryce Inn SH
(270) 563-5141. **$49-$55.** I-65, exit 38, 0.3 mi w. Ext corridors. **Pets:** Accepted.
SAVE 🖪 ⊠ 🖪 🖳 ⌫

VERSAILLES

▼▼▼ 1823 Historic Rose Hill Inn BB ✿
(859) 873-5957. **$109-$169, 7 day notice.** 233 Rose Hill. Just s on SR 33 (S Main St), then just w. Ext/int corridors. **Pets:** Dogs only. $15 one-time fee/room. Designated rooms.
⊠ 🖪 🖳

WILLIAMSTOWN

▲▲▲ ▼▼ Days Inn SH ✿
(859) 824-5025. **$49-$66, 3 day notice.** 211 SR 36 W. I-75, exit 154, just n. Ext corridors. **Pets:** Small, dogs only. $5 daily fee/pet. Designated rooms, no service, supervision.
SAVE 🖪 ⊠ 🖪 🖳 ⌫

WINCHESTER

▲▲▲ ▼▼▼ Best Western-Country Squire SH
(859) 744-7210. **$59-$69.** 1307 W Lexington Rd. I-64, exit 94 (US 60), 0.9 mi se. Ext corridors. **Pets:** Small. $5 daily fee/pet. Designated rooms, service with restrictions, supervision.
SAVE 🖪 ⊠ 🖪 🖳 ⌫

ALEXANDRIA

Best Western of Alexandria Inn & Suites & Conference Center SH
(318) 445-5530. **$67-$69.** 2720 W MacArthur Dr. 0.9 mi n of jct SR 28 and US 71/165 (MacArthur Dr). Ext/int corridors. **Pets:** Very small. $10 daily fee/pet. Designated rooms, service with restrictions, supervision.
SAVE

Clarion Hotel Alexandria SH
(318) 487-4261. **$65-$135.** 2716 N MacArthur Dr. 0.9 mi n of jct SR 28 and US 71/165 (MacArthur Dr). Ext/int corridors. **Pets:** Medium. $25 one-time fee/pet. Service with restrictions, supervision.
SAVE

Days Inn M
(318) 443-1841. **$53-$55.** 1146 MacArthur Dr. 0.7 mi s of jct SR 28 and US 71/165 (MacArthur Dr). Ext corridors. **Pets:** Small. $10 one-time fee/pet. Service with restrictions, supervision.
SAVE

La Quinta Inn & Suites-Alexandria SH
(318) 442-3700. **$85-$100.** 6116 W Calhoun Dr. I-49, exit 90 (Air Base Rd), just w. Int corridors. **Pets:** Accepted.

Ramada Limited SH
(318) 448-1611. **$65.** 742 MacArthur Dr. 0.4 mi s of jct SR 28 and US 71/165 (MacArthur Dr). Ext corridors. **Pets:** Medium. $25 deposit/room. Service with restrictions, supervision.
SAVE

Super 8 Motel M
(318) 445-6541. **$45-$60.** 700 MacArthur Dr. 0.4 mi s of jct SR 28 and US 71/65 (MacArthur Dr). Ext/int corridors. **Pets:** Medium, other species. $35 deposit/room. Service with restrictions, supervision.
SAVE

BATON ROUGE

AmeriSuites (Baton Rouge/East) SH
(225) 769-4400. **$85-$129.** 6080 Bluebonnet Blvd. I-10, exit 162. Int corridors. **Pets:** Small, other species. Service with restrictions.
SAVE

Baymont Inn & Suites Baton Rouge SH
(225) 291-6600. **$59-$79.** 10555 Rieger Rd. I-10, exit 163 (Siegen Ln), just n, then just e. Int corridors. **Pets:** Medium. $50 deposit/room. Designated rooms, service with restrictions, supervision.
SAVE

Chase Suites by Woodfin SH
(225) 927-5630. **$144-$179.** 5522 Corporate Blvd. I-10, exit 158, just n on College Dr, then just e. Ext corridors. **Pets:** Medium, other species. $150 deposit/room, $5 daily fee/pet. Service with restrictions, crate.
ASK

Comfort Inn SH
(225) 927-5790. **$64-$89.** 2445 S Acadian Thruway. I-10, exit 157B, just n. Int corridors. **Pets:** Medium, other species. $25 daily fee/pet. Designated rooms, service with restrictions, supervision.
ASK

La Quinta Inn-Baton Rouge M ✿
(225) 924-9600. **$76-$86.** 2333 S Acadian Thruway. I-10, exit 157B. Ext corridors. **Pets:** Other species. Service with restrictions, supervision.
SAVE

Motel 6 Baton Rouge Southeast #1124 M
(225) 291-4912. **Call for rates.** 10445 Rieger Rd. I-10, exit 163, just n. Ext corridors. **Pets:** Small, other species. Service with restrictions, supervision.

Residence Inn by Marriott-Baton Rouge SH
(225) 293-8700. **$149-$159.** 10333 N Mall Dr. I-10, exit 163 westbound, just s on Siegen Ln, then just e; eastbound, 0.5 mi to S Mall Dr, just e to Andrea (at Lowe's), then just n. Int corridors. **Pets:** $150 one-time fee/room. Service with restrictions, crate.
ASK

TownePlace Suites by Marriott SH
(225) 819-2112. **$75-$119.** 8735 Summa Ave. I-10, exit 160, 0.5 mi s to Summa Ave, 0.6 mi w. Int corridors. **Pets:** Accepted.
ASK

BOSSIER CITY

Best Western-Airline Motor Inn SH
(318) 742-6000. **$55-$95.** 1984 Airline Dr. I-20, exit 22 (Airline Dr), just n. Ext corridors. **Pets:** Accepted.

GuestHouse International SH
(318) 747-7700. **$49-$59.** 1836 Old Minden Rd. I-20, exit 21, just n. Ext corridors. **Pets:** Other species. $25 deposit/room. Service with restrictions, supervision.

Hampton Inn SH
(318) 752-1112. **$84-$94.** 1005 Gould Dr. I-20, exit 21. Int corridors. **Pets:** Accepted.

La Quinta Inn SH
(318) 747-4400. **$61-$85.** 309 Preston Blvd. I-20, exit 21, just n. Ext corridors. **Pets:** Accepted.

Microtel Inn & Suites SH
(318) 742-7882. **$54-$79.** 2713 Village Ln. I-20, exit 22 (Airline Dr), just s, then just w. Int corridors. **Pets:** $25 one-time fee/room. Service with restrictions, supervision.

Quality Inn & Suites SH
(318) 742-7890. **$69-$189.** 2717 Village Ln. I-20, exit 22 (Airline Dr), just s, then just w. Int corridors. **Pets:** Other species. $25 one-time fee/room. Service with restrictions.

Quality Inn of Bossier City SH
(318) 746-5050. **$60.** 4300 Industrial Dr. I-20, exit 23 (Industrial Dr). Ext corridors. **Pets:** Medium. $20 one-time fee/room. Designated rooms, service with restrictions, supervision.

Ramada Inn Bossier SH
(318) 746-8410. **$51-$83.** 750 Isle of Capri Blvd. I-20, exit 20A (Hamilton Rd). Ext corridors. **Pets:** Accepted.

Residence Inn by Marriott-Shreveport/Bossier City SH
(318) 747-6220. **$109-$165.** 1001 Gould Dr. I-20, exit 21, just ne. Ext corridors. **Pets:** Other species. $5 daily fee/room, $100 one-time fee/room. Service with restrictions.

BREAUX BRIDGE

Best Western of Breaux Bridge M
(337) 332-1114. **$70-$90.** 2088-B Rees St. I-10, exit 109 (Breaux Bridge). Ext corridors. **Pets:** Medium, other species. $20 daily fee/pet. Supervision.

CONVENT

Poche Plantation Bed & Breakfast BB
(225) 562-7728. **$99-$119, 7 day notice.** 6554 Louisiana Hwy 44. Jct SR 44 and 641; 10.1 mi s of Sunshine Bridge (SR 70), 10.2 mi n on SR 44. Ext corridors. **Pets:** $15 one-time fee/room. Service with restrictions.

DELHI

Days Inn SH
(318) 878-9000. **$65-$75.** 113 Snider Rd. I-20, exit 153. Ext corridors. **Pets:** Accepted.

DERIDDER

Stagecoach Inn SH
(337) 462-0022. **$57-$65.** 505 E 1st St. 2 mi on east side between US 171 NS. Ext corridors. **Pets:** Very small. $10 daily fee/pet. Service with restrictions, crate.

HAMMOND

Best Western Hammond Inn & Suites SH
(985) 419-2001. **$60-$80.** 107 Duo Dr. I-12, exit 40 (US 51), just ne. Ext corridors. **Pets:** Other species. $10 daily fee/room. Service with restrictions, supervision.

Michabelle-A Little Inn CI
(985) 419-0550. **$85-$125, 5 day notice.** 1106 S Holly St. I-12, exit 40 (US 51), 0.8 mi n, just e on Old Covington Hwy, then n, follow signs. Ext/int corridors. **Pets:** Accepted.

Rockwood Inn & Suites SH
(985) 345-1980. **$67-$115.** 42309 S Morrison Blvd. I-55, exit 28 (US 51), just e. Int corridors. **Pets:** Accepted.

IOWA

Howard Johnson Express Inn SH
(337) 582-2440. **$54-$60.** 107 E Frontage Rd. I-10, exit 43, just n, then just e. Int corridors. **Pets:** Medium, other species. $10 one-time fee/room. Service with restrictions, crate.

KINDER

Best Western Inn At Coushatta SH
(337) 738-4800. **$89-$119.** 12102 US Hwy 165 N. 5 mi n of jct US 190/165. Int corridors. **Pets:** Very small, other species. Service with restrictions, supervision.

Holiday Inn Express Hotel & Suites SH
(337) 738-3381. **$79-$109.** 11750 US Hwy 165. 5.2 mi n of jct US 190/165, 5.1 mi on US 165. Ext/int corridors. **Pets:** Accepted.

Super 8 Motel M
(337) 738-3366. **$55-$175.** 11586 US 165. 5.3 mi n of jct US 190/165. Ext corridors. **Pets:** Accepted.
A$K S6 X 6M e 8 9 2

LAFAYETTE

Best Suites of Lafayette SH
(337) 235-1367. **$87-$139.** 125 E Kaliste Saloom Rd. I-10, exit 103A, 1 mi w of jct of E Kaliste Saloom Rd and SW Evangeline Thruway (US 90). Int corridors. **Pets:** Accepted.
A$K S6 X e 8 9 2

Comfort Inn Lafayette SH
(337) 232-9000. **$79-$80.** 1421 SE Evangeline Thruway. 3 mi s of I-10 at jct US 90 (Evangeline Thruway). Int corridors. **Pets:** Large, other species. Service with restrictions, supervision.
A$K S6 X 9 8 9 11 2

Days Inn-Lafayette M
(337) 237-8880. **$55-$65.** 1620 N University. I-10, exit 101. Ext corridors. **Pets:** Other species. $10 daily fee/pet. Service with restrictions, crate.
A$K S6 X 8 2

Hilton Lafayette & Towers LH
(337) 235-6111. **$79-$179.** 1521 W Pinhook Rd. SR 182, 1.3 mi sw of US 90 (Evangeline Thruway). Int corridors. **Pets:** Small. $25 one-time fee/room. Designated rooms, service with restrictions, crate.
SAVE S6 X e 8 9 11 2

La Quinta Inn-Lafayette SH
(337) 233-5610. **$66-$76.** 2100 NE Evangeline Thruway. I-10, exit 103A, 0.3 mi s on US 167. Ext corridors. **Pets:** Other species. Service with restrictions.
SAVE X 9 8 9 2

Ramada Inn SH
(337) 235-0858. **$53-$70.** 120 E Kaliste Saloom Rd. I-10, exit 103A, 4.4 mi e on US 90 (Evangeline Thruway), 1 mi s. Ext corridors. **Pets:** Accepted.
A$K S6 X 8 9 11 2

Red Roof Inn M
(337) 233-3339. **$38-$51.** 1718 N University Ave. I-10, exit 101, just n. Ext corridors. **Pets:** Small. Service with restrictions, supervision.
SAVE X e

LAKE CHARLES

Best Suites of America SH
(337) 439-2444. **$89-$150.** 401 Lakeshore Dr. I-10, exit 29 (business district/tourist bureau) eastbound; exit 30B (Ryan St business district) westbound, just s to Pine, then just w. Int corridors. **Pets:** Accepted.
A$K S6 X 9 e 8 9 2

Travel Inn M
(337) 433-9461. **$39-$69, 3 day notice.** 1212 N Lake Shore Dr. I-10, exit 29 (business district/tourist bureau) eastbound; exit 30A westbound on west frontage road. Ext corridors. **Pets:** Accepted.
SAVE S6 X 11 2

MINDEN

Best Western Minden Inn SH
(318) 377-1001. **$50-$55.** 1411 Sibley Rd. I-20, exit 47, just n. Ext corridors. **Pets:** $7 daily fee/room. Service with restrictions, supervision.
SAVE S6 X 9 e 8 9 2

MONROE

Days Inn SH
(318) 345-2220. **$52-$66, 5 day notice.** 5650 Frontage Rd. I-20, exit 120, just s, 0.5 mi e on south service road. Ext corridors. **Pets:** Small. Designated rooms, service with restrictions, supervision.
SAVE S6 X 9 8 9 2

La Quinta Inn-Monroe SH
(318) 322-3900. **$65-$75.** 1035 Hwy 165 Bypass S. I-20, exit 118B, just ne on US 165 service road. Ext corridors. **Pets:** Accepted.
SAVE X 9 9 2

Residence Inn by Marriott SH
(318) 387-0210. **$104-$129.** 4960 Millhaven Rd. I-20, exit 120, just n of Pecanland Mall. Int corridors. **Pets:** Accepted.
A$K X 6M 9 e 8 9 2 X

MORGAN CITY

Holiday Inn-Morgan City SH
(985) 385-2200. **$90-$110.** 520 Roderick St. 1.5 mi s of jct US 90 and SR 70. Ext corridors. **Pets:** Medium, other species. $50 one-time fee/room. Service with restrictions, supervision.
SAVE S6 X 6M 9 e 8 9 11 2

NEW IBERIA

Best Western Inn & Suites SH
(337) 364-3030. **$62.** 2714 Hwy 14. 0.3 mi e of jct US 90. Ext/int corridors. **Pets:** Medium. $50 deposit/pet. Service with restrictions, supervision.
SAVE S6 X 8 9 11 2

NEW ORLEANS METROPOLITAN AREA

GRETNA

▼▼▼▼ **La Quinta Inn-New Orleans Westbank** SH
(504) 368-5600. **$80-$95.** 50 Terry Pkwy. S US 90 business route, exit 9A (Terry Pkwy); N US 90 (Westbank Expwy), exit 9 (Terry Pkwy/General DeGaulle). Ext corridors. **Pets:** Service with restrictions, crate.

KENNER

▲▲▲ ▼▼▼▼ **Comfort Suites New Orleans Airport Kenner** SH
(504) 466-6066. **$89-$179.** 2710 Idaho Ave. I-10, exit 223A (Williams Blvd), just s, just e on Veterans, then just s. Int corridors. **Pets:** Accepted.

▲▲▲ ▼▼▼▼ **Hilton New Orleans Airport** SH
(504) 469-5000. **$95-$320.** 901 Airline Dr. I-10, exit 223A (Williams Blvd), 2 mi s, then 0.8 mi w. Int corridors. **Pets:** Other species. $25 one-time fee/room. Service with restrictions, crate.

▼▼▼▼ **La Quinta Inn-New Orleans Airport** SH
(504) 466-1401. **$90-$100.** 2610 Williams Blvd. I-10, exit 223A (Williams Blvd), 0.3 mi s. Int corridors. **Pets:** Accepted.

LA PLACE

▲▲▲ ▼▼▼ **Best Western La Place Inn** SH
(985) 651-4000. **$79.** 4289 Main St. I-10, exit 209, just s. Ext corridors. **Pets:** Accepted.

METAIRIE

▲▲▲ ▼▼▼▼ **La Quinta Inn-New Orleans Causeway** M
(504) 835-8511. **$80-$95.** 3100 I-10 Service Rd. I-10, exit 228 (Causeway Blvd), just s. Ext corridors. **Pets:** Accepted.

▼▼▼▼ **La Quinta Inn-New Orleans Veterans** M
(504) 456-0003. **$80-$95.** 5900 Veterans Memorial Blvd. I-10, exit 225, just n. Ext/int corridors. **Pets:** Accepted.

NEW ORLEANS

▼▼▼▼ **1891 Castle Inn** BB
(504) 897-0540. **$100-$250, 14 day notice.** 1539 Fourth St. Between St. Charles and Prytania sts. Ext/int corridors. **Pets:** Accepted.

▲▲▲ ▼▼▼▼ **The 1896 O'Malley House Bed & Breakfast** BB
(504) 488-5896. **$99-$150, 30 day notice.** 120 S Pierce St. Just s of Canal St. Int corridors. **Pets:** Small, dogs only. $200 deposit/room, $10 daily fee/room. Service with restrictions.

▲▲▲ ▼▼▼▼ **Ambassador Hotel** SH
(504) 527-5271. **$49-$299.** 535 Tchoupitoulas St. Between Poydras and Lafayette; downtown. Int corridors. **Pets:** Large, other species. $25 daily fee/room. Designated rooms, service with restrictions.

▲▲▲ ▼▼▼ **Best Western Patio Downtown Motel** M
(504) 822-0200. **$69-$269.** 2820 Tulane Ave. I-10, exit 232, jct Carrollton and Tulane (US 61) aves, 1.3 mi e. Int corridors. **Pets:** Accepted.

▲▲▲ ▼▼▼▼ **Chateau Sonesta Hotel** LH
(504) 586-0800. **$99-$289, 3 day notice.** 800 Iberville St. Between Dauphine and Bourbon sts. Int corridors. **Pets:** $75 one-time fee/room. Service with restrictions, supervision.

▲▲▲ ▼▼▼▼ **Drury Inn & Suites-New Orleans** SH
(504) 529-7800. **$80-$120.** 820 Poydras St. Between Baronne and Carondelet sts. Int corridors. **Pets:** Large, other species. Service with restrictions, supervision.

▲▲▲ ▼▼▼▼ **Elysian Fields Inn** BB
(504) 948-9420. **$79-$125.** 930 Elysian Fields Ave. I-10, exit 237, 2 mi s. Int corridors. **Pets:** Small, other species. $25 one-time fee/pet. Crate.

▲▲▲ ▼▼▼ ▼▼▼ **The Fairmont New Orleans** LH
(504) 529-7111. **$90-$380.** 123 Baronne St. Between Canal and University sts; entrance on University St; downtown. Int corridors. **Pets:** Accepted.

▲▲▲ ▼▼▼▼ **French Quarter Courtyard Hotel** SH
(504) 522-7333. **$49-$299.** 1101 N Rampart St. Between Ursulines and Governor Nicholls sts. Ext/int corridors. **Pets:** $25 one-time fee/pet. Service with restrictions, crate.

▲▲▲ ▼▼▼▼ **Hilton New Orleans Riverside** LH
(504) 561-0500. **$229-$439, 3 day notice.** 2 Poydras St. At the Mississippi River. Int corridors. **Pets:** Accepted.

Hotel Monaco New Orleans SH ❖
(504) 561-0010. **$285-$335, 3 day notice.** 333 St. Charles Ave. Jct Perdido St. Int corridors. **Pets:** Other species. Crate.
SAVE ☒ 🖫 💻 ⏍

The Iberville Suites SH
(504) 523-2400. **$109-$295.** 910 Iberville St. Between Burgundy and Dauphine sts. Int corridors. **Pets:** Accepted.
SAVE ☒ 🖥 💻

La Quinta Inn & Suites-Downtown New Orleans SH
(504) 598-9977. **$103-$190.** 301 Camp St. Corner of Gravier and Camp sts; downtown. Int corridors. **Pets:** Accepted.
☒ 🖫M 🗇 🖟 🖥 💻 ⤢

La Quinta Inn-New Orleans Bullard SH
(504) 246-3003. **$60-$80.** 12001 I-10 Service Rd. I-10, exit 245 (Bullard Rd). Ext corridors. **Pets:** Accepted.
☒ 🖟 🖥 💻 ⤢

La Quinta Inn-New Orleans Crowder M
(504) 246-5800. **$60-$80.** 8400 I-10 Service Rd. I-10, exit 242 (Crowder Blvd). Ext corridors. **Pets:** Accepted.
SAVE ☒ 🖟 🖥 💻 ⤢

The Maison Orleans-Ritz Carlton SH
(504) 670-2900. **$346, 3 day notice.** 904 Iberville St. Between Burgundy and Dauphine sts. Int corridors. **Pets:** Accepted.
SAVE 🖫 ☒ 🖫M 🖟 ⏍

Motel 6- Six Flags Area M
(504) 240-2862. **$48-$56, 14 day notice.** 12330 I-10 Service Rd. I-10, exit 245 (Bullard Rd), just s, then 0.4 mi e. Int corridors. **Pets:** Small, other species. Service with restrictions, supervision.
🖫 ☒ 🖫M 🖟 ⤢

Omni Royal Crescent Hotel SH
(504) 527-0006. **$179-$349, 3 day notice.** 535 Gravier St. 0.3 mi w of Canal St; downtown. Int corridors. **Pets:** Accepted.
ASK 🖫 ☒ 🗇 🖟 🖥 💻 ☒

Omni Royal Orleans Hotel LH
(504) 529-5333. **$199-$349, 3 day notice.** 621 St. Louis St. At Royal and St. Louis sts. Int corridors. **Pets:** Small. $50 one-time fee/room. Service with restrictions, crate.
ASK 🖫 ☒ 🖟 🖥 💻 ⏍ ⤢

Radisson Hotel New Orleans LH
(504) 522-4500. **$89-$209, 3 day notice.** 1500 Canal St. Jct Lasalle and Canal sts; downtown. Int corridors. **Pets:** Accepted.
☒ 🗇 🖟 🖥 💻 ⏍ ⤢

Rathbone Inn BB
(504) 947-2100. **$59-$250.** 1227 Esplanade Ave. Just n of jct N Rampart and Esplanade Ave. Ext/int corridors. **Pets:** Accepted.
ASK 🖫 ☒ 🖥 💻

Residence Inn by Marriott SH
(504) 522-1300. **$169-$199, 3 day notice.** 345 St. Joseph's St. Jct Tchoupitoulas St. Int corridors. **Pets:** Accepted.
ASK ☒ 🖫M 🖥 💻 ⤢ ☒

Royal Sonesta Hotel New Orleans LH
(504) 586-0300. **$289-$409, 3 day notice.** 300 Bourbon St. Garage entrance on Conti or Bienville sts. Int corridors. **Pets:** Small. $50 one-time fee/room. Designated rooms, service with restrictions, supervision.
ASK 🖫 ☒ 🖫M 🗇 🖟 🖥 ⏍ ⤢

W French Quarter SH ❖
(504) 581-1200. **$134-$509.** 316 rue Chartres St. Between Conti and Bienville sts. Int corridors. **Pets:** Large, other species.
ASK 🖫 ☒ 🖟 💻 ⏍ ⤢

Windsor Court Hotel LH ❖
(504) 523-6000. **$210-$450.** 300 Gravier St. Between Magazine and Tchoucitoulas sts. Int corridors. **Pets:** Small. Service with restrictions, crate.
SAVE 🖫 ☒ 🗇 🖥 ⏍ ⤢ ☒

W New Orleans LH
(504) 525-9444. **$469-$1000, 3 day notice.** 333 Poydras St. Close to Riverfront area/Convention Center; jct Poydras and S Peters sts; downtown. Int corridors. **Pets:** Accepted.
SAVE ☒ 🖫M 🗇 🖟 💻 ⏍ ⤢

SLIDELL

La Quinta Inn-New Orleans Slidell SH
(985) 643-9770. **$61-$76.** 794 E I-10 Service Rd. I-10, exit 266 (Gause Blvd), just se. Ext corridors. **Pets:** Other species. Service with restrictions, supervision.
SAVE ☒ 🖟 🖥 💻 ⤢

❖ **END METROPOLITAN AREA** ❖

OPELOUSAS

Best Western of Opelousas SH
(337) 942-5540. **$60-$100.** 5791 I-49 S Service Rd. I-49, exit 18 (Creswell Ln), on west service road. Ext corridors. **Pets:** Medium, other species. $20 one-time fee/pet. Supervision.
SAVE 🖫 ☒ 🖟 🖥 ⤢

Days Inn & Suites SH
(337) 407-0004. **$75-$81.** 5761 I-49 S Service Rd. I-49, exit 18 (Creswell Ln). Ext corridors. **Pets:** Small. $20 one-time fee/pet. Service with restrictions, crate.
SAVE 🖫 ☒ 🖟 🖥 💻 ⤢

PORT ALLEN

🆔 🔷🔷 **Best Western Magnolia Manor** 🆂🅷
(225) 344-3638. **$65-$70.** 234 Lobdell Hwy. I-10, exit 151, just n. Int corridors. **Pets:** Accepted.
[SAVE] 🔊 ✕ 📶 💻 🏊

RAYVILLE

🆔 🔷🔷 **Ramada Limited** 🆂🅷
(318) 728-5985. **$64-$69.** 116 Cottonland Dr. I-20, exit 138, just s. Ext corridors. **Pets:** Accepted.
[SAVE] 🔊 ✕ 📶 💻 🏊

RUSTON

🔷🔷 **Econo Lodge** 🆂🅷 ❀
(318) 255-0354. **$44-$59.** 1301 Goodwin Rd. I-20, exit 85, just n on US 167, then just e on N Service Rd. Ext corridors. **Pets:** Other species. Service with restrictions, supervision.
[ASK] 🔊 ✕ 📶 📶 💻 📺 🍴 🏊 ⊠

🔷🔷 **Ramada Inn** 🆂🅷 ❀
(318) 255-5901. **$62, 3 day notice.** 401 N Service Rd. I-20, exit 85 on Frontage Rd; e of US 167. Ext corridors. **Pets:** Other species. Service with restrictions, supervision.
[ASK] 🔊 ✕ 📶 💻 🍴 🏊

ST. FRANCISVILLE

🔷🔷🔷 **Green Springs Inn & Cottages** 🅱🅱
(225) 635-4232. **$120-$180.** 7463 Tunica Trace. US 61, 4 mi n of jct US 61 and SR 10 to SR 66, 0.9 mi w. Ext/int corridors. **Pets:** Medium. Designated rooms, service with restrictions, crate.
✕ 📶 💻 📼

🔷🔷 **Lake Rosemound Inn Bed & Breakfast** 🅱🅱
(225) 635-3176. **$75-$125.** 10473 Lindsey Ln. US 61 n on SR 61, 3 mi w using Rosemound Loop, Sligo Rd, Lake Rosemound Rd and Lindsey Ln, follow signs. Ext/int corridors. **Pets:** Service with restrictions, supervision.
✕ ⊠

SCOTT

🔷🔷 **Howard Johnson** 🆂🅷
(337) 593-0849. **$70.** 103 Harley Davidson Dr. I-10, exit 97. Int corridors. **Pets:** Small. $25 deposit/pet. Service with restrictions, supervision.
[ASK] ✕ 📶 💻 🏊

SHREVEPORT

🔷🔷🔷 **Holiday Inn Downtown** 🅻🅷
(318) 222-7717. **$89-$129.** 102 Lake St. I-20, exit 19A (Spring St), just n. Int corridors. **Pets:** $25 deposit/room. Designated rooms, service with restrictions, supervision.
[ASK] 🔊 ✕ 📶 📶 📶 💻 🍴 🏊

🔷🔷 **Howard Johnson Express** 🆂🅷
(318) 636-0000. **$59-$89.** 2610 Claiborne Ave. I-20, exit 16A (Hearne Ave), just se. Ext corridors. **Pets:** Medium. $10 one-time fee/room. Service with restrictions, supervision.
[ASK] 🔊 ✕ 📶 💻 🏊

🔷🔷 **Jameson Inn** 🆂🅷
(318) 671-0731. **$76-$81.** 6715 Rasberry Ln. I-20, exit 10 (Pines Rd), 0.6 mi e on frontage road. Int corridors. **Pets:** Small. Service with restrictions, crate.
✕ 📶 📶 💻 🏊

🔷🔷🔷 **La Quinta Inn & Suites-Shreveport** 🆂🅷
(318) 671-1100. **$76-$106.** 6700 Financial Cir. I-20, exit 10. Int corridors. **Pets:** Medium. Service with restrictions, supervision.
✕ 📶 📶 📶 💻 🏊

🆔 🔷🔷 **Red Roof Inn** 🅼
(318) 938-5342. **$39-$57.** 7296 Greenwood Rd. I-20, exit 8, just nw. Ext corridors. **Pets:** Medium, other species. Service with restrictions, crate.
[SAVE] ✕ 📶

SULPHUR

🔷🔷🔷 **La Quinta Inn-Sulphur** 🅼
(337) 527-8303. **$66-$81.** 2600 S Ruth St. I-10, exit 20 (SR 27). Ext corridors. **Pets:** Other species. Supervision.
✕ 📶 📶 💻 🏊

TALLULAH

🆔 🔷🔷 **Days Inn** 🆂🅷
(318) 574-5200. **$64-$76.** 1603 Hwy 65. I-20, exit 171, just n. Ext corridors. **Pets:** Accepted.
[SAVE] 🔊 ✕ 📶 💻 🏊

WEST MONROE

🆔 🔷🔷🔷 **Quality Inn & Suites-West Monroe** 🆂🅷
(318) 387-2711. **$60-$85.** 503 Constitution Dr. I-20, exit 114 (Thomas Rd), just s to Constitution Dr, then 0.6 mi w. Int corridors. **Pets:** Small. $25 one-time fee/room. Service with restrictions, supervision.
[SAVE] 🔊 ✕ 📶 📶 📶 📶 💻 🏊

🆔 🔷🔷🔷 **Red Roof Inn** 🅼
(318) 388-2420. **$39-$54.** 102 Constitution Dr. I-20, exit 114 (Thomas Rd), just s. Ext corridors. **Pets:** Accepted.
[SAVE] ✕ 📶

MAINE

AUBURN

▼▼ A Fireside Inn & Suites 🆂🅷
(207) 777-1777. **$80-$120, 3 day notice.** 1777 Washington St. I-95 (Maine Tpke), exit 75, 5 mi s on US 202, SR 4 and 100. Ext/int corridors. **Pets:** Large. Service with restrictions.
🅰🆂🅺 🆂🔗 ⊠ 🈂 💻 🍴 🌊

AUGUSTA

🔴🔴🔴 ▼▼▼ Best Western Senator Inn & Spa 🆂🅷 🐾
(207) 622-5804. **$99-$259.** 284 Western Ave. I-95, exit 109 (Augusta-Winthrop) northbound; exit 109A southbound on US 202, SR 11 and 100. Ext/int corridors. **Pets:** Medium, other species. $50 deposit/room, $9 daily fee/pet. Designated rooms, service with restrictions, supervision.
🆂🅰🆅🅴 🆂🔗 ⊠ 🈂 💻 🍴 🌊 ⊠

▼▼▼ Comfort Inn 🆂🅷
(207) 623-1000. **$94-$189, 3 day notice.** 281 Civic Center Dr. I-95, exit 112B northbound; exit 112 southbound. Int corridors. **Pets:** Service with restrictions, supervision.
🅰🆂🅺 ⊠ 🔖 🈂 💻 🍴 🌊

🔴🔴🔴 ▼▼▼ Econo Lodge Inn & Suites 🆂🅷
(207) 622-6371. **$79-$119.** 390 Western Ave. I-95, exit 109 (Augusta-Winthrop) northbound; exit 109B southbound on US 202, SR 11 and 100. Ext corridors. **Pets:** Service with restrictions, crate.
🆂🅰🆅🅴 🆂🔗 ⊠ 🈂 💻 🍴 🌊

▼▼▼ Holiday Inn 🆂🅷
(207) 622-4751. **$94-$169, 3 day notice.** 110 Community Dr. I-95, exit 112A northbound; exit 112 southbound, just s on SR 8, 11 and 27. Int corridors. **Pets:** Large. Service with restrictions, supervision.
🅰🆂🅺 ⊠ 🈶 🔖 🐾 🈂 💻 🍴 🌊

BANGOR

▼▼ Best Inn 🆂🅷 🐾
(207) 942-1234. **$75-$110.** 570 Main St. Jct I-395. Int corridors. **Pets:** Service with restrictions, supervision.
🅰🆂🅺 🆂🔗 ⊠ 🈂 🍴

▼▼▼ Best Western White House 🆂🅷
(207) 862-3737. **$60-$123.** 155 Littlefield Ave. I-95, exit 180 (Coldbrook Rd), 5.5 mi s of downtown. Ext/int corridors. **Pets:** Other species. $100 deposit/room. Service with restrictions, supervision.
🅰🆂🅺 🆂🔗 ⊠ 🈂 💻 🌊

▼▼ Comfort Inn 🆂🅷
(207) 942-7899. **$69-$109.** 750 Hogan Rd. I-95, exit 187 (Hogan Rd), 0.5 mi w. Int corridors. **Pets:** Other species. $6 daily fee/pet. Service with restrictions, supervision.
🅰🆂🅺 🆂🔗 ⊠ 💻 🌊

▼▼ Days Inn 🆂🅷 🐾
(207) 942-8272. **$59-$99.** 250 Odlin Rd. I-95, exit 182B, 0.3 mi e on US 2 and SR 100. Int corridors. **Pets:** Other species. $6 one-time fee/room. Service with restrictions, supervision.
🅰🆂🅺 🆂🔗 ⊠ 🈶 🈂 💻 🌊

▼▼ Econo Lodge 🅼 🐾
(207) 945-0111. **$50-$99.** 327 Odlin Rd. I-95, exit 182B, just e on US 2 and SR 100. Int corridors. **Pets:** Other species. $6 one-time fee/room. Service with restrictions, supervision.
🅰🆂🅺 🆂🔗 ⊠ 🈶 🈂 💻

▼▼▼ Four Points by Sheraton Bangor 🆂🅷
(207) 947-6721. **$103-$159.** 308 Godfrey Blvd. At Bangor International Airport. Int corridors. **Pets:** Accepted.
🅰🆂🅺 🆂🔗 ⊠ 🈶 🈂 💻 🍴 🌊

◆▼▼ Holiday Inn-Bangor 🆂🅷
(207) 947-0101. **$121-$131.** 404 Odlin Rd. I-95, exit 182B at jct Odlin Rd and I-395. Int corridors. **Pets:** Accepted.
🅰🆂🅺 ⊠ 🈶 🈂 💻 🌊

◆▼▼ Holiday Inn Bangor-Civic Center 🆂🅷
(207) 947-8651. **$63-$119.** 500 Main St. Center. Int corridors. **Pets:** Other species. Designated rooms, service with restrictions, supervision.
🅰🆂🅺 🆂🔗 ⊠ 🈂 💻 🍴 🌊

🔴🔴🔴 ▼▼ Howard Johnson Inn 🆂🅷
(207) 947-5251. **$69-$99, 3 day notice.** 336 Odlin Rd. I-95, exit 182B at jct Odlin Rd and I-395. Int corridors. **Pets:** Accepted.
🆂🅰🆅🅴 🆂🔗 ⊠ 🈂 💻 🍴 🌊

🔴🔴🔴 ▼ Main Street Inn 🅼
(207) 942-5282. **$49-$59.** 480 Main St. I-95, exit 182A to jct I-395, exit 3B. Ext/int corridors. **Pets:** Designated rooms, service with restrictions, supervision.
🆂🅰🆅🅴 🆂🔗 ⊠

▼▼ Ramada Inn 🆂🅷
(207) 947-6961. **$79-$139.** 357 Odlin Rd. I-95, exit 182B at jct Odlin Rd and I-395. Int corridors. **Pets:** Accepted.
🅰🆂🅺 🆂🔗 ⊠ 🈂 💻 🍴 🌊

▼▼▼ Riverside Inn 🆂🅷
(207) 973-4100. **$79-$129.** 495 State St. Adjacent to Eastern Maine Medical Center. Int corridors. **Pets:** Accepted.
❌ 🅱 🖥

▼▼ Travelodge Ⓜ
(207) 942-6301. **$55-$105.** 482 Odlin Rd. I-95, exit 182B, just left. Ext corridors. **Pets:** Small. $10 daily fee/pet. Designated rooms, service with restrictions, supervision.
🅰🆂🅺 🆂🔟 ❌ 🅱 🖥

BAR HARBOR

🛆🅰🛆 ▼▼▼ Anchorage Motel Ⓜ
(207) 288-3959. **$54-$129, 3 day notice.** 51 Mt Desert St. In town on SR 3. Ext corridors. **Pets:** $15 daily fee/pet. Service with restrictions, supervision.
🆂🅰🆅🅴 ❌ 🅱

▼▼ A Wonder View Inn & Suites 🆂🅷
(207) 288-3358. **$49-$230, 3 day notice.** 50 Eden St. 0.5 mi w on SR 3. Ext corridors. **Pets:** $10 daily fee/pet. Service with restrictions, supervision.
❌ 🅱 🖥 🍴 🏊

🛆🅰🛆 ▼▼▼▼ Balance Rock Inn 1903 🅱🅱 ❀
(207) 288-2610. **$115-$625, 14 day notice.** 21 Albert Meadow. S on Main St, just e; center. Ext/int corridors. **Pets:** $30 daily fee/pet. Service with restrictions, supervision.
🆂🅰🆅🅴 ❌ 🅱 🏊

🛆🅰🛆 ▼▼▼▼ Best Western Inn 🆂🅷
(207) 288-5823. **$74-$140.** 452 State Hwy 3. 4.8 mi w. Ext corridors. **Pets:** Small, other species. Service with restrictions, supervision.
🆂🅰🆅🅴 🆂🔟 ❌ 🅱 🖥 🏊

▼▼ Days Inn Ⓜ
(207) 288-3321. **$89-$209.** 120 Eden St. 1 mi w on SR 3. Ext corridors. **Pets:** Accepted.
🅰🆂🅺 🆂🔟 ❌ 🅱

▼ Hutchins Mountain View Cottages 🅲🅰 ❀
(207) 288-4833. **$42-$96, 14 day notice.** 286 State Rt 3. 4 mi w. Ext corridors. **Pets:** Other species. Service with restrictions, supervision.
🅱 🖥 🏊 🅺 🅩

🛆🅰🛆 ▼▼▼▼ The Ledgelawn Inn 🅱🅱 ❀
(207) 288-4596. **$70-$325, 14 day notice.** 66 Mt Desert St. Center. Ext/int corridors. **Pets:** $30 daily fee/pet. Service with restrictions, supervision.
🆂🅰🆅🅴 ❌ 🏊

▼▼▼▼ Primrose Inn Bed and Breakfast 🅱🅱 ❀
(207) 288-4031. **$85-$215, 14 day notice.** 73 Mt Desert St. Center. Int corridors. **Pets:** Dogs only. $75 one-time fee/room. Designated rooms, supervision.
❌ 🅱 🖥

BATH

▼▼▼ Holiday Inn Bath/Brunswick 🆂🅷
(207) 443-9741. **$89-$179.** 139 Richardson St. 0.3 mi s on US 1. Int corridors. **Pets:** Medium. Designated rooms, service with restrictions, supervision.
🅰🆂🅺 🆂🔟 ❌ �figM 🅩 🅱 🖥 🍴 🏊 🅧

BELFAST

🛆🅰🛆 ▼▼▼▼ Belfast Bay Meadows Inn 🅱🅱 ❀
(207) 338-5715. **$75-$165, 14 day notice.** 192 Northport Ave (US 1). US 1, 2 mi s from jct SR 3. Ext/int corridors. **Pets:** $15 daily fee/pet. Designated rooms, service with restrictions, supervision.
🆂🅰🆅🅴 🆂🔟 ❌ 🅱 🍴

🛆🅰🛆 ▼▼▼ Belfast Harbor Inn 🆂🅷
(207) 338-2740. **$49-$129.** 91 Searsport Ave (Rt 1). On US 1, 1.2 mi n from jct SR 3. Ext/int corridors. **Pets:** Dogs only. $10 daily fee/pet. Service with restrictions, supervision.
🆂🅰🆅🅴 🆂🔟 ❌ 🏊

▼▼▼▼ Comfort Inn Ocean's Edge 🆂🅷
(207) 338-2090. **$79-$179.** 159 Searsport Ave. On US 1, 2 mi n from jct SR 3. Int corridors. **Pets:** Other species. $10 daily fee/room. Designated rooms, service with restrictions, supervision.
🅰🆂🅺 🆂🔟 ❌ �figM 🅩 🅧 🅱 🖥 🍴 🏊 🅧

🛆🅰🛆 ▼▼▼ Gull Motel Ⓜ
(207) 338-4030. **$39-$89, 3 day notice.** US Route 1. On US 1, 3 mi n from jct SR 3. Ext corridors. **Pets:** Large. $10 daily fee/pet. Service with restrictions.
🆂🅰🆅🅴 ❌ 🅱

🛆🅰🛆 ▼▼▼ Seascape Motel & Cottages Ⓜ
(207) 338-2130. **$49-$123, 3 day notice.** 202 Searsport Ave. On US 1, 3 mi n from jct SR 3. Ext corridors. **Pets:** Small. $10 one-time fee/pet. Designated rooms, service with restrictions, supervision.
🆂🅰🆅🅴 🆂🔟 ❌ 🅱 🏊

BETHEL

▼▼▼ Briar Lea Inn & Restaurant 🅲🅸
(207) 824-4717. **$69-$119.** 150 Mayville Rd (US 2). 1 mi n of jct US 2, SR 5 and 26. Int corridors. **Pets:** Accepted.
🅰🆂🅺 🆂🔟 ❌ 🍴

▼▼ The Inn At the Rostay Ⓜ
(207) 824-3111. **$48-$120, 14 day notice.** 186 Mayville Rd (US 2). On US 2, 2 mi e. Ext corridors. **Pets:** Large, other species. $10 one-time fee/room. Designated rooms, service with restrictions, supervision.
🅰🆂🅺 🆂🔟 ❌ 🅱 🍴 🏊

🛆🅰🛆 ▼▼▼▼ L'Auberge Country Inn & Bistro 🅲🅸
(207) 824-2774. **$99-$189, 14 day notice.** 22 Mill Hill Rd. Center of village. Int corridors. **Pets:** Accepted.
🆂🅰🆅🅴 ❌ 🍴 🅺 🅦 🅩

BOOTHBAY

▼▼ Hillside Acres Cabins & Motel 🆂🅷
(207) 633-3411. **$50-$85.** 301 Adams Pond Rd. US 1, 9 mi s on SR 27, then just w. Ext/int corridors. **Pets:** Designated rooms, service with restrictions, supervision.
❌ 🅱 🖥 🏊 🅺 🅩

▼▼▼ Kenniston Hill Inn 🅱🅱
(207) 633-2159. **$75-$135, 14 day notice.** 988 Wiscasset Rd. US 1 to SR 27, 10 mi s. Ext/int corridors. **Pets:** Medium. Designated rooms, service with restrictions, supervision.
🆂🔟 ❌ 🅦 🅩

White Anchor Inn M
(207) 633-3788. **$45-$79.** 609 Wiscasset Rd. US 1 to SR 27, 7.5 mi s. Ext/int corridors. **Pets:** $10 one-time fee/pet. Designated rooms, service with restrictions, supervision.
SAVE ⊠ 🖥

BOOTHBAY HARBOR

The Pines Motel M
(207) 633-4555. **$50-$95.** 30 Sunset Rd. 1 mi e of SR 27 via Atlantic Ave, on the east side of Boothbay Harbor. Ext corridors. **Pets:** Accepted.
SAVE 🐾 ⊠ 🖥 🏊

Welch House Inn BB
(207) 633-3431. **$75-$185, 14 day notice.** 56 McKown St. Center. Ext/int corridors. **Pets:** Accepted.
SAVE ⊠

BREWER

Brewer Motor Inn SH
(207) 989-4476. **$49-$59.** 359 Wilson St. I-95, exit 182A to I-395, exit 4, n on SR 15 to US 1A, then 0.7 mi e. Ext/int corridors. **Pets:** Designated rooms, service with restrictions, supervision.
SAVE 🐾 ⊠ 🍴

BRIDGTON

Pleasant Mountain Inn M 🌲
(207) 647-4505. **$55-$130.** N High St. On US 302, 3 mi w of center. Ext corridors. **Pets:** $10 daily fee/pet. Service with restrictions, crate.
SAVE 🐾 ⊠ 🖥 🖥 🍴

BRUNSWICK

Viking Motor Inn M 🌲
(207) 729-6661. **$59-$129.** 287 Bath Rd. US 1, exit Cooks Corner, left on Bath Rd, then 1 mi w. Ext/int corridors. **Pets:** Small. $10 daily fee/pet. Service with restrictions, supervision.
SAVE ⊠ 🖥

BRYANT POND

Mollyockett Motel & Swim Spa M
(207) 674-2345. **$70-$95.** 1132 S Main St. 1.3 mi n on SR 26, from jct SR 219. Ext/int corridors. **Pets:** Accepted.
ASK ⊠ 🖥 🖥 🏊 🐾

CALAIS

Calais Motor Inn SH
(207) 454-7111. **$54-$104.** 633 Main St. 0.5 mi s on US 1. Ext/int corridors. **Pets:** Accepted.
SAVE 🐾 ⊠ 🖥 🍴 🏊

International Motel M
(207) 454-7515. **$50-$80.** 626 Main St. 0.5 mi s on US 1. Ext corridors. **Pets:** Accepted.
SAVE 🐾 ⊠ 🖥 🖥

CAMDEN

Blue Harbor House, A Village Inn CI
(207) 236-3196. **$125-$205, 14 day notice.** 67 Elm St. On US 1; center. Ext/int corridors. **Pets:** $25 one-time fee/room. Designated rooms, service with restrictions, supervision.
⊠ 🍴

Camden Harbour Inn BB
(207) 236-4200. **Call for rates.** 83 Bayview St. Off US 1, 0.3 mi e; center. Int corridors. **Pets:** Accepted.
⊠ 🐕

Lord Camden Inn BB
(207) 236-4325. **$90-$220, 7 day notice.** 24 Main St. Center. Int corridors. **Pets:** Large, dogs only. $20 daily fee/pet. Designated rooms, service with restrictions, supervision.
SAVE 🐾 ⊠ 🖥 🖥

CAPE ELIZABETH

Inn By The Sea SH 🌲
(207) 799-3134. **$179-$639, 14 day notice.** 40 Bowery Beach Rd (SR 77). On SR 77, 7 mi s. Ext/int corridors. **Pets:** Other species. Designated rooms, supervision.
SAVE 🐾 ⊠ 🖥 🖥 🖥 🍴 🏊 🐾 🐕

CARIBOU

Caribou Inn & Convention Center SH 🌲
(207) 498-3733. **$68-$128, 14 day notice.** 19 Main St. 3 mi s on US 1. Int corridors. **Pets:** Other species.
SAVE 🐾 ⊠ 🖥 🖥 🍴 🏊 🐾

CASTINE

Pentagoet Inn CI
(207) 326-8616. **$95-$205, 14 day notice.** 26 Main St. Center. Int corridors. **Pets:** Accepted.
⊠ 🍴 🐕 🖥 🖥

CORNISH

Midway Motel M
(207) 625-8835. **$49-$79, 7 day notice.** 712 S Hiram Rd. 0.7 mi w on SR 25, just past jct SR 25. Ext/int corridors. **Pets:** Small, dogs only. $5 daily fee/pet. Service with restrictions, supervision.
⊠ 🖥

EAGLE LAKE

Overlook Motel & Lakeside Cabins M
(207) 444-4535. **$46-$150.** 3232 Aroostook Rd. On SR 11; center. Ext/int corridors. **Pets:** Other species. $3 daily fee/pet. Service with restrictions, supervision.
🖥 🖥 🐾

EAST BOOTHBAY

Smuggler's Cove Motor Inn SH
(207) 633-2800. **$69-$229.** 727 Ocean Point Rd. Jct SR 27, 4.5 mi e on SR 96. Ext corridors. **Pets:** Accepted.
SAVE ⊠ 🖥 🖥 🍴 🏊 🐾

EDGECOMB

Sheepscot River Inn SH 🌲
(207) 882-6343. **$79-$149.** 306 Eddy Rd. 1 mi w on US 1; on east side of Davies Bridge, 1 mi e of Wiscasset. Ext/int corridors. **Pets:** Other species. $10 daily fee/room. Designated rooms, service with restrictions, crate.
ASK 🐾 ⊠ 🖥 🖥 🍴 🐾

ELLSWORTH

◆◆ **Colonial Inn** [SH] 🐾
(207) 667-5548. **$58-$159.** 321 High St. 1.3 mi e on SR 3. Ext/int corridors. **Pets:** Medium, dogs only. Service with restrictions, supervision.
[A$K] [S D] ⊠ ♿ ▣ ☕ 🍴 🏊

◆◆ **Comfort Inn** [SH]
(207) 667-1345. **$59-$139.** 130 High St. Center. Int corridors. **Pets:** Accepted.
[A$K] [S D] ⊠ [♿M] ♿ ▣ ☕

[AAA] ◆◆ **Jasper's Motel** [SH]
(207) 667-5318. **$49-$99, 3 day notice.** 200 High St. 1 mi e on US 1 and SR 3. Ext corridors. **Pets:** Accepted.
[SAVE] [S D] ⊠ ▣ 🍴

[AAA] ◆◆ **Twilite Motel** [M]
(207) 667-8165. **$56-$94, 3 day notice.** 147 Bucksport Rd. Jct US 1A, 1.5 mi w on US 1/SR 3. Ext corridors. **Pets:** Medium, dogs only. $10 daily fee/pet. Designated rooms, service with restrictions, supervision.
[SAVE] ⊠ ▣ ☕

◆ **The White Birches** [SH]
(207) 667-3621. **$49-$99.** Rt 1. US 1, 1.5 mi n of jct SR 3. Ext corridors. **Pets:** Other species. Service with restrictions, crate.
[A$K] ⊠ ▣ 🍴

FARMINGTON

[AAA] ◆ **Mount Blue Motel** [M]
(207) 778-6004. **$48-$60.** 454 Wilton Rd. 2 mi w on US 2 and SR 4. Ext corridors. **Pets:** Accepted.
[SAVE] [S D] ⊠ ▣

FREEPORT

[AAA] ◆◆◆ **Best Western Freeport Inn** [SH]
(207) 865-3106. **$75-$150.** 31 US 1 S. I-295, exit 17, 1 mi n. Ext/int corridors. **Pets:** Other species. Designated rooms, service with restrictions.
[SAVE] [S D] ⊠ ▣ ☕ 🍴 🏊

◆◆ **Coastline Inn** [M]
(207) 865-3777. **$50-$150.** 537 US Rt 1. I-295, exit 20, 0.3 mi s. Ext corridors. **Pets:** Designated rooms, service with restrictions, supervision.
[A$K] [S D] ⊠ ▣ ☕

[AAA] ◆◆◆◆ **Harraseeket Inn** [CI] 🐾
(207) 865-9377. **$110-$275, 3 day notice.** 162 Main St. I-295, exit 22, 0.5 mi e. Int corridors. **Pets:** Dogs only. $25 daily fee/pet. Designated rooms, service with restrictions, supervision.
[SAVE] ⊠ [♿M] 👂 ♿ ▣ ☕ 🍴 🏊

GRAND LAKE STREAM

◆◆ **Leen's Lodge** [CA]
(207) 796-2929. **$100, 21 day notice.** 368 Bonney Brook Rd. 10 mi w off US 1, 2 mi n on gravel entry road. Ext corridors. **Pets:** Dogs only. Service with restrictions, crate.
[A$K] [S D] ▣ 🍴 ⊗ [no AC] [no TV] [no ☎]

◆◆ **Weatherby's-The Fisherman's Resort** [CA]
(207) 796-5558. **$108-$140, 21 day notice.** 1 Church St. 10 mi w off US 1. Ext corridors. **Pets:** Other species. $10 daily fee/pet. Crate.
[A$K] 🍴 ⊗ [no AC] [no TV] [no ☎]

GREENVILLE

◆◆ **Chalet Moosehead Lakefront Motel** [M]
(207) 695-2950. **$62-$125.** N Birch St. 1.5 mi w on SR 15. Ext corridors. **Pets:** Dogs only. $10 daily fee/pet. Designated rooms, service with restrictions, supervision.
⊠ ▣ ☕ ⊗

[AAA] ◆◆ **Kineo View Motor Lodge** [M]
(207) 695-4470. **$59-$99.** Overlook Dr. 2.5 mi s on SR 15. Ext corridors. **Pets:** $10 daily fee/room. Designated rooms, service with restrictions, supervision.
[SAVE] ⊠ ▣ ☕

HOULTON

[AAA] ◆ **Scottish Inns** [M]
(207) 532-2236. **$50-$75.** 239 Bangor St. I-95, exit 302, 1 mi s on US 1, then 1 mi sw on US 2A. Ext/int corridors. **Pets:** Accepted.
[SAVE] [S D] ⊠ ▣

KENNEBUNK

[AAA] ◆◆ **The Lodge at Kennebunk** [M]
(207) 985-9010. **$55-$89, 3 day notice.** 95 Alewive Rd. I-95 (Maine Tpke), exit 25 (Kennebunk), just n on SR 35. Ext corridors. **Pets:** $15 one-time fee/room. Designated rooms, service with restrictions.
[SAVE] [S D] ⊠ ▣ 🏊 ⊗

KENNEBUNKPORT

[AAA] ◆◆◆ **The Captain Jefferds Inn** [BB] 🐾
(207) 967-2311. **$110-$340, 14 day notice.** 5 Pearl St. Dock Square; 0.3 mi e on Maine St, just s; corner of Pearl and Pleasant sts. Ext/int corridors. **Pets:** Dogs only. $30 daily fee/room. Supervision.
[SAVE] ⊠ ▣

[AAA] ◆◆◆ **The Colony Hotel** [SH] 🐾
(207) 967-3331. **$135-$435, 3 day notice.** 140 Ocean Ave. Dock Square; 1 mi s. Int corridors. **Pets:** Other species. $25 daily fee/pet.
[SAVE] ⊠ 👂 ▣ 🍴 ⊗ [no AC]

[AAA] ◆◆◆ **Lodge At Turbat's Creek** [M]
(207) 967-8700. **$79-$169, 14 day notice.** 7 Turbat's Creek Rd. Dock Square; 0.5 mi e on Maine St, 0.6 mi ne on Wildes, then just se. Ext corridors. **Pets:** Accepted.
[SAVE] [S D] ⊠ [♿M] ▣ 🏊

[AAA] ◆◆◆◆ **The Yachtsman Lodge & Marina** [M]
(207) 967-2511. **$159-$314, 30 day notice.** 57 Ocean Ave. Dock Square; 0.3 mi e. Ext corridors. **Pets:** Medium, dogs only. $19 daily fee/pet. Designated rooms, supervision.
[SAVE] ⊠ ▣ ☕ ⊗

KITTERY

▼▼ **Enchanted Nights Bed & Breakfast** 🅱🅱 ✿
(207) 439-1489. **$47-$328, 15 day notice.** 29 Wentworth St.
I-95, exit 2 (Kittery), 1 mi s on SR 236, just w on SR 103.
Ext/int corridors. **Pets:** Other species. $10 one-time fee/
room. Supervision.
⊠ 🖬 🖵

LEWISTON

◈◈◈ ▼▼ **Chalet Motel** 🆂🅷
(207) 784-0600. **$60-$65.** 1243 Lisbon St. I-95 (Maine Tpke),
exit 80. Ext/int corridors. **Pets:** Accepted.
🆂🅰🆅🅴 🆂🔟 ⊠ 🖬 🍴 🔁 ⊠

▼▼ **Motel 6–1223** 🆂🅷
(207) 782-6558. **$45-$61.** 516 Pleasant St. I-95 (Maine
Tpke), exit 80, follow sign for Lisbon, just w. Ext/int corridors. **Pets:** Accepted.
🆂🔟 ⊠ 🔊 🔟

LINCOLNVILLE

▼ **Abbingtons Seaview Motel & Cottages** 🅼
(207) 236-3471. **$60-$130, 3 day notice.** Atlantic Hwy. US 1,
4 mi n of downtown Camden; 1.5 mi s of Lincolnville
Beach. Ext corridors. **Pets:** Other species. $10 daily fee/
pet. Designated rooms, supervision.
🅰🆂🅺 ⊠ 🖬 🖵 🔁

▼▼ **Pine Grove Cottages** 🅲🅰
(207) 236-2929. **$50-$150, 15 day notice.** 2076 Atlantic
Hwy. 2 mi s on US 1. Ext corridors. **Pets:** Other species. $7
daily fee/pet. Service with restrictions, supervision.
⊠ 🖬 🖵

LUBEC

◈◈◈ ▼▼ **The Eastland Motel** 🅼
(207) 733-5501. **$49-$69.** 395 County Rd. Jct US 1 and SR
189, 8.4 mi e on SR 189. Ext/int corridors. **Pets:** Medium,
dogs only. $10 daily fee/pet. Designated rooms, service with
restrictions, supervision.
🆂🅰🆅🅴 ⊠ 🖬

MACHIAS

◈◈◈ ▼▼ **The Bluebird Motel** 🅼
(207) 255-3332. **$52-$64, 3 day notice.** Dublin St. On US 1,
1 mi s. Ext corridors. **Pets:** Accepted.
🆂🅰🆅🅴 🆂🔟 ⊠ 🗺🅼 🖬

◈◈◈ ▼▼ **Machias Motor Inn** 🅼
(207) 255-4861. **$64-$80.** 26 E Main St. 0.5 mi e on US 1.
Ext corridors. **Pets:** Dogs only. $5 daily fee/pet. Service with
restrictions, supervision.
🆂🅰🆅🅴 ⊠ 🖬 🖵

MEDWAY

▼ **Katahdin Shadows Motel** 🅼
(207) 746-5162. **$49.** I-95, exit 244, 1.5 mi w on SR 157. Ext
corridors. **Pets:** Large. Supervision.
⊠ 🖬 🔁 ⊠

MILFORD

▼▼ **Milford Motel On The River** 🅼
(207) 827-3200. **$54-$89.** 154 Main Rd. 0.5 mi n on US 2.
Ext/int corridors. **Pets:** Large. Service with restrictions,
supervision.
⊠ 🖬

MILLINOCKET

▼▼ **Best Western Heritage Motor Inn** 🆂🅷
(207) 723-9777. **$69-$119.** 935 Central St. 0.8 mi e on SR
11 and 157. Int corridors. **Pets:** Service with restrictions,
supervision.
🅰🆂🅺 🆂🔟 ⊠ 🖵 🍴

◈◈◈ ▼▼ **The Katahdin Inn** 🆂🅷
(207) 723-4555. **$69-$99, 3 day notice.** 740 Central St. On
SR 157; center. Int corridors. **Pets:** Other species. Designated rooms, no service, supervision.
🆂🅰🆅🅴 ⊠ 🖬 🔁 ⊠

OGUNQUIT

▼▼ **Studio East Motor Inn** 🅼
(207) 646-7297. **$59-$159, 10 day notice.** 267 Main St. On
US 1; center. Ext corridors. **Pets:** Medium. $10 daily fee/
pet. Designated rooms, supervision.
⊠ 🖬

OLD ORCHARD BEACH

▼▼ **Beau Rivage Motel** 🅼
(207) 934-4668. **$49-$199, 14 day notice.** 54 E Grand Ave.
0.3 mi e of Old Orchard St. Ext corridors. **Pets:** Small, dogs
only. $25 deposit/pet, $10 daily fee/pet. Designated rooms,
service with restrictions, supervision.
⊠ 🗺 🖬 🔁

◈◈◈ ▼▼ **Old Colonial Motel** 🅼 ✿
(207) 934-9862. **$70-$220, 14 day notice.** 61 W Grand Ave.
On SR 9 (W Grand Ave), 0.5 mi w. Ext corridors.
Pets: Large, other species. $5 daily fee/pet. Designated
rooms, service with restrictions, crate.
🆂🅰🆅🅴 🆂🔟 ⊠ 🖬 🔁 ⊠

◈◈◈ ▼▼ **Sea View Motel** 🆂🅷
(207) 934-4180. **$50-$230, 3 day notice.** 65 W Grand Ave.
0.5 mi w on SR 9 (W Grand Ave). Ext corridors.
Pets: Medium. $100 deposit/pet, $10 daily fee/pet. Supervision.
🆂🅰🆅🅴 🆂🔟 ⊠ 🖬 🔁

▼▼ **Waves Oceanfront Resort** 🆂🅷
(207) 934-4949. **$70-$210, 3 day notice.** 87 W Grand Ave.
0.5 mi w on SR 9 (W Grand Ave). Ext corridors.
Pets: Accepted.
⊠ 🖬 🖵 🍴 🔁

ORONO

▼▼▼ **Best Western Black Bear Inn & Conference
Center** 🆂🅷
(207) 866-7120. **$89-$129.** 4 Godfrey Dr. I-95, exit 193 (Stillwater Ave). Int corridors. **Pets:** $5 daily fee/room. No serv-
ice, supervision.
🅰🆂🅺 ⊠ 🗺🅼 🖬 🖵

◈◈◈ ▼▼ **University Inn Academic Suites** 🆂🅷
(207) 866-4921. **$62-$79.** 5 College Ave. I-95, exit 191, 0.4
mi n on US 2, 8 mi n of Bangor. Int corridors. **Pets:** Other
species. Designated rooms, service with restrictions, supervision.
🆂🅰🆅🅴 ⊠ 🖬 🖵 🔁

PORTLAND

WWWW Doubletree Hotel 🔲
(207) 774-5611. **$85-$189.** 1230 Congress St. I-295, exit 5 northbound, w on SR 22; exit 5B southbound. Int corridors. **Pets:** Accepted.

(ASK) (S🌙) ✕ (&M) (🐾) 🔧 💻 🍴 ➰

WWWW Eastland Park Hotel 🔲
(207) 775-5411. **$129-$229.** 157 High St. At Congress Square; center. Int corridors. **Pets:** Accepted.

(SAVE) (S🌙) ✕ 🔧 💻 🍴 ✕

WWWW Embassy Suites Hotel 🔲
(207) 775-2200. **$129-$279, 3 day notice.** 1050 Westbrook St. At the Portland International Jetport. Int corridors. **Pets:** Other species. Designated rooms.

(SAVE) (S🌙) ✕ (&M) (🐾) 🔧 💻 🍴 ➰ ✕

WWWW Holiday Inn-West 🆂🅷
(207) 774-5601. **$110-$190.** 81 Riverside St. I-95 (Maine Tpke), exit 48. Int corridors. **Pets:** Designated rooms, service with restrictions, supervision.

(SAVE) (S🌙) ✕ (&M) (🐾) (🐾) 🔧 💻 🍴 ➰ ✕

WWWW Howard Johnson Plaza Hotel 🆂🅷
(207) 774-5861. **$80-$175.** 155 Riverside St. I-95 (Maine Tpke), exit 48, jct SR 25. Int corridors. **Pets:** $50 deposit/room. Service with restrictions, supervision.

(SAVE) (S🌙) ✕ 🔧 💻 🍴 ➰

WWWWW Portland Harbor Hotel 🆂🅷
(207) 775-9090. **$179-$299.** 468 Fore St. In the Old Port. Int corridors. **Pets:** Accepted.

(SAVE) (S🌙) ✕ (&M) 🍴

PRESQUE ISLE

WWW Northern Lights Motel Ⓜ �
(207) 764-4441. **$46-$68.** 72 Houlton Rd. 2 mi s on US 1. Ext corridors. **Pets:** Medium. Designated rooms, service with restrictions, supervision.

(SAVE) ✕ 🔧

WWW Presque Isle Inn & Convention Center 🆂🅷 �
(207) 764-3321. **$68-$128, 14 day notice.** 116 Main St. 1 mi s on US 1. Int corridors. **Pets:** Other species.

(SAVE) (S🌙) ✕ 🔧 💻 🍴 ➰

ROCKLAND

WWW Navigator Motor Inn 🆂🅷
(207) 594-2131. **$59-$115.** 520 Main St. On US 1. Ext corridors. **Pets:** Accepted.

(SAVE) (S🌙) ✕ 🔧 🍴

WWW Trade Winds Motor Inn 🆂🅷
(207) 596-6661. **$55-$149.** 2 Park Dr. On US 1; center. Ext/int corridors. **Pets:** Designated rooms, service with restrictions, supervision.

(SAVE) (S🌙) ✕ 🔧 🍴 ➰ ✕

RUMFORD

WWW Linnell Motel & RestInn Conference Center 🆂🅷
(207) 364-4511. **$60-$75.** 986 Prospect Ave. 2 mi w, just off US 2. Ext/int corridors. **Pets:** Medium. $15 daily fee/pet. Service with restrictions, supervision.

(SAVE) (S🌙) ✕ 🔧

WWW The Madison Motor Inn 🆂🅷
(207) 364-7973. **$79-$139, 14 day notice.** 1257 US Rt 2. 4 mi w. Ext corridors. **Pets:** Accepted.

(ASK) (S🌙) ✕ 🔧 💻 🍴 ➰ ✕

SACO

WWWW Hampton Inn 🆂🅷
(207) 282-7222. **$69-$139.** 48 Industrial Park Rd. I-95 (Maine Tpke), exit 36; I-195, exit 1. Int corridors. **Pets:** Service with restrictions, supervision.

(SAVE) (S🌙) ✕ (&M) (🐾) 🔧 💻 ➰

WWW Saco Motel Ⓜ
(207) 284-6952. **$40-$80, 3 day notice.** 473 Main St. I-95 (Maine Tpke), exit 36, 0.5 mi s on US 1. Ext corridors. **Pets:** Medium, dogs only. $5 daily fee/pet. Designated rooms, service with restrictions, supervision.

(ASK) (S🌙) ✕ 🔧 ➰

WWW Wagon Wheel Motel Ⓜ
(207) 284-6387. **$48-$95, 3 day notice.** 726 Portland Rd. 1.8 mi n on US 1; 0.8 mi n of jct I-95, exit 36. Ext corridors. **Pets:** Dogs only. Designated rooms, service with restrictions, supervision.

(ASK) (S🌙) ✕ 🔧 💻 ➰

SANFORD

WWW Super 8 Motel 🆂🅷
(207) 324-8823. **$57-$95.** 1892 Main St (Rt 109). I-95 (Maine Tpke), exit 19, 7 mi w. Int corridors. **Pets:** Other species. $15 daily fee/pet. Designated rooms, service with restrictions, supervision.

(ASK) (S🌙) ✕ (🐾)

SCARBOROUGH

WWW Pride Motel & Cottages 🆲🅰 �
(207) 883-4816. **$45-$115.** 677 US 1. I-95 (Maine Tpke), exit 36, 0.5 mi e to US 1, then 4.5 mi n. Ext corridors. **Pets:** Other species. $5 daily fee/room. Service with restrictions, supervision.

✕ 🔧 ➰ ✕

WWWW Residence Inn by Marriott 🆂🅷
(207) 883-0400. **$109-$219.** 800 Roundwood Dr. I-95 (Maine Tpke), exit 42, 1.5 mi n on Payne Rd. Int corridors. **Pets:** Accepted.

✕ (&M) (🐾) (🐾) 🔧 💻 ➰ ✕

WWWW TownePlace Suites by Marriott 🆂🅷 �
(207) 883-6800. **$109-$219.** 700 Roundwood Dr. I-95 (Maine Tpke), exit 42, 1.5 mi n on Payne Rd. Int corridors. **Pets:** Other species. $20 daily fee/room. Service with restrictions.

(ASK) (S🌙) ✕ (&M) (🐾) 🔧 💻 ➰

SEARSPORT

The Yardarm Motel M
(207) 548-2404. **$53-$100, 3 day notice.** 172 E Main St. 0.5 mi n on US 1. Ext corridors. **Pets:** Small, dogs only. Designated rooms, service with restrictions, supervision.

SKOWHEGAN

Breezy Acres Motel M
(207) 474-2703. **$58-$68.** 315 Waterville Rd. 1.5 mi s on US 201. Ext corridors. **Pets:** Accepted.

SOUTHPORT

The Lawnmere Inn CI
(207) 633-2544. **$89-$199, 14 day notice.** 65 Hendricks Hill Rd. 2 mi s of Boothbay Harbor on SR 27, just s of bridge to Southport Island. Ext/int corridors. **Pets:** Accepted.

SOUTH PORTLAND

AmeriSuites (Portland/Maine Mall) SH
(207) 775-3900. **$99-$229.** 303 Sable Oaks Dr. I-95 (Maine Tpke), exit 45, just n on Maine Mall Rd, then just w on Running Hill Rd. Int corridors. **Pets:** Medium, other species. $20 one-time fee/room. Service with restrictions, supervision.

Best Western Merry Manor Inn SH
(207) 774-6151. **$90-$160.** 700 Main St. I-95 (Maine Tpke), exit 45, 3 mi e on spur road to US 1, exit 7 spur road and US 1. Ext/int corridors. **Pets:** Large, other species. Service with restrictions, crate.

Coastline Inn M
(207) 772-3838. **$70-$130.** 80 John Roberts Rd. I-95 (Maine Tpke), exit 45 to Maine Mall Rd, right turn, continue to Philbrook Ave; corner of Philbrook Ave and John Roberts Rd. Ext corridors. **Pets:** Medium, other species. Service with restrictions, supervision.

Howard Johnson Hotel SH
(207) 775-5343. **$89-$164.** 675 Main St. I-95 (Maine Tpke), exit 45, 3 mi e on spur road to US 1, just n. Int corridors. **Pets:** Other species. Designated rooms, service with restrictions, supervision.

Portland Marriott Hotel & Golf Resort LH
(207) 871-8000. **$99-$219.** 200 Sable Oaks Dr. I-95 (Maine Tpke), exit 45, just n on Maine Mall Rd, then just w on Running Hill Rd. Int corridors. **Pets:** Accepted.

Sheraton South Portland LH
(207) 775-6161. **$119-$199.** 363 Maine Mall Rd. I-95 (Maine Tpke), exit 45. Int corridors. **Pets:** Accepted.

SPRUCE HEAD

Craignair Inn CI ☙
(207) 594-7644. **$60-$145, 14 day notice.** 5 Third St. 2.5 mi w on SR 73, 1.5 mi s on Clark Island Rd; 10 mi s of Rockland. Ext/int corridors. **Pets:** Medium. $10 daily fee/room. Designated rooms, service with restrictions, supervision.

WATERVILLE

Best Western Waterville SH
(207) 873-3335. **$89-$150.** 356 Main St. I-95, exit 130 (Main St). Int corridors. **Pets:** Accepted.

Budget Host Airport Inn SH
(207) 873-3366. **$40-$110.** 400 Kennedy Memorial Dr. I-95, exit 127, 0.3 mi e on SR 11 (Kennedy Memorial Dr). Ext/int corridors. **Pets:** Accepted.

Econo Lodge SH
(207) 872-5577. **$50-$95.** 455 Kennedy Memorial Dr. I-95, exit 127 on SR 11 Kennedy Memorial Dr) at Waterville-Oakland. Ext/int corridors. **Pets:** Dogs only. $5 daily fee/pet. Designated rooms, service with restrictions.

Holiday Inn SH
(207) 873-0111. **$119-$150.** 375 Main St. I-95, exit 130 (Main St) on SR 104. Int corridors. **Pets:** Accepted.

WELLS

Ne'r Beach Motel M
(207) 646-2636. **$44-$109, 7 day notice.** 395 Post Rd (Rt 1). US 1, 0.8 mi s of jct SR 9B. Ext corridors. **Pets:** Medium. $10 daily fee/pet. Designated rooms, supervision.

WESTPORT

The Squire Tarbox Inn CI
(207) 882-7693. **$122-$190, 14 day notice.** 1181 Main Rd. Jct US 1 and SR 144; in Wiscasset; 8.5 mi s on SR 144, follow signs. Ext/int corridors. **Pets:** Accepted.

WILTON

Whispering Pines Motel M ☙
(207) 645-3721. **$57-$105, 3 day notice.** 183 Lake Rd. SR 2, 1 mi w of jct SR 4. Ext corridors. **Pets:** Other species. $3 daily fee/pet. Designated rooms, supervision.

YARMOUTH

Down-East Village Motel SH
(207) 846-5161. **$65-$115.** 705 US Rt 1. I-295, exit 15 northbound; exit 17 southbound. Ext corridors. **Pets:** $8 daily fee/pet. Service with restrictions, supervision.

MARYLAND

BALTIMORE METROPOLITAN AREA

ABERDEEN

Four Points by Sheraton Aberdeen SH
(410) 273-6300. **$99.** 980 Hospitality Way. I-95, exit 85, just e on SR 22. Int corridors. **Pets:** Medium, other species. Designated rooms, service with restrictions, supervision.

Holiday Inn Chesapeake House SH
(410) 272-8100. **$104-$130.** 1007 Beards Hill Rd. I-95, exit 85, just e on SR 22. Int corridors. **Pets:** Medium. Service with restrictions, supervision.

Red Roof Inn M
(410) 273-7800. **$49-$72.** 988 Hospitality Way. I-95, exit 85, just e on SR 22. Ext corridors. **Pets:** Accepted.

ANNAPOLIS

Homestead Studio Suites Hotel-Annapolis SH
(410) 571-6600. **$94-$129.** 120 Admiral Cochrane Dr. 2.3 mi sw on US 50 and 301, exit 22, just s, then just e. Int corridors. **Pets:** Medium, other species. $25 daily fee/room. Service with restrictions, crate.

Loews Annapolis Hotel LH
(410) 263-7777. **$125-$299.** 126 West St. US 50 and 301, exit 24 eastbound; exit 24A westbound, 1.4 mi s on SR 70, just sw on Calvert St, then just w. Int corridors. **Pets:** Other species.

Radisson Hotel Annapolis LH
(410) 224-3150. **$79-$199.** 210 Holiday Ct. 2.3 mi sw on US 50 and 301, exit 22 to Riva Rd, then 0.3 mi n on Riva Rd. Int corridors. **Pets:** Medium. $75 deposit/room, $25 one-time fee/room. Designated rooms, service with restrictions, crate.

Residence Inn by Marriott-Annapolis SH
(410) 573-0300. **$99-$289.** 170 Admiral Cochrane Dr. 2.3 mi sw on US 50 and 301, exit 22 to Riva Rd, just s on Riva Rd, then just e. Ext corridors. **Pets:** Accepted.

ANNAPOLIS JUNCTION

TownePlace Suites by Marriott-Ft Meade/Baltimore M
(301) 498-7477. **$64-$139.** 120 National Business Pkwy. SR 295, exit Dorsey Run Rd, 2 mi n. Int corridors. **Pets:** Other species. $100 one-time fee/room.

BALTIMORE

Admiral Fell Inn SH
(410) 522-7377. **$119-$189.** 888 S Broadway. Corner of Broadway and Thames sts; facing the waterfront. Int corridors. **Pets:** Other species. Service with restrictions, crate.

Days Inn M
(410) 747-8900. **$59-$99.** 5701 Baltimore National Pike. I-695, exit 15A, just e. Int corridors. **Pets:** Accepted.

Peabody Court-A Clarion Hotel SH
(410) 727-7101. **$139-$275.** 612 Cathedral St. 612 Cathedral St and Mount Vernon Square. Int corridors. **Pets:** Small. $15 daily fee/pet, $35 one-time fee/room. Service with restrictions, crate.

COLUMBIA

Staybridge Suites by Holiday Inn Baltimore-Columbia SH
(410) 964-9494. **$89-$200.** 8844 Columbia 100 Pkwy. I-95, exit 43B, 4 mi w on SR 100, exit 1B. Int corridors. **Pets:** Accepted.

Wellesley Inn & Suites (Columbia) SH
(410) 872-2994. **$129-$139.** 8890 Stanford Blvd. I-95, exit 41B, 1.3 mi w on SR 175 (Little Patuxent Pkwy), 0.5 mi s on Snowden River Pkwy, just w on McGaw Rd, then 0.3 mi nw. Int corridors. **Pets:** Accepted.

EDGEWOOD

Best Western Invitation Inn SH ✿
(410) 679-9700. **$59-$99.** 1709 Edgewood Rd. I-95, exit 77A, just e on SR 24. Ext corridors. **Pets:** Other species. $50 deposit/room. Designated rooms, service with restrictions, crate.
SAVE 5o ✕ 🐾 🅾 🖥 🕭 🏊

Days Inn-Edgewood M
(410) 671-9990. **$59-$75.** 2116 Emmorton Park Rd. I-95, exit 77A, just e on SR 24. Ext corridors. **Pets:** Small, dogs only. $10 daily fee/pet. Designated rooms, service with restrictions, supervision.
SAVE 5o ✕ 🐾 🖥 🕭

ELLICOTT CITY

Residence Inn by Marriott Columbia SH ✿
(410) 997-7200. **$149.** 4950 Beaver Run. I-95, exit 43B, 4 mi w on SR 100, exit 1B (Executive Park Dr). Int corridors. **Pets:** Small. $10 daily fee/pet, $110 one-time fee/room. Service with restrictions, crate.
ASK 5o ᏏM 🐾 🖥 🕭 🏊 ✕

GLEN BURNIE

Days Inn-Glen Burnie SH
(410) 761-8300. **$79-$129.** 6600 Ritchie Hwy. I-695, exit 3B eastbound; exit 2 westbound, 0.5 mi s on SR 2. Ext corridors. **Pets:** $20 daily fee/room. Service with restrictions.
SAVE 5o ✕ 🐾 🖥 🕭 🏊

HANOVER

Red Roof Inn-BWI Parkway M
(410) 712-4070. **$54-$84.** 7306 Parkway Dr S. 0.7 mi w of SR 295, exit 100, w to exit 8, 0.5 mi se. Ext corridors. **Pets:** Accepted.
SAVE ✕ 🐾 🖥

JESSUP

Red Roof Inn-Columbia/Jessup M
(410) 796-0380. **$59-$84.** 8000 Washington Blvd. I-95, exit 41A, 0.3 mi s of jct US 1 and SR 175. Ext corridors. **Pets:** Accepted.
SAVE ✕ 🐾

LINTHICUM HEIGHTS

AmeriSuites (Baltimore/BWI Airport) SH
(410) 859-3366. **$119-$169.** 940 International Dr. I-695, exit 7A, 1 mi s on SR 295, just e on W Nursery Rd. Int corridors. **Pets:** Small. Designated rooms, service with restrictions, supervision.
SAVE 5o ✕ ᏏM 🐾 🖥 🕭 🏊

Comfort Inn Airport SH
(410) 789-9100. **$89-$129.** 6921 Baltimore Annapolis Blvd. I-695, exit 6A eastbound; exit 5 westbound, at jct SR 170 and 648. Int corridors. **Pets:** Medium. Service with restrictions, supervision.
SAVE 5o ✕ ᏏM 🐾 🖥 🕭 🍴 ✕

Comfort Suites-BWI Airport SH
(410) 691-1000. **$79-$209, 3 day notice.** 815 Elkridge Landing Rd. I-695, exit 7A, 1 mi s on SR 295, 1.3 mi e on W Nursery Rd. Int corridors. **Pets:** Small. $25 one-time fee/pet. Designated rooms, service with restrictions, crate.
SAVE 5o ✕ ᏏM 🖥 🕭 🖵 ✕

Hampton Inn BWI Airport SH
(410) 850-0600. **$104-$149.** 829 Elkridge Landing Rd. I-695, exit 7A, 1 mi s on SR 295, 1.3 mi e on W Nursery Rd, then just w. Int corridors. **Pets:** Accepted.
ASK 5o ✕ 🐾 🖥 🕭

Holiday Inn-BWI Airport LH
(410) 859-8400. **$89-$199.** 890 Elkridge Landing Rd. I-695, exit 7A, 1 mi s on SR 295, 1.3 mi e on W Nursery Rd, then 0.5 mi w. Int corridors. **Pets:** Large. $20 one-time fee/room. Service with restrictions, supervision.
SAVE 5o ✕ ᏏM 🐾 🅾 🖥 🕭 🍴 🏊

Homestead Studio Suites Hotel-Baltimore Washington Int'l Airport M ✿
(410) 691-2500. **$86-$111.** 939 International Dr. I-695, exit 7A, 1 mi s on SR 295, just e on W Nursery Rd. Ext corridors. **Pets:** Medium, other species. $25 daily fee/room. Service with restrictions, crate.
ASK 5o ✕ ᏏM 🐾 🅾 🖥 🕭

Homewood Suites by Hilton-BWI Airport SH
(410) 684-6100. **$109-$159.** 1181 Winterson Rd. I-695, exit 7A, 1 mi s on SR 295, 0.7 mi e on W Nursery Rd, then just n. Int corridors. **Pets:** Accepted.
ASK 5o ✕ ᏏM 🐾 🅾 🖥 🕭 🏊

Red Roof Inn-BWI Airport SH
(410) 850-7600. **$64-$99.** 827 Elkridge Landing Rd. I-695, exit 7A, 1 mi s on SR 295, 1.3 mi e on W Nursery Rd, then just w. Ext corridors. **Pets:** Accepted.
SAVE ✕ 🐾

Residence Inn by Marriott-BWI Airport SH ✿
(410) 691-0255. **$109-$189.** 1160 Winterson Rd. I-695, exit 7A, 1 mi s on SR 295, 0.7 mi e on W Nursery Rd, then just n. Int corridors. **Pets:** Medium, other species. $10 daily fee/pet, $100 one-time fee/pet. Service with restrictions, crate.
ASK 5o ✕ ᏏM 🐾 🖥 🕭 🏊 ✕

Sheraton International Hotel On BWI Airport SH
(410) 859-3300. **$89-$239.** 7032 Elm Rd. I-195, exit 1A, 0.5 mi n on SR 170, just e. Int corridors. **Pets:** Accepted.
SAVE 5o ✕ 🐾 🅾 🖥 🕭 🍴 🏊

Sleep Inn & Suites Airport SH
(410) 789-7223. **$79-$119.** 6055 Belle Grove Rd. I-695, exit 6A eastbound; exit 5 westbound, 0.3 mi n to jct SR 170/648. Int corridors. **Pets:** Medium. Service with restrictions, supervision.
SAVE 5o ✕ ᏏM 🐾 🅾 🖥 🕭

OWINGS MILLS

AmeriSuites (Baltimore/Owings Mills) SH
(410) 998-3630. **$99-$129.** 4730 Painters Mill Rd. I-795, exit 4 (Owings Mills Blvd), 0.5 mi s, 0.7 mi e on Red Run Blvd. Int corridors. **Pets:** Very small. $50 one-time fee/room. Service with restrictions, crate.

TIMONIUM

Red Roof Inn-Timonium M
(410) 666-0380. **$64-$89.** 111 W Timonium Rd. I-83, exit 16A northbound; exit 16 southbound, just e. Ext corridors. **Pets:** Accepted.

TOWSON

Ramada Inn-Towson/Baltimore SH
(410) 823-8750. **$60-$90.** 8712 Loch Raven Blvd. I-695, exit 29B, just e. Ext corridors. **Pets:** Accepted.

WESTMINSTER

The Boston Inn M
(410) 848-9095. **$50-$64.** 533 Baltimore Blvd. 0.9 mi se on SR 97/140 from jct SR 27. Ext corridors. **Pets:** Dogs only. $100 deposit/room. Service with restrictions, supervision.

🐾 END METROPOLITAN AREA 🐾

CUMBERLAND

Holiday Inn SH
(301) 724-8800. **$79-$109.** 100 S George St. I-68, exit 43C, just n; downtown. Int corridors. **Pets:** Large. $10 one-time fee/room. Service with restrictions, supervision.

Rocky Gap Lodge & Golf Resort LH
(301) 784-8400. **$109-$175, 3 day notice.** 16701 Lakeview Rd NE. I-68, exit 50, just n. Int corridors. **Pets:** Accepted.

DISTRICT OF COLUMBIA AREA

BETHESDA

Residence Inn by Marriott-Bethesda-Downtown LH
(301) 718-0200. **$239-$270.** 7335 Wisconsin Ave. I-495, exit 34, 2.5 mi s on SR 355; entrance on Waverly St. Int corridors. **Pets:** Medium. $10 daily fee/room, $200 one-time fee/room. Service with restrictions, supervision.

CAMP SPRINGS

Days Inn-Camp Springs/Andrews AFB SH
(301) 423-2323. **$64-$89.** 5001 Mercedes Blvd. I-95/495, exit 7B, 0.3 mi n on Auth Rd. Int corridors. **Pets:** Other species. $10 daily fee/pet. Service with restrictions, crate.

GAITHERSBURG

Comfort Inn Shady Grove SH
(301) 330-0023. **$69-$119.** 16216 Frederick Rd. I-270, exit 8, 1 mi e on Shady Grove Rd at jct SR 355. Int corridors. **Pets:** Service with restrictions, supervision.

Holiday Inn-Gaithersburg LH
(301) 948-8900. **$79-$119.** 2 Montgomery Village Ave. I-270, exit 11, 0.3 mi e. Int corridors. **Pets:** Accepted.

Homestead Studio Suites Hotel-Gaithersburg/Rockville SH 🐾
(301) 987-9100. **$86-$111.** 2621 Research Blvd. I-270, exit 8, just w, then just n. Int corridors. **Pets:** Medium, other species. $25 daily fee/room. Service with restrictions, crate.

Motel 6–1489 M
(301) 977-3311. **$61-$71.** 497 Quince Orchard Rd. I-270, exit 10 northbound; exit 11B southbound, just w. Ext corridors. **Pets:** Accepted.

Residence Inn by Marriott-Gaithersburg SH
(301) 590-3003. **$99-$179.** 9721 Washingtonian Blvd. I-270, exit 9B, just w to Fields Rd, 0.8 mi se, then just ne. Int corridors. **Pets:** Accepted.

Summerfield Suites by Wyndham-Gaithersburg SH 🐾
(301) 527-6000. **$99-$135.** 200 Skidmore Blvd. I-370, exit SR 355, just n to Westland Rd. Ext corridors. **Pets:** Large, other species. $200 one-time fee/room. Service with restrictions, crate.

▼▼▼ TownePlace Suites by
Marriott-Gaithersburg 🆂🅷
(301) 590-2300. **$59-$119.** 212 Perry Pkwy. I-270, exit 11,
just e on SR 124 to SR 355, 0.3 mi s, then 0.5 mi sw. Int
corridors. **Pets:** Accepted.
🄰🅂🄺 🅂🄳 ⌧ 🔊 🄼 📶 🛏 🍴 🖥 🏊

GERMANTOWN

▼▼ Homestead Studio Suites
Hotel-Germantown Ⓜ ❧
(301) 515-4500. **$73-$103.** 20141 Century Blvd. I-270, exit
15B, just w to Aircraft Dr, then just n. Ext corridors.
Pets: Medium, other species. $25 daily fee/room. Service
with restrictions, crate.
🄰🅂🄺 🅂🄳 ⌧ 🄼 📶 🛏 🖥

GREENBELT

▼▼▼ Residence Inn by Marriott-Greenbelt 🆂🅷
(301) 982-1600. **$129-$249, 3 day notice.** 6320 Golden Triangle Dr. I-95/495, exit 23, 0.5 mi sw of jct SR 201; off SR
193, just n on Walke Dr. Int corridors. **Pets:** Accepted.
🄰🅂🄺 🅂🄳 ⌧ 📶 🛏 🖥 🏊 ⌧

LANHAM

🄰🄰🄰 ▼▼▼ Red Roof Inn-Lanham Ⓜ
(301) 731-8830. **$59-$84.** 9050 Lanham Severn Rd. I-95/
495, exit 20A, 0.3 mi e on SR 450. Ext corridors.
Pets: Accepted.
🅂🄳 ⌧

LARGO

🄰🄰🄰 ▼▼▼ Doubletree Club Hotel Washington
DC-Largo 🄻🄷
(301) 773-0700. **$69-$149.** 9100 Basil Ct. I-95/495, exit 17A
(SR 202); off Capital Beltway. Int corridors. **Pets:** Accepted.
🅂🄳 🅂🄳 ⌧ 🄼 📶 🛏 🖥 🍴 🏊

LAUREL

🄰🄰🄰 ▼▼▼ Comfort Suites Hotel at Laurel
Lakes 🆂🅷
(301) 206-2600. **$109-$179.** 14402 Laurel Pl. Jct SR 198,
1.4 mi s on US 1. Int corridors. **Pets:** Accepted.
🅂🄳 🅂🄳 ⌧ 📶 🛏 🖥 🏊 ⌧

🄰🄰🄰 ▼▼ Quality Inn & Suites Laurel 🆂🅷
(301) 725-8800. **$95-$249.** One Second St. On US 1, 0.5 mi
n of jct SR 198. Ext/int corridors. **Pets:** Small. $15 daily
fee/room. Designated rooms, service with restrictions, crate.
🅂🄳 🅂🄳 ⌧ 🄼 🛏 🖥 🏊

🄰🄰🄰 ▼▼▼ Red Roof Inn-Laurel Ⓜ
(301) 498-8811. **$49-$84.** 12525 Laurel Bowie Rd. SR 295,
exit SR 197 (Laurel Bowie Rd), 0.3 mi w. Ext corridors.
Pets: Small. Service with restrictions, supervision.
🅂🄳 ⌧ 📶 🛏

ROCKVILLE

🄰🄰🄰 ▼▼▼ Best Western Washington Gateway
Hotel 🄻🄷
(301) 424-4940. **$69-$179.** 1251 W Montgomery Ave. I-270,
exit 6B, just w on SR 28. Int corridors. **Pets:** Medium. $10
daily fee/pet. Service with restrictions, crate.
🅂🄳 🅂🄳 ⌧ 📶 🄼 🛏 🖥 🏊

🄰🄰🄰 ▼▼▼ Quality Suites and Conference
Center 🆂🅷
(301) 840-0200. **$119-$179.** 3 Research Ct. I-270, exit 8, just
sw. Int corridors. **Pets:** Medium. $35 one-time fee/pet. Serv-
ice with restrictions, supervision.
🅂🄳 🅂🄳 ⌧ 📶 🄼 🛏 🖥 🏊

🄰🄰🄰 ▼▼▼ Red Roof Inn-Rockville 🆂🅷
(301) 987-0965. **$59-$89.** 16001 Shady Grove Rd. I-270, exit
8, 0.5 mi e. Ext corridors. **Pets:** Medium, other species.
Service with restrictions, supervision.
🅂🄳 ⌧ 🄼 📶 🄼 🍴

🄰🄰🄰 ▼▼▼ Woodfin Suites Hotel 🆂🅷
(301) 590-9880. **$124.** 1380 Piccard Dr. I-270, exit 8, 0.3 mi
s; 1 mi w of SR 355 via Redland Rd. Ext corridors.
Pets: Large, other species. $5 daily fee/pet. Designated
rooms, service with restrictions, supervision.
🅂🄳 🅂🄳 ⌧ 📶 🄼 🛏 🖥 🏊 ⌧

❧ END AREA ❧

EASTON

🄰🄰🄰 ▼▼▼ Comfort Inn Easton Ⓜ
(410) 820-8333. **$89-$109.** 8523 Ocean Gateway. US 50,
0.7 mi n of jct SR 331. Ext corridors. **Pets:** Accepted.
🅂🄳 🅂🄳 ⌧ 🖥 🏊

FREDERICK

▼▼▼ Frederick Residence Inn by Marriott 🆂🅷
(301) 360-0024. **$99-$124.** 5230 Westview Dr. I-270, exit
31B, 0.5 mi sw on SR 85, 0.3 mi n on Crestwood Blvd. Int
corridors. **Pets:** Accepted.
🄰🅂🄺 ⌧ 🄼 🛏 🖥 🏊 ⌧

🄰🄰🄰 ▼▼▼ Hampton Inn 🆂🅷
(301) 698-2500. **$79-$109.** 5311 Buckeystown Pike (SR 85).
I-270, exit 31B, 0.6 mi w via SR 85. Int corridors.
Pets: Accepted.
🅂🄳 🅂🄳 ⌧ 📶 🛏 🖥 🍴 🏊

▼▼▼ Holiday Inn Express-FSK Mall 🆂🅷
(301) 695-2881. **$71-$84.** 5579 Spectrum Dr. I-270, exit 31A,
just e on SR 85. Int corridors. **Pets:** Other species. $25
deposit/room. Service with restrictions, supervision.
🄰🅂🄺 🅂🄳 ⌧ 📶 🄼 🛏 🖥

▼▼▼▼ Holiday Inn-Francis Scott Key Mall **SH**
(301) 694-7500. **$89-$119.** 5400 Holiday Dr. I-270, exit 31A, just se of SR 85. Int corridors. **Pets:** Medium. Service with restrictions, supervision.
(ASK) (S🐾) (✕) (🔊) (📶) (📺) (🍴) (🏊) (🐾)

AAA ▼▼▼▼ Holiday Inn-Frederick/Ft Detrick **SH**
(301) 662-5141. **$68-$76.** 999 W Patrick St. Just w on US 40 from jct US 15. Ext corridors. **Pets:** Service with restrictions.
(SAVE) (S🐾) (✕) (🔊) (🈁) (📶) (📺) (🍴) (🏊) (🐾)

AAA ▼▼▼▼ MainStay Suites **SH**
(301) 668-4600. **$109.** 7310 Executive Way. I-270, exit 31B. Int corridors. **Pets:** Other species. $150 deposit/pet, $10 daily fee/pet. Service with restrictions, crate.
(SAVE) (S🐾) (✕) (🈁) (📶) (📺) (🏊)

AAA ▼▼▼ Quality Inn **SH**
(301) 695-6200. **$69-$99.** 420 Prospect Blvd. US 15, exit Jefferson St, just se. Int corridors. **Pets:** Other species. Service with restrictions, supervision.
(SAVE) (S🐾) (✕) (🔊) (📶) (📺) (🏊) (🐾)

FROSTBURG

AAA ▼▼▼ Days Inn & Suites **SH**
(301) 689-2050. **$69-$79.** 11100 New Georges Creek Rd. I-68, exit 34, 1 mi n on SR 36. Int corridors. **Pets:** Accepted.
(SAVE) (S🐾) (✕) (🔊) (📶) (📺)

GRANTSVILLE

▼▼▼▼ Holiday Inn **SH**
(301) 895-5993. **$60-$109.** 2541 Chestnut Ridge Rd. I-68, exit 22, just s on US 219. Int corridors. **Pets:** Accepted.
(ASK) (S🐾) (✕) (📶) (📺) (🍴) (🏊) (🐾)

▼▼▼ Walnut Ridge Bed & Breakfast **BB**
(301) 895-4248. **$85-$160, 7 day notice.** 92 Main St. I-68, exit 19, just n on SR 495, then 0.5 mi e on US 40. Ext/int corridors. **Pets:** Accepted.
(ASK) (S🐾) (✕) (📶) (📺)

GRASONVILLE

AAA ▼▼▼▼ Comfort Inn Kent Narrows **M** ✿
(410) 827-6767. **$79-$179.** 3101 Main St. US 50 and 301, exit 42; at Kent Narrows Bridge. Ext corridors. **Pets:** $25 one-time fee/room. Service with restrictions.
(SAVE) (S🐾) (✕) (🔊) (📶) (📺) (🏊) (🐾)

HAGERSTOWN

▼▼▼ Clarion Hotel & Conference Center Antietam Creek **SH**
(301) 733-5100. **$69-$89, 3 day notice.** 901 Dual Hwy. I-70, exit 32B, 2.3 mi w on US 40. Int corridors. **Pets:** Accepted.
(ASK) (S🐾) (✕) (🔊) (📶) (📺) (🍴) (🏊)

▼▼▼ Hagerstown Halfway Super 8 **M**
(301) 582-1992. **$47-$61.** 16805 Blake Rd. I-81, exit 5B, just w. Int corridors. **Pets:** Medium, other species. $10 deposit/pet, $15 one-time fee/pet. Designated rooms, service with restrictions, supervision.
(ASK) (S🐾) (✕) (🈁) (📶) (📺)

▼▼▼ Motel 6–1259 **M**
(301) 582-4445. **$45-$57.** 11321 Massey Blvd. I-81, exit 5, 0.5 mi e, 0.5 mi n of jct I-81 and 70. Ext corridors. **Pets:** Medium, other species. Service with restrictions, supervision.
(S🐾) (✕) (🈁) (🏊)

AAA ▼▼▼ Quality Inn Antietam Creek **SH**
(301) 733-2700. **$49-$89.** 1101 Dual Hwy. I-70, exit 32B, 2.2 mi w on US 40. Int corridors. **Pets:** Accepted.
(SAVE) (S🐾) (✕) (📶) (📺)

▼▼▼ Sleep Inn & Suites **SH**
(301) 766-9449. **$70-$130.** 18216 Col Henry K Douglas Dr. I-70, exit 29, just s. Int corridors. **Pets:** Other species. $10 daily fee/pet. Service with restrictions.
(ASK) (S🐾) (✕) (🈁) (📶) (📺) (🏊)

HANCOCK

AAA ▼▼ Best Value Inn **M**
(301) 678-6108. **$49-$56.** 2 Blue Hill Rd. I-70, exit 1B, 1.3 mi s on US 522. Ext corridors. **Pets:** Accepted.
(SAVE) (S🐾) (✕)

INDIAN HEAD

AAA ▼▼ Super 8 Motel **SH**
(301) 753-8100. **$58-$78.** 4694 Indian Head Hwy. SR 210, 0.6 mi s of jct SR 225. Int corridors. **Pets:** Small, dogs only. $6 daily fee/pet. Service with restrictions, supervision.
(SAVE) (S🐾) (✕) (🌓) (📶)

LA PLATA

AAA ▼▼▼▼ Best Western La Plata Inn **SH**
(301) 934-4900. **$69-$109.** 6900 Crain Hwy. Jct SR 6, 0.4 mi s on US 301. Int corridors. **Pets:** Medium. $25 one-time fee/room. Designated rooms, service with restrictions, supervision.
(SAVE) (S🐾) (✕) (♿) (🔊) (📶) (📺) (🏊)

LA VALE

AAA ▼▼▼ Oak Tree Inn **SH**
(301) 729-6700. **$69-$79.** 12310 Winchester Rd SW. I-68, exit 40, 0.6 mi s. Ext/int corridors. **Pets:** Other species. $5 daily fee/pet. Service with restrictions, supervision.
(SAVE) (S🐾) (✕) (🔊) (🈁) (📶) (📺)

AAA ▼▼▼ Super 8 Motel **M**
(301) 729-6265. **$54.** 1301 National Hwy. I-68, exit 40, 0.4 mi n. Int corridors. **Pets:** Accepted.
(SAVE) (S🐾) (✕) (📶)

LEXINGTON PARK

▼▼▼ Days Inn Lexington Park **M**
(301) 863-6666. **$123.** 21847 Three Notch Rd. On SR 235. Ext corridors. **Pets:** $8 daily fee/pet. Designated rooms, service with restrictions, supervision.
(ASK) (S🐾) (✕) (♿) (🔊) (📶) (📺) (🏊)

MCHENRY

◆◆ Comfort Inn **M**
(301) 387-4200. **$59-$119.** 2704 Deep Creek Dr. 1 mi s on US 219 from jct SR 42. Int corridors. **Pets:** Accepted.
(ASK) (S⊘) ⊠ 🏠 🔲

◆◆ Wisp Mountain Resort/Hotel & Conference Center **SH** ❀
(301) 387-5581. **$69-$219, 7 day notice.** 290 Marsh Hill Rd. 1 mi s on US 219 from jct SR 42, just w on Sang Run Rd, 0.3 mi s. Int corridors. **Pets:** Large. $50 one-time fee/room. Designated rooms, no service, supervision.
(ASK) (S⊘) ⊠ 🔗 🏠 🔲 🔲 🍴 🏊 ⊠

OCEAN CITY

◆◆ Best Western Sea Bay Inn **SH**
(410) 524-6100. **$29-$399, 3 day notice.** 6007 Coastal Hwy. Jct 60th St and Coastal Hwy. Int corridors. **Pets:** Large, other species. $50 deposit/room, $15 daily fee/pet. Supervision.
(ASK) (S⊘) ⊠ 🏠 🔲 🍴 🏊

◆◆ ◆◆◆ Clarion Resort Fontainebleau Hotel **LH** ❀
(410) 524-3535. **$119-$359, 3 day notice.** 10100 Coastal Hwy. 101st St and the ocean. Int corridors. **Pets:** Medium. $30 daily fee/pet. Designated rooms, service with restrictions, supervision.
(SAVE) (S⊘) ⊠ 🔗 🏠 🔲 🍴 🏊 ⊠

◆◆ ◆◆◆ Fenwick Inn **SH**
(410) 250-1100. **$49-$229, 3 day notice.** 13801 Coastal Hwy. 138th St and Coastal Hwy. Int corridors. **Pets:** Small. $10 daily fee/pet. Designated rooms, service with restrictions, supervision.
(SAVE) (S⊘) ⊠ 🏠 🔲 🍴 🏊

PERRYVILLE

◆◆◆ ◆◆◆ Comfort Inn **SH** ❀
(410) 642-2866. **$59-$89.** 61 Heather Ln. I-95, exit 93, just e. Ext corridors. **Pets:** Other species. $5 daily fee/pet. Designated rooms, service with restrictions, crate.
(SAVE) (S⊘) ⊠ 🔗 🏠 🔲

PRINCESS ANNE

◆◆◆ ◆◆◆ Waterloo Country Inn **CI** ❀
(410) 651-0883. **$125-$255, 7 day notice.** 28822 Mt. Vernon Rd. 3.3 mi w on SR 362 from jct US 13. Int corridors. **Pets:** Other species. Designated rooms, crate.
⊠ 🏠 🔲 🍴 🏊 ⊠

ROCK HALL

◆◆◆ ◆◆◆ Huntingfield Manor B&B **BB**
(410) 639-7779. **$110-$175, 5 day notice.** 4928 Eastern Neck Rd. 1.8 mi s on SR 445 from jct SR 20. Ext/int corridors. **Pets:** Designated rooms, service with restrictions, supervision.
⊠ 🏠 🔲 🏊 ⊠ 🕿

◆◆ Mariners Motel **M**
(410) 639-2291. **$65-$80.** 5681 S Hawthorne Ave. 0.3 mi e of SR 20. Ext corridors. **Pets:** Service with restrictions, supervision.
⊠ 🏠 🔲 🏊 ⊠

ST. MICHAELS

◆◆◆ ◆◆ The Parsonage Inn **BB**
(410) 745-5519. **$100-$195, 10 day notice.** 210 N Talbot St. 0.3 mi w on SR 33. Ext/int corridors. **Pets:** Accepted.
(SAVE) (S⊘) ⊠ ⊠ 🕿

SALISBURY

◆◆◆ ◆◆ Best Value Inn Salisbury **SH** ❀
(410) 742-7194. **$49-$149.** 2625 N Salisbury Blvd. US 13, 1 mi n of jct US 50. Ext corridors. **Pets:** $10 daily fee/pet. Service with restrictions, supervision.
(SAVE) ⊠ 🏠 🔲 🍴 🏊

◆◆◆ ◆◆ Best Western Salisbury Plaza **M**
(410) 546-1300. **$59-$129.** 1735 N Salisbury Blvd. US 13 business route, 1.5 mi n of US 50. Ext corridors. **Pets:** $10 daily fee/pet. Service with restrictions, supervision.
(SAVE) (S⊘) ⊠ 🏠 🔲 🏊

◆◆◆ ◆◆◆ Comfort Inn Salisbury **SH**
(410) 543-4666. **$60-$120.** 2701 N Salisbury Blvd. US 13, 0.5 mi n of jct US 13 business route and Bypass. Int corridors. **Pets:** Large. Service with restrictions, crate.
(SAVE) (S⊘) ⊠ 🔗 🏠 🔲 ⊠

SNOW HILL

◆◆◆ River House Inn **BB**
(410) 632-2722. **$120-$250, 7 day notice.** 201 E Market St. 1 mi w on SR 394 from jct SR 113. Ext/int corridors. **Pets:** Accepted.
(ASK) (S⊘) ⊠ 🏠 🔲 🕿

THURMONT

◆◆◆ Rambler Inn **M**
(301) 271-2424. **$62-$82.** US 15 at SR 550. Ext/int corridors. **Pets:** Medium, other species. Service with restrictions, supervision.
(SAVE) (S⊘) ⊠ 🏠

WALDORF

◆◆◆ Hampton Inn Waldorf **SH**
(301) 632-9600. **$96-$129.** 3750 Crain Hwy. On US 301; opposite St Charles Towne Plaza. Int corridors. **Pets:** Accepted.
(ASK) (S⊘) ⊠ (&M) 🏠 🔲 🏊

WHITEHAVEN

◆◆ Whitehaven Bed & Breakfast **BB**
(410) 873-3294. **$85-$100, 7 day notice.** 23844 River St. SR 352 to Whitehaven Rd, then w. Int corridors. **Pets:** Dogs only. Designated rooms, crate.
⊠ 🔲 🕅 🕿

WILLIAMSPORT

◆◆◆ ◆◆ Red Roof Inn **SH**
(301) 582-3500. **$49-$62.** 310 E Potomac St. I-81, exit 2, 0.3 mi sw on US 11. Ext corridors. **Pets:** Medium. Service with restrictions, supervision.
(SAVE) (S⊘) ⊠ 🔗 🏠 🏊

MASSACHUSETTS

CITY INDEX

AMHERST

◆◆◆◆ The Lord Jeffery Inn SH
(413) 253-2576. **$99-$159.** 30 Boltwood Ave. I-91, exit 19, 6 mi e. on SR 9 to Commons. Int corridors. **Pets:** $15 daily fee/pet. Designated rooms, service with restrictions, supervision.

[ASK] [S/] [✕] [🛏] [❄]

◆◆ University Lodge Ⓜ
(413) 256-8111. **$59-$139.** 345 N Pleasant St. 0.6 mi n. Ext corridors. **Pets:** Accepted.

[ASK] [S/] [✕] [💻]

AUBURN

◆◆◆ Baymont Inn & Suites Worcester-Auburn SH
(508) 832-7000. **$99-$119.** 446 Southbridge St. I-90, exit 10, 1.2 mi n on SR 12. Int corridors. **Pets:** Accepted.

[SAVE] [S/] [✕] [🛏] [💻]

BARRE

◆◆◆ Jenkins Inn CI ❀
(978) 355-6444. **$155-$185.** 7 West St. On SR 122 and 32. Int corridors. **Pets:** Dogs only. $5 daily fee/pet. Service with restrictions, supervision.

[SAVE] [S/] [✕] [💻] [❄]

BOSTON METROPOLITAN AREA

ANDOVER

◆◆◆◆ Hawthorn Suites-Andover SH ❀
(978) 475-6000. **$109-$139.** 4 Riverside Dr. I-93, exit 45, 0.5 mi e. Int corridors. **Pets:** Medium, other species. $10 daily fee/room, $50 one-time fee/room. Designated rooms, service with restrictions, crate.

[ASK] [✕] [♿] [🏋] [🐾] [🛏] [💻] [🏊] [✕]

◆◆◆ Residence Inn by Marriott Boston-Andover SH
(978) 683-0382. **$89-$189.** 500 Minuteman Rd. I-93, exit 45, 0.3 mi w, then 0.5 mi n. Int corridors. **Pets:** Other species. $10 daily fee/pet, $100 one-time fee/room. Service with restrictions.

[✕] [♿] [🏋] [💻] [🏊] [✕]

◆◆◆◆ Staybridge Suites Boston/Andover SH
(978) 686-2000. **$85-$153.** 4 Tech Dr. I-93, exit 45, just sw. Int corridors. **Pets:** Accepted.

[ASK] [S/] [✕] [♿] [🐾] [🛏] [💻] [🏊]

◆◆◆ Wyndham Andover LH
(978) 975-3600. **$99-$185.** 123 Old River Rd. I-93, exit 45, just e on River Rd. Int corridors. **Pets:** Small. $50 deposit/pet. Service with restrictions, supervision.

[SAVE] [S/] [✕] [♿] [🏋] [🛏] [💻] [🍴] [🏊] [✕]

BILLERICA

◆◆◆◆ Homewood Suites by Hilton SH ❀
(978) 670-7111. **$125-$152.** 35 Middlesex Tpke. I-95, exit 32B, 2.5 mi n. Int corridors. **Pets:** $150 one-time fee/pet. Service with restrictions.

[ASK] [S/] [✕] [♿] [🏋] [🛏] [💻] [🏊]

BOSTON

◆◆◆◆ Boston Harbor Hotel LH
(617) 439-7000. **Call for rates.** 70 Rowes Wharf. At Rowes Wharf. Int corridors. **Pets:** Accepted.

[✕] [♿] [🍴] [🏊] [✕]

◆◆◆ ◆◆ The Eliot Hotel SH
(617) 267-1607. **$255-$415.** 370 Commonwealth Ave. Corner of Commonwealth and Massachusetts aves. Int corridors. **Pets:** Other species. Service with restrictions, crate.

[SAVE] [✕] [♿] [🏋] [🍴]

◆◆◆ ◆◆ The Fairmont Copley Plaza Boston LH
(617) 267-5300. **$179-$499.** 138 St. James Ave. At Copley Square. Int corridors. **Pets:** Accepted.

[SAVE] [S/] [✕] [♿] [🏋] [🛏] [🍴]

Four Seasons Hotel
Boston 🄻🄷 ❖
(617) 338-4400. **$425-$815.** 200 Boylston St. Between Arlington and Charles sts. Int corridors. **Pets:** Small, other species. Designated rooms, service with restrictions, supervision.
[SAVE] ⊠ 🄼 ⬚ ⬚ 🍴 ⟿ ⊠

Hilton Boston Back Bay 🄻🄷
(617) 236-1100. **$99-$329.** 40 Dalton St. At Dalton and Belvidere sts. Int corridors. **Pets:** Small. $50 deposit/room. Service with restrictions, supervision.
⊠ ⬚ ⬚ ⬚ ⬚ ⟿

Hilton Boston Logan
Airport 🄻🄷
(617) 568-6700. **$99-$279.** 85 Terminal Rd. At General Edward Lawrence Logan International Airport. Int corridors. **Pets:** Other species. Designated rooms.
[SAVE] ⊠ 🄼 ⬚ ⬚ ⬚ ⬚ 🍴 ⟿ ⊠

Howard Johnson Hotel Fenway 🅂🄷
(617) 267-8300. **$109-$279.** 1271 Boylston St. I-90, exit Brookline Ave S, backing onto Fenway Park. Int corridors. **Pets:** Accepted.
⊠ ⬚ ⬚ 🍴 ⟿

Le Meridien 🄻🄷
(617) 451-1900. **$270-$375.** 250 Franklin St. Center; on Post Office Square. Int corridors. **Pets:** Accepted.
[ASK] ⊠ ⬚ ⬚ ⬚ 🍴 ⟿ ⊠

Marriott Residence Inn Boston
Harbor 🅂🄷 ❖
(617) 242-9000. **$200-$300.** 44 Charles River Ave. Just se of SR 99 at Charlestown Bridge. Int corridors. **Pets:** Other species. $150 one-time fee/room. Service with restrictions.
[ASK] [SAVE] ⊠ 🄼 ⬚ ⬚ ⬚ ⬚ ⟿

Omni Parker House 🄻🄷
(617) 227-8600. **$169-$319.** 60 School St. Corner of Tremont and School sts; northeast corner of Boston Common. Int corridors. **Pets:** Small. $50 one-time fee/room. Service with restrictions, crate.
[ASK] [SAVE] ⊠ ⬚ 🍴

Ramada Inn Boston 🅂🄷
(617) 287-9100. **$89-$269.** 800 William T Morrissey Blvd. I-93, exit 13 northbound, 0.5 mi sw; exit 12 southbound, follow signs. Int corridors. **Pets:** Other species. $50 deposit/room. Service with restrictions, supervision.
[SAVE] [SAVE] ⊠ ⬚ ⬚ ⟿

The Ritz-Carlton, Boston 🄻🄷
(617) 536-5700. **$275-$595.** 15 Arlington St. At Arlington and Newbury sts; overlooks the Public Gardens. Int corridors. **Pets:** Accepted.
⊠ ⬚ ⬚ 🍴 ⊠

The Ritz-Carlton Boston
Common 🅂🄷 ❖
(617) 574-7100. **$275-$595.** 10 Avery St. At Washington and Avery sts; 1 blk e of Boston Common. Int corridors. **Pets:** Large. $30 daily fee/room. Supervision.
⊠ 🄼 ⬚ ⬚ 🍴

Seaport Hotel 🄻🄷 ❖
(617) 385-4000. **$159-$289.** 1 Seaport Ln. At World Trade Center/Commonwealth Pier. Int corridors. **Pets:** Medium, other species. Service with restrictions, supervision.
[SAVE] [SAVE] ⊠ 🄼 ⬚ ⬚ ⬚ ⬚ 🍴 ⟿ ⊠

Sheraton Boston Hotel 🄻🄷 ❖
(617) 236-2000. **$149-$409, 7 day notice.** 39 Dalton St. I-90, exit 22. Int corridors. **Pets:** Medium, dogs only. Designated rooms, service with restrictions, supervision.
[ASK] [SAVE] ⊠ 🄼 ⬚ ⬚ ⬚ ⬚ 🍴 ⟿ ⊠

BOXBOROUGH

Holiday Inn Boxborough Woods 🅂🄷
(978) 263-8701. **$109-$229.** 242 Adams Pl. I-495, exit 28, just e on SR 111. Int corridors. **Pets:** Small. $25 one-time fee/pet. Designated rooms, service with restrictions, crate.
[ASK] [SAVE] ⊠ ⬚ ⬚ ⬚ 🍴 ⟿

BROOKLINE

Holiday Inn Brookline 🅂🄷
(617) 277-1200. **$169-$199.** 1200 Beacon St. 1 mi sw of Kenmore Square; at Beacon and St. Paul sts. Int corridors. **Pets:** Accepted.
[ASK] ⊠ 🄼 ⬚ ⬚ ⬚ ⬚ 🍴 ⟿

BURLINGTON

Four Points by Sheraton Burlington 🅂🄷
(781) 272-8800. **$99-$169.** 30 Wheeler Rd. I-95 and SR 128, exit 32B, just s. Int corridors. **Pets:** Accepted.
[ASK] [SAVE] ⊠ 🄼 ⬚ ⬚ ⬚ ⬚ 🍴 ⟿

Homestead Studio Suites
Hotel-Boston/Burlington 🅂🄷 ❖
(781) 359-9099. **$91-$105.** 40 South Ave. I-95 and SR 128, exit 32B, just n. Int corridors. **Pets:** Medium, other species. $25 daily fee/room. Service with restrictions, crate.
[ASK] [SAVE] ⊠ ⬚ ⬚ ⬚ ⬚

Staybridge Suites Boston-Burlington 🅂🄷
(781) 221-2233. **$116-$181.** 11 Old Concord Rd. I-95 and SR 128, exit 32B, just s on Middlesex Tpke. Int corridors. **Pets:** Accepted.
[ASK] [SAVE] ⊠ 🄼 ⬚ ⬚ ⬚ ⬚ ⟿

Summerfield Suites by
Wyndham-Boston/Burlington 🅂🄷 ❖
(781) 270-0800. **$99-$179.** 2 Van de Graaff Dr. I-95 and SR 128, exit 33A, just s on US 3, then 0.5 mi w on Wayside Rd. Int corridors. **Pets:** Medium. $5 daily fee/room, $150 one-time fee/room. Service with restrictions, crate.
[ASK] [SAVE] ⊠ 🄼 ⬚ ⬚ ⬚ ⬚ ⟿ ⊠

CAMBRIDGE

The Charles Hotel, Harvard
Square 🄻🄷
(617) 864-1200. **$179-$269.** One Bennett St. Corner of Eliot and Bennett sts; just s of Harvard Square. Int corridors. **Pets:** Medium. $50 one-time fee/pet. Service with restrictions, supervision.
[SAVE] [SAVE] ⊠ 🄼 ⬚ ⬚ ⬚ 🍴 ⟿ ⊠

▼▼▼▼ **Hotel @ MIT** 🆂🅷
(617) 577-0200. **$219-$329.** 20 Sidney St. On SR 2A, 1 mi n of the river. Int corridors. **Pets:** Service with restrictions, crate.

[X] [&M] [⊘] [⬩] [📶] [💻] [🍴]

🅐🅐🅐 ▼▼▼ ▼▼▼ **Hotel Marlowe** 🆂🅷 ❖
(617) 867-8000. **$119-$259.** 25 Edwin H Land Blvd. Just sw of jct SR 28. Int corridors. **Pets:** Other species. Service with restrictions, supervision.

[SAVE] [S📶] [X] [&M] [⊘] [⬩] [💻] [🍴]

▼▼▼▼ **Residence Inn by Marriott Cambridge** 🅛🅗
(617) 349-0700. **$249-$349.** 6 Cambridge Center. Corner of Ames St and Broadway. Int corridors. **Pets:** Other species. $10 daily fee/pet, $100 one-time fee/room. Service with restrictions.

[X] [&M] [⊘] [⬩] [📶] [💻] [🔀]

▼▼▼▼ **Sheraton Commander Hotel** 🆂🅷 ❖
(617) 547-4800. **$125-$315, 3 day notice.** 16 Garden St. Just n of Harvard Square. Int corridors. **Pets:** Medium, dogs only. Service with restrictions, supervision.

[ASK] [S📶] [X] [⊘] [⬩] [📶] [💻] [🍴]

CONCORD

▼▼ ▼ **Best Western at Historic Concord** 🆂🅷
(978) 369-6100. **$99-$139.** 740 Elm St. 1.8 mi w, just off SR 2 and 2A. Int corridors. **Pets:** Other species. $10 daily fee/room. Designated rooms, service with restrictions, supervision.

[ASK] [S📶] [X] [📶] [💻] [🔀]

DANVERS

▼▼▼▼ **Residence Inn by Marriott** 🆂🅷 ❖
(978) 777-7171. **$119-$149.** 51 Newbury St (Rt 1). US 1 N, just s of jct SR 114. Ext corridors. **Pets:** $10 daily fee/pet, $100 one-time fee/room. Service with restrictions, crate.

[ASK] [S📶] [X] [⬩] [📶] [💻] [🔀] [X]

🅐🅐🅐 ▼▼▼▼ **Sheraton Ferncroft Resort** 🅛🅗 ❖
(978) 777-2500. **$139-$159.** 50 Ferncroft Rd. I-95, exit 50, follow signs for US 1 S to Ferncroft Village. Int corridors. **Pets:** Medium, dogs only. Service with restrictions, supervision.

[SAVE] [X] [&M] [⊘] [⬩] [📶] [💻] [🍴] [🔀] [X]

▼▼▼▼ **TownePlace Suites by Marriott** 🆂🅷
(978) 777-6222. **$79-$149.** 238 Andover St. Southwest corner of jct US 1 and SR 114; SR 114 eastbound, enter just w of US 1 (no westbound entrance); US 1 southbound, enter through shopping center. Int corridors. **Pets:** Other species. $10 daily fee/room, $50 one-time fee/room. Designated rooms, service with restrictions, supervision.

[ASK] [X] [&M] [⊘] [⬩] [📶] [💻] [🔀]

DEDHAM

🅐🅐🅐 ▼▼▼▼ **Residence Inn by Marriott** 🆂🅷
(781) 407-0999. **$170.** 259 Elm St. I-95, exit 15A, 0.3 mi n on US 1, then 0.4 mi e. Int corridors. **Pets:** Other species. $10 daily fee/pet, $100 one-time fee/pet.

[SAVE] [X] [⊘] [⬩] [📶] [💻] [🔀] [X]

FOXBORO

▼▼▼▼ **Foxborough Residence Inn by Marriott** 🆂🅷 ❖
(508) 698-2800. **$119-$195.** 250 Foxborough Blvd. I-95, exit 7A, 0.6 mi s on SR 140, 0.7 mi e, then just n. Int corridors. **Pets:** Other species. $10 daily fee/room, $150 one-time fee/room. Service with restrictions, crate.

[X] [&M] [⬩] [📶] [💻] [🔀] [X]

FRAMINGHAM

▼▼ ▼ **Best Western Framingham** 🆂🅷
(508) 872-8811. **$99-$139.** 130 Worcester Rd. I-90 (Massachusetts Tpke), exit 13, 0.5 mi s to SR 9, 1 mi w of Speen St; just w of Shopper's World Mall. Int corridors. **Pets:** Accepted.

[ASK] [S📶] [X] [⬩] [💻] [🍴] [🔀]

🅐🅐🅐 ▼▼▼ **Red Roof Inn** 🅜
(508) 872-4499. **$66-$93.** 650 Cochituate Rd. I-90 (Massachusetts Tpke), exit 13, e on SR 9 in Natick, 0.8 mi n on Speen St, then just w on SR 30, follow signs for Massachusetts Tpke. Ext corridors. **Pets:** Accepted.

[SAVE] [X] [⬩] [💻]

▼▼▼▼ **Residence Inn by Marriott** 🆂🅷
(508) 370-0001. **$149-$219.** 400 Staples Dr. SR 9 W to Crossing Blvd, then s. Int corridors. **Pets:** Medium, other species. $150 one-time fee/room. Crate.

[ASK] [S📶] [X] [&M] [⊘] [⬩] [📶] [💻] [🔀]

FRANKLIN

▼▼▼▼ **Franklin Residence Inn by Marriott** 🆂🅷 ❖
(508) 541-8188. **$89-$179.** 4 Forge Pkwy. I-495, exit 17, 0.7 mi nw off SR 140 N. Int corridors. **Pets:** Other species. $10 daily fee/room, $100 one-time fee/room. Service with restrictions, crate.

[ASK] [X] [&M] [⊘] [⬩] [📶] [💻] [🔀]

🅐🅐🅐 ▼▼▼▼ **Hawthorn Suites Ltd** 🆂🅷
(508) 553-3500. **$99-$219.** 835 Upper Union St. I-495, exit 16, just s, then 0.3 mi e. Int corridors. **Pets:** Medium. $5 daily fee/room, $75 one-time fee/room. Service with restrictions, supervision.

[SAVE] [S📶] [X] [&M] [⊘] [⬩] [📶] [💻] [🔀] [X]

GLOUCESTER

▼▼ ▼ **Cape Ann Motor Inn** 🅜
(978) 281-2900. **$75-$250, 7 day notice.** 33 Rockport Rd. 2 mi n of terminus of SR 128 via SR 127A. Ext corridors. **Pets:** Large, other species. Service with restrictions, supervision.

[X] [⬩] [💻] [🏖]

🅐🅐🅐 ▼▼▼ **The Manor Inn** 🅑🅑
(978) 283-0614. **$69-$154.** 141 Essex Ave. On SR 133, 2.3 mi e of exit 14 (SR 128). Ext/int corridors. **Pets:** Other species. $15 daily fee/room. Designated rooms, service with restrictions, supervision.

[SAVE] [X]

LAWRENCE

▼▼▼▼ **Hampton Inn Boston/North Andover** SH ❀

(978) 975-4050. **$80-$130.** 224 Winthrop Ave. I-495, exit 42A, just s on SR 114. Int corridors. **Pets:** Other species. $15 daily fee/pet. Service with restrictions, supervision.

A$K S⦶ ✕ &M ⬡ 🛡 ❚ ▣

LYNN

▼▼▼▼ **Diamond District Inn** BB ❀

(781) 599-5122. **$145-$200, 14 day notice.** 142 Ocean St. 0.8 mi s of SR 129, eastern terminus of SR 129A via Wolcott St. Ext/int corridors. **Pets:** Small, dogs only. Designated rooms, supervision.

✕

MARLBOROUGH

▼▼▼▼ **Embassy Suites Hotel-Boston Marlborough** LH

(508) 485-5900. **$109-$169.** 123 Boston Post Rd W. I-495, exit 24B, 0.5 mi w, just off US 20. Int corridors. **Pets:** Accepted.

A$K S⦶ ✕ &M ⬡ &E ❚ ▣ 🍴 ▭

▼▼ **Homestead Studio Suites Hotel-Boston/Marlborough** SH ❀

(508) 490-9911. **$84-$92.** 19 Northborough Rd E. I-495, exit 24B, just w on US 20. Int corridors. **Pets:** Medium, other species. $25 daily fee/room. Service with restrictions, crate.

A$K S⦶ ✕ ⬡ &E ❚ ▣

MEDFORD

Ⓐ ▼▼▼▼ **AmeriSuites (Boston/Medford)** SH

(781) 395-8500. **$119-$179.** 116 Riverside Ave NE. I-93, exit 32, just sw via SR 60 and River St. Int corridors. **Pets:** Very small, other species. $50 one-time fee/room. Service with restrictions, crate.

SAVE S⦶ ✕ &M ⬡ &E ❚ ▣ ▭

NEWTON

▼▼▼▼ **Holiday Inn Newton** SH ❀

(617) 969-5300. **$139-$189.** 399 Grove St. I-95, exit 22, just e; 0.3 mi s of I-90 (Massachusetts Tpke). Int corridors. **Pets:** Small. $25 one-time fee/room. Service with restrictions, supervision.

A$K S⦶ ✕ ⬡ &E ❚ ▣ 🍴 ▭

▼▼▼▼ **Sheraton Newton Hotel** LH ❀

(617) 969-3010. **$99-$175.** 320 Washington St. I-90 (Massachusetts Tpke), exit 17 (SR 16). Int corridors. **Pets:** Medium, dogs only. Service with restrictions, supervision.

A$K S⦶ ✕ ⬡ &E ❚ ▣ 🍴 ▭

NORTH CHELMSFORD

▼▼▼▼ **Hawthorn Suites, LTD** SH

(978) 256-5151. **$109-$149.** 25 Research Pl. US 3, exit 32, 0.3 mi ne on SR 4. Int corridors. **Pets:** Medium. $10 daily fee/room, $50 one-time fee/room. Designated rooms.

A$K ✕ &M &E ❚ ▣ ▭

PEABODY

▼▼▼▼ **Homestead Studio Suites Hotel-Boston/Peabody** SH ❀

(978) 531-6632. **$109-$113.** 200 Jubilee Dr. SR 128, exit 28, just s to Centennial Dr, w to the end, n to Jubilee Dr, then 1.1 mi e. Int corridors. **Pets:** Medium, other species. $25 daily fee/room. Service with restrictions, crate.

A$K S⦶ ✕ ⬡ &E ❚ ▣ ▭

REVERE

▼▼▼▼ **Comfort Inn & Suites Boston Airport** SH

(781) 485-3600. **$99-$229.** 85 American Legion Hwy. Jct SR 1A and 60, 3 mi n of General Edward Lawrence Logan International Airport. Int corridors. **Pets:** Medium, other species. $10 daily fee/room. Designated rooms.

A$K S⦶ ✕ &E ❚ ▣ 🍴 ▭

▼▼▼▼ **Hampton Inn Boston Logan Airport** SH

(781) 286-5665. **$109-$189.** 230 Lee Burbank Hwy. On SR 1A; 1.9 mi n of General Edward Lawrence Logan International Airport; 0.6 mi s of terminus SR 60. Int corridors. **Pets:** Accepted.

A$K S⦶ ✕ &M ⬡ &E ❚ ▣ ▭

ROCKPORT

Ⓐ ▼▼▼ **Sandy Bay Motor Inn** SH

(978) 546-7155. **$90-$165, 7 day notice.** 183 Main St. 0.5 mi s on SR 127. Ext/int corridors. **Pets:** Accepted.

SAVE S⦶ ✕ ❚ 🍴 ▭ ✕

SALEM

▼▼▼▼ **Hawthorne Hotel** SH

(978) 744-4080. **$104-$189, 3 day notice.** 18 Washington Square W. On SR 1A. Int corridors. **Pets:** Other species. $8 daily fee/room. Service with restrictions, supervision.

A$K S⦶ ✕ ❚ 🍴

▼▼▼▼ **The Salem Inn** BB

(978) 741-0680. **$119-$230, 7 day notice.** 7 Summer St. On SR 114 at jct Essex St; SR 128, exit 25A, 3 mi e. Int corridors. **Pets:** Other species. $15 daily fee/pet. Designated rooms, service with restrictions, supervision.

✕ ▭

SAUGUS

Ⓐ ▼▼ **Red Roof Inn** SH

(781) 941-1400. **$79-$99.** 920 Broadway. I-95, exit 44 northbound; exit Main St/Saugus southbound to U-turn. Int corridors. **Pets:** Accepted.

SAVE ✕ &M ⬡ ❚

SUDBURY

▼▼▼▼ **Clarion Carriage House Inn** SH

(978) 443-2223. **$139-$250.** 738 Boston Post Rd. I-495, exit 24A, 4.7 mi w of jct SR 27 on US 20. Int corridors. **Pets:** Large, other species. $10 daily fee/pet. Service with restrictions, supervision.

A$K S⦶ ✕ ❚ ▣

TEWKSBURY

▼▼ **Motel 6 Boston-Tewksbury #1403** Ⓜ
(978) 851-8677. **$66-$76.** 95 Main St. I-495, exit 38, just s on SR 38. Ext corridors. **Pets:** Small. Service with restrictions, supervision.
⊠ 🐾 🏊

▼▼▼ Residence Inn by
Marriott-Boston/Tewksbury 🄢🄷 🐾
(978) 640-1003. **$79-$179.** 1775 Andover St. I-495, exit 39, 0.3 mi w on SR 133. Ext corridors. **Pets:** Other species. $10 daily fee/pet, $100 one-time fee/room. Service with restrictions, crate.
🄰🄺 🖃 ⊠ 🖫 🔏 🖎 🔒 🖥 🏊 🐾

▼▼▼ **TownePlace Suites by Marriott** 🄢🄷
(978) 863-9800. **$99-$159.** 20 International Pl. I-495, exit 39, 0.3 mi nw. Int corridors. **Pets:** Other species. $6.50 daily fee/room, $100 one-time fee/room. Service with restrictions, supervision.
🄰🄺 🖃 ⊠ 🖫 🔏 🖎 🔒 🖥 🏊

WALTHAM

▼▼ Homestead Studio Suites
Hotel-Boston/Waltham 🄢🄷 🐾
(781) 890-1333. **$105-$118.** 52 Fourth Ave. I-95, exit 27A, just se; behind The Westin, Waltham-Boston. Int corridors. **Pets:** Medium, other species. $25 daily fee/room. Service with restrictions, crate.
🄰🄺 🖃 ⊠ 🔏 🖎 🔒 🖥

🄰🄰🄰 ▼▼▼ Summerfield Suites by
Wyndham-Waltham/Boston 🄢🄷 🐾
(781) 290-0026. **$99-$219.** 54 Fourth Ave. I-95, exit 27A, just e; behind The Westin, Waltham-Boston. Int corridors. **Pets:** Medium, other species. $150 one-time fee/pet. Designated rooms.
🄢🄰🅅🄴 🖃 ⊠ 🖫 🔏 🖎 🔒 🖥 🏊 🐾

WESTFORD

▼▼▼ **Residence Inn by Marriott** 🄢🄷
(978) 392-1407. **$139-$189.** 7 Lan Dr. I-495, exit 32, just s, then 0.5 w on SR 110. Int corridors. **Pets:** Accepted.
🄰🄺 🖃 ⊠ 🖫 🔏 🔒 🖥 🏊 🐾

WOBURN

▼▼▼ **Radisson Hotel Woburn** 🄢🄷
(781) 935-8760. **$90-$200.** 15 Middlesex Canal Park Rd. I-95 and SR 128, exit 35, s via SR 38. Int corridors. **Pets:** Dogs only. $50 deposit/room. Service with restrictions, supervision.
🄰🄺 🖃 ⊠ 🖫 🔏 🖎 🔒 🖥 🍽 🏊

🄰🄰🄰 ▼▼▼ **Red Roof Inn Woburn** 🄢🄷
(781) 935-7110. **$75-$110.** 19 Commerce Way. I-95, exit 36, just n, then just w on Mishawum Rd. Int corridors. **Pets:** Accepted.
🄢🄰🅅🄴 ⊠ 🖎 🖫 🔒 🏊

▼▼▼ Residence Inn by
Marriott-Boston/Woburn 🄢🄷
(781) 376-4000. **$169.** 300 Presidential Way. I-93, exit 37C, just nw. Int corridors. **Pets:** Accepted.
🄰🄺 🖃 ⊠ 🖎 🔏 🖫 🔒 🖥 🏊

🐾 **END METROPOLITAN AREA** 🐾

BROCKTON

▼▼▼ **Residence Inn by Marriott** 🄢🄷
(508) 583-3600. **$89-$209.** 124 Liberty St. SR 24, exit 17B, just w, just s on Pearl St, then 0.3 mi se via Mill St connector. Int corridors. **Pets:** Other species. $10 daily fee/pet, $150 one-time fee/pet. Service with restrictions, crate.
🄰🄺 🖃 ⊠ 🖎 🖫 🔒 🖥 🏊

CAPE COD AREA

BUZZARDS BAY

🄰🄰🄰 ▼▼▼ **Bay Motor Inn** 🄒🄐
(508) 759-3989. **$51-$119, 10 day notice.** 223 Main St. SR 25, 0.5 mi w of Bourne rotary, exit 2. Ext corridors. **Pets:** $10 daily fee/room. Service with restrictions, supervision.
🄢🄰🅅🄴 🖃 🔒 🖥 🏊

CENTERVILLE

🄰🄰🄰 ▼▼▼ **The Inn at Centerville Corners** Ⓜ
(508) 775-7223. **$50-$160, 10 day notice.** 369 S Main St. 1 mi s of SR 28, jct Craigville Beach Rd. Ext corridors. **Pets:** Medium, dogs only. $5 daily fee/pet. Service with restrictions.
🄢🄰🅅🄴 ⊠ 🔒 🏊

FALMOUTH

▼▼ Capeside Cottage Bed & Breakfast 🄱🄱
(508) 548-6218. **$100-$180, 15 day notice.** 320 Woods Hole Rd. 2.2 mi s on SR 28. Int corridors. **Pets:** Accepted.
⊠ 🖧 ➔ 🆆 📞

🄰🄰🄰 ▼▼ Mariner Motel 🄼
(508) 548-1331. **$59-$159, 14 day notice.** 555 Main St. 0.5 mi e on SR 28. Ext corridors. **Pets:** Dogs only. $15 daily fee/pet. Supervision.
🆂🄰🅅🄴 ⊠ 🖧 ➔

HYANNIS

▼▼▼ Comfort Inn 🆂🄷 ❀
(508) 771-4804. **$89-$209.** 1470 Rt 132. US 6, exit 6, 1.3 mi se. Ext/int corridors. **Pets:** Large, other species. $50 deposit/room. Designated rooms, service with restrictions, crate.
🄰🅂🄺 🆂🄰 ⊠ 🖧 🖧 📺 ➔ ⊠

ORLEANS

🄰🄰🄰 ▼▼▼ Skaket Beach Motel 🄼 ❀
(508) 255-1020. **$53-$149.** 203 Cranberry Hwy (Rt 6A). US 6, exit 12, just e. Ext corridors. **Pets:** $9 daily fee/pet. Supervision.
🆂🄰🅅🄴 ⊠ 🖧 📺 ➔

PROVINCETOWN

▼▼▼ Bayshore & Chandler 🄲🄾
(508) 487-9133. **$100-$250.** 493 Commercial St. 0.8 mi e of Town Hall. Ext corridors. **Pets:** $15 daily fee/pet. Service with restrictions.
🖧 📺

🄰🄰🄰 ▼▼ Cape Inn 🆂🄷
(508) 487-1711. **$69-$179, 3 day notice.** 698 Commercial St. 1.5 mi se on SR 6A. Ext corridors. **Pets:** Accepted.
🆂🄰🅅🄴 🆂🄰 ⊠ 🖧 🖧 📺 🍴 ➔

▼▼ Surfside Hotel & Suites 🆂🄷 ❀
(508) 487-1726. **$89-$475.** 542-543 Commercial St. 1 mi e of Town Hall. Ext corridors. **Pets:** Medium, dogs only. $20 daily fee/pet. Designated rooms, service with restrictions, crate.
🄰🅂🄺 🆂🄰 ⊠ 🖧 📺 ➔

▼▼▼ White Wind Inn 🄱🄱
(508) 487-1526. **$80-$235, 14 day notice.** 174 Commercial St. Just w of Town Hall. Int corridors. **Pets:** Dogs only. $10 daily fee/pet. Designated rooms.
⊠ 🖧

SANDWICH

▼▼ The Earl of Sandwich Motel 🄼
(508) 888-1415. **$55-$109, 7 day notice.** 378 Rt 6A. At MM 5.1. Ext corridors. **Pets:** Other species. Designated rooms, service with restrictions, supervision.
⊠ 🖧 ➔

🄰🄰🄰 ▼▼ Sandwich Lodge & Resort 🄼
(508) 888-2275. **$59-$129, 7 day notice.** 54 Rt 6A. 1 mi w. Ext/int corridors. **Pets:** Other species. $15 one-time fee/pet. Designated rooms, service with restrictions, supervision.
🆂🄰🅅🄴 🆂🄰 ⊠ 🖧 ➔ ⊠

❀ **END AREA** ❀

DEERFIELD

▼▼▼ Deerfield Inn 🄲🄸
(413) 774-5587. **$125-$200, 7 day notice.** 81 Old Main St. Center. Int corridors. **Pets:** Medium, dogs only. $15 daily fee/pet. Designated rooms, service with restrictions, supervision.
🄰🅂🄺 🆂🄰 ⊠ 🍴

FITCHBURG

🄰🄰🄰 ▼▼▼ Best Western Royal Plaza Hotel & Trade Center 🄻🄷
(978) 342-7100. **$119-$139.** 150 Royal Plaza Dr. Just s on SR 31; SR 2, exit 28. Int corridors. **Pets:** Accepted.
🆂🄰🅅🄴 🆂🄰 ⊠ 🖧 🖧 📺 🍴 ➔ ⊠

GARDNER

▼▼ Super 8 Motel 🄼
(978) 630-2888. **$79-$105.** 22 Pearson Blvd. SR 2, exit 23, just n. Int corridors. **Pets:** Small. $11 daily fee/pet. Service with restrictions, supervision.
🄰🅂🄺 🆂🄰 ⊠ 🖧

GREENFIELD

🄰🄰🄰 ▼▼▼ The Brandt House B&B 🄱🄱 ❀
(413) 774-3329. **$100-$280.** 29 Highland Ave. I-91, exit 26, 1.8 mi e on SR 2A, then se via Cresent St. Int corridors. **Pets:** Dogs only. $25 one-time fee/pet. Service with restrictions, supervision.
🆂🄰🅅🄴 ⊠ 🖧

HADLEY

▼▼▼ Howard Johnson 🆂🄷
(413) 586-0114. **$69-$149.** 401 Russell St. I-91, exit 19 northbound, 4.3 mi e on SR 9; exit 24 southbound, 10 mi s on SR 116, then just w on SR 9. Int corridors. **Pets:** Medium, other species. $20 daily fee/room. Designated rooms, service with restrictions, supervision.
🄰🅂🄺 🆂🄰 ⊠ 🖧 🖧 📺 ➔

🄰🄰🄰 ▼▼▼ Quality Inn 🆂🄷
(413) 584-9816. **$55-$170.** 237 Russell St. I-91, exit 19 northbound; exit 20 southbound, 3 mi e on SR 9. Int corridors. **Pets:** Small, dogs only. $25 daily fee/pet. Supervision.
🆂🄰🅅🄴 🆂🄰 ⊠ 🖧 🖧 📺 ➔

HANCOCK

▼▼▼ Jericho Valley Inn Ⓜ
(413) 458-9511. **$68-$138, 14 day notice.** On SR 43, 5 mi s of jct US 7. Ext/int corridors. **Pets:** Designated rooms.
Ⓐ🆂🅺 🆂ⓓ ⊠ 🔒 🖵 🗪

LANESBORO

Ⓐ🅐🅐 ▼▼ Mt View Motel Ⓜ
(413) 442-1009. **$48-$145, 7 day notice.** 499 S Main St. 1 mi s on US 7. Ext corridors. **Pets:** Medium. $10 daily fee/pet. Designated rooms, service with restrictions, supervision.
🆂🅰🆅🅴 🆂ⓓ ⊠ 🔒

Ⓐ🅐🅐 ▼▼ The Weathervane Motel Ⓜ
(413) 443-3230. **$35-$125, 14 day notice.** 475 S Main St. 1.3 mi s on US 7. Ext corridors. **Pets:** Designated rooms, no service, supervision.
🆂🅰🆅🅴 🆂ⓓ ⊠ 🔒 🖵

LENOX

▼▼ Seven Hills Country Inn & Restaurant 🆂🅷 🐾
(413) 637-0060. **$85-$340.** 40 Plunkett St. Jct US 7/20, 0.6 mi e on US 20, then 0.8 mi s. Ext/int corridors. **Pets:** Other species. $20 daily fee/pet. Designated rooms.
⊠ 🅵 🔒 🖵 🍴 🗪 ⊠

MANSFIELD

Ⓐ🅐🅐 ▼▼ Red Roof Inn 🆂🅷
(508) 339-2323. **$72-$90.** 60 Forbes Blvd. I-95, exit 7A, 1.3 mi n of jct; I-495, exit 12, just off SR 140. Int corridors. **Pets:** Accepted.
🆂🅰🆅🅴 ⊠ 🅵 🔒 🗪

MIDDLEBORO

Ⓐ🅐🅐 ▼▼ Days Inn-Plymouth/Middleboro 🆂🅷 🐾
(508) 946-4400. **$66-$119.** 30 E Clark St. I-495, exit 4 at SR 105. Int corridors. **Pets:** $3 daily fee/pet. Service with restrictions, supervision.
🆂🅰🆅🅴 🆂ⓓ ⊠ 🅵 🔒 🖵 🗪

MILFORD

▼▼ Days Inn 🆂🅷
(508) 634-2499. **$60-$110.** 3 Fortune Blvd. I-495, exit 20, 0.3 mi s on SR 85, then just e. Int corridors. **Pets:** Accepted.
Ⓐ🆂🅺 🆂ⓓ ⊠ 🅵 🔒 🖵

▼▼▼ Holiday Inn Express 🆂🅷 🐾
(508) 634-1054. **$79-$129.** 50 Fortune Blvd. I-495, exit 20, just sw on SR 85, then just se. Int corridors. **Pets:** Other species. $25 one-time fee/room. Designated rooms, service with restrictions, supervision.
Ⓐ🆂🅺 🆂ⓓ ⊠ 🆖 🅐 🅵 🔒 🖵 🗪

ORANGE

Ⓐ🅐🅐 ▼▼ Executive Inn Ⓜ
(978) 544-8864. **$55-$85, 7 day notice.** 110 Daniel Shay Hwy. US 202, exit 16, just n of jct SR 2. Ext/int corridors. **Pets:** Medium. $7 daily fee/pet. Service with restrictions, supervision.
🆂🅰🆅🅴 🆂ⓓ ⊠ 🔒

PITTSFIELD

▼▼▼▼ Crowne Plaza Hotel and Resort Pittsfield Berkshires 🅻🅷
(413) 499-2000. **$145-$189.** 1 West St, Berkshire Common. Center. Int corridors. **Pets:** Accepted.
Ⓐ🆂🅺 🆂ⓓ ⊠ 🆖 🅐 🅵 🔒 🖵 🍴 🗪 ⊠

RAYNHAM

▼▼ Days Inn Taunton Ⓜ
(508) 824-8647. **$59-$109, 15 day notice.** 164 New State Hwy. SR 24, exit 13B, 0.8 mi w on US 44. Ext/int corridors. **Pets:** Small. Service with restrictions, supervision.
Ⓐ🆂🅺 🆂ⓓ ⊠ 🅵 🗪

REHOBOTH

▼▼▼▼ Five Bridge Inn Bed & Breakfast 🅱🅱 🐾
(508) 252-3190. **$88-$125.** 154 Pine St. 1.6 mi n of US 44, 3.3 mi w of jct SR 118; US 44, n on Blanding, e on Broad, n on Salisbury, then w. Int corridors. **Pets:** Medium, other species. $10 one-time fee/room. Designated rooms.
Ⓐ🆂🅺 🆂ⓓ ⊠ 🔒 🖵 🗪

SEEKONK

▼▼ Motel 6-1289 🆂🅷
(508) 336-7800. **$55-$75.** 821 Fall River Ave. I-195, exit 1, just n on SR 114A. Int corridors. **Pets:** Medium, other species. Service with restrictions, supervision.
🆂ⓓ ⊠ 🅐 🅵

SOMERSET

▼▼ Quality Inn-Fall River/Somerset 🆂🅷
(508) 678-4545. **$69-$159.** 1878 Wilbur Ave. Jct SR 103 and I-195, exit 4 eastbound; exit 4A westbound. Int corridors. **Pets:** Accepted.
Ⓐ🆂🅺 🆂ⓓ ⊠ 🔒 🖵 🗪 ⊠

SOUTHBOROUGH

Ⓐ🅐🅐 ▼▼▼ Red Roof Inn Ⓜ
(508) 481-3904. **$64-$89.** 367 Turnpike Rd. I-495, exit 23A, just e on SR 9. Ext corridors. **Pets:** Other species. Service with restrictions.
🆂🅰🆅🅴 ⊠ 🔒

SPRINGFIELD

Ⓐ🅐🅐 ▼▼▼ Holiday Inn 🅻🅷
(413) 781-0900. **$114-$149.** 711 Dwight St. I-291, exit 2A, just e. Int corridors. **Pets:** $35 one-time fee/room. Service with restrictions, supervision.
🆂🅰🆅🅴 🆂ⓓ ⊠ 🆖 🅐 🔒 🖵 🍴 🗪 ⊠

STURBRIDGE

Comfort Inn & Suites Colonial SH
(508) 347-3306. **$85-$215.** 215 Charlton Rd. I-90, exit 9, 0.5 mi e; I-84, exit 3A. Ext/int corridors. **Pets:** $15 daily fee/pet. Designated rooms, service with restrictions.

Days Inn M
(508) 347-3391. **$59-$140.** 66-68 Haynes St (SR 15). I-84, exit 2, 0.5 mi n, follow signs to SR 131, on I-84 service road. Ext/int corridors. **Pets:** Other species. $7 daily fee/room. Service with restrictions, crate.

Green Acres Motel M
(508) 347-3496. **$75-$119.** 2 Shepard Rd (SR 131). 1.4 mi s of jct US 20. Ext corridors. **Pets:** Service with restrictions, supervision.

Publick House Historic Inn & Country Lodge M
(508) 347-3313. **$79-$165.** 295 Main St. I-90, exit 9; I-84, exit 3B, 0.5 mi s of jct US 20. Ext/int corridors. **Pets:** Accepted.

Quality Inn & Conference Center SH
(508) 347-1978. **$59-$149.** 400 Haynes Rd (SR 15). I-84, exit 1, 0.5 mi w. Int corridors. **Pets:** Accepted.

Rodeway Inn M
(508) 347-9673. **$55-$145.** 172 Main St. On SR 131, 1.4 mi s of jct US 20. Ext corridors. **Pets:** $10 daily fee/pet. Service with restrictions, supervision.

Sturbridge Coach Motor Lodge M
(508) 347-7327. **$65-$135.** 408 Main St (US 20). I-90, exit 9, 0.8 mi w; I-84, exit 3B. Ext corridors. **Pets:** Medium. $10 one-time fee/room. Service with restrictions, supervision.

Sturbridge Host Hotel and Conference Center on Cedar Lake SH
(508) 347-7393. **$89-$169.** 366 Main St. I-90, exit 9, just w on US 20; I-84, exit 3B. Int corridors. **Pets:** Accepted.

Super 8 M
(508) 347-9000. **$49-$140.** 358 Main St. I-90, exit 9; I-84, exit 3B, on US 20. Ext corridors. **Pets:** Small. $10 daily fee/pet. Service with restrictions, supervision.

WESTBOROUGH

Residence Inn by Marriott Boston/Westborough SH
(508) 366-7700. **$89-$209.** 25 Connector Rd. I-495, exit 23B, just w on SR 9, exit Computer/Research Dr, 0.3 mi s. Ext/int corridors. **Pets:** Large, other species. $150 one-time fee/room. Designated rooms.

Wyndham Westborough LH
(508) 366-5511. **$99-$209.** 5400 Computer Dr. I-495, exit 23B, just w on SR 9, exit Computer/Research Dr. Int corridors. **Pets:** Medium. $50 deposit/room. Service with restrictions.

WEST SPRINGFIELD

Hampton Inn SH
(413) 732-1300. **$99-$159.** 1011 Riverdale St (US 5). I-91, exit 13B, 0.3 mi s. Int corridors. **Pets:** Other species. $75 one-time fee/room. Service with restrictions, supervision.

Red Roof Inn M
(413) 731-1010. **$57-$68.** 1254 Riverdale St. I-91, exit 13A. Ext corridors. **Pets:** Accepted.

Residence Inn by Marriott-West Springfield SH
(413) 732-9543. **$139, 7 day notice.** 64 Border Way. I-91, exit 13A, on US 5. Int corridors. **Pets:** Other species. $75 one-time fee/pet. Service with restrictions, crate.

WEST STOCKBRIDGE

Pleasant Valley Motel M
(413) 232-8511. **$49-$195, 12 day notice.** 42 Stockbridge Rd. I-90, exit B3 eastbound, 0.5 mi s on SR 22, then 3.5 mi e on SR 102; exit 1 westbound, 0.4 mi e. Ext corridors. **Pets:** Medium. $10 daily fee/pet. Designated rooms, service with restrictions, crate.

WILLIAMSTOWN

Cozy Corner Motel M
(413) 458-8006. **$49-$125, 10 day notice.** 284 Sand Springs Rd (US 7). On US 7, 1.5 mi n of jct SR 2. Ext corridors. **Pets:** Other species. $10 daily fee/pet. Service with restrictions, crate.

The Villager Motel M
(413) 458-4046. **$55-$125, 14 day notice.** 953 Simonds Rd. On US 7, 1.7 n of jct SR 2. Ext corridors. **Pets:** $10 daily fee/pet. Designated rooms, service with restrictions, supervision.

WORCESTER

Holiday Inn SH
(508) 852-4000. **$155-$179.** 500 Lincoln St. I-290, exit 20, 0.5 mi n on SR 70. Int corridors. **Pets:** Accepted.

MICHIGAN

ALANSON

Crooked River Lodge 🅂🄷
(231) 548-5000. **$105-$200.** 6845 US 31 N. On US 31, just
n. Int corridors. **Pets:** Medium, dogs only. $15 daily fee/pet.
Designated rooms, service with restrictions, supervision.

ALGONAC

Linda's Lighthouse Inn 🄱🄱
(810) 794-2992. **$95-$135, 7 day notice.** 5965 Pointe
Tremble Rd (SR 29). I-94, exit 243, 14 mi e. Int corridors.
Pets: $15 daily fee/pet. Service with restrictions, crate.

ALLENDALE

Sleep Inn & Suites 🅂🄷
(616) 892-8000. **$80-$150, 3 day notice.** 4869 Becker Dr.
I-96, exit 16, 6 mi s, then 2.5 mi e on SR 45. Int corridors.
Pets: Medium, other species. $10 daily fee/room. Desig-
nated rooms, supervision.

ALPENA

Holiday Inn 🅂🄷
(989) 356-2151. **$79-$99.** 1000 Hwy 23 N. On US 23, 1 mi
n. Int corridors. **Pets:** Accepted.

ANN ARBOR

Candlewood Suites 🅂🄷
(734) 663-2818. **$45-$169.** 701 Waymarket Way. I-94, exit
175 (Ann Arbor/Saline Rd), just e on Eisenhower Rd. Int
corridors. **Pets:** Large. $75 one-time fee/room. Service with
restrictions, supervision.

Hampton Inn-North 🅂🄷 🐾
(734) 996-4444. **$67-$80.** 2300 Green Rd. US 23, exit 41
(Plymouth Rd), just nw. Int corridors. **Pets:** Small. $25 one-
time fee/room. Designated rooms, service with restrictions,
supervision.

Hawthorn Suites 🅂🄷
(734) 327-0011. **$125-$225.** 3535 Green Rd. US 23, exit 41
(Plymouth Rd), just sw. Int corridors. **Pets:** Large. $75 one-
time fee/room. Service with restrictions.

Red Roof Inn 🄼
(734) 996-5800. **$57-$75.** 3621 Plymouth Rd. US 23, exit 41
(Plymouth Rd), just nw. Ext corridors. **Pets:** Accepted.

Residence Inn by Marriott 🅂🄷
(734) 996-5666. **Call for rates.** 800 Victor's Way. I-94, exit
177 (State St), just ne. Ext/int corridors. **Pets:** Large. $15
daily fee/pet. Service with restrictions.

Super 8 Motel 🅂🄷 🐾
(734) 741-8888. **$54-$99.** 2910 Jackson Ave. I-94, exit 172,
just e. Ext/int corridors. **Pets:** Medium. $15 daily fee/room.
Designated rooms, service with restrictions.

AU GRES

Best Western Pinewood Lodge 🅂🄷 🐾
(989) 876-4060. **$69-$79.** 510 W US 23. Just w on US 23.
Int corridors. **Pets:** Supervision.

BAD AXE

▼▼ ▼▼ Econo Lodge Inns & Suites SH
(989) 269-3200. **$59-$79.** 898 N Van Dyke Rd. Just s of jct SR 142 and SR 53 (Van Dyke Rd). Int corridors. **Pets:** Very small. Service with restrictions, supervision.
ASK ☒ ⇌

BARAGA

▼▼ Carla's Lake Shore Motel & Restaurant M
(906) 353-6256. **$45-$52.** 6 mi n on US 41. Ext corridors. **Pets:** Other species. $5 one-time fee/pet. Supervision.
ASK S🔒 ☒ 🛏 🍽

▼▼ Super 8 Motel SH
(906) 353-6680. **$54-$59.** 790 Michigan Ave. 1 mi w on SR 38. Int corridors. **Pets:** Medium. $5 one-time fee/pet. Designated rooms, service with restrictions, supervision.
ASK S🔒 ☒

BATTLE CREEK

▼▼▼ ▼▼ Baymont Inn & Suites-Battle Creek SH
(269) 979-5400. **$60-$100, 3 day notice.** 4725 Beckley Rd. I-94, exit 97, just sw. Int corridors. **Pets:** Accepted.
ASK S🔒 ☒ 🖉 🗲 🛏 🖵 ⇌

▼▼ Days Inn M
(269) 979-3561. **$40-$85.** 4786 Beckley Rd. I-94, exit 97. Ext corridors. **Pets:** Accepted.
ASK S🔒 ☒ 🛏

▼▼▼ ▼▼ McCamly Plaza Hotel LH
(269) 963-7050. **$159.** 50 Capital Ave SW. Downtown. Int corridors. **Pets:** Accepted.
ASK S🔒 ☒ 👤M 🖉 🗲 🖵 🍽 ⇌ ☒

BAY CITY

▼▼▼ ▼▼ AmericInn of Bay City SH
(989) 671-0071. **$66-$76.** 3915 3 Mile Rd. I-75, exit 164. Int corridors. **Pets:** Accepted.
ASK ☒ 🗲 🛏 🖵 ⇌

▼▼ ▼▼ Holiday Inn LH
(989) 892-3501. **$93.** 501 Saginaw St. Center line on I-75 business loop, SR 15 and 25; downtown. Int corridors. **Pets:** Other species. Service with restrictions, supervision.
ASK S🔒 ☒ 🗲 🖵 🍽 ⇌

BAY VIEW

🅰🅰🅰 ▼▼ ▼▼ Comfort Inn SH ❀
(231) 347-3220. **$60-$200.** 1314 US 31 N. Jct US 31 and SR 119. Int corridors. **Pets:** Other species. Service with restrictions, supervision.
SAVE S🔒 ☒ 🛏 🖵

BENTON HARBOR

🅰🅰🅰 ▼▼ ▼▼ Best Western T.C. Inn & Suites SH
(269) 925-1880. **$69-$119.** 1598 Mall Dr. I-94, exit 29 (Pipestone Rd), just n to Mall Dr, then just w. Int corridors. **Pets:** Accepted.
SAVE S🔒 ☒ 🛏 ⇌

▼▼ Motel 6–1141 M
(269) 925-5100. **$35-$55.** 2063 Pipestone Rd. I-94, exit 29 (Pipestone Rd), just nw. Ext corridors. **Pets:** Medium, other species. Service with restrictions, supervision.
S🔒 ☒ ⇌

▼▼ ▼▼ Ramada Inn SH
(269) 927-1172. **$79-$99.** 798 Ferguson Dr. I-94, exit 28, just sw. Int corridors. **Pets:** Accepted.
ASK S🔒 ☒ 🛏 🖵 🍽 ⇌ ☒

🅰🅰🅰 ▼▼ ▼▼ Red Roof Inn M
(269) 927-2484. **$42-$79.** 1630 Mall Dr. I-94, exit 29 (Pipestone Rd), just n, then just w. Ext corridors. **Pets:** Accepted.
SAVE ☒ 👤M 🖉 🛏

BIG RAPIDS

▼▼▼ ▼▼ ▼▼ Holiday Inn Hotel & Conference Center LH ❀
(231) 796-4400. **$85-$105.** 1005 Perry St. US 131, exit 139, 1.3 mi e on SR 20. Int corridors. **Pets:** $10 daily fee/pet. Service with restrictions, supervision.
ASK S🔒 ☒ 👤M 🗲 🛏 🖵 🍽 ⇌ ☒

BIRCH RUN

🅰🅰🅰 ▼▼ ▼▼ Super 8 Motel SH
(989) 624-4440. **$42-$70.** 9235 E Birch Run Rd. I-75, exit 136, just e. Int corridors. **Pets:** Designated rooms, service with restrictions, supervision.
SAVE S🔒 ☒ 🛏 ☒

BREVORT

▼▼ Chapel Hill Motel M
(906) 292-5521. **$37-$54, 3 day notice.** 4422 W US 2. Center. Ext/int corridors. **Pets:** Accepted.
☒ 🛏 🖵 ⇌

BRIDGEPORT

🅰🅰🅰 ▼▼ ▼▼ Baymont Inn & Suites-Frankenmuth/Bridgeport SH
(989) 777-3000. **$69-$99, 3 day notice.** 6460 Dixie Hwy. I-75, exit 144A. Int corridors. **Pets:** Accepted.
SAVE S🔒 ☒ 🗲 🛏 🖵 ⇌

BROOKLYN

▼▼ ▼▼ Super 8 Motel SH
(517) 592-0888. **$58-$130.** 155 Wamplers Rd. Jct SR 50 and SR 124; downtown. Int corridors. **Pets:** Accepted.
ASK S🔒 ☒ 👤M 🗲 🛏

CADILLAC

🅰🅰🅰 ▼▼ ▼▼ Best Value Inn of Cadillac SH
(231) 775-2458. **$59-$109.** 5676 E M55. On SR 55, 0.5 mi w of jct SR 115. Ext corridors. **Pets:** Accepted.
SAVE S🔒 ☒ 🛏 🖵 🍽 ⇌ ☒

🅰🅰🅰 ▼▼ Econo Lodge SH
(231) 775-6700. **$50-$95.** 2501 Sunnyside Dr. Jct SR 55 and 115. Ext/int corridors. **Pets:** $10 one-time fee/pet. Service with restrictions, supervision.
SAVE S🔒 ☒ 🛏 🖵

McGuires Resort 🏠
(231) 775-9947. **$79-$124, 7 day notice.** 7880 Mackinaw Tr. US 131, exit 177, 0.7 mi n, then 0.5 mi w. Int corridors. **Pets:** Medium. $15 daily fee/room. Designated rooms, service with restrictions, crate.

⟦SAVE⟧ ⟦✕⟧ ⟦⟧ ⟦⟧ ⟦⟧ ⟦🍴⟧ ⟦⟧ ⟦✕⟧

CASCADE

AmeriSuites Grand Rapids/Airport 🏠
(616) 940-8100. **$71-$129.** 5401 28th St Ct SE. I-96, exit 43B, just e on SR 11. Int corridors. **Pets:** Accepted.

⟦SAVE⟧ ⟦⟧ ⟦✕⟧ ⟦⟧ ⟦⟧ ⟦⟧ ⟦✕⟧

Baymont Inn-Grand Rapids Airport 🏠
(616) 956-3300. **$59-$99.** 2873 Kraft Ave SE. I-96, exit 43B, just e. Int corridors. **Pets:** Medium. Designated rooms, service with restrictions, crate.

⟦ASK⟧ ⟦⟧ ⟦⟧ ⟦⟧

Country Inn & Suites By Carlson of Grand Rapids 🏠 🐾
(616) 977-0909. **$65-$85.** 5399 28th St. I-96, exit 43B, just e on SR 11. Int corridors. **Pets:** Dogs only. Service with restrictions.

⟦ASK⟧ ⟦⟧ ⟦✕⟧ ⟦⟧ ⟦⟧ ⟦⟧ ⟦⟧ ⟦⟧ ⟦⟧

Exel Inn of Grand Rapids 🏠
(616) 957-3000. **$46-$66.** 4855 28th St SE. I-96, exit 43A, 0.5 mi w on SR 11. Int corridors. **Pets:** Accepted.

⟦SAVE⟧ ⟦⟧ ⟦✕⟧ ⟦⟧ ⟦⟧

Hampton Inn 🏠 🐾
(616) 956-9304. **$82-$97.** 4981 28th St SE. I-96, exit 43A, 0.5 mi w on SR 11. Int corridors. **Pets:** Other species. Service with restrictions, supervision.

⟦ASK⟧ ⟦⟧ ⟦✕⟧ ⟦⟧ ⟦⟧ ⟦⟧ ⟦⟧

Howard Johnson Express Inn & Suites 🏠
(616) 940-1777. **$59-$109.** 2985 Kraft Ave SE. I-96, exit 43B, just e. Int corridors. **Pets:** Medium. $25 daily fee/room. Designated rooms, service with restrictions, supervision.

⟦SAVE⟧ ⟦⟧ ⟦⟧ ⟦⟧

CEDARVILLE

Cedarville Inn 🏠
(906) 484-2266. **$79-$139.** 106 W M-134. On SR 134, just w of SR 129. Int corridors. **Pets:** Accepted.

⟦SAVE⟧ ⟦✕⟧ ⟦⟧ ⟦⟧ ⟦⟧ ⟦✕⟧

CHARLEVOIX

Sleep Inn 🏠
(231) 547-0300. **$60-$145, 3 day notice.** 800 Petoskey Ave. 1 mi n on US 31. Int corridors. **Pets:** Accepted.

⟦ASK⟧ ⟦⟧ ⟦✕⟧ ⟦⟧ ⟦⟧ ⟦⟧

CHARLOTTE

Super 8 Motel 🏠
(517) 543-8288. **$62-$72.** 828 E Shepherd St. I-69, exit 60, just w on SR 50. Int corridors. **Pets:** Accepted.

⟦SAVE⟧ ⟦⟧ ⟦✕⟧ ⟦⟧

CHEBOYGAN

Birch Haus Motel Ⓜ
(231) 627-5862. **$40-$60.** 1301 Mackinaw Ave. On US 23, 0.8 mi nw. Ext corridors. **Pets:** Medium. $5 daily fee/pet. Designated rooms, service with restrictions, supervision.

⟦SAVE⟧ ⟦✕⟧ ⟦⟧

Pine River Motel Ⓜ
(231) 627-5119. **$40-$80, 3 day notice.** 102 Lafayette. 0.5 mi e on US 23. Ext corridors. **Pets:** $10 one-time fee/pet. Service with restrictions, supervision.

⟦SAVE⟧ ⟦✕⟧ ⟦⟧

CHELSEA

Chelsea Comfort Inn & Conference Center 🏠
(734) 433-8000. **$94-$189.** 1645 Commerce Park Dr. I-94, exit 159, just n. Int corridors. **Pets:** Other species. Service with restrictions, supervision.

⟦ASK⟧ ⟦⟧ ⟦✕⟧ ⟦⟧ ⟦⟧ ⟦⟧ ⟦⟧ ⟦⟧

CHRISTMAS

Pair-A-Dice Inn 🏠
(906) 387-3500. **$69-$95, 3 day notice.** E7889 W M-28. On SR 28; center. Int corridors. **Pets:** Dogs only. $20 deposit/room. Service with restrictions, supervision.

⟦SAVE⟧ ⟦⟧ ⟦✕⟧ ⟦⟧ ⟦⟧

COLDWATER

Ramada Inn 🏠
(517) 278-2017. **$74-$129.** 1000 Orleans Blvd. I-69, exit 13, 0.3 mi w on E Chicago St, just n on N Michigan Ave, then just e. Int corridors. **Pets:** Medium, other species. $20 deposit/room. Service with restrictions, supervision.

⟦SAVE⟧ ⟦⟧ ⟦✕⟧ ⟦⟧ ⟦⟧ ⟦🍴⟧ ⟦⟧ ⟦✕⟧

Red Roof Inn 🏠 🐾
(517) 279-1199. **$49-$89.** 348 S Willowbrook Rd. I-69, exit 13, just e. Int corridors. **Pets:** Small. $25 deposit/room. Designated rooms, service with restrictions, supervision.

⟦ASK⟧ ⟦⟧ ⟦✕⟧ ⟦⟧ ⟦⟧

Super 8 Motel 🏠
(517) 278-8833. **$54-$73.** 600 Orleans Blvd. I-69, exit 13, 0.3 mi w on E Chicago St, just n on N Michigan Ave, then just e. Int corridors. **Pets:** Large, other species. Service with restrictions, supervision.

⟦SAVE⟧ ⟦⟧ ⟦✕⟧ ⟦⟧ ⟦⟧ ⟦⟧

COMSTOCK PARK

Swan Inn 🏠
(616) 784-1224. **$50-$80.** 5182 Alpine Ave. Jct I-96 and Alpine Ave, 3 mi n on SR 37. Ext corridors. **Pets:** Other species.

⟦✕⟧ ⟦⟧ ⟦⟧ ⟦🍴⟧ ⟦⟧

COPPER HARBOR

Lake Fanny Hooe Resort & Campground Ⓜ
(906) 289-4451. **$69-$84, 7 day notice.** 505 2nd St. Just s on Manganese Rd. Ext corridors. **Pets:** Other species. $6 daily fee/pet. Service with restrictions, supervision.

⟦✕⟧ ⟦⟧ ⟦⟧ ⟦✕⟧ ⟦⟧ ⟦⟧

DETROIT METROPOLITAN AREA

ALLEN PARK

Best Western Greenfield Inn 🅂🄷
(313) 271-1600. **$89-$149**. 3000 Enterprise Dr. I-94, exit 206 (Oakwood Blvd), just s. Int corridors. **Pets:** Small, dogs only. $100 deposit/pet. Designated rooms, service with restrictions, crate.

Holiday Inn Express & Suites 🅂🄷
(313) 323-3500. **$110-$130**. 3600 Enterprise Dr. I-94, exit 206 (Oakwood Blvd), just s. Int corridors. **Pets:** Small, dogs only. Designated rooms, service with restrictions, supervision.

AUBURN HILLS

AmeriSuites (Detroit/Auburn Hills) 🅂🄷 🐾
(248) 475-9393. **$109**. 1545 Opdyke Rd. I-75, exit 79 (University Dr), just w, then just n. Int corridors. **Pets:** Small, other species. Service with restrictions, supervision.

Hilton Suites Auburn Hills 🅂🄷
(248) 334-2222. **$89-$199**. 2300 Featherstone Rd. I-75, exit 79 (University Dr), just w, 0.5 mi s on Opdyke Rd, then just e. Int corridors. **Pets:** Accepted.

Homestead Studio Suites Hotel-Detroit/ Auburn Hills 🅂🄷 🐾
(248) 340-8888. **$69-$84**. 3315 University Dr. I-75, exit 79 (University Dr), 0.9 mi e. Int corridors. **Pets:** Medium, other species. $25 daily fee/room. Service with restrictions, crate.

Staybridge Suites 🅂🄷
(248) 322-4600. **$109-$169**. 2050 Featherstone Rd. I-75, exit 79 (University Dr), just w, 0.5 mi s on Opdyke Rd, just e. Int corridors. **Pets:** Other species. $75 one-time fee/room. Service with restrictions.

Wellesley Inn & Suites (Detroit/Auburn Hills) 🅂🄷
(248) 335-5200. **$69-$99**. 2100 Featherstone Rd. I-75, exit 79 (University Dr), just w, 0.5 mi s on Opdyke Rd, then just e. Int corridors. **Pets:** Medium, other species. Service with restrictions, crate.

BELLEVILLE

Comfort Inn 🅂🄷
(734) 697-8556. **$69-$129**. 45945 S I-94 Service Dr. I-94, exit 190 (Belleville Rd), just s. Int corridors. **Pets:** Accepted.

Red Roof Inn Metro Airport 🄼
(734) 697-2244. **$56-$64**. 45501 N I-94 Service Dr. I-94, exit 190 (Belleville Rd). Ext corridors. **Pets:** Large, other species. Service with restrictions, crate.

Super 8 Motel 🅂🄷
(734) 699-1888. **$50-$71**. 45707 S I-94 Service Dr. I-94, exit 190 (Belleville Rd), just s. Int corridors. **Pets:** Other species. $5 daily fee/room. Service with restrictions, crate.

BIRMINGHAM

Hamilton Hotel 🅂🄷 🐾
(248) 642-6200. **$99-$159**. 35270 Woodward Ave. Jct Woodward Ave and Maple Rd; center. Int corridors. **Pets:** $10 daily fee/room. Designated rooms, service with restrictions, supervision.

Holiday Inn Express Birmingham 🅂🄷
(248) 646-7300. **$160**. 34952 Woodward Ave. On SR 1, jct Woodward Ave and Maple Rd; center. Ext/int corridors. **Pets:** Accepted.

BLOOMFIELD HILLS

Radisson Kingsley Hotel 🅂🄷 🐾
(248) 644-1400. **$109-$179**. 39475 Woodward Ave. On SR 1 (Woodward Ave), just s of jct Long Lake Rd. Int corridors. **Pets:** Small. $20 daily fee/room. Designated rooms, service with restrictions.

CANTON

Baymont Inn & Suites Detroit-Canton 🅂🄷
(734) 981-1808. **$75**. 41211 Ford Rd. I-275, exit 25 (Ford Rd), just w on SR 153. Int corridors. **Pets:** Medium, other species. Service with restrictions, crate.

Motel 6–1070 🄼
(734) 981-5000. **$45-$62**. 41216 Ford Rd. I-275, exit 25, just w on SR 153 (Ford Rd). Ext corridors. **Pets:** Accepted.

Super 8 Motel-Canton 🅂🄷
(734) 722-8880. **$54-$60, 7 day notice**. 3933 Lotz Rd. I-275, exit 22, just e on US 12, then just s. Int corridors. **Pets:** Large, other species. $10 one-time fee/room. Service with restrictions, crate.

DEARBORN

Red Roof Inn-Dearborn 🄼
(313) 278-9732. **$64-$97**. 24130 Michigan Ave. Jct US 12 (Michigan Ave) and SR 24 (Telegraph Rd). Ext corridors. **Pets:** Medium. No service.

ⒶⒶⒶ ▼▼ ▼▼ The Ritz-Carlton, Dearborn 🏨
(313) 441-2000. **$135-$295.** 300 Town Center Dr. SR 39
(Southfield Frwy), between Ford Rd and Michigan Ave
exits, on Service Dr. Int corridors. **Pets:** Accepted.
[SAVE] [S🔥] [✕] [&M] [🌀] [📧] [📺] [💻] [🍴] [🏊] [🚫]

▼▼▼▼ TownePlace Suites 🔲 🐾
(313) 271-0200. **$99-$109.** 6141 Mercury Dr. SR 39 (Southfield Frwy), exit 7 (Ford Rd), just e, then 0.8 mi n. Int
corridors. **Pets:** Medium. $5 daily fee/room, $100 one-time
fee/room. Service with restrictions.
[✕] [&M] [📧] [💻] [🏊]

DETROIT

▼▼▼ Holiday Inn Express 🏨
(313) 887-7000. **$119-$159.** 1020 Washington Blvd. At corner of Washington Blvd and Michigan Ave. Int corridors.
Pets: Medium, dogs only. $25 daily fee/pet. Service with
restrictions, supervision.
[ASK] [S🔥] [✕] [📧] [💻] [🏊]

▼▼▼ Residence Inn By
      Marriott-Dearborn 🔲 🐾
(313) 441-1700. **$69-$199.** 5777 Southfield Service Dr. Just
w of Southfield Frwy at jct Ford Rd. Ext corridors.
Pets: Other species. $100 one-time fee/room. Service with
restrictions, crate.
[✕] [🌀] [📧] [💻] [🏊] [🚫]

FARMINGTON HILLS

▼▼▼ Candlewood Suites 🔲
(248) 324-0540. **$99-$144.** 37555 Hills Tech Dr. I-696, exit
I-96E/I-275S/SR 5, just s to SR 5 N, then 2 mi n to 12 Mile
Rd, 1.3 mi e on 12 Mile Rd, then 0.3 mi s on Halsted Rd.
Int corridors. **Pets:** Medium. $75 one-time fee/room. Serv-
ice with restrictions, supervision.
[ASK] [S🔥] [✕] [&M] [📧] [💻]

ⒶⒶⒶ ▼▼ Red Roof Inn-Farmington Hills M
(248) 478-8640. **$57-$71.** 24300 Sinacola Ct. I-96/275 and
SR 5, exit 165 (Grand River Ave), just w. Ext corridors.
Pets: Large, other species. Service with restrictions, crate.
[SAVE] [✕] [&M] [📧]

LAKE ORION

ⒶⒶⒶ ▼▼▼ Best Western Palace Inn 🔲
(248) 391-2755. **$100.** 2755 N Lapeer Rd. I-75, exit 81 (Lap-
eer Rd), 3.3 mi n. Ext/int corridors. **Pets:** Accepted.
[SAVE] [S🔥] [✕] [&M] [📧] [📺] [💻] [🏊] [🚫]

LIVONIA

ⒶⒶⒶ ▼▼▼ AmeriSuites
      (Detroit/Livonia) 🔲 🐾
(734) 953-9224. **$89-$129.** 19300 Haggerty Rd. I-275, exit
169A, just w on 7 Mile Rd. Int corridors. **Pets:** Medium,
other species. Service with restrictions, crate.
[SAVE] [S🔥] [✕] [📧] [📺] [💻] [🏊]

▼▼▼▼ Residence Inn Detroit-Livonia 🔲
(734) 462-4201. **$89-$144.** 17250 Fox Dr. I-275, exit 170 (6
Mile Rd), just nw. Int corridors. **Pets:** Other species. $200
one-time fee/room. Service with restrictions.
[ASK] [S🔥] [✕] [&M] [🌀] [📧] [📺] [💻] [🏊] [🚫]

MADISON HEIGHTS

ⒶⒶⒶ ▼▼ Red Roof Inn M
(248) 583-4700. **$52-$72.** 32511 Concord Dr. I-75, exit 65A,
just e, then just s. Ext corridors. **Pets:** Accepted.
[SAVE] [✕] [🌀] [📧]

▼▼▼ Residence Inn by Marriott-Madison
          Heights 🆑
(248) 583-4322. **$161-$339.** 32650 Stephenson Hwy. I-75,
exit 65B, just w, then just s. Ext corridors. **Pets:** Medium.
$75 one-time fee/room. Service with restrictions, supervi-
sion.
[ASK] [S🔥] [✕] [🌀] [📧] [💻] [🏊] [🚫]

NOVI

▼▼ TownePlace Suites 🔲
(248) 305-5533. **$69-$119.** 42600 11 Mile Rd. I-96, exit 162,
just s, 0.5 mi e on Crescent Dr, then just s on Town Center
Dr. Int corridors. **Pets:** Accepted.
[S🔥] [✕] [📧] [📺] [💻] [🏊]

PLYMOUTH

ⒶⒶⒶ ▼▼ Red Roof Inn-Plymouth M
(734) 459-3300. **$57-$74.** 39700 Ann Arbor Rd. I-275, exit
28, just e. Ext corridors. **Pets:** Large. Service with restrictions, supervision.
[SAVE] [✕] [🌀] [📧]

PONTIAC

▼▼▼ Residence Inn by Marriott
          Detroit/Pontiac 🔲
(248) 858-8664. **$159-$189.** 3333 Centerpoint Pkwy. I-75,
exit 75 (Square Lake Rd), w via Opdyke Rd. Int corridors.
Pets: Other species. $5 daily fee/room, $100 one-time fee/
room. Service with restrictions, crate.
[ASK] [S🔥] [✕] [🌀] [📧] [📺] [💻] [🏊] [🚫]

ROCHESTER HILLS

ⒶⒶⒶ ▼▼ Red Roof Inn M
(248) 853-6400. **$58-$78.** 2580 Crooks Rd. Jct Hall (SR 59)
and Crooks rds. Ext corridors. **Pets:** Medium, other species.
Service with restrictions, crate.
[SAVE] [✕] [🌀] [📧] [📺]

ROMULUS

ⒶⒶⒶ ▼▼ Baymont Inn & Suites
          Detroit-Airport 🔲
(734) 722-6000. **$79-$89.** 9000 Wickham Rd. I-94, exit 198
(Merriman Rd), just w. Int corridors. **Pets:** Medium, other
species. $50 deposit/room. Supervision.
[SAVE] [S🔥] [✕] [🌀] [📧] [💻]

▼▼▼ Detroit Metro Airport Marriott 🔲
(734) 729-7555. **$69-$139.** 30559 Flynn Dr. I-94, exit 198
(Merriman Rd). Int corridors. **Pets:** $75 one-time fee/room.
Service with restrictions, supervision.
[✕] [&M] [🌀] [📧] [📺] [💻] [🍴] [🏊]

AAA ◈◈◈◈ Four Points by Sheraton Detroit Metro
Airport SH ❀
(734) 729-9000. $89-$99. 8800 Wickham Rd. I-94, exit 198
(Merriman Rd). Int corridors. Pets: Medium, other species.
$100 deposit/room. Service with restrictions, supervision.

[SAVE] [✕] [⚡] [📶] [📶] [🍴] [≈]

◈◈ Super 8 Motel-Romulus SH
(734) 946-8808. $60, 7 day notice. 9863 Middlebelt Rd.
I-94, exit 199 (Middlebelt Rd), just s. Int corridors.
Pets: Medium. $25 one-time fee/pet. Service with restric-
tions, supervision.

[ASK] [S✓] [✕] [&M] [📶]

ROSEVILLE

AAA ◈◈◈◈ Baymont Inn & Suites
Detroit-Roseville SH
(586) 296-6910. $69-$89. 20675 13 Mile Rd. I-94, exit 232
(Little Mack Ave). Int corridors. Pets: Accepted.

[SAVE] [S✓] [✕] [⚡] [📶]

AAA ◈◈◈◈ Best Western Georgian Inn M
(586) 294-0400. $59-$179. 31327 Gratiot Ave. I-94, exit 232
(Little Mack Ave), just s, then 0.5 mi n on 13 Mile Rd, just n.
Ext corridors. Pets: Medium, dogs only. $8 daily fee/pet.
Service with restrictions.

[SAVE] [S✓] [✕] [📶] [📶] [🍴] [≈]

AAA ◈◈◈ Red Roof Inn M
(586) 296-0310. $45-$72. 31800 Little Mack Ave. I-94, exit
232 (Little Mack Ave), just n. Ext corridors. Pets: Medium,
other species. Service with restrictions, crate.

[SAVE] [✕] [⚡] [📶]

SOUTHFIELD

◈◈◈ Candlewood Suites SH
(248) 945-0010. $175. 1 Corporate Dr. SR 10 (Northwestern
Hwy), exit Lasher Rd, just e. Int corridors. Pets: Accepted.

[ASK] [S✓] [✕] [&M] [⚡] [📶] [📶]

◈◈◈ Hawthorn Suites Ltd SH
(248) 350-2400. $89-$134. 25100 Northwestern Hwy. SR 10
(Northwestern Hwy), exit 10 Mile Rd. Int corridors.
Pets: Medium. $150 one-time fee/room. Service with
restrictions, supervision.

[ASK] [S✓] [✕] [&M] [⚡] [📶] [📶] [≈]

◈◈◈ Holiday Inn-Southfield LH
(248) 353-7700. $121-$145. 26555 Telegraph Rd. I-696, exit
9, just s on US 24 (Telegraph Rd). Int corridors. Pets: Other
species. Designated rooms, service with restrictions, supervision.

[ASK] [S✓] [✕] [&M] [⚡] [📶] [📶] [🍴] [≈] [✕]

◈◈◈◈ Homestead Studio Suites
Hotel-Detroit/Southfield SH ❀
(248) 213-4500. $74-$89. 28500 Northwestern Hwy. I-696,
exit 9, just nw of jct US 24 (Telegraph Rd). Int corridors.
Pets: Medium, other species. $25 daily fee/room. Service
with restrictions, crate.

[ASK] [S✓] [✕] [&M] [⚡] [📶] [📶]

AAA ◈◈◈ Red Roof Inn-Southfield M
(248) 353-7200. $56-$71. 27660 Northwestern Hwy. I-696,
exit 9, just nw of Telegraph Rd. Ext corridors. Pets: Accepted.

[SAVE] [✕] [&M] [⚡] [📶]

SOUTHGATE

AAA ◈◈◈ Baymont Inn & Suites
Detroit-Southgate SH
(734) 374-3000. $79-$89. 12888 Reeck Rd. I-75, exit 37
(Northline Rd), just w. Int corridors. Pets: Medium. $50
deposit/room. Designated rooms, service with restrictions,
supervision.

[SAVE] [S✓] [✕] [⚡] [📶] [📶]

STERLING HEIGHTS

◈◈◈ TownePlace Suites SH
(586) 566-0900. $79-$129. 14800 Lakeside Cir. 1 mi e of jct
SR 53 (Van Dyke Ave) and SR 59 (Hall Rd). Int corridors.
Pets: $5 daily fee/room, $100 one-time fee/room. Service
with restrictions, crate.

[ASK] [S✓] [✕] [&M] [⚡] [📶] [📶] [≈]

TAYLOR

AAA ◈◈◈ Red Roof Inn-Taylor M
(734) 374-1150. $55-$80. 21230 Eureka Rd. I-75, exit 36
(Eureka Rd), just w. Ext corridors. Pets: Small. Service with
restrictions, supervision.

[SAVE] [✕]

TROY

◈◈◈◈ Drury Inn SH
(248) 528-3330. $113-$123. 575 W Big Beaver Rd. I-75, exit
69 (Big Beaver Rd), 0.3 mi e. Int corridors. Pets: Large,
other species. Service with restrictions, supervision.

[ASK] [✕] [⚡] [⚡] [📶] [📶] [🍴] [≈]

◈◈◈◈ Holiday Inn-Troy SH
(248) 689-7500. $69-$125. 2537 Rochester Ct. I-75, exit 67,
0.3 mi sw on Rochester Rd, just w. Int corridors.
Pets: Large. $5 daily fee/room. Service with restrictions,
crate.

[ASK] [S✓] [✕] [📶] [📶] [🍴] [≈]

AAA ◈◈◈ Red Roof Inn-Troy M
(248) 689-4391. $56-$76. 2350 Rochester Ct. I-75, exit 67,
0.3 mi sw. Ext corridors. Pets: Accepted.

[SAVE] [✕] [⚡]

◈◈◈◈ Residence Inn by Marriott SH
(248) 689-6856. $99-$159. 2600 Livernois Rd. I-75, exit 69
(Big Beaver Rd), 0.5 mi e, then 0.5 mi s. Ext corridors.
Pets: Accepted.

[ASK] [S✓] [✕] [⚡] [📶] [📶] [≈] [✕]

UTICA

AAA ◈◈◈◈ AmeriSuites (Detroit/Utica) SH
(586) 803-0100. $98-$107. 45400 Park Ave. Jct Van Dyke
Ave (SR 53) and Hall Rd (SR 59). Int corridors.
Pets: Accepted.

[SAVE] [S✓] [✕] [&M] [⚡] [📶] [≈]

 **Baymont Inn & Suites Detroit-Utica** 🆂🅷
(586) 731-4700. **$89-$159.** 45311 Park Ave. Jct of Van Dyke Ave (SR 53) and Hall Rd (SR 59), just n. Int corridors. **Pets:** Accepted.
🆂🅐🆅🆇🌀🅒🅿🔲🏊

▼▼▼▼ **Staybridge Suites-Utica** 🆂🅷
(586) 323-0101. **$149-$169.** 46155 Utica Park Blvd. Jct Van Dyke Ave (SR 53) and Hall Rd (SR 59), just n. Int corridors. **Pets:** Accepted.
🅐🆂🅺🆇🅒🅿🔲🏊

WARREN

 **Baymont Inn & Suites Detroit-Warren Tech Center** 🆂🅷
(586) 574-0550. **$67.** 30900 Van Dyke Ave. I-696, exit 23 (Van Dyke Ave), 2 mi n on SR 53. Int corridors. **Pets:** Accepted.
🆂🅐🆅🆇🌀🅒🅿🔲

▼▼▼▼ **Hawthorn Suites Ltd** 🆂🅷
(586) 264-8800. **$89-$169.** 7601 Chicago Rd. I-696, exit 23, 1.8 mi n on SR 53. Int corridors. **Pets:** $150 one-time fee/room. Service with restrictions, crate.
🅐🆂🅺🆇🅒🔲🏊

✿ END METROPOLITAN AREA ✿

DOUGLAS

▼▼▼▼ **AmericInn of Saugatuck/Douglas** 🆂🅷 ✿
(269) 857-8581. **$74-$254, 7 day notice.** 2905 Blue Star Hwy. I-196, exit 36, 1 mi n. Int corridors. **Pets:** Large, dogs only. $5 daily fee/pet. Designated rooms, service with restrictions, supervision.
🆇🆂🅼🌀🅒🅿🔲🏊

EAGLE HARBOR

 **Shoreline Resort** 🅼
(906) 289-4441. **$66-$77.** 201 Front St, F #2015. On SR 26. Ext corridors. **Pets:** Other species. $10 one-time fee/room. Service with restrictions, supervision.
🆂🅐🆅🔲🍽🆇🆑🅩

EAST LANSING

▼▼▼▼ **Residence Inn by Marriott** 🆂🅷
(517) 332-7711. **$79-$259.** 1600 E Grand River Ave. US 127, exit Grand River Ave, 2.6 mi se on SR 43. Ext corridors. **Pets:** Accepted.
🅐🆂🅺🆇🌀🅒🅿🔲🏊🆇

▼▼▼▼ **TownePlace Suites** 🆂🅷
(517) 203-1000. **$79-$94.** 2855 Hannah Blvd. I-96, exit 110 (Okemos Rd), 0.8 mi n, then 0.5 mi w, just n on Hagadorn Rd. Int corridors. **Pets:** Large. $100 one-time fee/room. Service with restrictions.
🅐🆂🅺🆇🅒🅿🔲🏊

▼▼▼▼ **Homewood Suites by Hilton** 🆂🅷
(586) 558-7870. **$79-$159.** 30180 N Civic Center Blvd. I-696, exit 23 (Van Dyke Rd), 2 mi n. Ext/int corridors. **Pets:** Accepted.
🅐🆂🅺🆇🅒🆂🅼🅒🅿🔲🏊

 **Red Roof Inn-Warren** 🅼
(586) 573-4300. **$55-$75.** 26300 Dequindre Rd. I-696, exit 20 (Dequindre Rd), just ne. Ext corridors. **Pets:** Large, other species. Service with restrictions, crate.
🆂🅐🆇🌀🅒

 **Residence Inn by Marriott** 🆂🅷
(586) 558-8050. **$94.** 30120 Civic Center Blvd. I-696, exit 23, 2 mi n on Van Dyke Ave. Ext/int corridors. **Pets:** Accepted.
🆂🅐🆇🌀🅒🅒🅿🔲🏊🆇

EAST TAWAS

 **Holiday Inn-Tawas Bay Resort** 🅻🅷
(989) 362-8601. **$76-$180, 3 day notice.** 300 E Bay St. On US 23 N. Int corridors. **Pets:** Accepted.
🆂🅐🆂🅺🆇🅒🅿🔲🍽🏊🆇

ESCANABA

 **Hiawatha Motel** 🅼
(906) 786-1341. **$45-$65.** 2400 Ludington St. 0.5 mi w on US 2/41. Ext corridors. **Pets:** Other species. $5 daily fee/pet. No service, supervision.
🆂🅐🆂🅺🆇🅒

FENTON

▼▼▼▼ **Holiday Inn Express Hotel & Suites** 🆂🅷
(810) 714-7171. **$79-$159.** 17800 Silver Pkwy. US 23, exit 78 (Owen Rd), just w, then 1 mi n. Int corridors. **Pets:** Small. Service with restrictions, supervision.
🅐🆂🅺🆇🅒🆂🅼🅒🅿🔲🏊

FLINT

▼▼▼ **AmericInn Flint** 🆂🅷 ✿
(810) 233-9000. **$66-$80, 7 day notice.** 6075 Hill 23 Dr. US 23, exit 90 (Hill Rd); I-75 N, exit 475 to Hill Rd exit, then 1.5 mi w. Int corridors. **Pets:** Large, other species. $50 deposit/pet. Designated rooms, service with restrictions, supervision.
🅐🆂🅺🆇🅒🅿🔲🏊🆇

(AAA) ▼▼▼ Baymont Inn & Suites-Flint SH
(810) 732-2300. **$49-$159.** 4160 Pier North Blvd. I-75, exit 122, just w on Pierson Rd. Int corridors. **Pets:** Accepted.
[SAVE] [S6] [X] [&] [█] [▣]

(AAA) ▼▼▼ Holiday Inn Express SH
(810) 238-7744. **$63-$209.** 1150 Robert T Longway Blvd. I-475, exit 8A. Int corridors. **Pets:** Accepted.
[SAVE] [S6] [X] [🐾] [█] [▣]

▼ Howard Johnson Lodge M
(810) 733-5910. **$49.** G-3277 Miller Rd. I-75, exit 117 south-bound; exit 117B northbound, just w. Ext corridors. **Pets:** Accepted.
[ASK] [S6] [X] [█] [▣] [≈]

(AAA) ▼▼▼ Red Roof Inn-Flint M
(810) 733-1660. **$50-$82.** G-3219 Miller Rd. I-75, exit 117B (Miller Rd), just w. Ext corridors. **Pets:** Small, other species. Service with restrictions, supervision.
[SAVE] [🐾] [&] [█]

▼▼▼ Residence Inn SH
(810) 424-7000. **$89-$149, 14 day notice.** 2202 W Hill Rd. US 23, exit 90 (Hill Rd), just e. Int corridors. **Pets:** Other species. $10 daily fee/room, $50 one-time fee/room. Service with restrictions, supervision.
[ASK] [S6] [X] [&M] [&] [█] [▣] [≈]

FRANKENMUTH

▼▼▼ Drury Inn & Suites SH
(989) 652-2800. **$93-$130.** 260 S Main St. On SR 83; center of downtown. Int corridors. **Pets:** Large, other species. Service with restrictions, supervision.
[ASK] [X] [&M] [&] [█] [▣] [≈]

GAYLORD

(AAA) ▼▼▼ Best Value Royal Crest Inn SH 🐾
(989) 732-6451. **$89-$99.** 803 S Otsego Ave. I-75, exit 279, 2.3 mi ne on I-75 business loop. Int corridors. **Pets:** $10 one-time fee/room. Service with restrictions, supervision.
[SAVE] [S6] [X] [█] [▣] [≈] [X]

(AAA) ▼▼▼ Best Western Alpine Lodge SH
(989) 732-2431. **$69-$109, 7 day notice.** 833 W Main St. I-75, exit 282, 0.3 mi e on SR 32. Ext/int corridors. **Pets:** Medium, dogs only. Service with restrictions, supervision.
[SAVE] [S6] [X] [█] [▣] [||] [≈] [X]

(AAA) ▼ Downtown Motel M
(989) 732-5010. **$46-$75.** 208 S Otsego Ave. I-75, exit 282, 0.5 mi e and 0.3 mi s on I-75 business loop. Ext/int corridors. **Pets:** Dogs only. $5 one-time fee/pet. Service with restrictions, supervision.
[SAVE] [S6] [X] [█]

(AAA) ▼ Timberly Motel M
(989) 732-5166. **$48-$84, 5 day notice.** 881 S Otsego Ave. I-75, exit 279, 2.5 mi n on I-75 business loop (Old US 27). Ext corridors. **Pets:** Medium, other species. $6 daily fee/pet. Designated rooms, service with restrictions, supervision.
[SAVE] [S6] [X]

GRAND MARAIS

(AAA) ▼ ArborGate Inn M
(906) 494-2681. **$50-$60.** Randolph Rd. Just e of SR 77. Ext corridors. **Pets:** Other species. Service with restrictions, supervision.
[SAVE] [S6] [X] [█] [K] [Z]

▼▼ Voyageur's Motel M
(906) 494-2389. **$73.** E Wilson St. 0.5 mi e of SR 77. Ext corridors. **Pets:** Accepted.
[X] [█] [▣] [X] [K]

GRAND RAPIDS

▼▼ Days Inn-Downtown LH
(616) 235-7611. **$79-$86.** 310 Pearl St NW. US 131, exit Pearl St; downtown. Int corridors. **Pets:** Other species. $10 daily fee/pet.
[ASK] [S6] [X] [█] [▣] [||] [≈]

▼▼▼ Homewood Suites by Hilton SH 🐾
(616) 285-7100. **$80-$116, 14 day notice.** 3920 Stahl Dr SE. I-96, exit 43A (28th St SW), 1.5 mi w to E Paris Ave, then just n. Int corridors. **Pets:** Other species. $5 daily fee/room, $80 one-time fee/pet. Designated rooms, service with restrictions.
[ASK] [S6] [X] [&M] [&] [█] [▣] [≈]

GRANDVILLE

▼▼▼ Residence Inn by Marriott Grand Rapids West SH
(616) 538-1100. **$104-$174.** 3451 Rivertown Point Ct SW. I-196, exit 67, 1.7 mi e. Int corridors. **Pets:** Small. $6 daily fee/pet, $150 one-time fee/room. Service with restrictions.
[S6] [X] [█] [▣] [≈] [X]

GRAYLING

(AAA) ▼▼▼ Holiday Inn SH 🐾
(989) 348-7611. **$79-$129.** 2650 S Business Loop. I-75 business loop, 0.8 mi s. Ext/int corridors. **Pets:** Other species. Service with restrictions.
[SAVE] [S6] [X] [&M] [&] [█] [▣] [||] [≈] [X]

(AAA) ▼ North Country Lodge M
(989) 348-8471. **$56-$160.** 617 N I-75 Business Loop. 1 mi n. Ext corridors. **Pets:** Accepted.
[SAVE] [X] [█]

▼▼ Super 8 Motel SH
(989) 348-8888. **$57-$99.** 5828 Nelson A Miles Pkwy. I-75, exit 251. Int corridors. **Pets:** $50 deposit/room, $5 one-time fee/pet. Designated rooms, service with restrictions, supervision.
[ASK] [X] [&] [█] [≈] [X]

HANCOCK

▼▼ Best Western Copper Crown Motel SH
(906) 482-6111. **$55-$57.** 235 Hancock Ave. On US 41 S; downtown. Ext/int corridors. **Pets:** $6 daily fee/room. Designated rooms.
[ASK] [S6] [X] [▣] [≈] [X]

HART

▼▼ Budget Host Hart Motel 🆂🅷
(231) 873-1855. **$49-$119.** 4143 Polk Rd. US 31, exit Mears/
Hart, just e on US 31 business route. Int corridors.
Pets: Small, dogs only. $25 deposit/room. Service with
restrictions, supervision.
🅰🆂🅺 🆂 🗙 🔳

▼▼▼ Comfort Inn 🆂🅷
(231) 873-3456. **$65-$179.** 2248 N Comfort Dr. US 31, exit
Mears/Hart, just e on US 31 business route. Int corridors.
Pets: Other species. $10 daily fee/pet. Service with restric-
tions, supervision.
🆂🅰🆅🅴 🆂 🗙 🖑 🔳 ⇔ 🗙

HOLLAND

▼▼▼▼ Best Western Kelly Inn &
Suites 🆂🅷
(616) 994-0400. **$85-$200.** 2888 W Shore Dr. US 31, exit
Felch St E, just n. Ext/int corridors. **Pets:** Accepted.
🆂🅰🆅🅴 🆂 🅖🅼 🖉 🖑 🖑 🔳 ⇔ 🗙

HOUGHTON

▼▼ Best Value King's Inn 🆂🅷
(906) 482-5000. **$67-$107.** 215 Shelden Ave. On US 41;
downtown. Int corridors. **Pets:** $8 daily fee/pet. Service with
restrictions, supervision.
🅰🆂🅺 🆂 🗙 🖑 🔳 ⇔ 🗙

▼▼▼ Best Western-Franklin Square Inn 🅻🅷
(906) 487-1700. **$91-$189.** 820 Shelden Ave. Center of
downtown. Int corridors. **Pets:** Large. $9 daily fee/pet. Des-
ignated rooms, service with restrictions, supervision.
🆂🅰🆅🅴 🆂 🗙 🖑 🔳 🍽 ⇔ 🗙

HOUGHTON LAKE

▼ Hillside Motel 🅼 🐾
(989) 366-5711. **$64-$74, 3 day notice.** 3419 W Houghton
Lake Dr. On SR 55, 6 mi e of US 27; 10 mi w of I-75. Ext
corridors. **Pets:** Other species. Supervision.
🅰🆂🅺 🆂 🗙 🖑

▼▼▼ Holiday Inn Express 🆂🅷
(989) 422-7829. **$69-$129.** 200 Cloverleaf Ln. Jct US 27 and
SR 55, just e. Int corridors. **Pets:** $25 one-time fee/room.
Service with restrictions, supervision.
🅰🆂🅺 🆂 🗙 🖉 🖑 ⇔ 🗙

HOWELL

▼▼ Best Western Howell 🅼
(517) 548-2900. **$135-$155.** 1500 Pinckney Rd. I-96, exit
137 (Pinkney Rd), just s on CR D19. Ext corridors.
Pets: Medium, dogs only. $10 daily fee/pet. Designated
rooms, service with restrictions, supervision.
🆂🅰🆅🅴 🆂 🗙 🖑 🔳 ⇔

▼ Kensington Inn 🅼
() [00ff][00be][00f0][00ec]. **$44-$59.** 124 Holiday Ln.
I-96, exit 137 (Pickney Rd), just n. Ext corridors.
Pets: Other species. $10 daily fee/pet. Designated rooms,
service with restrictions, supervision.
🆂🅰🆅🅴 🆂 🗙 🖑 ⇔

▼▼▼ Quality Inn Banquet & Conference
Center 🅼
(517) 546-6800. **$59-$89.** 125 Holiday Ln. I-96, exit 137
(Pickney Rd), just n. Int corridors. **Pets:** Other species. $15
daily fee/pet. Designated rooms, service with restrictions,
supervision.
🆂🅰🆅🅴 🆂 🗙 🖑 🔳 🍽 ⇔

IMLAY CITY

▼▼▼ Days Inn 🆂🅷
(810) 724-8005. **$59-$79, 14 day notice.** 6692 Newark Rd.
I-69, exit 168, 0.3 mi n, then w. Int corridors. **Pets:** Other
species. $8 one-time fee/room. Service with restrictions,
supervision.
🆂🅰🆅🅴 🆂 🗙 🖉 🖑 🔳 ⇔

▼▼ Super 8 Motel-Imlay City 🆂🅷
(810) 724-8700. **$59-$69.** 6951 Newark Rd. I-69, exit 168
(Van Dyke Rd), just n to Newark Rd, just e. Int corridors.
Pets: Other species. $10 one-time fee/pet. Service with
restrictions, supervision.
🅰🆂🅺 🗙 🖑

INDIAN RIVER

▼ Nor Gate Motel 🅼
(231) 238-7788. **$42-$48, 3 day notice.** 4846 S Straits Hwy.
I-75, exit 310, 0.3 mi w, then 2 mi s on Old US 27. Ext
corridors. **Pets:** Accepted.
🆂🅰🆅🅴 🗙 🖑 🔳 🗙

▼ Star Gate Motel 🅼 🐾
(231) 238-7371. **$44-$52, 3 day notice.** 4646 S Straits Hwy.
I-75, exit 310, 0.3 mi w, then 1.8 mi s on Old US 27. Ext
corridors. **Pets:** Medium, other species. $5 daily fee/pet.
Designated rooms, no service, supervision.
🆂🅰🆅🅴 🗙 🖑 🗙

IONIA

▼▼▼ Super 8 Motel 🆂🅷
(616) 527-2828. **$62-$75.** 7245 S State Rd. I-96, exit 67 (SR
66). Int corridors. **Pets:** Accepted.
🆂🅰🆅🅴 🗙 🅖🅼 🖉 🖑 🔳

IRON MOUNTAIN

▼ Budget Host Inn 🅼 🐾
(906) 774-6797. **$49-$55.** 1663 N Stephenson Ave. 1.5 mi
nw on US 2 and 141. Ext corridors. **Pets:** Medium. $5 daily
fee/room. Designated rooms, service with restrictions,
supervision.
🆂🅰🆅🅴 🆂 🗙 🖑

▼▼ Days Inn 🆂🅷
(906) 774-2181. **$55-$125.** W8176 S US 2. 1.8 mi e on US
2. Ext/int corridors. **Pets:** Dogs only. $6 one-time fee/pet.
Designated rooms, service with restrictions, supervision.
🅰🆂🅺 🆂 🗙 🖑 ⇔

▼ Guesthouse Inn 🆂🅷
(906) 774-6220. **$50.** 1609 S Stephenson Ave. 1 mi e on US
2. Ext/int corridors. **Pets:** Other species. Designated rooms,
service with restrictions.
🅰🆂🅺 🆂 🗙 🖑 🔳

▼▼ ▼▼ **Super 8 Motel** SH
(906) 774-3400. **$60-$70.** 2702 N Stephenson Ave. 2 mi nw on US 2 and 141. Int corridors. **Pets:** Other species. Designated rooms, service with restrictions, supervision.
(ASK) (S☜) (✕) (🛏) (💻) (🏊) (✕)

IRONWOOD

▼▼ ▼ **Crestview Motel** M ❀
(906) 932-4845. **$45-$75.** US 2. West edge. Ext corridors. **Pets:** $8 daily fee/room. No service, supervision.
(SAVE) (S☜) (✕) (🛏) (💻) (🏊)

▼▼ ▼ **Royal Motel** M
(906) 932-4230. **$41-$46, 7 day notice.** 715 W Cloverland Dr. 1 mi w on US 2. Ext corridors. **Pets:** Accepted.
(SAVE) (✕)

▼▼ **Super 8 Motel** M
(906) 932-3395. **$65-$108.** 160 E Cloverland Dr. Jct US 2 and US 2 business route. Int corridors. **Pets:** Medium, other species. $25 deposit/room. Service with restrictions, supervision.
(ASK) (S☜) (✕) (🛏) (💻) (✕)

ISHPEMING

▼▼ ▼▼ **Best Western Country Inn** SH
(906) 485-6345. **$72-$100.** 850 US 41 W. On US 41, just n of town. Int corridors. **Pets:** Designated rooms, service with restrictions, supervision.
(SAVE) (S☜) (✕) (💻) (🍴) (🏊) (✕)

JACKSON

▼▼▼▼ **Holiday Inn** SH
(517) 783-2681. **$76-$121.** 2000 Holiday Inn Dr. I-94, exit 138, just nw. Ext/int corridors. **Pets:** Medium. $15 daily fee/room. Designated rooms, service with restrictions, supervision.
(ASK) (S☜) (✕) (🍳) (🖥) (🛏) (💻) (🍴) (🏊) (✕)

▼▼ **Motel 6–1088** M
(517) 789-7186. **$45-$57.** 830 Royal Dr. I-94, exit 138, just se. Ext corridors. **Pets:** Accepted.
(S☜) (✕) (🍳) (🖥)

KALAMAZOO

▼▼ ▼▼ ▼ **Clarion Hotel** SH
(269) 385-3922. **$69-$179.** 3600 E Cork St. I-94, exit 80, just n. Int corridors. **Pets:** Accepted.
(SAVE) (S☜) (✕) (🛏) (💻) (🍴) (🏊) (✕)

▼▼ ▼ **Knights Inn** M
(269) 381-5000. **$50-$80.** 1211 S Westnedge Ave. I-94, exit 76B, 3 mi n, w on Park Place, then just s. Ext/int corridors. **Pets:** Very small, other species. $25 one-time fee/pet. Service with restrictions, supervision.
(SAVE) (S☜) (✕) (🛏)

▼▼ ▼▼ ▼ **Red Roof Inn-East** M
(269) 382-6350. **$48-$69.** 3701 E Cork St. I-94, exit 80, just nw. Ext corridors. **Pets:** Medium, other species. Service with restrictions, supervision.
(SAVE) (✕) (🖥) (🖥)

▼▼ ▼▼ ▼ **Red Roof Inn-West** SH
(269) 375-7400. **$51-$67.** 5425 W Michigan Ave. US 131, exit 36B, just nw. Ext corridors. **Pets:** Accepted.
(SAVE) (✕) (🖥) (🛏)

KENTWOOD

▼▼ ▼▼ ▼ **Best Western Midway Hotel** LH
(616) 942-2550. **$89-$109.** 4101 28th St SE. I-96, exit 43A, 1.5 mi w on SR 11. Int corridors. **Pets:** Medium. Designated rooms, service with restrictions, supervision.
(SAVE) (S☜) (✕) (🛏) (💻) (🍴) (🏊) (✕)

▼▼ ▼▼ ▼ **Comfort Inn** SH ❀
(616) 957-2080. **$65-$99.** 4155 28th St SE. I-96, exit 43A, 1.5 mi w on SR 11. Int corridors. **Pets:** Other species. Service with restrictions, crate.
(SAVE) (S☜) (✕) (🖥) (🛏) (💻)

▼▼▼▼ ▼ **Residence Inn by Marriott East** CO
(616) 957-8111. **$109-$145.** 2701 E Beltline Ave. Jct SR 11 and E Beltline Ave (SR 37). Ext corridors. **Pets:** Accepted.
(✕) (🍳) (🛏) (💻) (🏊) (✕)

▼▼▼▼ ▼ **Staybridge Suites by Holiday Inn** SH ❀
(616) 464-3200. **$79-$159.** 3000 Lake Eastbrook Blvd SE. I-96, exit 43A, 2 mi w on SR 11, then just s. Int corridors. **Pets:** $75 one-time fee/room.
(ASK) (S☜) (✕) (🛖) (🖥) (🛏) (💻) (🏊)

LAKE CITY

▼▼ ▼ **Northcrest Motel** M
(231) 839-2075. **$53-$72.** 1341 S Lakeshore. 1 mi s on SR 55 and 66. Ext corridors. **Pets:** Accepted.
(SAVE) (S☜) (💻) (🏊)

LAKESIDE

▼▼▼▼ ▼ **White Rabbit Inn** BB
(269) 469-4620. **$95-$155, 7 day notice.** 14634 Red Arrow Hwy. I-94, exit 6 (Union Pier Rd), 1 mi w, then 2 mi n. Ext corridors. **Pets:** Accepted.
(✕) (🛏) (💻) (🍳)

LANSING

▼▼ ▼▼ ▼ **Best Western Midway Hotel** SH
(517) 627-8471. **$86-$155.** 7711 W Saginaw Hwy. I-96/SR 43, exit 93B, just e. Int corridors. **Pets:** Small. $25 deposit/room. Designated rooms, service with restrictions, supervision.
(SAVE) (S☜) (✕) (🛏) (💻) (🍴) (🏊) (✕)

▼▼ ▼▼▼▼ **Hampton Inn of Lansing** SH ❀
(517) 627-8381. **$59-$79.** 525 N Canal Rd. I-96/SR 43, exit 93B, just e on Saginaw Hwy. Int corridors. **Pets:** Medium. $100 deposit/room. Designated rooms, service with restrictions, supervision.
(SAVE) (S☜) (✕) (🍳) (🛏) (💻)

▼▼ ▼▼▼▼ **Lansing's Quality Suites Hotel** SH
(517) 886-0600. **$99.** 901 Delta Commerce Dr. I-96/SR 43, exit 93B, 0.8 mi e on Saginaw St. Int corridors. **Pets:** Other species. $25 one-time fee/room. Designated rooms, service with restrictions.
(SAVE) (S☜) (✕) (🛏) (💻) (✕)

(AAA) ▼▼ ▼▼ Red Roof Inn-East M
(517) 332-2575. **$54-$72.** 3615 Dunckel Rd. Just e of I-496 and US 127, exit 11 (Jolly Rd). Ext corridors. **Pets:** Other species. Supervision.
[SAVE] [✕] [🔊] [📶]

(AAA) ▼▼ ▼▼ Red Roof Inn-West SH
(517) 321-7246. **$52-$67.** 7412 W Saginaw Hwy. I-96, exit 93B. Ext corridors. **Pets:** Accepted.
[SAVE] [✕]

▼▼ ▼▼ Residence Inn-Lansing West SH
(517) 886-5030. **$89-$110, 7 day notice.** 922 Delta Commerce Dr. I-96/SR 43, exit 93B, 0.8 mi e on Saginaw Hwy. Int corridors. **Pets:** Accepted.
[ASK] [S🔊] [✕] [🖥M] [🖥] [📶] [💻] [📶] [✕]

LUDINGTON

(AAA) ▼▼ ▼▼ ▼▼ Holiday Inn Express SH 🐾
(231) 845-7004. **$62-$349.** 5323 W US 10. Jct US 31, 1.3 mi w on US 10. Int corridors. **Pets:** Other species. $10 daily fee/pet. Designated rooms, service with restrictions, supervision.
[SAVE] [S🔊] [✕] [🖥] [📶] [💻] [📶] [✕]

(AAA) ▼▼ ▼▼ Super 8 Motel SH
(231) 843-2140. **$59-$229.** 5005 W US 10. Jct US 31, 1 mi w on US 10. Int corridors. **Pets:** Medium, dogs only. $25 deposit/room, $5 daily fee/room. Designated rooms, service with restrictions, supervision.
[SAVE] [S🔊] [✕] [🖥] [📶] [📶] [✕]

MACKINAW CITY

(AAA) ▼▼ ▼▼ ▼▼ Baymont Inn & Suites-Mackinaw City SH
(231) 436-7737. **$59-$199.** 109 S Nicolet St. I-75, exit 338. Int corridors. **Pets:** Medium. $50 deposit/room. Designated rooms, service with restrictions, supervision.
[SAVE] [S🔊] [✕] [🖥] [📶] [💻] [📶] [✕]

(AAA) ▼▼ Beachcomber Motel on the Water M
(231) 436-8451. **$37-$145, 3 day notice.** 1011 S Huron Ave. 1 mi s on US 23. Ext corridors. **Pets:** Small, dogs only. $5 daily fee/pet. Designated rooms, service with restrictions, supervision.
[SAVE] [S🔊] [✕] [📶]

(AAA) ▼▼ The Beach House CA
(231) 436-5353. **$39-$160, 14 day notice.** 11490 W US 23 St. 1.3 mi s. Ext corridors. **Pets:** Medium. $10 one-time fee/pet. Service with restrictions, supervision.
[SAVE] [📶] [📶] [✕] [🔊]

(AAA) ▼▼ Budget Inns-Starlite M 🐾
(231) 436-5959. **$28-$149, 3 day notice.** 116 Old US 31. I-75, exit 338 southbound, 0.3 mi e; exit 337 northbound, then just ne. Ext corridors. **Pets:** Small, dogs only. $15 daily fee/pet. Designated rooms, service with restrictions, crate.
[SAVE] [S🔊] [✕] [🖥] [📶] [✕]

(AAA) ▼▼ Capri Motel M
(231) 436-5498. **$39-$89.** 801 S Nicolet St. I-75, exit 338, just s. Ext corridors. **Pets:** $5 daily fee/room. Service with restrictions, supervision.
[SAVE] [S🔊] [✕] [📶] [✕]

(AAA) ▼▼ ▼▼ Days Inn M
(231) 436-5557. **$59-$159.** 825 S Huron Ave. I-75, exit 337 northbound, 0.5 mi n to US 23, 0.3 mi e; exit 338 southbound, 0.8 mi se on US 23. Ext corridors. **Pets:** Accepted.
[SAVE] [S🔊] [✕] [🖥] [📶] [💻] [🍴] [📶]

(AAA) ▼▼ ▼▼ Grand View Resort-Beachfront M
(231) 436-8100. **$38-$188, 3 day notice.** 1143 S Huron Ave. 1 mi s. Ext corridors. **Pets:** Accepted.
[SAVE] [S🔊] [✕] [🖥] [📶] [💻] [📶] [✕]

(AAA) ▼▼ ▼▼ ▼▼ Holiday Inn Express at the Bridge SH
(231) 436-7100. **$45-$259.** 364 Louvingny. I-75, exit 339. Int corridors. **Pets:** Accepted.
[SAVE] [S🔊] [✕] [🖥M] [🖥] [📶] [💻] [📶] [✕]

(AAA) ▼▼ Kings Inn M
(231) 436-5322. **$39-$99, 3 day notice.** 1020 S Nicolet St. I-75, exit 337 northbound, 0.5 mi n; exit 338 southbound, 0.5 mi s. Ext corridors. **Pets:** Small, dogs only. $15 daily fee/pet. Designated rooms, service with restrictions, supervision.
[SAVE] [S🔊] [✕] [🖥] [📶]

(AAA) ▼▼ Motel 6-Downtown M
(231) 436-8961. **$37-$169.** 206 N Nicolet St. I-75, exit 339; at bridge. Ext/int corridors. **Pets:** Small, dogs only. Designated rooms, no service, supervision.
[SAVE] [S🔊] [✕] [🖥] [📶]

▼▼ ▼▼ Ramada Inn Conference Resort LH
(231) 436-5535. **$79-$209.** 450 S Nicolet. I-75, exit 338. Int corridors. **Pets:** Other species. $15 one-time fee/pet. Service with restrictions, supervision.
[ASK] [S🔊] [✕] [🖥] [📶] [💻] [🍴] [📶] [✕]

(AAA) ▼▼ ▼▼ Super 8 Motel Bridgeview SH
(231) 436-5252. **$38-$179, 3 day notice.** 601 N Huron Ave. I-75, exit 339 northbound (Nicolet St), just n, then just e. Ext/int corridors. **Pets:** Accepted.
[SAVE] [S🔊] [✕] [🖥] [📶] [💻] [📶] [✕]

(AAA) ▼▼ ▼▼ Travelodge-Bayview M
(231) 436-7900. **$32-$188, 3 day notice.** 900 S Huron Ave. I-75, exit 337 northbound, 0.5 mi n to US 23, just e; exit 338 southbound, 0.7 mi se on US 23. Ext corridors. **Pets:** Accepted.
[SAVE] [S🔊] [✕] [🖥] [📶] [💻] [📶] [✕]

MANISTEE

(AAA) ▼▼ Hillside Motel M
(231) 723-2584. **$45-$125.** 1675 US 31 S. 1.5 mi s. Ext corridors. **Pets:** Small, dogs only. $5 daily fee/pet. Designated rooms, service with restrictions, supervision.
[SAVE] [✕] [🖥] [📶] [💻] [📶]

MANISTIQUE

▼▼ ▼▼ Best Western-The Breakers Motel M
(906) 341-2410. **Call for rates.** 1199 E Lakeshore Dr. 2 mi e on US 2. Ext corridors. **Pets:** Accepted.
[✕] [🖥] [📶] [💻] [📶] [✕]

AAA ▽▽▽ **Comfort Inn** SH
(906) 341-6981. **$69-$159.** 726 E Lakeshore Dr. 0.5 mi e on US 2. Int corridors. **Pets:** Other species. $10 daily fee/pet. Service with restrictions, supervision.
SAVE S🛏 ✕ 🛅 💻 ✕

AAA ▽ **Kewadin Casino Inn** SH
(906) 341-6911. **$45-$60.** Lakeshore Dr. 2.5 mi e on US 2. Int corridors. **Pets:** $10 daily fee/pet. Service with restrictions, supervision.
SAVE S🛏 ✕ 🛅 💻 ⤳

MARQUETTE

AAA ▽ **Birchmont Motel** M ❀
(906) 228-7538. **$45-$65.** 2090 US 41 S. On US 41 and SR 28, 4.3 mi s. Ext corridors. **Pets:** Other species. $6 daily fee/room. Designated rooms, service with restrictions, supervision.
SAVE ✕ 🛅 ⤳

▽▽ **Holiday Inn** LH
(906) 225-1351. **$120.** 1951 US 41 W. On US 41 and SR 28, 1.8 mi w. Int corridors. **Pets:** Other species. Designated rooms, service with restrictions, supervision.
ASK S🛏 ✕ 🐾 🛅 💻 🍴 ⤳ ✕

AAA ▽▽ **Nordic Bay Lodge** M ❀
(906) 226-7516. **$55-$110.** 1880 US 41 S. On US 41 and SR 28, 1.8 mi se. Ext corridors. **Pets:** Dogs only. Designated rooms, service with restrictions, supervision.
SAVE ✕ 🛅 💻 🍴 ✕

▽▽ **Ramada Inn** LH
(906) 228-6000. **$109-$119.** 412 W Washington St. 0.5 w on US 41 business route. Int corridors. **Pets:** Accepted.
ASK S🛏 ✕ 🛅 💻 🍴 ⤳ ✕

AAA ▽ **Travelodge** SH ❀
(906) 249-1712. **$69.** 1010 M-28 E. Jct US 41 S and SR 28 E. Int corridors. **Pets:** Other species. $6 daily fee/pet. Designated rooms, service with restrictions, supervision.
SAVE ✕ 🛅 💻 ⤳

MARSHALL

AAA ▽ **Arbor Inn of Historic Marshall** M
(269) 781-7772. **$50-$69.** 15435 W Michigan Ave. I-69, exit 36, just w. Ext corridors. **Pets:** Other species. $5 daily fee/pet. Designated rooms, service with restrictions, crate.
SAVE S🛏 ✕ 🛅 ⤳

MENOMINEE

AAA ▽▽ **Econo Lodge On The Bay** SH
(906) 863-4431. **$69-$149.** 2516 10th St. 1 mi n on US 41. Int corridors. **Pets:** Small. $25 daily fee/pet, $25 one-time fee/pet. Designated rooms, service with restrictions, supervision.
SAVE S🛏 ✕ 🛅 💻

MIDLAND

▽▽ **Best Western Valley Plaza Resort** LH
(989) 496-2700. **$83.** 5221 Bay City Rd. US 10, exit Midland/Bay City Rd. Int corridors. **Pets:** Accepted.
ASK S🛏 ✕ 🛅 💻 🍴 ⤳ ✕

AAA ▽▽ **Fairview Inn** SH
(989) 631-0070. **$68-$99.** 2200 W Wackerly St. Jct US 10 and Eastman Rd. Int corridors. **Pets:** Accepted.
SAVE S🛏 ✕ 🛅 ⤳

AAA ▽▽▽ **Holiday Inn** LH
(989) 631-4220. **$85-$199.** 1500 W Wackerly St. Jct US 10 and Eastman Rd. Ext/int corridors. **Pets:** Medium, dogs only. Designated rooms, service with restrictions.
SAVE S🛏 ✕ 🛅 💻 🍴 ⤳ ✕

▽▽▽ **Plaza Suites Hotel** SH
(989) 496-0100. **$105.** 5221 Bay City Rd. US 10, exit Midland/Bay City Rd. Int corridors. **Pets:** Accepted.
ASK S🛏 ✕ 🛅 💻

AAA ▽▽▽ **Sleep Inn of Midland** SH ❀
(989) 837-1010. **$79-$140.** 2100 W Wackerly. Jct US 10 and Eastman Rd. Int corridors. **Pets:** Other species. Designated rooms, service with restrictions, supervision.
SAVE ✕ 🐾 🐾 🛅 💻 ⤳

MONROE

AAA ▽▽▽ **Comfort Inn** SH
(734) 384-1500. **$55-$80.** 6500 Albain Rd. I-75, exit 11 (Laplaisance Rd), just w. Int corridors. **Pets:** Other species. $10 daily fee/pet. Service with restrictions, supervision.
SAVE S🛏 ✕ 🐾 🛅 💻 ⤳ ✕

AAA ▽▽▽ **Hometown Inn** M ❀
(734) 289-1080. **$60-$85.** 1885 Welcome Way. I-75, exit 15 (SR 50). Ext corridors. **Pets:** Medium. $25 one-time fee/pet. Service with restrictions, supervision.
SAVE S🛏 ✕ 🛅

MOUNT PLEASANT

▽▽▽ **Holiday Inn** SH
(989) 772-2905. **$89-$159, 3 day notice.** 5665 E Pickard Ave. Jct US 27 and SR 20 E. Ext/int corridors. **Pets:** Medium. Designated rooms, service with restrictions, supervision.
ASK S🛏 ✕ 🐾 🐾 🛅 💻 🍴 ⤳ ✕

MUNISING

AAA ▽ **Alger Falls Motel** M
(906) 387-3536. **$35-$65.** E9427 SR 28. 2 mi e on SR 28 and 94. Ext corridors. **Pets:** Small, dogs only. Designated rooms, service with restrictions, supervision.
SAVE S🛏 ✕ 🛅 ✕

AAA ▽▽ **Best Western** M
(906) 387-4864. **$59-$129, 3 day notice.** M-28. 3 mi e on SR 28. Ext/int corridors. **Pets:** Medium, other species. Designated rooms, service with restrictions, supervision.
SAVE S🛏 ✕ 🛅 💻 🍴 ⤳ ✕

▽▽▽ **Comfort Inn** SH
(906) 387-5292. **$75-$110, 3 day notice.** M-28 E. 1.5 mi e on SR 28. Int corridors. **Pets:** Designated rooms, service with restrictions, supervision.
ASK S🛏 ✕ 💻 ⤳ ✕

▼▼ Days Inn SH
(906) 387-2493. **$75-$110, 3 day notice.** On M-28. 0.5 mi e on SR 28. Int corridors. **Pets:** Designated rooms, service with restrictions, supervision.
[ASK] [S̄ᴅ] [✕] [🛏] [▣] [⇌] [⊠]

AAA ▼▼ Sunset Motel M
(906) 387-4574. **$45-$65.** 1315 Bay St. 1 mi e on E Munising Ave (CR 58). Ext corridors. **Pets:** Medium, dogs only. $10 one-time fee/pet. Designated rooms, service with restrictions, supervision.
[SAVE] [✕] [🛏] [▣] [⊠] [☎]

AAA ▼▼ Terrace Motel M ❖
(906) 387-2735. **$40-$55, 3 day notice.** 420 Prospect. 0.5 mi e, just off SR 28. Ext corridors. **Pets:** Medium, other species. $3 one-time fee/room. Designated rooms, service with restrictions, supervision.
[SAVE] [S̄ᴅ] [✕] [⊠] [K] [☎]

NORWAY

▼▼▼ AmericInn of Norway SH ❖
(906) 563-7500. **$76-$88.** W 6002 US Hwy 2. 0.7 mi w. Int corridors. **Pets:** Medium. $10 one-time fee/room. Designated rooms, service with restrictions, supervision.
[✕] [🛏] [▣] [⇌] [⊠]

PAW PAW

AAA ▼▼▼ Quality Inn & Suites SH ❖
(269) 655-0303. **$59-$129.** 153 Ampey Rd. I-94, exit 60, just nw. Int corridors. **Pets:** Other species. Service with restrictions, crate.
[SAVE] [S̄ᴅ] [✕] [&M] [🐾] [🔊] [🛏] [▣] [⇌]

PELLSTON

▼▼▼ Holiday Inn Express Pellston SH
(231) 539-7000. **$99-$239.** 1600 US 31 N. 1.2 mi n. Int corridors. **Pets:** Other species. $25 one-time fee/pet. Supervision.
[ASK] [S̄ᴅ] [✕] [&M] [🛏] [⇌] [⊠]

PETOSKEY

AAA ▼▼▼ Days Inn Petoskey M
(231) 348-3900. **$49-$159.** 1420 US 131 S. 1.3 mi s. Ext corridors. **Pets:** Accepted.
[SAVE] [S̄ᴅ] [✕] [🛏]

PLAINWELL

AAA ▼▼▼ Comfort Inn SH
(269) 685-9891. **$79-$200.** 622 Allegan St. US 131, exit 49A, just e. Int corridors. **Pets:** Medium. $10 daily fee/pet. Service with restrictions, supervision.
[SAVE] [S̄ᴅ] [✕] [🛏] [▣] [⇌]

PORTLAND

AAA ▼▼▼ Best Western American Heritage Inn SH
(517) 647-2200. **$79-$89.** 1681 Grand River Ave. I-96, exit 77, just n. Int corridors. **Pets:** Small, dogs only. $10 daily fee/pet. Service with restrictions, supervision.
[SAVE] [S̄ᴅ] [✕] [&M] [&] [🛏] [▣] [⇌] [⊠]

PRUDENVILLE

AAA ▼▼ Shea's Lake Front Lodge SH
(989) 366-5910. **$45-$63, 10 day notice.** 125 12th St. I-75, exit 227, 8 mi w on SR 55. Ext/int corridors. **Pets:** Very small. Service with restrictions, supervision.
[SAVE] [🛏] [▣] [⊠] [K] [☎]

SAGINAW

▼▼ Best Western–Saginaw LH
(989) 755-0461. **$59-$99.** 1408 S Outer Dr. I-75, exit 149B (SR 46). Int corridors. **Pets:** Other species. $25 one-time fee/room. Service with restrictions, supervision.
[ASK] [S̄ᴅ] [✕] [🛏] [▣] [⇌] [⊠]

▼▼▼ Four Points by Sheraton Saginaw LH
(989) 790-5050. **$69.** 4960 Towne Centre Rd. I-675, exit 6, just w on Tittabawassee Rd. Int corridors. **Pets:** Medium, other species. $50 one-time fee/pet. Designated rooms, service with restrictions.
[ASK] [S̄ᴅ] [✕] [🛏] [▣] [🍴] [⇌] [⊠]

▼▼ Motel 6 Saginaw M
(989) 754-8414. **$42-$61.** 966 S Outer Dr. I-75, exit 149B (SR 46). Ext corridors. **Pets:** Service with restrictions, supervision.
[✕] [🛏]

ST. IGNACE

▼▼ Bay View Motel M
(906) 643-9444. **$32-$76.** 1133 N State St. 3 mi n of bridge tollgate on I-75 business route. Ext corridors. **Pets:** Large, other species. $5 daily fee/pet. Designated rooms, service with restrictions, supervision.
[✕] [☎]

AAA ▼▼▼ Budget Host Inn SH
(906) 643-9666. **$58-$156.** 700 N State St. 1.8 mi n of bridge tollgate on I-75 business route. Ext/int corridors. **Pets:** Other species. $40 deposit/room. Designated rooms, service with restrictions, supervision.
[SAVE] [S̄ᴅ] [✕] [🛏] [⇌] [⊠]

AAA ▼▼▼ Econo Lodge Inn & Suites M
(906) 643-9688. **$49-$130.** 680 W US 2. Just e on I-75 business route and US 2. Ext/int corridors. **Pets:** Dogs only. $10 daily fee/room. Service with restrictions, supervision.
[SAVE] [S̄ᴅ] [✕] [🛏] [▣] [⇌] [⊠]

AAA ▼▼▼ Quality Inn St. Ignace SH
(906) 643-9700. **$70-$165.** 913 Boulevard Dr. Jct I-75 and US 2 W. Int corridors. **Pets:** Accepted.
[SAVE] [S̄ᴅ] [✕] [▣] [⇌] [⊠]

AAA ▼▼ Wayside Motel M
(906) 643-8944. **$40-$75.** 751 N State St. 2 mi n of bridge tollgate on I-75 business route. Ext corridors. **Pets:** Small, dogs only. $5 daily fee/pet. Designated rooms, service with restrictions, supervision.
[SAVE] [S̄ᴅ] [✕] [▣]

SAULT STE. MARIE

(AAA) ▼▼▼▼ Best Western Sault Ste Marie SH
(906) 632-2170. **$59-$109.** 4281 I-75 business loop. I-75, exit 392, 0.3 mi ne. Ext/int corridors. **Pets:** Accepted.
[SAVE] [S★] [✕] [🐾] [🛏] [💻] [≈] [✕]

(AAA) ▼ Budget Host Crestview Inn M
(906) 635-5213. **$49-$79.** 1200 Ashmun St. I-75, exit 392, 2.8 mi ne on I-75 business loop. Ext corridors. **Pets:** Large, other species. $5 one-time fee/room. Designated rooms, service with restrictions, supervision.
[SAVE] [S★] [✕] [🛏]

(AAA) ▼ La France Terrace Motel M
(906) 632-7823. **$42-$75.** 1608 Ashmun St. I-75, exit 392, 2.3 mi ne on I-75 business loop. Ext corridors. **Pets:** Dogs only. Designated rooms, service with restrictions, supervision.
[SAVE] [S★] [✕] [🛏] [≈]

(AAA) ▼▼ Mid-City Motel M
(906) 632-6832. **$46-$58.** 304 E Portage Ave. Just e of town, on I-75 business loop. Ext corridors. **Pets:** Accepted.
[SAVE] [S★] [✕]

▼ Royal Motel M
(906) 632-6323. **$46-$54.** 1707 Ashmun St. I-75, exit 392, 2 mi ne on I-75 business loop. Ext corridors. **Pets:** Small, dogs only. Service with restrictions, supervision.
[ASK] [S★] [✕] [💻]

(AAA) ▼ Sunset Motel M
(906) 632-3906. **$42-$46.** 8929 S Mackinaw Tr. I-75, exit 386, 0.3 mi e to jct SR 28 and CR H-63. Ext corridors. **Pets:** Accepted.
[SAVE] [✕] [🛏] [💻]

▼▼ Super 8 Motel SH
(906) 632-8882. **$49-$78.** 3826 I-75 Business Loop. I-75, exit 392, 0.5 mi ne. Int corridors. **Pets:** Other species. $50 deposit/room. Service with restrictions, supervision.
[ASK] [S★] [✕] [🐾]

SILVER CITY

▼▼▼ AmericInn Lodge & Suites LH
(906) 885-5311. **$79-$99.** 120 Lincoln Ave. On SR 107, 0.3 mi w of SR 64. Int corridors. **Pets:** Dogs only. $10 daily fee/pet. Designated rooms, service with restrictions, supervision.
[✕] [🐾] [🛏] [💻] [🍴] [≈] [✕]

▼▼ Mountain View Lodges CA
(906) 885-5256. **$119-$134, 14 day notice.** 237 SR 107. Jct SR 107 and 64, 0.8 mi w. Ext corridors. **Pets:** $25 one-time fee/room. Designated rooms, no service, supervision.
[✕] [🛏] [💻] [🐾]

(AAA) ▼▼▼ Tomlinson's Rainbow Lodging M
(906) 885-5348. **$55-$139, 7 day notice.** 2900 SR 64. SR 64, just e of jct SR 107. Ext corridors. **Pets:** Accepted.
[SAVE] [S★] [✕] [🛏] [💻] [✕]

SPRING LAKE

▼▼▼▼ Grand Haven Waterfront Holiday Inn LH
(616) 846-1000. **$129-$199.** 940 W Savidge St. On SR 104, just e of US 131. Int corridors. **Pets:** Accepted.
[ASK] [S★] [✕] [🐾] [🛏] [💻] [🍴] [≈] [✕]

STEVENSVILLE

(AAA) ▼▼▼▼ Baymont Inn & Suites-St. Joseph (Stevensville) SH
(269) 428-9111. **$59-$89.** 2601 W Marquette Woods Rd. I-94, exit 23, just w. Int corridors. **Pets:** Medium, other species. $50 deposit/pet. Service with restrictions, supervision.
[SAVE] [S★] [✕] [M] [🐾] [🛏] [💻]

▼▼▼ Hampton Inn SH
(269) 429-2700. **$99-$119.** 5050 Red Arrow Hwy. I-94, exit 23, just se. Int corridors. **Pets:** $50 deposit/room. Service with restrictions, supervision.
[ASK] [S★] [✕] [M] [🐾] [🛏] [💻] [≈]

(AAA) ▼▼▼ Park Inn International SH
(269) 429-3218. **$69-$119.** 4290 Red Arrow Hwy. I-94, exit 23, 0.5 mi n. Ext/int corridors. **Pets:** Large, other species. Service with restrictions, supervision.
[SAVE] [S★] [✕] [🐾] [🛏] [💻] [🍴] [≈] [✕]

STURGIS

(AAA) ▼ Green Briar Motor Lodge M
(269) 651-2361. **$32-$55.** 71381 S Centerville Rd. I-90, exit 121 (SR 66), 0.4 mi n. Ext corridors. **Pets:** Dogs only. $5 one-time fee/pet. Service with restrictions, supervision.
[SAVE] [S★] [✕] [≈]

SUTTONS BAY

▼ Red Lion Motor Lodge M
(231) 271-6694. **$75-$115.** 4290 S West Bay Shore Rd. 5 mi s on SR 22. Ext corridors. **Pets:** Medium. $10 daily fee/pet. Service with restrictions, supervision.
[✕] [🛏] [💻] [Z]

TAWAS CITY

(AAA) ▼ Tawas Motel-Resort M 🐾
(989) 362-3822. **$45-$85.** 1124 US 23 S. On US 23, 1.8 mi s. Ext corridors. **Pets:** Medium. Service with restrictions, crate.
[SAVE] [S★] [✕] [🛏] [💻] [≈] [✕]

TECUMSEH

▼ Tecumseh Inn Motel M 🐾
(517) 423-7401. **$55.** 1445 W Chicago Blvd. On SR 50, 1.5 mi w. Int corridors. **Pets:** Other species. $25 deposit/room.
[✕] [🛏] [💻] [🍴]

THREE RIVERS

▼▼ Super 8 Motel SH
(269) 279-8888. **$59-$89.** 711 US 131. Jct US 131 and SR 60 (Broadway St). Int corridors. **Pets:** Medium. $5 daily fee/pet. Service with restrictions, supervision.
[ASK] [S★] [✕] [M] [🐾] [🛏] [≈]

TRAVERSE CITY

Best Western Four Seasons M
(231) 946-8424. **$69-$169.** 305 Munson Ave. 2 mi e on US 31. Ext/int corridors. **Pets:** Medium. $10 daily fee/pet. Service with restrictions, supervision.

Holiday Inn LH
(231) 947-3700. **$109-$199.** 615 E Front St. 0.5 mi e on US 31. Int corridors. **Pets:** Accepted.

Motel 6-4065 SH
(231) 938-3002. **$42-$120, 7 day notice.** 1582 US 31 N. On US 31, 4.3 mi e. Int corridors. **Pets:** $6 daily fee/pet. Service with restrictions, supervision.

Quality Inn SH
(231) 929-4423. **$40-$170.** 1492 US 31 N. On US 31, 3.3 mi e. Ext/int corridors. **Pets:** $10 daily fee/room. Service with restrictions, supervision.

WALKER

Baymont Inn & Suites-Grand Rapids North SH
(616) 735-9595. **$79-$99.** 2151 Holton Ct NW. I-96, exit 28 (Walker Ave), just s. Int corridors. **Pets:** Small. $50 deposit/room. Designated rooms, service with restrictions, supervision.

WATERSMEET

Dancing Eagles Resort Lac Vieux Desert Casino LH
(906) 358-4949. **$60-$160.** N5384 US Hwy 45. 1.8 mi n of US 2. Int corridors. **Pets:** Medium. $100 deposit/room. Designated rooms, service with restrictions, supervision.

WEST BRANCH

Super 8 Motel SH
(989) 345-8488. **$66-$88.** 2596 Austin's Way. I-75, exit 212 (Cook Rd). Int corridors. **Pets:** Service with restrictions, supervision.

WHITEHALL

Lake Land Motel M
(231) 894-5644. **$40-$75.** 1002 E Colby St. On US 31 business route, 0.8 mi w of US 31. Ext corridors. **Pets:** $5 one-time fee/room. Service with restrictions.

WHITMORE LAKE

Best Western Whitmore Lake M
(734) 449-2058. **$75-$79.** 9897 Main St. US 23, exit 53, just e. Ext corridors. **Pets:** Medium, other species. $25 daily fee/pet. Designated rooms, service with restrictions, crate.

WYOMING

Super 8 Motel M
(616) 530-8588. **$54-$59.** 727 44th St SW. US 131, exit 79. Int corridors. **Pets:** Accepted.

MINNESOTA

CITY INDEX

AITKIN

40 Club Inn SH
(218) 927-2903. **$45-$89.** 950 2nd St NW. SR 210, 1 mi w of jct US 169. Int corridors. **Pets:** $5 daily fee/pet. Designated rooms, service with restrictions, supervision.

Ripple River Motel & RV Park M
(218) 927-3734. **$52-$85.** 701 Minnesota Ave S. US 169, 0.8 mi s of jct SR 210. Ext corridors. **Pets:** $10 daily fee/pet. Designated rooms, supervision.

ALBERT LEA

Albert Lea Countryside Inn Motel M
(507) 373-2446. **$40-$80, 3 day notice.** 2102 E Main St. I-35, exit 11, 1.3 mi w on CR 46. Ext/int corridors. **Pets:** $5 daily fee/pet. Service with restrictions, supervision.

Comfort Inn SH
(507) 377-1100. **$49-$89.** 810 Happy Trails Ln. I-35, exit 11, just se. Int corridors. **Pets:** Medium, other species. $25 one-time fee/pet. Designated rooms, service with restrictions, supervision.

Country Inn & Suites By Carlson SH
(507) 373-5513. **$79-$129.** 2214 E Main St. I-35, exit 12 southbound; exit 11 northbound, 1 mi w. Int corridors. **Pets:** Small, dogs only. $20 one-time fee/room. Designated rooms, service with restrictions, supervision.

Days Inn SH
(507) 373-8291. **$65-$80, 3 day notice.** 2301 E Main St. I-35, exit 11, 1 mi w on CR 46. Int corridors. **Pets:** Medium, other species. $8 daily fee/pet. Designated rooms, service with restrictions, supervision.

ALEXANDRIA

Country Inn & Suites By Carlson SH
(320) 763-9900. **$76-$109.** 5304 Hwy 29 S. I-94, exit 103, just sw. Int corridors. **Pets:** Very small. $10 one-time fee/pet. Designated rooms, service with restrictions, supervision.

Holiday Inn Alexandria SH
(320) 763-6577. **$80-$140.** 5637 State Hwy 29 S. I-94, exit 103, just s. Int corridors. **Pets:** Other species. Designated rooms, service with restrictions, crate.

Super 8 Motel SH
(320) 763-6552. **$64-$76, 3 day notice.** 4620 SR 29 S. I-94, exit 103, 0.3 mi n. Int corridors. **Pets:** Medium. $50 deposit/room, $6 one-time fee/pet. Service with restrictions, supervision.

AUSTIN

Country Side Inn SH
(507) 437-7774. **$45-$62.** 3303 Oakland Ave W. I-90, exit 175 (Oakland Ave), just nw. Int corridors. **Pets:** Other species. $5 one-time fee/room. Service with restrictions.

Days Inn SH
(507) 433-8600. **$69.** 700 16th Ave NW. I-90, exit 178A (4th St NW), just nw. Int corridors. **Pets:** Other species. $10 one-time fee/room. Designated rooms, service with restrictions, supervision.

▼▼▼▼ Holiday Inn & Austin Conference Center 🆂🅷
(507) 433-1000. **$99.** 1701 4th St NW. I-90, exit 178A (4th St NW), just nw. Int corridors. **Pets:** Other species. $10 one-time fee/room. Designated rooms, service with restrictions, supervision.
ASK 🆂 ✕ 🅔M 🖉 🛈 🖳 🍴 ➰ ✕

BABBITT

▼▼▼▼ Timber Bay Lodge & Houseboats 🅲🅰
(218) 827-3682. **$671-$1495 (weekly), 60 day notice.** 8347 Timber Bay Rd. 2.8 mi e of jct CR 21 via CR 70 and 623. Ext corridors. **Pets:** Other species. $15 daily fee/pet. No service, supervision.
🛈 🖳 ✕ 🅺 🖉

BAUDETTE

▼▼▼ AmericInn Lodge & Suites Lake of the Woods 🆂🅷
(218) 634-3200. **$72-$78.** 0.5 mi w on SR 11. Int corridors. **Pets:** Medium. $20 one-time fee/room. Designated rooms, no service, supervision.
ASK ✕ 🅔M 🖉 🖉 🛈 🖳 ➰ ✕

BAXTER

▼▼▼ Country Inn & Suites by Carlson 🆂🅷
(218) 828-2161. **$79-$95.** 15058 Dellwood Dr N. Jct SR 371 and 210, 1 mi n on SR 371. Int corridors. **Pets:** Dogs only. Service with restrictions, supervision.
ASK 🆂 ✕ 🅔M 🖉 🖉 🛈 🖳 ➰

BEMIDJI

⟨A⟩ ▼▼▼ Best Western Bemidji 🆂🅷 ❀
(218) 751-0390. **$45-$95.** 2420 Paul Bunyan Dr. Jct US 71 N and SR 197. Int corridors. **Pets:** Other species. Designated rooms, service with restrictions, supervision.
SAVE 🆂 ✕ 🖉 🛈 🖳 ➰ ✕

⟨A⟩ ▼▼▼ Ruttger's Birchmont Lodge 🅲🅰
(218) 444-3463. **$41-$235, 30 day notice.** 7598 Bemidji Rd NE. Jct SR 197, 3.6 mi n on CR 21 (Bemidji Ave N). Ext/int corridors. **Pets:** Other species. $10 daily fee/pet. Designated rooms, service with restrictions, supervision.
SAVE 🆂 ✕ 🛈 🖳 🍴 ➰ ✕

BIWABIK

⟨A⟩ ▼▼▼▼ The Lodge at Giants Ridge 🆂🅷
(218) 865-7170. **$69-$199, 14 day notice.** 6373 Wynne Creek Dr. 2.7 mi e on CR 135, then 4 mi e. Ext corridors. **Pets:** Other species. $25 one-time fee/room. Service with restrictions, supervision.
SAVE 🆂 ✕ 🖉 🛈 🖳 🍴 ➰ ✕

BLUE EARTH

⟨A⟩ ▼▼▼ AmericInn of Blue Earth 🆂🅷
(507) 526-4215. **$80-$150.** 1495 Domes Dr. I-90, exit 119 (US 169), just se. Int corridors. **Pets:** Medium, other species. $10 one-time fee/room. Designated rooms, service with restrictions, supervision.
SAVE 🆂 ✕ 🅔M 🖉 🛈 🖳 ➰

▼▼ Super 8 Motel 🆂🅷
(507) 526-7376. **$60-$70.** 1420 Giant Dr. I-90, exit 119 (US 169), just s. Int corridors. **Pets:** Other species. $5 one-time fee/pet. Designated rooms, service with restrictions, supervision.
ASK 🆂 ✕ 🛈 🖳

BRAINERD

▼▼ Brainerd Lakes Inn Ⓜ
(218) 829-0391. **$40-$80.** 1630 Fairview Rd N. On SR 210 and 371. Int corridors. **Pets:** Accepted.
ASK 🆂 ✕

⟨A⟩ ▼▼▼ Ramada Inn Brainerd 🆂🅷
(218) 829-1441. **$64-$95.** 2115 S 6th St. On SR 371 business route, 1.8 mi s of jct SR 210. Ext/int corridors. **Pets:** Small, other species. $10 daily fee/pet. Designated rooms, service with restrictions, supervision.
SAVE 🆂 ✕ 🖉 🛈 🖳 🍴 ➰ ✕

BRECKENRIDGE

⟨A⟩ ▼▼▼ Select Inn of Breckenridge/Wahpeton 🆂🅷 ❀
(218) 643-9201. **$49-$59.** 821 Hwy 75 N. Just sw of jct US 75 N and 210. Int corridors. **Pets:** Other species. $50 deposit/room, $10 one-time fee/room.
SAVE 🆂 ✕ 🖉 🛈 🖳 ➰

▼▼ South Haven Inn Ⓜ
(218) 643-3125. **$37-$41.** 1 mi s on jct US 75 and Minnesota Ave. Ext corridors. **Pets:** Small. No service, supervision.
ASK 🆂 ✕ 🛈 🖳

CALEDONIA

⟨A⟩ ▼▼▼ AmericInn Lodge & Suites 🆂🅷
(507) 725-8000. **$68-$78, 30 day notice.** 508 N Kruckow Ave. Just n of Main St on SR 44, then just w on Esch Dr. Int corridors. **Pets:** Accepted.
SAVE 🆂 ✕ 🛈 🖳 ➰

CANNON FALLS

⟨A⟩ ▼▼▼ Best Western Saratoga Inn 🆂🅷
(507) 263-7272. **$64-$99.** 31591 64th Ave. 1 mi s on US 52. Int corridors. **Pets:** Other species. $15 one-time fee/room. Designated rooms, service with restrictions, crate.
SAVE 🆂 ✕ 🛈 🖳 ➰

CLOQUET

▼▼ Super 8 Motel 🆂🅷
(218) 879-1250. **$66-$136.** 121 Big Lake Rd. I-35, exit 237 (SR 33), 2 mi nw. Int corridors. **Pets:** Accepted.
ASK 🆂 ✕ 🅔M 🖉 🛈

CROOKSTON

▼▼ Northland Inn of Crookston 🆂🅷
(218) 281-5210. **$69-$84.** 2200 University Ave. On US 2 W and 75 N, 1.5 mi n. Int corridors. **Pets:** Other species. $10 one-time fee/room. Supervision.
ASK 🆂 ✕ 🖉 🍴 ➰

DETROIT LAKES

Best Western Holland House & Suites SH
(218) 847-4483. **$79-$209, 3 day notice.** 615 Hwy 10 E. 1.3 mi se. Ext/int corridors. **Pets:** Accepted.
[SAVE] [X] [🐾] [🔌] [💻] [≈] [X]

Budget Host Inn M
(218) 847-4454. **$51-$96.** 895 Hwy 10 E. 1.5 mi se. Ext corridors. **Pets:** $10 daily fee/room. Designated rooms, service with restrictions.
[SAVE] [S☐] [X] [🔌] [💻]

DULUTH

AmericInn Hotel & Suites of Duluth/Proctor SH ❀
(218) 624-1026. **$75-$189.** 185 US 2. Jct I-35 and US 2, 0.8 mi n. Int corridors. **Pets:** Other species. $10 daily fee/room. Service with restrictions, supervision.
[ASK] [S☐] [X] [🐾] [☞] [🔌] [💻] [🍴] [≈]

Best Western Downtown Motel M
(218) 727-6851. **$39-$119.** 131 W 2nd St. 2nd St at 2nd Ave W; center. Ext/int corridors. **Pets:** Accepted.
[SAVE] [S☐] [X] [🔌] [💻]

Best Western Edgewater Motel M ❀
(218) 728-3601. **$69-$169.** 2400 London Rd. I-35, exit 258 (21st Ave E), just nw. Ext/int corridors. **Pets:** Small, dogs only. $6 daily fee/pet. Designated rooms, service with restrictions, supervision.
[SAVE] [S☐] [X] [🐾] [☞] [🔌] [💻] [≈] [X]

Days Inn-Duluth SH
(218) 727-3110. **$55-$135.** 909 Cottonwood Ave. SR 194, just n of jct US 53. Int corridors. **Pets:** Other species. Service with restrictions, supervision.
[ASK] [S☐] [X] [☞] [🔌]

Hawthorn Suites at Waterfront Plaza SH
(218) 727-4663. **$80-$230.** 325 Lake Ave S. In Canal Park area. Int corridors. **Pets:** $75 deposit/pet. Designated rooms, service with restrictions, supervision.
[SAVE] [S☐] [X] [🐾] [🌙] [☞] [🔌] [💻] [🍴] [≈] [X]

Radisson Hotel Duluth-Harborview LH
(218) 727-8981. **$109-$159.** 505 W Superior St. At 5th Ave W; center. Int corridors. **Pets:** Small, other species. $10 daily fee/room. Designated rooms, supervision.
[SAVE] [S☐] [X] [🔌] [💻] [🍴] [≈] [X]

ELY

Motel Ely-Budget Host M
(218) 365-3237. **$69-$89, 3 day notice.** 1047 E Sheridan St. SR 1 and 169. Ext corridors. **Pets:** Accepted.
[S☐] [X] [💻]

EVELETH

Super 8 Motel SH
(218) 744-1661. **$50-$109.** 1080 Industrial Park Dr. On US 53, 0.5 mi n of jct SR 37. Int corridors. **Pets:** Accepted.
[ASK] [S☐] [X] [🌙] [☞] [🔌] [💻] [≈] [X]

FAIRMONT

Comfort Inn SH
(507) 238-5444. **$60-$90.** 2225 N State St. I-90, exit 102 (SR 15), just sw. Int corridors. **Pets:** Medium. Designated rooms, service with restrictions.
[X] [🌙] [💻] [≈]

Holiday Inn SH
(507) 238-4771. **$70-$120.** 1201 Torgerson Dr. I-90, exit 102 (SR 15), just se. Int corridors. **Pets:** Medium. Designated rooms, service with restrictions.
[ASK] [S☐] [X] [🔌] [💻] [🍴] [≈] [X]

Super 8 Motel SH
(507) 238-9444. **$50-$80.** 1200 Torgerson Dr. I-90, exit 102 (SR 15), just se. Int corridors. **Pets:** Medium. Designated rooms, service with restrictions.
[ASK] [S☐] [X]

FARIBAULT

AmericInn Motel SH ❀
(507) 334-9464. **$73-$139.** 1801 Lavender Dr. I-35, exit 59 (SR 21), 0.3 mi e. Int corridors. **Pets:** Medium. Designated rooms, service with restrictions, crate.
[ASK] [S☐] [X] [🌙] [☞] [🔌] [💻] [≈] [X]

Days Inn & Suites SH
(507) 334-6835. **$50-$89.** 1920 Cardinal Ln. I-35, exit 59 (SR 21), just ne. Int corridors. **Pets:** $10 daily fee/room. Designated rooms, no service, supervision.
[ASK] [S☐] [X] [🌙] [🐾] [☞] [💻] [≈]

Select Inn M
(507) 334-2051. **$45-$57.** 4040 SR 60 W. I-35, exit 56, just w. Int corridors. **Pets:** Small. $5 daily fee/pet. Designated rooms, service with restrictions, supervision.
[SAVE] [S☐] [X] [☞] [🔌] [💻] [≈]

FERGUS FALLS

AmericInn Lodge & Suites SH ❀
(218) 739-3900. **$66-$125.** 526 Western Ave N. I-94, exit 54 (SR 210), just se. Int corridors. **Pets:** Other species. $50 deposit/room, $10 one-time fee/pet. Designated rooms, service with restrictions, supervision.
[SAVE] [X] [🌙] [🐾] [☞] [🔌] [💻] [≈] [X]

FINLAYSON

Banning Junction-North Country Inn SH
(320) 245-5284. **$52-$74.** 60671 State Hwy 23. I-35, exit 195 (SR 23), just ne. Int corridors. **Pets:** Accepted.
[ASK] [S☐] [X]

FOSSTON

Super 8 Motel SH
(218) 435-1088. **$60-$84.** 108 S Amber. US 2, 0.5 mi e. Int corridors. **Pets:** Dogs only. $5 daily fee/room. Supervision.
[ASK] [S☐] [X] [🔌]

GARRISON

▼▼▼▼ Garrison Inn & Suites by Ruttger's SH
(320) 692-4050. **$69-$129.** 9243 Hwy 169. SR 169, just s of jct SR 18. Int corridors. **Pets:** Accepted.
ASK ✕ 🛏 💻 ⚓

GAYLORD

▼▼ Gold Leaf Inn & Suites M
(507) 237-5860. **$52-$66.** 330 Main Ave E. 1.5 mi e. Int corridors. **Pets:** Medium, other species. Designated rooms, service with restrictions, supervision.
✕ 🏷 🛏

GRAND MARAIS

**⚑ ▼▼▼▼ Best Western Superior Inn &
Suites** SH
(218) 387-2240. **$69-$249, 3 day notice.** 104 1st Ave E. SR 61, just ne of center. Int corridors. **Pets:** Designated rooms, supervision.
SAVE ✕ 🗭 🏷 🛏 💻

▼▼▼ Gunflint Lodge VH ❖
(218) 388-2294. **$105-$459, 42 day notice.** 143 S Gunflint Lake. 43 mi n of Grand Marais, 0.8 mi e of jct CR 12 (Gunflint Tr) and 50. Ext corridors. **Pets:** Other species. $15 daily fee/pet.
🏷M 🛏 💻 🍽 ✕ 🐾 🐕

⚑ ▼▼▼ Nor'Wester Lodge and Outfitter CA
(218) 388-2252. **$560-$1390 (weekly), 60 day notice.** 7778 Gunflint Tr. 30 mi nw on CR 12 (Gunflint Tr) from jct SR 61. Ext corridors. **Pets:** Other species. $15 daily fee/pet. Designated rooms, no service, supervision.
SAVE 🛏 💻 ✕ 🐾 🐾 🐕

▼ Outpost Motel M
(218) 387-1833. **$45-$88.** 2935 SR 61 E. 9 mi ne. Ext corridors. **Pets:** $10 daily fee/pet. Supervision.
✕ 🛏 💻 🐾

⚑ ▼▼▼ Spruceglen Inn M
(218) 264-1020. **$39-$119, 3 day notice.** 310 E Hwy 61. On SR 61; just ne of center. Ext corridors. **Pets:** Accepted.
SAVE 🏷 ✕ 🛏 🐾

⚑ ▼▼ Super 8 Motel M
(218) 387-2448. **$45-$119, 3 day notice.** 1711 W Hwy 61. On SR 61, 1 mi sw. Ext/int corridors. **Pets:** Accepted.
SAVE 🏷 ✕ 🛏

⚑ ▼ Wedgewood Motel M
(218) 387-2944. **$45.** 1663 E Hwy 61. On SR 61, 2.5 mi ne. Ext corridors. **Pets:** Dogs only. Supervision.
SAVE 🏷 ✕ 🐾 🐕

GRAND RAPIDS

⚑ ▼▼▼ Budget Host Inn M
(218) 326-3457. **$55-$78, 7 day notice.** 311 E Hwy 2. Jct US 2 E and 169 N. Ext/int corridors. **Pets:** Accepted.
SAVE 🏷 ✕

⚑ ▼▼▼▼ Country Inn By Carlson SH ❖
(218) 327-4960. **$78-$124, 30 day notice.** 2601 Hwy 169 S. US 2, 2 mi s. Int corridors. **Pets:** Medium, dogs only. Service with restrictions, supervision.
SAVE 🏷 ✕ 🏷M 🗭 🏷 🛏 💻 ⚓

⚑ ▼▼▼▼ Sawmill Inn M
(218) 326-8501. **$76-$99.** 2301 S Pokegama Ave. US 2, 2 mi s on US 169. Ext/int corridors. **Pets:** Supervision.
SAVE 🏷 ✕ 🗭 🛏 💻 🍽 ⚓ ✕

HARMONY

▼▼ Country Lodge Motel SH
(507) 886-2515. **$85.** 525 Main Ave N. 0.4 mi n on US 52. Int corridors. **Pets:** Accepted.
🏷 ✕ 🏷 🛏 💻

HINCKLEY

⚑ ▼▼▼ Days Inn SH
(320) 384-7751. **$50-$120.** 104 Grindstone Ct. I-35, exit 183 (SR 48), just e. Int corridors. **Pets:** $10 daily fee/pet. Service with restrictions.
SAVE 🏷 ✕ 🏷 🛏 💻 ⚓

⚑ ▼▼▼ Hinckley Gold Pine Inn M
(320) 384-6112. **$39-$75.** 325 Fire Monument. I-35, exit 183 (SR 48), just w. Ext/int corridors. **Pets:** Accepted.
SAVE 🏷 ✕ 🗭 🛏 💻

INTERNATIONAL FALLS

▼▼ Hilltop Motel M
(218) 283-2505. **$45-$79.** 2002 2nd Ave W. US 53, 1 mi s of jct US 53 and SR 11. Ext corridors. **Pets:** Medium, dogs only. $10 daily fee/pet. Designated rooms, service with restrictions, supervision.
ASK 🏷 ✕

▼▼▼ Holiday Inn SH
(218) 283-8000. **$99-$175, 3 day notice.** 1500 US 71 W. 1.5 mi w on US 71 and SR 11 W. Int corridors. **Pets:** Designated rooms, service with restrictions, crate.
ASK 🏷 ✕ 🏷 🛏 💻 🍽 ⚓ ✕

JACKSON

⚑ ▼ Budget Host Inn Praire Winds M ❖
(507) 847-2020. **$40-$65.** 950 US 71. I-90, exit 73 (US 71), 0.4 mi s. Ext corridors. **Pets:** Other species. $4 daily fee/pet. Designated rooms, service with restrictions, supervision.
SAVE ✕ 🏷M 🛏

▼▼ Super 8 Motel SH
(507) 847-3498. **$65-$109.** 2025 Hwy 71 N. I-90, exit 73 (US 71), just n. Int corridors. **Pets:** $6 daily fee/pet. Designated rooms, service with restrictions, supervision.
ASK 🏷 ✕ 🏷M 🏷 🛏

LITCHFIELD

▼▼ ScotWood Motel M
(320) 693-2496. **$82-$189, 3 day notice.** 1017 E Frontage Rd. On US 12. Int corridors. **Pets:** Accepted.
ASK 🏷 ✕ 🛏 ⚓

LITTLE FALLS

AAA ▼◆▼◆▼ **Country Inn & Suites By Carlson** SH
(320) 632-1000. **$79-$94.** 209 16th St NE. Just ne of jct SR 10 and 27. Int corridors. **Pets:** Accepted.
SAVE 🆂 ⊗ ⟨🄼 ⟨🄹 🆓 🄳 ➔

LONG PRAIRIE

AAA ▼◆▼◆▼ **Budget Host Inn** M
(320) 732-6118. **$50-$69, 3 day notice.** 417 Lake St. On US 71 and SR 27, just s of jct SR 287. Ext corridors. **Pets:** $5 daily fee/pet. Designated rooms, service with restrictions, supervision.
SAVE 🆂 ⊗ 🄳 🄳

LUTSEN

▼◆▼◆ **Lutsen Lodging Company** SH
(218) 663-7244. **$59-$134, 46 day notice.** 360 Ski Hill Rd. On CR 36 (Ski Hill Rd), 1.3 mi n of jct SR 61. Int corridors. **Pets:** Accepted.
ASK 🆂 ⊗ 🄳 ⊗

AAA ▼◆▼◆▼ **Solbakken Resort** M ❖
(218) 663-7566. **$49-$255, 14 day notice.** 4874 W SR 61. On SR 61, 1.3 mi n of jct CR 4 (Caribou Tr). Ext corridors. **Pets:** Other species. $12 daily fee/pet. Designated rooms, service with restrictions, supervision.
SAVE ⊗ 🄳 🄳 🄳 ⊗ 🄺

MANKATO

AAA ▼◆▼◆▼ **Best Western Hotel, Restaurant & Conference Center** SH ❖
(507) 625-9333. **$70-$99.** 1111 Range St. 1.3 mi n on US 169. Int corridors. **Pets:** Designated rooms, service with restrictions, crate.
SAVE 🆂 ⊗ 🄳 🄳 🄳 ➔ ⊗

▼◆▼◆ **Comfort Inn** SH
(507) 388-5107. **$64-$109.** 131 Apache Pl. Just s of jct US 14 and SR 22 S. Int corridors. **Pets:** Accepted.
ASK 🆂 ⊗ 🄳 🄳 🄳 ➔ ⊗

▼◆▼◆▼ **Grandstay Residential Suites** SH
(507) 388-8688. **$80-$99.** 1000 Raintree Rd. 1.3 mi s of jct US 14 and SR 22, on CR 3. Int corridors. **Pets:** Accepted.
⊗ 🄳 🄳 🄳 🄳 ➔

▼◆▼◆ **Holiday Inn** SH
(507) 345-1234. **$65-$115.** 101 E Main St. Main St at Riverfront Dr; downtown. Int corridors. **Pets:** Accepted.
ASK 🆂 ⊗ 🄼 🄹 🄳 🄳 🄳 🄳 ➔ ⊗

▼◆▼◆ **Super 8 Motel** SH
(507) 387-4041. **$44-$89.** RR 7. Jct US 169 N and 14, just n. Int corridors. **Pets:** Large, dogs only. $100 deposit/room. Designated rooms, service with restrictions, supervision.
ASK 🆂 ⊗

MARSHALL

AAA ▼◆▼◆▼ **Best Western Marshall Inn** SH
(507) 532-3221. **$73-$99.** 1500 E College Dr. SR 19, just w of jct SR 23. Int corridors. **Pets:** Other species. $10 one-time fee/pet. Service with restrictions, crate.
SAVE 🆂 ⊗ 🄳 🄳 🄳 🄳 ➔ ⊗

▼◆▼◆ **Comfort Inn** SH
(507) 532-3070. **$75-$90.** 1511 E College Dr. SR 19, w of jct SR 23. Int corridors. **Pets:** Other species. $5 one-time fee/room. Service with restrictions, crate.
ASK 🆂 ⊗ 🄼 🄹 🄳 🄳 🄳 ➔

▼◆▼◆ **Super 8 Motel** SH
(507) 537-1461. **$65-$75.** 1106 E Main St. 0.3 mi se on US 59 from jct SR 23. Int corridors. **Pets:** Large. $50 deposit/room, $10 one-time fee/pet. Designated rooms, service with restrictions, supervision.
ASK 🆂 ⊗ 🄹 🄳

MCGREGOR

▼◆▼◆ **Country Meadows Inn** SH
(218) 768-7378. **$60-$109.** Jct SR 65 and 210. Int corridors. **Pets:** Accepted.
⊗ 🄹 🄳 🄳 ➔

MILACA

▼◆▼◆ **Super 8 Motel** SH
(320) 983-2660. **Call for rates.** 215 10th Ave SE. Jct SR 23 and 169. Int corridors. **Pets:** Accepted.
⊗ 🄼 🄹 🄳

<hr>

MINNEAPOLIS-ST. PAUL METROPOLITAN AREA

ARDEN HILLS

AAA ▼◆▼◆▼ **Super 8 Arden Hills/Minneapolis/St. Paul** SH
(651) 484-6557. **$60-$87.** 1125 Red Fox Rd. I-694, exit 43A (Lexington Ave), just sw. Int corridors. **Pets:** Small. $50 deposit/room, $8 daily fee/pet. Service with restrictions, crate.
SAVE 🆂 ⊗ 🄳 🄳

BLOOMINGTON

AAA ▼◆▼◆▼ **AmeriSuites (Minneapolis/Mall of America)** SH
(952) 854-0700. **$99-$139.** 7800 International Dr. I-494, exit 1B (34th Ave), just sw. Int corridors. **Pets:** Accepted.
SAVE 🆂 ⊗ 🄼 🄹 🄳 🄳 ➔

(AAA) (W)(W) **Baymont Inn Minneapolis-Airport (Bloomington)** SH
(952) 881-7311. **$74-$84.** 7815 Nicollet Ave S. I-494, exit 4A (Nicollet Ave), just s. Int corridors. **Pets:** Other species. No service, supervision.
(SAVE) (S🔒) (X) (🔊) (🛏) (💻)

(AAA) (W)(W) **Clarion Hotel Bloomington** SH
(952) 830-1300. **$83-$93.** 5151 American Blvd W. I-494, exit 6B (France Ave), just se of SR 100, 1 mi w on frontage road. Int corridors. **Pets:** Medium. $10 daily fee/room. Designated rooms, service with restrictions, crate.
(SAVE) (S🔒) (X) (🔊) (🛏) (💻) (🍴) (✕)

(AAA) (W)(W)(W) **Days Inn Bloomington** SH
(952) 835-7400. **$64-$79.** 7851 Normandale Lake Blvd. I-494, exit 7 (SR 100), just ne. Int corridors. **Pets:** Accepted.
(SAVE) (S🔒) (X) (👤M) (💺) (💻) (🏊)

(AAA) (W)(W)(W) **Hilton Minneapolis-St. Paul Airport** LH
(952) 854-2100. **$79-$89.** 3800 E 80th St. I-494, exit 1B (34th Ave), just se. Int corridors. **Pets:** Accepted.
(SAVE) (X) (👤M) (🔊) (💺) (🛏) (💻) (🍴) (🏊) (✕)

(W)(W)(W) **Homewood Suites by Hilton** SH
(952) 854-0900. **$129-$159.** 2261 Killebrew Dr. I-494, exit 2A (24th Ave), 1 mi s, just w. Int corridors. **Pets:** Accepted.
(ASK) (S🔒) (X) (💺) (🛏) (💻) (🏊)

(W)(W)(W) **Hospitality Inn & Suites** SH
(952) 854-1687. **$69-$99.** 1601 79th St E. I-494, exit 3, 0.5 mi s. Int corridors. **Pets:** Small. $20 daily fee/pet. Designated rooms, service with restrictions, crate.
(ASK) (S🔒) (X) (🛏) (💻) (🍴) (🏊)

(AAA) (W)(W)(W) **Radisson Hotel South & Plaza Tower** LH
(952) 835-7800. **$79-$139.** 7800 Normandale Blvd. I-494, exit 7 (SR 100). Int corridors. **Pets:** Medium. $100 deposit/room, $40 one-time fee/room. Service with restrictions, crate.
(SAVE) (S🔒) (X) (💺) (🛏) (💻) (🍴) (🏊) (✕)

(AAA) (W)(W)(W) **Ramada Inn Airport & Thunderbird Convention Center** SH
(952) 854-3411. **$79-$99.** 2201 E 78th St. I-494, exit 2A (24th Ave), just s. Int corridors. **Pets:** Large, other species. $5 daily fee/pet. Designated rooms, service with restrictions, supervision.
(SAVE) (S🔒) (X) (👤M) (🔊) (🛏) (💻) (🍴) (🏊) (✕)

(W)(W)(W) **Residence Inn by Marriott** SH
(952) 876-0900. **$129-$189.** 7850 Bloomington Ave S. I-494, exit 3, on south frontage road. Int corridors. **Pets:** Other species. $50 one-time fee/room.
(ASK) (S🔒) (X) (🔊) (💺) (🛏) (💻) (🏊)

(AAA) (W)(W)(W)(W) **Sofitel Minneapolis** LH ✿
(952) 835-1900. **$184-$234.** 5601 W 78th St. Just nw of jct I-494 and SR 100, access via SR 100 and Industrial Blvd. Int corridors. **Pets:** Medium. Service with restrictions.
(SAVE) (S🔒) (X) (👤M) (🔊) (💺) (🛏) (🍴) (✕)

(W)(W)(W) **Staybridge Suites By Holiday Inn** SH
(952) 831-7900. **$149-$239.** 8150 Bridge Rd. I-494, exit 6B (France Ave), just se of SR 100, 1 mi w on frontage road. Int corridors. **Pets:** Other species. $75 one-time fee/room. Service with restrictions, crate.
(ASK) (S🔒) (X) (👤M) (🔊) (💺) (🛏) (💻) (🏊)

BROOKLYN CENTER

(AAA) (W)(W) **Baymont Inn & Suites Minneapolis-Brooklyn Center** SH
(763) 561-8400. **$59-$79.** 6415 James Cir N. I-94/694, exit 34 (Shingle Creek Pkwy), just ne. Int corridors. **Pets:** Accepted.
(SAVE) (S🔒) (X) (🔊) (🛏) (💻)

(W)(W) **Comfort Inn** SH
(763) 560-7464. **$69-$99.** 1600 James Cir N. I-694, exit 34 (Shingle Creek Pkwy), just ne. Int corridors. **Pets:** Accepted.
(ASK) (S🔒) (X) (👤M) (🔊) (💺) (🛏) (💻) (✕)

(AAA) (W)(W)(W) **Hilton Minneapolis North** SH
(763) 566-8000. **$62-$172.** 2200 Freeway Blvd. I-94/694, exit 34 (Shingle Creek Pkwy). Int corridors. **Pets:** Medium. $15 daily fee/pet. Service with restrictions, supervision.
(SAVE) (S🔒) (X) (💺) (🛏) (💻) (🍴) (🏊) (✕)

BROOKLYN PARK

(AAA) (W)(W)(W) **Sleep Inn** SH
(763) 971-8000. **$79-$99.** 7011 Northland Cir. I-94/694, exit 30 (Boone Ave), just ne. Int corridors. **Pets:** $50 deposit/room, $10 daily fee/room. Designated rooms, service with restrictions, crate.
(SAVE) (S🔒) (X) (👤M) (💺) (🛏) (💻) (🏊)

BURNSVILLE

(AAA) (W)(W)(W) **Red Roof Inn** M 🐾
(952) 890-1420. **$40-$80.** 12920 Aldrich Ave S. I-35 W, exit 2 (Burnsville Pkwy), just sw. Ext corridors. **Pets:** Medium. Service with restrictions, supervision.
(SAVE) (X) (🔊)

(W)(W) **Super 8 Motel** M
(952) 894-3400. **$52-$67.** 1101 Burnsville Pkwy. I-35 W, exit 2 (Burnsville Pkwy), just sw. Int corridors. **Pets:** Dogs only. $10 one-time fee/pet. Service with restrictions, supervision.
(ASK) (S🔒) (X)

CHANHASSEN

(AAA) (W)(W)(W) **AmericInn Motel & Suites** SH
(952) 934-3888. **$101-$195.** 570 Pond Promenade. Just se of jct SR 5 and 101 N. Int corridors. **Pets:** Small, other species. $100 deposit/room, $30 one-time fee/room. Designated rooms, service with restrictions, supervision.
(SAVE) (S🔒) (X) (👤M) (💺) (🛏) (💻) (🏊) (✕)

CHISAGO CITY

(W)(W) **Super 8 Motel-Chisago City/Lindstrom** SH
(651) 257-8088. **$49-$75.** 11490 Lake Ln (Hwy 8). 1.3 mi ne. Int corridors. **Pets:** Accepted.
(ASK) (S🔒) (X) (🛏)

COON RAPIDS

(AAA) ▼▼▼▼ Comfort Inn-Northtown SH
(763) 785-4746. **$49-$95.** 9052 University Ave NE. Just ne of jct US 10, exit University Ave. Int corridors. **Pets:** Small. $10 daily fee/pet. Designated rooms, service with restrictions, supervision.

SAVE SØ ⊠ 🖬 🖵 ⤸

(AAA) ▼▼▼▼ Country Suites By Carlson SH
(763) 780-3797. **$105-$115.** 155 Coon Rapids Blvd. 0.5 mi e of SR 610. Int corridors. **Pets:** Small, other species. $10 daily fee/room. Designated rooms, service with restrictions, crate.

SAVE SØ ⊠ 🐾 🖳 🖬 🖵 ⤸

EAGAN

▼▼▼▼ Homestead Studio Suites
Hotel-Minneapolis/Eagan SH 🐾
(651) 905-1778. **$64-$79.** 3015 Denmark Ave. I-35 E, exit 98 (Lone Oak Rd), just se. Int corridors. **Pets:** Medium, other species. $25 daily fee/room. Service with restrictions, crate.

ASK SØ ⊠ 🐾 🖳 🖬 🖵

(AAA) ▼▼▼ Microtel Inn SH
(651) 405-0988. **$45-$70.** 3000 Denmark Ave. I-35 E, exit 98 (Lone Oak Rd), just se. Int corridors. **Pets:** Small. $25 one-time fee/room. Designated rooms, service with restrictions, supervision.

SAVE SØ ⊠ 🖳 🖬 🖵

▼▼▼▼ Residence Inn by Marriott-Mpls/St. Paul
Airport SH
(651) 688-0363. **$99-$119.** 3040 Eagandale Pl. I-35 E, exit 98 (Lone Oak Rd), just sw. Ext corridors. **Pets:** Accepted.

ASK SØ ⊠ 🐾 🖵 ⤸ ⊠

▼▼▼▼ Staybridge Suites SH
(651) 994-7810. **$69-$199, 3 day notice.** 4675 Rahncliff Rd. I-35 E, exit 93 (Cliff Rd), just w, then just s. Int corridors. **Pets:** Medium, other species. $75 one-time fee/room. Service with restrictions.

ASK SØ ⊠ 🐾 🖳 🖬 🖵 ⤸

▼▼▼▼ TownePlace Suites SH
(651) 994-4600. **$49-$129.** 3615 Crestridge Dr. I-35, exit 71 (Pilot Knob Rd), just se. Int corridors. **Pets:** Accepted.

ASK SØ ⊠ 🖬 🖵 ⤸

EDEN PRAIRIE

(AAA) ▼▼▼▼ AmeriSuites (Minneapolis/Eden
Prairie) SH
(952) 944-9700. **$79-$99.** 11369 Viking Dr. I-494, exit 11A westbound to Prairie Center Dr, then nw; eastbound follow US 212 (Flying Cloud Dr). Int corridors. **Pets:** Accepted.

SAVE SØ ⊠ 🖳M 🖳 🖬 🖵 ⤸

▼▼▼▼ Homestead Studio Suites
Hotel-Minneapolis/Eden Prairie SH 🐾
(952) 942-6818. **$64-$79.** 11905 Technology Dr. Just sw of jct I-494 and US 212 (Flying Cloud Dr). Int corridors. **Pets:** Medium, other species. $25 daily fee/room. Service with restrictions, crate.

ASK SØ ⊠ 🖳M 🖳 🖬 🖵

▼▼▼▼ The Residence Inn by Marriott-Minneapolis
SW SH
(952) 829-0033. **$104-$113.** 7780 Flying Cloud Dr. On US 169 S and 212 (Flying Cloud Dr), at jct I-494. Int corridors. **Pets:** Accepted.

⊠ 🖬 🖵 ⤸ ⊠

▼▼▼▼ TownePlace Suites By Marriott SH
(952) 942-6001. **$49-$109.** 11588 Leona Rd. Se of jct US 212 (Flying Cloud Dr) and I-494. Int corridors. **Pets:** Accepted.

ASK SØ ⊠ 🖬 🖵 ⤸

EDINA

▼▼▼▼ Residence Inn Minneapolis-Edina SH
(952) 893-9300. **$109-$161.** 3400 Edinborough Way. I-494, exit 6B (France Ave), 0.3 mi n to Minnesota Dr, then just e. Int corridors. **Pets:** Accepted.

ASK ⊠ 🖬 🖵

ELK RIVER

▼▼▼ AmericInn Motel M
(763) 441-8554. **Call for rates.** 17432 Hwy 10. 1.5 mi se on US 10/169. Int corridors. **Pets:** Accepted.

⊠ 🖳 🖵

FRIDLEY

▼▼▼ Best Western Kelly Inn SH
(763) 571-9440. **Call for rates.** 5201 Central Ave NE. I-694, exit 38 (Central Ave/SR 65), 0.3 mi s. Ext/int corridors. **Pets:** Accepted.

⊠ 🐾 🖳 🖬 🖵 ⤸ ⊠

HASTINGS

(AAA) ▼▼▼▼ Country Inn & Suites By
Carlson SH
(651) 437-8870. **$79-$149.** 300 33rd St. Just e of US 61. Int corridors. **Pets:** Other species. $75 deposit/room, $10 daily fee/room. Designated rooms, service with restrictions.

SAVE SØ ⊠ 🖳 🖬 🖵 ⤸

LAKEVILLE

▼▼▼▼ Comfort Inn SH
(952) 898-3700. **$69-$150.** 10935 176th St W. I-35, exit 85 (SR 50), just se. Int corridors. **Pets:** Accepted.

⊠ 🖳M 🖳 🖬 🖵 ⤸

(AAA) ▼▼▼ Super 8 Conference Center SH
(952) 469-1134. **$79-$111.** 20800 Kenrick Ave. I-35, exit 81 (CR 70), just se. Int corridors. **Pets:** Other species. Service with restrictions, supervision.

SAVE SØ ⊠ 🖳 🖬 🍴 ⤸

MAPLE GROVE

▼▼▼▼ Staybridge Suites Minneapolis-Maple
Grove SH
(763) 494-8856. **$125-$150.** 7821 Elm Creek Blvd. Just ne of jct I-94/494/694. Int corridors. **Pets:** Medium. $75 one-time fee/pet. Designated rooms, service with restrictions, crate.

ASK SØ ⊠ 🖳M 🐾 🖳 🖬 🖵 ⤸ ⊠

MINNEAPOLIS

▼▼▼▼ Hilton Minneapolis [LH]
(612) 376-1000. **$95-$309.** 1001 Marquette Ave. Between S 10th and S 11th sts. Int corridors. **Pets:** Medium. $100 deposit/room. Service with restrictions, crate.
(ASK) (S$) (✕) (🐾) (🛏) (🏋) (🖥) (📺) (▥) (➳) (✗)

▼▼▼▼ Holiday Inn Minneapolis Metrodome [LH]
(612) 333-4646. **Call for rates.** 1500 Washington Ave S. Jct Washington and S 15th aves. Int corridors. **Pets:** Accepted.
(✕) (🐾) (🛏) (🏋) (🖥) (📺) (➳) (✗)

(AAA) ▼▼▼▼ Millenium Hotel
Minneapolis [LH] 🐾
(612) 332-6000. **$79-$129.** 1313 Nicollet Mall. Jct of Nicollet Ave and Grant St. Int corridors. **Pets:** $25 daily fee/pet. Service with restrictions, supervision.
(SAVE) (S$) (✕) (LM) (🐾) (🛏) (🏋) (📺) (➳) (✗)

▼▼▼▼ Minneapolis Marriott City Center [LH]
(612) 349-4000. **$179-$249.** 30 S 7th St. Between Hennepin and Nicollet aves; in City Center Shopping Complex. Int corridors. **Pets:** Large, other species. $350 deposit/room. Service with restrictions, crate.
(✕) (LM) (🐾) (🛏) (🏋) (📺) (✗)

(AAA) ▼▼▼▼▼ Radisson Plaza Hotel
Minneapolis [LH]
(612) 339-4900. **$94-$194.** 35 S 7th St. Between Nicollet and Hennepin aves. Int corridors. **Pets:** Accepted.
(SAVE) (S$) (✕) (LM) (🐾) (🛏) (🏋) (🖥) (📺) (✗)

▼▼▼▼ Residence Inn Milwaukee Road
Depot [SH]
(612) 340-1300. **Call for rates.** 425 S 2nd St. Jct S 2nd St and 5th Ave S. Int corridors. **Pets:** Accepted.
(✕) (🐾) (🏋) (🛏) (🖥) (✗)

MINNETONKA

▼▼▼▼ Minneapolis Marriott-Southwest [LH]
(952) 935-5500. **$139-$159.** 5801 Opus Pkwy. Just nw of jct US 169 and Cross Town SR 62, exit Bren Rd off US 169. Int corridors. **Pets:** Large, other species. $250 deposit/pet. Service with restrictions, supervision.
(ASK) (S$) (✕) (🐾) (🛏) (🖥) (📺) (➳) (✗)

MONTICELLO

(AAA) ▼▼▼ Best Western Silver Fox Inn [SH]
(763) 295-4000. **$72-$140.** 1114 Cedar St. I-94, exit 193, 0.3 mi se. Int corridors. **Pets:** Accepted.
(SAVE) (S$) (✕) (🛏) (🖥) (📺)

▼▼▼ Days Inn [SH]
(763) 295-1111. **$60-$80.** 200 E Oakwood Dr. I-94, exit 193, 0.3 mi se. Int corridors. **Pets:** Medium. $10 daily fee/pet. Designated rooms, service with restrictions, supervision.
(ASK) (S$) (✕) (🛏) (🖥)

OAKDALE

▼▼▼▼ Wingate Inn [SH] 🐾
(651) 578-8466. **$69-$165.** 970 Helena Ave N. I-694, exit 57, just e, then just s. Int corridors. **Pets:** Medium. $50 deposit/room. Designated rooms, service with restrictions, crate.
(ASK) (S$) (✕) (LM) (🐾) (🖥) (🛏) (🖥)

PLYMOUTH

(AAA) ▼▼▼▼ Best Western Kelly Inn [SH]
(763) 553-1600. **$79-$119.** 2705 N Annapolis Ln. I-494, exit 22 (SR 55), just e. Int corridors. **Pets:** Other species. Designated rooms, service with restrictions, crate.
(SAVE) (S$) (✕) (🖥) (🛏) (🖥) (📺) (➳) (✗)

(AAA) ▼▼▼▼ Radisson Hotel & Conference Center
Minneapolis [LH] 🐾
(763) 559-6600. **$75-$127.** 3131 Campus Dr. I-494, exit 22 (SR 55), just e to CR 61 (Northwest Blvd), 0.8 mi nw. Int corridors. **Pets:** $50 deposit/pet. Service with restrictions.
(SAVE) (S$) (✕) (🐾) (🖥) (🖥) (📺) (✗)

(AAA) ▼▼▼ Red Roof Inn [M] 🐾
(763) 553-1751. **$55-$86.** 2600 Annapolis Ln N. I-494, exit 22 (SR 55), just se. Ext corridors. **Pets:** Large, other species. Service with restrictions, supervision.
(SAVE) (✕)

RICHFIELD

▼▼▼▼ Candlewood Suites [SH]
(612) 869-7704. **$105-$135.** 351 W 77th St. I-494, exit 4B (Lyndale Ave), just ne. Int corridors. **Pets:** Medium. $150 one-time fee/room. Service with restrictions, supervision.
(ASK) (S$) (✕) (LM) (🐾) (🖥) (🛏) (🖥)

ROGERS

▼▼▼ AmericInn Motel & Suites [SH]
(763) 428-4346. **Call for rates.** 21800 Industrial Blvd. I-94, exit 207 (SR 101). Int corridors. **Pets:** Accepted.
(✕) (🖥) (🛏) (🖥) (➳)

ROSEVILLE

▼▼▼▼ Residence Inn [SH] 🐾
(651) 636-0680. **$129-$169.** 2985 Centre Pointe Dr. I-35 W, exit 25A (CR C), just se. Int corridors. **Pets:** Medium, other species. $150 one-time fee/room. Service with restrictions, crate.
(ASK) (S$) (✕) (LM) (🖥) (🛏) (🖥) (➳) (✗)

ST. LOUIS PARK

(AAA) ▼▼▼ Lakeland Inn [SH]
(952) 926-6575. **$50-$70.** 4025 Hwy 7. SR 7, 0.5 mi e of SR 100. Int corridors. **Pets:** Medium. $5 daily fee/pet. Designated rooms, service with restrictions, supervision.
(SAVE) (S$) (✕) (🛏)

▼▼▼▼ TownePlace Suites-Minneapolis West [SH]
(952) 847-6900. **$64-$94.** 1400 Zarthan Ave S. I-394, exit 5 (Park Place Blvd), 0.3 mi w on 16th, then just n. Int corridors. **Pets:** Accepted.
(ASK) (S$) (✕) (🛏) (🖥) (➳)

ST. PAUL

(AAA) ▼▼▼▼ Best Western Kelly Inn [SH]
(651) 227-8711. **$89-$119.** 161 St. Anthony Ave. Jct I-35 E and 94. Int corridors. **Pets:** Other species. Designated rooms, service with restrictions, supervision.
(SAVE) (S$) (✕) (🖥) (🛏) (🖥) (📺) (➳)

(AAA) ▼▼▼ Exel Inn of St. Paul 🆂🅷 ❀
(651) 771-5566. **$46-$76.** 1739 Old Hudson Rd. I-94, exit 245 (White Bear Ave), just nw. Int corridors. **Pets:** Small. Designated rooms, service with restrictions, supervision.
🆂🅰🆅🅴 🆂🅾 ⊠ 🖉 🔲 💻

SHAKOPEE

(AAA) ▼▼▼ Hearthside Extended Stay Studios by Villager 🆂🅷
(952) 277-0100. **$59-$69.** 3910 12th Ave. Just nw of US 169. Int corridors. **Pets:** Small. $10 daily fee/pet. Service with restrictions, supervision.
🆂🅰🆅🅴 🆂🅾 ⊠ 🔲

(AAA) ▼▼▼▼ Park Inn & Suites International 🆂🅷
(952) 445-3644. **$79-$119.** 1244 Canterbury Rd. Just nw of US 169. Int corridors. **Pets:** Small. $10 daily fee/room. Service with restrictions, crate.
🆂🅰🆅🅴 🆂🅾 ⊠ 🖉 🔲 💻 🍽 🏊 🗙

STILLWATER

(AAA) ▼▼▼▼ Best Western Stillwater Inn 🆂🅷
(651) 430-1300. **$59-$101, 30 day notice.** 1750 W Frontage Rd. SR 36 at Washington Ave, 3 mi sw. Int corridors. **Pets:** Medium. $10 daily fee/pet. Service with restrictions, supervision.
🆂🅰🆅🅴 🆂🅾 ⊠ 🅼 🦽 🔲 💻 🏊

TAYLORS FALLS

(AAA) ▼▼▼ The Springs Country Inn 🅼
(651) 465-6565. **$58-$69.** 361 Government St. US 8 and SR 95, just w. Ext corridors. **Pets:** Accepted.
🆂🅰🆅🅴 ⊠ 🔲

WACONIA

▼▼▼ Super 8 Motel 🅼
(952) 442-5147. **$56-$65.** 301 E Frontage Rd. On SR 5 at jct CR 10. Int corridors. **Pets:** Large. $10 daily fee/pet. Designated rooms, service with restrictions, supervision.
🅰🆂🅺 🆂🅾 ⊠ 🖉 🦽 🔲 💻

WHITE BEAR LAKE

(AAA) ▼▼▼▼ Best Western White Bear Country Inn 🆂🅷
(651) 429-5393. **$89-$109.** 4940 N Hwy 61. Jct SR 96, 1 mi n. Int corridors. **Pets:** $10 daily fee/room. Service with restrictions, supervision.
🆂🅰🆅🅴 🆂🅾 ⊠ 🔲 💻 🍽 🏊 🗙

WOODBURY

(AAA) ▼▼▼▼ Holiday Inn Express Hotels & Suites 🆂🅷
(651) 702-0200. **$109.** 9840 Norma Ln. I-94, exit 251, just sw. Int corridors. **Pets:** Accepted.
🆂🅰🆅🅴 🆂🅾 ⊠ 🦽 🔲 💻 🏊 🗙

(AAA) ▼▼▼ Red Roof Inn 🅼
(651) 738-7160. **$45-$80.** 1806 Wooddale Dr. I-494, exit 59 (Valley Creek Rd), just se. Ext corridors. **Pets:** Accepted.
🆂🅰🆅🅴 ⊠ 🖉

❖ END METROPOLITAN AREA ❖

MONTEVIDEO

▼▼▼ Country Inn & Suites by Carlson 🆂🅷
(320) 269-8000. **$75-$145.** 1805 E Hwy 7. On SR 7. Int corridors. **Pets:** Accepted.
🅰🆂🅺 🆂🅾 ⊠ 🔲 💻 🏊

MOORHEAD

(AAA) ▼▼▼ Days Inn 🆂🅷
(218) 287-7100. **$72-$102.** 600 30th Ave SW. I-94, exit 1A (US 75), just sw. Int corridors. **Pets:** Other species. $25 one-time fee/pet. Designated rooms, service with restrictions, supervision.
🆂🅰🆅🅴 ⊠ 🔲 💻 🍽 🏊 🗙

(AAA) ▼▼▼ Motel 75 🆂🅷
(218) 233-7501. **$45-$51.** 810 Belsly Blvd. I-94, exit 1A (US 75), 0.5 mi s. Int corridors. **Pets:** Large, other species. Designated rooms, service with restrictions, supervision.
🆂🅰🆅🅴 🆂🅾 ⊠

(AAA) ▼▼▼ Travelodge & Suites 🆂🅷
(218) 233-5333. **$45-$80, 7 day notice.** 3027 S Frontage Rd. Just s of US 10 E. Int corridors. **Pets:** Designated rooms, service with restrictions, supervision.
🆂🅰🆅🅴 🆂🅾 ⊠ 🅼 🦽 🔲 💻 🏊

MORRIS

(AAA) ▼▼▼ Best Western Prairie Inn 🆂🅷
(320) 589-3030. **$45-$83.** 200 SR 28 E. Jct US 59 and SR 28, just sw. Int corridors. **Pets:** Accepted.
🆂🅰🆅🅴 🆂🅾 ⊠ 🔲 💻 🍽 🏊

NEW ULM

▼▼▼ Holiday Inn 🆂🅷
(507) 359-2941. **$60-$145.** 2101 S Broadway. SR 15/68, 1.8 mi se. Int corridors. **Pets:** Accepted.
🅰🆂🅺 ⊠ 🔲 💻 🍽 🏊 🗙

(AAA) ▼▼▼ Microtel Inn & Suites 🆂🅷
(507) 354-9800. **$68.** 424 20th St S. Just e of jct SR 15/68 and CR 37. Int corridors. **Pets:** Small. $10 daily fee/pet. Designated rooms, service with restrictions, crate.
🆂🅰🆅🅴 🆂🅾 ⊠ 🅼 🖉 🦽 🔲 💻 🏊

 **Super 8 Motel** SH
(507) 359-2400. **Call for rates.** 1901 S Broadway. SR 15/68 at jct 20th St S, 1.5 mi se. Int corridors. **Pets:** Accepted.
⊠ 🏋 🐾 🔒

NISSWA

▽ **Nisswa Motel** M
(218) 963-7611. **$49-$80.** 5370 Merrill Ave. Just sw of Main St; center. Ext corridors. **Pets:** Medium, dogs only. $5 daily fee/pet. Designated rooms, service with restrictions.
ASK ⊠ 🔒 🖵

OLIVIA

▽▽ **The Sheep Shedde Inn** SH
(320) 523-5000. **$55-$65.** 2425 W Lincoln Ave. Just e of jct US 71 and 212. Int corridors. **Pets:** Other species. $5 one-time fee/room. Service with restrictions, supervision.
⊠ 🔒 🖵 🍽

ONAMIA

▽▽ **Econo Lodge** SH
(320) 532-3838. **Call for rates.** 40847 US 169. On US 169; 6 mi n. Int corridors. **Pets:** Accepted.
⊠ 🐾 🔒 🖵

▽▽▽ **Eddy's Lake Mille Lacs Resort** SH
(320) 532-3657. **$40-$160.** 41334 Shakopee Lake Rd. SR 26, 6 mi n on US 169. Int corridors. **Pets:** Accepted.
ASK ⊠ 🏋 🔒 🖵 🍽 🏊 🎾

ORR

▽▽ **North Country Inn** SH
(218) 757-3778. **$56-$85.** 4483 Hwy 53. 0.3 mi s. Int corridors. **Pets:** $10 one-time fee/pet. Service with restrictions, supervision.
⊠ 🏋 🔒 🎾

ORTONVILLE

▽▽ **Econo Lodge** M
(320) 839-2414. **Call for rates.** RR 2, Box 25D. Jct US 12 and 75, 0.3 mi n. Int corridors. **Pets:** Accepted.
⊠ 🐾 🔒 🖵

OWATONNA

▽▽▽ **Country Inn & Suites By Carlson** SH
(507) 455-9295. **$69-$99.** 130 Allen Ave SW. I-35, exit 41 (Bridge St), just se. Int corridors. **Pets:** Accepted.
ASK 🏊 ⊠ 🏋 🐾 🛢 🔒 🖵 🏊

PERHAM

▽▽ **Super 8 Motel** SH
(218) 346-7888. **$66-$73.** 106 Jake St SE. SR 78, just nw of jct US 10. Int corridors. **Pets:** Large. $5 daily fee/pet. Service with restrictions, supervision.
ASK 🏊 ⊠ 🔒

PINE RIVER

▽▽ **Econo Lodge** M
(218) 587-4499. **$69-$89, 3 day notice.** 2684 SR 371 SW. 1 mi s. Ext corridors. **Pets:** Other species. $5 daily fee/room. Service with restrictions, supervision.
ASK 🏊 ⊠ 🖵 🎾

RED WING

🅰🅰🅰 ▽▽▽ **Best Western Quiet House & Suites** SH
(651) 388-1577. **$109.** 752 Withers Harbor Dr. 1.5 mi n on US 61, at Withers Harbor Dr; opposite side of US 61 from Pottery Mall. Ext/int corridors. **Pets:** Medium. $17 daily fee/pet. Designated rooms, service with restrictions, supervision.
SAVE 🏊 ⊠ 🏋 🛢 🔒 🖵 🏊

▽▽ **Days Inn** M
(651) 388-3568. **$52-$91.** 955 E 7th St. US 61/63, 1.7 mi se. Ext corridors. **Pets:** Other species. $7 daily fee/pet. Service with restrictions, supervision.
ASK ⊠ 🔒 🖵 🏊

ROCHESTER

▽▽ **Days Inn-South** M
(507) 286-1001. **$49-$69.** 111 28th St SE. Jct US 52 and 63 (Broadway), 0.5 mi n. Int corridors. **Pets:** Accepted.
ASK 🏊 ⊠ 🐾 🛢 🔒

▽▽ **Econo Lodge** M
(507) 288-1855. **$55.** 519 3rd Ave SW. Just s of Mayo Clinic, 3rd Ave SW at 5th St SW. Ext corridors. **Pets:** Accepted.
🏊 ⊠ 🐾 🔒 🖵

▽▽ **Econo Lodge-South** SH
(507) 282-9905. **$55-$65.** 1850 S Broadway. Jct US 52 and 63 (Broadway), 1 mi s. Int corridors. **Pets:** Other species. Designated rooms, service with restrictions.
ASK 🏊 ⊠ 🐾 🛢 🔒 🖵

🅰🅰🅰 ▽▽▽ **Executive Suites and Economy Inn by Kahler** SH
(507) 289-8646. **$65-$99.** 9 NW 3rd Ave. Just n of Mayo Clinic. Int corridors. **Pets:** Accepted.
SAVE 🏊 ⊠ 🐾 🛢 🔒 🖵 🍽 🏊 🎾

▽▽▽ **Holiday Inn South** SH
(507) 288-1844. **$77-$97.** 1630 S Broadway. On US 63 (Broadway), 0.5 mi s of jct US 14. Ext/int corridors. **Pets:** Accepted.
ASK 🏊 ⊠ 🐾 🔒 🖵 🍽 🏊 🎾

🅰🅰🅰 ▽▽▽ **The Kahler Grand Hotel** LH
(507) 282-2581. **$89-$149.** 20 2nd Ave SW. Opposite Mayo Clinic and Methodist Hospital. Int corridors. **Pets:** Accepted.
SAVE 🏊 ⊠ 🐾 🛢 🔒 🖵 🍽 🏊 🎾

▽▽▽ **Marriott Hotel** LH
(507) 280-6000. **$159-$199.** 101 1st Ave SW. Just e of Mayo Clinic. Int corridors. **Pets:** Accepted.
⊠ 🐾 🛢 🔒 🖵 🍽 🏊 🎾

🅰🅰🅰 ▽▽▽ **Microtel Inn & Suites** SH
(507) 286-8780. **$51-$62.** 4210 Hwy 52 N. US 52, exit 41st St NW, just w. Int corridors. **Pets:** Accepted.
SAVE 🏊 ⊠ 🏋 🐾 🛢 🔒 🖵

🅰🅰🅰 ▽▽▽ **Quality Inn & Suites** SH
(507) 282-8091. **$85.** 1620 1st Ave SE. On US 63 (Broadway) from jct US 14, 0.5 mi s, just e on 16th St, then just s. Ext/int corridors. **Pets:** Other species.
SAVE 🏊 ⊠ 🐾 🔒 🖵

Radisson Plaza Hotel 🏨 ❖
(507) 281-8000. **$155-$185.** 150 S Broadway. On US 63 (Broadway); downtown. Int corridors. **Pets:** Medium. Service with restrictions, crate.
[SAVE] 🛢️ ✕ 🎇 🖥️ 🍴 🏊 ✕

Super 8 Motel-South #1 🆂🅷
(507) 288-8288. **$65-$79.** 1230 S Broadway. Jct of US 63 (Broadway) and 14. Int corridors. **Pets:** Accepted.
[ASK] 🛢️ ✕ 🎇 🖥️ 🖥️ 🏊

ST. CLOUD

AmericInn Motel & Suites 🆂🅷
(320) 253-6337. **$90-$116.** 4385 Clearwater Rd. I-94, exit 171 (CR 75), just ne. Int corridors. **Pets:** $10 daily fee/pet. Service with restrictions, supervision.
[SAVE] 🛢️ ✕ 🎇 🖥️ 🖥️ 🏊

Best Western Americanna Inn & Conference Center 🆂🅷
(320) 252-8700. **$54-$121.** 520 S US Hwy 10. Jct SR 23, 0.3 mi s. Ext/int corridors. **Pets:** Other species. $10 daily fee/pet. Service with restrictions.
[SAVE] 🛢️ ✕ 🎇 🖥️ 🖥️ 🍴 🏊 ✕

Best Western Kelly Inn 🆂🅷
(320) 253-0606. **$82-$145.** 100 4th Ave S. SR 23 at 4th Ave S; center. Int corridors. **Pets:** Other species. Designated rooms, service with restrictions, supervision.
[SAVE] 🛢️ ✕ 🎇 🖥️ 🖥️ 🍴 🏊 ✕

Country Inn & Suites By Carlson 🆂🅷
(320) 259-8999. **$73-$95.** 235 S Park Ave. Jct SR 15 and 23 W, just w. Int corridors. **Pets:** Small. $10 daily fee/pet. Designated rooms, service with restrictions, supervision.
[SAVE] 🛢️ ✕ 🎇 🖥️ 🖥️ 🏊

Holiday Inn Express 🆂🅷
(320) 240-8000. **$63-$89.** 4322 Clearwater Rd. I-94, exit 171 (CR 75), just ne. Int corridors. **Pets:** Service with restrictions, supervision.
[ASK] 🛢️ ✕ 🎇 🖥️ 🖥️ 🏊 ✕

Holiday Inn Hotel & Suites 🆂🅷
(320) 253-9000. **$68-$110.** 75 S 37th Ave. Jct SR 15 and 23. Int corridors. **Pets:** Other species. Service with restrictions, supervision.
[ASK] 🛢️ ✕ 🎇 🖥️ 🖥️ 🍴 🏊 ✕

Quality Inn Waterpark 🆂🅷
(320) 253-4444. **$49-$129.** 70 37th Ave S. Jct SR 15 and 23, just e. Int corridors. **Pets:** Accepted.
[ASK] 🛢️ ✕ 🎇 🖥️ 🖥️ 🏊

Ramada Limited & Suites 🆂🅷
(320) 253-3200. **$70-$175.** 121 Park Ave S. Jct SR 15 and 23, just w. Int corridors. **Pets:** Small. $6 daily fee/pet. Service with restrictions, supervision.
[SAVE] 🛢️ ✕ 🎇 🖥️ 🖥️ 🏊

Thrifty Motel Ⓜ
(320) 253-6320. **$32-$44.** 130 14th Ave NE. Jct US 10 and SR 23, 0.3 mi e. Int corridors. **Pets:** $5 daily fee/pet. Service with restrictions, supervision.
✕ 🎇 🖥️

SAUK CENTRE

AmericInn Lodge & Suites 🆂🅷 ❖
(320) 352-2800. **$69-$128.** 1230 Timberlane Dr. I-94, exit 127, just ne. Int corridors. **Pets:** Medium, dogs only. $50 deposit/room, $10 one-time fee/pet. Designated rooms, service with restrictions, supervision.
[SAVE] ✕ 🎇 🖥️ 🖥️ 🏊 ✕

SHERBURN

Four Columns Inn 🅱🅱
(507) 764-8861. **$80-$90 (no credit cards).** 668 140th St. I-90, exit 87, 1.6 mi n on SR 4, then just w on CR 132. Int corridors. **Pets:** Accepted.
✕

SILVER BAY

Mariner Motel Ⓜ ❖
(218) 226-4488. **$50-$70, 3 day notice.** 46 Outer Dr. Just w off SR 61; at traffic signal. Ext corridors. **Pets:** Dogs only. $5 daily fee/pet. Service with restrictions, supervision.
[SAVE] ✕ 🖥️ 🖥️ 🎿

SLEEPY EYE

Best Western Inn of Seven Gables 🆂🅷
(507) 794-5390. **$99-$104.** 1100 E Main St. US 14, 0.8 mi e of jct CR 4 and US 14. Int corridors. **Pets:** Accepted.
[SAVE] 🛢️ ✕ 🖥️ 🖥️ 🏊

SPICER

Northern Inn Hotel & Suites 🆂🅷
(320) 796-2091. **$59-$119.** 154 Lake Ave S. On SR 23; center. Int corridors. **Pets:** Medium. $10 daily fee/pet. Designated rooms, service with restrictions, supervision.
✕ 🖥️ 🖥️ 🏊

THIEF RIVER FALLS

C'mon Inn 🆂🅷
(218) 681-3000. **$54-$76.** 1586 Hwy 59 SE. 1 mi se. Int corridors. **Pets:** Designated rooms, service with restrictions, supervision.
[ASK] 🛢️ ✕ 🖥️ 🖥️ 🏊

Hartwood Motel Ⓜ
(218) 681-2640. **$33-$40.** 1010 N Main Ave. Jct US 59 and SR 32, 0.5 mi n on SR 32. Ext/int corridors. **Pets:** Accepted.
[SAVE] ✕ 🖥️

TOFTE

AmericInn Lodge & Suites 🆂🅷
(218) 663-7899. **$69-$229, 7 day notice.** 7261 W SR 61. On SR 61. Int corridors. **Pets:** Accepted.
[SAVE] 🛢️ ✕ 🎇 🖥️ 🖥️ 🏊 ✕

Bluefin Bay on Lake Superior 🅲🅾 ❖
(218) 663-7296. **$65-$525, 7 day notice.** 7198 W SR 61. On SR 61. Ext corridors. **Pets:** Other species. $20 one-time fee/room. Designated rooms, service with restrictions, supervision.
✕ 🖥️ 🖥️ 🍴 🏊 ✕ 🎿

TWO HARBORS

AAA ♦♦♦♦ **Superior Shores Resort** CO ❖
(218) 834-5671. **$49-$439, 14 day notice.** 1521 Superior Shores Dr. On SR 61, 1.5 mi n of center. Ext/int corridors. **Pets:** $25 deposit/room. Designated rooms, service with restrictions, supervision.
SAVE ⊠ 🛢 💻 🍴 ➔ ⊠

VIRGINIA

♦♦♦♦ **AmericInn Lodge & Suites** SH ❖
(218) 741-7839. **$67-$113.** 5480 Mountain Iron Dr. US 53, just s of jct US 169. Int corridors. **Pets:** $100 deposit/room. Designated rooms, service with restrictions, supervision.
⊠ 🔊M 🔊 🛢 💻 ➔ ⊠

♦ **Lakeshor Motor Inn Downtown** M
(218) 741-3360. **$50-$68.** 404 6th Ave N. Just n of Chestnut St; center. Ext corridors. **Pets:** Small, dogs only. Designated rooms, service with restrictions, supervision.
🔊 ⊠ 🛢 💻

AAA ♦♦♦ **Park Inn** SH
(218) 749-1000. **$70-$94.** 502 Chestnut St. Jct 5th Ave W; downtown. Int corridors. **Pets:** Accepted.
SAVE 🔊 ⊠ 🛢 💻 🍴 ➔

♦ **Ski-View Motel** M
(218) 741-8918. **$40-$48.** 903 N 17th St. Jct US 53 and 169, 0.5 mi n on US 53, 0.7 mi e on 9th St N, then 0.5 mi n on 9th Ave W. Ext/int corridors. **Pets:** $5 daily fee/room. Service with restrictions, supervision.
⊠ 💻

WABASHA

♦♦♦♦ **AmericInn Lodge & Suites** SH
(651) 565-5366. **$69-$169.** 150 Commerce Dr. Just ne of jct US 61 and SR 60. Int corridors. **Pets:** Accepted.
⊠ 🔊 🛢 💻 ➔

WALKER

♦♦♦♦ **Country Inn & Suites By Carlson** SH
(218) 547-1400. **$69-$93.** 442 Walker Bay Blvd. 1 mi s on SR 371. Int corridors. **Pets:** Other species. $50 deposit/room. Service with restrictions, crate.
ASK 🔊 ⊠ 🔊M 🛢 💻 ➔

WARROAD

♦♦ **Can-Am Motel** SH
(218) 386-3807. **$56-$67.** 406 Main Ave NE. 1 mi w on SR 11. Int corridors. **Pets:** Accepted.
ASK 🔊 ⊠ 🔊M 🔊

♦♦ **The Patch Motel** M
(218) 386-2723. **$56-$67.** Hwy 11 W. 1 mi w. Int corridors. **Pets:** Accepted.
ASK 🔊 ⊠ 🔊M 🔊 🛢 ➔

WILLMAR

♦♦♦♦ **Comfort Inn** SH
(320) 231-2601. **$80-$90.** 2200 E US 12. 1.8 mi e. Int corridors. **Pets:** Accepted.
ASK 🔊 ⊠ 🔊 🛢 💻 ➔ ⊠

♦♦♦ **Days Inn-Willmar** SH
(320) 231-1275. **$53-$69.** 225 28th St SE. 2.3 mi e on US 12. Int corridors. **Pets:** Accepted.
ASK 🔊 ⊠ 🔊 🛢 💻

♦♦♦ **Holiday Inn & Willmar Conference Center** SH
(320) 235-6060. **$83-$120.** 2100 US 12 E. 1.8 mi e. Int corridors. **Pets:** Small. $50 deposit/room. Designated rooms, service with restrictions, supervision.
ASK 🔊 ⊠ 🔊 🛢 💻 🍴 ➔ ⊠

WINDOM

♦♦ **Super 8 of Windom** M
(507) 831-1120. **$59-$65.** 222 3rd Ave S. Jct US 71 and SR 60, just n. Int corridors. **Pets:** Accepted.
ASK 🔊 ⊠ 🛢 💻

WINONA

AAA ♦♦♦ **Best Western Riverport Inn & Suites** SH
(507) 452-0606. **$70-$110.** 900 Bruski Dr. Jct US 14/61 and SR 43. Int corridors. **Pets:** Other species. $15 daily fee/room. Designated rooms, service with restrictions, supervision.
SAVE 🔊 ⊠ 🛢 💻 🍴 ➔

♦♦♦ **Holiday Inn Hotel and Suites** SH
(507) 453-0303. **$99-$179.** 1025 Hwy 61 E. Jct SR 43, just sw. Int corridors. **Pets:** Medium, other species. $26 one-time fee/room. Designated rooms, service with restrictions, supervision.
ASK ⊠ 🔊M 🔊 🛢 💻 🍴 ➔ ⊠

♦♦ **Quality Inn** SH
(507) 454-4390. **$89-$99.** 956 Mankato Ave. Jct US 14/61 and SR 43. Ext/int corridors. **Pets:** Accepted.
ASK 🔊 ⊠ 🛢 💻 🍴 ➔ ⊠

WORTHINGTON

♦♦ **AmericInn Motel** SH
(507) 376-4500. **$69-$109, 7 day notice.** 1475 Darling Dr. I-90, exit 43 (US 59), just se. Int corridors. **Pets:** Other species. $10 one-time fee/room. Designated rooms, service with restrictions, supervision.
⊠ 🔊M 🔊 🔊 🛢 💻 ➔ ⊠

♦♦ **Days Inn** SH
(507) 376-6155. **$62-$87.** 207 Oxford St. I-90, exit 42, 1 mi se on SR 266. Ext/int corridors. **Pets:** Accepted.
ASK 🔊 ⊠ 🔊M 🔊 🛢 💻 ➔

ABERDEEN

Best Western Aberdeen Inn
(662) 369-4343. **$59-$78.** 801 E Commerce St. Jct US 45 and SR 25. Ext corridors. **Pets:** Small. Designated rooms, service with restrictions, supervision.

BATESVILLE

Comfort Inn
(662) 563-1188. **$55-$90.** 290 Power Dr. I-55, exit 243B, just ne on frontage road. Ext corridors. **Pets:** Medium. $7 one-time fee/pet. Service with restrictions, supervision.

BAY ST. LOUIS

Key West Inn
(228) 466-0444. **$45-$60.** 1000 Hwy 90. 2.5 mi e of jct SR 603. Ext corridors. **Pets:** Accepted.

BILOXI

Father Ryan House Bed & Breakfast Inn
(228) 435-1189. **$100-$130.** 1196 Beach Blvd. I-110, exit 1B, 0.8 mi w on US 90. Ext/int corridors. **Pets:** Accepted.

Holiday Inn Express
(228) 388-1000. **$65-$135.** 2416 Beach Blvd. I-110, exit 1B, 5.5 mi w on US 90. Ext corridors. **Pets:** Accepted.

BOONEVILLE

Super 8 Motel
(662) 720-1688. **$65.** 110 Hospitality Ave. Jct US 45 and SR 4/30, 1.7 mi e to SR 145, then 0.5 mi s. Int corridors. **Pets:** Small. $5 daily fee/room. Service with restrictions, supervision.

BROOKHAVEN

Best Western-Brookhaven
(601) 835-1053. **$49-$58.** 749 Magee Dr. I-55, exit 40, 0.3 mi e, just ne. Ext corridors. **Pets:** Medium. $5 one-time fee/pet. Service with restrictions, crate.

CANTON

Best Western-Canton Inn
(601) 859-8600. **$58.** 137 Soldier Colony Rd. I-55, exit 119. Int corridors. **Pets:** Accepted.

CLARKSDALE

Econo Lodge
(662) 621-1110. **$55-$65.** 350 S State St. On US 61. Ext corridors. **Pets:** Accepted.

Hampton Inn
(662) 627-9292. **$64-$68.** 710 S State St. US 61, 1 mi s of jct US 49. Ext/int corridors. **Pets:** Small. $5 daily fee/room. Service with restrictions, supervision.

CLEVELAND

Comfort Inn of Cleveland
(662) 843-4060. **$55.** 721 N Davis Ave. On US 61, 1 mi n of jct US 61 and SR 8. Ext corridors. **Pets:** Accepted.

COLUMBIA

Comfort Inn
(601) 731-9955. **$69-$79.** 820 Hwy 98 Bypass. Just e of jct US 98 Bypass and SR 13. Int corridors. **Pets:** Other species. $25 deposit/room. Service with restrictions, supervision.

COLUMBUS

Master Hosts Inns & Suites
(662) 328-5202. **$45-$60.** 506 Hwy 45 N. US 82, exit US 45 N, just s. Ext corridors. **Pets:** Accepted.

CORINTH

Comfort Inn
(662) 287-4421. **$45-$55.** 2101 Hwy 72 W. Jct US 72 and 45, just e. Ext corridors. **Pets:** Other species. $25 deposit/room.

DIAMONDHEAD

Ramada Inn Diamondhead SH
(228) 255-1300. **$59-$95.** 103 Live Oak Dr. I-10, exit 16, just nw. Ext/int corridors. **Pets:** Accepted.
SAVE 🛁 ⊠ ⬚ ⬚ 💻 ⑪ ⋙ ⊠

D'IBERVILLE

Wingate Inn D'Iberville/Biloxi SH
(228) 396-0036. **$79-$109.** 3641 Sangani Dr. I-10, exit 46B, just ne. Int corridors. **Pets:** Accepted.
ASK 🛁 ⊠ ⬚ ⬚ 💻 ⋙

FOREST

Apple Tree Inn SH
(601) 469-2640. **$55-$61.** SR 35. I-20, exit 88, just n on SR 35. Ext corridors. **Pets:** Service with restrictions.
SAVE 🛁 ⊠ ⬚ 💻 ⑪ ⋙

Comfort Inn SH 🐾
(601) 469-2100. **$55-$60.** 1250 Hwy 35 S. I-20, exit 88, just n. Ext corridors. **Pets:** Very small. $12 daily fee/pet. Service with restrictions, supervision.
SAVE ⊠ ⬚ 💻 ⋙

GREENVILLE

Key West Inn SH
(662) 332-5800. **$58.** 344 S Walnut St. US 82, 1.8 mi n on Broadway, 0.4 mi w on Central; corner of Central and Walnut. Ext corridors. **Pets:** Accepted.
ASK 🛁 ⊠ ⬚ⁿ ⬚ ⬚ ⬚ 💻 ⋙

GREENWOOD

Comfort Inn SH
(662) 453-5974. **$64-$74.** 401 Hwy 82 W. On US 82; in town center. Ext corridors. **Pets:** Accepted.
ASK 🛁 ⊠ ⬚ 💻 ⋙

GRENADA

Best Western Grenada SH 🐾
(662) 226-7816. **$54-$89, 5 day notice.** 1750 Sunset Dr. I-55, exit 206, just ne on frontage road. Ext corridors. **Pets:** $5 daily fee/pet. Service with restrictions, supervision.
SAVE 🛁 ⊠ ⬚ 💻 ⑪ ⋙

Country Inn & Suites by Carlson SH
(662) 227-8444. **$64-$89.** 255 SW Frontage Rd. I-55, exit 206, southwest corner. Int corridors. **Pets:** Small. $25 one-time fee/pet. Service with restrictions, supervision.
ASK 🛁 ⊠ ⬚ 💻 ⋙

Holiday Inn SH
(662) 226-2851. **$67-$71.** 1796 Sunset Dr. I-55, exit 206, just ne on frontage road. Ext/int corridors. **Pets:** Medium, other species. Designated rooms, service with restrictions.
ASK 🛁 ⊠ ⬚ 💻 ⑪ ⋙ ⊠

GULFPORT

Best Western Seaway Inn SH
(228) 864-0050. **$50-$120.** 9475 Hwy 49. I-10, exit 34A, just sw. Ext corridors. **Pets:** Medium. $10 daily fee/pet. No service, supervision.
SAVE 🛁 ⊠ ⬚ⁿ ⬚ ⬚ 💻 ⋙

Crystal Inn SH
(228) 822-9600. **$89-$109.** 9379 Canal Rd. I-10, exit 31, just sw. Int corridors. **Pets:** Accepted.
ASK 🛁 ⊠ ⬚ ⬚ 💻 ⋙ ⊠

GuestHouse International Inn SH
(228) 868-8500. **$59-$109.** 9375 Hwy 49. I-10, exit 34A, just sw. Ext corridors. **Pets:** Accepted.
ASK 🛁 ⊠ ⬚ 💻 ⋙

Holiday Inn Express SH
(228) 864-7222. **$49-$99, 3 day notice.** 9435 Hwy 49. I-10, exit 34A, just sw. Ext corridors. **Pets:** Small. $35 one-time fee/room. Service with restrictions, supervision.
⊠ ⬚ⁿ ⬚ ⬚ 💻

Holiday Inn I-10/Airport SH
(228) 868-8200. **$49-$89, 3 day notice.** 9415 Hwy 49. I-10, exit 34A, just sw. Ext corridors. **Pets:** Accepted.
ASK 🛁 ⊠ ⬚ ⬚ 💻 ⑪ ⋙

HATTIESBURG

Comfort Inn University SH
(601) 264-1881. **$69-$89.** 6541 US Hwy 49. I-59, exit 67A, just s. Ext/int corridors. **Pets:** Other species. $25 one-time fee/pet. Service with restrictions, supervision.
ASK 🛁 ⊠ ⬚ 💻 ⋙

Hampton Inn of Hattiesburg SH
(601) 264-8080. **$72-$85.** 4301 Hardy St. I-59, exit 65, just nw. Ext/int corridors. **Pets:** Small, dogs only. Designated rooms, no service, supervision.
SAVE 🛁 ⊠ ⬚ ⬚ 💻 ⋙

Holiday Inn-Hattiesburg SH
(601) 268-2850. **$75.** 6563 Hwy 49 N. I-59, exit 67A, just se. Int corridors. **Pets:** Accepted.
SAVE 🛁 ⊠ 💻 ⑪ ⋙

Inn on the Hill SH
(601) 599-2001. **$65-$89.** 6595 Hwy 49 N. I-59, exit 67A, just se. Ext corridors. **Pets:** Accepted.
SAVE 🛁 ⊠ ⬚ 💻 ⑪ ⋙

HORN LAKE

Drury Inn & Suites-Memphis South SH
(662) 349-6622. **$73-$105.** 735 Goodman Rd W. I-55, exit 289, just sw. Int corridors. **Pets:** Large, other species. Service with restrictions, supervision.
ASK ⊠ ⬚ⁿ ⬚ ⬚ ⬚ 💻 ⋙

JACKSON

Best Suites of America-Jackson SH
(601) 899-9000. **$84-$100.** 5411 I-55 N. I-55, exit 102A northbound; exit 102 southbound, s on west service road. Int corridors. **Pets:** Accepted.
SAVE 🛁 ⊠ ⬚ ⬚ ⬚ 💻 ⋙

🔺 ▼▼▼▼ Clarion Hotel & Convention Center SH
(601) 969-2141. $59-$109. 400 Greymont Ave. I-55, exit 96B, just w, then just s. Ext/int corridors. Pets: Other species. $25 one-time fee/room. Service with restrictions, supervision.
[SAVE] [S🐾] [✕] [🔒] [🔲] [🔲] [🍴] [≈]

🔺 ▼▼▼▼ Crowne Plaza Hotel and Resort Jackson LH
(601) 969-5100. $75-$149. 200 E Amite St. I-55, exit 96B (High St), w to State St, 0.4 mi s to Amite St, then just w; downtown. Int corridors. Pets: Accepted.
[SAVE] [S🐾] [✕] [&M] [🖊] [🔒] [🔲] [🍴] [≈]

▼▼▼ The Edison Walthall Hotel LH
(601) 948-6161. $89-$99. 225 E Capitol St. I-55, exit 96A (Pearl St), 0.8 mi w; between West and Lamar St; downtown. Ext/int corridors. Pets: Accepted.
[ASK] [✕] [🔒] [🔲] [🍴] [≈]

▼▼▼ Holiday Inn Hotel & Suites LH
(601) 366-9411. $85-$105. 5075 I-55 N. I-55, exit 102A, s on west frontage road. Ext/int corridors. Pets: $100 deposit/pet, $25 one-time fee/room. Service with restrictions.
[ASK] [S🐾] [✕] [🔒] [🔒] [🔲] [🍴] [≈]

▼▼▼ Jameson Inn SH
(601) 206-8923. $72-$77. 585 Beasley Rd. I-55, exit 102, just w. Int corridors. Pets: Small. Service with restrictions, crate.
[✕] [&M] [🖊] [🔒] [🔒] [🔲] [≈]

🔺 ▼▼▼▼ La Quinta Inn-Jackson North SH
(601) 957-1741. $55-$75. 616 Briarwood Dr. I-55, exit 102 northbound, just ne. Ext corridors. Pets: Small, other species. Service with restrictions, supervision.
[SAVE] [✕] [🔒] [🔲] [≈]

▼▼ Microtel Inn & Suites SH
(601) 352-8282. $50-$68. 614 Monroe St. I-55, exit 96B (High St), just nw. Int corridors. Pets: Accepted.
[ASK] [S🐾] [✕] [🔒] [≈]

🔺 ▼▼▼▼ Quality Inn & Suites SH
(601) 969-2230. $59-$89. 400 Greymont Ave. I-55, exit 96B (High St), just w, then just s. Ext corridors. Pets: Accepted.
[SAVE] [S🐾] [✕] [🖊] [🔒] [🔲] [🍴] [≈]

🔺 ▼▼▼ Red Roof Inn Fairgrounds M
(601) 969-5006. $42-$59. 700 Larson St. I-55, exit 96B (High St), just ne. Ext corridors. Pets: Medium, other species. Service with restrictions, supervision.
[SAVE] [✕] [🖊] [🔒]

▼▼▼▼ Residence Inn by Marriott SH
(601) 355-3599. $94-$104. 881 E River Pl. I-55, exit 96C, just e. Ext corridors. Pets: Accepted.
[ASK] [✕] [🖊] [🔒] [🔒] [🔲] [≈] [✕]

🔺 ▼▼▼ Sleep Inn SH
(601) 354-3900. $55-$60, 7 day notice. 2620 Hwy 80 W. I-20, exit 42B, just nw off Ellis Ave. Int corridors. Pets: Accepted.
[SAVE] [S🐾] [✕] [🖊] [🔒]

KOSCIUSKO

🔺 ▼▼▼ Best Western Parkway Inn SH
(662) 289-6252. $52-$66. 1052 Veterans Memorial Dr/Hwy 35 Bypass. Just sw of jct SR 35 and Natchez Trace Pkwy. Ext corridors. Pets: Accepted.
[SAVE] [S🐾] [✕] [🔒] [🔲] [≈]

MCCOMB

🔺 ▼▼▼ Days Inn McComb SH
(601) 684-5566. $49-$79. 2298 Delaware Ave. I-55, exit 17, just nw. Ext corridors. Pets: Accepted.
[SAVE] [S🐾] [✕] [🔒] [🔲] [🍴] [≈]

MERIDIAN

▼▼▼▼ Baymont Inn & Suites Meridian SH
(601) 693-2300. $74-$79. 1400 Roebuck Dr. I-20/59, exit 153, just s. Int corridors. Pets: Accepted.
[ASK] [S🐾] [✕] [🔒] [🔲] [≈]

▼▼ Econo Lodge M
(601) 693-9393. $39-$54. 2405 S Frontage Rd. I-20/59, exit 153, 0.5 mi sw. Ext corridors. Pets: Accepted.
[ASK] [S🐾] [✕] [🔲]

▼▼ Econo Lodge of Meridian SH
(601) 485-3254. $45-$55. 109 US Hwy 11 & 80. I-20/59, exit 154 eastbound; exit 154B eastbound, just n to Frontage Rd, then just e. Ext corridors. Pets: Medium. $20 one-time fee/room. Designated rooms, service with restrictions.
[ASK] [S🐾] [✕] [🖊] [🔒] [🔲]

🔺 ▼▼▼ Holiday Inn Northeast SH
(601) 485-5101. $85-$105. 111 US 11 & 80. I-20/59, exit 154 westbound, just n to frontage road, then just e; exit 154B eastbound. Ext corridors. Pets: Accepted.
[SAVE] [S🐾] [✕] [&M] [🖊] [🔒] [🔒] [🔲] [🍴] [≈]

▼▼ Jameson Inn SH
(601) 483-3315. $74-$79. 524 Bonita Lakes Dr. I-20/59, exit 154 southbound; exit 154A northbound, just s. Ext corridors. Pets: Small. Service with restrictions, crate.
[✕] [&M] [🖊] [🔒] [🔒] [≈]

▼▼▼▼ Quality Inn SH
(601) 693-4521. $75-$80. 1401 Roebuck Dr. I-20/59, exit 153, just s. Ext corridors. Pets: Accepted.
[ASK] [S🐾] [✕] [🖊] [🔲] [≈]

NEWTON

🔺 ▼▼▼ Days Inn M
(601) 683-3361. $70-$75. 261 Eastside Dr. I-20, exit 109, just s on SR 15. Ext corridors. Pets: Accepted.
[SAVE] [S🐾] [✕] [🔒] [🔲] [≈]

OCEAN SPRINGS

▼▼▼▼ Comfort Inn Biloxi/Ocean Springs SH
(228) 818-0300. $49-$159. 7827 Lamar Poole Rd. I-10, exit 50, just nw on service road. Int corridors. Pets: Accepted.
[ASK] [S🐾] [✕] [&M] [🖊] [🔒] [🔲] [≈]

▼▼▼▼ **Holiday Inn Express** 🆂🅷
(228) 875-7555. **$69-$150.** 7304 Washington Ave. I-10, exit 50, 0.4 mi s on SR 609. Ext corridors. **Pets:** Accepted.
🅰🆂🅺 Ⓢ 🗙 Ⓛ🅼 📺 🔌 💻 🏊

▼▼ **Ramada Limited** 🆂🅷
(228) 872-2323. **$74-$139.** 8011 Tucker Rd. I-10, exit 50, just n. Ext corridors. **Pets:** Accepted.
🅰🆂🅺 Ⓢ 🗙 📺 🔌 💻 🏊

OLIVE BRANCH

▼▼▼▼ **Comfort Inn** 🆂🅷
(662) 895-0456. **$66.** 7049 Enterprise. Just w of US 78 on SR 302. Int corridors. **Pets:** $10 one-time fee/pet. Service with restrictions, supervision.
🅰🆂🅺 Ⓢ 🗙 📺 🔌 💻 🏊

▼▼▼▼ **Whispering Woods Hotel and Conference Center** 🅻🅷
(662) 895-2941. **$90-$100.** 11200 E Goodman Rd. 3 mi e of jct US 78. Int corridors. **Pets:** Accepted.
🅰🆂🅺 Ⓢ 🗙 📺 🔌 💻 🍴 🏊 🗙

OXFORD

▼▼ **Days Inn** 🆂🅷
(662) 234-9500. **$50-$150.** 1101 Frontage Rd. SR 6, exit Lamar. Ext corridors. **Pets:** Medium. $10 one-time fee/room. Service with restrictions, supervision.
🅰🆂🅺 Ⓢ 🗙 🔌 💻 🍴 🏊

PASS CHRISTIAN

🅐🅐🅐 ▼▼▼▼ **Harbour Oaks Inn** 🅱🅱
(228) 452-9399. **$83-$128, 7 day notice.** 126 W Scenic Dr. Just off US 90. Int corridors. **Pets:** Dogs only. $20 one-time fee/room. Designated rooms, service with restrictions, supervision.
🆂🅰🆅🅴 🗙

PEARL

▼▼▼▼ **Jameson Inn** 🆂🅷
(601) 932-6030. **$72-$77.** 434 Riverwind Dr. I-20, exit 48, just nw. Int corridors. **Pets:** Small. Service with restrictions, crate.
🗙 Ⓛ🅼 📺 🔌 💻 🏊

🅐🅐🅐 ▼▼▼▼ **La Quinta Inn & Suites** 🆂🅷
(601) 664-0065. **$60-$65.** 501 S Pearson Rd. I-20, exit 48, just s. Int corridors. **Pets:** Accepted.
🆂🅰🆅🅴 Ⓢ 🗙 📺 🔌 💻 🏊

PHILADELPHIA

▼▼ **Deluxe Inn & Suites** 🆂🅷
(601) 656-0052. **$39-$89.** 1004 Central Dr. Jct SR 15 and 16. Ext corridors. **Pets:** Medium. $10 daily fee/pet. Service with restrictions, crate.
🅰🆂🅺 Ⓢ 🗙 Ⓛ🅼 🔌 💻 🏊

PICAYUNE

▼▼▼▼ **Days Inn** 🆂🅷
(601) 799-1339. **$54-$109.** 450 S Lofton Dr. I-59, exit 4, just nw. Ext corridors. **Pets:** Medium, other species. $5 daily fee/pet. Service with restrictions, supervision.
🅰🆂🅺 Ⓢ 🗙 📺 🔌 💻 🏊

RICHLAND

▼▼ **Days Inn** 🅼
(601) 932-5553. **$55-$70.** 1035 US Hwy 49 S. I-20, exit 47A, 4 mi s on US 49. Ext corridors. **Pets:** Medium. $5 daily fee/pet. Service with restrictions, supervision.
🅰🆂🅺 Ⓢ 🗙 🔌

▼▼ **Executive Inn & Suites** 🆂🅷
(601) 664-3456. **$49-$59.** 390 Hwy 49 S. I-20, exit 47, just s. Ext corridors. **Pets:** Medium. $15 deposit/pet, $5 one-time fee/pet. Service with restrictions, supervision.
🅰🆂🅺 Ⓢ 🗙 📺 🔌 💻 🏊

RIDGELAND

▼▼▼▼ **Drury Inn & Suites** 🆂🅷
(601) 956-6100. **$85-$105.** 610 E County Line Rd. I-55, exit 103 (County Line Rd), just w. Int corridors. **Pets:** Large, other species. Service with restrictions, supervision.
🅰🆂🅺 🗙 Ⓛ🅼 🅿 🔌 📺 💻 🏊

▼▼ **GuestHouse International Inn of Jackson** 🆂🅷
(601) 956-6203. **$54-$74.** 839 Ridgewod Rd. I-55, exit 103, just ne. Ext corridors. **Pets:** Accepted.
🅰🆂🅺 Ⓢ 🗙 📺 🔌 💻 🏊

🅐🅐🅐 ▼▼▼ **Red Roof Inn Ridgeland** 🅼
(601) 956-7707. **$43-$56.** 810 Adcock St. I-55, exit 103, just ne on Frontage Rd. Ext corridors. **Pets:** Medium, other species. Service with restrictions, crate.
🆂🅰🆅🅴 🗙 🔌 📺

SARDIS

▼▼ **Knights Inn** 🆂🅷 🐾
(662) 487-2424. **$36-$48.** 598 E Lee St. I-55, exit 252. Ext corridors. **Pets:** Other species. Service with restrictions, supervision.
🅰🆂🅺 Ⓢ 🗙 📺 🔌 💻 🍴 🏊

STARKVILLE

▼▼▼ **Comfort Suites Starkville** 🆂🅷
(662) 324-9595. **$89-$129.** 801 Russell St. 0.5 mi w of jct US 82 and SR 12. Int corridors. **Pets:** Small. Service with restrictions, supervision.
🅰🆂🅺 Ⓢ 🗙 📺 🔌 💻 🏊

TUNICA

🅐🅐🅐 ▼▼▼▼ **Best Western Tunica North** 🆂🅷
(662) 363-6711. **$49-$149.** 7500 Casino Strip Resort Blvd. Jct of US 61 and SR 304. Int corridors. **Pets:** Accepted.
🆂🅰🆅🅴 Ⓢ 🗙 Ⓛ🅼 🅿 📺 🔌 💻 🏊

Key West Inn Tunica SH
(662) 363-0021. **$45-$145.** 11635 Hwy 61 N. US 61, 0.3 mi n of SR 304. Ext corridors. **Pets:** Very small. $10 daily fee/pet. Service with restrictions, supervision.

TUPELO

Days Inn M
(662) 842-0088. **$48-$65.** 1015 N Gloster St. Old US 45, w on McCullough Blvd (Old US 78) to N Gloster St, just n. Ext corridors. **Pets:** Small. $20 deposit/room. Service with restrictions, supervision.

Howard Johnson Express Inn SH
(662) 842-8811. **$39-$99.** 923 N Gloster St. On SR 145 (Old US 45), just s of McCullough Blvd (Old US 78). Ext corridors. **Pets:** Accepted.

Jameson Inn M
(662) 840-2380. **$67-$72.** 879 Mississippi Dr. US 45, exit Barnes Crossing, 1 mi sw. Ext corridors. **Pets:** Small. Service with restrictions, crate.

Red Roof Inn Tupelo M
(662) 844-1904. **$43-$54.** 1500 McCullough Blvd. On McCullough Blvd (Old US 78), just w of jct SR 145 (Old US 45). Ext corridors. **Pets:** Small. No service, supervision.

Super 8 Motel M
(662) 842-0448. **$43-$55.** 3898 McCullough Blvd. On McCullough Blvd (Old US 78), exit 81, just ne. Ext corridors. **Pets:** Small. $5 daily fee/pet. Designated rooms, service with restrictions, supervision.

VICKSBURG

Battlefield Inn SH ❖
(601) 638-5811. **$50-$75.** 4137 I-20 N Frontage Rd. I-20, exit 4B, 1 mi ne. Ext/int corridors. **Pets:** Other species. $5 daily fee/pet. Service with restrictions.

The Corners Bed & Breakfast Inn BB
(601) 636-7421. **$90-$130, 3 day notice.** 601 Klein St. I-20, exit 1A, 2.3 mi n on Washington St, just w. Ext/int corridors. **Pets:** Accepted.

Econo Lodge of Vicksburg M
(601) 634-8766. **$50-$70.** 3330-A Clay St. I-20, exit 4B (Clay St), just n. Ext corridors. **Pets:** Accepted.

Hampton Inn of Vicksburg SH
(601) 636-6100. **$70-$85.** 3332 Clay St. I-20, exit 4B (Clay St), just n. Ext corridors. **Pets:** Other species. No service, supervision.

Jameson Inn SH
(601) 619-7799. **$68-$73.** 3975 S Frontage Rd. I-20, exit 4A, on southeast frontage road. Ext corridors. **Pets:** Accepted.

Motel 6 SH
(601) 638-5077. **Call for rates.** 4127 N Frontage Rd. I-20, exit 4B (Clay St), just ne on Frontage Rd. Int corridors. **Pets:** Accepted.

WIGGINS

Best Western Woodstone SH
(601) 928-1616. **$52-$69.** 535 Frontage Dr E. At the jct of US 49 and SR 26. Int corridors. **Pets:** Accepted.

YAZOO CITY

Comfort Inn SH
(662) 746-6444. **$67.** 1600 Jerry Clower Blvd. US 49 E, 1.8 mi n of jct US 49 W. Int corridors. **Pets:** Accepted.

CITY INDEX

ARNOLD

▼▼▼ Drury Inn-St. Louis/Arnold SH
(636) 296-9600. **$72-$100.** 1201 Drury Ln. I-55, exit 191 (SR 141), 0.3 mi e. Int corridors. **Pets:** Large, other species. Service with restrictions, supervision.
ASK ✕ 🛁 💻 ➷

AVA

▼▼ Ava Super 8 SH
(417) 683-1343. **$55-$110.** 1711 S Jefferson St. Jct SR 5 S and 76. Int corridors. **Pets:** Other species. $25 deposit/ room. Designated rooms, service with restrictions, supervision.
ASK ✕ 🛁 💻

BELTON

▲▲▲ ▼▼▼ Econo Lodge M
(816) 322-1222. **$50-$65.** 222 Peculiar Dr. Jct of US 71 and SR 58. Ext corridors. **Pets:** Accepted.
SAVE 🛇 ✕ 🛁 💻 ➷

BETHANY

▼▼ Family Budget Inn M
(660) 425-7915. **$45-$49, 3 day notice.** 4014 Miller St. I-35, exit 92. Int corridors. **Pets:** $20 deposit/room, $5 daily fee/ room. Service with restrictions, supervision.
ASK 🛇 ✕ 🐾 🛁 ➷

BOLIVAR

▲▲▲ ▼ Welcome Inn M
(417) 326-5268. **$30-$45.** 4710 S 128th Rd, S Hwy 13. On Frontage Rd, 0.3 mi s of jct SR 13, 83 and 15 business route. Ext corridors. **Pets:** $5 daily fee/pet. Service with restrictions, crate.
SAVE 🛇 ✕ 🛁 ➷

BRANSON

▲▲ ▼▼ 1st Inn Gold SH
(417) 334-7000. **$40-$159, 3 day notice.** 2719 W Hwy 76. 2.5 mi w of jct US 65. Ext/int corridors. **Pets:** Accepted.
SAVE 🛇 ✕ 🛁 ➷

▼▼ Atrium Inn SH
(417) 336-6000. **$45-$75.** 3005 Green Mountain Dr. 2.5 mi w on SR 76 (Country Music Blvd) from jct US 65 and SR 76 (Country Music Blvd), 0.4 mi s. Ext corridors. **Pets:** Other species. $10 one-time fee/room. Service with restrictions.
ASK 🛇 ✕ 🛁 💻 ➷

▲▲▲ ▼▼▼ Best Western Branson Rustic Oak SH
(417) 334-6464. **$55-$79.** 403 W Main (Hwy 76). 0.3 mi e from SR 76 (Country Music Blvd) and US 65. Ext corridors. **Pets:** Accepted.
SAVE 🛇 ✕ 🗘 🛁 💻 ➷

▲▲▲ ▼▼▼ ▼▼▼ Chateau on the Lake Resort & Convention Center LH
(417) 334-1161. **$134-$294, 3 day notice.** 415 N State Hwy 265. Just n of jct SR 165 and 265. Int corridors. **Pets:** Small. $20 one-time fee/room. Designated rooms, service with restrictions, supervision.
SAVE 🛇 ✕ 🛒 🗘 🍽 🛁 💻 🍴 ➷ ✕

▲▲▲ ▼▼▼ Days Inn of Branson SH
(417) 334-5544. **$40-$80.** 3524 Keeter St. Jct SR 376, 0.5 mi e on SR 76 (Country Music Blvd), then 0.3 mi w. Ext corridors. **Pets:** $10 daily fee/pet. Service with restrictions, crate.
SAVE 🛇 ✕ 🗘 🍽 🛁 💻 ➷

▼▼ ▼▼ Dogwood Inn SH
(417) 334-5101. **$30-$55.** 1420 Hwy 76 W. Jct US 65, 1 mi w on SR 76 (Country Music Blvd). Ext/int corridors. **Pets:** Other species. $10 daily fee/pet. Service with restrictions, supervision.
ASK 🛇 ✕ 🗘 🛁 💻 🍴 ➷

WWWW Holiday Inn Express Hotel & Suites SH
(417) 336-1100. **$57-$93.** 1970 W Hwy 76. 1.8 mi w of jct
US 65 and SR 76 (Country Music Blvd). Int corridors.
Pets: Small. $25 one-time fee/room. Designated rooms,
service with restrictions, supervision.

WWWW Hotel Grand Victorian SH
(417) 336-2935. **$69-$109.** 2325 W Hwy 76. SR 76 (Country
Music Blvd), 2.6 mi w of US 65. Int corridors. **Pets:** Small,
other species. $25 one-time fee/room. Designated rooms,
service with restrictions, crate.

WWW Howard Johnson SH
(417) 336-5151. **$49-$89.** 3027-A W Hwy 76. On SR 76
(Country Music Blvd), 4 mi w of US 65. Ext corridors.
Pets: $10 daily fee/pet. Service with restrictions, crate.

WW Ramada Limited SH
(417) 337-5207. **$39-$99.** 2316 Shepherd of the Hills Expwy.
Jct SR 76, 1.3 mi e. Ext corridors. **Pets:** Other species. $10
daily fee/room. Service with restrictions, crate.

WWW Residence Inn by Marriott SH
(417) 336-4077. **$69-$189.** 280 Wildwood Dr S. 2 mi w on
US 76, just s. Int corridors. **Pets:** Other species. $10 daily
fee/room, $50 one-time fee/room. Service with restrictions,
crate.

WW Rock View Resort M
(417) 334-4678. **$51-$84, 21 day notice.** 1049 Park View
Dr. Jct US 65, 4.4 mi w on SR 165, 0.3 mi s via Dale Dr,
then 0.7 mi w. Ext corridors. **Pets:** Other species. $7 daily
fee/pet. Designated rooms, no service, supervision.

WWW Scenic Hills Inn SH
(417) 336-8855. **$37-$55.** 2422 Shepherd of the Hills Expwy.
Jct SR 76, 1.1 mi e. Int corridors. **Pets:** Medium. $5 daily
fee/room. Designated rooms, service with restrictions, crate.

**WWW Settle Inn Resort & Conference
Center SH**
(417) 335-4700. **$58-$119.** 3050 Green Mountain Dr. Jct SR
76 and US 65, 3 mi w on SR 76, 0.8 mi s. Int corridors.
Pets: Other species. $10 daily fee/pet. Designated rooms,
service with restrictions, supervision.

WW White Wing Resort M ✿
(417) 338-2318. **$35-$123, 21 day notice.** 1028 Jakes
Creek Tr. Jct SR 76 and 265, 0.6 mi w, 1 mi s on Indian
Point Rd, then 1 mi e. Ext corridors. **Pets:** Dogs only. $25
one-time fee/pet.

BRANSON WEST

WW Shady Acre Motel M
(417) 338-2316. **$36.** 8722 Hwy 76. Jct SR 265, 1.1 mi w.
Ext corridors. **Pets:** Accepted.

BUFFALO

WWW Goodnite Inn M
(417) 345-2345. **$36-$45.** 642 S Ash. US 65, just s of jct SR
32. **Pets:** Accepted.

BUTLER

WW Days Inn SH
(660) 679-4544. **Call for rates.** 100 S Fran Ave. Just e of jct
US 71 and SR 52. Int corridors. **Pets:** Accepted.

WW Super 8 Motel–Butler M
(660) 679-6183. **$40-$80.** 1114 W Fort Scott St. Just e of jct
US 71 and SR 52. Ext corridors. **Pets:** Medium, other
species. $5 daily fee/pet. Service with restrictions, supervi-
sion.

CAMERON

WWW Best Western Acorn Inn M
(816) 632-2187. **$58-$78.** 2210 E US 36. I-35, exit 54, 0.3 mi
e. Ext corridors. **Pets:** Accepted.

WWW Comfort Inn SH ✿
(816) 632-5655. **$60-$85.** 1803 Comfort Ln. I-35, exit 54, just
e. Int corridors. **Pets:** Medium. Designated rooms, service
with restrictions, supervision.

WWW Econo Lodge M
(816) 632-6571. **$41-$60.** 220 E Grand. I-35, exit 54, 0.5 mi
w on US 36, then just s on US 69. Ext corridors.
Pets: Accepted.

WW Super 8 Motel SH
(816) 632-8888. **$60.** 1710 N Walnut St. I-35, exit 54, 0.5 mi
w on US 36. Int corridors. **Pets:** Medium. $10 one-time
fee/pet. Designated rooms, service with restrictions, supervision.

CANTON

WW Comfort Inn Canton SH
(573) 288-8800. **$64-$119.** 1701 Oak St. US 61, exit CR-P,
just e. Int corridors. **Pets:** Large. $20 deposit/room. Desig-
nated rooms, service with restrictions, supervision.

CAPE GIRARDEAU

WW Drury Lodge-Cape Girardeau SH
(573) 334-7151. **$80-$101.** 104 S Vantage Dr. I-55, exit 96
(William St), just e. Ext/int corridors. **Pets:** Large, other
species. Service with restrictions, supervision.

▼▼▼▼ **Drury Suites-Cape Girardeau** SH
(573) 339-9500. **$93-$106.** 3303 Campster Dr. I-55, exit 96 (William St), just w. Int corridors. **Pets:** Large, other species. Service with restrictions, supervision.
ASK ⊠ &M ⚷ 🖱 ❚ ▣ ⇌ ⊠

▼▼▼▼ **Hampton Inn-Cape Girardeau** SH
(573) 651-3000. **$88-$105.** 103 Cape W Pkwy. I-55, exit 96 (William St), 0.3 mi sw. Int corridors. **Pets:** Accepted.
ASK ⊠ &M ⚷ 🖱 ❚ ▣

▼▼ **Pear Tree Inn by Drury-Cape Girardeau** SH
(573) 334-3000. **$67-$86.** 3248 William St. I-55, exit 96 (William St), just e. Int corridors. **Pets:** Large, other species. Service with restrictions, supervision.
ASK ⊠ ▣ ⇌

▼▼▼▼ **Victorian Inn & Suites** SH
(573) 651-4486. **$79-$99.** 3265 William St. I-55, exit 96 (William St), just e. Ext/int corridors. **Pets:** Accepted.
ASK S⦶ ⊠ &M ⚷ 🖱 ❚ ▣ ⇌ ⊠

CARTHAGE

🆑 ▼▼▼ **Days Inn** M
(417) 358-2499. **$45-$58.** 2244 Grand Ave. Just n of jct SR HH. Ext corridors. **Pets:** Medium. $10 one-time fee/room. Designated rooms, service with restrictions, crate.
SAVE S⦶ ⊠ ❚ ⇌

🆑 ▼▼▼ **Econo Lodge** SH
(417) 358-3900. **$57-$62.** 1441 W Central. On SR 96, at jct US 71. Ext/int corridors. **Pets:** Medium. $5 daily fee/pet. Designated rooms, service with restrictions, supervision.
SAVE S⦶ ⊠ 🖱 ❚ ⇌

CASSVILLE

▼ **Budget Inn** M
(417) 847-4196. **$38-$58.** Hwy 112/248. On SR 76, 86 and 112, just e of jct SR 248; downtown. Ext corridors. **Pets:** Very small. $10 deposit/pet. Service with restrictions, supervision.
ASK S⦶ ⊠ ❚ ▣ ⇌

▼▼ **Super 8 Motel** SH
(417) 847-4888. **$54-$58.** 101 S Hwy 37. Just s of jct SR 76, 86 and 37 business route. Int corridors. **Pets:** Accepted.
ASK S⦶ ⊠ &M ❚ ⇌

CHILLICOTHE

▼▼ **Best Western Inn** SH
(660) 646-0572. **$54-$72.** 1020 S Washington St. Jct US 36 and 65. Ext/int corridors. **Pets:** Other species. $10 daily fee/pet. Service with restrictions.
ASK S⦶ ⊠ &M ❚ ▣ ⇌

▼▼ **Chillicothe Super 8 Motel** SH
(660) 646-7888. **$60-$81, 3 day notice.** 580 Old Hwy 36 E. Jct US 36 and 65, 0.8 mi e. Int corridors. **Pets:** Medium, other species. $10 one-time fee/pet. Crate.
ASK S⦶ ⊠ ❚

CLINTON

🆑 ▼▼◆ **Motel USA Inn** M
(660) 885-2267. **$35-$55.** 1508 N 2nd St. Jct of SR 7 and 13. Ext corridors. **Pets:** Small, dogs only. $10 daily fee/pet. Designated rooms, no service, supervision.
SAVE S⦶ ⊠ ❚

COLUMBIA

▼▼▼◆ **Drury Inn-Columbia** SH
(573) 445-1800. **$92-$137.** 1000 Knipp St. I-70, exit 124 (Stadium Blvd), just s. Int corridors. **Pets:** Large, other species. Service with restrictions, supervision.
ASK ⊠ ⚷ ❚ ▣ ⇌

▼▼▼▼ **Holiday Inn Express** SH
(573) 449-4422. **$86-$102.** 801 Keene St. I-70, exit 128A, just se. Int corridors. **Pets:** Small. Service with restrictions, supervision.
ASK S⦶ ⊠ &M ⚷ 🖱 ❚ ▣ ⇌

🆑 ▼▼▼▼ **Holiday Inn Select Executive Center** LH
(573) 445-8531. **$79.** 2200 I-70 Dr SW. I-70, exit 124 (Stadium Blvd), just w. Int corridors. **Pets:** Designated rooms, service with restrictions, crate.
SAVE S⦶ ⊠ &M ⚷ 🖱 ❚ ▣ ¶ ⇌ ⊠

🆑 ▼▼▼ **Quality Inn Columbia** SH
(573) 449-2491. **$69-$99.** 1612 N Providence Rd. I-70, exit 126 (Providence Rd). Ext/int corridors. **Pets:** Accepted.
SAVE S⦶ ⊠ &M ❚ ▣ ⇌ ⊠

▼▼ **Ramada Inn & Conference Center** SH
(573) 449-0051. **Call for rates.** 1100 Vandiver Dr. I-70, exit 127 (US 63). Int corridors. **Pets:** Accepted.
⊠ &M ⚷ 🖱 ❚ ▣ ¶ ⇌

🆑 ▼▼▼ **Red Roof Inn-Columbia** M
(573) 442-0145. **$45-$68.** 201 E Texas Ave. I-70, exit 126 (Providence Rd), just n. Ext corridors. **Pets:** Medium. Service with restrictions, supervision.
SAVE ⊠ 🖱

🆑 ▼▼▼ **Travelodge** M ❀
(573) 449-1065. **$59-$89, 3 day notice.** 900 Vandiver Dr. I-70, exit 127 (US 63), just n. Ext corridors. **Pets:** Medium. $5 daily fee/pet. Designated rooms, service with restrictions, crate.
SAVE S⦶ ⊠ ❚ ▣ ⇌

▼▼▼ **Wingate Inn** SH ❀
(573) 817-0500. **$89-$129.** 3101 Wingate Ct. I-70, exit 128A, just s to I-70 Dr SE, 0.3 mi e to Keene St, 0.3 mi s, then just w. Int corridors. **Pets:** Small. $15 one-time fee/pet. Service with restrictions.
ASK S⦶ ⊠ &M 🖱 ❚ ▣ ⇌

CONCORDIA

🆑 ▼▼▼ **Days Inn of Concordia** M
(660) 463-7987. **$54-$99.** 301 NW 3rd St. I-70, exit 58, just s to 3rd St, then just w. Ext/int corridors. **Pets:** Accepted.
SAVE S⦶ ⊠ ❚ ⇌

CUBA

(AAA) ▼▼▼ Best Western Cuba Inn M
(573) 885-7707. **$55-$75.** 246 Hwy P. I-44, exit 208, just ne. Ext corridors. **Pets:** Small. $10 one-time fee/room. Designated rooms, service with restrictions, supervision.
[SAVE] [S🐾] [✕] [🛏] [💻] [⇌]

FESTUS

▼▼ Drury Inn St. Louis/Festus SH
(636) 933-2400. **$67-$92.** 1001 Veterans Blvd. I-55, exit 175, just e. Int corridors. **Pets:** Large, other species. Service with restrictions, supervision.
[ASK] [✕] [🛏] [💻] [⇌]

FULTON

▼▼▼ Loganberry Inn Bed & Breakfast BB ❀
(573) 642-9229. **$95-$175, 14 day notice.** 310 W 7th St. 1 mi e of jct US 54 and CR F, n on Westminster, then just e. Int corridors. **Pets:** Other species. $10 daily fee/room. Designated rooms, service with restrictions, crate.
[ASK] [✕] [🛏]

GRAY SUMMIT

▼▼ Best Western Diamond Inn Motel M
(636) 742-3501. **$64-$99.** 2875 Hwy 100. I-44, exit 253. Ext corridors. **Pets:** Accepted.
[ASK] [S🐾] [✕] [🐾] [🛏] [💻] [⇌]

HANNIBAL

(AAA) ▼▼▼ Hannibal Travelodge M
(573) 221-4100. **$46-$82.** 500 Mark Twain Ave. I-72, exit 157, 0.6 mi se on US Business Rt 36/SR 29. Ext corridors. **Pets:** Other species. $5 one-time fee/pet. Designated rooms, service with restrictions, crate.
[SAVE] [S🐾] [✕] [🛏] [💻] [⇌]

HARRISONVILLE

(AAA) ▼▼▼ Best Western Harrisonville M
(816) 884-3200. **$64-$92.** 2201 N Rockhaven Rd. Just n of jct US 71 and SR 291. Ext corridors. **Pets:** Small. $10 daily fee/pet. Designated rooms, service with restrictions, supervision.
[SAVE] [S🐾] [✕] [🛏] [💻] [⇌]

▼ Budget Host Caravan Motel M
(816) 884-4100. **$39-$60.** 1705 Hwy 291 N. Just n of jct US 71. Ext corridors. **Pets:** Medium. Service with restrictions, supervision.
[ASK] [S🐾] [✕] [🛏]

(AAA) ▼ Slumber Inn Motel M
(816) 884-3100. **$37-$47, 7 day notice.** 21400 E 275th St. Jct US 71 and SR 7 S (Clinton exit), just w. Ext corridors. **Pets:** Medium. $5 daily fee/pet. Service with restrictions, supervision.
[SAVE] [S🐾] [✕] [🛏] [⇌]

HAYTI

▼▼▼ Drury Inn & Suites-Hayti SH
(573) 359-2702. **$72-$110.** 1317 Hwy 84. I-55, exit 19 (US 412/SR 84), just w. Int corridors. **Pets:** Large, other species. Service with restrictions, supervision.
[ASK] [✕] [🐾] [🛏] [💻] [⇌]

HIGGINSVILLE

▼▼ Super 8 Motel-Higginsville SH
(660) 584-7781. **$56-$70.** 6471 Oakview Ln. I-70, exit 49 (SR 13), just se. Int corridors. **Pets:** Other species. $10 deposit/room, $5 daily fee/pet. Service with restrictions, supervision.
[ASK] [S🐾] [✕] [🛏]

HOUSTON

▼▼ Southern Inn Motel SH
(417) 967-4591. **$45-$50.** 1493 S Hwy 63. 1.3 mi s on US 63. Ext corridors. **Pets:** Accepted.
[ASK] [S🐾] [✕] [🛏]

JACKSON

▼▼▼ Drury Inn & Suites-Jackson SH
(573) 243-9200. **$74-$91.** 225 Drury Ln. I-55, exit 105 (SR 61), 0.3 mi w. Int corridors. **Pets:** Large, other species. Service with restrictions, supervision.
[ASK] [✕] [📶] [🐾] [🛏] [💻] [⇌]

JEFFERSON CITY

(AAA) ▼▼▼ Capitol Plaza Hotel LH
(573) 635-1234. **$89-$94.** 415 W McCarty St. On US 50 and 63 S, just e of jct US 54. Int corridors. **Pets:** $50 deposit/room, $5 one-time fee/room. Service with restrictions, crate.
[SAVE] [S🐾] [✕] [🐾] [🛏] [💻] [🍴] [⇌] [✗]

(AAA) ▼▼▼ Ramada Inn-Jefferson City SH
(573) 635-7171. **$72-$82.** 1510 Jefferson St. US 54, exit Ellis Blvd, 0.5 mi nw. Ext/int corridors. **Pets:** $10 daily fee/room. Service with restrictions, crate.
[SAVE] [S🐾] [✕] [🐾] [🛏] [💻] [🍴] [⇌]

JOPLIN

(AAA) ▼▼▼ Baymont Inn & Suites SH
(417) 623-0000. **$66-$86.** 3510 S Range Line Rd. I-44, exit 8B, just n. Ext/int corridors. **Pets:** Accepted.
[SAVE] [S🐾] [✕] [🐾] [🛏] [💻] [⇌]

(AAA) ▼▼▼ Best Western Oasis Inn & Suites SH
(417) 781-6776. **$59-$79.** 3508 S Range Line Rd. I-44, exit 8B, just nw. Ext corridors. **Pets:** Medium. $10 daily fee/room. Service with restrictions, supervision.
[SAVE] [S🐾] [✕] [🛏] [💻] [⇌]

▼▼▼ Drury Inn & Suites-Joplin SH
(417) 781-8000. **$85-$115.** 3601 Range Line Rd. I-44, exit 8B, just ne. Int corridors. **Pets:** Large, other species. Service with restrictions, supervision.
[ASK] [✕] [🐾] [🛏] [💻] [⇌] [✗]

(AAA) ▼▼▼▼ Holiday Inn SH
(417) 782-1000. **$134-$144.** 3615 Range Line Rd. I-44, exit
8B, just ne. Int corridors. **Pets:** Medium. $25 deposit/room.
Designated rooms, service with restrictions, supervision.
[SAVE] [S] [X] [] [] [] [] [] []

▼ Motel 6–427 M
(417) 781-6400. **$39-$52.** 3031 S Range Line Rd. I-44, exit
8B, 1 mi n. Ext corridors. **Pets:** Small, other species. Service with restrictions, supervision.
[S] [X] [] []

▼▼▼ Ramada Inn SH
(417) 781-0500. **$88-$99.** 3320 Range Line Rd. I-44, exit 8B,
0.4 mi n. Int corridors. **Pets:** Accepted.
[ASK] [S] [X] [] [] [] [] [] []

(AAA) ▼▼ Sleep Inn SH
(417) 782-1212. **$69.** I-44 & State Hwy 43 S. I-44, exit 4, just
s. Int corridors. **Pets:** Medium. $10 one-time fee/room.
Service with restrictions, supervision.
[SAVE] [S] [X] [] []

▼▼ Super 8 Motel-Joplin M
(417) 782-8765. **$49-$75.** 2830 E 36th St. I-44, exit 8B, just
n. Int corridors. **Pets:** Accepted.
[ASK] [S] [X] []

KANSAS CITY METROPOLITAN AREA

BLUE SPRINGS

▼▼ ▼▼ Days Inn & Suites SH
(816) 224-1122. **$50-$86.** 3120 NW Jefferson Rd. I-70, exit
18, just n to NW Jefferson St, then 0.5 mi e. Int corridors.
Pets: Other species. $5 daily fee/pet. Designated rooms,
service with restrictions.
[ASK] [S] [X] [M] [] [] []

(AAA) ▼▼ ▼ Sleep Inn SH
(816) 224-1199. **$60-$65.** 451 NW Jefferson St. I-70, exit 20,
just n on SR 7 to NW Jefferson St, then just e. Int corridors.
Pets: $5 one-time fee/room. Supervision.
[SAVE] [S] [X] [M] [] [] [] []

GRAIN VALLEY

(AAA) ▼▼ ▼ Travelodge Kansas City M
(816) 224-3420. **$59.** 105 Sunny Lane Dr. I-70, exit 24, just
n. Ext corridors. **Pets:** Other species. $5 daily fee/pet. Serv-
ice with restrictions, supervision.
[SAVE] [S] [X] [] [] []

INDEPENDENCE

(AAA) ▼▼ ▼ Best Western Truman Inn M
(816) 254-0100. **$64-$99.** 4048 S Lynn Court Dr. I-70, exit
12, just n on Noland Rd, then just w. Ext corridors.
Pets: Small. $30 deposit/room, $6 daily fee/room. Designated rooms, service with restrictions, supervision.
[SAVE] [S] [X] [] []

(AAA) ▼▼ ▼ Red Roof Inn M
(816) 373-2800. **$45-$70.** 13712 E 42nd Terrace. I-70, exit
12 (Noland Rd), just sw. Ext corridors. **Pets:** Large. Service
with restrictions, supervision.
[SAVE] [X] [M] []

▼ Super 8 Motel SH
(816) 833-1888. **$44-$89.** 4032 S Lynn Court Dr. I-70, exit
12, just nw. Int corridors. **Pets:** Small. $30 deposit/room, $6
daily fee/room. Designated rooms, service with restrictions,
supervision.
[ASK] [S] [X] [] []

KANSAS CITY

**(AAA) ▼▼▼▼ AmeriSuites (Kansas
City/Airport) SH**
(816) 891-0871. **$85-$89.** 7600 NW 97th Terr. I-29, exit 10,
just sw. Int corridors. **Pets:** Accepted.
[SAVE] [S] [X] [] [] []

**(AAA) ▼▼ ▼ Baymont Inn & Suites Kansas City
South SH**
(816) 822-7000. **$69-$89.** 8601 Hillcrest Rd. I-435, exit 69
(87th St). Int corridors. **Pets:** Small. Designated rooms,
service with restrictions, supervision.
[SAVE] [S] [X] [M] [] [] []

▼▼ ▼ Chase Suites by Woodfin SH
(816) 891-9009. **$139-$149.** 9900 NW Prairie View Rd. I-29,
exit 10. Ext corridors. **Pets:** Accepted.
[ASK] [S] [X] [] [] [] [] [] []

▼▼ ▼ Days Inn M
(816) 746-1666. **$65-$180.** 11120 NW Ambassador Dr. I-29,
exit 12, just e, then s. Int corridors. **Pets:** Accepted.
[ASK] [S] [X] [] [] [] [] []

**▼▼▼ Drury Inn & Suites-Kansas City
Airport SH**
(816) 880-9700. **$90-$110.** 7900 NW Tiffany Springs Pkwy.
I-29, exit 10, just w. Int corridors. **Pets:** Large, other spe-
cies. Service with restrictions, supervision.
[ASK] [X] [M] [] [] [] [] [] []

**▼▼▼ Drury Inn & Suites-Kansas City
Stadium SH**
(816) 923-3000. **$75-$110.** 3830 Blue Ridge Cutoff. I-70, exit
9 (Blue Ridge Cutoff), just nw. Int corridors. **Pets:** Large,
other species. Service with restrictions, supervision.
[ASK] [X] [M] [] [] [] []

**(AAA) ▼▼ ▼▼ Embassy Suites Hotel KCI
Airport SH**
(816) 891-7788. **$99-$209.** 7640 NW Tiffany Springs Pkwy.
I-29, exit 10, just e. Int corridors. **Pets:** Small, other species.
$50 deposit/room. Service with restrictions, supervision.
[SAVE] [S] [X] [M] [] [] [] [] [] []

AAA ▼▼▼ ▼▼▼ The Fairmont Kansas City at the Plaza LH ❖
(816) 756-1500. **$109-$255.** 401 Ward Pkwy. Corner of Wornall and Ward Pkwy. Int corridors. **Pets:** Dogs only. $25 daily fee/room. Service with restrictions, supervision.
SAVE ✕ 🐾 ❚❙ ➔ ✕

AAA ▼▼▼▼ Hampton Inn SH
(816) 483-7900. **$70-$93.** 1051 N Cambridge Ave. I-435, exit 57, just w to Cambridge Ave, then just s. Int corridors. **Pets:** Medium. $10 one-time fee/pet. Designated rooms, service with restrictions, supervision.
SAVE S✕ ✕ 🐾 🖼 ❚ ➔ ➔ ✕

AAA ▼▼▼ Holiday Inn Express Westport Plaza SH
(816) 931-1000. **$119-$129.** 801 Westport Rd. Int corridors. **Pets:** Other species. $25 one-time fee/pet. Crate.
SAVE S✕ ✕ ➔M 🐾 ❚ ➔

▼▼▼▼ Holiday Inn-Sports Complex SH
(816) 353-5300. **$99-$149.** 4011 Blue Ridge Cutoff. I-70, exit 9 (Blue Ridge Cutoff), just se. Int corridors. **Pets:** Accepted.
ASK S✕ ✕ 🐾M 🐾 🖼 ❚ ➔ ➔ ✕

▼▼▼▼ Homestead Studio Suites Hotel-Kansas City/Country Club Plaza SH ❖
(816) 531-2212. **$77-$97.** 4535 Main St. Just ne of Country Club Plaza. Int corridors. **Pets:** Medium, other species. $25 daily fee/room. Service with restrictions, crate.
ASK S✕ ✕ 🐾M 🖼 ❚ ➔ ❚❙

▼▼▼ Homestead Studio Suites Hotel-Kansas City/KCI Airport SH ❖
(816) 891-8500. **$68-$88.** 9701 N Shannon Ave. I-29, exit 10. Int corridors. **Pets:** Medium, other species. $25 daily fee/room. Service with restrictions, crate.
ASK S✕ ✕ 🐾M 🐾 🖼 ❚ ➔ ➔

AAA ▼▼▼▼ Homewood Suites by Hilton SH
(816) 880-9880. **$89-$159.** 7312 NW Polo Dr. I-29, exit 10, just e. Int corridors. **Pets:** Small, other species. $50 one-time fee/room. Service with restrictions, crate.
SAVE S✕ ✕ 🐾 🖼 ❚ ➔ ➔ ✕

▼▼▼▼ Kansas City Marriott Downtown LH
(816) 421-6800. **$169-$240.** 200 W 12th St. Just s of I-70, US 24 and 40. Int corridors. **Pets:** Accepted.
ASK ✕ 🐾 🖼 ❚ ➔ ❚❙ ➔ ✕

▼▼▼▼ Quality Inn & Suites Airport SH
(816) 587-6262. **$61-$71.** 6901 NW 83rd St. I-29, exit 8. Int corridors. **Pets:** Medium. Service with restrictions, supervision.
ASK S✕ ✕ 🖼 ❚ ➔ ➔

▼▼▼▼ Radisson Hotel Kansas City Airport SH
(816) 464-2423. **$59-$109.** 11828 NW Plaza Cir. I-29, exit 13, just se. Int corridors. **Pets:** Small. $10 daily fee/room. Designated rooms, service with restrictions, supervision.
ASK S✕ ✕ 🐾M 🐾 ❚ ➔ ❚❙ ➔ ✕

AAA ▼▼▼ ▼▼▼ Red Roof Inn-North M
(816) 452-8585. **$54-$74.** 3636 NE Randolph Rd. I-435, exit 55B northbound; exit 55 southbound, just e on SR 210, then just n. Ext corridors. **Pets:** Medium. Service with restrictions, supervision.
SAVE ✕ 🐾M 🐾

▼▼▼▼ Residence Inn by Marriott Union Hill SH
(816) 561-3000. **$119-$199, 3 day notice.** 2975 Main St. Just e of 31st St. Ext corridors. **Pets:** Small, other species. $5 daily fee/room, $50 one-time fee/room. Service with restrictions, crate.
ASK S✕ ✕ 🐾 🖼 ❚ ➔ ➔ ✕

▼▼ ▼▼ Sleep Inn SH
(816) 891-0111. **$45-$99.** 7611 NW 97th Terrace. I-29, exit 10, just sw. Int corridors. **Pets:** Medium. $10 daily fee/room. Service with restrictions, supervision.
ASK S✕ ✕ 🐾M 🐾 🖼 ❚ ➔

AAA ▼▼▼▼ Westin Crown Center LH
(816) 474-4400. **$159-$249.** 1 Pershing Rd. 0.5 mi s. Int corridors. **Pets:** Accepted.
SAVE ✕ 🐾M 🐾 🖼 ❚ ➔ ❚❙ ➔ ✕

KEARNEY

▼▼ ▼▼ Kearney Super 8 Motel SH
(816) 628-6800. **Call for rates.** 210 Platte Clay Way. I-35, exit 26, just e on SR 92, then just n. Int corridors. **Pets:** Medium, dogs only. $10 one-time fee/pet. Service with restrictions, supervision.
✕ ❚

LEE'S SUMMIT

▼▼▼▼ Summit Inn and Suites SH
(816) 525-1400. **$54-$129.** 625 NW Murray Rd. I-470, exit 7A, just s of jct US 50 (Chipman Rd exit). Int corridors. **Pets:** Medium, other species. Service with restrictions, supervision.
ASK S✕ ✕ 🐾 🖼 ❚ ➔ ❚❙ ➔

LIBERTY

AAA ▼▼▼ Days Inn M
(816) 781-8770. **$55-$65, 3 day notice.** 209 N 291 Hwy. I-35, exit 16, 0.7 mi e on SR 152, then just n on SR 291. Ext corridors. **Pets:** Small. $15 daily fee/pet. Service with restrictions, supervision.
SAVE S✕ ✕ ❚ ➔ ➔

NORTH KANSAS CITY

AAA ▼▼▼ Baymont Inn & Suites Kansas City North SH
(816) 221-1200. **$69-$99.** 2214 Taney Rd. I-29/35, exit 6A, just e on SR 210, then just n. Int corridors. **Pets:** Accepted.
SAVE S✕ ✕ 🐾 ❚ ➔

▼▼ Days Inn-North SH
(816) 421-6000. **$57-$77.** 2232 Taney Rd. I-29/35, exit 6A, just e on SR 210, then just n. Int corridors. **Pets:** Medium, dogs only. $10 one-time fee/room. Service with restrictions, supervision.
ASK S✕ ✕ 🐾M 🐾 🖼 ➔

OAK GROVE (JACKSON COUNTY)

Econo Lodge M
(816) 690-3681. **$59.** 410 SE 1st St. I-70, exit 28, just s on Broadway, just e on SE 4th St, then just n. Ext corridors. **Pets:** Small. $5 daily fee/pet. Service with restrictions.
[SAVE] [S6] [X] [H]

PLATTE CITY

Comfort Inn-KCI M
(816) 858-5430. **$70-$120.** 1200 Hwy 92. I-29, exit 18, 1 mi w. Int corridors. **Pets:** Accepted.
[SAVE] [S6] [X] [hand] [key] [H] [tv] [pool]

❖ END METROPOLITAN AREA ❖

KIMBERLING CITY

Kimberling Heights Resort M
(417) 779-4158. **$48-$59.** 9687 State Hwy 13. On US 13, 1.5 mi s. Ext corridors. **Pets:** Large, other species. Service with restrictions, supervision.
[SAVE] [S6] [H] [tv] [pool] [Z]

Kimberling Inn Resort & Conference Center SH
(417) 739-4311. **Call for rates.** 11863 St Hwy 13. On SR 13. Ext corridors. **Pets:** Accepted.
[X] [H] [tv] [fork] [pool] [X]

KINGDOM CITY

Super 8 Motel-Kingdom City M
(573) 642-2888. **$59-$72.** 3370 Gold Ave. I-70, exit 148 (US 54), 0.3 mi s. Int corridors. **Pets:** Other species. $5 daily fee/pet. Service with restrictions, supervision.
[ASK] [S6] [X] [M] [hand] [H]

KIRKSVILLE

Comfort Inn M
(660) 665-2205. **$59-$104.** 2209 N Baltimore. US 63 N. Int corridors. **Pets:** Service with restrictions, crate.
[ASK] [S6] [X] [M] [hand] [H] [tv]

Shamrock Inn M
(660) 665-8352. **$45-$50.** 2521 S Business 63. 0.3 mi w jct US 63 and Business Rt 63. Ext corridors. **Pets:** Medium. $10 daily fee/pet. Service with restrictions, supervision.
[ASK] [S6] [X] [H] [tv] [pool]

Super 8 Motel-Kirksville M
(660) 665-8826. **$51-$75.** 1101 Country Club Dr. On US 63 and SR 6. Int corridors. **Pets:** Accepted.
[ASK] [S6] [X] [H]

LAKE OZARK

Holiday Inn SunSpree Resort & Conference Center LH ❖
(573) 365-2334. **$90-$176, 3 day notice.** 120 Holiday Ln. 2.6 mi s of Bagnell Dam on US 54 business route. Ext/int corridors. **Pets:** Other species. $50 deposit/pet, $6 daily fee/pet. Supervision.
[SAVE] [S6] [X] [M] [hand] [key] [H] [tv] [fork] [pool] [X]

LAMAR

Blue Top Inn M ❖
(417) 682-3333. **$39-$52.** 65 SE 1st Ln. Just se of jct US 71 and 160. Ext corridors. **Pets:** Other species. $25 deposit/room. Service with restrictions.
[ASK] [S6] [X] [H] [tv] [pool]

LEBANON

Best Western Wyota Inn SH
(417) 532-6171. **$58-$65.** 1225 Milk Creek Rd. I-44, exit 130. Ext corridors. **Pets:** Medium. $10 daily fee/pet. Designated rooms, service with restrictions, supervision.
[SAVE] [S6] [X] [H] [tv] [fork] [pool]

LICKING

Best Value Inn SH
(573) 674-4809. **$42-$44.** 209 S Hwy 63. On US 63. Ext corridors. **Pets:** $5 daily fee/pet. Service with restrictions, crate.
[ASK] [S6] [X] [key]

LOUISIANA

River's Edge Motel M
(573) 754-4522. **$50-$60, 5 day notice.** 201 Mansion St. On US 54 at Champ Clark Bridge. Ext corridors. **Pets:** Medium, dogs only. $10 deposit/room. Service with restrictions, supervision.
[SAVE] [S6] [X] [H] [tv]

MACON

Best Western Inn M
(660) 385-2125. **$57.** 28933 Sunset Dr. On Outer Rd S at US 36 and Long Branch Lake exit. Ext corridors. **Pets:** Other species. $20 deposit/pet. Service with restrictions, supervision.
[ASK] [S6] [X] [H] [tv] [pool]

Super 8 Motel SH
(660) 385-5788. **$56-$65.** 203 E Briggs Dr. Jct US 63 and 36. Int corridors. **Pets:** Dogs only. $10 daily fee/pet. Service with restrictions, supervision.
[ASK] [S6] [X] [H] [tv]

MARSHFIELD

Holiday Inn Express SH
(417) 859-6000. **$72-$88.** 1301 Banning St. I-44, exit 100 (SR 38), on southeast corner. Int corridors. **Pets:** Small. $20 deposit/room. Designated rooms, no service, supervision.
[ASK] [S6] [X] [M] [H] [tv] [pool]

MARSTON

◆◆ **Super 8 Motel** [M]
(573) 643-9888. **$55.** 501 SE Outer Rd. I-55, exit 40, just se. Int corridors. **Pets:** Accepted.
[ASK] [SD] ⊠ ▣ ☕

MARYVILLE

◆◆ **Super 8 Motel-Maryville** [SH]
(660) 582-8088. **$44-$48.** 222 Summit Dr. 2 mi s on US 71. Int corridors. **Pets:** Large, other species. $10 deposit/room. Service with restrictions, supervision.
[ASK] [SD] ⊠ ▣ ☕

MINER

[AAA] ◆◆ **Best Western Coach House Inn** [SH]
(573) 471-9700. **$65-$130.** 220 S Interstate Dr. I-55, exit 67, just e, 0.5 mi s on Interstate Dr (frontage road). Int corridors. **Pets:** Small. $25 one-time fee/room. Designated rooms, service with restrictions, supervision.
[SAVE] [SD] ⊠ 🦻 ▣ ☕ 🏊

◆◆◆ **Drury Inn-Sikeston** [SH]
(573) 471-4100. **$77-$93.** 2602 E Malone. I-55, exit 67, just sw. Int corridors. **Pets:** Large, other species. Service with restrictions, supervision.
[ASK] ⊠ [♿M] 🦻 ♿ ▣ ☕ 🏊

◆◆ **Pear Tree Inn by Drury-Sikeston** [SH]
(573) 471-8660. **$58-$82.** 2602 Rear E Malone. I-55, exit 67, just sw. Ext corridors. **Pets:** Large, other species. Service with restrictions, supervision.
[ASK] ⊠ [♿M] 🦻 ☕ 🏊

MOBERLY

◆◆◆ **Best Western Moberly Inn** [SH]
(660) 263-6540. **$69-$71.** 1200 Hwy 24 E. Jct US 24 and 63. Ext/int corridors. **Pets:** Medium, dogs only. $30 one-time fee/room. Service with restrictions, supervision.
[ASK] [SD] ⊠ [♿M] ▣ ☕ 🍴 🏊

MONETT

◆◆ **Days Inn** [SH]
(417) 235-8039. **$60-$69.** 868 Hwy 60. On US 60, 1.3 mi e of jct SR 37. Ext corridors. **Pets:** Accepted.
[ASK] [SD] ⊠ 🦻 ▣ ☕ 🏊

MOUNTAIN GROVE

[AAA] ◆◆ **Best Western Ranch House Inn** [M]
(417) 926-3152. **$49-$58.** 111 E 17th St. Jct US 60 and 95, just s. Ext corridors. **Pets:** Accepted.
[SAVE] [SD] ⊠ ☕ 🏊

◆◆ **Days Inn of Mountain Grove** [SH]
(417) 926-5555. **$54-$59, 3 day notice.** 300 E 19th St. Jct US 60 and 95, just se. Ext corridors. **Pets:** Accepted.
[ASK] [SD] ⊠ 🏊

MOUNT VERNON

[AAA] ◆ **Budget Host Ranch Motel** [M]
(417) 466-2125. **$45-$50.** 1015 E Mt Vernon Blvd. I-44, exit 46, just n. Ext corridors. **Pets:** Accepted.
[SAVE] [SD] ⊠ 🏊

◆◆ **Super 8** [SH]
(417) 461-0230. **$61-$90.** 1200 E Industrial Blvd. I-44, exit 46, just n, then just se. Int corridors. **Pets:** Small. $10 one-time fee/room. Service with restrictions, supervision.
[ASK] [SD] ⊠ ♿ ▣ 🏊

NEOSHO

◆◆ **Super 8 Motel-Neosho** [SH]
(417) 455-1888. **$52-$69.** 3085 Gardner/Edgewood Dr. Just s of jct US 60B and 71B. Int corridors. **Pets:** Small. $10 daily fee/pet. Service with restrictions, supervision.
[ASK] [SD] ⊠ 🦻 ▣

NEVADA

[AAA] ◆ **Econo Lodge** [M]
(417) 667-3351. **$40-$75.** 1401 E Austin Blvd. Just e of jct US 54 and US 71 business route. Ext corridors. **Pets:** $5 one-time fee/pet. Service with restrictions, supervision.
[SAVE] [SD] ⊠ ▣ ☕ 🏊

◆◆ **Welk-Um Inn & Suites** [SH]
(417) 667-6777. **$42-$60.** 2345 Marvel Dr. US 71 business route, just w of jct US 71, exit Camp Clark and Nevada. Ext/int corridors. **Pets:** Small, other species. $5 daily fee/room. Designated rooms, service with restrictions, crate.
[ASK] [SD] ⊠ ▣ ☕ 🏊

NEW FLORENCE

◆◆ **Days Inn Booneslick Lodge** [SH]
(573) 835-7777. **$50-$72.** 403 Booneslick Rd. I-70, exit 175, just w. Int corridors. **Pets:** Other species. $20 deposit/pet, $5 daily fee/pet. Service with restrictions, supervision.
[ASK] [SD] ⊠ 🏊

OSAGE BEACH

[AAA] ◆◆ **Best Western Dogwood Hills Resort Inn** [SH]
(573) 348-1735. **$46-$129, 7 day notice.** 1252 State Hwy KK. 0.5 mi n US 54. Ext corridors. **Pets:** Large. $25 one-time fee/room. Service with restrictions.
[SAVE] [SD] ⊠ ▣ ☕ 🍴 🏊

[AAA] ◆◆ **Lake Chateau Resort** [M]
(573) 348-2791. **$49-$145, 3 day notice.** 5066 Hwy 54. Just s of Grand Glaize Bridge. Ext corridors. **Pets:** Medium. $10 one-time fee/pet. Designated rooms, service with restrictions, supervision.
[SAVE] [SD] ⊠ ▣ ☕ 🍴 🏊 🏋

[AAA] ◆ **Scottish Inns** [M]
(573) 348-3123. **$35-$90, 3 day notice.** 5404 Hwy 54. 1 mi w of Grand Glaize Bridge. Ext/int corridors. **Pets:** Small. $5 daily fee/pet. Designated rooms, service with restrictions, supervision.
[SAVE] ⊠ 🏊

POPLAR BLUFF

◆◆◆ **Drury Inn-Poplar Bluff** [SH]
(573) 686-2451. **$78-$94.** 2220 N Westwood Blvd. On US 67, 1.4 mi s from jct US 60 E. Int corridors. **Pets:** Large, other species. Service with restrictions, supervision.
[ASK] ⊠ 🦻 ▣ ☕ 🏊

▼▼ Pear Tree Inn by Drury-Poplar Bluff M
(573) 785-7100. **$58-$75.** 2218 N Westwood Blvd. On US 67, 1.4 mi s from jct US 60 E. Ext corridors. **Pets:** Large, other species. Service with restrictions, supervision.
[ASK] [✕] [🐾] [💻] [≈]

RICH HILL

⚑⚑ Apache Motel M
(417) 395-2161. **$36-$40.** Hwys 71 and B. Just e of jct US 71 and CR B. Ext corridors. **Pets:** Accepted.
[SAVE] [S6] [✕]

ROLLA

⚑⚑ ▼▼▼ Best Western Coachlight M
(573) 341-2511. **$48-$85.** 1403 Martin Springs Dr. Jct I-44 and Business Rt 44 S, exit 184. Ext corridors. **Pets:** Small. $20 deposit/room. Service with restrictions, crate.
[SAVE] [S6] [✕] [🛏] [💻] [≈]

▼▼ Days Inn M
(573) 341-3700. **$50-$85.** 1207 Kingshighway. I-44, exit 184, just s. Ext corridors. **Pets:** Other species. Service with restrictions, crate.
[ASK] [S6] [✕] [≈]

▼▼ Drury Inn SH
(573) 364-4000. **$65-$96.** 2006 N Bishop. I-44, exit 186 (US 63), just ne. Ext/int corridors. **Pets:** Large, other species. Service with restrictions, supervision.
[ASK] [✕] [🛏] [💻] [≈]

⚑⚑ ▼▼▼ Econo Lodge M
(573) 341-3130. **$50-$65.** 1417 Martin Springs Dr. I-44, exit 184, just n. Ext corridors. **Pets:** Medium, other species. Designated rooms, service with restrictions, crate.
[SAVE] [S6] [✕] [🛏] [💻] [≈]

▼▼ Holiday Inn Express SH
(573) 364-8200. **$83.** 1507 Martin Springs Dr. I-44, exit 184. Int corridors. **Pets:** Small. $10 daily fee/pet. Designated rooms, service with restrictions, supervision.
[ASK] [S6] [✕] [🐾] [🛏] [💻] [≈]

⚑⚑ ▼▼ Super 8 Motel-Rolla M
(573) 364-4156. **$45-$55.** 1201 Kingshighway. I-44, exit 184, just ne. Ext/int corridors. **Pets:** $5 one-time fee/pet. Supervision.
[SAVE] [S6] [✕] [🛏]

ST. CLAIR

⚑⚑ ▼▼▼ Budget Lodging M
(636) 629-1000. **$49-$79.** 866 S Outer Rd W. I-44, exit 240, just w. Ext/int corridors. **Pets:** Medium. $5 daily fee/pet. Designated rooms, service with restrictions, supervision.
[SAVE] [S6] [✕] [🛏] [💻] [≈]

ST. JOSEPH

▼▼▼ Drury Inn-St. Joseph SH
(816) 364-4700. **$70-$90.** 4213 Frederick Blvd. I-29, exit 47. Int corridors. **Pets:** Large, other species. Service with restrictions, supervision.
[ASK] [✕] [♿] [🐾] [🛏] [💻] [≈]

⚑⚑ ▼▼▼ Ramada Inn LH 🐾
(816) 233-6192. **$68.** 4016 Frederick Blvd. I-29, exit 47. Int corridors. **Pets:** Other species. $25 deposit/pet. Designated rooms, supervision.
[SAVE] [S6] [✕] [🛏] [💻] [🍴] [≈] [✕]

▼▼▼ St. Joseph Riverfront Historic District Hotel LH
(816) 279-8000. **$69-$119.** 102 S Third St. I-229, exit Edmond St northbound; exit Felix St southbound; downtown. Int corridors. **Pets:** Accepted.
[ASK] [S6] [✕] [♿] [🐾] [🛏] [💻] [🍴] [≈] [✕]

ST. LOUIS METROPOLITAN AREA

BRIDGETON

⚑⚑ ▼▼ Red Roof Inn-Bridgeton M
(314) 291-3350. **$44-$72.** 3470 Hollenberg Dr. I-270, exit 20B (St Charles Rock Rd), 0.4 mi w. Ext corridors. **Pets:** Medium. Designated rooms, service with restrictions, crate.
[SAVE] [✕] [♿]

CHESTERFIELD

▼▼▼ Doubletree Hotel & Conference Center SH 🐾
(636) 532-5000. **$71-$125.** 16625 Swingley Ridge Rd. I-64, exit 19A (Chesterfield Pkwy), 0.5 mi w. Int corridors. **Pets:** Large. Service with restrictions, supervision.
[ASK] [S6] [✕] [🐾] [🛏] [💻] [🍴] [≈] [✕]

▼▼▼ Homewood Suites by Hilton SH
(636) 530-0305. **$99-$129.** 840 Chesterfield Pkwy W. I-64, exit 20, 1 mi n. Int corridors. **Pets:** Accepted.
[ASK] [S6] [✕] [♿] [🛏] [💻] [≈]

CLAYTON

⚑⚑ ▼▼▼▼ The Ritz-Carlton, St. Louis LH
(314) 863-6300. **$239-$249.** 100 Carondelet Plaza. I-64, exit 32, 1.2 mi n on Hanley Rd, just e. Int corridors. **Pets:** Accepted.
[SAVE] [S6] [✕] [🐾] [🛏] [💻] [🍴] [≈] [✕]

⚑⚑ ▼▼▼ Sheraton Clayton Plaza Hotel SH
(314) 863-0400. **$199-$239.** 7730 Bonhomme Ave. I-64/US 40, exit 31 (Brentwood Blvd), 1.3 mi n, 0.7 mi e. Int corridors. **Pets:** Small. Service with restrictions, crate.
[SAVE] [S6] [✕] [🐾] [♿] [🛏] [💻] [🍴] [≈]

CREVE COEUR

▼▼▼▼ Drury Inn & Suites-St. Louis/Creve
     Coeur SH
(314) 989-1100. $112-$132. 11980 Olive Blvd. I-270, exit 14
(Olive Blvd). Int corridors. Pets: Large, other species. Service with restrictions, supervision.
ASK ✕ &M 🐾 🚪 💻 🌊

EDMUNDSON

▼▼▼▼ Drury Inn-St. Louis Airport SH
(314) 423-7700. $99-$124. 10490 Natural Bridge Rd. I-70,
exit 236 (Lambert Airport), just se. Int corridors.
Pets: Large, other species. Service with restrictions, supervision.
ASK ✕ &M 🐾 🚪 💻 🌊

EUREKA

▲▲▲ ▼▼▼▼ Holiday Inn at Six Flags SH 🐾
(636) 938-6661. $94-$244. 4901 Six Flags Rd. I-44, exit 261
(Allenton Rd). Ext/int corridors. Pets: Large, other species.
$10 one-time fee/room. Service with restrictions, crate.
SAVE S🐾 ✕ 🚪 💻 🍴 🌊 🌊

FENTON

▼▼▼▼ Drury Inn & Suites St. Louis Fenton SH
(636) 343-7822. $82-$117. 1088 S Hwy Dr. I-44, exit 274
(Bowles Ave), just se. Int corridors. Pets: Large, other species. Service with restrictions, supervision.
ASK ✕ 🐾 🚪 💻 🌊

▼▼▼▼ Pear Tree Inn by Drury-Fenton SH
(636) 343-8820. $72-$100. 1100 S Hwy Dr. I-44, exit 274
(Bowles Ave), just s. Int corridors. Pets: Large, other species. Service with restrictions, supervision.
ASK ✕ 🐾 🚪 💻 🌊

▼▼ ▼▼ Towne Place Suites by Marriott SH
(636) 305-7000. $82-$135. 1662 Fenton Business Park Ct.
I-44, exit 275 westbound; exit 274 eastbound, to S Highway
Dr, then just s. Int corridors. Pets: Accepted.
ASK S🐾 ✕ &M 🐾 ⛳ 🚪 💻 🌊

FORISTELL

▲▲▲ ▼▼▼ Best Western West 70 Inn SH
(636) 673-2900. $60-$70, 14 day notice. 12 Hwy W. I-70,
exit 203 (CR W), just n. Int corridors. Pets: $10 daily fee/
pet. Service with restrictions, supervision.
SAVE S🐾 ✕ 🚪 💻 🌊

HAZELWOOD

▲▲▲ ▼▼▼ Baymont Inn & Suites St.
     Louis-Airport SH
(314) 731-4200. $69-$89. 318 Taylor Rd. I-270, exit 25B
(Lindberg Blvd N), just s. Int corridors. Pets: Accepted.
SAVE S🐾 ✕ 🐾 🚪 💻

▼▼ ▼▼ Fairfield Inn by Marriott-St.
     Louis/Hazelwood SH
(314) 731-7700. $49-$99. 9079 Dunn Rd. I-270, exit 25
(Lindbergh Blvd), just n to Douglas Palmer Rd, then just e.
Ext/int corridors. Pets: Accepted.
ASK S🐾 ✕ 🐾 ⛳ 🚪 🌊

▼▼▼▼ La Quinta Inn-Airport SH
(314) 731-3881. $76-$96. 5781 Campus Ct. I-270, exit 23
(McDonnell Blvd), just s. Int corridors. Pets: Accepted.
ASK S🐾 ✕ 🐾 🚪 💻 🌊

KIRKWOOD

▲▲▲ ▼▼▼▼ Best Western Kirkwood Inn SH
(314) 821-3950. $79-$109. 1200 S Kirkwood Rd. I-44, exit
277B (Lindbergh Blvd), just n. Int corridors. Pets: Medium.
$10 daily fee/pet. Designated rooms, service with restric-
tions, supervision.
SAVE S🐾 ✕ 🐾 🚪 💻 🌊

MARYLAND HEIGHTS

▼▼▼▼ ClubHouse Inn & Suites SH
(314) 205-8000. $59-$139. 1970 Craig Rd. I-270, exit 16A
(Page Ave), 0.8 mi e to Lackland Rd exit, 0.3 mi w to Craig
Rd, then just s. Int corridors. Pets: Small. $10 daily fee/
room. Service with restrictions, supervision.
ASK S🐾 ✕ &M 🐾 ⛳ 🚪 💻 🌊 🌊

▲▲▲ ▼▼▼▼ Comfort Inn Westport SH
(314) 878-1400. $59-$109. 12031 Lackland Rd. I-270, exit
16A (Page Ave), just e to Lackland Rd, then just w. Int
corridors. Pets: Medium. $35 one-time fee/room. Desig-
nated rooms, service with restrictions, supervision.
SAVE S🐾 ✕ 🐾 ⛳ 🚪 💻 🍴 🌊

▼▼▼▼ Drury Inn & Suites-St. Louis
     Westport SH
(314) 576-9966. $88-$108. 12220 Dorsett Rd. I-270, exit 17
(Dorsett Rd), just se. Int corridors. Pets: Large, other species. Service with restrictions, supervision.
ASK ✕ 🐾 🚪 💻 🌊

▼▼▼▼ Harrah's Hotel at Riverport Casino
     Center SH
(314) 770-8100. $59-$169. 777 Casino Center Dr. I-70, exit
231 (Earth City Expwy), 1 mi s to Casino Center Dr, 1.2 mi
nw. Int corridors. Pets: Small, dogs only. $15 one-time fee/
room. No service, supervision.
ASK ✕ &M 🐾 ⛳ 🚪 💻

▲▲▲ ▼▼ ▼▼ Red Roof Inn-Westport M
(314) 991-4900. $44-$69. 11837 Lackland Rd. I-270, exit
16A (Page Ave), 1.5 mi se. Ext corridors. Pets: Medium.
Service with restrictions, crate.
SAVE ✕ &M 🐾 ⛳

▲▲▲ ▼▼▼▼ Staybridge Suites SH
(314) 878-1555. $69-$139. 1855 Craigshire Rd. I-270, exit
16A (Page Ave), 0.8 mi e, exit Lackland Rd, 1 mi w, then s
via Lackland and Craigshire rds. Ext corridors.
Pets: Medium. $150 one-time fee/pet. Designated rooms,
service with restrictions, crate.
SAVE S🐾 ✕ 🐾 🚪 💻 🌊 🌊

MEHLVILLE

▼▼▼▼ Holiday Inn St. Louis-South I-55 SH
(314) 894-0700. $99-$134. 4234 Butler Hill Rd. I-55, exit 195
(Butler Hill Rd), just se. Ext/int corridors. Pets: Accepted.
ASK S🐾 ✕ 🐾 ⛳ 🚪 💻 🍴 🌊 🌊

O'FALLON

AAA ◆◆◆ **Comfort Inn & Suites** SH
(636) 696-8000. **$79-$149, 7 day notice.** 100 Comfort Inn
Ct. I-70, exit 219, just sw. Int corridors. **Pets:** Other species.
$10 daily fee/room. Designated rooms, service with restrictions, crate.
[SAVE] [S⌀] [✕] [✍] [🛏] [▭] [🍽] [✕]

RICHMOND HEIGHTS

◆◆◆ **Residence Inn By Marriott-St. Louis**
Galleria SH 🐾
(314) 862-1900. **$84-$189.** 1100 McMorrow Ave. I-170, exit
1C (Brentwood Ave) northbound; exit Brentwood Ave southbound, 0.5 mi e of Galleria via Galleria Pkwy. Ext corridors.
Pets: Large, other species. $10 daily fee/room, $50 one-
time fee/room. Service with restrictions, crate.
[ASK] [S⌀] [✕] [&M] [🅿] [✍] [🛏] [▭] [🍽] [✕]

ST. ANN

◆◆◆ **Hampton Inn-St. Louis Airport** SH
(314) 427-3400. **$103-$123.** 10800 Pear Tree Ln. I-70, exit
236, just sw. Int corridors. **Pets:** Accepted.
[ASK] [✕] [🛏] [▭] [🍽]

ST. CHARLES

AAA ◆◆◆ **Comfort Suites-St. Charles** SH 🐾
(636) 949-0694. **$84-$115.** 1400 S Fifth St. I-70, exit 229
(Fifth St), just ne. Int corridors. **Pets:** Other species. Service
with restrictions, crate.
[SAVE] [S⌀] [✕] [✍] [🛏] [▭] [🍽]

ST. LOUIS

◆◆◆ **Drury Inn & Suites St. Louis Convention**
Center LH
(314) 231-8100. **$108-$118.** 711 N Broadway. I-70, exit
250B, at convention center. Int corridors. **Pets:** Large, other
species. Service with restrictions, supervision.
[ASK] [✕] [🛏] [▭] [🍽] [🍽] [✕]

◆◆◆ **Drury Inn St. Louis/Union Station** SH
(314) 231-3900. **$128-$150.** 201 S 20th St. Just e of Jefferson Ave; between Market St and Clark Ave. Int corridors.
Pets: Large, other species. Service with restrictions, supervision.
[ASK] [✕] [🅿] [✍] [🛏] [▭] [🍽] [🍽]

◆◆◆ **Drury Plaza Hotel-St. Louis At the**
Arch SH
(314) 231-3003. **$133-$153.** 2 S Fourth St. I-70, 250B
(Stadium/Memorial Dr), just w on Pine to Broadway, just s
to Walnut St, just e to Fourth St, then just n. Int corridors.
Pets: Large, other species. Service with restrictions, super-
vision.
[ASK] [✕] [&M] [✍] [🛏] [▭] [🍽] [🍽]

◆◆◆ **Four Points by Sheraton St. Louis**
Downtown LH
(314) 516-9300. **$159-$269.** 310 S 4th St. Just w of Gateway Arch. Int corridors. **Pets:** Accepted.
[ASK] [S⌀] [✕] [🛏] [▭] [🍽] [🍽]

◆◆◆ **Hampton Inn St. Louis/Union Station** SH
(314) 241-3200. **$122-$132.** 2211 Market St. I-64/US 40, exit
39, just n on Jefferson Ave, then just e. Int corridors.
Pets: Accepted.
[ASK] [✕] [🛏] [▭] [🍽] [✕]

◆◆◆ **Holiday Inn-Forest Park** SH
(314) 645-0700. **$99-$145.** 5915 Wilson Ave. I-44, exit 286
(Hampton Ave), just se. Int corridors. **Pets:** Other species.
$75 deposit/room, $25 one-time fee/pet. Service with
restrictions.
[ASK] [S⌀] [✕] [&M] [🅿] [✍] [🛏] [▭] [🍽] [🍽]

◆◆◆ **Omni Majestic Hotel** SH
(314) 436-2355. **$139-$159.** 1019 Pine St. Between 10th
and 11th sts. Int corridors. **Pets:** Small, dogs only. $25
one-time fee/room. Service with restrictions, crate.
[ASK] [S⌀] [✕] [🅿] [🛏] [▭] [🍽]

AAA ◆◆◆ **Red Roof Inn-Hampton** M
(314) 645-0101. **$73-$109.** 5823 Wilson Ave. I-44, exit 286
(Hampton Ave), 0.3 mi se. Ext corridors. **Pets:** Medium,
other species. Service with restrictions, supervision.
[SAVE] [✕] [🅿] [🛏]

AAA ◆◆◆ ◆◆◆ **Renaissance Grand Hotel St.**
Louis LH
(314) 621-9600. **$169-$209.** 800 Washington Ave. Across
from America's Center (Convention Center). Int corridors.
Pets: $45 one-time fee/room. Service with restrictions,
crate.
[SAVE] [✕] [&M] [🅿] [✍] [🛏] [▭] [🍽] [🍽]

◆◆◆ ◆◆◆ **The Renaissance St. Louis Suites**
Hotel SH
(314) 621-9700. **Call for rates.** 827 Washington Ave. Next to
America's Center (Convention Center). Int corridors.
Pets: $45 one-time fee/room. Service with restrictions,
crate.
[✕] [&M] [🅿] [✍] [🛏] [▭] [🍽] [✕]

◆◆◆ ◆◆◆ **Sheraton St. Louis City Center Hotel &**
Suites LH 🐾
(314) 231-5007. **$239-$249.** 400 S 14th St. I-40, exit 39B
(14th St), just ne. Int corridors. **Pets:** Medium, dogs only.
$75 deposit/room. Designated rooms, service with restric-
tions.
[ASK] [S⌀] [✕] [&M] [🅿] [✍] [🛏] [▭] [🍽] [🍽] [✕]

◆◆◆ ◆◆◆ **The Westin St. Louis** LH 🐾
(314) 621-2000. **$339.** 811 Spruce St. Just w of Busch Sta-
dium. Int corridors. **Pets:** Medium. Service with restrictions,
crate.
[ASK] [S⌀] [✕] [&M] [🅿] [✍] [▭] [🍽]

ST. PETERS

◆◆◆ ◆◆◆ **Drury Inn-St. Charles/St. Peters** SH
(636) 397-9700. **$92-$114.** 170 Westfield Dr. I-70, exit 222
(Mid Rivers Mall Dr), just se. Int corridors. **Pets:** Large,
other species. Service with restrictions, supervision.
[ASK] [✕] [&M] [🅿] [✍] [🛏] [▭] [🍽]

▼▼▼ **Holiday Inn Select of St. Peters/St. Charles** 🆂🅷
(636) 928-1500. **$75-$94, 30 day notice.** 4341 Veteran's Memorial Pkwy. I-70, exit 225 (Cave Springs), 0.5 mi w. Int corridors. **Pets:** Accepted.
🅰🆂🅺 Ⓢ🅾 ⊗ 🖥 💷 🍴 🛬 ⊠

WENTZVILLE

🅰🅰🅰 ▼▼▼ **Holiday Inn-Wentzville** 🆂🅷
(636) 327-7001. **$59-$85.** 900 Corporate Pkwy. I-70, exit 212A, 0.3 mi w on service road. Int corridors. **Pets:** Other species. $35 deposit/room. Designated rooms, service with restrictions, supervision.
🆂🅰🆅🅴 Ⓢ🅾 ⊗ ⊘ 🖥 💷 🍴 🛬

✿ END METROPOLITAN AREA ✿

ST. ROBERT

🅰🅰🅰 ▼▼▼ **Best Western Montis Inn** Ⓜ
(573) 336-4299. **$55-$79.** 14086 Hwy Z. I-44, exit 163, just se. Ext corridors. **Pets:** Medium. Service with restrictions, crate.
🆂🅰🆅🅴 Ⓢ🅾 ⊗ 🖥 💷 🛬

🅰🅰🅰 ▼▼▼ **Red Roof Inn** Ⓜ
(573) 336-2510. **$65-$70.** 129 St Robert Blvd. I-44, exit 161, just nw. Int corridors. **Pets:** Small. Designated rooms, service with restrictions, supervision.
🆂🅰🆅🅴 Ⓢ🅾 ⊗ ⓘ 🖥 🛬

SEDALIA

▼▼▼ **The Hotel Bothwell** 🆂🅷
(660) 826-5588. **$49-$179, 3 day notice.** 103 E 4th St. Corner of 4th St and S Ohio; downtown. Int corridors. **Pets:** Accepted.
🅰🆂🅺 Ⓢ🅾 ⊗ 🖥 💷 🍴

SPRINGFIELD

🅰🅰🅰 ▼▼▼ **Baymont Inn & Suites** 🆂🅷
(417) 889-8188. **$66-$86.** 3776 S Glenstone Ave. On US 60. Int corridors. **Pets:** Accepted.
🆂🅰🆅🅴 Ⓢ🅾 ⊗ 🅜 ⊘ ⓘ 🖥 💷 🛬

🅰🅰🅰 ▼▼▼ **Best Western Coach House Inn** Ⓜ
(417) 862-0701. **$59-$79.** 2535 N Glenstone Ave. I-44, exit 80A, just s. Ext corridors. **Pets:** $10 one-time fee/room. No service, supervision.
🆂🅰🆅🅴 Ⓢ🅾 ⊗ 🖥 💷 🛬 ⊠

🅰🅰🅰 ▼▼▼ **Best Western Route 66 Rail Haven** Ⓜ
(417) 866-1963. **$54-$74.** 203 S Glenstone Ave. I-44, exit 80A, 3 mi s. Ext corridors. **Pets:** $10 one-time fee/room. Service with restrictions, supervision.
🆂🅰🆅🅴 Ⓢ🅾 ⊗ 🅜 🖥 🛬

🅰🅰🅰 ▼▼▼ **Super 8 Motel-Wentzville** 🆂🅷
(636) 327-5300. **$49-$60.** 4 Pantera Dr. I-70, exit 208 (Pearce Blvd), on S Outer Rd. Int corridors. **Pets:** Very small, dogs only. $50 deposit/room, $7 one-time fee/pet. Service with restrictions, supervision.
🆂🅰🆅🅴 Ⓢ🅾 ⊗ ⊘ 🛬

▼▼▼ **Clarion Hotel** 🆂🅷 ✿
(417) 883-6550. **$75-$85, 30 day notice.** 3333 S Glenstone Ave. On US 60 (James River Expwy), 0.5 mi n. Int corridors. **Pets:** Medium, other species. $10 daily fee/room. Service with restrictions, crate.
🅰🆂🅺 Ⓢ🅾 ⊗ 🅜 ⊘ 🦽 🖥 💷 🍴 🛬

🅰🅰🅰 ▼▼▼ **Comfort Suites** 🆂🅷
(417) 886-5090. **$70-$90.** 1260 E Independence St. US 60 (James River Expwy), exit National Ave. Ext corridors. **Pets:** Accepted.
🆂🅰🆅🅴 Ⓢ🅾 ⊗ ⊘ 🖥 💷 🛬

▼▼▼ **Days Inn** 🆂🅷 ✿
(417) 862-0153. **$84-$199.** 621 W Sunshine Ave. US 65, exit Sunshine St, 3 mi w. Int corridors. **Pets:** Large, other species. $15 daily fee/pet. Service with restrictions, supervision.
🅰🆂🅺 Ⓢ🅾 ⊗ 🅜 🦽 🖥 💷 🛬

▼▼▼ **Drury Inn & Suites-Springfield** 🆂🅷
(417) 863-8400. **$86-$125.** 2715 N Glenstone Ave. I-44, exit 80A (Glenstone Ave), just s. Int corridors. **Pets:** Large, other species. Service with restrictions, supervision.
🅰🆂🅺 ⊗ 🅜 ⊘ 🦽 🖥 💷 🛬

▼▼▼ **Howard Johnson Express Inn** 🆂🅷 ✿
(417) 890-6060. **$69-$79.** 2535 S Campbell. US 65, exit Sunshine St, 5 mi s, just e. Int corridors. **Pets:** Other species. $15 daily fee/pet. Service with restrictions.
🅰🆂🅺 Ⓢ🅾 ⊗ 🅜 ⓘ 🖥 💷 🛬

🅰🅰🅰 ▼▼▼ **Lamplighter Inn Convention Center North** 🆂🅷
(417) 869-3900. **$54-$74.** 2820 N Glenstone Ave. I-44, exit 80A, just se. Ext/int corridors. **Pets:** Medium, dogs only. $25 deposit/room. Designated rooms, service with restrictions, supervision.
🆂🅰🆅🅴 Ⓢ🅾 ⊗ 🅜 🦽 🖥 💷 🛬

🅰🅰🅰 ▼▼▼ **Merigold Inn** Ⓜ
(417) 881-2833. **$44-$68.** 2006 S Glenstone Ave. On Business Rt US 65, just s of CR D. Ext corridors. **Pets:** Small, dogs only. $10 daily fee/pet. Supervision.
🆂🅰🆅🅴 Ⓢ🅾 ⊗ 🛬

▼ Plaza Inn Ⓜ
(417) 862-4301. **$40-$50, 10 day notice.** 2933 N Glenstone Ave. I-44, exit 80, just s, then 0.3 mi w. Ext corridors. **Pets:** Very small, dogs only. $10 daily fee/pet. Service with restrictions, supervision.
[ASK] [S☼] [✕] [🖥] [≈]

▼▼▼ Red Lion Inn North 🆂🅷
(417) 520-8800. **Call for rates.** 1610 E Evergreen. I-44, exit 80A. Int corridors. **Pets:** Accepted.
[✕] [🅼] [🖉] [🖥] [💻] [≈]

🅐🅐🅐 ▼▼ Red Roof Inn Ⓜ
(417) 831-2100. **$37-$54.** 2655 N Glenstone Ave. I-44, exit 80A, just s. Ext corridors. **Pets:** Large, other species. Service with restrictions.
[SAVE] [✕] [🖉] [🖥]

🅐🅐🅐 ▼▼▼▼ Residence Inn-Springfield 🆂🅷 ❀
(417) 890-0020. **$99-$169.** 1303 E Kingsley St. Int corridors. **Pets:** Other species. $50 one-time fee/room. Service with restrictions.
[SAVE] [S☼] [✕] [🅼] [🖉] [🖥] [💻] [≈] [✕]

▼▼▼▼ Sheraton Hawthorn Park Hotel 🆂🅷 ❀
(417) 831-3131. **$74-$139.** 2431 N Glenstone Ave. I-44, exit 80A, just s. Int corridors. **Pets:** Medium, other species. $50 one-time fee/pet. Service with restrictions, supervision.
[ASK] [S☼] [✕] [🖉] [🖥] [💻] [🍽] [≈] [✕]

▼▼ Sleep Inn of Springfield 🆂🅷
(417) 886-2464. **$69-$105.** 233 E Camino Alto. US 60 (James River Expwy), exit Campbell Ave, just se. Int corridors. **Pets:** Medium, dogs only. $10 daily fee/pet. Designated rooms, service with restrictions, supervision.
[ASK] [S☼] [✕] [🖉] [🖥] [💻] [≈]

🅐🅐🅐 ▼▼▼▼ University Plaza Hotel 🅻🅷
(417) 864-7333. **$99-$159.** 333 John Q Hammons Pkwy. 0.5 mi e on St. Louis St. Int corridors. **Pets:** Accepted.
[SAVE] [S☼] [✕] [🅼] [🖉] [🖥] [💻] [🍽] [≈] [✕]

STE. GENEVIEVE

🅐🅐🅐 ▼ Family Budget Inn 🆂🅷
(573) 543-2272. **$43-$50.** 17030 New Bremen Rd. I-55, exit 143, just w on SR M. Ext/int corridors. **Pets:** Medium. $20 deposit/pet, $5 daily fee/pet. Service with restrictions, crate.
[SAVE] [S☼] [✕] [🖥] [≈]

SULLIVAN

🅐🅐🅐 ▼▼▼ Super 8 Motel-Sullivan Ⓜ
(573) 468-8076. **$44-$54.** 601 N Service Rd. I-44, exit 225, just ne. Int corridors. **Pets:** Accepted.
[SAVE] [S☼] [✕] [🖥] [💻]

SWEET SPRINGS

▼ People's Choice Motel Ⓜ
(660) 335-6315. **$34-$41.** 1001 N Locust St. I-70, exit 66, just se. Ext corridors. **Pets:** $20 deposit/room. Service with restrictions, supervision.
[ASK] [S☼] [✕]

▼▼ Super 8 Motel 🆂🅷
(660) 335-4888. **$60-$70.** 208 W 40 Hwy. I-70, exit 66, just se. Int corridors. **Pets:** Large. $20 deposit/pet, $5 daily fee/pet. Service with restrictions, supervision.
[ASK] [S☼] [✕] [🖥]

TIPTON

▼ Twin Pine Motel Ⓜ ❀
(660) 433-5525. **$40-$60.** 442 Hwy 50 W. On US 50 and SR 5, just w. Ext corridors. **Pets:** Designated rooms, service with restrictions, supervision.
[✕] [🖥]

TRENTON

▼▼ Super 8 Motel 🆂🅷
(660) 359-2988. **Call for rates.** 1845A E 28th St. US 65, 1 mi n of jct SR 6 and US 65. Int corridors. **Pets:** Accepted.
[✕]

WAPPAPELLO

▼▼ Millers Motor Lodge Ⓜ
(573) 222-8579. **$42-$89, 7 day notice.** 8920 Hwy T. 2 mi s of Wappapello Dam, on CR T. Ext corridors. **Pets:** Accepted.
[🖥] [💻] [≈] [✕]

WARRENSBURG

▼▼ University Inn 🆂🅷
(660) 747-5125. **$55-$75.** 403 E Russell Ave. Jct US 50 and SR 13. Ext corridors. **Pets:** Medium. $5 daily fee/pet. Designated rooms, service with restrictions, supervision.
[ASK] [S☼] [✕] [🖥] [💻] [🍽] [≈]

WARSAW

▼▼ Super 8 Motel-Warsaw 🆂🅷
(660) 438-2882. **$65-$85.** Commercial St & 7 Hwy. US 65 and SR 7, exit Clinton. Ext corridors. **Pets:** Medium, dogs only. $20 deposit/pet, $5 one-time fee/pet. Service with restrictions, supervision.
[ASK] [S☼] [✕] [🖥] [≈]

WEST PLAINS

🅐🅐🅐 ▼▼▼ Ramada Inn 🆂🅷 ❀
(417) 256-8191. **$69.** 1301 Preacher Roe Blvd. 2 mi sw at jct US 160 and 63 Bypass. Ext/int corridors. **Pets:** $10 daily fee/pet. Service with restrictions, supervision.
[SAVE] [S☼] [✕] [🖥] [💻] [🍽] [≈]

MONTANA

BELGRADE

▼▼▼▼ Gallatin River Lodge 🆂🅷 ❀
(406) 388-0148. **$170-$270, 7 day notice.** 9105 Thorpe Rd. I-90, exit 298, 2.7 mi s on SR 85, 1 mi w on Valley Center Rd (gravel), then 0.5 mi s, follow sign. Int corridors. **Pets:** $20 daily fee/pet. Designated rooms, service with restrictions, supervision.
🗙 🍽 🖾 🐾

▼▼▼ Holiday Inn Express 🆂🅷
(406) 388-0800. **$90-$100.** 6261 Jack Rabbit Ln. I-90, exit 298, just s on SR 85. Int corridors. **Pets:** Accepted.
🅰🆂🅺 🆂🄳 🗙 🖾ᴹ 🖾 🖪 💻 🍽

⨁ ▼▼▼▼ La Quinta Inn & Suites 🆂🅷
(406) 388-2222. **$49-$109.** 6445 Jackrabbit Ln. I-90, exit 298, just s on SR 85. Int corridors. **Pets:** Service with restrictions, supervision.
🆂🄰🆅🅴 🆂🄳 🗙 🖾 🖪 💻 🌊 🐾

BIGFORK

⨁ ▼▼▼▼ Mountain Lake Lodge 🆂🅷
(406) 837-3800. **$85-$292, 7 day notice.** 1950 Sylvan Dr. On US 35, 5 mi s. Ext corridors. **Pets:** Medium. $15 daily fee/pet. Designated rooms.
🆂🄰🆅🅴 🆂🄳 🗙 🖾ᴹ 🖪 💻 🍽 🌊 🐾

⨁ ▼▼▼ Timbers Motel 🅼 ❀
(406) 837-6200. **$46-$93, 7 day notice.** 8540 Hwy 35. Just n on US 35 from jct of SR 209. Ext corridors. **Pets:** Medium, dogs only. $5.35 daily fee/pet. Designated rooms, service with restrictions, supervision.
🆂🄰🆅🅴 🗙 🖾 💻 🌊

BIG SKY

⨁ ▼▼▼ 320 Guest Ranch 🆁🄰
(406) 995-4283. **$100-$338, 30 day notice.** 205 Buffalo Horn Creek Rd. 11.8 mi s on US 191. Ext corridors. **Pets:** Other species. $10 daily fee/pet. Service with restrictions, supervision.
🆂🄰🆅🅴 🆂🄳 🗙 🖪 💻 🍽 🗙 🐾

⨁ ▼▼▼▼ Best Western Buck's T-4 Lodge 🆂🅷
(406) 995-4111. **$89-$144, 7 day notice.** 46625 Gallatin Rd. US 191, 1 mi s of Big Sky entrance. Ext/int corridors. **Pets:** Large, other species. $5 daily fee/pet. Service with restrictions, supervision.
🆂🄰🆅🅴 🆂🄳 🗙 🖾 🖪 💻 🍽 🗙

▼▼▼▼ Comfort Inn at Big Sky 🅼
(406) 995-2333. **$69-$149.** 47214 Gallatin Rd. US 191, 0.7 mi s of Big Sky entrance. Int corridors. **Pets:** Accepted.
🅰🆂🅺 🆂🄳 🗙 🖾ᴹ 🖾 🖪 💻 🌊 🗙

⨁ ▼▼▼▼ Rainbow Ranch Lodge 🅼 ❀
(406) 995-4132. **$145-$295.** 42950 Gallatin Rd. 5 mi s on US 191. Ext corridors. **Pets:** Dogs only. $40 daily fee/pet. Supervision.
🆂🄰🆅🅴 🆂🄳 🗙 🍽 🗙 🐾

BIG TIMBER

▼ Big Timber Budget Host 🅼
(406) 932-4943. **$58-$88.** 600 W 2nd St. I-90, exit 367, just n, then 0.6 mi e. Int corridors. **Pets:** Small. $10 daily fee/pet. Designated rooms, service with restrictions, supervision.
🗙 🖪

BILLINGS

⨁ ▼▼▼▼ Best Western Billings 🆂🅷
(406) 248-9800. **$69-$119.** 5610 S Frontage Rd. I-90, exit 446, just s. Ext/int corridors. **Pets:** Accepted.
🆂🄰🆅🅴 🆂🄳 🗙 🖾ᴹ 🖾 🖪 💻 🌊

⨁ ▼▼▼▼ Best Western Ponderosa Inn 🆂🅷
(406) 259-5511. **$65-$80, 3 day notice.** 2511 1st Ave N. On I-90 business loop; downtown. Ext/int corridors. **Pets:** Accepted.
🆂🄰🆅🅴 🆂🄳 🗙 🏊 🖪 💻 🍽 🌊

▼▼▼▼ Billings Hotel and Convention Center 🆂🅷
(406) 248-7151. **$69-$79.** 1223 Mullowney Ln. I-90, exit 446, just s. Int corridors. **Pets:** Accepted.
🅰🆂🅺 🆂🄳 🗙 🖪 💻 🍽 🌊 🗙

⨁ ▼▼▼ The Billings Inn 🆂🅷 ❀
(406) 252-6800. **$48-$78.** 880 N 29th St. I-90, exit 27th St, 2 mi n, just w on 9th Ave. Int corridors. **Pets:** Other species. $5 daily fee/pet. Designated rooms, service with restrictions, supervision.
🆂🄰🆅🅴 🆂🄳 🗙 🖪 💻

▼▼ Billings Super 8 Motel 🆂🅷
(406) 248-8842. **$48-$78.** 5400 Southgate Dr. I-90, exit 447, just n on S Billings Blvd, 0.8 mi w on King Ave, then just s on Parkway Ln. Int corridors. **Pets:** Medium. $20 deposit/room. Designated rooms, service with restrictions, supervision.
🅰🆂🅺 🆂🄳 🗙 🖾ᴹ 🏊 🖪 💻

AAA ▼▼▼ Cherry Tree Inn **M**
(406) 252-5603. **$50-$55.** 823 N Broadway. I-90, exit 450, 2 mi n on 27th St, just w on 9th Ave. Int corridors. **Pets:** Other species. Service with restrictions, crate.
SAVE S⊘ ✕ 🛏 💻

▼▼▼ Comfort Inn of Billings **SH**
(406) 652-5200. **$59-$99.** 2030 Overland Ave. I-90, exit 446, 0.5 mi n, then just s. Int corridors. **Pets:** Medium, other species. $20 one-time fee/room. Designated rooms, service with restrictions, supervision.
ASK S⊘ ✕ ⓛM 🖉 🛏 💻 ⇆

▼▼ Days Inn **M**
(406) 252-4007. **$55-$130.** 843 Parkway Ln. I-90, exit 447, just n on S Billings Blvd, 0.8 mi w on King Ave, then just s on Parkway Ln. Int corridors. **Pets:** Large, other species. $5 daily fee/pet. Service with restrictions, supervision.
ASK S⊘ ✕ 👞 🛏 💻

▼ Dude Rancher Lodge **M**
(406) 259-5561. **$45-$80.** 415 N 29th St. Just w of the 400 block of N 27th st; downtown. Ext/int corridors. **Pets:** Medium. $5 daily fee/room. Designated rooms, service with restrictions, supervision.
ASK S⊘ ✕ 🛏 💻 🍽

▼▼▼ Hampton Inn **SH**
(406) 248-4949. **$74-$104.** 5110 Southgate Dr. I-90, exit 447, just n on Billings Blvd, just w on King Ave, then 0.4 mi sw. Int corridors. **Pets:** Accepted.
ASK S⊘ ✕ ⓛM 🖉 👞 🛏 💻 ⇆

AAA ▼▼▼ Hilltop Inn **SH**
(406) 245-5000. **$62-$72.** 1116 N 28th St. I-90, exit 450, 2 mi n, just w on 11th Ave, then just n. Int corridors. **Pets:** Other species. $5 daily fee/pet. Service with restrictions, supervision.
SAVE S⊘ ✕ ⓛM 🛏 💻

▼▼▼ The Historic Northern Hotel **LH**
(406) 245-5121. **$89-$99.** 19 N 28th St. Downtown. Int corridors. **Pets:** Accepted.
ASK S⊘ ✕ 🖉 🛏 💻 🍽

AAA ▼▼▼ Holiday Inn Grand Montana Billings **LH**
(406) 248-7701. **$69-$109.** 5500 Midland Rd. I-90, exit 446. Int corridors. **Pets:** Small, other species. $25 one-time fee/room. Designated rooms, service with restrictions.
SAVE S⊘ ✕ ⓛM 🖉 👞 🛏 💻 🍽 ⇆ 🐾

▼▼▼ Howard Johnson Express Inn **SH**
(406) 248-4656. **$59-$99, 7 day notice.** 1001 S 27th St. I-90, exit 450, just n on SR 3 (S 27th St). Int corridors. **Pets:** Other species. $100 deposit/room. Designated rooms, service with restrictions, supervision.
ASK S⊘ ✕ ⓛM 🖉 👞 🛏 💻

AAA ▼▼ Kelly Inn **SH**
(406) 252-2700. **$62-$89.** 5425 Midland Rd. I-90, exit 446, just se. Ext/int corridors. **Pets:** Medium, other species. Service with restrictions, supervision.
SAVE S⊘ ✕ 👞 🛏 💻 ⇆

▼▼▼ Quality Inn Homestead **SH**
(406) 652-1320. **$59-$99.** 2036 Overland Ave. I-90, exit 446, n on King Ave W, just s, first stoplight. Int corridors. **Pets:** Large. $25 deposit/room. Service with restrictions, supervision.
ASK S⊘ ✕ 🛏 💻 ⇆ 🐾

▼▼ Red Roof Inn–#269 **SH**
(406) 248-7551. **$41-$67.** 5353 Midland Rd. I-90, exit 446, 0.5 mi se. Int corridors. **Pets:** Medium, other species. Service with restrictions, supervision.
✕ ⓛM 🖉 👞 🛏 ⇆

AAA ▼▼▼ Rimview Inn **M**
(406) 248-2622. **$55-$65.** 1025 N 27th St. I-90, exit 450, 2 mi n. Ext/int corridors. **Pets:** Dogs only. $5 one-time fee/pet. Service with restrictions, supervision.
SAVE ✕ 🛏

▼▼▼ Sheraton Downtown Billings Hotel **LH** ❖
(406) 252-7400. **$119-$169.** 27 N 27th St. I-90 business loop and SR 3. Int corridors. **Pets:** Small, dogs only. $25 deposit/room, $25 one-time fee/room. Service with restrictions, supervision.
ASK S⊘ ✕ 👞 🛏 💻 🍽 ⇆ 🐾

BOZEMAN

▼▼ Best Value Inn **SH**
(406) 585-7888. **$44-$84.** 817 Wheat Dr. I-90, exit 306, just n. Int corridors. **Pets:** Accepted.
ASK ✕ ⓛM 👞 🛏 ⇆

▼▼ Bozeman Days Inn **SH**
(406) 587-5251. **$49-$99.** 1321 N 7th. I-90, exit 306, just s. Int corridors. **Pets:** Large, other species. $5 daily fee/pet. Service with restrictions, supervision.
ASK S⊘ ✕ 👞 🛏 💻 🐾

AAA ▼▼▼ Bozeman Inn **M**
(406) 587-3176. **$39-$79.** 1235 N 7th Ave. I-90, exit 306, just s. Ext corridors. **Pets:** Other species. $5 one-time fee/room. Service with restrictions.
SAVE S⊘ ✕ 🛏 💻 ⇆

▼▼ Bozeman Super 8 **SH**
(406) 586-1521. **$50-$74.** 800 Wheat Dr. I-90, exit 306, just n, then just w. Int corridors. **Pets:** Other species. $5 daily fee/room. Designated rooms.
ASK S⊘ ✕

AAA ▼▼▼ Bozeman's Western Heritage Inn **SH**
(406) 586-8534. **$44-$88.** 1200 E Main St. I-90 business loop, exit 309, 0.5 mi w. Int corridors. **Pets:** Dogs only. $5 daily fee/room. Designated rooms, service with restrictions, supervision.
SAVE S⊘ ✕ 🛏 🐾

AAA ▼▼▼ Holiday Inn Bozeman **SH**
(406) 587-4561. **$89-$159.** 5 Baxter Ln. I-90, exit 306, just s of jct I-90. Int corridors. **Pets:** Service with restrictions, supervision.
SAVE ✕ 👞 🛏 💻 🍽 ⇆ 🐾

▼▼ ▼▼ Microtel Inn & Suites 🆂🅷
(406) 586-3797. **$59-$89.** 612 Nikles Dr. I-90, exit 306, just ne. Int corridors. **Pets:** $10 one-time fee/room. Designated rooms, service with restrictions, supervision.
Ⓐ🆂🅺 🆂🅳 ⊠ ✆ 🅱 ▭ ⇌ ⊠

ⒶⒶ ▼▼ Rainbow Motel Ⓜ
(406) 587-4201. **$45-$75.** 510 N 7th Ave. I-90, exit 306, 0.8 mi s. Ext corridors. **Pets:** Accepted.
🆂🅰🆅🅴 ⊠ 🅱 ▭ ⇌

▼▼ ▼▼ Ramada Limited Ⓜ
(406) 585-2626. **$49-$149.** 2020 Wheat Dr. I-90, exit 306, just n, then just w. Int corridors. **Pets:** Very small, dogs only. $10 one-time fee/pet. Service with restrictions, supervision.
Ⓐ🆂🅺 🆂🅳 ⊠ 🅱 ▭ ⇌

ⒶⒶ ▼▼▼ Royal "7" Budget Inn Ⓜ ❀
(406) 587-3103. **$45-$66.** 310 N 7th Ave. I-90, exit 306, 0.8 mi s on I-90 business loop. Ext corridors. **Pets:** Designated rooms, service with restrictions, supervision.
🆂🅰🆅🅴 🆂🅳 ⊠ 🅱 ⇌

BROWNING

ⒶⒶ ▼▼ Western Motel Ⓜ
(406) 338-7572. **$45-$95.** 121 Central Ave E. On US 2; center of town. Ext corridors. **Pets:** Medium, other species. $25 deposit/room. Supervision.
🆂🅰🆅🅴 ⊠ 🅱

BUTTE

ⒶⒶ ▼▼▼▼ Best Western Butte Plaza Inn 🆂🅷
(406) 494-3500. **$77-$99.** 2900 Harrison Ave. I-90/15, exit 127 (Harrison Ave). Int corridors. **Pets:** Other species. $50 deposit/pet. Designated rooms, service with restrictions, supervision.
🆂🅰🆅🅴 🆂🅳 ⊠ 🅱 ▭ 🍴 ⇌ ⊠

▼▼▼ Comfort Inn of Butte Ⓜ
(406) 494-8850. **$75-$99.** 2777 Harrison Ave. I-90/15, exit 127 (Harrison Ave), just s. Int corridors. **Pets:** Medium, other species. $5 daily fee/pet. Service with restrictions, supervision.
Ⓐ🆂🅺 🆂🅳 ⊠ 🖉 🅲 🅱 ▭ ⇌ ⊠

▼▼▼▼ Days Inn 🆂🅷
(406) 494-7000. **$70-$139.** 2700 Harrison Ave. I-90/15, exit 127 (Harrison Ave), just n. Int corridors. **Pets:** Medium. Designated rooms, service with restrictions, supervision.
Ⓐ🆂🅺 🆂🅳 ⊠ 🅻🅼 🖉 🅲 🅱 ▭ ⇌

ⒶⒶ ▼▼▼ Ramada Inn Copper King 🆂🅷
(406) 494-6666. **$55-$65.** 4655 Harrison Ave S. I-90/15, exit 127A, 2 mi s on SR 2 (Harrison Ave). Int corridors. **Pets:** Accepted.
🆂🅰🆅🅴 🆂🅳 ⊠ 🅻🅼 🖉 🅱 ▭ 🍴 ⇌ ⊠

▼▼▼▼ Red Lion Hotel 🆂🅷
(406) 494-7800. **$59-$119.** 2100 Cornell Ave. I-90/15, exit 127B (Harrison Ave), just n, then just e. Int corridors. **Pets:** $25 deposit/room. Service with restrictions, supervision.
Ⓐ🆂🅺 🆂🅳 ⊠ 🖉 🅲 🅱 ▭ 🍴 ⇌ ⊠

ⒶⒶ ▼▼ Rocker Inn Ⓜ
(406) 723-5464. **$45-$57.** 122001 W Brown's Gulch Rd. I-90/15, exit 122 (Rocker). Int corridors. **Pets:** Medium. $5 daily fee/pet. Designated rooms, service with restrictions, supervision.
🆂🅰🆅🅴 ⊠ 🅱

▼▼▼ Super 8 Motel of Butte Ⓜ
(406) 494-6000. **$53-$78.** 2929 Harrison Ave. I-90/15, exit 127 (Harrison Ave), just s. Int corridors. **Pets:** Dogs only. $50 deposit/room, $5 daily fee/pet. Designated rooms, service with restrictions, supervision.
Ⓐ🆂🅺 🆂🅳 ⊠

CHINOOK

ⒶⒶ ▼▼ Chinook Motor Inn 🆂🅷
(406) 357-2248. **$55-$68.** 100 Indiana St. On US 2. Int corridors. **Pets:** Accepted.
🆂🅰🆅🅴 🆂🅳 ⊠ ▭ 🍴

CHOTEAU

▼▼ Big Sky Motel Ⓜ
(406) 466-5318. **Call for rates.** 209 S Main Ave. Just s of town center on US 89. Ext corridors. **Pets:** Accepted.
⊠ 🅱

COLSTRIP

▼▼▼ Super 8 Motel of Colstrip LLC Ⓜ
(406) 748-3400. **$55-$85.** 6227 Main St. SR 39. Int corridors. **Pets:** Accepted.
Ⓐ🆂🅺 🆂🅳 ⊠ 🅱 ▭

COLUMBUS

▼▼ Super 8 of Columbus 🆂🅷
(406) 322-4101. **$65-$99.** 602 8th Ave N. I-90, exit 408, just s on SR 78. Int corridors. **Pets:** Other species. $5 one-time fee/room. Service with restrictions, supervision.
Ⓐ🆂🅺 🆂🅳 ⊠ 🅻🅼 🖉 🅲 🅱 ▭

CONRAD

▼▼ Super 8 Motel 🆂🅷
(406) 278-7676. **$65-$99.** 215 N Main. I-15, exit 339, just w. Int corridors. **Pets:** Medium, other species. $50 deposit/pet, $5 daily fee/pet. Service with restrictions, supervision.
Ⓐ🆂🅺 🆂🅳 ⊠ 🖉 🅱 ▭

CUT BANK

ⒶⒶ ▼▼▼ Glacier Gateway Inn 🆂🅷
(406) 873-5544. **$56-$74.** 1121 E Railroad St. US 2, just e from town center. Int corridors. **Pets:** Accepted.
🆂🅰🆅🅴 🆂🅳 ⊠ 🅱

ⒶⒶ ▼▼▼ Glacier Gateway Plaza Ⓜ
(406) 873-2566. **$65-$84.** 1130 E Main St. Just e of town center on US 2. Int corridors. **Pets:** Accepted.
🆂🅰🆅🅴 🆂🅳 ⊠ 🅱 ⇌

DEER LODGE

444 ▼▼▼ Super 8 Motel Ⓜ
(406) 846-2370. **$61-$80.** 1150 N Main St. I-90, exit 184, 0.3 mi s. Int corridors. **Pets:** Other species. $10 daily fee/pet. Designated rooms, service with restrictions, supervision.
SAVE S🔟 ✕ 🛏 🖵

DILLON

444 ▼▼▼ Best Western Paradise Inn Ⓜ
(406) 683-4214. **$51-$79.** 650 N Montana St. I-15, exit 63, 0.3 mi s on SR 41. Ext corridors. **Pets:** Other species. Service with restrictions, supervision.
SAVE S🔟 ✕ 🖵 🍽 ➰

▼▼ Comfort Inn of Dillon Ⓜ
(406) 683-6831. **$65-$99.** 450 N Interchange. I-15, exit 63. Int corridors. **Pets:** Medium, other species. $5 daily fee/pet. Service with restrictions, supervision.
A$K S🔟 ✕ 🍳 🛏 🖵 ➰

▼▼▼ GuestHouse International Inns & Suites 🆂🅷
(406) 683-3636. **$69-$89.** 580 Sinclair St. I-15, exit 63. Int corridors. **Pets:** Other species. $10 one-time fee/room. Service with restrictions, supervision.
A$K S🔟 ✕ ♿M 🍳 🛏 🖵 ➰

444 ▼▼ Sundowner Motel Ⓜ
(406) 683-2375. **$38-$43.** 500 N Montana St. I-15, exit 63, just s. Ext corridors. **Pets:** Other species. Designated rooms, service with restrictions, supervision.
SAVE ✕ 🛏

▼▼ Super 8 Motel Ⓜ
(406) 683-4288. **$56-$70.** 550 N Montana St. I-15, exit 63, just n on US 91. Int corridors. **Pets:** $25 deposit/pet. Designated rooms, service with restrictions, supervision.
A$K S🔟 ✕ 🛏

EAST GLACIER PARK

444 ▼▼ Dancing Bears Inn LLC Ⓜ
(406) 226-4402. **$45-$120.** 40 Montana Ave. Just off US 2, follow signs; center. Ext/int corridors. **Pets:** Medium, other species. $25 deposit/room. Supervision.
SAVE ✕ 🛏 🖵

ENNIS

444 ▼▼▼▼ El Western Cabins & Lodges 🅲🅰
(406) 682-4217. **$62-$115, 3 day notice.** US Hwy 287 S. 0.8 mi s. Ext corridors. **Pets:** Large, dogs only. $10 daily fee/pet. Supervision.
SAVE ✕ 🛏 🖵 ✕ 🅺

444 ▼▼▼ Fan Mountain Inn Ⓜ
(406) 682-5200. **$48-$70, 10 day notice.** 204 N Main. US 287, just nw of city center. Ext corridors. **Pets:** Accepted.
SAVE ✕ ♿M 🍳 🛏

444 ▼▼ Riverside Motel & Outfitters Ⓜ
(406) 682-4240. **$68-$108.** 346 Main St. US 287, e of town. Ext corridors. **Pets:** $10 daily fee/pet. Service with restrictions, crate.
SAVE ✕ 🍳 🛏 🖵 ✕ 🅺

▼▼ Sportsman's 🅲🅰 ❀
(406) 682-4242. **$45-$80, 5 day notice.** 310 US Hwy 287 N. US 287, just nw of city center. Ext corridors. **Pets:** Other species. $5 daily fee/pet. Designated rooms, service with restrictions, supervision.
✕ 🛏 🖵 🍽

FORSYTH

444 ▼▼▼ Best Western Sundowner Inn Ⓜ
(406) 346-2115. **$69-$79.** 1018 Front St. I-94, exit 95, 0.5 mi nw on north frontage road. Ext corridors. **Pets:** Other species. $7 daily fee/pet. Service with restrictions, supervision.
SAVE S🔟 ✕ 🛏 🖵

444 ▼▼▼ Rails Inn Motel 🆂🅷
(406) 346-2242. **$62-$67.** 3rd & Front sts. I-94, exit 93, just n, 0.5 mi e on frontage road. Int corridors. **Pets:** Accepted.
SAVE S🔟 ✕ 🛏 🍽

444 ▼▼ Restwel Motel Ⓜ
(406) 346-2771. **$45-$60.** 810 Front St. I-94, exit 95, 0.8 mi nw on north frontage road. Ext corridors. **Pets:** $5 daily fee/pet. Designated rooms, service with restrictions, supervision.
SAVE S🔟 ✕ 🍳 🛏

444 ▼▼ Westwind Motor Inn Ⓜ
(406) 346-2038. **$60-$65.** 225 Westwind Ln. I-94, exit 93, 0.3 mi n. Int corridors. **Pets:** Accepted.
SAVE S🔟 ✕ 🛏

GARDINER

444 ▼▼▼▼ Best Western by Mammoth Hot Springs 🆂🅷
(406) 848-7311. **$45-$119.** S Hwy 89. 0.5 mi n. Ext/int corridors. **Pets:** Other species. $5 daily fee/pet. Designated rooms, service with restrictions, supervision.
SAVE S🔟 ✕ 🍳 🛏 🖵 🍽 ➰ ✕

444 ▼▼ Yellowstone River Motel Ⓜ
(406) 848-7303. **$45-$85.** 14 E Park St. Just e of US 89. Ext corridors. **Pets:** Accepted.
SAVE S🔟 ✕ ♿M 🛏 🖵 ✕

▼▼ Yellowstone Super 8-Gardiner 🆂🅷
(406) 848-7401. **$50-$190.** Hwy 89 S. On US 89. Int corridors. **Pets:** Accepted.
A$K S🔟 ✕ 🛏 🖵 ➰

GLASGOW

▼▼ Cottonwood Inn 🆂🅷
(406) 228-8213. **$63-$73.** 45 1st Ave NE. 0.5 mi e of center on US 2. Int corridors. **Pets:** Service with restrictions, supervision.
A$K S🔟 ✕ 🛏 🍽 ➰

GLENDIVE

444 ▼▼▼ Best Western Jordan Inn 🆂🅷
(406) 377-5555. **$72-$106, 10 day notice.** 223 N Merrill Ave. I-94, exit 215, on I-94 business loop; downtown. Ext/int corridors. **Pets:** Small. $5 daily fee/room. Designated rooms, service with restrictions, supervision.
SAVE S🔟 ✕ 🛏 🖵 🍽 ➰

▼▼ Super 8 Glendive **M**
(406) 365-5671. **$48-$69.** 1904 Merrill Ave. I-94, exit 215, just n. Int corridors. **Pets:** Other species. $5 one-time fee/room. Service with restrictions, supervision.
⊠

GREAT FALLS

◈◈ ▼▼▼▼ Best Western Heritage Inn **SH**
(406) 761-1900. **$79-$109.** 1700 Fox Farm Rd. I-15, exit 278, 0.8 mi e on 10th Ave S and US 87/89 and SR 3/200. Int corridors. **Pets:** Medium. Service with restrictions, supervision.
SAVE ⓢ ⊠ ⊘ 🖥 🖵 ⊪ ⊇ ⊠

◈◈ ▼▼ Central Motel **M**
(406) 453-0161. **$45-$75, 7 day notice.** 715 Central Ave W. I-15, exit 280 (Central Ave), 0.7 mi e. Ext corridors. **Pets:** Medium. $10 daily fee/pet. Service with restrictions, supervision.
SAVE ⓢ ⊠ 🖥 🖵

▼▼ ◈ Comfort Inn Great Falls **SH**
(406) 454-2727. **$65-$95.** 1120 9th St S. I-15, exit 278, 3 mi e on 10th Ave S and US 87/89 and SR 3/200, then just s. Int corridors. **Pets:** Accepted.
ASK ⓢ ⊠ 🗚 ⊘ 🖥 🖵 ⊇

▼▼ ▼▼ Days Inn of Great Falls **M**
(406) 727-6565. **$63-$87.** 101 14th Ave NW. I-15, exit 280 (Central Ave), 1.3 mi e on Central Ave/Business 15, 0.8 mi n on 3rd St NW, then just w. Int corridors. **Pets:** Dogs only. $5 daily fee/room. Designated rooms, service with restrictions, supervision.
ASK ⓢ ⊠ ⊘ 🖥 🖵

◈◈ ▼▼ ◈ The Great Falls Inn **SH** ❖
(406) 453-6000. **$66-$71.** 1400 28th St S. I-15, exit 278, 5.3 mi e on 10th Ave s, 0.3 mi s on 26th St S, then just e on 15th Ave S. Int corridors. **Pets:** Medium. $5 daily fee/pet. Service with restrictions, crate.
SAVE ⓢ ⊠ 🗚 ⊘ 🖥 🖵

▼▼ ▼▼ Great Falls Super 8 Motel **SH**
(406) 727-7600. **$50-$79.** 1214 13th St S. I-15, exit 278, 2.7 mi e on 10th Ave S and US 87/89 and SR 3/200, then just s. Int corridors. **Pets:** Accepted.
ASK ⓢ ⊘ 🖥 🖵

◈◈ ▼▼▼▼ Hampton Inn **SH**
(406) 453-2675. **$79-$99.** 2301 14th St SW. I-15, exit 278, just sw. Int corridors. **Pets:** Medium. $10 one-time fee/room. Service with restrictions, supervision.
SAVE ⊠ 🗚 ⊘ 🖥 🖵 ⊇

▼▼▼▼ Holiday Inn **LH**
(406) 727-7200. **$89-$109.** 400 10th Ave S. I-15, exit 278, 2 mi e on 10th Ave S, just s. Int corridors. **Pets:** Medium, dogs only. $10 daily fee/pet. Designated rooms, service with restrictions, supervision.
ASK ⓢ ⊠ ⊘ 🖥 🖵 ⊪ ⊇

◈◈ ▼▼▼ Howard Johnson Ponderosa Inn **SH**
(406) 761-3410. **$55-$90.** 220 Central Ave. Downtown. Ext/int corridors. **Pets:** Accepted.
SAVE ⓢ ⊠ 🖥 🖵 ⊪ ⊇

◈◈ ▼▼▼ La Quinta Inn & Suites **SH**
(406) 761-2600. **$79-$119.** 600 River Dr S. I-15, exit 278, 1.7 mi e on 10th Ave S, then 0.8 mi n. Int corridors. **Pets:** Small. Service with restrictions, supervision.
SAVE ⓢ ⊠ 🗚 ⊘ 🖾 🖥 🖵 ⊇ ⊠

◈◈ ▼▼ Motel 6 #4238 **M**
(406) 453-1602. **$48-$59.** 2 Treasure State Dr. I-15, exit 278, 0.8 mi e on 10th Ave S and US 87/89 and SR 3/200; next to Best Western. Int corridors. **Pets:** Service with restrictions, supervision.
SAVE ⓢ ⊠ ⊘ 🖵

◈◈ ▼▼ Plaza Inn **M**
(406) 452-9594. **$50-$75, 7 day notice.** 1224 10th Ave S. I-15, exit 278, 2.4 mi e on 10th Ave S and US 87/89 and SR 3/200. Ext corridors. **Pets:** Medium. $10 daily fee/pet. Service with restrictions, supervision.
SAVE ⊠ 🖥

◈◈ ▼▼ Ski's Western Motel **M**
(406) 453-3281. **$50-$75, 7 day notice.** 2420 10th Ave S. I-15, exit 278, 5.2 mi e on 10th Ave S and US 87/89 and SR 3/200. Ext corridors. **Pets:** Medium. $10 daily fee/pet. Service with restrictions, supervision.
SAVE ⓢ ⊠ 🖥

HAMILTON

▼▼ ◈ Comfort Inn of Hamilton **SH** ❖
(406) 363-6600. **$65-$99.** 1113 N 1st St. N of city center on US 93. Int corridors. **Pets:** Other species. $4 daily fee/pet. Service with restrictions, supervision.
ASK ⓢ ⊠ 🗚 ⊘ 🖥 🖵

HARDIN

◈◈ ▼▼▼ American Inn of Hardin **SH**
(406) 665-1870. **$46-$79.** 1324 N Crawford Ave. I-90, exit 495, just s on SR 47. Ext corridors. **Pets:** Large, other species. $5 daily fee/room. Designated rooms, service with restrictions, supervision.
SAVE ⓢ ⊠ ⊘ 🖥 🖵 ⊪ ⊇ ⊠

▼▼ ▼▼ Western Motel **M**
(406) 665-2296. **$33-$75.** 830 W 3rd St. I-90, exit 495 eastbound, 1.3 mi s on SR 47 and CR 313, just e; exit 497 westbound, 0.3 mi w on I-90 business loop, continue straight on 3rd St for 0.7 mi. Ext corridors. **Pets:** Other species. $2.50 daily fee/pet. Designated rooms, service with restrictions, supervision.
⊠ 🖥

HARLOWTON

▼▼ Corral Motel **M**
(406) 632-4331. **$45-$50, 3 day notice.** 0.5 mi e at jct US 12 and 191. Ext corridors. **Pets:** Medium, dogs only. $5 one-time fee/pet. Service with restrictions, supervision.
⊠ 🖥

HELENA

▼▼▼ **Barrister Bed & Breakfast** BB ❖
(406) 443-7330. **$95-$110, 4 day notice.** 416 N Ewing. I-15, exit 192 (Prospect Ave), 1.5 mi sw via Prospect and Montana aves to 9th Ave, 0.8 mi w, then just s. Int corridors. **Pets:** Other species.
ASK ✕ ✆

▼▼▼ **Best Western Helena Great Northern Hotel** SH
(406) 457-5500. **$135-$155.** 835 Great Northern Blvd. I-15, exit 193 (Cedar St), just e of jct Lyndale and Benton aves; downtown. Int corridors. **Pets:** Accepted.
ASK S∅ ✕ &M ⌒ &' 🖥 🖳 ⇆ ✕

▼▼▼ **Comfort Inn of Helena** SH
(406) 443-1000. **$54-$89.** 750 N Fee St. I-15, exit 192 (Prospect Ave), just n. Int corridors. **Pets:** Accepted.
ASK S∅ ✕ &M 🖥 🖳 ⇆

▼▼ **Days Inn Helena** SH
(406) 442-3280. **$63-$95.** 2001 Prospect Ave. I-15, exit 192 (Prospect Ave), just w. Int corridors. **Pets:** Other species. $10 daily fee/room. Designated rooms, no service, supervision.
ASK S∅ ✕ &M ⌒ &' 🖥 🖳 ✕

▼▼▼ **Elkhorn Mountain Inn** SH
(406) 442-6625. **$66-$76.** 1 Jackson Creek Rd. I-15, exit 187 (Montana City), just w. Int corridors. **Pets:** Other species. $5 daily fee/pet. Supervision.
SAVE S∅ ✕ &M &' 🖥 🖳

▼▼▼ **Hampton Inn-Helena** SH
(406) 443-5800. **$69-$99.** 3000 Hwy 12 E. I-15, exit 192 eastbound; exit 192A westbound, just e on SR 12/287, then just n. Int corridors. **Pets:** Small. $20 one-time fee/room. No service, supervision.
✕ &M ⌒ &' 🖥 🖳 ⇆

▼▼ **Helena's Country Inn & Suites** M
(406) 443-2300. **$49-$129.** 2101 E 11th Ave. I-15, exit 192 B (Capitol), just sw. Ext/int corridors. **Pets:** Dogs only. $6 daily fee/pet. Designated rooms, service with restrictions, supervision.
SAVE S∅ ✕ 🖥 🖳 ⇆

▼▼▼ **Red Lion Colonial Hotel** SH ❖
(406) 443-2100. **$65-$96.** 2301 Colonial Dr. I-15, exit 192 southbound; exit 192B northbound. Int corridors. **Pets:** Large. $20 one-time fee/room. Service with restrictions.
ASK S∅ ✕ 🖥 🖳 ⑪ ⇆

▼▼ **Super 8 Motel** SH ❖
(406) 443-2450. **$50-$60.** 2200 11th Ave. I-15, exit Capitol area southbound; exit west business district northbound on US 12. Int corridors. **Pets:** Other species. Designated rooms, service with restrictions.
ASK S∅ ✕ ⌒ &' 🖥 🖳

▼▼▼ **Wingate Inn** SH
(406) 449-3000. **$90-$110.** 2007 Oakes. I-15, exit 193, just sw. Int corridors. **Pets:** Accepted.
ASK S∅ ✕ &M ⌒ &' 🖥 🖳 ⇆

HUNGRY HORSE

AAA ▼▼▼ **Mini Golden Inns Motel** M
(406) 387-4313. **$56-$96, 45 day notice.** 8955 US 2 E. East end of town. Ext corridors. **Pets:** Accepted.
SAVE ✕ &M &' 🖥 🖳

KALISPELL

AAA ▼▼▼ **Aero Inn** M
(406) 755-3798. **$42-$81.** 1830 US 93 S. 1.3 mi s on US 93 from jct of US 2. Int corridors. **Pets:** Other species. $10 deposit/room. Designated rooms, service with restrictions, supervision.
SAVE S∅ ✕ ⌒ &' 🖥 ⇆

▼▼▼ **Days Inn Kalispell** SH
(406) 756-3222. **$57-$101.** 1550 Hwy 93 N. 1.3 mi n on US 93 from jct of US 2. Int corridors. **Pets:** Accepted.
ASK S∅ ✕ 🖥

AAA ▼▼▼ **Four Seasons Motor Inn** SH ❖
(406) 755-6123. **$52-$98.** 350 N Main St. US 93, just n of jct US 2. Ext/int corridors. **Pets:** Other species. Designated rooms, service with restrictions, supervision.
SAVE S∅ ✕ 🖥 🖳 ⑪

AAA ▼▼ **Glacier Gateway Motel** M
(406) 755-3330. **$59-$94, 3 day notice.** 264 N Main St. Northwest corner of jct US 2 and 93. Ext corridors. **Pets:** Medium, dogs only. $8 daily fee/pet. Designated rooms, service with restrictions, supervision.
SAVE ✕ 🖥 🖳

▼▼ **Kalispell/Glacier Int'l Airport area Super 8 Motel** SH
(406) 755-1888. **$57-$113.** 1341 1st Ave E. 1.2 mi s on US 93 from jct of US 2. Int corridors. **Pets:** Other species. $10 daily fee/room. Service with restrictions, crate.
ASK S∅ ✕ &M ⌒ 🖥 🖳

▼▼ **Kalispell Grand Hotel** SH
(406) 755-8100. **$69-$96.** 100 Main St. On US 93; downtown. Int corridors. **Pets:** Service with restrictions.
ASK S∅ ✕ ⑪

AAA ▼▼▼ **La Quinta Inn & Suites** SH
(406) 257-5255. **$59-$159.** 255 Montclair Dr. Jct US 93 and 2, 1 mi e. Int corridors. **Pets:** Large, other species. Service with restrictions, supervision.
SAVE S∅ ✕ &M ⌒ &' 🖥 🖳 ⇆ ✕

AAA ▼▼▼ **Red Lion Inn Kalispell** SH
(406) 755-6700. **$69-$129.** 1330 Hwy 2 W. 1 mi w on US 2 from jct of US 93. Int corridors. **Pets:** Medium. $15 one-time fee/room. Designated rooms, service with restrictions, supervision.
SAVE S∅ ✕ 🖥 🖳 ⑪ ⇆

AAA ▼▼▼ **WestCoast Kalispell Center** SH
(406) 751-5050. **$90-$127.** 20 N Main St. Just s on US 93 from jct of US 2. Int corridors. **Pets:** $15 deposit/room. Designated rooms, service with restrictions, supervision.
SAVE S∅ ✕ &M 🖥 🖳 ⑪ ⇆ ✕

▲▲▲ ▼▼▼ WestCoast Outlaw
Hotel-Kalispell 🆂🅷
(406) 755-6100. **$80-$117.** 1701 Hwy 93 S. 1.4 mi s on US 93 from jct US 2. Int corridors. **Pets:** Accepted.
🆂🅰🆅🅴 🆂🅳 ⊠ 🅱 🖵 🍴 🌊 ⊠

LAKESIDE

▼▼ Sunrise Vista Inn 🅼
(406) 844-0231. **$72-$125, 10 day notice.** 7005 US 93. North edge of town on US 93. Ext corridors. **Pets:** Accepted.
🅰🆂🅺 ⊠ 🅱 🖵

LAUREL

▼▼▼ Laurel Super 8 🆂🅷
(406) 628-6888. **$67-$99.** 205 SE 4th St. I-90, exit 434, just n, just e. Int corridors. **Pets:** Medium, dogs only. $10 one-time fee/pet. Designated rooms, service with restrictions, supervision.
🅰🆂🅺 🆂🅳 ⊠ 🅶🅼 🎨 🎳 🅱 🖵 🌊

LEWISTOWN

▲▲▲ ▼ B & B Motel 🅼
(406) 538-5496. **$40-$60.** 520 E Main St. Downtown. Ext corridors. **Pets:** Dogs only. $3 daily fee/pet. Designated rooms, service with restrictions, supervision.
🆂🅰🆅🅴 ⊠ 🅱

LIBBY

▼ Sandman Motel 🅼 🐾
(406) 293-8831. **$39-$62.** 688 US Hwy 2 W. Just w on US 2 from jct SR 37. Ext corridors. **Pets:** Medium, other species. $20 deposit/room. Designated rooms, service with restrictions, supervision.
🅰🆂🅺 🆂🅳 ⊠ 🅱

▲▲▲ ▼▼▼ Super 8 Motel 🆂🅷
(406) 293-2771. **$50-$78.** 448 US 2 W. Just w on US 2 from jct SR 37. Int corridors. **Pets:** Other species. $10 one-time fee/room. Designated rooms, service with restrictions, supervision.
🆂🅰🆅🅴 🆂🅳 ⊠ 🎨 🌊

LINCOLN

▲▲▲ ▼▼▼ Leeper's Ponderosa Motel 🅼
(406) 362-4333. **$47-$52, 3 day notice.** Hwy 200 & 1st Ave. Just w on SR 200. Ext corridors. **Pets:** $5 daily fee/pet. Designated rooms, service with restrictions, supervision.
🆂🅰🆅🅴 ⊠ 🅱 🖵 🅰🅲

LIVINGSTON

▲▲▲ ▼▼▼ Best Western Yellowstone Inn &
Conference Center 🆂🅷 🐾
(406) 222-6110. **$49-$129.** 1515 W Park St. I-90, exit 333, just n. Int corridors. **Pets:** Other species. $10 daily fee/room. Service with restrictions.
🆂🅰🆅🅴 🆂🅳 ⊠ 🅱 🖵 🍴 🌊

▲▲▲ ▼ Del Mar Motel Inc 🅼
(406) 222-3120. **$42-$74, 3 day notice.** 1201 Hwy 10 W. I-90, exit 330, 1.9 mi e on I-90 business loop. Ext corridors. **Pets:** Other species. $5 daily fee/pet. Designated rooms, service with restrictions, supervision.
🆂🅰🆅🅴 🆂🅳 ⊠ 🅱 🖵 🌊 ⊠

▲▲▲ ▼▼▼ Econo Lodge 🆂🅷
(406) 222-0555. **$45-$99.** 111 Rogers Ln. I-90, exit 333, just n on US 89, then just w. Int corridors. **Pets:** Other species. $5 daily fee/pet. Service with restrictions, supervision.
🆂🅰🆅🅴 🆂🅳 ⊠ 🅶🅼 🎨 🎳 🅱 🖵 🌊

▲▲▲ ▼▼▼ Travelodge Livingston 🅼
(406) 222-6320. **$59-$110.** 102 Rogers Ln. I-90, exit 333, just n. Ext/int corridors. **Pets:** Other species. $5 one-time fee/pet. Designated rooms, service with restrictions, supervision.
🆂🅰🆅🅴 ⊠ 🅱 🍴 🌊

LOLO

▼▼ Days Inn 🆂🅷 🐾
(406) 273-2121. **$55-$99.** 11225 US 93 S. North edge of town. Ext/int corridors. **Pets:** Dogs only. $10 daily fee/pet. Service with restrictions, supervision.
⊠ 🅶🅼 🅱 🖵

MILES CITY

▲▲▲ ▼▼▼ Best Western War Bonnet Inn 🅼
(406) 234-4560. **$78.** 1015 S Haynes Ave. I-94, exit 138 (Broadus), 0.3 mi n. Ext corridors. **Pets:** $5 daily fee/pet. Designated rooms, service with restrictions, supervision.
🆂🅰🆅🅴 🆂🅳 ⊠ 🅱 🖵 🌊 ⊠

▼▼▼ GuestHouse International Inn &
Suites 🆂🅷
(406) 232-3661. **$65-$139.** 3111 Steel St. I-94, exit 138 (Broadus), just s. Int corridors. **Pets:** Large, other species. $10 daily fee/room. Designated rooms, service with restrictions, supervision.
🅰🆂🅺 🆂🅳 ⊠ 🅶🅼 🎳 🅱 🖵 🌊

MISSOULA

▲▲▲ ▼▼ Best Inn & Conference
Center-South 🆂🅷
(406) 251-2665. **$65-$89.** 3803 Brooks St. I-90, exit 101 (Reserve St), 5 mi s to Brooks (US 93), just w. Int corridors. **Pets:** Medium, other species. $7 daily fee/room. Designated rooms.
🆂🅰🆅🅴 🆂🅳 ⊠ 🅶🅼 🎨 🎳 🅱 🖵

▼▼ Best Inn North 🆂🅷
(406) 542-7550. **$65-$89.** 4953 N Reserve St. I-90 W, exit 101 (Reserve St), just s. Int corridors. **Pets:** Medium, other species. $7 daily fee/room. Designated rooms.
🅰🆂🅺 🆂🅳 ⊠ 🎨 🎳 🅱 🖵

▲▲▲ ▼▼▼ Best Western Grant Creek Inn 🆂🅷
(406) 543-0700. **$85-$169.** 5280 Grant Creek Rd. I-90, exit 101 (Reserve St), just n. Int corridors. **Pets:** Small. $20 daily fee/room. Service with restrictions, supervision.
🆂🅰🆅🅴 🆂🅳 ⊠ 🅶🅼 🎨 🎳 🅱 🖵 🌊 ⊠

▼▼ Campus Inn M
(406) 549-5134. **$40-$120.** 744 E Broadway. I-90, exit 105 (Van Buren St), just s to Broadway, just w. Ext/int corridors. **Pets:** Other species. $6 daily fee/pet. Service with restrictions, supervision.

⊠ 🕗 🛋 🔲 ⊇

▼▼▼ Comfort Inn SH
(406) 542-0888. **$70-$160, 7 day notice.** 4545 N Reserve St. I-90, exit 101 (Reserve St), 0.5 mi s. Int corridors. **Pets:** Medium. $10 daily fee/room. Service with restrictions, supervision.

A$K S🔒 ⊠ &M 🕗 🛋 🔲 🔲 ⊇

▲▲▲ ▼▼▼ Days Inn/Missoula Airport SH
(406) 721-9776. **$61-$84.** 8600 Truck Stop Rd. I-90, exit 96, just n. Int corridors. **Pets:** Other species. $5 daily fee/pet. Service with restrictions, supervision.

SAVE S🔒 ⊠ 🔲

▲▲▲ ▼▼▼ Doubletree Hotel Missoula/Edgewater SH
(406) 728-3100. **$104-$189.** 100 Madison. I-90, exit 105 (Van Buren St), just s, then w on Front St. Int corridors. **Pets:** Accepted.

SAVE ⊠ &M 🕗 🛋 🔲 🔲 🍴 ⊇

▲▲▲ ▼▼ Downtown Motel M
(406) 549-5191. **$40-$49.** 502 E Broadway. I-90, exit 105 (Van Buren St), just w. Ext corridors. **Pets:** Accepted.

SAVE ⊠ 🔲 🔲

▲▲▲ ▼▼▼ Executive Inn SH
(406) 543-7221. **$59-$79.** 201 E Main St. I-90, exit 104 (Orange St), 0.5 mi s to Broadway, 0.5 mi e to Washington, just s to Main St, just w. Ext corridors. **Pets:** $50 deposit/room. Service with restrictions, crate.

SAVE S🔒 ⊠ 🔲 🔲 ⊇

▼▼ Family Inn M
(406) 543-7371. **$62-$76.** 1031 E Broadway. I-90, exit 105 (Van Buren St), just s, then just e. Ext corridors. **Pets:** Accepted.

A$K S🔒 ⊠ 🔲 ⊇

▼▼▼ Hampton Inn SH ❀
(406) 549-1800. **$75-$119.** 4805 N Reserve St. I-90, exit 101 (Reserve St), just s. Int corridors. **Pets:** Other species. $10 one-time fee/room. Designated rooms.

A$K S🔒 ⊠ &M 🕗 🛋 🔲 ⊇

▼▼▼ Holiday Inn Missoula-Parkside SH
(406) 721-8550. **$69-$119, 3 day notice.** 200 S Pattee St. I-90, exit 104 (Orange St), 0.5 mi s to Broadway, just e to Pattee St, then just s. Int corridors. **Pets:** Large. $25 one-time fee/room. Designated rooms, service with restrictions, supervision.

A$K S🔒 ⊠ 🕗 🔲 🔲 🍴 ⊇ ⊠

▼▼ Microtel Inn & Suites SH
(406) 543-0959. **$50-$90.** 5059 N Reserve St. I-90, exit 101 (Reserve St), just s. Int corridors. **Pets:** Accepted.

⊠ &M 🕗 🛋 🔲 🔲

▲▲▲ ▼▼▼ Ramada Limited SH
(406) 721-3610. **$85.** 801 N Orange St. I-90, exit 104 (Orange St), just s. Int corridors. **Pets:** Small. $10 one-time fee/room. Service with restrictions, supervision.

SAVE S🔒 ⊠ 🔲

▼▼ Red Lion Inn SH
(406) 728-3300. **$79-$129.** 700 W Broadway. I-90, exit 104 (Orange St), just s, then just w. Ext corridors. **Pets:** $5 daily fee/pet. Service with restrictions, crate.

A$K ⊠ 🕗 🔲 🔲 ⊇

▲▲▲ ▼▼▼ Redwood Lodge M
(406) 721-2110. **$65-$75.** 8060 Hwy 93 N. I-90, exit 96, just s. Ext corridors. **Pets:** Other species. Service with restrictions, supervision.

SAVE S🔒 ⊠ 🔲

▲▲▲ ▼ Royal Motel M
(406) 542-2184. **$36-$48.** 338 Washington St. I-90, exit 105 (Van Buren St), just s, then 0.5 mi w on Broadway. Ext corridors. **Pets:** Large. $4 daily fee/pet. Designated rooms, service with restrictions, supervision.

SAVE ⊠ 🔲

▲▲▲ ▼▼▼ Ruby's Inn & Convention Center SH ❀
(406) 721-0990. **$70-$120.** 4825 N Reserve St. I-90, exit 101 (Reserve St), just s. Ext/int corridors. **Pets:** Other species. $5 one-time fee/pet. Service with restrictions.

SAVE ⊠ &M 🕗 🛋 🔲 🔲 ⊇ ⊠

▼▼ Sleep Inn SH
(406) 543-5883. **$55-$85.** 3425 Dore Ln. I-90, exit 101 (Reserve St), 5 mi s, then just e on Brooks St. Int corridors. **Pets:** Other species. $5 daily fee/room. Designated rooms, service with restrictions, supervision.

A$K S🔒 ⊠ &M 🕗 🛋 🔲 🔲 ⊇

▲▲▲ ▼▼▼ Southgate Inn SH ❀
(406) 251-2250. **$45-$85.** 3530 Brooks St. I-90, exit 101 (Reserve St), 5 mi s to Brooks St, just e. Ext corridors. **Pets:** Other species. $5 daily fee/pet. Designated rooms, service with restrictions, supervision.

SAVE S🔒 ⊠ 🔲 🔲 ⊇ ⊠

▼▼ Super 8-Brooks St SH
(406) 251-2255. **$52-$75.** 3901 Brooks St. I-90, exit 101 (Reserve St), 5 mi s, just w. Int corridors. **Pets:** Large, dogs only. $5 daily fee/pet. Service with restrictions, supervision.

A$K S🔒 ⊠ 🔲

▲▲▲ ▼▼▼ Travelers Inn Motel M
(406) 728-8330. **$49-$69.** 4850 N Reserve St. I-90, exit 101 (Reserve St), just s. Ext corridors. **Pets:** Small, dogs only. $3 daily fee/pet. Designated rooms, service with restrictions, supervision.

SAVE S🔒 ⊠ 🔲

OVANDO

▼▼▼ Lake Upsata Guest Ranch RA
(406) 793-5890. **$180-$440, 30 day notice.** 201 Lower Lakeside Ln. 7.5 mi w on SR 200 to MM 38, 3.4 mi n on Woodworth Rd, then 1 mi e. Ext corridors. **Pets:** Accepted.

⊠ 🔲 🔲 ⊠ 🎿 🐾 🎣

POLSON

▼▼ Bayview Inn M
(406) 883-3120. **$40-$80.** 914 Hwy 93. Just s; downtown. Ext corridors. **Pets:** Accepted.

A$K S🔒 ⊠ 🔲 🔲

RED LODGE

♦♦♦ Best Western Lu Pine Inn SH
(406) 446-1321. **$69-$99.** 702 S Hauser. 0.4 mi s, just w of US 212. Int corridors. **Pets:** Other species. Service with restrictions, supervision.
ASK SÃ ✕ 🔒 🖵 ⇌ ✕

♦♦♦ Comfort Inn of Red Lodge SH
(406) 446-4469. **$50-$99.** 612 N Broadway. Jct US 212 and SR 78, north entrance. Int corridors. **Pets:** Other species. $25 deposit/room. Designated rooms, service with restrictions, supervision.
ASK SÃ ✕ 🔒 &M ⚹ 🔒 🖵 ⇌

♦♦♦ Super 8 of Red Lodge M
(406) 446-2288. **$50-$100, 30 day notice.** 1223 S Broadway Ave. Just s on US 212. Ext/int corridors. **Pets:** Other species. $5 daily fee/pet. Supervision.
SAVE SÃ ✕ 🔒 🖵 ⇌

♦♦♦ Yodeler Motel M
(406) 446-1435. **$49-$79.** 601 S Broadway. Just s on US 212. Ext corridors. **Pets:** Dogs only. $10 one-time fee/pet. Designated rooms, service with restrictions, supervision.
SAVE SÃ ✕ 🔒 🖵

RONAN

♦ Starlite Motel M
(406) 676-7000. **$58-$71.** 18 Main St SW. Just w of jct US 93 and Main St. Ext corridors. **Pets:** Accepted.
ASK SÃ ✕ 🔒 🖵

ST. IGNATIUS

♦ Sunset Motel M
(406) 745-3900. **$62-$72.** 32670 Hwy 93. Just s of downtown, exit on US 93. Ext corridors. **Pets:** Medium, dogs only. $5 daily fee/room. Service with restrictions, supervision.
✕ 🔒 🗘

ST. REGIS

♦♦ Little River Motel M
(406) 649-2713. **$35-$65.** 50 Old US Hwy 10 W. I-90, exit 33, just n to flashing light, just w, then just sw. Ext corridors. **Pets:** Small. $5 daily fee/pet. Service with restrictions, supervision.
SAVE SÃ ✕ 🔒 🗘 🗘

SEELEY LAKE

♦♦♦ Wilderness Gateway Inn M
(406) 677-2095. **$43-$61.** 2996 Hwy 83 N. South end of town on SR 83. Ext corridors. **Pets:** $5 daily fee/pet. Supervision.
SAVE SÃ ✕

SHELBY

♦♦ Comfort Inn of Shelby SH
(406) 434-2212. **$65-$99.** 50 Frontage Rd. I-15, exit 363, just e, then just s on McKinley Ave. Int corridors. **Pets:** Medium, other species. $5 daily fee/pet. Service with restrictions, supervision.
ASK SÃ ✕ ⚹ ⚹ 🔒 🖵 ✕

♦♦♦ Crossroads Inn M
(406) 434-5134. **$52-$60, 7 day notice.** 1200 Roosevelt Hwy. Just w of town center on US 2. Int corridors. **Pets:** Other species. $10 daily fee/pet. Designated rooms, service with restrictions, supervision.
SAVE ✕ ⚹ 🔒 ⇌

♦♦♦ O'Haire Manor Motel M
(406) 434-5555. **$50-$65.** 204 2nd St S. Just s of Main St via Maple St. Ext/int corridors. **Pets:** $5 daily fee/pet. Service with restrictions, supervision.
SAVE SÃ ✕ 🔒

SHERIDAN

♦♦ Moriah Motel M
(406) 842-5491. **$48-$56.** 220 S Main St. SR 287 S. Ext corridors. **Pets:** Other species. $7 one-time fee. Service with restrictions, supervision.
✕ 🔒

SIDNEY

♦♦♦ Richland Motor Inn M
(406) 433-6400. **$70-$80.** 1200 S Central Ave. 1.5 mi n of jct SR 200 and 16. Int corridors. **Pets:** $50 deposit/room, $5 daily fee/pet. Designated rooms, service with restrictions, supervision.
SAVE SÃ ✕ 🔒 🖵 ✕

SUPERIOR

♦♦♦ Budget Host Big Sky Motel M
(406) 822-4831. **$48-$60.** 103 4th Ave E. I-90, exit 47, just n. Ext corridors. **Pets:** Accepted.
SAVE SÃ ✕ 🔒

THOMPSON FALLS

♦♦ The Riverfront M
(406) 827-3460. **$69-$107.** 4907 Scenic SR 200 W. 1 mi w of city center. Ext corridors. **Pets:** Medium. $7 daily fee/pet. Designated rooms, service with restrictions, supervision.
✕ 🔒 🖵 ✕

THREE FORKS

♦♦♦ Broken Spur Motel M
(406) 285-3237. **$48-$66.** 124 W Elm (Hwy 2). I-90, exit 278 westbound, 1.3 mi sw on SR 2; exit 274 eastbound, 1 mi s on SR 287 to jct SR 2, 3 mi se on SR 2. Ext corridors. **Pets:** Other species. $5 daily fee/pet. Service with restrictions, supervision.
SAVE SÃ ✕ 🔒

♦♦ Fort Three Forks Motel & RV Park M
(406) 285-3233. **$66-$85.** 10776 Hwy 287. I-90, exit 274. Ext corridors. **Pets:** Accepted.
✕ 🔒

VICTOR

♦♦ Wildlife Adventures RA ❀
(406) 642-3262. **$105-$170, 30 day notice.** 1765 Pleasant View DR. Jct US 93 and Fifth St, 0.9 mi w, 3.2 mi s. Int corridors. **Pets:** Other species. $15 daily fee/pet. Service with restrictions.
ASK ✕ ✕ 🗘 🗘 🗘

WEST YELLOWSTONE

(AAA) ▼▼▼▼ Best Western Cross Winds Motor Inn SH
(406) 646-9557. **$42-$124, 3 day notice.** 201 Firehole Ave. Just w of US 191 and 287, on US 20 at Dunraven St and Firehole Ave. Ext corridors. **Pets:** Dogs only. Designated rooms, service with restrictions, supervision.
SAVE Sᴅ ✕ 🖥 🖳 ⊇

(AAA) ▼▼▼▼ Best Western Desert Inn M
(406) 646-7376. **$49-$139, 3 day notice.** 133 Canyon Ave. US 191 at jct US 20, corner of Canyon and Firehole aves. Int corridors. **Pets:** Dogs only. Designated rooms, service with restrictions, supervision.
SAVE Sᴅ ✕ ᴸᴹ 🖐 🖉 🖥 🖳 ⊇

(AAA) ▼▼▼▼ Days Inn West Yellowstone SH
(406) 646-7656. **$69-$165, 14 day notice.** 301 Madison Ave. W off US 191; just nw of park entrance. Ext/int corridors. **Pets:** Accepted.
SAVE Sᴅ ✕ ᴸᴹ 🖉 🖥 🖳 🖳 ⊇ ✕

(AAA) ▼▼▼▼ Gray Wolf Inn & Suites M
(406) 646-0000. **$59-$139.** 250 S Canyon Ave. Just w of Yellowstone National Park entrance. Int corridors. **Pets:** Other species. $50 deposit/room. Designated rooms, service with restrictions, supervision.
SAVE Sᴅ ✕ ᴸᴹ 🖐 🖉 🖥 🖳 ⊇

(AAA) ▼ Hebgen Lake Mountain Inn SH
(406) 646-5100. **$95-$140, 10 day notice.** 15475 Hebgen Lake Rd. 8 mi n on US 191, w at jct US 191/287, then 7 mi w on US 287. Ext corridors. **Pets:** Medium, dogs only. Service with restrictions.
SAVE Sᴅ ✕ 🖳 🖳 ✕

(AAA) ▼▼▼▼ Kelly Inn SH
(406) 646-4544. **$59-$149.** 104 S Canyon Ave. S of jct US 191, 287 and 20, just w of park entrance. Ext/int corridors. **Pets:** Other species. Service with restrictions, supervision.
SAVE Sᴅ ✕ 🖉 🖥 🖳 ⊇

(AAA) ▼ Roundup Motel & Dude Motor Inn M
(406) 646-7301. **$45-$119, 3 day notice.** 3 Madison Ave. Just n of park entrance. Ext corridors. **Pets:** $50 deposit/pet, $5 daily fee/pet. Designated rooms, service with restrictions, crate.
SAVE Sᴅ ✕ 🖥 🖳 ⊇

(AAA) ▼▼▼▼ Stage Coach Inn SH
(406) 646-7381. **$49-$139.** 209 Madison Ave. Corner of Dunraven St and Madison Ave, just w of park entrance. Ext/int corridors. **Pets:** Designated rooms, service with restrictions, supervision.
SAVE Sᴅ ✕ 🖉 🖉 🖥 🖳 🖳 ✕

(AAA) ▼▼▼▼ Three Bear Motor Lodge M
(406) 646-7353. **$50-$99.** 217 Yellowstone Ave. Just w of park entrance. Ext/int corridors. **Pets:** Large, other species. $5 one-time fee/pet. Service with restrictions, supervision.
SAVE ✕ 🖥 🖳 🖳 ⊇ ✕

(AAA) ▼▼▼ Travelers Lodge M
(406) 646-9561. **$79-$95, 14 day notice.** 225 Yellowstone Ave. Just w of park entrance. Ext corridors. **Pets:** Accepted.
SAVE ✕ 🖉 🖥 ⊇

(AAA) ▼▼▼ Yellowstone Country Inn SH
(406) 646-7622. **$39-$129, 30 day notice.** 234 Firehole Ave. On US 20 and 191, just w of Canyon Ave, corner of Firehole Ave and Electric St. Ext/int corridors. **Pets:** $50 deposit/pet, $10 daily fee/pet. Designated rooms, service with restrictions, crate.
SAVE Sᴅ ✕ 🖥 🖳 🖳 ⊇ ✕

(AAA) ▼▼▼ Yellowstone Lodge SH
(406) 646-0020. **$49-$129.** 251 S Electric St. Just w of park entrance. Int corridors. **Pets:** Other species. $100 deposit/room. Designated rooms, service with restrictions, crate.
SAVE Sᴅ ✕ 🖉 🖥 🖳 ⊇

WHITEFISH

(AAA) ▼▼▼ Bay Point on the Lake CO
(406) 862-2331. **$89-$165, 30 day notice.** 300 Bay Point Dr. Jct US 93 and SR 487, 0.6 mi n on SR 487 to Skyles Pl, 0.3 mi w to Dakota Ave, 0.3 mi n, then just w. Ext corridors. **Pets:** Other species. Designated rooms, no service, supervision.
SAVE Sᴅ ✕ 🖥 🖳 ⊇ ✕

▼▼ Cheap Sleep Motel SH
(406) 862-5515. **$40-$70.** 6400 Hwy 93 S. US 93, 1 mi s. Int corridors. **Pets:** Medium, other species. $5 daily fee/pet. Service with restrictions, supervision.
✕ ⊇

(AAA) ▼▼▼ Kristianna Mountain Homes CO
(406) 862-2860. **$138-$308.** 3842 Winter Ln. Jct US 93 and SR 487, 2.4 mi n on SR 487, at flashing light go 5.2 mi on Big Mountain Rd, just n on Gelande, then just w on Kristanna Close. Ext/int corridors. **Pets:** Accepted.
SAVE ✕ 🖥 🖳 ✕ 🔧

▼▼▼ North Forty Resort CA
(406) 862-7740. **$69-$215, 14 day notice.** 3765 Hwy 40 W. 2.5 mi e on SR 40 from jct of US 93. Ext corridors. **Pets:** Other species. $10 daily fee/pet. Designated rooms, supervision.
✕ 🖥 🖳 ✕ 🔧

(AAA) ▼▼▼▼ Pine Lodge SH 🐾
(406) 862-7600. **$75-$130.** 920 Spokane Ave. 1 mi s on US 93. Int corridors. **Pets:** Service with restrictions, supervision.
SAVE Sᴅ ✕ ᴸᴹ 🖉 🖉 🖥 🖳 ⊇

(AAA) ▼▼▼ Super 8 Motel SH
(406) 862-8255. **$49-$89.** 800 Spokane Ave. 1 mi s on US 93 from jct of SR 487. Int corridors. **Pets:** Dogs only. $5 daily fee/pet. Designated rooms, service with restrictions, supervision.
SAVE Sᴅ ✕

WHITE SULPHUR SPRINGS

▼▼▼▼ All Seasons Super 8 Motel M
(406) 547-8888. **$48-$58.** 808 3rd Ave SW. On US 89, south end of town. Int corridors. **Pets:** $20 deposit/pet, $2 daily fee/pet. Service with restrictions, supervision.
ASK Sᴅ ✕ ᴸᴹ 🖉 🖥

AINSWORTH

Comfort Inn SH
(402) 387-1050. **$69-$105.** 1124 E 4th St. 0.5 mi e on US 20. Int corridors. **Pets:** Accepted.

Super 8 Motel SH
(402) 387-0700. **$45-$50.** 1025 E 4th St. 0.5 mi e on US 20. Int corridors. **Pets:** Accepted.

ALLIANCE

Days Inn of Alliance SH
(308) 762-8000. **$56-$71.** 117 Cody Ave. Jct US 385 and SR 2, 1.1 mi w, just s. Int corridors. **Pets:** Medium. $5 daily fee/pet. Designated rooms, service with restrictions, supervision.

Sunset Motel & RV Park M
(308) 762-8660. **$44-$65.** 1210 W Hwy 2. Jct US 385, 1 mi e. Ext/int corridors. **Pets:** Medium, dogs only. $5 daily fee/pet. Service with restrictions, supervision.

AURORA

Budget Host, Ken's Motel M
(402) 694-3141. **$38-$40.** 1515 11th St. I-80, exit 332, 3 mi n on SR 14, then 0.3 mi w on US 34. Ext corridors. **Pets:** Accepted.

BEATRICE

Beatrice Super 8 Motel SH
(402) 228-8808. **$59-$64.** 3721 N 6th St. 1 mi n on US 77. Int corridors. **Pets:** Other species. $10 daily fee/pet. Supervision.

Holiday Inn Express Hotel & Suites SH
(402) 228-7000. **$63-$73.** 4005 N 6th St. 1 mi n on US 77. Int corridors. **Pets:** Other species. $25 deposit/room, $25 one-time fee/room. Designated rooms, service with restrictions, crate.

BELLEVUE

American Family Inn M
(402) 291-0804. **$52-$62.** 1110 Fort Crook Rd S. US 75, 0.3 mi n of jct SR 370 and Fort Crook Rd. Ext corridors. **Pets:** Accepted.

Best Western White House Inn SH
(402) 293-1600. **$59-$109.** 305 Fort Crook Rd N. US 75, 1.8 mi n of jct of SR 370 and Fort Crook Rd N. Int corridors. **Pets:** Accepted.

Days Inn SH
(402) 292-3800. **$61-$185.** 1811 Hillcrest Dr. Jct US 75 and SR 370, 0.8 mi on SR 370. Int corridors. **Pets:** Medium, dogs only. $35 one-time fee/pet. Designated rooms, service with restrictions, supervision.

Settle Inn and Suites SH
(402) 292-1155. **$69-$99.** 2105 Pratt Ave. US 75, exit Cornhusker, just w. Int corridors. **Pets:** Small, other species. $10 daily fee/room. Designated rooms, service with restrictions, supervision.

CENTRAL CITY

Super 8 Motel SH
(308) 946-5055. **$46-$55.** 1701 31st St. SR 14, 1 mi s of jct US 30. Ext/int corridors. **Pets:** Accepted.

CHADRON

Best Western West Hills Inn SH
(308) 432-3305. **$56-$97.** 1100 W 10th St. Jct US 385 and 20. Ext/int corridors. **Pets:** Medium. Service with restrictions, supervision.

Chadron Super 8 Motel SH
(308) 432-4471. **$45-$103, 7 day notice.** 840 W Hwy 20. 0.8 mi w on US 20, just e of jct US 385. Int corridors. **Pets:** Accepted.

Grand Westerner Motel M
(308) 432-5595. **$39-$52.** 1050 W Hwy 20. 0.8 mi w on US 20, just e of jct US 385. Ext corridors. **Pets:** Accepted.

△△△ ▽▽ Westerner Motel M
(308) 432-5577. **$39-$52.** 300 Oak St. On US 20, 0.5 mi e of jct US 385 and SR 87. Ext corridors. **Pets:** Other species. Designated rooms, service with restrictions, supervision.
[SAVE] [S▲] [✕] [🛈]

COLUMBUS

▽▽ Days Inn SH
(402) 564-2527. **$54-$61.** 371 33rd Ave. Jct US 30 and 81, 1 mi s. Int corridors. **Pets:** Accepted.
[ASK] [S▲] [✕] [🛈]

▽▽ Sleep Inn & Suites Hotel SH
(402) 562-5200. **$64-$111.** 303 23rd St. On US 30, 2 mi e of jct US 30 and 81; east side of town. Int corridors. **Pets:** Accepted.
[ASK] [S▲] [✕] [&M] [🗏] [✎] [🛈] [▭] [⤳]

▽▽ Super 8 Motel-Columbus SH
(402) 563-3456. **$49-$59.** 3324 20th St. On US 30/81, just s. Int corridors. **Pets:** Small. $10 one-time fee/pet. Service with restrictions, supervision.
[ASK] [S▲] [✕] [🗏]

COZAD

▽▽ Motel 6-Cozad–4091 SH ❀
(308) 784-4900. **$43-$72.** 809 S Meridian. I-80, exit 222. Int corridors. **Pets:** Other species. Service with restrictions, supervision.
[✕]

CRETE

▽▽ Super 8 Motel SH
(402) 826-3600. **$61-$88.** 1880 W 12th St. 1.3 mi sw at jct SR 33/103. Int corridors. **Pets:** Small. $5 daily fee/pet. Service with restrictions, supervision.
[ASK] [S▲] [✕] [✎] [🛈]

FAIRBURY

△△△ ▽▽ Capri Motel M
(402) 729-3317. **$40-$55.** 1100 14th St. On US 136 at jct SR 15. Ext/int corridors. **Pets:** Medium, other species. $10 deposit/room. Service with restrictions, supervision.
[SAVE] [✕] [🛈] [▭]

FREMONT

▽▽ Comfort Inn SH
(402) 721-1109. **$64-$89.** 1649 E 23rd Ave. 2 mi e on US 30, just e of Business Rt US 275. Int corridors. **Pets:** Other species. $5 one-time fee/room. Service with restrictions.
[ASK] [S▲] [✕] [🗏] [🛈] [▭] [⤳]

△△△ ▽▽ Holiday Lodge SH
(402) 727-1110. **$49-$76, 14 day notice.** 1220 E 23rd St. US 30, jct Business Rt US 275 and 30. Ext/int corridors. **Pets:** Small, other species. $25 deposit/room. Designated rooms, supervision.
[SAVE] [S▲] [✕] [🛈] [▭] [¶] [⤳] [✕]

FULLERTON

▽▽▽ The Fullerton Inn M ❀
(308) 536-2699. **$54-$58.** S Hwy 14. Just s of center. Int corridors. **Pets:** $5 deposit/room. Service with restrictions, supervision.
[ASK] [S▲] [✕] [&M]

GERING

▽▽ Microtel Inn & Suites SH
(308) 436-1950. **$60-$65.** 1130 M St. On SR 92, 1 mi e of SR 71. Int corridors. **Pets:** Other species. $10 one-time fee/room. Service with restrictions.
[ASK] [S▲] [✕] [&M] [✎] [🛈] [▭]

GOTHENBURG

△△△ ▽▽▽ Gothenburg Super 8 SH
(308) 537-2684. **$50-$80.** 401 Platte River Dr. I-80, exit 211, just n. Int corridors. **Pets:** Accepted.
[SAVE] [S▲] [✕] [✎] [🛈] [⤳]

GRAND ISLAND

▽▽ Days Inn SH
(308) 384-8624. **$55-$75.** 2620 N Diers Ave. Off W Capital Ave, 4.8 mi nw on US 281 at jct SR 2. Ext/int corridors. **Pets:** $15 daily fee/pet, $15 one-time fee/pet. Designated rooms, service with restrictions, supervision.
[ASK] [S▲] [✕] [🗏] [✎] [🛈]

▽▽▽▽ Holiday Inn-Interstate 80 SH ❀
(308) 384-7770. **$64-$109.** 7838 S US Hwy 281. I-80, exit 312 (US 281). Int corridors. **Pets:** Other species. $15 daily fee/room. Service with restrictions, supervision.
[ASK] [✕] [&M] [🗏] [✎] [🛈] [▭] [¶] [⤳] [✕]

△△△ ▽▽▽ Howard Johnson Riverside Inn & Conference Center SH ❀
(308) 384-5150. **$61-$81.** 3333 Ramada Rd. I-80, exit 312 (US 281) eastbound, 5 mi n to US 34, 2 mi e to Locust St; exit 318 westbound, 3 mi n to US 34, 5 mi w to Locust St. Ext/int corridors. **Pets:** Other species. $10 one-time fee/room. Designated rooms, service with restrictions, crate.
[SAVE] [S▲] [✕] [🛈] [▭] [¶] [⤳] [✕]

▽▽ Oak Grove Inn SH
(308) 384-1333. **$35.** 3205 S Locust St. I-80, exit 312 (US 281) eastbound, 5 mi n to US 34, 2 mi e; exit 318 westbound, 3 mi n to US 34, then 5 mi w. Int corridors. **Pets:** Other species. $10 one-time fee/room. Service with restrictions.
[ASK] [S▲] [✕]

▽▽ Super 8 SH
(308) 384-4380. **$55-$58.** 2603 S Locust St. I-80, exit 312 (US 281) eastbound, 5 mi n to US 34, 2 mi e to Locust St, then 0.5 mi n; exit 318 westbound, 3 mi n to US 34, 5 mi w to Locust St, then 0.5 mi n. Int corridors. **Pets:** Service with restrictions, supervision.
[ASK] [✕] [🛈] [▭] [⤳]

▼▼ Travelodge SH
(308) 382-5003. **$51.** 1311 S Locust St. I-80, exit 312 (US 281) eastbound, 5 mi n to US 34, 2 mi e to Locust St, then 1 mi n; exit 318 westbound, 3 mi n to US 34, 5 mi w to Locust St, then 1 mi n. Int corridors. **Pets:** Other species. $6 one-time fee/room. Service with restrictions, supervision.
(A$K) (S.) (X) (🌙) 🔒 💻

⚠ ▼▼ USA Inns of America M
(308) 381-0111. **$55-$67.** 7000 S Nine Bridge Rd. I-80, exit 312 (US 281). Ext/int corridors. **Pets:** Medium. $5 daily fee/pet. Designated rooms, service with restrictions, supervision.
(SAVE) (S.) (X) 🔒 💻

HASTINGS

⚠ ▼▼▼ Holiday Inn-Hastings SH 🐾
(402) 463-6721. **$70-$130.** 2205 Osborne Dr E. Jct US 34 and 281, 2 mi n on US 34. Ext/int corridors. **Pets:** Small, other species. $25 deposit/room. Service with restrictions, crate.
(SAVE) (S.) (X) (⚅M) (🌙) (🌙) 🔒 💻 🍴 ⊠ ⊠

⚠ ▼▼▼ Midlands Lodge M 🐾
(402) 463-2428. **$39-$54, 7 day notice.** 910 W J St. Jct US 6, 34 and 281. Ext corridors. **Pets:** Other species. Service with restrictions, supervision.
(SAVE) (S.) (X) 🔒 ⊠

▼▼ Super 8 SH
(402) 463-8888. **$47-$89.** 2200 N Kansas Ave. Jct US 34 and 281, 2 mi n on US 34. Int corridors. **Pets:** Medium, other species. Service with restrictions, supervision.
(X) (🌙) (🌙)

HOLDREGE

▼▼ Super 8 SH
(308) 995-2793. **$59-$99, 7 day notice.** 420 Broadway. US 183, 0.5 mi w on US 6/34. Int corridors. **Pets:** Medium. $10 daily fee/room. Service with restrictions, supervision.
(A$K) (S.) (X) 🔒 ⊠ ⊠

KEARNEY

⚠ ▼▼▼ Best Western Inn of Kearney SH
(308) 237-5185. **$69-$88.** 1010 3rd Ave. I-80, exit 272 (SR 44), 1 mi n, then just w. Ext/int corridors. **Pets:** Accepted.
(SAVE) (S.) (X) (🌙) 🔒 🍴 ⊠ ⊠

⚠ ▼▼▼ Ramada Inn-Kearney SH
(308) 237-3141. **$92-$99.** 301 2nd Ave. I-80, exit 272 (SR 44), 0.7 mi n. Int corridors. **Pets:** $10 one-time fee/pet. Designated rooms, service with restrictions, supervision.
(SAVE) (S.) (X) 🔒 💻 🍴 ⊠ ⊠

KIMBALL

▼▼ Days Inn-Kimball M
(308) 235-4671. **Call for rates.** 611 E 3rd St. I-80, exit 20, 1.5 ne on SR 71, then 0.5 mi e on US 30. Ext corridors. **Pets:** Accepted.
(X) 🔒 💻 ⊠

LEXINGTON

⚠ ▼▼ Budget Host Minute Man Motel M
(308) 324-5544. **$39-$50, 3 day notice.** 801 Plum Creek Pkwy. I-80, exit 237, 2 mi n on US 283. Ext corridors. **Pets:** Medium, dogs only. $5 daily fee/pet. Designated rooms, no service, supervision.
(SAVE) (X)

▼▼ Days Inn SH
(308) 324-6440. **$55-$85.** 2506 Plum Creek Pkwy. I-80, exit 237, 0.6 mi n on US 283. Int corridors. **Pets:** Small, dogs only. $6 daily fee/pet. Designated rooms, service with restrictions, supervision.
(A$K) (S.) (X) 🔒

⚠ ▼▼▼ Holiday Inn Express Hotel & Suites SH
(308) 324-9900. **$59-$109.** 2605 Plum Creek Pkwy. I-80, exit 237, 0.5 mi n on US 283. Int corridors. **Pets:** Medium. $10 one-time fee/room. Designated rooms, service with restrictions, supervision.
(SAVE) (S.) (X) (⚅M) (🌙) (🌙) 🔒 💻 ⊠

LINCOLN

⚠ ▼▼▼ Baymont Inn & Suites SH
(402) 477-1100. **$73-$75.** 3939 N 26th St. I-80, exit 403, 1.7 mi s. Int corridors. **Pets:** Small. Service with restrictions, supervision.
(SAVE) (S.) (X) (⚅M) (🌙) (🌙) 🔒 💻 ⊠ ⊠

⚠ ▼▼▼ Best Western Villager Courtyard & Gardens Hotel SH 🐾
(402) 464-9111. **$58-$69.** 5200 O St. 3 mi e on US 6 city route and 34. Ext corridors. **Pets:** Medium, other species. $25 deposit/room. Service with restrictions, crate.
(SAVE) (S.) (X) (⚅M) (🌙) (🌙) 🔒 💻 🍴 ⊠ ⊠

▼▼▼ Chase Suites Hotel SH
(402) 483-4900. **$129-$169.** 200 S 68th St Pl. On US 34, 4.3 mi e, just s of jct 68th St. Ext corridors. **Pets:** Medium, other species. $5 daily fee/pet, $150 one-time fee/pet. Designated rooms, service with restrictions, crate.
(A$K) (S.) (X) (⚅M) (🌙) (🌙) 🔒 💻 ⊠ ⊠

▼▼ Comfort Inn of Lincoln SH
(402) 475-2200. **$54-$84.** 2940 NW 12th St. I-80, exit 399 (airport); enter at Perkins Restaurant. Int corridors. **Pets:** Accepted.
(A$K) (S.) (X) (🌙) 🔒 💻

⚠ ▼▼▼ Country Inns & Suites By Carlson SH
(402) 476-5353. **$89-$99.** 5353 N 27th St. I-80, exit 403, 1.5 mi s. Int corridors. **Pets:** Accepted.
(SAVE) (S.) (X) (⚅M) (🌙) 🔒 💻 🍴 ⊠

▼▼ Days Inn SH
(402) 475-3616. **$49-$75.** 2920 NW 12th St. I-80, exit 399. Int corridors. **Pets:** Medium. $50 deposit/room. Designated rooms, service with restrictions, supervision.
(A$K) (S.) (X) (🌙) (🌙) 🔒 💻

◆◆◆ ▼▼▼ **Days Inn South** 🆂🅷
(402) 423-7111. **$53-$68.** 1140 Calvert St. 2.5 mi s on SR 2. Ext/int corridors. **Pets:** Small, dogs only. $5 daily fee/pet. Designated rooms, service with restrictions, supervision.
[SAVE] 🆂 ⊠ 📶 📺

▼▼▼ **Hawthorn Suites Ltd** 🆂🅷
(402) 464-4400. **Call for rates.** 216 N 48th St. 2.5 mi e on US 6 and 34; just ne of jct O St; entrance off of 48th St. Int corridors. **Pets:** Accepted.
⊠ 🐾 🖩 📶 📺 ≈

▼▼▼ **Holiday Inn Express** 🆂🅷 🐾
(402) 435-0200. **$76-$97.** 1133 Belmont Ave. I-80, exit 401A; 2 mi s on I-180, exit 2 (Cornhusker Hwy), then just e. Int corridors. **Pets:** Other species. Service with restrictions, crate.
[ASK] 🆂 ⊠ &M 🐾 🖩 📶 📺 ≈ ⊠

▼▼▼ **Settle Inn & Suites** 🆂🅷
(402) 435-8100. **$59-$99.** 2800 Husker Cir. I-80, exit 403, just s to Wildcat Dr, just e, then just n. Int corridors. **Pets:** Accepted.
[ASK] 🆂 ⊠ &M 🖩 📶 📺 ≈

▼▼▼ **Staybridge Suites Lincoln-I-80** 🆂🅷
(402) 438-7829. **$85-$199.** 2701 Fletcher Ave. I-80, exit 403, 0.4 mi s on N 27th St. Int corridors. **Pets:** Other species. $75 one-time fee/room.
[ASK] ⊠ &M 🖩 📶 📺 ≈ ⊠

▼▼▼ **Super 8 Motel-Lincoln/Cornhusker** 🆂🅷
(402) 467-4488. **$53-$65.** 2545 Cornhusker Hwy. I-80, exit 403, 2 mi s. Int corridors. **Pets:** Other species. $10 one-time fee/room. Service with restrictions, supervision.
[ASK] 🆂 ⊠ &M 🐾 🖩 📶 📺

◆◆◆ ▼▼▼ **Town House Motel** 🆂🅷
(402) 475-3000. **$55-$85, 7 day notice.** 1744 M St. Downtown. Int corridors. **Pets:** Accepted.
[SAVE] 🆂 ⊠ 🐾 📶 📺

MCCOOK

▼▼▼ **Days Inn & Suites McCook** 🆂🅷 🐾
(308) 345-7115. **$45-$85.** 901 N Hwy 83. Jct US 6 and 34, 0.3 mi n. Int corridors. **Pets:** Other species. Service with restrictions, supervision.
[ASK] 🆂 ⊠ 📶 📺 ≈

▼▼▼ **Holiday Inn Express** 🆂🅷
(308) 345-4505. **$67-$88.** 1 Holiday Bison Dr. On US 83, just n of jct US 6 and 34. Int corridors. **Pets:** Medium. Service with restrictions, supervision.
[ASK] 🆂 ⊠ &M 🐾 📶

▼ **Super 8 Motel** 🅼
(308) 345-1141. **$49.** 1103 E B St. Jct US 6 and 34, 0.5 mi e. Ext corridors. **Pets:** Accepted.
[ASK] 🆂 ⊠

MORRILL

▼▼ **Oak Tree Inn** 🆂🅷 🐾
(308) 247-2111. **$55-$65.** 707 E Webster. 0.5 mi e. Ext/int corridors. **Pets:** $5 one-time fee/room.
[ASK] 🆂 ⊠ &M 🐾 📶 🍴 ⊠

NEBRASKA CITY

◆◆◆ ▼▼▼ **Apple Inn** 🆂🅷
(402) 873-5959. **$54-$64.** 502 S 11th. Center. Ext/int corridors. **Pets:** Small, dogs only. $5 daily fee/pet. Designated rooms, service with restrictions, supervision.
[SAVE] 🆂 ⊠ 🐾 📶 📺 ≈

NORFOLK

▼▼ **Howard Johnson-White House Inn** 🆂🅷
(402) 371-3133. **$55-$60.** 2206 Market Ln. On US 275 Bypass, 1 mi w of US 81. Int corridors. **Pets:** $20 deposit/pet, $5 daily fee/pet. Designated rooms, service with restrictions, supervision.
[ASK] 🆂 ⊠ 🐾 &M 📶 📺 ⊠

◆◆◆ ▼▼▼ **Norfolk Country Inn** 🆂🅷 🐾
(402) 371-4430. **$62.** 1201 S 13th St. Jct US 275 Bypass and US 81. Ext corridors. **Pets:** Other species. Designated rooms, service with restrictions.
[SAVE] 🆂 ⊠ 🐾 📶 📺 🍴 ≈

▼▼ **Super 8 Motel-Norfolk** 🆂🅷
(402) 379-2220. **$49-$59.** 1223 Omaha Ave. Jct of US 81 and 275, just e. Int corridors. **Pets:** Designated rooms, service with restrictions, supervision.
[ASK] 🆂 ⊠ 🐾 📶 📺

NORTH PLATTE

◆◆◆ ▼▼▼ **Best Value Travelers Inn** 🅼
(308) 534-4020. **$36-$55.** 602 E 4th St. I-80, exit 177 (US 83), 1.5 mi n, then just e. Ext corridors. **Pets:** Medium, other species. Service with restrictions, supervision.
[SAVE] 🆂 ⊠ 📶 ≈

◆◆◆ ▼▼▼ **Best Western Chalet Lodge** 🅼
(308) 532-2313. **$49-$76.** 920 N Jeffers St. I-80, exit 177, 2 mi n on US 30 and 83. Ext corridors. **Pets:** Other species. $5 daily fee/pet. Service with restrictions, supervision.
[SAVE] 🆂 ⊠ 📶 📺 ≈

◆◆◆ ▼▼▼ **Holiday Inn Express Hotel & Suites** 🆂🅷
(308) 532-9500. **$75-$150.** 300 Holiday Frontage Rd. I-80, exit 177 (US 83), just s. Int corridors. **Pets:** Other species. $12 one-time fee/room. Designated rooms, service with restrictions, crate.
[SAVE] 🆂 ⊠ &M 🐾 🖩 📶 📺 ≈ ⊠

▼▼ **Howard Johnson Inn** 🆂🅷
(308) 532-0130. **$49-$84.** 1211 S Dewey. I-80, exit 177, 0.5 mi n on US 83. Ext corridors. **Pets:** Other species. $10 one-time fee/room. Service with restrictions, supervision.
[ASK] 🆂 ⊠ 📶 🍴 ≈

◆◆◆ ▼▼▼ **Quality Inn & Suites** 🆂🅷
(308) 532-9090. **$65-$155.** 2102 S Jeffers St. I-80, exit 177 (US 83), just n. Ext/int corridors. **Pets:** $10 daily fee/pet. Designated rooms.
[SAVE] 🆂 ⊠ &M 🐾 🖩 📶 📺 🍴 ≈ ⊠

△△△ ▽▼▽ Ramada Limited 🆂🅷 ✿
(308) 534-3120. **$55-$75.** 3201 S Jeffers St. I-80, exit 177
(US 83), 0.3 mi s. Int corridors. **Pets:** Medium, other species. $10 daily fee/pet. Designated rooms, service with
restrictions, supervision.
(SAVE) (S🔊) ⊠ 🖥 📺 🍴 ≈

OGALLALA

△△△ ▽▼▽▼ Best Western Stagecoach Inn 🆂🅷
(308) 284-3656. **$58-$95.** 201 Stagecoach Tr. I-80, exit 126,
just ne on Frontage Rd. Ext corridors. **Pets:** Accepted.
(SAVE) (S🔊) ⊠ 🖥 📺 🍴 ≈ ⊠

△△△ ▽▼▽ Days Inn 🅼 ✿
(308) 284-6365. **$50-$65.** 601 Stagecoach Tr. I-80, exit 126,
just ne on frontage road. Int corridors. **Pets:** Dogs only. $6
daily fee/room. Crate.
(SAVE) (S🔊) ⊠ 🖥

▽▼▽▽ Holiday Inn Express 🆂🅷
(308) 284-2266. **$65-$95.** 501 Stagecoach Dr. I-80, exit 126,
just n, just e on service road. Ext/int corridors.
Pets: Accepted.
(ASK) (S🔊) ⊠ 🗂 🖉 🖥

▽▼▽▽ Ogallala Comfort Inn 🆂🅷
(308) 284-4028. **$60-$100.** 110 Pony Express Rd. I-80, exit
126, just s. Ext/int corridors. **Pets:** Accepted.
(ASK) (S🔊) ⊠ 🗂 🖥 📺 ≈

OMAHA

△△△ ▽▼▽▽ Baymont Inn Omaha 🆂🅷
(402) 592-5200. **$59-$89.** 10760 M St. I-80, exit 445 (L St
E), 0.3 mi; entry off 108th St. Int corridors. **Pets:** Medium,
other species. Designated rooms, service with restrictions,
crate.
(SAVE) (S🔊) ⊠ 🗂 🖥 📺

▽▼▽▽ Best Western Redick Plaza Hotel 🅻🅷
(402) 342-1500. **$89-$149.** 1504 Harney St. Downtown. Int
corridors. **Pets:** Accepted.
(ASK) (S🔊) ⊠ 🗂 🖥 📺 🍴 ⊠

△△△ ▽▼▽▽ Best Western Settle Inn 🆂🅷 ✿
(402) 431-1246. **$69-$109.** 650 N 109th Ct. I-680 N, exit 3
(Dodge St W), 0.8 mi to 108th St to 108th Ave and N Old
Mill Rd exit, just n on 108th Ave, then just w on Mill Valley
Rd. Int corridors. **Pets:** $10 daily fee/room. Designated
rooms, service with restrictions.
(SAVE) ⊠ 🗂 🖉 🖥 📺 ≈

▽▼▽▽ Candlewood Suites 🆂🅷
(402) 758-2848. **$71-$85.** 360 S 108th Ave. I-680, exit 3
(Dodge St W), 0.7 mi to 108th St, then 0.8 mi s. Int corridors. **Pets:** Medium. $150 one-time fee/pet. Service with
restrictions, supervision.
(ASK) (S🔊) ⊠ (L🅼) 🗂 🖉 🖥 📺

▽▼▽▽ Clarion Hotel-West 🆂🅷
(402) 895-1000. **$65-$149.** 4888 S 118th St. I-80, exit 445 (L
St W), 0.3 mi w on US 275/SR 92, then just s on 120th St.
Int corridors. **Pets:** Other species. $10 daily fee/room. Serv-
ice with restrictions, crate.
(ASK) ⊠ (S🔊) ⊠ (L🅼) 🗂 🖉 🖥 📺 🍴 ≈ ⊠

▽▼▽▽ ClubHouse Inn & Suites 🆂🅷
(402) 496-7500. **$99-$119.** 11515 Miracle Hills Dr. I-680, exit
3 (Dodge St W), 0.8 mi w to 114th St N, then 0.8 mi nw. Int
corridors. **Pets:** Other species. Service with restrictions,
crate.
(ASK) (S🔊) ⊠ 🗂 🖥 📺 ≈

**▽▼▽▽ Crowne Plaza Hotel and Resort Omaha-Old
      Mill 🅻🅷**
(402) 496-0850. **$79-$139.** 655 N 108th Ave. I-680, exit 3
(Dodge St W), 0.7 mi to 108th St to 108th Ave and N Old
Mill Rd exits, then just n. Int corridors. **Pets:** Accepted.
(ASK) ⊠ 🗂 🖉 🖥 📺 🍴 ≈ ⊠

**△△△ ▽▼▽▽ Doubletree Guest Suites
      Omaha 🅻🅷**
(402) 397-5141. **$69-$159.** 7270 Cedar St. I-80, exit 449
(72nd St), 1.3 mi n. Int corridors. **Pets:** Accepted.
(SAVE) ⊠ 🗂 🖉 🖥 📺 🍴 ≈ ⊠

▽▼▽ Econo Lodge West Dodge 🅼
(402) 391-7100. **$54-$74.** 7833 Dodge St. I-680, exit 3
(Dodge St E), 2.2 mi e. Ext corridors. **Pets:** Medium. $10
one-time fee/room. Designated rooms, service with restrictions.
(ASK) (S🔊) ⊠ 🖥 📺 ≈

▽▼▽▽ Hampton Inn-Omaha Central 🆂🅷
(402) 391-8129. **$78-$82.** 3301 S 72nd St. I-80, exit 449
(72nd St), just n. Ext/int corridors. **Pets:** Accepted.
(ASK) (S🔊) ⊠ (L🅼) 🗂 🖉 🖥 📺

▽▼▽▽ Hampton Inn-Southwest 🆂🅷
(402) 593-2380. **$67-$71, 30 day notice.** 10728 L St. I-80,
exit 445 (L St E), just n on 108th St, then e. Int corridors.
Pets: Medium, other species. Service with restrictions,
supervision.
(ASK) ⊠ 🖥 📺 ≈

△△△ ▽▼▽▽ Hawthorn Suites 🆂🅷
(402) 331-0101. **$99-$149.** 11025 M St. I-80, exit 445 (L St),
0.3 mi e, just s on 108th St, then just w. Ext corridors.
Pets: Medium. $6 daily fee/pet. Service with restrictions,
crate.
(SAVE) (S🔊) ⊠ 🗂 🖥 📺 ≈ ⊠

▽▼▽▽ Holiday Inn Central 🅻🅷
(402) 393-3950. **$99-$169.** 3321 S 72nd St. I-80, exit 449
(72nd St), just n. Int corridors. **Pets:** Medium, other species.
$25 one-time fee/pet. Designated rooms, service with
restrictions, supervision.
(ASK) (S🔊) ⊠ (L🅼) 🗂 🖉 🖥 📺 🍴 ≈ ⊠

▽▼▽▽ Holiday Inn Express Hotel & Suites 🆂🅷
(402) 339-8111. **$77-$86, 30 day notice.** 10729 J St. I-80,
exit 445 (L St E), 0.3 mi e. Int corridors. **Pets:** Medium,
other species. $10 daily fee/room. Designated rooms, serv-
ice with restrictions, supervision.
(ASK) ⊠ (L🅼) 🗂 🖉 🖥 📺 ≈

△△△ ▽▼▽▽ La Quinta Inn 🆂🅷
(402) 493-1900. **$60-$85.** 3330 N 104th Ave. I-680, exit 4
(Maple St), just w to 108th St, just n to Bedford, then just e.
Int corridors. **Pets:** Service with restrictions, supervision.
(SAVE) ⊠ 🗂 🖥 📺 ≈

Motel 6–161 M
(402) 331-3161. **$45-$59.** 10708 M St. I-80, exit 445 (L St E), 0.4 mi e; entry on 108th St. Ext corridors. **Pets:** Medium, other species. Service with restrictions, supervision.

Ramada Inn-Airport SH
(402) 342-5100. **$83-$85.** 2002 E Locust St. I-480 E, exit 14th St (downtown), 2.5 mi n, follow signs. Ext/int corridors. **Pets:** Accepted.

Ramada Inn Executive Center SH
(402) 397-3700. **$69-$89.** 3650 S 72nd St. I-80, exit 449 (72nd St). Int corridors. **Pets:** Accepted.

Ramada Limited SH
(402) 896-9500. **$68-$90, 5 day notice.** 9505 S 142nd St. I-80, exit 440. Int corridors. **Pets:** Small, dogs only. $10 daily fee/pet. Service with restrictions, supervision.

Red Lion Hotel Omaha LH
(402) 397-7030. **$79-$128.** 7007 Grover St. I-80, exit 449 (72nd St), just n, just e. Int corridors. **Pets:** Accepted.

Relax Inn Motel & Suites M
(402) 731-7300. **$48-$56.** 4578 S 60th St. I-80, exit 450 (60th St), 0.8 mi s. Ext corridors. **Pets:** Very small, other species. $20 deposit/room, $6 daily fee/pet. Service with restrictions, supervision.

Satellite Motel M
(402) 733-7373. **$44-$56.** 6006 L St. I-80, exit 450 (60th St), 0.8 mi s; just n of US 275 and SR 92. Ext/int corridors. **Pets:** Very small, other species. $20 deposit/room, $6 daily fee/pet. Designated rooms, service with restrictions, supervision.

Sheraton Omaha Hotel LH
(402) 342-2222. **$199.** 1615 Howard St. Downtown. Int corridors. **Pets:** Accepted.

Super 8 Motel-Omaha/West L SH
(402) 339-2250. **$55-$65.** 10829 M St. I-80, exit 445 (L St E), just e; entry off 108th St. Int corridors. **Pets:** Other species. $10 daily fee/pet. Designated rooms, service with restrictions, supervision.

O'NEILL

Elms Motel M
(402) 336-3800. **$38-$45.** 414 E Hwy 20. 1 mi se on US 20/275. Ext corridors. **Pets:** Medium, dogs only. Service with restrictions, supervision.

Golden Hotel SH
(402) 336-4436. **$39-$55.** 406 E Douglas St. Jct US 20/275/281; center. Ext/int corridors. **Pets:** Medium. $7 daily fee/pet. Service with restrictions, supervision.

Holiday Inn Express Hotel & Suites SH
(402) 336-4500. **$60-$75.** 1020 E Douglas St. 0.4 mi e on US 20/275. Int corridors. **Pets:** Accepted.

Super 8 Motel-O'Neill SH
(402) 336-3100. **$49-$65.** 106 E Hwy 20. 0.5 mi e on US 20/275. Int corridors. **Pets:** Small, dogs only. $10 daily fee/pet. Designated rooms, service with restrictions, supervision.

OSHKOSH

Shady Rest Motel M
(308) 772-4115. **$38-$40.** 102 Main St. On US 26. Ext corridors. **Pets:** Service with restrictions, supervision.

PAXTON

Paxton Days Inn M
(308) 239-4510. **$55-$70.** 851 Paxton Rd. I-80, exit 145, just n. Ext corridors. **Pets:** Other species. $10 one-time fee/room.

ST. PAUL

Super 8 Motel SH
(308) 754-4554. **$58-$70.** 116 Howard Ave. Just e of downtown, jct US 281. Ext/int corridors. **Pets:** Accepted.

SCOTTSBLUFF

Capri Motel M
(308) 635-2057. **$37-$41.** 2424 Ave I. 1.5 mi nw, just s of 27th St. Ext corridors. **Pets:** Other species. $5 daily fee/room. Service with restrictions.

Lamplighter American Inn SH
(308) 632-7108. **$38-$42.** 606 E 27th St. US 26 business route, 0.5 mi e of jct SR 71, just s. Int corridors. **Pets:** Dogs only. $6 daily fee/pet. Service with restrictions, supervision.

SEWARD

Seward Super 8 M
(402) 643-3388. **$49-$56.** 1329 Progressive Rd. I-80, exit 379, 3 mi n on SR 15. Ext/int corridors. **Pets:** Accepted.

SIDNEY

AmericInn Motel & Suites of Sidney SH
(308) 254-0100. **$84-$149.** 645 Cabela Dr. I-80, exit 59, just nw. Int corridors. **Pets:** Accepted.

(AAA) ▼ Best Value Sidney Motor Lodge M
(308) 254-4581. **$46-$68.** 2031 Illinois St. On US 30; west end of town. Ext corridors. **Pets:** Medium, other species. Designated rooms, service with restrictions, supervision.
[SAVE] [S6] [X] [blank]

(AAA) ▼▼▼ Days Inn SH
(308) 254-2121. **$54-$80, 7 day notice.** 3042 Silverberg Dr. I-80, exit 59, just n. Int corridors. **Pets:** Medium. $10 daily fee/pet. Designated rooms, service with restrictions, supervision.
[SAVE] [X] [blank] [pool]

▼▼▼ Holiday Inn & Conference Center SH
(308) 254-2000. **$80-$110, 3 day notice.** 664 Chase Blvd. I-80, exit 59, just s. Int corridors. **Pets:** Accepted.
[ASK] [X] [&M] [icons] [blank] [blank] [TI] [pool] [X]

SOUTH SIOUX CITY

▼▼▼▼ Marina Inn Conference Center SH
(402) 494-4000. **$89-$109, 3 day notice.** 4th & B sts. I-29, exit 148, on banks of Missouri River (e at stop light by Nebraska side of bridge). Int corridors. **Pets:** Accepted.
[ASK] [S6] [X] [&M] [icons] [blank] [blank] [TI] [pool]

SYRACUSE

▼▼▼▼ Sleep Inn & Suites SH
(402) 269-2700. **Call for rates.** 130 N 30th Rd. Jct SR 2, 1 mi n on SR 50. Int corridors. **Pets:** Accepted.
[X] [&M] [icons] [blank] [blank] [pool]

VALENTINE

**▼▼▼▼ Holiday Inn Express Hotel &
   Suites SH** 🐾
(402) 376-3000. **$59-$109.** 803 E Hwy 20. Jct US 20/83, 0.5 mi se. Int corridors. **Pets:** Small, other species. $10 daily fee/pet. Designated rooms, service with restrictions, supervision.
[ASK] [S6] [X] [&M] [icons] [blank] [blank] [pool] [X]

(AAA) ▼▼▼ Motel Raine M
(402) 376-2030. **$38-$58.** US 20 W. On US 20, 0.5 mi sw. Ext corridors. **Pets:** Accepted.
[SAVE] [S6] [X] [blank]

(AAA) ▼▼▼ Trade Winds Motel M 🐾
(402) 376-1600. **$44-$69.** E Hwy 20 & 83. Jct US 20/83, 1 mi se. Ext corridors. **Pets:** $3 daily fee/pet. Service with restrictions, supervision.
[SAVE] [S6] [X] [blank] [blank] [pool]

WAHOO

▼▼ Super 8 Motel-Wahoo SH
(402) 443-1288. **Call for rates.** 950 N Chestnut. On US 77 and SR 92, just se of downtown. Ext/int corridors. **Pets:** Accepted.
[X] [&M] [blank] [blank]

YORK

(AAA) ▼▼▼ Best Western Palmer Inn M
(402) 362-5585. **$48-$71.** 2426 S Lincoln Ave. I-80, exit 353, 1 mi n on US 81. Ext corridors. **Pets:** Accepted.
[SAVE] [S6] [X] [blank] [blank] [pool]

▼▼ Yorkshire Motel M
(402) 362-6633. **$44-$70.** 3402 S Lincoln Ave. I-80, exit 353, 0.5 mi n on US 81. Ext/int corridors. **Pets:** Accepted.
[ASK] [S6] [X] [blank]

NEVADA

AMARGOSA VALLEY

▼▼▼▼ Longstreet Inn, Casino & RV Park ⓈⒽ
(775) 372-1777. **$70-$100.** 373 Stateline. 7 mi n of jct SR 127 and 190 (Death Valley Jct) on SR 373; 15 mi s of jct SR 95 and 373 on SR 373. Int corridors. **Pets:** Cats only. $50 deposit/pet. Service with restrictions, supervision.
[A$K] [S🔥] [✕] [🍴] [🏊]

BATTLE MOUNTAIN

ⓐ ▼▼▼ Battle Mountain Inn Ⓜ
(775) 635-5200. **$49-$59.** 650 W Front St. I-80, exit 229 or 233, 0.5 mi e. Ext corridors. **Pets:** Accepted.
[SAVE] [S🔥] [✕] [🛏] [💻]

ⓐ ▼▼▼ Big Chief Motel Ⓜ
(775) 635-2416. **$39-$49.** 434 W Front St. I-80, exit 229 or 233, just n. Ext corridors. **Pets:** Other species. $5 daily fee/pet. Designated rooms, service with restrictions, supervision.
[SAVE] [S🔥] [✕] [🗐] [🛏] [💻] [🏊]

ⓐ ▼▼▼ Comfort Inn Ⓜ
(775) 635-5880. **$56-$89.** 521 E Front St. I-80, exit 229 or 233, just n. Int corridors. **Pets:** Accepted.
[SAVE] [S🔥] [✕] [🗐] [🛏] [💻] [🏊]

BEATTY

▼ Burro Inn Ⓜ
(775) 553-2225. **$40.** Third St & Hwy 95. 4 blks s on SR 95. Ext corridors. **Pets:** $25 deposit/room, $5 daily fee/pet. Designated rooms, service with restrictions, supervision.
[A$K] [S🔥] [✕] [🗐] [🍴]

▼ Phoenix Inn Ⓜ
(775) 553-2250. **$31-$50.** 350 First St. Just off SR 95. Ext corridors. **Pets:** $5 daily fee/pet. Designated rooms, service with restrictions, supervision.
[A$K] [S🔥] [✕] [🛏]

ⓐ ▼▼ Stagecoach Hotel Casino & RV Park Ⓜ
(775) 553-2419. **$40-$48.** Hwy 95 N. North end of town, west side of US 95. Ext/int corridors. **Pets:** Medium, other species. $10 deposit/pet, $5 one-time fee/pet. Designated rooms, service with restrictions, crate.
[SAVE] [✕] [🗜] [🛏] [🍴] [🏊]

CARLIN

ⓐ ▼▼▼ Comfort Inn Ⓜ
(775) 754-6110. **$59-$89.** 1018 Fir St. I-80, exit 280, just s. Int corridors. **Pets:** Accepted.
[SAVE] [S🔥] [✕] [🗜] [🗐] [🛏] [💻]

CARSON CITY

ⓐ ▼▼ Best Value Inn Ⓜ
(775) 882-2007. **$33-$199.** 2731 S Carson St. 1.3 mi s on US 50 and 395. Ext corridors. **Pets:** Other species. $50 deposit/room. Service with restrictions, supervision.
[SAVE] [S🔥] [✕] [🛏] [🏊]

ⓐ ▼▼▼ Best Western Trailside Inn Ⓜ
(775) 883-7300. **$55-$179.** 1300 N Carson St. 0.5 mi n on US 395. Ext corridors. **Pets:** Other species. $10 daily fee/room. Service with restrictions, supervision.
[SAVE] [S🔥] [✕] [🛏] [💻] [🏊]

ⓐ ▼ Carson City Super 8 Ⓜ
(775) 883-7800. **$34-$199.** 2829 S Carson. South end of town. Int corridors. **Pets:** Large. $10 daily fee/pet. Designated rooms, service with restrictions, supervision.
[SAVE] [S🔥] [✕] [🛏]

ⓐ ▼▼▼ Days Inn Ⓜ
(775) 883-3343. **$50-$140.** 3103 N Carson St. US 395 N, north end of city. Ext corridors. **Pets:** Dogs only. $10 one-time fee/pet. Designated rooms, service with restrictions, supervision.
[SAVE] [S🔥] [✕] [🛏] [💻]

ELKO

ⓐ ▼▼▼▼ Best Western Gold Country Motor Inn Ⓜ
(775) 738-8421. **$69-$109.** 2050 Idaho St. I-80, exit 303, just s. Ext corridors. **Pets:** Accepted.
[SAVE] [S🔥] [✕] [🗜M] [🗐] [🗜] [🛏] [💻] [🍴] [🏊]

▼▼▼ Elko Inn Express Ⓜ
(775) 738-7261. **$64.** 837 Idaho St. I-80, exit 301 or 303, 1 mi s. Ext corridors. **Pets:** Accepted.
[A$K] [S🔥] [✕] [🗐] [🛏] [🏊]

ⓐ ▼▼▼ High Desert Inn ⓈⒽ
(775) 738-8425. **$69.** 3015 Idaho St. I-80, exit 303, just s. Ext/int corridors. **Pets:** Accepted.
[SAVE] [S🔥] [✕] [🗐] [🛏] [💻] [🍴] [🏊]

ⓐ ▼▼▼▼ Holiday Inn Express Hotel & Suites Ⓜ
(775) 777-0990. **$99-$109.** 3019 Idaho St. I-80, exit 303, just s. Int corridors. **Pets:** Accepted.
[SAVE] [S🔥] [✕] [🗜M] [🗐] [🗜] [🛏] [💻]

ⓐ ▼▼▼ Oak Tree Inn Ⓜ
(775) 777-2222. **$59-$79.** 95 Spruce Rd. I-80, exit 301, just n. Int corridors. **Pets:** Accepted.
[SAVE] [S🔥] [✕] [🗜M] [🗜] [🛏] [💻]

(AAA) ▼▼▼▼ Red Lion Inn & Casino SH
(775) 738-2111. **$89-$119.** 2065 Idaho St. I-80, exit 303, just
s. Int corridors. **Pets:** Other species. $15 one-time fee/
room. Service with restrictions, crate.
[SAVE] [S6] [X] [&M] [🐾] [🛏] [🍴] [🏊]

(AAA) ▼▼▼ Thunderbird Motel M
(775) 738-7115. **$59-$69.** 345 Idaho St. I-80, exit 301 or 303,
1 mi s. Ext corridors. **Pets:** Accepted.
[SAVE] [S6] [X] [🐾] [🛏] [🏊]

ELY

(AAA) ▼▼ Fireside Inn M 🐾
(775) 289-3765. **$46.** McGill Hwy. 2 mi n on US 95. Ext
corridors. **Pets:** Medium. $5 daily fee/pet. Service with
restrictions, supervision.
[SAVE] [S6] [X] [🛏] [💻]

**(AAA) ▼▼▼ Historic Hotel Nevada & Gambling
Hall** SH
(775) 289-6665. **$30-$48.** 501 Aultman St. Downtown. Int
corridors. **Pets:** Service with restrictions, supervision.
[SAVE] [S6] [X] [🛏] [🍴]

**(AAA) ▼▼▼▼ Ramada Inn-Copper Queen
Casino** M
(775) 289-4884. **$69-$110.** 805 Great Basin Blvd. 0.3 mi s of
jct US 6, 50 and 93. Ext/int corridors. **Pets:** Other species.
Service with restrictions.
[SAVE] [S6] [X] [&M] [🛏] [💻] [🍴] [🏊]

FALLON

(AAA) ▼▼▼ Comfort Inn M
(775) 423-5554. **$60-$160.** 1830 W Williams Ave. US 50, 1
mi w of US 95. Int corridors. **Pets:** Accepted.
[SAVE] [S6] [X] [&M] [✍] [🛏] [🏊]

▼▼ Microtel Inn & Suites M
(775) 428-0300. **Call for rates.** 1051 W Williams Ave. Just w
of US 95. Int corridors. **Pets:** Accepted.
[S6] [X] [&M] [✍] [🛏]

(AAA) ▼▼ Motel 6 M
(775) 423-2277. **$46-$63, 7 day notice.** 1705 S Taylor St.
0.5 mi s of US 50. Ext corridors. **Pets:** Small, dogs only.
Service with restrictions, supervision.
[SAVE] [S6] [X] [🏊]

▼▼▼ Western Motel M
(775) 423-5118. **$41.** 125 S Carson St. US 95, just e. Ext
corridors. **Pets:** Accepted.
[SAVE] [S6] [X] [🛏] [🏊]

FERNLEY

(AAA) ▼▼▼ Best Western Fernley Inn M
(775) 575-6776. **$68-$88.** 1405 E Newlands Dr. I-80, exit 48,
just s. Ext corridors. **Pets:** $7 one-time fee/pet. Designated
rooms, service with restrictions, supervision.
[SAVE] [S6] [X] [&M] [🐾] [🛏] [💻] [🏊]

GARDNERVILLE

(AAA) ▼▼▼ Topaz Lodge M
(775) 266-3338. **$55-$75.** 1979 US 395 S. US 395 S at
Topaz Lake, 22 mi s. Ext corridors. **Pets:** Small, dogs only.
$10 daily fee/pet. Designated rooms, service with restric-
tions.
[SAVE] [X] [🍴] [🏊]

(AAA) ▼▼▼ Westerner Motel M
(775) 782-3602. **$40-$65.** 1353 US 395 N. US 395 S; end of
town. Ext corridors. **Pets:** Other species. Designated
rooms, service with restrictions, supervision.
[SAVE] [X] [🛏] [💻] [🏊]

HAWTHORNE

(AAA) ▼▼▼ El Capitan Resort Casino M
(775) 945-3321. **$54-$60.** 540 F St. Just n of US 95. Ext
corridors. **Pets:** Accepted.
[SAVE] [X] [🛏] [🍴] [🏊]

JACKPOT

(AAA) ▼▼▼▼ Horseshu Hotel & Casino SH
(775) 755-7777. **$29-$85.** 1385 Hwy 93. On SR 93. Int corridors. **Pets:** Other species. Designated rooms, service with
restrictions.
[SAVE] [X] [💻] [🍴] [🏊] [X]

▼▼ West Star Resort M 🐾
(775) 755-2600. **$32-$75.** Hwy 93 & Poker St. Just w of SR
93. Int corridors. **Pets:** Medium. $5 daily fee/pet. Desig-
nated rooms, service with restrictions.
[ASK] [X] [&M] [✍] [💻]

NEARBY CALIFORNIA
LAKE TAHOE AREA

STATELINE

(AAA) ▼▼▼ ▼▼ Harveys Casino & Resort LH
(775) 588-2411. **$121-$230, 3 day notice.** US 50, in casino
center. Int corridors. **Pets:** Accepted.
[SAVE] [X] [&M] [✍] [💻] [🍴] [🏊] [X]

▼▼▼▼ Lake Village Resort CO
(775) 589-6065. **$145-$425, 30 day notice.** 301 Hwy 50.
Near casino center. Ext corridors. **Pets:** Accepted.
[ASK] [S6] [X] [🛏] [💻] [🏊] [X] [🎿]

🐾 END AREA 🐾

LAS VEGAS METROPOLITAN AREA

BOULDER CITY

Best Western Lighthouse Inn & Resort M
(702) 293-6444. **$49-$99.** 110 Ville Dr. 1 mi e on US 93. Ext corridors. **Pets:** Accepted.

El Rancho Boulder Motel M
(702) 293-1085. **$80.** 725 Nevada Way. On US 93. Ext corridors. **Pets:** Accepted.

Super 8 Motel M
(702) 294-8888. **$50-$100.** 704 Nevada Way. On US 93. Ext corridors. **Pets:** Medium, dogs only. $10 daily fee/pet. Service with restrictions, supervision.

ECHO BAY

Echo Bay Resort M
(702) 394-4000. **$85-$115, 3 day notice.** 4 mi e of SR 167; on Lake Mead. Int corridors. **Pets:** Dogs only. $50 deposit/pet, $10 daily fee/pet. Service with restrictions, supervision.

HENDERSON

Green Valley Ranch LH
(702) 617-7777. **$159-$450.** 2300 S Paseo Verde Dr. I-215, exit Green Valley Pkwy, just s. **Pets:** Accepted.

Hawthorn Inn & Suites M
(702) 568-7800. **$79-$139.** 910 S Boulder Hwy. S of Lake Mead Blvd. Int corridors. **Pets:** Accepted.

Residence Inn-Green Valley M
(702) 434-2700. **$114-$144.** 2190 Olympic Ave. I-215, exit Green Valley Pkwy N. Int corridors. **Pets:** Accepted.

The Ritz-Carlton, Lake Las Vegas LH
(702) 567-4700. **$199-$589.** 1610 Lake Las Vegas Pkwy. I-215, e to end, n on Lake Las Vegas Pkwy, then 0.5 mi on right. Int corridors. **Pets:** Accepted.

INDIAN SPRINGS

Indian Springs Motor Hotel M
(702) 879-3700. **$39-$45.** 300 Tonopah Hwy. On US 95, 45 mi n of Las Vegas. Int corridors. **Pets:** Small, other species. $5 daily fee/pet. Crate.

LAS VEGAS

AmeriSuites (Las Vegas/Paradise Road) SH
(702) 369-3366. **$59-$159.** 4520 Paradise Ave. Cross streets Harmon and Paradise, e of the Strip. Int corridors. **Pets:** Accepted.

Best Western Main Street Inn M
(702) 382-3455. **$39-$149.** 1000 N Main St. I-15, exit 43E northbound; exit 44E southbound. Ext corridors. **Pets:** Large, other species. $8 daily fee/pet. Service with restrictions.

Best Western Nellis Motor Inn M
(702) 643-6111. **$54-$200.** 5330 E Craig Rd. I-15, exit 48 eastbound, 7 mi ne; 0.3 mi from Nellis AFB. Ext corridors. **Pets:** Other species. $10 daily fee/pet. Service with restrictions, supervision.

Best Western Parkview Inn M
(702) 385-1213. **$49-$149.** 921 Las Vegas Blvd N. I-15, exit US 93-95, 0.3 mi n at Washington. Ext corridors. **Pets:** Medium, other species. $8 daily fee/pet. Service with restrictions, supervision.

Candlewood Suites SH
(702) 836-3660. **$89-$209.** 4034 S Paradise Rd. I-15, exit E Flamingo Rd to Paradise Rd, just ne. Int corridors. **Pets:** Accepted.

Comfort Inn M
(702) 399-1500. **$69-$299.** 910 E Cheyenne Ave. I-15, exit 46 (Cheyenne Ave W). Int corridors. **Pets:** Accepted.

Crowne Plaza LH
(702) 369-4400. **$99-$259, 3 day notice.** 4255 S Paradise Rd. I-15, exit Flamingo Rd, 0.5 mi e to Paradise Rd, 0.3 mi s. Int corridors. **Pets:** Accepted.

Four Seasons Hotel Las Vegas LH
(702) 632-5000. **$250-$500.** 3960 Las Vegas Blvd S. I-15, exit E Tropicana Ave, just s on the Strip. Int corridors. **Pets:** Small, dogs only. Designated rooms, service with restrictions, supervision.

Hampton Inn Las Vegas M
(702) 360-5700. **$59-$99, 30 day notice.** 7100 Cascade Valley Ct. I-95, exit W Cheyenne Ave, just s on Tenaya Way. Int corridors. **Pets:** Small. $25 one-time fee/pet. Service with restrictions, supervision.

▼▼◆▼ **Hawthorn Suites-Las Vegas** M
(702) 739-7000. **$69-$309.** 5051 Duke Ellington Way. I-15, exit E Tropicana Ave, 0.8 mi e to Duke Ellington Way, then just s. Ext corridors. **Pets:** Accepted.

◆◆◆ ▼▼◆▼ **Holiday Inn Express** M
(702) 256-3766. **$69-$150.** 8669 W Sahara Ave. I-15, exit Sahara Ave, 6.5 mi w at Durango. Int corridors. **Pets:** Dogs only. $20 one-time fee/pet. Designated rooms, service with restrictions, supervision.

▼▼◆▼ **Holiday Inn Express Hotel & Suites N Las Vegas** M
(702) 649-3000. **$62-$80.** 4540 Donovan Way. I-15, exit W Craig Rd. Int corridors. **Pets:** Accepted.

▼▼ **Homestead Studio Suites** M
(702) 369-1414. **$60.** 3045 S Maryland Pkwy. I-15, exit Sahara Ave E, just s. Int corridors. **Pets:** Accepted.

▼ **Howard Johnson Airport Inn** M
(702) 798-2777. **$59-$159, 7 day notice.** 5100 Paradise Rd. I-15, exit E Tropicana Ave, 1.8 mi to Paradise Rd, then 0.3 mi s. Ext corridors. **Pets:** $50 one-time fee/pet. Designated rooms, service with restrictions, supervision.

◆◆◆ ▼▼◆ **Howard Johnson Las Vegas Strip** M
(702) 388-0301. **$39-$159.** 1401 Las Vegas Blvd S. I-15, exit Las Vegas Blvd, just n. Ext/int corridors. **Pets:** Small. $10 daily fee/pet. Designated rooms, service with restrictions.

◆◆◆ ▼▼◆ **La Quinta Inn** M
(702) 798-7736. **$59-$250.** 4975 S Valley View Blvd. I-15, exit Tropicana Ave W. Int corridors. **Pets:** Designated rooms, service with restrictions, supervision.

▼▼◆▼ **La Quinta Inn Convention Center** M
(702) 796-9000. **$80-$110.** 3970 Paradise Rd. I-15, exit E Flamingo Rd, 0.8 mi s of convention center; 0.5 mi e of the Strip. Int corridors. **Pets:** Accepted.

▼▼◆▼ **La Quinta Inn-Nellis** M ❀
(702) 632-0229. **$79-$139.** 4288 N Nellis Blvd. I-15, exit Craig St, e to N Las Vegas Blvd. Int corridors. **Pets:** Large, other species. $25 one-time fee/pet. Service with restrictions.

▼▼◆▼ **La Quinta Las Vegas NW Tech Center** M
(702) 360-1200. **$71-$96.** 7101 Cascade Valley Ct. US 95, exit W Cheyenne Ave. Int corridors. **Pets:** Other species. Service with restrictions.

◆◆◆ ▼▼◆ **La Quinta Suites** M
(702) 243-0356. **$79-$199.** 9570 W Sahara Ave. Just w of Fort Apache. Int corridors. **Pets:** Large. Designated rooms, service with restrictions, supervision.

▼▼◆ **Motel 6 Boulder Highway** M
(702) 457-8051. **$36-$81.** 4125 Boulder Hwy. Just s of Sahara Ave. Ext corridors. **Pets:** Medium, other species. Service with restrictions, supervision.

▼▼◆▼ **Residence Inn-Hughes Center** M
(702) 650-0040. **$99-$300.** 370 Hughes Center Dr. I-15, exit Paradise Rd. Int corridors. **Pets:** Medium. $10 daily fee/room, $50 one-time fee/room.

▼◆▼▼ **Residence Inn Las Vegas Convention Center** M
(702) 796-9300. **$119-$289.** 3225 Paradise Rd. Opposite the convention center. Ext corridors. **Pets:** Medium, other species. $10 daily fee/pet, $50 one-time fee/room. Designated rooms, service with restrictions, crate.

▼▼◆ **Super 8 Motel Las Vegas Strip** M
(702) 794-0888. **$61-$225.** 4250 S Koval Ln. I-15, exit S Koval Ln. Int corridors. **Pets:** $15 daily fee/pet. Designated rooms, service with restrictions, supervision.

◆◆◆ ▼▼◆▼ **Wellesley Inn & Suites (Las Vegas/ East Flamingo)** M
(702) 731-3111. **$49-$79.** 1550 E Flamingo Rd. I-15, exit E Flamingo Rd, then 2 mi. Int corridors. **Pets:** Accepted.

LAUGHLIN

▼▼◆▼ **Don Laughlin's Riverside Resort Hotel & Casino** LH
(702) 298-2535. **$39-$199, 7 day notice.** 1650 S Casino Dr. 2 mi s of Davis Dam. Int corridors. **Pets:** Accepted.

MESQUITE

▼▼ **Budget Inn & Suites** M
(702) 346-7444. **$49-$69.** 390 N Sandhill. I-15, exit 122. Ext corridors. **Pets:** Medium. $10 daily fee/room. Designated rooms, service with restrictions, supervision.

▼▼ **Virgin River Hotel Casino Bingo** M
(702) 346-7777. **$19-$99.** 100 Pioneer Blvd. I-15, exit 122, just w. Ext corridors. **Pets:** Medium, other species. $25 deposit/room. Designated rooms, service with restrictions, supervision.

OVERTON

▼▼◆▼ **Best Western North Shore Inn at Lake Mead** M
(702) 397-6000. **$55-$69.** 520 N Moapa Valley Blvd. I-15, exit 93, 10 mi ne on SR 169. Int corridors. **Pets:** Medium. $10 daily fee/room. Designated rooms, service with restrictions, supervision.

PAHRUMP

AAA ▼▼▼ **Best Western Pahrump Station** M
(775) 727-5100. **$51-$129.** 1101 S Hwy 160. Downtown. Ext corridors. **Pets:** Accepted.
[SAVE] [S🐾] [✕] [🐾] [📱] [💻] [🏊]

AAA ▼▼▼ **Saddle West Hotel & Casino** M
(775) 727-1111. **$46-$61.** 1220 S Hwy 160. Downtown. Ext corridors. **Pets:** Medium. $100 deposit/room. Designated rooms, service with restrictions, supervision.
[SAVE] [S🐾] [✕] [🐾M] [🐾] [📱] [💻] [🍴] [🏊]

❖ **END METROPOLITAN AREA** ❖

LOVELOCK

▼▼▼▼ **Ramada Inn-Sturgeon's Casino** M ❖
(775) 273-2971. **$53-$59.** 1420 Cornell Ave. I-80, exit 105 or 107, just n. Ext corridors. **Pets:** Other species. $5 one-time fee/room. Designated rooms, service with restrictions, supervision.
[ASK] [S🐾] [✕] [🐾M] [🐾] [📱] [💻] [🍴] [🏊]

MINDEN

AAA ▼▼▼▼ **Best Western Minden Inn** M
(775) 782-7766. **$59-$129.** 1795 Ironwood Dr. US 395, exit Ironwood Dr W, 0.5 mi n of jct US 395 and SR 88. Ext corridors. **Pets:** Large, dogs only. $15 daily fee/pet. Service with restrictions.
[SAVE] [S🐾] [✕] [🐾] [📱] [💻] [🏊]

▼▼▼ **Holiday Lodge** M
(775) 782-2288. **$38-$49.** 1591 US 395 N. Center. Ext corridors. **Pets:** Large, dogs only. $20 deposit/pet, $5 daily fee/pet. Designated rooms, supervision.
[✕] [📱] [🏊]

RENO

AAA ▼▼▼ **A&A's Rodeway Inn & Spa** M ❖
(775) 786-2500. **$36-$169.** 2050 Market St. I-395, exit W Mill St. Int corridors. **Pets:** Other species. $50 deposit/pet. Service with restrictions, supervision.
[SAVE] [S🐾] [✕] [📱] [💻] [🏊]

AAA ▼▼▼▼ **Best Western Airport Plaza**
Hotel SH ❖
(775) 348-6370. **$79-$249.** 1981 Terminal Way. US 395, exit E Plumb Villanova. Int corridors. **Pets:** Medium. $50 deposit/room, $10 daily fee/pet. Designated rooms, supervision.
[SAVE] [S🐾] [✕] [🐾M] [🐾] [📱] [💻] [🍴] [🏊] [✕]

AAA ▼▼ **Days Inn** M
(775) 786-4070. **$30-$185.** 701 E 7th St. I-80, exit Wells Ave, just s. Ext corridors. **Pets:** Other species. $10 daily fee/pet. Designated rooms.
[SAVE] [S🐾] [✕] [📱] [🏊]

AAA ▼▼ **Easy 8 Motel** M
(775) 322-4588. **$39-$200.** 255 W 5th St. I-80, exit Keystone, 4 blks e. Ext corridors. **Pets:** Accepted.
[SAVE] [S🐾] [✕]

▼▼▼ **Golden Phoenix Hotel & Casino** LH
(775) 785-7100. **$29-$79.** 255 N Sierra St. I-80, exit S Virginia St. Int corridors. **Pets:** Accepted.
[ASK] [S🐾] [✕] [🐾M] [🐾] [📱] [💻] [🍴]

AAA ▼▼▼▼ **Holiday Inn-Downtown** SH ❖
(775) 786-5151. **$69-$299.** 1000 E 6th St. I-80, exit Wells Ave, 12 blks e. Int corridors. **Pets:** Medium. $15 daily fee/pet. Designated rooms, service with restrictions, supervision.
[SAVE] [S🐾] [✕] [🐾] [📱] [💻] [🍴] [🏊]

▼▼▼ **La Quinta Inn** M
(775) 348-6100. **$71-$96.** 4001 Market St. US 395, exit airport northbound; exit Villanova Dr southbound. Ext corridors. **Pets:** Small, other species. Service with restrictions, supervision.
[✕] [🐾M] [🐾] [📱] [💻] [🏊]

AAA ▼▼▼ **Reno Downtown Travelodge** M
(775) 329-3451. **$29-$199.** 655 W 4th St. I-80, exit Keystone, just e. Ext corridors. **Pets:** Other species. $8 daily fee/room. Designated rooms, service with restrictions, supervision.
[SAVE] [S🐾] [✕] [📱] [💻] [🏊]

AAA ▼▼▼▼ **Residence Inn by Marriott** M
(775) 853-8800. **$109-$209.** 9845 Gateway Dr. US 395, exit S Meadows Pkwy, then e. Int corridors. **Pets:** Accepted.
[SAVE] [S🐾] [✕] [🐾M] [🐾] [📱] [💻] [🏊] [✕]

AAA ▼▼▼ **Seasons Inn** M
(775) 322-6000. **$38-$129.** 495 West St. Corner of West and 5th sts; 1 blk w of casinos. Ext corridors. **Pets:** Accepted.
[SAVE] [✕]

AAA ▼▼▼ **Super 8 Motel at Meadow Wood**
Courtyard M ❖
(775) 829-4600. **$49-$139.** 5851 S Virginia St. US 395 at S McCarran Blvd. Ext corridors. **Pets:** Other species. $10 daily fee/pet. Designated rooms, service with restrictions.
[SAVE] [S🐾] [✕] [🐾M] [🐾] [📱] [💻] [🍴] [🏊]

AAA ▼▼ **Super 8 Motel (Miners Inn)** M
(775) 329-3464. **$39-$140.** 1651 N Virginia St. Opposite University of Nevada. Ext corridors. **Pets:** $10 daily fee/pet. Designated rooms, service with restrictions, supervision.
[SAVE] [S🐾] [✕] [📱] [🏊]

▼▼ **Travelodge Airport** M ❖
(775) 786-2506. **$35-$190.** 2050-B Market St. I-395, exit W Mill St, just w. Int corridors. **Pets:** Other species. $50 deposit/pet. Service with restrictions, supervision.
[ASK] [S🐾] [✕] [📱] [💻] [🏊]

▼▼ **Truckee River Lodge** M 🐾
(775) 786-8888. **$48.** 501 W 1st St. I-80, exit Virginia St, just w. Ext/int corridors. **Pets:** Other species. $10 daily fee/pet. Service with restrictions, supervision.
[ASK] [S🐾] [✕] [📱] [💻] [🍴]

AAA ▽ Vagabond Inn **M** ❀
(775) 825-7134. **$50-$79.** 3131 S Virginia St. 2.5 mi s on US 395. Ext corridors. **Pets:** Other species. $10 daily fee/room. Designated rooms, service with restrictions.
SAVE Sb X 🗎 🖥 💻 🏊

TONOPAH

AAA ▽▽▽ Best Western Hi-Desert Inn **M**
(775) 482-3511. **$69-$89.** 320 Main St. On US 6 and 95. Int corridors. **Pets:** Dogs only. Designated rooms, service with restrictions, supervision.
SAVE Sb X 🗎 🖥 💻 🏊

AAA ▽▽▽ Jim Butler Motel **M**
(775) 482-3577. **$50-$56.** 100 S Main St. On US 6 and 95; downtown. Ext corridors. **Pets:** Accepted.
SAVE Sb X 🗎

▽▽ Ramada Inn-Tonopah Station **M**
(775) 482-9777. **$50-$58.** 1100 Main St. On US 6 and 95. Int corridors. **Pets:** Other species. Service with restrictions.
ASK Sb X 🗎 🍴

UNIONVILLE

▽▽ Old Pioneer Garden **BB**
(775) 538-7585. **$95.** 2805 Unionville Rd. I-80, exit 149, 16 mi s, then 2.5 mi w. Int corridors. **Pets:** Service with restrictions, supervision.
X 🗎 🖥

WELLS

AAA ▽▽▽ Best Western Sage Inn **M**
(775) 752-3353. **$49-$65.** 576 6th St. I-80, exit 352, 0.5 mi n. Ext corridors. **Pets:** Accepted.
SAVE Sb X 🗎 💻 🏊

AAA ▽▽▽ Super 8 Motel **M**
(775) 752-3384. **$49-$69.** 930 6th St. I-80, 0.5 mi w of jct US 93. Ext corridors. **Pets:** Accepted.
SAVE Sb X 🗎 🏊

WEST WENDOVER

▽▽ Wendover Super 8 **M**
(775) 664-2888. **$40-$100.** 1325 Wendover Blvd. I-80, exit 410, 0.5 mi w. Int corridors. **Pets:** Accepted.
ASK Sb X 🗎 🗎

WINNEMUCCA

AAA ▽▽▽ Best Western Gold Country Inn **M**
(775) 623-6999. **$89-$119.** 921 W Winnemucca Blvd. I-80, exit 176 or 178, just s. Int corridors. **Pets:** Accepted.
SAVE Sb X 🗎 🏊

AAA ▽▽▽ Best Western Holiday Motel **M**
(775) 623-3684. **$59-$94.** 670 W Winnemucca Blvd. I-80, exit 176 or 178, just s. Ext corridors. **Pets:** Other species. $20 deposit/pet. Service with restrictions, supervision.
SAVE Sb X 🗎 💻 🏊

AAA ▽▽▽ Days Inn **M**
(775) 623-3661. **$59-$99.** 511 W Winnemucca Blvd. I-80, exit 176 or 178, just s. Ext corridors. **Pets:** $10 one-time fee/room. Service with restrictions, supervision.
SAVE Sb X 🗎 💻 🏊

▽▽ Holiday Inn Express **M**
(775) 625-3100. **$59-$99, 30 day notice.** 1987 W Winnemucca Blvd. I-80, exit 176, just s. Int corridors. **Pets:** Other species. $40 deposit/pet, $10 one-time fee/pet. Service with restrictions, supervision.
ASK X 🗎 🖥 🗎

AAA ▽▽▽ Red Lion Hotel & Casino **SH**
(775) 623-2565. **$89-$119.** 741 W Winnemucca Blvd. I-80, exit 176 or 178, just s. Int corridors. **Pets:** Accepted.
SAVE Sb X 🗎 🖥 💻 🍴 🏊

AAA ▽▽ Scott Shady Court Motel **M**
(775) 623-3646. **$38-$55.** 400 First St. I-80, exit 176 or 178, 0.3 mi n on Pavilion. Ext corridors. **Pets:** Service with restrictions, supervision.
SAVE 💻 🏊

▽▽ Super 8 Motel **M**
(775) 625-1818. **$48-$62.** 1157 W Winnemucca Blvd. I-80, exit 176, 0.5 mi e. Int corridors. **Pets:** Other species. $50 deposit/room, $10 daily fee/room. Service with restrictions, supervision.
ASK Sb X 🗎

AAA ▽▽▽ Town House Motel **M**
(775) 623-3620. **$40-$58.** 375 Monroe St. I-80, exit 176 or 178, just s. Ext corridors. **Pets:** Medium. Service with restrictions, supervision.
SAVE Sb X 🗎 💻 🏊

▽▽ Val-U Motel **M**
(775) 623-5248. **$45-$49.** 125 E Winnemucca Blvd. I-80, exit 178, just s. Int corridors. **Pets:** Service with restrictions, supervision.
ASK Sb X 🗎 🏊

BARTLETT

The Villager Motel M
(603) 374-2742. **$49-$159, 10 day notice.** US 302. 1 mi e on US 302; 1.3 mi w of Attitash Mountain. Ext corridors. **Pets:** Accepted.

BETHLEHEM

The Mulburn Inn at Bethlehem BB
(603) 869-3389. **$90-$175, 14 day notice.** 2370 Main St. I-93, exit 40, 3.5 mi e on US 302. Int corridors. **Pets:** Other species. $15 one-time fee/pet. Designated rooms, supervision.

CAMPTON

Super 8 Motel SH
(603) 536-3520. **Call for rates.** 1513 US 3. I-93, exit 27, just ne. Int corridors. **Pets:** Accepted.

CHESTERFIELD

Chesterfield Inn CI
(603) 256-3211. **$150-$250, 5 day notice.** 399 Cross Rd. I-91, exit 3, 2 mi e on SR 9. Ext/int corridors. **Pets:** Other species. Service with restrictions, supervision.

CLAREMONT

Best Budget Inn M
(603) 542-9567. **$53-$70, 3 day notice.** 24 Sullivan St. Just n of jct SR 11/12/103/120; center. Ext corridors. **Pets:** Medium, dogs only. $15 daily fee/pet. Designated rooms, service with restrictions, supervision.

COLEBROOK

Northern Comfort Motel M
(603) 237-4440. **$64-$74, 3 day notice.** Rt 3. 1.5 mi s. Ext corridors. **Pets:** $5 daily fee/pet. No service, supervision.

CONCORD

Best Western Concord Inn & Suites SH
(603) 228-4300. **$59-$199.** 97 Hall St. I-93, exit 13, just n on Main St, then 0.5 mi w. Int corridors. **Pets:** Small. $10 daily fee/pet. Service with restrictions, supervision.

Concord Comfort Inn SH
(603) 226-4100. **$59-$119.** 71 Hall St. I-93, exit 13, just n on Main St, then 0.3 mi w. Int corridors. **Pets:** Accepted.

CONWAY

White Deer Motel M
(603) 447-5366. **$49-$149, 3 day notice.** 379 White Mountain Hwy. 2.1 mi s of jct US 302, 0.5 mi n of village center on SR 16. Ext/int corridors. **Pets:** Other species. $35 deposit/room, $10 daily fee/pet. Designated rooms, supervision.

DOVER

Days Inn M
(603) 742-0400. **$80-$140.** 481 Central Ave. Spaulding Tpke, exit 7, 2 mi n on SR 108; downtown. Ext/int corridors. **Pets:** Other species. $50 deposit/room. Service with restrictions, supervision.

DURHAM

Hickory Pond Inn & Golf Course BB
(603) 659-2227. **$119-$139, 3 day notice.** 1 Stagecoach Rd. 2.8 mi s on SR 108. Int corridors. **Pets:** Accepted.

EATON CENTER

Inn at Crystal Lake CI
(603) 447-2120. **$89-$239, 14 day notice.** 2356 Eaton Rd. On SR 153; center. Ext/int corridors. **Pets:** Accepted.

FRANCONIA

△△△ ▽▽▽ Franconia Village Hotel Resort & Conference Center **SH**
(603) 823-7422. **$59-$119, 3 day notice.** 87 Wallace Hill Rd. I-93, exit 38, just e. Int corridors. **Pets:** Other species. Service with restrictions, crate.

[SAVE] [S🐾] [✕] [🔒] [💻] [🍴] [🏊] [✕]

△△△ ▽▽▽ Gale River Motel **M** ❀
(603) 823-5655. **$75-$105, 7 day notice.** 1 Main St. I-93, exit 38, 0.8 mi n on SR 18. Ext corridors. **Pets:** Medium, other species. $10 daily fee/pet. Designated rooms, service with restrictions, supervision.

[SAVE] [✕] [🔒] [💻] [🏊] [✕]

GORHAM

▽▽▽ Colonial Comfort Inn **M**
(603) 466-2732. **$48-$130, 3 day notice.** 370 Main St. Jct US 2 and SR 16. Ext corridors. **Pets:** Service with restrictions, supervision.

[✕] [🔒] [🍴]

▽▽▽ Moose Brook Motel **M**
(603) 466-5400. **$39-$79, 5 day notice.** 65 Lancaster Rd. Jct SR 16, 0.5 mi w on US 2. Ext corridors. **Pets:** Medium. $5 one-time fee/pet. Designated rooms, service with restrictions, supervision.

[✕] [🔒] [🏊]

▽▽▽ Mt Madison Motel **M**
(603) 466-3622. **$47-$124, 3 day notice.** 365 Main St. 1.2 mi n on US 2 and SR 16. Ext corridors. **Pets:** Accepted.

[ASK] [S🐾] [✕] [🔒] [🏊]

▽▽▽ Royalty Inn **SH**
(603) 466-3312. **$61-$102.** 130 Main St. On US 2 and SR 16; center. Ext/int corridors. **Pets:** Other species. $5 daily fee/room. Designated rooms, service with restrictions, supervision.

[✕] [🔒M] [🔒] [💻] [🍴] [🏊] [✕]

△△△ ▽▽▽ Top Notch Inn **M** ❀
(603) 466-5496. **$44-$142.** 265 Main St. On US 2 and SR 16; center. Ext/int corridors. **Pets:** Medium, dogs only. Designated rooms, service with restrictions, supervision.

[SAVE] [S🐾] [✕] [🔒] [🔒] [💻] [🏊]

▽▽▽ Town & Country Motor Inn **SH**
(603) 466-3315. **$58-$96.** US Rt 2. 0.5 mi e of jct SR 16. Ext/int corridors. **Pets:** $6 daily fee/pet. Service with restrictions, crate.

[✕] [🔒] [🍴] [🏊] [✕]

HAMPTON

▽▽▽▽ Lamie's Inn & Tavern **CI** ❀
(603) 926-0330. **$95-$145, 3 day notice.** 490 Lafayette Rd. Jct SR 27 on US 1. Int corridors. **Pets:** Medium, other species. $50 deposit/pet, $10 daily fee/pet. Designated rooms, service with restrictions, supervision.

[ASK] [S🐾] [✕] [🔒] [🔒] [🍴]

HAMPTON FALLS

△△△ ▽▽▽▽ Hampton Falls Inn **M**
(603) 926-9545. **$69-$169.** 11 Lafayette Rd. I-95, exit 1, 0.5 mi e on SR 107, 1 mi n on US 1. Int corridors. **Pets:** Medium, dogs only. $50 deposit/pet. Designated rooms, service with restrictions, supervision.

[SAVE] [S🐾] [✕] [🔒] [🍴] [🏊]

HANOVER

△△△ ▽▽▽ Chieftain Motor Inn **M**
(603) 643-2550. **$100-$150.** 84 Lyme Rd. I-91, exit 13; SR 10, 2.5 mi n. Ext corridors. **Pets:** Dogs only. $20 one-time fee/room. Designated rooms, service with restrictions, crate.

[SAVE] [✕] [🔒] [🏊] [✕]

HARTS LOCATION

▽▽▽▽ Notchland Inn **CI**
(603) 374-6131. **$190-$300, 14 day notice.** US 302. From Bartlett, 6.4 mi w. Int corridors. **Pets:** Other species. $10 daily fee/pet. Designated rooms, service with restrictions, crate.

[✕] [🍴] [✕]

KEENE

▽▽▽▽ Best Western Sovereign Hotel **SH**
(603) 357-3038. **$69-$195.** 401 Winchester St. SR 10, just s of jct SR 12 and 101. Int corridors. **Pets:** Other species. $10 one-time fee/pet. Service with restrictions, supervision.

[ASK] [S🐾] [✕] [🎱] [🔒] [💻] [🍴] [🏊]

▽▽▽▽ Holiday Inn Express **SH**
(603) 352-7616. **$100-$180.** 175 Key Rd. SR 101, just n, via Winchester St, then 0.3 mi w. Int corridors. **Pets:** Accepted.

[✕] [🔒M] [🎱] [🔒] [🔒] [💻] [🏊]

△△△ ▽▽▽ Super 8 Keene **M**
(603) 352-9780. **$70-$150.** 3 Ashbrook Rd. Jct SR 9 and 12, just w. Int corridors. **Pets:** Other species. $20 one-time fee/room. Service with restrictions, supervision.

[SAVE] [S🐾] [✕] [🔒M] [🔒]

LEBANON

▽▽▽▽ Days Inn **M**
(603) 448-5070. **$89-$189.** 135 SR 120. I-89, exit 18, 0.8 mi n. Ext/int corridors. **Pets:** Accepted.

[ASK] [S🐾] [✕] [🔒]

▽▽▽▽ Residence Inn by Marriott-Lebanon **SH**
(603) 643-4511. **$149-$299.** 32 Centerra Pkwy. I-89, exit 18, 2.5 mi n on SR 120. Int corridors. **Pets:** Accepted.

[ASK] [S🐾] [✕] [🔒M] [🎱] [🔒] [🔒] [💻] [🏊]

LINCOLN

△△△ ▽▽▽ Parker's Motel **M**
(603) 745-8341. **$39-$99, 3 day notice.** US 3. I-93, exit 33 (US 3), 2 mi ne. Ext corridors. **Pets:** $5 daily fee/pet. Designated rooms, service with restrictions.

[SAVE] [S🐾] [✕] [🔒] [🏊] [✕]

LISBON

▼▼▼ Ammonoosuc Inn 🆑
(603) 838-6118. **$65-$130, 14 day notice.** 641 Bishop Rd. US 302 and SR 10, just nw on Lyman Rd, then 1 mi sw. Int corridors. **Pets:** Accepted.
ASK Sᴅ ✕ 🍴 ✕ 🖊 📺 🖊

LITTLETON

🔼🔼 ▼▼▼ Eastgate Motor Inn Ⓜ
(603) 444-3971. **$49-$99.** 335 Cottage St. I-93, exit 41, just e. Ext/int corridors. **Pets:** Accepted.
SAVE ✕ 🍴 🖊 ✕

▼▼ Historic Thayers Inn 🆂🅷
(603) 444-6469. **$59-$99.** 111 Main St. I-93, exit 42, 1.3 mi e on US 302 and SR 10; center. Int corridors. **Pets:** Accepted.
Sᴅ ✕ 🖥

▼▼ Littleton Motel Ⓜ
(603) 444-5780. **$58-$82.** 166 Main St. I-93, exit 42, 1.2 mi e on US 302 and SR 10; center. Ext corridors. **Pets:** Medium. $10 one-time fee/room. Supervision.
✕ 🖥 🖊

LOUDON

▼▼▼ Lovejoy Farm Bed & Breakfast 🅱🅱
(603) 783-4007. **$99-$109, 14 day notice.** 268 Lovejoy Rd. Jct SR 106 and 129, just w on SR 129, just nw on Village Rd, then 1.2 mi n. Int corridors. **Pets:** Medium. Designated rooms, supervision.
✕ ✕ 🖊 🖊

MANCHESTER

▼▼▼ Center of New Hampshire-Holiday Inn 🅻🅷
(603) 625-1000. **$109-$179.** 700 Elm St. Jct Granite St; downtown. Int corridors. **Pets:** Large. $25 one-time fee/pet. Service with restrictions, supervision.
ASK Sᴅ ✕ 🚭 🖊 🖥 🖥 🖥 🍴 🖊 ✕

▼▼▼ Holiday Inn Express Hotel & Suites–Manchester Airport 🆂🅷
(603) 669-6800. **$129-$159.** 1298 S Porter St. I-293, exit 1. Int corridors. **Pets:** Large, other species. $50 deposit/room. Service with restrictions, crate.
ASK Sᴅ ✕ 🚭 🖊 🖥 🖥 🖊

▼▼ TownePlace Suites by Marriott 🆂🅷 ✿
(603) 641-2288. **$119-$139.** 686 Huse Rd. I-293, exit 1, 0.5 mi se on SR 28. Int corridors. **Pets:** Other species. $175 one-time fee/room.
ASK Sᴅ ✕ 🚭 🖊 🖥 🖥 🖥 🖊

MERRIMACK

▼▼ Days Inn Merrimack Ⓜ
(603) 429-4600. **$60-$80.** 242 Daniel Webster Hwy. Everett Tpke, exit 11, just e, then 0.7 mi s on US 3. Int corridors. **Pets:** Accepted.
ASK Sᴅ ✕ 🚭 🖊 🖊 🖥 🖥

▼▼▼ Residence Inn by Marriott 🆂🅷
(603) 424-8100. **$89-$159.** 246 Daniel Webster Hwy. Everett Tpke, exit 11, just e, then 0.6 mi s on US 3. Ext/int corridors. **Pets:** Accepted.
ASK Sᴅ ✕ 🚭 🖊 🖊 🖥 🖥 🖊 ✕

NASHUA

▼▼▼ Holiday Inn Nashua 🆂🅷
(603) 888-1551. **$75-$150.** 9 Northeastern Blvd. US 3 (Everett Tpke), exit 4, just w, then 0.3 mi n. Int corridors. **Pets:** Small, other species. $25 one-time fee/room. No service, supervision.
ASK Sᴅ ✕ 🚭 🖊 🖥 🖥 🍴 🖊

▼▼▼ Nashua Marriott 🅻🅷
(603) 880-9100. **$89-$150.** 2200 Southwood Dr. US 3 (Everett Tpke) exit 8, just w. Int corridors. **Pets:** Medium. Service with restrictions, supervision.
ASK ✕ 🚭 🖊 🖥 🖥 🖥 🍴 🖊 ✕

🔼🔼 ▼▼▼ Red Roof Inn Ⓜ
(603) 888-1893. **$54-$84.** 77 Spitbrook Rd. US 3 (Everett Tpke), exit 1, just e. Ext corridors. **Pets:** Medium, other species. Service with restrictions, supervision.
SAVE ✕ 🚭 🖊 🖊 🖥

NEWBURY

🔼🔼 ▼▼▼ Best Western Sunapee Lake Lodge 🆂🅷
(603) 763-2010. **$99-$289, 14 day notice.** 1403 Rt 103. Jct SR 103B, just e. Int corridors. **Pets:** $8 daily fee/pet. Designated rooms, supervision.
SAVE Sᴅ ✕ 🚭 🖊 🖊 🖥 🖥 🖊 ✕

NEW CASTLE

🔼🔼 ▼▼▼▼ Wentworth By The Sea Marriott Hotel & Spa 🅻🅷
(603) 422-7322. **$159-$369, 3 day notice.** 588 Wentworth Rd. On SR 1B, 2 mi e of SR 1A. Ext/int corridors. **Pets:** Medium. Service with restrictions, supervision.
SAVE ✕ 🖥 🍴 🖊 ✕

NORTH CONWAY

🔼🔼 ▼▼▼ Cranmore Mt Lodge 🅱🅱 ✿
(603) 356-2044. **$60-$350, 14 day notice.** 859 Kearsarge Rd. On US 302, e at traffic light, then 1.3 mi, follow signs; from n, 1.2 mi e on Hurricane Mountain Rd, follow signs; village center. Ext/int corridors. **Pets:** Dogs only. $25 one-time fee/room. Designated rooms, service with restrictions.
SAVE ✕ 🖥 🖥 🖊 ✕

🔼🔼 ▼▼▼ North Conway Mountain Inn Ⓜ
(603) 356-2803. **$59-$169, 3 day notice.** 2114 White Mountain Hwy. 1 mi s on US 302 and SR 16; village center. Ext corridors. **Pets:** Dogs only.
SAVE ✕

▼▼▼ Spruce Moose Lodge and Cottages 🅱🅱 ✿
(603) 356-6239. **$49-$149, 21 day notice.** 207 Seavey St. US 302 and SR 16, 0.5 mi e; village center. Ext/int corridors. **Pets:** Dogs only. $100 deposit/room. Service with restrictions, crate.
Sᴅ ✕ 🖥 🖥

PITTSBURG

▼▼ ▼▼ The Glen **CA**
(603) 538-6500. **$180-$220 (no credit cards), 7 day notice.**
118 Glen Rd. 8.1 mi n on US 3, then 0.7 mi se via Varney
Rd, follow signs. Ext/int corridors. **Pets:** Accepted.
⊠ 🖬 🖵 🍴 ⊠ 🐾 🅌 🗷

PLYMOUTH

▼▼▼▼ The Common Man Inn & Spa **SH**
(603) 536-2200. **$69-$189, 3 day notice.** 231 Main St. I-93,
exit 26, on US 3. Int corridors. **Pets:** Accepted.
ASK 🕏 ⊠ 🖑 🖬 🍴 🍻 ⊠

PORTSMOUTH

▼▼ ▼▼ Meadowbrook Inn **M** 🐾
(603) 436-2700. **$69-$129.** 549 US Hwy 1 Bypass. I-95, exit
5; jct US 1 Bypass and Portsmouth Traffic Circle. Ext/int
corridors. **Pets:** Medium, other species. $50 deposit/room,
$10 one-time fee/pet. Designated rooms, supervision.
ASK 🕏 ⊠ 🖬 🍻

▼▼▼▼ Residence Inn by Marriott **SH**
(603) 436-8880. **$159-$289.** 1 International Dr. SR 4/16, exit
1, just s. Int corridors. **Pets:** Other species. $200 one-time
fee/room. Service with restrictions, supervision.
ASK 🕏 ⊠ 🖑 🖉 🅳 🖬 🖵 🍻 ⊠

ROCHESTER

AAA ▼▼▼ Anchorage Inn **M**
(603) 332-3350. **$49-$129.** 13 Wadleigh Rd. Jct Spaulding
Tpke and SR 125, exit 12. Ext corridors. **Pets:** Accepted.
SAVE 🕏 ⊠ 🖬 🍻

SALEM

AAA ▼▼ Red Roof Inn **M**
(603) 898-6422. **$51-$72.** 15 Red Roof Ln. I-93, exit 2, just
se. Ext corridors. **Pets:** Accepted.
SAVE ⊠ 🖑 🖉

SUGAR HILL

▼▼▼▼ The Hilltop Inn **BB** 🐾
(603) 823-5695. **$90-$195, 8 day notice.** 1348 Main St. I-93,
exit 38, 0.5 mi n on SR 18, then 2.8 mi w on SR 117. Int
corridors. **Pets:** Dogs only. $10 daily fee/room. Supervision.
⊠ 🖬 ⊠ 🅌 🅌

SUNAPEE

▼▼▼▼ Dexter's Inn **BB** 🐾
(603) 763-5571. **$125-$175, 14 day notice.** 258 Stagecoach
Rd. Jct SR 103B and 11, 0.4 mi w on SR 11, 1.75 mi s
(Winn Hill Rd). Ext/int corridors. **Pets:** Other species. $10
daily fee/pet. Designated rooms.
ASK 🕏 ⊠ 🖬 🖵 🍻 ⊠ 🅌

TAMWORTH

▼▼▼▼ Tamworth Inn **CI**
(603) 323-7721. **$115-$280.** 15 Cleveland Hill Rd. Jct SR 16
and 113, 3 mi w on SR 113; center. Int corridors.
Pets: Accepted.
⊠ 🍴 🍻 ⊠ 🅌 🗷

THORNTON

▼▼ Shamrock Motel **M**
(603) 726-3534. **$40-$60, 7 day notice.** 2913 US 3. I-93,
exit 29, 2.3 mi n. Ext corridors. **Pets:** Accepted.
ASK 🕏 ⊠ 🖬 🍻 🅌 🗷

WEST LEBANON

AAA ▼▼▼ Airport Economy Inn **M**
(603) 298-8888. **$63-$115.** 45 Airport Rd. I-89, exit 20 (SR
12A), just s, then just e. Int corridors. **Pets:** $10 daily fee/
pet. Designated rooms, service with restrictions, supervision.
SAVE 🕏 ⊠ 🖬 🍻

▼▼▼▼ Fireside Inn and Suites **SH**
(603) 298-5906. **$99-$149.** 25 Airport Rd. I-89, exit 20 (SR
12A), just s. Int corridors. **Pets:** $10 daily fee/pet. Desig-
nated rooms, service with restrictions, supervision.
ASK 🕏 ⊠ 🖉 🖬 🖵 🍴 🍻

WOLFEBORO

▼▼ ▼▼ The Lake Motel **M**
(603) 569-1100. **$119-$139, 14 day notice.** 280 S Main St.
0.5 mi se on SR 28. Ext/int corridors. **Pets:** Accepted.
🖬 ⊠

WOODSVILLE

AAA ▼▼ All Seasons Motel **M** 🐾
(603) 747-2157. **$50-$75.** 36 Smith St. Jct SR 10, 0.4 mi w
on US 302, then 0.3 mi se. Ext corridors. **Pets:** $5 daily
fee/pet. Designated rooms, service with restrictions, supervision.
SAVE 🕏 ⊠ 🖬 🍻 ⊠

AAA ▼▼ ▼▼ Nootka Lodge **M** 🐾
(603) 747-2418. **$55-$140.** Jct 10 & 302. Jct SR 10 and US
302. Ext corridors. **Pets:** $5 daily fee/pet. Designated
rooms, service with restrictions, supervision.
SAVE 🕏 ⊠ 🖬 🍻 ⊠

NEW JERSEY

ATLANTIC CITY METROPOLITAN AREA

HAMMONTON

AAA ◊◊◊ Ramada Inn of Hammonton **M**
(609) 561-5700. **$59-$110.** 308 S White Horse Pike (US 30).
Atlantic City Expwy, exit 28, 3 mi n on SR 54, then 1 mi e.
Ext corridors. **Pets:** Medium. $15 daily fee/pet. Service with
restrictions, supervision.
SAVE Sb ✕ 📶 💻 ➰

SOMERS POINT

◊◊◊◊ Residence Inn by Marriott **SH**
(609) 927-6400. **$129-$289.** 900 Mays Landing Rd. Garden
State Pkwy, exit 30 southbound; exit 29 northbound, 1 mi e.
Ext corridors. **Pets:** Large, other species. $100 one-time
fee/room. Service with restrictions, crate.
✕ 🐾 📶 📶 💻 ➰

❀ END METROPOLITAN AREA ❀

BASKING RIDGE

AAA ◊◊◊◊ The Inn at Somerset Hills **SH** ❀
(908) 580-1300. **$129-$225.** 80 Allen Rd. I-78, exit 33, 0.3 mi
n on CR 525, then 0.3 mi w. Int corridors. **Pets:** Large,
other species. $25 daily fee/room. Designated rooms, serv-
ice with restrictions, crate.
SAVE Sb ✕ 🐾 📶 📶 💻 🍽

◊◊◊◊ Olde Mill Inn **SH**
(908) 221-1100. **$135-$145.** 225 US 202 & N Maple Ave.
I-287, exit 30B (2nd ramp). Ext/int corridors.
Pets: Accepted.
ASK Sb ✕ 🐾 📶 📶 💻 🍽

BEACH HAVEN

AAA ◊◊◊ Engleside Inn **SH**
(609) 492-1251. **$90-$404, 30 day notice.** 30 Engleside
Ave. 6.9 mi s of SR 72 Cswy to Engleside Ave, then just e.
Ext corridors. **Pets:** Other species. $10 daily fee/pet. Des-
ignated rooms, service with restrictions.
SAVE ✕ 📶 📶 💻 🍽 ➰

BRIDGEWATER

◊◊◊◊ Marriott Bridgewater Hotel **LH**
(908) 927-9300. **$89-$275.** 700 Commons Way. I-287, exit
17 to US 202/206 S, 0.5 mi to Commons Way, then 0.4 mi
e. Int corridors. **Pets:** Accepted.
ASK Sb ✕ 🐾 📶 📶 💻 🍽 ➰

◊◊◊◊ Summerfield Suites by
Wyndham-Bridgewater **SH**
(908) 725-0800. **$119-$169.** 530 Rt 22 E. I-287, exit 14B
northbound; exit 17 southbound to US 22 W, then 0.8 mi.
Ext corridors. **Pets:** Accepted.
ASK Sb ✕ 🐾 📶 📶 📶 💻 ➰ ✕

CRANBURY

◊◊◊◊ Residence Inn by
Marriott/Cranbury **SH** ❀
(609) 395-9447. **$159-$189.** 2662 Rt 130. New Jersey Tpke,
exit 8A to SR 32 W toward town, 2 mi w on S River Rd. Int
corridors. **Pets:** Large, other species. $175 one-time fee/
room. Service with restrictions.
✕ 🐾 📶 📶 📶 💻 ➰ ✕

DENVILLE

AAA ◊◊◊◊ Hampton Inn-The Inn At
Denville **SH**
(973) 664-1050. **$119-$149, 7 day notice.** 350 Morris Ave.
I-80, exit 37 westbound, just s on Green Pond Rd, then just
e; exit 37 eastbound, just n on Hibernia Ave, then just e. Int
corridors. **Pets:** Medium, other species. $20 daily fee/pet.
Service with restrictions.
SAVE Sb ✕ 📶 🐾 📶 📶 💻 ➰ ✕

EAST BRUNSWICK

◊◊◊◊ Hilton East Brunswick **LH**
(732) 828-2000. **$99-$269.** 3 Tower Center Blvd. New Jersey
Tpke, exit 9 (SR 18 N), first right on service road. Int
corridors. **Pets:** Accepted.
ASK Sb ✕ 📶 🐾 📶 💻 🍽 ➰ ✕

◊◊◊ Motel 6, East Brunswick **SH**
(732) 390-4545. **$62-$75.** 244 Rt 18 N. New Jersey Tpke,
exit 9 (SR 18) to SR 18 S, 1 mi, exit at Edgeboro Rd, w at
U-turn, then just e. Ext/int corridors. **Pets:** Service with
restrictions, supervision.
Sb ✕ 📶 🐾 📶 📶

EAST HANOVER

(AAA) ▼▼▼▼ Ramada Inn & Conference Center SH
(973) 386-5622. **$79-$109.** 130 Rt 10 W. I-287, exit 39, 3 mi e. Int corridors. **Pets:** Accepted.
[SAVE] [S&] [X] [&M] [⌖] [&] [H] [▦] [¶]

EAST RUTHERFORD

▼▼ Homestead Studio Suites
Hotel-Meadowlands/East Rutherford SH ❀
(201) 939-8866. **$92-$109.** 300 SR 3 E. New Jersey Tpke, exit 16W (from western spur), sports complex right after toll. Int corridors. **Pets:** Medium, other species. $25 daily fee/room. Service with restrictions, crate.
[ASK] [S&] [X] [&M] [⌖] [&] [H] [▦]

(AAA) ▼▼▼▼ Sheraton (East
Rutherford/Meadowlands) LH
(201) 896-0500. **$109-$169.** 2 Meadowlands Plaza. New Jersey Tpke, exit 16W (from western spur), sports complex right after toll to Sheraton Plaza Dr. Int corridors. **Pets:** Accepted.
[SAVE] [S&] [X] [&M] [⌖] [&] [H] [▦] [¶] [➔] [X]

EDISON

(AAA) ▼ Red Roof Inn M ❀
(732) 248-9300. **$72-$76.** 860 New Durham Rd. I-287, exit 2A northbound, 0.3 mi w via Bridge St, then left; exit 3 southbound, just w. Ext corridors. **Pets:** Medium, other species. Service with restrictions, supervision.
[SAVE] [X] [&M] [⌖]

▼▼▼ Sheraton Edison LH ❀
(732) 225-8300. **$85-$189.** 125 Raritan Center Pkwy. New Jersey Tpke, exit 10, 0.5 mi se on CR 514, keep right after tolls. Int corridors. **Pets:** Small. $20 daily fee/room. Service with restrictions.
[ASK] [S&] [X] [&M] [⌖] [&] [H] [▦] [¶] [➔] [X]

(AAA) ▼▼▼ Wellesley Inn (Edison) M
(732) 287-0171. **$109.** 831 US 1 S. 1.3 mi s of I-287. Int corridors. **Pets:** Accepted.
[SAVE] [S&] [X] [&] [H] [▦]

ELIZABETH

(AAA) ▼▼▼▼ Hilton Newark Airport LH
(908) 351-3900. **$99-$279.** 1170 Spring St. New Jersey Tpke, exit 13A, on US 1 and 9 N, U-turn on McClellan St. Int corridors. **Pets:** Accepted.
[SAVE] [X] [&M] [⌖] [&] [H] [▦] [¶] [➔] [X]

▼▼▼▼ Residence Inn by Marriott SH ❀
(908) 352-4300. **$89-$179.** 83 Glimcher Realty Way. New Jersey Tpke, exit 13A, after toll follow signs to Jersey Garden Blvd, 1 mi, left on Kapkowski Rd, then just e. Int corridors. **Pets:** $10 daily fee/room, $50 one-time fee/room. Designated rooms, service with restrictions.
[ASK] [X] [&M] [⌖] [&] [H] [▦] [➔]

FAIR LAWN

(AAA) ▼▼▼▼ AmeriSuites (Fair Lawn/Paramus) SH
(201) 475-3888. **$159-$194.** 41-01 Broadway (Rt 4 W). Garden State Pkwy, exit 161 northbound, 0.7 mi w; exit 163 southbound. Int corridors. **Pets:** Small, other species. Designated rooms, service with restrictions, crate.
[SAVE] [S&] [X] [&M] [⌖] [&] [H] [▦] [➔]

FLEMINGTON

▼▼ The Ramada Inn M ❀
(908) 782-7472. **$102-$145.** 250 Hwy 202 & SR 31. 0.5 mi s of the circle. Ext corridors. **Pets:** Medium. $10 daily fee/pet. Service with restrictions, crate.
[ASK] [S&] [X] [⌖] [H] [▦] [¶] [➔]

HAZLET

(AAA) ▼▼▼ Wellesley Inn (Hazlet) SH
(732) 888-2800. **$129-$189.** 3215 SR 35 N. Garden State Pkwy, exit 117, 1.5 mi s on SR 35, U-turn on Hazlet Ave. Int corridors. **Pets:** Medium, other species. Service with restrictions.
[SAVE] [S&] [X] [&M] [⌖] [&] [H] [▦]

JERSEY CITY

▼▼▼▼ Candlewood Suites SH
(201) 659-2500. **Call for rates.** 21 Second St. Corner of Hudson St. Int corridors. **Pets:** Accepted.
[X] [&] [H] [▦]

LAWRENCEVILLE

(AAA) ▼▼▼ Howard Johnson Inn M
(609) 896-1100. **$75-$110.** 2995 Rt 1 S. On US 1 southbound, 0.5 mi s of I-295. Ext/int corridors. **Pets:** Medium. $10 daily fee/pet. Service with restrictions, crate.
[SAVE] [S&] [X] [⌖] [H] [▦] [➔]

(AAA) ▼▼▼ Red Roof Inn-Princeton M
(609) 896-3388. **$50-$75.** 3203 Brunswick Pike (US 1). I-295, exit 67A, just n. Ext corridors. **Pets:** Medium. No service, supervision.
[SAVE] [X] [⌖] [&]

LEDGEWOOD

(AAA) ▼▼▼ Days Inn SH
(973) 347-5100. **$92-$102, 3 day notice.** 1691 US 46 W. I-80, exit 27, 2 mi e (thru US 206 N and 183 N). Int corridors. **Pets:** $50 deposit/room. Service with restrictions.
[SAVE] [S&] [X] [⌖] [&] [H] [¶] [➔]

LYNDHURST

▼▼▼ Quality Inn Meadowlands SH
(201) 933-9800. **$79-$159.** 10 Polito Ave. New Jersey Tpke, exit 16W (SR 3 W), s on SR 17 S. Int corridors. **Pets:** $100 deposit/room. Service with restrictions, supervision.
[ASK] [S&] [X] [⌖] [H] [▦] [¶] [X]

MAHWAH

▼▼▼▼ Homewood Suites by Hilton 🆂🅷
(201) 760-9994. **$139-$159, 30 day notice.** 375 Corporate Dr. I-278, exit 66, 1.7 mi on SR 17 S to MacArthur Blvd, then 0.4 mi w. Int corridors. **Pets:** Accepted.
🅰🆂🅺 💲🔟 ✖ 🐾 🔌 🛏 🖵 🌊

🔷🔷🔷 ▼▼▼▼ Sheraton Crossroads Hotel 🅻🅷
(201) 529-1660. **$209-$231.** 1 International Blvd (Rt 17). I-287, exit 66, at SR 17 N. Int corridors. **Pets:** Accepted.
🆂🅰🆅🅴 💲🔟 ✖ 🐾 🛏 🖵 🍽 🌊 ✖

MIDDLETOWN

🔷🔷🔷 ▼▼▼ Howard Johnson Inn 🅼 🐾
(732) 671-3400. **$108-$179.** 750 Hwy 35 S. Garden State Pkwy, exit 114, 2 mi on Red Hill Rd, 1 mi s on King's Hwy to SR 35, then 0.3 mi s. Int corridors. **Pets:** Large, other species. $22 daily fee/room. Service with restrictions, supervision.
🆂🅰🆅🅴 💲🔟 ✖ 🐾 🛏 🖵 🌊

MONMOUTH JUNCTION

🔷🔷🔷 ▼ Red Roof Inn/North Princeton 🅼
(732) 821-8800. **$51-$75.** 208 New Rd. On US 1 S. Ext corridors. **Pets:** Large, other species. Service with restrictions, crate.
🆂🅰🆅🅴 ✖ 🐾

🔷🔷🔷 ▼▼▼ Residence Inn by Marriott 🆂🅷 🐾
(732) 329-9600. **$109-$169.** 4225 Rt 1 S. 0.5 mi s of Raymond Rd. Int corridors. **Pets:** Other species. $20 daily fee/room. Service with restrictions.
🆂🅰🆅🅴 💲🔟 ✖ 🅶🅼 🐾 🔌 🛏 🖵 🌊 ✖

MORRISTOWN

🔷🔷🔷 ▼▼▼▼ Summerfield Suites by Wyndham-Morristown 🆂🅷
(973) 971-0008. **$105-$199.** 194 Park Ave. SR 24, exit 2A (Morristown), stay in far left lane. Int corridors. **Pets:** Medium. $150 one-time fee/room. Designated rooms, service with restrictions.
🆂🅰🆅🅴 💲🔟 ✖ 🅶🅼 🐾 🔌 🛏 🖵 🌊 ✖

NEWARK

▼▼▼▼ Hilton Gateway 🅻🅷
(973) 622-5000. **$119-$309.** Raymond Blvd. New Jersey Tpke, exit 15E, 3 mi w via Raymond Blvd. Int corridors. **Pets:** Accepted.
🅰🆂🅺 💲🔟 ✖ 🐾 🔌 🛏 🖵 🍽 🌊

NORTH BERGEN

▼▼▼ Days Inn 🆂🅷
(201) 348-3600. **$109-$185.** 2750 Tonnelle Ave (US 1 & 9). Jct SR 3, 0.4 mi s. Int corridors. **Pets:** Large. $50 deposit/room. Designated rooms, service with restrictions, supervision.
🅰🆂🅺 💲🔟 ✖ 🐾 🔌 🛏 🖵 🍽

PARK RIDGE

▼▼▼▼ Park Ridge Marriott Hotel 🅻🅷
(201) 307-0800. **$209-$229.** 300 Brae Blvd. Garden State Pkwy S, U-turn thru Food Fuel Service Plaza; exit 172 northbound, right 300 yds on Grand Ave, then 0.5 mi s on Mercedes. Int corridors. **Pets:** Accepted.
✖ 🐾 🔌 🛏 🖵 🍽 🌊 ✖

PARSIPPANY

▼▼▼▼ Embassy Suites 🅻🅷 🐾
(973) 334-1440. **$319.** 909 Parsippany Blvd. I-80, exit 42 to US 202 N, just ne of jct US 202 and 46 W. Int corridors. **Pets:** $20 daily fee/pet. Designated rooms, service with restrictions, supervision.
💲🔟 ✖ 🐾 🔌 🛏 🖵 🍽 🌊 ✖

▼▼▼▼ Hilton Parsippany 🅻🅷
(973) 267-7373. **$89-$277.** 1 Hilton Ct. I-287, exit 39 northbound; exit 39B southbound, 1.3 mi w on SR 10; in Hilton Court. Int corridors. **Pets:** Accepted.
✖ 🐾 🔌 🛏 🖵 🍽 🌊 ✖

🔷🔷🔷 ▼▼▼ Red Roof Inn 🅼
(973) 334-3737. **$66-$86.** 855 US 46 E. I-80, exit 47 westbound; exit 45 eastbound, then 0.5 mi e. Ext corridors. **Pets:** Medium, other species. Service with restrictions, crate.
🆂🅰🆅🅴 ✖ 🐾 🔌

NEARBY PENNSYLVANIA
PHILADELPHIA METROPOLITAN AREA

BORDENTOWN

🔷🔷🔷 ▼▼ Imperial Inn 🅼 🐾
(609) 298-3355. **$50-$75.** 3312 Rt 206 S. New Jersey Tpke, exit 7, 0.8 mi s. Ext corridors. **Pets:** Medium, dogs only. $5 daily fee/room. Service with restrictions, crate.
🆂🅰🆅🅴 💲🔟 ✖ 🛏

CARNEYS POINT

▼▼▼▼ Holiday Inn Express Hotel & Suites 🆂🅷
(856) 351-9222. **$100-$110.** 506 Pennsville-Auburn Rd. I-295, exit 2B, just e. Int corridors. **Pets:** Accepted.
🅰🆂🅺 💲🔟 ✖ 🐾 🔌 🛏 🖵

CHERRY HILL

🔷🔷🔷 ▼▼▼▼ Holiday Inn-Cherry Hill 🆂🅷
(856) 663-5300. **$85-$149.** Rt 70 & Sayer Ave. I-295, exit 34B, 2.5 mi w. Int corridors. **Pets:** Small, other species. $75 deposit/room. Service with restrictions, supervision.
🆂🅰🆅🅴 💲🔟 ✖ 🐾 🔌 🛏 🖵 🍽 🌊

▼▼▼▼ Residence Inn by Marriott 🆂🅷
(856) 429-6111. **$149.** 1821 Old Cuthbert Rd. I-295, exit 34A, just e to Marlkress Rd jughandle, back to Old Cuthbert Rd, then just n. Ext corridors. **Pets:** Accepted.
🅰🆂🅺 💲🔟 ✖ 🐾 🛏 🖵 🌊 ✖

DEPTFORD

▼▼▼ Residence Inn by Marriott-Deptford 🅂🄷
(856) 686-9188. **$129.** 1154 Hurffville Rd. SR 42, exit Deptford, Woodbury, Runnemede to CR 544, just e to CR 415. Int corridors. **Pets:** Accepted.
🄰🅂🄺 🆂 ⊠ 🄯 🄴 🄱 🄿 🏊 🆇

HADDONFIELD

▼▼▼ Haddonfield Inn 🄱🄱 ❀
(856) 428-2195. **$129-$259, 14 day notice.** 44 W End Ave. I-295, exit 28, 0.7 mi n on SR 168, 2.6 mi e on Kings Hwy, then just n. Int corridors. **Pets:** Dogs only. $15 daily fee/pet. Designated rooms.
⊠ 🄴 🄱

MOUNT HOLLY

▲▲ ▼▼▼ Best Western Burlington Inn 🅂🄷
(609) 261-3800. **$84-$119, 3 day notice.** Box 2020, Rt 541, RD 1. New Jersey Tpke, exit 5, just n. Int corridors. **Pets:** Accepted.
🅂🄰🆅🄴 🆂 ⊠ 🄯 🄱 🄿 🏊

MOUNT LAUREL

▲▲ ▼▼▼▼ AmeriSuites (Mt. Laurel/Philadelphia) 🅂🄷
(856) 840-0770. **$59-$149.** 8000 Crawford Pl. New Jersey Tpke, exit 4, 1 mi se on SR 73; I-295, exit 36A, 1.7 mi se on SR 73. Int corridors. **Pets:** Accepted.
🅂🄰🆅🄴 🆂 ⊠ 🄰🄼 🄴 🄱 🄿 🏊

▼▼▼ Candlewood Suites 🅂🄷
(856) 642-7567. **$139.** 4000 Crawford Pl. New Jersey Tpke, exit 4, 1 mi s on SR 73 S. Int corridors. **Pets:** Medium. $75 one-time fee/pet. Service with restrictions.
🄰🅂🄺 🆂 ⊠ 🄱 🄿

▼▼▼ Radisson Hotel Mount Laurel 🄻🄷
(856) 234-7300. **$107.** 915 Rt 73 N. New Jersey Tpke, exit 4, northeast corner; I-295, exit 36A, just se. Int corridors. **Pets:** Accepted.
⊠ 🄯 🄴 🄱 🄿 🍴 🏊 🆇

▲▲ ▼ Red Roof Inn 🄼
(856) 234-5589. **$50-$70.** 603 Fellowship Rd. New Jersey Tpke, exit 4, just nw on SR 73 to Fellowship Rd, then just s; I-295, exit 36A, just se on SR 73 to Fellowship Rd, then just s. Ext corridors. **Pets:** Accepted.
🅂🄰🆅🄴 ⊠ 🄯

▼▼▼ Summerfield Suites by Wyndham-Mount Laurel 🅂🄷
(856) 222-1313. **$99-$169.** 3000 Crawford Pl. New Jersey Tpke, exit 4, 1 mi s on SR 73; I-295, exit 36A, 1.5 mi s on SR 73. Ext corridors. **Pets:** Accepted.
🄰🅂🄺 🆂 ⊠ 🄰🄼 🄯 🄴 🄱 🄿 🏊 🆇

❖   **END METROPOLITAN AREA**   ❖

PHILLIPSBURG

▼▼▼ Clarion Hotel & Conference Center 🄼
(908) 454-9771. **$89-$129.** 1314 US Rt 22. I-78, exit 3, just n. Ext/int corridors. **Pets:** Accepted.
🄰🅂🄺 🆂 ⊠ 🄰🄼 🄯 🄴 🄱 🄿 🍴 🏊

PRINCETON

▲▲ ▼▼▼ AmeriSuites (Princeton/Carnegie Center West) 🅂🄷
(609) 720-0200. **$149-$179.** 3565 US 1 S. 1.5 mi s of jct SR 526 and 571. Int corridors. **Pets:** Accepted.
🅂🄰🆅🄴 🆂 ⊠ 🄰🄼 🄴 🄱 🄿 🏊

▲▲ ▼▼▼ Holiday Inn Princeton 🅂🄷
(609) 520-1200. **$99-$165.** 100 Independence Way. I-295, exit 67A (SR 1) northbound; exit 67 (SR 1) southbound, 7 mi n. Int corridors. **Pets:** Accepted.
🅂🄰🆅🄴 🆂 ⊠ 🄯 🄴 🄱 🄿 🍴 🏊

▲▲ ▼▼▼ Staybridge Suites 🅂🄷
(609) 951-0009. **$125-$195.** 4375 US 1 S. Just past Ridge Rd. Ext corridors. **Pets:** Accepted.
🅂🄰🆅🄴 🆂 ⊠ 🄯 🄴 🄱 🄿 🏊 🆇

RAMSEY

▲▲ ▼▼▼ Best Western 🅂🄷
(201) 327-6700. **$79-$155.** 1315 Rt 17 S. Jct I-287 and SR 17 S, 3 mi s. Int corridors. **Pets:** Medium. $10 one-time fee/room. Service with restrictions, supervision.
🅂🄰🆅🄴 🆂 ⊠ 🄱 🄿 🍴

▲▲ ▼▼▼ Wellesley Inn (Ramsey) 🅂🄷
(201) 934-9250. **$99-$189.** 946 Rt 17 N. At Airmont Rd. Int corridors. **Pets:** Small. Designated rooms, no service, supervision.
🅂🄰🆅🄴 🆂 ⊠ 🄰🄼 🄯 🄴 🄱 🄿

ROCKAWAY

▼▼ Best Western-The Inn at Rockaway 🅂🄷
(973) 625-1200. **$119.** 14 Green Pond Rd. I-80, exit 37, just n. Int corridors. **Pets:** Accepted.
🄰🅂🄺 🆂 ⊠ 🄯 🄿 🏊

SECAUCUS

▲▲ ▼▼▼ AmeriSuites (Secaucus/Meadowlands) 🅂🄷
(201) 422-9480. **$129-$159.** 575 Park Plaza Dr. New Jersey Tpke, exits 16E, 17 or 16W via SR 3 to Harmon Meadow Blvd, then just w. Int corridors. **Pets:** Accepted.
🅂🄰🆅🄴 🆂 ⊠ 🄰🄼 🄯 🄴 🄱 🄿

▼▼▼ Homestead Studio Suites
Hotel-Meadowlands/Secaucus 🅂🅷 ✥
(201) 553-9700. **$109-$127.** 1 Park Plaza Dr. New Jersey
Tpke, exit 16E northbound; exit 17E southbound, 0.3 mi e.
Int corridors. **Pets:** Medium, other species. $25 daily fee/
room. Service with restrictions, crate.

Ⓐ🅢🅚 🆂🅓 ✖ 🕭ᴹ 🕭 🗲 🗎 🖵 🛲

🆊🆊🆊 ▼▼▼ Radisson Suite Hotel
Meadowlands 🅻🅷
(201) 863-8700. **$139-$165.** 350 Rt 3 W, at Mill Creek.
Between eastern and western spurs of New Jersey Tpke,
exits 16E, 17 or 16W via SR 3 W and Harmon Meadow
Blvd. Int corridors. **Pets:** Accepted.

🆂🅐🆅🅴 🆂🅓 ✖ 🕭 🗎 🖵 🍴 🛲

🆊🆊🆊 ▼▼▼ Red Roof Inn-Meadowlands Ⓜ ✥
(201) 319-1000. **$75-$90.** 15 Meadowlands Pkwy. Between
eastern and western spurs of New Jersey Tpke, exits 16E,
17 or 16W to SR 3, exit Meadowlands Pkwy. Ext corridors.
Pets: Medium. Service with restrictions, crate.

🆂🅐🆅🅴 ✖ 🗲

SOMERSET

🆊🆊🆊 ▼▼▼▼ Holiday Inn-Somerset 🅂🅷 ✥
(732) 356-1700. **$65-$154.** 195 Davidson Ave. I-287, exit 10
(CR 527), just n (direction Bound Brook), then 0.5 mi sw. Int
corridors. **Pets:** Other species. Service with restrictions,
crate.

🆂🅐🆅🅴 🆂🅓 ✖ 🕭ᴹ 🕭 🗲 🗎 🖵 🍴 🛲

▼▼▼▼ Residence Inn by Marriott-Somerset 🅂🅷
(732) 627-0881. **$159.** 37 World Fair Dr. I-287, exit 10 (CR
527), left on ramp (CR 527 S/Easton Ave) 0.3 mi, then 0.5
mi w. Int corridors. **Pets:** Accepted.

Ⓐ🅢🅚 🆂🅓 ✖ 🕭ᴹ 🕭 🗲 🗎 🖵 🛲

🆊🆊🆊 ▼▼▼▼ Staybridge Suites 🅂🅷
(732) 356-8000. **$109-$129.** 260 Davidson Ave. I-287, exit
10 (CR 527), just n (direction Bound Brook) to Davidson
Ave, then 0.8 mi sw. Ext corridors. **Pets:** Medium. $250
one-time fee/room. Service with restrictions, crate.

🆂🅐🆅🅴 🆂🅓 ✖ 🕭 🗎 🖵 🛲 ✖

SOUTH PLAINFIELD

▼▼▼▼ Holiday Inn 🅂🅷
(908) 753-5500. **$154-$164.** 4701 Stelton Rd. I-287, exit 5,
just s. Int corridors. **Pets:** Other species. Service with
restrictions, supervision.

Ⓐ🅢🅚 🆂🅓 ✖ 🕭 🗎 🖵 🍴 🛲 ✖

SPRINGFIELD

🆊🆊🆊 ▼▼▼▼ Holiday Inn Springfield 🅂🅷
(973) 376-9400. **$135-$150.** 304 Rt 22 W. Garden State
Pkwy, exit 140 northbound, 4 mi w; exit 140A southbound.
Int corridors. **Pets:** Service with restrictions, crate.

🆂🅐🆅🅴 🆂🅓 ✖ 🕭 🗎 🖵 🍴 🛲

TINTON FALLS

🆊🆊🆊 ▼▼ Red Roof Inn Ⓜ ✥
(732) 389-4646. **$60-$100.** 11 Centre Plaza. Garden State
Pkwy, exit 105, just right at 1st light after toll. Ext corridors.
Pets: Medium. Designated rooms, service with restrictions,
supervision.

🆂🅐🆅🅴 ✖ 🕭ᴹ 🗲

▼▼▼▼ Residence Inn by Marriott 🅂🅷
(732) 389-8100. **$159-$229.** 90 Park Rd. Garden State
Pkwy, exit 105, 1st jughandle after toll, immediate left before
Courtyard by Marriott, just n, then e. Ext corridors.
Pets: Other species. $175 one-time fee/pet. Service with
restrictions.

Ⓐ🅢🅚 🆂🅓 ✖ 🕭 🗲 🗎 🖵 🛲 ✖

▼▼▼▼ Sunrise Suites Hotel 🅂🅷
(732) 389-4800. **$95-$175.** 3 Centre Plaza. Garden State
Pkwy, exit 105, 1st right at Hope Rd after toll. Ext/int corridors. **Pets:** Accepted.

Ⓐ🅢🅚 🆂🅓 ✖ 🗎 🖵 🛲 ✖

TOMS RIVER

🆊🆊🆊 ▼▼▼▼ Howard Johnson Hotel-Toms
River 🅂🅷 ✥
(732) 244-1000. **$85-$199.** 955 Hooper Ave. Garden State
Pkwy, exit 82, 1 mi e on SR 37. Int corridors. **Pets:** Large,
other species. $50 daily fee/pet. Designated rooms, service
with restrictions, supervision.

🆂🅐🆅🅴 🆂🅓 ✖ 🗎 🖵 🍴 🛲

VINELAND

▼▼▼▼ Ramada Inn Vineland 🅂🅷
(856) 696-3800. **$75-$85.** 2216 W Landis Ave. SR 55, exit
32A, just e. Int corridors. **Pets:** Medium. $10 daily fee/room.
Designated rooms, service with restrictions, supervision.

Ⓐ🅢🅚 🆂🅓 ✖ 🗎 🖵 🍴 🛲

WANTAGE

▼▼▼ High Point Country Inn Ⓜ ✥
(973) 702-1860. **$80-$90.** 1328 SR 23 N. 1 mi n of Colesville
Village Center. Ext corridors. **Pets:** Other species. $15 one-
time fee/room.

✖ 🗎 🛲

WARREN

▼▼▼▼ Somerset Hills Hotel 🅂🅷 ✥
(908) 647-6700. **$129-$225.** 200 Liberty Corner Rd. I-78, exit
33, just n on CR 525. Int corridors. **Pets:** $25 daily fee/
room. Designated rooms, service with restrictions, crate.

Ⓐ🅢🅚 🆂🅓 ✖ 🕭 🗎 🖵 🍴 🛲 ✖

WAYNE

🆊🆊🆊 ▼▼▼▼ Wellesley Inn (Wayne) 🅂🅷
(973) 696-8050. **$119, 7 day notice.** 1850 Rt 23 & Ratzer
Rd. I-80, exit 53 (Butler-Verona) westbound to SR 23 N, 3
mi to Ratzer Rd (service road); exit 54 eastbound to Mini-
sink Rd to U-turn for I-80 W to exit 53. Int corridors.
Pets: Small. Service with restrictions, supervision.

🆂🅐🆅🅴 🆂🅓 ✖ 🕭ᴹ 🕭 🗲 🗎 🖵 🛲

WEEHAWKEN

 **Sheraton Suites on the Hudson** 🅛🅗 ❖
(201) 617-5600. **$199-$349.** 500 Harbor Blvd. I-495 E toward
Lincoln Tunnel, exit Weekawken/Hoboken, bear right at bottom of hill, then 0.4 mi e to Lincoln Harbor Complex. Int
corridors. **Pets:** Small, dogs only. $50 one-time fee/room.
Service with restrictions, supervision.

🆂🅰🆅🅴 ⌁ ✖ 🕗 🐾 🔳 🖵 ⫿ ⇝

WHIPPANY

🔷 🔷 **Homestead Studio Suites**
     Hotel-Hanover/Parsippany 🆂🅷 ❖
(973) 463-1999. **$91-$100.** 125 Rt 10 E. I-287, exit 39, 3.6
mi e. Int corridors. **Pets:** Medium, other species. $25 daily
fee/room. Service with restrictions, crate.

🅰🆂🅺 ⌁ ✖ ⌂ 🕗 🐾 🔳 🖵

🔷 🔷🔷 **Summerfield Suites by**
     Wyndham-Parsippany/Whippany 🆂🅷
(973) 605-1001. **$89-$189.** 1 Ridgedale Ave. I-287, exit 39,
just nw. Int corridors. **Pets:** Large, other species. $150 one-
time fee/room. Supervision.

🆂🅰🆅🅴 ⌁ ✖ ⌂ 🕗 🐾 🔳 🖵 ⇝

🔷 🔷🔷 **Wellesley Inn (Whippany)** 🆂🅷
(973) 539-8350. **$124-$134, 7 day notice.** 1255 Rt 10 E.
I-287, exit 39B southbound; exit 39 northbound, just w. Int
corridors. **Pets:** Accepted.

🆂🅰🆅🅴 ⌁ ✖ 🕗 🐾 🔳 🖵 ⇝

WILDWOOD CREST

🔷 🔷 **Carriage Stop Motel** 🅜
(609) 522-6400. **Call for rates.** 400 E St. Paul Ave. Garden
State Pkwy, exit 4B, 3 mi se on SR 47, then 1.6 mi s on
Atlantic Ave. Ext corridors. **Pets:** Accepted.

🔳 🖵 ⇝ ✖

WOODBRIDGE

🔷 🔷 **Homestead Studio Suites**
     Hotel-Woodbridge 🆂🅷 ❖
(732) 442-8333. **$84-$96.** 1 Hoover Way. New Jersey Tpke,
exit 11, 1.4 mi to US 9 N, then just w on King George Post
Rd. Int corridors. **Pets:** Medium, other species. $25 daily
fee/room. Service with restrictions, crate.

🅰🆂🅺 ⌁ ✖ ⌂ 🕗 🐾 🔳 🖵

NEW MEXICO

ABIQUIU

▼▼▼▼ Casa del Rio BB
(505) 753-2035. **$99-$125, 21 day notice.** Hwy 84, MM 199.46. 2.3 mi n from jct US 285, then just e on gated drive. Ext/int corridors. **Pets:** Accepted.

ASK ✕ 🐾 🛏 🎣 📺 🔒

ALAMOGORDO

⚫⚫⚫ ▼▼▼▼ Best Western Desert Aire Inn SH
(505) 437-2110. **$58-$109.** 1021 S White Sands Blvd. 1.5 mi s of jct US 54/70 and 82. Ext corridors. **Pets:** $50 deposit/room, $10 one-time fee/room. Service with restrictions, supervision.

SAVE S6 ✕ 🔒 🛏 💻 🏊 ✕

▼▼▼ Holiday Inn Express-Alamogordo SH
(505) 437-7100. **$59-$65.** 1401 S White Sands Blvd. 1.6 mi s of jct US 54/70 and 82. Int corridors. **Pets:** Accepted.

ASK S6 ✕ 🅼 🔒 🏊

▼▼▼ Super 8 Motel-Alamogordo SH
(505) 434-4205. **$53-$73.** 3204 N White Sands Blvd. Just s of jct US 54/70 and 82. Int corridors. **Pets:** Medium, other species. Designated rooms, service with restrictions, supervision.

ASK S6 ✕ 🛏

ALBUQUERQUE

⚫⚫⚫ ▼▼▼▼ The Airport University Inn SH
(505) 247-0512. **$79-$99, 8 day notice.** 1901 University Blvd SE. I-25, exit 222A, southbound; exit 222 northbound, just e. Int corridors. **Pets:** Large, other species. $100 deposit/room. Designated rooms, service with restrictions, crate.

SAVE S6 ✕ 🔒 🛏 💻 🍴 🏊

⚫⚫⚫ ▼▼▼▼ AmeriSuites
(Albuquerque/Airport) SH
(505) 242-9300. **$99.** 1400 Sunport Place Blvd SE. I-25, exit 221, 0.3 mi e to University Blvd exit, just n to Woodward Rd. Int corridors. **Pets:** Medium, other species. Service with restrictions, crate.

SAVE S6 ✕ 🅼 🔒 🎣 🛏 💻 🏊

⚫⚫⚫ ▼▼▼▼ AmeriSuites
(Albuquerque/Midtown) SH
(505) 881-0544. **$59-$89.** 2500 Menaul Blvd NE. I-40, exit 160, just n to Menaul Blvd, 0.6 mi w. Int corridors. **Pets:** Accepted.

SAVE S6 ✕ 🅼 🎣 🔒 🛏 💻 🏊

⚫⚫⚫ ▼▼▼▼ AmeriSuites
(Albuquerque/Uptown) SH
(505) 872-9000. **$69-$99.** 6901 Arvada Ave NE. I-40, exit 162 westbound; exit 162B eastbound, 0.7 mi n. Int corridors. **Pets:** Accepted.

SAVE S6 ✕ 🅼 🎣 🔒 🛏 💻 🏊

⚫⚫⚫ ▼▼▼▼ Baymont Inn & Suites Albuquerque
North SH
(505) 345-7500. **$64-$119.** 7439 Pan American Frwy NE. I-25, exit 231, just w. Int corridors. **Pets:** Medium. Designated rooms, service with restrictions, supervision.

SAVE S6 ✕ 🎣 🛏 💻 🏊

⚫⚫⚫ ▼▼▼ Best Western American Motor
Inn SH
(505) 298-7426. **$59-$79.** 12999 Central Ave NE. I-40, exit 167, 0.3 mi w on Central Ave westbound; exit 166 right on Juan Tabo, left on Central Ave, then 0.5 mi eastbound. Ext corridors. **Pets:** Accepted.

SAVE S6 ✕ 🛏 💻 🍴 🏊

⚫⚫⚫ ▼▼▼ Best Western InnSuites Hotel &
Suites-Airport Albuquerque SH
(505) 242-7022. **$59-$109.** 2400 Yale Blvd SE. I-25, exit 222 northbound; exit 222A southbound, 1 mi e, then just s. Int corridors. **Pets:** Accepted.

SAVE S6 ✕ 🎣 🛏 💻 🏊 ✕

⚫⚫⚫ ▼▼▼▼ Brittania & W E Mauger Estate Bed &
Breakfast BB ❀
(505) 242-8755. **$89-$209, 10 day notice.** 701 Roma Ave NW. I-25, exit 225, 1 mi w, just s on 7th Ave. Int corridors. **Pets:** Small, dogs only. $30 one-time fee/room. Supervision.

SAVE S6 ✕ 🛏 💻

▼▼▼ Candlewood Suites SH
(505) 888-3424. **$59-$95.** 3025 Menaul Blvd NE. I-40, exit 160, just n to Menaul Blvd, 0.5 mi w. Int corridors. **Pets:** Medium, other species. $75 one-time fee/room. Service with restrictions.

ASK S6 ✕ 🅼 🎣 🛏 💻

AAA ▼▼▼ Comfort Inn-Airport SH
(505) 243-2244. **$49-$99.** 2300 Yale Blvd SE. I-25, exit 222A southbound; exit 222 northbound, 1 mi n, then just s. Ext/int corridors. **Pets:** Medium. $10 daily fee/room. Designated rooms, service with restrictions.

[SAVE] [S⌀] [✕] [&M] [♋] [⌂] [⇌]

▼▼▼ Comfort Inn & Suites SH
(505) 822-1090. **$59-$79.** 5811 Signal Ave NE. I-25, exit 233, just e via Alameda. Int corridors. **Pets:** Other species. $10 daily fee/pet. Service with restrictions, supervision.

[ASK] [S⌀] [✕] [&M] [♋] [⌂] [⏢] [⇌]

AAA ▼▼▼ Comfort Inn East M ☙
(505) 294-1800. **$59-$69.** 13031 Central Ave NE. I-40, exit 167, just w. Ext corridors. **Pets:** Very small, other species. $3 daily fee/room. Service with restrictions, crate.

[SAVE] [S⌀] [✕] [&M] [♋] [⌂] [⏢] [⊟] [▯] [⏢] [⇌]

▼▼ Comfort Inn-Midtown SH
(505) 881-3210. **$59-$69.** 2015 Menaul Blvd NE. I-25, exit 225 northbound, 1.6 mi n of Frontage Rd to Menaul Blvd, then just e; exit 227 (Commanche Rd) southbound s on Frontage Rd, 0.8 mi n to Menaul Blvd, then just e. Ext corridors. **Pets:** Medium. $10 daily fee/pet. Designated rooms, service with restrictions, supervision.

[ASK] [S⌀] [✕] [⊟] [▯] [⇌]

▼▼▼ Country Inn & Suites SH
(505) 246-9600. **$62-$69.** 2601 Mulberry SE. I-25, exit 222, just e. Int corridors. **Pets:** Accepted.

[ASK] [S⌀] [✕] [⇌]

▼▼ Days Inn-Hotel Circle SH
(505) 275-3297. **$48-$80.** 10321 Hotel Cir NE. I-40, exit 165 (Eubank Blvd), just n. Ext corridors. **Pets:** Medium, other species. $10 daily fee/pet. Service with restrictions, supervision.

[ASK] [S⌀] [✕] [⇌]

▼▼▼ Days Inn West M
(505) 836-3297. **$52-$55.** 6031 Iliff Rd NW. I-40, exit 155, just s on Coors Rd, then just w. Ext corridors. **Pets:** Accepted.

[ASK] [S⌀] [✕] [&M] [♋] [⌂] [⇌]

AAA ▼▼▼ Econo Lodge SH ☙
(505) 243-1321. **$42-$99.** 817 Central Ave NE. I-25, 224A northbound; exit 224B southbound, just e. Ext corridors. **Pets:** Medium, other species. $25 deposit/pet. Designated rooms, service with restrictions, supervision.

[SAVE] [S⌀] [✕] [⊟] [▯] [⇌]

AAA ▼▼▼ Econo Lodge Old Town SH
(505) 243-8475. **$40-$95.** 2321 Central Ave NW. I-40, exit 157A, 0.6 mi s on Rio Grande Blvd, then 0.4 mi w. Ext corridors. **Pets:** Medium, dogs only. $10 daily fee/pet. Designated rooms, service with restrictions, crate.

[SAVE] [S⌀] [✕] [⊟] [▯] [⇌]

▼▼ Equus Hotel Suites M ☙
(505) 883-8888. **$54-$59.** 2401 Wellsley Dr NE. I-40, exit 160, just n to Menaul Blvd, just w, then just s. Ext corridors. **Pets:** Large, other species. $5 daily fee/pet. Designated rooms, service with restrictions, crate.

[ASK] [S⌀] [✕] [⊟] [▯]

AAA ▼▼▼ Hacienda Antigua B & B BB
(505) 345-5399. **$129-$300, 10 day notice.** 6708 Tierra Dr NW. I-25, exit 230 (Osuna Dr), 2 mi w, just n. Ext/int corridors. **Pets:** Accepted.

[SAVE] [S⌀] [✕] [⊟] [▯] [⇌]

AAA ▼▼▼ Hampton Inn-North SH
(505) 344-1555. **$49-$99.** 5101 Ellison NE. I-25, exit 231, just w. Ext corridors. **Pets:** Other species. Service with restrictions, supervision.

[SAVE] [S⌀] [✕] [&M] [♋] [⌂] [⊟] [▯] [⇌]

▼▼▼ Hawthorn Inn & Suites SH
(505) 242-1555. **$64-$189.** 1511 Gibson Blvd SE. I-25, exit 222, northbound; exit 222A southbound, just e. Int corridors. **Pets:** Medium, other species. Designated rooms, supervision.

[ASK] [S⌀] [✕] [&M] [♋] [⌂] [⊟] [▯] [⏢] [⇌]

AAA ▼▼▼ Holiday Inn Express M ☙
(505) 275-8900. **$80.** 10330 Hotel Ave NE. I-40, exit 165 (Eubank Blvd), 2 blks n. Ext corridors. **Pets:** Other species. $5 daily fee/room. Service with restrictions, supervision.

[SAVE] [S⌀] [✕] [♋] [⌂] [⊟] [▯] [⇌] [✕]

AAA ▼▼▼ Holiday Inn Express-West SH
(505) 836-8600. **$72.** 6100 Iliff Rd NW. I-40, exit 155, just sw. Ext/int corridors. **Pets:** Small. $25 one-time fee/pet. Service with restrictions, supervision.

[SAVE] [S⌀] [✕] [&M] [♋] [⌂] [⊟] [▯] [⇌] [✕]

▼▼▼ Holiday Inn-Mountain View SH
(505) 884-2511. **$69.** 2020 Menaul Blvd NE. I-40, exit 160, 0.3 mi n to Menaul Blvd, 1 mi w. Int corridors. **Pets:** Other species. $20 one-time fee/room. Service with restrictions, supervision.

[ASK] [S⌀] [✕] [&M] [♋] [⌂] [▯] [⏢] [⇌] [✕]

▼▼▼ The Hotel Blue SH
(505) 924-2400. **$79-$109.** 717 Central Ave NW. 8th and Central Ave; downtown. Ext corridors. **Pets:** Accepted.

[ASK] [S⌀] [✕] [♋] [⌂] [⊟] [▯] [⇌]

▼▼▼ Howard Johnson Express Inn SH
(505) 828-1600. **$59, 4 day notice.** 7630 Pan American Frwy NE. I-25, exit 231, 0.8 mi n on frontage road. Int corridors. **Pets:** Other species. $5 daily fee/pet. Service with restrictions, supervision.

[ASK] [S⌀] [✕] [♋] [⌂] [⇌]

▼▼▼ Howard Johnson Hotel & Convention Center SH
(505) 296-4852. **$39-$60.** 15 Hotel Cir NE. I-40, exit 165, just n. Int corridors. **Pets:** Large, other species. $10 one-time fee/pet. Designated rooms, service with restrictions, supervision.

[ASK] [✕] [♋] [⌂] [⊟] [▯] [⏢] [⇌]

▼▼▼ La Quinta Inn-Airport SH
(505) 243-5500. **$75-$85.** 2116 Yale Blvd SE. I-25, exit 222, northbound; exit 222A southbound, 1 mi e. Ext/int corridors. **Pets:** Accepted.

[ASK] [✕] [&M] [♋] [⌂] [⊟] [▯] [⇌]

▼▼▼ La Quinta Inn & Suites-West SH
(505) 839-1744. **$89-$109.** 6101 Iliff Rd NW. I-40, exit 155, just sw. Int corridors. **Pets:** Accepted.

[ASK] [S⌀] [✕] [&M] [♋] [⌂] [⊟] [▯] [⇌]

(AAA) ▼▼▼ La Quinta Inn North SH
(505) 821-9000. **$69-$89.** 5241 San Antonio Dr NE. I-25, exit 231, just e. Ext corridors. **Pets:** Other species. Service with restrictions, crate.

▼▼▼ La Quinta Inn San Mateo SH
(505) 884-3591. **$59-$79.** 2424 San Mateo Blvd NE. I-40, exit 161 westbound; exit 161B eastbound, just n. Ext corridors. **Pets:** Large, other species. Service with restrictions, supervision.

▼▼▼ Le Baron Courtyard & Suites SH
(505) 884-0250. **$49.** 2120 Menaul Blvd NE. I-40, exit 160, just n to Menaul Blvd, 0.8 mi w. Ext corridors. **Pets:** Medium, other species. $25 one-time fee/room.

▼▼ Microtel Inn & Suites SH
(505) 836-1686. **$59-$69.** 9910 Avalon NW. I-40, exit 153, just s on western edge of city. Int corridors. **Pets:** Accepted.

▼ Motel 6–1349 M
(505) 243-8017. **$41-$55.** 1000 Avenida Cesar Chavez. I-25, exit 223, just w. Ext corridors. **Pets:** Accepted.

(AAA) ▼▼▼ Motel 76 SH
(505) 836-3881. **$34-$39.** 1521 Coors Blvd NW. I-40, exit 155 (Coors Blvd), just s. Ext corridors. **Pets:** Other species. $25 deposit/pet. Service with restrictions, supervision.

(AAA) ▼▼▼ Plaza Inn Albuquerque SH
(505) 243-5693. **$89-$99.** 900 Medical Arts NE. I-25, exit 225, just e. Int corridors. **Pets:** Other species. $25 one-time fee/room. Service with restrictions, crate.

▼▼▼ Radisson Hotel & Conference Center LH
(505) 888-3311. **$119-$129.** 2500 Carlisle Blvd NE. I-40, exit 160, just n. Ext/int corridors. **Pets:** Accepted.

▼▼▼ Ramada Limited SH
(505) 858-3297. **$54-$79.** 5601 Alameda Blvd NE. I-25, exit 233, just w. Int corridors. **Pets:** Accepted.

(AAA) ▼▼▼ Red Roof Inn SH
(505) 831-3400. **$41-$56.** 6015 Iliff Rd NW. I-40, exit 155 (Coors Blvd), just s, then just w. Ext corridors. **Pets:** Accepted.

▼▼▼ Residence Inn by Marriott SH ❀
(505) 881-2661. **$79-$199.** 3300 Prospect Dr NE. I-40, exit 160, just n to Menaul Blvd, just w. Ext corridors. **Pets:** Other species. $10 daily fee/room, $50 one-time fee/room. Service with restrictions.

▼▼▼ Residence Inn North by Marriott SH
(505) 761-0200. **$109-$149.** 4331 The Lane at 25 NE. I-25, exit 229 (Jefferson St), just w, just n to The Lane, then just e. Int corridors. **Pets:** Small. $50 one-time fee/pet. Designated rooms, service with restrictions, supervision.

(AAA) ▼▼▼ Silver Moon Lodge M
(505) 243-1773. **$59-$63.** 918 Central Ave SW. I-40, exit 157B, 1 mi s, then just e. Ext corridors. **Pets:** Small. $10 one-time fee/pet. Designated rooms, service with restrictions, supervision.

▼▼ Sleep Inn Airport SH
(505) 244-3325. **$65-$86.** 2300 International Ave SE. I-25, exit 222, northbound; exit 222A southbound, 1 mi e to Yale Blvd, then just n. Int corridors. **Pets:** Medium, other species. $50 deposit/room. Designated rooms, service with restrictions, supervision.

(AAA) ▼ Stardust Inn M
(505) 243-2891. **$30-$65.** 801 Central Ave NE. I-25, 224A northbound; exit 224B southbound, just e. Ext corridors. **Pets:** Medium. $25 deposit/room, $3 daily fee/pet. Service with restrictions, supervision.

▼▼▼ Sun Village Corporate Suites CO
(505) 842-6640. **$60-$90, 3 day notice.** 801 Locus NE. From University Blvd, just w on Indian School Rd, then just n. Ext corridors. **Pets:** Accepted.

▼▼ Super 8 Motel East SH
(505) 271-4807. **$52-$65.** 450 Paisano NE. I-40, exit 166, just n to Copter, then just s. Int corridors. **Pets:** Other species. $5 daily fee/pet. Designated rooms, service with restrictions, supervision.

▼▼ Super 8 Motel of Albuquerque SH
(505) 888-4884. **$50-$85.** 2500 University Blvd NE. I-25, exit 225 northbound, 1.9 mi n on frontage road to Menaul Blvd, then just e; exit 227 (Comanche Rd) southbound, 0.9 mi s to Menaul Blvd, then just e. Int corridors. **Pets:** Other species. $5 daily fee/pet. Designated rooms, service with restrictions, supervision.

▼▼ Super 8 Motel West (Albuquerque) SH
(505) 836-5560. **$52-$65.** 6030 Iliff Rd NW. I-40, exit 155, 0.5 mi s. Int corridors. **Pets:** Other species. $5 daily fee/pet. Designated rooms, service with restrictions, supervision.

(AAA) ▼▼▼ TownePlace Suites SH ❀
(505) 232-5800. **$59-$79.** 2400 Centre Ave SE. I-25, exit 222 northbound; exit 222A southbound, 1 mi e to Yale Blvd, at ne jct of Gibson and Yale blvds. **Pets:** Other species. $10 daily fee/pet, $50 one-time fee/room. Service with restrictions, crate.

Ⓐ ▼▼▼ Travelodge Ⓜ
(505) 292-4878. **$45-$75.** 13139 Central Ave NE. I-40, exit 167, just w. Ext corridors. **Pets:** Accepted.
[SAVE] [✕] [▭]

ALGODONES

Ⓐ ▼▼▼▼ Hacienda Vargas Bed and Breakfast Inn ⒷⒷ ❖
(505) 867-9115. **$89-$149, 10 day notice.** 1431 SR 313 (El Camino Real). I-25, exit 248, 0.5 mi w. Int corridors. **Pets:** Other species. $5 daily fee/pet. Designated rooms, crate.
[SAVE] [S6] [✕] [W] [☎]

ALTO

▼▼ High Country Lodge Ⓒ
(505) 336-4321. **$89-$130, 7 day notice.** Hwy 48. Center. Ext corridors. **Pets:** Small, dogs only. $11 one-time fee/pet. Supervision.
[🛏] [▭] [☞] [✕] [🎿]

▼▼ Rancho Ruidoso Condominiums Ⓒ
(505) 336-8103. **$85-$165, 14 day notice.** 6 Little Creek Rd. Jct SR 48, 4.2 mi e on Little Creek Rd (SR 220), then just s at sign. Ext corridors. **Pets:** Accepted.
[🛏] [▭] [☞] [🎿] [☎]

ARROYO SECO

▼▼▼▼ Adobe and Stars B & B ⒷⒷ
(505) 776-2776. **$185-$200, 60 day notice.** 584 SR 150. 1.1 mi ne on SR 150 at Valdez Rd. Ext/int corridors. **Pets:** Accepted.
[ASK] [S6] [✕] [🛏] [🎿] [W]

ARTESIA

Ⓐ ▼▼▼ Artesia Inn Ⓜ
(505) 746-9801. **$45-$55.** 1820 S 1st St. 1.5 mi s on US 285. Ext corridors. **Pets:** $10 one-time fee/room. Service with restrictions, supervision.
[SAVE] [S6] [✕] [🛏] [▭] [☞]

Ⓐ ▼▼▼▼ Holiday Inn Express-Artesia Ⓢ
(505) 748-3904. **$75-$95.** 2210 W Main. 1.6 mi w of jct US 82 and 285. Int corridors. **Pets:** Small, dogs only. $20 one-time fee/pet. Service with restrictions, supervision.
[SAVE] [S6] [✕] [&M] [📶] [🍴] [🛏] [▭] [☞]

BELEN

Ⓐ ▼▼▼▼ Best Western-Belen Ⓢ
(505) 861-3181. **$68-$78.** 2111 Camino del Llano Blvd. I-25, exit 191, just w. Ext/int corridors. **Pets:** Accepted.
[SAVE] [S6] [✕] [🍴] [🛏] [▭] [☞]

▼▼▼▼ Holiday Inn Express Ⓢ
(505) 861-5000. **$73-$89.** 2110 Camino del Llano. I-25, exit 191, just w. Int corridors. **Pets:** $10 daily fee/room. Service with restrictions, supervision.
[ASK] [✕] [&M] [🍴] [🛏] [▭] [☞]

BERNALILLO

▼▼▼ Days Inn Ⓢ
(505) 771-7000. **$50-$100.** 107 N Camino del Pueblo. I-25, exit 242, just w. Int corridors. **Pets:** Small. $30 deposit/pet. Service with restrictions, supervision.
[ASK] [S6] [✕] [☞]

▼▼▼▼ La Hacienda Grande ⒷⒷ ❖
(505) 867-1887. **$109-$139, 10 day notice.** 21 Barros Rd. I-25, exit 242, 0.3 mi w to Camino del Pueblo, then 0.5 mi n. Ext/int corridors. **Pets:** Other species. Designated rooms, no service, crate.
[ASK] [S6] [✕]

▼▼ Quality Inn & Suites Ⓢ
(505) 771-9500. **$45-$80.** 210 N Hill Rd. I-25, exit 242, just w. Int corridors. **Pets:** Very small, dogs only. $10 daily fee/pet. Designated rooms, service with restrictions, supervision.
[ASK] [S6] [✕] [&M] [🛏] [▭]

BLOOMFIELD

▼▼ Super 8 Motel Ⓜ
(505) 632-8886. **$50.** 525 W Broadway Blvd. Jct of US 64 and SR 44. Int corridors. **Pets:** Other species. $10 one-time fee/pet. Service with restrictions, supervision.
[ASK] [S6] [✕] [📶] [🛏]

CARLSBAD

Ⓐ ▼▼▼▼ Best Western Stevens Inn Ⓢ ❖
(505) 887-2851. **$99.** 1829 S Canal St. 1 mi s on US 62, 180 and 285. Ext corridors. **Pets:** $10 daily fee/room. Service with restrictions, supervision.
[SAVE] [S6] [✕] [🍴] [🛏] [▭] [🍴] [☞]

Ⓐ ▼▼▼ Carlsbad Inn Ⓜ
(505) 887-1171. **$36-$49.** 2019 S Canal St. 1.5 mi s on US 62, 180 and 285. Ext corridors. **Pets:** Medium, other species. $5 daily fee/pet. Designated rooms, service with restrictions, supervision.
[SAVE] [S6] [✕] [🛏] [☞]

▼▼▼▼ Comfort Inn Ⓢ
(505) 887-1994. **$65-$80.** 2429 W Pierce St. N on US 285. Int corridors. **Pets:** Accepted.
[ASK] [S6] [✕] [&M] [🍴] [🛏] [▭] [☞]

Ⓐ ▼▼▼ Continental Inn Ⓜ
(505) 887-0341. **$36-$59.** 3820 National Parks Hwy. 3.5 mi sw on US 62 and 180. Ext corridors. **Pets:** Medium, other species. $5 one-time fee/pet. Designated rooms, service with restrictions, supervision.
[SAVE] [S6] [✕] [🛏] [☞]

Ⓐ ▼▼▼▼ Days Inn of Carlsbad Ⓢ
(505) 887-7800. **$60-$69.** 3910 National Parks Hwy. 3.5 mi sw on US 62 and 180. Ext corridors. **Pets:** Small, dogs only. $10 daily fee/pet. Service with restrictions, supervision.
[SAVE] [S6] [✕] [&M] [📶] [🛏] [☞]

▼▼▼▼ Holiday Inn Carlsbad SH
(505) 885-8500. **$85-$156.** 601 S Canal St. On US 62, 180 and 285, Canal St at Lee St; center. Ext corridors. **Pets:** Other species. $25 one-time fee/room. Service with restrictions, supervision.

ASK S⊘ ✕ ⎕M ⌂ ⌘ ⎕ ⌷ ⍟ ⎯ ✕

⏵⏵⏵ ▼▼▼▼ Quality Inn SH ✿
(505) 887-2861. **$59-$79.** 3706 National Parks Hwy. 3 mi sw on US 62 and 180. Ext corridors. **Pets:** Large, other species. Designated rooms, service with restrictions.

SAVE S⊘ ✕ ⌂ ⌘ ⎕ ⍟ ⎯

⏵⏵⏵ ▼ Stagecoach Inn M
(505) 887-1148. **$44-$52.** 1819 S Canal St. 1 mi s on US 62, 180 and 285. Ext corridors. **Pets:** Medium. $5 daily fee/pet. Designated rooms, service with restrictions, supervision.

SAVE S⊘ ✕ ⌘ ⍟ ⎯

CHAMA

⏵⏵⏵ ▼▼▼▼ Vista del Rio Lodge M
(505) 756-2138. **$60-$90.** 2595 US Hwy 84/64. 0.5 mi s of SR 17. Ext corridors. **Pets:** Small. Service with restrictions, supervision.

SAVE S⊘ ✕ ⌘ ⎕ ✕ ⌗

CHIMAYO

▼▼ Casa Escondida Bed & Breakfast BB ✿
(505) 351-4805. **$85-$145, 14 day notice.** 64 CR 0100. SR 68, 7.1 mi e on SR 76, then 0.5 mi nw on CR 100, follow signs. Ext/int corridors. **Pets:** Other species. $15 daily fee/pet. Designated rooms, service with restrictions, supervision.

✕ ⌘ ⍟ ⌗

CIMARRON

⏵⏵⏵ ▼ Cimarron Inn & RV Park M
(505) 376-2268. **$48-$55.** 212 10th St. On US 64. Ext corridors. **Pets:** Medium, other species. $5 one-time fee/room. Service with restrictions, supervision.

SAVE ✕ ⌘ ⎕ ⌗

CLAYTON

⏵⏵⏵ ▼▼▼▼ Best Western Kokopelli Lodge SH
(505) 374-2589. **$69-$125, 7 day notice.** 702 S 1st St. US 87, 0.5 mi se of jct US 56 and 64. Ext corridors. **Pets:** Accepted.

SAVE S⊘ ✕ ⌂ ⌘ ⎕ ⍟ ⎯ ✕

⏵⏵⏵ ▼▼ Days Inn & Suites SH
(505) 374-0133. **$69-$129.** 1120 S 1st St. US 87, 1 mi s of jct US 56 and 64. Int corridors. **Pets:** $5 daily fee/pet. Service with restrictions, supervision.

SAVE S⊘ ✕ ⌂ ⌘ ⎕ ⎯

▼▼ Super 8 Motel M
(505) 374-8127. **$55-$70.** 1425 S 1st St. US 87, 1 mi se of jct US 56 and 64. Int corridors. **Pets:** Accepted.

ASK S⊘ ✕ ⌂

CLOUDCROFT

⏵⏵⏵ ▼▼▼▼ The Lodge SH
(505) 682-2566. **$99-$319, 14 day** [n]
82, 0.3 mi s. Int corridors. **Pets:** O[ther]
time fee/room. Designated rooms, s[ervice with]
supervision.

SAVE ✕ ⎕M ⌂ ⌘ ⎕ ⍟ ⎯ ✕

CLOVIS

⏵⏵⏵ ▼▼ Comfort Inn SH
(505) 762-4591. **$59-$69.** 1616 Mabry Dr. 1 mi e on US 60, 70 and 84. Ext corridors. **Pets:** Large, other species. $10 one-time fee/room. Service with restrictions, supervision.

SAVE S⊘ ✕ ⌘ ⎕ ⎯

⏵⏵⏵ ▼ Econo Lodge M
(505) 763-3439. **$59-$69.** 1400 E Mabry Dr. 0.5 mi e on US 60,70 and 84. Ext corridors. **Pets:** Small. $5 one-time fee/pet. No service, supervision.

SAVE S⊘ ✕ ⌂ ⌘ ⎕ ⎯

▼▼▼ Holiday Inn Clovis SH
(505) 762-4491. **$80.** 2700 E Mabry Dr. 1.5 mi e on US 60, 70 and 84. Ext corridors. **Pets:** Accepted.

ASK S⊘ ✕ ⎕M ⌂ ⌂ ⌘ ⎕ ⍟ ⎯ ✕

▼▼ Howard Johnson Expressway Inn SH
(505) 769-1953. **$52-$66.** 2920 Mabry Dr. US 60/70/84, just e. Int corridors. **Pets:** Accepted.

ASK S⊘ ✕ ⌘ ⎕ ⎯

CORRALES

▼▼▼ Yours Truly Bed & Breakfast BB
(505) 898-7027. **$180, 3 day notice.** 160 Paseo de Corrales. Jct SR 528 and 448 (Corrales Rd), 1.7 mi n on Corrales Rd/SR 448, left on Meadowlark Ln 1 mi, just right on Loma Largo. Int corridors. **Pets:** Accepted.

S⊘ ✕

DEMING

▼▼ Best Western Mimbres Valley Inn SH ✿
(505) 546-4544. **$49-$75.** 1500 W Pine. I-10, exit 81, just e. Ext corridors. **Pets:** Small, other species. $5 daily fee/pet. Designated rooms, service with restrictions, supervision.

ASK S⊘ ✕ ⌘ ⎕ ⎯

⏵⏵⏵ ▼ Days Inn M ✿
(505) 546-8813. **$45-$55.** 1601 E Pine St. I-10, exit 85 westbound, 2 mi w on business loop; exit 82 eastbound, 1 mi e on business loop. Ext corridors. **Pets:** Small. $5 daily fee/pet. Service with restrictions, supervision.

SAVE S⊘ ✕ ⌘ ⎕ ⍟ ⎯

⏵⏵⏵ ▼▼ Grand Motor Inn SH
(505) 546-2632. **$48.** 1721 E Pine St. I-10, exit 81, just e. Ext corridors. **Pets:** Other species. Service with restrictions, supervision.

SAVE S⊘ ✕ ⌘ ⍟ ⎯

⏵⏵⏵ ▼▼▼ Holiday Inn SH
(505) 546-2661. **$59-$89.** 4600 Motel Dr. I-10, exit 85, just w. Ext corridors. **Pets:** Accepted.

SAVE S⊘ ✕ ⎕M ⌂ ⌂ ⌘ ⎕ ⍟ ⎯

▼▼ Wagon Wheel Motel Ⓜ 🐾
(505) 546-2681. **$29-$35.** 1109 W Pine St. I-10, exit 81, just e. Ext corridors. **Pets:** Medium, dogs only. Designated rooms, no service, supervision.
SAVE ⊠ 🖥

EDGEWOOD

▼▼▼▼ Alta Mae's Heritage Inn 🅱🅱
(505) 281-5000. **$95-$115, 14 day notice.** 1950 Old Route 66. I-40, exit 187, just s to stop sign, then just e. Ext corridors. **Pets:** Accepted.
ASK 🖫 ⊠ ⊠

ELEPHANT BUTTE

🆔 **▼▼▼** Marina Suites Motel Ⓜ
(505) 744-5269. **$65-$80, 7 day notice.** 200 Country Club Dr. I-25, exit 83, 4.7 mi e. Ext corridors. **Pets:** $10 deposit/pet. Designated rooms, service with restrictions, supervision.
SAVE 🖫 🖥 🖳 🖎

🆔 **▼▼▼** Quality Inn Ⓜ
(505) 744-5431. **$70-$90, 3 day notice.** 401 Hwy 195. I-25, exit 83, 4 mi e. Ext corridors. **Pets:** Other species. $15 one-time fee/pet. Service with restrictions, supervision.
SAVE 🖫 ⊠ 🖳M 🖎 🖥 🖳 🍴 🏊

ESPANOLA

▼▼ Comfort Inn 🆂🅷
(505) 753-2419. **$54-$134.** 604-B S Riverside Dr. US 84 and 285, just s of jct SR 68. Int corridors. **Pets:** Accepted.
ASK 🖫 ⊠ 🖥 🖳 🏊

▼▼ Espanola Days Inn 🆂🅷
(505) 747-1242. **$50-$75.** 807 S Riverside Dr. US 84 and 285, 0.7 mi s of jct SR 68. Ext corridors. **Pets:** Other species. $5 one-time fee/pet. Service with restrictions, supervision.
ASK 🖫 ⊠

🆔 **▼▼▼** Super 8 Motel 🆂🅷
(505) 753-5374. **$49-$119.** 811 S Riverside Dr. US 84 and 285, 0.5 mi s of jct SR 68. Int corridors. **Pets:** Accepted.
SAVE 🖫 ⊠ 🖥

FARMINGTON

🆔 **▼▼▼▼** Best Western Inn & Suites 🆂🅷
(505) 327-5221. **$89-$109.** 700 Scott Ave. 0.8 mi e on US 64 at Bloomfield Blvd and Scott Ave. Int corridors. **Pets:** $10 one-time fee/room. Service with restrictions, supervision.
SAVE 🖫 ⊠ 🖎 🖥 🖳 🍴 🏊 ⊠

🆔 **▼▼▼** Comfort Inn Ⓜ
(505) 325-2626. **$69-$89.** 555 Scott Ave. 0.8 mi e on US 64 (Bloomfield Blvd), just n. Int corridors. **Pets:** Accepted.
SAVE 🖫 ⊠ 🖥 🖳 🏊

▼▼ Days Inn Ⓜ
(505) 325-3700. **$50, 3 day notice.** 1901 E Broadway. 1.7 mi e on US 64 (Bloomfield Blvd). Int corridors. **Pets:** Accepted.
ASK 🖫 ⊠ 🖳M 🖎 🖎 🖥 🖳

▼▼▼▼ Holiday Inn Express Ⓜ
(505) 325-2545. **$71-$151.** 2110 Bloomfield Blvd. 1.6 mi e on US 64 (Bloomfield Blvd). Int corridors. **Pets:** Accepted.
ASK 🖫 ⊠ 🖳M 🖎 🖎 🖥 🖳 🏊

▼▼▼▼ Holiday Inn of Farmington 🆂🅷
(505) 327-9811. **$64.** 600 E Broadway. 0.8 mi e on US 64 at Bloomfield Blvd and Scott Ave. Int corridors. **Pets:** Medium. $25 one-time fee/room. Designated rooms, service with restrictions, supervision.
ASK 🖫 ⊠ 🖎 🖥 🖳 🍴 🏊 ⊠

🆔 **▼▼▼▼** La Quinta Inn Ⓜ
(505) 327-4706. **$71-$91.** 675 Scott Ave. 0.8 mi e on US 64 at Bloomfield Blvd and Scott Ave. Ext corridors. **Pets:** Service with restrictions.
SAVE 🖫 ⊠ 🖳M 🖎 🖥 🖳 🏊

🆔 **▼▼▼** Super 8 Motel Ⓜ
(505) 325-1813. **$45-$85, 3 day notice.** 1601 E Broadway. Just n of jct SR 44. Int corridors. **Pets:** Accepted.
SAVE 🖫 ⊠ 🖎 🖥

GALLUP

🆔 **▼▼▼▼** Best Western Inn & Suites 🆂🅷 🐾
(505) 722-2221. **$72-$135.** 3009 US 66 W. I-40, exit 16, 1 mi e. Int corridors. **Pets:** Medium, other species. $10 one-time fee/room. Designated rooms, service with restrictions, supervision.
SAVE 🖫 ⊠ 🖥 🖳 🍴 🏊 ⊠

🆔 **▼▼▼** Best Western Royal Holiday Motel 🆂🅷
(505) 722-4900. **$59-$104.** 1903 W Hwy 66. I-40, exit 20, 0.5 mi s to US 66, 0.8 mi w. Int corridors. **Pets:** Medium, other species. $10 daily fee/pet. Service with restrictions, supervision.
SAVE 🖫 ⊠ 🖥 🖳 🏊

🆔 **▼▼▼▼** Comfort Inn Ⓜ
(505) 722-0982. **$49-$99.** 3208 US 66 W. I-40, exit 16, 0.3 mi e. Int corridors. **Pets:** Small. $5 daily fee/pet. Designated rooms, service with restrictions, supervision.
SAVE 🖫 ⊠ 🖥 🖳 🏊

▼▼▼ Days Inn-West 🆂🅷
(505) 863-6889. **$49-$69, 7 day notice.** 3201 W Hwy 66. I-40, exit 16, 0.3 mi e. Ext corridors. **Pets:** Medium. $5 daily fee/pet. Designated rooms, service with restrictions, supervision.
ASK 🖫 ⊠ 🖥 🖳 🏊

🆔 **▼▼▼** Econo Lodge 🆂🅷
(505) 722-3800. **$35-$50.** 3101 US 66 W. I-40, exit 16, 0.8 mi e. Int corridors. **Pets:** Accepted.
SAVE 🖫 ⊠

🆔 **▼▼▼** Gallup Travelodge 🆂🅷
(505) 722-2100. **$44-$69, 7 day notice.** 3275 US 66 W. I-40, exit 16, just e. Int corridors. **Pets:** Medium. $5 daily fee/pet. Designated rooms, service with restrictions, supervision.
SAVE 🖫 ⊠ 🖳M 🖎 🖳 🏊

AAA ▼▼▼ Ramada Limited SH
(505) 726-2700. **$59-$89, 7 day notice.** 1440 W Maloney Ave. I-40, exit 20, 1 mi w. Int corridors. **Pets:** Medium. $5 daily fee/pet. Designated rooms, service with restrictions, supervision.
SAVE 🛎 ⊗ 🅰M 🛏 🔲 ⇌

AAA ▼▼ Red Roof Inn M
(505) 722-7765. **$36-$60.** 3304 W Hwy 66. I-40, exit 16, just se. Ext corridors. **Pets:** Large. $5 daily fee/pet. Designated rooms, service with restrictions, supervision.
SAVE 🛎 ⊗ 🛏 🔲 ⇌

AAA ▼▼ Road Runner Motel M
(505) 863-3804. **$37.** 3012 Hwy 66 E. I-40, exit 26, 1 mi w. Ext corridors. **Pets:** Other species. Service with restrictions.
SAVE 🛎 ⊗ 🍴 ⇌

AAA ▼▼▼ Sleep Inn SH
(505) 863-3535. **$55-$75, 7 day notice.** 3820 E US 66. I-40, exit 26, just e. Int corridors. **Pets:** Accepted.
SAVE 🛎 ⊗ 🅰M 🛁 🔲 ⇌

AAA ▼▼▼ Super 8 Motel M
(505) 722-5300. **$45-$56.** 1715 W US 66. I-40, exit 20, s to US 66, 0.5 mi w. Int corridors. **Pets:** Accepted.
SAVE 🛎 ⊗ 🛏 🔲 ⇌

GRANTS

AAA ▼▼▼ Best Western Inn & Suites SH
(505) 287-7901. **$69-$89.** 1501 E Santa Fe Ave. I-40, exit 85, just w. Int corridors. **Pets:** Medium. $10 one-time fee/room. Designated rooms, service with restrictions, supervision.
SAVE 🛎 ⊗ 🛁 🛏 🔲 🍴 ⇌ 🔲

▼▼▼▼ Comfort Inn SH
(505) 287-8700. **$49-$69, 7 day notice.** 1551 E Santa Fe Ave. I-40, exit 85, 0.3 mi n. Int corridors. **Pets:** Medium. $5 daily fee/pet. Designated rooms, service with restrictions, supervision.
ASK 🛎 ⊗ 🅰M 🛏 🔲 ⇌

AAA ▼▼▼ Days Inn SH
(505) 287-8883. **$60-$90.** 1504 E Santa Fe Ave. I-40, exit 85, 0.3 mi n. Ext corridors. **Pets:** Accepted.
SAVE 🛎 ⊗

AAA ▼▼▼ Grants Travelodge SH
(505) 287-7800. **$44-$59, 7 day notice.** 1608 E Santa Fe Ave. I-40, exit 85, 0.3 mi n. Ext corridors. **Pets:** Medium. $5 daily fee/pet. Designated rooms, service with restrictions, supervision.
SAVE 🛎 ⊗ 🅰M 🛁 🔲 ⇌

AAA ▼▼▼ Holiday Inn Express SH
(505) 285-4676. **$60-$90.** 1496 E Sante Fe Ave. I-40, exit 85, 0.3 mi n. Ext/int corridors. **Pets:** Accepted.
SAVE 🛎 ⊗ 🛏 🔲 ⇌

AAA ▼▼▼ Sands Motel M
(505) 287-2996. **$40-$43.** 112 McArthur St. I-40, exit 85, 1.5 mi w on Business Loop 40. Ext corridors. **Pets:** $5 one-time fee/pet. Service with restrictions, supervision.
SAVE 🛎 ⊗ 🛏

▼▼ ▼ Super 8 Grants SH
(505) 287-8811. **$40-$55, 7 day notice.** 1604 E Santa Fe Ave. I-40, exit 85, just n. Ext corridors. **Pets:** Accepted.
ASK 🛎 ⊗ 🔲 ⇌

HOBBS

AAA ▼▼▼ Best Western Executive Inn SH
(505) 397-7171. **$61-$80.** 309 N Marland Blvd. US 62/180 and Snyder St. Ext corridors. **Pets:** Accepted.
SAVE 🛎 ⊗ 🛏 🔲 ⇌

AAA ▼▼▼ Days Inn M
(505) 397-6541. **$55-$65, 3 day notice.** 211 N Marland Blvd. 2 mi e on US 62 and 180. Ext corridors. **Pets:** Small. $10 one-time fee/pet. Designated rooms, service with restrictions, supervision.
SAVE 🛎 ⊗ 🔲 🛁 🛏 🔲 ⇌

AAA ▼▼▼ Econo Lodge SH
(505) 397-3591. **$44-$54.** 619 N Marland Blvd. 2.5 mi e on US 62 and 180. Ext corridors. **Pets:** Accepted.
SAVE 🛎 ⊗ 🛏 🔲 ⇌

AAA ▼▼▼ Howard Johnson-Hobbs SH
(505) 397-3251. **$55-$75.** 501 N Marland Blvd. 2.5 mi e on US 62 and 180. Ext/int corridors. **Pets:** Accepted.
SAVE 🛎 ⊗ 🛁 🛏 🔲 🍴 ⇌

▼▼ Rodeway Inn M
(505) 393-4101. **$50-$65.** 200 N Marland Blvd. On US 62/180, 2 mi e. Ext corridors. **Pets:** Accepted.
ASK 🛎 ⊗ 🛏 🔲 ⇌

LAS CRUCES

AAA ▼▼▼▼ Baymont Inn & Suites Las Cruces SH
(505) 523-0100. **$49-$64.** 1500 Hickory Dr. I-10, exit 140, just se of jct I-25 and Avenida de Mesilla. Int corridors. **Pets:** Medium. $50 deposit/pet. Service with restrictions, supervision.
SAVE 🛎 ⊗ 🅰M 🛁 🛏 🔲 ⇌

AAA ▼▼▼▼ Best Western Mesilla Valley Inn SH
(505) 524-8603. **$62-$89.** 901 Avenida de Mesilla. I-10, exit 140, just n. Ext/int corridors. **Pets:** Medium, other species.
SAVE 🛎 ⊗ 🔲 🛏 🔲 🍴 ⇌

AAA ▼▼▼▼ Best Western Mission Inn SH
(505) 524-8591. **$69-$89.** 1765 S Main St. I-10, exit 142, 1 mi n. Ext corridors. **Pets:** Accepted.
SAVE ⊗ 🛏 🔲 🍴 ⇌

AAA ▼▼▼ Hampton Inn SH
(505) 526-8311. **$75.** 755 Avenida de Mesilla. I-10, exit 140. Ext corridors. **Pets:** Accepted.
SAVE 🛎 ⊗ 🛏 🔲 ⇌

▼▼▼▼ Hilton Las Cruces LH
(505) 522-4300. **$89-$94.** 705 S Telshore Blvd. I-25, exit 3 (Lohman Dr), just e. Int corridors. **Pets:** Medium, dogs only. $20 daily fee/room. Designated rooms, service with restrictions, supervision.
ASK 🛎 ⊗ 🅰M 🔲 🛏 🔲 🍴 ⇌

◆◆◆◆ Holiday Inn de Las Cruces SH
(505) 526-4411. **$95.** 201 E University Ave. I-10, exit 142, just n. Int corridors. **Pets:** Other species. $25 one-time fee/room. Service with restrictions, supervision.

ASK S⭐ ✕ &M 🐾 & 🛏 💻 ¶ ≋

◆◆◆◆ Holiday Inn Express SH
(505) 527-9947. **$49-$149.** 2200 S Valley Dr. I-10, exit 142, 2 blks w. Ext corridors. **Pets:** Accepted.

ASK S⭐ ✕ &M 🐾 🛏 💻 ≋

◆◆◆◆ La Quinta Inn-Las Cruces SH
(505) 524-0331. **$70-$80.** 790 Avenida de Mesilla. I-10, exit 140. Int corridors. **Pets:** Medium, other species. Service with restrictions.

ASK S⭐ ✕ &M 🐾 🛏 💻 ≋

◆◆◆◆ Lundeen's Inn of the Arts BB ✿
(505) 526-3326. **$77.** 618 S Alameda Blvd. Center. Int corridors. **Pets:** Medium. $15 one-time fee/pet. Service with restrictions, crate.

ASK ✕

◆◆ Motel 6–363 M
(505) 525-1010. **$42-$55.** 235 La Posada Ln. I-10, exit 142, just n. Ext corridors. **Pets:** Accepted.

S⭐ ✕ &M 🐾 & 🛏 💻 ≋

◆◆ Royal Host Motel M
(505) 524-8536. **$38-$42, 4 day notice.** 2146 W Picacho St. I-10, exit 139, 1 mi n, then 0.5 mi e on I-10 business route (Picacho St). Ext corridors. **Pets:** Medium. $15 daily pet. No service, supervision.

✕ 🛏 ≋

◆◆ Super 8 Motel M
(505) 523-8695. **$41-$45.** 245 La Posada Ln. I-10, exit 142, 2.8 mi s on US 80, 85 and 180. Int corridors. **Pets:** Medium, other species. $15 one-time fee/pet. Service with restrictions, supervision.

ASK S⭐ ✕ 🛏

◆◆ Teakwood Inn & Suites SH
(505) 526-4441. **$50-$100.** 2600 S Valley Dr. I-10, exit 142. Int corridors. **Pets:** Large, other species. $10 one-time fee/pet. Service with restrictions, supervision.

ASK S⭐ ✕ 🐾 🛏 ≋

◆◆◆◆ TRH Smith Mansion Bed and Breakfast BB
(505) 525-2525. **$89, 7 day notice.** 909 N Alameda Blvd. Center. Int corridors. **Pets:** Accepted.

ASK ✕

LAS VEGAS

◆◆◆ ◆◆◆◆ Comfort Inn SH
(505) 425-1100. **$70-$100.** 2500 N Grand Ave. I-25, exit 347, just sw, US 85 and I-25 business route. Int corridors. **Pets:** Other species. Designated rooms, service with restrictions, supervision.

SAVE S⭐ ✕ & 💻 ≋

◆◆◆ ◆◆◆ El Camino Motel M
(505) 425-5994. **$50-$65.** 1152 N Grand Ave. I-25, exit 345, 0.3 mi w, US 85 and I-25 business route. Ext corridors. **Pets:** Very small, dogs only. $6 daily fee/pet. Designated rooms, service with restrictions, supervision.

SAVE S⭐ ✕ ¶

◆◆◆ Inn on the Santa Fe Trail M ✿
(505) 425-6791. **$59-$84.** 1133 N Grand Ave. I-25, exit 345, 0.5 mi n; I-25 business route and US 84, 0.3 mi w. Ext corridors. **Pets:** $5 daily fee/room. Service with restrictions, supervision.

SAVE S⭐ ✕ 🛏 💻 ¶ ≋

◆◆◆ ◆◆◆ Plaza Hotel CI
(505) 425-3591. **$86-$116.** 230 Plaza. I-25, exit 343W, just w, follow signs to Old Town Plaza. Int corridors. **Pets:** $10 daily fee/pet. Designated rooms, service with restrictions, supervision.

SAVE S⭐ ✕ 🛏 💻 ¶

LORDSBURG

◆◆◆ ◆◆◆ Best Western-Western Skies Inn SH
(505) 542-8807. **$62-$80.** 1303 S Main St. I-10, exit 22, just s. Ext corridors. **Pets:** $10 daily fee/pet. Designated rooms, service with restrictions, supervision.

SAVE S⭐ ✕ 🛏 💻 ¶ ≋

◆◆◆◆ Holiday Inn Express SH
(505) 542-3666. **$67-$74, 5 day notice.** 1408 S Main St. I-10, exit 22, just s. Ext corridors. **Pets:** Accepted.

ASK S⭐ ✕ &M & 🛏 💻 ≋

LOS ALAMOS

◆◆◆ ◆◆◆ Los Alamos Inn SH
(505) 662-7211. **$79-$99.** 2201 Trinity Dr. Center. Int corridors. **Pets:** Accepted.

SAVE ✕ 🛏 💻 ¶ ≋

LOS LUNAS

◆◆ Days Inn SH
(505) 865-5995. **$53-$66.** 1919 Main St SW. I-25, exit 203, just s to entrance at southeast corner. Int corridors. **Pets:** Other species. $15 daily fee/room. Service with restrictions, crate.

ASK S⭐ ✕ 🛏 💻 ≋

◆◆ Western Skies Inn & Suites SH
(505) 865-0001. **$59-$69.** 2258 Sun Ranch Village Loop. I-25, exit 203, just n. Int corridors. **Pets:** Small. $5 daily fee/pet. Designated rooms, service with restrictions, supervision.

ASK S⭐ ✕ &M & ≋

LOVINGTON

◆◆◆ ◆◆◆ Lovington Inn SH
(505) 396-5346. **$59-$74.** 1600 W Ave D. Jct of US 82 and SR 18, 1 mi w. Ext corridors. **Pets:** Small. $10 deposit/pet. Service with restrictions, supervision.

SAVE S⭐ ✕ & 🛏 💻 ¶

MESILLA

▼▼ Meson de Mesilla 🄲
(505) 525-9212. **$65-$140.** 1803 Avenida de Mesilla. I-10, exit 140, 0.4 mi s. Int corridors. **Pets:** Accepted.
⊠ 🖥 🍴 ⌫

MORIARTY

🄰🄰🄰 ▼▼▼ Days Inn 🅂🄷
(505) 832-4451. **$43-$59.** 1809 Route 66 W. I-40, exit 194. Int corridors. **Pets:** $5 daily fee/pet. No service, supervision.
🆂🄰🅅🄴 🅂🄳 ⊠ 🖥

🄰🄰🄰 ▼▼▼ Econo Lodge 🅂🄷
(505) 832-4457. **$41-$69.** 1316 Route 66 W. I-40, exit 194, 0.5 mi se on US 66 and I-40 business loop. Int corridors. **Pets:** Other species. $5 daily fee/pet. Service with restrictions, supervision.
🆂🄰🅅🄴 🅂🄳 ⊠ 🖥 💻

🄰🄰🄰 ▼▼▼▼ Holiday Inn Express 🅂🄷
(505) 832-5000. **$96.** 1507 Route 66. I-40, exit 194, 0.4 mi e. Int corridors. **Pets:** Medium. $10 one-time fee/room. No service, supervision.
🆂🄰🅅🄴 ⊠ 🔊🄼 🖥 💻 ⌫

▼▼ Motel 6 #4069 🅂🄷
(505) 832-6666. **$46.** 109 Route 66 E. I-40, exit 197, 1 mi e, then 0.5 mi e. Int corridors. **Pets:** Accepted.
⊠ 🔊🄼 📶 🐾 ⌫

🄰🄰🄰 ▼ Sunset Motel 🄼
(505) 832-4234. **$43-$49.** 501 Old Route 66. I-40, exit 197, 1 mi w, then 0.5 mi e. Ext corridors. **Pets:** Accepted.
🆂🄰🅅🄴 🅂🄳 ⊠ 🖥 💻

🄰🄰🄰 ▼▼ Super 8 Motel 🅂🄷
(505) 832-6730. **$49-$65.** 1611 W Old Route 66. I-40, exit 194, 0.5 mi e on Central Ave. Int corridors. **Pets:** Other species. $20 deposit/room. Designated rooms, service with restrictions, supervision.
🆂🄰🅅🄴 🅂🄳 ⊠ 🐾 🖥

PINOS ALTOS

▼▼ Bear Creek Motel & Cabins 🄲🄰
(505) 388-4501. **$89-$159, 14 day notice.** 88 Main St. 1 mi n on SR 15. Ext corridors. **Pets:** Small. $10 daily fee/pet. No service.
🖥 💻 🎿

PLACITAS

▼▼▼▼ Hacienda de Placitas Inn of the Arts 🄱🄱
(505) 867-0082. **$109-$209, 14 day notice.** 491 Hwy 165. I-25, exit 242, 4.9 mi e. Ext corridors. **Pets:** Accepted.
⊠ 🖥 💻 ⌫

POJOAQUE PUEBLO

🄰🄰🄰 ▼▼▼▼ Cities of Gold Hotel 🅂🄷
(505) 455-0515. **$75-$95.** 10A Cities of Gold Rd. On US 84/265, just n. Int corridors. **Pets:** Other species. $25 deposit/room. Designated rooms.
🆂🄰🅅🄴 🅂🄳 ⊠ 🔊🄼 🐾 🖥 💻 🍴

RANCHOS DE TAOS

🄰🄰🄰 ▼ Budget Host Inn 🄼
(505) 758-2524. **$48-$70.** 1798 Paseo Del Pueblo Sur. On SR 68; center. Ext corridors. **Pets:** Other species. $5 one-time fee/room. Service with restrictions, crate.
🆂🄰🅅🄴 🅂🄳 ⊠ 🖥 💻

RATON

🄰🄰🄰 ▼▼▼ Budget Host Raton 🄼
(505) 445-3655. **$43-$54.** 136 Canyon Dr. I-25, exit 454, 0.8 mi s on I-25 business loop. Ext corridors. **Pets:** Medium. $2 daily fee/pet. Service with restrictions, supervision.
🆂🄰🅅🄴 🅂🄳 ⊠ 🔊🄼 🖥

▼ The Pass Inn
(505) 445-3641. **$42-$52.** 308 Canyon Dr. I-25, exit 454, 0.8 mi s. Ext corridors. **Pets:** Medium, other species. Service with restrictions, supervision.
🄰🅂🄺 🅂🄳 ⊠ 🖥

RIO RANCHO

**🄰🄰🄰 ▼▼▼ Best Western Rio Rancho Inn &
Conference Center** 🅂🄷
(505) 892-1700. **$64-$99.** 1465 Rio Rancho Blvd. I-25, exit 233 (Alameda Blvd), 6.5 mi w; I-40, exit 155, 10 mi n on Coors Rd/Coors Bypass to SR 528, 1 mi n. Ext corridors. **Pets:** Accepted.
🆂🄰🅅🄴 🅂🄳 ⊠ 📶 🖥 💻 🍴 ⌫

🄰🄰🄰 ▼▼▼ Days Inn 🄼
(505) 892-8800. **$50-$65.** 4200 Crestview Dr. I-25, exit 233 (Alameda Blvd), 8 mi w on SR 528; I-40, exit 155, then 8 mi n on Coors Rd (SR 448). Ext corridors. **Pets:** Accepted.
🆂🄰🅅🄴 🅂🄳 ⊠ 🖥 ⌫

▼▼▼▼ Ramada Limited Hotel 🅂🄷
(505) 892-5998. **$55.** 4081 High Resort Blvd. I-25, exit 233 (Alameda Blvd), 8 mi w; I-40, exit 155, 8 mi n on Coors Rd (SR 448). Int corridors. **Pets:** Accepted.
🄰🅂🄺 🅂🄳 ⊠ 🖥 💻 ⌫

▼▼ Rio Rancho Super 8 Motel 🅂🄷
(505) 896-8888. **$56-$61.** 4100 Barbara Loop. I-25, exit 233 (Alameda Blvd), 0.5 mi w, 3.8 mi nw on SR 528, just e. Int corridors. **Pets:** $8 daily fee/pet. Service with restrictions, supervision.
🄰🅂🄺 🅂🄳 ⊠

**🄰🄰🄰 ▼▼▼▼ Wellesley Inn & Suites
(Albuquerque/North)** 🅂🄷
(505) 892-7900. **$72-$225.** 2221 Rio Rancho Blvd. I-25, exit 233 (Alameda Blvd), 6 mi w (becomes SR 528/Rio Rancho Blvd). Int corridors. **Pets:** Small. Designated rooms, service with restrictions, supervision.
🆂🄰🅅🄴 🅂🄳 ⊠ 📶 🖥 💻 ⌫ 🐾

ROSWELL

🄰🄰🄰 ▼▼▼ Best Western El Rancho Palacio 🅂🄷
(505) 622-2721. **$60-$75, 7 day notice.** 2205 N Main St. 1.8 mi n on US 70 and 285. Ext corridors. **Pets:** Service with restrictions, supervision.
🆂🄰🅅🄴 🅂🄳 ⊠ 🖥 💻 ⌫

(AAA) ▼▼▼ Best Western Sally Port Inn & Suites SH
(505) 622-6430. **$89-$100, 7 day notice.** 2000 N Main St. 1.5 mi n on US 70 and 285. Int corridors. **Pets:** Other species. $10 daily fee/pet. Designated rooms, service with restrictions, supervision.
SAVE S6 X 🗄 💻 🍴 🏊 🐾

(AAA) ▼▼▼ Budget Inn-North M ❖
(505) 623-6050. **$35-$45.** 2101 N Main St. 1.8 mi n on US 70 and 285. Ext corridors. **Pets:** Medium. $5 daily fee/pet. Designated rooms, service with restrictions, supervision.
SAVE S6 X 🗄 🏊

(AAA) ▼▼▼ Budget Inn West SH
(505) 623-3811. **$32-$50.** 2200 W 2nd St. 2 mi w on US 70 and 380. Ext corridors. **Pets:** Small, dogs only. $2 daily fee/pet. Service with restrictions, supervision.
SAVE S6 X 🗄 🏊

(AAA) ▼▼▼ Comfort Inn SH
(505) 623-4567. **$69-$109, 5 day notice.** 3595 N Main St. On US 70 and 285, 3 mi n. Int corridors. **Pets:** Small. Service with restrictions, supervision.
SAVE S6 X 🔥 🖐 🗄 💻 🏊

(AAA) ▼▼▼ Days Inn SH
(505) 623-4021. **$55-$75, 7 day notice.** 1310 N Main St. 0.8 mi n on US 70 and 285. Ext corridors. **Pets:** Service with restrictions, supervision.
SAVE S6 X 🕐 🗄 💻 🍴 🏊

(AAA) ▼▼▼ Frontier Motel M ❖
(505) 622-1400. **$36-$44.** 3010 N Main St. 2.5 mi n on US 70 and 285. Ext corridors. **Pets:** Service with restrictions, supervision.
SAVE S6 X 🗄 🏊

(AAA) ▼▼▼ Leisure Inn SH
(505) 622-2575. **$36-$65.** 2700 W 2nd St. 2.5 mi w on US 70 and 380. Ext corridors. **Pets:** Small, dogs only. $4 daily fee/pet. Designated rooms, service with restrictions, supervision.
SAVE S6 X 🗄 💻 🏊 🐾

(AAA) ▼▼▼ National 9 Inn M
(505) 622-0110. **$35-$37.** 2001 N Main St. 1.5 mi n on US 70 and 285. Ext corridors. **Pets:** Other species. $5 daily fee/pet. Service with restrictions.
SAVE S6 X 🗄 🏊

▼▼▼ Ramada Limited SH
(505) 623-9440. **$59-$68.** 2803 W 2nd St. 2.5 mi w on US 70 and 380. Ext/int corridors. **Pets:** Accepted.
ASK S6 X 🗄 🏊

▼▼ Western Inn M
(505) 623-9425. **$50-$225.** 2331 N Main St. Jct US 70/285/ 380, 2.2 mi n. Ext corridors. **Pets:** Accepted.
ASK S6 X 🗄 💻 🏊

RUIDOSO

▼▼▼▼ Hawthorn Suites Golf & Convention Resort SH
(505) 258-5500. **$113-$133.** 107 Sierra Blanca Dr. 2.5 mi n on SR 48. Int corridors. **Pets:** Designated rooms, service with restrictions, supervision.
ASK S6 X 🕐 🖐 🗄 💻 🏊 🐾

▼▼ Travelodge SH
(505) 378-4471. **$45-$129.** 159 W Hwy 70. Jct of US 70 and SR 48 (the "Y"). Ext corridors. **Pets:** Small. $10 daily fee/ pet. Designated rooms, service with restrictions, supervision.
ASK S6 X 🗄 💻 🏊

▼▼▼ Village Lodge Suites CO
(505) 258-5442. **$129-$250, 30 day notice.** 1000 Mechem Dr. 2 mi n on SR 48. Ext corridors. **Pets:** Small. $10 one-time fee/room. Designated rooms, crate.
ASK S6 X 🗄 💻

SANTA FE

(AAA) ▼▼▼ Alexander's Inn BB ❖
(505) 986-1431. **$85-$190, 14 day notice.** 529 E Palace Ave. 6 blks e of The Plaza. Ext/int corridors. **Pets:** Other species. $25 one-time fee/pet. Service with restrictions.
SAVE X 🗄 💻 🐾

(AAA) ▼▼▼ Best Western of Santa Fe SH
(505) 438-3822. **$45-$125, 7 day notice.** 3650 Cerrillos Rd. I-25, exit 278, 2.8 mi n. Int corridors. **Pets:** Accepted.
SAVE S6 X 🕐 🗄 🏊

(AAA) ▼▼ Bishop's Lodge Resort LH
(505) 983-6377. **$209-$409, 14 day notice.** N Bishop's Lodge Rd. 3.5 mi n of jct Paseo De Peralta. Ext/int corridors. **Pets:** Other species. $150 deposit/room. Service with restrictions.
SAVE S6 X 🕐 🗄 💻 🍴 🏊 🐾

(AAA) ▼ Cactus Lodge Motel M
(505) 471-7699. **$44-$85.** 2864 Cerrillos Rd. 3.8 mi sw on US 85. Ext corridors. **Pets:** Accepted.
SAVE S6 X 🗄

(AAA) ▼▼▼ Camel Rock Suites CO
(505) 989-3600. **$89-$99, 3 day notice.** 3007 S St Frances Dr. I-25, exit 282, 0.8 mi n on S Saint Francis Dr, just e on Zia via access drive. Ext corridors. **Pets:** Small, dogs only. $100 deposit/room, $25 one-time fee/room. Designated rooms, service with restrictions, supervision.
SAVE S6 X 🔥 🕐 🖐 🗄 💻

▼▼▼ Casapueblo Inn BB
(505) 988-4455. **$129-$279, 3 day notice.** 138 Park Ave. Intersection of Guadalupe and Park; center. Ext corridors. **Pets:** Large. $50 one-time fee/room. Service with restrictions, crate.
ASK S6 X 🖐 🗄 💻

(AAA) ▼▼▼ Comfort Inn SH
(505) 474-7330. **$69-$139.** 4312 Cerrillos Rd. I-25, exit 278, 1.6 mi n. Int corridors. **Pets:** Other species. Service with restrictions, supervision.
SAVE S6 X 🕐 🖐 🗄 💻 🏊

🔷 💎💎 💎💎 Eldorado Hotel 🏩
(505) 988-4455. **$169-$1500, 3 day notice.** 309 W San Francisco. Just w of The Plaza at Sandoval St. Int corridors. **Pets:** Other species. $50 one-time fee/pet. Service with restrictions.
SAVE 🆓 ✕ 🔧M 🗐 🖵 🍴 ⊇ ✕

🔷 💎💎 💎💎 El Paradero Bed & Breakfast 🅱🅱
(505) 988-1177. **$75-$160, 14 day notice.** 220 W Manhattan Ave. 0.3 mi s on Cerrillos Rd, just e. Ext/int corridors. **Pets:** Accepted.
SAVE ✕ 🔧 🖥 🖵

💎💎 💎💎 The Hacienda at Hotel Santa Fe 🆂🅷 🐾
(505) 955-7800. **$199-$499, 3 day notice.** 1501 Paseo de Peralta. At Cerrillos Rd, 0.6 mi s of The Plaza. Int corridors. **Pets:** Medium, dogs only. $20 daily fee/pet. Service with restrictions, supervision.
ASK 🆓 ✕ 🖵 🍴 ⊇

💎💎 💎💎 Hacienda Nicholas 🅱🅱
(505) 986-1431. **$100-$175, 14 day notice.** 320 E Marcy St. 4 blks e of The Plaza. Ext/int corridors. **Pets:** Accepted.
✕

🔷 💎💎💎 Hampton Inn Santa Fe 🆂🅷
(505) 474-3900. **$59-$129.** 3625 Cerrillos Rd. I-25, exit 278B, 2.5 mi n. Int corridors. **Pets:** Accepted.
SAVE ✕ 🔧M 🗐 🖥 🖵 ⊇ ✕

🔷 💎💎💎 Hotel Plaza Real 🆂🅷
(505) 988-4900. **$139-$299, 3 day notice.** 125 Washington Ave. Just ne of The Plaza; center. Ext corridors. **Pets:** Accepted.
SAVE 🆓 🗐 🖥 🖵

🔷 💎💎💎 Hotel Santa Fe 🆂🅷 🐾
(505) 982-1200. **$119-$499.** 1501 Paseo de Peralta. At Cerrillos Rd, 0.6 mi s of The Plaza. Int corridors. **Pets:** Medium, dogs only. $20 daily fee/pet. Designated rooms, service with restrictions, supervision.
SAVE 🆓 ✕ 🗐 🍴 ⊇ ✕

🔷 💎💎💎 Inn On The Alameda 🆂🅷 🐾
(505) 984-2121. **$129-$275, 3 day notice.** 303 E Alameda Ave. 4 blks e of The Plaza; at jct Paseo De Peralta. Ext/int corridors. **Pets:** Small, other species. $20 daily fee/pet. Designated rooms.
SAVE 🆓 ✕ 🗐 🖥 🖵 ✕

🔷 💎💎💎 La Quinta Inn 🆂🅷
(505) 471-1142. **$79-$119.** 4298 Cerrillos Rd. I-25, exit 278, 1.8 mi n. Int corridors. **Pets:** Medium, other species. Service with restrictions, supervision.
SAVE 🆓 ✕ 🗐 🖥 🖵 ⊇

💎💎💎 Las Palomas 🅼
(505) 988-4455. **$129-$239, 3 day notice.** 460 W San Francisco St. Just w of jct Guadalupe St. Ext corridors. **Pets:** Accepted.
ASK 🆓 ✕ 🗐 🖥 🖵 ⊇ ✕

💎💎 Motel 6–150 🅼
(505) 473-1380. **$45-$71.** 3007 Cerrillos Rd. I-25, exit 278B, 3.8 mi n. Ext corridors. **Pets:** Accepted.
🆓 ✕ 🖥 🖵 ⊇

💎💎💎 The Old Santa Fe Inn 🅼 🐾
(505) 995-0800. **$79-$299, 3 day notice.** 320 Galisteo St. Just sw of Historic Santa Fee Plaza; center. Ext/int corridors. **Pets:** $25 one-time fee/room. Designated rooms, service with restrictions, crate.
ASK 🆓 ✕ 🗐 🖥 🖵

🔷 💎💎💎 Park Inn & Suites 🆂🅷
(505) 471-3000. **$79-$84.** 2907 Cerrillos Rd. I-25, exit 278, 7 mi n. Ext corridors. **Pets:** Medium, other species. $100 deposit/pet. Service with restrictions, supervision.
SAVE 🆓 ✕ 🖥 🖵 ⊇ ✕

🔷 💎💎 Pecos Trail Inn 🅼
(505) 982-1943. **$79-$149, 5 day notice.** 2239 Old Pecos Tr. I-25, exit 284, 0.8 mi n on CR 466 (Old Pecos Tr). Ext corridors. **Pets:** Accepted.
SAVE 🆓 ✕ 🖥 🖵 🍴 ⊇

🔷 💎💎 Quality Inn 🆂🅷
(505) 471-1211. **$65-$115.** 3011 Cerrillos Rd. I-25, exit 278B, 3.8 mi n. Int corridors. **Pets:** Medium, other species. Service with restrictions, supervision.
SAVE 🆓 ✕ 🖥 🖵 🍴 ⊇

🔷 💎💎 Ramada Limited 🆂🅷
(505) 471-4000. **$49-$129.** 3450 Cerrillos Rd. I-25, exit 278, 3 mi n. Int corridors. **Pets:** Accepted.
SAVE ✕ 🔧M 🖥 🖵

💎💎 Residence Inn by Marriott 🆂🅷
(505) 988-7300. **$139-$239.** 1698 Galisteo St. I-25, exit 282, 1.7 mi n on St Francis Dr to St Michaels Dr, just e. Ext corridors. **Pets:** Accepted.
ASK 🆓 ✕ 🗐 🖥 🖵 ⊇

💎💎 Rio Vista Suites 🅲🅾
(505) 982-6636. **Call for rates.** 527 E Alameda St. 0.5 mi e of center. Ext corridors. **Pets:** Accepted.
✕ 🖥 🖵

💎💎 Santa Fe Plaza Travelodge 🆂🅷
(505) 982-3551. **$59-$150.** 646 Cerrillos Rd. 0.8 mi sw of The Plaza. Ext/int corridors. **Pets:** Accepted.
ASK 🆓 ✕ 🗐 🖥 🖵 ⊇

SANTA ROSA

🔷 💎💎 Best Western Adobe Inn 🆂🅷
(505) 472-3446. **$58-$80, 3 day notice.** 1501 Historic Route 66. I-40, exit 275. Ext corridors. **Pets:** Medium, other species. No service, supervision.
SAVE 🆓 ✕ 🖵 ⊇

🔷 💎💎💎 Best Western Santa Rosa Inn 🅼 🐾
(505) 472-5877. **$55-$75.** 3022 Historic Route 66. I-40, exit 277, 0.5 mi w. Ext corridors. **Pets:** Medium. Designated rooms, service with restrictions, supervision.
SAVE 🆓 ✕ 🖥 🖵 ⊇

💎💎💎 Comfort Inn 🆂🅷
(505) 472-5570. **$59-$89.** 3343 E Historic Route 66. I-40, exit 277, 0.3 mi w. Ext corridors. **Pets:** Medium, other species. $10 one-time fee/pet. Designated rooms, service with restrictions, supervision.
ASK 🆓 ✕ 🖥 🖵 ⊇

Days Inn of Santa Rosa SH
(505) 472-5985. **$45-$70.** 1830 Historic Route 66. I-40, exit 275. Ext corridors. **Pets:** Other species. $5 one-time fee/pet. Designated rooms, no service, supervision.

Holiday Inn Express SH
(505) 472-5411. **$69-$89.** 3300 Historic Route 66. I-40, exit 277, 0.3 mi w. Int corridors. **Pets:** Medium. Designated rooms, service with restrictions, supervision.

La Quinta SH
(505) 472-4800. **$73-$90.** 1701 Historic Route 66. I-40, exit 275, just e. Int corridors. **Pets:** Other species. Service with restrictions, supervision.

Motel 6–273 M
(505) 472-3045. **$41-$55.** 3400 Historic Route 66. I-40, exit 277, 0.3 mi w. Ext corridors. **Pets:** Accepted.

Super 8 Motel-Santa Rosa M
(505) 472-5388. **$50-$62.** 1201 Historic Route 66. I-40, exit 275, just w. Int corridors. **Pets:** Accepted.

SILVER CITY

The Drifter Motel SH
(505) 538-2916. **$45-$50.** 711 Silver Heights Blvd. On US 180 and SR 90, 1.3 mi ne. Ext corridors. **Pets:** Accepted.

Econo Lodge Silver City SH
(505) 534-1111. **$45-$70.** 1120 Hwy 180 E. 1.5 mi ne on US 180 and SR 90. Int corridors. **Pets:** Medium, other species. $20 deposit/room, $7 daily fee/pet. Service with restrictions, supervision.

Holiday Inn Express SH
(505) 538-2525. **$80-$90.** 1103 Superior St. 3 mi ne on US 180 and SR 90. Int corridors. **Pets:** Small, dogs only. $150 deposit/pet. Designated rooms, service with restrictions, supervision.

Holiday Motor Hotel SH
(505) 538-3711. **$42-$46.** 3420 Hwy 180 E. 3 mi ne on jct US 180 and SR 90. Ext corridors. **Pets:** Accepted.

Super 8 Motel SH
(505) 388-1983. **$39-$52, 5 day notice.** 1040 E Hwy 180. 1.5 mi ne on US 180 and SR 90. Int corridors. **Pets:** Accepted.

SOCORRO

Econo Lodge SH
(505) 835-1500. **$39-$65.** 713 California Ave. I-25, exit 150, 1 mi s. Ext corridors. **Pets:** Small, dogs only. $5 daily fee/pet. Designated rooms, service with restrictions, supervision.

Holiday Inn Express SH
(505) 838-0556. **$90-$130.** 1100 California Ave NE. Center. Ext/int corridors. **Pets:** Medium, other species. $10 daily fee/room. Designated rooms.

Motel 6 #392 SH
(505) 835-4300. **$38-$55.** 807 S US 85. I-25, exit 147. Ext corridors. **Pets:** Accepted.

TAOS

Adobe Sun God Lodge M
(505) 758-3162. **$49-$99.** 919 Paseo del Pueblo Sur. SR 68, 1.8 mi sw of jct US 64 and Taos Plaza. Ext corridors. **Pets:** Large, other species. $10 one-time fee/room. Service with restrictions, supervision.

American Artists Gallery House Bed & Breakfast BB
(505) 758-4446. **$95-$225, 14 day notice.** 132 Frontier Ln. SR 68, 1 mi sw of jct US 64 and Taos Plaza, 0.3 mi e. Ext/int corridors. **Pets:** Dogs only. $10 daily fee/pet, $25 one-time fee/pet. Designated rooms, service with restrictions, supervision.

Brooks Street Inn Bed and Breakfast BB
(505) 758-1489. **$89-$169, 14 day notice.** 119 Brooks St. 0.5 mi n on US 64 from jct SR 68 and Taos Plaza, just e. Ext/int corridors. **Pets:** Small, dogs only. $10 daily fee/pet. Designated rooms, service with restrictions, supervision.

Burch Street Casitas CA
(505) 737-9038. **$69-$139, 21 day notice.** 310 Burch St. US 64, just e of jct SR 68, just s. Ext corridors. **Pets:** Medium. $25 one-time fee/pet. No service, supervision.

Casa Encantada BB
(505) 758-7477. **$110-$195, 10 day notice.** 416 Liebert St. Jct SR 68 and Taos Plaza, 0.6 mi e on US 64, then just s. Ext corridors. **Pets:** Other species. $15 daily fee/room. Service with restrictions.

Casa Europa Inn & Gallery BB
(505) 758-9798. **$125-$185, 14 day notice.** 840 Upper Ranchitos Rd. 1.7 mi s from jct US 64. Ext/int corridors. **Pets:** Large, dogs only. Designated rooms, service with restrictions, supervision.

El Pueblo Lodge M
(505) 758-8700. **$69-$89, 7 day notice.** 412 Paseo del Pueblo Norte. US 64, 0.5 mi n of jct SR 68 and Taos Plaza. Ext corridors. **Pets:** Other species. $10 daily fee/pet. Service with restrictions, crate.

Fechin Inn ◆
(505) 751-1000. **$114-$512, 3 day notice.** 227 Paseo del Pueblo Norte. Just n on US 64 of jct SR 68 and Taos Plaza; center. Int corridors. **Pets:** Small, dogs only. $50 one-time fee/pet. Designated rooms, service with restrictions, supervision.

Holiday Inn Don Fernando de Taos
(505) 758-4444. **$99-$185.** 1005 Paseo del Pueblo Sur. SR 68, 1.8 mi sw of jct US 64 and Taos Plaza. Ext corridors. **Pets:** Accepted.

Inn On The Rio
(505) 758-7199. **$99-$129, 15 day notice.** 910 Kit Carson Rd. US 64, 1.5 mi e of jct SR 68 and Taos Plaza. Ext corridors. **Pets:** Dogs only. $25 one-time fee/room. Designated rooms, service with restrictions, supervision.

Orinda Bed & Breakfast
(505) 758-8581. **$89-$145, 14 day notice.** 461 Valverde. 0.5 mi ne of Taos Plaza; center. Ext/int corridors. **Pets:** Medium, dogs only. $10 daily fee/pet. Designated rooms, service with restrictions, supervision.

Quality Inn
(505) 758-2200. **$59-$109, 3 day notice.** 1043 Paseo del Pueblo Sur. SR 68, 2 mi sw of jct US 64 and Taos Plaza. Ext/int corridors. **Pets:** Other species. $7 daily fee/pet. Designated rooms, service with restrictions, supervision.

Ramada Inn de Taos
(505) 758-2900. **$55-$99.** 615 Paseo del Pueblo Sur. SR 68, 1 mi sw of jct US 64 and Taos Plaza. Ext corridors. **Pets:** Accepted.

Sagebrush Inn
(505) 758-2254. **$85-$125, 3 day notice.** 1508 Paseo del Pueblo Sur. SR 68, 3 mi sw of jct US 64 and Taos Plaza. Ext corridors. **Pets:** Other species. $7 daily fee/room. Designated rooms, supervision.

San Geronimo Lodge ◆
(505) 751-3776. **$95-$150, 10 day notice.** 1101 Witt Rd. Jct US 64 and SR 68, 1.3 mi e on US 64 E (Kit Carson Rd), 0.6 mi s; center. Ext/int corridors. **Pets:** $10 one-time fee/room. Designated rooms, service with restrictions, crate.

THOREAU

Zuni Mountain Lodge
(505) 862-7769. **$95 (no credit cards), 3 day notice.** 40 W Perch Dr. I-40, exit 53, 13 mi s on SR 612, then w. Ext/int corridors. **Pets:** Medium, other species. Service with restrictions.

TRUTH OR CONSEQUENCES

Best Western Hot Springs Motor Inn ◆
(505) 894-6665. **$50-$70.** 2270 N Date St. I-25, exit 79. Ext corridors. **Pets:** Other species. Service with restrictions.

Holiday Inn
(505) 894-1660. **$60-$85.** 2250 N Date St. I-25, exit 79, just e. Int corridors. **Pets:** Medium, other species. Supervision.

Super 8 Motel
(505) 894-7888. **$60.** 2151 N Date St. I-25, exit 79, just s. Int corridors. **Pets:** Accepted.

TUCUMCARI

Americana Motel
(505) 461-0431. **$26-$42.** 406 E Tucumcari Blvd. I-40, exit 332, 1.5 mi n on SR 18, 0.5 mi e on US 66. Ext corridors. **Pets:** Accepted.

Best Western Discovery Inn
(505) 461-4884. **$58-$84.** 200 E Estrella. I-40, exit 332. Ext corridors. **Pets:** Accepted.

Best Western Pow Wow Inn
(505) 461-0500. **$54-$69.** 801 W Tucumcari Blvd. I-40, exit 332, 1.5 mi n on SR 18, 0.5 mi w on US 66. Ext corridors. **Pets:** Accepted.

Budget Inn
(505) 461-4139. **$30-$40.** 824 W Tucumcari Blvd. I-40, exit 332, 1 mi n to Tucumari Blvd, 1 mi w. Ext corridors. **Pets:** Medium. $5 one-time fee/room. Service with restrictions, supervision.

Comfort Inn
(505) 461-4094. **$55-$85, 7 day notice.** 2800 E Tucumcari Blvd. I-40, exit 335, 0.5 mi w. Ext corridors. **Pets:** Medium. $6 daily fee/pet. Service with restrictions, supervision.

Days Inn
(505) 461-3158. **$53-$70.** 2623 S First St. I-40, exit 332, just n. Ext/int corridors. **Pets:** Other species. $5 daily fee/pet. Service with restrictions, supervision.

Friends Inn
(505) 461-0330. **$30-$40.** 315 E Tucumcari Blvd. I-40, exit 332, n to Tucumcari Blvd, then just e. Ext corridors. **Pets:** Accepted.

Holiday Inn
(505) 461-3780. **$79-$99.** 3716 E Tucumcari Blvd. I-40, exit 335, 0.3 mi w on US 66. Ext corridors. **Pets:** Accepted.

(AAA) ▼▼▼ Howard Johnson Express Inn SH
(505) 461-2747. **$49-$59.** 3604 E Route 66. I-40, exit 335, 0.5 mi w. Int corridors. **Pets:** Accepted.
(SAVE) (S🐾) (X) (🛏) (💻)

(AAA) ▼▼▼ Microtel Inn-Tucumcari SH
(505) 461-0600. **$45-$70.** 2420 S 1st St. I-40, exit 332, just n. Int corridors. **Pets:** Other species. $6 daily fee/pet. Designated rooms, service with restrictions, supervision.
(SAVE) (S🐾) (X) (🖊) (🛏) (💻) (🏊)

(AAA) ▼▼▼ Rodeway Inn East M ❀
(505) 461-0360. **$61-$91.** 1023 E Tucumcari Blvd. I-40, exit 333, n to Tucumcari Blvd, then 0.6 mi w. Ext corridors. **Pets:** Other species. $10 daily fee/pet. Service with restrictions, supervision.
(SAVE) (S🐾) (X) (🛏) (💻) (🏊)

(AAA) ▼▼▼ Safari Motel M ❀
(505) 461-3642. **$38-$44, 5 day notice.** 722 E Tucumcari Blvd. I-40, exit 332, 1.5 mi n on 1st St, 0.4 mi e on US 66. Ext corridors. **Pets:** Other species. $5 daily fee/pet. Designated rooms, service with restrictions, supervision.
(SAVE) (S🐾) (X) (🛏) (🏊)

▼▼ Super 8 Motel M
(505) 461-4444. **$45-$75.** 4001 E Tucumcari Blvd. I-40, exit 335, just w. Int corridors. **Pets:** Small. $5 one-time fee/pet. Service with restrictions, supervision.
(ASK) (S🐾) (X) (🛏) (🏊)

(AAA) ▼▼▼ Tucumcari Travelodge SH
(505) 461-1401. **$40-$51.** 1214 E Tucumcari Blvd. I-40, exit 333, 1.5 mi n on Mountain Rd, then 0.5 mi w. Ext corridors. **Pets:** Accepted.
(SAVE) (S🐾) (X) (🛏) (💻)

VAUGHN

(AAA) ▼▼▼ Bel-Air Motel M
(505) 584-2241. **$38-$44.** 1004 US 54/60/285. 1 mi e on US 54, 60 and 285. Ext corridors. **Pets:** Medium. Service with restrictions, supervision.
(SAVE) (X) (💻)

(AAA) ▼▼▼ Oak Tree Inn SH
(505) 584-8733. **$60.** Jct State Hwy 54/60 & 285. 1.5 mi e on US 54, 60 and 285. Int corridors. **Pets:** Accepted.
(SAVE) (X) (♿M) (🗞) (🖊) (🛏) (💻) (🍴)

WHITES CITY

(AAA) ▼▼▼▼ Best Western Cavern Inn SH
(505) 785-2291. **$65-$105.** 17 Carlsbad Caverns Hwy. US 62 and 180 at SR 7. Ext corridors. **Pets:** Small, other species. $10 one-time fee/room. Service with restrictions, supervision.
(SAVE) (S🐾) (X) (🗞) (💻) (🏊) (🐾X)

NEW YORK

ALBANY

(AAA) ▼▼▼ Albany Mansion Hill Inn & Restaurant BB ✿
(518) 465-2038. **$175, 5 day notice.** 115 Philip St at Park Ave. I-787, exit 3B (Madison Ave/US 20 W) to Philip St, 0.4 mi s. Ext/int corridors. **Pets:** Medium, other species. Service with restrictions, supervision.
[SAVE] [S◇] [✕] [🖥] [📶] [🍴]

(AAA) ▼▼▼ Best Western Sovereign Hotel Albany SH
(518) 489-2981. **$89-$149.** 1228 Western Ave. I-90, exit 2, 0.7 mi s, follow signs to US 20 (Western Ave). Int corridors. **Pets:** Small. $10 one-time fee/pet. Service with restrictions, crate.
[SAVE] [S◇] [✕] [📶] [🐾] [🖥] [📶] [🍴] [🏊]

▼▼▼ CrestHill Suites SH ✿
(518) 454-0007. **$119-$289.** 1415 Washington Ave. I-90, exit 2 westbound, just s on Fuller Rd, then just e; eastbound, just e. Int corridors. **Pets:** Medium, other species. $150 one-time fee/pet. Service with restrictions, supervision.
[ASK] [S◇] [✕] [&M] [🐾] [🖥] [📶] [🏊]

(AAA) ▼▼▼ Regency Inn & Suites SH
(518) 462-6555. **$70-$129.** 416 Southern Blvd. On SR 9W; I-87, exit 23. Ext/int corridors. **Pets:** Accepted.
[SAVE] [S◇] [✕] [🖥] [📶] [✕]

▼▼▼ TownePlace Suites-Albany SH
(518) 435-1900. **$100-$180.** 1379 Washington Ave. I-90, exit 2 westbound, just s on Fuller Rd, then 0.6 mi e; eastbound, just e. Int corridors. **Pets:** Accepted.
[ASK] [S◇] [✕] [&M] [🐾] [🖥] [📶] [🏊]

ALEXANDRIA BAY

(AAA) ▼▼▼ ▼▼▼ Riveredge Resort-Hotel SH
(315) 482-9917. **$99-$338, 15 day notice.** 17 Holland St. I-81, exit 50N, 4.9 mi n on SR 12, 0.6 mi e on Walton, then just ne. Int corridors. **Pets:** Medium, dogs only. $20 daily fee/pet. Designated rooms, service with restrictions, supervision.
[SAVE] [✕] [🐾] [🖥] [📶] [🍴] [🏊] [✕]

ANGELICA

▼▼▼ Angelica Inn B&B BB
(585) 466-3063. **$75-$125, 14 day notice.** 64 W Main St. SR 17, exit 31, 0.5 mi w. Ext/int corridors. **Pets:** Accepted.
[✕] [🖥] [📶] [🐾]

APALACHIN

▼▼ The Dolphin Inn SH
(607) 625-4441. **$55-$70.** 7666 SR 434. SR 17, exit 66, just e. Int corridors. **Pets:** Other species. $10 one-time fee/pet. Crate.
[ASK] [S◇] [✕] [&] [🖥]

AUBURN

(AAA) ▼▼▼ Auburn Microtel Inn & Suites SH
(315) 253-5000. **$70-$120.** 12 Seminary Ave. Jct SR 34/38, just e on US 20/SR 5; center. Int corridors. **Pets:** $15 one-time fee/pet. Designated rooms, service with restrictions, supervision.
[SAVE] [✕] [&M] [🐾] [&] [🖥] [📶]

Holiday Inn-Auburn/Finger Lakes SH

(315) 253-4531. **$67-$102.** 75 North St. SR 34, just n of US 20/SR 5. Int corridors. **Pets:** Medium, other species. $10 daily fee/room. Designated rooms, service with restrictions, supervision.

SAVE S X M H D TI A

Sleepy Hollow Motel M ❖

(315) 704-0343. **$49-$109, 10 day notice.** 3401 E Genesee St. US 20, 1 mi e. Ext corridors. **Pets:** Other species. $15 daily fee/pet. Designated rooms, service with restrictions, crate.

X H D

AVERILL PARK

La Perla at the Gregory House Country Inn & Restaurant CI

(518) 674-3774. **$90-$135, 7 day notice.** 3016 SR 43. Center. Int corridors. **Pets:** Accepted.

ASK S X TI A

BALDWINSVILLE

Microtel Inn & Suites SH

(315) 635-9556. **$50-$100.** 131 Downer St. SR 690, exit SR 31 W, 0.6 mi e. Int corridors. **Pets:** Other species. $5 daily fee/pet. Service with restrictions, crate.

SAVE S X M ₤ H D

BATAVIA

Comfort Inn SH

(585) 344-9999. **$69-$189.** 4371 Federal Dr. I-90, exit 48, just n on SR 98. Int corridors. **Pets:** Other species. $10 daily fee/room. Supervision.

SAVE S X M ₤ H D A

Days Inn SH

(585) 343-6000. **$49-$109.** 200 Oak St. I-90, exit 48, just s. Ext/int corridors. **Pets:** $10 one-time fee/pet. Service with restrictions, supervision.

SAVE S X H TI A

Holiday Inn-Darien Lake SH

(585) 344-2100. **$59-$129.** 8250 Park Rd. I-90, exit 48, just w. Int corridors. **Pets:** Small, dogs only. Service with restrictions, supervision.

SAVE S X H D TI A X

Park Oak Inn M

(585) 343-7921. **$45-$110.** 301 Oak St. I-90, exit 48, just n. Int corridors. **Pets:** Medium, other species. $4 daily fee/pet. Service with restrictions, supervision.

SAVE S X H

Ramada Limited SH

(585) 343-1000. **$49-$119.** 8204 Park Rd. I-90, exit 48, just w. Int corridors. **Pets:** Accepted.

SAVE S X D TI A

Red Carpet M

(585) 343-2311. **$42-$120.** 8212 Park Rd. I-90, exit 48, just w. Ext/int corridors. **Pets:** Accepted.

ASK S X H D

BATH

Bath Super 8 SH

(607) 776-2187. **$66-$86, 3 day notice.** 333 W Morris St. I-86, exit 38, just n. Int corridors. **Pets:** Medium, other species. Service with restrictions, supervision.

ASK S X H

Days Inn SH

(607) 776-7644. **$80-$89, 30 day notice.** 330 W Morris St. I-86, exit 38, just n. Int corridors. **Pets:** Other species. Service with restrictions, supervision.

ASK S X H D A

BELLPORT

The Great South Bay Inn BB

(631) 286-8588. **$115-$150, 7 day notice.** 160 S Country Rd. SR 27, exit 56, 2.2 mi s on Station Rd, then just e. Int corridors. **Pets:** Small. $15 daily fee/pet. Service with restrictions, supervision.

X Z

BINGHAMTON

Carousel Inn SH

(607) 722-2412. **$72-$99.** 65 Front St. I-81, exit 5, 2 mi s; SR 17 E, exit 72, 1 mi s. Int corridors. **Pets:** Small. $15 daily fee/pet. Designated rooms, service with restrictions, supervision.

SAVE S X H D A

Comfort Inn SH

(607) 722-5353. **$69-$199.** 1156 Front St. I-81, exit 6, just n of Broome Community College. Int corridors. **Pets:** Medium, other species. $15 one-time fee/room. Designated rooms, service with restrictions, crate.

SAVE S X H D

Days Inn SH

(607) 724-3297. **$90-$100.** 1000 Front St. I-81, exit 5, 1 mi n on US 11 (Front St). Int corridors. **Pets:** Large, other species. $5 daily fee/room. Designated rooms, service with restrictions, supervision.

ASK S X M H D A

Holiday Inn Arena LH ❖

(607) 722-1212. **$89-$300.** 2-8 Hawley St. Downtown. Int corridors. **Pets:** $25 one-time fee/room. Designated rooms, service with restrictions, crate.

ASK S X M H D TI A

Motel 6—1222 SH

(607) 771-0400. **$41-$55.** 1012 Front St. I-81, exit 6 southbound, 2 mi s on US 11 (Front St); exit 5 northbound, 1 mi n on US 11 (Front St). Int corridors. **Pets:** Accepted.

S X M ₤

Super 8 Motel-Binghamton SH ❖

(607) 773-8111. **$45-$54, 3 day notice.** 650 Old Front St. I-81, exit 5, to access road. Int corridors. **Pets:** Large, other species. $35 deposit/room. Service with restrictions, supervision.

SAVE S X H

BOONVILLE

Headwaters Motor Lodge M
(315) 942-4493. **$59-$65, 3 day notice.** 13524 Rt 12. Jct SR 12 and 120, 0.7 mi n. Int corridors. **Pets:** Service with restrictions, supervision.
[SAVE] [S⌖] [✕] [⊟]

BRIGHTON

Wellesley Inn (Rochester/South) SH
(585) 427-0130. **$55-$105.** 797 E Henrietta Rd. I-390, exit 16 northbound; exit 16B (Henrietta Rd) southbound, just s on SR 15A S. Int corridors. **Pets:** Accepted.
[SAVE] [S⌖] [✕] [⌖] [✎] [⊟] [⊡]

BROCKPORT

Holiday Inn Express SH
(585) 395-1000. **$89-$139.** 4908 Lake Rd S. Just s of jct SR 31 and 19. Int corridors. **Pets:** Other species. $15 one-time fee/room. No service, supervision.
[SAVE] [S⌖] [✕] [&M] [⊟] [⊡]

BUFFALO METROPOLITAN AREA

AMHERST

Buffalo Marriott-Niagara LH
(716) 689-6900. **$129-$189.** 1340 Millersport Hwy. I-290, exit 5B, 0.5 mi n on SR 263 (Millersport Hwy). Int corridors. **Pets:** Other species. $50 one-time fee/room. Designated rooms, supervision.
[SAVE] [S⌖] [✕] [&M] [∅] [✎] [⊟] [⊡] [◎] [⊠] [✕]

Lord Amherst Motor Hotel M
(716) 839-2200. **$75-$109.** 5000 Main St. I-290, exit 7A, just w on SR 5. Ext/int corridors. **Pets:** Designated rooms, service with restrictions, supervision.
[SAVE] [S⌖] [✕] [&M] [⊟] [⊡] [◎] [⊠]

Red Roof Inn M
(716) 689-7474. **$47-$89.** 42 Flint Rd. I-290, exit 5B, 0.5 mi n on SR 263 (Millersport Hwy). Ext corridors. **Pets:** Accepted.
[SAVE] [✕] [&M] [⊟]

Super 8 Motel-Amherst/Buffalo/Niagara Falls SH
(716) 688-0811. **$44-$74.** 1 Flint Rd. I-290, exit 5B, 0.5 mi n on SR 263 (Millersport Hwy), just w. Int corridors. **Pets:** Other species. $10 daily fee/pet. Service with restrictions, supervision.
[ASK] [S⌖] [✕] [⊟]

BLASDELL

Econo Lodge South M
(716) 825-7530. **$54-$99.** 4344 Milestrip Rd. I-90, exit 56, just e on SR 179. Ext corridors. **Pets:** $6 daily fee/room. Designated rooms, service with restrictions, supervision.
[SAVE] [S⌖] [✕] [∅] [⊟] [⊡]

McKinley's Hotel & Banquet SH
(716) 648-5700. **$74-$159, 3 day notice.** S 3950 McKinley Pkwy. I-90, exit 56, 0.4 mi e on SR 179, then 0.8 mi s. Int corridors. **Pets:** Accepted.
[SAVE] [S⌖] [✕] [✎] [⊟] [⊡]

BOWMANSVILLE

Red Roof Inn-Buffalo Airport M
(716) 633-1100. **$43-$81.** 146 Maple Dr. Just e of SR 78, just n of entrance to I-90 (New York Thruway), exit 49. Ext corridors. **Pets:** Medium, other species. Service with restrictions, supervision.
[SAVE] [✕] [∅]

BUFFALO

Best Western Inn-On The Avenue SH
(716) 886-8333. **$109-$159.** 510 Delaware Ave. Between Virginia and Allen sts; downtown. Int corridors. **Pets:** Small, dogs only. $100 deposit/room. Designated rooms, service with restrictions.
[SAVE] [S⌖] [✕] [✎] [⊟] [⊡]

Holiday Inn-Downtown SH
(716) 886-2121. **$69-$149.** 620 Delaware Ave. Between Allen and North sts; downtown. Int corridors. **Pets:** Accepted.
[SAVE] [✕] [⊟] [⊡] [◎] [⊠]

CHEEKTOWAGA

Homewood Suites by Hilton SH
(716) 685-0700. **$109-$199.** 760 Dick Rd. SR 33, exit Dick Rd, 0.3 mi sw. Int corridors. **Pets:** Accepted.
[✕] [✎] [⊟] [⊡] [◎]

Residence Inn by Marriott SH
(716) 892-5410. **$99-$179.** 107 Anderson Rd. I-90, exit 52 westbound, stay to the left off exit ramp. Int corridors. **Pets:** Other species. $10 daily fee/room, $100 one-time fee/room. Service with restrictions, supervision.
[ASK] [S⌖] [✕] [&M] [∅] [✎] [⊟] [⊡] [◎] [⊠]

CLARENCE

Asa Ransom House CI
(716) 759-2315. **$98-$175, 7 day notice.** 10529 Main St. Jct SR 78 (Transit Rd), 5.3 mi e on SR 5 (Main St). Int corridors. **Pets:** Large, dogs only. $50 deposit/room. Designated rooms, service with restrictions.
[SAVE] [S⌖] [✕] [&M] [⊟] [⊡] [◎] [⊠]

GRAND ISLAND

Chateau Motor Lodge M
(716) 773-2868. **$35-$79, 3 day notice.** 1810 Grand Island Blvd. I-190, exit 18A northbound, 0.5 mi n on SR 324 W. Ext corridors. **Pets:** Medium. $9 daily fee/pet. Service with restrictions, supervision.

Cinderella Motel M
(716) 773-2872. **$46-$75, 3 day notice.** 2797 Grand Island Blvd. I-190, exit 19 northbound, 1.3 mi w on SR 324; exit 20B southbound, just e on SR 324. Ext corridors. **Pets:** Small. Service with restrictions, supervision.

HAMBURG

Comfort Inn & Suites SH
(716) 648-2922. **$74-$189.** 3615 Commerce Pl. I-90, exit 57, just w. Int corridors. **Pets:** Small. $25 deposit/pet, $10 daily fee/pet. Service with restrictions, supervision.

Holiday Inn Hamburg SH
(716) 649-0500. **$65-$109.** 5440 Camp Rd. I-90, exit 57, 0.3 mi e se on SR 75. Int corridors. **Pets:** Accepted.

Red Roof Inn M
(716) 648-7222. **$43-$80.** 5370 Camp Rd. I-90, exit 57, just se on SR 75. Ext corridors. **Pets:** Accepted.

Tallyho-tel M
(716) 648-2000. **$25-$125.** 5245 Camp Rd. I-90, exit 57, just nw on SR 75. Ext corridors. **Pets:** Other species. $15 one-time fee/pet. Service with restrictions, supervision.

KENMORE

Super 8-Buffalo/Niagara Falls SH
(716) 876-4020. **$48-$75.** 1288 Sheridan Dr. I-190, exit 15, 1.5 mi e. Int corridors. **Pets:** Medium. Service with restrictions, supervision.

SPRINGVILLE

Microtel Inn & Suites SH
(716) 592-3141. **$44-$79, 30 day notice.** 270 S Cascade Dr. On SR 219 S (Cascade Dr). Int corridors. **Pets:** Other species. $10 daily fee/room. Service with restrictions, crate.

TONAWANDA

Days Inn M
(716) 835-5916. **$45-$125.** 1120 Niagara Falls Blvd. I-290, exit 3 (Niagara Falls Blvd), 1.3 mi s on US 62. Ext corridors. **Pets:** Other species. Service with restrictions.

Microtel-Tonawanda SH
(716) 693-8100. **$43-$75, 3 day notice.** 1 Hospitality Centre Way. I-290, exit 1B; I-290 E, exit 1, 0.5 mi e on Crestmount Ave, just n on SR 384 (Delaware St). Int corridors. **Pets:** $10 daily fee/pet. Service with restrictions, crate.

WILLIAMSVILLE

Microtel-Lancaster SH
(716) 633-6200. **$42-$79, 3 day notice.** 50 Freeman Rd. I-90, exit 49 (SR 78 N), just n, then just e. Int corridors. **Pets:** Accepted.

Residence Inn by Marriott Buffalo/Amherst M
(716) 632-6622. **$99-$169.** 100 Maple Rd. I-290, exit 5B, just e on Maple Rd from jct SR 263 (Millersport Hwy). Ext corridors. **Pets:** Other species. $10 daily fee/pet, $75 one-time fee/room. Service with restrictions, crate.

❖   **END METROPOLITAN AREA**   ❖

CANANDAIGUA

Canandaigua Inn on the Lake SH
(585) 394-7800. **$94-$144, 3 day notice.** 770 S Main St. I-90, exit 44, jct SR 332, just s across US 20 and SR 5. Int corridors. **Pets:** Accepted.

Econo Lodge Canandaigua SH
(585) 394-9000. **$49-$109, 3 day notice.** 170 Eastern Blvd. Jct SR 332, 5 and US 20, 0.5 mi e. Int corridors. **Pets:** Other species. Service with restrictions, supervision.

CANASTOTA

Days Inn SH
(315) 697-3309. **$59-$129.** N Peterboro St. I-90, exit 34, on SR 13. Int corridors. **Pets:** Service with restrictions, supervision.

CATSKILL

Quality Inn & Conference Center SH
(518) 943-5800. **$69-$249.** 704 Rt 23B. I-87, exit 21, just w. Int corridors. **Pets:** Medium. $20 daily fee/pet. Designated rooms, service with restrictions, crate.

CICERO

Budget Inn M
(315) 458-3510. **$55-$120.** 901 S Bay Rd. I-481, exit 10, just s. Ext corridors. **Pets:** Medium. $10 daily fee/pet. Service with restrictions, supervision.
[ASK] [SD] [X] [H]

CLINTON

The Hedges BB ❖
(315) 853-3031. **$120-$150, 5 day notice.** 180 Sanford Ave. College St, 0.3 mi n on Elm St. Int corridors. **Pets:** Dogs only. Service with restrictions, supervision.
[X] [H] [P] [≈]

COBLESKILL

Best Western Inn of Cobleskill SH
(518) 234-4321. **$74-$179.** 121 Burgin Dr. I-88, exit 21 eastbound on SR 7, 0.8 mi e of jct SR 10; exit 22 westbound. Int corridors. **Pets:** Medium. $15 daily fee/room.
[SAVE] [SD] [X] [&M] [⌂] [H] [P] [¶] [≈]

COLONIE

Albany Super 8 Motel M
(518) 869-8471. **$60-$85.** 1579 Central Ave. I-87, exit 2W, just nw on SR 5 W. Ext corridors. **Pets:** Small. $25 deposit/room. Designated rooms, supervision.
[ASK] [SD] [X] [H]

Ambassador Motor Inn M
(518) 456-6982. **Call for rates.** 1600 Central Ave. I-87, exit 2W, 0.8 mi w; on SR 5, then 5.4 mi w. Ext corridors. **Pets:** Accepted.
[X]

Ramada Limited M ❖
(518) 456-0222. **$79-$140.** 1630 Central Ave. I-87, exit 2W, 0.8 mi w, then 5.5 mi w on SR 5. Ext corridors. **Pets:** Medium. $10 one-time fee/room. Designated rooms, service with restrictions.
[SAVE] [SD] [X] [H] [P]

Red Roof Inn M
(518) 459-1971. **$56-$92.** 188 Wolf Rd. I-87, exit 4, just se to Wolf Rd, then just sw. Ext corridors. **Pets:** Accepted.
[SAVE] [X] [&M] [H]

CORNING

Radisson Hotel Corning SH
(607) 962-5000. **$110-$160.** 125 Denison Pkwy E. On SR 17; center. Int corridors. **Pets:** Accepted.
[X] [H] [P] [¶] [≈]

Staybridge Suites by Holiday Inn SH
(607) 936-7800. **$119-$199.** 201 Townley Ave. SR 17, exit 46, just s. Int corridors. **Pets:** Accepted.
[ASK] [SD] [X] [&M] [⌂] [&] [H] [P] [≈] [X]

CORTLAND

Comfort Inn SH
(607) 753-7721. **$89-$189.** 2 1/2 Locust Ave. I-81, exit 11, just e. Int corridors. **Pets:** Medium. $10 one-time fee/room. Designated rooms, service with restrictions, crate.
[ASK] [SD] [X] [H] [P] [¶]

Econo Lodge M
(607) 756-2856. **$52-$155.** 10 Church St. I-81, exit 11, 0.8 mi s on US 11. Ext corridors. **Pets:** Accepted.
[SAVE] [SD] [X] [H]

Quality Inn Cortland SH
(607) 756-5622. **$79-$179.** 188 Clinton St. I-81, exit 11, just n. Int corridors. **Pets:** $10 daily fee/room. Service with restrictions, supervision.
[ASK] [SD] [X] [P]

CUBA

Cuba Coachlight Motel M
(585) 968-1992. **$49-$59.** 1 N Branch Rd. US 86, exit 28, n to N Branch Rd, then e. Int corridors. **Pets:** Other species. $5 daily fee/room. Service with restrictions, crate.
[SAVE] [SD] [X] [H]

DELHI

Buena Vista Motel M
(607) 746-2135. **$72-$85.** 18718 State Hwy 28. Jct SR 10, 0.8 mi e. Ext corridors. **Pets:** Dogs only. $10 daily fee/pet. Designated rooms, service with restrictions, supervision.
[SAVE] [SD] [X] [H]

DE WITT

Econo Lodge M
(315) 446-3300. **$65-$120, 3 day notice.** 3400 Erie Blvd E. I-481, exit 3W, 1.2 mi w on SR 5 W. Ext corridors. **Pets:** Medium. $10 daily fee/pet. Service with restrictions, supervision.
[SAVE] [SD] [X] [H] [P]

DIAMOND POINT

Hillview Cottages CA
(518) 668-5787. **$65-$99, 30 day notice.** 3647 Lake Shore Dr. I-87, exit 22, 3.3 mi n on SR 9N. Ext corridors. **Pets:** Other species. Service with restrictions, supervision.
[X] [H] [P] [≈] [X]

DOVER PLAINS

Old Drovers Inn CI ❖
(845) 832-9311. **$150-$475, 14 day notice.** 196 E Duncan Hill Rd. 3 mi s of SR 22 on Old Rt 22 (CR 6). Int corridors. **Pets:** Small. $25 daily fee/pet. No service, supervision.
[X] [¶] [W] [Z]

DUNKIRK

Best Western Dunkirk/Fredonia SH
(716) 366-7100. **$69-$139.** 3912 Vineyard Dr. I-90, exit 59, just w. Int corridors. **Pets:** $10 daily fee/pet. Service with restrictions, supervision.
[SAVE] [SD] [X] [&] [H] [P] [≈]

Comfort Inn SH
(716) 672-4450. **$59-$139.** 3925 Vineyard Dr. I-90, exit 59, just w of jct SR 60. Int corridors. **Pets:** $10 daily fee/pet. Service with restrictions, supervision.
[SAVE] [SD] [X] [&] [H] [P]

(AAA) ▼▼▼ Days Inn Dunkirk-Fredonia SH ❖
(716) 673-1351. **$60-$125.** 10455 Bennett Rd. I-90, exit 59, just s on SR 60. Ext/int corridors. **Pets:** Other species. Designated rooms, service with restrictions, supervision.
SAVE 🛇 ✕ 🖥 💷 🍴 🏊

(AAA) ▼▼▼▼ Ramada Inn & Conference
Center SH
(716) 366-8350. **$99-$199.** 30 Lake Shore Dr E. Jct SR 60, 0.3 mi w on SR 5. Int corridors. **Pets:** Accepted.
SAVE 🛇 ✕ 🐾 🖥 💷 🍴 🏊 ✕

EAST HAMPTON

▼▼ Dutch Motel & Cottages M
(631) 324-4550. **$70-$285, 60 day notice.** 488 Montauk Hwy. 1.3 mi e on SR 27 E (Montauk Hwy). Ext corridors. **Pets:** Accepted.
🖥

EAST SYRACUSE

▼▼▼▼ CrestHill Suites SH
(315) 432-5595. **$119-$259.** 6410 New Venture Gear Dr. I-90, exit 35 (Carrier Cir) to SR 298 E, just s. Int corridors. **Pets:** Other species. $125 one-time fee/room. Service with restrictions, supervision.
ASK 🛇 ✕ 🐾 🖥 💷 🏊

▼▼ East Syracuse Super 8 SH
(315) 432-5612. **$50-$80.** 6620 Old Collamer Rd. I-90, exit 35 (Carrier Cir), just e on SR 298, then just n. Int corridors. **Pets:** Accepted.
ASK 🛇 ✕ 🖥 🐾 🖥 💷 🖥

▼▼▼▼ Holiday Inn East-Carrier Circle SH
(315) 437-2761. **$79-$109.** 6555 Old Collamer Rd. I-90, exit 35 (Carrier Cir) to SR 298 E to Collamer Rd, just n. Ext/int corridors. **Pets:** Medium. $25 one-time fee/room. Designated rooms, service with restrictions, supervision.
ASK 🛇 ✕ 🐾 🖥 💷 🍴 🏊 ✕

(AAA) ▼▼▼ Microtel Inn Syracuse SH
(315) 437-3500. **$43-$83.** 6608 Old Collamer Rd. I-90, exit 35 (Carrier Cir) to SR 298 E. Int corridors. **Pets:** Small. $25 one-time fee/pet. Designated rooms, service with restrictions, supervision.
SAVE 🛇 ✕ 🖥 🐾

▼▼▼▼ Residence Inn By Marriott SH
(315) 432-4488. **Call for rates.** 6420 Yorktown Cir. I-90, exit 35 (Carrier Cir) to SR 298 E, just e to Old Collamer Rd, 0.5 mi n. Ext corridors. **Pets:** Accepted.
✕ 🐾 🖥 🖥 💷 🏊 ✕

ELLICOTTVILLE

(AAA) ▼▼ The Jefferson Inn of Ellicottville BB
(716) 699-5869. **$89-$199, 30 day notice.** 3 Jefferson St. Western jct US 219 and SR 242, just n; eastern jct US 219 and 242, 0.8 mi w. Ext/int corridors. **Pets:** Dogs only. $15 daily fee/pet. Designated rooms, no service.
SAVE ✕ 🖥 💷

ELMIRA

(AAA) ▼▼▼ Coachman Motor Lodge M
(607) 733-5526. **$70, 3 day notice.** SR 17, exit 56 (Church St), 0.5 mi w, 0.5 mi s on Madison Ave, then 1.4 mi s. Ext corridors. **Pets:** Large. Service with restrictions, supervision.
SAVE 🛇 🖥 💷

ENDICOTT

(AAA) ▼▼▼ Kings Inn M ❖
(607) 754-8020. **$57-$125.** 2603 E Main St. SR 17 W, exit 69, 2.4 mi w on SR 17C; SR 17 E, exit 67N, 1.3 mi e. Ext corridors. **Pets:** Other species. $5 daily fee/room. Designated rooms, service with restrictions, supervision.
SAVE 🛇 ✕ 🖥 💷 🏊

FALCONER

(AAA) ▼▼ Red Roof Inn
Jamestown/Falconer SH
(716) 665-3670. **$54-$78.** 1980 E Main St. I-86, exit 13, just w. Int corridors. **Pets:** Accepted.
SAVE ✕

FARMINGTON

(AAA) ▼▼▼ Budget Inn M
(585) 924-5020. **$54-$79, 3 day notice.** 6001 Rt 96. I-90, exit 44, 1 mi s on SR 332, then just e. Ext corridors. **Pets:** Small, dogs only. $10 daily fee/pet. Service with restrictions, crate.
SAVE 🛇 ✕ 🖥 💷

FISHKILL

▼▼▼ Homestead Studio Suites
Hotel-Fishkill SH ❖
(845) 897-2800. **$118-$127.** 25 Merritt Blvd. I-84, exit 13, just n. Int corridors. **Pets:** Medium, other species. $25 daily fee/room. Service with restrictions, crate.
ASK 🛇 ✕ 🐾 🖥 🖥 💷

▼▼▼▼ Residence Inn by Marriott SH
(845) 896-5210. **$139-$179.** 14 Schuyler Blvd. I-84, exit 13, just n. Ext corridors. **Pets:** Accepted.
ASK 🛇 ✕ 🖥 🐾 🖥 💷 🏊 ✕

(AAA) ▼▼▼ Wellesley Inn (Fishkill) SH
(845) 896-4995. **$103.** 20 Schuyler Blvd & Rt 9. I-84, exit 13, just n. Int corridors. **Pets:** Small. Designated rooms, service with restrictions, supervision.
SAVE 🛇 ✕ 🖥 🐾 🖥 💷

FREEPORT

(AAA) ▼▼ Freeport Motor Inn & Boatel M
(516) 623-9100. **$105-$115.** 445 S Main St. 1 mi s from SR 27 (Sunrise Hwy). Ext corridors. **Pets:** Accepted.
SAVE ✕ 🖥

FULTON

◤◤ Riverside Inn 🆂🅷
(315) 593-2444. **$59-$109, 7 day notice.** 930 S First St. On SR 481. Int corridors. **Pets:** Other species. $100 deposit/room, $5 daily fee/room. Service with restrictions, supervision.
🅰🆂🅺 🆂🅾 ✖ 🛑 🖥 🍽 ⌁

GATES

◤◤ Comfort Inn Central 🆂🅷
(585) 436-4400. **$79-$94, 3 day notice.** 395 Buell Rd. I-390, exit 18B (SR 204), 0.3 mi w; opposite entrance to Rochester-Monroe County Airport. Int corridors. **Pets:** Accepted.
🅰🆂🅺 🆂🅾 ✖ 🗲 🛑 🖥

◆ ◤◤◤ Holiday Inn-Rochester Airport 🆂🅷
(585) 328-6000. **$109-$141.** 911 Brooks Ave. I-390, exit 18A (SR 204), just e. Int corridors. **Pets:** Medium. $25 deposit/room. Designated rooms, service with restrictions, supervision.
🆂🅰🆅🅴 ✖ 🗲 🛑 🖥 🍽 ⌁ ✖

◤ Motel 6 Rochester-Airport #1221 🆂🅷
(585) 436-2170. **$41-$66.** 155 Buell Rd. Just s. Int corridors. **Pets:** Other species. Service with restrictions, supervision.
🆂🅾 ✖ 🗲

GENEVA

◆ ◤◤◤ Ramada Inn Geneva Lakefront 🆂🅷
(315) 789-0400. **$99-$170.** 41 Lakefront Dr. I-90, exit 42, 8 mi s on SR 14. Int corridors. **Pets:** $10 daily fee/pet. Service with restrictions, supervision.
🆂🅰🆅🅴 🆂🅾 ✖ 🗲 🛑 🖥 🍽 ⌁

GREAT NECK

◆ ◤◤◤ The Andrew Hotel 🆂🅷
(516) 482-2900. **$165-$215.** 75 N Station Plaza. Jct SR 25A, 0.8 mi n on Middle Neck Rd, then just e. Int corridors. **Pets:** Small, dogs only. $150 one-time fee/pet. Service with restrictions, supervision.
🆂🅰🆅🅴 🆂🅾 ✖ 🛑 🍽

◤◤◤ Inn at Great Neck 🆂🅷
(516) 773-2000. **$219-$259.** 30 Cutter Mill Rd. Jct SR 25A, 0.8 mi n on Middle Neck Rd, then just w. Int corridors. **Pets:** Accepted.
🅰🆂🅺 🆂🅾 ✖ 🗲 🗲 🛑 🖥 🍽

GREECE

◆ ◤◤ Comfort Inn-West 🆂🅷
(585) 621-5700. **$84,** 1501 W Ridge Rd. Jct SR 390 and 104 (Ridge Rd), 0.5 mi e. Int corridors. **Pets:** Large, other species. $10 one-time fee/room. Service with restrictions.
🆂🅰🆅🅴 🆂🅾 ✖ 🛑 🖥

◤◤◤ Hampton Inn-Rochester North 🆂🅷 🐾
(585) 663-6070. **$94-$109, 7 day notice.** 500 Center Place Dr. I-390, exit 24A, just e on SR 104 (Ridge Rd), then just n on Buckman Rd. Int corridors. **Pets:** Small. Service with restrictions, supervision.
🅰🆂🅺 🆂🅾 ✖ 🔣 🗲 🛑 🖥

◤◤◤ Residence Inn by Marriott-West 🆂🅷
(585) 865-2090. **$109-$219.** 500 Paddy Creek Cir. I-390, exit 24A, just e on SR 104 (Ridge Rd), then just s on Hoover Dr, then just w. Int corridors. **Pets:** Accepted.
🆂🅾 ✖ 🗲 🛑 🖥 ⌁ ✖

◆ ◤◤ Wellesley Inn (Rochester/North) 🆂🅷
(585) 621-2060. **$55-$105.** 1635 W Ridge Rd. I-390, exit 24A, just e on SR 104 (Ridge Rd). Int corridors. **Pets:** Medium, other species. Service with restrictions.
🆂🅰🆅🅴 🆂🅾 ✖ 🔣🅼 🗲 🗲 🛑 🖥

GREENE

◤◤ Serenity Farms 🅱🅱 🌸
(607) 656-4659. **$69-$89, 7 day notice.** 386 Pollard Rd. I-81, exit 8, 1.2 mi s, 11 mi e on SR 206, 4.1 mi n on SR 12 to King Rd, 2.7 mi n, then 1.5 mi e. Int corridors. **Pets:** Other species. $89 daily fee/room.
🅰🆂🅺 🆂🅾 ✖ 🛑 🖥 ⌁ 🗲

HANCOCK

◤◤ Smith's Colonial Motel 🅼
(607) 637-2989. **$60-$105.** 23085 State Hwy 97. SR 17, exit 87. Ext corridors. **Pets:** Accepted.
✖

HAUPPAUGE

◤◤◤ Residence Inn by Marriott 🆂🅷 🌸
(631) 724-4188. **$179-$299.** 850 Veterans Memorial Hwy. I-495, exit 57, 1.2 mi nw. Int corridors. **Pets:** Large, other species. $10 daily fee/pet, $100 one-time fee/pet. Service with restrictions.
🅰🆂🅺 🆂🅾 ✖ 🗲 🛑 🖥 ⌁ ✖

◆ ◤◤◤ Wyndham Wind Watch Hotel & Hamlet Golf Club 🅻🅷
(631) 232-9800. **$174-$204.** 1717 Motor Pkwy. I-495, exit 57, just n to Motor Pkwy, 1.3 mi ne. Int corridors. **Pets:** Accepted.
🆂🅰🆅🅴 🆂🅾 ✖ 🔣🅼 🗲 🛑 🖥 🍽 ⌁ ✖

HENRIETTA

◤◤ Econo Lodge-Rochester South 🆂🅷
(585) 427-2700. **$82, 3 day notice.** 940 Jefferson Rd. I-390, exit 14A southbound; exit 14 northbound, just w on SR 252 (Jefferson Rd). Int corridors. **Pets:** Accepted.
🅰🆂🅺 🆂🅾 ✖ 🗲 🛑 🖥

◤◤ Homewood Suites by Hilton-Rochester/Henrietta 🆂🅷
(585) 334-9150. **$119-$135.** 2095 Hylan Dr. I-390, exit 13, just e. Int corridors. **Pets:** Medium, other species. $75 one-time fee/room. Service with restrictions.
🅰🆂🅺 🆂🅾 ✖ 🔣🅼 🗲 🗲 🛑 🖥 ⌁

◆ ◤◤◤ Microtel-Rochester 🆂🅷
(585) 334-3400. **$37-$69.** 905 Lehigh Station Rd. I-390, exit 12 northbound; exit 12A southbound, just w on SR 253. Int corridors. **Pets:** $10 one-time fee/room. Service with restrictions, supervision.
🆂🅰🆅🅴 🆂🅾 ✖ 🛑

(AAA) ▼▼▼ Ramada Inn Rochester SH
(585) 475-9190. **$79.** 800 Jefferson Rd. I-390, exit 14A southbound; exit 14 northbound, 0.5 mi w on SR 252 (Jefferson Rd). Int corridors. **Pets:** Accepted.
🅢🅐🅥🅔 🅢🏧 ⊠ 🛢 💻 🍴 ⇒

(AAA) ▼▼▼ Red Roof Inn-Henrietta M
(585) 359-1100. **$48-$75.** 4820 W Henrietta Rd. I-390, exit 12 northbound; exit 12A southbound, 0.5 mi w on SR 253, then just s on SR 15 (W Henrietta Rd). Ext corridors. **Pets:** Accepted.
🅢🅐🅥🅔 ⊠ 🛢

▼▼▼▼ Residence Inn by Marriott M ❀
(585) 272-8850. **$179-$189.** 1300 Jefferson Rd. I-390, exit 14A southbound, 0.5 mi e on SR 252 (Jefferson Rd); exit 14 northbound, just n on 15A, then 0.5 mi e on SR 252 (Jefferson Rd). Ext corridors. **Pets:** Other species. $125 one-time fee/room.
🄰🅂🄺 🅢🏧 ⊠ 🖉 🛢 💻 ⇒ ⊠

▼▼▼▼ R I T Inn & Conference Center SH
(585) 359-1800. **$85-$115.** 5257 W Henrietta Rd. I-390, exit 12 northbound; exit 12A southbound, 0.5 mi w on SR 253, then 0.7 mi s. Int corridors. **Pets:** Accepted.
🄰🅂🄺 🅢🏧 ⊠ 🖉 🛢 💻 🍴 ⇒ ⊠

HERKIMER

(AAA) ▼▼▼ Herkimer Motel M
(315) 866-0490. **$68-$88.** 100 Marginal Rd. I-90, exit 30, just n on SR 28. Ext/int corridors. **Pets:** Service with restrictions, supervision.
🅢🅐🅥🅔 🅢🏧 ⊠ 🖉 🛢 💻 ⇒

(AAA) ▼ Inn Towne Motel M
(315) 866-1101. **$45-$150.** 227 N Washington St. 1 mi n on SR 28, just w; downtown. Ext corridors. **Pets:** Medium, dogs only. $10 daily fee/pet. Designated rooms, service with restrictions, supervision.
🅢🅐🅥🅔 🅢🏧 ⊠ 🛢

HORNELL

(AAA) ▼▼▼ Econo Lodge M
(607) 324-0800. **$44-$69.** 7462 Seneca Rd. Jct I-86 and SR 36, exit 34, just s to SR 21, just e to Seneca Rd, then just s. Ext/int corridors. **Pets:** Other species. $7 daily fee/room. Service with restrictions, crate.
🅢🅐🅥🅔 🅢🏧 🛢 💻 🍴

HORSEHEADS

▼▼▼▼ Hilton Garden Inn Elmira/Corning SH
(607) 795-1111. **$99-$150, 3 day notice.** 35 Arnot Rd. SR 17, exit 51A westbound; exit 51 eastbound. Int corridors. **Pets:** Small. $20 one-time fee/pet. Designated rooms, service with restrictions, supervision.
🄰🅂🄺 🅢🏧 ⊠ 🖉 🛢 💻 🍴 ⇒

HUNTER

(AAA) ▼▼▼▼ Hunter Inn SH
(518) 263-3777. **$79-$295, 14 day notice.** Rt 23A. Jct SR 296, 1.9 mi e. Int corridors. **Pets:** Accepted.
🅢🅐🅥🅔 ⊠ 🛢 ⊠

ITHACA

(AAA) ▼▼▼▼ Holiday Inn-Executive Tower SH ❀
(607) 272-1000. **$126-$135, 30 day notice.** 222 S Cayuga St. Just n from SR 96B. Int corridors. **Pets:** Other species. $15 one-time fee/room. Service with restrictions, supervision.
🅢🅐🅥🅔 🅢🏧 ⊠ 🖉 🛢 💻 🍴 ⇒

(AAA) ▼▼▼ Meadow Court Inn M
(607) 273-3885. **$50-$195.** 529 S Meadow St. 1.5 mi s on SR 13 and 96. Ext/int corridors. **Pets:** $100 deposit/pet, $10 daily fee/pet. Designated rooms, service with restrictions, crate.
🅢🅐🅥🅔 ⊠ 🌢 🖉 🛢 💻 🍴

JAMESTOWN

(AAA) ▼▼▼▼ Comfort Inn SH
(716) 664-5920. **$149-$169.** 2800 N Main St Extension. I-86, exit 12, just s. Int corridors. **Pets:** Other species. $10 one-time fee/room. Service with restrictions, supervision.
🅢🅐🅥🅔 🅢🏧 ⊠ 🛢 💻

JOHNSON CITY

(AAA) ▼▼▼▼ Best Western of Johnson City SH
(607) 729-9194. **$65-$105.** 569 Harry L Dr. SR 17, exit 70N, 0.3 mi n. Int corridors. **Pets:** Accepted.
🅢🅐🅥🅔 🅢🏧 ⊠ 🛢 💻

(AAA) ▼▼▼ Red Roof Inn-Binghamton M
(607) 729-8940. **$43-$72.** 590 Fairview St. SR 17, exit 70N, 0.3 mi n, just n on Reynolds Rd. Ext corridors. **Pets:** Accepted.
🅢🅐🅥🅔 ⊠ 🛢

JOHNSTOWN

▼▼▼▼ Holiday Inn SH ❀
(518) 762-4686. **$94-$145.** 308 N Comrie Ave. Jct SR 30A and 29 E, 1.3 mi n. Ext/int corridors. **Pets:** Designated rooms, service with restrictions, supervision.
🄰🅂🄺 🅢🏧 ⊠ 🌢 🖉 🛢 💻 🍴 ⇒

LAKE GEORGE

▼▼▼ Balmoral Motel M
(518) 668-2673. **$49-$225, 14 day notice.** 444 Canada St. I-87, exit 22, 0.3 mi s on US 9. Ext corridors. **Pets:** Accepted.
⊠ 🛢 💻 ⇒

▼▼▼ Green Haven M
(518) 668-2489. **$54-$109, 10 day notice.** 3136 Lake Shore Dr. I-87, exit 22, 0.8 mi n on SR 9N. Ext corridors. **Pets:** Dogs only. $10 one-time fee/pet. Service with restrictions, supervision.
⊠ 🛢 💻 ⇒ ⊠

▼▼▼ Lake Haven Motel M
(518) 668-2260. **$49-$139, 10 day notice.** 442 Canada St. I-87, exit 22, 0.4 mi s on SR 9. Ext corridors. **Pets:** Medium. $10 daily fee/pet. Designated rooms, service with restrictions, supervision.
⊠ 🛢 💻 ⇒

Travelodge of Lake George **M**
(518) 668-5421. **$74-$164.** 2011 SR 9. I-87, exit 21. Ext/int corridors. **Pets:** Small, dogs only. $20 daily fee/pet. Designated rooms, service with restrictions, supervision.
[SAVE] [S6] [X] [H] [D] [T] [~]

LAKE LUZERNE

Luzerne Court **M**
(518) 696-2734. **$66-$195, 14 day notice.** 508 Lake Ave. I-87, exit 21, 8.7 mi s on SR 9N. Ext corridors. **Pets:** Accepted.
[SAVE] [X] [H] [T] [~] [Z]

LAKE PLACID

Art Devlin's Olympic Motor Inn, Inc **M**
(518) 523-3700. **$58-$148, 10 day notice.** 350 Main St. 0.5 mi e on SR 86. Ext corridors. **Pets:** Dogs only. Service with restrictions, supervision.
[SAVE] [X] [H] [~]

Best Western Golden Arrow Hotel **SH**
(518) 523-3353. **$99-$199, 30 day notice.** 150 Main St. On SR 86; center. Int corridors. **Pets:** Small. $100 deposit/room, $50 one-time fee/pet. Designated rooms, service with restrictions, supervision.
[SAVE] [X] [∅] [H] [D] [T] [~] [X]

Edge of the Lake Motel **M**
(518) 523-9430. **$49-$129.** 56 Saranac Ave. 0.5 mi w on SR 86. Ext/int corridors. **Pets:** $10 daily fee/pet. Service with restrictions, supervision.
[SAVE] [H] [D] [~] [X]

Hilton Lake Placid Resort **SH**
(518) 523-4411. **$79-$289, 7 day notice.** 1 Mirror Lake Dr. 0.3 mi w on SR 86. Int corridors. **Pets:** Accepted.
[ASK] [S6] [X] [&M] [∅] [&] [H] [D] [T] [~] [X]

Howard Johnson Resort Inn **SH**
(518) 523-9555. **$85-$190.** 90 Saranac Ave. 0.5 mi w on SR 86. Ext/int corridors. **Pets:** Service with restrictions, supervision.
[SAVE] [S6] [X] [∅] [H] [D] [T] [~] [X]

Lake Placid Ramada Inn **SH**
(518) 523-2587. **$79-$169, 3 day notice.** 8-12 Saranac Ave. 0.3 mi w on SR 86. Int corridors. **Pets:** Accepted.
[SAVE] [S6] [X] [∅] [H] [D] [T] [~]

Lake Placid Resort Hotel & Golf Club/ Holiday Inn **SH**
(518) 523-2556. **$69-$249, 30 day notice.** 1 Olympic Dr. Downtown. Ext/int corridors. **Pets:** $25 one-time fee/room. Designated rooms, service with restrictions, supervision.
[X] [∅] [H] [D] [T] [~] [X]

Swiss Acres Inn **SH**
(518) 523-3040. **$49-$98, 7 day notice.** 189 Saranac Ave. 1 mi w on SR 86. Ext/int corridors. **Pets:** $20 one-time fee/room. Service with restrictions, supervision.
[SAVE] [S6] [X] [H] [D] [T] [~] [X]

LANSING

The Clarion University Hotel & Conference Center **SH**
(607) 257-2000. **$99-$269.** On SR 13, N of Ithaca, exit Triphammer Rd, then just s. Int corridors. **Pets:** Medium. $20 one-time fee/room. Designated rooms, service with restrictions, supervision.
[ASK] [S6] [X] [H] [D] [T] [~] [X]

Econo Lodge **SH**
(607) 257-1400. **$66-$135.** 2303 N Triphammer Rd. Intersection of SR 13 and Triphammer Rd. Int corridors. **Pets:** Small. $10 daily fee/pet. Designated rooms, service with restrictions, supervision.
[SAVE] [S6] [X] [H] [D]

Ramada Inn-Airport **SH**
(607) 257-3100. **$109-$269.** 2310 N Triphammer Rd. Jct SR 13 and 34, 3.5 mi n on SR 13, exit Triphammer Rd, then just w. Int corridors. **Pets:** Medium. $20 one-time fee/room. Designated rooms, service with restrictions, supervision.
[ASK] [S6] [X] [&] [H] [D] [T] [~] [X]

LATHAM

Century House Restaurant & Hotel **SH**
(518) 785-0931. **$115-$225.** 997 New Loudon Rd. I-87, exit 7 (SR 7), just e; 0.5 mi n on US 9 (New Loudon Rd). Int corridors. **Pets:** Supervision.
[SAVE] [X] [H] [D] [T] [~] [X]

Comfort Inn At Albany Airport **SH** ❖
(518) 783-1900. **$89-$109.** 20 Airport Park Blvd. I-87, exit 4, 2.2 mi nw on Albany Shaker Rd, just se. Int corridors. **Pets:** $10 daily fee/room. Designated rooms, service with restrictions, supervision.
[ASK] [S6] [X] [H] [D] [T]

Hampton Inn-Latham **SH**
(518) 785-0000. **$104-$164.** 981 New Loudon Rd. I-87, exit 7 (SR 7), just n on US 9 (New Loudon Rd). Int corridors. **Pets:** Accepted.
[ASK] [S6] [X] [&M] [H] [D] [~]

Holiday Inn Express-Airport **SH**
(518) 783-6161. **$80-$130.** 946 New Loudon Rd. I-87, exit 7 (SR 7) on US 9 N, then just n. Ext corridors. **Pets:** Accepted.
[SAVE] [S6] [X] [∅] [H] [D] [~]

Microtel Inn **SH**
(518) 782-9161. **$47-$119.** 7 Rensselaer Ave. I-87, exit 6, just w. Int corridors. **Pets:** Small. $10 daily fee/pet. Service with restrictions, supervision.
[SAVE] [S6] [X] [&M] [&] [H] [D]

Residence Inn by Marriott Albany Airport **SH**
(518) 783-0600. **$149-$209.** 1 Residence Inn Dr. I-87, exit 6, 2 mi w on SR 7. Ext corridors. **Pets:** Other species. $100 one-time fee/pet. Service with restrictions, crate.
[ASK] [S6] [X] [∅] [H] [D] [~] [X]

LITTLE FALLS

(AAA) ▼▼▼ Best Western Little Falls Motor Inn 🆂🅷
(315) 823-4954. **$65-$105.** 20 Albany St. On SR 5 and 167. Int corridors. **Pets:** Other species. $10 deposit/pet. Designated rooms, service with restrictions, crate.
[SAVE] [S🐾] [✕] [🖥] [🍴]

LIVERPOOL

(AAA) ▼▼▼▼ Best Western Inn & Suites 🆂🅷
(315) 701-4400. **$99-$169.** 136 Transistor Pkwy. I-90, exit 37 (Electronics Pkwy), just n; I-81, exit 25 (7th North St), 1.3 mi w, just n on Electronics Pkwy, then just w. Int corridors. **Pets:** Small, dogs only. $100 deposit/pet, $25 one-time fee/pet. Designated rooms, service with restrictions, supervision.
[SAVE] [S🐾] [✕] [🖥] [🖥] [🌊]

▼▼▼ Holiday Inn Syracuse Airport 🅻🅷
(315) 457-1122. **$114-$139.** 441 Electronics Pkwy. I-90, exit 37 (Electronics Pkwy); I-81, exit 25 (7th North St), 1.3 mi nw. Int corridors. **Pets:** Medium, other species. Designated rooms, service with restrictions, crate.
[ASK] [S🐾] [✕] [♿] [🐕] [🐾] [🖥] [🖥] [🍴] [🌊] [✕]

▼▼▼ Homewood Suites 🆂🅷
(315) 451-3800. **$109-$219.** 275 Elwood Davis Rd. I-81, exit 25 (7th North St), 1 mi w; I-90, exit 36. Int corridors. **Pets:** Accepted.
[ASK] [S🐾] [✕] [🖥] [🖥] [🌊] [✕]

(AAA) ▼▼▼ Knights Inn 🅼 ❀
(315) 453-6330. **$44-$129.** 430 Electronics Pkwy. I-90, exit 37 (Electronics Pkwy), just s; I-81, exit 25 (7th North St), 1.3 mi nw, just s. Ext corridors. **Pets:** Large. $8 daily fee/pet. Service with restrictions, supervision.
[SAVE] [S🐾] [✕] [🖥]

▼▼ Super 8 Motel Syracuse/Liverpool 🆂🅷
(315) 451-8888. **$69-$99.** 421 7th North St. I-81, exit 25 (7th North St), just nw; I-90, exit 36. Int corridors. **Pets:** Large, other species. Designated rooms, service with restrictions, supervision.
[ASK] [S🐾] [✕]

LONG LAKE

(AAA) ▼▼▼ Journey's End Cottages 🄲🄰
(518) 624-5381. **$550-$750 (weekly), 60 day notice.** Deerland Rd (Rt 30). On SR 30/28, 1 mi s. Ext corridors. **Pets:** Accepted.
[SAVE] [🖥] [🖥] [✕] [🄺] [☎]

▼▼ Long View Lodge 🄲🄸
(518) 624-2862. **$65-$95, 7 day notice.** Deerland Rd (Rt 30). On SR 30/28, 2.2 mi s. Ext/int corridors. **Pets:** Accepted.
[✕] [🖥] [🍴] [✕] [🄺]

LOWMAN

(AAA) ▼▼▼ Red Jacket Motor Inn 🅼
(607) 734-1616. **$36-$65, 3 day notice.** Rt 17. SR 17, just e from CR 8; between MM 195 and 196. Ext corridors. **Pets:** Dogs only. $10 daily fee/pet. No service, supervision.
[SAVE] [S🐾] [✕] [♿] [🖥] [🍴] [🌊]

MALONE

(AAA) ▼▼▼ Four Seasons Motel 🅼
(518) 483-3490. **$45-$79.** 236 W Main St. 1 mi w on US 11. Ext corridors. **Pets:** Other species. Designated rooms, service with restrictions, supervision.
[SAVE] [S🐾] [✕] [♿] [🖥] [🌊]

▼▼ Sunset Inn 🅼
(518) 483-3367. **$50-$75.** 3899 US 11. 1.5 mi e. Ext corridors. **Pets:** Service with restrictions, crate.
[ASK] [S🐾] [✕] [♿] [🖥] [🌊]

(AAA) ▼▼▼ Super 8 Motel at Jons 🆂🅷
(518) 483-8123. **$67-$89.** 42 Finney Blvd. On SR 30; just s of jct US 11. Int corridors. **Pets:** Medium. Service with restrictions, supervision.
[SAVE] [✕] [♿🅼] [♿]

MASSENA

(AAA) ▼▼▼▼ Econo Lodge-Meadow View Motel 🆂🅷
(315) 764-0246. **$72-$99.** 15054 SR 37. On SR 37 W, 2.7 mi sw. Ext/int corridors. **Pets:** Small. $5 daily fee/pet. Designated rooms, service with restrictions.
[SAVE] [S🐾] [✕] [♿] [🖥] [🍴]

MCGRAW

(AAA) ▼▼▼ Cortland Days Inn 🆂🅷
(607) 753-7594. **$59-$125.** 3775 US Rt 11. I-81, exit 10 (McGraw/Cortland), just n. Int corridors. **Pets:** Small, dogs only. $10 daily fee/pet. Designated rooms, service with restrictions, supervision.
[SAVE] [S🐾] [✕] [🖥]

MIDDLETOWN

▼▼▼ Super 8 Motel 🆂🅷
(845) 692-5828. **$90-$99, 30 day notice.** 563 Rt 211 E. I-84, exit 4W, 0.5 mi w on SR 17 to exit 120, then 0.3 mi e. Int corridors. **Pets:** Other species. $25 deposit/room. Service with restrictions, supervision.
[ASK] [S🐾] [✕] [♿]

MONTOUR FALLS

(AAA) ▼ Relax Inn 🅼
(607) 535-7183. **$39-$89, 3 day notice.** 100 Clawson Blvd. Jct SR 14 and 224. Ext corridors. **Pets:** Dogs only. $10 daily fee/pet. Designated rooms, service with restrictions, supervision.
[SAVE] [S🐾] [✕] [♿]

NEW HAMPTON

▼▼ Days Inn 🅼
(845) 374-2411. **$59-$119.** 4939 Rt 17M. I-84, 0.8 mi e on US 6 and SR 17M. Ext/int corridors. **Pets:** Large. Service with restrictions, supervision.
[ASK] [S🐾] [✕] [♿] [🖥] [🌊]

NEW HARTFORD

▼▼▼ Holiday Inn Utica 🆂🅷
(315) 797-2131. **$129-$169.** 1777 Burrstone Rd. I-90 (New York Thruway), exit 31, 4.5 mi w on SR 5 W and 12 S, exit Burrstone Rd, then 1 mi nw. Ext/int corridors. **Pets:** Accepted.
[ASK] [S🐾] [✕] [🐾] [♿] [🖥] [🍴] [🌊] [✕]

NEW YORK METROPOLITAN AREA

LONG ISLAND CITY

AAA ▼▼▼ **Holiday Inn Express** SH
(718) 706-6700. **$149-$169.** 3805 Hunters Point Ave. In Long Island City; I-278, exit I-495 (Midtown tunnel) eastbound, exit 15 (Van Dam St), just n to Hunters Point Blvd, w on Greenpoint Ave, n at 39th St; I-278 westbound, exit 35 (. Int corridors. **Pets:** Accepted.
SAVE S◐ ✕ ⌖ ⌨ ▤ ▭

MOUNT KISCO

AAA ▼▼▼ **Holiday Inn** SH ❀
(914) 241-2600. **$119-$149.** 1 Holiday Inn Dr. Saw Mill River Pkwy, exit 37, just e. Int corridors. **Pets:** Medium. $10 daily fee/pet. Service with restrictions, supervision.
SAVE S◐ ✕ &M ⌖ ⌨ ▤ ▭ �𝄐 ⚓

NANUET

▼▼▼ **Candlewood Suites** SH
(845) 371-4445. **$139-$179.** 20 Overlook Blvd. I-287/87, exit 14 (SR 59 W) to New Clarkstown Rd. Int corridors. **Pets:** Accepted.
ASK S◐ ✕ ⌖ ▤ ▭ ⚓

AAA ▼▼▼ **Days Inn Nanuet** SH
(845) 623-4567. **$79-$129.** 367 W Rte 59. I-287/87, exit 14 (SR 59 W), just w. Ext/int corridors. **Pets:** Large. $10 daily fee/pet. Service with restrictions.
SAVE S◐ ✕ ▤ ▭ ⚓

NEW YORK

▼▼▼ **Beekman Tower Hotel** SH
(212) 355-7300. **$225-$299.** 3 Mitchell Pl. 49th St and 1st Ave. Int corridors. **Pets:** Accepted.
✕ ⌖ ⌨ ▤ ▭ ⚓

▼▼▼ ▼▼ **The Benjamin Hotel** SH
(212) 715-2500. **$334-$479.** 125 E 50th St. Between Lexington and 3rd aves. Int corridors. **Pets:** Accepted.
✕ ⌖ ▤ ▭ ⚓ ⚔

▼▼▼ ▼▼ **The Carlyle** SH
(212) 744-1600. **$410-$610.** 35 E 76th St. At Madison Ave. Int corridors. **Pets:** Accepted.
✕ ⌖ ⌨ ▤ ▭ ⚓ ⚔

▼▼▼ **Crowne Plaza at the United Nations** LH
(212) 986-8800. **$209-$369.** 304 E 42nd St. Between 1st and 2nd aves. Int corridors. **Pets:** Small. $500 deposit/room. Service with restrictions, crate.
ASK S◐ ✕ ⌖ ⌨ ▭ ⚓ ⚔

▼▼▼ **Crowne Plaza Times Square Manhattan** LH
(212) 977-4000. **$169-$229.** 1605 Broadway. 49th St and Broadway. Int corridors. **Pets:** Accepted.
ASK ✕ &M ⌖ ⌨ ▤ ▭ ⚓ ⚓ ⚔

▼▼ **Eastgate Tower Hotel** SH
(212) 687-8000. **$224-$324.** 222 E 39th St. Between 2nd and 3rd aves. Int corridors. **Pets:** Accepted.
✕ &M ⌖ ⌨ ▤ ▭ ⚓

▼▼▼ ▼▼ **Embassy Suites Hotel New York** LH
(212) 945-0100. **$159-$359.** 102 N End Ave. Between Murray and Vesey sts. Int corridors. **Pets:** $75 one-time fee/room. Service with restrictions, supervision.
✕ ⌖ ▤ ▭ ⚓

▼▼▼ ▼▼ **Four Seasons Hotel, New York** LH ❀
(212) 758-5700. **$575-$675.** 57 E 57th St. Between Park and Madison aves. Int corridors. **Pets:** Very small. Service with restrictions, crate.
ASK ✕ &M ⌖ ⌨ ▤ ▭ ⚓ ⚔

AAA ▼▼▼ **Hampton Inn Chelsea** SH ❀
(212) 414-1000. **$169-$224.** 108 W 24th St. Between 6th (Ave of the Americas) and 7th aves. Int corridors. **Pets:** Small. $20 one-time fee/room. Service with restrictions, supervision.
SAVE S◐ ✕ ⌖ ⌨ ▤ ▭

▼▼▼ ▼▼ **Hilton New York** LH
(212) 586-7000. **$199-$529.** 1335 Ave of the Americas. Between 53rd and 54th sts. Int corridors. **Pets:** Small, other species. Designated rooms, service with restrictions, supervision.
✕ ⌖ &M ▤ ▭ ⚓

▼▼▼ ▼▼ **Hilton Times Square** LH
(212) 840-8222. **$179-$449.** 234 W 42nd St. Between 7th and 8th aves. Int corridors. **Pets:** Medium. $100 deposit/room. Service with restrictions, supervision.
ASK S◐ ✕ &M ⌖ ⌨ ▤ ▭ ⚓

AAA ▼▼▼ **The Holiday Inn Martinique on Broadway** SH
(212) 736-3800. **$199-$299.** 49 W 32nd St. Corner of Broadway. Int corridors. **Pets:** Small, dogs only. $50 deposit/pet. Service with restrictions, crate.
SAVE ✕ &M ⌖ ⌨ ▤ ▭ ⚓

▼▼▼ ▼▼ **Holiday Inn Wall Street Hotel** LH
(212) 232-7700. **$199-$369.** 15 Gold St. Corner of Gold and Platt sts. Int corridors. **Pets:** Small, other species. $10 daily fee/pet. Service with restrictions.
ASK S◐ ✕ &M ⌖ ⌨ ▤ ▭ ⚓

▼▼▼ ▼▼ **Hotel Plaza Athenee** SH ❀
(212) 734-9100. **$525-$675.** 37 E 64th St. Between Madison and Park aves. Int corridors. **Pets:** Small. Designated rooms, no service.
ASK ✕ ▤ ▭ ⚓ ⚔

▼▼▼ ▼▼ **Hotel Wales** SH ❀
(212) 876-6000. **$239-$745.** 1295 Madison Ave. Between 92 E and 93 E sts. Int corridors. **Pets:** $75 deposit/pet. Service with restrictions.
ASK S◐ ✕ ⌖ ▤ ▭ ⚓ ⚔

▼▼▼ ▼▼ **Inter-Continental Central Park South New York** SH
(212) 757-1900. **$239-$615.** 112 Central Park S. Between 6th (Ave of the Americas) and 7th aves. Int corridors. **Pets:** Accepted.
✕ ⌖ ▤ ▭ ⚓ ⚔

▼▼▼▼ **Jolly Hotel Madison Towers** 🅛🅗
(212) 802-0600. **$214-$265.** 22 E 38th St. Between Park and Madison aves. Int corridors. **Pets:** Medium, other species. Designated rooms, service with restrictions, supervision.
(A$K) (S🖋) (✕) (🖋) (🯄) (🍴)

▼▼▼ ▼▼▼ **Le Parker Meridien New York** 🅛🅗 🐾
(212) 245-5000. **$380-$505.** 118 W 57th St. Between 6th (Ave of the Americas) and 7th aves; vehicle entrance on 56th St. Int corridors. **Pets:** Other species. Service with restrictions.
(A$K) (✕) (🖋) (🯄) (🍴) (🛶) (✕)

▼▼▼▼ **The Lowell Hotel** 🅢🅗 🐾
(212) 838-1400. **$525-$585.** 28 E 63rd St. Between Park and Madison aves. Int corridors. **Pets:** Medium.
(🖋) (🯄) (🯄) (🍴) (✕)

▼▼▼▼ **The Mansfield** 🅢🅗
(212) 944-6050. **$245-$350.** 12 W 44th St. Between 5th and 6th (Ave of the Americas) aves. Int corridors. **Pets:** Accepted.
(A$K) (S🖋) (✕)

▼▼▼▼ **The Mark, New York** 🅢🅗
(212) 744-4300. **$600-$2500.** 25 E 77th St. Madison Ave at E 77th St. Int corridors. **Pets:** Accepted.
(✕) (🖋) (🍴) (✕)

🅐🅐🅐 ▼▼▼ **The Mayflower Hotel On The Park** 🅢🅗
(212) 265-0060. **$230-$270.** 15 Central Park W. At 61st St. Int corridors. **Pets:** Medium. Designated rooms, service with restrictions, supervision.
(SAVE) (S🖋) (✕) (🖋) (🯄) (🍴)

▼▼▼▼ **The Metropolitan** 🅢🅗
(212) 752-7000. **$209-$339.** 569 Lexington Ave. At E 51st St. Int corridors. **Pets:** Accepted.
(A$K) (S🖋) (✕) (🖋M) (🖋) (🯄) (🍴)

🅐🅐🅐 ▼▼▼ ▼▼▼ **Millenium Hilton** 🅛🅗
(212) 693-2001. **$179-$499.** 55 Church St. Between Dey and Fulton sts. Int corridors. **Pets:** Medium, dogs only. $175 deposit/room. Service with restrictions, supervision.
(SAVE) (✕) (🖋) (🯄) (🍴) (🛶)

🅐🅐🅐 ▼▼▼▼ **Millennium Broadway** 🅛🅗
(212) 768-4400. **$329-$479.** 145 W 44th St. Between 6th (Ave of the Americas) and 7th aves. Int corridors. **Pets:** Accepted.
(SAVE) (S🖋) (✕) (🖋M) (🯄) (🖋) (💻) (🍴)

🅐🅐🅐 ▼▼▼ ▼▼▼ **The Muse** 🅢🅗 🐾
(212) 485-2400. **$369-$449.** 130 W 46th St. Between 6th (Ave of the Americas) and 7th aves. Int corridors. **Pets:** Other species.
(SAVE) (✕) (🖋) (🯄) (💻) (🍴)

▼▼▼▼ **New York Marriott Marquis** 🅛🅗
(212) 398-1900. **$199-$700.** 1535 Broadway. Between 45th and 46th sts; motor entrance on 46th St. Int corridors. **Pets:** Small, other species. Service with restrictions, supervision.
(S🖋) (✕) (🯄) (🖋) (🯄) (💻) (🍴)

🅐🅐🅐 ▼▼▼ ▼▼▼ **The New York Palace** 🅛🅗
(212) 888-7000. **$475-$770.** 455 Madison Ave. Between 50th and 51st sts. Int corridors. **Pets:** Accepted.
(SAVE) (✕) (🖋M) (🯄) (🖋) (🯄) (💻) (🍴) (✕)

🅐🅐🅐 ▼▼▼▼ **Novotel New York** 🅛🅗
(212) 315-0100. **$179-$369.** 226 W 52nd St. At Broadway. Int corridors. **Pets:** Medium, other species. Service with restrictions, crate.
(SAVE) (S🖋) (✕) (🯄) (🍴)

🅐🅐🅐 ▼▼▼▼ **The Peninsula New York** 🅛🅗 🐾
(212) 956-2888. **$440-$640.** 700 5th Ave. At 55th St. Int corridors. **Pets:** Small.
(SAVE) (✕) (🯄) (🖋) (🯄) (🍴) (🛶) (✕)

▼▼▼▼ **The Pierre New York–A Four Seasons Hotel** 🅢🅗
(212) 838-8000. **$405-$905.** 2 E 61st St. At 5th Ave. Int corridors. **Pets:** Accepted.
(✕) (🖋M) (🯄) (🖋) (🯄) (🍴) (✕)

▼▼ ▼▼ **Plaza Fifty Hotel** 🅢🅗 🐾
(212) 751-5710. **$249-$419.** 155 E 50th St. Between 3rd and Lexington aves. Int corridors. **Pets:** Other species. $250 deposit/room. Service with restrictions, crate.
(✕) (🯄) (🯄) (💻)

🅐🅐🅐 ▼▼▼ ▼▼▼ **The Regency Hotel** 🅛🅗
(212) 759-4100. **$239-$419.** 540 Park Ave. At 61st St. Int corridors. **Pets:** Accepted.
(SAVE) (S🖋) (✕) (🖋M) (🯄) (🖋) (🯄) (🍴)

▼▼ ▼▼ **The Regent Wall Street** 🅢🅗
(212) 845-8600. **$525-$550.** 55 Wall St. Corner of William and Wall sts. Int corridors. **Pets:** Accepted.
(A$K) (✕) (🯄) (🖋) (🍴) (✕)

🅐🅐🅐 ▼▼▼ ▼▼▼ **Renaissance New York Hotel Times Square** 🅛🅗
(212) 765-7676. **$249-$369.** 2 Times Square, 7th Ave at W 48th St. Broadway and 7th Ave; auto access from 7th Ave, s of W 48th St. Int corridors. **Pets:** Accepted.
(SAVE) (✕) (🯄) (💻) (🍴)

🅐🅐🅐 ▼▼▼▼ **The Ritz-Carlton New York, Battery Park** 🅢🅗 🐾
(212) 344-0800. **$350-$475.** Two West St. Jct Battery Pl. Int corridors. **Pets:** Small. $30 daily fee/pet.
(SAVE) (✕) (🖋M) (🯄) (🖋) (🍴)

🅐🅐🅐 ▼▼▼▼ **The Ritz-Carlton New York, Central Park** 🅛🅗 🐾
(212) 308-9100. **$425-$875.** 50 Central Park S. Between 5th and 6th (Ave of the Americas) aves. Int corridors. **Pets:** Medium, dogs only. Service with restrictions.
(SAVE) (✕) (🖋M) (🯄) (🖋) (🯄) (💻) (🍴)

🅐🅐🅐 ▼▼ ▼▼ **The Roger Smith Hotel** 🅢🅗
(212) 755-1400. **$169-$255.** 501 Lexington Ave. Between 47th and 48th sts. Int corridors. **Pets:** Accepted.
(SAVE) (S🖋) (✕) (🯄) (🖋) (💻) (🍴)

(AAA) ▼▼▼▼▼ The St. Regis-New York 🏨
(212) 753-4500. **$610-$6000.** 2 E 55th St. Between Madison and 5th aves. Int corridors. **Pets:** Accepted.
⟦SAVE⟧ ⟦✕⟧ ⟦&M⟧ ⟦🐾⟧ ⟦🖥⟧ ⟦🍴⟧ ⟦✕⟧

▼▼▼▼ The Shoreham Hotel 🏨 ❀
(212) 247-6700. **$169-$1500.** 33 W 55th St. Between 5th and 6th (Ave of the Americas) aves. Int corridors. **Pets:** Medium. $100 deposit/room. Designated rooms.
⟦ASK⟧ ⟦SÆ⟧ ⟦✕⟧ ⟦&M⟧ ⟦🐾⟧ ⟦🖥⟧ ⟦🍴⟧ ⟦✕⟧

(AAA) ▼▼▼▼ Sofitel New York 🏨
(212) 354-8844. **$289.** 45 W 44th St. Between 5th and 6th (Ave of the Americas) aves. Int corridors. **Pets:** Accepted.
⟦SAVE⟧ ⟦SÆ⟧ ⟦✕⟧ ⟦🐾⟧ ⟦🖥⟧ ⟦🍴⟧

▼▼▼▼ The SoHo Grand Hotel 🏨
(212) 965-3000. **Call for rates.** 310 W Broadway. Jct Grand St; in SoHo District. Int corridors. **Pets:** Accepted.
⟦🍴⟧

▼▼▼▼ Southgate Tower Suite Hotel 🏨
(212) 563-1800. **$224-$334.** 371 7th Ave. At 31st St. Int corridors. **Pets:** Accepted.
⟦✕⟧ ⟦🐾⟧ ⟦🖥⟧ ⟦🍴⟧

(AAA) ▼▼▼▼ The Stanhope Park Hyatt New York 🏨
(212) 774-1234. **$279-$499.** 995 5th Ave. At 81st St. Int corridors. **Pets:** Accepted.
⟦SAVE⟧ ⟦✕⟧ ⟦🐾⟧ ⟦🖥⟧ ⟦🍴⟧ ⟦✕⟧

▼▼▼▼ Surrey Hotel 🏨
(212) 288-3700. **$334-$479.** 20 E 76th St. E 76th St and Madison Ave. Int corridors. **Pets:** Accepted.
⟦✕⟧ ⟦🐾⟧ ⟦🖥⟧ ⟦🍴⟧

▼▼▼▼ Swissotel The Drake, New York 🏨
(212) 421-0900. **$240-$290.** 440 Park Ave. At 56th St; between Park and Madison aves. Int corridors. **Pets:** Accepted.
⟦ASK⟧ ⟦✕⟧ ⟦🐾⟧ ⟦🖥⟧ ⟦🍴⟧ ⟦✕⟧

▼▼▼▼ Tribeca Grand Hotel 🏨
(212) 519-6600. **Call for rates.** 2 Ave of the Americas. 6th Ave (Ave of the Americas) and White St. Int corridors. **Pets:** Accepted.
⟦✕⟧ ⟦🖥⟧ ⟦🍴⟧

▼▼▼ Trump International Hotel & Tower 🏨
(212) 299-1000. **$550-$625.** 1 Central Park W. Jct Central Park S; at Columbus Circle. Int corridors. **Pets:** Very small, dogs only. $250 one-time fee/room. Service with restrictions, crate.
⟦✕⟧ ⟦🐾⟧ ⟦🖥⟧ ⟦🍴⟧ ⟦➰⟧ ⟦✕⟧

▼▼▼ The Westin 🏨
(212) 201-2700. **$179-$519.** 270 W 43rd St. Corner of 8th Ave. Int corridors. **Pets:** Accepted.
⟦ASK⟧ ⟦SÆ⟧ ⟦✕⟧ ⟦🐾⟧ ⟦🖥⟧ ⟦🍴⟧ ⟦✕⟧

▼▼▼ W New York 🏨
(212) 755-1200. **$449-$509.** 541 Lexington Ave. At 49th St. Int corridors. **Pets:** Accepted.
⟦ASK⟧ ⟦SÆ⟧ ⟦✕⟧ ⟦&M⟧ ⟦🐾⟧ ⟦🖥⟧ ⟦🍴⟧

▼▼▼ W New York Times Square 🏨
(212) 930-7400. **$489-$539.** 1567 Broadway at 47th St. Corner of 47th St. Int corridors. **Pets:** Accepted.
⟦ASK⟧ ⟦SÆ⟧ ⟦✕⟧ ⟦&M⟧ ⟦🐾⟧ ⟦🖥⟧ ⟦🍴⟧

▼▼▼ W New York-Union Square 🏨
(212) 253-9119. **$579-$1900.** 201 Park Ave S. At 17th St. Int corridors. **Pets:** Accepted.
⟦ASK⟧ ⟦SÆ⟧ ⟦✕⟧ ⟦&M⟧ ⟦🐾⟧ ⟦🖥⟧ ⟦🍴⟧

PEEKSKILL

(AAA) ▼▼▼ Peekskill Inn 🅜
(914) 739-1500. **$117-$130.** 634 Main St. Jct US 6 and 9, e to top of Main St. Ext corridors. **Pets:** Accepted.
⟦SAVE⟧ ⟦SÆ⟧ ⟦✕⟧ ⟦🖥⟧ ⟦🍴⟧ ⟦➰⟧

STATEN ISLAND

▼▼▼ Hilton Garden Inn Staten Island 🏨
(718) 477-2400. **$139-$159.** 1100 South Ave. I-278 westbound, exit 6 (South Ave), then just s; I-278 eastbound, exit 5 to SR 440 S, exit South Ave, 1 mi n to Lois Ln, then just w. Int corridors. **Pets:** Accepted.
⟦ASK⟧ ⟦SÆ⟧ ⟦✕⟧ ⟦🐾⟧ ⟦🖥⟧ ⟦🍴⟧ ⟦➰⟧ ⟦✕⟧

▼▼▼ The Staten Island Hotel 🏨
(718) 698-5000. **$154.** 1415 Richmond Ave. I-278, exit Richmond Ave, 0.5 mi se. Int corridors. **Pets:** Designated rooms, service with restrictions, supervision.
⟦ASK⟧ ⟦SÆ⟧ ⟦✕⟧ ⟦🖥⟧ ⟦🍴⟧

SUFFERN

(AAA) ▼▼▼ Wellesley Inn (Suffern) 🏨
(845) 368-1900. **$79-$119.** 17 N Airmont Rd. I-87/287, exit 14B, just s. Int corridors. **Pets:** Accepted.
⟦SAVE⟧ ⟦SÆ⟧ ⟦✕⟧ ⟦&M⟧ ⟦🐾⟧ ⟦🖥⟧

TARRYTOWN

▼▼▼ Hilton of Tarrytown 🏨
(914) 631-5700. **$119-$229.** 455 S Broadway. I-287/87 (New York Thruway), exit 9, then just s on US 9. Int corridors. **Pets:** Accepted.
⟦ASK⟧ ⟦SÆ⟧ ⟦✕⟧ ⟦🐾⟧ ⟦🖥⟧ ⟦🍴⟧ ⟦➰⟧ ⟦✕⟧

WHITE PLAINS

▼▼▼ Renaissance Westchester Hotel 🏨
(914) 694-5400. **$119-$221.** 80 W Red Oak Ln. I-287 (Cross Westchester Exwy), exit 9N-S eastbound, 0.5 mi e on Westchester Ave, just n on Kenilworth Rd, then 0.7 mi w on Westchester Ave; westbound, 0.8 mi w on Westchester Ave. Int corridors. **Pets:** Accepted.
⟦ASK⟧ ⟦✕⟧ ⟦&M⟧ ⟦🐾⟧ ⟦🖥⟧ ⟦🍴⟧ ⟦➰⟧ ⟦✕⟧

▼▼▼ Summerfield Suites By Wyndham-Westchester 🏨 ❀
(914) 251-9700. **$109-$329.** 101 Corporate Park Dr. I-287 (Cross Westchester Exwy), exit 9A eastbound, 0.6 mi e on Westchester Ave, then 0.3 mi n; exit 9N-S westbound, 0.9 mi w on Westchester Ave. Int corridors. **Pets:** Supervision.
⟦ASK⟧ ⟦SÆ⟧ ⟦✕⟧ ⟦🐾⟧ ⟦🖥⟧ ⟦🍴⟧ ⟦➰⟧ ⟦✕⟧

NIAGARA FALLS METROPOLITAN AREA

LOCKPORT

WW Best Western Lockport Inn M
(716) 434-6151. **$69-$129.** 515 S Transit St. 1 mi s on SR
78. Int corridors. **Pets:** Other species. $5 daily fee/room.
Service with restrictions, crate.

ASK S⍥ ✕ 🛏 ▣ ⑪ ⇶

NEWFANE

W Lake Ontario Motel M
(716) 778-5004. **$49-$65.** 3330 Lockport-Olcott Rd. 2.5 mi n
of jct SR 104 on SR 78. Int corridors. **Pets:** Other species.
$5 daily fee/room. Service with restrictions, supervision.

ASK ✕ 🛏

NIAGARA FALLS

WWW Best Western Summit Inn SH
(716) 297-5050. **$59-$159.** 9500 Niagara Falls Blvd. I-190,
exit 22, 2.1 mi e on US 62 S. Int corridors. **Pets:** Medium.
$8 daily fee/room. Designated rooms, service with restrictions, supervision.

SAVE S⍥ ✕ 🛏 ▣ ⇶

WW Budget Host Inn M
(716) 283-3839. **$49-$149.** 6621 Niagara Falls Blvd. I-190,
exit 22, just e on US 62 S. Ext corridors. **Pets:** Small. $15
deposit/room. Service with restrictions, supervision.

SAVE S⍥ ✕ 🛏 ⇶

**WWW Howard Johnson Hotel (Closest to the
Falls) SH ✽**
(716) 285-5261. **$55-$175.** 454 Main St. I-190, exit 21 (Robert Moses Pkwy), 2 mi e, just n to Rainbow Blvd, then just
s. Int corridors. **Pets:** Other species. $10 daily fee/pet.
Service with restrictions, crate.

SAVE S⍥ ✕ 🚹 🛏 ▣ ⇶

WWW Quality Hotel and Suites "At the Falls" SH
(716) 282-1212. **$79-$299.** 240 Rainbow Blvd. Downtown.
Int corridors. **Pets:** Other species. $20 daily fee/pet. Service
with restrictions, supervision.

ASK S⍥ ✕ ⊘ 🛏 ▣ ⑪ ⇶

W Travelers Budget Inn M
(716) 297-3228. **$45-$135.** 9001 Niagara Falls Blvd. I-190,
exit 22, 1.7 mi e. Ext corridors. **Pets:** Accepted.

ASK S⍥ ✕ 🛏

✽ END METROPOLITAN AREA ✽

NORTH SYRACUSE

**WWWW Doubletree Club Hotel/Syracuse
Airport SH**
(315) 457-4000. **$75-$139.** 6701 Buckley Rd. I-81, exit 25
(7th North St), 0.8 mi w; I-90, exit 36. Int corridors.
Pets: Accepted.

ASK S⍥ ✕ ⊘ 🛏 ▣ ⑪ ⇶ ⊠

WW Quality Inn North M
(315) 451-1212. **$69-$139.** 1308 Buckley Rd. I-81, exit 25
(7th North St), 0.3 mi w, then just n. Ext/int corridors.
Pets: Accepted.

SAVE S⍥ ✕ 🛏 ▣ ⑪ ⇶

NORWICH

WW Super 8 Motel of Norwich SH
(607) 336-8880. **$65-$115, 7 day notice.** 6067 SR 12. On
SR 12, 0.9 mi n. Int corridors. **Pets:** Service with restrictions, supervision.

ASK S⍥ ✕

OGDENSBURG

WWW Quality Inn Gran-View M ✽
(315) 393-4550. **$80-$169.** 6765 State Hwy 37. On SR 37
W, 3 mi sw. Ext/int corridors. **Pets:** $10 one-time fee/room.
Designated rooms, supervision.

SAVE S⍥ ✕ 🛏 ▣ ⑪ ⇶ ⊠

WWWW The Stonefence Resort & Motel M
(315) 393-1545. **$77-$132.** 7191 SR 37. Jct SR 68 W, 0.5 mi
w. Ext/int corridors. **Pets:** Accepted.

SAVE ✕ 🛏 ▣ ⑪ ⇶ ⊠

OLD FORGE

WW Best Western Sunset Inn M
(315) 369-6836. **$49-$239, 7 day notice.** 2752 SR 28. 0.3
mi s. Ext/int corridors. **Pets:** Accepted.

ASK S⍥ ✕ 🛏 ▣ ⇶ ⊠

ONEONTA

**WWWW Holiday Inn Oneonta/Cooperstown
Area SH ✽**
(607) 433-2250. **$79-$189.** 5206 State Hwy 23. I-88, exit 15
(SR 23 and 28), 1.5 mi e. Int corridors. **Pets:** Small. Designated rooms, supervision.

SAVE S⍥ ✕ ⊘ 🐾 🛏 ▣ ⑪ ⇶ ⊠

WW Super 8 Motel SH
(607) 432-9505. **$62-$150, 3 day notice.** 4973 SR 23. I-88,
exit 15 (SR 23 and 28), 0.3 mi e. Int corridors. **Pets:** Large.
Service with restrictions, supervision.

ASK S⍥ ✕ 🚹 🛏

OWEGO

WWW Sunrise Motel M
(607) 687-5667. **$51-$55.** 3778 Waverly Rd. SR 17, exit 64
(SR 96 N) across river w to SR 17C, then 2 mi s. Ext
corridors. **Pets:** Accepted.

SAVE S⍥ ✕

PAINTED POST

⟨AAA⟩ ▼▼ Best Western Lodge on the Green M
(607) 962-2456. **$50-$100.** 3171 Canada Rd. SR 17, exit 44, s to Gang Mills exit, then n. Ext corridors. **Pets:** Other species. Service with restrictions.
[SAVE] [S◇] [✕] [🛄] [▣] [❸] [≈]

▼▼ Econo Lodge SH
(607) 962-4444. **$45-$120.** 200 Robert Dann Dr. Jct US 15 and SR 17, exit 44, s to Gang Mills exit. Int corridors. **Pets:** $10 daily fee/pet. Service with restrictions, supervision.
[ASK] [S◇] [✕] [&M] [🐾] [🛄] [▣]

⟨AAA⟩ ▼ Erwin Motel M
(607) 962-7411. **$42-$79, 3 day notice.** Rt 417. US 15, exit Erwin Addison, 0.5 mi e. Ext corridors. **Pets:** $10 daily fee/room. Supervision.
[SAVE] [✕] [🛄] [≈]

PEMBROKE

▼▼ Darien Lakes Econo Lodge SH 🐾
(585) 599-4681. **$44-$119.** 8493 SR 77. I-90, exit 48A, just s. Int corridors. **Pets:** Other species. $20 deposit/room. Designated rooms, service with restrictions, supervision.
[ASK] [S◇] [✕] [🛄] [▣]

PINE VALLEY

⟨AAA⟩ ▼▼▼ Best Western Marshall Manor M
(607) 739-3891. **$50-$87.** 3527 Watkins Rd. SR 17, exit 52, 5 mi n on SR 14. Ext corridors. **Pets:** Large. $4 daily fee/pet. Service with restrictions, crate.
[SAVE] [S◇] [✕] [🛄] [▣] [≈]

PLAINVIEW

▼▼▼ Residence Inn by Marriott SH
(516) 433-6200. **$209-$375.** 9 Gerhard Rd. I-495, exit 44, 1.6 mi s on SR 135, exit 10, then just e on Old Country Rd. Int corridors. **Pets:** Accepted.
[✕] [&M] [🐾] [🛄] [▣] [❸] [≈] [✕]

PLATTSBURGH

⟨AAA⟩ ▼▼▼ Baymont Inn & Suites Plattsburgh SH
(518) 562-4000. **$60-$90.** 16 Plaza Blvd. I-87, exit 37, just w. Int corridors. **Pets:** Medium, other species. Designated rooms, service with restrictions, supervision.
[SAVE] [S◇] [✕] [&M] [🐾] [❧] [🛄] [▣] [≈]

⟨AAA⟩ ▼▼▼ Best Western The Inn at Smithfield SH 🐾
(518) 561-7750. **$69-$104.** 446 Rt 3. I-87, exit 37, just w. Int corridors. **Pets:** Supervision.
[SAVE] [S◇] [✕] [🛄] [▣] [❸] [≈] [✕]

PORT JERVIS

⟨AAA⟩ ▼▼ Comfort Inn SH
(845) 856-6611. **$70-$180.** 2247 Greenville Tpke. I-84, exit 1, just se. Int corridors. **Pets:** Small. $20 one-time fee/room. Designated rooms, service with restrictions, crate.
[SAVE] [S◇] [✕] [🛄] [▣] [≈]

PULASKI

⟨AAA⟩ ▼ Redwood Motel M
(315) 298-4717. **$52-$59.** 3723 SR 13. I-81, exit 36, just e. Ext/int corridors. **Pets:** $20 deposit/room. Service with restrictions, supervision.
[SAVE] [✕] [🛄] [❸] [≈]

RHINEBECK

▼▼▼ Beekman Arms & Delamater Inn and Conference Center CI
(845) 876-7077. **$115-$250, 7 day notice.** 6387 Mill St (Rt 9). Jct US 9 and SR 308. Ext/int corridors. **Pets:** Accepted.
[✕] [❦] [🛄] [▣] [❸]

RICHMONDVILLE

▼▼ Econo Lodge Cobleskill/Richmondville M
(518) 294-7739. **$59-$175.** 555 Ploss Rd. I-88, exit 20, just e on SR 7, then just s. Ext corridors. **Pets:** Other species. $15 daily fee/pet. Service with restrictions, supervision.
[ASK] [S◇] [✕] [🛄] [▣]

RIVERHEAD

▼▼▼ Best Western East End SH
(631) 369-2200. **$139-$229.** 1830 SR 25. I-495, exit 72 (SR 25 E). Int corridors. **Pets:** Accepted.
[ASK] [S◇] [✕] [❦] [🛄] [▣] [❸] [≈]

ROCHESTER

⟨AAA⟩ ▼▼▼ Crowne Plaza Hotel and Resort Rochester LH
(585) 546-3450. **$69-$139.** 70 State St. Downtown. Int corridors. **Pets:** Accepted.
[SAVE] [S◇] [✕] [🐾] [🛄] [▣] [❸] [≈]

ROCK HILL

⟨AAA⟩ ▼▼▼ The Lodge at Rock Hill SH
(845) 796-3100. **$99-$189.** 283 Rock Hill Dr. SR 17, exit 109, just e. Int corridors. **Pets:** $25 one-time fee/pet. Supervision.
[SAVE] [S◇] [✕] [🐾] [❦] [🛄] [▣] [≈]

ROCKVILLE CENTRE

⟨AAA⟩ ▼▼▼ Holiday Inn SH 🐾
(516) 678-1300. **$159.** 173 Sunrise Hwy. On SR 27, between N Village and N Centre aves. Ext corridors. **Pets:** $15 daily fee/room. Service with restrictions.
[SAVE] [S◇] [✕] [&M] [🐾] [❦] [🛄] [▣] [❸] [≈]

ROME

▽▽ Adirondack Thirteen Pines Motel M
(315) 337-4930. **$45-$60, 3 day notice.** 7353 River Rd. Jct SR 49, 0.5 mi e on SR 365. Ext corridors. **Pets:** Other species. No service, supervision.
(ASK) (S⊘) 🛏 🌊 🗵

ⒶⒶⒶ ▽▽ Inn at the Beeches M
(315) 336-1776. **$79-$125.** 7900 Turin Rd. Jct SR 46, 2 mi n on SR 26 (Turin Rd). Ext corridors. **Pets:** Accepted.
(SAVE) (S⊘) 🗵 🛏 🍴 🌊

ROSCOE

ⒶⒶⒶ ▽▽ Roscoe Motel M
(607) 498-5220. **$55-$65.** 2054 Old Rt 17. SR 17, exit 94, 0.5 mi n on SR 206, then just w. Ext corridors. **Pets:** $10 daily fee/pet. Service with restrictions.
(SAVE) 🛏 💻

ROTTERDAM

▽▽ Super 8 Schenectady SH
(518) 355-2190. **$55-$80, 5 day notice.** 3083 Carman Rd. I-890, exit 9 (Curry Rd), 0.4 mi w; I-90, exit 25. Int corridors. **Pets:** Small, dogs only. $10 daily fee/pet. Designated rooms, service with restrictions, supervision.
(ASK) (S⊘) 🗵

SACKETS HARBOR

▽▽ Ontario Place Hotel SH
(315) 646-8000. **$69-$150, 3 day notice.** 103 General Smith Dr. Center. Int corridors. **Pets:** Medium. $10 daily fee/pet. Designated rooms, service with restrictions, supervision.
🗵 🛏 💻

SALAMANCA

▽▽▽ Holiday Inn Express Hotel &
Suites SH 🐾
(716) 945-7600. **$104-$179.** 779 Broad St. I-86, exit 20, just n. Int corridors. **Pets:** Other species. $50 deposit/pet. Service with restrictions, supervision.
(ASK) (S⊘) 🗵 ♿ 🛏 💻 🌊 🗵

SARANAC LAKE

ⒶⒶⒶ ▽▽ Adirondack Motel M
(518) 891-2116. **$55-$160.** 248 Lake Flower Ave. 0.7 mi e on SR 86. Ext corridors. **Pets:** Dogs only. $10 daily fee/room. Service with restrictions, supervision.
(SAVE) (S⊘) 🗵 🛏 💻 🗵

ⒶⒶⒶ ▽▽▽ Best Western Mountain Lake
Inn SH
(518) 891-1970. **$70-$150.** 487 Lake Flower Ave. 0.8 mi e on SR 86. Int corridors. **Pets:** $20 one-time fee/room. Designated rooms, supervision.
(SAVE) (S⊘) 🗵 (⊾M) 💻 🍴 🌊

ⒶⒶⒶ ▽▽ The Hotel Saranac of Paul Smith's
College SH
(518) 891-2200. **$99-$140, 3 day notice.** 101 Main St. Center. Int corridors. **Pets:** Other species. $15 daily fee/pet. Service with restrictions, supervision.
(SAVE) (S⊘) 🗵 🗁 🛏 💻 🍴

▽▽ Lake Flower Inn M
(518) 891-2310. **$48-$108, 14 day notice.** 234 Lake Flower Ave. 0.6 mi e on SR 86. Ext corridors. **Pets:** Accepted.
🗵 🛏 🌊 🗵

ⒶⒶⒶ ▽▽▽ Lake Side Motel M
(518) 891-4333. **$59-$109, 7 day notice.** 256 Lake Flower Ave. 0.6 mi e on SR 86. Ext corridors. **Pets:** Accepted.
(SAVE) (S⊘) 🗵 🛏 🌊 🗵

SARATOGA SPRINGS

▽▽▽▽ Holiday Inn SH
(518) 584-4550. **$125-$499.** 232 Broadway. On US 9, jct SR 50. Int corridors. **Pets:** Other species. Service with restrictions.
(ASK) (S⊘) 🗵 🗁 🛏 💻 🍴 🌊

ⒶⒶⒶ ▽▽▽▽ Union Gables Bed & Breakfast BB
(518) 584-1558. **$130-$300, 14 day notice.** 55 Union Ave. I-87, exit 14, 1.5 mi w. Int corridors. **Pets:** Accepted.
(SAVE) 🗵 🛏

SCHENECTADY

▽▽ Days Inn SH
(518) 370-3297. **$54-$99.** 167 Nott Terrace. Jct State St (SR 5) and Nott Terrace, 2 blks e; downtown. Int corridors. **Pets:** Accepted.
(ASK) (S⊘) 🗵 🗁 🛏 💻

▽▽▽▽ Holiday Inn-Downtown Schenectady SH
(518) 393-4141. **$109-$129.** 100 Nott Terrace. Jct State St (SR 5) and Nott Terrace, 2 blks e; center. Int corridors. **Pets:** Accepted.
(ASK) (S⊘) 🗵 🛏 💻 🍴 🌊 🗵

SCHROON LAKE

ⒶⒶⒶ ▽ Blue Ridge Motel M 🐾
(518) 532-7521. **$79-$89, 14 day notice.** 2455 US Rt 9. I-87, exit 28, 4 mi n. Ext/int corridors. **Pets:** $10 daily fee/pet. Service with restrictions, supervision.
(SAVE) (S⊘) 🗵 🛏 💻 🌊 🗵

SOUTHAMPTON

▽▽▽ Southampton Inn SH
(631) 283-6500. **$119-$489, 30 day notice.** 91 Hill St. 0.3 mi n from corner of Main St and Jobs Ln. Ext corridors. **Pets:** Accepted.
(ASK) (S⊘) 🗵 ♿ 🛏 🍴 🌊 🗵

SYLVAN BEACH

▽▽ Cinderella's Comfort Sleep Suites M
(315) 762-4280. **$59-$179, 16 day notice.** 1208 N Main St. On SR 13; center. Ext corridors. **Pets:** Medium. $75 deposit/room. Service with restrictions, supervision.
(ASK) (S⊘) 🗵 🛏 💻 🍴

SYRACUSE

▽▽▽ Best Western Fairgrounds SH
(315) 484-0044. **$85-$99, 14 day notice.** 670 State Fair Blvd. I-690, exit 7, 1.3 mi nw, just past fairgrounds. Int corridors. **Pets:** Small. $25 one-time fee/room. Supervision.
(ASK) (S⊘) 🗵 (⊾M) ♿ 🛏 💻 🍴

WWW Comfort Inn Fairgrounds SH
(315) 453-0045. $79-$179. 7010 Interstate Island Rd. I-90, exit 39 to I-690 E, exit 2 (Jones Rd), just sw. Int corridors. **Pets:** Other species. $15 one-time fee/room. Service with restrictions, supervision.
ASK SD X H P

AAA WWW Econo Lodge
University/Downtown M
(315) 425-0015. $55-$80. 454 James St. Downtown. Ext corridors. **Pets:** Medium. $10 daily fee/pet. Service with restrictions, supervision.
SAVE SD X H

AAA WWWW Holiday Inn/Farrell Road SH
(315) 457-8700. $69-$139. 100 Farrell Rd. I-90, exit 39 to I-690 E, exit John Glenn Blvd. Int corridors. **Pets:** Accepted.
SAVE SD X ⌀ ⌂ H P ¶ ⇌

AAA WWW Red Roof Inn M
(315) 437-3309. $45-$73. 6614 N Thompson Rd. I-90, exit 35 (Carrier Cir), just n. Ext corridors. **Pets:** Medium, other species. Supervision.
SAVE X ⌀ ⌂ H

AAA WWWWW Sheraton Syracuse University Hotel & Conference Center LH ❀
(315) 475-3000. $289-$370. 801 University Ave. I-81, exit 18. Int corridors. **Pets:** Medium, dogs only. Designated rooms, service with restrictions, supervision.
SAVE X H P ¶ ⇌ X

TICONDEROGA

AAA WW Circle Court Motel M
(518) 585-7660. $57-$75. 6 Montcalm St. SR 9N; at Liberty Monument traffic circle. Ext corridors. **Pets:** $5 daily fee/room. Service with restrictions, supervision.
SAVE SD X H P

TROY

AAA WWW Best Western-Rensselaer Inn SH
(518) 274-3210. $84-$119. 1800 6th Ave. I-787, exit 9 E, 0.5 mi e, exit downtown, 0.5 mi s. Int corridors. **Pets:** Accepted.
SAVE SD X H P ¶ ⇌

UTICA

AAA WW A-1 Motel M
(315) 735-6698. $45-$60, 3 day notice. 238 N Genesee St. I-90 (New York Thruway), exit 31, just s. Int corridors. **Pets:** Dogs only. $5 daily fee/pet. Service with restrictions, supervision.
SAVE SD X H

WWWW Best Western Gateway Adirondack Inn SH
(315) 732-4121. $89-$190. 175 N Genesee St. I-90 (New York Thruway), exit 31, 0.5 mi s. Int corridors. **Pets:** Service with restrictions, crate.
ASK SD X ⌀ H P

AAA WWW Red Roof Inn M
(315) 724-7128. $50-$94. 20 Weaver St. I-90 (New York Thruway), exit 31. Ext corridors. **Pets:** Accepted.
SAVE X H

VALATIE

AAA WWW Blue Spruce Inn & Suites M
(518) 758-9711. $70-$95, 3 day notice. 3093 Rt 9. I-90 (New York Thruway), exit 12, 4 mi s on US 9 via New York Thruway Extension, exit B1. Ext corridors. **Pets:** Service with restrictions, supervision.
SAVE SD X H P ¶ ⇌

VESTAL

WWWW Holiday Inn at the University SH
(607) 729-6371. $109-$129. 4105 Vestal Pkwy. SR 17, exit 70S, 2.5 mi s on US 201 to SR 434 W, then right on Bunn Hill Rd. Ext/int corridors. **Pets:** Accepted.
ASK SD X ⌂M H P ¶ ⇌

WARRENSBURG

WWW Super 8 Warrensburg M
(518) 623-2811. $65-$120. 3619 SR 9. I-87, exit 23, just w. Int corridors. **Pets:** Accepted.
ASK SD X

WATERLOO

AAA WWWW Holiday Inn Waterloo-Seneca Falls SH
(315) 539-5011. $65-$130. 2468 SR 414. I-90 (New York Thruway), exit 41, 4 mi s, just n of jct SR 414/5 and US 20. Int corridors. **Pets:** Medium, other species. Service with restrictions, supervision.
SAVE SD X H P ¶ ⇌ X

AAA WWW Microtel Inn & Suites SH
(315) 539-8438. $56-$87. 1966 Rt 5 & 20. I-90 (New York Thruway), exit 41, 4 mi s on SR 414, then just e. Int corridors. **Pets:** $5 daily fee/room. Supervision.
SAVE SD X ⌂M ⌂ H

WATERTOWN

WW Best Western Carriage House Inn SH ❀
(315) 782-8000. Call for rates. 300 Washington St. Center. Int corridors. **Pets:** Medium. $10 daily fee/pet. Designated rooms, service with restrictions.
X H P ¶ ⇌

AAA WWW Ramada Inn SH
(315) 788-0700. $74-$109. 6300 Arsenal St. I-81, exit 45, just w. Int corridors. **Pets:** Other species. $200 deposit/room. Service with restrictions, crate.
SAVE SD X H P ¶ ⇌ X

WATKINS GLEN

AAA WWW Anchor Inn and Marina M ❀
(607) 535-4159. $69-$135, 10 day notice. 3425 Salt Point Rd. 1.2 mi n on SR 14. Ext corridors. **Pets:** Other species. $25 deposit/pet. Service with restrictions, supervision.
SAVE SD X ⌂ H X

AAA WWW Budget Inn M
(607) 535-4800. $48-$125. 435 S Franklin St. On SR 14. Ext corridors. **Pets:** Very small, dogs only. $10 daily fee/pet. Designated rooms, service with restrictions, supervision.
SAVE SD X H

AAA ▽▽ Chieftain Motel **M** ❀
(107) 535-4759. **$59-$135, 10 day notice.** 3815 State Rt 14. Jct SR 14A, 3 mi n. Ext corridors. **Pets:** Other species. $25 deposit/pet. Service with restrictions, supervision.
[SAVE] [$6] [✕] [🛋] [🖥] [💻] [⇌]

WELLSVILLE

AAA ▽ Long-Vue Motel **M**
(585) 593-2450. **$44-$90.** 5081 Rt 417 W. Jct SR 19, 3 mi w. Ext corridors. **Pets:** Service with restrictions, supervision.
[SAVE] [✕] [🛋] [🖥]

WEST COXSACKIE

AAA ▽▽▽ Best Western New Baltimore Inn **SH**
(518) 731-8100. **$84-$144.** 12600 Rt 9 W. I-87 (New York Thruway), exit 21B, 0.5 mi s. Int corridors. **Pets:** Other species. $5 daily fee/pet.
[SAVE] [$6] [✕] [🛋] [🖥] [💻] [⇌] [✕]

WESTMORELAND

AAA ▽ Carriage Motor Inn **M**
(315) 853-3561. **$42-$65, 5 day notice.** 5370 SR 233. I-90, exit 32, just n. Ext corridors. **Pets:** Medium. $20 deposit/room, $5 daily fee/room. Service with restrictions, supervision.
[SAVE] [$6] [✕] [🛋]

WILMINGTON

AAA ▽ Grand View Motel **M**
(518) 946-2209. **$59-$99.** HC 2, Box 121A (SR 86). On SR 86, 1 mi e. Ext corridors. **Pets:** Small, dogs only. Designated rooms, service with restrictions, supervision.
[SAVE] [$6] [✕] [⇌] [✕]

AAA ▽▽ Hungry Trout Resort **M**
(518) 946-2217. **$69-$179, 7 day notice.** Rt 86. On SR 86, 2 mi w. Ext corridors. **Pets:** Accepted.
[SAVE] [✕] [🛋] [🖥] [🍴] [⇌] [✕]

AAA ▽▽▽ Ledge Rock at Whiteface Mountain **M**
(518) 946-2379. **$69-$139, 10 day notice.** Placid Rd (SR 86). On SR 86, 3 mi w. Ext corridors. **Pets:** Medium. $10 one-time fee/pet. Service with restrictions, crate.
[SAVE] [$6] [✕] [🛋] [🖥] [💻] [⇌] [✕]

▽▽ Mountain Brook Lodge **M**
(518) 946-2262. **$55-$99.** Rt 86. Center. Ext corridors. **Pets:** Large. $2 daily fee/room. Service with restrictions, crate.
[✕] [🛋] [🖥] [⇌]

AAA ▽▽ North Pole Motor Inn **M**
(518) 946-7733. **$49-$99, 7 day notice.** SR 86. On SR 86, just w of jct CR 431. Ext corridors. **Pets:** Dogs only. $3 daily fee/pet. Service with restrictions, supervision.
[SAVE] [✕] [🛋] [🖥] [⇌] [✕]

NORTH CAROLINA

CITY INDEX

ABERDEEN

ⒶⒶⒶ ▼▼▼ Best Western Pinehurst Motor Inn Ⓜ ❀
(910) 944-2367. **$70-$80.** 1500 Sandhills Blvd. Jct of US 15
and 501, 0.3 mi s on US 1. Ext corridors. **Pets:** Dogs only.
$10 daily fee/room. Service with restrictions, crate.

▼ Motel 6-1234 Ⓜ
(910) 944-5633. **$42-$53.** 1408 Sandhills Blvd. Jct US 15
and 501, 0.3 mi s on US 1. Ext corridors. **Pets:** Accepted.

ANDREWS

**▼▼▼ Hawkesdene House Bed & Breakfast Inn
and Cottages** ⒷⒷ
(828) 321-6027. **$85-$125, 3 day notice.** 381 Phillips Creek
Rd. US 19 business route, 3.2 mi s on Cherry St, then 0.5
mi s. Ext/int corridors. **Pets:** $50 one-time fee/pet. Desig-
nated rooms, no service, supervision.
🚫 🛏 💻

ARCHDALE

▼▼ Best Western Archdale Inn ⓈⒽ
(336) 861-3000. **$59-$175.** 1202 Liberty Rd. I-85, exit 113,
just w. Int corridors. **Pets:** Accepted.
ⒶⓈⓀ 🆂 ✕ 🛏 💻 ≈

ASHEBORO

ⒶⒶⒶ ▼▼ Comfort Inn ⓈⒽ
(336) 626-3680. **$49-$99.** 242 Lake Crest Rd. US 64, just w
on SR 42. Ext corridors. **Pets:** Accepted.
SAVE 🆂 ✕ 🛏 💻 ≈

ⒶⒶⒶ ▼▼▼ Ramada Limited Ⓜ ❀
(336) 626-4414. **$45-$70.** 825 W Dixie Dr. I-220, US 64
E/SR 49 N Raleigh, just e. Int corridors. **Pets:** Medium. $20
one-time fee/room. Designated rooms, service with restrictions, supervision.
SAVE 🆂 ✕ 🛏 💻 ≈

ASHEVILLE

**ⒶⒶⒶ ▼▼▼ Best Western of Asheville Biltmore
East** Ⓜ
(828) 298-5562. **$49-$99.** 501 Tunnel Rd. I-240, exit 7, 0.5
mi e on SR 70. Ext corridors. **Pets:** Small, dogs only. $10
one-time fee/pet. Service with restrictions, supervision.
SAVE 🆂 ✕ 🛏 💻 ≈

▼▼ Comfort Inn River Ridge ⓈⒽ ❀
(828) 298-9141. **$59-$179.** 800 Fairview Rd. I-240, exit 8; jct
I-40 and US 74. Int corridors. **Pets:** Service with restrictions, supervision.
ⒶⓈⓀ 🆂 ✕ 🍴 🛏 💻 ≈ ✕

**ⒶⒶⒶ ▼▼▼ Comfort Suites-Biltmore Square
Mall** ⓈⒽ
(828) 665-4000. **$65-$130.** 890 Brevard Rd. I-26, exit 2, 0.3
mi w. Int corridors. **Pets:** Other species. $20 daily fee/room.
Designated rooms, service with restrictions, crate.
SAVE 🆂 ✕ 🛏 💻 ≈

ⒶⒶⒶ ▼▼▼ Days Inn-Asheville Mall Ⓜ ❀
(828) 252-4000. **$30-$179.** 201 Tunnel Rd. I-240, exit 6, 0.5
mi e, on south side of road. Ext corridors. **Pets:** Other
species. $15 daily fee/pet. Service with restrictions.
SAVE ✕ 🍴 🛏 💻 ≈

ⒶⒶⒶ ▼▼▼ Days Inn-Biltmore East ⓈⒽ
(828) 298-4000. **$35-$139.** 1435 Tunnel Rd. I-40, exit 55,
just n. Int corridors. **Pets:** Small, other species. $15 daily
fee/pet. Service with restrictions.
SAVE 🆂 ✕ 🍴 🛏 💻 ≈

**▼▼▼ Holiday Inn-Biltmore East at the Blue Ridge
Parkway** ⓈⒽ
(828) 298-5611. **$59-$149.** 1450 Tunnel Rd. I-40, exit 55, just
n. Int corridors. **Pets:** Large, other species. $10 daily fee/
pet. Designated rooms, service with restrictions, supervision.
ⒶⓈⓀ 🆂 ✕ 🛏 💻 🍴 ≈

ⒶⒶⒶ ▼ The Log Cabin Motor Court ⒸⒶ
(828) 645-6546. **$50-$250, 14 day notice.** 330 Weaverville
Hwy. 4 mi n on US 19 and 23, exit New Bridge northbound,
then 1 mi n on Weaverville Hwy; exit New Stock Rd southbound, 1 mi s. Ext corridors. **Pets:** Other species. $15 daily
fee/pet. No service.
SAVE 🛏 💻 Ⓩ

▼ Motel 6–1134 Ⓜ
(828) 299-3040. **$39-$57.** 1415 Tunnel Rd. I-40, exit 55. Ext
corridors. **Pets:** Accepted.

AAA ▼▼▼ **The Pines Cottages** CA
(828) 645-9661. **$55-$165, 14 day notice.** 346 Weaverville Hwy. 4 mi n on US 19 and 23, exit New Bridge northbound, 1.1 mi n on Weaverville Hwy; exit New Stock Rd southbound, 1 mi s. Ext corridors. **Pets:** Other species. $50 deposit/pet. Service with restrictions.
SAVE ⊟ ▣ K Z

AAA ▼▼▼ **Red Roof Inn-West** M
(828) 667-9803. **$38-$79.** 16 Crowell Rd. I-40, exit 44, just n on US 19 and 23, just w on old Haywood Rd, then just s. Ext corridors. **Pets:** Large, other species. Service with restrictions, crate.
SAVE ⊠ ☞ ⊟

AAA ▼▼▼ **Super 8 East** SH ❀
(828) 298-7952. **$39-$119.** 1329 Tunnel Rd. I-40, exit 55, 0.3 mi w. Ext corridors. **Pets:** Large, other species. $20 one-time fee/pet. Service with restrictions, supervision.
SAVE S☐ ⊠ ⊟ ⇌ ⊠

BANNER ELK

▼▼▼ **Banner Elk Inn Bed & Breakfast** BB
(828) 898-6223. **$165, 30 day notice.** 407 Main St E. Jct SR 184 and 194, 0.3 mi n on SR 194. Int corridors. **Pets:** Service with restrictions, supervision.
⊠ ⊟ ▣ K

▼▼▼ **Holiday Inn/Banner Elk-Boone Area** SH ❀
(828) 898-4571. **$75-$160, 3 day notice.** 1615 Tynecastle Hwy. 1 mi se on SR 184. Ext corridors. **Pets:** Other species. $25 deposit/room. Designated rooms, service with restrictions.
ASK S☐ ⊠ ☞M ☞ ⊟ ▣ ¶ ⇌

BURLINGTON

AAA ▼▼▼▼ **Holiday Inn** SH
(336) 229-5203. **$89-$250.** 2444 Maple Ave. I-40/85, exit 145, just n. Int corridors. **Pets:** Medium. $50 one-time fee/room. Service with restrictions, supervision.
SAVE S☐ ⊠ ☞M ☞ ⊟ ▣ ¶ ⇌

▼▼ **Motel 6–1257** SH
(336) 226-1325. **$40-$53.** 2155 Hanford Rd. I-40/85, exit 145, just s, then just w. Ext corridors. **Pets:** Accepted.
S☐ ⊠ ☞ ☞ ⇌

AAA ▼▼▼ **Red Roof Inn** SH
(336) 227-1270. **$45-$120, 3 day notice.** 2133 W Hanford Rd. I-40/85, exit 145, just s on SR 49, then just w. Int corridors. **Pets:** Medium. Service with restrictions, supervision.
SAVE S☐ ⊠ ⊟ ▣ ⇌

CARY

▼▼▼ **Candlewood Suites** SH
(919) 468-4222. **$119-$139.** 1020 Buck Jones Rd. I-40, exit 293, 0.3 mi sw on US 1 and 64 W, just w, then 0.5 mi n. Int corridors. **Pets:** Large, other species. $12 daily fee/room. Service with restrictions, supervision.
ASK ⊠ ☞ ☞ ⊟ ⊟

▼▼▼ **Comfort Suites Hotel** SH
(919) 852-4318. **$69-$109.** 350 Asheville Ave. US 1 and 64, exit 98A, 0.8 mi e on Tryon Rd, then just n. Int corridors. **Pets:** Accepted.
ASK S☐ ⊠ ☞M ☞ ⊟ ▣ ⇌ ⊠

▼▼▼ **La Quinta Inn & Suites** SH
(919) 851-2850. **$69-$99.** 191 Crescent Commons. US 1 and 64, exit 98A, 0.5 mi e on Tryon Rd, just n. Int corridors. **Pets:** Accepted.
ASK S☐ ⊠ ☞M ☞ ☞ ⊟ ▣ ⇌

AAA ▼▼▼ **Red Roof Inn** SH ❀
(919) 469-3400. **$44-$69.** 1800 Walnut St. I-40, exit 293, 0.3 mi sw on US 1 and 64 W; exit Cary-Walnut St, just e. Int corridors. **Pets:** Large, cats only. Service with restrictions, supervision.
SAVE ⊠ ☞M ☞ ☞ ⊟

▼▼▼ **Residence Inn** SH
(919) 851-4080. **Call for rates.** 2900 Regency Pkwy. US 1 and 64, exit 98A, 0.5 mi e on Tryon Rd, just s. Int corridors. **Pets:** Other species. $10 daily fee/room, $50 one-time fee/room. Service with restrictions.
⊠ ☞M ☞ ⊟ ▣ ⇌ ⊠

CASHIERS

▼▼▼ **High Hampton Inn & Country Club** SH
(828) 743-2411. **$184-$310, 10 day notice.** 1525 Hwy S. Jct US 64, 1.5 mi s on SR 107. Ext/int corridors. **Pets:** Accepted.
¶ ⊠ K P Z

CHAPEL HILL

AAA ▼▼▼▼ **Carolina Inn** SH
(919) 933-2001. **$99-$224.** 211 Pittsboro St. Jct Columbia and Franklin sts, 0.3 mi s on SR 86. Int corridors. **Pets:** Small, other species. $75 one-time fee/room. Designated rooms, service with restrictions, crate.
SAVE ⊠ ☞ ☞ ⊟ ▣ ¶

AAA ▼▼▼ **The Siena Hotel** SH
(919) 929-4000. **$109-$235.** 1505 E Franklin St. I-40, exit 270, 2 mi s on US 15/501. Int corridors. **Pets:** Medium, dogs only. $75 one-time fee/pet. Service with restrictions.
SAVE S☐ ⊠ ☞M ☞ ☞ ⊟ ¶

CHARLOTTE METROPOLITAN AREA

CHARLOTTE

AAA ▼▼▼▼ **AmeriSuites (Charlotte/Airport)** SH
(704) 423-9931. **$69-$149.** 2950 Oak Lake Blvd. I-85, exit 33 (Billy Graham Pkwy), then exit Tyvola/Coliseum, 0.3 mi s. Int corridors. **Pets:** Accepted.
SAVE S☐ ⊠ ⊟ ▣ ⇌

AAA ▼▼▼▼ **AmeriSuites (Charlotte/Arrowood)** SH
(704) 522-8400. **$77.** 7900 Forest Point Blvd. I-77, exit 3 southbound; exit 2 northbound, just e. Int corridors. **Pets:** Small. Service with restrictions, crate.
SAVE S☐ ⊠ ☞M ☞ ☞ ⊟ ▣ ⇌

▼▼▼▼ Clarion Hotel 🆂🅷
(704) 523-1400. **$70.** 321 W Woodlawn Rd. I-77, exit 6B, just w. Int corridors. **Pets:** Accepted.
(ASK) 🆂 ⊠ 🖫 🕮 📶 🖥 💻 🍴 ➔ ⊠

▼▼▼▼ Comfort Inn Carowinds 🆂🅷
(803) 548-5200. **$54-$90.** 3725 Avenue of the Carolinas. I-77, exit 90, just w. Int corridors. **Pets:** Accepted.
(ASK) 🆂 ⊠ 📶 🖥 💻 ➔

▲▲▲ ▼▼▼ Comfort Inn-Executive Park 🆂🅷 🐾
(704) 525-2626. **$49.** 5822 Westpark Dr. I-77, exit 5 (Tyvola Rd), just e, then 0.4 mi s. Int corridors. **Pets:** Medium, other species. $25 one-time fee/room. Service with restrictions, crate.
(SAVE) 🆂 ⊠ 📶 🖥 🖥 💻 ➔

▲▲▲ ▼▼▼▼ Drury Inn & Suites-Charlotte North 🆂🅷
(704) 593-0700. **$87-$107.** 415 West WT Harris Blvd. I-85, exit 45A, just e. Int corridors. **Pets:** Large, other species. Service with restrictions, supervision.
(SAVE) ⊠ 🕮 📶 🖥 🖥 💻 ➔

▼▼▼▼ Holiday Inn Airport 🆂🅷
(704) 394-4301. **$79.** 2707 Little Rock Rd. I-85, exit 32, just e. Int corridors. **Pets:** Medium. $25 one-time fee/pet. Designated rooms, service with restrictions, supervision.
(ASK) 🆂 ⊠ 📶 🖥 💻 🍴 ➔

▼▼▼▼ Holiday Inn at University Executive Park 🆂🅷
(704) 547-0999. **$63-$99.** 8520 University Executive Park Dr. I-85, exit 45A, 0.3 mi e, then s. Int corridors. **Pets:** Other species. $25 one-time fee/pet. Designated rooms, service with restrictions.
(ASK) 🆂 ⊠ 🕮 📶 🖥 🖥 💻 🍴 ➔

▼▼ Homestead Studio Suites Hotel-Charlotte/Coliseum 🆂🅷 🐾
(704) 676-0083. **$54-$64.** 710 Yorkmont Rd. I-77, exit 6B, 0.3 mi w. Ext corridors. **Pets:** Medium, other species. $25 daily fee/room. Service with restrictions, crate.
(ASK) 🆂 ⊠ 🖥 🖥 💻

▲▲▲ ▼▼▼ La Quinta Inn-Airport 🅼
(704) 393-5306. **$65-$95.** 3100 I-85 S Service Rd. I-85, exit 33 (Billy Graham Pkwy), just w, then just n. Ext/int corridors. **Pets:** Other species. Service with restrictions.
(SAVE) 🆂 ⊠ 🕮 📶 🖥 💻 ➔

▼▼▼▼ La Quinta Inn & Suites-Charlotte Coliseum 🆂🅷
(704) 523-5599. **$59-$89.** 4900 S Tryon St. I-77, exit 6B, just w. Int corridors. **Pets:** Accepted.
(ASK) 🆂 ⊠ 🕮 📶 🖥 🖥 💻 ➔

▼▼ MainStay Suites 🆂🅷
(704) 521-3232. **$79.** 7926 Forest Pine Dr. I-77, exit 3, just e. Int corridors. **Pets:** $100 one-time fee. Service with restrictions.
(ASK) 🆂 ⊠ 🕮 📶 🖥 🖥 💻 ➔

▲▲▲ ▼▼▼ ▼▼▼ Omni Charlotte Hotel 🅻🅷
(704) 377-0400. **$179-$339.** 132 E Trade St. I-77, exit 10B (Trade St E); I-277, exit College St; jct Trade and Tryon sts. Int corridors. **Pets:** Accepted.
(SAVE) 🆂 ⊠ 🕮 🖥 💻 🍴 ➔ ⊠

▼▼ Ramada Inn Merchandise Mart 🅼
(704) 377-1501. **$69.** 3000 E Independence Blvd. 3.5 mi e on US 74. Ext corridors. **Pets:** Accepted.
(ASK) 🆂 ⊠ 🕮 📶 🖥 🖥 💻 🍴 ➔

▲▲▲ ▼▼▼ Red Roof Inn-Airport 🅼 🐾
(704) 392-2316. **$44-$64.** 3300 S I-85 Service Rd. I-85, exit 33 (Billy Graham Pkwy), just w, then just s. Ext corridors. **Pets:** Medium. Service with restrictions, supervision.
(SAVE) ⊠ 🕮 📶 🖥

▼▼▼▼ Residence Inn by Marriott 🆂🅷 🐾
(704) 547-1122. **Call for rates.** 8503 N Tryon St. I-85, exit 45A, 0.3 mi e, then just s. Ext corridors. **Pets:** Medium. $100 one-time fee/room. Service with restrictions.
⊠ 🕮 📶 🖥 🖥 💻 ➔ ⊠

▼▼▼▼ Residence Inn by Marriott-Charlotte Uptown 🆂🅷
(704) 340-4000. **$119-$149.** 404 S Mint St. I-77, exit 10 (Trade St), 0.5 mi e, then just s. Int corridors. **Pets:** Accepted.
(ASK) ⊠ 🕮 📶 🖥 💻

▼▼▼▼ Residence Inn by Marriott-Piper Glen 🆂🅷
(704) 319-3900. **$89-$109.** 5115 Piper Station Dr. I-485, exit 59 (Tyvola Rd), just s, then e. Int corridors. **Pets:** Accepted.
(ASK) 🆂 ⊠ 🕮 📶 🖥 🖥 💻 ➔ ⊠

▼▼▼▼ Residence Inn by Marriott-Tyvola Executive Park 🅲🅾
(704) 527-8110. **$79-$109.** 5816 Westpark Dr. I-77, exit 5 (Tyvola Rd), just e, then 0.4 mi s. Ext/int corridors. **Pets:** Accepted.
(ASK) 🆂 ⊠ 🕮 📶 🖥 🖥 💻 ➔ ⊠

▲▲▲ ▼▼▼ ▼▼ Sheraton Charlotte Airport Plaza Hotel 🅻🅷 🐾
(704) 392-1200. **$94.** 3315 I-85 S at Billy Graham Pkwy. I-85, exit 33 (Billy Graham Pkwy), just e. Int corridors. **Pets:** Medium. Service with restrictions, crate.
(SAVE) 🆂 ⊠ 🕮 📶 🖥 🖥 💻 🍴 ➔ ⊠

▲▲▲ ▼▼▼ Sleep Inn 🆂🅷
(704) 549-4544. **$59-$69.** 8525 N Tryon St. I-85, exit 45A, 0.3 mi e on WT Harris Blvd, just s on US 29. Int corridors. **Pets:** Large, other species. $25 one-time fee/room. Service with restrictions, supervision.
(SAVE) 🆂 ⊠ 🕮 📶 🖥 🖥 💻 ➔

▼▼▼▼ Staybridge Suites Charlotte-Ballantyne 🆂🅷 🐾
(704) 248-5000. **$110-$120.** 15735 John J Delaney Dr. I-485, exit 61, just s. Int corridors. **Pets:** $150 one-time fee/room. Designated rooms, service with restrictions, supervision.
(ASK) 🆂 ⊠ 🕮 📶 🖥 🖥 💻 ➔ ⊠

▼▼▼ **Summerfield Suites by Wyndham-Charlotte Airport** SH
(704) 525-2600. **$79-$99.** 4920 S Tryon St. I-77, exit 6B, just w. Int corridors. **Pets:** Accepted.
ASK S🛏 ✕ 🚹M 🌙 🈁 🛋 ➿ 🐾

▼▼▼ **TownePlace Suites by Marriott** SH ❀
(704) 227-2000. **$59-$79.** 7805 Forest Point Blvd. I-77, exit 3 southbound; exit 2 northbound, just e. Int corridors. **Pets:** Medium. $10 daily fee/room, $100 one-time fee/room. Service with restrictions, crate.
ASK S🛏 ✕ 🚹M 🌙 🈁 🛋 ➿

▼▼▼ **TownePlace Suites by Marriott** SH
(704) 548-0388. **$79-$94.** 8710 Research Dr. I-85, exit 45 B, just w, then n. Ext corridors. **Pets:** Accepted.
ASK S🛏 ✕ 🈁 🛋 ➿

CORNELIUS

▼▼ **Best Western Lake Norman** SH
(704) 896-0660. **$74-$89, 14 day notice.** 19608 Liverpool Pkwy. I-77, exit 28, just w, then s. Int corridors. **Pets:** Small. $20 one-time fee/pet. Designated rooms, service with restrictions, supervision.
ASK S🛏 ✕ 🈁 🛋 ➿ 🐾

▼▼ **Holiday Inn Lake Norman** SH
(704) 892-9120. **$79-$99.** 19901 Holiday Ln. I-77, exit 28, just e, then just n. Ext corridors. **Pets:** Large, other species. $25 one-time fee/room. Service with restrictions.
ASK S🛏 ✕ 🈁 🛋 🍴 ➿

HUNTERSVILLE

▼▼▼ **Candlewood Suites** SH
(704) 895-3434. **$79-$159.** 16530 Northcross Dr. I-77, exit 25 (Sam Kurr Rd), just w, then s. Int corridors. **Pets:** Accepted.
ASK S🛏 ✕ 🈁 🛋

▼▼▼ **Ramada Limited** SH
(704) 892-6597. **$39.** 16825 Caldwell Creek Dr. I-77, exit 25 (Sam Kurr Rd), just e, then n. Int corridors. **Pets:** Accepted.
ASK S🛏 ✕ 🈁 🛋

▼▼▼ **Residence Inn by Marriott-Lake Norman** SH
(704) 584-0000. **$89-$199.** 16830 Kenton Dr. I-77, exit 25 (Sam Kurr Rd), 1 mi w, then just n. Int corridors. **Pets:** Accepted.
ASK S🛏 ✕ 🚹M 🌙 🈁 🛋 ➿ 🐾

PINEVILLE

▼▼▼ **Quality Suites** SH
(704) 889-7095. **$85-$129.** 9840 Pineville Matthews Rd. I-485, exit 64B, 0.3 mi s on SR 51. Int corridors. **Pets:** Accepted.
ASK S🛏 ✕ 🚹M 🌙 🈁 🛋 ➿

❖   **END METROPOLITAN AREA**   ❖

CHEROKEE

AAA ▼▼▼ **Best Western Great Smokies Inn** M
(828) 497-2020. **$49-$119.** 1636 Acquoni Rd. US 441 N, 2.5 mi n; downtown. Ext corridors. **Pets:** Large. $10 daily fee/room. Designated rooms, service with restrictions, supervision.
SAVE S🛏 ✕ 🌙 🈁 🛋 🍴 ➿

AAA ▼ **Pioneer Motel** M
(828) 497-2435. **$38-$78, 7 day notice.** 0.8 mi w on US 19 S. Ext corridors. **Pets:** Accepted.
SAVE S🛏 ✕ 🈁 🛋 ➿ 🐾

CLAYTON

▼▼▼▼ **Quality Inn & Suites** SH
(919) 773-1110. **$52-$110.** 126 Cleveland Crossing Dr. I-40, exit 312, just n, then just e. Int corridors. **Pets:** Accepted.
ASK S🛏 ✕ 🈁 🛋 ➿

▼▼ **Sleep Inn** SH
(919) 772-7771. **$50-$66, 5 day notice.** 105 Commerce Pkwy. I-40, exit 312, just s. Int corridors. **Pets:** Medium. $25 one-time fee/pet. Service with restrictions, supervision.
ASK S🛏 ✕ 🚹M 🌙 🈁 🛋 ➿

▼▼ **Super 8 Motel** SH
(919) 661-1991. **$58-$120.** 101 Leone Ct. I-40, exit 312, just n. Ext corridors. **Pets:** Accepted.
ASK S🛏 ✕ 🈁 🛋 ➿

CLEMMONS

▼▼ **The Village Inn Golf & Conference Center** SH
(336) 766-9121. **$69.** 6205 Ramada Dr. I-40, exit 184, just s, then just e. Int corridors. **Pets:** Accepted.
ASK S🛏 ✕ 🌙 🈁 🛋 🍴 ➿

DORTCHES

▼▼ **Econo Lodge/Dortches** M
(252) 937-6300. **$50-$70.** 5350 Dortches Blvd. I-95, exit 141, just w, then just n on service road. Ext corridors. **Pets:** Accepted.
ASK S🛏 ✕ 🌙 🈁 🛋 🍴 ➿

DUNN

▼▼ **Jameson Inn** M
(910) 891-5758. **$66-$71.** 901 Jackson Rd. I-95, exit 73, just w, then just s. Ext corridors. **Pets:** Small. Service with restrictions, crate.
✕ 🚹M 🌙 🈁 🛋 ➿

DURHAM

AAA ▼▼▼ **Best Value Carolina Duke Inn** M
(919) 286-0771. **$49-$99.** 2517 Guess Rd. I-85, exit 175, just e. Ext corridors. **Pets:** $3 daily fee/pet. Designated rooms, service with restrictions, crate.
SAVE S🛏 ✕ 🌙 🈁 ➿

AAA ▼▼▼ Best Western Skyland Inn 🅼 ❀
(919) 383-2508. **$62-$74, 7 day notice.** 5400 US 70 W.
I-85, exit 170, 0.3 mi e on US 70, then just n. Ext corridors.
Pets: Large, other species. $10 daily fee/pet. Service with
restrictions, supervision.
🆂🅰🆅🅴 🆂🔟 ❌ 🎟 🍽 💻 🌊

▼▼▼ Candlewood Suites 🆂🅷
(919) 484-9922. **$60-$110.** 1818 E NC Hwy 54. I-40, exit
278, just s, then just w. Int corridors. **Pets:** Accepted.
🅰🆂🅺 🆂🔟 ❌ 🔌 🎵 🎟 🍽 💻 ❎

▼▼▼ Homestead Studio Suites
      Hotel-Durham/University 🅼 ❀
(919) 402-1700. **$54-$64.** 1920 Ivy Creek Blvd. I-40, exit
270, 2 mi n on US 15 and 501, then just e on Martin Luther
King Jr Pkwy; in University Place. Ext corridors.
Pets: Medium, other species. $25 daily fee/room. Service
with restrictions, crate.
🅰🆂🅺 🆂🔟 ❌ 🎵 🎟 🍽

▼▼ Homestead Studio Suites Hotel-Raleigh/
     Durham/Research Triangle Park 🆂🅷 ❀
(919) 544-9991. **$44-$59.** 4515 NC Hwy 55. I-40, exit 278,
just s. Ext corridors. **Pets:** Medium, other species. $25 daily
fee/room. Service with restrictions, crate.
🅰🆂🅺 🆂🔟 ❌ 🎵 🎟 🍽 💻

▼▼▼ La Quinta Inn & Suites 🆂🅷
(919) 401-9660. **$79-$99.** 4414 Chapel Hill Blvd. I-40, exit
270, 1.7 mi n on US 15/501. Int corridors. **Pets:** Accepted.
🅰🆂🅺 🆂🔟 ❌ 🔌 🎵 🎟 🍽 💻 🌊

▼▼▼ La Quinta Inn & Suites RTP 🆂🅷
(919) 484-1422. **$65-$85.** 1910 W Park Dr. I-40, exit 278,
just n, then just e. Int corridors. **Pets:** Accepted.
🅰🆂🅺 🆂🔟 ❌ 🔌 🎵 🎟 🍽 💻 🌊

▼▼▼ Residence Inn 🆂🅷
(919) 361-1266. **$149.** 201 Residence Inn Blvd. I-40, exit
278, just s. Ext/int corridors. **Pets:** Accepted.
🅰🆂🅺 🆂🔟 ❌ 🔌 🎵 🎟 🍽 💻 🌊 ❎

▼▼ Sleep Inn-RTP 🆂🅷
(919) 993-3393. **$89, 7 day notice.** 5208 New Page Rd.
I-40, exit 282, just s. Int corridors. **Pets:** Medium. Service
with restrictions, crate.
🅰🆂🅺 🆂🔟 ❌ 🔌 🎟 💻

AAA ▼▼▼▼ Wellesley Inn & Suites (Durham
          Research Triangle Park) 🆂🅷
(919) 998-0400. **$69-$99.** 4919 S Miami Blvd. I-40, exit 281,
just s. Int corridors. **Pets:** Accepted.
🆂🅰🆅🅴 🆂🔟 ❌ 🔌 🎵 🎟 🍽 💻

▼▼▼▼ Wingate Inn-RTP/RDU Airport 🆂🅷
(919) 941-2854. **$79-$119.** 5223 Page Rd. I-40, exit 282, just
s. Int corridors. **Pets:** Accepted.
🅰🆂🅺 🆂🔟 ❌ 🎟 💻 ❎

▼▼▼▼ Wyndham Garden Hotel-RTP/RDU
          Airport 🆂🅷
(919) 941-6066. **$84-$134.** 4620 S Miami Blvd. I-40, exit
281, just n. Int corridors. **Pets:** $50 one-time fee/room. Des-
ignated rooms, service with restrictions, crate.
🅰🆂🅺 🆂🔟 ❌ 🎵 🎟 🍽 💻 🍽 🌊 ❎

EDEN

▼▼▼ Jameson Inn 🆂🅷
(336) 627-0472. **$66-$71.** 716 Linden Dr. Just w of Moore-
head Memorial Hospital. Ext corridors. **Pets:** Small. Service
with restrictions, crate.
❌ 🔌 🎟 💻 🌊

ELIZABETH CITY

AAA ▼▼▼ Quality Inn 🆂🅷
(252) 338-3951. **$66-$97.** 522 S Hughes Blvd. Jct Halstead
Blvd and US 17 Bypass. Ext corridors. **Pets:** Medium. $25
one-time fee/room. Service with restrictions, supervision.
🆂🅰🆅🅴 🆂🔟 ❌ 🎟 🍽 💻 🍽 🌊

FAYETTEVILLE

AAA ▼▼▼ Comfort Inn I-95 🅼
(910) 323-8333. **$66-$91.** 1957 Cedar Creek Rd. I-95, exit
49, just w. Ext corridors. **Pets:** Medium, other species. Designated rooms, service with restrictions, supervision.
🆂🅰🆅🅴 🆂🔟 ❌ 🎵 🎟 🍽 💻 🌊

▼▼▼ Fayetteville Inn & Suites 🆂🅷
(910) 486-8300. **$65-$120.** 3136 Bordeaux Park Dr. Jct I-95
business route/US 301, 1.7 mi w on Owen Dr, then just s.
Int corridors. **Pets:** Very small, other species. Designated
rooms, service with restrictions, crate.
🅰🆂🅺 🆂🔟 ❌ 🔌 🎟 🍽 💻 🌊

▼▼▼▼ Holiday Inn Bordeaux 🆂🅷
(910) 323-0111. **$95-$109.** 1707 Owen Dr. Jct I-95 business
route/US 301 S, 2.3 mi w. Ext/int corridors. **Pets:** Accepted.
🅰🆂🅺 🆂🔟 ❌ 🎵 🎟 🍽 💻 🍽 🌊

AAA ▼▼▼▼ Holiday Inn I-95 🆂🅷 ❀
(910) 323-1600. **$81.** 1944 Cedar Creek Rd. I-95, exit 49,
just w. Ext/int corridors. **Pets:** Medium, other species. $20
one-time fee/room. Designated rooms, service with restrictions.
🆂🅰🆅🅴 🆂🔟 ❌ 🎵 🎟 🍽 💻 🍽 🌊

▼▼ Motel 6 🅼
(910) 485-8122. **$40-$56.** 2076 Cedar Creek Rd. I-95, exit
49, just e. Ext corridors. **Pets:** Medium, other species. Service with restrictions, supervision.
❌ 🎵 🌊

AAA ▼▼▼ Red Roof Inn 🆂🅷
(910) 321-1460. **$60-$70.** 1569 Jim Johnson Rd. I-95, exit
49, just w on SR 53, then just n. Int corridors.
Pets: Accepted.
🆂🅰🆅🅴 ❌ 🔌 🎵 🎟 🌊

FLETCHER

▼▼▼▼ Holiday Inn Asheville-Airport 🆂🅷
(828) 684-1213. **$100-$120.** 550 Airport Rd. I-26, exit 9, just
e. Int corridors. **Pets:** Medium. $50 one-time fee/room.
Service with restrictions, supervision.
🅰🆂🅺 ❌ 🎵 🎵 🎟 💻 🍽 🌊

FOREST CITY

▼▼ Jameson Inn SH
(828) 287-8788. **$68-$73.** 164 Jameson Inn Dr. US 74 Bypass, exit 181, 1.8 mi nw on US 74A. Ext corridors. **Pets:** Small. Service with restrictions, crate.
⊠ ⓜ 🐾 🐾 🛏 💻 🗘

FRANKLIN

▼ Colonial Inn M
(828) 524-6600. **$40-$85.** 3157 Georgia Rd. US 441 Bypass, 2.4 mi s on US 441 and 23. Ext corridors. **Pets:** Accepted.
ASK Sð ⊠ 🐾 🛏 🗘

▼ Days Inn-Franklin M
(828) 524-6491. **$59-$104.** 1320 E Main St. Jct US 23 and 441 Bypass, just nw on US 441 business route. Ext corridors. **Pets:** Medium. $15 one-time fee/pet. No service, supervision.
ASK Sð ⊠ 🛏 🗘

▲▲▲ ▼ Franklin Motel M
(828) 524-4431. **$40-$70, 3 day notice.** 17 W Palmer St. Jct US 441 Bypass, 1 mi n on US 441 business route; downtown. Ext corridors. **Pets:** Medium. $20 one-time fee/room. No service, supervision.
SAVE Sð ⊠ 🐾 🛏 🗘

▼▼ Microtel M
(828) 349-9000. **$39-$99.** 81 Allman Dr. Jct US 441 Bypass, 0.4 mi s on US 441 and 23. Int corridors. **Pets:** Other species. $20 one-time fee/room.
ASK Sð ⊠ 🐾 🛏 🗘

▼ Mountainside Vacation Lodging M
(828) 524-6209. **$60-$75, 7 day notice.** 8356 Sylva Rd. 4.8 mi n on US 441 and 23. Ext corridors. **Pets:** Medium, dogs only. $5 daily fee/pet. Service with restrictions, crate.
⊠ 🛏 💻 🗇

GARNER

▼▼ Holiday Inn Express SH
(919) 662-4890. **$90.** 1595 Mechanical Blvd. I-40, exit 298A, 2.3 mi e on US 70, then just n. Int corridors. **Pets:** Small. $15 daily fee/pet. Designated rooms, service with restrictions, supervision.
ASK Sð ⊠ 🐾 🛏

GOLDSBORO

▼▼▼ Best Western Goldsboro Inn M
(919) 735-7911. **$55-$65.** 801 US 70 E Bypass. 2 mi e on US 70 E Bypass, exit Williams St, follow service road. Ext corridors. **Pets:** Large, dogs only. $10 daily fee/pet. Service with restrictions, supervision.
ASK Sð ⊠ 🐾 🛏 💻 🍴 🗘

▼▼ Jameson Inn SH
(919) 778-9759. **$72-$77.** 1408 S Harding Dr. US 70 E Bypass, exit Spence Ave, just n on Best Rd, then just e. Int corridors. **Pets:** Small. Service with restrictions, crate.
⊠ ⓜ 🐾 🛏 💻 🗘

GREENSBORO

▲▲▲ ▼▼▼ AmeriSuites
(Greensboro/Wendover) SH
(336) 852-1443. **$69-$125.** 1619 Stanley Rd. I-40, exit 214 westbound; exit 214B eastbound, just s, then just e. Int corridors. **Pets:** Large. $20 deposit/room. Designated rooms, service with restrictions.
SAVE Sð ⊠ 🐾 🐾 🛏 💻 🗘

▼▼ Biltmore Greensboro Hotel SH
(336) 272-3474. **$95-$195.** 111 W Washington St. Just s of town center on Elm St, then just w; downtown. Int corridors. **Pets:** Accepted.
ASK Sð ⊠ 🛏 💻

▼▼▼ Drury Inn & Suites-Greensboro SH
(336) 856-9696. **$87-$107.** 3220 High Point Rd. I-40, exit 217, just s. Int corridors. **Pets:** Large, other species. Service with restrictions, supervision.
ASK ⊠ 🐾 🐾 🛏 💻 🗘

▼▼▼ La Quinta Inn & Suites SH
(336) 316-0100. **$101-$126.** 1201 Lanada Rd. I-40, exit 214 westbound; exit 214A eastbound, just s, then just e. Int corridors. **Pets:** Accepted.
ASK Sð ⊠ ⓜ 🐾 🐾 🛏 💻 🗘

▲▲▲ ▼▼▼ Red Roof Inn Greensboro-Airport M
(336) 271-2636. **$42-$59.** 615 Regional Rd S. I-40, exit 210, just s on SR 68 via service road. Ext corridors. **Pets:** Accepted.
SAVE ⊠ ⓜ 🐾 🐾 🛏

▼▼▼ Residence Inn by Marriott SH
(336) 294-8600. **$94-$144.** 2000 Veasley St. I-40, exit 217, 0.3 mi s, then 0.4 mi w. Ext corridors. **Pets:** Other species. $150 one-time fee/room.
⊠ 🐾 🛏 💻 🗘 🗙

GREENVILLE

▼▼ Jameson Inn M
(252) 752-7382. **$64-$69.** 920 Crosswinds St. US 264, 2 mi e on Stantonsburg Rd, 0.5 mi s on Memorial Dr. Ext corridors. **Pets:** Small. Service with restrictions, crate.
⊠ ⓜ 🐾 🛏 💻 🗘

▲▲▲ ▼ Travelodge M
(252) 355-5699. **$40-$55.** 3435 S Memorial Dr. Jct US 264 Alternate Rt and SR 11, 0.3 mi s. Ext corridors. **Pets:** Small, dogs only. $6 daily fee/pet. Designated rooms, service with restrictions, supervision.
SAVE Sð ⊠ 🛏 💻

HAYESVILLE

▼▼ Chatuge Mountain Inn M
(828) 389-9340. **$50-$80.** 4238 Hwy 64 E. Jct SR 69, 4.2 mi e on US 64. Ext corridors. **Pets:** Accepted.
ASK Sð ⊠ 🛏 💻

▼▼ Deerfield Inn M 🌸
(828) 389-8272. **$45-$70.** 40 Chatuge Ln. 3 mi e on US 64. Ext corridors. **Pets:** Other species. $10 daily fee/pet. Designated rooms.
ASK Sð ⊠ 🛏

HENDERSON

▼▼ Jameson Inn 🆂🅷
(252) 430-0247. **$73-$78.** 400 N Cooper Dr. I-85, exit 213, just w, then just n. Int corridors. **Pets:** Small. Service with restrictions, crate.
✖ 🅼 🕗 🖭 🛏 🖵 🏊

▼▼ Lamplight Inn 🅱🅱 🌼
(252) 438-6311. **$75-$120, 5 day notice.** 1680 Flemingtown Rd. I-85, exit 220, 1.5 mi nw. Int corridors. **Pets:** Small. $10 deposit/pet. Service with restrictions, supervision.
🅰🆂🅺 🆂 ✖ 🗙 🖃

HENDERSONVILLE

◈ ▼▼ Best Western Hendersonville Inn Ⓜ 🌼
(828) 692-0521. **$39-$109.** 105 Sugarloaf Rd. I-26, exit 18A, just e. Ext corridors. **Pets:** Other species. $10 one-time fee/room. Service with restrictions, supervision.
🆂🅰🆅🅴 🆂 ✖ 🛏 🖵 🍽 🏊

◈ ▼▼ Comfort Inn Ⓜ
(828) 693-8800. **$45-$139.** 206 Mitchell Dr. I-26, exit 18B, just w. Ext corridors. **Pets:** Medium, other species. $10 daily fee/pet. Service with restrictions.
🆂🅰🆅🅴 🆂 ✖ 🕗 🛏 🖵 🏊

HICKORY

▼▼ Jameson Inn Ⓜ
(828) 304-0410. **$68-$73.** 1120 13th Ave Dr SE. I-40, exit 125, just s, then 0.4 mi w. Ext corridors. **Pets:** Small. Service with restrictions, crate.
✖ 🅼 🕗 🛏 🖵 🏊

◈ ▼▼ Park Inn Gateway Conference Center 🆂🅷
(828) 328-5101. **$89-$99.** 909 US 70 SW. I-40, exit 123, just n on US 321, then just e at jct US 70 E. Ext/int corridors. **Pets:** Very small, dogs only. $250 deposit/room. Designated rooms, service with restrictions, crate.
🆂🅰🆅🅴 🆂 ✖ 🕗 🕗 🛏 🖵 🏊

◈ ▼ Red Roof Inn Hickory Ⓜ
(828) 323-1500. **$46-$66.** 1184 Lenoir Rhyne Blvd. I-40, exit 125, just n. Ext corridors. **Pets:** Accepted.
🆂🅰🆅🅴 ✖ 🕗 🕗 🛏

HIGHLANDS

▼▼▼ Kelsey & Hutchinson Lodge 🆂🅷 🌼
(828) 526-4746. **$111-$278, 7 day notice.** 450 Spring St. Just s of US 64 (Main St), just e of 4th St. Ext corridors. **Pets:** $20 daily fee/pet. Designated rooms, service with restrictions.
✖ 🛏 🖵 🗙

◈ ▼▼ Mountain High Lodge Ⓜ
(828) 526-2790. **$59-$200, 7 day notice.** 200 Main St. Downtown. Ext corridors. **Pets:** Accepted.
🆂🅰🆅🅴 🆂 ✖ 🛏 🖵

HILLSBOROUGH

◈ ▼▼ Microtel Inn & Suites 🆂🅷
(919) 245-3102. **$49-$79.** 120 Old Dogwood St. I-85, exit 164, just w, then n. Int corridors. **Pets:** Accepted.
🆂🅰🆅🅴 ✖ 🛏 🖵

JACKSONVILLE

▼▼ Super 8 Motel 🆂🅷
(910) 455-6888. **$55-$65.** 2149 N Marine Blvd. 2.8 mi n on US 17. Int corridors. **Pets:** Dogs only. $10 one-time fee/room. Designated rooms, service with restrictions, supervision.
🅰🆂🅺 🆂 ✖ 🛏 🖵 🏊

JONESVILLE

◈ ▼▼▼ Comfort Inn 🆂🅷
(336) 835-9400. **$64-$96.** 1633 Winston Rd. I-77, exit 82, just w. Ext corridors. **Pets:** Other species. $10 daily fee/pet. Designated rooms, service with restrictions, supervision.
🆂🅰🆅🅴 🆂 ✖ 🅼 🕗 🛏 🖵 🏊 🗙

◈ ▼▼▼ Holiday Inn Express 🆂🅷
(336) 835-6000. **$59-$119.** 1713 NC 67 Hwy. I-77, exit 82, just e. Int corridors. **Pets:** Small. $10 daily fee/pet. Service with restrictions, supervision.
🆂🅰🆅🅴 🆂 ✖ 🅼 🕗 🕗 🛏 🖵 🏊

LAURINBURG

▼▼▼ Hampton Inn 🆂🅷
(910) 277-1516. **$64-$67.** 115 Hampton Cir. Just s on US 15/401 Bypass from jct US 74/501, then just e. Int corridors. **Pets:** Accepted.
🆂 ✖ 🕗 🕗 🛏 🖵 🏊

▼▼ Jameson Inn Ⓜ
(910) 277-0080. **$66-$71.** 14 Jameson Inn Ct. Just n on US 15 and 401 Bypass from US 74 and 501 Bypass. Ext corridors. **Pets:** Small. Service with restrictions, crate.
✖ 🛏 🖵 🏊

LENOIR

▼▼ Jameson Inn Ⓜ
(828) 758-1200. **$66-$71.** 350 Wilkesboro Blvd. Jct US 321, 0.4 mi ne on SR 18. Ext corridors. **Pets:** Small. Service with restrictions, crate.
✖ 🅼 🛏 🖵 🏊

LEXINGTON

▼▼ Quality Inn 🆂🅷
(336) 249-0111. **$60-$65, 7 day notice.** 418 Piedmont Dr. I-85, exit 96, 3.5 mi w on US 64. Ext corridors. **Pets:** Accepted.
🅰🆂🅺 🆂 ✖ 🛏 🖵 🏊

LINCOLNTON

▼▼ Days Inn Ⓜ
(704) 735-8271. **$54.** 614 Clark Dr. US 321, exit 24, 1 mi w on SR 150. Ext corridors. **Pets:** Other species. $10 daily fee/room. No service, supervision.
✖ 🛏 🖵 🏊

LITTLE SWITZERLAND

◈ ▼▼▼ Switzerland Inn 🅲🅸
(828) 765-2153. **$180, 7 day notice.** Jct SR 226A and Blue Ridge Pkwy, MM 334. Ext/int corridors. **Pets:** Accepted.
🆂🅰🆅🅴 🆂 ✖ 🛏 🖵 🍽 🏊 🗙

LUMBERTON

AAA ♦♦♦ Best Western Inn M
(910) 618-9799. **$59-$99.** 201 Jackson Ct. I-95, exit 22, just e, then just s. Ext corridors. **Pets:** Small. $10 daily fee/pet. Service with restrictions, supervision.
⬛ ⬛ ⬛ ⬛ ⬛ ⬛ ⬛

AAA ♦♦♦ Quality Inn and Suites SH
(910) 738-8261. **$50-$75.** 3608 Kahn Dr. I-95, exit 20, just e, enter at K-Mart entrance, then just w. Ext/int corridors. **Pets:** Accepted.
⬛ ⬛ ⬛ ⬛ ⬛ ⬛ ⬛

MAGGIE VALLEY

♦ Applecover Inn Motel M
(828) 926-9100. **$40-$109, 3 day notice.** 4077 Soco Rd. US 19, 4.5 mi w of US 276. Ext corridors. **Pets:** Accepted.
⬛ ⬛

♦♦ Quality Inn M
(828) 926-0201. **$39-$129.** 70 Soco Rd. US 19, just w of US 276. Int corridors. **Pets:** Accepted.
⬛ ⬛ ⬛ ⬛ ⬛ ⬛

MOCKSVILLE

♦♦♦♦ Days Inn & Suites SH ❧
(336) 751-5966. **$55-$85.** 629 Madison Rd. I-40, exit 170, just s on US 601. Int corridors. **Pets:** $10 daily fee/pet. Designated rooms, service with restrictions, crate.
⬛ ⬛ ⬛ ⬛ ⬛ ⬛ ⬛ ⬛ ⬛

MOREHEAD CITY

♦♦♦♦ Holiday Inn Express Hotel & Suites SH
(252) 247-5001. **$75-$125.** 5063 Executive Dr. Jct US 70 and SR 58. Int corridors. **Pets:** Accepted.
⬛ ⬛ ⬛ ⬛ ⬛ ⬛ ⬛ ⬛

MORGANTON

♦♦♦♦ Comfort Inn & Suites SH
(828) 430-4000. **$55-$145.** 1273 Burkemont Ave. I-40, exit 103, just s. Int corridors. **Pets:** Very small. $25 daily fee/room. Service with restrictions, supervision.
⬛ ⬛ ⬛ ⬛ ⬛ ⬛ ⬛ ⬛ ⬛

MORRISVILLE

AAA ♦♦♦♦ AmeriSuites (Raleigh/RDU Airport-RTP) SH
(919) 405-2400. **$79-$129.** 200 Airgate Dr. I-40, exit 284 and 284B, just n, just w on Pleasant Grove Church Rd, then just s. Int corridors. **Pets:** Small, dogs only. Designated rooms, service with restrictions, crate.
⬛ ⬛ ⬛ ⬛ ⬛ ⬛ ⬛ ⬛

AAA ♦♦♦♦ Baymont Inn & Suites Raleigh-Airport SH
(919) 481-3600. **$79-$109.** 1001 Aerial Center Pkwy. I-40, exit 284 and 284A, 0.3 mi s. Int corridors. **Pets:** Accepted.
⬛ ⬛ ⬛ ⬛ ⬛ ⬛ ⬛ ⬛

♦♦♦♦ La Quinta Inn & Suites-Airport SH
(919) 461-1771. **$69-$109.** 1001 Hospitality Ct. I-40, exit 284 and 284A, just s. Int corridors. **Pets:** Small, other species. Service with restrictions, supervision.
⬛ ⬛ ⬛ ⬛ ⬛ ⬛ ⬛ ⬛ ⬛

♦♦♦♦ Staybridge Suites Raleigh Durham Airport SH
(919) 468-0180. **$80-$150, 3 day notice.** 1012 Airport Blvd. I-40, exit 284 and 284A, just s; enter between Hampton Inn and Holiday Inn Express. Int corridors. **Pets:** $125 one-time fee/room. Designated rooms, service with restrictions.
⬛ ⬛ ⬛ ⬛ ⬛ ⬛ ⬛ ⬛ ⬛ ⬛

MURPHY

AAA ♦♦♦♦ Best Western of Murphy M
(828) 837-3060. **$59-$109.** 1522 Andrews Rd. US 74, 19 and SR 129, exit Andrews Rd. Ext corridors. **Pets:** Very small. $10 daily fee/pet. Service with restrictions, supervision.
⬛ ⬛ ⬛ ⬛ ⬛ ⬛

AAA ♦♦♦♦ Comfort Inn M
(828) 837-8030. **$59-$119.** 754 Hwy 64 W. US 64 W, 19 S, 74 W and 129 S. Ext corridors. **Pets:** Accepted.
⬛ ⬛ ⬛ ⬛ ⬛

OUTER BANKS AREA

KILL DEVIL HILLS

AAA ♦♦♦ Ramada Inn Outer Banks Resort & Conference Center SH
(252) 441-2151. **$73-$245.** 1701 S Virginia Dare Tr. SR 12 (Beach Rd), at MM 9.5. Int corridors. **Pets:** Other species. $10 daily fee/pet. Service with restrictions, supervision.
⬛ ⬛ ⬛ ⬛ ⬛ ⬛ ⬛ ⬛

♦♦ Travelodge-Nags Head Beach SH
(252) 441-0411. **$39-$289, 3 day notice.** 804 N Virginia Dare Tr. SR 12 (Beach Rd), at MM 8.1. Ext/int corridors. **Pets:** Medium, other species. $20 daily fee/pet. Designated rooms, service with restrictions, crate.
⬛ ⬛ ⬛ ⬛ ⬛ ⬛

OCRACOKE

AAA ♦♦♦ The Anchorage Inn SH
(252) 928-1101. **$79-$155, 3 day notice.** 205 Irving Garrish Hwy (SR 12). From Cedar Island Ferry on SR 12, just n. Ext corridors. **Pets:** $10 daily fee/room. Designated rooms, service with restrictions, supervision.
⬛ ⬛ ⬛ ⬛ ⬛ ⬛

PINEHURST

Homewood Suites by Hilton SH
(910) 255-0300. **$99-$200.** 250 Central Park Ave. Jct SR 5 and 211; in Olmsted Village. Int corridors. **Pets:** Other species. $50 one-time fee/room. Service with restrictions.

PINE KNOLL SHORES

AmeriSuites (Atlantic Beach) SH
(252) 247-5118. **$81-$179.** 118 Salter Path Rd. SR 58, at MM 5. Int corridors. **Pets:** Medium, dogs only. Designated rooms, service with restrictions, supervision.

RALEIGH

AmeriSuites (Raleigh/Wake Forest Rd) SH
(919) 877-9997. **$69-$99.** 1105 Navaho Dr. I-440, exit 10 (Wake Forest Rd), just n, then just w. Int corridors. **Pets:** Accepted.

Best Western Raleigh North SH
(919) 872-5000. **$62-$89.** 2715 Capital Blvd. I-440, exit 11 and 11B, just n on US 1. Int corridors. **Pets:** $50 one-time fee/pet. Service with restrictions, supervision.

Candlewood Suites-Crabtree SH
(919) 789-4840. **$59.** 4433 Lead Mine Rd. I-440, exit 7 (Glenwood Ave), just w, then just n. Int corridors. **Pets:** Medium, dogs only. $125 one-time fee/room. Designated rooms, service with restrictions, crate.

Holiday Inn-Crabtree LH
(919) 782-8600. **$90-$140.** 4100 Glenwood Ave. I-440, exit 7 (Glenwood Ave), just w on US 70. Int corridors. **Pets:** Medium, other species. $50 one-time fee/room. Service with restrictions, supervision.

Holiday Inn Raleigh-North LH
(919) 872-3500. **$59-$102.** 2805 Highwoods Blvd. I-440, exit 11 southbound; exit 11B northbound, just n on US 1. Int corridors. **Pets:** Accepted.

Homestead Studio Suites Hotel-Raleigh/Crabtree Valley SH ☙
(919) 510-8551. **$49-$59.** 4810 Bluestone Dr. I-440, exit 7 (Glenwood Ave), 1 mi w on US 70, then just s. Ext corridors. **Pets:** Medium, other species. $25 daily fee/room. Service with restrictions, crate.

Homestead Studio Suites Hotel-Raleigh/North SH ☙
(919) 981-7353. **$49-$59.** 3531 Wake Forest Rd. I-440, exit 10 (Wake Forest Rd), 0.5 mi n. Ext corridors. **Pets:** Medium, other species. $25 daily fee/room. Service with restrictions, crate.

Homestead Studio Suites Hotel-Raleigh/Northeast SH ☙
(919) 807-9970. **$79-$94.** 2601 Appliance Ct. I-440, exit 11, just n on US 1, then just e. Int corridors. **Pets:** Medium, other species. $25 daily fee/room. Service with restrictions, crate.

La Quinta Inn & Suites SH
(919) 785-0071. **$65-$85.** 2211 Summit Park Ln. I-440, exit 7B, just n to Blue Ridge Rd, then just e. Int corridors. **Pets:** Service with restrictions, supervision.

Quality Suites Hotel SH
(919) 876-2211. **$59-$115.** 4400 Capital Blvd. I-440, exit 11 and 11B, 2.5 mi n on US 1. Int corridors. **Pets:** Accepted.

Red Roof Inn-North M
(919) 878-9310. **$49-$64.** 3201 Wake Forest Rd. I-440, exit 10 (Wake Forest Rd), just n, then just w. Ext corridors. **Pets:** Accepted.

Red Roof Inn-South SH
(919) 833-6005. **$52-$64.** 1813 S Saunders St. I-40, exit 298B, just n. Int corridors. **Pets:** Medium, other species. Crate.

Residence Inn by Marriott SH ☙
(919) 878-6100. **$79-$129.** 1000 Navaho Dr. I-440, exit 10 (Wake Forest Rd), just n, then w. Ext corridors. **Pets:** Medium. $100 one-time fee/room. Service with restrictions, supervision.

Residence Inn By Marriott Crabtree SH
(919) 279-3000. **Call for rates.** 2200 Summit Park Ln. I-440, exit 7B, just n to Blue Ridge Rd, then just e. Int corridors. **Pets:** Accepted.

REIDSVILLE

Ramada Inn SH
(336) 342-0341. **$65-$120, 3 day notice.** 2100 Barnes St. US 29 business route, exit 149 (Barnes St), just n. Ext corridors. **Pets:** Small. $10 daily fee/pet. Service with restrictions, supervision.

ROANOKE RAPIDS

Jameson Inn M
(252) 533-0022. **$66-$71.** 101 Old Farm Rd. I-95, exit 173, 0.5 mi w on US 158, then just s. Ext corridors. **Pets:** Small. Service with restrictions, crate.

ROBBINSVILLE

Microtel Inn & Suites SH
(828) 479-6772. **$40-$80, 14 day notice.** 111 Rodney Orr Bypass (US 129). Center of downtown. Int corridors. **Pets:** Accepted.

ROCKY MOUNT

AAA ▼▼▼ **Best Western Inn I-95 Gold Rock M**
(252) 985-1450. **$56-$95.** 7095 NC 4. I-95, exit 145, just e.
Ext corridors. **Pets:** Medium, other species. $5 daily fee/pet.
Service with restrictions, supervision.
SAVE ✕ 🔓 🖥 🏊

AAA ▼▼▼ **Comfort Inn** SH
(252) 937-7765. **$73-$78.** 200 Gateway Blvd. I-95, exit 138,
1 mi e on US 64, exit Winstead Ave, then just s. Int corridors. **Pets:** Medium, other species. $25 one-time fee/room.
Service with restrictions, crate.
SAVE 🅂🄳 ✕ 🖉 🔓 🖥 🏊

▼▼▼ **Quality Inn & Suites** SH
(252) 977-0101. **$40-$75.** 7688 NC Hwy 48. I-95, exit 145,
just e. Int corridors. **Pets:** $25 one-time fee/pet. Designated
rooms, service with restrictions, supervision.
ASK 🅂🄳 ✕ 🔓 🖥 🏊

AAA ▼▼▼ **Red Roof Inn** SH
(252) 984-0907. **$44-$57.** 1370 N Weslyan Blvd. Jct US 64
Bypass, 1.5 mi n on US 301. Int corridors. **Pets:** Medium,
other species. Service with restrictions, supervision.
SAVE ✕ 🖉 🔓 🏊

AAA ▼▼▼▼ **Residence Inn by Marriott** SH ❧
(252) 451-5600. **$149-$169.** 230 Gateway Blvd. I-95, exit
138, 1 mi e on US 64, exit Winstead Ave, then just s. Int
corridors. **Pets:** Other species. $100 one-time fee/room.
Service with restrictions.
SAVE 🅂🄳 ✕ 🔓🄼 🖉 🔓 🖥 🏊 ✕

ROWLAND

▼▼▼ **Holiday Inn Express M**
(910) 422-3377. **$59-$99.** 14733 US Hwy 301. I-95, exit 1B,
just w. Ext corridors. **Pets:** $10 one-time fee/pet. Service
with restrictions, supervision.
ASK 🅂🄳 ✕ 🖉 🔓 🖥 🏊

SALISBURY

▼▼▼▼ **Hampton Inn** SH
(704) 637-8000. **$79-$139.** 1001 Klumac Rd. I-85, exit 75,
just w. Int corridors. **Pets:** Other species. Service with
restrictions, supervision.
ASK 🅂🄳 ✕ 🖉 🔓 🖥 🏊

SANFORD

▼▼ **Jameson Inn** SH
(919) 708-7400. **$65-$70.** 2614 S Horner Blvd. 2.5 mi s on
SR 87. Ext corridors. **Pets:** Small. Service with restrictions,
crate.
✕ 🔓🄼 🔓 🖥 🏊

SMITHFIELD

▼▼ **Jameson Inn M**
(919) 989-5901. **$66-$71.** 125 S Equity Dr. I-95, exit 95, just
w, then just n. Ext corridors. **Pets:** Small. Service with
restrictions, crate.
✕ 🔓🄼 🖉 🔓 🖥 🏊

AAA ▼▼▼ **Log Cabin Motel M**
(919) 934-1534. **$40-$42.** 2491 US 70 E (Business Route).
I-95, exit 95, 0.5 mi e. Ext corridors. **Pets:** Accepted.
SAVE ✕ 🔓 🍴 🏊

AAA ▼▼▼ **Super 8 Motel** SH
(919) 989-8988. **$53-$99.** 735 Industrial Park Dr. I-95, exit
95, just w on US 70, then just n. Int corridors. **Pets:** Small,
other species. $4 daily fee/room. Designated rooms, service
with restrictions, supervision.
SAVE 🅂🄳 ✕ 🔓🄼 🖉 🔓 🔓 🖥 🏊

SPRING LAKE

▼▼ **Super 8 Motel M**
(910) 436-8588. **$45-$70, 14 day notice.** 256 S Main St. Jct
SR 24, just s. Int corridors. **Pets:** Accepted.
ASK 🅂🄳 ✕ 🖉 🔓

SPRUCE PINE

AAA ▼▼▼▼ **Richmond Inn** BB
(828) 765-6993. **$65-$125, 7 day notice.** 51 Pine Ave. Exit
off US 19 E and 226 to Oak Ave, just n on Walnut Ave,
follow signs; center. Int corridors. **Pets:** Accepted.
SAVE ✕ 🄺 🎵 🎿

STATESVILLE

AAA ▼▼▼ **Best Western Statesville Inn** SH
(704) 881-0111. **$59-$150.** 1121 Morland Dr. I-77, exit 49A,
just e on US 70 E. Ext/int corridors. **Pets:** Other species.
$15 one-time fee/room. Service with restrictions, supervi-
sion.
SAVE 🅂🄳 ✕ 🔓 🔓 🖥

▼▼ **Holiday Inn Express Hotel & Suites M**
(704) 872-4101. **$69-$79.** 740 Sullivan Rd. I-40, exit 151, just
s. Ext corridors. **Pets:** Small. $25 one-time fee/pet. Service
with restrictions, supervision.
ASK 🅂🄳 ✕ 🔓🄼 🖉 🔓 🖥 🏊

AAA ▼▼▼ **Super 8 Motel M**
(704) 878-9888. **$48-$110.** 1125 Greenland Rd. I-77, exit
49A, just e. Ext/int corridors. **Pets:** Small, dogs only. $5
daily fee/pet. Designated rooms, service with restrictions,
supervision.
SAVE 🅂🄳 ✕ 🖉

WASHINGTON

AAA ▼▼ **Econo Lodge M** ❧
(252) 946-7781. **$45-$65.** 1220 W 15th. US 17, 1 mi n at jct
US 264. Ext corridors. **Pets:** Small. $10 daily fee/pet. Des-
ignated rooms, service with restrictions, crate.
SAVE 🅂🄳 ✕ 🖉 🔓 🖥

WELDON

AAA ▼▼ **Days Inn M**
(252) 536-4867. **$59-$64, 3 day notice.** 1611 Julian Alls-
brook Hwy. I-95, exit 173, just e on US 158. Ext corridors.
Pets: Accepted.
SAVE 🅂🄳 ✕ 🖉 🔓 🏊

WILLIAMSTON

WWW Hampton Inn SH
(252) 809-1100. **$79-$89.** 1099 Hampton Ct. US 64, exit 514, just s on US 17, then just w. Int corridors. **Pets:** Accepted.
ASK S⬤ ✕ ⬤ 🖥 💻 ➰

WWW Holiday Inn SH
(252) 792-3184. **$62-$79.** 101 East Blvd. US 64, exit 514, 1.5 mi n on US 17. Ext/int corridors. **Pets:** Medium. $25 deposit/room. Service with restrictions, supervision.
ASK S⬤ ✕ ⬤ 🖥 💻 ¶¶ ➰

WILMINGTON

AAA WWW Comfort Inn Wilmington SH
(910) 791-4841. **$74-$124.** 151 S College Rd. US 17, just s on SR 132. Int corridors. **Pets:** Other species. $25 one-time fee/pet. Designated rooms, service with restrictions, crate.
SAVE S⬤ ✕ ⬤ 🖥 💻 ➰

WW Days Inn M ✿
(910) 799-6300. **$44-$99.** 5040 Market St. 3.5 mi n on US 17 and 74. Ext corridors. **Pets:** Other species. $15 daily fee/room. Service with restrictions, crate.
ASK S⬤ ✕ ⬤ 🖥 💻 ¶¶ ➰

WWW Hilton Wilmington Riverside LH
(910) 763-5900. **$89-$209.** 301 N Water St. On Cape Fear River waterfront. Int corridors. **Pets:** Accepted.
ASK S⬤ ✕ ⬤ ⬤ 🖥 ¶¶ ➰

WW Jameson Inn SH
(910) 452-5660. **$73-$78.** 5102 Dunlea Ct. 0.5 mi s on US 17 (Market St) from SR 132, then just w on New Centre Dr. Int corridors. **Pets:** Small. Service with restrictions, crate.
✕ ⬤ 🖥 💻 ➰

WWW MainStay Suites SH
(910) 392-1741. **$80-$100.** 5229 Market St. 4 mi n on US 17 and 74. Int corridors. **Pets:** Accepted.
ASK S⬤ ✕ ⬤ ⬤ 🖥 💻

WWW Residence Inn-Landfall Business Center SH
(910) 256-0098. **$84-$199.** 1200 Culbreth Dr. 2.8 mi e on US 74 from jct SR 132, 0.4 mi n on Military Cutoff Rd, then just e. Int corridors. **Pets:** Large, other species. $85 one-time fee/room. Service with restrictions, supervision.
ASK S⬤ ✕ ⬤ ⬤ 🖥 💻 ➰ ✕

WW The Wilmington Inn M
(910) 799-1440. **$39-$129.** 4903 Market St. On US 17 and 74. Ext corridors. **Pets:** Accepted.
ASK S⬤ ✕ ⬤ ➰

WILSON

WWW Holiday Inn Express & Suites SH ✿
(252) 246-1588. **$65-$84.** 2308 Montgomery Dr. US 264, exit 40, 3.2 mi e on SR 42, then just n. Int corridors. **Pets:** Other species. $15 one-time fee/pet. Service with restrictions.
ASK S⬤ ✕ ⬤ 🖥 💻 ➰

WINSTON-SALEM

AAA WWWW Augustus T Zevely Inn BB
(336) 748-9299. **$80-$125.** 803 S Main St. In Old Salem Historical District. Ext/int corridors. **Pets:** Accepted.
SAVE ✕ ⬤

AAA WWWW Best Western Salem Inn & Suites SH
(336) 725-8561. **$75-$109.** 127 S Cherry St. I-40 business route, exit 5C (Cherry St) eastbound; exit 5D westbound, just s. Ext corridors. **Pets:** $25 one-time fee/room. Designated rooms, service with restrictions, crate.
SAVE S⬤ ✕ ⬤ 🖥 💻 ¶¶ ➰

AAA WWWW The Hawthorne Inn & Conference Center SH
(336) 777-3000. **$59-$89.** 420 High St. I-40 business route, exit 5C (Cherry St) eastbound, just e; exit 5C (Cherry St) westbound, just w on 1st St, just s on Marshall St. Int corridors. **Pets:** Medium. $15 daily fee/room. Designated rooms, service with restrictions.
SAVE S⬤ ✕ ⬤M ⬤ ⬤ 🖥 💻 ¶¶ ➰

AAA WWWW Holiday Inn Select SH
(336) 767-9595. **$99-$129.** 5790 University Pkwy. US 52, exit 115B, just s. Int corridors. **Pets:** Accepted.
SAVE S⬤ ✕ ⬤ 🖥 💻 ¶¶ ➰

WWWW La Quinta Inns & Suites SH
(336) 765-8777. **$71-$101.** 2020 Griffith Rd. I-40, exit 189, just s on Stratford Rd, just e on Hanes Mall Blvd. Int corridors. **Pets:** Small, other species. Service with restrictions, supervision.
ASK S⬤ ✕ ⬤M ⬤ ⬤ 🖥 💻 ➰

WWWW Residence Inn by Marriott CO
(336) 759-0777. **$89-$159.** 7835 N Point Blvd. US 52 N, exit 115B, 2 mi s on University Pkwy, just e. Ext corridors. **Pets:** Accepted.
ASK S⬤ ✕ ⬤ 🖥 💻 ➰ ✕

YANCEYVILLE

WWW Days Inn SH
(336) 694-9494. **$55-$125.** 1858 NC Hwy 86 N. Jct US 158 W, just s. Ext corridors. **Pets:** $10 daily fee/pet. Service with restrictions, supervision.
ASK S⬤ ✕ ⬤ 🖥 ➰

BEULAH

AmericInn Motel & Suites SH
(701) 873-2220. **$70-$125.** 2100 2nd Ave NW. Jct SR 49/200, 1.2 mi s. Int corridors. **Pets:** $100 deposit/room. Service with restrictions, supervision.

BISMARCK

Best Western Doublewood Inn SH
(701) 258-7000. **$81-$109.** 1400 E Interchange Ave. I-94, exit 159 (US 83), just s. Int corridors. **Pets:** Large. $10 daily fee/room. Designated rooms, service with restrictions, supervision.

Best Western Ramkota Hotel SH
(701) 258-7700. **$79.** 800 S 3rd St. Just s of jct I-94 business loop and S 3rd St. Int corridors. **Pets:** $10 daily fee/room. Designated rooms, service with restrictions, supervision.

Comfort Inn SH
(701) 223-1911. **$56-$80.** 1030 Interstate Ave. I-94, exit 159 (US 83), 0.3 mi nw. Int corridors. **Pets:** Large. Service with restrictions, supervision.

Days Inn-Bismarck SH
(701) 223-9151. **$55-$75, 14 day notice.** 1300 E Capitol Ave. I-94, exit 159 (US 83), just s. Int corridors. **Pets:** Other species. $10 one-time fee/room. Supervision.

Expressway Inn SH
(701) 222-2900. **$57-$79.** 200 Bismarck Expwy. Jct I-94 business loop (Bismarck Expwy) and S 3rd St. Int corridors. **Pets:** $5 one-time fee/pet. Designated rooms, service with restrictions, supervision.

Kelly Inn SH
(701) 223-8001. **$61-$81.** 1800 N 12 St. I-94, exit 159 (US 83), 0.3 mi s. Int corridors. **Pets:** Designated rooms, service with restrictions, supervision.

Radisson Hotel Bismarck LH
(701) 255-6000. **$99.** 605 E Broadway Ave. Jct 6th St; center. Int corridors. **Pets:** Supervision.

Select Inn SH
(701) 223-8060. **$45-$60.** 1505 Interchange Ave. I-94, exit 159 (US 83), just se. Int corridors. **Pets:** $25 deposit/room, $5 daily fee/room. Service with restrictions, supervision.

BOWMAN

North Winds Lodge M
(701) 523-5641. **$40-$58.** 503 Hwy 85 S. On US 85, just s of US 12. Ext corridors. **Pets:** Accepted.

CARRINGTON

Chieftain Conference Center SH
(701) 652-3131. **$58-$80.** 60 4th Ave S. Jct US 52 and 281, 0.5 mi e on US 52, just s of jct SR 200. Ext/int corridors. **Pets:** Small. $5 daily fee/pet. Designated rooms, service with restrictions, supervision.

Super 8 Motel SH
(701) 652-3982. **$49-$60.** 101 4th Ave S. Jct US 52 and 281, 0.5 mi e on US 52, then just s of jct SR 200. Int corridors. **Pets:** Medium. $5 daily fee/pet. Designated rooms, supervision.

DEVILS LAKE

Comfort Inn SH
(701) 662-6760. **$55-$69.** 215 Hwy 2 E. Jct US 2 and SR 20. Int corridors. **Pets:** $10 deposit/room. Service with restrictions, supervision.

Days Inn Devils Lake SH
(701) 662-5381. **$58-$85, 14 day notice.** 1109 Hwy 20 S. On SR 20, just s of jct US 2. Ext corridors. **Pets:** Accepted.

Trails West Motel M
(701) 662-5011. **$42-$43.** 309 1st St W. 0.8 mi sw on US 2. Int corridors. **Pets:** $5 daily fee/pet. Service with restrictions, supervision.

DICKINSON

AmericInn Motel & Suites of Dickinson SH
(701) 225-1400. **$72-$112.** 229 15th St W. I-94, exit 61, just ne. Int corridors. **Pets:** Other species. Designated rooms, service with restrictions, supervision.

▼▼ Comfort Inn SH
(701) 264-7300. **$66-$160.** 493 Elk Dr. I-94, exit 61, just nw of jct SR 22. Int corridors. **Pets:** Other species. Service with restrictions, supervision.
(ASK) (S🐾) (✕) (🐾M) (🎬) (💺) (🔒) (💻) (🏊)

▲▲▲ ▼▼▼ Hartfiel Inn BB
(701) 225-6710. **$79.** 509 3rd Ave W. I-94, exit 61, 0.8 mi s on SR 22. Int corridors. **Pets:** Accepted.
(SAVE) (✕) (💻)

FARGO

▼▼ Airport/Dome Days Inn & Suites SH
(701) 232-0000. **$65-$95.** 1507 19th Ave N. I-29, exit 67, 1.2 mi e. Int corridors. **Pets:** $15 one-time fee/room. Designated rooms, crate.
(ASK) (S🐾) (✕) (🎬) (💺) (🔒) (💻) (🏊)

▲▲▲ ▼▼▼ Americinn Lodge & Suites SH
(701) 234-9946. **$71-$134.** 1423 35th St SW. I-29, exit 64 (13th Ave S), just se. Int corridors. **Pets:** Other species. $10 one-time fee/room. Designated rooms, service with restrictions, supervision.
(SAVE) (✕) (🎬) (💺) (🔒) (💻) (🏊) (✕)

▲▲▲ ▼▼▼ Best Western Fargo Doublewood Inn SH
(701) 235-3333. **$79-$179.** 3333 13th Ave S. I-29, exit 64 (13th Ave S), 0.3 mi e. Int corridors. **Pets:** Other species.
(SAVE) (S🐾) (✕) (🐾M) (🎬) (💺) (🔒) (💻) (🍴) (🏊) (✕)

▲▲▲ ▼▼▼ Best Western Kelly Inn SH ❀
(701) 282-2143. **$64-$89.** 3800 Main Ave. I-29, exit 65 (Main Ave), just w. Ext/int corridors. **Pets:** Medium. Service with restrictions, supervision.
(SAVE) (S🐾) (✕) (🎬) (💺) (🔒) (💻) (🍴) (🏊) (✕)

▼▼▼ Comfort Inn East SH
(701) 280-9666. **$59-$99.** 1407 35th St S. I-29, exit 64 (13th Ave S), just se. Int corridors. **Pets:** Designated rooms, service with restrictions, crate.
(ASK) (S🐾) (✕) (🎬) (🔒) (💻) (🏊)

▼▼▼ Comfort Inn West SH
(701) 282-9596. **$59-$99.** 3825 9th Ave SW. I-29, exit 64 (13th Ave S), just nw. Int corridors. **Pets:** Accepted.
(ASK) (S🐾) (✕) (🔒) (💻) (🏊)

▼▼▼ Comfort Suites SH
(701) 237-5911. **$64-$99.** 1415 35th St SW. I-29, exit 64 (13th Ave S), just se. Int corridors. **Pets:** Dogs only. Service with restrictions, supervision.
(ASK) (S🐾) (✕) (🐾M) (🎬) (💺) (🔒) (💻) (🏊) (✕)

▼▼ Econo Lodge of Fargo SH
(701) 232-3412. **$49-$74.** 1401 35th St S. I-29, exit 64 (13th Ave S), just se. Int corridors. **Pets:** Accepted.
(ASK) (S🐾) (✕) (🎬) (💺) (🔒) (💻)

▼▼ Expressway Inn SH
(701) 235-3141. **$70.** 1340 21st Ave S. I-94, exit 351, just sw. Ext/int corridors. **Pets:** Medium. $5 daily fee/room. Designated rooms, service with restrictions, crate.
(ASK) (S🐾) (✕) (🐾M) (🎬) (💺) (🔒) (💻) (🍴) (🏊) (✕)

▲▲▲ ▼▼▼ Holiday Inn SH
(701) 282-2700. **$79-$130.** 3803 13th Ave S. I-29, exit 64 (13 Ave S), just nw. Int corridors. **Pets:** Service with restrictions, supervision.
(SAVE) (S🐾) (✕) (🐾M) (🎬) (💺) (🔒) (💻) (🍴) (🏊) (✕)

▼▼▼ Holiday Inn Express Fargo SH
(701) 282-2000. **$89.** 1040 40th St S. I-29, exit 64 (13th Ave S), just nw. Int corridors. **Pets:** Large, other species. $10 one-time fee/room. Service with restrictions, supervision.
(ASK) (S🐾) (✕) (🐾M) (🎬) (💺) (🔒) (💻) (🏊) (✕)

▲▲▲ ▼▼▼ Kelly Inn 13th Avenue SH
(701) 277-8821. **$75-$109.** 4207 13th Ave SW. I-29, exit 64 (13th Ave S), 0.5 mi w. Ext/int corridors. **Pets:** Accepted.
(SAVE) (S🐾) (✕) (🐾M) (🎬) (💺) (🔒) (💻) (🏊)

▼▼▼ MainStay Suites SH
(701) 277-4627. **$79-$89.** 1901 44th St SW. I-94, exit 348, just n, just e. Int corridors. **Pets:** Designated rooms, service with restrictions, supervision.
(ASK) (S🐾) (✕) (🐾M) (🎬) (💺) (🔒) (💻) (🏊) (✕)

▼ Motel 6 #1158 M
(701) 232-9251. **$39-$55.** 1202 36th S. I-29, exit 64 (13th Ave S), just n on east frontage road. Int corridors. **Pets:** Other species. Service with restrictions, supervision.
(S🐾) (✕) (💺) (🔒) (🏊)

▲▲▲ ▼ Motel 75 SH
(701) 232-1321. **$45-$51.** 3402 14th Ave S. I-29, exit 64 (13th Ave S), just se. Int corridors. **Pets:** Large, other species. Designated rooms, service with restrictions, supervision.
(SAVE) (S🐾) (✕) (🔒)

▲▲▲ ▼▼▼ Radisson Hotel Fargo LH
(701) 232-7363. **$74-$119.** 201 5th St N. Corner of 2nd Ave N; downtown. Int corridors. **Pets:** Accepted.
(SAVE) (S🐾) (✕) (🐾M) (🎬) (💻) (🍴) (✕)

▼▼ Sleep Inn SH
(701) 281-8240. **$64-$69.** 1921 44 St SW. I-94, exit 348 (45th St), just n, then just e. Int corridors. **Pets:** Designated rooms, service with restrictions, supervision.
(ASK) (S🐾) (✕) (🐾M) (💺) (🔒) (💻) (🏊) (✕)

FORT TOTTEN

▼▼▼ Totten Trail Historic Inn BB
(701) 766-4874. **$72-$110.** Fort Totten Historic Site. Jct SR 2 and CR 7, 1 mi e. Int corridors. **Pets:** Accepted.
(ASK) (✕) (W)

GRAND FORKS

▲▲▲ ▼ Best Value Inn of Grand Forks M
(701) 775-0555. **$44-$68.** 1000 N 42nd St. I-29, exit 141 (Gateway Dr), jct US 2, then just se. Int corridors. **Pets:** Other species. $25 deposit/pet, $6 daily fee/pet. Designated rooms, service with restrictions, supervision.
(SAVE) (S🐾) (✕)

▼▼ Best Western Town House SH
(701) 746-5411. **$59-$89.** 710 1st Ave N. I-29, exit 140, 3 mi e; downtown. Int corridors. **Pets:** Designated rooms, service with restrictions, supervision.
(ASK) (S🐾) (✕) (🎬) (🔒) (💻) (🍴) (🏊) (✕)

▼▼ Days Inn 🆂🅷
(701) 775-0060. **$54-$84.** 3101 34th St S. I-29, exit 138, 0.5 mi e. Int corridors. **Pets:** Small. Designated rooms, service with restrictions, supervision.
🅰🅎 🆂👁 ⊠ 🕽 🖵

▲▲ ▼▼ Econo Lodge 🆂🅷
(701) 746-6666. **$42-$59.** 900 N 43 St. I-29, exit 141 (Gateway Dr), just se. Ext/int corridors. **Pets:** Other species. $5 daily fee/room. Service with restrictions, supervision.
🆂🅰🆅🅴 🆂👁 ⊠ 🕽 🖵

▼▼ Travelodge 🆂🅷
(701) 772-8151. **$54-$74.** 2100 S Washington St. I-29, exit 140 (Demers Ave), 2.5 mi e, then 1.5 mi s. Int corridors. **Pets:** Small, dogs only. $3 daily fee/room. Designated rooms, service with restrictions, supervision.
🅰🅎 🆂👁 ⊠ 🖰 🕽 🖵 🏊 ⊠

JAMESTOWN

▼▼ Comfort Inn 🆂🅷
(701) 252-7125. **$69-$99.** 811 20 St SW. I-94, exit 258 (US 281), just n, then just w. Int corridors. **Pets:** Accepted.
🅰🅎 🆂👁 ⊠ 🕽 🖵 🏊

▲▲ ▼ Ranch House Motel 🅼
(701) 252-0222. **$35-$46.** 408 Business Loop W. I-94, exit 258 (US 281), 0.8 mi n. Ext/int corridors. **Pets:** $3 daily fee/pet. Designated rooms, service with restrictions, supervision.
🆂🅰🆅🅴 ⊠ 🕽 🏊

KENMARE

▼▼ Quilt Inn 🆂🅷
(701) 385-4100. **$50.** 1232 N Central Ave. Just n on US 52. Int corridors. **Pets:** Accepted.
🅰🅎 🆂👁 ⊠ 🕽 🏊

MANDAN

▲▲ ▼▼▼ Best Western Seven Seas Inn & Conference Center 🆂🅷
(701) 663-7401. **$79-$150.** 2611 Old Red Tr. I-94, exit 152, just nw. Int corridors. **Pets:** Other species.
🆂🅰🆅🅴 🆂👁 ⊠ 🖰🅼 🖰 🖰 🕽 🖵 🍽 🏊 ⊠

MEDORA

▲▲ ▼▼▼ Americinn Motel & Suites 🆂🅷
(701) 623-4800. **$61-$199.** 75 E River Rd. I-94, exit 24, just se of downtown. Int corridors. **Pets:** Accepted.
🆂🅰🆅🅴 🆂👁 ⊠ 🖰🅼 🖰 🕽 🖵 🏊 ⊠

MINOT

▲▲ ▼▼▼ Best Western Kelly Inn 🆂🅷
(701) 852-4300. **$64-$149.** 1510 26th Ave SW. US 2 and 52 Bypass at 16th St SW. Ext/int corridors. **Pets:** Other species. Designated rooms, service with restrictions, crate.
🆂🅰🆅🅴 🆂👁 ⊠ 🕽 🖵 🏊 ⊠

▲▲ ▼▼▼ Comfort Inn 🆂🅷
(701) 852-2201. **$60-$150.** 1515 22nd Ave SW. US 2 and 52 Bypass at 16th St SW. Int corridors. **Pets:** Other species. Service with restrictions, crate.
🆂🅰🆅🅴 🆂👁 ⊠ 🖰 🕽 🖵 🏊 ⊠

▲▲ ▼▼▼ Dakota Inn 🆂🅷
(701) 838-2700. **$49.** 2401 US 2 & 52 Bypass. Jct US 83, 1 mi w. Int corridors. **Pets:** Accepted.
🆂🅰🆅🅴 🆂👁 ⊠ 🖰 🖰 🏊 ⊠

▼▼▼ Holiday Inn Riverside Minot 🅻🅷
(701) 852-2504. **$67-$84.** 2200 Burdick Expwy E. 1.3 mi e on US 2 business route (Burdick Expwy E). Int corridors. **Pets:** Very small, dogs only. Designated rooms, service with restrictions, supervision.
🅰🅎 🆂👁 ⊠ 🖰 🖰 🕽 🖵 🍽 🏊 ⊠

▲▲ ▼▼▼ International Inn 🆂🅷
(701) 852-3161. **$65-$95, 3 day notice.** 1505 N Broadway. 1.5 mi n on US 83. Int corridors. **Pets:** Large. Designated rooms, supervision.
🆂🅰🆅🅴 🆂👁 ⊠ 🖰 🖰 🕽 🖵 🍽 🏊 ⊠

NEW TOWN

▼▼ 4 Bears Lodge 🆂🅷
(701) 627-4018. **$55-$70.** 202 Frontage Rd. 4 mi w. Int corridors. **Pets:** Accepted.
🆂👁 ⊠ 🕽 🖵 🍽 🏊 ⊠

VALLEY CITY

▲▲ ▼▼▼▼ Americinn Lodge & Suites 🆂🅷 ✤
(701) 845-5551. **$66-$136.** 280 Winter Show Rd SE. I-94, exit 292, just ne. Int corridors. **Pets:** $10 daily fee/room. Designated rooms, service with restrictions, supervision.
🆂🅰🆅🅴 ⊠ 🖰🅼 🖰 🖰 🕽 🖵 🏊 ⊠

▼▼ Super 8 Motel-Valley City 🅼
(701) 845-1140. **$50-$63.** 822 11th St. I-94, exit 292, just nw. Int corridors. **Pets:** $5 daily fee/pet. Designated rooms, service with restrictions.
🅰🅎 🆂👁 ⊠

▲▲ ▼▼▼ Wagon Wheel Inn & Suites 🆂🅷
(701) 845-5333. **$50-$62.** 455 Winter Show Rd. I-94, exit 292, just ne. Ext/int corridors. **Pets:** Medium. Designated rooms, service with restrictions, supervision.
🆂🅰🆅🅴 ⊠ 🖰 🕽 🖵 🏊

WAHPETON

▼▼▼▼ Americinn Lodge & Suites 🆂🅷
(701) 642-8365. **$79-$99.** 2029 Two-Ten Dr. 1 mi n on SR 210 Bypass. Int corridors. **Pets:** Medium. Designated rooms, service with restrictions, supervision.
🅰🅎 🆂👁 ⊠ 🖰 🖰 🕽 🖵 🏊 ⊠

▼▼ Comfort Inn 🆂🅷
(701) 642-1115. **$54-$79.** 209 13th St S. SR 13, 0.3 mi e of jct SR 210 Bypass. Int corridors. **Pets:** Accepted.
🅰🅎 🆂👁 ⊠ 🕽 🖵 🏊

▼▼▼▼ Hospitality Inn & Suites 🆂🅷
(701) 642-5000. **$69-$89.** 1800 Two-Ten Dr. 1 mi n on SR 210 Bypass. Int corridors. **Pets:** Medium. Designated rooms, service with restrictions, supervision.
🅰🅎 🆂👁 ⊠ 🖰🅼 🖰 🕽 🖵 🏊 ⊠

▼▼ Wahpeton Super 8 SH ❀
(701) 642-8731. **$44-$75, 3 day notice.** 995 21st Ave N. 1.5
mi n on SR 210 Bypass. Int corridors. **Pets:** Other species.
$5 daily fee/room. Service with restrictions, supervision.
ASK ✕ ❖ ❚¶ ➣

WATFORD CITY

◆◆◆ ▼ McKenzie Inn M
(701) 444-3980. **$47.** 132 SW 3rd St. US 85, just w of SR
23. Ext corridors. **Pets:** Medium. Designated rooms, service
with restrictions, supervision.
SAVE S❖ ✕ ❖

WEST FARGO

▼▼ West Fargo Days Inn SH
(701) 281-0000. **$55-$67.** 525 E Main Ave. I-29, exit 65, 2.3
mi w. Int corridors. **Pets:** Medium. $15 one-time fee/room.
Designated rooms, service with restrictions, crate.
ASK S❖ ✕ ❀ ❖ ❚ ➣

WILLISTON

◆◆◆ ▼▼ El Rancho Motor Hotel SH
(701) 572-6321. **$47-$54.** 1623 2nd Ave W. US 2 and 85 N
Bypass, 1 mi n. Ext/int corridors. **Pets:** Other species. Designated rooms, service with restrictions, supervision.
SAVE S❖ ✕ ❖ ❚ ❚¶

◆◆◆ ▼▼ Super 8 Motel SH
(701) 572-8371. **$48-$58, 10 day notice.** 2324 2nd Ave W.
1.3 mi n on US 2 and 85 Bypass. Int corridors. **Pets:** $5
daily fee/pet. Service with restrictions, supervision.
SAVE S❖ ✕ ❀ ➣

OHIO

AKRON

Days Inn Akron South/Airport M
(330) 644-1204. **$50-$70.** 3237 S Arlington Rd. I-77, exit 120, just s. Ext corridors. **Pets:** Accepted.
ASK S0 X 🔒 ➰

Holiday Inn Express Akron South Convention Center SH
(330) 644-7126. **$79-$119.** 2940 Chenoweth Rd. I-77, exit 120, just n. Int corridors. **Pets:** Accepted.
SAVE S0 X 📶 🔒 💻 ➰

Red Roof Inn-Akron South M
(330) 644-7748. **$43-$65.** 2939 S Arlington Rd. I-77, exit 120, just n. **Pets:** Accepted.
SAVE X

ALLIANCE

Holiday Inn Express Hotel & Suites SH
(330) 821-6700. **$71-$90.** 2341 W State St. 2 mi w on US 62. Int corridors. **Pets:** Accepted.
ASK S0 X 📶 🔒 💻 ➰

Super 8 Motel M
(330) 821-5688. **$50-$67.** 2330 W State St. 2 mi w on US 62. Ext corridors. **Pets:** Other species. $5 daily fee/pet. Service with restrictions.
SAVE S0 X 📶 🔒 ➰

AMHERST

Country Hearth Inn M
(440) 985-1428. **$50-$80.** 934 N Leavitt Rd. SR 58, 0.3 mi n of SR 2. Ext/int corridors. **Pets:** $10 daily fee/pet. Service with restrictions, supervision.
ASK S0 X 🔒 💻 ➰

ASHLAND

Days Inn M
(419) 289-0101. **$45-$76.** 1423 CR 1575. I-71, exit 186, just w. Ext corridors. **Pets:** Other species. Service with restrictions, crate.
SAVE S0 X 🔒 💻 ➰

The Surrey Inn SH
(419) 289-7700. **$59-$199, 4 day notice.** 1065 Claremont Ave. 1 mi s. Int corridors. **Pets:** Medium. $30 deposit/room. Designated rooms, service with restrictions, supervision.
ASK X 🔒 💻

ASHTABULA

Cedars Motel M
(440) 992-5406. **$70-$80.** 2015 W Prospect Rd. Jct SR 11, 3 mi w on US 20. Ext corridors. **Pets:** Other species. $5 daily fee/pet. Service with restrictions, supervision.
SAVE X 🔒

Ho Hum Motel M 🐾
(440) 969-1136. **$55-$80.** 3801 N Ridge Rd W. I-90, exit 223, 3 mi n on SR 45, 1 mi e on SR 20. Ext corridors. **Pets:** Other species. $5 daily fee/pet. Service with restrictions, supervision.
SAVE X 🔒

ATHENS

Budget Host-Coach Inn M
(740) 594-2294. **$41-$85, 3 day notice.** 100 Albany Rd (Hwy 50 W). US 50 W, just past Richland Ave exit; US 50 E, e on Township Rd 60. Ext corridors. **Pets:** Small, dogs only. $10 daily fee/pet. Designated rooms, service with restrictions, supervision.
SAVE X 🔒

AAA ▼▼▼ **Super 8 Motel** SH
(740) 594-4900. **$50-$130, 21 day notice.** 2091 E State St.
US 33, exit State St, 2.7 mi e. Int corridors. **Pets:** $5 daily
fee/pet. Designated rooms, service with restrictions, crate.
SAVE S X

AUSTINBURG

AAA ▼▼▼▼ **Comfort Inn-Ashtabula** SH ❀
(440) 275-2711. **$65-$82.** 1860 Austinburg Rd. I-90, exit 223,
just n. Int corridors. **Pets:** Other species. $10 one-time fee/
room. Designated rooms, service with restrictions, crate.
SAVE S X

AUSTINTOWN

AAA ▼▼▼ **Austintown Super 8 Motel** M
(330) 793-7788. **$48-$79.** 5280 76 Dr. I-80, exit 223, just s
on SR 46. Int corridors. **Pets:** Accepted.
SAVE X

AAA ▼▼▼ **Best Western Meander Inn** SH
(330) 544-2378. **$79-$150.** 870 N Canfield-Niles Rd. I-80,
exit 223, 0.3 mi s on SR 46. Int corridors. **Pets:** Other
species. $10 daily fee/pet. Service with restrictions, supervision.
SAVE S X

▼▼▼ **Days Inn Youngstown West** SH
(330) 793-9851. **Call for rates.** 1051 N Canfield-Niles Rd.
I-80, exit 229, just n. Int corridors. **Pets:** Accepted.
X

AAA ▼▼▼ **Econo Lodge** M
(330) 270-2865. **$50-$65.** I-80, exit 223, just s on SR 46. Ext
corridors. **Pets:** Accepted.
SAVE S X

AAA ▼▼▼ **Motel 6–4066** M
(330) 793-9305. **$65-$69.** 5431 76 Dr. I-80, exit 223, just s
on SR 46. Ext corridors. **Pets:** Accepted.
SAVE S X

BEAVERCREEK

▼▼▼▼ **Residence Inn by Marriott
Beavercreek** SH
(937) 427-3914. **$109-$169.** 2779 Fairfield Commons. I-675,
exit 17. Int corridors. **Pets:** Large, other species. $100 one-
time fee/room. Service with restrictions, crate.
ASK S X

BELLEFONTAINE

▼▼▼▼ **Woodland Hotel** SH
(937) 593-8515. **$59-$99.** 1134 N Main St. Jct US 33 and
SR 68. Ext/int corridors. **Pets:** Accepted.
ASK S X

BLUFFTON

AAA ▼▼▼▼ **Comfort Inn** SH
(419) 358-6000. **$65-$100.** 117 Commerce Ln. I-75, exit 142,
just w on SR 103. Int corridors. **Pets:** Medium, other species. $15 one-time fee/pet. Service with restrictions.
SAVE X

BOARDMAN

AAA ▼▼ **Days Inn** M
(330) 758-2371. **$36-$85, 3 day notice.** 8392 Market St.
I-76, exit 232, 1.8 mi n on SR 7. Ext corridors. **Pets:** $5
daily fee/pet. Service with restrictions, supervision.
SAVE S X

▼▼▼ **Microtel Inn Youngstown** SH
(330) 758-1816. **$44-$55.** 7393 South Ave. Jct I-68 and US
224, 0.3 mi w. Int corridors. **Pets:** Other species. $25 one-
time fee/pet. Service with restrictions, supervision.
ASK S X

AAA ▼▼▼ **Ramada Limited** SH
(330) 549-0157. **$59-$79.** 9988 Market St. 0.5 mi n on SR 7.
Int corridors. **Pets:** $10 daily fee/pet. No service, supervi-
sion.
SAVE X

BOWLING GREEN

AAA ▼▼ **Days Inn** M ❀
(419) 352-5211. **$59-$69.** 1550 E Wooster St. I-75, exit 181,
just w. Ext corridors. **Pets:** Other species. $5 daily fee/
room. Service with restrictions.
SAVE S X

AAA ▼▼▼ **Quality Inn & Suites** SH
(419) 352-2521. **$59-$109.** 1630 E Wooster St. I-75, exit
181, just w. Int corridors. **Pets:** Medium, other species. $10
daily fee/room. Service with restrictions, supervision.
SAVE S X

BROOKVILLE

AAA ▼▼▼ **Brookville Days Inn** M
(937) 833-4003. **$60.** 100 Parkview Dr. I-70, exit 21. Ext
corridors. **Pets:** Other species. $10 daily fee/pet. Desig-
nated rooms, no service.
SAVE S X

BRUNSWICK

▼▼▼ **Sleep Inn** SH
(330) 273-1112. **$42-$58.** 1435 S Carpenter Rd. I-71, exit
226, just w. Ext corridors. **Pets:** Accepted.
ASK S X

CAMBRIDGE

▼▼ **Best Western Cambridge** SH
(740) 439-3581. **$35-$65.** 1945 Southgate Pkwy. I-70, exit
178, 0.3 mi n on SR 209. Ext corridors. **Pets:** Accepted.
ASK S X

▼▼ **Budget Host Deer Creek Motel** M
(740) 432-6391. **$36-$62.** 2321 Southgate Pkwy. I-70, exit
178, just n on SR 209. Ext corridors. **Pets:** Accepted.
ASK S X

AAA ▼▼ **Budget Inn** M
(740) 432-2304. **$30-$50.** 6405 Glenn Hwy. I-70, exit 176, e
on US 40. Ext/int corridors. **Pets:** Small. $7 daily fee/pet.
Designated rooms, service with restrictions, supervision.
SAVE S X

(AAA) ▼▼▼▼ Comfort Inn [SH]
(740) 435-3200. **$64-$135.** 2327 Southgate Pkwy. I-70, exit 178, just n on SR 209. Int corridors. **Pets:** Medium, other species. $10 one-time fee/pet. Designated rooms, service with restrictions, supervision.
[SAVE] [S6] [X] [!] [H] [P] [~]

▼▼▼▼ Holiday Inn Cambridge/Salt Fork Area [SH]
(740) 432-7313. **$65-$95.** 2248 Southgate Pkwy. I-70, exit 178, just n on SR 209. Int corridors. **Pets:** Medium. Service with restrictions, supervision.
[ASK] [S6] [X] [7] [H] [P] [TI] [~] [X]

▼▼ Super 8 Motel-Cambridge [SH]
(740) 435-8080. **$46-$79.** 8779 Georgetown Rd. I-70, exit 178, just n. Ext corridors. **Pets:** Small. $10 daily fee/room. No service, supervision.
[ASK] [S6] [X] [P]

CANTON

(AAA) ▼▼▼▼ Best Suites of America [SH]
(330) 499-1011. **$75-$93.** 4914 Everhard Rd. I-77, exit 109, 1 mi w. Int corridors. **Pets:** Accepted.
[SAVE] [X] [6M] [7] [H] [P] [~]

(AAA) ▼▼▼ Red Roof Inn [M]
(330) 499-1970. **$43-$68.** 5353 Inn Circle Ct NW. I-77, exit 109, just w on Everhard Rd. Ext corridors. **Pets:** Large. Service with restrictions, crate.
[SAVE] [X] [7]

▼▼▼▼ Residence Inn By Marriott [SH]
(330) 493-0004. **$89-$130.** 5325 Broadmoor Cir NW. I-77, exit 109, 0.5 mi e on Everhard Rd. Int corridors. **Pets:** Accepted.
[ASK] [S6] [X] [6M] [7] [H] [P] [~] [X]

CARROLLTON

▼▼▼▼ Carrollton Days Inn [SH]
(330) 627-9314. **$74-$80.** 1111 Canton Rd. On SR 43, 0.5 mi n of SR 39. Int corridors. **Pets:** Other species. $20 one-time fee/pet. Service with restrictions, supervision.
[ASK] [S6] [X] [H] [P] [~]

CEDARVILLE

▼▼▼▼ Hearthstone Inn & Suites [SH]
(937) 766-3000. **$94-$119.** 10 S Main St. I-70, exit 54, 11 mi s. Int corridors. **Pets:** Small, dogs only. $15 daily fee/pet. Service with restrictions, supervision.
[ASK] [X] [H] [P]

CHILLICOTHE

▼▼▼▼ Christopher Inn & Suites [SH]
(740) 774-6835. **$56-$86.** 30 N Plaza Blvd. US 35, exit Bridge St. Int corridors. **Pets:** Medium. $5 daily fee/room. Service with restrictions, crate.
[ASK] [S6] [X] [!] [H] [P] [~] [X]

▼▼▼▼ Comfort Inn [SH]
(740) 775-3500. **$62-$82.** 20 N Plaza Blvd. Jct US 35 and 23 business route. Int corridors. **Pets:** Accepted.
[X] [7] [H] [P] [~]

▼▼ Country Hearth Inn [M]
(740) 775-2500. **$59.** 1135 E Main St. Jct US 35 and 50. Ext/int corridors. **Pets:** Accepted.
[ASK] [S6] [X] [H] [P] [~]

▼▼ Days Inn Chillicothe [SH]
(740) 775-7000. **$62-$76.** 1250 N Bridge St. US 35, exit Bridge St, 0.8 mi n. Int corridors. **Pets:** $5 daily fee/room. Service with restrictions, crate.
[ASK] [S6] [X] [H] [P] [~]

Cincinnati Metropolitan Area

BATAVIA

▼▼▼▼ Hampton Inn-Cincinnati Eastgate [SH]
(513) 752-8584. **$71-$109.** 858 Eastgate North Dr. I-275, exit 63B (SR 32), just e, just n on Gleneste Withamsville Rd, then just w; beind the Longhorn Steak House. Int corridors. **Pets:** Medium, other species. Service with restrictions, crate.
[ASK] [S6] [X] [6M] [7] [H] [P] [~]

(AAA) ▼▼▼▼ Holiday Inn-Cincinnati Eastgate [SH]
(513) 752-4400. **$120-$251.** 4501 Eastgate Blvd. I-275, exit 63B (SR 32) to Eastgate Mall exit. Int corridors. **Pets:** Supervision.
[SAVE] [S6] [X] [7] [H] [P] [TI] [~]

BLUE ASH

(AAA) ▼▼▼ AmeriSuites (Cincinnati/Blue Ash) [SH]
(513) 489-3666. **$79-$109.** 11435 Reed-Hartman Hwy. I-275, exit 47, 0.8 mi s. Int corridors. **Pets:** Small, other species. Service with restrictions, supervision.
[SAVE] [S6] [X] [6M] [7] [H] [P] [~]

▼▼▼ Homestead Studio Suites Hotel-Cincinnati/ Blue Ash [SH] ❀
(513) 985-9992. **$79-$94.** 4630 Creek Rd. I-275, exit 47, 2.3 mi s on Reed-Hartman Hwy, just e. Int corridors. **Pets:** Medium, other species. $25 daily fee/room. Service with restrictions, crate.
[ASK] [S6] [X] [7] [6'] [H] [P] [~] [X]

(AAA) ▼▼▼ Red Roof Inn Northeast (Blue Ash) [M]
(513) 793-8811. **$46-$72.** 5900 Pfeiffer Rd. I-71, exit 15, just w. Ext corridors. **Pets:** Accepted.
[SAVE] [X] [6M] [6'] [H]

▼▼▼ **Residence Inn by Marriott-Blue Ash** 🆂🅷 🐾
(513) 530-5060. **$119-$139.** 11401 Reed-Hartman Hwy. I-275, exit 47, 0.8 mi s. Ext corridors. **Pets:** Other species. $75 one-time fee/room. Service with restrictions, crate.
(ASK) 🆂🔟 ⊠ &M 🕖 🅔 🔒 💻 ⇌ ⊠

▼▼▼ **TownePlace Suites by Marriott Blue Ash** 🆂🅷
(513) 469-8222. **$79-$95.** 4650 Cornell Rd. I-275, exit 47, 0.9 mi s on Reed-Hartman Hwy, just w. Int corridors. **Pets:** Accepted.
(ASK) 🆂🔟 ⊠ 🅔 🔒 💻 ⇌

CHERRY GROVE

🔺🔺🔺 ▼▼ **Red Roof Inn Cincinnati East** Ⓜ
(513) 528-2741. **$44-$74.** 4035 Mt. Carmel-Tobasco Rd. I-275, exit 65, just n. Ext corridors. **Pets:** Medium. Service with restrictions, crate.
(SAVE) ⊠ 🅔 🔒

CINCINNATI

🔺🔺🔺 ▼▼▼ **Garfield Suites Hotel** 🆂🅷
(513) 421-3355. **$169-$199.** 2 Garfield Pl. Corner of Vine and 8th sts. Int corridors. **Pets:** Medium. $100 one-time fee/room. Designated rooms, service with restrictions, crate.
(SAVE) 🆂🔟 ⊠ 🕖 🔒 💻 🍽

🔺🔺🔺 ▼▼▼ **Millennium Hotel Cincinnati** 🅻🅷
(513) 352-2100. **$179.** 141 W 6th St. Between Elm and Race sts. Int corridors. **Pets:** Accepted.
(SAVE) 🆂🔟 ⊠ 🅔 💻 🍽 ⇌

🔺🔺🔺 ▼▼▼ **The Vernon Manor Hotel** 🅻🅷
(513) 281-3300. **$110-$180.** 400 Oak St. I-71, exit 2 (Reading Rd) northbound, 1 mi n; exit 3 (Taft Rd) southbound, just n on Reading Rd, then w. Int corridors. **Pets:** Accepted.
(SAVE) 🆂🔟 ⊠ 🕖 🅔 🔒 🍽

▼▼▼ ▼▼ **The Westin Cincinnati** 🅻🅷
(513) 621-7700. **$150-$155.** 21 E 5th St. Between Vine and Walnut sts. Int corridors. **Pets:** Accepted.
(ASK) ⊠ &M 🕖 🅔 💻 🍽 ⇌

FAIRFIELD

▼▼▼ **Holiday Inn Express** 🆂🅷 🐾
(513) 860-2900. **$89-$159.** 6755 Fairfield Business Park Dr. I-275, exit 41 (SR 4), 1.5 mi n on SR 4. Int corridors. **Pets:** Small. Designated rooms, service with restrictions, supervision.
(ASK) 🆂🔟 ⊠ &M 🕖 🅔 🔒 💻 ⇌

FOREST PARK

🔺🔺🔺 ▼▼▼ **AmeriSuites (Cincinnati/North)** 🆂🅷
(513) 825-9035. **$89-$119.** 12001 Chase Plaza Dr. I-275, exit 39, just s, then just w. Int corridors. **Pets:** Accepted.
(SAVE) 🆂🔟 ⊠ 🕖 🔒 💻 ⇌

▼▼▼ **Lees Inn & Suites Cincinnati** 🆂🅷
(513) 825-9600. **$99-$109.** 11967 Chase Plaza Dr. I-275, exit 39, just s on Winton Rd. Int corridors. **Pets:** Accepted.
(ASK) 🆂🔟 ⊠ &M 🅔 🔒 💻 ⇌ ⊠

HAMILTON

▼▼▼ **The Hamiltonian Hotel** 🆂🅷
(513) 896-6200. **$74-$84.** 1 Riverfront Plaza. Just off High St, on Front St. Int corridors. **Pets:** Accepted.
(ASK) 🆂🔟 ⊠ 🕖 🔒 💻 🍽 ⇌

KENWOOD

▼▼▼ **Hannaford Suites Hotel Cincinnati NE** 🆂🅷
(513) 936-0525. **$109.** 5900 E Galbraith Rd. I-71, exit 12, 0.5 mi e, then just n. Int corridors. **Pets:** Accepted.
(ASK) 🆂🔟 ⊠ 🔒 💻 ⇌

MASON

🔺🔺🔺 ▼▼▼ **AmeriSuites (Cincinnati/Deerfield Crossing)** 🆂🅷
(513) 754-0003. **$89-$139.** 5070 Natorp Blvd. I-71, exit 19, 0.5 mi w. Int corridors. **Pets:** Medium, other species. Service with restrictions, crate.
(SAVE) 🆂🔟 ⊠ 🅔 🔒 💻 ⇌

🔺🔺🔺 ▼▼▼ **Baymont Inn & Suites Cincinnati-Mason/near Kings Island** 🆂🅷
(513) 459-1111. **$69-$109.** 9918 Escort Dr. I-71, exit 19, just w, then just s. Int corridors. **Pets:** Medium. $50 deposit/room. Designated rooms, service with restrictions, supervision.
(SAVE) 🆂🔟 ⊠ 🕖 🅔 🔒 💻 ⇌

🔺🔺🔺 ▼▼▼ **Holiday Inn Express Kings Island** Ⓜ
(513) 398-8075. **$79-$259.** 5589 Kings Mills Rd. I-71, exit 25, just w, then just s. Ext corridors. **Pets:** Accepted.
(SAVE) 🆂🔟 ⊠ &M 🕖 🅔 🔒 💻 ⇌ ⊠

▼▼▼ **Ramada Limited Kings Island Area** 🆂🅷
(513) 336-7911. **$58-$85.** 9665 Mason-Montgomery Rd. I-71, exit 19, just w. Int corridors. **Pets:** Small, other species. Service with restrictions, crate.
(ASK) 🆂🔟 ⊠ &M 🅔 🔒 💻 ⇌

▼▼▼ **Red Roof Inn-Kings Island** Ⓜ
(513) 398-3633. **$49-$129.** 9847 Bards Rd. I-71, exit 19, just w. Ext corridors. **Pets:** Accepted.
(ASK) 🆂🔟 ⊠ &M 🕖 🅔 🔒 💻 ⇌

▼▼▼ **TownePlace Suites by Marriott** 🆂🅷
(513) 774-0610. **$69-$99, 7 day notice.** 9369 Waterstone Blvd. I-71, exit 19, 0.5 mi e on Fields-Ertel Rd, then 0.9 mi n. Int corridors. **Pets:** Other species. $100 one-time fee/room. Service with restrictions, supervision.
(ASK) 🆂🔟 ⊠ 🅔 🔒 💻 ⇌

MIDDLETOWN

▼▼▼ **The Manchester Inn & Conference Center** 🆂🅷
(513) 422-5481. **$82-$157.** 1027 Manchester Ave. Just w of SR 4 and 73. Int corridors. **Pets:** Medium. $25 deposit/pet. Service with restrictions, supervision.
(ASK) 🆂🔟 ⊠ 🔒 💻 🍽

▽▽▽ **Ramada Inn Middletown** 🅂🄷
(513) 424-1201. **$75, 14 day notice.** I-75, exit 32, just e. Int corridors. **Pets:** Small. $10 daily fee/pet. Designated rooms, service with restrictions, supervision.
🄰🅂🄺 🅂🄳 ⊠ 🗚 🗚 🗚 🗚 🗚 ≋

▽▽ **Super 8 Motel Middletown** 🅂🄷
(513) 422-4888. **$49-$69.** 3553 Commerce Dr. I-75, exit 32, just e, then just n. Int corridors. **Pets:** Accepted.
🄰🅂🄺 🅂🄳 ⊠ 🗚

MOUNT ORAB

▽▽▽ **Best Inn** 🅂🄷
(937) 444-6666. **$69-$150.** 100 Leininger St. Jct US 68 and SR 32, just n on US 68. Int corridors. **Pets:** Accepted.
🄰🅂🄺 🅂🄳 ⊠ 🗚 🗚 🗚 ≋ 🗚

NORWOOD

▽▽▽ **Howard Johnson East** 🅂🄷
(513) 631-8500. **$59-$69.** 5410 Ridge Rd. I-71, exit 8 south-bound; exit 8B northbound, 0.4 mi nw. Int corridors. **Pets:** Other species.
🄰🅂🄺 🅂🄳 ⊠ 🗚 🗚 ≋

▽▽ **Motel 6 Cincinnati Central (Norwood)** 🄼
(513) 531-6589. **$47-$73.** 5300 Kennedy Ave. I-71, exit 8 southbound; exit 8B northbound; corner of Highland. Ext corridors. **Pets:** Accepted.
⊠ 🗚

SHARONVILLE

🄰🄰🄰 ▽▽▽ **Homewood Suites by Hilton-Cincinnati North** 🅂🄷
(513) 772-8888. **$98-$116.** 2670 E Kemper Rd. I-275, exit 44, jct Mosteller Rd. Int corridors. **Pets:** Large, other species. $15 daily fee/room. Service with restrictions.
🅂🄰🅅🄴 🅂🄳 ⊠ 🗚 🗚 ≋ 🗚

🄰🄰🄰 ▽▽▽ **Red Roof Inn-Sharon Road** 🄼
(513) 771-5552. **$44-$64.** 2301 E Sharon Rd. I-75, exit 15, just e. Ext corridors. **Pets:** Accepted.
🅂🄰🅅🄴 ⊠ 🗚 🗚

▽▽▽ **Residence Inn by Marriott** 🄼
(513) 771-2525. **$89-$119.** 11689 Chester Rd. I-75, exit 15, 0.3 mi w on Sharon Rd, then 1 mi n. Ext corridors. **Pets:** Large. $15 daily fee/pet. Service with restrictions.
🄰🅂🄺 🅂🄳 ⊠ 🗚 🗚 ≋ 🗚

▽▽▽ **Signature Inn Cincinnati North** 🅂🄷
(513) 772-7877. **$72-$81.** 11385 Chester Rd. I-75, exit 15, just w on Sharon Rd, then 0.5 mi n. Int corridors. **Pets:** Small. Service with restrictions, crate.
⊠ 🗚 🗚 🗚 🗚 ≋

▽▽▽ **Woodfield Suites Cincinnati-Sharonville** 🅂🄷
(513) 771-0300. **$99-$199.** 11029 Dowlin Dr. I-75, exit 15, just e. Int corridors. **Pets:** Large. $50 deposit/room, $10 daily fee/room. Service with restrictions, supervision.
🄰🅂🄺 🅂🄳 ⊠ 🗚 🗚 🗚 🗚 🗚 ≋ 🗚

SPRINGDALE

🄰🄰🄰 ▽▽ **Baymont Inn & Suites Cincinnati North** 🅂🄷
(513) 671-2300. **$59-$89.** 12150 Springfield Pike. I-275, exit 41, just n. Int corridors. **Pets:** Accepted.
🅂🄰🅅🄴 🅂🄳 ⊠ 🗚 🗚 🗚

WILMINGTON

▽▽▽ **Holiday Inn Express** 🅂🄷
(937) 382-5858. **$80-$115.** 155 Holiday Dr. 1.6 mi e on US 22. Int corridors. **Pets:** Accepted.
🄰🅂🄺 🅂🄳 ⊠ 🗚 🗚 🗚 🗚 🗚 ≋ 🗚

🄰🄰🄰 ▽▽▽ **Ramada Plaza-Wilmington** 🄻🄷
(937) 283-3200. **$99.** 123 Gano Rd. I-71, exit 50, just w. Int corridors. **Pets:** $250 deposit/room. Service with restrictions, supervision.
🅂🄰🅅🄴 🅂🄳 ⊠ 🗚 🗚 🗚 🗚 🗚 ≋

CLEVELAND METROPOLITAN AREA

BEACHWOOD

▽▽▽ **Holiday Inn-Beachwood** 🅂🄷
(216) 831-3300. **$89-$119.** 3750 Orange Pl. I-271, exit Chagrin Blvd, just e. Int corridors. **Pets:** Small, dogs only. $50 deposit/room. Service with restrictions, supervision.
🄰🅂🄺 🅂🄳 ⊠ 🗚 🗚 🗚 🗚 🗚 ≋ 🗚

▽▽ **Homestead Studio Suites Hotel-Cleveland/Beachwood** 🅂🄷 🐾
(216) 896-5555. **$69-$94.** 3625 Orange Pl. I-271, exit Chagrin Blvd, just e. Int corridors. **Pets:** Medium, other species. $25 daily fee/room. Service with restrictions, crate.
🄰🅂🄺 🅂🄳 ⊠ 🗚 🗚 🗚

▽▽▽ **Residence Inn by Marriot Cleveland-Beachwood** 🅂🄷
(216) 831-3030. **$129-$189.** 3628 Park East Dr. Jct US 422 and I-271, exit Chagrin Blvd, just w. Int corridors. **Pets:** Other species. $250 one-time fee/room. Service with restrictions, crate.
⊠ 🗚 🗚 🗚 🗚 🗚 ≋ 🗚

BROADVIEW HEIGHTS

🄰🄰🄰 ▽▽ **Tallyho-tel** 🄼
(440) 526-0640. **$35.** 4501 E Royalton Rd. I-77 and SR 82, exit 149B southbound; exit 149 northbound. Ext corridors. **Pets:** Accepted.
🅂🄰🅅🄴 🅂🄳 ⊠ 🗚 ≋

CLEVELAND

▼▼▼▼ Airport Sheraton Cleveland Hotel 🆂🅷
(216) 267-1500. **$109-$280.** 5300 Riverside Dr. I-71, exit 237, follow signs; just s of I-480 on SR 237. Int corridors. **Pets:** Accepted.

🅰🆂🅺 🆂🔂 ✖ 🔣ᴹ 🌀 🎿 🔲 🔳 🍴 ⇆ ✖

㊙ ▼▼▼▼ Baymont Inn & Suites Cleveland-Airport 🆂🅷
(216) 251-8500. **$69-$79.** 4222 W 150th St. I-71, exit 240, just n. Int corridors. **Pets:** Accepted.

🆂🅰🆅🅴 🆂🔂 ✖ 🌀 🔲 🔳

㊙ ▼▼▼ Cleveland Airport Marriott 🅻🅷
(216) 252-5333. **$59-$169.** 4277 W 150th St. I-71, exit 240, just s. Int corridors. **Pets:** Other species. $50 one-time fee/room. Service with restrictions, supervision.

🆂🅰🆅🅴 ✖ 🌀 🎿 🔲 🔳 🍴 ⇆

▼▼▼▼ Residence Inn by Marriott 🆂🅷
(216) 443-9043. **$139-$179.** 527 Prospect Ave. Int corridors. **Pets:** Other species. $250 one-time fee/room. Service with restrictions.

🅰🆂🅺 🆂🔂 ✖ 🔲 🔳 ✖

㊙ ▼▼▼▼▼ The Ritz-Carlton, Cleveland 🅻🅷
(216) 623-1300. **$269-$279.** 1515 W 3rd St. In Tower City Center (3rd St side). Int corridors. **Pets:** Accepted.

🆂🅰🆅🅴 ✖ 🌀 🎿 🔲 🔳 🍴 ⇆ ✖

INDEPENDENCE

㊙ ▼▼▼▼ AmeriSuites (Cleveland So/Independence) 🆂🅷
(216) 328-1060. **$79-$119.** 6025 Jefferson Dr. I-77, exit Rockside Rd, just w to W Creek Rd, then just n. Int corridors. **Pets:** Designated rooms, service with restrictions.

🆂🅰🆅🅴 🆂🔂 ✖ 🔣ᴹ 🌀 🎿 🔲 🔳 ⇆

㊙ ▼▼▼ Baymont Inn & Suites Cleveland-Independence 🆂🅷
(216) 447-1133. **$59-$79.** 6161 Quarry Ln. I-77, exit Rockside Rd, just e. Int corridors. **Pets:** Accepted.

🆂🅰🆅🅴 🆂🔂 ✖ 🌀 🔲 🔳

㊙ ▼▼▼ Red Roof Inn 🅼
(216) 447-0030. **$55-$71.** 6020 Quarry Ln. I-77, exit Rockside Rd, just e. Ext corridors. **Pets:** Medium, other species. Service with restrictions, supervision.

🆂🅰🆅🅴 ✖ 🌀 🎿

▼▼▼▼ Residence Inn by Marriott 🆂🅷
(216) 520-1450. **$114-$149.** 5101 W Creek Rd. I-77, exit Rockside Rd, just w to W Creek Rd, then just n. Ext corridors. **Pets:** Medium. $200 one-time fee/room. Service with restrictions, supervision.

✖ 🌀 🎿 🔲 🔳 ⇆ ✖

LAKEWOOD

▼▼ Days Inn 🆂🅷
(216) 226-4800. **$59-$69.** 12019 Lake Ave. I-90, exit 166, 1 mi n on W 117th St, then just w. **Pets:** $100 deposit/room. Service with restrictions, supervision.

🅰🆂🅺 🆂🔂

▼▼ Travelodge 🆂🅷
(216) 221-9000. **$59-$69.** 11837 Edgewater Dr. I-90, exit 166, 1 mi n on W 117th St, just w. Int corridors. **Pets:** $100 deposit/room. Service with restrictions, supervision.

🅰🆂🅺 🆂🔂 ✖ 🔲 🔳

MACEDONIA

㊙ ▼▼▼▼ Baymont Inn & Suites Cleveland-Macedonia 🆂🅷
(330) 468-5400. **$74-$99.** 268 E Highland Rd. I-271, exit 18, just s; I-80/90 (Ohio Tpke), exit 180, just n. Int corridors. **Pets:** Large, other species. $50 deposit/room. Designated rooms, service with restrictions, supervision.

🆂🅰🆅🅴 🆂🔂 ✖ 🔣ᴹ 🌀 🎿 🔲 🔳 ⇆

▼▼ Knights Inn-Cleveland/Macedonia 🅼
(330) 467-1981. **$40-$75.** 240 E Highland Rd. I-271, exit 18, just s; I-80/90 (Ohio Tpke), exit 180, 3 mi n. Ext corridors. **Pets:** Medium, other species. No service, supervision.

🅰🆂🅺 🆂🔂 ✖ 🔲 🔳 ⇆

MAYFIELD HEIGHTS

㊙ ▼▼▼ Baymont Inn & Suites-Cleveland (Mayfield Heights) 🆂🅷 🐾
(440) 442-8400. **$69-$99.** 1421 Golden Gate Blvd. I-271, exit Mayfield, 0.3 mi w off US 322. Int corridors. **Pets:** Large, other species. $10 daily fee/room. Service with restrictions, supervision.

🆂🅰🆅🅴 🆂🔂 ✖ 🌀 🔲 🔳

MEDINA

㊙ ▼▼ Best Value Inn Cleveland-Medina 🅼
(330) 722-4335. **$56-$89, 14 day notice.** 5200 Montville Dr. I-71, exit 218, just e. Ext corridors. **Pets:** Accepted.

🆂🅰🆅🅴 🆂🔂 ✖ 🔲 ⇆

▼▼ Motel 6 4112 🆂🅷
(330) 723-3322. **Call for rates.** 3122 EastPointe Dr. I-71, exit 218, just w. Int corridors. **Pets:** Medium. Service with restrictions, supervision.

✖ ⇆

MIDDLEBURG HEIGHTS

㊙ ▼▼▼▼ Comfort Inn-Cleveland Airport 🆂🅷
(440) 234-3131. **$69-$139.** 17550 Rosbough Dr. I-71, exit 235, 0.3 mi w to Engle Rd, then 0.3 mi n. Int corridors. **Pets:** $10 daily fee/room, $35 one-time fee/room. Service with restrictions, supervision.

🆂🅰🆅🅴 🆂🔂 ✖ 🔣ᴹ 🔲 🔳 ⇆

㊙ ▼▼▼ Red Roof Inn-Middleburg Heights 🆂🅷
(440) 243-2441. **$49-$61.** 17555 Bagley Rd. I-71, exit 235, just w. Ext/int corridors. **Pets:** Medium. No service, crate.

🆂🅰🆅🅴 ✖

▼▼▼▼ Residence Inn by Marriott 🆂🅷
(440) 234-6688. **$109-$159.** 17525 Rosbough Dr. I-71, exit 235, just w on Bagley Rd, then just n on Engle Rd. Ext/int corridors. **Pets:** Accepted.

🅰🆂🅺 🆂🔂 ✖ 🎿 🔲 🔳 ✖

▼▼▼▼ TownePlace Suites 🆂🅷
(440) 816-9300. **$39-$109.** 7325 S Engle Rd. I-71, exit 235, just w on Bagley Rd. Int corridors. **Pets:** Accepted.
🄰🅂🄺 🆂🄰 ⨉ 🎿 🔋 🖥 🏊

NORTH OLMSTED

**▼▼ ▼▼ Homestead Studio Suites Hotel-Cleveland/
     Airport/North Olmsted** 🆂🅷 🐾
(440) 777-8585. **$44-$59.** 24851 Country Club Blvd. I-480, exit 6B, just n on SR 252. Ext corridors. **Pets:** Medium, other species. $25 daily fee/room. Service with restrictions, crate.
⨉ 🕭 🎿 🔋 🖥

**🄰🄰🄰 ▼▼▼▼ Radisson Hotel Cleveland
     Airport** 🆂🅷
(440) 734-5060. **$75-$109.** 25070 Country Club Blvd. I-480, exit 6B, just n on SR 252. Int corridors. **Pets:** Large, other species. $50 deposit/room. Service with restrictions, supervision.
🅂🄰🆅🄴 🆂🄰 ⨉ 🕭 🎿 🔋 🖥 🍽 🏊 ⨯

NORTH RIDGEVILLE

**🄰🄰🄰 ▼▼ Travelers Inn, Cleveland/North
     Ridgeville** 🄼
(440) 327-6311. **$40-$61.** 32751 Lorain Rd. I-80, exit 152, 0.6 mi ne on SR 10. Ext corridors. **Pets:** Accepted.
🅂🄰🆅🄴 🆂🄰 ⨉ 🖥

STRONGSVILLE

▼▼▼▼ Motel 6-Strongsville 🄼
(440) 238-0170. **$45-$65.** 15385 Royalton Rd. I-71, exit 231A, just e; I-76 (Ohio Tpke), exit 161, 1 mi s. Ext corridors. **Pets:** Accepted.
⨉ 🎿

TWINSBURG

▼▼ ▼▼ Twinsburg Super 8 Motel 🆂🅷
(330) 425-2889. **$47-$99.** 8848 Twins Hills Dr. I-480, exit 36, just w on SR 82. Int corridors. **Pets:** $5.34 daily fee/pet. Service with restrictions, supervision.
🄰🅂🄺 🆂🄰 ⨉ 🔋

WESTLAKE

🄰🄰🄰 ▼▼▼▼ Red Roof Inn-Westlake 🄼
(440) 892-7920. **$49-$84.** 29595 Clemens Rd. I-90, exit 156, just n. Ext corridors. **Pets:** Medium, other species. Service with restrictions, supervision.
🅂🄰🆅🄴 ⨉ 🎿 🔋

▼▼▼▼ Residence Inn by Marriott 🆂🅷
(440) 892-2254. **$105-$159.** 30100 Clemens Rd. I-90, exit 156, just n. Ext corridors. **Pets:** Accepted.
🄰🅂🄺 🆂🄰 ⨉ 🎿 🔋 🖥 🏊 ⨯

WICKLIFFE

🄰🄰🄰 ▼▼▼▼ Clarion Hotel Cleveland East 🆂🅷
(440) 585-2750. **$89-$140.** 28500 Euclid Ave. I-90, exit 186, just n. Int corridors. **Pets:** $10 one-time fee/room. Service with restrictions, supervision.
🅂🄰🆅🄴 🆂🄰 ⨉ 🎿 🔋 🖥 🍽 🏊 ⨯

WILLOUGHBY

🄰🄰🄰 ▼▼▼▼ Red Roof Inn-East 🄼 🐾
(440) 946-9872. **$45-$81.** 4166 SR 306. I-90, exit 193, just s. Ext corridors. **Pets:** Large. Service with restrictions, supervision.
🅂🄰🆅🄴 ⨉ 🎿 🕭

🐾   **END METROPOLITAN AREA**   🐾

CLYDE

▼▼▼▼ Red Roof Inn 🆂🅷
(419) 547-6660. **$54-$109.** 1363 W McPherson Hwy. 1 mi w on SR 20. Int corridors. **Pets:** Small, dogs only. $50 deposit/pet. Designated rooms, service with restrictions, supervision.
🄰🅂🄺 🆂🄰 ⨉ 🔋 🏊

COLUMBUS METROPOLITAN AREA

COLUMBUS

**🄰🄰🄰 ▼▼▼▼ AmeriSuites
     (Columbus/Worthington)** 🆂🅷
(614) 846-4355. **$94-$125.** 7490 Vantage Dr. I-270, exit 23, just ne. Int corridors. **Pets:** Small, other species. Designated rooms, service with restrictions, supervision.
🅂🄰🆅🄴 🆂🄰 ⨉ 🕭 🎿 🔋 🖥 🏊

🄰🄰🄰 ▼▼▼▼ Best Western Columbus North 🆂🅷
(614) 888-8230. **$70-$80.** 888 E Dublin-Granville Rd. I-71, exit 117, 0.5 mi w on SR 161. Int corridors. **Pets:** Very small, other species. $25 deposit/room. Service with restrictions, crate.
🅂🄰🆅🄴 🆂🄰 ⨉ 🎿 🔋 🖥 🍽 🏊 ⨯

🄰🄰🄰 ▼▼▼▼ Columbus Marriott North 🆂🅷
(614) 885-1885. **$139-$149.** 6500 Doubletree Ave. I-71, exit 117, 0.3 mi w on SR 161, then 0.8 mi on Busch Blvd to Kingsmill Pkwy. Int corridors. **Pets:** Accepted.
🅂🄰🆅🄴 🆂🄰 ⨉ 🕭 🎿 🎿 🔋 🖥 🍽 🏊 ⨯

▼▼▼▼ Comfort Suites West 🆂🅷
(614) 870-7658. **$59-$79.** 5547 Keim Cir. I-70, exit 91B, just n on Renner Rd. Int corridors. **Pets:** Accepted.
[A$K] [S🐾] [✕] [🛏] [💻] [🏊]

◈◈◈ ▼▼▼ Days Inn Fairgrounds Ⓜ 🐾
(614) 299-4300. **$50-$70.** 1700 Clara St. I-71, exit 111, just w. Ext corridors. **Pets:** Large, other species. $10 one-time fee/room. Service with restrictions, supervision.
[SAVE] [S🐾] [✕] [🛏] [💻] [🏊]

▼▼▼▼ Doubletree Guest Suites 🅻🅷
(614) 228-4600. **$99-$214.** 50 S Front St. Corner of Front and State sts, just n. Int corridors. **Pets:** Accepted.
[A$K] [✕] [🐾] [🛏] [💻] [🍽]

▼▼▼▼ Drury Inn & Suites-Columbus Convention Center 🆂🅷
(614) 221-7008. **$93-$113.** 88 E Nationwide Blvd. 0.3 mi n on US 23. Int corridors. **Pets:** Large, other species. Service with restrictions, supervision.
[A$K] [✕] [🅼] [🐾] [🗝] [🛏] [💻] [🏊]

▼▼▼▼ Drury Inn & Suites-Columbus Northwest 🆂🅷
(614) 798-8802. **$93-$113.** 6170 Parkcenter Cir. I-270, exit 15 (Tuttle Crossing), just e. Int corridors. **Pets:** Large, other species. Service with restrictions, supervision.
[A$K] [✕] [🛏] [💻] [🏊]

◈◈◈ ▼▼▼▼ Holiday Inn Columbus East Airport Area 🆂🅷
(614) 868-1380. **$99-$109.** 4560 Hilton Corporate Dr. I-70, exit 107. Int corridors. **Pets:** Accepted.
[SAVE] [S🐾] [✕] [🅼] [🗝] [🛏] [💻] [🍽] [🏊] [✕]

◈◈◈ ▼▼▼▼ Holiday Inn-Columbus/Worthington Area 🅻🅷
(614) 885-3334. **$137.** 175 Hutchinson Ave. I-270, exit 23, just n of jct US 23 N. Int corridors. **Pets:** Accepted.
[SAVE] [S🐾] [✕] [🅼] [🐾] [🗝] [🛏] [💻] [🍽] [🏊] [✕]

◈◈◈ ▼▼▼▼ Holiday Inn on the Lane 🆂🅷
(614) 294-4848. **$99-$109.** 328 W Lane Ave. 0.5 mi e of SR 315, exit Lane Ave. Int corridors. **Pets:** $25 one-time fee/room. Designated rooms, service with restrictions, supervision.
[SAVE] [S🐾] [✕] [🅼] [🐾] [🛏] [💻] [🍽] [🏊] [✕]

◈◈◈ ▼▼▼ Knights Inn-Columbus East Ⓜ
(614) 864-0600. **$50-$90.** 4320 Groves Rd. I-70, exit 107, just sw. Ext corridors. **Pets:** Medium. $35 deposit/pet. Service with restrictions, supervision.
[SAVE] [S🐾] [✕] [🛏]

▼▼▼ Microtel Inn-Columbus/Worthington 🆂🅷
(614) 436-0556. **$43-$70.** 7500 Vantage Dr. I-270, exit 23, just n of US 23 N. Int corridors. **Pets:** Medium, other species. $10 one-time fee/pet.
[A$K] [S🐾] [✕] [🅼]

▼▼▼ Motel 6 OSU #1491 Ⓜ
(614) 846-8520. **$41-$53.** 750 Morse Rd. I-71, exit 116. Ext corridors. **Pets:** Accepted.
[S🐾] [✕] [🅼] [🗝]

◈◈◈ ▼▼▼ Red Roof Inn-OSU 🆂🅷
(614) 267-9941. **$59-$69.** 441 Ackerman Rd. SR 315, exit Ackerman Rd, 0.3 mi e. Ext corridors. **Pets:** Small, other species. Service with restrictions, supervision.
[SAVE] [✕]

◈◈◈ ▼▼▼ Red Roof Inn-West Ⓜ
(614) 878-9245. **$51-$75.** 5001 Renner Rd. I-70, exit 91 eastbound; exit 91B westbound, just nw. Ext corridors. **Pets:** Large. Service with restrictions, supervision.
[SAVE] [✕] [🅼] [🗝] [🛏]

▼▼▼▼ Residence Inn by Marriott 🆂🅷
(614) 885-0799. **$109-$139.** 7300 Huntington Park Dr. I-270, exit 23, just e of Vantage Dr. Int corridors. **Pets:** Accepted.
[A$K] [✕] [🗝] [🛏] [💻] [🏊] [✕]

▼▼▼▼ The Residence Inn by Marriott-Columbus North 🆂🅷 🐾
(614) 431-1819. **$89-$114.** 6191 W Zumstein Dr. I-71, exit 117, 0.3 mi w on SR 161, 0.4 mi n on Busch Blvd, Shapter and Mediterranean Ave. Ext corridors. **Pets:** Other species. $100 one-time fee/room. Service with restrictions.
[A$K] [S🐾] [✕] [🗝] [🛏] [💻] [🏊] [✕]

▼▼▼▼ Residence Inn by Marriott-Columbus Southeast 🆂🅷
(614) 864-8844. **$109-$179.** 2084 S Hamilton Rd. I-70, exit 107, just e. Ext corridors. **Pets:** Other species. $5 daily fee/room, $100 one-time fee/room.
[A$K] [S🐾] [✕] [🅼] [🗝] [🛏] [💻] [🏊] [✕]

▼▼▼▼ Residence Inn by Marriott Easton 🆂🅷
(614) 414-1000. **$139-$209.** 3999 Easton Loop W. I-270, exit 33, 1 mi w, then just n. Int corridors. **Pets:** Accepted.
[A$K] [✕] [🗝] [🛏] [💻] [🏊] [✕]

▼▼▼ Signature Inn Columbus North 🆂🅷
(614) 890-8111. **$78-$87.** 6767 Schrock Hill Ct. I-270, exit 27, n off Cleveland Ave; enter off Schrock Rd. Int corridors. **Pets:** Small. Service with restrictions, crate.
[✕] [🐾] [🛏] [💻] [🏊]

▼▼▼ TownePlace Suites by Marriott 🆂🅷
(614) 885-1557. **$70-$95.** 7272 Huntington Park Dr. I-270, exit 23, just e of Vantage Dr. Int corridors. **Pets:** Other species. $100 one-time fee/room. Service with restrictions, supervision.
[A$K] [S🐾] [✕] [🗝] [🛏] [💻] [🏊]

◈◈◈ ▼▼▼▼ The University Plaza Hotel & Conference Center 🆂🅷
(614) 267-7461. **$109-$129.** 3110 Olentangy River Rd. 0.5 mi s of N Broadway, exit off SR 315. Int corridors. **Pets:** Medium. $10 deposit/room. Service with restrictions, crate.
[SAVE] [S🐾] [✕] [🛏] [💻] [🍽] [🏊]

◈◈◈ ▼▼▼▼ Wellesley Inn & Suites (Columbus/Polaris) 🆂🅷
(614) 431-5522. **$89-$109.** 8555 Lyra Dr. I-71, exit 121, just w on Polaris Pkwy. Int corridors. **Pets:** Small. Service with restrictions, crate.
[SAVE] [S🐾] [✕] [🅼] [🗝] [🛏] [💻] [🏊]

(AAA) ▼▼▼ ▼▼▼ **The Westin Great Southern Columbus** 🄻🄷
(614) 228-3800. **$115-$155.** 310 S High St. Corner of Main and High sts. Int corridors. **Pets:** Accepted.
[SAVE] [S🄳] [✕] [🐾] [📺] [🖥] [🍽]

DELAWARE

▼▼ ◆ **Delaware Hotel** 🅂🄷 ❧
(740) 363-1262. **$59-$85.** 351 S Sandusky St. 0.5 mi e. Int corridors. **Pets:** $20 one-time fee/pet. Designated rooms, service with restrictions, supervision.
[ASK] [S🄳] [✕] [🖥] [🛄] [📺]

(AAA) ▼ **Travelodge** 🄼
(740) 369-4421. **$58-$72.** 1001 US Rt 23 N. 0.5 mi n of downtown. Ext/int corridors. **Pets:** Other species. $10 daily fee/room. Service with restrictions, supervision.
[SAVE] [S🄳] [✕] [🖥] [📺]

DUBLIN

(AAA) ▼▼▼ **AmeriSuites (Columbus/Dublin)** 🅂🄷
(614) 799-1913. **$79-$109.** 6161 Park Center Cir. I-270, exit 15 (Tuttle Crossing Blvd), just e. Int corridors. **Pets:** Accepted.
[SAVE] [S🄳] [✕] [&M] [🐾] [📺] [🖥] [📺] [🛄]

(AAA) ▼▼ ▼▼ **Baymont Inn & Suites Columbus-Dublin** 🅂🄷
(614) 792-8300. **$59-$89.** 6145 Park Center Cir. I-270, exit 15 (Tuttle Crossing Blvd), just e. Int corridors. **Pets:** Medium, other species. $50 deposit/room. Designated rooms, service with restrictions, supervision.
[SAVE] [S🄳] [✕] [&M] [📺] [🖥] [📺]

(AAA) ▼▼▼ ▼ **Columbus Marriott Northwest** 🄻🄷
(614) 791-1000. **$100-$180.** 5605 Paul Blazer Memorial Pkwy. I-270, exit 15 (Tuttle Crossing Blvd), 0.3 mi e. Int corridors. **Pets:** Accepted.
[SAVE] [✕] [&M] [🐾] [📺] [🖥] [📺] [🍽] [🛄]

▼▼▼▼ **Homewood Suites by Hilton** 🅂🄷 ❧
(614) 791-8675. **$129, 14 day notice.** 5300 Parkcenter Ave. I-270, exit 15, just e. Int corridors. **Pets:** Small. $10 daily fee/room, $50 one-time fee/room. Designated rooms, service with restrictions, crate.
[ASK] [S🄳] [✕] [&M] [🐾] [📺] [🖥] [📺] [🛄] [✕🐾]

(AAA) ▼▼ ◆ **Red Roof Inn-Dublin** 🄼
(614) 764-3993. **$56-$72.** 5125 Post Rd. I-270, exit 17A, just ne. Ext corridors. **Pets:** Accepted.
[SAVE] [✕] [&M] [🖥]

(AAA) ▼▼▼ ▼ **Residence Inn by Marriott** 🅂🄷
(614) 791-0403. **$79-$129.** 435 Metro Pl S. I-270, exit 17A, 0.5 mi s to Frantz Rd, then 0.5 mi w. Ext/int corridors. **Pets:** Accepted.
[SAVE] [✕] [&M] [🐾] [📺] [🖥] [📺] [🛄] [✕🐾]

▼▼▼▼ **Staybridge Suites by Holiday Inn** 🅂🄷
(614) 734-9882. **$109.** 6095 Emerald Pkwy. I-270, exit 15 (Tuttle Crossing Blvd), just w. Int corridors. **Pets:** Small. $100 one-time fee/room. No service.
[ASK] [S🄳] [✕] [🖥] [📺] [🛄] [✕🐾]

(AAA) ▼▼▼ ▼ **Wellesley Inn & Suites (Columbus/Dublin)** 🅂🄷
(614) 760-0245. **$85-$125.** 5530 Tuttle Crossing Blvd. I-270, exit 15 (Tuttle Crossing Blvd), 0.3 mi w. Int corridors. **Pets:** Accepted.
[SAVE] [S🄳] [✕] [&M] [🐾] [🖥] [📺]

▼▼▼▼ **Woodfin Suites Hotel** 🅂🄷
(614) 766-7762. **$99-$129.** 4130 Tuller Rd. I-270, exit 20, 0.3 mi s on Sawmill Rd via Dublin Center Dr. Ext corridors. **Pets:** Accepted.
[ASK] [S🄳] [✕] [🐾] [🖥] [📺]

(AAA) ▼▼▼▼ **Wyndham Dublin** 🅂🄷
(614) 764-2200. **$99-$129.** 600 Metro Pl N. I-270, exit 17A, just e, then s on Frantz Rd. Int corridors. **Pets:** Accepted.
[SAVE] [S🄳] [✕] [🖥] [📺] [🍽] [🛄]

GAHANNA

▼▼ ▼ **TownePlace Suites by Marriott** 🅂🄷
(614) 861-1400. **$79-$109.** 695 Taylor Rd. I-270, exit 37, just w to Morrison Rd, just s to Taylor Rd, then just w. Int corridors. **Pets:** Accepted.
[ASK] [S🄳] [✕] [🐾] [🐾] [🖥] [📺] [🛄]

GROVE CITY

(AAA) ▼▼ ▼ **Best Western Executive Inn** 🄼
(614) 875-7770. **$53-$68.** 4026 Jackpot Rd. I-71, exit 100, just e. Ext corridors. **Pets:** Small, dogs only. $9 daily fee/pet. Designated rooms, service with restrictions, supervision.
[SAVE] [S🄳] [✕] [🖥] [📺] [🛄]

▼▼ ▼ **Motel 6-South Columbus #1492** 🄼
(614) 875-8543. **$45-$55.** 1900 Stringtown Rd. I-71, exit 100, just w. Ext corridors. **Pets:** Accepted.
[S🄳] [✕] [🐾]

HEATH

(AAA) ▼▼ ▼ **Best Western Amber Inn** 🅂🄷 ❧
(740) 522-1165. **$59-$120.** 733 Hebron Rd. I-70, exit 129B, 7 mi n on SR 79. Ext corridors. **Pets:** Medium. $5 daily fee/room. Service with restrictions, supervision.
[SAVE] [S🄳] [✕] [🖥] [📺] [🍽] [🛄]

HEBRON

▼▼ ▼ **Red Roof Inn** 🅂🄷
(740) 467-7663. **Call for rates.** 10668 Lancaster Rd SW. I-70, exit 126, just s. Int corridors. **Pets:** Large, other species. Service with restrictions, supervision.
[✕] [&M] [🐾]

HILLIARD

▼▼▼ ▼ **Comfort Suites-Columbus** 🅂🄷
(614) 529-8118. **$75-$95.** 3831 Park Mill Run Dr. I-270, exit 13A northbound; exit 13 southbound. Int corridors. **Pets:** Accepted.
[ASK] [S🄳] [✕] [&M] [🐾] [🐾] [🖥] [📺]

▼▼▼▼ **Homewood Suites by**
     Hilton-Columbus/Hilliard SH
(614) 529-4100. **$89-$109.** 3841 Park Mill Run Dr. I-270, exit
13 southbound; exit 13A northbound. Int corridors.
Pets: Small. Service with restrictions, supervision.
(ASK) 🅢 ✕ 🚿 ⚙ 🅱 🖃 ⚓ ✕

LANCASTER

(AAA) ▼▼▼ **Best Western Lancaster Inn** SH ✿
(740) 653-3040. **$67-$75, 3 day notice.** 1858 N Memorial
Dr. 2 mi nw on US 33. Ext/int corridors. **Pets:** Small. $10
daily fee/pet. Service with restrictions, crate.
(SAVE) 🅢 ✕ 🅱 🖃 🍴 ⚓

(AAA) ▼▼ **Knights Inn** M
(740) 687-4823. **$55-$85.** 1327 River Valley Blvd. 2 mi nw
on US 33. Ext corridors. **Pets:** Accepted.
(SAVE) 🅢 ✕ 🅱

MARYSVILLE

▼▼ **Days Inn Marysville** SH
(937) 644-8821. **$69, 7 day notice.** 16510 Square Dr. Just e
of US 36, exit off US 33. Ext corridors. **Pets:** $10 one-time
fee/room. Service with restrictions.
(ASK) 🅢 ✕ 🅱 🖃

REYNOLDSBURG

(AAA) ▼▼▼ **Best Western Columbus**
     East SH ✿
(614) 864-1280. **$62-$67.** 2100 Brice Rd. I-70, exit 110 westbound; exit 110B eastbound, just n. Int corridors.
Pets: Other species. Service with restrictions, crate.
(SAVE) 🅢 ✕ 🏍 🅱 🖃 🍴 ⚓

(AAA) ▼▼▼ **La Quinta Inn** SH
(614) 866-6456. **$79-$89.** 2447 Brice Rd. I-70, exit 110 westbound; exit 110B eastbound, 0.3 mi n. Int corridors.
Pets: Accepted.
(SAVE) ✕ 🅱 🖃 ⚓

(AAA) ▼▼▼ **Red Roof Inn-East** M
(614) 864-3683. **$52-$69.** 2449 Brice Rd. I-70, exit 110 westbound; exit 110B eastbound. Ext corridors. **Pets:** Accepted.
(SAVE) ✕ 🏍

SUNBURY

(AAA) ▼▼▼ **Days Inn of Sunbury** SH
(740) 362-6159. **$60-$70.** 7323 SR 37 E. I-71, exit 131, just
w. Int corridors. **Pets:** Accepted.
(SAVE) 🅢 ✕ 🏍 🅱 ⚓

▼▼▼▼ **Hampton Inn-Columbus/Delaware** SH
(740) 363-4700. **$89-$120.** 7329 SR 36 & 37. I-71, exit 131,
just nw. Int corridors. **Pets:** Accepted.
(ASK) 🅢 ✕ 🚿 🚿 🏍 🅱 ⚓

WORTHINGTON

▼▼ **Motel 6** M
(614) 431-2525. **$45-$60.** 7474 N High St. I-270, exit 23, jct
US 23 N, just n. Ext corridors. **Pets:** Accepted.
🅢 ✕

✿ END METROPOLITAN AREA ✿

CONNEAUT

(AAA) ▼▼▼ **Days Inn of Conneaut** SH
(440) 593-6000. **$55-$85.** 600 Days Blvd. I-90, exit 241, 0.3
mi n. Int corridors. **Pets:** $5 daily fee/room. Designated
rooms, service with restrictions, crate.
(SAVE) ✕ 🖃 ⚓

CUYAHOGA FALLS

(AAA) ▼▼▼▼ **Akron Sheraton Suites Cuyahoga**
     Falls SH ✿
(330) 929-3000. **$114-$199.** 1989 Front St. SR 8, exit Broad
Blvd, just w. Int corridors. **Pets:** Large, other species. $50
one-time fee/room. Service with restrictions, supervision.
(SAVE) 🅢 ✕ 🚿 🚿 🅱 🖃 🍴 ⚓ ✕

(AAA) ▼▼ **Economy Inn** M
(330) 929-8200. **$63-$109.** 1070 Graham Rd. SR 8, exit
Graham Rd, just w. Ext corridors. **Pets:** Small, dogs only.
$10 one-time fee/pet. Designated rooms, service with
restrictions, crate.
(SAVE) 🅢 ✕ 🅱

DAYTON

▼▼▼ **Dayton Marriott Hotel** LH ✿
(937) 223-1000. **$69-$149.** 1414 S Patterson Blvd. I-75, exit
51 (Edwin C Moses Blvd), 1 mi e. Int corridors. **Pets:** Other
species. $50 one-time fee/room. Designated rooms, service
with restrictions, crate.
🅢 ✕ 🚿 🏍 🅱 🖃 🍴 ⚓ ✕

▼▼ **Howard Johnson Express Inn** SH
(937) 454-0550. **$68-$81.** 7575 Poe Ave. I-75, exit 60 (Little
York Rd) northbound, just n; southbound, n on Miller Ln,
then n on Little York Rd. Int corridors. **Pets:** $50 deposit/
pet. Service with restrictions, supervision.
(ASK) 🅢 ✕ 🚿 🅱 🖃 ⚓

▼▼ **Motel 6-603** SH
(937) 898-3606. **$39-$53.** 7130 Miller Ln. I-75, exit 60 (Little
York Rd). Ext corridors. **Pets:** Small, other species. Service
with restrictions, supervision.
🅢 ✕ 🏍 ⚓

▼▼ **Ramada Inn-North** SH
(937) 890-9500. **$60-$85.** 4079 Little York Rd. I-75, exit 60
(Little York Rd), 0.5 mi s of jct I-70. Ext/int corridors.
Pets: Accepted.
(ASK) 🅢 ✕ 🚿 🅱 🖃 🍴 ⚓

▲▲▲ ▽▽▽ Red Roof Inn-North SH
(937) 898-1054. **$39-$69.** 7370 Miller Ln. I-75, exit 60 (Little York Rd); 0.5 mi s of jct I-70. Ext corridors. **Pets:** Other species. Service with restrictions, crate.

[SAVE] [✕] [🐾] [🖼] [🛏]

▽▽▽ Residence Inn by Marriott-Dayton North SH
(937) 898-7764. **$119-$169.** 7070 Poe Ave. I-75, exit 60 (Little York Rd). Ext corridors. **Pets:** Large, other species. $200 one-time fee/room. Service with restrictions.

[ASK] [✕] [🐾] [🖼] [🛏] [💻] [≈] [✕]

DOVER

▽ Hospitality Inn M ❀
(330) 364-7724. **$40-$75.** 889 Commercial Pkwy. I-77, exit 83, just e. Ext corridors. **Pets:** Other species. $10 one-time fee/pet. Service with restrictions, supervision.

[ASK] [S🐾] [✕] [🐾] [🛏] [≈]

EATON

▲▲▲ ▽▽ Econo Lodge M
(937) 456-5959. **$40-$80.** 6161 Rt 127 N. I-70, exit 10 (US 127). Ext corridors. **Pets:** Small. $10 daily fee/pet. Designated rooms, no service, supervision.

[SAVE] [S🐾] [✕] [🛏] [💻]

ELYRIA

▽▽ Comfort Inn SH
(440) 324-7676. **$64-$159.** 739 Leona St. I-80, exit 145, just n on SR 57, exit Midway Blvd. Int corridors. **Pets:** Accepted.

[ASK] [S🐾] [✕] [🛏] [💻]

▽▽▽ Super 8 Motel SH ❀
(440) 323-7488. **$49-$104.** 910 Lorain Blvd. I-80, exit 145, 0.5 mi s on SR 57. Int corridors. **Pets:** $10 one-time fee/room. Service with restrictions, supervision.

[ASK] [S🐾] [✕] [🐾] [💻] [≈]

ENGLEWOOD

▽▽▽ Holiday Inn-Dayton Northwest Airport SH
(937) 832-1234. **$99-$125.** 10 Rockridge Rd. I-70, exit 29. Int corridors. **Pets:** Small, dogs only. $15 one-time fee/room. Designated rooms, service with restrictions, supervision.

[ASK] [S🐾] [✕] [🛏] [💻] [🍴] [≈]

▽▽ Super 8 Motel-Englewood M
(937) 832-3350. **$40-$99.** 15 Rockridge Rd. I-70, exit 29, just n. Ext corridors. **Pets:** Small. $10 daily fee/pet. Service with restrictions.

[ASK] [S🐾] [✕]

FAIRBORN

▲▲▲ ▽▽▽▽ Comfort Inn-Wright Patterson SH
(937) 879-7666. **$64-$114.** 616 N Broad St. I-675, exit 24, 1.8 sw on SR 444. Int corridors. **Pets:** Other species. $75 one-time fee/room. Service with restrictions, crate.

[SAVE] [S🐾] [✕] [🐾] [🛏] [💻] [≈]

▽▽▽ Hawthorn Inn & Suites SH
(937) 754-9109. **$84-$98.** 730 E Xenia Dr. I-675, exit 23, just w. Int corridors. **Pets:** Other species. $125 one-time fee/pet. Service with restrictions, crate.

[ASK] [S🐾] [✕] [🐾] [🖼] [🛏] [💻]

▲▲▲ ▽▽▽ Homewood Suites by Hilton-Fairborn/Dayton SH
(937) 429-0600. **$129-$149.** 2750 Presidential Dr. I-675, exit 17 (N Fairfield Rd). Ext/int corridors. **Pets:** $100 one-time fee/pet. Service with restrictions, crate.

[SAVE] [S🐾] [✕] [🐾] [🛏] [💻] [≈]

▽▽▽ Ramada Limited & Suites SH ❀
(937) 490-2000. **$95-$110.** 2540 University Blvd. I-675, exit 17 (N Fairfield Rd), just n, 0.5 mi sw on Colonel Glenn Hwy. Int corridors. **Pets:** Small. $50 deposit/pet, $10 daily fee/pet. Service with restrictions, supervision.

[ASK] [S🐾] [✕] [🛏] [💻] [≈]

▲▲▲ ▽▽▽ Red Roof Inn-Fairborn SH
(937) 426-6116. **$54-$68.** 2580 Colonel Glenn Hwy. I-675, exit 17 (N Fairfield Rd). Ext corridors. **Pets:** Accepted.

[SAVE] [✕] [🐾] [🛏] [💻]

FAIRLAWN

▲▲▲ ▽▽ Akron Super 8 Motel SH
(330) 666-8887. **$35-$79.** 79 Rothrock Rd. I-77, exit 137A, just e. Int corridors. **Pets:** Medium, other species. $5 daily fee/pet. Service with restrictions, crate.

[SAVE] [S🐾] [✕] [🐾] [🛏] [💻]

▽▽ Motel 6 Akron North M
(330) 666-0566. **$39-$64.** 99 Rothrock Rd. I-77, exit 137A, just e. Ext corridors. **Pets:** Accepted.

[✕] [🐾]

▽▽▽ The Residence Inn by Marriott SH ❀
(330) 666-4811. **$109-$119.** 120 W Montrose Ave. I-77, exit 137B, just w. Ext corridors. **Pets:** Medium, other species. $75 one-time fee/room. Service with restrictions.

[ASK] [S🐾] [✕] [🛏] [💻] [≈] [✕]

FINDLAY

▲▲▲ ▽▽ Econo Lodge M
(419) 422-0154. **$35-$65.** 316 Emma St. I-75, exit 157, just w. Ext corridors. **Pets:** Medium. $10 daily fee/pet. Service with restrictions, crate.

[SAVE] [S🐾] [✕] [🛏] [💻]

▲▲▲ ▽ Rodeway Inn M
(419) 424-1133. **$44-$54.** 1901 Broad Ave. I-75, exit 159, 0.5 mi e. Ext corridors. **Pets:** Accepted.

[SAVE] [S🐾] [✕] [🛏] [💻] [≈]

▽▽ Super 8 Motel-Findlay SH
(419) 422-8863. **$45-$64.** 1600 Fox St. I-75, exit 159, just e. Int corridors. **Pets:** Accepted.

[ASK] [S🐾] [✕] [🐾] [🛏]

FOSTORIA

AAA ◆ **Days Inn** **M**
(419) 435-6511. **$56-$70.** 737 Independence Rd. SR 12, 1 mi w of SR 23. Ext corridors. **Pets:** Medium, other species. $25 deposit/pet. Service with restrictions, supervision.
[SAVE] [S🐾] [✕] [🛏] [🖵]

FREDERICKTOWN

◆◆◆◆ **Heartland Country Resort** [BB] ❧
(419) 768-9300. **$125-$175, 7 day notice.** 3020 Township Rd 190. I-71, exit 151, 2 mi e on SR 95, 2 mi s on SR 314, then 1 mi e on SR 179. Int corridors. **Pets:** Other species. $15 daily fee/room. Crate.
[ASK] [✕] [🛏] [🖵] [⊇]

FREMONT

AAA ◆◆◆ **Comfort Inn & Suites** [SH] ❧
(419) 355-9300. **$84-$211.** 840 Sean Dr. I-80/90, exit 91, 2 mi s on SR 53. Int corridors. **Pets:** Other species. $15 one-time fee/pet. Designated rooms, service with restrictions, supervision.
[SAVE] [S🐾] [✕] [🖑] [🛏] [🖵] [⊇]

AAA ◆◆◆ **Holiday Inn-Fremont** [SH]
(419) 334-2682. **$89-$129.** 3422 Port Clinton Rd. I-80/90, exit 91, just s. Int corridors. **Pets:** Other species. Designated rooms, service with restrictions, supervision.
[SAVE] [S🐾] [✕] [⫶M] [🛏] [🖵] [🍴] [⊇] [⊠]

GALION

◆ **Hometown Inn** **M**
(419) 468-9909. **$50-$175.** 172 N Portland Way. 1 mi w on SR 598, n of jct SR 309/61/19. Ext/int corridors. **Pets:** Other species. $10 daily fee/room. Service with restrictions, supervision.
[ASK] [S🐾] [✕] [🛏]

GALLIPOLIS

AAA ◆ **William Ann Motel** **M**
(740) 446-3373. **$50-$65.** 918 2nd Ave. 0.8 mi n on SR 7. Ext corridors. **Pets:** Accepted.
[SAVE] [✕] [🛏]

GREEN

◆◆ **Super 8 Motel** [SH]
(330) 899-9888. **$55-$70.** 1605 Corporate Woods Pkwy. I-77, exit 118, just w. **Pets:** $6 daily fee/pet. Service with restrictions, crate.
[ASK] [S🐾] [✕] [🛏] [🖵] [⊇]

GREENVILLE

AAA ◆◆◆ **Greenville Inn** [SH]
(937) 548-3613. **$65-$85, 3 day notice.** 851 E Martin. Jct US 36 and 127, 0.3 mi w on SR 571. Int corridors. **Pets:** Medium. $75 deposit/room. Service with restrictions, crate.
[SAVE] [S🐾] [✕] [🔊] [🛏] [🖵] [🍴]

HOLLAND

◆◆ **Cross Country Inn** **M**
(419) 866-6565. **$47-$54.** 1201 E Mall Dr. I-475, exit 8, just w on SR 2. Ext corridors. **Pets:** Accepted.
[ASK] [S🐾] [✕] [🖑] [⊇]

AAA ◆◆◆ **Red Roof Inn Toledo/Holland** **M**
(419) 866-5512. **$44-$61.** 1214 Corporate Dr. I-475, exit 8, just e on Holland-Sylvania Rd, then just n to Trust Dr. Ext corridors. **Pets:** Other species. Service with restrictions, crate.
[SAVE] [✕] [🔊] [🛏]

◆◆◆ **Residence Inn by Marriott** [SH]
(419) 867-9555. **$89-$129.** 6101 Trust Dr. I-475, exit 8, just e to Holland-Sylvania Rd, then just n. Ext corridors. **Pets:** Other species. $10 daily fee/room, $50 one-time fee/room. Service with restrictions, supervision.
[ASK] [S🐾] [✕] [🔊] [🛏] [🖵] [⊇] [⊠]

HUBER HEIGHTS

◆ **Travelodge** **M**
(937) 236-9361. **$50-$70, 7 day notice.** 7911 Brandt Pike. I-70, exit 38, just s at SR 201. Ext/int corridors. **Pets:** Accepted.
[ASK] [S🐾] [✕] [🛏] [🖵] [⊇]

HURON

AAA ◆ **Plantation Motel** **M**
(419) 433-4790. **$38-$95, 3 day notice.** 2815 E Cleveland Rd. 3 mi e on US 6. Ext corridors. **Pets:** Other species. $7 daily fee/pet. Service with restrictions, supervision.
[SAVE] [✕] [🛏] [🖵] [⊇]

JACKSON

◆ **Knights Inn** **M**
(740) 286-2135. **$48-$62.** 404 Chillicothe St. 0.7 mi n on US 35 business route. Ext corridors. **Pets:** Other species. $20 deposit/pet.
[ASK] [S🐾] [✕] [🛏]

JEFFERSONVILLE

AAA ◆◆◆ **AmeriHost Inn-Jeffersonville North** [SH]
(740) 426-6400. **$74-$86.** 10160 Carr Rd NW. I-71, exit 69 (SR 41). Int corridors. **Pets:** Accepted.
[SAVE] [S🐾] [✕] [⫶M] [🖑] [🛏] [🖵] [⊇]

KENT

◆◆ **Alden Inn** **M**
(330) 678-9927. **$45-$55.** I-76, exit 33. Ext/int corridors. **Pets:** Accepted.
[ASK] [S🐾] [✕] [🛏]

AAA ◆◆◆ **Ramada Inn-Akron/Kent** [SH] ❧
(330) 678-0101. **$59-$99.** 4363 SR 43. I-76, exit 33. Ext corridors. **Pets:** Large, other species. $50 deposit/room. Service with restrictions, crate.
[SAVE] [S🐾] [✕] [🔊] [🛏] [🖵] [🍴] [⊇] [⊠]

Super 8 Motel SH
(330) 678-8817. **$44-$74.** 4380 Edson Rd. I-76, exit 33. Int corridors. **Pets:** Other species. $5 one-time fee/pet. Service with restrictions, supervision.
ASK S✗ 🐾 🖥

LIMA

Motel 6-586 M
(419) 228-0456. **$41-$53.** 1800 Harding Hwy. I-75, exit 125, just e, jct SR 117 and 309. Ext corridors. **Pets:** Accepted.
S✗ ⌨

LISBON

Lisbon Inn SH
(330) 420-0111. **$79-$89.** 40952 SR 154. SR 11, exit SR 154, just w. Int corridors. **Pets:** Other species. $10 daily fee/pet. Service with restrictions, supervision.
SAVE S✗ 🐾 🖥

LOGAN

Shawnee Inn M
(740) 385-5674. **$55-$65, 3 day notice.** 30916 Lake Logan Rd. SR 664, just s of US 33. Ext corridors. **Pets:** Medium. $5 daily fee/pet. Designated rooms, service with restrictions, supervision.
SAVE S✗ 🖥

LOUDONVILLE

Little Brown Inn M
(419) 994-5525. **$46-$73.** 940 S Market St. 1 mi s on SR 3. Int corridors. **Pets:** Accepted.
✗ 🖥

MANSFIELD

AmeriHost Inn Mansfield SH
(419) 756-6670. **$59-$179.** 180 E Hanley Rd. I-71, exit 169, jct SR 13. Int corridors. **Pets:** $25 deposit/room. Service with restrictions, supervision.
SAVE S✗ 🐾 ⌨ 🖥 ≈ ✗

Baymont Inn & Suites Mansfield SH
(419) 774-0005. **$79-$99.** 120 Stander Ave. I-71, exit 169. Int corridors. **Pets:** Accepted.
SAVE S✗ ⌨M 🐾 ⌨ 🖥 ≈

Comfort Inn North SH
(419) 529-1000. **$65-$130.** 500 N Trimble Rd. Jct US 30. Int corridors. **Pets:** Accepted.
ASK S✗ 🐾 🖥 ≈ ✗

Econo Lodge SH
(419) 589-3333. **$34-$60.** 1017 Koogle Rd. I-71, exit 176, just e. Int corridors. **Pets:** Medium. $5 daily fee/pet. Service with restrictions, supervision.
SAVE S✗ 🖥 ≈

Knights Inn M
(419) 529-2100. **$44-$95.** 555 N Trimble Rd. Jct US 30. Ext corridors. **Pets:** Accepted.
ASK S✗ 🐾 🖥

Spruce Hill Inn & Cottages CA
(419) 756-2200. **$99-$125, 3 day notice.** 3230 O'Possum Run Rd. I-71, exit 169, just s to O'Possum Run Rd; by Exxon station. Ext corridors. **Pets:** $25 daily fee/pet. No service.
ASK S✗ 🖥 🖥

Super 8 Motel SH
(419) 756-8875. **$58-$90, 14 day notice.** 2425 Interstate Cir. I-71, exit 169. Int corridors. **Pets:** Other species. $50 deposit/room. Designated rooms, service with restrictions, supervision.
ASK S✗ 🐾 🖥

MARIETTA

Econo Lodge M
(740) 374-8481. **$49-$79.** 702 Pike St. I-77, exit 1. Ext corridors. **Pets:** $7 daily fee/pet. Service with restrictions, supervision.
SAVE S✗ 🖥 ≈

Knights Inn M
(740) 373-7373. **$49-$65.** 506 Pike St. I-77, exit 1. Ext corridors. **Pets:** $5 one-time fee/pet. Service with restrictions, crate.
SAVE S✗ 🖥 ≈

The Lafayette Hotel LH
(740) 373-5522. **$65-$125, 3 day notice.** 101 Front St. Center. Int corridors. **Pets:** Other species. $100 deposit/room. Supervision.
ASK S✗ 🖥 🖥 🍴

Super 8 Motel-Marietta SH
(740) 374-8888. **$40-$60.** 46 Acme St. I-77, exit 1, just w. Int corridors. **Pets:** Medium. $5 daily fee/pet. Designated rooms, service with restrictions, supervision.
ASK S✗ 🐾 🖥

MARION

Comfort Inn-Marion SH
(740) 389-5552. **$49-$69.** 256 James Way. Jct US 23 and SR 95. Int corridors. **Pets:** Accepted.
ASK S✗ 🐾 ⌨ 🖥 ≈

MASSILLON

Hampton Inn-Canton/Massillon SH
(330) 834-1144. **$79-$109.** 44 First St SW. Downtown. Int corridors. **Pets:** Accepted.
ASK S✗ ⌨M 🖥

MAUMEE

Arrowhead Super 8 Toledo SH 🐾
(419) 897-3800. **$45-$69.** 1390 Arrowhead Rd. I-475, exit 6, just e. Int corridors. **Pets:** Medium, other species. $10 one-time fee/room. Service with restrictions, supervision.
SAVE ✗ 🐾 ⌨ 🖥

Comfort Inn Toledo West/Maumee SH
(419) 893-2800. **$85.** 1426 S Reynolds Rd. I-80/90, exit 59, just s. Int corridors. **Pets:** Small. $10 daily fee/room. Service with restrictions, supervision.
SAVE S✗ 🖥 ≈

▼▼▼▼ **Country Inn & Suites By Carlson of Toledo** SH
(419) 893-8576. **$65-$85.** 541 W Dussel Dr. I-475, exit 6, just e. Int corridors. **Pets:** Accepted.
[ASK] [S] [✕] [⌖] [⌘] [🔒] [💻] [⇌]

ⓐⓐⓐ ▼▼▼ **Days Inn-Toledo/Maumee** M
(419) 897-6900. **$34-$69.** 1704 Tollgate Dr. I-80/90, exit 59, just s. Ext corridors. **Pets:** Large. $10 daily fee/room. Designated rooms, service with restrictions, supervision.
[SAVE] [S] [✕] [⌖] [⌘] [⇌]

ⓐⓐⓐ ▼▼▼ **Econ Lodge-Toledo/Maumee** M
(419) 893-9960. **$40-$72.** 150 Dussel Dr. I-80/90, exit 59, just s. Ext corridors. **Pets:** Other species. $25 deposit/room. Designated rooms, service with restrictions, crate.
[SAVE] [S] [✕] [⌖] [🔒] [💻] [⇌]

▼▼▼▼ **Homewood Suites by Hilton-Toledo/Maumee** SH
(419) 897-0980. **$116, 3 day notice.** 1410 Arrowhead Rd. I-475, exit 6, just e. Int corridors. **Pets:** Accepted.
[ASK] [S] [✕] [⌖] [⌘] [🔒] [💻] [⇌] [✕]

ⓐⓐⓐ ▼▼▼ **Red Roof Inn-Maumee** M ❖
(419) 893-0292. **$46-$72.** 1570 S Reynolds Rd. I-80/90, exit 59, just s. Ext/int corridors. **Pets:** Other species. Service with restrictions.
[SAVE] [✕] [⌖] [⌘] [🔒]

MENTOR

ⓐⓐⓐ ▼▼▼▼ **Best Western Lawnfield Inn & Suites** SH ❖
(440) 205-7378. **$69-$129.** 8434 Mentor Ave. I-90, exit 193, 2 mi n on SR 306, then 2 mi e. Int corridors. **Pets:** Medium. Service with restrictions, crate.
[SAVE] [S] [✕] [⌖M] [🔒] [💻] [⇌]

▼▼▼▼ **Residence Inn by Marriott** SH
(440) 392-0800. **$85-$125.** 5660 Emerald Ct. Jct SR 2 and Heisley Rd, just s. Int corridors. **Pets:** Other species. $250 one-time fee/room. Service with restrictions.
[ASK] [S] [✕] [⌘] [🔒] [💻] [⇌] [✕]

▼▼ **Studio 6 #6019** M ❖
(440) 946-0749. **$53-$63.** 7677 Reynolds Rd. Just s of SR 2 on SR 306. Ext corridors. **Pets:** Small, other species. $10 daily fee/pet. Service with restrictions, crate.
[✕] [⌖M] [⌘] [🔒] [💻]

▼▼ **Super 8 Motel** SH
(440) 951-8558. **Call for rates.** 7325 Palisades Pkwy. On SR 306, just s of SR 2. Int corridors. **Pets:** Accepted.
[✕] [🔒]

MIAMISBURG

▼▼▼▼ **Holiday Inn-Dayton Mall** SH
(937) 434-8030. **$109-$139.** 31 Prestige Plaza Dr. I-75, exit 44, just e on SR 725. Int corridors. **Pets:** Small. $25 one-time fee/room. Service with restrictions, supervision.
[ASK] [S] [✕] [⌖] [🔒] [💻] [🍴] [⇌] [✕]

▼▼▼▼ **Homewood Suites by Hilton-Dayton South** SH
(937) 432-0000. **$89-$129.** 3100 Contemporary Ln. I-75, exit 44, just e on SR 725. Int corridors. **Pets:** Other species. $250 deposit/room, $10 daily fee/room, $50 one-time fee/room. Service with restrictions, supervision.
[ASK] [S] [✕] [⌖] [⌘] [🔒] [💻] [⇌]

ⓐⓐⓐ ▼▼▼ **Red Roof Inn-South** SH
(937) 866-0705. **$44-$64.** 222 Byers Rd. I-75, exit 44, just w on SR 725. Ext corridors. **Pets:** Medium. Service with restrictions, supervision.
[SAVE] [✕] [⌖] [⌘] [🔒]

▼▼▼▼ **Residence Inn by Marriott-Dayton South** SH
(937) 434-7881. **$129-$150.** 155 Prestige Pl. I-75, exit 44, just e on SR 725. Ext corridors. **Pets:** Accepted.
[S] [✕] [⌘] [🔒] [💻] [⇌]

▼▼▼▼ **Signature Inn Dayton South** SH
(937) 865-0077. **$78-$87.** 250 Byers Rd. I-75, exit 44, just w on SR 725. Int corridors. **Pets:** Small. Service with restrictions, crate.
[✕] [⌖] [🔒] [💻] [⇌]

MILAN

▼▼ **Motel 6-4016** SH ❖
(419) 499-8001. **$34-$144, 3 day notice.** 11406 US 250 N. I-80/90, exit 118, 1.5 mi n. Int corridors. **Pets:** Large, other species. Service with restrictions, crate.
[ASK] [S] [✕] [⌘] [⇌]

MONTPELIER

▼▼ **Ramada Inn & Suites** SH
(419) 485-5555. **$99.** 13508 SR 15. I-80/90, exit 13, just s. Int corridors. **Pets:** Other species. Service with restrictions, supervision.
[ASK] [S] [✕] [⌖] [🔒] [💻] [🍴] [⇌] [✕]

MORAINE

▼▼▼▼ **Holiday Inn Hotel & Suites** SH
(937) 294-1471. **$94-$129.** 2455 Dryden Rd. I-75, exit 50A. Int corridors. **Pets:** Medium, other species. $10 daily fee/room. Service with restrictions, crate.
[ASK] [S] [✕] [⌖] [⌘] [🔒] [💻] [🍴] [⇌] [✕]

ⓐⓐⓐ ▼▼▼ **Super 8 Motel-Moraine** M ❖
(937) 298-0380. **$39-$99, 7 day notice.** 2450 Dryden Rd. I-75, exit 50A. Ext corridors. **Pets:** Medium, other species. $10 one-time fee/room. Service with restrictions, supervision.
[SAVE] [S] [✕] [🔒] [⇌]

MOUNT GILEAD

ⓐⓐⓐ ▼▼ **Knights Inn** M
(419) 946-6010. **$42-$57.** 5898 SR 95. I-71, exit 151, 0.3 mi w. Ext corridors. **Pets:** Dogs only. $15 deposit/room. Service with restrictions, supervision.
[SAVE] [✕] [🔒]

MOUNT VERNON

▼▼▼ Holiday Inn Express **SH**
(740) 392-1900. **$72-$150, 14 day notice.** 11555 Upper Gilchrist Rd. 3 mi e on US 36. Int corridors. **Pets:** Other species. Designated rooms, service with restrictions, supervision.

⊗ 🗟ᴹ 🖾 🗋 💻 ⊐

NEWCOMERSTOWN

▼▼▼ Hampton Inn **SH** ☙
(740) 498-9800. **$69-$114, 7 day notice.** 200 Morris Crossing. I-77, exit 65, 0.8 mi w. Int corridors. **Pets:** Medium, other species. Service with restrictions, crate.

🗚🗚🗲 🗟 ⊗ 🗋 💻 ⊐

NEW PHILADELPHIA

▼ Days Inn-New Philadelphia **SH**
(330) 339-6644. **$53-$65.** 1281 W High St. I-77, exit 81, just e. Int corridors. **Pets:** Accepted.

🗚🗚🗲 🗟 ⊗ 🗐 ⊐

▼◆▼ Hampton Inn **SH** ☙
(330) 339-7000. **$75-$85.** 1299 W High St. I-77, exit 81, just e. **Pets:** Very small, dogs only. $50 deposit/room. Service with restrictions, supervision.

🗚🗚🗲 🗟 ⊗ 🗟ᴹ 🗲 🗋 💻 ⊐ ⊗

▼ Motel 6–254 **M**
(330) 339-6446. **$35-$47.** 181 Bluebell Dr SW. I-77, exit 81, 0.4 mi e. Ext corridors. **Pets:** Accepted.

🗟 ⊗ 🖾 ⊐

▼▼▼ Schoenbrunn Inn by Christopher **SH**
(330) 339-4334. **$69-$99.** 1186 W High Ave. I-77, exit 81, 0.6 mi e. Int corridors. **Pets:** Accepted.

🗚🗚🗲 🗟 ⊗ 🖾 🗋 💻 ⊐ ⊗

NEWTON FALLS

▼ Rodeway Inn **M** ☙
(330) 872-0988. **$35-$75.** 4248 SR 5. I-80, exit 209, just w. Ext corridors. **Pets:** Other species. $5 daily fee/pet. Service with restrictions.

🗚🗚🗲 🗟 ⊗ 🗋

NORTH CANTON

▼▼ Super 8 Motel Canton North **M**
(330) 492-5030. **$40-$60.** 3950 Convenience Cir NW. I-77, exit 109 southbound, 0.3 mi e on Everhard, 0.3 mi s on Whipple; exit 109A northbound, 0.3 mi s on Whipple. Ext corridors. **Pets:** Accepted.

🗚🗚🗲 🗟 ⊗ 🗋 💻 ⊐

NORTH LIMA

▼ Rodeway Inn **M**
(330) 549-3988. **$40-$85.** 10650 Market St. I-76, exit 232, 0.3 mi s on SR 7. Ext corridors. **Pets:** Accepted.

🗚🗚🗲 🗟 ⊗ 🗋 💻

▼ Super 8 Motel **M**
(330) 549-2187. **Call for rates.** 10076 Market St. I-76, exit 232, 0.4 mi n. Ext corridors. **Pets:** Accepted.

⊗ 🗋 ⊐

NORTHWOOD

▼▼ Comfort Inn South **SH** ☙
(419) 666-2600. **$60-$85.** 2426 Oregon Rd. I-75, exit 198, just e. Int corridors. **Pets:** Small, other species. $10 daily fee/room. Service with restrictions, supervision.

🗚🗚🗲 🗟 ⊗ 🗋 💻 🕎

NORWALK

▼▼ Econo Lodge **M**
(419) 668-5656. **$38-$138.** 342 Milan Ave. 3 mi n on SR 250; 6 mi s of I-80/90 (Ohio Tpke), on SR 250. Ext corridors. **Pets:** Small, dogs only. $50 deposit/pet, $25 one-time fee/pet. Designated rooms, service with restrictions, supervision.

🗚🗚🗲 🗟 ⊗ 🗋 💻 ⊐

OBERLIN

▼▼▼ Oberlin Inn **CI**
(440) 775-1111. **$109-$179.** 7 N Main St. On SR 58; jct College and Main sts; center. Int corridors. **Pets:** Small. Designated rooms, service with restrictions, crate.

🗚🗚🗲 🗟 ⊗ 🗋 💻 🕎

OREGON

▼▼▼ Comfort Inn East **SH**
(419) 691-8911. **$69-$74.** 2930 Navarre Ave. I-280, exit 7, just n on access road, then 0.5 mi e on SR 2 (Navarre Ave). Int corridors. **Pets:** Other species. $10 one-time fee/room. Designated rooms, service with restrictions, supervision.

🗚🗚🗲 🗟 ⊗ 🗐 🗋 💻 ⊐

▼▼▼ Sleep Inn & Suites **SH**
(419) 697-7800. **$74-$79.** 1761 Meijer Cir. I-280, exit 6. Int corridors. **Pets:** $12 one-time fee/pet. Designated rooms, service with restrictions, supervision.

🗚🗚🗲 🗟 ⊗ 🖾 🗋 💻 ⊐

PERRYSBURG

AAA ▼▼▼ Baymont Inn & Suites Toledo-Perrysburg **SH** ☙
(419) 872-0000. **$69-$79.** 1154 Professional Dr. I-75, exit 193, just w. Int corridors. **Pets:** Large, other species. $50 deposit/room. Designated rooms, service with restrictions, supervision.

SAVE 🗟 ⊗ 🗐 🖾 🗋 💻

AAA ▼▼▼ Howard Johnson Inn Toledo South **M** ☙
(419) 837-5245. **$44-$74.** 3555 Hanley Rd. I-80/90 (Ohio Tpke), exit 71 to I-280, exit 1B. Ext/int corridors. **Pets:** Other species. $10 daily fee/pet. Service with restrictions, crate.

SAVE 🗟 ⊗ 🗐 🗋 💻 ⊐

AAA ▼ Red Carpet Inn **M**
(419) 872-2902. **$40-$50.** 26054 N Dixie Hwy. I-475, exit 2, just s. Ext corridors. **Pets:** Accepted.

SAVE 🗟 ⊗ 🗋

PIQUA

▼▼▼ Comfort Inn-Piqua **SH**
(937) 778-8100. **$61-$90.** 987 E Ash St. I-75, exit 82. Int corridors. **Pets:** Medium. $25 deposit/room. Designated rooms, service with restrictions, crate.
(ASK) 🛏 ✕ 🖊 🐾 🖥 🖦 🐾

▼▼▼ La Quinta Inn-Piqua **SH**
(937) 615-0140. **Call for rates.** 950 E Ash St. I-75, exit 82, just w. Int corridors. **Pets:** Accepted.
✕ 🐾 🖥 🖦 🐾

POLAND

AAA ▼▼ Red Roof Inn **SH**
(330) 758-1999. **$43-$76.** 1051 Tiffany S. I-680, exit 11, just w. Int corridors. **Pets:** Accepted.
(SAVE) ✕ 🖊 🐾 🖥 🖦

▼▼▼ Residence Inn-Youngstown **SH**
(330) 726-1747. **$110-$120.** 7396 Tiffany S. I-680, exit 11, just w. Int corridors. **Pets:** Accepted.
(ASK) 🛏 ✕ 🖊 🐾 🖥 🖦 🐾 ✕

PORT CLINTON

AAA ▼▼ Commodore Perry Inn &
Suites **SH** ❀
(419) 732-2645. **$49-$219.** 255 W Lakeshore Dr. Just n of the bridge. Int corridors. **Pets:** Medium. $15 one-time fee/pet. Service with restrictions, crate.
(SAVE) 🛏 ✕ 🐾 🖥 🍴 🐾

▼▼ Country Hearth Inn **M**
(419) 732-2111. **$81-$130.** 1815 E Perry St. 1.2 mi e on SR 163, w of jct SR 2. Ext/int corridors. **Pets:** Accepted.
(ASK) 🛏 ✕ 🖥 🖦 🐾

RIO GRANDE

▼ College Hill Motel **M**
(740) 245-5326. **Call for rates.** 10987 State Rt 588. US 35, exit Rio Grande. Ext corridors. **Pets:** Accepted.
✕ 🖥

ST. CLAIRSVILLE

AAA ▼▼ Knights Inn-St.
Clairsville/Wheeling **M**
(740) 695-5038. **$45-$68.** 51260 National Rd. I-70, exit 218, 0.5 mi ne on US 40. Ext corridors. **Pets:** Medium, other species. $5 one-time fee/room. Service with restrictions, crate.
(SAVE) 🛏 ✕ 🖊 🖥 🖦 🐾

AAA ▼▼ Red Roof Inn **M**
(740) 695-4057. **$44-$76.** 68301 Red Roof Ln. I-70, exit 218, just n. Ext corridors. **Pets:** Large, other species. Service with restrictions, supervision.
(SAVE) ✕ 🖥

ST. MARYS

AAA ▼▼▼ AmeriHost Inn-St. Marys **SH**
(419) 394-2710. **$67-$84.** 1410 Commerce Dr. Jct US 33 and SR 29, just s. Int corridors. **Pets:** Small. $35 daily fee/pet. Designated rooms, service with restrictions, supervision.
(SAVE) 🛏 ✕ 🖊 🐾 🖥 🖦 🐾

AAA ▼▼ S & W Motel & Suites **SH**
(419) 394-2341. **$55-$99.** 1321 Celina Rd. SR 29, 0.8 mi w on SR 703. Ext corridors. **Pets:** $10 daily fee/pet. Designated rooms, service with restrictions, supervision.
(SAVE) 🛏 ✕ 🖥 🖦 🐾 ✕

SANDUSKY

▼▼ Best Budget Inn **M**
(419) 625-7252. **$35-$149.** 5918 Milan Rd. Jct US 250 and SR 2. Ext/int corridors. **Pets:** Accepted.
(ASK) 🛏 ✕ 🖥 🐾

▼▼ Clarion Inn Sandusky **SH**
(419) 625-6280. **$60-$160.** 1119 Sandusky Mall Blvd. On US 250, 1.5 mi n of SR 2. Int corridors. **Pets:** Medium. $100 deposit/pet. Service with restrictions, supervision.
(ASK) 🛏 ✕ 🖊 🖥 🖦 🍴 🐾 ✕

SEVILLE

AAA ▼▼◆ Super 8 Motel-Seville **SH**
(330) 769-8880. **$55-$89.** 6116 Speedway Dr. Jct SR 224 and Lake Rd. Int corridors. **Pets:** Small. $20 one-time fee/pet. Service with restrictions, supervision.
(SAVE) 🛏 ✕ 🖦 🐾 🖥

SIDNEY

AAA ▼▼▼ Comfort Inn **SH**
(937) 492-3001. **$70-$90.** 1959 W Michigan Ave. I-75, exit 92, on SR 47. Int corridors. **Pets:** Small, other species. $25 deposit/pet. Service with restrictions, supervision.
(SAVE) 🛏 ✕ 🖥 🖦 🐾

▼▼ Days Inn Sidney **M**
(937) 492-1104. **$50-$72.** 420 Folkerth Ave. I-75, exit 92, at SR 47. Ext corridors. **Pets:** Medium. $5 daily fee/pet. Service with restrictions, supervision.
(ASK) 🛏 ✕ 🖥 🍴 🐾

AAA ▼▼▼ Holiday Inn **SH**
(937) 492-1131. **$89.** 400 Folkerth Ave. I-75, exit 92, just w. Int corridors. **Pets:** Small. $50 deposit/pet. Designated rooms, service with restrictions, supervision.
(SAVE) 🛏 ✕ 🖊 🖥 🖦 🍴 🐾

SPRINGFIELD

AAA ▼ Knights Inn **M**
(937) 325-8721. **$36-$52.** 2207 W Main St. I-70, exit 52, 1.7 mi n on US 68, then just e on US 40. Ext corridors. **Pets:** $10 daily fee/room. Service with restrictions, supervision.
(SAVE) 🛏 ✕ 🖥 🐾

(AAA) ▼▼▼▼ The "New" Courtyard by Marriott
Springfield Ohio SH
(937) 322-3600. $95. 100 S Fountain Ave. I-70, exit 54, 2 mi n on SR 72, follow Limestone St; downtown. Int corridors. Pets: Medium. Service with restrictions, crate.
SAVE S/b ✕ ☞ ☐ ☐ ⑪

(AAA) ▼▼▼ Ramada Limited SH
(937) 328-0123. $79-$89. 319 E Leffel Ln. I-70, exit 54, just n. Int corridors. Pets: $10 daily fee/pet. Service with restrictions, supervision.
SAVE S/b ✕ ☞ ☐ ☐ ⇌

(AAA) ▼▼▼ Red Roof Inn SH
(937) 325-5356. $59-$99. 155 W Leffel Ln. I-70, exit 54, just n, then w. Int corridors. Pets: Small. $10 one-time fee/pet. No service, supervision.
SAVE S/b ✕ ☐ ☐ ⇌

STRASBURG

(AAA) ▼▼▼▼ Ramada Limited Dover/Strasburg SH
(330) 878-1400. $60-$110. 509 S Wooster Ave. I-77, exit 87, 0.4 mi n on US 250 and SR 21. Int corridors. Pets: $10 daily fee/room. Service with restrictions, supervision.
SAVE S/b ✕ Ⓜ ☞ Ⓚ ☐ ☐ ⇌

STREETSBORO

▼▼ Comfort Inn SH
(330) 626-5511. $65-$135. 9789 SR 14. I-80, exit 187, 0.5 mi s. Int corridors. Pets: Large. $25 one-time fee/room. Service with restrictions, crate.
ASK S/b ✕ ☐ ☐

▼▼ Microtel Inn & Suites of Streetsboro SH
(330) 422-1234. $50-$119. 9371 SR 14. I-80, exit 187, 1.2 mi s. Int corridors. Pets: Medium. $25 one-time fee/room. Service with restrictions, supervision.
ASK S/b ✕ Ⓚ ☐ ☐ ⇌

▼▼ TownePlace Suites by Marriott SH
(330) 422-1855. $79-$159. 795 Mondial Pkwy. I-80, exit 187, 0.8 mi s. Int corridors. Pets: Medium, other species. $100 one-time fee/pet.
ASK ✕ ☐ ☐ ⇌

SWANTON

▼▼ Super 8 Toledo Airport SH
(419) 865-2002. $69. 10753 Airport Hwy. I-80/90, exit 3A, just s, then e. Int corridors. Pets: Other species. Service with restrictions, supervision.
ASK S/b ✕ Ⓚ ☐

TIFFIN

▼▼▼ Holiday Inn Express SH
(419) 443-5100. $79. 78 Shaffer Park Dr. Just w of mall. Int corridors. Pets: $20 one-time fee/room. Service with restrictions, supervision.
ASK S/b ✕ ☐ ☐ ⇌

▼▼▼ Quality Inn SH
(419) 447-6313. $65-$70. 1927 S SR 53. Jct US 224 and SR 53, 2 mi sw. Ext/int corridors. Pets: Medium. $10 daily fee/pet. Designated rooms, service with restrictions, crate.
ASK S/b ✕ ☞ Ⓚ ☐ ☐ ⑪ ⇌

TOLEDO

(AAA) ▼▼▼ Comfort Inn-North SH
(419) 476-0170. $64-$69. 445 E Alexis Rd. I-75, exit 210, 2 mi w on SR 184; just e of jct US 24 and SR 184. Int corridors. Pets: Other species. $10 daily fee/room. Designated rooms, service with restrictions, supervision.
SAVE S/b ✕ ☞ ☐ ☐

(AAA) ▼▼▼▼ Radisson Hotel Toledo SH
(419) 241-3000. $139. 101 N Summit St. Between Jefferson and Monroe sts; downtown. Int corridors. Pets: Accepted.
SAVE S/b ✕ ☐ ⑪

▼▼▼ Ramada Inn & Suites SH
(419) 242-8885. Call for rates. 141 N Summit St. Between Jefferson and Monroe sts; downtown. Int corridors. Pets: Medium. $50 one-time fee/pet. Service with restrictions, supervision.
✕ ☞ ☐ ☐ ⑪ ⇌

(AAA) ▼▼▼ Red Roof Inn Toledo University M
(419) 536-0118. $47-$67. 3530 Executive Pkwy. I-475, exit 17, 0.5 mi s on Secor Rd, then just e. Ext corridors. Pets: Large, other species. Service with restrictions, supervision.
SAVE ✕ ☞ Ⓚ ☐

TROY

▼ Knights Inn Troy M
(937) 339-1515. $50. 30 Troy Town Dr. I-75, exit 74, just w on SR 41. Ext corridors. Pets: Accepted.
ASK S/b ✕ ☐ ☐ ✕

▼▼▼ Residence Inn By Marriott SH
(937) 440-9303. $79-$119. 87 Troy Town Dr. I-75, exit 74, just w on SR 41. Int corridors. Pets: Large, other species. $200 one-time fee/room. Service with restrictions.
ASK S/b ✕ ☞ Ⓚ ☐ ☐ ⇌ ✕

UHRICHSVILLE

(AAA) ▼▼▼ Best Western Country Inn M
(740) 922-0774. $49-$70. 111 McCauley Dr. US 250, exit McCauley Dr. Ext corridors. Pets: $15 daily fee/room. Service with restrictions, supervision.
SAVE S/b ✕ ☞ ☐ ☐

URBANA

(AAA) ▼▼▼ Logan Lodge Motel M
(937) 652-2188. $45-$70. 2551 S US Hwy 68. 1.3 mi s. Ext corridors. Pets: $15 daily fee/room. Service with restrictions, supervision.
SAVE S/b ✕ ☐ ⇌

VANDALIA

(AAA) ▼▼▼ Travelodge Dayton Airport M
(937) 898-8321. $60-$110. 75 Corporate Center Dr. Off National Rd. Ext corridors. Pets: Small. $10 daily fee/pet. Designated rooms, service with restrictions, supervision.
SAVE S/b ✕ ☐ ☐ ⇌

VERMILION

▼▼▼▼ Holiday Inn Express SH
(440) 967-8770. **$89-$149.** 2417 SR 60. Jct SR 2 and 60. Int corridors. **Pets:** Medium, other species. $40 deposit/room. Service with restrictions, crate.
[ASK] [S◑] [✕] [⌖] [◔] [🛏] [▣] [≈]

ⒶⒶⒶ ▼ Motel Plaza M ❀
(440) 967-3191. **$65-$89.** 4645 Liberty Ave. On US 6, 2 mi e of SR 60. Ext corridors. **Pets:** Dogs only. $25 deposit/pet. Service with restrictions, supervision.
[SAVE] [S◑] [✕] [🛏] [▣]

WADSWORTH

ⒶⒶⒶ ▼ Legacy Inn M
(330) 336-6671. **$42-$51, 3 day notice.** 810 High St. I-76, exit 9, just s. Ext corridors. **Pets:** Medium. Service with restrictions, crate.
[SAVE] [S◑] [✕] [🛏] [≈]

WAPAKONETA

ⒶⒶⒶ ▼▼▼ Best Western Wapakoneta SH
(419) 738-8181. **$99.** 1510 Saturn Dr. I-75 business loop at jct I-75, exit 111. Int corridors. **Pets:** Accepted.
[SAVE] [S◑] [✕] [⌖] [🛏] [▣] [≈]

▼▼▼ Super 8 Motel-Wapakoneta SH
(419) 738-8810. **$48.** 1011 Lunar Dr. I-75 business loop at jct I-75, exit 111. Ext/int corridors. **Pets:** Accepted.
[ASK] [S◑] [✕] [🛏] [▣]

ⒶⒶⒶ ▼▼▼ Travelodge SH
(419) 739-9600. **$40-$50.** 413 Apollo Dr. I-75, exit 111, just w. Ext corridors. **Pets:** Dogs only. $5 one-time fee/pet. Service with restrictions, supervision.
[SAVE] [S◑] [✕] [🛏] [▣]

WARREN

ⒶⒶⒶ ▼▼ Best Western M
(330) 392-2515. **$59-$71.** Mahoning Ave. 0.3 mi n of Courthouse Square. Ext corridors. **Pets:** Accepted.
[SAVE] [S◑] [✕] [🛏] [▣] [≈]

ⒶⒶⒶ ▼▼▼ Comfort Inn SH
(330) 393-1200. **$60-$80.** 136 N Park Ave. Downtown; east side of Courthouse Square. Int corridors. **Pets:** Medium. $10 daily fee/pet. Service with restrictions, supervision.
[SAVE] [S◑] [✕] [🛏] [▣] [⌑]

WAUSEON

ⒶⒶⒶ ▼▼▼ Best Western Del Mar M
(419) 335-1565. **$65-$159.** 8319 SR 108. I-80/90, exit 34, just s. Ext corridors. **Pets:** Medium. $17 one-time fee/pet. Service with restrictions, supervision.
[SAVE] [S◑] [✕] [⌖] [◔] [🛏] [▣] [≈]

WOOSTER

ⒶⒶⒶ ▼▼▼ Econo Lodge M ❀
(330) 264-8883. **$59-$69.** 2137 E Lincoln Way. US 30, 3 mi e. Ext corridors. **Pets:** Medium. $10 daily fee/pet. No service, supervision.
[SAVE] [S◑] [✕] [⌖] [🛏] [▣] [≈]

▼▼▼ The Wooster Inn CI
(330) 263-2660. **$80-$150.** 801 E Wayne Ave. 0.5 mi e on Liberty St, 1 mi n on Beall Ave. Int corridors. **Pets:** $15 daily fee/pet. Service with restrictions.
[✕] [🛏] [⌑] [✕]

XENIA

▼▼ Regency Inn SH
(937) 372-9954. **$47-$52.** 600 Little Main St. 1 mi w. Ext corridors. **Pets:** Small, other species. $5.65 daily fee/pet. Service with restrictions, crate.
[ASK] [S◑] [✕] [🛏] [▣]

YOUNGSTOWN

▼ Days Inn M
(330) 759-3410. **$49-$79, 14 day notice.** 1610 Motor Inn Dr. I-80, exit 229, just n. Ext corridors. **Pets:** Other species. $10 daily fee/pet. Service with restrictions, supervision.
[ASK] [S◑] [✕] [🛏] [▣] [≈]

ZANESVILLE

ⒶⒶⒶ ▼▼ Best Western Town House SH
(740) 452-4511. **$54-$94.** 135 N 7th St. I-70, exit 155, on SR 60 via signs; downtown. Ext corridors. **Pets:** Other species. $10 one-time fee/room. Designated rooms.
[SAVE] [S◑] [✕] [⌖] [🛏] [▣] [⌑]

ⒶⒶⒶ ▼▼▼ Comfort Inn SH
(740) 454-4144. **$64-$159.** 500 Monroe St. I-70, exit 155 westbound; exit 7th St eastbound, e on Elberon to light, just n on Underwood. Int corridors. **Pets:** Medium, other species. $10 one-time fee/room. Designated rooms, service with restrictions, supervision.
[SAVE] [S◑] [✕] [⌖] [◔] [🛏] [▣] [≈] [✕]

ⒶⒶⒶ ▼▼▼▼ Holiday Inn Conference Center SH
(740) 453-0771. **$69-$99.** 4645 E Pike. I-70, exit 160, on US 22 and 40. Int corridors. **Pets:** Small. Designated rooms, supervision.
[SAVE] [S◑] [✕] [⌖] [◔] [🛏] [▣] [⌑] [≈] [✕]

▼▼▼ Red Roof Inn SH ❀
(740) 453-6300. **$57-$72.** 4929 E Pike. I-70, exit 160, just s. Int corridors. **Pets:** Medium, other species. Service with restrictions, supervision.
[ASK] [S◑] [✕] [◔] [◔] [🛏] [≈]

ⒶⒶⒶ ▼▼▼ Super 8 Motel-Zanesville SH ❀
(740) 455-3124. **$49-$95.** 2440 National Rd. I-70, exit 152, just n. Int corridors. **Pets:** Medium. $10 daily fee/pet. Service with restrictions, supervision.
[SAVE] [S◑] [✕] [⌖] [🛏]

ⒶⒶⒶ ▼▼ Travelodge SH
(740) 453-0611. **$48-$70, 14 day notice.** 58 N 6th St. I-70, exit 155, on US 22 and SR 60 at Market St. Ext/int corridors. **Pets:** Medium. $8 one-time fee/pet. Supervision.
[SAVE] [S◑] [✕] [🛏] [▣]

OKLAHOMA

CITY INDEX

ALTUS

▲▲▲ ▼▼▼ Best Western Altus SH
(580) 482-9300. **$64-$74.** 2804 N Main St. 2 mi n on US 283. Ext corridors. **Pets:** Medium, other species. Service with restrictions, crate.

SAVE S X ▮ ▯ ▭ X

▼ Days Inn M
(580) 477-2300. **Call for rates.** 3202 N Main St. 2.3 mi n on US 283. Ext corridors. **Pets:** Accepted.

X ▮ ▯

ARDMORE

▲▲▲ ▼▼▼ Best Western Inn SH
(580) 223-7525. **$58-$70, 14 day notice.** 6 Holiday Dr. I-35, exit 31A, just ne. Int corridors. **Pets:** Small. $6 daily fee/pet. Designated rooms, service with restrictions, supervision.

SAVE S X ▮ ▯ ▭

▼▼ Comfort Inn SH
(580) 226-1250. **$69-$79.** 2700 W Broadway. I-35, exit 31A, just e. Int corridors. **Pets:** Other species. Service with restrictions.

X ▮ ▯ ▭

▼▼▼ Holiday Inn SH
(580) 223-7130. **$65.** 2705 Holiday Dr. I-35, exit 31A, just e. Ext corridors. **Pets:** Small. $10 one-time fee/room. Service with restrictions, supervision.

ASK S X ✎ ▮ ▯ ▯ ▭

▼▼ La Quinta Inn SH
(580) 223-7976. **$68-$74, 4 day notice.** 2432 Veterans Blvd. I-35, exit 33, just e. Ext corridors. **Pets:** Small. Service with restrictions, supervision.

ASK S X ✎ ▮ ▯ ▭

▼ Microtel Inn & Suites SH
(580) 224-2600. **$48.** 1904 Cooper Dr. I-35, exit 32, just w. Int corridors. **Pets:** Accepted.

ASK S X ✎ ▭ ▮ ▯

▼▼ Super 8 Motel SH
(580) 223-2201. **$40-$60, 7 day notice.** 2120 Veterans Blvd. I-35, exit 33, just e. Int corridors. **Pets:** Medium. $5 daily fee/pet. Service with restrictions, supervision.

ASK S X ▮ ▭

BARTLESVILLE

▼▼ Econo Lodge M
(918) 333-0710. **$59-$69.** 3910 SE Nowata Rd. Just e of jct US 60 and 75. Ext corridors. **Pets:** Very small, dogs only. $10 daily fee/pet. Service with restrictions, supervision.

ASK S X ▮ ▭

▼▼ Holiday Inn SH
(918) 333-8320. **$85.** 1410 SE Washington Blvd. Just s of jct US 75 and 60 W. Int corridors. **Pets:** Medium. $75 deposit/room. Service with restrictions, crate.

ASK S X ▮ ▯ ▯ ▭

▼▼ Super 8 Motel M ❀
(918) 335-1122. **$48, 7 day notice.** 211 SE Washington Blvd (US 75). 0.7 mi n of jct US 60 and 75. Ext/int corridors. **Pets:** Service with restrictions, crate.

ASK X ▮ ▯

BIG CABIN

▼▼ Big Cabin Super 8 M
(918) 783-5888. **$51-$57.** 30954 S Hwy 69. I-44, exit 283, just ne. Ext/int corridors. **Pets:** Other species. $20 deposit/room. Designated rooms, service with restrictions.

ASK S X ▮ ▭

BLACKWELL

▲▲▲ ▼▼▼ Comfort Inn SH
(580) 363-7000. **$69, 5 day notice.** 1201 N 44th St. I-35, exit 222, just ne. Int corridors. **Pets:** Small. $10 daily fee/pet. Designated rooms, service with restrictions, supervision.

SAVE S X ✎ ▮ ▯ ▭

BROKEN BOW

▼ Microtel Inn SH
(580) 584-7708. **$64.** 1701 S Park Dr. 1 mi s. Int corridors. **Pets:** Accepted.

ASK S X ▮ ▯ ▭

CHECOTAH

▼▼ Days Inn of Eufaula M
(918) 689-3999. **Call for rates.** Hwy 69 & 150. Just w of jct US 69 and SR 150. Ext corridors. **Pets:** Accepted.

X ✎ ▮

Lake Eufaula Inn M
(918) 473-2376. **$19-$79.** SR 150 & I-40. I-40, exit 259, just s. Ext corridors. **Pets:** Service with restrictions, supervision.

CHICKASHA

Best Western Inn SH
(405) 224-4890. **$55-$65.** 2101 S 4th St. I-44, exit 80, just nw. Ext/int corridors. **Pets:** Very small, other species. $10 one-time fee/pet. Service with restrictions, crate.

DUNCAN

Chisholm Suite Hotel SH
(580) 255-0551. **$77.** 1204 N Hwy 81. Center. Int corridors. **Pets:** Accepted.

DURANT

Comfort Inn & Suites of Durant SH
(580) 924-8881. **Call for rates.** 2112 W Main St. US 75/69, exit US 70, just e. Int corridors. **Pets:** Medium. $10 one-time fee/pet. Service with restrictions, supervision.

ELK CITY

Bedford Inn M
(580) 225-6775. **Call for rates.** 2004 S Main. I-40, exit 38, just ne. Ext corridors. **Pets:** $5 daily fee/pet. Service with restrictions, supervision.

Budget Host Inn M
(580) 225-1811. **$40-$45, 3 day notice.** 2000 W 3rd St. I-40, exit 41 westbound, 4 mi nw; exit 32 eastbound, 5 mi ne. Ext corridors. **Pets:** Accepted.

Holiday Inn SH
(580) 225-6637. **$68-$88.** 101 Meadow Ridge Dr. I-40, exit 38, just sw. Ext/int corridors. **Pets:** Accepted.

Ramada Inn SH
(580) 225-8140. **Call for rates.** 102 B J Hughes Access Rd. I-40, exit 38, just s. Ext corridors. **Pets:** Accepted.

Travelodge M ❖
(580) 225-6661. **$33-$40.** 2500 E Hwy 66. I-40, exit 41, 0.5 mi nw. Ext corridors. **Pets:** $5 daily fee/pet. Service with restrictions, supervision.

ENID

Best Western Inn of Enid SH
(580) 242-7110. **$70-$75.** 2818 S Van Buren St. 1.7 mi s of jct US 412 and 81. Int corridors. **Pets:** Small, dogs only. $5 daily fee/pet. Service with restrictions, supervision.

Comfort Inn SH
(580) 234-1200. **Call for rates.** 210 N Van Buren St. 0.7 mi n on US 81. Ext/int corridors. **Pets:** Small, other species. $7 daily fee/pet. Designated rooms, service with restrictions, supervision.

ERICK

Comfort Inn SH
(580) 526-8124. **$81, 5 day notice.** 1001 N Sheb Wooley. I-40, exit 7, just nw. Ext corridors. **Pets:** Small. $6 daily fee/pet. Designated rooms, service with restrictions, supervision.

FREDERICK

Scottish Inns M ❖
(580) 335-2129. **$30-$50.** 1015 S Main St. 1 mi s. Ext corridors. **Pets:** Designated rooms, service with restrictions, supervision.

Tanglewood Motel M
(580) 335-7557. **$38-$42.** 1123 S Main. 1 mi s. Ext corridors. **Pets:** Accepted.

GUYMON

Ambassador Inn SH
(580) 338-5555. **$50-$60.** Hwy 64 N at 21st. 1.5 mi n on US 64 and SR 136. Ext corridors. **Pets:** Accepted.

Best Western Townsman Inn SH ❖
(580) 338-6556. **$55-$95.** 212 NE Hwy 54. 0.8 mi se. Ext corridors. **Pets:** Small, other species. Designated rooms, no service, crate.

Econo Lodge M
(580) 338-5431. **$55-$65.** 923 Hwy 54 E. Just s of jct US 64. Ext corridors. **Pets:** Small. $8 one-time fee/pet. Service with restrictions, supervision.

Guymon Super 8 SH
(580) 338-0507. **$50-$88.** 1201 Hwy 54 NE. Jct US 54 and 64. Int corridors. **Pets:** Other species. Service with restrictions, supervision.

HENRYETTA

Gateway Inn M ❖
(918) 652-4448. **$38-$40.** 903 E Trudgeon St. I-40, exit 240B, 0.5 mi n. Ext/int corridors. **Pets:** Medium, other species. $3 daily fee/pet. Service with restrictions, crate.

Green Country Inn M
(918) 652-9988. **$38-$40.** 2004 Old Hwy 75 W. I-40, exit 237, just ne. Ext corridors. **Pets:** Accepted.

IDABEL

▼▼▼▼ Comfort Suites 🆂🅷
(580) 286-9393. **$75-$85.** 400 SE Lincoln Blvd. Just s of jct US 70 and 259. Int corridors. **Pets:** $15 daily fee/pet. Service with restrictions, supervision.

(A$K) (S🌀) (✕) (🖉) 🖥 💻 🏊

▼ Microtel Inn 🆂🅷
(580) 286-4466. **$64.** 2906 NW Texas St. 1.5 mi w on US 70. Int corridors. **Pets:** Small. $20 deposit/pet. Service with restrictions, supervision.

(A$K) (S🌀) (✕) (🖉) 🖥

LAWTON

▼▼ Best Western Hotel 🆂🅷
(580) 353-0200. **$78-$109.** 1125 E Gore Blvd. I-44, exit 37, just e. Ext/int corridors. **Pets:** Accepted.

(A$K) (S🌀) (✕) 🖥 💻 (🍴) 🏊 (✕)

▼▼ Ramada Inn 🆂🅷
(580) 355-7155. **$62-$66.** 601 NW 2nd St. I-44, exit 37 northbound; exit 39B southbound. Ext/int corridors. **Pets:** Medium. $15 one-time fee/pet. Service with restrictions, supervision.

(A$K) (S🌀) (✕) 🖥 💻 (🍴) 🏊

(AAA) ▼▼▼▼ Red Lion Hotel 🆂🅷
(580) 353-1682. **$61-$73.** 3134 NW Cache Rd. I-44, exit 39A, 2.5 mi w. Ext corridors. **Pets:** $25 one-time fee/room. Service with restrictions, supervision.

(SAVE) (S🌀) (✕) 🖥 💻 (🍴) 🏊 (✕)

MCALESTER

▼▼▼▼ Best Western Inn of McAlester 🆂🅷
(918) 426-0115. **$65-$75.** 1215 George Nigh Expwy. 3 mi s on US 69. Ext corridors. **Pets:** Accepted.

(A$K) (S🌀) (✕) (🕭) 🖥 💻 🏊

▼▼▼▼ Holiday Inn Express Hotel & Suites 🆂🅷
(918) 302-0001. **$91.** 650 George Nigh Expwy. 1.2 mi s on US 69. Int corridors. **Pets:** Accepted.

(A$K) (S🌀) (✕) (🖉) 🖥 💻 🏊

▼▼ Microtel Inn 🆂🅷
(918) 429-0910. **$44-$59.** 1400 S George Nigh. 3.3 mi s on US 69. Int corridors. **Pets:** Other species. $10 one-time fee/room. Service with restrictions, supervision.

(A$K) (S🌀) (✕) (🖉) 🖥 💻 🏊

▼▼ Super 8 Motel Ⓜ
(918) 426-5400. **$50-$65.** 2400 S Main. Just n of jct US 69 and 69 business route. Ext corridors. **Pets:** Accepted.

(✕) 🖥 🏊

MIAMI

(AAA) ▼▼ Best Western Inn of Miami 🆂🅷 🐾
(918) 542-6681. **$64-$79.** 2225 E Steve Owens Blvd. I-44, exit 313, just w. Ext corridors. **Pets:** Medium, other species. Service with restrictions, crate.

(SAVE) (S🌀) (✕) 🖥 💻 (🍴) 🏊

MUSKOGEE

(AAA) ▼▼▼▼ Days Inn of Muskogee Ⓜ
(918) 683-3911. **$59-$69.** 900 S 32nd St. 3 mi s on US 64 and 69. Ext corridors. **Pets:** Very small. $5 daily fee/pet. Service with restrictions, supervision.

(SAVE) (S🌀) (✕) 🖥 💻 🏊

OKLAHOMA CITY METROPOLITAN AREA

DEL CITY

(AAA) ▼▼▼▼ La Quinta Inn-East 🆂🅷
(405) 672-0067. **$65-$85.** 5501 Tinker Diagonal Rd. I-40, exit 156A (Sooner Ave), just nw. Ext/int corridors. **Pets:** Other species. Service with restrictions.

(SAVE) (S🌀) (✕) (🖉) 🖥 💻 🏊

EDMOND

(AAA) ▼▼▼▼ Best Western Edmond Inn &
Suites 🆂🅷
(405) 216-0300. **$65-$125.** 2700 E 2nd St. I-35, exit 141, 1.1 mi w. Int corridors. **Pets:** Accepted.

(SAVE) (S🌀) (✕) 🖥 💻 🏊

(AAA) ▼▼▼▼ Ramada Plaza Hotel 🆂🅷
(405) 341-3577. **$79.** 930 E 2nd St. I-35, exit 141, 2.3 mi w. Int corridors. **Pets:** Accepted.

(SAVE) (S🌀) (✕) (🖉) 🖥 💻 (🍴) 🏊

EL RENO

(AAA) ▼▼▼▼ Best Western Hensley's 🆂🅷
(405) 262-6490. **$50-$70.** 2701 S Country Club Rd. I-40, exit 123, just s. Ext corridors. **Pets:** Medium, other species. $25 deposit/room, $5 one-time fee/room. Service with restrictions, supervision.

(SAVE) (S🌀) (✕) (🖉) 🖥 💻 🏊

GUTHRIE

(AAA) ▼▼▼▼ Best Western Territorial Inn 🆂🅷
(405) 282-8831. **$65-$90.** 2323 Territorial Tr. I-35, exit 157, just sw. Int corridors. **Pets:** Small, other species. Service with restrictions, supervision.

(SAVE) (S🌀) (✕) (🖉) 🖥 💻 🏊

MIDWEST CITY

▼▼▼▼ AmeriSuites (Midwest City/Tinker Air Force
Base) 🆂🅷
(405) 737-7777. **$95-$105.** 5701 Tinker Diagonal Rd. I-40, exit 156A. Int corridors. **Pets:** Medium. Service with restrictions, crate.

(A$K) (S🌀) (✕) (🅼) (🖉) (🖉) 🖥 💻 🏊

▼ Studio 6 **M**
(405) 737-8851. **$44.** 5801 Tinker Diagonal. I-40, exit 156A, just ne. Ext corridors. **Pets:** Accepted.
ASK S6 ☒ ⊞ ▣ ⇌

MOORE

🔷 ▼▼ Microtel Inn & Suites **SH**
(405) 799-8181. **$52-$69.** 2400 S Service Rd. I-35, exit 116, just s on east service road. Int corridors. **Pets:** Accepted.
SAVE S6 ☒ ♿ ⊞ ▣ ⇌

▼▼ Super 8 Motel **M**
(405) 794-4030. **Call for rates.** 1520 N Service Rd. I-35, exit 118, just ne. Ext corridors. **Pets:** Accepted.
☒ ⊞

NORMAN

▼▼ Days Inn **SH**
(405) 360-4380. **$45-$55.** 609 N Interstate Dr. I-35, exit 110, on east service road, 0.5 mi s. Ext corridors. **Pets:** Accepted.
ASK S6 ☒ 🌀 ⊞ ▣ ⇌

▼▼▼ La Quinta Inn & Suites **SH**
(405) 579-4000. **$85-$105.** 930 Ed Noble Dr. I-35, exit 108B (Lindsey), just nw. Int corridors. **Pets:** Small. Service with restrictions, supervision.
ASK S6 ☒ ♿ ⊞ ▣ ⇌

🔷 ▼▼▼ The Residence Inn by
    Marriott **SH** 🐾
(405) 366-0900. **$89-$109.** 2681 Jefferson St. I-35, exit 108A, just se. Ext corridors. **Pets:** Other species. $75 one-time fee/pet. Service with restrictions, supervision.
SAVE S6 ☒ 🌀 ⊞ ▣ ⇌ ☒

OKLAHOMA CITY

🔷 ▼▼▼ AmeriSuites (Oklahoma
    City/Airport) **SH**
(405) 682-3900. **$80-$109.** 1818 S Meridian Ave. I-40, exit 145, 1 mi s. Int corridors. **Pets:** Accepted.
SAVE S6 ☒ 🌀 ♿ ⊞ ▣ ⇌

🔷 ▼▼▼ AmeriSuites (Oklahoma City/Quail
    Springs) **SH**
(405) 749-1595. **$99-$104, 17 day notice.** 3201 W Memorial Rd. John Kilpatrick Tpke, exit May Ave, 0.4 mi w on north service road. Int corridors. **Pets:** Accepted.
SAVE S6 ☒ ♿ ⊞ ▣ ⇌

🔷 ▼▼▼ Best Western Saddleback Inn **LH**
(405) 947-7000. **$94.** 4300 SW 3rd St. I-40, exit 145, just ne. Ext/int corridors. **Pets:** Small. $25 deposit/room. Service with restrictions, crate.
SAVE S6 ☒ 🌀 ⊞ ▣ 🍴 ⇌ ☒

▼▼▼ Clarion Meridian Hotel and Convention
    Center **SH**
(405) 942-8511. **$85.** 737 S Meridian Ave. I-40, exit 145 (Meridian Ave), just s. Ext/int corridors. **Pets:** Accepted.
ASK S6 ☒ ♿M 🌀 ♿ ⊞ ▣ ⇌

🔷 ▼▼▼ Comfort Inn at Founders Tower **SH**
(405) 810-1100. **$69-$149.** 5704 Mosteller Dr. 0.5 mi e of jct SR 74 and 3. Int corridors. **Pets:** Accepted.
SAVE S6 ☒ ♿ ⊞ ▣

🔷 ▼▼▼ Comfort Inn North **SH**
(405) 478-7282. **$65-$74.** 4625 NE 120th. I-35, exit 137 (122nd St), just sw. Int corridors. **Pets:** Large, other species. $10 daily fee/pet. Service with restrictions, supervision.
SAVE S6 ☒ ♿ ⊞ ▣ ⇌

▼▼▼ Days Inn & Suites North **SH**
(405) 478-2554. **$50-$85, 15 day notice.** 12013 N I-35 Service Rd. I-35, exit 137, just sw. Ext/int corridors. **Pets:** Accepted.
ASK ☒ ⊞ ▣ ⇌

🔷 ▼▼▼ Days Inn West **SH**
(405) 942-8294. **$49, 7 day notice.** 504 S Meridian Ave. I-40, exit 145 (Meridian Ave), just ne. Ext corridors. **Pets:** Other species. $10 one-time fee/room. Service with restrictions.
SAVE S6 ☒ ⊞ ▣ ⇌

🔷 ▼▼▼ Econo Lodge **SH**
(405) 942-5955. **$55-$65.** 4601 SW 3rd. I-40, exit 145 (Meridian Ave), just nw. Ext corridors. **Pets:** Accepted.
SAVE S6 ☒ ▣ ⇌

▼▼▼ Embassy Suites **LH**
(405) 682-6000. **$99-$169.** 1815 S Meridian Ave. I-40, exit 145 (Meridian Ave), 1 mi s. Int corridors. **Pets:** Medium. $35 one-time fee/room. Service with restrictions, crate.
ASK S6 ☒ 🌀 ⊞ ▣ 🍴 ⇌ ☒

▼▼▼ Four Points by Sheraton Oklahoma
    City **SH**
(405) 681-3500. **$72.** 6300 Terminal Dr. I-40, exit 145 (Meridian Ave), 4 mi s. Int corridors. **Pets:** Accepted.
ASK S6 ☒ ♿ ⊞ ▣ 🍴 ⇌

🔷 ▼▼▼ Hampton Inn OKC Airport **SH**
(405) 682-2080. **$97-$117, 7 day notice.** 1905 S Meridian Ave. I-40, exit 145 (Meridian Ave), 1 mi s. Int corridors. **Pets:** Small. $25 one-time fee/room. Service with restrictions, crate.
SAVE S6 ☒ 🌀 ⊞ ▣ ⇌

🔷 ▼▼▼ Hilton Northwest **LH**
(405) 848-4811. **$62-$159.** 2945 Northwest Expwy. 0.5 mi e of jct SR 74 and 3. Ext/int corridors. **Pets:** Small. $15 one-time fee/pet. Designated rooms, service with restrictions, supervision.
SAVE S6 ☒ 🌀 ♿ ⊞ ▣ 🍴 ⇌

▼▼▼ Holiday Inn Express-Quail Springs **SH**
(405) 755-8686. **$75-$95.** 13520 Plaza Terrace. John Kilpatrick Tpke, exit May Ave, just e on south frontage road. Int corridors. **Pets:** $10 one-time fee/pet. Designated rooms, service with restrictions, supervision.
ASK S6 ☒ ♿ ⊞ ▣ ⇌

▼▼▼ Holiday Inn Hotel & Suites **SH**
(405) 843-5558. **$109-$250.** 6200 N Robinson. I-44, exit 127, just nw. Ext/int corridors. **Pets:** Accepted.
ASK S6 ☒ ♿ ⊞ ▣ 🍴 ⇌

♨ ▼▼▼ Howard Johnson Express Inn-Airport M

(405) 943-9841. **$42-$59.** 400 S Meridian Ave. I-40, exit 145 (Meridian Ave), just n. Int corridors. **Pets:** Other species. $6 daily fee/pet. Designated rooms, service with restrictions, crate.

SAVE S6 ⊠ 🐾 🖥 💻 ➿

▼▼▼ La Quinta Inn & Suites SH

(405) 773-5575. **$89-$109.** 4829 Northwest Expwy. 1.9 mi w of jct SR 74 and 3. Int corridors. **Pets:** Other species. No service, supervision.

ASK S6 ⊠ 🐾 🖥 💻 ➿

▼▼▼ La Quinta Inn-South SH

(405) 631-8661. **$59-$69.** 8315 I-35 S. I-35, exit 121A (82nd St), just sw. Ext corridors. **Pets:** Other species. Service with restrictions, supervision.

ASK S6 ⊠ 🐾 🖥 💻 ➿

♨ ▼▼▼ La Quinta Oklahoma City Airport SH

(405) 942-0040. **$69-$89.** 800 S Meridian Ave. I-40, exit 145 (Meridian Ave), just se. Ext/int corridors. **Pets:** Accepted.

SAVE S6 ⊠ 🖥 💻 ⓣ ➿

▼▼ Microtel Inn and Suites SH

(405) 942-0011. **$55-$60, 14 day notice.** 624 S MacArthur. I-40, exit 144 (MacArthur), just s. Int corridors. **Pets:** Accepted.

ASK S6 ⊠ 🖥 💻 ➿

▼ Motel 6–1182 M

(405) 478-4030. **$37-$52.** 12121 Northeast Expwy. I-35, exit 137, just sw. Ext corridors. **Pets:** Small. Service with restrictions, supervision.

S6 ⊠ 🐾 🖥 ➿

▼ Motel 6 Airport–116 M

(405) 946-6662. **$39-$55.** 820 S Meridian Ave. I-40, exit 145 (Meridian Ave), just se. Ext corridors. **Pets:** Accepted.

S6 ⊠ 🐾 🖥 ➿

▼▼ Motel 6 West–1128 SH

(405) 947-6550. **$42-$57.** 4200 I-40 Service Rd. I-40, exit 145 (Meridian Ave), just e on south frontage road. Ext/int corridors. **Pets:** Accepted.

S6 ⊠ 🖥 ➿

▼▼▼ Oklahoma City Marriott LH

(405) 842-6633. **$119-$149.** 3233 Northwest Expwy. Just e of jct SR 74 and 3. Int corridors. **Pets:** Accepted.

ASK ⊠ 🐾 🖥 🖥 💻 ⓣ ➿ ⊠

▼▼▼ Oklahoma City Residence Inn South-Crossroads Mall SH

(405) 634-9696. **$99-$140, 14 day notice.** 1111 E I-240 Service Rd. I-240, exit 4C eastbound, 0.4 mi nw; exit 5 westbound, 0.8 mi nw. Int corridors. **Pets:** Other species. $5 daily fee/room, $75 one-time fee/room. Service with restrictions, supervision.

ASK S6 🖥 🖥 💻 ➿

♨ ▼▼ Quality Inn SH 🐾

(405) 632-6666. **$73.** 7800 CA Henderson Blvd. I-240, exit 2A, just s. Ext corridors. **Pets:** Medium, dogs only. $10 one-time fee/pet. Service with restrictions.

SAVE S6 ⊠ 🐾 🖥 🖥 💻 ➿

♨ ▼▼▼ Quality Inn at Frontier City SH

(405) 478-0400. **$50-$100.** 12001 N I-35 Service Rd. I-35, exit 137, just sw. Ext corridors. **Pets:** Small. $10 daily fee/pet. Service with restrictions, supervision.

SAVE S6 ⊠ 🖥 🖥 💻 ➿

▼▼▼ Ramada Limited SH

(405) 948-8000. **$55-$59, 15 day notice.** 2727 W I-44 Service Rd. I-44, exit 124, just n. Int corridors. **Pets:** Accepted.

ASK S6 ⊠ 🖥 🖥 💻 ➿

♨ ▼▼▼▼ Renaissance Oklahoma City Hotel LH

(405) 228-8000. **$109-$179.** 10 N Broadway Ave. Sheridan and Broadway aves; downtown. Int corridors. **Pets:** Accepted.

SAVE S6 ⊠ 🖥M 🐾 🖥 🖥 💻 ⓣ ➿ ⊠

▼▼▼ Residence Inn by Marriott-West SH

(405) 942-4500. **$81.** 4361 W Reno Ave. I-40, exit 145 (Meridian Ave), 0.3 mi n, then e. Ext corridors. **Pets:** Other species. $25 daily fee/pet. Service with restrictions, supervision.

ASK S6 ⊠ 🐾 🖥 💻 ➿ ⊠

♨ ▼▼▼▼ The Waterford Marriott LH

(405) 848-4782. **$116.** 6300 Waterford Blvd. I-44, exit 125A, 1.4 mi n. Int corridors. **Pets:** Small. $35 one-time fee/room. Service with restrictions, crate.

SAVE S6 ⊠ 🐾 🖥 🖥 💻 ⓣ ➿ ⊠

PURCELL

♨ ▼▼ Econo Lodge M

(405) 527-5603. **$60-$70.** 2122 Hwy 74 S. I-35, exit 91, just e. Ext corridors. **Pets:** Small. $5 daily fee/pet. Service with restrictions, supervision.

SAVE S6 ⊠ 🐾 🖥

SHAWNEE

♨ ▼▼ Best Western Cinderella Motor Inn SH

(405) 273-7010. **$55.** 623 Kickapoo Spur. I-40, exit 185, 2.8 mi s, just w on US 270 business route. Ext/int corridors. **Pets:** Medium, other species. $10 daily fee/pet. Designated rooms, service with restrictions, supervision.

SAVE S6 ⊠ 🐾 🖥 💻 ⓣ ➿

▼▼ Motel 6–1236 M

(405) 275-5310. **$45-$59.** 4981 N Harrison. I-40, exit 186, just ne. Int corridors. **Pets:** Accepted.

S6 ⊠ 🐾 🖥 ➿

YUKON

♨ ▼▼▼ Best Western Inn & Suites Yukon SH

(405) 265-2995. **$59-$74.** 11440 W I-40 Service Rd. I-40, exit 138, just sw. Ext/int corridors. **Pets:** Other species. $25 deposit/room. Supervision.

SAVE S6 ⊠ 🐾 🖥 🖥 💻 ➿

♨ ▼▼▼ Yukon Super 8 SH

(405) 324-1000. **$39-$59.** 321 N Mustang Rd. I-40, exit 138, just n. Ext corridors. **Pets:** Other species. Service with restrictions.

SAVE S6 ⊠ 🖥 ➿

OKMULGEE

AAA ▽▽▽ Best Western Okmulgee SH
(918) 756-9200. **$69-$95.** 3499 N Wood Dr. Just n of jct US
75 and SR 56. Int corridors. **Pets:** Very small. $50 deposit/
pet. Service with restrictions, supervision.
SAVE S/ ✕ (·) 🛏 🖵 ⑪ ↩

PAULS VALLEY

AAA ▽▽▽ Days Inn SH
(405) 238-7548. **$60-$70.** 2606 W Grant Ave. I-35, exit 72,
just e. Int corridors. **Pets:** Accepted.
SAVE S/ ✕ 🛏

PERRY

**AAA ▽▽▽ Best Western Cherokee Strip
Motel** SH ✿
(580) 336-2218. **$54-$60, 3 day notice.** I-35 & US 77. I-35,
exit 185, just e. Ext corridors. **Pets:** Other species. $15
deposit/pet. Service with restrictions, supervision.
SAVE S/ ✕ 🖵 ⑪ ↩

PRYOR

▽▽▽▽ Comfort Inn & Suites SH
(918) 476-6660. **$63-$108.** 307 Mid America Dr. 5 mi s on
US 69. Int corridors. **Pets:** Medium, dogs only. $10 daily
fee/pet. Service with restrictions, supervision.
ASK S/ ✕ (·) 🛏 🖵 ↩

▽ Microtel Inn & Suites SH
(918) 476-4661. **$47, 7 day notice.** 315 Mid America Dr. 5.1
mi s on US 69. Int corridors. **Pets:** $20 deposit/pet. Crate.
ASK ✕ ⊘ (·) 🛏 🖵

ROLAND

▽▽ Days Inn of Roland SH
(918) 427-1000. **Call for rates.** 207 Cherokee Blvd. I-40, exit
325, just ne. Int corridors. **Pets:** Accepted.
✕ ⊘ (·) 🛏 ↩

SALLISAW

▽▽ Microtel Inn & Suites SH
(918) 774-0400. **$49-$79, 3 day notice.** 710 S Kerr Blvd.
I-40, exit 308, just n. Int corridors. **Pets:** Accepted.
ASK S/ ✕ (·) 🛏 🖵 ↩

SAVANNA

AAA ▽▽▽ Travelodge M
(918) 548-3506. **$35-$47.** Hwy 69 & Panola. 2 mi sw of jct
Indian Nation Tpke. Ext corridors. **Pets:** Accepted.
SAVE S/ ✕ 🛏 🖵 ↩

SAYRE

▽▽▽▽ AmericInn Lodge & Suites of Sayre SH
(580) 928-2700. **$66-$127.** 2405 S El Camino. I-40, exit 20,
just n. Int corridors. **Pets:** Small. $10 one-time fee/room.
Designated rooms, service with restrictions, supervision.
✕ (M) (·) 🛏 🖵 ↩

STILLWATER

AAA ▽▽▽ Best Western Stillwater SH
(405) 377-7010. **$65-$99.** 600 E McElroy. 1 mi n on US 177
(Perkins Rd). Int corridors. **Pets:** Accepted.
SAVE S/ ✕ ⊘ 🛏 🖵 ⑪ ↩ ⊠

▽▽▽▽ Holiday Inn SH
(405) 372-0800. **$71-$155.** 2515 W 6th Ave. 1.8 mi w on SR
51. Ext/int corridors. **Pets:** Medium, other species. Service
with restrictions, supervision.
ASK S/ ✕ 🛏 🖵 ⑪ ↩ ⊠

TAHLEQUAH

▽▽ Oak Hill Motel and Suites M
(918) 458-1200. **$39-$79.** 2600 S Muskogee Pl. Just s on
US 62 from jct SR 51. Ext corridors. **Pets:** Medium, other
species. $7 daily fee/room. Designated rooms, service with
restrictions.
ASK S/ ✕ 🛏 🖵 ⑪ ↩

TULSA METROPOLITAN AREA

BROKEN ARROW

AAA ▽▽▽ Holiday Inn Tulsa South SH
(918) 258-7085. **$64.** 2600 N Aspen. Broken Arrow Expwy
(SR 51), exit 145th Ave. Int corridors. **Pets:** Accepted.
SAVE S/ ✕ ⊘ 🛏 🖵 ↩

CATOOSA

AAA ▽▽▽ Super 8 M
(918) 266-7000. **$44-$51.** 19250 Timbercrest Cir. I-44, exit
240A, just nw. Ext corridors. **Pets:** Other species. Service
with restrictions, supervision.
SAVE S/ ✕ ↩

CLAREMORE

AAA ▽▽▽ Claremore Motor Inn M
(918) 342-4545. **$45-$55.** 1709 N Lynn Riggs. 1.2 mi n on
SR 66. Ext/int corridors. **Pets:** Very small. $5 daily fee/pet.
Service with restrictions, supervision.
SAVE S/ ✕ 🛏

▽▽▽▽ Days Inn Claremore SH
(918) 343-3297. **$48-$64.** 1720 S Lynn Riggs. 1.6 mi s on
SR 66. Int corridors. **Pets:** Other species. $10 daily fee/pet.
Supervision.
ASK S/ ✕ ⊘ 🛏 🖵 ↩

▽▽ Microtel Inn & Suites SH
(918) 343-2868. **$52-$92.** 10600 E Mallard Lake Rd. 2.6 mi
s on SR 66. Int corridors. **Pets:** Accepted.
ASK S/ ✕ (·) 🛏 🖵 ↩

AAA ▼▼◆ Super 8 Motel 🆂🅷
(918) 341-2323. **$59-$69.** 1100 E Will Rogers Blvd. I-44, exit 255, just w. Ext/int corridors. **Pets:** Very small. $5 daily fee/pet. Service with restrictions, supervision.
🆂🅰🆅🅴 �!️ ✖ ▤

AAA ▼◆ Travel Inn 🅼
(918) 341-3254. **$40-$42.** 812 E Will Rogers Blvd. I-44, exit 255, 0.5 mi w. Ext corridors. **Pets:** Accepted.
🆂🅰🆅🅴 🌡️ ✖ ▤

GLENPOOL

AAA ▼▼◆ Best Western Glenpool/Tulsa 🆂🅷
(918) 322-5201. **$61-$99.** 14831 S Casper St. I-44, exit 224, 9.5 mi s on US 75. Ext corridors. **Pets:** Very small. $50 deposit/pet. Service with restrictions, supervision.
🆂🅰🆅🅴 🌡️ ✖ ▤ 🖥️ 🏊

SAND SPRINGS

AAA ▼▼◆ Best Western Sand Springs Inn & Suites 🆂🅷
(918) 245-4999. **$64-$74.** 211 S Lake Dr. Off SR 51, US 64 and 412, exit 81st W Ave, just sw. Ext/int corridors. **Pets:** Accepted.
🆂🅰🆅🅴 🌡️ ✖ ▤ 🖥️ 🏊

SAPULPA

▼▼ Sapulpa Super 8 🆂🅷
(918) 227-3300. **Call for rates.** 1505 New Sapulpa Rd. 0.5 mi e on SR 66. Int corridors. **Pets:** Accepted.
✖ 🔖 🏊

TULSA

AAA ▼▼◆▼ AmeriSuites (Tulsa/Hyde Park) 🆂🅷
(918) 491-4010. **$66-$109.** 7037 S Zurich Ave. I-44, exit 229 (Yale Ave/SR 66), 3 mi s to 71st St, then just e. Int corridors. **Pets:** Other species. Service with restrictions.
🆂🅰🆅🅴 🌡️ ✖ 🔖 🖥️ ▤ 🖥️ 🏊

AAA ▼▼◆▼ Baymont Inn & Suites Tulsa 🆂🅷
(918) 488-8777. **$59-$89.** 4530 E Skelly Dr. I-44, exit 229 (Yale Ave/SR 66), just s, then w. Int corridors. **Pets:** Accepted.
🆂🅰🆅🅴 🌡️ ✖ 🔖 ▤ 🖥️ 🏊

AAA ▼▼◆▼ Best Western Trade Winds Central Inn 🆂🅷
(918) 749-5561. **$59-$79.** 3141 E Skelly Dr. I-44, exit 228 (Harvard Ave), on northwest frontage road. Ext/int corridors. **Pets:** Very small. $10 one-time fee/pet. Service with restrictions, crate.
🆂🅰🆅🅴 🌡️ ✖ 🔖 ▤ 🖥️ 🍴 🏊

▼▼◆▼ Cambridge Suites 🆂🅷
(918) 664-7241. **$109.** 8181 E 41st St. 1.7 mi w of US 169. Ext corridors. **Pets:** Medium, other species. $75 one-time fee/room. Service with restrictions, supervision.
🅰🆂🅺 🌡️ ✖ 🔖 ▤ 🖥️ 🏊 🚫

AAA ▼◆▼ Days Inn-Tulsa West 🆂🅷
(918) 446-1561. **$50.** 5525 W Skelly Dr. I-44, exit 222B eastbound, just w on south service road; exit 222A westbound, just e on south service road. Ext/int corridors. **Pets:** Small. $8 daily fee/pet. Service with restrictions, supervision.
🆂🅰🆅🅴 🌡️ ✖ ▤ 🏊

▼▼▼▼ Doubletree Hotel At Warren Place 🅻🅷
(918) 495-1000. **$99-$139.** 6110 S Yale Ave. I-44, exit 229 (Yale Ave/SR 66), 1.3 mi s. Int corridors. **Pets:** Accepted.
🅰🆂🅺 🌡️ ✖ 🔖 ▤ 🖥️ 🍴 🏊 🚫

▼▼▼▼ Doubletree Hotel Downtown Tulsa 🅻🅷
(918) 587-8000. **$72-$153.** 616 W 7th St. 7th St and Houston. Int corridors. **Pets:** Accepted.
🅰🆂🅺 ✖ 🔖 ▤ 🖥️ 🍴 🏊

▼▼▼▼ Holiday Inn Express-Tulsa 🆂🅷
(918) 459-5321. **$75-$95.** 9010 E 71st St. US 169, exit 71st St, 1 mi w. Int corridors. **Pets:** Small. $50 one-time fee/room. Service with restrictions, supervision.
🅰🆂🅺 🌡️ ✖ 🔖 🖥️ ▤ 🖥️ 🏊

▼▼▼▼ Holiday Inn-International Airport 🆂🅷
(918) 437-7660. **$86-$96, 7 day notice.** 1010 N Garnett Rd. I-244, exit 14 (Garnett Rd), just n. Int corridors. **Pets:** Medium, dogs only. $15 one-time fee/room. Crate.
🅰🆂🅺 🌡️ ✖ 🔖 ▤ 🖥️ 🍴 🏊 🚫

▼▼▼▼ Holiday Inn Select 🆂🅷
(918) 622-7000. **$74.** 5000 E Skelly Dr. I-44, exit 229 (Yale Ave/SR 66), on south frontage road. Ext/int corridors. **Pets:** Small. $25 one-time fee/room. Service with restrictions, crate.
🅰🆂🅺 🌡️ ✖ 🔖 ▤ 🖥️ 🍴 🏊

AAA ▼▼▼▼ Hotel Ambassador 🆂🅷 ✿
(918) 587-8200. **$149-$225.** 1324 S Main St. 14th and Main St. Int corridors. **Pets:** Other species. $25 one-time fee/room. Designated rooms, service with restrictions.
🅰🆂🅺 🌡️ ✖ 🔖 ▤ 🖥️ 🍴

AAA ▼▼▼▼ La Quinta Inn 41st St 🆂🅷
(918) 665-0220. **$59-$79.** 10829 E 41st St. US 169, exit E 41st St. Ext corridors. **Pets:** Accepted.
🆂🅰🆅🅴 ✖ 🔖 ▤ 🖥️ 🏊

AAA ▼▼▼▼ La Quinta Inn Airport 🆂🅷
(918) 836-3931. **$61-$75.** 35 N Sheridan Rd. I-244, exit 11 (Sheridan Rd). Ext corridors. **Pets:** Other species. Service with restrictions, supervision.
🆂🅰🆅🅴 🌡️ ✖ 🔖 ▤ 🖥️ 🏊

▼▼▼▼ La Quinta Inn-Tulsa South 🆂🅷
(918) 254-1626. **$65-$75.** 12525 E 52nd St S. Broken Arrow Expwy (SR 51), exit 129th and 51st sts, just s. Ext corridors. **Pets:** Small. Service with restrictions, supervision.
🅰🆂🅺 🌡️ ✖ 🔖 ▤ 🖥️ 🏊

▼◆ Microtel Inn & Suites 🆂🅷
(918) 858-3775. **$52-$99.** 4531 E 21st St. Just w of 21st St and Yale Ave. Int corridors. **Pets:** $25 one-time fee/room. Service with restrictions, supervision.
🅰🆂🅺 🌡️ ✖ 🔖 ▤ 🖥️

◆◆ **Microtel Inn & Suites** SH
(918) 234-9100. **$49-$89, 3 day notice.** 16518 E Admiral Pl. I-44, exit 238 (161st Ave), just s. Int corridors. **Pets:** Small. $10 daily fee/pet. Service with restrictions, supervision.
ASK SÓ ✕ 🐾 🐾 🖥 💻

◆◆ **Ramada Inn** SH
(918) 743-9811. **$64-$79.** 3131 E 51st. I-44, exit 228 (Harvard Ave), just sw. Ext/int corridors. **Pets:** Medium, other species. $50 deposit/pet. Designated rooms, service with restrictions, crate.
ASK SÓ ✕ 🐾 🖥 💻 ⊇

◆◆◆ ◆◆ **Renaissance Tulsa Hotel & Convention Center** LH
(918) 307-2600. **$139-$209.** 6808 S 107th E Ave. Jct US 169 and 71st St, just ne. Int corridors. **Pets:** Small, other species. Service with restrictions, crate.
SAVE SÓ ✕ ♿M 🐾 🖥 💻 🍴 ⊇ ✕

◆◆◆◆ **Residence Inn by Marriott Tulsa** SH
(918) 250-4850. **$99-$139, 14 day notice.** 11025 E 73rd St. US 169, exit 71st St, just e. Int corridors. **Pets:** Accepted.
ASK SÓ ✕ 🖥 💻 ⊇ ✕

◆◆◆◆ **Sheraton Tulsa Hotel** LH
(918) 627-5000. **$79.** 10918 E 41st St. Just e of US 169. Int corridors. **Pets:** Accepted.
ASK SÓ ✕ 🐾 ♿ 🖥 💻 🍴 ⊇ ✕

◆◆ **Sleep Inn & Suites Tulsa** SH
(918) 663-2777. **$73-$109.** 8021 E 33rd St S. I-44, exit 231 eastbound; exit 232 (Memorial Dr) westbound, just sw. Int corridors. **Pets:** Small, dogs only. $10 one-time fee/room. Service with restrictions, supervision.
ASK SÓ ✕ 🐾 ♿ 🖥 💻 ⊇ ✕

◆◆◆◆ **Staybridge Suites** SH 🐾
(918) 461-2100. **$89-$139.** 11111 E 73rd St. Just se of jct US 169 and 71st St. Int corridors. **Pets:** Small, dogs only. $75 one-time fee/pet. Designated rooms, service with restrictions, supervision.
ASK SÓ ✕ ♿M 🐾 🖥 💻 ⊇ ✕

◆◆◆ ◆◆ **Super 8 Airport** SH
(918) 836-1981. **$45-$60.** 6616 E Archer. I-244, exit 11 (Sheridan Rd), just e. Ext corridors. **Pets:** Medium. $5 daily fee/pet. Service with restrictions, supervision.
SAVE SÓ ✕ 🖥 ⊇

◆◆◆ ◆◆ **Super 8 Motel** SH
(918) 446-6000. **$41-$51.** 5811 S 49th West Ave. I-44, exit 222A, just e on south service road. Ext corridors. **Pets:** Accepted.
SAVE SÓ ✕ ⊇

◆◆◆◆ **Tulsa Hilton Southern Hills** LH
(918) 492-5000. **$69-$179.** 7902 S Lewis. I-44, exit 227, 3 mi s. Int corridors. **Pets:** $50 one-time fee/room. Service with restrictions.
ASK SÓ ✕ 🐾 ♿ 🖥 💻 🍴 ⊇

❖ **END METROPOLITAN AREA** ❖

WEATHERFORD

◆◆◆ ◆◆◆ **Best Western Mark Motor Hotel** SH
(580) 772-3325. **$51-$79.** 525 E Main St. I-40, exit 82, 0.5 mi n. Ext corridors. **Pets:** Accepted.
SAVE SÓ ✕ 🐾 ♿ 🖥 💻 ⊇

OREGON

ALBANY

Best Western Albany Inn SH
(541) 928-6322. **$79-$89.** 315 Airport Rd SE. I-5, exit 234B southbound; exit 234 northbound, just w, then just s. Ext corridors. **Pets:** Designated rooms, supervision.

Days Inn & Suites SH
(541) 928-5050. **$54-$75, 7 day notice.** 1100 Price Rd SE. I-5, exit 233, just e, then just n. Int corridors. **Pets:** $10 one-time fee/pet. Designated rooms, service with restrictions, supervision.

Holiday Inn Express Hotel & Suites SH
(541) 928-8820. **$95-$145.** 105 Opal Ct NE. I-5, exit 234A southbound; exit 234 northbound, 0.4 mi e. Int corridors. **Pets:** Accepted.

La Quinta Inn & Suites SH
(541) 928-0921. **$67-$141.** 251 Airport Rd SE. I-5, exit 234B southbound; exit 234 northbound, just w. Int corridors. **Pets:** Other species. Service with restrictions, supervision.

Motel 6 #4124 SH
(541) 926-4233. **$64-$68.** 2735 E Pacific Blvd. I-5, exit 234, 0.5 mi e. Ext corridors. **Pets:** Medium, other species. Service with restrictions, supervision.

Phoenix Inn Suites-Albany SH
(541) 926-5696. **$79-$99.** 3410 Spicer Rd SE. I-5, exit 233, just e. Int corridors. **Pets:** Other species. $30 one-time fee/room. Service with restrictions, crate.

ASHLAND

Best Western Bard's Inn SH
(541) 482-0049. **$80-$184.** 132 N Main St. Just n on SR 99 (N Main St) from Downtown Plaza. Ext/int corridors. **Pets:** Large, other species. $15 daily fee/pet. Designated rooms, service with restrictions, supervision.

Best Western Windsor Inn SH
(541) 488-2330. **$79-$139, 3 day notice.** 2520 Ashland St. I-5, exit 14, just e. Ext corridors. **Pets:** Small. $15 daily fee/pet. No service, supervision.

Cedarwood Inn M
(541) 488-2000. **$59-$105, 3 day notice.** 1801 Siskiyou Blvd. I-5, exit 14, 0.5 mi w on SR 66, s on Tolman Creek Blvd, then just n. Ext corridors. **Pets:** Small. $10 daily fee/pet. Designated rooms, service with restrictions, supervision.

Flagship Inn of Ashland M
(541) 482-2641. **$59-$98, 3 day notice.** 1193 Siskiyou Blvd. I-5, exit 14, 1.1 mi w on SR 66, just n on SR 99 (Siskiyou Blvd). Ext corridors. **Pets:** Accepted.

Knights Inn Motel M
(541) 482-5111. **$52-$78, 3 day notice.** 2359 Hwy 66. I-5, exit 14, just w. Ext corridors. **Pets:** Other species. $10 daily fee/pet. Designated rooms, service with restrictions, supervision.

La Quinta Inn & Suites SH
(541) 482-6932. **$69-$139.** 434 Valley View Rd. I-5, exit 19, just w. Int corridors. **Pets:** Other species. Service with restrictions, supervision.

Plaza Inn & Suites At Ashland Creek 🆂🅷

(541) 488-8900. **$69-$139.** 98 Central Ave. I-5, exit 19, 0.5 mi w, 1.9 mi s on SR 99 (N Main St), just e on Water St, then just n. Int corridors. **Pets:** Accepted.

Super 8 Motel-Ashland 🆂🅷

(541) 482-8887. **$44-$108.** 2350 Ashland St. I-5, exit 14, just w. Int corridors. **Pets:** Accepted.

Timbers Motel Ⓜ ❀

(541) 482-4242. **$46-$96, 3 day notice.** 1450 Ashland St. I-5, exit 14, 0.8 mi w. Ext corridors. **Pets:** Other species. Designated rooms, service with restrictions, crate.

Windmill Inn & Suites of Ashland 🆂🅷 ❀

(541) 482-8310. **$59-$142.** 2525 Ashland St. I-5, exit 14, just e. Int corridors. **Pets:** Large, other species. Designated rooms, service with restrictions, supervision.

ASTORIA

Best Western Astoria Inn 🆂🅷

(503) 325-2205. **$69-$299.** 555 Hamburg Ave. On US 101/ 26, at east end of Young's Bay Bridge. Int corridors. **Pets:** Other species. $10 daily fee/room. Service with restrictions, crate.

Clementine's Bed & Breakfast 🅱🅱

(503) 325-2005. **$70-$160, 7 day notice.** 847 Exchange St. At 8th and Exchange sts; downtown. Int corridors. **Pets:** Accepted.

Crest Motel Ⓜ

(503) 325-3141. **$63-$138.** 5366 Leif Erickson Dr. 4 mi e of Astoria Bridge on US 30. Ext corridors. **Pets:** Other species. Service with restrictions, supervision.

Red Lion Inn Ⓜ

(503) 325-7373. **$69-$129.** 400 Industry St. Just w of Astoria Bridge on US 30, just n on Basin St (Caution: do not turn onto Astoria-Megler Bridge). Ext corridors. **Pets:** $10 daily fee/room. Crate.

BAKER CITY

Best Western Sunridge Inn 🆂🅷 ❀

(541) 523-6444. **$74-$90, 5 day notice.** 1 Sunridge Ln. I-84, exit 304, just w. Int corridors. **Pets:** Medium. $15 daily fee/room. Designated rooms, service with restrictions, supervision.

Geiser Grand Hotel 🆂🅷 ❀

(541) 523-1889. **$89-$139.** 1996 Main St. I-84, exit 304, 0.9 mi w on Campbell St, then 0.3 mi s; downtown. Int corridors. **Pets:** Other species. $15 daily fee/pet. Service with restrictions, crate.

BANDON

Best Western Inn at Face Rock 🆂🅷 ❀

(541) 347-9441. **$88-$254.** 3225 Beach Loop Dr. 1 mi s on US 101, 0.8 mi w on Seabird Rd, just s. Ext corridors. **Pets:** $15 one-time fee/pet. Designated rooms, supervision.

Driftwood Motel Ⓜ

(541) 347-9022. **$70-$100, 3 day notice.** 460 Hwy 101. On US 101; center. Ext corridors. **Pets:** Dogs only. $10 one-time fee/pet. Designated rooms, service with restrictions, supervision.

BEND

Bend Super 8 Motel 🆂🅷 ❀

(541) 388-6888. **$53-$73, 3 day notice.** 1275 S Business Hwy 97. US 97, exit 139 (Reed Market Rd), then just s; jct US 20 E, 3.5 mi s on US Business 97. Int corridors. **Pets:** Other species. $5 daily fee/room. Service with restrictions, supervision.

Best Western Inn & Suites of Bend 🆂🅷

(541) 382-1515. **$79-$129, 3 day notice.** 721 NE 3rd St. On US Business 97, just s of jct US 20. Ext corridors. **Pets:** Other species. $10 daily fee/room. Designated rooms, service with restrictions, supervision.

Cricketwood Country Bed & Breakfast 🅱🅱 ❀

(541) 330-0747. **$90-$130, 5 day notice.** 63520 Cricketwood Rd. 3.8 mi se on Deschutes Market Rd, 0.5 mi e on Hamehook Rd, 0.5 mi on Repine Rd, then just n. Ext/int corridors. **Pets:** Dogs only. $10 daily fee/room. Designated rooms, no service.

Entrada Lodge 🆂🅷

(541) 382-4080. **$69-$99.** 19221 SW Century Dr. 5.7 mi w on Mt Bachelor Rt via Division/Colorado from jct US 20 W/97 N. Ext corridors. **Pets:** Accepted.

Hampton Inn 🆂🅷

(541) 388-4114. **$79-$109.** 15 NE Butler Market Rd. US 97, exit 136, just n. Ext corridors. **Pets:** Medium. $10 daily fee/pet. Designated rooms, service with restrictions, supervision.

Holiday Inn Express Hotel & Suites 🆂🅷 ✿
(541) 317-8500. **$65-$159.** 20615 Grandview Dr. On US 97; north end of town. Int corridors. **Pets:** Other species. $10 daily fee/pet. Service with restrictions, crate.

La Quinta Inn 🆂🅷 ✿
(541) 388-2227. **$59-$150.** 61200 S Business Hwy 97. 3 mi s on US Business 97 from jct US 20 E. Int corridors. **Pets:** Other species. Service with restrictions, supervision.

Plaza Motel Ⓜ
(541) 382-1621. **$44-$89.** 1430 NW Hill St. US 97, exit 137 (Revere Ave), just s; downtown. Ext corridors. **Pets:** Small, dogs only. $10 one-time fee/room. Service with restrictions, supervision.

Quality Inn 🆂🅷 ✿
(541) 318-0848. **$59-$99.** 20600 Grandview Dr. On US 97; north end of town. Int corridors. **Pets:** Medium, other species. $10 daily fee/room. Service with restrictions, supervision.

Red Lion Inn/North 🆂🅷
(541) 382-7011. **$64-$84.** 1415 NE 3rd St. US 97, just n of jct US 20. Ext corridors. **Pets:** Accepted.

Red Lion Inn/South 🆂🅷 ✿
(541) 382-8384. **$64-$84.** 849 NE 3rd St. US 97, just s of jct US 20. Ext corridors. **Pets:** Other species. Service with restrictions.

The Riverhouse Resort Hotel 🆂🅷
(541) 389-3111. **$79-$135.** 3075 N Business 97. US 97, exit 136 (Butler Market Rd) northbound, just n; exit 135B southbound. Ext/int corridors. **Pets:** Accepted.

Rodeway Inn 🆂🅷
(541) 382-2211. **$39-$89.** 3705 N US Hwy 97 business loop. 2 mi n on US 97 business loop. Ext corridors. **Pets:** Dogs only. $5 one-time fee/room. Designated rooms, service with restrictions, supervision.

Sleep Inn of Bend 🆂🅷
(541) 330-0050. **$69-$89.** 600 NE Bellevue. On US 20 E, 2 mi e of jct US 97. Int corridors. **Pets:** Medium. $8 one-time fee/pet. Service with restrictions, supervision.

BOARDMAN

Econo Lodge Ⓜ
(541) 481-2375. **$55-$80.** 105 SW Front St. I-84, exit 164, just s. Ext corridors. **Pets:** Other species. Designated rooms, service with restrictions, supervision.

BROOKINGS

Best Western Beachfront Inn 🆂🅷
(541) 469-7779. **$99-$195.** 16008 Boat Basin Rd. South end on US 101, 1 mi w on Lower Harbor Rd. Ext corridors. **Pets:** Large, other species. $5 daily fee/pet. Designated rooms, service with restrictions, supervision.

Westward Motel Ⓜ
(541) 469-7471. **$39-$79, 3 day notice.** 1026 Chetco Ave. North end on US 101. Ext corridors. **Pets:** Small, dogs only. $8 daily fee/pet. Supervision.

BURNS

Best Inn Ⓜ ✿
(541) 573-1700. **$47-$67.** 999 Oregon Ave. 1 mi w on US 395/20 from jct SR 78. Ext/int corridors. **Pets:** Small. $20 deposit/pet, $5 daily fee/pet. Designated rooms, service with restrictions, supervision.

Days Inn Ponderosa Ⓜ
(541) 573-2047. **$43-$58.** 577 W Monroe St. Just w on US 395/20 from jct SR 78. Ext corridors. **Pets:** Medium. $10 daily fee/pet. Designated rooms, service with restrictions, supervision.

Silver Spur Motel Ⓜ
(541) 573-2077. **$50.** 789 N Broadway. US 395/20, at edge of town. Ext corridors. **Pets:** Dogs only. $10 daily fee/pet. Designated rooms, supervision.

CANNON BEACH

Hallmark Resort at Cannon Beach 🆂🅷
(503) 436-1566. **$99-$329, 3 day notice.** 1400 S Hemlock St. US 101, exit Sunset Blvd, just s. Ext corridors. **Pets:** Accepted.

Haystack Resort Motel Ⓜ ✿
(503) 436-1577. **$109-$219, 3 day notice.** 3339 S Hemlock St. US 101, exit Tolovana Park, just w. Ext corridors. **Pets:** Other species. $10 daily fee/pet. Designated rooms, service with restrictions, supervision.

Inn at Cannon Beach Ⓜ ✿
(503) 436-9085. **$99-$219, 3 day notice.** 3215 S Hemlock St. US 101, exit Tolovana Park, just w, then just n. Ext corridors. **Pets:** $10 daily fee/pet. Designated rooms, service with restrictions, supervision.

Ocean Lodge 🆂🅷 ✿
(503) 436-2241. **$169-$299, 3 day notice.** 2864 S Pacific. US 101, exit Tolovana Park, 1 mi s, then just w on Chisana. Ext/int corridors. **Pets:** Other species. $25 daily fee/pet. Designated rooms, service with restrictions, supervision.

AAA ▼▼▼▼ Surfsand Resort & Meeting
Facility **M** ❀
(503) 436-2274. **$99-$349, 3 day notice.** Ocean Front & Gower. US 101, exit 2nd Cannon Beach; downtown. Ext corridors. **Pets:** Other species. $12 daily fee/pet. Designated rooms, supervision.
[SAVE] [S▲] [X] [◇] [&] [🔒] [💻] [¶] [➳] [✕] [🐾]

AAA ▼▼▼▼ Tolovana Inn **CO** ❀
(503) 436-2211. **$65-$289, 3 day notice.** 3400 S Hemlock St. 2 mi s off US 101 Beach Loop. Ext corridors. **Pets:** Large. $10 daily fee/pet. Designated rooms, service with restrictions, supervision.
[SAVE] [S▲] [X] [🔒] [💻] [➳] [✕] [🐾]

CANYONVILLE

AAA ▼▼▼▼ Best Western Canyonville Inn &
Suites **SH**
(541) 839-4200. **$65-$139.** 200 Creekside Rd. I-5, exit 99, just nw. Int corridors. **Pets:** Small. $15 daily fee/room. Designated rooms, service with restrictions, supervision.
[SAVE] [S▲] [X] [&] [🔒] [💻] [➳]

CASCADE LOCKS

AAA ▼▼▼▼ Best Western Columbia River
Inn **SH** ❀
(541) 374-8777. **$64-$129.** 735 WaNaPa St. I-84, exit 44. Int corridors. **Pets:** Other species. $10 daily fee/pet. Designated rooms, service with restrictions, supervision.
[SAVE] [S▲] [X] [&M] [◇] [&] [🔒] [💻] [➳]

COOS BAY

AAA ▼▼▼▼ Best Western Holiday Motel **SH**
(541) 269-5111. **$74-$159.** 411 N Bayshore Dr. Just n of downtown on US 101. Ext/int corridors. **Pets:** Small, dogs only. $10 daily fee/pet. Service with restrictions, supervision.
[SAVE] [S▲] [X] [&] [🔒] [💻] [➳]

▼▼▼ Edgewater Inn **M**
(541) 267-0423. **$75-$100.** 275 E Johnson Ave. Just s of downtown on US 101, then e. Ext/int corridors. **Pets:** Accepted.
[ASK] [S▲] [X] [&M] [◇] [🔒] [💻] [➳] [✕]

▼▼▼ Motel 6–1244 **SH**
(541) 267-7171. **$43-$65.** 1445 Bayshore Dr. 0.6 mi n of downtown on US 101. Ext corridors. **Pets:** Service with restrictions, supervision.
[S▲] [X] [◇] [&] [🔒] [💻]

AAA ▼▼▼ Red Lion Hotel **SH**
(541) 267-4141. **$144-$188.** 1313 N Bayshore Dr. 0.5 mi n of downtown on US 101. Ext corridors. **Pets:** Other species. Service with restrictions, crate.
[SAVE] [S▲] [X] [&M] [◇] [🔒] [💻] [¶] [➳] [✕]

COQUILLE

▼▼▼ Myrtle Lane Motel **M**
(541) 396-2102. **$45.** 787 N Central Blvd. SR 42, 0.4 mi n. Ext corridors. **Pets:** Small. $4 daily fee/pet. Designated rooms, service with restrictions, supervision.
[X] [&] [🔒] [🐾]

CORVALLIS

AAA ▼▼▼ Days Inn **SH**
(541) 754-7474. **$62-$82.** 1113 NW 9th St. 1.3 mi n. Int corridors. **Pets:** Medium, other species. $5 daily fee/pet. Designated rooms, service with restrictions, supervision.
[SAVE] [S▲] [X] [◇] [🔒] [➳]

▼▼▼ Holiday Inn Express On The
River **SH** ❀
(541) 752-0800. **$69-$85.** 781 NE 2nd St. I-5, exit 228, 9.8 mi w on SR 34, 0.4 mi nw on SR 99 W, then just n. Int corridors. **Pets:** Other species. $15 daily fee/room. Designated rooms, service with restrictions, supervision.
[ASK] [S▲] [X] [◇] [&] [🔒] [💻] [➳]

AAA ▼▼▼ Motel 6 **SH**
(541) 758-9125. **$59-$89.** 935 NW Garfield. 1.5 mi n on 9th St; downtown. Int corridors. **Pets:** Accepted.
[SAVE] [S▲] [X] [&M] [◇] [&] [🔒] [💻]

▼▼▼ Super 8 Motel **SH**
(541) 758-8088. **$63-$77.** 407 NW 2nd St. US 20, just n of jct SR 34; downtown. Int corridors. **Pets:** Other species. $25 deposit/pet. Designated rooms, service with restrictions, supervision.
[ASK] [S▲] [X] [&M] [◇] [&] [🔒] [➳]

COTTAGE GROVE

AAA ▼▼▼ Comfort Inn **SH**
(541) 942-9747. **$59-$79, 3 day notice.** 845 Gateway Blvd. I-5, exit 174, just w. Ext/int corridors. **Pets:** Other species. $10 daily fee/pet. Designated rooms, service with restrictions, supervision.
[SAVE] [S▲] [X] [◇] [🔒] [💻] [➳]

AAA ▼▼▼▼ Holiday Inn Express **SH**
(541) 942-1000. **$69-$89, 3 day notice.** 1601 Gateway Blvd. I-5, exit 174, just w. Int corridors. **Pets:** Medium, dogs only. $10 one-time fee/pet. Service with restrictions, supervision.
[SAVE] [S▲] [X] [◇] [&] [🔒] [➳]

AAA ▼▼▼ Village Green Resort **M**
(541) 942-2491. **$69-$109.** 725 Row River Rd. I-5, exit 174, just e. Ext corridors. **Pets:** Medium. $30 one-time fee/pet. Designated rooms, service with restrictions, supervision.
[SAVE] [S▲] [X] [🔒] [💻] [➳]

CRESCENT

AAA ▼▼▼ Woodsman Country Lodge **M**
(541) 433-2710. **$45-$47.** 136740 Hwy 97 N. Center. Ext corridors. **Pets:** Medium, other species. $10 daily fee/pet. Designated rooms, service with restrictions, supervision.
[SAVE] [X] [🔒] [💻]

CRESWELL

AAA ▼▼▼▼ Best Western Creswell Inn **M** ❀
(541) 895-3341. **$64-$119.** 345 E Oregon Ave. I-5, exit 182, just w. Ext corridors. **Pets:** $10 deposit/pet, $10 one-time fee/pet. Designated rooms, service with restrictions, supervision.
[SAVE] [S▲] [X] [🔒] [💻] [➳]

DALLAS

Best Western Dallas Inn & Suites SH
(503) 623-6000. **$79-$89.** 250 Orchard Dr. SR 223, just n. Int corridors. **Pets:** Accepted.

THE DALLES

Best Western River City Inn SH ❧
(541) 296-9107. **$62-$89.** 112 W 2nd. I-84, exit 84 eastbound; exit 85 westbound, just s; downtown. Ext/int corridors. **Pets:** Small, other species. $10 daily fee/pet. Designated rooms, service with restrictions.

Comfort Inn Columbia Gorge SH ❧
(541) 298-2800. **$60-$129.** 351 Lone Pine Dr. I-84, exit 87, just n. Int corridors. **Pets:** Small, other species. $15 daily fee/pet. Service with restrictions, supervision.

DEPOE BAY

Crown Pacific Inn M
(541) 765-7773. **$95-$125.** 50 NE Bechill St. Center. Ext/int corridors. **Pets:** Medium. $10 daily fee/pet. Designated rooms, service with restrictions, supervision.

Gracie's Sea Hag Inn BB ❧
(541) 765-2322. **$99-$150, 3 day notice.** 235 SE Bay View Ave. US 101, just e on SE Bay St. Int corridors. **Pets:** Large. $9 daily fee/pet. Designated rooms, service with restrictions, supervision.

ENTERPRISE

Ponderosa Motel M
(541) 426-3186. **$67-$76.** 102 E Greenwood St. Center of town. Ext corridors. **Pets:** Dogs only. $10 one-time fee/pet. Supervision.

The Wilderness Inn M
(541) 426-4535. **$51-$65.** 301 W North St. Corner of NW 2nd. Ext corridors. **Pets:** Accepted.

EUGENE

Best Western Greentree Inn SH ❧
(541) 485-2727. **$80-$94.** 1759 Franklin Blvd. I-5, exit 194B southbound to I-105, then University of Oregon Rt; exit 192 northbound, 1.2 mi w. Ext/int corridors. **Pets:** $50 deposit/pet. Service with restrictions, supervision.

Best Western New Oregon Motel SH ❧
(541) 683-3669. **$80-$94.** 1655 Franklin Blvd. I-5, exit 194B southbound to I-105, then University of Oregon Rt; exit 192 northbound, 1.3 mi w. Ext/int corridors. **Pets:** $50 deposit/pet. Service with restrictions, supervision.

Courtesy Inn M
(541) 345-3391. **$45-$80.** 345 W 6th Ave. I-5, exit 194B, 2 mi w on I-105 (to end of freeway), to 7th Ave, just e to Lincoln, then just n; downtown at Lincoln and 6th Ave. Ext corridors. **Pets:** Very small, dogs only. $7 daily fee/pet. Service with restrictions, supervision.

Days Inn M
(541) 342-6383. **$55-$113.** 1859 Franklin Blvd. I-5, exit 192 northbound, 1 mi w; exit 194B southbound to I-105, follow University of Oregon signs. Ext/int corridors. **Pets:** Accepted.

Eugene Red Lion Hotel SH ❧
(541) 342-5201. **$69-$99.** 205 Coburg Rd. I-5, exit 194B southbound, 1.3 mi w on I-105, exit 2 (Coburg Rd), just n. Ext corridors. **Pets:** Accepted.

Eugene/Springfield Residence Inn by Marriott SH
(541) 342-7171. **$114-$124.** 25 Club Rd. I-5, exit 194B southbound, 1.3 mi w on I-105, exit 2 (Coburg Rd), just s, just w on Centennial Blvd, then just se. Int corridors. **Pets:** Medium, other species. $50 one-time fee/room. Service with restrictions.

Franklin Inn M
(541) 342-4804. **$44-$79.** 1857 Franklin Blvd. I-5, exit 192 northbound, 1 mi w; exit 194B southbound to I-105, follow University of Oregon signs. Ext corridors. **Pets:** Medium, dogs only. $10 daily fee/pet. Designated rooms, service with restrictions, supervision.

Hilton Eugene LH ❧
(541) 342-2000. **$124-$169.** 66 E 6th Ave. At 6th Ave and Oak St; center. Int corridors. **Pets:** Medium, other species. $25 one-time fee/room. Service with restrictions.

La Quinta Inn & Suites Waterfront SH ❧
(541) 344-8335. **$81-$135.** 155 Day Island Rd. I-5, exit 194B southbound, 1.3 mi w on I-105, exit 2 (Coburg Rd), just s, just w on Centennial Rd, then 0.5 mi se on Country Club Rd. Int corridors. **Pets:** Other species. $50 deposit/room. Service with restrictions, supervision.

Motel 6-36 M
(541) 687-2395. **$47-$63.** 3690 Glenwood Dr. I-5, exit 191, just sw. Ext corridors. **Pets:** Accepted.

QQQ ▼▼▼ Quality Inn & Suites M ❖
(541) 342-1243. **$56-$108.** 2121 Franklin Blvd. I-5, exit 192 northbound, just w; exit 194B southbound to I-105, exit University of Oregon Rt. Ext corridors. **Pets:** Medium. $5 daily fee/pet. Service with restrictions, supervision.
[SAVE] [S🐾] [✕] [🔒] [💻] [🚭]

▼▼▼ Ramada Inn-Eugene SH
(541) 342-5181. **$65-$108.** 225 Coburg Rd. I-5, exit 194B southbound, 1.3 mi w on I-105, exit 2 (Coburg Rd), then just s. Ext/int corridors. **Pets:** $15 one-time fee/pet. Service with restrictions, supervision.
[ASK] [S🐾] [✕] [🍽] [🖥] [🔒] [💻] [🍴] [🚭]

▼▼▼▼ The Valley River Inn SH
(541) 687-0123. **$200.** 1000 Valley River Way. I-5, exit 194B southbound, 2.5 mi w on I-105, exit 1, follow the Valley River Center signs, just s of mall. Int corridors. **Pets:** Service with restrictions, supervision.
[ASK] [S🐾] [✕] [🍽] [🖥] [🔒] [💻] [🍴] [🚭] [✕]

FLORENCE

QQQ ▼▼ Best Western Pier Point Inn SH
(541) 997-7191. **$75-$149.** 85625 Hwy 101. Jct SR 126, 1 mi s. Ext/int corridors. **Pets:** Accepted.
[SAVE] [S🐾] [✕] [🍽] [🔒] [💻] [🍴] [🚭]

QQQ ▼ Oceanbreeze Motel M
(541) 997-2642. **$39-$109.** 85165 Hwy 101 S. SR 126, 2 mi s. Ext corridors. **Pets:** Dogs only. $50 deposit/room, $10 daily fee/pet. Supervision.
[SAVE] [✕] [🔒] [💻] [🎞]

QQQ ▼ Old Town Inn M
(541) 997-7131. **$57-$96.** 170 Hwy 101. SR 126, 0.5 mi s. Ext corridors. **Pets:** $10 one-time fee/pet. Designated rooms, service with restrictions, supervision.
[SAVE] [S🐾] [✕] [💻] [🎞]

QQQ ▼▼▼ Park Motel M ❖
(541) 997-2634. **$47-$129.** 85034 Hwy 101 S. SR 126, 2.2 mi s. Ext corridors. **Pets:** Other species. $8 daily fee/pet. Service with restrictions, supervision.
[SAVE] [S🐾] [✕] [🔒] [💻] [🎞]

GARIBALDI

▼▼▼▼ Inn at Garibaldi SH
(503) 322-3338. **$59-$119.** 502 Garibaldi Ave. On US 101 at jct 5th St; center. Int corridors. **Pets:** Accepted.
[ASK] [S🐾] [✕] [🖥] [🔒] [🚭] [✕]

GEARHART

QQQ ▼▼▼ Gearhart By The Sea Resort CO
(503) 738-8331. **$63-$150, 7 day notice.** 1157 N Marion. 1 mi w off US 101 via City Center exit (Pacific Way). Ext corridors. **Pets:** Medium. $11 daily fee/pet. Designated rooms, service with restrictions, supervision.
[SAVE] [S🐾] [✕] [🔒] [💻] [🚭] [🎞]

GLENEDEN BEACH

QQQ ▼▼▼ ▼▼▼ Salishan Lodge & Golf Resort LH ❖
(541) 764-2371. **$179-$319, 3 day notice.** 7760 Hwy 101 N. Just e of US 101; center. Ext corridors. **Pets:** Other species. $25 one-time fee/pet. Designated rooms, service with restrictions, supervision.
[SAVE] [S🐾] [✕] [🍽] [🖥] [🔒] [💻] [🍴] [🚭] [✕] [🎞]

GLIDE

QQQ ▼▼▼ Steelhead Run B & B and Fine Art Gallery BB ❖
(541) 496-0563. **$58-$125, 7 day notice.** 23049 N Umpqua (Hwy 138). I-5, exit 124, 0.8 mi s, just n to SR 138, then 18 mi e to MM 20. Ext/int corridors. **Pets:** Other species. $20 daily fee/room. Designated rooms, crate.
[SAVE] [S🐾] [✕] [🔒] [💻] [✕]

GOLD BEACH

QQQ ▼▼ Econo Lodge at Gold Beach M
(541) 247-6606. **$40-$125.** 29171 Ellensburg Ave. On US 101, south end of town. Ext corridors. **Pets:** Accepted.
[SAVE] [S🐾] [✕] [🔒] [💻] [🎞]

QQQ ▼▼▼ Inn of The Beachcomber M ❖
(541) 247-6691. **$65-$180.** 29266 Ellensburg Ave. On US 101, south end of town. Ext/int corridors. **Pets:** Small, dogs only. $25 one-time fee/pet. Designated rooms, service with restrictions, supervision.
[SAVE] [S🐾] [✕] [🔒] [💻] [🚭]

QQQ ▼▼▼ Ireland's Rustic Lodges CA
(541) 247-7718. **$55-$95.** 29330 Ellensburg Ave. On US 101; center. Ext corridors. **Pets:** Accepted.
[SAVE] [✕] [🔒] [💻] [🎞] [🔌]

QQQ ▼▼▼ Jot's Resort M ❖
(541) 247-6676. **$50-$180.** 94360 Wedderburn Loop. Just w of US 101, north end of bridge. Ext corridors. **Pets:** Other species. $10 daily fee/pet. Service with restrictions, supervision.
[SAVE] [✕] [🍽] [🔒] [💻] [🍴] [🚭] [✕] [🎞]

▼▼ ▼▼▼ Motel 6-4047 M
(541) 247-4533. **$55-$78.** 94433 Jerry's Flat Rd. On US 101, north end of town. Ext corridors. **Pets:** Large, other species. Service with restrictions, supervision.
[✕] [🔒] [💻] [🎞]

▼▼ ▼▼ Sand 'n Sea Motel M
(541) 247-6658. **$49-$109.** 29362 Ellensburg Ave. On US 101; center. Ext/int corridors. **Pets:** Accepted.
[ASK] [S🐾] [✕] [🖥] [🔒] [💻] [🎞]

QQQ ▼▼▼ Shore Cliff Inn M
(541) 247-7091. **$50-$95.** 29346 Ellensburg Ave. On US 101; center. Ext corridors. **Pets:** Accepted.
[SAVE] [✕] [🔒] [💻] [🎞]

GOVERNMENT CAMP

Mt. Hood Inn SH
(503) 272-3205. **$149-$169.** 87450 E Government Camp. 0.5 mi w of center. Int corridors. **Pets:** Other species. $10 daily fee/pet. Service with restrictions, supervision.

GRANTS PASS

Best Western Grants Pass Inn SH
(541) 476-1117. **$73-$116.** 111 NE Agness Ave. I-5, exit 55, just w. Ext corridors. **Pets:** Other species. $5 daily fee/room. Service with restrictions, supervision.

Best Western Inn at the Rogue SH
(541) 582-2200. **$60-$120.** 8959 Rogue River Hwy. I-5, exit 48, just w. Int corridors. **Pets:** Other species. $20 daily fee/pet. Designated rooms, service with restrictions, supervision.

Comfort Inn SH
(541) 479-8301. **$70-$114.** 1889 NE 6th St. I-5, exit 58, just s on SR 99. Int corridors. **Pets:** Other species. $100 deposit/room. Service with restrictions, supervision.

Holiday Inn Express SH
(541) 471-6144. **$79-$129.** 105 NE Agness Ave. I-5, exit 55, just w. Int corridors. **Pets:** Large, other species. $5 daily fee/pet. Designated rooms, service with restrictions, supervision.

Knights Inn Motel M
(541) 479-5595. **$50-$105.** 104 SE 7th St. I-5, exit 58, 1.5 mi s on SR 99 to G St, 1 blk e. Ext corridors. **Pets:** Medium, dogs only. $20 deposit/pet, $10 daily fee/pet. Service with restrictions.

La Quinta Inn & Suites SH
(541) 472-1808. **$67-$130.** 243 NE Morgan Ln. I-5, exit 58, 0.4 mi s on SR 99, just e on Hillcrest Dr to SR 99 northbound, then just n. Int corridors. **Pets:** Large. Service with restrictions, supervision.

Motel 6–253 M
(541) 474-1331. **$45-$60.** 1800 NE 7th St. I-5, exit 58, 0.3 mi s on SR 99. Ext corridors. **Pets:** Small, other species. Service with restrictions, supervision.

Redwood Motel M
(541) 476-0878. **$50-$200.** 815 NE 6th St. I-5, exit 58, 1.2 mi s on SR 99. Ext corridors. **Pets:** Small, dogs only. $10 daily fee/pet. Service with restrictions, supervision.

Riverside Inn Resort SH
(541) 476-6873. **$69-$129.** 971 SE 6th St. I-5, exit 58, 2.5 mi s on SR 99. Ext corridors. **Pets:** $10 daily fee/pet. Designated rooms, service with restrictions, supervision.

Sunset Inn M
(541) 479-3305. **$50-$135.** 1400 NW 6th St. I-5, exit 58, 0.6 mi s on SR 99. Ext corridors. **Pets:** Medium, dogs only. $25 deposit/room, $5 daily fee/pet. Designated rooms, service with restrictions, supervision.

Super 8 Motel-Grants Pass M
(541) 474-0888. **$54-$80.** 1949 NE 7th St. I-5, exit 58, 0.4 mi s on SR 99, just e on Hillcrest Dr to SR 99 northbound, then just n. Int corridors. **Pets:** Other species. $25 deposit/room. Service with restrictions, supervision.

Sweet Breeze Inn M
(541) 471-4434. **$58-$100.** 1627 NE 6th St. I-5, exit 58, 0.4 mi s on SR 99. Ext/int corridors. **Pets:** Small. Designated rooms, service with restrictions, supervision.

Travelodge M
(541) 479-6611. **$59-$69.** 1950 NW Vine St. I-5, exit 58, just s on SR 99. Ext corridors. **Pets:** Small. $5 daily fee/pet. Designated rooms, service with restrictions, supervision.

HALSEY

Best Western Pioneer Lodge M
(541) 369-2804. **$69-$81.** 33180 SR 228. I-5, exit 216, just e. Ext corridors. **Pets:** $5 daily fee/pet.

HERMISTON

Oak Tree Inn SH
(541) 567-2330. **$59-$99.** 1110 SE 4th St. 0.4 mi s on US 395, just w. Int corridors. **Pets:** $10 daily fee/pet. Service with restrictions, crate.

Oxford Suites SH
(541) 564-8000. **$69-$115.** 1050 N First. 0.3 mi n on US 395. Int corridors. **Pets:** Small, dogs only. $20 one-time fee/pet. Designated rooms, service with restrictions, supervision.

HINES

Comfort Inn M
(541) 573-3370. **$57-$69.** 504 N Hwy 20. On US 20 (Hines/Burns). Int corridors. **Pets:** Small, dogs only. $10 one-time fee/pet. Designated rooms, service with restrictions, supervision.

HOOD RIVER

Best Western Hood River Inn SH
(541) 386-2200. **$79-$139.** 1108 E Marina Way. I-84, exit 64, just n, then just e. Int corridors. **Pets:** Medium, dogs only. $12 daily fee/room. Service with restrictions, supervision.

⚠⚠ ▽▽▽▽ Columbia Gorge Hotel 🅲🅸
(541) 386-5566. **$179-$399, 14 day notice.** 4000 Westcliff Dr. I-84, exit 62, just w of overpass. Int corridors. **Pets:** Accepted.
[SAVE] [✕] [🛏] [🍴]

⚠⚠ ▽▽▽ Meredith Gorge Motel Ⓜ
(541) 386-1515. **$53-$79.** 4300 Westcliff Dr. I-84, exit 62, just n, then 0.8 mi w. Ext corridors. **Pets:** Accepted.
[SAVE] [S🐾] [✕] [🛏] [🖥]

⚠⚠ ▽ Vagabond Lodge Ⓜ
(541) 386-2992. **$49-$82.** 4070 Westcliff Dr. I-84, exit 62, just n, then just w. Ext corridors. **Pets:** Small. $5 daily fee/pet. Designated rooms, service with restrictions, supervision.
[SAVE] [✕] [🛏] [🖥]

JACKSONVILLE

⚠⚠ ▽▽▽▽ Jacksonville Inn 🅲🅸
(541) 899-1900. **$145-$189, 3 day notice.** 175 E California St. At California and 5th (SR 238) sts; center. Ext/int corridors. **Pets:** Dogs only. Service with restrictions, supervision.
[SAVE] [S🐾] [✕] [🛏] [🖥] [🍴] [✕]

▽▽ The Stage Lodge Ⓜ ✤
(541) 899-3953. **$109-$185, 7 day notice.** 830 N 5th St. On N 5th St (SR 238), 0.3 mi ne. Ext corridors. **Pets:** Medium. $15 daily fee/pet. Designated rooms, service with restrictions, supervision.
[ASK] [S🐾] [✕] [✍] [🛏] [🖥]

JOHN DAY

⚠⚠ ▽▽▽ Best Western John Day Inn Ⓜ
(541) 575-1700. **$74-$94.** 315 W Main St. Just w on US 26 and 395. Ext corridors. **Pets:** Small. $5 daily fee/pet. Designated rooms, service with restrictions, crate.
[SAVE] [S🐾] [✕] [✍] [🛏] [🖥] [≈]

⚠⚠ ▽▽▽ Dreamers Lodge Ⓜ
(541) 575-0526. **$45-$65.** 144 N Canyon Blvd. Just n of jct US 26 and 395. Ext corridors. **Pets:** Other species. $5 one-time fee/pet. Service with restrictions, supervision.
[SAVE] [S🐾] [✕] [🛏] [🖥]

JOSEPH

⚠⚠ ▽▽▽▽ Manuel Bronze Bear Bed & Breakfast 🅱🅱
(541) 432-2233. **$159, 30 day notice.** 208 S East St. Just s on S Main St, just e on E Third St, then just n; downtown. Ext/int corridors. **Pets:** Accepted.
[SAVE] [✕] [☎]

KLAMATH FALLS

⚠⚠ ▽▽▽ Best Western Klamath Inn 🆂🅷
(541) 882-1200. **$78-$81.** 4061 S 6th St. Just w on 6th St (SR 140) from jct SR 140 E/39 S and SR 39 N/US 97 business route. Ext corridors. **Pets:** Accepted.
[SAVE] [S🐾] [✕] [✍] [🖐] [🛏] [🖥] [≈]

⚠⚠ ▽▽▽ Maverick Motel Ⓜ
(541) 882-6688. **$39-$59.** 1220 Main St. US 97 N to City Center exit, 0.3 mi e. Ext corridors. **Pets:** Designated rooms, service with restrictions, supervision.
[SAVE] [S🐾] [✕] [🛏] [≈]

▽ Motel 6–226 🆂🅷
(541) 884-2110. **$41-$69.** 5136 S 6th St. 0.5 mi e on 6th St (SR 140) E from jct SR 39/US 97 business route. Ext corridors. **Pets:** Accepted.
[S🐾] [✕] [🖐] [✍] [👞] [≈]

⚠⚠ ▽ Oregon Motel 8 Ⓜ
(541) 883-3431. **$47-$100.** 5225 Hwy 97 N. On US 97, between MM 270 and 271, east side of highway. Ext corridors. **Pets:** Medium. $10 one-time fee/room. Designated rooms, service with restrictions, supervision.
[SAVE] [S🐾] [✕] [🛏] [🖥] [≈]

⚠⚠ ▽▽▽ Quality Inn 🆂🅷
(541) 882-4666. **$79-$99.** 100 Main St. Just e of US 97, exit City Center. Ext corridors. **Pets:** Accepted.
[SAVE] [S🐾] [✕] [🖐] [✍] [👞] [🛏] [🖥] [🍴] [≈]

▽▽ Red Lion Inn 🆂🅷
(541) 882-8864. **$62-$89.** 3612 S 6th St. 0.3 mi w on 6th St (SR 140) from jct SR 140 E/39 S and SR 39 N/US 97 business route. Ext corridors. **Pets:** $50 deposit/room. Service with restrictions.
[ASK] [S🐾] [✕] [✍] [👞] [🛏] [🖥] [🍴] [≈] [✕]

▽▽▽▽ The Running Y Ranch Resort 🆂🅷
(541) 850-5500. **$119-$269, 3 day notice.** 5500 Running Y Rd. On SR 140, 7.2 mi n from jct US 66 and SR 140. Int corridors. **Pets:** Large, other species. $20 daily fee/room. Designated rooms, service with restrictions.
[ASK] [S🐾] [✕] [🖐] [✍] [👞] [🛏] [🖥] [🍴] [≈] [✕]

▽▽ Super 8 Motel 🆂🅷
(541) 884-8880. **$75, 5 day notice.** 3805 Hwy 97. On US 97, 2 mi n. Int corridors. **Pets:** Accepted.
[ASK] [S🐾] [✕] [🖐] [🛏]

LA GRANDE

⚠⚠ ▽▽▽ Howard Johnson Inn 🆂🅷
(541) 963-7195. **$77.** 2612 Island Ave. I-84, exit 261, just e. Ext/int corridors. **Pets:** $10 one-time fee/room. Designated rooms, service with restrictions, supervision.
[SAVE] [S🐾] [✕] [✍] [🛏] [🖥] [≈] [✕]

⚠⚠ ▽ Royal Motor Inn Ⓜ ✤
(541) 963-4154. **$40-$50.** 1510 Adams Ave. I-84, exit La Grande on US 30, just n of jct SR 82; downtown. Ext corridors. **Pets:** Medium, other species. $10 one-time fee/room. Designated rooms, service with restrictions, supervision.
[SAVE] [S🐾] [✕] [✍] [🛏]

LAKEVIEW

⚠⚠ ▽▽▽▽ Best Western Skyline Motor Lodge 🆂🅷
(541) 947-2194. **$99-$129.** 414 N G St. Jct US 395 and SR 140. Ext corridors. **Pets:** Small. $10 one-time fee/pet. Designated rooms, service with restrictions, supervision.
[SAVE] [S🐾] [✕] [✍] [🛏] [🖥] [≈]

LA PINE

▼▼▼ **Best Western Newberry Station** SH
(541) 536-5130. **$89-$119.** 16515 Reed Rd. North end of town, just off SR 97. Int corridors. **Pets:** Accepted.
(ASK) (S📶) (✕) (&M) (🐕) 📖 🖵 🏊

LINCOLN CITY

🔷 ▼▼▼ **Coho Inn** M
(541) 994-3684. **$62-$162.** 1635 NW Harbor. US 101, exit N 17th St, just w. Ext corridors. **Pets:** Small, other species. $8 daily fee/pet. Designated rooms, service with restrictions, supervision.
(SAVE) (✕) 📖 🖵 (K)

🔷 ▼▼ **Crown Pacific Inn Express** SH
(541) 994-7559. **$50-$100.** 1070 SE 1st St. On US 101 near D River. Int corridors. **Pets:** Medium. $10 daily fee/pet. Designated rooms, service with restrictions, supervision.
(SAVE) (S📶) (✕) 📖 🖵 (K)

🔷 ▼▼ **Lincoln City Inn** M
(541) 996-4400. **$59-$79.** 1091 SE 1st St. On US 101 at D River. Int corridors. **Pets:** Medium, dogs only. $10 one-time fee/room. Service with restrictions, supervision.
(SAVE) (S📶) (✕) (&M) (🐕) 📖 🖵

🔷 ▼▼▼▼ **The O'dysius Hotel** SH ❀
(541) 994-4121. **$149-$319.** 120 NW Inlet Ct. On US 101 at D River; center. Int corridors. **Pets:** Small, dogs only. $10 daily fee/pet. Designated rooms, service with restrictions, supervision.
(SAVE) (S📶) (✕) (🐕) 📖 🖵 (✕) (K)

MADRAS

🔷 ▼▼ **Best Western Rama Inn** M ❀
(541) 475-6141. **$69-$89.** 12 SW 4th St. On US 97/26 southbound; downtown. Ext corridors. **Pets:** Medium. $20 one-time fee/room. Supervision.
(SAVE) (S📶) (✕) (&M) (🐕) 📖 🖵 🏊

MCMINNVILLE

▼▼▼ **Red Lion Inn & Suites** SH
(503) 472-1500. **$97-$134.** 2535 NE Cumulus Ave. Jct SR 99 W, 3.7 mi e on SR 18 E. Int corridors. **Pets:** Accepted.
(ASK) (S📶) (✕) (&M) (🐕) 📖 🖵 🏊

MEDFORD

🔷 ▼▼▼▼ **Best Western Horizon Inn** SH
(541) 779-5085. **$77-$125, 3 day notice.** 1154 E Barnett Rd. I-5, exit 27, just e. Ext corridors. **Pets:** Other species. $10 daily fee/room. Service with restrictions, supervision.
(SAVE) (S📶) (✕) (🐕) (🐕) 📖 🖵 🏊 (✕)

🔷 ▼▼ **Cedar Lodge Motor Inn** M
(541) 773-7361. **$52-$72.** 518 N Riverside Ave. I-5, exit 27, 0.5 mi w on Barnett Rd, then 1.2 mi n on SR 99. Ext corridors. **Pets:** Small. $20 deposit/room. Service with restrictions, supervision.
(SAVE) (S📶) (✕) 📖 🏊

🔷 ▼▼▼ **Comfort Inn Medford North** SH ❀
(541) 772-9500. **$69-$119.** 1100 Hilton Rd. I-5, exit 30 northbound, then just n on Biddle Rd; southbound, follow signs for Biddle Rd, then just n. Int corridors. **Pets:** Other species. $50 deposit/room, $20 daily fee/pet. Designated rooms, service with restrictions, supervision.
(SAVE) (S📶) (✕) (🐕) (🐕) 📖 🖵 🏊

🔷 ▼▼ **Knights Inn** M
(541) 773-3676. **$50-$66.** 500 N Riverside Ave. I-5, exit 27, 0.4 mi w on Barnett Rd, then 1.2 mi n on SR 99. Ext corridors. **Pets:** Accepted.
(SAVE) (S📶) (✕) (🐕) 📖 🏊

🔷 ▼▼▼ **Medford Inn** SH
(541) 773-8266. **$61-$98.** 1015 S Riverside Ave. I-5, exit 27, 0.4 mi w, then just n. Ext corridors. **Pets:** Small. $100 deposit/pet. Service with restrictions, supervision.
(SAVE) (S📶) (✕) (🐕) (🐕) 📖 🖵 🏊

▼▼ **Motel 6-Medford North–739** M
(541) 779-0550. **$49-$67.** 2400 Biddle Rd. I-5, exit 30 northbound, just s; southbound, follow signs. Ext corridors. **Pets:** Other species. Service with restrictions, supervision.
(S📶) (✕) (🐕) (🐕) 📖 🏊

▼▼ **Motel 6-Medford South–89** M
(541) 773-4290. **$45-$63.** 950 Alba Dr. I-5, exit 27, just e on Barnett Rd, then just n. Ext corridors. **Pets:** Other species. Service with restrictions, supervision.
(S📶) (✕) (&M) (🐕) (🐕) 📖 🏊

🔷 ▼▼▼ **Pear Tree Motel & RV Park** M
(541) 535-4445. **$69-$95.** 300 Pear Tree Ln. I-5, exit 24, 1 blk e, just s to Frontage Rd, then just n. Ext corridors. **Pets:** Small, dogs only. $10 daily fee/room. Service with restrictions, supervision.
(SAVE) (S📶) (✕) (🐕) 📖 🏊

🔷 ▼▼▼ **Red Lion Hotel** SH
(541) 779-5811. **$69-$79.** 200 N Riverside Ave. I-5, exit 27, 0.4 mi w on Barnett Rd, then 1 mi n. Ext corridors. **Pets:** Other species. $25 deposit/room. Service with restrictions, supervision.
(SAVE) (✕) (&M) (🐕) 📖 🖵 🍴 🏊

🔷 ▼▼▼▼ **Windmill Inn of Medford** SH ❀
(541) 779-0050. **$69-$89.** 1950 Biddle Rd. I-5, exit 30 northbound, just s; southbound, follow signs for Biddle Rd, then just s. Int corridors. **Pets:** Medium. Designated rooms, service with restrictions.
(SAVE) (S📶) (✕) (🐕) (🐕) 📖 🏊 (✕)

MYRTLE POINT

🔷 ▼▼ **Myrtle Trees Motel** M
(541) 572-5811. **$50-$56.** 1010 8th St (Hwy 42). On SR 42, 0.5 mi e. Ext corridors. **Pets:** Accepted.
(SAVE) (S📶) (✕) 📖 (K)

NEWBERG

▼▼▼ **Travelodge Suites** 🆂🅷
(503) 537-5000. **$58-$88.** 2816 Portland Rd. North end on SR 99 W. Int corridors. **Pets:** $5 daily fee/pet. Service with restrictions, supervision.
🄰🅂🄺 🆂🄳 ⊠ 🛏 ▣ 🏊 ⊠

NEWPORT

🔷🔷🔷 ▼▼▼ **The Best Western Agate Beach Inn** 🆂🅷 ❖
(541) 265-9411. **$79-$149.** 3019 N Coast Hwy. US 20, 1.5 mi n on US 101. Int corridors. **Pets:** Medium, other species. $15 one-time fee/pet. Designated rooms, service with restrictions, supervision.
🆂🄰🆅🄴 🆂🄳 ⊠ 🄰 🛏 ▣ 🍴 🏊 ⊠ 🎬

🔷🔷🔷 ▼▼▼ **Econo Lodge** Ⓜ ❖
(541) 265-7723. **$44-$99.** 606 SW Coast Hwy 101. 0.5 mi s of US 20. Ext/int corridors. **Pets:** Medium. $5 one-time fee/room. Service with restrictions, supervision.
🆂🄰🆅🄴 🆂🄳 ⊠ 🄰 🛏 🎬

🔷🔷🔷 ▼▼▼▼ **Hallmark Resort** 🆂🅷 ❖
(541) 265-2600. **$79-$179.** 744 SW Elizabeth St. US 20, 0.7 mi s on US 101, just w on SW Bay St. Ext corridors. **Pets:** $5 daily fee/pet. Service with restrictions, supervision.
🆂🄰🆅🄴 ⊠ 🄼 🄰 🄴 🛏 ▣ 🍴 🏊 ⊠ 🎬

🔷🔷🔷 ▼▼▼▼ **La Quinta Inn & Suites** 🆂🅷 ❖
(541) 867-7727. **$64-$149.** 45 SE 32nd St. US 101, just s of Yaquina Bay Bridge. Int corridors. **Pets:** Other species. Designated rooms, service with restrictions, supervision.
🆂🄰🆅🄴 🆂🄳 ⊠ 🄼 🄰 🄴 🛏 ▣ 🏊 ⊠

▼▼▼ **Val-U Inn** Ⓜ ❖
(541) 265-6203. **Call for rates.** 531 SW Fall St. US 20, 0.5 mi s on US 101, just w. Int corridors. **Pets:** Dogs only. $10 daily fee/room. Designated rooms, service with restrictions, supervision.
⊠ 🛏 ▣ 🎬

🔷🔷🔷 ▼▼▼ **Whaler Motel** Ⓜ ❖
(541) 265-9261. **$79-$159.** 155 SW Elizabeth St. Just s on US 101 from jct US 20, just w on SW 2nd. Ext corridors. **Pets:** Dogs only. $5 daily fee/pet. Designated rooms, service with restrictions, supervision.
🆂🄰🆅🄴 🆂🄳 ⊠ 🄼 🄰 🄴 🛏 ▣ 🏊 🎬

NORTH BEND

🔷🔷🔷 ▼▼▼ **Ramada Inn** Ⓜ
(541) 756-3191. **$69-$111.** 1503 Virginia Ave. 0.5 mi w of US 101. Ext/int corridors. **Pets:** Accepted.
🆂🄰🆅🄴 🆂🄳 ⊠ 🄼 🄰 🄴 🛏 ▣ 🍴

OAKRIDGE

🔷🔷🔷 ▼▼▼▼ **Best Western Oakridge Inn** Ⓜ ❖
(541) 782-2212. **$69-$89, 3 day notice.** 47433 SR 58. West end of SR 58. Ext corridors. **Pets:** Large, dogs only. $10 one-time fee/pet. Service with restrictions, supervision.
🆂🄰🆅🄴 🆂🄳 ⊠ 🄼 🄰 🛏 ▣ 🎬

ONTARIO

🔷🔷🔷 ▼▼▼▼ **Best Western Inn & Suites** 🆂🅷
(541) 889-2600. **$56-$169.** 251 Goodfellow St. I-84, exit 376B, just ne. Int corridors. **Pets:** Small. $20 one-time fee/room. Designated rooms, service with restrictions, supervision.
🆂🄰🆅🄴 🆂🄳 ⊠ 🄰 🛏 ▣ 🏊

🔷🔷🔷 ▼▼▼ **Carlile Motel** Ⓜ ❖
(541) 889-8658. **$38-$67, 14 day notice.** 589 N Oregon St (SR 201 & 30). I-84, exit 374, 1.5 mi se; Business Rt 30 and SR 201. Ext corridors. **Pets:** $5 one-time fee/pet. Service with restrictions, supervision.
🆂🄰🆅🄴 🆂🄳 ⊠ 🛏 ▣

🔷🔷🔷 ▼▼▼▼ **Holiday Inn–Ontario, OR** 🆂🅷 ❖
(541) 889-8621. **$75-$85.** 1249 Tapadera Ave. I-84, exit 376B, just ne. Int corridors. **Pets:** Small, other species. $10 one-time fee/room. Designated rooms, service with restrictions, supervision.
🆂🄰🆅🄴 🆂🄳 ⊠ 🄰 🄴 🛏 ▣ 🍴 🏊

🔷🔷🔷 ▼▼ **Holiday Motel** 🆂🅷
(541) 889-9188. **$46-$50.** 615 E Idaho. I-84, exit 376A, just nw. Ext corridors. **Pets:** Accepted.
🆂🄰🆅🄴 🆂🄳 ⊠ 🍴 🎬

PACIFIC CITY

🔷🔷🔷 ▼▼▼▼ **Inn at Cape Kiwanda** Ⓜ ❖
(503) 965-7001. **$109-$239.** 33105 Cape Kiwanda Dr. Just w on Pacific Ave, 1 mi n. Ext corridors. **Pets:** Other species. $15 daily fee/pet. Designated rooms, service with restrictions, supervision.
🆂🄰🆅🄴 🆂🄳 ⊠ 🄼 ▣ ⊠ 🎬

🔷🔷🔷 ▼▼ **Pacific City Inn** 🆂🅷
(503) 965-6464. **$55-$99.** 35280 Brooten Rd. Center. Ext corridors. **Pets:** Dogs only. $15 daily fee/pet. Designated rooms, service with restrictions, supervision.
🆂🄰🆅🄴 🆂🄳 ⊠ 🛏 ▣ 🎬

PENDLETON

🔷🔷🔷 ▼▼▼ **Best Western Pendleton Inn** 🆂🅷
(541) 276-2135. **$66-$125.** 400 SE Nye Ave. I-84, exit 210, just se. Int corridors. **Pets:** Accepted.
🆂🄰🆅🄴 🆂🄳 ⊠ 🄼 🄴 🛏 ▣ 🏊

🔷🔷🔷 ▼▼▼ **Econo Lodge** Ⓜ
(541) 276-8654. **$53-$59.** 620 SW Tutuilla Rd. I-84, exit 209, just s on US 395. Ext corridors. **Pets:** Small. $7 daily fee/pet. Designated rooms, service with restrictions, supervision.
🆂🄰🆅🄴 🆂🄳 ⊠ 🛏 ▣

🔷🔷🔷 ▼▼▼▼ **Holiday Inn Express** 🆂🅷
(541) 966-6520. **$74-$95.** 600 SE Nye Ave. I-84, exit 210, just se. Int corridors. **Pets:** Other species. $20 deposit/room, $10 one-time fee/room. Designated rooms, service with restrictions, supervision.
🆂🄰🆅🄴 🆂🄳 ⊠ 🄴 🛏 ▣ 🎬

▼▼▼▼ **Oxford Suites** SH
(541) 276-6000. **$89-$149.** 2400 SW Court Pl. I-84, exit 209, just n on US 395, at northwest corner. Int corridors. **Pets:** Small. $20 one-time fee/room. Designated rooms, service with restrictions, supervision.
ASK SO ✕ &M 🐾 &' 🛏 💻 ⌇

AAA ▼▼▼ **Red Lion Hotel** SH
(541) 276-6111. **$66-$86.** 304 SE Nye Ave. I-84, exit 210, just s. Ext/int corridors. **Pets:** $25 deposit/room. Designated rooms, service with restrictions, supervision.
SAVE ✕ 🐾 &' 🛏 💻 🍴 ⌇ ✕

▼▼ **Super 8 Motel** SH
(541) 276-8881. **Call for rates.** 601 SE Nye Ave. I-84, exit 210. Int corridors. **Pets:** Other species. $50 deposit/room, $10 daily fee/pet. Service with restrictions, supervision.
✕ 🐾 🛏 ⌇

AAA ▼▼▼ **Travelodge** M
(541) 276-7531. **$69-$89.** 411 SW Dorion Ave. I-84, exit 209, just w of town center on corner of SW 4th St; downtown. Ext corridors. **Pets:** Medium, dogs only. $10 daily fee/room. Designated rooms, service with restrictions, supervision.
SAVE SO ✕ 🛏 ⌇

▼▼ **Wildhorse Resort Hotel & Casino** SH
(541) 276-0355. **$65-$175.** 72779 Hwy 331. I-84, exit 216, 0.6 mi n. Int corridors. **Pets:** Large. $10 one-time fee/room. Designated rooms, service with restrictions, supervision.
ASK SO ✕ &' 🛏 💻 🍴 ⌇ ✕

PORTLAND METROPOLITAN AREA

BEAVERTON

AAA ▼▼▼▼ **Best Western Greenwood Inn & Suites** M
(503) 643-7444. **$69-$109.** 10700 SW Allen Blvd. SR 217, exit Allen Blvd, just e. Ext/int corridors. **Pets:** Accepted.
SAVE SO ✕ &M 🐾 &' 🛏 💻 🍴 ⌇ ✕

▼▼ **Homestead Studio Suites Hotel-Beaverton** M 🐾
(503) 690-3600. **$59-$79.** 875 SW 158th Ave. US 26, exit 65 westbound, just s on Cornell Rd, 1.1 mi se on 158th Ave; eastbound, just straight on feeder road, then same directions as westbound. Ext corridors. **Pets:** Medium, other species. $25 daily fee/room. Service with restrictions, crate.
ASK SO ✕ &' 🛏 💻

▼▼▼ **Homewood Suites By Hilton** SH 🐾
(503) 614-0900. **$89-$149.** 15525 NW Gateway Ct. US 26, exit 65, s on 158th Ave, just e on Waterhouse Ave. Int corridors. **Pets:** Medium. $75 one-time fee/pet. Service with restrictions, supervision.
ASK SO ✕ &M 🐾 &' 🛏 💻 ⌇

CLACKAMAS

AAA ▼▼▼ **Clackamas Inn** SH
(503) 650-5340. **$59-$109.** 16010 SE 82nd Dr. I-205, exit 12A southbound; exit 12 northbound (SR 212). Int corridors. **Pets:** $10 daily fee/room. Supervision.
SAVE SO ✕ 🛏 ⌇

GLADSTONE

▼▼▼▼ **Oxford Suites** SH
(503) 722-7777. **$89-$109.** 75 82nd Dr. I-205, exit 11, just w. Int corridors. **Pets:** Small, dogs only. $25 one-time fee/pet. Service with restrictions, supervision.
ASK SO ✕ &M 🐾 &' 🛏 💻 ⌇

GRESHAM

AAA ▼▼▼▼ **Best Western Pony Soldier Inn** SH
(503) 665-1591. **$79-$98.** 1060 NE Cleveland Ave. I-84, exit 16, 2.7 mi s on NE 238th, just w on Division St, then just n; I-205, exit 19, 5.5. mi e on Division St, then just n. Int corridors. **Pets:** Small. Service with restrictions, supervision.
SAVE SO ✕ 🐾 🛏 💻 ⌇ ✕

AAA ▼▼▼ **Hawthorn Inn & Suites** SH
(503) 492-4000. **$64-$82.** 2323 NE 181st Ave. I-84, exit 13, just e. Int corridors. **Pets:** Accepted.
SAVE SO ✕ &M 🐾 &' 🛏 💻 ⌇ ✕

AAA ▼▼ **Sleep Inn-Portland Gresham** SH
(503) 618-8400. **$54-$85.** 2261 NE 181st Ave. I-84, exit 13, just s. Int corridors. **Pets:** Accepted.
SAVE SO ✕ &M &' 🛏 💻 ⌇

AAA ▼▼ **Super 8 Motel** M
(503) 661-5100. **$54-$69.** 121 NE 181st Ave. I-84, exit 13, 1.3 mi s. Int corridors. **Pets:** Small, other species. $10 daily fee/pet. Designated rooms, service with restrictions, supervision.
SAVE SO ✕ 🐾 🛏 💻

HILLSBORO

AAA ▼▼▼▼ **Candlewood Suites** SH 🐾
(503) 681-2121. **$64-$109.** 3133 NE Shute Rd. US 26, exit 61, 1.2 mi s. Int corridors. **Pets:** Medium. $75 one-time fee/room. Service with restrictions, supervision.
SAVE SO ✕ 🐾 &' 🛏 💻 ✕

AAA ▼▼▼▼ **Red Lion Hotel Hillsboro** SH 🐾
(503) 648-3500. **$57-$73.** 3500 NE Cornell Rd. US 26, exit 62, 1.1 mi s on Cornelius Pass Rd, then 2.5 mi w. Int corridors. **Pets:** Other species. $5 daily fee/pet. Service with restrictions, crate.
SAVE SO ✕ 🐾 🛏 💻 🍴 ⌇ ✕

▼▼▼ Residence Inn by Marriott Portland
West 🆂🅷 ❀
(503) 531-3200. **$99-$159.** 18855 NW Tanasbourne Dr. US
26, exit 64, just s. Ext/int corridors. **Pets:** Other species.
$10 daily fee/room.
🔗 🔗 🔗 🔗 🔗 🔗 🔗 🔗 🔗 🔗

▼▼▼ TownePlace Suites by Marriott-Portland
Hillsboro 🆂🅷
(503) 268-6000. **$60-$105.** 6550 NE Brighton St. US 26, exit
62, just s; 1 mi on Cornelius Pass Rd, 0.7 mi w on Cornell
Rd, just n on 229th Ave, then just w. Ext/int corridors.
Pets: Small, other species. $10 daily fee/pet.
🔗 🔗 🔗 🔗 🔗 🔗 🔗 🔗 🔗 🔗

🆔 ▼ Travelodge 🅼
(503) 640-4791. **$42.** 622 SE 10th Ave. 0.5 mi e on SR 8.
Ext corridors. **Pets:** Other species. $10 daily fee/pet. Des-
ignated rooms, service with restrictions, crate.
🔗 🔗 🔗 🔗 🔗

🆔 ▼▼▼ Wellesley Inn & Suites
(Portland/Hillsboro) 🆂🅷
(503) 439-0706. **$105.** 19311 NW Cornell Rd. US 26, exit 64,
0.5 mi s on 185th Ave, 0.4 mi w. Int corridors.
Pets: Medium. Service with restrictions, crate.
🔗 🔗 🔗 🔗 🔗 🔗 🔗 🔗

KING CITY

🆔 ▼▼▼ Best Western Northwind Inn &
Suites 🆂🅷
(503) 431-2100. **$74-$140.** 16105 SW Pacific Hwy. I-5, exit
292, just nw on SR 217, exit SR 99 W, then 2.5 mi s. Int
corridors. **Pets:** Medium. $5 daily fee/pet. Service with
restrictions, supervision.
🔗 🔗 🔗 🔗 🔗 🔗 🔗 🔗 🔗

LAKE OSWEGO

🆔 ▼▼▼ Crowne Plaza Hotel 🆂🅷
(503) 624-8400. **$99-$139.** 14811 Kruse Oaks Dr. I-5, exit
292, just e. Int corridors. **Pets:** Medium. $10 daily fee/pet.
Service with restrictions, crate.
🔗 🔗 🔗 🔗 🔗 🔗 🔗 🔗 🔗 🔗 🔗

🆔 ▼▼▼ Phoenix Inn Suites-Lake
Oswego 🆂🅷 ❀
(503) 624-7400. **$79-$109.** 14905 SW Bangy Rd. I-5, exit
292 southbound; exit 292B northbound, just e, then just s.
Int corridors. **Pets:** Other species. $15 one-time fee/pet.
Service with restrictions, supervision.
🔗 🔗 🔗 🔗 🔗 🔗 🔗 🔗 🔗 🔗

▼◈▼ Residence Inn by Marriott-Portland
South 🆂🅷 ❀
(503) 684-2603. **$99-$199.** 15200 SW Bangy Rd. I-5, exit
292, just e, then 0.3 mi s. Ext corridors. **Pets:** Other species. $10 daily fee/pet.
🔗 🔗 🔗 🔗 🔗 🔗 🔗 🔗 🔗 🔗

OREGON CITY

🆔 ▼▼▼ Rivershore Hotel 🆂🅷 ❀
(503) 655-7141. **$64-$84.** 1900 Clackamette Dr. I-205, exit 9,
just n. Int corridors. **Pets:** Other species. $5 daily fee/pet.
Service with restrictions, crate.
🔗 🔗 🔗 🔗 🔗 🔗 🔗 🔗

PORTLAND

🆔 ▼▼▼ ▼▼▼ 5TH Avenue Suites
Hotel 🅻🅷 ❀
(503) 222-0001. **$119-$189.** 506 SW Washington St. At SW
5th Ave and SW Washington St. Int corridors. **Pets:** Service
with restrictions, supervision.
🔗 🔗 🔗 🔗 🔗 🔗 🔗 🔗 🔗

🆔 ▼▼▼ ▼▼▼ The Benson Hotel, a Coast
Hotel 🅻🅷 ❀
(503) 228-2000. **$120-$200.** 309 SW Broadway. At SW
Broadway and Oak. Int corridors. **Pets:** $50 one-time fee/
room. Designated rooms, service with restrictions.
🔗 🔗 🔗 🔗 🔗 🔗 🔗

🆔 ▼▼▼ Best Western Inn at the
Meadows 🆂🅷
(503) 286-9600. **$79-$99.** 1215 N Hayden Meadows Dr. I-5,
exit 306B, just e. Int corridors. **Pets:** Other species. $22
one-time fee/room. Service with restrictions.
🔗 🔗 🔗 🔗 🔗 🔗

▼▼▼ Country Inn & Suites at Portland
Airport 🆂🅷 ❀
(503) 255-2700. **$75-$85.** 7205 NE Alderwood Rd. I-205, exit
24A (Airport Way) northbound; exit 24 southbound, 1 mi w
on Airport Way, then just sw on NE 82nd Ave. Int corridors.
Pets: Other species. $25 one-time fee/room. Designated
rooms, service with restrictions, supervision.
🔗 🔗 🔗 🔗 🔗 🔗 🔗 🔗

🆔 ▼▼ ▼ Days Inn-Portland North 🆂🅷 ❀
(503) 289-1800. **$70-$80.** 9930 N Whitaker Rd. I-5, exit
306B (Delta Park), just e. Int corridors. **Pets:** Other species.
$15 one-time fee/room. Service with restrictions.
🔗 🔗 🔗 🔗 🔗 🔗

🆔 ▼▼▼ Doubletree Hotel-Columbia
River 🅻🅷
(503) 283-2111. **$79-$129.** 1401 N Hayden Island Dr. I-5,
exit 308, just w. Int corridors. **Pets:** Small. $35 one-time
fee/room. Service with restrictions.
🔗 🔗 🔗 🔗 🔗 🔗 🔗 🔗 🔗 🔗 🔗

🆔 ▼▼▼ Doubletree Hotel-Jantzen Beach 🅻🅷
(503) 283-4466. **$89-$129.** 909 N Hayden Island Dr. I-5, exit
308, just e. Int corridors. **Pets:** Small. $35 one-time fee/
room. Service with restrictions.
🔗 🔗 🔗 🔗 🔗 🔗 🔗 🔗 🔗 🔗 🔗

▼◈▼ Doubletree Hotel Portland
Downtown 🆂🅷 ❀
(503) 221-0450. **$79-$139.** 310 SW Lincoln. I-5 to I-405, exit
4th Ave, just n, then just e. Ext/int corridors. **Pets:** Other
species. $25 deposit/pet. Service with restrictions, crate.
🔗 🔗 🔗 🔗 🔗 🔗 🔗 🔗 🔗 🔗

▼▼▼ Four Points by Sheraton Portland Downtown 🆂🅷
(503) 221-0711. **$69-$109.** 50 SW Morrison. At Morrison and Naito Pkwy (formerly Front Ave). Int corridors. **Pets:** Accepted.

▼▼▼ ▼▼▼ The Heathman Hotel 🆂🅷 ❧
(503) 241-4100. **$159-$650.** 1001 SW Broadway. At SW Broadway and Salmon. Int corridors. **Pets:** Medium. $25 one-time fee/pet. Service with restrictions, supervision.

▼▼▼ Hotel Lucia 🆂🅷 ❧
(503) 225-1717. **$145-$170.** 400 SW Broadway. At SW Broadway and Stark. Int corridors. **Pets:** Dogs only. $100 deposit/pet.

🔼🔼🔼 ▼▼▼▼ Hotel Vintage Plaza 🆂🅷 ❧
(503) 228-1212. **$119-$189.** 422 SW Broadway. At Broadway and Washington St. Int corridors. **Pets:** Other species. Service with restrictions, supervision.

🔼🔼🔼 ▼▼▼▼ La Quinta Inn & Suites 🆂🅷
(503) 382-3820. **$69-$89.** 11207 NE Holman St. I-205, exit 24B northbound; exit 24 southbound, just e on Airport Way. Int corridors. **Pets:** Large, other species. Service with restrictions, crate.

🔼🔼🔼 ▼▼▼ La Quinta Inn & Suites Portland Northwest 🆂🅷
(503) 497-9044. **$66-$91.** 4319 NW Yeon. I-405, exit 3 (US 30) northbound, 2.5 mi w; exit 302B southbound, 2.5 mi w on US 30. Int corridors. **Pets:** Accepted.

🔼🔼🔼 ▼▼▼ La Quinta Inn Convention Center 🆂🅷
(503) 233-7933. **$75-$135.** 431 NE Multnomah. I-5, exit 302A, just e, then just s on Martin Luther King Blvd. Int corridors. **Pets:** Other species. Service with restrictions, crate.

🔼🔼🔼 ▼▼▼ Mallory Hotel 🆂🅷 ❧
(503) 223-6311. **$100-$165.** 729 SW 15th Ave. I-5 to I-405, exit Salmon St northbound, just n on 14th Ave, w on Morrison, then s; exit Couch-Burnside southbound; at SW 15th and Yamhill. Int corridors. **Pets:** Other species. $10 one-time fee/room.

▼▼▼ The Mark Spencer Hotel 🆂🅷 ❧
(503) 224-3293. **$149.** 409 SW 11th Ave. Jct SW Stark Ave. Int corridors. **Pets:** Other species. $25 one-time fee/room. Service with restrictions.

🔼🔼🔼 ▼▼▼ Marriott City Center 🅻🅷
(503) 226-6300. **$99-$159.** 520 SW Broadway. At Washington and SW Broadway. Int corridors. **Pets:** Accepted.

▼▼▼ Oxford Suites 🆂🅷
(503) 283-3030. **$89-$169.** 12226 N Jantzen Dr. I-5, exit 308, just e on Hayden Island Dr. Int corridors. **Pets:** Small. $25 one-time fee/pet. Service with restrictions, supervision.

🔼🔼🔼 ▼▼▼ Park Lane Suites 🅼
(503) 226-6288. **$99-$149.** 809 SW King Ave. I-405, exit Burnside southbound, 0.5 mi w, then just s; exit Everett northbound, 0.4 mi w on Glisan, just s on NW 21st Ave, then just w on Burnside. Ext corridors. **Pets:** Accepted.

🔼🔼🔼 ▼▼▼ The Portlander Inn 🆂🅷
(503) 345-0300. **$66.** 10350 N Vancouver Way. I-5, exit 307, follow signs for Marine Dr E, just ne, then 0.7 mi se. Int corridors. **Pets:** Medium. $35 one-time fee/room. Designated rooms, no service, supervision.

🔼🔼🔼 ▼▼▼ Quality Inn Portland Airport 🆂🅷
(503) 256-4111. **$70-$90.** 8247 NE Sandy Blvd. I-84, exit 5, 1.5 mi n on 82nd Ave. Ext/int corridors. **Pets:** Accepted.

🔼🔼🔼 ▼▼▼ Red Lion Inn & Suites-Portland Airport 🆂🅷
(503) 252-6397. **$64-$81.** 5019 NE 102nd Ave. I-205, exit 23A, just e on NE Sandy Blvd. Int corridors. **Pets:** Other species. $15 one-time fee/room. Service with restrictions.

▼▼▼ Residence Inn by Marriott-Lloyd Center 🆂🅷
(503) 288-1400. **$119-$139.** 1710 NE Multnomah. I-5, exit 302A, 1.3 mi e on Weidler St, just s on 15th Ave; I-84, exit 1 (Lloyd Center) westbound, just n on 13th St, then just e. Ext corridors. **Pets:** Accepted.

▼▼▼ Residence Inn Portland Downtown at RiverPlace 🆂🅷 ❧
(503) 552-9500. **$229.** 2115 SW River Pkwy. At SW Moody and SW River Pkwy; on the Willamette River Waterfront. Int corridors. **Pets:** Large, other species. $10 daily fee/pet.

🔼🔼🔼 ▼▼▼▼ RiverPlace Hotel 🆂🅷 ❧
(503) 228-3233. **$149-$239.** 1510 SW Harbor Way. At Naito Pkwy (formerly Front Ave) and SW Harbor Way. Int corridors. **Pets:** Other species. $45 one-time fee/room.

▼▼▼ Sheraton Portland Airport Hotel 🅻🅷
(503) 281-2500. **$89-$178.** 8235 NE Airport Way. I-205, exit 24A northbound; exit 24 southbound, 1.5 mi w. Int corridors. **Pets:** Medium. $50 one-time fee/room. Service with restrictions, supervision.

▼▼▼ Staybridge Suites Portland-Airport 🆂🅷
(503) 262-8888. **$104-$164.** 11936 NE Glenn Widing Dr. I-205, exit 24B northbound; exit 24 southbound, just e. Int corridors. **Pets:** Medium, other species. $10 daily fee/pet, $25 one-time fee/pet. Service with restrictions.

(AAA) ▼▼▼ Travelodge Suites Portland M
(503) 788-9394. **$66-$82.** 7740 SE Powell Blvd. I-205, exit
19, 1 mi w. Ext/int corridors. **Pets:** Medium. Service with
restrictions, supervision.
[SAVE] [S𝟘] [✕] [🛏] [💻]

(AAA) ▼▼▼▼ The Westin Portland LH ❋
(503) 294-9000. **$119-$169.** 750 SW Alder. At Park Ave and
SW Alder. Int corridors. **Pets:** Dogs only. Designated rooms,
service with restrictions.
[SAVE] [S𝟘] [✕] [🛏M] [🌀] [❄] [🛏] [💻] [🍽] [✕]

TIGARD

▼▼▼▼ Embassy Suites Hotel-Portland Washington
Square LH ❋
(503) 644-4000. **$89-$159.** 9000 SW Washington Square
Rd. SR 217, exit Progress/Scholls Ferry Rd, just e, then just
s on Hall Blvd. Int corridors. **Pets:** Other species. $50 one-
time fee/room. Designated rooms, service with restrictions,
supervision.
[ASK] [S𝟘] [✕] [🛏M] [🌀] [❄] [🛏] [💻] [🍽] [🏊] [✕]

▼▼▼ Homestead Studio Suites Hotel-Tigard/Lake
Oswego SH ❋
(503) 670-0555. **$59-$79.** 13009 SW 68th Pkwy. SR 217,
exit 72nd St, just ne, just e on Hampton St, then just s. Ext
corridors. **Pets:** Medium, other species. $25 daily fee/room.
Service with restrictions, crate.
[ASK] [S𝟘] [✕] [🌀] [❄] [🛏] [💻]

▼▼▼ Shilo Inn-Portland I-5 South SH
(503) 639-2226. **$69-$99.** 7300 SW Hazel Fern Rd. I-5, exit
290, just w, then just s. Ext corridors. **Pets:** $10 daily fee/
room. Service with restrictions, supervision.
[ASK] [S𝟘] [✕] [🌀] [🛏] [💻] [🏊] [✕]

TROUTDALE

(AAA) ▼▼▼▼ Comfort Inn & Suites SH
(503) 669-6500. **$139.** 477 NW Phoenix Dr. I-84, exit 17. Int
corridors. **Pets:** Accepted.
[SAVE] [S𝟘] [✕] [🌀] [🛏] [💻] [🏊]

▼▼▼▼ Holiday Inn Express SH
(503) 492-2900. **$69-$89.** 1000 NW Graham Rd. I-84, exit
17, on north frontage road. Int corridors. **Pets:** Small. $10
one-time fee/pet. Service with restrictions, supervision.
[✕] [🌀] [❄] [🛏] [💻]

▼ Motel 6-Portland Troutdale-407 M
(503) 665-2254. **$39-$55.** 1610 NW Frontage Rd. I-84, exit
17. Ext corridors. **Pets:** Other species. Service with restrictions, supervision.
[S𝟘] [✕] [🛏M] [🌀] [❄] [🏊]

(AAA) ▼▼ Portland/Troutdale Travelodge SH ❋
(503) 666-6623. **$44-$59.** 23705 NE Sandy Blvd. I-84, exit
16, just n. Int corridors. **Pets:** Other species. $5 daily fee/
pet. Service with restrictions, supervision.
[SAVE] [S𝟘] [✕] [❄] [🛏] [💻] [🍽]

TUALATIN

(AAA) ▼▼▼▼ La Quinta Inn & Suites SH
(503) 612-9952. **$69-$89.** 7640 SW Warm Springs St. I-5,
exit 289, 0.3 mi w on Nyberg Rd, just s on SW Martinazzi
Ave, then just e. Int corridors. **Pets:** Large. Service with
restrictions, supervision.
[SAVE] [S𝟘] [✕] [🛏M] [🌀] [❄] [🛏] [💻] [🏊]

(AAA) ▼▼▼▼ The Sweetbrier Inn & Suites SH
(503) 692-5800. **$74-$89.** 7125 SW Nyberg Rd. I-5, exit 289,
just e. Ext/int corridors. **Pets:** Large, other species. $25
deposit/room. Service with restrictions.
[SAVE] [S𝟘] [✕] [🛏M] [🌀] [❄] [🛏] [💻] [🍽] [🏊] [✕]

WILSONVILLE

(AAA) ▼▼▼▼ Best Western Willamette Inn SH
(503) 682-2288. **$69-$85.** 30800 SW Parkway Ave. I-5, exit
283, just e, then just s. Int corridors. **Pets:** Small, other
species. Designated rooms, service with restrictions, supervision.
[SAVE] [S𝟘] [✕] [🛏M] [🛏] [💻] [🏊] [✕]

(AAA) ▼▼▼ Comfort Inn SH
(503) 682-9000. **$100.** 8855 SW Citizens Dr. I-5, exit 283,
just e, then just n on Town Center Loop W. Int corridors.
Pets: Other species. $10 daily fee/room. Service with
restrictions, supervision.
[SAVE] [S𝟘] [✕] [🛏M] [🌀] [❄] [🛏] [💻] [🏊]

▼▼▼ Days Inn & Suites SH
(503) 682-3184. **$55-$95.** 8815 SW Sun Pl. I-5, exit 286, just
e. Int corridors. **Pets:** Accepted.
[ASK] [S𝟘] [✕] [🌀] [🛏] [💻] [🏊]

(AAA) ▼▼▼ Holiday Inn-Wilsonville SH
(503) 682-2211. **$79-$124.** 25425 SW 95th Ave. I-5, exit 286,
just w. Int corridors. **Pets:** Other species. $15 daily fee/
room. Service with restrictions.
[SAVE] [S𝟘] [✕] [🛏M] [🌀] [❄] [🛏] [💻] [🍽] [🏊]

❋ **END METROPOLITAN AREA** ❋

PORT ORFORD

(AAA) ▼ Sea Crest Motel M ❋
(541) 332-3040. **$48-$75.** 44 Hwy 101. On US 101, 1 mi s.
Ext corridors. **Pets:** Medium. $4 daily fee/room. Designated
rooms, service with restrictions, supervision.
[SAVE] [✕] [🛏] [💻] [🎬]

PRINEVILLE

▼▼▼ Best Western Prineville Inn SH
(541) 447-8080. **$68-$99.** 1475 NE 3rd St. 1.4 mi e on US
26 from SR 126. Int corridors. **Pets:** Accepted.
[ASK] [S𝟘] [✕] [🛏M] [🛏] [💻] [🏊]

▼▼▼▼ **Stafford Inn** 🅂🄷
(541) 447-7100. **$69-$79.** 1773 NE 3rd St. On US 26. Int corridors. **Pets:** $25 one-time fee/room. Designated rooms, service with restrictions, supervision.
🄰🄢🄺 🆂🄳 ⊠ 🕭 🕭 🖥 🌊

PROSPECT

▼▼ **Prospect Historical Hotel-Motel & Dinner House** 🄼 🐾
(541) 560-3664. **$50-$150.** 391 Mill Creek Dr. Off SR 62; center. Ext/int corridors. **Pets:** Other species. Designated rooms, service with restrictions, supervision.
⊠ 🕭 🖥 🍴 🐾

REDMOND

▼▼▼▼ **Comfort Suites-Airport** 🅂🄷
(541) 504-8900. **$84-$164.** 2243 SW Yew Ave. US 97, just w. Int corridors. **Pets:** Small. $25 one-time fee/pet. Service with restrictions, supervision.
🄰🄢🄺 🆂🄳 ⊠ 🕭 🕭 🖥 🌊

▼▼▼▼ **Eagle Crest Resort** 🅂🄷
(541) 923-2453. **$77-$157.** 1522 Cline Falls Rd. 5 mi w on SR 126, 1 mi s. Int corridors. **Pets:** Accepted.
🄰🄢🄺 🆂🄳 ⊠ 🄼 🌀 🕭 🕭 🖥 🍴 🌊 🐾

🔺🔺🔺 ▼▼ ▼ **Motel 6 Redmond-4076** 🅂🄷
(541) 923-2100. **$51-$75.** 2247 S Hwy 97. 1 mi s on US 97 from jct SR 126 W. Int corridors. **Pets:** Accepted.
🅂🄰🅅🄴 ⊠ 🄼 🌀 🕭 🕭

🔺🔺🔺 ▼▼ ▼ **Redmond Inn** 🄼 🐾
(541) 548-1091. **$55-$70.** 1545 Hwy 97 S. 0.5 mi s on US 97 from jct SR 126 W. Ext corridors. **Pets:** Other species. $5 daily fee/pet. Service with restrictions, supervision.
🅂🄰🅅🄴 🆂🄳 ⊠ 🕭 🖥 🌊

▼▼ ▼▼ **Redmond Super 8 Motel** 🅂🄷
(541) 548-8881. **$45-$72, 3 day notice.** 3629 21st Place SW. US 97, exit Yew Ave. Int corridors. **Pets:** Accepted.
🄰🄢🄺 ⊠ 🄼 🌀 🕭 🌊

REEDSPORT

🔺🔺🔺 ▼▼ **Anchor Bay Inn** 🄼
(541) 271-2149. **$50-$77.** 1821 Winchester Ave (Hwy 101). On US 101, 0.8 mi s of jct SR 38. Ext corridors. **Pets:** Other species. $7 daily fee/pet. Designated rooms, supervision.
🅂🄰🅅🄴 🆂🄳 ⊠ 🕭 🖥 🌊 🐾

🔺🔺🔺 ▼▼▼▼ **Best Western Salbasgeon Inn** 🄼
(541) 271-4831. **$73-$165.** 1400 Hwy Ave 101 S. Just s on US 101 from jct SR 38. Ext corridors. **Pets:** Medium, dogs only. $5 one-time fee/pet. Designated rooms, service with restrictions, supervision.
🅂🄰🅅🄴 🆂🄳 ⊠ 🕭 🖥 🌊

🔺🔺🔺 ▼▼ **Economy Inn** 🄼
(541) 271-3671. **$35-$90.** 1593 Highway Ave 101. On US 101; center. Ext corridors. **Pets:** Accepted.
🅂🄰🅅🄴 ⊠ 🕭 🌊 🐾

🔺🔺🔺 ▼▼ ▼ **Salbasgeon Inn of the Umpqua** 🅂🄷
(541) 271-2025. **$68-$160.** 45209 Hwy 38. 7.3 mi e on SR 38 from jct US 101. Ext corridors. **Pets:** Medium, dogs only. $5 one-time fee/pet. Service with restrictions, supervision.
🅂🄰🅅🄴 🆂🄳 ⊠ 🕭 🖥 🐾

ROCKAWAY BEACH

🔺🔺🔺 ▼▼▼ **Sea Treasures Inn** 🄼
(503) 355-8220. **$59-$99.** 301 N Miller St. Jct 3rd Ave N; center. Ext corridors. **Pets:** Accepted.
🅂🄰🅅🄴 ⊠ 🕭 🖥 🐾

🔺🔺🔺 ▼▼ ▼ **Silver Sands Motel** 🄼
(503) 355-2206. **$74-$146.** 215 S Pacific St. US 101, exit S 2nd Ave, just w. Ext corridors. **Pets:** Dogs only. $5 one-time fee/pet. Designated rooms, service with restrictions, supervision.
🅂🄰🅅🄴 🆂🄳 ⊠ 🄼 🕭 🖥 🌊 🐾 🐾

🔺🔺🔺 ▼▼ ▼ **Tradewinds Motel** 🄼 🐾
(503) 355-2112. **$47-$125, 4 day notice.** 523 N Pacific St. Just w of US 101, off N 6th Ave. Ext corridors. **Pets:** Dogs only. $10 daily fee/pet. Designated rooms, service with restrictions, supervision.
🅂🄰🅅🄴 ⊠ 🕭 🖥 🐾

ROSEBURG

🔺🔺🔺 ▼▼▼ **Best Western Garden Villa Inn** 🄼
(541) 672-1601. **$69-$94.** 760 NW Garden Valley Blvd. I-5, exit 125, just w. Ext corridors. **Pets:** Accepted.
🅂🄰🅅🄴 🆂🄳 ⊠ 🌀 🕭 🕭 🖥 🌊

🔺🔺🔺 ▼▼▼▼ **Holiday Inn Express** 🅂🄷 🐾
(541) 673-7517. **$69-$94.** 375 W Harvard Blvd. I-5, exit 124, just e. Ext/int corridors. **Pets:** Other species. Designated rooms, service with restrictions, supervision.
🅂🄰🅅🄴 🆂🄳 ⊠ 🄼 🌀 🕭 🕭 🖥 🌊

🔺🔺🔺 ▼▼▼ **Howard Johnson Express Inn** 🄼
(541) 673-5082. **$50-$69.** 978 NE Stephen St. I-5, exit 125, 0.6 mi e on Garden Valley Blvd, 0.4 mi s. Ext corridors. **Pets:** Accepted.
🅂🄰🅅🄴 🆂🄳 ⊠ 🕭 🖥

🔺🔺🔺 ▼▼▼▼ **Quality Inn** 🅂🄷
(541) 673-5561. **$69-$109.** 427 NW Garden Valley Blvd. I-5, exit 125, just e. Ext corridors. **Pets:** Large, other species. $100 deposit/room, $5 daily fee/room. Designated rooms, service with restrictions, supervision.
🅂🄰🅅🄴 🆂🄳 ⊠ 🌀 🕭 🕭 🖥 🌊

🔺🔺🔺 ▼▼ ▼ **Roseburg Travelodge** 🄼 🐾
(541) 672-4836. **$65-$89.** 315 W Harvard Blvd. I-5, exit 124, just e. Ext corridors. **Pets:** Large, other species. $10 daily fee/room. Designated rooms, service with restrictions, supervision.
🅂🄰🅅🄴 🆂🄳 ⊠ 🕭 🖥 🌊

🔺🔺🔺 ▼▼ **Shady Oaks Motel** 🄼
(541) 672-2608. **$40-$48.** 2954 Old Hwy 99 S. I-5, exit 120, 0.5 mi n. Ext corridors. **Pets:** Accepted.
🅂🄰🅅🄴 ⊠ 🕭

▼▼ ▼▼ Sleep Inn and Suites 🆂🅷 ❀

(541) 464-8338. **$49-$84.** 2855 NW Edenbower Blvd. I-5, exit 127, just n. Int corridors. **Pets:** $7 daily fee/room. Service with restrictions, crate.

(A$K) 🆂🅳 ✕ 🐾 🅲 🖥 💻 🏊

▼▼ ▼▼ Super 8 Motel 🆂🅷

(541) 672-8880. **$51-$65.** 3200 NW Aviation Dr. I-5, exit 127, just n. Int corridors. **Pets:** Medium. $25 deposit/pet. Service with restrictions, supervision.

(A$K) 🆂🅳 ✕ 🅺🅼 🐾 🅲 🖥 🏊

ⒶⒶⒶ ▼▼▼▼ Windmill Inn of Roseburg 🆂🅷 ❀

(541) 673-0901. **$70-$88.** 1450 NW Mulholland Dr. I-5, exit 125, just e. Int corridors. **Pets:** Other species. Designated rooms, service with restrictions, crate.

(SAVE) 🆂🅳 ✕ 🐾 🅲 🖥 💻 🏊 ✕

ST. HELENS

ⒶⒶⒶ ▼▼▼▼ Best Western Oak Meadows Inn 🆂🅷

(503) 397-3000. **$69-$129.** 585 S Columbia River Hwy. South end of town on US 30. Int corridors. **Pets:** Medium. $10 one-time fee/room. Service with restrictions, supervision.

(SAVE) 🆂🅳 ✕ 🅲 🖥 💻 🏊

SALEM

ⒶⒶⒶ ▼▼▼▼ Best Western New Kings Inn 🆂🅷

(503) 581-1559. **$72-$85.** 1600 Motor Ct NE. I-5, exit 256, just e. Ext corridors. **Pets:** Accepted.

(SAVE) 🆂🅳 ✕ 🅺🅼 🐾 🅲 🖥 💻 🏊 ✕

ⒶⒶⒶ ▼▼▼▼ Best Western Pacific Hwy Inn 🆂🅷

(503) 390-3200. **$71-$89.** 4646 Portland Rd NE. I-5, exit 258, just e. Ext corridors. **Pets:** Accepted.

(SAVE) 🆂🅳 ✕ 🅺🅼 🐾 🅲 🖥 💻 🏊

ⒶⒶⒶ ▼▼▼ Holiday Inn Express 🆂🅷

(503) 391-7000. **$71-$114.** 890 Hawthorne Ave SE. I-5, exit 253, just w, then just n. Int corridors. **Pets:** Accepted.

(SAVE) 🆂🅳 ✕ 🐾 🅲 🖥 💻 🏊

ⒶⒶⒶ ▼▼▼ Holiday Lodge 🅼 ❀

(503) 585-2323. **$44-$58.** 1400 Hawthorne Ave NE. I-5, exit 256, just w, then just s. Ext corridors. **Pets:** Medium, dogs only. $10 daily fee/room. Designated rooms, service with restrictions, supervision.

(SAVE) ✕ 🅲 🖥 🏊

▼▼ Motel 6-1343 🅼

(503) 371-8024. **$43-$57.** 1401 Hawthorne Ave NE. I-5, exit 256, just w, then just s. Ext corridors. **Pets:** Other species. Service with restrictions, supervision.

🆂🅳 ✕ 🐾 🅲 🏊

ⒶⒶⒶ ▼▼▼▼ Phoenix Inn Suites-North Salem 🆂🅷

(503) 581-7004. **$79-$99.** 1590 Weston Ct NE. I-5, exit 256, just w, then just s. Int corridors. **Pets:** Accepted.

(SAVE) 🆂🅳 ✕ 🅺🅼 🐾 🅲 🖥 💻 🏊

ⒶⒶⒶ ▼▼▼▼ Phoenix Inn Suites-South Salem 🆂🅷 ❀

(503) 588-9220. **$79-$99.** 4370 Commercial SE. I-5, exit 252, 1.5 mi w on Kuebler Rd, then 0.7 mi n. Int corridors. **Pets:** Medium, other species. $10 daily fee/room. Designated rooms, supervision.

(SAVE) 🆂🅳 ✕ 🅺🅼 🐾 🅲 🖥 💻 🏊 ✕

▼▼▼▼ Red Lion Hotel 🆂🅷

(503) 370-7888. **$59-$109.** 3301 Market St NE. I-5, exit 256, just w. Int corridors. **Pets:** Accepted.

(A$K) 🆂🅳 ✕ 🐾 🅲 🖥 💻 🍽 🏊 ✕

▼▼▼▼ Residence Inn by Marriott Salem 🆂🅷 ❀

(503) 585-6500. **$89-$129.** 640 Hawthorne Ave SE. I-5, exit 253, just w, then n. Int corridors. **Pets:** Large, other species. $150 one-time fee/room. Designated rooms, service with restrictions, crate.

(A$K) 🆂🅳 ✕ 🅺🅼 🐾 🅲 🖥 💻 🏊 ✕

ⒶⒶⒶ ▼▼▼▼ Salem Inn 🆂🅷

(503) 588-0515. **$79-$119.** 1775 Freeway Ct NE. I-5, exit 256, just w. Int corridors. **Pets:** Other species. $50 deposit/room, $10 daily fee/pet. Service with restrictions, supervision.

(SAVE) 🆂🅳 ✕ 🅺🅼 🐾 🅲 🖥 💻 🏊

▼▼ ▼▼ Salem Super 8 🆂🅷 ❀

(503) 370-8888. **$54-$76.** 1288 Hawthorne Ave NE. I-5, exit 256, just w, then just s. Int corridors. **Pets:** Other species. $10 one-time fee/pet. Designated rooms, service with restrictions.

(A$K) 🆂🅳 ✕ 🅺🅼 🐾 🅲 🖥 💻 🏊

ⒶⒶⒶ ▼▼▼ Travelodge Salem Capital 🅼

(503) 581-2466. **$49-$69.** 1555 State St. I-5, exit 253, just w on SR 22/99 (Mission St), 0.7 mi n on Hawthorne Ave SE, then 1.6 mi w. Ext corridors. **Pets:** Accepted.

(SAVE) 🆂🅳 ✕ 🐾 🅲 🖥 💻 🏊

SANDY

▼▼▼▼ Best Western Sandy Inn 🆂🅷

(503) 668-7100. **$81-$114.** 37465 Hwy 26. West side of town. Int corridors. **Pets:** Dogs only. $10 daily fee/pet. Service with restrictions, supervision.

(A$K) 🆂🅳 ✕ 🅺🅼 🐾 🅲 🖥 💻 🏊

SEASIDE

ⒶⒶⒶ ▼▼▼▼ Best Western Ocean View Resort 🆂🅷

(503) 738-3334. **$59-$375.** 414 N Prom. US 101, exit 1st Ave, just w, just n on Necanicum Dr, then just w on 4th Ave. Ext/int corridors. **Pets:** Medium. $20 daily fee/pet. Designated rooms, service with restrictions, supervision.

(SAVE) 🆂🅳 ✕ 🐾 🅲 🖥 💻 🍽 🏊 🎿

ⒶⒶⒶ ▼▼▼▼ Comfort Inn Boardwalk 🆂🅷 ❀

(503) 738-3011. **$79-$249.** 545 Broadway. US 101, exit Ave A, just w; downtown. Ext/int corridors. **Pets:** Other species. $10 deposit/pet. Service with restrictions.

(SAVE) ✕ 🅺🅼 🐾 🅲 🖥 💻 🏊

🔺 ▽▽ Seaside Convention Center
Inn M ❄️
(503) 738-9581. **$109-$189, 3 day notice.** 441 2nd Ave. US 101, exit 1st Ave, 0.4 mi w. Ext/int corridors. **Pets:** $10 daily fee/pet. Service with restrictions, crate.
[SAVE] [S🔒] [✖] [🅼] [🖥] [🖩] [🏊]

🔺 ▽▽▽ Sea Side Oceanfront Inn Bed &
Breakfast Hotel BB
(503) 738-6403. **$95-$295, 5 day notice.** 581 S Prom. US 101, exit Ave G, 0.6 mi w, then just n. Int corridors. **Pets:** Medium. $25 daily fee/pet. Designated rooms, service with restrictions, supervision.
[SAVE] [✖] [🖥] [🖩] [🍴]

SHADY COVE

▽▽▽▽ The Edgewater Inn on the Rogue
River M
(541) 878-3171. **$67-$158.** 7800 Rogue River Dr. Off SR 62. Ext corridors. **Pets:** Medium. $8 daily fee/pet. Service with restrictions, crate.
[ASK] [S🔒] [✖] [🎮] [🅼] [🖥] [🖩] [🏊] [✖]

SISTERS

▽▽ ▽▽ Aspen Meadow Lodge BB
(541) 549-4312. **$89-$169 (no credit cards), 3 day notice.** 68733 Junipine Ln. 1 mi e on SR 126 (Redmond Hwy) from jct SR 126 and US 20. Ext corridors. **Pets:** Accepted.
[ASK] [S🔒] [✖] [🖥] [🏊] [🎫]

🔺 ▽▽▽▽ Best Western Ponderosa
Lodge SH ❄️
(541) 549-1234. **$79-$169.** 500 Hwy 20 W. West end of town, just w on US 20 from jct SR 242. Ext corridors. **Pets:** $10 daily fee/pet. Designated rooms, service with restrictions, supervision.
[SAVE] [✖] [🎮] [🖥] [🖩] [🏊]

▽▽ ▽▽ Comfort Inn at Sisters SH
(541) 549-7829. **$90-$130.** 540 Hwy 20 W. West end of town, just w on US 20 from jct SR 242. Ext corridors. **Pets:** $25 daily fee/pet. Designated rooms, service with restrictions, supervision.
[ASK] [S🔒] [✖] [🅼] [🅼] [🖥] [🖩] [🏊]

🔺 ▽▽▽▽ Conklin's Guest House BB
(541) 549-0123. **$70-$150 (no credit cards), 3 day notice.** 69013 Camp Polk Rd. East end of town, just w on US 20 from jct SR 126, then 0.5 mi n on Locust Rd. Int corridors. **Pets:** Accepted.
[SAVE] [✖] [🅼] [🅼] [🖥] [🏊] [🎾] [🎫]

SPRINGFIELD

▽▽ ▽▽ Clarion Hotel/Eugene-Springfield SH
(541) 726-8181. **$94-$139.** 3280 Gateway St. I-5, exit 195A, just e, then just s. Ext/int corridors. **Pets:** Medium, other species. $25 one-time fee/room. Service with restrictions, supervision.
[ASK] [S🔒] [✖] [🎮] [🅼] [🖥] [🖩] [🍴] [🏊]

🔺 ▽▽▽ Comfort Suites
Eugene/Springfield SH
(541) 746-5359. **$59-$145.** 969 Kruse Way. I-5, exit 195A, just e. Int corridors. **Pets:** Dogs only. $10 daily fee/room. Designated rooms, service with restrictions, supervision.
[SAVE] [S🔒] [✖] [🎮] [🅼] [🖥] [🖩] [🏊]

🔺 ▽▽▽▽ Holiday Inn Express SH
(541) 746-8471. **$69-$109.** 3480 Hutton St. I-5, exit 195A, just e. Int corridors. **Pets:** Medium, dogs only. $10 daily fee/room. Designated rooms, service with restrictions, supervision.
[SAVE] [S🔒] [✖] [🎮] [🅼] [🖥] [🖩] [🏊]

▽▽ Motel 6 #418 M
(541) 741-1105. **$43-$57.** 3752 International Ct. I-5, exit 195A, just e, then just n on Gateway St. Ext corridors. **Pets:** Accepted.
[S🔒] [✖] [🅼] [🅼] [🏊]

🔺 ▽▽ ▽ Motel Orleans SH
(541) 746-1314. **$54-$89.** 3315 Gateway St. I-5, exit 195A, just e, then just s. Int corridors. **Pets:** Accepted.
[SAVE] [S🔒] [✖] [🅼] [🖥] [🖩]

🔺 ▽▽ ▽ Village Inn SH
(541) 747-4546. **$62.** 1875 Mohawk Blvd. I-5, exit 194A (SR 126), 2.5 mi e, then just n. Ext corridors. **Pets:** Small. Service with restrictions, supervision.
[SAVE] [S🔒] [✖] [🖥] [🖩] [🍴] [🏊]

SUMMER LAKE

▽▽▽▽ Summer Lake Inn CI
(541) 943-3983. **$105-$275, 14 day notice.** 47531 Hwy 31. 10 mi s; between MM 81 and 82. Ext corridors. **Pets:** Dogs only. $10 one-time fee/pet. Supervision.
[✖] [🖥] [🖩] [🍴] [✖] [🎫]

SUNRIVER

🔺 ▽▽▽ ▽▽▽ Sunriver Resort LH
(541) 593-1000. **$119-$179, 21 day notice.** 1 Center Dr. 2 mi w of US 97. Ext corridors. **Pets:** Accepted.
[SAVE] [S🔒] [✖] [🎮] [🅼] [🖥] [🖩] [🍴] [🏊] [✖]

SUTHERLIN

▽▽ ▽▽ Sutherlin Inn SH ❄️
(541) 459-6800. **$49-$99.** 1400 Hospitality Pl. I-5, exit 136, just se. Int corridors. **Pets:** Other species. $10 daily fee/room. Service with restrictions, supervision.
[✖] [🅼] [🖥] [🖩]

🔺 ▽▽ ▽ Umpqua Regency Inn M
(541) 459-1424. **$61-$74.** 150 Myrtle St. I-5, exit 136, just e. Ext corridors. **Pets:** Other species. $5 daily fee/pet. Service with restrictions, supervision.
[SAVE] [S🔒] [✖] [🖥] [🖩] [🏊]

SWEET HOME

Sweet Home Inn **M**
(541) 367-5137. **$64-$74, 3 day notice.** 805 Long St. Just e of jct US 20 and SR 228, just s on 10th Ave, then just w. Ext corridors. **Pets:** Large, dogs only. $10 one-time fee/pet. Service with restrictions, supervision.

TILLAMOOK

Mar-Clair Inn **M**
(503) 842-7571. **$55-$82.** 11 Main Ave. US 101, just n of jct SR 6. Ext/int corridors. **Pets:** Small, dogs only. $10 one-time fee/room. Service with restrictions, supervision.

WALDPORT

Alsea Manor Motel **M** ❀
(541) 563-3249. **$43-$78.** 190 SW Hwy 101. SR 34, just s on US 101; downtown. Ext corridors. **Pets:** Small, dogs only. $5 daily fee/room. Designated rooms, service with restrictions, supervision.

WELCHES

The Resort at the Mountain **LH**
(503) 622-3101. **$99-$450, 3 day notice.** 68010 E Fairway Ave. 0.8 mi s of US 26 on Welches Rd. Ext corridors. **Pets:** Accepted.

WHEELER

Wheeler on the Bay Lodge and Marina **M**
(503) 368-5858. **$68-$135, 3 day notice.** 580 Marine Dr. On US 101; center. Ext corridors. **Pets:** Small. $25 deposit/pet, $10 daily fee/pet. Service with restrictions, supervision.

WINSTON

Sweet Breeze Inn II **M**
(541) 679-2420. **$62-$68.** 251 NE Main St. I-5, exit 119, 3 mi w. Ext corridors. **Pets:** Accepted.

WOODBURN

Best Western Woodburn **SH**
(503) 982-6515. **$75-$115.** 2887 Newberg Hwy. I-5, exit 271, just e. Int corridors. **Pets:** Medium. $10 daily fee/pet. Designated rooms, service with restrictions, supervision.

La Quinta Inn & Suites **SH**
(503) 982-1727. **$62-$84.** 120 Arney Rd NE. I-5, exit 271, just w. Int corridors. **Pets:** Medium. Service with restrictions, supervision.

YACHATS

The Adobe Resort **SH** ❀
(541) 547-3141. **$75-$225.** 1555 Hwy 101. 0.5 mi n. Int corridors. **Pets:** Other species. $10 daily fee/pet. Designated rooms, service with restrictions.

The Dublin House **M**
(541) 547-3200. **$49-$160.** 251 W 7th St. US 101 at 7th St; downtown. Ext corridors. **Pets:** Accepted.

Fireside Motel **SH** ❀
(541) 547-3636. **$60-$140.** 1881 Hwy 101 N. On US 101, 0.6 mi n. Ext corridors. **Pets:** Other species. $9 daily fee/pet. Service with restrictions, supervision.

Shamrock Lodgettes **CA** ❀
(541) 547-3312. **$59-$149, 3 day notice.** 105 Hwy 101 S. On US 101, just s. Ext corridors. **Pets:** $6 daily fee/pet. Designated rooms, supervision.

CITY INDEX

ABBOTTSTOWN

▼▼▼▼ The Inn at the Altland House ◨
(717) 259-9535. **$99-$150.** Center Square Rt 30. Jct SR 194. Int corridors. **Pets:** Medium, other species. $10 one-time fee/room. Service with restrictions.
[SAVE] [✕] [🛎] [🍴]

ALLENTOWN

▼▼◆ Allentown Howard Johnson Inn & Suites ▣
(610) 439-4000. **$49-$199.** 3220 Hamilton Blvd. I-78, exit 54 (Hamilton Blvd), 0.8 mi n on US 22. Int corridors. **Pets:** $20 one-time fee/room. Designated rooms, service with restrictions, supervision.
[SAVE] [Sᴅ] [✕] [&M] [⌖] [🖊] [🛎] [💻] [🌊]

▼▼ Allenwood Motel Ⓜ ❀
(610) 395-3707. **$59-$125.** 1058 Hausman Rd. I-476, exit 56, 0.5 mi e on US 22, then 0.8 mi s on SR 309; I-78, exit 53, 1 mi n on SR 309, w on Tilghman St to light, then 0.8 mi n to end. Ext corridors. **Pets:** Medium. $10 daily fee/pet. Designated rooms, no service, supervision.
[SAVE] [Sᴅ] [✕] [🛎]

▼▼▼▼ Crowne Plaza Allentown ▣
(610) 433-2221. **$89-$199.** 904 Hamilton Blvd. 9th St and Hamilton Blvd; downtown. Int corridors. **Pets:** Accepted.
[SAVE] [Sᴅ] [✕] [⌖] [🛎] [💻] [🍴] [🌊] [✕]

▼▼ Days Inn Conference Center ▣ ❀
(610) 395-3731. **$75-$150.** 1151 Bulldog Dr. I-476, exit 56, 0.5 mi e on US 22, then 0.6 mi n on SR 309 via Bulldog Dr access road. Ext/int corridors. **Pets:** Other species. $15 daily fee/room. Designated rooms, service with restrictions, crate.
[ASK] [Sᴅ] [✕] [&M] [⌖] [🖊] [🛎] [💻] [🍴] [🌊] [✕]

▼▼▼ Four Points by Sheraton Hotel & Suites Lehigh Valley Airport ▣
(610) 266-1000. **$82-$99, 14 day notice.** 3400 Airport Rd. On SR 987 N (Airport Rd), 0.5 mi n of jct US 22. Int corridors. **Pets:** Accepted.
[ASK] [Sᴅ] [✕] [&M] [⌖] [🖊] [🛎] [💻] [🍴] [🌊]

▼▼▼ Microtel Inn ▣
(610) 266-9070. **$64-$74, 3 day notice.** 1880 Steelstone Rd. US 22, exit Airport Rd S. Int corridors. **Pets:** Accepted.
[ASK] [Sᴅ] [✕] [&M] [⌖] [🖊] [🛎] [💻]

▼▼▼ Red Roof Inn Ⓜ
(610) 264-5404. **$45-$73.** 1846 Catasauqua Rd. US 22, exit Airport Rd S, just s. Ext corridors. **Pets:** Medium, other species. Service with restrictions, supervision.
[SAVE] [✕] [&M] [⌖] [🖊] [🛎]

▼▼▼▼ Staybridge Suites Allentown-Airport ▣
(610) 443-5000. **$99-$169.** 1787-A Airport Rd. US 22, exit Airport Rd S, 0.3 mi s. Int corridors. **Pets:** Accepted.
[SAVE] [Sᴅ] [✕] [&M] [⌖] [🖊] [🛎] [💻] [🌊] [✕]

WWW Super 8 Motel-Allentown 🆂🅷
(610) 435-7880. **$60-$90.** 1715 Plaza Ln. US 22, exit 15th
St, just n. Int corridors. **Pets:** $10 daily fee/pet. Service with
restrictions, supervision.
🅰🆂🅺 🆂🅳 ✕ 🔗 🔋 🖥

ALTOONA

AAA WWW Econo Lodge 🅼
(814) 944-3555. **$63.** 2906 Pleasant Valley Blvd. I-99/US
220, exit 32 (Frankstown Rd), 0.4 mi w, then 0.5 mi n. Ext
corridors. **Pets:** Other species. No service, crate.
🆂🅰🆅🅴 🆂🅳 ✕ 🔋 🖥 🍴

WWW Motel 6 🅼
(814) 946-7601. **$47-$62.** 1500 Sterling St. I-99/US 220, exit
31 (Plank Rd), just n. Ext corridors. **Pets:** Medium, other
species. Service with restrictions, supervision.
🆂🅳 ✕ 🦽 🐾

WWW Super 8 Motel Altoona 🅼
(814) 942-5350. **$50-$80, 14 day notice.** 3535 Fairway Dr.
I-99/US 220, exit 32 (Frankstown Rd), just w. Int corridors.
Pets: Medium. $6 daily fee/pet. Service with restrictions,
supervision.
🅰🆂🅺 🆂🅳 ✕ 🦽 🔋

BARKEYVILLE

AAA WWW Comfort Inn-Barkeyville 🅼 🐾
(814) 786-7901. **$54-$75.** 137 Gibb Rd. I-80, exit 29, just n
on SR 8. Ext corridors. **Pets:** Dogs only. $10 one-time
fee/room. Designated rooms, service with restrictions,
supervision.
🆂🅰🆅🅴 🆂🅳 ✕ 🔋 🖥

WW Super 8 Motel-Barkeyville 🅼
(814) 786-8375. **$48-$69, 3 day notice.** 1010 Dholu Rd.
I-80, exit 29, just n. Int corridors. **Pets:** $5 daily fee/pet.
Designated rooms, service with restrictions, supervision.
🅰🆂🅺 🆂🅳 ✕ 🔗 🔋

BEDFORD

AAA WWWW Best Western Bedford Inn 🆂🅷 🐾
(814) 623-9006. **$70-$85.** 4517 Business Rt 220. I-70/76
(Pennsylvania Tpke), exit 146, 0.3 mi n. Ext/int corridors.
Pets: Medium, other species. $50 deposit/room, $10 daily
fee/room. Service with restrictions, supervision.
🆂🅰🆅🅴 🆂🅳 ✕ 🔗 🔋 🖥 🍴 🐾 ✕

AAA WW Budget Host Inn 🅼
(814) 623-8107. **$35-$80.** 4378 Business Rt 220 N. I-70/76
(Pennsylvania Tpke), exit 146, just n. Ext corridors.
Pets: $5 one-time fee/pet. Service with restrictions.
🆂🅰🆅🅴 🆂🅳 ✕ 🔋

AAA WW Janey Lynn Motel 🅼
(814) 623-9515. **$35-$75.** 3567 Business Rt 220. I-70/76
(Pennsylvania Tpke), exit 146, 1.6 mi s. Ext corridors.
Pets: $5 daily fee/pet. Service with restrictions, supervision.
🆂🅰🆅🅴 🆂🅳 ✕ 🔋

AAA WW Motel Town House 🅼
(814) 623-5138. **$40-$65.** 200 S Richard St. I-70/76 (Pennsylvania Tpke), exit 146, 2.5 mi s on US 220 business
route. Ext corridors. **Pets:** Accepted.
🆂🅰🆅🅴 🆂🅳 ✕ 🔋

AAA WWWW Quality Inn Bedford 🆂🅷
(814) 623-5188. **$69-$80.** 4407 Business Rt 220 N. I-70/76
(Pennsylvania Tpke), exit 11, just n. Ext/int corridors.
Pets: Large. $10 daily fee/room. Designated rooms, service
with restrictions, crate.
🆂🅰🆅🅴 🆂🅳 ✕ 🔋 🖥 🍴 🐾

AAA WW Super 8 Motel 🅼
(814) 623-5880. **$55-$70, 3 day notice.** 4498 Business Rt
220 N. I-70/76 (Pennslyvania Tpke), exit 146, 0.3 mi n. Int
corridors. **Pets:** Accepted.
🆂🅰🆅🅴 🆂🅳 ✕ 🔋

AAA WWW Travelodge 🅼 🐾
(814) 623-7800. **$45-$65.** 4271 Business Rt 220. I-70/76
(Pennsylvania Tpke), exit 146, just s. Ext/int corridors.
Pets: Large, other species. $7 one-time fee/pet. Designated
rooms, crate.
🆂🅰🆅🅴 🆂🅳 ✕ 🔋 🖥

BETHEL

AAA WWWW Comfort Inn-Bethel/Midway 🆂🅷
(717) 933-8888. **$69-$129.** 41 Diner Dr. I-78, exit 16. Int
corridors. **Pets:** Other species. $10 daily fee/pet. Desig-
nated rooms, service with restrictions, supervision.
🆂🅰🆅🅴 🆂🅳 ✕ 🦽 🦽 🔋 🖥 🐾

BETHLEHEM

WWWW Comfort Inn 🆂🅷 🐾
(610) 865-6300. **$65-$129.** 3191 Highfield Dr. US 22, exit SR
191, just s. Ext/int corridors. **Pets:** Other species. $10 daily
fee/pet. Designated rooms, service with restrictions, supervision.
🅰🆂🅺 🆂🅳 ✕ 🔗 🔋 🖥

WWW Comfort Suites 🆂🅷
(610) 882-9700. **$79-$139.** 120 W 3rd St. W 3rd St and
Brodhead Ave (3rd St exit from SR 378); center. Int corridors. **Pets:** Designated rooms, supervision.
🅰🆂🅺 🆂🅳 ✕ 🔗 🔋 🖥 🍴

**WWWW Holiday Inn Bethlehem at the Gateway
Conference Center** 🆂🅷
(610) 866-5800. **$125.** 300 Gateway Dr. US 22, exit Center
St and SR 512. Ext/int corridors. **Pets:** Small, dogs only.
$50 one-time fee/room. Service with restrictions, supervi-
sion.
🅰🆂🅺 🆂🅳 ✕ 🦽 🔗 🦽 🔋 🖥 🍴 🐾

WWWW Residence Inn by Marriott 🆂🅷
(610) 317-2662. **$89-$124.** 2180 Motel Dr. US 22, exit Aiport
Rd S, 0.8 mi se on Catasauqua Rd. Int corridors.
Pets: Accepted.
✕ 🔗 🦽 🔋 🖥 🐾 ✕

BLOOMSBURG

**AAA WWW Econo Lodge at
Bloomsburg** 🆂🅷 🐾
(570) 387-0490. **$61-$89, 3 day notice.** 189 Columbia Mall
Dr. I-80, exit 232, just n on SR 42. Int corridors.
Pets: Large, other species. $25 one-time fee/room. Desig-
nated rooms, service with restrictions, supervision.
🆂🅰🆅🅴 🆂🅳 ✕ 🔗 🔋 🖥

▼▼▼ The Inn at Turkey Hill 🇨🇮 ❀
(570) 387-1500. **$109-$115.** 991 Central Rd. I-80, exit 236 eastbound; exit 236A westbound, just s. Ext/int corridors. **Pets:** Other species. $15 one-time fee/room. Designated rooms, supervision.

⊠ 🛢 🖳 🍴

BLUE MOUNTAIN

🔷 ▼▼▼ Kenmar Motel 🅼
(717) 423-5915. **$60-$75.** 17788 Cumberland Hwy. I-76, exit 201, just e on SR 997 N. Ext corridors. **Pets:** Dogs only. $5 daily fee/pet. Designated rooms, service with restrictions, supervision.

SAVE 🆂 ⊠ 🛢 ⇔

BOYERTOWN

▼ Mel-Dor Motel 🅼 ❀
(610) 367-2626. **$50-$53.** 1 Spring Garden Dr. SR 100, exit New Berlinville, 1 mi n. Ext corridors. **Pets:** Small, dogs only. $5 daily fee/pet. Service with restrictions, supervision.

⊠ 🛢 ⊠

BRADFORD

🔷 ▼▼▼ Best Western Bradford Inn 🆂🅷
(814) 362-4501. **$77-$149.** 100 Davis St S. US 219, exit Forman St southbound, just s; exit Elm St northbound. Ext/int corridors. **Pets:** $10 daily fee/pet. Designated rooms, service with restrictions.

SAVE ⊠ 🛢 🖳 🍴 ⇔

▼▼ ▼▼ Glendorn 🇨🇮 ❀
(814) 362-6511. **$495-$695, 30 day notice.** 1000 Glendorn Dr. Main and Corydon, 4.3 mi w to W Corydon, follow signs. Ext/int corridors. **Pets:** Large, dogs only. $75 daily fee/pet. Designated rooms, service with restrictions, supervision.

ASK 🛢 🖳 🍴 ⇔ ⊠

BREEZEWOOD

🔷 ▼▼▼ Breezewood Ramada Inn 🆂🅷 ❀
(814) 735-4005. **$49-$79.** 16620 Lincoln Hwy. I-70 (Pennsylvania Tpke), exit 147, just e on US 30; I-76 (Pennsylvania Tpke), exit 161. Int corridors. **Pets:** Service with restrictions.

SAVE 🆂 ⊠ 🛢 🖳 🍴 ⇔ ⊠

🔷 ▼▼▼ Comfort Inn of Breezewood 🅼
(814) 735-2200. **$45-$75.** 16550 Lincoln Hwy. I-70 (Pennsylvania Tpke), exit 147, just n on US 30; I-76 (Pennsylvania Tpke), exit 161. Int corridors. **Pets:** Small, other species. $10 daily fee/pet. Designated rooms, service with restrictions, supervision.

SAVE 🆂 ⊠ ⬚ 🖳 ⇔

🔷 ▼ Wiltshire Motel 🅼
(814) 735-4361. **$44-$46.** 140 S Breezewood Rd. I-70 (Pennsylvania Tpke), exit 147, just w on US 30; I-76 (Pennsylvania Tpke), exit 161. Ext corridors. **Pets:** Small, dogs only. Service with restrictions, supervision.

SAVE ⊠ 🖳

BROOKVILLE

🔷 ▼ Budget Host Gold Eagle Inn 🅼
(814) 849-7344. **$45-$70.** 250 W Main St. I-80, exit 78, 0.5 mi s on SR 36. Ext corridors. **Pets:** Service with restrictions, crate.

SAVE ⊠ 🛢 🖳 🍴

🔷 ▼▼ Holiday Inn Express 🅼
(814) 849-8381. **$69-$89.** 235 Allegheny Blvd. I-80, exit 78, just s on SR 36. Int corridors. **Pets:** $10 one-time fee/pet. Service with restrictions, crate.

SAVE 🆂 ⊠

▼▼ Super 8 Motel 🅼
(814) 849-8840. **$56-$66.** 251 Allegheny Blvd. I-80, exit 78, just n on SR 36. Int corridors. **Pets:** Medium. $50 deposit/room. Designated rooms, service with restrictions, supervision.

ASK 🆂 ⊠ 🛢

CAMBRIDGE SPRINGS

🔷 ▼▼ Riverside Inn 🇨🇮
(814) 398-4645. **$55-$160.** 1 Fountain Ave. I-79, exit 154, 2.9 mi e on SR 198, then 8.4 mi n on US 19. Int corridors. **Pets:** Supervision.

SAVE ⊠ 🛢 🍴 ⇔ ⊠ 🍽

CAMP HILL

▼▼▼ Radisson Penn Harris Hotel & Convention Center 🆂🅷
(717) 763-7117. **$175.** 1150 Camp Hill Bypass. Jct US 11, 15 and Erford Rd. Ext/int corridors. **Pets:** Accepted.

ASK 🆂 ⊠ 🅼 🎵 🎼 🛢 🖳 🍴 ⇔

CARLISLE

🔷 ▼▼▼ Clarion Hotel and Convention Center 🅻🅷
(717) 243-1717. **$89-$179.** 1700 Harrisburg Pike. I-81, exit 52 southbound; exit 52A northbound, 0.4 mi n; I-76 (Pennsylvania Tpke), exit 226, 1.2 mi n. Int corridors. **Pets:** Accepted.

SAVE 🆂 ⊠ 🛢 🖳 🍴 ⇔ ⊠

▼▼▼ Comfort Suites Hotel 🆂🅷
(717) 960-1000. **$99-$174.** 10 S Hanover St. Just s of the square; downtown. Int corridors. **Pets:** Small, other species. $10 daily fee/pet. Service with restrictions, crate.

ASK 🆂 ⊠ 🅼 🎼 🛢 🖳 🍴

🔷 ▼▼▼ Days Inn & Suites-Carlisle 🆂🅷
(717) 258-4147. **$70-$165.** 101 Alexander Spring Rd. I-81, exit 45, just sw. Int corridors. **Pets:** Medium, other species. $10 daily fee/room. Designated rooms, service with restrictions, supervision.

SAVE 🆂 ⊠ 🅼 🎼 🛢 🖳 ⇔

🔷 ▼▼▼ Econo Lodge 🅼
(717) 249-7775. **$53-$65.** 1460 Harrisburg Pike. I-81, exit 52 southbound; exit 52A northbound; I-76 (Pennsylvania Tpke), exit 226, 0.8 mi n. Ext corridors. **Pets:** Small, other species. $10 daily fee/pet. Designated rooms, service with restrictions, crate.

SAVE 🆂 ⊠ 🖳 ⊠

Hampton Inn Carlisle SH
(717) 240-0200. **$79-$119.** 1164 Harrisburg Pike. I-76 (Pennsylvania Tpke), exit 226, just n; I-81, exit 52 southbound; exit 52B northbound, 0.8 mi s. Int corridors. **Pets:** Medium. $15 one-time fee/room. Supervision.

Holiday Inn Carlisle SH
(717) 245-2400. **$99-$175.** 1450 Harrisburg Pike. I-81, exit 52 southbound; exit 52A northbound, just se; I-76 (Pennsylvania Tpke), exit 226, 0.8 mi n. Int corridors. **Pets:** Accepted.

Quality Inn Carlisle SH
(717) 243-6000. **$70-$75.** 1255 Harrisburg Pike. I-81, exit 52 southbound; exit 52B northbound; I-76 (Pennsylvania Tpke), exit 226, 0.8 mi n. Int corridors. **Pets:** Designated rooms, service with restrictions, crate.

Ramada Ltd SH ✿
(717) 243-8585. **$58-$69.** 1252 Harrisburg Pike. I-81, exit 52 southbound; exit 52B northbound; I-76 (Pennsylvania Tpke), exit 226, 1 mi n on US 11. Ext/int corridors. **Pets:** Other species. $10 daily fee/pet. Designated rooms, service with restrictions, crate.

Rodeway Inn M
(717) 249-2800. **$50-$125, 7 day notice.** 1239 Harrisburg Pike. I-81, exit 52 southbound; exit 52B northbound, 0.3 mi s; I-76 (Pennsylvania Tpke), exit 226, 0.8 mi s. Ext corridors. **Pets:** Medium. $8 daily fee/pet. Designated rooms, service with restrictions, crate.

Sleep Inn Carlisle SH
(717) 249-8863. **$56-$139.** 5 E Garland Dr. I-81, exit 47 northbound, just ne; exit 47A southbound. Int corridors. **Pets:** $10 daily fee/pet. Supervision.

Super 8 Motel M
(717) 245-9898. **$50-$70, 14 day notice.** 100 Alexander Spring Rd. I-81, exit 45, just se. Int corridors. **Pets:** Large, other species. $6 daily fee/pet. Service with restrictions, supervision.

CHAMBERSBURG

Best Western Chambersburg M
(717) 262-4994. **$59-$139.** 211 Walker Rd. I-81, exit 16, just w on US 30, then just n. Int corridors. **Pets:** Small. $9 daily fee/pet. Service with restrictions, supervision.

Chambersburg Travelodge M
(717) 264-4187. **$40-$89.** 565 Lincoln Way E. I-81, exit 16, 0.8 mi w on US 30. Ext corridors. **Pets:** Other species. $5 daily fee/pet. Service with restrictions, supervision.

Comfort Inn-Chambersburg SH
(717) 263-6655. **$59-$89.** 3301 Black Gap Rd. I-81, exit 20, just e, then just s on SR 997. Int corridors. **Pets:** Medium, other species. $10 daily fee/room. Designated rooms, service with restrictions, supervision.

Days Inn M
(717) 263-1288. **$65-$109.** 30 Falling Spring Rd. I-81, exit 16, just e on US 30. Int corridors. **Pets:** Medium, other species. $10 daily fee/pet. Designated rooms, service with restrictions, supervision.

Econo Lodge M
(717) 264-8005. **$60-$70.** 1110 Sheller Ave. I-81, exit 14, just w on SR 316. Int corridors. **Pets:** Other species. $10 one-time fee/pet. Service with restrictions, supervision.

Quality Inn & Suites M
(717) 263-3400. **$59-$89.** 1095 Wayne Ave. I-81, exit 14, just w on SR 316. Ext/int corridors. **Pets:** Accepted.

CLARION

Holiday Inn SH
(814) 226-8850. **$75-$99.** 45 Holiday Inn Rd. I-80, exit 62, 0.5 mi n on SR 68. Int corridors. **Pets:** $10 one-time fee/room. Service with restrictions, supervision.

Microtel Inn & Suites-Clarion M ✿
(814) 227-2700. **$49-$79.** 151 Hotel Dr. I-80, exit 62. Int corridors. **Pets:** Designated rooms, service with restrictions, supervision.

Super 8 M ✿
(814) 226-4550. **$45-$75.** 135 Hotel Rd. I-80, exit 62, just n. Ext corridors. **Pets:** Large, other species. Designated rooms, service with restrictions, supervision.

CLARKS SUMMIT

Comfort Inn-Clarks Summit/Scranton SH
(570) 586-9100. **$69-$150.** 811 Northern Blvd. I-81, exit 194 on US 6 and 11; I-476 (Pennsylvania Tpke), exit 131. Int corridors. **Pets:** Accepted.

Ramada Plaza Hotel SH
(570) 586-2730. **$79-$149.** 820 Northern Blvd. I-81, exit 194; I-476 (Pennsylvania Tpke), exit 131, 0.3 mi w on US 6 and 11. Int corridors. **Pets:** Accepted.

CLEARFIELD

Budget Inn M
(814) 765-2639. **$36-$59.** Rt 322 E. I-80, exit 120, 1.5 mi sw
on SR 879, then 1.2 mi e. Ext/int corridors. **Pets:** $5 one-
time fee/pet. Designated rooms, service with restrictions,
supervision.

Super 8 Motel-Clearfield M
(814) 768-7580. **$52-$60.** Rt 879. I-80, exit 120, just s. Int
corridors. **Pets:** Accepted.

COOPERSBURG

Econo Lodge M
(610) 282-1212. **$40-$79.** 321 Rt 309 S. On SR 309; center.
Ext corridors. **Pets:** Very small. $10 daily fee/pet. Service
with restrictions.

DANVILLE

Hampton Inn SH
(570) 271-2500. **$99-$139.** 97 Valley School Rd. I-80, exit
224, just s on SR 54. Int corridors. **Pets:** Medium. $25
one-time fee/pet. Designated rooms, service with restrictions, crate.

Quality Inn & Suites
       Danville M
(570) 275-5100. **$59-$139.** 15 Valley West Rd. I-80, exit 224,
just n on SR 54. Int corridors. **Pets:** Small. $25 one-time
fee/room. Designated rooms, service with restrictions,
supervision.

DICKSON CITY

Days Inn Scranton SH
(570) 383-9979. **$68-$130.** 1946 Scranton-Carbondale Hwy.
I-81, exit 191A, 2 mi e on US 6; I-476 (Pennsylvania Tpke
Northeast Extension), exit 131 (Clarks Summit), 4.5 mi e on
US 6. Int corridors. **Pets:** Other species. $20 one-time fee/
room. Service with restrictions, supervision.

Residence Inn by Marriott-Scranton SH
(570) 343-5121. **$79-$170.** 947 Viewmont Dr. I-81, exit 190,
just e, follow signs. Int corridors. **Pets:** Large, other species.
$100 one-time fee/pet. Service with restrictions, supervision.

DOUGLASSVILLE

Econo Lodge M
(610) 385-3016. **$49-$89.** 387 Ben Franklin Hwy (Rt 422) W.
From Pottstown, 6 mi w on US 422; from Reading, 8 mi e
on US 422. Ext corridors. **Pets:** $12 daily fee/pet. Desig-
nated rooms, service with restrictions, supervision.

DU BOIS

Holiday Inn DuBois SH
(814) 371-5100. **$72.** US 219 & I-80. I-80, exit 97, just s. Int
corridors. **Pets:** Other species. Designated rooms, service
with restrictions.

DUNMORE

Days Inn SH
(570) 348-6101. **$49-$125.** 1226 O'Neill Hwy. I-81, exit 188,
just e at SR 347. Int corridors. **Pets:** Medium. $5 daily
fee/pet. Service with restrictions, supervision.

EASTON

Best Western Easton Inn SH
(610) 253-9131. **$59-$99.** 185 S 3rd St. I-78, exit 75, 1 mi n,
follow signs; US 22, exit 4th St (SR 611), just e to 3rd St,
then 0.5 mi s; downtown. Int corridors. **Pets:** Small. $50
deposit/room. Designated rooms, service with restrictions,
crate.

Days Inn SH
(610) 253-0546. **$50-$150.** 2555 Nazareth Rd. US 22, exit
25th St, just e on N Service Rd. Int corridors.
Pets: Medium. $10 daily fee/pet. Designated rooms, service
with restrictions, supervision.

EBENSBURG

Comfort Inn SH
(814) 472-6100. **$77-$90.** 111 Cook Rd. Jct US 219, just e
on US 22. Int corridors. **Pets:** Other species. $25 deposit/
room, $8 daily fee/pet. Designated rooms, supervision.

ERIE

Best Western Erie Inn & Suites SH
(814) 864-1812. **$49-$129, 7 day notice.** 7820 Perry Hwy.
I-90, exit 27, just n. Int corridors. **Pets:** Other species. $10
one-time fee/pet. Designated rooms, service with restrictions, crate.

Country Inn & Suites SH
(814) 864-5810. **$49-$130, 3 day notice.** 8040 Oliver Rd.
I-90, exit 24, just s, then 0.5 mi w. Int corridors. **Pets:** Small.
$25 one-time fee/pet. Service with restrictions, supervision.

Days Inn SH
(814) 868-8521. **$50-$110.** 7415 Schultz Rd. I-90, exit 27,
just n. Int corridors. **Pets:** Accepted.

Homewood Suites by Hilton SH
(814) 866-8292. **$109-$129, 14 day notice.** 2084 Interchange Rd. I-79, exit 180, just e. Int corridors. **Pets:** Other
species. $75 one-time fee/room. Service with restrictions.

💎 Microtel Inn-Erie Ⓜ
(814) 864-1010. **$44-$79.** 8100 Peach St. I-90, exit 24, just s. Int corridors. **Pets:** Other species. $10 one-time fee/room. Designated rooms, service with restrictions, supervision.
(ASK) (S) (X) (🐾) (✦) (📞)

💎💎 Motel 6 Ⓜ
(814) 864-4811. **$49-$100.** 7875 Peach St. I-90, exit 24, just n. Int corridors. **Pets:** Accepted.
(ASK) (S) (X) (📞) (🏊)

🔶 💎💎 Red Roof Inn Ⓜ
(814) 868-5246. **$43-$88.** 7865 Perry Hwy. I-90, exit 27, just n. Ext/int corridors. **Pets:** Large, other species. Service with restrictions, supervision.
(SAVE) (X) (📞)

💎💎💎 Residence Inn by Marriott 🅢🅗
(814) 864-2500. **$109-$159.** 8061 Peach St. I-90, exit 24, just s. Int corridors. **Pets:** Accepted.
(ASK) (S) (X) (🐾) (✦) (📞) (💻) (🏊) (X)

FAYETTEVILLE

🔶 💎 Rite Spot Motel Ⓜ
(717) 352-2144. **$35-$70.** 5651 Lincoln Way E. On US 30, 1 mi w of jct SR 997. Ext corridors. **Pets:** Medium, other species. $5 daily fee/pet. Designated rooms, no service, supervision.
(SAVE) (S) (X) (📞) (💻)

FOGELSVILLE

💎 Cloverleaf Motel Ⓜ
(610) 395-3367. **$40-$55.** I-78, exit 49A, 0.3 mi s on SR 100, left at 1st traffic light, then immediate left on service road. Ext corridors. **Pets:** Medium. $15 daily fee/room. Designated rooms, service with restrictions, supervision.
(X) (🐾) (📞) (💻)

🔶 💎💎💎 Comfort Inn Lehigh
Valley-West 🅢🅗 ❀
(610) 391-0344. **$80-$120.** I-78, exit 49B (SR 100), just n. Int corridors. **Pets:** Other species. $25 one-time fee/pet. Designated rooms, service with restrictions.
(SAVE) (S) (X) (🐾) (📞) (💻)

💎💎💎 Holiday Inn Conference Center 🅢🅗
(610) 391-1000. **$79-$139.** 7736 Adrienne Dr. I-78, exit 49A, 0.3 mi s on SR 100. Int corridors. **Pets:** Other species. $10 daily fee/pet. Designated rooms, service with restrictions, supervision.
(ASK) (S) (X) (♿M) (🐾) (📞) (💻) (🍴) (🏊)

🔶 💎💎💎 Sleep Inn 🅢🅗
(610) 395-6603. **$59-$99.** I-78, exit 49A, 0.3 mi s on SR 100, left at 1st traffic light, then immediate left on service road. Int corridors. **Pets:** Medium. $15 one-time fee/pet. Designated rooms, service with restrictions, supervision.
(SAVE) (S) (X) (♿M) (🐾) (✦) (📞) (💻)

FRACKVILLE

🔶 💎💎💎 Econo Lodge Ⓜ
(570) 874-3838. **$45-$75.** 501 S Middle St. I-81, exit 124B, 0.4 mi n on SR 61. Ext corridors. **Pets:** Accepted.
(SAVE) (S) (X) (📞) (💻)

🔶 💎💎 Granny's Motel & Restaurant 🅢🅗
(570) 874-0408. **$39-$45.** I-81, exit 124B. I-81, exit 124B, 0.3 mi nw on SR 61, then 0.3 mi n on Altamont Blvd. Ext/int corridors. **Pets:** Accepted.
(SAVE) (X) (📞) (💻) (🍴)

💎💎 Motel 6–4043 Ⓜ
(570) 874-1223. **$49-$50, 7 day notice.** 701 Altamont Blvd. I-81, exit 124B, 0.3 mi nw on SR 61, then 0.3 mi n. Ext/int corridors. **Pets:** Accepted.
(X) (📞)

FRANKLIN

💎 Franklin Super 8 Motel 🅢🅗
(814) 432-2101. **$60-$65.** 847 Allegheny Ave. 2 mi on SR 8. Int corridors. **Pets:** $10 deposit/room. Service with restrictions, supervision.
(ASK) (X) (📞)

GALETON

💎 Pine Log Motel Ⓜ
(814) 435-6400. **$65-$80, 3 day notice.** 5156 US Rt 6 W. 9 mi w. Ext corridors. **Pets:** Accepted.
(ASK) (S) (X) (📞) (X) (🎾)

GETTYSBURG

🔶 💎💎 Best Inn Ⓜ
(717) 334-3188. **$48-$110.** 301 Steinwehr Ave. 1 mi s on US 15 business route, just s of jct SR 134. Ext/int corridors. **Pets:** Medium, dogs only. Service with restrictions, supervision.
(SAVE) (S) (X) (🏊)

💎💎 Gettysburg Travelodge Ⓜ
(717) 334-9281. **$69-$165.** 613 Baltimore St. On SR 97 at US 15 business route. Ext/int corridors. **Pets:** Other species. Service with restrictions, supervision.
(ASK) (S) (X) (✦) (📞) (💻)

💎💎💎 Holiday Inn-Battlefield 🅢🅗
(717) 334-6211. **$100-$250.** 516 Baltimore St. Jct US 15 business route and SR 97. Ext/int corridors. **Pets:** Accepted.
(ASK) (S) (X) (✦) (📞) (💻) (🍴) (🏊)

🔶 💎 Red Carpet Inn-Perfect Rest Motel Ⓜ
(717) 334-1345. **$40-$135, 30 day notice.** 2450 Emmitsburg Rd. 4.5 mi s on US 15 business route. Ext corridors. **Pets:** Dogs only. $5 daily fee/pet. Designated rooms, service with restrictions, supervision.
(SAVE) (S) (X) (📞) (🏊)

GRANTVILLE

🔶 💎💎💎 Econo Lodge Ⓜ
(717) 469-0631. **$45-$90, 30 day notice.** 252 Bow Creek Rd. I-81, exit 80. Ext corridors. **Pets:** Small. $6 daily fee/pet. Designated rooms, service with restrictions, supervision.
(SAVE) (S) (X) (🐾) (📞) (💻)

💎💎💎 Holiday Inn Harrisburg-Hershey Area,
I-81 🅢🅗
(717) 469-0661. **$89-$209.** 604 Station Rd. I-81, exit 80. Int corridors. **Pets:** Other species. Service with restrictions, crate.
(ASK) (S) (X) (♿M) (🐾) (✦) (📞) (💻) (🍴) (🏊) (X)

GREENCASTLE

◆◆◆ ▼▼▼ Comfort Inn SH
(717) 597-8164. **$50-$75.** 50 Pine Dr. I-81, exit 3, just s on US 11. Int corridors. **Pets:** $6 daily fee/pet. Designated rooms, service with restrictions, supervision.
SAVE SÒ ⊠ 🖬 🖵 ⊗

GROVE CITY

▼▼ Old Arbor Rose BB
(724) 458-6425. **$70-$80, 7 day notice.** 114 W Main St. Just e. Int corridors. **Pets:** Accepted.
⊠ 🄿 🄲

HANOVER

▼▼ Howard Johnson Inn M
(717) 646-1000. **$40-$60.** 1080 Carlisle St. 1.5 mi n on SR 94, then just e. Ext corridors. **Pets:** Other species. $10 daily fee/pet. Service with restrictions.
ASK SÒ ⊠ ᏜM 🖬 🖵 ⊇

HARRISBURG

◆◆◆ ▼▼ Baymont Inn & Suites Harrisburg-Airport SH
(717) 939-8000. **$79-$109.** 990 Eisenhower Blvd. I-283, exit 2, just se; I-76 (Pennsylvania Tpke), exit 247, 1 mi n. Int corridors. **Pets:** Other species. Designated rooms, service with restrictions, supervision.
SAVE SÒ ⊠ 🄿 🖬 🖵

◆◆◆ ▼▼ Best Western Capital Plaza SH
(717) 545-9089. **$76-$90.** 150 Nationwide Dr. I-81, exit 69, just n. Ext/int corridors. **Pets:** Dogs only. Service with restrictions, supervision.
SAVE SÒ ⊠ 🄿 🖬 🖵 ⊇

◆◆◆ ▼▼▼ Best Western Harrisburg/Hershey Hotel & Suites SH
(717) 652-7180. **$83-$94.** 300 N Mountain Rd. I-81, exit 72. Int corridors. **Pets:** $5 daily fee/pet. Designated rooms, service with restrictions.
SAVE SÒ ⊠ 🄿 🄶 🖬 🖵 🍽 ⊇ ⊗

▼▼▼ Comfort Inn Harrisburg East SH
(717) 561-8100. **$81-$116.** 4021 Union Deposit Rd. I-83, exit 48, just w. Int corridors. **Pets:** Accepted.
ASK SÒ ⊠ 🄿 🄶 🖬 🖵 ⊇

◆◆◆ ▼▼▼ Comfort Inn Harrisburg/Hershey SH
(717) 540-8400. **$69-$189.** 7744 Linglestown Rd. I-81, exit 77, 0.5 mi w. Int corridors. **Pets:** Other species. $10 daily fee/room. Designated rooms, service with restrictions, supervision.
SAVE SÒ ⊠ 🄿 🄶 🖬 🖵 ⊇ ⊗

◆◆◆ ▼▼▼ Comfort Inn-Riverfront SH ❀
(717) 233-1611. **$69-$149.** 525 S Front St. I-83, exit 43, 0.5 mi n. Ext/int corridors. **Pets:** $10 daily fee/pet. Designated rooms, service with restrictions, crate.
SAVE SÒ ⊠ 🄿 🖬 🖵 🍽 ⊇

▼▼ Days Inn-Harrisburg Airport SH ❀
(717) 939-4147. **$69-$109.** I-76 (Pennsylvania Tpke), exit 247, just n; I-283, exit 1B (Highspire). Ext corridors. **Pets:** Dogs only. $50 deposit/room. Service with restrictions, supervision.
ASK SÒ ⊠ 🄿 🖬 🖵 ⊇

▼ Greenlawn Motel M
(717) 652-1530. **$59-$99.** 7490 Allentown Blvd. W of jct SR 39 and US 22. Ext corridors. **Pets:** Other species. $10 one-time fee/pet. Service with restrictions.
ASK SÒ ⊠ 🖬

◆◆◆ ▼▼▼▼ Harrisburg-Hershey Marriott LH
(717) 564-5511. **$84-$225.** 4650 Lindle Rd. I-283, exit 2, just e. Int corridors. **Pets:** Other species. $50 one-time fee/room.
SAVE ⊠ ᏜM 🄿 🄶 🖬 🖵 🍽 ⊇ ⊗

◆◆◆ ▼▼▼▼ Holiday Inn Express Hotel & Suites SH
(717) 657-2200. **$79-$139.** 5680 Allentown Blvd. I-81, exit 72, just s on S Mountain Rd, then just w on SR 22. Int corridors. **Pets:** Accepted.
SAVE SÒ ⊠ ᏜM 🄿 🄶 🖬 🖵 ⊇

▼▼▼▼ Holiday Inn Harrisburg East-Airport SH
(717) 939-7841. **$69-$199, 4 day notice.** 4751 Lindle Rd. I-283, exit 2, just e. Int corridors. **Pets:** Accepted.
ASK SÒ ⊠ 🄿 🖬 🖵 🍽 ⊇ ⊗

◆◆◆ ▼▼▼▼ Quality Inn SH
(717) 540-9339. **$59-$129.** 200 N Mountain Rd. I-81, exit 72A northbound; exit 72 southbound. Int corridors. **Pets:** Other species. Service with restrictions, crate.
SAVE SÒ ⊠ 🄿 🖬 🖵

▼▼▼ Ramada Limited SH
(717) 545-6944. **Call for rates.** 7965 Jonestown Rd. I-81, exit 77, just s. Int corridors. **Pets:** Accepted.
⊠ 🖬 ⊇

◆◆◆ ▼▼▼ Red Roof Inn-North M
(717) 657-1445. **$45-$78.** 400 Corporate Cir. I-81, exit 69, just n on Progress Ave. Ext/int corridors. **Pets:** Accepted.
SAVE ⊠ 🄿 🄶 🖬

◆◆◆ ▼▼▼ Red Roof Inn-South M
(717) 939-1331. **$46-$78.** 950 Eisenhower Blvd. I-283, exit 2, just e. Ext/int corridors. **Pets:** Accepted.
SAVE ⊠ 🄿 🄶

▼▼▼ Residence Inn by Marriott Harrisburg-Hershey SH
(717) 561-1900. **$169-$249.** 4480 Lewis Rd. US 322, exit Penhar Dr, just e. Ext corridors. **Pets:** $10 daily fee/pet, $100 one-time fee/room. Service with restrictions, supervision.
ASK SÒ ⊠ 🄿 🖬 🖵 ⊇ ⊗

◆◆◆ ▼▼▼ Sleep Inn SH
(717) 540-9100. **$59-$149.** 7930 Linglestown Rd. I-81, exit 77. Int corridors. **Pets:** Other species. $10 one-time fee/pet. Service with restrictions, supervision.
SAVE SÒ ⊠ 🄿 🖬 🖵

(AAA) ▼▼ Super 8 Motel-North M
(717) 233-5891. **$65-$139.** 4125 N Front St. I-81, exit 66, 0.8 mi n. Ext corridors. **Pets:** Accepted.
[SAVE] [Sᴅ] [✕] [🛏] [🍴] [⚓]

▼▼▼ Wingate Inn SH
(717) 985-1600. **$109.** 1344 Eisenhower Blvd. I-76 (Pennsylvania Tpke), exit 247, just n; I-283, exit 1B (Highspire), just w, then 0.5 mi n. Int corridors. **Pets:** Accepted.
[ASK] [Sᴅ] [✕] [ᴸᴹ] [🐾] [🐾] [🛏] [💻]

HAZLETON

(AAA) ▼▼▼ Best Western Genetti Lodge SH
(570) 454-2494. **$65-$110.** 32nd & N Church St. I-80, exit 262, 6 mi s on SR 309. Ext/int corridors. **Pets:** Medium. $10 one-time fee/pet. Service with restrictions, supervision.
[SAVE] [Sᴅ] [✕] [🐾] [🛏] [💻] [⚓]

(AAA) ▼▼ Hazleton Motor Inn M
(570) 459-1451. **$35-$50.** 615 E Broad St. I-81, exit 143, 2 mi n on SR 924, then 1 mi s on SR 93. Int corridors. **Pets:** $5 daily fee/pet. Service with restrictions, supervision.
[SAVE] [Sᴅ] [✕] [🛏]

HERSHEY

(AAA) ▼▼▼ Best Western Inn-Hershey SH
(717) 533-5665. **$69-$229.** US 422 & Sipe Ave. Jct US 322, just e. Ext/int corridors. **Pets:** Other species. Designated rooms, service with restrictions, supervision.
[SAVE] [Sᴅ] [✕] [🐾] [🛏] [💻] [⚓]

(AAA) ▼▼▼ Comfort Inn SH
(717) 566-2050. **$90-$259.** 1200 Mae St. Jct US 322, 422 and SR 39 (Hershey Park Dr); just off Hershey Park Dr. Int corridors. **Pets:** Medium. $10 daily fee/room, $25 one-time fee/room. Service with restrictions, supervision.
[SAVE] [Sᴅ] [✕] [ᴸᴹ] [🐾] [🛏] [💻] [⚓]

(AAA) ▼▼▼ Hampton Inn & Suites SH
(717) 533-8400. **$119-$259.** 749 E Chocolate Ave. 0.9 mi e on US 422. Int corridors. **Pets:** Small. $10 daily fee/pet. Designated rooms, service with restrictions, supervision.
[SAVE] [Sᴅ] [✕] [ᴸᴹ] [🐾] [🐾] [🛏] [💻] [⚓] [✕]

(AAA) ▼▼▼ Holiday Inn Express SH
(717) 583-0500. **$99-$209.** Just nw of jct US 322, 422 and SR 39 (Hershey Park Dr); just off Hershey Park Dr. Int corridors. **Pets:** Medium. $50 deposit/pet. Designated rooms, service with restrictions, crate.
[SAVE] [Sᴅ] [✕] [ᴸᴹ] [🐾] [🐾] [🛏] [💻] [⚓] [✕]

HUNTINGDON

▼▼ Huntingdon Motor Inn M
(814) 643-1133. **$50-$65.** Motor Inn Rd. On US 22 at SR 26. Ext corridors. **Pets:** Accepted.
[✕] [🐾] [🛏] [💻]

INDIANA

(AAA) ▼▼▼ Best Western University Inn SH
(724) 349-9620. **$74-$99.** 1545 Wayne Ave. 0.6 mi n of US 422, exit Wayne Ave. Int corridors. **Pets:** Accepted.
[SAVE] [Sᴅ] [✕] [🛏] [💻] [⚓]

▼▼▼ Holiday Inn Holidome SH
(724) 463-3561. **$79-$119.** 1395 Wayne Ave. US 422, exit Wayne Ave, 1 mi n. Ext/int corridors. **Pets:** Service with restrictions, supervision.
[ASK] [Sᴅ] [✕] [🐾] [🛏] [💻] [🍴] [⚓] [✕]

JONESTOWN

▼▼▼ Days Inn Lebanon/Lickdale SH ✿
(717) 865-4064. **$60-$135, 3 day notice.** 3 Everest Ln. I-81, exit 90. Int corridors. **Pets:** Other species. $10 one-time fee/room. Service with restrictions, crate.
[ASK] [Sᴅ] [✕] [🐾] [🛏] [💻]

▼▼▼ Red Carpet Inn & Suites-Jonestown SH
(717) 865-6600. **$48-$72.** 16 Marsenna Ln. I-81, exit 90, just w. Int corridors. **Pets:** Accepted.
[ASK] [Sᴅ] [✕] [🛏] [⚓]

▼▼▼ Strawberry Patch Bed & Breakfast BB
(717) 865-7219. **$125-$168, 21 day notice.** 115 Moores Rd. I-81, exit 90, 2.8 mi s on SR 72, 1 mi e on Jonestown Rd, 0.8 mi s on S Lancaster St, then just e. Ext/int corridors. **Pets:** Accepted.
[ASK] [Sᴅ] [✕] [✕]

KITTANNING

▼▼▼ Comfort Inn SH
(724) 543-5200. **$69-$89.** 13 Hilltop Plaza. SR 28, exit 19A. Int corridors. **Pets:** Small. $25 deposit/pet. Service with restrictions, crate.
[ASK] [Sᴅ] [✕] [🐾] [🛏] [💻] [⚓]

(AAA) ▼▼▼ Quality Inn Royle SH
(724) 543-1159. **$59-$90.** 405 Butler Rd. SR 28, exit I-422 W (Belmont). Ext/int corridors. **Pets:** Accepted.
[SAVE] [Sᴅ] [✕] [🐾] [🛏] [💻]

(AAA) ▼▼ Rodeway Inn Kittanning M ✿
(724) 543-1100. **$58-$63.** US 422 E. E of jct Business Rt US 422, SR 66 and 28. Ext corridors. **Pets:** Medium, dogs only. $25 deposit/room, $5 one-time fee/pet. Service with restrictions, supervision.
[SAVE] [Sᴅ] [✕] [🛏] [💻]

KUTZTOWN

(AAA) ▼▼▼ Campus Inn M
(610) 683-8721. **$55-$75, 3 day notice.** 15080 Kutztown Rd. US 222, exit Kutztown Rd/Virginsville, 1 mi e. Ext corridors. **Pets:** Accepted.
[SAVE] [Sᴅ] [✕] [🛏] [⚓]

(AAA) ▼▼▼ Lincoln Motel M
(610) 683-3456. **$50-$70, 3 day notice.** 12 Lincoln Dr. US 222, exit Kutztown Rd/Virginsville. Ext corridors. **Pets:** Accepted.
[SAVE] [Sᴅ] [✕] [🛏]

LAMAR

(AAA) ▼▼▼ Comfort Inn of Lamar SH
(570) 726-4901. **$79-$142.** 31 Comfort Inn Ln. I-80, exit 173, just n on SR 64. Int corridors. **Pets:** Medium. $10 daily fee/pet. Designated rooms, service with restrictions, supervision.
[SAVE] [Sᴅ] [✕] [🛏] [💻] [⚓]

LAUREL HIGHLANDS METROPOLITAN AREA

CHALK HILL

▼▼▼▼ Historic Summit Inn LH
(724) 438-8594. **$89-$299, 3 day notice.** On US 40; center. Int corridors. **Pets:** Accepted.
(ASK) (S/D) (X) (⬛) (⬛) (⬛) (⬛) (🏊) (⊗)

AAA ▼▼▼◆ The Lodge at Chalk Hill M
(724) 438-8880. **$60-$78.** Just w. Ext corridors. **Pets:** Other species. $10 daily fee/pet. Designated rooms, service with restrictions, supervision.
(SAVE) (X) (⬛) (⬛) (⊗)

GREENSBURG

▼▼▼▼ Four Points by Sheraton SH
(724) 836-6060. **$99-$129.** 100 Sheraton Dr. I-76 (Pennsylvania Tpke), exit 75, 5.6 mi on US 119 N, 3 mi e on US 30, then just n. Int corridors. **Pets:** Medium, other species. $10 daily fee/room. Service with restrictions, crate.
(ASK) (S/D) (X) (⬛) (⬛) (⬛) (⬛) (🏊) (⊗)

▼▼ Knights Inn-Greensburg M
(724) 836-7100. **$53-$95.** 1215 S Main St. I-76 (Pennsylvania Tpke), exit 75, 4 mi on US 119; just s of US 30. Ext corridors. **Pets:** Accepted.
(ASK) (S/D) (X) (⬛) (⬛) (🏊)

JOHNSTOWN

▼▼▼▼ Comfort Inn & Suites SH
(814) 266-3678. **$65-$135.** 455 Theatre Dr. US 219, exit Elton (SR 756), just e. Int corridors. **Pets:** $25 deposit/room, $15 daily fee/pet. Designated rooms, service with restrictions, supervision.
(ASK) (S/D) (X) (⬛M) (🎦) (⬛) (⬛) (🏊)

▼▼ Econo Lodge M
(814) 536-1114. **$56-$75.** 430 Napoleon Pl. Jct SR 271 and 403; downtown. Int corridors. **Pets:** Service with restrictions, supervision.
(ASK) (S/D) (X) (⬛M) (🎦) (⬛) (⬛) (⬛)

▼▼▼▼ Holiday Inn Downtown SH
(814) 535-7777. **$94-$115.** 250 Market St. Corner of Market and Vine sts; downtown. Int corridors. **Pets:** Accepted.
(ASK) (S/D) (X) (⬛) (⬛) (⬛) (⬛) (🏊) (⊗)

▼▼ Holiday Inn Express Johnstown M
(814) 266-8789. **$85-$100.** 1440 Scalp Ave. US 219, exit Windber (SR 56 E), just e. Int corridors. **Pets:** Accepted.
(ASK) (S/D) (X) (⬛M) (🎦) (⬛) (⬛)

▼▼ Sleep Inn SH
(814) 262-9292. **$59-$75.** 453 Theatre Dr. US 219, exit Elton (SR 756), just e. Int corridors. **Pets:** $25 deposit/room, $15 daily fee/pet. Designated rooms, service with restrictions, supervision.
(ASK) (S/D) (X) (⬛M) (🎦) (⬛) (⬛) (⬛)

▼▼ Super 8 Motel Johnstown SH
(814) 535-5600. **$43-$48, 4 day notice.** 627 Solomon Run Rd. US 219, exit Galleria Dr, just w. Int corridors. **Pets:** Accepted.
(ASK) (S/D) (X) (⬛) (⬛)

LIGONIER

AAA ▼▼▼▼ Lady of the Lake Bed & Breakfast BB ❀
(724) 238-6955. **$75-$135, 30 day notice.** 157 Rt 30 E. US 30 E, just w of jct SR 711; beside Idlewild Park. Ext/int corridors. **Pets:** Medium, other species. $20 deposit/pet. Designated rooms, service with restrictions, supervision.
(SAVE) (X) (⬛) (⬛) (🏊) (⊗) (🐾)

NEW STANTON

AAA ▼▼▼ Quality Inn New Stanton SH
(724) 925-6755. **$47-$77.** 110 N Main St/Byers Ave. I-76 (Pennsylvania Tpke), exit 75, just w; I-70 (Pennsylvania Tpke), exit 57, just ne. Int corridors. **Pets:** Accepted.
(SAVE) (S/D) (X) (⬛) (⬛) (⬛)

▼▼ Super 8 Motel-New Stanton M ❀
(724) 925-8915. **$56-$72.** 103 Bair Blvd. I-76 (Pennslyvania Tpke), exit 75, 0.6 mi sw; I-70 (Pennslyvania Tpke), exit 57. Int corridors. **Pets:** Medium. $10 daily fee/pet. Designated rooms, service with restrictions, supervision.
(X) (⬛)

SOMERSET

AAA ▼▼▼▼ Best Western Executive Inn SH
(814) 445-3996. **$45-$120.** 165 Water Works Rd. I-70/76 (Pennsylvania Tpke), exit 110, just e. Int corridors. **Pets:** Large, other species. $7 daily fee/pet. Designated rooms, service with restrictions, supervision.
(SAVE) (S/D) (X) (⬛) (⬛) (⬛) (⊗)

AAA ▼▼ Budget Host Inn M
(814) 445-7988. **$40-$85, 7 day notice.** 799 N Center Ave. I-70/76 (Pennsylvania Tpke), exit 110, 0.3 mi s. Ext corridors. **Pets:** Very small. $7 daily fee/pet. No service, supervision.
(SAVE) (S/D) (X) (⬛)

AAA ▼▼ The Budget Inn M
(814) 443-6441. **$32-$75.** 736 N Center Ave. I-70/76 (Pennsylvania Tpke), exit 110, 0.4 mi s. Ext corridors. **Pets:** Accepted.
(SAVE) (S/D) (X) (⬛)

▼▼ Days Inn-Somerset M
(814) 445-9200. **$45-$100.** 220 Water Works Rd. I-70/76 (Pennsylvania Tpke), exit 110, just e. Ext corridors. **Pets:** Accepted.
(ASK) (S/D) (X) (⬛) (⬛)

AAA ▼▼ Dollar Inn M
(814) 445-2977. **$35-$65.** 1146 N Center Ave. I-70/76 (Pennsylvania Tpke) exit 110, just e via Water Works Rd, then just n on SR 601, at top of hill. Ext corridors. **Pets:** Accepted.
(SAVE) (S/D) (X) (⬛)

▼▼ Glades Pike Inn 🅱🅱
(814) 443-4978. **$70-$110, 7 day notice.** 2684 Glades Pike. I-70/76 (Pennsylvania Tpke), exit 110, 7.9 mi w on SR 31. Int corridors. **Pets:** Other species. $5 daily fee/pet. Crate.
🅰🆂🅺 🆂 ✖ ✖ 🕭

🆔 ▼▼▼ Holiday Inn 🆂🅷
(814) 445-9611. **$89-$109.** 202 Harmon St. I-70/76 (Pennsylvania Tpke), exit 110, just s. Int corridors. **Pets:** Medium, other species. $50 one-time fee/room. Designated rooms, service with restrictions, supervision.
🆂🅰🆅🅴 🆂 ✖ 🖋 💻 🍴 🏊

▼▼▼ The Inn at Georgian Place 🅱🅱
(814) 443-1043. **$95-$185, 7 day notice.** 800 Georgian Place Dr. I-70/76 (Pennsylvania Tpke), exit 110, just e via Water Works Rd, then 0.5 mi n on SR 601. Int corridors. **Pets:** No service, supervision.
🅰🆂🅺 🆂 ✖ 🍴

▼▼▼ Knights Inn Ⓜ
(814) 445-8933. **$60.** 585 Ramada Rd. I-70/76 (Pennsylvania Tpke), exit 110, just s. Ext corridors. **Pets:** Other species. Service with restrictions, crate.
🅰🆂🅺 🆂 ✖ 🖋 💻 🏊

🆔 ▼▼▼ Ramada Inn 🆂🅷
(814) 443-4646. **$59-$109.** 215 Ramada Rd. I-70/76 (Pennsylvania Tpke), exit 110, just s. Int corridors. **Pets:** Accepted.
🆂🅰🆅🅴 🆂 ✖ 🖋 💻 🍴 🏊 ✖

▼▼ Super 8 Motel Ⓜ
(814) 445-8788. **$44-$88.** 125 Lewis Dr. I-70/76 (Pennsylvania Tpke), exit 110, just s. Int corridors. **Pets:** Other species. Service with restrictions, supervision.
🅰🆂🅺 🆂 ✖ 🖋 💻

UNIONTOWN

▼▼ Holiday Inn 🆂🅷
(724) 437-2816. **$74-$129.** 700 W Main St. 1.8 mi w on US 40. Int corridors. **Pets:** Accepted.
🅰🆂🅺 🆂 ✖ 🖋 🌀 🖋 💻 🍴 🏊 ✖

❖ END METROPOLITAN AREA ❖

LEBANON

🆔 ▼▼▼ Quality Inn-Lebanon/Hershey 🆂🅷
(717) 273-6771. **$99-$119.** 625 Quentin Rd. 0.5 mi s on SR 72. Ext/int corridors. **Pets:** Medium, other species. $5 daily fee/pet. Designated rooms, service with restrictions, supervision.
🆂🅰🆅🅴 🆂 ✖ 🆖 🖋 🖋 🖋 💻 🍴 🏊 ✖

LEWISBURG

🆔 ▼▼ Days Inn-Lewisburg 🆂🅷
(570) 523-1171. **$80-$96, 3 day notice.** US Rt 15. 0.5 mi n of jct SR 45. Ext corridors. **Pets:** Other species. Service with restrictions, crate.
🆂🅰🆅🅴 🆂 ✖ 🖋 💻 🏊

LINCOLN FALLS

▼▼ Morgan Century Farm 🅱🅱
(570) 924-4909. **$85-$125, 3 day notice.** Rt 154. In village; on SR 154. Ext/int corridors. **Pets:** Small. $5 one-time fee/room. Designated rooms, service with restrictions, supervision.
🆂 ✖ 🖋 💻 🕭

MANSFIELD

▼▼▼ Comfort Inn 🆂🅷
(570) 662-3000. **$69-$119.** 300 Gateway Dr. Jct US 6 and 15. Int corridors. **Pets:** Accepted.
🅰🆂🅺 🆂 ✖ 🖋 💻 ✖

🆔 ▼ West's Deluxe Motel Ⓜ
(570) 659-5141. **$50-$60.** Rt 15, 2848 S Main St. 3.5 mi s. Ext corridors. **Pets:** Accepted.
🆂🅰🆅🅴 🆂 ✖ 🖋 💻 🏊

MEADVILLE

▼ Days Inn Conference Center 🆂🅷
(814) 337-4264. **$49-$159.** 18360 Conneaut Lake Rd. I-79, exit 147A, just e on US 322. Int corridors. **Pets:** Accepted.
🅰🆂🅺 🆂 ✖ 🖋 💻 🍴 🏊

▼▼ Motel 6 Ⓜ
(814) 724-6366. **$54-$100.** 11237 Shaw Ave. I-79, exit 147A, just e on US 322. Int corridors. **Pets:** Accepted.
🅰🆂🅺 🆂 ✖ 🖋

▼ Super 8 Motel Ⓜ
(814) 333-8883. **$57-$67.** 17259 Conneaut Lake Rd. I-79, exit 147B, just w on US 322. Ext/int corridors. **Pets:** Medium, other species. $50 deposit/room. Service with restrictions, supervision.
🅰🆂🅺 🆂 ✖ 🖋

MECHANICSBURG

🆔 ▼▼▼ Comfort Inn Capital City 🆂🅷
(717) 766-3700. **$79-$179.** 1012 Wesley Dr. I-76 (Pennsylvania Tpke), exit 236 (US 15), 1 mi n to Wesley Dr exit, then just w. Int corridors. **Pets:** Accepted.
🆂🅰🆅🅴 🆂 ✖ 🆖 🖋 🖋 💻 🏊

🆔 ▼▼▼▼ Hampton Inn-Harrisburg West 🆂🅷
(717) 691-1300. **$99-$154, 14 day notice.** 4950 Ritter Rd. I-76 (Pennsylvania Tpke), exit 236 (US 15), 1 mi n to Rossmoyne Rd exit. Int corridors. **Pets:** Other species. Designated rooms, service with restrictions, supervision.
🆂🅰🆅🅴 🆂 ✖ 🆖 🖋 💻 🏊 ✖

(AAA) ▼▼▼ Holiday Inn Harrisburg-West SH
(717) 697-0321. **$94-$134, 3 day notice.** 5401 Carlisle Pike. Jct Carlisle Pike and US 11, just w. Ext corridors. **Pets:** $10 one-time fee/room. Service with restrictions, crate.
SAVE Sↄ ⊠ 🔒 📺 🍴 ⤳ ⊠

MERCER

(AAA) ▼ Colonial Inn Motel M
(724) 662-5600. **$33-$40.** 383 N Perry Hwy. I-80, exit 15, 3 mi n; I-79, exit 121, 4 mi w on SR 62 S, then 0.5 mi n on US 19. Ext corridors. **Pets:** Other species. $4 daily fee/pet. Service with restrictions, supervision.
SAVE ⊠ 🔒 📺

▼▼▼ Howard Johnson Inn SH
(724) 748-3030. **$82-$83.** 835 Perry Hwy. I-80, exit 15, just n on US 19. Int corridors. **Pets:** Accepted.
ASK Sↄ ⊠ 🅿 🔒 📺 🍴 ⤳ ⊠

MIFFLINVILLE

▼▼ Super 8 Motel M
(570) 759-6778. **$51-$90, 3 day notice.** 450 3rd St. I-80, exit 242, just n on SR 339. Ext corridors. **Pets:** Dogs only. $10 one-time fee/room. Service with restrictions, supervision.
ASK Sↄ ⊠

MILESBURG

▼▼▼ Holiday Inn SH
(814) 355-7521. **$75-$180, 7 day notice.** Rt 150. I-80, exit 158, 0.4 mi n. Int corridors. **Pets:** Other species. Service with restrictions, supervision.
ASK Sↄ ⊠ 🅼 🅿 🕸 🔒 📺 🍴 ⤳ ⊠

MOOSIC

(AAA) ▼▼ Rodeway Inn-Scranton M 🐾
(570) 457-6713. **$45-$110, 15 day notice.** 4130 Birney Ave. I-81, exit 182B southbound, 0.7 mi w, then 2.3 mi s on US 11; exit 180 northbound, just n on US 11. Ext corridors. **Pets:** Other species. $10 daily fee/pet. Service with restrictions, supervision.
SAVE Sↄ ⊠ 🕸 🔒 📺

MORGANTOWN

(AAA) ▼▼▼ Holiday Inn SH
(610) 286-3000. **$109-$119.** 6170 Morgantown Rd. I-76, exit 298, just s on SR 10. Int corridors. **Pets:** Medium. $10 daily fee/room. Designated rooms, service with restrictions, supervision.
SAVE Sↄ ⊠ 🅿 🔒 📺 🍴 ⤳ ⊠

NEW COLUMBIA

(AAA) ▼▼▼ New Columbia Comfort Inn SH
(570) 568-8000. **$74-$84, 3 day notice.** 330 Commerce Park Dr. I-80, exit 210A (US 15/New Columbia), just s. Int corridors. **Pets:** Large, other species.
SAVE Sↄ ⊠ 🅼 🔒 📺 🍴 ⤳

NEW CUMBERLAND

(AAA) ▼▼▼ Days Inn Harrisburg South SH 🐾
(717) 774-4156. **$59-$115, 14 day notice.** 353 Lewisberry Rd. I-83, exit 39A, just ne; I-76 (Pennsylvania Tpke), exit 242, 0.5 mi s. Int corridors. **Pets:** $15 daily fee/pet. Designated rooms, service with restrictions, supervision.
SAVE Sↄ ⊠ 🔒 📺 ⤳

(AAA) ▼▼▼ Holiday Inn Hotel & Conference Center-Harrisburg SH
(717) 774-2721. **$69-$89.** 148 Sheraton Dr. I-83, exit 40A, just se. Int corridors. **Pets:** Accepted.
SAVE Sↄ ⊠ 🕸 🔒 📺 🍴 ⤳ ⊠

PENNSYLVANIA DUTCH COUNTRY AREA

ADAMSTOWN

▼▼▼ The Barnyard Inn B & B and Suites BB 🐾
(717) 484-1111. **$85-$100, 10 day notice.** 2145 Old Lancaster Pike. 1 mi ne via Main St/Old Lancaster Pike; SR 272, just w on Willow St to Main St, 1 mi n bearing left at fork, then just n. Int corridors. **Pets:** Medium, other species. $20 one-time fee/room. Designated rooms.
ASK ⊠ 🔒 📺 🗺

(AAA) ▼▼▼ Black Forest Inn M
(717) 484-4801. **$49-$109.** 500 Lancaster Ave. I-76 (Pennsylvania Tpke), exit 286, 2.8 mi n on SR 272. Ext corridors. **Pets:** Small, dogs only. $15 daily fee/pet. Designated rooms, service with restrictions, supervision.
SAVE Sↄ ⊠ 🔒

DENVER

(AAA) ▼▼▼ Black Horse Lodge and Suites SH
(717) 336-7563. **$69-$139.** 2180 N Reading Rd. I-76 (Pennsylvania Tpke), exit 286, 1 mi w to SR 272, then 0.3 mi n. Ext/int corridors. **Pets:** Other species. Service with restrictions, supervision.
SAVE Sↄ ⊠ 🔒 📺 🍴 ⤳

(AAA) ▼▼▼ Comfort Inn SH
(717) 336-4649. **$69-$159, 3 day notice.** 2017 N Reading Rd. I-76 (Pennsylvania Tpke), exit 286, 1 mi w to SR 272, then just s. Int corridors. **Pets:** Medium, dogs only. $20 daily fee/room. Designated rooms, service with restrictions, supervision.
SAVE Sↄ ⊠ 🅿 🔒 📺

EPHRATA

AAA ▼▼▼▼ Historic Smithton Inn 🅱🅱
(717) 733-6094. **$85-$150, 14 day notice.** 900 W Main St. On US 322, just w of jct SR 272. Int corridors. **Pets:** Dogs only. Designated rooms, supervision.
[SAVE] [✕] [🛏] [🕅] [✆]

LANCASTER

AAA ▼▼▼▼ Best Western Eden Resort Inn & Suites 🅻🅷
(717) 569-6444. **$79-$169.** 222 Eden Rd. Jct US 30 (Lincoln Hwy) and SR 272 (Oregon Pike). Ext/int corridors. **Pets:** Medium, other species. $20 one-time fee/pet. Designated rooms, service with restrictions, crate.
[SAVE] [S💰] [✕] [⅃M] [🚭] [✆] [🛏] [💻] [🍴] [🏊] [✕🐾]

AAA ▼▼▼▼ Hawthorn Inn & Suites 🆂🅷
(717) 290-7100. **$69-$139.** 2045 Lincoln Hwy E. Jct US 30 E and Lincoln Hwy. Int corridors. **Pets:** Large. $25 one-time fee/room. Service with restrictions, crate.
[SAVE] [S💰] [✕] [🚭] [✆] [🛏] [💻]

AAA ▼▼▼▼ Holiday Inn Visitors Center 🆂🅷
(717) 299-2551. **$89-$119.** 521 Greenfield Rd. 3.3 mi e on US 30 (Lincoln Hwy), exit Greenfield Rd, just n. Ext/int corridors. **Pets:** Small. $25 one-time fee/room. Designated rooms, service with restrictions, supervision.
[SAVE] [S💰] [✕] [⅃M] [🚭] [✆] [🛏] [💻] [🍴] [🏊] [✕🐾]

▼▼▼ Lancaster Host Resort & Conference Center 🅻🅷 🐾
(717) 299-5500. **$109-$150.** 2300 Lincoln Hwy E. On US 30 (Linoln Hwy), 5 mi e. Int corridors. **Pets:** Medium. $25 one-time fee/room. Designated rooms, service with restrictions, supervision.
[ASK] [S💰] [✕] [🚭] [🛏] [💻] [🍴] [🏊] [✕🐾]

AAA ▼▼▼ Lancaster Travelodge & Conference Center 🆂🅷
(717) 393-0771. **$49-$99.** 1492 Lititz Pike. US 30 (Lincoln Hwy), exit Lititz Pike (SR 501), just s. Ext corridors. **Pets:** Medium. $30 daily fee/pet. Designated rooms, service with restrictions, supervision.
[SAVE] [S💰] [✕] [✆] [🛏] [💻] [🍴] [🏊]

AAA ▼▼▼▼ Ramada Inn Brunswick Conference Center 🅻🅷
(717) 397-4801. **$69-$99, 3 day notice.** 151 N Queen St. Center. Int corridors. **Pets:** Accepted.
[SAVE] [S💰] [✕] [🚭] [✆] [🛏] [💻] [🍴] [🏊]

LITITZ

▼▼▼▼ General Sutter Inn 🅲🅸 🌸
(717) 626-2115. **$88-$115.** 14 E Main St. Jct SR 501 and 772; downtown. Int corridors. **Pets:** Other species. $10 one-time fee/pet. Service with restrictions, supervision.
[✕] [🍴]

MANHEIM

AAA ▼▼▼ Rodeway Inn-Penns Woods 🅼
(717) 665-2755. **$42-$70.** 2931 Lebanon Rd. I-76 (Pennsylvania Tpke), exit 266, just s on SR 72. Ext corridors. **Pets:** Medium, other species. $5 daily fee/pet. Service with restrictions, supervision.
[SAVE] [S💰] [✕] [🏊]

MOUNTVILLE

AAA ▼▼▼▼ MainStay Suites 🆂🅷
(717) 285-2500. **$85-$195.** 314 Primrose Ln. US 30 (Lincoln Hwy), exit Mountville. Int corridors. **Pets:** Medium, other species. $100 deposit/room, $10 daily fee/room. Service with restrictions, crate.
[SAVE] [S💰] [✕] [⅃M] [🚭] [✆] [🛏] [💻] [🏊]

NEW HOLLAND

AAA ▼▼ The Hollander Motel 🅼
(717) 354-4377. **$49-$69, 3 day notice.** 320 E Main St. Just e on SR 23. Ext corridors. **Pets:** Small. $5 daily fee/pet. Service with restrictions, supervision.
[SAVE] [S💰] [✕]

STRASBURG

AAA ▼▼▼ Carriage House Motor Inn 🅼
(717) 687-7651. **$49-$99.** 144 E Main St. 0.3 mi e on SR 896 and 741. Ext corridors. **Pets:** Accepted.
[SAVE] [S💰] [✕] [🛏]

AAA ▼▼▼▼ Netherlands Inn & Spa 🅲🅸
(717) 687-7691. **$149-$179, 3 day notice.** One Historic Dr. 0.5 mi n on SR 896; 2.5 mi s of US 30 (Lincoln Hwy). Ext/int corridors. **Pets:** Accepted.
[SAVE] [✕] [🛏] [💻] [🍴] [🏊] [✕🐾]

PHILADELPHIA METROPOLITAN AREA

BENSALEM

AAA ▼▼▼▼ Holiday Inn-Philadelphia Northeast 🆂🅷
(215) 638-1500. **$99-$139.** 3499 Street Rd. I-276 (Pennsylvania Tpke), exit 351, just s on US 1, then 0.3 mi e on SR 132. Ext/int corridors. **Pets:** Large. $25 deposit/room. Service with restrictions, supervision.
[SAVE] [S💰] [✕] [🚭] [🛏] [💻] [🍴] [🏊]

AAA ▼▼▼▼ Sleep Inn & Suites-Bensalem 🆂🅷
(215) 244-2300. **$69-$149.** 3427 Street Rd. I-276 (Pennsylvania Tpke), exit 351, just s on US 1, then 0.3 mi e on SR 132. Int corridors. **Pets:** Accepted.
[SAVE] [S💰] [✕] [⅃M] [🚭] [✆] [🛏] [💻]

BERWYN

♦♦♦ **Residence Inn by Marriott** [SH]
(610) 640-9494. **$164-$189.** 600 W Swedesford Rd. US 202, exit Valley Forge Rd, then 1 mi s. Ext corridors. **Pets:** $150 one-time fee/room. Service with restrictions, supervision.
[A$K] [S/D] ☒ 🦻 ♿ ▣ 📺 🏊 🏋

CHADDS FORD

[AAA] ♦♦♦ **Brandywine River Hotel** [SH]
(610) 388-1200. **$125-$169.** Rt 1 & 100. Jct US 1 and SR 100, 2 mi w of US 202. Int corridors. **Pets:** Small, dogs only. $150 deposit/room, $20 daily fee/pet. Designated rooms, service with restrictions, crate.
[SAVE] ☒ 🦻 ♿ ▣ 📺

CONSHOHOCKEN

♦♦♦ **Residence Inn by Marriott Philadelphia/Conshohocken** [SH]
(610) 828-8800. **$109-$169.** 191 Washington St. I-76 (Schuylkill Expwy), exit 332; I-476, exit 16 (SR 23), 0.3 mi over Fayette Bridge to Elm St, then just se along the river. Int corridors. **Pets:** Other species. $20 daily fee/room.
[S/D] ☒ ♿M 🦻 ♿ ▣ 📺 🏊 🏋

EAST NORRITON

♦♦♦ **Summerfield Suites Hotel by Wyndham-Plymouth Meeting East Norriton** [SH]
(610) 313-9990. **$99-$198.** 501 E Germantown Pike. I-476, exit 20; I-276 (Pennsylvania Tpke), exit 333, 2.5 mi w. Int corridors. **Pets:** Accepted.
[A$K] [S/D] ☒ 🦻 ♿ ▣ 📺 🏊

ERWINNA

♦♦♦ **Golden Pheasant Inn** [CI] 🐾
(610) 294-9595. **$95-$175, 21 day notice.** 763 River Rd. SR 32, 0.5 mi n of jct Dark Hollow Rd. Ext/int corridors. **Pets:** Medium, other species. $20 daily fee/pet. Designated rooms, service with restrictions, crate.
[A$K] [S/D] ☒ ▣ 📺 🍴 🏋

ESSINGTON

[AAA] ♦♦♦ **Comfort Inn Airport** [SH]
(610) 521-9800. **$68-$150.** 53 Industrial Hwy. I-95, exit 9A, 0.3 mi sw on SR 291. Int corridors. **Pets:** Small, other species. $10 daily fee/pet. Service with restrictions, crate.
[SAVE] [S/D] ☒ ♿M 🦻 ▣ 📺

[AAA] ♦♦ **Red Roof Inn-Airport** [M]
(610) 521-5090. **$73-$95.** 49 Industrial Hwy. I-95, exit 9A, 0.3 mi sw on SR 291. Ext corridors. **Pets:** Medium. Service with restrictions, supervision.
[SAVE] ☒ ♿M 🦻 ♿

EXTON

[AAA] ♦♦♦ **Holiday Inn Express** [SH]
(610) 524-9000. **$87-$116.** 120 N Pottstown Pike. I-76 (Pennsylvania Tpke), exit 312, 3 mi s at jct Business Rt US 30 and SR 100. Int corridors. **Pets:** Accepted.
[SAVE] [S/D] ☒ ♿M 🦻 ▣ 📺 🏊

HORSHAM

♦♦♦ **Homestead Studio Suites Hotel-Horsham/ Willow Grove** [SH] 🐾
(215) 956-9966. **$99-$109.** 537 Dresher Rd. I-276 (Pennsylvania Tpke), exit 343, 1.5 mi n on SR 611 (Easton Rd), just w on Horsham Rd, then 0.5 mi s. Int corridors. **Pets:** Medium, other species. $25 daily fee/room. Service with restrictions, crate.
[A$K] [S/D] ☒ ♿M 🦻 ♿ ▣ 📺

♦♦♦ **Horsham/Willow Grove NAS JRB Days Inn Business Place** [SH]
(215) 674-2500. **$89-$119.** 245 Easton Rd. I-276 (Pennsylvania Tpke), exit 343, 1 mi n. Int corridors. **Pets:** Accepted.
[A$K] [S/D] ☒ 🦻 ♿ ▣ 📺

♦♦♦ **Residence Inn by Marriott-Willow Grove** [SH]
(215) 443-7330. **$164-$185.** 3 Walnut Grove Dr. I-276 (Pennsylvania Tpke), exit 343, 1 mi n on SR 611 (Easton Rd), then 1.3 mi w on Dresher Rd. Ext corridors. **Pets:** Accepted.
[A$K] ☒ ♿M 🦻 ♿ ▣ 📺 🏊 🏋

KING OF PRUSSIA

♦♦♦ **Homestead Studio Suites Hotel-King of Prussia** [SH] 🐾
(610) 962-9000. **$80-$90.** 400 American Ave. I-76 (Pennsylvania Tpke), exit 326 (Valley Forge); Schuylkill Expwy, exit 328A (Mall Blvd), 1.3 mi n on N Gulph Rd, then 1 mi ne on 1st Ave. Int corridors. **Pets:** Medium, other species. $25 daily fee/room. Service with restrictions, crate.
[A$K] [S/D] ☒ ♿M 🦻 ♿ ▣ 📺

[AAA] ♦♦♦ **MainStay Suites** [SH] 🐾
(484) 690-3000. **$129-$169.** 440 American Ave. I-76 (Pennsylvania Tpke), exit 326 (Valley Forge); Schuylkill Expwy, exit 328A (Mall Blvd), 1.3 mi n on N Gulph Rd, 1 mi ne on 1st Ave, then just e. Int corridors. **Pets:** Medium. $15 daily fee/pet. Service with restrictions, crate.
[SAVE] [S/D] ☒ ♿M ♿ ▣ 📺 🏊

KULPSVILLE

♦♦♦ **Best Western-The Inn at Towamencin** [SH]
(215) 368-3800. **$104-$109.** 1750 Sumneytown Pike. I-476, exit 31, just e. Int corridors. **Pets:** Accepted.
[A$K] [S/D] ☒ 🦻 ▣ 📺 🍴 🏊 🏋

LANGHORNE

[AAA] ♦♦ **Red Roof Inn-Oxford Valley** [M]
(215) 750-6200. **$60-$103.** 3100 Cabot Blvd W. I-95, exit 46A (Oxford Valley Rd), just e off US 1 N; 0.5 mi n of Sesame Place. Ext corridors. **Pets:** Large, other species. Service with restrictions, supervision.
[SAVE] ☒ 🦻 ♿

LIONVILLE

♦♦♦ **Hampton Inn** [SH]
(610) 363-5555. **$89-$99.** 4 N Pottstown Pike. I-76 (Pennsylvania Tpke), exit 312, 0.5 mi s; jct SR 113 and 100. Int corridors. **Pets:** Accepted.
[A$K] ☒ ♿M 🦻 ▣ 📺 🏊

▼▼▼▼ Residence Inn by Marriott-Exton 🆂🅷
(610) 594-9705. **$94-$129, 14 day notice.** 10 N Pottstown Pike. I-76 (Pennsylvania Tpke), exit 312, 1 mi s on SR 100. Int corridors. **Pets:** Accepted.
[ASK] 🛇 ✕ 🖑 🛢 💻 ➤ ✕

MALVERN

▼▼▼▼ Homestead Studio Suites
Hotel-Malvern 🆂🅷 ☙
(610) 695-9200. **$109-$119.** 8 E Swedesford Rd. Just w of US 202 and SR 29 N. Int corridors. **Pets:** Medium, other species. $25 daily fee/room. Service with restrictions, crate.
[ASK] 🛇 ✕ 🗂 🖑 🛢 💻

▼▼▼▼ Homewood Suites by Hilton 🆂🅷
(610) 296-3500. **$169-$209.** 12 E Swedesford Rd. US 202, exit SR 29 N, just w. Int corridors. **Pets:** Other species. $25 one-time fee/room. Service with restrictions, crate.
[ASK] 🛇 ✕ 🖑ᴹ 🗂 🖑 🛢 💻 ➤

🅰🅰🅰 ▼▼▼▼ Staybridge Suites 🆂🅷
(610) 296-4343. **$129-$179.** 20 Morehall Rd. Jct US 30 and SR 29, just nw. Ext/int corridors. **Pets:** Medium. $75 one-time fee/room. Service with restrictions, supervision.
[SAVE] 🛇 ✕ 🗂 🛢 💻 ➤ ✕

NEW HOPE

▼▼▼▼ 1870 Wedgwood Inn of New Hope 🅱🅱
(215) 862-2570. **$105-$275, 10 day notice.** 111 W Bridge St (SR 179). 0.5 mi w of SR 32; downtown. Ext/int corridors. **Pets:** Small, dogs only. $50 deposit/pet, $20 daily fee/pet. Service with restrictions, supervision.
✕ 🛢 💻

▼▼▼▼ Aaron Burr House Inn & Conference
Center 🅱🅱
(215) 862-2520. **$99-$205, 10 day notice.** 80 W Bridge St (SR 179). 0.5 mi w of SR 32; at W Bridge and Chestnut sts. Int corridors. **Pets:** Small, dogs only. $20 daily fee/pet. Service with restrictions, supervision.
✕ 🛢 🕖

🅰🅰🅰 ▼▼▼▼ Best Western New Hope Inn 🆂🅷
(215) 862-5221. **$89-$169.** 6426 Lower York Rd. 2 mi s on US 202, 1 mi w of jct SR 179. Ext corridors. **Pets:** Small. $20 daily fee/room. Designated rooms, service with restrictions, supervision.
[SAVE] 🛇 ✕ 🗂 🛢 💻 🍽 ➤ ✕

🅰🅰🅰 ▼▼▼ The New Hope Motel in the
Woods 🅼 ☙
(215) 862-2800. **$69-$149, 14 day notice.** 400 W Bridge St. 1 mi s on SR 179, e of jct US 202. Ext corridors. **Pets:** Medium, dogs only. $25 one-time fee/pet. Service with restrictions, supervision.
[SAVE] 🛇 ✕ 🛢 ➤

PHILADELPHIA

🅰🅰🅰 ▼▼▼▼ Best Western Center City Hotel 🆂🅷
(215) 568-8300. **$125-$145.** 501 N 22nd St. Just n of Benjamin Franklin Pkwy. Int corridors. **Pets:** Small. $10 one-time fee/pet. Service with restrictions, crate.
[SAVE] 🛇 ✕ 🗂 🛢 💻 🍽 ➤

🅰🅰🅰 ▼▼▼▼ Best Western Independence Park
Inn 🆂🅷 ☙
(215) 922-4443. **$125-$214.** 235 Chestnut St. Between 2nd and 3rd sts. Int corridors. **Pets:** Small, other species. $50 one-time fee/pet. Service with restrictions, crate.
[SAVE] 🛇 ✕ 🗂 🛢 💻

▼▼▼ The Doubletree Hotel
Philadelphia 🅻🅷 ☙
(215) 893-1600. **$139-$209.** Broad & Locust sts. Int corridors. **Pets:** Large. $50 deposit/room. Designated rooms, service with restrictions, supervision.
[ASK] 🛇 ✕ 🗂 🖑 🛢 💻 🍽 ➤ ✕

🅰🅰🅰 ▼▼▼▼ Four Seasons Hotel 🅻🅷
(215) 963-1500. **$330-$2600.** 1 Logan Square. Corner of 18th St and Benjamin Franklin Pkwy. Int corridors. **Pets:** Accepted.
[SAVE] ✕ 🖑ᴹ 🗂 🖑 🛢 💻 🍽 ➤ ✕

🅰🅰🅰 ▼▼▼▼ Hampton Inn-Center City 🅻🅷
(215) 665-9100. **$99-$169.** 1301 Race St. At 13th and Race sts. Int corridors. **Pets:** Small, dogs only. $100 deposit/room, $20 daily fee/room. Service with restrictions, supervision.
[SAVE] 🛇 ✕ 🖑 🛢 💻 ➤

🅰🅰🅰 ▼▼▼▼ Loews Philadelphia Hotel 🅻🅷 ☙
(215) 627-1200. **$170-$245.** 1200 Market St. Corner of 12th and Market sts. Int corridors. **Pets:** Other species. Designated rooms, service with restrictions.
[SAVE] 🛇 ✕ 🖑ᴹ 🗂 🖑 🛢 💻 🍽 ➤ ✕

🅰🅰🅰 ▼▼▼ Marriott Residence Inn Center City
Philadelphia 🅻🅷
(215) 557-0005. **$159-$239.** 1 E Penn Square. Market and Juniper sts. Int corridors. **Pets:** Other species. $200 one-time fee/room. Service with restrictions.
[SAVE] ✕ 🗂 🖑 🛢 💻 ➤

▼▼▼▼ Philadelphia Airport Residence Inn 🆂🅷
(215) 492-1611. **$89-$169.** 4630 Island Ave. I-95, exit 13 northbound; exit 15 southbound, 0.3 mi e on SR 291. Ext/int corridors. **Pets:** Accepted.
[ASK] 🛇 ✕ 🖑ᴹ 🗂 🖑 🛢 💻 ➤ ✕

🅰🅰🅰 ▼▼▼▼ Philadelphia Downtown Marriott
Hotel 🅻🅷
(215) 625-2900. **$229-$309.** 1201 Market St. Between 12th and 13th sts. Int corridors. **Pets:** Accepted.
[SAVE] ✕ 🗂 🖑 🛢 💻 🍽 ➤ ✕

🅰🅰🅰 ▼▼▼▼ The Radisson Plaza-Warwick Hotel
Philadelphia 🅻🅷
(215) 735-6000. **$139-$180.** 1701 Locust St. Jct 17th and Locust sts. Int corridors. **Pets:** Accepted.
[SAVE] 🛇 ✕ 🗂 🛢 💻 🍽

🅰🅰🅰 ▼▼▼▼ The Rittenhouse Hotel and
Condominium
Residences 🅻🅷 ☙
(215) 546-9000. **$380-$420.** 210 W Rittenhouse Square. On Rittenhouse Square. Int corridors. **Pets:** Service with restrictions, supervision.
[SAVE] ✕ 🖑ᴹ 🗂 🖑 🍽 ➤ ✕

▼▼▼▼▼ **The Ritz-Carlton Philadelphia** 🏠
(215) 523-8000. **Call for rates.** Ten Avenue of the Arts. Chestnut and Broad sts. Int corridors. **Pets:** Accepted.

⊠ 🐾 🐾 🖥 🍴 ⊠

▼▼▼▼ **Sofitel Philadelphia** 🏠
(215) 569-8300. **$179-$199.** 120 S 17th St. Jct Sansom and 17th sts. Int corridors. **Pets:** Small, dogs only. $50 one-time fee/room. Service with restrictions, supervision.

🅰🆂🅺 🐾 ⊠ 🐾 🐾 🐾 🍴

🔼🔼🔼 ▼▼▼▼ **The Westin Philadelphia** 🏠
(215) 563-1600. **$389-$950.** 99 S 17th St at Liberty Pl. On 17th St; between Market and Chestnut sts. Int corridors. **Pets:** Accepted.

🆂🅰🆅🅴 🐾 ⊠ 🐾 🐾 🖥 🍴 ⊠

🔼🔼🔼 ▼▼▼▼ **Wyndham Philadelphia at Franklin Plaza** 🏠
(215) 448-2000. **$99-$179.** 2 Franklin Plaza. Jct 17th and Race sts. Int corridors. **Pets:** Accepted.

🆂🅰🆅🅴 🐾 ⊠ 🐾 🐾 🖥 🖥 🍴 🏊 ⊠

POTTSTOWN

▼▼▼▼ **Comfort Inn** 🆂🅷
(610) 326-5000. **$69-$99.** 99 Robinson St. SR 100, 1 mi n of jct US 422. Int corridors. **Pets:** Large, other species. $50 deposit/pet. Service with restrictions, supervision.

🅰🆂🅺 🐾 ⊠ 🐾 🐾 🐾 🖥 🏊

🔼🔼🔼 ▼▼▼ **Days Inn** Ⓜ
(610) 970-1101. **$42-$79.** 29 High St. Just off SR 663, 0.5 mi e of jct SR 100. Ext corridors. **Pets:** Medium, other species. $10 daily fee/room. Service with restrictions, supervision.

🆂🅰🆅🅴 🐾 ⊠ 🖥

QUAKERTOWN

🔼🔼🔼 ▼▼▼ **Rodeway Inn Quakertown** Ⓜ
(215) 536-7600. **$59-$89.** 1920 John Fries Hwy (SR 663). I-476 (Pennsylvania Tpke), exit 44, just e. Ext corridors. **Pets:** Medium, other species. $8 one-time fee/pet. Service with restrictions.

🆂🅰🆅🅴 ⊠ 🖥 🖥

TREVOSE

🔼🔼🔼 ▼▼▼ **Red Roof Inn** Ⓜ
(215) 244-9422. **$57-$80.** 3100 Lincoln Hwy. I-276 (Pennsylvania Tpke), exit 351, 0.5 mi s on US 1 at US 132. Ext corridors. **Pets:** Medium. Service with restrictions, crate.

🆂🅰🆅🅴 ⊠ 🐾 🐾

WEST CHESTER

🔼🔼🔼 ▼▼▼ **Microtel Inn & Suites** 🆂🅷
(610) 738-9111. **$69-$84.** 500 Willowbrook Ln. Just se of US 202, exit Matlack St. Int corridors. **Pets:** $10 daily fee/pet. Service with restrictions, supervision.

🆂🅰🆅🅴 🐾 ⊠ 🐾 🐾 🐾 🖥 🖥

❖ END METROPOLITAN AREA ❖

PHILIPSBURG

🔼🔼🔼 ▼ **Main Liner Motel** Ⓜ
(814) 342-2004. **$36-$55.** 1896 Philipsburg Bigler Hwy. 1 mi w of jct SR 53 N. Ext corridors. **Pets:** Small. $10 one-time fee/pet. Designated rooms, no service, supervision.

🆂🅰🆅🅴 🐾 ⊠ 🖥

PIGEON

▼ **The Forest Lodge & Campground** Ⓜ 🐾
(814) 927-8790. **$45-$60.** SR 66, 6 mi n of Marienville. Ext corridors. **Pets:** Other species. $8 daily fee/pet. Designated rooms, service with restrictions, supervision.

🅰🆂🅺 🐾 ⊠ 🖥 🖥

PINE GROVE

🔼🔼🔼 ▼▼▼ **Comfort Inn** 🆂🅷
(570) 345-8031. **$59-$109.** SR 443. I-81, exit 100. Int corridors. **Pets:** Medium, other species. $10 daily fee/pet. Designated rooms, service with restrictions, supervision.

🆂🅰🆅🅴 🐾 ⊠ 🐾 🐾 🖥 🏊

🔼🔼🔼 ▼▼▼ **Econo Lodge** 🆂🅷
(570) 345-4099. **$45-$85.** 419 Suedberg Rd. I-81, exit 100, just e on SR 443. Ext/int corridors. **Pets:** Other species. $20 daily fee/pet. Designated rooms.

🆂🅰🆅🅴 ⊠ 🐾 🖥 🖥

PITTSBURGH METROPOLITAN AREA

BEAVER FALLS

▼▼▼▼ **Holiday Inn** 🆂🅷 🐾
(724) 846-3700. **$99-$129.** 7195 Eastwood Rd. I-76 (Pennsylvania Tpke), exit 13, just n. Int corridors. **Pets:** $50 one-time fee/room. Service with restrictions, supervision.

🅰🆂🅺 🐾 ⊠ 🐾 🖥 🖥 🍴 🏊 ⊠

BETHEL PARK

▼▼▼▼ **Windsor Court of South Hills** 🆂🅷
(412) 833-5300. **$85.** 164 Ft Couch Rd. 1 mi n on US 19. Int corridors. **Pets:** Accepted.

🅰🆂🅺 🐾 ⊠ 🐾 🐾 🖥 🖥 🍴 🏊

BRADDOCK HILLS

🔼🔼🔼 ▼▼▼▼ **Holiday Inn Parkway East** 🆂🅷
(412) 247-2700. **$109-$119.** 915 Brinton Rd. I-376, exit 8B, 0.3 mi n. Int corridors. **Pets:** Accepted.

🆂🅰🆅🅴 🐾 ⊠ 🐾 🖥 🖥 🍴 🏊

BRIDGEVILLE

Knights Inn-Pittsburgh/Bridgeville M
(412) 221-8110. **$50-$55.** 111 Hickory Grade Rd. I-79, exit 54 (SR 50). Ext corridors. **Pets:** Small. $10 daily fee/pet. Designated rooms, service with restrictions, supervision.

BUTLER

Comfort Inn SH
(724) 287-7177. **$69-$109.** 1 Comfort Ln. 4 mi s on SR 8. Int corridors. **Pets:** Medium, other species. $10 daily fee/pet. Service with restrictions, supervision.

Super 8 Motel M
(724) 287-8888. **$50-$55.** 138 Pittsburgh/SR 8. 2 mi s on SR 8. Int corridors. **Pets:** Medium. $5 deposit/pet. Service with restrictions, supervision.

CANONSBURG

Super 8 Motel M
(724) 873-8808. **$52-$64.** 8 Curry Ave. I-79, exit 45, follow signs. Int corridors. **Pets:** Small, other species. Service with restrictions, supervision.

CORAOPOLIS

Hampton Inn Hotel Airport SH
(412) 264-0020. **$99-$119.** 8514 University Blvd. Business Rt SR 60, 0.5 mi n. Int corridors. **Pets:** Medium. Service with restrictions, supervision.

Holiday Inn-Pittsburgh Airport LH ✿
(412) 262-3600. **$79-$159.** 8256 University Blvd. Busines Rt SR 60, 1 mi n. Int corridors. **Pets:** Small. $25 one-time fee/room. Designated rooms, service with restrictions, crate.

La Quinta Inn-Airport SH ✿
(412) 269-0400. **$76-$87.** 1433 Beers School Rd. 1 mi n of Business Rt SR 60. Int corridors. **Pets:** Medium. Service with restrictions, supervision.

Red Roof Inn Pittsburgh Airport M
(412) 264-5678. **$46-$61.** 1454 Beers School Rd. 0.5 mi n of Business Rt SR 60. Ext corridors. **Pets:** Accepted.

CRANBERRY TOWNSHIP

AmeriSuites (Pittsburgh/Cranberry) SH
(724) 779-7900. **$79-$124.** 136 Emeryville Dr. I-76 (Pennsylvania Tpke), exit 28; I-79, exit 76 northbound; exit 78 southbound, 0.3 mi s on US 19. Int corridors. **Pets:** Small. Service with restrictions, supervision.

Hampton Inn Cranberry SH
(724) 776-1000. **$94-$109.** 210 Executive Dr. I-76 (Pennsylvania Tpke) exit 28, 0.5 mi n on US 19, then 0.3 mi w on Freedom Rd; I-79, exit 78 southbound, 0.5 mi w on Freedom Rd. Int corridors. **Pets:** $10 daily fee/pet. Service with restrictions, supervision.

Holiday Inn Express SH
(724) 772-1000. **$84.** 20003 Rt 19. I-76 (Pennsylvania Tpke), exit 28, jct US 19 and I-76 (Pennsylvania Tpke); I-79, exit 76 northbound; exit southbound, just s. Int corridors. **Pets:** Accepted.

Red Roof Inn-Cranberry Township-Pittsburgh North M
(724) 776-5670. **$55-$71.** 20009 Rt 19. I-76 (Pennsylvania Tpke) exit 28; I-79, exit 76 northbound; exit 78 southbound. Ext corridors. **Pets:** Other species. Service with restrictions, crate.

DELMONT

Super 8 Motel M
(724) 468-4888. **$51-$55.** 180 Sheffield Dr. SR 66, just s of US 22. Int corridors. **Pets:** Other species. $5 daily fee/pet. Service with restrictions, crate.

GIBSONIA

Comfort Inn Gibsonia M
(724) 444-8700. **$59-$69.** 5137 Rt 8. I-76 (Pennsylvania Tpke), exit 39, just n. Ext corridors. **Pets:** Large, other species. $6 daily fee/pet. Service with restrictions, supervision.

GREEN TREE

Hampton Inn Hotel Green Tree SH
(412) 922-0100. **$109-$119.** 555 Trumbull Dr. I-279, exit 4A to jct US 22 and 30, 1 mi nw via Mansfield Ave. Int corridors. **Pets:** Medium, other species. Service with restrictions, supervision.

Hawthorn Suites SH
(412) 279-6300. **$149-$179.** 700 Mansfield Ave. I-279, exit 4A to jct US 22 and 30, 1.5 mi nw. Ext corridors. **Pets:** Accepted.

Holiday Inn-Greentree Pittsburgh Central SH
(412) 922-8100. **$69-$109.** 401 Holiday Dr. I-279, exit 4A to jct US 22 and 30, 1 mi nw via Mansfield Ave. Int corridors. **Pets:** Accepted.

HARMARVILLE

Days Inn Harmarville M ❀
(412) 828-5400. **$45-$54, 14 day notice.** 6 Landings Dr. I-76 (Pennsylvania Tpke), exit 48, just s on Freeport Rd. Ext corridors. **Pets:** Other species. Service with restrictions, supervision.
(ASK) (S🛏) (✕) (🖨)

MARS

Comfort Inn SH
(724) 772-2700. **$59-$105.** 924 Sheraton Dr. I-76 (Pennsylvania Tpke), exit 28; I-79, exit 76 northbound; exit 78 southbound, 0.5 mi s on US 19. Int corridors. **Pets:** Medium. $10 one-time fee/room. Designated rooms, service with restrictions, supervision.
(ASK) (S🛏) (✕) (⌖) (🖨) (💻)

MONROEVILLE

Comfort Inn Pittsburgh East SH
(412) 244-1600. **$69-$109.** 699 Rodi Rd. Jct I-376 and US 22, exit 11, 8 mi e. Int corridors. **Pets:** Medium, other species. Service with restrictions, supervision.
(ASK) (S🛏) (✕) (🖨) (💻) (🍴) (🏊) (🐾)

Days Inn-Monroeville M
(412) 856-1610. **$40-$71.** 2727 Mosside Blvd. I-76 (Pennsylvania Tpke), exit 57; I-376, exit 14A, 1 mi s on SR 48. Ext corridors. **Pets:** Dogs only. $25 daily fee/pet. Service with restrictions, supervision.
(ASK) (S🛏) (✕) (🖨)

Hampton Inn Monroeville/Pittsburgh SH
(412) 380-4000. **$104-$134.** 3000 Mosside Blvd. I-76 (Pennsylvania Tpke), exit 57; I-376, exit 14A, 0.3 mi s on SR 48. Int corridors. **Pets:** Accepted.
(ASK) (✕) (⌖) (🅿) (🖨) (💻) (🏊)

Holiday Inn Pittsburgh-Monroeville SH
(412) 372-1022. **$79-$139.** 2750 Mosside Blvd. I-76 (Pennsylvania Tpke), exit 57, 0.4 mi s on SR 48; I-376, exit 14A, 0.4 mi s on SR 48. Int corridors. **Pets:** Accepted.
(SAVE) (S🛏) (✕) (⌖) (🅿) (🖨) (💻) (🍴) (🏊)

Red Roof Inn-Monroeville M
(412) 856-4738. **$54-$74.** 2729 Mosside Blvd. I-76 (Pennsylvania Tpke), exit 57; I-376, exit 14A, 0.8 mi s on SR 48. Ext corridors. **Pets:** Other species. Service with restrictions, supervision.
(SAVE) (✕)

Super 8 Motel Pittsburgh/Monroeville M
(724) 733-8008. **$49-$57.** 1807 Rt 286. I-76 (Pennsylvania Tpke), exit 57; I-376, exit 14A, 2 mi e on US 22 E, then 2 mi e. Int corridors. **Pets:** Other species. $5 daily fee/room. Service with restrictions, crate.
(ASK) (S🛏) (✕) (🖨)

MOON RUN

AmeriSuites (Pittsburgh/Airport) SH
(412) 494-0202. **$109-$119.** 6011 Campbells Run Rd. Jct US 22 and 30, exit Moon Run Rd, just w. Int corridors. **Pets:** Very small, dogs only. Service with restrictions, supervision.
(SAVE) (S🛏) (✕) (🖨M) (⌖) (🅿) (🖨) (💻) (🏊)

Comfort Inn-Pittsburgh Airport SH
(412) 787-2600. **$58-$95.** US 22 and 30, jct SR 60; 4 mi w of jct I-279 and 79. Ext/int corridors. **Pets:** Other species. $7 daily fee/pet. Designated rooms.
(SAVE) (S🛏) (✕) (⌖) (🖨) (🍴)

Comfort Suites SH
(412) 494-5750. **Call for rates.** 750 Aten Rd. SR 60, exit 2 (Montour Run Rd). Int corridors. **Pets:** Accepted.
(✕) (🖨) (💻) (🏊)

MainStay Suites Pittsburgh Airport SH
(412) 490-7343. **$62-$71.** 1000 Park Lane Dr. SR 60, exit 2 (Montour Run Rd), just w on Cliff Mine Rd, then just s. Int corridors. **Pets:** Medium, other species. $100 deposit/pet, $10 daily fee/pet. Supervision.
(ASK) (S🛏) (✕) (🅿) (🖨) (💻)

Red Roof Inn South Airport M
(412) 787-7870. **$45-$65.** 6404 Steubenville Pike. I-79, exit 60A, 3.2 mi w on SR 60. Ext/int corridors. **Pets:** Accepted.
(SAVE) (✕) (⌖) (🅿) (💻)

Residence Inn-Pittsburgh Airport SH
(412) 787-3300. **$129-$169.** 1500 Park Lane Dr. SR 60, exit 2 (Montour Run Rd), just w on Cliff Mine Dr to Summit Park Dr, just s to Park Lane Dr, then just e. Int corridors. **Pets:** Accepted.
(ASK) (✕) (🖨M) (⌖) (🅿) (🖨) (💻) (🏊) (🐾)

Sleep Inn Pittsburgh Airport SH
(412) 859-4000. **$59-$129.** 2500 Marketplace Blvd. SR 60, exit 2 (Montour Run Rd), 0.5 mi e, then 0.5 mi n. Int corridors. **Pets:** Small, other species. $25 daily fee/room. Supervision.
(SAVE) (S🛏) (✕) (⌖) (🅿) (💻) (🏊)

Wyndham Pittsburgh Airport LH
(412) 788-8800. **$99-$149.** 777 Aten Rd. SR 60, exit 2 (Montour Run Rd). Int corridors. **Pets:** Accepted.
(SAVE) (S🛏) (✕) (🖨) (💻) (🍴) (🏊) (🐾)

NEW KENSINGTON

Clarion Hotel SH
(724) 335-9171. **$74-$94, 3 day notice.** 300 Tarentum Bridge Rd. SR 366, 1.5 mi s of SR 28, exit 14; at south end of Tarentum Bridge. Int corridors. **Pets:** Accepted.
(ASK) (S🛏) (✕) (⌖) (🖨) (💻) (🍴) (🏊)

PITTSBURGH

Days Inn Pittsburgh M ❀
(412) 531-8900. **$49-$90.** 1150 Banksville Rd. 3.5 mi s on US 19. Ext/int corridors. **Pets:** Medium, dogs only. $25 deposit/pet. Service with restrictions.
(SAVE) (S🛏) (✕) (⌖) (🖨) (🍴) (🏊)

Hilton Pittsburgh LH
(412) 391-4600. **$84-$249.** 600 Commonwealth Pl. On Commonwealth Pl; in Gateway Center. Int corridors. **Pets:** Accepted.
(SAVE) (S🛏) (✕) (🖨M) (⌖) (🅿) (🖨) (💻) (🍴)

AAA ♦♦♦ Holiday Inn Pittsburgh North Hills SH
(412) 366-5200. **$119-$159.** 4859 McKnight Rd. 7 mi n. Int corridors. **Pets:** Accepted.
SAVE S♦ ✕ 🐾 🐾 🖥 💻 ¶¶ 🏊

AAA ♦♦♦♦ Holiday Inn Select University Center SH
(412) 682-6200. **$135-$145.** 100 Lytton Ave. Just nw of 5th Ave. Int corridors. **Pets:** Accepted.
SAVE ✕ 🐾 🖥 💻 ¶¶ 🏊

♦♦♦ Pittsburgh Comfort Inn SH
(412) 922-7555. **$59-$79.** 4770 Steubenville Pike. I-79, exit 60A, just s on Steubenville Pike (SR 60). Int corridors. **Pets:** Accepted.
ASK S♦ ✕ 🐾 🐾 🖥 💻

AAA ♦♦♦♦ Residence Inn by Marriott SH 🐾
(412) 621-2200. **$109-$149.** 3896 Bigelow Blvd. On SR 380. Int corridors. **Pets:** Other species. $10 daily fee/room. Designated rooms, service with restrictions, supervision.
SAVE ✕ 🐾 🖥 💻 🏊 ✕

♦♦♦ The Westin Convention Center Pittsburgh LH
(412) 281-3700. **$149-$229.** 1000 Penn Ave. At Liberty Center; adjacent to convention center. Int corridors. **Pets:** Accepted.
✕ 🐾 🖥 💻 ¶¶ 🏊 ✕

♦♦♦♦ Wyndham Garden Hotel Pittsburgh University Place LH
(412) 683-2040. **$119-$129.** 3454 Forbes Ave. Just w of Bundary St. Int corridors. **Pets:** $200 deposit/room. Designated rooms, service with restrictions, supervision.
ASK S♦ ✕ 🐾 🖥 💻 ¶¶

WASHINGTON

AAA ♦♦♦ Ramada Inn SH
(724) 225-9750. **$60-$95.** 1170 W Chestnut St. I-70, exit 15, 0.5 mi e on US 40. Ext/int corridors. **Pets:** Small. $30 one-time fee/room. Designated rooms, service with restrictions, crate.
SAVE S♦ ✕ 🖥 💻 ¶¶ 🏊

AAA ♦♦♦ Red Roof Inn M
(724) 228-5750. **$45-$65.** 1399 W Chestnut St. I-70, exit 15, just e on US 40. Ext/int corridors. **Pets:** Accepted.
SAVE ✕ 🐾 🖥

🐾 **END METROPOLITAN AREA** 🐾

PITTSTON

AAA ♦♦♦ Knights Inn-Scranton/Pittston M
(570) 654-6020. **$40-$75.** 310 SR 315. I-81, exit 175 northbound, just s on SR 315; exit 175A southbound; I-476 (Northeast Extension Pennslyvania Tpke), exit 115. Ext corridors. **Pets:** Very small. Service with restrictions, supervision.
SAVE S♦ ✕ 🖥

AAA ♦♦♦ Super 8 Motel SH
(570) 654-3301. **$55-$65.** 307 Rt 315 Hwy. I-81, exit 48 northbound, just s on SR 315; exit 48A southbound and 37 (Northeast Pennsylvania Tpke). Int corridors. **Pets:** Very small, other species. $10 one-time fee/room. Service with restrictions, supervision.
SAVE S♦ ✕ 🐾 🖥

POCONO MOUNTAINS AREA

BLAKESLEE

AAA ♦♦♦ Best Western Inn-Blakeslee/Pocono SH
(570) 646-6000. **$80-$190.** New Ventures Business Park. I-80, exit 284, just n. Int corridors. **Pets:** Small. $50 deposit/pet. Service with restrictions, supervision.
SAVE S♦ ✕ 🐾 🐾 🐾 💻 🏊

AAA ♦♦♦♦ Blue Berry Mountain Inn BB
(570) 646-7144. **$90-$135, 30 day notice.** Thomas Rd. I-80, exit 284, 3 mi n on SR 115, just n on Thomas Rd, then to the end of Edmund Dr. Int corridors. **Pets:** Medium, other species. $10 one-time fee/pet. Designated rooms, service with restrictions, supervision.
SAVE S♦ ✕ 🖥 💻 🏊 ✕ ✕

EAST STROUDSBURG

AAA ♦♦♦♦ Budget Motel SH
(570) 424-5451. **$64-$99, 3 day notice.** I-80, exit 308. I-80, exit 308, just se on Greentree Rd. Ext/int corridors. **Pets:** $25 deposit/pet. Designated rooms, service with restrictions, supervision.
SAVE S♦ ✕ 🖥 ¶¶

♦♦♦ Super 8 Motel M
(570) 424-7411. **$58-$118.** 340 Greentree Rd. I-80, exit 308, just se. Int corridors. **Pets:** Accepted.
ASK S♦ ✕ 🐾 🖥

HAMLIN

WWW Comfort Inn SH
(570) 689-4148. **$70-$150.** SR 191. I-84, exit 17, just n. Int corridors. **Pets:** Accepted.
[SAVE] [S6] [X] [H] [P] [X]

HAWLEY

WWW The Falls Port Inn & Restaurant CI
(570) 226-2600. **$70-$120, 3 day notice.** 330 Main Ave. At Main Ave (US 6) and Church St; downtown. Int corridors. **Pets:** $20 one-time fee/room.
[SAVE] [X] [H] [Z]

LAKE HARMONY

WWW Ramada Inn-Pocono SH
(570) 443-8471. **$80-$175.** I-80, exit 277; I-476 (Northeast Extension Pennsylvania Tpke), exit 95, 0.5 mi e. Int corridors. **Pets:** Small. $50 deposit/room. Service with restrictions, supervision.
[SAVE] [S6] [X] [🐾] [♿] [H] [P] [H] [🏊] [X]

MATAMORAS

**WWW Best Western Inn at Hunt's
        Landing SH**
(570) 491-2400. **$89-$159.** 120 Rt 6 & 209. I-84, exit 53. Int corridors. **Pets:** Medium. $10 daily fee/pet. Designated rooms, service with restrictions, supervision.
[SAVE] [S6] [X] [🐾] [H] [P] [H] [🏊] [X]

MILFORD

WWW Cliff Park Inn & Golf Course CI
(570) 296-6491. **$175-$225, 14 day notice.** 155 Cliff Park Rd. I-84, exit 46, 2 mi e on US 6, just s on 6th St, 1.5 mi w on SR 2001, then 0.5 mi s. Int corridors. **Pets:** Accepted.
[SAVE] [X] [H] [X]

WWW Milford Motel M
(570) 296-6411. **$50-$95, 3 day notice.** 591 Rt 6 & 209. On US 6 and 209 N, 0.7 mi e. Ext corridors. **Pets:** Dogs only. $8 daily fee/pet. Designated rooms, service with restrictions, supervision.
[SAVE] [S6] [X] [H]

WWW Red Carpet Inn-Milford M 🐾
(570) 296-9444. **$65-$115, 7 day notice.** 240 Rt 6. I-84, exit 46, just s. Ext corridors. **Pets:** Small. $7 daily fee/pet. Designated rooms, no service, supervision.
[SAVE] [S6] [X] [H]

WW Scottish Inns M
(570) 491-4414. **$45-$90.** 274 Rt 6 & 209. I-84, exit 53, 1 mi s. Ext corridors. **Pets:** Accepted.
[SAVE] [S6] [X] [H] [P]

🐾 END AREA 🐾

PUNXSUTAWNEY

WW Pantall Hotel SH
(814) 938-6600. **$59.** 135 E Mahoning St. On US 119 and SR 36; downtown. Int corridors. **Pets:** Supervision.
[ASK] [S6] [X] [H]

READING

WWW Airport Lodge & Suites SH
(610) 736-0400. **$45-$70.** 2017 Bernville Rd. US 222, exit SR 183, 2 mi s. Int corridors. **Pets:** Accepted.
[ASK] [S6] [X] [H]

**WWW Best Western Dutch Colony Inn &
        Suites SH**
(610) 779-2345. **$84-$108.** 4635 Perkiomen Ave. US 422, 0.3 mi e of jct US 422 business route. Ext/int corridors. **Pets:** Accepted.
[SAVE] [S6] [X] [🐾] [♿] [H] [P] [H] [🏊] [X]

WW Econo Lodge M
(610) 378-1145. **$59-$69.** 2310 Fraver Dr. US 222 business route (5th St); just s of Warren St Bypass (SR 12 E). Ext corridors. **Pets:** Medium. $10 daily fee/pet. Service with restrictions, crate.
[ASK] [S6] [X] [H] [P]

ST. MARYS

WWW Comfort Inn SH
(814) 834-2030. **$54-$90.** 195 Comfort Ln. SR 255, south end of town. Int corridors. **Pets:** Other species. Service with restrictions, supervision.
[ASK] [S6] [X] [♿] [H] [P] [🏊]

WWW Towne House Inn CI
(814) 781-1556. **$53-$85.** 138 Center St. Just n of "Diamond" and jct SR 255 and 120; downtown. Int corridors. **Pets:** Accepted.
[SAVE] [S6] [X] [♿] [H] [P] [H] [🏊]

SELINSGROVE

WWW Comfort Inn SH
(570) 374-8880. **$69-$169.** 710 S US Hwy 11 & 15. Just n of jct US 522. Int corridors. **Pets:** Accepted.
[SAVE] [S6] [X] [H] [P] [🏊]

SHAMOKIN DAM

WWW Hampton Inn SH
(570) 743-2223. **$119-$169.** 3 Stettler Ave. US 11 and 15, 1 mi s of jct SR 61. Int corridors. **Pets:** Other species. $25 one-time fee/room. Designated rooms, service with restrictions, supervision.
[SAVE] [S6] [X] [&M] [🐾] [♿] [H] [P] [🏊]

AAA **WW** Quality Inn & Suites **M**
(570) 743-1111. **$69-$199.** 2 Susquehanna Tr. US 11 and 15; just n of jct SR 61. Ext corridors. **Pets:** Accepted.
SAVE S X 🕯 💻 🔄

SHARTLESVILLE

AAA **W** Dutch Motel **M**
(610) 488-1479. **$45-$65.** 1 Motel Dr. I-78, exit 23, just nw. Ext corridors. **Pets:** $5 daily fee/pet. Designated rooms, no service.
SAVE S X 🕯 💻

SHICKSHINNY

WW The Blue Heron Bed & Breakfast **BB**
(570) 864-3740. **$55-$95 (no credit cards).** 1270 Bethel Hill Rd. Jct US 11, 6.2 mi n on SR 239, then 2 mi n on CR 4016 (Harveyville/Bethel Hill Rd). Int corridors. **Pets:** Accepted.
X X M W

SLIPPERY ROCK

W Evening Star Motel **M** 🐾
(724) 794-3211. **$49-$55.** 915 New Castle Rd. I-79, exit 105, 0.5 mi e on SR 108. Ext corridors. **Pets:** $5 daily fee/pet. Service with restrictions, supervision.
S X 🕯 💻

SOUTH WILLIAMSPORT

AAA **WWW** Ridgemont Motel **M**
(570) 321-5300. **$43-$53.** 637 US 15 Hwy. 1.2 mi s. Ext corridors. **Pets:** Accepted.
SAVE S X 🕯

STATE COLLEGE

WW The Autoport Motel & Restaurant Inc **SH**
(814) 237-7666. **$69-$99.** 1405 S Atherton St. US 322 business route, 1.4 mi e of jct SR 26. Ext/int corridors. **Pets:** Other species. $10 daily fee/pet. Designated rooms, service with restrictions, crate.
ASK S X 🕯 💻 🍴 🔄

AAA **WWW** Days Inn Penn State **LH**
(814) 238-8454. **$59-$250, 30 day notice.** 240 S Pugh St. Just e of SR 26 northbound, 0.4 mi n of jct US 322 business route; downtown. Int corridors. **Pets:** Accepted.
SAVE X 🗐 🖉 🕯 💻 🍴 🔄

AAA **W** Happy Valley Motor Inn **M**
(814) 234-1111. **$37-$48, 14 day notice.** 1245 S Atherton St. 1.3 mi e on US 322 business route. Ext/int corridors. **Pets:** Other species. $20 one-time fee/room. Service with restrictions, supervision.
SAVE S X 🕯

WW Motel 6 State College **M**
(814) 234-1600. **$49-$56.** 1274 N Atherton St. US 322 business route, 1 mi w of jct SR 26. Int corridors. **Pets:** Accepted.
S X 🕯M 🖉 🗐 🕯

WW Nittany Budget Motel **M**
(814) 238-0015. **$49-$52.** 2070 Cato Ave. SR 26, 2.6 mi s of jct US 322 business route. Ext corridors. **Pets:** Other species. $10 daily fee/pet. Designated rooms, service with restrictions, supervision.
ASK S X 🖉 🕯

AAA **WWW** Ramada Inn-State College **LH**
(814) 238-3001. **$103-$175.** 1450 S Atherton St. US 322 business route, 1.4 mi e of jct SR 26. Ext/int corridors. **Pets:** Accepted.
SAVE S X 💻 🍴 🔄 🕸

WW Super 8 State College **SH**
(814) 237-8005. **$49-$89.** 1663 S Atherton St. US 322 business route, 1.6 mi e of jct SR 26. Int corridors. **Pets:** Accepted.
ASK S X 🕯 💻 🕸

TOWN HILL

W Days Inn **SH**
(814) 735-3860. **$53-$68.** 9648 Old 126. I-70, exit 156, just n. Int corridors. **Pets:** Accepted.
ASK S X 🍴

WARREN

AAA **WWW** Holiday Inn of Warren **SH**
(814) 726-3000. **$72-$100.** 210 Ludlow St. 1.5 mi w on US 6, exit Ludlow St. Int corridors. **Pets:** Small. Service with restrictions, supervision.
SAVE S X 🖉 🕯 💻 🍴 🔄

W Warren Super 8 Motel **SH**
(814) 723-8881. **$56-$66.** 204 Struthers St. 1.5 mi w on US 6, exit Ludlow St, w on Allegheny, then s. Ext/int corridors. **Pets:** $25 deposit/pet. Designated rooms, service with restrictions, supervision.
ASK S X 🕯 💻

WAYNESBORO

AAA **WWW** Best Western of Waynesboro **M**
(717) 762-9113. **$69-$85, 7 day notice.** 239 W Main St. 0.5 mi w on SR 16. Ext corridors. **Pets:** Medium, other species. $20 daily fee/pet. Designated rooms, service with restrictions.
SAVE S X 🕯 💻 🍴

WAYNESBURG

WWW Comfort Inn **SH**
(724) 627-3700. **$59-$150, 10 day notice.** 100 Comfort Ln. I-79, exit 14, just e. Int corridors. **Pets:** Medium. $25 one-time fee/pet. Service with restrictions, supervision.
ASK S X 🖉 🕯 💻

WW Econo Lodge **M**
(724) 627-5544. **$51-$65.** 350 Miller Ln. I-79, exit 14, just w. Ext corridors. **Pets:** Accepted.
ASK S X 🕯 💻

WW Super 8 Motel-Waynesburg **M**
(724) 627-8880. **$54-$64.** 100 Stanley Dr. I-79, exit 14, just w. Int corridors. **Pets:** Other species. Service with restrictions, supervision.
ASK S X 🕯 💻

WELLSBORO

⬥⬥ ▽▽▽ Canyon Motel M
(570) 724-1681. **$61-$99.** 18 East Ave. Just e on US 6 and SR 660. Ext/int corridors. **Pets:** Other species. $10 daily fee/room. Designated rooms, crate.

[SAVE] [S♦] [✕] [⌕] [🍴] [📺] [⇌] [✕]

WEST HAZLETON

▽▽▽▽ Comfort Inn Hazleton West
Hazleton SH ⬥
(570) 455-9300. **$106-$170.** 58 SR 93. I-81, exit 145, 0.3 mi se; I-80, exit 256, 3.8 mi se. Int corridors. **Pets:** Other species. Designated rooms, service with restrictions, supervision.

[ASK] [S♦] [✕] [⌕] [🍴] [📺] [🍴]

⬥⬥ ▽▽▽▽ Forest Hill Inn M
(570) 459-2730. **$55.** 18202 SR 93. I-81, exit 145, 0.3 mi se; I-80, exit 256, 3.8 mi se. Ext corridors. **Pets:** Other species. Service with restrictions, supervision.

[SAVE] [S♦] [✕]

WEST MIDDLESEX

▽▽ ▽▽ Super 8 Motel-West Middlesex/Sharon SH
(724) 528-3888. **$55-$80.** 3369 New Castle Rd. I-80, exit 4B (SR 18), just s. Int corridors. **Pets:** Small, dogs only. $10 daily fee/pet. Designated rooms, service with restrictions, supervision.

[ASK] [S♦] [✕] [⌕] [🍴]

WILKES-BARRE

⬥⬥ ▽▽▽▽ Best Western Genetti Hotel &
Conference Center LH
(570) 823-6152. **$104-$269.** 77 E Market St. Market and Washington sts; downtown. Int corridors. **Pets:** Accepted.

[SAVE] [S♦] [✕] [🍴] [📺] [🍴] [⇌]

⬥⬥ ▽▽ ▽ Days Inn SH
(570) 826-0111. **$53-$75.** 760 Kidder St. I-81, exit 170B, exit 1 (SR 309 S business route), just w; I-76 (Pennsylvania Tpke), exit 105, exit 1 (SR 115 N). Int corridors. **Pets:** Other species. $5 daily fee/pet. Service with restrictions, supervision.

[SAVE] [S♦] [✕] [🍴]

▽▽ ▽▽▽ Holiday Inn SH ⬥
(570) 824-8901. **$79.** 880 Kidder St. I-81, exit 170B, exit 1 (SR 309 S business route). Ext corridors. **Pets:** Other species. Service with restrictions, crate.

[ASK] [S♦] [✕] [⌕] [🍴] [📺] [🍴] [⇌]

⬥⬥ ▽▽ ▽ Red Roof Inn M
(570) 829-6422. **$49-$58.** 1035 Hwy 315. I-81, exit 170B, jct SR 115, 0.7 mi w, exit 1 (SR 309 S business route) to SR 315, then just n. Ext corridors. **Pets:** Medium, other species. No service, supervision.

[SAVE] [✕] [⌕] [🍴]

WILLIAMSPORT

⬥⬥ ▽▽ ▽ Genetti Hotel & Suites SH
(570) 326-6600. **$71-$101, 7 day notice.** 200 W Fourth St. Jct William St; downtown. Int corridors. **Pets:** Large, other species. Service with restrictions, crate.

[SAVE] [S♦] [✕] [🍴] [📺] [🍴] [⇌]

▽▽▽▽ Holiday Inn-Williamsport M ⬥
(570) 326-1981. **$79-$99.** 1840 E 3rd St. I-180, exit 25 (Faxon St), just e; 1 mi w of W 3rd St. Ext corridors. **Pets:** Medium, other species. Service with restrictions, supervision.

[ASK] [S♦] [✕] [🍴] [📺] [🍴] [⇌] [✕]

▽▽▽▽ Radisson Hotel Williamsport SH ⬥
(570) 327-8231. **$100-$134.** 100 Pine St. Jct US 220 and SR 15 S; downtown. Int corridors. **Pets:** Medium. Designated rooms, service with restrictions, supervision.

[ASK] [S♦] [✕] [🍴] [📺] [🍴] [⇌]

WIND GAP

⬥⬥ ▽▽ ▽ Travel Inn of Wind Gap M
(610) 863-4146. **$50-$90, 3 day notice.** 499 E Moorestown Rd. SR 512, e of jct SR 33, exit Bath/Wind Gap. Ext corridors. **Pets:** Dogs only. $5 daily fee/pet. Designated rooms, service with restrictions, supervision.

[SAVE] [S♦] [✕] [🍴]

WYOMISSING

▽▽ ▽ Econo Lodge SH
(610) 378-5105. **$55-$80.** 635 Spring St. Just off US 422, exit Papermill Rd. Int corridors. **Pets:** Small. $10 daily fee/pet. Service with restrictions, supervision.

[ASK] [S♦] [✕] [⌕] [🍴] [📺]

▽▽▽▽ Homewood
Suites-Reading/Wyomissing SH
(610) 736-3100. **$149-$299.** 2801 Papermill Rd. US 422, exit Papermill Rd, 1.8 mi nw; US 222, exit Spring Ridge Rd. Int corridors. **Pets:** Accepted.

[ASK] [S♦] [✕] [⌕] [⌕] [🍴] [🍴] [📺] [⇌] [✕]

⬥⬥ ▽▽▽▽ The Inn at Reading SH
(610) 372-7811. **$99-$129.** 1040 Park Rd. US 222, exit N Wyomissing Blvd, just n, then 0.3 mi e. Int corridors. **Pets:** Accepted.

[SAVE] [S♦] [✕] [⌕] [🍴] [📺] [🍴] [⇌] [✕]

▽▽▽▽ Sheraton Reading Hotel SH ⬥
(610) 376-3811. **$98-$104.** 1741 W Papermill Rd. US 422, exit Papermill Rd. Int corridors. **Pets:** Other species. $10 one-time fee/room.

[ASK] [S♦] [✕] [⌕] [⌕] [🍴] [📺] [🍴] [⇌] [✕]

⬥⬥ ▽▽▽▽ Wellesley Inn (Reading) SH
(610) 374-1500. **$89-$139.** 910 Woodland Rd. US 422 W, exit Papermill Rd, just e. Int corridors. **Pets:** Small, other species. $10 daily fee/pet. Designated rooms, service with restrictions, supervision.

[SAVE] [S♦] [✕] [⌕] [⌕] [🍴] [📺]

WYSOX

▼▼▼▼ Comfort Inn SH
(570) 265-5691. **$99-$119.** US 6. Center. Int corridors. **Pets:** Other species. $12 one-time fee/room. Service with restrictions, supervision.

YORK

▼▼▼ Four Points by Sheraton Hotel and Suites SH
(717) 846-4940. **$137-$225.** 1650 Toronita St. I-83, exit 9E, just e; on US 30. Int corridors. **Pets:** Medium. $25 one-time fee/pet. Designated rooms, service with restrictions.

▼▼▼ Holiday Inn Holidome & Conference Center SH
(717) 846-9500. **$88-$134.** 2000 Loucks Rd. I-83, exit 21B northbound, 2.5 mi w on US 30, then just n; exit 22 southbound, 0.5 mi s on SR 181, 2.2 mi w on US 30, then just n. Int corridors. **Pets:** Accepted.

◆◆◆ ▼▼▼▼ Holiday Inn York I-83 & Rt 30 SH
(717) 845-5671. **$89-$119.** 334 Arsenal Rd. I-83, exit 21A northbound; exit 21 southbound, just e on US 30. Ext corridors. **Pets:** Medium, dogs only. Designated rooms, service with restrictions, supervision.

◆◆◆ ▼▼▼ Red Roof Inn M
(717) 843-8181. **$45-$73.** 323 Arsenal Rd. I-83, exit 21A northbound; exit 21 southbound; just e on US 30. Ext corridors. **Pets:** Large, other species. Service with restrictions, supervision.

▼▼ Super 8 Motel M
(717) 852-8686. **$46-$66.** 40 Arsenal Rd. I-83, exit 21B northbound, 0.3 mi w on US 30; exit 21 southbound, 0.5 mi s on SR 181 to US 30. Int corridors. **Pets:** Accepted.

CRANSTON

AAA **WWW** Days Inn **M**
(401) 942-4200. **$79-$109, 14 day notice.** 101 New London Ave. I-95, exit 14B to SR 37, exit 2B westbound, then 0.5 mi. Ext corridors. **Pets:** Service with restrictions, supervision.
[SAVE] [S] [X]

MIDDLETOWN

WW The Bay Willows Inn **M** ❄
(401) 847-8400. **$39-$179, 7 day notice.** 1225 Aquidneck Ave. Jct SR 138 and 138A. Ext corridors. **Pets:** Other species. $25 deposit/room, $10 daily fee/room. Designated rooms, service with restrictions.
[X] [H]

AAA **WWW** Howard Johnson Inn-Newport **M**
(401) 849-2000. **$44-$239.** 351 W Main Rd. On SR 114, 0.3 mi s of jct SR 138. Int corridors. **Pets:** Other species. $5 daily fee/pet. Designated rooms, service with restrictions, supervision.
[SAVE] [S] [X] [&M] [?] [?] [H] [P] [≈] [X]

WWW SeaView Inn **M** ❄
(401) 846-5000. **$59-$219, 7 day notice.** 240 Aquidneck Ave (SR 138A). Jct SR 214. Ext corridors. **Pets:** Other species. $25 deposit/room, $10 daily fee/room. Designated rooms, service with restrictions.
[X] [H] [P]

NEWPORT

AAA **WWWW** Beech Tree Inn **BB**
(401) 847-9794. **$125-$325, 14 day notice.** 34 Rhode Island Ave. Just e of SR 114, 0.8 mi s of jct SR 138. Int corridors. **Pets:** Large. Designated rooms, service with restrictions.
[SAVE] [X] [H]

PORTSMOUTH

AAA **WWW** Founder's Brook Motel & Suites **M**
(401) 683-1244. **$59-$145, 3 day notice.** 314 Boyd's Ln. Jct SR 24, exit Mt. Hope Blvd, on SR 138. Ext corridors. **Pets:** Medium. $10 one-time fee/pet. Supervision.
[SAVE] [S] [X] [H]

PROVIDENCE

AAA **WWW** **WWW** The Westin Providence **LH** ❄
(401) 598-8000. **$419-$1700.** One W Exchange St. I-95, exit 22A; downtown. Int corridors. **Pets:** Small, dogs only. $50 one-time fee/room. Service with restrictions, supervision.
[SAVE] [S] [X] [&M] [?] [?] [P] [T] [≈] [X]

WAKEFIELD

WWWW The Kings' Rose Bed & Breakfast Inn **BB**
(401) 783-5222. **$140-$170 (no credit cards), 7 day notice.** 1747 Mooresfield Rd (SR 138). I-95, exit 3A, 11 mi e on SR 138, then 3.3 mi w of US 1. Int corridors. **Pets:** Supervision.
[X]

WARWICK

WWWW Crowne Plaza Hotel at the Crossings **LH**
(401) 732-6000. **$139-$189.** 801 Greenwich Ave. I-95, exit 12A southbound; exit 12 northbound, 0.3 mi e on SR 5. Int corridors. **Pets:** Large, other species. $50 deposit/room. Designated rooms, service with restrictions, crate.
[ASK] [S] [X] [&M] [?] [H] [P] [T] [≈] [X]

AAA **WWW** Holiday Inn Express Hotel & Suites **SH** ❄
(401) 736-5000. **$109-$159.** 901 Jefferson Blvd. I-95, exit 13A, 0.6 mi e. Int corridors. **Pets:** Other species. $50 deposit/room. Service with restrictions.
[SAVE] [S] [X] [&M] [?] [?] [H] [P] [≈]

WW Homestead Studio Suites Hotel-Providence/Airport/Warwick **SH** ❄
(401) 732-6667. **$105-$123.** 268 Metro Center Blvd. I-95, exit 12A, 0.4 mi e on SR 113, 0.4 mi n on SR 5, then 0.4 mi e. Int corridors. **Pets:** Medium, other species. $25 daily fee/room. Service with restrictions, crate.
[ASK] [S] [X] [&M] [?] [?] [H] [P] [X]

WWW Homewood Suites by Hilton **SH** ❄
(401) 738-0008. **$139-$209.** 33 International Way. I-95, exit 13, 0.4 mi n on Jefferson Blvd, then 0.5 mi w on Kilvert St toward Metro Center Blvd. Int corridors. **Pets:** Medium, dogs only. $50 one-time fee/pet. Designated rooms, service with restrictions, supervision.
[ASK] [S] [X] [&M] [?] [?] [H] [P] [≈] [X]

WWW Residence Inn by Marriott **SH**
(401) 737-7100. **$99-$229.** 500 Kilvert St. I-95, exit 13 to Jefferson Blvd, 0.4 mi n, then 0.5 mi w. Ext corridors. **Pets:** Accepted.
[ASK] [S] [X] [?] [H] [P] [≈] [X]

WWWW Sheraton Providence Airport Hotel **LH** ❄
(401) 738-4000. **$119-$165.** 1850 Post Rd. I-95, exit 13, on US 1. Int corridors. **Pets:** Medium, dogs only. $50 one-time fee/room. Service with restrictions, supervision.
[ASK] [X] [&M] [?] [?] [H] [P] [T] [≈]

WOONSOCKET

WWWW Holiday Inn Express Hotel & Suites **SH**
(401) 769-5000. **$125-$155.** 194 Fortin Dr. I-295, exit 9 on SR 122, 3.5 mi n via SR 146/99/122. Int corridors. **Pets:** Medium. $10 daily fee/pet. Designated rooms, service with restrictions, supervision.
[ASK] [S] [X] [&M] [?] [?] [H] [P] [≈]

SOUTH CAROLINA

AIKEN

Best Western Executive Inn M
(803) 649-3968. **$48-$75, 7 day notice.** 3560 Richland Ave W. Jct SR 19/US 1/78, 2.5 mi w on US 1/78. Ext corridors. **Pets:** Accepted.

Comfort Suites SH
(803) 641-1100. **$60-$80, 3 day notice.** 3608 Richland Ave W. 2.3 mi w on US 1 and 78. Ext corridors. **Pets:** Medium, other species. $6 daily fee/pet. Service with restrictions, supervision.

Days Inn-Downtown M
(803) 649-5524. **$42-$175.** 1204 Richland Ave W. 0.5 mi w on US 1 and 78. Ext corridors. **Pets:** Very small. $10 daily fee/pet. Service with restrictions, supervision.

Holiday Inn Express SH
(803) 648-0999. **$90.** 155 Colony Pkwy/Whiskey Rd. Jct US 1/78/SR 19, 1.8 mi s on SR 19. Ext corridors. **Pets:** Accepted.

Ramada Ltd SH 🐾
(803) 648-6821. **$49-$75.** 1850 Richland Ave W. 1.8 mi w on US 1 and 78. Ext corridors. **Pets:** Small. $8 daily fee/pet. Designated rooms, service with restrictions.

Sleep Inn SH
(803) 644-9900. **$49-$79.** 1002 Monterey Dr. Jct US 78 and SR 302/19 (Whiskey Rd), 0.5 mi s on SR 19, then just e. Int corridors. **Pets:** Accepted.

Town & Country Inn BB 🐾
(803) 642-0270. **$70-$125.** 2340 Sizemore Cir. Jct US 78 and SR 302/19 (Whiskey Rd), 2.3 mi s on SR 19, then just w. Int corridors. **Pets:** Other species.

ANDERSON

Days Inn M
(864) 375-0375. **$57-$65.** 1007 Smith Mill Rd. I-85, exit 19A, jct US 76, just se. Ext corridors. **Pets:** Accepted.

Holiday Inn Express SH
(864) 231-0231. **$65-$150.** 103 Anderson Business Park. I-85, exit 27, just s on SR 81. Int corridors. **Pets:** Small, dogs only. $25 one-time fee/room. Service with restrictions, supervision.

Jameson Inn SH
(864) 375-9800. **$70-$75.** 128 Interstate Blvd. I-85, exit 19B, jct US 76, just nw on frontage road. Ext corridors. **Pets:** Small. Service with restrictions, crate.

La Quinta Inn SH
(864) 225-3721. **$71-$91.** 3430 Clemson Blvd. I-85, exit 19A, 2.5 mi se on US 76. Ext corridors. **Pets:** Accepted.

BEAUFORT

Ramada Limited of Beaufort SH
(843) 524-2144. **$75-$95.** 2001 Boundary St. I-95, exit 33 (Point South/US 17), jct SR 281/US 21, just w on US 21. Ext corridors. **Pets:** Accepted.

BLUFFTON

Holiday Inn Express Hotel & Suites SH
(843) 757-2002. **$70-$100.** 35 Bluffton Rd. Jct William Hilton Pkwy (US 278/Bluffton Rd US 46), just se. Int corridors. **Pets:** $25 one-time fee/pet. Service with restrictions.

CAMDEN

Colony Inn M
(803) 432-5508. **$55-$59.** 2020 W DeKalb St. Jct US 521/1/601, 1.6 mi w on US 1/601. Ext/int corridors. **Pets:** Medium. Designated rooms, service with restrictions, supervision.

CAYCE

Ramada Limited Airport SH
(803) 794-7500. **$55-$65.** 3020 Charleston Hwy. I-26, exit 115 (US 21), just s. Ext corridors. **Pets:** $10 one-time fee/ room. Service with restrictions.

Riverside Inn M
(803) 939-4688. **$55-$60.** 111 Knox Abbott Dr. US 21, just w of Congaree River Bridge. Ext corridors. **Pets:** Accepted.

CHARLESTON METROPOLITAN AREA

CHARLESTON

▼▼▼ **Best Western Sweetgrass Inn** M
(843) 571-6100. **$69-$149.** 1540 Savannah Hwy. US 17 S, 3.6 mi w of Ashley River Bridge; jct I-526 W (end) and US 17 N, 1.7 mi e. Ext corridors. **Pets:** Accepted.

ASK [SA] [X] [fridge] [microwave] [coffee] 🏊

▼▼ **Howard Johnson Riverfront** SH
(843) 722-4000. **$59-$129.** 250 Spring St. I-26, exit 221A (US 17 S), 1.2 mi sw; just e of Ashley River. Int corridors. **Pets:** $20 daily fee/room. Designated rooms, service with restrictions.

ASK [SA] [X] [fridge] [microwave] [11] 🏊

AAA **▼▼▼** **Indigo Inn** SH
(843) 577-5900. **$99-$210.** 1 Maiden Ln. Corner of Meeting and Pinckney sts. Ext corridors. **Pets:** Medium, other species. $20 daily fee/pet. Designated rooms, service with restrictions, crate.

[SAVE] [X] [coffee]

▼▼▼▼ **Residence Inn by Marriott** SH
(843) 571-7979. **$99-$199.** 90 Ripley Point Dr. US 17 S, just over Ashley River Bridge to Albermarle Rd, then just s. Int corridors. **Pets:** Medium, dogs only. $75 one-time fee/pet. Designated rooms, service with restrictions, supervision.

ASK [SA] [X] [microwave] [coffee] [grill] [fridge] [microwave] 🏊 [X]

▼▼▼▼ **Town & Country Inn & Conference Center** SH
(843) 571-1000. **$69-$129.** 2008 Savannah Hwy. US 17 S, 3.5 mi nw of Ashley River Bridge; jct I-526 W (end) and US 17 N, just se. Ext corridors. **Pets:** Medium. Service with restrictions, supervision.

ASK [SA] [X] [fridge] [microwave] [11] 🏊 [X]

MOUNT PLEASANT

▼▼ **Comfort Inn East** SH
(843) 884-5853. **$59-$139.** 310 Hwy 17 (Johnnie Dodds Blvd). US 17, 0.7 mi n of Cooper River Bridge. Ext corridors. **Pets:** Small, dogs only. $10 one-time fee/pet. Service with restrictions, crate.

ASK [SA] [X] [fridge] [microwave] 🏊

▼▼▼▼ **MainStay Suites Mount Pleasant** SH
(843) 881-1722. **$49-$249.** 400 McGrath Darby Blvd. Base of Cooper River Bridge, just ne on US 17, then just n. Int corridors. **Pets:** Accepted.

ASK [SA] [X] [microwave] [grill] [fridge] [microwave] 🏊

AAA **▼▼▼** **Red Roof Inn #7242** M
(843) 884-1411. **$45-$79.** 301 Johnnie Dodds Blvd. Just e of base of Cooper River Bridge, on US 17, then just s on McGrath-Darby Blvd. Ext corridors. **Pets:** Medium, other species. Service with restrictions, supervision.

[SAVE] [X] [coffee] [grill] [fridge] 🏊

▼▼▼ **Residence Inn by Marriott** SH ❄
(843) 881-1599. **$89-$199.** 1116 Isle of Palms Connector. I-526, exit Georgetown/US 17 N, 1.4 mi ne on US 17 to SR 517 Isle of Palms Connector, then just se. Int corridors. **Pets:** Small, other species. $75 one-time fee/room. Service with restrictions.

ASK [SA] [X] [microwave] [fridge] [microwave] 🏊 [X]

▼▼ **Sleep Inn Mt Pleasant** SH ❄
(843) 856-5000. **$39-$149.** 299 Wingo Way. Just e of base of Cooper River Bridge, then just n at McGrath-Darby Blvd. Int corridors. **Pets:** Other species. $10 one-time fee/room. Service with restrictions, crate.

ASK [SA] [X] [microwave] [coffee] [grill] [fridge] 🏊

NORTH CHARLESTON

AAA **▼▼▼** **Best Western Charleston Airport Hotel** SH ❄
(843) 744-1621. **$59-$79.** 6099 Fain St. I-26, exit 211A (W Aviation Ave), just w. Ext corridors. **Pets:** Small, other species. $25 one-time fee/room. Designated rooms.

[SAVE] [SA] [X] [coffee] [grill] [fridge] [microwave] [11] 🏊

▼▼ **Charleston Super 8 Motel** M
(843) 572-2228. **$60-$95, 7 day notice.** 2311 Ashley Phosphate Rd. I-26, exit 209 (Ashley Phosphate Rd), just e. Ext corridors. **Pets:** Medium. $15 daily fee/room. Service with restrictions, crate.

ASK [SA] [X] [fridge] 🏊

▼▼ **Comfort Inn Coliseum** M
(843) 554-6485. **$70-$90.** 5055 N Arco Ln. I-26, exit 213A/B (Montague Ave), just s, then nw. Ext corridors. **Pets:** Accepted.

ASK [SA] [X] [coffee] [fridge] [microwave] 🏊

▼▼ **Homestead Studio Suites Hotel-Charleston/Airport** SH ❄
(843) 740-3440. **$94-$109.** 5045 N Arco Ln. I-26, exit 213A/B (Montague Ave), just nw. Int corridors. **Pets:** Medium, other species. $25 daily fee/room. Service with restrictions, crate.

ASK [SA] [X] [microwave] [coffee] [grill] [fridge] [microwave] 🏊

AAA **▼▼▼** **La Quinta Inn** SH
(843) 797-8181. **$55-$85.** 2499 La Quinta Ln. I-26, exit 209A/B (Ashley Phosphate Rd), just w. Ext corridors. **Pets:** Accepted.

[SAVE] [SA] [X] [coffee] [fridge] [microwave] 🏊

▼▼ **Motel 6** M
(843) 572-6590. **$41-$59.** 2551 Ashley Phosphate Rd. I-26, exit 209 (Ashley Phosphate), just w. Ext corridors. **Pets:** Small, other species. Service with restrictions, supervision.

[SA] [X] [grill] 🏊

AAA **▼▼▼** **Red Roof Inn** M
(843) 572-9100. **$44-$61.** 7480 Northwoods Blvd. I-26, exit 209 (Ashley Phosphate Rd), just e, then just n. Ext corridors. **Pets:** Medium. Service with restrictions, supervision.

[SAVE] [X] [coffee] [grill] [fridge]

Residence Inn by Marriott SH
(843) 572-5757. **$154.** 7645 Northwoods Blvd. I-26, exit 209 (Ashley Phosphate Rd), just e, then n. Ext corridors. **Pets:** Other species. $75 one-time fee/room. Service with restrictions.

[ASK] [S₀] [X] [⌀] [🛏] [💻] [➳] [⊠]

Sheraton North Charleston LH ✿
(843) 747-1900. **$77-$97.** 4770 Goer Dr. I-26, exit 213A/B (Montague Ave), just ne. Int corridors. **Pets:** Medium. $20 one-time fee/room. Designated rooms, service with restrictions, supervision.

[SAVE] [S₀] [X] [⌀] [🛏] [💻] [¶] [➳]

Sleep Inn Charleston North SH
(843) 572-8400. **$59-$79, 14 day notice.** 7435 Northside Dr. I-26, exit 209 (Ashley Phosphate Rd), just w. Int corridors. **Pets:** Accepted.

[ASK] [S₀] [X] [🛏] [💻]

ST. STEPHEN

Econo Lodge SH
(843) 567-7397. **$56-$66.** 3986 Byrnes Dr. Center. Int corridors. **Pets:** Medium. $25 deposit/pet. Service with restrictions, supervision.

[X] [🛏] [💻] [➳]

SUMMERVILLE

Holiday Inn Express-Charleston/Summerville SH
(843) 875-3300. **$59-$75, 30 day notice.** 120 Holiday Inn Dr. I-26, exit 199A (US 17 alternate route), just w. Int corridors. **Pets:** Accepted.

[ASK] [S₀] [X] [&M] [⌀] [♿] [💻] [➳]

Woodlands Resort & Inn CI ✿
(843) 875-2600. **$295-$425, 7 day notice.** 125 Parsons Rd. I-26, exit 199A, 2 mi s on US 17 alternate route, 1.5 mi w on W Richardson Ave (SR 165), just s. Int corridors. **Pets:** Service with restrictions.

[SAVE] [S₀] [X] [⌀] [¶] [➳] [⊠]

✿ END METROPOLITAN AREA ✿

CHERAW

Days Inn–Cheraw M
(843) 537-5554. **$50-$90.** 820 Market St. US 52 and 1, jct SR 9. Ext corridors. **Pets:** Small. $10 daily fee/pet. Service with restrictions, supervision.

[SAVE] [S₀] [X] [🛏] [💻] [➳]

Jameson Inn M
(843) 537-5625. **$68-$73.** 885 Chesterfield Hwy. Jct US 1 and 52, 1.5 mi n on SR 9. Ext corridors. **Pets:** Small. Service with restrictions, supervision.

[X] [♿] [🛏] [💻] [➳]

CLEMSON

Ramada Inn of Clemson SH
(864) 654-7501. **$59-$79.** 1310 Tiger Blvd. I-85, exit 19B; jct US 76 and SR 123. Int corridors. **Pets:** Small, other species. $10 daily fee/pet. Service with restrictions, supervision.

[SAVE] [S₀] [X] [♿] [🛏] [💻] [¶] [➳]

CLINTON

Comfort Inn SH
(864) 833-5558. **$55-$75.** 105 Trade St. I-26, exit 52, just e, then n. Ext corridors. **Pets:** Small. $10 one-time fee/pet. Service with restrictions, supervision.

[SAVE] [S₀] [X] [⌀] [🛏] [💻] [➳]

COLUMBIA

AmeriSuites (Columbia/Northeast) SH
(803) 736-6666. **$69-$89.** 7525 Two Notch Rd. I-20, exit 74 (Two Notch Rd), just n; I-77, exit 17 (Two Notch Rd), 0.5 mi s. Int corridors. **Pets:** Accepted.

[SAVE] [S₀] [X] [⌀] [♿] [🛏] [💻] [➳]

Baymont Inn & Suites Columbia NE/Ft. Jackson Area SH
(803) 736-6400. **$59-$89.** 1538 Horseshoe Dr. I-20, exit 74 (Two Notch Rd), just n; I-77, exit 17 (Two Notch Rd), 0.5 mi s. Int corridors. **Pets:** Small. $50 deposit/room. Designated rooms, service with restrictions, supervision.

[SAVE] [S₀] [X] [⌀] [🛏] [💻] [➳]

Best Inn SH
(803) 798-9590. **$55-$75.** 1335 Garner Ln. I-20, exit 65 (US 176), just ne. Ext corridors. **Pets:** Accepted.

[ASK] [S₀] [X] [⌀] [🛏] [💻] [➳]

Best Western Fort Jackson SH
(803) 695-0666. **$69-$99.** 240 E Exchange Blvd. I-77, exit 9A (US 76/378), just se on US 76/378, then just s. Int corridors. **Pets:** Accepted.

[SAVE] [S₀] [X] [&M] [♿] [🛏] [💻] [➳]

Chestnut Cottage Bed & Breakfast BB
(803) 256-1718. **$125-$225, 15 day notice.** 1718 Hampton St. SR 12 (Taylor St), just s, between Henderson and Barnwell sts. Int corridors. **Pets:** Accepted.

[ASK] [X] [🛏] [💻]

Days Inn M
(803) 754-4408. **$45-$60.** 133 Plumbers Rd. I-20, exit 71 (Wilson Blvd), just n, then just e. Ext corridors. **Pets:** Other species. $8 daily fee/pet. Service with restrictions, supervision.

[ASK] [S₀] [X] [➳]

Days Inn SH
(803) 798-5101. **$47-$59.** 911 Bush River Rd. I-26, exit 108 (Bush River Rd), just e. Int corridors. **Pets:** Accepted.

[ASK] [S₀] [X] [⌀] [🛏] [💻] [➳]

Holiday Inn Express Hotel & Suites SH
(803) 419-3558. **$82.** 1011 Clemson Frontage Rd. I-20, exit 80 (Clemson Rd), just n. Int corridors. **Pets:** Accepted.
ASK 🛇 📶 🖭 🖭 🌊

Holiday Inn-Northeast SH
(803) 736-3000. **$100.** 7510 Two Notch Rd. I-20, exit 74 (Two Notch Rd), just n; I-77, exit 17 (Two Notch Rd), 0.5 mi s. Int corridors. **Pets:** Small. $25 one-time fee/pet. Service with restrictions.
SAVE 🛇 📶 🖭 🖭 🍴 🌊 🛇

Microtel Inn SH
(803) 736-3237. **$53-$68.** 1520 Barbara Dr. I-20, exit 74 (Two Notch Rd), just n; I-77, exit 17 (Two Notch Rd), 0.5 mi s. Int corridors. **Pets:** Medium. $7 daily fee/pet. Supervision.
ASK 🛇 🛇 🖭 🖭 📶

Microtel Inn & Suites Harbison Area SH
(803) 772-1914. **$45-$55, 10 day notice.** 411 Piney Grove Rd. I-26, exit 104 (Piney Grove Rd), just sw. Int corridors. **Pets:** Medium. $10 one-time fee/pet. Service with restrictions, crate.
ASK 🛇 🛇 🌊 🛇 🖭 📶 🖭

Motel 6 SH
(803) 736-3900. **$44-$48.** 7541 Nates Rd. I-20, exit 74 (US 1), just n, then just e; I-77, exit 17 (US 1), 0.5 mi s, then e. Int corridors. **Pets:** Accepted.
🛇 🛇 🌊 🛇 🌊

Ramada Plaza Hotel SH
(803) 736-5600. **$94.** 8105 Two Notch Rd. I-77, exit 17 (Two Notch Rd), just ne. Int corridors. **Pets:** Other species. $75 deposit/room. Service with restrictions.
SAVE 🛇 🛇 🛇 🖭 🖭 🖭 🍴 🌊 🛇

Red Roof Inn-West M
(803) 798-9220. **$37-$49.** 10 Berryhill Rd. I-26, exit 106A westbound; exit 106 eastbound, just w. Ext corridors. **Pets:** Accepted.
SAVE 🛇 🛇 🖭

Residence Inn by Marriott SH
(803) 779-7000. **$79-$159.** 150 Stoneridge Dr. I-126, exit Greystone Blvd, just n, then just e. Ext corridors. **Pets:** Medium, other species. $10 daily fee/room, $50 one-time fee/room. Designated rooms, service with restrictions, supervision.
ASK 🛇 🛇 🛇 🖭 🖭 🖭 🌊 🛇

Sheraton Hotel & Conference Center LH
(803) 731-0300. **$89-$169.** 2100 Bush River Rd. I-20, exit 63 (Bush River Rd), just e; I-26, exit 108, 0.7 mi w. Int corridors. **Pets:** Accepted.
SAVE 🛇 🛇 🛇 🛇 🖭 🖭 🖭 🍴 🌊 🛇

Super 8 SH
(803) 772-7275. **$55-$75.** 773 St Andrews Rd. I-26, exit 106A westbound; exit 106 eastbound, just w. Ext corridors. **Pets:** Accepted.
ASK 🛇 🛇 🖭 🖭 🌊

TownePlace Suites by Marriott SH 🐾
(803) 781-9391. **$74-$79.** 350 Columbiana Dr. I-26, exit 103 (Harbison Blvd), just sw, then nw. Int corridors. **Pets:** Other species. $20 daily fee/room, $65 one-time fee/room. Service with restrictions.
ASK 🛇 🛇 🛇 🛇 🖭 🖭 🌊

DUNCAN

Days Inn SH
(864) 433-1122. **$52-$85.** 1386 E Main St. I-85, exit 63, just w on SR 290. Ext corridors. **Pets:** $25 one-time fee/room. Designated rooms, service with restrictions.
ASK 🛇 🛇 🛇 🖭 🖭 🌊

Hampton Inn & Suites Greenville/Duncan SH
(864) 486-8100. **$81-$129.** 108 Spartangreen Blvd. I-85, exit 63, just e. Int corridors. **Pets:** Accepted.
ASK 🛇 🛇 🖭 🖭 🌊

EASLEY

Jameson Inn SH
(864) 306-9000. **$70-$75.** 211 Dayton School Rd. Jct US 123 and SR 93, 1.2 mi ne on US 123; jct US 123 and SR 153, 1.5 mi sw. Ext corridors. **Pets:** Small. Service with restrictions, crate.
🛇 🛇 🖭 🖭 🌊

FLORENCE

Country Hearth Inn M
(843) 662-9421. **$45-$55.** 831 S Irby St. 1.3 mi s on US 301 and 52. Ext corridors. **Pets:** Accepted.
SAVE 🛇 🛇 🖭 🖭 🍴 🌊

Econo Lodge M
(843) 665-8558. **$39-$49.** 1811 W Lucas St. I-95, exit 164, just e. Ext corridors. **Pets:** Accepted.
ASK 🛇 🛇 🖭 🖭 🌊

Holiday Inn Express Civic Center M
(843) 664-2400. **$69-$99.** 150 Dunbarton Dr. I-95, exit 160A (I-20 business route), 0.3 mi e. Ext corridors. **Pets:** Accepted.
ASK 🛇 🛇 🛇 🛇 🖭 🖭 🌊

Holiday Inn Hotel & Suites SH
(843) 665-4555. **$89.** 1819 W Lucas St. I-95, exit 164, just e on US 52. Ext corridors. **Pets:** Medium. Designated rooms, service with restrictions.
SAVE 🛇 🛇 🌊 🛇 🛇 🖭 🖭 🍴 🌊

Howard Johnson Express Inn & Suites M 🐾
(843) 664-9494. **$65-$72.** 3821 Bancroft Rd. I-95, exit 157, 0.4 mi e on US 76. Ext corridors. **Pets:** Medium. $10 one-time fee/room. Service with restrictions, crate.
SAVE 🛇 🛇 🛇 🖭 🖭 🌊

Motel 6 #1250 M
(843) 667-6100. **$35-$48.** 1834 W Lucas St. I-95, exit 164, just e. Ext corridors. **Pets:** Small, other species. Service with restrictions, supervision.
🛇 🛇 🛇 🌊

❤❤ Ramada Inn 🆂🅷
(843) 669-4241. **$63, 3 day notice.** 2038 W Lucas St. I-95, exit 164, just w. Ext/int corridors. **Pets:** Accepted.
(A$K) 🆂🅳 ❌ 🍴 💻 🍴 🏊 ❌

AAA ❤❤ Red Roof Inn Ⓜ
(843) 678-9000. **$40-$54.** 2690 David McLeod Blvd. I-95, exit 160A (I-20 business route), 0.4 mi e, on service road. Ext corridors. **Pets:** Medium. Service with restrictions, supervision.
(SAVE) ❌ (𝖫ᴹ) 🅳 🔥

AAA ❤❤ Thunderbird Inn Ⓜ
(843) 669-1611. **$44-$49.** 2004 W Lucas St. I-95, exit 164, just w. Ext corridors. **Pets:** Accepted.
(SAVE) 🆂🅳 ❌ 🍴 🍴 🏊

THE GRAND STRAND AREA

GEORGETOWN

AAA ❤❤ Carolinian Inn 🆂🅷
(843) 546-5191. **$59-$79.** 706 Church St. US 17, 0.7 mi se of jct US 17/17 alternate route/701. Ext corridors. **Pets:** Service with restrictions.
(SAVE) 🆂🅳 ❌ 🅳 🍴 💻 🏊

❤❤ Jameson Inn Georgetown 🆂🅷
(843) 546-6090. **$72-$77.** 120 Church St. US 17, just w of the Intracoastal Waterway Bridge. Ext corridors. **Pets:** Small. Service with restrictions, crate.
❌ 🅳 🅳 🍴 💻 🏊

LITTLE RIVER

❤❤❤ Holiday Inn Hotel & Suites at Coquina Harbor 🆂🅷
(843) 281-9400. **$59-$199, 3 day notice.** 722 Hwy 17. At Coquina Harbor. Int corridors. **Pets:** Accepted.
(A$K) 🆂🅳 ❌ 🍴 💻 🍴 🏊

MYRTLE BEACH

AAA ❤❤ El Dorado Motel Ⓜ 🐾
(843) 626-3559. **$27-$125, 21 day notice.** 2800 S Ocean Blvd. 28th Ave S and S Ocean Blvd. Ext corridors. **Pets:** Small, dogs only. $10 daily fee/pet. Designated rooms, service with restrictions, supervision.
(SAVE) 🆂🅳 ❌ 🍴 💻 🏊 ❌

AAA ❤❤❤ La Quinta Inn & Suites 🆂🅷
(843) 916-8801. **$69-$169.** 1561 21st Ave N. US 17 Bypass, just e. Int corridors. **Pets:** Small. Service with restrictions, supervision.
(SAVE) 🆂🅳 ❌ (𝖫ᴹ) 🅳 🅳 🍴 💻 🏊

AAA ❤ Mariner Ⓜ
(843) 449-5281. **$39-$149.** 7003 N Ocean Blvd. 71st Ave N and N Ocean Blvd. Ext corridors. **Pets:** Accepted.
(SAVE) 🆂🅳 ❌ 🍴 🏊 ❌

AAA ❤❤ Red Roof Inn & Suites 🆂🅷
(843) 626-4444. **$31-$89.** 2801 S Kings Hwy. US 17 business route and 28th Ave S. Int corridors. **Pets:** Large. Service with restrictions, supervision.
(SAVE) ❌ 🅳 🍴 💻 🏊

AAA ❤❤ Sea Mist Oceanfront Resort 🅻🅷
(843) 448-1551. **$32-$167, 14 day notice.** 1200 S Ocean Blvd. 12th Ave S and S Ocean Blvd. Ext/int corridors. **Pets:** $50 one-time fee/pet. Designated rooms, service with restrictions, crate.
(SAVE) ❌ 🅳 🅳 🍴 🍴 🏊 ❌

❤❤❤ Staybridge Suites-Fantasy Harbour 🆂🅷 🐾
(843) 903-4000. **$79-$179.** 3163 Outlet Blvd. 1 mi w on US 501. Int corridors. **Pets:** Medium. $75 one-time fee/room. Designated rooms, service with restrictions, supervision.
(A$K) 🆂🅳 ❌ 🅳 🅳 🍴 💻 🏊 ❌

AAA ❤❤ St. John's Inn Ⓜ
(843) 449-5251. **$36-$109, 7 day notice.** 6803 N Ocean Blvd. 68th Ave N and N Ocean Blvd. Ext corridors. **Pets:** Accepted.
(SAVE) 🆂🅳 ❌ 🍴 🏊 ❌

NORTH MYRTLE BEACH

AAA ❤❤ Red Roof Inn 🆂🅷
(843) 280-4555. **$39-$79.** 1601-B Hwy 17 N. Jct US 17 and SR 9, just s. Int corridors. **Pets:** Small. $25 deposit/pet. Designated rooms, service with restrictions, supervision.
(SAVE) 🆂🅳 ❌ 🍴 🏊

PAWLEYS ISLAND

❤❤ Hammock Inn Ⓜ
(843) 237-4261. **$59-$125, 3 day notice.** 7903 Ocean Hwy. 1 mi s on US 17. Ext corridors. **Pets:** Small, dogs only. Service with restrictions, supervision.
(A$K) 🆂🅳 ❌ 🍴 💻 🍴 🏊

GAFFNEY

AAA ❤❤ Comfort Inn Ⓜ
(864) 487-4200. **$63-$75.** 143 Corona Dr. I-85, exit 92, just w of SR 11. Ext corridors. **Pets:** $10 one-time fee/room. Service with restrictions, crate.
(SAVE) 🆂🅳 ❌ 🅳 🍴 💻 🏊

❤❤ Jameson Inn Ⓜ
(864) 489-0240. **$66-$71.** 101 Stuard St. I-85, exit 92, just e at jct SR 11. Ext corridors. **Pets:** Small. Service with restrictions, crate.
❌ 🍴 💻 🏊

🐾 **END AREA** 🐾

GREENVILLE

AAA ▼▼▼▼ **AmeriSuites**
        (Greenville/Haywood) SH
(864) 232-3000. **$59-$109.** 40 W Orchard Park Dr. I-385, exit 39 (Haywood Rd), just n, then w. Int corridors. **Pets:** Small, other species. $40 one-time fee/room. Designated rooms, service with restrictions.
SAVE S⊘ ✕ &M ⊘ ✍ 🖥 🖵 ⇆

AAA ▼▼▼ **Comfort Inn Executive Center** SH
(864) 271-0060. **$55.** 540 N Pleasantburg Dr. I-385, exit 40 (US 291), just w, then just s. Ext corridors. **Pets:** Accepted.
SAVE S⊘ ✕ ⊘ 🖥 ⇆

▼▼▼▼ **Comfort Suites-Greenville/Greer** SH
(864) 213-9331. **$62-$79.** 2681 Dry Pocket Rd. I-85, exit 54 (Pelham Rd), just nw, 0.3 mi ne on The Parkway to Parkway Rd, then 0.3 mi e. Int corridors. **Pets:** Accepted.
ASK S⊘ ✕ ⊘ ✍ 🖥 🖵 ⇆ ✕

▼▼▼ **Crowne Plaza Hotel and Resort**
        Greenville SH
(864) 297-6300. **$120-$160.** 851 Congaree Rd. I-385, exit 37, just w, then n. Int corridors. **Pets:** Accepted.
ASK S⊘ ✕ &M ⊘ ✍ 🖥 🖵 ⊓ ⇆ ✕

▼▼▼ **Days Inn** SH
(864) 288-6221. **$55-$100.** 831 Congaree Rd. I-385, exit 37, just w, then n. Int corridors. **Pets:** $15 one-time fee/pet. Service with restrictions, supervision.
ASK S⊘ ✕ ⊘ 🖥 ⇆

▼▼▼▼ **GuestHouse International Suites Plus** SH
(864) 297-0099. **$59-$82.** 48 McPrice Ct. I-385, exit 39 (Haywood Rd), just n, then just e on Orchard Park Rd, just s. Ext corridors. **Pets:** Designated rooms, service with restrictions, crate.
ASK S⊘ ✕ ⊘ 🖥 🖵 ⇆ ✕

▼▼▼▼ **Hilton Greenville and Towers** SH
(864) 232-4747. **$79-$169.** 45 W Orchard Park Dr. I-385, exit 39 (Haywood Rd), just n, then w. Int corridors. **Pets:** Accepted.
ASK S⊘ ✕ &M ⊘ 🖥 🖵 ⊓ ⇆ ✕

▼▼▼▼ **Holiday Inn Augusta Rd/I-85** SH ❀
(864) 277-8921. **$110-$145.** 4295 Augusta Rd. I-85, exit 46, just s. Int corridors. **Pets:** $30 one-time fee/room. Service with restrictions, crate.
ASK S⊘ ✕ &M ⊘ ✍ 🖥 🖵 ⊓ ⇆

▼▼▼▼ **Holiday Inn Express Hotel & Suites** SH
(864) 678-5555. **$72.** 1036 Woodruff Rd. I-85, exit 51A, 0.5 mi n on SR 146. Int corridors. **Pets:** Accepted.
ASK S⊘ ✕ &M ⊘ 🖥 ⇆

AAA ▼▼▼▼ **La Quinta Inn** SH
(864) 297-3500. **$55-$75.** 31 Old Country Rd. I-85, exit 51A, just n on SR 146. Ext corridors. **Pets:** Accepted.
SAVE S⊘ ✕ ⊘ 🖥 🖵 ⇆

▼▼▼▼ **La Quinta Inns & Suites-Greenville**
        Haywood SH
(864) 233-8018. **$65-$85.** 65 W Orchard Park Dr. I-385, exit 39 (Haywood Rd), just n, then w. Int corridors. **Pets:** Accepted.
ASK S⊘ ✕ ⊘ ✍ 🖥 🖵 ⇆

AAA ▼▼▼▼ **MainStay Suites-Greenville** SH
(864) 987-5566. **$70-$80.** 2671 Dry Pocket Rd. I-85, exit 54 (Pelham Rd), just nw on Pelham Rd, 0.3 mi ne on The Parkway to Parkway Rd, then 0.3 mi e. Int corridors. **Pets:** Other species. $7 daily fee/pet. Service with restrictions, supervision.
SAVE S⊘ ✕ ⊘ ✍ 🖥 🖵 ⇆ ✕

▼▼ **Microtel Inn & Suites** SH
(864) 297-3811. **$49-$59, 7 day notice.** 1024 Woodruff Rd. I-85, exit 51A, 0.5 mi n on SR 146. Int corridors. **Pets:** Accepted.
ASK S⊘ ✕ ✍ 🖥 🖵

AAA ▼▼▼▼ **The Phoenix Greenville's Inn** SH
(864) 233-4651. **$95-$120, 3 day notice.** 246 N Pleasantburg Dr. I-385, exit 40B, 0.6 mi s on SR 291. Ext corridors. **Pets:** Medium, other species. Service with restrictions, supervision.
SAVE S⊘ ✕ ⊘ 🖥 🖵 ⊓ ⇆

AAA ▼▼ **Red Roof Inn** M
(864) 297-4458. **$38-$54.** 2801 Laurens Rd. I-85, exit 48A, just s on frontage road to dead end. Ext corridors. **Pets:** Accepted.
SAVE ✕ ⊘

AAA ▼▼▼▼ **Sleep Inn** SH ❀
(864) 240-2006. **$59-$109, 3 day notice.** 231 N Pleasantburg Dr. I-385, exit 40B, 0.6 mi s on SR 291. Int corridors. **Pets:** Medium. $20 one-time fee/room. Service with restrictions, crate.
SAVE S⊘ ✕ &M 🖥

GREENWOOD

▼▼ **Days Inn** SH
(864) 223-1818. **$55-$75, 3 day notice.** 230 Birchtree Dr. Jct US 25/US 25 Bypass (SR 72 NE), just ne on US 25 Bypass (SR 72 NE), then just s. Int corridors. **Pets:** Accepted.
ASK ✕ 🖥 🖵

HARDEEVILLE

AAA ▼▼▼ **Comfort Inn** M
(843) 784-2188. **$50-$106.** US 17 & I-95. I-95, exit 5 (US 17), just n. Ext/int corridors. **Pets:** Other species. $10 daily fee/pet. Service with restrictions, crate.
SAVE S⊘ ✕ ⇆

HILTON HEAD ISLAND

AAA ▼▼▼ **Comfort Inn** SH ❀
(843) 842-6662. **$59-$169.** 2 Tanglewood Dr. Over bridge, 7.9 mi sw on Cross Island Pkwy (toll), 1.3 mi se on Pope Ave to Coligny Cir, then just sw. Int corridors. **Pets:** Small, dogs only. $10 daily fee/pet, $25 one-time fee/pet. Service with restrictions, supervision.
SAVE S⊘ ✕ ⊘ 🖥 🖵 ⇆ ✕

AAA ▼▼▼▼ **Holiday Inn Express** SH
(843) 842-8888. **$50-$100.** 40 Waterside Dr. US 278, exit Pope Rd, 0.7 mi se. Ext corridors. **Pets:** Medium, dogs only. $40 one-time fee/room. Service with restrictions, crate.
SAVE S⊘ ✕ ⊘ ✍ 🖥 🖵 ⇆

▼▼ Motel 6 **M** ❀
(843) 785-2700. **$42-$66.** 830 William Hilton Pkwy. J Wilton
Graves Bridge, 9 mi e on US 278 business route. Ext
corridors. **Pets:** Large, other species. Service with restrictions, supervision.

🅰️ 🅲️ 🆗 🆎 ➿

▼▼▼▼ Quality Inn & Suites of Hilton Head
   Island **SH**
(843) 681-3655. **$59-$129, 3 day notice.** 200 Museum St.
3.3 mi e of J Wilton Graves Bridge on US 278. Ext corridors. **Pets:** Accepted.

🅰️🆂🅺 ❎ 🆎 🆗 🆎 ➿

◈◈◈ ▼▼◈ Red Roof Inn-Hilton Head **M**
(843) 686-6808. **$44-$94.** 5 Regency Pkwy. Over bridge, 9
mi e on US 278; between Shipyard Plantation and Palmetto
Dunes. Ext corridors. **Pets:** Accepted.

🆂🅰️🆅🅴 ❎ 🆎 🆎 ➿

IRMO

◈◈◈ ▼▼▼▼ AmeriSuites (Columbia/I-26) **SH**
(803) 407-1560. **$69-$89.** 1130 Kinley Rd. I-26, exit 102B,
just e, then n. Int corridors. **Pets:** Accepted.

🆂🅰️🆅🅴 🆂🅰️ ❎ 🆗🅼 🆎 🅲️ 🆎 🆗 ➿

◈◈◈ ▼▼▼◈ Wellesley Inn & Suites
   (Columbia/I-26) **SH**
(803) 781-8590. **$59-$89.** 1170 Kinley Rd. I-26, exit 102B,
just e, then n. Int corridors. **Pets:** Accepted.

🆂🅰️🆅🅴 🆂🅰️ ❎ 🆗🅼 🆎 🅲️ 🆎 🆗 ➿

LAKE CITY

▼▼ Days Inn **M** ❀
(843) 394-3269. **$65.** 170 S Ron McNair Blvd (US 52). I-95,
exit 135, jct US 52/378 business route, just s. Ext corridors.
Pets: Medium. $10 daily fee/pet. Designated rooms, no
service, supervision.

🅰️🆂🅺 🆂🅰️ ❎ 🆎 ➿

LANCASTER

▼▼ Jameson Inn **M**
(803) 283-1188. **$67-$72.** 114 Commerce Blvd. Jct SR 9
Bypass and US 521, 1 mi w on SR 9 Bypass. Ext corridors.
Pets: Small. Service with restrictions, crate.

❎ 🆗🅼 🆎 🅲️ 🆎 🆗 ➿

LANDRUM

▼▼▼▼ The Red Horse Inn **CA** ❀
(864) 909-1575. **$105-$235, 7 day notice.** 310 N Campbell
Rd. Jct SR 14, 1 mi w on SR 11, 1 mi s on Tugaloo Rd. Ext
corridors. **Pets:** Medium. $50 deposit/pet, $20 one-time fee/
pet. Designated rooms, service with restrictions, supervision.

🅰️🆂🅺 🆂🅰️ ❎ 🆎 🆗 ❌

LUGOFF

▼▼▼▼ Ramada Limited **M**
(803) 438-1807. **$60.** 542 Hwy 601 S. I-20, exit 92 (US 601),
just n. Ext corridors. **Pets:** Small. $5 daily fee/room. Desig-
nated rooms, service with restrictions, supervision.

🅰️🆂🅺 🆂🅰️ ❎ 🆎 ➿

▼▼ Travel Inn **SH**
(803) 438-4961. **$35-$85.** 928 Hwy 1 S. I-20, exit 92 (US
601), 2.8 mi n. Ext corridors. **Pets:** Large, other species.
$10 daily fee/pet. Designated rooms, no service, supervi-
sion.

🅰️🆂🅺 🆂🅰️ ❎ 🆎 🆗 ➿

MANNING

◈◈◈ ▼▼▼ Best Western Palmetto Inn **SH**
(803) 473-4021. **$59.** 2825 Paxville Hwy. I-95, exit 119 (US
261), just se. Ext corridors. **Pets:** Small, other species. $5
daily fee/pet. Service with restrictions, supervision.

🆂🅰️🆅🅴 🆂🅰️ ❎ 🆎 🆗 ➿

◈◈◈ ▼▼▼ Comfort Inn **SH**
(803) 473-7550. **$66-$70.** Hwy 261 & I-95. I-95, exit 119 (SR
261), just se. Ext corridors. **Pets:** Other species. $8 one-
time fee/room. Service with restrictions, supervision.

🆂🅰️🆅🅴 🆂🅰️ ❎ 🆎 🆎 🆗 ➿

◈◈◈ ▼▼▼▼ Ramada Limited **SH** ❀
(803) 473-5135. **$46-$85.** 2816 Paxville Hwy. I-95, exit 119
(SR 261), just se. Ext corridors. **Pets:** Other species. Service with restrictions.

🆂🅰️🆅🅴 🆂🅰️ ❎ 🆎 🆎 🆗 🆎 ➿

NEWBERRY

◈◈◈ ▼▼▼ Best Western Newberry Inn **SH**
(803) 276-5850. **$50-$60.** 11701 S Carolina Hwy 34. I-26,
exit 74 (SR 34), just ne. Ext corridors. **Pets:** Small, dogs
only. $5 daily fee/pet. Service with restrictions, supervision.

🆂🅰️🆅🅴 🆂🅰️ ❎ 🆎 🆗 ➿

ORANGEBURG

◈◈◈ ▼▼▼ Comfort Inn & Suites **SH**
(803) 531-9200. **$62-$72.** 3671 St Matthews Rd. I-26, exit
145A (US 601), just sw. Ext corridors. **Pets:** Other species.
$10 one-time fee/pet. Designated rooms, service with
restrictions.

🆂🅰️🆅🅴 🆂🅰️ ❎ 🆎 🅲️ 🆎 🆗 ➿

◈◈◈ ▼▼▼ Days Inn **SH**
(803) 534-0500. **$58-$85.** 3402 Five Chop Rd. I-26, exit
154B (US 301), just e. Ext corridors. **Pets:** Other species.
$7 one-time fee/pet. Designated rooms, service with restric-
tions, supervision.

🆂🅰️🆅🅴 🆂🅰️ ❎ 🅲️ 🆎 🆗 🍴 ➿

▼▼ Jameson Inn Orangeburg **SH**
(803) 534-1611. **$66-$71.** 2350 Chestnut St NE. I-26, exit
145A (US 601), 3.9 mi sw to jct US 601 and 21/178
Bypass, then 2 mi nw. Ext corridors. **Pets:** Small. Service
with restrictions, crate.

❎ 🅲️ 🆎 🆗 ➿

◈◈◈ ▼▼▼ Orangeburg Days Inn **SH** ❀
(803) 531-2590. **$45-$150.** 3691 St Matthews Rd. I-26, exit
145A (US 601), just sw. Ext corridors. **Pets:** Medium. $7
daily fee/pet. Service with restrictions, supervision.

🆂🅰️🆅🅴 🆂🅰️ ❎ 🆎 🆗 ➿

AAA WWWW Quality Inn & Suites **SH** ❀
(803) 531-4600. **$55-$100.** 1415 John C Calhoun Dr. I-26, exit 154A (US 301) northbound, 8.6 mi nw; exit 145A (US 601) southbound, 5.9 mi sw. Ext corridors. **Pets:** $10 one-time fee/pet. Service with restrictions, crate.

`SAVE` `SD` `X` `GM` `F` `B` `D` `TI` `~`

POINT SOUTH

WWWW Holiday Inn Express Point
     South/Yemassee **SH**
(843) 726-9400. **$85-$89.** 40 Frampton Dr. I-95, exit 33, just ne on US 17. Int corridors. **Pets:** Accepted.

`ASK` `SD` `X` `GM` `&` `B` `D` `~`

RIDGELAND

WWWW Comfort Inn **M**
(843) 726-2121. **$50-$75.** Hwy 336 & I-95. I-95, exit 21, just nw. Ext/int corridors. **Pets:** Accepted.

`ASK` `SD` `X` `D` `B` `D` `~`

AAA WWWW Ramada Limited Ridgeland **M**
(843) 717-9595. **$59-$90.** Hwy 336 & I-95. I-95, exit 21, just nw. Ext corridors. **Pets:** Medium. $50 deposit/pet, $10 daily fee/pet. No service, supervision.

`SAVE` `X` `B` `D` `~`

ROCK HILL

AAA WWWWW Best Western Inn **M**
(803) 329-1330. **$60-$90.** 1106 N Anderson Rd. I-77, exit 82B, 0.6 mi w on US 21 to US 21 Bypass. Int corridors. **Pets:** Other species. $10 daily fee/room. Service with restrictions.

`SAVE` `SD` `X` `B` `D` `~`

WWWWW The Book & the Spindle **BB**
(803) 328-1913. **$95-$425, 14 day notice.** 626 Oakland Ave. I-77, exit 82B, 3.1 mi s on US 21; before Aiken. Int corridors. **Pets:** Small, other species. $10 deposit/room. Service with restrictions, crate.

`X` `B` `D` `Z`

AAA WWWWW Holiday Inn **SH**
(803) 329-1122. **$59-$99.** 2640 N Cherry Rd. I-77, exit 82A, just e. Int corridors. **Pets:** Accepted.

`SAVE` `SD` `X` `&` `B` `D` `TI` `~`

ST. GEORGE

AAA WWW American Inn **M**
(843) 563-2360. **$40-$55.** 125 Motel Dr. I-95, exit 77 (US 78), just e. Ext corridors. **Pets:** Dogs only. Designated rooms, no service, supervision.

`SAVE` `SD` `X` `B` `~`

AAA WWW WWW Best Western-St. George **SH**
(843) 563-2277. **$59-$79, 10 day notice.** 104 Interstate Dr. I-95, exit 77 (US 78), just w. Ext corridors. **Pets:** Accepted.

`SAVE` `SD` `X` `D` `~`

AAA WWW WWW Comfort Inn **SH**
(843) 563-4180. **$61-$91.** 139 Motel Dr. I-95, exit 77 (US 78), just e. Ext corridors. **Pets:** Other species. $10 one-time fee/room. Service with restrictions.

`SAVE` `SD` `X` `D` `~`

AAA WWW Econo Lodge **M**
(843) 563-4195. **$50-$65.** 5971 W Jim Bilton Blvd. I-95, exit 77 (US 78), just e. Ext corridors. **Pets:** Small. $5 daily fee/pet. Designated rooms, service with restrictions, supervision.

`SAVE` `SD` `X` `B` `D` `~`

WWW WWW Peach Tree Inn **SH**
(843) 636-9393. **Call for rates.** 111 Connors Dr. I-95, exit 82 (US 178), just se. Ext corridors. **Pets:** Accepted.

`X` `&` `B` `D`

WWW WWW Quality Inn-St. George **SH** ❀
(843) 563-4581. **$49-$59.** 6014 W Jim Bilton Blvd. I-95, exit 77 (US 78), just e. Ext corridors. **Pets:** Medium. $10 daily fee/room. Service with restrictions, supervision.

`ASK` `SD` `X` `&` `D` `~`

SANTEE

AAA WWWW Comfort Inn **SH**
(803) 854-3221. **$50-$75.** 249 Britain St. I-95, exit 98 (SR 6), just nw, then just s. Ext corridors. **Pets:** $10 one-time fee/room. Designated rooms, service with restrictions, supervision.

`SAVE` `X` `D` `&` `B` `D` `~`

WWW WWW Days Inn **SH**
(803) 854-2175. **$45-$50.** 9074 Old Hwy 6. I-95, exit 98 (SR 6), just se. Ext corridors. **Pets:** Small. $6 daily fee/pet. Designated rooms, no service, supervision.

`ASK` `SD` `X` `D` `B` `D` `~`

AAA WWW WWW Howard Johnson Express Inn **M**
(803) 854-3870. **$48-$62.** 9112 Old #6 Hwy. I-95, exit 98 (SR 6), 0.4 mi se. Ext corridors. **Pets:** Accepted.

`SAVE` `SD` `X` `B` `D` `~`

WWW WWW Super 8 Motel **M**
(803) 854-3456. **$39-$44.** 9125 Old Hwy 6. I-95, exit 98 (SR 6), 0.4 mi se. Ext corridors. **Pets:** Accepted.

`X` `B` `D` `~`

SENECA

WWW WWW Jameson Inn **M**
(864) 888-8300. **$67-$72.** 226 Hi-Tech Rd. Jct US 76 and SR 28/123, 1 mi s. Ext corridors. **Pets:** Small. Service with restrictions, crate.

`X` `GM` `D` `&` `B` `D` `~`

SIMPSONVILLE

WWW WWW Days Inn **SH** ❀
(864) 963-7701. **$55-$75.** 45 Ray E Talley Ct. I-385, exit 27, 0.4 mi s, then just e. Ext corridors. **Pets:** Large. $10 daily fee/pet. Designated rooms, service with restrictions, supervision.

`ASK` `SD` `X` `B` `D` `~`

SPARTANBURG

WWW WWW Brookwood Inn Spartanburg **SH**
(864) 576-6080. **$45-$79.** 4930 College Dr. I-85, exit 69 northbound, just n on I-85 business route, exit 1, just w, then n on the frontage road; I-85 business route, exit 1 southbound. Ext corridors. **Pets:** Accepted.

`ASK` `SD` `X` `D` `B` `D` `~`

▼▼▼ **Holiday Inn Express Hotel & Suites** SH
(864) 699-7777. **$85.** 895 Spartan Blvd. I-26, exit 21B (US 29), just e, then 1 mi on Blackstock Rd. Int corridors. **Pets:** Other species. $35 one-time fee/room. Service with restrictions, supervision.

ASK Sᴅ ✕ ♪ ⟨ꞏ⟩ 🖥 🖂 ≈

SUMMERTON

▼▼ **Days Inn of Summerton** M
(803) 485-2865. **$33-$75.** 18 Bluff Blvd. I-95, exit 108, just n. Ext corridors. **Pets:** Medium. Service with restrictions, supervision.

ASK Sᴅ ✕ 🖥 🖂 ≈

SUMTER

▼▼▼ **Magnolia House** BB ✿
(803) 775-6694. **$85-$105.** 230 Church St. US 76 business route/521 (Broad St), just s; between Broad and Haynsworth sts. Int corridors. **Pets:** Other species. $10 one-time fee/pet. Supervision.

✕

⟨AAA⟩ ▼▼▼▼ **Ramada Inn** SH ✿
(803) 775-2323. **$75-$85.** 226 N Washington St. US 76 business route/521 (Broad St), just n. Ext corridors. **Pets:** Medium. $50 deposit/room, $8 daily fee/room. Service with restrictions.

SAVE Sᴅ ✕ ♪ 🖥 🖂 🍴 ≈

TURBEVILLE

⟨AAA⟩ ▼▼▼ **Days Inn** SH
(843) 659-8060. **$43-$100.** Hwy 378. I-95, exit 135 (US 378), just e. Ext corridors. **Pets:** Accepted.

SAVE Sᴅ ✕ ≈

⟨AAA⟩ ▼▼ **Knights Inn-Turbeville** M
(843) 659-2175. **$39-$80.** 7840 Myrtle Beach Hwy. I-95, exit 135 (US 378), just e. Ext corridors. **Pets:** Other species. $5 one-time fee/room. Service with restrictions.

SAVE Sᴅ ✕ 🖥 🍴 ≈

WALTERBORO

⟨AAA⟩ ▼▼▼ **Best Western of Walterboro** SH ✿
(843) 538-3600. **$49-$89.** 1428 Sniders Hwy. I-95, exit 53 (SR 63), just e. Ext corridors. **Pets:** Small. $6 daily fee/pet. Designated rooms, service with restrictions, supervision.

SAVE Sᴅ ✕ ♪ 🖥 ≈

⟨AAA⟩ ▼▼▼ **Econo Lodge** SH
(843) 538-3830. **$45-$85.** 1145 Sniders Hwy. I-95, exit 53 (SR 63), just e. Ext corridors. **Pets:** Medium, other species. $10 daily fee/pet. Designated rooms, service with restrictions, supervision.

SAVE Sᴅ ✕ 🖥 🖂

▼▼▼ **Howard Johnson Express** SH
(843) 538-5473. **$40-$60.** 1286 Sniders Hwy. I-95, exit 53 (SR 63), just e. Ext corridors. **Pets:** Medium, other species. $5 daily fee/pet. Designated rooms, service with restrictions, supervision.

ASK Sᴅ ✕ ♪ ⟨ꞏ⟩ 🖥 ≈

⟨AAA⟩ ▼▼ **Rice Planters Inn** M
(843) 538-8964. **$35-$39.** I-95 & SR 63. I-95, exit 53 (SR 63), just e. Ext corridors. **Pets:** Accepted.

SAVE Sᴅ ✕ ≈

⟨AAA⟩ ▼▼▼ **Super 8 Motel** M
(843) 538-5383. **$41-$56, 7 day notice.** 1972 Bells Hwy. I-95, exit 57 (SR 64), just nw. Ext corridors. **Pets:** Small, other species. $5 daily fee/pet. Designated rooms, service with restrictions, supervision.

SAVE Sᴅ ✕ 🖥 ≈

⟨AAA⟩ ▼▼ **Thunderbird Inn** M
(843) 538-2503. **$33-$43.** I-95, exit 53 (SR 63), just e. Ext corridors. **Pets:** Medium, other species. Service with restrictions, supervision.

SAVE Sᴅ ✕

WINNSBORO

▼▼ **Days Inn** M
(803) 635-1447. **$47-$60, 7 day notice.** 1894 US Hwy 321 Bypass. I-77, exit 34 (SR 34), 6.5 mi w, at jct US 321/SR 34/213. Ext corridors. **Pets:** Medium. $5 daily fee/pet. Designated rooms, service with restrictions, supervision.

ASK Sᴅ ✕ ♪ 🖥 ≈

⟨AAA⟩ ▼▼▼ **Fairfield Motel** M
(803) 635-3458. **$40-$50.** 115 S 321 Bypass. Jct SR 213/US 321 S Bypass, 1.8 mi n. Ext corridors. **Pets:** Small, dogs only. $5 daily fee/pet. Service with restrictions, supervision.

SAVE Sᴅ ✕ 🖥 ≈

SOUTH DAKOTA

CITY INDEX

ABERDEEN

◆◆ ◆◆ Aberdeen East Super 8 Motel SH
(605) 229-5005. **Call for rates.** 2405 6th Ave SE. 1.8 mi e on US 12. Int corridors. **Pets:** Medium, dogs only. $6 daily fee/pet. Designated rooms, service with restrictions, supervision.

◆◆ ◆◆ Aberdeen North Super 8 Motel SH
(605) 226-2288. **Call for rates.** 770 NW Hwy 281. On US 281, 1.5 mi nw. Int corridors. **Pets:** Medium, dogs only. $6 daily fee/pet. Designated rooms, service with restrictions, supervision.

◆◆ ◆◆ Aberdeen West Super 8 Motel SH
(605) 225-1711. **Call for rates.** 714 S Hwy 281. Jct US 12 and 281. Int corridors. **Pets:** Medium, dogs only. $6 daily fee/pet. Designated rooms, service with restrictions, supervision.

◆◆ ◆◆ ◆ AmericInn Lodge & Suites of Aberdeen SH
(605) 225-4565. **$79-$189.** 310 Centennial St. 2.2 mi e on US 12, just n. Int corridors. **Pets:** Accepted.

◆◆ ◆◆ ◆ Best Western Ramkota Hotel SH
(605) 229-4040. **$84.** 1400 8th Ave NW. 1.5 mi nw on US 281. Ext/int corridors. **Pets:** Medium, other species. Designated rooms, supervision.

◆◆ ◆◆ ◆ Comfort Inn SH
(605) 226-0097. **$59-$69.** 2923 6th Ave SE. 2 mi e on US 12. Int corridors. **Pets:** Accepted.

◆◆ ◆◆ ◆ Holiday Inn Express Hotel & Suites SH
(605) 725-4000. **$79-$155.** 3310 7th Ave SE. 2.1 mi e on US 12. Int corridors. **Pets:** Small, dogs only. $50 deposit/pet, $5 daily fee/pet. No service, supervision.

◆◆ ◆◆ ◆ Ramada Inn SH
(605) 225-3600. **$74-$84.** 2727 6th Ave SE. 2 mi e on US 12. Ext/int corridors. **Pets:** Medium. Designated rooms, supervision.

BERESFORD

◆◆ ◆◆ Super 8 Motel SH
(605) 763-2001. **$47-$58.** 1410 W Cedar. I-29, exit 47, just e. Int corridors. **Pets:** Other species. $5 one-time fee/room. Service with restrictions, supervision.

BLACK HILLS AREA

BELLE FOURCHE

◆◆ Ace Motel M
(605) 892-2612. **$28-$48.** 109 6th Ave. 0.5 mi n via US 85, just e, just s of US 212 Bypass. Ext corridors. **Pets:** Medium. $4 one-time fee/pet. Designated rooms, service with restrictions, supervision.

◆◆ ◆ Lariat Motel M
(605) 892-2601. **$30-$45.** 1033 Elkhorn. 0.8 mi e of US 85 on Business 212 (State St). Ext corridors. **Pets:** Medium. $3 daily fee/room. Service with restrictions, supervision.

BLACK HAWK

◆◆ ◆◆ Black Hawk Super 8 SH
(605) 787-4844. **Call for rates.** 7900 Stagestop Rd. I-90, exit 48, just s. Int corridors. **Pets:** Accepted.

CUSTER

◆◆ ◆◆ ◆ Bavarian Inn Motel SH
(605) 673-2802. **$48-$112, 3 day notice.** 1000 N 5th St. 1 mi n on US 16 and 385. Ext/int corridors. **Pets:** Accepted.

◆◆ ◆◆ ◆ Chief Motel M
(605) 673-2318. **$39-$88.** 120 Mt. Rushmore Rd. Just w on US 16. Ext corridors. **Pets:** Accepted.

◆◆ ◆◆ ◆ Rocket Motel M
(605) 673-4401. **$34-$64.** 211 Mt. Rushmore Rd. On US 16; center. Ext corridors. **Pets:** Other species. $5 daily fee/room. Supervision.

◆ **The Roost Resort** CA
(605) 673-2326. **$49-$158, 10 day notice.** US 16 A. 2 mi e on US Alternate Rt 16. Ext corridors. **Pets:** Other species. $50 deposit/room. No service, supervision.

[X] [🔒] [📺] [☎]

◆◆ **Super 8 Custer** SH
(605) 673-2200. **$45-$109.** 415 W Mt. Rushmore Rd. US 16, 0.8 mi w. Int corridors. **Pets:** Other species. $5 daily fee/pet. Designated rooms, supervision.

[ASK] [S6] [X] [➿]

DEADWOOD

◆◆◆ ◆ **Budget Host Jackpot Inn** M
(605) 578-7791. **$33-$70.** US Hwy 385. 0.3 mi s of jct US 385 and 85. Int corridors. **Pets:** Small, dogs only. $50 deposit/room, $5 daily fee/pet. Designated rooms, service with restrictions, supervision.

[SAVE] [S6] [X] [➿]

◆◆◆ ◆◆ **Deadwood Gulch Resort** SH
(605) 578-1294. **$39-$225.** 12 Timm Ln. 0.7 mi s on US 85 S. Ext/int corridors. **Pets:** Accepted.

[SAVE] [S6] [X] [🔒] [📺] [🍴] [➿] [X]

◆◆◆ ◆◆◆ **First Gold Hotel** SH
(605) 578-9777. **$59-$159.** 270 Main St. 0.7 mi n on US 85. Int corridors. **Pets:** Small. $50 deposit/room. Designated rooms, service with restrictions, supervision.

[SAVE] [S6] [X] [🔒] [📺] [🍴]

HILL CITY

◆◆◆ ◆◆◆◆ **Best Western Golden Spike Inn** SH
(605) 574-2577. **$59-$137.** 106 Main St. Just n on US 16 and 385. Ext/int corridors. **Pets:** $10 one-time fee/pet. Designated rooms, service with restrictions, supervision.

[SAVE] [S6] [X] [🔒] [📺] [🍴] [➿] [X]

◆◆◆ ◆◆◆ **Lantern Inn** M
(605) 574-2582. **$44-$120, 3 day notice.** 430 E Main St. On north side of town, on US 16/385. Ext corridors. **Pets:** Small. $10 daily fee/pet. Designated rooms, supervision.

[SAVE] [S6] [X] [🔒] [➿]

◆◆◆ ◆◆◆◆ **The Lodge at Palmer Gulch** SH
(605) 574-2525. **$50-$192, 10 day notice.** 12620 SR 244. On SR 244, 5 mi w of Mt. Rushmore. Int corridors. **Pets:** Other species. Designated rooms, service with restrictions, supervision.

[SAVE] [S6] [X] [🔒] [📺] [🍴] [➿] [X]

HOT SPRINGS

◆◆◆ ◆◆◆ **Budget Host Hills Inn** M
(605) 745-3130. **$52-$142.** 640 S 6th St. 0.5 mi se off US 18 and 385. Ext corridors. **Pets:** Accepted.

[SAVE] [S6] [X] [🔒] [➿]

◆◆◆ ◆◆◆ **Comfort Inn** SH
(605) 745-7378. **$69-$159.** 737 S 6th St. 0.5 mi se off US 18 and 385. Int corridors. **Pets:** Medium. Designated rooms, service with restrictions, supervision.

[SAVE] [S6] [X] [&M] [🔒] [📺] [➿]

◆◆◆ ◆◆◆ **Hot Springs Super 8 Motel** SH
(605) 745-3888. **$54-$116.** 800 Mammoth St. US 18 Bypass. Int corridors. **Pets:** Medium, other species. $25 deposit/room, $10 one-time fee/room. Service with restrictions, supervision.

[SAVE] [S6] [X] [📺] [🔒]

KEYSTONE

◆◆◆ ◆◆◆ **Powder House Lodge** CA
(605) 666-4646. **$55-$175.** 24125 Hwy 16A. 1.5 mi n. Ext corridors. **Pets:** Accepted.

[SAVE] [🔒] [📺] [🍴] [➿]

◆◆◆ ◆◆◆ **Rushmore Express** M
(605) 666-4483. **$61-$159.** 320 Old Cemetary Rd. S on US 16A to Tramway, then just e. Ext/int corridors. **Pets:** Accepted.

[SAVE] [X] [📺] [🔒] [📺]

LEAD

◆◆◆ ◆◆◆ **Golden Hills Inn** SH
(605) 584-1800. **$34-$92.** 900 Miners Ave. US 85 and 14A; center. Int corridors. **Pets:** $25 deposit/room. Service with restrictions, supervision.

[SAVE] [S6] [X] [&M] [📺] [🔒] [🍴]

◆◆◆ ◆◆◆ **Palace Hotels, Palace Express** SH
(605) 584-2000. **$34-$92, 3 day notice.** 395 Glendale Dr. US 14A, 0.3 mi n. Int corridors. **Pets:** $25 deposit/room. Service with restrictions, supervision.

[SAVE] [S6] [X] [📺] [&M] [🔒]

PIEDMONT

◆◆◆ ◆◆◆ **Elk Creek Resort & Lodge** M
(605) 787-4884. **$49-$99, 14 day notice.** 8220 Elk Creek Rd. I-90, exit 46, 1 mi e. Ext corridors. **Pets:** Accepted.

[SAVE] [S6] [X] [🔒] [📺] [➿] [X]

RAPID CITY

◆◆◆ ◆◆◆◆ **Alex Johnson Hotel** SH
(605) 342-1210. **$82-$160, 3 day notice.** 523 6th St. I-90, exit 57, s on I-190, left at Omaha; downtown. Int corridors. **Pets:** Small. $25 one-time fee/room. Designated rooms, service with restrictions, supervision.

[SAVE] [S6] [X] [📺] [🔒] [📺] [🍴]

◆◆◆ ◆◆◆◆ **Comfort Inn & Suites** SH
(605) 718-4444. **$84-$199.** 915 Fairmont Blvd. 1.4 mi s on US 16. Int corridors. **Pets:** Accepted.

[SAVE] [S6] [X] [&M] [📺] [🔒] [🔒] [📺] [➿] [X]

◆◆◆ ◆◆◆ **Econo Lodge of Rapid City** SH ❀
(605) 342-6400. **$52-$119.** 625 E Disk Dr. I-90, exit 59 (Lacrosse St), just ne. Ext/int corridors. **Pets:** Other species. $10 daily fee/room. Designated rooms, service with restrictions, supervision.

[ASK] [S6] [X] [🔒] [📺] [➿] [X]

◆◆◆ ◆◆◆ **Fair Value Inn** M
(605) 342-8118. **$38-$72.** 1607 Lacrosse St. I-90, exit 59 (Lacrosse St), 0.3 mi s. Ext corridors. **Pets:** Very small, dogs only. Designated rooms, service with restrictions, supervision.

[SAVE] [S6] [X]

⬥⬥ ▼▼ Foothills Inn SH
(605) 348-5640. **$29-$119.** 1625 N Lacrosse St. I-90, exit 59 (Lacrosse St), just s. Int corridors. **Pets:** $10 one-time fee/room. Designated rooms, service with restrictions, crate.
🅂🄰🅅🄴 🆂 ✕ ⬛ ➷

⬥⬥ ▼▼ Gold Star Motel M
(605) 341-7051. **$36-$68.** 801 E North. I-90, exit 60, 1.5 mi sw on I-90 business loop, 1.2 mi s, then just e, from exit 59 (Lacrosse St). Ext corridors. **Pets:** Medium, other species. $5 daily fee/pet. Service with restrictions, supervision.
🅂🄰🅅🄴 🆂 ✕ 🖵

▼▼▼ Holiday Inn Express Hotel & Suites, I-90 SH
(605) 355-9090. **$70-$225.** 645 E Disk Dr. I-90, exit 59, just ne. Int corridors. **Pets:** Accepted.
🄰🅂🄺 🆂 ✕ ♿ 🗘 🄫 ⬛ 🖵 ➷ ✕

⬥⬥ ▼▼▼ Holiday Inn-Rushmore Plaza LH
(605) 348-4000. **$69-$134.** 505 N 5th St. I-90, exit 58, 1.3 mi s on Haines. Int corridors. **Pets:** Accepted.
🅂🄰🅅🄴 🆂 ✕ ♿ 🗘 🄫 ⬛ 🖵 🍴 ➷ ✕

⬥⬥ ▼▼ Microtel Inn & Suites SH
(605) 348-2523. **$59-$125.** 1740 Rapp St. I-90, exit 59 (Lacrosse St), just se. Int corridors. **Pets:** Small, other species. $10 daily fee/room. Designated rooms, supervision.
🅂🄰🅅🄴 🆂 ✕ ♿ 🗘 🄫 ⬛ 🖵 ➷

▼▼ Motel 6-352 M ♣
(605) 343-3687. **$40-$78.** 620 E Latrobe St. I-90, exit 59 (Lacrosse St). Ext corridors. **Pets:** Service with restrictions, supervision.
🆂 ✕ 🄫 ⬛ ➷

▼▼ Quality Inn SH
(605) 342-3322. **$69-$129.** 1902 Lacrosse St. I-90, exit 59 (Lacrosse St), just s. Ext/int corridors. **Pets:** Large. $10 daily fee/room. Service with restrictions, crate.
🄰🅂🄺 🆂 ✕ ♿ ⬛ 🖵 ➷ ✕

⬥⬥ ▼▼▼ Ramada Inn Gold Key SH
(605) 342-1300. **$69-$199.** 1721 N Lacrosse St. I-90, exit 59 (Lacrosse St), just s. Int corridors. **Pets:** Large. $10 one-time fee/room. Designated rooms, service with restrictions, crate.
🅂🄰🅅🄴 🆂 ✕ ♿ ⬛ 🖵 ➷ ✕

⬥⬥ ▼▼▼ Red Roof Inn SH
(605) 343-5434. **$60-$120.** 620 Howard St. I-90, exit 58, just nw of Haines Ave. Int corridors. **Pets:** Medium. Designated rooms, service with restrictions, supervision.
🅂🄰🅅🄴 🆂 ✕ ➷

⬥⬥ ▼▼ Rodeway Inn SH
(605) 342-1303. **$45-$189.** 2208 Mt. Rushmore Rd. 1 mi s on US 16. Ext corridors. **Pets:** Other species. Designated rooms, service with restrictions.
🅂🄰🅅🄴 🆂 ✕ ⬛ 🖵 🍴 ➷

▼▼ Super 8 Motel-North SH
(605) 348-8070. **$40-$170, 14 day notice.** 2124 Lacrosse St. I-90, exit 59 (Lacrosse St), just n. Int corridors. **Pets:** Medium. $7 daily fee/pet. Service with restrictions, supervision.
🄰🅂🄺 🆂 ✕ ♿ 🗘 🄫 ⬛

⬥⬥ ▼▼ Super 8 Motel-South SH
(605) 342-4911. **$45-$105.** 2520 Tower Rd. 1.4 mi s on US 16. Int corridors. **Pets:** Accepted.
🅂🄰🅅🄴 🆂 ✕ ⬛

⬥⬥ ▼▼ Thrifty Motor Inn M
(605) 342-0551. **$38-$72.** 1303 Lacrosse St. I-90, exit 59 (Lacrosse St), 0.5 mi s. Ext corridors. **Pets:** Very small, dogs only. Designated rooms, service with restrictions, supervision.
🅂🄰🅅🄴 🆂 ✕

ROCKERVILLE

▼ Rockerville Trading Post & Motel M ♣
(605) 341-4880. **$55-$75, 3 day notice.** 13525 Main St. Center. Ext corridors. **Pets:** Dogs only. $5 daily fee/room. Designated rooms, service with restrictions, supervision.
🆂 ✕ ➷

SPEARFISH

⬥⬥ ▼▼ Best Western Black Hills Lodge SH
(605) 642-7795. **$60-$160.** 540 E Jackson. I-90, exit 12, just s. Ext/int corridors. **Pets:** Other species. $5 daily fee/pet. Designated rooms, service with restrictions, supervision.
🅂🄰🅅🄴 🆂 ✕ 🗘 ⬛ ➷ ✕

▼▼ Days Inn SH
(605) 642-7101. **$62-$98.** 240 Ryan Rd. I-90, exit 10, 1.2 mi s. Ext/int corridors. **Pets:** Medium. $10 daily fee/pet. Service with restrictions, supervision.
🄰🅂🄺 🆂 ✕

⬥⬥ ▼▼▼ Holiday Inn Hotel & Convention Center SH
(605) 642-4683. **$72-$105, 30 day notice.** 305 N 27th St. I-90, exit 14 (Spearfish Canyon), just n. Ext/int corridors. **Pets:** Medium, other species. $10 one-time fee/pet. Service with restrictions, supervision.
🅂🄰🅅🄴 🆂 ✕ ♿ 🗘 🄫 ⬛ 🖵 🍴 ➷ ✕

⬥⬥ ▼ Royal Rest Motel M
(605) 642-3842. **$30-$50.** 444 Main St. On US 14/85; downtown. Ext corridors. **Pets:** Medium. Service with restrictions, supervision.
🅂🄰🅅🄴 🆂 ✕ ⬛

⬥⬥ ▼▼▼ Spearfish Canyon Lodge SH
(605) 584-3435. **$79-$275, 5 day notice.** Hwy 14A at Savoy. I-90, exit 14 (Spearfish Canyon), 13 mi s. Int corridors. **Pets:** $15 daily fee/room. Service with restrictions, supervision.
🅂🄰🅅🄴 🆂 ✕ ⬛ 🖵 🍴 ✕

⬥⬥ ▼▼▼ Travelodge of Spearfish M
(605) 642-4676. **$45-$110.** 346 W Kansas St. Follow signs off Main St; downtown. Ext corridors. **Pets:** Accepted.
🅂🄰🅅🄴 ✕ ⬛ 🖵 ➷

STURGIS

Best Western of Sturgis SH
(605) 347-3604. **$49-$109.** 2431 S Junction Ave. I-90, exit 32. Ext/int corridors. **Pets:** $20 deposit/room. Designated rooms, service with restrictions, supervision.

BRANDON

Holiday Inn Express of Brandon SH
(605) 582-2901. **$79-$119.** 1105 N Split Rock Blvd. I-90, exit 406, just s. Int corridors. **Pets:** Other species. $10 one-time fee/pet. Designated rooms, service with restrictions, crate.

BROOKINGS

Brookings Super 8 Motel SH
(605) 692-6920. **$50-$110.** 3034 Lefevre Dr. I-29, exit 132, just e. Int corridors. **Pets:** $5 daily fee/pet. Service with restrictions, supervision.

BUFFALO

Tipperary Lodge M
(605) 375-3721. **$46-$55.** 604 1st St W. 0.5 mi n on US 85, turn at sign. Int corridors. **Pets:** Other species. Designated rooms, service with restrictions, supervision.

CANISTOTA

Best Western U-Bar Motel M
(605) 296-3466. **$42-$80.** 130 Ash St. I-90, exit 368, 6 mi s, follow signs. Ext corridors. **Pets:** Accepted.

CHAMBERLAIN

Alewel's Lake Shore Motel M
(605) 234-5566. **$27-$64.** 115 N River St. Just n of US 16 bridge (the northernmost bridge). Ext corridors. **Pets:** Medium. Service with restrictions, supervision.

Bel Aire Motel M
(605) 734-5595. **$40-$64, 4 day notice.** 312 E King St. On US 16 and I-90 business loop; downtown. Ext/int corridors. **Pets:** Accepted.

Best Western Lee's Motor Inn SH
(605) 734-5575. **$45-$90.** 220 W King St. On US 17 and I-90 business loop; downtown. Ext/int corridors. **Pets:** Very small. No service, supervision.

END AREA

Days Inn SH
(605) 347-3027. **$58-$90, 14 day notice.** I-90, exit 30, jct US 14A. Ext/int corridors. **Pets:** Medium, other species. $10 daily fee/pet. Designated rooms, service with restrictions, supervision.

Cedar Shore Resort SH
(605) 734-6376. **$70-$150.** 1500 Shoreline Dr. I-90, exit 260, 2.5 mi e on Business Rt 90, 1 mi ne on Mickelson county road, follow signs. Int corridors. **Pets:** Other species. $10 deposit/pet. Service with restrictions, supervision.

Holiday Inn Express SH
(605) 734-5593. **$70-$150.** 100 W Hwy 16. I-90, exit 260, just n. Int corridors. **Pets:** Accepted.

Oasis Inn SH
(605) 734-6061. **$51-$119.** 1100 E Hwy 16. I-90, exit 260, 0.4 mi e on US 16 and I-90 business loop. Ext/int corridors. **Pets:** Other species. Service with restrictions, supervision.

DELL RAPIDS

Super 8 Motel SH
(605) 428-4288. **$44-$69.** 510 N Hwy 77. I-29, exit 98 (SR 115), 3 mi e, then just n. Int corridors. **Pets:** Small. $6 daily fee/pet. Designated rooms, service with restrictions, supervision.

DE SMET

De Smet Super 8 SH
(605) 854-9388. **$89-$129.** 288 Hwy 14 E. US 14, just e. Int corridors. **Pets:** $8 daily fee/pet. Designated rooms, service with restrictions, supervision.

FAITH

Prairie Vista Inn SH
(605) 967-2343. **$65-$85.** Hwy 212 & E 1st. On US 212; at east city edge. Int corridors. **Pets:** Medium. $10 daily fee/pet. Designated rooms, service with restrictions, supervision.

FAULKTON

Super 8 Motel SH
(605) 598-4567. **$50-$60.** 700 Main St. On US 212; center. Int corridors. **Pets:** Accepted.

FLANDREAU

⚠ ▼▼▼▼ Royal River Casino & Hotel 🆂🅷
(605) 997-3746. **$60-$199.** 607 S Veterans St. I-29, exit 114, 7 mi e, follow signs. Int corridors. **Pets:** Other species. $50 deposit/room. Designated rooms, service with restrictions, supervision.
(SAVE) (S🐾) ✕ (&M) (🐾) 🖬 🖵 (🍴) 🌊

FORT PIERRE

⚠ ▼▼▼ Fort Pierre Motel Ⓜ ❀
(605) 223-3111. **$50-$58, 3 day notice.** 211 S 1st Ave. On US 83, 1.2 mi s of jct US 14. Ext corridors. **Pets:** Other species. Supervision.
(SAVE) ✕ 🖬

▼▼▼▼ Holiday Inn Express Hotel & Suites 🆂🅷
(605) 223-9045. **$90-$100.** 110 E Stanley Rd. On US 83, just s of jct US 14/SR 34. Int corridors. **Pets:** Medium, dogs only. $5 daily fee/pet. Designated rooms, service with restrictions, supervision.
(ASK) (S🐾) ✕ (&M) (🐾) (&') 🖬 🖵 🌊

FORT THOMPSON

▼▼ Lode Star Motel 🆂🅷
(605) 245-2899. **Call for rates.** E Hwy 34. Just e of jct SR 47/34. Int corridors. **Pets:** Accepted.
✕ (&')

FREEMAN

▼▼ Super 8 Motel 🆂🅷
(605) 925-4888. **Call for rates.** 1019 S Hwy 81. On US 81, just s. Int corridors. **Pets:** Accepted.
✕ (&') 🖬

HURON

▼▼▼▼ Best Western of Huron 🆂🅷 ❀
(605) 352-2000. **$56-$93.** 2000 Dakota Ave. 1.3 mi s on SR 37. Ext/int corridors. **Pets:** Medium. $10 daily fee/room. Service with restrictions, supervision.
(ASK) (S🐾) ✕ (&M) (🐾) (&') 🖬 🖵

⚠ ▼▼▼▼ The Crossroads Hotel & Convention Center 🆂🅷
(605) 352-3204. **$80-$145, 3 day notice.** 100 4th St. Just w of Dakota Ave; downtown. Int corridors. **Pets:** $15 daily fee/room. Service with restrictions, supervision.
(SAVE) (S🐾) ✕ (&M) 🖬 🖵 (🍴) 🌊 (✕̸)

▼▼▼▼ Holiday Inn Express 🆂🅷
(605) 352-6655. **$70-$75.** 100 21st St SW. 1.3 mi s on SR 37. Ext/int corridors. **Pets:** $25 one-time fee/room. Supervision.
(ASK) (S🐾) ✕ (&M) (🐾) (&') 🖬 🖵 (✕̸)

INTERIOR

⚠ ▼▼ Badlands Budget Host Motel Ⓜ
(605) 433-5335. **$46-$58.** Jct SR 44 and 377, 2 mi s of Badlands National Park. Ext corridors. **Pets:** Accepted.
(SAVE) 🖵 🌊 (✓)

KADOKA

⚠ ▼▼ Best Value Dakota Inn Ⓜ
(605) 837-2151. **$50-$70.** I-90, exit 150, just n. Ext/int corridors. **Pets:** Medium, other species. $5 one-time fee/pet. Designated rooms, service with restrictions, supervision.
(SAVE) (S🐾) ✕ 🖬 🖵 🌊

⚠ ▼▼▼ Best Western H & H El Centro Motel Ⓜ ❀
(605) 837-2287. **$52-$120.** 105 E Hwy 16. 1.5 mi w on I-90 business route from exit 152, 1.3 mi e from exit 150. Ext corridors. **Pets:** Other species. Designated rooms, service with restrictions, crate.
(SAVE) (S🐾) ✕ 🖵 (🍴) 🌊 (✕̸)

⚠ ▼▼ West Motel Ⓜ
(605) 837-2427. **$34-$70.** 306 Hwy 16 W. I-90, exit 150, 1 mi e on I-90 business route. Ext corridors. **Pets:** Other species. $5 daily fee/room, $5 one-time fee/room. Service with restrictions, supervision.
(SAVE) ✕

KIMBALL

⚠ ▼▼ Travlers Motel Ⓜ
(605) 778-6215. **$38-$60.** 720 S Main. I-90, exit 284, just n on SR 45. Ext corridors. **Pets:** Other species. $5 daily fee/pet. Supervision.
(SAVE) ✕

MADISON

▼▼ Super 8 Motel 🆂🅷
(605) 256-6931. **Call for rates.** 219 N Highland Ave. Jct US 81/SR 34. Int corridors. **Pets:** Accepted.
✕ (&') 🖬

MITCHELL

▼▼ AmericInn Motel & Suites 🆂🅷
(605) 996-9700. **$68-$100.** 1421 S Burr St. I-90, exit 332, just n. Int corridors. **Pets:** Small, other species. $5 daily fee/pet. Designated rooms, service with restrictions, supervision.
(ASK) (S🐾) ✕ (&M) (&') 🖬 🖵 🌊

⚠ ▼▼▼▼ Hampton Inn 🆂🅷
(605) 995-1575. **$72-$123.** 1920 Highland Way. I-90, exit 332, just se. Int corridors. **Pets:** Large, dogs only. $20 daily fee/room. Service with restrictions, supervision.
(SAVE) (S🐾) ✕ (&M) (🐾) (&') 🖬 🖵 🌊

⚠ ▼▼▼▼ Holiday Inn 🆂🅷
(605) 996-6501. **$70-$150.** 1525 W Havens St. I-90, exit 330, 0.5 mi n. Ext/int corridors. **Pets:** Other species. $10 daily fee/room. Service with restrictions, crate.
(SAVE) (S🐾) ✕ (&M) (🐾) 🖵 (🍴) 🌊 (✕̸)

⚠ ▼▼▼▼ Kelly Inn & Suites 🆂🅷 ❀
(605) 995-0500. **$69-$114.** 1010 Cabela Dr. I-90, exit 332, just sw. Ext/int corridors. **Pets:** Other species. Service with restrictions, supervision.
(SAVE) ✕ (&') 🖬 🖵 🌊 (✕̸)

△△△ ▼▼▼ Thunderbird Lodge M
(605) 996-6645. **$45-$79.** 1601 S Burr St. I-90, exit 332, just n. Ext/int corridors. **Pets:** Medium, other species. $10 daily fee/room. Designated rooms, service with restrictions, supervision.
(SAVE) (S⌂) (✕) (&M) (❂)

MOBRIDGE

△△△ ▼▼▼ Best Value Wrangler Inn SH
(605) 845-3641. **$60-$78.** 820 W Grand Crossing. 0.5 mi w on US 12. Ext/int corridors. **Pets:** Dogs only. Service with restrictions, supervision.
(SAVE) (S⌂) (✕) (❂) (¶) (🐾) (✕)

MURDO

△△△ ▼▼▼ Best Western Graham's M
(605) 669-2441. **$59-$110.** 301 W 5th. On I-90 business loop, 0.5 mi w of jct US 83; I-90, exits 191 and 192. Ext corridors. **Pets:** Service with restrictions, supervision.
(SAVE) (S⌂) (✕) (💻) (🐾)

△△△ ▼▼▼▼ Days Inn Range Country SH
(605) 669-2425. **$69-$125.** 302 W 5th. I-90 business loop, 0.5 mi w of jct US 83, exits 192 and 191. Ext/int corridors. **Pets:** Designated rooms, supervision.
(SAVE) (S⌂) (✕) (❂) (🐾)

NORTH SIOUX CITY

▼▼▼ Econo Lodge SH
(605) 232-9600. **$49-$84, 3 day notice.** 110 Sodrac Dr. I-29, exit 2, just w. Int corridors. **Pets:** Accepted.
(ASK) (S⌂) (✕) (&·) (❂) (💻)

▼▼▼▼ Hampton Inn SH
(605) 232-9739. **$59-$79.** 101 S Sodrac Dr. I-29, exit 2, just w. Int corridors. **Pets:** Medium, other species. $20 one-time fee/room. Designated rooms, service with restrictions, supervision.
(ASK) (S⌂) (✕) (&M) (❂) (💻) (🐾)

△△△ ▼▼▼ Super 8 Motel SH
(605) 232-4716. **$50-$90.** 1300 River Dr. I-29, exit 2, just w. Int corridors. **Pets:** Other species. $5 daily fee/pet. Designated rooms, service with restrictions, supervision.
(SAVE) (S⌂) (✕) (❂) (💻)

PICKSTOWN

▼▼▼ Fort Randall Inn M
(605) 487-7801. **$55.** 103 Hwy 18/281. On US 18/281; just e of the dam. Ext corridors. **Pets:** Other species. Service with restrictions.
(ASK) (S⌂) (✕) (❂)

PIERRE

▼▼▼▼ Best Western Ramkota Hotel SH
(605) 224-6877. **$89-$91.** 920 W Sioux Ave. 1 mi w on US 14/83. Ext/int corridors. **Pets:** Designated rooms, service with restrictions.
(ASK) (S⌂) (✕) (&M) (❂) (&·) (❂) (💻) (¶) (🐾) (✕)

△△△ ▼▼▼ Comfort Inn SH
(605) 224-0377. **$52-$109.** 410 W Sioux Ave. 0.3 mi w on US 14/83 and SR 34. Int corridors. **Pets:** Medium, dogs only. $10 daily fee/pet. Designated rooms, service with restrictions, supervision.
(SAVE) (S⌂) (✕) (&M) (&·) (❂) (💻) (🐾)

▼▼ Days Inn SH 🐾
(605) 224-0411. **$55-$95.** 520 W Sioux Ave. 0.5 mi w on US 14/83 and SR 34. Int corridors. **Pets:** $5 daily fee/pet. Designated rooms, service with restrictions, supervision.
(ASK) (S⌂) (✕) (❂) (&·) (❂) (💻)

△△△ ▼▼▼▼ Governor's Inn SH 🐾
(605) 224-4200. **$69-$109.** 700 W Sioux Ave. 0.8 mi w on US 14/83 and SR 34. Ext/int corridors. **Pets:** Dogs only. $5 daily fee/room. Service with restrictions, supervision.
(SAVE) (S⌂) (✕) (❂) (&·) (❂) (💻) (🐾) (✕)

▼▼ Kelly Inn SH
(605) 224-4140. **$52-$65.** 713 W Sioux Ave. 0.8 mi w on US 14/83. Int corridors. **Pets:** Other species. No service, supervision.
(ASK) (S⌂) (✕) (&·) (❂) (💻)

▼▼ Super 8 Motel SH
(605) 224-1617. **$45-$70.** 320 W Sioux Ave. 0.3 mi w on US 14/83 and SR 34. Int corridors. **Pets:** Medium. $5 daily fee/pet. Service with restrictions, crate.
(ASK) (S⌂) (✕) (&·) (❂)

PLANKINTON

▼▼ Super 8 Motel SH
(605) 942-7722. **$45-$80.** 801 S Main St. I-90, exit 308, just n. Int corridors. **Pets:** Medium, other species. $8 daily fee/pet. Service with restrictions, supervision.
(ASK) (S⌂) (✕)

SIOUX FALLS

▼▼ Baymont Inn SH 🐾
(605) 362-0835. **$59-$115.** 3200 Meadow Ave. I-29, exit 77 (41st St), just w. Int corridors. **Pets:** Other species. $10 daily fee/room. Service with restrictions, supervision.
(ASK) (S⌂) (✕) (&M) (❂) (&·) (❂) (💻) (🐾)

▼▼▼▼ Best Western Ramkota Hotel & Conference Center SH
(605) 336-0650. **$89-$139.** 3200 W Maple. I-29, exit 81 (Airport/Russell St), just e. Ext/int corridors. **Pets:** Service with restrictions, crate.
(ASK) (S⌂) (✕) (&M) (❂) (&·) (❂) (💻) (¶) (🐾) (✕)

▼▼▼ Comfort Inn North SH
(605) 331-4490. **$55-$139.** 5100 N Cliff Ave. I-90, exit 399 (Cliff Ave), 0.3 mi s. Int corridors. **Pets:** Other species. $10 daily fee/pet. Service with restrictions, supervision.
(ASK) (S⌂) (✕) (&M) (❂) (❂) (💻) (🐾)

▼▼▼ Comfort Inn South SH
(605) 361-2822. **$64-$94.** 3216 S Carolyn Ave. I-29, exit 77 (41st St), just e, then n. Int corridors. **Pets:** $25 deposit/pet, $6 daily fee/pet. Service with restrictions, supervision.
(ASK) (S⌂) (✕) (❂) (❂) (💻) (🐾)

WWWW Comfort Suites SH
(605) 362-9711. **$74-$109.** 3208 S Carolyn Ave. I-29, exit 77 (41st St), just e, then n. Int corridors. **Pets:** Large. $10 daily fee/room. Designated rooms, service with restrictions, supervision.

(ASK) (S$) (X) (🐾) (🔧) (💻) (🏊)

WWWW Country Inn & Suites By Carlson SH
(605) 373-0153. **$69-$89.** 200 E 8th St. Just e of Phillips Ave; downtown. Int corridors. **Pets:** Medium. $10 daily fee/room. Designated rooms, service with restrictions, crate.

(ASK) (S$) (X) (&M) (🐾) (🌙) (🔧) (💻) (🍽) (🏊)

WWW Days Inn Airport SH
(605) 331-5959. **$70-$149.** 5001 N Cliff Ave. I-90, exit 399 (Cliff Ave), just s. Int corridors. **Pets:** Accepted.

(SAVE) (S$) (X) (&M) (🌙) (🔧) (💻)

WWWW Homewood Suites By Hilton SH
(605) 338-8585. **$99-$189.** 3620 W Avera Dr. I-229, exit 1C, just s. Int corridors. **Pets:** Accepted.

(SAVE) (S$) (X) (&M) (🐾) (🌙) (🔧) (💻) (🏊) (⊠)

WWWW Kelly Inn SH 🐾
(605) 338-6242. **$67-$99.** 3101 W Russell St. I-29, exit 81 (Airport/Russell St), just e. Ext/int corridors. **Pets:** Large, other species. No service, supervision.

(SAVE) (S$) (X) (🐾) (🌙) (🔧) (💻) (⊠)

WWW Microtel Inn & Suites SH
(605) 361-7484. **$48-$100.** 2901 S Carolyn Ave. I-29, exit 77 (41st St), just e, then n. Int corridors. **Pets:** Other species. $15 one-time fee/room. Service with restrictions, supervision.

(SAVE) (S$) (X) (&M) (🐾) (🌙) (🔧) (💻)

W Motel 6–0162 M
(605) 336-7800. **$37-$57.** 3009 W Russell St. I-29, exit 81 (Airport/Russell St), just e. Ext corridors. **Pets:** Accepted.

(S$) (X) (&M) (🌙) (🔧) (💻)

W Ramada Limited SH
(605) 330-0000. **Call for rates.** 407 S Lyons Ave. I-29, exit 79 (12th St), just e. Int corridors. **Pets:** Accepted.

(X) (&M) (🌙) (🔧) (💻) (🏊) (⊠)

WWW Red Roof Inn SH
(605) 361-1864. **$60-$95.** 3500 S Gateway Blvd. I-29, exit 77 (41st St), just w. Int corridors. **Pets:** Small. Designated rooms, service with restrictions, supervision.

(ASK) (S$) (X) (🌙) (🔧) (💻)

WWWW Residence Inn by Marriott SH 🐾
(605) 361-2202. **$80-$170, 14 day notice.** 4509 W Empire Pl. I-29, exit 77 (41st St), 0.5 mi se. Int corridors. **Pets:** Other species. $5 daily fee/pet, $25 one-time fee/room.

(ASK) (S$) (X) (&M) (🐾) (🌙) (🔧) (💻) (🏊) (⊠)

WW Sleep Inn SH
(605) 339-3992. **$50-$79.** 1500 N Kiwanis Ave. I-29, exit 81 (Airport/Russell St), 0.7 mi e. Int corridors. **Pets:** Medium. $10 daily fee/room. Designated rooms, service with restrictions, crate.

(ASK) (S$) (X) (&M) (🌙) (🔧) (💻) (🏊)

W Super 8/I-90/Airport East SH
(605) 339-9212. **$55-$90.** 4808 N Cliff Ave. I-90, exit 399 (Cliff Ave), 0.3 mi s. Int corridors. **Pets:** Small, dogs only. $10 one-time fee/room. Designated rooms, service with restrictions, crate.

(ASK) (S$) (X) (🔧) (💻)

WWW TownePlace Suites by Marriott SH
(605) 361-2626. **$69-$129.** 4545 W Homefield Dr. I-29, exit 78 (26th St), just w. Int corridors. **Pets:** Small, other species. $5 daily fee/room, $25 one-time fee/room. Designated rooms, service with restrictions, supervision.

(SAVE) (S$) (X) (&M) (🌙) (🔧) (💻) (🏊)

VERMILLION

WW Comfort Inn SH
(605) 624-8333. **$59-$79.** 701 W Cherry St. I-29, exit 26, 7.5 mi w on Business Rt SR 50. Int corridors. **Pets:** Medium. $5 daily fee/pet. Service with restrictions, supervision.

(ASK) (S$) (X) (🔧) (💻) (🏊) (⊠)

WALL

WWW Best Western Plains Motel M
(605) 279-2145. **$49-$150.** 712 Glenn St. I-90, exit 110, just n. Ext corridors. **Pets:** Other species. $10 one-time fee/pet. Service with restrictions, supervision.

(SAVE) (S$) (X) (💻) (🏊)

WWW Econo Lodge M
(605) 279-2121. **$69-$125.** 804 Glenn St. I-90, exit 110, just nw. Ext corridors. **Pets:** Accepted.

(SAVE) (S$) (X) (🔧) (💻) (🏊)

WW Sunshine Inn M
(605) 279-2178. **$48-$79.** 608 Main St. Downtown. Ext corridors. **Pets:** Other species. $5 one-time fee/room.

(SAVE) (S$) (X)

WATERTOWN

WWWW Best Western Ramkota Hotel SH
(605) 886-8011. **$89-$99.** 1901 9th Ave SW. I-29, exit 177 (US 212), 4 mi w. Int corridors. **Pets:** Accepted.

(ASK) (S$) (X) (🌙) (🔧) (💻) (🍽) (🏊) (⊠)

WW Comfort Inn SH 🐾
(605) 886-3010. **$60-$114.** 800 35th St Cir. I-29, exit 177 (US 212). Ext/int corridors. **Pets:** $10 one-time fee/room. Service with restrictions, supervision.

(ASK) (S$) (X) (&M) (🌙) (🔧) (💻) (🏊)

WWWW Country Inn & Suites By Carlson SH
(605) 886-8900. **$75-$85.** 3400 8th Ave SE. I-29, exit 177 (US 212), just w. Int corridors. **Pets:** Small. $20 one-time fee/room. Designated rooms, service with restrictions, supervision.

(SAVE) (S$) (X) (&M) (🌙) (🔧) (💻) (🏊)

WWW Days Inn SH
(605) 886-3500. **$56-$80, 14 day notice.** 2900 9th Ave SE. I-29, exit 177 (US 212), 0.5 mi w. Ext/int corridors. **Pets:** Large, other species. $10 one-time fee/room. Service with restrictions, supervision.

(SAVE) (S$) (X) (&M) (🌙) (🔧) (💻) (🏊) (⊠)

▼▼▼▼ **Holiday Inn Express Hotel & Suites** SH
(605) 882-3636. **$65-$89, 3 day notice.** 3900 9th Ave SE.
I-29, exit 177 (US 212), just e. Int corridors. **Pets:** Other
species. $10 daily fee/pet. Designated rooms, service with
restrictions, supervision.

ASK SÒ ⊠ ⫶ ⊞ ⬜ ⮐ ⊠

ⒶⒶⒶ ▼▼▼▼ **Travelers Inn Motel** SH ⚘
(605) 882-2243. **$44-$48.** 920 14th St SE. I-29, exit 177, 1.5
mi w, then just s. Int corridors. **Pets:** Large, other species.
$6 daily fee/pet. Designated rooms.

SAVE SÒ ⊠ ⫶ ⊞

ⒶⒶⒶ ▼▼▼▼ **Travel Host Motel** M
(605) 886-6120. **$48-$54.** 1714 9th Ave SW. I-29, exit 177
(US 212), 4 mi w. Int corridors. **Pets:** Accepted.

SAVE ⊠ ⊞

YANKTON

▼▼▼▼ **Best Western Kelly Inn-Yankton** SH
(605) 665-2906. **$89-$249.** 1607 Hwy 50 E. On US 50, 1.8
mi e. Ext/int corridors. **Pets:** Medium, other species. Designated rooms, service with restrictions, supervision.

ASK SÒ ⊠ ⫶M ⟲ ⫶ ⊞ ⬜ ⊪ ⮐ ⊠

▼▼ **Days Inn** SH
(605) 665-8717. **$60-$75.** 2410 Broadway. US 81, 1.7 mi n.
Int corridors. **Pets:** Medium, dogs only. $10 daily fee/room.
Service with restrictions, supervision.

ASK SÒ ⊠ ⊞

▼▼ **Lewis & Clark Resort** M
(605) 665-2680. **$50-$199 (no credit cards), 30 day notice.**
43496 Lake Shore Dr. 4 mi w on SR 52; in Lewis and Clark
State Park, turn into park, just w of Marina. Ext corridors.
Pets: Accepted.

⊠ ⫶ ⊞ ⬜ ⮐ ⊠ ⫶

ⒶⒶⒶ ▼▼▼▼ **Ramada Limited** SH
(605) 665-8053. **$69.** 2118 Broadway. US 81, 1.4 mi n. Int
corridors. **Pets:** Accepted.

SAVE SÒ ⊠ ⊞ ⬜

CITY INDEX

ALCOA

▼▼▼▼ Jameson Inn Alcoa SH

(865) 984-6800. **$72-$74.** 206 Corporate Pl. US 129, just s. Int corridors. **Pets:** Small. Service with restrictions, crate.

ATHENS

▼▼ Motel 6 SH

(423) 745-4441. **$34-$49.** 2002 Whittaker Rd. I-75, exit 49, just e on SR 30. Int corridors. **Pets:** Accepted.

▼▼ Ramada Inn SH

(423) 745-1212. **$73-$99.** 115 CR 247. I-75, exit 52, just w. Ext corridors. **Pets:** Accepted.

BOLIVAR

⬥⬥⬥ ◈ The Bolivar Inn M

(731) 658-3372. **$35-$45.** 626 W Market St. Jct US 64 and SR 18; downtown. Ext corridors. **Pets:** Service with restrictions, supervision.

▼▼ ◈ Rodeway Inn SH

(731) 658-7888. **$40-$70, 3 day notice.** 916 W Market St. Jct US 64 and SR 18. Ext corridors. **Pets:** Accepted.

BRENTWOOD

⬥⬥⬥ ▼▼▼ AmeriSuites
(Nashville/Brentwood) SH

(615) 661-9477. **$59-$79.** 202 Summit View Dr. I-65, exit 74A. Int corridors. **Pets:** Large, other species. Service with restrictions, crate.

▼▼▼▼ Baymont Inn & Suites SH

(615) 376-4666. **$62-$69.** 111 Penn Warren Dr. I-65, exit 74B, 1.5 mi w, just s on West Park. Int corridors. **Pets:** Other species. Service with restrictions, crate.

▼▼▼▼ Candlewood Suites SH

(615) 309-0600. **$79.** 5129 Virginia Way. I-65, exit 74B, 0.5 mi w, 0.5 mi s on Franklin Rd, 1.2 mi w on Marilyn Way, just s on Wade Cir, then just s. Int corridors. **Pets:** Accepted.

▼▼▼▼ Hilton Suites Brentwood LH

(615) 370-0111. **$89-$119.** 9000 Overlook Blvd. I-65, exit 74B, 0.5 mi s on US 31, e on Church St. Int corridors. **Pets:** Accepted.

⬥⬥⬥ ▼▼▼▼ MainStay Suites-Brentwood SH

(615) 371-8477. **$60-$80.** 107 Brentwood Blvd. I-65, exit 74B, 1 mi w. Int corridors. **Pets:** Small. $100 deposit/pet. Designated rooms, service with restrictions.

▼▼▼ Residence Inn Brentwood M ❀

(615) 371-0100. **$94-$99.** 206 Ward Cir. I-65, exit 74B, 0.3 mi s on Franklin Pike Cir (US 31 S), 0.5 mi w on Maryland Way. Ext/int corridors. **Pets:** Small, other species. $150 one-time fee/room. Service with restrictions.

▼▼▼ Sleep Inn SH

(615) 376-2122. **$59-$79.** 1611 Service Merchandise Blvd. I-65, exit 69 northbound, 0.4 mi, just n; exit 69W southbound, just n. Int corridors. **Pets:** Other species. $10 daily fee/room. Service with restrictions.

BROWNSVILLE

▼▼ Days Inn SH

(731) 772-3297. **$46-$82.** 2530 Anderson Ave. I-40, exit 56. Ext corridors. **Pets:** Accepted.

▼▼▼▼ Holiday Inn Express SH

(731) 772-4030. **$60.** 120 Sunny Hill Cove. I-40, exit 56. Int corridors. **Pets:** Accepted.

BUCKSNORT

⟨AAA⟩ ▼ Travel Inn
(931) 729-5450. **$40-$55.** 5032 Hwy 230 W. I-40, exit 152. Ext corridors. **Pets:** $10 deposit/pet. No service, supervision.

SAVE ⓢ ✕ 🖵

BULLS GAP

▼▼ Super 8 Motel SH
(423) 235-4112. **$48-$60.** 90 Speedway Ln. I-81, exit 23. Ext corridors. **Pets:** $10 daily fee/room. Designated rooms, service with restrictions, supervision.

ASK ⓢ ✕ 🦮 🖬 🐾

BUTLER

▼▼▼ Iron Mountain Inn B&B and Creekside Chalet BB
(423) 768-2446. **$150-$300, 20 day notice.** 138 Moreland Dr. 1.6 mi w on Pine Orchard Rd from SR 67 at Stout Store, follow signs; 13 mi w on SR 67 from US 421 in Mountain City, then follow sign at Stout Store area. Ext/int corridors. **Pets:** Other species. $100 deposit/room. Designated rooms, no service, supervision.

ASK ⓢ ✕ 🖬 🖵

CARYVILLE

⟨AAA⟩ ▼ Budget Host Inn
(423) 562-9595. **$29-$46.** 115 Woods Ave. I-75, exit 134, just w. Ext corridors. **Pets:** Accepted.

SAVE ⓢ ✕

▼▼ Super 8 Motel of Caryville SH
(423) 562-8476. **$35-$65.** 200 John McGhee Blvd. I-75, exit 134, just e, then just s on CR 116. Ext corridors. **Pets:** Small. $5 daily fee/pet. Designated rooms, service with restrictions, supervision.

ASK ⓢ ✕ 🐾

CENTERVILLE

▼▼ Days Inn SH
(931) 729-5600. **$45-$60.** 634 David St. On SR 100, 3 mi w of jct SR 48. Int corridors. **Pets:** Accepted.

ASK ⓢ ✕ 🐾 🖬 🖵 🍴 🐾

CHATTANOOGA

⟨AAA⟩ ▼▼▼ Baymont Inn & Suites-Chattanooga SH
(423) 821-1090. **$45-$100.** 3540 Cummings Hwy. I-24, exit 174, 0.4 mi s. Int corridors. **Pets:** Accepted.

SAVE ⓢ ✕ 🦮 🖬 🖵 🐾

▼▼ Best Inn-Hamilton Mall Area SH
(423) 894-5454. **$43-$95.** 7717 Lee Hwy. I-75, exit 7B northbound; exit 7 southbound, 6.5 mi n of jct I-24. Ext corridors. **Pets:** Accepted.

✕ 🐾 🖬 🖵 🐾

⟨AAA⟩ ▼▼ Best Western Royal Inn SH
(423) 821-6840. **$55-$90.** 3644 Cummings Hwy. I-24, exit 174, 0.4 mi s. Ext corridors. **Pets:** Small. $10 daily fee/pet. Designated rooms, service with restrictions, supervision.

SAVE ⓢ ✕ 🖬 🖵 🐾

▼▼ Chattanooga/Aquarium Super 8 Motel SH
(423) 821-8880. **$45-$110, 14 day notice.** 20 Birmingham Hwy. I-24, exit 174. Int corridors. **Pets:** Medium. $10 one-time fee/pet. Service with restrictions, supervision.

ASK ⓢ ✕ 🖬

▼▼▼ Chattanooga Marriott at the Convention Center LH ❀
(423) 756-0002. **$94-$113.** 2 Carter Plaza. I-24 to US 27 N, exit 1A (M L King Blvd). Int corridors. **Pets:** Medium, other species. $15 daily fee/room. Designated rooms.

ASK ⓢ ✕ 🦮 🐕 🖬 🖵 🍴 🐾 🐾

▼▼▼ Days Inn Airport SH
(423) 899-2288. **$37-$45.** 7725 Lee Hwy. I-75, exit 7A southbound; exit 7 northbound. Int corridors. **Pets:** Accepted.

ASK ⓢ ✕ 🖬 🐾

⟨AAA⟩ ▼▼ Days Inn-Lookout Mountain Tiftonia West SH
(423) 821-6044. **$48-$78.** 3801 Cummings Hwy. I-24, exit 174, just n. Ext corridors. **Pets:** Other species. $10 daily fee/pet. Designated rooms, service with restrictions, supervision.

SAVE ⓢ ✕ 🐕 🖬 🐾

⟨AAA⟩ ▼▼▼ La Quinta Inn SH
(423) 855-0011. **$59-$85.** 7015 Shallowford Rd. I-75, exit 5 (Shallowford Rd), just w. Ext corridors. **Pets:** Medium, other species. Service with restrictions.

SAVE ⓢ ✕ 🐕 🦮 🖵 🐾

▼▼ Microtel Inn-Chattanooga SH
(423) 510-0761. **$31-$45.** 7014 McCutcheon Rd. I-75, exit 5 (Shallowford Rd), just w, 0.3 mi n on Shallowford Village Dr, then just w. Int corridors. **Pets:** Very small, other species. $25 one-time fee/room. No service, supervision.

ASK ⓢ ✕ 🦮

▼▼ Motel 6 Downtown SH
(423) 265-7300. **$34-$58.** 2440 Williams St. I-24, exit 178 (Market St). Int corridors. **Pets:** Small. Designated rooms, service with restrictions, supervision.

✕ 🦮 🖬

⟨AAA⟩ ▼▼ Red Roof Inn-Chattanooga SH
(423) 899-0143. **$42-$62.** 7014 Shallowford Rd. I-75, exit 5 (Shallowford Rd), just w. Ext corridors. **Pets:** Medium, other species. Service with restrictions, supervision.

SAVE ✕

▼▼ Residence Inn by Marriott SH
(423) 266-0600. **$109-$149.** 215 Chestnut St. US 27, exit 1C (4th St), just n. Int corridors. **Pets:** Accepted.

ASK ⓢ ✕ 🦮 🐕 🐾 🖬 🖵 🐾 🐾

CLARKSVILLE

▼▼ Days Inn North SH
(931) 552-1155. **$45-$80, 7 day notice.** 130 Westfield Ct. I-24, exit 4, just s. Ext corridors. **Pets:** Small. $5 daily fee/room. Designated rooms, service with restrictions, supervision.

ASK ⓢ ✕ 🦮 🖬 🐾

▼▼ **Days Inn of Clarksville** 🆂🅷 ❀
(931) 358-3194. **$50-$60.** 1100 Hwy 76 Connector Rd. I-24, exit 11. Ext corridors. **Pets:** Medium, other species. Service with restrictions, supervision.
🅰🆂🅺 🆂🅾 ✕ 🎛 🏊

▼▼▼ **GuestHouse International Inn** 🆂🅷
(931) 552-8060. **$49-$57.** 3083B Wilma Rudolph Blvd. I-24, exit 4, just s. Ext corridors. **Pets:** Accepted.
🅰🆂🅺 🆂🅾 ✕ 🅶🅼 🎛 🏊 🏊

🅰🅰🅰 ▼▼▼ **Holiday Inn-I-24** 🆂🅷
(931) 648-4848. **$69-$89.** 3095 Wilma Rudolph Blvd. I-24, exit 4, just s. Ext corridors. **Pets:** Other species. $10 daily fee/room. Designated rooms, service with restrictions, supervision.
🆂🅰🆅🅴 🆂🅾 ✕ 🅶 🎛 🏊 🍴 🏊 🏊

▼▼ **Ramada Limited** 🆂🅷
(931) 552-0098. **$39-$65, 14 day notice.** 3100 Wilma Rudolph Blvd. I-24, exit 4. Ext corridors. **Pets:** Small. $30 deposit/room, $5 daily fee/pet. Designated rooms, service with restrictions, supervision.
🅰🆂🅺 🆂🅾 ✕ 🎛 🏊

▼▼ **Red Roof Inn** 🆂🅷
(931) 905-1555. **$45-$79.** 197 Holiday Dr. I-24, exit 4, just se. Ext corridors. **Pets:** Medium. Designated rooms, service with restrictions, supervision.
🅰🆂🅺 🆂🅾 ✕ 🎛 🏊

CLEVELAND

▼▼ **Douglas Inn & Suites** 🆂🅷
(423) 559-5579. **$69-$99.** 2600 Westside Dr NW. I-75, exit 25, just s on SR 60, just e. Ext/int corridors. **Pets:** Other species. $10 daily fee/pet. Service with restrictions, supervision.
🅰🆂🅺 🆂🅾 ✕ 🎛 🏊

🅰🅰🅰 ▼▼▼ **Holiday Inn Mountain View** 🆂🅷
(423) 472-1500. **$69.** 2400 Executive Park Dr. I-75, exit 25. Ext/int corridors. **Pets:** Accepted.
🆂🅰🆅🅴 🆂🅾 ✕ 🎵 🎛 🏊 🍴 🏊

▼▼▼ **Jameson Inn** 🆂🅷
(423) 614-5583. **$67-$71.** 360 Paul Huff Pkwy. I-75, exit 27, 1 mi e. Ext corridors. **Pets:** Small. Service with restrictions, crate.
✕ 🎛 🏊 🏊

▼▼ **Ramada Limited** 🆂🅷
(423) 472-5566. **$52-$67.** 156 James Asbury Dr. I-75, exit 27. Ext corridors. **Pets:** Accepted.
🅰🆂🅺 🆂🅾 ✕ 🅶 🎛 🏊 🏊

🅰🅰🅰 ▼▼ **Super 8 Motel** 🆂🅷
(423) 476-5555. **$50-$55.** 163 Bernham Dr. I-75, exit 27, just w on Paul Huff Pkwy, then s. Ext/int corridors. **Pets:** Other species. $5 daily fee/pet. Service with restrictions, supervision.
🆂🅰🆅🅴 🆂🅾 ✕ 🅶 🎛 🏊 🏊

CLINTON

▼▼ **Best Western Clinton Inn** 🅼
(865) 457-2311. **$44-$120.** 720 Park Pl. I-75, exit 122, just w. Ext corridors. **Pets:** $5 daily fee/pet. Service with restrictions, supervision.
🅰🆂🅺 🆂🅾 ✕ 🅶🅼 🎛 🏊 🏊

▼▼ **Holiday Inn Express Hotel & Suites** 🅼
(865) 457-2233. **$79-$109, 21 day notice.** 141 Buffalo Rd. I-75, exit 122, just w. Ext corridors. **Pets:** Small. $10 daily fee/pet. No service, supervision.
🅰🆂🅺 🆂🅾 ✕ 🅶🅼 🅶 🎛 🏊 🏊

COLUMBIA

🅰🅰🅰 ▼▼ **Best Value Inn** 🆂🅷
(931) 381-1410. **$49-$59, 3 day notice.** 1548 Bear Creek Pike. I-65, exit 46, just w. Ext corridors. **Pets:** Large, other species. $5 one-time fee/pet. Service with restrictions, supervision.
🆂🅰🆅🅴 🆂🅾 ✕ 🎛

🅰🅰🅰 ▼ **James K Polk Motel** 🅼
(931) 388-4913. **$39.** 1111 Nashville Hwy. Jct SR 412 and US 31, just n. Ext corridors. **Pets:** $5 one-time fee/pet. Service with restrictions, supervision.
🆂🅰🆅🅴 ✕ 🎛 🏊

▼▼ **Jameson Inn** 🆂🅷
(931) 388-3326. **$72-$74.** 715 James M Campbell Blvd. 0.9 mi w jct SR 50 and US 31. Int corridors. **Pets:** Small. Service with restrictions, crate.
✕ 🎛 🏊 🏊

COOKEVILLE

🅰🅰🅰 ▼▼ **Alpine Lodge & Suites** 🆂🅷
(931) 526-3333. **$40-$54.** 2021 E Spring St. I-40, exit 290, just s. Int corridors. **Pets:** Medium, other species. $5 daily fee/room. Designated rooms, service with restrictions, supervision.
🆂🅰🆅🅴 🆂🅾 ✕ 🎵 🎛 🏊 🏊

🅰🅰🅰 ▼▼▼ **Baymont Inn & Suites Cookeville** 🆂🅷
(931) 525-6668. **$55-$95.** 1151 S Jefferson Ave. I-40, exit 387. Int corridors. **Pets:** Other species. Service with restrictions, crate.
🆂🅰🆅🅴 🆂🅾 ✕ 🅶🅼 🅶 🎛 🏊 🏊

▼▼▼ **Best Western Thunderbird Motel** 🆂🅷
(931) 526-7115. **$50-$85.** 900 S Jefferson Ave. I-40, exit 287. Ext corridors. **Pets:** Accepted.
🅰🆂🅺 🆂🅾 ✕ 🅶🅼 🅶 🎛 🏊

🅰🅰🅰 ▼▼▼ **Comfort Suites** 🆂🅷
(931) 372-1881. **$59-$64.** 1035 Interstate Dr. I-40, exit 287, 0.5 mi n. Int corridors. **Pets:** Medium, other species. $10 one-time fee/room. Service with restrictions.
🆂🅰🆅🅴 🆂🅾 ✕ 🅶 🎛 🏊 🏊 🏊

▼▼ **Days Inn** 🆂🅷
(931) 528-1511. **$34-$88, 14 day notice.** 1296 S Walnut Ave. I-40, exit 287. Ext corridors. **Pets:** Medium. $5 one-time fee/pet. Designated rooms, service with restrictions.
🅰🆂🅺 🆂🅾 ✕ 🎛 🏊 🏊

△△△ ▼▼▼ Econo Lodge 🆂🅷 ❀
(931) 528-1040. **$35-$65.** 1100 S Jefferson Ave. I-40, exit
287. Ext corridors. **Pets:** Medium, other species. $5 daily
fee/pet. Designated rooms, service with restrictions, supervision.
🆂🅰🆅🅴 🆂🅾 ✕ 🖥 🖵 🏊

▼▼ Holiday Inn 🆂🅷
(931) 526-7125. **$59-$89.** 970 S Jefferson Ave. I-40, exit
287. Ext/int corridors. **Pets:** Accepted.
🅰🆂🅺 🆂🅾 ✕ &ᴹ 🖥 🍴 🏊

CORNERSVILLE

△△△ ▼▼▼ Econo Lodge 🅼
(931) 293-2111. **$60-$70.** 3731 Pulaski Hwy. I-65, exit 22 at
jct US 31A. Ext corridors. **Pets:** Accepted.
🆂🅰🆅🅴 🆂🅾 ✕ 🖵 🏊

CROSSVILLE

△△△ ▼▼▼ Ramada Limited 🆂🅷
(931) 484-7581. **$79-$89.** 4083 Hwy 127 N. I-40, exit 317,
just n. Ext corridors. **Pets:** Accepted.
🆂🅰🆅🅴 🆂🅾 ✕ 🖥 🖵 🏊

△△△ ▼ Scottish Inn 🅼
(931) 484-8122. **$35-$90, 10 day notice.** 3406 N Main St.
I-40, exit 317, 0.9 mi s. Ext corridors. **Pets:** Accepted.
🆂🅰🆅🅴 🆂🅾 ✕ 🖥

CUMBERLAND GAP

▼▼▼ Cumberland Gap Inn 🆂🅷
(423) 869-3996. **$69-$145.** 630 Brooklyn St. Center of town.
Ext corridors. **Pets:** Accepted.
🅰🆂🅺 🆂🅾 ✕ 🖥 🖵 🏊

▼▼ Ramada Inn of Cumberland Gap 🆂🅷 ❀
(423) 869-3631. **$45-$89.** Hwy 58. On US 58, just e of jct
US 25 E. Int corridors. **Pets:** Other species. $25 one-time
fee/pet. Service with restrictions.
🅰🆂🅺 🆂🅾 ✕ 🖥 🖵 🍴 🏊

DANDRIDGE

▼▼ Tennessee Mountain Inn 🆂🅷
(865) 397-9437. **$45-$100, 14 day notice.** 531 Patriot Dr.
I-40, exit 417, just n. Ext corridors. **Pets:** Accepted.
🅰🆂🅺 🆂🅾 ✕ 🏊

DAYTON

△△△ ▼▼▼ Best Western Dayton 🆂🅷
(423) 775-6560. **$65-$105.** 7835 Rhea County Hwy. 1 mi n
on US 27. Ext corridors. **Pets:** Small. $5 daily fee/pet.
Designated rooms, service with restrictions, crate.
🆂🅰🆅🅴 🆂🅾 ✕ 🖥 🖵 🍴 🏊 ✕🖵

△△△ ▼ Days Inn 🅼
(423) 775-9718. **$55-$85.** 3914 Rhea County Hwy. 1 mi s on
US 27. Ext corridors. **Pets:** $3 daily fee/room. Service with
restrictions, supervision.
🆂🅰🆅🅴 🆂🅾 ✕ 🖥

DECHERD

▼▼ Jameson Inn 🆂🅷
(931) 962-0130. **$65-$67.** 1838 Decherd Blvd. Jct Main St
and SR 41A, just s. Ext corridors. **Pets:** Small. Service with
restrictions, crate.
✕ 🖥 🖵 🏊

DICKSON

△△△ ▼▼▼ Best Western Executive Inn 🆂🅷
(615) 446-0541. **$40-$60.** 2338 Hwy 46. I-40, exit 172, just n.
Ext corridors. **Pets:** Small, dogs only. $10 daily fee/pet.
Designated rooms, service with restrictions, supervision.
🆂🅰🆅🅴 🆂🅾 ✕ 🖥 🖵 🏊

△△△ ▼▼▼ Days Inn 🆂🅷
(615) 740-7475. **$49-$69.** 2415 Hwy 46 S. I-40, exit 172, just
s. Ext corridors. **Pets:** Small, cats only. $20 deposit/pet.
Designated rooms, service with restrictions, supervision.
🆂🅰🆅🅴 🆂🅾 ✕ 🖥 🏊

△△△ ▼▼▼ Holiday Inn 🆂🅷
(615) 446-9081. **$62, 7 day notice.** 2420 Hwy 46 S. I-40,
exit 172, just s. Ext corridors. **Pets:** Accepted.
🆂🅰🆅🅴 🆂🅾 ✕ 🎱 🖥 🖵 🍴 🏊

▼▼ Motel 6 #4226 🆂🅷
(615) 446-2423. **$41-$51.** 2325 Hwy 46 S. I-40, exit 172, just
n. Ext corridors. **Pets:** No service, supervision.
🅰🆂🅺 🆂🅾 ✕ 🎱 🖥 🏊

▼▼▼ Super 8 Motel 🆂🅷
(615) 446-1923. **$49-$59, 14 day notice.** 150 Suzanne Dr.
I-40, exit 172, just n on SR 46, then just e. Int corridors.
Pets: $10 daily fee/pet. Service with restrictions, supervi-
sion.
🅰🆂🅺 🆂🅾 ✕ 🖥 🖵 🏊

DYERSBURG

▼▼ Best Western Dyersburg 🆂🅷
(731) 285-8601. **$69.** 770 Hwy 51 Bypass W. I-155, exit 13,
0.5 mi s, jct of US 51 Bypass and SR 78. Ext corridors.
Pets: Accepted.
🅰🆂🅺 🆂🅾 ✕ 🎱 🅶 🖥 🖵 🍴 🏊

△△△ ▼▼▼ Comfort Inn 🆂🅷
(731) 285-6951. **$69, 10 day notice.** 815 Reelfoot Dr. I-155,
exit 13, just s. Ext corridors. **Pets:** Small. $10 daily fee/
room. Designated rooms, service with restrictions, supervision.
🆂🅰🆅🅴 🆂🅾 ✕ 🖥 🖵 🏊

▼▼ Four Seasons Inn 🆂🅷
(731) 287-0044. **$40.** 2331 Lake Rd. I-155, exit 13, 0.5 mi s.
Ext corridors. **Pets:** Accepted.
🅰🆂🅺 🆂🅾 ✕ 🖥

▼▼▼ Hampton Inn 🆂🅷
(731) 285-4778. **$74-$84.** 2750 Mall Loop Rd. I-155, exit 13,
just s. Int corridors. **Pets:** Medium. Service with restrictions,
supervision.
🅰🆂🅺 ✕ &ᴹ 🎱 🅶 🖥 🖵 🏊

EAST RIDGE

AAA **WWW** Best Value Inn **SH**
(423) 894-6110. **$37-$59.** 639 Camp Jordan Pkwy. I-75, exit 1 (Ringgold Rd), 0.3 mi e. Ext/int corridors. **Pets:** Accepted.
SAVE S X B D Y

WWW Howard Johnson Plaza Hotel **SH**
(423) 892-8100. **$50-$90.** 6700 Ringgold Rd. I-75, exit 1 (Ringgold Rd). Int corridors. **Pets:** Medium. Designated rooms, service with restrictions, supervision.
ASK S X B Y

WW Ramada Limited **SH**
(423) 894-1860. **$46-$64.** 6650 Ringgold Rd. I-75, exit 1 (Ringgold Rd). Int corridors. **Pets:** Small, other species. $5 daily fee/room. Service with restrictions, supervision.
ASK S X

ELIZABETHTON

WW Americourt **SH**
(423) 542-4466. **$54-$200.** 1515 US 19 E Bypass. 1 mi e on US 19 E Bypass and US 321. Int corridors. **Pets:** Accepted.
ASK S X B D

ERWIN

WWW Holiday Inn Express **SH**
(423) 743-4100. **$69-$109.** 2002 Temple Hill Rd. US 19 W and 23, exit 15, just e. Int corridors. **Pets:** Medium. $15 daily fee/pet. Designated rooms, service with restrictions, supervision.
ASK S X B D

FAIRVIEW

AAA **WWW** Deerfield Inn & Suites **SH**
(615) 799-4700. **$49-$79.** 1407 Hwy 96 N. I-40, exit 182. Ext corridors. **Pets:** Small. $8 daily fee/pet. Service with restrictions, supervision.
SAVE X B D

FARRAGUT

WWW Baymont Inn & Suites-Knoxville West **SH**
(865) 671-1010. **$60-$96.** 11341 Campbell Lakes. I-40/75, exit 373 (Campbell Station Rd). Int corridors. **Pets:** Other species. Service with restrictions, crate.
ASK S X B D

AAA **WWW** Super 8 **SH**
(865) 675-5566. **$49-$94.** 11748 Snyder Rd. I-40/75, exit 373 (Campbell Station Rd), just ne. Ext corridors. **Pets:** Small. $6 daily fee/pet. Designated rooms, service with restrictions, supervision.
SAVE S X B D

FAYETTEVILLE

WW Best Western-Fayetteville Inn **SH**
(931) 433-0100. **$63-$68.** 3021 Thornton Taylor Pkwy. 0.7 mi e of US 431, on US 64 and 231 Bypass. Ext corridors. **Pets:** Other species. $10 one-time fee/room.
ASK S X B D Y

FRANKLIN

AAA **WWW** AmeriSuites (Nashville/Cool Springs) **SH**
(615) 771-8900. **$84-$99.** 650 Bakers Bridge Ave. I-65, exit 69 (Gallerria Blvd), 0.5 mi s, then just e. Int corridors. **Pets:** Accepted.
SAVE S X B D

AAA **WWW** Baymont Inn & Suites Nashville-Franklin **M**
(615) 791-7700. **$79-$109.** 4207 Franklin Commons Ct. I-65, exit 65, just e. Int corridors. **Pets:** Medium. Service with restrictions, supervision.
SAVE S X B D

WW Best Western Franklin Inn **SH**
(615) 790-0570. **$40-$80, 14 day notice.** 1308 Murfreesboro Rd. I-65, exit 65, just w. Ext corridors. **Pets:** Medium. $10 one-time fee/pet. Service with restrictions.
ASK S X B D

AAA **WWW** Comfort Inn **M**
(615) 791-6675. **$49-$125.** 4206 Franklin Commons Ct. I-65, exit 65, just e. Ext corridors. **Pets:** Accepted.
SAVE S X B D

AAA **WWW** Days Inn **SH**
(615) 790-1140. **$60-$75.** 4217 S Carothers Rd. I-65, exit 65, just e. Ext corridors. **Pets:** Very small. $10 daily fee/pet. Service with restrictions, supervision.
SAVE S X B D

WW Holiday Inn Express Hotel & Suites **M**
(615) 591-6660. **$99-$159.** 4202 Franklin Commons Ct. I-65, exit 65, just e. Int corridors. **Pets:** $25 daily fee/pet. Designated rooms, service with restrictions, crate.
ASK S X B D

WW Homestead Studio Suites Hotel-Nashville/ Cool Springs/Brentwood **SH**
(615) 771-7600. **$49-$64.** 680 Bakers Bridge Ave. I-65, exit 69 (Galleria Blvd). Ext corridors. **Pets:** Medium, other species. $25 daily fee/room. Service with restrictions, crate.
ASK S X B D

WWW Namaste Acres Country Ranch Inn **BB**
(615) 791-0333. **$85-$95, 5 day notice.** 5436 Leipers Creek. SR 96, 5 mi w; SR 46, 6 mi sw, 1.9 mi s. Ext/int corridors. **Pets:** Other species. $10 one-time fee/room. No service, supervision.
X B D

WWW Ramada Limited & Suites **SH**
(615) 791-4004. **$49-$99.** 6210 Hospitality Dr. I-65, exit 65, 1 mi e. Int corridors. **Pets:** Small, other species. $10 daily fee/room. Service with restrictions.
ASK S X B D

WW Super 8 **SH**
(615) 794-7591. **$49-$110, 3 day notice.** 1307 Murfreesboro Rd. I-65, exit 65, just w. Ext corridors. **Pets:** Very small. Service with restrictions, supervision.
ASK S X B D

GALLATIN

▼▼ Jameson Inn M
(615) 451-4494. **$66-$68.** 1001 Village Green Crossing. 2 mi s on US 31. Ext corridors. **Pets:** Medium. Service with restrictions, crate.

GATLINBURG

✦✦ ▼▼▼ Greenbrier Valley Resorts At Cobbly Nob CA
(865) 436-2015. **$110-$400, 14 day notice.** 3629 E Parkway. 10.8 mi e on US 321 N (E Parkway). Ext corridors. **Pets:** Dogs only. $100 deposit/pet, $10 daily fee/pet. Designated rooms, no service, crate.

SAVE ✕ 🛏 🖵 🏊

✦✦ ▼▼▼ Holiday Inn SunSpree Resort LH ❀
(865) 436-9201. **$59-$139.** 520 Historic Nature Tr. US 441, 1 mi e at traffic light 8. Ext/int corridors. **Pets:** Small, other species. $15 one-time fee/pet. Designated rooms, service with restrictions, supervision.

SAVE S✕ ✕ ⚐M ⚐ ⚐ 🛏 🖵 🍴 🏊

✦✦ ▼▼▼ Microtel-Gatlinburg SH
(865) 436-0107. **$34-$94, 3 day notice.** 211 Historic Nature Tr. US 441, traffic light 8, just e. Int corridors. **Pets:** Medium. $10 one-time fee/pet. Service with restrictions, supervision.

SAVE S✕ ✕ ⚐M ⚐ 🛏

▼ Terrace Motel M
(865) 436-4965. **$55-$80, 7 day notice.** 396 Parkway. US 441, between traffic lights 2 and 3. Ext corridors. **Pets:** Accepted.

ASK S✕ 🛏 🏊

GREENEVILLE

✦✦ ▼▼▼▼ Comfort Inn of Greeneville SH
(423) 639-4185. **$63-$77.** 1790 E Andrew Johnson Hwy. US 11 E, 2.9 mi ne. Ext/int corridors. **Pets:** Accepted.

SAVE ✕ 🛏 🖵 🏊

▼▼▼ Jameson Inn SH
(423) 638-7511. **$69-$71.** 3160 E Andrew Johnson Hwy. US 11 E, 3.6 mi ne. Int corridors. **Pets:** Small. Service with restrictions, crate.

✕ 🛏 🖵 🏊

HARRIMAN

✦✦ ▼▼▼ Best Western Sundancer Motor Lodge M
(865) 882-6200. **$49-$60.** 120 Childs Rd. I-40, exit 347, just n. Ext corridors. **Pets:** Accepted.

SAVE S✕ ✕ 🛏 🖵

✦✦ ▼▼▼▼ Holiday Inn Express M
(865) 882-5340. **$65-$95.** 1845 S Roane St. I-40, exit 347, just s. Ext corridors. **Pets:** Other species. $25 one-time fee/room. No service, supervision.

SAVE S✕ ✕ ⚐M ⚐ 🛏 🖵 🏊

✦✦ ▼▼▼ Super 8 Motel M
(865) 882-6600. **$49-$55.** 1867 S Roane St. I-40, exit 347, 0.3 mi s on US 27/SR 61. Ext corridors. **Pets:** Medium. $5 daily fee/pet. Service with restrictions, supervision.

SAVE S✕ ✕ 🛏 🏊

HENDERSONVILLE

✦✦ ▼▼▼▼ AmeriSuites (Nashville/Hendersonville) SH
(615) 826-4301. **$79-$104.** 330 E Main St. US 31, 1 mi n. Int corridors. **Pets:** Accepted.

SAVE S✕ ✕ ⚐M 🛏 🖵 🏊

HURRICANE MILLS

✦✦ ▼▼▼ Best Western of Hurricane Mills M ❀
(931) 296-4251. **$60-$90.** 15542 Hwy 13 S. I-40, exit 143. Ext corridors. **Pets:** Medium. $10 daily fee/pet. Service with restrictions, crate.

SAVE S✕ ✕ ⚐ 🛏 🖵 🏊

✦✦ ▼▼▼▼ Holiday Inn Express SH
(931) 296-2999. **$67-$89.** 15368 Hwy 13 S. I-40, exit 143, just n. Int corridors. **Pets:** Other species. Service with restrictions, supervision.

SAVE S✕ ✕ ⚐ 🛏 🏊

JACKSON

✦✦ ▼▼▼ Baymont Inn & Suites Jackson SH
(731) 664-1800. **$69-$89.** 2370 N Highland Ave. I-40, exit 82A. Int corridors. **Pets:** Medium. $50 deposit/room. Designated rooms, service with restrictions, supervision.

SAVE S✕ ✕ 🛏 🖵 🏊

▼▼ Days Inn SH
(731) 668-3444. **$39-$53.** 1919 US 45 Bypass. I-40, exit 80A, just s. Ext corridors. **Pets:** Accepted.

ASK S✕ ✕ 🛏 🏊

▼▼ Days Inn-West SH
(731) 668-4840. **$40-$46, 7 day notice.** 2239 Hollywood Dr. I-40, exit 79. Ext corridors. **Pets:** Other species. $5 daily fee/pet. Designated rooms, service with restrictions, supervision.

ASK S✕ ✕ 🛏 🏊

▼▼▼ Doubletree Hotel Jackson LH
(731) 664-6900. **$89-$99.** 1770 Hwy 45 Bypass. I-40, exit 80A, 0.5 mi s. Int corridors. **Pets:** Large. $5 one-time fee/pet. Designated rooms, service with restrictions, crate.

ASK S✕ ✕ ⚐ 🛏 🖵 🍴 🏊

▼▼▼ Jameson Inn SH
(731) 660-8651. **$72-$74.** 1292 Vann Dr. I-40, exit 80B, 0.6 mi w. Int corridors. **Pets:** Small. Service with restrictions, crate.

✕ 🛏 🖵 🏊

✦✦ ▼▼▼ Old Hickory Inn SH
(731) 668-4222. **$44-$48.** 1849 Hwy 45 Bypass. I-40, exit 80A, 0.3 mi s. Ext corridors. **Pets:** Very small. $10 daily fee/pet. Designated rooms, service with restrictions, supervision.

SAVE S✕ ✕ 🛏 🖵 🏊

JELLICO

▼▼ **Best Western Holiday Plaza Motel** 🆂🅷
(423) 784-7241. **$49-$85.** 133 Holiday Dr. I-75, exit 160, just w. Ext corridors. **Pets:** Accepted.

🅰🆂🅺 🆂🔟 ⊠ 💻 ⌫

▼▼ **Days Inn** 🆂🅷
(423) 784-7281. **$39-$55.** US 25 W. I-75, exit 160, just w. Ext corridors. **Pets:** Accepted.

🅰🆂🅺 🆂🔟 ⊠ 💻 🍴 ⌫

JOHNSON CITY

▼▼▼ **Best Western Johnson City Hotel &**
Conference Center 🆂🅷 ✿
(423) 282-2161. **$68-$99, 30 day notice.** 2406 N Roan St. I-26, exit 35A northbound; exit 35 southbound, just e. Ext/int corridors. **Pets:** Medium. $15 one-time fee/pet. Designated rooms, service with restrictions, crate.

🅰🆂🅺 🆂🔟 ⊠ 🤚 🈁 💻 🍴 ⌫

▼▼ **Comfort Inn of Johnson City** 🆂🅷
(423) 928-9600. **$65-$110.** 1900 S Roan St. I-181, exit 31, just w on US 321. Ext corridors. **Pets:** Accepted.

🅰🆂🅺 🆂🔟 ⊠ 🈁 💻 ⌫

▼▼ **Holiday Inn-Johnson City** 🆂🅷
(423) 282-4611. **$93-$110.** 101 W Springbrook Dr. I-181, exit 35A northbound; exit 35 southbound, just e on N Roan St, just n. Int corridors. **Pets:** Other species. $50 deposit/room. Designated rooms, service with restrictions, crate.

🅰🆂🅺 ⊠ 🎵 🈁 💻 🍴 ⌫

▼▼ **Jameson Inn** 🆂🅷
(423) 282-0488. **$67-$69.** 119 Pinnacle Dr. I-181, exit 38, just w on CR 354, then just s. Ext corridors. **Pets:** Small. Service with restrictions, crate.

⊠ 🤚 🈁 💻 ⌫

🅰🅰🅰 ▼▼▼ **Red Roof Inn-Johnson City** 🆂🅷
(423) 282-3040. **$43-$66.** 210 Broyles Dr. I-181, exit 35B northbound; exit 35 southbound, just w on N Roan St, then s. Ext corridors. **Pets:** Accepted.

🆂🅰🆅🅴 ⊠ 🎵 🈁

▼▼ **Sleep Inn** 🆂🅷
(423) 915-0081. **$66-$68.** 2020 Franklin Terrace Ct. I-181, exit 36, just w, then just n, follow signs; must enter on Oakland Ave at the light. Int corridors. **Pets:** Other species. Service with restrictions, crate.

🅰🆂🅺 🆂🔟 ⊠ 🅼 🎵 🤚 🈁 💻

KINGSPORT

▼▼▼ **Jameson Inn** 🆂🅷
(423) 230-0534. **$76-$78.** 3004 Bay Meadow Pl. I-81, exit 51. Int corridors. **Pets:** Small. Service with restrictions.

⊠ 🈁 💻 ⌫

▼▼▼ **La Quinta Inn-Kingsport** 🆂🅷
(423) 323-0500. **$59-$89.** 10150 Airport Pkwy. I-81, exit 63, just e. Int corridors. **Pets:** Accepted.

🅰🆂🅺 🆂🔟 ⊠ 🅼 🎵 🤚 🈁 💻 ⌫

▼▼ **Sleep Inn** 🆂🅷
(423) 279-1811. **$66.** 200 Hospitality Pl. I-81, exit 63, just s. Int corridors. **Pets:** Accepted.

🅰🆂🅺 🆂🔟 ⊠ 🤚 🈁 💻

KINGSTON

🅰🅰🅰 ▼▼ **Comfort Inn of Kingston** Ⓜ
(865) 376-4965. **$50-$80.** 905 N Kentucky St. I-40, exit 352, 0.3 mi s. Ext corridors. **Pets:** Medium. $10 one-time fee/room. Service with restrictions, supervision.

🆂🅰🆅🅴 🆂🔟 ⊠ 🈁

🅰🅰🅰 ▼▼ **Days Inn** Ⓜ
(865) 376-2069. **$55-$100.** 495 Gallaher Rd. I-40, exit 356, just n. Ext corridors. **Pets:** Medium. $10 daily fee/pet. Service with restrictions, supervision.

🆂🅰🆅🅴 🆂🔟 ⊠ 🎵 🈁 ⌫

KINGSTON SPRINGS

🅰🅰🅰 ▼▼ **Best Western Harpeth Inn** 🆂🅷
(615) 952-3961. **$45-$75.** 116 Luy Ben Hills Rd. I-40, exit 188, just n. Ext corridors. **Pets:** Accepted.

🆂🅰🆅🅴 ⊠ 🎵 🈁 💻 ⌫

KNOXVILLE

🅰🅰🅰 ▼▼▼ **The Clarion Inn** 🆂🅷
(865) 687-8989. **$69-$99.** 5634 Merchant Center Blvd. I-75, exit 108 (Merchant Dr), 0.5 mi w, then 0.5 mi n. Int corridors. **Pets:** Small. $10 one-time fee/room. Service with restrictions, supervision.

🆂🅰🆅🅴 🆂🔟 ⊠ 🅼 🎵 🤚 🈁 💻 ⌫

▼▼▼ **ClubHouse Inn & Suites Knoxville** 🆂🅷
(865) 531-1900. **$79-$109.** 208 Market Place Ln. I-40/75, exit 378 (Cedar Bluff Rd). Int corridors. **Pets:** Accepted.

🅰🆂🅺 🆂🔟 ⊠ 🅼 🎵 🤚 🈁 💻 🍴 ⌫

🅰🅰🅰 ▼▼ **Days Inn West** Ⓜ
(865) 966-5801. **$40-$90.** 326 Lovell Rd. I-40/75, exit 374. Ext corridors. **Pets:** Accepted.

🆂🅰🆅🅴 🆂🔟 ⊠ 🎵 🤚 🈁 💻 ⌫

🅰🅰🅰 ▼▼ **Econo Lodge West** Ⓜ
(865) 693-6061. **$50-$99.** 9240 Park West Blvd. I-40/75, exit 378 (Cedar Bluff Rd), just n to Park West Blvd, then just w. Ext corridors. **Pets:** Medium. $5 daily fee/pet. Service with restrictions, supervision.

🆂🅰🆅🅴 🆂🔟 ⊠ 🈁 💻 ⌫

▼▼▼ **Hampton Inn-Knoxville West at Cedar**
Bluff Ⓜ
(865) 693-1101. **$84-$104.** 9128 Executive Park Blvd. I-40/75, exit 378 (Cedar Bluff Rd). Ext/int corridors. **Pets:** Small. Designated rooms, service with restrictions, supervision.

🅰🆂🅺 🆂🔟 ⊠ 🅼 🎵 🤚 🈁 💻 ⌫

🅰🅰🅰 ▼▼▼ **Hilton Knoxville Downtown** 🅻🅷
(865) 523-2300. **$89.** 501 W Church Ave. Between Locust and Walnut sts; downtown. Int corridors. **Pets:** Accepted.

🆂🅰🆅🅴 🆂🔟 ⊠ 🅼 🎵 🤚 🈁 💻 🍴 ⌫

(AAA) ▼▼▼ **Holiday Inn-Central/Papermill Road** LH
(865) 584-3911. **$113-$129, 3 day notice.** 1315 Kirby Rd. I-40/75, exit 383 (Papermill Rd). Int corridors. **Pets:** Accepted.
SAVE S🐾 ✕ 🐾M 🖉 🐾 🛏 💻 🍽 ⊇

▼▼ **Knights Inn-North** M 🐾
(865) 687-3500. **$40-$65.** 6730 N Central Avenue Pike. I-75, exit 110 (Callahan Dr), just e. Ext corridors. **Pets:** Dogs only. $10 daily fee/pet. Service with restrictions, supervision.
ASK S🐾 ✕ 🛏

(AAA) ▼▼▼ **La Quinta Inn** SH
(865) 690-9777. **$69-$89.** 258 Peters Rd N. I-40, exit 378 (Cedar Bluff Rd). Ext corridors. **Pets:** Medium, other species. Service with restrictions, crate.
SAVE S🐾 ✕ 🐾M 🖉 🛏 💻 ⊇

▼▼ **Microtel** M
(865) 531-8041. **$44-$75.** 309 N Peters Rd. I-40/75, exit 378 (Cedar Bluff Rd), 0.5 mi s, just w. Int corridors. **Pets:** Medium, other species. $10 one-time fee/room. Designated rooms, service with restrictions.
ASK S🐾 ✕ 🐾M 🖉

▼▼ **Motel 6-1252** M
(865) 675-7200. **$36-$52.** 402 Lovell Rd. I-40/75, exit 374 (Lovell Rd). Ext corridors. **Pets:** Accepted.
S🐾 ✕ 🐾M 🖉 🐾 ⊇

▼▼ **Motel 6 #1482** M
(865) 689-7100. **$40-$53.** 5640 Merchant Center Blvd. I-75, exit 108 (Merchant Dr). Ext corridors. **Pets:** Accepted.
S🐾 ✕ 🖉

▼▼ **Quality Inn North** M
(865) 689-6600. **$50-$70.** 6712 Central Ave Pike. I-75, exit 110 (Callahan Dr), just e. Ext/int corridors. **Pets:** Other species. Service with restrictions, supervision.
ASK S🐾 ✕ 🛏 💻 ⊇

▼▼▼ **Radisson Summit Hill** SH 🐾
(865) 522-2600. **$135.** 401 Summit Hill Dr. Corner of jct Walnut St; downtown. Int corridors. **Pets:** Large. $25 one-time fee/room. Service with restrictions, crate.
ASK S🐾 ✕ 🖉 🐾 🛏 💻 🍽 ⊇

(AAA) ▼▼ **Ramada Limited-East** M
(865) 546-7271. **$70-$100, 3 day notice.** 722 Brakebill Rd. I-40, exit 398 (Strawberry Plains), just n. Ext corridors. **Pets:** Accepted.
SAVE S🐾 ✕ 🐾M 🛏 💻 ⊇

(AAA) ▼▼ **Red Roof Inn-West** M
(865) 691-1664. **$44-$54.** 209 Advantage Pl. I-40/75, exit 378 (Cedar Bluff Rd), just sw. Ext corridors. **Pets:** Accepted.
SAVE ✕ 🐾M 🖉 🛏

▼▼▼ **Signature Inn Cedar Bluff** SH
(865) 531-7444. **$84-$89.** 209 Market Place Ln. I-40/75, exit 378 (Cedar Bluff Rd). Int corridors. **Pets:** Small. Service with restrictions, crate.
ASK S🐾 ✕ 🐾M 🛏 💻 ⊇

▼▼ **Super 8 Motel-Knoxville** M
(865) 584-8511. **$45-$75.** 6200 Papermill Rd. I-40/75, exit 383 (Papermill Rd), 0.3 mi e. Ext corridors. **Pets:** Large, other species. Service with restrictions, supervision.
ASK S🐾 ✕ 🐾M 🖉 🛏 💻 ⊇

LAWRENCEBURG

▼▼ **Best Western Villa Inn** SH
(931) 762-4448. **$69-$89.** 2126 N Locust Ave. On US 43, 2.2 mi n of jct US 64. Ext corridors. **Pets:** Small. $10 daily fee/pet. Service with restrictions, supervision.
ASK ✕ 🛏 💻 ⊇

LEBANON

(AAA) ▼▼▼ **Best Western Executive Inn** M 🐾
(615) 444-0505. **$49-$122.** 631 S Cumberland St. I-40, exit 238, 0.5 mi n. Ext/int corridors. **Pets:** Small. Service with restrictions.
SAVE S🐾 ✕ 🐾M 🛏 💻 ⊇

▼▼ **Comfort Inn** M
(615) 444-1001. **$49-$89.** 829 S Cumberland St. I-40, exit 238. Ext corridors. **Pets:** $5 one-time fee/pet. Designated rooms, crate.
ASK S🐾 ✕ 🛏 💻 ⊇

▼▼ **Days Inn** M
(615) 444-5635. **$40-$70, 3 day notice.** 914 Murfreesboro Rd. I-40, exit 238. Ext corridors. **Pets:** Small. $5 one-time fee/room. Service with restrictions, supervision.
ASK S🐾 ✕ 🛏 ⊇

▼▼▼ **GuestHouse International Inn** M
(615) 449-5781. **$37-$129.** 822 S Cumberland St. I-40, exit 238. Ext corridors. **Pets:** Medium, other species. $8 daily fee/pet. Service with restrictions, crate.
ASK S🐾 ✕ 🛏 💻 ⊇

(AAA) ▼▼▼ **Hampton Inn** M
(615) 444-7400. **$59-$89.** 704 S Cumberland St. I-40, exit 238. Ext corridors. **Pets:** Medium. $50 deposit/pet. Designated rooms, service with restrictions, supervision.
SAVE S🐾 ✕ 🐾M 🖉 🛏 💻 ⊇ ✕

▼▼ **Super 8 Motel** M
(615) 444-5637. **$40-$70, 3 day notice.** 914 Murfreesboro Rd. I-40, exit 238. Ext corridors. **Pets:** Small. $5 one-time fee/room. Service with restrictions, supervision.
ASK S🐾 ✕ 🛏 ⊇

LENOIR CITY

(AAA) ▼▼▼ **Days Inn** M
(865) 986-2011. **$52-$70.** 1110 Hwy 321 N. I-75, exit 81, just e. Ext corridors. **Pets:** Small. $10 one-time fee/pet. Service with restrictions, supervision.
SAVE S🐾 ✕ 🛏 ⊇

(AAA) ▼▼ **Econo Lodge** M
(865) 986-0295. **$59-$82.** 1211 Hwy 321 N. I-75, exit 81, just w. Ext corridors. **Pets:** Small. $6 daily fee/pet. Designated rooms, service with restrictions, supervision.
SAVE S🐾 ✕ 🖉 🛏 ⊇

LOUDON

Knights Inn Ⓜ
(865) 458-5855. **$45-$69.** 15100 Hwy 72. I-75, exit 72, just w. Ext corridors. **Pets:** Large. $5 daily fee/pet. Service with restrictions, supervision.

Super 8 Motel 🆂🅷
(865) 458-5669. **$59-$64.** 12452 Hwy 72 N. I-75, exit 72, just e. Ext corridors. **Pets:** Small. Service with restrictions, crate.

MANCHESTER

Country Inn & Suites 🆂🅷
(931) 728-7551. **$59-$63, 10 day notice.** 126 Expressway Dr. I-24, exit 114, just w. Int corridors. **Pets:** Small. Service with restrictions, supervision.

Days Inn & Suites 🆂🅷
(931) 728-9530. **$59, 5 day notice.** 2259 Hillsboro Blvd. I-24, exit 114, just w. Ext corridors. **Pets:** Medium, dogs only. $7 daily fee/pet. Service with restrictions, supervision.

Econo Lodge Ⓜ
(931) 728-6023. **$50-$75, 5 day notice.** 890 Interstate Dr. I-24, exit 110, just n on SR 53. Ext corridors. **Pets:** Medium. $5 daily fee/pet. Designated rooms, service with restrictions, supervision.

Ramada Inn 🆂🅷
(931) 728-0800. **$39-$69.** 2314 Hillsboro Blvd. I-24, exit 114, just n. Ext corridors. **Pets:** Accepted.

MCMINNVILLE

Best Western McMinnville Inn 🆂🅷
(931) 473-7338. **$49-$69.** 2545 Sparta Hwy. I-24, exit 111, n on SR 55 to US 70 S Bypass. Ext corridors. **Pets:** Accepted.

MEMPHIS METROPOLITAN AREA

COLLIERVILLE

Comfort Inn 🆂🅷
(901) 853-1235. **$74-$99.** 1230 W Poplar Ave. 2.5 mi w on SR 57 and US 72. Ext corridors. **Pets:** Other species. $10 one-time fee/room. Service with restrictions, supervision.

CORDOVA

Quality Suites-Wolfchase 🆂🅷
(901) 386-4600. **$79-$165, 7 day notice.** 8166 Varnavas Dr. I-40, exit 16, 0.3 mi s on Germantown Pkwy, then e. Int corridors. **Pets:** Accepted.

COVINGTON

Comfort Inn 🆂🅷
(901) 475-0380. **$70-$85.** 901 Hwy 51 N. 1 mi n of jct US 59. Ext corridors. **Pets:** Small, other species. $10 daily fee/pet.

GERMANTOWN

Comfort Inn & Suites-Germantown 🆂🅷 ❖
(901) 757-7800. **$59-$114, 7 day notice.** 7787 Wolf River Blvd. I-40, exit 16, 5 mi s on Germantown Pkwy. Int corridors. **Pets:** Other species. Service with restrictions, supervision.

Homewood Suites by Hilton-Germantown 🆂🅷
(901) 751-2500. **$119.** 7855 Wolf River Pkwy. I-40, exit 16, 5.8 mi s on CR 177 at jct of Germantown Pkwy and Wolf River Blvd. Int corridors. **Pets:** Large, other species. $100 one-time fee/room.

Residence Inn 🆂🅷
(901) 751-2500. **$89-$114.** 9314 Poplar Ave. I-240, exit 15 (Poplar Ave), 7 mi e. Int corridors. **Pets:** Small, other species. $100 one-time fee/room. Service with restrictions.

LAKELAND

Super 8 Motel 🆂🅷
(901) 372-4575. **$56-$75, 7 day notice.** 9779 Huff Puff Rd. I-40, exit 20. Ext corridors. **Pets:** Medium, dogs only. $20 daily fee/pet. No service, supervision.

MEMPHIS

AmeriSuites (Memphis/Cordova) 🆂🅷
(901) 371-0010. **$89-$99.** 7905 Giacosa Pl. I-40, exit 16, just n on Germantown Rd, then just w. Int corridors. **Pets:** Accepted.

AmeriSuites (Memphis/Primacy Pkwy) 🆂🅷
(901) 680-9700. **$99-$129.** 1220 Primacy Pkwy. I-240, exit 15 (Poplar Ave), 0.3 mi e, s on Ridgeway, just w, then just s. Int corridors. **Pets:** Accepted.

Baymont Inn & Suites Memphis-Airport SH
(901) 396-5411. **$69-$89.** 3005 Millbranch Rd. I-240, exit 24, just s. Int corridors. **Pets:** Accepted.

Baymont Inn & Suites Memphis East SH
(901) 377-2233. **$59-$89.** 6020 Shelby Oaks Dr. I-40, exit 12, just n. Int corridors. **Pets:** Accepted.

Comfort Inn Airport/Graceland SH
(901) 345-3344. **$50-$90.** 1581 E Brooks Rd. I-55, exit 5A (Brooks Rd), 0.3 mi e. Ext corridors. **Pets:** $10 daily fee/pet. Service with restrictions, supervision.

Comfort Suites SH
(901) 365-2575. **$75-$300, 7 day notice.** 2575 Thousand Oaks Dr. I-240, exit 18. Int corridors. **Pets:** Service with restrictions, crate.

Drury Inn & Suites-Memphis Northeast SH
(901) 373-8200. **$72-$94.** 1556 Sycamore View. I-40, exit 12, just n. Int corridors. **Pets:** Large, other species. Service with restrictions, supervision.

Hampton Inn & Suites SH
(901) 762-0056. **$95-$109.** 962 S Shady Grove Rd. I-240, exit 15 (Poplar Ave), 0.5 mi e. Int corridors. **Pets:** Accepted.

Hawthorn Suites SH
(901) 682-1722. **$79-$129.** 1070 Ridge Lake Blvd. I-240, exit 15 (Poplar Ave), just e, then n under overpass. Int corridors. **Pets:** Accepted.

Holiday Inn-Sycamore View SH
(901) 388-7050. **$89-$119.** 6101 Shelby Oaks Dr. I-40, exit 12, just n. Int corridors. **Pets:** Other species. $25 one-time fee/pet. Service with restrictions, crate.

Holiday Inn-University of Memphis SH
(901) 678-8200. **$125-$145, 3 day notice.** 3700 Central Ave. I-240 E, exit 20B, 1.7 mi w on Getwell, 0.3 mi n on Park, 1 mi w on Goodlett, then just w; follow signs to university. Int corridors. **Pets:** Accepted.

Homestead Studio Suites Hotel-Memphis/Airport SH
(901) 344-0010. **$49-$59.** 2541 Corporate Ave E. I-240, exit 23B (Airways Blvd S), just s to Democrat Rd, just w to Nonconnah Blvd, 0.4 mi n to Corporate Ave, follow signs. Int corridors. **Pets:** Medium, other species. $25 daily fee/room. Service with restrictions, crate.

Homestead Studio Suites Hotel-Memphis/Poplar SH
(901) 767-5522. **$69-$84.** 6500 Poplar Ave. I-240, exit 15 (Poplar Ave), 1 mi e. Int corridors. **Pets:** Medium, other species. $25 daily fee/room. Service with restrictions, crate.

Homewood Suites SH
(901) 763-0500. **$139-$169.** 5811 Poplar Ave. I-240, exit 15 (Poplar Ave). Ext/int corridors. **Pets:** Medium. $150 one-time fee/room. Service with restrictions, supervision.

La Quinta Inn & Suites SH
(901) 374-0330. **$59-$89.** 1236 Primacy Pkwy. I-240, exit 15 (Poplar Ave), 0.3 mi e, s on Ridgeway, then w, just s. Int corridors. **Pets:** Accepted.

La Quinta Inn-East SH
(901) 382-2323. **$55-$75.** 6068 Macon Cove Rd. I-40, exit 12, just s. Ext corridors. **Pets:** Accepted.

Marriott Residence Inn SH
(901) 685-9595. **$79-$139.** 6141 Old Poplar Pike. I-240, exit 15 (Poplar Ave), 0.5 mi e. Ext/int corridors. **Pets:** $100 one-time fee/room. Designated rooms, service with restrictions.

Motel 6-459 SH
(901) 382-8572. **$41-$54.** 1321 Sycamore View. I-40, exit 12, just e. Ext corridors. **Pets:** Accepted.

Red Roof Inn-East SH
(901) 388-6111. **$44-$54.** 6055 Shelby Oaks Dr. I-40, exit 12, just n. Ext corridors. **Pets:** Accepted.

Red Roof Inn-South SH
(901) 363-2335. **$44-$54.** 3875 American Way. I-240, exit 20 (Getwell Rd), then just s. Ext corridors. **Pets:** Accepted.

The Ridgeway Inn SH
(901) 766-4000. **$75-$150.** 5679 Poplar Ave. I-240, exit 15 (Poplar Ave), just w. Int corridors. **Pets:** Accepted.

Wellesley Inn & Suites (Memphis/ Horizon Center) SH
(901) 380-1525. **$54-$84.** 2520 Horizon Lake Dr. I-40, exit 16B (Germantown), just n, then just w. Int corridors. **Pets:** Accepted.

❖ **END METROPOLITAN AREA** ❖

MONTEAGLE

▼▼▼▼ **Best Western Smoke House Lodge** SH
(931) 924-2091. **$59-$90.** 850 W Main St. I-24, exit 134. Ext corridors. **Pets:** Accepted.

ASK SÒ X 🐾 🔥 🛏 🖥 🍴 ⇌ ⊠

MORRISTOWN

▼▼▼▼ **Comfort Suites** SH 🐾
(423) 585-4000. **$66-$139, 5 day notice.** 3660 W Andrew Johnson Hwy. 3 mi w on US 11 E; downtown. Int corridors. **Pets:** Small, dogs only. $10 daily fee/pet. Service with restrictions, crate.

ASK SÒ X 🐾 🛏 🖥 ⇌ ⊠

▲▲▲ ▼▼▼ **Days Inn** M
(423) 587-2200. **$45-$65.** 2512 E Andrew Johnson Hwy. I-81, exit 8, 6 mi n on US 25 E to exit 2B (Greenville-Morristown), then just w. Ext corridors. **Pets:** Accepted.

SAVE SÒ X 🛏 ⇌

▼▼▼▼ **Holiday Inn** SH
(423) 581-8700. **$69-$79.** 3304 W Andrew Johnson Hwy. 2.5 mi w on US 11 E; downtown. Ext corridors. **Pets:** Other species. $10 one-time fee/pet. Designated rooms, service with restrictions, supervision.

ASK SÒ X 🐾 🛏 🖥 🍴 ⇌

▼▼▼▼ **Holiday Inn Morristown Conference Center** SH
(423) 587-2400. **$75-$80.** 5435 S Davy Crockett Pkwy. I-81, exit 8, just n. Int corridors. **Pets:** Medium, other species. $15 one-time fee/room. Service with restrictions, supervision.

ASK SÒ X 🛏 🖥 🍴 ⇌

▼▼ **Super 8 Motel** SH
(423) 318-8888. **$45-$60.** 5400 S Davy Crockett Pkwy. I-81, exit 8, just n. Int corridors. **Pets:** $9 one-time fee/pet. Service with restrictions, supervision.

ASK SÒ X 🔥 🛏 🖥

MOUNT JULIET

▼▼ **Microtel Inn & Suites** SH
(615) 773-3600. **$47-$73, 10 day notice.** 1000 Hershel Dr. I-40, exit 226. Int corridors. **Pets:** Accepted.

ASK SÒ X 🛏 🖥 ⇌

MURFREESBORO

▼▼▼▼ **Best Inn & Suites** SH
(615) 890-1006. **$49-$149.** 2135 S Church St. I-24, exit 81 westbound; exit 81B eastbound. Int corridors. **Pets:** Medium. Service with restrictions.

ASK SÒ X 🔥 🛏 🖥 ⇌

▲▲▲ ▼▼▼ **Best Western Chaffin Inn** M 🐾
(615) 895-3818. **$56-$98, 6 day notice.** 168 Chaffin Pl. I-24, exit 78B. Ext corridors. **Pets:** Small. $12 daily fee/pet. Designated rooms, service with restrictions, supervision.

SAVE SÒ X 🛏 🖥 ⇌

▼▼▼▼ **Hampton Inn** SH 🐾
(615) 896-1172. **$69-$119.** 2230 Armory Dr. I-24, exit 78B, just n. Ext corridors. **Pets:** Medium. $10 daily fee/pet. Designated rooms, service with restrictions, crate.

ASK SÒ X 🔥 🐾 🛏 🖥 ⇌

▼▼▼▼ **Holiday Inn Holidome** SH
(615) 896-2420. **Call for rates.** 2227 Old Fort Pkwy. I-24, exit 78B. Ext/int corridors. **Pets:** Accepted.

X 🐾 🛏 🖥 🍴 ⇌ ⊠

▲▲▲ ▼▼▼ **Howard Johnson Express Inn** SH
(615) 896-5522. **$40-$99.** 2424 S Church St. I-24, exit 81A eastbound; exit 81 westbound. Int corridors. **Pets:** Small. $5 daily fee/pet. Service with restrictions, supervision.

SAVE SÒ X 🛏 🖥 🍴 ⇌

▲▲▲ ▼▼▼ **Quality Inn** SH
(615) 848-9030. **$45-$79.** 118 Westgate Blvd. I-24, exit 81A eastbound; exit 81 westbound. Int corridors. **Pets:** Small. $5 daily fee/pet. Service with restrictions, supervision.

SAVE SÒ X 🛏 🖥 ⇌

▲▲▲ ▼▼▼ **Ramada Limited** SH
(615) 896-5080. **$60-$109.** 1855 S Church St. I-24, exit 81. Int corridors. **Pets:** Accepted.

SAVE X 🛏 🖥 ⇌

NASHVILLE METROPOLITAN AREA

GOODLETTSVILLE

▲▲▲ ▼▼▼▼ **Baymont Inn & Suites-Nashville North** SH
(615) 851-1891. **$59-$125.** 120 Cartwright St. I-65, exit 97 (Long Hollow Pike), just w. Int corridors. **Pets:** Small. Designated rooms, service with restrictions, supervision.

SAVE SÒ X 🔥 🐾 🔥 🛏 🖥 ⇌

▲▲▲ ▼▼▼▼ **Best Western Fairwinds Inn** M
(615) 851-1067. **$55-$99, 3 day notice.** 100 Northcreek Blvd. I-65, exit 97 (Long Hollow Pike), 0.5 mi e. Ext corridors. **Pets:** Small. $10 daily fee/pet. Service with restrictions, supervision.

SAVE SÒ X 🛏 🖥 ⇌

▲▲▲ ▼▼▼ **Red Roof Inn-Nashville North** M
(615) 859-2537. **$42-$52.** 110 Northgate Dr. I-65, exit 97 (Long Hollow Pike), 0.5 mi e. Ext corridors. **Pets:** Accepted.

SAVE X 🔥 🐾

HERMITAGE

▼▼▼ Comfort Inn M
(615) 889-5060. **$65-$75, 3 day notice.** 5768 Old Hickory Blvd. I-40, exit 221 westbound; exit 221B eastbound, just n. Ext corridors. **Pets:** Accepted.

NASHVILLE

▲▲▲ ▼▼▼ AmeriSuites (Nashville/Airport) SH
(615) 493-5200. **$109-$149.** 721 Royal Pkwy. I-40, exit 216C (Donelson Pike). Int corridors. **Pets:** Medium. Service with restrictions, supervision.

▲▲▲ ▼▼▼ Baymont Inn & Suites Nashville-Airport SH
(615) 885-3100. **$69-$99.** 531 Donelson Pike. I-40, exit 216C (Donelson Pike), 0.3 mi n. Int corridors. **Pets:** Medium, other species. $10 daily fee/room. No service.
[SAVE] [S] [X] [✏] [🔒] [💻] [≈]

▲▲▲ ▼ Best Value Inn M
(615) 226-9805. **$30-$70.** 2403 Brick Church Pike. I-65, exit 87 (Trinity Ln), just nw. Ext corridors. **Pets:** Medium. $10 daily fee/pet. Designated rooms, no service, crate.
[SAVE] [S] [X]

▲▲▲ ▼▼▼ Best Western Downtown Music Row SH ✿
(615) 242-1631. **$59-$119.** 1407 Division St. I-40, exit 209, just w. Int corridors. **Pets:** Small, other species. $5 daily fee/pet.
[SAVE] [S] [X] [🔒] [💻] [≈]

▼▼▼ ClubHouse Inn & Suites SH
(615) 883-0500. **$89-$94.** 2435 Atrium Way. Briley Pkwy to exit 7 (Elm Hill Pike), then just e. Int corridors. **Pets:** Small. Service with restrictions, supervision.
[ASK] [S] [X] [🔒] [💻] [≈]

▲▲▲ ▼▼▼ Comfort Inn Opryland M
(615) 889-0086. **$55-$99.** 2516 Music Valley Dr. I-40, exit 215 (Briley Pkwy), 4 mi n; I-65, exit 90, exit McGavock Pike off Briley Pkwy. Int corridors. **Pets:** Small. Service with restrictions, crate.
[SAVE] [S] [X] [💻] [≈]

▲▲▲ ▼▼▼ Days Inn Bell Road M
(615) 731-7800. **$65-$99.** 510 Collins Park Dr. I-24, exit 59 (Bell Rd). Ext corridors. **Pets:** Accepted.
[SAVE] [S] [X] [✏] [🔒] [💻] [≈]

▲▲▲ ▼▼▼ Days Inn Vanderbilt SH
(615) 327-0922. **$79-$88, 5 day notice.** 1800 West End Ave. I-40, exit 209A westbound; exit 209B eastbound. Ext/int corridors. **Pets:** Medium. $10 daily fee/pet. Service with restrictions, supervision.
[SAVE] [S] [X] [🔒] [💻] [≈]

▼▼▼ Days Inn West SH
(615) 356-9100. **$55-$58.** 269 White Bridge Pk. I-40, exit 204, just s. Ext corridors. **Pets:** Small. $5 daily fee/pet. No service.
[ASK] [S] [X] [🔒]

▲▲▲ ▼▼▼ Doubletree Hotel Downtown Nashville LH
(615) 244-8200. **$79-$209.** 315 4th Ave N. Corner of Union St and 4th Ave. Int corridors. **Pets:** Accepted.
[SAVE] [S] [X] [✏] [🔒] [💻] [🍴] [≈]

▲▲▲ ▼▼▼ Drury Inn & Suites-Nashville Airport SH
(615) 902-0400. **$86-$96.** 555 Donelson Pike. I-40, exit 216 (Donelson Pike). Int corridors. **Pets:** Medium. Service with restrictions, crate.
[SAVE] [X] [S,M] [✏] [🔒] [💻] [≈]

▼▼▼ Drury Inn-Nashville South SH
(615) 834-7170. **$68-$88.** 341 Harding Pl. I-24, exit 56 (Harding Pl). Ext corridors. **Pets:** Large, other species. Service with restrictions, supervision.
[ASK] [X] [S,M] [✏] [✏] [🔒] [💻] [≈]

▲▲▲ ▼▼▼ Embassy Suites LH
(615) 871-0033. **$98-$153.** 10 Century Blvd. I-40, exit 215 (Briley Pkwy N), then exit 7 (Elm Hill Pike), 0.3 mi e to McGavock Pike, 0.3 mi s to Century Blvd, then 0.3 mi w. Int corridors. **Pets:** Small. $10 daily fee/pet. Service with restrictions, supervision.
[SAVE] [S] [X] [S,M] [✏] [🔒] [💻] [🍴] [≈] [X]

▲▲▲ ▼▼ Fiddlers Inn SH
(615) 885-1440. **$50-$78.** 2410 Music Valley Dr. I-40, exit 215B (Briley Pkwy), 4 mi n to exit 11 (McGavock Pike), then just w. Ext corridors. **Pets:** Small, other species. Service with restrictions, supervision.
[SAVE] [X] [🔒] [💻] [≈]

▲▲▲ ▼▼▼ GuestHouse Inn of Music Valley SH
(615) 885-4030. **$69-$109.** 2420 Music Valley Dr. Briley Pkwy, exit 12B, 0.3 mi w, then 0.3 mi n. Int corridors. **Pets:** Accepted.
[SAVE] [S] [X] [🔒] [💻] [≈]

▼▼▼ Hampton Inn Briley Parkway M
(615) 871-0222. **$65-$82.** 2350 Elm Hill Pike. I-40, exit 215B (Briley Pkwy), to exit 7 (Elm Hill Pike). Ext corridors. **Pets:** Accepted.
[ASK] [S] [X] [S,M] [✏] [💻] [≈]

▲▲▲ ▼▼▼▼ The Hermitage Hotel LH
(615) 244-3121. **$265-$400.** 231 6th Ave N. Center. Int corridors. **Pets:** Accepted.
[SAVE] [S] [X] [🔒] [🍴]

▼▼▼ Holiday Inn Select-Vanderbilt SH
(615) 327-4707. **$84-$134.** 2613 West End Ave. I-40, exit 209B eastbound; exit 209A westbound, w on Broadway. Int corridors. **Pets:** $100 deposit/room, $25 one-time fee/room. Service with restrictions.
[ASK] [S] [X] [S,M] [✏] [🔒] [💻] [🍴] [≈]

▼▼▼ Holiday Inn-The Crossings SH ✿
(615) 731-2361. **$70-$99.** 201 Crossings Pl. I-24, exit 60, 0.5 mi e. Int corridors. **Pets:** Other species. Service with restrictions, supervision.
[ASK] [S] [X] [S,M] [✏] [✏] [🔒] [💻] [🍴] [≈]

▼▼▼ **Homestead Studio Suites**
Hotel-Nashville/Airport Ⓜ ❖
(615) 316-9020. **$54-$64.** 727 McGavock Pike. I-40, exit 215B (Briley Pkwy), 1 mi n to exit 7 (Elm Hill Pike), just e. Ext corridors. **Pets:** Medium, other species. $25 daily fee/room. Service with restrictions, crate.
(ASK) (S̄d) (✕) (&M) (🐾) (🔧) (🍴) (💻)

▼▼▼ **Homewood Suites by Hilton** SH
(615) 884-8111. **$99-$129.** 2640 Elm Hill Pike. I-40, exit 216C (Donelson Pike). Int corridors. **Pets:** Small. $200 one-time fee/room. Service with restrictions, supervision.
(ASK) (S̄d) (✕) (&M) (🐾) (🔧) (💻) (🐾)

▼▼ **Howard Johnson Inn** SH
(615) 352-7080. **$55-$62.** 6834 Charlotte Pike. I-40, exit 201, 0.4 mi e on US 70. Int corridors. **Pets:** Small. $5 daily fee/pet. Service with restrictions, supervision.
(ASK) (S̄d) (✕) (🔧) (💻) (🐾)

ⒶⒶⒶ ▼▼▼▼ **La Quinta Inn Nashville Airport** Ⓜ
(615) 885-3000. **$71-$81.** 2345 Atrium Way. I-40, exit 215B (Briley Pkwy), 1 mi n to exit 7 (Elm Hill Pike), e to Atrium Way, then 0.3 mi n. Int corridors. **Pets:** Medium, other species. Service with restrictions, supervision.
(SAVE) (S̄d) (✕) (&M) (🐾) (💻) (🐾)

ⒶⒶⒶ ▼▼▼▼ **La Quinta Inn-South** SH
(615) 834-6900. **$55-$75.** 4311 Sidco Dr. I-65, exit 78A. Ext corridors. **Pets:** Small, other species. No service, supervision.
(SAVE) (S̄d) (✕) (&M) (🔧) (💻) (🐾)

ⒶⒶⒶ ▼▼ ▼▼ **Loews Vanderbilt Hotel**
Nashville LH ❖
(615) 320-1700. **$139-$219.** 2100 West End Ave. I-40, exit 209 (Broadway), 1.3 mi w. Int corridors. **Pets:** Other species. Service with restrictions, supervision.
(SAVE) (S̄d) (✕) (🐾) (🔧) (🔧) (💻) (🍴)

▼▼ **Motel 6-156** SH
(615) 333-9933. **$35-$49.** 95 Wallace Rd. I-24, exit 56 (Harding Pl). Ext corridors. **Pets:** Accepted.
(S̄d) (✕) (🐾)

▼▼ **Music Valley Inn** SH
(615) 889-8235. **Call for rates.** 2500 Music Valley Dr. Briley Pkwy, exit 12. Int corridors. **Pets:** Accepted.
(✕) (💻) (🐾)

▼▼ **Pear Tree Inn-Nashville South** SH
(615) 834-4242. **$55-$71.** 343 Harding Pl. I-24, exit 56 (Harding Pl). Ext corridors. **Pets:** Large, other species. Service with restrictions, supervision.
(ASK) (✕) (🐾) (💻) (🐾)

ⒶⒶⒶ ▼▼▼ **The Quarters Motor Inn** Ⓜ
(615) 731-5990. **$45-$99.** 1100 Bell Rd. I-24, exit 59 (Bell Rd), just w. Ext corridors. **Pets:** Medium, other species. Designated rooms, service with restrictions, supervision.
(SAVE) (S̄d) (✕) (🔧)

ⒶⒶⒶ ▼▼▼ **Red Roof Inn** SH
(615) 889-0090. **$60-$80.** 2460 Music Valley Dr. I-40, exit 215B (Briley Pkwy), 4 mi n to exit 11 (McGavock Pike). Int corridors. **Pets:** Large, other species. Crate.
(SAVE) (S̄d) (✕) (🔧) (🐾)

ⒶⒶⒶ ▼▼▼ **Red Roof Inn Airport** Ⓜ
(615) 872-0735. **$44-$59.** 510 Claridge Dr. I-40, exit 216C (Donelson Pike), 0.3 mi n. Ext corridors. **Pets:** Large, other species. Service with restrictions, supervision.
(SAVE) (✕) (🐾)

ⒶⒶⒶ ▼▼▼ **Red Roof Inn South** SH
(615) 832-0093. **$45-$65.** 4271 Sidco Dr. I-65, exit 78. Ext corridors. **Pets:** Accepted.
(SAVE) (✕) (&M) (🐾)

▼▼▼ **Residence Inn** Ⓜ
(615) 889-8600. **$99-$115.** 2300 Elm Hill Pike. I-40, exit 215B (Briley Pkwy), 1.5 mi n. Ext corridors. **Pets:** Other species. $50 one-time fee/room. Service with restrictions.
(✕) (🔧) (🔧) (💻) (🐾)

ⒶⒶⒶ ▼▼▼▼ **Sheraton Music City Hotel** LH ❖
(615) 885-2200. **$89-$159.** 777 McGavock Pike. I-40, exit 215B (Briley Pkwy), 1 mi n to exit 7 (Elm Hill Pike), 0.5 mi e, then s. Int corridors. **Pets:** Other species. Service with restrictions, supervision.
(SAVE) (S̄d) (✕) (🔧) (💻) (🍴) (🐾) (🔧)

ⒶⒶⒶ ▼▼▼ **Super 8** SH
(615) 834-0620. **$38-$49.** 350 Harding Pl. I-24, exit 56. Int corridors. **Pets:** Medium, other species. $5 daily fee/room. Supervision.
(SAVE) (S̄d) (✕) (🔧) (💻) (🐾)

ⒶⒶⒶ ▼▼▼ **Super 8 Motel-West** SH
(615) 356-6005. **$55-$80.** 6924 Charlotte Pike. I-40, exit 201. Ext corridors. **Pets:** Medium, other species. $10 daily fee/pet. Service with restrictions, crate.
(SAVE) (S̄d) (✕) (🔧)

ⒶⒶⒶ ▼▼▼▼ **Union Station-A Wyndham Historic**
Hotel SH
(615) 726-1001. **$139-$149.** 1001 Broadway. I-40, exit 209A, just ne. Int corridors. **Pets:** Accepted.
(SAVE) (S̄d) (✕) (🔧) (💻) (🍴)

❖ **END METROPOLITAN AREA** ❖

NEWPORT

ⒶⒶⒶ ▼▼▼▼ **Best Western Newport Inn** Ⓜ
(423) 623-8713. **$45-$130.** 1015 Cosby Hwy. I-40, exit 435, just w. Ext corridors. **Pets:** Accepted.
(SAVE) (S̄d) (✕) (&M) (🐾) (🔧) (💻) (🐾)

ⒶⒶⒶ ▼▼▼▼ **Comfort Inn** Ⓜ
(423) 623-5355. **$39-$159.** 1149 Smokey Mountain Ln. I-40, exit 432B. Int corridors. **Pets:** Small. $10 daily fee/pet. Service with restrictions, supervision.
(SAVE) (S̄d) (✕) (&M) (🔧) (🔧) (💻) (🐾)

▽▽▽ Holiday Inn 🆂🅷
(423) 623-8622. **$64-$72.** 1010 Cosby Hwy. I-40, exit 435. Ext/int corridors. **Pets:** Medium. Service with restrictions, supervision.
🅰🆂🅺 🆂🅱 ⊗ 🎦 🛆 🖵 🍴 ➳ ⊠

▽▽ Motel 6-4090 Ⓜ
(423) 623-1850. **$35-$70.** 255 Heritage Blvd. I-40, exit 435, just n, then turn right. Int corridors. **Pets:** Large, other species. Designated rooms, service with restrictions, supervision.
⊗ 🅼 🖟 ➳

ⒶⒶⒶ ▽ Relax Inn Ⓜ
(423) 625-1521. **$55-$60, 3 day notice.** 1148 W Hwy 25-70. I-40, exit 432B. Ext corridors. **Pets:** Small, dogs only. $4 daily fee/pet. Service with restrictions, supervision.
🆂🅰🆅🅴 🆂🅱 ⊗ 🛆

OAK RIDGE

▽▽▽ Comfort Inn Ⓜ
(865) 481-8200. **$67-$80.** 433 S Rutgers Ave. 0.9 mi se of SR 95 on SR 62. Int corridors. **Pets:** Accepted.
🅰🆂🅺 🆂🅱 ⊗ 🅼 🛆 🖵 ➳

▽▽▽ Jameson Inn Ⓜ
(865) 483-6809. **$76-$81.** 216 S Rutgers Ave. Jct SR 95 and 62, 0.9 mi se on SR 62 to Rutgers Ave, then 0.7 mi n. Int corridors. **Pets:** Small. Service with restrictions, crate.
⊗ 🛆 🖵 ➳

ONEIDA

▽ The Galloway Inn Ⓜ
(423) 569-8835. **$26-$39.** 299 Galloway Dr. Jct SR 63, 3.3 mi n on US 27, just e. Ext corridors. **Pets:** Accepted.
🅰🆂🅺 🆂🅱 ⊗ 🛆 🖵

OOLTEWAH

▽ Super 8 Motel 🆂🅷
(423) 238-5951. **$45-$50.** 5111 Hunter Rd. I-75, exit 11, jct US 11 and 64. Ext corridors. **Pets:** Accepted.
🅰🆂🅺 🆂🅱 ⊗ 🛆 ➳

PARIS

▽▽▽ Hampton Inn 🆂🅷
(731) 642-2838. **$57-$69, 15 day notice.** 1510 E Wood St. 1.5 mi ne on US 79. Ext corridors. **Pets:** Accepted.
🅰🆂🅺 🆂🅱 ⊗ 🅼 🛆 🖵 ➳

PIGEON FORGE

ⒶⒶⒶ ▽▽▽▽ Grand Resort Hotel & Convention Center 🆂🅷
(865) 453-1000. **$49-$149, 3 day notice.** 3171 Parkway. On US 441. Ext/int corridors. **Pets:** Accepted.
🆂🅰🆅🅴 🆂🅱 ⊗ 🛆 🖵 🍴 ➳

▽▽▽▽ Holiday Inn Resort 🆂🅷 🐾
(865) 428-2700. **$89-$169.** 3230 Parkway. Just w of US 441. Int corridors. **Pets:** Small. $15 one-time fee/pet. Service with restrictions, supervision.
🅰🆂🅺 🆂🅱 ⊗ 🎦 🛆 🖵 🍴 ➳

ⒶⒶⒶ ▽▽▽ Microtel Ⓜ 🐾
(865) 429-0150. **$30-$100, 5 day notice.** 202 Emert St. On US 441, just w between traffic lights 7 and 8. Int corridors. **Pets:** $15 daily fee/pet. Designated rooms, service with restrictions.
🆂🅰🆅🅴 🆂🅱 ⊗ 🅼 🛆 ➳

▽▽▽ Microtel Suites @ Music Road Ⓜ 🐾
(865) 453-1116. **$35-$120.** 2045 Parkway. On US 441, between traffic lights 1 and 1A. Int corridors. **Pets:** $15 one-time fee/pet. Designated rooms, service with restrictions.
🅰🆂🅺 🆂🅱 ⊗ 🅼 🛆 🖵 ➳

▽▽▽ Motel 6 #4021 Ⓜ
(865) 908-1244. **$24-$79, 3 day notice.** 336 Henderson Chapel Rd. On US 441, just w of traffic light 1. Int corridors. **Pets:** Small. Service with restrictions.
⊗ 🅼 🖟 🛆 ➳

▽▽▽ National Parks Resort Lodge 🆂🅷
(865) 453-4106. **$29-$140.** 2385 Parkway. On US 441 at traffic light 1. Int corridors. **Pets:** $20 one-time fee/room. Designated rooms, service with restrictions, supervision.
🅰🆂🅺 ⊗ 🛆 ➳

ⒶⒶⒶ ▽▽▽ Smoky Shadows Motel & Conference Center 🆂🅷
(865) 453-7155. **$39-$129.** 4215 Parkway. On US 441, just s of traffic light 9. Ext/int corridors. **Pets:** Small. $10 one-time fee/room. Service with restrictions, crate.
🆂🅰🆅🅴 🆂🅱 ⊗ 🛆 🖵 ➳

POWELL

ⒶⒶⒶ ▽▽▽ Comfort Inn Ⓜ
(865) 938-5500. **$55-$85.** 323 E Emory Rd. I-75, exit 112. Ext corridors. **Pets:** Small, other species. $10 daily fee/room. Service with restrictions, crate.
🆂🅰🆅🅴 🆂🅱 ⊗ 🛆 ➳

PULASKI

ⒶⒶⒶ ▽▽ Super 8 Motel 🆂🅷
(931) 363-4501. **$45-$69.** 2400 Hwy 64 E. I-65, exit 14, just e. Ext corridors. **Pets:** Accepted.
🆂🅰🆅🅴 🆂🅱 ⊗ 🛆 ➳

ROGERSVILLE

▽▽▽ Holiday Inn Express 🆂🅷
(423) 272-1842. **$72.** 7139 Hwy 11 W. Jct SR 66 and US 11, just sw. Int corridors. **Pets:** Very small. $10 daily fee/pet. Designated rooms, service with restrictions, supervision.
🅰🆂🅺 🆂🅱 ⊗ 🖟 🛆 🖵 ➳

SELMER

▽▽ Super 8 Motel-Selmer 🆂🅷
(731) 645-8880. **$50-$120.** 644 Mulberry Ave. Jct SR 64 and 45, just s on SR 45. Ext corridors. **Pets:** $25 deposit/room. Service with restrictions, supervision.
🅰🆂🅺 🆂🅱 ⊗ 🛆 ➳

SEVIERVILLE

ⓐ ◈◈◈◈ **Best Western Dumplin Valley Inn** 🆂🅷
(865) 933-3467. **$39-$109.** 3426 Winfield Dunn Pkwy. I-40, exit 407, 0.3 mi s. Ext corridors. **Pets:** Other species. $10 daily fee/pet. Designated rooms, service with restrictions, crate.

🆂🅰🆅🅴 Ⓢ🄍 ⊠ 🖉 🖥 💻 ➳

◈◈◈◈ **Holiday Inn Express Hotel & Suites** 🆂🅷
(865) 933-9448. **$59-$179.** 2863 Winfield Dunn Pkwy. I-40, exit 407, 2 mi s. Int corridors. **Pets:** Accepted.

🄰🅂🄺 Ⓢ🄍 ⊠ 🄶🄼 🖉 🄲 🖥 💻 ➳

SMYRNA

◈◈◈◈ **Days Inn** 🆂🅷 ❀
(615) 355-6161. **$55-$63.** 1300 Plaza Dr. I-24, exit 66, 2 mi ne. Ext corridors. **Pets:** $10 daily fee/pet. Designated rooms, service with restrictions, crate.

🄰🅂🄺 Ⓢ🄍 ⊠ 🖥 ➳

SWEETWATER

ⓐ ◈◈◈◈ **Best Western Sweetwater Inn** 🆂🅷
(423) 337-3541. **$69-$105.** 1421 Murray's Chapel Rd. I-75, exit 60, just w. Ext/int corridors. **Pets:** Very small. Designated rooms, service with restrictions, supervision.

🆂🅰🆅🅴 Ⓢ🄍 ⊠ 🖥 💻 🍴 ➳

ⓐ ◈◈ **Budget Host Inn** 🆂🅷
(423) 337-9357. **$42-$46.** 207 Hwy 68. I-75, exit 60. Ext corridors. **Pets:** Accepted.

🆂🅰🆅🅴 Ⓢ🄍 ⊠ 🖥

ⓐ ◈◈◈ **Comfort Inn** 🆂🅷
(423) 337-6646. **$50-$70.** 731 S Main St. On US 11, jct SR 68. Ext/int corridors. **Pets:** Small. $5 daily fee/pet. Service with restrictions, supervision.

🆂🅰🆅🅴 Ⓢ🄍 ⊠ 🖥 💻 ➳

ⓐ ◈◈◈ **Comfort Inn West** 🆂🅷
(423) 337-3353. **$55-$85.** 249 Hwy 68. I-75, exit 60, just e. Ext/int corridors. **Pets:** Medium. $5 daily fee/pet. Service with restrictions, supervision.

🆂🅰🆅🅴 Ⓢ🄍 ⊠ 🖥 💻 ➳

ⓐ ◈◈◈ **Days Inn** 🆂🅷
(423) 337-4200. **$55-$69.** 229 Hwy 68. I-75, exit 60, just e. Ext corridors. **Pets:** Small. $10 daily fee/pet. Service with restrictions, supervision.

🆂🅰🆅🅴 Ⓢ🄍 ⊠ 🖥 💻 ➳

TOWNSEND

ⓐ ◈◈◈◈ **Best Western Valley View Lodge** 🆂🅷
(865) 448-2237. **$45-$100.** 7726 E Lamar Alexander Pkwy. On US 321; center. Ext corridors. **Pets:** Small, dogs only. $10 one-time fee/room. Service with restrictions, crate.

🆂🅰🆅🅴 Ⓢ🄍 ⊠ 🖉 🖥 💻 ➳

◈◈◈◈ **Maple Leaf Lodge** 🅱🅱
(865) 448-6000. **$120-$170, 14 day notice.** 137 Apple Valley Way. On US 321, 2 mi n. Ext/int corridors. **Pets:** Accepted.

⊠ 🖥 💻 🈲

TULLAHOMA

◈◈ **Jameson Inn** 🆂🅷
(931) 455-7891. **$65-$67.** 2113 N Jackson St. From town, 3 mi n on SR 41A (N Jackson St). Ext corridors. **Pets:** Small. Service with restrictions, crate.

⊠ 🄲 🖥 💻 ➳

VONORE

◈◈◈◈ **Grand Vista Hotel & Suites** 🆂🅷 ❀
(423) 884-6200. **$90.** 117 Grand Vista Dr. I-75, exit 172, 14 mi e. Int corridors. **Pets:** Small. $5 daily fee/room. Designated rooms, supervision.

🄰🅂🄺 Ⓢ🄍 ⊠ 🄶🄼 🖉 🄲 🖥 💻 ➳

WHITE HOUSE

ⓐ ◈◈◈ **Days Inn Whitehouse** 🆂🅷
(615) 672-3746. **$35-$70.** 1009 Hwy 76. I-65, exit 108, just w. Ext corridors. **Pets:** Medium. $5 daily fee/pet. Designated rooms, service with restrictions, supervision.

🆂🅰🆅🅴 Ⓢ🄍 ⊠ 🖥 💻 ➳

◈◈◈◈ **Holiday Inn Express** 🆂🅷
(615) 672-7200. **$49-$69.** 354 Hester Ln. I-65, exit 108, just e. Ext corridors. **Pets:** Medium, other species. $5 one-time fee/pet. Service with restrictions, supervision.

🄰🅂🄺 Ⓢ🄍 ⊠ 🄶🄼 🄲 🖥 💻 ➳

WHITE PINE

ⓐ ◈◈◈ **Days Inn** 🄼
(865) 674-2573. **$48-$57.** 3670 Roy Messer Hwy. I-81, exit 4, just w. Ext corridors. **Pets:** Small. $10 daily fee/pet. Designated rooms, service with restrictions, crate.

🆂🅰🆅🅴 Ⓢ🄍 ⊠ 🖥

WHITEVILLE

◈◈ **Super 8** 🆂🅷
(731) 254-8884. **$60.** 2040 Hwy 64. US 64 and SR 179. Ext corridors. **Pets:** Other species. $5 daily fee/pet. Service with restrictions, supervision.

🄰🅂🄺 Ⓢ🄍 ⊠ 🄶🄼 🄲 🖥

WILDERSVILLE

ⓐ ◈◈◈ **Best Western Crossroads Inn** 🆂🅷
(731) 968-2532. **$45-$61.** 21045 Hwy 22 N. I-40, exit 108, just s. Ext corridors. **Pets:** Small, other species. $10 daily fee/pet. Service with restrictions, supervision.

🆂🅰🆅🅴 Ⓢ🄍 ⊠ 🖥 💻 ➳

TEXAS

CITY INDEX

ABILENE

▼▼▼▼ Ambassador Suites Hotel SH
(325) 698-1234. **$104-$109.** 4250 Ridgemont Dr. 0.3 mi s of US 83/84, exit Ridgemont Dr. Ext/int corridors. **Pets:** Accepted.

ASK ⬡ ✕ ▤ 🖵 🍴 ⊃ ⊠

▼▼ Antilley Inn M
(325) 695-3330. **$55-$57.** 6550 S Hwy 83. US 83/84, exit Antilley Rd. Ext corridors. **Pets:** Medium. $10 one-time fee/room. Service with restrictions.

ASK ⬡ ✕ ▤ 🖵 ⊃

▼▼▼ Best Western Abilene Inn & Suites SH
(325) 672-5501. **Call for rates.** 350 I-20 W. I-20, exit 286C, just n. Int corridors. **Pets:** Accepted.

✕ ⬡ ▤ 🖵 ⊃

▲▲▲ ▼▼▼ Best Western Mall South SH
(325) 695-1262. **$75-$85.** 3950 Ridgemont Dr. US 83/84, exit Ridgemont Dr, just s. Ext corridors. **Pets:** $10 daily fee/pet. Service with restrictions, supervision.

SAVE ⬡ ✕ ⬡ ▤ 🖵 ⊃

▲▲▲ ▼▼▼ Budget Host Colonial Inn M ✿
(325) 677-2683. **$35-$40.** 3210 Pine St. Jct I-20 and US 83 business route, exit 286A. Ext/int corridors. **Pets:** Medium. $10 daily fee/pet. Designated rooms, service with restrictions, supervision.

SAVE ⬡ ✕ ⬡ ▤ 🖵 ⊃

▲▲▲ ▼▼ Civic Plaza Hotel SH
(325) 676-0222. **$49-$125.** 505 Pine St. Downtown. Ext corridors. **Pets:** Small. $20 one-time fee/room. Service with restrictions, supervision.

SAVE ⬡ ✕ ▤ 🖵 🍴 ⊃

▲▲▲ ▼▼▼▼ Comfort Suites SH
(325) 795-8500. **$89-$164.** 3165 S Danville Dr. I-20, exit 279, s on US 83/84/277 to Southwest Dr, then just e. Int corridors. **Pets:** Medium, other species. $30 one-time fee/room. Service with restrictions, supervision.

SAVE ⬡ ✕ ⬡M ⬡ ⬡ ▤ 🖵 ⊃

▼▼▼ Days Inn M
(325) 672-6433. **$55-$60.** 1702 E Hwy 20. I-20, exit 288. Ext corridors. **Pets:** $10 one-time fee/pet. Service with restrictions, supervision.

ASK ✕ ⬡ ▤ 🖵 ⊃

▼▼ Econo Lodge M

(325) 673-5424. **$50-$60.** 1633 W Stamford. S Frontage Rd off I-20 and US 80, exit 285 eastbound; exit 286A westbound. Ext corridors. **Pets:** Small. $10 daily fee/pet. Service with restrictions, supervision.

(ASK) (S&) (✕) (🖥) (💻) (≈)

▼▼ Executive Inn M

(325) 677-2200. **$60-$70.** 1650 I-20 E. I-20, exit 288. Ext corridors. **Pets:** Accepted.

(S&) (✕) (🖥) (💻) (≈)

◆◆◆ ▼▼▼▼ La Quinta Inn-Abilene SH

(325) 676-1676. **$66-$81.** 3501 W Lake Rd. I-20, exit 286C. Ext corridors. **Pets:** Medium. Service with restrictions, supervision.

(SAVE) (S&) (✕) (🌀) (🖥) (💻) (≈)

▼▼ Regency Inn & Suites SH

(325) 695-7700. **$54-$79.** 3450 S Clack St. 5 mi sw on US 83/84, exit Southwest Dr. Int corridors. **Pets:** Other species. $15 daily fee/room. Service with restrictions, supervision.

(ASK) (S&) (✕) (🖥) (💻) (🍴) (≈)

▼▼ Super 8 Motel M

(325) 673-5251. **$55-$70.** 1525 E I-20. I-20, exit 288. Ext corridors. **Pets:** Large, other species. $5 daily fee/pet. Service with restrictions, supervision.

(ASK) (S&) (✕) (🖥) (💻) (≈)

▼▼ Whitten Inn Expo SH ☙

(325) 677-8100. **$48-$68.** 840 Hwy 80 E. I-20, exit 292A, 3 mi w on Business Rt 20. Ext corridors. **Pets:** Other species. Service with restrictions.

(ASK) (S&) (✕) (🖥) (💻) (🍴) (≈)

▼▼ Whitten Inn University SH ☙

(325) 673-5271. **$39-$65.** 1625 Hwy 351. I-20, exit 288. Ext corridors. **Pets:** Other species.

(ASK) (S&) (✕) (&M) (🌀) (🖾) (🖥) (💻) (≈)

ALAMO

◆◆◆ ▼▼▼ Super 8 Motel SH

(956) 787-9444. **$49-$79, 7 day notice.** 714 N Alamo Rd. US 83, exit FM 907, just n. Ext corridors. **Pets:** Medium. Service with restrictions, supervision.

(SAVE) (S&) (✕) (🖥) (≈)

ALPINE

◆◆◆ ▼▼▼ Oak Tree Inn SH

(432) 837-5711. **$70-$77.** 2407 E Holland (Hwy 90/67). US 90, 2 mi e. Int corridors. **Pets:** Medium. $5 one-time fee/pet. Service with restrictions, supervision.

(SAVE) (S&) (✕) (&M) (🌀) (🖾) (🖥) (💻)

◆◆◆ ▼▼▼▼ Ramada Limited SH

(432) 837-1100. **$85-$95.** 2800 W Hwy 90. On US 90, 2 mi n. Int corridors. **Pets:** Accepted.

(SAVE) (S&) (✕) (&M) (🌀) (🖾) (🖥) (💻) (≈)

ALVIN

◆◆◆ ▼▼▼ Country Hearth Inn M

(281) 331-0335. **$55-$58.** 1588 S Hwy 35 Bypass. CR 35 Bypass, 0.5 mi sw of SR 6. Ext corridors. **Pets:** Medium. $10 daily fee/pet. Designated rooms, service with restrictions, supervision.

(SAVE) (S&) (✕) (🖥) (💻) (≈)

AMARILLO

◆◆◆ ▼▼▼▼ Ambassador Hotel LH

(806) 358-6161. **$99-$139.** 3100 I-40 W. I-40, exit 68, just w on north frontage road. Int corridors. **Pets:** $29 one-time fee/pet. Service with restrictions, crate.

(SAVE) (S&) (✕) (🌀) (🖥) (💻) (🍴) (≈) (🖾)

◆◆◆ ▼▼▼▼ Best Western Amarillo Inn SH

(806) 358-7861. **$62-$82, 30 day notice.** 1610 Coulter Dr. I-40, exit 65 (Coulter Dr), 0.6 mi n. Ext/int corridors. **Pets:** Small, other species. $10 one-time fee/pet. No service, supervision.

(SAVE) (S&) (✕) (&M) (🖥) (💻) (🍴) (≈)

◆◆◆ ▼▼▼▼ Best Western Santa Fe SH ☙

(806) 372-1885. **$68-$105.** 4600 I-40 E. I-40, exit 73 (Eastern St) eastbound; exit 73 (Bolton St) westbound, U-turn on south frontage road. Int corridors. **Pets:** Medium. $10 one-time fee/pet. Service with restrictions, supervision.

(SAVE) (S&) (✕) (🖥) (💻) (≈)

◆◆◆ ▼▼ Big Texan Motel M

(806) 372-5000. **$60-$65.** 7701 I-40 E. I-40, exit 75 (Lakeside Dr), 0.3 mi w on north frontage road. Ext corridors. **Pets:** Accepted.

(SAVE) (S&) (✕) (🖥) (🍴) (≈)

◆◆◆ ▼▼▼▼ Clarion Hotel Amarillo Airport SH

(806) 373-3303. **$60-$80, 14 day notice.** 7909 I-40 E. I-40, exit 75 (Lakeside Dr), just nw. Int corridors. **Pets:** Accepted.

(SAVE) (S&) (✕) (🌀) (🖥) (💻) (🍴) (≈)

◆◆◆ ▼▼▼▼ Comfort Inn-East SH

(806) 376-9993. **$49-$119.** 1515 I-40 E. I-40, exit 71 (Ross-Osage), just w on north frontage road. Ext corridors. **Pets:** $10 daily fee/room. No service, supervision.

(SAVE) (S&) (✕) (🌀) (🖥) (💻) (≈)

◆◆◆ ▼▼▼▼ Days Inn SH

(806) 379-6255. **$49-$99, 4 day notice.** 1701 I-40 E. I-40, exit 71 (Ross-Osage), just w on north frontage road. Int corridors. **Pets:** Other species. $10 one-time fee/pet. Service with restrictions.

(SAVE) (S&) (✕) (🌀) (🖥) (💻) (≈)

▼▼▼▼ Days Inn South SH

(806) 468-7100. **$55-$79.** 8601 Canyon Dr. I-27, exit 116, just n on east service road. Int corridors. **Pets:** Accepted.

(ASK) (S&) (✕) (🖾) (🖥) (💻) (≈)

◆◆◆ ▼▼▼▼ Hampton Inn SH

(806) 372-1425. **$49-$109.** 1700 I-40 E. I-40, exit 71 (Ross-Osage), just e on south frontage road. Int corridors. **Pets:** Other species. Service with restrictions, supervision.

(SAVE) (S&) (✕) (🌀) (🖥) (💻) (≈)

▼▼▼▼ Holiday Inn Express SH
(806) 356-6800. **$109-$139.** 3411 I-40 W. I-40, exit 67, 0.3 mi e on south frontage road. Int corridors. **Pets:** Other species. $25 one-time fee/room. Supervision.
⊠ 🐾 🛎 📼

▼▼▼▼ Holiday Inn-I-40 SH
(806) 372-8741. **$119-$125.** 1911 I-40 at Ross-Osage. I-40, exit 71 (Ross-Osage), on north frontage road. Int corridors. **Pets:** Other species. $25 one-time fee/room. Service with restrictions, supervision.
(ASK) SD ⊠ 🐾 🛎 📼 ▥ ⟲ ⊠

▲▲▲ ▼▼▼▼ La Quinta Inn-Amarillo-Medical Center SH
(806) 352-6311. **$65-$95.** 2108 S Coulter Dr. I-40, exit 65 (Coulter Dr), just n. Ext corridors. **Pets:** Accepted.
(SAVE) SD ⊠ 🅼 🐾 🛎 📼 ⟲

▼▼▼▼ La Quinta Inn East-Amarillo SH
(806) 373-7486. **$66-$102.** 1708 I-40 E. I-40, exit 71 (Ross-Osage), just e on south frontage road. Ext corridors. **Pets:** Accepted.
(ASK) SD ⊠ 🐾 🛎 📼 ⟲

▼▼ Motel 6 Amarillo East M
(806) 374-6444. **$40-$55.** 3930 I-40 E. I-40, exit 72B, on eastbound frontage road. Ext corridors. **Pets:** Other species. Service with restrictions, supervision.
SD ⊠ ⟲

▼▼ Motel 6 Amarillo West #1146 M
(806) 359-7651. **$35-$52.** 6030 I-40 W. I-40, exit 66 (Bell St), just w, on north frontage road. Ext corridors. **Pets:** Other species. Service with restrictions, supervision.
SD ⊠ 🐾 ⟲

▲▲▲ ▼▼▼▼ Quality Inn & Suites SH
(806) 335-1561. **$79-$89.** 1803 Lakeside Dr. I-40, exit 75 (Lakeside Dr), just n. Ext/int corridors. **Pets:** Accepted.
(SAVE) SD ⊠ 🐾 🛎 📼 ⟲

▼▼ Ramada Limited SH
(806) 374-2020. **$48-$76.** 1620 I-40 E. I-40, exit 71 (Ross-Osage), just e on south frontage road. Ext corridors. **Pets:** Large. $10 one-time fee/pet. Designated rooms, service with restrictions, supervision.
(ASK) SD ⊠ 🛎 ⟲

▼▼▼▼ Residence Inn-Amarillo SH
(806) 354-2978. **$130-$160, 14 day notice.** 6700 I-40 W. I-40, exit 66 (Bell St), 0.5 mi w on north frontage road. Int corridors. **Pets:** Accepted.
(ASK) SD ⊠ 🅼 🐾 🛎 🛎 📼 ⟲ ⊠

▲▲▲ ▼▼▼ Sleep Inn Amarillo SH
(806) 372-6200. **$75-$120, 7 day notice.** 2401 I-40 E. I-40, exit 72A (Nelson), 0.3 mi w on north frontage road. Int corridors. **Pets:** Accepted.
(SAVE) SD ⊠ 🅼 🐾 🛎 🛎 📼 ⟲

ANGLETON

▲▲▲ ▼▼▼▼ Best Western Angelton Inn M
(979) 849-5822. **$70-$110.** 1809 N Velasco (Business Rt 288). 1.5 mi n of jct SR 35 and Business Rt 288, e of SR 288. Ext corridors. **Pets:** Small. $25 one-time fee/pet. Service with restrictions, supervision.
(SAVE) SD ⊠ 🛎 📼 ⟲

ANTHONY

▲▲▲ ▼▼▼▼ Holiday Inn Express SH
(915) 886-3333. **$79-$89.** 9401 S Desert Blvd. I-10, exit 0. Ext corridors. **Pets:** Small, dogs only. $75 one-time fee/room. Designated rooms, service with restrictions, supervision.
(SAVE) SD ⊠ 🅼 🐾 🛎 📼 ⟲ ⊠

ARLINGTON

▲▲▲ ▼▼▼ AmeriSuites (Dallas/Arlington) SH
(817) 649-7676. **$59-$99.** 2380 East Rd to Six Flags St. I-30, exit 30 (SR 360), 0.5 mi sw. Int corridors. **Pets:** Service with restrictions, supervision.
(SAVE) SD ⊠ 🐾 🛎 📼 ⟲

▼▼▼▼ Arlington TownePlace Suites by Marriott SH
(817) 861-8728. **$79-$89.** 1709 E Lamar Ave. 2 mi w of SR 360. Int corridors. **Pets:** Accepted.
(ASK) SD ⊠ 🅼 🐾 🛎 📼 ⟲

▲▲▲ ▼▼▼▼ Baymont Inn & Suites-Arlington SH
(817) 633-2400. **$59-$119, 14 day notice.** 2401 Diplomacy Dr. I-30, exit 30 (SR 360), 0.5 mi s; off SR 360, exit Six Flags Dr northbound; exit Ave H/Lamar Blvd southbound, on southbound service road. Int corridors. **Pets:** Small. $50 deposit/room. Service with restrictions, supervision.
(SAVE) SD ⊠ 🅼 🐾 🛎 📼 ⟲

▲▲▲ ▼▼▼ Country Inn & Suites By Carlson SH ✿
(817) 261-8900. **$59-$129.** 1075 Wet'N Wild Way. I-30, exit 28 (Collins St/SR 157), just e. Ext corridors. **Pets:** Very small, dogs only. $50 deposit/pet, $10 daily fee/pet. Designated rooms, service with restrictions, supervision.
(SAVE) SD ⊠ 🅼 🐾 🛎 📼 ⟲

▲▲▲ ▼▼▼ Days Inn Ballpark at Arlington/Six Flags SH
(817) 261-8444. **$40-$96, 3 day notice.** 910 N Collins St. I-30, exit 28 (Collins St/SR 157), 1 mi s. Int corridors. **Pets:** Medium. $10 daily fee/pet. Service with restrictions, crate.
(SAVE) SD ⊠ 🛎 ⟲

▼▼▼▼ Hawthorn Suites Hotel SH
(817) 640-1188. **$59-$199.** 2401 Brookhollow Plaza Dr. I-30, exit 30 (SR 360), just n to Lamar Blvd, just w to Brookhollow Plaza Dr, then just n. Ext corridors. **Pets:** Medium. $50 one-time fee/pet. Service with restrictions, crate.
(ASK) SD ⊠ 🐾 🛎 📼 ⟲ ⊠

▼▼ Homestead Studio Suites
Hotel-Arlington 🆂🅷 🐾
(817) 633-7588. $49-$59. 1221 N Watson Rd. Jct SR 360, exit Ave K/Brown Blvd. Ext corridors. Pets: Medium, other species. $25 daily fee/room. Service with restrictions, crate.
[ASK] [S🅳] [✕] [�] [🔌] [🖥] [🛁] [💻] [⚓]

▼▼▼ Homewood Suites-Arlington 🆂🅷
(817) 633-1594. $109-$159. 2401 East Rd to Six Flags St. I-30, exit 30 (SR 360), 0.5 mi sw. Int corridors. Pets: Accepted.
[ASK] [S🅳] [✕] [�] [🔌] [🖥] [🛁] [💻] [⚓]

▼▼ Howard Johnson Express Inn 🆂🅷
(817) 461-1122. $59-$99. 2001 E Copeland Rd. I-30, exit 30 (SR 360) westbound, just s to Six Flags Dr, just w to Copeland Rd, then 0.9 mi w; exit 29 (Ball Pkwy) eastbound. Int corridors. Pets: Medium. $5 daily fee/pet. Service with restrictions, crate.
[ASK] [S🅳] [✕] [🛁] [💻] [⚓]

▼▼▼ La Quinta Inn & Suites South
Arlington 🆂🅷
(817) 467-7756. $102-$131. 4001 Scott's Legacy. I-20, exit 450 (Matlock Rd) on southbound service road. Int corridors. Pets: Accepted.
[ASK] [S🅳] [✕] [🔌] [🔌] [🛁] [💻] [⚓]

🅰🅰🅰 ▼▼▼ La Quinta Inn-Arlington-Conference
Center 🆂🅷
(817) 640-4142. $76-$115. 825 N Watson Rd. I-30, exit 30 (SR 360), exit Six Flags Dr northbound; exit Ave H/Lamar Blvd southbound. Ext corridors. Pets: Medium, other species. Designated rooms, service with restrictions, crate.
[SAVE] [S🅳] [✕] [🔌] [🔌] [🛁] [💻] [⚓] [✕]

▼ Motel 6–122 🆂🅷
(817) 649-0147. $40-$55. 2626 E Randol Mill Rd. Jct SR 360 and Randol Mill Rd. Ext corridors. Pets: Accepted.
[S🅳] [✕] [⚓]

▼▼ Residence Inn by Marriott 🆂🅷
(817) 649-7300. $129-$199. 1050 Brookhollow Plaza Dr. I-30, exit 30 (SR 360), just n to Lamar Blvd, then just w. Int corridors. Pets: Accepted.
[ASK] [S🅳] [✕] [�] [🔌] [🔌] [🛁] [💻] [⚓] [✕]

🅰🅰🅰 ▼▼ Sleep Inn Main Gate-Six Flags 🆂🅷
(817) 649-1010. $76-$110. 750 Six Flags Dr. I-30, exit 30 (SR 360), 0.5 mi s. Int corridors. Pets: Small, other species. $10.75 daily fee/pet. Service with restrictions, supervision.
[SAVE] [S🅳] [✕] [🔌] [🛁] [💻] [⚓]

AUSTIN

🅰🅰🅰 ▼▼▼ AmeriSuites (Austin/Airport) 🆂🅷
(512) 386-7600. $79. 7601 Ben White Blvd. I-35, exit 230B (Ben White Blvd), 3.2 mi e. Int corridors. Pets: Small. $25 one-time fee/room. Service with restrictions, supervision.
[SAVE] [S🅳] [✕] [🔌] [🔌] [🛁] [💻] [✕]

🅰🅰🅰 ▼▼▼ AmeriSuites (Austin/Arboretum) 🆂🅷
(512) 231-8491. $159-$179. 3612 Tudor Dr. Jct US 183 and SR 360, 1 blk w to Stonelake Blvd, 0.5 mi s to Tudor Blvd, then just e. Int corridors. Pets: Medium, other species. Service with restrictions.
[SAVE] [S🅳] [✕] [🔌] [🔌] [🛁] [💻] [⚓]

🅰🅰🅰 ▼▼▼▼ AmeriSuites (Austin/North
Central) 🆂🅷 🐾
(512) 323-2121. $99-$129. 7522 N I-35. I-35, exit 240A, on west frontage road. Int corridors. Pets: Large. Service with restrictions, crate.
[SAVE] [S🅳] [✕] [�] [🔌] [🔌] [🛁] [💻] [⚓]

▼▼▼▼ Austin Marriott at the Capitol 🅻🅷
(512) 478-1111. $129-$199. 701 E 11th St. I-35, exit 234B, 0.3 mi e. Int corridors. Pets: Small, dogs only. Service with restrictions.
[S🅳] [✕] [🔌] [🔌] [🛁] [💻] [🍴] [⚓] [✕]

🅰🅰🅰 ▼▼▼▼ Best Value Inn & Suites 🆂🅷 🐾
(512) 617-4900. $60-$80. 6911 I-35 N. I-35, exit 238A, on east frontage road. Ext corridors. Pets: Other species. $15 one-time fee/room. Service with restrictions.
[SAVE] [S🅳] [✕] [🔌] [🔌] [🛁] [💻] [⚓]

🅰🅰🅰 ▼▼▼▼ Best Western Atrium North 🆂🅷
(512) 339-7311. $49-$99. 7928 Gessner Dr. I-35, exit 240A, 0.4 mi w on Anderson Ln. Int corridors. Pets: Small. $25 deposit/room. Service with restrictions, supervision.
[SAVE] [S🅳] [✕] [🛁] [💻] [⚓]

▼▼▼ Best Western Seville Plaza Inn 🆂🅷
(512) 447-5511. $59-$89. 4323 I-35 S. I-35, exit 230A (Stassney Rd) southbound; exit 230 (Ben White Blvd) northbound. Int corridors. Pets: Small. $50 deposit/room. Service with restrictions, supervision.
[ASK] [S🅳] [✕] [🔌] [🛁] [💻] [🍴] [⚓]

▼▼▼ Candlewood Suites Austin Northwest 🆂🅷
(512) 338-1611. $72-$89. 9701 Stonelake Blvd. Jct US 183 and SR 360, on northwest corner. Int corridors. Pets: Accepted.
[ASK] [S🅳] [✕] [�] [🔌] [🔌] [🛁] [💻]

▼▼▼ Candlewood Suites-South 🆂🅷
(512) 444-8882. $137-$157. 4320 S IH-35. I-35, exit 230 northbound; exit 230B southbound, on southbound frontage road. Int corridors. Pets: Accepted.
[ASK] [S🅳] [✕] [�] [🔌] [🔌] [🛁] [💻]

▼▼▼ Clarion Inn & Suites Conference
Center 🆂🅷
(512) 444-0561. $69-$139. 2200 S I-35. I-35, exit 232A (Oltorf Blvd), on west side access road. Ext/int corridors. Pets: Accepted.
[ASK] [S🅳] [✕] [🔌] [🔌] [🛁] [💻] [🍴] [⚓]

▼▼▼ Crowne Plaza 🅻🅷
(512) 480-8181. $109-$159. 500 N I-35. I-35, exit 234B southbound; exit 234C northbound, on southbound frontage road. Int corridors. Pets: Medium. $50 one-time fee/room. Service with restrictions, supervision.
[✕] [🔌] [🔌] [🛁] [💻] [🍴] [⚓]

🅰🅰🅰 ▼▼▼ Days Inn Austin North 🆂🅷
(512) 835-4311. $57-$67, 3 day notice. 820 E Anderson Ln. I-35, exit 240A, on east frontage road. Int corridors. Pets: Small. $50 one-time fee/room. Designated rooms, service with restrictions, crate.
[SAVE] [S🅳] [✕] [🔌] [🔌] [🛁] [💻] [⚓]

(AAA) ▼▼▼ Days Inn University-Downtown M
(512) 478-1631. **$59-$99.** 3105 N I-35. I-35, exit 236A at 32nd St (from lower level). Ext corridors. **Pets:** Small. $8 one-time fee/room. Service with restrictions, supervision.
SAVE (SD) ✕ 🖥 💻 🏊

▼▼▼ Doubletree Club Hotel SH
(512) 479-4000. **$79-$149.** 1617 I-35 N. I-35, exit Martin Luther King Jr Blvd, just n on northbound frontage road. Int corridors. **Pets:** Small, other species. $15 daily fee/pet. Service with restrictions, supervision.
ASK ✕ 📶 🖥 🖨 💻 🍴 🏊

▼▼▼ DoubleTree Guest Suites-Austin LH
(512) 478-7000. **$109-$249.** 303 W 15th St. Just nw of capitol; center. Int corridors. **Pets:** Accepted.
✕ 📶 🖥 💻 🍴 🏊 🍽

(AAA) ▼▼▼ Doubletree Hotel Austin LH
(512) 454-3737. **$89-$179.** 6505 I-35 N. I-35, exit 238A, on east frontage road. Int corridors. **Pets:** Accepted.
SAVE (SD) ✕ 🖥M 📶 🖨 🖥 💻 🍴 🏊

▼▼▼ ▼▼ The Driskill LH 🐾
(512) 474-5911. **$185-$340.** 604 Brazos St. Jct 6th St. Int corridors. **Pets:** Small, other species. $50 one-time fee/room. Designated rooms, service with restrictions, crate.
ASK ✕ 📶 🖨 🍴

▼▼▼ Drury Inn & Suites-Austin North SH
(512) 467-9500. **$89-$109.** 6711 I-35 N. I-35, exit 238A, on east frontage road. Int corridors. **Pets:** Large, other species. Service with restrictions, supervision.
ASK ✕ 🖨 🖥 💻 🏊

▼▼▼ Drury Inn Austin-Highland Mall SH
(512) 454-1144. **$82-$102.** 919 E Koenig Ln. I-35, exit 238A, on west frontage road. Int corridors. **Pets:** Large, other species. Service with restrictions, supervision.
ASK ✕ 🖥M 🖥 💻 🏊

▼▼▼ Econo Lodge SH
(512) 458-4759. **Call for rates.** 6201 Hwy 290 E. I-35, exit 238, 0.3 mi e of jct I-35 and US 290 E. Ext corridors. **Pets:** Accepted.
✕ 🖥 💻 🏊

▼▼▼ Embassy Suites Hotel-Downtown LH
(512) 469-9000. **$109-$219.** 300 S Congress Ave. Just s of Congress Ave Bridge. Int corridors. **Pets:** Medium. $25 one-time fee/pet. Service with restrictions, supervision.
ASK (SD) ✕ 📶 🖨 🖥 💻 🍴 🏊 🍽

(AAA) ▼▼ Exel Inn Of Austin SH
(512) 462-9201. **$49-$79.** 2711 I-35 S. I-35, exit 231 (Woodward Ave) southbound; exit 232A (Oltorf St) northbound, on northbound frontage road; just n of jct I-35 and US 290/SR 71. Int corridors. **Pets:** Large, other species. Service with restrictions, supervision.
SAVE (SD) ✕ 📶 🖨 🖥 💻 🏊

▼▼▼ Four Points by Sheraton SH 🐾
(512) 836-8520. **$126-$128.** 7800 I-35 N. I-35, exit 240A, on west frontage road. Int corridors. **Pets:** Large, other species. $50 deposit/pet. Service with restrictions, crate.
ASK (SD) ✕ 🖨 🖥 💻 🍴 🏊

▼▼▼ ▼▼ Four Seasons Hotel LH
(512) 478-4500. **$245-$395.** 98 San Jacinto Blvd. Bordering Town Lake. Int corridors. **Pets:** Accepted.
✕ 📶 🖨 🖥 💻 🍴 🏊 🍽

▼▼▼ Hampton Inn Northwest SH
(512) 349-9898. **$79-$109.** 3908 W Braker Ln. 1 mi n of US 183 on Loop 1 (Mo-Pac Blvd) to Braker Ln exit. Int corridors. **Pets:** Accepted.
ASK (SD) ✕ 🖥M 📶 🖨 💻

▼▼▼ Hawthorn Suites Austin Central SH
(512) 459-3335. **$79-$164.** 935 La Posada Dr. I-35, exit 238A, just off east frontage road. Ext corridors. **Pets:** Accepted.
ASK (SD) ✕ 📶 🖨 🖥 💻 🏊 🍽

▼▼▼ Hawthorn Suites Austin South SH
(512) 440-7722. **$59-$138.** 4020 I-35 S. I-35, exit 230B (Ben White Blvd/SR 71) southbound; exit 231 (Woodward Dr) northbound, just n of jct SR 71, US 290 and I-35, on southbound frontage road. Ext corridors. **Pets:** Accepted.
ASK (SD) ✕ 📶 🖨 🖥 💻 🏊 🍽

(AAA) ▼▼▼ Hawthorn Suites Ltd-Austin-Bergstrom International Airport SH
(512) 247-6166. **$69-$149.** 7800 E Riverside Dr. I-35, exit 230B (Ben White Blvd/SR 71), 3.2 mi e. Int corridors. **Pets:** Accepted.
SAVE (SD) ✕ 🖥M 📶 🖨 🖥 💻 🏊 🍽

▼▼▼ Hawthorn Suites Northwest SH
(512) 343-0008. **$79-$129.** 8888 Tallwood Dr. Just sw of jct US 183 and Loop 1 (Mo-Pac Blvd). Ext corridors. **Pets:** Accepted.
ASK (SD) ✕ 🖥M 📶 🖨 🏊 🍽

(AAA) ▼▼▼ Hilton Austin North LH
(512) 451-5757. **$89-$179.** 6000 Middle Fiskville Rd. I-35, exit 238A, just off west frontage road. Int corridors. **Pets:** Other species. $50 deposit/room. Service with restrictions, supervision.
SAVE (SD) ✕ 🖥M 📶 🖨 🖥 💻 🍴 🏊

(AAA) ▼▼▼ Holiday Inn Airport South SH
(512) 448-2444. **$89-$99.** 3401 I-35 S. I-35, exit 231 (Woodward St) southbound; exit 230 (Ben White Blvd/SR 71) northbound, on northbound frontage road. Ext/int corridors. **Pets:** Small. $25 one-time fee/room. Designated rooms, service with restrictions, crate.
SAVE (SD) ✕ 📶 🖨 🖥 💻 🍴 🏊 🍽

▼▼▼ Holiday Inn Northwest/Arboretum SH 🐾
(512) 343-0888. **$59-$109.** 8901 Business Park Dr. Jct US 183 and Loop 1 (Mo-Pac Blvd), on southwest corner. Int corridors. **Pets:** Medium, other species. $25 one-time fee/room. Designated rooms, service with restrictions, crate.
ASK (SD) ✕ 📶 🖨 🖥 💻 🍴 🏊

(AAA) ▼▼▼ Holiday Inn-Town Lake LH
(512) 472-8211. **$129.** 20 N I-35. I-35, exit 233. Int corridors. **Pets:** $100 deposit/room, $25 one-time fee/room. Service with restrictions, crate.
SAVE (SD) ✕ 📶 🖨 💻 🍴 🏊 🍽

▼▼▼ Homestead Studio Suites
Hotel-Austin/Arboretum 🆂🅷 ❧
(512) 837-6677. **$54-$64.** 9100 Waterford Centre Blvd. US 183, exit Burnet Rd; on westbound frontage road. Ext corridors. **Pets:** Medium, other species. $25 daily fee/room. Service with restrictions, crate.

🄰🅂🄺 🆂🄳 ⊠ 🄴 🄱 💻

▼▼▼ Homestead Studio Suites Hotel-Austin/
Downtown/Town Lake 🆂🅷 ❧
(512) 476-1818. **$74-$84.** 507 S First St. I-35, exit 234B southbound; exit 234A northbound, 1.8 mi w on Caesar Chavez/E First St, then 0.5 mi s. Int corridors. **Pets:** Medium, other species. $25 daily fee/room. Service with restrictions, crate.

🄰🅂🄺 🆂🄳 ⊠ 🄳 🄴 🄱 💻

▼▼▼ Homewood Suites by Hilton Arboretum
NW 🆂🅷
(512) 349-9966. **Call for rates.** 3908 Braker Ln. US 183 N to Loop 1 (Mo-Pac Blvd), 1.5 mi n to Braker Ln; on northwest corner. Int corridors. **Pets:** Other species. $10 daily fee/room.

⊠ 🅓🄼 🄳 🄴 🄱 💻 ⇌ ⊠

▼▼▼ La Quinta Capitol 🆂🅷
(512) 476-1166. **$100-$130.** 300 E 11 St. Just e of state capitol building. Ext/int corridors. **Pets:** Other species. Service with restrictions, supervision.

🄰🅂🄺 🆂🄳 ⊠ 🄳 🄴 🄱 💻 ⇌

🄐🄐🄐 ▼▼▼▼ La Quinta Inn & Suites at
Austin-Airport 🆂🅷
(512) 386-6800. **$75-$100.** 7625 E Ben White Blvd. I-35, exit 230B (Ben White Blvd/SR 71), 3.8 mi e. Int corridors. **Pets:** Accepted.

🆂🄰🆅🄴 🆂🄳 ⊠ 🅓🄼 🄳 🄴 🄱 💻 ⇌

🄐🄐🄐 ▼▼▼▼ La Quinta Inn & Suites-Austin North
Mopac 🆂🅷
(512) 832-2121. **$86-$120.** 11901 N Mo-Pac Blvd. US 183, 2 mi n on Loop 1 (Mo-Pac Blvd) to Duval exit. Int corridors. **Pets:** Medium. Service with restrictions, supervision.

🆂🄰🆅🄴 🆂🄳 ⊠ 🅓🄼 🄳 🄴 🄱 💻 ⇌

🄐🄐🄐 ▼▼▼▼ La Quinta Inn-Highland Mall 🆂🅷
(512) 459-4381. **$71-$86.** 5812 I-35 N. I-35, exit 238A, on west frontage road. Ext corridors. **Pets:** Accepted.

🆂🄰🆅🄴 🆂🄳 ⊠ 🄳 🄴 🄱 💻 ⇌

🄐🄐🄐 ▼▼▼▼ La Quinta Inn IH35 at Ben
White 🆂🅷
(512) 443-1774. **$71-$86.** 4200 I-35 S. I-35, exit 230B (Ben White Blvd/SR 71) southbound; exit 230 northbound, just s of jct I-35, US 290 and SR 71, on frontage road. Ext corridors. **Pets:** Accepted.

🆂🄰🆅🄴 🆂🄳 ⊠ 🅓🄼 🄳 🄴 🄱 💻 ⇌

🄐🄐🄐 ▼▼▼▼ La Quinta Inn-North 🆂🅷
(512) 452-9401. **$71-$86.** 7100 I-35 N. I-35, exit 239, on west frontage road. Ext corridors. **Pets:** Service with restrictions, crate.

🆂🄰🆅🄴 🆂🄳 ⊠ 🄳 🄴 🄱 💻 ⇌

▼▼▼▼ La Quinta Inn Oltorf 🆂🅷 ❧
(512) 447-6661. **$71-$86.** 1603 E Oltorf Blvd. I-35, exit 232A (Oltorf Blvd), just s. Ext/int corridors. **Pets:** Small, other species. Service with restrictions, supervision.

🄰🅂🄺 🆂🄳 ⊠ 🄳 🄴 🄱 💻 ⇌

▼▼▼▼ La Quinta SW 🆂🅷
(512) 899-3000. **$120-$140.** 4424 S Loop 1 (Mo-Pac Blvd). Jct Loop 1 (Mo-Pac Blvd), US 290 and SR 71 E, on southbound frontage road. Int corridors. **Pets:** Accepted.

🄰🅂🄺 🆂🄳 ⊠ 🅓🄼 🄳 🄳 🄴 🄱 💻 ⇌

▼▼▼▼ The Mansion at Judge's Hill 🆂🅷 ❧
(512) 495-1800. **$99-$295, 3 day notice.** 1900 Rio Grande. Jct Rio Grande and Martin Luther King Blvd. Int corridors. **Pets:** Other species. $75 deposit/room. Designated rooms, crate.

🄰🅂🄺 🆂🄳 ⊠ 🍴

▼ Motel 6 Austin North–360 🄼
(512) 339-6161. **$41-$55.** 9420 N I-35. I-35, exit 241 (Rundberg St), just w. Ext corridors. **Pets:** Small, other species. Service with restrictions, supervision.

🆂🄳 ⊠ 🄳 ⇌

▼▼ Motel 6 Central #1118 🄼
(512) 467-9111. **$43-$55.** 5330 I-35 N. I-35, exit 238A, on west frontage road. Ext corridors. **Pets:** Accepted.

🆂🄳 ⊠ 🄳 ⇌

▼▼ Northpark Executive Suite Hotel 🆂🅷
(512) 452-9391. **$75-$129.** 7685 Northcross Dr. Loop 1 (Mo-Pac Blvd), exit Anderson Rd, just e to Northcross Dr, then just s. Ext corridors. **Pets:** Accepted.

🄰🅂🄺 🆂🄳 ⊠ 🄳 🄴 🄱 💻 ⇌

🄐🄐🄐 ▼▼▼▼ Omni Austin Hotel & Suites 🄻🄷
(512) 476-3700. **$139-$379.** 700 San Jacinto Blvd. 8th St and San Jacinto Blvd. Int corridors. **Pets:** Accepted.

🆂🄰🆅🄴 🆂🄳 ⊠ 🅓🄼 🄳 🄳 🄴 🄱 💻 🍴 ⇌ ⊠

▼▼▼ Omni Austin Hotel Southpark 🆂🅷
(512) 448-2222. **$179.** 4140 Governor's Row. I-35, exit 230B (Ben White Blvd/SR 71) southbound; exit 230 northbound, on east frontage road. Int corridors. **Pets:** Accepted.

🄰🅂🄺 🆂🄳 ⊠ 🄳 🄴 🄱 💻 🍴 ⇌ ⊠

▼▼ Ramada Limited Austin North 🆂🅷
(512) 836-0079. **$49-$99.** 9121 N I-35. I-35, exit 241 northbound; exit 240A southbound, on east frontage road. Int corridors. **Pets:** $10 daily fee/pet. Service with restrictions, supervision.

🄰🅂🄺 🆂🄳 ⊠ 🄱 ⇌

▼▼▼ Red Lion Hotel Austin 🆂🅷
(512) 323-5466. **$69-$99.** 6121 I-35 N. I-35, exit 238A, on east frontage road. Int corridors. **Pets:** Large, other species. Service with restrictions, crate.

🄰🅂🄺 🆂🄳 ⊠ 🄳 🄴 🄱 💻 🍴 ⇌

🄐🄐🄐 ▼▼▼ Red Roof Inn Austin North 🄼
(512) 835-2200. **$44-$54.** 8210 I-35 N. I-35, exit 241, on west frontage road. Ext corridors. **Pets:** Large. Service with restrictions, crate.

🆂🄰🆅🄴 ⊠ 🄳 🄳 🍴 ⇌

🔺 ♦♦♦ Red Roof Inn-Austin South 🆂🅷
(512) 448-0091. **$44-$59.** 4701 I-35 S. I-35, exit 230B (Ben White Blvd/SR 71) southbound; exit 229 (Stassney Rd) northbound, on northbound frontage road. Int corridors. **Pets:** Medium, other species. Service with restrictions, supervision.

🆂🅰🆅🅴 ✖ ♿ 🐾 ♻ 🛏 🌊

🔺 ♦♦♦ Renaissance Austin Hotel 🅻🅷 ❀
(512) 343-2626. **$179-$199.** 9721 Arboretum Blvd. Jct US 183 and SR 360; southwest corner. Int corridors. **Pets:** Service with restrictions, supervision.

🆂🅰🆅🅴 🆂🅳 ✖ ♿ 🐾 🛏 🌊 🍴 🌊 ✖

♦♦♦ Residence Inn Austin South 🆂🅷
(512) 912-1100. **$119-$159.** 4537 S I-35. I-35, exit 229 (Stassney Rd) southbound; exit 230 (Ben White Blvd/SR 71) northbound, on northbound frontage road. Int corridors. **Pets:** Accepted.

🅰🆂🅺 ✖ 🐾 ♻ 🛏 🌊 🌊 ✖

♦♦♦ Residence Inn by Marriott-Austin North 🆂🅷
(512) 977-0544. **$119-$169.** 12401 N Lamar Blvd. I-35, exit 245, just w. Int corridors. **Pets:** $75 one-time fee/room. Service with restrictions.

🅰🆂🅺 🆂🅳 ✖ ♿ 🐾 ♻ 🛏 🌊 🌊 ✖

♦♦♦ Staybridge Suites Hotel 🆂🅷
(512) 349-0888. **$69-$161.** 10201 Stonelake Blvd. Jct US 183 and SR 360; northwest corner. Int corridors. **Pets:** Accepted.

🅰🆂🅺 🆂🅳 ✖ ♿ 🐾 ♻ 🛏 🌊 🌊 ✖

♦♦♦ Studio 6-Austin Midtown #6033 🅼 ❀
(512) 458-5453. **$47-$61.** 937 Camino La Costa. I-35, exit 238A, on east frontage road. Ext corridors. **Pets:** $25 deposit/pet, $10 daily fee/room. Service with restrictions.

✖ 🐾 ♻ 🛏 🌊

🔺 ♦♦ Super 8 Austin North 🆂🅷
(512) 339-1300. **$52-$62.** 8128 N I-35. I-35, exit 241, on west frontage road. Int corridors. **Pets:** Accepted.

🆂🅰🆅🅴 🆂🅳 ✖ 🐾 🛏 🌊 🌊

🔺 ♦ Super 8 Central 🅼
(512) 472-8331. **$59-$89.** 1201 N I-35. I-35, exit 234, at 12th St. Ext corridors. **Pets:** Accepted.

🆂🅰🆅🅴 🆂🅳 ✖ ♻ 🛏 🌊 🌊

🔺 ♦♦♦ Wellesley Inn & Suites (Austin/N Mopac) 🆂🅷
(512) 833-0898. **$65-$75.** 2700 Gracy Farms Ln. 2 mi n of US 183 on Loop 1 (Mo-Pac Blvd), exit Burnet Rd (FM 1325). Int corridors. **Pets:** Accepted.

🆂🅰🆅🅴 🆂🅳 ✖ ♻ 🛏 🌊 🌊

🔺 ♦♦♦ Wellesley Inn & Suites (Austin/North) 🆂🅷
(512) 339-6005. **$62.** 8221 N I-35. I-35, exit 241, on east frontage road. Int corridors. **Pets:** Very small, other species. Service with restrictions, supervision.

🆂🅰🆅🅴 🆂🅳 ✖ ♻ 🛏 🌊 🌊

🔺 ♦♦♦ Wellesley Inn & Suites (Austin/NW) 🆂🅷
(512) 219-6500. **$72.** 12424 Research Blvd. US 183, exit Oak Knoll, on eastbound frontage road. Int corridors. **Pets:** Very small, other species. Service with restrictions, supervision.

🆂🅰🆅🅴 🆂🅳 ✖ ♿ 🐾 ♻ 🛏 🌊 🌊

BANDERA

🔺 ♦♦♦ Bandera Lodge Motel 🆂🅷
(830) 796-3093. **$60-$90.** 700 Hwy 16 S. 1 mi s on SR 16; 7 mi s of jct SR 173. Ext corridors. **Pets:** Accepted.

🆂🅰🆅🅴 🆂🅳 ✖ 🛏 🍴 🌊

BASTROP

♦♦♦ Holiday Inn Express Hotel and Suites 🆂🅷
(512) 321-1900. **$71-$80.** 491 Agnes St. Jct SR 71/95, 2 mi w. Int corridors. **Pets:** Medium. $25 one-time fee/room. Designated rooms, service with restrictions, supervision.

🅰🆂🅺 🆂🅳 ✖ ♿ 🐾 ♻ 🛏 🌊

BEAUMONT

🔺 ♦♦♦ Best Western Beaumont Inn 🅼
(409) 898-8150. **$53-$59, 14 day notice.** 2155 N 11th St. I-10, exit 853B (11th St), just n. Ext corridors. **Pets:** Small. Service with restrictions, supervision.

🆂🅰🆅🅴 🆂🅳 ✖ 🛏 🌊 🌊

🔺 ♦♦♦ Best Western Jefferson Inn 🅼
(409) 842-0037. **$56-$62.** 1610 I-10 S. I-10, exit 851 (College St), westbound service road, 0.5 mi s of jct US 90. Ext corridors. **Pets:** Small. Service with restrictions, supervision.

🆂🅰🆅🅴 🆂🅳 ✖ 🛏 🌊 🌊

♦♦♦ Hilton Beaumont 🆂🅷
(409) 842-3600. **$79-$109.** 2355 I-10 S. I-10, exit 850 (Washington Blvd), on eastbound service road. Int corridors. **Pets:** $50 deposit/room, $50 one-time fee/room. Designated rooms, service with restrictions, supervision.

✖ 🐾 ♻ 🛏 🌊 🍴 🌊

🔺 ♦♦♦ Holiday Inn Atrium Plaza 🅻🅷
(409) 842-5995. **$89-$99.** 3950 I-10 S. I-10, exit 848 (Walden Rd), just n. Int corridors. **Pets:** Other species. $25 one-time fee/room. Service with restrictions, supervision.

🆂🅰🆅🅴 🆂🅳 ✖ 🐾 ♻ 🛏 🌊 🍴 🌊 ✖

🔺 ♦♦♦ Holiday Inn Beaumont Midtown 🆂🅷
(409) 892-2222. **$109.** 2095 N 11th St. I-10, exit 853B (11th St), just n. Int corridors. **Pets:** Accepted.

🆂🅰🆅🅴 ✖ ♿ 🐾 ♻ 🛏 🌊 🍴 🌊

♦♦♦ La Quinta Inn-Beaumont 🅼
(409) 838-9991. **$69-$82.** 220 I-10 N. I-10, exit 852B (Calder Ave) eastbound, on eastbound service road; exit 852A (Laurel Ave) westbound, on eastbound service road. Ext corridors. **Pets:** Small, other species. Service with restrictions.

🅰🆂🅺 🆂🅳 ✖ 🐾 ♻ 🛏 🌊 🌊

(AAA) ▼▼▼ Super 8 Beaumont 🆂🅷
(409) 899-3040. **$46-$48.** 2850 I-10 E. I-10, exit 853B (11th St), on westbound service road. Int corridors. **Pets:** Medium, other species. Service with restrictions, crate.
[SAVE] [S🐾] [✕] [🛏] [➳]

BEDFORD

(AAA) ▼▼▼▼ Holiday Inn-DFW-Airport West 🆂🅷
(817) 267-3181. **$59-$69.** 3005 W Airport Frwy. SR 183, just e of jct SR 121, exit Murphy Dr N. Int corridors. **Pets:** Accepted.
[SAVE] [S🐾] [✕] [&M] [🏊] [🛏] [💻] [🍴] [➳]

(AAA) ▼▼▼▼ La Quinta Inn-Bedford 🆂🅷 ❀
(817) 267-5200. **$67-$82.** 1450 Airport Frwy. SR 121/183, 0.3 mi e of jct Bedford Rd/Forest Ridge Dr exit. Ext corridors. **Pets:** Medium, other species. Service with restrictions.
[SAVE] [S🐾] [✕] [🏊] [🛏] [💻] [➳]

▼▼ Super 8 Motel-Bedford 🆂🅷
(817) 545-8108. **$55.** 1800 Airport Frwy. SR 183 at Bedford Rd, exit Forest Ridge Dr. Int corridors. **Pets:** Accepted.
[ASK] [S🐾] [✕] [&M] [🐾] [🛏]

BEEVILLE

▼▼ Beeville Days Inn 🆂🅷
(361) 358-4000. **$54.** 400 A S US 181 Bypass. 0.3 mi s of jct US 59 and 181. Ext corridors. **Pets:** Accepted.
[ASK] [S🐾] [✕] [🛏] [➳]

▼▼ Best Western Texan Inn 🆂🅷
(361) 358-9999. **Call for rates.** 2001 Hwy 59. US 181 at US 59, just e. Ext/int corridors. **Pets:** Accepted.
[✕] [💻] [➳]

BELTON

(AAA) ▼▼▼ Budget Host Inn 🆂🅷 ❀
(254) 939-0744. **$40-$52.** 1520 S I-35. I-35, exit 292 southbound; exit 293A northbound. Ext corridors. **Pets:** Small. Service with restrictions, supervision.
[SAVE] [S🐾] [✕] [🛏] [💻] [➳]

▼▼ Ramada Limited 🆂🅷
(254) 939-3745. **$62-$72.** 1102 E 2nd Ave. I-35, exit 294A southbound; exit 294B northbound. Ext corridors. **Pets:** No service, crate.
[ASK] [S🐾] [✕] [🛏] [💻] [➳]

▼▼ River Forest Inn 🆂🅷
(254) 939-5711. **$45-$75.** 1414 E 6th Ave. I-35, exit 294B. Ext corridors. **Pets:** Small, dogs only. $20 deposit/room. No service, supervision.
[ASK] [S🐾] [✕] [🛏] [➳]

BENBROOK

▼▼ Motel 6-4051 🆂🅷
(817) 249-8885. **$50-$75.** 8601 Benbrook Blvd (Hwy 377 S). I-20, exit 429A, 0.7 mi s. Int corridors. **Pets:** Small. Service with restrictions, supervision.
[ASK] [✕] [&M] [🐾] [🛏] [➳]

BIG SPRING

(AAA) ▼▼▼ Super 8 Motel Ⓜ
(432) 267-1601. **$46-$108.** 700 W I-20. I-20, exit 177, just n. Ext corridors. **Pets:** Accepted.
[SAVE] [S🐾] [✕] [🏊] [🛏] [💻] [➳]

BOERNE

(AAA) ▼▼▼ Best Western Texas Country Inn 🆂🅷
(830) 249-9791. **$69-$85.** 35150 I-10 W. I-10, exit 540 (SR 46). Ext corridors. **Pets:** Accepted.
[SAVE] [S🐾] [✕] [💻] [➳]

BONHAM

(AAA) ▼ 5 Star Inn Ⓜ
(903) 583-3121. **$46-$51.** 1515 Old Ector Rd. Jct SR 121 S and SR 56 W. Ext corridors. **Pets:** Medium. $10 deposit/room. Designated rooms, service with restrictions, supervision.
[SAVE] [S🐾] [✕] [🛏] [💻] [➳]

BORGER

(AAA) ▼▼▼ Best Western Borger Inn 🆂🅷
(806) 274-7050. **$83-$120.** 206 S Cedar. Jct SR 136 and 207, just n. Int corridors. **Pets:** Very small. $10 daily fee/pet. Service with restrictions, supervision.
[SAVE] [S🐾] [✕] [🐾] [🛏] [💻] [➳]

BOWIE

(AAA) ▼▼ Days Inn 🆂🅷
(940) 872-5426. **$45-$65, 3 day notice.** 2436 S US 287. Jct SR 59. Ext corridors. **Pets:** Medium, other species. $5 daily fee/pet. Designated rooms, service with restrictions, supervision.
[SAVE] [S🐾] [✕] [🛏] [➳]

(AAA) ▼ Park's Inn Ⓜ
(940) 872-1111. **$46-$60.** 708 W Wise St. 0.5 mi n of jct SR 59; downtown. Ext corridors. **Pets:** Medium. $5 daily fee/pet. No service, supervision.
[SAVE] [S🐾] [✕] [🛏] [➳]

BRADY

(AAA) ▼▼▼ Best Western Brady Inn 🆂🅷
(325) 597-3997. **$55-$75.** 2200 S Bridge St. 1.1 mi s on US 87/377. Ext corridors. **Pets:** Accepted.
[SAVE] [S🐾] [✕] [🛏] [💻] [➳]

(AAA) ▼▼▼ Days Inn Ⓜ ❀
(325) 597-0789. **$49-$79, 10 day notice.** 2108 S Bridge St. 1 mi s on US 87/377 at US 190. Ext corridors. **Pets:** Medium, other species.
[SAVE] [S🐾] [✕] [🛏] [💻] [➳]

BRENHAM

(AAA) ▼▼▼▼ Best Western Inn of Brenham 🆂🅷
(979) 251-7791. **$65-$109.** 1503 Hwy 290 E. 0.7 mi w of jct US 290 E and SR 577 eastbound; westbound 1.3 mi e of jct SR 36 and US 290. Ext corridors. **Pets:** Accepted.
[SAVE] [S🐾] [✕] [🛏] [💻] [🍴] [➳]

▼▼▼▼ Comfort Suites 🆂🅷
(979) 421-8100. **$62-$107.** 2350 S Day St. US 290, exit SR 36 S, just n on Business Rt 36. Int corridors. **Pets:** Accepted.

🅰🆂🅺 🆂🅾 ✖ 🛅 💻 ➴

BROWNFIELD

▼▼▼ Best Western Caprock Inn 🆂🅷
(806) 637-9471. **Call for rates.** 321 Lubbock Rd. Jct US 385 and 82, 2 blks n. Ext corridors. **Pets:** Accepted.

✖ 📶 🛅 💻 ➴

BROWNSVILLE

▼▼▼▼ Four Points by Sheraton 🆂🅷
(956) 547-1500. **$99-$129.** 3777 North Expwy. US 77 and 83, exit McAllen Rd, 0.5 mi s on west frontage road. Int corridors. **Pets:** Small. $125 one-time fee/room. Service with restrictions.

🅰🆂🅺 🆂🅾 ✖ 🐾 🛅 💻 🍴 ➴ ✖

▼▼▼▼ Residence Inn by Marriott 🆒
(956) 350-8100. **$105-$169.** 3975 North Expwy. US 83 and 77 Expwy, exit McAllen Rd. Int corridors. **Pets:** Medium, other species. $5 daily fee/pet, $50 one-time fee/pet. Designated rooms, service with restrictions.

✖ 📶 📶 🛅 💻 ➴ ✖

BROWNWOOD

▼▼▼ Best Western 🅼
(325) 646-3511. **$49-$69.** 410 E Commerce. On US 67/84/377; just n of jct Main Ave. Ext corridors. **Pets:** Accepted.

🅰🆂🅺 ✖ 📶 🛅 💻 ➴

▼▼▼ Days Inn-Brownwood 🆂🅷
(325) 646-2551. **$49-$74.** 515 E Commerce St. On US 67/84/377, 0.4 mi n of jct Main Ave. Ext corridors. **Pets:** Other species. $15 one-time fee/room. Service with restrictions.

🅰🆂🅺 🆂🅾 ✖ 🛅 💻 ➴

BURLESON

🅰🅰🅰 ▼▼▼ Comfort Suites 🆂🅷
(817) 426-6666. **$79-$89.** 321 S Burleson Blvd. I-35, exit 36 (Renfro St) westbound, 0.6 mi s on frontage road east of interstate. Int corridors. **Pets:** Medium. $10 daily fee/pet. Designated rooms, service with restrictions, supervision.

🆂🅰🆅🅴 🆂🅾 ✖ 📶 📶 🛅 💻 ➴

🅰🅰🅰 ▼▼ Days Inn 🆂🅷
(817) 447-1111. **$65-$75, 3 day notice.** 329 S Burleson Blvd. I-35, exit 36 (Renfro St), just w to east frontage road, 0.5 mi s. Ext corridors. **Pets:** Accepted.

🆂🅰🆅🅴 🆂🅾 ✖ 🛅 ➴

CANTON

🅰🅰🅰 ▼▼▼ Best Western Canton Inn 🆂🅷
(903) 567-6591. **$55-$165.** 2251 N Trade Days Blvd. Jct I-20 and SR 19, exit 527. Ext corridors. **Pets:** Small, other species. $5 daily fee/pet. Service with restrictions, supervision.

🆂🅰🆅🅴 🆂🅾 ✖ 🛅 💻 ➴

▼▼▼ Holiday Inn Express 🆂🅷
(903) 567-0909. **$55-$165.** 2406 N Trade Days Blvd. I-20, exit 527. Ext corridors. **Pets:** Accepted.

🅰🆂🅺 🆂🅾 ✖ 📶 📶 🛅 ➴

CANYON

🅰🅰🅰 ▼▼▼ Holiday Inn Express Hotel & Suites 🆂🅷
(806) 655-4445. **$72-$98.** 2901 4th Ave. I-27, exit 106, 2 mi w. Int corridors. **Pets:** Other species. $10 one-time fee/room. Service with restrictions, supervision.

🆂🅰🆅🅴 🆂🅾 ✖ 📶 📶 🛅 💻 ➴

CEDAR PARK

▼▼ Comfort Inn 🆂🅷
(512) 259-1810. **$70-$100.** 300 E Whitestone Blvd. I-35, exit 256, 8 mi w on FM 1431. Int corridors. **Pets:** Other species. $10 daily fee/pet. Service with restrictions, supervision.

🅰🆂🅺 🆂🅾 ✖ 📶 📶 🛅 💻 ➴

CENTER

▼▼ Best Western Center Inn 🆂🅷
(936) 598-3384. **$79, 7 day notice.** 1005 Hurst St. On US 96, jct SR 87. Ext corridors. **Pets:** Accepted.

🅰🆂🅺 🆂🅾 ✖ 🛅 💻 ➴

CHILDRESS

🅰🅰🅰 ▼▼▼▼ Best Western Childress 🅼
(940) 937-6353. **$70-$80.** 1801 Ave F NW (Hwy 287). On US 287, just s of jct US 62/83. Ext corridors. **Pets:** Medium. $10 daily fee/pet. Service with restrictions, supervision.

🆂🅰🆅🅴 🆂🅾 ✖ 🛅 💻 ➴

▼▼▼▼ Comfort Inn 🆂🅷
(940) 937-6363. **$69-$94.** 1804 Ave F NW (Hwy 287). US 287, just s of jct US 62/83. Ext corridors. **Pets:** Large, other species. $5 daily fee/pet. Service with restrictions, supervision.

🅰🆂🅺 🆂🅾 ✖ 📶 🐾 🛅 💻 ➴

🅰🅰🅰 ▼▼ Econo Lodge 🆂🅷
(940) 937-3695. **$48-$70.** 1612 Ave F NW Hwy 287. On US 287, just s of jct US 62/83. Ext corridors. **Pets:** Medium. $5 daily fee/pet. Designated rooms, service with restrictions, supervision.

🆂🅰🆅🅴 🆂🅾 ✖ 💻 ➴

🅰🅰🅰 ▼▼▼ Super 8 Motel Childress 🅼 🐾
(940) 937-8825. **$70-$100.** 411 Ave F NE (Hwy 287 S). Jct US 83/287, just w. Ext corridors. **Pets:** Other species. $10 one-time fee/pet. Designated rooms, service with restrictions, supervision.

🆂🅰🆅🅴 🆂🅾 ✖ 📶 🛅 ➴

CISCO

▼▼ Best Western Inn Cisco 🅼 🐾
(254) 442-3735. **$59-$64.** 1898 Hwy 206 W. I-20, exit 330. Ext corridors. **Pets:** $10 daily fee/pet. Service with restrictions.

🅰🆂🅺 🆂🅾 ✖ 🛅 💻 ➴

CLARENDON

Western Skies Motel M
(806) 874-3501. **$45-$50, 7 day notice.** 800 W 2nd St. 0.5 mi nw on US 287 and SR 70. Ext corridors. **Pets:** Medium, dogs only. $5 daily fee/room. Designated rooms, service with restrictions, supervision.

CLAUDE

L A Motel M
(806) 226-4981. **$40-$50, 5 day notice.** Hwy 287/200 E 1st St. 0.3 mi s. Ext corridors. **Pets:** Small. $5 daily fee/pet. Designated rooms, no service, supervision.

CLEBURNE

Comfort Inn SH
(817) 641-4702. **$79-$89.** 2117 N Main St. On SR 174, just s of jct US 67. Int corridors. **Pets:** Medium. $10 daily fee/room. Service with restrictions, supervision.

Sagamar Inn M
(817) 556-3631. **$60, 3 day notice.** 2107 N Main St. US 67, exit SR 174 (Main St), just e. Ext corridors. **Pets:** Medium, dogs only. $15 deposit/room. Service with restrictions, supervision.

CLUTE

La Quinta Inn M
(979) 265-7461. **$72-$87.** 1126 Hwy 332 W. 3.5 mi e of jct SR 288 and 332. Ext corridors. **Pets:** Other species. Service with restrictions.

Mainstay Suites Clute/Lake Jackson SH
(979) 388-9300. **$99-$139.** 1003 W Hwy 332. Just w of jct SR 288. Int corridors. **Pets:** Small. $100 deposit/room. Service with restrictions, supervision.

COLLEGE STATION

Holiday Inn-College Station SH
(979) 693-1736. **$79.** 1503 S Texas Ave. 1.3 mi s of jct CR 60. Int corridors. **Pets:** Medium. $15 one-time fee/pet. Service with restrictions, crate.

La Quinta Inn SH
(979) 696-7777. **$76-$96.** 607 Texas Ave. Just s on jct CR 60/SR 6 business route to Live Oak St, just e. Ext corridors. **Pets:** Accepted.

Manor House Inn SH
(979) 764-9540. **$67-$99.** 2504 Texas Ave S. 2.4 mi s of jct CR 60. Ext corridors. **Pets:** Accepted.

Ramada Inn SH
(979) 693-9891. **$69-$125, 3 day notice.** 1502 Texas Ave S. 1.3 mi s of jct CR 60. Int corridors. **Pets:** Small, other species. $15 one-time fee/pet. Service with restrictions, supervision.

TownePlace Suites By Marriott SH
(979) 260-8500. **Call for rates.** 1300 E University Dr. SR 6, exit University Dr, 1 mi w. Ext corridors. **Pets:** Accepted.

COLUMBUS

Country Hearth Inn SH
(979) 732-6293. **$70-$80.** 2436 Hwy 71 S. I-10, exit 696 (SR 71). Ext corridors. **Pets:** Very small, dogs only. $10 one-time fee/room. Designated rooms, service with restrictions, supervision.

Holiday Inn Express Hotel & Suites SH
(979) 733-9300. **$69-$89.** 4321 I-10. I-10, exit 696 (SR 71), just w on westbound service road. Int corridors. **Pets:** $40 deposit/room, $10 daily fee/pet. No service, supervision.

CONWAY

Budget Host S & S Motel M
(806) 537-5111. **$40, 3 day notice.** I-40 & SR 207. I-40, exit 96 (SR 207), 0.3 mi w on southbound access road. Ext corridors. **Pets:** Accepted.

COPPERAS COVE

Howard Johnson Express Inn SH
(254) 547-2345. **$54-$69.** 302 W US 190. On US 190, jct Georgetown Rd, 0.4 mi w of jct US 190 and SR 116. Ext corridors. **Pets:** Accepted.

CORPUS CHRISTI

Best Western Garden Inn M
(361) 241-6675. **$64-$139, 7 day notice.** 11217 I-37. I-37, exit 11B (Violet Rd), on southbound access road. Ext corridors. **Pets:** Small. $5 one-time fee/pet. Service with restrictions.

Best Western Marina Grand Hotel SH
(361) 883-5111. **$69-$195.** 300 N Shoreline Dr. Center of downtown. Int corridors. **Pets:** $25 one-time fee/pet. Service with restrictions, supervision.

Christy Estate Suites CO
(361) 854-1091. **$109-$169.** 3942 Holly Rd. SR 358, exit Weber Rd, 0.5 mi s. Ext/int corridors. **Pets:** Large. $500 deposit/room. Designated rooms, service with restrictions, crate.

Clarion Hotel SH
(361) 883-6161. **$74-$84.** 5224 I-37 (Navigation Blvd). I-37, exit 3A (Navigation Blvd), on northbound access lane. Ext corridors. **Pets:** Small, other species. $25 one-time fee/room. Service with restrictions, supervision.

Days Inn SH
(361) 888-8599. **$40-$130.** 901 Navigation Blvd. I-37, exit 3A (Navigation Blvd), just w. Ext corridors. **Pets:** Small. $10 daily fee/pet. Designated rooms, service with restrictions.

Days Inn Corpus Christi South SH
(361) 854-0005. **$69-$169.** 2838 S Padre Island Dr. On SR 358 westbound access road, 0.4 mi w, exit Kostoryz Rd. Ext corridors. **Pets:** Accepted.

Drury Inn-Corpus Christi SH
(361) 289-8200. **$72-$92.** 2021 N Padre Island Dr. I-37, exit SR 358, just se at Leopard St. Int corridors. **Pets:** Large, other species. Service with restrictions, supervision.

Holiday Inn-Emerald Beach LH
(361) 883-5731. **$115-$179.** 1102 S Shoreline Blvd. 1.5 mi s on bay from downtown marina. Ext/int corridors. **Pets:** Accepted.

Holiday Inn-Padre Island Drive LH
(361) 289-5100. **$79-$129.** 5549 Leopard St. Jct SR 358 and Leopard St, 5.5 mi w. Int corridors. **Pets:** Accepted.

La Quinta Inn-Corpus Christi-North SH
(361) 888-5721. **$70-$90.** 5155 I-37 N. I-37, exit 3A (Navigation Blvd), on southbound access road. Ext corridors. **Pets:** Other species. Service with restrictions.

La Quinta Inn-South SH
(361) 991-5730. **$69-$95.** 6225 S Padre Island Dr. SR 358 Expwy, exit Airline Rd. Ext corridors. **Pets:** Other species. Supervision.

Motel 6 Lantana–231 M
(361) 289-9397. **$35-$53.** 845 Lantana St. I-37, exit 4B (Lantana St), on southbound access road. Ext corridors. **Pets:** Accepted.

Motel 6 SPI Drive–413 SH
(361) 991-8858. **$39-$55.** 8202 S Padre Island Dr. S Padre Island Dr at Paul Jones St. Ext corridors. **Pets:** Accepted.

Ramada Limited SH ❀
(361) 289-5861. **$44-$149.** 5501 I-37 at McBride Ln. I-37, exit 3A (Navigation St), take loop to McBride Ln, then just n. Int corridors. **Pets:** Medium. $10 daily fee/pet. Designated rooms, service with restrictions, crate.

Red Roof Inn Corpus Christi Airport M
(361) 289-6925. **$42-$175.** 6301 I-37. I-37, exit 5 (Corn Products Rd), southbound access road. Ext corridors. **Pets:** Small. $10 deposit/pet. Service with restrictions, supervision.

Surfside Condominium Apartments CO
(361) 949-8128. **$120-$155, 3 day notice.** 15005 Windward Dr. Park Rd 22 on N Padre Island Dr, jct Whitecap Blvd, just e. Ext corridors. **Pets:** Medium. $15 daily fee/pet. Designated rooms, service with restrictions, supervision.

DALHART

Best Western Nursanickel Motel SH
(806) 244-5637. **$58-$78.** 102 Scott Ave (Hwy 87 S). Just s of jct US 54 and 87. Ext corridors. **Pets:** Small, dogs only. $8 one-time fee/pet. Designated rooms, service with restrictions, supervision.

Budget Inn M
(806) 244-4557. **$36-$69.** 415 Liberal St (Hwy 54). US 54, just e of US 87 and 385. Ext corridors. **Pets:** Medium. Service with restrictions, supervision.

Comfort Inn M
(806) 249-8585. **$70-$90.** 1110 Hwy 54 E. 0.5 mi e of jct US 54 and 87. Ext corridors. **Pets:** Medium. Designated rooms, service with restrictions, supervision.

Days Inn SH ❀
(806) 244-5246. **$85-$109.** 701 Liberal St (Hwy 54). 0.5 mi e on US 54. Int corridors. **Pets:** Medium, other species. Designated rooms, service with restrictions, supervision.

Holiday Inn Express SH
(806) 249-1145. **$79-$99.** 801 Liberal St (Hwy 54). 1 mi e of jct US 54 and 87. Int corridors. **Pets:** Service with restrictions, supervision.

Sands Motel M
(806) 244-4568. **$30-$70.** 301 Liberal St (Hwy 54). US 54, just e of US 87 and 385. Ext corridors. **Pets:** Service with restrictions, supervision.

Super 8 Motel M
(806) 249-8526. **$54-$64.** 403 Tanglewood Rd. Jct US 87/54, 0.5 mi e. Int corridors. **Pets:** Small. $25 deposit/pet. Designated rooms, service with restrictions, supervision.

DALLAS METROPOLITAN AREA

ADDISON

Best Western Addison/Galleria Hotel & Suites SH
(972) 386-4800. **$69-$129.** 15200 Addison Rd. Just n of Belt Line Rd. Int corridors. **Pets:** Accepted.

Comfort Inn Hotel by the Galleria SH
(972) 701-0881. **$49-$99.** 14975 Landmark Blvd. Jct Beltway Rd and Landmark Blvd, just s. Int corridors. **Pets:** $25 deposit/room. Service with restrictions.

Comfort Suites SH
(972) 503-6500. **$69.** 4555 Belt Line Rd. Just ne of jct Midway and Belt Line rds. Int corridors. **Pets:** Small. $50 one-time fee/room. Service with restrictions, crate.

Crowne Plaza North Dallas/Near the Galleria LH
(972) 980-8877. **$109-$159.** 14315 Midway Rd. 0.8 mi s of jct Belt Line and Midway rds. Int corridors. **Pets:** Accepted.

Homewood Suites by Hilton SH
(972) 788-1342. **$109-$129.** 4451 Belt Line Rd. Just e of jct Belt Line and Midway rds. Ext/int corridors. **Pets:** Accepted.

La Quinta Inn & Suites-Dallas Addison SH
(972) 404-0004. **$60-$100.** 14925 Landmark Blvd. Jct Belt Line Rd and Landmark Blvd, just s. Int corridors. **Pets:** Other species. Service with restrictions, crate.

Summerfield Suites by Wyndham SH
(972) 661-3113. **$149.** 4900 Edwin Lewis Dr. Just n of jct Belt Line Rd and Quorum Dr to Edwin Lewis Dr, just w. Ext/int corridors. **Pets:** Accepted.

CARROLLTON

Red Roof Inn-Carrollton M
(972) 245-1700. **$38-$51.** 1720 S Broadway. I-35 E, exit 442 (Valwood Pkwy), just ne. Ext corridors. **Pets:** Large, other species. Service with restrictions, supervision.

THE COLONY

Comfort Suites SH
(972) 668-5555. **$89.** 4796 Memorial Dr. Just n of jct SR 121. Int corridors. **Pets:** Very small. $10 daily fee/pet. Service with restrictions, supervision.

DALLAS

AmeriSuites (Dallas/Near the Galleria) SH
(972) 716-2001. **$99-$109.** 5229 Spring Valley Rd. Jct Dallas Pkwy, just e. Int corridors. **Pets:** Accepted.

AmeriSuites (Dallas/Park Central) SH
(972) 458-1224. **$99-$119.** 12411 N Central Expwy. US 75, exit 8B (Coit Rd) northbound; exit 8 (Coit Rd), on southbound access road. Int corridors. **Pets:** Medium, other species. No service, supervision.

Best Western Dallas Telecom Area Suites SH
(972) 669-0478. **$79-$89.** 13636 Goldmark Dr. US 75, exit 22 (Midpark Rd). Ext/int corridors. **Pets:** Other species. $25 one-time fee/pet.

Bristol House Suites Dallas-Park Central SH
(972) 391-0000. **$114-$129.** 7880 Alpha Rd. I-635, exit 19B (Coit Rd), 0.3 mi n, then just w. Int corridors. **Pets:** Other species. $125 one-time fee/room. Service with restrictions.

Candlewood Dallas Market Center SH
(214) 631-3333. **$74-$84.** 7930 N Stemmons Frwy. I-35, exit 433B (Mockingbird Ln), just w. Int corridors. **Pets:** Small, other species. $75 one-time fee/pet. Service with restrictions, crate.

Candlewood Suites-Dallas Galleria SH 🐾
(972) 233-6888. **$69-$119.** 13939 Noel Rd. Jct Dallas Pkwy and Spring Valley, just e to Noel Rd, then just s. Int corridors. **Pets:** Medium, other species. $50 one-time fee/pet. Service with restrictions, crate.

Candlewood Suites Dallas North/Richardson SH
(972) 669-9606. **$69-$99.** 12525 Greenville Ave. I-635, exit 18A (Greenville Ave), just n. Int corridors. **Pets:** Accepted.

Crowne Plaza Hotel and Resort Dallas Market Center LH
(214) 630-8500. **$119-$179.** 7050 Stemmons Frwy. I-35 E, exit 433B northbound; exit 432B southbound. Int corridors. **Pets:** Accepted.

Crowne Plaza Suites Hotel and Resort Dallas Park Central LH
(972) 233-7600. **$79-$139.** 7800 Alpha Rd. I-635, exit 19C (Coit Rd) eastbound; exit 19B (Coit Rd) westbound, 0.3 mi nw of jct US 75. Int corridors. **Pets:** Accepted.

▲▲▲ ▼▼▼▼ Dallas Marriott Suites Market Center 🆂🅷

(214) 905-0050. **$79-$199.** 2493 N Stemmons Frwy. I-35, exit 431 (Motor St). Int corridors. **Pets:** Medium. $50 one-time fee/room. Service with restrictions.

🆂🅰🆅🅴 🆂🅾 ✕ 🅡🅼 🕖 🄺 🯄 🖵 🍴 🏊

▼▼▼ Drury Inn & Suites-Dallas North 🆂🅷

(972) 484-3330. **$74-$97.** 2421 Walnut Hill Ln. I-35 E, exit 438 (Walnut Hill Ln). Int corridors. **Pets:** Large, other species. Service with restrictions, supervision.

🄰🆂🅺 ✕ 🕖 🯄 🖵 🏊

▼▼▼ Embassy Suites Dallas-Market Center 🅻🅷

(214) 630-5332. **$99-$219.** 2727 Stemmons Frwy. I-35 E, exit 432 (Inwood Rd). Int corridors. **Pets:** Medium. $25 one-time fee/pet. Service with restrictions.

🄰🆂🅺 🆂🅾 ✕ 🕖 🄺 🯄 🖵 🍴 🏊 🗙

▼▼▼▼ The Fairmont Dallas 🅻🅷

(214) 720-2020. **$159-$309.** 1717 N Akard St. Corner of Ross Ave and N Akard St. Int corridors. **Pets:** Accepted.

🄰🆂🅺 🆂🅾 ✕ 🅡🅼 🕖 🄺 🯄 🖵 🍴 🏊

▼▼ Hawthorn Suites Hotel-Dallas-Market Center 🆂🅷

(214) 688-1010. **$79-$159.** 7900 Brookriver Dr. I-35 E, exit 433B (Mockingbird Ln), just se. Ext corridors. **Pets:** Accepted.

🄰🆂🅺 🆂🅾 ✕ 🕖 🯄 🖵 🏊

▼▼▼ Holiday Inn Express-Love Field 🆂🅷

(214) 350-5577. **$69-$79.** 2370 W Northwest Hwy. I-35 E, exit 436 (W Northwest Hwy), 0.8 mi e. Int corridors. **Pets:** Accepted.

🄰🆂🅺 🆂🅾 ✕ 🕖 🄺 🯄 🖵

▼▼▼ Holiday Inn Express Park Central 🆂🅷

(972) 907-9500. **$65-$75.** 13185 Central Expwy. US 75 N, exit 22 (Midpart Rd). Int corridors. **Pets:** Accepted.

🄰🆂🅺 🆂🅾 ✕ 🕖 🄺 🯄 🖵 🏊

▲▲▲ ▼▼▼▼ Holiday Inn Select Dallas Central 🅻🅷

(214) 373-6000. **$129-$350.** 10650 N Central Expwy. N US 75, exit 6 (Walnut Hill Ln/Meadow Rd). Int corridors. **Pets:** Medium. $50 one-time fee/room. Service with restrictions, supervision.

🆂🅰🆅🅴 🆂🅾 ✕ 🕖 🄺 🯄 🖵 🍴 🏊

▼▼ Homestead Studio Suites Hotel-Dallas/North Addison/Tollway 🆂🅷 🐾

(972) 447-1800. **$44-$54.** 17425 North Dallas Pkwy. On North Dallas Tollway, exit Trinity Mills, just s of jct Trinity Mills and Dallas Pkwy, on southbound access road. Ext corridors. **Pets:** Medium, other species. $25 daily fee/room. Service with restrictions, crate.

🄰🆂🅺 🆂🅾 ✕ 🄺 🯄 🖵

▼▼ Homestead Studio Suites Hotel-Dallas/North/ Park Central 🆂🅷 🐾

(972) 663-1800. **$54-$64.** 12121 Coit Rd. I-635, exit 19C (Coit Rd), 0.7 mi s. Ext corridors. **Pets:** Medium, other species. $25 daily fee/room. Service with restrictions, crate.

🄰🆂🅺 🆂🅾 ✕ 🕖 🄺 🖵

▼▼▼ Homestead Studio Suites Hotel-Dallas/Plano 🆂🅷 🐾

(972) 248-2233. **$69-$79.** 18470 North Dallas Pkwy. North Dallas Tollway, exit Frankford, just ne. Int corridors. **Pets:** Medium, other species. $25 daily fee/room. Service with restrictions, crate.

🄰🆂🅺 🆂🅾 ✕ 🅡🅼 🕖 🯄 🖵 🏊

▼▼▼ Homewood Suites by Hilton 🆂🅷

(214) 819-9700. **$86.** 2747 N Stemmons Frwy. I-35, exit 432 (Inwood Rd). Int corridors. **Pets:** Accepted.

🄰🆂🅺 🆂🅾 ✕ 🅡🅼 🄺 🯄 🖵 🏊

▼▼▼ Homewood Suites by Hilton-I-635 🆂🅷

(972) 437-6966. **$109, 7 day notice.** 9169 Markville Dr. I-635, exit 18A (Greenville Ave S), just s, then just e. Int corridors. **Pets:** Medium. $100 one-time fee/room. Service with restrictions, crate.

🄰🆂🅺 🆂🅾 ✕ 🯄 🖵 🏊 🗙

▼▼▼▼ Hotel Crescent Court 🅻🅷

(214) 871-3200. **$365-$2500.** 400 Crescent Ct. Corner of Crescent Ct and McKinney Ave; uptown. Int corridors. **Pets:** Accepted.

✕ 🯄 🍴 🏊 🗙

▼▼▼ Hotel Dallas Mockingbird 🆂🅷

(214) 634-8850. **$49-$109.** 1893 W Mockingbird Ln. I-35 E, exit 433C (Mockingbird Ln), 0.8 mi e. Int corridors. **Pets:** Accepted.

🄰🆂🅺 🆂🅾 ✕ 🕖 🯄 🖵 🍴 🏊 🗙

▲▲▲ ▼▼▼▼ Hotel St. Germain 🅲🅸 🐾

(214) 871-2516. **$290-$650, 7 day notice.** 2516 Maple Ave. Woodall Rogers Pkwy, exit Pearl St, 0.3 mi n. Int corridors. **Pets:** Small, dogs only. $50 daily fee/pet. Designated rooms, service with restrictions, supervision.

🆂🅰🆅🅴 🖵 🍴

▼▼▼ Hotel ZaZa 🆂🅷

(214) 468-8399. **$275-$2000.** 2332 Leonard St. Jct Maple Ave/Routh St and McKinney Ave, northeast corner. Int corridors. **Pets:** Accepted.

✕ 🅡🅼 🯄 🖵 🍴 🏊 🗙

▼▼▼ La Quinta Inn & Suites-Dallas Northwest 🆂🅷

(214) 904-9955. **$59-$79.** 2380 W Northwest Hwy. I-35, exit 436 (W Northwest Hwy), 0.8 mi e. Int corridors. **Pets:** Accepted.

🄰🆂🅺 🆂🅾 ✕ 🕖 🯄 🖵 🏊

▼▼▼ La Quinta Inn & Suites near North Park Mall 🆂🅷 🐾

(214) 361-8200. **$86-$121.** 10001 N Central Expwy. I-75, exit 6 (Walnut Hill Ln/Meadow Rd) northbound, 0.5 mi n to Meadow Rd, U-turn under highway; exit 7 (Royal Meadow Rd) southbound, 1 mi s on feeder. Int corridors. **Pets:** Small. Service with restrictions, supervision.

🄰🆂🅺 🆂🅾 ✕ 🅡🅼 🯄 🖵 🏊

▼▼▼ La Quinta Inn-Dallas-City Place 🆂🅷

(214) 821-4220. **$80-$100.** 4440 N Central Expwy. N off US 75, exit 2 (Henderson-Knox) northbound; exit 1B (Haskell/Blackburn) southbound. Ext corridors. **Pets:** Accepted.

🄰🆂🅺 🆂🅾 ✕ 🕖 🯄 🖵 🏊

▼▼▼▼ La Quinta Inn-Dallas-East 🆂🅷
(214) 324-3731. **$66-$81.** 8303 E R L Thornton Frwy. I-30, exit 52A (Jim Miller Rd). Ext corridors. **Pets:** Accepted.
[A$K] [S🐾] [✕] [🐾ᴹ] [⚡] [🛏] [💻] [🛍]

▼▼▼▼ La Quinta Inn Love Field 🆂🅷
(214) 630-5701. **$60-$80.** 1625 Regal Row. I-35 E, exit 434B (Regal Row). Ext corridors. **Pets:** Accepted.
[A$K] [S🐾] [✕] [🐾] [⚡] [💻] [🛍]

▲▲▲ ▼▼▼▼ La Quinta Inn-Richardson 🆂🅷
(972) 234-1016. **$50-$70.** 13685 N Central Expwy. US 75 N, exit 22 (Midpark Rd). Ext/int corridors. **Pets:** Supervision.
[SAVE] [S🐾] [✕] [🐾] [⚡] [💻] [🛍]

▼▼▼▼ Magnolia Hotel Dallas 🅻🅷
(214) 915-6500. **$159-$230.** 1401 Commerce St. Corner of Commerce and Akard sts. Int corridors. **Pets:** Accepted.
[A$K] [S🐾] [✕] [🐾] [⚡] [🛏] [💻] [✕]

▲▲▲ ▼▼▼▼ The Mansion On Turtle Creek 🅻🅷 🐾
(214) 559-2100. **$400-$2400.** 2821 Turtle Creek Blvd. 2 mi nw; entrance on Gillespie St. Int corridors. **Pets:** Large, other species. $100 one-time fee/room. Service with restrictions.
[SAVE] [✕] [⚡] [🛏] [💻] [🍴] [🛍] [✕]

▼▼▼▼ The Melrose Hotel 🆂🅷 🐾
(214) 521-5151. **$249-$1500.** 3015 Oak Lawn Ave. I-35 E, exit 430, 0.8 mi n, entrance off Cedar Springs, just n. Int corridors. **Pets:** Other species. $50 deposit/room.
[A$K] [S🐾] [✕] [🛏] [💻] [🍴]

▼▼ Motel 6 #1479 🅼
(214) 388-8741. **$47-$65.** 8108 E R L Thornton Frwy. I-30, exit 52A (Jim Miller Rd). Ext corridors. **Pets:** Accepted.
[S🐾] [✕] [🐾]

▼▼ Motel 6 #1493 🆂🅷 🐾
(972) 506-8100. **$41-$54.** 10335 Gardner Rd. I-35 E, exit 436, just sw of jct Loop 12 (Northwest Hwy) and Spur 348; 0.8 mi w of I-35 E and US 77. Ext corridors. **Pets:** Other species. Service with restrictions, supervision.
[✕] [🐾]

▼▼ Motel 6–560 🆂🅷
(972) 620-2828. **$39-$51.** 2753 Forest Ln. I-635, exit 26 (Josey Ln) eastbound; exit 25 (Josey Ln) westbound, just s to Forest Ln, just w. Ext corridors. **Pets:** Accepted.
[S🐾] [✕] [⚡] [🛍]

▼ Motel 6 Forest Lane-South #1119 🅼
(972) 484-9111. **$39-$53.** 2660 Forest Ln. I-635, exit 26 (Josey Ln) eastbound, 0.5 mi s to Forest Ln, just w; exit 25 (Josey Ln) westbound, just s to Forest Ln, just w. Ext corridors. **Pets:** Other species. Service with restrictions, supervision.
[S🐾] [✕] [🐾] [🛍]

▲▲▲ ▼▼▼▼ Radisson Hotel Central/Dallas 🅻🅷
(214) 750-6060. **$139-$159.** 6060 N Central Expwy. US 75, exit 3 (Mockingbird Ln). Int corridors. **Pets:** Medium, other species. $50 deposit/room. Supervision.
[SAVE] [S🐾] [✕] [🐾] [⚡] [🛏] [💻] [🍴] [🛍] [✕]

▲▲▲ ▼▼▼ Red Roof Inn-Market Center 🅼
(214) 638-5151. **$44-$54.** 1550 Empire Central Dr. I-35 E, exit 434A (Empire Central Dr), 0.3 mi e. Ext corridors. **Pets:** Accepted.
[SAVE] [✕] [🐾]

▲▲▲ ▼▼▼ ▼▼▼ Renaissance Dallas Hotel 🅻🅷 🐾
(214) 631-2222. **$89-$199.** 2222 Stemmons Frwy. I-35 E, exit 430B (Market Center Blvd), 0.3 mi nw on access road. Int corridors. **Pets:** $25 deposit/pet. Service with restrictions, supervision.
[SAVE] [S🐾] [✕] [🐾] [🛏] [💻] [🍴] [🛍] [✕]

▼▼▼▼ Residence Inn by Marriott at Dallas Central 🆂🅷
(214) 750-8220. **Call for rates.** 10333 N Central Expwy. I-75 N, exit 6 (Meadow Rd) northbound; exit 7 (Royal Ln) southbound. Ext corridors. **Pets:** Accepted.
[✕] [🐾] [🛏] [💻] [🛍] [✕]

▼▼▼▼ Residence Inn by Marriott-Dallas Market Center 🆂🅷
(214) 631-2472. **$79-$119.** 6950 N Stemmons Frwy. I-35 E, exit 432B (Commonwealth), on northbound frontage road. Ext/int corridors. **Pets:** Medium, other species. $50 one-time fee/room. Service with restrictions.
[A$K] [S🐾] [✕] [🐾] [⚡] [🛏] [💻] [🛍] [✕]

▼▼▼▼ Residence Inn by Marriott-Dallas Park Central 🆂🅷 🐾
(972) 503-1333. **Call for rates.** 7642 LBJ Frwy. I-635, exit 20 (Hillcrest), just e, on eastbound access road. Int corridors. **Pets:** Other species. $75 one-time fee/room. Service with restrictions.
[✕] [🐾ᴹ] [🐾] [⚡] [🛏] [💻] [🛍] [✕]

▲▲▲ ▼▼▼▼ Sheraton Dallas Brookhollow Hotel 🅻🅷
(214) 630-7000. **$59-$119.** 1241 W Mockingbird Ln. I-35 E, exit 433B, just nw of jct I-35 E and W Mockingbird Ln. Int corridors. **Pets:** Accepted.
[SAVE] [S🐾] [✕] [🐾] [⚡] [🛏] [💻] [🍴] [🛍]

▼▼▼▼ Sheraton Suites Market Center-Dallas 🅻🅷
(214) 747-3000. **$229.** 2101 Stemmons Frwy. Nw off I-35 E and US 77, exit 430B (Market Center Blvd). Int corridors. **Pets:** Service with restrictions.
[A$K] [S🐾] [✕] [🐾] [⚡] [🛏] [💻] [🍴] [🛍]

▼▼▼▼ Sterling Hotel Dallas 🆂🅷
(214) 634-8550. **$69-$79.** 1055 Regal Row. Southeast corner of jct SR 183 and Regal Row. Int corridors. **Pets:** Accepted.
[A$K] [S🐾] [✕] [🐾] [⚡] [🛏] [💻] [🍴] [🛍] [✕]

▲▲▲ ▼▼▼ Wellesley Inn & Suites (Dallas/Park Central) 🆂🅷
(972) 671-7722. **$69-$79.** 9019 Vantage Point Rd. I-635, exit 18A (Greenville Ave), just sw. Ext corridors. **Pets:** Small. Service with restrictions, crate.
[SAVE] [S🐾] [✕] [🐾ᴹ] [⚡] [🛏] [💻]

▼▼▼▼ **The Westin City Center, Dallas** 🄛🄷
(214) 979-9000. **$99-$149.** 650 N Pearl St. Between San Jacinto and Bryan St, 0.3 mi w of US 75 Central Expwy. Int corridors. **Pets:** Accepted.

〔ASK〕 〔S🌓〕 ✕ 🕖 🏃 📳 📠 📺 🍴 ✕

▼▼▼ ▼▼▼ **The Westin Galleria, Dallas** 🄛🄷
(972) 934-9494. **$199-$359.** 13340 Dallas Pkwy. Just n of jct I-635 and N Dallas Pkwy. Int corridors. **Pets:** Accepted.

✕ 🅱M 🕖 🏃 📳 📠 🍴 ⇌

▼▼▼ ▼▼▼ **The Westin Park Central**
Dallas 🄛🄷 ❀
(972) 385-3000. **$239-$259.** 12720 Merit Dr. I-635, exit 19C (Coit Rd) eastbound; exit 19B (Coit Rd) westbound, 0.3 mi w of jct US 75. Int corridors. **Pets:** Medium, dogs only. Service with restrictions.

〔ASK〕 〔S🌓〕 ✕ 🅱M 🕖 🏃 📳 📠 🍴 ⇌ ✕

▼▼▼▼ **Wingate Inn** 🅂🄷
(214) 267-8400. **$89-$109.** 8650 N Stemmons Frwy. I-35, exit 434A (Empire Central), just n. Int corridors. **Pets:** Accepted.

〔ASK〕 〔S🌓〕 ✕ 🅱M 🏃 📳 📠 ⇌

DENTON

🅰 ▼▼▼ **Exel Inn of Denton** 🅂🄷
(940) 383-1471. **$43-$65.** 4211 I-35 E N. Jct US 380 and I-35, exit 469, just n. Int corridors. **Pets:** Small. Designated rooms, service with restrictions, supervision.

〔SAVE〕 〔S🌓〕 ✕ 🕖 📳 📠 ⇌

▼▼▼ ▼ **La Quinta Inn-Denton** 🅂🄷
(940) 387-5840. **$72-$95.** 700 Fort Worth Dr. I-35 E, exit 465B (Fort Worth Dr), just n. Ext corridors. **Pets:** Accepted.

〔ASK〕 〔S🌓〕 ✕ 🅱M 🕖 🏃 📳 📠 ⇌

▼▼▼ ▼ **Radisson Hotel Denton & Eagle Point Golf**
Club 🅂🄷
(940) 565-8499. **$129-$149.** 2211 I-35 E N. Off I-35 E and US 77, exit 466B (Ave D), 2.5 mi sw. Int corridors. **Pets:** Small, other species. $100 deposit/room. Service with restrictions, crate.

〔ASK〕 〔S🌓〕 ✕ 📳 📠 🍴 ⇌

DESOTO

🅰 ▼▼▼ **Red Roof Inn Dallas/DeSoto** 🅂🄷
(972) 224-7100. **$41-$54.** 1401 N Beckley Dr. I-35, exit 416, just s. Ext/int corridors. **Pets:** Medium. Designated rooms, service with restrictions, supervision.

〔SAVE〕 ✕ 🕖 📳

DUNCANVILLE

▼ **Motel 6-#1130** 🅂🄷
(972) 296-0345. **$41-$55.** 202 Jellison Blvd. I-20, exit 462A (Duncanville Rd). Ext/int corridors. **Pets:** Accepted.

〔S🌓〕 ✕ 🏃 📳 ⇌

FARMERS BRANCH

🅰 ▼▼▼ **Best Western Dallas North** 🅂🄷
(972) 241-8521. **$54-$74.** 13333 N Stemmons Frwy. I-35 E, exit 441 (Valley View Ln), on west side of frontage road. Ext/int corridors. **Pets:** Accepted.

〔SAVE〕 〔S🌓〕 ✕ 📳 📠 🍴 ⇌

🅰 ▼▼▼ **Days Inn–North Dallas** 🅂🄷
(972) 488-0800. **$45-$53.** 13313 Stemmons Frwy. I-35 E, exit 441 (Valley View Ln), on west side of frontage road. Int corridors. **Pets:** Accepted.

〔SAVE〕 〔S🌓〕 ✕ 🏃 📳 📠 ⇌

🅰 ▼▼▼ **La Quinta**
Inn-Dallas-Northwest-Farmers
Branch 🅂🄷
(972) 620-7333. **$60-$75.** 13235 Stemmons Frwy N. I-35 E, exit 441 (Valley View Ln), on west side of frontage road. Ext corridors. **Pets:** Other species. No service.

〔SAVE〕 〔S🌓〕 ✕ 🕖 🏃 📳 📠 ⇌

🅰 ▼▼▼ ▼▼▼ **Omni Dallas Hotel Parkwest** 🄛🄷
(972) 869-4300. **$189.** 1590 LBJ Frwy. Nw off I-635, 1.5 mi w of jct I-35 E, exit 29 (Luna Rd). Int corridors. **Pets:** Accepted.

〔SAVE〕 ✕ 🕖 🏃 📳 📠 🍴 ⇌ ✕

GARLAND

🅰 ▼▼▼ **Best Western Lakeview Inn** 🅂🄷
(972) 303-1601. **$55-$79.** 1635 E I-30 at Chaha Rd. I-30, exit 62 (Chaha Rd). Ext corridors. **Pets:** Other species. $10 daily fee/pet. Service with restrictions, supervision.

〔SAVE〕 〔S🌓〕 ✕ 📳 📠 ⇌

▼▼▼▼ **Comfort Inn** 🅂🄷
(972) 613-5000. **$53.** 12670 E Northwest Hwy. I-635, exit 11B, just s. Ext corridors. **Pets:** Accepted.

〔ASK〕 〔S🌓〕 ✕ 🕖 📳 📠 ⇌

🅰 ▼▼▼ ▼ **La Quinta Inn-Dallas-LBJ**
Northeast-Garland 🅂🄷
(972) 271-7581. **$66-$86.** 12721 I-635. I-635, exit 11B, just nw. Ext/int corridors. **Pets:** Small. No service, crate.

〔SAVE〕 〔S🌓〕 ✕ 🕖 📳 📠 ⇌

🅰 ▼▼▼ **Microtel Inn & Suites** 🅂🄷
(972) 270-7200. **$40-$85.** 1901 Pendleton Dr. I-635, exit 11B, just n to Pendleton Dr, then just e. Int corridors. **Pets:** Accepted.

〔SAVE〕 〔S🌓〕 ✕ 🅱M 🏃 📳 📠

▼ **Motel 6-0620** 🅂🄷
(972) 226-7140. **$39-$53.** 436 W I-30. I-30, exit 58 (Belt Line Rd). Ext corridors. **Pets:** Accepted.

〔S🌓〕 ✕ 🏃 ⇌

GRAND PRAIRIE

🅰 ▼▼▼ **AmeriSuites (Dallas/Grand**
Prairie) 🅂🄷
(972) 988-6800. **$109-$119.** 1542 N Hwy 360. SR 360, exit J/K aves. Int corridors. **Pets:** Accepted.

〔SAVE〕 〔S🌓〕 ✕ 🅱M 🏃 📳 📠 ⇌

🅰 ▼▼▼ ▼ **La Quinta Inn-Dallas-Grand Prairie**
(Six Flags) 🅂🄷
(972) 641-3021. **$66-$86.** 1410 NW 19th St. I-30, exit 32, just e. Ext corridors. **Pets:** Accepted.

〔SAVE〕 〔S🌓〕 ✕ 🅱M 🕖 🏃 📳 📠 ⇌

▼▼ Motel 6–446 [SH]
(972) 642-9424. **$35-$53.** 406 E Safari Pkwy. I-30, exit 34 (Belt Line Rd), just n to Safari Pkwy, 0.6 mi w. Ext corridors. **Pets:** Accepted.

[S$] [X] [&] [📷] [📖] [≈]

GREENVILLE

▼▼ Best Western Inn & Suites [SH]
(903) 454-1792. **$64-$74.** 1216 I-30 W. I-30, exit 94B. Ext/int corridors. **Pets:** Accepted.

[A$K] [S$] [X] [📷] [📖] [≈]

▼▼▼ Holiday Inn Express Hotel & Suites [SH]
(903) 454-8680. **$89-$125.** 2901 Mustang Crossing. I-30, exit 93A. Int corridors. **Pets:** Accepted.

[A$K] [S$] [X] [&M] [&] [📷] [📖] [≈]

IRVING

⚠️⚠️⚠️ ▼▼▼▼ AmeriSuites (Dallas Las Colinas/Hidden Ridge) [SH]
(972) 910-0302. **$89-$119.** 333 W John Carpenter Frwy. SR 114, exit Hidden Ridge. Int corridors. **Pets:** Medium, other species. Service with restrictions, supervision.

[SAVE] [S$] [X] [&M] [📷] [&] [📷] [📖] [≈]

⚠️⚠️⚠️ ▼▼▼▼ AmeriSuites (Dallas Las Colinas/Walnut Hill) [SH]
(972) 550-7400. **$69-$109.** 5455 Green Park Dr. SR 114, exit Walnut Hill Ln. Int corridors. **Pets:** Very small. Service with restrictions, crate.

[SAVE] [S$] [X] [&M] [📷] [&] [📷] [📖] [≈]

▼▼▼▼ Candlewood Las Colinas [SH]
(972) 714-9990. **$95-$114.** 5300 Greenpark Dr. SR 114, exit Walnut Hill Ln, just s. Int corridors. **Pets:** Accepted.

[A$K] [S$] [X] [&M] [📷] [&] [📷] [📖]

▼▼▼ Dallas Las Colinas TownePlace Suites [SH]
(972) 550-7796. **$80.** 900 W Walnut Hill Ln. SR 114, exit Walnut Hill Ln, then w. Int corridors. **Pets:** Accepted.

[A$K] [S$] [X] [&M] [📷] [&] [📷] [📖] [≈]

▼▼▼▼ Drury Inn & Suites–DFW Airport [SH]
(972) 986-1200. **$75-$104.** 4210 W Airport Frwy. SR 183, exit Esters Rd, on southbound access road. Int corridors. **Pets:** Large, other species. Service with restrictions, supervision.

[A$K] [X] [📷] [📷] [📖] [≈]

⚠️⚠️⚠️ ▼▼▼▼▼ Four Seasons Resort & Club [LH] 🐾
(972) 717-0700. **$315-$460.** 4150 N MacArthur Blvd. Se off SR 114, 1.5 mi s of exit MacArthur Blvd. Int corridors. **Pets:** Very small. Service with restrictions, supervision.

[SAVE] [X] [&M] [📷] [&] [📷] [📖] [🍴] [≈] [X]

▼▼▼▼ Hampton Inn–DFW Airport South [SH]
(972) 986-3606. **$102-$112.** 4340 W Airport Frwy. SR 183, exit Valley View Ln, on southbound access road. Int corridors. **Pets:** Accepted.

[A$K] [X] [📷] [&] [📷] [📖] [≈]

⚠️⚠️⚠️ ▼▼▼▼ Harvey Hotel-DFW Airport [LH]
(972) 929-4500. **$119-$149.** 4545 W John Carpenter Frwy. Nw off SR 114, exit Esters Rd. Int corridors. **Pets:** Accepted.

[SAVE] [S$] [X] [📷] [📷] [📖] [🍴] [≈]

⚠️⚠️⚠️ ▼▼▼▼ Harvey Suites-DFW Airport [SH]
(972) 929-4499. **$110-$152.** 4550 W John Carpenter Frwy. SR 114, exit Freeport Pkwy, on southbound service road. Int corridors. **Pets:** Accepted.

[SAVE] [S$] [X] [&M] [📷] [&] [📷] [📖] [≈] [X]

⚠️⚠️⚠️ ▼▼▼▼ Holiday Inn Select DFW Airport South [LH]
(972) 399-1010. **$69-$99.** 4440 W Airport Frwy. SR 183, exit Valley View Ln, on southbound access road. Int corridors. **Pets:** Accepted.

[SAVE] [S$] [X] [📷] [&] [📷] [📖] [🍴] [≈] [X]

▼▼ Homestead Studio Suites Hotel-Dallas/DFW Airport North [SH] 🐾
(972) 929-3333. **$54-$64.** 7825 Heathrow Dr. SR 114, exit MacArthur Blvd, 0.5 mi s, just e. Int corridors. **Pets:** Medium, other species. $25 daily fee/room. Service with restrictions, crate.

[X] [📷] [📖]

▼▼ Homestead Studio Suites Hotel-Dallas/Las Colinas [SH] 🐾
(972) 756-0458. **$54-$64.** 5315 Carnaby St. SR 114, exit MacArthur Blvd, 0.5 mi s, then just e on Meadow Creek. Ext corridors. **Pets:** Medium, other species. $25 daily fee/room. Service with restrictions, crate.

[X] [📷] [📖]

▼▼▼▼ Homewood Suites by Hilton Las Colinas [SH]
(972) 556-0665. **$139-$199, 4 day notice.** 4300 Wingren Dr. Ne off SR 114, exit O'Connor Rd/Wingren Dr eastbound; exit Rochelle Rd westbound. Ext/int corridors. **Pets:** Accepted.

[A$K] [S$] [X] [&M] [📷] [📖] [≈] [X]

▼▼▼▼ La Quinta Inn & Suites DFW Airport North [SH]
(972) 915-4022. **$76-$106.** 4850 W John Carpenter Frwy. SR 114, exit Freeport Pkwy, on eastbound service road. Int corridors. **Pets:** Small, dogs only.

[A$K] [S$] [X] [&M] [📷] [&] [📷] [📖] [≈]

▼▼▼▼ La Quinta Inn-DFW-South [SH]
(972) 252-6546. **$76-$106.** 4105 W Airport Frwy. 3 mi nw off SR 183, exit Esters Rd; on northbound access road. Int corridors. **Pets:** Accepted.

[A$K] [S$] [X] [&] [📷] [📖] [≈]

▼▼▼▼ MainStay Suites Hotel DFW Airport South [SH]
(972) 257-5400. **$79-$99.** 2323 Imperial Dr. SR 183, exit Story Rd, 0.6 mi w on westbound access road. Int corridors. **Pets:** Accepted.

[A$K] [S$] [X] [&M] [📷] [&] [📷] [📖]

▼▼ Motel 6 #1274 DFW North [M]
(972) 915-3993. **$43-$55.** 7800 Heathrow Dr. Nw off SR 114, exit Freeport Pkwy. Int corridors. **Pets:** Accepted.

[S$] [X] [&] [📷] [≈]

◆◆ Motel 6–1335 **SH**
(972) 438-4227. **$39-$49.** 510 S Loop 12. S Loop 12, exit SR 356 (Irving Blvd). Ext corridors. **Pets:** Accepted.
🆂🅳 ⊠ 🐾

◆◆ Motel 6/DFW Airport South #1476 **SH**
(972) 570-7500. **$35-$55.** 2611 W Airport Frwy. SR 183, exit Story Rd. Int corridors. **Pets:** Accepted.
🆂🅳 ⊠ 🐾 ➔

🅰🅰🅰 ◆◆◆◆ Omni Mandalay Hotel at Las Colinas **LH** 🐾
(972) 556-0800. **$109-$249.** 221 E Las Colinas Blvd. Nw off SR 114, exit O'Connor Rd. Int corridors. **Pets:** Medium, dogs only. $50 one-time fee/room. Designated rooms, service with restrictions, supervision.
🆂🅰🆅🅴 🆂🅳 ⊠ 🐾 🅼 🍴 ➔ ⊠

◆◆ Park Inn & Suites DFW North **SH**
(972) 929-4008. **$49-$119.** 4100 W John Carpenter Frwy. Nw off SR 114, exit Esters Rd, just s to Reese St, just e. Ext corridors. **Pets:** Accepted.
🅰🆂🅺 🆂🅳 ⊠ 🐾 🅼 🅼 ➔

◆◆◆ Radisson Hotel-DFW Airport South **SH**
(972) 513-0800. **$109-$139.** 4600 W Airport Frwy. SR 183, exit Valley View Ln, 3.3 mi nw. Int corridors. **Pets:** Accepted.
🅰🆂🅺 🆂🅳 ⊠ 🅼 🅼 🍴 ➔

🅰🅰🅰 ◆◆ Red Roof Inn/DFW Airport North **M**
(972) 929-0020. **$45-$63.** 8150 Esters Blvd. SR 114, exit Esters Blvd, just n. Ext corridors. **Pets:** Medium. Service with restrictions, supervision.
🆂🅰🆅🅴 ⊠ 🐾 🅼 🅼

◆◆◆ Residence Inn by Marriott at Las Colinas **SH**
(972) 580-7773. **$132-$149, 10 day notice.** 950 W Walnut Hill Ln. SR 114, exit MacArthur Blvd, 0.5 mi s, then just e. Ext corridors. **Pets:** Accepted.
🅰🆂🅺 🆂🅳 ⊠ 🅼 🐾 🅼 🅼 🅼 ➔ ⊠

◆◆◆ Residence Inn by Marriott-DFW/Irving **SH**
(972) 871-1331. **$94-$159.** 8600 Esters Blvd. SR 114, exit Esters Blvd, 0.9 mi n. Int corridors. **Pets:** Accepted.
🅰🆂🅺 ⊠ 🅼 🐾 🅼 🅼 🅼 ⊠

◆◆◆ Sheraton Grand Hotel **LH**
(972) 929-8400. **$112.** 4440 W John Carpenter Frwy. SR 114, exit Esters Blvd, just s. Int corridors. **Pets:** Accepted.
🅰🆂🅺 🆂🅳 ⊠ 🅼 🐾 🅼 🅼 🅼 🍴 ➔ ⊠

◆◆◆ Staybridge Suites Dallas-Las Colinas **SH**
(972) 465-9400. **$130-$150.** 1201 Executive Cir. SR 114, exit MacArthur Blvd, just s to W Walnut Hill Ln, then just w. Int corridors. **Pets:** Accepted.
🅰🆂🅺 🆂🅳 ⊠ 🐾 🅼 🅼 ➔

◆◆◆ Summerfield Suites Hotel-Las Colinas **SH**
(972) 831-0909. **$85-$148.** 5901 N MacArthur Blvd. SR 114, exit MacArthur Blvd, jct MacArthur Blvd and SR 114, northwest corner. Ext corridors. **Pets:** Medium. $200 one-time fee/room. Service with restrictions.
🅰🆂🅺 🆂🅳 ⊠ 🅼 🅼 🅼 ➔ ⊠

◆◆ Super 8 Motel DFW Airport North/Irving **SH**
(214) 441-9000. **$49-$65.** 4770 W John Carpenter Frwy (SR 114). SR 114, exit Freeport Pkwy. Int corridors. **Pets:** $5 daily fee/pet.
🅰🆂🅺 🆂🅳 ⊠ 🅼 🐾 🅼 🅼

🅰🅰🅰 ◆◆◆◆ Wellesley Inn & Suites (Dallas/Las Colinas) **SH**
(972) 751-0808. **$79-$149.** 5401 Green Park Dr. SR 114, exit Walnut Hill Ln, just s. Int corridors. **Pets:** Medium, other species. Service with restrictions, crate.
🆂🅰🆅🅴 🆂🅳 ⊠ 🅼 🐾 🅼 🅼 🅼 ➔

LEWISVILLE

◆◆◆ Comfort Suites **SH** 🐾
(972) 315-6464. **$59-$75.** 755A Vista Ridge Mall Dr. I-35 E, exit 448A, 0.5 mi s of jct I-35 and Round Grove Rd on southbound service road to Vista Ridge Mall Dr, just w. Int corridors. **Pets:** Other species. $50 one-time fee/room. Service with restrictions.
🅰🆂🅺 🆂🅳 ⊠ 🐾 🅼 🅼 🅼 ➔

◆◆◆ La Quinta Inn-Dallas-Lewisville **SH**
(972) 221-7525. **$61-$86.** 1657 S Stemmons Frwy. I-35 E, exit 449, just w. Ext corridors. **Pets:** Other species. Service with restrictions.
🅰🆂🅺 🆂🅳 ⊠ 🅼 🐾 🅼 🅼 ➔

◆◆ Microtel Inn & Suites **SH**
(972) 434-0447. **Call for rates.** 881 S Stemmons Frwy. I-35 E, exit 451, just w. Int corridors. **Pets:** Accepted.
⊠ 🐾 🅼 🅼 🅼

◆◆ Motel 6-1288 **SH**
(972) 436-5008. **$40-$52.** 1705 Lakepointe Dr. I-35 E, exit 449, just n on access road. Int corridors. **Pets:** Service with restrictions, supervision.
🆂🅳 ⊠ 🐾 🅼 ➔

◆◆◆ Residence Inn-Dallas/Lewisville **SH** 🐾
(972) 315-3777. **$125-$130, 7 day notice.** 755C Vista Ridge Mall Dr. I-33 E, exit 448A, 0.5 mi s on service road; jct I-35 and Round Grove Rd to Vista Ridge Rd, just w. Int corridors. **Pets:** Other species. $20 daily fee/room, $200 one-time fee/room. Service with restrictions, supervision.
🅰🆂🅺 🆂🅳 ⊠ 🅼 🐾 🅼 🅼 🅼 ➔ ⊠

◆◆ Super 8-Lewisville/Dallas North/Airport **M**
(972) 221-7511. **$45-$50.** 1305 S Stemmons Frwy. I-35 E, exit 450, just sw. Ext corridors. **Pets:** Medium. $5 daily fee/pet, $5 one-time fee/pet. Designated rooms, service with restrictions, supervision.
🅰🆂🅺 🆂🅳 ⊠ 🅼 🅼 ➔

MCKINNEY

◆◆ Days Inn McKinney **SH**
(972) 548-8888. **$60-$75.** 2104 N Central Expwy. US 75, 0.5 mi n of jct US 380, exit 41. Ext corridors. **Pets:** Medium. $5 daily fee/pet. Service with restrictions, supervision.
🅰🆂🅺 🆂🅳 ⊠ 🅼 ➔

MESQUITE

▲▲▲ ▼▼▼▼ Hampton Inn and Suites at Rodeo Center SH
(972) 329-3100. **$84-$106.** 1700 Rodeo Dr. I-635, exit 4 (Military Pkwy), 0.5 mi s on Hickory Tree Rd. Int corridors. **Pets:** Accepted.
SAVE S X 占M 占 🔒 🖳 ⇌

▲▲▲ ▼▼▼ Super 8 Motel SH
(972) 289-5481. **$46-$66.** 121 Grand Junction. I-635, exit 4 (Military Pkwy). Ext corridors. **Pets:** Accepted.
SAVE S X 🔒 🖳 ⇌

MIDLOTHIAN

▲▲▲ ▼▼▼▼ Best Western Midlothian Inn SH
(972) 775-1891. **$64-$74, 3 day notice.** 220 N Hwy 67. On US 67, just n of jct US 287. Ext corridors. **Pets:** Medium, other species. $25 deposit/pet. Service with restrictions, crate.
SAVE S X 🔒 🖳 ⇌

PLANO

▲▲▲ ▼▼▼▼ AmeriSuites (Dallas/Plano) SH ❀
(972) 378-3997. **$89-$109.** 3100 Dallas Pkwy. Dallas Pkwy, exit Park Blvd northbound; exit Parker Blvd southbound, on northbound service road. Int corridors. **Pets:** Medium, other species. Crate.
SAVE S X 占 🕭 占 🔒 🖳 ⇌

▼▼▼▼ Best Western Park Suites Hotel SH
(972) 578-2243. **$85-$100, 5 day notice.** 640 Park Blvd E. US 75, exit 29A northbound, just e; exit 29 southbound, 0.5 mi s on access road, just e on 15th St, then 0.5 mi n on access road. Int corridors. **Pets:** Medium, dogs only. $25 one-time fee/pet. Designated rooms, service with restrictions, crate.
A$K S X 占M 🕭 🔒 🖳 ⇌

▼▼▼▼ Candlewood Suites-Plano SH
(972) 618-5446. **$69-$99.** 4701 Legacy Dr. Jct SR 289 (Preston Rd) and Legacy Dr, just e. Int corridors. **Pets:** Medium. $10 daily fee/room. Service with restrictions.
A$K S X 🕭 🔒

▼▼▼▼ Hampton Inn Plano SH
(972) 519-1000. **$59.** 4901 Old Shepherd Pl. 0.4 mi n of jct Preston Rd and W Plano Pkwy, just e. Int corridors. **Pets:** Small. $50 one-time fee/room. Service with restrictions, crate.
A$K S X 🗲 🔒 🖳 ⇌

▲▲▲ ▼▼▼▼ Holiday Inn-Plano SH
(972) 881-1881. **$89-$109.** 700 Central Pkwy E. Just e of US 75; 0.3 mi ne of jct FM 544, exit 29A. Int corridors. **Pets:** Other species. $100 deposit/room, $25 one-time fee/room. Service with restrictions, crate.
SAVE X 🗲 🔒 🖳 🕇 ⇌ 🖂

▼▼▼ Homestead Studio Suites Hotel-Dallas/ Plano/Legacy Park SH ❀
(972) 596-9966. **$69-$84.** 4709 W Plano Pkwy. Just n of jct Plano Pkwy and Preston Rd, just e. Int corridors. **Pets:** Medium, other species. $25 daily fee/room. Service with restrictions, crate.
A$K S X 🗲 🕭 🔒 🖳 ⇌

▼▼▼▼ Homewood Suites by Hilton SH
(972) 758-8800. **$129.** 4705 Old Shepherd Pl. Jct Plano Pkwy and SR 289 (Preston Rd), 0.4 mi n, then just e. Int corridors. **Pets:** Small, other species. $75 one-time fee/room. Service with restrictions, supervision.
A$K S X 占M 🕭 🗲 🔒 🖳 ⇌ 🖂

▼▼▼▼ La Quinta Inn & Suites-West Plano SH
(972) 599-0700. **$66-$110.** 4800 W Plano Pkwy. Just n of jct SR 289 (Preston Rd), just e. Int corridors. **Pets:** Accepted.
A$K S X 占M 🕭 🗲 🔒 🖳 ⇌

▲▲▲ ▼▼▼▼ La Quinta Inn-Plano SH
(972) 423-1300. **$61-$75.** 1820 N Central Expwy. US 75, exit 29A, just ne. Ext corridors. **Pets:** Accepted.
SAVE S X 占M 🕭 🗲 🔒 ⇌

▼▼▼ Motel 6-1121 SH
(972) 578-1626. **$41-$55.** 2550 N Central Expwy. US 75, exit 29A (Park Blvd) northbound; exit 29 southbound, 1 mi n of jct Park Rd (SR 544), on east side of US 75. Ext corridors. **Pets:** Accepted.
S X 🕭 🗲 ⇌

▼▼▼ Ramada Limited SH
(972) 424-5568. **$43-$55.** 621 Central Pkwy E. Just e of US 75; exit 29A northbound; exit 29 southbound, 0.5 mi s on access road, just e on 15th St, then 0.5 mi n on access road. Int corridors. **Pets:** Accepted.
A$K S X 🔒 🖳 ⇌

▲▲▲ ▼▼▼ Red Roof Inn Dallas-Plano SH
(972) 881-8191. **$39-$60.** 301 Ruisseau Dr. SR 75, exit 30 (Parker Rd), 0.5 mi w to Premier, then just n. Ext/int corridors. **Pets:** Accepted.
SAVE S X 占M 🕭 🗲 🔒

▼▼▼▼ Residence Inn by Marriott Dallas/Plano SH
(972) 473-6761. **$132-$189.** 5001 White Stone Ln. North Dallas Tollway, exit Spring Creek Pkwy, 1.9 mi e, then n on Preston Rd; between Spring Creek Pkwy and Tennyson. Int corridors. **Pets:** Accepted.
A$K S X 🔒 🖳 ⇌ 🖂

▲▲▲ ▼▼▼ Sleep Inn Plano SH
(972) 867-1111. **$49-$69.** 4801 W Plano Pkwy. Just n of jct SR 289 (Preston Rd) and N Plano Pkwy, just e. Int corridors. **Pets:** Small. $25 one-time fee/room. Service with restrictions, supervision.
SAVE S X 占M 🕭 🗲 🔒 🖳 ⇌

▼▼▼ Super 8 Motel-Plano SH
(972) 423-8300. **$45-$59.** 1704 N Central Expwy. US 75, exit 29A northbound, just e; exit 29 southbound, 0.5 mi s on access road, just e on 15th St, then just n on access road. Int corridors. **Pets:** Accepted.
A$K S X 占M 🕭

▼▼▼ TownePlace Suites by Marriott SH
(972) 943-8200. **$84-$94.** 5005 Whitestone Ln. North Dallas Tollway, exit Spring Creek Pkwy, 1.9 mi e, just n on Preston Rd to Whitestone Ln, then just w. Int corridors. **Pets:** Other species. $150 one-time fee/room. Service with restrictions.
A$K S X 占M 🗲 🔒 🖳 ⇌

Wellesley Inn & Suites (Dallas/Plano) SH

(972) 378-9978. **$79-$89.** 2900 Dallas Pkwy. Dallas Pkwy, exit Park Blvd northbound; exit Parker Blvd southbound, on northbound service road. Int corridors. **Pets:** Accepted.

RICHARDSON

Hampton Inn SH

(972) 234-5400. **$69.** 1577 Gateway Blvd. US 75, exit 26 (Campbell Rd), 0.4 mi s on access road, just w, then 0.5 mi s. Int corridors. **Pets:** Other species. Service with restrictions, crate.

Homestead Studio Suites Dallas/Richardson SH

(972) 479-0500. **$69-$79.** 901 E Campbell Rd. US 75, exit 26 (Campbell Rd), just e. Int corridors. **Pets:** Medium, other species. $25 daily fee/room. Service with restrictions, crate.

Renaissance Dallas-Richardson Hotel LH

(972) 367-2000. **$89-$169.** 900 E Lookout Dr. US 75, exit 26 (Campbell Rd), just e to Glenville Dr, 0.8 mi n to Lookout Dr, then just w. Int corridors. **Pets:** Small. $50 deposit/pet. Service with restrictions, supervision.

Residence Inn by Marriott Richardson SH

(972) 669-5888. **$99-$159.** 1040 Waterwood Dr. US 75, exit 26 (Campbell Rd), just e to Greenville Ave, 0.4 mi n to Glenville Rd, then just w. Int corridors. **Pets:** Accepted.

ROANOKE

Comfort Suites Roanoke SH

(817) 490-1455. **$79-$300.** 801 Byron Nelson Blvd/W Hwy 114 Bus. I-35, exit 70 (SR 114), 3.4 mi e, exit Rufe/Snow, just se. Int corridors. **Pets:** Very small, other species. $20 one-time fee/pet. Service with restrictions, supervision.

Speedway Sleep Inn & Suites SH

(817) 491-3120. **$60-$90.** 13471 Raceway Dr. I-35, exit 70 (SR 114), just e, then just s. Int corridors. **Pets:** Accepted.

TERRELL

Best Inn M ❀

(972) 563-2676. **$49-$65.** 309 I-20 E. Jct SR 35 and I-20, exit 501. Ext corridors. **Pets:** Small, other species. $5 one-time fee/pet. Service with restrictions, supervision.

WAXAHACHIE

Best Western Gingerbread Inn SH

(972) 937-4202. **$72-$82, 4 day notice.** 200 N I-35 E. I-35 E and US 287 business route, 1.8 mi s of jct US 287, exit 401B. Ext corridors. **Pets:** Accepted.

Super 8 Motel SH

(972) 938-9088. **$75.** 400 I-35 E. I-35 E, exit 401B. Int corridors. **Pets:** Accepted.

❀ END METROPOLITAN AREA ❀

DECATUR

Best Western Decatur Inn M

(940) 627-5982. **$60-$80.** 1801 S Hwy 287. 0.6 mi s of jct Business Rt SR 380. Ext corridors. **Pets:** Accepted.

Comfort Inn SH

(940) 627-6919. **$59-$110.** 1709 S US 287. 0.6 mi s of jct Business Rt SR 380. Ext corridors. **Pets:** Accepted.

DEL RIO

Best Western Inn of Del Rio SH

(830) 775-7511. **$69-$135, 7 day notice.** 810 Vetrans Blvd. 0.8 mi nw on US 90, 277 and 377. Ext corridors. **Pets:** Accepted.

Days Inn and Suites SH

(830) 775-0585. **$59-$79.** 3808 Veterans Blvd. 3.5 mi nw on US 90. Ext corridors. **Pets:** Medium, other species. $15 daily fee/room. Service with restrictions.

Holiday Inn Express & Suites SH

(830) 775-2933. **$69.** 3616 Veterans Blvd. 3.2 mi nw on US 90. Ext/int corridors. **Pets:** Small. $25 deposit/pet. Designated rooms, service with restrictions, crate.

La Quinta Inns-Del Rio SH ❀

(830) 775-7591. **$69-$81.** 2005 Veterans Blvd. 1.8 mi nw on US 90, 277 and 377. Ext/int corridors. **Pets:** Service with restrictions, supervision.

Motel 6 Del Rio #323 SH

(830) 774-2115. **$35-$49.** 2115 Ave F. Jct US 90/277 and Garner Dr. Ext corridors. **Pets:** Accepted.

Ramada Inn SH ❀

(830) 775-1511. **$89-$105.** 2101 Veterans Blvd. 1.8 mi nw on US 90, 277 and 377. Ext/int corridors. **Pets:** Small, other species. Designated rooms, service with restrictions, crate.

DIBOLL

(AAA) ▼▼▼ Best Western Diboll Inn SH
(936) 829-2055. **$56-$69.** 910 N Temple Dr. 0.8 mi n on US 59 and Loop 210 and SR 1818. Ext corridors. **Pets:** Accepted.
[SAVE] [S6] [X] [🛏] [📺] [≈]

DONNA

(AAA) ▼▼▼ Howard Johnson Express Inn-Suites SH
(956) 464-4656. **$44-$80.** 602 N Victoria Rd. US 83, exit Victoria Rd. Ext corridors. **Pets:** Small, other species. $50 deposit/pet, $5 daily fee/pet. Designated rooms, service with restrictions, crate.
[SAVE] [S6] [X] [🛏] [📺] [❖] [≈] [X]

DUMAS

(AAA) ▼▼▼ Econo Lodge SH
(806) 935-9098. **$49-$96.** 1719 S Dumas Ave. US 287, 2 mi s of US 87 and SR 152. Int corridors. **Pets:** Accepted.
[SAVE] [S6] [X] [🛏]

▼▼▼▼ Holiday Inn Express SH
(806) 935-4000. **$69-$99.** 1525 S Dumas Ave. US 87, 1.1 mi s of US 87 and SR 152. Int corridors. **Pets:** Other species. $15 one-time fee/room. Service with restrictions, supervision.
[ASK] [S6] [X] [🛏] [📺] [≈]

(AAA) ▼▼▼ Super 8 Motel M ❖
(806) 935-6222. **$60-$89.** 119 W 17th St. US 287, 2 mi s of jct US 87 and SR 152. Ext corridors. **Pets:** Small. $10 one-time fee/pet. Designated rooms, service with restrictions, supervision.
[SAVE] [S6] [X] [🛏] [📺]

EAGLE PASS

(AAA) ▼▼▼▼ Best Western SH
(830) 758-1234. **$84-$90.** 1923 Loop 431. US 57, jct Loop 431 (US 277). Ext corridors. **Pets:** Accepted.
[SAVE] [S6] [X] [❖] [🛏] [📺] [≈]

(AAA) ▼▼▼▼ Holiday Inn Express Hotel & Suites SH
(830) 757-3050. **$85-$90.** 2007 Loop 431. 1.5 mi n on Loop 431 (US 277). Int corridors. **Pets:** Accepted.
[SAVE] [S6] [X] [❖M] [❖] [🛏] [📺] [≈]

▼▼▼▼ La Quinta Inn-Eagle Pass SH
(830) 773-7000. **$71-$86.** 2525 E Main St. US 57 and 277 at jct Loop 431. Ext corridors. **Pets:** Service with restrictions, crate.
[X] [❖] [🛏] [📺] [≈]

▼▼ Super 8 Motel SH
(830) 773-9531. **$50-$60.** 2150 N US Hwy 277. On US 277, 4 mi n. Ext corridors. **Pets:** Accepted.
[ASK] [S6] [X] [❖] [❖] [🛏] [≈]

EARLY

(AAA) ▼▼▼ Post Oak Inn M
(325) 643-5621. **$65-$75.** 606 Early Blvd. On SR 377 at Northline. Ext corridors. **Pets:** Accepted.
[SAVE] [X] [🛏] [📺] [≈]

EASTLAND

▼▼▼ The Eastland BB
(254) 629-8397. **$70-$135.** 112 N Lamar St. I-20, exit 343, 1.7 mi n to Lamar St, just e; downtown. Int corridors. **Pets:** Accepted.
[ASK] [X] [📺] [⊘]

▼▼ Super 8 Motel & RV Park M
(254) 629-3336. **$59-$79.** 3900 I-20 E. I-20, exit 343, on north service road. Ext corridors. **Pets:** Small. $5 daily fee/room. Designated rooms, service with restrictions, supervision.
[ASK] [S6] [X] [🛏] [📺] [≈]

EDINBURG

(AAA) ▼▼▼ Super 8-Edinburg SH
(956) 381-1688. **$49-$79.** 202 N Hwy 281. I-281, exit 107 (University Dr), just n. Ext corridors. **Pets:** Accepted.
[SAVE] [S6] [X] [🛏] [≈]

EL PASO

(AAA) ▼▼▼▼ AmeriSuites (El Paso/Airport) SH
(915) 771-0022. **$79-$115.** 6030 Gateway Blvd E. I-10, exit 24B (Geronimo St) westbound, 0.6 mi to Trowbridge, U-turn under interstate, then just e. Int corridors. **Pets:** Accepted.
[SAVE] [S6] [X] [❖M] [❖] [❖] [🛏] [📺] [≈]

(AAA) ▼▼▼ Baymont Inn & Suites El Paso East SH
(915) 591-3300. **$49-$64.** 7944 Gateway Blvd E. I-10, exit 28B. Int corridors. **Pets:** Medium. $50 deposit/room. Designated rooms, service with restrictions, supervision.
[SAVE] [S6] [X] [❖M] [❖] [❖] [🛏] [📺] [≈]

(AAA) ▼▼▼ Baymont Inn & Suites El Paso West SH
(915) 585-2999. **$44-$64.** 7620 N Mesa St. I-10, exit 11 (Mesa St). Int corridors. **Pets:** Accepted.
[SAVE] [S6] [X] [❖] [🛏] [📺] [≈]

(AAA) ▼▼▼ Best Western Airport Inn SH
(915) 779-7700. **$68.** 7144 Gateway E. I-10, exit 26 (Hawkins Blvd), on eastbound frontage road. Ext corridors. **Pets:** Accepted.
[SAVE] [S6] [X] [❖] [❖] [🛏] [📺] [≈]

(AAA) ▼▼▼ Best Western Sunland Park Inn M
(915) 587-4900. **$54-$63.** 1045 Sunland Park Dr. I-10, exit 13, just s. Ext corridors. **Pets:** Very small. $25 daily fee/pet. Designated rooms, service with restrictions, supervision.
[SAVE] [S6] [X] [🛏] [📺] [≈]

▼▼▼ Camino Real Hotel, El Paso LH
(915) 534-3000. **$139-$159.** 101 S El Paso St. Center. Int corridors. **Pets:** Small. $25 one-time fee/pet. Service with restrictions, crate.
[ASK] [S6] [X] [❖] [🛏] [📺] [❖] [≈]

▼▼▼▼ **Chase Suites by Woodfin** SH
(915) 772-8000. **$95-$135, 10 day notice.** 6791 Montana Ave. I-10, exit 25 (Airway Blvd), 1 mi n, then just e. Ext corridors. **Pets:** Accepted.
ASK S📶 ✕ 🖥 ▦ ➰ ✕̸

▼▼▼ **Comfort Inn Airport East** SH
(915) 594-9111. **Call for rates.** 900 Yarbrough Dr. I-10, exit 28B. Ext corridors. **Pets:** Accepted.
✕ 🖥 ▦ ➰

▼▼▼ **Comfort Suites** SH
(915) 587-5300. **$69-$85.** 949 Sunland Park Dr. I-10, exit 13. Int corridors. **Pets:** Accepted.
ASK S📶 ✕ 🗝 🖥 ▦ ➰ ✕̸

AAA ▼▼▼ **Days Inn** M
(915) 845-3500. **$49-$79.** 5035 S Desert Blvd. I-10, exit 11 (Mesa St) eastbound; exit 9 (Redd) northbound, 1.5 mi e on eastbound service road. Ext corridors. **Pets:** Medium, dogs only. $25 one-time fee/pet. Designated rooms, service with restrictions, supervision.
SAVE S📶 ✕ 🖥 ➰

AAA ▼▼▼ **Econo Lodge** M
(915) 778-3311. **$55-$60.** 6363 Montana Ave. I-10, exit 24 (Geronimo St) westbound; exit 24B (Geronimo St) eastbound, 0.5 mi n, then 0.5 mi e. Ext corridors. **Pets:** Medium. $10 one-time fee/pet. Service with restrictions, supervision.
SAVE S📶 ✕ ▦ ➰

▼▼▼▼ **Hawthorn Inn & Suites** SH
(915) 778-6789. **$120-$140.** 6789 Boeing. 7 mi e on US 62 and 180 to Airway Blvd, then just n. Int corridors. **Pets:** Accepted.
ASK S📶 ✕ 🗝 🌀 🗝 🖥 ▦ ➰

▼▼▼▼ **Hilton El Paso Airport** LH
(915) 778-4241. **$114-$132.** 2027 Airway Blvd. I-10, exit 25 (Airway Blvd), 1.3 mi n. Int corridors. **Pets:** Large. $200 deposit/room. Service with restrictions, supervision.
✕ 🌀 🗝 🖥 ▦ 🍴 ➰ ✕̸

AAA ▼▼▼▼ **Holiday Inn Sunland Park** SH
(915) 833-2900. **$104.** 900 Sunland Park Dr. I-10, exit 13. Ext corridors. **Pets:** Accepted.
SAVE S📶 ✕ 🖥 ▦ 🍴 ➰

▼▼▼ **Howard Johnson Inn** SH
(915) 591-9471. **$62-$72.** 8887 Gateway Blvd W. I-10, exit 26 (Hawkins Blvd). Int corridors. **Pets:** Service with restrictions, supervision.
ASK S📶 ✕ 🖥 ▦ 🍴 ➰

▼▼▼▼ **La Quinta Inn-El Paso-Airport** M
(915) 778-9321. **$69-$84.** 6140 Gateway Blvd E. I-10, exit 24B (Geronimo St). Ext corridors. **Pets:** Accepted.
ASK S📶 ✕ 🌀 🗝 🖥 ▦ ➰

▼▼▼ **La Quinta Inn-El Paso-Cielo Vista** M
(915) 593-8400. **$67-$81.** 9125 Gateway Blvd W. I-10, exit 28B westbound; exit 27 eastbound. Ext corridors. **Pets:** Accepted.
ASK S📶 ✕ 🌀 🖥 ▦ ➰

▼▼▼▼ **La Quinta Inn-El Paso-Lomaland** M
(915) 591-2244. **$52-$72.** 11033 Gateway Blvd W. I-10, exit 29 eastbound; exit 30 westbound, 1 mi w. Ext corridors. **Pets:** Medium. Service with restrictions, supervision.
ASK S📶 ✕ 🗝 🌀 🗝 🖥 ▦ ➰

AAA ▼▼▼▼ **La Quinta Inn-El Paso-West** M
(915) 833-2522. **$70-$85.** 7550 Remcon Cir. I-10, exit 11 (Mesa St). Ext corridors. **Pets:** Medium. Service with restrictions, supervision.
SAVE S📶 ✕ 🌀 🗝 🖥 ▦ ➰

▼▼▼ **Microtel Inn & Suites** SH
(915) 772-3650. **$55-$93, 14 day notice.** 2001 Airway Blvd. I-10, exit 25 (Airway Blvd), 1.3 mi n. Int corridors. **Pets:** Small, other species. $100 deposit/pet. Service with restrictions.
ASK S📶 ✕ 🗝 🌀 🖥 ▦

▼▼▼▼ **Quality Inn & Suites** SH
(915) 772-3300. **$69-$89.** 6099 Montana Ave. I-10, exit 24 (Geronimo St) westbound; exit 24B (Geronimo St) eastbound, 0.5 mi n. Ext corridors. **Pets:** Accepted.
ASK S📶 ✕ 🗝 🖥 ▦ 🍴 ➰

AAA ▼▼▼▼ **Red Roof Inn West** SH
(915) 587-9977. **$41-$61.** 7530 Remcon Cir. I-10, exit 11 (Mesa St). Ext/int corridors. **Pets:** Accepted.
SAVE ✕ 🗝 🌀 🗝 🖥 ▦

▼▼▼ **Sleep Inn** SH
(915) 585-7577. **$49-$70.** 953 Sunland Park Dr. I-10, exit 13. Int corridors. **Pets:** Accepted.
ASK S📶 ✕ 🗝 🖥 ▦ ➰

▼▼▼ **Travelodge** M
(915) 833-2613. **$50-$70.** 7815 N Mesa St. I-10, exit 11 (Mesa St). Ext corridors. **Pets:** Accepted.
ASK S📶 ✕ 🖥 ▦ ➰

AAA ▼▼▼ **Travelodge Hotel El Paso City Center** SH
(915) 544-3333. **$45-$90.** 409 E Missouri St. I-10, exit 19A, just s. Int corridors. **Pets:** Medium. $50 deposit/room. Service with restrictions.
SAVE S📶 ✕ 🖥 ▦ 🍴 ➰

AAA ▼▼▼ **Travelodge La Hacienda Airport** M
(915) 772-4231. **$40-$77.** 6400 Montana Ave. I-10, exit 24 (Geronimo St) westbound; exit 24B (Geronimo St) eastbound, 0.5 mi n, then 0.5 mi e. Ext corridors. **Pets:** $10 daily fee/pet. Designated rooms, no service, supervision.
SAVE S📶 ✕ 🗝 🖥 ▦ 🍴 ➰

EULESS

AAA ▼▼▼▼ **La Quinta Inn-DFW Airport West-Euless** SH
(817) 540-0233. **$66-$81.** 1001 W Airport Frwy. SR 183, just e of FM 157, exit Industrial Blvd. Ext corridors. **Pets:** Other species. Service with restrictions.
SAVE S📶 ✕ 🌀 🖥 ▦ ➰

▼▼ ▼▼ Microtel Inn and Suites **SH**
(817) 545-1111. **$52-$65.** 901 W Airport Frwy. SR 183, exit Industrial Blvd (FM 157), just e. Int corridors. **Pets:** Medium, dogs only. $25 deposit/room. Service with restrictions, supervision.

(ASK) (S🐾) (✕) (&M) (🐾) 🛏 💻 ⊇

▼▼ Motel 6-Euless #1345 **SH**
(817) 545-0141. **$37-$51.** 110 Airport Frwy. SR 183, exit Euless/Main St, on westbound access road. Ext corridors. **Pets:** Accepted.

(S🐾) (✕) (🐾) ⊇

FORT STOCKTON

(AAA) ▼▼▼▼ Atrium West Inn **SH**
(432) 336-6666. **$69-$129.** 1305 N Hwy 285. I-10, exit 257, just s. Ext corridors. **Pets:** Small. $5 daily fee/pet. Designated rooms, service with restrictions, supervision.

(SAVE) (S🐾) (✕) 🛏 💻 ⊇ (✕)

(AAA) ▼▼▼▼ Best Western Swiss Clock Inn **SH**
(432) 336-8521. **$68-$78, 7 day notice.** 3201 W Dickinson Blvd. I-10, exit 256, 0.5 mi e. Ext corridors. **Pets:** Accepted.

(SAVE) (S🐾) (✕) (🐾) 💻 🍽 ⊇

(AAA) ▼▼▼▼ Comfort Inn of Fort Stockton **SH**
(432) 336-8531. **$66-$76.** 3200 W Dickinson Blvd. I-10, exit 256, just s. Int corridors. **Pets:** $6 daily fee/room. Service with restrictions, supervision.

(SAVE) (S🐾) (✕) (🐾) 🛏 💻 ⊇

(AAA) ▼▼▼▼ Days Inn **SH**
(432) 336-7500. **$56-$76.** 1408 N US Hwy 285. I-10, exit 257, just s. Ext corridors. **Pets:** Very small. Service with restrictions, supervision.

(SAVE) (S🐾) (✕) (🐾) 🛏 ⊇

▼▼ ▼▼ Econo Lodge **M**
(432) 336-9711. **$38-$43.** 800 E Dickinson Blvd. I-10, exit 261, 1.3 mi w on I-20 business route. Ext corridors. **Pets:** Accepted.

(ASK) (S🐾) (✕) 🛏 ⊇

(AAA) ▼▼▼▼ Holiday Inn Express **SH**
(432) 336-5955. **$62-$95.** 1308 N US Hwy 285. I-10, exit 257, just s. Ext corridors. **Pets:** Medium. $8 daily fee/room. Designated rooms, service with restrictions.

(SAVE) (S🐾) (✕) (🐾) 🛏 💻 ⊇

(AAA) ▼▼▼▼ La Quinta Inn-Fort Stockton **SH**
(432) 336-9781. **$58-$68.** 1537 N Hwy 285. I-10, exit 257. Ext corridors. **Pets:** Accepted.

(SAVE) (S🐾) (✕) (🐾) (🐾) 💻 ⊇

FORT WORTH

(AAA) ▼▼▼▼ AmeriSuites (Ft Worth/Cityview) **SH**
(817) 361-9797. **$105-$115.** 5900 Cityview Blvd. I-20, exit 431 (Bryant Irvin Rd). Int corridors. **Pets:** Small. Service with restrictions, crate.

(SAVE) (S🐾) (✕) (&M) (🐾) (🐾) 🛏 💻 ⊇

▼▼▼ ▼▼▼ The Ashton Hotel **SH**
(817) 332-0100. **$250-$770.** 610 Main St. Jct 6th and Main sts; center. Int corridors. **Pets:** Accepted.

(✕) (🐾) 🍽

▼▼▼ ▼▼▼ Candlewood Suites **SH**
(817) 838-8229. **$55-$95.** 5201 Endicott Ave. I-820, exit 17B, just s. Int corridors. **Pets:** Accepted.

(ASK) (S🐾) (✕) (🐾) 🛏 💻

▼▼▼ ▼▼▼ Hampton Inn & Suites-FW Alliance
Airport **SH**
(817) 439-0400. **Call for rates.** 13600 North Frwy. I-35 W, exit 66 (Westport Pkwy). Int corridors. **Pets:** Accepted.

(✕) (&M) (🐾) (🐾) 🛏 💻 ⊇

(AAA) ▼▼▼▼ Holiday Inn Express Hotel &
Suites **SH**
(817) 292-4900. **$94-$164.** 4609 City Lake Blvd W. I-20, exit 431. Int corridors. **Pets:** $25 one-time fee/room. Service with restrictions, crate.

(SAVE) (✕) (🐾) (🐾) 🛏 💻 ⊇

▼▼▼ ▼▼▼ Holiday Inn Express Hotel & Suites-Fort
Worth West **SH**
(817) 560-4200. **$89-$129.** 2730 Cherry Ln. I-30, exit 7A. Int corridors. **Pets:** Accepted.

(ASK) (S🐾) (✕) 🛏 💻 ⊇

(AAA) ▼▼▼▼ Holiday Inn Ft. Worth South &
Conference Center **SH**
(817) 293-3088. **$80-$90.** 100 Altamesa E Blvd. I-35, exit 44. Int corridors. **Pets:** Accepted.

(SAVE) (S🐾) (✕) (🐾) 🛏 💻 🍽 ⊇

(AAA) ▼▼▼▼ Holiday Inn North/Conference
Center **SH**
(817) 625-9911. **$65-$99.** 2540 Meacham Blvd. I-35 W, exit 56A. Int corridors. **Pets:** Accepted.

(SAVE) (S🐾) (✕) (🐾) 🛏 💻 🍽 ⊇

▼▼▼ ▼▼▼ Homestead Studio Suites Hotel-Fort
Worth/Medical Center **SH** 🐾
(817) 338-4808. **$64-$74.** 1601 River Run. I-30, exit 12 (University Dr), just s. Ext corridors. **Pets:** Medium, other species. $25 daily fee/room. Service with restrictions, crate.

(ASK) (S🐾) (✕) (🐾) 🛏 💻

▼▼▼ ▼▼▼ La Quinta Inn & Suites-Fort Worth
North **SH** 🐾
(817) 222-2888. **$86-$106.** 4700 North Frwy. I-35 W, exit 56A, just n. Int corridors. **Pets:** Medium. Service with restrictions, supervision.

(ASK) (S🐾) (✕) (🐾) (🐾) 🛏 💻 ⊇

▼▼▼ ▼▼▼ La Quinta Inn & Suites Fort Worth
Southwest **SH**
(817) 370-2700. **$96-$116.** 4900 Bryant Irving Rd. I-20, exit 431. Int corridors. **Pets:** Small. Service with restrictions.

(ASK) (S🐾) (✕) (&M) (🐾) (🐾) 🛏 💻 ⊇

(AAA) ▼▼▼▼ La Quinta Inn-Fort Worth West
Medical Center **SH** 🐾
(817) 246-5511. **$66-$80.** 7888 I-30 W. I-30, exit 7A. Ext/int corridors. **Pets:** Small, other species. Service with restrictions, supervision.

(SAVE) (S🐾) (✕) (🐾) (🐾) 🛏 💻 ⊇

Motel 6–#117 **SH**
(817) 244-9740. **$35-$51.** 8701 I-30 W. I-30, exit 6, just s on Las Vegas. Ext corridors. **Pets:** Small. Service with restrictions, supervision.

Motel 6 East–1341 **SH**
(817) 834-7361. **$35-$49.** 1236 Oakland Blvd. I-30, exit 18. Ext corridors. **Pets:** Accepted.

The Renaissance Worthington Hotel **LH**
(817) 870-1000. **$132-$209.** 200 Main St. Northwest corner of 2nd and Main sts. Int corridors. **Pets:** Accepted.

Residence Inn-Alliance Airport **SH**
(817) 750-7000. **$69-$250.** 13400 North Frwy. I-35 W, exit 66. Int corridors. **Pets:** Large. $6 daily fee/pet, $175 one-time fee/room. Designated rooms, service with restrictions, crate.

Residence Inn By Marriott Fort Worth-River Plaza **SH**
(817) 870-1011. **$138-$179.** 1701 S University Dr. I-30, exit 12 (University Dr), 0.4 mi s. Ext corridors. **Pets:** Accepted.

Residence Inn by Marriott-Fossil Creek **SH**
(817) 439-1300. **$69-$114.** 5801 Sandshell. I-35 W, exit 58 (Western Center Blvd) northbound to Sandshell, 0.7 mi s; southbound, take first road to the right through strip center, just s to Sandshell, 0.7 mi s. Int corridors. **Pets:** Accepted.

TownePlace Suites by Marriott-Fort Worth **SH**
(817) 732-2224. **$76-$109.** 4200 International Plaza Dr. I-20, exit 433. Int corridors. **Pets:** Medium, other species. $50 one-time fee/room. Service with restrictions, crate.

FREDERICKSBURG

Best Western Fredericksburg **SH**
(830) 992-2929. **$79-$95.** 314 E Highway St. Jct US 87 and 290, 6 blks s. Int corridors. **Pets:** Small, dogs only. $10 daily fee/pet. Service with restrictions, supervision.

Comfort Inn **SH**
(830) 997-9811. **$80-$90.** 908 S Adams St. 0.8 mi sw on SR 16; 0.8 mi sw of jct US 87 and 290. Ext corridors. **Pets:** Accepted.

Dietzel Motel **M**
(830) 997-3330. **$49-$79.** 1141 W US 290. 1 mi w on US 290 at US 87. Ext corridors. **Pets:** Other species. $7 one-time fee/pet. Designated rooms, service with restrictions.

Frontier Inn & RV Park **M**
(830) 997-4389. **$46-$150.** 1704 US Hwy 290 W. US 290, 1 mi w. Ext corridors. **Pets:** Accepted.

Holiday Inn Express **SH**
(830) 990-4200. **$84-$109.** 1220 N Hwy 87. 1 mi w on US 290 at US 87. Int corridors. **Pets:** Accepted.

Sunset Inn **M**
(830) 997-9581. **$64-$69.** 900 S Adams St. 0.8 mi sw of jct US 290 and SR 16. Ext corridors. **Pets:** Medium, dogs only. No service, crate.

Super 8 Fredericksburg **M**
(830) 997-6568. **$65-$110.** 514 E Main St. US 290, just e of jct US 87. Ext corridors. **Pets:** Other species. $10 one-time fee/room. Service with restrictions, supervision.

FULTON

Best Western Inn by the Bay **M**
(361) 729-8351. **$90-$95.** 3902 N Hwy 35. SR 35, 0.5 mi n of jct Business Rt SR 35 and FM 3063. Ext corridors. **Pets:** Other species. $5 daily fee/pet. Service with restrictions, supervision.

GAINESVILLE

Best Western Southwinds **M**
(940) 665-7737. **$55-$79.** 2103 N I-35. I-35, exit 499 northbound, 1.4 mi n on access road to S Frontage Rd; exit 498B southbound. Ext corridors. **Pets:** Dogs only. $7 daily fee/pet. Service with restrictions, crate.

Budget Host Inn **M**
(940) 665-2856. **$40.** 1900 N I-35. I-35, exit 499 northbound; exit 498B southbound. Ext corridors. **Pets:** Medium. No service.

GALVESTON

La Quinta Inn **SH**
(409) 763-1224. **$80-$199.** 1402 Seawall Blvd. Seawall Blvd at 14th St. Ext corridors. **Pets:** Accepted.

GEORGETOWN

La Quinta-Georgetown-Sun City **SH**
(512) 869-2541. **$67-$86.** 333 I-35 N. I-35, exit 264 northbound; exit 262 southbound; on west frontage road. Ext corridors. **Pets:** Other species. Service with restrictions.

GEORGE WEST

Best Western George West Executive Inn SH
(361) 449-3300. **$70-$75.** 208 N Nueces St. Just n of US 59 on SR 281. Ext corridors. **Pets:** Small. $40 deposit/pet. Service with restrictions, supervision.
SAVE ᏚᏫ ☒ Ꮵ Ꭾ ▣ ⩘

GIDDINGS

Ramada Limited M
(979) 542-9666. **$75.** 4002 E Austin St. 2.5 mi e on US 290. Ext corridors. **Pets:** Accepted.
SAVE ᏚᏫ ☒ Ꭾ ▣ ⩘

Super 8 Motel M
(979) 542-5791. **$49-$59.** 3556 E Austin St. 2 mi e on US 290. Ext corridors. **Pets:** Accepted.
SAVE ᏚᏫ ☒ Ꭾ ▣ ⩘

GLEN ROSE

Best Western Dinosaur Valley Inn & Suites SH
(254) 897-4818. **$85-$375.** 1311 NE Big Ben Tr. On US 67. Int corridors. **Pets:** Medium, dogs only. $40 one-time fee/room. Service with restrictions, crate.
SAVE ☒ ᎮᎷ Ꮵ Ꭾ ▣ ⩘ ☒

GRANBURY

Comfort Inn SH
(817) 573-2611. **$75-$190.** 1201 Plaza Dr N. 2 mi e on US 377 Bypass. Ext corridors. **Pets:** Accepted.
SAVE ᏚᏫ ☒ Ꮵ Ꭾ ▣ ⩘

Days Inn and Suites SH
(817) 573-2691. **$49-$89.** 1339 N Plaza Dr. 2 mi e on US 377 Bypass. Ext corridors. **Pets:** Other species. $20 one-time fee/room. Service with restrictions, supervision.
ASK ☒ Ꮵ Ꭾ ▣ ⩘

Plantation Inn on the Lake SH
(817) 573-8846. **$65-$95.** 1451 E Pearl St. 0.3 mi w of Business Rt US 377 at US 377 Bypass. Ext/int corridors. **Pets:** Medium. $10 one-time fee/pet. Service with restrictions, supervision.
SAVE ᏚᏫ ☒ Ꭾ ▣ ⩘

GRAPEVINE

AmeriSuites (Dallas/DFW Airport North) SH
(972) 691-1199. **$89-$119.** 2220 Grapevine Mills Cir W. SR 121 N, exit Bass Pro Dr. Int corridors. **Pets:** Large. $50 one-time fee/pet. Designated rooms, service with restrictions.
SAVE ᏚᏫ ☒ ᎮᎷ ⩗ Ꮵ Ꭾ ▣ ⩘

Embassy Suites Outdoor World LH ✿
(972) 724-2600. **$99-$259, 3 day notice.** 2401 Bass Pro Dr. US 121, exit Bass Pro Dr. Int corridors. **Pets:** Small. $250 deposit/room. Service with restrictions, supervision.
SAVE ᏚᏫ ☒ ᎮᎷ Ꮵ Ꭾ ▣ 🍴 ⩘ ☒

Homewood Suites of Grapevine SH
(972) 691-2427. **$125-$134, 14 day notice.** 2214 Grapevine Mills Cir W. SR 121 N, exit Bass Pro Dr. Int corridors. **Pets:** Accepted.
ASK ᏚᏫ ☒ ᎮᎷ Ꮵ Ꭾ ▣ ⩘ ☒

Super 8 Motel-Grapevine SH
(817) 329-7222. **$59-$79.** 250 E Hwy 114. SR 114, exit Main St. Int corridors. **Pets:** Medium. $100 deposit/room, $10 daily fee/pet. Designated rooms, service with restrictions, supervision.
ASK ᏚᏫ ☒ ᎮᎷ ⩗ Ꮵ Ꭾ ▣ ⩘

HARLINGEN

Country Inn & Suites by Carlson SH 🐾
(956) 428-0043. **$64-$94.** 3825 S Expwy 83. US 83 and 77 Expwy, exit Ed Carrey. Int corridors. **Pets:** Medium. $25 one-time fee/pet. Designated rooms, service with restrictions, supervision.
ASK ᏚᏫ ☒ Ꮵ Ꭾ ▣ ⩘ ☒

Howard Johnson Inn SH
(956) 425-7070. **$62-$67, 7 day notice.** 6779 W Expwy 83. Jct US 77, 2.3 mi w on US 83, exit Stuart Place Rd. Ext corridors. **Pets:** Medium, other species. Service with restrictions, crate.
ASK ᏚᏫ Ꭾ ▣ 🍴 ⩘

La Quinta Inn-Harlingen SH
(956) 428-6888. **$81-$101.** 1002 S Expwy 83. US 83 and 77 Expwy, exit M St. Ext corridors. **Pets:** Other species. Service with restrictions, supervision.
ASK ᏚᏫ ☒ ᎮᎷ ⩗ Ꭾ ▣ ⩘

Super 8 Motel SH
(956) 412-8873. **$45-$55.** 1115 S Expwy 83. US 83 and 77 Expwy, exit M St, just n. Int corridors. **Pets:** Medium, other species. $5 daily fee/pet. Service with restrictions, crate.
SAVE ᏚᏫ ☒ Ꭾ ▣ ⩘

HEARNE

Oak Tree Inn SH
(979) 279-5599. **$75-$125, 7 day notice.** 1051 N Market St. 0.6 mi n of jct US 79 and SR 6. Ext/int corridors. **Pets:** Accepted.
SAVE ᏚᏫ ☒ Ꮵ Ꭾ

HENDERSON

Best Western Inn of Henderson SH
(903) 657-9561. **$65-$85.** 1500 Hwy 259 S. 2 mi s on US 259, 0.7 mi s of jct US 79 and 259 S. Ext/int corridors. **Pets:** Very small, other species. $10 daily fee/pet. Designated rooms, service with restrictions, crate.
SAVE ᏚᏫ ☒ Ꭾ ▣ ⩘

HEREFORD

Best Western Red Carpet Inn SH
(806) 364-0540. **$62-$75.** 830 W 1st St. Just w of jct US 385 and 60. Ext corridors. **Pets:** Small. Service with restrictions.
ASK ᏚᏫ ☒ Ꭾ ▣ ⩘

HILLSBORO

🔷🔷🔷 ▽▽▽ Best Western Hillsboro Inn Ⓜ
(254) 582-8465. **$65-$71.** 307 I-35. I-35, exit 368A northbound; exit 368B southbound, just w. Ext corridors. **Pets:** Medium. Service with restrictions, supervision.
[SAVE] [S🐾] [✕] [🛏] [☕] [🏊]

▽▽ Motel 6–4136 SH
(254) 580-9000. **$53-$57.** 1506 Hillview Dr. I-35, exit 368 southbound; exit 368A northbound. Int corridors. **Pets:** Very small. Service with restrictions, supervision.
[ASK] [S🐾] [✕] [&M] [🛏] [🏊]

HONDO

🔷🔷🔷 ▽▽🔷 Hondo Executive Inn Ⓜ 🐾
(830) 426-2535. **$45-$65.** 102 E 19th St. On US 90 W. Ext corridors. **Pets:** $10 one-time fee/pet. Designated rooms, service with restrictions, supervision.
[SAVE] [S🐾] [✕] [&] [🛏] [☕] [🏊]

🔷🔷🔷 ▽▽▽ Whitetail Lodge Ⓜ
(830) 426-3031. **$56-$86.** 401 Hwy 90 E. Jct SR 173. Ext corridors. **Pets:** Small, dogs only. $10 daily fee/pet. Designated rooms, service with restrictions, supervision.
[SAVE] [S🐾] [✕] [🛏] [🏊]

HOUSTON METROPOLITAN AREA

BAYTOWN

🔷🔷🔷 ▽▽▽▽ Baymont Inn & Suites Houston-Baytown SH
(281) 421-7300. **$54-$74.** 5215 I-10 E. I-10, exit 792 (Garth Rd). Int corridors. **Pets:** Accepted.
[SAVE] [S🐾] [✕] [🎵] [&] [🛏] [☕] [🏊]

🔷🔷🔷 ▽▽▽ Holiday Inn Express SH
(281) 421-7200. **$79-$89.** 5222 I-10 E. I-10, exit 792 (Garth Rd). Int corridors. **Pets:** $10 one-time fee/pet.
[SAVE] [S🐾] [✕] [&M] [🎵] [&] [🛏] [☕] [🏊]

🔷🔷🔷 ▽▽▽▽ La Quinta Inn-Baytown Ⓜ
(281) 421-5566. **$67-$82.** 4911 I-10 E. I-10, exit 792 (Garth Rd). Ext corridors. **Pets:** Small. Service with restrictions, supervision.
[SAVE] [S🐾] [✕] [🎵] [🛏] [☕] [🏊]

▽▽ Motel 6–1136 Ⓜ
(281) 576-5777. **$42-$55.** 8911 Hwy 146. I-10, exit 797 (SR 146). Ext corridors. **Pets:** Accepted.
[S🐾] [✕] [&] [🛏] [🏊]

▽▽ Quality Inn Baytown SH
(281) 427-7481. **$53, 7 day notice.** 300 S Hwy 146 business route. I-10, exit 797 (SR 146), 5.5 mi sw, 2.2 mi s on Business Rt 146 (Alexander Rd). Ext corridors. **Pets:** Small. Service with restrictions, supervision.
[ASK] [S🐾] [✕] [🛏] [☕] [🍴] [🏊]

CHANNELVIEW

▽▽ Best Western Houston East Ⓜ
(281) 452-1000. **$52.** 15919 I-10 E. I-10, exit 783 westbound; exit 784 eastbound. Ext corridors. **Pets:** Small, other species. $10 one-time fee/pet. Designated rooms, service with restrictions, crate.
[ASK] [S🐾] [✕] [🛏] [☕] [🍴] [🏊]

▽▽ Travelodge Suites Ⓜ
(281) 862-0222. **$65.** 15831 2nd St. I-10, exit 783 (Sheldon Rd) eastbound, just n, then just e on 2nd St; westbound, 0.8 mi on Frontage Rd. Ext corridors. **Pets:** $15 one-time fee/room. Service with restrictions, supervision.
[ASK] [S🐾] [✕] [🛏] [☕] [🏊]

CONROE

🔷🔷🔷 ▽▽▽▽ Baymont Inn-Conroe SH
(936) 539-5100. **$69-$74, 30 day notice.** 1506 I-45 S. I-45, exit 85 (Gladstell St) northbound; exit 84 (Frazier St) southbound. Int corridors. **Pets:** Medium. $10 daily fee/room. Service with restrictions, crate.
[SAVE] [S🐾] [✕] [🎵] [&] [🛏] [☕] [🏊]

HOUSTON

▽▽▽▽ America's Inn Ⓜ
(713) 270-9559. **$50.** 10552 Southwest Frwy. Sw on US 59, 1 mi sw of Bissonnet St exit. Ext corridors. **Pets:** Accepted.
[ASK] [S🐾] [✕] [🎵] [🛏] [☕] [🏊]

🔷🔷🔷 ▽▽▽▽ AmeriSuites (Houston/Hobby Airport) Ⓜ
(713) 943-1713. **$99-$109.** 7922 Mosley Rd. I-45, exit 36 (Airport Blvd/College Rd), off southbound service road. Int corridors. **Pets:** Medium, dogs only. Service with restrictions, crate.
[SAVE] [S🐾] [✕] [&M] [&] [🛏] [☕] [🏊]

🔷🔷🔷 ▽▽▽▽ AmeriSuites (Houston Intercontinental Airport/Greenspoint) SH
(281) 820-6060. **$119-$129.** 300 Ronan Park Pl. Sam Houston Pkwy (Beltway 8), exit Imperial Valley westbound, 0.8 mi w on frontage road; exit Hardy Toll Rd eastbound, turn under parkway, 1.2 mi w on west frontage road. Int corridors. **Pets:** Small, other species. $50 deposit/room. Service with restrictions, supervision.
[SAVE] [S🐾] [✕] [&M] [&] [🛏] [☕] [🏊]

🔷🔷🔷 ▽▽▽▽ Baymont Inn & Suites Houston-Greenspoint SH
(281) 875-2000. **$59-$71.** 12701 North Frwy. I-45, exit 61 (Greens Rd), on southbound frontage road; northbound, just w on Greens Rd, just n on Northborough, then just e on Glenborough. Int corridors. **Pets:** Large. $50 deposit/room. Service with restrictions, crate.
[SAVE] [S🐾] [✕] [🎵] [&] [🛏] [☕] [🏊]

🔷🔷🔷 ▽▽▽▽ Baymont Inn & Suites Houston Northwest SH
(713) 680-8282. **$64-$79.** 11130 Northwest Frwy. US 290 W, exit W 34th St, on southeast corner. Int corridors. **Pets:** Accepted.
[SAVE] [S🐾] [✕] [&] [🛏] [☕] [🏊]

(AAA) ▼▼▼▼ Baymont Inn & Suites Houston Southwest SH
(713) 784-3838. **$59-$84.** 6790 Southwest Frwy. US 59 (Southwest Frwy), exit Hillcroft St/W Park eastbound; exit Hillcroft St westbound. Int corridors. **Pets:** Accepted.
SAVE 🛏 ✕ 🅿 🔌 💻 ➹

(AAA) ▼▼▼▼ Best Western Park Place Suites Near Houston Medical Center SH
(713) 796-1000. **$109-$159.** 1400 Old Spanish Tr. I-610, exit 1C (Kirby Dr), 0.9 mi n, then just e. Int corridors. **Pets:** Accepted.
SAVE 🛏 ✕ 🅿 🔌 💻 ➹

▼▼▼ Candlewood Suites Houston by the Galleria SH
(713) 839-9411. **$129-$159.** 4900 Loop Central Dr. I-610, exit 7 (Fournace Pl), on northbound frontage road. Int corridors. **Pets:** Accepted.
ASK 🛏 ✕ 🔌 💻

▼▼▼ Candlewood Suites-Town & Country SH
(713) 464-2677. **$109.** 10503 Town & Country Way. I-10, exit 755 eastbound, 1.1 mi on frontage road to Town & Country Blvd, 0.4 mi s; exit 756A westbound, U-turn under I-10, just e to Town & Country Blvd, 0.4 mi s. Int corridors. **Pets:** Accepted.
ASK 🛏 ✕ 🅱 🅿 🔌 💻 ➹

▼▼▼ Candlewood Suites-Westchase SH
(713) 780-7881. **$49-$109.** 4033 W Sam Houston Pkwy S. Sam Houston Pkwy (Beltway 8), exit Westpark, southeast corner of Westpark and Sam Houston Pkwy (Beltway 8) on northbound frontage road. Int corridors. **Pets:** Accepted.
ASK 🛏 ✕ 🅱 🅿 🔌 💻

▼▼ Champions Lodge Motel M
(281) 587-9171. **$44-$57.** 4726 FM 1960 W. I-45, exit 66 (FM 1960), 4.7 mi sw. Ext corridors. **Pets:** Other species. $10 daily fee/room. Service with restrictions.
ASK 🛏 ✕ 🔌 ➹

(AAA) ▼▼▼ Comfort Inn Galleria/Westchase SH
(713) 783-1400. **$69-$89.** 9041 Westheimer Rd. Just w of jct Fondren. Ext corridors. **Pets:** Medium, other species. $25 one-time fee/room. Service with restrictions.
SAVE 🛏 ✕ 🔌 💻 ➹

(AAA) ▼▼▼▼ Comfort Suites Galleria SH
(713) 787-0004. **$109-$206.** 6221 Richmond Ave. US 59, exit Hillcroft, 1 mi n to Richmond Ave, 0.6 mi e. Int corridors. **Pets:** Small. $25 one-time fee/pet. Service with restrictions.
SAVE 🛏 ✕ 🅿 🔌 💻 ➹

(AAA) ▼▼▼▼ Crowne Plaza Hotel and Resort Brookhollow Hotel LH
(713) 462-9977. **$149.** 12801 Northwest Frwy. Nw on US 290, exit Hollister Rd, 0.7 mi e on south service road. Ext/int corridors. **Pets:** Medium. $25 one-time fee/pet. Service with restrictions, crate.
SAVE 🛏 ✕ 🏊 🔌 🔌 💻 🍴 ➹ ✕

▼▼ Days Inn-Houston North M
(281) 820-1500. **Call for rates.** 9025 North Frwy. I-45, exit 57A (Gulf Bank Rd). Ext corridors. **Pets:** Accepted.
✕ 🔌 ➹

▼▼▼ Doubletree Guest Suites LH
(713) 961-9000. **$89-$239.** 5353 Westheimer Rd. I-610, exit 8C (Westheimer Rd) northbound; exit 9A (San Felipe/ Westheimer rds) southbound, 0.8 mi w. Int corridors. **Pets:** Other species. $75 deposit/room, $25 one-time fee/ room. Service with restrictions.
ASK 🛏 ✕ 🏊 🔌 🔌 💻 🍴 ➹ ✕

(AAA) ▼▼▼▼ Doubletree Hotel at Allen Center LH
(713) 759-0202. **$149-$339.** 400 Dallas St. At Dallas and Bagby sts. Int corridors. **Pets:** Small. $35 one-time fee/pet. Service with restrictions, supervision.
SAVE 🛏 ✕ 🏊 🔌 🔌 💻 🍴

▼▼▼▼ Drury Inn & Suites-Houston Hobby SH
(713) 941-4300. **$91-$111.** 7902 Mosley Rd. I-45, exit 36 (Airport Blvd/College Rd) off southbound service road. Int corridors. **Pets:** Large, other species. Service with restrictions, supervision.
ASK ✕ 🅱 🏊 🔌 🔌 💻 ➹

▼▼▼ Drury Inn & Suites-Houston Near Galleria SH
(713) 963-0700. **$115-$120.** 1615 W Loop S. I-610, exit 9 (San Felipe Rd) northbound; exit 9A (San Felipe/ Westheimer rds) southbound, on east service road. Int corridors. **Pets:** Large, other species. Service with restrictions, supervision.
ASK ✕ 🅱 🏊 🔌 🔌 💻 ➹

▼▼▼ Drury Inn & Suites Houston West SH
(281) 558-7007. **$82-$106.** 1000 N Hwy 6. I-10, exit 751 (Addicks/SR 6), just n on SR 6. Int corridors. **Pets:** Large, other species. Service with restrictions, supervision.
ASK ✕ 🔌 🔌 💻 ➹

(AAA) ▼▼▼ Executive Inn & Suites Houston/Hobby Airport M
(713) 645-7666. **$52-$180.** 6711 Telephone Rd. I-610, exit 33, 2.1 mi s; 0.5 mi s of jct Telephone and Bellfort rds. Ext corridors. **Pets:** Small, other species. $8 daily fee/room. Designated rooms, service with restrictions, supervision.
SAVE 🛏 ✕ 🔌

(AAA) ▼▼▼▼ Four Seasons Hotel Houston LH
(713) 650-1300. **$295-$350.** 1300 Lamar St. Lamar St and Austin. Int corridors. **Pets:** Accepted.
SAVE ✕ 🏊 🔌 🔌 💻 🍴 ➹ ✕

(AAA) ▼▼ Grant's Palm Court Inn M
(713) 668-8000. **$55-$75.** 8200 S Main St. I-610, exit 2 (Main St), 1.4 mi ne. Ext corridors. **Pets:** Medium, dogs only. Service with restrictions, crate.
SAVE 🛏 ✕ ➹

(AAA) ▼▼▼▼ Hampton Inn I-10 East SH
(713) 673-4200. **$69-$92.** 828 Mercury Dr. I-10, exit 776A (Mercury Dr), just n. Int corridors. **Pets:** Medium. $25 one-time fee/room. Service with restrictions, crate.
SAVE 🛏 ✕ 🏊 🔌 💻 ➹

▼▼▼▼ **Holiday Inn Express Hotel & Suites-I45/**
West Rd SH
(832) 554-5000. **$71-$80.** 10137 North Frwy. I-45, exit 59
(West Rd), on southbound frontage road. Int corridors.
Pets: Large. $50 deposit/room. Service with restrictions,
crate.

ASK SD ✕ ✑ ☷ ▤ ⛱

▼▼▼▼ **Holiday Inn Express Hotel &**
Suites-Intercontinental SH
(281) 372-1000. **$109.** 1330 N Sam Houston Pkwy. Off Sam
Houston Pkwy (Beltway 8), exit Aldine Westfield eastbound,
0.8 mi e on service road; exit Hardy Toll Rd westbound,
U-turn, then 1 mi e on service road. Int corridors.
Pets: Small. $25 one-time fee/pet. Service with restrictions,
supervision.

ASK SD ✕ ✑ ☷ ▤ ⛱

▼▼▼▼ **Holiday Inn Hotel and Suites Galleria** SH
(713) 681-5000. **$119-$139.** 7787 Katy Frwy. I-10, exit 762
(Antoine Dr) westbound; exit 761 (Antoine Dr) eastbound,
on eastbound service road. Int corridors. **Pets:** Accepted.

ASK SD ✕ ✑ ☷ ▤ ⛱

▼▼▼ **Holiday Inn Houston Intercontinental**
Airport LH
(281) 449-2311. **$89-$159.** 15222 John F Kennedy Blvd. Jct
N Sam Houston Pkwy (Beltway 8) E and John F Kennedy
Blvd. Int corridors. **Pets:** Other species. $25 one-time fee/
room. Service with restrictions, crate.

ASK SD ✕ ✑ ☷ ▤ ☷ ⛱ ✕

▼▼▼▼ **Holiday Inn Select-Greenway Plaza** SH
(713) 523-8448. **$65-$99.** 2712 Southwest Frwy. US 59, exit
Kirby Dr. Int corridors. **Pets:** Accepted.

ASK SD ✕ ✑ ☷ ▤ ☷ ⛱

▼▼▼▼ **Holiday Inn Select I-10** SH
(281) 558-5580. **$130-$188.** 14703 Park Row. I-10, exit 751
(Addicks Rd/SR 6), just n. Int corridors. **Pets:** Accepted.

ASK SD ✕ ✑ ☷ ▤ ☷ ⛱ ✕

▼▼▼▼ **Homestead Studio Suites Hotel-Houston/**
Galleria Area SH ✿
(713) 960-9660. **$79-$89.** 2300 W Loop S. Loop 610, exit 9A
(San Felipe/Westheimer rds) southbound; exit 9 (San Felipe
Rd) northbound, on southbound frontage road. Int corridors.
Pets: Medium, other species. $25 daily fee/room. Service
with restrictions, crate.

ASK SD ✕ ✑ ☷ ▤

▼▼ ▼▼ **Homestead Studio Suites Hotel-Houston/**
Medical Center/Reliant Park SH ✿
(713) 797-0000. **$58-$78.** 7979 Fannin St. I-610, exit 1B, 0.8
mi n. Ext corridors. **Pets:** Medium, other species. $25 daily
fee/room. Service with restrictions, crate.

ASK SD ✕ ✑ ☷ ▤

▼▼ ▼▼ **Homestead Studio Suites**
Hotel-Houston/Willowbrook SH ✿
(281) 397-9922. **$54-$64.** 13223 Champions Center Dr. Jct
SR 249 and FM 1960 W, 0.9 mi e to Champion Center Dr,
just n to Champion Center Plaza, then just w. Ext corridors.
Pets: Medium, other species. $25 daily fee/room. Service
with restrictions, crate.

ASK SD ✕ ✑ ✑ ✑ ☷ ▤

▼▼▼▼ **Homewood Suites by Hilton** SH
(281) 486-7677. **$139-$189.** 401 Bay Area Blvd. I-45, exit 26
(Bay Area Blvd), 1 mi e. Int corridors. **Pets:** Accepted.

ASK SD ✕ ✑ ✑ ☷ ▤ ⛱ ✕

▼▼▼▼ **Homewood Suites Hotel-Willowbrook**
Mall SH
(281) 955-5200. **$119-$169, 14 day notice.** 7655 W FM
1960. Just e of jct SR 249 and FM 1960. Int corridors.
Pets: Other species. $100 one-time fee/room. No service.

ASK SD ✕ ✑ ✑ ☷ ▤ ⛱

▼▼▼▼ **Hotel Sofitel Houston** LH
(281) 445-9000. **$99-$209.** 425 N Sam Houston Pkwy E.
Sam Houston Pkwy (Beltway 8), exit Imperial Valley Dr
westbound; exit Hardy Toll Rd eastbound, on westbound
frontage road. Int corridors. **Pets:** Medium. $200 deposit/
room, $50 one-time fee/room. Service with restrictions,
crate.

ASK SD ✕ ☷ ▤ ☷ ⛱ ✕

ⒶⒶⒶ ▼▼▼▼ **Houston Hobby Airport Marriott** LH
(713) 943-7979. **$179-$199.** 9100 Gulf Frwy. I-45, exit 36
(Airport Blvd/College Rd), on west service road. Int corridors. **Pets:** Accepted.

SAVE SD ✕ ✑ ✑ ☷ ▤ ☷ ⛱

ⒶⒶⒶ ▼▼▼▼ **Houston Marriott Medical Center**
Hotel LH
(713) 796-0080. **$89-$199.** 6580 Fannin St. I-610, exit 2
(Main St), 2.5 mi ne to Holcombe St, 0.3 mi e, then just n.
Int corridors. **Pets:** Accepted.

SAVE SD ✕ ✑M ✑ ✑ ☷ ▤ ☷ ⛱

▼▼▼ ▼▼▼ **InterContinental Houston** LH
(713) 627-7600. **$279-$515.** 2222 W Loop S. I-610, exit 9
(San Felipe Rd) northbound; exit 9A (San Felipe/
Westheimer rds) southbound. Int corridors. **Pets:** Accepted.

ASK SD ✕ ✑ ✑ ☷ ▤ ☷ ⛱ ✕

▼▼▼▼ **La Quinta Inn & Suites** SH
(281) 219-2000. **$105-$130.** 15510 John F Kennedy Blvd.
Sam Houston Pkwy (Beltway 8), exit John F Kennedy Blvd/
Vickery, just n. Int corridors. **Pets:** Accepted.

ASK ✕ ✑M ✑ ☷ ▤ ⛱

▼▼▼▼ **La Quinta Inn & Suites Houston-Galleria**
Area SH
(713) 355-3440. **$80-$150.** 1625 W Loop S. I-610, exit 9
(San Felipe Rd) northbound; exit 9A (San Felipe/
Westheimer rds) southbound, on northbound service road.
Int corridors. **Pets:** Small, other species. Service with
restrictions, supervision.

ASK SD ✕ ✑M ✑ ✑ ☷ ▤ ⛱

▼▼▼▼ **La Quinta Inn & Suites Park 10** SH
(281) 646-9200. **$90-$110.** 15225 Katy Frwy. I-10, exit 748
(Barker Cypress Rd) eastbound, 2.6 mi on eastbound service road; exit 751 (SR 6) westbound, just s to Grisby Rd,
0.5 mi w. Int corridors. **Pets:** Accepted.

ASK SD ✕ ✑ ✑ ☷ ▤ ⛱

ⒶⒶⒶ ▼▼▼▼ **La Quinta Inn-BrookHollow** M
(713) 688-2581. **$66-$81.** 11002 Northwest Frwy. Nw on US
290, exit Magnum-Dacoma. Ext corridors. **Pets:** Large.
Service with restrictions, supervision.

SAVE SD ✕ ✑ ✑ ☷ ▤ ⛱

La Quinta Inn-Greenway Plaza SH
(713) 623-4750. **$80-$100.** 4015 Southwest Frwy. Sw off US 59 (Southwest Frwy), exit Weslayan. Ext/int corridors. **Pets:** Accepted.

La Quinta Inn-Houston-Astrodome SH
(713) 668-8082. **$77-$107.** 9911 Buffalo Speedway. I-610, exit 2 (Buffalo Speedway/S Main St), just s. Ext corridors. **Pets:** Service with restrictions, supervision.

La Quinta Inn-Houston-Cy-Fair SH
(281) 469-4018. **$77-$93.** 13290 FM 1960 W. Just w of jct US 290 and FM 1960. Ext corridors. **Pets:** Medium, other species. Service with restrictions, supervision.

La Quinta Inn-Houston East M
(713) 453-5425. **$65-$80.** 11999 East Frwy. I-10, exit 778A (Federal Rd) eastbound; exit 776B (Holland Ave) westbound, just n. Ext corridors. **Pets:** Accepted.

La Quinta Inn-Houston-Hobby Airport M
(713) 941-0900. **$65-$80.** 9902 Gulf Frwy. I-45 S, exit 36 (Airport Blvd/College Rd), just s on southbound frontage road. Ext/int corridors. **Pets:** Accepted.

La Quinta Inn-Houston-I-45 North(Loop 1960) M
(281) 444-7500. **$67-$82.** 17111 North Frwy. I-45, exit 66, southbound service road, 0.4 mi s of jct FM 1960 and I-45. Ext corridors. **Pets:** Accepted.

La Quinta Inn-Wilcrest M
(713) 932-0808. **$60-$80.** 11113 Katy Frwy. I-10, exit 754 (Kirkwood Dr) westbound; exit 755 (Wilcrest Rd) eastbound, on eastbound service road. Ext corridors. **Pets:** Other species. Service with restrictions, crate.

La Quinta Inn-Wirt Rd M
(713) 688-8941. **$70-$87.** 8017 Katy Frwy. I-10, exit 761A (Wirt Rd), on eastbound frontage road. Ext corridors. **Pets:** Accepted.

The Lovett Inn BB
(713) 522-5224. **$85-$275, 3 day notice.** 501 Lovett Blvd. I-610, exit Westheimer Rd, 4.5 mi e to Montrose Blvd, just s to Lovett Blvd, then just e. Ext/int corridors. **Pets:** Other species. Designated rooms, service with restrictions, crate.

Marriott-West Loop-By The Galleria LH
(713) 960-0111. **$86-$229.** 1750 W Loop S. I-610, exit 9 (San Felipe Rd) northbound, just w; exit 9A (San Felipe/ Westheimer rds) southbound; entrance from San Felipe Rd or service road. Int corridors. **Pets:** Accepted.

Motel 6–1140 M
(713) 937-7056. **$41-$55.** 16884 Northwest Frwy. US 290, exit Jones Rd westbound; exit Senate Ave eastbound, on westbound frontage road. Ext corridors. **Pets:** Accepted.

Motel 6–1401 M
(713) 334-9188. **$47-$59.** 2900 W Sam Houston Pkwy S. Sam Houston Pkwy (Beltway 8), exit Westheimer Rd. Int corridors. **Pets:** Accepted.

Omni Houston Hotel LH
(713) 871-8181. **$315-$399.** Four Riverway. I-610, exit 10 (Woodway Dr), 0.3 mi w. Int corridors. **Pets:** Accepted.

Omni Houston Westside LH
(281) 558-8338. **$71-$184.** 13210 Katy Frwy. I-10, exit 753A (Eldridge St), just n. Int corridors. **Pets:** Accepted.

Radisson Hotel Astrodome Convention Center LH
(713) 795-8477. **$129-$279.** 8686 Kirby Dr. I-610, exit 1C (Kirby Dr). Int corridors. **Pets:** Accepted.

Ramada Limited/S.H. 249 M
(281) 970-5000. **$90.** 18836 Tomball Pkwy. SR 249, exit Grant, on northbound frontage road. Ext corridors. **Pets:** Medium, other species. $10 daily fee/pet. Designated rooms, service with restrictions, crate.

Ramada Plaza Hotel Near the Galleria SH
(713) 688-2222. **$90-$100.** 7611 Katy Frwy. I-10, exit 762 (Silber Rd), on eastbound frontage road. Int corridors. **Pets:** Accepted.

Red Roof Inn Hobby Airport SH
(713) 943-3300. **$44-$54.** 9005 Airport Blvd. I-45, exit 36 (Airport Blvd/College Rd), just w. Int corridors. **Pets:** Accepted.

Red Roof Inn Houston West SH
(281) 579-7200. **$44-$62.** 15701 Park Ten Pl. I-10, exit 751 (Addicks Rd/SR 6), 0.8 mi on west frontage road. Ext/int corridors. **Pets:** Medium. Service with restrictions, supervision.

Red Roof Inns SH
(713) 939-0800. **$44-$64.** 12929 Northwest Frwy. US 290, exit Hollister and Tidwell rds, on eastbound service road. Ext/int corridors. **Pets:** Accepted.

Red Roof Inns M
(713) 785-9909. **$48-$59.** 2960 W Sam Houston Pkwy S. SW Sam Houston Pkwy (Beltway 8), exit Westheimer Rd. Ext/int corridors. **Pets:** Medium, other species. Service with restrictions, crate.

▼▼▼▼ **Residence Inn by Marriott** SH 🌺
(713) 840-9757. **$99-$299.** 2500 McCue. I-610, exit 8C (Westheimer Rd) northbound; exit 9A (San Felipe/ Westheimer rds) southbound, just w to McCue, then just n. Ext/int corridors. **Pets:** Medium, other species. $100 one-time fee/room.

Ⓐ🅢🅚 🅢🅓 ⌧ 🄲 🖬 🖳 🏊 ⌧

▼▼▼ **Residence Inn by Marriott Houston**
Westchase SH
(713) 974-5454. **$132-$180.** 9965 Westheimer Rd. Sam Houston Pkwy (Beltway 8), exit Westheimer Rd, 0.7 mi e to Elmside Dr, just s. Int corridors. **Pets:** Accepted.

Ⓐ🅢🅚 🅢🅓 ⌧ 🄲 🖬 🖳 🏊 ⌧

▼▼▼ **Residence Inn by Marriott-Medical**
Center/Reliant Park SH
(713) 660-7993. **$139-$179.** 7710 Main St. I-610, exit 2 (S Main St/Buffalo Speedway), 1.5 mi n. Ext corridors. **Pets:** Accepted.

Ⓐ🅢🅚 🅢🅓 ⌧ 🖬 🖳 🏊 ⌧

▼▼▼ **Residence Inn by Marriott**
Willowbrook SH
(832) 237-2002. **$120-$170, 14 day notice.** 7311 W Greens Rd. SR 249, exit Greens Rd, just e. Int corridors. **Pets:** Other species. $10 daily fee/room, $75 one-time fee/ room. Service with restrictions, supervision.

Ⓐ🅢🅚 🅢🅓 ⌧ 🄲 🖬 🖳 🏊 ⌧

▼▼▼ **Residence Inn-Houston Clear Lake** SH
(281) 486-2424. **$139-$179.** 525 Bay Area Blvd. I-45 S, exit 26 (Bay Area Blvd), 1.2 mi e. Ext/int corridors. **Pets:** Accepted.

Ⓐ🅢🅚 🅢🅓 ⌧ 🄳 🄲 🖬 🖳 🏊 ⌧

▼▼ **Robin's Nest Bed & Breakfast Inn** BB
(713) 528-5821. **$110-$150, 7 day notice.** 4104 Greeley St. US 59 (Southwest Frwy), exit Richmond Ave, just e, then just n. Int corridors. **Pets:** Accepted.

Ⓐ🅢🅚 🅢🅓 ⌧ 🖬

▼ **Rodeway Inn-Southwest Freeway** M
(713) 526-1071. **Call for rates.** 3135 Southwest Frwy. US 59 (Southwest Frwy), exit Buffalo Speedway, on eastbound service road. Ext corridors. **Pets:** Accepted.

⌧ 🖬 🖳 🏊

Ⓐ🅐🅐 ▼▼▼▼ **The St. Regis, Houston** SH 🌺
(713) 840-7600. **$430, 3 day notice.** 1919 Briar Oaks Ln. I-610, exit 9A (San Felipe/Westheimer rds), 0.3 mi e. Int corridors. **Pets:** Medium. $25 deposit/room. Service with restrictions, crate.

🆂🅰🆅🅴 🅢🅓 ⌧ 🄳 🄲 🖬 🖳 🍴 🏊 ⌧

Ⓐ🅐🅐 ▼▼▼ **Sheraton Houston Brook**
Hollow LH
(713) 688-0100. **$239-$259.** 3000 N Loop W. Jct I-610 and US 290, exit 13C (TC Jester), just nw. Int corridors. **Pets:** Accepted.

🆂🅰🆅🅴 🅢🅓 ⌧ 🄳 🄲 🖬 🖳 🍴 🏊 ⌧

▼▼▼ **Staybridge Suites by Holiday Inn**
Houston-Near The Galleria SH
(713) 355-8888. **$79-$149.** 5190 Hidalgo St. I-610, exit 9A (San Felipe/Westheimer rds) southbound; exit 8C (Westheimer Rd) northbound, 0.4 mi w to Sage Rd, just s. Int corridors. **Pets:** Accepted.

Ⓐ🅢🅚 🅢🅓 ⌧ 🄶🄼 🖬 🖳 🏊

▼▼ **Studio 6 #6043** M
(281) 579-6959. **$45-$58.** 1255 Hwy 6 N. I-10, exit 751 (Addicks Rd/SR 6), just n. Ext corridors. **Pets:** Accepted.

⌧ 🄲 🖬 🖳

▼▼ **Studio 6-Cypress Station #6037** M
(281) 580-2221. **$43-$53.** 220 Bammel-Westfield Rd. I-45, exit 66, southbound frontage road, then just w. Ext corridors. **Pets:** Accepted.

⌧ 🄳 🄲 🖬 🖳

▼▼ **Studio 6-Houston Hobby South #6039** M
(281) 929-5400. **$45-$71.** 12700 Featherwood. I-45, exit 33 (Fuqua St) southbound, stay in right lane and cross over I-45, just e to Featherwood, then just s. Ext corridors. **Pets:** Accepted.

⌧ 🄲 🖬 🖳

▼▼▼ **Super 8-Houston-Gessner** M
(713) 772-3626. **$49-$59, 3 day notice.** 8201 Southwest Frwy. Sw on US 59, exit Gessner St. Ext corridors. **Pets:** Accepted.

Ⓐ🅢🅚 🅢🅓 ⌧ 🄳 🖬 🖳 🏊

▼▼ **Super 8 Motel** SH
(281) 866-8686. **$69-$89.** 609 W FM 1960. I-45, exit 66 (FM 1960) southbound; exit 66A northbound, just w. Int corridors. **Pets:** Medium. $25 deposit/pet. Designated rooms, service with restrictions, supervision.

Ⓐ🅢🅚 🅢🅓 ⌧ 🖬 🏊

▼▼ **TownePlace Suites by Marriott (I-10**
West) SH
(281) 646-0058. **$60-$120.** 15155 Katy Frwy. I-10, exit 751, just s on SR 6 to Grisby Rd, then w. Int corridors. **Pets:** Medium. $5 daily fee/pet, $200 one-time fee/room. Designated rooms, service with restrictions, crate.

Ⓐ🅢🅚 🅢🅓 ⌧ 🄲 🖬 🖳 🏊

▼▼▼ **TownePlace Suites Houston-Northwest**
Freeway (US 290) SH
(713) 690-4035. **$60-$90.** 12820 Northwest Frwy (US 290). US 290, exit Bingle/43rd St eastbound; exit Bingle/ Pinemont/43rd St westbound; on westbound feeder. Int corridors. **Pets:** Other species. $10 daily fee/room, $100 one-time fee/room.

⌧ 🄶🄼 🄲 🖬 🖳 ⌧

▼▼▼ **The Warwick** SH 🌺
(713) 526-1991. **$179-$189.** 5701 Main St. Jct Main and Ewing sts, just n of Herman Park. Int corridors. **Pets:** Other species. $100 one-time fee/room. Service with restrictions.

Ⓐ🅢🅚 🅢🅓 ⌧ 🄶🄼 🄳 🄲 🖬 🖳 🍴 🏊 ⌧

Wellesley Inn & Suites (Houston/Memorial) 🆂🅷
(713) 263-9770. **$55-$159.** 7855 Katy Frwy. I-10, exit 762 (Antoine Dr) westbound; exit 761B (Antoine Dr) eastbound, on eastbound service road. Int corridors. **Pets:** Small, other species. Service with restrictions, supervision.
🆂🅰🆅🅴 🆂🅳 ⊠ 🅺 🔒 📺 ⊋

Wellesley Inn & Suites (Houston/Reliant Park Medical Ctr) 🆂🅷
(713) 794-0800. **$109-$119.** 1301 S Braeswood Blvd. I-610, exit 1B, 1.5 mi n, just e. Int corridors. **Pets:** Accepted.
🆂🅰🆅🅴 🆂🅳 ⊠ 🅺 🔒 📺 ⊋ ⊠

The Westin Galleria, Houston 🅻🅷 ❀
(713) 960-8100. **$299-$349.** 5060 W Alabama St. I-610 S, exit San Felipe/Westheimer rds, 0.5 mi s on Frontage Rd to Westheimer Rd, 0.5 mi w on Westheimer Rd to Sage Rd, 1 blk s to W Alabama St, then 1 blk e. Int corridors. **Pets:** Medium, dogs only. Designated rooms, service with restrictions, supervision.
🆂🅰🆅🅴 🆂🅳 ⊠ 🅼 🅺 🔒 📺 🍴 ⊋

The Westin Oaks, Houston 🅻🅷 ❀
(713) 960-8100. **$299-$349.** 5011 Westheimer Rd. I-610, exit 8C (Westheimer Rd) northbound; exit 9A (San Felipe/ Westheimer rds) southbound, just w. Int corridors. **Pets:** Medium, dogs only. Designated rooms, service with restrictions, supervision.
🆂🅰🆅🅴 🆂🅳 ⊠ 🅺 📺 🍴 ⊋

KATY

Best Western-Houston West 🅼
(281) 392-9800. **$59, 3 day notice.** 22455 I-10 (Katy Frwy). I-10, exit 743 (Grand Pkwy), just e on eastbound service road. Ext corridors. **Pets:** Medium. $10 daily fee/pet. Service with restrictions, crate.
🆂🅰🆅🅴 🆂🅳 ⊠ 🔒 📺 ⊋

Holiday Inn Express Katy 🆂🅷
(281) 395-4800. **Call for rates.** 22105 Katy Frwy. I-10, exit 743 (Grand Pkwy) westbound; exit 745 (Mason Rd) eastbound, on eastbound frontage road. Int corridors. **Pets:** Accepted.
⊠ 🅼 🅺 🔒 📺 ⊋

LA PORTE

La Quinta Inn-La Porte 🅼
(281) 470-0760. **$72-$87.** 1105 Hwy 146 S. Jct SR 146, exit Fairmont Pkwy. Ext corridors. **Pets:** Accepted.
🅰🆂🅺 🆂🅳 ⊠ 🎾 🔒 📺 ⊋

NASSAU BAY

Holiday Inn Houston/Nasa 🆂🅷
(281) 333-2500. **$115.** 1300 NASA Rd One. I-45, exit 25, 2.5 mi e. Ext/int corridors. **Pets:** Accepted.
🅰🆂🅺 🆂🅳 ⊠ 🎾 🔒 📺 🍴 ⊋

ROSENBERG

Holiday Inn Express Hotel & Suites 🆂🅷
(281) 342-7888. **$69-$89.** 27927 Southwest Frwy. US 59, exit SR 36, just se of jct. Int corridors. **Pets:** Accepted.
🅰🆂🅺 🆂🅳 ⊠ 🅼 🅺 🔒 📺 ⊋

STAFFORD

Days Inn 🆂🅷
(281) 240-8100. **$60.** 4630 Techniplex Dr. US 59, exit Kirkwood Rd, just s to Techniplex Dr, then just w. Int corridors. **Pets:** Small. $25 deposit/pet. Designated rooms, service with restrictions, supervision.
🅰🆂🅺 🆂🅳 ⊠ 🅺 🔒

La Quinta Inn-Stafford 🆂🅷
(281) 240-2300. **$66-$86.** 12727 Southwest Frwy. US 59 eastbound service road, exit Corporate Dr southbound; exit Airport Blvd/Kirkwood Rd northbound. Int corridors. **Pets:** Medium, other species. Service with restrictions.
🆂🅰🆅🅴 🆂🅳 ⊠ 🎾 🔒 📺 ⊋

Residence Inn by Marriott Sugarland 🆂🅷
(281) 277-0770. **$129.** 12703 Southwest Frwy. US 59, exit Corporate Dr southbound; exit Airport Blvd/Kirkwood Rd northbound. Int corridors. **Pets:** Accepted.
🅰🆂🅺 🆂🅳 ⊠ 🔒 📺 ⊋ ⊠

Studio 6 #6044 🅼
(281) 240-6900. **$45-$58.** 12827 Southwest Frwy. US 59, exit US 90 and SR 41 alternate route northbound, follow frontage road; exit Corporate Dr southbound, follow frontage road. Ext corridors. **Pets:** Accepted.
⊠ 🅺 🔒 📺

Wellesley Inn & Suites (Houston/Stafford) 🆂🅷
(281) 240-0025. **$79-$89.** 4726 Sugar Grove Blvd. US 59, exit W Airport Blvd/Kirkwood Dr, just w on Frontage Rd to Sugar Grove Blvd, then just n. Ext corridors. **Pets:** Small, other species. Service with restrictions, supervision.
🆂🅰🆅🅴 🆂🅳 ⊠ 🅺 🔒 📺 ⊋

SUGAR LAND

Drury Inn & Suites-Houston/Sugar Land 🆂🅷
(281) 277-9700. **$91-$111.** 13770 Southwest Frwy. Sw on US 59, exit Sugarland/Alternate Rt US 90, exit Sugar Creek Blvd northbound. Int corridors. **Pets:** Large, other species. Service with restrictions, supervision.
🅰🆂🅺 ⊠ 🎾 🅺 🔒 📺 ⊋

Holiday Inn Express Sugar Land 🆂🅷
(281) 565-6655. **$79.** 14444 Southwest Frwy. US 59, exit Sugarland/Alternate Rt US 90 southbound, on southbound frontage road; exit Williams Trace northbound, 1.2 mi n on frontage road to Dairy Ashford/Sugarcreek, then U-tur. Int corridors. **Pets:** Accepted.
🅰🆂🅺 🆂🅳 ⊠ 🅺 🔒 📺 ⊋

WEBSTER

⨁ ▼▼▼▼ Wellesley Inn & Suites (Houston/ NASA Clear Lake) SH
(281) 338-7711. **$85-$139.** 720 W Bay Area Blvd. I-45, exit 26 (Bay Area Blvd), just e. Int corridors. **Pets:** Small, other species. Service with restrictions, crate.
[SAVE] [S6] [X] [⌖] [Ⓚ] [🛏] [💻] [🏊]

THE WOODLANDS

▼▼▼▼ Drury Inn & Suites-Houston The Woodlands SH
(281) 362-7222. **$82-$102.** 28099 I-45 N. I-45, exit 78 southbound; exit 77 northbound, on west service road. Int corridors. **Pets:** Large, other species. Service with restrictions, supervision.
[ASK] [X] [&M] [⌖] [Ⓚ] [🛏] [💻] [🏊]

⨁ ▼▼▼▼ La Quinta Inn-Houston-Woodlands SH
(281) 367-7722. **$67-$82.** 28673 I-45 N. I-45, exit 78 southbound; exit 79 northbound, on southbound frontage road. Ext/int corridors. **Pets:** Accepted.
[SAVE] [S6] [X] [⌖] [Ⓚ] [🛏] [💻] [🏊]

▼▼▼▼ Residence Inn-The Woodlands SH ❖
(281) 292-3252. **$105.** 1040 Lake Front Cir. I-45, exit 78 southbound; exit 79 northbound, 0.8 mi s of jct I-45 and Research Forest Dr, just w. Int corridors. **Pets:** $10 daily fee/room, $75 one-time fee/room. Service with restrictions.
[ASK] [S6] [X] [Ⓚ] [🛏] [💻] [🏊] [🏊]

❖ END METROPOLITAN AREA ❖

HUNTSVILLE

▼▼▼▼ Holiday Inn Express (Sam Houston) SH
(936) 293-8800. **$62-$99, 14 day notice.** 201 W Hill Park Cir. I-45, exit 116, just w on US 190. Ext corridors. **Pets:** Accepted.
[ASK] [S6] [X] [&M] [Ⓚ] [🛏] [💻] [🏊]

⨁ ▼▼▼▼ La Quinta Inn-Huntsville SH
(936) 295-6454. **$71-$86.** 124 I-45 N. I-45, exit 116. Ext corridors. **Pets:** Accepted.
[SAVE] [S6] [X] [⌖] [💻] [🏊]

HURST

⨁ ▼▼▼▼ AmeriSuites (Ft Worth/Hurst) SH
(817) 577-3003. **$89-$99.** 1601 Hurst Town Center Dr. SR 183, exit Precinct Line Rd, just n to Thousand Oaks, then just w. Int corridors. **Pets:** Small. Service with restrictions, supervision.
[SAVE] [S6] [X] [&M] [⌖] [Ⓚ] [🛏] [💻] [🏊]

JASPER

⨁ ▼▼▼▼ Best Western Inn Of Jasper SH
(409) 384-7767. **$57.** 205 W Gibson. US 190 and SR 63, 0.5 mi w of jct US 96. Ext corridors. **Pets:** Accepted.
[SAVE] [S6] [X] [🛏] [💻] [🏊]

▼▼▼ Ramada Inn Jasper SH
(409) 384-9021. **$58-$79.** 239 E Gibson (US 190). US 190 and SR 63, just w of jct US 96. Ext corridors. **Pets:** Other species. $25 deposit/room. Service with restrictions.
[ASK] [S6] [X] [🛏] [💻] [🍴] [🏊]

JUNCTION

▼▼ ▼▼ Days Inn SH
(325) 446-3730. **$66-$70, 7 day notice.** 111 S Martinez St. I-10, exit 457, 0.3 mi s. Ext corridors. **Pets:** Medium. $4 daily fee/pet. Service with restrictions, supervision.
[ASK] [S6] [X] [🛏] [💻] [🏊]

▼▼ The Hills Motel M
(325) 446-2567. **$38-$42.** 1520 N Main St. I-10, exit 456, 1.3 mi s on US 377. Ext corridors. **Pets:** Medium. Service with restrictions, supervision.
[X] [🛏] [🏊]

KERRVILLE

⨁ ▼▼▼▼ Best Western Sunday House Inn SH
(830) 896-1313. **$70-$109.** 2124 Sidney Baker St. I-10, exit 508 (SR 16), just s. Ext corridors. **Pets:** Small. $10 daily fee/pet. Designated rooms, service with restrictions, supervision.
[SAVE] [S6] [X] [💻] [🍴] [🏊]

⨁ ▼▼ Budget Inn M
(830) 896-8200. **$45-$65.** 1804 Sidney Baker St. I-10, exit 508 (SR 16), 0.5 mi s on SR 16. Ext corridors. **Pets:** Small, dogs only. $5 one-time fee/pet. Designated rooms, service with restrictions, supervision.
[SAVE] [S6] [X] [🛏] [🏊]

▼▼▼▼ Days Inn of Kerrville M
(830) 896-1000. **$64-$94.** 2000 Sidney Baker St. I-10, exit 508 (SR 16), 0.5 mi s. Ext/int corridors. **Pets:** Accepted.
[ASK] [S6] [X] [Ⓚ] [🛏] [💻] [🏊]

▼▼ ▼▼ Econo Lodge of Kerrville SH
(830) 896-1711. **$45-$129.** 2145 Sidney Baker St. I-10, exit 508, just s on SR 16. Int corridors. **Pets:** Very small. $15 daily fee/pet. Designated rooms, no service, supervision.
[ASK] [S6] [X] [🛏] [💻] [🍴] [🏊]

⨁ ▼▼▼▼ Y. O. Ranch Resort Hotel & Conference Center LH
(830) 257-4440. **$108-$119, 3 day notice.** 2033 Sidney Baker St. I-10, exit 508 (SR 16), 0.3 mi s. Ext/int corridors. **Pets:** Service with restrictions.
[SAVE] [S6] [X] [⌖] [🛏] [💻] [🏊] [🏊]

KILLEEN

▲▲▲ ▼▼ Holiday Inn Express SH
(254) 554-2727. **$59-$95.** 1602 E Center Expwy. US 190, exit Trimmier Rd. Ext corridors. **Pets:** Medium. Service with restrictions, supervision.

SAVE ✕ 🅱 💻

▼▼▼▼ La Quinta Inn-Killeen SH
(254) 526-8331. **$76-$86.** 1112 Fort Hood St. US 190, exit Fort Hood St, on westbound access road. Ext corridors. **Pets:** Accepted.

ASK S�} ✕ 🔌 🅱 💻 🏊

KINGSVILLE

▼▼ Holiday Inn M
(361) 595-5753. **Call for rates.** 3430 Hwy 77 S. On US 77, 1.5 mi s. Ext corridors. **Pets:** Accepted.

✕ 💻 🍴 🏊

▲▲▲ ▼▼▼ Super 8 Motel M
(361) 592-6471. **$59-$79, 7 day notice.** 105 S 77 Bypass. 0.8 mi e on US 77. Ext corridors. **Pets:** Very small. $25 one-time fee/pet. Designated rooms, no service, supervision.

SAVE S�} ✕ 🅱 💻 🏊

LAKE JACKSON

▼▼▼▼ Chertel Brazosport Hotel & Conference Center SH
(979) 297-1161. **$132-$161.** 925 Hwy 332. 2.8 mi e of jct SR 288 and 332. Int corridors. **Pets:** Other species. $100 deposit/room. Designated rooms, service with restrictions, supervision.

ASK S�} ✕ 🅱 💻 🍴 🏊

▼▼ ▼ Super 8 Motel-Lake Jackson M
(979) 297-3031. **$50-$55.** 915 Hwy 332. 3 mi e of jct SR 288 and 332. Ext corridors. **Pets:** Small. $15 daily fee/pet. Service with restrictions, supervision.

ASK S�} ✕ 🅱 💻 🏊

LAKEWAY

▲▲▲ ▼▼▼▼ Lakeway Inn Conference Resort LH
(512) 261-6600. **$109-$229, 3 day notice.** 101 Lakeway Dr. Jct FM 620 and Lakeway Blvd W to Lakeway Dr, then n, follow signs. Ext/int corridors. **Pets:** Large. $100 deposit/room. Designated rooms, service with restrictions, crate.

SAVE S�} ✕ LM 🔌 🔲 🅱 💻 🍴 🏊 ✕

LAMESA

▲▲▲ ▼ Budget Host Inn M
(806) 872-2118. **$44-$46, 3 day notice.** 901 S Dallas Ave (US 87). Jct US 87 and 180, 0.7 mi s. Ext corridors. **Pets:** Accepted.

SAVE S�} ✕ 🅱 🏊

▼▼ Shiloh Inn M
(806) 872-6721. **$40-$53.** 1707 Lubbock Hwy. Jct US 87 and 180, 1 mi n. Ext corridors. **Pets:** Accepted.

✕ 🅱 💻 🏊

LAREDO

▲▲▲ ▼▼▼ Fiesta Inn M
(956) 723-3603. **$72.** 5240 San Bernardo Ave. I-35, exit 3B (Mann Rd), on southbound access road. Ext corridors. **Pets:** Small. $25 one-time fee/room. Service with restrictions, supervision.

SAVE ✕ 🅱 🏊

▼▼▼▼ La Quinta Inn-Laredo SH
(956) 722-0511. **$90-$106.** 3610 Santa Ursula Ave. I-35, exit 2 (US 59). Ext corridors. **Pets:** Accepted.

ASK S�} ✕ 🅱 💻 🏊

▼▼ Motel 6–1107 M
(956) 722-8133. **$52-$64.** 5920 San Bernardo Ave. I-35, exit 4 (Del Mar Blvd/Santa Maria Ave). Ext/int corridors. **Pets:** Accepted.

S�} ✕ 🔲 🏊

▼▼ Motel 6 South-142 M
(956) 725-8187. **$52-$63.** 5310 San Bernardo Ave. I-35, exit 3B (Mann Rd). Ext corridors. **Pets:** Accepted.

S�} ✕ 🏊

▲▲▲ ▼▼▼ Red Roof Inn Laredo M
(956) 712-0733. **$54-$74.** 1006 W Calton Rd. I-35, exit 3A, 0.3 mi w. Ext/int corridors. **Pets:** Large, other species. Service with restrictions, supervision.

SAVE ✕ 🔲 🅱 🏊

▲▲▲ ▼▼▼▼ Rio Grande Plaza Hotel SH
(956) 722-2411. **$89-$99.** One S Main Ave. I-35, exit 1, just w of International Bridge. Int corridors. **Pets:** $100 deposit/room. Service with restrictions, crate.

SAVE S�} ✕ 🔌 🅱 💻 🍴 🏊

LITTLEFIELD

▲▲▲ ▼ Crescent Park Motel M
(806) 385-4464. **$47-$65.** 2000 Hall Ave. Jct US 84, 0.3 mi n on SR 385. Ext corridors. **Pets:** Accepted.

SAVE S�} ✕ 🅱 💻

LLANO

▲▲▲ ▼▼ Best Western Llano SH
(325) 247-4101. **$56-$79, 4 day notice.** 901 W Young St. 1 mi w on SR 71 and 29. Ext corridors. **Pets:** Small. $5 daily fee/pet. Service with restrictions, supervision.

SAVE S�} ✕ 🅱 💻 🏊

LOCKHART

▲▲▲ ▼▼▼ Best Western Plum Creek Inn M
(512) 398-4911. **$75-$95, 7 day notice.** 2001 Hwy 183 S. US 183 S, 1 mi s. Ext corridors. **Pets:** Accepted.

SAVE S�} ✕ 🅱 💻 🍴 🏊

LONGVIEW

▼▼▼▼ Hampton Inn SH
(903) 758-0959. **Call for rates.** 112 S Access Rd. I-20, exit 595A. Ext corridors. **Pets:** Accepted.

✕ LM 🅱 💻 🏊

La Quinta Inn 🆂🅷
(903) 757-3663. **$63-$79.** 502 S Access Rd. I-20, exit 595.
Ext corridors. **Pets:** Other species. Service with restrictions.

LUBBOCK

Best Western Lubbock Windsor Inn 🆂🅷
(806) 762-8400. **$69-$109.** 5410 I-27. 3.5 mi s on I-27, exit
1B southbound; U-turn at exit 1A (50th St) northbound. Int
corridors. **Pets:** $25 deposit/room, $8 daily fee/room. Service with restrictions, supervision.

Days Inn Texas Tech 🆂🅷
(806) 747-7111. **$54-$89, 3 day notice.** 2401 4th St. I-27,
exit 4 (4th St), 1.5 mi w. Ext corridors. **Pets:** Dogs only.
Service with restrictions, supervision.

Econo Lodge 🆂🅷
(806) 747-3525. **$49-$99, 5 day notice.** 5401 Ave Q. I-27,
exit 1A (US 84/Ave Q), 0.5 mi w. Ext/int corridors.
Pets: Medium. $25 deposit/pet, $8 daily fee/pet. Designated rooms, service with restrictions, supervision.

Holiday Inn Park Plaza 🆂🅷
(806) 797-3241. **$72-$82.** 3201 S Loop 289. 5 mi s on Loop
289, exit Indiana, on south frontage road. Ext/int corridors.
Pets: Accepted.

La Quinta Inn-Lubbock-Civic Center 🆂🅷
(806) 763-9441. **$73-$93.** 601 Ave Q. 0.8 mi nw on US 84.
Ext corridors. **Pets:** Supervision.

La Quinta Inn-Lubbock-Medical Center 🆂🅷
(806) 792-0065. **$76-$96.** 4115 Brownfield Hwy. 3.3 mi sw;
2.5 mi ne of Loop 289 on US 62 and 82. Int corridors.
Pets: Other species. Supervision.

Lubbock Super 8 Motel 🅼
(806) 762-8726. **$48-$70, 7 day notice.** 501 Ave Q. 1 mi nw
on US 84. Ext corridors. **Pets:** $25 deposit/room, $6 daily
fee/pet. Service with restrictions, supervision.

Motel 6 Lubbock #298 🆂🅷
(806) 745-5541. **$41-$55.** 909 66th St. I-27, exit 1 northbound; exit 1B southbound, on westbound frontage road.
Ext corridors. **Pets:** Other species. Service with restrictions,
supervision.

Ramada Inn and Conference Center 🆂🅷
(806) 745-2208. **$54-$95, 30 day notice.** 6624 I-27. 3.8 mi s
on I-27 and US 87; just w of jct Loop 289, exit 1B southbound. Int corridors. **Pets:** Dogs only. $25 one-time fee/
room. Service with restrictions, supervision.

Residence Inn by Marriott 🆂🅷
(806) 745-1963. **$114.** 2551 S Loop 289. Loop 289, exit
University, 3 mi s, south frontage road. Ext corridors.
Pets: Medium, other species. $50 one-time fee/room. Service with restrictions, crate.

LUFKIN

Days Inn 🆂🅷
(936) 639-3301. **$77-$87.** 2130 S 1st St. 0.3 mi s of jct US
59 and Loop 287. Ext/int corridors. **Pets:** Small. $25
deposit/pet, $25 one-time fee/pet. Service with restrictions.

La Quinta Inn-Lufkin 🆂🅷
(936) 634-3351. **$76-$86.** 2119 S 1st St. US 59, exit Carriageway northbound, 0.3 mi s of jct S Loop 287 and US 59
business route. Ext corridors. **Pets:** Service with restrictions.

MADISONVILLE

Western Lodge 🅼
(936) 348-7654. **$45-$50.** 2007 E Main St. I-45, exit 142, 0.3
mi w. Ext corridors. **Pets:** Very small. $5 daily fee/room.
Supervision.

MARATHON

The Gage Hotel 🅲🅸
(432) 386-4205. **$69-$155.** Hwy 90. US 90; center. Ext/int
corridors. **Pets:** $15 daily fee/pet. Service with restrictions,
supervision.

MARBLE FALLS

Best Western Marble Falls Inn 🆂🅷
(830) 693-5122. **$59-$109.** 1403 Hwy 281 N. 0.4 mi n of jct
SR 281 and FM 1431. Ext/int corridors. **Pets:** Medium. $10
one-time fee/pet. Designated rooms, service with restrictions, crate.

MARSHALL

Best Western Executive Inn 🆂🅷
(903) 935-0707. **$79-$99.** 5201 E End Blvd S. I-20, exit 617,
just n on US 59. Ext corridors. **Pets:** Small, dogs only. $15
daily fee/pet. Designated rooms, service with restrictions,
supervision.

MCALLEN

Drury Inn 🆂🅷
(956) 687-5100. **$77-$101.** 612 W Expwy 83. US 83, exit
2nd St, northwest frontage road. Int corridors. **Pets:** Large,
other species. Service with restrictions, supervision.

Drury Suites-McAllen 🆂🅷
(956) 682-3222. **$103-$113.** 228 W Expwy 83. At US 83 and
6th St. Int corridors. **Pets:** Large, other species. Service
with restrictions, supervision.

▼▼▼ Hampton Inn-McAllen 🆂🅷
(956) 682-4900. **$92-$112.** 300 W Expwy 83. US 83, exit 2nd St, northwest frontage road. Int corridors. **Pets:** Accepted.

(A$K) (✕) 🛢 🖃 🏊

🅐🅐🅐 ▼▼▼▼ La Quinta Inn-McAllen 🆂🅷
(956) 687-1101. **$73.** 1100 S 10th St. 1.5 mi s on SR 336 (S 10th St); just n of jct US 83. Ext corridors. **Pets:** Accepted.
(SAVE) (S🖬) (✕) (🖬M) 🕼 🖃 🛢 🖃 🏊

▼▼▼ Posada Ana Inn 🆂🅷
(956) 631-6700. **$65-$75.** 620 W Expwy 83. US 83, exit 2nd St, on northwest frontage road. Int corridors. **Pets:** Large, other species. Service with restrictions, supervision.

(A$K) (✕) 🖃

▼▼▼ Residence Inn by Marriott 🆂🅷
(956) 994-8626. **$89-$94.** 220 W Expwy 83. US 83, exit 2nd St, just w, then just n on 2nd St. Int corridors. **Pets:** Accepted.

(A$K) (S🖬) (✕) 🛢 🖃 🏊 (✕)

🅐🅐🅐 ▼▼▼ Super 8 Motel 🆂🅷
(956) 682-1190. **$49-$79.** 1420 E Jackson Ave. US 83, exit Jackson Ave/Sam Houston St, just s. Int corridors. **Pets:** Very small. Supervision.

(SAVE) (S🖬) (✕) 🛢 🏊

MEMPHIS

🅐🅐🅐 ▼▼▼ Executive Inn 🅼
(806) 259-3583. **$45-$60, 7 day notice.** 1600 Boykin Dr. On US 287, 1.3 mi n of jct SR 256. Ext corridors. **Pets:** Small. $5 daily fee/pet. Service with restrictions, supervision.

(SAVE) (S🖬) (✕) 🛢 (🍴) 🏊

MIDLAND

🅐🅐🅐 ▼▼▼▼ Best Western Atrium Inn 🆂🅷
(432) 694-7774. **$59-$89.** 3904 W Wall St. I-20, exit 134, 1 mi n on Midkiff Rd, 0.3 mi w on I-20 business route. Ext/int corridors. **Pets:** $5 daily fee/room. Service with restrictions, crate.

(SAVE) (S🖬) (✕) 🕼 🛢 🖃 🏊 (✕)

▼▼▼▼ Holiday Inn 🆂🅷
(432) 697-3181. **$59-$64.** 4300 W Wall St. I-20, exit 134 (Midkiff Rd), 1 mi n to I-20 business loop, 0.7 mi w. Ext/int corridors. **Pets:** Accepted.

(A$K) (S🖬) (✕) 🛢 🖃 (🍴) 🏊 (✕)

🅐🅐🅐 ▼▼▼▼ La Quinta Inn-Midland 🆂🅷
(432) 697-9900. **$59-$79.** 4130 W Wall St. I-20, exit 131, 0.9 mi n on SR 250 Loop to exit 1A; 1.2 mi e on I-20 business route. Ext corridors. **Pets:** Other species. Service with restrictions, supervision.

(SAVE) (S🖬) (✕) 🕼 🛢 🖃 🏊

▼▼▼▼ Plaza Inn 🆂🅷
(432) 686-8733. **$65.** 4108 N Big Spring St. I-20, exit 144, 6.1 mi on SR 250 Loop to SR 349 (Big Spring St), just s on SR 349. Ext corridors. **Pets:** Small. $25 one-time fee/room. Designated rooms, service with restrictions, supervision.

(A$K) (S🖬) (✕) 🕼 🛢 🖃 🏊

🅐🅐🅐 ▼▼▼ Ramada Limited 🆂🅷
(432) 699-4144. **$59-$69.** 3100 W Wall St. 2 mi w on I-20 business loop. Int corridors. **Pets:** Accepted.

(SAVE) (S🖬) (✕) 🛢 🖃 🏊

🅐🅐🅐 ▼▼▼ Sleep Inn 🆂🅷
(432) 689-6822. **$59-$79.** 3828 W Wall St. I-20, exit 134 (Midkiff Rd), 1 mi n to Wall St, just w. Int corridors. **Pets:** Accepted.

(SAVE) (S🖬) (✕) 🕼 🛢 🖃 🏊

MINERAL WELLS

🅐🅐🅐 ▼▼▼▼ Best Western Clubhouse Inn & Suites 🆂🅷
(940) 325-2270. **$79-$159.** 4410 Hwy 180 E. Jct US 180 and SR 1195; in East Mineral Wells. Int corridors. **Pets:** Large, other species. $10 one-time fee/pet. Service with restrictions, supervision.

(SAVE) (S🖬) (✕) (🖬M) 🕼 🛢 🖃 🏊

MONAHANS

🅐🅐🅐 ▼▼▼ Best Western Colonial Inn 🅼
(432) 943-4345. **$50-$64.** 702 W I-20. I-20, exit 80, just s. Ext/int corridors. **Pets:** Medium, other species. Service with restrictions, supervision.

(SAVE) (S🖬) (✕) 🕼 🖃 (🍴) 🏊

MOUNT PLEASANT

🅐🅐🅐 ▼▼▼▼ Best Western Mt. Pleasant Inn 🆂🅷
(903) 572-5051. **$74-$84.** 102 Burton St. I-30 and Business Rt US 271, exit 162. Ext corridors. **Pets:** Small, dogs only. $10 daily fee/pet. Service with restrictions, supervision.

(SAVE) (S🖬) (✕) 🕼 🛢 🖃 🏊

▼▼▼▼ Holiday Inn Express Hotel & Suites 🆂🅷
(903) 577-3800. **$76-$110.** 2306 Greenhill Rd. I-30, exit 162, just n. Int corridors. **Pets:** Small. $50 deposit/pet. Service with restrictions, supervision.

(A$K) (S🖬) (✕) (🖬M) 🕼 🛢 🖃 🏊

▼▼▼ Ramada Inn-Mt. Pleasant 🆂🅷
(903) 572-6611. **$49-$55.** 2502 W Ferguson Rd. I-30, exit 160. Ext corridors. **Pets:** Accepted.

(A$K) (✕) 🛢 🖃 (🍴) 🏊

🅐🅐🅐 ▼▼▼ Super 8 🅼
(903) 572-9808. **$50-$70.** 204 Lakewood Dr. I-30, exit 162 eastbound; exit 162A westbound. Ext corridors. **Pets:** $10 daily fee/pet. Service with restrictions, supervision.

(SAVE) (S🖬) (✕) 🛢 🏊

MOUNT VERNON

🅐🅐🅐 ▼▼▼ Super 8 Motel of Mount Vernon 🆂🅷
(903) 588-2882. **$50.** 401 W I-30. I-30, exit 146 (SR 37). Ext corridors. **Pets:** $5 daily fee/room. Service with restrictions, supervision.

(SAVE) (S🖬) (✕) 🕼 🛢 🖃

MULESHOE

(AAA) ▼▼▼ Economy Inn M
(806) 272-4261. **$46.** 2701 W American Blvd. US 70/84, just w. Ext corridors. **Pets:** Accepted.
SAVE S☐ ☒ ☐

NACOGDOCHES

(AAA) ▼▼▼▼ La Quinta Inn-Nacogdoches SH
(936) 560-5453. **$66-$76.** 3215 South St. US 59, jct Loop 224 and US 59 business route, south of town. Ext corridors. **Pets:** Other species. Service with restrictions.
SAVE S☐ ☒ ☐ ☐ ☐ ☐

NEDERLAND

▼▼ Best Western-Airport Inn M ❄
(409) 727-1631. **$60-$69.** 200 Memorial Hwy 69. US 69, 96 and 287, exit Nederland Ave. Ext corridors. **Pets:** Small, dogs only. $20 one-time fee/pet. Service with restrictions, supervision.
ASK S☐ ☒ ☐ ☐ ☐ ☐

NEW BOSTON

(AAA) ▼▼▼ Best Western Inn of New Boston SH
(903) 628-6999. **$64-$99.** 1024 N Center. I-30, exit 201, on westbound access road. Ext corridors. **Pets:** Accepted.
SAVE S☐ ☒ ☐ ☐ ☐ ☐

NOCONA

▼▼ Nocona Hills Motel and Resort M ❄
(940) 825-3161. **$40-$46.** 100 E Huron Cir. 6 mi w of Saint Jo; US 82 to jct SR 1815, 4.6 mi n on SR 1815, 2.7 mi w on SR 1956, 2.4 mi n on SR 3301, then 0.6 mi w on Nocona Dr. Ext corridors. **Pets:** Large. $5 daily fee/pet. Service with restrictions, crate.
ASK S☐ ☒ ☐ ☐ ☒

NORTH RICHLAND HILLS

(AAA) ▼▼▼ Ramada Limited SH
(817) 485-2750. **$40-$69, 3 day notice.** 7920 Bedford-Euless Rd. I-820, exit 22A (Colleyville/SR 26) eastbound, just n on SR 26 under expressway to Bedford-Euless Rd, just e; exit Bedford-Euless Rd (SR 183) westbound, 0.4 mi w. Ext corridors. **Pets:** Accepted.
SAVE ☒ ☐ ☐ ☐ ☐

▼▼ Studio 6 #6034 M
(817) 788-6000. **$43-$51.** 7450 NE Loop 820. I-820, exit 21 (Holiday Ln), 0.4 mi e on south access road. Ext corridors. **Pets:** Accepted.
☒ ☐ ☐ ☐ ☐

ODEM

(AAA) ▼▼▼ Days Inn-Odem M
(361) 368-2166. **$60-$110.** 1505 Voss Ave (US 77). US 77, 1 mi s of jct 631. Ext corridors. **Pets:** Accepted.
SAVE S☐ ☒ ☐ ☐

ODESSA

▼▼▼ Best Western Garden Oasis SH
(432) 337-3006. **Call for rates.** 110 W I-20. Jct I-20 and US 385, exit 116. Ext/int corridors. **Pets:** Accepted.
☒ ☐ ☐ ☐ ☐ ☐ ☒

(AAA) ▼▼▼ Days Inn SH
(432) 335-8000. **$54-$64.** 3075 E Business Loop 20. I-20, exit 121, 0.7 mi n on Loop 338, then 0.5 mi w. Int corridors. **Pets:** Other species. $25 deposit/room. Service with restrictions, crate.
SAVE S☐ ☒ ☐ ☐

▼▼ Holiday Inn Express Hotel & Suites SH
(432) 333-3931. **$58.** 3001 E Business I-20. I-20, exit 121, 0.7 mi n on Loop 338, then 0.5 mi w. Ext/int corridors. **Pets:** Medium, other species. $25 deposit/room. Service with restrictions, crate.
ASK S☐ ☒ ☐ ☐ ☐ ☒

▼▼▼ Holiday Inn Hotel & Suites SH
(432) 362-2311. **$64.** 6201 E Business I-20. I-20, exit 121, 0.8 mi n on Loop 338, then 1 mi e. Ext/int corridors. **Pets:** Medium, other species. $25 deposit/room. Service with restrictions, crate.
ASK S☐ ☒ ☐ ☐ ☐ ☐ ☒

▼▼▼ La Quinta Inn-Odessa SH ❄
(432) 333-2820. **$70-$80.** 5001 E Business Loop I-20. I-20, exit 121, 0.8 mi n on Loop 338, then just w. Ext corridors. **Pets:** Service with restrictions, supervision.
ASK S☐ ☒ ☐ ☐ ☐ ☐

▼▼ Motel 6 Odessa #439 M
(432) 333-4025. **$37-$48.** 200 E I-20 Service Rd. I-20, exit 116, on eastbound frontage road. Ext corridors. **Pets:** Accepted.
S☐ ☐

OZONA

(AAA) ▼▼ Best Value Inn M
(325) 392-2631. **$45-$59.** 820 11th St. I-10, exit 365 westbound to SR 163, 1 mi n; exit 363 eastbound to Loop 466, 2 mi e. Ext corridors. **Pets:** Medium, other species. $5 one-time fee/pet. Service with restrictions, supervision.
SAVE S☐ ☒

(AAA) ▼ Travelodge M
(325) 392-2656. **$55-$65.** 8 11th St. I-10, exit 368 westbound, 2 mi w; exit 365 eastbound to Loop 466, 1 mi e. Ext corridors. **Pets:** Other species. $5 daily fee/pet. Service with restrictions, supervision.
SAVE S☐ ☒ ☐ ☐ ☐

PALESTINE

(AAA) ▼▼▼ Best Western Palestine Inn SH
(903) 723-4655. **$52-$68.** 1601 W Palestine Ave. Jct US 287/SR 19, 0.7 mi sw on US 79. Ext corridors. **Pets:** Small, dogs only. $5 one-time fee/pet. Service with restrictions, supervision.
SAVE S☐ ☒ ☐ ☐ ☐ ☐ ☐

PARIS

Best Western Inn of Paris 🅂🄷
(903) 785-5566. **$55-$68.** 3755 NE Loop 286. Jct US 82 and E Loop 286, just n. Ext corridors. **Pets:** Medium, other species. Service with restrictions, supervision.
🆂🄰🆅🄴 🆂🄳 ⊗ 🄰 🄴 🄰 🄴 ≈

PECOS

Best Western Swiss Clock Inn Ⓜ
(432) 447-2215. **$68-$70.** 133 S Frontage Rd, I-20 W. 1 mi w of jct US 285; 1 mi e of jct I-20 and SR 17, exit 40. Ext corridors. **Pets:** Small. Designated rooms, no service, supervision.
🆂🄰🆅🄴 🆂🄳 ⊗ 🄰 🄴 🄰 🄴 🄸🄸 ≈

LAURA LODGE Ⓜ
(432) 445-4924. **$40-$48.** 1000 E Business 20. I-20, exit 42 (US 285), 1 mi nw to Business Rt I-20, 0.5 mi e. Ext corridors. **Pets:** Small. $10 daily fee/pet. Designated rooms, service with restrictions, supervision.
🆂🄰🆅🄴 🆂🄳 ⊗ 🄴 🄴 ≈

Oak Tree Inn 🅂🄷
(432) 447-0180. **$64-$91.** 22 N Frontage Rd. I-20, exit 42, just w on north access road. Int corridors. **Pets:** Medium. $10 one-time fee/room. No service.
🆂🄰🆅🄴 🆂🄳 ⊗ 🄰 🄴 🄴

Quality Inn 🅂🄷
(432) 445-5404. **$61-$86, 7 day notice.** 4002 S Cedar St. Jct I-20 and US 285. Int corridors. **Pets:** Small. $10 daily fee/pet. Designated rooms, service with restrictions, crate.
🄰🆂🄺 🆂🄳 ⊗ 🄴 🄴 🄸🄸 ≈

PLAINVIEW

Best Western Conestoga 🅂🄷
(806) 293-9454. **$42-$53.** 600 N I-27. I-27, exit 49, just s of US 70 on east access road. Ext corridors. **Pets:** Small, other species. $7 one-time fee/pet. Service with restrictions, supervision.
🆂🄰🆅🄴 🆂🄳 ⊗ 🄰 🄴 🄴 ≈

Holiday Inn Express Hotel & Suites 🅂🄷
(806) 296-9900. **$90-$150.** 4213 W 13th St. I-27, exit 49 northbound, just w to Mesa, then just n; exit 50 southbound, just s to 13th St, then just w. Int corridors. **Pets:** Small. $20 one-time fee/pet. Service with restrictions, supervision.
🄰🆂🄺 🆂🄳 ⊗ 🄶🄼 🄴 🄴 🄴 ≈

Plainview Hotel 🅂🄷
(806) 293-4181. **$65-$70.** 4005 Olton Rd. I-27, exit 49. Ext/int corridors. **Pets:** Accepted.
🄰🆂🄺 🆂🄳 ⊗ 🄴 🄴 ≈

PORT ISABEL

Southwind Inn Ⓜ
(956) 943-3392. **$40-$120.** 600 Davis St. Queen Isabella Cswy to Musina, then 3 blks n. Ext corridors. **Pets:** Accepted.
🆂🄰🆅🄴 🆂🄳 ⊗ 🄴 🄴 ≈

PORTLAND

Comfort Inn 🅂🄷
(361) 643-2222. **$75-$114.** 1703 N Hwy 181. US 181 W access road, exit FM 3239 northbound; exit Lang St southbound. Ext corridors. **Pets:** Very small, other species. $6 daily fee/pet. Designated rooms, service with restrictions, supervision.
🆂🄰🆅🄴 🆂🄳 ⊗ 🄴 🄴 ≈

POST

Best Western Post Inn 🅂🄷
(806) 495-9933. **$65-$70.** 1011 N Broadway. 1 mi n on US 84. Int corridors. **Pets:** Small, dogs only. $50 deposit/pet, $10 one-time fee/pet. Designated rooms, service with restrictions, supervision.
🄰🆂🄺 ⊗ 🄴 🄴 ≈

ROBSTOWN

Days Inn 🅂🄷
(361) 387-9416. **$52-$100.** 320 Hwy 77 S. On US 77, 1 mi s. Ext corridors. **Pets:** Accepted.
🆂🄰🆅🄴 🆂🄳 ⊗ 🄴 ≈

ROCKPORT

Laguna Reef Hotel 🄲🄾 🐾
(361) 729-1742. **$80-$350.** 1021 Water St. 0.5 mi s, just e of Business Rt SR 35; entrance on S Austin St. Ext corridors. **Pets:** Medium, other species. $50 deposit/pet. Service with restrictions, supervision.
🆂🄰🆅🄴 🆂🄳 ⊗ 🄴 🄴 ≈ ⊗

The Village Inn Ⓜ
(361) 729-6370. **$55-$70.** 503 N Austin St. Just w of jct SR 35 and Business Rt SR 35. Ext corridors. **Pets:** Other species. $10 daily fee/pet. Designated rooms, service with restrictions, crate.
🆂🄰🆅🄴 🆂🄳 ⊗ 🄴 🄴 ≈

ROUND ROCK

AmeriSuites (Austin/Round Rock) 🅂🄷
(512) 733-2599. **$69-$99.** 2340 I-35 N. I-35, exit 254, on west frontage road. Int corridors. **Pets:** Accepted.
🆂🄰🆅🄴 🆂🄳 ⊗ 🄴 🄴 ≈

Baymont Inn & Suites Austin-Round Rock 🅂🄷
(512) 246-2800. **$74-$99.** 150 Parker Dr. I-35, exit 250, on west frontage road. Int corridors. **Pets:** Accepted.
🆂🄰🆅🄴 🆂🄳 ⊗ 🄶🄼 🄰 🄴 🄴 🄴 ≈

Best Western Executive Inn 🅂🄷
(512) 255-3222. **$55-$79.** 1851 N I-35. I-35, exit 253 northbound; exit 253A U-turn southbound. Ext corridors. **Pets:** Very small.
🆂🄰🆅🄴 🆂🄳 ⊗ 🄶🄼 🄰 🄴 🄴 ≈

Candlewood Suites 🅂🄷
(512) 828-0899. **$64-$108.** 521 S I-35. I-35, exit 252A, just n on northbound frontage road. Int corridors. **Pets:** Other species. $25 one-time fee/room. Service with restrictions, crate.
🄰🆂🄺 ⊗ 🄰 🄴 🄴

▼▼▼▼ **Days Inn and Suites** SH
(512) 246-0055. **$59-$79.** 1802 S I-35. I-35, exit 251, just s. Ext/int corridors. **Pets:** Accepted.
(ASK) (S☉) (✕) (⚡) (⊟) (💻) (⇆)

(AAA) ▼▼▼▼ **La Quinta Inn-Austin-Round Rock** SH
(512) 255-6666. **$80-$90.** 2004 I-35 S. I-35, exit 254, on west frontage road. Int corridors. **Pets:** Accepted.
(SAVE) (S☉) (✕) (⌖) (⊟) (💻) (⇆)

(AAA) ▼▼▼ **Red Roof Inn** SH
(512) 310-1111. **$44-$64.** 1990 I-35 N. I-35, exit 254, on west frontage road. Int corridors. **Pets:** Medium. Service with restrictions, supervision.
(SAVE) (✕) (⊟) (⇆)

▼▼▼ **Residence Inn by Marriott** SH 🐾
(512) 733-2400. **$107.** 2505 S I-35. I-35, exit 250 southbound; exit 251 northbound, on east frontage road. Int corridors. **Pets:** Other species. $5 daily fee/pet, $50 one-time fee/room. Service with restrictions, crate.
(ASK) (S☉) (✕) (⌖M) (⌖) (⚡) (⊟) (💻) (⇆) (✕)

▼▼▼ **Staybridge Suites Austin-Round Rock** SH 🐾
(512) 733-0942. **$109-$179.** 520 I-35 S. I-35, exit 252B northbound; exit 252AB southbound, on west frontage road. Int corridors. **Pets:** Small. $50 deposit/pet. Service with restrictions.
(ASK) (S☉) (✕) (⌖M) (⚡) (⌖) (⊟) (💻) (⇆)

SAN ANGELO

▼▼ **Benchmark Comfort Inn** SH
(325) 944-2578. **$75-$105.** 2502 Loop 306. Loop 306, exit Knickebocker Rd. Ext corridors. **Pets:** Medium. $25 one-time fee/room. Service with restrictions, crate.
(ASK) (S☉) (✕) (⊟) (💻) (⇆)

(AAA) ▼▼▼▼ **Best Western San Angelo** SH
(325) 223-1273. **$70-$75.** 3017 W Loop 306. Loop 306, exit College Hills Blvd, just s. Ext corridors. **Pets:** Very small. $25 deposit/pet. Service with restrictions, supervision.
(SAVE) (S☉) (✕) (⌖) (⊟) (💻) (⇆)

▼▼▼▼ **Holiday Inn Convention Center Hotel** SH
(325) 658-2828. **$109-$169.** 441 Rio Concho Dr. US 87 to Concho Ave, 0.5 mi e; downtown. Int corridors. **Pets:** Small, other species. $50 one-time fee/room. Service with restrictions, supervision.
(ASK) (S☉) (✕) (⚡) (⊟) (💻) (🍴) (⇆)

(AAA) ▼▼▼ **Howard Johnson San Angelo** SH
(325) 653-2995. **$60.** 415 W Beauregard. Just w on US 67 business route at jct US 87 southbound. Ext/int corridors. **Pets:** Accepted.
(SAVE) (S☉) (✕) (⊟) (💻) (🍴) (⇆)

(AAA) ▼▼▼▼ **La Quinta Inn-San Angelo** SH
(325) 949-0515. **$71-$91.** 2307 Loop 306. Loop 306, exit Knickerbocker Rd, just s. Ext corridors. **Pets:** Accepted.
(SAVE) (S☉) (✕) (⚡) (⊟) (💻) (⇆)

▼▼ **Motel 6 San Angelo #229** M
(325) 653-1323. **$39-$52.** 311 N Bryant Blvd. Just n on US 87. Ext corridors. **Pets:** Accepted.
(S☉) (✕) (⌖) (⊟) (💻) (⇆)

(AAA) ▼▼ **Super 8 Motel** M
(325) 653-1323. **$50-$55.** 1601 S Bryant Blvd. US 87 and 277 at Ave L. Ext/int corridors. **Pets:** Small, dogs only. $25 deposit/pet. Service with restrictions, supervision.
(SAVE) (S☉) (✕) (⊟) (⇆)

SAN ANTONIO METROPOLITAN AREA

ELMENDORF

(AAA) ▼▼▼ **San Antonio Inn & Suites** SH 🐾
(210) 633-1833. **$49-$63.** 13800 I-37 S. I-37, exit 130, on northbound access lane. Ext corridors. **Pets:** Large, other species. $5 one-time fee/room. Service with restrictions, supervision.
(SAVE) (S☉) (✕) (⊟) (💻) (⇆)

FLORESVILLE

(AAA) ▼▼▼▼ **Best Western Floresville Inn** SH
(830) 393-0443. **$62-$79.** 1720 S 10th St. US 181, just s of downtown. Ext corridors. **Pets:** Small. $10 daily fee/room. Service with restrictions.
(SAVE) (S☉) (✕) (⊟) (💻) (⇆)

LIVE OAK

▼▼▼ **La Quinta-Inn-San Antonio-Toepperwein** SH
(210) 657-5500. **$69-$109.** 12822 I-35 N. I-35, exit 170B (Toepperwein), on northbound access road. Ext/int corridors. **Pets:** Accepted.
(ASK) (S☉) (✕) (⌖M) (⊟) (💻) (⇆)

NEW BRAUNFELS

(AAA) ▼▼▼▼ **Best Western Inn & Suites** SH
(830) 625-7337. **$44-$149.** 1493 I-35 N. I-35, exit 190, on southbound access lane. Ext/int corridors. **Pets:** Accepted.
(SAVE) (S☉) (✕) (⌖) (💻) (⇆)

▼▼▼ **Executive Inn & Suites** SH
(830) 625-3932. **$39-$199.** 808 Hwy 46 S. I-35, exit 189, just e. Ext corridors. **Pets:** Accepted.
(ASK) (S☉) (✕) (⌖M) (⌖) (⊟) (💻) (⇆)

(AAA) ▼▼▼▼ **Holiday Inn** SH
(830) 625-8017. **$109-$199.** 1051 I-35 E. I-35, exit 189, on southbound access road. Ext corridors. **Pets:** Accepted.
(SAVE) (S☉) (✕) (⌖M) (⊟) (💻) (🍴) (⇆)

(AAA) ▼▼▼ **Rodeway Inn** SH
(830) 629-6991. **$49-$129.** 1209 I-35 E. I-35, exit 189, on southbound access road. Ext corridors. **Pets:** Small, other species. $10 deposit/pet. Service with restrictions, supervision.
(SAVE) (S☉) (✕) (⊟) (💻) (⇆)

▼▼▼ Super 8 Motel-New Braunfels 🅼
(830) 629-1155. $49-$129. 510 Hwy 46 S. I-35, exit 189 (SR 46), just e. Ext corridors. Pets: Medium. $10 daily fee/pet. Service with restrictions, supervision.
Ⓐ🆂🅆 🆂🅓 ⊠ 🗄 🖵 🛏

SAN ANTONIO

🄰🄰🄰 ▼▼▼ Alamo Travelodge 🆂🅷 🐾
(210) 222-1000. $45-$99. 405 Broadway. US 281, exit Broadway. Ext corridors. Pets: Medium, dogs only. $5 daily fee/pet. Designated rooms, service with restrictions.
🆂🅆 🆂🅓 ⊠ 🗄 🖵 🍽 🛏

🄰🄰🄰 ▼▼▼▼ AmeriSuites (San
                    Antonio/Airport) 🆂🅷
(210) 930-2333. $89-$99. 7615 Jones Maltberger Rd. US 281, exit Jones Maltsberger Rd, inside Loop 410. Int corridors. Pets: Accepted.
🆂🅆 🆂🅓 ⊠ 🖋 🗄 🖵 🛏

🄰🄰🄰 ▼▼▼▼ AmeriSuites (San
                    Antonio/Riverwalk) 🆂🅷
(210) 227-6854. $159-$199. 601 S St. Mary's St. I-35, exit Durango St, 0.9 mi e. Int corridors. Pets: Small. $15 deposit/pet. Service with restrictions, crate.
🆂🅆 🆂🅓 ⊠ 🖋 🗄 🖵 🛏

🄰🄰🄰 ▼▼▼▼ Arbor House Suites Bed &
                    Breakfast 🄱🄱
(210) 472-2005. $95-$225, 3 day notice. 109 Arciniega St. Just n of Durango St; near La Villita. Ext/int corridors. Pets: Medium, other species. Service with restrictions.
🆂🅆 ⊠ 🗄 🖵

🄰🄰🄰 ▼▼▼▼ Best Western Fiesta Inn 🆂🅷
(210) 696-2400. $50-$130. 13535 I-10 W. I-10, exit 557 westbound; exit 558 eastbound, on westbound access road. Ext corridors. Pets: Accepted.
🆂🅆 🆂🅓 ⊠ 🖋 🗄 🖵 🛏

🄰🄰🄰 ▼▼▼▼ Best Western Ingram Park Inn 🆂🅷
(210) 520-8080. $50-$130. 6855 NW Loop 410. I-410, exit 10 westbound; exit 11 eastbound; on westbound access road. Ext corridors. Pets: Accepted.
🆂🅆 🆂🅓 ⊠ 🗄 🖵 🛏

🄰🄰🄰 ▼▼▼▼ Best Western Posada Ana Inn San
                    Antonio Medical Center 🆂🅷
(210) 561-9300. $77-$110. 9411 Wurzbach Rd. I-10 NW, exit 561 (Wurzbach Rd), on eastbound access road. Int corridors. Pets: Accepted.
🆂🅆 ⊠ 🗄 🖵 🛏

🄰🄰🄰 ▼▼▼▼ Brackenridge House B & B 🄱🄱
(210) 271-3442. $110-$200, 14 day notice. 230 Madison. King William Historic District. Ext/int corridors. Pets: Other species. Designated rooms, service with restrictions.
🆂🅆 ⊠ 🗄 🖵

▼▼▼ Candlewood Suites Hotel 🆂🅷
(210) 615-0550. $109. 9350 I-10 W. I-10 W, exit 561 (Wurzbach Rd), eastbound access road between Wurzbach Rd and Callaghan. Int corridors. Pets: $75 one-time fee/room. Service with restrictions.
Ⓐ🆂🅆 ⊠ 🖋 🗄 🖵 🛏

🄰🄰🄰 ▼▼▼▼ Comfort Inn Sea World 🆂🅷
(210) 684-8606. $64-$139. 4 Piano Pl. I-410, exit 13B (Evers Rd), 0.5 mi e of jct Evers Rd, eastbound access road. Ext corridors. Pets: Small. $10 daily fee/pet. No service, supervision.
🆂🅆 🆂🅓 ⊠ 🗄 🖵 🛏

▼▼▼ Days Inn Coliseum 🆂🅷
(210) 225-4040. $45-$110. 3443 I-35 N. I-35, exit 160 (Splashtown), on southbound access road. Ext corridors. Pets: Medium, other species. $25 one-time fee/pet. Designated rooms, service with restrictions.
Ⓐ🆂🅆 🆂🅓 ⊠ 🗄 🖵 🛏

▼▼▼ Days Inn-Downtown Laredo St 🆂🅷
(210) 271-3334. $49-$109. 1500 I-35 S. I-10/35, exit 154 (Laredo St). Ext/int corridors. Pets: Medium, other species. $25 one-time fee/pet. Designated rooms, service with restrictions.
Ⓐ🆂🅆 🆂🅓 ⊠ 🗄 🖵 🛏

▼▼▼▼ Drury Inn & Suites San Antonio
                    Airport 🆂🅷
(210) 308-8100. $82-$107. 95 NE Loop 410. I-410, exit 21A (Jones Maltsberger Rd), 1.8 mi w of airport. Int corridors. Pets: Large, other species. Service with restrictions, supervision.
Ⓐ🆂🅆 ⊠ 🅼 🖋 🗄 🖵 🛏

▼▼▼▼ Drury Inn & Suites-San Antonio
                    Northwest 🆂🅷
(210) 561-2510. $85-$122. 9806 I-10 W. I-10, exit Wurzbach Rd, on southeast corner. Int corridors. Pets: Large, other species. Service with restrictions, supervision.
Ⓐ🆂🅆 ⊠ 🗄 🖵 🛏

▼▼▼▼ Drury Inn & Suites San Antonio
                    Riverwalk 🆂🅷
(210) 212-5200. $130-$173. 201 N St. Mary's St. Just s of College St. Int corridors. Pets: Large, other species. Service with restrictions, supervision.
Ⓐ🆂🅆 ⊠ 🖋 🗄 🖵 🍽 🛏

▼▼▼▼ Drury Inn San Antonio Northeast 🆂🅷
(210) 654-1144. $80-$100. 8300 I-35 N. I-35, exit 165 (Walzem Rd), northbound access road. Ext/int corridors. Pets: Large, other species. Service with restrictions, supervision.
Ⓐ🆂🅆 ⊠ 🅼 🗄 🖵 🛏

▼▼▼ Econo Lodge Airport 🅼
(210) 247-4774. $57-$74. 2635 NE Loop 410. I-410, exit 25B (Perrin-Beitel Rd), on westbound access lane. Ext/int corridors. Pets: Accepted.
Ⓐ🆂🅆 🆂🅓 ⊠ 🛏

▼▼▼▼ Four Points by Sheraton Riverwalk
                    North 🄻🄷
(210) 223-9461. $89-$119. 110 Lexington Ave. 0.3 mi s of jct Lexington Ave and I-35. Int corridors. Pets: Accepted.
Ⓐ🆂🅆 🆂🅓 ⊠ 🗄 🖵 🍽 🛏

▼▼▼▼ Hampton Inn-San Antonio Airport 🆂🅷
(210) 366-1800. $90-$120. 8818 Jones Maltsberger Rd. I-410, exit 21B (Jones Maltsberger Rd), on westbound access road. Int corridors. Pets: Medium. No service.
Ⓐ🆂🅆 ⊠ 🖉 🖵 🛏

(AAA) ▼▼▼ Hampton Inn Six Flags Area SH ❖
(210) 561-9058. **$79-$99.** 11010 I-10 W. I-10, exit 560 westbound; exit 559 (Huebner Rd) eastbound. Int corridors. **Pets:** Other species. $10 one-time fee/pet. Service with restrictions, supervision.

▼▼▼ Hawthorn Suites Riverwalk SH
(210) 527-1900. **$129-$189.** 830 N St. Mary's St. Just n of Navarro St. Int corridors. **Pets:** Medium. $25 one-time fee/room. Service with restrictions, crate.

▼▼▼ Hill Country Inn & Suites SH
(210) 599-4204. **$66.** 2383 NE Loop 410. I-410, exit 24B (Perrin Beitel Rd) eastbound; exit 25A (Starcrest) westbound. Ext corridors. **Pets:** Accepted.

▼▼▼ Hilton Palacio del Rio LH
(210) 222-1400. **$98-$256.** 200 S Alamo St. Adjacent to convention center. Int corridors. **Pets:** Medium. $25 one-time fee/pet. Service with restrictions, crate.

(AAA) ▼▼▼ Hilton San Antonio Airport LH
(210) 340-6060. **$79-$265.** 611 NW Loop 410. I-410, exit San Pedro Ave, on westbound access road. Int corridors. **Pets:** Accepted.

▼▼▼ Holiday Inn Crockett Hotel LH
(210) 225-6500. **$199, 3 day notice.** 320 Bonham St. Center. Ext/int corridors. **Pets:** Accepted.

▼▼▼ Holiday Inn-Downtown-Market Square SH
(210) 225-3211. **$119-$139.** 318 W Durango St. I-35, exit Durango St, 2 blks e. Int corridors. **Pets:** Accepted.

▼▼▼ Holiday Inn Express SH
(210) 599-0999. **$79-$209.** 11939 N I-35. I-35, exit 170, on southbound access road, 0.5 mi s to Judson Rd exit. Ext corridors. **Pets:** Very small. $10 daily fee/pet. Service with restrictions, crate.

▼▼▼ Holiday Inn Express-San Antonio Airport SH
(210) 308-6700. **$103-$123.** 91 NE Loop 410. I-410, exit 21A (Jones Maltsberger Rd) eastbound; exit 20B westbound, on westbound access road between San Pedro Ave and Jones Maltsberger Rd. Int corridors. **Pets:** Accepted.

▼▼▼ Holiday Inn-Northeast SH
(210) 226-4361. **$95.** 3855 I-35 N. I-35, exit 162 (Binz-Engleman Rd) southbound; exit 161 northbound, on southbound access road. Ext corridors. **Pets:** Very small. $50 one-time fee/room. Service with restrictions, crate.

▼▼▼ Holiday Inn Riverwalk SH
(210) 224-2500. **$149-$179.** 217 N St. Mary's St. Houston St, just s. Int corridors. **Pets:** Medium, other species. $25 one-time fee/room. Service with restrictions, supervision.

▼▼▼ Holiday Inn Select SH
(210) 349-9900. **$129.** 77 NE Loop 410. I-410, exit 20B (McCullough St), on westbound access road. Int corridors. **Pets:** Large. $100 deposit/room, $25 one-time fee/room. Service with restrictions, supervision.

▼▼ HomeGate Studios & Suites SH
(210) 342-4800. **$49-$69.** 11221 San Pedro Ave. I-410, exit US 281 (San Pedro Ave), 2.3 mi n on US 281, exit Nakoma, on west frontage road. Ext corridors. **Pets:** Accepted.

▼▼ Homestead Studio Suites Hotel-San Antonio/Airport M ❖
(210) 491-9009. **$54-$74.** 1015 Central Pkwy S. I-410, exit US 281 (San Pedro Ave), 4 mi n on US 281, exit Bitters Rd, on northbound access road. Ext corridors. **Pets:** Medium, other species. $25 daily fee/room. Service with restrictions, crate.

(AAA) ▼▼ Howard Johnson Coliseum SH
(210) 229-9220. **$50-$120.** 2755 I-35 N. I-35, exit 159B (Walters Ave), southbound access road. Ext corridors. **Pets:** Accepted.

▼▼ Howard Johnson Express Inn Fiesta SH
(210) 558-7152. **$59-$99.** 13279 I-10 W. I-10 NW, exit 557 westbound; exit 558 eastbound, on westbound access road. Ext corridors. **Pets:** Accepted.

(AAA) ▼▼ Knights Inn Windsor Park M
(210) 646-6336. **$59-$89.** 6370 I-35 N. I-410/35, exit Rittiman Rd, on northbound access road. Ext corridors. **Pets:** Small. $10 one-time fee/room. Designated rooms, service with restrictions, crate.

(AAA) ▼▼▼ La Mansion del Rio LH ❖
(210) 518-1000. **$219-$369, 3 day notice.** 112 College St. Just s on the Riverwalk. Ext/int corridors. **Pets:** Medium. Service with restrictions, supervision.

▼▼▼ La Quinta Inn-Convention Center SH
(210) 222-9181. **$115-$155.** 1001 E Commerce St. 0.5 mi ne. Ext/int corridors. **Pets:** Accepted.

(AAA) ▼▼▼ La Quinta Inn Market Square SH
(210) 271-0001. **$89-$139.** 900 Dolorosa. I-10/35, exit Durango St, just n on Santa Rosa St, then just w on Nueva St. Ext corridors. **Pets:** Accepted.

△△△ ▽▽▽▽ La Quinta Inn-San Antonio-Ingram Park 🆂🅷 🐾
(210) 680-8883. **$62-$122.** 7134 NW Loop 410. I-410, exit 10 (Culebra Rd), on eastbound access road. Ext corridors. **Pets:** Other species. Service with restrictions, supervision.
(SAVE) (S🔳) ✕ 🅱 🔲 🔁

▽▽▽▽ La Quinta Inn-San Antonio-Lackland 🆂🅷
(210) 674-3200. **$71-$91.** 6511 Military Dr W. Southwest of jct US 90 and Military Dr W. Ext corridors. **Pets:** Accepted.
(ASK) (S🔳) ✕ 🅱 🔲 🔁

▽▽▽▽ La Quinta Inn-San Antonio-Vance Jackson 🆂🅷 🐾
(210) 734-7931. **$71-$95.** 5922 NW Expwy. I-10, exit 565B eastbound; exit 565C (Vance Jackson Rd) westbound, on eastbound access road. Ext corridors. **Pets:** Other species. Service with restrictions.
(ASK) (S🔳) ✕ 🅱 🔲 🔁

▽▽▽▽ La Quinta Inn-San Antonio-Windsor Park 🆂🅷
(210) 653-6619. **$71-$101.** 6410 I-35 N. I-35, exit 163B northbound, on I-35 northbound access road between Rittiman and Eisenhauer rds; exit 164A (Rittiman Rd) southbound. Ext corridors. **Pets:** Accepted.
(ASK) (S🔳) ✕ 🅱 🔲 🔁

△△△ ▽▽▽▽ La Quinta Inn-San Antonio-Wurzbach 🆂🅷 🐾
(210) 593-0338. **$69-$99.** 9542 I-10 W. I-10, exit Wurzbach Rd, just e on eastbound access road. Ext corridors. **Pets:** Other species. Service with restrictions, supervision.
(SAVE) (S🔳) ✕ 🅱 🔲 🔁

▽▽▽▽ La Quinta Inns-San Antonio Airport 🆂🅷 🐾
(210) 342-3738. **$89-$109.** 850 Halm. I-410, exit US 281 S, southwest corner. Int corridors. **Pets:** Other species. Service with restrictions, crate.
(ASK) (S🔳) ✕ 🅱 🔲 🔁

▽▽ Motel 6–1122 🅼
(210) 225-1111. **$45-$65.** 211 N Pecos St. I-10/35, exit 155 B (Pecos St), on I-10 E/35 S access road. Ext corridors. **Pets:** Accepted.
(S🔳) ✕ 🄺 🅱 🔁

▽▽ Motel 6–134 🅼
(210) 650-4419. **$35-$49.** 9503 I-35 N. I-35, exit 167A (Randolf Blvd) southbound; exit 167 (Starlight Terrace) northbound. Ext corridors. **Pets:** Accepted.
(S🔳) ✕ 🔁

▽▽ Motel 6–651 🅼
(210) 673-9020. **$35-$51.** 2185 SW Loop 410. I-410, exit 7 (Marbach Rd), on westbound access road. Ext corridors. **Pets:** Accepted.
(S🔳) ✕ 🔄 🄺 🅱 🔁

▽▽▽▽ Motel 6 East #183 🆂🅷
(210) 333-1850. **$35-$48.** 138 N W W White Rd. I-10, exit 580 (W W White Rd), just off westbound access road. Ext corridors. **Pets:** Accepted.
(S🔳) ✕ 🔁

▽▽▽▽ Motel 6 Fort Sam Houston 🅼
(210) 661-8791. **$35-$50.** 5522 N PanAm Expwy. I-35/410, exit 164 (Rittiman Rd), just s of Rittiman Rd on northbound access lane, just off Goldfield St. Ext corridors. **Pets:** Accepted.
(ASK) (S🔳) ✕ 🄺 🔁

▽▽▽▽ Motel 6 Northeast #1188 🅼
(210) 653-8088. **$35-$55.** 4621 E Rittiman Rd. I-35/410, exit 164 (Rittiman Rd), on north side. Ext corridors. **Pets:** Small, other species. No service, supervision.
(S🔳) ✕ 🄺

▽▽▽▽ Motel 6 Northwest #1123 🅼
(210) 593-0013. **$45-$59.** 9400 Wursbach Rd. I-10, exit Wurzbach Rd, 1 blk s. Ext corridors. **Pets:** Accepted.
(S🔳) ✕ 🔁

▽▽▽▽ Pear Tree Inn San Antonio Airport 🆂🅷
(210) 366-9300. **$78-$94.** 143 NE Loop 410. Loop 410 W, exit 21 (Jones Maltsberger Rd), on westbound access road, between San Pedro Ave and Jones Maltsberger Rd. Int corridors. **Pets:** Large, other species. Service with restrictions, supervision.
(ASK) ✕ 🅱 🔲 🔁

△△△ ▽▽▽▽ ▽▽▽▽ Plaza San Antonio, A Marriott Hotel 🅻🅷
(210) 229-1000. **$169-$279.** 555 S Alamo St. Opposite convention center and Hemisfair Plaza. Int corridors. **Pets:** Accepted.
(SAVE) ✕ 🄼 🔄 🔲 🍴 🔁 🚫

▽▽▽▽ Quality Inn & Suites 🆂🅷
(210) 359-7200. **$55-$95.** 222 S W W White Rd. I-10, exit 580 (W W White Rd), 0.4 mi s. Ext corridors. **Pets:** Accepted.
(ASK) (S🔳) ✕ ♿ 🅱 🔲 🔁

△△△ ▽▽▽▽ Quality Inn & Suites Coliseum 🆂🅷
(210) 224-3030. **$59.** 3817 I-35 N. I-35, exit 161 (Binz-Engleman Rd), follow signs to I-35 S access road northbound, exit Binz-Engleman Rd, continue straight southbound. Int corridors. **Pets:** Accepted.
(SAVE) (S🔳) ✕ 🅱 🔲 🔁

△△△ ▽▽▽▽ Red Roof Inn Lackland 🆂🅷 🐾
(210) 675-4120. **$46-$66.** 6861 Hwy 90 W. Ne jct of US 90 and Military Dr W; access via Renwick St, off Military Dr, just n of jct US 90. Ext corridors. **Pets:** Other species. Service with restrictions, supervision.
(SAVE) (S🔳) ✕ 🅱 🔁

△△△ ▽▽▽▽ Red Roof Inn-San Antonio Airport 🅼
(210) 340-4055. **$44-$61.** 333 Wolfe Rd. On southbound access road, just s of US 281 at Isom Rd. Ext/int corridors. **Pets:** Medium. Service with restrictions, crate.
(SAVE) ✕ 🄼 🔄 🅱

△△△ ▽▽▽▽ Red Roof Inn San Antonio (Downtown) 🅼
(210) 229-9973. **$54-$94.** 1011 E Houston St. I-37, exit 141 northbound; exit 141B southbound. Int corridors. **Pets:** Accepted.
(SAVE) ✕ 🅱 🔁

Red Roof Inn San Antonio (NW-SeaWorld) SH
(210) 509-3434. **$43-$78.** 6880 NW Loop 410. I-410, exit 10B (Alamo Downs Pkwy), on eastbound access road. Ext/int corridors. **Pets:** Accepted.
SAVE ⊠ 🔥ᴹ 🐾 ⊇

Residence Inn Alamo Plaza SH
(210) 212-5555. **$169-$236.** 425 Bonham St. I-37/281, exit Commerce St, just w to Bowie St, 4 blks n. Int corridors. **Pets:** Small, other species. $10 daily fee/pet. No service, supervision.
ASK ⊠ 🖥 🖵 ⊇

Residence Inn by Marriott SH
(210) 231-6000. **$149-$299.** 628 S Santa Rosa. I-10/35, exit Durango St, 0.5 mi e. Int corridors. **Pets:** $20 one-time fee/room. Service with restrictions, crate.
ASK 🔥 ⊠ 🔥ᴹ 🖥 🖵 ⊇ ⊠

Residence Inn NW/Six Flags SH
(210) 561-9660. **$109-$199.** 4041 Bluemel Rd. I-10, exit Wurzbach Rd, 0.3 mi w on eastbound access road. Ext corridors. **Pets:** Medium. $100 one-time fee/room. Service with restrictions, supervision.
ASK 🔥 ⊠ 🖵 ⊇ ⊠

Residence Inn San Antonio-Airport SH
(210) 805-8118. **$134-$229.** 1014 NE Loop 410. On Loop 410, exit Broadway St, 0.4 mi e on access road. Ext corridors. **Pets:** Accepted.
ASK 🔥 ⊠ 🔥ᴹ 🖵 ⊇ ⊠

Rodeway Inn-Six Flags Fiesta SH
(210) 698-3991. **$39-$109.** 19793 I-10 W. I-10, exit 554 (Camp Bullis), on eastbound access road. Ext corridors. **Pets:** Accepted.
SAVE 🔥 ⊠ 🖥 🖵 ⊇

Sleep Inn San Antonio SH
(210) 344-5400. **$55-$95.** 8318 I-10 W. I-10, exit 561 (Callaghan Rd), on eastbound access road. Int corridors. **Pets:** Accepted.
SAVE 🔥 ⊠ 🔥ᴹ 🖵 ⊇

Staybridge Suites by Holiday Inn San Antonio NW-Colonnade SH
(210) 558-9009. **$96-$208.** 4320 Spectrum One. I-10 W, exit 560 (Wurzbach Rd), follow westbound access road through light, then just n. Int corridors. **Pets:** $75 one-time fee/room. Service with restrictions, crate.
ASK 🔥 ⊠ 🔥ᴹ 🖥 🖵 ⊇ ⊠

Staybridge Suites San Antonio-Airport SH
(210) 341-3220. **$148-$178.** 66 NE Loop 410. I-410, exit 20B (McCullough St), on eastbound access lane. Int corridors. **Pets:** Accepted.
ASK ⊠ 🔥ᴹ 🖥 🖵 ⊇

Studio 6 #6046 M
(210) 691-0121. **$49-$74.** 11802 I-10 W. I-10, exit 558 (De Zavala), on eastbound access road. Ext corridors. **Pets:** Accepted.
⊠ 🔥 🖵

Studio 6 #6047 M
(210) 349-3100. **$49-$74.** 7719 Louis Pasteur Ct. Loop 410, 1.5 mi nw on Fredericksburg Rd to Louis Pasteur Ct. Ext corridors. **Pets:** Accepted.
⊠ 🔥 🖵

Super 8 Motel Downtown North M
(210) 227-8888. **$48-$88.** 3617 N PanAm Expwy. I-35, exit 160 (Splashtown), on southbound access road. Ext corridors. **Pets:** Small. $50 deposit/pet, $8 daily fee/pet. Designated rooms, no service, supervision.
ASK 🔥 ⊠ 🔥ᴹ 🖥 ⊇

Super 8 Motel of San Antonio Airport SH
(210) 637-1033. **$35-$75.** 11027 I-35 N. I-35, exit 168 (Weidner Rd), on southbound access road. Int corridors. **Pets:** Large, other species. $50 deposit/room. Designated rooms, service with restrictions, supervision.
ASK 🔥 ⊠ ⊇

Super 8 Motel-Six Flags Fiesta SH
(210) 696-6916. **$55-$75.** 5319 Casa Bella. I-10, exit 557 westbound; exit 558 eastbound, on westbound access road. Int corridors. **Pets:** Small. $5 daily fee/pet. Service with restrictions, supervision.
ASK 🔥 ⊠ 🔥 🖥 ⊇

Wellesley Inn (San Antonio/Airport) SH
(210) 653-9110. **$65-$95.** 2635 NE Loop 410. I-410, exit 25B (Perrin-Beitel Rd), on westbound access lane. Ext/int corridors. **Pets:** Accepted.
SAVE 🔥 ⊠ 🖥 🖵 ⊇

Westin Riverwalk Hotel LH 🌸
(210) 224-6500. **$329-$419.** 420 W Market St. 2 blks w of Navarro St. Int corridors. **Pets:** Medium, dogs only. Designated rooms, service with restrictions, supervision.
ASK 🔥 ⊠ 🔥ᴹ 🎧 🔥 🖥 🖵 🍴 ⊇ ⊠

Woodfield Suites San Antonio-Downtown SH
(210) 212-5400. **$99-$149.** 100 W Durango Blvd. I-35, exit 155B (Durango Blvd), 3 blks e of jct E Flores St. Int corridors. **Pets:** Accepted.
ASK 🔥 ⊠ 🔥ᴹ 🎧 🔥 🖥 🖵 ⊇ ⊠

SEGUIN

Best Western of Seguin SH
(830) 379-9631. **$65-$99.** 1603 I-10 & Hwy 46. I-10, exit 607 (SR 46). Ext corridors. **Pets:** Accepted.
SAVE 🔥 ⊠ 🖥 🖵 ⊇

Holiday Inn Seguin SH
(830) 372-0860. **$94-$116.** 2950 N 123 Bypass. I-10, exit 610 (SR 123). Ext corridors. **Pets:** Small. $25 one-time fee/room. Service with restrictions, supervision.
ASK 🔥 ⊠ 🎧 🔥 🖥 🖵 🍴 ⊇

▼▼ Super 8 Motel of Seguin SH
(830) 379-6888. **$49-$120.** 1525 N Hwy 46. I-10, exit 607
(SR 46). Int corridors. **Pets:** Accepted.
[ASK] [S☼] [✕] [♿] [🛏] [💻]

UNIVERSAL CITY

▲▲▲ ▼▼ Clarion Suites Hotel SH
(210) 655-9491. **$79-$159.** 13101 E Loop, 1604 N. Loop
1604 at Pat Booker Rd; 0.8 mi e of I-35. Ext corridors.
Pets: Medium. $25 one-time fee/room. Designated rooms,
service with restrictions, crate.
[SAVE] [S☼] [✕] [♿] [💻] [⤳]

❀ END METROPOLITAN AREA ❀

SANDERSON

▼ Budget Inn M
(432) 345-2541. **$38-$48, 3 day notice.** Hwy 90 E. Just e of
center. Ext corridors. **Pets:** Accepted.
[ASK] [S☼] [✕] [🛏]

▲▲▲ ▼ Desert Air Motel M
(432) 345-2572. **$34-$39.** 806 W Oak. 0.5 mi w on US 90,
just e of jct US 285. Ext corridors. **Pets:** Accepted.
[SAVE] [S☼] [🛏]

SAN MARCOS

▲▲▲ ▼▼ Best Western San Marcos SH
(512) 754-7557. **$59-$99.** 917 I-35 N. I-35, exit 204B, on
westside access road. Int corridors. **Pets:** Small. $10 daily
fee/pet. Service with restrictions, supervision.
[SAVE] [S☼] [✕] [🛏] [💻] [⤳]

▼▼ Days Inn SH
(512) 353-5050. **$35-$125.** 1005 I-35 N. I-35, exit 205 northbound; exit 204B southbound; on southbound frontage
road, jct SR 80. Ext corridors. **Pets:** Accepted.
[ASK] [✕] [🛏] [⤳]

▲▲▲ ▼▼▼ La Quinta Inn-San Marcos SH
(512) 392-8800. **$66-$105.** 1619 I-35 N. I-35, exit 206. Ext/int
corridors. **Pets:** Accepted.
[SAVE] [S☼] [✕] [☾M] [🔌] [♿] [🛏] [💻] [⤳]

▲▲▲ ▼▼ Ramada Limited SH
(512) 395-8000. **$34-$139.** 1701 I-35 N. I-35, exit 206 (Aqua-
rina Spring). Ext corridors. **Pets:** Very small. $10 daily fee/
pet. Service with restrictions, supervision.
[SAVE] [S☼] [✕] [🛏] [💻] [⤳]

▲▲▲ ▼▼ Red Roof Inn SH
(512) 754-8899. **$44-$130.** 817 I-35 N. I-35, exit 204B southbound; exit 205 northbound on westside access road. Int
corridors. **Pets:** Large. $25 deposit/room. Service with
restrictions, supervision.
[SAVE] [S☼] [✕] [♿] [🛏] [⤳]

SEMINOLE

▲▲▲ ▼▼ Raymond Motor Inn M
(432) 758-3653. **$40-$45.** 301 W Ave A. 0.3 mi w on US 62
and 180. Ext corridors. **Pets:** Other species. $5 one-time
fee/pet. Service with restrictions, supervision.
[SAVE] [S☼] [✕] [🛏]

SHAFTER

▼▼▼ Cibolo Creek Ranch RA
(432) 229-3737. **Call for rates.** US Hwy 67 N. On US 67, 6
mi n; 33 mi s from Marfa. Ext corridors. **Pets:** Accepted.
[✕] [♿] [💻] [🍴] [⤳] [☒] [W] [☑]

SHAMROCK

▼ Budget Host-Blarney Inn M
(806) 256-2101. **$35-$45.** 402 E 12th St, Rt 66. I-40, exit 164
westbound; exit 161 or 163 eastbound, just e of US 83. Ext
corridors. **Pets:** Accepted.
[ASK] [S☼] [✕] [🛏]

▲▲▲ ▼ Econo Lodge M
(806) 256-2111. **$48-$70.** 1006 E 12th St. I-40, exit 164
westbound; exit 161 or 163 eastbound, just e of US 83. Ext
corridors. **Pets:** Small. $5 daily fee/pet. Service with restric-
tions, supervision.
[SAVE] [S☼] [✕] [🛏] [💻] [⤳]

▲▲▲ ▼▼▼ Irish Inn SH
(806) 256-2106. **$49-$58.** 301 I-40 E. I-40, exit 163, 0.3 mi e
on north service road. Ext/int corridors. **Pets:** Medium, other
species. $9 one-time fee/room. Service with restrictions,
crate.
[SAVE] [S☼] [✕] [🔌] [🛏] [💻] [🍴] [⤳]

▲▲▲ ▼ The Western Motel M
(806) 256-3244. **$39-$59.** 104 E 12th St. Business Rt I-40
and US 83. Ext corridors. **Pets:** Medium. $5 daily fee/pet.
Service with restrictions, supervision.
[SAVE] [S☼] [✕] [🍴]

SHERMAN

▼▼▼ Comfort Suites of Sherman SH
(903) 893-0499. **$89-$129.** 2900 US Hwy 75 N. US 75, exit
63, 0.3 mi s of jct US 82. Int corridors. **Pets:** Accepted.
[ASK] [S☼] [✕] [♿] [🛏] [💻] [⤳]

▼▼▼ La Quinta Inn & Suites Sherman SH
(903) 870-1122. **$90-$110.** 2912 US 75 N. US 75, exit 63, jct
US 82, just sw. Int corridors. **Pets:** Accepted.
[ASK] [S☼] [✕] [♿] [🛏] [💻] [⤳]

SNYDER

▲▲▲ ▼▼ Best Western Snyder Inn M
(325) 574-2200. **$70-$80.** 810 E Coliseum Dr. 1.5 mi w of
US 84/80. Ext corridors. **Pets:** Medium. $25 one-time fee/
room. Service with restrictions, crate.
[SAVE] [S☼] [✕] [🛏] [💻] [⤳]

AAA WWWW Purple Sage Motel M ❀
(325) 573-5491. **$52-$70.** 1501 E Coliseum. 1 mi w on US 180 from jct US 84. Ext corridors. **Pets:** Other species. Service with restrictions, crate.
[SAVE] [So] [X] [🔋] [💻] [🏊]

SONORA

AAA WWW Best Value Inn-Twin Oaks Motel M
(325) 387-2551. **$45-$50.** 907 N Crockett Ave. I-10, exit 400 westbound; exit 399 eastbound, 0.5 mi e, then 0.3 mi s on US 277. Ext corridors. **Pets:** Accepted.
[SAVE] [So] [X] [🔋]

WWWW Best Western Sonora Inn SH
(325) 387-9111. **$68-$90.** 270 Hwy 277 N. I-10, exit 400. Ext corridors. **Pets:** Accepted.
[X] [🐾] [🔋] [💻] [🏊]

AAA WWW Days Inn M ❀
(325) 387-3516. **$59-$69.** 1312 N Service Rd. I-10, exit 400, just n. Ext corridors. **Pets:** Other species. $4 daily fee/room. Service with restrictions.
[SAVE] [So] [X] [🔋] [💻] [🍴] [🏊]

AAA WWW Holiday Host Motel M
(325) 387-2532. **$40-$50.** 127 Loop 467 (Hwy 290). Loop 467, exit 404 westbound, 3 mi w; exit 399 eastbound, 3 mi e. Ext corridors. **Pets:** No service, supervision.
[SAVE] [So] [X] [🔋] [🏊]

SOUTH PADRE ISLAND

AAA WWWW Best Western Fiesta Isles Hotel SH
(956) 761-4913. **$39-$249.** 5701 Padre Blvd. 3 mi n of Queen Isabella Cswy. Ext corridors. **Pets:** Accepted.
[SAVE] [So] [X] [🔋] [💻] [🏊]

WWW Days Inn SH
(956) 761-7831. **$59-$250, 15 day notice.** 3913 Padre Blvd. 2.6 mi n of Queen Isabella Cswy. Ext corridors. **Pets:** Other species. $25 one-time fee/room. Crate.
[ASK] [So] [X] [🔋] [💻]

AAA WWWW Econo Lodge SH
(956) 761-8500. **$29-$299, 14 day notice.** 3813 Padre Blvd. 2.6 mi n of Queen Isabella Cswy. Int corridors. **Pets:** Accepted.
[SAVE] [So] [X] [🔋] [🏊]

AAA WWWW Ramada Limited SH
(956) 761-4097. **$49-$299.** 4109 Padre Blvd. 2 mi n from Queen Isabella Cswy. Ext corridors. **Pets:** Small, dogs only. Designated rooms, service with restrictions, supervision.
[SAVE] [So] [X] [🔋] [💻] [🏊]

WWW Super 8 Motel SH
(956) 761-6300. **$40-$340.** 4205 Padre Blvd. 2.7 mi n of Queen Isabella Cswy. Ext corridors. **Pets:** Very small. $10 daily fee/pet. Designated rooms, service with restrictions, supervision.
[ASK] [So] [X] [🔋🅜] [🐾] [🔋] [🏊]

WWW The Tiki Condominium Hotel CO
(956) 761-2694. **$79-$155.** 6608 Padre Blvd. 3.8 mi n of Queen Isabella Cswy. Ext corridors. **Pets:** Small. $2 daily fee/pet, $35 one-time fee/pet. Designated rooms, service with restrictions, supervision.
[ASK] [So] [X] [🔋] [💻] [🏊] [X]

STEPHENVILLE

WWW Days Inn SH
(254) 968-3392. **$55-$69.** 701 E South Loop. On US 377, just s of jct US 281. Ext corridors. **Pets:** Accepted.
[ASK] [So] [X] [🔋] [💻] [🏊]

WWWW Holiday Inn Stephenville SH
(254) 968-5256. **$89-$99.** 2865 W Washington St. 1.5 mi s on US 377/167. Ext corridors. **Pets:** Accepted.
[ASK] [So] [X] [🐾] [🔋] [💻] [🍴] [🏊]

SULPHUR SPRINGS

WWWW Best Western Trail Dust Inn SH
(903) 885-7515. **$74-$109.** 1521 Shannon Rd. Jct I-30 and Loop 301, exit 127. Ext/int corridors. **Pets:** Accepted.
[ASK] [So] [X] [🔋] [💻] [🏊]

AAA WWWW Comfort Suites SH
(903) 438-0918. **$74-$99.** 1521 E Industrial. I-30, exit 127, just n. Int corridors. **Pets:** Accepted.
[SAVE] [So] [X] [🔋🅜] [🐾] [🔋] [💻] [🏊]

WWWW Holiday Inn SH
(903) 885-0562. **$79-$99.** 1495 E Industrial Dr. I-30, exit 127. Ext/int corridors. **Pets:** Accepted.
[ASK] [So] [X] [🔋] [💻] [🍴] [🏊]

SWEETWATER

AAA WWWW Comfort Inn SH
(325) 235-5234. **$59-$125.** 216 SE Georgia Ave. I-20, exit 244. Ext corridors. **Pets:** Small. $50 deposit/room. Service with restrictions, supervision.
[SAVE] [So] [X] [🐾] [🔋🅜] [🔋] [💻] [🏊]

AAA WWWW Holiday Inn SH
(325) 236-6887. **$79-$119.** 500 NW Georgia St. I-20, exit 244, just w of jct SR 70 on north access road. Ext/int corridors. **Pets:** Other species. $25 one-time fee/room. Service with restrictions, crate.
[SAVE] [So] [X] [🔋] [💻] [🍴] [🏊]

AAA WWWW Ranch House Motel & Restaurant SH
(325) 236-6341. **$49-$65.** 301 SW Georgia Ave. I-20, exit 244, just w of jct SR 70 on south access road. Ext/int corridors. **Pets:** Medium, other species. Designated rooms, service with restrictions, crate.
[SAVE] [So] [X] [🔋] [💻] [🍴] [🏊]

TEMPLE

WWW Days Inn SH
(254) 774-9223. **$69-$79.** 1104 N General Bruce Dr. I-35, exit 302 (Nugent Ave). Ext corridors. **Pets:** Small. $7 daily fee/pet. Designated rooms, service with restrictions, crate.
[ASK] [So] [X] [🐾] [🔋] [💻] [🏊]

♦♦ **Howard Johnson Express Inn & Suites** [SH]
(254) 778-5521. **$64.** 1912 S 31st St. 0.4 mi ne of jct Loop 363, US 190 and SR 36. Ext corridors. **Pets:** Accepted.
[ASK] [SD] ☒ ▣ ☕

[AAA] ♦♦♦ **La Quinta Inn-Temple** [SH] 🐾
(254) 771-2980. **$67-$82.** 1604 W Barton Ave. SR 53, just e, jct I-35 and US 81, exit 301. Ext/int corridors. **Pets:** Other species. Service with restrictions, supervision.
[SAVE] [SD] ☒ ▣ ☕ 🏊

♦ **Motel 6–257** [SH]
(254) 778-0272. **$35-$48.** 1100 N General Bruce Dr. I-35, exit 302 (Nugent Ave), just s on access road, follow signs. Ext corridors. **Pets:** Accepted.
[SD] ☒ 🏊

[AAA] ♦♦ **Super 8 Motel** [SH]
(254) 778-0962. **$50-$60, 7 day notice.** 5505 S General Bruce Dr. I-35, exit 297 (Midway Dr). Ext corridors. **Pets:** Very small, dogs only. $5 one-time fee/pet. Designated rooms, service with restrictions, supervision.
[SAVE] [SD] ☒ ▣ ☕ 🏊

TERLINGUA

[AAA] ♦♦ **Big Bend Motor Inn** [M]
(432) 371-2218. **$75-$87, 7 day notice.** 300 N Jim Wright Frwy. SR 118, 2 mi from entrance of Big Bend National Park. Ext corridors. **Pets:** Accepted.
[SAVE] ☒ ▣ ☕

TEXARKANA

[AAA] ♦♦ **Ameri-Star Inn & Suites** [SH]
(903) 792-6688. **$50-$90.** 5105 State Line Ave. I-30, exit 223A, just sw. Ext corridors. **Pets:** Accepted.
[SAVE] [SD] ☒ ▣ ☕ 🏊

[AAA] ♦♦ **Best Western Northgate Motor Lodge** [SH]
(903) 793-6565. **$58-$69.** 400 W 53rd St. I-30, exit 223B, on northwest frontage road. Int corridors. **Pets:** Accepted.
[SAVE] [SD] ☒ ▣ ☕ 🏊

[AAA] ♦♦♦ **Four Points Hotel Sheraton Texarkana** [SH]
(903) 792-3222. **$75-$105.** 5301 N State Line Ave. I-30, exit 223B. Int corridors. **Pets:** Small, dogs only. $50 one-time fee/room. Designated rooms, service with restrictions, supervision.
[SAVE] [SD] ☒ ♿M ▣ ☕ 🍴 🏊

[AAA] ♦♦♦ **Holiday Inn Express** [SH]
(903) 792-3366. **$71-$79, 14 day notice.** 5401 N State Line Ave. I-30, exit 223B, 0.3 mi n on US 71. Int corridors. **Pets:** Accepted.
[SAVE] ☒ ▣ ☕ 🏊

[AAA] ♦♦♦ **La Quinta Inn-Texarkana** [SH]
(903) 794-1900. **$71-$81.** 5201 State Line Ave. I-30, exit 223A, sw of jct US 59 and 71. Ext corridors. **Pets:** Accepted.
[SAVE] [SD] ☒ ▣ ☕ 🏊

♦ **Motel 6–201** [SH]
(903) 793-1413. **$39-$50.** 1924 Hampton Rd. I-30, exit 222 (Summerhill Rd). Ext corridors. **Pets:** Other species. Service with restrictions, supervision.
[SD] ☒ 🏊

TEXAS CITY

♦♦♦ **La Quinta Inn** [SH]
(409) 948-3101. **$70-$85.** 1121 Hwy 146 N. Jct SR 146 S and FM 1764, 5 mi se of I-45, exit 16 southbound; exit 15 northbound. Ext corridors. **Pets:** Accepted.
[ASK] [SD] ☒ 👂 ▣ ☕ 🏊

THREE RIVERS

♦♦ **Bass Inn** [M]
(361) 786-3521. **$35-$45.** Hwy 72 W. SR 72, 7.5 mi w of jct US 281. Ext corridors. **Pets:** Accepted.
[ASK] [SD] ☒ ▣ ☕ 🏊

TULIA

♦♦ **Select Inn of Tulia** [M]
(806) 995-3248. **$54-$64.** Rt 1, Box 60. I-27, exit 74. Ext corridors. **Pets:** Accepted.
[ASK] ☒ ♿M ▣ ☕

TYLER

[AAA] ♦♦ **Best Western Inn & Suites** [SH]
(903) 595-2681. **$65-$99.** 2828 W NW Loop 323. Jct US 69 N and Loop 323. Ext corridors. **Pets:** Medium. $10 daily fee/pet. Service with restrictions, supervision.
[SAVE] [SD] ☒ ▣ ☕ 🏊

♦♦♦ **Holiday Inn Select** [SH]
(903) 561-5800. **$139.** 5701 S Broadway. 1.1 mi s of jct Loop 323 and US 69 (S Broadway). Int corridors. **Pets:** Small. $50 one-time fee/pet. Service with restrictions, supervision.
[ASK] [SD] ☒ 👂 ♿ ▣ ☕ 🍴 🏊 ✂

[AAA] ♦♦♦ **La Quinta Inn** [SH]
(903) 561-2223. **$75-$95.** 1601 W SW Loop 323. 1 mi w of S US 69. Ext corridors. **Pets:** Accepted.
[SAVE] ☒ 👂 ☕ 🏊

♦♦♦ **Radisson Hotel Tyler** [SH]
(903) 597-1301. **$79-$99.** 2843 W NW Loop 323. Just w of jct US 69. Int corridors. **Pets:** Accepted.
[ASK] [SD] ☒ ♿M ▣ ☕ 🍴 🏊

♦♦ **Ramada Tyler Conference Center** [SH]
(903) 593-3600. **$109.** 3310 Troup Hwy. 3.5 mi se on SR 110, 0.3 mi n of jct E Loop 323. Ext corridors. **Pets:** Other species. $20 one-time fee/room. Service with restrictions.
[ASK] [SD] ☒ ♿ ▣ ☕ 🍴 🏊

♦♦♦ **Residence Inn by Marriott** [SH]
(903) 595-5188. **$76.** 3303 Troup Hwy. 3.5 mi se on SR 110, 0.3 mi n of jct E Loop 323. Ext corridors. **Pets:** $50 one-time fee/room. Service with restrictions, supervision.
[ASK] ☒ ♿ ▣ ☕ 🏊 ✂

UVALDE

Inn of Uvalde SH
(830) 278-4511. **$88-$93.** 920 E Main St. 0.5 mi e on US 90. Ext corridors. **Pets:** Large. Service with restrictions, supervision.

VAN HORN

Best Western American Inn M
(432) 283-2030. **$55-$95.** 1309 W Broadway. I-10, exit 138, 1 mi e. Ext corridors. **Pets:** Accepted.

Best Western Inn of Van Horn M
(432) 283-2410. **$55-$85.** 1705 W Broadway. I-10, exit 138, 0.3 mi e, 1 mi w on US 80. Ext corridors. **Pets:** Other species. $6 one-time fee/room. Designated rooms, service with restrictions, supervision.

Budget Inn M
(432) 283-2019. **$30-$45.** 1303 W Broadway. I-10, exit 138, 0.7 mi e. Ext corridors. **Pets:** Small. $3 daily fee/pet, $3 one-time fee/pet. Designated rooms, service with restrictions, supervision.

Days Inn M
(432) 283-1007. **$57-$62, 15 day notice.** 600 E Broadway St. I-10, exit 140B, just w. Ext corridors. **Pets:** Medium. $6 daily fee/pet. Designated rooms, no service, supervision.

Economy Inn M
(432) 283-2754. **$32-$55.** 1500 W Broadway St. I-10, exit 138, 0.5 mi e on US 80. Ext corridors. **Pets:** Medium. $5 one-time fee/room. No service, crate.

Holiday Inn Express SH
(432) 283-7444. **$69-$99.** 1905 SW Frontage Rd. I-10, exit 138 (Golf Course Dr). Ext corridors. **Pets:** Small, other species. Service with restrictions, supervision.

Motel 6-4024 M
(432) 283-2992. **$51-$55.** 1805 W Broadway St. I-10, exit 138. Ext corridors. **Pets:** Other species. Service with restrictions, supervision.

Ramada Limited SH
(432) 283-2780. **$68-$78.** 200 Golf Course Dr. I-10, exit 138 (Golf Course Dr). Ext/int corridors. **Pets:** Other species. $6 daily fee/pet. Service with restrictions, supervision.

Van Horn Super 8 M
(432) 283-2282. **$57-$62, 15 day notice.** 1807 E Service Rd. I-10, exit 138 (Golf Course Dr). Ext corridors. **Pets:** Medium. $6 daily fee/pet. Designated rooms, no service, supervision.

VEGA

Best Western Country Inn M ✿
(806) 267-2131. **$69-$79.** 1800 W Vega Blvd. 0.5 mi w on US 40 business loop. Ext corridors. **Pets:** Large. Service with restrictions, supervision.

VERNON

Best Western Village Inn M
(940) 552-5417. **$59-$69.** 1615 Expwy. US 287, exit Main St, just w. Ext/int corridors. **Pets:** Very small, other species. $5 one-time fee/pet. Service with restrictions, supervision.

VICTORIA

Comfort Inn SH
(361) 574-9393. **$75-$85, 30 day notice.** 1906 Houston Hwy. 3.5 mi ne on US 59. Ext corridors. **Pets:** Small, dogs only. $25 deposit/room, $5 daily fee/pet. Service with restrictions, supervision.

Holiday Inn Holidome SH
(361) 575-0251. **$90-$140.** 2705 E Houston Hwy (Business Rt 59). On Business Rt US 59, 2.5 mi ne. Ext/int corridors. **Pets:** Small. $125 deposit/room. Designated rooms, service with restrictions, supervision.

La Quinta Inn-Victoria M
(361) 572-3585. **$71-$91.** 7603 N Navarro St (US 77 N). 4 mi n on US 77 at Loop 463. Ext corridors. **Pets:** Accepted.

WACO

Best Western Old Main Lodge SH
(254) 753-0316. **$89-$99.** I-35 & 4th St. I-35 and US 81, exit 335A (4th-5th sts). Ext corridors. **Pets:** Small. Service with restrictions, supervision.

Best Western Waco Mall SH
(254) 776-3194. **Call for rates.** 6624 Hwy 84 W. On US 84, 0.3 mi w of jct SR 6 and Loop 340. Ext corridors. **Pets:** Small. $10 one-time fee/pet. Service with restrictions, supervision.

Days Inn SH
(254) 799-8585. **$79-$89.** 1504 I-35. I-35, exit 338B (Behrens Cir), just n. Ext corridors. **Pets:** Accepted.

Hawthorn Suites SH
(254) 799-9989. **$85-$110.** 1508 I-35 N. I-35, exit 338B southbound; exit 339 northbound, on southbound access road. Int corridors. **Pets:** $10 daily fee/pet. Service with restrictions, crate.

Holiday Inn-Waco I-35 SH
(254) 753-0261. **$100.** 1001 Martin Luther King Blvd. I-35, exit 335C (Lake Brazos Dr), just n. Int corridors. **Pets:** Accepted.

▼▼▼▼ La Quinta Inn-Waco SH
(254) 752-9741. **$76-$91.** 1110 S 9th St. I-35, exit 334 (17th St) southbound; exit 334A (18th St) northbound. Ext corridors. **Pets:** Small. Service with restrictions.
ASK SÓ ⊠ 🖉 🖪 💻 ➡

▼▼▼▼ Residence Inn-Waco SH
(254) 714-1386. **$120.** 501 S University Parks Dr. I-35, exit 335B, 0.3 mi w. Int corridors. **Pets:** Other species. $10 daily fee/pet, $150 one-time fee/room. Service with restrictions, crate.
ASK SÓ ⊠ 🖉 🖾 🖪 💻 ➡ ⊠

▼▼ Super 8 Motel-Waco SH ❀
(254) 754-1023. **$59-$79.** 1320 S Jack Kultgen Frwy. I-35, exit 334, just e. Int corridors. **Pets:** Large. $7 one-time fee/pet. Designated rooms, service with restrictions, supervision.
ASK SÓ ⊠

WEATHERFORD

▼▼ Best Western Santa Fe Inn SH
(817) 594-7401. **$69-$89.** 1927 Santa Fe Dr. I-20, exit 409 (Clear Lake Rd/FM 2552), 0.3 mi nw. Ext corridors. **Pets:** Accepted.
ASK SÓ ⊠ 🖪 💻 🍴 ➡

⒜ ▼▼▼ Hampton Inn SH
(817) 599-4800. **$80-$150.** 2524 S Main St. I-20, exit 408. Int corridors. **Pets:** Medium. $10 daily fee/pet. No service, supervision.
SAVE SÓ ⊠ 🖉 🖾 🖪 💻 ➡

⒜ ▼▼▼ Holiday Inn Express & Suites SH
(817) 599-3700. **$80-$160.** 2500 S Main St. I-20, exit 408. Ext corridors. **Pets:** Medium. $10 daily fee/pet. No service, supervision.
SAVE SÓ ⊠ 🖉 🖪 💻 ➡

▼▼▼ Weatherford Comfort Suites SH
(817) 599-3300. **$85-$159, 3 day notice.** 210 Alford Dr. I-20, exit 408, just s on SR 171, just w. Int corridors. **Pets:** Accepted.
ASK SÓ ⊠ 🖾 🖾 🖪 💻 ➡

WELLINGTON

▼ Cherokee Inn & Restaurant M
(806) 447-2508. **$34-$48.** 1105 Houston. US 83, just n of jct FM 338. Ext corridors. **Pets:** Accepted.
ASK SÓ ⊠ 🍴

WESLACO

⒜ ▼▼▼ Best Western Palm Aire Motor Inn & Suites SH
(956) 969-2411. **$54-$111.** 415 S International Blvd. US 83, exit International Blvd. Ext corridors. **Pets:** Small. Service with restrictions, supervision.
SAVE SÓ ⊠ 🖉 🖪 💻 🍴 ➡ ⊠

⒜ ▼▼▼ Super 8 Motel SH
(956) 969-9920. **$50-$69.** 1702 E Expwy 83. US 83, exit Airport Dr. Ext corridors. **Pets:** $10 daily fee/pet. Designated rooms, service with restrictions.
SAVE SÓ ⊠ 🖪 ➡

WICHITA FALLS

⒜ ▼▼▼ Best Western Wichita Falls Inn SH
(940) 766-6881. **$55-$69.** 1032 Central Frwy. I-44, exit 2, just w. Ext corridors. **Pets:** Small, other species. $10 daily fee/room. Service with restrictions, supervision.
SAVE SÓ ⊠ 🖪 💻 ➡

▼▼▼ Comfort Inn & Suites SH
(940) 767-5653. **$64, 3 day notice.** 1740 Maurine St. US 287, exit Maurine St, just e. Ext/int corridors. **Pets:** $10 one-time fee/pet. Service with restrictions, crate.
ASK SÓ ⊠ 🖾 🖾 🖪 💻 ➡

▼▼▼ Hampton Inn SH
(940) 766-3300. **$59-$89, 7 day notice.** 1317 Kenley Ave. I-44, exit 2, just w. Int corridors. **Pets:** Medium. $30 one-time fee/room. Service with restrictions, crate.
ASK SÓ ⊠ 🖪 💻 ➡

▼▼▼ Hawthorn Suites Limited SH
(940) 692-7900. **$84-$149.** 1917 N Elmwood Ave. US 281 S, exit Southwest Pkwy (CR 319), 2.3 mi w to Kemp, 2 blks n to Elmwood Ave, then just e. Int corridors. **Pets:** Accepted.
⊠ 🖾 🖉 🖾 🖪 ➡

⒜ ▼▼▼ La Quinta Inn-Wichita Falls SH
(940) 322-6971. **$69-$79.** 1128 Central Frwy N. I-44, exit 2, just w. Ext corridors. **Pets:** Other species. Service with restrictions, crate.
SAVE SÓ ⊠ 🖉 🖪 💻 ➡

▼▼ Motel 6 #130 M
(940) 322-8817. **$41-$57.** 1812 Maurine St. I-44, exit 2, just e. Ext corridors. **Pets:** Service with restrictions, supervision.
⊠ 🖉 🖾 ➡

▼▼▼ Quality Inn and Suites M
(940) 322-2477. **$59-$69.** 1750 Maurine St. I-44, exit 2, just e. Int corridors. **Pets:** $10 one-time fee/pet. Service with restrictions, crate.
ASK SÓ ⊠ 🖾 🖾 🖪 💻 ➡

▼▼▼ Radisson Hotel LH
(940) 761-6000. **$89.** 100 Central Frwy. I-287, exit 1C, on west side access road. Int corridors. **Pets:** Accepted.
ASK SÓ ⊠ 🖪 💻 🍴 ➡

⒜ ▼▼▼ Ramada Limited M
(940) 855-0085. **$55.** 3209 Northwest Frwy. US 287, exit Beverly (CR 11), just w. Ext corridors. **Pets:** Accepted.
SAVE SÓ ⊠ 🖾 🖪 💻 ➡

⒜ ▼▼▼ Towne Crest Inn M
(940) 322-1182. **$41-$49.** 1601 8th St. US 287, exit Broad St/Business, w on 9th St, 1 blk n on Brook to 8th St, then just e. Ext corridors. **Pets:** Accepted.
SAVE SÓ ⊠ 🖪 💻

ZAPATA

⒜ ▼▼▼ Best Western Inn by the Lake SH
(956) 765-8403. **$72.** Hwy 83 S. On US 83, 0.5 mi se. Ext corridors. **Pets:** Medium. $5 daily fee/pet. Crate.
SAVE SÓ ⊠ 🖪 💻 ➡

UTAH

AMERICAN FORK

▼▼▼▼ Quality Inn & Suites Ⓜ
(801) 763-8383. **$64-$89.** 712 S Utah Valley Dr. I-15, exit 279. Int corridors. **Pets:** Small, other species. $25 deposit/pet. Service with restrictions, crate.
ⒶⓈⓀ 🛏 ✕ 🄴 🎁 💻 🏊

BEAVER

ⒶⒶⒶ ▼▼▼ Best Western Butch Cassidy Inn Ⓜ
(435) 438-2438. **$52-$105.** 161 S Main St. I-15, exit 109 or 112, just e. Ext corridors. **Pets:** Other species. $5 daily fee/pet. Service with restrictions, supervision.
Ⓢ🛏 ✕ 🄴 🎁 🏊 ✕

ⒶⒶⒶ ▼▼▼ Best Western Paradise Inn Ⓜ
(435) 438-2455. **$51-$79.** 1451 N 300 W. I-15, exit 112, just e; north end of town. Ext corridors. **Pets:** Crate.
Ⓢ 🛏 ✕ 💻 🍴 🏊

▼▼▼ Country Inn Ⓜ 🌸
(435) 438-2484. **$42-$55.** 1450 N 300 W. I-15, exit 112, 2 blks e. Ext corridors. **Pets:** Small. $20 deposit/pet. Supervision.
✕ 🎁

ⒶⒶⒶ ▼▼▼ DeLano Motel Ⓜ 🌸
(435) 438-2418. **$34-$42.** 480 N Main St. I-15, exit 109 or 112, just e; north end of town. Ext corridors. **Pets:** Medium, dogs only. $3 one-time fee/pet. Service with restrictions, supervision.
Ⓢ 🛏 ✕ 🎁

▼▼▼ Motel 6 Beaver Ⓜ
(435) 438-1666. **$42-$56.** 1345 N 450 W. I-15, exit 112, just se. Int corridors. **Pets:** Accepted.
ⒶⓈⓀ 🛏 ✕ 🄴 🎁 🏊

▼▼▼ Quality Inn Ⓜ
(435) 438-5426. **$55-$75.** 781 W 1800 S. I-15, exit 109, just w. Int corridors. **Pets:** Small. Designated rooms, service with restrictions, supervision.
ⒶⓈⓀ 🛏 ✕ 💻 🏊

▼▼ Sleepy Lagoon Motel Ⓜ
(435) 438-5681. **$40-$60.** 882 S Main St. I-15, exit 109 or 112, 0.5 mi n. Ext corridors. **Pets:** Other species. $5 one-time fee/room. No service, supervision.
ⒶⓈⓀ 🛏 ✕ 🎁 🏊

BICKNELL

ⒶⒶ ▼▼▼ Aquarius Motel and Restaurant Ⓜ
(435) 425-3835. **$39-$43.** 240 W Main St. SR 24, 9 mi w of Capitol Reef National Park; downtown. Ext/int corridors. **Pets:** Large, other species. $5 daily fee/pet. Service with restrictions, crate.
Ⓢ 🛏 ✕ 🎁 💻 🍴 🏊

BLANDING

ⒶⒶ ▼▼▼ Best Western Gateway Inn Ⓜ
(435) 678-2278. **$43-$89.** 88 E Center St. East side on US 191. Ext corridors. **Pets:** Accepted.
Ⓢ 🛏 ✕ 💻 🏊

ⒶⒶ ▼▼▼ Four Corners Inn Ⓜ
(435) 678-3257. **$52-$66.** 131 E Center St. On US 191. Ext corridors. **Pets:** Accepted.
Ⓢ 🛏 ✕ 🎁

BLUFF

ⒶⒶ ▼ Kokopelli Inn Ⓜ
(435) 672-2322. **$38-$48.** 161 E Main St. On US 191. Int corridors. **Pets:** Medium. $10 daily fee/pet. Service with restrictions, supervision.
Ⓢ 🛏 ✕

ⒶⒶ ▼▼▼ Recapture Lodge Ⓜ 🌸
(435) 672-2281. **$38-$56.** 220 E Main St. On US 191. Ext corridors. **Pets:** Other species. Service with restrictions, supervision.
Ⓢ 🛏 ✕ 🌀 🎁 💻 🏊 ✕ 🄯

BOULDER

▼▼▼ Boulder Mountain Lodge Ⓜ 🌸
(435) 335-7460. **$75-$186, 15 day notice.** 20 N Hwy 12. Jct SR 12 and Burr Tr. Ext/int corridors. **Pets:** Dogs only. $8.50 daily fee/pet. Designated rooms, service with restrictions, supervision.
✕ 🎁 💻 🍴 ✕

BRIGHAM CITY

(AAA) ▼▼▼ Howard Johnson Inn M
(435) 723-8511. **$51-$70.** 1167 S Main St. I-15 and 84, exit 364 (Logan and Brigham City), 2 mi e on US 89 and 91. Ext corridors. **Pets:** Accepted.
SAVE Sᴅ ✕ ⁊ ⛭ ▣ ⩏

BRYCE

(AAA) ▼▼▼▼ Best Western Ruby's Inn SH
(435) 834-5341. **$49-$115.** UT Hwy 63. SR 63, 1 mi s of SR 12, 1 mi n of Bryce Canyon National Park entrance. Ext/int corridors. **Pets:** $100 deposit/room. Service with restrictions, supervision.
SAVE Sᴅ ✕ ⓶ᴍ ⁊ ⁊ ⛭ ▣ ⑪ ⩏ ⊠

▼▼▼ Bryce Canyon Resort M
(435) 834-5351. **$39-$120.** 13500 E Hwy 12. Jct of SR 12 and 63. Ext corridors. **Pets:** $15 daily fee/pet. Designated rooms, service with restrictions.
ASK Sᴅ ✕ ⛭ ▣ ⑪ ⩏

(AAA) ▼▼▼ Bryce View Lodge M
(435) 834-5180. **$45-$70.** SR 63. Ext corridors. **Pets:** $100 deposit/room. Service with restrictions, supervision.
SAVE Sᴅ ✕ ⛭ ▣ ⩏ ⊠

CANNONVILLE

▼▼ Grand Staircase Inn M
(435) 679-8400. **$39-$89.** 105 N Kodachrome Dr. Center of town. Ext/int corridors. **Pets:** Accepted.
ASK Sᴅ ✕ ⁊

CEDAR CITY

(AAA) ▼▼▼ Best Value Inn M
(435) 586-6557. **$34-$79.** 323 S Main St. Cross streets 300 S and Main sts; downtown. Ext corridors. **Pets:** Large. $7 daily fee/pet. Service with restrictions, supervision.
SAVE Sᴅ ✕ ⛭ ▣ ⩏

(AAA) ▼▼▼▼ Cedar Rest Motel M
(435) 586-9471. **$35-$70.** 479 S Main St. I-15, exit 59, just e. Ext corridors. **Pets:** Accepted.
SAVE Sᴅ ✕ ⛭

▼▼▼▼ Comfort Inn M
(435) 586-2082. **$47-$80, 7 day notice.** 250 N 1100 W. I-15, exit 59, just e. Ext corridors. **Pets:** Other species. Designated rooms, service with restrictions, crate.
ASK Sᴅ ✕ ⁊ ⛭ ▣ ⩏

(AAA) ▼▼▼▼ Days Inn M
(435) 867-8877. **$49-$89.** 1204 S Main St. I-15, exit 57, 0.4 mi e. Ext corridors. **Pets:** Small. $5 daily fee/pet. Service with restrictions, supervision.
SAVE Sᴅ ✕ ⁊ ⛭ ⩏

▼▼▼ Motel 6 of Cedar City–4041 M
(435) 586-9200. **$40-$58.** 1620 W 200 N. I-15, exit 59, just w. Int corridors. **Pets:** Medium, other species. Designated rooms, service with restrictions, supervision.
Sᴅ ✕ ⁊

▼▼▼ Ramada Limited M
(435) 586-9916. **$45-$99.** 281 S Main St. I-15, exit 57, just e. Ext corridors. **Pets:** Medium. $10 daily fee/pet. Service with restrictions, supervision.
ASK Sᴅ ✕ ⛭ ▣ ⩏

▼▼ Super 8 Motel M
(435) 586-8880. **$52-$69.** 145 N 1550 W. I-15, exit 59, just w. Int corridors. **Pets:** Medium. $6 daily fee/pet. Service with restrictions, supervision.
ASK Sᴅ ✕ ⓶ᴍ ⁊ ⛭ ⩏

(AAA) ▼▼ Valu-Inn M
(435) 586-9114. **$30-$45.** 344 S Main St. I-15, exit 57, just e. Ext corridors. **Pets:** Accepted.
SAVE Sᴅ ✕ ⛭

CLEARFIELD

▼▼▼ Clearfield Super 8 M
(801) 825-8000. **$45-$85.** 572 N Main St. I-15, exit 338, just w. Int corridors. **Pets:** Other species. $50 deposit/room, $10 daily fee/room. Service with restrictions.
ASK Sᴅ ✕ ⁊ ⁊ ⛭

COALVILLE

▼▼▼ Best Western Holiday Hills M
(435) 336-4444. **$69-$99.** 210 S 200 W. I-80, exit 164, just w. Int corridors. **Pets:** Other species. $15 daily fee/pet. Service with restrictions, supervision.
ASK Sᴅ ✕ ⁊ ⛭ ▣ ⩏ ⊠

DELTA

(AAA) ▼▼▼ Best Western Motor Inn M
(435) 864-3882. **$58-$72.** 527 E Topaz Blvd. US 6, at jct US 50. Ext corridors. **Pets:** Other species. $25 one-time fee/room. Designated rooms, supervision.
SAVE Sᴅ ✕ ⁊ ⛭ ▣ ⩏

DUCK CREEK VILLAGE

▼▼▼ Duck Creek Village Inn M
(435) 682-2565. **$64-$84, 7 day notice.** Hwy 14. 30 mi e of Cedar City on SR 14; 10 mi w of US 89. Ext corridors. **Pets:** Accepted.
ASK Sᴅ ✕ ⛭ ▣ ⑪ ⓚ ⓩ

(AAA) ▼▼▼ Pinewoods Resort M
(435) 682-2512. **$90-$150, 30 day notice.** 121 Duck Greek Ridge Rd. Just s of SR 14 via Cedar Mountain Rd, 31 mi e of Cedar City; 10 mi w of jct US 89. Ext/int corridors. **Pets:** Medium. $25 deposit/room, $10 daily fee/pet. Designated rooms, supervision.
SAVE Sᴅ ✕ ⛭ ▣ ⑪ ⊠ ⓚ ⓩ

ESCALANTE

▼▼ Rainbow Country Bed & Breakfast BB
(435) 826-4567. **$45-$75, 3 day notice.** 586 E 300 S. Just off SR 12, south end of town. Int corridors. **Pets:** $5 daily fee/room. Service with restrictions, supervision.
ASK Sᴅ ✕ ⓦ ⓩ

FILLMORE

◆◆◆ ▼▼▼ Best Western Paradise Resort M
(435) 743-6895. **$51-$79.** 905 N Main St. I-15, exit 167, just e. Ext corridors. **Pets:** No service, supervision.
⬛ ⬛ ⬛ ⬛ ⬛ ⬛ ⬛

▼▼▼ Inn at Apple Creek M
(435) 743-4334. **$50-$76, 3 day notice.** 940 S Hwy 99. I-15, exit 163, just e. Int corridors. **Pets:** Medium. $6 daily fee/room. Designated rooms, service with restrictions, supervision.
⬛ ⬛ ⬛ ⬛ ⬛ ⬛ ⬛

GARDEN CITY

▼▼ Canyon Cove Inn M
(435) 946-3565. **$45-$125.** 315 W Logan Hwy. 3 blks w of downtown. Int corridors. **Pets:** Accepted.
⬛ ⬛ ⬛ ⬛ ⬛

GLENDALE

▼▼ Historic Smith Hotel Bed &
   Breakfast BB ❖
(435) 648-2156. **$44-$70.** 295 N Main St. US 89, north end of town. Int corridors. **Pets:** Large, other species. $5 one-time fee/pet. Designated rooms, service with restrictions.
⬛ ⬛ ⬛ ⬛ ⬛

GREEN RIVER

▼▼▼ Holiday Inn Express M
(435) 564-4439. **$55-$85.** 965 E Main. I-70, exit 162, 1.8 mi w; exit 158 eastbound, 2.8 mi e on business loop. Int corridors. **Pets:** Other species. $5 daily fee/room. Designated rooms, service with restrictions, supervision.
⬛ ⬛ ⬛ ⬛ ⬛ ⬛

▼ Motel 6 M
(435) 564-3436. **$35-$61.** 946 E Main St. Ext corridors. **Pets:** Accepted.
⬛ ⬛ ⬛ ⬛ ⬛

▼▼▼ Ramada Limited M ❖
(435) 564-8441. **$45-$75.** 1117 E Main St. I-70, exit 162, 1 mi nw. Ext/int corridors. **Pets:** Other species. $5 one-time fee/pet. Service with restrictions, supervision.
⬛ ⬛ ⬛ ⬛ ⬛ ⬛

▼▼▼ Super 8 Motel M
(435) 564-8888. **$45-$70.** 1248 E Main St. I-70, exit 162. Int corridors. **Pets:** Accepted.
⬛ ⬛ ⬛ ⬛ ⬛ ⬛ ⬛

HATCH

◆◆◆ ▼▼▼ Riverside Resort & RV Park M ❖
(435) 735-4223. **$45-$80, 3 day notice.** 594 US Hwy 89. On US 89, 1 mi n. Ext corridors. **Pets:** Other species. $50 deposit/room. Designated rooms, service with restrictions, supervision.
⬛ ⬛ ⬛ ⬛ ⬛ ⬛ ⬛

HEBER CITY

◆◆◆ ▼▼▼ National 9 High Country Inn M
(435) 654-0201. **$54-$66.** 1000 S Main St. On US 40 E. Ext corridors. **Pets:** Accepted.
⬛ ⬛ ⬛ ⬛

◆◆◆ ▼▼▼ Swiss Alps Inn M
(435) 654-0722. **$55-$90.** 167 S Main St. On US 40. Ext corridors. **Pets:** Medium. Designated rooms, service with restrictions, supervision.
⬛ ⬛ ⬛ ⬛ ⬛ ⬛ ⬛

HUNTSVILLE

▼▼ Jackson Fork Inn BB
(801) 745-0051. **$75-$125, 3 day notice.** 7345 E 900 S. On SR 39. Int corridors. **Pets:** Small. $20 one-time fee/room. Supervision.
⬛ ⬛ ⬛ ⬛

HURRICANE

◆◆◆ ▼▼▼ Motel 6–4050 M
(435) 635-4010. **$54-$75.** 650 W State. Just w on SR 9. Ext corridors. **Pets:** Very small. $50 deposit/pet. Designated rooms, service with restrictions, supervision.
⬛ ⬛ ⬛ ⬛

▼▼ Super 8 M
(435) 635-0808. **$39-$78.** 65 S 700 W. Just s of SR 9. Ext corridors. **Pets:** Accepted.
⬛ ⬛ ⬛ ⬛ ⬛ ⬛ ⬛

▼▼ Travelodge M
(435) 635-4647. **$36-$89.** 280 W State. Just w on SR 9. Ext corridors. **Pets:** Small. $10 daily fee/pet. Designated rooms, service with restrictions, supervision.
⬛ ⬛ ⬛ ⬛ ⬛ ⬛

KANAB

◆◆◆ ▼▼ Aikens Lodge National 9 M
(435) 644-2625. **$33-$57.** 79 W Center St. On US 89. Ext corridors. **Pets:** Small, dogs only. $10 one-time fee/pet. Designated rooms, service with restrictions, supervision.
⬛ ⬛ ⬛ ⬛ ⬛ ⬛

◆◆◆ ▼▼▼ Best Western Red Hills M
(435) 644-2675. **$47-$109.** 125 W Center St. Ext/int corridors. **Pets:** Accepted.
⬛ ⬛ ⬛ ⬛ ⬛ ⬛ ⬛ ⬛

◆◆◆ ▼▼ Bob-Bon Inn M
(435) 644-5094. **$29-$65, 3 day notice.** 236 Hwy 89 N. On US 89. Ext corridors. **Pets:** $10 one-time fee/pet. Designated rooms, supervision.
⬛ ⬛ ⬛ ⬛

▼▼▼ Clarion-Victorian Charm Inn M ❖
(435) 644-8660. **$69-$159.** 190 N Hwy 89. North end of town. Int corridors. **Pets:** Small, dogs only. $10 one-time fee/room. Designated rooms, service with restrictions, supervision.
⬛ ⬛ ⬛ ⬛

▼ **Color Country Inn** Ⓜ
(435) 644-2164. **$50.** 1550 S US 89A. On US 89A, 1.5 mi s. Int corridors. **Pets:** Other species. Supervision.
🅰🅢🅚 🆂🅾 ⊗

▼ **Four Seasons Motel & Restaurant** Ⓜ
(435) 644-2635. **$49-$79.** 36 N 300 W. Ext corridors. **Pets:** Medium.
🅰🅢🅚 🆂🅾 ⊗ 🗄 🍴 ≈

▼▼ **Holiday Inn Express** Ⓜ
(435) 644-8888. **$59-$99.** 815 E Hwy 89. On US 89, just e. Int corridors. **Pets:** Large, other species. $10 daily fee/room. Designated rooms, service with restrictions, crate.
🅰🅢🅚 🆂🅾 ⊗ 🗔 🖃 ≈

🆔 ▼ **Kanab Mission Motel** Ⓜ
(435) 644-5373. **$42-$47.** 386 E 300 S. E on US 89. Int corridors. **Pets:** Accepted.
🆂🅰🆅🅴 🆂🅾 ⊗

🆔 ▼▼ **Parry Lodge** Ⓜ
(435) 644-2601. **$40-$78.** 89 E Center St. On US 89, corner of 100 E; center. Ext/int corridors. **Pets:** Other species. $8 daily fee/pet. Designated rooms, service with restrictions, crate.
🆂🅰🆅🅴 🆂🅾 ⊗ 🗄 🖃 🍴 ≈

🆔 ▼ **Quail Park Lodge** Ⓜ
(435) 644-5094. **$29-$65, 3 day notice.** 125 Hwy 89 N. On US 89. Ext corridors. **Pets:** $10 daily fee/pet, $10 one-time fee/pet. Designated rooms, supervision.
🆂🅰🆅🅴 🆂🅾 ⊗ 🗄 ≈

🆔 ▼ **Sun N Sand Motel** Ⓜ 🐾
(435) 644-5050. **$30-$46.** 347 S 100 E. Jct US 89 and 89A. Ext corridors. **Pets:** Medium, other species. $10 deposit/room. Designated rooms.
🆂🅰🆅🅴 🆂🅾 ⊗ 🗄 ≈

▼▼ **Super 8** Ⓜ
(435) 644-5500. **$41-$78.** 70 S 200 W. Just s off US 89. Ext corridors. **Pets:** Other species. $50 deposit/room, $6 daily fee/pet. Service with restrictions, supervision.
🅰🅢🅚 🆂🅾 ⊗ 🗄 ≈

🆔 ▼▼ **Treasure Trail** Ⓜ
(435) 644-2687. **$32-$58.** 150 W Center St. Center of downtown. Ext corridors. **Pets:** Accepted.
🆂🅰🆅🅴 🆂🅾 ⊗ 🗄 ≈

LAKE POWELL

🆔 ▼▼▼ **Defiance House Lodge-Bullfrog Marina** Ⓜ
(435) 684-3000. **$108-$128.** Bullfrog Marina. 70 mi s of Hanksville; 44 mi s off SR 95 on SR 276. Int corridors. **Pets:** Accepted.
🆂🅰🆅🅴 🆂🅾 ⊗ 🖃 🍴 ⊗

LAYTON

🆔 ▼▼▼ **Comfort Inn** Ⓜ
(801) 544-5577. **$56-$89.** 877 N 400 W. I-15, exit 334, then e. Int corridors. **Pets:** Accepted.
🆂🅰🆅🅴 🆂🅾 ⊗ 🗔 🗄 🖃 ≈

▼▼▼▼ **Hampton Inn** Ⓜ
(801) 775-8800. **$89-$109.** 1700 Woodland Park Dr. I-15, exit 335, 0.3 mi se. Int corridors. **Pets:** Medium, other species. $150 deposit/room. Designated rooms, service with restrictions, supervision.
🅰🅢🅚 🆂🅾 ⊗ 🗔 🗄 🖃 ≈

▼▼▼ **Holiday Inn Express** Ⓜ
(801) 773-3773. **$79-$129.** 1695 Woodland Park Dr. I-15, exit 335, 0.3 mi se. Int corridors. **Pets:** Accepted.
🅰🅢🅚 🆂🅾 ⊗ 🗔 🗄 🖃 ≈

🆔 ▼▼▼ **La Quinta Inn** Ⓜ
(801) 776-6700. **$65-$75.** 1965 N 1200 W. I-15, exit 335, 1 blk e; corner of Antelope Dr and Angel Rd. Int corridors. **Pets:** Accepted.
🆂🅰🆅🅴 ⊗ 🗔 🗄 🖃 ≈ ⊗

▼▼▼ **TownePlace Suites** Ⓜ
(801) 779-2422. **$99.** 1743 Woodland Park Dr. I-15, exit 335, 0.3 mi se. Int corridors. **Pets:** Other species. $12 daily fee/room, $75 one-time fee/room. Service with restrictions, crate.
🅰🅢🅚 🆂🅾 ⊗ 🗔 🗄 🖃 ≈

LEHI

🆔 ▼▼▼ **Best Western Timpanogos Inn** Ⓜ 🐾
(801) 768-1400. **$49-$75.** 195 S 850 E. I-15, exit 282, southwest side. Int corridors. **Pets:** Other species. $10 one-time fee/pet. Supervision.
🆂🅰🆅🅴 🆂🅾 ⊗ 🗔 🗄 🖃 ≈

▼▼ **Motel 6-1405** Ⓜ
(801) 768-2668. **$35-$45.** 210 S 1200 E. I-15, exit 282, just e. Int corridors. **Pets:** Accepted.
🆂🅾 ⊗ 🗔 🗄 🖃 ≈

🆔 ▼▼▼ **Super 8** Ⓜ
(801) 766-8800. **$45-$79.** 125 S 850 E. I-15, exit 282, southwest side. Int corridors. **Pets:** Other species. $50 deposit/room. Service with restrictions, supervision.
🆂🅰🆅🅴 🆂🅾 ⊗ 🗔 🗄 🖃 ≈

LOGAN

🆔 ▼▼▼ **Best Western Weston Inn** Ⓜ
(435) 752-5700. **$59-$99.** 250 N Main St. On US 89 and 91; downtown. Ext corridors. **Pets:** Medium. $5 daily fee/pet. Designated rooms, service with restrictions, supervision.
🆂🅰🆅🅴 🆂🅾 ⊗ 🗔 🗄 🖃 ≈ ⊗

▼▼ **Logan Days Inn** Ⓜ
(435) 753-5623. **$40-$88.** 364 S Main St. On US 89 and 91. Ext corridors. **Pets:** Accepted.
🅰🅢🅚 🆂🅾 ⊗ 🗄 ≈

▼▼ **Logan Super 8** Ⓜ
(435) 753-8883. **$47-$80.** 865 S Hwy 89 and 91. South end of town. Int corridors. **Pets:** Accepted.
🅰🅢🅚 🆂🅾 ⊗ 🗄 ≈

▼▼▼ **Ramada Limited** Ⓜ
(435) 787-2060. **$51-$75.** 2002 S Hwy 89 and 91. South end of town. Int corridors. **Pets:** Other species. $50 deposit/pet. Service with restrictions, supervision.
🅰🅢🅚 🆂🅾 ⊗ 🗄 🗔 🖃 ≈ ⊗

MANTI

▼▼▼▼ **Manti Country Village** M
(435) 835-9300. **$54-$82.** 145 N Main St. On US 89. Ext corridors. **Pets:** Accepted.
⊠ 🖬 🍽

MARYSVALE

▼▼ **Big Rock Candy Mountain Resort** M
(435) 326-2000. **$59-$99.** 4479 N Hwy 89. On US 89, 6 mi n. Ext corridors. **Pets:** Accepted.
ASK 🖬 ⊠ 🖬 🖵 🍽 ⊠

MEXICAN HAT

▲▲▲ ▼▼▼ **San Juan Inn & Trading Post** M
(435) 683-2220. **$40-$72.** Hwy 163 & San Juan River. On US 163. Ext corridors. **Pets:** Dogs only. Designated rooms, service with restrictions, supervision
SAVE 🖬 ⊠ 🍽 ⊠

MIDWAY

▼▼▼▼ **The Kastle Inn Bed & Breakfast** BB
(435) 657-1250. **$89-$159, 7 day notice.** 1220 Interlaken Ln. Ext/int corridors. **Pets:** Accepted.
ASK 🖬 ⊠ 🗶

MILFORD

▲▲▲ ▼▼▼ **Oak Tree Inn** M
(435) 387-5266. **$60.** 777 W Hwy 21. Int corridors. **Pets:** Large. $10 daily fee/pet. Service with restrictions.
SAVE 🖬 ⊠ ✎ 🖬 🖵 🍽

MOAB

▲▲▲ ▼▼▼ **Adventure Inn Moab** M
(435) 259-6122. **$39-$68.** 512 N Main St. US 191 N. Ext corridors. **Pets:** $50 deposit/room, $10 one-time fee/pet. Supervision.
SAVE 🖬 ⊠ 🖬

▲▲▲ ▼▼▼ **Apache Motel** M
(435) 259-5727. **$29-$89.** 166 S 400 E. Just e off US 191. Ext corridors. **Pets:** Medium. Designated rooms, service with restrictions, supervision.
SAVE 🖬 ⊠ 🖬 🛋

▼▼▼▼ **Best Inn of Moab** M
(435) 259-8848. **$35-$65.** 988 N Main St. 1 mi n on US 191. Int corridors. **Pets:** Medium, dogs only. $10 daily fee/room. Supervision.
ASK 🖬 ⊠ ✎ 🖬 🛋

▲▲▲ ▼▼▼▼ **Big Horn Lodge** M
(435) 259-6171. **$34-$89.** 550 S Main St. South end of town. Ext corridors. **Pets:** Other species. $5 daily fee/pet. Designated rooms, service with restrictions, supervision.
SAVE 🖬 ⊠ 🖬 🖵 🍽 🛋

▲▲▲ ▼▼ **Bowen Motel** M
(435) 259-7132. **$35-$65.** 169 N Main St. Downtown. Ext corridors. **Pets:** Medium. $20 deposit/room, $5 daily fee/pet. Supervision.
SAVE 🖬 ⊠ 🖬 🛋

▲▲▲ ▼▼▼▼ **Cedar Breaks Condos** CO
(435) 259-7830. **$55-$95, 7 day notice.** 400 East & Center St. Just s off US 191. Ext corridors. **Pets:** Dogs only. $10 daily fee/pet. Designated rooms, service with restrictions, supervision.
SAVE ⊠ 🖬 🖵

▼▼▼▼ **Comfort Suites** M
(435) 259-5252. **$69-$119.** 800 S Main St. Int corridors. **Pets:** Medium. Designated rooms, service with restrictions, crate.
ASK 🖬 ⊠ ✎ 🖬 🖵 🛋 ⊠

▲▲▲ ▼▼▼▼ **The Gonzo Inn** M
(435) 259-2515. **$80-$299, 14 day notice.** 100 W 200 S. Downtown. Ext/int corridors. **Pets:** $25 one-time fee/room. Designated rooms, service with restrictions, supervision.
SAVE 🖬 ⊠ ✎ 🖬 🖵 🛋

▼▼▼ **Kokopelli Lodge** M
(435) 259-7615. **$35-$75.** 72 S 100 E. Downtown. Ext corridors. **Pets:** Other species. $5 daily fee/pet. Service with restrictions, supervision.
ASK 🖬 ⊠ 🖬 🖵

▼▼▼▼ **La Quinta Inns** M
(435) 259-8700. **$63-$90.** 815 S Main St. South end of town. Int corridors. **Pets:** Other species. $10 one-time fee/room. Designated rooms, service with restrictions, supervision.
ASK 🖬 ⊠ ✎ 🖬 🖵 🛋

▼▼ **Microtel Inn** M
(435) 259-5145. **$30-$100.** 71 W 200 N. Cross streets 100 W and 200 N; downtown. Int corridors. **Pets:** Medium, other species. $10 one-time fee/room. Designated rooms, service with restrictions, supervision.
ASK 🖬 ⊠ ✎ ✎ 🖬 🖵 🛋

▼▼▼ **Moab Valley Inn** M 🐾
(435) 259-4419. **$57-$135.** 711 S Main St. 1 mi s on US 191. Int corridors. **Pets:** $5 daily fee/room. Designated rooms, service with restrictions, supervision.
ASK 🖬 ⊠ ✎ 🖬 🖵 🛋 ⊠

▼▼▼ **Motel 6 Moab** M
(435) 259-6686. **$29-$99.** 1089 N Main St. North end of town, west side of street. Int corridors. **Pets:** Medium. $100 deposit/room. Designated rooms, service with restrictions, supervision.
ASK 🖬 ⊠ ✎ ✎ 🛋

▲▲▲ ▼▼▼▼ **Red Cliffs Adventure Lodge** CI
(435) 259-2002. **$79-$169, 30 day notice.** Milepost 14 Hwy 128. 14 mi e on SR 128 from jct US 191. Ext corridors. **Pets:** Large. $20 daily fee/pet. Designated rooms, service with restrictions, supervision.
SAVE 🖬 ⊠ ✎ 🖬 🖵 🍽 🛋 ⊠

▼▼ **Red Rock Lodge & Suites** M
(435) 259-5431. **$29-$95, 7 day notice.** 51 N 100 W. Just w of Main St. Ext/int corridors. **Pets:** Other species. $5 daily fee/room. Designated rooms, service with restrictions.
ASK 🖬 ⊠ 🖬 🖵 🛋

[AAA] ♦♦ **Red Stone Inn** [M] 🐾
(435) 259-3500. **$34-$80.** 535 S Main St. Downtown. Int corridors. **Pets:** Other species. $5 daily fee/pet. Designated rooms, service with restrictions, supervision.
[SAVE] [SD] 🚭 ▣ 💻

♦♦ **Rustic Inn** [M]
(435) 259-6177. **$30-$75.** 120 E 100 S. Ext corridors. **Pets:** Accepted.
🚭 ▣ 💻 🏊

[AAA] ♦ **Silver Sage Inn** [M]
(435) 259-4420. **$25-$54.** 840 S Main. Int corridors. **Pets:** $10 deposit/pet. Service with restrictions.
[SAVE] 🚭 💻

♦♦ **Sleep Inn** [M]
(435) 259-4655. **$39-$109.** 1051 S Main St. South end of town. Int corridors. **Pets:** Other species. Designated rooms, service with restrictions, supervision.
[A$K] [SD] 🚭 [&M] 👂 ♿ ▣ 💻 🏊

[AAA] ♦♦♦ **Super 8 Motel, Moab** [M]
(435) 259-8868. **$30-$99.** 889 N Main St. US 191, 1 mi n. Int corridors. **Pets:** Accepted.
[SAVE] [SD] 🚭 👂 ▣ 🏊

[AAA] ♦♦ **The Virginian Motel** [M]
(435) 259-5951. **$29-$79.** 70 E 200 S. Just e of US 191. Ext corridors. **Pets:** Other species. $10 daily fee/pet. Service with restrictions, supervision.
[SAVE] [SD] 🚭 ♿ ▣ 💻

MONTICELLO

[AAA] ♦♦♦ **Best Western Wayside Inn** [M]
(435) 587-2261. **$49-$95.** 173 E Central St. On US 491, just e of US 191. Ext corridors. **Pets:** Accepted.
[SAVE] [SD] 🚭 👂 ▣ 💻 🏊

♦♦♦ **Go West Inn & Suites** [M]
(435) 587-2489. **$39-$68.** 649 N Main St. On US 194 N; end of town. Int corridors. **Pets:** Accepted.
🚭 ▣ 🏊

MOUNT CARMEL JUNCTION

[AAA] ♦♦♦ **Best Western Thunderbird Resort** [M]
(435) 648-2203. **$51-$102.** Jct US 89 and 9. Ext corridors. **Pets:** Accepted.
[SAVE] [SD] 🚭 💻 🍴 🏊

[AAA] ♦♦ **Golden Hills Motel** [M]
(435) 648-2268. **$31-$49.** 4473 S State St. US 89, jct SR 9. Ext corridors. **Pets:** $3 one-time fee/pet. No service, supervision.
[SAVE] 🚭 🏊

NEPHI

[AAA] ♦♦ **Best Western Paradise Inn** [M]
(435) 623-0624. **$45-$67.** 1025 S Main St. I-15, exit 222, 0.5 mi n. Ext corridors. **Pets:** Small. $25 deposit/room, $5 daily fee/pet. Designated rooms, service with restrictions, supervision.
[SAVE] [SD] 🚭 ▣ 💻 🏊

♦♦ **Motel 6** [M]
(435) 623-0666. **$40-$49.** 2195 S Main St. I-15, exit 222, just s. Int corridors. **Pets:** Accepted.
[A$K] [SD] 🚭 ▣ 🏊

[AAA] ♦♦♦ **Roberta's Cove Motor Inn** [M]
(435) 623-2629. **$45-$50.** 2250 S Main St. I-15, exit 222, just s. Ext corridors. **Pets:** $5 daily fee/pet. Designated rooms, supervision.
[SAVE] [SD] 🚭 👂 ▣ 💻 🏊

[AAA] ♦♦ **Safari Motel** [M]
(435) 623-1071. **$38-$47, 5 day notice.** 413 S Main St. I-15, exit 222, 3 mi nw. Ext corridors. **Pets:** Accepted.
[SAVE] [SD] 🚭 ▣ 🏊

OGDEN

♦♦♦ **Best Rest Inn** [M]
(801) 393-8644. **$49-$69.** 1206 W 2100 S. I-15, exit 346, just e. Ext corridors. **Pets:** Accepted.
[A$K] [SD] 🚭 👂 ♿ ▣ 🍴 🏊

[AAA] ♦♦♦ **Best Western High Country Inn** [M]
(801) 394-9474. **$69-$89.** 1335 W 12th St. I-15, exit 347 (12th St), then e. Ext corridors. **Pets:** Other species.
[SAVE] [SD] 🚭 👂 ▣ 💻 🍴 🏊 🏋

♦♦♦ **Comfort Suites of Ogden** [M]
(801) 621-2545. **$74-$150.** 2250 S 1200 W. I-15, exit 346E. Int corridors. **Pets:** Accepted.
[A$K] [SD] 🚭 👂 ♿ ▣ 💻 🍴 🏊 🏋

♦♦♦ **Days Inn of Ogden** [M] 🐾
(801) 399-5671. **$49-$69.** 3306 Washington Blvd. I-15, exit 344A, 1.5 mi e via 31st St, then s. Ext/int corridors. **Pets:** Medium. $5 daily fee/pet. Service with restrictions, supervision.
[A$K] [SD] 🚭 ▣ 💻 🍴 🏊 🏋

♦♦♦ **Holiday Inn Express Hotel & Suites** [M] 🐾
(801) 392-5000. **$74-$150.** 2245 S 1200 W. I-15, exit 346E, just e. Int corridors. **Pets:** Other species. $50 deposit/room. Service with restrictions, crate.
[A$K] [SD] 🚭 👂 ♿ ▣ 💻 🏊 🏋

♦♦ **Ogden Lodge** [M]
(801) 394-4563. **$39-$45.** 2110 Washington Blvd. Cross street 21st St; downtown. Ext corridors. **Pets:** Accepted.
[A$K] [SD] 🚭 ▣ 💻 🏊

[AAA] ♦♦ **Red Roof Inn** [M] 🐾
(801) 627-2880. **$44-$54.** 1500 W Riverdale Rd. I-15, exit 343 southbound, 2 mi via Riverdale Rd; exit 342 northbound, 1 mi via Riverdale Rd. Ext/int corridors. **Pets:** Medium. Designated rooms, service with restrictions, supervision.
[SAVE] 🚭 ♿ ▣ 🏊

♦♦ **Super 8 Motel** [M] 🐾
(801) 731-7100. **$41-$44.** 1508 W 2100 S. I-15, exit 346, just w. Int corridors. **Pets:** Other species. $20 deposit/room. Service with restrictions, supervision.
[A$K] [SD] 🚭 👂 ♿

△△△ ▽▽▽ Western Colony Inn M
(801) 627-1332. **$35-$40.** 234 24th St. City center. Ext corridors. **Pets:** Accepted.
[SAVE] [S/] [✕] [📞]

△△△ ▽▽▽ Western Inn-Ogden M
(801) 731-6500. **$58-$68.** 1155 S 1700 W. I-15, exit 347, just w. Int corridors. **Pets:** Other species. $10 one-time fee/room. Designated rooms, service with restrictions, supervision.
[SAVE] [S/] [✕] [🐾] [↕] [📞] [🖥]

OLD LA SAL

▽▽▽ Mt. Peale Inn & Spa BB ❄
(435) 686-2284. **$65-$95, 14 day notice.** 1415 E Hwy 46. 14 mi e from jct US 191 and SR 46. Ext/int corridors. **Pets:** Dogs only. $35 one-time fee/pet. Designated rooms, no service, supervision.
[ASK] [S/] [✕] [📞] [🖥] [🍴] [✕] [K] [☎]

OREM

△△△ ▽▽▽▽ La Quinta Inn M
(801) 235-9555. **$49-$89.** 1100 W 780 N. I-15, exit 275, east side. Int corridors. **Pets:** Other species. Service with restrictions, supervision.
[SAVE] [S/] [✕] [🐾] [↕] [📞] [🖥] [☞]

△△△ ▽▽▽▽ La Quinta Inn & Suites M
(801) 226-0440. **$75-$85.** 521 W University Pkwy. I-15, exit 272, to 12th St S, 1 mi e. Int corridors. **Pets:** Small. Service with restrictions, supervision.
[SAVE] [✕] [🐾] [↕] [📞] [🖥] [☞]

PANGUITCH

▽▽▽ Adobe Sands Motel M ❄
(435) 676-8874. **$38-$52.** 390 N Main St. Downtown. Ext corridors. **Pets:** Small, dogs only. Service with restrictions, supervision.
[ASK] [S/] [✕]

▽▽▽ Bryce Junction Inn M
(435) 676-2221. **Call for rates.** 3068 E Hwy 12. 7 mi se on SR 12; 15 mi w of Bryce Caynon. Int corridors. **Pets:** Accepted.
[S/] [✕]

△△△ ▽▽▽ Bryce Way Motel M
(435) 676-2400. **$40-$55.** 429 N Main St. On US 89. Ext corridors. **Pets:** Accepted.
[SAVE] [S/] [✕] [📞] [🖥]

△△△ ▽▽▽ Color Country Motel M ❄
(435) 676-2386. **$35-$62.** 526 N Main St. On US 89. Ext corridors. **Pets:** Medium, other species. $10 one-time fee/pet. Designated rooms, service with restrictions.
[SAVE] [✕] [☞]

▽▽ ▽▽ Harold's Place Cabins CA ❄
(435) 676-2350. **$45-$60.** 3066 Hwy 12. 7 mi se on SR 12; 17 mi w of Bryce Canyon. Ext corridors. **Pets:** Medium. $20 deposit/room. Designated rooms, service with restrictions.
[ASK] [S/] [✕] [🖥] [🍴] [☎]

△△△ ▽▽▽ Horizon Motel M ❄
(435) 676-2651. **$35-$99.** 730 N Main St. US 89. Ext corridors. **Pets:** Small, dogs only. $15 one-time fee/room. Designated rooms, service with restrictions, supervision.
[SAVE] [S/] [✕] [📞] [🖥]

△△△ ▽▽▽ Marianna Inn Motel M
(435) 676-8844. **$30-$75.** 699 N Main St. On SR 89. Ext corridors. **Pets:** Accepted.
[SAVE] [S/] [✕] [🖥]

▽▽▽ ▽▽ Silverado Wild West "Movie Town" M
(435) 676-8770. **$79-$108, 60 day notice.** 3900 S Hwy 89. 0.3 mi n of jct SR 12 and 89, 5 mi s off Panguitch on US 89, 17 mi w of Bryce Canyon. Ext corridors. **Pets:** Accepted.
[ASK] [S/] [✕] [📞] [🍴] [☞] [☎]

PARK CITY

△△△ ▽▽▽▽ Best Western Landmark Inn M ❄
(435) 649-7300. **$109-$169.** 6560 N Landmark Dr. I-80, exit 145, 5 mi n of Park City at Kimball Junction. Int corridors. **Pets:** Large, other species. $25 deposit/room, $10 daily fee/room. Designated rooms, service with restrictions, supervision.
[SAVE] [S/] [✕] [&M] [🐾] [📞] [🖥] [☞] [☎]

△△△ ▽▽▽▽ Holiday Inn Express Hotel & Suites M
(435) 658-1600. **$72-$269, 7 day notice.** 1501 W Ute Blvd. I-80, exit 145, 5 mi n of Park City at Kimball Junction. Int corridors. **Pets:** Medium, other species. $50 deposit/room. Service with restrictions, supervision.
[SAVE] [S/] [✕] [🐾] [↕] [📞] [🖥] [☞] [☎]

△△△ ▽▽▽▽ The Radisson Inn Park City SH
(435) 649-5000. **$69-$215, 30 day notice.** 2121 Park Ave. I-80, exit Kimball Junction; north end of town. Int corridors. **Pets:** Accepted.
[SAVE] [S/] [✕] [🐾] [📞] [🖥] [🍴] [☞] [☎]

PAROWAN

△△△ ▽▽▽▽ Days Inn M
(435) 477-3326. **$49-$85.** 625 W 200 S. I-15, exit 75, 1.5 mi e. Ext corridors. **Pets:** Accepted.
[SAVE] [S/] [✕] [📞] [☞] [☎]

PAYSON

▽▽▽▽ Comfort Inn M
(801) 465-4861. **$79-$100.** 830 N Main St. I-15, exit 254, just e. Int corridors. **Pets:** Large, other species. $20 deposit/room. Service with restrictions, supervision.
[ASK] [S/] [✕] [🐾] [📞] [🖥] [☞] [☎]

PRICE

△△△ ▽▽▽ Budget Host Inn M
(435) 637-2424. **$45-$59.** 145 N Carbonville Rd. US 6, exit 240, just e. Ext corridors. **Pets:** Accepted.
[SAVE] [S/] [✕] [📞] [🖥] [☞]

▼▼ National 9-Price River Inn M
(435) 637-7000. **$41-$54.** 641 W Price River Dr. US 6, exit
240. Ext/int corridors. **Pets:** Accepted.
(ASK) (S) (X) (🔌) (💻)

PROVO

▲▲ ▼ Colony Inn Suites-National 9 M
(801) 374-6800. **$45-$62.** 1380 S University Ave. I-15, exit
266. Ext corridors. **Pets:** Accepted.
(SAVE) (S) (X) (🔌) (≈)

▼▼▼ Days Inn M
(801) 375-8600. **$54-$89, 14 day notice.** 1675 N 200 W.
I-15, exit 272, 3.5 mi e on University Pkwy. Ext corridors.
Pets: Other species. $5 one-time fee/room. Service with
restrictions.
(ASK) (S) (X) (🚲) (🎿) (🔌) (💻) (≈)

▼▼▼ Econo Lodge Provo Airport M
(801) 373-0099. **$45-$68.** 1625 W Center St. I-15, exit 268
southbound, 0.3 mi w; exit 268B northbound, 0.3 mi w. Ext
corridors. **Pets:** Large, other species. $8 daily fee/pet. Serv-
ice with restrictions, supervision.
(ASK) (S) (X) (🔌) (💻)

▼▼▼ Hampton Inn M 🐾
(801) 377-6396. **$49-$95.** 1511 S 40 E. I-15, exit 266, just e.
Int corridors. **Pets:** Other species. $25 one-time fee/room.
Service with restrictions, supervision.
(ASK) (S) (X) (🚲) (🎿) (🔌) (💻) (≈)

▼▼▼▼ La Quinta Inn of Provo M
(801) 374-6020. **$65-$69.** 1555 N Canyon Rd. I-15, exit 272,
3.5 mi e. Int corridors. **Pets:** Accepted.
(ASK) (S) (X) (🚲) (🎿) (🔌) (💻) (≈)

▲▲▲ ▼ Provo Travelers Inn M
(801) 373-8248. **$40-$70.** 469 W Center St. I-15, exit 268
southbound; exit 268A northbound. Ext corridors.
Pets: Medium. $50 deposit/pet, $5 daily fee/pet. Service
with restrictions, supervision.
(SAVE) (S) (X) (🔌) (≈)

▼▼▼ Residence Inn by Marriott M
(801) 374-1000. **$99-$129.** 252 W 2230 N. I-15, exit 272, 3.1
mi e via University Pkwy. Int corridors. **Pets:** Accepted.
(ASK) (S) (X) (🔌) (🚲) (🎿) (🔌) (💻) (≈) (X)

▼▼▼ Sleep Inn M
(801) 377-6597. **$49-$79.** 1505 S 40 E. I-15, exit 266, just e.
Int corridors. **Pets:** Other species. $10 daily fee/pet. Service
with restrictions, supervision.
(ASK) (S) (X) (🚲) (🎿) (🔌) (💻)

RICHFIELD

▲▲▲ ▼▼▼ Best Western AppleTree Inn M
(435) 896-5481. **$49-$79.** 145 S Main St. I-70, exit 37 or 40;
center of downtown. Ext corridors. **Pets:** Accepted.
(SAVE) (S) (X) (🚲) (🔌) (💻) (≈)

▲▲▲ ▼▼▼ Budget Host Nights Inn M
(435) 896-8228. **$36-$48.** 69 S Main St. I-70, exit 37 or 40;
center of downtown. Ext corridors. **Pets:** Accepted.
(SAVE) (S) (X) (🔌) (≈)

▲▲▲ ▼▼▼ Days Inn SH
(435) 896-6476. **$55-$90.** 333 N Main St. I-70, exit 40, just s
on US 89. Int corridors. **Pets:** Small, other species. $50
deposit/room, $10 one-time fee/room. Designated rooms,
service with restrictions, supervision.
(SAVE) (S) (X) (🔌) (💻) (🍴) (≈) (X)

▼▼ Luxury Inn M
(435) 893-0100. **$39-$79.** 1335 N Main St. North end of
town. Int corridors. **Pets:** Accepted.
(ASK) (S) (X) (🎿) (🔌) (≈)

▲▲▲ ▼ New West Motel M
(435) 896-5450. **$33-$37.** 447 S Main St. I-70, exit 37 or 40;
downtown. Ext corridors. **Pets:** Accepted.
(SAVE) (S) (X) (🔌) (🔌)

▼▼▼ Richfield Travelodge M
(435) 896-9271. **$52-$82.** 647 S Main St. I-70, exit 37; south
end of town. Int corridors. **Pets:** Small. $15 deposit/room,
$5 one-time fee/room. Designated rooms, service with
restrictions, supervision.
(ASK) (S) (X) (🔌) (💻) (🍴) (≈)

▲▲▲ ▼▼▼ Romanico Inn M
(435) 896-8471. **$33-$44.** 1170 S Main St. I-70, exit 37, just
n. Ext corridors. **Pets:** Accepted.
(SAVE) (S) (X) (🔌)

ROOSEVELT

▲▲▲ ▼▼▼ Frontier Motel M
(435) 722-2201. **$43-$55.** 75 S 200 E. On US 40. Ext corridors. **Pets:** Small, dogs only. Service with restrictions,
supervision.
(SAVE) (S) (X) (🔌) (🍴) (≈)

▲▲▲ ▼▼▼ Western Hills Motel M
(435) 722-5115. **$35-$45.** 737 E 200 N. On US 40. Ext
corridors. **Pets:** Small. $500 deposit/pet. Designated rooms,
no service, supervision.
(SAVE) (S) (X) (🔌)

ST. GEORGE

▼▼▼ An Olde Penny Farthing Inn Bed &
Breakfast BB 🐾
(435) 673-7755. **$60-$130, 7 day notice.** 278 N 100 W.
Historic District. Int corridors. **Pets:** Other species. $20
deposit/pet. Designated rooms, service with restrictions,
supervision.
(X) (🎿) (🔌) (🔌)

▲▲▲ ▼▼▼ Atkin's Singletree Inn M 🐾
(435) 673-6161. **$46-$99.** 260 E St George Blvd. I-15, exit 8,
1.5 mi w. Ext corridors. **Pets:** $15 one-time fee/pet. Desig-
nated rooms, no service, supervision.
(SAVE) (S) (X) (🔌) (≈)

▼▼ The Bluffs Inn & Suites M
(435) 628-6699. **$49-$99.** 1140 S Bluff St. I-15, exit 6 (Bluff
St), just w. Ext corridors. **Pets:** $15 daily fee/pet. Desig-
nated rooms, supervision.
(X) (🎿) (🔌) (💻) (≈)

▼▼▼▼ **Budget Inn & Suites** Ⓜ
(435) 673-6661. **$40-$142.** 1221 S Main St. I-15, exit 6 (Bluff St), just w. Ext corridors. **Pets:** Accepted.
ASK 🐾 ⊗ 🛏 🍴 💻 🏊 ⊗

🔴 ▼▼▼ **Comfort Suites** Ⓜ
(435) 673-7000. **$65-$119.** 1239 S Main St. I-15, exit 6 (Bluff St), just w. Ext corridors. **Pets:** Small, dogs only. $10 daily fee/room. Designated rooms, service with restrictions, supervision.
SAVE 🐾 📞 🛏 💻 🏊 ⊗

▼▼▼▼ **Crystal Inn St. George** 🅂🄷
(435) 688-7477. **$99-$139.** 1450 S Hilton Dr. I-15, exit 6 (Bluff St), just w. Int corridors. **Pets:** Small. $25 one-time fee/room. Service with restrictions, supervision.
ASK 🐾 ⊗ 🛏 💻 🍴 🏊 ⊗

🔴 ▼▼▼ ▼▼▼ **Green Valley Spa & Coyote Inn** 🅂🄷
(435) 628-8060. **$200-$1000, 14 day notice.** 1871 W Canyon View Dr. Bluff and S Main sts, 4 mi sw via Hilton Dr to Tonaquint Dr, to Dixie Dr, then to Canyon View Dr. Ext corridors. **Pets:** Small. $25 daily fee/pet. Service with restrictions, supervision.
SAVE ⊗ 🛏 💻 🏊 ⊗

🔴 ▼▼▼ **Howard Johnson Express Inn & Suites** Ⓜ
(435) 628-8000. **$49-$135.** 1040 S Main St. I-15, exit 6 (Bluff St), just w, then just e. Ext corridors. **Pets:** Other species. $20 deposit/room. Designated rooms, supervision.
SAVE 🐾 ⊗ 🛏 💻 🏊

🔴 ▼▼▼ **Red Cliffs Inn & Suites** Ⓜ
(435) 673-3537. **$49-$129.** 912 Red Cliffs Dr. I-15, exit 10, just e. Ext/int corridors. **Pets:** Small. $25 deposit/room. Designated rooms, service with restrictions, supervision.
SAVE 🐾 ⊗ 🛏 💻 🍴 🏊

▼▼▼ **Seven Wives Inn** 🅱🅱
(435) 628-3737. **$85-$250, 7 day notice.** 217 N 100 W. I-15, exit 8, 2.1 mi w, then right on 100 W. Ext/int corridors. **Pets:** Other species. $25 one-time fee/room. Designated rooms.
ASK ⊗ 🛏 🍴 🏊

▼▼ **Suntime Inn** Ⓜ
(435) 673-6181. **$34-$79.** 420 E St. George Blvd. Cross streets 400 E and St. George Blvd; downtown. Ext corridors. **Pets:** Accepted.
ASK 🐾 ⊗ 🛏 🏊

▼▼ **Super 8 Motel** Ⓜ
(435) 688-8383. **$39-$78.** 915 S Bluff St. I-15, exit 6 (Bluff St), just w. Int corridors. **Pets:** Accepted.
ASK 🐾 ⊗ 🏊

SALINA

▼▼ **Henry's Hideway** Ⓜ
(435) 529-7467. **$40-$50.** 60 N State St. I-70, exit 54, 1.7 mi n on US 89; downtown. Ext corridors. **Pets:** Accepted.
ASK 🐾 ⊗ 🛏 🏊

▼▼ **Luxury Inn** Ⓜ
(435) 529-1300. **$39-$79, 5 day notice.** 1400 S State. I-70, exit 54, just n. Int corridors. **Pets:** Very small. $5 daily fee/pet. Designated rooms, service with restrictions, supervision.
ASK 🐾 ⊗ 🛏 🏊

▼ **Ranch Motel** Ⓜ
(435) 529-7789. **$40-$48.** 80 N State St. On US 89; near town center. Ext/int corridors. **Pets:** Other species. $6 one-time fee/pet. Service with restrictions, supervision.
ASK 🐾 ⊗ 🛏

🔴 ▼▼▼ **Scenic Hills Super 8** Ⓜ 🐾
(435) 529-7483. **$50-$62.** 75 E 1500 S. I-70, exit 54, just n. Ext corridors. **Pets:** Other species. $10 daily fee/room. Designated rooms, service with restrictions, supervision.
SAVE 🐾 ⊗ 🛏 🏊

SALT LAKE CITY METROPOLITAN AREA

BOUNTIFUL

🔴 ▼▼▼ **Country Inn & Suites** Ⓜ
(801) 292-8100. **$69-$159.** 999 N 500 W. I-15, exit 321. Int corridors. **Pets:** Other species. $100 deposit/pet. Service with restrictions, supervision.
SAVE 🐾 ⊗ 📞 🛏 🛏 💻 🏊

DRAPER

▼▼▼▼ **Holiday Inn Express** Ⓜ
(801) 571-2511. **$59-$79.** 12033 S Factory Outlet Dr. I-15, exit 294, just n; on east side of interstate. Int corridors. **Pets:** Medium, other species. $30 deposit/room. Service with restrictions, crate.
ASK 🐾 ⊗ 🛏 💻

▼▼ **Ramada Limited** Ⓜ
(801) 571-1122. **$59-$79.** 12605 S Minuteman Dr. I-15, exit 294, 0.3 mi s on frontage road. Int corridors. **Pets:** Accepted.
ASK 🐾 ⊗ 📞 🛏 🛏 💻

MIDVALE

🔴 ▼▼▼ **Best Western Executive Inn** Ⓜ
(801) 566-4141. **$70.** 280 W 7200 S. I-15, exit 301, just e. Int corridors. **Pets:** Accepted.
SAVE 🐾 ⊗ 📞 🛏 💻 🏊

▼▼▼ Candlewood Suites Hotel **M**
(801) 567-0111. **$89-$129.** 6990 S Park Centre Dr. I-15, exit 301, 2.5 mi via 7200 S and Fort Union Blvd. Int corridors. **Pets:** Accepted.
ASK S✕ ⌂ ♿ 🛏 💻

AAA ▼▼▼▼ La Quinta Inn **M**
(801) 566-3291. **$69-$79.** 7231 S 440 W. I-15, exit 301, just e. Int corridors. **Pets:** Other species. Service with restrictions, crate.
SAVE ✕ ⌂ ♿ 🛏 💻 ⇌

AAA ▼▼▼▼ National 9 Discovery Inn **M**
(801) 561-2256. **$45-$74.** 380 W 7200 S. I-15, exit 301, just e. Ext corridors. **Pets:** Medium, other species. $10 deposit/room, $5 daily fee/room. Designated rooms, service with restrictions, supervision.
SAVE S✕ ⌂ 🛏 💻 ⇌

AAA ▼▼▼ Super 8 **M**
(801) 255-5559. **$54-$79.** 7048 S 900 E. I-15, exit 301, 1.5 mi e on 7200 S to 900 E. Int corridors. **Pets:** $100 deposit/room. Service with restrictions, supervision.
SAVE S✕ ⌂ ♿ 🛏 💻

MURRAY

▼▼▼▼ Holiday Inn Express **M**
(801) 268-2533. **$80.** 4465 S Century Dr. I-15, exit 304, just w. Int corridors. **Pets:** Accepted.
ASK S✕ ⌂ 🛏 💻 ⇌

▼▼▼▼ Reston Hotel **M**
(801) 264-1054. **$69-$79.** 5335 College Dr. I-15, exit 303, 0.3 mi w. Int corridors. **Pets:** Accepted.
ASK S✕ ⌂ 🛏 ⇌

▼▼ Studio 6 **M**
(801) 685-2102. **$49-$59.** 975 E 6600 S. I-215, exit 9 on 900 E, 0.5 mi e. Ext corridors. **Pets:** Other species. $10 daily fee/room. Service with restrictions, crate.
✕ ⌂ ♿ 🛏 💻

NORTH SALT LAKE

AAA ▼▼▼▼ Best Western Cottontree Inn **M**
(801) 292-7666. **$60-$140.** 1030 N 400 E. I-15, exit 318, just e. Int corridors. **Pets:** Accepted.
SAVE S✕ ⌂ 🛏 💻 ⇌

SALT LAKE CITY

AAA ▼▼▼▼ Airport Comfort Inn **SH**
(801) 746-5200. **$69-$89.** 200 N Admiral Byrd Rd. I-80, exit 113, 0.8 mi ne via 5600 W, Amelia Earhart Dr, then s. Int corridors. **Pets:** Medium, other species. $15 one-time fee/room. Designated rooms, service with restrictions, crate.
SAVE S✕ ⌂ 🛏 💻 ¶ ⇌

▼▼ Alpine Executive Suites **CO**
(801) 533-8184. **$99-$109, 10 day notice.** 164 S 900 E. Cross streets 200 S and 900 E. Int corridors. **Pets:** Medium, dogs only. $300 deposit/room, $10 daily fee/pet. Designated rooms, service with restrictions, supervision.
ASK S✕ 🛏 💻

▼▼▼ Best Western Airport Inn **M**
(801) 539-5005. **$69-$99, 14 day notice.** 315 N Admiral Byrd Rd. I-80, exit 113, 0.8 m ne via 5600 W and Amelia Earhart Dr, then s. Int corridors. **Pets:** Medium, other species. $15 daily fee/pet. Designated rooms, service with restrictions, supervision.
ASK S✕ ♿ 🛏 💻 ⇌

AAA ▼▼▼ Best Western Garden Inn **SH**
(801) 521-2930. **$64-$109.** 154 W 600 S. Between cross streets 100-200 W. Ext/int corridors. **Pets:** Other species. $50 deposit/pet. Designated rooms, service with restrictions, supervision.
SAVE S✕ ⌂ ♿ 🛏 💻 ¶ ⇌

AAA ▼▼▼ Best Western Salt Lake
Plaza **LH** 🐾
(801) 521-0130. **$69-$129, 3 day notice.** 122 W S Temple Dr. W of Temple Square. Int corridors. **Pets:** Medium, other species. $11 daily fee/pet. Designated rooms, service with restrictions, supervision.
SAVE S✕ ⌂ 🛏 💻 ¶ ⇌

▼▼▼▼ Candlewood Suite Hotel **M**
(801) 359-7500. **$69-$99.** 2170 W N Temple. Temple Square, 3 mi w. Int corridors. **Pets:** Accepted.
ASK S✕ ⌂ ♿ 🛏 💻

▼▼▼▼ Chase Suite Hotel by Woodfin **M**
(801) 532-5511. **$98-$128.** 765 E 400 S. Ext corridors. **Pets:** Medium. $50 deposit/room, $5 daily fee/room. Designated rooms, service with restrictions, supervision.
ASK ✕ ⌂ ♿ 🛏 💻 ⇌ ✕

AAA ▼▼▼ City Creek Inn **M**
(801) 533-9100. **$48-$74.** 230 W N Temple Dr. Cross street 200 W. Ext corridors. **Pets:** Accepted.
SAVE S✕ ⌂ ♿

▼▼▼▼ Days Inn-Salt Lake City Airport **M**
(801) 539-8538. **$60-$140.** 1900 W N Temple. W of Temple 59, 2.5 mi. Int corridors. **Pets:** Other species. $20 deposit/room. Designated rooms, service with restrictions, supervision.
ASK S✕ ⌂ ♿ 🛏 💻 ⇌

▼▼ Econo Lodge Downtown **M**
(801) 363-0062. **$54-$64.** 715 W N Temple. W from Temple Square, 1 mi. Ext corridors. **Pets:** Accepted.
ASK S✕ 🛏 💻 ⇌

AAA ▼▼▼▼ Hilton Salt Lake City Airport **LH**
(801) 539-1515. **$79-$159.** 5151 Wiley Post Way. I-80, exit 114 westbound, 0.4 mi nw via Wright Brothers Dr and Wiley Post; exit 113 eastbound, 1.3 mi ne via 5600 W, Amelia Earhart Dr then s on Charles Lindbergh Dr. Int corridors. **Pets:** Large, other species. $50 deposit/pet. Designated rooms, service with restrictions, crate.
SAVE S✕ ⌂ ♿ 🛏 💻 ¶ ⇌ ✕

▼▼ ▼▼▼ Hilton Salt Lake City Center **LH**
(801) 328-2000. **$79-$209.** 255 S W Temple Dr. Int corridors. **Pets:** Accepted.
ASK S✕ ⌂ ♿ 🛏 💻 ¶ ⇌ ✕

Holiday Inn-Downtown SH
(801) 359-8600. **$110-$145.** 999 S Main St. Cross streets 900 S & Main St. Int corridors. **Pets:** Medium. $35 one-time fee/room. Designated rooms, service with restrictions, supervision.

ASK S X 🔒 🖨 💻 🍴 🏊 ⊗

Homestead Studio Suites Hotel-Salt Lake City/Sugar House M ❀
(801) 474-0771. **$72-$92.** 1220 E 2100 S. Cross streets 1300 E and 2100 S Sugarhouse. Ext corridors. **Pets:** Medium, other species. $25 daily fee/room. Service with restrictions, crate.

ASK S X 🔒 🖨 💻

Hotel Monaco LH ❀
(801) 595-0000. **$199-$220.** 15 W 200 S. Cross streets 200 S and Main St. Int corridors. **Pets:** Other species. Service with restrictions, crate.

SAVE S X 🔒 🖨 💻 🍴 ⊗

Howard Johnson Express Inn M ❀
(801) 521-3450. **$49-$79.** 121 N 300 W. At N Temple. Ext/int corridors. **Pets:** Small. Designated rooms, service with restrictions, supervision.

SAVE S X 🔒 🖨 💻 🏊

La Quinta Inn & Suites Salt Lake City Airport M
(801) 366-4444. **$69-$99.** 4905 W Wiley Post Way. I-80, exit 113 eastbound, 2 mi ne via 5600 W, Amelia Earhart Dr, s on Wright Brothers Dr, then 2 mi to Wiley Post Way; exit 114 westbound, 0.3 mi nw. Int corridors. **Pets:** Service with restrictions, supervision.

SAVE X 🔒 🖨 💻 🏊

Microtel Inn & Suites M ❀
(801) 236-2800. **$48-$58.** 61 N Tommy Thompson Rd. I-80, exit 114 westbound, n on Wright Brothers Dr, e on Wiley Post Way; exit 113 eastbound, 2.4 mi ne via 5600 W, Amelia Earhart Dr, then s. Int corridors. **Pets:** Supervision.

SAVE S X 🔒 🖨 💻

Red Lion Hotel Salt Lake Downtown LH
(801) 521-7373. **$159-$169.** 161 W 600 S. At W Temple and 600 S. Int corridors. **Pets:** Medium, other species. $10 daily fee/pet. Service with restrictions, supervision.

ASK S X 🔒 🖨 💻 🍴 🏊 ⊗

Residence Inn by Marriott at The Cottonwoods M
(801) 453-0430. **$71-$239.** 6425 S 3000 E. I-215 S, exit 6200 S, 0.3 mi se. Int corridors. **Pets:** Other species. $150 one-time fee/room. Service with restrictions.

ASK S X 🔒 🖨 💻 🏊 ⊗

Residence Inn by Marriott-City Center SH
(801) 355-3300. **$109-$209.** 285 W 300 S. Cross streets 300 W and 300 S (Broadway). Int corridors. **Pets:** Small, other species. $20 daily fee/pet, $200 one-time fee/pet. Service with restrictions, crate.

X 🔒 🖨 💻 🏊 ⊗

Residence Inn by Marriott Salt Lake City Airport SH
(801) 532-4101. **$119, 7 day notice.** 4883 W Douglas Corrigon Way. I-80, exit 114 westbound, via Wright Brothers Dr; exit 113 eastbound, via Amelia Earhart and Wright Brothers drs, then 2.6 mi se. Int corridors. **Pets:** Other species. $50 one-time fee/room. Service with restrictions, crate.

ASK S X 🔒 🖨 💻 🏊 ⊗

Saltair Bed & Breakfast BB
(801) 533-8184. **$79-$109, 10 day notice.** 164 S 900 E. Cross streets 900 E and 200 S. Ext/int corridors. **Pets:** Accepted.

ASK S X 🖨 💻

Salt Lake City Centre Travelodge M
(801) 531-7100. **$59, 7 day notice.** 524 S W Temple. Cross streets 500 S and Temple. Ext corridors. **Pets:** Small. $20 one-time fee/room. Designated rooms, supervision.

ASK S X 🔒 🖨 💻 🏊

Salt Lake Travelodge At Temple Square M
(801) 533-8200. **$75.** 144 W N Temple. Just n of Genealogical Library. Ext/int corridors. **Pets:** Large, other species. Service with restrictions, crate.

ASK S X 🖨 💻

Sheraton City Centre LH
(801) 401-2000. **$70-$119.** 150 W 500 S. At 200 W and 500 S. Int corridors. **Pets:** Accepted.

ASK S X 🔒 🖨 💻 🍴 🏊 ⊗

The Skyline Inn M
(801) 582-5350. **$55-$77.** 2475 E 1700 S. E off Foothill Dr. Ext corridors. **Pets:** Accepted.

SAVE S X 🔒 🖨 🏊

Super 8 Airport M
(801) 533-8878. **$79.** 223 N Jimmy Doolittle Rd. I-80, exit 113, 0.7 mi ne via 5600 W, Amelia Earhart Dr and Admiral Byrd Rd, then e. Int corridors. **Pets:** $50 deposit/room. Service with restrictions, supervision.

SAVE S X 🔒 🖨 💻 🏊

SANDY

Best Western Cotton Tree Inn M
(801) 523-8484. **$84-$150.** 10695 S Auto Mall Dr. I-15, exit 297 E, 0.3 mi e. Int corridors. **Pets:** Accepted.

SAVE S X 🔒 🖨 💻

Comfort Inn M
(801) 255-4919. **$65-$109.** 8955 S 255 West. I-15, exit 298, just ne, follow signs. Int corridors. **Pets:** Large, other species. $10 daily fee/pet. Service with restrictions, crate.

ASK S X 🔒 🖨 💻

Country Inn & Suites M
(801) 553-1151. **$92.** 10499 S Jordan Gate Way. I-15, exit 297 W, 1 mi w via 10600 S to Jordan Gate Way, then n. Int corridors. **Pets:** Accepted.

SAVE S X 🔒 🖨 💻 🏊 ⊗

Residence Inn by Marriott M ❀
(801) 561-5005. **$109-$209.** 270 W 10000 S. From Stare St, 0.3 mi w on 10000 S. Int corridors. **Pets:** Other species. $150 one-time fee/room. Service with restrictions, crate.

ASK S X 🔒 🖨 💻 🏊 ⊗

▼▼▼▼ **Sandy Comfort Suites** Ⓜ
(801) 495-1317. **$84-$109.** 10680 S Auto Mall Dr. I-15, exit 297 E, 0.3 mi e. Int corridors. **Pets:** Large, other species. $10 daily fee/pet. Service with restrictions, supervision.

🈂️ 🔊 ✕ 🖉 🖉 🚪 🖥 ➳

▼▼ **Sleep Inn** Ⓜ
(801) 572-2020. **$50-$79.** 10676 S 300 W. I-15, exit 297 W, just w. Int corridors. **Pets:** Other species. $50 deposit/room. Designated rooms, service with restrictions, supervision.

🈂️ 🔊 ✕ 🚪 🖥 🏊

▼▼▼▼ **Super 8 Motel Sandy/South Jordan** Ⓜ
(801) 553-8888. **$45-$79.** 10722 S 300 W. I-15, exit 297 W, just w. Int corridors. **Pets:** Medium, other species. $50 deposit/room. Service with restrictions, supervision.

🈂️ 🔊 ✕ 🖉 🖉 🚪 🖥 ➳

SOUTH SALT LAKE

▼▼▼▼ **Days Inn-Central** Ⓜ
(801) 486-8780. **$59-$89.** 315 W 3300 S. W from State St, 0.3 mi; I-15, just e. Ext corridors. **Pets:** Accepted.

🈂️ 🔊 ✕ 🖉 🚪 🖥 ➳ ✕

▼▼▼▼ **Ramada Limited Salt Lake City** Ⓜ
(801) 486-2400. **$75.** 2455 S State St. Cross street Morris Ave. Int corridors. **Pets:** Cats only. Service with restrictions, supervision.

🈂️ 🔊 ✕ 🖉 🚪 🖥 ➳

TAYLORSVILLE

▼▼ **Homestead Studio Suites Hotel-Salt Lake City/Mid Valley** Ⓜ ❀
(801) 269-9292. **$50-$70.** 5683 S Redwood Rd. I-215, exit 13, 0.5 mi n. Ext corridors. **Pets:** Medium, other species. $25 daily fee/room. Service with restrictions, crate.

🈂️ 🔊 ✕ 🖉 🖉 🚪 🖥

WEST VALLEY CITY

🔺 ▼▼▼▼ **Baymont Inn & Suites Salt Lake City-West Valley City** Ⓜ
(801) 886-1300. **$64-$84.** 2229 W City Center Ct. I-215, exit 18, just e. Int corridors. **Pets:** Accepted.

🈂️ 🔊 ✕ 🖉 🖉 🚪 🖥 ➳

▼▼▼▼ **La Quinta Inn & Suites** Ⓜ
(801) 954-9292. **$59-$99, 10 day notice.** 3540 S 2200 W. I-215, exit 18; east side. Int corridors. **Pets:** Accepted.

🈂️ 🔊 ✕ 🖉 🚪 🖥 ➳

▼▼ **Parkway Suites** Ⓜ
(801) 977-0800. **$79.** 3580 W Parkway Blvd. Cross streets 2700 S and 3600 W. Ext corridors. **Pets:** Accepted.

🈂️ ✕ 🚪 🖥

▼▼ **Sleep Inn** Ⓜ ❀
(801) 975-1888. **$59.** 3440 S 2200 W. I-215, exit 18, just e. Int corridors. **Pets:** $6 daily fee/room. Service with restrictions, supervision.

🈂️ 🔊 ✕ 🖉 🖉 🚪 🖥 ➳

WOODS CROSS

▼▼▼▼ **Hampton Inn** Ⓜ
(801) 296-1211. **$69-$84.** 2393 S 800 W. I-15, exit 318, just w of freeway. Int corridors. **Pets:** Medium. $25 deposit/room. Service with restrictions, supervision.

🈂️ 🔊 ✕ 🖉 🚪 🖥 ➳

❀ **END METROPOLITAN AREA** ❀

SCIPIO

▼▼ **Super 8** Ⓜ
(435) 758-9188. **$55-$65.** 230 W 400 N. I-15, exit 188, just ne. Int corridors. **Pets:** Accepted.

🈂️ 🔊 ✕ 🖉 🚪 🖥 ➳

SPANISH FORK

🔺 ▼▼▼ **Western Inn** Ⓜ
(801) 798-9400. **$54-$65.** 632 Kirby Ln. I-15, exit 261 southbound, 0.5 mi e; exit 260 northbound, 1 mi ne. Int corridors. **Pets:** $10 one-time fee/room. Service with restrictions, supervision.

🈂️ 🔊 ✕ 🚪

SPRINGDALE

🔺 ▼▼▼▼ **Best Western Zion Park Inn** Ⓜ
(435) 772-3200. **$62-$109.** 1215 Zion Park Blvd. 2 mi s of park entrance. Int corridors. **Pets:** Small. $25 one-time fee/room. Designated rooms, service with restrictions, supervision.

🈂️ 🔊 ✕ 🖉 🖉 🚪 🖥 🍴 ➳ ✕

▼▼▼ **Canyon Ranch Motel** 🄲🄰 ❀
(435) 772-3357. **$68-$88.** 668 Zion Park Blvd. SR 9, just s of south gate to Zion National Park. Ext corridors. **Pets:** Dogs only. $10 one-time fee/pet. Service with restrictions, supervision.

✕ 🚪 🖥 ➳

🔺 ▼▼▼▼ **Driftwood Lodge** Ⓜ
(435) 772-3262. **$72-$109.** 1515 Zion Park Blvd. SR 9, 2 mi s of south gate to Zion National Park. Ext corridors. **Pets:** Other species. $10 one-time fee/room. Designated rooms, service with restrictions, supervision.

🈂️ 🔊 ✕ 🚪 🖥 ➳

▼▼▼▼ **Majestic View Lodge** 🅂🄷
(435) 772-0665. **$89-$199.** 2400 Zion Park Blvd. 3 mi s of park entrance. Ext corridors. **Pets:** Small, dogs only. $50 deposit/pet. Designated rooms, service with restrictions, supervision.

🈂️ 🔊 ✕ 🚪 🖥 ➳ ✕

SPRINGVILLE

AAA ▼▼▼ Best Western CottonTree Inn M
(801) 489-3641. **$59-$94, 14 day notice.** 1455 N 1750 W.
I-15, exit 265, just e; just s of Provo. Int corridors.
Pets: Other species. $10 one-time fee/room. Service with
restrictions.
[SAVE] [S&] [X] [🖉] [📠] [🖥] [🖥] [≈]

▼▼▼ Days Inn M
(801) 491-0300. **$65-$70.** 520 S 2000 W. I-15, exit 263. Int
corridors. **Pets:** Accepted.
[ASK] [S&] [X] [📠] [🖥] [🖥] [≈]

TICABOO

▼▼ Ticaboo Resort M
(435) 788-2110. **$49-$99.** 84533 Hwy 276. Jct SR 95 and
276, 28 mi s. Int corridors. **Pets:** Accepted.
[ASK] [S&] [X] [🍴] [≈]

TORREY

▼▼ Cactus Hill Ranch Motel M
(435) 425-3578. **$45-$75, 3 day notice.** 830 S 1000 E. 5 mi
s of SR 24 at Teasdale; 5 mi w of SR 12, exit Teasdale; 13
mi w of Capitol Reef National Park, 2 mi se of Town Center.
Ext corridors. **Pets:** Medium. Service with restrictions,
supervision.
[X] [🖥] [🖥]

▼▼ Rim Rock Inn M
(435) 425-3398. **$49-$59.** 2523 E Hwy 24. 2.5 mi e of jct SR
12 and 24; east end of town. Ext corridors. **Pets:** Accepted.
[ASK] [S&] [X] [📠] [🍴]

▼▼ Torrey/Capitol Reef-Super 8 M ❀
(435) 425-3688. **$39-$78.** 600 E Hwy 24. On SR 24, 0.3 mi
w of SR 12; 3.3 mi w of Capitol Reef National Park. Int
corridors. **Pets:** Medium. $10 daily fee/pet. Designated
rooms, service with restrictions, supervision.
[X] [📠] [🖥] [🖥] [≈]

AAA ▼▼▼ Torrey Days Inn M
(435) 425-3111. **$60-$70.** 675 E Hwy 24. Jct SR 12 and 24.
Int corridors. **Pets:** Medium, other species. $50 deposit/
room, $10 one-time fee/room. Designated rooms, service
with restrictions, supervision.
[SAVE] [S&] [X] [📠] [🖥] [≈]

AAA ▼▼▼▼ Wonderland Inn M
(435) 425-3775. **$40-$70.** Jct SR 12 & 24. Jct SR 12 and 24;
3 mi w of Capitol Reef National Park. Ext corridors.
Pets: Accepted.
[SAVE] [S&] [X] [📠] [🍴] [≈]

TREMONTON

AAA ▼▼▼ Sandman Motel M
(435) 257-5675. **$51-$60.** 585 W Main St. I-15/84, exit 379,
2.1 mi ne to 4-way stop, then 1.5 mi w; I-15 S, exit 383, 0.6
mi e to 4-way stop, s to Main St, then 0.5 mi w; I-84, exit
40, 1.5 mi e. Ext corridors. **Pets:** Accepted.
[SAVE] [S&] [X]

TROPIC

▼▼ Doug's Country Inn Motel M
(435) 679-8632. **$25-$50.** 141 N Main St. On SR 12; center.
Int corridors. **Pets:** Accepted.
[ASK] [S&] [X] [🍴]

AAA ▼▼▼ World Host Bryce Valley Inn M
(435) 679-8811. **$40-$90.** 199 N Main St. SR 12, 10 mi e of
Bryce Canyon Park. Ext/int corridors. **Pets:** Accepted.
[SAVE] [S&] [X] [🖥] [🍴]

VERNAL

AAA ▼▼▼ Econolodge M
(435) 789-2000. **$45-$75, 14 day notice.** 311 E Main St. Ext
corridors. **Pets:** $5 daily fee/pet. Service with restrictions,
supervision.
[SAVE] [S&] [X] [📠] [🖥]

▼▼ Motel 6 M
(435) 789-0666. **$40-$56.** 1092 W Hwy 40. Int corridors.
Pets: Other species. $5 daily fee/room. Service with restric-
tions, supervision.
[X] [🖉] [📠] [🖥] [≈]

▼▼ Rodeway Inn M
(435) 789-8172. **$38-$55.** 590 W Main St. US 40. Ext corridors. **Pets:** $5 daily fee/pet. Service with restrictions, super-
vision.
[ASK] [S&] [X] [📠] [🖥] [🍴]

▼ Sage Motel & Restaurant M ❀
(435) 789-1442. **$45-$80.** 54 W Main St. Center. Ext corridors. **Pets:** Other species. $5 daily fee/pet. Designated
rooms, service with restrictions.
[X] [📠] [🍴]

WELLINGTON

▼▼ National 9 Inn SH
(435) 637-7980. **$44-$59.** 50 S 700 E. On US 6. Ext/int
corridors. **Pets:** Other species. $5 daily fee/pet. Service with
restrictions, supervision.
[ASK] [S&] [X] [📠] [🍴] [≈]

WENDOVER

▼▼▼▼ Days Inn of Wendover M
(435) 665-2215. **$59-$99.** 685 E Wendover Blvd. I-80, exit 2.
Int corridors. **Pets:** Accepted.
[ASK] [S&] [X] [🖉] [📠] [≈]

▼▼▼ Econo Lodge M
(435) 665-2226. **$55-$85.** 295 E Wendover Blvd. I-80, exit 2.
Ext/int corridors. **Pets:** Accepted.
[ASK] [S&] [X] [📠] [≈]

▼ Western Ridge Motel M
(435) 665-2211. **$21-$64.** 895 E Wendover Blvd. I-80, exit 2.
Ext corridors. **Pets:** Designated rooms, service with restrictions, supervision.
[ASK] [S&] [X] [📠] [≈]

VERMONT

ALBURG

♥♥ Ransom Bay Inn BB
(802) 796-3399. **$75.** 4 Center Bay Rd. 0.5 mi s on US 2, from jct SR 78. Int corridors. **Pets:** Small. Designated rooms, no service, supervision.
⊠ 🅿 🅩

BARRE

◆◆ ♥♥♥ The Hollow Inn & Motel M
(802) 479-9313. **$90-$135, 3 day notice.** 278 S Main St. Jct US 302, 1 mi s on SR 14; I-89, exit 6, 4.3 mi e on SR 63, 0.7 mi n on SR 14. Ext/int corridors. **Pets:** Accepted.
SAVE 🆂 🔒 💻 ➔ ⊠

BENNINGTON

◆◆ ♥♥♥ Apple Valley Inn & Cafe M
(802) 442-6588. **$45-$94.** 979 US Hwy 7 S. Jct SR 9, 1.8 mi s. Ext/int corridors. **Pets:** Accepted.
SAVE 🆂 ⊠ 🔒 🍴 ➔

◆◆ ♥♥♥ Bennington Motor Inn M ❖
(802) 442-5479. **$73-$108, 10 day notice.** 143 W Main St. Jct US 7, 0.4 mi w on SR 9. Ext corridors. **Pets:** $20 daily fee/room. Designated rooms, service with restrictions, supervision.
SAVE ⊠ 🔒 💻

◆◆ ♥♥♥ Darling Kelly's Motel M
(802) 442-2322. **$43-$105, 3 day notice.** 357 US 7 S. Jct SR 9 and US 7, 1.2 mi s. Ext corridors. **Pets:** Dogs only. $5 daily fee/pet. Designated rooms, supervision.
SAVE 🆂 ⊠ 🔒 ➔

◆◆ ♥♥♥ Fife 'N Drum Motel M ❖
(802) 442-4074. **$47-$112, 3 day notice.** 693 US Rt 7 S. Jct SR 9 and US 7, 1.6 mi s. Ext corridors. **Pets:** Medium, dogs only. $6 daily fee/pet. Designated rooms, service with restrictions, supervision.
SAVE 🆂 ⊠ 🔒 💻 ➔ ⊠

♥♥♥ Knotty Pine Motel M
(802) 442-5487. **$51-$95.** 130 Northside Dr (SR 7A). Jct SR 9, 1.2 mi n on US 7, then just n on Historic SR 7A. Ext corridors. **Pets:** Accepted.
⊠ 🔒 💻 ➔

◆◆ ♥♥♥ Vermonter Motor Lodge M
(802) 442-2529. **$80-$129.** 2968 West Rd. 3.9 mi w on SR 9, from jct US 7. Ext corridors. **Pets:** Medium. $10 one-time fee/pet. No service, crate.
SAVE 🆂 ⊠ 🔒 ⊠

BRANDON

◆◆ ♥♥♥ Brandon Motor Lodge M ❖
(802) 247-9594. **$55-$95.** 2095 Franklin St. 2 mi s on US 7. Ext corridors. **Pets:** Medium, dogs only. $5 daily fee/room. Designated rooms, supervision.
SAVE ⊠ 🔒 ⊠

♥♥♥ The Lilac Inn CI
(802) 247-5463. **$140-$325, 30 day notice.** 53 Park St. Just e on SR 73. Int corridors. **Pets:** Accepted.
ASK 🆂 ⊠ 🍴 🅩

BRATTLEBORO

◆◆ ♥♥♥ Colonial Motel & Spa SH
(802) 257-7733. **$130.** 889 Putney Rd. I-91, exit 3, just e on SR 9, then 0.5 mi s on US 5. Ext corridors. **Pets:** Other species. $10 daily fee/room. Service with restrictions, supervision.
SAVE 🆂 ⊠ 🔒 💻 🍴 ➔ ⊠

◆◆ ♥♥♥ Super 8 Motel M
(802) 254-8889. **$50-$115.** 1043 Putney Rd. I-91, exit 3, just e on SR 9, then just s on US 5. Int corridors. **Pets:** Other species. Service with restrictions, supervision.
SAVE ⊠ 🆎 🔒

BURLINGTON

◆◆ ♥♥♥ Town & Country Motel M ❖
(802) 862-5786. **$59-$109, 3 day notice.** 490 Shelburne Rd. I-89, exit 13, just n on US 7 N. Ext corridors. **Pets:** Dogs only. $10 daily fee/pet. Designated rooms, service with restrictions.
SAVE ⊠ 🔒 💻

CAVENDISH

◆◆ ♥♥♥ Clarion Hotel at Cavendish Pointe SH
(802) 226-7688. **$89-$289, 14 day notice.** 2940 SR 103. On SR 103, just n of jct SR 131. Int corridors. **Pets:** $20 daily fee/room. Designated rooms, supervision.
SAVE 🆂 ⊠ 🔒 💻 🍴 ➔ ⊠

CHESTER

♦♦ The Stone Hearth Inn **CI**
(802) 875-2525. **$79-$159, 14 day notice.** 698 Rt 11 W. 1.5
mi w. Int corridors. **Pets:** Medium. $35 one-time fee/pet.
Designated rooms, service with restrictions, supervision.

CHITTENDEN

♦♦♦ The Mountain Top Inn & Resort **CI**
(802) 483-2311. **$115-$415, 21 day notice.** 195 Mountain
Top Rd. Jct US 4, 1.8 mi n on Meadowlake Dr, 2.8 mi e on
Chittenden Rd, then 2 mi n. Ext/int corridors.
Pets: Accepted.

COLCHESTER

♦♦ Days Inn **SH**
(802) 655-0900. **$50-$175.** 23 College Pkwy. I-89, exit 15
northbound, just e on SR 15; exit 16 southbound, 1.1 mi s
on US 7, then 1 mi e on SR 15. Int corridors. **Pets:** Dogs
only. $20 deposit/room, $10 daily fee/pet. Designated
rooms, service with restrictions, supervision.

♦♦♦ Hampton Inn & Conference Center **SH**
(802) 655-6177. **$99-$159.** 42 Lower Mountain View Dr. I-89,
exit 16, just n on US 7. Int corridors. **Pets:** Designated
rooms, service with restrictions, supervision.

♦♦ Motel 6 **SH**
(802) 654-6860. **$45-$91.** 74 S Park Dr. I-89, exit 16, just s
on US 7. Int corridors. **Pets:** Other species. Service with
restrictions, crate.

CRAFTSBURY COMMON

♦♦♦ Inn on the Common **CI**
(802) 586-9619. **$109-$239, 30 day notice.** 1162 N Crafts-
bury Rd. Center. Ext/int corridors. **Pets:** Accepted.

ESSEX JUNCTION

♦♦♦ ♦♦♦♦ The Inn at Essex **SH** ❀
(802) 878-1100. **$169-$499, 7 day notice.** 70 Essex Way.
SR 289, exit 10, then 0.3 mi s. Int corridors. **Pets:** Other
species. $300 deposit/room, $25 daily fee/pet. Designated
rooms, service with restrictions.

♦♦♦♦ The Wilson Inn **SH** ❀
(802) 879-1515. **$65-$239.** 10 Kellogg Rd. I-89, exit 15
northbound, 2.1 mi e on SR 15, then 0.5 mi n on Susie
Wilson Rd; exit 16 southbound, 1 mi s on US 7, 2.8 mi e on
SR 15, then 0.5 mi n on Susie Wilson Rd. Int corridors.
Pets: Other species. $10 daily fee/room. Designated
rooms.

FAIRLEE

♦♦♦ ♦♦ Silver Maple Lodge & Cottages **BB**
(802) 333-4326. **$64-$89, 14 day notice.** 520 US 5 S. I-91,
exit 15, 0.5 mi s. Ext/int corridors. **Pets:** Other species.
Designated rooms.

FERRISBURG

♦♦♦ ♦♦ Skyview Motel **M** ❀
(802) 877-3410. **$50-$95, 3 day notice.** 2956 US Rt 7. On
US 7, 0.3 mi s. Ext corridors. **Pets:** Other species. $15 daily
fee/pet. No service, supervision.

FLETCHER

♦♦♦ The Inn at Buck Hollow Farm **BB** ❀
(802) 849-2400. **$73-$93, 14 day notice.** 2150 Buck Hollow
Rd. 6.4 mi n of jct SR 104 via Buck Hollow Rd. Int corridors. **Pets:** Crate.

JAMAICA

♦♦♦ ♦♦♦ Three Mountain Inn **CI** ❀
(802) 874-4140. **$145-$345, 10 day notice.** 3732 Main St.
On SR 30; center. Ext/int corridors. **Pets:** Dogs only. $75
deposit/pet, $25 one-time fee/pet. Designated rooms, serv-
ice with restrictions, supervision.

JEFFERSONVILLE

♦♦ Deer Run Motor Inn **M**
(802) 644-8866. **$85, 15 day notice.** 80 Deer Run Loop. 0.7
mi e on SR 15. Ext/int corridors. **Pets:** Medium. $10 daily
fee/pet. Service with restrictions, supervision.

KILLINGTON

♦♦♦ ♦♦ Butternut on the Mountain **SH**
(802) 422-2000. **$58-$205, 30 day notice.** 63 Weathervane
Rd. Jct SR 100/US 4, 1.1 mi s on Killington Rd, then just e.
Ext/int corridors. **Pets:** Accepted.

♦♦♦ ♦♦♦♦ The Cascades Lodge **SH**
(802) 422-3731. **$79-$229, 21 day notice.** 58 Old Mill Rd.
3.6 mi s on Killington Rd, from jct SR 100/US 4, then just e.
Int corridors. **Pets:** Other species. $10 daily fee/room. Des-
ignated rooms, crate.

♦♦♦ ♦♦ Val Roc Motel **M** ❀
(802) 422-3881. **$59-$120, 14 day notice.** 8006 US 4. 5.9
mi e on US 4, from jct SR 100 N. Ext/int corridors.
Pets: Other species. $5 daily fee/pet. Service with restric-
tions.

LUDLOW

△△△ ▽▽▽ Timber Inn Motel M
(802) 228-8666. **$69-$179, 14 day notice.** 112 Rt 103 S. On SR 103 S, 1 mi e. Ext corridors. **Pets:** Dogs only. $10 daily fee/pet. Designated rooms, crate.
(SAVE) (S⌀) ⊠ 🛢 ▣ ⊇ ⊠

MENDON

▽▽▽▽ Cortina Inn and Resort SH ❖
(802) 773-3333. **$119-$229.** 103 US 4. Jct SR 100 N, 3 mi w. Int corridors. **Pets:** Other species. $10 daily fee/pet. Designated rooms, service with restrictions, supervision.
(ASK) (S⌀) ⊠ 🖉 🛢 ▣ 🍴 ⊇ ⊠

△△△ ▽▽▽ Econo Lodge-Killington Area SH
(802) 773-6644. **$45-$135, 7 day notice.** 51 US 4. Jct US 7, 5.3 mi e. Int corridors. **Pets:** $10 one-time fee/room. Designated rooms, service with restrictions, supervision.
(SAVE) (S⌀) ⊠ 🛢 ▣ ⊇ ⊠

△△△ ▽▽▽ Mendon Mountainview Resort Lodge SH ❖
(802) 773-4311. **$59-$169, 7 day notice.** 78 US 4. On US 4, 6 mi e of jct US 7. Int corridors. **Pets:** Medium, dogs only. $50 deposit/room. Designated rooms, service with restrictions, crate.
(SAVE) (S⌀) ⊠ 🛢 ⊇ ⊠

△△△ ▽▽ Red Carpet Inn M
(802) 775-5577. **$54-$135, 14 day notice.** 119 Rt 4. Jct SR 100 N, 3 mi w. Ext corridors. **Pets:** Medium. Designated rooms, no service.
(SAVE) (S⌀) ⊠ 🛢 ▣ ⊇ ⊠

MIDDLEBURY

△△△ ▽▽▽▽ The Middlebury Inn SH ❖
(802) 388-4961. **$88-$395, 3 day notice.** 14 Court Square. On US 7; center. Ext/int corridors. **Pets:** Designated rooms, service with restrictions, crate.
(SAVE) (S⌀) ⊠ 🖉 ✒ 🛢 ▣ 🍴

MONTPELIER

△△△ ▽▽ Econo Lodge M
(802) 223-5258. **$55-$75.** 101 Northfield St. Just s of jct US 302/SR 12. Ext corridors. **Pets:** Medium. $10 daily fee/room. Service with restrictions.
(SAVE) ⊠ 🛢 ▣ 🍴

NEWFANE

▽▽▽▽ Four Columns Inn CI
(802) 365-7713. **$125-$340, 14 day notice.** 21 West St. Just w of SR 30; center. Int corridors. **Pets:** Accepted.
⊠ 🍴 ⊇

NORTH HERO

△△△ ▽▽▽ Shore Acres Inn SH
(802) 372-8722. **$105-$195, 10 day notice.** 237 Shore Acres Dr. 1 mi s on US 2. Ext/int corridors. **Pets:** Other species. $10 deposit/pet. Service with restrictions, supervision.
(SAVE) ⊠ 🛢 🍴 ⊠ 🗲

PERU

▽▽▽ Johnny Seesaw's CI ❖
(802) 824-5533. **$80-$150, 14 day notice.** 3574 Vt Rt 11. 2.1 mi e on SR 11, from jct SR 30 S. Ext/int corridors. **Pets:** Other species. $10 daily fee/pet.
🛢 🍴 ⊇ ⊠

PUTNEY

▽▽▽▽ The Putney Inn SH
(802) 387-5517. **$78-$158.** 57 Putney Landing Rd. I-91, exit 4, just e. Ext corridors. **Pets:** $10 daily fee/pet. Supervision.
(ASK) (S⌀) ⊠ ▣ 🍴

RUTLAND

△△△ ▽▽▽▽ Holiday Inn Rutland/Killington LH
(802) 775-1911. **$139-$299.** 476 US Rt 7 S. 2.4 mi s on US 7, from US 4 W; 0.4 mi n, US 7 from US 4 E. Int corridors. **Pets:** Other species. $10 daily fee/pet. Service with restrictions, supervision.
(SAVE) (S⌀) ⊠ ⌂M 🖉 🛢 ▣ 🍴 ⊇ ⊠

△△△ ▽▽▽ Ramada Limited of Rutland SH ❖
(802) 773-3361. **$49-$179.** 253 S Main St, US 7. 1.3 mi s on US 7, from US 4 W; 1.5 mi n US 7, from US 4 E. Int corridors. **Pets:** $25 one-time fee/pet. Designated rooms, service with restrictions, supervision.
(SAVE) (S⌀) ⊠ 🛢 ▣ ⊇

▽▽▽▽ Red Roof Inn Rutland-Killington SH
(802) 775-4303. **$69-$179, 14 day notice.** 401 US Hwy 7 S. On US 7/4. Int corridors. **Pets:** Medium. Service with restrictions, supervision.
(ASK) (S⌀) ⊠ ✒ 🛢 ▣ ⊇ ⊠

△△△ ▽▽ Rodeway Inn M
(802) 775-2575. **$39-$165, 5 day notice.** 138 N Main St. US 7, 0.5 mi n of jct US 4 E. Ext corridors. **Pets:** Small. $10 daily fee/pet. Service with restrictions, supervision.
(SAVE) (S⌀) ⊠ 🛢 ⊇

△△△ ▽▽ Royal Motel M
(802) 773-9176. **$52-$109, 7 day notice.** 115 Woodstock Ave. Jct US 7, 0.5 mi e on US 4 (Woodstock Ave). Ext/int corridors. **Pets:** Large, other species. $10 daily fee/pet. Designated rooms, no service, supervision.
(SAVE) (S⌀) ⊠ 🛢 ⊇

ST. ALBANS

△△△ ▽▽▽ Econo Lodge M
(802) 524-5956. **$55-$109.** 287 S Main St. I-89, exit 19, 1 mi w to US 7, then 0.5 mi s. Ext/int corridors. **Pets:** Small. $10 daily fee/pet. Service with restrictions, supervision.
(SAVE) (S⌀) ⊠ 🛢 ▣

ST. JOHNSBURY

▽▽▽ Fairbanks Inn M ❖
(802) 748-5666. **$69-$169.** 401 Western Ave. I-91, exit 21, 1 mi e on US 2. Ext corridors. **Pets:** Dogs only. $5 daily fee/pet. Designated rooms, service with restrictions, supervision.
(ASK) (S⌀) ⊠ 🛢 ▣ ⊇

▼▼ Holiday Motel & Annex M
(802) 748-8192. $49-$139. 222 Hastings St. Jct US 5 and
Alternate 5. Ext/int corridors. Pets: Medium, dogs only. Designated rooms, service with restrictions, supervision.
ASK SÓ ☒ 🛏 🗷

SHAFTSBURY

▼ Serenity Motel CA
(802) 442-6490. $65-$80. 4379 Rt 7A. 3.3 mi n on Historic
SR 7A, from jct SR 67. Ext corridors. Pets: Large, other
species. Designated rooms, supervision.
☒ 🛏 🖵

SOUTH BURLINGTON

▼▼ Anchorage Inn SH
(802) 863-7000. $60-$110. 108 Dorset St. I-89, exit 14E, just
e on US 2 to Dorset St, then 0.3 mi s. Int corridors.
Pets: Dogs only. $50 deposit/room. Designated rooms,
service with restrictions, supervision.
ASK SÓ ☒ 🛏 🖵 🗷

▼▼▼ Best Western Windjammer Inn &
Conference Center SH ❀
(802) 863-1125. $89-$154. 1076 Williston Rd. I-89, exit 14E,
0.3 mi e on US 2. Int corridors. Pets: $5 daily fee/pet.
Designated rooms, service with restrictions, supervision.
ASK SÓ ☒ ᏦM 🎵 🎿 🛏 🖵 🍴 🗷 🏞

🏧 ▼▼▼ Clarion Hotel and Suites SH ❀
(802) 658-0250. $109-$199. 1117 Williston Rd. I-89, exit 14E,
just e on US 2. Int corridors. Pets: Other species. $50
deposit/room. Service with restrictions, supervision.
SAVE SÓ ☒ ᏦM 🎵 🎿 🛏 🖵 🍴 🗷

▼▼▼ Comfort Inn SH
(802) 865-3400. $69-$159. 1285 Williston Rd. I-89, exit 14E,
0.5 mi e on US 2. Int corridors. Pets: Other species. $10
daily fee/room. Service with restrictions.
ASK SÓ ☒ ᏦM 🎵 🛏 🖵 🗷

🏧 ▼▼▼ Hawthorn Suites Hotel SH ❀
(802) 860-1212. $105-$190, 7 day notice. 401 Dorset St.
I-89, exit 14E, just e on US 2, then 0.8 mi s. Int corridors.
Pets: Other species. $5 daily fee/pet. Designated rooms,
service with restrictions, crate.
SAVE SÓ ☒ ᏦM 🛏 🖵 🗷 🏞

🏧 ▼▼▼ Holiday Inn Burlington LH
(802) 863-6363. $84-$188. 1068 Williston Rd. I-89, exit 14E,
just e on US 2. Int corridors. Pets: Accepted.
SAVE SÓ ☒ ᏦM 🎵 🛏 🖵 🍴 🗷

▼▼▼ MainStay Suites SH
(802) 860-1986. $109-$199. 1702 Shelburne Rd. I-89, exit
13 to US 7, then 1.5 mi s. Int corridors. Pets: Accepted.
ASK SÓ ☒ 🛏 🖵

🏧 ▼▼▼ Sheraton Burlington Hotel &
Conference Center LH
(802) 865-6600. $159-$249. 870 Williston Rd. I-89, exit 14W,
just w on US 2. Int corridors. Pets: Accepted.
SAVE ☒ 🎵 🛏 🖵 🍴 🗷 🏞

🏧 ▼▼▼ Smart Suites SH
(802) 860-9900. $99-$199. 1700 Shelburne Rd. I-89, exit 13
to US 7, then 1.5 mi s. Int corridors. Pets: Accepted.
SAVE SÓ ☒ 🛏 🖵

SOUTH WOODSTOCK

🏧 ▼▼▼ Kedron Valley Inn CI
(802) 457-1473. $109-$327, 7 day notice. Rt 106. Jct US 4,
5 mi s. Ext/int corridors. Pets: Accepted.
SAVE ☒ 🛏 🖵 🍴 🗷 🏞

SPRINGFIELD

▼▼▼ Holiday Inn Express SH
(802) 885-4516. $109-$169. 818 Charlestown Rd. I-91, exit
7. Int corridors. Pets: Accepted.
ASK SÓ ☒ ᏦM 🎿 🛏 🖵 🍴 🗷

STOWE

▼▼▼ 1066 Ye Olde England Inne CI ❀
(802) 253-7558. $119-$359, 15 day notice. 433 Mountain
Rd. 0.4 mi w on SR 108, from jct SR 100. Ext/int corridors.
Pets: Large, other species. $10 daily fee/pet. Designated
rooms, service with restrictions.
ASK SÓ ☒ 🎿 🛏 🖵 🍴 🏞 🗷

🏧 ▼▼▼ Andersen Lodge-An Austrian Inn CI
(802) 253-7336. $68-$198, 4 day notice. 3430 Mountain Rd.
3.5 mi w on SR 108, from jct SR 100. Int corridors.
Pets: Dogs only. $5 deposit/pet. Service with restrictions,
supervision.
SAVE SÓ ☒ 🛏 🍴 🏞 🗷

🏧 ▼▼▼ Commodores Inn LH
(802) 253-7131. $98-$198, 7 day notice. 823 S Main St. Jct
SR 108, 0.8 mi s on SR 100. Int corridors. Pets: Accepted.
SAVE SÓ ☒ 🎿 🛏 🍴 🏞 🗷

▼▼▼ Edson Hill Manor CI
(802) 253-7371. $99-$199, 15 day notice. 1500 Edson Hill
Rd. Jct SR 100, 3.5 mi w on SR 108, then 1.3 mi n. Ext/int
corridors. Pets: Dogs only. Service with restrictions, supervision.
☒ 🍴 🏞 🗷

🏧 ▼▼▼ Green Mountain Inn CI
(802) 253-7301. $105-$225, 14 day notice. 18 S Main St.
Jct SR 108 on SR 100; center. Ext/int corridors.
Pets: Accepted.
SAVE SÓ ☒ 🛏 🖵 🍴 🏞 🗷

🏧 ▼▼▼ Hob Knob Inn & Restaurant M
(802) 253-8549. $75-$210, 14 day notice. 2364 Mountain
Rd. Jct SR 100, 2.5 mi w on SR 108. Ext/int corridors.
Pets: $15 daily fee/pet. Designated rooms, service with
restrictions, crate.
SAVE ☒ 🛏 🖵 🍴 🏞

🏧 ▼▼▼ Honeywood Country Lodge M
(802) 253-4124. $65-$179, 15 day notice. 4527 Mountain
Rd. Jct SR 100, 4.5 mi w on SR 108. Ext corridors.
Pets: Accepted.
SAVE SÓ ☒ 🛏 🖵 🗷

(AAA) ▼▼▼ Innsbruck Inn at Stowe M
(802) 253-8582. **$69-$169, 14 day notice.** 4361 Mountain Rd. 4.5 mi w on SR 108, from jct SR 100. Ext/int corridors. **Pets:** Accepted.
[SAVE] [S▲] [X] [🛏] [💻] [🏊] [X]

(AAA) ▼▼▼▼ The Mountain Road Resort at Stowe M
(802) 253-4566. **$115-$260, 15 day notice.** 1007 Mountain Rd. 1 mi w on SR 108, from jct SR 100. Ext corridors. **Pets:** Accepted.
[SAVE] [S▲] [X] [🛏] [💻] [🏊] [X]

▼▼ Notch Brook Condominiums CO
(802) 253-4882. **$51-$107, 15 day notice.** 1229 Notch Brook Rd. 5.1 mi w on SR 108, from jct SR 100, then 1.3 mi n. Ext corridors. **Pets:** Accepted.
[X] [🛏] [💻] [🏊] [X] [🐾]

▼▼▼ Ten Acres Lodge CI
(802) 253-7638. **$149-$600, 30 day notice.** 14 Barrows Rd. Jct SR 100, 2.1 mi w on SR 108, then 0.5 mi s on Luce Hill Rd. Ext/int corridors. **Pets:** Accepted.
[ASK] [S▲] [X] [🛏] [💻] [🍴] [🏊] [X]

(AAA) ▼▼▼▼ Topnotch at Stowe Resort & Spa LH ✿
(802) 253-8585. **$175-$355, 14 day notice.** 4000 Mountain Rd. 4.2 mi w on SR 108, from jct SR 100. Ext/int corridors. **Pets:** Dogs only. Supervision.
[SAVE] [X] [🛏] [💻] [🍴] [🏊] [X]

STRATTON MOUNTAIN

▼▼▼ Stratton Mountain Inn LH
(802) 297-2500. **$69-$289, 14 day notice.** 61 Middle Ridge Rd. Jct SR 30, 4 mi s on Stratton Mountain Rd, then just e. Int corridors. **Pets:** Accepted.
[ASK] [S▲] [X] [💻] [🍴] [🏊] [X]

WARREN

(AAA) ▼▼ PowderHound Inn & Condominiums CO ✿
(802) 496-5100. **$84-$129, 14 day notice.** 203 Powderhound Rd. On SR 100, 0.3 mi s of jct Sugarbush Access Rd. Ext corridors. **Pets:** Other species. $5 daily fee/pet. Service with restrictions.
[SAVE] [S▲] [X] [🛏] [💻] [🍴] [🏊] [🐾]

WEST BRATTLEBORO

▼ Molly Stark Motel M
(802) 254-2440. **$45-$80.** 829 Marlboro Rd. I-91, exit 2, 3.3 mi w on SR 9. Ext corridors. **Pets:** Large, dogs only. $8 one-time fee/pet. Supervision.
[X] [🛏] [💻]

WEST DOVER

(AAA) ▼▼▼ The Gray Ghost Inn SH ✿
(802) 464-2474. **$77-$84, 14 day notice.** 290 Rt 100 N. 7.8 mi n on SR 100, from jct SR 9. Int corridors. **Pets:** Dogs only. Service with restrictions, supervision.
[SAVE] [S▲] [X] [X] [🐾] [🖊]

(AAA) ▼▼▼ Snow Goose Inn BB
(802) 464-3984. **$95-$360, 14 day notice.** 259 Rt 100. 7.5 mi n on SR 100, from jct SR 9. Int corridors. **Pets:** Other species. $25 daily fee/pet. Service with restrictions.
[SAVE] [S▲] [X] [🛏] [🖊]

WESTMORE

(AAA) ▼▼▼▼ WilloughVale Inn on Lake Willoughby CI
(802) 525-4123. **$79-$219, 14 day notice.** 793 VT Rt 5A. Just s on SR 5A, from jct SR 16. Ext/int corridors. **Pets:** Medium. $20 daily fee/pet. Designated rooms, service with restrictions, supervision.
[SAVE] [X] [🛏] [💻] [🍴] [X]

WHITE RIVER JUNCTION

(AAA) ▼▼▼ Best Western at the Junction SH
(802) 295-3015. **$79-$159.** 306 N Harland Rd (US 5). Jct I-89 and 91. Int corridors. **Pets:** Accepted.
[SAVE] [S▲] [X] [🛏] [💻] [🏊] [X]

WILLISTON

▼▼▼ TownePlace Suites by Marriott SH
(802) 878-5900. **$109-$189.** 66 Zephyr Rd. I-89, exit 12, 1.1 mi n on SR 2A. Int corridors. **Pets:** Accepted.
[X] [🔊M] [🔧] [🛏] [💻] [🏊] [X]

WOODSTOCK

(AAA) ▼▼ Braeside Motel M
(802) 457-1366. **$68-$108, 15 day notice.** 432 US 4 E (Woodstock Rd). 1 mi e. Ext corridors. **Pets:** Accepted.
[SAVE] [X] [🛏] [🏊]

VIRGINIA

ALTAVISTA

▼▼▼ Comfort Suites Hotel SH ☙
(434) 369-4000. **$83-$122, 7 day notice.** 1558 Main St. US 29 business route, exit US 29. Int corridors. **Pets:** Medium, other species. $10 one-time fee/room. Designated rooms, service with restrictions.
ASK S⊘ ✕ 🖬 💻 🍽 ➰

BEDFORD

▲▲▲ ▼▼▼ Days Inn SH
(540) 586-8286. **$50-$65.** 921 Blue Ridge Ave. Jct US 221, 1.5 mi w, on US 460. Ext corridors. **Pets:** Small. Designated rooms, service with restrictions.
SAVE S⊘ ✕ 🖬 💻 🍽 ➰

BIG STONE GAP

▲▲▲ ▼ Country Inn Motel M
(276) 523-0374. **$50.** 627 Gilley Ave. US 23, 1 mi w on US 23 business route and 58A. Ext corridors. **Pets:** Small, dogs only. $3 daily fee/pet. Service with restrictions, crate.
SAVE S⊘ ✕ 🖬

BLACKSBURG

▼▼ Best Western Red Lion Inn SH
(540) 552-7770. **$75-$175.** 900 Plantation Rd. 1.7 mi w on SR 685; jct US 460 Bypass and Prices Fork Rd. Ext corridors. **Pets:** Accepted.
S⊘ ✕ 💻 🍽 ➰

▼▼▼ Clay Corner Inn Bed & Breakfast BB ☙
(540) 953-2604. **$99-$129.** 401 Clay St SW. US 460 and 460 business route, 2.8 mi w on US 460 business route, 0.3 mi s, then just e. Int corridors. **Pets:** Dogs only. $20 daily fee/pet. Service with restrictions, supervision.
✕ ➰

▲▲▲ ▼▼▼▼ Comfort Inn SH
(540) 951-1500. **$60-$150, 7 day notice.** 3705 S Main St. 3.5 mi s on US 460, jct US 460 Bypass. Int corridors. **Pets:** Other species. Service with restrictions, supervision.
SAVE S⊘ ✕ 🖬 💻 ➰

BRISTOL

▲▲▲ ▼ Econo Lodge M
(276) 466-2112. **$44-$350.** 912 Commonwealth Ave. I-81, exit 3, 1.5 mi e. Ext corridors. **Pets:** Dogs only. $10 daily fee/pet. Designated rooms, service with restrictions, supervision.
SAVE S⊘ ✕ 🗗 🖬 💻

▼▼▼ Holiday Inn Hotel & Suites LH
(276) 466-4100. **$109.** 3005 Linden Dr. I-81, exit 7, just w. Int corridors. **Pets:** Accepted.
ASK S⊘ ✕ 🄜 🖬 💻 🍽 ➰

▲▲▲ ▼▼▼▼ La Quinta Inn SH
(276) 669-9353. **$61-$81.** 1014 Old Airport Rd. I-81, exit 7. Ext corridors. **Pets:** Other species. Service with restrictions, crate.
SAVE ✕ 🄜 🄓 🖬 💻 ➰

▼▼ Microtel Inn & Suites SH
(276) 669-8164. **$59-$64, 14 day notice.** 131 Bristol E Rd. I-81, exit 7 northbound, just w; southbound, just e. Int corridors. **Pets:** Other species. $10 one-time fee/room. Service with restrictions, supervision.
ASK S⊘ ✕ 🖬 💻 ➰

▼▼ Motel 6 SH
(276) 466-6060. **$54.** 21561 Clear Creek Rd. I-81, exit 7, 0.3 mi w. Int corridors. **Pets:** Accepted.
ASK S⊘ ✕ 🄜 🄓

▼▼ Super 8 Motel SH
(276) 466-8800. **$50-$275, 45 day notice.** 2139 Lee Hwy. I-81, exit 5, just s. Int corridors. **Pets:** Medium, other species. $7 one-time fee/pet. Service with restrictions, supervision.
ASK S⊘ ✕ 🖬

BUENA VISTA

▲▲▲ ▼ Buena Vista Motel M
(540) 261-2138. **$44-$65.** 447 E 29th St. I-81, exit 188A, 4.3 mi e on US 60, 0.4 mi w of Blue Ridge Pkwy. Ext corridors. **Pets:** Accepted.
SAVE S⊘ ✕ 🖬

BURKEVILLE

(AAA) ▼▼▼▼ **Comfort Inn Burkeville** SH
(434) 767-3750. **$75-$145.** 419 N Agnew St. On US 460, just e of jct US 360. Int corridors. **Pets:** Very small. $20 one-time fee/pet. Service with restrictions, supervision.
SAVE S☺ ✕ (&) 🛏 💻 ¶¶ ⇌

CAPE CHARLES

(AAA) ▼▼▼▼ **Best Western Sunset Beach**
Resort SH ❧
(757) 331-1776. **$64-$109.** 32246 Lankford Hwy. US 13, just n of the Chesapeake Bay Bridge Tunnel. Ext corridors. **Pets:** Other species. $10 daily fee/room. Designated rooms, service with restrictions.
SAVE S☺ ✕ &M (&) 🛏 💻 ¶¶ ⇌ ⊠

CHARLOTTESVILLE

(AAA) ▼▼▼▼ **Comfort Inn** SH
(434) 293-6188. **$73-$93.** 1807 Emmet St. Jct US 250 Bypass, just n on US 29. Int corridors. **Pets:** Accepted.
SAVE S☺ ✕ 🐾 🛏 💻 ⇌

▼▼▼▼ **Days Inn University Area** SH
(434) 293-9111. **$65-$99.** 1600 Emmet St. I-64, exit 118B (US 29), just n of jct US 250 Bypass. Ext corridors. **Pets:** Other species. $10 daily fee/pet. Service with restrictions, crate.
ASK S☺ ✕ 🛏 💻 ¶¶ ⇌

(AAA) ▼▼▼▼ **Doubletree Hotel**
Charlottesville SH ❧
(434) 973-2121. **$79-$109.** 990 Hilton Heights Rd. I-64, exit 118B (US 29), 4 mi n of jct US 250 Bypass. Int corridors. **Pets:** Other species. $50 one-time fee/pet. Designated rooms, service with restrictions.
SAVE ✕ 🐾 (&) 🛏 💻 ¶¶ ⇌ ⊠

(AAA) ▼▼ **Econo Lodge-University** M
(434) 296-2104. **$46-$160.** 400 Emmet St. Jct US 250 Bypass, 1 mi s on US 29 business route. Ext corridors. **Pets:** Dogs only. $10 daily fee/pet. Designated rooms, service with restrictions, supervision.
SAVE S☺ ✕ 🐾 🛏 💻 ⇌

▼▼▼▼ **Holiday**
Inn-Monticello/Charlottesville LH ❧
(434) 977-5100. **$69-$129.** 1200 5th St SW. I-64, exit 120, just n on SR 631. Int corridors. **Pets:** Large, other species. $10 one-time fee/pet. Service with restrictions, supervision.
ASK S☺ ✕ 🐾 🛏 💻 ¶¶ ⇌

(AAA) ▼▼▼▼ **Omni Charlottesville Hotel** LH
(434) 971-5500. **$119-$159.** 235 W Main St. I-64, exit 120, 2.3 mi n on SR 631; downtown. Int corridors. **Pets:** Small. $50 one-time fee/room. Service with restrictions, supervision.
SAVE S☺ ✕ 🐾 🛏 💻 ¶¶ ⇌ ⊠

▼▼▼▼ **Quality Inn-University Area** SH
(434) 971-3746. **$65-$99.** 1600 Emmet St. US 29, just n of jct US 250 Bypass, just e on Holiday Dr. Ext corridors. **Pets:** Other species. $10 daily fee/pet. Service with restrictions, crate.
ASK S☺ ✕ 🛏 💻

(AAA) ▼▼▼▼ **Red Roof Inn of Charlottesville** SH
(434) 295-4333. **$69-$94.** 1309 W Main St. US 29 (Emmet St), 1 mi e on US 250 (University Ave). Int corridors. **Pets:** Accepted.
SAVE ✕ 🐾 (&) 🛏

(AAA) ▼▼▼▼ **Residence Inn by Marriott** SH
(434) 923-0300. **$114.** 1111 Millmont St. I-64, exit 118B (US 29), 2.5 mi n SR 29/250 E, just s on Barracks Rd. Int corridors. **Pets:** Medium, other species. $200 one-time fee/room. Service with restrictions.
SAVE S☺ ✕ (&) 🛏 💻 ⇌ ⊠

(AAA) ▼▼▼ **Super 8 Motel** SH
(434) 973-0888. **$49-$89.** 390 Greenbrier Dr. US 29, 1 mi n of US 250 Bypass. Int corridors. **Pets:** Accepted.
SAVE S☺ ✕

CHRISTIANSBURG

(AAA) ▼▼▼ **Econo Lodge** M
(540) 382-6161. **$47-$139.** 2430 Roanoke St. I-81, exit 118, just w on US 11/460. Ext corridors. **Pets:** Small. $10 daily fee/pet. Service with restrictions, supervision.
SAVE S☺ ✕ &M 🛏 💻 ⇌

▼▼▼ **Super 8 Motel-Christiansburg West** SH
(540) 382-5813. **$51-$63.** 55 Laurel St NE. I-81, exit 118, 1 mi w on US 11/460, then 3.5 mi nw on US 460 Bypass; at jct SR 114. Int corridors. **Pets:** $20 one-time fee/pet. Service with restrictions, supervision.
ASK S☺ ✕ 🛏

COLLINSVILLE

(AAA) ▼▼▼ **Knights Inn** M
(276) 647-3716. **$54-$60.** 2357 Virginia Ave. Jct US 58, 3 mi n on US 220 business route. Ext corridors. **Pets:** Dogs only. $8 daily fee/pet. Designated rooms, service with restrictions, supervision.
SAVE S☺ ✕ 🛏 ⇌

▼▼▼ **Quality Inn-Dutch Inn Hotel and Convention**
Center SH
(276) 647-3721. **$75-$90.** 2360 Virginia Ave. Jct US 58, 3 mi n on US 220 business route. Ext corridors. **Pets:** Medium. $5 daily fee/pet. Service with restrictions, crate.
ASK S☺ ✕ 🛏 💻 ¶¶ ⇌

COVINGTON

▼▼ **Best Value Inn** M
(540) 962-7600. **$71-$85.** 908 Valley Ridge Rd. I-64, exit 16, just ne. Ext corridors. **Pets:** Large. $10 one-time fee/room. Service with restrictions, supervision.
ASK S☺ ✕ 🛏 💻

▼▼▼ **Best Western Mountain View** SH
(540) 962-4951. **$87-$92.** 820 E Madison St. I-64, exit 16, just n. Ext corridors. **Pets:** Large. $10 one-time fee/room. Service with restrictions, supervision.
ASK S☺ ✕ 🛏 💻 ¶¶ ⇌

▼▼▼ **Comfort Inn** M
(540) 962-2141. **$87-$99.** 203 Interstate Dr. I-64, exit 16, just sw. Int corridors. **Pets:** Other species. $10 one-time fee/room. Service with restrictions, supervision.
ASK S☺ ✕ 🛏 💻 ⇌

CULPEPER

◆◆ **Comfort Inn-Culpeper** [SH]
(540) 825-4900. **$79-$129.** 890 Willis Ln. 2 mi s on US 29 business route, jct US 29, then just e. Ext corridors. **Pets:** Large, other species. $15 daily fee/pet. Service with restrictions.
[ASK] [SD] ⊠ 👂 ☎ 📺 🏊

DALEVILLE

[AAA] ◆◆ **Best Western-Coachman Inn Roanoke/Daleville** [SH]
(540) 992-1234. **$75-$85.** 437 Roanoke Rd. I-81, exit 150B, just nw on US 220. Ext corridors. **Pets:** Accepted.
[SAVE] [SD] ⊠ 👂 ☎ 📺 🏊 ⊗

DANVILLE

[AAA] ◆◆ **Ramada Inn Stratford** [SH]
(434) 793-2500. **$90.** 2500 Riverside Dr. US 58, just e of jct US 29 business route. Ext corridors. **Pets:** Large, other species. $15 daily fee/pet. Service with restrictions, supervision.
[SAVE] [SD] ⊠ ♿M ♿ ☎ 📺 🍴 🏊

DISTRICT OF COLUMBIA AREA

ALEXANDRIA

◆◆◆ **Executive Club Suites** [SH]
(703) 739-2582. **$124-$164.** 610 Bashford Ln. Off George Washington Memorial Pkwy. Int corridors. **Pets:** Accepted.
[ASK] [SD] ⊠ ☎ 📺 🏊

◆◆ **Hawthorn Suites LTD-Alexandria** [LH]
(703) 370-1000. **$125-$150.** 420 N Van Dorn St. I-395, exit 3A, 0.3 mi e on SR 236 to S Van Dorn St, then 0.5 mi n. Int corridors. **Pets:** Medium, other species. $100 one-time fee/room. Service with restrictions.
[ASK] [SD] ⊠ 👂 ♿ ☎ 📺 🏊

◆◆◆ **Hilton Alexandria Old Town** [LH]
(703) 837-0440. **$119-$259.** 1767 King St. I-95/495, exit 176B, 0.5 mi n on SR 241, 0.5 mi e on SR 236, just ne on Diagonal Rd; in Old Town. Int corridors. **Pets:** Accepted.
[ASK] [SD] ⊠ 👂 ♿ 📺 🍴 🏊

◆◆◆ **Holiday Inn Eisenhower Metro** [LH]
(703) 960-3400. **$109-$169.** 2460 Eisenhower Ave. I-95/495, exit 176B, immediate e on Pershing Ave, then s on Stovall Rd, jct Telegraph Rd (SR 214 N) and I-95/495. Int corridors. **Pets:** Accepted.
[ASK] [SD] ⊠ 👂 ♿ ☎ 📺 🍴 🏊

[AAA] ◆◆◆ **Holiday Inn Select-Old Town** [LH]
(703) 549-6080. **$179-$229.** 480 King St. On SR 7; between S Pitt and S Royal sts; just sw of City Hall. Int corridors. **Pets:** Accepted.
[SAVE] [SD] ⊠ 👂 📺 🍴 🏊 ⊗

◆◆ **Homestead Studio Suites Hotel-Alexandria** [SH] 🐾
(703) 329-3399. **$100-$124.** 200 Blue Stone Rd. I-95/495, exit 174 (Eisenhower Ave Connector), just n to Eisenhower Ave, then 1.2 mi e. Int corridors. **Pets:** Medium, other species. $25 daily fee/room. Service with restrictions, crate.
[ASK] [SD] ⊠ ♿M 👂 ♿ ☎ 📺

[AAA] ◆◆ **Red Roof Inn-Alexandria** [M]
(703) 960-5200. **$67-$99.** 5975 Richmond Hwy. I-95/495, exit 177A, 0.5 mi s on US 1. Ext corridors. **Pets:** Large. Service with restrictions, crate.
[SAVE] ⊠ ♿M ♿ ☎

[AAA] ◆◆◆ **Residence Inn by Marriott Alexandria-Old Town** [LH]
(703) 548-5474. **$119-$309.** 1456 Duke St. I-95/495, exit 176, 0.5 mi n on SR 241, 0.7 mi e on SR 236. Int corridors. **Pets:** Medium. $10 daily fee/room, $150 one-time fee/room. Designated rooms, service with restrictions, crate.
[SAVE] [SD] ⊠ ♿M 👂 ♿ ☎ 📺 🏊

[AAA] ◆◆◆ **Washington Suites-Alexandria** [LH]
(703) 370-9600. **$89-$199.** 100 S Reynolds St. I-395, exit 3A, 0.8 mi e on SR 236 E (Duke St), just s. Int corridors. **Pets:** Medium, other species. $10 daily fee/pet. Designated rooms, service with restrictions, crate.
[SAVE] [SD] ⊠ ♿M 👂 ♿ ☎ 📺 🍴 🏊 ⊗

ARLINGTON

[AAA] ◆◆ **Best Western Washington Key Bridge** [LH]
(703) 522-0400. **$79-$139.** 1850 N Fort Meyer Dr. I-66, exit 73, just sw of Key Bridge. Int corridors. **Pets:** $25 one-time fee/room. Service with restrictions, crate.
[SAVE] ⊠ ☎ 📺 🏊

◆◆ **Executive Club Suites-Arlington** [SH]
(703) 522-2582. **$124-$164.** 108 S Courthouse Rd. I-395, exit 8A northbound; exit 8 southbound, 1 mi nw on Washington Blvd to Second St; 0.3 mi se of US 50. Ext corridors. **Pets:** Accepted.
[ASK] [SD] ⊠ ☎ 📺 🏊 ⊗

[AAA] ◆◆◆ **Quality Hotel Courthouse Plaza** [LH]
(703) 524-4000. **$169-$189.** 1200 N Courthouse Rd. 1.5 mi sw of Theodore Roosevelt Bridge on US 50. Ext/int corridors. **Pets:** Medium. $10 daily fee/pet, $35 one-time fee/pet. Designated rooms, service with restrictions, crate.
[SAVE] [SD] ⊠ 👂 ♿ ☎ 📺 🍴 🏊

[AAA] ◆◆ **Quality Inn-Iwo Jima** [SH]
(703) 524-5000. **$89-$159, 7 day notice.** 1501 Arlington Blvd. 1 mi w of Theodore Roosevelt Bridge on US 50. Ext/int corridors. **Pets:** Dogs only. $10 daily fee/pet. Designated rooms, service with restrictions, supervision.
[SAVE] [SD] ⊠ ☎ 📺 🍴 🏊

Residence Inn by Marriott-Pentagon City 🄻🄷
(703) 413-6630. **$219.** 550 Army Navy Dr. I-395, exit 8C, just 1 mi s of 14th St Bridge. Int corridors. **Pets:** Other species. $8 daily fee/room, $200 one-time fee/room. Service with restrictions, supervision.

The Ritz-Carlton, Pentagon City 🄻🄷
(703) 415-5000. **$349-$3500.** 1250 S Hayes St. 1 mi s of 14th St Bridge. Int corridors. **Pets:** Accepted.

The Virginian Suites 🄱🄱
(703) 522-9600. **$119-$159.** 1500 Arlington Blvd. 1 mi w of Theodore Roosevelt Bridge, on US 50. Int corridors. **Pets:** Accepted.

CHANTILLY

AmeriSuites (Dulles Airport South/Chantilly) 🅂🄷
(703) 961-8160. **$104.** 4994 Westone Plaza Dr. I-66, exit 53, 2 mi n on SR 28, just w on Westfields Blvd; 1.7 mi s of jct SR 28 and US 50. Int corridors. **Pets:** Other species. Designated rooms, service with restrictions, supervision.

Holiday Inn Select Chantilly-Dulles Expo Center 🄻🄷
(703) 815-6060. **$89-$199.** 4335 Chantilly Shopping Center. I-66, exit 53, 3 mi n on SR 28, 1 mi s of jct US 50 and SR 28. Int corridors. **Pets:** Accepted.

Homestead Studio Suites Hotel-Dulles/Chantilly 🄼 ❀
(703) 263-3361. **$68-$93.** 4504 Brookfield Corporate Dr. I-66, exit 53, 3 mi n on SR 28; jct SR 28 and 50, 1 mi s. Ext corridors. **Pets:** Medium, other species. $25 daily fee/room. Service with restrictions, crate.

TownePlace Suites by Marriott-Chantilly 🅂🄷
(703) 709-0453. **$109-$144.** 14036 Thunderbolt Pl. Jct SR 28, just e on US 50. Int corridors. **Pets:** Accepted.

DUMFRIES

Holiday Inn Express-Dumfries 🅂🄷 ❀
(703) 221-1141. **$72-$99.** 17133 Dumfries Rd. I-95, exit 152B, just w on SR 234 N. Ext/int corridors. **Pets:** Other species. Designated rooms, service with restrictions.

FAIRFAX

Comfort Inn University Center 🄻🄷 ❀
(703) 591-5900. **$79-$139.** 11180 Main St. I-66, exit 57A, 0.8 mi se on US 50, 0.5 mi nw of jct US 29. **Pets:** Other species. Service with restrictions, supervision.

Holiday Inn Fairfax-Fair Oaks Mall 🄻🄷
(703) 352-2525. **$79-$139.** 11787 Lee Jackson Memorial Hwy. I-66, exit 57B, jct US 50. Int corridors. **Pets:** Medium, other species. $25 one-time fee/room. Designated rooms, service with restrictions, supervision.

Homestead Studio Suites Hotel-Fair Oaks 🅂🄷 ❀
(703) 273-3444. **$73-$97.** 12104 Monument Dr. I-66, exit 57B, 0.8 mi w on US 50, then 0.3 mi s on SR 620 (West Ox Rd), just se. Ext corridors. **Pets:** Medium, other species. $25 daily fee/room. Service with restrictions, crate.

Homestead Studio Suites Hotel-Falls Church/Merrifield 🅂🄷 ❀
(703) 204-0088. **$91-$115.** 8281 Willow Oaks Corporate Dr. I-495, exit 50A, just w on US 50 to Gallows Rd, then just s. Ext corridors. **Pets:** Medium, other species. $25 daily fee/room. Service with restrictions, crate.

Residence Inn by Marriott-Fairlakes 🅂🄷
(703) 266-4900. **$152.** 12815 Fair Lakes Pkwy. I-66, exit 55 (Fairfax County Pkwy N), just w. Int corridors. **Pets:** Medium. $150 one-time fee/pet. Service with restrictions, supervision.

FALLS CHURCH

Fairfax-Merrifield Residence Inn by Marriott 🅂🄷 ❀
(703) 573-5200. **$194-$224.** 8125 Gatehouse Rd. I-495, exit 50A, just w to SR 640 N. Int corridors. **Pets:** $150 one-time fee/room. Service with restrictions.

Homewood Suites by Hilton-Falls Church 🄻🄷 ❀
(703) 560-6644. **$89-$199.** 8130 Porter Rd. I-495, exit 50A, just w to SR 650, 0.4 mi n of SR 650. Int corridors. **Pets:** Medium. $100 one-time fee/room. Service with restrictions, crate.

TownePlace Suites by Marriott-Falls Church 🅂🄷
(703) 237-6172. **$89-$199.** 205 Hillwood Ave. I-495, exit 50B, 2.5 mi e on US 50, 0.6 mi n on Annandale Rd, then e. Int corridors. **Pets:** Accepted.

HERNDON

Hawthorn Suites 🅂🄷
(703) 437-5000. **$129-$169.** 467 Herndon Pkwy. SR 267 (Dulles Toll Rd), exit 11 (Fairfax County Pkwy). Int corridors. **Pets:** Accepted.

Hilton Washington Dulles Airport 🄻🄷
(703) 478-2900. **$89-$209.** 13869 Park Center Rd. SR 267 (Dulles Toll Rd), exit 9, 3 mi s on SR 28. Int corridors. **Pets:** Accepted.

Holiday Inn Express–Reston/Herndon SH
(703) 478-9777. **$79-$129.** 485 Elden St. 0.3 mi e on SR 606. Int corridors. **Pets:** $10 daily fee/pet, $25 one-time fee/pet. Designated rooms, service with restrictions, supervision.

Homewood Suites by Hilton SH
(703) 793-1700. **$109-$259.** 2185 Fox Mill Rd. SR 267 (Dulles Toll Rd), exit 10, 0.5 mi s on SR 657, just w. Int corridors. **Pets:** Accepted.

Residence Inn by Marriott-Herndon/Reston SH
(703) 435-0044. **$79-$169.** 315 Elden St. 0.5 mi e on SR 606. Int corridors. **Pets:** Accepted.

Staybridge Suites SH
(703) 713-6800. **$109-$155.** 13700 Coppermine Rd. SR 267 (Dulles Toll Rd), exit 10, 0.7 mi s on Centerville Rd (SR 657), 0.4 mi w. Ext corridors. **Pets:** Accepted.

LEESBURG

Holiday Inn at Carradoc Hall SH
(703) 771-9200. **$59-$89.** 1500 E Market St. 2 mi e on SR 7. Int corridors. **Pets:** Large. $25 deposit/pet. Service with restrictions, supervision.

LORTON

Comfort Inn Gunston Corner SH
(703) 643-3100. **$89-$109.** 8180 Silverbrook Rd. I-95, exit 163, just w. Int corridors. **Pets:** Small, other species. $25 one-time fee/pet. Service with restrictions, supervision.

MANASSAS

Best Western Battlefield Inn SH
(703) 361-8000. **$69-$175, 14 day notice.** 10820 Balls Ford Rd. I-66, exit 47A westbound; exit 47 eastbound, just s on SR 234, then just w. Ext corridors. **Pets:** Accepted.

Red Roof Inn-Manassas M
(703) 335-9333. **$64-$84.** 10610 Automotive Dr. I-66, exit 47 eastbound; exit 47A westbound, just s on SR 234, then just e on Balls Ford Rd. Ext corridors. **Pets:** Accepted.

MCLEAN

Best Western Tysons Westpark Hotel LH
(703) 734-2800. **$69-$169, 7 day notice.** 8401 Westpark Dr. I-495, exit 47A, 1.3 mi w on SR 7. Int corridors. **Pets:** Large. Designated rooms, service with restrictions, crate.

Staybridge Suites by Holiday Inn-McLean/ Tysons Corner LH
(703) 448-5400. **$149-$229.** 6845 Old Dominion Dr. I-495, exit 46B, 2 mi n on SR 123, 0.3 mi e on SR 309. Int corridors. **Pets:** Accepted.

RESTON

Homestead Studio Suites Hotel-Reston ✿
(703) 707-9700. **$95-$120.** 12190 Sunset Hills Rd. SR 267 (Dulles Toll Rd), exit 12 (Reston Pkwy), just n, then just w. Ext corridors. **Pets:** Medium, other species. $25 daily fee/ room. Service with restrictions, crate.

SPRINGFIELD

Comfort Inn Washington DC/Springfield SH ✿
(703) 922-9000. **$69-$109, 30 day notice.** 6560 Loisdale Ct. I-95, exit 169A, just e on SR 644 E; I-395 and 495, 0.7 mi s. Int corridors. **Pets:** Large, other species. Service with restrictions, supervision.

Hampton Inn Washington DC/Springfield SH ✿
(703) 924-9444. **$75-$114.** 6550 Loisdale Ct. I-95, exit 169A, just e on SR 644 E; jct I-395 and 495, 0.6 mi s. Int corridors. **Pets:** Large, other species. Service with restrictions.

STERLING

Hampton Inn-Dulles/Cascades SH
(703) 450-9595. **$59-$119.** 46331 McClellan Way. SR 28 N, 5 mi to exit 7E, SR 7 to Cascade Pkwy. Int corridors. **Pets:** Accepted.

Hampton Inn Washington-Dulles Airport SH
(703) 471-8300. **$59-$109.** 45440 Holiday Dr. SR 267 (Dulles Toll Rd), exit 9B, 1.8 mi n on SR 28, then just ne. Ext corridors. **Pets:** Accepted.

Holiday Inn Washington Dulles International Airport SH
(703) 471-7411. **$69-$169.** 1000 Sully Rd. SR 28, 1.8 mi n of SR 267 (Dulles Toll Rd), exit 9B. Ext/int corridors. **Pets:** Accepted.

Homestead Studio Suites Hotel-Dulles/Sterling SH ✿
(703) 904-7575. **$68-$93.** 45350 Catalina Ct. SR 267 (Dulles Toll Rd), exit 9B, 0.8 mi n on SR 28, just w on SR 606. Ext corridors. **Pets:** Medium, other species. $25 daily fee/room. Service with restrictions, crate.

▼▼▼ TownePlace Suites by Marriott at Dulles
Airport [SH]
(703) 707-2017. **$59-$119.** 22744 Holiday Park Dr. SR 267
(Dulles Toll Rd), exit 9B, 1.8 mi n on SR 28, then just ne. Int
corridors. **Pets:** $10 daily fee/room. Service with restrictions.

ASK S▼ ✕ 🖉 🖾 🖬 🖵 ⊇

VIENNA

♣♣♣ ▼▼▼ Comfort Inn Tysons Corner [M]
(703) 448-8020. **$70-$160.** 1587 Spring Hill Rd. I-495, exit
47A, 1.8 mi w on SR 7, just s on Spring Hill Rd, just e of jct
SR 267 (Dulles Toll Rd). Ext corridors. **Pets:** Accepted.

SAVE S▼ ✕ 🖬 🖵 ⊇

▼▼ Homestead Studio Suites Hotel-Tysons
Corner [SH] ♣
(703) 356-6300. **$109-$133.** 8201 Old Courthouse Rd. I-495,
exit 47A, 0.6 mi w on SR 7, then just s on Gallows Rd. Int
corridors. **Pets:** Medium, other species. $25 daily fee/room.
Service with restrictions, crate.

ASK S▼ ✕ 🖾M 🖾 🖬 🖵

▼▼▼ Residence Inn by Marriott-Tysons
Corner [SH]
(703) 893-0120. **$189-$259.** 8616 Westwood Center Dr.
I-495, exit 47A, 1.9 mi w on SR 7, just s. Ext corridors.
Pets: Accepted.

ASK S▼ ✕ 🖬 🖵 ⊇ ✕

▼▼▼ Residence Inn by Marriott Tysons
Corner-Mall [SH]
(703) 917-0800. **$119-$179.** 8400 Old Courthouse Rd. I-495,
exit 46A, 1.1 mi s on SR 123; 0.3 mi s of jct SR 7 and 123.
Int corridors. **Pets:** Other species. $100 one-time fee/room.

ASK ✕ 🖾M 🖉 🖾 🖬 🖵 ⊇

WOODBRIDGE

♣♣♣ ▼▼▼ Quality Inn at Potomac Mills [SH]
(703) 494-0300. **$60-$120.** 1109 Horner Rd. I-95, exit 161
southbound, 1.5 mi s on US 1, just n on SR 123, then just
s; exit 160A northbound, 0.5 mi s on SR 123, then just s. Int
corridors. **Pets:** Medium. $20 daily fee/pet. Service with
restrictions.

SAVE S▼ ✕ 🖉 🖬 🖵 ⊇

❀   **END AREA**   ❀

DUBLIN

▼▼▼ Comfort Inn-Dublin [SH]
(540) 674-1100. **$52-$75.** 4424 Cleburne Blvd. I-81, exit 98,
just e. Int corridors. **Pets:** Accepted.

ASK S▼ ✕ 🖉 🖬 🖵 ⊇

EMPORIA

♣♣♣ ▼▼▼▼ Best Western Emporia [SH]
(434) 634-3200. **$55-$75, 7 day notice.** 1100 W Atlantic St.
I-95, exit 11B, just w on US 58. Ext corridors. **Pets:** Other
species. $10 one-time fee/room. Service with restrictions.

SAVE S▼ ✕ 🖾 🖬 🖵 ⊇

♣♣♣ ▼▼▼▼ Comfort Inn [SH]
(434) 348-3282. **$52-$70.** 1411 Skippers Rd. I-95, exit 8, just
e on US 301. Ext corridors. **Pets:** Medium. Designated
rooms, service with restrictions, supervision.

SAVE S▼ ✕ 🖬 🖵 🍴 ⊇

▼▼▼ Days Inn-Emporia [SH]
(434) 634-9481. **$65-$75.** 921 W Atlantic St. I-95, exit 11B,
just w on US 58. Ext corridors. **Pets:** Medium. $8 daily
fee/pet. Designated rooms, service with restrictions, supervision.

ASK S▼ ✕ 🖬 ⊇

♣♣♣ ▼▼▼ Hampton Inn [SH]
(434) 634-9200. **$64-$76.** 1207 W Atlantic St. I-95, exit 11B,
just w on US 58. Ext corridors. **Pets:** Accepted.

SAVE S▼ ✕ 🖉 🖬 🖵 ⊇

♣♣♣ ▼▼ Knights Inn [M]
(434) 535-8535. **$35-$60.** 3173 Sussex Dr. I-95, exit 17, 0.5
mi s on US 301. Ext corridors. **Pets:** Accepted.

SAVE S▼ ✕ 🖬 ⊇

FANCY GAP

♣♣♣ ▼▼▼ Doe Run Lodge [SH]
(276) 398-2212. **$99-$234, 7 day notice.** MM 189.2 on Blue
Ridge Pkwy; 10 mi n from US 52 (parkway entrance). Ext
corridors. **Pets:** Accepted.

SAVE ✕ 🖬 🖵 🍴 ⊇ ✕

FREDERICKSBURG

♣♣♣ ▼▼▼▼ Best Western Central Plaza [M]
(540) 786-7404. **$63-$77.** 3000 Plank Rd. I-95, exit 130B on
SR 3. Ext corridors. **Pets:** Small. Designated rooms, service
with restrictions, supervision.

SAVE ✕ 🖾M 🖬 🖵

♣♣♣ ▼▼▼▼ Best Western Fredericksburg [SH]
(540) 371-5050. **$62-$89.** 2205 William St. I-95, exit 130A,
0.3 mi e on SR 3. Ext corridors. **Pets:** Designated rooms,
service with restrictions, crate.

SAVE S▼ ✕ 🖾M 🖬 🖵 ⊇

♣♣♣ ▼▼▼ Dunning Mills Inn All Suites
Hotel [SH]
(540) 373-1256. **$59-$79.** 2305 C Jefferson Davis Hwy. I-95,
exit 126, 3 mi n on US 1. Ext corridors. **Pets:** Accepted.

SAVE S▼ ✕ 🖬 🖵 ⊇

♣♣♣ ▼▼▼▼ Hampton Inn [SH] ♣
(540) 371-0330. **$82-$105.** 2310 William St. I-95, exit 130A
on SR 3 E. Ext corridors. **Pets:** Small, other species. Designated rooms, service with restrictions, crate.

SAVE S▼ ✕ 🖬 🖵 ⊇

♣♣♣ ▼▼▼ Holiday Inn-Fredericksburg
North [SH]
(540) 371-5550. **$70-$90.** 564 Warrenton Rd. I-95, exit 133,
just nw on US 17. Ext corridors. **Pets:** Accepted.

SAVE S▼ ✕ 🖬 🖵 🍴 ⊇ ✕

ⓌⓌ ▽▽▽▽ Holiday Inn Select Fredericksburg 🅛🅗
(540) 786-8321. **$119-$139.** 2801 Plank Rd. I-95, exit 130B on SR 3. Int corridors. **Pets:** Accepted.
SAVE ✕ ♿Ⓜ 🐾 🛏 💻 🍴 ⚊

ⓌⓌ ▽ Howard Johnson Hotel 🆂🅗 ❀
(540) 898-1800. **$70-$130.** 5327 Jefferson Davis Hwy. I-95, exit 126. Int corridors. **Pets:** Small, other species. $10 one-time fee/pet. Service with restrictions, supervision.
SAVE 🆂 ✕ 🐾 🛏 💻 ⚊

ⓌⓌ ▽▽▽▽ Quality Inn Fredericksburg 🆂🅗 ❀
(540) 373-0000. **$52-$70.** 543 Warrenton Rd. I-95, exit 133, just n on US 17. Ext corridors. **Pets:** Other species. $8 daily fee/pet. Service with restrictions.
SAVE 🆂 ✕ 💻 🍴 ⚊

ⓌⓌ ▽▽▽ Ramada Inn South 🆂🅗
(540) 898-1102. **$49-$109.** 5324 Jefferson Davis Hwy. I-95, exit 126, just n on US 1. Ext/int corridors. **Pets:** Medium. $50 deposit/room, $25 one-time fee/room. Designated rooms, service with restrictions, supervision.
SAVE 🆂 ✕ 🛏 💻 🍴 ⚊ ✕

FRONT ROYAL

ⓌⓌ ▽ Bluemont Inn Ⓜ
(540) 635-9447. **$42-$115, 3 day notice.** 1525 N Shenandoah Ave. I-66, exit 6, 1.8 mi s on US 340/522. Ext corridors. **Pets:** Large. Service with restrictions, supervision.
SAVE 🆂 ✕ 🛏 💻

ⓌⓌ ▽ Budget Inn Ⓜ ❀
(540) 635-2196. **$39-$75.** 1122 N Royal Ave. I-66, exit 6, 2.2 mi s on US 340/522 and SR 55. Ext corridors. **Pets:** Medium. $10 daily fee/pet. Service with restrictions, supervision.
SAVE 🆂 ✕ 🛏

ⓌⓌ ▽ Relax Inn Ⓜ
(540) 635-4101. **$50-$75.** 1801 Shenandoah Ave. I-66, exit 6, 1.5 mi s on US 340/522. Ext corridors. **Pets:** $5 daily fee/pet. Service with restrictions, supervision.
SAVE 🆂 ✕ 🛏 💻 ⚊

ⓌⓌ ▽ Scottish Inn Ⓜ
(540) 636-6168. **$45-$85.** 533 S Royal Ave. I-66, exit 6, 3.8 mi s on US 340, at jct SR 55. Ext corridors. **Pets:** Service with restrictions, supervision.
SAVE 🆂 ✕ 🛏 💻

ⓌⓌ ▽ Twi-Lite Motel Ⓜ
(540) 635-4148. **$45-$89, 3 day notice.** 53 W 14th St. I-66, exit 6, 2.3 mi s on US 340/522. Ext corridors. **Pets:** Accepted.
SAVE ✕ 🛏 ⚊

GLADE SPRING

ⓌⓌ ▽▽▽ Swiss Inn Motel & Suites Ⓜ
(276) 429-5191. **$45-$65.** 33361 Lee Hwy. I-81, exit 29, just e. Ext corridors. **Pets:** Dogs only. $7 daily fee/room. Service with restrictions, supervision.
SAVE 🆂 ✕ 🛏

GREENVILLE

ⓌⓌ ▽▽▽ Budget Host-Historic Hessian House 🆂🅗
(540) 337-1231. **$40-$75, 3 day notice.** 3554 Lee Jackson Hwy. I-81, exit 213, 0.3 mi e. Ext corridors. **Pets:** Very small. $6 daily fee/pet. Designated rooms, service with restrictions, crate.
SAVE 🆂 ✕ 🛏 💻 ✕

GRUNDY

ⓌⓌ Comfort Inn 🆂🅗
(276) 935-5050. **$59-$140, 7 day notice.** US 460. On US 460, 0.5 mi e. Int corridors. **Pets:** Accepted.
ASK 🆂 ✕ ♿Ⓜ 🐾 🛏 💻

HAMPTON ROADS AREA

CHESAPEAKE

ⓌⓌ ▽▽ Days Inn-Chesapeake Ⓜ
(757) 487-8861. **$75-$100.** 1439 George Washington Hwy. I-64, exit 296, 2.5 mi n on US 17. Ext/int corridors. **Pets:** Accepted.
SAVE 🆂 ✕ 🛏 💻

ⓌⓌ ▽▽ Red Roof Inn Ⓜ
(757) 523-0123. **$44-$79.** 724 Woodlake Dr. I-64, exit 289A, just n to Woodlake Dr, then just e. Ext corridors. **Pets:** Accepted.
SAVE ✕ 🛏

ⓌⓌ ▽▽ Super 8 Motel Ⓜ ❀
(757) 686-8888. **$49-$64.** 3216 Churchland Blvd. I-664, exit 9B, 1 mi s on SR 17. Int corridors. **Pets:** Other species. Designated rooms, service with restrictions, crate.
ASK 🆂 ✕ ♿Ⓜ 🛏

ⓌⓌ ▽▽ TownePlace Suites By Marriott Ⓜ
(757) 523-5004. **$89-$179.** 2000 Old Greenbriar Rd. I-64, exit 289A, just n. Int corridors. **Pets:** Accepted.
✕ ♿Ⓜ 🐾 🛏 💻 ⚊

GLOUCESTER

ⓌⓌ ▽▽ Comfort Inn Gloucester 🆂🅗
(804) 695-1900. **$69-$99.** 6639 Forest Hill Ave. US 17, just s. Int corridors. **Pets:** Medium, dogs only. $10 daily fee/pet. Designated rooms, service with restrictions, crate.
ASK 🆂 ✕ 🛏 💻 ⚊

HAMPTON

ⓌⓌ ▽▽ Candlewood Suites 🆂🅗
(757) 766-8976. **Call for rates.** 401 Butler Farm Rd. I-64, exit 261B (Hampton Roads Center Pkwy) eastbound; exit 261 (Magruder Blvd) westbound, then n. Int corridors. **Pets:** Large, other species. $75 one-time fee/room. Service with restrictions, supervision.
✕ ♿Ⓜ 🐾 🛏 💻

▼▼▼ Holiday Inn Hampton Hotel & Conference Center 🅛🄷
(757) 838-0200. **$59-$129.** 1815 W Mercury Blvd. I-64, exit 263A. Ext/int corridors. **Pets:** $25 one-time fee/pet. Service with restrictions, supervision.

(A$K) (S🐾) (✕) (🤚M) (🏷) (🍴) (📞) (🍴) (🏊) (✕)

🔺🔺🔺 ▼▼▼▼ La Quinta Inn 🅢🄷
(757) 827-8680. **$59-$99.** 2138 W Mercury Blvd. I-64, exit 263B (Mercury Blvd), just s. Ext/int corridors. **Pets:** Accepted.

(SAVE) (✕) (🤚M) (🏷) (♿) (🍴) (📞) (🏊)

🔺🔺🔺 ▼▼▼▼ Quality Inn & Suites Conference Center 🅢🄷
(757) 838-5011. **$90-$150.** 1809 W Mercury Blvd. I-64, exit 263B (Mercury Blvd), jct SR 58. Int corridors. **Pets:** Accepted.

(SAVE) (S🐾) (✕) (🤚M) (🏷) (♿) (🍴) (📞) (🍴) (🏊)

NEWPORT NEWS

▼◆▼ Comfort Inn 🅢🄷
(757) 249-0200. **$69-$129.** 12330 Jefferson Ave. I-64, exit 255A, just s on Clarie Ln (mall parking lot). Int corridors. **Pets:** Other species. $10 daily fee/pet. Designated rooms, service with restrictions, supervision.

(A$K) (S🐾) (✕) (🤚M) (🏷) (🍴) (📞) (🏊)

🔺🔺🔺 ▼▼▼ Days Inn 🅢🄷
(757) 874-0201. **$53-$85.** 14747 Warwick Blvd. I-64, exit 250A (SR 105/Ft Eustis Blvd S), 2.5 mi to US 60 E, Warwick Blvd on US 60. Ext corridors. **Pets:** Other species. $10 daily fee/pet. Service with restrictions, supervision.

(SAVE) (S🐾) (✕) (🍴) (📞) (🏊)

🔺🔺🔺 ▼▼▼▼ Days Inn-Oyster Point 🅢🄷
(757) 873-6700. **$69-$89.** 11829 Fishing Point Dr. I-64, exit 255A, 2.5 mi s to Thimble Shoals Dr E, 1 blk to property. Int corridors. **Pets:** Other species. $10 daily fee/pet. Service with restrictions, supervision.

(SAVE) (S🐾) (✕) (🏷) (🍴) (📞) (🏊)

🔺🔺🔺 ▼▼▼ Host Inn 🄼
(757) 599-3303. **$49-$90, 3 day notice.** 985 J Clyde Morris Blvd. I-64, exit 258B, 0.8 mi n. Ext corridors. **Pets:** Medium. $10 daily fee/pet. Designated rooms, no service, supervision.

(SAVE) (✕) (🍴) (🏊)

NORFOLK

🔺🔺🔺 ▼▼▼ ▼▼▼ Bed & Breakfast at the Page House Inn 🅑🅑
(757) 625-5033. **$140-$160, 7 day notice.** 323 Fairfax Ave. I-264, exit 9, 1.4 mi n on Waterside Dr to Olney Rd, just w to Mowbray Arch, then just s; in the Ghent historic district. Int corridors. **Pets:** Accepted.

(SAVE) (✕) (🍴) (✕)

🔺🔺🔺 ▼▼▼ Clarion Hotel James Madison 🅢🄷
(757) 622-6682. **$89-$129.** 345 Granby St. Jct Freemason St; downtown. Int corridors. **Pets:** $25 one-time fee/room. Service with restrictions, supervision.

(SAVE) (S🐾) (✕) (♿) (🍴) (📞) (🍴)

🔺🔺🔺 ▼▼▼▼ Quality Suites Lake Wright 🅢🄷
(757) 461-6251. **$109-$159, 3 day notice.** 6280 Northampton Blvd. I-64, exit 282, just w on US 13. Int corridors. **Pets:** Other species. $35 one-time fee/room. Service with restrictions, crate.

(SAVE) (S🐾) (✕) (🤚M) (♿) (🍴) (📞) (🍴)

🔺🔺🔺 ▼▼▼▼ Radisson Hotel Norfolk 🅢🄷
(757) 627-5555. **$79-$199.** 700 Monticello Ave. Jct Brambleton Ave and St Pauls Blvd; downtown. Int corridors. **Pets:** Small. $25 deposit/room. Designated rooms, service with restrictions, crate.

(SAVE) (S🐾) (✕) (🏷) (♿) (🍴) (📞) (🍴) (🏊)

🔺🔺🔺 ▼▼▼ Sleep Inn Lake Wright 🅢🄷
(757) 461-1133. **$89-$139, 3 day notice.** 6280 Northampton Blvd. I-64, exit 282, just w on US 13. Int corridors. **Pets:** Other species. $25 one-time fee/room. Service with restrictions, crate.

(SAVE) (S🐾) (✕) (🤚M) (♿) (🍴) (📞) (🏊)

🔺🔺🔺 ▼▼▼▼ Tazewell Hotel and Suites 🅢🄷
(757) 623-6200. **$119-$169, 3 day notice.** 245 Granby St. Jct Tazewell St; downtown. Int corridors. **Pets:** Accepted.

(SAVE) (S🐾) (✕) (♿) (🍴) (📞) (🍴)

PORTSMOUTH

▼◆▼ Holiday Inn-Olde Towne Portsmouth 🅢🄷 🐾
(757) 393-2573. **$91-$132.** 8 Crawford Pkwy. Just nw from High St. Int corridors. **Pets:** Large. Service with restrictions, crate.

(A$K) (S🐾) (✕) (♿) (🍴) (📞) (🍴) (🏊)

VIRGINIA BEACH

🔺🔺🔺 ▼▼▼▼ Days Inn Oceanfront 🅢🄷 🐾
(757) 428-7233. **$55-$250, 3 day notice.** 3107 Atlantic Ave. I-264, 0.8 mi n of terminus, just n of jct Laskin Rd (SR 58) at 32nd St. Int corridors. **Pets:** Other species. $15 daily fee/pet. Designated rooms, service with restrictions, crate.

(SAVE) (S🐾) (✕) (🍴) (📞) (🍴) (🏊)

🔺🔺🔺 ▼▼▼▼ DoubleTree Hotel Virginia Beach 🅢🄷 🐾
(757) 422-8900. **$79-$229, 3 day notice.** 1900 Pavilion Dr. I-264, exit 22 (Birdneck Rd). Int corridors. **Pets:** Other species. $25 one-time fee/room. Service with restrictions, supervision.

(SAVE) (S🐾) (✕) (🏷) (🍴) (📞) (🍴) (🏊)

🔺🔺🔺 ▼▼▼ Flagship Motel 🄼
(757) 425-6422. **$40-$175.** 512 Atlantic Ave. I-264, 1 mi s of terminus; at Atlantic Ave and 6th St. Ext corridors. **Pets:** $30 one-time fee/pet. Designated rooms, service with restrictions, crate.

(SAVE) (S🐾) (✕) (🍴) (📞) (🏊)

🔺🔺🔺 ▼▼▼▼ La Quinta Inn 🅢🄷
(757) 497-6620. **$71-$135.** 192 Newtown Rd. I-64, exit 284B to I-264 (Virginia Beach-Norfolk Expwy), exit Newtown Rd S. Int corridors. **Pets:** Large, other species. Service with restrictions.

(SAVE) (✕) (🤚M) (🍴) (📞) (🏊)

AAA ▽▽▽ **Ramada Plaza Resort**
Oceanfront 🅛🅗 ❀
(757) 428-7025. **$69-$225, 3 day notice.** Atlantic Ave and 57th St. I-264, 2.2 mi n of terminus. Int corridors. **Pets:** Large. $10 daily fee/pet. Designated rooms, service with restrictions, crate.
SAVE 🆂🄳 ✕ 🅂🄼 🔒 💻 🍽 ➰ ✕

AAA ▽▽▽ **Red Roof Inn VA Beach (Norfolk**
Airport) 🅜
(757) 460-6700. **$50-$180, 15 day notice.** 5745 Northampton Blvd. I-64, exit 282, 1 mi n on US 13 (Northampton Blvd). Ext corridors. **Pets:** Small, dogs only. $15 one-time fee/room. Designated rooms, no service, supervision.
SAVE 🆂🄳 ✕ 🔒 ➰

AAA ▽▽▽ **Red Roof Inn-Virginia Beach** 🅜
(757) 490-0225. **$44-$99.** 196 Ballard Ct. I-64/264, exit 284B (Newtown Rd). Ext corridors. **Pets:** Accepted.
SAVE ✕ 🔒 ➰

▽▽▽ **The Thunderbird Motor Lodge** 🅢🅗
(757) 428-3024. **$39-$209, 3 day notice.** 3410 Atlantic Ave. I-264, 1.2 mi n of terminus; at Atlantic Ave and 35th St. Ext/int corridors. **Pets:** Small, other species. $10 daily fee/pet. Designated rooms, service with restrictions.
ASK 🆂🄳 ✕ 🔒 🍽 ➰

▽▽▽ **TownePlace Suites By Marriott** 🅢🅗
(757) 490-9367. **$55-$190.** 5757 Cleveland St. I-64, exit 284B to I-264 (Virginia Beach-Norfolk Expwy), exit Newtown Rd N. Int corridors. **Pets:** Medium. $125 one-time fee/room. Service with restrictions, crate.
ASK 🆂🄳 ✕ 🅂🄼 🔒 💻 ➰

❀ **END AREA** ❀

HARRISONBURG

▽ **Belle Meade Red Carpet Inn** 🅜
(540) 434-6704. **$40-$65, 4 day notice.** 3210 S Main St. I-81, exit 243, just nw. Ext corridors. **Pets:** Accepted.
ASK 🆂🄳 ✕ 🔒 ➰

AAA ▽▽▽ **Comfort Inn** 🅢🅗
(540) 433-6066. **$87-$103.** 1440 E Market St. I-81, exit 247A, just e. Int corridors. **Pets:** Other species. Service with restrictions, supervision.
SAVE 🆂🄳 ✕ 🅃 🔒 💻 ➰

AAA ▽▽▽ **Days Inn Harrisonburg** 🅢🅗 ❀
(540) 433-9353. **$54-$170.** 1131 Forest Hill Rd. I-81, exit 245, just e. Int corridors. **Pets:** Large, dogs only. $10 daily fee/pet. Service with restrictions, supervision.
SAVE 🆂🄳 ✕ 🅃 🔒 💻 ➰ ✕

AAA ▽▽▽ **Four Points by Sheraton** 🅢🅗
(540) 433-2521. **$69-$109.** 1400 E Market St. I-81, exit 247A, just e on US 33. Int corridors. **Pets:** Medium.
SAVE 🆂🄳 ✕ 🅃 🔒 💻 🍽 ➰

AAA ▽▽ **Harrisonburg Econo Lodge** 🅜
(540) 433-2576. **$60-$100.** 1703 E Market St. I-81, exit 247A, 0.5 mi e on US 33. Ext/int corridors. **Pets:** Small. Designated rooms, service with restrictions, supervision.
SAVE 🆂🄳 ✕ 🔒 ➰

▽▽▽ **Jameson Inn** 🅢🅗
(540) 442-1515. **$73-$77.** 1881 Evelyn Byrd Ave. I-81, exit 247A, just e. Int corridors. **Pets:** Small. Service with restrictions, crate.
✕ 🅃 🔒 💻 ➰

AAA ▽▽ **Ramada Inn** 🅢🅗
(540) 434-9981. **$80-$90.** 1 Pleasant Valley Rd. I-81, exit 243, just w, then just n on US 11. Ext corridors. **Pets:** Small, dogs only. $10 one-time fee/room. Service with restrictions, supervision.
SAVE 🆂🄳 ✕ 🅃 🔒 💻 🍽 ➰

AAA ▽▽▽ **Super 8 Motel** 🅜
(540) 433-8888. **$44-$145.** 3330 S Main St. I-81, exit 243, just e, then just s on US 11. Int corridors. **Pets:** Medium. $20 deposit/pet, $10 daily fee/pet. Service with restrictions, supervision.
SAVE 🆂🄳 ✕ 🔒

AAA ▽▽▽ **The Village Inn** 🅢🅗 ❀
(540) 434-7355. **$59-$69.** 4979 S Valley Pike. I-81, exit 240 southbound, 0.6 mi w on SR 257, then 1.5 mi n on US 11; exit 243 northbound, just w to US 11, then 1.7 mi s. Ext corridors. **Pets:** $6 daily fee/pet. Service with restrictions, crate.
SAVE ✕ 🔒 💻 ➰ ✕

HILLSVILLE

AAA ▽▽▽ **Holiday Inn Express** 🅢🅗 ❀
(276) 728-2120. **$69-$175.** 85 Airport Rd. I-77, exit 14, just w on US 58 and 221. Ext corridors. **Pets:** Small, other species. $10 daily fee/pet. Designated rooms, service with restrictions, supervision.
SAVE 🆂🄳 ✕ 🅂🄼 🔒 💻 ➰

▽ **Red Carpet Inn** 🅜
(276) 728-9118. **$37-$131.** 2666 Old Galax Pike. I-77, exit 14, just n. Int corridors. **Pets:** Accepted.
ASK 🆂🄳 ✕ 🔒 💻

HOPEWELL

AAA ▽▽▽ **Econo Lodge** 🅢🅗
(804) 541-4849. **$59-$79, 7 day notice.** 4096 Oaklawn Blvd. I-295, exit 9A, just e. Int corridors. **Pets:** Very small, dogs only. Service with restrictions, supervision.
SAVE 🆂🄳 ✕ 🅂🄼 🔒 💻

HOT SPRINGS

▽▽ **Roseloe Motel** 🅜
(540) 839-5373. **$60-$80.** 590 US 220 N. 3 mi n. Ext corridors. **Pets:** Medium. $10 one-time fee/room. Crate.
✕ 🔒 💻

IRVINGTON

▼▼▼ **The Hope and Glory Inn** 🄱🄱 ☙
(804) 438-6053. **$185-$325, 14 day notice.** 65 Tavern Rd.
Just w of CR 200 on King Carter Dr. Ext/int corridors.
Pets: Medium. $30 daily fee/pet. Designated rooms, service
with restrictions, crate.
⊠ 🍴 ⊠ 🅦

KESWICK

▼▼▼▼ **Keswick Hall at Monticello** 🆂🅷
(434) 979-3440. **$315-$705, 3 day notice.** 701 Club Dr. I-64,
exit 129, just n. Int corridors. **Pets:** Accepted.
⊠ Ⓜ 🖥 🍴 ➳ ⊠

KEYSVILLE

🄰🄰🄰 ▼▼▼ **Sheldon's Motel** 🆂🅷
(434) 736-8434. **$50-$72.** 1450 Four Locust Hwy. 1.3 mi n
on US 15 and 360 business route. Ext corridors.
Pets: Other species. Service with restrictions, crate.
🆂🅰🆅🅴 🆂 ⊠ 🖥 🍴

LAWRENCEVILLE

▼▼▼ **Brunswick Mineral Springs B & B Circa
1785** 🄱🄱
(434) 848-4010. **$85-$155, 5 day notice.** 14910 Western
Mill Rd. 5 mi e on US 58, 1 mi s on SR 712, then just e. Int
corridors. **Pets:** Accepted.
🄰🅂🄺 ⊠ 🖥 🖵

LEXINGTON

🄰🄰🄰 ▼▼▼▼ **Best Western Inn at Hunt Ridge** 🆂🅷
(540) 464-1500. **$69-$150, 7 day notice.** 25 Willow Springs
Rd. I-64, exit 55, just n on US 11 to SR 39; I-81, exit 191,
0.6 mi w. Int corridors. **Pets:** Small, other species. $25
one-time fee/room. Service with restrictions, supervision.
🆂🅰🆅🅴 🆂 ⊠ Ⓜ 🖥 ⊠ 🖥 🖵 🍴 ➳

🄰🄰🄰 ▼▼▼▼ **Comfort Inn-Virginia Horse
Center** 🆂🅷
(540) 463-7311. **$54-$125, 7 day notice.** 62 Comfort Way.
I-64, exit 55, just s on US 11; I-81, exit 191, 0.6 mi w. Int
corridors. **Pets:** Other species. $25 one-time fee/room.
Designated rooms, service with restrictions, supervision.
🆂🅰🆅🅴 🆂 ⊠ 🖥 🖵 ➳

▼▼▼ **Days Inn Keydet General** 🆂🅷
(540) 463-2143. **$50-$85, 3 day notice.** 325 W Midland Tr.
I-81, exit 188B, 4.5 mi on US 60 W; I-64, exit 50, 5 mi e on
US 60. Ext/int corridors. **Pets:** Medium, dogs only. $6 daily
fee/pet. Designated rooms, service with restrictions, supervision.
🄰🅂🄺 🆂 ⊠ 🖥

🄰🄰🄰 ▼▼▼ **Econo Lodge** Ⓜ
(540) 463-7371. **$48-$89.** 65 Econo Ln. I-81, exit 191, just s
on US 11. Ext corridors. **Pets:** Accepted.
🆂🅰🆅🅴 🆂 ⊠ 🖥 🖵

🄰🄰🄰 ▼▼▼▼ **Holiday Inn Express** 🆂🅷
(540) 463-7351. **$55-$130, 7 day notice.** 850 N Lee Hwy.
I-64, exit 55, just s on US 11; I-81, exit 191, 1.6 mi w. Ext
corridors. **Pets:** Accepted.
🆂🅰🆅🅴 🆂 ⊠ 🖥 🖥 🖵

🄰🄰🄰 ▼▼▼ **Howard Johnson Inn** 🆂🅷
(540) 463-9181. **$65-$130.** 2836 N Lee Hwy. I-81, exit 195,
just s on US 11. Int corridors. **Pets:** $7 daily fee/pet. No
service, supervision.
🆂🅰🆅🅴 🆂 ⊠ 🗗 🖥 🖵 🍴 ➳

▼▼▼ **Ramada Inn Lexington** 🆂🅷
(540) 463-6400. **$60-$76.** 2814 N Lee Hwy. I-81, exit 195,
just sw on US 11. Int corridors. **Pets:** $8 daily fee/pet.
Service with restrictions, supervision.
🄰🅂🄺 🆂 ⊠ 🗗 🖼 🖥 🖵 🍴 ➳

LURAY

🄰🄰🄰 ▼▼▼▼ **Best Western Intown of Luray** 🆂🅷
(540) 743-6511. **$65-$110.** 410 W Main St. 0.3 mi w on US
211 business route. Ext corridors. **Pets:** Other species. $20
daily fee/pet. Service with restrictions, supervision.
🆂🅰🆅🅴 🆂 ⊠ 🖥 🖵 🍴 ➳

▼▼▼ **Days Inn-Luray** 🆂🅷
(540) 743-4521. **$50-$100.** 138 Whispering Hill Rd. US 211
Bypass, 1.7 mi e of jct US 340. Ext corridors.
Pets: Medium. $10 daily fee/pet. Designated rooms, service
with restrictions, crate.
🄰🅂🄺 🆂 ⊠ 🍴 ➳

LYNCHBURG

🄰🄰🄰 ▼▼▼ **Best Western Lynchburg** Ⓜ
(434) 237-2986. **$74-$150, 14 day notice.** 2815 Candlers
Mountain Rd. Jct US 29 and 460. Ext corridors.
Pets: Small. $25 one-time fee/room. Designated rooms,
service with restrictions, crate.
🆂🅰🆅🅴 🆂 ⊠ 🗗 🖥 🖵 ➳

🄰🄰🄰 ▼▼▼▼ **Comfort Inn** 🆂🅷
(434) 847-9041. **$66-$79.** 3125 Albert Lankford Dr. US 29,
exit 7, 2.5 mi s. Int corridors. **Pets:** Accepted.
🆂🅰🆅🅴 🆂 ⊠ 🖥 🖵 ➳

🄰🄰🄰 ▼▼▼▼ **Holiday Inn Select** 🆂🅷
(434) 528-2500. **$79-$99.** 601 Main St. US 29 Expwy, exit 1
(Main St); center of downtown. Int corridors.
Pets: Accepted.
🆂🅰🆅🅴 🆂 ⊠ 🖥 🖵 🍴 ➳

MARION

🄰🄰🄰 ▼▼▼ **Best Western-Marion** 🆂🅷
(276) 783-3193. **$40-$55, 15 day notice.** 1424 N Main St.
I-81, exit 47, 0.3 mi s on US 11. Ext corridors.
Pets: Medium. $25 deposit/room. Designated rooms,
supervision.
🆂🅰🆅🅴 🆂 ⊠ 🗗 🖥 🖵 🍴 ➳

▼▼▼ **Econo Lodge** 🆂🅷
(276) 783-6031. **$40-$60, 15 day notice.** 1424 N Main St.
I-81, exit 47, 0.3 mi s on US 11. Ext corridors.
Pets: Medium. $25 deposit/room. Designated rooms,
supervision.
🄰🅂🄺 🆂 ⊠ 🗗 🖥 🖵

MARTINSVILLE

▼▼ Best Lodge Ⓜ
(276) 647-3941. **$45-$55, 30 day notice.** 1985 Virginia Ave. Jct US 58, 2.5 mi n on US 220 business route. Ext corridors. **Pets:** Medium. $7 daily fee/pet. Designated rooms, service with restrictions, supervision.
ⒶⓈⓀ 🛏 ⊠ 🖥 🖳

ⒶⒶⒶ ▼▼▼ Best Western Martinsville Inn 🆂🅷
(276) 632-5611. **$79-$119.** US 220 Business Route S. Jct US 58, 2.3 mi n. Ext corridors. **Pets:** Accepted.
🆂🅰🆅🅴 🛏 ⊠ 🖥 🖳 🍴 🏊

▼▼ Super 8 Motel Ⓜ
(276) 666-8888. **$54-$71.** 1044 N Memorial Blvd. Jct US 58, 1.5 mi n on US 220 business route. Int corridors. **Pets:** Accepted.
ⒶⓈⓀ 🛏 ⊠ 🖥

MAX MEADOWS

ⒶⒶⒶ ▼▼▼ Comfort Inn 🆂🅷
(276) 637-4281. **$69-$89.** 2594 E Lee Hwy. I-77/81, exit 80, just w. Int corridors. **Pets:** Accepted.
🆂🅰🆅🅴 🛏 ⊠ 🛏 🖥 🖳 🏊

MIDDLETOWN

ⒶⒶⒶ ▼▼ Super 8 Motel Ⓜ
(540) 868-1800. **$55-$125.** 2120 Relaince Rd. I-81, exit 302. Int corridors. **Pets:** Medium. $10 daily fee/pet. Designated rooms, service with restrictions, supervision.
🆂🅰🆅🅴 🛏 ⊠ 🏊

MINT SPRING

▼ Armstrong Family Motel & Restaurant Ⓜ
(540) 337-2611. **$50-$75, 7 day notice.** 210 White Hill Rd. I-81, exit 217, just w on SR 654. Ext corridors. **Pets:** Accepted.
ⒶⓈⓀ 🛏 ⊠ 🖥 🖳 🍴 🏊

▼▼ Days Inn-Staunton Ⓜ
(540) 337-3031. **$59-$119.** 372 White Hill Rd. I-81, exit 217, just e on SR 654. Ext corridors. **Pets:** Medium, other species. $6 daily fee/pet. Designated rooms, service with restrictions, supervision.
ⒶⓈⓀ 🛏 ⊠ 🖥 🖳 🏊

MOUNT JACKSON

ⒶⒶⒶ ▼▼▼ Best Western-Shenandoah Valley 🆂🅷
(540) 477-2911. **$70-$95, 3 day notice.** 250 Conickville Rd. I-81, exit 273, just e. Ext corridors. **Pets:** Other species. $10 daily fee/pet. Designated rooms, service with restrictions, crate.
🆂🅰🆅🅴 🛏 ⊠ 🖳 🍴 🏊

▼▼▼ The Widow Kip's 🅱🅱 🐾
(540) 477-2400. **$90-$125, 5 day notice.** 355 Orchard Dr. I-81, exit 273, 1.5 mi s on US 11, just w on SR 263, then just sw on SR 698. Int corridors. **Pets:** Other species. $10 deposit/pet. Designated rooms, service with restrictions, crate.
ⒶⓈⓀ 🛏 ⊠ 🖥 🖳 🏊

NATURAL BRIDGE

▼ Relax Inn Ⓜ
(540) 291-2143. **$39-$89, 3 day notice.** 4852 S Lee Hwy. I-81, exit 180A, just se. Ext corridors. **Pets:** Small, dogs only. $10 one-time fee/pet. Designated rooms, service with restrictions, supervision.
⊠ 🖥

NEW CHURCH

▼▼▼ The Garden & The Sea Inn 🅲🅸 🐾
(757) 824-0672. **$75-$195, 10 day notice.** 4188 Nelson Rd. US 13, 0.3 mi n, just w on CR 710 (Nelson Rd). Int corridors. **Pets:** Other species.
ⒶⓈⓀ 🛏 ⊠ 🖥 🖳 🍴 ✉

NEW MARKET

ⒶⒶⒶ ▼ Budget Inn Ⓜ
(540) 740-3105. **$29-$69, 3 day notice.** 2192 Old Valley Pike. I-81, exit 264, 1 mi n on US 11. Ext corridors. **Pets:** Small. $5 one-time fee/pet. Designated rooms, no service, supervision.
🆂🅰🆅🅴 🛏 ⊠ 🖥

ⒶⒶⒶ ▼▼ Days Inn 🆂🅷 🐾
(540) 740-4100. **$60-$80.** 9360 George Collins Pkwy. I-81, exit 264, just w on US 211. Ext corridors. **Pets:** Other species. $5 daily fee/pet. Service with restrictions, supervision.
🆂🅰🆅🅴 🛏 ⊠ 🏊

PETERSBURG

ⒶⒶⒶ ▼▼▼ Best Western-Steven Kent 🆂🅷 🐾
(804) 733-0600. **$45-$100.** 12205 S Crater Rd. I-95, exit 45, jct US 301. Ext/int corridors. **Pets:** Small. $10 daily fee/pet. Designated rooms, service with restrictions, supervision.
🆂🅰🆅🅴 🛏 ⊠ 🖥 🖳 🍴 🏊 ⊠

ⒶⒶⒶ ▼▼▼ Comfort Inn 🆂🅷
(804) 732-2900. **$65-$99.** 11974 S Crater Rd. I-95, exit 45, n on US 301. Ext corridors. **Pets:** Medium, other species. $10 daily fee/room, $10 one-time fee/room. Designated rooms, service with restrictions, crate.
🆂🅰🆅🅴 🛏 ⊠ 🖥 🖳 🏊

ⒶⒶⒶ ▼▼▼ Days Inn 🆂🅷
(804) 733-4400. **$60-$80.** 12208 S Crater Rd. I-95, exit 45, jct US 301. Ext corridors. **Pets:** $10 daily fee/pet. Designated rooms, service with restrictions, supervision.
🆂🅰🆅🅴 🛏 ⊠ 🖥 🖳 🏊

ⒶⒶⒶ ▼▼▼ Econo Lodge-South 🆂🅷
(804) 862-2717. **$39-$129.** 16905 Parkdale Rd. I-95, exit 41, just e. Ext corridors. **Pets:** Accepted.
🆂🅰🆅🅴 🛏 ⊠ 🖥 🖳 🍴 🏊

ⒶⒶⒶ ▼▼▼ Quality Inn 🆂🅷
(804) 733-1776. **$60-$110, 3 day notice.** 405 E Washington St. I-95, exit 52 southbound; exit 50D northbound; I-85, exit 69; downtown. Ext corridors. **Pets:** Medium, other species. $5 daily fee/pet. Service with restrictions.
🆂🅰🆅🅴 🛏 ⊠ 🖥 🖳 🍴 🏊

PULASKI

▼▼ Days Inn SH
(540) 980-2230. **$45-$120, 9 day notice.** 3063 Old Rt 100 Rd. I-81, exit 94, just e. Ext/int corridors. **Pets:** Accepted.

ASK SÓ ⊠ 🖀

RADFORD

AAA ▼▼▼▼ Best Western Radford Inn SH
(540) 639-3000. **$76-$95.** 1501 Tyler Ave. I-81, exit 109, 2.7 mi nw on SR 177. Int corridors. **Pets:** Medium, other species. $40 deposit/room, $10 one-time fee/room. Designated rooms, service with restrictions, supervision.

SAVE SÓ ⊠ 🖀 🖵 ⑪ 🛥 🗵

RAPHINE

▼▼ Days Inn-Shenandoah Valley M
(540) 377-2604. **$54-$94.** 584 Oakland Cr. I-81, exit 205, just sw. Int corridors. **Pets:** Other species. $5 daily fee/pet. Designated rooms, service with restrictions, supervision.

ASK SÓ ⊠ 🖀 🛥

RICHMOND METROPOLITAN AREA

CARMEL CHURCH

▼▼ Red Roof Inn SH
(804) 448-2828. **$44-$74.** 23500 Welcome Way Dr. I-95, exit 104 (SR 207), just w. Int corridors. **Pets:** Large, other species. Designated rooms, service with restrictions, crate.

ASK SÓ ⊠ ⑦ 🖧 🖀 ⑪ 🛥

CHESTER

AAA ▼▼▼▼ Comfort Inn-Richmond/Chester SH
(804) 751-0000. **$69-$99.** 2100 W Hundred Rd. I-95, exit 61A, just e on SR 10. Int corridors. **Pets:** Medium. Designated rooms, service with restrictions, supervision.

SAVE SÓ ⊠ 🖧 🖀 🖵 ⑪ 🛥

DOSWELL

AAA ▼▼▼ Best Western-Kings Quarters SH
(804) 876-3321. **$34-$169, 3 day notice.** 16102 Theme Park Way. I-95, exit 98, just e on SR 30; at entrance to theme park. Ext corridors. **Pets:** Accepted.

SAVE SÓ ⊠ 🖧 🖀 🖵 ⑪ 🛥 🗵

GLEN ALLEN

AAA ▼▼▼▼ AmeriSuites
(Richmond/Innsbrook) SH
(804) 747-9644. **$81-$91.** 4100 Cox Rd. I-64, exit 178B, SR 250/W Broad St, 0.5 mi e to Dominion Blvd, just n. Int corridors. **Pets:** Small, other species. Service with restrictions, supervision.

SAVE SÓ ⊠ ⑦ 🖀 🖵 🛥

▼▼ Homestead Studio Suites
Hotel-Richmond/Innsbrook M
(804) 747-9898. **$54-$64.** 10961 W Broad St. I-64, exit 178B, just e on W Broad St, just s on Cox Rd. Ext corridors. **Pets:** Medium, other species. $25 daily fee/room. Service with restrictions, crate.

ASK SÓ ⊠ 🖀 🖵

▼▼▼ Homewood Suites Hotel Richmond West
End SH
(804) 217-8000. **$99-$299.** 4100 Innslake Dr. I-64, exit 178B, just e on W Broad St to Cox Rd, just n. Int corridors. **Pets:** Accepted.

ASK SÓ ⊠ 🖧 ⑦ 🖧 🖀 🖵 🛥

▼▼▼ Residence Inn by Marriott SH
(804) 762-9852. **$79-$109.** 3940 Westerre Pkwy. I-64, exit 180, n on Gaskins Rd to W Broad St. Int corridors. **Pets:** Other species. $100 one-time fee/room. Service with restrictions.

ASK SÓ ⊠ 🖧 🖧 🖀 🖵 🛥 🗵

▼▼▼ TownePlace Suites by Marriott M
(804) 747-5253. **$44-$109.** 4231 Park Place Ct. I-64, exit 178B, just e on W Broad St to Cox Rd, just n to Innslake Dr. Int corridors. **Pets:** Accepted.

ASK SÓ ⊠ 🖧 🖧 🖀 🖵 🛥

RICHMOND

AAA ▼▼▼ AmeriSuites
(Richmond/Arboretum) SH
(804) 560-1566. **$69-$129.** 201 Arboretum Pl. Jct Powhite Pkwy (US 76) and Midlothian Tpke (US 60), just w; enter at the Arboretum Pl. Int corridors. **Pets:** Small. Service with restrictions, crate.

SAVE SÓ ⊠ 🖧 ⑦ 🖧 🖀 🖵 🛥

▼▼▼ Candlewood Suites SH
(804) 271-0016. **$79.** 4301 Commerce Rd. I-95, exit 69, just n. Int corridors. **Pets:** Accepted.

ASK SÓ ⊠ 🖧 🖧 🖀 🖵

AAA ▼▼▼▼ Commonwealth Park Suites SH
(804) 343-7300. **$89-$109.** 901 Bank St. Jct 9th and Bank sts; across the green from the state capitol. Int corridors. **Pets:** Accepted.

SAVE SÓ ⊠ 🖧 🖵

▼▼ Days Inn-West Broad SH
(804) 282-3300. **$49-$129.** 2100 Dickens Rd. I-64, exit 183B westbound; exit 183 eastbound, 0.3 mi e on W Broad St, just n. Int corridors. **Pets:** Accepted.

ASK SÓ ⊠ ⑦ 🖀 🖵 🛥

AAA ▼▼▼▼ Holiday Inn-Richmond North SH
(804) 266-8753. **$99, 14 day notice.** 801 E Parham Rd. I-95, exit 83B. Int corridors. **Pets:** Small, other species. $25 one-time fee/room. Service with restrictions, supervision.

SAVE SÓ ⊠ 🖧 ⑦ 🖧 🖀 🖵 🛥

▼▼▼ **Homestead Studio Suites
Hotel-Richmond/Midlothian** 🆂🅷 🐾
(804) 272-1800. **$69-$79.** 241 Arboretum Pl. Jct Powhite Pkwy (US 76) and Midlothian Tpke (US 60), just w; enter at the Arboretum Pl. Int corridors. **Pets:** Medium, other species. $25 daily fee/room. Service with restrictions, crate.
(ASK) (S🅓) (✕) (🖦M) (🔊) (🖘) (🛢) (🖵)

🆀🅰🅰 ▼▼▼▼▼ **The Jefferson Hotel** 🅻🅷 🐾
(804) 788-8000. **$285-$335.** 101 W Franklin St. Franklin and Adams sts; center. Int corridors. **Pets:** $35 daily fee/room. Designated rooms, service with restrictions, crate.
(SAVE) (S🅓) (✕) (🔊) (🖘) (🛢) (🍴) (🛌) (✕)

▼▼▼ **Omni Richmond Hotel** 🅻🅷
(804) 344-7000. **$209-$229.** 100 S 12th St. I-95, exit 74A; I-195, exit Canal St. Int corridors. **Pets:** Small. $50 one-time fee/room. Service with restrictions, crate.
(ASK) (S🅓) (✕) (🔊) (🖘) (🛢) (🖵) (🍴) (🛌)

🆀🅰🅰 ▼▼▼▼ **Quality Inn West End** 🆂🅷
(804) 346-0000. **$69-$159.** 8008 W Broad St. I-64, exit 183C westbound; exit 183 eastbound, 1.5 mi w. Int corridors. **Pets:** Medium, other species. $10 daily fee/room, $35 one-time fee/room. Service with restrictions, supervision.
(SAVE) (S🅓) (✕) (🖘) (🛢) (🖵) (🛌)

▼▼▼▼ **Radisson Hotel Historic
Richmond** 🆂🅷 🐾
(804) 644-9871. **$139.** 301 W Franklin St. Franklin St at Madison. Int corridors. **Pets:** Medium, other species. $25 one-time fee/room. Service with restrictions, crate.
(ASK) (S🅓) (✕) (🖘) (🛢) (🖵) (🍴) (🛌)

▼▼▼▼ **Residence Inn by Marriott** 🆂🅷
(804) 285-8200. **$101-$129.** 2121 Dickens Rd. I-64, exit 183B, 0.3 mi e, just n of US 60 (Broad St). Ext corridors. **Pets:** Accepted.
(ASK) (S🅓) (✕) (🔊) (🖘) (🛢) (🖵) (🛌) (✕)

🆀🅰🅰 ▼▼▼▼ **Wyndham Richmond Airport** 🆂🅷
(804) 226-4300. **$94-$99.** 4700 S Laburnum Ave. I-64, exit 195, 0.5 mi s. Int corridors. **Pets:** Small. $50 one-time fee/pet. Service with restrictions, supervision.
(SAVE) (S🅓) (✕) (🖘) (🛢) (🖵) (🍴) (🛌) (✕)

SANDSTON

▼▼▼▼ **Holiday Inn-Airport** 🆂🅷
(804) 222-6450. **$74-$84.** 5203 Williamsburg Rd. I-64, exit 195, 1.5 mi s to Williamsburg Rd, then just e. Ext/int corridors. **Pets:** Accepted.
(ASK) (S🅓) (✕) (🖘) (🛢) (🖵) (🍴) (🛌)

🆀🅰🅰 ▼▼▼ **Microtel Inn & Suites** 🆂🅷
(804) 737-3322. **$53-$62.** 6000 Audubon Dr. I-64, exit 197A (Sandston-RIC Airport), just s. Int corridors. **Pets:** Other species. $15 one-time fee/pet. Service with restrictions, supervision.
(SAVE) (S🅓) (✕) (🖦M) (🔊) (🖘) (🛢) (🖵)

▼▼▼▼ **Wingate Inn Richmond Airport** 🆂🅷
(804) 222-1499. **$69-$99.** 491 International Centre Dr. I-64, exit 197A (Sandston-RIC Airport), just s to Audobon Dr, then just n. Int corridors. **Pets:** Accepted.
(ASK) (S🅓) (✕) (🖦M) (🖘) (🛢) (🖵) (🛌)

🐾 **END METROPOLITAN AREA** 🐾

ROANOKE

🆀🅰🅰 ▼▼▼▼ **AmeriSuites (Roanoke/Valley View
Mall)** 🆂🅷
(540) 366-4700. **$59-$149.** 5040 Valley View Blvd. I-581, exit 3E, just e, then just s via shopping center exit. Int corridors. **Pets:** Small, other species. Service with restrictions, supervision.
(SAVE) (S🅓) (✕) (🖦M) (🔊) (🖘) (🛢) (🖵) (🛌)

🆀🅰🅰 ▼▼▼ **Best Western Inn at Valley View** 🆂🅷
(540) 362-2400. **$69-$125, 7 day notice.** 5050 Valley View Blvd. I-581, exit 3E, just e, then just s via shopping center exit. Int corridors. **Pets:** $20 one-time fee/room. Designated rooms, service with restrictions, supervision.
(SAVE) (✕) (🖘) (🛢) (🖵) (🛌)

🆀🅰🅰 ▼▼▼ **Clarion Hotel Roanoke
Airport** 🆂🅷 🐾
(540) 362-4500. **$89-$139.** 3315 Ordway Dr. I-581, exit 3W, just w to Ordway Dr, then 0.6 mi n via service road. Int corridors. **Pets:** $10 daily fee/room, $25 one-time fee/room. Designated rooms, service with restrictions, crate.
(SAVE) (S🅓) (✕) (🔊) (🖘) (🛢) (🖵) (🛌) (✕)

▼▼▼ **Days Inn** 🆂🅷
(540) 366-0341. **$49-$99, 3 day notice.** 8118 Plantation Rd. I-81, exit 146, just e on SR 115. Ext/int corridors. **Pets:** Other species. $15 one-time fee/room. Service with restrictions, supervision.
(ASK) (S🅓) (✕) (🖘) (🛢) (🖵) (🍴) (🛌)

🆀🅰🅰 ▼▼▼▼ **MainStay Suites Roanoke
Airport** 🆂🅷
(540) 527-3030. **$64-$140, 7 day notice.** 5080 Valley View Blvd. I-581, exit 3E, just n. Int corridors. **Pets:** Small, other species. $25 daily fee/room. Designated rooms, service with restrictions, supervision.
(SAVE) (S🅓) (✕) (🖘) (🛢) (🖵)

🆀🅰🅰 ▼▼▼ **Rodeway Inn-Civic Center** 🆂🅷
(540) 981-9341. **$38-$100.** 526 Orange Ave NE. I-581, exit 4E, jct US 400 and 11, just n. Ext corridors. **Pets:** Dogs only. $10 daily fee/pet. Designated rooms, service with restrictions, supervision.
(SAVE) (S🅓) (✕) (🔊) (🖘) (🛢) (🖵)

▼▼▼ **Super 8 Motel** 🆂🅷
(540) 563-8888. **$55-$65, 3 day notice.** 6616 Thirlane Rd. I-581, exit 25, s on SR 117 (Peters Creek Rd), just w. Int corridors. **Pets:** Small, other species. $10 deposit/pet. Service with restrictions, supervision.
(ASK) (S🅓) (✕) (🖘)

(AAA) ▼▼▼ **Wyndham Roanoke Airport** [LH]
(540) 563-9300. **$79-$99.** 2801 Hershberger Rd. I-581, exit 3W, just w to Ordway Dr, just n via service road. Int corridors. **Pets:** Large, other species. $25 one-time fee/pet. Designated rooms, service with restrictions, supervision.
[SAVE] [🐾] [✕] [🐕] [💻] [🍴] [🏊] [✕]

ROCKY MOUNT

(AAA) ▼▼ **Franklin Motel** [M]
(540) 483-9962. **$45-$80.** 20281 Virgil H Goode Hwy. 6.5 mi n on US 220. Ext corridors. **Pets:** Very small. $10 daily fee/pet. Designated rooms, service with restrictions, supervision.
[SAVE] [🐾] [✕] [🐕]

SALEM

(AAA) ▼ **Blue Jay Budget Host Inn** [M] ❧
(540) 380-2080. **$32-$80, 3 day notice.** 5399 W Main St. I-81, exit 132, just e, then 0.3 mi n on US 11/460. Ext corridors. **Pets:** Medium. $5 daily fee/pet. Designated rooms, service with restrictions, supervision.
[SAVE] [🐾] [✕] [🐕] [🏊]

▼▼ **Econo Lodge-Roanoke/Salem** [M]
(540) 389-0280. **$37-$64.** 301 Wildwood Rd. I-81, exit 137, just e on SR 112. Ext corridors. **Pets:** Medium. $6 one-time fee/pet. Designated rooms, service with restrictions, crate.
[ASK] [🐾] [✕] [🐕]

(AAA) ▼▼▼ **Quality Inn Roanoke/Salem** [SH]
(540) 562-1912. **$56-$85.** 179 Sheraton Dr. I-81, exit 141, 0.4 mi e on SR 419. Int corridors. **Pets:** Medium. $15 daily fee/pet. Designated rooms, service with restrictions, crate.
[SAVE] [🐾] [✕] [🐕] [💻] [🏊] [✕]

▼▼▼ **Salem Ramada Inn & Conference Center** [SH]
(540) 389-7061. **$59-$79.** 1671 Skyview Rd. I-81, exit 137, just w on SR 112, then just n. Ext corridors. **Pets:** Accepted.
[ASK] [🐾] [✕] [🐕] [🐕] [💻] [🍴] [🏊]

SOUTH BOSTON

▼▼▼ **Holiday Inn-Express** [SH]
(434) 575-4000. **$89-$99.** 1074 Bill Tuck Hwy. Just e on US 58, from jct US 501. Int corridors. **Pets:** Small. $20 daily fee/pet. Service with restrictions, supervision.
[ASK] [🐾] [✕] [🔥] [⛳] [🐕] [💻] [🏊]

(AAA) ▼▼▼ **Quality Inn Howard House** [SH]
(434) 572-4311. **$45-$99.** 2001 Seymour Dr. Jct US 58, 501 and 360, 1 mi e on US 360. Ext corridors. **Pets:** Medium. $10 daily fee/pet. Designated rooms, service with restrictions.
[SAVE] [🐾] [✕] [🐕] [💻] [🍴] [🏊]

SOUTH HILL

▼▼ **Comfort Inn** [SH]
(434) 447-2600. **$56-$72.** 918 E Atlantic St. I-85, exit 12B, just w. Ext corridors. **Pets:** Accepted.
[ASK] [🐾] [✕] [🐕]

▼▼ **Econo Lodge** [M]
(434) 447-7116. **$35-$75.** 623 E Atlantic St. I-85, exit 12B, 0.5 mi w on US 58. Ext corridors. **Pets:** Medium, other species. $10 daily fee/room. Service with restrictions, supervision.
[ASK] [🐾] [✕] [🐕] [💻]

STAFFORD

(AAA) ▼▼▼ **Days Inn Aquia-Quantico** [SH]
(540) 659-0022. **$72-$89.** 2868 Jefferson Davis Hwy. I-95, exit 143A, jct US 1 and SR 610. Ext corridors. **Pets:** Accepted.
[SAVE] [🐾] [✕] [🐕] [💻] [🏊]

STAUNTON

▼▼▼ **Ashton Country House** [BB] ❧
(540) 885-7819. **$90-$150, 7 day notice.** 1205 Middlebrook Ave. I-81, exit 220, 1 mi to SR 252 (Middlebrook Ave), 0.3 mi n. Int corridors. **Pets:** Other species. $10 daily fee/room. Service with restrictions.
[ASK] [🐾] [✕] [🐕]

(AAA) ▼▼▼ **Comfort Inn** [SH]
(540) 886-5000. **$69-$119.** 1302 Richmond Ave. I-81, exit 222, just w on US 250. Int corridors. **Pets:** Small. $10 daily fee/pet. Designated rooms, service with restrictions, supervision.
[SAVE] [🐾] [✕] [🐕] [🐕] [💻] [🏊]

▼▼ **Days Inn–Business Place** [SH]
(540) 248-0888. **$64-$91.** 273-D Bells Ln. I-81, exit 225, just w. Ext corridors. **Pets:** Other species. $10 daily fee/room. Designated rooms, supervision.
[ASK] [🐾] [✕] [🐕] [🐕] [💻] [🏊]

(AAA) ▼▼▼ **Econo Lodge Staunton** [M]
(540) 885-5158. **$56-$86.** 1031 Richmond Ave. I-81, exit 222, 0.7 mi w on US 250. Ext/int corridors. **Pets:** Medium. $10 one-time fee/pet. Service with restrictions, supervision.
[SAVE] [🐾] [✕] [🐕] [💻]

(AAA) ▼▼▼ **Holiday Inn Golf & Conference Center** [SH]
(540) 248-6020. **$79-$160.** 152 Fairway Ln. I-81, exit 225, 0.3 mi w on SR 275 (Woodrow Wilson Pkwy). Int corridors. **Pets:** Accepted.
[SAVE] [🐾] [✕] [🐕] [🐕] [💻] [🍴] [🏊]

(AAA) ▼▼▼ **Quality Inn-Conference Center** [SH] ❧
(540) 248-5111. **$55-$95.** 96 Baker Ln. I-81, exit 225, just e on SR 275 (Woodrow Wilson Pkwy). Ext corridors. **Pets:** Other species. $5 daily fee/room. Designated rooms, service with restrictions, supervision.
[SAVE] [🐾] [✕] [🐕] [💻] [🏊]

(AAA) ▼▼ **Sleep Inn** [SH]
(540) 887-6500. **$54-$120, 7 day notice.** 222 Jefferson Hwy. I-81, exit 222, just e on US 250. Int corridors. **Pets:** Service with restrictions, supervision.
[SAVE] [🐾] [✕] [⛳] [🐕] [💻]

(AAA) ▼▼◆ Super 8 Motel M
(540) 886-2888. **$56-$86.** 1015 Richmond Rd. I-81, exit 222, 1.2 mi w on US 250. Int corridors. **Pets:** Medium. $10 one-time fee/pet. Service with restrictions, supervision.
[SAVE] [S⊘] [✕] [☐]

STEPHENS CITY

(AAA) ▼▼◆▼ Comfort Inn-Stephens City SH
(540) 869-6500. **$69-$85.** 167 Town Run Ln. I-81, exit 307, just se. Int corridors. **Pets:** Other species. $10 daily fee/pet. Service with restrictions, supervision.
[SAVE] [S⊘] [✕] [⌖] [☐] [▣] [⇌]

STONY CREEK

(AAA) ▼▼◆▼ Sleep Inn & Suites SH
(434) 246-5100. **$60-$99.** 11019 Blue Star Hwy. I-95, exit 33, 0.3 mi s on SR 301. Int corridors. **Pets:** $7 daily fee/room. Service with restrictions, supervision.
[SAVE] [S⊘] [✕] [⌖] [☐] [▣] [⇌]

STRASBURG

(AAA) ▼▼◆▼ Hotel Strasburg CI
(540) 465-9191. **$85-$185.** 213 Holliday St. I-81, exit 298, 2.2 mi s on US 11, just s. Int corridors. **Pets:** Other species. Service with restrictions, crate.
[SAVE] [S⊘] [✕] [¶]

THORNBURG

▼▼◆▼ Holiday Inn Express SH
(540) 582-1097. **$89-$109.** 6409 Dan Bell Ln. I-95, exit 118 (SR 606), just w. Ext corridors. **Pets:** Small. $10 daily fee/pet. Service with restrictions, supervision.
[ASK] [S⊘] [✕] [⌖M] [⌖] [☐] [▣] [⇌]

TROUTVILLE

(AAA) ▼▼◆▼ Comfort Inn Troutville SH
(540) 992-5600. **$44-$94, 7 day notice.** 2545 Lee Hwy S. I-81, exit 150A, just s on US 11. Int corridors. **Pets:** Small. $20 one-time fee/pet. Service with restrictions, crate.
[SAVE] [S⊘] [✕] [☐] [▣] [⇌]

(AAA) ▼▼◆▼ Travelodge Roanoke North M
(540) 992-6700. **$40-$75.** 2619 Lee Hwy S. I-81, exit 150A, just e, then just s on US 11. Ext corridors. **Pets:** Medium. $6 daily fee/pet. Designated rooms, service with restrictions, supervision.
[SAVE] [S⊘] [✕] [☐] [▣] [⇌] [✕]

VERONA

(AAA) ▼▼◆▼ Ramada Limited SH
(540) 248-8981. **$39-$155.** 70 Lodge Ln. I-81, exit 227, just w, then just n. Ext corridors. **Pets:** Accepted.
[SAVE] [S⊘] [✕] [⌖] [▣] [⇌]

WARRENTON

(AAA) ▼▼◆▼ Comfort Inn SH
(540) 349-8900. **$69-$99.** 7379 Comfort Inn Dr. 1.5 mi n on US 15/29, on service road. Ext/int corridors. **Pets:** $10 daily fee/pet. Designated rooms, crate.
[SAVE] [S⊘] [✕] [☐] [▣] [⇌] [✕]

▼▼◆▼ Hampton Inn SH
(540) 349-4200. **$89-$120.** 501 Blackwell Rd. 1 mi n on US 29 business route and US 211. Ext corridors. **Pets:** Other species. Service with restrictions, supervision.
[ASK] [S⊘] [✕] [⌖M] [⌖] [☐] [▣] [⇌]

(AAA) ▼▼◆ Howard Johnson Inn-Warrenton M
(540) 347-4141. **$80-$100.** 6 Broadview Ave. US 17/29 business route, jct US 211 W. Int corridors. **Pets:** Medium. $10 daily fee/pet. Service with restrictions, supervision.
[SAVE] [S⊘] [✕] [☐] [▣] [⇌]

WARSAW

▼▼◆▼ Best Western Warsaw SH
(804) 333-1700. **$66-$84.** 4522 Richmond Rd. US 360, just w of town. Int corridors. **Pets:** Accepted.
[ASK] [S⊘] [✕] [◈] [☐] [▣] [⇌]

WAYNESBORO

(AAA) ▼▼◆ Days Inn Waynesboro M
(540) 943-1101. **$54-$89.** 2060 Rosser Ave. I-64, exit 94, 0.5 mi n on US 340. Ext corridors. **Pets:** Other species. $10 daily fee/room. Service with restrictions.
[SAVE] [S⊘] [✕] [☐] [▣] [⇌]

(AAA) ▼▼◆ Quality Inn Waynesboro SH
(540) 942-1171. **$79-$109.** 640 W Broad St. I-64, exit 96, 3 mi w on SR 624, jct US 250 and 340. Ext/int corridors. **Pets:** $10 daily fee/pet. Service with restrictions, supervision.
[SAVE] [S⊘] [✕] [⌖] [☐] [▣] [⇌]

(AAA) ▼▼◆ Super 8 Motel SH
(540) 943-3888. **$60-$81.** 2045 Rosser Ave. I-64, exit 94, n on US 340 to Lew DeWitt Blvd, just w to Apple Tree Ln. Int corridors. **Pets:** Other species. $5 daily fee/pet. Service with restrictions, supervision.
[SAVE] [S⊘] [✕] [⌖] [☐]

Williamsburg, Jamestown & Yorktown Metropolitan Area

WILLIAMSBURG

[AAA] ♦♦ **Best Western Colonial Capitol Inn** [SH]
(757) 253-1222. **$59-$129, 3 day notice.** 111 Penniman Rd. Just n of jct US 60 and SR 5. Int corridors. **Pets:** Small. $10 one-time fee/room. Service with restrictions.
[SAVE] [SD] ☒ ♿M ♿ ▣ ☕ 🏊

[AAA] ♦♦♦ **Best Western Patrick Henry Inn** [SH]
(757) 229-9540. **$49-$169, 3 day notice.** 249 E York St NW. E on US 60 at jct SR 5 and 31, 1 blk from Colonial Williamsburg. Int corridors. **Pets:** Large, other species. $15 one-time fee/room. Service with restrictions.
[SAVE] [SD] ☒ ♿M ♿ ▣ ☕ 🍴 🏊

[AAA] ♦♦ **Best Western Williamsburg** [SH]
(757) 229-3003. **$69-$129, 3 day notice.** 7411 Pocahontas Tr. 2 mi e on US 60 at jct SR 199. Ext corridors. **Pets:** Small. $10 daily fee/pet. Designated rooms, no service, crate.
[SAVE] [SD] ☒ ♿M ♿ ▣ 🏊

[AAA] ♦♦♦ **Best Western Williamsburg Westpark Hotel** [SH]
(757) 229-1134. **$39-$99.** 1600 Richmond Rd. Jct US 60 (Richmond Rd) and SR 612 (Ironbound Rd). Ext/int corridors. **Pets:** Other species. $10 daily fee/room. Service with restrictions, crate.
[SAVE] [SD] ☒ ▣ ☕ 🏊

[AAA] ♦♦ **Days Inn Colonial Downtown** [SH]
(757) 229-5060. **$39-$119, 3 day notice.** 902 Richmond Rd. Just w of Colonial Williamsburg on US 60. Ext corridors. **Pets:** Small. $15 daily fee/pet. Designated rooms, service with restrictions, supervision.
[SAVE] [SD] ☒ ▣ 🏊

♦♦♦ **Four Points by Sheraton Hotel & Suites Williamsburg Historic District** [SH]
(757) 229-4100. **$54-$144, 3 day notice.** 351 York St. US 60 E, 0.3 mi se of jct SR 5 and 31. Ext/int corridors. **Pets:** Medium. $25 one-time fee/pet. Designated rooms, service with restrictions, supervision.
[A$K] [SD] ☒ ♿M 🦻 ♿ ▣ ☕ 🍴 🏊 🏋

[AAA] ♦♦♦ **Holiday Inn Patriot** [SH] 🐾
(757) 565-2600. **$59-$159.** 3032 Richmond Rd. I-64, exit 234 (SR 199 E) to US 60, 2.5 mi e. Int corridors. **Pets:** Medium. $10 daily fee/room.
[SAVE] [SD] ☒ 🦻 ▣ ☕ 🍴 🏊 🏋

[AAA] ♦♦♦ **La Quinta Inn** [M]
(757) 253-1663. **$46-$126.** 119 Bypass Rd. US 60 Bypass Rd, 0.3 mi e of Richmond Rd. Ext corridors. **Pets:** Medium, other species. $30 one-time fee/room. Service with restrictions.
[SAVE] [SD] ☒ ♿M 🦻 ▣ ☕ 🏊

[AAA] ♦♦ **Quarterpath Inn** [M]
(757) 220-0960. **$39-$119, 3 day notice.** 620 York St. I-64, exit 242 (SR 199 W), 0.6 mi w to US 60 E, just w. Ext corridors. **Pets:** Other species. Service with restrictions.
[SAVE] [SD] ☒ ▣ 🏊

[AAA] ♦♦♦ **Ramada Inn 1776** [SH] 🐾
(757) 220-1776. **$44-$129.** 725 Bypass Rd. US 60 (Bypass Rd), 0.5 mi w of jct SR 132. Int corridors. **Pets:** Other species. Service with restrictions.
[SAVE] [SD] ☒ ♿M ▣ ☕ 🍴 🏊 🏋

♦♦♦ **Residence Inn by Marriott Williamsburg** [SH]
(757) 941-2000. **$89-$189.** 1648 Richmond Rd. US 60, just w of jct Bypass Rd. Int corridors. **Pets:** Large, other species. $6 daily fee/room, $250 one-time fee/room. Service with restrictions.
[A$K] ☒ ♿M ♿ ▣ ☕ 🏊 🏋

[AAA] ♦♦ **Super 8 Motel-Colonial/Historical** [SH]
(757) 253-1087. **$40-$90, 3 day notice.** 1233 Richmond Rd. 2 mi w of Colonial Williamsburg restored area, jct Lafayette St. Int corridors. **Pets:** Small, dogs only. $10 daily fee/pet. Designated rooms, service with restrictions, supervision.
[SAVE] [SD] ☒ ♿ ▣ 🏊

YORKTOWN

♦♦♦ **Candlewood Suites-Yorktown** [SH]
(757) 952-1120. **$129-$189.** 329 Commonwealth Dr. I-64, exit 256B (Victory Blvd), just n, then just e. Int corridors. **Pets:** Large. $150 one-time fee/room. Service with restrictions.
[A$K] [SD] ☒ ♿M ♿ ▣ ☕ 🏊

[AAA] ♦♦♦ **TownePlace Suites by Marriott** [SH]
(757) 874-8884. **$89-$169.** 200 Cybernetics Way. I-64, exit 256B, e to Kiln Creek Pkwy. Int corridors. **Pets:** Other species. $100 one-time fee/room. Service with restrictions, crate.
[SAVE] [SD] ☒ ♿M ♿ ▣ ☕ 🏊

🐾 **End Metropolitan Area** 🐾

WINCHESTER

⚠ ▼▼▼ Best Western Lee-Jackson Motor Inn 🆂🅷
(540) 662-4154. **$57-$69.** 711 Millwood Ave. I-81, exit 313B, just nw on US 50/522/17. Ext corridors. **Pets:** $5 one-time fee/pet. Designated rooms, service with restrictions, supervision.
🆂🅰🆅🅴 🆂🅾 ⊗ 🎬 💻 🍽 🏊

⚠ ▼▼▼ Days Inn 🆂🅷
(540) 667-1200. **$55-$69.** 2951 Valley Ave. I-81, exit 310, just w, then 1.8 mi n on US 11. Ext corridors. **Pets:** $8 daily fee/pet. Service with restrictions, supervision.
🆂🅰🆅🅴 🆂🅾 ⊗ 🎬 🍽 🏊

▼ Mohawk Motel 🅼
(540) 667-1410. **$46.** 2754 Northwestern Pike. I-81, exit 317, 3 mi s on SR 37, 1.7 mi w on US 50. Ext corridors. **Pets:** $10 daily fee/pet. Designated rooms, service with restrictions, supervision.
🅰🆂🅺 🆂🅾 ⊗

⚠ ▼▼ Quality Inn East 🆂🅷
(540) 667-2250. **$58-$75.** 603 Millwood Ave. I-81, exit 313 northbound; exit 313B southbound, 0.5 mi nw on US 50/522/17. Ext corridors. **Pets:** Large, other species. $8 daily fee/pet. Service with restrictions.
🆂🅰🆅🅴 🆂🅾 ⊗ 🎬 💻 🏊

⚠ ▼▼ Red Roof Inn 🆂🅷
(540) 667-5000. **$58-$77.** 991 Millwood Pike. I-81, exit 313 northbound; exit 313A southbound, just se on US 50/17. Ext corridors. **Pets:** Other species. Service with restrictions, supervision.
🆂🅰🆅🅴 🆂🅾 ⊗ 🎬 💻

▼▼ Super 8 Motel 🆂🅷
(540) 665-4450. **$60-$69.** 1077 Millwood Pike. I-81, exit 313 northbound; exit 313A southbound, 0.3 mi se on US 50/17. Int corridors. **Pets:** Other species. $7 daily fee/pet. Service with restrictions, supervision.
🅰🆂🅺 🆂🅾 ⊗

⚠ ▼ Tourist City Motel 🅼 ❀
(540) 662-9011. **$37-$42, 5 day notice.** 214 Millwood Ave. I-81, exit 313 northbound; exit 313B southbound, 1 mi nw on US 50/522. Ext corridors. **Pets:** Small. $4 daily fee/pet. Designated rooms, no service, supervision.
🆂🅰🆅🅴 🆂🅾 ⊗ 🎬

⚠ ▼▼▼ Travelodge of Winchester 🆂🅷
(540) 665-0685. **$66-$77.** 160 Front Royal Pike. I-81, exit 313 northbound; exit 313A southbound, just s on US 522. Int corridors. **Pets:** Other species. $5 daily fee/pet. Designated rooms, service with restrictions, supervision.
🆂🅰🆅🅴 🆂🅾 ⊗ 🔈 🎬 💻 🏊

WOODSTOCK

⚠ ▼ Budget Host Inn 🅼
(540) 459-4086. **$48.** 1290 S Main St. I-81, exit 283, 0.8 mi se on SR 42, then 0.6 mi s on US 11. Ext corridors. **Pets:** Service with restrictions, crate.
🆂🅰🆅🅴 🆂🅾 ⊗ 🎬 🏊

⚠ ▼▼▼▼ Comfort Inn Shenandoah 🆂🅷
(540) 459-7600. **$74-$90.** 1011 Motel Dr. I-81, exit 283, just e. Int corridors. **Pets:** Other species. Service with restrictions, supervision.
🆂🅰🆅🅴 🆂🅾 ⊗ 🎱 🎬 💻 🏊

⚠ ▼▼ Ramada Inn 🆂🅷
(540) 459-5000. **$58-$69, 30 day notice.** 1130 Motel Dr. I-81, exit 283, just e on SR 42. Int corridors. **Pets:** Medium. $10 daily fee/pet. Designated rooms, supervision.
🆂🅰🆅🅴 🆂🅾 ⊗ 🎬 💻 🍽 🏊

WYTHEVILLE

⚠ ▼▼ Best Western Wytheville Inn 🆂🅷
(276) 228-7300. **$50-$100, 14 day notice.** 355 Nye Rd. I-77, exit 41, just e. Int corridors. **Pets:** $6 daily fee/pet. Designated rooms, service with restrictions, supervision.
🆂🅰🆅🅴 🆂🅾 ⊗ 🎬 💻 🏊

▼ Budget Host Inn/Interstate Inn 🅼
(276) 228-8618. **$39-$65.** 705 Chapman Rd. I-77/81, exit 73, just w. Ext corridors. **Pets:** Small, other species. $5 daily fee/pet. Service with restrictions, supervision.
🅰🆂🅺 🆂🅾 ⊗ 🎬

▼▼ Days Inn 🆂🅷
(276) 228-5500. **$50-$85.** 150 Malin Dr. I-81, exit 73, just w. Ext corridors. **Pets:** Medium. $5 daily fee/pet. Service with restrictions, supervision.
🅰🆂🅺 🆂🅾 ⊗ 🔈

⚠ ▼▼▼ Econo Lodge 🅼
(276) 228-5517. **$39-$115.** 1160 E Main St. I-81, exit 73, 0.8 mi w. Ext corridors. **Pets:** Medium, dogs only. $10 daily fee/pet. Designated rooms, service with restrictions, supervision.
🆂🅰🆅🅴 🆂🅾 ⊗ 🔈 🎬 💻

▼▼ Holiday Inn 🆂🅷
(276) 228-5483. **$65-$110.** 1800 E Main St. I-81, exit 73, just w. Ext/int corridors. **Pets:** Accepted.
🅰🆂🅺 🆂🅾 ⊗ 🔈 🎱 🎬 💻 🍽 🏊

▼▼ Ramada Inn 🆂🅷
(276) 228-6000. **$59-$109.** 955 Peppers Ferry Rd. I-77, exit 41, just e. Ext corridors. **Pets:** Medium. Service with restrictions.
🅰🆂🅺 🆂🅾 ⊗ 💻 🍽 🏊

⚠ ▼▼▼ Red Carpet Inn 🅼
(276) 228-5525. **$45-$120.** 280 Lithia Rd. I-81/77, exit 73, just w. Ext corridors. **Pets:** Very small. $6 daily fee/pet. Designated rooms, no service, supervision.
🆂🅰🆅🅴 ⊗ 🎬

▼▼ Super 8 Motel 🆂🅷
(276) 228-6620. **$59-$70.** 130 Nye Cir. I-77, exit 41, just e. Ext corridors. **Pets:** Large, other species. $10 one-time fee/room. Designated rooms, service with restrictions.
🅰🆂🅺 🆂🅾 ⊗

▼▼ Travelodge 🅼
(276) 228-3188. **$45-$110.** 140 Lithia Rd. I-77/81, exit 73, on US 11. Ext/int corridors. **Pets:** $5 daily fee/pet. Designated rooms, service with restrictions, supervision.
🅰🆂🅺 🆂🅾 ⊗ 🎬 💻

CITY INDEX

ABERDEEN

▼▼▼ **GuestHouse International Inn &
Suites** 🆂🅷 ❖
(360) 537-7460. **$70-$150.** 701 E Heron St. Just e on US
12, cross street to Kansas St; downtown. Int corridors.
Pets: Other species. $50 deposit/room, $10 daily fee/pet.
Service with restrictions, crate.
(ASK) 🆂🔟 ✕ 🗾 🎨 🎁 🖥 ⚿

🔷🔷🔷 ▼▼▼ **Olympic Inn** Ⓜ
(360) 533-4200. **$65-$85, 7 day notice.** 616 W Heron St.
0.5 mi w; downtown. Ext corridors. **Pets:** Medium. $5 daily
fee/pet. Supervision.
(SAVE) 🆂🔟 ✕ 🎁

▼▼ **Red Lion Inn** Ⓜ
(360) 532-5210. **$64-$89.** 521 W Wishkah. 0.5 mi w on US
101 N. Ext corridors. **Pets:** Other species. Service with
restrictions.
(ASK) 🆂🔟 ✕ 🖨 🗾 🎁 🖥

AIRWAY HEIGHTS

▼▼ **Microtel Inn & Suites** 🆂🅷
(509) 242-1200. **$44-$109.** 1215 S Garfield Rd. I-90, exit 277
to SR 2, 4 mi w. Int corridors. **Pets:** Accepted.
(ASK) ✕ 🗾 🎨 🎁 🖥

ANACORTES

🔷🔷🔷 ▼▼▼ **Anaco Inn** 🆂🅷
(360) 293-8833. **$59-$105, 3 day notice.** 905 20th St. Just s
of downtown. Ext/int corridors. **Pets:** Accepted.
(SAVE) 🆂🔟 ✕ 🎁 🖥

🔷🔷🔷 ▼▼▼ **Anacortes Inn** Ⓜ
(360) 293-3153. **$65-$77.** 3006 Commercial Ave. Just s of
downtown. Ext corridors. **Pets:** Accepted.
(SAVE) 🆂🔟 ✕ 🎁 🖥 ⚿

🔷🔷🔷 ▼▼▼ **Fidalgo Country Inn** 🆂🅷 ❖
(360) 293-3494. **$89-$109.** 7645 SR 20. Jct SR 20. Ext/int
corridors. **Pets:** Medium. $10 daily fee/pet. Designated
rooms, supervision.
(SAVE) 🆂🔟 ✕ 🎨🅜 🗾 🎁 🖥 ⚿

▼▼ **Islands Inn** Ⓜ
(360) 293-4644. **$69-$150.** 3401 Commercial Ave. Just s of
downtown. Ext corridors. **Pets:** Dogs only. $5 daily fee/
room. Service with restrictions, supervision.
(ASK) 🆂🔟 ✕ 🎁 🖥 🍴 ⚿

BELLINGHAM

🔷🔷🔷 ▼▼▼ **Best Western Lakeway Inn** 🆂🅷 ❖
(360) 671-1011. **$79-$119.** 714 Lakeway Dr. I-5, exit 253
(Lakeway Dr), just se. Int corridors. **Pets:** Small. $10 daily
fee/room. Designated rooms, service with restrictions,
supervision.
(SAVE) 🆂🔟 ✕ 🗾 🎁 🖥 🍴 ⚿ ✕

▼▼▼ **The Chrysalis Inn & Spa** 🆂🅷
(360) 756-1005. **$159-$185, 10 day notice.** 804 10th St. I-5,
exit 250, 1.3 mi nw on Old Fairhaven Pkwy, 0.6 mi n via
12th and 11th sts, just w on Taylor Ave, then just n. Int
corridors. **Pets:** Very small, dogs only. $50 one-time fee/pet.
Service with restrictions, supervision.
(ASK) 🆂🔟 ✕ 🎁 🖥 🍴

🔷🔷🔷 ▼▼▼ **Fairhaven Village Inn** 🆂🅷 ❖
(360) 733-1311. **$109-$159.** 1200 10th St. I-5, exit 250, 1.5
mi w. Int corridors. **Pets:** Medium. $20 daily fee/pet. Service
with restrictions, supervision.
(SAVE) 🆂🔟 ✕ 🎨🅜 🗾 🎨 🎁 🖥

▼▼▼ **Holiday Inn Express-Bellingham** 🆂🅷 ❖
(360) 671-4800. **$84-$119.** 4160 Guide Meridian St. I-5, exit
256A, 0.7 mi e. Int corridors. **Pets:** Large, other species.
$10 one-time fee/room. Designated rooms, service with
restrictions, supervision.
(ASK) 🆂🔟 ✕ 🎨🅜 🗾 🎨 🎁 🖥 ⚿

◆◆◆ Hotel Bellwether SH
(360) 392-3100. **$125-$800, 3 day notice.** One Bellwether Way. I-5, exit 253 (Lakeway Dr), 0.9 mi nw via Lakeway Dr and E Holly St, just w on Bay St, 0.6 mi n on W Chestnut St, then just w. Int corridors. **Pets:** $65 one-time fee/room. Designated rooms, service with restrictions.
(ASK) (S6) (X) (💻) (🍴) (🐾)

◆◆ Motel 6-44 M
(360) 671-4494. **$43-$65.** 3701 Byron Ave. I-5, exit 252, just nw. Ext corridors. **Pets:** Other species. Service with restrictions, supervision.
(S6) (X) (&M) (🐾)

◆◆◆ ◆ Quality Inn Baron Suites SH
(360) 647-8000. **$85-$180.** 100 E Kellogg Rd. I-5, exit 256A, 1 mi ne via Guide Meridian St. Ext/int corridors. **Pets:** Medium. $25 one-time fee/room. Designated rooms, service with restrictions, crate.
(SAVE) (S6) (X) (🐕) (🔒) (💻) (🐾)

◆◆◆ Shangri-La Downtown Motel M
(360) 733-7050. **$39-$59.** 611 E Holly St. I-5, exit 253 (Lakeway Dr), 0.3 mi nw. Ext corridors. **Pets:** Cats only. $5 one-time fee/pet. Designated rooms, supervision.
(SAVE) (S6) (X) (🔒) (🐾)

◆◆◆ ◆ Travel House Inn M
(360) 671-4600. **$44-$89.** 3750 Meridian St. I-5, exit 256A, just w. Ext corridors. **Pets:** Other species. $6 daily fee/pet. Service with restrictions, supervision.
(SAVE) (S6) (X) (🔒) (🐾)

◆◆ Val-U Inn SH
(360) 671-9600. **$56-$80.** 805 Lakeway Dr. I-5, exit 253 (Lakeway Dr), just ne. Int corridors. **Pets:** Medium, dogs only. $5 daily fee/pet. Designated rooms, service with restrictions, supervision.
(ASK) (S6) (X) (🔒)

BLAINE

◆◆◆ ◆◆◆ ◆ Semiahmoo Resort SH
(360) 318-2000. **$139-$409, 7 day notice.** 9565 Semiahmoo Pkwy. I-5, exit 270, 9.5 mi nw on Semiahmoo Spit. Int corridors. **Pets:** Accepted.
(SAVE) (S6) (X) (🐕) (🔒) (💻) (🍴) (🐾) (🐾)

BREMERTON

◆◆◆ ◆ Flagship Inn SH
(360) 479-6566. **$65-$79.** 4320 Kitsap Way. 3.5 mi w of ferry terminal; SR 3, exit Kitsap Way, 0.5 mi e. Int corridors. **Pets:** Small. $6 daily fee/pet. Supervision.
(SAVE) (S6) (X) (🔒) (💻) (🐾)

◆◆ ◆◆ Howard Johnson Plaza Hotel & Conference Center SH
(360) 373-9900. **$79-$172.** 5640 Kitsap Way. SR 3, exit Kitsap Way, just nw. Int corridors. **Pets:** Accepted.
(ASK) (S6) (X) (🔒) (💻) (🍴) (🐾) (🐾)

◆◆◆ ◆◆◆ ◆ Illahee Manor Bed & Breakfast BB
(360) 698-7555. **$115-$215, 10 day notice.** 6680 Illahee Rd NE. SR 3, exit East Bremerton, 4.9 mi se on Wheaton Way (SR 303), 1.2 mi e on McWilliams Rd, just n on East Rd, 0.3 mi e on 3rd St, then just n. Ext/int corridors. **Pets:** Accepted.
(SAVE) (S6) (X) (🔒) (💻) (🔐) (✂️)

◆◆◆ ◆ Midway Inn SH
(360) 479-2909. **$59-$99.** 2909 Wheaton Way. SR 303, 2 mi n. Int corridors. **Pets:** Small. $150 deposit/room, $15 daily fee/room. Designated rooms, service with restrictions, supervision.
(SAVE) (S6) (X) (🔒) (💻)

◆◆◆ Super 8 Motel SH
(360) 377-8881. **$68-$81.** 5068 Kitsap Way. 4.2 mi w of ferry terminal; SR 3, exit Kitsap Way, just ne. Int corridors. **Pets:** Accepted.
(ASK) (S6) (X) (&M)

BUCKLEY

◆◆◆ ◆◆◆ Mt View Inn SH
(360) 829-1100. **$85-$95, 7 day notice.** 29405 SR 410 E. On SR 410 at jct of SR 165. Int corridors. **Pets:** Small, dogs only. $20 one-time fee/pet. Designated rooms, service with restrictions, supervision.
(SAVE) (S6) (X) (🔒) (🐾)

BURLINGTON

◆◆◆ ◆◆◆ Cocusa Motel M
(360) 757-6044. **$63-$92.** 370 W Rio Vista. I-5, exit 230, just e. Ext corridors. **Pets:** $10 one-time fee/room. Designated rooms, supervision.
(SAVE) (S6) (X) (🔐) (🔒) (💻) (🐾)

CASHMERE

◆◆◆ ◆◆◆ Village Inn Motel M
(509) 782-3522. **$49-$64, 7 day notice.** 229 Cottage Ave. On Business Rt US 2 and 97; downtown. Ext corridors. **Pets:** Small, dogs only. $10 daily fee/pet. Designated rooms, service with restrictions, supervision.
(SAVE) (S6) (X) (🔒)

CASTLE ROCK

◆◆◆ ◆◆◆ Timberland Inn & Suites M
(360) 274-6002. **$60-$125.** 1271 Mount St. Helens Way. I-5, exit 49, just ne. Ext corridors. **Pets:** Small, dogs only. $10 daily fee/pet. Designated rooms, service with restrictions, supervision.
(SAVE) (S6) (X) (🔒) (💻)

CENTRALIA

◆◆◆ Motel 6-394 M
(360) 330-2057. **$37-$53.** 1310 Belmont Ave. I-5, exit 82, 0.6 mi nw. Ext corridors. **Pets:** Accepted.
(S6) (X) (🔐) (🐾)

CHEHALIS

◆◆◆ ◆◆◆ ◆ Best Western Park Place Inn & Suites SH
(360) 748-4040. **$74-$114.** 201 SW Interstate Ave. I-5, exit 76, just se. Int corridors. **Pets:** Very small, dogs only. $10 daily fee/pet. Service with restrictions, crate.
(SAVE) (S6) (X) (&M) (🔐) (🔒) (💻) (🐾)

CHELAN

(AAA) ◈◈◈◈ **Best Western Lakeside Lodge** SH
(509) 682-4396. **$79-$309, 7 day notice.** W 2312 Woodin Ave. West end of town. Ext corridors. **Pets:** Small, dogs only. $10 daily fee/pet. Designated rooms, service with restrictions, supervision.
[SAVE] [S♦] [✕] [🐾] [🛋] [🛁] [💻] [🏊] [⊗]

CHEWELAH

(AAA) ◈◈ **Nordlig Motel** M
(509) 935-6704. **$54-$59.** W 101 Grant St. North edge of town on US 395. Ext corridors. **Pets:** Other species. $3 one-time fee/room. Supervision.
[SAVE] [S♦] [✕] [🛁]

CLE ELUM

(AAA) ◈◈◈ **Cle Elum Travelers Inn** M
(509) 674-5535. **$42-$110.** 1001 E 1st St. I-90, exit 85, 1 mi w on SR 903. Ext/int corridors. **Pets:** Small. $5 daily fee/pet. Service with restrictions, supervision.
[SAVE] [S♦] [✕] [🐾] [🛁]

◈◈ **Stewart Lodge** M
(509) 674-4548. **$48-$78.** 805 W 1st St. I-90, exit 84 eastbound, just n; exit westbound, 0.6 mi w. Ext corridors. **Pets:** Other species. $5 one-time fee/room. Supervision.
[ASK] [✕] [🐾] [🛁] [🏊]

◈◈ **Timber Lodge Inn** M
(509) 674-5966. **$55-$75.** 301 W 1st St. I-90, exit 84 eastbound, 1 mi ne; exit westbound, just w; downtown. Ext/int corridors. **Pets:** Large, other species. $10 one-time fee/pet. Designated rooms, service with restrictions.
[ASK] [S♦] [✕] [🛁]

(AAA) ◈ **Wind Blew Inn Motel** M
(509) 674-2294. **$45-$65.** 811 Hwy 970. I-90, exit 85, just w. Ext corridors. **Pets:** Accepted.
[SAVE] [✕] [🐾] [🛁] [💻]

COLVILLE

(AAA) ◈◈◈ **Colville Comfort Inn** SH
(509) 684-2010. **$65-$125.** 166 NE Canning Dr. 1.5 mi n on US 395. Int corridors. **Pets:** $50 deposit/room, $5 daily fee/room. Service with restrictions, supervision.
[SAVE] [S♦] [✕] [🛁M] [🐾] [🐾] [🛁] [💻] [🏊]

CONCRETE

(AAA) ◈◈◈◈ **Ovenell's Heritage Inn B&B and Log Cabins** CA
(360) 853-8494. **$100-$120, 3 day notice.** 46276 Concrete Sauk Valley Rd. 0.5 mi w of downtown on SR 20, 2 mi se. Ext/int corridors. **Pets:** Other species. $10 daily fee/pet. Designated rooms, service with restrictions, supervision.
[SAVE] [✕] [🛁] [💻] [⊗]

COUGAR

◈ **Lone Fir Resort** M 🐾
(360) 238-5210. **$40.** 16806 Lewis River Rd. Center. Ext corridors. **Pets:** Other species. $15 one-time fee/room. Service with restrictions, supervision.
[ASK] [S♦] [✕] [🛁] [💻] [🏊] [🌅]

COULEE DAM

(AAA) ◈◈◈ **Coulee House Motel** M
(509) 633-1101. **$65-$120.** 110 Roosevelt Way. Just e of river bridge. Ext corridors. **Pets:** Other species. $15 daily fee/pet. Service with restrictions, supervision.
[SAVE] [S♦] [✕] [🛁] [💻] [🏊]

DAYTON

◈◈◈ **The Weinhard Hotel** SH
(509) 382-4032. **$75-$150, 7 day notice.** 235 E Main St. Downtown. Int corridors. **Pets:** Accepted.
[ASK] [✕] [🍴]

EAST WENATCHEE

◈◈◈ **Cedars Inn, East Wenatchee** SH
(509) 886-8000. **$77-$87.** 80 Ninth St NE. Just e of SR 28. Int corridors. **Pets:** Medium. $6 daily fee/room. Designated rooms, service with restrictions, supervision.
[ASK] [S♦] [✕] [🛁] [🏊]

EATONVILLE

(AAA) ◈◈◈ **Mill Village Motel** M
(360) 832-3200. **$55-$70.** 210 Center St E. Downtown. Ext corridors. **Pets:** Small. $10 daily fee/room. Designated rooms, supervision.
[SAVE] [✕] [🐾] [🛁] [💻]

ELLENSBURG

(AAA) ◈◈◈◈ **Best Western Lincoln Inn & Suites** SH
(509) 925-4244. **$89-$129.** 211 W Umptanum Rd. I-90, exit 109, just n, then just w. Int corridors. **Pets:** Dogs only. $10 daily fee/room. Service with restrictions, supervision.
[SAVE] [S♦] [✕] [🛁M] [🐾] [🐾] [🛁] [💻] [🏊] [⊗]

◈◈◈◈ **Ellensburg Comfort Inn** SH
(509) 925-7037. **$70-$155.** 1722 Canyon Rd. I-90, exit 109. Int corridors. **Pets:** Large, other species. $10 one-time fee/pet. Service with restrictions, supervision.
[ASK] [S♦] [✕] [🐾] [🐾] [🛁] [💻] [🏊]

(AAA) ◈◈◈ **Ellensburg Inn** SH 🐾
(509) 925-9801. **$70-$89.** 1700 Canyon Rd. I-90, exit 109, just n. Int corridors. **Pets:** $6 one-time fee/room. Designated rooms, service with restrictions, supervision.
[SAVE] [S♦] [✕] [🛁] [💻] [🍴] [🏊]

(AAA) ◈◈◈ **I-90 Inn Motel** M
(509) 925-9844. **$52-$70.** 1390 Dollar Way Rd. I-90, exit 106, just n. Ext corridors. **Pets:** Accepted.
[SAVE] [S♦] [✕] [🛁]

◈◈ **Nites Inn** M
(509) 962-9600. **$54.** 1200 S Ruby. I-90, exit 109, 0.5 mi n. Ext corridors. **Pets:** Other species. $8 one-time fee/pet. Service with restrictions, supervision.
[ASK] [S♦] [✕] [🛁] [💻]

ENUMCLAW

ⒶⒶⒶ ▼▼ Best Western Park Center 🆂🅷
(360) 825-4490. **$75-$85.** 1000 Griffin Ave. Downtown. Ext
corridors. **Pets:** Medium. $10 daily fee/pet. Designated
rooms, service with restrictions, supervision.
🆂🅰🆅🅴 ⊠ 🛢 💻 🍽

EPHRATA

▼▼ Ephrata Travelodge Ⓜ
(509) 754-4651. **$50-$75.** 31 Basin St SW. On SR 28; downtown. Ext corridors. **Pets:** Other species. $5 daily fee/room.
Service with restrictions, supervision.
🄰🅂🄺 🆂🅱 ⊠ 🛢 💻 ➤

FERNDALE

▼▼ Ferndale Super 8 🆂🅷
(360) 384-8881. **$49-$64, 15 day notice.** 5788 Barrett Ave.
I-5, exit 262, just ne. Int corridors. **Pets:** Accepted.
🄰🅂🄺 🆂🅱 ⊠ 🅂🄼 🅔 🛢 ➤

▼▼ Slater Heritage House 🅱🅱
(360) 384-4273. **Call for rates.** 1371 W Axton Rd. I-5, exit
262, 1 mi e. Int corridors. **Pets:** Accepted.
⊠ 🛢 🅺 🆉

FORKS

ⒶⒶⒶ ▼▼ Forks Motel Ⓜ
(360) 374-6243. **$52-$95, 7 day notice.** 351 US 101 (Forks
Ave S). Just s. Ext corridors. **Pets:** Medium. $10 daily
fee/pet. Designated rooms.
🆂🅰🆅🅴 ⊠ 🛢 ➤

▼▼ Manitou Lodge 🅱🅱 🐾
(360) 374-6295. **$100-$160, 14 day notice.** 813 Kilmer Rd.
8 mi sw on SR 110 (LaPush Rd), 1 mi w on Mora Rd, then
1 mi n. Ext/int corridors. **Pets:** Other species. $10 daily
fee/room. Designated rooms, supervision.
⊠ 💻 🅧 🅺 🅦 🆉

▼▼ Miller Tree Inn Bed & Breakfast 🅱🅱
(360) 374-6806. **$75-$180, 7 day notice.** 654 E Division St.
0.3 mi e of US 101 (S Forks Ave). Ext/int corridors.
Pets: Other species. $10 daily fee/pet. Designated rooms,
service with restrictions, crate.
⊠ 🛢 💻 🅺 🆉

ⒶⒶⒶ ▼▼ Olympic Suites Inn Ⓜ
(360) 374-5400. **$54-$89.** 800 Olympic Dr. North end of
town, just ne off US 101 (S Forks Ave). Ext corridors.
Pets: Accepted.
🆂🅰🆅🅴 🆂🅱 ⊠ 🛢 💻 🅺

FREELAND

▼▼ Harbour Inn Motel Ⓜ
(360) 331-6900. **$68-$95.** 1606 Main St. Just e of SR 525.
Ext corridors. **Pets:** Dogs only. $10 daily fee/pet. Desig-
nated rooms, service with restrictions, supervision.
⊠ 🛢 💻 🅺

KALALOCH

ⒶⒶⒶ ▼▼ Kalaloch Lodge 🄲🄰
(360) 962-2271. **$127-$264, 3 day notice.** 157151 US 101.
At MM 157. Ext/int corridors. **Pets:** Accepted.
🆂🅰🆅🅴 ⊠ 🛢 💻 🍽 🅺 🆉

KALAMA

▼▼ Best Value Kalama River Inn Ⓜ
(360) 673-2855. **$54-$65.** 602 NE Frontage Rd. I-5, exit 30
northbound, 0.4 mi n; exit southbound, 0.4 mi s. Ext corridors. **Pets:** Medium. $5 one-time fee/pet. Designated
rooms, service with restrictions, supervision.
🄰🅂🄺 🆂🅱 ⊠ 🛢

KELSO

ⒶⒶⒶ ▼▼ Best Western Aladdin 🆂🅷
(360) 425-9660. **$68-$88.** 310 Long Ave. I-5, exit 39, 1.1 mi
w via Allen St and W Main St, then just n on 5th Ave. Int
corridors. **Pets:** Small, dogs only. $10 daily fee/pet. Service
with restrictions, supervision.
🆂🅰🆅🅴 🆂🅱 ⊠ 🛢 💻 ➤

▼▼▼ GuestHouse Inn & Suites 🆂🅷 🐾
(360) 414-5953. **$66-$190.** 501 Three Rivers Dr. I-5, exit 39,
0.3 mi w on Allen St, then 0.3 mi s. Int corridors.
Pets: Other species. $50 deposit/room, $10 one-time fee/
room. Service with restrictions, supervision.
🄰🅂🄺 🆂🅱 ⊠ 🄌 🅔 🛢 💻 ➤

▼ Motel 6-43 Ⓜ
(360) 425-3229. **$41-$63.** 106 Minor Rd. I-5, exit 39, 0.3 mi
ne. Ext corridors. **Pets:** Accepted.
🆂🅱 ⊠ 🅔 🛢 ➤

ⒶⒶⒶ ▼▼ Red Lion Hotel
  Kelso/Longview 🆂🅷 🐾
(360) 636-4400. **$49-$79.** 510 Kelso Dr. I-5, exit 39, 0.3 mi
se. Int corridors. **Pets:** Large, other species. Designated
rooms, service with restrictions, supervision.
🆂🅰🆅🅴 🆂🅱 ⊠ 🄌 🅔 🛢 💻 🍽 ➤

▼▼ Super 8 Motel 🆂🅷 🐾
(360) 423-8880. **$44-$71.** 250 Kelso Dr. I-5, exit 39, just sw.
Int corridors. **Pets:** Other species. $15 deposit/pet, $10
one-time fee/room. Service with restrictions, supervision.
🄰🅂🄺 🆂🅱 ⊠ 🅂🄼 🅔 🛢 ➤

KENNEWICK

ⒶⒶⒶ ▼▼▼ Best Value Clearwater Inn 🆂🅷
(509) 735-2242. **$68.** 5616 W Clearwater Ave. US 395, 1.9
mi w. Int corridors. **Pets:** Accepted.
🆂🅰🆅🅴 🆂🅱 ⊠ 🄌 🅔 🛢 💻

ⒶⒶⒶ ▼▼▼ Best Western Kennewick Inn 🆂🅷
(509) 586-1332. **$89-$149.** 4001 W 27th Ave. I-82, exit 113,
0.8 mi n. Int corridors. **Pets:** Medium, other species. $10
one-time fee/room. Designated rooms, service with restrictions, supervision.
🆂🅰🆅🅴 🆂🅱 ⊠ 🅂🄼 🄌 🅔 🛢 💻 ➤ ⊠

▼▼▼▼ Comfort Inn **M**
(509) 783-8396. **$65-$150.** 7801 W Quinault Ave. 0.5 mi s on Columbia Center Blvd from SR 240. Int corridors. **Pets:** Dogs only. $10 daily fee/pet. Service with restrictions, crate.

(ASK) (S6) (X) (&M) (🖊) (&) (🛏) (💻) (🏊)

▼▼ Days Inn Kennewick **SH**
(509) 735-9511. **$44-$104.** 2811 W 2nd Ave. Jct US 395 and Clearwater Ave, just s, then just w. Ext/int corridors. **Pets:** Small, dogs only. $5 one-time fee/room. Designated rooms, service with restrictions, supervision.

(ASK) (S6) (X) (🛏) (💻) (🏊)

▼▼ Kennewick Super 8 **SH**
(509) 736-6888. **$60.** 626 Columbia Center Blvd. 1.1 mi s of SR 240. Int corridors. **Pets:** $10 one-time fee/room. Service with restrictions, supervision.

(ASK) (S6) (X) (&M) (🖊) (&) (🛏) (🏊)

Ⓐ ▼▼▼▼ La Quinta Inn & Suites **SH**
(509) 736-3326. **$59-$109.** 4220 W 27th Pl. I-82, exit 113 (US 395), 0.8 mi n. Int corridors. **Pets:** Service with restrictions, supervision.

(SAVE) (S6) (X) (&M) (🖊) (&) (🛏) (💻) (🏊) (X)

▼▼▼▼ Red Lion Hotel Columbia
Center–Kennewick **SH**
(509) 783-0611. **$79-$89.** 1101 N Columbia Center Blvd. SR 240, 0.5 mi s. Int corridors. **Pets:** Other species. $30 deposit/room. Service with restrictions, supervision.

(ASK) (X) (&M) (🖊) (🛏) (💻) (🍴) (🏊)

Ⓐ ▼▼▼ Tapadera Inn **M**
(509) 783-6191. **$78-$130.** 300A N Ely St. On US 395, jct Clearwater Ave. Ext corridors. **Pets:** Small, dogs only. $7 daily fee/pet. Designated rooms, service with restrictions, supervision.

(SAVE) (S6) (X) (🛏) (🏊)

▼▼ Travelodge Extended Stay **SH**
(509) 735-6385. **$59-$68.** 321 N Johnson St. US 395, just w on Clearwater Ave, then just n. Int corridors. **Pets:** Accepted.

(ASK) (S6) (X) (🛏) (💻) (🏊)

LACEY

Ⓐ ▼▼▼ Days Inn **SH**
(360) 493-1991. **$60-$90.** 120 College St SE. I-5, exit 109, just sw. Int corridors. **Pets:** Large. $10 daily fee/pet. Service with restrictions, crate.

(SAVE) (S6) (X) (🖊) (&) (🛏)

LA CONNER

Ⓐ ▼▼▼▼ La Conner Country Inn **SH**
(360) 466-3101. **$82-$130.** 107 S 2nd St. At 2nd and Morris sts; downtown. Ext/int corridors. **Pets:** Other species. $20 one-time fee/room. Service with restrictions, supervision.

(SAVE) (S6) (X) (&) (💻) (🍴) (🐾)

LANGLEY

▼▼▼▼ Island Tyme Bed & Breakfast **BB** 🐾
(360) 221-5078. **$85-$140, 7 day notice.** 4940 S Bayview Rd. SR 525 at MM 15, just e on Marshview, then 2.1 mi n. Int corridors. **Pets:** Other species. Designated rooms, supervision.

(X) (🐾)

LEAVENWORTH

Ⓐ ▼▼▼▼ Der Ritterhof Motor Inn **SH** 🐾
(509) 548-5845. **$74-$90, 3 day notice.** 190 US 2. 0.3 mi w. Ext corridors. **Pets:** Dogs only. $10 daily fee/pet. Service with restrictions.

(SAVE) (S6) (X) (🖊) (🛏) (💻) (🏊) (X)

▼▼ The Evergreen Inn **M** 🐾
(509) 548-5515. **$65-$135.** 1117 Front St. US 2, just s. Ext corridors. **Pets:** $10 daily fee/room. Service with restrictions, supervision.

(X) (🛏) (💻) (X)

▼▼▼▼ Howard Johnson Express Inn **M** 🐾
(509) 548-4326. **$79-$139.** 405 W US 2. West end of town. Ext corridors. **Pets:** $12 daily fee/pet. Designated rooms, service with restrictions, supervision.

(ASK) (S6) (X) (🛏) (💻) (🏊)

Ⓐ ▼▼▼▼ Obertal Inn **M**
(509) 548-5204. **$59-$139.** 922 Commercial St. Off US 2; center. Ext corridors. **Pets:** Large, other species. $10 one-time fee/pet. Designated rooms, service with restrictions.

(SAVE) (S6) (X) (🛏) (💻)

▼▼ River's Edge Lodge **M**
(509) 548-7612. **$66-$81, 7 day notice.** 8401 US 2. 3.5 mi e. Ext corridors. **Pets:** Accepted.

(X) (🛏) (💻) (🏊)

Ⓐ ▼▼▼▼ Rodeway Inn & Suites **SH**
(509) 548-7992. **$69-$119.** 185 US 2. 0.3 mi w. Ext corridors. **Pets:** Large, other species. $12 daily fee/pet. Designated rooms, service with restrictions, crate.

(SAVE) (S6) (X) (&M) (🖊) (&) (🛏) (💻) (🏊) (X)

LIBERTY LAKE

▼▼▼▼ Comfort Inn Liberty Lake **SH**
(509) 340-3333. **$55-$110.** 2327 N Madson Rd. I-90, exit 296, 1 mi e on Appleway, just n. Int corridors. **Pets:** Accepted.

(ASK) (S6) (X) (&M) (🖊) (&) (🛏) (💻) (🏊)

LONG BEACH

Ⓐ ▼▼▼ Anchorage Cottages **CA**
(360) 642-2351. **$55-$113.** 2209 Boulevard N. Just w of SR 103. Ext corridors. **Pets:** Accepted.

(SAVE) (X) (🛏) (💻) (🐾) (🖊)

Ⓐ ▼▼▼ The Breakers **CO**
(360) 642-4414. **$89-$99.** 26th & SR 103. North end of downtown. Ext corridors. **Pets:** Dogs only. $10 daily fee/room. Supervision.

(SAVE) (S6) (X) (🛏) (💻) (🏊) (X) (🐾)

[AAA] ♦♦ **Edgewater Inn** [SH]
(360) 642-2311. **$59-$139, 3 day notice.** 409 10th St SW. Just w of SR 103. Ext/int corridors. **Pets:** Large. $8 daily fee/pet. Designated rooms, service with restrictions, supervision.
[SAVE] ⊠ ♿ ▣ 📺 🍴 [AC]

[AAA] ♦♦ **Our Place at the Beach** [M]
(360) 642-3793. **$42-$86.** 1309 South Blvd. South end of town. Ext corridors. **Pets:** Medium. $5 deposit/pet. Service with restrictions, supervision.
[SAVE] [S/D] ⊠ ▣ 📺 ⚒ [AC]

[AAA] ♦♦ **Shaman Motel** [M]
(360) 642-3714. **$54-$99, 7 day notice.** 115 3rd St SW. Downtown. Ext corridors. **Pets:** $5 one-time fee/pet. Service with restrictions, supervision.
[SAVE] ⊠ ▣ 📺 🏊 [AC]

[AAA] ♦♦ **Super 8 Motel** [SH]
(360) 642-8988. **$59-$129.** 500 Ocean Beach Blvd. On SR 103; downtown. Int corridors. **Pets:** Dogs only. $5 daily fee/room. Service with restrictions, supervision.
[SAVE] [S/D] ⊠ [♿M] 👂 ▣ 📺 [AC]

LONGVIEW

[AAA] ♦♦ **Hudson Manor Inn** [M]
(360) 425-1100. **$42-$52.** 1616 Hudson St. Downtown. Ext corridors. **Pets:** Accepted.
[SAVE] [S/D] ⊠ ▣ 📺

[AAA] ♦♦♦ **Ramada Limited Longview** [SH]
(360) 414-1000. **$69-$109, 14 day notice.** 723 7th Ave. I-5, exit 36, 3 mi w on SR 432. Int corridors. **Pets:** Other species. $15 one-time fee/room. Service with restrictions, supervision.
[SAVE] [S/D] ⊠ [♿M] 👂 ♿ ▣ 📺 🏊

[AAA] ♦ **The Townhouse Motel** [M]
(360) 423-7200. **$44-$57, 3 day notice.** 744 Washington Way. Downtown. Ext corridors. **Pets:** $7 one-time fee/pet. Supervision.
[SAVE] [S/D] ⊠ ▣ 📺 🏊

MOCLIPS

♦♦ **Hi Tide Ocean Beach Resort** [CO] 🐾
(360) 276-4142. **$95-$180, 3 day notice.** 4890 Railroad Ave. SR 109, 0.8 mi nw on beach at 6th and Railroad sts. Ext corridors. **Pets:** Medium, dogs only. $12 daily fee/pet. Service with restrictions, supervision.
[A$K] [S/D] ⊠ ▣ 📺 [AC] ☎

[AAA] ♦♦ **Ocean Crest Resort** [M] 🐾
(360) 276-4465. **$50-$175, 7 day notice.** 4651 SR 109 N. South edge of town. Ext corridors. **Pets:** Small, other species. $15 daily fee/pet. Service with restrictions, supervision.
[SAVE] [S/D] ⊠ ♿ ▣ 📺 🍴 🏊 ⚒ [AC]

MONTESANO

[AAA] ♦♦ **Monte Square Motel** [M] 🐾
(360) 249-4424. **$59-$99.** 100 Brumfield Ave W. US 12, exit SR 107 (Montesano/Raymond), just nw. Ext corridors. **Pets:** Dogs only. $10 daily fee/pet. Designated rooms, service with restrictions, supervision.
[SAVE] [S/D] ⊠ [♿M] ▣ 📺

MORTON

[AAA] ♦♦♦ **The Seasons Motel** [M]
(360) 496-6835. **$55-$70.** 200 Westlake Ave. Jct SR 7 and US 12. Ext corridors. **Pets:** Accepted.
[SAVE] ⊠ ▣ 📺

MOSES LAKE

[AAA] ♦♦♦ **Best Western Hallmark Inn** [SH] 🐾
(509) 765-9211. **$74-$94.** 3000 Marina Dr. I-90, exit 176, just nw. Int corridors. **Pets:** Other species. Service with restrictions, supervision.
[SAVE] [S/D] ⊠ [♿M] 👂 ▣ 📺 🍴 🏊 ⚒

♦♦♦ **Holiday Inn Express** [SH]
(509) 766-2000. **$67-$99.** 1745 E Kittleson. I-90, exit 179, just n. Int corridors. **Pets:** Large. Designated rooms, service with restrictions, supervision.
[A$K] [S/D] ⊠ [♿M] ♿ ▣ 📺 🏊

♦♦ **Inn at Moses Lake** [SH]
(509) 766-7000. **$59-$79.** 1741 E Kittleson. I-90, exit 179, just n. Int corridors. **Pets:** Medium. Designated rooms, service with restrictions, supervision.
[A$K] [S/D] ⊠ ▣

♦♦ **Moses Lake Super 8** [SH]
(509) 765-8886. **$54-$64.** 449 Melva Ln. I-90, exit 176, just n. Int corridors. **Pets:** Large, other species. $15 deposit/room, $10 one-time fee/room. Service with restrictions.
[A$K] [S/D] ⊠ ▣ 🏊

♦♦♦ **Shilo Inn Suites-Moses Lake** [SH]
(509) 765-9317. **$75-$100.** 1819 E Kittleson. I-90, exit 179, just n. Int corridors. **Pets:** Accepted.
[A$K] [S/D] ⊠ [♿M] 👂 ▣ 📺 🏊 ⚒

MOUNT VERNON

[AAA] ♦♦ **Best Western College Way Inn** [M]
(360) 424-4287. **$68-$87.** 300 W College Way. I-5, exit 227, just w. Ext corridors. **Pets:** Other species. $10 daily fee/room. Service with restrictions, supervision.
[SAVE] [S/D] ⊠ 👂 ▣ 📺 🏊

[AAA] ♦♦♦ **Best Western Cotton Tree Inn & Convention Center** [SH]
(360) 428-5678. **$89-$99.** 2300 Market St. I-5, exit 227, 0.3 mi e on College Way, then 0.5 mi n on Riverside Dr. Int corridors. **Pets:** Dogs only. $10 one-time fee/room. Designated rooms, service with restrictions, supervision.
[SAVE] [S/D] ⊠ [♿M] 👂 ▣ 📺 🏊

[AAA] ♦♦♦ **Comfort Inn-Mount Vernon** [SH]
(360) 428-7020. **$70-$130.** 1910 Freeway Dr. I-5, exit 227, just w on College Way, then just n. Ext corridors. **Pets:** $10 daily fee/room. Designated rooms, service with restrictions, supervision.
[SAVE] [S/D] ⊠ ▣ 📺 🏊

OAK HARBOR

[AAA] ♦♦ **Acorn Motor Inn** [SH]
(360) 675-6646. **$46-$98.** 31530 SR 20. On SR 20 at jct 300th Ave W (SE Barrington Dr). Int corridors. **Pets:** Other species. $10 daily fee/pet. Designated rooms, service with restrictions, supervision.
[SAVE] [S/D] ⊠ ▣

(AAA) ▼▼▼ Best Western Harbor Plaza SH
(360) 679-4567. **$109-$149, 3 day notice.** 33175 SR 20.
Just n. Int corridors. **Pets:** Medium, dogs only. $15 daily
fee/room. Designated rooms, service with restrictions,
supervision.
[SAVE] [S🐾] ✕ [&M] [🌙] [🛏] [💻] [🐾]

OCEAN PARK

(AAA) ▼ Ocean Park Resort M
(360) 665-4585. **$67-$98, 10 day notice.** 25904 R St. Just e
of SR 103; downtown. Ext corridors. **Pets:** Small, other
species. $7 daily fee/pet. Designated rooms, service with
restrictions, supervision.
[SAVE] ✕ [🛏] [💻] [🐾] [✕] [K] [Z]

OCEAN SHORES

(AAA) ▼▼▼ The Grey Gull Resort CO
(360) 289-3381. **$80-$335, 3 day notice.** 651 Ocean Shores
Blvd NW. Just s of Shores Mall. Ext corridors.
Pets: Accepted.
[SAVE] [S🐾] ✕ [🛏] [💻] [🐾] [K]

(AAA) ▼▼▼ The Nautilus CO
(360) 289-2722. **$70-$150.** 835 Ocean Shores Blvd NW.
North end of town. Ext corridors. **Pets:** Dogs only. $20
one-time fee/pet. Supervision.
[SAVE] [S🐾] ✕ [🛏] [💻] [K]

(AAA) ▼▼▼ The Polynesian Condominium
Resort CO ❀
(360) 289-3361. **$99-$199.** 615 Ocean Shores Blvd NW.
Just s of Shores Mall. Ext/int corridors. **Pets:** Other species.
$15 daily fee/pet. Designated rooms, service with restric-
tions, supervision.
[SAVE] [S🐾] ✕ [🌙] [🛏] [💻] [🍴] [🐾] [✕] [K]

OKANOGAN

(AAA) ▼▼▼ Ponderosa Motor Lodge M ❀
(509) 422-0400. **$46-$51.** 1034 S 2nd Ave. 0.3 mi n on SR
215 from jct SR 20. Ext corridors. **Pets:** Other species.
Service with restrictions, crate.
[SAVE] [S🐾] ✕ [🛏] [💻] [🐾]

OLYMPIA

(AAA) ▼▼▼ Ramada Inn Governor House SH
(360) 352-7700. **$140.** 621 S Capitol Way. I-5, exit 105 (City
Center) northbound; exit 105A southbound, 0.4 mi w on
14th Ave, then 0.6 mi n; downtown. Int corridors.
Pets: Large. $50 one-time fee/room. Service with restric-
tions, supervision.
[SAVE] [S🐾] ✕ [🌙] [🛏] [💻] [🍴] [🐾] [✕]

▼▼▼ Red Lion Hotel Olympia SH
(360) 943-4000. **$99-$119.** 2300 Evergreen Park Dr SW. I-5,
exit 104, 0.5 mi nw, via US 101 and Cooper Point Rd N
exit. Int corridors. **Pets:** $45 one-time fee/room. Designated
rooms, supervision.
[ASK] [S🐾] ✕ [🛏] [💻] [🍴] [🐾]

OLYMPIC NATIONAL PARK

(AAA) ▼▼▼ Lake Crescent Lodge SH
(360) 928-3211. **$93, 3 day notice.** 416 Lake Crescent Rd.
22 mi w of Port Angeles on US 101. Ext/int corridors.
Pets: Accepted.
[SAVE] ✕ [🛏] [💻] [🍴] [✕] [K] [W] [Z]

▼▼▼ Log Cabin Resort CA
(360) 928-3325. **$50-$120, 3 day notice.** 3183 E Beach Rd.
3.3 mi nw of US 101 (MM 232). Ext corridors.
Pets: Accepted.
✕ [🛏] [💻] [🍴] [✕] [K] [W] [Z]

OMAK

(AAA) ▼▼▼ Motel Nicholas M ❀
(509) 826-4611. **$42-$46.** 527 E Grape Ave. 0.8 mi n on SR
215 business route, 0.3 mi w of US 97, on north exit to
Omak. Ext corridors. **Pets:** Small, dogs only. $3 daily fee/
pet. Designated rooms, service with restrictions, supervision.
[SAVE] [S🐾] ✕ [🛏] [💻]

(AAA) ▼▼▼ Omak Inn M
(509) 826-3822. **$66-$76.** 912 Koala Dr. On US 97, just n of
Riverside Dr. Int corridors. **Pets:** Small, dogs only. $25 daily
fee/pet. Service with restrictions, supervision.
[SAVE] [S🐾] ✕ [🛏] [💻] [🐾]

▼▼ Rodeway Inn & Suites M
(509) 826-0400. **$45-$80.** 122 N Main St. Downtown. Ext
corridors. **Pets:** Dogs only. $5 daily fee/pet. Designated
rooms, service with restrictions.
[ASK] [S🐾] ✕ [🐾] [🛏] [💻] [🐾]

OTHELLO

(AAA) ▼▼▼ Best Western Lincoln Inn SH
(509) 488-5671. **$70-$85.** 1020 E Cedar St. Just off Main St
at 10th and Cedar sts. Int corridors. **Pets:** Large, dogs only.
$10 daily fee/pet. Service with restrictions, supervision.
[SAVE] [S🐾] ✕ [🛏] [💻] [🐾]

PACIFIC BEACH

(AAA) ▼▼▼ Sandpiper Beach Resort CO
(360) 276-4580. **$90-$210, 14 day notice.** 4159 SR 109. 1.8
mi s. Ext corridors. **Pets:** Other species. $10 daily fee/pet.
Service with restrictions, supervision.
[SAVE] ✕ [🛏] [💻] [K] [W] [Z]

PACKWOOD

▼▼ Inn of Packwood M
(360) 494-5500. **$60-$70.** 13032 US 12. Center. Ext corridors. **Pets:** Medium, other species. $5 one-time fee/pet.
Designated rooms, service with restrictions, supervision.
[ASK] [S🐾] ✕ [🛏] [💻] [🐾]

PASCO

▼▼ Budget Inn M
(509) 546-2010. **$48-$55.** 1520 N Oregon St. I-182, exit 14A
(SR 395 S). Ext corridors. **Pets:** Medium. $20 deposit/room.
Service with restrictions, supervision.
[ASK] [S🐾] ✕ [🛏] [🐾]

▼▼▼ Red Lion Hotel Pasco 🏨
(509) 547-0701. **$114-$154.** 2525 N 20th Ave. I-182, exit 12B, just n. Int corridors. **Pets:** Large, other species. Service with restrictions, crate.
[ASK] [S⊘] [✕] [GM] [♨] [🐾] [✦] [💻] [🍴] [⤻]

▲▲▲ ▼▼▼ Sleep Inn 🏨
(509) 545-9554. **$65-$105.** 9930 Bedford St. I-182, exit 7, just ne. Int corridors. **Pets:** Small. $15 daily fee/pet. Service with restrictions, supervision.
[SAVE] [S⊘] [✕] [GM] [♨] [🐾] [✦] [💻] [⤻]

PORT ANGELES

▲▲▲ ▼▼▼ The Pond Motel Ⓜ
(360) 452-8422. **$40-$70, 3 day notice.** 1425 W US 101. 2 mi w. Ext corridors. **Pets:** Accepted.
[SAVE] [S⊘] [✕] [✦] [💻] [♬] [✦]

▲▲▲ ▼▼▼ Portside Inn Ⓜ
(360) 452-4015. **$49-$159, 3 day notice.** 1510 E Front St. Front St at Alder, on east side. Ext corridors. **Pets:** Medium. $25 deposit/room, $10 one-time fee/room. Designated rooms, service with restrictions, supervision.
[SAVE] [S⊘] [✕] [✦] [💻] [⤻]

▲▲▲ ▼▼▼▼ Red Lion Hotel Port
Angeles 🏨 🐾
(360) 452-9215. **$80-$143.** 221 N Lincoln St. On US 101 westbound, at the ferry landing. Ext/int corridors. **Pets:** Large, other species. Service with restrictions, crate.
[SAVE] [S⊘] [✕] [♨] [✦] [✦] [💻] [🍴] [⤻]

▲▲▲ ▼▼▼ Riviera Inn Ⓜ
(360) 417-3955. **$49-$99, 3 day notice.** 535 E Front St. On US 101 W; downtown. Ext corridors. **Pets:** Medium, dogs only. $25 daily fee/room. Designated rooms, no service, supervision.
[SAVE] [✕] [✦] [♬]

▼▼▼ Super 8 Motel Ⓜ
(360) 452-8401. **$67-$93.** 2104 E 1st St. 1.8 mi e of downtown, just s of US 101. Int corridors. **Pets:** Other species. $15 deposit/room, $10 one-time fee/room. Service with restrictions, supervision.
[ASK] [✕] [GM] [✦]

NEARBY OREGON
PORTLAND METROPOLITAN AREA

VANCOUVER

▼▼▼▼ Best Inn & Suites 🏨
(360) 696-0516. **$65-$85.** 7001 NE Hwy 99. I-5, exit 4, 0.8 mi se. Int corridors. **Pets:** Medium. $10 daily fee/pet. Service with restrictions, supervision.
[ASK] [S⊘] [✕] [♨] [✦] [💻] [⤻]

▲▲▲ ▼▼▼▼ Comfort Inn 🏨
(360) 574-6000. **$59-$119.** 13207 NE 20th Ave. I-5, exit 7, just e; I-205, exit 36, just w. Int corridors. **Pets:** Large, other species. $10 daily fee/room. Service with restrictions, supervision.
[SAVE] [S⊘] [✕] [♨] [✦] [💻] [⤻]

▼▼▼ Ferryman's Inn Ⓜ
(360) 574-2151. **$63-$68.** 7901 NE 6th Ave. I-5, exit 4, just nw. Ext/int corridors. **Pets:** Other species. $5 daily fee/pet. Designated rooms, service with restrictions, supervision.
[ASK] [S⊘] [✕] [GM] [♨] [✦] [⤻]

▼▼▼▼ Homewood Suites by Hilton 🏨 🐾
(360) 750-1100. **$98-$134.** 701 SE Columbia Shores Blvd. SR 14, exit 1, just s. Ext/int corridors. **Pets:** Other species. $10 daily fee/pet, $25 one-time fee.
[ASK] [S⊘] [✕] [✦] [✦] [💻] [⤻] [✕]

▼▼▼▼ Red Lion Hotel at the Quay,
Vancouver 🏨
(360) 694-8341. **$59-$99.** 100 Columbia St. 0.5 mi s on dock at foot of Columbia St. Int corridors. **Pets:** Medium. $25 one-time fee/pet. Service with restrictions, crate.
[ASK] [S⊘] [✕] [GM] [♨] [✦] [✦] [💻] [🍴] [⤻] [✕]

▼▼▼▼ Red Lion Inn At Salmon Creek 🏨
(360) 566-1100. **$79.** 1500 NE 134th St. I-5, exit 7, just w; I-205, exit 36, 0.5 mi w. Int corridors. **Pets:** Large, other species. $25 one-time fee/room. Service with restrictions, crate.
[ASK] [S⊘] [✕] [GM] [✦] [✦] [💻] [⤻]

▼▼▼▼ Residence Inn Vancouver 🏨 🐾
(360) 253-4800. **$159-$189.** 8005 NE Parkway Dr. I-205, exit 30 (SR 500 W), 0.5 mi w to Thurston Way, just n to NE Parkway Dr, then just w. Ext corridors. **Pets:** Other species. $15 daily fee/pet.
[ASK] [S⊘] [✕] [GM] [♨] [✦] [💻] [⤻] [✕]

▼▼▼▼ Staybridge Suites
Vancouver-Portland 🏨 🐾
(360) 891-8282. **$105-$145.** 7301 NE 41st St. I-205, exit 30 (SR 500 W), 1 mi w to NE Andresen Rd, just n to NE 40th St, just e to NE 72nd St, just n to NE 41st St, then just e. Int corridors. **Pets:** Large, other species. $50 deposit/room, $10 daily fee/pet. Designated rooms, service with restrictions.
[ASK] [S⊘] [✕] [GM] [♨] [✦] [✦] [💻] [⤻] [✕]

▲▲▲ ▼▼▼ Vancouver Days Inn Ⓜ 🐾
(360) 256-7044. **$45-$69.** 221 NE Chkalov Dr. I-205, exit 28 (Mill Plain E), just ne. Ext corridors. **Pets:** Small. $50 deposit/room, $10 daily fee/room. Designated rooms, service with restrictions, supervision.
[SAVE] [S⊘] [✕] [✦] [💻] [⤻]

🐾   **END METROPOLITAN AREA**   🐾

PORT ORCHARD

▼▼▼▼ Days Inn SH
(360) 895-7818. **$79-$109.** 220 Bravo Terrace. SR 16, exit Sedgwick, just e. Int corridors. **Pets:** Other species. $10 daily fee/pet. Service with restrictions, supervision.
[ASK] [S⊘] [✕] [🐾] [🛏] [🍴] [🖥] [🛏] [≈]

PORT TOWNSEND

▲▲ ▼▼▼▼ Bishop Victorian Hotel SH
(360) 385-6122. **$99-$209, 3 day notice.** 714 Washington St. Corner of Washington and Quincy sts. Int corridors. **Pets:** Accepted.
[SAVE] [S⊘] [✕] [🍴] [🖥] [🥬]

▼▼▼▼ Harborside Inn SH
(360) 385-7909. **$70-$115.** 330 Benedict St. Just e of SR 20. Ext corridors. **Pets:** Small, dogs only. $5 daily fee/pet. Designated rooms, service with restrictions, supervision.
[✕] [🐾] [🍴] [🖥] [≈] [🥬]

▲▲ ▼▼▼▼ Palace Hotel SH ✿
(360) 385-0773. **$59-$289.** 1004 Water St. Downtown. Int corridors. **Pets:** Large, other species. $10 one-time fee/pet. Service with restrictions, supervision.
[SAVE] [S⊘] [✕] [🍴] [🖥] [🥬]

▲▲ ▼▼▼▼ The Swan Hotel M
(360) 385-1718. **$80-$190, 3 day notice.** 216 Monroe St. Downtown. Ext corridors. **Pets:** Dogs only. $15 daily fee/pet. Designated rooms, service with restrictions, supervision.
[SAVE] [S⊘] [✕] [🍴] [🖥] [🥬]

POULSBO

▲▲ ▼▼▼▼ Poulsbo Inn M
(360) 779-3921. **$88-$115.** 18680 SR 305. SR 3, 2.3 mi e. Ext corridors. **Pets:** Medium. $10 daily fee/pet. Designated rooms, service with restrictions, crate.
[SAVE] [S⊘] [✕] [SM] [🐾] [🍴] [🖥] [≈] [🥬]

PROSSER

▼▼▼▼ Best Western Prosser Inn SH
(509) 786-7977. **$99-$109, 14 day notice.** 225 Merlot Dr. I-82, exit 80, just s. Int corridors. **Pets:** Accepted.
[ASK] [✕] [SM] [🐾] [🍴] [🖥] [≈]

▼▼▼▼ Inn at Horse Heaven SH
(509) 786-7090. **$109-$139, 14 day notice.** 259 Merlot Dr. I-82, exit 80, just s, then just e. Int corridors. **Pets:** Accepted.
[ASK] [✕] [SM] [🐾] [🍴] [🖥] [≈]

PULLMAN

▲▲ ▼▼▼▼ Hawthorn Inn & Suites SH
(509) 332-0928. **$89-$99.** 928 NW Olsen St. 1.6 mi e on SR 270 from US 195. Int corridors. **Pets:** Large, other species. $15 one-time fee/room. Designated rooms, service with restrictions, supervision.
[SAVE] [S⊘] [✕] [🐾] [🛏] [🍴] [🖥] [≈] [🥬]

▲▲ ▼▼▼▼ Holiday Inn Express Hotel & Suites SH ✿
(509) 334-4437. **$94.** SE 1190 Bishop Blvd. Jct US 195 business route, 0.5 mi s, then 1 mi e on SR 270. Int corridors. **Pets:** Large, other species. Designated rooms, service with restrictions.
[SAVE] [S⊘] [✕] [SM] [🐾] [🛏] [🍴] [🖥] [≈] [🥬]

▼▼▼▼ Quality Inn Paradise Creek SH
(509) 332-0500. **$74-$114.** 1400 SE Bishop Blvd. Jct US 195 business route, just s, then 1 mi e on SR 270. Int corridors. **Pets:** Accepted.
[ASK] [S⊘] [✕] [🐾] [🍴] [🖥] [≈] [🥬]

QUINAULT

▲▲ ▼▼▼▼ Lake Quinault Lodge SH
(360) 288-2900. **$68-$180, 3 day notice.** 345 S Shore Rd. 2 mi off US 101. Ext/int corridors. **Pets:** Other species. $10 daily fee/room. Designated rooms, service with restrictions, supervision.
[SAVE] [S⊘] [✕] [🖥] [🍴] [≈] [🥬] [K] [✆]

QUINCY

▼▼ Traditional Inns M
(509) 787-3525. **$63-$68.** 500 F St SW. West end of town on SR 28. Ext corridors. **Pets:** Very small, dogs only. $5 daily fee/pet. Supervision.
[ASK] [S⊘] [✕] [🍴]

REPUBLIC

▲▲ ▼▼▼ Prospector Inn SH ✿
(509) 775-3361. **$52-$98.** 979 S Clark Ave. Downtown. Int corridors. **Pets:** Other species. $10 daily fee/pet. Designated rooms, service with restrictions, supervision.
[SAVE] [S⊘] [✕] [🍴] [🥬]

RICHLAND

▼▼ Days Inn M
(509) 943-4611. **$54-$74.** 615 Jadwin Ave. I-182, exit 5B, 0.9 mi n, just w of SR 240 business route; downtown. Ext corridors. **Pets:** Other species. $10 daily fee/room.
[ASK] [S⊘] [✕] [🍴] [🖥] [≈]

▼▼ Red Lion Hotel Richland Hanford House SH
(509) 946-7611. **$78-$124.** 802 George Washington Way. I-182, exit 5B, 1.3 mi n on SR 240 business route. Ext/int corridors. **Pets:** Large. $20 deposit/room. Service with restrictions, crate.
[ASK] [✕] [SM] [🐾] [🛏] [🍴] [🖥] [🍴] [≈] [🥬]

▲▲ ▼▼▼▼ Royal Hotel SH
(509) 946-4121. **$69-$99.** 1515 George Washington Way. I-182, exit 5B, 2.5 mi n. Int corridors. **Pets:** Accepted.
[SAVE] [S⊘] [✕] [SM] [🐾] [🛏] [🍴] [🖥] [≈] [🥬]

RIMROCK

▼▼ Game Ridge Motel M
(509) 672-2212. **$75-$110, 7 day notice.** 27350 US Hwy 12. Downtown. Ext corridors. **Pets:** Accepted.
[ASK] [S⊘] [✕] [🍴] [🖥] [🥬] [K] [✆]

RITZVILLE

Colwell Best Value Inn M
(509) 659-1620. **$56-$74.** 501 W 1st Ave. I-90, exit 220, 0.9 mi n; downtown. Ext corridors. **Pets:** Medium, other species. $25 deposit/pet, $5 daily fee/pet. Designated rooms, no service, supervision.

La Quinta Inn SH
(509) 659-1007. **$49-$89.** 1513 Smitty's Blvd. I-90, exit 221, just n. Int corridors. **Pets:** Accepted.

Top Hat Motel M
(509) 659-1100. **$38-$48.** 210 E 1st Ave. I-90, exit 221, 1 mi ne via Division St. Ext corridors. **Pets:** Medium, dogs only. $500 one-time fee/room. Designated rooms, service with restrictions, supervision.

SAN JUAN ISLANDS AREA

DEER HARBOR

Deer Harbor Inn CI
(360) 376-4110. **$119-$129, 14 day notice.** 33 Inn Ln. 8 mi sw of ferry landing, 4 mi sw of Westsound Marina. Ext/int corridors. **Pets:** Accepted.

EASTSOUND

Outlook Inn on Orcas Island SH
(360) 376-2200. **$64-$265, 7 day notice.** 171 Main St. In Eastsound; downtown. Ext/int corridors. **Pets:** Accepted.

FRIDAY HARBOR

Lakedale Resort SH
(360) 378-2350. **$120-$265, 30 day notice.** 4313 Roche Harbor Rd. 4 mi n of Friday Harbor via Tucker Ave. Ext/int corridors. **Pets:** Accepted.

LOPEZ ISLAND

Lopez Islander SH
(360) 468-2233. **$89-$159, 14 day notice.** 2864 Fisherman Bay Rd. From ferry landing, 4.8 mi s via Ferry Rd and Fisherman Bay Rd. Ext corridors. **Pets:** Small. $10 daily fee/pet. Service with restrictions, supervision.

SEATTLE METROPOLITAN AREA

ARLINGTON

Crossroads Inn SH
(360) 403-7222. **$62-$79.** 5200 172nd St NE. I-5, exit 206, 1 mi e. Int corridors. **Pets:** Accepted.

AUBURN

Days Inn M
(253) 939-5950. **$74-$79.** 1521 D St NE. SR 167, exit 15th St NW, 0.9 mi e, just n. Ext corridors. **Pets:** Medium. $25 one-time fee/pet. Service with restrictions, supervision.

Travelodge Suites SH
(253) 833-7171. **$59-$99.** Nine 16th St NW. SR 167, exit 15th St NW, 0.8 mi e, then just n on A St NE. Int corridors. **Pets:** Other species. $10 daily fee/pet. Service with restrictions, crate.

Val-U Inn SH
(253) 735-9600. **$60-$105.** Nine 14th St NW. SR 167, exit 15th St NW, 0.8 mi e, just s on A St NE, then just w. Int corridors. **Pets:** Accepted.

BAINBRIDGE ISLAND

Island Country Inn M
(206) 842-6861. **$99-$119.** 920 Hildebrand Ln NE. 0.8 mi n of ferry dock on SR 305, just w on High School Rd, just s. Ext corridors. **Pets:** Other species. $10 daily fee/pet. Designated rooms, service with restrictions, supervision.

BELLEVUE

Candlewood Suites Hotel SH
(425) 373-1212. **$79-$145.** 15805 SE 37th St. I-90, exit 11 westbound; exit 11A (156 N Ave SE) eastbound, 0.9 mi s se on south frontage road. Int corridors. **Pets:** Large, other species. $10 daily fee/pet, $75 one-time fee/room. Service with restrictions.

Days Inn Bellevue SH
(425) 643-6644. **$82-$97.** 3241 156th Ave SE. I-90, exit 11 westbound; exit 11A (156th Ave SE) eastbound, just ne. Ext corridors. **Pets:** Accepted.

Embassy Suites Hotel Bellevue LH
(425) 644-2500. **$89-$199.** 3225 158th Ave SE. I-90, exit 11 westbound; exit 11A (156th Ave SE) eastbound, just ne. Int corridors. **Pets:** Medium. $50 daily fee/pet. Designated rooms, service with restrictions, supervision.

▼▼ ▼▼ **Homestead Studio Suites**
Hotel-Bellevue/Factoria Ⓜ ❖
(425) 865-8680. **$74-$99.** 3700 132nd Ave SE. I-90, exit 11A
westbound; exit 10B eastbound, 0.5 mi se. Ext corridors.
Pets: Medium, other species. $25 daily fee/room. Service
with restrictions, crate.

⟨A$K⟩ ⟨S🐾⟩ ⟨✕⟩ ⟨🌀⟩ ⟨🐾⟩ ⟨🛏⟩ ⟨💻⟩

▼▼ ▼▼ **Homestead Studio Suites**
Hotel-Redmond/Bellevue Ⓜ ❖
(425) 885-6675. **$104-$133.** 15805 NE 28th St. I-405, exit 14
(SR 520), 3.3 mi e, exit 148th Ave NE (south exit), just e on
24th St, just ne on Bel-Red Rd, just n on 156th Ave, then
just e. Ext corridors. **Pets:** Medium, other species. $25 daily
fee/room. Service with restrictions, crate.

⟨A$K⟩ ⟨S🐾⟩ ⟨✕⟩ ⟨🌀⟩ ⟨🐾⟩ ⟨🛏⟩ ⟨💻⟩

◆◆◆ ▼▼ ▼▼ **La Residence Suite Hotel** 🅂🄷
(425) 455-1475. **$105-$145.** 475 100th Ave SE. I-405, exit
13B, 0.9 mi w on NE 8th St, just s. Int corridors.
Pets: Accepted.

⟨SAVE⟩ ⟨S🐾⟩ ⟨✕⟩ ⟨🛏⟩ ⟨💻⟩

◆◆◆ ▼▼ ▼▼ **Ramada Inn Bellevue Center** 🅂🄷
(425) 455-1515. **$79-$150.** 818 112th Ave NE. I-405, exit
13B, 0.3 mi nw. Ext/int corridors. **Pets:** Accepted.

⟨SAVE⟩ ⟨S🐾⟩ ⟨✕⟩ ⟨🌀⟩ ⟨🛏⟩ ⟨💻⟩ ⟨🏊⟩

▼▼ ▼▼ **Red Lion Bellevue Inn** 🅂🄷
(425) 455-5240. **$159-$175.** 11211 Main St. I-405, exit 12,
0.4 mi n on 114th St. Int corridors. **Pets:** Small. $25 one-
time fee/pet. Designated rooms, service with restrictions,
supervision.

⟨A$K⟩ ⟨S🐾⟩ ⟨✕⟩ ⟨🌀⟩ ⟨🛏⟩ ⟨💻⟩ ⟨🍴⟩ ⟨🏊⟩

▼▼ ▼▼ **The Residence Inn By Marriott,**
Bellevue-Redmond 🅂🄷 ❖
(425) 882-1222. **$89-$179.** 14455 NE 29th Pl. I-405, exit 14
(SR 520), 2.3 mi e to 148th Ave NE (north exit), just nw. Ext
corridors. **Pets:** Other species. $20 daily fee/pet. Service
with restrictions.

⟨A$K⟩ ⟨✕⟩ ⟨🌀⟩ ⟨🛏⟩ ⟨💻⟩ ⟨🏊⟩ ⟨✕⟩

BOTHELL

▼▼ ▼▼ **Residence Inn by Marriott Seattle**
NE 🅂🄷 ❖
(425) 485-3030. **$129-$179.** 11920 NE 195th St. I-405, exit
24, 0.4 mi ne. Ext corridors. **Pets:** $15 daily fee/pet. Service
with restrictions, supervision.

⟨A$K⟩ ⟨S🐾⟩ ⟨✕⟩ ⟨🌀⟩ ⟨🛏⟩ ⟨💻⟩ ⟨🏊⟩ ⟨✕⟩

DUPONT

▼▼ ▼▼ **GuestHouse Inn & Suites** 🅂🄷
(253) 912-8900. **$79-$150.** 1609 McNeil St. I-5, exit 118, 0.6
mi w. Int corridors. **Pets:** Large. $10 daily fee/pet. Service
with restrictions, supervision.

⟨A$K⟩ ⟨S🐾⟩ ⟨✕⟩ ⟨🅜⟩ ⟨🌀⟩ ⟨🛏⟩ ⟨💻⟩ ⟨🏊⟩

EDMONDS

◆◆◆ ▼▼ ▼▼ **Edmonds Harbor Inn &**
Suites 🅂🄷 ❖
(425) 771-5021. **$89-$129.** 130 W Dayton St. Just s at Port
of Edmonds. Ext/int corridors. **Pets:** Large. $10 daily fee/
room. Designated rooms.

⟨SAVE⟩ ⟨S🐾⟩ ⟨✕⟩ ⟨🌀⟩ ⟨🛏⟩ ⟨💻⟩

◆◆◆ ▼▼ **K & E Motor Inn** Ⓜ
(425) 778-2181. **$44-$74, 3 day notice.** 23921 Hwy 99. I-5,
exit 177, 1 mi w, 0.3 mi n of jct SR 99 and 104. Ext
corridors. **Pets:** Small, other species. $10 daily fee/room.
Service with restrictions.

⟨SAVE⟩ ⟨S🐾⟩ ⟨✕⟩ ⟨🛏⟩

◆◆◆ ▼▼ ▼▼ **Travelodge Seattle North** Ⓜ
(425) 771-8008. **$59-$109.** 23825 Hwy 99. I-5, exit 177, 1 mi
w, 0.3 mi n at jct SR 99 and 104. Ext corridors.
Pets: Medium. $25 one-time fee/pet. Service with restric-
tions, supervision.

⟨SAVE⟩ ⟨S🐾⟩ ⟨✕⟩ ⟨🛏⟩ ⟨💻⟩

EVERETT

◆◆◆ ▼▼ ▼▼ **Best Western Cascadia Inn** 🅂🄷
(425) 258-4141. **$59-$129.** 2800 Pacific Ave. I-5, exit 193
northbound; exit 194 southbound, just w. Int corridors.
Pets: Accepted.

⟨SAVE⟩ ⟨S🐾⟩ ⟨✕⟩ ⟨🐾⟩ ⟨🛏⟩ ⟨💻⟩ ⟨🏊⟩

▼▼ ▼▼ **Days Inn** 🅂🄷
(425) 355-1570. **$65-$75.** 1602 SE Everett Mall Way. I-5, exit
189 northbound, 0.5 mi w on SR 527, 0.5 mi s; exit southbound, 0.7 mi s. Ext corridors. **Pets:** Medium, dogs only.
$10 one-time fee/pet. Designated rooms, service with
restrictions, supervision.

⟨A$K⟩ ⟨S🐾⟩ ⟨✕⟩ ⟨🛏⟩ ⟨💻⟩ ⟨🏊⟩

◆◆◆ ▼▼ ▼▼ **Quality Inn Hotel & Conference**
Center 🅂🄷
(425) 337-2900. **$99-$109.** 101 128th St SE. I-5, exit 186,
just e. Int corridors. **Pets:** Accepted.

⟨SAVE⟩ ⟨S🐾⟩ ⟨✕⟩ ⟨🌀⟩ ⟨🛏⟩ ⟨💻⟩ ⟨🍴⟩ ⟨🏊⟩

FEDERAL WAY

◆◆◆ ▼▼ ▼▼ **Federal Way Comfort Inn** 🅂🄷
(253) 529-0101. **$69-$149.** 31622 Pacific Hwy S. I-5, exit
143, 0.5 mi w on 320th St, just n on 20th Ave, then just w
on 316th Pl. Int corridors. **Pets:** Large, other species. $20
one-time fee/room. Service with restrictions, crate.

⟨SAVE⟩ ⟨S🐾⟩ ⟨✕⟩ ⟨🌀⟩ ⟨🐾⟩ ⟨🛏⟩ ⟨💻⟩ ⟨🏊⟩ ⟨✕⟩

▼▼ ▼▼ **Federal Way Super 8** 🅂🄷
(253) 838-8808. **$54-$64.** 1688 S 348th St. I-5, exit 142B,
just w. Int corridors. **Pets:** Medium. $10 daily fee/pet. Serv-
ice with restrictions, supervision.

⟨A$K⟩ ⟨S🐾⟩ ⟨✕⟩ ⟨🛏⟩

▼▼ ▼▼ ▼▼ **La Quinta Inn & Suites** 🅂🄷
(253) 529-4000. **$99-$119.** 32124 25th Ave S. I-5, exit 143,
just sw. Int corridors. **Pets:** Small, dogs only. Designated
rooms, service with restrictions, supervision.

⟨A$K⟩ ⟨S🐾⟩ ⟨✕⟩ ⟨🛏⟩ ⟨💻⟩ ⟨🍴⟩ ⟨🏊⟩

▼▼▼▼ Quality Inn & Suites 🆂🅷
(253) 835-4141. **$83-$93.** 1400 S 348th St. I-5, exit 142B, 0.5 mi w. Int corridors. **Pets:** Accepted.
(A$K) (S🔒) (✕) (👟M) (🏊) (🐾) (📶) (💻) (≈)

FIFE

🅰🅰🅰 ▼ Best Inn & Suites 🅼
(253) 922-9520. **$50-$65.** 3100 Pacific Hwy E. I-5, exit 136B northbound; exit 136 southbound, just nw. Ext corridors. **Pets:** Small, dogs only. $50 deposit/room, $10 daily fee/pet. Designated rooms, no service, supervision.
(SAVE) (S🔒) (✕) (📶) (💻) (≈)

🅰🅰🅰 ▼▼▼ Comfort Inn 🅼
(253) 926-2301. **$65-$89.** 5601 Pacific Hwy E. I-5, exit 137, just e. Ext corridors. **Pets:** Other species. $15 one-time fee/room. Designated rooms, service with restrictions, crate.
(SAVE) (S🔒) (✕) (📶) (💻)

🅰🅰🅰 ▼▼▼▼ Ramada Limited 🅼
(253) 926-1000. **$45-$79.** 3501 Pacific Hwy E. I-5, exit 136B northbound; exit 136 southbound, just ne. Ext corridors. **Pets:** Accepted.
(SAVE) (S🔒) (✕) (📶) (💻)

🅰🅰🅰 ▼▼▼ Royal Coachman Inn 🅼 🐾
(253) 922-2500. **$62-$81.** 5805 Pacific Hwy E. I-5, exit 137, just ne. Ext corridors. **Pets:** $25 deposit/room. Service with restrictions, crate.
(SAVE) (S🔒) (✕) (📶) (💻)

GIG HARBOR

🅰🅰🅰 ▼▼▼ Best Western Wesley Inn 🆂🅷 🐾
(253) 858-9690. **$109-$194.** 6575 Kimball Dr. SR 16, exit City Center, just e on Pioneer Way, then 0.3 mi s. Int corridors. **Pets:** Large, other species. $10 daily fee/pet. Designated rooms, service with restrictions, supervision.
(SAVE) (S🔒) (✕) (👟M) (🔑) (📶) (💻) (≈)

🅰🅰🅰 ▼▼▼▼ The Inn at Gig Harbor 🆂🅷
(253) 858-1111. **$115-$199.** 3211 56th St NW. SR 16, exit Olympic Dr, just w, then 0.4 mi n. Int corridors. **Pets:** Medium, other species. $15 one-time fee/room. Designated rooms, service with restrictions, crate.
(SAVE) (S🔒) (✕) (👟M) (🔑) (📶) (💻) (🍽) (≈)

ISSAQUAH

▼ Motel 6–295 🅼
(425) 392-8405. **$55-$75.** 1885 15th PL NW. I-90, exit 15, 0.3 mi n on Renton Issaquah Rd, then just w on NW Sammamish Rd. Ext corridors. **Pets:** Accepted.
(S🔒) (✕) (🔑) (≈)

KENT

🅰🅰🅰 ▼▼▼▼ Comfort Inn Kent 🆂🅷
(253) 872-2211. **$69-$149.** 22311 84th Ave S. SR 167, exit 84th Ave S, 0.3 mi n. Int corridors. **Pets:** Small. $50 deposit/room, $10 daily fee/pet. Service with restrictions, crate.
(SAVE) (S🔒) (✕) (📶) (💻) (≈)

▼▼ Days Inn South Seattle/Kent 🆂🅷
(253) 854-1950. **$54-$69.** 1711 W Meeker St. I-5, exit 149 southbound; exit 149A northbound, 2.3 mi ne via Kent/Des Moines Rd (SR 516) and Meeker St. Int corridors. **Pets:** Accepted.
(A$K) (S🔒) (✕) (📶) (💻)

🅰🅰🅰 ▼▼▼ Howard Johnson Inn 🅼
(253) 852-7224. **$69-$99.** 1233 N Central. SR 167, exit 84th Ave S, just s. Ext corridors. **Pets:** Other species. $10 daily fee/pet. Service with restrictions, supervision.
(SAVE) (S🔒) (✕) (📶) (💻) (≈) (🚫)

▼▼▼ La Quinta Inn Kent 🆂🅷
(253) 520-6670. **$59-$79.** 25100 74th Ave S. I-5, exit 149, 2.5 mi se via SR 516 to 74th Ave. Int corridors. **Pets:** Small. $25 one-time fee/pet. Service with restrictions, supervision.
(A$K) (S🔒) (✕) (🏊) (🔑) (📶) (💻) (≈) (🚫)

▼▼▼ TownePlace Suites by Marriott-Seattle Southcenter 🆂🅷
(253) 796-6000. **$75-$95.** 18123 72nd Ave S. I-405, exit 1 (SR 181), 1.6 mi s on W Valley Hwy, just e on S 180th, then just s. Ext corridors. **Pets:** Accepted.
(A$K) (S🔒) (✕) (👟M) (🏊) (🔑) (📶) (💻) (≈) (🚫)

▼▼ Val U Inn 🆂🅷 🐾
(253) 872-5525. **$79-$84.** 22420 84th Ave S. SR 167, exit 84th Ave S, then just n. Int corridors. **Pets:** Small, dogs only. $5 daily fee/pet. Designated rooms, service with restrictions, supervision.
(A$K) (S🔒) (✕) (📶)

KIRKLAND

▼▼▼ La Quinta Inn 🆂🅷
(425) 828-6585. **$89-$125.** 10530 NE Northup Way. I-405, exit 14 (SR 520) via 108th Ave exit, s on 108th St, then just w. Int corridors. **Pets:** Other species. Service with restrictions.
(✕) (🏊) (🔑) (📶) (💻) (≈)

▼ Motel 6–687 🅼
(425) 821-5618. **$55-$71.** 12010 120th PI NE. I-405, exit 20B northbound; exit 20 southbound, just se. Ext corridors. **Pets:** Other species. Service with restrictions, supervision.
(S🔒) (✕) (🏊) (🔑) (≈)

🅰🅰🅰 ▼▼▼ The Woodmark Hotel on Lake Washington 🅻🅷
(425) 822-3700. **$215-$285.** 1200 Carillon Point. On Lake Washington Blvd, 1 mi n of SR 520. Int corridors. **Pets:** Accepted.
(SAVE) (S🔒) (✕) (🏊) (💻) (🍽) (🚫)

LAKEWOOD

🅰🅰🅰 ▼▼▼ Best Western Lakewood Motor Inn 🅼
(253) 584-2212. **$78-$98.** 6125 Motor Ave SW. I-5, exit 125, 2 mi nw via Bridgeport to Gravelly Lake Dr, just left. Ext corridors. **Pets:** Accepted.
(SAVE) (S🔒) (✕) (👟M) (🏊) (🔑) (📶) (💻) (≈)

Howard Johnson Express Inn M ✿
(253) 589-8800. **$49-$64.** 4215 Sharondale St SW. I-5, exit 127 (S Tacoma Way), just w on SR 512, 0.8 m s on S Tacoma Way, then just w. Ext corridors. **Pets:** $20 one-time fee/pet. Service with restrictions.
SAVE ⓢⓓ ✕ 🖵 🖬 🖳

Ramada Inn M
(253) 588-5241. **$72-$99.** 9920 S Tacoma Way. I-5, exit 127 (S Tacoma Way), 0.3 mi nw. Ext corridors. **Pets:** Accepted.
SAVE ⓢⓓ ✕ 🖬 🖳

LYNNWOOD

Embassy Suites Hotels Seattle North/Lynnwood LH
(425) 775-2500. **$89-$169.** 20610 44th Ave W. I-5, exit 181A northbound, just e; exit 181 southbound, just w on 196th St SW, then 0.4 mi s. Int corridors. **Pets:** Accepted.
ASK ⓢⓓ ✕ ⓛⓜ 🖉 🖵 🖬 🖳 📺 🍴 ⚓ ✕

La Quinta Lynnwood SH
(425) 775-7447. **$89-$134.** 4300 Alderwood Mall Blvd. I-5, exit 181A northbound, just w; exit 181 southbound, 0.5 mi sw via 196th St and 44th Ave SW, just e. Int corridors. **Pets:** Medium, other species. Service with restrictions, supervision.
ASK ⓢⓓ ✕ 🖬 🖳 ⚓

The Residence Inn by Marriott-Seattle North SH
(425) 771-1100. **$89-$149.** 18200 Alderwood Mall Pkwy. I-5, exit 183, just w on 164th St SW, then 1.5 mi se on 28th St W; just n of Alderwood Mall Shopping Center. Ext corridors. **Pets:** Large. $10 daily fee/pet. Service with restrictions, crate.
ASK ⓢⓓ ✕ 🖉 🖬 🖳 ⚓ ✕

MARYSVILLE

Best Western Tulalip Inn SH
(360) 659-4488. **$59-$109.** 3228 Marine Dr NE. I-5, exit 199, just w. Int corridors. **Pets:** Accepted.
SAVE ⓢⓓ ✕ ⓛⓜ 🖉 🖵 🖬 🖳 🍴 ⚓

The Village Motor Inn SH
(360) 659-0005. **$59-$129.** 235 Beach Ave. I-5, exit 199, just se. Int corridors. **Pets:** Small. $12 daily fee/pet. Service with restrictions, crate.
SAVE ⓢⓓ ✕ 🖬 🖳

MONROE

Best Western Baron Inn SH
(360) 794-3111. **$75-$130.** 19233 US 2. West end of town. Int corridors. **Pets:** Medium, other species. $25 one-time fee/room. Service with restrictions, supervision.
SAVE ⓢⓓ ✕ 🖵 🖬 🖳 ⚓

MOUNTLAKE TERRACE

Studio 6 #6042 M ✿
(425) 771-3139. **$65-$80.** 6017 244th St SW. I-5, exit 177, just ne. Ext corridors. **Pets:** Small. $10 daily fee/room, $50 one-time fee/room. Service with restrictions, supervision.
ⓢⓓ ✕ ⓛⓜ 🖉 🖵 🖬 🖳

MUKILTEO

TownePlace Suites by Marriott-Mukilteo SH
(425) 551-5900. **$79-$99.** 8521 Mukilteo Speedway. Just se of jct 84th St SW and SR 535 (Mukilteo Speedway). Ext corridors. **Pets:** Accepted.
ASK ⓢⓓ ✕ ⓛⓜ 🖉 🖵 🖬 🖳 ⚓ ✕

PUYALLUP

Best Western Park Plaza SH
(253) 848-1500. **$117-$132.** 620 S Hill Park Dr. SR 512, exit S Hill/Eatonville, just w. Int corridors. **Pets:** Accepted.
SAVE ⓢⓓ ✕ ⓛⓜ 🖵 🖬 🖳 ⚓

Holiday Inn Express Hotel & Suites Puyallup SH ✿
(253) 848-4900. **$114-$119.** 812 S Hill Park Dr. SR 512, exit S Hill/Eatonville, just w. Int corridors. **Pets:** Small, dogs only. $25 one-time fee/room. Service with restrictions, supervision.
SAVE ⓢⓓ ✕ 🖉 🖬 🖳 ⚓

REDMOND

Residence Inn by Marriott Redmond Town Center SH
(425) 497-9226. **$189.** 7575 164th Ave NE. I-405, exit 14 (SR 520), 5 mi e to West Lake Sammamish Pkwy, just n to Leary Way, just e to Bear Creek Pkwy, just s to 74th Ave, just w to 163rd Ave, then just n. Int corridors. **Pets:** Accepted.
ASK ✕ 🖬 🖳 ⚓ ✕

RENTON

Holiday Inn Select Seattle-Renton SH
(425) 226-7700. **$139-$169.** One S Grady Way. I-405, exit 2 (Renton/Rainier Ave), at jct SR 167 N. Int corridors. **Pets:** Medium. $50 deposit/pet. Service with restrictions, crate.
SAVE ⓢⓓ ✕ 🖉 🖬 🖳 🍴 ⚓

Travelodge of Renton SH
(425) 251-9591. **$55-$79.** 3700 E Valley Rd. SR 167, exit E Valley Rd, just nw. Int corridors. **Pets:** Other species. $10 daily fee/pet. No service, supervision.
SAVE ⓢⓓ ✕ 🖬 🖳

SEATAC

Coast Gateway Hotel SH
(206) 248-8200. **$78-$93, 7 day notice.** 18415 International Blvd. On SR 99. Int corridors. **Pets:** Other species. Designated rooms.
SAVE ⓢⓓ ✕ ⓛⓜ 🖉 🖬 🖳

Doubletree Hotel Seattle Airport LH
(206) 246-8600. **$69-$145.** 18740 International Blvd. On SR 99. Int corridors. **Pets:** Accepted.
SAVE ⓢⓓ ✕ 🖉 🖵 🖬 🖳 🍴 ⚓

🔺 ▼▼▼ Hilton Seattle Airport & Conference Center LH
(206) 244-4800. **$89-$179.** 17620 International Blvd. On SR 99. Int corridors. **Pets:** Accepted.

[SAVE] [Sd] [✕] [🔊] [🔇] [🔋] [💻] [🍴] [🏊] [✕]

▼▼▼ Holiday Inn Express Hotel & Suites-Seatac-Airport SH
(206) 824-3200. **$99-$134.** 19621 International Blvd. On SR 99. Int corridors. **Pets:** $125 deposit/room, $10 daily fee/pet. Designated rooms, service with restrictions, crate.

[ASK] [Sd] [✕] [🔋] [💻]

🔺 ▼▼▼ Holiday Inn Sea-Tac LH
(206) 248-1000. **$119-$159.** 17338 International Blvd. On SR 99. Int corridors. **Pets:** Small, other species. $20 daily fee/room. Designated rooms.

[SAVE] [Sd] [✕] [🔊M] [🔇] [🔋] [💻] [🍴] [🏊]

🔺 ▼▼▼ La Quinta Inn-Sea Tac Intl SH ✿
(206) 241-5211. **$95-$109.** 2824 S 188th St. On SR 99. Int corridors. **Pets:** Other species. Service with restrictions, supervision.

[SAVE] [✕] [🔇] [🔋] [💻] [🏊]

▼ Motel 6-1332 M
(206) 246-4101. **$45-$65.** 16500 International Blvd. On SR 99. Ext corridors. **Pets:** Accepted.

[Sd] [✕] [🔇]

▼ Motel 6-90 SH
(206) 241-1648. **$45-$63.** 18900 47th Ave S. I-5, exit 152, just sw. Int corridors. **Pets:** Service with restrictions, supervision.

[Sd] [✕] [🔇] [🔊] [🔋] [🏊]

▼▼▼ Red Lion Hotel Seattle Airport SH
(206) 246-5535. **$89-$149.** On SR 99. Int corridors. **Pets:** Other species. Service with restrictions, supervision.

[ASK] [Sd] [✕] [🔇] [🔋] [💻] [🍴] [✕]

🔺 ▼▼ Red Roof Inn SH
(206) 248-0901. **$49-$69.** 16838 International Blvd. On SR 99. Int corridors. **Pets:** Other species. Service with restrictions, supervision.

[SAVE] [Sd] [✕] [🔋]

▼▼▼ Seattle Marriott Sea-Tac Airport LH
(206) 241-2000. **$129-$164.** 3201 S 176th St. Just e of SR 99. Int corridors. **Pets:** Accepted.

[ASK] [✕] [🔇] [🔊] [🔋] [💻] [🍴] [🏊] [✕]

▼▼ Super 8 Motel Sea-Tac SH
(206) 433-8188. **$59-$89.** 3100 S 192nd St. Just e of SR 99. Int corridors. **Pets:** Other species. $25 deposit/room. Service with restrictions, supervision.

[ASK] [Sd] [✕]

SEATTLE

🔺 ▼▼▼ ▼▼▼ The Alexis Hotel LH ✿
(206) 624-4844. **$225-$319.** 1007 1st Ave. Corner of Madison St and 1st Ave. Int corridors. **Pets:** Large, other species. Service with restrictions, crate.

[SAVE] [Sd] [✕] [🔊] [🔇] [💻] [🍴] [✕]

🔺 ▼▼▼ Aurora Seafair Inn M
(206) 524-3600. **$65-$95.** 9100 Aurora Ave N. I-5, exit 172, 1.5 mi w on N 85th St, just n. Ext corridors. **Pets:** Small. $5 daily fee/pet. Designated rooms, service with restrictions, supervision.

[SAVE] [Sd] [✕] [🔋]

🔺 ▼▼▼ Best Western Evergreen Inn SH ✿
(206) 361-3700. **$84-$149.** 13700 Aurora Ave N. I-5, exit 175, 1.1 mi w on NE 145th St, then 0.3 mi s. Int corridors. **Pets:** Other species. $10 daily fee/pet. Service with restrictions, supervision.

[SAVE] [Sd] [✕] [🔋] [💻] [✕]

🔺 ▼▼▼ Best Western Executive Inn/Seattle SH
(206) 448-9444. **$120-$165.** 200 Taylor Ave N. I-5, exit 166, 1 mi w; near Seattle Center; just w of SR 99. Int corridors. **Pets:** Accepted.

[SAVE] [Sd] [✕] [🔊M] [🔇] [🔊] [🔋] [💻] [🍴]

🔺 ▼▼▼ Crowne Plaza Seattle LH
(206) 464-1980. **$220-$298.** 1113 6th Ave. Corner of 6th Ave and Seneca St. Int corridors. **Pets:** Dogs only. $50 one-time fee/room. Service with restrictions, supervision.

[SAVE] [Sd] [✕] [🔇] [🔋] [💻] [🍴]

▼▼▼ The Edgewater LH
(206) 728-7000. **$189-$415.** 2411 Alaskan Way-Pier 67. On waterfront at Pier 67. Int corridors. **Pets:** Accepted.

[ASK] [Sd] [✕] [🔇] [💻] [🍴] [✕]

▼▼▼ Executive Pacific Plaza Hotel SH ✿
(206) 623-3900. **$99-$109.** 400 Spring St. 4th Ave at Spring St. Int corridors. **Pets:** Small, dogs only. Service with restrictions.

[ASK] [Sd] [✕] [🔇] [🔋] [💻] [🔊]

🔺 ▼▼▼▼ The Fairmont Olympic Hotel, Seattle LH ✿
(206) 621-1700. **$295-$435.** 411 University St. At 4th Ave and University St. Int corridors. **Pets:** Small, other species. Designated rooms, service with restrictions.

[SAVE] [✕] [🔇] [🔊] [🔋] [💻] [🍴] [🏊] [✕]

▼▼▼ Homewood Suites by Hilton-Seattle/Downtown SH ✿
(206) 281-9393. **$109-$189.** 206 Western Ave W. I-5, exit 167 (Mercer St), 0.3 mi w, 0.5 mi s on Fairview, 1 mi w on Denny Way, then just n. Int corridors. **Pets:** Other species. $20 daily fee/pet.

[ASK] [Sd] [✕] [🔋] [💻]

🔺 ▼▼▼ Hotel Monaco LH ✿
(206) 621-1770. **$219-$299.** 1101 4th Ave. Corner of 4th Ave and Spring St. Int corridors. **Pets:** Other species. Crate.

[SAVE] [Sd] [✕] [🔇] [🔋] [💻] [🍴] [✕]

🔺 ▼▼▼ ▼▼▼ Hotel Vintage Park LH ✿
(206) 624-8000. **$179-$269.** 1100 5th Ave. Corner of Spring St and 5th Ave. Int corridors. **Pets:** Other species. Service with restrictions, crate.

[SAVE] [Sd] [✕] [🔇] [🍴]

(AAA) ▼▼▼▼ La Quinta Inn & Suites SH
(206) 624-6820. **$79-$149.** 2224 8th Ave. At 8th Ave and Blanchard. Int corridors. **Pets:** Service with restrictions, supervision.
SAVE Sₒ ✕ 🐾 🖥 ⬛ ✕

▼ Motel 6-736 M
(206) 824-9902. **$45-$61.** 20651 Military Rd. I-5, exit 151, just s. Ext corridors. **Pets:** Other species. Service with restrictions, supervision.
Sₒ ✕ 🐾 🖥 ⬛ ≈

(AAA) ▼▼▼▼ Ramada Inn Seattle at
Northgate SH 🐾
(206) 365-0700. **$109-$139.** 2140 N Northgate Way. I-5, exit 173, just nw. Ext corridors. **Pets:** Other species. Service with restrictions, crate.
SAVE Sₒ ✕ 🐾 🖥 ⬛ ≈

(AAA) ▼▼▼▼ Red Lion Hotel on Fifth
Avenue-Seattle LH
(206) 971-8000. **$119-$239.** 1415 5th Ave. Between Pike and Union sts. Int corridors. **Pets:** Medium. $50 one-time fee/room. Supervision.
SAVE Sₒ ✕ 🐾 🖥 &M 🖥 ⬛ ❙❙

▼▼ Residence Inn by Marriott Seattle
Downtown SH
(206) 624-6000. **$109-$169.** 800 Fairview Ave N. I-5, exit 167 (Mercer St), south end of Lake Union. Int corridors. **Pets:** $10 daily fee/pet.
ASK Sₒ ✕ 🐾 🖥 ⬛ ≈ ✕

(AAA) ▼▼▼▼ Sheraton Seattle Hotel &
Towers LH 🐾
(206) 621-9000. **$129-$269.** 1400 6th Ave. Corner of 6th Ave and Pike St. Int corridors. **Pets:** Large. Service with restrictions, supervision.
SAVE Sₒ ✕ 🐾 &M 🖥 ⬛ ❙❙ ≈ ✕

(AAA) ▼▼▼▼ Sorrento Hotel SH 🐾
(206) 622-6400. **$275.** 900 Madison St. I-5, exit Madison St, just e; at 9th Ave and Madison St. Int corridors. **Pets:** Other species. Designated rooms, service with restrictions, supervision.
SAVE Sₒ ✕ ⬛ ❙❙

(AAA) ▼▼▼ Travelodge by the Space Needle SH
(206) 441-7878. **$89-$169.** 200 6th Ave N. I-5, exit 167 (Mercer St), just n on Fairview Ave, just w via Valley and Broad sts, just s on 5th Ave, then just e on John St. Int corridors. **Pets:** Dogs only. $10 daily fee/room. Service with restrictions, supervision.
SAVE Sₒ ✕ 🐾 🖥 ⬛ ≈

(AAA) ▼▼▼▼ University Inn SH 🐾
(206) 632-5055. **$109-$139.** 4140 Roosevelt Way NE. I-5, exit 169, 0.5 mi e, then just s. Int corridors. **Pets:** Medium, dogs only. $10 daily fee/room. Designated rooms, service with restrictions, supervision.
SAVE Sₒ ✕ 🐾 🖥 ⬛ ❙❙ ≈

▼▼▼▼ Vance Hotel SH
(206) 441-4200. **$139.** 620 Stewart St. At 7th Ave and Stewart St. Int corridors. **Pets:** $25 one-time fee/room. Designated rooms, service with restrictions, supervision.
ASK Sₒ ✕ &M 🐾 &M 🖥 ⬛ ❙❙

(AAA) ▼▼▼▼ The Westin Seattle LH 🐾
(206) 728-1000. **$129-$199.** 1900 5th Ave. At 5th Ave and Stewart St. Int corridors. **Pets:** Medium, dogs only. Service with restrictions.
SAVE Sₒ ✕ &M 🐾 🖥 ⬛ ❙❙ ≈

SNOHOMISH

(AAA) ▼▼▼ Inn At Snohomish M
(360) 568-2208. **$65-$105.** 323 2nd St. East end of town. Ext corridors. **Pets:** Other species. $150 deposit/room. Service with restrictions, crate.
SAVE Sₒ ✕ 🖥 ⬛

TACOMA

(AAA) ▼▼▼▼ Best Western Tacoma Inn M 🐾
(253) 535-2880. **$79-$109.** 8726 S Hosmer St. I-5, exit 128 northbound, just se; exit 129 southbound, just e on 72nd St, then 1.2 mi s. Ext corridors. **Pets:** $20 one-time fee/room. Designated rooms, service with restrictions, crate.
SAVE Sₒ ✕ 🐾 &M 🖥 ⬛ ❙❙ ≈ ✕

▼▼▼▼ La Quinta Inn & Suites & Conference
Center SH 🐾
(253) 383-0146. **$99-$119.** 1425 E 27th St. I-5, exit 135 southbound; exit 134 northbound, just n. Int corridors. **Pets:** Dogs only. Service with restrictions, crate.
✕ 🐾 🖥 ⬛ ❙❙ ≈

(AAA) ▼▼▼▼ Sheraton Tacoma Hotel LH 🐾
(253) 572-3200. **$199.** 1320 Broadway Plaza. I-5, exit 133 (City Center) to I-705 N, exit A St, left on 11th, then left; downtown. Int corridors. **Pets:** Large. $250 deposit/room. Service with restrictions, crate.
SAVE Sₒ ✕ 🐾 🖥 ⬛ ❙❙

TUKWILA

(AAA) ▼▼▼▼ Comfort Suites Tukwila SH 🐾
(425) 227-7200. **$96-$131, 7 day notice.** 7200 Fun Center Way. I-405, exit 1 (SR 181), just n on Interurban Ave, then just e. Int corridors. **Pets:** Medium. $15 one-time fee/room. Designated rooms, service with restrictions, crate.
SAVE Sₒ ✕ &M 🐾 &M 🖥 ⬛ ≈ ✕

▼▼ Homestead Studio Suites
Hotel-Seattle/Southcenter M 🐾
(425) 235-7160. **$56-$81.** 15635 W Valley Hwy. I-405, exit 1 (SR 181), just s. Ext corridors. **Pets:** Medium, other species. $25 daily fee/room. Service with restrictions, crate.
ASK Sₒ ✕ &M 🐾 &M 🖥 ⬛

▼▼▼▼ Homewood Suites by Hilton SH
(206) 433-8000. **$109-$149.** 6955 Fort Dent Way. I-405, exit 1 (SR 181), just ne. Ext/int corridors. **Pets:** $20 daily fee/pet. Service with restrictions, supervision.
ASK Sₒ ✕ 🐾 🖥 ⬛ ≈ ✕

▼▼ Ramada Limited Sea-Tac Airport SH
(206) 244-8800. **$69-$109.** 13916 Tukwila International Blvd. I-5, exit 158 southbound, 2 mi s; exit 154 (SR 158 W) northbound, just w; exit 99 N, 1 mi n. Int corridors. **Pets:** Small. $20 daily fee/pet. Service with restrictions, supervision.
ASK Sₒ ✕ 🖥 ⬛

**AAA ▼▼▼ Residence Inn by Marriott-Seattle
South SH**
(425) 226-5500. **$115-$145.** 16201 W Valley Hwy. I-405, exit
1 (SR 181), just s. Ext corridors. **Pets:** Accepted.
[SAVE] [S🐾] [✕] [🔥M] [🎦] [🚫] [🛏] [💻] [🏊] [🚫]

VASHON

▼▼ The Swallow's Nest Guest Cottages CA ❀
(206) 463-2646. **$65-$250.** 6030 SW 248th St. From north
end Ferry Landing, 7.8 mi s on Vashon Hwy; from south
end (Tahlequah) Ferry Landing, 5.8 mi n on Vashon Hwy,
1.4 mi w on Quartermaster Dr, 1.5 mi s on Dockton Rd, 0.4
mi. Ext corridors. **Pets:** Other species. $10 daily fee/pet.
Designated rooms, service with restrictions, supervision.
[✕] [🛏] [💻] [🐾]

▼▼ Van Gelder's Retreat CA
(206) 463-3684. **$85-$120.** 18522 Beall Rd SW. From north
end Ferry Landing, 4.6 mi s on Vashon Hwy; from south
end (Tahlequah) Ferry Landing, 9 mi n on Vashon Hwy, 0.5
mi e on SW Bank Rd, then 0.6 mi s. Ext corridors.
Pets: Other species. Designated rooms, no service, supervision.
[ASK] [S🐾] [✕] [🎦] [🛏] [💻] [🐾] [🐾]

❀ END METROPOLITAN AREA ❀

SEDRO-WOOLLEY

AAA ▼▼▼ Three Rivers Inn M
(360) 855-2626. **$79-$83.** 210 Ball St. On SR 20, just w of jct
SR 9 N. Ext corridors. **Pets:** Small, other species. $10
one-time fee/pet. Service with restrictions, supervision.
[SAVE] [S🐾] [✕] [🔥M] [🛏] [💻] [🍴] [🐾]

SEQUIM

AAA ▼▼▼ Econo Lodge SH
(360) 683-7113. **$65-$104.** 801 E Washington St. US 101,
exit Sequim Ave, 0.4 mi n, then 0.6 mi e; east end of
downtown. Int corridors. **Pets:** Other species. $10 one-time
fee/pet. No service.
[SAVE] [S🐾] [✕] [🎦] [🛏]

AAA ▼▼▼ Ramada Limited SH
(360) 683-1775. **$59-$119.** 1095 E Washington St. US 101,
exit Sequim Ave, 0.4 mi n, then 0.9 mi e; east end of
downtown. Int corridors. **Pets:** Other species. $10 daily fee/
pet. Service with restrictions, supervision.
[SAVE] [✕] [🛏] [💻] [🐾]

AAA ▼▼▼ Sequim Bay Lodge M
(360) 683-0691. **$65-$113, 7 day notice.** 268522 US 101.
3.2 mi se of town. Ext corridors. **Pets:** Accepted.
[SAVE] [S🐾] [✕] [🎦] [🛏] [💻] [🐾]

AAA ▼▼▼ Sequim West Inn M
(360) 683-4144. **$68-$115.** 740 W Washington St. US 101,
exit River Rd, 0.9 mi ne via River Rd and W Washington St.
Ext corridors. **Pets:** Small, dogs only. $10 daily fee/pet.
Service with restrictions, supervision.
[SAVE] [S🐾] [✕] [🛏] [💻]

SHELTON

▼▼ Super 8 Motel of Shelton SH
(360) 426-1654. **$56-$82, 3 day notice.** 2943 Northview Cir.
US 101, exit Wallace-Kneeland Blvd, just se. Int corridors.
Pets: Small. $20 daily fee/pet. Service with restrictions,
supervision.
[ASK] [S🐾] [✕] [🛏] [💻]

SILVERDALE

▼▼ Cimarron Motel SH
(360) 692-7777. **$79-$89.** 9734 NW Silverdale Way. Downtown. Int corridors. **Pets:** Small, dogs only. $10 deposit/
room. Designated rooms, service with restrictions,
supervision.
[ASK] [S🐾] [✕] [🛏] [💻]

▼▼▼▼ Red Lion Hotel Silverdale SH
(360) 698-1000. **$107-$127.** 3073 NW Bucklin Hill Rd. On
the shoreline at north end of Dyes Inlet. Int corridors.
Pets: Dogs only. $20 daily fee/room. Designated rooms,
service with restrictions, crate.
[ASK] [S🐾] [✕] [🎦] [🛏] [💻] [🍴] [🐾] [🚫]

SKYKOMISH

AAA ▼▼▼ SkyRiver Inn M ❀
(360) 677-2261. **$83-$115, 14 day notice.** 333 River Dr E.
16 mi w of Stevens Pass on US 2; south end of Skykomish
River Bridge. Ext/int corridors. **Pets:** Other species. $5 daily
fee/pet. Service with restrictions.
[SAVE] [✕] [🛏] [💻]

SNOQUALMIE PASS

AAA ▼▼▼ Best Western Summitt Inn SH
(425) 434-6300. **$109-$199, 3 day notice.** 603 SR 906. I-90,
exit 52 eastbound, 0.3 mi e; exit 53 westbound, 0.3 mi w.
Int corridors. **Pets:** Other species. $15 one-time fee/room.
Designated rooms, no service.
[SAVE] [S🐾] [✕] [🛏] [💻] [🍴] [🐾]

SOAP LAKE

▼▼▼ Notaras Lodge M
(509) 246-0462. **$65-$110.** 236 E Main Ave. Just w of SR
17. Ext corridors. **Pets:** Accepted.
[✕] [🛏] [💻]

SOUTH BEND

▼▼▼ The Russell House BB
(360) 875-6487. **$75-$100, 7 day notice.** 902 E Water St.
0.5 mi s on Harrison. Int corridors. **Pets:** Accepted.
[ASK] [S🐾] [✕] [🔥]

SPOKANE

▼▼ Alpine Motel 🅼 ❁
(509) 928-2700. **$50-$75.** 18815 E Cataldo. I-90, exit 293, just n. Ext corridors. **Pets:** Other species. $10 daily fee/pet. Designated rooms, service with restrictions, supervision.

🄰🅂🄺 🎦 ✕ 🔳 🛢 ✕

⨀ ▼▼ Apple Tree Inn 🅼 ❁
(509) 466-3020. **$49-$59.** 9508 N Division St. Jct of US 2 and 395, just n. Ext/int corridors. **Pets:** Small, dogs only. $10 daily fee/pet. Designated rooms, service with restrictions, crate.

🆂🅰🆅🅴 🎦 ✕ 🛢 ⇌

▼▼ Best Value Thunderbird Inn 🅼
(509) 747-2011. **$79-$109.** 120 W 3rd Ave. I-90, exit 281 (Division St), just n, then just w on 2nd Ave. Ext corridors. **Pets:** Small. $10 daily fee/pet. Service with restrictions, supervision.

🄰🅂🄺 🎦 ✕ 🖌 🛢 🖥 ⇌

⨀ ▼◆ Best Western Pheasant Hill 🆂🅷
(509) 926-7432. **$89-$109.** 12415 E Mission. I-90, exit 289, just se. Int corridors. **Pets:** Dogs only. $10 daily fee/pet. Designated rooms, service with restrictions, supervision.

🆂🅰🆅🅴 🎦 ✕ 🖴 🖌 🛢 🖥 ⇌

⨀ ▼◆ Best Western Trade Winds North 🅼 ❁
(509) 326-5500. **$64-$120, 14 day notice.** 3033 N Division St. I-90, exit 281 (Division St), 2.3 mi n on US 2 and 395 (Division St). Ext/int corridors. **Pets:** Other species. Service with restrictions, supervision.

🆂🅰🆅🅴 ✕ 🛢 🖥 ⇌

⨀ ▼▼ Broadway Inn & Suites 🆂🅷 ❁
(509) 535-7185. **$39-$129.** 6309 E Broadway. I-90, exit 286, just w. Ext/int corridors. **Pets:** Other species. Service with restrictions, crate.

🆂🅰🆅🅴 🎦 ✕ 🖌 🛢 🖥 ⇌

⨀ ▼▼ Clinic Center Inn 🅼
(509) 747-6081. **$38-$46.** 702 S McClellan St. I-90, exit 281 (Division St) eastbound, just s to 5th, just w to Browne, just sw, then just s; exit westbound, just n to 2nd, just w to Browne, 0.5 mi s to Ninth, just e, then just s. Ext corridors. **Pets:** Other species. $5 daily fee/pet. Supervision.

🆂🅰🆅🅴 🖥

▼▼ Comfort Inn North 🆂🅷 ❁
(509) 467-7111. **$47-$89.** 7111 N Division St. I-90, exit 281 (Division St), 4.6 mi n. Int corridors. **Pets:** Large. $7 daily fee/pet. Designated rooms, service with restrictions, supervision.

🄰🅂🄺 🎦 ✕ 🖥 ⇌ ✕

▼▼ Comfort Inn Valley 🆂🅷
(509) 924-3838. **$59-$99.** 905 N Sullivan Rd. I-90, exit 291B, just s. Int corridors. **Pets:** Accepted.

🄰🅂🄺 🎦 ✕ 🛢 🖥 ⇌

⨀ ▼▼▼ The Davenport Hotel 🅻🅷 ❁
(509) 455-8888. **$155-$235.** 10 S Post St. Downtown. Int corridors. **Pets:** Other species.

🆂🅰🆅🅴 🎦 ✕ 🖴 🖌 🖌 🛢 🍽 ⇌ ✕

⨀ ▼▼ Days Inn Spokane Airport 🆂🅷
(509) 747-2021. **$69-$79.** 4212 W Sunset Blvd. I-90, exit 277A eastbound, 1 mi on Garden Spring Rd; exit 277 westbound, just n on Rustle. Ext corridors. **Pets:** Accepted.

🆂🅰🆅🅴 🎦 ✕ 🖌 🛢 🍽 ⇌

▼▼▼ Doubletree Hotel Spokane City Center 🅻🅷
(509) 455-9600. **$174-$514.** 322 N Spokane Falls Ct. I-90, exit 281 (Division St), just n; downtown. Int corridors. **Pets:** Accepted.

🄰🅂🄺 🎦 ✕ 🖌 🛢 🖥 🍽 ⇌

▼▼▼ Holiday Inn Express-Valley 🆂🅷 ❁
(509) 927-7100. **$79-$169.** 9220 E Mission. I-90, exit 287, just s. Ext/int corridors. **Pets:** Dogs only. Designated rooms, service with restrictions, supervision.

🄰🅂🄺 🎦 ✕ 🖴 🖌 🖌 🛢 🖥 ⇌ ✕

▼▼ Holiday Inn Spokane Airport 🆂🅷 ❁
(509) 838-1170. **$89-$119.** 1616 S Windsor Dr. I-90, exit 277 westbound; exit 277B eastbound, just w on US 2, then just s. Int corridors. **Pets:** Medium. $20 one-time fee/room. Designated rooms, service with restrictions, supervision.

🄰🅂🄺 🎦 ✕ 🖴 🖌 🖌 🛢 🖥 🍽 ⇌

▼▼ Howard Johnson Inn 🆂🅷
(509) 838-6630. **$50-$100.** 211 S Division St. I-90, exit 281 (Division St), just n. Int corridors. **Pets:** Small. $10 daily fee/pet. Designated rooms, service with restrictions, supervision.

🄰🅂🄺 🎦 ✕ 🖌 🛢 🖥

⨀ ▼▼▼ La Quinta Inn & Suites 🆂🅷
(509) 893-0955. **$59-$89.** 3808 N Sullivan Rd. I-90, exit 291B, 1.3 mi n. Int corridors. **Pets:** Other species. Service with restrictions, supervision.

🆂🅰🆅🅴 🎦 ✕ 🖴 🖌 🖌 🛢 🖥 ⇌

⨀ ▼▼▼ Madison Inn 🆂🅷 ❁
(509) 474-4200. **$64-$69.** 15 W Rockwood Blvd. I-90, exit 281 (Division St) eastbound, just e to Cowley, 0.4 mi s, then just w; westbound, just n to 2nd Ave, just w to Browne, 0.5 mi s to Ninth, then just e. Int corridors. **Pets:** Other species. $5 daily fee/pet. Designated rooms, service with restrictions, supervision.

🆂🅰🆅🅴 🎦 ✕ 🖴 🖌 🛢 🖥

⨀ ▼▼ Mirabeau Park Hotel and Convention Center 🆂🅷
(509) 924-9000. **$69-$129.** 1100 N Sullivan Rd. I-90, exit 291B, just s. Int corridors. **Pets:** Other species. Service with restrictions.

🆂🅰🆅🅴 🎦 ✕ 🖌 🛢 🖥 🍽 ⇌ ✕

▼▼▼ Oxford Suites-Downtown Spokane 🆂🅷
(509) 353-9000. **$89-$149.** 115 W North River Dr. I-90, exit 281 (Division St), 1 mi n, then just n. Int corridors. **Pets:** Small, dogs only. $15 one-time fee/pet. Designated rooms, service with restrictions, supervision.

🄰🅂🄺 🎦 ✕ 🖌 🖌 🛢 🖥 ⇌ ✕

▼▼▼ Oxford Suites Spokane Valley 🆂🅷
(509) 847-1000. **$99-$139.** 15015 E Indiana Ave. I-90, exit 291A eastbound; exit 291B westbound, just nw. Int corridors. **Pets:** Medium. $10 daily fee/room. Service with restrictions, supervision.

🄰🅂🄺 🎦 ✕ 🖴 🖌 🖌 🛢 🖥 ⇌ ✕

Quality Inn Oakwood SH
(509) 467-4900. **$63-$80.** 7919 N Division St. I-90, exit 281 (Division St), 6.5 mi n. Int corridors. **Pets:** Small. $20 one-time fee/room. Designated rooms, service with restrictions, supervision.

Quality Inn Valley Suites SH
(509) 928-5218. **$89-$177.** 8923 E Mission. I-90, exit 287. Int corridors. **Pets:** Medium. $50 deposit/room. Designated rooms, service with restrictions, supervision.

Ramada Inn Airport SH
(509) 838-5211. **$93-$99.** 8909 Airport Dr. I-90, exit 277B eastbound; exit 277 westbound, 3.4 mi n. Int corridors. **Pets:** Medium. Service with restrictions, supervision.

Ramada Limited M
(509) 838-8504. **$59-$69.** 123 S Post St. I-90, exit 280B (Lincoln St), just n to 1st Ave W, just e to Post St, then just s. Ext corridors. **Pets:** Accepted.

Ramada Limited Suites SH
(509) 468-4201. **$79-$89.** 9601 N Newport Hwy. US 2 and 395, just n on Newport Hwy (US 2). Int corridors. **Pets:** Accepted.

Red Lion Hotel at the Park–Spokane LH ❀
(509) 326-8000. **$79-$109.** 303 W North River Dr. I-90, exit 281 (Division St), 1.5 mi n on US 195, then just w. Int corridors. **Pets:** Large, other species. Designated rooms, service with restrictions.

Red Lion River Inn–Spokane SH ❀
(509) 326-5577. **$69-$99.** N 700 Division St. I-90, exit 281 (Division St), 0.8 mi n; downtown. Int corridors. **Pets:** Other species. $75 deposit/room. Service with restrictions, supervision.

Residence Inn by Marriott SH ❀
(509) 892-9300. **$80-$125.** 15915 E Indiana. I-90, exit 291 westbound, just e; exit 291B eastbound, just n, then just e. Int corridors. **Pets:** Small. $10 daily fee/pet, $50 one-time fee/pet. Designated rooms, service with restrictions, supervision.

Shangri-La Motel M
(509) 747-2066. **$41-$46.** 2922 W Government Way. I-90, exit 277A eastbound; exit 277 westbound, Garden Springs Rd to Sunset Blvd, 1 mi e to Government Way, just n to Hartson. Ext corridors. **Pets:** Dogs only. Supervision.

Super 8 Motel SH
(509) 928-4888. **$50-$80.** N 2020 Argonne Rd. I-90, exit 287, just n. Int corridors. **Pets:** Accepted.

Super 8 West SH
(509) 838-8800. **$69-$79.** 11102 W Westbow Blvd. I-90, exit 272 (Medical Lake), just s. Int corridors. **Pets:** Accepted.

Travelodge SH ❀
(509) 623-9727. **$60-$99.** W 33 Spokane Falls Blvd. I-90, exit 281 (Division St), 0.5 mi n, just w. Int corridors. **Pets:** Medium, other species. $10 daily fee/pet. Designated rooms, service with restrictions.

Travelodge Hotel SH
(509) 838-1471. **$65-$70.** W 4301 Sunset Blvd. I-90, exit 277A eastbound, 1 mi n on Garden Springs Rd; exit 277 westbound, just n on Rustle. Int corridors. **Pets:** Accepted.

STEVENSON

Dolce Skamania Lodge LH ❀
(509) 427-7700. **$169-$359, 5 day notice.** 1131 SW Skamania Lodge Way. West of town on SR 14. Int corridors. **Pets:** $50 one-time fee/room. Designated rooms, service with restrictions, supervision.

SULTAN

Dutch Cup Motel M
(360) 793-2215. **$68-$76, 7 day notice.** 918 Main St. Jct US 2 and Main St. Ext corridors. **Pets:** Medium, other species. $8 daily fee/room. Service with restrictions, supervision.

SUNNYSIDE

Rodeway Inn SH
(509) 837-5781. **$89-$109.** 3209 Picard Pl. I-82, exit 69, just n. Int corridors. **Pets:** $10 daily fee/pet. Service with restrictions, supervision.

TOPPENISH

Best Western Lincoln Inn SH ❀
(509) 865-7444. **$79-$119.** 515 S Elm St. I-82, exit 50, 3.1 mi e. Int corridors. **Pets:** Small, dogs only. $10 daily fee/pet. Designated rooms, service with restrictions, supervision.

TUMWATER

Best Western Tumwater Inn SH
(360) 956-1235. **$70-$85.** 5188 Capitol Blvd. I-5, exit 102, just e. Int corridors. **Pets:** Other species. $5 daily fee/room.

Comfort Inn and Conference Center SH ❀
(360) 352-0691. **$79-$85.** 1620 74th Ave SW. I-5, exit 101, just se. Int corridors. **Pets:** $10 daily fee/pet. Service with restrictions, crate.

▼▼▼▼ GuestHouse Inn & Suites SH
(360) 943-5040. **$85-$105.** 1600 74th Ave SW. I-5, exit 101, just se. Int corridors. **Pets:** Accepted.
(ASK) (S⊘) (✕) (&M) (⊘) (🖈) (🛏) (💻) (⇄)

▼ Motel 6–77 M
(360) 754-7320. **$43-$55.** 400 W Lee St. I-5, exit 102, just e on Trosper Rd, just s on Capital Blvd, then just w. Ext corridors. **Pets:** Accepted.
(S⊘) (✕) (🖈) (🛏) (⇄)

TWISP

AAA ▼▼▼ Idle-A-While Motel M ❀
(509) 997-3222. **$46-$89, 5 day notice.** 505 N SR 20. Just n of town. Ext corridors. **Pets:** Dogs only. $5 daily fee/pet. Service with restrictions, supervision.
(SAVE) (S⊘) (✕) (🛏) (💻) (⇄)

UNION GAP

▼▼▼▼ Best Western Ahtanum Inn SH
(509) 248-9700. **$99-$119.** 2408 Rudkin Rd. I-82, exit 36, just n. Int corridors. **Pets:** Accepted.
(ASK) (S⊘) (✕) (&M) (🛏) (💻) (⇄) (⊠)

AAA ▼▼▼▼ Quality Inn-Yakima Valley M 🐾
(509) 248-6924. **$69-$119.** 12 E Valley Mall Blvd. I-82, exit 36, just s. Ext corridors. **Pets:** Small, dogs only. $10 daily fee/pet. Designated rooms, service with restrictions, supervision.
(SAVE) (S⊘) (✕) (&M) (⊘) (🖈) (🛏) (💻) (⇄)

▼▼ Super 8 Motel Yakima SH
(509) 248-8880. **$60-$71.** 2605 Rudkin Rd. I-82, exit 36, just s. Int corridors. **Pets:** $25 deposit/room. Service with restrictions, crate.
(ASK) (S⊘) (✕) (⊘) (⇄)

WALLA WALLA

AAA ▼▼▼ Best Western Walla Walla Suites Inn SH
(509) 525-4700. **$74-$119.** 7 E Oak St. US 12, exit 2nd Ave, just s. Int corridors. **Pets:** Dogs only. $10 daily fee/pet. Service with restrictions, crate.
(SAVE) (S⊘) (✕) (&M) (⊘) (🖈) (🛏) (💻) (⇄)

AAA ▼ Budget Inn M
(509) 529-4410. **$55-$75.** 305 N 2nd St. US 12, exit 2nd Ave, 0.3 mi s. Ext corridors. **Pets:** Medium. $7 daily fee/pet. Service with restrictions, supervision.
(SAVE) (S⊘) (✕) (🛏) (⇄)

▼▼▼ Holiday Inn Express SH
(509) 525-6200. **$69-$129.** 1433 W Pine St. US 12, exit Pendleton/Prescott. Int corridors. **Pets:** Accepted.
(ASK) (S⊘) (✕) (🛏) (💻) (⇄) (⊠)

▼▼ Howard Johnson Express Inn SH ❀
(509) 529-4360. **$89-$129, 14 day notice.** 325 E Main. US 12, exit 2nd St, 0.5 mi s just e. Ext/int corridors. **Pets:** Large. Designated rooms, service with restrictions, supervision.
(ASK) (S⊘) (✕) (🛏) (💻) (⇄) (⊠)

AAA ▼▼▼▼ La Quinta Inn SH
(509) 525-2522. **$59-$99.** 520 N 2nd Ave. US 12, exit 2nd St, just s. Int corridors. **Pets:** Other species. Service with restrictions, supervision.
(SAVE) (S⊘) (✕) (⊘) (🛏) (💻) (⇄) (⊠)

▼▼ Walla Walla Super 8 SH
(509) 525-8800. **$46-$74.** 2315 Eastgate St N. US 12, exit Wilbur, just s. Int corridors. **Pets:** Accepted.
(ASK) (S⊘) (✕) (&M) (⊘) (🖈) (🛏) (⇄)

AAA ▼▼▼ Walla Walla Travelodge M
(509) 529-4940. **$75-$85.** 421 E Main. US 12, exit 2nd Ave, 0.5 mi s, then just e. Ext/int corridors. **Pets:** Medium. $7 daily fee/pet. Service with restrictions, supervision.
(SAVE) (S⊘) (✕) (🛏) (💻) (⇄)

WENATCHEE

▼▼ Avenue Motel M
(509) 663-7161. **$47-$66, 5 day notice.** 720 N Wenatchee Ave. On US 2 business loop; just nw of downtown. Ext/int corridors. **Pets:** Dogs only. $5 daily fee/room. Service with restrictions, supervision.
(✕) (🛏) (💻) (⇄)

AAA ▼▼▼▼ Coast Wenatchee Center Hotel LH
(509) 662-1234. **$95-$125.** 201 N Wenatchee Ave. Downtown. Int corridors. **Pets:** $10 daily fee/room. Service with restrictions, supervision.
(SAVE) (S⊘) (✕) (🛏) (💻) (🍴) (⇄)

▼▼▼ Comfort Inn SH
(509) 662-1700. **$81-$99.** 815 N Wenatchee Ave. Downtown. Int corridors. **Pets:** $10 daily fee/pet. Service with restrictions, supervision.
(ASK) (S⊘) (✕) (🖈) (🛏) (💻) (⇄)

▼▼▼ Holiday Inn Express SH
(509) 663-6355. **$75-$99.** 1921 N Wenatchee Ave. Northwest side of town. Int corridors. **Pets:** Accepted.
(ASK) (S⊘) (✕) (&M) (⊘) (🖈) (🛏) (💻) (⇄)

AAA ▼▼▼▼ La Quinta Inn & Suites SH ❀
(509) 664-6565. **$55-$90, 7 day notice.** 1905 N Wenatchee Ave. West end of town. Int corridors. **Pets:** Other species. Designated rooms, service with restrictions, supervision.
(SAVE) (S⊘) (✕) (⊘) (🖈) (🛏) (💻) (⇄) (⊠)

AAA ▼▼▼ Orchard Inn SH
(509) 662-3443. **$50-$65.** 1401 N Miller St. 1.5 mi n on US 2. Int corridors. **Pets:** Dogs only. $10 daily fee/pet. Designated rooms, service with restrictions, supervision.
(SAVE) (S⊘) (✕) (🛏) (⇄)

AAA ▼▼▼▼ Red Lion Hotel Wenatchee LH
(509) 663-0711. **$59-$95.** 1225 N Wenatchee Ave. Just nw of downtown. Int corridors. **Pets:** Accepted.
(SAVE) (S⊘) (✕) (⊘) (🛏) (💻) (🍴) (⇄)

WESTPORT

▼▼ CoHo Motel M
(360) 268-0111. **$52-$75, 3 day notice.** 2501 N Nyhus. Just e of boat basin. Ext corridors. **Pets:** Very small. $10 daily fee/pet. Designated rooms, service with restrictions, supervision.
(✕) (🛏) (⊠) (🐾)

▼▼ Windjammer Motel M ✻
(360) 268-9351. **$45-$50.** 461 E Pacific Ave. Downtown. Ext corridors. **Pets:** $10 daily fee/pet. Service with restrictions, supervision.
⊠ 📠 💻 📺 🏊

WINTHROP

AAA ▼▼▼ Best Western Cascade Inn M ✻
(509) 996-3100. **$65-$159, 3 day notice.** 960 SR 20. 0.8 mi e. Ext corridors. **Pets:** Small, dogs only. $10 daily fee/pet. Designated rooms, service with restrictions, supervision.
SAVE 🔊 ⊠ 📠 💻 🏊 🏊

AAA ▼▼▼ River Run Inn M
(509) 996-2173. **$70-$110, 7 day notice.** 27 Rader Rd. 0.5 mi w of town on SR 20. Ext corridors. **Pets:** Dogs only. $10 daily fee/pet. Service with restrictions, supervision.
SAVE ⊠ 📠 💻 🏊 🏊

AAA ▼▼▼ Winthrop Inn M ✻
(509) 996-2217. **$65-$95.** 960 SR 20. 1 mi e. Int corridors. **Pets:** Medium, dogs only. $10 daily fee/pet. Supervision.
SAVE 🔊 ⊠ 📠 🏊 🏊

WOODLAND

AAA ▼▼▼ Econo Lodge M
(360) 225-6548. **$54-$74.** 1500 Atlantic St. I-5, exit 21, just ne. Ext corridors. **Pets:** $10 daily fee/pet. Supervision.
SAVE 🔊 ⊠ 📠 🏊

AAA ▼▼▼ Lewis River Inn M
(360) 225-6257. **$56-$73.** 1100 Lewis River Rd. I-5, exit 21, just e. Ext corridors. **Pets:** $6 daily fee/pet. Designated rooms, service with restrictions, supervision.
SAVE 🔊 ⊠ 📠 💻

YAKIMA

▼▼ Cedars Inn and Suites M
(509) 452-8101. **$51-$67.** 1010 East A St. I-82, exit 33B eastbound; exit 33 westbound, just w to 9th St, just n to A St, then just e. Ext corridors. **Pets:** Small, dogs only. $7 daily fee/pet. Service with restrictions, supervision.
ASK 🔊 ⊠ 📠

AAA ▼▼▼ Comfort Suites-Yakima SH
(509) 249-1900. **$89-$129.** 3702 Fruitvale Blvd. US 12, exit 40th Ave, just s. Int corridors. **Pets:** Very small, dogs only. $10 daily fee/pet. Service with restrictions, supervision.
SAVE 🔊 ⊠ 📺 📠 🗂 📠 💻 🏊

▼▼▼ Holiday Inn Express Yakima SH
(509) 249-1000. **$55-$85.** 1001 East A St. I-82, exit 33B eastbound; exit 33 westbound, just w to 9th St, just n to A St, then just e. Int corridors. **Pets:** Small, dogs only. $6 daily fee/room. Supervision.
⊠ 📺 🗂 📠 📠 🏊

▼▼▼ Oxford Inn SH
(509) 457-4444. **$69.** 1603 E Yakima Ave. I-82, exit 33 west-bound, just e; exit 33B eastbound. Int corridors. **Pets:** Accepted.
ASK 🔊 ⊠ 📺 🗂 📠 📠 💻 🏊 🏊

▼▼▼ Oxford Suites SH
(509) 457-9000. **$89-$199.** 1701 E Yakima Ave. I-82, exit 33 westbound; exit 33B eastbound. Int corridors. **Pets:** Small. $20 one-time fee/room. Service with restrictions.
ASK 🔊 ⊠ 📺 🗂 📠 📠 💻 🏊 🏊

▼▼ Ramada Limited M
(509) 453-0391. **$59-$99.** 818 N 1st St. I-82, exit 31, 1.2 mi s. Ext corridors. **Pets:** Accepted.
ASK 🔊 ⊠ 🗂 📠 📠 💻 🏊

▼▼▼ Red Lion Hotel Yakima Center SH
(509) 248-5900. **$79-$119.** 607 E Yakima Ave. I-82, exit 33 westbound; exit 33B eastbound, 0.8 mi w. Ext/int corridors. **Pets:** Medium. $5 daily fee/pet. Service with restrictions, crate.
ASK 🔊 ⊠ 🗂 📠 💻 🍴 🏊

▼▼▼ Red Lion Hotel Yakima Gateway SH
(509) 452-6511. **$89-$129.** 9 N 9th St. I-82, exit 33 west-bound; exit 33B eastbound, just s. Int corridors. **Pets:** Large. $5 daily fee/pet. Service with restrictions, crate.
ASK 🔊 ⊠ 🗂 📠 💻 🍴 🏊

▼▼ Yakima Valley Conference Center & Hotel SH
(509) 248-7850. **$67-$149.** 1507 N 1st St. I-82, exit 31, 0.5 mi s. Int corridors. **Pets:** Small. $15 one-time fee/pet. Service with restrictions, supervision.
⊠ 🗂 📺 🗂 📠 💻 🍴 🏊 🏊

ZILLAH

▼▼▼ Comfort Inn SH
(509) 829-3399. **$69-$159.** 911 Vintage Valley Pkwy. I-82, exit 52, just n. Int corridors. **Pets:** Other species. $10 daily fee/pet.
ASK 🔊 ⊠ 🗂 📺 📠 💻 🏊

CITY INDEX

BARBOURSVILLE

▼▼▼ Comfort Inn-Barboursville SH
(304) 733-2122. **$119-$279.** 249 Mall Rd. I-64, exit 20, 0.4 mi n. Int corridors. **Pets:** Small. $20 one-time fee/pet. Service with restrictions, supervision.

BECKLEY

◆◆◆ ▼▼▼ Best Western Four Seasons Inn SH
(304) 252-0671. **$69-$109.** 1939 Mall Rd. I-64/77, exit 44, just e on SR 3. Ext/int corridors. **Pets:** Small. $5 daily fee/pet. Designated rooms, service with restrictions, supervision.

▼▼ Comfort Inn SH 🐾
(304) 255-2161. **$65-$100.** 1909 Harper Rd. I-64/77, exit 44, 0.3 mi e on SR 3. Ext/int corridors. **Pets:** Other species. Service with restrictions, crate.

[icons]

◆◆◆ ▼▼▼ Country Inn & Suites By Carlson SH
(304) 252-5100. **$81-$140.** 2120 Harper Rd. I-64/77, exit 44, just w on SR 3. Int corridors. **Pets:** Small. $25 one-time fee/pet. Designated rooms, service with restrictions, supervision.

[icons]

▼▼ Microtel Inn SH
(304) 256-2000. **$45-$80.** 2130 Harper Rd. I-64/77, exit 44. Int corridors. **Pets:** Other species. $25 one-time fee/room. Designated rooms, service with restrictions, crate.

[icons]

◆◆◆ ▼▼▼ Park Inn & Suites SH
(304) 255-9091. **$63-$99.** 134 Harper Park Dr. I-64/77, exit 44, just w on SR 3. Int corridors. **Pets:** Medium. $10 one-time fee/pet. Service with restrictions, supervision.

[icons]

BLUEFIELD

▼▼▼ East River Mountain Inn SH
(304) 325-5421. **$68-$83.** 3175 E Cumberland Rd. I-77, exit 1, 3.8 mi nw via US 52/460, then 0.7 mi n on US 52. Ext corridors. **Pets:** Accepted.

[icons]

◆◆◆ ▼▼ Econo Lodge M
(304) 327-8171. **$44-$135.** 3400 Cumberland Rd. I-77, exit 1, 3.8 mi nw via US 52/460, 0.4 mi n on US 52. Ext corridors. **Pets:** Dogs only. $10 daily fee/pet. Designated rooms, service with restrictions, supervision.

[icons]

◆◆◆ ▼▼▼ Holiday Inn-On The Hill SH
(304) 325-6170. **$75-$110.** 3350 Big Laurel Hwy. I-77, exit 1, 3.8 mi nw via US 52/460. Int corridors. **Pets:** Medium. Service with restrictions.

[icons]

BRIDGEPORT

◆◆◆ ▼▼▼ Holiday Inn Clarksburg-Bridgeport SH
(304) 842-5411. **$62-$79.** 100 Lodgeville Rd. I-79, exit 119, just e on US 50. Int corridors. **Pets:** Accepted.

[icons]

▼▼▼ Knights Inn-Clarksburg M 🐾
(304) 842-7115. **$54-$85.** 1235 W Main St. I-79, exit 119, 0.3 mi e on US 50. Ext corridors. **Pets:** Large, other species. Service with restrictions.

[icons]

▼▼▼ Sleep Inn M
(304) 842-1919. **$69.** 115 Tolley Dr. I-79, exit 119, just e on US 50. Int corridors. **Pets:** Accepted.

[icons]

CHAPMANVILLE

▼▼▼ Rodeway Inn M
(304) 855-7182. **$53-$55.** Rt 10/119. Jct US 119, just s on SR 10. Ext/int corridors. **Pets:** Medium. $5 daily fee/pet. Service with restrictions, supervision.

[icons]

CHARLESTON

▼▼▼ Days Inn Charleston East M
(304) 925-1010. **Call for rates.** 6400 MacCorkle Ave. I-77, exit 95, just s on SR 61. Int corridors. **Pets:** Accepted.

[icons]

▼▼▼ Holiday Inn Express Civic Center SH
(304) 345-0600. **$86-$100.** 100 Civic Center Dr. I-64, exit 58B eastbound; exit 58C westbound, just s; downtown. Int corridors. **Pets:** Small. $15 one-time fee/pet. Designated rooms, service with restrictions, supervision.

[icons]

Knights Inn-Charleston East M
(304) 925-0451. **$45-$60.** 6401 MacCorkle Ave SE. I-77, exit 95, just s on SR 61. Ext corridors. **Pets:** Medium. $15 one-time fee/room. Service with restrictions, crate.

Red Roof Inn-Kanawha City M
(304) 925-6953. **$44-$59.** 6305 SE MacCorkle Ave. I-77, exit 95, just s on SR 61. Ext corridors. **Pets:** Accepted.

CROSS LANES

Comfort Inn West Charleston SH
(304) 776-8070. **$69-$79.** 102 Racer Dr. I-64, exit 47, just s. Int corridors. **Pets:** Other species. $10 daily fee/pet. Designated rooms, service with restrictions, supervision.

DAVIS

Deerfield Village Resort-Canaan Valley CO
(304) 866-4698. **$140-$275, 10 day notice.** Cortland Ln. 7 mi s on SR 32. Ext corridors. **Pets:** Medium, other species. $75 one-time fee/pet. No service, supervision.

ELKINS

Best Country Inn & Suites M
(304) 636-7711. **$58-$120, 3 day notice.** Route 219/250 S. 0.9 mi s of SR 219. Ext/int corridors. **Pets:** Other species. $10 daily fee/room. Service with restrictions.

Cheat River Lodge & Inn CA
(304) 636-2301. **$68-$83, 30 day notice.** Rt 1, Box 115, Faulkner Rd. 4.8 mi e on US 33, then 1.5 mi ne. Ext corridors. **Pets:** Other species. $10 daily fee/pet. Service with restrictions, supervision.

Econo Lodge M
(304) 636-5311. **$50-$75.** US 33 E. 1 mi e. Ext/int corridors. **Pets:** Accepted.

Elkins Days Inn SH
(304) 637-4667. **$65-$89, 3 day notice.** 1200 Harrison Ave. 1 mi w on US 33/250/SR 92; downtown. Int corridors. **Pets:** Other species. $5 daily fee/pet. Service with restrictions, supervision.

FAIRMONT

Days Inn SH
(304) 366-5995. **$47-$95, 21 day notice.** 228 Middletown Rd. I-79, exit 132, just se on US 250, then just s. Ext corridors. **Pets:** Small, dogs only. $10 one-time fee/pet. Designated rooms, service with restrictions, supervision.

Holiday Inn Fairmont SH
(304) 366-5500. **$59-$99.** 930 E Grafton Rd. I-79, exit 137, just e. Int corridors. **Pets:** Accepted.

Red Roof Inn M
(304) 366-6800. **$42-$49.** 50 Middletown Rd. I-79, exit 132, 0.3 mi s on US 250, just w, then just s. Ext corridors. **Pets:** Accepted.

Super 8 Motel M
(304) 363-1488. **$57-$77.** 2208 Pleasant Valley Rd. I-79, exit 133, just e. Int corridors. **Pets:** Service with restrictions, crate.

FAYETTEVILLE

White Horse Bed & Breakfast BB
(304) 574-1400. **Call for rates (no credit cards).** 120 Fayette Ave. US 19, 0.4 mi e on Court St, just n. Ext/int corridors. **Pets:** Accepted.

HUNTINGTON

Red Roof Inn SH
(304) 733-3737. **$42-$59.** 5190 US Rt 60 E. I-64, exit 15, just s. Ext corridors. **Pets:** Medium, other species. Service with restrictions, crate.

HURRICANE

Red Roof Inn M
(304) 757-6392. **$42-$64.** 500 Putnam Village Dr. I-64, exit 39, just n on SR 34, just e. Ext corridors. **Pets:** Medium, other species. Service with restrictions, supervision.

Super 8 Motel-Hurricane M
(304) 562-3346. **$40-$56, 7 day notice.** 419 Hurricane Creek Rd. I-64, exit 34, just s. Ext corridors. **Pets:** Accepted.

JANE LEW

Wilderness Plantation Inn SH
(304) 884-7806. **$57-$65.** Rt 7 Berlin Rd. I-79, exit 105, just e, then 0.3 mi s. Ext corridors. **Pets:** $7 daily fee/pet. Service with restrictions, supervision.

KEYSER

Keyser Inn M
(304) 788-0913. **$49-$75.** Rt 220 S. On US 220, 2.3 mi s. Int corridors. **Pets:** Medium. $20 one-time fee/room. Service with restrictions, supervision.

LEWISBURG

Brier Inn SH
(304) 645-7722. **$54-$100.** 540 N Jefferson St. I-64, exit 169, just s on US 219. Ext corridors. **Pets:** Large, other species. $10 daily fee/pet. Designated rooms, crate.

🔷 🔷🔷 Days Inn SH
(304) 645-2345. **$55-$150, 3 day notice.** 635 N Jefferson St. I-64, exit 169, 0.3 mi n on US 219. Ext corridors. **Pets:** Small. $10 daily fee/pet. Designated rooms, service with restrictions, supervision.
SAVE 🔵 ❎ 🛏 💻

🔷🔷 Super 8 Motel SH
(304) 647-3188. **$57-$67.** 550 N Jefferson St. I-64, exit 169, just s on US 219. Int corridors. **Pets:** Accepted.
ASK 🔵 ❎ 🐾 🛏

MARTINSBURG

🔷🔷 Days Inn Martinsburg SH
(304) 263-1800. **$51-$62, 5 day notice.** 209 Viking Way. I-81, exit 13, just e on W King St (CR 15). Ext/int corridors. **Pets:** Medium. Service with restrictions, supervision.
ASK 🔵 ❎ 🛏 💻

🔷 🔷🔷 Econo Lodge M
(304) 274-2181. **$60-$65.** 5595 Hammonds Mill Rd. I-81, exit 20, just e. Ext/int corridors. **Pets:** Other species. Service with restrictions, supervision.
SAVE 🔵 ❎ 💻

🔷 🔷 Economy Inn M
(304) 267-2994. **$40-$58.** 1616 Winchester Ave (US 11 S). I-81, exit 12, 0.3 mi e on SR 45, 0.3 mi s. Ext corridors. **Pets:** Very small. $5 daily fee/pet. Designated rooms, no service, supervision.
SAVE ❎ 🛏 🐾

🔷🔷🔷 Hampton Inn SH
(304) 267-2900. **$74-$94.** 975 Foxcroft Ave. I-81, exit 12, just e on SR 45, then just n. Int corridors. **Pets:** Other species. Service with restrictions, supervision.
ASK ❎ 🐾 👶 💻 🐾

🔷🔷🔷 Holiday Inn Martinsburg SH
(304) 267-5500. **$69-$99.** 301 Foxcroft Ave. I-81, exit 13, just e on W King St (CR 15). Int corridors. **Pets:** Other species. Service with restrictions, supervision.
ASK 🔵 ❎ 🐾 👶 🛏 💻 🍴 🐾 ❌

🔷 🔷🔷 Knights Inn-Martinsburg M
(304) 267-2211. **$55-$65.** 1997 Edwin Miller Blvd. I-81, exit 16E, 0.4 mi e on SR 9. Ext corridors. **Pets:** Large, other species. $5 daily fee/pet. Designated rooms, service with restrictions.
SAVE 🔵 ❎ 🛏

🔷🔷 Martinsburg Travelodge M
(304) 263-8811. **$69-$99.** 94 McMillan Ct. I-81, exit 16E, just e. Ext/int corridors. **Pets:** $10 daily fee/pet. Designated rooms, service with restrictions, supervision.
ASK 🔵 ❎ 🛏 💻 🐾 ❌

🔷 🔷 Relax Inn M 🐾
(304) 263-0831. **$30-$59, 3 day notice.** 1022 Winchester Ave (US 11 N). I-81, exit 12, 0.3 mi e on SR 45, then just n. Ext corridors. **Pets:** $5 daily fee/pet. Service with restrictions, supervision.
SAVE ❎ 🛏 🐾

🔷 🔷 Scottish Inns M
(304) 267-2935. **$40-$60.** 1024 Winchester Ave (US 11 N). I-81, exit 12, 0.3 mi e on SR 45, just n. Ext corridors. **Pets:** Medium. $5 daily fee/pet. Designated rooms, no service, supervision.
SAVE 🔵 ❎ 🛏 🐾

MINERALWELLS

🔷🔷 Microtel Inn SH
(304) 489-3892. **$45-$55.** 104 Nickolette Rd. I-77, exit 170, just w. Int corridors. **Pets:** Accepted.
❎ 🛏

MORGANTOWN

🔷 🔷 Friends Inn M
(304) 599-4850. **$53-$125, 7 day notice.** 452 Country Club Rd. I-79, exit 155, s on US 19 to SR 705, then e on University Ave. Ext corridors. **Pets:** Medium. $5 daily fee/pet. Designated rooms, service with restrictions, supervision.
SAVE 🔵 ❎ 👶 🛏 💻

🔷 🔷🔷🔷 Ramada Inn and Conference Center SH
(304) 296-3431. **$87-$92, 3 day notice.** US Rt 119, I-68 & I-79. I-68, exit 1, 0.3 mi n. Int corridors. **Pets:** Medium. Designated rooms, service with restrictions, crate.
SAVE 🔵 ❎ 🛏 💻 🍴 🐾 ❌

NITRO

🔷 Econo Lodge M
(304) 755-8341. **$50-$56.** 4115 1st Ave. I-64, exit 45, 0.8 mi e on SR 25. Ext corridors. **Pets:** Medium, other species. $10 daily fee/pet. Designated rooms, service with restrictions, supervision.
ASK 🔵 ❎ 🛏 💻

PARKERSBURG

🔷 🔷 Expressway Motor Inn M
(304) 485-1851. **$45-$50.** 6333 Emerson Ave. I-77, exit 179, 0.4 mi sw on SR 68. Ext corridors. **Pets:** $5 daily fee/pet. Service with restrictions, supervision.
SAVE 🔵 ❎ 🛏 💻

🔷🔷 Red Roof Inn M 🐾
(304) 485-1741. **$44-$61.** 3714 E 7th St. I-77, exit 176, just w on US 50. Ext corridors. **Pets:** Other species. Service with restrictions.
❎ 🛏 💻

PHILIPPI

🔷🔷 Philippi Lodging M
(304) 457-5888. **$55-$95, 3 day notice.** Rt 4, Box 155. 2.5 mi s on US 250. Int corridors. **Pets:** Large, other species.
ASK 🔵 ❎ 🔵 🐾 🛏

PRINCETON

🔷 🔷🔷🔷 Days Inn M
(304) 425-8100. **$51-$68, 3 day notice.** 347 Meadowfield Ln. I-77, exit 9, 0.3 mi w on US 460, just s on Ambrose Ln, then just e. Ext corridors. **Pets:** Accepted.
SAVE 🔵 ❎ 🐾 🛏 💻 🐾

⚠ ▼▼▼ Ramada Limited 🅂🄷
(304) 425-8711. **$53-$70, 3 day notice.** 1115 Oakvale Rd. I-77, exit 9, just w, then just ne via service road. Ext corridors. **Pets:** Accepted.

🆂🄰🅅🄴 💲🄳 ⊠ 🎁 💻 🏊

▼▼ Sleep Inn 🅂🄷 ❀
(304) 431-2800. **$57-$125.** 1015 Oakvale Rd. I-77, exit 9, just w on US 460, then just n via service road. Int corridors. **Pets:** Other species. Service with restrictions, crate.

🄰🅂🄺 💲🄳 ⊠ 🐾 📶 🎁 💻 🏊

⚠ ▼▼ Town-N-Country Motel 🄼
(304) 425-8156. **$35-$70, 3 day notice.** 805 Oakvale Rd. I-77, exit 9, 0.3 mi w on US 460. Ext corridors. **Pets:** Accepted.

🆂🄰🅅🄴 💲🄳 ⊠ 🏊

RIPLEY

⚠ ▼▼▼▼ Best Western McCoys Inn & Conference Center 🅂🄷
(304) 372-9122. **$69-$79, 3 day notice.** 701 W Main St. I-77, exit 138, just e. Ext/int corridors. **Pets:** Accepted.

🆂🄰🅅🄴 💲🄳 ⊠ 🐾 💻 🍽 🏊

▼▼ Ripley Super 8 Motel 🄼
(304) 372-8880. **$60-$70.** 102 Duke Dr. I-77, exit 138, just e on SR 33. Int corridors. **Pets:** Accepted.

🄰🅂🄺 💲🄳 ⊠ 🐾 🎁 💻

SOUTH CHARLESTON

▼▼▼ Ramada Plaza Hotel Charleston 🅂🄷
(304) 744-4641. **$69.** 400 2nd Ave. I-64, exit 56, just nw. Int corridors. **Pets:** Accepted.

🄰🅂🄺 💲🄳 ⊠ 🐾 🎁 💻 🍽 🏊 ⊠

STAR CITY

▼▼ Econo Lodge-Coliseum 🅂🄷
(304) 599-8181. **$49-$75.** 3506 Monongahela Blvd. I-79, exit 155, 1.4 mi s on US 119/SR 7. Ext corridors. **Pets:** Medium. Designated rooms, service with restrictions, supervision.

⊠ 🎁 💻

⚠ ▼▼▼ Holiday Inn Morgantown 🅂🄷
(304) 599-1680. **$66-$100.** 1400 Saratoga Ave. I-79, exit 155, 1.7 mi s on US 119/SR 7. Ext corridors. **Pets:** Accepted.

🆂🄰🅅🄴 💲🄳 ⊠ 🆖 🐾 📶 🎁 💻 🍽 🏊

SUMMERSVILLE

⚠ ▼▼ Best Western Summersville Lake Motor Lodge 🅂🄷
(304) 872-6900. **$56-$95.** 1203 S Broad St. US 19 and Broad St; 0.6 mi s of jct SR 39. Ext corridors. **Pets:** Medium. $7 daily fee/pet. Service with restrictions, supervision.

🆂🄰🅅🄴 💲🄳 ⊠ 🎁 💻

⚠ ▼▼▼ Comfort Inn 🅂🄷
(304) 872-6500. **$60-$145, 30 day notice.** 903 Industrial Dr N. US 19, 1.9 mi n of jct SR 39. Int corridors. **Pets:** Small, other species. $5 daily fee/pet. Designated rooms, service with restrictions, supervision.

🆂🄰🅅🄴 💲🄳 ⊠ 🐾 📶 🎁 💻 🏊 ⊠

⚠ ▼▼▼ Sleep Inn of Summersville 🅂🄷
(304) 872-4500. **$49-$95.** 701 Professional Park Dr. US 19, 1.7 mi n of jct SR 39. Int corridors. **Pets:** Small, other species. $5 daily fee/pet. Designated rooms, service with restrictions, supervision.

🆂🄰🅅🄴 💲🄳 ⊠ 🐾 📶 🎁 💻 🏊

TRIADELPHIA

⚠ ▼▼▼ Holiday Inn Express Wheeling East 🅂🄷
(304) 547-1380. **$69-$109.** I-70, exit 11. Int corridors. **Pets:** Medium. $10 daily fee/pet. Designated rooms, service with restrictions, supervision.

🆂🄰🅅🄴 💲🄳 ⊠ 🐾 📶 🎁 🏊

WEIRTON

▼▼▼ Holiday Inn 🅂🄷
(304) 723-5522. **$115-$129.** 350 Three Springs Dr. 4.5 mi e on US 22, exit Three Springs Dr. Int corridors. **Pets:** Medium. $50 one-time fee/room. Service with restrictions, supervision.

🄰🅂🄺 💲🄳 ⊠ 🐾 📶 🎁 💻 🍽 🏊 ⊠

WESTON

⚠ ▼▼▼ Comfort Inn 🅂🄷
(304) 269-7000. **$49-$99.** I-79 & Rt 33 E. I-79, exit 99, just e on US 33. Ext corridors. **Pets:** $10 daily fee/room. Designated rooms, service with restrictions, supervision.

🆂🄰🅅🄴 💲🄳 ⊠ 🐾 📶 🎁 💻 🏊

WHEELING

⚠ ▼▼▼ Best Western Wheeling Inn 🅂🄷
(304) 233-8500. **$65-$74.** 949 Main St. I-70, exit 1A, just s; downtown. Ext corridors. **Pets:** Accepted.

🆂🄰🅅🄴 💲🄳 ⊠ 🐾 🎁 💻 🍽 ⊠

CITY INDEX

ABBOTSFORD

▼▼ Sleep Inn SH
(715) 223-3337. **$69-$84.** 300 E Elderberry Rd. SR 29, exit 132 (SR 13), just se. Int corridors. **Pets:** Other species. $50 deposit/room, $15 daily fee/pet. Service with restrictions, crate.

(ASK) (S₆) ✕ 🛇 🛇 🛇 🛇 🛇

ALGOMA

◈◈ ▼▼ Algoma Beach Motel & Condos SH
(920) 487-2828. **$59-$259, 3 day notice.** 1500 Lake St. Jct SR 22 and 72; 2 mi n on SR 22. Ext/int corridors. **Pets:** Dogs only. $15 daily fee/pet. Designated rooms, service with restrictions, crate.

(SAVE) (S₆) ✕ 🛇 🛇

▼▼ Scenic Shore Inn M ❖
(920) 487-3214. **$44-$59, 3 day notice.** 2221 Lake St. Jct SR 54, 0.8 mi s on SR 42. Ext corridors. **Pets:** Small, dogs only. Service with restrictions, crate.

✕ 🛇 🛇

ANTIGO

▼▼ Super 8 Motel-Antigo SH
(715) 623-4188. **$59-$85.** 535 Century Ave. On US 45 at jct SR 64 E. Int corridors. **Pets:** Dogs only. $15 daily fee/pet. Designated rooms, service with restrictions, supervision.

(ASK) (S₆) ✕ 🛇 🛇 🛇 🛇 🛇

APPLETON

◈◈ ▼▼ Best Western Midway Hotel SH
(920) 731-4141. **$89-$109.** 3033 W College Ave. US 41, exit 137 (SR 125), 0.5 mi e. Int corridors. **Pets:** $10 daily fee/room. Designated rooms, service with restrictions, supervision.

(SAVE) (S₆) ✕ 🛇 🛇 🛇 🛇 🛇 🛇

▼▼ Budgetel Inn Appleton M
(920) 734-6070. **$54-$84.** 3920 W College Ave. US 41, exit 137 (SR 125), just e. Ext/int corridors. **Pets:** Medium. $25 deposit/room. Service with restrictions, supervision.

(ASK) (S₆) ✕ 🛇 🛇 🛇

▼▼▼ Comfort Suites Comfort Dome SH
(920) 730-3800. **$100-$140.** 3809 W Wisconsin Ave. US 41, exit 138 (Wisconsin Ave), just e. Int corridors. **Pets:** Large, other species. Service with restrictions, crate.

(ASK) (S₆) ✕ 🛇 🛇 🛇 🛇 🛇

◈◈ ▼▼▼ Country Inn & Suites By Carlson SH
(920) 830-3240. **$69-$200.** 355 Fox River Dr. US 41, exit 137 (W SR 125), just nw. Int corridors. **Pets:** Medium. Designated rooms, service with restrictions, crate.

(SAVE) (S₆) ✕ 🛇 🛇 🛇 🛇 🛇

◈◈ ▼▼▼ Exel Inn of Appleton M
(920) 733-5551. **$42-$62.** 210 Westhill Blvd. US 41, exit 137 (SR 125), just e. Int corridors. **Pets:** Small, other species. Designated rooms, service with restrictions, supervision.

(SAVE) (S₆) ✕ 🛇 🛇

◈◈ ▼▼▼ Microtel Inn & Suites SH
(920) 997-3121. **$63-$73.** 321 Metro Dr. US 41, exit 137 (W SR 125), just nw. Int corridors. **Pets:** Medium, dogs only. $10 daily fee/room. Designated rooms, service with restrictions, supervision.

(SAVE) ✕ 🛇 🛇 🛇

▼▼▼ Residence Inn by Marriott SH ❖
(920) 954-0570. **$109, 3 day notice.** 310 Metro Dr. US 41, exit 137 (W SR 125), just nw on Mall Dr. Int corridors. **Pets:** Other species. $200 one-time fee/pet. Service with restrictions, crate.

(ASK) (S₆) ✕ 🛇 🛇 🛇 🛇 🛇 🛇

▼▼▼▼ **Woodfield Suites Appleton** 🆂🅷
(920) 734-7777. **$94-$114.** 3730 W College Ave. US 41, exit 137 (SR 125), just e. Int corridors. **Pets:** Accepted.
🅰🆂🅺 💲🐾 ⊠ 🛏 💻 🏊 🔀

ARCADIA

▼ **RKD Motel** Ⓜ
(608) 323-3338. **$50.** 915 E Main St. On SR 95, 0.6 mi w of jct SR 93. Ext corridors. **Pets:** Medium, dogs only. $5 daily fee/pet. Designated rooms, service with restrictions, supervision.
⊠ 🛏 💻

ASHLAND

🆔🆔🆔 ▼▼▼ **AmericInn of Ashland** 🆂🅷
(715) 682-9950. **$79-$139.** 3009 Lakeshore Dr E. On US 2, 2.1 mi e of jct SR 13 S. Int corridors. **Pets:** Accepted.
🆂🅰🆅🅴 💲🐾 ⊠ ✎ 🛏 💻 🏊 🔀

▼▼ **Super 8 Motel** 🆂🅷
(715) 682-9377. **$45-$120.** 1610 W Lakeshore Dr. On US 2 at jct 16th Ave. Int corridors. **Pets:** Other species. $50 deposit/room, $10 daily fee/pet. Supervision.
🅰🆂🅺 💲🐾 ⊠ 🖭 🎵 ✎ 🛏 💻 🏊

BALDWIN

▼▼ **Super 8 Motel** 🆂🅷
(715) 684-2700. **$63-$78.** 2110 10th Ave. I-94, exit 19 (US 63), just se. Int corridors. **Pets:** Medium, other species. Service with restrictions, supervision.
🅰🆂🅺 💲🐾 ⊠ ✎ 🛏 🏊

BARABOO

🆔🆔🆔 ▼▼▼ **Park Plaza Baraboo** 🆂🅷
(608) 356-6422. **$79-$159.** 626 W Pine St. On US 12, 0.3 mi n of SR 33. Int corridors. **Pets:** Accepted.
🆂🅰🆅🅴 💲🐾 ⊠ 🖭 🛏 💻 🍴 🏊 🔀

BEAVER DAM

▼▼▼ **AmericInn Lodge & Suites** 🆂🅷
(920) 356-9000. **$75-$120.** 325 Seippel Blvd. US 151, exit 134 (CR B/Industrial Dr). Int corridors. **Pets:** $10 daily fee/pet. Designated rooms, service with restrictions.
🅰🆂🅺 💲🐾 ⊠ ✎ 🛏 💻 🏊

▼▼ **Super 8 Motel** 🆂🅷
(920) 887-8880. **$57-$77.** 711 Park Ave. US 151, exit 132 (SR 33), just w. Int corridors. **Pets:** Other species. $50 deposit/pet. Designated rooms, service with restrictions, supervision.
🅰🆂🅺 💲🐾 ⊠ 🎵

BELOIT

▼▼ **Comfort Inn of Beloit** 🆂🅷
(608) 362-2666. **$59-$109.** 2786 Milwaukee Rd. I-90, exit 185A, just w at jct I-43 and SR 81. Int corridors. **Pets:** Medium, other species. $10 daily fee/pet. Designated rooms, supervision.
🅰🆂🅺 💲🐾 ⊠ 🎵 🛏 💻 🏊

🆔🆔🆔 ▼▼▼ **Econo Lodge** Ⓜ
(608) 364-4000. **$45-$75.** 2956 Milwaukee Rd. I-90, exit 185A, 0.3 mi w. Ext/int corridors. **Pets:** $10 daily fee/pet. Designated rooms, service with restrictions, supervision.
🆂🅰🆅🅴 💲🐾 ⊠ 💻 🍴

▼▼ **Super 8 Motel** 🆂🅷
(608) 365-8680. **$59-$79.** 3002 Milwaukee Rd. I-90, exit 185A, just w at jct I-43 and SR 81. Int corridors. **Pets:** Accepted.
🅰🆂🅺 💲🐾 ⊠ 🚹Ⓜ 🛏

BERLIN

🆔🆔🆔 ▼▼▼ **Best Western Countryside** Ⓜ
(920) 361-4411. **$74-$119.** 227 Ripon Rd. On SR 49, at jct CR F. Int corridors. **Pets:** Very small, dogs only. $15 one-time fee/pet. Designated rooms, service with restrictions, supervision.
🆂🅰🆅🅴 💲🐾 ⊠ 🛏 💻

BLACK RIVER FALLS

🆔🆔🆔 ▼▼▼ **Best Western-Arrowhead Lodge &**
Suites 🆂🅷 ❄
(715) 284-9471. **$58-$96.** 600 Oasis Rd. I-94, exit 116, at jct SR 54. Int corridors. **Pets:** Large, other species. Service with restrictions, supervision.
🆂🅰🆅🅴 💲🐾 ⊠ 🎵 ✎ 🛏 💻 🍴 🏊 🔀

🆔🆔🆔 ▼▼▼ **Days Inn** 🆂🅷
(715) 284-4333. **$69-$89.** 919 Hwy 54 E. I-94, exit 116, just w. Int corridors. **Pets:** $10 daily fee/pet. Designated rooms, service with restrictions, supervision.
🆂🅰🆅🅴 💲🐾 ⊠ ✎ 🛏 💻 🏊 🔀

BOULDER JUNCTION

▼▼▼▼ **White Birch Village** 🆅🅷
(715) 385-2182. **$600-$1500 (weekly) (no credit cards), 30 day notice.** 8764 Hwy K. On CR K, 8 mi se. Ext corridors. **Pets:** Accepted.
⊠ 🛏 💻 🔀

CABLE

🆔🆔🆔 ▼▼▼ **Lakewoods Resort** 🆂🅷
(715) 794-2561. **$95-$350, 30 day notice.** 21540 CR M. On CR M, 8 mi e. Ext/int corridors. **Pets:** Accepted.
🆂🅰🆅🅴 ⊠ 🎵 ✎ 🛏 💻 🍴 🏊 🔀

CADOTT

▼▼ **Countryside Motel** Ⓜ
(715) 289-4000. **$45-$80.** 545 Lavorata Rd. SR 29, exit 91 (SR 27), just s. Int corridors. **Pets:** Small, dogs only. Designated rooms, service with restrictions, supervision.
⊠

CAMERON

▼▼ **Viking Motel** Ⓜ
(715) 458-2111. **$55-$66.** 201 S 1st St. On US 8 and CR SS. Ext corridors. **Pets:** Other species. Designated rooms, service with restrictions, supervision.
🅰🆂🅺 💲🐾 ⊠ 💻

CAMP DOUGLAS

🆔🆔🆔 ▼▼ **K & K Motel** Ⓜ
(608) 427-3100. **$60-$65.** 219 Hwy 12 & 16. I-90/94, exit 55, just s. Ext corridors. **Pets:** Accepted.
🆂🅰🆅🅴 💲🐾 ⊠ 🛏

CHIPPEWA FALLS

▼▼ Americinn Motel & Suites 🆂🅷 ❖
(715) 723-5711. **$74-$94.** 11 W South Ave. 2 mi s on SR 124, access via CR J. Int corridors. **Pets:** Other species. Designated rooms, service with restrictions, supervision.
🆂🅾 ⊠ 🗗 🐾 🗗 🗗 ➿

Ⓐ ▼▼ Park Inn 🆂🅷
(715) 723-2281. **$89-$119.** 1009 W Park Ave. Jct SR 124 and CR J. Ext/int corridors. **Pets:** Accepted.
🆂🅰🆅🅴 🆂🅾 ⊠ 🗗 🗗 🍽 ➿

COLUMBUS

▼▼ The Columbus Super 8 🆂🅷
(920) 623-8800. **$59-$84.** 219 Industrial Dr. US 151, exit 118 (SR 16/60), just ne. Int corridors. **Pets:** Medium, other species. $50 deposit/room, $10 one-time fee/room. Designated rooms, service with restrictions, supervision.
🅰🆂🅺 🆂🅾 ⊠ 🐾 🗗 ➿

CRIVITZ

▼▼ Shaffer Park Resort Ⓜ
(715) 854-2186. **$49-$72, 14 day notice.** N 7217 Shaffer Rd. 5 mi w on CR W. Ext corridors. **Pets:** Medium, dogs only. $6 daily fee/pet. Designated rooms, service with restrictions, supervision.
🗗 🗗 🍽 ⊠ 🕿

DE FOREST

▼▼▼ Holiday Inn Express 🆂🅷 ❖
(608) 846-8686. **$74-$109.** 7184 Morrisonville Rd. I-90/94, exit 126 (CR V), just e. Int corridors. **Pets:** Large, other species. $20 one-time fee/room. Designated rooms, service with restrictions, crate.
🅰🆂🅺 🆂🅾 ⊠ 🐾 🗗 🗗 🗗 ➿

DE PERE

▼▼ Kress Inn 🆂🅷
(920) 403-5100. **$104-$124.** 300 Grant St. US 41, exit 163 (Main St), 1 mi e, then just s on 3rd St. Int corridors. **Pets:** Accepted.
🅰🆂🅺 🆂🅾 ⊠ 🐾 🗗 🗗 🗗

DODGEVILLE

Ⓐ ▼▼▼ Best Western Quiet House & Suites 🆂🅷
(608) 935-7739. **$99-$118.** 1130 N Johns St. On US 18, just e of jct SR 23. Int corridors. **Pets:** $15 daily fee/pet. Designated rooms, supervision.
🆂🅰🆅🅴 🆂🅾 ⊠ 🐾 🗗 🗗 🗗 ➿

Ⓐ ▼ Pine Ridge Motel Ⓜ ❖
(608) 935-3386. **$30-$65.** 405 CR YZ. On CR YZ, 0.5 mi e of jct SR 23. Ext corridors. **Pets:** Very small, dogs only. $8 one-time fee/pet. Designated rooms, service with restrictions, supervision.
🆂🅰🆅🅴 🆂🅾 ⊠ 🗗

Ⓐ ▼▼ Super 8 Motel of Dodgeville 🆂🅷
(608) 935-3888. **$46-$80, 12 day notice.** 1308 Johns St. Just n of US 18. Int corridors. **Pets:** $50 deposit/room. Service with restrictions, supervision.
🆂🅰🆅🅴 🆂🅾 ⊠ 🐾 🗗

DOOR COUNTY AREA

ELLISON BAY

Ⓐ ▼▼ Parkside Inn Ⓜ ❖
(920) 854-9050. **$69-$99, 7 day notice.** 11946 Hwy 42. On SR 42, 0.3 mi s. Ext corridors. **Pets:** Dogs only. $10 daily fee/room. Designated rooms, service with restrictions.
🆂🅰🆅🅴 ⊠ 🗗

FISH CREEK

▼ Julie's Park Cafe & Motel Ⓜ
(920) 868-2999. **$41-$106, 10 day notice.** 4020 Hwy 42. On SR 42, 0.3 mi n. Ext corridors. **Pets:** Other species. $15 daily fee/pet. Designated rooms, supervision.
🅰🆂🅺 🆂🅾 ⊠ 🗗 🍽

GILLS ROCK

▼▼ Harbor House Inn 🅱🅱 ❖
(920) 854-5196. **$49-$185, 21 day notice.** 12666 SR 42. On SR 42; center. Ext/int corridors. **Pets:** $20 daily fee/pet. Service with restrictions, supervision.
⊠ 🗗 ⊠ 🕿

▼ Maple Grove Motel Ⓜ ❖
(920) 854-2587. **Call for rates.** 809 SR 42. On SR 42, 0.3 mi e, 1.5 mi w of car ferry. Ext corridors. **Pets:** Dogs only. $10 daily fee/pet. Service with restrictions, crate.
⊠ 🗗 🗗 🕿

STURGEON BAY

▼▼ Super 8 Motel 🆂🅷
(920) 743-9211. **$51-$101, 30 day notice.** 409 Green Bay Rd. 1 mi s on Business Rt SR 42/57. Int corridors. **Pets:** Medium, dogs only. $20 deposit/room. Designated rooms, service with restrictions, crate.
🅰🆂🅺 🆂🅾 ⊠ 🐾 🗗 ➿

❖   END AREA   ❖

EAGLE RIVER

AAA ▼▼▼ **Days Inn** SH
(715) 479-5151. **$76-$97.** 844 Railroad St N. 0.5 mi n on US 45. Int corridors. **Pets:** Medium, other species. $10 daily fee/room. Designated rooms, service with restrictions, supervision.
(SAVE) (S6) ✕ ⌂ ⌂ ▣ ▣ ⌖ ✕

AAA ▼ **Traveler's Inn Motel** M
(715) 479-4403. **$45-$80.** 309 Wall St. Center of downtown. Ext/int corridors. **Pets:** Medium. $10 daily fee/pet. Designated rooms, service with restrictions, crate.
(SAVE) (S6) ✕ ⌂ ▣

EAST TROY

AAA ▼▼▼ **Country Inn & Suites** SH ❀
(262) 642-2100. **$80-$139.** 2921 O'Leary Ln. I-43, exit 36, at jct SR 120. Int corridors. **Pets:** Medium, dogs only. Designated rooms, service with restrictions, supervision.
(SAVE) (S6) ✕ ⌂M ⌂ ⌂ ▣ ▣ ⌖

EAU CLAIRE

▼▼▼ **AmericInn Motel & Suites** SH
(715) 874-4900. **$59-$135, 7 day notice.** 6200 Texaco Dr. I-94, exit 59, jct US 12. Int corridors. **Pets:** Designated rooms, service with restrictions, supervision.
(ASK) (S6) ✕ ⌂ ⌂ ▣ ▣ ⌖ ✕

▼▼ **Comfort Inn** SH
(715) 833-9798. **$69-$119.** 3117 Craig Rd. I-94, exit 65, 1.3 mi n on SR 37, just s of jct US 12. Int corridors. **Pets:** Accepted.
(ASK) (S6) ✕ ⌖ ⌂ ▣ ⌖

AAA ▼▼▼ **Country Inn & Suites By Carlson** SH
(715) 832-7289. **$85-$102.** 3614 Gateway Dr. I-94, exit 70, 0.8 mi n on US 53, then just ne on CR AA (Golf Rd). Int corridors. **Pets:** Accepted.
(SAVE) (S6) ✕ ⌖ ⌂ ⌂ ▣ ⌖

▼▼▼ **Days Inn-West** SH
(715) 874-5550. **$50-$100.** 6319 Truax Ln. I-94, exit 59, jct US 12. Int corridors. **Pets:** $25 deposit/room. Designated rooms, service with restrictions, crate.
(ASK) (S6) ✕ ⌂ ⌂ ▣ ⌖

▼▼▼ **Econo Lodge** SH
(715) 833-8818. **$45-$125.** 4608 Royal Dr. I-94, exit 68, just n on SR 93, just w on Golf Rd, then just s. Int corridors. **Pets:** Dogs only. Designated rooms, service with restrictions, supervision.
(ASK) (S6) ✕ ⌂ ▣

AAA ▼▼ **Exel Inn of Eau Claire** SH
(715) 834-3193. **$45-$65.** 2305 Craig Rd. I-94, exit 65, 1.3 mi n on SR 37, just w of jct US 12. Int corridors. **Pets:** Small, other species. Designated rooms, supervision.
(SAVE) (S6) ✕ ⌂ ▣

▼▼▼ **Heartland Inn** SH
(715) 839-7100. **$75-$85.** 4075 Commonwealth Ave. I-94, exit 70, 0.8 mi n on US 53, just w on CR AA (Golf Rd), then just s. Int corridors. **Pets:** $5 daily fee/room. Designated rooms, service with restrictions, supervision.
(ASK) (S6) ✕ ⌂ ▣ ⌖

▼▼▼ **Holiday Inn Campus Area** SH
(715) 835-2211. **$75-$125.** 2703 Craig Rd. I-94, exit 65, 1.3 mi n on SR 37, just w of jct US 12. Int corridors. **Pets:** Accepted.
(ASK) (S6) ✕ ⌂M ⌂ ⌂ ▣ ⌸ ⌖ ✕

AAA ▼▼ **Maple Manor Motel** M
(715) 834-2618. **$37-$49.** 2507 S Hastings Way. I-94, exit 70, 3 mi n on US 53, exit US 12 (Clairemont Ave), just se, follow signs for Storrs Ave. Ext corridors. **Pets:** Accepted.
(SAVE) (S6) ✕ ⌂ ▣ ⌸

AAA ▼▼▼ **Park Inn & Suites International** SH
(715) 838-9989. **$109-$119.** 3340 Mondovi Rd. I-94, exit 65, just n. Int corridors. **Pets:** Accepted.
(SAVE) (S6) ✕ ⌂M ⌂ ⌂ ▣ ⌖ ✕

▼▼▼ **The Plaza Hotel & Suites** SH
(715) 834-3181. **$69-$179.** 1202 W Clairemont Ave. I-94, exit 65, 1.3 mi n on SR 37, just w of jct US 12. Int corridors. **Pets:** Other species. $15 one-time fee/room. Service with restrictions, crate.
(ASK) (S6) ✕ ⌖ ⌂ ⌂ ▣ ⌸ ⌖ ✕

AAA ▼▼▼ **Ramada Inn Convention Center** LH
(715) 835-6121. **$70-$110.** 205 S Barstow St. S Barstow at Gibson sts; downtown. Int corridors. **Pets:** Other species. $10 one-time fee/room. Designated rooms, service with restrictions.
(SAVE) (S6) ✕ ⌂ ▣ ⌸ ⌖

EDGERTON

▼▼▼ **Comfort Inn** SH
(608) 884-2118. **$49-$175.** 11102 Goede Rd. I-90, exit 163, just e. Int corridors. **Pets:** Accepted.
(ASK) (S6) ✕ ⌂ ⌂ ▣ ⌖

FENNIMORE

▼▼ **Fenmore Hills Motel** SH
(608) 822-3281. **$62-$70.** 5814 Hwy 18 W. 2.4 mi w. Int corridors. **Pets:** Service with restrictions, supervision.
(S6) ✕ ⌂

FITCHBURG

AAA ▼▼▼ **Quality Inn & Suites** SH
(608) 274-7200. **$79-$129.** 2969 Cahill Main. US 12/18, exit 260 (Fish Hatchery/CR D), then 1.5 mi s at jct CR PD. Int corridors. **Pets:** Accepted.
(SAVE) (S6) ✕ ⌂ ▣ ⌖ ✕

FOND DU LAC

AAA ▼▼▼ **Baymont Inn & Suites-Fond du Lac** SH ❀
(920) 921-4000. **$79-$159.** 77 Holiday Ln. Sw of jct US 41 and 151. Int corridors. **Pets:** Other species. $10 one-time fee/room.
(SAVE) (S6) ✕ ⌂ ▣ ⌖ ✕

▼▼▼▼ **Holiday Inn** SH
(920) 923-1440. **$120-$210.** 625 W Rolling Meadows Dr. On US 151, just sw of jct US 41. Int corridors. **Pets:** Other species. $200 deposit/room. Designated rooms, service with restrictions, supervision.

ASK SÁ ✕ 🐾 🖥 💻 ❀ ✕

♦♦♦ ▼▼▼ **Microtel Inn & Suites** SH
(920) 929-4000. **$45-$80.** 920 S Military Rd. Jct US 41 and 151. Int corridors. **Pets:** Other species. $11 one-time fee/room. Service with restrictions, crate.

SAVE ✕ 🐾 🖥 💻 ✕

♦♦♦ ▼▼▼ **Ramada Plaza Hotel** LH
(920) 923-3000. **$69-$189.** 1 N Main St. Downtown. Int corridors. **Pets:** Accepted.

SAVE SÁ ✕ 🖥 💻 ❀ ✕

▼▼ ▼▼ **Super 8 Motel** SH
(920) 922-1088. **$56-$61.** 391 N Pioneer Rd. US 41, exit SR 23, just n on east frontage road (CR VV). Int corridors. **Pets:** Medium, dogs only. $10 one-time fee/room. Designated rooms, service with restrictions, supervision.

ASK SÁ ✕ 🐾 🖥

GREEN BAY

♦♦♦ ▼▼▼▼ **AmericInn** SH
(920) 434-9790. **$65-$140, 30 day notice.** 2032 Velp Ave. US 41, exit 170, 0.3 mi w. Int corridors. **Pets:** Medium. $10 daily fee/room. Designated rooms, service with restrictions, supervision.

SAVE SÁ ✕ 🐾 🐾 🖥 💻 ❀

♦♦♦ ▼▼▼ **Baymont Inn-Green Bay** SH
(920) 494-7887. **$70-$120.** 2840 S Oneida St. US 41, exit 164 (Oneida St), just e. Int corridors. **Pets:** Accepted.

SAVE SÁ ✕ 🖥 💻

♦♦♦ ▼▼ **Bay Motel** M
(920) 494-3441. **$45-$60.** 1301 S Military Ave. US 41, exit 167 (Lombardi Ave), 0.4 mi e to Marlee, then 0.6 mi n. Ext corridors. **Pets:** Accepted.

SAVE ✕ 🖥 🍴

♦♦♦ ▼▼▼ **Days Inn-Lambeau Field** SH
(920) 498-8088. **$54-$99.** 1978 Holmgren Way. US 41, exit 167 (Lombardi Ave), 1.4 mi e, just s. Int corridors. **Pets:** Small. $10 daily fee/room. Service with restrictions, supervision.

SAVE SÁ ✕ 🐾 🖥 💻 ❀

♦♦♦ ▼▼▼ **Exel Inn of Green Bay** SH
(920) 499-3599. **$46-$66.** 2870 Ramada Way. US 41, exit 164 (Oneida St), just e. Int corridors. **Pets:** Small. Designated rooms, supervision.

SAVE SÁ ✕ 🖥 💻

▼▼▼▼ **Holiday Inn City Centre** LH
(920) 437-5900. **$89-$109.** 200 Main St. Downtown. Int corridors. **Pets:** Designated rooms, service with restrictions, supervision.

ASK SÁ ✕ 🐾 💻 🍴 ❀ ✕

♦♦♦ ▼▼▼▼ **Ramada Plaza Green Bay** LH
(920) 499-0631. **$93-$124.** 2750 Ramada Way. US 41, exit 164 (Oneida St), just e to Ramada Way, then 0.3 mi n. Int corridors. **Pets:** Accepted.

SAVE SÁ ✕ 🐾 🖥 💻 🍴 ❀ ✕

▼▼▼▼ **Residence Inn by Marriott** SH
(920) 435-2222. **$99-$159.** 335 W St Joseph St. SR 172, exit Riverside Dr, 1.1 mi n on SR 57, then just e. Ext corridors. **Pets:** Accepted.

ASK SÁ ✕ 🖥 💻 ❀ ✕

♦♦♦ ▼▼▼ **Super 8 Motel** SH
(920) 494-2042. **$67-$79, 3 day notice.** 2868 S Oneida St. US 41, exit 164 (Oneida St), just e. Int corridors. **Pets:** Other species. $25 deposit/room. Service with restrictions, supervision.

SAVE ✕ 🐾 🖥

HAYWARD

▼▼▼▼ **AmericInn of Hayward** SH
(715) 634-2700. **$66-$139.** 15601 US Hwy 63. On US 63, just n of jct SR 77. Int corridors. **Pets:** Medium. $5 daily fee/pet. Designated rooms, service with restrictions, supervision.

ASK SÁ ✕ 🐾 🖥 💻 ❀ ✕

♦♦♦ ▼▼▼ **Best Western Northern Pine Inn** SH
(715) 634-4959. **$59-$119, 3 day notice.** 9966 N Hwy 27. On SR 27 S, 1.7 mi s of jct US 63. Ext/int corridors. **Pets:** Accepted.

SAVE SÁ ✕ 🖥 💻 ❀ ✕

▼▼▼▼ **Comfort Suites** SH
(715) 634-0700. **$70-$165.** 15586 CR B. On CR B, 0.5 mi s of jct SR 27. Int corridors. **Pets:** Accepted.

✕ 🐾 🐾 🖥 💻 ❀ ✕

▼▼▼▼ **Ross' Teal Lake Lodge and Teal Wing Golf Club** CA
(715) 462-3631. **$130-$350.** 12425 N Ross Rd. On SR 77, 20 mi ne of jct US 63. Ext corridors. **Pets:** Other species. $5 daily fee/pet. Service with restrictions, supervision.

✕ 🖥 🍴 ❀ ✕ 🎾 ✉

▼▼ ▼▼ **Super 8 Motel** SH
(715) 634-2646. **$50-$75.** 10444 N SR 27. On SR 27, 0.3 mi s of jct US 63. Ext/int corridors. **Pets:** Dogs only. Designated rooms, service with restrictions, supervision.

ASK SÁ ✕ ❀

HUDSON

▼▼ ▼▼ **Comfort Inn** SH
(715) 386-6355. **$59-$79.** 811 Dominion Dr. I-94, exit 2 (CR F), 1 mi w on south frontage road (Crestview Dr). Int corridors. **Pets:** Medium. $50 deposit/room. Service with restrictions, supervision.

ASK SÁ ✕ 🖥 💻 ❀

♦♦♦ ▼▼▼ **Super 8 Motel of Hudson** SH
(715) 386-8800. **$72-$104.** 808 Dominion Dr. I-94, exit 2 (CR F), 1 mi w on south frontage road (Crestview Dr). Int corridors. **Pets:** Medium. Designated rooms, service with restrictions, supervision.

SAVE SÁ ✕ 🖥 💻 ❀

HURLEY

Days Inn of Hurley SH
(715) 561-3500. **$69-$87.** 850 10th Ave N. S of jct US 2 and 51. Int corridors. **Pets:** $10 daily fee/room. Designated rooms, service with restrictions, supervision.

JANESVILLE

Baymont Inn & Suites-Janesville SH
(608) 758-4545. **$62-$80.** 616 Midland Rd. I-90, exit 175B (SR 11), just ne. Int corridors. **Pets:** Medium. $10 one-time fee/room. Designated rooms, service with restrictions, supervision.

Best Western Janesville SH
(608) 756-4511. **$69-$199.** 3900 Milton Ave. I-90, exit 171A (SR 26), just e. Int corridors. **Pets:** Large, other species. $10 daily fee/pet. Designated rooms, service with restrictions, supervision.

Microtel Inn SH
(608) 752-3121. **$46-$76.** 3121 Wellington Pl. I-90, exit 171C (US 14), just se. Int corridors. **Pets:** Other species. $10 one-time fee/room. Service with restrictions, crate.

Select Inn SH
(608) 754-0251. **$42-$52.** 3520 Milton Ave. I-90, exit 171A (SR 26), just sw. Int corridors. **Pets:** Other species. $5 daily fee/room. Supervision.

JEFFERSON

Rodeway Inn M
(920) 674-4404. **$55-$99, 30 day notice.** 1456 S Ryan Ave. On SR 26, 1.2 mi s of jct US 18. **Pets:** Medium, other species. $20 deposit/pet, $10 daily fee/pet. Service with restrictions, supervision.

JOHNSON CREEK

Days Inn-Johnson Creek SH
(920) 699-8000. **$68-$90.** W4545 Linmar Ln. I-94, exit 267 (SR 26), just ne. Int corridors. **Pets:** $75 deposit/room. Service with restrictions, supervision.

KAUKAUNA

Settle Inn SH
(920) 766-0088. **$60-$82.** 1201 Maloney Rd. US 41, exit 148, just e. Int corridors. **Pets:** $3 daily fee/room. Designated rooms, service with restrictions, supervision.

KENOSHA

Country Inn & Suites By Carlson SH
(262) 857-3680. **$82-$127.** 7011 122nd Ave. I-94, exit 344 (SR 50), just nw. Int corridors. **Pets:** Small, dogs only. $10 one-time fee/room. Service with restrictions, supervision.

Holiday Inn Express-Harborside SH
(262) 658-3281. **$99-$175.** 5125 6th Ave. Just ne of jct SR 32 and 158; downtown. Int corridors. **Pets:** Accepted.

KEWAUNEE

The Historic Karsten Inn SH
(920) 388-3800. **$59-$149, 3 day notice.** 122 Ellis St. Center. Int corridors. **Pets:** Medium, other species. $25 one-time fee/room. Designated rooms, service with restrictions, crate.

LA CROSSE

Days Inn Hotel & Conference Center SH ❖
(608) 783-1000. **$79-$99.** 101 Sky Harbour Dr. I-90, exit 2, just sw; on French Island. Int corridors. **Pets:** Medium. $10 daily fee/pet. Designated rooms, service with restrictions, supervision.

Exel Inn of La Crosse SH
(608) 781-0400. **$43-$63.** 2150 Rose St. I-90, exit 3, 0.8 mi s on US 53. Int corridors. **Pets:** Small. Designated rooms, service with restrictions, supervision.

The Radisson Hotel La Crosse LH ❖
(608) 784-6680. **$139-$179.** 200 Harborview Plaza. Just w of US 53; downtown. Int corridors. **Pets:** Other species. Designated rooms, service with restrictions.

LAKE DELTON

Lake Delton Travelodge SH
(608) 355-0700. **Call for rates.** E 10892 Fern Dell Rd. I-90/94, exit 92 (US 12), just s. Int corridors. **Pets:** Accepted.

LAND O'LAKES

Sunrise Lodge CA
(715) 547-3684. **$165-$180, 21 day notice.** 5894 W Shore Dr. 2 mi s on US 45, 2.8 mi e on CR E, then 1 mi n. Ext corridors. **Pets:** Service with restrictions, crate.

LUCK

Luck Country Inn SH
(715) 472-2000. **$50-$77.** 10 Robertson Rd. Jct SR 35 and 48. Int corridors. **Pets:** Small, dogs only. Service with restrictions, supervision.

MADISON

Baymont Inn & Suites-Madison West SH ❖
(608) 831-7711. **$69-$109, 14 day notice.** 8102 Excelsior Dr. US 12 and 14, exit 253 (Old Sauk Rd), just nw. Int corridors. **Pets:** Other species. Designated rooms, service with restrictions.

Best Western East Towne Suites SH
(608) 244-2020. **$77-$99.** 4801 Annamark Dr. I-90/94, exit 135A, just sw on US 151. Int corridors. **Pets:** Other species. $20 deposit/room. Designated rooms, service with restrictions, supervision.
SAVE SÃ X Ã H 🗭 ≈

Best Western West Towne Suites SH
(608) 833-4200. **$59-$109.** 650 Grand Canyon Dr. US 12 and 14, exit 255 (Gammon Rd), just e on Odana Rd, then just sw. Int corridors. **Pets:** Accepted.
ASK SÃ X H 🗭

Clarion Suites Central SH
(608) 284-1234. **$89-$184.** 2110 Rimrock Rd. US 12 and 18, exit 262 (Rimrock Rd), just nw. Int corridors. **Pets:** Large. $25 daily fee/pet. Service with restrictions, crate.
SAVE SÃ X Ã H 🗭 ≈

Comfort Suites SH
(608) 836-3033. **$89-$250.** 1253 John Q Hammons Dr. US 12 and 14, exit 252 (Greenway Blvd), just sw. Int corridors. **Pets:** Service with restrictions.
ASK SÃ X Ã H 🗭 ≈ X

Crowne Plaza Hotel and Resort LH
(608) 244-4703. **$99-$209.** 4402 E Washington Ave. I-90/94, exit 135A, 0.4 mi w on US 151. Int corridors. **Pets:** Medium. $15 daily fee/room. Designated rooms, service with restrictions.
SAVE SÃ X Ã H 🗭 ⫚ ≈ X

Days Inn-Madison SH
(608) 223-1800. **$68-$83.** 4402 E Broadway Service Rd. US 12 and 18, exit 266 (US 51), just ne. Int corridors. **Pets:** $75 deposit/room. Service with restrictions, supervision.
SAVE SÃ X Ã H 🗭 ≈

Econo Lodge of Madison SH
(608) 241-4171. **$49-$79.** 4726 E Washington Ave. I-90/94, exit 135A, just w on US 151. Int corridors. **Pets:** Medium, other species. $10 daily fee/room. Service with restrictions, supervision.
SAVE SÃ X Ã H 🗭

Exel Inn of Madison SH
(608) 241-3861. **$46-$76.** 4202 E Towne Blvd. I-90/94, exit 135A, 0.5 mi w on US 151. Int corridors. **Pets:** Small. Designated rooms, service with restrictions, supervision.
SAVE SÃ X H 🗭

GrandStay Residential Suites SH
(608) 241-2500. **$89.** 5317 High Crossing Blvd. US 51, exit 98A, just e, then 0.5 mi s. Int corridors. **Pets:** Other species. $50 deposit/room. Designated rooms, service with restrictions, crate.
ASK SÃ X Ã Ã Ã H 🗭 ≈ X

Holiday Inn Express-Madison SH
(608) 255-7400. **$85-$115.** 722 John Nolen Dr. US 12 and 18, exit 263 (John Nolen Dr), just ne. Int corridors. **Pets:** Small, other species. Designated rooms, service with restrictions, supervision.
SAVE SÃ X Ã Ã H 🗭 ≈

Holiday Inn Madison East SH
(608) 244-2481. **$79-$149.** 3841 E Washington Ave. I-90/94, exit 135A, 1 mi w on US 151. Int corridors. **Pets:** Medium. $15 daily fee/room. Service with restrictions.
SAVE SÃ X Ã Ã H 🗭 ⫚ ≈ X

Microtel Inn & Suites SH
(608) 242-9000. **$51-$59.** 2139 E Springs Dr. I-90/94, exit 135A, just s, then 0.5 mi e. Int corridors. **Pets:** Medium. $25 one-time fee/pet. Designated rooms, service with restrictions, supervision.
SAVE SÃ X H 🗭

Red Roof Inn-Madison M
(608) 241-1787. **$40-$75.** 4830 Hayes Rd. I-90/94, exit 135A, just sw on US 151. Ext corridors. **Pets:** Accepted.
SAVE X Ã Ã

Residence Inn SH
(608) 244-5047. **$89-$129, 7 day notice.** 4862 Hayes Rd. I-90/94, exit 135A, just sw on US 151. Int corridors. **Pets:** Medium. $5 daily fee/room, $50 one-time fee/room. Designated rooms, service with restrictions, supervision.
ASK SÃ X Ã Ã H 🗭 ≈ X

Residence Inn By Marriott-Madison West CO
(608) 833-8333. **$119-$169.** 501 D'Onofrio Dr. US 12 and 14, exit 254 (Mineral Point Rd), 0.4 mi e, then just s. Ext corridors. **Pets:** Other species. $200 one-time fee/pet. Service with restrictions.
ASK SÃ X Ã Ã H 🗭 ≈ X

Select Inn SH
(608) 249-1815. **$46-$75.** 4845 Hayes Rd. I-90/94, exit 135A, just sw on US 151. Int corridors. **Pets:** Other species. $25 deposit/room, $50 daily fee/pet. Service with restrictions, supervision.
SAVE SÃ X Ã H 🗭

Staybridge Suites SH
(608) 241-2300. **$119.** 3301 City View Dr. US 151, exit 98A, just e, then 0.5 mi s on High Crossing Blvd. Int corridors. **Pets:** Accepted.
SAVE X Ã Ã H 🗭 ≈ X

Super 8 Motel SH
(608) 258-8882. **$49-$99.** 1602 W Beltline Hwy. US 12 and 18, exit 260B (CR D), just w on north frontage road. Int corridors. **Pets:** $5 daily fee/room. Service with restrictions, supervision.
SAVE SÃ X Ã Ã H 🗭

Woodfield Suites-Madison SH
(608) 245-0123. **$109-$129.** 5217 E Terrace Dr. US 151, exit 98B (American Pkwy), just sw. Int corridors. **Pets:** Large. $50 deposit/pet, $10 daily fee/pet. Service with restrictions, supervision.
ASK SÃ X ⫚ Ã Ã H 🗭 ≈

MANITOWOC

Comfort Inn SH
(920) 683-0220. **$54-$99.** 2200 S 44th St. I-43, exit 149, just e. Int corridors. **Pets:** Other species. Service with restrictions, supervision.
ASK SÃ X H 🗭

▼▼▼▼ Holiday Inn 🄻🄷
(920) 682-6000. **$95-$115.** 4601 Calumet Ave. I-43, exit 149, just e. Int corridors. **Pets:** Other species. $200 deposit/room. Designated rooms, service with restrictions, supervision.
🄰🄢🄺 🆂🐾 ⊠ 🄴 🄸 💻 🍴 ⇌ 🆇

MARSHFIELD

🄰🄰🄰 ▼ Park Motel 🄼
(715) 387-1741. **$42-$46, 3 day notice.** 1806 S Roddis Ave. 1 mi s on SR 13. Ext corridors. **Pets:** $10 one-time fee/pet. Service with restrictions, supervision.
🆂🄰🅅🄴 🆂🐾 ⊠ 🄸

MAUSTON

🄰🄰🄰 ▼▼▼ Country Inn By Carlson 🆂🄷
(608) 847-5959. **$74-$97.** 1001 SR 82. I-90/94, exit 69, just ne. Int corridors. **Pets:** $5 one-time fee/pet. Service with restrictions, supervision.
🆂🄰🅅🄴 🆂🐾 ⊠ 🄸 💻 ⇌

▼▼ Super 8 Motel 🄼
(608) 847-2300. **$58-$89, 7 day notice.** 1001A Hwy 82 E. I-90/94, exit 69, just ne. Int corridors. **Pets:** Other species. $5 daily fee/pet. Service with restrictions, supervision.
⊠ 🄸 💻 ⇌

MENOMONIE

🄰🄰🄰 ▼▼▼ Country Inn & Suites 🆂🄷
(715) 235-5664. **$79-$99.** 320 Oak Ave. I-94, exit 41 (SR 25), just se. Int corridors. **Pets:** Dogs only. $15 daily fee/pet. Designated rooms, service with restrictions, supervision.
🆂🄰🅅🄴 🆂🐾 ⊠ 🄴 🄸 💻 ⇌

▼▼ Menomonie Motel 6 #4109 🆂🄷
(715) 235-6901. **$44-$58.** 2100 Stout St. I-94, exit 41 (SR 25), just se. Int corridors. **Pets:** Medium. Service with restrictions, supervision.
⊠ 🄴

▼▼ Super 8 Motel-Menomonie 🆂🄷
(715) 235-8889. **$49-$90.** 1622 N Broadway. I-94, exit 41 (SR 25), just s. Int corridors. **Pets:** Dogs only. $10 daily fee/room. Designated rooms, service with restrictions, supervision.
🄰🄢🄺 🆂🐾 ⊠ 🄐 🄸 ⇌

MERRILL

▼▼▼ AmericInn Lodge & Suites of
Merrill 🆂🄷 🐾
(715) 536-7979. **$79-$139.** 3300 E Main St. US 51, exit 208, 0.5 mi w on SR 64. Int corridors. **Pets:** $10 daily fee/pet. Designated rooms, supervision.
🄰🄢🄺 🆂🐾 ⊠ 🄴 🄸 💻 ⇌

🄰🄰🄰 ▼▼ Pine Ridge Inn 🆂🄷
(715) 536-9526. **$42-$85.** 200 S Pine Ridge. I-39, exit 208, just w. Int corridors. **Pets:** $5 daily fee/pet. Service with restrictions, supervision.
🆂🄰🅅🄴 🆂🐾 ⊠ 🄸 💻 ⇌

🄰🄰🄰 ▼▼ Super 8 Motel 🆂🄷
(715) 536-6880. **$67-$121.** 3209 E Main St. I-39, exit 208, 0.5 mi w on SR 64. Int corridors. **Pets:** Accepted.
🆂🄰🅅🄴 🆂🐾 ⊠ 🄴🄼 🄴 🄸 💻 ⇌ 🆇

MIDDLETON

🄰🄰🄰 ▼▼▼ Marriott Madison West 🄻🄷
(608) 831-2000. **$98-$179.** 1313 John Q Hammons Dr. US 12 and 14, exit 252 (Greenway Blvd), then just w. Int corridors. **Pets:** Small. Service with restrictions, supervision.
🆂🄰🅅🄴 ⊠ 🄐 🄸 💻 🍴 ⇌ 🆇

🄰🄰🄰 ▼▼▼ Staybridge Suites by Holiday
Inn 🆂🄷
(608) 664-5888. **$119.** 7790 Elmwood Ave. US 12 and 14, exit University Ave, just nw. Int corridors. **Pets:** Accepted.
🆂🄰🅅🄴 ⊠ 🄴🄼 🄴 🄸 💻 ⇌ 🆇

MILWAUKEE METROPOLITAN AREA

BROOKFIELD

🄰🄰🄰 ▼▼▼ Baymont Inn & Suites
Milwaukee-Brookfield 🆂🄷
(262) 782-9100. **$59-$99.** 20391 W Bluemound Rd. I-94, exit 297, just e on US 18. Int corridors. **Pets:** Medium. $50 deposit/room. Designated rooms, service with restrictions, supervision.
🆂🄰🅅🄴 🆂🐾 ⊠ 🄐 🄸 💻

▼▼▼ Homestead Studio Suites
Hotel-Milwaukee/Brookfield 🆂🄷 🐾
(262) 782-9300. **$54-$69.** 325 N Brookfield Rd. I-94, exit 297, 1.1 mi e on US 18, just e. Int corridors. **Pets:** Medium, other species. $25 daily fee/room. Service with restrictions, crate.
🄰🄢🄺 🆂🐾 ⊠ 🄐 🄴 🄸 💻

▼▼▼ TownePlace Suites by Marriott 🆂🄷 🐾
(262) 784-8450. **$59-$99.** 600 N Calhoun Rd. I-94, exit 297 eastbound, 2.1 mi e on US 18; exit 301B westbound, 1.5 mi n on Moorland Rd, then 0.4 mi w on US 18. Int corridors. **Pets:** Other species. $75 one-time fee/room. Service with restrictions.
🄰🄢🄺 🆂🐾 ⊠ 🄸 💻 ⇌

DELAFIELD

🄰🄰🄰 ▼▼▼ Baymont Inn & Suites
Milwaukee-Delafield 🆂🄷
(262) 646-8500. **$64-$79.** 2801 Hillside Dr. I-94, exit 287, just s on SR 83, then just e. Int corridors. **Pets:** Accepted.
🆂🄰🅅🄴 🆂🐾 ⊠ 🄴🄼 🄐 🄴 🄸 💻 ⇌

GERMANTOWN

Holiday Inn Express Milwaukee NW-Germantown SH
(262) 255-1100. **$69-$109.** W 177 N9675 Riversbend Ln. US 41 and 45, exit CR Q (County Line Rd), then just w. Int corridors. **Pets:** Accepted.

Super 8 Motel-Germantown/Milwaukee SH ❖
(262) 255-0880. **$69-$89.** N96 W17490 County Line Rd. US 41 and 45, exit CR Q (County Line Rd), then just w. Int corridors. **Pets:** Medium. $5 daily fee/pet. Service with restrictions, supervision.

GLENDALE

Baymont Inn Milwaukee-Glendale SH
(414) 964-8484. **$69-$94.** 5110 N Port Washington Rd. I-43, exit 78A (Silver Spring Dr), 0.4 mi se. Int corridors. **Pets:** Large. $50 deposit/room. Service with restrictions, supervision.

Exel Inn of Milwaukee Northeast SH
(414) 961-7272. **$61-$91.** 5485 N Port Washington Rd. I-43, exit 78A (Silver Spring Dr), just se. Int corridors. **Pets:** Accepted.

Residence Inn by Marriott SH
(414) 352-0070. **$89-$299.** 7275 N Port Washington Rd. I-43, exit 80 (Good Hope Rd), just e. Ext corridors. **Pets:** Other species. $6 daily fee/room, $175 one-time fee/room. Service with restrictions.

Woodfield Suites Milwaukee-Glendale SH
(414) 962-6767. **$109-$199.** 5423 N Port Washington Rd. I-43, exit 78A (Silver Spring Dr), just se. Int corridors. **Pets:** Accepted.

HARTFORD

Super 8 Motel-Hartford SH
(262) 673-7431. **$65-$150.** 1539 E Sumner St. On SR 60, 1.1 mi e of center. Int corridors. **Pets:** Small. $10 daily fee/pet. Designated rooms, service with restrictions, supervision.

JACKSON

Hawthorn Inn and Suites of Jackson SH
(262) 677-1133. **$74-$119.** W227 N16890 Tillie Lake Ct. Nw of jct US 45 and SR 60. Int corridors. **Pets:** Accepted.

MEQUON

Best Western Quiet House & Suites SH
(262) 241-3677. **$95-$105.** 10330 N Port Washington Rd. I-43, exit 85 (Mequon Rd), just w on SR 167, then 1 mi s. Int corridors. **Pets:** Other species. $15 daily fee/pet. Designated rooms, service with restrictions, supervision.

The Chalet Motel of Mequon M ❖
(262) 241-4510. **$69-$159.** 10401 N Port Washington Rd. I-43, exit 85 (Mequon Rd), just w on SR 167, then 1 mi s. Ext corridors. **Pets:** Other species. $10 daily fee/room. Designated rooms, service with restrictions, supervision.

MILWAUKEE

Baymont Inn & Suites Milwaukee NW SH
(414) 535-1300. **$79-$99.** 5442 N Lovers Lane Rd. US 45, exit 46 (Silver Spring Rd), just se. Int corridors. **Pets:** Medium, other species. $50 deposit/room. Designated rooms, service with restrictions, supervision.

Best Western Inn Towne Hotel LH ❖
(414) 224-8400. **$59-$119.** 710 N Old World 3rd St. Corner of Wisconsin Ave and N Old World 3rd St. Int corridors. **Pets:** Medium, other species. $50 deposit/room. Designated rooms, service with restrictions.

Hotel Metro-Milwaukee SH
(414) 272-1937. **$169-$259.** 411 E Mason St. Corner of Mason and Milwaukee sts. Int corridors. **Pets:** Small. $25 daily fee/pet. Designated rooms, service with restrictions, supervision.

OAK CREEK

Baymont Inn & Suites Milwaukee-Airport SH
(414) 762-2266. **$54-$99.** 7141 S 13th St. I-94, exit 320, just se on Rawson Ave (CR BB). Int corridors. **Pets:** Medium. Designated rooms, service with restrictions, supervision.

Comfort Suites Milwaukee Airport SH
(414) 570-1111. **$89-$249.** 6362 S 13th St. I-94, exit 319, just e on College Ave (CR 22), then just s. Int corridors. **Pets:** $5 deposit/pet. Service with restrictions, supervision.

Exel Inn of Milwaukee South SH
(414) 764-1776. **$41-$69.** 1201 W College Ave. I-94, exit 319, just e. Int corridors. **Pets:** Accepted.

MainStay Suites Oak Creek SH
(414) 571-8800. **$69-$199.** 1001 W College Ave. I-94, exit 319, just e. Int corridors. **Pets:** $15 one-time fee/room. Service with restrictions, crate.

[AAA] ♦ **Red Roof Inn-Milwaukee** [M]
(414) 764-3500. **$41-$71.** 6360 S 13th St. I-94, exit 319, just e on College Ave (CR 22). Ext corridors. **Pets:** Small. Service with restrictions, crate.
[SAVE] ⊠ 🦻 ☎

PORT WASHINGTON

[AAA] ♦♦♦ **Best Western Harborside** [SH]
(262) 284-9461. **$69-$169.** 135 E Grand Ave. On SR 43, waterfront of Lake Michigan; downtown. Int corridors. **Pets:** Medium. $25 one-time fee/room. Designated rooms, service with restrictions, supervision.
[SAVE] [SD] ⊠ ♿ ☎ ☕ 🍴 🏊 ⚒

WAUKESHA

[AAA] ♦♦♦ **Best Western Waukesha Grand** [SH]
(262) 524-9300. **$75-$95.** 2840 N Grandview Blvd. I-94, exit 293, just s on CR T. Int corridors. **Pets:** Accepted.
[SAVE] [SD] ⊠ ♿M ♿ ☎ ☕ 🏊

[AAA] ♦♦ **Ramada Limited** [SH]
(262) 547-7770. **$55-$145.** 2111 E Moreland Blvd. I-94, exit 297, 1 mi w on US 18. Int corridors. **Pets:** $25 deposit/pet, $5 daily fee/pet. Designated rooms, service with restrictions, supervision.
[SAVE] [SD] ⊠ ♿ ☎ ☕ 🏊 ⚒

[AAA] ♦♦ **Select Inn** [SH]
(262) 786-6015. **$49-$80.** 2510 Plaza Ct. I-94, exit 297, just w on CR JJ (Bluemound Rd). Int corridors. **Pets:** Medium. $25 deposit/room, $5 daily fee/room. Designated rooms, service with restrictions, supervision.
[SAVE] [SD] ⊠ ♿ ☎ ☕

WAUWATOSA

[AAA] ♦♦ **Exel Inn of Milwaukee West** [SH]
(414) 257-0140. **$53-$84.** 115 N Mayfair Rd. I-94, exit 304B, just n on SR 100. Int corridors. **Pets:** Small, other species. Designated rooms, service with restrictions, supervision.
[SAVE] [SD] ⊠ ☎ ☕

🐾 **END METROPOLITAN AREA** 🐾

MINERAL POINT

♦♦♦ **Comfort Inn** [SH]
(608) 987-4747. **$50-$150.** 1345 Business Park Rd. On US 151, 0.6 mi n of jct SR 23 and 39. Int corridors. **Pets:** Medium. $25 deposit/room. Designated rooms, service with restrictions, crate.
[A$K] [SD] ⊠ ♿ ☎ ☕ 🏊

[AAA] ♦ **Redwood Motel** [M]
(608) 987-2317. **$45-$59.** 625 Dodge St. On US 151, just n of jct SR 23 and 39. Int corridors. **Pets:** Accepted.
[SAVE] [SD] ⊠

MINOCQUA

[AAA] ♦♦♦ **AmericInn of Minocqua** [SH]
(715) 356-3730. **$69-$159.** 700 Hwy 51. On US 51; center. Int corridors. **Pets:** Accepted.
[SAVE] [SD] ⊠ ♿ ☎ ☕ 🏊

♦♦ **Comfort Inn-Minocqua** [SH] 🐾
(715) 358-2588. **$49-$99.** 8729 US 51 N. On US 51 at jct SR 70 W. Int corridors. **Pets:** Other species. $10 daily fee/room. Designated rooms, service with restrictions, supervision.
[A$K] [SD] ⊠ ☎ ☕ 🏊 ⚒

[AAA] ♦♦ **Lakeview Motor Lodge** [M]
(715) 356-5208. **$41-$116.** 311 E Park Ave. North end of US 51 bridge; downtown. Ext/int corridors. **Pets:** Medium. $8 daily fee/pet. Service with restrictions, supervision.
[SAVE] [SD] ⊠ ☎ ☕ ⚒

[AAA] ♦ **Super 8 Motel** [M]
(715) 356-9541. **$65-$90.** 8730 Hwy 51 N. On US 51 at jct SR 70 W. Ext/int corridors. **Pets:** Other species. $10 one-time fee/room. Designated rooms, service with restrictions.
[SAVE] [SD] ⊠ ☎ ☕

MONONA

[AAA] ♦♦♦ **AmericInn of Madison South/Monona** [SH] 🐾
(608) 222-8601. **$79-$159.** 101 W Broadway. US 12 and 18, exit 265 (Monona Dr), just nw. Int corridors. **Pets:** Other species. $5 daily fee/room. Service with restrictions.
[SAVE] [SD] ⊠ ♿ ☎ ☕ 🏊 ⚒

MOSINEE

♦♦ **Comfort Inn** [SH]
(715) 355-4449. **$59-$79.** 1510 County Hwy XX. I-39, exit 185 (US Business Rt 51), just se. Int corridors. **Pets:** Small, dogs only. $30 one-time fee/room. Designated rooms, service with restrictions, crate.
[A$K] [SD] ⊠ 🦻 ☎ ☕ 🏊

NEENAH

♦♦ **Days Inn of Fox Cities** [M]
(920) 720-9020. **$56-$100.** 495 S Greenbay Rd. US 41, exit 131 (Winneconne Ave), just e, then just n. Int corridors. **Pets:** Accepted.
[A$K] [SD] ⊠ ☎ 🏊

♦♦♦ **Holiday Inn Neenah Riverwalk** [SH]
(920) 725-8441. **$89-$126.** 123 E Wisconsin Ave. US 41, exit 132 (Main St), 2 mi e; downtown. Int corridors. **Pets:** Accepted.
[A$K] ⊠ 🦻 ☎ ☕ 🍴 🏊

NEW LISBON

[AAA] ♦♦ **Edge O' the Wood Motel** [M]
(608) 562-3705. **$35-$80.** W 7396 Frontage Rd. I-90/94, exit 61 (SR 80), just e. Ext corridors. **Pets:** Accepted.
[SAVE] [SD] ⊠ ☎ ☕ 🏊 ⚒

ΦΦΦ ▼▼▼ Travelodge of New Lisbon SH
(608) 562-5141. **$55-$110.** 1700 E Bridge St. I-90/94, exit 61 (SR 80), just ne. Int corridors. **Pets:** $50 deposit/room. Designated rooms, service with restrictions, supervision.
SAVE 🐾 ✕ 🐕 🛏 💻 🏊

NEW LONDON

▼▼▼▼ AmericInn Lodge & Suites of New London SH
(920) 982-5700. **$69-$99.** 1404 N Shawano St. US 45, exit US 54, just n. Int corridors. **Pets:** Small, dogs only. $10 one-time fee/pet. Designated rooms, service with restrictions, supervision.
ASK 🐾 ✕ 🐕 🐕 🛏 💻 🏊

ΦΦΦ ▼▼▼ RidgeMark Inns SH 🐾
(920) 982-7907. **$42-$115.** 1409 N Shawano St. US 45, exit US 54, just n. Int corridors. **Pets:** Dogs only. $8 daily fee/pet. Service with restrictions, supervision.
SAVE 🐾 ✕ 🛏 💻 🏊

NEW RICHMOND

▼▼ AmericInn Motel SH
(715) 246-3993. **$69-$134.** 1020 S Knowles Ave. Just s on SR 65. Int corridors. **Pets:** Other species. $25 deposit/room. Service with restrictions, supervision.
ASK 🐾 ✕ 🐕 🛏 💻 🏊 ✕

▼▼ Super 8 Motel SH
(715) 246-7829. **$59-$89.** 1561 Dorset Ln. Just s on SR 65. Int corridors. **Pets:** $15 daily fee/room. Designated rooms, service with restrictions, supervision.
ASK 🐾 ✕ 🐕 🛏

ONALASKA

ΦΦΦ ▼▼▼ Baymont Inn & Suites LaCrosse-Onalaska SH 🐾
(608) 783-7191. **$74-$109.** 3300 Kinney Coulee Rd N. I-90, exit 5, just ne. Int corridors. **Pets:** $5 daily fee/pet. Designated rooms, service with restrictions, supervision.
SAVE 🐾 ✕ 🐕 🐕 🐕 🛏 💻 🏊

▼▼ Comfort Inn SH
(608) 781-7500. **$69-$119.** 1223 Crossing Meadows Dr. I-90, exit 4, just e on SR 157, then e on CR SS. Int corridors. **Pets:** Small, other species. Designated rooms, no service, supervision.
ASK 🐾 ✕ 🐕 🛏 💻 🏊

▼▼▼ Holiday Inn Express SH
(608) 783-6555. **$99-$129.** 9409 Hwy 16. I-90, exit 5, 1 mi e. Int corridors. **Pets:** Small, other species. Designated rooms, service with restrictions, supervision.
ASK 🐾 ✕ 🐕 🛏 💻 🏊

ΦΦΦ ▼▼▼ Microtel Inn SH
(608) 783-0833. **$49-$62.** 3240 N Kinney Coulee Rd. I-90, exit 5, just ne. Int corridors. **Pets:** Small, other species. $5 daily fee/room. Designated rooms, service with restrictions, supervision.
SAVE 🐾 ✕ 🐕 🛏

OSCEOLA

ΦΦΦ ▼▼◆ River Valley Inn SH
(715) 294-4060. **$65-$120.** 1030 Cascade St. Just n on SR 35. Int corridors. **Pets:** Accepted.
SAVE 🐾 ✕ 🛏 💻 🏊

OSHKOSH

ΦΦΦ ▼▼◆ Baymont Inn Oshkosh SH
(920) 233-4190. **$59-$79.** 1950 Omro Rd. US 41, exit 119, at jct SR 21. Int corridors. **Pets:** Small. $50 deposit/room. Designated rooms, supervision.
SAVE 🐾 ✕ 🐕 🛏 💻

▼▼▼ Hawthorn Inn & Suites SH
(920) 303-1133. **$99-$299.** 3105 S Washburn St. US 41, exit 116 (SR 44), just w, then just s. Int corridors. **Pets:** Accepted.
ASK 🐾 ✕ 🐕 🐕 🛏 💻 🍴 🏊

▼◆▼◆ Holiday Inn Express Hotel & Suites SH
(920) 303-1300. **$99-$229.** 2251 Westowne Ave. US 41, exit 119, 0.4 mi sw of jct SR 21. Int corridors. **Pets:** Accepted.
ASK 🐾 ✕ 🐕 🛏 💻 🏊 ✕

ΦΦΦ ▼◆ Oshkosh Travelodge M
(920) 233-4300. **$42-$59.** 1015 S Washburn St. US 41, exit 117, just sw. Ext corridors. **Pets:** Other species. $10 one-time fee/room. Service with restrictions, supervision.
SAVE 🐾 ✕ 🛏 💻 🏊

PHILLIPS

▼▼ Super 8 Motel SH
(715) 339-2898. **$50-$65.** 726 S Lake Ave. 0.6 mi s on SR 13. Int corridors. **Pets:** Designated rooms, service with restrictions, supervision.
ASK 🐾 ✕

PLATTEVILLE

▼▼ Mound View Inn SH
(608) 348-9518. **$50-$70.** 1755 E Hwy 151. On US 151, 2 mi n of jct SR 80/81 N. Int corridors. **Pets:** Accepted.
✕ 🐕 🛏 ✕

ΦΦΦ ▼▼▼ Super 8 Motel SH
(608) 348-8800. **$58-$90.** 100 Hwy 80/81 S. Jct US 151 and SR 80. Int corridors. **Pets:** Accepted.
SAVE 🐾 ✕ 🛏 💻 ✕

PLEASANT PRAIRIE

ΦΦΦ ▼▼▼ Baymont Inn Kenosha-Pleasant Prairie SH
(262) 857-7911. **$58-$98.** 7540 118th Ave. I-94, exit 344 (SR 50), just e. Int corridors. **Pets:** Medium. $25 deposit/room. Designated rooms, service with restrictions, crate.
SAVE 🐾 ✕ 🐕 🛏 💻

ΦΦΦ ▼▼▼▼ Hawthorn Suites LTD Hotel SH 🐾
(262) 942-6000. **$89-$159.** 7887 94th Ave. I-94, exit 344 (SR 50), 1.5 mi e, then 0.3 mi s. Int corridors. **Pets:** Other species. $50 one-time fee/room. Service with restrictions.
SAVE 🐾 ✕ 🐕 🐕 🐕 🛏 💻 🏊 ✕

PORTAGE

▼▼▼ **Super 8 Motel-Portage** 🆂🅷
(608) 742-8330. **$49-$89.** 3000 New Pinery. I-39, exit 92, just s. Int corridors. **Pets:** Dogs only. $10 daily fee/room. Service with restrictions, supervision.
🅰🆂🅺 🆂🅾 ⊠ 🕝 🛗

PRAIRIE DU CHIEN

🔷 ▼▼▼ **Best Western Quiet House &**
Suites 🆂🅷
(608) 326-4777. **$99-$129.** US 18 and SR 35. On US 18, 1.9 mi e of jct SR 27 N. Ext/int corridors. **Pets:** Accepted.
🆂🅰🆅🅴 🆂🅾 ⊠ 🛗 💻 🌊

🔷 ▼▼▼ **Bridgeport Inn** 🆂🅷
(608) 326-6082. **$87-$129.** Hwy 18, 35 & 60 S. On US 18, 2.2 mi e of jct SR 27 N. Int corridors. **Pets:** Medium. $15 daily fee/pet. Designated rooms, service with restrictions, supervision.
🆂🅰🆅🅴 ⊠ 🛗 🌊

🔷 ▼▼▼ **Brisbois Motor Inn** 🅼
(608) 326-8404. **$59-$89.** 533 N Marquette Rd. On SR 35 N, 0.5 mi n of jct US 18/SR 35 S and 27 N. Ext/int corridors. **Pets:** Accepted.
🆂🅰🆅🅴 🆂🅾 ⊠ 🛗 💻 🌊

🔷 ▼▼▼ **Super 8 Motel** 🆂🅷
(608) 326-8777. **$69-$79.** 1930 S Marquette Rd. On US 18, 1.9 mi e of jct SR 27 N. Ext/int corridors. **Pets:** Accepted.
🆂🅰🆅🅴 🆂🅾 ⊠ 🛗

RACINE

🔷 ▼ **Knights Inn** 🅼
(262) 886-6667. **$50-$70.** 1149 Oakes Rd. I-94, exit 333, 4 mi e on SR 20. Ext corridors. **Pets:** Accepted.
🆂🅰🆅🅴 ⊠ 🕝 🛗 💻

🔷 ▼▼ **Microtel Inn & Suites** 🆂🅷
(262) 554-8855. **$62-$73, 14 day notice.** 5419 Durand Ave. On SR 11, 0.5 mi e of jct SR 31. Int corridors. **Pets:** Medium. $10 one-time fee/pet. Designated rooms, service with restrictions, supervision.
🆂🅰🆅🅴 🆂🅾 ⊠ 🆕🅼 🕝 🅲 🛗 💻

▼▼▼ **Racine Marriott Hotel** 🅻🅷
(262) 886-6100. **$150.** 7111 Washington Ave. I-94, exit 333, 4 mi e on SR 20. Int corridors. **Pets:** Accepted.
🅰🆂🅺 🆂🅾 ⊠ 🕝 🛗 💻 🍽 🌊 🍴

▼▼ **Super 8-Racine** 🆂🅷
(262) 884-0486. **$55-$70.** 7141 Kinzie Ave. I-94, exit 333, 4 mi e on SR 20. Int corridors. **Pets:** Accepted.
🅰🆂🅺 🆂🅾 ⊠ 🅲 🛗

REEDSBURG

🔷 ▼ **Copper Springs Motel** 🅼 🐾
(608) 524-4312. **$44-$68, 5 day notice.** E7278 Hwy 23 & 33. 2 mi e on SR 23 and 33. Ext corridors. **Pets:** Other species. $10 daily fee/pet. Designated rooms, supervision.
🆂🅰🆅🅴 ⊠ 🛗 💻

RHINELANDER

▼▼▼ **AmericInn of Rhinelander** 🆂🅷
(715) 369-9600. **$59-$99.** 648 W Kemp St. On Business Rt US 8, 0.3 mi e of jct SR 47. Int corridors. **Pets:** Designated rooms, service with restrictions, supervision.
⊠ 🕝 🅲 🛗 💻 🌊 🍴

🔷 ▼▼▼ **Best Western Claridge Motor Inn** 🅻🅷
(715) 362-7100. **$84-$160.** 70 N Stevens St. On SR 17; center. Int corridors. **Pets:** Accepted.
🆂🅰🆅🅴 🆂🅾 ⊠ 🛗 💻 🍽 🌊 🍴

▼▼ **Comfort Inn** 🆂🅷 🐾
(715) 369-1100. **$65-$107.** 1490 Lincoln St. On Business Rt US 8, 2.6 mi e of jct SR 47. Int corridors. **Pets:** Medium, other species. $25 deposit/pet, $10 daily fee/pet. Designated rooms, service with restrictions, supervision.
🅰🆂🅺 🆂🅾 ⊠ 🛗 💻 🍴

▼▼ **Holiday Acres Resort** 🅻🅷
(715) 369-1500. **$69-$289, 15 day notice.** 4060 S Shore Dr. 4.5 mi e on Business Rt US 8, 2.3 mi n on W Lake George Rd. Ext/int corridors. **Pets:** Other species. $14 daily fee/pet. Designated rooms, service with restrictions, supervision.
🆂🅾 ⊠ 🛗 💻 🍽 🌊 🍴

🔷 ▼▼▼ **Holiday Inn Express** 🆂🅷
(715) 369-3600. **$69-$119.** 668 W Kemp St. On Business Rt US 8, just e of jct SR 47. Int corridors. **Pets:** Medium, other species. $50 one-time fee/room. Designated rooms, service with restrictions, supervision.
🆂🅰🆅🅴 🆂🅾 ⊠ 🆖🅼 🅲 🛗 💻 🌊 🍴

RICE LAKE

🔷 ▼▼▼ **Currier's Lakeview Resort**
Motel 🅼 🐾
(715) 234-7474. **$52-$87.** 2010 E Sawyer St. Jct CR 0, 1.5 mi n on CR SS, 1 mi e, then n on CR C. Ext/int corridors. **Pets:** Other species. Crate.
🆂🅰🆅🅴 🆂🅾 ⊠ 🛗 💻 🍴

▼▼ **Microtel Inn & Suites** 🅼
(715) 736-2010. **$45-$65.** 2771 Decker Dr. US 53, exit 140 (CR 0), just ne. Int corridors. **Pets:** Other species. $10 one-time fee/room. Designated rooms, service with restrictions, supervision.
🅰🆂🅺 🆂🅾 ⊠ 🅲 🛗 💻

RICHLAND CENTER

▼▼ **Super 8 Motel-Richland Center** 🆂🅷
(608) 647-8988. **$75-$90.** 100 Foundry Dr. 0.9 mi e on US 14. Int corridors. **Pets:** Accepted.
🅰🆂🅺 🆂🅾 ⊠ 🛗 💻 🌊 🍴

RIVER FALLS

▼▼ **Super 8 Motel** 🆂🅷
(715) 425-8388. **$82-$92.** 1207 St. Croix St. On SR 65, 0.5 mi w jct SR 35. Int corridors. **Pets:** Accepted.
🅰🆂🅺 🆂🅾 ⊠ 🛗 💻 🌊

ST. CROIX FALLS

Holiday Inn Express Hotel & Suites SH
(715) 483-5775. **$65-$115.** 2190 E US Hwy 8. On US 8, 1.3 mi e of jct SR 35 S. Int corridors. **Pets:** Small, other species. $20 daily fee/pet. Service with restrictions, supervision.
SAVE S X A H P H

ST. GERMAIN

North Woods Rest Motel M
(715) 479-8770. **$49, 3 day notice.** 8083 Hwy 70 E. On SR 70, 0.8 mi e. Ext corridors. **Pets:** Accepted.
H P

SHAWANO

Super 8 Motel-Shawano SH
(715) 526-6688. **$55-$95.** 211 Waukechon St. 1.2 mi e on SR 29 business route. Int corridors. **Pets:** $25 deposit/room. Service with restrictions, supervision.
ASK S X P H P

SHEBOYGAN

AmericInn of Sheboygan SH
(920) 208-8130. **$76-$300.** 3664 S Taylor Dr. I-43, exit 123, just e. Int corridors. **Pets:** $50 deposit/room, $7 daily fee/pet. Designated rooms, no service, crate.
SAVE S X P H P H

Baymont Inn Sheboygan SH
(920) 457-2321. **$69-$109.** 2932 Kohler Memorial Dr. I-43, exit 126, 1 mi e on SR 23. Int corridors. **Pets:** Medium, other species. Service with restrictions, supervision.
SAVE S X P H P

Comfort Inn-Sheboygan SH
(920) 457-7724. **$55-$95.** 4332 N 40th St. I-43, exit 128, 0.3 mi e on Business Rt 42. Int corridors. **Pets:** $10 daily fee/pet. Designated rooms, service with restrictions, supervision.
ASK S X P H P H

Super 8 Motel SH
(920) 458-8080. **$59-$74.** 3402 Wilgus Rd. I-43, exit 126, just ne. Int corridors. **Pets:** Dogs only. $10 one-time fee/room. Service with restrictions, supervision.
ASK S X H P

SIREN

The Lodge at Crooked Lake SH
(715) 349-2500. **$69-$109.** 24271 SR 35 N. On SR 35, 0.5 mi n of jct SR 70. Int corridors. **Pets:** Dogs only. $50 deposit/room. Service with restrictions, supervision.
SAVE S X H P H P

Pine Wood Motel M
(715) 349-5225. **$39-$55.** 23862 Hwy 35 S. On SR 35, 0.3 mi s of jct SR 70 W and CR B E. Ext corridors. **Pets:** Small, dogs only. $25 deposit/room. Supervision.
SAVE X H

SPARTA

Best Nights Inn M
(608) 269-3066. **$39-$139.** 303 W Wisconsin St. I-90, exit 25 (SR 27), 0.5 mi s. Ext corridors. **Pets:** Medium, other species. $50 deposit/room. Designated rooms, service with restrictions, crate.
SAVE S X H P H

Country Inn By Carlson SH
(608) 269-3110. **$75-$130.** 737 Avon Rd. I-90, exit 25 (SR 27), just n. Int corridors. **Pets:** Medium, other species. $5 daily fee/pet. Service with restrictions, supervision.
SAVE S X M H P H

Super 8 Sparta SH
(608) 269-8489. **$75-$87.** 716 Avon Rd. I-90, exit 25 (SR 27), just n. Int corridors. **Pets:** Small. $5 one-time fee/pet. Service with restrictions, supervision.
X H P H

SPOONER

Best Western American Heritage Inn SH
(715) 635-9770. **$79-$99.** 101 Maple St. On SR 70 at jct US 63, 1 mi w of US 53. Int corridors. **Pets:** Small, other species. $50 deposit/pet, $10 daily fee/pet. Designated rooms, service with restrictions, supervision.
SAVE S X P H P H

Country House Motel & RV Park M
(715) 635-8721. **$59-$109.** 717 S River St. On US 63, 0.5 mi s of jct SR 70. Ext/int corridors. **Pets:** Dogs only. $4 daily fee/pet. Designated rooms, service with restrictions, supervision.
SAVE X M A P H P H

STEVENS POINT

Baymont Inn & Suites Stevens Point SH
(715) 344-1900. **$54-$74, 18 day notice.** 4917 Main St. I-39, exit 158B (US 10), just w. Int corridors. **Pets:** Accepted.
SAVE S X A H P H

Country Inn & Suites By Carlson SH
(715) 345-7000. **$64-$139.** 301 Division St N. I-39, exit 161, on US 51 business route, 0.6 mi s. Int corridors. **Pets:** $25 one-time fee/room. Designated rooms, service with restrictions, supervision.
SAVE S X P H P H

Point Motel M
(715) 344-8312. **$38-$48.** 209 Division St. I-39, exit 161 (US 51 business route), 0.7 mi s. Ext corridors. **Pets:** Medium. $5 daily fee/pet. Designated rooms, service with restrictions, supervision.
ASK S X H P

STURTEVANT

Holiday Inn Express-Racine SH
(262) 884-0200. **$69-$99.** 13339 Hospitality Ct. I-94, exit 333 (SR 20), just se. Int corridors. **Pets:** Small. Designated rooms, service with restrictions, supervision.
SAVE S X M A P H P H

SUN PRAIRIE

ⒶⒶⒶ ◊ McGovern's Motel & Suites Ⓜ
(608) 837-7321. **$56-$80.** 820 W Main St. On US 151, exit 101, 1.2 mi ne. Ext/int corridors. **Pets:** Medium, dogs only. $5 daily fee/pet. Service with restrictions, supervision.
🆂🅰🆅🅴 🆂🅳 ⊗ 🖥 💻 🍴

SUPERIOR

ⒶⒶⒶ ◊◊◊ Barkers Island Inn 🆂🅷
(715) 392-7152. **$67-$210.** 300 Marina Dr. Just ne of US 2/53; on Barkers Island. Int corridors. **Pets:** Medium. $50 deposit/room, $10 daily fee/pet. Designated rooms, service with restrictions, supervision.
🆂🅰🆅🅴 🆂🅳 ⊗ 🖥 💻 🍴 ≈ 🚫

◊◊◊ Best Western Bay Walk Inn 🆂🅷
(715) 392-7600. **$59-$119.** 1405 Susquehanna Ave. Just e of US 2 on Belknap St. Int corridors. **Pets:** Designated rooms, service with restrictions, supervision.
🅰🆂🅺 🆂🅳 ⊗ 🖥 💻 ≈ 🚫

ⒶⒶⒶ ◊◊◊ Best Western Bridgeview Motor Inn 🆂🅷
(715) 392-8174. **$49-$135.** 415 Hammond Ave. 0.8 mi n at south end of Blatnik Bridge. Int corridors. **Pets:** Accepted.
🆂🅰🆅🅴 🆂🅳 ⊗ 🖥 💻 ≈ 🚫

◊ Days Inn-Superior/Bayfront 🆂🅷
(715) 392-4783. **$59-$119.** 110 Harborview Pkwy. Just n of jct US 2/53. Ext/int corridors. **Pets:** $50 deposit/room, $10 daily fee/room. Designated rooms, service with restrictions, supervision.
🅰🆂🅺 🆂🅳 ⊗ 🕹 🖥 💻 🍴 ≈ 🚫

◊ Stockade Motel Ⓜ
(715) 398-3585. **Call for rates.** 1610 E 2nd St. On US 2/53, 2.8 mi se. Ext corridors. **Pets:** Accepted.
⊗ 💻

ⒶⒶⒶ ◊◊◊ Superior Inn 🆂🅷
(715) 394-7706. **$85-$120.** 525 Hammond Ave. 0.8 mi n at south end of Blatnik Bridge. Int corridors. **Pets:** Other species. Designated rooms, service with restrictions, supervision.
🆂🅰🆅🅴 🆂🅳 ⊗ 🖥 💻 ≈

THORP

ⒶⒶⒶ ◊◊◊ AmericInn Lodge & Suites 🆂🅷
(715) 669-5959. **$76-$131.** 203 1/2 W Hill St. US 29, exit 108 (SR 73), just nw. Int corridors. **Pets:** Small. $10 daily fee/pet. Service with restrictions, supervision.
🆂🅰🆅🅴 ⊗ 🕹 🖥 💻 ≈

TOMAH

◊◊ Comfort Inn-Tomah 🆂🅷
(608) 372-6600. **$64-$114.** 305 Wittig Rd. I-94, exit 143 (SR 21), just w. Int corridors. **Pets:** Accepted.
🅰🆂🅺 🆂🅳 ⊗ 🖥 🖥 💻 ≈

◊◊ Econo Lodge 🆂🅷
(608) 372-9100. **$41-$145.** 2005 N Superior Ave. I-94, exit 143 (SR 21), just w. Ext/int corridors. **Pets:** Accepted.
🅰🆂🅺 🆂🅳 ⊗ 🖥 🖥 💻 ≈

◊◊ Holiday Inn 🆂🅷 ❀
(608) 372-3211. **$89-$115.** 1017 E McCoy Blvd. I-94, exit 143 (SR 21), just e. Int corridors. **Pets:** Service with restrictions, supervision.
🅰🆂🅺 🆂🅳 ⊗ 🖥 💻 🍴 ≈ 🚫

ⒶⒶⒶ ◊◊◊ Lark Inn Ⓜ ❀
(608) 372-5981. **$59-$91.** 229 N Superior Ave. I-94, exit 143 (SR 21), 1.5 mi s on US 12; I-90, exit 41, 2 mi n on US 12. Ext/int corridors. **Pets:** Other species. $6 daily fee/pet. Designated rooms, supervision.
🆂🅰🆅🅴 🆂🅳 ⊗ 🖥 💻

◊◊◊ Super 8 Motel-Tomah 🆂🅷
(608) 372-3901. **$48-$78.** 1008 E McCoy Blvd. I-94, exit 143 (SR 21), just e. Int corridors. **Pets:** $10 one-time fee/room. Designated rooms, service with restrictions, supervision.
🅰🆂🅺 🆂🅳 ⊗ 🕹 🖥 💻

TOMAHAWK

ⒶⒶⒶ ◊◊◊ Comfort Inn 🆂🅷
(715) 453-8900. **$63-$115.** 1738 E Comfort Dr. US 51, exit 229. Int corridors. **Pets:** Other species. $15 one-time fee/room. Designated rooms, service with restrictions, supervision.
🆂🅰🆅🅴 🆂🅳 ⊗ 🕹🅼 🕹 🖥 💻 ≈

◊◊ Super 8 Motel-Tomahawk 🆂🅷
(715) 453-5210. **$53-$89.** 108 W Mohawk Dr. On US 51 business route, 0.6 mi n of downtown. Int corridors. **Pets:** $25 deposit/room. Service with restrictions, supervision.
🅰🆂🅺 🆂🅳 🕹 🖥 ≈ 🚫

VERONA

◊◊ Super 8 Motel-Verona/Madison 🆂🅷 ❀
(608) 848-7829. **$66-$75.** 131 Horizon Dr. US 18 and 151, exit 94 southbound; exit 89 northbound, just n. Int corridors. **Pets:** Other species. $6 one-time fee/room. Service with restrictions.
🅰🆂🅺 🆂🅳 ⊗ 🖥 💻 ≈ 🚫

WATERFORD

ⒶⒶⒶ ◊◊◊ Baymont Inns & Suites-Waterford 🆂🅷
(262) 534-4100. **$66-$98.** 750 Fox Ln. On SR 36, 1 mi s of jct SR 164. Int corridors. **Pets:** Medium. $50 deposit/room. Designated rooms, service with restrictions, supervision.
🆂🅰🆅🅴 🆂🅳 ⊗ 🕹 🖥 💻 ≈

WATERTOWN

◊◊ Econo Lodge 🆂🅷
(920) 261-9010. **$59-$79.** 700 E Main St. On US 16 and SR 19. Int corridors. **Pets:** $10 daily fee/pet. Designated rooms, service with restrictions, supervision.
🅰🆂🅺 🆂🅳 ⊗ 🖥 🍴

◊◊ Holiday Inn Express 🆂🅷
(920) 262-1910. **$79-$109.** 101 Aviation Way. On SR 26, 1.5 mi s of jct SR 19. Int corridors. **Pets:** Large, dogs only. $100 deposit/room, $5 one-time fee/pet. Designated rooms, service with restrictions, supervision.
🅰🆂🅺 🆂🅳 ⊗ 🕹 🖥 💻 ≈ 🚫

▼▼ ▼▼ **Super 8 Motel** SH
(920) 261-1188. **$68-$83.** 1730 S Church St. On SR 26, 1.5 mi s of jct SR 19. Int corridors. **Pets:** $75 deposit/room. Service with restrictions, supervision.
ASK SO X 🖥 💻 ⇌

WAUPACA

◬◬ ▼▼▼ **Baymont Inn & Suites** SH
(715) 258-9212. **$129-$149.** 110 Grand Seasons Dr. Jct US 10 and SR 54. Int corridors. **Pets:** Medium, other species. $50 deposit/room. Designated rooms, supervision.
SAVE SO X 🐾 🔧 🖥 💻 ⇌ 🗙

WAUPUN

▼▼ **Inn Town Motel** M
(920) 324-4211. **$48-$52.** 27 S State St. US 151, exit 146 (SR 49), 1.3 mi w. Ext corridors. **Pets:** Accepted.
X 🖥 💻

WAUSAU

◬◬ ▼▼▼ **Baymont Inn-Wausau** SH
(715) 842-0421. **$59-$94.** 1910 Stewart Ave. I-39, exit 192, just e. Int corridors. **Pets:** Other species. $50 deposit/room. Designated rooms, service with restrictions, supervision.
SAVE SO X 🐾 🖥 💻 ⇌

◬◬ ▼▼▼ **Days Inn-Wausau** SH
(715) 355-5501. **$69-$130.** 4700 Rib Mountain Dr. I-39, exit 188, just e. Int corridors. **Pets:** Other species. $10 daily fee/room. Designated rooms, service with restrictions, supervision.
SAVE SO X 🖥 💻 ⇌

◬◬ ▼▼▼ **Exel Inn of Wausau** M
(715) 842-0641. **$45-$65.** 116 S 17th Ave. I-39, exit 192, just e. Int corridors. **Pets:** Small. Designated rooms, service with restrictions, supervision.
SAVE SO X 🖥 💻

▼▼ ▼▼ **Plaza Hotel & Suites** SH
(715) 845-4341. **$75-$169.** 201 N 17th Ave. I-39, exit 193, just e. Int corridors. **Pets:** Accepted.
ASK SO X 🐾 🔧 🖥 💻 🍴 ⇌ 🗙

▼▼ ▼▼ **Rib Mountain Inn** SH
(715) 848-2802. **$69-$449, 3 day notice.** 2900 Rib Mountain Way. I-39, exit 190 (CR NN), 1 mi w. Ext/int corridors. **Pets:** Other species. $10 daily fee/pet. Service with restrictions.
ASK SO 🔧 🖥 💻 🗙

◬◬ ▼▼▼ **Super 8 Motel** SH
(715) 848-2888. **$45-$79.** 2006 Stewart Ave W. I-39, exit 192, just e. Int corridors. **Pets:** Other species. $5 daily fee/pet. Designated rooms, service with restrictions, supervision.
SAVE SO X 🐾 🔧 🖥 💻 ⇌

WAUTOMA

▼▼ ▼▼ **AmericInn** SH
(920) 787-5050. **$77-$177.** W7696 SR 21/73. On SR 21 and 73, 1.2 mi e. Int corridors. **Pets:** Accepted.
ASK SO X 🔧M 🔧 🖥 💻 ⇌

▼▼ ▼▼ **Super 8 Motel-Wautoma** SH
(920) 787-4811. **$63-$79.** W7607 SR 21 and 73. On SR 21 and 73, 1.5 mi e. Int corridors. **Pets:** Other species. $25 deposit/room. Service with restrictions, supervision.
ASK SO X 🖥 ⇌

WEST SALEM

▼▼▼▼ **AmericInn** SH
(608) 786-3340. **$89-$149.** 125 Buol Rd. I-90, exit 12, just sw on CR C. Int corridors. **Pets:** Accepted.
ASK SO X 🔧 🖥 💻 ⇌

WHITEWATER

▼▼▼▼ **AmeriHost Inn & Suites** SH
(262) 472-9400. **$74-$79.** 1355 W Main St. On US 12, 0.5 mi w of jct SR 59 W. Int corridors. **Pets:** Other species. $20 deposit/pet, $10 one-time fee/pet. Service with restrictions, supervision.
ASK SO X 🔧M 🐾 🔧 🖥 💻 ⇌ 🗙

▼▼ ▼▼ **Super 8 Motel** SH
(262) 472-9400. **$49-$114.** 917 E Milwaukee St. On US 12, just e of jct SR 59 E. Int corridors. **Pets:** Accepted.
ASK SO X 🔧M 🖥

WINDSOR

◬◬ ▼▼▼▼ **Days Inn** SH
(608) 846-7473. **$54-$65.** 6311 Rostad Cir. I-90/94, exit 131 (SR 19). Int corridors. **Pets:** Accepted.
SAVE SO X 🔧M 🔧 🖥 💻 ⇌ 🗙

▼▼ ▼▼ **Super 8 Motel-Windsor/North Madison** SH
(608) 846-3971. **$49-$100.** 4506 Lake Cir. I-90/94, exit 131 (SR 19). Int corridors. **Pets:** $10 one-time fee/room. Designated rooms, service with restrictions, supervision.
ASK SO X 🖥 💻

WISCONSIN DELLS

◬◬ ▼▼▼ **Baker's Sunset Bay Resort** SH
(608) 254-8406. **$54-$225, 7 day notice.** 921 Canyon Rd. I-90/94, exit 92 (US 12), 0.5 mi w, right on E Adams St, right on Canyon Rd, then 0.8 mi on left. Ext/int corridors. **Pets:** Accepted.
SAVE X 🔧 🖥 💻 ⇌ 🗙

◬◬ ▼▼▼ **Black Hawk Motel** M 🐾
(608) 254-7770. **$35-$140, 3 day notice.** 720 Race St. I-90/94, exit 87 (SR 13), 2 mi e on SR 13, 16 and 23. Ext corridors. **Pets:** Small, other species. $5 one-time fee/pet. Service with restrictions, crate.
SAVE SO X 🔧 🖥 💻 ⇌ 🗙

▼▼ **Bridge View Motel** M
(608) 254-6114. **$49-$99, 3 day notice.** 1020 River Rd. Just n of SR 13 (Broadway); center. Ext corridors. **Pets:** Small. $10 daily fee/pet. Designated rooms, service with restrictions, crate.
ASK SO X 🔧 ⇌

▲▲▲ ▼▼ **Day's End Motel** 🅼
(608) 254-8171. **$34-$124, 3 day notice.** N 604 Hwy 12-16.
I-90/94, exit 85 (US 12), 0.8 mi nw. Ext corridors.
Pets: Other species. $7 daily fee/pet. Designated rooms,
service with restrictions, crate.
⟦SAVE⟧ ⟦S🐕⟧ ⟦✕⟧ 🛎 💻 ⟦🔁⟧ ⟦🐾⟧

▲▲▲ ▼▼▼ **Howard Johnson Hotel and Antiqua
        Bay Waterpark** 🆂🅷
(608) 254-8306. **$89-$140, 3 day notice.** 655 Frontage Rd.
I-90/94, exit 87 (SR 13), just e. Int corridors. **Pets:** Dogs
only. $10 daily fee/pet. Designated rooms, service with
restrictions, supervision.
⟦SAVE⟧ ⟦S🐕⟧ ⟦✕⟧ ⟦🏊⟧ 🛎 💻 ⟦🍽⟧ ⟦🐾⟧ ⟦🔁⟧

▼▼ **Rodeway Inn** 🆂🅷
(608) 254-6492. **$65-$150.** 350 W Munroe Ave. I-90/94, exit
89 (SR 23 N), 0.4 mi e. Int corridors. **Pets:** Medium. $10
daily fee/pet. Designated rooms, service with restrictions,
supervision.
⟦ASK⟧ ⟦S🐕⟧ ⟦✕⟧ ⟦♿M⟧ ⟦🏊⟧ 🛎 💻 ⟦🐾⟧

▼▼ **Super 8 Motel** 🆂🅷
(608) 254-6464. **$56-$165.** 800 CR H. I-90/94, exit 87 (SR
13), just e. Int corridors. **Pets:** Medium, other species. Service with restrictions, supervision.
⟦✕⟧ ⟦🏊⟧ 💻 ⟦🐾⟧ ⟦🔁⟧

WISCONSIN RAPIDS

▲▲▲ ▼▼▼ **Best Western Rapids Motor Inn** 🆂🅷
(715) 423-3211. **$62-$76.** 911 Huntington Ave. 0.5 mi s on
SR 13 of jct SR 54. Int corridors. **Pets:** Accepted.
⟦SAVE⟧ ⟦S🐕⟧ ⟦✕⟧ 🛎 💻

▲▲▲ ▼▼▼ **Hotel Mead** 🅻🅷
(715) 423-1500. **$119-$224.** 451 E Grand Ave. Just e of
downtown. Int corridors. **Pets:** Accepted.
⟦SAVE⟧ ⟦S🐕⟧ ⟦✕⟧ ⟦🏊⟧ ⟦🏊⟧ 🛎 💻 ⟦🍽⟧ ⟦🐾⟧ ⟦🔁⟧

▼▼ **Super 8 Motel** 🆂🅷
(715) 423-8080. **$53-$68.** 3410 8th St S. 1.9 mi s on SR 13
of jct SR 54 W. Int corridors. **Pets:** Dogs only. $10 one-time
fee/room. Service with restrictions, supervision.
⟦ASK⟧ ⟦S🐕⟧ ⟦✕⟧ ⟦🏊⟧ 🛎 💻

WITTENBERG

▼▼▼ **Comfort Inn & Wilderness Conference
        Center** 🆂🅷 🐾
(715) 253-3755. **$57-$137.** W17267 Red Oak Ln. US 29,
exit 198, just se. Int corridors. **Pets:** Other species. $20
one-time fee/room. Designated rooms, service with restrictions, supervision.
⟦ASK⟧ ⟦S🐕⟧ ⟦✕⟧ ⟦♿M⟧ ⟦🏊⟧ 🛎 💻 ⟦🐾⟧

WYOMING

AFTON

▼ The Corral CA
(307) 885-5424. **$50-$55.** 161 Washington St (US Hwy 89). On US 89; center. Ext corridors. **Pets:** Small. Service with restrictions, supervision.
⊠ 🖥

⚠ ▼▼ Hi Country Inn M
(307) 885-3856. **$95-$100, 5 day notice.** 689 S Washington St (US Hwy 89). On US 89, 0.8 mi s. Ext corridors. **Pets:** Accepted.
SAVE S🔊 ⊠ 🖥 ➹ ⊠ 🅚

⚠ ▼ Lazy B Motel M ❖
(307) 885-3187. **$65-$75.** 219 Washington St (US Hwy 89). On US 89; center. Ext corridors. **Pets:** Other species. Service with restrictions, supervision.
SAVE S🔊 ⊠ 🖥 ➹

▼▼ Mountain Inn M
(307) 885-3156. **$65-$85.** 83542 Hwy 89. On US 89, 1.5 mi s. Ext corridors. **Pets:** Other species. $5 daily fee/pet. Supervision.
A$K S🔊 ⊠ 🖥 🖵 ➹ ⊠ 🅚

ALPINE

⚠ ▼▼▼ Best Western Flying Saddle Lodge M
(307) 654-7561. **$116-$180.** 118878 Jct US 26 & 89. 0.5 mi e of jct US 26 and 89. Ext corridors. **Pets:** $50 deposit/room. Service with restrictions, supervision.
SAVE S🔊 ⊠ 🖥 🖵 🍴 ➹ ⊠

BUFFALO

▼ Arrowhead Motel M ❖
(307) 684-9453. **$35-$60.** 749 Fort St. Jct US 16, 87 and Business Loop I-25, 0.6 mi w. Ext corridors. **Pets:** Other species. $5 daily fee/pet. Supervision.
⊠ 🖥

▼ Canyon Motel M ❖
(307) 684-2957. **$34-$60.** 997 Fort St. Jct US 16/87/ Business Loop I-25, 0.9 mi w on US 16. Ext corridors. **Pets:** Other species. $3 one-time fee/pet. Service with restrictions, supervision.
A$K S🔊 ⊠ 🖥

▼▼▼ Comfort Inn SH
(307) 684-9564. **$45-$120.** 65 Hwy 16 E. I-25, exit 299 (US 16), just e; I-90, exit 58, 1.3 mi w. Ext/int corridors. **Pets:** Medium, other species. $5 daily fee/pet. Designated rooms, service with restrictions, supervision.
A$K S🔊 ⊠ 🖵

▼ Mountain View Motel & Campground CA
(307) 684-2881. **$35-$99, 7 day notice.** 585 Fort St. Jct US 16/87 and Business Loop I-25, 0.4 mi w on US 16. Ext corridors. **Pets:** Medium. $10 one-time fee/room. Designated rooms, service with restrictions, supervision.
⊠ 🖥 🖵

⚠ ▼▼▼ Super 8 Motel of Buffalo SH
(307) 684-2531. **$55-$120, 3 day notice.** 655 E Hart St. I-25, exit 299 (US 16), just w; I-90, exit 58, 1.3 mi w. Int corridors. **Pets:** Large, other species. $6 daily fee/pet. Designated rooms, service with restrictions, supervision.
SAVE S🔊 ⊠ ⊠

⚠ ▼▼▼ Wyoming Motel M ❖
(307) 684-5505. **$27-$97.** 610 E Hart St. I-25, exit 299 (US 16), just w; I-90, exit 58, 1.3 mi w. Ext corridors. **Pets:** Designated rooms, service with restrictions, supervision.
SAVE ⊠ 🖥 🖵 ➹

⚠ ▼▼▼ Z-Bar Motel CA
(307) 684-5535. **$40-$67, 30 day notice.** 626 Fort St. Jct US 16, 87 and Business Loop I-25, 0.5 mi w on US 16. Ext corridors. **Pets:** Other species. $4 daily fee/pet. Service with restrictions, supervision.
SAVE S🔊 ⊠ 🖥 🖵

CASPER

▼▼ Days Inn Casper SH
(307) 234-1159. **$72-$86.** 301 E 'E' St. I-25, exit 188A, just w. Int corridors. **Pets:** Accepted.
A$K S🔊 ⊠ 🖥 🖵 ➹

⚠ ▼▼▼ Hearthside SH
(307) 232-5100. **$68-$108.** 111 S Wilson St. I-25, exit 186, 0.5 mi s to 1st St, then 0.4 mi w. Int corridors. **Pets:** Accepted.
SAVE S🔊 ⊠ 🖥 🖵

⚠ ▼▼▼▼ Holiday Inn SH
(307) 235-2531. **$99-$109, 3 day notice.** 300 W 'F' St. I-25, exit 188A, just e. Int corridors. **Pets:** Accepted.
SAVE S🔊 ⊠ 📶M 🗔 🖥 🖵 🍴 ➹ ⊠

(AAA) ▼▼ **Parkway Plaza Hotel & Convention Centre** SH
(307) 235-1777. **$90-$95.** 123 W 'E' St. I-25, exit 188A, just w. Ext/int corridors. **Pets:** Other species. $35 deposit/room. Designated rooms, service with restrictions.
[SAVE] [S6] [X] [cM] [🛏] [💻] [🍴] [🏊] [🐾]

(AAA) ▼▼ **Quality Inn & Suites** SH ❖
(307) 266-2400. **$70-$95.** 821 N Poplar St. I-25, exit 188B, just e. Int corridors. **Pets:** Other species. $5 daily fee/room. Designated rooms, service with restrictions, supervision.
[SAVE] [S6] [X] [cM] [🛏] [💻]

▼▼▼ **Radisson Hotel Casper** LH
(307) 266-6000. **$89-$105.** 800 N Poplar St. I-25, exit 188B, just e. Int corridors. **Pets:** Accepted.
[ASK] [S6] [X] [cM] [cM] [🛏] [💻] [🍴] [🏊] [🐾]

▼▼ **Super 8 Motel** SH ❖
(307) 266-3480. **$57-$62.** 3838 CY Ave. I-25, exit 188B, 1.7 mi w on S Poplar St (SR 220), 1.8 mi n. Int corridors. **Pets:** Other species. $3 one-time fee/pet. Designated rooms, service with restrictions, supervision.
[ASK] [S6] [X] [🛏] [💻]

CHEYENNE

(AAA) ▼▼▼ **Best Western Hitching Post Inn Resort & Conference Center** SH ❖
(307) 638-3301. **$89-$159.** 1700 W Lincolnway. I-25, exit 9, 0.8 mi e on I-80 business loop/US 30. Ext/int corridors. **Pets:** Medium. $50 deposit/room. Service with restrictions, supervision.
[SAVE] [S6] [X] [cM] [cM] [cM] [🛏] [💻] [🍴] [🏊] [🐾]

▼▼ **Comfort Inn of Cheyenne** SH ❖
(307) 638-7202. **$79-$109.** 2245 Etchepare Dr. I-25, exit 7, just w. Int corridors. **Pets:** Medium, other species. $20 deposit/pet. Service with restrictions, supervision.
[ASK] [S6] [X] [cM] [cM] [🛏] [💻]

▼▼ **Days Inn Cheyenne** SH
(307) 778-8877. **$64-$89.** 2360 W Lincolnway. I-25, exit 9, just e on US 30/I-80 business loop. Int corridors. **Pets:** Other species. $25 deposit/room. Service with restrictions, supervision.
[ASK] [S6] [X] [cM] [cM] [🛏] [💻]

(AAA) ▼▼ **Express Inn** SH
(307) 632-7556. **$44-$140, 7 day notice.** 2512 W Lincolnway. I-25, exit 9, just e. Int corridors. **Pets:** Accepted.
[SAVE] [S6] [X] [cM] [🛏] [🐾]

▼ **Fleetwood Motel** M
(307) 638-8908. **$47-$59, 7 day notice.** 3800 E Lincolnway. I-80, exit 364, 1.2 mi n on N College Dr (SR 212), just w on I-80/US 30 business loop. Ext corridors. **Pets:** Accepted.
[ASK] [S6] [X] [🛏] [🐾]

(AAA) ▼▼▼ **Holiday Inn Cheyenne Dream in the West** SH
(307) 638-4466. **$69-$189.** 204 W Fox Farm Rd. I-80, exit 362, just s. Int corridors. **Pets:** Large, other species. $25 deposit/pet, $25 one-time fee/pet. Service with restrictions, supervision.
[SAVE] [X] [cM] [cM] [🛏] [💻] [🍴] [🏊] [🐾]

(AAA) ▼▼▼▼ **La Quinta Inn Cheyenne** SH
(307) 632-7117. **$70-$90.** 2410 W Lincolnway. I-25, exit 9, just e. Int corridors. **Pets:** Accepted.
[SAVE] [X] [cM] [🛏] [💻] [🐾]

(AAA) ▼▼▼▼ **Nagle Warren Mansion B & B** BB
(307) 637-3333. **$118-$138, 3 day notice.** 222 E 17th St. I-80, exit 362, 1.2 mi n on I-25 business loop/US 85/87 business route, just e; downtown. Int corridors. **Pets:** Medium, other species. $20 daily fee/pet. Designated rooms, supervision.
[SAVE] [X] [cM] [🐾]

(AAA) ▼▼ **Oak Tree Inn** SH
(307) 778-6620. **$65-$100.** 1625 Stillwater. 1.2 mi e of jct Dell Range Blvd and Yellowstone Rd, 0.4 mi s. Ext/int corridors. **Pets:** Small, other species. $10 one-time fee/pet. Service with restrictions, supervision.
[SAVE] [S6] [X] [🛏] [🍴]

▼▼▼ **The Plains Hotel** SH
(307) 638-3311. **$79-$209.** 1600 Central Ave. I-80, exit 362, 1 mi n on I-180/I-25 business loop/US 85/87 business route, just w on I-80 business loop/US 30; downtown. Int corridors. **Pets:** Medium, other species. Designated rooms, service with restrictions, supervision.
[ASK] [S6] [cM] [🛏] [💻] [🍴]

▼▼ **Porch Swing Bed & Breakfast** BB ❖
(307) 778-7182. **$85, 30 day notice.** 502 E 24th St. I-80, exit 362, 1.8 mi n on I-25 business loop/US 85/87 business route, just e; downtown. Int corridors. **Pets:** Large, other species. Service with restrictions.
[X] [cM]

(AAA) ▼▼▼ **Windy Hills Guest House** BB ❖
(307) 632-6423. **$98-$200, 3 day notice.** 393 Happy Jack Rd. I-25, exit 10B, 22 mi w on SR 210 (Happy Jack Rd), 1 mi s on private gravel road. Ext corridors. **Pets:** Dogs only. $50 deposit/pet. Designated rooms, no service, supervision.
[SAVE] [S6] [X] [🛏] [💻] [cM] [cM]

CHUGWATER

▼▼ **Super 8 Motel-Chugwater** SH
(307) 422-3248. **$52-$80.** 100 Buffalo Dr. I-25, exit 54, just ne. Int corridors. **Pets:** Medium, other species. $10 daily fee/pet. Designated rooms, supervision.
[ASK] [S6] [X] [🍴] [🐾]

CODY

(AAA) ▼▼▼ **Beartooth Inn** M ❖
(307) 527-5505. **$69-$131.** 2513 Greybull Hwy. 1.5 mi e on US 14/16/20. Ext/int corridors. **Pets:** Medium, dogs only. Designated rooms, service with restrictions, supervision.
[SAVE] [S6] [X] [🛏] [💻]

(AAA) ▼▼▼▼ **Best Western Sunset Motor Inn** SH
(307) 587-4265. **$55-$139.** 1601 8th St. 0.8 mi w on US 14/16/20. Ext corridors. **Pets:** Medium, other species. $15 one-time fee/pet. Designated rooms, service with restrictions, supervision.
[SAVE] [S6] [X] [cM] [🛏] [💻] [🍴] [🏊] [🐾]

AAA **WW** Big Bear Motel **M**
(307) 587-3117. **$39-$70.** 139 W Yellowstone Hwy. 2 mi w on US 14/16/20, from city center. Ext corridors. **Pets:** Accepted.
SAVE S♦ ✕ ➹ ✆

AAA **WWW** Cody Motor Lodge **M** ❀
(307) 527-6291. **$55-$120.** 1455 Sheridan Ave. Just w on US 14/16/20 and SR 120. Int corridors. **Pets:** Other species. Designated rooms, supervision.
SAVE S♦ ✕

WWW Cody Super 8 Motel **M**
(307) 527-6214. **$68-$169.** 730 Yellowstone Rd. On US 14/16, 1 mi w of city center. Int corridors. **Pets:** Accepted.
ASK S♦ ✕ ∅ 🅷 🖥

WWWW Green Gables Inn **M**
(307) 587-6886. **$49-$99.** 1636 Central Ave. Just e on US 14/16/20 and SR 120. Ext corridors. **Pets:** Small, dogs only. $25 deposit/room. Service with restrictions, supervision.
ASK S♦ ✕ 🖥

AAA **WWW** Skyline Motor Inn **M**
(307) 587-4201. **$38-$74.** 1919 17th St. 0.8 mi e on US 14/16/20 and SR 120. Ext corridors. **Pets:** Accepted.
SAVE ✕ ➹

WWW Sunrise Motor Inn **M**
(307) 587-5566. **$45-$110.** 1407 8th St. 0.8 mi w on US 14/16/20. Ext corridors. **Pets:** Small, dogs only. Service with restrictions, supervision.
ASK S♦ ✕ ∅ 🖥 ➹

DOUGLAS

AAA **WWW** Best Western Douglas Inn & Conference Center **SH**
(307) 358-9790. **$75-$95.** 1450 Riverbend Dr. I-25, exit 140, 0.8 mi e. Int corridors. **Pets:** Medium. $25 deposit/room. Designated rooms, service with restrictions, supervision.
SAVE S♦ ✕ ⅏ ∅ 🅷 🖥 🍴 ➹ ✕

DUBOIS

WWW Bald Mountain Inn **M**
(307) 455-2844. **$45-$125, 3 day notice.** 1349 W Ramshorn St. 1.6 mi w on US 26 and 287. Ext corridors. **Pets:** Accepted.
✕ 🅷 🖥 ✕ 🅺

AAA **WWW** Black Bear Country Inn **M**
(307) 455-2344. **$45-$65.** 505 N Ramshorn St. 0.5 mi w on US 26 and 287. Ext corridors. **Pets:** Dogs only. $300 one-time fee/pet. Service with restrictions, supervision.
SAVE S♦ ✕ 🅷 🅺

AAA **WWW** Branding Iron Inn **CA**
(307) 455-2893. **$40-$90.** 401 W Ramshorn St. 0.3 mi w on US 26 and 287. Ext corridors. **Pets:** Dogs only. $10 daily fee/pet. Service with restrictions, supervision.
SAVE ✕ 🅷 🖥 🅺

WWW Chinook Winds Mt. Lodge **M**
(307) 455-2987. **$45-$70.** 640 S First St. 0.8 mi e on US 26 and 287. Ext corridors. **Pets:** Other species. $5 daily fee/room. Service with restrictions, supervision.
ASK S♦ ✕ 🅷 ✕ 🅺

WWW Pinnacle Buttes Lodge & Campground **M**
(307) 455-2506. **$40-$95, 14 day notice.** 3577 US Hwy 26 W. 20 mi w on US 26 and 287. Ext corridors. **Pets:** Accepted.
🖥 🍴 ➹ ✕ 🅺 ✆

WWW Riverside Inn & Campground **M**
(307) 455-2337. **$40-$50.** 5810 US Hwy 26. 3 mi e of town center on US 26 and 287. Ext corridors. **Pets:** Medium, dogs only. $5 daily fee/pet. Designated rooms, service with restrictions, supervision.
S♦ ✕ 🅷 🖥 ✕ 🅺 📺 ✆

AAA **WWW** Stagecoach Motor Inn **SH** ❀
(307) 455-2303. **$44-$74.** 103 Ramshorn St. On US 26 and 287; center. Ext corridors. **Pets:** Small, dogs only. $10 daily fee/pet. Designated rooms, service with restrictions, supervision.
SAVE ✕ ⅏ 🅷 🖥 ➹ ✕ 🅺

EVANSTON

WWW Comfort Inn **SH**
(307) 789-7799. **$65-$99.** 1931 Harrison Dr. I-80, exit 3 (Harrison Dr). Int corridors. **Pets:** Other species. $10 daily fee/room. Designated rooms, service with restrictions, supervision.
ASK S♦ ✕ ⅏ 🅷 🖥 ➹

AAA **WWW** Prairie Inn **M**
(307) 789-2920. **$50-$65.** 264 Bear River Dr. I-80, exit 6, 0.3 mi n. Ext/int corridors. **Pets:** Small. $5 daily fee/pet. Designated rooms, service with restrictions, supervision.
SAVE ✕ 🅷

WWW Rendezvous Lodge **SH**
(307) 789-2220. **$65-$150.** 339 Wasatch Rd. I-80, exit 3 (Harrison Dr), just n to Wasatch Rd. Int corridors. **Pets:** Accepted.
ASK S♦ ✕ 🅷 🖥 🍴

EVANSVILLE

WWWW Comfort Inn-Casper **SH**
(307) 235-3038. **$65-$95.** 480 Lathrop Rd. I-25, exit 185, just e. Int corridors. **Pets:** Medium. Designated rooms, service with restrictions, supervision.
ASK S♦ ✕ ⅏ ∅ ⅏ 🅷 🖥 ➹

GILLETTE

AAA **WWW** Best Western Tower West Lodge **SH**
(307) 686-2210. **$49-$159.** 109 N US Hwy 14-16. I-90, exit 124, just n. Int corridors. **Pets:** Accepted.
SAVE S♦ ✕ ⅏ 🅷 🖥 🍴 ➹ ✕

WWWW Holiday Inn Express Hotel & Suites **SH**
(307) 686-9576. **$83-$159.** 1908 Cliff Davis Dr. I-90, exit 126. Int corridors. **Pets:** Other species. Service with restrictions, crate.
ASK S♦ ✕ ⅏ ∅ ⅏ 🅷 🖥 ➹

GLENROCK

◉◉◉ ▽▽ All American Inn M
(307) 436-2772. **$50-$60.** 500 W Aspen. I-25, exit 165, 2.2 mi n. Ext corridors. **Pets:** Accepted.
SAVE ⊠ ⊟

GRAND TETON NATIONAL PARK

◉◉◉ ▽▽▽▽ Flagg Ranch Resort LH
(307) 543-2861. **$150-$165, 7 day notice.** US 89 and 191; 2 mi s of Yellowstone National Park south entrance; 5 mi n of Grand Teton National park north entrance. Ext corridors. **Pets:** Other species. $10 daily fee/pet. Service with restrictions, crate.
SAVE ⊠ ⌖M ⊘ ⌖ 🖵 ⑪ ⊠ 🐾 🖩

▽▽▽ Jackson Lake Lodge LH
(307) 543-2811. **$137-$240, 7 day notice.** 5 mi nw of Moran at jct US 89 and 287. Ext/int corridors. **Pets:** Accepted.
⊠ ⌖M ⊘ ⌖ ⊟ 🖵 ➴ ⊠ 🐾 🖩

▽▽▽ Signal Mountain Lodge SH
(307) 543-2831. **$98-$250, 4 day notice.** Teton Park Rd, 2 mi s of US 89, 191 and 287. Ext corridors. **Pets:** Other species. $5 daily fee/pet. Designated rooms, service with restrictions, crate.
⊠ ⊟ 🖵 ⑪ ⊠ 🐾 🖩

GREEN RIVER

◉◉◉ ▽▽ Coachman Inn Motel M 🐾
(307) 875-3681. **$40-$49.** 470 E Flaming Gorge Way. I-80, exit 89, just e on I-80 business loop. Ext corridors. **Pets:** Small, dogs only. $10 one-time fee/pet. Designated rooms, service with restrictions, supervision.
SAVE S⊘ ⊠ ⊟

◉◉◉ ▽▽▽ Oak Tree Inn SH
(307) 875-3500. **$64-$79.** 1170 W Flaming Gorge Way. I-80, exit 89, just s. Ext/int corridors. **Pets:** Other species. $5 daily fee/pet. Service with restrictions, crate.
SAVE S⊘ ⊠ ⌖M ⊘ ⌖ ⊟ 🖵 ⑪

GREYBULL

◉◉◉ ▽▽ Antler Motel M
(307) 765-4404. **$40-$60.** 1116 N 6th St. 0.8 mi w on US 14/16/20. Ext corridors. **Pets:** Dogs only. $10 daily fee/pet. Designated rooms, service with restrictions, supervision.
SAVE S⊘ ⊠ ⊟ 🖵

◉◉◉ ▽▽▽ Yellowstone Motel M
(307) 765-4456. **$52-$79, 3 day notice.** 247 Greybull Ave. 0.4 mi e on US 14. Ext corridors. **Pets:** Accepted.
SAVE S⊘ ⊠ ⊟ 🖵 ➴

GUERNSEY

▽▽ The Bunkhouse Motel M
(307) 836-2356. **$51.** 350 W Whalen. On US 26; center. Ext corridors. **Pets:** Large, other species. $10 one-time fee/room. Designated rooms, service with restrictions, supervision.
⊠ ⊟

HULETT

◉◉◉ ▽▽ Hulett Motel M
(307) 467-5220. **$65-$85.** 202 Main St. SR 24 at north end of town. Ext corridors. **Pets:** Accepted.
SAVE ⊠

JACKSON

◉◉◉ ▽▽▽▽ 49'er Inn and Suites (Quality Inn and Suites) SH
(307) 733-7550. **$60-$199, 14 day notice.** 330 W Pearl St. Just w and just s of town square. Ext/int corridors. **Pets:** Other species. Designated rooms, service with restrictions, supervision.
SAVE S⊘ ⊠ ⊘ ⌖ ⊟ 🖵 ⊠

◉◉◉ ▽▽▽ Antler Inn SH
(307) 733-2535. **$75-$110, 14 day notice.** 43 W Pearl St. Just s of town square. Ext/int corridors. **Pets:** Dogs only. Designated rooms, service with restrictions, supervision.
SAVE ⊠ ⊟ 🖵

◉◉◉ ▽▽▽▽ Cowboy Village Resort CA
(307) 733-3121. **$89-$179.** 120 S Flat Creek Dr. 0.3 mi w on Broadway to Flat Creek Dr, just s; downtown. Ext corridors. **Pets:** Accepted.
SAVE S⊘ ⊠ ⊟ 🖵

◉◉◉ ▽▽▽ Elk Country Inn SH 🐾
(307) 733-2364. **$60-$126, 14 day notice.** 480 W Pearl St. Just w, then just s of town square. Ext/int corridors. **Pets:** Large, other species. Designated rooms, service with restrictions, supervision.
SAVE ⊠ ⊟ 🖵 ⊠

◉◉◉ ▽▽▽ Jackson Hole Lodge SH
(307) 733-2992. **$104-$124, 14 day notice.** 420 W Broadway. 0.3 mi w on US 26/89/191. Ext corridors. **Pets:** Medium, other species. $50 deposit/pet. Designated rooms, service with restrictions, supervision.
SAVE S⊘ ⊠ ⊟ 🖵 ➴ ⊠

◉◉◉ ▽▽▽ Painted Buffalo Inn SH
(307) 733-4340. **$70-$159.** 400 W Broadway. Just w of town square. Ext corridors. **Pets:** Large. $10 one-time fee/room. Service with restrictions, supervision.
SAVE S⊘ ⊠ ⌖M ⊟ ➴

◉◉◉ ▽▽▽ Snow King Resort LH
(307) 733-5200. **$140-$720.** 400 E Snow King Ave. Just se of town square. Int corridors. **Pets:** Medium. $50 one-time fee/room. Designated rooms, service with restrictions, supervision.
SAVE S⊘ ⊠ ⌖ ⊟ 🖵 ⑪ ➴ ⊠

LANDER

▽▽▽ Baldwin Creek Bed & Breakfast CA
(307) 332-7608. **$65-$95, 14 day notice.** 2343 Baldwin Creek Rd. 4.8 mi w on Baldwin Creek Rd from jct US 287. Ext/int corridors. **Pets:** Large. $5 daily fee/room. Designated rooms, supervision.
⊠ ⊟ 🐾 🖩 🐾

▲▲▲ ▼▼▼ Budget Host Pronghorn Lodge SH
(307) 332-3940. **$46-$90.** 150 E Main St. Just n of jct US 287 and SR 789. Ext corridors. **Pets:** Accepted.
SAVE S❑ ✕ ❷ ❶ ❏ ❙❙

▲▲▲ ▼ Holiday Lodge M
(307) 332-2511. **$48-$54.** 210 McFarlane Dr. Just e of jct US 287 and SR 789. Ext corridors. **Pets:** $10 daily fee/pet. Service with restrictions, supervision.
SAVE ✕ ❶

▲▲▲ ▼ Silver Spur Motel M ❖
(307) 332-5189. **$35-$55.** 1240 W Main St. 1.5 mi n on US 287. Ext corridors. **Pets:** Other species. $5 daily fee/pet. Designated rooms, service with restrictions, supervision.
SAVE S❑ ✕ ❶ ❏ ➴

LARAMIE

▲▲▲ ▼▼▼ 1st Inn Gold SH
(307) 742-3721. **$57-$99, 15 day notice.** 421 Boswell. I-80, exit 313, just n on US 287. Ext/int corridors. **Pets:** Accepted.
SAVE S❑ ✕ ❙❙ ➴

▼▼▼▼ Best Western Center Hotel SH
(307) 742-6611. **$89-$199, 14 day notice.** 2313 Soldier Springs Rd. I-80, exit 313, just s on US 287. Ext/int corridors. **Pets:** Accepted.
ASK S❑ ✕ ❶ ❏ ❙❙ ➴

▼▼▼ Days Inn SH
(307) 745-5678. **$65-$105.** 1368 McCue St. I-80, exit 310, just e. Int corridors. **Pets:** Medium. $15 daily fee/pet. Designated rooms, service with restrictions, supervision.
ASK S❑ ✕ ♿M ❷ ♿ ❶ ❏ ➴

▲▲▲ ▼▼▼ Gas Lite Inn Motel M ❖
(307) 742-6616. **$46-$66.** 960 N 3rd St. I-80, exit 313, 1.6 mi n on US 287; downtown. Ext corridors. **Pets:** Other species. $5 one-time fee/room. Supervision.
SAVE S❑ ✕ ❶ ➴

▲▲▲ ▼▼▼ Howard Johnson Inn SH
(307) 742-8371. **$57-$128.** 1555 Snowy Range Rd. I-80, exit 311, just s. Ext corridors. **Pets:** Other species. $10 daily fee/room. Designated rooms, service with restrictions, supervision.
SAVE S❑ ✕ ❶ ❏ ❙❙ ➴

▲▲▲ ▼ Sunset Inn M
(307) 742-3741. **$52-$75.** 1104 S 3rd St. I-80, exit 313, just n on US 287. Ext corridors. **Pets:** Accepted.
SAVE S❑ ✕ ❶ ➴

▲▲▲ ▼▼▼ Travelodge Downtown M
(307) 742-6671. **$45-$65.** 165 N 3rd St. I-80, exit 313, 1 mi n on US 287; downtown. Ext corridors. **Pets:** $50 deposit/room. Designated rooms, service with restrictions, supervision.
SAVE S❑ ✕ ❶ ❏

LUSK

▼ Town House Motel M
(307) 334-2376. **$40-$68.** 525 S Main St. On US 20/85, just n. Ext corridors. **Pets:** Other species. $5 one-time fee/pet. Designated rooms, service with restrictions.
ASK S❑ ✕ ❶ ❏

NEWCASTLE

▲▲▲ ▼ Auto Inn Motel M
(307) 746-2734. **$42-$69.** 2503 W Main St. West end of town on US 16. Ext corridors. **Pets:** Other species. $5 daily fee/pet. Designated rooms, service with restrictions, crate.
SAVE ✕ ❶

▲▲▲ ▼▼▼ Pines Motel M
(307) 746-4334. **$42-$75.** 248 E Wentworth St. Just e from jct US Business Rt 16; downtown. Ext corridors. **Pets:** Medium. $5 one-time fee/pet. Service with restrictions, supervision.
SAVE S❑ ✕ ❶ ❏

▲▲▲ ▼▼▼ Sage Motel M
(307) 746-2724. **$42-$60, 3 day notice.** 1227 S Summit Ave. 0.3 mi s of jct US 16 on US 85, just w. Ext corridors. **Pets:** Small, other species. $5 daily fee/pet. Designated rooms, service with restrictions, supervision.
SAVE S❑ ✕ ❶ ❏

PAINTER

▼ Hunter Peak Ranch RA
(307) 587-3711. **$115-$150, 90 day notice.** 4027 Crandall Rd. SR 296, 5 mi s of US 212; 40 mi n of SR 120. Ext corridors. **Pets:** Medium. $10 daily fee/pet. Designated rooms, no service, supervision.
✕ ❶ ❏ ❙❙ ❎ ♿ ♿ ➰

PINEDALE

▲▲▲ ▼▼▼ Best Western Pinedale Inn SH
(307) 367-6869. **$69-$129, 30 day notice.** 850 W Pine St. 0.5 mi n on US 191. Int corridors. **Pets:** Designated rooms, service with restrictions, supervision.
SAVE S❑ ✕ ❶ ❏ ➴

▲▲▲ ▼▼▼ The Lodge at Pinedale SH
(307) 367-8800. **$75-$108.** 1054 W Pine St. 0.7 mi n on US 191. Int corridors. **Pets:** Accepted.
SAVE S❑ ✕ ❶ ➴

▲▲▲ ▼ Sun Dance Motel M
(307) 367-4336. **$45-$105.** 148 E Pine St. US 191; city center. Ext corridors. **Pets:** Designated rooms, service with restrictions, supervision.
SAVE S❑ ✕ ❶ ❏ ♿

POWELL

▼▼ Kings Inn SH
(307) 754-5117. **$58-$87.** 777 E 2nd St. 0.3 mi e on US 14A. Ext corridors. **Pets:** Accepted.
ASK S❑ ✕ ❶ ❏ ❙❙ ➴

RAWLINS

◆◆◆ ▼▼▼▼ Best Western CottonTree Inn SH
(307) 324-2737. **$84-$119, 14 day notice.** 2221 W Spruce
St. I-80, exit 211, just n. Ext/int corridors. **Pets:** Medium,
other species. $10 daily fee/room. Designated rooms, serv-
ice with restrictions, supervision.
SAVE S♦ ✕ ⎙ ⊟ ▣ ⟨¶ ⊛ ⊠

◆◆◆ ▼▼▼ The Lodge at Rawlins SH
(307) 324-2783. **$50-$80.** 1801 E Cedar. I-80, exit 215, just
w of jct US 287. Int corridors. **Pets:** Accepted.
SAVE S♦ ✕ ⊟ ▣ ⟨¶ ⊛

RIVERTON

▼▼ Days Inn SH ✿
(307) 856-9677. **$50-$90.** 909 W Main St. 0.5 mi nw on US
26. Ext corridors. **Pets:** Medium. $5 daily fee/pet. Desig-
nated rooms, service with restrictions, supervision.
ASK S♦ ✕ ⊛ ⊟

◆◆◆ ▼▼▼ Holiday Inn Convention
     Center SH ✿
(307) 856-8100. **$79-$109.** 900 E Sunset Dr. 0.8 mi ne on
US 26/SR 789. Int corridors. **Pets:** $20 one-time fee/room.
Designated rooms, service with restrictions, crate.
SAVE S♦ ✕ ⊛M ⊟ ▣ ⟨¶ ⊛

▼▼ Paintbrush Motel M
(307) 856-9238. **$46-$49.** 1550 N Federal Blvd. 1.3 mi ne on
US 26/SR 789. Ext corridors. **Pets:** Accepted.
✕ ⊟

▼▼ Super 8 Motel SH
(307) 857-2400. **$45-$70, 7 day notice.** 1040 N Federal
Blvd. 1 mi ne on US 26/SR 789. Int corridors. **Pets:** Other
species. $5 daily fee/pet. Service with restrictions, supervi-
sion.
ASK S♦ ✕ ⊟

◆◆◆ ▼ Thunderbird Motel M
(307) 856-9201. **$36-$52.** 302 E Fremont. Just n of US 26;
downtown. Ext corridors. **Pets:** Medium, dogs only. $4 daily
fee/pet. Service with restrictions.
SAVE S♦ ✕ ⊟

▼▼▼ Tomahawk Motor Lodge M ✿
(307) 856-9205. **$57-$65.** 208 E Main St. On US 26; downtown. Ext/int corridors. **Pets:** Other species. $25 deposit/
pet, $10 one-time fee/pet. Crate.
ASK S♦ ✕ ⊟ ▣

ROCK SPRINGS

◆◆◆ ▼ Budget Host Inn M
(307) 362-6673. **$45-$70.** 1004 Dewar Dr. I-80, exit 102
(Dewar Dr), 1.3 mi se. Ext corridors. **Pets:** $5 daily fee/pet.
Designated rooms, service with restrictions, supervision.
SAVE S♦ ✕ ⊟

▼▼▼ Comfort Inn SH
(307) 362-9490. **$70-$82.** 1670 Sunset Dr. I-80, exit 102
(Dewar Dr), 0.3 mi s, then just w. Ext corridors.
Pets: Accepted.
ASK S♦ ✕ ⊛ ⊟ ▣ ⊛ ⊠

▼▼▼ Econo Lodge SH
(307) 382-4217. **$55-$75, 7 day notice.** 1635 Elk St. I-80,
exit 104 (Elk St), just n. Ext corridors. **Pets:** Accepted.
ASK S♦ ✕ ⊟ ▣ ⊛

▼▼▼ Holiday Inn SH
(307) 382-9200. **$75-$110.** 1675 Sunset Dr. I-80, exit 102
(Dewar Dr), 0.3 mi sw. Ext/int corridors. **Pets:** Accepted.
ASK S♦ ✕ ⊛ ⊟ ▣ ⟨¶ ⊛ ⊠

▼ Motel 6-395 M
(307) 362-1850. **$35-$59.** 2615 Commercial Way. I-80, exit
102 (Dewar Dr), n to Foothills Blvd, just e. Ext corridors.
Pets: Other species. Service with restrictions, supervision.
S♦ ✕ ⊛ ⊟ ⊛

▼▼▼ Ramada Limited SH
(307) 362-1770. **$70-$95.** 2717 Dewar Dr. I-80, exit 102
(Dewar Dr), just n. Int corridors. **Pets:** Other species. $5
daily fee/pet. Designated rooms, service with restrictions,
supervision.
ASK S♦ ✕ ⊛ ⊟ ▣ ⊛

◆◆◆ ▼ Springs Motel M
(307) 362-6683. **$40-$64.** 1525 9th St. I-80, exit 107, 0.3 mi
w. Ext corridors. **Pets:** Accepted.
SAVE S♦ ✕

SARATOGA

▼▼▼ Hacienda Motel M
(307) 326-5751. **$56-$76.** 1500 S First St. 0.5 mi s on SR
130. Int corridors. **Pets:** $5 daily fee/pet. Designated rooms,
service with restrictions, supervision.
ASK S♦ ✕ ⊟

SHERIDAN

◆◆◆ ▼▼▼ Best Western Sheridan Center SH
(307) 674-7421. **$59-$149.** 612 N Main St. I-90, exit 20, 1.7
mi s. Ext/int corridors. **Pets:** Accepted.
SAVE S♦ ✕ ⊛ ⊟ ▣ ⟨¶ ⊛

◆◆◆ ▼ Budget Host Inn M
(307) 674-7496. **$50-$70, 10 day notice.** 2007 N Main St.
I-90, exit 20, 0.7 mi s; on I-90 business loop. Ext corridors.
Pets: Medium. $5 daily fee/pet. Designated rooms, service
with restrictions, supervision.
SAVE S♦ ✕ ⊟ ▣

◆◆◆ ▼▼▼ Holiday Inn Atrium & Convention
     Center SH ✿
(307) 672-8931. **$79-$119.** 1809 Sugarland Dr. I-90, exit 25,
0.3 mi nw. Int corridors. **Pets:** Other species. $50 deposit/
room. Service with restrictions, supervision.
SAVE ✕ ⊛ ⊛ ⊟ ▣ ⟨¶ ⊛ ⊠

SUNDANCE

◆◆◆ ▼▼▼▼ Best Western Inn at Sundance SH
(307) 283-2800. **$57-$114.** 2719 E Cleveland. I-90, exit 189,
just n, then just w on I-90 business loop. Int corridors.
Pets: Other species. $5 daily fee/pet. Service with restric-
tions, supervision.
SAVE S♦ ✕ ▣ ⊛

(AAA) ▼▼▼ Budget Host Arrowhead Motel M ❖
(307) 283-3307. **$39-$69.** 214 Cleveland. I-90 business loop and US 14. Ext corridors. **Pets:** Medium, dogs only. Designated rooms, service with restrictions, supervision.
SAVE S X

(AAA) ▼▼▼ Sundance Mountain Inn M
(307) 283-3737. **$58-$97, 14 day notice.** 26 SR 585. I-90, exit 187, 0.4 mi n. Ext corridors. **Pets:** $5 daily fee/pet. Service with restrictions, supervision.
SAVE S X ⊟ ⬛ ≈

THERMOPOLIS

▼▼ Holiday Inn of the Waters SH ❖
(307) 864-3131. **$89-$139.** 115 E Park St. In Hot Springs State Park. Ext/int corridors. **Pets:** Other species. Service with restrictions, supervision.
ASK X ⊘ ⬛ ⬛ ⦀ ≈ X

TORRINGTON

(AAA) ▼▼▼ Kings Inn SH
(307) 532-4011. **$46-$60.** 1555 Main St. Just s of jct US 26 and 85. Int corridors. **Pets:** Accepted.
SAVE S X ⊟ ⬛ ⦀ ≈

▼▼ Maverick Motel M
(307) 532-4064. **$42-$46.** US 26 W. 1.7 mi w on US 26/85. Ext corridors. **Pets:** Service with restrictions, supervision.
ASK S X ⊟ ⬛

UCROSS

(AAA) ▼▼▼ The Ranch at Ucross RA
(307) 737-2281. **$199-$299, 3 day notice.** 2673 US Hwy 14 E. Jct US 14/16, 0.5 mi w on US 14. Ext/int corridors. **Pets:** $250 deposit/room. Service with restrictions, supervision.
SAVE S X ⦀ ≈ X �𝒲

WAPITI

(AAA) ▼▼▼ Green Creek Inn M
(307) 587-5004. **$40-$70.** 2908 Yellowstone Hwy. 2.8 mi w on US 14/16/20. Ext corridors. **Pets:** Other species. $5 daily fee/pet. Service with restrictions, supervision.
SAVE S X Ⓩ

WHEATLAND

(AAA) ▼▼▼▼ Best Western Torchlite Motor Inn SH
(307) 322-4070. **$48-$80.** 1809 N 16th St. I-25, exit 78, just e; 1.5 mi n on US 87/I-25 business loop (16th St). Ext corridors. **Pets:** Other species. $20 deposit/pet, $5 daily fee/pet. Service with restrictions, supervision.
SAVE S X ⊟ ⬛ ≈ X

▼▼ Motel West Winds M
(307) 322-2705. **$43-$58.** 1756 South Rd. I-25, exit 78, just e; 0.4 mi n on US 87/I-25 business loop (16th St). Ext corridors. **Pets:** Other species. Service with restrictions, supervision.
ASK X ⊟ ⬛

(AAA) ▼▼ Vimbo's Motel M
(307) 322-3842. **$44-$77.** 203 16th St. I-25, exit 78, just e; just n on US 87/I-25 business loop (16th St). Ext/int corridors. **Pets:** Accepted.
SAVE X ⊟ ⦀

WILSON

▼▼ Sassy Moose Inn of Jackson Hole BB
(307) 733-1277. **$79-$189, 30 day notice.** 3859 Miles Rd. 2 mi n on SR 390 from jct SR 22; 5 mi s from Teton Village; 6 mi nw from Jackson. Int corridors. **Pets:** Accepted.
X 𝒦 Ⓩ

WORLAND

▼▼ Days Inn M
(307) 347-4251. **$55-$90.** 500 N 10th St. 0.5 mi n on US 20. Ext corridors. **Pets:** Small. $5 daily fee/pet. Designated rooms, service with restrictions, supervision.
ASK S X ⊟ ⬛

YELLOWSTONE NATIONAL PARK

(AAA) ▼▼▼ Elephant Head Lodge CA ❖
(307) 587-3980. **$99-$125, 30 day notice.** 1170 Yellowstone Hwy. 7 mi e of east entrance. Ext corridors. **Pets:** Other species.
SAVE S X ⊟ ⬛ ⦀ X 𝒦 𝒲 Ⓩ

Canada

ALBERTA

ATHABASCA

CAA ♦♦♦ Best Western Athabasca Inn SH
(780) 675-2294. **$109-$139.** 5211 41st Ave. 1 km s on Hwy 2. Int corridors. **Pets:** Accepted.
[SAVE] [icons]

BANFF

♦♦♦ Banff Rocky Mountain Resort CO
(403) 762-5531. **$150-$430, 3 day notice.** 1029 Banff Ave. Banff Ave and Tunnel Mountain Rd; just s of Trans-Canada Hwy 1. Ext corridors. **Pets:** $15 daily fee/pet. Service with restrictions.
[ASK] [icons]

CAA ♦♦♦ Best Western Siding 29 Lodge SH
(403) 762-5575. **$95-$305.** 453 Marten St. 1.3 km ne off Banff Ave. Int corridors. **Pets:** Supervision.
[SAVE] [icons]

CAA ♦♦♦ Castle Mountain Chalets CA
(403) 762-3868. **$125-$330, 14 day notice.** 32 km w on Trans-Canada Hwy 1, at Castle jct, 1 km ne on Hwy 1A (Bow Valley Pkwy). Ext corridors. **Pets:** Accepted.
[SAVE] [icons]

CAA ♦♦♦ ♦♦♦ The Fairmont Banff Springs LH
(403) 762-2211. **$219-$629, 3 day notice.** 405 Spray Ave. Just s on Banff Ave over the bridge, 0.5 km e. Int corridors. **Pets:** Other species. $40 one-time fee/pet. Designated rooms, supervision.
[SAVE] [icons]

♦♦♦ Johnston Canyon Resort CA
(403) 762-2971. **$89-$274.** Hwy 1A. 24 km nw on Hwy 1A (Bow Valley Pkwy). Ext corridors. **Pets:** Accepted.
[ASK] [icons]

CAA ♦♦♦ Red Carpet Motor Inn M
(403) 762-4184. **$69-$150.** 425 Banff Ave. 1 km ne. Ext/int corridors. **Pets:** Large, other species. Service with restrictions, supervision.
[SAVE] [icons]

BROOKS

CAA ♦♦♦ Best Western Brooks Inn SH
(403) 363-0080. **$119-$139.** 115 Fifteenth Ave W. Just s off Trans-Canada Hwy 1. Ext/int corridors. **Pets:** Accepted.
[SAVE] [icons]

♦♦ Heritage Inn SH
(403) 362-6666. **$90-$95.** 1217 2nd St W. Hwy 873, 0.8 km s of jct Trans-Canada Hwy 1. Int corridors. **Pets:** $10 daily fee/pet. Designated rooms, service with restrictions, crate.
[ASK] [icons]

♦♦♦ Holiday Inn Express Hotel & Suites SH
(403) 362-7440. **$115-$131.** 1307 2nd St W. Trans-Canada Hwy 1, exit 2nd St W. Int corridors. **Pets:** Accepted.
[ASK] [icons]

♦♦ Super 8 Motel-Brooks SH
(403) 362-8000. **$76-$95.** 1240 Cassils Rd E. Trans-Canada Hwy 1, 0.3 km sw on SR 542, exit E Brooks. Ext/int corridors. **Pets:** Other species. $5 daily fee/room. Designated rooms, service with restrictions, supervision.
[ASK] [icons]

CALGARY METROPOLITAN AREA

AIRDRIE

CAA ♦♦♦ Super 8 Motel-Airdrie SH
(403) 948-4188. **$75-$94.** 815 E Lake Blvd. Hwy 2, exit E Airdrie, 0.8 km e on Hwy 587 E, then 1.8 km s. Int corridors. **Pets:** Other species. $10 one-time fee/room. Designated rooms, service with restrictions, supervision.
[SAVE] [icons]

CALGARY

CAA ♦♦♦ Best Western Hospitality Inn LH ❀
(403) 278-5050. **$109-$179.** 135 Southland Dr SE. On Hwy 2A (MacLeod Tr); corner of Southland Dr. Int corridors. **Pets:** Medium, other species. Designated rooms, service with restrictions, crate.
[SAVE] [icons]

CAA ♦♦♦ Best Western Village Park Inn SH
(403) 289-0241. **$99-$189.** 1804 Crowchild Tr NW. Just ne of jct Trans-Canada Hwy 1 and Crowchild Tr. Int corridors. **Pets:** Medium, other species. Service with restrictions.
[SAVE] [icons]

♦♦♦ Blackfoot Inn SH ❀
(403) 252-2253. **$99-$165, 3 day notice.** 5940 Blackfoot Tr SE. At 58th Ave SE; access to property from 58th Ave only. Int corridors. **Pets:** Other species. Designated rooms, service with restrictions, supervision.
[ASK] [icons]

ⒸⒶ ▼▼▼▼ **Calgary Marriott Hotel** 🅻🅷 ❀
(403) 266-7331. **$199-$299.** 110 9th Ave SE. Jct 9th Ave and Centre St. Int corridors. **Pets:** Other species. Service with restrictions, supervision.
(save) ☒ 🎧 🖊 🛏 💻 🍴 🔚 ☒

ⒸⒶ ▼▼▼ **Calgary Westways Guest**
      House 🅱🅱 ❀
(403) 229-1758. **$89-$139, 7 day notice.** 216 25th Ave SW. 1.7 km s on Hwy 2A (MacLeod Tr S), 0.5 km w. Int corridors. **Pets:** Large, other species. $10 daily fee/pet.
(save) 🅢🅓 ☒

ⒸⒶ ▼▼▼ **Carriage House Inn** 🆂🅷
(403) 253-1101. **$89-$129, 3 day notice.** 9030 MacLeod Tr S. On Hwy 2A (MacLeod Tr); corner of 90th Ave SW. Int corridors. **Pets:** Medium. $10 daily fee/room. Designated rooms, service with restrictions, crate.
(save) 🅢🅓 ☒ 🛏 💻 🍴 🔚 ☒

ⒸⒶ ▼▼▼ **Coast Plaza Hotel & Conference**
      Centre 🅻🅷 ❀
(403) 248-8888. **$125-$180.** 1316 33rd St NE. Just s of jct 16th Ave (Trans-Canada Hwy 1) and 36th St NE, just w on 12th Ave NE. Int corridors. **Pets:** Medium. $20 one-time fee/room. Service with restrictions, supervision.
(save) ☒ 🅛🅜 🛏 💻 🍴 🔚 ☒

ⒸⒶ ▼▼▼ **Days Inn & Conference Centre** 🆂🅷
(403) 243-5531. **$79-$199.** 3828 MacLeod Tr S. Corner of MacLeod Tr and 38th Ave SE. Int corridors. **Pets:** Medium. $10 daily fee/room. Designated rooms, service with restrictions, supervision.
(save) 🅢🅓 ☒ 🛏 💻 🍴 🔚

▼▼▼ **Days Inn Calgary Airport** 🆂🅷
(403) 250-3297. **$99-$119.** 2799 Sunridge Way NE. Barlow Tr, just e of Sunridge Way NE. Int corridors. **Pets:** Small, dogs only. $10 daily fee/pet. Designated rooms, service with restrictions, crate.
(ASK) 🅢🅓 ☒ 🅛🅜 🛏 💻 🔚 ☒

▼▼▼ **Days Inn-Calgary West** 🆂🅷
(403) 289-1961. **$59-$130, 3 day notice.** 1818 16th Ave NW. 5.2 km nw on 16th Ave NW (Trans-Canada Hwy 1). Int corridors. **Pets:** Accepted.
(ASK) 🅢🅓 ☒ 🛏 💻 🍴 🔚

▼▼▼ **Delta Bow Valley** 🅻🅷
(403) 266-1980. **$99-$159.** 209 4th Ave SE. 1st St SE and 4th Ave SE. Int corridors. **Pets:** Large, other species. Designated rooms, service with restrictions, supervision.
(ASK) 🅢🅓 ☒ 💻 🍴 🔚 ☒

ⒸⒶ ▼▼▼ **Delta Calgary Airport** 🅻🅷 ❀
(403) 291-2600. **$129-$189.** 2001 Airport Rd NE. At Calgary International Airport. Int corridors. **Pets:** Medium. $25 daily fee/pet. Designated rooms, supervision.
(save) 🅢🅓 ☒ 🛏 💻 🍴 🔚 ☒

ⒸⒶ ▼▼ **Econo Lodge South** 🅼
(403) 252-4401. **$89-$129.** 7505 MacLeod Tr S. Corner of MacLeod Tr and 75th Ave. Ext/int corridors. **Pets:** Small. $10 daily fee/pet. Designated rooms, service with restrictions, supervision.
(save) 🅢🅓 ☒ 🛏 💻 🔚

ⒸⒶ ▼▼ **Elbow River Inn & Casino** 🆂🅷
(403) 269-6771. **$109-$129.** 1919 MacLeod Tr SE. Jct MacLeod Tr and 1st St SE. Int corridors. **Pets:** Accepted.
(save) 🅢🅓 ☒ 🍴

▼▼▼▼ **The Fairmont Palliser** 🅻🅷 ❀
(403) 262-1234. **$109-$339.** 133 9th Ave SW. 9th Ave SW and 1st St SW. Int corridors. **Pets:** Medium. $25 daily fee/pet. Service with restrictions, crate.
(ASK) 🅢🅓 ☒ 💻 🍴 🔚 ☒

▼▼▼ **Glenmore Inn and Convention Centre** 🆂🅷
(403) 279-8611. **$145.** 2720 Glenmore Tr SE. 3 km e of Hwy 2 (Deerfoot Tr), exit Glenmore Tr E; at Ogden Rd. Int corridors. **Pets:** Designated rooms, service with restrictions, supervision.
🅢🅓 ☒ 🛏 💻 🍴 ☒

ⒸⒶ ▼▼▼ **Greenwood Inn Hotels** 🆂🅷
(403) 250-8855. **$99-$139.** 3515 26th St NE. From Barlow Tr N, just e on 32nd Ave NE, then just n. Int corridors. **Pets:** Accepted.
(save) ☒ 🎧 🛏 💻 🍴 🔚 ☒

▼▼ **Hawthorn Hotel & Suites** 🅻🅷
(403) 263-0520. **$220, 3 day notice.** 618 5th Ave SW. Corner of 5th Ave SW and 6th St. Int corridors. **Pets:** Medium. $12 daily fee/pet. Designated rooms, service with restrictions, crate.
(ASK) 🅢🅓 ☒ 🛏 💻 🍴 🔚 ☒

ⒸⒶ ▼▼▼ **Holiday Inn Calgary Airport** 🆂🅷
(403) 230-1999. **$94-$114.** 1250 McKinnon Dr NE. 1 km e of jct Hwy 2 (Deerfoot Tr) and 16th Ave NE (Trans-Canada Hwy 1). Int corridors. **Pets:** Medium. Supervision.
(save) ☒ 🛏 💻 🍴 🔚

▼▼▼ **Holiday Inn Calgary Downtown** 🅻🅷
(403) 266-4611. **$129.** 119 12th Ave SW. At 1st St SW; centre. Int corridors. **Pets:** Accepted.
(ASK) ☒ 🅛🅜 🎧 🛏 💻 🍴 🔚

▼▼▼ **Holiday Inn Express Hotel & Suites Calgary**
      South 🆂🅷
(403) 225-3000. **$166-$249.** 12025 Lake Frasier Dr SE. Hwy 2 (Deerfoot Tr), exit Anderson Rd w, then just s on MacLeod Tr. Int corridors. **Pets:** Accepted.
(ASK) 🅢🅓 ☒ 🛏 💻 🔚 ☒

ⒸⒶ ▼▼▼ **Holiday Inn Express University** 🆂🅷
(403) 289-6600. **$85-$115.** 2227 Banff Tr NW. 16th Ave (Trans-Canada Hwy 1) and Banff Tr NW. Int corridors. **Pets:** Other species. Designated rooms, service with restrictions, supervision.
(save) 🅢🅓 ☒ 🅛🅜 🎧 🛏 💻

▼▼▼ **Marriott Residence Inn-Calgary**
      Airport 🆂🅷
(403) 735-3336. **$129-$179.** 2622 39th Ave NE. Corner of Barlow Tr and 39th Ave NE. Int corridors. **Pets:** Accepted.
(ASK) ☒ 🅛🅜 🎧 🛏 💻 🔚 ☒

ⒸⒶ ▼▼ **Quality Inn University** 🆂🅷
(403) 289-1973. **$89-$219, 3 day notice.** 2359 Banff Tr NW. Just n of jct Trans-Canada Hwy 1 and Crowchild Tr. Ext/int corridors. **Pets:** Accepted.
(save) 🅢🅓 ☒ 🛏 💻 🍴 🔚 ☒

(AA) ♦♦♦ **Radisson Hotel Calgary Airport** SH
(403) 291-4666. **$219-$239.** 2120 16th Ave NE. 0.5 km e of
jct 16th Ave NE (Trans-Canada Hwy 1) and Hwy 2 (Deerfoot Tr). Int corridors. **Pets:** $10 one-time fee/pet. Desig-
nated rooms, service with restrictions, supervision.
[SAVE] [S☼] [✕] [&M] [🖥] [🖥] [🛒] [➤]

♦♦♦♦ **Sandman Hotel Downtown Calgary** LH
(403) 237-8626. **$105-$190.** 888 7th Ave SW. Corner of 7th
Ave SW and 8th St. Int corridors. **Pets:** Small, other species. $10 daily fee/room. Service with restrictions, supervi-
sion.
[ASK] [S☼] [✕] [🖥] [🖥] [🛒] [➤]

(AA) ♦♦♦ ♦♦♦ **Sheraton Suites Calgary Eau**
Claire LH ✿
(403) 266-7200. **$225-$395.** 255 Barclay Parade SW. At 3rd
St SW and 2nd Ave SW. Int corridors. **Pets:** Medium, dogs
only. Designated rooms, service with restrictions, crate.
[SAVE] [S☼] [✕] [✍] [🖥] [🖥] [🛒] [➤] [✕]

(AA) ♦♦ ♦♦ **Super 8 Motel Calgary Airport** SH
(403) 291-9888. **$75-$138.** 3030 Barlow Tr NE. Corner of
32nd Ave and Barlow Tr NE. Int corridors. **Pets:** Medium,
dogs only. $10 daily fee/pet. Service with restrictions, super-
vision.
[SAVE] [S☼] [✕] [🖥]

(AA) ♦♦ ♦♦ **Super 8 Motel-Motel Village** M
(403) 289-9211. **$59-$169.** 1904 Crowchild Tr NW. Just n of
jct Trans-Canada Hwy 1 and Crowchild Tr. Ext corridors.
Pets: Small, dogs only. $10 daily fee/pet. Supervision.
[SAVE] [S☼] [✕] [🖥] [🖥] [➤]

(AA) ♦♦ ♦♦ **Travelodge Hotel Calgary Airport** SH
(403) 291-1260. **$89-$149.** 2750 Sunridge Blvd NE. Barlow
Tr, then e. Int corridors. **Pets:** Other species. Service with
restrictions, crate.
[SAVE] [S☼] [✕] [🖥] [🖥] [🛒] [➤]

(AA) ♦♦ ♦♦ **Travelodge Hotel Calgary Macleod**
Trail SH ✿
(403) 253-7070. **$99-$179.** 9206 MacLeod Tr S. On Hwy 2
(Deerfoot Tr) at 90th Ave SW. Int corridors. **Pets:** Medium.
$12 daily fee/pet. Designated rooms, service with restric-
tions, supervision.
[SAVE] [S☼] [✕] [🖥] [🖥] [🛒] [➤]

(AA) ♦♦ ♦♦ ♦♦ ♦♦ **The Westin Calgary** LH ✿
(403) 266-1611. **$99-$319.** 320 4th Ave SW. Corner of 4th
Ave SW and 3rd St. Int corridors. **Pets:** Large, other species. Service with restrictions.
[SAVE] [✕] [&M] [✍] [🖥] [🛒] [➤] [✕]

♦♦ ♦♦ **Wingate Inn** SH ✿
(403) 514-0099. **$155-$175.** 400 Midpark Way. Hwy 2A
(MacLeod Tr), 0.5 km e on Sun Valley, 0.3 km n on Midpark
Way, then just s. Int corridors. **Pets:** Small. $25 daily fee/
room. Designated rooms, service with restrictions, crate.
[ASK] [S☼] [✕] [✍] [🖥] [🛒] [➤] [✕]

COCHRANE

♦♦ ♦♦ **Bow River Inn** M
(403) 932-7900. **$69-$169.** 3 West Side Dr. Hwy 1A, 1 km
sw on Hwy 22. Ext corridors. **Pets:** Medium. $7 daily fee/
pet. Designated rooms, service with restrictions, supervision.
[ASK] [S☼] [✕] [🖥] [🖥]

STRATHMORE

(AA) ♦♦ ♦♦ ♦♦ **Best Western Strathmore Inn** SH
(403) 934-5777. **$85-$169.** 550 Hwy 1. Trans-Canada Hwy
1, jct SR 817; centre. Int corridors. **Pets:** Medium. $10
one-time fee/room. Designated rooms, service with restrictions, supervision.
[SAVE] [S☼] [✕] [🖥] [🖥] [➤]

♦♦ ♦♦ **Super 8 Motel** M
(403) 934-1808. **$80-$125.** 450 Westlake Rd. Just n on SR
817. Ext/int corridors. **Pets:** Accepted.
[ASK] [S☼] [✕] [🖥] [🖥]

✿   END METROPOLITAN AREA   ✿

CAMROSE

♦♦ ♦♦ **Norsemen Inn** SH
(780) 672-9171. **$85-$99.** 6505 48th Ave. Hwy 13 (48th Ave)
at 65th St; west end of town. Int corridors. **Pets:** Accepted.
[✕] [🖥] [🛒]

♦♦ ♦♦ **The Travellers Inn** M
(780) 672-3377. **$60-$100.** 6216 48th Ave. Hwy 13 E (48th
Ave) at 62nd St. Ext corridors. **Pets:** Accepted.
[ASK] [S☼] [✕] [🖥] [🖥]

CANMORE

(AA) ♦♦ ♦♦ ♦♦ **Banff Boundary Lodge** CO
(403) 678-9555. **$100-$270, 4 day notice.** 1000 Harvie
Heights Rd. Just e of Banff National Park east gate, parallel
to Trans-Canada Hwy 1, exit Harvie Heights Rd. Ext corridors. **Pets:** Medium, other species. $15 daily fee/pet. Des-
ignated rooms, service with restrictions.
[SAVE] [S☼] [✕] [🖥] [🖥] [🎦]

(AA) ♦♦ ♦♦ **Canadian Rockies Chalets** CO
(403) 678-3799. **$99-$269, 3 day notice.** 1206 Bow Valley
Tr. 5.8 km e of Banff National Park east gate on Hwy 1A
(Bow Valley Tr); Trans-Canada Hwy 1, exit Canmore. Ext
corridors. **Pets:** Other species. $15 daily fee/pet. Desig-
nated rooms, service with restrictions.
[SAVE] [S☼] [✕] [🖥] [🖥] [🎦]

(AA) ♦♦ ♦♦ **Radisson Hotel & Conference**
Center SH ✿
(403) 678-3625. **$109-$289.** 511 Bow Valley Tr. Trans-
Canada Hwy 1, exit Canmore; 6 km e of Banff National
Park east gate on Hwy 1A (Bow Valley Tr). Ext/int corridors.
Pets: $10 daily fee/pet. Designated rooms, service with
restrictions, supervision.
[SAVE] [S☼] [✕] [🖥] [🖥] [🛒] [➤] [✕]

Ⓐ ♥♥♥ **Residence Inn by Marriott** 🅂🄷
(403) 678-3400. **$149-$274.** 91 Three Sisters Dr. Trans-Canada Hwy 1, exit Three Sisters Pkwy, then 4 km n. Int corridors. **Pets:** Accepted.

[SAVE] [S⌀] [✕] [&M] [🖉] [🐾] [🖬] [🖳] [🛋] [✕]

Ⓐ ♥♥♥ **Rocky Mountain Ski Lodge** 🅼
(403) 678-5445. **$60-$125.** 1711 Bow Valley Tr. Trans-Canada Hwy 1, exit Canmore; 4.8 km e of Banff National Park east gate on Hwy 1A (Bow Valley Tr). Ext corridors. **Pets:** Medium, other species. $5 daily fee/room. Designated rooms, service with restrictions, crate.

[SAVE] [S⌀] [✕] [🖬] [🖳] [✕]

Ⓐ ♥♥♥ **Rundle Mountain Lodge** 🅼 🐾
(403) 678-5322. **$64-$135.** 1723 Bow Valley Tr. Trans-Canada Hwy 1, exit Canmore; 4.8 km e of Banff National Park east gate on Hwy 1A (Bow Valley Tr). Ext corridors. **Pets:** Other species. $7 daily fee/pet. Designated rooms, service with restrictions, supervision.

[SAVE] [✕] [🖬] [🖳] [🛋] [🕻]

Ⓐ ♥ **Rundle Ridge Chalets** 🄲🄰
(403) 678-5387. **$79-$184.** 1100 Harvie Heights Rd. Trans-Canada Hwy 1, exit Harvie Heights Rd; 1 km e of Banff National Park east gate. Ext corridors. **Pets:** Large, other species. $10 daily fee/pet. Designated rooms, service with restrictions, supervision.

[SAVE] [S⌀] [✕] [🖬] [🕻] [✆]

Ⓐ ♥ **The Stockade Log Cabins** 🄲🄰
(403) 678-5212. **$78-$225.** 1050 Harvie Heights Rd. Trans-Canada Hwy 1, exit Harvie Heights Rd; 1 km e of Banff National Park east gate. Ext corridors. **Pets:** Accepted.

[SAVE] [S⌀] [✕] [🖬] [🖳] [🕻] [✆]

Ⓐ ♥♥♥ **Windtower Mountain Lodge** 🄲🄾 🐾
(403) 609-6600. **$89-$399, 3 day notice.** 160 Kananaskis Way. Trans-Canada Hwy 1, exit 1A (Bow Valley Tr), 1 km w, then n at Montane Dr. Int corridors. **Pets:** Other species. $5 one-time fee/room. Designated rooms, supervision.

[SAVE] [S⌀] [✕] [🖬] [🖳] [🕻] [🕻]

CLARESHOLM

♥♥ **Bluebird Motel** 🅼 🐾
(403) 625-3395. **$62-$72.** 5505 1st St W. 0.5 km n on Hwy 2. Ext corridors. **Pets:** Other species. Designated rooms, service with restrictions, crate.

[A$K] [S⌀] [✕] [🖬] [🖳]

DEAD MAN'S FLATS

Ⓐ ♥ **Pigeon Mountain Motel** 🅼
(403) 678-5756. **$75-$120, 4 day notice.** 250 1st Ave. On Trans-Canada Hwy 1. Ext corridors. **Pets:** Accepted.

[SAVE] [S⌀] [✕] [🖬] [🖳] [🕻]

DRUMHELLER

Ⓐ ♥♥ **Best Western Jurassic Inn** 🅼
(403) 823-7700. **$109-$159.** 1103 Hwy 9 S. Hwy 9, se access to town. Ext/int corridors. **Pets:** Accepted.

[SAVE] [S⌀] [✕] [🖬] [🖳] [🕻] [🛋]

♥♥ **Super 8 Motel** 🅼
(403) 823-8887. **$99-$169.** 600-680 2nd St SE. Off Hwy 9. Int corridors. **Pets:** Accepted.

[A$K] [S⌀] [✕] [🖬] [🖳] [🛋]

EDMONTON METROPOLITAN AREA

EDMONTON

♥♥ **Alberta Place Suite Hotel** 🄲🄾
(780) 423-1565. **$155-$185.** 10049 103rd St. Just s of Jasper Ave. Int corridors. **Pets:** Other species. $10 daily fee/pet. Designated rooms, service with restrictions.

[A$K] [S⌀] [✕] [🖬] [🖳] [🕻] [🛋] [✕]

♥ **Argyll Plaza Hotel** 🅂🄷
(780) 438-5876. **$79-$139.** 9933 63rd Ave. 63rd Ave at 99th St. Int corridors. **Pets:** Accepted.

[A$K] [S⌀] [✕] [🖬] [🖳] [🕻]

Ⓐ ♥♥♥ **Best Western Cedar Park Inn** 🅂🄷
(780) 434-7411. **$109-$139.** 5116 Gateway Blvd. Hwy 2 (Gateway Blvd) at 51st Ave. Int corridors. **Pets:** Accepted.

[SAVE] [S⌀] [✕] [🖳] [🕻] [🛋]

Ⓐ ♥♥♥ **Chateau Louis Hotel & Conference Centre** 🅂🄷
(780) 452-7770. **$109-$199, 3 day notice.** 11727 Kingsway. On Kingsway and 117th St. Int corridors. **Pets:** Accepted.

[SAVE] [S⌀] [✕] [&M] [🖉] [&] [🖬] [🖳] [🕻]

♥♥ **Comfort Inn West** 🅂🄷
(780) 484-4415. **$90-$104, 3 day notice.** 17610 100th Ave. At 176th St. Int corridors. **Pets:** $10 daily fee/pet. Service with restrictions, supervision.

[A$K] [S⌀] [✕] [🖬] [🖳] [🕻]

♥♥♥ **Crowne Plaza-Chateau Lacombe** 🄻🄷
(780) 428-6611. **$140.** 10111 Bellamy Hill. Jct 101st St, MacDonald Dr and Bellamy Hill. Int corridors. **Pets:** Small. Designated rooms, service with restrictions, crate.

[A$K] [S⌀] [✕] [&M] [🖬] [🕻]

♥♥♥ **Delta Edmonton Centre Suite Hotel** 🄻🄷
(780) 429-3900. **$155-$205.** 10222 102nd St. At 102nd St at 103rd Ave. Int corridors. **Pets:** Designated rooms, service with restrictions, crate.

[✕] [🖉] [&] [🖳] [🕻] [✕]

Ⓐ ♥♥♥ **Delta Edmonton South Hotel and Conference Centre** 🄻🄷
(780) 434-6415. **$109-$159.** 4404 Gateway Blvd. Jct Calgary Tr (Hwy 2) and Whitemud Dr. Int corridors. **Pets:** $10 one-time fee/room. Designated rooms, service with restrictions, supervision.

[SAVE] [✕] [🖬] [🖳] [🕻] [🛋] [✕]

▼▼▼▼ Executive Royal Inn West Edmonton 🆂🅷
(780) 484-6000. **$95-$189.** 10010 178th St. Corner of 178th St and 100th Ave. Int corridors. **Pets:** Small. $15 daily fee/room. Designated rooms, service with restrictions, supervision.

[ASK] [✕] [📶] [💻] [🍴] [✕]

Ⓒ🅐🅐 ▼▼▼ ▼▼▼ The Fairmont Hotel
Macdonald 🅻🅷
(780) 424-5181. **$159-$189.** 10065 100th St. Just s of Jasper Ave. Int corridors. **Pets:** Accepted.

[SAVE] [📶] [✕] [&M] [💻] [🍴] [⇌] [✕]

Ⓒ🅐🅐 ▼▼▼▼ Greenwood Inn Hotels 🆂🅷
(780) 431-1100. **$99-$139.** 4485 Gateway Blvd. Hwy 2 (Gateway Blvd), just n of Whitemud Dr. Int corridors. **Pets:** Accepted.

[SAVE] [✕] [&M] [🏊] [⛳] [📶] [💻] [🍴] [⇌] [✕]

▼▼▼▼ Holiday Inn Convention Centre 🆂🅷
(780) 468-5400. **$119-$199.** 4520 76th Ave. Hwy 14, just s via 50th St exit, then just e. Int corridors. **Pets:** Small. $15 daily fee/room. Service with restrictions, supervision.

[ASK] [📶] [✕] [🏊] [📶] [💻] [🍴] [⇌] [✕]

Ⓒ🅐🅐 ▼▼▼ Holiday Inn The Palace 🆂🅷
(780) 438-1222. **$95-$180.** 4235 Gateway Blvd. Just s of Whitemud Dr. Int corridors. **Pets:** $10 daily fee/pet. Designated rooms, service with restrictions, supervision.

[SAVE] [📶] [✕] [💻] [🍴]

▼▼▼▼ The Mayfield Inn & Suites, Edmonton 🅻🅷
(780) 484-0821. **$111-$279.** 16615 109th Ave. 1.6 km n of jct Hwy 2 and 16A on Mayfield Rd. Int corridors. **Pets:** $15 daily fee/room. Service with restrictions, supervision.

[ASK] [📶] [✕] [📶] [💻] [🍴] [⇌] [✕]

Ⓒ🅐🅐 ▼▼▼▼ Super 8 Hotel 🆂🅷 ❀
(780) 433-8688. **$98-$139.** 3610 Gateway Blvd. Jct 36th Ave. Int corridors. **Pets:** Other species. $10 daily fee/pet. Service with restrictions, crate.

[SAVE] [📶] [✕] [&M] [📶] [💻] [⇌] [✕]

▼▼▼▼ The Sutton Place Hotel 🅻🅷
(780) 428-7111. **$99-$259.** 10235 101st St. 102nd Ave at 101st St. Int corridors. **Pets:** Medium. $50 one-time fee/room. Designated rooms, service with restrictions, supervision.

[ASK] [📶] [✕] [💻] [🍴] [⇌] [✕]

▼▼▼▼ Thornton Court Hotel 🅻🅷
(780) 423-9999. **$79-$219.** One Thornton Ct. Just s of Jasper Ave at Thornton Ct and 99th St. Int corridors. **Pets:** $10 daily fee/room. Service with restrictions, crate.

[ASK] [📶] [✕] [📶] [💻] [🍴] [✕]

Ⓒ🅐🅐 ▼▼▼ Travelodge Beverly Crest 🆂🅷
(780) 474-0456. **$77-$97.** 3414 118th Ave. 8 km e of Capilano Dr, 1 km s from W Hwy 16 (Yellowhead Tr) on Victoria Tr exit. Int corridors. **Pets:** Other species. Service with restrictions, supervision.

[SAVE] [✕] [💻] [🍴]

Ⓒ🅐🅐 ▼▼▼▼ Travelodge Edmonton South 🆂🅷
(780) 436-9770. **$79-$115.** 10320 45th Ave S. Jct Calgary Tr (Hwy 2) and 45th Ave, just n of Whitemud Dr. Int corridors. **Pets:** Large. $10 daily fee/pet. Designated rooms, service with restrictions, supervision.

[SAVE] [📶] [✕] [📶] [💻] [⇌]

▼▼▼▼ The Varscona Hotel 🆂🅷
(780) 434-6111. **$225-$305.** 8208 106th St. Corner of 82nd Ave (Whyte Ave) and 106th St. Int corridors. **Pets:** Medium, other species. $35 one-time fee/pet. Designated rooms, service with restrictions, supervision.

[ASK] [📶] [✕] [💻] [🍴]

▼▼▼▼ The Westin Edmonton 🅻🅷 ❀
(780) 426-3636. **$289.** 10135 100th St. 101st Ave at 100th St. Int corridors. **Pets:** Other species. Service with restrictions.

[✕] [🏊] [💻] [🍴] [⇌] [✕]

▼▼▼▼ Wingate Inn Edmonton West 🆂🅷
(780) 443-1000. **$99-$162.** 18220 100th Ave. 100th Ave at 182nd St. Int corridors. **Pets:** Accepted.

[ASK] [📶] [✕] [&M] [📶] [💻] [⇌] [✕]

LEDUC

▼▼▼ Edmonton International Airport-Super 8
Motel 🆂🅷
(780) 986-8000. **$79-$95.** 8004 Sparrow Crescent. Hwy 2, exit N Business Section, 32 km s. Int corridors. **Pets:** Medium. $10 daily fee/pet. Designated rooms, service with restrictions, supervision.

[ASK] [📶] [✕] [📶] [💻]

▼▼▼▼ Executive Royal Inn Hotel & Conference
Centre 🆂🅷
(780) 986-1840. **$125.** 8450 Sparrow Dr. Hwy 2, 1 km e. Int corridors. **Pets:** Small. $20 daily fee/room. Designated rooms, service with restrictions, supervision.

[ASK] [📶] [✕] [&M] [📶] [💻] [🍴]

NISKU

Ⓒ🅐🅐 ▼▼▼▼ Holiday Inn Express-Edmonton
International Airport 🆂🅷
(780) 955-1000. **$93-$169.** 1102 4th St. Hwy 2, exit Edmonton International Airport/Nisku Business Park (10th Ave), 0.8 km e. Int corridors. **Pets:** Other species. $10 daily fee/pet. Designated rooms, service with restrictions, crate.

[SAVE] [📶] [✕] [&M] [🏊] [⛳] [📶] [💻]

▼▼▼ Nisku Inn & Conference Centre-Edmonton
Airport 🆂🅷
(780) 955-7744. **$143-$183.** 1103 4th St. Hwy 2, exit Edmonton International Airport/Nisku Business Park (10th Ave), 0.5 km e. Int corridors. **Pets:** Large, other species. $20 daily fee/pet. Designated rooms, service with restrictions, supervision.

[ASK] [📶] [✕] [&M] [📶] [💻] [🍴] [⇌]

SHERWOOD PARK

Ⓒ🅐🅐 ▼▼▼ Franklin's Inn 🆂🅷
(780) 467-1234. **$75-$85.** 2016 Sherwood Dr. At Granada Blvd. Int corridors. **Pets:** Accepted.

[SAVE] [✕] [📶] [💻] [🍴]

(AA) ▼▼▼▼ Ramada Limited-Edmonton East/
Sherwood Park SH
(780) 467-6727. **$105-$129.** 30 Broadway Blvd. Hwy 14, 1.5 km e on Baseline Rd, 0.4 km n on Broadmoor Blvd; Hwy 16, exit Broadmoor Blvd, 2.5 km s. Int corridors. **Pets:** Medium. $200 deposit/room, $10 daily fee/pet. Designated rooms, service with restrictions, supervision.
SAVE S🐾 ✕ 🖁M 🛏 🖳

(AA) ▼▼▼▼ Roadking Inns SH
(780) 464-1000. **$89-$99.** 26 Strathmoor Dr. Just sw of Hwy 16, exit Broadmoor Blvd. Int corridors. **Pets:** $200 deposit/room. Designated rooms, service with restrictions, crate.
SAVE S🐾 ✕ 🛏 🖳 🍴

SPRUCE GROVE

▼▼▼ Royal Inn Express Hotel SH
(780) 962-6050. **$88-$110.** 20 Westgrove Dr. I-16A, just n. Int corridors. **Pets:** Small, dogs only. $10 daily fee/pet. Designated rooms, service with restrictions, supervision.
ASK S🐾 ✕ 🛏 🖳

❖ END METROPOLITAN AREA ❖

EDSON

▼▼▼ Best Western High Road Inn SH
(780) 712-2378. **$119.** 300 52nd St. On 2nd Ave; centre. Int corridors. **Pets:** Other species. $10 daily fee/pet. Designated rooms, supervision.
ASK S🐾 ✕ 🛏 🖳 🍴 🏊 🐾✕

▼▼ Super 8 Motel SH
(780) 723-2500. **$78-$108.** 4300 2nd Ave. 1.1 km e on Hwy 16. Int corridors. **Pets:** Accepted.
✕ 🛏 🖳

FORT MACLEOD

(AA) ▼ Sunset Motel M
(403) 553-4448. **$42-$62.** 104 Hwy 3W. 1 km w on Hwy 2 and 3. Ext corridors. **Pets:** Other species. Service with restrictions, supervision.
SAVE S🐾 ✕ 🛏 🖳

FORT MCMURRAY

▼▼ Quality Hotel & Conference Centre Fort
McMurray SH
(780) 791-7200. **$109-$159.** 424 Gregoire Dr. Hwy 63, 1 km e at Gregoire Dr. Int corridors. **Pets:** Medium, other species. Designated rooms, service with restrictions, crate.
ASK S🐾 ✕ 🛏 🖳 🍴 🏊

▼▼ Super 8 Motel SH
(780) 799-8450. **$119-$130.** 321 Sakitawaw Tr. Just w of Hwy 63, 5 km s. Int corridors. **Pets:** Very small, other species. $10 daily fee/pet. Designated rooms, service with restrictions, crate.
ASK S🐾 ✕ 🛏 🖳 🍴

STONY PLAIN

▼▼▼ Ramada Inn & Suites SH
(780) 963-0222. **$76-$187.** 3301 43rd Ave. Hwy 16A, exit Dunmore Rd, just s. Ext/int corridors. **Pets:** Medium, other species. $4 daily fee/pet. Designated rooms, service with restrictions, supervision.
ASK ✕ 🛏 🖳 🍴 🏊

▼▼ Stony Convention Inn SH
(780) 963-3444. **$73-$82.** 4620 48th St. Hwy 16A, exit Stony Plain Rd, 0.8 km s on SR 779. Int corridors. **Pets:** Other species. $50 deposit/room. Designated rooms, service with restrictions, supervision.
ASK S🐾 ✕ 🛏 🖳 🍴

GRANDE PRAIRIE

(AA) ▼▼▼ Best Western Grande Prairie Hotel &
Suites SH
(780) 402-2378. **$99-$119.** 10745 117th Ave. Corner of 107th and 117th aves. Int corridors. **Pets:** Large, other species. $10 one-time fee/room. Designated rooms, service with restrictions, supervision.
SAVE S🐾 ✕ 🐕 🛏 🖳 🍴 🏊

▼▼ Quality Hotel & Conference Centre Grande
Prairie SH
(780) 539-6000. **$79-$139.** 11201 100th Ave. 2.9 km w on Hwy 2. Int corridors. **Pets:** Accepted.
ASK S🐾 ✕ 🛏 🖳 🍴

▼▼▼ Service Plus Inns and Suites SH ❖
(780) 538-3900. **$99-$250.** 10810 107th Ave. 2.2 km w on Hwy 2, just n. Int corridors. **Pets:** Medium. $10 one-time fee/room. Designated rooms, service with restrictions, supervision.
S🐾 ✕ 🖋 🛏 🖳 🏊 🐾✕

▼▼ Stanford Inn SH ❖
(780) 539-5678. **$74.** 11401 100th Ave. 2.8 km w on Hwy 2. Ext/int corridors. **Pets:** Other species. $5 daily fee/pet. Service with restrictions, supervision.
ASK S🐾 ✕ 🛏 🖳 🍴 🐾✕

HIGH RIVER

▼▼ Heritage Inn SH
(403) 652-3834. **$80-$85.** 1104 11th Ave SE. Trans-Canada Hwy 2, exit 23, 2 km w of Hwy 2. Int corridors. **Pets:** Other species. $10 daily fee/room. Designated rooms, service with restrictions, supervision.
ASK S🐾 ✕ 🛏 🖳 🍴 🏊

Ⓐ ▼▼▼ Super 8 Motel 🅂🄷 🐾
(403) 652-4448. **$99-$159.** 1601 13th Ave SE. Trans-Canada Hwy 2, exit High River, just w. Int corridors. **Pets:** Other species. $10 daily fee/room. Designated rooms, service with restrictions.
[SAVE] [S⚡] [✕] [&M] [🖊] [🖥] [🛏] [🖨]

HINTON

▼▼ ▼▼ Best Western White Wolf Inn 🅂🄷
(780) 865-7777. **$77-$170.** 828 Carmichael Ln. At west end of town; just off Hwy 16. Ext corridors. **Pets:** $10 daily fee/room. Supervision.
[A$K] [S⚡] [✕] [🖊] [🖥] [🖨]

Ⓐ ▼▼ ▼▼ Crestwood Hotel 🅂🄷
(780) 865-4001. **$79-$109.** 678 Carmichael Ln. 1 km w on Hwy 16. Int corridors. **Pets:** Accepted.
[SAVE] [S⚡] [✕] [🖊] [🖥] [🍴] [🛏]

▼▼▼ Ramada Limited & Suites 🅂🄷
(780) 865-2575. **$91-$123.** 500 Smith St. 6 km e on Hwy 16. Ext/int corridors. **Pets:** Accepted.
[✕] [🖊] [🖥]

▼▼ ▼▼ Super 8 Motel 🅂🄷
(780) 817-2228. **$79-$125.** 284 Smith St. 1.6 km e on Hwy 16. Int corridors. **Pets:** Large, other species. $10 daily fee/pet. Designated rooms, service with restrictions.
[A$K] [S⚡] [✕] [&M] [🖊] [🛏]

JASPER

Ⓐ ▼▼ ▼▼ Amethyst Lodge 🅂🄷
(780) 852-3394. **$61-$218.** 200 Connaught Dr. 0.5 km e. Ext/int corridors. **Pets:** Medium. Designated rooms, service with restrictions, supervision.
[SAVE] [S⚡] [✕] [🖥] [🍴]

▼▼▼▼ The Fairmont Jasper Park Lodge 🄻🄷 🐾
(780) 852-3301. **$189-$529, 3 day notice.** Lodge Rd. 4.8 km ne via Hwy 16; 3.2 km se off highway via Maligne Rd, follow signs for lodge. Ext corridors. **Pets:** Other species. $30 daily fee/room. Service with restrictions, supervision.
[✕] [&] [🖊] [🖥] [🍴] [🛏] [🖨] [🐾]

Ⓐ ▼▼ ▼▼ Jasper Inn Alpine Resort 🅂🄷
(780) 852-4461. **$109-$300, 3 day notice.** 98 Geikie St. 1.2 km ne at Geikie and Bonhomme sts. Ext/int corridors. **Pets:** Other species. $10 one-time fee/room. Designated rooms, supervision.
[SAVE] [S⚡] [✕] [🖊] [🖥] [🍴] [🛏] [🖨] [🐾]

Ⓐ ▼▼▼▼ Lobstick Lodge 🅂🄷
(780) 852-4431. **$70-$223.** 94 Geikie St. 1.2 km ne at Geikie and Juniper sts. Int corridors. **Pets:** Medium, other species. Designated rooms, service with restrictions, supervision.
[SAVE] [S⚡] [✕] [🖊] [🖥] [🍴] [🖨] [🐾]

Ⓐ ▼▼ ▼▼ Marmot Lodge 🄼
(780) 852-4471. **$65-$223.** 86 Connaught Dr. 1.6 km ne. Ext corridors. **Pets:** Medium, other species. Designated rooms, service with restrictions, supervision.
[SAVE] [S⚡] [✕] [🖊] [🖥] [🍴] [🛏]

▼▼ ▼▼ Patricia Lake Bungalows 🄲🄰
(780) 852-3560. **$81-$250, 7 day notice.** Pyramid Lake Rd. 4.8 km nw via Pyramid Lake Rd. Ext corridors. **Pets:** Medium, dogs only. $15 one-time fee/room. Designated rooms, service with restrictions, supervision.
[✕] [🖊] [🖥] [🖨] [🐾] [🛏]

▼▼ ▼▼ Sunwapta Falls Resort 🄼
(780) 852-4852. **$89-$199.** Hwy 93. 55 km s on Icefields Pkwy (Hwy 93). Ext corridors. **Pets:** Accepted.
[✕] [🖊] [🖥] [🍴] [🖨] [🐾] [🛏]

KANANASKIS

Ⓐ ▼▼▼ Delta Lodge at Kananaskis 🄻🄷 🐾
(403) 591-7711. **$89-$329, 3 day notice.** Kanaskis Village. Trans-Canada Hwy 1, 23.5 km s on Hwy 40 (Kananaskis Tr), then 3 km on Kananaskis Village access road, follow signs. Int corridors. **Pets:** $100 one-time fee/room. Designated rooms, service with restrictions, supervision.
[SAVE] [S⚡] [✕] [&] [🖥] [🍴] [🛏] [🖨]

LAKE LOUISE

▼▼ ▼▼ The Fairmont Chateau Lake Louise 🄻🄷 🐾
(403) 522-3511. **$199-$839, 3 day notice.** 111 Lake Louise Dr. 3 km up the hill from the village. Int corridors. **Pets:** Medium. $25 daily fee/pet. Designated rooms, service with restrictions, supervision.
[A$K] [S⚡] [✕] [🖥] [🍴] [🛏] [🖨]

▼▼ ▼▼ Lake Louise Inn 🅂🄷
(403) 522-3791. **$134-$274, 7 day notice.** 210 Village Rd. Just w of 4-way stop. Ext/int corridors. **Pets:** Other species. $100 deposit/room. Designated rooms, service with restrictions, supervision.
[A$K] [S⚡] [✕] [🖊] [🖥] [🍴] [🛏] [🖨]

LETHBRIDGE

▼▼ ▼▼ Comfort Inn 🅂🄷
(403) 320-8874. **$95-$135.** 3226 Fairway Plaza Rd S. Southeast end of city; Mayor Magrath Dr, exit n at Scenic Dr. Int corridors. **Pets:** Large, other species. $10 daily fee/pet. Designated rooms, service with restrictions, crate.
[A$K] [S⚡] [✕] [🖊] [🖥] [🛏]

Ⓐ ▼▼ ▼▼ Days Inn Lethbridge 🅂🄷
(403) 327-6000. **$94-$160.** 100 3rd Ave S. Corner of 3rd Ave and Scenic Dr; centre. Ext/int corridors. **Pets:** Other species. Designated rooms, service with restrictions, supervision.
[SAVE] [S⚡] [✕] [🖊] [🖥] [🛏]

Ⓐ ▼▼ ▼▼ Econo Lodge-Lethbridge 🄼
(403) 328-5591. **$70-$80.** 1124 Mayor Magrath Dr S. Hwy 3, 4 or 5, exit Mayor Magrath Dr S. Ext corridors. **Pets:** Accepted.
[SAVE] [S⚡] [✕] [🖊] [🖥]

Ⓐ ▼▼▼▼ Lethbridge Lodge Hotel and Conference Centre 🄻🄷
(403) 328-1123. **$109-$159.** 320 Scenic Dr. Scenic Dr at 4th Ave S; centre. Int corridors. **Pets:** Other species. $30 one-time fee/room. Service with restrictions, supervision.
[SAVE] [S⚡] [✕] [🖊] [🖥] [🍴] [🛏]

▼▼▼▼ Ramada Hotel and Suites 🆂🅷
(403) 380-5050. **$99-$159.** 2375 Mayor Magrath Dr S. 4.5 km se on Hwy 4 and 5, exit Mayor Magrath Dr S. Int corridors. **Pets:** Accepted.
🅰🆂🅺 🆂🅾 ⊠ 🔒 🖵 🍽 🏊 🏋

▼▼ Thriftlodge 🅼
(403) 328-4436. **$56-$66, 3 day notice.** 1142 Mayor Magrath Dr S. 4 km se on Hwy 4 and 5, exit Mayor Magrath Dr S. Ext corridors. **Pets:** Medium. $7 daily fee/room. Designated rooms, service with restrictions, supervision.
🆂🅰🆅🅴 🆂🅾 ⊠ 🔒 🏊

LLOYDMINSTER

▼▼ Best Western Wayside Inn 🆂🅷
(780) 875-4404. **$106-$225.** 5411 44th St. 0.8 km w on Hwy 16 from jct Hwy 17. Int corridors. **Pets:** Other species. $5 daily fee/pet. Designated rooms, service with restrictions, supervision.
🅰🆂🅺 🆂🅾 ⊠ 🔒 🖵 🍽 🏊

▼▼ Tropical Inn 🆂🅷
(780) 875-7000. **$89-$103.** 5621 44th St. Jct Hwy 16 and 17, 1 km w. Int corridors. **Pets:** Other species. Designated rooms, service with restrictions, supervision.
🆂🅰🆅🅴 🆂🅾 ⊠ 🔒 🖵 🍽 🏊 🏋

MEDICINE HAT

▼▼▼▼ Best Western Inn 🆂🅷
(403) 527-3700. **$109-$269.** 722 Redcliff Dr. On Trans-Canada Hwy 1; 0.4 km w of jct Hwy 3 access 7th St SW. Ext/int corridors. **Pets:** Medium, other species. Designated rooms, service with restrictions, supervision.
🅰🆂🅺 🆂🅾 ⊠ 🅶🅼 🔒 🖵 🏊 🏋

▼▼▼ Imperial Inn 🅼
(403) 527-8811. **$68-$84.** 3282 13th Ave SE. 3.6 km se; just n off Trans-Canada Hwy 1. Ext/int corridors. **Pets:** Other species. $100 deposit/room, $5 daily fee/room. Designated rooms, service with restrictions, supervision.
🆂🅰🆅🅴 🆂🅾 ⊠ 🔒 🖵 🍽 🏊 🏋

▼▼▼ Medicine Hat Lodge Hotel Casino & Convention Centre 🅻🅷
(403) 529-2222. **$99-$129.** 1051 Ross Glen Dr SE. East end approach to city on Trans-Canada Hwy 1, at jct Dunmore Rd. Int corridors. **Pets:** Other species. Designated rooms, service with restrictions, supervision.
🅰🆂🅺 ⊠ 🔒 🖵 🍽 🏊 🏋

▼▼ Ranchmen Motel 🅼
(403) 527-2263. **$44-$48.** 1617 Bomford Crescent SW. Trans-Canada Hwy 1 at 16th St SW. Ext corridors. **Pets:** Small, dogs only. $5 daily fee/room. Designated rooms, service with restrictions.
⊠ 🔒 🖵

▼▼▼ Super 8 Motel 🆂🅷
(403) 528-8888. **$70-$91.** 1280 Trans-Canada Way SE. Trans-Canada Way at 13 Ave SE; just n off Trans-Canada Hwy 1. Ext/int corridors. **Pets:** Other species. $5 daily fee/pet. Designated rooms, service with restrictions, crate.
🅰🆂🅺 🆂🅾 ⊠ 🅶🅼 🔒 🖵 🏊

▼▼▼ Travelodge Hotel Medicine Hat 🆂🅷
(403) 527-2275. **$105-$115.** 1100 Redcliff Dr SW. 2.8 km sw on Trans-Canada Hwy 1 at jct Hwy 3. Ext/int corridors. **Pets:** Other species. $7 deposit/room. Designated rooms, service with restrictions, supervision.
🆂🅰🆅🅴 🆂🅾 ⊠ 🔒 🖵 🍽 🏊 🏋

PEACE RIVER

▼▼▼ Traveller's Motor Hotel 🆂🅷
(780) 624-3621. **$69-$109.** 9510 100th St. Just off Hwy 2 S, exit town centre. Ext/int corridors. **Pets:** Other species. $100 deposit/room. Designated rooms, service with restrictions, supervision.
🆂🅰🆅🅴 🆂🅾 ⊠ 🅶🅼 🔒 🖵 🍽

PINCHER CREEK

▼▼ Heritage Inn 🆂🅷
(403) 627-5000. **$89-$95.** 919 Waterton Ave (Hwy 6). SR 3, 4.7 km s on SR 6. Int corridors. **Pets:** Medium. $10 daily fee/pet. Designated rooms, service with restrictions, supervision.
🅰🆂🅺 🆂🅾 ⊠ 🔒 🖵 🍽

RED DEER

▼▼▼▼ Holiday Inn 67 Street 🆂🅷
(403) 342-6567. **$90-$100.** 6500 67th St. 3.2 km nw, 0.8 km e of Hwy 2, exit 67th St. Int corridors. **Pets:** Small, other species. $15 daily fee/pet. Designated rooms, service with restrictions, supervision.
🆂🅰🆅🅴 🆂🅾 ⊠ 🔒 🖵 🍽 🏊 🏋

▼▼▼▼ Holiday Inn Express-Red Deer 🆂🅷 ✿
(403) 343-2112. **$119.** 2803 50th Ave. 1.8 km e on Hwy 2A (Gaetz Ave). Int corridors. **Pets:** Small. $15 daily fee/room. Designated rooms, service with restrictions, supervision.
🆂🅰🆅🅴 🆂🅾 ⊠ 🔒 🖵 🏊 🏋

▼▼▼▼ Red Deer Lodge Hotel & Conference Centre 🅻🅷
(403) 346-8841. **$89.** 4311 49th Ave. Corner of 43rd St and 49th Ave; centre. Int corridors. **Pets:** $10 daily fee/pet. Designated rooms, service with restrictions, crate.
🆂🅰🆅🅴 🆂🅾 ⊠ 🔒 🖵 🍽 🏊 🏋

▼▼▼▼ Sandman Hotel Red Deer 🆂🅷
(403) 343-7400. **$99-$119.** 2818 Gaetz Ave. 2 km n. Int corridors. **Pets:** Medium. $10 daily fee/room. Service with restrictions, crate.
🅰🆂🅺 🆂🅾 ⊠ 🅶🅼 🔒 🖵 🍽 🏊

▼▼▼▼ Service Plus Inns and Suites 🆂🅷
(403) 342-4445. **$94-$99.** 6853 66th St. 3.6 km nw, 0.5 km e of Hwy 2, exit 67th St. Int corridors. **Pets:** Other species. $10 daily fee/room. Designated rooms, service with restrictions, supervision.
🆂🅰🆅🅴 🆂🅾 ⊠ 🔒 🖵 🍽 🏊 🏋

▼▼ Stanford Inn 🆂🅷
(403) 347-5551. **$80-$95.** 4707 Ross St. Hwy 2, exit Gaetz Ave to 49th St, just e. Int corridors. **Pets:** Designated rooms, service with restrictions, supervision.
🅰🆂🅺 🆂🅾 ⊠ 🔒 🖵 🍽

(CAA) ▼▼▼ **Travelodge Red Deer** SH
(403) 346-2011. **$99-$125.** 2807 50th Ave. 1.8 km s on Hwy 2A (Gaetz Ave). Ext/int corridors. **Pets:** Accepted.
SAVE S☉ ✕ ⊟ ▣ ❔ ⊵

ROCKY MOUNTAIN HOUSE

(CAA) ▼ **Chinook Inn** M
(403) 845-2833. **$75-$85.** 5321 59th Ave. 1.3 km w on Hwy 11, then s. Int corridors. **Pets:** $10 daily fee/room. Designated rooms, supervision.
SAVE S☉ ✕ ⊟ ▣

(CAA) ▼▼▼ **Holiday Inn Express** SH
(403) 845-2871. **$89-$99.** 4715 45th St. Just nw of jct 47th Ave and 45th St. Int corridors. **Pets:** Accepted.
SAVE S☉ ✕ ⊟ ▣

TABER

▼▼▼ **Heritage Inn** SH
(403) 223-4424. **$86-$88.** 4830 46th Ave. 1 km e of jct Hwy 3 and 36 S, on Hwy 3. Int corridors. **Pets:** Other species. $5 daily fee/pet. Designated rooms, service with restrictions, supervision.
ASK S☉ ✕ ⊟ ▣ ❔ ⊠

VALLEYVIEW

▼ **Raven Motor Inn** M
(780) 524-3383. **$63-$70.** 4606 50th St. Jct Hwy 49 and 43. Ext corridors. **Pets:** Accepted.
ASK S☉ ✕ ⊟ ▣ ⊵

WATERTON PARK

(CAA) ▼▼▼ **Bayshore Inn** M ❀
(403) 859-2211. **$99-$199, 3 day notice.** 111 Waterton Ave. Centre. Ext corridors. **Pets:** $50 deposit/room. Designated rooms, service with restrictions.
SAVE ✕ ⊟ ▣ ❔ ✖

(CAA) ▼▼▼ **Waterton Lakes Lodge** LH
(403) 859-2150. **$129-$239.** 101 Clematis Ave. Centre. Ext/int corridors. **Pets:** Medium, other species. $20 daily fee/room. Designated rooms, service with restrictions, supervision.
SAVE ✕ ⟁M ✍ ⊟ ▣ ❔ ⊵ ⊠

WETASKIWIN

▼▼ **Best Western Wayside Inn** SH
(780) 352-6681. **$89.** 4103 56 St. Just n of Hwy 13 W, on Hwy 2A. Int corridors. **Pets:** Medium, other species. $100 deposit/room. Designated rooms, supervision.
ASK S☉ ✕ ▣ ❔

▼▼ **Super 8 Motel** SH
(780) 361-3808. **$79-$89.** 3820 56th St. On Hwy 2A, just s of jct Hwy 13 W. Ext/int corridors. **Pets:** Large, other species. $100 deposit/room. Designated rooms, service with restrictions, supervision.
ASK S☉ ✕ ⟁M ⊟

WHITECOURT

(CAA) ▼▼▼ **Quality Inn** SH
(780) 778-5477. **$55-$75, 7 day notice.** 5420 49th Ave. On Hwy 43, 0.5 km e of Hwy 32. Int corridors. **Pets:** Other species. Designated rooms.
SAVE S☉ ✕ ⊟ ▣ ❔ ⊠

CITY INDEX

100 MILE HOUSE

▼▼ 100 Mile House Super 8 Ⓜ
(250) 395-8888. **$79-$88.** 989 Alder Ave. 1 km s on Hwy 97.
Ext corridors. **Pets:** Accepted.
[ASK] [S6] [✕] [🛏] [▣]

▼▼ Ramada Limited Ⓜ
(250) 395-2777. **$84-$94.** 917 Alder Rd. 1 km s on Hwy 97.
Int corridors. **Pets:** Accepted.
[ASK] [S6] [✕] [🛏] [▣]

▼▼ Red Coach Inn SH
(250) 395-2266. **$79-$97.** 170 Cariboo Hwy N. On Hwy 97,
on the north end of town. Ext/int corridors. **Pets:** Accepted.
[ASK] [S6] [✕] [6M] [🛏] [▣] [🍴] [≈]

108 MILE HOUSE

**CAA ▼▼◆ 108 Resort & Conference
Centre** LH
(250) 791-5211. **$90-$120.** 4816 Telqua Dr. From Hwy 97,
1.6 km nw on access road, follow signs. Ext corridors.
Pets: Accepted.
[SAVE] [S6] [✕] [6M] [🛏] [▣] [🍴] [X]

ABBOTSFORD

▼▼◆ Coast Abbotsford Hotel & Suites LH
(604) 853-1880. **$115-$120.** 2020 Sumas Way. Trans-
Canada Hwy 1, exit 92 (Town Centre), just n on Hwy 11. Int
corridors. **Pets:** $10 daily fee/pet. Service with restrictions,
supervision.
[ASK] [S6] [✕] [🛏] [▣] [🍴] [≈]

CAA ▼▼◆ Holiday Inn Express LH
(604) 859-6211. **$69-$94.** 2073 Clearbrook Rd. Trans-
Canada Hwy 1, exit 87 (Clearbrook Rd). Ext/int corridors.
Pets: Accepted.
[SAVE] [S6] [✕] [6M] [🛏] [▣] [🍴] [≈] [X]

**▼▼◆ Ramada Inn & Conference
Centre-Abbotsford** LH ✿
(604) 870-1050. **$160-$250.** 36035 N Parallel Rd. Trans-
Canada Hwy 1, exit 95 (Whatcom Rd). Int corridors.
Pets: Other species. $10 daily fee/pet. Designated rooms,
service with restrictions, crate.
[ASK] [S6] [✕] [6M] [⚡] [🛏] [▣] [🍴] [≈] [X]

CAA ▼▼◆ Super 8 Motel Abbotsford Ⓜ
(604) 853-1141. **$70-$120.** 1881 Sumas Way. Trans-Canada
Hwy 1, exit 92 (Town Centre), just n on Hwy 11. Ext corridors. **Pets:** Accepted.
[SAVE] [S6] [✕] [🛏] [▣]

BARRIERE

**CAA ▼▼◆ Mountain Springs Motel & RV
Park** Ⓜ
(250) 672-0090. **$48-$62.** 4253 Yellowhead Hwy. 1 km s on
Hwy 5 (Yellowhead Hwy). Ext corridors. **Pets:** Accepted.
[SAVE] [S6] [✕] [🛏] [▣]

BLUE RIVER

▼▼ Glacier Mountain Lodge SH
(250) 673-2393. **$79-$119.** 869 Shell Rd. On Hwy 5 (Yellowhead Hwy) at Shell Rd, follow signs. Int corridors. **Pets:** $10
daily fee/room. Designated rooms, service with restrictions,
supervision.
[ASK] [S6] [✕] [🛏]

▼▼◆ Mike Wiegele Helicopter Skiing SH
(250) 673-8381. **$85-$295, 3 day notice.** 1 Harwood Dr. On
Hwy 5 (Yellowhead Hwy) at Harwood Dr, follow signs. Ext
corridors. **Pets:** Accepted.
[ASK] [✕] [🛏] [▣] [🍴] [X]

BOWEN ISLAND

▼▼ Wildwood Lane Cottages CA ✿
(604) 947-2253. **$125-$200, 14 day notice.** 1291 Adams
Rd. From ferry terminal, 5.6 km w on Grafton Rd, then 1 km
n. Ext corridors. **Pets:** $20 daily fee/room. Supervision.
[ASK] [S6] [✕] [🛏] [▣] [🏧]

CACHE CREEK

(AA) 🔻🔻 **Bonaparte Motel** M ✿
(250) 457-9693. **$60-$95.** 1395 Hwy 97 N. 1 km n of jct Trans-Canada Hwy 1. Ext corridors. **Pets:** Other species. $10 daily fee/pet. No service, supervision.
SAVE ✕ 🛢 ➛

CAMPBELL RIVER

(AA) 🔻🔻🔻 **Best Western Austrian Chalet** M
(250) 923-4231. **$94-$164.** 462 S Island Hwy. 3.2 km s on Island Hwy 19A. Ext/int corridors. **Pets:** Medium, other species. $5 daily fee/pet. Designated rooms, service with restrictions, supervision.
SAVE S🔒 ✕ 🛢 🖥 ➛ ✕ 🐾

💎 **Campbell River Lodge Fishing & Adventure Resort** M 🐾
(250) 287-7446. **$59-$94, 3 day notice.** 1760 Island Hwy. On Island Hwy 19A, 2 km nw of downtown; just e from Hwy 19 and 28. Ext/int corridors. **Pets:** Medium. $10 daily fee/ pet. Designated rooms, service with restrictions, supervision.
✕ 🛢 🍴 🐾

🔻 **Campbell River Super 8** M
(250) 286-6622. **$66-$90.** 340 S Island Hwy. 3 km s on Island Hwy 19A. Int corridors. **Pets:** Medium, dogs only. $6 daily fee/pet. Designated rooms, service with restrictions, supervision.
ASK S🔒 ✕ 🛢 ➛

🔻🔻🔻 **Ramada Hotel & Suites** SH
(250) 286-1131. **$109-$299.** 261 Island Hwy. On Island Hwy 19A, 2 km s. Int corridors. **Pets:** Medium, other species. $8 daily fee/pet. Designated rooms, service with restrictions, supervision.
ASK S🔒 ✕ 🛢 🖥 🍴 ➛ 🐾

🔻 **Rustic Motel** M
(250) 286-6295. **$85-$90.** 2140 N Island Hwy. Just n of jct Hwy 19 S and 28. Ext corridors. **Pets:** Other species. $5 daily fee/pet. Service with restrictions, supervision.
✕ 🛢 🖥

CHASE

🔻🔻 **Chase Country Inn Motel** M
(250) 679-3333. **$59-$95, 3 day notice.** 576 Coburn St. Trans-Canada Hwy 1 and Coburn St. Ext corridors. **Pets:** Accepted.
ASK S🔒 ✕ 🛢 🖥 🍴

🔻🔻 **Quaaout Lodge Resort** SH
(250) 679-3090. **$75-$180.** Trans-Canada Hwy 1, exit Squilax Bridge, 2.5 km w on Little Shuswap Rd. Int corridors. **Pets:** $10 daily fee/pet. Designated rooms, service with restrictions.
S🔒 ✕ 🐾 🛢 🖥 🍴 ➛ 🐾

CHEMAINUS

💎 **Chemainus Fuller Lake Motel** M
(250) 246-3282. **$75-$95, 3 day notice.** 9300 Smiley Rd. On Trans-Canada Hwy 1 and Henry Rd. Ext corridors. **Pets:** Accepted.
✕ 🛢 🐾

CHILLIWACK

(AA) 🔻🔻🔻 **Best Western Rainbow Country Inn** LH
(604) 795-3828. **$94-$130.** 43971 Industrial Way. Trans-Canada Hwy 1, exit 116 (Lickman Rd). Int corridors. **Pets:** Accepted.
SAVE S🔒 ✕ 🛢 🖥 🍴 ➛

(AA) 🔻🔻🔻 **Chilliwack Travelodge** LH
(604) 792-4240. **$60-$90.** 45466 Yale Rd W. Trans-Canada Hwy 1, exit 119B eastbound; exit 119A westbound, then just n. Int corridors. **Pets:** Medium. $5 daily fee/room. Designated rooms, service with restrictions, supervision.
SAVE S🔒 ✕ 🛢 🖥 🍴 ➛

🔻🔻 **Comfort Inn** M
(604) 858-0636. **$82-$113.** 45405 Luckakuck Way. Trans-Canada Hwy 1, exit 119A eastbound; exit 119B westbound, s on Vedder Rd, then 1 km w. Int corridors. **Pets:** Medium, other species. $5 daily fee/room. Designated rooms, service with restrictions, supervision.
ASK S🔒 ✕ 🐾 🖥

(AA) 🔻🔻🔻 **Rhombus Hotels & Resorts-Downtown Chilliwack** LH
(604) 795-4788. **$78-$130.** 45920 First Ave. Trans-Canada Hwy 1, exit 119B eastbound; exit 119A westbound, 3 km n, then just w; downtown. Int corridors. **Pets:** Accepted.
SAVE S🔒 ✕ 🐾 🛢 🖥 🍴 ➛ ✕

CHRISTINA LAKE

🔻🔻 **New Horizon Motel** M
(250) 447-9312. **$79-$135, 60 day notice.** 2037 Hwy 3. Just e. Ext corridors. **Pets:** Accepted.
✕ 🛢 🖥 ✕

CLEARWATER

(AA) 🔻 **Jasper Way Inn Motel on beautiful Dutch Lake** M
(250) 674-3345. **$51-$95.** 57 E Old N Thompson Hwy. 1 km w on Old N Thompson Hwy, just off Hwy 5 (Yellowhead Hwy). Ext corridors. **Pets:** Accepted.
SAVE S🔒 ✕ 🛢 🖥 ✕

COURTENAY

🔻🔻 **The Coast Westerly Hotel** SH 🐾
(250) 338-7741. **$119-$169.** 1590 Cliffe Ave. 1 km n on Cliffe Ave (Hwy 19A) from jct Island Hwy connector. Int corridors. **Pets:** Large. $50 deposit/room, $10 daily fee/pet. Service with restrictions, supervision.
ASK S🔒 ✕ 🐾 🛢 🖥 🍴 ➛ ✕

🔻🔻🔻 **Kingfisher Oceanside Resort & Spa** SH
(250) 338-1323. **$129-$425, 7 day notice.** 4330 S Island Hwy. From Hwy 19, exit 101, follow signs to Island Hwy 19A, then 1 km s. Ext corridors. **Pets:** Accepted.
✕ 🐾 🛢 🖥 🍴 ➛ ✕ 🐾

(AA) 🔻 **Travelodge Courtenay** M
(250) 334-4491. **$83-$103.** 2605 S Island Hwy (Cliffe Ave). 1.8 km s of downtown, on Island Hwy 19A. Ext corridors. **Pets:** Accepted.
SAVE S🔒 ✕ 🛢 🖥 ➛ 🐾

CRANBROOK

**▼▼▼ ▼▼▼ Delta St. Eugene Mission
Resort** 🏠 ❀
(250) 420-2000. **$109-$199.** 7731 Mission Rd. Hwy 3, exit
Kimberley/Airport (Hwy 95A) to Mission Rd, 4.5 km n. Int
corridors. **Pets:** Medium. $15 daily fee/room. Designated
rooms, service with restrictions, crate.
🅰🆂🅺 🆂 ⊗ 🛑 🖵 🍽 ⇌ ⊗

▼▼ ▼▼ Heritage Inn 🆂🅷
(250) 489-4301. **$98-$105.** 803 Cranbrook St N. Hwy 3 and
95; centre. Int corridors. **Pets:** Accepted.
🅰🆂🅺 🆂 ⊗ 🛑 🖵 🍽 ⇌ ⊗

▼▼ ▼▼ Model A Inn Ⓜ ❀
(250) 489-4600. **$80-$175.** 1908 Cranbrook St N. 2.5 km n
on Hwy 3 and 95. Ext corridors. **Pets:** $5 daily fee/pet.
Designated rooms, service with restrictions, supervision.
🆂🅰🆅🅴 🆂 ⊗ 🛑 🖵

Ⓐ ▼▼ ▼▼ Super 8 Motel 🆂🅷
(250) 489-8028. **$90-$105, 30 day notice.** 2370 Cranbrook
St N. Just w of jct Hwy 93 and 95, corner of 30th Ave. Int
corridors. **Pets:** Accepted.
🆂🅰🆅🅴 🆂 ⊗ 🅲🅼 🛑

CRESTON

▼▼ Downtowner Motor Inn 🆂🅷
(250) 428-2238. **$45-$66.** 1218 Canyon St. Corner of 12th
Ave N. Int corridors. **Pets:** $4 daily fee/pet.
⊗ 🛑

Ⓐ ▼▼ Skimmerhorn Inn Ⓜ ❀
(250) 428-4009. **$65-$86.** 2711 Hwy 3. On Hwy 3, 0.8 km e.
Ext corridors. **Pets:** Medium, dogs only. $5 daily fee/pet.
Service with restrictions, supervision.
🆂🅰🆅🅴 ⊗ 🛑 🖵 ⇌

Ⓐ ▼▼ ▼▼ Sunset Motel Ⓜ
(250) 428-2229. **$69-$79.** 2705 Canyon St, Hwy 3 E. 1 km e
on Hwy 3. Ext corridors. **Pets:** Accepted.
🆂🅰🆅🅴 ⊗ 🛑 🖵 ⇌

DAWSON CREEK

Ⓐ ▼▼ ▼▼ Dawson Creek Super 8 🆂🅷 ❀
(250) 782-8899. **$83-$97.** 1440 Alaska Ave. Just s of jct Hart
Hwy 97 S and Alaska Hwy 97 N. Int corridors. **Pets:** Other
species. $10 daily fee/pet. Designated rooms, service with
restrictions, supervision.
🆂🅰🆅🅴 🆂 ⊗ 🛑 🖵

DUNCAN

**Ⓐ ▼▼ ▼▼ Best Western Cowichan Valley
Inn** 🆂🅷
(250) 748-2722. **$95-$129.** 6474 Trans-Canada Hwy 1. 3 km
n. Int corridors. **Pets:** Accepted.
🆂🅰🆅🅴 🆂 ⊗ 🛑 🖵 🍽 ⇌

▼▼ Falcon Nest Motel Ⓜ
(250) 748-8188. **$50-$67.** 5867 Trans-Canada Hwy 1. 1.5
km n. Ext corridors. **Pets:** Small, dogs only. $10 daily fee/
pet. Designated rooms, service with restrictions, supervision.
🆂 ⊗ 🛑 🖵 ⇌

**▼▼▼ ▼▼▼ Travelodge Silver Bridge Inn
Duncan** 🆂🅷 ❀
(250) 748-4311. **$99-$189.** 140 Trans-Canada Hwy 1. Just n
of the Silver Bridge. Ext corridors. **Pets:** Other species. $10
daily fee/pet.
🅰🆂🅺 🆂 ⊗ 🛑 🖵 🍽

ENDERBY

**Ⓐ ▼▼ ▼▼ Howard Johnson Inn Fortunes
Landing** 🆂🅷
(250) 838-6825. **$79-$89.** 1510 George St. 1 km n on Hwy
97A. Ext corridors. **Pets:** Accepted.
🆂🅰🆅🅴 🆂 ⊗ 🛑 🖵 🍽 ⇌

FERNIE

**Ⓐ ▼▼▼ ▼▼▼ Best Western Fernie Mountain
Lodge** 🆂🅷
(250) 423-5500. **$114-$329.** 1622 7th Ave. I-3, exit 7th Ave,
on Hwy 3; east end of Fernie. Int corridors. **Pets:** Small.
$10 daily fee/pet. Designated rooms, service with restric-
tions, supervision.
🆂🅰🆅🅴 🆂 ⊗ 🛑 🖵 🍽 ⇌

Ⓐ ▼▼ ▼▼ Little Log Inn Ⓜ
(250) 423-4696. **$59-$99, 14 day notice.** 141 Commerce
Rd. 1.8 km e on Hwy 3. Ext corridors. **Pets:** Accepted.
🆂🅰🆅🅴 🆂 ⊗ 🖵 🍽 🅰🅲

Ⓐ ▼▼▼ ▼▼▼ Park Place Lodge 🆂🅷
(250) 423-6871. **$99-$229.** 742 Hwy 3. At 7th St. Int corridors. **Pets:** Accepted.
🆂🅰🆅🅴 🆂 ⊗ 🛑 🖵 🍽 ⇌ ⊗

Ⓐ ▼▼▼ ▼▼▼ Riverside Mountain Lodge 🅲🅾
(250) 423-5000. **$59-$199, 30 day notice.** 100 Riverside
Way. Hwy 3, 2 km w. Ext/int corridors. **Pets:** Accepted.
🆂🅰🆅🅴 🆂 ⊗ 🛑 🖵 🍽 ⇌ ⊗

▼▼ ▼▼ Super 8 Motel-Fernie 🆂🅷
(250) 423-6788. **$72-$82.** 2021 Hwy 3. 1.5 km w. Int corridors. **Pets:** Accepted.
🅰🆂🅺 🆂 ⊗ 🛑 ⊗

FIELD

▼▼ ▼▼ Kicking Horse Lodge 🆂🅷
(250) 343-6303. **$79-$172, 7 day notice.** 100 Centre St.
Centre. Ext corridors. **Pets:** Accepted.
⊗ 🛑 🖵 🍽 ⊗ 🅰🅲 🗝

FORT ST. JOHN

Ⓐ ▼▼▼ ▼▼▼ Best Western Coachman Inn 🆂🅷
(250) 787-0651. **$89-$110.** 8540 Alaska Rd. 2 km s on Hwy
97. Int corridors. **Pets:** Other species. $15 daily fee/room.
Designated rooms, supervision.
🆂🅰🆅🅴 🆂 ⊗ 🛑 🖵 🍽

Ⓐ ▼▼▼ ▼▼▼ Quality Inn Northern Grand 🏠
(250) 787-0521. **$109-$129.** 9830 100th Ave. Centre. Int corridors. **Pets:** Large. $15 one-time fee/pet. Designated
rooms.
🆂🅰🆅🅴 🆂 ⊗ 🛑 🖵 🍽 ⇌ ⊗

▼▼▼ **Ramada Limited** 🆂🅷
(250) 787-0779. **$106-$116.** 10103 98th Ave. Corner of 100th Ave; centre of downtown. Int corridors. **Pets:** Accepted.
🅰🆂🅺 🆂👼 ⊗ 🅰🅼 ⟨🐾⟩ 🔒 💻 🍽

FORT STEELE

🆎 ▼▼▼ **Bull River Guest Ranch** 🆁🅰
(250) 429-3760. **$95-$110.** Hwy 95, 21.9 km se of Ft Steele on Ft Steele-Wardner Rd, 12 km ne on gravel road, follow signs; Hwy 3 W, 41 km e of Cranbrook, use Ft Steele Rd. Ext corridors. **Pets:** Accepted.
🆂🅰🆅🅴 🔒 💻 ⊗ 🅺 🆆 🍽

GIBSONS

▼▼ **Cedars Inn** 🅼
(604) 886-3008. **$96-$106.** 895 Gibsons Way. Hwy 101 and Shaw Rd; 6 km n from ferry terminal. Ext/int corridors. **Pets:** Accepted.
🅰🆂🅺 🆂👼 ⊗ 🔒 💻 ⟷ ⊗

GOLD BRIDGE

▼▼▼ **Morrow Chalets** 🅲🅰
(250) 238-2462. **$200-$300, 30 day notice.** 8 km n from the Tyaughton Lake turnoff, follow signs. Ext corridors. **Pets:** Other species. Supervision.
⊗ 🔒 🅺 🆆

GOLDEN

▼ **Golden Gate Motel** 🅼
(250) 344-2252. **$45-$75.** 1408 Golden View Rd. On Trans-Canada Hwy 1, 1.5 km e of jct Hwy 95. Ext corridors. **Pets:** Medium. $5 daily fee/pet. Service with restrictions, supervision.
🅰🆂🅺 🆂👼 ⊗ 🔒

▼▼ **Golden Rim Motor Inn** 🅼
(250) 344-2216. **$69-$105.** 1416 Golden View Rd. 1.5 km e on Trans-Canada Hwy 1 from jct Hwy 95. Ext corridors. **Pets:** Medium. $6 daily fee/pet. Service with restrictions, supervision.
🅰🆂🅺 🆂👼 ⊗ 🔒 💻 🍽 ⟷ ⊗

🆎 ▼▼▼ **Hillside Lodge & Chalets** 🅲🅰
(250) 344-7281. **$108-$135, 5 day notice.** 1740 Seward Frontage Rd. 15 km w on Hwy 1, follow signs n off highway. Ext corridors. **Pets:** Accepted.
🆂🅰🆅🅴 ⊗ 🔒 💻 ⊗ 🅺 🆉

🆎 ▼ **Rondo Motel** 🅼
(250) 344-5295. **$58-$88.** 824 Park Dr. Jct Trans-Canada Hwy 1 and 95, 2 km s on 10th Ave, just w on Park Dr; downtown. Ext corridors. **Pets:** Medium, other species. $6 daily fee/pet. Designated rooms, service with restrictions, supervision.
🆂🅰🆅🅴 ⊗ 🔒

GRAND FORKS

▼▼ **Ramada Limited** 🅼
(250) 442-2127. **$99-$109, 14 day notice.** 2729 Central Ave. West end of town on Hwy 3. Ext corridors. **Pets:** Very small. $15 daily fee/pet. Service with restrictions, supervision.
🅰🆂🅺 🆂👼 ⊗ 🔒 💻 🍽 ⟷

🆎 ▼ **Western Traveller Motel** 🅼
(250) 442-5566. **$59-$79.** 1591 Central Ave. West end of town on Hwy 3. Ext corridors. **Pets:** Small, dogs only. $7 daily fee/pet. Designated rooms, service with restrictions, supervision.
🆂🅰🆅🅴 🆂👼 ⊗ 🔒 💻

GULF ISLANDS NATIONAL PARK RESERVE
METROPOLITAN AREA

QUADRA ISLAND

▼▼▼▼ **April Point Resort & Marina** 🅻🅷
(250) 285-2222. **Call for rates.** 900 April Point Rd. From Campbell River terminal; n on Ferry Rd, 1 km to Pidcock and April Point rds, then 3.2 km n. Ext corridors. **Pets:** Accepted.
⊗ 🔒 💻 🍽 ⊗ 🅺 🆉

SALTSPRING ISLAND

▼▼ **Harbour House** 🆂🅷
(250) 537-5571. **$59-$295.** 121 Upper Ganges Rd. 1 km n on Lower Ganges Rd, then just e, towards Long Harbour ferry terminal. Ext/int corridors. **Pets:** Accepted.
🅰🆂🅺 🆂👼 ⊗ 🅰🅼 ⟨🐾⟩ 💻 🍽 🅺

▼▼ **Seabreeze Inne** 🅼 ❀
(250) 537-4145. **$69-$189, 14 day notice.** 101 Bittancourt Rd. From Ganges township, 1 km s on Fulford-Ganges Rd. Ext corridors. **Pets:** Dogs only. $20 daily fee/pet. Designated rooms, service with restrictions, supervision.
⊗ 🔒 💻 ⊗ 🅺

SATURNA

▼▼▼ **Saturna Lodge & Restaurant** 🅲🅸
(250) 539-2254. **$120-$195, 14 day notice.** 130 Payne Rd. From BC ferry terminal, just s on Narvaez Bay Rd, then just e, follow signs. Int corridors. **Pets:** Small. $15 daily fee/pet. Designated rooms.
🅰🆂🅺 🆂👼 ⊗ 🍽 🅺 🆆 🆉

❀   END METROPOLITAN AREA   ❀

HARRISON HOT SPRINGS

▼▼▼▼ Harrison Hot Springs Resort &
Spa LH ❖
(604) 796-2244. **$219-$394, 3 day notice.** 100 Esplanade
Ave. Just w. Int corridors. **Pets:** Medium. $100 one-time
fee/room. Designated rooms, service with restrictions,
supervision.
SAVE S⌂ ✕ ⬛ ❚❙ ⮌ ✕

HOPE

▼▼ Alpine Motel M
(604) 869-9931. **$64-$85.** 505 Old Hope-Princeton Way. Hwy
5, exit 173 westbound; exit 170 eastbound, just n from
lights. Ext corridors. **Pets:** Small. $50 deposit/room, $10
daily fee/room. No service, supervision.
SAVE S⌂ ✕ ⬛ ⬛

▼ Best Continental Motel M
(604) 869-9726. **$55-$80.** 860 Fraser Ave. Hwy 5, exit 170 to
downtown; at Fort St. Ext corridors. **Pets:** Small. $6 daily
fee/pet. No service, supervision.
SAVE S⌂ ✕ ⬛

▼ Inn Towne Motel M
(604) 869-7276. **$65-$110.** 510 Trans-Canada Hwy. Hwy 5,
exit 170, 1 km n to downtown. Ext corridors.
Pets: Accepted.
SAVE S⌂ ✕ ⬛ ⮌

▼▼▼ Quality Inn M
(604) 869-9951. **$70-$95.** 350 Old Hope-Princeton Way. Hwy
5, exit 173 westbound; exit 170 eastbound, just n from
lights. Int corridors. **Pets:** Small. Service with restrictions,
supervision.
SAVE S⌂ ✕ ⬛M ⬛ ⬛ ⮌

▼ Swiss Chalets M
(604) 869-9020. **Call for rates.** 456 Trans-Canada Hwy. Hwy
5, exit 170, 1 km n to downtown. Ext corridors.
Pets: Accepted.
✕ ⬛

INVERMERE

▼▼▼ Best Western Invermere Inn SH
(250) 342-9246. **$85-$125.** 1310 7th Ave. 3 km w of Hwy 93
and 95 at Invermere exit; centre. Int corridors.
Pets: Accepted.
SAVE S⌂ ✕ ⬛ ❚❙

KAMLOOPS

▼▼▼ Accent Inns M ❖
(250) 374-8877. **$89-$139.** 1325 Columbia St W. Trans-
Canada Hwy 1, exit 369 (Columbia St) eastbound at Notre
Dame Dr; exit 370 (Summit Dr) westbound at Notre Dame
Dr. Ext corridors. **Pets:** Other species. $10 daily fee/room.
Designated rooms, service with restrictions, supervision.
SAVE S⌂ ✕ ⬛M ⬛ ⬛ ⮌ ✕

▼ A Super View Motel M
(250) 374-8100. **Call for rates.** 1200 Rogers Way. Trans-
Canada Hwy 1, exit 368 (Hillside Ave), just s. Ext corridors.
Pets: Accepted.
✕ ⬛ ⬛ ⮌

▼ Casa Marquis Motor Inn M
(250) 372-7761. **$45-$85, 3 day notice.** 530 Columbia St.
Corner of 5th Ave and Columbia St, just n via City Centre;
downtown. Ext corridors. **Pets:** Small, dogs only. $20
deposit/room, $10 daily fee/pet. Designated rooms, service
with restrictions, supervision.
ASK S⌂ ✕ ⬛ ⬛

▼▼▼ Courtesy Motel M
(250) 372-8533. **$75-$89.** 1773 Trans-Canada Hwy E. 2.4
km e on Trans-Canada Hwy 1, south side of service access
road. Ext corridors. **Pets:** Accepted.
ASK S⌂ ✕ ⬛ ⬛ ⮌

▼▼ Days Inn LH
(250) 374-5911. **$99-$119.** 1285 Trans-Canada Hwy W.
Trans-Canada Hwy 1, exit 368 (Hillside Ave), just s. Int
corridors. **Pets:** Accepted.
ASK ✕ ⬛ ⬛ ❚❙

▼▼ Grandview Motel M ❖
(250) 372-1312. **$55-$89.** 463 Grandview Terrace. Trans-
Canada Hwy 1, exit 369 (Columbia St) eastbound, 2 km n;
exit 370 (Summit Dr) westbound to Columbia St via City
Centre. Ext corridors. **Pets:** Medium. $5 daily fee/pet. Des-
ignated rooms, service with restrictions, supervision.
SAVE S⌂ ✕ ⬛ ⬛ ⮌

▼▼ Hospitality Inn M
(250) 374-4164. **$61-$89.** 500 W Columbia St. Trans-
Canada Hwy 1, exit 369 (Columbia St) eastbound, 2 km n;
exit 370 (Summit Dr) westbound to Columbia St via City
Centre. Ext corridors. **Pets:** Medium. $10 deposit/room.
Designated rooms, service with restrictions.
SAVE S⌂ ✕ ⬛ ⬛ ❚❙ ⮌

▼▼ Kamloops Super 8 Motel M
(250) 374-8688. **$59-$91.** 1521 Hugh Allan Dr. Trans-
Canada Hwy 1, exit 367 (Pacific Way). Int corridors.
Pets: Accepted.
SAVE S⌂ ✕ ⬛M

▼▼ Ramada Inn-Kamloops SH
(250) 374-0358. **$69-$109.** 555 W Columbia St. Trans-
Canada Hwy 1, exit 369 (Columbia St) eastbound, 2 km n;
exit 370 (Summit Dr) westbound to Columbia St via City
Centre. Ext/int corridors. **Pets:** Medium, other species. $10
daily fee/pet. Designated rooms, service with restrictions,
crate.
SAVE S⌂ ✕ ⬛ ⬛ ❚❙ ⮌ ✕

▼▼ Ranchland Motel M
(250) 828-8787. **$50-$67.** 2357 Trans-Canada Hwy E. 4.5
km e on Trans-Canada Hwy 1, exit River Rd, then just w
along service access road. Ext corridors. **Pets:** Medium.
$10 daily fee/pet. Designated rooms, service with restric-
tions, supervision.
ASK S⌂ ✕ ⬛ ⬛

▼▼ Scott's Inn & Restaurant M
(250) 372-8221. **$55-$90.** 551 11th Ave. Trans-Canada Hwy
1, exit 369 (Columbia St) eastbound, 5 km n; exit City
Centre westbound, 1.6 km s on Columbia St. Ext corridors.
Pets: Small. $6 daily fee/pet. Designated rooms, service
with restrictions, supervision.
SAVE S⌂ ✕ ⬛ ⬛ ❚❙ ⮌

▼▼ The Thompson Hotel & Conference Centre 🆂🅷
(250) 374-1999. **$69-$139.** 650 Victoria St. Trans-Canada Hwy 1, exit 369 (Columbia St) eastbound to City Centre; exit 370 (Summit Dr) westbound, then just n on 6th Ave; downtown. Int corridors. **Pets:** Designated rooms, service with restrictions, crate.

(ASK) 🆂 ⊠ 🔋 🖵 🍽 ⊷ ⊠

Ⓐ ▼ Thriftlodge Ⓜ
(250) 374-2488. **$37-$58.** 2459 Trans-Canada Hwy 1 E. 4.8 km e on Trans-Canada Hwy 1, just e of jct River Rd along service access road, follow signs. Ext corridors. **Pets:** Small. Designated rooms, service with restrictions, supervision.

(SAVE) ⊠ ⊷

KELOWNA

Ⓐ ▼▼▼ Accent Inns 🆂🅷 ✿
(250) 862-8888. **$99-$159.** 1140 Harvey Ave. Corner of Hwy 97 N (Harvey Ave) and Gordon Dr. Ext corridors. **Pets:** Medium. $10 daily fee/room. Designated rooms, service with restrictions, supervision.

(SAVE) 🆂 ⊠ 🆓 🔋 🖵 🍽 ⊷ ⊠

Ⓐ ▼▼▼ Best Western Inn-Kelowna 🅻🅷 ✿
(250) 860-1212. **$109-$269.** 2402 Hwy 97 N. 1 km s of jct Hwy 33 and 97 N (Harvey Ave); corner of Leckie Rd. Ext/int corridors. **Pets:** Medium, other species. $15 daily fee/room. Designated rooms, service with restrictions, crate.

(SAVE) 🆂 ⊠ 🆓 🔋 🖵 🍽 ⊷ ⊠

▼▼ Comfort Inn 🆂🅷
(250) 769-2355. **$69-$139.** 1655 Westgate Rd. Jct Hwy 97 (Harvey Ave) and Bartley Rd, s to Ross Rd. Int corridors. **Pets:** Medium. $10 daily fee/pet. Designated rooms, supervision.

(ASK) 🆂 ⊠ 🔋 🖵 ⊷

▼▼◆▼ The Grand Okanagan Lakefront Resort & Conference Centre 🅻🅷
(250) 763-4500. **$149-$449, 3 day notice.** 1310 Water St. Hwy 97 (Harvey Ave), 1 km w. Int corridors. **Pets:** Accepted.

(ASK) 🆂 ⊠ 🆓 🔋 🖵 🍽 ⊷ ⊠

▼▼ The Hotel Eldorado 🆂🅷
(250) 763-7500. **$179-$339, 7 day notice.** 500 Cook Rd. Hwy 97 (Harvey Ave), 4 km s on Pandosy which becomes Lakeshore Rd, just w. Int corridors. **Pets:** Accepted.

(ASK) ⊠ 🍽 ⊠

▼▼ Town & Country Motel Ⓜ
(250) 860-7121. **$64-$130.** 2629 Hwy 97 N. 0.5 km n on Hwy 97 N (Harvey Ave) from jct Hwy 33. Ext corridors. **Pets:** Small. $10 daily fee/pet. Designated rooms, service with restrictions, supervision.

(ASK) 🆂 ⊠ 🆓 🔋 🖵 ⊷

▼▼ Vineyard Inn Ⓜ
(250) 860-5703. **$59-$139.** 2486 Hwy 97 N. Southwest corner of jct Hwy 97 (Harvey Ave) and 33. Ext corridors. **Pets:** Small, dogs only. $5 daily fee/pet. Supervision.

(ASK) 🆂 ⊠ 🔋 🖵 ⊷ ⊠

KIMBERLEY

▼▼ Inn of the Rockies 🆂🅷
(250) 427-2266. **$79-$99.** 300 Wallinger Ave. Centre. Int corridors. **Pets:** Accepted.

(ASK) 🆂 ⊠ 🔋 🖵 🍽

Ⓐ ▼▼◆▼ Trickle Creek Residence Inn by Marriott 🆂🅷 ✿
(250) 427-5175. **$104-$229.** 500 Stemwinder Dr. Hwy 95A, 3.1 km w on Ross St, follow signs for Alpine Village, then just e. Int corridors. **Pets:** $25 one-time fee/pet. Designated rooms, service with restrictions.

(SAVE) ⊠ ⊘ 🆓 🔋 🖵 🍽 ⊷ ⊠

LADYSMITH

▼ Seaview Marine Resort 🅲🅰
(250) 245-3768. **$70-$80, 14 day notice.** 11111 Chemainus Rd. 2.5 km s on Trans-Canada Hwy 1, 3 km se. Ext corridors. **Pets:** Medium, dogs only. Service with restrictions, supervision.

⊠ 🔋 🖵 🎣 🖉

LOGAN LAKE

▼ Logan Lake Lodge 🆂🅷
(250) 523-9466. **$60-$65, 7 day notice.** 111 Chartrand Ave. Centre at Meadow Creek Rd and Chartrand Cresent. Int corridors. **Pets:** Other species. $15 one-time fee/room. Designated rooms, supervision.

(ASK) 🆂 ⊠ 🖵 🍽 🎣

MADEIRA PARK

▼▼◆▼ Sunshine Coast Resort 🅲🅾 ✿
(604) 883-9177. **$85-$185, 21 day notice.** 12695 Sunshine Coast (Hwy 101). Just n of Madeira Park Rd, follow signs. Ext/int corridors. **Pets:** $15 daily fee/pet. Designated rooms, supervision.

⊠ 🆓 🆓 🔋 🖵 ⊠ 🎣

MANNING PARK

▼▼ Manning Park Resort 🆂🅷
(250) 840-8822. **$69-$159, 14 day notice.** Hwy 3. Crowsnest Hwy 3, midway between Hope and Princeton. Ext/int corridors. **Pets:** Medium, other species. $25 one-time fee/room. Designated rooms, service with restrictions.

⊠ 🔋 🖵 🍽 ⊠ 🎣

MCBRIDE

Ⓐ ▼▼ North Country Lodge Ⓜ
(250) 569-0001. **$59-$99.** 868 Frontage Rd N. Just w of village main exit, on Hwy 16 north service road. Ext corridors. **Pets:** Accepted.

(SAVE) 🆂 ⊠ 🔋 🖵 🍽

MERRITT

Ⓐ ▼▼▼ Best Western Nicola Inn 🆂🅷
(250) 378-4253. **$75-$115.** 4025 Walters St. Hwy 5, exit 290, 1 km w. Ext corridors. **Pets:** Very small. $20 daily fee/pet. Designated rooms, service with restrictions, supervision.

(SAVE) 🆂 ⊠ 🔋 🖵 🍽 ⊷

⬨ ▽▽ Merritt Motor Inn Ⓜ
(250) 378-9422. **$65-$90.** 3561 Voght St. Hwy 5, exit 290, just w. Ext corridors. **Pets:** Accepted.
[SAVE] [S∅] [✕] [🛏] [📺] [🍴] [≈]

▽▽ Merritt Travelodge Ⓜ
(250) 378-8830. **$65-$89.** 3581 Voght St. Hwy 5, exit 290, just w. Int corridors. **Pets:** Accepted.
[ASK] [S∅] [✕] [🛏] [📺] [🍴] [≈]

▽▽ Ramada Limited 🆂🅷
(250) 378-3567. **$80-$100.** 3571 Voght St. Hwy 5, exit 290, just w. Ext corridors. **Pets:** Other species. $5 daily fee/pet. Designated rooms, service with restrictions, supervision.
[ASK] [S∅] [✕] [🛏] [📺] [≈] [✕]

NAKUSP

⬨ ▽▽ The Selkirk Inn 🆂🅷
(250) 265-3666. **$45-$75.** 210 W 6th Ave. Just n. Int corridors. **Pets:** Small. $20 deposit/room, $8 daily fee/pet. Designated rooms, service with restrictions, supervision.
[SAVE] [✕] [🛏] [📺]

NANAIMO

⬨ ▽▽ Best Western Northgate Inn 🆂🅷
(250) 390-2222. **$79-$129.** 6450 Metral Dr. Hwy 19A (Island Hwy), just w on Aulds Rd, then just s. Int corridors. **Pets:** Accepted.
[SAVE] [S∅] [✕] [🛏] [📺] [🍴] [✕]

▽▽ Harbourview Days Inn 🆂🅷
(250) 754-8171. **$89-$120.** 809 Island Hwy S. On Island Hwy 1, 2 km s. Int corridors. **Pets:** Medium. $5 daily fee/pet. Designated rooms, service with restrictions, supervision.
[ASK] [S∅] [✕] [🛏] [📺] [🍴] [≈]

⬨ ▽▽▽ Ramada Limited On Long Lake 🆂🅷 ❀
(250) 758-1144. **$109-$169.** 4700 Island Hwy N. 5 km n on Hwy 19A (Island Hwy) from Departure Bay ferry terminal. Ext corridors. **Pets:** Other species. $20 one-time fee/pet. Supervision.
[SAVE] [S∅] [✕] [&M] [🛏] [📺] [✕]

⬨ ▽▽▽ Travelodge Nanaimo Ⓜ ❀
(250) 754-6355. **$83-$105.** 96 Terminal Ave N. Jct Hwy 19A (Terminal Ave) and Island Hwy 1, access from either highway. Int corridors. **Pets:** Medium. $10 one-time fee/pet. Service with restrictions, supervision.
[SAVE] [S∅] [✕] [🛏] [📺]

NANOOSE BAY

▽▽ Schooner Cove Resort & Marina at Fairwinds 🆂🅷 ❀
(250) 468-7691. **$89-$149.** 3521 Dolphin Dr. Island Hwy 1, 8.5 km se, follow signs via Powderpoint Rd (becoming Fairwinds Dr). Int corridors. **Pets:** Medium. $10 daily fee/room. Designated rooms, service with restrictions, crate.
[ASK] [S∅] [✕] [&M] [🛏] [🍴] [≈] [✕] [🎾]

NARAMATA

▽▽ The Village Motel Ⓜ
(250) 496-5535. **$50-$104, 14 day notice.** 244 Robinson Dr. 14 km n on Naramata Rd from Penticton. Ext corridors. **Pets:** Accepted.
[✕] [🛏] [📺] [🎾] [🎾]

NELSON

⬨ ▽▽▽ Best Western Baker Street Inn & Convention Centre 🆂🅷
(250) 352-3525. **$109-$259.** 153 Baker St. Jct of Hwy 6 and 3A. Int corridors. **Pets:** Accepted.
[SAVE] [S∅] [✕] [&M] [🛏] [📺] [🍴]

NEW DENVER

▽▽ Sweet Dreams Guesthouse & Dining 🅲🅸
(250) 358-2415. **$80-$95, 7 day notice.** 702 Eldorado St. 0.4 km w of Hwy 6 on Slocan Ave. Int corridors. **Pets:** Accepted.
[ASK] [S∅] [✕] [🍴] [✕] [🎾] [🎾] [🎾]

PARKSVILLE

⬨ ▽▽▽ Best Western Bayside Inn 🅻🅷
(250) 248-8333. **$89-$189.** 240 Dogwood St. Island Hwy 19, exit Parksville, 8 km n on Hwy 19A. Int corridors. **Pets:** Dogs only. $15 daily fee/pet. Designated rooms, service with restrictions, supervision.
[SAVE] [S∅] [✕] [&M] [📺] [🍴] [≈] [✕]

▽▽ Skylite Motel Ⓜ ❀
(250) 248-4271. **$62-$129.** 459 E Island Hwy. Island Hwy 19, exit Parksville, 3.5 km n on Hwy 19A. Ext corridors. **Pets:** Other species. Service with restrictions, supervision.
[ASK] [S∅] [✕] [🛏] [🎾]

⬨ ▽▽▽ Tigh-Na-Mara Resort Spa & Conference Centre 🅻🅷
(250) 248-2072. **$89-$299, 5 day notice.** 1095 E Island Hwy. Island Hwy 19, exit Parksville, 2 km n on Hwy 19A. Ext corridors. **Pets:** Other species. $2 daily fee/pet. Designated rooms, service with restrictions, supervision.
[SAVE] [✕] [🛏] [📺] [🍴] [≈] [✕] [🎾]

▽▽ Travelodge Parksville 🆂🅷
(250) 248-2232. **$90-$189.** 424 W Island Hwy. Island Hwy 19, exit Parksville, 8 km n on Hwy 19A. Int corridors. **Pets:** Large, other species. $10 daily fee/pet. Designated rooms, service with restrictions, supervision.
[ASK] [S∅] [✕] [&M] [📺] [≈]

⬨ ▽▽▽ V.I.P. Motel Ⓜ ❀
(250) 248-3244. **$84-$129, 7 day notice.** 414 W Island Hwy. Island Hwy 19, exit Parksville, 6.5 km n on Hwy 19A. Ext corridors. **Pets:** Other species. Service with restrictions, supervision.
[SAVE] [S∅] [✕] [🛏] [📺] [🎾]

PARSON

▽▽ Timber Inn & Chalets 🆂🅷
(250) 348-2228. **$65-$95, 30 day notice.** 3483 Hwy 95. Just off Hwy 95 in Parson; 34 km s of Golden. Ext/int corridors. **Pets:** Accepted.
[✕] [🛏] [📺] [🍴] [✕] [🎾] [🎾] [🎾]

PENTICTON

▼▼ ▼▼ Best Western Inn at Penticton 🆂🅷
(250) 493-0311. **$79-$199.** 3180 Skaha Lake Rd. 4 km s.
Ext corridors. **Pets:** Accepted.
🅰🆂🅺 🆂🐾 ⊠ 🛏 🖵 ¶¶ ⊅

▼▼ ▼▼ Days Inn Penticton 🆂🅷 🐾
(250) 493-6616. **$89-$199, 7 day notice.** 152 Riverside Dr.
Hwy 97, just n. Int corridors. **Pets:** Medium. $10 daily fee/
pet. Designated rooms, service with restrictions, supervision.
🅰🆂🅺 🆂🐾 ⊠ 🛏 🖵 ⊅ 🐾⊠

▼▼ ▼▼ Golden Sands Resort 🅲🅾
(250) 492-4210. **$69-$265, 14 day notice.** 1028 Lakeshore
Dr W. Riverside Dr and Lakeshore Dr W. Ext corridors.
Pets: Accepted.
🅰🆂🅺 🆂🐾 ⊠ 🛏 🖵 ⊅

**🅰🅰 ▼▼▼▼▼ Penticton Lakeside Resort, Convention
Centre & Casino** 🅻🅷 🐾
(250) 493-8221. **$149-$255.** 21 Lakeshore Dr W. Main St at
Lakeshore Dr W. Int corridors. **Pets:** Other species. $10
daily fee/room. Service with restrictions, supervision.
🆂🅰🆅🅴 🆂🐾 ⊠ 🛏 🖵 ¶¶ ⊅ 🐾⊠

🅰🅰 ▼▼ ▼▼ Penticton Slumber Lodge 🅼
(250) 492-4008. **$78-$130, 7 day notice.** 274 Lakeshore Dr
W. Corner of Lakeshore Dr and Winnipeg St; Hwy 97, n on
Riverside, 1.5 km e. Ext corridors. **Pets:** Accepted.
🆂🅰🆅🅴 🆂🐾 ⊠ 🗞🅼 🛏 🖵 ⊅

🅰🅰 ▼▼ ▼▼ Spanish Villa Resort 🅼
(250) 492-2922. **$68-$165, 7 day notice.** 890 Lakeshore Dr
W. Corner of Power St and Lakeshore Dr W. Ext corridors.
Pets: Accepted.
🆂🅰🆅🅴 ⊠ 🛏 🖵 ⊅

▼▼ ▼▼ Super 8 Motel Penticton 🆂🅷
(250) 492-3829. **$80-$105.** 1706 Main St. Jct Main St and
Industrial. Ext/int corridors. **Pets:** Small, other species. $10
daily fee/pet. Designated rooms, service with restrictions,
crate.
🅰🆂🅺 🆂🐾 ⊠ 🛏 🖵 ⊅ 🐾⊠

▼▼ ▼▼ Waterfront Inn 🅼
(250) 492-8228. **$55-$125, 30 day notice.** 3688 Parkview
St. Hwy 97 to Channel Pkwy and Skaha Lake Rd, just ne to
Lee Ave, then just s. Ext corridors. **Pets:** Accepted.
⊠ 🛏 🖵

PORT ALBERNI

🅰🅰 ▼▼▼▼▼ Best Western Barclay Hotel 🅻🅷
(250) 724-7171. **$89-$149.** 4277 Stamp Ave. Johnston Rd
(Hwy 4), just s on Gertrude St. Int corridors. **Pets:** Small.
$10 daily fee/room, $20 one-time fee/room. Designated
rooms, service with restrictions, supervision.
🆂🅰🆅🅴 🆂🐾 ⊠ 🛏 🖵 ¶¶ ⊅ 🐾⊠

▼▼▼▼▼ Coast Hospitality Inn 🆂🅷
(250) 723-8111. **$100-$145.** 3835 Redford St. 3.2 km sw of
jct Hwy 4 via City Centre/Port Alberni South Rt. Int corridors. **Pets:** Accepted.
🅰🆂🅺 🆂🐾 ⊠ 🖵 ¶¶

▼▼ Riverside Motel 🅼
(250) 724-9916. **$55-$93.** 5065 Roger St. Johnston Rd (Hwy
4), just s on Gertrude St, then just w. Ext corridors.
Pets: Accepted.
🅰🆂🅺 🆂🐾 ⊠ 🛏 🖵 🅰🅲 🖂

PORT HARDY

▼▼ Airport Inn 🆂🅷
(250) 949-9434. **$75-$120.** 4030 Byng Rd. Hwy 19, 5 km ne,
follow signs. Int corridors. **Pets:** Other species. Supervision.
⊠ 🛏 🖵 ¶¶ 🅰🅲

▼▼ ▼▼ Glen Lyon Inn 🆂🅷
(250) 949-7115. **$75-$105.** 6435 Hardy Bay Rd. Hwy 19, 1.5
km n. Ext corridors. **Pets:** Medium. $5 daily fee/room. Des-
ignated rooms, service with restrictions, supervision.
⊠ 🛏 🖵 ¶¶ 🅰🅲

🅰🅰 ▼▼ Pioneer Inn 🆂🅷
(250) 949-7271. **$54-$115.** 8405 Byng Rd. Hwy 19, 1 km w,
follow signs. Ext corridors. **Pets:** Accepted.
🆂🅰🆅🅴 ⊠ 🛏 🖵 ¶¶ 🅰🅲

POWELL RIVER

▼▼▼▼▼ Powell River Town Centre Hotel 🆂🅷 🐾
(604) 485-3000. **$109-$154.** 4660 Joyce Ave. 0.8 km e on
Duncan St (BC ferry terminal), then 1 km n. Int corridors.
Pets: Large. $10 daily fee/pet. Service with restrictions,
supervision.
🅰🆂🅺 🆂🐾 ⊠ ¶¶

PRINCE GEORGE

🅰🅰 ▼▼ ▼▼ P.G. Hi-Way Motel 🅼
(250) 564-6869. **$55-$70.** 1737 20th Ave. Jct Hwy 97, 1.2
km e on Trans-Canada Hwy 16 (Yellowhead Hwy). Ext
corridors. **Pets:** Medium. $10 daily fee/pet. Designated
rooms, service with restrictions, supervision.
🆂🅰🆅🅴 🆂🐾 ⊠ 🛏 🖵

PRINCE RUPERT

🅰🅰 ▼▼ Aleeda Motel 🆂🅷
(250) 627-1367. **$55-$80.** 900 3rd Ave W. Corner of 3rd Ave
W and 8th St. Int corridors. **Pets:** Medium, other species.
$5 daily fee/pet. Service with restrictions, supervision.
🆂🅰🆅🅴 🆂🐾 ⊠ 🅰🅲

▼▼ Howard Johnson Highliner Plaza Hotel 🅻🅷
(250) 624-9060. **$103-$130.** 815 1st Ave W. Corner of 1st
Ave W and 7th St; downtown. Int corridors. **Pets:** Medium.
Designated rooms, service with restrictions, supervision.
🅰🆂🅺 🆂🐾 ⊠ 🛏 🖵 ¶¶ 🅰🅲

PRINCETON

🅰🅰 ▼▼▼▼▼ Best Western Princeton Inn 🅼
(250) 295-3537. **$89-$119.** 169 Hwy 3. On Hwy 3. Ext corridors. **Pets:** Medium, other species. $10 daily fee/pet. Des-
ignated rooms, service with restrictions, supervision.
🆂🅰🆅🅴 🆂🐾 ⊠ 🛏 🖵 ⊅ 🐾⊠

QUALICUM BEACH

♦♦ ♦♦♦ Old Dutch Inn (By The Sea) 🅂🄷
(250) 752-6914. **$69-$109.** 2690 Island Hwy W. Hwy 19, exit Qualicum Beach/Port Alberni, 4 km on Memorial Ave at jct Hwy 19A. Int corridors. **Pets:** Accepted.

🄰🅂🄺 🆂🔴 ⊠ 🔋 💻 🍽 ⊷ 🐾

QUESNEL

🅐🅐 ♦♦♦ Talisman Inn 🄼 🐾
(250) 992-7247. **$65-$81.** 753 Front St. Hwy 97, 1 km n of Carson Ave. Int corridors. **Pets:** Other species. Designated rooms, service with restrictions, supervision.

🅂🄰🅅🄴 🆂🔴 ⊠ 🔋 💻

RADIUM HOT SPRINGS

🅐🅐 ♦♦♦ Cedar Motel 🄼
(250) 347-9463. **$45-$82.** 7593 Main St W. Hwy 93 and 95, just s of jct Hwy 93, on service road (Main St). Ext corridors. **Pets:** Medium. $5 daily fee/pet. Designated rooms, service with restrictions, supervision.

🅂🄰🅅🄴 🆂🔴 ⊠ 🔋 💻

♦♦ ♦♦ Chalet Europe 🄼
(250) 347-9305. **$85-$155.** 5063 Madsen Rd. Hwy 93 and 95, just e, 1 km off Hwy 93 up the hill. Ext corridors. **Pets:** Accepted.

🄰🅂🄺 🆂🔴 ⊠ 🔋 💻 ⊠

♦♦ Lido Motel 🄼 🐾
(250) 347-9533. **$45-$75.** 4876 McKay St. Hwy 93 and 95 S, Stanley St W to Main St W, then s. Ext corridors. **Pets:** $5 daily fee/pet. Supervision.

⊠ 🔋 💻 ⊘

♦♦♦ ♦ Sunrise Suites Motel 🄲🄾
(250) 347-0008. **$70-$140, 4 day notice.** 7371 Prospector Ave. Hwy 93 and 95, 0.7 km n on Hwy 95, just sw. Ext corridors. **Pets:** Accepted.

🄰🅂🄺 🆂🔴 ⊠ 🔋 💻 ⊠ 🐾

♦♦ Sunset Motel 🄼
(250) 347-9863. **$60-$105, 3 day notice.** 4883 McKay St. Hwy 93 and 95 S, w to service road (Main St), just s. Ext corridors. **Pets:** Other species.

🄰🅂🄺 🆂🔴 ⊠ 🔋 💻 ⊘

REVELSTOKE

🅐🅐 ♦♦♦♦ Best Western Wayside Inn 🅂🄷
(250) 837-6161. **$89-$149.** 1901 LaForme Blvd. North side of Trans-Canada Hwy 1, at intersection nearest east end of Columbia River Bridge. Ext/int corridors. **Pets:** Other species. Designated rooms, no service.

🅂🄰🅅🄴 🆂🔴 ⊠ 🅂🄼 🔋 💻 🍽 ⊷

**🅐🅐 ♦♦♦♦ The Coast Hillcrest Resort
Hotel** 🄻🄷 🐾
(250) 837-3322. **$110-$180.** 2100 Oak Dr. 4.3 km e on Trans-Canada Hwy 1, 0.9 km sw. Int corridors. **Pets:** Large. $15 one-time fee/room. Designated rooms, service with restrictions, supervision.

🅂🄰🅅🄴 🆂🔴 ⊠ 🔋 💻 🍽 ⊠

🅐🅐 ♦♦♦ Monashee Lodge 🄼
(250) 837-6778. **$45-$86.** 1601 3rd St W. South side of Trans-Canada Hwy 1, just e of Columbia River Bridge at Victoria Rd, then just se on Wright Ave. Ext corridors. **Pets:** Accepted.

🅂🄰🅅🄴 ⊠ 🔋 💻

🅐🅐 ♦♦♦♦ The Regent Inn 🅂🄷
(250) 837-2107. **$109-$149.** 112 1st St E. 2 km s from Trans-Canada Hwy 1 at Victoria Rd; downtown. Int corridors. **Pets:** Small, dogs only. $10 daily fee/room. Designated rooms, supervision.

🅂🄰🅅🄴 🆂🔴 ⊠ 🍽 ⊠

🅐🅐 ♦♦ Swiss Chalet Motel 🄼
(250) 837-4650. **$54-$82.** 1101 Victoria Rd. 1 km s from Trans-Canada Hwy 1. Ext corridors. **Pets:** Accepted.

🅂🄰🅅🄴 ⊠ 🔋 💻

ROSSLAND

♦♦ Thriftlodge Rossland 🄼
(250) 362-7364. **$64-$89, 3 day notice.** 1199 Nancy Green Hwy. 1 km w on Hwy 3B, at jct of Hwy 22. Ext corridors. **Pets:** Other species. $5 daily fee/pet. Designated rooms, service with restrictions, supervision.

🄰🅂🄺 🆂🔴 ⊠ 🔋 💻

SALMON ARM

♦♦♦♦ Holiday Inn Express Hotel & Suites 🅂🄷
(250) 832-7711. **$99-$189.** 1090 22nd St NE. 0.5 mi on Trans-Candada Hwy 1. Int corridors. **Pets:** Medium. $10 daily fee/pet. Designated rooms, service with restrictions, supervision.

🄰🅂🄺 🆂🔴 ⊠ 🅂🄼 🄲🄼 🔋 💻 ⊷ ⊠

♦♦♦ Super 8 Motel 🅂🄷
(250) 832-8812. **$69-$90.** 2901 10th Ave NE. 1 km e on Trans-Canada Hwy 1. Int corridors. **Pets:** Accepted.

🄰🅂🄺 🆂🔴 ⊠ 🅂🄼 🔋

SICAMOUS

♦♦ ♦♦ Sicamous Super 8 Motel 🅂🄷 🐾
(250) 836-4988. **$84-$143.** 1120 Riverside Ave. Trans-Canada Hwy 1, s on Hwy 97A, then just w on Main St to traffic circle, then just s. Ext corridors. **Pets:** $10 daily fee/room. Service with restrictions, supervision.

🄰🅂🄺 🆂🔴 ⊠ 🅂🄼 🔋

SILVERTON

♦♦ ♦♦ William Hunter Cabins 🄲🄰
(250) 358-2844. **$75-$98, 10 day notice.** 303 Lake Ave. Centre. Ext corridors. **Pets:** Supervision.

🆂🔴 ⊠ 🔋 💻 ⊠ 🐾

SMITHERS

🅐🅐 ♦♦♦♦ Aspen Motor Inn 🅂🄷
(250) 847-4551. **$76-$96.** 4628 Yellowhead Hwy. 1.5 km w on Hwy 16 (Yellowhead Hwy). Ext corridors. **Pets:** Medium, other species. $7 daily fee/pet. Designated rooms, service with restrictions, supervision.

🅂🄰🅅🄴 🆂🔴 ⊠ 🔋 💻 🍽 ⊷

SQUAMISH

(CAA) ▼▼/▼▼ **Best Western Sea To Sky** SH
(604) 898-4874. **$89-$159.** 40330 Tantalus Way. 4.5 km n on Hwy 99 at Garibaldi Way. Int corridors. **Pets:** Small. $15 one-time fee/room. Designated rooms, service with restrictions, supervision.
SAVE ⚫ ✕ 🚪 💻 🍴

SUMMERLAND

(CAA) ▼▼ **Summerland Motel** M
(250) 494-4444. **$55-$99, 10 day notice.** 2107 Tait St. 5 km s on Hwy 97. Ext corridors. **Pets:** Dogs only. $10 daily fee/pet. Service with restrictions, supervision.
SAVE ✕ 🚪 💻 ➰

SUN PEAKS

(CAA) ▼▼/▼▼ **Delta Sun Peaks Resort** LH
(250) 578-6000. **$99-$259, 7 day notice.** 3240 Village Way. Hwy 5, 31 km ne on Todd Mountain Rd, follow signs to village. Int corridors. **Pets:** Other species. $15 daily fee/pet. Service with restrictions, supervision.
SAVE ⚫ ✕ &M 💻 ➰ ✕

TERRACE

(CAA) ▼▼/▼ **Best Western Terrace Inn** SH
(250) 635-6133. **$79-$114.** 4553 Greig Ave. Hwy 16, just e on Greig Ave, follow City Centre signs. Int corridors. **Pets:** Small, other species. $10 daily fee/pet. Supervision.
SAVE ⚫ ✕ 🚪 💻 🍴

(CAA) ▼▼/▼ **Coast Inn of the West** SH 🐾
(250) 638-8141. **$85-$115.** 4620 Lakelse Ave. Hwy 16 to City Centre, 0.5 km e to Emerson, just n. Int corridors. **Pets:** Medium, other species. Service with restrictions, supervision.
SAVE ✕ 💻 🍴

TOFINO

(CAA) ▼▼/▼▼ **Best Western Tin Wis Resort Lodge** LH
(250) 725-4445. **$129-$199.** 1119 Pacific Rim Hwy. 3.5 km s on Hwy 4. Ext corridors. **Pets:** Accepted.
SAVE ✕ &M 🚪 💻 🍴 🐾

(CAA) ▼▼/▼▼ **Long Beach Lodge Resort** SH
(250) 725-2442. **$159-$489, 7 day notice.** 1441 Pacific Rim Hwy. 7.5 km s on Hwy 4. Int corridors. **Pets:** Accepted.
SAVE ✕ 🚪 💻 🍴 🐾

(CAA) ▼▼/▼▼ **Wickaninnish Inn** LH 🐾
(250) 725-3100. **$260-$1500, 7 day notice.** Osprey Ln at Chesterman Beach. 4.3 km e on Hwy 4. Int corridors. **Pets:** Dogs only. $40 daily fee/pet. Designated rooms, service with restrictions, crate.
SAVE ✕ &M 💻 🍴 ✕ 🐾

VALEMOUNT

(CAA) ▼▼/▼ **Canoe Mountain Lodge** SH
(250) 566-9171. **$85-$136.** 1465 5th Ave. Just e of Hwy 5 (Yellowhead Hwy). Int corridors. **Pets:** Accepted.
SAVE ⚫ ✕ 🚪 💻

▼▼/▼ **Holiday Inn Valemount Lodge** SH
(250) 566-0086. **$89-$180.** 1950 Hwy 5 S. 1.5 km s on Hwy 5 (Yellowhead Hwy). Int corridors. **Pets:** $35 one-time fee/room. Designated rooms, service with restrictions, supervision.
ASK ⚫ ✕ &M 📷 🐾 🚪 💻 🍴 ➰ ✕

VANCOUVER METROPOLITAN AREA

BURNABY

(CAA) ▼▼/▼▼ **Accent Inns** SH 🐾
(604) 473-5000. **$109-$169.** 3777 Henning Dr. Trans-Canada Hwy 1, exit 28 (Grandview Hwy), just n on Boundary Rd. Ext corridors. **Pets:** Small, dogs only. $10 daily fee/room. Designated rooms, service with restrictions, crate.
SAVE ⚫ ✕ &M 🐾 🚪 💻 🍴 ✕

(CAA) ▼▼/▼▼ **Best Western Kings Inn and Conference Centre** SH
(604) 438-1383. **$89-$159.** 5411 Kingsway. Trans-Canada Hwy 1, exit 29 (Willingdon Ave S), 3 km s to Kingsway, then 2 km e. Ext corridors. **Pets:** $10 daily fee/pet. Service with restrictions, supervision.
SAVE ⚫ ✕ 🚪 💻 🍴 ➰

(CAA) ▼▼/▼▼ **Hilton Vancouver Metrotown** LH
(604) 438-1200. **$135-$217.** 6083 McKay Ave. Trans-Canada Hwy 1, exit 29 (Willingdon Ave S), 3 km S to Kingsway, then just e. Int corridors. **Pets:** Large. $75 one-time fee/room. Designated rooms, service with restrictions.
SAVE ✕ &M 📷 🚪 💻 🍴 ➰

▼▼/▼ **Lake City Motor Inn** M
(604) 294-5331. **$79-$104.** 5415 Lougheed Hwy. Boundary Rd, 3 km e on Lougheed Hwy at Holdom Ave; entrance on north side of highway. Ext corridors. **Pets:** Very small, other species. $5 daily fee/pet. Designated rooms, service with restrictions, supervision.
✕ 🚪 ➰

COQUITLAM

(CAA) ▼▼/▼ **Holiday Inn Coquitlam/Vancouver** SH
(604) 931-4433. **$89-$159.** 631 Lougheed Hwy. Trans-Canada Hwy 1, exit 37 (Gaglardi Way) eastbound, 3.5 km e on Lougheed Hwy (Hwy 7); exit 44 (Coquitlam) westbound, then 3 km w on Lougheed Hwy (Hwy 7). Ext/int corridors. **Pets:** Accepted.
SAVE ⚫ ✕ &M 🚪 💻 🍴 ➰

DELTA

The Coast Tsawwassen Inn SH
(604) 943-8221. **$99-$119.** 1665 56th St. Hwy 99, exit 28
(Tsawwassen Ferries), 8 km w on Hwy 17; 5 km from the
Island ferry terminal. Int corridors. **Pets:** Small. $10 daily
fee/pet. Service with restrictions, supervision.

River Run Cottages BB
(604) 946-7778. **$130-$210, 21 day notice.** 4551 River Rd
W. Hwy 17, 2.5 km n on Ladner Trunk Rd which becomes
47A St and then becomes River Rd W. Ext corridors.
Pets: Dogs only. $20 daily fee/pet. Designated rooms, serv-
ice with restrictions, supervision.

Southlands House Inn BB
(604) 943-1846. **Call for rates.** 1160 Boundary Bay Rd. Hwy
99, exit 28 (Tsawwassen Ferries), 8 km w on Hwy 17, 2 km
s on 52nd St, 1 km e on 12th Ave. Int corridors.
Pets: Accepted.

LANGLEY

Best Value Westward Inn M
(604) 534-9238. **$59-$77.** 19650 Fraser Hwy. Trans-Canada
Hwy 1, exit 58 (200th St/Langley City), 5 km s on 200th St,
1 km w on Hwy 10, then just w. Ext corridors. **Pets:** Other
species. $4 daily fee/room. Service with restrictions, super-
vision.

Best Western Langley Inn SH
(604) 530-9311. **$99-$119.** 5978 Glover Rd. Trans-Canada
Hwy 1, exit 66 (232nd St), 6 km s, follow signs. Int corridors. **Pets:** Accepted.

**Holiday Inn Express Hotel &
Suites** SH
(604) 882-2000. **$105-$115.** 8750 204th St. Trans-Canada
Hwy 1, exit 58 (200th St), just e on 88th Ave. Int corridors.
Pets: Medium. $10 daily fee/pet. Service with restrictions,
supervision.

Sandman Hotel Langley SH
(604) 888-7263. **$89-$119, 7 day notice.** 8855 202nd St.
Trans-Canada Hwy 1, exit 58 (200th St), just e on 88th Ave.
Int corridors. **Pets:** Accepted.

Sleep Inn Langley M
(604) 514-3111. **$79-$119.** 6722 Glover Rd. Trans-Canada
Hwy, exit 66 (232nd St), 4 km s on Glover Rd, follow signs.
Int corridors. **Pets:** Accepted.

Travelodge-Langley City M
(604) 533-4431. **$69-$89.** 21653 Fraser Hwy. Trans-Canada
Hwy 1, exit 66 (232nd St), 6 km s, 1 km se on Langley
Bypass, then 1.5 km e to 216 St. Ext corridors.
Pets: Medium, dogs only. $50 deposit/room, $10 daily fee/
pet. Supervision.

MAPLE RIDGE

Travelodge Maple Ridge SH
(604) 467-1511. **$85-$99.** 21650 Lougheed Hwy. 2 km w on
Lougheed Hwy (Hwy 7) from downtown. Int corridors.
Pets: Accepted.

MISSION

**Best Western Mission City
Lodge** SH
(604) 820-5500. **$79-$120.** 32281 Lougheed Hwy. Just w of
Hwy 11, corner of Lougheed Hwy (Hwy 7) and Hurd St. Int
corridors. **Pets:** Medium. $10 daily fee/pet. Designated
rooms, supervision.

NORTH VANCOUVER

**Holiday Inn Express Vancouver North
Shore** LH
(604) 987-4461. **$99-$139, 30 day notice.** 1800 Capilano
Rd. Trans-Canada Hwy 1, exit 14 (Capilano Rd), then 1.5
km s; from north end of Lions Gate Bridge, 1 km e on
Marine Dr, then just n. Ext corridors. **Pets:** Small. $100
deposit/room. Designated rooms, service with restrictions,
crate.

**Holiday Inn Hotel & Suites North
Vancouver** LH
(604) 985-3111. **$99-$169.** 700 Old Lillooet Rd. Trans-
Canada Hwy 1, exit 22 (Mt Seymour Pkwy), follow signs.
Int corridors. **Pets:** Dogs only. $20 daily fee/pet. Designated
rooms, service with restrictions, supervision.

RICHMOND

Accent Inns SH
(604) 273-3311. **$89-$119.** 10551 St Edwards Dr. Hwy 99,
exit 39 (Bridgeport/Airport) northbound to St Edwards Dr;
exit 39A (Richmond/Airport) southbound. Ext corridors.
Pets: Large. $10 daily fee/room. Designated rooms, service
with restrictions, crate.

Best Western Abercorn Inn SH
(604) 270-7576. **$79-$139.** 9260 Bridgeport Rd. Hwy 99, exit
39 (Bridgeport/Airport) northbound; exit 39A (Richmond/
Airport) southbound. Int corridors. **Pets:** Medium, other species. $15 daily fee/room. Service with restrictions.

**Best Western Richmond Hotel &
Convention Center** LH
(604) 273-7878. **$89-$129.** 7551 Westminster Hwy. Corner
of Minoru Rd and Westminster Hwy. Int corridors.
Pets: Other species. Service with restrictions.

ⒸⒶⒶ ▼▼▼ Comfort Inn Vancouver Airport 🆂🅷
(604) 278-5161. $84-$154. 3031 #3 Rd. Hwy 99, exit 39 (Bridgeport/Airport) northbound; exit 39A (Richmond/Airport) southbound. Int corridors. Pets: $10 daily fee/pet. Designated rooms, service with restrictions, supervision.

🆂🅰🆅🅴 S🗑 ✕ 🖵 🍽 🛳

ⒸⒶⒶ ▼▼▼ Delta Vancouver Airport 🅻🅷 🐾
(604) 278-1241. $99-$139. 3500 Cessna Dr. Corner of Russ Baker Way and Cessna Dr; near the Moray Bridge. Int corridors. Pets: Medium. $30 one-time fee/room. Service with restrictions, supervision.

🆂🅰🆅🅴 S🗑 ✕ 🗆M 🖵 🍽 🛳 ✕

ⒸⒶⒶ ▼▼▼ ▼▼▼ The Fairmont Vancouver
Airport 🅻🅷 🐾
(604) 207-5200. $169-$354. 3111 Grant McConachie Way. In Vancouver International Airport. Int corridors. Pets: Other species. $25 daily fee/room. Service with restrictions, supervision.

🆂🅰🆅🅴 S🗑 ✕ 🗆M 📶 🖵 🍽 🛳 ✕

▼▼▼ Park Plaza 🅻🅷
(604) 278-9611. $99-$139. 10251 St Edwards Dr. Hwy 99, exit 39 (Bridgeport/Airport) northbound to St Edwards Dr; exit 39A (Richmond/Airport) southbound. Int corridors. Pets: Large. Service with restrictions.

🅰🆂🅺 S🗑 ✕ 🗆M 🎦 🍽 🛳 ✕

ⒸⒶⒶ ▼▼▼ Ramada Plaza 🅻🅷
(604) 278-9611. $99-$139. 10251 St Edwards Dr. Hwy 99, exit 39 (Bridgeport/Airport) northbound to St Edwards Dr; exit 39A (Richmond/Airport) southbound. Int corridors. Pets: Large. Service with restrictions.

🆂🅰🆅🅴 S🗑 ✕ 🗆M 📶 🖵 🍽 🛳 ✕

▼▼ Sandman Hotel Vancouver Airport 🆂🅷
(604) 303-8888. $69-$159. 3233 St. Edwards Dr. Hwy 99, exit 39 (Bridgeport/Airport) northbound to St. Edwards Dr; exit 39A (Richmond/Airport) southbound. Int corridors. Pets: Medium. $10 daily fee/pet. Designated rooms, service with restrictions, crate.

🅰🆂🅺 S🗑 ✕ 🗆M 📶 🖵 🍽 🛳

ⒸⒶⒶ ▼▼▼ Vancouver Airport Marriott 🅻🅷
(604) 276-2112. $119-$159. 7571 Westminster Hwy. Corner of Minoru Rd and Westminster Hwy. Int corridors. Pets: Large, other species. $30 one-time fee/room. Service with restrictions, supervision.

🆂🅰🆅🅴 S🗑 ✕ 🗆M 📶 🖵 🍽 🛳

SURREY

ⒸⒶⒶ ▼▼▼ Days Hotel-Vancouver Surrey 🆂🅷
(604) 588-9511. $93-$106. 9850 King George Hwy. Jct Fraser Hwy (Hwy 1A) and Hwy 99A (King George Hwy). Int corridors. Pets: Large, other species. $10 daily fee/room. Designated rooms, service with restrictions, crate.

🆂🅰🆅🅴 S🗑 ✕ 📶 🖵 🍽 🛳 ✕

▼▼ Ramada Hotel & Suites
Surrey/Guildford 🆂🅷
(604) 930-4700. $69-$89. 10410 158th St. Trans-Canada Hwy 1, exit 50 (160th St), just w on 104th Ave. Int corridors. Pets: $50 one-time fee/room. Service with restrictions, supervision.

🅰🆂🅺 S🗑 ✕ 🗆M 🎦 📶 🖵 🍽 🛳

▼▼▼ Ramada Limited Surrey-Langley 🆂🅷 🐾
(604) 576-8388. $94-$124. 19225 Hwy 10. Trans-Canada Hwy 1, exit 58, 5 km s on 200th St, then 2 km w on Rt 10; corner of 192nd St and Rt 10. Int corridors. Pets: Other species. $10 daily fee/pet.

🅰🆂🅺 S🗑 ✕ 🗆M 🎦 📶 🖵 🍽 🛳

ⒸⒶⒶ ▼▼◆ Sheraton Guildford Hotel
Surrey 🅻🅷 🐾
(604) 582-9288. $69-$109. 15269 104th Ave. Trans-Canada Hwy 1, exit 48 eastbound, 1 km s on 152 St, then just e; exit 50 westbound, then just w. Int corridors. Pets: Medium. Service with restrictions, supervision.

🆂🅰🆅🅴 ✕ 🖵 🍽 🛳

VANCOUVER

▼▼▼ 2400 Motel 🅼
(604) 434-2464. $55-$125. 2400 Kingsway. 7.2 km se on Hwy 1A and 99A (Kingsway). Ext corridors. Pets: Other species. $5 daily fee/pet. Designated rooms, service with restrictions, crate.

✕ 📶 🕷

ⒸⒶⒶ ▼▼▼ Best Western Chateau Granville 🅻🅷
(604) 669-7070. $139-$219. 1100 Granville St. Between Davie and Helmcken sts. Int corridors. Pets: Small. $25 one-time fee/pet. Designated rooms, service with restrictions, supervision.

🆂🅰🆅🅴 S🗑 ✕ 🗆M 📶 🖵 🍽

ⒸⒶⒶ ▼▼▼ Best Western Downtown
Vancouver 🅻🅷
(604) 669-9888. $99-$219. 718 Drake St. Corner of Drake and Granville sts. Int corridors. Pets: Small. $100 deposit/room. Designated rooms.

🆂🅰🆅🅴 S🗑 ✕ 🗆M 📶 🖵 ✕

ⒸⒶⒶ ▼▼▼ Best Western Sands 🆂🅷 🐾
(604) 682-1831. $119-$239. 1755 Davie St. Between Bidwell and Denman sts. Int corridors. Pets: Large. $10 daily fee/pet. Designated rooms, supervision.

🆂🅰🆅🅴 S🗑 ✕ 📶 🖵 🍽

ⒸⒶⒶ ▼▼▼ Bosmans Hotel 🆂🅷
(604) 682-3171. $119-$129. 1060 Howe St. Between Nelson and Helmcken sts. Int corridors. Pets: Accepted.

🆂🅰🆅🅴 S🗑 ✕ 🍽 🛳

ⒸⒶⒶ ▼▼▼ Comfort Inn Downtown 🆂🅷
(604) 605-4333. $89-$239. 654 Nelson St. Between Granville and Seymour sts. Int corridors. Pets: Medium. $25 one-time fee/room. Service with restrictions, crate.

🆂🅰🆅🅴 S🗑 ✕ 🖵

ⒸⒶⒶ ▼▼▼ Crowne Plaza Hotel Georgia 🅻🅷
(604) 682-5566. $129-$199. 801 W Georgia St. Between Howe and Hornby sts. Int corridors. Pets: Other species. Service with restrictions.

🆂🅰🆅🅴 ✕ 🗆M 🖵 🍽

ⒸⒶⒶ ▼▼▼ Delta Vancouver Suites 🅻🅷 🐾
(604) 689-8188. $159-$269. 550 W Hastings St. Between Seymour and Richards sts; entrance in alley way. Int corridors. Pets: Other species. Service with restrictions, supervision.

🆂🅰🆅🅴 ✕ 🗆M 🎦 🖵 🍽 🛳 ✕

▼▼▼ ▼▼▼ **The Fairmont Hotel Vancouver** 🏨 ❀
(604) 684-3131. **$197-$337.** 900 W Georgia St. Corner of Burrard at W Georgia St; enter from Hornby St. Int corridors. **Pets:** Other species. $25 daily fee/room. Designated rooms, service with restrictions, supervision.
ASK 🛏 ✕ ♿ ▤ 🍴 ≈ ✕

▼▼▼ ▼▼▼ **The Fairmont Waterfront** 🏨 ❀
(604) 691-1991. **$169-$339.** 900 Canada Place Way. Howe St at Cordova St. Int corridors. **Pets:** Other species. $25 daily fee/room. Service with restrictions, supervision.
ASK 🛏 ✕ ♿ ▤ 🍴 ≈ ✕

Ⓐ ▼▼▼ ▼▼▼ **Four Seasons Hotel Vancouver** 🏨 ❀
(604) 689-9333. **$200-$380.** 791 W Georgia St. Howe and W Georgia sts. Int corridors. **Pets:** Small, other species. Designated rooms, service with restrictions, supervision.
SAVE ✕ ♨ 🍴 ≈ ✕

▼▼▼ ▼▼ **The Georgian Court Hotel** 🏨
(604) 682-5555. **$115-$260.** 773 Beatty St. Between Georgia and Robson sts. Int corridors. **Pets:** $20 one-time fee/room. Service with restrictions, supervision.
ASK 🛏 ✕ ▤ 🍴 ✕

Ⓐ ▼▼▼ ▼ **Granville Island Hotel** 🏨
(604) 683-7373. **$150-$230.** 1253 Johnston St. Granville Island; below the bridge, follow signs. Int corridors. **Pets:** Other species. $25 daily fee/pet. Designated rooms, service with restrictions, supervision.
SAVE 🛏 ✕ ♿ ▤ 🍴 ✕

▼▼ ▼▼ **Holiday Inn Express Vancouver** 🏨
(604) 254-1000. **$129-$350.** 2889 E Hastings St. Corner of Renfrew and E Hastings sts. Int corridors. **Pets:** Small. $25 daily fee/pet. Service with restrictions, supervision.
ASK 🛏 ✕ 🛢 ▤ 🍴

Ⓐ ▼▼▼ ▼▼ **Holiday Inn Vancouver Downtown Hotel & Suites** 🏨
(604) 684-2151. **$139-$289.** 1110 Howe St. Between Helmcken and Davie sts. Int corridors. **Pets:** Service with restrictions, supervision.
SAVE 🛏 ✕ ♿ 🛢 ▤ 🍴 ≈ ✕

Ⓐ ▼▼▼ ▼▼▼ **Hotel Le Soleil** 🏨
(604) 632-3000. **$155-$275.** 567 Hornby St. Between Dunsmuir and Pender sts. Int corridors. **Pets:** Dogs only. $75 one-time fee/room. Service with restrictions, crate.
SAVE 🛏 ✕ ♿ ▤ 🍴

▼ **The London Guard Motel** Ⓜ
(604) 430-4646. **$49-$75.** 2227 Kingsway. 6.8 km se on Hwy 1A and 99A (Kingsway). Ext corridors. **Pets:** Accepted.
✕ 🛢 🎞

Ⓐ ▼▼▼ ▼ **Marriott Residence Inn, Vancouver** 🏨
(604) 688-1234. **$107-$197.** 1234 Hornby St. Between Drake and Davie sts. Int corridors. **Pets:** Accepted.
SAVE 🛏 ✕ ♿ 🛢 ▤ 🍴 ≈

Ⓐ ▼▼▼ ▼▼▼ **Metropolitan Hotel** 🏨 ❀
(604) 687-1122. **$185-$359.** 645 Howe St. Between Georgia and Dunsmuir sts. Int corridors. **Pets:** Medium. $50 one-time fee/room.
SAVE 🛏 ✕ ♿ ♨ ▤ 🍴 ≈ ✕

Ⓐ ▼▼▼ ▼▼▼ **Pacific Palisades Hotel** 🏨 ❀
(604) 688-0461. **$290-$390.** 1277 Robson St. Between Jervis and Bute sts. Int corridors. **Pets:** $25 one-time fee/room. Service with restrictions, supervision.
SAVE 🛏 ✕ ♿ ♨ 🛢 ▤ 🍴 ≈ ✕

Ⓐ ▼▼▼ ▼▼ **Pan Pacific Vancouver** 🏨
(604) 662-8111. **$390-$540.** 300-999 Canada Place. Motor entrance off Burrard St. Int corridors. **Pets:** Other species. $30 daily fee/room. Service with restrictions, crate.
SAVE 🛏 ✕ ♿ ▤ 🍴 ≈ ✕

Ⓐ ▼▼ ▼ **Quality Hotel Downtown-The Inn at False Creek** 🏨
(604) 682-0229. **$89-$229.** 1335 Howe St. Between Drake and Pacific sts. Int corridors. **Pets:** Small. $15 daily fee/pet. Service with restrictions, supervision.
SAVE 🛏 ✕ ♿ 🛢 🛢 ▤ 🍴 ≈

Ⓐ ▼▼▼ ▼ **Ramada Inn & Suites Downtown Vancouver** 🏨
(604) 685-1111. **$99-$199.** 1221 Granville St. Between Davie and Drake sts. Int corridors. **Pets:** Other species. $20 daily fee/pet. Service with restrictions, supervision.
SAVE 🛏 ✕ 🛢 ▤ 🍴

Ⓐ ▼▼ ▼ **Ramada Vancouver Centre** 🅂🄷
(604) 872-8661. **$130-$170.** 898 W Broadway. Between Laurel and Willow sts. Int corridors. **Pets:** Medium, other species. $100 deposit/room. Designated rooms, service with restrictions, supervision.
SAVE 🛏 ✕ ♿ 🛢 ▤ 🍴

Ⓐ ▼▼▼ ▼ **Renaissance Vancouver Hotel Harbourside** 🏨 ❀
(604) 689-9211. **$129-$229.** 1133 W Hastings St. Between Bute and Thurlow sts. Int corridors. **Pets:** Large. $25 one-time fee/pet. Service with restrictions, supervision.
SAVE 🛏 ✕ ♿ ▤ 🍴 ≈ ✕

▼▼ ▼▼ **Sandman Hotel Downtown Vancouver** 🏨
(604) 681-2211. **$109-$199.** 180 W Georgia St. Between Cambie and Beatty sts. Int corridors. **Pets:** Medium. $20 daily fee/pet. Designated rooms, service with restrictions, supervision.
ASK 🛏 ✕ ▤ 🍴 ≈

Ⓐ ▼▼▼ ▼▼ **Sheraton Vancouver Wall Centre Hotel** 🏨
(604) 331-1000. **$165-$429.** 1088 Burrard St. Between Helmcken and Comox sts. Int corridors. **Pets:** Accepted.
SAVE 🛏 ✕ ♿ 🛢 🛢 ▤ 🍴 ≈ ✕

Ⓐ ▼▼▼ ▼▼ **The Sutton Place Hotel** 🏨 ❀
(604) 682-5511. **$179-$450, 3 day notice.** 845 Burrard St. Between Smythe and Robson sts. Int corridors. **Pets:** Other species. $150 one-time fee/room. Service with restrictions, supervision.
SAVE 🛏 ✕ ♿ ♨ ▤ 🍴 ≈ ✕

▼ Sylvia Hotel 🆂🅷
(604) 681-9321. **$75-$225.** 1154 Gilford St. Beach Ave and Gilford St; across from English Bay. Int corridors. **Pets:** Accepted.
☒ 🍽 🅰🅲

Ⓒ🅐 ▼▼ ▼▼ **Vancouver Marriott Pinnacle** 🅻🅷
(604) 684-1128. **$199-$339.** 1128 W Hastings St. Between Thurlow and Bute sts. Int corridors. **Pets:** Accepted.
🆂🅰🆅🅴 🆂🅰 ☒ 🅰🅼 🖥 💻 🍽 🏊 ☒

Ⓒ🅐 ▼▼ ▼▼ **The Westin Bayshore Resort &**
Marina 🅻🅷 ❁
(604) 682-3377. **$350-$660.** 1601 Bayshore Dr. W Georgia and Cardero sts. Int corridors. **Pets:** Medium, dogs only. Service with restrictions, supervision.
🆂🅰🆅🅴 🆂🅰 ☒ 🅰🅼 📶 💻 🍽 🏊 ☒

Ⓒ🅐 ▼▼ ▼▼ **The Westin Grand** 🅻🅷 ❁
(604) 602-1999. **$199-$429.** 433 Robson St. Between Homer and Richards sts. Int corridors. **Pets:** Medium, dogs only. $50 one-time fee/pet. Service with restrictions, supervision.
🆂🅰🆅🅴 🆂🅰 ☒ 🅰🅼 🖥 💻 🍽 🏊 ☒

❁   **END METROPOLITAN AREA**   ❁

VERNON

Ⓒ🅐 ▼▼ ▼▼ **Best Western Vernon Lodge &**
Conference Centre 🆂🅷 ❁
(250) 545-3385. **$92-$134.** 3914 32nd St. 1.5 km n on Hwy 97 (32nd St). Int corridors. **Pets:** Other species. $10 daily fee/room. Designated rooms, service with restrictions, supervision.
🆂🅰🆅🅴 🆂🅰 ☒ 🅰🅼 🖥 💻 🍽 🏊

Ⓒ🅐 ▼▼ ▼▼ **Best Western Villager Motor Inn** 🆂🅷
(250) 549-2224. **$75-$110.** 5121 26th St. 2.5 km n on 27th St. Ext/int corridors. **Pets:** Medium. $10 daily fee/pet. Designated rooms, supervision.
🆂🅰🆅🅴 🆂🅰 ☒ 🖥 💻 🏊

Ⓒ🅐 ▼▼ ▼▼ **Schell Motel** 🅼
(250) 545-1351. **$70-$150.** 2810 35th St. Corner of 35th St and 30th Ave; centre. Ext corridors. **Pets:** Accepted.
🆂🅰🆅🅴 🆂🅰 ☒ 🖥 💻 🏊

Ⓒ🅐 ▼▼ ▼▼ **Tiki Village Motor Inn** 🅼 ❁
(250) 503-5566. **$79-$145, 3 day notice.** 2408 34th St. Jct Hwy 97 (32nd St) and 6 (25th Ave), just w. Ext corridors. **Pets:** Dogs only. $10 one-time fee/pet. Service with restrictions, supervision.
🆂🅰🆅🅴 🆂🅰 ☒ 🖥 💻 🍽 🏊 ☒

▼▼ ▼▼ **Vernon Travelodge** 🆂🅷
(250) 545-2161. **$79-$89.** 3000 28th Ave. Hwy 97 (32nd St), just e on 28th Ave, near Polson Park. Ext corridors. **Pets:** Accepted.
🅰🆂🅺 🆂🅰 ☒ 🖥 💻 🏊

VICTORIA METROPOLITAN AREA

MALAHAT

▼▼ **Malahat Bungalows Motel** 🅼
(250) 478-3011. **$50-$140, 3 day notice.** Trans-Canada Hwy 1, 26 km n of Victoria. Ext corridors. **Pets:** Medium, other species. $10 daily fee/pet. Service with restrictions, supervision.
☒ 🖥 ☒ 🅰🅲 🅰

SAANICHTON

Ⓒ🅐 ▼▼ ▼▼ **Quality Inn Waddling Dog** 🆂🅷
(250) 652-1146. **$79-$139.** 2476 Mt Newton Crossroad. Corner of Hwy 17 and Mt Newton Crossroad. Int corridors. **Pets:** Dogs only. $10 daily fee/pet. Service with restrictions, supervision.
🆂🅰🆅🅴 🆂🅰 ☒ 💻 🍽

Ⓒ🅐 ▼▼ ▼▼ **Super 8 Victoria/Saanichton** 🆂🅷
(250) 652-6888. **$70-$135.** 2477 Mt Newton Crossroad. Just e of Hwy 17. Int corridors. **Pets:** $10 one-time fee/room. Service with restrictions, supervision.
🆂🅰🆅🅴 🆂🅰 ☒ 🅰🅼 🖥 💻

SIDNEY

Ⓒ🅐 ▼▼ ▼▼ **Best Western Emerald Isle Motor**
Inn 🆂🅷 ❁
(250) 656-4441. **$119-$179.** 2306 Beacon Ave. Hwy 17, exit Sidney, just e. Int corridors. **Pets:** Other species. $20 one-time fee/pet. Designated rooms, service with restrictions, supervision.
🆂🅰🆅🅴 🆂🅰 ☒ 🅰🅼 🖥 💻 🍽

▼▼ ▼▼ **The Cedarwood Inn & Suites** 🆂🅷
(250) 656-5551. **$79-$245.** 9522 Lochside Dr. Hwy 17, just e on McTavish Rd, then 1.4 km n. Ext corridors. **Pets:** Small. $15 daily fee/pet. Service with restrictions, supervision.
☒ 🖥 💻 🅰🅲

▼▼ ▼▼ **Shoal Harbour Inn & Latch Dining**
Room 🆂🅷 ❁
(250) 656-6622. **$119-$339, 7 day notice.** 2328 Harbour Rd. Beacon Ave, 2 km n on Resthaven Dr, then 1 km e. Int corridors. **Pets:** $30 daily fee/room. Designated rooms, service with restrictions.
🅰🆂🅺 🆂🅰 ☒ 🅰🅼 🎬 🖥 💻 🍽 🅰🅲

ⓒ ▼▼ **Victoria Airport Travelodge**
Sidney ⬛

(250) 656-1176. **$79-$145.** 2280 Beacon Ave. Just e of Hwy 17, exit Sidney. Int corridors. **Pets:** Large, other species. $50 deposit/room, $10 daily fee/room. Designated rooms, service with restrictions, supervision.

⬛ ⬛ ⬛ ⬛ ⬛ ⬛

SOOKE

▼▼ **Ocean Wilderness Inn & Spa** ⬛

(250) 646-2116. **$99-$175, 7 day notice.** 109 W Coast Rd. 14 km w on Hwy 14. Ext/int corridors. **Pets:** Other species. $15 daily fee/pet. Service with restrictions, supervision.

⬛ ⬛ ⬛ ⬛ ⬛ ⬛ ⬛

ⓒ ▼▼▼ **Sooke Harbour House** ⬛

(250) 642-3421. **$193-$445, 14 day notice.** 1528 Whiffen Spit Rd. 2 km w on Hwy 14. Ext/int corridors. **Pets:** Accepted.

⬛ ⬛ ⬛ ⬛ ⬛ ⬛ ⬛ ⬛ ⬛

VICTORIA

ⓒ ▼▼▼ **Accent Inns** ⬛

(250) 475-7500. **$99-$159.** 3233 Maple St. 3 km n on Blanshard St (Hwy 17); corner of Blanchard St and Cloverdale Ave. Ext corridors. **Pets:** Small, other species. $10 daily fee/room. Designated rooms, service with restrictions, supervision.

⬛ ⬛ ⬛ ⬛ ⬛ ⬛ ⬛

ⓒ ▼▼ **Blue Ridge Inns** ⬛

(250) 388-4345. **$69-$109.** 3110 Douglas St. Between Finlayson St and Speed Ave. Ext corridors. **Pets:** $10 daily fee/room. Designated rooms, service with restrictions, supervision.

⬛ ⬛ ⬛ ⬛ ⬛ ⬛ ⬛ ⬛

▼▼▼ **Chateau Victoria Hotel and**
Suites ⬛

(250) 382-4221. **$86-$379.** 740 Burdett Ave. Between Douglas St and Fairfield Rd. Int corridors. **Pets:** Dogs only. $15 daily fee/pet. Designated rooms, service with restrictions, crate.

⬛ ⬛ ⬛ ⬛ ⬛

ⓒ ▼▼▼ **Comfort Inn & Suites** ⬛

(250) 388-7861. **$69-$139.** 101 Island Hwy. Douglas St, 5 km w on Gorge Rd, then just s on Admirals Rd. Ext/int corridors. **Pets:** Dogs only. $10 daily fee/pet. Service with restrictions, supervision.

⬛ ⬛ ⬛ ⬛ ⬛ ⬛

ⓒ ▼▼ **Dashwood Seaside Manor** ⬛ ⬛

(250) 385-5517. **$85-$295, 14 day notice.** 1 Cook St. 1 km e of Douglas St on Dallas Rd. Int corridors. **Pets:** Medium. $25 one-time fee/pet. Designated rooms.

⬛ ⬛ ⬛ ⬛ ⬛ ⬛ ⬛

ⓒ ▼▼▼ **Days Inn on the Harbour** ⬛ ⬛

(250) 386-3451. **$99-$223.** 427 Belleville St. Entrance on Oswego at Quebec sts. Int corridors. **Pets:** $10 daily fee/room. Designated rooms, service with restrictions.

⬛ ⬛ ⬛ ⬛ ⬛ ⬛ ⬛ ⬛ ⬛

ⓒ ▼▼▼▼ **Delta Victoria Ocean Pointe Resort**
& Spa ⬛ ⬛

(250) 360-2999. **$318-$478.** 45 Songhees Rd. Just w of Johnson St Bridge, Esquimalt at Tyee rds. Int corridors. **Pets:** Dogs only. Service with restrictions, supervision.

⬛ ⬛ ⬛ ⬛ ⬛ ⬛ ⬛ ⬛ ⬛

ⓒ ▼▼▼ **Executive House Hotel** ⬛ ⬛

(250) 388-5111. **$85-$189.** 777 Douglas St. Between Blanshard and Douglas sts; downtown. Int corridors. **Pets:** Medium, other species. $15 daily fee/pet.

⬛ ⬛ ⬛ ⬛ ⬛ ⬛ ⬛ ⬛

▼▼▼▼ **The Fairmont Empress** ⬛

(250) 384-8111. **$169-$539.** 721 Government St. Government St at Wharf St, just n of the Parliament buildings. Int corridors. **Pets:** Accepted.

⬛ ⬛ ⬛ ⬛ ⬛ ⬛ ⬛ ⬛ ⬛ ⬛

ⓒ ▼▼▼ **Harbour Towers Hotel &**
Suites ⬛ ⬛

(250) 385-2405. **$99-$435.** 345 Quebec St. Between Oswego and Pendray sts. Int corridors. **Pets:** Medium. $15 daily fee/room. Service with restrictions, supervision.

⬛ ⬛ ⬛ ⬛ ⬛ ⬛ ⬛ ⬛ ⬛ ⬛

ⓒ ▼▼▼▼ **Hotel Grand Pacific** ⬛ ⬛

(250) 386-0450. **$119-$319.** 463 Belleville St. Belleville at Menzies St; downtown. Int corridors. **Pets:** Small. $60 one-time fee/room. Designated rooms, service with restrictions, supervision.

⬛ ⬛ ⬛ ⬛ ⬛ ⬛ ⬛ ⬛ ⬛

▼▼▼ **Howard Johnson Hotel & Suites** ⬛

(250) 704-4656. **$109-$199.** 4670 Elk Lake Dr. Hwy 17, just w on Royal Oak Dr, then just n. Ext/int corridors. **Pets:** Accepted.

⬛ ⬛ ⬛ ⬛ ⬛ ⬛ ⬛ ⬛ ⬛

ⓒ ▼▼ **Howard Johnson Hotel-City**
Centre ⬛

(250) 382-2151. **$55-$189.** 310 Gorge Rd E. Douglas St, 1.4 km w. Int corridors. **Pets:** $10 one-time fee/pet. Designated rooms, service with restrictions, crate.

⬛ ⬛ ⬛ ⬛ ⬛ ⬛ ⬛

ⓒ ▼▼▼ **The Magnolia Hotel &**
Spa ⬛ ⬛

(250) 381-0999. **$169-$309.** 623 Courtney St. Corner of Courtney and Gordon sts. Int corridors. **Pets:** Medium. $60 one-time fee/room. Service with restrictions, crate.

⬛ ⬛ ⬛ ⬛ ⬛ ⬛

ⓒ ▼▼▼ **Oxford Castle Inn** ⬛

(250) 388-6431. **$70-$158.** 133 Gorge Rd E. Douglas St, 2 km w. Int corridors. **Pets:** Small, dogs only. $15 daily fee/pet. Service with restrictions, supervision.

⬛ ⬛ ⬛ ⬛ ⬛ ⬛ ⬛

ⓒ ▼▼ **Robin Hood Motel** ⬛

(250) 388-4302. **$51-$89.** 136 Gorge Rd E. Douglas St, 2.4 km w. Ext corridors. **Pets:** Dogs only. $5 daily fee/pet. Designated rooms, service with restrictions, supervision.

⬛ ⬛ ⬛ ⬛ ⬛ ⬛

▼▼▼ Ryan's Bed & Breakfast BB
(250) 389-0012. **$119-$229, 10 day notice.** 224 Superior St. Between Montreal and Oswego sts. Int corridors. **Pets:** Accepted.
⊠ 𝐾 ☎

ⓐ ▼▼▼ Travelodge Victoria SH
(250) 388-6611. **$59-$175.** 229 Gorge Rd E. Douglas St, 2 km w. Ext corridors. **Pets:** Medium, other species. $10 daily fee/pet. Designated rooms, service with restrictions.
SAVE S☆ ⊠ 🖬 🖵 🍴 ⇝

❖ END METROPOLITAN AREA ❖

WESTBANK

▼▼▼ Holiday Inn SH ❀
(250) 768-8879. **$115-$155, 7 day notice.** 2569 Dobbin Rd. Hwy 97 (Dobbin Rd) and Herbert Rd. Int corridors. **Pets:** $10 daily fee/room. Designated rooms, service with restrictions, supervision.
ASK S☆ ⊠ 🖬 🖵 🍴 ⇝

WHISTLER

ⓐ ▼▼▼ Best Western Listel Whistler Hotel SH
(604) 932-1133. **$199-$329, 30 day notice.** 4121 Village Green. Hwy 99, just e on Village Gate Blvd, then follow Whistler Way. Int corridors. **Pets:** $15 daily fee/pet. Designated rooms, service with restrictions, supervision.
SAVE S☆ ⊠ 🖬 🖵 🍴 ⇝

ⓐ ▼▼▼ Crystal Lodge SH ❀
(604) 932-2221. **$180-$320, 30 day notice.** 4154 Village Green. Hwy 99, just e on Village Gate Blvd, then follow Whistler Way. Int corridors. **Pets:** Medium, dogs only. $20 daily fee/pet. Designated rooms, service with restrictions, supervision.
SAVE S☆ ⊠ 🖬 🖵 🍴 ⇝ ⊠

ⓐ ▼▼▼ Delta Whistler Resort LH ❀
(604) 932-1982. **$139-$699.** 4050 Whistler Way. Hwy 99, just e on Village Gate Blvd, then follow Whistler Way. Int corridors. **Pets:** $20 daily fee/room. Service with restrictions, supervision.
SAVE S☆ ⊠ 🖬 🖵 🍴 ⇝ ⊠

ⓐ ▼▼▼ Delta Whistler Village Suites LH ❀
(604) 905-3987. **$139-$1149, 45 day notice.** 4308 Main St. Hwy 99, just e on Village Gate Blvd, just n on Northlands Blvd, then just e. Int corridors. **Pets:** $15 daily fee/room. Service with restrictions.
SAVE S☆ ⊠ 🖬 🖵 🍴 ⇝ ⊠

ⓐ ▼▼ Edgewater Lodge M ❀
(604) 932-0688. **$125-$320, 14 day notice.** 8020 Alpine Way. 4 km n of Whistler Village via Hwy 99, e on Alpine Way. Ext corridors. **Pets:** Dogs only. $20 one-time fee/pet. Service with restrictions, supervision.
SAVE S☆ ⊠ 🍴 𝐾

ⓐ ▼▼▼ The Fairmont Chateau Whistler LH ❀
(604) 938-8000. **$134-$799, 30 day notice.** 4599 Chateau Blvd. Hwy 99, 1 km e on Lorimer Rd, then just w on Blackcomb Way. Int corridors. **Pets:** $30 daily fee/room. Service with restrictions, supervision.
SAVE ⊠ 🖬 𝐾 🖵 🍴 ⇝ ⊠

▼▼▼ Residence Inn by Marriott CO ❀
(604) 905-3400. **$139-$499, 30 day notice.** 4899 Painted Cliff Rd. Hwy 99, 1 km e on Lorimer Rd (Upper Village), just se on Blackcomb Way, then just w, follow road all the way to the end. Int corridors. **Pets:** Other species. $25 daily fee/pet. Service with restrictions, supervision.
ASK S☆ ⊠ 🖬 🖵 ⇝ 𝐾

ⓐ ▼▼▼ Summit Lodge SH ❀
(604) 932-2778. **$119-$720, 21 day notice.** 4359 Main St. Hwy 99, just n on Village Gate Blvd, then just w on Northlands Blvd. Int corridors. **Pets:** Other species. Service with restrictions, crate.
SAVE S☆ ⊠ 🖬 🖵 ⇝ ⊠

ⓐ ▼▼▼ Tantalus Resort Lodge CO ❀
(604) 932-4146. **$119-$749, 14 day notice.** 4200 Whistler Way. Hwy 99, just e on Village Gate Blvd, then follow Whistler Way to the end. Int corridors. **Pets:** $15 one-time fee/room. Supervision.
SAVE S☆ ⊠ 🖬 🖵 ⇝ ⊠ 𝐾

WILLIAMS LAKE

▼▼ Drummond Lodge Motel M ❀
(250) 392-5334. **$68-$88.** 1405 Cariboo Hwy. 1 km s on Hwy 97. Ext corridors. **Pets:** Medium. $7 one-time fee/pet. Service with restrictions, supervision.
⊠ 🖬 🖵

▼▼ Williams Lake Super 8 Motel M
(250) 398-8884. **$69-$76.** 1712 Broadway Ave S. 2 km s on Hwy 97. Int corridors. **Pets:** Other species. $7 daily fee/pet. Supervision.
ASK S☆ ⊠ 🖬 🖵

MANITOBA

BRANDON

▼▼ Comfort Inn SH ✿
(204) 727-6232. **$70-$89.** 925 Middleton Ave. Northside Trans-Canada Hwy 1 service road, between Hwy 10 N and 10 S, just e of McDonald's Restaurant. Int corridors. **Pets:** Other species. $10 daily fee/room. Designated rooms, service with restrictions, supervision.

(ASK) (S☉) (✕) (☾M) (☐) (▣)

ⒸⒶⒶ ▼ Rodeway Inn Motel SH
(204) 728-7230. **$57-$62.** 300 18th St N. On Hwy 10 S, 3.2 km s of Trans-Canada Hwy 1. Ext/int corridors. **Pets:** $3 daily fee/room. Service with restrictions, supervision.

(SAVE) (S☉) (✕) (☐) (▣)

▼▼ Royal Oak Inn & Suites SH
(204) 728-5775. **$90-$93.** 3130 Victoria Ave. 5 km s of Trans-Canada Hwy 1; 1.4 km w of jct Hwy 10 (18th St) and 1A (Victoria Ave). Int corridors. **Pets:** Medium, other species. $10 daily fee/room. Designated rooms, service with restrictions, supervision.

(ASK) (S☉) (✕) (☐) (▣) (�ⓘ) (➿) (✕)

▼▼ Super 8 Motel Brandon SH
(204) 729-8024. **$81.** 1570 Highland Ave. On Trans-Canada Hwy 1, south service road, just e of Hwy 10 (18th St). Int corridors. **Pets:** Designated rooms, service with restrictions, supervision.

(ASK) (S☉) (✕) (☾M) (☐) (▣) (➿)

ⒸⒶⒶ ▼▼▼ Victoria Inn SH ✿
(204) 725-1532. **$83-$159.** 3550 Victoria Ave. 5 km s of Trans-Canada Hwy 1; 1.8 km w of jct Hwy 10 (18th St) and 1A (Victoria Ave). Int corridors. **Pets:** $10 daily fee/pet. Service with restrictions, supervision.

(SAVE) (✕) (☐) (▣) (�☐) (➿) (✕)

CHURCHILL

▼▼ Polar Inn & Suites M
(204) 675-8878. **$135-$180, 14 day notice.** 153 Kelsey Blvd. Centre. Int corridors. **Pets:** Crate.

(ASK) (S☉) (✕) (☐) (▣) (K)

▼▼ The Tundra Inn SH
(204) 675-8831. **$105-$185.** 34 Franklin St. Centre. Int corridors. **Pets:** Medium. Service with restrictions, supervision.

(✕) (☐) (▣) (K)

DAUPHIN

▼ Canway Inn & Suites SH
(204) 638-5102. **$79.** 1601 Main St S. 2.4 km s on Hwy 5A and 10A (Main St). Ext/int corridors. **Pets:** Accepted.

(ASK) (S☉) (✕) (☐) (▣) (☐) (➿)

FLIN FLON

ⒸⒶⒶ ▼▼▼ Victoria Inn North SH
(204) 687-7555. **$98.** 160 Hwy 10A N. Jct Hwy 10 and 10A, 1 km nw (eastern approach to city). Int corridors. **Pets:** Accepted.

(SAVE) (☐) (▣) (☐) (➿)

HECLA

▼▼ Solmundson Gesta Hus BB
(204) 279-2088. **$55-$80.** On Hwy 8; in Hecla Village. Int corridors. **Pets:** Medium, other species. $10 one-time fee/room. Supervision.

(ASK) (S☉) (✕) (☑)

NEEPAWA

▼▼ Bay Hill Inns & Suites M
(204) 476-8888. **$73-$89.** 160 Main St W. Hwy 16, just w of jct Rt 5. Int corridors. **Pets:** Medium. $20 deposit/room. Designated rooms, supervision.

(ASK) (S☉) (✕) (☐) (☐) (➿)

THE PAS

ⒸⒶⒶ ▼▼ Wescana Inn SH
(204) 623-5446. **$85.** 439 Fischer Ave. On Hwy 10, just s. Ext/int corridors. **Pets:** Medium. Service with restrictions, crate.

(SAVE) (S☉) (✕) (☐) (▣) (☐)

PORTAGE LA PRAIRIE

▼▼ Super 8 M ✿
(204) 857-8883. **$69-$73.** 1.5 km w on Trans-Canada Hwy 1A. Int corridors. **Pets:** Other species. Designated rooms, service with restrictions, crate.

(ASK) (S☉) (✕) (☐) (▣) (➿)

▼ Westgate Inn Motel M
(204) 239-5200. **$49-$55.** 1010 Saskatchewan Ave E. 1 km e on Trans-Canada Hwy 1A. Ext corridors. **Pets:** Other species. Designated rooms, service with restrictions, supervision.

(ASK) (S☉) (✕) (☐)

RUSSELL

▼▼ The Russell Inn Hotel & Conference Centre SH
(204) 773-2186. **$90-$93.** Hwy 16 Russell. 1.2 km se on Hwy 16 and 83. Ext/int corridors. **Pets:** Accepted.

(ASK) (S☉) (✕) (☐) (▣) (☐) (➿) (✕)

STEINBACH

▼▼▼ Days Inn SH
(204) 320-9200. **$80-$85.** 75 Hwy 12 N. Jct Trans-Canada Hwy 1 and 12, 20 km s. Int corridors. **Pets:** Other species. $10 one-time fee/room. Designated rooms, service with restrictions, crate.

(ASK) (✕) (☾) (☐) (▣) (➿)

THOMPSON

Country Inn & Suites By Carlson SH ❀
(204) 778-8879. **$105.** 70 Thompson Dr N. Just w of Hwy 6.
Int corridors. **Pets:** Medium. $10 daily fee/pet. Designated
rooms, service with restrictions, supervision.
(ASK) [icons]

WINKLER

Heartland Inn & Conference Centre SH
(204) 325-4381. **$80-$88.** 851 Main St N. Main St and Hwy
14; centre. Int corridors. **Pets:** Accepted.
(ASK) [icons]

WINNIPEG METROPOLITAN AREA

WINNIPEG

Best Western Victoria Inn SH
(204) 786-4801. **$99.** 1808 Wellington Ave. At Berry St. Int
corridors. **Pets:** $10 one-time fee/pet. Designated rooms,
service with restrictions, supervision.
(SAVE) [icons]

Carlton Inn SH
(204) 942-0881. **$78-$88.** 220 Carlton St. Just s off Metro Rt
85 (Portage Ave). Int corridors. **Pets:** Other species. Service with restrictions, crate.
(SAVE) [icons]

Clarion Hotel & Suites SH
(204) 774-5110. **$129-$239.** 1445 Portage Ave. Jct Empress
St. Int corridors. **Pets:** Other species. $10 daily fee/pet.
Designated rooms, service with restrictions.
(ASK) [icons]

Comfort Inn SH
(204) 783-5627. **$85-$102.** 1770 Sargent Ave. At Sargent
Ave and King Edward St. Int corridors. **Pets:** $5 daily fee/
room. Designated rooms, service with restrictions, crate.
(ASK) [icons]

Comfort Inn SH
(204) 269-7390. **$80-$98.** 3109 Pembina Hwy. Just n of jct
Perimeter Hwy 100 and 75. Int corridors. **Pets:** Medium. $5
daily fee/room. Designated rooms, service with restrictions,
supervision.
(SAVE) [icons]

Country Inn & Suites By Carlson SH
(204) 783-6900. **$110-$115, 14 day notice.** 730 King
Edward St. Just s of jct Wellington Ave. Int corridors.
Pets: Accepted.
(ASK) [icons]

Days Inn SH
(204) 586-8525. **$109.** 550 McPhillips St. Just n of Logan
Ave. Int corridors. **Pets:** Medium. $10 daily fee/pet. Desig-
nated rooms, service with restrictions, supervision.
(SAVE) [icons]

Delta Winnipeg LH
(204) 942-0551. **$89-$159.** 350 St. Mary Ave. At Hargrave
St. Int corridors. **Pets:** Dogs only. $20 one-time fee/room.
Designated rooms, service with restrictions, crate.
(SAVE) [icons]

The Fairmont Winnipeg LH ❀
(204) 957-1350. **$97-$229.** 2 Lombard Pl. Just e of corner
Portage Ave and Main St. Int corridors. **Pets:** Medium. $25
daily fee/room. Service with restrictions, supervision.
(SAVE) [icons]

Gordon Downtowner Motor Hotel SH
(204) 943-5581. **$81-$89.** 330 Kennedy St. Kennedy St at
Ellice Ave. Int corridors. **Pets:** Accepted.
(SAVE) [icons]

Greenwood Inn SH
(204) 775-9889. **$149-$159.** 1715 Wellington Ave. Wellington
Ave at Century St. Int corridors. **Pets:** Other species. Designated rooms, service with restrictions, crate.
(SAVE) [icons]

Holiday Inn Winnipeg South SH
(204) 452-4747. **$110-$159.** 1330 Pembina Hwy. At
McGillivray Blvd. Int corridors. **Pets:** Other species. Designated rooms, supervision.
(ASK) [icons]

**Place Louis Riel All-Suite
Hotel** LH ❀
(204) 947-6961. **$95-$145.** 190 Smith St. At St. Mary's Ave;
downtown. Int corridors. **Pets:** Large. $10 daily fee/room.
Crate.
(SAVE) [icons]

Radisson Hotel Winnipeg Downtown LH
(204) 956-0410. **$84-$124.** 288 Portage Ave. At Smith St. Int
corridors. **Pets:** Medium. Service with restrictions, supervision.
(ASK) [icons]

Ramada Marlborough Hotel SH
(204) 942-6411. **$120-$160.** 331 Smith St. Just n off Metro
Rt 85 (Portage Ave); downtown. Int corridors.
Pets: Accepted.
(ASK) [icons]

Sheraton Hotel LH
(204) 942-5300. **$89-$159.** 161 Donald St. At York Ave. Int
corridors. **Pets:** Accepted.
(SAVE) [icons]

Super 8 SH
(204) 269-8888. **$90-$99.** 1714 Pembina Hwy. 1 km n of jct
Bishop Grandin Blvd. Int corridors. **Pets:** Other species.
Designated rooms, service with restrictions.
(ASK) [icons]

Travelodge SH
(204) 255-6000. **$81-$96.** 20 Alpine Ave. Just e of jct Fermor
Ave and St. Anne's Rd. Int corridors. **Pets:** Small. $6 daily
fee/room. Designated rooms, service with restrictions.
(SAVE) [icons]

NEW BRUNSWICK

BATHURST

▼▼▼ Atlantic Host Hotel SH
(506) 548-3335. **$80-$92.** 1450 Vanier Blvd. Hwy 11, exit 310 (Vanier Blvd). Int corridors. **Pets:** Small. Designated rooms, no service, supervision.
SD ⊠ 🖵 🍴 🏊 ⊠

▼▼ Comfort Inn SH
(506) 547-8000. **$74-$99, 7 day notice.** 1170 St Peter's Ave. 3.4 km n on Rt 134 (St Peter's Ave). Int corridors. **Pets:** Service with restrictions, supervision.
ASK SD ⊠ 🖵

▼▼▼ Danny's Inn & Conference Centre SH
(506) 546-6621. **$76-$86.** Hwy 11, exit 310 (Vanier Blvd) northbound to Rt 134 (St Peter's Ave), 4 km n; exit 318 southbound to Rt 134 (St Peter's Ave), 3.8 km s. Ext/int corridors. **Pets:** Accepted.
SD ⊠ 🖬 🖵 🍴 🏊 ⊠

▼▼ Lakeview Inn & Suites SH
(506) 548-4949. **$90-$92.** 777 St Peter's Ave. 3 km n on Rt 134 (St Peter's Ave). Int corridors. **Pets:** Accepted.
ASK SD ⊠ 🖥M 🖬 🖵

▼▼ Le Chateau Bathurst Hotel SH
(506) 546-6691. **$62-$118.** 80 Main St. On Rt 134 (St Peter's Ave) and Rt 7; centre. Ext/int corridors. **Pets:** Accepted.
ASK SD ⊠ 🖵 🍴 🏊 ⊠

BOUCTOUCHE

▼▼▼▼ Les Chalets Chebooktoosk CA
(506) 743-1999. **$180, 25 day notice.** 23 Acadie St. 1 km e on Rt 134; centre. Ext corridors. **Pets:** Accepted.
ASK ⊠ 🖬 🖵 🎞

CAMPBELLTON

▼▼ Comfort Inn SH
(506) 753-4121. **$92-$130.** 111 Val D'amour Rd. Hwy 11, exit 415, 1 km e on Sugarloaf St W. Ext/int corridors. **Pets:** Other species. Service with restrictions, crate.
ASK SD ⊠ 🖬 🖵

CAA ▼▼ Howard Johnson SH
(506) 753-4133. **$110.** 157 Water St. Hwy 134; in City Centre Complex. Int corridors. **Pets:** Accepted.
SAVE SD ⊠ 🖬 🖵 🍴

COCAGNE

▼▼ Cocagne Motel M
(506) 576-6657. **$55-$90.** Hwy 11, exit 15, 1 km n on Rt 535. Ext corridors. **Pets:** Small. Service with restrictions, crate.
🖬 🎞

DALHOUSIE

▼▼▼▼ Best Western Manoir Adelaide SH
(506) 684-5681. **$109-$149, 15 day notice.** 385 Adelaide St. Centre. Int corridors. **Pets:** Accepted.
ASK SD ⊠ 🖬 🖵

EDMUNDSTON

▼▼▼ Comfort Inn SH
(506) 739-8361. **$82-$146.** 5 Bateman Ave. Trans-Canada Hwy 2, exit 18 (Herbert Blvd). Int corridors. **Pets:** Large, other species. Service with restrictions.
ASK SD ⊠ 🖵

▼▼▼ Days Inn Edmundston SH
(506) 263-0000. **$89-$149.** 10 rue Mathieu. 8 km e on Trans-Canada Hwy 2, exit 26. Int corridors. **Pets:** Small. $10 daily fee/pet. Designated rooms, service with restrictions, supervision.
ASK SD ⊠ 🖬 🖵

FREDERICTON

▼▼ Auberge Wandlyn Inn SH
(506) 462-4444. **$100-$130, 7 day notice.** 958 Prospect St. Rt 8, exit 3 (Hanwell Rd) eastbound; exit 5 (Smythe St) westbound. Ext/int corridors. **Pets:** Small. $300 deposit/room. Designated rooms, service with restrictions, supervision.
ASK SD ⊠ 🖬 🖵 🍴 🏊

▼▼ City Motel SH
(506) 450-9900. **$95-$115.** 1216 Regent St. Trans-Canada Hwy 2, exit 285A and B eastbound; exit 285B westbound, 3.3 km n on Rt 101 (Regent St). Int corridors. **Pets:** Accepted.
ASK SD ⊠ 🍴

▼▼ Comfort Inn SH
(506) 453-0800. **$100-$199.** 797 Prospect St. Rt 8, exit 3 (Hanwell Rd) eastbound; exit 5 (Smythe St) westbound. Int corridors. **Pets:** Other species. Designated rooms, service with restrictions, supervision.
ASK SD ⊠ 🖬 🖵

CAA ▼▼▼▼ Delta Fredericton LH 🐾
(506) 457-7000. **$259-$339.** 225 Woodstock Rd. 1.6 km n on Rt 102; centre. Int corridors. **Pets:** Designated rooms, service with restrictions, supervision.
SAVE SD ⊠ 🖥M 🖬 🖵 🍴 🏊 ⊠

▼▼▼ Holiday Inn Fredericton SH
(506) 363-5111. **$109-$189, 30 day notice.** 35 Mactaquac Rd (Hwy 102). Trans-Canada Hwy 2, exit 258 eastbound, 11 km e on Rt 102; exit 294 westbound, 30 km w on Rt 102. Ext/int corridors. **Pets:** Accepted.
ASK ⊠ 🖥M 🖬 🖵 🍴 🏊 ⊠

▼▼ Lakeview Inn & Suites-Fredericton SH
(506) 459-0035. **$109-$125.** 665 Prospect St. Rt 8, exit 3 (Hanwell Rd). Int corridors. **Pets:** $50 deposit/room, $4 daily fee/pet. Designated rooms, service with restrictions, crate.
ASK SD ⊠ 🖬 🖵

▼▼▼▼ Lord Beaverbrook Hotel 🄻🄷
(506) 455-3371. **$109.** 659 Queen St. Centre. Int corridors.
Pets: Large. $15 daily fee/pet. No service.
ASK 🔊 ✕ 💻 🍴 ➰ ⊠

▼▼▼▼ Ramada Hotel Fredericton 🅂🄷 🐾
(506) 460-5500. **$119-$149, 14 day notice.** 480 Riverside
Dr. On Rt 105 at the north end of Princess Margaret Bridge.
Int corridors. **Pets:** Designated rooms, service with restrictions, supervision.
ASK 🔊 ✕ 🔋 💻 🍴 ➰ ⊠

GRAND FALLS

▼▼▼▼ Auberge Pres-du-Lac Inn 🅂🄷
(506) 473-1300. **$80-$115.** 10039 Trans-Canada Hwy 2. 4
km w. Ext/int corridors. **Pets:** Small. Designated rooms,
service with restrictions, supervision.
🔊 ✕ 🔋 🍴 ➰ ⊠

▼▼ Hilltop Motel & Restaurant 🅂🄷
(506) 473-2684. **$70-$99.** 131 Madawaska Rd. Trans-
Canada Hwy 2, exit 75, 2.4 km e. Ext corridors.
Pets: Accepted.
🔊 ✕ 🔋 🍴

MIRAMICHI

▼▼ Comfort Inn 🅂🄷
(506) 622-1215. **$89-$115, 3 day notice.** 201 Edward St. 1
km w on Rt 8. Int corridors. **Pets:** Service with restrictions,
supervision.
ASK 🔊 ✕ 🔋 💻

▼▼ Lakeview Inn & Suites 🅂🄷
(506) 627-1999. **$85-$105.** 333 King George Hwy. 1.8 km w
on Rt 8. Int corridors. **Pets:** Medium, other species. $50
deposit/room. Designated rooms, service with restrictions,
supervision.
ASK 🔊 ✕ 🔋 💻

**▼▼▼ Rodd Miramichi River-A Rodd Signature
Hotel** 🅂🄷
(506) 773-3111. **$98-$189.** 1809 Water St. Hwy 11, exit 120,
0.6 km e. Int corridors. **Pets:** $10 daily fee/pet. Service with
restrictions.
ASK 🔊 ✕ 🄼 ⬚ 🔋 💻 🍴 ➰

MONCTON

🄰🄰 ▼▼▼ Beacon Light Motel 🄼
(506) 384-1734. **$79-$99.** 1062 Mountain Rd. Trans-Canada
Hwy 2, exit 454 (Mapleton Rd), 2.8 km to Rt 126 (Mountain
Rd), then just s. Ext/int corridors. **Pets:** Accepted.
SAVE ✕ 🔋 🍴 ➰

▼▼ Colonial Inns 🅂🄷
(506) 382-3395. **$94.** 42 Highfield St. 1 blk n of Main St;
centre. Ext/int corridors. **Pets:** Small. Designated rooms,
service with restrictions, supervision.
ASK 🔊 ✕ 🔋 💻 🍴 ➰

▼▼ Comfort Inn 🅂🄷
(506) 859-6868. **$85-$165.** 20 Maplewood Dr. Trans-Canada
Hwy 2, exit 459A onto Hwy 115 S, left on Rt 134 E (Lewis-
ville Rd). Int corridors. **Pets:** Medium. Service with restrictions, supervision.
ASK 🔊 ✕ 💻

▼▼ Comfort Inn 🅂🄷
(506) 384-3175. **$75-$155.** 2495 Mountain Rd. Trans-
Canada Hwy 2, exit 450. Int corridors. **Pets:** Accepted.
ASK 🔊 ✕ 🔋 💻

▼▼ Country Inn & Suites By Carlson 🅂🄷
(506) 852-7000. **$125-$175.** 2475 Mountain Rd. Trans-
Canada Hwy 2, exit 450. Int corridors. **Pets:** Other species.
$50 deposit/room, $10 daily fee/room. Designated rooms,
service with restrictions, crate.
ASK 🔊 ✕ 🔋 💻

▼▼▼ Holiday Inn Express 🅂🄷
(506) 384-1050. **$109-$134.** 2515 Mountain Rd. Trans-
Canada Hwy 2, exit 450. Ext/int corridors. **Pets:** Accepted.
ASK ✕ 🄼 🗊 💻 🍴 ➰ ⊠

**▼▼ Howard Johnson Brunswick Plaza Hotel &
Conference Centre** 🄻🄷
(506) 854-6340. **$109-$159.** 1005 Main St. Highfield and
Main sts. Int corridors. **Pets:** Accepted.
ASK 🔊 ✕ 💻 🍴 ➰

▼▼ Nor-West Motel 🄼
(506) 384-1222. **$80-$150.** 1325 Mountain Rd. Trans-
Canada Hwy 2, exit 450, 5.2 km se on Rt 126 (Mountain
Rd). Ext/int corridors. **Pets:** Accepted.
ASK 🔊 ✕ 🍴

▼▼ Rodd Park House Inn 🅂🄷
(506) 382-1664. **$77-$163.** 434 Main St. 1 km e on Rt 106.
Ext/int corridors. **Pets:** Accepted.
ASK 🔊 ✕ 💻 🍴 ➰

ROTHESAY

▼▼▼ Shadow Lawn Inn 🄲🄸
(506) 847-7539. **$109-$195, 3 day notice.** 3180 Rothesay
Rd. Hwy 1, exit 137B eastbound; exit 137A westbound,
follow signs for Rothesay Rd and Rt 100, 1.6 km left on Old
Hampton Rd (Rt 100), then left. Int corridors.
Pets: Accepted.
✕ 🔋 💻 🍴

SACKVILLE

▼▼ Coastal Inn Sackville 🅂🄷
(506) 536-0000. **$99-$115.** 15 Wright St. Trans-Canada Hwy
2, exit 504. Int corridors. **Pets:** Designated rooms, service
with restrictions, supervision.
ASK 🔊 ✕

🄰🄰 ▼▼▼ Marshlands Inn 🄲🄸
(506) 536-0170. **$79-$109.** 55 Bridge St. On Hwy 106; centre. Int corridors. **Pets:** Accepted.
SAVE ✕ 🍴 🅇

ST. ANDREWS

▼▼▼ The Fairmont Algonquin 🄻🄷 🐾
(506) 529-8823. **$97-$329, 3 day notice.** 184 Adolphus St.
Off Hwy 127. Int corridors. **Pets:** Small, other species. $25
daily fee/room. Designated rooms, supervision.
ASK ✕ 🔋 💻 🍴 ➰ ⊠

▼▼ St. Andrews Cottages 🄲🄰
(506) 529-8555. **$79-$139.** 3907 Rt 127. On Hwy 127, 2.5
km n. Ext corridors. **Pets:** Accepted.
✕ 🔋 ➰ 🅇

(AA) ▼▼▼▼ The Windsor House of St. Andrews **CI**
(506) 529-3330. **$125-$300, 14 day notice.** 132 Water St.
Centre. Int corridors. **Pets:** Dogs only. Service with restrictions, crate.

(SAVE) (S6) (✕) (♈) (AC)

ST. GEORGE

▼▼ Lake Digdeguash Four Season Chalets **CA**
(506) 755-2737. **$115 (no credit cards), 60 day notice.** Jct
Hwy 1, 9 km w on Rt 760 to entry road, 1.5 km e on gravel
entry road. Ext corridors. **Pets:** Medium. Designated rooms,
service with restrictions, supervision.

(▣) (✕) (AC) (♈) (Z)

SAINT JOHN

▼ Colonial Inns **SH**
(506) 652-3000. **$94.** 175 City Rd. Adjacent to Hwy 1, exit
123. Ext/int corridors. **Pets:** Medium. Service with restrictions, supervision.

(ASK) (S6) (✕) (♦) (♈) (➔)

▼▼ Comfort Inn **SH**
(506) 674-1873. **$120-$155.** 1155 Fairville Blvd. Hwy 1, exit
117 westbound; exit 119 eastbound, left turn. Int corridors.
Pets: Accepted.

(ASK) (S6) (✕) (▣)

▼▼ Country Inn & Suites **SH**
(506) 635-0400. **$105-$160.** 1011 Fairville Blvd. Hwy 1, exit
119B eastbound, left on Catherwood Dr, left at lights; exit
119A westbound. Int corridors. **Pets:** $15 one-time fee/room.
Designated rooms, service with restrictions, supervision.

(ASK) (S6) (✕) (♦) (▣)

(AA) ▼▼▼ Delta Brunswick **LH**
(506) 648-1981. **$105-$169.** 39 King St. Centre of downtown. Int corridors. **Pets:** Other species. $50 one-time fee/
pet. Service with restrictions, crate.

(SAVE) (S6) (✕) (▣) (♈) (➔) (✕)

▼▼▼ Hilton Saint John **LH**
(506) 693-8484. **$119-$139.** One Market Square. Hwy 1, exit
122 at Market Square. Int corridors. **Pets:** Accepted.

(✕) (▣) (♈) (➔) (✕)

(AA) ▼▼▼▼ Howard Johnson Hotel **SH**
(506) 642-2622. **$89-$165.** 400 Main St/Chesley Dr. 1 km w
on Hwy 1; north end Chesley Dr, exit 121; off Harbour
Bridge. Int corridors. **Pets:** Large, other species. Designated rooms, service with restrictions.

(SAVE) (S6) (✕) (♦) (▣) (➔) (✕)

▼ Island View Motel **M**
(506) 672-1381. **$45-$65.** 1726 Manawagonish Rd. 1.8 km w
on Rt 100. Ext corridors. **Pets:** Accepted.

(ASK) (✕) (♦) (AC)

▼ Regent Motel **M**
(506) 672-8273. **$50-$55.** 2121 Ocean West Way. Hwy 1, exit
112 eastbound, 2.4 km e on Rt 100; exit 114 westbound onto
exit 96W, 0.5 km w on Rt 100. Ext corridors. **Pets:** Accepted.

(ASK) (S6) (✕) (♦) (AC) (Z)

ST-LEONARD

(AA) ▼▼ Daigle's Motel **SH**
(506) 423-6351. **$76-$94.** 68 rue DuPont. On Hwy 17, 1 km s
of Trans-Canada Hwy 2, exit 58. Ext corridors. **Pets:** Accepted.

(SAVE) (S6) (✕) (♈) (➔)

ST. STEPHEN

▼ St. Stephen Inn **SH**
(506) 466-1814. **$55-$100.** 99 King St. On Hwy 1; centre.
Ext/int corridors. **Pets:** Accepted.

(ASK) (S6) (✕) (♈)

SHEDIAC

▼▼ Gaudet Chalets & Motel **M**
(506) 533-8877. **$75-$109, 30 day notice.** 14 Belleview
Heights. On Rt 133, 2.4 km w of Rt 15, exit 37. Ext corridors. **Pets:** Accepted.

(✕) (♦) (▣) (AC)

SUSSEX

▼▼ Econo Lodge **SH**
(506) 433-2220. **$65-$100.** 1015 Main St. Hwy 1, exit 192
eastbound; exit 198 westbound, left towards Sussex Corner; centre. Ext corridors. **Pets:** $10 daily fee/pet. Service
with restrictions, supervision.

(ASK) (S6) (✕) (▣) (♈)

▼▼ Pine Cone Motel **M**
(506) 433-3958. **$65-$75.** 12808 Rt 114. Hwy 1, exit 198, 2
km e on Hwy 114 towards Penobsquis. Ext corridors.
Pets: Small. Designated rooms, service with restrictions,
supervision.

(✕) (Z)

(AA) ▼▼▼ Quality Inn Fairway **SH** ❖
(506) 433-3470. **$85-$135.** Hwy 1 at Sussex. Hwy 1, exit
193. Ext/int corridors. **Pets:** Small. $10 one-time fee/pet.
Designated rooms, service with restrictions, supervision.

(SAVE) (S6) (✕) (▣) (♈) (➔)

WOODSTOCK

▼▼ Econo Lodge **SH** ❖
(506) 328-8876. **$85-$149.** 268 Rt 555. 4.8 km w on Trans-
Canada Hwy 2, exit 188 (Houlton Rd) at jct Hwy 95. Ext/int
corridors. **Pets:** Other species. Designated rooms, service
with restrictions, crate.

(ASK) (S6) (✕) (▣) (♈) (➔)

▼▼ Panorama Motel **M**
(506) 328-3315. **Call for rates.** Trans-Canada Hwy 2, exit
188 (Houlton Rd). Ext/int corridors. **Pets:** Accepted.

(✕) (➔) (✕)

(AA) ▼ Stiles Motel Hill View **SH**
(506) 328-6671. **$80-$105, 3 day notice.** 827 Main St.
Trans-Canada Hwy 2, exit 185 eastbound, 2.5 km e; exit
188 (Houlton Rd) westbound, 5.5 km via Rt 555 and 103
(Main St). Ext corridors. **Pets:** Accepted.

(SAVE) (S6) (✕) (♈)

YOUNGS COVE ROAD

(AA) ▼ McCready's Motel **M**
(506) 362-2916. **$55-$65, 7 day notice.** 10995 Rt 10. Trans-
Canada Hwy 2, exit 365, just w. Ext corridors.
Pets: Accepted.

(SAVE) (♈) (AC) (Z)

CHANNEL-PORT-AUX-BASQUES

St. Christopher's Hotel 🆂🅷
(709) 695-7034. **$75-$100.** 146 Caribou Rd. Trans-Canada Hwy 1, exit Port Aux Basques (downtown), follow signs 2 km. Int corridors. **Pets:** Designated rooms, service with restrictions, supervision.

🅰🆂🅺 🆂🗙 📵 📺 🍴

CLARENVILLE

Restland Motel 🆂🅷
(709) 466-7636. **$74-$82.** Memorial Dr. Centre. Ext/int corridors. **Pets:** Accepted.

🅰🆂🅺 🆂🗙 📵 🍴 🅺

St. Jude Hotel 🆂🅷
(709) 466-1717. **$88-$95.** On Trans-Canada Hwy 1; centre. Int corridors. **Pets:** Large. $40 deposit/room. Designated rooms, service with restrictions, supervision.

🅰🆂🅺 🆂🗙 📵 📺 🍴

CORNER BROOK

Comfort Inn 🆂🅷
(709) 639-1980. **$95-$115.** 41 Maple Valley Rd. Trans-Canada Hwy 1, exit 5 eastbound; exit 6 westbound, via Confederation Ave. Int corridors. **Pets:** Other species. Service with restrictions, supervision.

🅰🆂🅺 🆂🗙 📺 🍴

Holiday Inn Corner Brook 🅻🅷
(709) 634-5381. **$95-$105.** 48 West St. Centre. Int corridors. **Pets:** Other species.

🅰🆂🅺 🗙 📵 📺 🍴 🏊

COW HEAD

Shallow Bay Motel & Cabins 🆂🅷
(709) 243-2471. **$85-$105.** Hwy 430, 4 km w towards the ocean, follow signs. Ext/int corridors. **Pets:** Accepted.

🅰🆂🅺 🆂🗙 📵 🍴 🏊 🅺

GANDER

Albatross Hotel 🆂🅷
(709) 256-3956. **$88-$89.** On Trans-Canada Hwy 1. Ext/int corridors. **Pets:** Large, other species. Service with restrictions, crate.

🗙 📵 📺 🍴

Comfort Inn 🆂🅷
(709) 256-3535. **$129-$139.** 112 Trans-Canada Hwy 1. Centre. Ext/int corridors. **Pets:** Small. Service with restrictions, supervision.

🅰🆂🅺 🆂🗙 📵 📺 🍴

Hotel Gander 🆂🅷
(709) 256-3931. **$95.** 100 Trans-Canada Hwy 1. Centre. Int corridors. **Pets:** Medium, other species. Designated rooms, service with restrictions, supervision.

🅰🆂🅺 🆂🗙 📵 📺 🍴 🏊

Sinbad's Hotel & Suites 🆂🅷
(709) 651-2678. **$86-$172, 30 day notice.** Bennett Dr. Centre. Ext corridors. **Pets:** Other species. Service with restrictions, supervision.

🅰🆂🅺 🆂🗙 📵 📺 🍴

GRAND FALLS-WINDSOR

Mount Peyton Hotel 🆂🅷
(709) 489-2251. **$94-$206.** 214 Lincoln Rd. 1 km ne on Trans-Canada Hwy 1. Ext/int corridors. **Pets:** Accepted.

🗙 📺 🍴

L'ANSE AU CLAIR

Northern Light Inn 🆂🅷
(709) 931-2332. **$85-$150.** Rt 510. On Rt 510; centre. Int corridors. **Pets:** Accepted.

🅰🆂🅺 🆂🗙 📵 🍴

ST. JOHN'S

Best Western Travellers Inn 🆂🅷
(709) 722-5540. **$75-$97.** 199 Kenmount Rd. 4.8 km w on Trans-Canada Hwy 1. Ext/int corridors. **Pets:** Medium, other species. Service with restrictions, supervision.

🆂🅰🆅🅴 🆂🗙 📵 📺 🍴 🏊 🅺

Delta St John's Hotel and Conference Centre 🅻🅷
(709) 739-6404. **$159-$214.** 120 New Gower St. Centre. Int corridors. **Pets:** Very small. $50 deposit/room. Designated rooms, service with restrictions, supervision.

🅰🆂🅺 🗙 📺 🍴 🏊 🗙

The Fairmont Newfoundland 🅻🅷 🐾
(709) 726-4980. **$165-$281.** Cavendish Square. Centre. Int corridors. **Pets:** Small, other species. $25 daily fee/room. Designated rooms, service with restrictions, crate.

🗙 📺 🍴 🏊 🗙

Holiday Inn-St. John's 🅻🅷
(709) 722-0506. **$151-$169.** 180 Portugal Cove Rd. Trans-Canada Hwy 1, exit 47A, 1.4 km s. Ext/int corridors. **Pets:** Accepted.

🗙 🅖🅼 🅖 📺 🍴 🏊

STEPHENVILLE

Holiday Inn Stephenville 🆂🅷
(709) 643-6666. **$148-$158.** 44 Queen St. Centre. Int corridors. **Pets:** Accepted.

🅰🆂🅺 🆂🗙 🗙 📺 🍴

YELLOWKNIFE

◆◆ **Yellowknife Super 8 Motel** M
(867) 669-8888. **$139-$149.** 308 Old Airport Rd. 2 km s on
Franklin, 1 km w; in Walmart Plaza. Int corridors. **Pets:** $25
one-time fee/room. Designated rooms, service with restrictions.
ASK 5₀ ✕ 🖥 💻

NOVA SCOTIA

AMHERST

▼▼▼ **Auberge Wandlyn Inn** 🆂🅷
(902) 667-3331. **$109-$122.** Victoria St. Trans-Canada Hwy 104, exit 3, 1 km w. Ext/int corridors. **Pets:** Other species. Designated rooms, service with restrictions, supervision.
🄰🅂🄺 🅂🄾 ⊠ 🄱 💻 🍴 ⊷

▼▼ **Comfort Inn** 🆂🅷
(902) 667-0404. **$105-$160.** 143 Albion St S. Trans-Canada Hwy 104, exit 4, 1.5 km n on Rt 2. Int corridors. **Pets:** Service with restrictions, crate.
🄰🅂🄺 🅂🄾 ⊠ 💻

ANNAPOLIS ROYAL

▼▼ **Annapolis Royal Inn** 🄼
(902) 532-2323. **$89-$150.** 1 km w on Hwy 1. Ext corridors. **Pets:** Service with restrictions, crate.
🄰🅂🄺 🅂🄾 ⊠ 💻

▼▼ **Champlain Motel** 🄼
(902) 532-5473. **$69-$115.** RR 2. 4.2 km w on Hwy 1. Ext corridors. **Pets:** Service with restrictions, crate.
🄰🅂🄺 🅂🄾 ⊠ 🄱 💻 ⊷

ANTIGONISH

🄰🄰 ▼▼▼ **Maritime Inn Antigonish** 🆂🅷
(902) 863-4001. **$98-$159.** 158 Main St. Centre. Ext/int corridors. **Pets:** Other species. Service with restrictions, supervision.
🅂🄰🅅🄴 ⊠ 💻 🍴

AULD'S COVE

🄰🄰 ▼▼▼ **The Cove Motel & Restaurant** 🄼
(902) 747-2700. **$105-$109.** 227 Auld's Cove. 1 km n off Trans-Canada Hwy 104, 3 km w of Canso Cswy. Ext corridors. **Pets:** Medium, dogs only. Designated rooms, service with restrictions, crate.
🅂🄰🅅🄴 ⊠ 💻 🍴 ⊠

BADDECK

▼▼▼▼ **McIntyre's Housekeeping Cottages** 🄲🄰
(902) 295-1133. **$68-$140, 4 day notice.** 8908 Hwy 105. On Trans-Canada Hwy 105, 5 km w. Ext corridors. **Pets:** Other species. $7 daily fee/pet. Service with restrictions, crate.
⊠ 🄱 💻 ⊠ 🄪 🄩

🄰🄰 ▼▼▼ **Silver Dart Lodge & MacNeil House** 🆂🅷
(902) 295-2340. **$103-$155, 3 day notice.** 257 Hwy 205. Trans-Canada Hwy 105, exit 8, 1 km e on Rt 205 (Shore Rd). Ext/int corridors. **Pets:** Small, other species. $15 daily fee/room. Designated rooms, service with restrictions, supervision.
🅂🄰🅅🄴 ⊠ 🄱 💻 🍴 ⊷ ⊠

BRIDGETOWN

▼▼ **Bridgetown Motor Inn** 🆂🅷
(902) 665-4403. **$69-$79.** 396 Granville St. Hwy 101, exit 20, 1 km w on Rt 1. Ext corridors. **Pets:** Accepted.
⊠ 🍴 ⊷

BRIDGEWATER

▼▼ **Auberge Wandlyn Inn** 🆂🅷
(902) 543-7131. **$99-$129.** 50 North St. 1 km e on Hwy 325; Hwy 103, exit 12 to North St. Int corridors. **Pets:** Accepted.
🄰🅂🄺 ⊠ 🄱 💻 🍴 ⊷

▼▼ **Comfort Inn** 🆂🅷
(902) 543-1498. **$95-$170.** 49 North St. Hwy 103, exit 12, 1.7 km s on Rt 10. Int corridors. **Pets:** Other species. Service with restrictions, supervision.
🄰🅂🄺 🅂🄾 ⊠ 🄼 💻

CHESTER

▼▼ **Windjammer Motel** 🄼
(902) 275-3567. **$60-$75.** 4070 Rt 3. 1 km w. Ext corridors. **Pets:** Service with restrictions, supervision.
🅂🄾 ⊠ 🄱 🍴

CHETICAMP

🄰🄰 ▼▼ **Parkview Motel, Dining Room & Lounge** 🄼
(902) 224-3232. **$79-$109, 7 day notice.** 16546 Cabot Tr. 7.2 km n at West Gate Cape Breton Highlands National Park. Ext corridors. **Pets:** Accepted.
🅂🄰🅅🄴 ⊠ 🄱 💻 🍴 🄩

CHURCH POINT

▼▼ **Le Manoir Samson Inn** 🄼
(902) 769-2526. **$100-$125.** 1768 Rt 1. On Hwy 1; centre. Ext corridors. **Pets:** Accepted.
⊠ 🄱 💻 🄪

DARTMOUTH

▼▼▼ Comfort Inn SH ❖
(902) 463-9900. **$115-$149.** 456 Windmill Rd. Hwy 111, exit
Shannon Park. Int corridors. **Pets:** Designated rooms, service with restrictions, supervision.
[ASK] [S🐾] [✕] [▣]

▼▼ Country Inn & Suites By Carlson SH
(902) 465-4000. **$95-$150.** 101 Yorkshire Ave Ext. Hwy 111,
exit Princess Margret Blvd. Int corridors. **Pets:** Medium. $50
deposit/pet, $5 daily fee/pet. Designated rooms, no service,
supervision.
[ASK] [S🐾] [✕] [✚] [▣]

⊕A ▼▼▼ Holiday Inn-Harbourview LH
(902) 463-1100. **$119-$189.** 99 Wyse Rd. Adjacent to Angus
L MacDonald Bridge. Int corridors. **Pets:** Small. $25 one-
time fee/room. Designated rooms, service with restrictions,
supervision.
[SAVE] [S🐾] [✕] [✚] [▣] [↑↓] [⇌]

⊕A ▼▼▼ Park Place Ramada Plaza Hotel LH
(902) 468-8888. **$109-$129.** 240 Brownlow Ave. From Murray Mackay Bridge, 1.2 km n on Hwy 111, exit 3 (Burnside
Dr). Int corridors. **Pets:** Small. $50 deposit/room. Desig-
nated rooms, service with restrictions, supervision.
[SAVE] [S🐾] [✕] [✚M] [▣] [↑↓] [⇌] [✕]

⊕A ▼▼▼ Quality Inn-Mic Mac SH
(902) 469-5850. **$100-$160.** 313 Prince Albert Rd. Hwy 111,
exit 6A, 1 blk s. Int corridors. **Pets:** Medium. Designated
rooms, service with restrictions, supervision.
[SAVE] [S🐾] [✕] [✚] [▣] [↑↓]

DIGBY

⊕A ▼▼▼ Admiral Digby Inn SH
(902) 245-2531. **$70-$200.** 441 Shore Rd. Hwy 101, exit 26,
2.5 km n, follow St John Ferry signs, 5 km w on Victoria
Rd, 1 km e of ferry terminal. Ext corridors. **Pets:** Medium.
Designated rooms, service with restrictions, supervision.
[SAVE] [✕] [✚] [▣] [↑↓] [⇌]

DINGWALL

▼▼ Markland Coastal Resort CA
(902) 383-2246. **$169-$339, 7 day notice.** 802 Dingwall Rd.
Follow signs marked "Resort" to end of winding road. Ext
corridors. **Pets:** Medium. Designated rooms, service with
restrictions, supervision.
[✕] [✚] [▣] [↑↓] [⇌]

HALIFAX

▼▼▼ Airport Hotel Halifax SH
(902) 873-3000. **$154.** 60 Bell Blvd. Hwy 102, exit 6. Int
corridors. **Pets:** Accepted.
[ASK] [S🐾] [✕] [✚] [▣] [↑↓] [⇌] [✕]

⊕A ▼▼▼▼ Casino Nova Scotia Hotel LH
(902) 421-1700. **$109-$300.** 1919 Upper Water St. Adjacent
to historic properties; centre. Int corridors. **Pets:** Accepted.
[SAVE] [S🐾] [✕] [✚M] [✦] [✚] [▣] [↑↓] [⇌] [✕]

▼▼ Chebucto Inn SH
(902) 453-4330. **$75-$145.** 6151 Lady Hammond Rd. Jct
Hwy 111 and Rt 2, 0.7 km e. Ext corridors. **Pets:** Accepted.
[✕] [↑↓]

⊕A ▼▼▼▼ Citadel Halifax Hotel LH
(902) 422-1391. **$124-$259.** 1960 Brunswick St. Between
Cogswell and Duke sts. Int corridors. **Pets:** Accepted.
[SAVE] [✕] [✚] [▣] [↑↓] [⇌] [✕]

⊕A ▼▼▼▼ Delta Barrington LH ❖
(902) 429-7410. **$139-$209.** 1875 Barrington St. Between
Cogswell and Duke sts. Int corridors. **Pets:** Other species.
Service with restrictions, crate.
[SAVE] [✕] [▣] [↑↓] [⇌] [✕]

⊕A ▼▼▼▼ Delta Halifax LH ❖
(902) 425-6700. **$139-$209.** 1990 Barrington St. Corner of
Cogswell and Barrington sts. Int corridors. **Pets:** Other species. Service with restrictions, supervision.
[SAVE] [✕] [▣] [↑↓] [⇌] [✕]

⊕A ▼▼▼ Econo Lodge & Suites SH ❖
(902) 443-0303. **$79-$139.** 560 Bedford Hwy. On Rt 2 (Bedford Hwy), 9.6 km w. Int corridors. **Pets:** $10 one-time
fee/pet. Designated rooms, service with restrictions, supervision.
[SAVE] [S🐾] [✕] [✚M] [▣] [↑↓] [⇌]

▼▼ Esquire Motel M
(902) 835-3367. **$60-$90.** 771 Bedford Hwy. Hwy 102, exit
4A, 5.3 km e on Rt 2 (Bedford Hwy). Ext corridors.
Pets: Dogs only. Service with restrictions, supervision.
[ASK] [S🐾] [✕] [✚] [▣] [↑↓] [✕]

⊕A ▼▼▼ Holiday Inn Express SH ❖
(902) 445-1100. **$139-$169, 14 day notice.** 133 Kearney
Lake Rd. Hwy 102, exit 2. Int corridors. **Pets:** Medium. $25
one-time fee/room. Designated rooms, service with restrictions, supervision.
[SAVE] [S🐾] [✕] [✚M] [✦] [✚] [▣] [↑↓]

**⊕A ▼▼▼ Holiday Inn Select-Halifax
Centre** LH
(902) 423-1161. **$149-$209.** 1980 Robie St. Jct Quinpool St.
Int corridors. **Pets:** Accepted.
[SAVE] [S🐾] [✕] [▣] [↑↓] [⇌] [✕]

▼▼ Howard Johnson Hotel Halifax LH
(902) 477-5611. **$139-$149.** 20 St Margaret's Bay Rd. On
Hwy 3, 1 km w of Armdale traffic circle. Ext/int corridors.
Pets: Service with restrictions, supervision.
[ASK] [S🐾] [✕] [✚] [▣] [↑↓] [⇌]

▼▼▼ Lakeview Inn & Suites SH
(902) 450-3020. **$120-$200.** 98 Chain Lake Dr. Hwy 102,
exit 2A eastbound; Hwy 103, exit 2. Int corridors.
Pets: Medium. $100 deposit/room, $10 daily fee/pet. Designated rooms, service with restrictions, crate.
[ASK] [S🐾] [✕] [✚M] [✚] [▣] [↑↓]

⊕A ▼▼▼ The Lord Nelson Hotel & Suites LH
(902) 423-6331. **$169-$249.** 1515 S Park St. Corner of Park
St and Spring Garden Rd; centre. Int corridors. **Pets:** Large,
other species. Service with restrictions, supervision.
[SAVE] [S🐾] [✕] [✚] [▣] [↑↓]

(AA) 🚩🚩 The Prince George
Hotel 🔲 ❀
(902) 425-1986. **$139-$209.** 1725 Market St. Between Prince and Carmichael sts. Int corridors. **Pets:** Other species. Service with restrictions, supervision.
🆘 ⊠ 🔳 🔲 🍴 ⇌ ⊠

🚩 Travelers Motel **M**
(902) 835-3394. **$55-$82.** 773 Bedford Hwy. Hwy 102, exit 4A, 5.3 km e on Rt 2 (Bedford Hwy). Ext corridors. **Pets:** Designated rooms, service with restrictions, supervision.
🆘 ⊠ 🔳 🔲

(AA) 🚩🚩 The Westin Nova Scotian 🔲 ❀
(902) 421-1000. **$199-$255.** 1181 Hollis St. Between Barrington and Lower Water sts. Int corridors. **Pets:** Medium, other species. Service with restrictions, supervision.
🆘 🆘 ⊠ 🔳 🔲 🍴 ⇌ ⊠

INGONISH BEACH

🚩🚩 Keltic Lodge 🔲
(902) 285-2880. **$114-$373, 3 day notice.** Middle Head Peninsula. Inside the Cape Breton Highlands National Park; off Cabot Tr main highway. Ext/int corridors. **Pets:** Other species. Designated rooms, service with restrictions.
🆘 ⊠ 🔳 🔲 🍴 ⇌ ⊠

KEMPTVILLE

🚩🚩 Trout Point Lodge 🔲
(902) 749-7629. **$222-$343, 21 day notice.** 289 Trout Point Rd. 11 km e on Rt 203, 3.5 km n on gravel entry road. Ext corridors. **Pets:** $100 deposit/room. Designated rooms, service with restrictions, supervision.
🆘 🆘 ⊠ 🍴 ⊠ 🔳 🔲 🔲

KENTVILLE

(AA) 🚩 Allen's Motel **M**
(902) 678-2683. **$57-$75.** 384 Park St. Hwy 101, exit 14, 3 km e on Rt 1. Ext corridors. **Pets:** Accepted.
🆘 🆘 ⊠ 🔳 🔲

🚩🚩 Auberge Wandlyn Inn 🔲
(902) 678-8311. **$110-$125.** 7270 Hwy 1. Hwy 101, exit 14. Ext/int corridors. **Pets:** $12 daily fee/room. Service with restrictions, supervision.
🆘 🆘 ⊠ 🔳 🔲 🍴 ⇌

(AA) 🚩 Sun Valley Motel **M**
(902) 678-7368. **$50-$70.** 905 Park St. Hwy 101, exit 14, 0.8 km e, then 3.2 km w on Rt 1. Ext corridors. **Pets:** Accepted.
🆘 🆘 ⊠ 🔳 🔲 🔳 🔲

LISCOMB

🚩🚩 Liscombe Lodge 🔲
(902) 779-2307. **$129, 3 day notice.** RR #1. On Hwy 7. Ext/int corridors. **Pets:** Accepted.
🆘 ⊠ 🔳 🔲 🍴 ⇌ ⊠ 🔳

LUNENBURG

(AA) 🚩🚩 Boscawen Inn 🔲
(902) 634-3325. **$100-$215, 3 day notice.** 150 Cumberland St. Centre. Int corridors. **Pets:** Accepted.
🆘 ⊠ 🍴 🔳

🚩🚩 Homeport Motel & Inn **M**
(902) 634-8234. **$69-$125.** 167 Victoria Rd. 1 km w on Rt 3. Ext corridors. **Pets:** Accepted.
🆘 🆘 ⊠ 🔳 🔲

🚩🚩🚩 Lunenburg Arms Hotel 🔲 ❀
(902) 640-4040. **$89-$249, 14 day notice.** 94 Pelham St. Corner of Pelham and Duke sts; centre. Int corridors. **Pets:** Accepted.
⊠ 🔳 🔳 🔲 🍴

MAHONE BAY

🚩🚩🚩 Bayview Pines Country Inn 🔲 ❀
(902) 624-9970. **$90-$110, 3 day notice.** 678 Oakland Rd Indian Point. Hwy 103, exit 10, 2 km w on Rt 3 to Kedy's Landing, 6 km e of Mahone Bay. Ext/int corridors. **Pets:** Designated rooms, service with restrictions, supervision.
⊠ 🔳 🔲 🔳 🔲

MAVILLETTE

🚩🚩 Cape View Motel & Cottages **M**
(902) 645-2258. **$62-$74, 3 day notice.** Rt 1, 32 km ne of Yarmouth; centre. Ext corridors. **Pets:** Service with restrictions, supervision.
🆘 ⊠ 🔳 🔳 🔲

MIDDLETON

🚩🚩 Mid-Valley Motel 🔲
(902) 825-3433. **$85-$125.** 121 Main St. 1 km w on Rt 1; Hwy 101, exit 18. Ext corridors. **Pets:** Other species. $5 daily fee/room.
⊠ 🔳 🍴 ⇌

NEW GLASGOW

🚩🚩 Comfort Inn 🔲
(902) 755-6450. **$90-$150.** 740 Westville Rd. On Hwy 289, just e of jct Trans-Canada Hwy 104, exit 23. Int corridors. **Pets:** Other species. Service with restrictions, supervision.
🆘 🆘 ⊠ 🔳 🔲

🚩🚩 Country Inn & Suites By Carlson 🔲 ❀
(902) 928-1333. **$119-$150.** 700 Westville Rd. On Hwy 289, just e of jct Trans-Canada Hwy 104, exit 23. Int corridors. **Pets:** Other species. $50 deposit/room, $5 daily fee/room. Service with restrictions, supervision.
🆘 🆘 ⊠ 🔳 🔲

NEW HARBOUR

🚩🚩🚩 Lonely Rock Seaside Bungalows 🔲
(902) 387-2668. **$100-$195, 14 day notice.** 150 New Harbour Rd. Rt 316, 0.7 km s. Ext corridors. **Pets:** Dogs only. No service, crate.
⊠ 🔳 🔲 🔳 🔳 🔲

NORTH SYDNEY

CAA ♦♦♦ **Clansman Motel** SH
(902) 794-7226. **$79-$125.** 9 Baird St. Hwy 125, exit 2, just e on King St. Ext/int corridors. **Pets:** Accepted.
SAVE 🏊 ⊠ 🍽 💻 ¶ ➳

PARRSBORO

♦♦♦ **The Sunshine Inn** M
(902) 254-3135. **$76-$150.** 3.2 km n on Rt 2. Ext corridors. **Pets:** Accepted.
⊠ 🍽 ⊠ ☎

PICTOU

♦♦♦ **Willow House Inn** BB
(902) 485-5740. **$55-$75.** 11 Willow St. Corner of Willow and Church sts; centre. Int corridors. **Pets:** Accepted.
⊠ ☎

PORT DUFFERIN

♦♦♦ **Marquis of Dufferin Seaside Inn** M
(902) 654-2696. **$66-$76.** On Hwy 7. Ext corridors. **Pets:** Other species. $30 deposit/room, $10 daily fee/room. No service, crate.
⊠ ¶ ⊠ 🏌 ☎

PORT HASTINGS

♦♦♦ **Econo Lodge MacPuffin** M
(902) 625-0621. **$69-$109.** 373 Hwy 4. 1.6 km n on Hwy 4, 1.6 km s of Canso Cswy. Ext corridors. **Pets:** Other species. Service with restrictions, crate.
ASK 🏊 ⊠ 💻 ¶ ➳

PORT HAWKESBURY

CAA ♦♦♦ **Maritime Inn Port Hawkesbury** SH
(902) 625-0320. **$87-$135.** 717 Reeves St. 6.4 km e of Canso Cswy on Hwy 4. Ext/int corridors. **Pets:** $50 deposit/room. Designated rooms, service with restrictions, supervision.
SAVE ⊠ 🍽 💻 ¶ ➳

SCOTSBURN

♦♦♦♦ **Stonehame Lodge & Chalets** CA
(902) 485-3468. **$69-$175.** Rt 256, 12 km w of Pictou via Rt 376, last 2 km on gravel entry road. Ext corridors. **Pets:** Large, other species. Service with restrictions, crate.
🏊 ⊠ 🍽 💻 ➳ ⊠ 🏌

SHELBURNE

CAA ♦♦♦ **MacKenzie's Motel & Cottages** M
(902) 875-2842. **$60-$85.** 260 Water St. Hwy 103, exit 26, 1.5 km e on Rt 3. Ext corridors. **Pets:** Accepted.
SAVE 🏊 ⊠ 🍽 💻 ➳

SMITHS COVE

♦♦♦ **Hedley House Inn By The Sea** SH
(902) 245-2500. **$79-$199.** RR 1. Hwy 101, exit 25 eastbound; exit 24 westbound. Ext corridors. **Pets:** Very small. Crate.
⊠ 🍽 💻 ¶ 🏌 ☎

CAA ♦♦♦ **Mountain Gap Inn** SH
(902) 245-5841. **$122-$138, 3 day notice.** 217 Hwy 1, Smiths Cove. Hwy 101, exit 25 eastbound; exit 24 westbound. Ext corridors. **Pets:** Service with restrictions, crate.
SAVE 🏊 ⊠ 🍽 💻 ¶ ➳ ⊠

SYDNEY

♦♦♦ **Cambridge Suites Hotel** LH
(902) 562-6500. **$149-$169.** 380 Esplanade. Hwy 4, 5 km e of jct Hwy 125, exit 6E; downtown. Int corridors. **Pets:** Accepted.
ASK 🏊 ⊠ 🍽 💻 ¶

♦♦♦ **Comfort Inn** SH
(902) 562-0200. **$95-$160.** 368 Kings Rd. Hwy 4, 3.5 km e of jct Hwy 125, exit 6E. Int corridors. **Pets:** Other species. Designated rooms, service with restrictions, supervision.
ASK 🏊 ⊠ 💻

CAA ♦♦♦♦ **Days Inn Sydney** SH
(902) 539-6750. **$89-$119.** 480 Kings Rd. Hwy 4, 2.8 km e of jct Hwy 125, exit 6E. Int corridors. **Pets:** Accepted.
SAVE 🏊 ⊠ 💻 ➳ ⊠

♦♦♦♦ **Delta Sydney** LH
(902) 562-7500. **$149-$169.** 300 Esplanade. Hwy 4, 5.5 km e of jct Hwy 125, exit 6E; downtown. Int corridors. **Pets:** Large, other species. Designated rooms, service with restrictions.
ASK 🏊 ⊠ 🍽 💻 ¶ ➳ ⊠

♦♦♦ **Quality Inn Sydney** SH ❀
(902) 539-8101. **$89-$190.** 560 Kings Rd. Hwy 4, 3.3 km e of jct Hwy 125. Int corridors. **Pets:** Designated rooms, service with restrictions, supervision.
ASK 🏊 ⊠ 💻 ¶ ➳

SYDNEY MINES

♦♦♦♦ **Gowrie House Country Inn** CI
(902) 544-1050. **$85-$295, 3 day notice.** 139 Shore Rd. Hwy 105, exit 21E, 3 km n on Rt 305. Ext/int corridors. **Pets:** Other species. Designated rooms, service with restrictions.
⊠ 🍽 💻 ¶

TRURO

♦♦♦ **Comfort Inn** SH
(902) 893-0330. **$105-$156.** 12 Meadow Dr. Trans-Canada Hwy 102, exit 14. Int corridors. **Pets:** Other species. Service with restrictions, supervision.
ASK 🏊 ⊠ 💻

♦♦♦ **Howard Johnson Hotel and Convention Centre** SH
(902) 895-1651. **$84-$99.** 437 Prince St. Centre. Ext/int corridors. **Pets:** Service with restrictions, supervision.
ASK 🏊 ⊠ 🍽 💻 ¶ ➳

CAA ♦♦ **The Palliser Motel** M
(902) 893-8951. **$59-$75, 3 day notice.** 103/104 Tidal Bore Rd. Trans-Canada Hwy 102, exit 14; Trans-Canada Hwy 104, exit 15, 3.2 km s. Ext corridors. **Pets:** Accepted.
SAVE ⊠ ¶ ☎

▼▼▼▼ Super 8 Motel SH
(902) 895-8884. **$99-$179.** 85 Treaty Tr. Hwy 102, exit 13A. Int corridors. **Pets:** Small, dogs only. Designated rooms, service with restrictions, supervision.
ASK S🄳 ✕ ᴍ 🄳 🄳 🖵 ≋

WESTERN SHORE

CAA ▼▼▼▼ Oak Island Resort & Spa SH
(902) 627-2600. **$79-$149, 3 day notice.** 55 Vaughn Rd. Hwy 103, exit 9 or 10, follow signs on Rt 3, 10 km e of Mahone Bay. Int corridors. **Pets:** Accepted.
SAVE S🄳 ✕ ᴍ 🄳 🄳 🖵 ⊺⊺ ≋ ✕

WHITE POINT

▼▼ White Point Beach Resort SH
(902) 354-2711. **$95-$170, 3 day notice.** 75 White Point Rd 2. Hwy 103, exit 20A, 9 km w on Rt 3. Ext/int corridors. **Pets:** Other species. Designated rooms.
✕ 🄳 🖵 ⊺⊺ ≋ ✕

YARMOUTH

CAA ▼▼▼ Best Western Mermaid M ✿
(902) 742-7821. **$69-$190.** 545 Main St. Corner of Main St and Starrs Rd. Ext corridors. **Pets:** Large. Designated rooms, service with restrictions, crate.
SAVE S🄳 ✕ 🖵 ≋ 🄰

▼▼ Capri Motel M
(902) 742-7168. **$59-$180.** 8-12 Herbert St. Corner of Hebert and Main sts. Ext corridors. **Pets:** Large. Service with restrictions, crate.
ASK S🄳 ✕ 🄳 🖵

▼▼ Comfort Inn SH
(902) 742-1119. **$80-$180.** 96 Starrs Rd. Jct Hwy 101 E and Hwy 3. Int corridors. **Pets:** Other species. Designated rooms, service with restrictions, crate.
ASK S🄳 ✕ 🖵

CAA ▼ Lakelawn Motel M
(902) 742-3588. **$74-$99.** 641 Main St. 1 km n on Hwy 1. Ext/int corridors. **Pets:** Small, dogs only. Designated rooms, service with restrictions, supervision.
SAVE S🄳 ✕ 🄰 ✕

▼▼ Rodd Colony Harbour Inn SH ✿
(902) 742-9194. **$84-$139.** 6 Forest St. At ferry terminal. Int corridors. **Pets:** Medium. Service with restrictions, crate.
ASK S🄳 ✕ 🄳 🖵 ⊺⊺ 🄰

▼▼▼▼ Rodd Grand Yarmouth-A Rodd Signature Hotel LH
(902) 742-2446. **$121-$215.** 417 Main St. Near centre of downtown. Int corridors. **Pets:** Accepted.
ASK S🄳 ✕ 🄳 🖵 ⊺⊺ ≋ ✕

▼▼ Voyageur Motel M
(902) 742-7157. **$79-$99.** 4.8 km ne on Hwy 1. Ext corridors. **Pets:** Small. $10 daily fee/pet. Designated rooms, service with restrictions, supervision.
✕ 🄳 🄰

ONTARIO

AJAX

♦♦♦ Super 8 Motel-Ajax SH
(905) 428-6884. **$99-$139.** 210 Westney Rd S. Jct of Bayly St from Hwy 401, exit Westney Rd, 1 km s. Int corridors. **Pets:** Accepted.
ASK S X ▣ ⇥

ARNPRIOR

♦ Country Squire Motel M
(613) 623-6556. **$59-$75.** 111 Staye Court Dr. Hwy 17, exit White Lake Rd N. Ext corridors. **Pets:** Accepted.
X ▤

BANCROFT

♦♦ Best Western Sword Motor Inn M
(613) 332-2474. **$99-$139.** 146 Hastings St. On Hwy 62 N; centre. Ext/int corridors. **Pets:** Small. $15 deposit/pet. Designated rooms, service with restrictions, supervision.
SAVE S X ▤ ▣ ⑪ ⇥ X

BARRIE

♦♦♦ Holiday Inn Barrie SH
(705) 728-6191. **$139-$189.** 20 Fairview Rd. 1.6 km s at jct Hwy 400 and 27, exit 94 (Essa Rd). Int corridors. **Pets:** Other species. Service with restrictions, supervision.
SAVE S X ▤ ▣ ⑪ ⇥ X

♦♦ Travelodge Barrie SH
(705) 734-9500. **$99-$129.** 55 Hart Dr. Hwy 400, exit 96A E (Dunlop St). Int corridors. **Pets:** Other species. $20 deposit/room. Designated rooms, service with restrictions.
ASK S X ▤ ▣ ⑪ ⇥

BARRY'S BAY

♦ Mountain View Motel M
(613) 756-2757. **$59-$89.** 18508 Hwy 60 E. 4 km e on Hwy 60. Ext corridors. **Pets:** Accepted.
ASK S X ▤ ▣

BAYFIELD

♦♦♦♦ The Little Inn of Bayfield CI
(519) 565-2611. **$175-$297, 3 day notice.** 26 Main St. Hwy 21, exit Main St, jct Catherine St. Int corridors. **Pets:** Medium. $25 one-time fee/room. Designated rooms, service with restrictions, supervision.
SAVE X ⑪

♦♦ The Martha Ritz House CI
(519) 565-2325. **$115, 3 day notice.** 27 Main St. Hwy 21, exit Main St; jct of Catherine St. Int corridors. **Pets:** Accepted.
ASK S ⑪ W Z

BELLEVILLE

♦♦♦ Best Western Belleville SH
(613) 969-1112. **$110-$130.** 387 N Front St. Hwy 401, exit 543A, 0.5 km s on Hwy 62 (N Front St). Int corridors. **Pets:** Accepted.
SAVE S X ▤ ▣ ⇥

♦♦ Comfort Inn SH 🐾
(613) 966-7703. **$109-$129.** 200 N Park St. Hwy 401, exit 543A, 1 km s on Hwy 62 (N Front St). Int corridors. **Pets:** Large. Service with restrictions, crate.
ASK S X ▤ ▣

♦♦ Quality Inn Belleville SH
(613) 962-9211. **Call for rates.** 407 N Front St. Hwy 401, exit 543A, just s on Hwy 62 (N Front St). Int corridors. **Pets:** Accepted.
X ▤ ▣ ⇥

♦♦♦ Ramada Inn on the Bay SH 🐾
(613) 968-3411. **$165-$210, 3 day notice.** 11 Bay Bridge Rd. Hwy 2, 0.5 km s. Int corridors. **Pets:** Medium. Designated rooms, service with restrictions, supervision.
ASK S X ▤ ▣ ⑪ ⇥ X

BLIND RIVER

▼ Lakeview Inn M
(705) 356-0800. **$69-$72, 4 day notice.** 143 Causley St. On Hwy 17, just e of Hwy 557. Ext corridors. **Pets:** Medium. Service with restrictions, supervision.

ASK S✗ ⊞ ⏻

BRACEBRIDGE

ⒸⒶⒶ ▼▼ Travelodge Bracebridge M
(705) 645-2235. **$89-$169.** 320 Taylor Rd. Hwy 11, exit 189 (Hwy 42/Taylor Rd), 1 km w. Ext corridors. **Pets:** Medium, other species. $10 one-time fee/pet. Service with restrictions, supervision.

SAVE S✗ ⊞ ⏻ ⇔ ⊠

BRAMPTON

ⒸⒶⒶ ▼▼ Comfort Inn SH
(905) 452-0600. **$99-$119.** 5 Rutherford Rd S. Hwy 401, exit Hwy 410 N, 11 km to Hwy 7 E (Queen St), 1 km w. Int corridors. **Pets:** Small. Designated rooms, service with restrictions, supervision.

SAVE S✗ ⊞ ⏻

ⒸⒶⒶ ▼▼▼▼ Holiday Inn Select
Toronto-Brampton LH
(905) 792-9900. **$189-$209.** 30 Peel Centre Dr. Hwy 410 N, exit 7 (Queen St), 2 km e. Int corridors. **Pets:** Accepted.

SAVE S✗ ⊞ ⏻ ⇔ ⊠

▼▼ Motel 6 #1902 SH
(905) 451-3313. **$70-$88.** 160 Steelwell Rd. Hwy 410, exit Steeles Ave E, s on Tomken, then just w. Int corridors. **Pets:** Small, other species. Service with restrictions, supervision.

S✗

BRANTFORD

▼▼▼ Comfort Inn SH
(519) 753-3100. **$91-$134.** 58 King George Rd. Just s of jct Hwy 403 and 24. Int corridors. **Pets:** Accepted.

ASK S✗ ⊞ ⏻

ⒸⒶⒶ ▼▼▼ Days Inn SH 🐾
(519) 759-2700. **$102-$112.** 460 Fairview Dr. Hwy 403, exit Wayne Gretzky Pkwy, 0.8 km n. Int corridors. **Pets:** Other species. $15 one-time fee/room. Service with restrictions.

SAVE S✗ ⊞ ⏻

BRIGHTON

▼ Presquile Beach Motel M
(613) 475-1010. **$55-$99.** 243 Main St W. Hwy 401, exit 509, 4 km s on Hwy 30, 2 km w on Hwy 2. Ext corridors. **Pets:** Other species. Supervision.

✗ ⊞ ⏻

BROCKVILLE

ⒸⒶⒶ ▼▼ Best Western White House Motel M
(613) 345-1622. **$69-$109.** RR 1, 1843 Hwy 2 E. Hwy 401, exit 698, 1.7 km s on N Augusta Rd, 1.5 km e on Hwy 2 (King St W). Ext corridors. **Pets:** Medium. $10 daily fee/pet. Service with restrictions, supervision.

SAVE S✗ ⊞ ⏻ ⇔

▼▼ Comfort Inn SH
(613) 345-0042. **$89-$124.** 7777 Kent Blvd. Hwy 401, exit 696, just nw. Int corridors. **Pets:** Other species. $5 daily fee/pet. Service with restrictions, crate.

ASK S✗ ✗ ⊞ ⏻

BURLINGTON

ⒸⒶⒶ ▼▼▼ Burlington on the Lake Travelodge
Hotel LH 🐾
(905) 681-0762. **$149-$154.** 2020 Lakeshore Rd. Jct of Brant. Int corridors. **Pets:** Large, other species. $5 daily fee/pet. Designated rooms, service with restrictions.

SAVE S✗ ✗ ⊞ ⏻ ⇔ ⊠

ⒸⒶⒶ ▼▼▼ Comfort Inn SH
(905) 639-1700. **$85-$135.** 3290 S Service Rd. QEW, exit Walker's Line Rd westbound, just s to Harvester Rd, then just w; exit Guelph Line Rd eastbound, just s to Harvester Rd, then just e. Int corridors. **Pets:** Service with restrictions.

SAVE S✗ ⊞ ⏻

▼▼ Motel 6 Canada #1900 SH
(905) 331-1955. **$68-$83.** 4345 N Service Rd. QEW, exit Walker's Line Rd N to N Service Rd. Int corridors. **Pets:** Accepted.

S✗ ✗ ⊞

CAMBRIDGE

▼▼ Comfort Inn SH 🐾
(519) 658-1100. **$101-$136.** 220 Holiday Inn Dr. Hwy 401, exit 282, just n to Groh Ave. Int corridors. **Pets:** Service with restrictions, supervision.

ASK S✗ ⊞ ⏻

ⒸⒶⒶ ▼▼▼▼ Langdon Hall Country House Hotel
& Spa CI 🐾
(519) 740-2100. **$229-$629, 7 day notice.** RR 33. Hwy 401, exit 275 to Homer Watson Blvd (Fountain St), 1 km s to Blair Rd, follow signs 1 km to Langdon Dr. Ext/int corridors. **Pets:** $50 one-time fee/room. Designated rooms.

SAVE ✗ ⊞ ⏻ ⇔ ⊠

ⒸⒶⒶ ▼▼▼ Super 8 Motel–Cambridge SH
(519) 622-1070. **$78-$128.** 650 Hespeler Rd. Hwy 401, exit 282, 1 km n. Int corridors. **Pets:** Small. Designated rooms, service with restrictions, supervision.

SAVE S✗ ⊞ ⏻ ⇔

▼▼ Travelodge Cambridge SH
(519) 622-1180. **$74-$149.** 605 Hespeler Rd. Hwy 401, exit 282, 1 km s. Int corridors. **Pets:** Small, other species. $100 deposit/room. Designated rooms, service with restrictions, supervision.

ASK S✗ ⊞ ⏻

CHAPLEAU

▼ Riverside Motel M
(705) 864-0440. **$74-$89.** 116 Cherry St. Corner of Grey and Cherry sts. Ext corridors. **Pets:** Other species. $10 one-time fee/room. Service with restrictions, supervision.

ASK S✗ ✗ ⊞ ⏻

CHATHAM

W W Comfort Inn 🆂🅷
(519) 352-5500. **$94-$117.** 1100 Richmond St. Hwy 401, exit 81 (Bloomfield Rd), 5 km n to Richmond St (Hwy 2). Int corridors. **Pets:** Accepted.
🅰🆂🅺 🔊 ⊗ 🖥 💻

W W Travelodge Chatham 🅼
(519) 436-1200. **$112-$122.** 555 Bloomfield Rd. Hwy 401, exit 81 (Bloomfield Rd), 5 km n. Int corridors. **Pets:** $25 deposit/room. Service with restrictions, supervision.
🅰🆂🅺 🔊 ⊗ 🖥 💻

CHATSWORTH

W W Key Motel 🅼
(519) 794-2350. **$60-$80.** 317051 Hwy 6/10. On Hwy 6 and 10. Ext/int corridors. **Pets:** Accepted.
⊗ 🖥 ➰ ⊠

CHESLEY

🅐🅰 **W** Cedarbrae Bed & Breakfast Inn 🅱🅱
(519) 363-9667. **$60-$85, 7 day notice.** 1748 Bruce CR 10. 0.5 km e of 1st Ave (business district). Int corridors. **Pets:** Accepted.
🆂🅰🆅🅴 🔊 ⊗ ⊠ 🎿 📺 ✈

COBOURG

🅐🅰 **W W W** Best Western Cobourg Inn and Convention Centre 🆂🅷
(905) 372-2105. **$122-$200, 3 day notice.** 930 Burnham St. Hwy 401, exit 472 (Burnham St). Int corridors. **Pets:** Service with restrictions, supervision.
🆂🅰🆅🅴 🔊 ⊗ 🖥 💻 🍽 ➰

W W Comfort Inn 🆂🅷 ❧
(905) 372-7007. **$100-$125.** 121 Densmore Rd. Hwy 401, exit 474, just se. Int corridors. **Pets:** Supervision.
🅰🆂🅺 🔊 ⊗ 🖥 💻

CORNWALL

🅐🅰 **W W W** Best Western Parkway Inn & Conference Centre 🆂🅷
(613) 932-0451. **$119-$139.** 1515 Vincent Massey Dr. Hwy 401, exit 789 (Brookdale Ave), 2.8 km s, just w. Int corridors. **Pets:** Designated rooms, service with restrictions.
🆂🅰🆅🅴 🔊 ⊗ 💻 🍽 ➰

🅐🅰 **W** Econo Lodge 🆂🅷
(613) 936-1996. **$65-$85, 7 day notice.** 1142 Brookdale Ave. Hwy 401, exit 789 (Brookdale Ave), 3 km s. Ext/int corridors. **Pets:** Small, other species. $10 daily fee/pet. Designated rooms, supervision.
🆂🅰🆅🅴 🔊 ⊗ 🖥

W W Holiday Inn Express 🆂🅷
(613) 937-0111. **$102.** 1625 Vincent Massey Dr. Hwy 401, exit 789 (Brookdale Ave), 2.8 km s, then 0.7 km w. Int corridors. **Pets:** $15 one-time fee/room. Designated rooms, service with restrictions, supervision.
🅰🆂🅺 🔊 ⊗ 🖥 💻 ➰

🅐🅰 **W W W** Ramada Inn & Conference Centre 🆂🅷 ❧
(613) 933-8000. **$95-$149.** 805 Brookdale Ave. Hwy 401, exit 789 (Brookdale Ave), 4 km s. Int corridors. **Pets:** Small. Designated rooms, supervision.
🆂🅰🆅🅴 🔊 ⊗ 🖥 💻 🍽 ➰ ⊠

DRYDEN

🅐🅰 **W W W** Best Western Motor Inn 🆂🅷
(807) 223-3201. **$90-$100.** 349 Government St. On Hwy 17. Ext/int corridors. **Pets:** Other species. Designated rooms, service with restrictions, supervision.
🆂🅰🆅🅴 🔊 ⊗ 🖥 💻 🍽 ➰ ⊠

W W Comfort Inn 🅼
(807) 223-3893. **$85-$146.** 522 Government St. On Hwy 17. Int corridors. **Pets:** Accepted.
🅰🆂🅺 🔊 ⊗ 🖥 💻

🅐🅰 **W W W** Holiday Inn Express Dryden 🆂🅷
(807) 223-3000. **$99-$129.** 585 Government St. On Hwy 17. Int corridors. **Pets:** Other species. $10 daily fee/room. Designated rooms, service with restrictions, supervision.
🆂🅰🆅🅴 🔊 ⊗ 🖥 💻 ➰

ELLIOT LAKE

W Dunlop Lake Lodge 🆂🅷
(705) 848-8090. **$68, 7 day notice.** 74 Dunlop Lake Rd. Hwy 17, 38.8 km n on Hwy 108, 0.8 km w, follow signs. Int corridors. **Pets:** Accepted.
🅰🆂🅺 🔊 ⊗ 🍽 ⊠ 🎿

FONTHILL

W Hipwell's Motel 🅼
(905) 892-3588. **$52-$80.** 299 Regional Rd 20. 1.6 km w; centre. Ext corridors. **Pets:** $5 daily fee/pet. Service with restrictions, supervision.
⊗ 🖥 🍽 ➰

GANANOQUE

🅐🅰 **W** Travelodge 1000 Islands 🅼
(613) 382-4282. **$54-$199.** 555 King St E. Hwy 401, exit 647 eastbound; exit 648 westbound, 1.5 km w on Hwy 2 (King St). Ext corridors. **Pets:** Medium. $25 deposit/room. Designated rooms, service with restrictions, supervision.
🆂🅰🆅🅴 🔊 ⊗ 🍽 ➰

GRIMSBY

W W W Super 8 Motel-Grimsby 🆂🅷
(905) 309-8800. **$69-$169.** 11 Windward Dr. QEW, exit 74 (Casablanca N). Int corridors. **Pets:** $10 daily fee/pet. Service with restrictions, supervision.
🅰🆂🅺 🔊 ⊗ 🖥 💻 ➰

GUELPH

🅐🅰 **W W W** Comfort Inn Guelph 🆂🅷
(519) 763-1900. **$113-$136.** 480 Silvercreek Pkwy. Jct Hwy 6 and 7. Int corridors. **Pets:** Medium. Designated rooms, service with restrictions, supervision.
🆂🅰🆅🅴 🔊 ⊗ 🖥 💻

(CAA) ▼▼▼ Holiday Inn-Guelph 🏨 ❀
(519) 836-0231. **$135-$189.** 601 Scottsdale Dr. Jct Hwy 6 N and Stone Rd E, 8 km n of jct Hwy 401. Int corridors. **Pets:** Other species. Service with restrictions, crate.
SAVE 🛏 ✕ 🗄 💻 🍴 🏊 🏋

(CAA) ▼▼ Ramada Hotel & Conference
        Centre SH
(519) 836-1240. **$112-$124.** 716 Gordon St. Jct Gordon St and Stone Rd, 8 km n of Hwy 401 via Brock Rd. Int corridors. **Pets:** Other species. Designated rooms, service with restrictions, supervision.
SAVE 🛏 ✕ 🗄 💻 🍴 🏊

HAMILTON

(CAA) ▼▼▼ Sheraton Hamilton 🏨
(905) 529-5515. **$99-$155.** 116 King St W. On Hwy 6 and 8 westbound; downtown. Int corridors. **Pets:** Accepted.
SAVE 🛏 ✕ 🚹 🗄 💻 🍴 🏊 🏋

HANOVER

(CAA) ▼▼▼ Victorian Manor Bed &
        Breakfast BB
(519) 364-1117. **$75-$95.** 500 9th Ave. Just n of 10th St. Int corridors. **Pets:** Accepted.
SAVE 🛏 ✕ 📺 🍴

HAWKESBURY

▼▼▼ Best Western L'Heritage SH
(613) 632-5941. **$95-$100.** 1575 Tupper St. Jct Hwy 34, 3 km e on Hwy 17. Int corridors. **Pets:** Small. Designated rooms, service with restrictions, supervision.
ASK 🛏 ✕ 🗄 💻 🍴

HUNTSVILLE

▼▼ Comfort Inn SH
(705) 789-1701. **$102-$157.** 86 King William St. Jct Hwy 60. Int corridors. **Pets:** Other species. Designated rooms, service with restrictions, supervision.
ASK 🛏 ✕ 🗄

▼▼ Tulip Inn M ❀
(705) 789-4001. **$90-$130.** 211 Arrowhead Park Rd. Hwy 11, exit 226 (Muskoka Rd 3), follow signs for Arrowhead Park. Ext corridors. **Pets:** Service with restrictions, supervision.
ASK ✕ 🗄 💻

INGERSOLL

▼▼▼ Travelodge Ingersoll SH
(519) 425-1100. **$95-$109.** 20 Samnah Crescent. Hwy 401, exit 216 (Culloden Rd). Int corridors. **Pets:** Other species.
ASK 🛏 ✕ 🗄 💻 🏊

IRON BRIDGE

▼▼ Red Top Motor Inn M
(705) 843-2100. **$63-$69.** 22133 Hwy 17. 0.5 km w. Ext corridors. **Pets:** Other species. Service with restrictions.
ASK 🛏 ✕ 🍴 🏊

JORDAN

(CAA) ▼▼ Best Western Beacon Harborside Resort
        & Conference Centre SH
(905) 562-4155. **$69-$199.** 2793 Beacon Blvd. QEW, exit 57. Int corridors. **Pets:** Small, other species. $10 daily fee/room. Designated rooms, service with restrictions, supervision.
SAVE 🛏 ✕ 💻 🍴 🏊 🏋

KAPUSKASING

▼▼ Comfort Inn SH ❀
(705) 335-8583. **$107-$116.** 172 Government Rd E. Hwy 11, corner of Burnell Rd. Int corridors. **Pets:** $10 daily fee/room. Designated rooms, supervision.
ASK 🛏 ✕ 🗄 💻

KENORA

▼▼▼ Best Western Lakeside Inn & Convention
        Centre SH
(807) 468-5521. **$111-$136.** 470 First Ave S. Centre. Int corridors. **Pets:** Medium, other species. Service with restrictions, supervision.
ASK 🛏 ✕ 💻 🍴 🏊

▼▼ Comfort Inn M ❀
(807) 468-8845. **$92-$115.** 1230 Hwy 17 E. 1.5 km e. Int corridors. **Pets:** Other species. Designated rooms, service with restrictions.
ASK 🛏 ✕ 🗄 💻

▼▼ Days Inn SH
(807) 468-2003. **$98-$115.** 920 Hwy 17 E. On Hwy 17, 1 km e. Ext/int corridors. **Pets:** Accepted.
ASK 🛏 ✕ 🗄 💻 🏊 🏋

(CAA) ▼▼ Kenora Travelodge SH
(807) 468-3155. **$98-$110.** 800 Hwy 17 E. 1 km e. Int corridors. **Pets:** Designated rooms, service with restrictions, supervision.
SAVE 🛏 ✕ 🗄 💻 🍴 🏊 🏋

(CAA) ▼ Whispering Pines Motel M
(807) 548-4025. **$65-$77.** 5 km w of jct Hwy 17 and 71, on Hwy 17; 15 km e on Hwy 17 from Kenora Centre. Ext corridors. **Pets:** Accepted.
SAVE 🛏 ✕ 🗄 💻 📺

KINGSTON

▼▼ Comfort Inn SH
(613) 549-5550. **$95-$155.** 1454 Princess St. Hwy 401, exit 613 (Sydenham Rd), 4 km se. Int corridors. **Pets:** Accepted.
ASK 🛏 ✕ 🗄 💻

(CAA) ▼▼ Comfort Inn SH
(613) 546-9500. **$95-$155.** 55 Warne Crescent. Hwy 401, exit 617 (Division St), 0.5 km s to Dalton Ave. Int corridors. **Pets:** Accepted.
SAVE 🛏 ✕ 🗄 💻

(CAA) ▼ The Executive Motel M
(613) 549-1620. **$62-$115, 3 day notice.** 794 Hwy 2 E. Hwy 401, exit 623, 8 km s, then 2 km e. Ext corridors. **Pets:** Accepted.
SAVE ✕ 🗄 🏊

(CAA) ▼▼▼ **Howard Johnson Confederation Place Hotel** SH ❀
(613) 549-6300. **$129-$229.** 237 Ontario St. Centre of downtown. Int corridors. **Pets:** Medium. $20 daily fee/room. Designated rooms, service with restrictions.
SAVE S🐾 ⊠ 🛏 🖥 ¶ ⊇

(CAA) ▼▼▼ **Peachtree Inn** SH
(613) 546-4411. **$95-$105.** 1187 Princess St. Hwy 401, exit 615, 4 km sw. Int corridors. **Pets:** Designated rooms, service with restrictions, supervision.
SAVE S🐾 ⊠ 🛏 🖥

KIRKLAND LAKE

▼▼ **Comfort Inn** SH
(705) 567-4909. **$80-$155.** 455 Government Rd W. Rt 66, just w of town centre. Int corridors. **Pets:** Other species. Designated rooms.
ASK S🐾 ⊠ 🛏 🖥

KITCHENER

(CAA) ▼▼▼▼ **Four Points by Sheraton Kitchener** LH
(519) 744-4141. **$99-$155.** 105 King St E. Corner of King and Benton sts; downtown. Int corridors. **Pets:** $25 daily fee/room. Designated rooms, service with restrictions, supervision.
SAVE S🐾 ⊠ 🖥 ¶ ⊇ ⊠

(CAA) ▼▼▼▼ **Holiday Inn-Kitchener** LH
(519) 893-1211. **$89-$149.** 30 Fairway Rd S. Hwy 401, exit 278. 5.6 km w via Hwy 8 W to Weber St exit, just e on King St. Int corridors. **Pets:** Medium. Designated rooms, service with restrictions, supervision.
SAVE S🐾 ⊠ 🛏 🖥 ¶ ⊇ ⊠

▼▼ **The Howard Johnson Hotel** SH
(519) 893-1234. **$79-$129.** 1333 Weber St E. Hwy 401, exit 278, 6.4 km w to Kitchener on Hwy 8 W, exit Weber St W. Ext/int corridors. **Pets:** Medium. $15 daily fee/room. Designated rooms, service with restrictions, crate.
ASK S🐾 ⊠ 🛏 🖥 ¶ ⊇ ⊠

▼▼ **Mornington Crescent B&B** BB
(519) 743-4557. **$75-$110.** 11 Sunbridge Crescent. Hwy 86 N, exit University E, 1 km to Bridge St S, 0.5 km s to Bridal Tr, then just e. Int corridors. **Pets:** Other species. Supervision.
⊠ 🛏 🖥 ⊇ ⊠

(CAA) ▼▼▼▼ **Radisson Hotel Kitchener** SH
(519) 894-9500. **$99-$149.** 2960 King St E. Hwy 401, exit 35, 6 km w on Hwy 8 W, exit Weber St. Int corridors. **Pets:** Other species. Service with restrictions, supervision.
SAVE S🐾 ⊠ 🛏 🖥 ¶ ⊇

LEAMINGTON

▼▼▼ **Comfort Inn** SH
(519) 326-9071. **$105-$130.** 279 Erie St S. Just s of jct Talbot and Erie sts; on direct route to Point Pelee National Park. Int corridors. **Pets:** Medium. $10 daily fee/room. Designated rooms, service with restrictions, supervision.
ASK S🐾 ⊠ 🖥

(CAA) ▼▼▼ **Ramada Limited Leamington** SH
(519) 325-0260. **$99-$169.** 201 Erie St N. 1 km n of Talbot. Int corridors. **Pets:** $10 daily fee/pet. Designated rooms, service with restrictions, supervision.
SAVE S🐾 ⊠ 🗝 🛏 🖥 ⊇

(CAA) ▼▼ **Sun Parlor Motel** M
(519) 326-6131. **$58-$90, 7 day notice.** 135 Talbot St W. On Hwy 3, 1 km w of Erie St. Ext corridors. **Pets:** $10 daily fee/room. Designated rooms, service with restrictions, supervision.
SAVE ⊠ 🛏

LISTOWEL

(CAA) ▼▼▼ **Country Inn Motel** M
(519) 291-1580. **$89-$175.** RR1 Hwy 23 N-8500 Rd 164. On Hwy 23 N, 3.5 km n of Main St. Ext/int corridors. **Pets:** Medium. Service with restrictions, supervision.
SAVE S🐾 ⊠ 🛏 🖥 ⊠

LONDON

(CAA) ▼▼▼▼ **Best Western Lamplighter Inn & Conference Centre** SH
(519) 681-7151. **$129-$159.** 591 Wellington Rd S. 3.7 km n off Hwy 401, exit 186. Int corridors. **Pets:** Accepted.
SAVE S🐾 ⊠ 🛏 🖥 ¶ ⊇ ⊠

▼▼▼ **Comfort Inn** SH
(519) 685-9300. **$91-$135.** 1156 Wellington Rd. Hwy 401, exit 186B (Wellington Rd), just n. Int corridors. **Pets:** Designated rooms, service with restrictions, supervision.
ASK S🐾 ⊠ 🛏 🖥

▼▼ **Days Inn London** SH ❀
(519) 681-1240. **$79-$109.** 1100 Wellington Rd S. Hwy 401, exit 186B (Wellington Rd), 1.5 km n. Int corridors. **Pets:** Designated rooms, service with restrictions, crate.
ASK S🐾 ⊠ 🛏 🖥 ¶ ⊇

(CAA) ▼▼▼▼ **Delta London Armouries** LH
(519) 679-6111. **$109-$169.** 325 Dundas St. On Hwy 2. Int corridors. **Pets:** Other species. Designated rooms, service with restrictions, crate.
SAVE S🐾 ⊠ 🛏 🖥 ¶ ⊇ ⊠

(CAA) ▼▼▼ **London Executive Suites Hotel** SH
(519) 679-3932. **$79-$139.** 362 Dundas St. Between Waterloo and Colburne sts. Int corridors. **Pets:** $75 one-time fee/room. Service with restrictions.
SAVE S🐾 ⊠ 🛏 🖥

▼▼▼▼ **Marriott Residence Inn-London** SH
(519) 433-7222. **Call for rates.** 383 Colborne St. Jct of King St. Int corridors. **Pets:** Accepted.
⊠ 🗝 🛏 🖥 ⊠

(CAA) ▼▼▼▼ **Quality Suites** SH
(519) 680-1024. **$115-$155.** 1120 Dearness Dr. Hwy 401, exit 186B (Wellington Rd N), 1.6 km. Int corridors. **Pets:** Accepted.
SAVE S🐾 ⊠ 🛏 🖥

(AA) ▼▼▼ StationPark All Suite Hotel LH
(519) 642-4444. **$169.** 242 Pall Mall St. Hwy 401, exit 186B (Wellington Rd N), 9 km to Pall Mall St. Int corridors. **Pets:** Other species. Designated rooms, service with restrictions.
SAVE S⊘ ✕ ▣ ¶¶ ✕

MARATHON

(AA) ▼ Peninsula Inn M
(807) 229-0651. **$78-$88, 3 day notice.** On Hwy 17, 2.4 km w of jct Hwy 626. Ext corridors. **Pets:** Small. Designated rooms, service with restrictions, supervision.
SAVE ✕ 日 ¶¶

MASSEY

▼ Mohawk Motel Canada M
(705) 865-2722. **$59-$75.** 335 Sable St. Centre. Ext/int corridors. **Pets:** Medium. $6 daily fee/room. Designated rooms, service with restrictions, supervision.
ASK S⊘ ✕ 日 ▣

MCKELLAR

(AA) ▼▼▼▼ The Inn at Manitou SH
(705) 389-2171. **$270-$437, 30 day notice.** 81 The Inn Rd. Hwy 124, exit McKellar Centre Rd, 8 km s, follow signs. Ext corridors. **Pets:** Very small. Designated rooms, no service.
SAVE ✕ 日 ¶¶ ⇌ ✕

MIDLAND

▼▼ Comfort Inn SH
(705) 526-2090. **$88-$114.** 980 King St. Jct King St and Hwy 12. Int corridors. **Pets:** Accepted.
ASK S⊘ ✕ 日 ▣

MINDEMOYA

(AA) ▼ Mindemoya Motel M
(705) 377-4779. **$79-$107, 3 day notice.** 6375 Hwy 542. In Mindemoya; 1 km w of jct Hwy 551 and 542. Ext corridors. **Pets:** Small, dogs only. $10 daily fee/pet. Designated rooms, service with restrictions, supervision.
SAVE S⊘ ✕ 日 ▣

MISSISSAUGA

(AA) ▼▼▼ Comfort Inn Airport West SH ❀
(905) 624-6900. **$99-$129.** 1500 Matheson Blvd. Hwy 401, exit Dixie Rd, then s. Int corridors. **Pets:** Other species. Designated rooms, service with restrictions, supervision.
SAVE S⊘ ✕ 日 ▣ ¶¶

(AA) ▼▼▼ Comfort Inn & Suites SH
(905) 823-8600. **$129-$199.** 2085 N Sheridan Way. QEW to Erin Mills Pkwy, n to N Sheridan Way, then w. Int corridors. **Pets:** Medium. Service with restrictions, supervision.
SAVE S⊘ ✕ ⑸ ⑹ 日 ▣ ⇌

(AA) ▼▼▼ Comfort Inn Mississauga SH
(905) 858-8600. **$90.** 2420 Surveyor Rd. Hwy 401, exit Erin Mills Pkwy, 2 km s. Int corridors. **Pets:** Medium. $10 daily fee/pet. Designated rooms, service with restrictions, supervision.
SAVE S⊘ ✕ 日 ▣

(AA) ▼▼▼ Delta Meadowvale Resort and
       Conference Centre LH
(905) 821-1981. **$99-$179.** 6750 Mississauga Rd. Hwy 401 W, exit 336 (Mississauga Rd), just s. Int corridors. **Pets:** Accepted.
SAVE ✕ ▣ ¶¶ ⇌ ✕

(AA) ▼▼▼▼ Delta Toronto Airport West LH
(905) 624-1144. **$125-$159.** 5444 Dixie Rd. 1 km s of jct Hwy 401 and Dixie Rd. Int corridors. **Pets:** Other species. Service with restrictions, crate.
SAVE S⊘ ✕ 日 ▣ ¶¶ ⇌ ✕

(AA) ▼▼▼▼ Hampton Inn & Suites Toronto
       Airport SH
(905) 671-4730. **$169-$199.** 3279 Caroga Dr. Hwy 401, exit Dixon Rd, 3.5 km w to Bresler Rd. Int corridors. **Pets:** Accepted.
SAVE S⊘ ✕ ⑹ ⑸ 日 ▣ ⇌

(AA) ▼▼▼▼ Holiday Inn Toronto West SH
(905) 890-5700. **$119-$155.** 100 Britannia Rd E. Jct Hwy 401 and 10; Hwy 401, exit Hwy 10 S (Hurontario St). Int corridors. **Pets:** Medium. Designated rooms, service with restrictions.
SAVE S⊘ ✕ 日 ▣ ¶¶ ⇌ ✕

▼▼ Motel 6 #1910 SH
(905) 814-1664. **$71-$83.** 2935 Argentia Rd. Hwy 401, exit 333 (Winston Churchill Blvd), just s. Int corridors. **Pets:** Small, other species. Designated rooms, service with restrictions, supervision.
S⊘ ✕ ⑹ ⑸ 日

▼▼▼ Novotel Hotel Mississauga LH
(905) 896-1000. **$119-$169.** 3670 Hurontario St. On Hwy 10 at Burnhamthorpe Rd; Hwy 401, exit Hwy 10 S (Hurontario St), then 5 km. Int corridors. **Pets:** Large, other species. $15 daily fee/room. Service with restrictions, crate.
ASK S⊘ ✕ ▣ ¶¶ ⇌ ✕

(AA) ▼▼▼ Quality Hotel Airport SH
(905) 567-2577. **$89-$129.** 5599 Ambler Dr. Hwy 401, exit 346 (S Dixie Rd), w on Aerowood, just n. Int corridors. **Pets:** Designated rooms, service with restrictions, supervision.
SAVE S⊘ ✕ 日 ▣ ¶¶ ⇌

(AA) ▼▼▼ Radisson Hotel
       Toronto-Mississauga LH
(905) 858-2424. **$109-$159.** 2501 Argentia Rd. Sw of Hwy 401 and Mississauga Rd, corner of Derry and Argentia rds. Int corridors. **Pets:** Accepted.
SAVE S⊘ ✕ 日 ▣ ¶¶ ⇌ ✕

▼▼▼ Residence Inn by Marriott SH
(905) 567-2577. **$189.** 7005 Century Ave. Hwy 401, exit Erin Mills/Mississauga Rd, s to Argentia Rd. Int corridors. **Pets:** Medium. $200 one-time fee/room. Service with restrictions, supervision.
ASK S⊘ ✕ ⑹ ⑸ 日 ▣ ⇌

(CAA) ▼▼▼▼ **Sandalwood Suites Hotel** SH
(905) 238-9600. **$99-$204.** 5050 Orbitor Dr. Jct Eglinton Ave and Renforth Dr, 2.3 km w on Eglinton Ave. Int corridors. **Pets:** Medium. $8 daily fee/pet. Designated rooms, service with restrictions.
[SAVE] [S⬦] [✕] [🛏] [💻]

(CAA) ▼▼▼ ▼▼▼ **Sheraton Gateway Hotel In Toronto International Airport** LH
(905) 672-7000. **$99-$309.** Box 3000. In Toronto Pearson International Airport. Int corridors. **Pets:** Accepted.
[SAVE] [S⬦] [✕] [&M] [💻] [🍴] [🏊] [✕]

▼▼▼ ▼▼▼ **Stage West All Suite Hotel & Theatre Restaurant** LH
(905) 238-0159. **$179-$199.** 5400 Dixie Rd. 1 km s of Hwy 401. Int corridors. **Pets:** Accepted.
[ASK] [✕] [🛏] [💻] [🍴] [🏊] [✕]

▼▼ **Studio 6 Mississauga #1908** M
(905) 502-8897. **$91-$101.** 60 Brittannia Rd E. Jct Hwy 101 and 10; from Hwy 401, exit 3, Hwy 10 S (Hurontario St). **Pets:** Accepted.
[S⬦] [✕] [&] [🛏] [💻]

▼▼▼▼ **Toronto Airport Hilton** LH
(905) 677-9900. **$124-$280.** 5875 Airport Rd. Hwy 401, exit Dixon Rd, 3.5 km w; 1 km from Toronto Pearson International Airport. Int corridors. **Pets:** Accepted.
[ASK] [✕] [💻] [🍴] [🏊]

MONETVILLE

▼▼ ▼▼ **Memquisit Lodge** CA
(705) 898-2355. **$79-$150, 21 day notice.** 506 Memquisit Rd. 20.8 km ne on west arm of Lake Nipissing, on Hwy 64 and Memquisit Lodge Rd; 36.8 km sw off Hwy 17, on Hwy 64. Ext corridors. **Pets:** Accepted.
[🛏] [💻] [🍴] [✕] [🅺] [🆉]

MORRISBURG

(CAA) ▼▼ ▼▼ **The McIntosh Country Inn & Conference Centre** SH
(613) 543-3788. **$79-$199.** 12495 Hwy 2E. Hwy 401, exit 750, 2 km s on Rt 31, 1 km e. Int corridors. **Pets:** Designated rooms, supervision.
[SAVE] [S⬦] [✕] [🛏] [💻] [🍴] [🏊] [✕]

NEWMARKET

▼▼ ▼▼ **Comfort Inn** SH
(905) 895-3355. **$90-$140.** 1230 Journey's End Cir. Hwy 404, exit 51 (Davis Dr). Int corridors. **Pets:** Other species. Designated rooms, service with restrictions, supervision.
[ASK] [S⬦] [✕] [🛏] [💻]

NIAGARA FALLS METROPOLITAN AREA

FORT ERIE

▼▼ ▼▼ **Comfort Inn** SH
(905) 871-8500. **$79-$115.** 1 Hospitality Dr. QEW, exit 2 (Berti St) westbound; exit 1B (Concession Rd S) eastbound. Int corridors. **Pets:** Other species. $10 one-time fee/pet. Service with restrictions, crate.
[✕] [🛏] [💻]

NIAGARA FALLS

(CAA) ▼▼ ▼▼ **Best Western Fallsview** SH
(905) 356-0551. **$79-$299, 3 day notice.** 6289 Fallsview Blvd. Jct Niagara Pkwy, just n on Murray St. Ext/int corridors. **Pets:** Service with restrictions, supervision.
[SAVE] [S⬦] [✕] [💻] [🍴] [🏊] [✕]

(CAA) ▼▼ ▼▼ **Camelot Inn** M
(905) 354-3754. **$39-$199.** 5640 Stanley Ave. Just n of Hwy 20; just s of Hwy 420. Ext corridors. **Pets:** Other species. $50 deposit/pet. Service with restrictions.
[SAVE] [S⬦] [✕] [🛏] [🏊] [🆉]

▼▼ ▼▼ **Econo Lodge Near the Falls** M
(905) 358-6243. **$50-$195.** 6000 Stanley Ave. 1.3 km w on Hwy 20, just s. Ext/int corridors. **Pets:** Accepted.
[ASK] [S⬦] [✕] [🛏] [🏊]

(CAA) ▼▼ ▼▼ **Flamingo Motor Inn** M
(905) 356-4646. **$49-$179, 7 day notice.** 7701 Lundy's Ln. QEW, 3.4 km w on Hwy 20. Ext corridors. **Pets:** Accepted.
[SAVE] [S⬦] [✕] [🛏] [🏊]

(CAA) ▼▼▼▼ **Glengate Hotel** SH
(905) 357-1333. **$65-$300.** 5534 Stanley Ave. Jct Hwy 420. Int corridors. **Pets:** Accepted.
[SAVE] [S⬦] [✕] [🛏] [💻]

(CAA) ▼▼ **Niagara Parkway Court Motel** M
(905) 295-3331. **$39-$199.** 3708 Main St. 2.5 km s of the falls on the Niagara Pkwy. Ext corridors. **Pets:** Medium. $10 one-time fee/pet. Designated rooms, service with restrictions.
[SAVE] [S⬦] [✕] [🛏] [💻] [🆉]

(CAA) ▼▼▼▼ **Peninsula Inn & Resort** SH
(905) 354-8812. **$59-$209.** 7373 Niagara Square Dr. QEW, exit McLeod Rd, just w. Int corridors. **Pets:** Very small. $10 daily fee/pet. Designated rooms, service with restrictions, supervision.
[SAVE] [S⬦] [✕] [&M] [🛏] [💻] [🍴] [✕]

▼▼ **Pilgrim Motor Inn** M
(905) 374-7777. **$58-$149.** 4955 Clifton Hill. Just s of jct Victoria Ave. Int corridors. **Pets:** Small, dogs only. $100 deposit/room. Service with restrictions, crate.
[ASK]

(CAA) ▼▼ ▼▼ **Sheraton Fallsview Hotel & Conference Centre** LH
(905) 374-1077. **$99-$349.** 6755 Fallsview Blvd. Near Minolta Tower. Int corridors. **Pets:** Accepted.
[SAVE] [S⬦] [✕] [&M] [🛏] [💻] [🍴] [🏊] [✕]

(CAA) ▼▼ ▼▼ **Stanley Motor Inn** M
(905) 358-9238. **$60-$150.** 6220 Stanley Ave. 2 blks from the falls, w of Skylon Tower. Ext/int corridors. **Pets:** Accepted.
[SAVE] [✕] [🛏] [🕁] [🗗]

(CAA) ▼▼ **Thriftlodge Clifton Hill** M
(905) 357-4330. **$59-$369.** 4945 Clifton Hill. Just s on jct Victoria Ave. Ext corridors. **Pets:** Medium. Service with restrictions, supervision.
[SAVE] [S🗖] [✕] [🛏] [🖵]

NIAGARA-ON-THE-LAKE

▼▼ ▼▼ **Gate House Hotel** CI
(905) 468-3263. **$145-$250.** 142 Queen St. Jct Gate. Int corridors. **Pets:** Small. $20 one-time fee/pet. Service with restrictions.
[🕁]

▼▼ ▼▼ ▼▼ **Harbour House Hotel** SH 🐾
(905) 468-4683. **$195-$395, 7 day notice.** 85 Melville St. Jct of Ricardo St. Int corridors. **Pets:** Dogs only. $25 one-time fee/room. Supervision.
[ASK] [S🗖] [✕] [🖵]

(CAA) ▼▼ ▼▼ ▼▼ **The Pillar & Post Inn** CI
(905) 468-2123. **$150-$365.** 48 John St. 13 km from QEW, just n on Hwy 55, then just e. Ext/int corridors. **Pets:** Accepted.
[SAVE] [✕] [🛏] [🕁] [🕁] [✕]

ST. CATHARINES

(CAA) ▼▼ ▼▼ **Comfort Inn** SH
(905) 687-8890. **$94-$149.** 2 Dunlop Dr. QEW, exit 46 (Lake St), between Lake and Geneva sts. Int corridors. **Pets:** Designated rooms, service with restrictions, supervision.
[SAVE] [S🗖] [✕] [🕁M] [🛏] [🖵] [🕁]

(CAA) ▼▼ ▼▼ **Holiday Inn, St. Catharines/Niagara** SH
(905) 934-8000. **$169-$299.** 2 N Service Rd. QEW, exit 46 (Lake St), just e. Int corridors. **Pets:** Small. $15 daily fee/pet. Designated rooms, supervision.
[SAVE] [S🗖] [✕] [🛏] [🖵] [🕁] [🕁] [✕]

(CAA) ▼▼ ▼▼ **Howard Johnson Hotel & Conference Centre** SH
(905) 934-5400. **$89-$289.** 89 Meadowvale Dr. Jct QEW and exit 46 (Lake St). Int corridors. **Pets:** Medium, dogs only. $10 one-time fee/room. Designated rooms, service with restrictions, supervision.
[SAVE] [S🗖] [✕] [🛏] [🖵] [🕁] [🕁] [✕]

(CAA) ▼▼ ▼▼ ▼▼ **Quality Hotel Parkway Convention Centre** LH
(905) 688-2324. **$89-$299.** 327 Ontario St. Jct QEW and exit 47 (Ontario St), 0.8 km s. Int corridors. **Pets:** Service with restrictions, supervision.
[SAVE] [S🗖] [✕] [🛏] [🖵] [🕁] [🕁] [✕]

(CAA) ▼▼ ▼▼ ▼▼ **The Travelodge St. Catharines** M
(905) 688-1646. **$89-$169.** 420 Ontario St. QEW, exit 47 (Ontario St). Ext corridors. **Pets:** Service with restrictions, crate.
[SAVE] [S🗖] [✕] [🛏] [🖵] [🕁] [🕁]

THOROLD

▼▼ ▼▼ **Four Points by Sheraton St. Catharines** LH
(905) 984-8484. **$147-$289.** 3530 Schmon Pkwy. Hwy 406, exit St. David's Rd W. Int corridors. **Pets:** Other species. $10 daily fee/room. Designated rooms, service with restrictions, crate.
[ASK] [S🗖] [✕] [🕁] [🛏] [🖵] [🕁] [🕁] [✕]

WELLAND

▼▼ ▼▼ **Comfort Inn** SH
(905) 732-4811. **$83-$111.** 870 Niagara St. 2.5 km n. Int corridors. **Pets:** Other species. $10 daily fee/room. Designated rooms, service with restrictions, supervision.
[ASK] [✕] [🛏] [🖵]

🌸   **END METROPOLITAN AREA**   🌸

NORTH BAY

(CAA) ▼▼ ▼▼ **Best Western North Bay** SH 🐾
(705) 474-5800. **$99-$199.** 700 Lakeshore Dr. Hwy 11, exit Lakeshore Dr, 4 km n on Hwy 11B. Int corridors. **Pets:** Large, other species. Service with restrictions, crate.
[SAVE] [S🗖] [✕] [🛏] [🖵] [🕁] [🕁] [✕]

▼▼ ▼▼ ▼▼ **Clarion Resort Pinewood Park** SH 🐾
(705) 472-0810. **$152-$172.** 201 Pinewood Park Dr. Hwy 11, exit Lakeshore Dr, immediate turn s onto Pinewood Park Dr, then 0.7 km. Int corridors. **Pets:** Other species. Service with restrictions, crate.
[ASK] [S🗖] [✕] [🛏] [🖵] [🕁] [🕁] [✕]

▼▼ ▼▼ **Comfort Inn** SH
(705) 494-9444. **$95-$149.** 676 Lakeshore Dr. Hwy 11B, exit Lakeshore Dr, 4 km n of jct Hwy 11. Int corridors. **Pets:** Other species. Service with restrictions, crate.
[ASK] [S🗖] [✕] [🛏] [🖵]

▼▼ ▼▼ **Comfort Inn-Airport** SH
(705) 476-5400. **$109-$144.** 1200 O'Brien St. 3 km e on Hwy 11 and 17 Bypass at O'Brien St exit. Int corridors. **Pets:** Service with restrictions, supervision.
[ASK] [S🗖] [✕] [🛏] [🖵]

(CAA) ▼▼▼ **Super 8** SH
(705) 495-4551. **$87-$98.** 570 Lakeshore Dr. Hwy 11, exit Lakeshore Dr, 4.5 km n, on Hwy 11B. Int corridors. **Pets:** Medium, other species. Service with restrictions, supervision.
[SAVE] [S⭘] [✕] [✍] [🖥]

▼▼ **Travelodge-Airport** SH
(705) 495-1133. **$109-$149.** 1525 Seymour St. Jct Hwy 11, 17 and Seymour St. Int corridors. **Pets:** Accepted.
[✕] [🖥] [💻] [➰]

OAKVILLE

▼▼▼▼ **Days Inn Toronto West/Oakville** SH
(905) 829-8444. **Call for rates.** 2937 Sherwood Heights Dr. QEW, exit 124 (Winston Churchill Blvd), 1 km s. Int corridors. **Pets:** Accepted.
[✕] [✍] [🖥] [💻] [➰]

▼▼▼▼ **Holiday Inn Oakville Centre** SH
(905) 842-5000. **$109-$139.** 590 Argus Rd. QEW, exit Trafalgar Rd, then s. Int corridors. **Pets:** Accepted.
[ASK] [S⭘] [✕] [🖥] [💻] [🍴] [➰] [✕]

(CAA) ▼▼▼▼ **Quality Hotel & Suites-Oakville** SH
(905) 847-6667. **$99-$175.** 754 Bronte Rd. QEW, exit 111 (Bronte Rd/Hwy 25), 0.4 km s. Int corridors. **Pets:** Accepted.
[SAVE] [S⭘] [✕] [🖥] [💻] [🍴] [➰] [✕]

ORILLIA

▼▼ **Comfort Inn** SH ✿
(705) 327-7744. **$110-$128.** 75 Progress Dr (RR 1). Hwy 11 N, exit Hwy 12, s on Memorial Ave; corner of Progress Dr and Memorial Ave. Int corridors. **Pets:** Medium, other species. $10 one-time fee/room. Designated rooms, service with restrictions, crate.
[ASK] [S⭘] [✕] [🖥] [💻]

(CAA) ▼▼▼ **Econo Lodge** SH
(705) 326-3554. **$65-$109.** 265 Memorial Ave. 0.5 km n of Hwy 12. Int corridors. **Pets:** Accepted.
[SAVE] [S⭘] [✕] [🖥] [💻]

OSHAWA

▼▼ **Comfort Inn** SH
(905) 434-5000. **$109-$136.** 605 Bloor St W. Hwy 401, exit 416 (Park Rd), s to Bloor St, 0.8 km w. Int corridors. **Pets:** Medium. Service with restrictions.
[ASK] [S⭘] [✕] [🖥] [💻]

(CAA) ▼▼▼▼ **Holiday Inn Oshawa** SH
(905) 576-5101. **$119-$179.** 1011 Bloor St E. Hwy 401, exit 419 (Harmony Rd). Int corridors. **Pets:** Medium. $10 one-time fee/room. Designated rooms, service with restrictions, supervision.
[SAVE] [S⭘] [✕] [🖥] [💻] [🍴] [➰] [✕]

▼▼ **Oshawa Travelodge** SH
(905) 436-9500. **$99-$129.** 940 Champlain Ave. Hwy 401, exit 412 (Thickson Rd N). Int corridors. **Pets:** Small. $25 one-time fee/pet. Designated rooms, service with restrictions, supervision.
[ASK] [S⭘] [✕] [🖥] [💻] [➰]

OTTAWA METROPOLITAN AREA

OTTAWA

(CAA) ▼▼▼ **Adam's Airport Inn** SH
(613) 738-3838. **$94-$99.** 2721 Bank St. Jct Hunt Club Rd and Bank St, 1 km s. Int corridors. **Pets:** Accepted.
[SAVE] [✕] [🖥] [💻]

(CAA) ▼▼▼ **Best Western Barons Hotel & Conference Centre** SH
(613) 828-2741. **$135-$180.** 3700 Richmond Rd. Hwy 417, exit 130, 2 km s. Int corridors. **Pets:** Medium, other species. $25 one-time fee/room. Supervision.
[SAVE] [S⭘] [✕] [🖥] [💻] [🍴] [➰] [✕]

(CAA) ▼▼▼▼ **Bostonian Executive Suites** SH
(613) 594-5757. **$149-$179.** 341 MacLaren St. Between Bank and O'Connor sts. Int corridors. **Pets:** Accepted.
[SAVE] [S⭘] [✕] [🖥] [💻]

(CAA) ▼▼▼▼ **Cartier Place Suite Hotel** SH
(613) 236-5000. **$109-$229.** 180 Cooper St. Between Elgin and Cartier sts. Int corridors. **Pets:** Large. $15 daily fee/room.
[SAVE] [S⭘] [✕] [🖥] [💻] [🍴] [➰] [✕]

(CAA) ▼▼▼ **Comfort Inn** SH
(613) 744-2900. **$95-$145.** 1252 Michael St. Hwy 417, exit 115 (St. Laurent Blvd N) eastbound, just n to Lemieux St, just e to Labelle St, then just e; westbound, just n to Labelle St, then just e. Int corridors. **Pets:** Medium, other species. Designated rooms, service with restrictions, supervision.
[SAVE] [S⭘] [✕] [🖥] [💻]

(CAA) ▼▼▼ **Days Inn-Downtown (Ottawa)** SH
(613) 789-5555. **$109-$139.** 319 Rideau St. Between Nelson St and King Edward Ave. Ext/int corridors. **Pets:** Other species. Designated rooms, service with restrictions, supervision.
[SAVE] [S⭘] [✕] [🖥] [💻] [🍴]

▼▼▼▼ **The Days Inn Ottawa West** SH
(613) 726-1717. **$99-$120.** 350 Moodie Dr. Hwy 417, exit 134, 1.5 km s. Int corridors. **Pets:** $10 daily fee/room. Crate.
[✕] [🖥] [💻] [🍴]

(CAA) ▼▼▼▼ **Delta Ottawa Hotel and Suites** LH ✿
(613) 238-6000. **$119-$159.** 361 Queen St. Corner of Lyon St. Int corridors. **Pets:** Other species. $50 one-time fee/pet. Service with restrictions.
[SAVE] [S⭘] [✕] [🖥] [💻] [🍴] [➰] [✕]

Ⓐ ▼▼ **Econo Lodge-Ottawa East/Orleans** Ⓜ
(613) 745-1531. **$85-$110.** 2098 Montreal Rd. Hwy 417, exit 113, 2.5 km e on Hwy 174 to Montreal Rd W exit. Ext corridors. **Pets:** Large, other species. $5 daily fee/pet. Service with restrictions, crate.
SAVE Ⓢ ⊠ 🛏 💻

Ⓐ ▼▼▼▼ **Fairmont Chateau**
Laurier 🅛🅗 ❀
(613) 241-1414. **$169-$229.** 1 Rideau St. Just e of Parliament buildings. Int corridors. **Pets:** Small. $25 daily fee/pet. Designated rooms, service with restrictions, supervision.
SAVE ⊠ 🅛🅜 🛏 💻 🍽 ≈ ⊠

Ⓐ ▼▼▼▼ **Les Suites Hotel Ottawa** 🅛🅗
(613) 232-2000. **$169-$209.** 130 Besserer St. Between Nicholas and Waller sts. Int corridors. **Pets:** Accepted.
SAVE Ⓢ ⊠ 🛏 🅛🅜 💻 🍽 ≈ ⊠

Ⓐ ▼▼▼▼ **Lord Elgin Hotel** 🅛🅗
(613) 235-3333. **$135-$165.** 100 Elgin St. Between Laurier Ave and Slater St. Int corridors. **Pets:** Designated rooms, service with restrictions, supervision.
SAVE ⊠ 🛏 💻 🍽 ≈ ⊠

▼▼ **The Mirada Inn** Ⓜ
(613) 741-1102. **$99-$110.** 545 Montreal Rd. Jct St. Laurent Blvd, just e. Ext/int corridors. **Pets:** $100 deposit/room. Designated rooms, service with restrictions, crate.
ASK Ⓢ ⊠ 🛏 🍽 ≈

▼▼▼ **Novotel Ottawa Hotel** 🅛🅗
(613) 230-3033. **$150-$167.** 33 Nicholas St. Corner of Daly Ave. Int corridors. **Pets:** Small.
ASK ⊠ 💻 🍽 ≈ ⊠

Ⓐ ▼▼▼▼ **Ottawa Marriott** 🅛🅗
(613) 238-1122. **$119-$159.** 100 Kent St. Corner of Queen St. Int corridors. **Pets:** Other species. Service with restrictions, crate.
SAVE Ⓢ ⊠ 🛏 💻 🍽 ≈ ⊠

Ⓐ ▼▼▼▼ **Quality Hotel Ottawa,**
Downtown 🅢🅗 ❀
(613) 789-7511. **$135-$149.** 290 Rideau St. Corner of King Edward Ave. Int corridors. **Pets:** Medium. Designated rooms, service with restrictions, crate.
SAVE Ⓢ ⊠ 🛏 💻 🍽

Ⓐ ▼▼▼▼ **Radisson Hotel Ottawa Parliament**
Hill 🅢🅗
(613) 236-1133. **$129-$189.** 402 Queen St. Corner of Bay and Queen sts. Int corridors. **Pets:** Accepted.
SAVE Ⓢ ⊠ 🛏 💻 🍽

▼▼▼ **Ramada Hotel & Suites** 🅛🅗
(613) 238-1331. **$122.** 111 Cooper St. Corner of Cartier St. Int corridors. **Pets:** Other species. Crate.
⊠ 🛏 💻 🍽

Ⓐ ▼▼▼ **Residence Inn by Marriott** 🅢🅗
(613) 231-2020. **$139-$279.** 161 Laurier Ave W. Corner of Elgin St. Int corridors. **Pets:** $150 one-time fee/pet. Service with restrictions.
SAVE Ⓢ ⊠ 🛏 💻 ≈ ⊠

▼▼ **Rideau Heights Motor Inn** Ⓜ
(613) 226-4152. **$89-$109.** 72 Rideau Heights Dr. Hwy 16 (Prince of Wales Dr), 0.5 km n of Hunt Club Rd. Ext corridors. **Pets:** Small. $20 daily fee/pet. Designated rooms, service with restrictions, supervision.
ASK Ⓢ ⊠ 🛏 💻

Ⓐ ▼▼▼ **Southway Inn of Ottawa** 🅢🅗
(613) 737-0811. **$112-$128, 3 day notice.** 2431 Bank St. On Hwy 31, corner of Hunt Club Rd. Int corridors. **Pets:** $5 daily fee/room. Service with restrictions, supervision.
SAVE Ⓢ ⊠ 🛏 💻 🍽 ≈ ⊠

Ⓐ ▼▼ **Travelodge** 🅢🅗
(613) 745-1133. **$99-$149.** 1486 Innes Rd. Hwy 417, exit 112 (Innes Rd), just e. Int corridors. **Pets:** Accepted.
SAVE Ⓢ ⊠ 🛏 💻 🍽 ≈

Ⓐ ▼▼ **Webb's Motel** Ⓜ
(613) 728-1881. **$95, 3 day notice.** 1705 Carling Ave. 0.5 km n on Maitland Ave from jct Hwy 417, exit 126, then 0.5 km e. Ext/int corridors. **Pets:** Service with restrictions, supervision.
SAVE ⊠ 🛏

▼▼▼ **The Westin, Ottawa** 🅛🅗 ❀
(613) 560-7000. **$169-$199.** 11 Colonel By Dr. Corner of Rideau St. Int corridors. **Pets:** Small. Designated rooms, service with restrictions, supervision.
⊠ 🎲 🅕 💻 🍽 ≈ ⊠

❀ **END METROPOLITAN AREA** ❀

OWEN SOUND

▼▼▼ **Comfort Inn** 🅢🅗
(519) 371-5500. **$93-$114.** 955 9th Ave E. Jct Hwy 6, 10, 21 and 26. Int corridors. **Pets:** Accepted.
ASK Ⓢ ⊠ 🛏 💻

▼▼▼ **Days Inn Hotel and Convention**
Centre 🅢🅗
(519) 376-1551. **$89-$169.** 950 6th St E. Jct Hwy 6 and 10. Int corridors. **Pets:** $20 daily fee/pet. Service with restrictions, crate.
ASK Ⓢ ⊠ 🛏 💻 🍽 ≈ ⊠

Ⓐ ▼▼▼ **Owen Sound Inn** 🅢🅗
(519) 371-3011. **$45-$150.** 485 9th Ave E. Jct Hwy 6, 10, 26 and 21; follow Hwy 6 and 10, 1 km s. Int corridors. **Pets:** Accepted.
SAVE Ⓢ ⊠ 🛏

▼▼▼ **Travelodge** 🅢🅗
(519) 371-9297. **$99-$130, 15 day notice.** 880 10th St E. Jct of Hwy 6, 10, 21 and 26. Int corridors. **Pets:** Accepted.
ASK Ⓢ ⊠ 🛏 💻

PARRY SOUND

(CAA) ▼▼▼ **Best Western Georgian Inn** SH
(705) 746-5837. **$120-$150.** 48 Joseph St. Hwy 69, exit 224 (Bowes St), 2 km w, Bowes St becomes Seguin, 0.5 km w, Church St e 1 km, Church St becomes Joseph St, 0.5 km e. Ext/int corridors. **Pets:** Large. Designated rooms, service with restrictions, supervision.
[SAVE] [SÐ] [✕] [🛏] [💲] [🍽] [🏊] [✕🍽]

▼▼ **Comfort Inn** SH
(705) 746-6221. **$103-$157.** 120 Bowes St. Hwy 224, exit 224 (Bowes St), just w. Int corridors. **Pets:** Designated rooms, service with restrictions, supervision.
[✕] [💲]

PEMBROKE

▼ **Colonial Fireside Inn** M
(613) 732-3623. **$63-$93.** 1350 Pembroke St W. Jct Hwy 17, 5 km n on Forest Lea Rd, then just e. Ext corridors. **Pets:** Small. $5 daily fee/pet. Designated rooms, service with restrictions, supervision.
[✕] [🛏] [💲] [🏊]

▼▼ **Comfort Inn** SH
(613) 735-1057. **$89-$159.** 959 Pembroke St E. 1.6 km e of town centre on Old Hwy 17. Int corridors. **Pets:** Accepted.
[ASK] [SÐ] [✕] [🛏] [💲]

PETERBOROUGH

(CAA) ▼▼▼ **Comfort Inn & Suites** SH
(705) 740-7000. **$115-$135.** 1209 Lansdowne St W. 0.6 km w of jct Hwy 28. Int corridors. **Pets:** Accepted.
[SAVE] [SÐ] [✕] [🛏] [💲] [🍽] [🏊]

▼▼ **King Bethune Guest House &**
   Spa BB 🐾
(705) 743-4101. **$104-$129, 14 day notice.** 270 King St. From Charlotte and George St to King St, then just w. Int corridors. **Pets:** Other species. $10 daily fee/pet. No service, supervision.
[✕] [🛏] [💲]

(CAA) ▼▼▼ **Quality Inn** SH
(705) 748-6801. **$110-$130.** 1074 Lansdowne St W. 3 km from jct Hwy 115 and bypass. Int corridors. **Pets:** Medium. Designated rooms, service with restrictions, supervision.
[SAVE] [SÐ] [✕] [🛏] [💲]

▼ **Robyn's Motel** M
(705) 745-3225. **$60-$65.** 1136 Hwy 7E. On Hwy 7, 2.5 km e of Television Rd. Ext corridors. **Pets:** Accepted.
[ASK] [SÐ] [✕] [🛏]

PICKERING

(CAA) ▼▼▼ **Comfort Inn** SH
(905) 831-6200. **$114-$119.** 533 Kingston Rd. Hwy 401, exit 394 N (White's Rd) to Hwy 2, 0.5 km w. Int corridors. **Pets:** Designated rooms, service with restrictions, supervision.
[SAVE] [✕] [🛏] [💲]

PLANTAGENET

▼▼ **Motel De Champlain** M
(613) 673-5220. **$80-$90.** 200 Hwy 17. Jct CR 9. Ext/int corridors. **Pets:** Accepted.
[ASK] [✕] [🛏] [🍽]

PORT HOPE

(CAA) ▼▼▼ **Comfort Inn** SH
(905) 885-7000. **$99-$195.** Hwy 401 & 28. Hwy 401, exit 464, just n. Int corridors. **Pets:** Accepted.
[SAVE] [SÐ] [✕] [🛏] [💲]

PROVIDENCE BAY

(CAA) ▼ **Huron Sands Motel** M
(705) 377-4616. **$69-$79.** 5216 Hwy 551. In Providence Bay; on Hwy 551, 27.2 km w of South Baymouth, via 10th Side Rd, follow signs; centre. Ext corridors. **Pets:** Other species. Service with restrictions, supervision.
[SAVE] [✕] [🛏] [🍽] [🐾]

RENFREW

(CAA) ▼▼▼ **The Renfrew Inn** SH
(613) 432-8109. **$104-$114.** 760 Gibbons Rd. Hwy 17, exit O'Brien Rd. Int corridors. **Pets:** Accepted.
[SAVE] [SÐ] [✕] [🛏] [💲] [🍽] [🏊] [✕🍽]

RICHARDS LANDING

▼ **The Clansmen Motel** M
(705) 246-2581. **Call for rates.** 1430 Richard St. Hwy 17 to Hwy 548, follow signs. Ext corridors. **Pets:** Accepted.
[✕] [🛏] [💲] [🏊] [✕🍽] [🎿]

ROSSPORT

▼▼ **The Willows Inn Bed & Breakfast** BB
(807) 824-3389. **$80-$125.** 1 Main St. Centre. Int corridors. **Pets:** Designated rooms, service with restrictions, supervision.
[✕] [🎿]

ST. THOMAS

▼▼ **Comfort Inn** SH
(519) 633-4082. **$85-$111.** 100 Centennial Ave. 6.5 km e on Hwy 3. Int corridors. **Pets:** $10 one-time fee/pet. Service with restrictions, supervision.
[ASK] [SÐ] [✕] [🛏] [💲]

SARNIA

(CAA) ▼▼▼▼ **Best Western Guildwood Inn** SH
(519) 337-7577. **$109-$119.** 1400 Venetian Blvd. 1 km e of Bluewater Bridge. Ext/int corridors. **Pets:** Service with restrictions, supervision.
[SAVE] [SÐ] [✕] [🛏] [💲] [🍽] [🏊]

▼▼▼▼ **Holiday Inn-Sarnia** SH
(519) 336-4130. **$100-$190.** 1498 Venetian Blvd. East of Bluewater Bridge. Int corridors. **Pets:** Medium. $25 one-time fee/room. Designated rooms, no service, supervision.
[ASK] [SÐ] [✕] [🛏] [💲] [🍽] [🏊] [✕🍽]

SAULT STE. MARIE

⬥ 🔷🔷🔷🔷 Algoma's Water Tower Inn SH
(705) 949-8111. **$119-$165.** 360 Great Northern Rd. Jct Hwy 17 and Second Line. Int corridors. **Pets:** Large. Designated rooms, service with restrictions, supervision.

[SAVE] [S🔆] [✕] [🛏] [💻] [🍴] [🚐] [✕]

🔷 Ambassador Motel M
(705) 759-6199. **$49-$94.** 1275 Great Northern Rd. 6.4 km n on Hwy 17. Ext corridors. **Pets:** Other species. $5 daily fee/pet, $5 one-time fee/pet. Designated rooms, service with restrictions, supervision.

[✕] [🛏] [💻] [🚐] [✕]

⬥ 🔷 Bel-Air Motel M
(705) 945-7950. **$60-$90.** 398 Pim St. 2 km n on Hwy 17B. Ext corridors. **Pets:** Small. $5 daily fee/pet. Designated rooms, no service.

[SAVE] [S🔆] [✕] [🛏]

⬥ 🔷 Catalina Motel M ❀
(705) 945-9260. **$105-$108.** 259 Great Northern Rd. 3.2 km n on Hwy 17B. Ext corridors. **Pets:** $10 daily fee/pet. Designated rooms, service with restrictions, crate.

[SAVE] [S🔆] [✕] [🛏] [💻]

🔷🔷 Comfort Inn SH
(705) 759-8000. **$75-$139.** 333 Great Northern Rd. 3.6 km n on Hwy 17B. Ext/int corridors. **Pets:** Large. Supervision.

[ASK] [S🔆] [✕] [🛏] [💻]

🔷🔷🔷 Glenview Vacation Cottages CA
(705) 759-3436. **$115-$150, 5 day notice.** 2611 Great Northern Rd. 9.6 km n on Hwy 17. Ext corridors. **Pets:** Small. $5 daily fee/room. Designated rooms, service with restrictions, crate.

[ASK] [✕] [🛏] [💻] [🚐] [✕]

⬥ 🔷🔷🔷 Holiday Inn SH ❀
(705) 949-0611. **$115-$189.** 208 St. Marys River Dr. On the waterfront. Int corridors. **Pets:** Other species. Designated rooms, service with restrictions, supervision.

[SAVE] [S🔆] [✕] [🛏] [💻] [🍴] [🚐] [✕]

⬥ 🔷 Northlander Motel M
(705) 254-6452. **$50-$80.** 243 Great Northern Rd. 3 km n on Hwy 17B. Ext corridors. **Pets:** Accepted.

[SAVE] [S🔆] [✕] [🛏] [💻]

🔷 Satelite Motel M
(705) 759-2897. **$50-$95.** 248 Great Northern Rd. 3 km n on Hwy 17B. Ext corridors. **Pets:** Medium, other species. $5 daily fee/room. Service with restrictions.

[✕] [🛏]

⬥ 🔷🔷🔷 Travelodge SH
(705) 759-1400. **$109-$130.** 332 Bay St. Opposite Station Mall. Int corridors. **Pets:** Medium. Designated rooms, service with restrictions, supervision.

[SAVE] [S🔆] [✕] [🛏] [💻]

SHARBOT LAKE

⬥ 🔷🔷 Sharbot Lake Country Inn M
(613) 279-2198. **$100.** 14152 Hwy 38. 3.5 km s of jct Hwy 7. Ext corridors. **Pets:** Medium, dogs only. $10 daily fee/pet. Service with restrictions, supervision.

[SAVE] [✕] [🍴] [📞]

SIMCOE

🔷🔷 Comfort Inn SH
(519) 426-2611. **$85-$150.** 85 Queensway E. 0.5 km e on Hwy 3. Int corridors. **Pets:** Designated rooms, service with restrictions, supervision.

[ASK] [S🔆] [✕] [🛏] [💻]

🔷 Travelodge Simcoe SH
(519) 426-4751. **$110-$190.** 385 Queensway W (Hwy 3). 1 km w on Hwy 3. Ext/int corridors. **Pets:** $10 daily fee/pet. Service with restrictions, supervision.

[ASK] [S🔆] [✕] [🛏] [💻] [🚐] [✕]

SMITHS FALLS

🔷 Roger's Motel M
(613) 283-5200. **$70-$90.** 178 Lombard St. 1.6 km s on Hwy 15. Ext corridors. **Pets:** $10 daily fee/pet. Designated rooms, service with restrictions, crate.

[ASK] [S🔆] [✕] [🛏]

STRATFORD

🔷🔷🔷 Arden Park Hotel SH
(519) 275-2936. **$94-$225.** 552 Ontario St. Jct of Romeo St. Int corridors. **Pets:** Small. Designated rooms, service with restrictions, supervision.

[✕] [🛏] [💻] [🍴] [🚐]

SUDBURY

⬥ 🔷🔷🔷 Best Western Downtown Sudbury Centre-Ville SH
(705) 673-7801. **$94-$145.** 151 Larch St. Centre. Int corridors. **Pets:** Accepted.

[SAVE] [S🔆] [✕] [💻]

🔷🔷 Comfort Inn SH
(705) 522-1101. **$103-$140.** 2171 Regent St S. 5 km s on Hwy 46. Int corridors. **Pets:** Designated rooms, service with restrictions, supervision.

[ASK] [S🔆] [✕] [🛏] [💻]

🔷🔷 Comfort Inn SH
(705) 560-4502. **$90-$165.** 440 Second Ave N. The Kingsway at Second Ave. Int corridors. **Pets:** Medium, dogs only. Designated rooms, service with restrictions, supervision.

[ASK] [S🔆] [✕] [🔆M] [🛏] [💻]

⬥ 🔷🔷🔷 Quality Inn & Conference Center SH
(705) 675-1273. **$90-$115.** 390 Elgin St S. Jct Hwy 55 and 80 (Paris St), 0.5 km s, then just e. Int corridors. **Pets:** Medium. Designated rooms, service with restrictions, supervision.

[SAVE] [S🔆] [✕] [🛏] [💻] [🍴] [🚐]

ΨΨ ΨΨ Ramada Inn & Convention Centre SH
(705) 675-1123. **$99-$150.** 85 St. Anne Rd. Jct St. Anne Rd and Notre Dame Ave; downtown. Int corridors. **Pets:** $20 one-time fee/room. Designated rooms, service with restrictions, supervision.
ASK S⊙ ✕ 📻 🖵 ⑾ ⇄

CAA ΨΨ ΨΨ Travelodge Hotel Sudbury SH
(705) 522-1100. **$109-$159.** 1401 Paris St. 1.5 km n of jct Hwy 69 (Regent St). Int corridors. **Pets:** Other species. Designated rooms, service with restrictions, supervision.
SAVE S⊙ ✕ 📻 🖵 ⑾ ⇄

THESSALON

CAA ΨΨ Carolyn Beach Motor Inn M
(705) 842-3330. **$70-$95.** 1 Lakeside Dr. Just w on Hwy 17 jct Hwy 17B. Ext corridors. **Pets:** Large. $10 daily fee/pet. Service with restrictions, supervision.
SAVE S⊙ ✕ 📻 🖵 ⑾ ⊠

THUNDER BAY

**CAA ΨΨ ΨΨ Best Western Crossroads Motor
Inn** SH
(807) 577-4241. **$105-$140.** 655 W Arthur St. Jct Hwy 61, 17 and 11, just e. Int corridors. **Pets:** Accepted.
SAVE S⊙ ✕ 📻 🖵

**CAA ΨΨ ΨΨ Best Western Nor'Wester Resort
Hotel** SH ❖
(807) 473-9123. **$129-$250, 30 day notice.** 2080 Hwy 61. 9.2 km sw of jct Hwy 11, 17 and 61, exit Loch Lomond Rd. Int corridors. **Pets:** Medium. Designated rooms, service with restrictions, crate.
SAVE S⊙ ✕ 📻 🖵 ⑾ ⇄ ⊠

ΨΨ ΨΨ Comfort Inn M
(807) 475-3155. **$105-$144.** 660 W Arthur St. Jct Hwy 11, 17 and 61, just e. Int corridors. **Pets:** Other species. Service with restrictions, supervision.
ASK S⊙ ✕ 📻 🖵

CAA ΨΨ ΨΨ Super 8 Motel SH
(807) 344-2612. **$70-$95.** 439 Memorial Ave. Jct Hwy 11, 17 and Harbour Expwy, 3 km e on Harbour Expwy, then 2 km n. Int corridors. **Pets:** Designated rooms, service with restrictions, supervision.
SAVE S⊙ ✕ 📻

ΨΨ ΨΨ Victoria Inn SH
(807) 577-8481. **$110.** 555 W Arthur St. 0.8 km e of jct Hwy 11B, 17B and 61 (western access to town). Int corridors. **Pets:** Other species. $5 daily fee/pet. Designated rooms, service with restrictions.
ASK S⊙ ✕ 📻 🖵 ⑾ ⇄ ⊠

TILLSONBURG

CAA ΨΨ ΨΨ Super 8 Motel-Tillsonburg SH
(519) 842-7366. **$95-$100.** 92 Simcoe St. Hwy 19, just e. Int corridors. **Pets:** Service with restrictions, supervision.
SAVE S⊙ ✕ 📻 🖵 ⑾

TIMMINS

ΨΨ ΨΨ Comfort Inn SH
(705) 264-9474. **$101-$132, 15 day notice.** 939 Algonquin Blvd E. Hwy 101, 0.5 km e of Hwy 655. Int corridors. **Pets:** Accepted.
ASK S⊙ ✕ 📻 🖵

TORONTO METROPOLITAN AREA

MARKHAM

ΨΨ ΨΨ ΨΨ Comfort Inn SH
(905) 477-6077. **$115-$118.** 8330 Woodbine Ave. Hwy 401, exit 375, 9 km n; Hwy 404, exit Hwy 7, just e, then s. Int corridors. **Pets:** Accepted.

ASK S⊙ ✕ 📻 🖵 ⇄

**CAA ΨΨ ΨΨ ΨΨ Howard Johnson Hotel
Toronto-Markham** SH
(905) 479-5000. **$89-$159.** 555 Cochrane Dr. Hwy 404 N, exit Hwy 7E, to East Valhalla Dr. Int corridors. **Pets:** $50 deposit/room. Service with restrictions, supervision.
SAVE S⊙ ✕ 📻 🖵 ⑾ ⇄ ⊠

**CAA ΨΨ ΨΨ ΨΨ Radisson Hotel
Toronto-Markham** LH
(905) 477-2010. **$119-$149.** 50 E Valhalla Dr. Hwy 404, exit Hwy 7, then e. Int corridors. **Pets:** Medium. $25 one-time fee/room. Service with restrictions, crate.

SAVE S⊙ ✕ 📻 🖵 ⑾ ⇄ ⊠

ΨΨ ΨΨ ΨΨ Residence Inn by Marriott SH
(905) 707-7933. **$159-$169.** 55 Minthorn Blvd. Directly s of jct Hwy 7 and Leslie. Int corridors. **Pets:** Medium. $8 daily fee/pet. Designated rooms, service with restrictions, supervision.
ASK S⊙ ✕ 🖊 📻 🖵 ⇄

ΨΨ ΨΨ ΨΨ Staybridge Suites SH ❖
(905) 771-9333. **$159-$179.** 355 S Park Rd. Jct Hwy 404 and 7, w on Hwy 7, then e. Int corridors. **Pets:** Other species. $75 one-time fee/room. Service with restrictions, supervision.
ASK S⊙ ✕ 🖊 📻 🖵 ⇄

TORONTO

CAA ΨΨ ΨΨ ΨΨ Carlingview Airport Inn SH
(416) 675-5303. **$99-$149.** 221 Carlingview Dr. QEW, exit Hwy 427 N to Dixon Rd E, 1 km to Carlingview Dr, then just s. Ext/int corridors. **Pets:** Other species. $15 daily fee/room. Service with restrictions.
SAVE S⊙ ✕ 📻 🖵 ⑾

ⓐⓐ ▼▼▼ **Comfort Inn** 🅂🄷
(416) 736-4700. **$90-$120.** 66 Norfinch Dr. Hwy 400, exit Finch Ave E, then just n. Int corridors. **Pets:** Small. Designated rooms, service with restrictions, supervision.
🆂🅰🆅🅴 🆂💰 ⊠ 🛏 💻 🍴

▼▼▼ **Crowne Plaza Toronto Don Valley** 🄻🄷
(416) 449-4111. **$149-$199.** 1250 Eglinton Ave E. Don Valley Pkwy, exit 375 (Wynford Dr); jct Don Valley Pkwy and Eglinton Ave E. Int corridors. **Pets:** Accepted.
🄰🅂🄺 🆂💰 ⊠ 🖱 🛏 💻 🍴 ➰ ⊠

ⓐⓐ ▼ **Days Inn Toronto West Lakeshore** 🅂🄷
(416) 532-9900. **$79-$119.** 14 Roncesvalles Ave. Jct of King St W/Queen St W and the Queensway. Int corridors. **Pets:** Very small. $10 daily fee/pet. Designated rooms, no service, supervision.
🆂🅰🆅🅴 🆂💰 ⊠ 🛏 💻 🍴

ⓐⓐ ▼▼▼ **Delta Chelsea Hotel** 🄻🄷 🐾
(416) 595-1975. **$109-$165.** 33 Gerrard St W. W of Yonge St, just s of College St. Int corridors. **Pets:** Small. Service with restrictions, supervision.
🆂🅰🆅🅴 ⊠ 🛏 💻 🍴 ➰ ⊠

▼▼▼ **Delta Toronto East** 🄻🄷
(416) 299-1500. **$139-$199.** 2035 Kennedy Rd. Just ne of jct Hwy 401 and Kennedy Rd, exit 379. Int corridors. **Pets:** $30 one-time fee/room. Designated rooms, service with restrictions, crate.
⊠ 💻 🍴 ➰ ⊠

ⓐⓐ ▼▼▼▼ **Doubletree International Plaza Hotel Toronto Airport** 🄻🄷
(416) 244-1711. **$99-$258.** 655 Dixon Rd. Jct Hwy 27 N, just w of jct Hwy 401. Int corridors. **Pets:** Medium. $100 deposit/room. Service with restrictions, supervision.
🆂🅰🆅🅴 🆂💰 ⊠ 🛏 💻 🍴 ➰ ⊠

ⓐⓐ ▼▼▼▼ **The Fairmont Royal York** 🄻🄷
(416) 368-2511. **$159-$329.** 100 Front St W. QEW/Gardiner Expwy, exit n on York or Bay sts; entrance on Wellington St. Int corridors. **Pets:** Large, other species. $25 daily fee/room. Service with restrictions, supervision.
🆂🅰🆅🅴 🆂💰 ⊠ 🎗 🛏 💻 🍴 ➰ ⊠

ⓐⓐ ▼▼▼▼ **Four Seasons Hotel** 🄻🄷
(416) 964-0411. **$355.** 21 Avenue Rd. Corner of Avenue Rd and Cumberland Ave. Int corridors. **Pets:** Accepted.
🆂🅰🆅🅴 ⊠ 🛏 🍴 ➰ ⊠

▼▼ ▼▼ **Hilton Toronto** 🄻🄷
(416) 869-3456. **$239-$394, 3 day notice.** 145 Richmond St W. Jct of University Ave. Int corridors. **Pets:** Small, other species. $50 one-time fee/room. Service with restrictions, supervision.
🄰🅂🄺 ⊠ 🖱 🛏 💻 🍴 ➰ ⊠

ⓐⓐ ▼▼▼▼ **Holiday Inn On King** 🄻🄷 🐾
(416) 599-4000. **$199-$289.** 370 King St W. Between Spadina Ave and Peter St. Int corridors. **Pets:** Large, other species.
🆂🅰🆅🅴 🆂💰 ⊠ 🖱 🛏 💻 🍴 ➰ ⊠

▼▼▼ ▼▼▼ **Hotel Inter-Continental Toronto** 🄻🄷
(416) 960-5200. **$300.** 220 Bloor St W. Just w of Avenue Rd. Int corridors. **Pets:** Accepted.
🄰🅂🄺 🆂💰 ⊠ 🛏 💻 🍴 ➰ ⊠

ⓐⓐ ▼▼▼ ▼▼▼ **Le Royal Meridien King Edward Hotel** 🄻🄷 🐾
(416) 863-3131. **$230-$250.** 37 King St E. Just e of Yonge St. Int corridors. **Pets:** Small. $50 one-time fee/room. Service with restrictions, supervision.
🆂🅰🆅🅴 🆂💰 ⊠ 🍴

▼▼▼ ▼▼▼ **Metropolitan Hotel** 🄻🄷 🐾
(416) 977-5000. **$330.** 108 Chestnut St. Just s of Dundas St. Int corridors. **Pets:** Medium. Service with restrictions, supervision.
🄰🅂🄺 ⊠ 🛏 💻 🍴 ➰ ⊠

▼▼▼ **Montecassino Hotel & Suites** 🅂🄷
(416) 630-8100. **$139-$159.** 3710 Chesswood Dr. On Chesswood Dr at Sheppard Ave. Int corridors. **Pets:** Accepted.
🄰🅂🄺 🆂💰 ⊠ 🛏 💻 🍴

▼▼▼ **Novotel Toronto Centre** 🄻🄷
(416) 367-8900. **Call for rates.** 45 The Esplanade. Just ne of Gardiner Expwy via Yonge St. Int corridors. **Pets:** Accepted.
⊠ 🛏 💻 🍴 ➰ ⊠

▼▼▼ **Novotel Toronto North York** 🄻🄷
(416) 733-2929. **$99-$139.** 3 Park Home Ave. Hwy 401, exit Yonge St, 1 km n, then just w. Int corridors. **Pets:** Accepted.
🄰🅂🄺 🆂💰 ⊠ 🛏 💻 🍴 ➰

ⓐⓐ ▼▼ ▼▼ **Quality Hotel & Suites Toronto Airport East** 🅂🄷
(416) 240-9090. **$89-$199.** 2180 Islington Ave. Hwy 401, exit 356. Int corridors. **Pets:** Accepted.
🆂🅰🆅🅴 🆂💰 ⊠ 🛏 💻 🍴

ⓐⓐ ▼▼ ▼ **Quality Hotel Downtown** 🅂🄷
(416) 367-5555. **$119-$179.** 111 Lombard St. West side of Jarvis St; between Adelaide and Lombard sts, 1 km n off Gardiner Expwy at Jarvis St exit. Int corridors. **Pets:** Small. Service with restrictions, supervision.
🆂🅰🆅🅴 🆂💰 ⊠ 🛏 💻

ⓐⓐ ▼▼▼ **Quality Hotel Midtown** 🅂🄷
(416) 968-0010. **$119-$179.** 280 Bloor St W. Just w of St. George. Int corridors. **Pets:** Service with restrictions, supervision.
🆂🅰🆅🅴 🆂💰 ⊠ 💻 🍴

ⓐⓐ ▼▼▼▼ **Quality Suites Toronto Airport** 🄻🄷
(416) 674-8442. **$109-$189.** 262 Carlingview Dr. 1 km w of jct Hwy 27 N and Dixon Rd. Int corridors. **Pets:** Other species. Supervision.
🆂🅰🆅🅴 🆂💰 ⊠ 🛏 💻 🍴

ⓐⓐ ▼▼▼▼ **Radisson Suite Hotel Toronto Airport** 🄻🄷
(416) 242-7400. **$129-$189.** 640 Dixon Rd. Just e of jct Hwy 27; 0.3 km w of jct Hwy 401. Int corridors. **Pets:** Accepted.
🆂🅰🆅🅴 🆂💰 ⊠ 💻 🍴

♦♦♦♦ Ramada Hotel Toronto Airport 🄻🄷
(416) 621-2121. **$139-$199.** 2 Holiday Dr. Hwy 427, exit Holiday Dr southbound; exit Burnhamthorpe Rd northbound. Int corridors. **Pets:** Medium, other species. $8 one-time fee/pet. Designated rooms, service with restrictions, supervision.
🄰🅂🄺 🖪 ⊗ 🖥 💻 🍴 ⇔ ⊠

🄒🄐🄐 ♦♦♦ ♦♦♦ The Sheraton Centre Toronto
Hotel 🄻🄷 ❀
(416) 361-1000. **$129-$369.** 123 Queen St W. Opposite Toronto Civic Centre and City Hall. Int corridors. **Pets:** Medium. Service with restrictions, crate.
🅂🄰🅅🄴 🖪 ⊗ 🅶🄼 🖥 💻 🍴 ⇔ ⊠

♦♦♦ ♦♦♦ SoHo Metropolitan 🅂🄷
(416) 599-8800. **$275-$460.** 318 Wellington St W. Jct of Blue Jays Way. Int corridors. **Pets:** Medium, other species. Service with restrictions, crate.
🄰🅂🄺 ⊗ 💻 🍴 ⇔ ⊠

🄒🄐🄐 ♦♦♦ ♦♦♦ The Sutton Place Hotel 🄻🄷
(416) 924-9221. **$199-$415.** 955 Bay St. Jct of Wellesley St. Int corridors. **Pets:** Small, other species. $150 deposit/room. Crate.
🅂🄰🅅🄴 🖪 ⊗ 🖥 💻 🍴 ⇔ ⊠

🄒🄐🄐 ♦♦♦ ♦♦♦ Travelodge Hotel Toronto Airport
(Dixon Road) 🅂🄷
(416) 674-2222. **$104-$148, 7 day notice.** 925 Dixon Rd. Corner of Carlingview Dr and Dixon Rd. Int corridors. **Pets:** $25 one-time fee/pet. Designated rooms, service with restrictions, supervision.
🅂🄰🅅🄴 🖪 ⊗ 🖥 💻 🍴 ⇔ ⊠

♦♦♦ ♦♦♦ Travelodge Hotel Toronto Yorkdale 🄻🄷
(416) 636-4656. **$119-$149.** 2737 Keele St. Jct Hwy 401 and Keele St N. Int corridors. **Pets:** Accepted.
🄰🅂🄺 🖪 ⊗ 🖥 💻 🍴 ⇔ ⊠

🄒🄐🄐 ♦♦♦ ♦♦♦ Travelodge Toronto East 🅂🄷 ❀
(416) 299-9500. **$109-$149.** 20 Milner Business Ct. Jct Hwy 401 and Markham Rd, just n on Markham Rd. Int corridors. **Pets:** Other species.
🅂🄰🅅🄴 ⊗ 🖥 💻 🍴 ⇔

🄒🄐🄐 ♦♦♦ Travelodge Toronto North (North
York) 🅂🄷
(416) 663-9500. **$99-$149.** 50 Norfinch Dr. Hwy 400, exit Finch Ave E. Int corridors. **Pets:** Accepted.
🅂🄰🅅🄴 🖪 ⊗ 🖥 💻 🍴 ⇔

♦♦♦ ♦♦♦ Windsor Arms 🅂🄷
(416) 971-9666. **$295.** 18 St. Thomas St. Jct of Bloor St. Int corridors. **Pets:** Small. Service with restrictions, supervision.
🄰🅂🄺 ⊗ 🍴 ⇔ ⊠

🄒🄐🄐 ♦♦♦ ♦♦♦ Wyndham Bristol Place-Toronto
Airport 🄻🄷
(416) 675-9444. **$139-$215.** 950 Dixon Rd. 3 km w of jct Hwy 401. Int corridors. **Pets:** Accepted.
🅂🄰🅅🄴 🖪 ⊗ 💻 🍴 ⇔

❀   **END METROPOLITAN AREA**   ❀

TRENTON
♦♦ ♦♦ Comfort Inn 🅂🄷 ❀
(613) 965-6660. **$97-$124.** 68 Monogram Pl. Hwy 401, exit 526 (Glen Miller Rd S). Int corridors. **Pets:** Other species. Designated rooms, service with restrictions, supervision.
🄰🅂🄺 🖪 ⊗ 🅶🄼 🖥 💻

♦♦♦ ♦♦♦ Holiday Inn Trenton 🅂🄷
(613) 394-4855. **$140-$150.** 99 Glen Miller Rd. Hwy 401, exit 526 (Glen Miller Rd S). Int corridors. **Pets:** Medium. $5 daily fee/room. Designated rooms, service with restrictions, supervision.
🄰🅂🄺 🖪 ⊗ 🖥 💻 🍴 ⇔ ⊠

TWEED
♦♦ Park Place Motel 🄼
(613) 478-3134. **$59.** 43 Victoria St. Hwy 37, 0.5 km s of centre. Ext corridors. **Pets:** Service with restrictions.
🖥

WALLACEBURG
🄒🄐🄐 ♦♦ ♦♦ Super 8 Motel 🅂🄷
(519) 627-0781. **$69-$99.** 76 McNaughton Ave. On Hwy 40 (McNaughton Ave), south side of town. Int corridors. **Pets:** $10 daily fee/pet. Supervision.
🅂🄰🅅🄴 🖪 ⊗ 🖥

WASAGA BEACH
♦♦ Kingsbridge Inn 🄼
(705) 429-6364. **$60-$220, 60 day notice.** 268 Main St. Hwy 92, just n. Ext corridors. **Pets:** Small. $100 deposit/room, $20 daily fee/room. Designated rooms, service with restrictions, crate.
⊗ 🖥 💻 ⇔ ⊠ 🅩

WATERLOO
♦♦ ♦♦ Comfort Inn 🅂🄷
(519) 747-9400. **$99-$149.** 190 Weber St N. East side off Weber St, 0.3 km s of University Ave (Hwy 86). Int corridors. **Pets:** Supervision.
🄰🅂🄺 🖪 ⊗ 🖥 💻 🍴

♦♦♦ ♦♦♦ Les Diplomates B&B (Executive Guest
House) 🄱🄱
(519) 725-3184. **$110-$149.** 100 Blythwood Rd. Hwy 86 N, exit King St, s to Columbia, w to Hazel St, then e. Ext/int corridors. **Pets:** Accepted.
🄰🅂🄺 🖪 ⊗ 🖥

▼▼▼ The Waterloo Inn & Conference Centre 🆂🅷
(519) 884-0220. **$129-$149.** 475 King St N. 3 km n on King St, jct Hwy 86. Int corridors. **Pets:** Medium. $15 daily fee/pet. Designated rooms, service with restrictions, supervision.

WAWA

▼ Kinniwabi Pines Motel/Cottages 🅼
(705) 856-7302. **$50-$68.** 52 Hwy 17. Hwy 17, 5.3 km s of jct Hwy 101. Ext corridors. **Pets:** $8 daily fee/pet. Designated rooms, service with restrictions, supervision.

▼ Parkway Motel 🅼
(705) 856-7020. **$52-$63.** 938 Hwy 17. Hwy 17, 4 km s of jct Hwy 101. Ext corridors. **Pets:** Accepted.

▼ Sportsman's Motel 🅼
(705) 856-2272. **$75-$79.** 45 Mission Rd. Hwy 101, 2.4 km e of jct Hwy 17. Ext corridors. **Pets:** Medium. $10 daily fee/room. Designated rooms, service with restrictions, supervision.

Ⓐ ▼ Wawa Northern Lights Motel & Chalets 🅼
(705) 856-1900. **$79-$99.** 80 Hwy 17 N. 8 km n of jct Hwy 101. Ext corridors. **Pets:** Other species. Supervision.

WESTPORT

▼▼▼ Stepping Stone Inn 🅱🅱
(613) 273-3806. **$80-$175, 10 day notice.** 328 Centreville Rd. Jct Hwy 42 and CR 10, 3 km s on CR 10, follow signs. Int corridors. **Pets:** Accepted.

WHITBY

▼ ▼ Motel 6 #1907 🆂🅷
(905) 665-8883. **$71-$91.** 165 Consumers Dr. Hwy 401, exit 410 (Brock St/Hwy 12), just ne. Int corridors. **Pets:** Accepted.

Ⓐ ▼▼▼ Quality Suites 🆂🅷
(905) 432-8800. **$145-$199.** 1700 Champlain Ave. Hwy 401, exit 412 (Thickson Rd), 0.5 km n to Champlain, just 1 km e. Int corridors. **Pets:** Accepted.

WHITEFISH FALLS

Ⓐ ▼▼▼▼ The Island Lodge 🅲🅰
(705) 285-4343. **$164-$184 (no credit cards), 21 day notice.** In Whitefish Falls; parking and dock, just w of Hwy 6 (phone for boat at Espanola or Little Current). Ext corridors. **Pets:** Accepted.

WINDSOR

▼▼▼ Comfort Inn 🆂🅷
(519) 966-7800. **$105-$160.** 2955 Dougall Ave. 5.3 km s on Hwy 3B, off Hwy 401 via Detroit-Windsor Tunnel exit. Int corridors. **Pets:** Other species. $10 daily fee/room. Service with restrictions, supervision.

Ⓐ ▼▼▼▼ Hampton Inn and Suites 🆂🅷
(519) 972-0770. **$129-$159.** 1840 Huron Church Rd. 1.5 km n of EC Row Expwy. Int corridors. **Pets:** Service with restrictions, supervision.

Ⓐ ▼▼▼▼ Hilton Windsor 🅻🅷
(519) 973-5555. **$129-$199.** 277 Riverside Dr W. 1 km w of Detroit-Windsor Tunnel; 1 km e of Ambassador Bridge; downtown. Int corridors. **Pets:** Accepted.

Ⓐ ▼▼▼▼ Holiday Inn Select 🅻🅷
(519) 966-1200. **$139-$179.** 1855 Huron Church Rd. Jct Huron Church and Malden rds; 1.5 km n of EC Row Expwy. Int corridors. **Pets:** Other species. $25 deposit/room. Service with restrictions, supervision.

Ⓐ ▼▼▼▼ Quality Suites Windsor 🆂🅷
(519) 977-9707. **$249.** 250 Dougall Ave. Jct Dougall Ave and Chatham St; downtown. Int corridors. **Pets:** Accepted.

Ⓐ ▼▼▼▼ Radisson Riverfront Hotel 🅻🅷
(519) 977-9777. **$129-$199.** 333 Riverside Dr W. 1 km w of Detroit-Windsor Tunnel; 1 km e of Ambassador Bridge. Int corridors. **Pets:** Very small. Service with restrictions, crate.

▼▼▼ Royal Marquis Hotel 🆂🅷
(519) 966-1900. **$100-$120, 7 day notice.** 590 Grand Marais Rd E. Just n of Devonshire Mall and the EC Row Expwy. Int corridors. **Pets:** Accepted.

WOODSTOCK

Ⓐ ▼▼▼▼ Quality Hotel and Suites 🆂🅷
(519) 537-5586. **$299.** 580 Bruin Blvd. Hwy 401, exit 232, just n; w of Hwy 59. Int corridors. **Pets:** $50 deposit/room. Service with restrictions, supervision.

▼▼ Super 8 Motel 🆂🅷
(519) 421-4588. **$80-$150.** 560 Norwich Ave. Jct Hwy 401 and 59, exit 232, just n. Int corridors. **Pets:** Service with restrictions, supervision.

WYOMING

▼ ▼ Country View Motel and RV Camping Resort 🅼
(519) 845-3394. **$64-$69, 7 day notice.** 4569 London Line. Hwy 402, exit 25, 1 km s on Hwy 21 to Hwy 22, then just e. Ext corridors. **Pets:** Small. $10 daily fee/pet. Designated rooms, service with restrictions, supervision.

PRINCE EDWARD ISLAND

CITY INDEX

CAVENDISH

◆◆◆ Bay Vista Motor Inn M
(902) 963-2225. **$49-$95, 3 day notice.** 9517 Cavendish Rd. Jct Rt 13, 4.8 km w on Rt 6. Ext corridors. **Pets:** Small. $4 daily fee/room. Service with restrictions, supervision.
⊠ 🖥 ⇒ ☎

◆◆ Cavendish Bosom Buddies Cottages CA
(902) 963-3449. **$80-$280, 14 day notice.** RR 1. Jct Rt 6 and 13, 0.6 km e on Rt 6. Ext corridors. **Pets:** Large. Service with restrictions, supervision.
⊠ 🖥 ⊠ 🐾 ☎

CAA ◆◆◆ Cavendish Maples Cottages CA
(902) 963-2818. **$105-$270, 30 day notice.** Jct Rt 6 and 13, 2.5 km w on Rt 6. Ext corridors. **Pets:** Small. Designated rooms, service with restrictions, supervision.
SAVE 🖥 ⇒ ⊠ 🐾 ☎

CHARLOTTETOWN

CAA ◆◆◆ Best Western Charlottetown SH
(902) 892-2461. **$144-$224.** 238 Grafton St. Centre. Int corridors. **Pets:** Small. $100 deposit/room. Designated rooms, service with restrictions, supervision.
SAVE 📶 ⊠ 🦽 🎦 🔔 🖥 🖵 🍴 ⇒ ⊠

◆◆◆ Comfort Inn SH
(902) 566-4424. **$109-$159.** 112 Trans-Canada Hwy 1. Trans-Canada Hwy 1, 4.5 km w. Int corridors. **Pets:** Service with restrictions, supervision.
ASK 📶 ⊠ 🖵

◆◆ Delta Prince Edward LH
(902) 566-2222. **$121-$202.** 18 Queen St. Centre. Int corridors. **Pets:** Accepted.
ASK 📶 ⊠ 🖵 🍴 ⇒ ⊠

◆◆ Econo Lodge M
(902) 368-1110. **$69-$109, 30 day notice.** 20 Lower Malpeque Rd. Jct of Trans-Canada Hwy 1 and Lower Malpeque Rd, 4.5 km w. Ext/int corridors. **Pets:** Medium, other species. $100 deposit/room. Designated rooms, service with restrictions, crate.
ASK 📶 ⊠ 🔔 🖥 🖵 ⇒

CAA ◆◆◆ Holiday Inn Express Hotel & Suites SH
(902) 892-1201. **$99-$166.** 200 Trans-Canada Hwy. On Trans-Canada Hwy 1, 4.8 km w. Int corridors. **Pets:** Accepted.
SAVE 📶 ⊠ 🦽 🎦 🔔 🖥 🖵 ⇒ ⊠

◆◆ Quality Inn Charlottetown SH
(902) 894-8572. **$140-$261.** 150 Euston St. Centre. Int corridors. **Pets:** Accepted.
ASK 📶 ⊠ 🔔 🖥 🖵 🍴

◆◆◆ Rodd Charlottetown-A Rodd Signature Hotel SH
(902) 894-7371. **$103-$230.** Kent & Pownal sts. Centre. Int corridors. **Pets:** Large. Service with restrictions, supervision.
ASK 📶 ⊠ 🔔 🖥 🖵 🍴 ⇒ ⊠

◆◆ Rodd Confederation Inn & Suites M
(902) 892-2481. **$70-$120.** Trans-Canada Hwy 1. On Trans-Canada Hwy 1, 4 km w. Ext/int corridors. **Pets:** Accepted.
ASK 📶 ⊠ 🔔 🖥 🖵 🍴 ⇒

◆◆ Rodd Royalty Inn SH
(902) 894-8566. **$81-$170.** Intersection Hwy 1 & 2. 4 km w on Trans-Canada Hwy 1. Ext/int corridors. **Pets:** Medium. Designated rooms.
ASK 📶 ⊠ 🔔 🖥 🖵 🍴 ⇒

CORNWALL

◆ Sunny King Motel M
(902) 566-2209. **$50-$118.** On Hwy 1; centre. Ext corridors. **Pets:** Large, dogs only. Designated rooms, service with restrictions, supervision.
ASK 📶 ⊠ 🔔 🖥 🖵 ⇒ 🐾

MAYFIELD

◆◆ Quality Inn Mayfield M
(902) 963-2213. **$89-$175.** On Rt 13, 6 km w of Cavendish; centre. Ext/int corridors. **Pets:** Accepted.
ASK 📶 ⊠ 🔔 🖥 🖵 ⇒

MONTAGUE

◆◆◆ Rodd Marina Inn & Suites SH
(902) 838-4075. **$73-$153.** 115 Sackville St. Centre. Int corridors. **Pets:** $10 daily fee/room. Designated rooms, service with restrictions, supervision.
ASK 📶 ⊠ 🦽 🔔 🖥 🖵

NORTH RUSTICO

◆ St. Lawrence Motel M
(902) 963-2053. **$45-$149, 14 day notice.** On Gulf Shore Rd. Ext corridors. **Pets:** Accepted.
⊠ 🔔 🖥 🖵 ⊠ 🐾 ☎

RICHMOND

◆◆◆ Caernarvon Cottages, BB in Bayside CA
(902) 854-3418. **$150, 30 day notice.** 4697 Hwy 12, RR 1. Jct Hwy 2 and Rt 131, 10 km e. Ext/int corridors. **Pets:** Designated rooms, service with restrictions, supervision.
🔔 🖵 🐾

ROSENEATH

▼▼▼ **Rodd Brudenell River-A Rodd Signature Resort** 🇱🇭
(902) 652-2332. **$119-$226, 3 day notice.** Jct Rt 4 and 3, 5.5 km e on Rt 3. Ext/int corridors. **Pets:** Accepted.
(ASK) (S/O) (X) (🔒) (💻) (🍴) (➤) (❌)

ST. PETERS

▼▼ **Greenwich Gate Lodge** Ⓜ
(902) 961-3496. **$69-$129, 7 day notice.** Rt 2. Jct Rt 2 and 16; centre. Ext corridors. **Pets:** Small, dogs only. Service with restrictions, supervision.
(ASK) (S/O) (X) (🔒) (💻)

SUMMERSIDE

▼▼ **Econo Lodge** 🇸🇭
(902) 436-9100. **$80-$140.** 80 All Weather Hwy. Jct Hwy 1A and 2, 5 km w on Hwy 2. Int corridors. **Pets:** Other species. Designated rooms, service with restrictions, supervision.
(ASK) (X) (🔒) (💻) (🍴) (➤)

Ⓐ ▼▼▼ **Quality Inn Garden of the Gulf** Ⓜ
(902) 436-2295. **$82-$279, 7 day notice.** 618 Water St. 1.6 km e on Hwy 11. Ext/int corridors. **Pets:** Designated rooms, service with restrictions, supervision.
(SAVE) (S/O) (X) (🔒) (💻) (➤)

WOODSTOCK

▼▼ **Rodd Mill River Resort** 🇸🇭
(902) 859-3555. **$80-$178, 3 day notice.** Rt 180. On Rt 136, just e of jct Rt 2. Int corridors. **Pets:** Accepted.
(ASK) (S/O) (X) (💻) (🍴) (➤) (❌)

QUEBEC

ALMA

▼▼ Comfort Inn SH
(418) 668-9221. **$82-$91.** 870 ave du Pont S. On Hwy 169; centre of town. Int corridors. **Pets:** Accepted.
ASK SD X H

▼▼ Hotel Motel Les Cascades M
(418) 662-6547. **$55-$70.** 140 ave du Pont N. On Hwy 169, just n of bridge; centre. Ext/int corridors. **Pets:** Accepted.
ASK SD X 🖵 TI

AYLMER

▼▼▼ Chateau Cartier Relais-Resort LH
(819) 778-0000. **$115-$165.** 1170 chemin Aylmer. On Hwy 148, 1 km w of Champlain Bridge. Int corridors. **Pets:** $25 one-time fee/room. Designated rooms, service with restrictions, supervision.
ASK SD X H 🖵 TI 🛥 🗙

BAIE-COMEAU

▼▼ Comfort Inn SH
(418) 589-8252. **$108-$119.** 745 boul Lafleche. On Rt 138. Int corridors. **Pets:** Service with restrictions, supervision.
ASK X H

▼▼▼ Hotel Le Manoir SH
(418) 296-3391. **$89-$109.** 8 ave Cabot. Rt 138, 4.4 km e, follow signs. Int corridors. **Pets:** Accepted.
ASK SD X 🖵 TI 🗙

BAIE-ST-PAUL

▼▼ Hotel Baie-Saint-Paul SH
(418) 435-3683. **$64-$129, 3 day notice.** 911 boul Mgr-de-Laval. On Rt 138, 0.5 km e of Rt 362. Int corridors. **Pets:** Dogs only. $5 daily fee/room. Service with restrictions, supervision.
X H 🖵 TI

BERTHIERVILLE

▼▼ Days Inn Berthierville SH
(450) 836-1621. **$82-$165.** 760 rue Gadoury. Hwy 40, exit 144. Ext/int corridors. **Pets:** Medium. Designated rooms, service with restrictions, supervision.
ASK SD X H 🖵

CHICOUTIMI

▼▼ Comfort Inn SH
(418) 693-8686. **$85-$98.** 1595 boul Talbot. Jct Rt 170, 2.8 km n. Int corridors. **Pets:** Medium. Service with restrictions, supervision.
ASK SD X H 🖵

▼▼ Hotel La Sagueneenne SH
(418) 545-8326. **$78-$103.** 250 des Sagueneens. Just w of jct Rt 175 (boul Talbot). Int corridors. **Pets:** Small. Service with restrictions, supervision.
ASK SD X H 🖵 TI 🛥

COWANSVILLE

▼▼ Days Inn-Cowansville SH ❀
(450) 263-7331. **$70-$95.** 111 place Jean-Jacques Bertrand. Hwy 10, exit 68, 15.9 km s on Rt 139. Int corridors. **Pets:** Service with restrictions, supervision.
ASK SD X 🖵 TI

DRUMMONDVILLE

(CAA) ▼▼▼ Best Western Hotel Universel SH
(819) 478-4971. **$109-$239.** 915 rue Hains. Hwy 20, exit 177, 0.3 km s on boul St-Joseph, then just e. Int corridors. **Pets:** Accepted.
SAVE SD X H 🖵 TI 🛥

▼▼ Comfort Inn SH
(819) 477-4000. **$87-$123, 3 day notice.** 1055 rue Hains. Hwy 20, exit 177, 0.5 km s on boul St-Joseph, then just w. Int corridors. **Pets:** Designated rooms, service with restrictions, supervision.
ASK SD X H 🖵

GASPE

▼▼▼ Hotel des Commandants SH
(418) 368-3355. **$99-$135.** 178 rue de la Reine. Rt 132, 0.5 km e of bridge; centre. Ext/int corridors. **Pets:** Small. Designated rooms, service with restrictions, supervision.
X H 🖵 TI 🗙

▼▼ Motel Adams M
(418) 368-2244. **$89-$99.** 20 rue Adams. Corner of rue Jacques Cartier; centre. Ext/int corridors. **Pets:** Very small. Service with restrictions, supervision.
X H 🖵 TI

GATINEAU

ⒶⒶ ♦♦ Comfort Inn Gatineau 🅂🄷
(819) 243-6010. $98-$135. 630 boul La Gappe. Hwy 50, exit 140, 2 km e. Int corridors. Pets: Designated rooms, service with restrictions, supervision.
[SAVE] [S❄] [✕] [🛏] [🖳]

GRANBY

♦♦ Hotel Le Castel 🅂🄷
(450) 378-9071. $65-$120. 901 rue Principale. On Rt 112, 1 km e of jct Rt 139; Hwy 10, exit 68. Int corridors. Pets: Accepted.
[ASK] [✕] [🛏] [🖳] [¶¶] [⇀]

HULL

ⒶⒶ ♦♦♦♦ Four Points by Sheraton & Conference Centre Gatineau-Ottawa 🄻🄷
(819) 778-6111. $99-$189. 35 rue Laurier. Corner rue Victoria, across from Canadian Museum of Civilization. Int corridors. Pets: Small. $100 deposit/room. Designated rooms, service with restrictions, supervision.
[SAVE] [S❄] [✕] [🛏] [🖳] [¶¶] [⇀]

ⒶⒶ ♦♦♦♦ Holiday Inn Plaza la Chaudiere 🄻🄷
(819) 778-3880. $112. 2 rue Montcalm. 0.8 km w of Portage Bridge at jct Rt 148 and rue Montcalm. Int corridors. Pets: Large. Service with restrictions, supervision.
[SAVE] [S❄] [✕] [🛏] [🖳] [¶¶] [⇀] [✕]

LA MALBAIE

ⒶⒶ ♦♦♦♦ Fairmont Le Manoir Richelieu 🄻🄷
(418) 665-3703. $149-$299. 181 rue Richelieu. On Rt 362, 4.1 km w of jct Rt 138. Int corridors. Pets: Accepted.
[SAVE] [S❄] [✕] [🛏] [🖳] [¶¶] [⇀] [✕]

LA POCATIERE

♦♦ Motel Le Pocatois 🄼
(418) 856-1688. $65-$79. 235 Rt 132. Hwy 20, exit 439, 0.8 km s. Ext/int corridors. Pets: Small. Service with restrictions, supervision.
[S❄] [✕] [🛏] [¶¶]

LENNOXVILLE

ⒶⒶ ♦ La Paysanne Motel 🄼
(819) 569-5585. $70-$80. 42 rue Queen. On Rt 143. Ext/int corridors. Pets: Accepted.
[SAVE] [S❄] [✕] [¶¶] [⇀]

LOUISEVILLE

♦♦♦ Gite du Carrefour et Maison historique J.L.L. Hamelin 🄱🄱
(819) 228-4932. $75-$85 (no credit cards), 15 day notice. 11 ave St-Laurent ouest. On Rt 138; Hwy 40, exit 174 westbound; exit 166 eastbound; centre. Int corridors. Pets: Accepted.
[ASK] [✕] [K] [W] [☎]

MAGOG

♦♦ Auberge Memphre 🅂🄷
(819) 847-2222. $137-$147. 1007 Merry N. Hwy 10, exit 118, 1.6 km s on Rt 141. Int corridors. Pets: Accepted.
[✕] [🖳] [¶¶] [⇀]

MARIA

♦♦ Hotel Honguedo 🅂🄷
(418) 759-3488. $82-$145. 548 boul Perron. On Rt 132, in town centre. Ext/int corridors. Pets: Accepted.
[ASK] [S❄] [✕] [🛏] [🖳] [¶¶] [⇀]

MATANE

ⒶⒶ ♦ Motel La Marina 🄼
(418) 562-3234. $50-$73. 1032 ave du Phare ouest. On Rt 132. Ext corridors. Pets: Dogs only. Supervision.
[SAVE] [✕] [🛏] [🖳] [⇀] [K]

MONTEBELLO

♦♦ ♦♦ Fairmont Le Chateau Montebello 🄻🄷 ❖
(819) 423-6341. $179-$269, 3 day notice. 392 rue Notre-Dame. On Rt 148. Int corridors. Pets: Other species. $35 daily fee/pet. Service with restrictions, crate.
[ASK] [S❄] [✕] [🛏] [🖳] [¶¶] [⇀] [✕]

MONTMAGNY

♦♦♦ Manoir des Erables 🄲🄸
(418) 248-0100. $89-$160, 10 day notice. 220 boul Tache est (Rt 132). Hwy 20, exit 376, 2.2 km e on Rt 228, 1.5 km e. Ext/int corridors. Pets: Small, other species. $15 daily fee/pet. Designated rooms, service with restrictions, crate.
[✕] [🖳] [¶¶] [⇀] [✕]

MONTREAL METROPOLITAN AREA

BOUCHERVILLE

♦♦ Comfort Inn 🄼
(450) 641-2880. $111-$150. 96 boul de Mortagne. Hwy 20, exit 92, just n. Int corridors. Pets: Small. Designated rooms, service with restrictions, supervision.
[ASK] [S❄] [✕] [🖳]

BROSSARD

♦♦ Comfort Inn 🅂🄷
(450) 678-9350. $84-$92. 7863 boul Taschereau. Rt 134, 1.5 km w of Hwy 10, exit boul Taschereau ouest. Int corridors. Pets: Accepted.
[ASK] [S❄] [✕] [🛏]

DORVAL

Ⓐ ▼▼▼ Comfort Inn Dorval 𝐒𝐇
(514) 636-3391. **$100-$130.** 340 ave Michel-Jasmin. Hwy 520, exit 2 eastbound; exit 1 westbound, 0.3 km along service road to ave Marshall, follow to ave Michel-Jasmin. Int corridors. **Pets:** Designated rooms, service with restrictions.
𝐒𝐀𝐕𝐄 🐾 ✕ 🗄

Ⓐ ▼▼▼ Hampton Inn & Suites 𝐒𝐇
(514) 633-8243. **$140-$175.** 1900 route Transcanadienne (Hwy 40). Hwy 40, exit 55, 0.8 km e of boul Sources on south side service road. Int corridors. **Pets:** Other species. $50 deposit/room. Designated rooms, service with restrictions.
𝐒𝐀𝐕𝐄 🐾 ✕ 🅼 🗄 💻 ➤

Ⓐ ▼▼▼ Travelodge Dorval Airport 𝐒𝐇 🐾
(514) 631-4537. **$93-$148.** 1010 chemin Herron. Hwy 20, exit 54 westbound, just s on boul Fenelon to ave Dumont, follow to chemin Herron; exit 56 eastbound, 1.7 km along service road. Int corridors. **Pets:** $40 deposit/room. Designated rooms, service with restrictions.
𝐒𝐀𝐕𝐄 🐾 ✕ 🗄 💻 ✕

LAVAL

▼▼ Comfort Inn 𝐒𝐇
(450) 686-0600. **$105-$123.** 2055 Autoroute des Laurentides. Hwy 15, exit 8, e on boul St-Martin, 0.7 km n on boul Le Corbusier, w on boul Tessier. Int corridors. **Pets:** Other species. Service with restrictions, supervision.
𝐀𝐒𝐊 🐾 ✕ 🗄 🍴

▼▼ Econo Lodge 𝐒𝐇
(450) 681-6411. **$90-$169.** 1981 boul Cure Labelle. Hwy 15, exit 8 northbound; exit 10 southbound, 2.2 km w on boul St-Martin ouest, then 0.5 km n. Ext/int corridors. **Pets:** Designated rooms, service with restrictions, supervision.
𝐀𝐒𝐊 🐾 ✕ 🗄 💻 ➤

Ⓐ ▼▼▼ Quality Suites Laval 𝐒𝐇
(450) 686-6777. **$127-$146.** 2035 Autoroute des Laurentides. Hwy 15, exit 8, e on boul St-Martin, 0.7 km n on boul Le Corbusier, w on boul Tessier. Int corridors. **Pets:** Other species. Service with restrictions, crate.
𝐒𝐀𝐕𝐄 🐾 ✕ 🗄 💻

LONGUEUIL

▼▼ Days Inn Longueuil 𝐒𝐇
(450) 677-8911. **$80-$99, 3 day notice.** 2800 boul Marie-Victorin. Hwy 20/Rt 132, exit 15 eastbound, follow signs for boul Marie-Victorin est; exit 90 westbound from Pont-Tunnel Louis-Hippolyte-Lafontaine. Int corridors. **Pets:** Small. Service with restrictions.
𝐀𝐒𝐊 🐾 ✕ 💻 🍴

▼▼▼ Holiday Inn Montreal-Longueuil 𝐒𝐇
(450) 646-8100. **$119-$169, 10 day notice.** 900 rue St-Charles est. Rt 132, exit 11. Int corridors. **Pets:** Other species. Service with restrictions, supervision.
𝐀𝐒𝐊 🐾 ✕ 🗄 💻 🍴 ➤

MONTREAL

Ⓐ ▼▼▼ Chateau Versailles Hotel 𝐒𝐇 🐾
(514) 933-3611. **$205-$300.** 1659 rue Sherbrooke ouest. Corner rue St-Mathieu. Int corridors. **Pets:** $15 daily fee/room. Designated rooms, service with restrictions, supervision.
𝐒𝐀𝐕𝐄 🐾 ✕ 💻

▼▼▼ Crowne Plaza Montreal Centre 𝐋𝐇
(514) 842-8581. **$139-$189.** 505 Sherbrooke est. Between rue Berri and St-Hubert. Int corridors. **Pets:** Small. Service with restrictions, supervision.
𝐀𝐒𝐊 🐾 ✕ 💻 🍴 ➤ ✕

Ⓐ ▼▼▼ Delta Montreal 𝐋𝐇
(514) 286-1986. **$169-$330.** 475 ave President Kennedy. Corner rue City Councillors. Int corridors. **Pets:** $30 one-time fee/room. Designated rooms, service with restrictions, crate.
𝐒𝐀𝐕𝐄 🐾 ✕ 🗄 💻 🍴 ➤ ✕

Ⓐ ▼▼▼ Fairmont The Queen Elizabeth 𝐋𝐇 🐾
(514) 861-3511. **$159-$199.** 900 boul Rene-Levesque ouest. Between rue Universite and Mansfield. Int corridors. **Pets:** Small, other species. $25 daily fee/room. Service with restrictions, supervision.
𝐒𝐀𝐕𝐄 ✕ 🅼 🗄 💻 🍴 ➤ ✕

Ⓐ ▼▼▼ Four Points by Sheraton Montreal Centre-Ville 𝐋𝐇
(514) 842-3961. **$149-$159.** 475 rue Sherbrooke ouest. Between rue Durocher and Aylmer. Int corridors. **Pets:** Service with restrictions, supervision.
𝐒𝐀𝐕𝐄 🐾 ✕ 🗄 💻 🍴 ✕

Ⓐ ▼▼▼▼ Hilton Montreal Bonaventure 𝐋𝐇
(514) 878-2332. **$159-$269.** 900 rue de La Gauchetiere W, Ste 10750. Corner of Mansfield and de la Gauchetiere. Int corridors. **Pets:** Accepted.
𝐒𝐀𝐕𝐄 🐾 ✕ 🗄 💻 🍴 ➤ ✕

▼▼▼ Holiday Inn Montreal-Midtown 𝐋𝐇
(514) 842-6111. **$119-$169.** 420 rue Sherbrooke ouest. Between rue Bleury and City Councillors. Int corridors. **Pets:** Small. Designated rooms, service with restrictions, supervision.
𝐀𝐒𝐊 🐾 ✕ 🗄 💻 🍴 ➤ ✕

▼▼▼ Hotel Gault 𝐒𝐇
(514) 904-1616. **$349.** 449 rue Ste-Helene. Just s of rue Notre-Dame. Int corridors. **Pets:** Medium, other species. $8 daily fee/pet. Service with restrictions, crate.
✕ 🗄

▼▼▼▼ Hotel Inter-Continental Montreal 𝐋𝐇
(514) 987-9900. **$280-$425.** 360 rue St-Antoine ouest. Corner of rue St-Pierre. Int corridors. **Pets:** Accepted.
𝐀𝐒𝐊 ✕ 🗄 💻 🍴 ➤ ✕

▼▼▼ Hotel Le Germain 𝐒𝐇
(514) 849-2050. **$230-$290.** 2050 rue Mansfield. Just n of ave President Kennedy. Int corridors. **Pets:** $30 daily fee/pet. Supervision.
✕ 🗄 💻 🍴

▼▼▼ ▼▼▼ Hotel Le St-James SH ❖
(514) 841-3111. **$400-$675.** 355 rue St-Jacques ouest. Corner of rue St-Pierre. Int corridors. **Pets:** Small. Service with restrictions, supervision.
⊠

Ⓒ▲ ▼▼▼▼ Hotel Maritime Plaza LH
(514) 932-1411. **$169-$329.** 1155 rue Guy. Corner of boul Rene-Levesque; centre. Int corridors. **Pets:** Accepted.
SAVE S🐾 ⊠ 🛅 💻 ¶ 🏊

▼▼▼▼ Hotel Omni Mont-Royal LH
(514) 284-1110. **$160-$329.** 1050 rue Sherbrooke ouest. Corner rue Peel. Int corridors. **Pets:** Accepted.
A$K ⊠ 🐾 🛅 ¶ 🏊 ⊠

Ⓒ▲ ▼▼▼▼ Hyatt Regency Montreal LH
(514) 285-1450. **$165-$239.** 1255 rue Jeanne-Mance CP 130. Corner rue Ste-Catherine. Int corridors. **Pets:** Accepted.
SAVE S🐾 ⊠ &M 🛅 💻 ¶ 🏊 ⊠

▼▼▼▼ La Presidence Appartements De Luxe CO
(514) 842-9988. **$129-$169.** 505 rue Sherbrooke est. Between rue Berri and St-Hubert. Int corridors. **Pets:** Medium. Service with restrictions, supervision.
A$K S🐾 ⊠ 🛅 💻 ¶ 🏊 ⊠

Ⓒ▲ ▼▼▼ ▼▼▼ Le Centre Sheraton LH ❖
(514) 878-2000. **$299-$650.** 1201 boul Rene-Levesque ouest. Between rue Drummond and Stanley. Int corridors. **Pets:** Medium. Service with restrictions, supervision.
SAVE ⊠ 🐾 🛅 💻 ¶ 🏊 ⊠

Ⓒ▲ ▼▼▼▼ Le Meridien Versailles-Montreal SH ❖
(514) 933-8111. **$169-$285.** 1808 rue Sherbrooke ouest. Corner rue St-Mathieu. Int corridors. **Pets:** $15 daily fee/room. Designated rooms, service with restrictions, supervision.
SAVE S🐾 ⊠ 🛅 💻

Ⓒ▲ ▼▼▼ ▼▼▼ Le Saint-Sulpice Hotel Montreal SH
(514) 288-1000. **$239-$489.** 414 rue St-Sulpice. Just n of rue St-Paul. Int corridors. **Pets:** Accepted.
SAVE ⊠ 🛅 💻 ¶

▼▼▼▼ Le Square Phillips Hotel & Suites SH
(514) 393-1193. **$165-$315.** 1193 Place Phillips. Between rue Ste-Catherine and boul Rene-Levesque. Int corridors. **Pets:** Medium. Service with restrictions, supervision.
A$K S🐾 ⊠ 🛅 💻 🏊

Ⓒ▲ ▼▼▼ ▼▼▼ Loews Hotel Vogue LH ❖
(514) 285-5555. **$152-$428.** 1425 rue de la Montagne. Between rue Ste-Catherine and boul de Maisonneuve. Int corridors. **Pets:** Other species. Designated rooms.
SAVE S🐾 ⊠ 🛅 ¶

Ⓒ▲ ▼▼▼▼ Marriott Residence Inn-Montreal Downtown SH
(514) 982-6064. **$140-$425.** 2045 rue Peel. Between rue Sherbrooke and boul de Maisonneuve. Int corridors. **Pets:** Medium. $250 one-time fee/room. Service with restrictions, crate.
SAVE S🐾 ⊠ 🛅 💻 🏊

▼▼▼▼ Novotel Montreal Centre LH
(514) 861-6000. **$159-$240.** 1180 rue de la Montagne. Between rue Ste-Catherine and boul Rene-Levesque. Int corridors. **Pets:** Accepted.
A$K S🐾 ⊠ 🛅 ¶ ⊠

Ⓒ▲ ▼▼▼▼ Quality Hotel Downtown Montreal SH
(514) 849-1413. **$164-$330.** 3440 ave du Parc. Between rue Sherbrooke and Milton. Int corridors. **Pets:** Accepted.
SAVE S🐾 ⊠ 🛅 💻 ¶

Ⓒ▲ ▼▼▼▼ Residence Inn by Marriott Montreal Westmount LH
(514) 935-9224. **$109-$149.** 2170 ave Lincoln. Just e of rue Atwater. Int corridors. **Pets:** Small. $250 one-time fee/pet. Service with restrictions, supervision.
SAVE S🐾 ⊠ &M 🛅 💻 🏊

▼▼▼ ▼▼▼ The Ritz-Carlton, Montreal LH ❖
(514) 842-4212. **$198-$445.** 1228 rue Sherbrooke ouest. Corner de la Montagne. Int corridors. **Pets:** $150 one-time fee/room. Service with restrictions, supervision.
⊠ ¶ ⊠

▼▼▼ ▼▼▼ Sofitel Montreal SH
(514) 285-9000. **$199-$500.** 1155 rue Sherbrooke ouest. Corner of rue Stanley. Int corridors. **Pets:** Medium. $20 daily fee/pet. Designated rooms, service with restrictions, supervision.
A$K S🐾 ⊠ 🛅 ¶ ⊠

Ⓒ▲ ▼▼ Travelodge Montreal Centre SH
(514) 874-9090. **$109-$129.** 50 boul Rene-Levesque ouest. Between rue Clark and St-Urbain. Int corridors. **Pets:** Accepted.
SAVE ⊠ 💻 ¶

POINTE-CLAIRE

Ⓒ▲ ▼▼ ▼▼ Comfort Inn SH
(514) 697-6210. **$99-$175.** 700 boul St-Jean. Hwy 40, exit 52, 0.3 km s. Int corridors. **Pets:** Accepted.
SAVE S🐾 ⊠ 🛅 💻

Ⓒ▲ ▼▼▼▼ Holiday Inn Pointe-Claire Montreal Airport LH
(514) 697-7110. **$125-$179.** 6700 Transcanadienne. Hwy 40, exit 52, south side service road. Int corridors. **Pets:** Accepted.
SAVE S🐾 ⊠ 🛅 💻 ¶ 🏊 ⊠

Ⓒ▲ ▼▼▼▼ Quality Suites SH
(514) 426-5060. **$119-$159.** 6300 Rt Transcanadienne. Hwy 40, exit 52, south side service road; westbound, follow signs for boul St-Jean sud and Hwy 40 est to access south side service road. Int corridors. **Pets:** Designated rooms, service with restrictions, crate.
SAVE S🐾 ⊠ &M 🛅 💻 ¶

ROSEMERE

(CAA) ▼▼▼ **Hotel Le Rivage** SH
(450) 437-2171. **$79-$249.** 125 boul LaBelle. Hwy 15, exit 19, 1.4 km e on Rt 344, then 0.5 km s. Int corridors. **Pets:** Accepted.
[SAVE] [X] [⊟] [≈]

ST-LAURENT

▼▼▼ **Holiday Inn Aeroport Montreal** SH
(514) 739-3391. **$143.** 6500 Cote-de-Liesse. Hwy 520, exit 5 eastbound on south side service road; exit westbound to rue Ness, follow signs for rue Hickmore and Hwy 520 E. Ext/int corridors. **Pets:** Other species. Service with restrictions, supervision.
[ASK] [S⚡] [X] [⚿M] [⊟] [▣] [|1] [≈] [X]

(CAA) ▼▼▼ **Quality Hotel Dorval** SH
(514) 731-7821. **$145, 7 day notice.** 7700 Cote-de-Liesse. Hwy 520, exit 4 eastbound on south side service road; exit Montee-de-Liesse westbound. Int corridors. **Pets:** Medium. $20 one-time fee/pet. Designated rooms, service with restrictions, supervision.
[SAVE] [S⚡] [X] [⊟] [▣] [|1] [≈] [X]

(CAA) ▼▼▼ **Ramada Montreal Airport Hotel** SH
(514) 733-8818. **$129-$159, 7 day notice.** 7300 Cote-de-Liesse. Hwy 520, exit 4 eastbound on south side service road; exit Montee-de-Liesse westbound. Int corridors. **Pets:** Medium. Designated rooms, service with restrictions, supervision.
[SAVE] [S⚡] [X] [⊟] [▣] [|1] [≈]

❧ END METROPOLITAN AREA ❧

MONT-TREMBLANT

(CAA) ▼▼▼ **Le Grand Lodge**
Mont-Tremblant SH ❧
(819) 425-2734. **$120-$640, 8 day notice.** 2396 rue Labelle. Jct Hwy 117 and 327, 1.5 km s. Int corridors. **Pets:** Medium. $25 daily fee/room. Designated rooms, service with restrictions, supervision.
[SAVE] [X] [⊟] [▣] [|1] [≈] [X]

NEW RICHMOND

▼▼▼ **Hotel Francis** M
(418) 392-4485. **$75-$99.** 210 chemin Pardiac. Just s of Rt 132. Ext/int corridors. **Pets:** Small. $10 one-time fee/pet. Designated rooms, service with restrictions, supervision.
[ASK] [S⚡] [X] [⊟] [▣] [|1] [≈] [X]

NORTH HATLEY

(CAA) ▼▼▼▼ **Auberge Hatley** CI
(819) 842-2451. **$290-$590, 14 day notice.** CP 330-325 Virgin Hill Rd. Hwy 55, exit 29, 11 km e on Rt 108. Int corridors. **Pets:** Supervision.
[SAVE] [|1] [≈] [X]

(CAA) ▼▼▼▼ **Le Coeur d'Or B&B** BB
(819) 842-4363. **$104-$288, 7 day notice.** 85 School St. Centre. Ext/int corridors. **Pets:** Accepted.
[SAVE] [X] [⊟] [▣] [Z]

PASPEBIAC

▼▼▼ **Auberge Du Parc Inn** SH
(418) 752-3355. **$79-$135.** 68 boul Gerard D Levesque ouest. On Rt 132; centre. Ext corridors. **Pets:** Accepted.
[X] [|1] [≈] [X] [⚿]

PERCE

▼ **Au Pic de l'Aurore** CA
(418) 782-2151. **$59-$135.** 1 Rt 132. 2 km e from village. Ext corridors. **Pets:** Medium. Service with restrictions, supervision.
[X] [⊟] [▣] [⚿]

▼▼▼ **Hotel La Normandie** SH
(418) 782-2112. **$79-$209.** 221 Rt 132 ouest. Centre. Int corridors. **Pets:** Accepted.
[X] [⊟] [▣] [|1] [⚿]

▼▼▼ **Hotel/Motel Le Mirage** M
(418) 782-5151. **$69-$148, 7 day notice.** 288 Rt 132 ouest. On Rt 132. Ext corridors. **Pets:** Very small, dogs only. Service with restrictions, supervision.
[X] [⊟] [≈]

▼▼ **Hotel Motel Manoir de Perce** SH
(418) 782-2022. **$65-$148, 7 day notice.** 212 Rt 132. Centre. Ext/int corridors. **Pets:** Small. Service with restrictions, supervision.
[X] [⊟] [|1]

PINE HILL

(CAA) ▼▼▼ **Hotel du Lac Carling** LH
(450) 533-9211. **$225-$275, 14 day notice.** 2255 Rt 327. 5 km n. Int corridors. **Pets:** Accepted.
[SAVE] [S⚡] [X] [⊟] [▣] [|1] [≈] [X]

PORTNEUF

▼▼ **Hotel Le Portneuvois** SH
(418) 286-6400. **$70.** 101 rue Simeon-Delisle. Hwy 40, exit 261, then 0.5 km s on rue Provencher. Int corridors. **Pets:** Other species. Supervision.
[ASK] [X] [⊟] [▣]

QUEBEC METROPOLITAN AREA

BEAUPORT

▼▼ Comfort Inn SH
(418) 666-1226. **$85-$145.** 240 boul Ste-Anne. Hwy 440, exit Francois-de-Laval. Int corridors. **Pets:** No service, supervision.
ASK S♂ ✕ 🛏 💻

BEAUPRE

CAA ▼▼▼ Hotel Val des Neiges LH
(418) 827-5711. **$99-$169.** 201 rue Val-des-Neiges. Just off Hwy 360. Int corridors. **Pets:** Accepted.
SAVE S♂ ✕ 🛏 💻 🍴 ⇔ ✕

L'ANCIENNE-LORETTE

▼▼ Comfort Inn SH
(418) 872-5900. **$80-$145.** 1255 boul Duplessis. Jct boul Duplessis and Wilfrid-Hamel (Hwy 138). Int corridors. **Pets:** No service, supervision.
ASK S♂ ✕ 🛏 💻

LEVIS

▼▼ Comfort Inn SH
(418) 835-5605. **$87-$165.** 10 du Vallon est. Hwy 20, exit 325S eastbound; exit 325 westbound. Int corridors. **Pets:** Accepted.
ASK S♂ ✕ 🛏 💻

QUEBEC

CAA ▼▼▼ Delta Quebec LH
(418) 647-1717. **$99-$279.** 690 boul Rene-Levesque est. Just w of boul Honore-Mercier. Int corridors. **Pets:** Medium. $30 one-time fee/room. Designated rooms, service with restrictions, supervision.
SAVE S♂ ✕ 🛏 💻 🍴 ⇔ ✕

CAA ▼▼▼ Hilton Quebec LH
(418) 647-2411. **$135-$315.** 1100 boul Rene-Levesque est. Corner of ave Dufferin. Int corridors. **Pets:** Small. Designated rooms, service with restrictions, crate.
SAVE ✕ 🛏 💻 🍴 ⇔ ✕

CAA ▼▼▼ Hotel Quality Suites Quebec SH
(418) 622-4244. **$120-$175, 30 day notice.** 1600 rue Bouvier. Hwy 40, exit 312 N (Pierre Bertrand nord), 2 km w of jct Rt 358. Int corridors. **Pets:** Accepted.
SAVE S♂ ✕ 💻

CAA ▼▼ L'Hotel du Vieux Quebec SH
(418) 692-1850. **$99-$255.** 1190 rue St-Jean. Corner of rue de l'Hotel-Dieu. Int corridors. **Pets:** Designated rooms, service with restrictions, supervision.
SAVE ✕ 🛏 🍴

CAA ▼▼▼▼ Loews Le Concorde LH
(418) 647-2222. **$119-$295.** 1225 Cours du General-de-Montcalm. Corner of Grande Allee est. Int corridors. **Pets:** Accepted.
SAVE S♂ ✕ 🛏 💻 🍴 ⇔ ✕

ST-FERREOL-LES-NEIGES

CAA ▼▼ Chalets Montmorency Condominiums CO
(418) 826-2600. **$89-$129.** 1768 ave Royale. On Hwy 360. Ext corridors. **Pets:** Dogs only. $25 daily fee/pet. No service, supervision.
SAVE S♂ ✕ 🛏 💻 ⇔ ✕

CAA ▼▼ Chalets-Village Mont-Sainte-Anne CA
(418) 826-3331. **$895-$9950 (weekly), 60 day notice.** 1815 boul Les Neiges. On north side of Hwy 360; village center. Ext corridors. **Pets:** Other species. $100 one-time fee/room. Designated rooms, no service, supervision.
SAVE 🛏 💻 ✕ AC

STE-FOY

▼▼ Comfort Inn de l'Aeroport SH
(418) 872-5038. **$87-$110.** 7320 boul Wilfrid-Hamel. Hwy 138, 1.5 km w of boul Duplessis. Int corridors. **Pets:** Small, other species. Designated rooms, service with restrictions, supervision.
ASK S♂ ✕ 🛏 💻

▼▼▼ Hotel Clarion Quebec LH
(418) 653-4901. **$99-$239.** 3125 boul Hochelaga. Autoroute 73, exit 136 (Hochelaga ouest). Int corridors. **Pets:** Small. Designated rooms, service with restrictions, supervision.
ASK S♂ ✕ 🛏 💻 🍴 ⇔ ✕

▼ Motel Oncle Sam M
(418) 872-1488. **$45-$129.** 7025 boul Wilfrid-Hamel. On Hwy 138 at jct boul Duplessis. Ext corridors. **Pets:** Accepted.
✕ 🛏 ⇔

❈ END METROPOLITAN AREA ❈

RIMOUSKI

▼▼ Comfort Inn SH
(418) 724-2500. **$98-$108.** 455 boul St-Germain ouest. On Rt 132. Int corridors. **Pets:** Service with restrictions, supervision.
ASK S♂ ✕ 🛏 💻

RIVIERE-DU-LOUP

▼▼ Comfort Inn SH
(418) 867-4162. **$101-$166.** 85 boul Cartier. Hwy 20, exit 507, just sw; Hwy 185, exit 96 (Fraserville). Int corridors. **Pets:** Accepted.
ASK S♂ ✕ 💻

ROBERVAL

(CAA) ▼▼▼ Hotel Chateau Roberval LH
(418) 275-7511. **$89-$139.** 1225 boul Marcotte. On Hwy 169; centre. Int corridors. **Pets:** Small. $25 deposit/pet. Service with restrictions, supervision.
[SAVE] ⊠ 🗲 💻 🍴 🏊 ⊠

ROUYN-NORANDA

▼▼ Comfort Inn SH
(819) 797-1313. **$75-$77.** 1295 rue Lariviere. On Rt 117, 4 km s from town centre. Int corridors. **Pets:** Accepted.
[ASK] 🏊 ⊠ 🗲 💻

▼ Motel Mistral M
(819) 762-0884. **$70-$80.** 903 rue Lariviere. On Rt 117, 2 km s from town centre. Ext/int corridors. **Pets:** Accepted.
[ASK] 🏊 ⊠ 🗲 🍴

ST-ANTOINE-DE-TILLY

▼▼▼ Manoir de Tilly CI
(418) 886-2407. **$150-$220.** 3854 chemin de Tilly. Jct Hwy 20, exit 291, 8.5 km n on Rt 273; centre. Int corridors. **Pets:** Very small, dogs only. $15 daily fee/pet. Designated rooms, service with restrictions, crate.
🍴 ⊠

ST-FAUSTIN-LAC-CARRE

▼ Motel sur la Colline M
(819) 688-2102. **$75-$85, 14 day notice.** 357 Rt 117. On Rt 117, 4 km n of exit for city. Ext/int corridors. **Pets:** Medium. $15 daily fee/pet. Designated rooms, service with restrictions, supervision.
[ASK] 🏊 ⊠ 🗲 💻 🏊

ST-FELICIEN

▼▼▼ Hotel du Jardin LH
(418) 679-8422. **$87-$180.** 1400 boul du Jardin. On Hwy 167. Int corridors. **Pets:** Large, other species. Service with restrictions, supervision.
[ASK] 🏊 ⊠ 🗲 🍴 🏊 ⊠

ST-HONORE

▼ Motel Jasper M
(418) 497-2322. **$60-$70.** 657 Rt 185. On Rt 185. Ext corridors. **Pets:** Accepted.
[ASK] 🏊 ⊠ 🍴

ST-HYACINTHE

▼▼▼ Hotel des Seigneurs Saint-Hyacinthe LH
(450) 774-3810. **$109-$129.** 1200 rue Johnson. Hwy 20, exit 130S, just e on Gauvin St from boul Laframboise. Int corridors. **Pets:** Small, other species. Designated rooms, service with restrictions, crate.
[ASK] 🏊 ⊠ 🗲 💻 🍴 🏊 ⊠

ST-JEAN-PORT-JOLI

▼▼ Auberge du Faubourg M
(418) 598-6455. **$89-$105, 10 day notice.** 280 ave de Gaspe ouest (Rt 132). 2.4 km w on Rt 132 from jct Rt 204; Hwy 20, exit 414. Ext corridors. **Pets:** Small, other species. $15 daily fee/pet. Service with restrictions, supervision.
[ASK] ⊠ 🗲 💻 🍴 🏊 ⊠ 🐾

ST-JEAN-SUR-RICHELIEU

▼▼ Comfort Inn SH
(450) 359-4466. **$89-$129.** 700 rue Gadbois. Hwy 35, exit 9, e on rue Pierre-Caisse. Int corridors. **Pets:** Accepted.
[ASK] 🏊 ⊠ 🗲 🏊

▼▼ Hotel Relais Gouverneur
St-Jean-sur-Richelieu SH
(450) 348-7376. **$72-$140.** 725 boul du Seminaire nord. Hwy 35, exit 7. Int corridors. **Pets:** Accepted.
[ASK] 🏊 ⊠ 🗲 💻 🍴 🏊

SALABERRY-DE-VALLEYFIELD

▼▼▼ Hotel Plaza Valleyfield LH
(450) 373-1990. **$109-$114.** 40 ave du Centenaire. Corner of rue St-Laurent; centre. Int corridors. **Pets:** Accepted.
⊠ 🗲 💻 🍴 🏊 ⊠

SEPT-ILES

▼▼ Comfort Inn SH
(418) 968-6005. **$96-$103.** 854 boul Laure. 4.5 km w on Rt 138. Int corridors. **Pets:** Accepted.
[ASK] 🏊 ⊠ 🗲

SHAWINIGAN

▼▼ Auberge Escapade Inn SH
(819) 539-6911. **$78-$99.** 3383 rue Garnier. Hwy 55, exit 217, then 0.5 km n on Rt 351. Ext/int corridors. **Pets:** Small. $10 daily fee/pet. Designated rooms, supervision.
⊠ 🗲 🍴

▼▼▼ Auberge Gouverneur & Convention Center
Shawinigan SH
(819) 537-6000. **$170.** 1100 Promenade-du-St-Maurice. Hwy 55 N, exit 211, 4.4 km n on Hwy 153, follow signs. Int corridors. **Pets:** Large. Supervision.
[ASK] 🏊 ⊠ 🗲 💻 🍴 🏊 ⊠

(CAA) ▼▼▼ Comfort Inn & Suites SH
(819) 536-2000. **$72-$99.** 500 boul du Capitaine. Hwy 55, exit 211, 4.4 km n on Hwy 153, then 2 km s on Rt 157. Int corridors. **Pets:** Service with restrictions, supervision.
[SAVE] 🏊 ⊠ 🗲 💻

SHAWINIGAN-SUD

▼ Motel Safari M
(819) 536-2664. **$75.** 4500 12 ieme ave. Hwy 55, exit 211, then 4.4 km n on Hwy 153, then 6.6 km s on Rt 157. Ext/int corridors. **Pets:** Accepted.
[ASK] 🏊 ⊠ 🗲

SHERBROOKE

♦♦ Comfort Inn SH
(819) 564-4400. **$83-$105.** 4295 boul Bourque. Hwy 410, exit 4, 1.5 km w on Rt 112. Ext/int corridors. **Pets:** Medium. Designated rooms, service with restrictions, supervision.
ASK SO X

♦♦♦ Delta Sherbrooke Hotel and Conference Centre LH
(819) 822-1989. **$93-$143.** 2685 rue King ouest. Hwy 410, exit 4E, 1 km e on Rt 112. Int corridors. **Pets:** $30 one-time fee/room. Service with restrictions, supervision.
X 🛏 💻 🍽 ➰ ❌

STE-ANNE-DES-MONTS

CAA ♦♦♦ Motel Beaurivage M
(418) 763-2291. **$55-$160.** 245 1ere Ave ouest. Just off Rt 132. Ext/int corridors. **Pets:** Accepted.
SAVE X 🛏 💻 🍽 🏊

STE-MARTHE

♦♦♦ Auberge des Gallant CI
(450) 459-4241. **$150-$350, 14 day notice.** 1171 chemin St-Henri. 8.5 km w on chemin St-Henri from Hwy 201. Int corridors. **Pets:** Medium. $25 daily fee/room. Designated rooms, supervision.
X 💻 🍽 ➰ ❌

THETFORD MINES

♦♦ Comfort Inn SH
(418) 338-0171. **$95-$107.** 123 boul Smith sud. On Rt 112. Int corridors. **Pets:** Accepted.
ASK SO X 🛏

TROIS-RIVIERES

♦♦♦ Delta Trois-Rivieres Hotel and Conference Center LH 🐾
(819) 376-1991. **$89.** 1620 rue Notre-Dame. Corner of rue St-Roch; centre. Int corridors. **Pets:** $50 one-time fee/room. Service with restrictions, supervision.
ASK SO X 🛏 💻 🍽 ➰ ❌

♦♦ Hotel Du Roy Trois-Rivieres SH
(819) 379-3232. **$70-$75.** 3600 boul Royal. On Hwy 138, 2 km e of Pont Laviolette and jct Hwy 55. Ext/int corridors. **Pets:** Accepted.
X 🛏 💻 🍽 ➰

TROIS-RIVIERES-OUEST

♦♦ Comfort Inn SH
(819) 371-3566. **$92-$102.** 6255 rue Corbeil. Hwy 55, exit 183 (boul Jean XXIII), 2 km n of Laviolette Bridge, then 0.5 km e. Int corridors. **Pets:** Accepted.
ASK SO X 🛏 💻

CAA ♦♦ Days Inn SH
(819) 377-4444. **$80-$140.** 3155 boul St-Jean. Hwy 55, exit 183 (boul Jean XXIII), 0.5 km w, then 0.4 km n. Int corridors. **Pets:** $10 daily fee/pet. Designated rooms, service with restrictions, crate.
SAVE SO X 🛏 💻

VAL-D'OR

♦♦ Comfort Inn SH
(819) 825-9360. **$100-$105.** 1665 3 ieme ave. In town centre. Int corridors. **Pets:** Other species. Service with restrictions, supervision.
ASK SO X 🛏 💻

♦♦ Hotel Forestel LH
(819) 825-5660. **$76-$100.** 1001 3 ieme Ave est. On Rt 117 N. Int corridors. **Pets:** Other species. Service with restrictions, supervision.
ASK SO X 🛏 💻 🍽 ➰

♦♦ Hotel-Motel Econo Lodge Val-d'Or SH
(819) 825-0090. **$75-$81.** 1159 3 ieme Ave. On Rt 117 N; in town centre,. Ext/int corridors. **Pets:** No service, supervision.
ASK SO X 🛏 💻

♦♦♦ Motel L'Escale Hotel Suite SH
(819) 824-2711. **$90-$120.** 1100 rue L'Escale. In town centre. Ext/int corridors. **Pets:** Accepted.
X 🛏 💻 🍽

SASKATCHEWAN

CARONPORT

The Pilgrim Inn SH
(306) 756-5002. **$77.** Hwy 1 W. Jct Main Access; on Trans-Canada Hwy 1. Int corridors. **Pets:** Accepted.

ESTEVAN

(CAA) **Perfect Inns & Suites** SH
(306) 634-8585. **$84-$99.** 134 2nd Ave. Just n of jct Hwy 39 E and 2nd Ave. Int corridors. **Pets:** Accepted.

FOAM LAKE

La Vista Motel M
(306) 272-3341. **$60.** Jct Hwy 16 & 310. On Hwy 16. Int corridors. **Pets:** Accepted.

KINDERSLEY

(CAA) **Best Western Westridge Inn** SH
(306) 463-4687. **$79, 7 day notice.** 100 12 Ave NW. Jct of Hwy 7 and 21. Ext/int corridors. **Pets:** Small. Service with restrictions, supervision.

MOOSE JAW

(CAA) **Capone's Hideaway Theme Motel** M
(306) 692-6422. **$63-$78.** 1 Main St N. Jct Manitoba St E. Ext corridors. **Pets:** Accepted.

(CAA) **Comfort Inn** SH
(306) 692-2100. **$89-$180.** 155 Thatcher Dr W. Just w of jct Main St. Int corridors. **Pets:** $30 one-time fee/room. Designated rooms, service with restrictions, supervision.

Heritage Inn SH
(306) 693-7550. **$99-$100.** 1590 Main St N. 1.5 km s of jct Trans-Canada Hwy 1 and 2; access from Hwy 2 via Thatcher Dr. Int corridors. **Pets:** $10 daily fee/room. Service with restrictions, supervision.

(CAA) **Prairie Oasis Motel** M
(306) 693-8888. **$72.** 955 Thatcher Dr E. Just s of jct Trans-Canada Hwy 1 and Thatcher Dr E. Ext corridors. **Pets:** Designated rooms, service with restrictions, crate.

Super 8 Motel-Moose Jaw M
(306) 692-8888. **$70-$80.** 1706 Main St N. 1.5 km s of jct Trans-Canada Hwy 1; access from Hwy 2 via Thatcher Dr. Int corridors. **Pets:** Other species. $30 daily fee/room, $30 one-time fee/room. Designated rooms, service with restrictions, supervision.

NORTH BATTLEFORD

Super 8 Motel SH
(306) 446-8888. **$65-$74, 14 day notice.** 1006 Hwy 16 Bypass. 0.5 km nw of jct Hwy 16. Int corridors. **Pets:** Other species. Designated rooms, service with restrictions, supervision.

Tropical Inn SH
(306) 446-4700. **$71-$129.** 1001 Hwy 16 Bypass. Corner of Battleford Rd and Hwy 16 Bypass. Int corridors. **Pets:** Accepted.

PRINCE ALBERT

Comfort Inn SH
(306) 763-4466. **$95-$112.** 3863 2nd Ave W. 2.3 km s at jct Hwy 2 and Marquis Rd. Int corridors. **Pets:** Other species. Service with restrictions, supervision.

Super 8 SH
(306) 953-0088. **$75-$91.** 4444 2nd Ave W. Just s of jct Hwy 2 and Marquis Rd. Int corridors. **Pets:** Small. Designated rooms, service with restrictions, supervision.

Travelodge Prince Albert SH
(306) 764-6441. **$74-$135, 7 day notice.** 3551 2nd Ave W. 2.2 km s at jct Hwy 2 and Marquis Rd. Ext/int corridors. **Pets:** Other species. Service with restrictions, crate.

REGINA

(CAA) **Comfort Inn** SH
(306) 789-5522. **$87-$91.** 3221 E Eastgate Dr. Trans-Canada Hwy 1, 2 km e of Ring Rd, at eastern approach to Regina. Int corridors. **Pets:** Accepted.

Country Inn & Suites By Carlson SH
(306) 789-9117. **$91-$96, 3 day notice.** 3321 Eastgate Bay. Trans-Canada Hwy 1, 2 km e of Ring Rd, at eastern approach to city. Int corridors. **Pets:** Small, other species. Designated rooms, service with restrictions, crate.

(CAA) ▼▼▼▼ **Radisson Plaza Hotel Saskatchewan** LH ❀
(306) 522-7691. **$124-$134.** 2125 Victoria Ave. Victoria Ave at Scarth St; centre. Int corridors. **Pets:** $30 one-time fee/room. Designated rooms, service with restrictions, crate.
[SAVE] [✕] [&M] [🛏] [💻] [🍴] [✕]

▼▼ **Ramada Hotel & Convention Centre** LH ❀
(306) 569-1666. **$96-$190.** 1818 Victoria Ave. Victoria Ave and Broad St; centre of downtown. Int corridors. **Pets:** $12 one-time fee/room. Service with restrictions, supervision.
[ASK] [So] [✕] [🛏] [💻] [🍴] [🏊] [✕]

(CAA) ▼▼▼▼ **Regina Inn Hotel & Conference Centre** LH
(306) 525-6767. **$95-$105.** 1975 Broad St. Jct Victoria Ave; centre of downtown. Int corridors. **Pets:** Designated rooms, service with restrictions, supervision.
[SAVE] [✕] [🛏] [💻] [🍴]

▼ **Regina Super 8** SH
(306) 789-8833. **$66-$70.** 2730 Victoria Ave E. Trans-Canada Hwy 1, 1.6 km e of Ring Rd, at eastern approach to Regina. Int corridors. **Pets:** Accepted.
[ASK] [So] [✕] [&M] [🛏]

▼▼ **Travelodge Regina East** SH
(306) 565-0455. **$80-$109.** 1110 Victoria Ave E. Trans-Canada Hwy 1, just w of Ring Rd, at eastern approach to city. Int corridors. **Pets:** Accepted.
[ASK] [So] [✕] [🛏] [💻] [🏊]

SASKATOON

(CAA) ▼▼ **Best Western Inn & Suites** SH
(306) 244-5552. **$79-$125, 14 day notice.** 1715 Idylwyld Dr N. 2.6 km n on Hwy 11 (Idylwyld Dr). Ext/int corridors. **Pets:** Medium. Service with restrictions, supervision.
[SAVE] [So] [✕] [🛏] [💻] [🍴]

(CAA) ▼▼▼ **Colonial Square Motel** SH
(306) 343-1676. **$79-$84.** 1301 8th St E. Just w of Cumberland St. Ext/int corridors. **Pets:** Medium, other species. $5 daily fee/room. Designated rooms, service with restrictions, crate.
[SAVE] [So] [✕] [💻]

(CAA) ▼▼ **Comfort Inn** SH
(306) 934-1122. **$82-$95.** 2155 Northridge Dr. 3 km n; just ne of jct Hwy 11 (Idylwyld Dr) and Circle Dr. Int corridors. **Pets:** Designated rooms, service with restrictions, supervision.
[SAVE] [So] [✕] [&M] [🛏] [💻]

▼▼▼▼ **Country Inn & Suites By Carlson** SH
(306) 934-3900. **$88-$94.** 617 Cynthia St. Just w of jct Hwy 11 (Idylwyld Dr) and Circle Dr. Int corridors. **Pets:** Accepted.
[ASK] [So] [✕] [&M] [🛏] [💻]

▼▼▼▼ **Delta Bessborough** LH
(306) 244-5521. **$109-$179.** 601 Spadina Crescent E. At 21st St E; centre of downtown. **Pets:** Service with restrictions, crate.
[ASK] [So] [✕] [🛏] [💻] [🍴] [🏊] [✕]

▼▼ **Heritage Inn** SH
(306) 665-8121. **$78-$95.** 102 Cardinal Crescent. Jct Circle and Airport drs. Int corridors. **Pets:** Other species. $10 daily fee/pet. Designated rooms, service with restrictions, supervision.
[ASK] [So] [✕] [🛏] [💻] [🍴] [🏊]

▼▼▼ **Holiday Inn Express Hotel & Suites** SH
(306) 384-8844. **$90-$119.** 315 Idylwyld Dr N. Jct 25th St W. Int corridors. **Pets:** Small, other species. $10 daily fee/room. Service with restrictions, supervision.
[ASK] [So] [✕] [&M] [🛏] [💻] [🏊]

▼▼ **Quality Hotel** LH
(306) 244-2311. **$105-$119.** 90 22nd St E. Just e of jct Hwy 11 (Idylwyld Dr), 1st and 22nd sts. Int corridors. **Pets:** Accepted.
[ASK] [So] [✕] [🛏] [💻] [🍴] [🏊] [✕]

(CAA) ▼▼▼▼ **Radisson Hotel Saskatoon** LH
(306) 665-3322. **$115-$249.** 405 20th St E. At 4th Ave S; centre. Int corridors. **Pets:** Accepted.
[SAVE] [So] [✕] [&M] [🛏] [💻] [🍴] [🏊] [✕]

▼▼ **Ramada Hotel & Golf Dome** LH
(306) 665-6500. **$130-$175, 10 day notice.** 806 Idylwyld Dr N. 4 km s of jct Circle Dr. Int corridors. **Pets:** Other species. Designated rooms, service with restrictions, supervision.
[So] [✕] [🛏] [💻] [🍴] [🏊]

▼▼▼ **Sandman Hotel** LH
(306) 477-4844. **$110-$115.** 310 Circle Dr W. Jct Ave C N. Int corridors. **Pets:** Small. $5 daily fee/room. Service with restrictions, supervision.
[ASK] [So] [✕] [🛏] [💻] [🍴] [🏊]

(CAA) ▼▼▼▼ **Saskatoon Inn Hotel & Conference Centre** LH
(306) 242-1440. **$109.** 2002 Airport Dr. Jct Circle and Airport drs. Int corridors. **Pets:** Service with restrictions, supervision.
[SAVE] [So] [✕] [🛏] [💻] [🍴] [🏊]

(CAA) ▼▼▼▼ **Saskatoon Travelodge Hotel** LH
(306) 242-8881. **$124-$154.** 106 Circle Dr W. 3 km n, just w of jct Hwy 11 (Idylwyld Dr). Int corridors. **Pets:** Accepted.
[SAVE] [So] [✕] [🛏] [💻] [🍴] [🏊] [✕]

▼▼ **Super 8** SH
(306) 384-8989. **$85-$87.** 706 Circle Dr E. 2 km e of jct Hwy 11 (Idylwyld Dr). Ext/int corridors. **Pets:** Other species. $5 one-time fee/room. Service with restrictions, crate.
[ASK] [So] [✕] [🛏] [💻]

(CAA) ▼ **Thriftlodge** M ❀
(306) 244-2191. **$69-$89, 3 day notice.** 1825 Idylwyld Dr N. 0.2 km s of Cirlce Dr N. Ext corridors. **Pets:** Small, dogs only. $10 one-time fee/room. Designated rooms, service with restrictions, supervision.
[SAVE] [So] [✕] [🛏] [💻]

SHAUNAVON

▼ **Hidden Hilten Motel** M
(306) 297-4166. **$48-$63.** 352 5th St W. 0.5 km e from jct Hwy 13 and 37, just n. Ext corridors. **Pets:** Crate.
[✕] [🛏] [💻]

SWIFT CURRENT

Ⓐ Ⓦ Caravel Motel M ✿
(306) 773-8385. **$48-$59, 3 day notice.** 705 N Service Rd E. Just e of Central Ave. Ext corridors. **Pets:** Small. Designated rooms, service with restrictions, supervision.

SAVE SD X ⊟ ⊡

Ⓦ Ⓦ Comfort Inn SH
(306) 778-3994. **$71-$108, 30 day notice.** 1510 S Service Rd E. Trans-Canada Hwy 1, just w of 22nd Ave NE. Int corridors. **Pets:** Accepted.

ASK SD X ⊟ ⊡

Ⓦ Rainbow Motel M
(306) 778-3331. **$43-$55.** 210 South Service Rd E. Trans-Canada Hwy 1, exit George St to South Service Rd, just e. Ext corridors. **Pets:** Small, dogs only. $5 daily fee/pet. Designated rooms, service with restrictions, supervision.

ASK SD X ⊟ ⊡

Ⓐ Ⓦ Rodeway Inn Motel SH
(306) 773-4664. **$54.** 1200 S Service Rd E. Trans-Canada Hwy 1, just w of 22nd Ave NE. Ext/int corridors. **Pets:** Small. Designated rooms, service with restrictions, supervision.

SAVE SD X ⊟ ⊞

Ⓐ Ⓦ Safari Motel M
(306) 773-4608. **$46-$56, 3 day notice.** 810 S Service Rd E. 1 km w of jct Hwy 1 and 4, on S Service Rd. Ext corridors. **Pets:** $5 one-time fee/pet. No service, supervision.

SAVE SD X ⊟ ⊡

Ⓦ Ⓦ Super 8 Motel SH
(306) 778-6088. **$74-$90, 14 day notice.** 405 N Service Rd E. Just e of Central Ave. Int corridors. **Pets:** Accepted.

ASK SD X ⊟ ⊡ ⇝

Ⓐ Ⓦ Ⓦ Swift Current Travelodge M
(306) 773-3101. **$80-$120.** Trans-Canada Hwy 1 E. Just e of Central Ave, on N Service Rd. Ext corridors. **Pets:** $10 daily fee/pet. Designated rooms, service with restrictions, supervision.

SAVE SD X ⊟ ⊡ ⇝

Ⓐ Ⓦ Westwind Motel M
(306) 773-1441. **$52-$64.** N Service Rd W. Trans-Canada Hwy 1, 0.5 km w of Central Ave. Ext corridors. **Pets:** Other species. Designated rooms, service with restrictions, supervision.

SAVE SD X ⊟ ⊞ ⇝

WEYBURN

Ⓐ Ⓦ Ⓦ Perfect Inns & Suites M
(306) 842-2691. **$57-$82.** 238 Sims Ave. 0.5 km w of jct Hwy 35 and 39. Ext/int corridors. **Pets:** Accepted.

SAVE X ⊟ ⊡

Ⓐ Ⓦ Ⓦ Weyburn Inn SH
(306) 842-6543. **$68, 7 day notice.** 5 Government Rd. Centre. Ext/int corridors. **Pets:** Accepted.

SAVE SD X ⊟ ⊡ ⊞ ⇝ X

YORKTON

Ⓦ Ⓦ Ⓦ Comfort Inn & Suites SH
(306) 783-0333. **$69-$149.** 22 Dracup Ave. Just w of jct Hwy 9, 10 and 16 (Yellowhead Hwy). Int corridors. **Pets:** $5 daily fee/room. Designated rooms, service with restrictions, supervision.

ASK SD X ⊟ ⊡ ⇝

Ⓦ Ⓦ Holiday Inn SH
(306) 783-9781. **$67-$80.** 100 Broadway St E. On Hwy 9, 10 and 16 (Yellowhead Hwy); downtown. Int corridors. **Pets:** Accepted.

ASK SD X ⊟ ⊡ ⊞ ⇝ X

Ⓦ Imperial 400 Yorkton SH
(306) 783-6581. **$65-$149.** 207 Broadway Ave E. Jct Hwy 9, 10 and 16 (Yellowhead Hwy). Ext/int corridors. **Pets:** Designated rooms, service with restrictions, supervision.

ASK SD X ⊟ ⊡ ⊞ ⇝

Ⓦ Ⓦ Travelodge Yorkton SH
(306) 783-6571. **$99-$189.** 345 Broadway W. West end of town, just e of Agriplex (Hwy 10A). Ext/int corridors. **Pets:** Medium. $50 deposit/room. Designated rooms, service with restrictions, supervision.

ASK SD X ⊟ ⊡ ⊞ ⇝

YUKON TERRITORY

DAWSON CITY

⬥⬥ Bonanza Gold Motel M
(867) 993-6789. **$99-$119.** 2.4 km s on Hwy 2. Ext corridors.
Pets: Accepted.

⊠ 🐾 📶 💻 🍴 🍽

(CAA) ⬥⬥ Westmark Inn Dawson City M
(867) 993-5542. **$116.** 5th Ave & Harper. At 5th and Harper
sts; downtown. Ext/int corridors. **Pets:** Accepted.

SAVE S⬥ ⊠ 💻 🍴 🍽

HAINES JUNCTION

(CAA) ⬥⬥ Alcan Motor Inn M
(867) 634-2371. **$100-$150.** Jct of Alaska and Haines hwys
(1 and 3). Ext corridors. **Pets:** Other species. $7.50 daily
fee/pet. Designated rooms, service with restrictions, supervision.

SAVE ⊠ 📶 💻

WHITEHORSE

(CAA) ⬥⬥ High Country Inn SH 🐾
(867) 667-4471. **$89-$189, 3 day notice.** 4051 4th Ave. 0.6
km e of Main St. Int corridors. **Pets:** Large. $10 daily fee/
pet. Designated rooms, service with restrictions, crate.

SAVE S⬥ ⊠ 📶 💻 🍴

(CAA) ⬥ The Town and Mountain Hotel SH
(867) 668-7644. **$69-$99.** 401 Main St. Downtown. Int corridors. **Pets:** Other species. $10 daily fee/pet. Designated
rooms, service with restrictions.

SAVE S⬥ ⊠ 📶 💻 🍴 🍽

(CAA) ⬥⬥ Westmark Whitehorse Hotel &
Conference Centre SH
(867) 393-9700. **$116-$119.** 201 Wood St. At 2nd Ave; centre. Int corridors. **Pets:** Medium. Designated rooms, service
with restrictions.

SAVE S⬥ ⊠ 🐾 🔇 🐾 📶 💻 🍴 🍽